Books of Related Interest from the IEEE Press . . .

TRELLIS CODING
Christian Schlegel
1997   Hardcover   304 pp   IEEE Order No. PC4069   ISBN 0-7803-1052-7

CLAUDE E. SHANNON: COLLECTED PAPERS
Edited by Neil Sloane
1993   Hardcover   968 pp   IEEE Order No. PC3319   ISBN 0-7803-0434-9

AN INTRODUCTION TO STATISTICAL COMMUNICATION THEORY: An IEEE Classic Reissue
David Middleton
1996   Hardcover   1184 pp   IEEE Order No. PC5648   ISBN 0-7803-1178-7

FUNDAMENTALS OF CONVOLUTIONAL CODING
Rolf Johannesson and Kamil Sh. Zigangirov
1999   Hardcover   448 pp   IEEE Order No. PC5739   ISBN 0-7803-3483-3

REED-SOLOMON CODES AND THEIR APPLICATIONS
Vijay Bhargava and Stephen B. Wicker
1994   Hardcover   336 pp   IEEE Order No. PC3749   ISBN 0-7803-1025-X

DIGITAL TRANSMISSION ENGINEERING
John B. Anderson
1998   Hardcover   400 pp   IEEE Order No. PC5714   ISBN 0-7803-3457-4

INFORMATION THEORY

INFORMATION THEORY

50 Years of Discovery

Edited by

Sergio Verdú
Princeton University

Steven W. McLaughlin
Georgia Institute of Technology

IEEE Information Theory Society, *Sponsor*

IEEE PRESS

A Selected Reprint Volume

The Institute of Electrical and Electronics Engineers, Inc., New York

This book and other books may be purchased at a discount
from the publisher when ordered in bulk quantities. Contact:

IEEE Press Marketing
Attn: Special Sales
Piscataway, NJ 08855-1331
Fax: (732) 981-9334

For more information about IEEE PRESS products, visit the
IEEE Home Page: http://www.ieee.org/press

All articles are reprinted with permission from
IEEE Transactions on Information Theory,
Vol. 4, No. 6, pp. 2042–2772, October 1998.

© 2000 by the Institute of Electrical and Electronics Engineers, Inc.
3 Park Avenue, 17th Floor, New York, NY 10016-5997

Printed in the United States of America

10   9   8   7   6   5   4   3   2   1

ISBN 0-7803-5363-3

IEEE Order Number PC5804

Library of Congress Cataloging-in-Publication Data

Information theory : 50 years of discovery / edited by Sergio Verdú
   Steven W. McLaughlin
      "Published under the sponsorship of the IEEE Information Theory Society."
         p.   cm.
      Includes bibliographical references and index.
      ISBN 0-7803-5363-3
      1. Information theory.   I. Verdú, Sergio, 1958–
   II. McLaughlin, Steven W., 1962–
   Q367 . I525 2000
   003' .54—dc21
                                                  99-10125
                                                      CIP

Contents

Contents

Contents

Preface

THIS book is a collection of tutorial and retrospective papers on key subjects from communications, signal processing, computer science, probability and statistics and, of course, information theory. The authors are all major contributors to the subjects about which they have written, and many are pioneers in their respective fields. The topics range from the practical (data and image compression, error control coding, data storage, detection and estimation, coded modulation, quantum computing, and wavelets) to the more theoretical (minimum description principle and zero-error information theory). One of the great strengths of this book is the comprehensive collection of references. We anticipate that this book will be of use to both academic and industry researchers and engineers alike. In academics, these papers can be launching points for new students as well as discussion references for courses in coding and information theory.

The articles in this book originally appeared in October 1998 as a special issue of the *IEEE Transactions on Information Theory*. This special issue commemorated the 50th anniversary of Claude Shannon's original 1948 paper that single-handedly started information theory. Sergio Verdú edited the issue and did a splendid job commissioning and gathering the 25 papers in that issue. The Information Theory Society decided to reprint this issue because they believe researchers in communications, signal processing, and computing will find the tutorial papers interesting and vital to introducing themselves, colleagues, and students to the topics addressed.

The book comes with a CD-ROM that contains various items of interest. Of particular note are the author, subject, and transaction indexes of the IEEE Transactions of Information Theory Digital Library. Here you will find a complete listing of, and hyperlinks to, all papers that have appeared in the *IEEE Transactions on Information Theory* since its inception in 1953. You can browse the electronic versions (PDF files) of all papers by consulting the online digital library at http://galaxy.ucsd.edu.

We hope you enjoy the papers.

Steven W. McLaughlin
School of Electrical and Computer Engineering

Guest Editorial

INFORMATION Theory is one of the few scientific disciplines fortunate enough to have a precise date of birth. This special commemorative issue of the IEEE TRANSACTIONS ON INFORMATION THEORY celebrates the 50th anniversary of Claude E. Shannon's "A Mathematical Theory of Communication," published in July and October 1948.

With communication engineering at the epicenter of the bombshell, the sensational aftermath of Shannon's paper soon reached Mathematics, Physics, Statistics, Computing, and Cryptology. Even Economics, Biology, Linguistics, and other fields in the natural and social sciences felt the ripples of Shannon's new theory. Although Information Theory eventually failed to become the "theory of everything" that a few had envisioned, it thrived in its natural habitat of information compression, transmission, and processing.

Claude Shannon became an instant celebrity of the post-war industrial age with articles in the popular press that had the foresight to proclaim the far-reaching importance of Information Theory, e.g.:[1]

> Great scientific theories, like great symphonies and great novels, are among man's proudest—and rarest—creations. What sets the scientific theory apart from and, in a sense, above the other creations is that it may profoundly and rapidly alter man's view of his world... Within the last five years a new theory has appeared that seems to bear some of the same hallmarks of greatness... It may be no exaggeration to say that man's progress in peace, and security in war, depend more on fruitful applications of information theory than on physical demonstrations, either in bombs or power plants, that Einstein's famous equation works.

Today, in addition to Shannon's theory of fundamental limits of information transmission and compression, Information Theory encompasses the design of compression, coding, signaling, detection, and classification techniques that underlie contemporary information transmission, storage and processing technologies. With the inexorable advance of technology, Shannon's fundamental limits become increasingly relevant to the design of systems in which resources such as bandwidth, energy, time, and space are at a premium.

This issue contains 25 papers written by a total of 57 authors, who were invited to offer tutorial perspectives on the development and state-of-the-art of the major fields under the purview of the IEEE TRANSACTIONS ON INFORMATION THEORY. Targeted to a wide audience and destined to become classic references, the articles in this issue are invaluable sources for specialists and novices alike.

Without aiming to be exhaustive, the topics selected for this issue provide a snapshot of some of the most dynamic research fields in Information Theory today. The interdisciplinary nature of Information Theory is evident from the list of invited authors, in which we find engineers, mathematicians, computer scientists, probabilists, statisticians, and physicists.

Calderbank's personal perspective on the past, present, and future of coding theory covers the major trends in Hamming and Euclidean spaces as well as the impact of coding beyond reliable communication through noisy channels. The overview by Costello, Hagenauer, Imai, and Wicker illustrates the rich variety of practical applications of error control codes in space communication, voiceband modems, data storage, broadcasting, mobile communication, and network protocols. Forney and Ungerboeck give an account of the basic principles and techniques responsible for the greatest technological success story of coding theory: the pursuit of the capacity of the linear Gaussian channel. Blake, Heegard, Hoeholdt, and Wei offer a self-contained introduction to the theory of algebraic-geometry codes—a class of codes with great, but yet unrealized, practical potential, which has been championed by a number of algebraic coding theorists over the last two decades. As surveyed in the paper by Delsarte and Levenshtein, the unifying tools provided by the combinatorial theory of association schemes have led to important advances in algebraic coding theory over the last 25 years.

The survey by the Guest Editor spans the three major fields founded by Shannon in 1948, namely, lossless data compression algorithms and their fundamental limits, the capacity of noisy channels, and the asymptotic theory of lossy data compression.

Over the last decade, the theory of pattern recurrence times (pioneered by Kac in 1947) has emerged as a powerful tool in the analysis and design of universal lossless data compression algorithms. Wyner, Ziv, and Wyner present a general approach to pattern matching in problems of classification, distribution estimation, entropy estimation, lossless compression, and prediction. In fact, the strong link between compression and prediction of finite-alphabet time series was recognized by Shannon in the early days of Information Theory. Merhav and Feder give a survey of universal prediction of both probabilistically modeled sources and individual deterministic sequences.

Shannon foresaw in 1948 that some communication channels would require the addition of redundancy to the data, not (only) to combat channel noise, but to avoid transmitting certain forbidden sequences. Data-recording systems are prime examples of such channels. Immink, Siegel, and Wolf give

Publisher Item Identifier S 0018-9448(98)08038-9.

[1] "The Information Theory," *Fortune*, pp. 136–158, Dec. 1953.

a comprehensive account of the fundamental limits on the redundancy of constrained sequences, and the progress in constructing algorithms that approach those limits.

In 1956 a new branch of combinatorics sprang up from Shannon's definition of the capacity of a graph. Körner and Orlitsky survey the major results on zero-error capacity, zero-error source coding, interactive communication, and protocol complexity. At the intersection of large deviations and combinatorics, the information-theoretic method of types enjoys much popularity in dealing with discrete memoryless sources, channels and hypothesis testing problems. Csiszár gives an overview of the basic tools and achievements of this method. Determining the fundamental limits of sources and channels with memory often calls for ergodic-theoretic tools. Conversely, Information Theory has proved to be instrumental in the proof of key results in ergodic theory. The many facets of the interplay between Information Theory and ergodic theory are discussed in the tutorial paper by Shields.

Jamming and fading are some of the impairments under which the statistical description of the channel available to encoder and/or decoder may be incomplete. Lapidoth and Narayan give a systematic exposition of the existing coding theorems for compound and arbitrarily varying channels. Much has been done and much remains to be done in the field of reliable and efficient communication through time-varying channels. Coding, equalization, and capacity of fading channels are reviewed by Biglieri, Proakis, and Shamai.

Multiuser information theory, founded by Shannon in 1960, has seen a number of fundamental contributions over the last three decades. However, several key canonical problems have defied many efforts. Cover summarizes the progress achieved in the partial solution of the broadcast channel he introduced in 1972. Since the 1970's, information theorists have been responsible for key advances in data networking. However, the information theory of communication networks remains at an embryonic stage. Ephremides and Hajek offer a broad view of networking from an information-theoretic perspective.

The timely tutorial survey of quantum information theory by Bennett and Shor gives an accessible introduction to compression, transmission and cryptography for quantum-mechanical models.

Gray and Neuhoff give a definitive exposition of the historical development of the principles and practice of quantization. The asymptotic theory of analog-to-digital conversion, known as rate-distortion theory, was pioneered by Shannon in 1948 and 1959. Its development is surveyed by Berger and Gibson with emphasis on its first three decades and on the subsequent impact that Information Theory has had on the state-of-the-art in audio, image, and video compression. Many of those algorithms are based on modern harmonic analysis and, in particular, the theory of wavelets. The team of Donoho, Daubechies, DeVore, and Vetterli assembles a broad array of expertise in a forward-looking paper on the use of wavelets and other transform techniques in lossy source coding.

Statistical inference methods in imaging are surveyed by O'Sullivan, Blahut, and Snyder highlighting the important role that Information Theory has played and is expected to play in the development of modeling and estimation techniques. Systems with several sensors connected to a central controller through a capacity-constrained channel give rise to decentralized statistical inference problems with a distinct Shannon-theoretic flavor. Although key open problems remain, the considerable progress in this two-decade-old field is synthesized by Han and Amari.

Information Theory is having a major impact on the field of Statistics thanks to the minimum description length principle put forth around 1980 by Rissanen. Barron, Rissanen, and Yu give an introduction to the subject and to its applications in data compression and statistical inference. Focussing on the two-class classification paradigm, the tutorial survey by Kulkarni, Lugosi, and Venkatesh serves as an introduction to statistical pattern recognition and learning theory—a field with a distinguished tradition in this journal. The detection of signals embedded in noise is another field that has supplied major contributions to the TRANSACTIONS ON INFORMATION THEORY. Kailath and Poor concentrate on two major subfields of interest in communication theory: the structure of the likelihood ratio, and sequence detection.

It is a pleasure to acknowledge those people who, in addition to the authors, have been instrumental in making this publication possible. The initiative to publish a Golden Jubilee Special Issue is due to Robert Calderbank, past Editor-in-Chief, who appointed the Guest Editor and offered valuable advice in the selection of topics and authors. The flawless production of the issue is the result of the generous efforts of our Publications Editor, Steve McLaughlin. Nela Rybowicz, Senior Associate Editor at IEEE Periodicals, has added one more item to her long list of services to the IEEE TRANSACTIONS ON INFORMATION THEORY. Under severe time constraints, the referees provided unusually insightful and thorough reviews. Aaron Wyner's enthusiasm for this project meant a lot to us. His posthumous article leads this issue.

United in the spirit of Claude Shannon's legacy, we celebrate one of the towering scientific achievements of the twentieth century. This commemorative issue is a proud testimony of the great accomplishments of five fascinating decades and of the vibrancy of our field today. Let the second 50 years of Information Theory begin.

SERGIO VERDÚ
Guest Editor

On the Role of Pattern Matching in Information Theory

Aaron D. Wyner, *Fellow, IEEE*, Jacob Ziv, *Fellow, IEEE*, and Abraham J. Wyner, *Member, IEEE*

(Invited Paper)

In Memory of Aaron D. Wyner (1939–1997)

Abstract— In this paper, the role of pattern matching information theory is motivated and discussed. We describe the relationship between a pattern's recurrence time and its probability under the data-generating stochastic source. We show how this relationship has led to great advances in universal data compression. We then describe nonasymptotic uniform bounds on the performance of data-compression algorithms in cases where the size of the training data that is available to the encoder is not large enough so as to yield the asymptotic compression: the Shannon entropy. We then discuss applications of pattern matching and universal compression to universal prediction, classification, and entropy estimation.

Index Terms— Information theory, source coding, universal data compression.

I. INTRODUCTION

THE self-information of a random event or a random message is a term coined by C. E. Shannon who defined it to be "minus the logarithm of the probability of the random event." The Shannon "entropy" of the stochastic source that generated the event is the expectation of the self-information.

Shannon discovered that the entropy of a stochastic source has a clear and important physical meaning: on average, it is the smallest number of bits that it takes to faithfully represent or communicate events generated from the stochastic source.

Suppose, for example, we are interested in finding efficient representations of incoming random messages or random events. In a broad sense, we consider three possible circumstances.

- The source distribution is completely known.
- The source distribution is unknown, but it belongs to a parameterized family of probability distributions.
- The source distribution is known to be stationary and ergodic, but no other information is available.

Manuscript received December 1, 1997; revised May 30, 1998. This work was supported in part by the Bi-national US-Israel Science fund. The work of A. J. Wyner was supported by the National Science Foundation under Grant DMS-9508933.

A. D. Wyner (deceased) was with Bell Laboratories, Lucent Technologies.

J. Ziv is with the Department of Electrical Engineering, Technion–Israel Institute of Technology, 32000 Haifa, Israel.

A. J. Wyner was with the Department of Statistics, University of California at Berkeley, Berkeley, CA 94720 USA. He is now with the Department of Statistics, Wharton School, University of Pennsylvania, Philadelphia, PA 19104 USA.

Publisher Item Identifier S 0018-9448(98)06082-9.

If the source distribution is completely known then there is a wide variety of efficient and practical solutions. Shannon himself showed how to find a code which assigns to every random message a codeword whose length is nearly the self-information (log likelihood) of the message.[1] Consider then the situation where the source's underlying probability law is *not* completely known, which is indeed the case when dealing with practical information sources. The obvious way to proceed is by the "plug-in" approach: This involves estimation of the source distribution, which is then used in the coding algorithm in place of the unknown distribution. If, for example, the source distribution is not specified completely but is known to be a member of a parametric family then the unknown parameters are readily estimated from the message itself or from training data. The actual representation can be accomplished by finding a Shannon code that uses codewords whose lengths are nearly the self-information of messages with respect to the estimated measure, instead of the true measure. With enough data the estimate will be sufficiently close to the truth and the representation will be nearly optimal. On the other hand, as we shall see, conventional methods for estimating the source probability measure are not always optimal and are rarely practical in universal settings where no prior information is available. Consequently, we propose the following general question:

Can we find an appropriate and universal way to estimate the probability measure that governs the generation of messages by the source?

This is a question of wide-ranging interest to scientists, mathematicians, and engineers (for perhaps different reasons). We will attempt to answer this question from the point of view of information theory.

A natural (frequentist) understanding of the probability of an event begins with a long realization from a stochastic source, which we will assume to be stationary and ergodic. The number of occurrences of a random event when divided by the length of the realization, is nearly the probability of the event. Thus the time between events, called the recurrence time, is on average inversely proportional to its probability of occurrence. For example, suppose we observed a monkey typing at a typewriter. The number of occurrences of the

---

[1] We call this the Shannon code. See [1] for a description.

1

pattern "CLAUDESHANNON" in the monkey manuscript is expected to be the probability of the pattern multiplied by the number of letters in the manuscript. Therefore, the time, measured in letters, that it will take the monkey to type the pattern "CLAUDESHANNON" is simply the inverse of the probability of the pattern. Since the probability of the pattern is easily seen to be 2^{-13} the average recurrence time is 2^{13}. This is accurately expressed by Kac's lemma which states that the expected time until the recurrence of a fixed pattern in a stationary ergodic sequence is the inverse of the pattern's probability. We can rewrite the quantity 26^{13} as $2^{13 \log 26}$ which in turn is equal to $2^{\ell H}$, where ℓ is the length of the pattern and H is defined to be $\log_2 26$.[2] Thus for this pattern, the expected log of the recurrence time divided by the length of the pattern is not more than H. For some source distributions it is possible to find the distribution of the recurrence time for any fixed pattern using probabilistic and analytical techniques [32], [33].

In the above discussion, we delt with the recurrence time for any fixed pattern. The information theorist, on the other hand, is interested in random messages and the recurrence time of random patterns.

Let us introduce some notation: The random variables X_i are assumed to take values in a finite alphabet $\boldsymbol{A}$ with $|\boldsymbol{A}| = A \leq \infty$. For any positive integer ℓ we write

$$X_1^\ell = X_1, X_2, \cdots, X_\ell.$$

For stationary sources, define the ℓth-order-per-letter entropy

$$H\left(X_1^\ell\right) = -\frac{1}{\ell} E \log P\left(X_1^\ell\right).$$

The entropy rate is defined to be

$$H = \lim_{\ell \to \infty} H\left(X_1^\ell\right). \tag{1}$$

We define N_ℓ to be the time of the first recurrence of X_1^ℓ in the stochastic source. That is, N_ℓ is the smallest integer N so that a copy of X_1^ℓ equals $X_{N+1}^{N+\ell}$. The asymptotic equipartition theorem (AEP) implies that for ℓ large enough the random pattern is with high probability *typical* which means that minus the log of the probability of X_1^ℓ divided by ℓ is nearly its expected value H. Thus for almost every pattern (the typical ones) Kac's theorem implies that the log of the recurrence time divided by ℓ is nearly H. This is stated formally in the following theorem:

A Recurrence Time Theorem [8]–[10]: Let N_ℓ be the first recurrence of pattern X_1^ℓ in a stationary, ergodic, finite-alphabet source. Then

$$\lim_{\ell \to \infty} \frac{\log N_\ell}{\ell} = H \text{ with probability } 1. \tag{2}$$

In light of this result,[3] it should not be at all surprising that matching a pattern onto its first recurrence, moving backward into the suffix of the string, turns out to be an important device

[2] All logarithms will be base 2.

[3] **Historical Note:** Convergence in probability and half of an almost sure extension appeared first in [8]. A complete proof of almost sure convergence first appeared in [9]. A short proof can be found in [10].

for generating an efficient estimate for the probability of the pattern.

What *is* surprising is that the recurrence time may be the *only* available tool for estimating probabilities while other more "intuitive" estimates are useless. There is, of course, a significant practical problem: For a given sequence of letters X_1^n and a fixed ℓ, it may be that $N_\ell > n$. To avoid this uncertainty, we turn the problem inside out and consider a different kind of pattern matching.

Define L_n to be the "longest match" of any prefix of the incoming sequence X_1^∞ into the sequence X_{-n+1}^0 of the n most recent observations. Mathematically, the longest match behaves like the recurrence time since

$$\{N_\ell > n\} = \{L_n < \ell\}.$$

The following result is the match length equivalent of the recurrence time theorem.

A Match Length Theorem [8]: Let L_n be the longest match of the incoming sequence X_1^∞ into the past n observations X_{-n+1}^0. Then

$$\lim_{n \to \infty} \frac{L_n}{\log n} = \frac{1}{H} \text{ in probability.} \tag{3}$$

Let us motivate this result by establishing directly the relationship between the longest match and the probability of the pattern. Taking our lead from renewal theory, we introduce the stopping time $T = T_n$ equal to the smallest k such that $-\log P(X_1^k | X_{-n+1}^0) \geq \log n$. For most sources it follows (informally) that $-\log P(X_1^T | X_{-n+1}^0) \approx \log n$. Now consider a pattern of length $\ell = T + \delta$, where δ is any positive integer. From the linearity of expectations it is easy to see that if $S_n(X_1^\ell)$ is the number of occurrences of X_1^ℓ in X_{-n+1}^0 then

$$ES_n\left(X_1^\ell\right) = nEP\left(X_1^\ell\right) \approx EP\left(X_{T+1}^{T+\delta} \mid X_1^T\right). \tag{4}$$

For δ large the right-hand side of (4) is small which implies that strings longer than T are not expected to appear even once in the past n observations; this in turn implies that $L_n < \ell$. Now let $\ell = T - \delta$. Then

$$ES_n\left(X_1^\ell\right) = nEP\left(X_1^\ell\right) \approx EP\left(X_{T-\delta+1}^T \mid X_1^{T-\delta}\right)^{-1}. \tag{5}$$

If δ is large then the right-hand side of (5) is *large* which implies that we expect many occurrences of X_1^ℓ in the past n observations; this in turn implies that $L_n > \ell$.

Taken together, we have shown that the longest match is likely to be sandwiched between $T - \delta$ and $T + \delta$. To prove this precisely we would need to show 1) if the expected number of pattern occurrences is larg, than the probability of at least one occurrence is close to one; and 2) that the maximum conditional probability of any pattern goes to zero sufficiently fast. For sources with vanishing memory these conditions are satisfied, and the random variable $\Delta = |L_n - T|$ is not too large [14].

In summary, we have established the connection between the match length and the probability of a pattern: the longest match is approximately the first prefix of X_1^∞ whose probability is less than $\frac{1}{n}$.

We shall see, in Section II, that that this approach is efficient and enormously practical. Consequently, pattern matching has blossomed into an important tool for information theorists, especially when no knowledge of the underlying probability measure is available.

In this paper we describe the role of pattern matching in information theory. In Section II, we develop a general way to use recurrence times and patterns to estimate a probability measure, specifically in order to construct, improve, and analyze universal coding algorithms. We show how pattern-matching-based data compression algorithms can achieve optimal compression rates. We then show how some string-matching algorithms for universal data compression are not only asymptotically optimal when the length of the training set tends to infinity, but are also optimal for intermediate amounts of training data. In Sections III and IV we consider applications of pattern matching and recurrence times to problems of classification, prediction, and entropy estimation.

II. UNIVERSAL DATA COMPRESSION

As mentioned earlier, C. E. Shannon was the first one to point out that for a given source, the entropy is the lowest average number of bits per input letter that a noiseless (i.e., error-free) encoder can achieve. Indeed, for a given source code, let $L(X_1^\ell)$ denote the length function of X_1^ℓ defined to be the number of bits that represent X_1^ℓ. It is well known (see, for example [1]) that

$$E \frac{L(X_1^\ell)}{\ell} \geq H(X_1^\ell). \qquad (6)$$

Let $L(X_1^\ell)$ be the length function associated with the application of the Shannon coding algorithm, which can easily be applied when the source probabilities are known. This length function satisfies

$$-\log P(X_1^\ell) \leq L(X_1^\ell) \leq -\log P(X_1^\ell) + 1$$

hence

$$H(X_1^\ell) \leq \frac{1}{\ell} EL(X_1^\ell) \leq H(X_1^\ell) + \frac{1}{\ell}.$$

Thus with ℓ going to infinity, it follows that H is the lowest ACHIEVABLE average number of bits per source letter for any given stationary source.

Sometimes, no *a priori* information about the underlying statistics of the source is available. To formulate a representation of our random event in such a circumstance we can utilize various different universal data compression algorithms that take the following forms:

A) Universal data-compression algorithms that operate on the input sequence that is to be compressed. These algorithms may be adaptable to empirical statistics generated by the sequence itself.

B) Universal data-compression algorithms that utilize a finite "training sequence" which was either emitted by the same source, or some other finite binary vector that conveys some description of the statistics of the source.

C) Universal data compression algorithms that utilize a training set, but are also adaptable to statistics generated from the sequence itself.

Let us begin our exploration of universal data compression algorithms of type (A). Our goal is to compress a given sequence of n letters using those letters and no other information. Let

$$X_1^n = X_1, X_2, \cdots X_n \qquad (7)$$

and let

$$\tilde{Q}(x_1^\ell) \triangleq \frac{1}{n-\ell+1} \sum_{i=1}^{n-\ell+1} 1\{X_i^{i+\ell-1} = x_1^\ell\}. \qquad (8)$$

The quantity defined in (5) is called the ℓth-order empirical probability measure. We also define $\tilde{H}(X_1^\ell)$ to be the entropy rate of the empirical probability $\tilde{Q}$.

Now, by the concavity of the entropy function and Jensen's inequality, it follows that

$$E\tilde{H}(X_1^\ell) = \frac{1}{\ell} E\left\{ -\sum_{\alpha^\ell} \tilde{Q}(X_1^\ell) \log \tilde{Q}(X_1^\ell) \right\} \leq H(X_1^\ell). \qquad (9)$$

By [2] and [3], for any ℓ (smaller than n) one can, for example, empirically evaluate $\tilde{Q}(X_1^\ell)$ for each ℓ vector and then apply the appropriate Shannon coding algorithm on consecutive ℓ-blocks. (The description of $\{\tilde{Q}(X_1^\ell)\}$ takes about $A^\ell \log n$ bits.) The length function may therefore be upper-bounded by

$$L(X_1^n) = A^\ell \log n + \sum_{i=0}^{\frac{n}{\ell}-1} L(X_{i\ell+1}^{i+\ell}) \qquad (10)$$

where it is assumed that ℓ divides n and that the length function $L(X_{i\ell+1}^{i+\ell})$ is that produced by the Shannon coding algorithm. It therefore follows that if we let $\ell \leq \log n$, then

$$-\log \tilde{Q}(X_1^\ell) \leq L(X_1^\ell) \leq -\log \tilde{Q}(X_1^\ell) + 1 + o(n).$$

If we further assume that $\ell \ll \log n$ then the per-letter cost of describing $\tilde{Q}$ tends to zero. Thus taking expectation in (10), it follows that

$$\frac{1}{n} EL(X_1^n) \leq H(X_1^\ell) + \frac{1}{\ell} + \frac{o(n)}{n}. \qquad (11)$$

Thus the expected compression of the sequence X_1^n is very nearly $H(X_1^\ell)$.

This will be good if $H(X_1^\ell)$ is close to H. If ℓ is such that $H(X_1^\ell)$ is not close to H we may try to close the gap by increasing ℓ. But increasing ℓ will sharply increase the length of the description of the empirical distribution! Good sense dictates that we try to find the ℓ that achieves the shortest overall representation. It was a similar approach that led J. Rissanen to suggest the MDL (i.e. Minimum Description Length, see [12]) as an alternative to Shannon's self-information for an individual sequence.

At first glance this approach appears to solve the compression problem completely; but there are drawbacks. For any ℓ, the compression $H(X_1^\ell)$ is achieved by introducing a *coding delay* of n letters. This means that no decoding is possible until the entire n-block has been encoded. Furthermore, if there also exists a training set, then this approach will not necessarily yield the best compression.

Finally, if the source belongs to a parametric family, more efficient coding schemes (as well as achievable lower bounds) do exist (see [3]).

3

We now introduce an alternative approach to data compression which is optimal in a very general sense, since:

- no knowledge of the source is required;
- the coding delay is not long;
- it is simple and easy to implement.

The approach uses pattern matching.

Universal Data Compression with a Training Sequence

Rather than to generate the empirical statistics from the incoming data to be compressed, one can use past data which was emitted by the source or some other description of the source in order to generate an appropriate encoder for the incoming data (this is case (B) above). With that an mind we propose that the encoder be fed with two inputs:

a) The incoming data X_1^ℓ.
b) A *training sequence* that consists of N_0 letters, emitted by the very same source. For example, the training sequence may consist of the most recent N_0 letters, $X_{-N_0+1}^0$, prior to the incoming sequence X_1^ℓ. If the training set is shifted with incoming data, then the training set is called a *sliding window*. If the training sequence is not shifted then the training set is called a *fixed database*.

Our first attempt at data compression in this setting is the most intuitive approach: the plug-in method. Given the training sequence of length N_0, we choose an integer ℓ and then compute the relative frequency $\tilde{Q}(X_1^\ell)$ of all ℓ-vectors. Assuming that the empirical distribution is the true probability law we then encode incoming ℓ-blocks using a Shannon code, or better still, the appropriate Huffman code. The expected compression ratio in this case will be nearly $-E \log \tilde{Q}(X_1^\ell)$. The primary concern is whether it is possible to make the expected compression ratio close to $H(X_1^\ell)$. This may not be the case since $-\frac{1}{\ell} E \log \tilde{Q}(X_1^\ell)$ is *not* lower-bounded by $H(X_1^\ell)$. In fact, if X_1^ℓ is generated independently of the training sequence $X_{-N_0+1}^0$ then it follows that

$$-\frac{1}{\ell} E \log \tilde{Q}(X_1^\ell) \geq H(X_1^\ell) \tag{12}$$

by the concavity of the logarithmic function.

Thus in general, the highly intuitive plug-in approach, based on frequency counting, does not always work if the length N_0 of the training sequence is not large, even though the distance between $-E \log \tilde{Q}(X_1^\ell)/\ell$ and $H(X_1^\ell)$ goes to zero with N_0 very quickly for most sources. We therefore have to seek other encoding methods for intermediate values of N_0. To this end, we resume our investigation of the connection between a sequence's probability and its recurrence time. Our first task is to define the first recurrence of a pattern looking backwards into the suffix of a training sequence:

Definition: Let $N_\ell(X_{-N_0+1}^\ell)$ be the *smallest* integer $N \geq 1$ such that $X_1^\ell = X_{-N+1}^{-N+\ell}$, provided that $N \leq N_0$. If no such N can be found, we let $N_\ell(X_{-N_0+1}^\ell) \triangleq N_0$.

We will often wish to evaluate the expected recurrence time conditional on the opening sequence. To this end, let $E_{X_1^\ell}(\cdot)$

denote the conditional expectation $E(\cdot | X_1^\ell)$. The following simple lemma forms the basis of an enormously powerful tool.

Kac's Lemma [4], [6], [19]: For all stationary ergodic sources, the expected recurrence time into a training sequence of length N_0 can be bounded by

$$E_{X_1^\ell}\{N_\ell(X_{-N_0+1}^\ell)\} \leq \frac{1}{P(X_1^\ell)}. \tag{13}$$

Equality is achieved for $N_0 \to \infty$. It then follows by convexity that

$$\frac{1}{\ell} E \log N_\ell(X_{-N_0+1}^\ell) \leq H(X_1^\ell). \tag{14}$$

Here is a possible coding algorithm (following [5]), which is a simplified variant of the Lempel–Ziv (LZ) algorithm [11]: encode each block of length ℓ into a binary sequence. The first bit of this sequence will be a "yes–no" flag to indicate if $N_\ell(X_{-N_0+1}^\ell) < N_0$. If "yes," then a copy of the sequence X_1^ℓ occurs in $X_{-N_0+1}^\ell$. In that case, we append the binary encoding of the pointer $N_\ell(X_{-N_0+1}^\ell)$ to the location of its most recent occurrence. If there is no such occurrence (the flag is "no"), then we append the binary encoding of the ordinal number of the vector X_1^ℓ in A^ℓ (which requires $\ell \log A$ bits). We define the length function $L(X_1^\ell | X_{-N_0+1}^0)$ to be the total number of bits in the binary sequence. It is roughly equal to

1) $L(X_1^\ell | X_{-N_0+1}^0) \approx \log N_\ell(X_{-N_0+1}^\ell) + O(\log \log N_0)$,
   if $N_\ell(X_{-N_0+1}^\ell) < N_0$
2) $L(X_1^\ell | X_{-N_0+1}^0) \approx \ell \log A$ (no compression),
   otherwise.

Recurrence Time Coding Theorem: Let δ be some arbitrary small positive number. For any $R > 0$ and any stationary ergodic source (assume that $A = 2$), we define the set

$$T_R = \{x_1^\ell : P(x_1^\ell) < 2^{-R\ell}\}.$$

Let

$$B_\ell = \min[R : \Pr\{T_R\} \leq \delta].$$

For N_0 sufficiently large and any ℓ such that $B_\ell \leq \frac{\log N_0}{\ell} - \delta$

$$\frac{1}{\ell} EL(X_1^\ell | X_{-N_0+1}^0) \leq H(X_1^\ell) + O\left(\frac{\log \ell}{\ell}\right) + \delta. \tag{15}$$

Proof: Consider any N_0 and ℓ for which $B_\ell \leq \frac{\log N_0}{\ell} - \delta$. If $X_1^\ell \notin T_{B_\ell}$ then the encoding takes at most $\log N_\ell + O(\log \log N_0)$ bits if $N_\ell \leq N_0$. Otherwise, the encoding takes at most ℓ bits. Thus

$$EL(X_1^\ell) \leq E \log N_\ell + O(\log \log N_0)$$
$$+ \ell \Pr\{X_1^\ell \notin T_{B_\ell}, N_\ell > N_0\}$$
$$+ \ell \Pr\{X_1^\ell \in T_{B_\ell}\}.$$

For any sequence $X_1^\ell \notin T_{B_\ell}$ the Markov inequality implies that

$$\Pr\{N_\ell > N_0 | X_1^\ell\} \leq \frac{E_{X_1^\ell} N_\ell}{N_0}.$$

4

Applying Kac's lemma to $X_1^\ell \notin T_{B_\ell}$ with the smallest probability implies

$$\Pr\{X_1^\ell \notin T_{B_\ell}, N_\ell > N_0\} \leq \max_{X_1^\ell \notin T_{B_\ell}} \frac{1}{\Pr\{X_1^\ell\} N_0}$$

$$\leq \frac{2^{B_\ell}}{N_0} \leq 2^{-\delta\ell}.$$

Thus

$$\frac{1}{\ell} EL(X_1^\ell \mid X_{-N_0+1}^0)$$

$$\leq H(X_1^\ell) + O\left(\frac{\log\log N_0}{\ell}\right) + \delta + 2^{-\delta\ell}. \quad (16)$$

Now (16) holds for all ℓ and N_0 with $B_\ell \leq \frac{\log N_0}{\ell} - \delta$. If N_0 is sufficiently large it follows from the AEP, for any δ, that

$$B_\ell \leq \frac{\log N_0}{\ell} - \delta, \quad \text{for} \quad \ell = \frac{\log N_0}{H + 2\delta}$$

(15) follows.

Discussion: We measure performance in terms of the compression ratio. The recurrence time coding encodes each ℓ-block using $L(X_1^\ell)$ bits. Thus the per-block compression ratio is $\frac{L(X_1^\ell)}{\ell}$. We would like to measure the average per-block compression ratio. Since the algorithm encodes fixed-length blocks into variable-length strings, the average compression ratio must be $\frac{EL(X_1^\ell)}{\ell}$. We point out that if the encoding mapped variable length blocks into variable length binary strings, then the block length ℓ would be random. In this case, the expected compression can be defined as *either* $\frac{EL(X_1^\ell)}{E\ell}$ or $E\frac{L(X_1^\ell)}{\ell}$. The distinction is real since the definitions result in possibly different compression ratios, corresponding to sound operational motivations, albeit distinct (see [14] and [29] for a discussion).

The practical result of the coding theorem is that the recurrence time provides a basic tool for construction of a workable universal algorithm in the sense that as N_0 tends to infinity the compression ratio will tend to $H(X_1^\ell)$. For most sources, the plug-in method may satisfy the same result.

There is a complication with this algorithm: For any given N_0 the algorithm is effective only for those ℓ with $B_\ell \leq \frac{\log N_0}{\ell} - \delta$. It is, therefore, essential to know the values of B_ℓ in order to design the appropriate algorithm. The plug-in approach has a similar problem: if the blocklength is too short you waste data; but if it is too long, the method fails outright.

This problem is solved by replacing this universal Fixed-to-Variable (F-V) scheme by a sliding-window version of the universal LZ-77 algorithm [6] which is Variable-to-Variable (V-V); it encodes blocks of variable length into variable-length codes. This algorithm does not require the user to choose a blocklength. The fixed-length ℓ-blocks are replaced by variable-length blocks defined using the "longest match" idea. More formally, we define

$$L_{N_0} = \max\{k : X_1^k = X_{-i}^{k-i-1} \text{ for some } 0 \leq i \leq N_0\}.$$

The blocklength L_{N_0} is the longest prefix of the incoming data that matches a contiguous substring in the training set. In this context, the sequence $X_1^{L_{N_0}}$ is called a *phrase*, and L_{N_0} is the *phrase length*. As before, the encoding of each phrase

is the binary representation of the location of the match, plus additional bits to encode L_{N_0} as a binary string. That is, if $L(X_1^\ell) = L(X_1^\ell | X_{-N_0+1}^0)$ is the length of the binary encoding of X_1^ℓ with $\ell = L_{N_0}$, then

$$L(X_1^\ell) \approx \log N_0 + O(\log\log N_0).$$

In another version of the LZ algorithm, LZ-78, the training sequence itself is parsed into *unique* phrases. This eliminates the need to encode the phrase lengths, although the incoming data is parsed into phrases that are shorter than in LZ-77. The coding in either version is optimal as N_0 tends to infinity, with an encoding delay that is also variable (i.e., the encoding cannot proceed until at least $L_{N_0} + 1$ letters are observed), but is on average $O(\log N_0)$.

Perhaps the most significant advantage of the LZ algorithm over the recurrence-time algorithm that is described above is that there are no choices for the encoder since the encoding delay is entirely data-driven. The fixed-length blocks are replaced by variable-length blocks which are "just right" automatically: Successive variable-length phrases are all approximately equiprobable with common probability $\frac{1}{N_0}$. Furthermore, the approach is also very practical since no explicit estimate of the probability needs to be computed. There is a small price: The phrase length needs to be encoded, although a clever encoding (see [16]) can make even these extra bits negligible.

A Match Length Coding Theorem: Let L_{N_0} be the longest match of the incoming sequence X_1^∞ into the past N_0 observations $X_{-N_0+1}^0$. For N_0 sufficiently large

expected compression ratio

$$= \frac{EL(X_1^\ell)}{EL_{N_0}} = H + \frac{H\log\log N_0}{\log N_0} + o\left(\frac{\log\log N_0}{\log N_0}\right). \quad (17)$$

Proof: For N_0 sufficiently large it follows from (3) that each phrase is approximately $\frac{\log N_0}{H}$ letters long. The encoding of each phrase requires $\log N_0$ bits to encode the location of the match in the training sequence and an additional $\log L_{N_0} + o(\log\log L_{N_0})$ bits to encode the phrase length. If we form the compression ratio as indicated, we have the result.

We remark that we have not formally proven the convergence of the LZ-77 algorithm (any variant). This would require a convergence theorem that holds jointly for all phrases. This is harder to prove (although intuitively true) since consecutive phrases are not independent even if the source itself is memoryless. See [6], [14], [24], [30], and [34] for complete proofs and useful results.

In summary, we have seen how the recurrence time is closely related to Shannon's self-information and Shannon's entropy. We now know how to construct practical universal coding algorithms without *a priori* information about the source probability law. We also have a new interpretation of the Shannon self-information: "the logarithm of the recurrence time."

5

*Nonasymptotic Universal Data Compression
with a Training Sequence*

Indeed, the Lempel-Ziv algorithm is optimal in the limit as the length of the training sequence tends to infinity. What is not at all clear, however, is if, in cases where the memory which is constrained to some "reasonable" finite value N_0 and a delay that is $O(\log N_0)$, one cannot achieve better compression.

In general, a sliding-window data compression algorithm with a training sequence of N_0 letters, encodes substrings (phrases) of $\cdots X_{-2}, X_{-1}, X_0, X_1 \cdots X_i \cdots$ into binary strings. Let $\{s = i\}$ denote the event that a phrase has ended at X_{i-1} and thus X_i is the first letter of the next phrase. Conditional on $\{s = i\}$, let the training data be a sequence $Y_{-N_0+i}^{i-1}$ (of length N_0 letters). In most applications, the sequence $Y_{-N_0+i}^{i-1}$ is $X_{-N_0+i}^{i-1}$ ("sliding-window" case). On the other hand, by introducing $Y_{-N_0+i}^{i-1}$ we may consider other cases. The training set for fixed-database algorithms is always a fixed vector $Y_{-N_0+1}^{0}$, that may or may not be the first N_0 observations of X. We will, however, insist that the distribution of $Y_{-N_0+i}^{i-1}$ be the same as $X_{-N_0+i}^{i-1}$.

A *code* consists of a collection of words

$$C_i = C(Y_{-N_0+i}^{i-1}, s = i) = \{X_1^j; 1 \le j \le \tau\}$$

that satisfy the property that no word is a prefix of any other word, and any sequence $X_1^k;; k \ge \tau$ has a word in C_i as its prefix. Here τ is the maximum allowable delay (i.e., the maximal length of a codeword in any of the codebooks C_s). Since we have assumed stationarity we may restrict our attention to the case $\{s = 1\}$. Each codeword X_1^j in C_1 is mapped into a distinct binary vector of length $L(X_1^j | Y_{-N_0+1}^0; s = 1)$ ("length function"), where

$$\sum_{X_1^j \in C_1} 2^{-L(X_1^j | Y_{-N_0+1}^0; s=1)} \le 1.$$

We now introduce the random variable K defined to be the largest integer k such that X_{-k}^1 is a substring of $Y_{-N_0+1}^0$. If no such k is found, K is defined to be zero. Thus K is the length of the longest match moving backwards into the past N_0 observations. We point out that the random variable K has the same distribution as the LZ-77 phrase lengths. Consider the "constrained conditional entropy" defined to be

$$H(X_1 \mid X_{-K}^0) = -E[\log P(X_1 \mid X_{-K}^0)].$$

It follows from (3) that $K = O(\log N_0)$ which implies that $H(X_1 | X_{-K}^0)$ converges to H as N_0 tends to infinity.

Our main results, presented below, connect the optimal performance of universal compression algorithms (as measured by either definition of the expected compression ratio) to the constrained conditional entropy.

Claims:

a) Let $C_v(N_0)$ be the expected compression ratio for any universal coding algorithm, with a training sequence of length N_0 and a variable length (V-V) delay $\tau = O(\log N_0)$. There exists a *fixed* blocklength universal algorithm (F-V) with a training-sequence of length about N_0, a blocklength ℓ, and an expected compression ratio C_f that satisfies

$$|C_f(N_0) - C_v(N_0)| < O\left(\frac{\log \log N_0}{\ell}\right).$$

b) At least for some ergodic sources, the expected compression ratio $C(N_0)$ that may be achieved by *any* sliding-window universal coding algorithm with a window of length N_0 and a delay of no more than $\tau = O(\log N_0)$, satisfies the following lower bound:

$$C(N_0) > H(X_1 \mid X_{-K}^0) - O\left(\frac{\log \log N_0}{\ell}\right) > H.$$

for $O(\log \log N_0) \le \ell < O(\log N_0)$

c) Consider the LZ family of universal data-compression algorithms. These are all compression algorithms that are "dictionary-type" algorithms in the sense that they encode incoming strings by referring to entries in a "dictionary" of phrases from a training sequence of length N_0.

If the training-data $Y_{-N_0+1}^0$ is independent of the incoming data and the source is stationary and ergodic, then the expected per-letter compression ratio $C(N_0)$ satisfies the following lower bound:

$$C(N_0) > H(X_1 \mid X_{-K}^0) - O\left(\frac{\log \log N_0}{\ell}\right)$$

for any $\ell \le \log N_0$. The above lower bound holds also for the LZ sliding-window algorithm [6] for sources with "vanishing memory" (e.g., Markov sources) [17].

d) The Hershkovitz–Ziv (HZ) sliding-window context algorithm [7] is essentially "optimal" in the sense of Claim b) above and achieves an expected compression ratio $C_{HZ}(N_0)$ upper-bounded by

$$C_{HZ}(N_0) < H(X_1 \mid X_{-K+\ell-1}^0) + O\left(\frac{\log \log N_0}{\ell}\right).$$

for $O(\log \log N_0) \le \ell < O(\log N_0)$.
This holds for *any* ergodic source.

We leave the proof of claims a) and c) to the Appendix. The proofs of claims b) and d) follow from claim a) and [7].

Discussion: Claims a)–d) are best understood against the background of what is known already about the LZ algorithms. As indicated earlier, there are two standard implementations of the algorithm: the LZ-77 and the LZ-78. Brushing aside minor differences in implementation, it is known that the LZ-77 algorithm (with a training sequence of length n) achieves a compression ratio equal to $H + \frac{H \log \log n}{\log n}$ when applied to sources with vanishing memory (see [14]). The LZ-78 is slightly better (at least asymptotically) since it is known (see [18]) that it achieves a compression ratio equal to $H + O\left(\frac{1}{\log n}\right)$ when applied to memoryless sources. It is also known to be no worse than $H + O\left(\frac{1}{\log n}\right)$ (see [20]) for Markov sources. In [16] it was demonstrated that the LZ-77 algorithm can achieve the efficiency of the LZ-78 algorithm but only if modified. As informative as these results may be, they are nevertheless all asymptotic in character. They indicate that

6

eventually the compression ratio will be within a specified distance from the entropy. In contrast, claims a)–d) establish a nonasymptotic standard of optimal efficiency. Let us examine each claim in turn:

In a) we learn that all universal-coding algorithms that parse incoming data into variable-length phrases can be adapted to parse using fixed phrases of length ℓ. We prove the claim by construction leaving the proof for the Appendix. Of course, it should be pointed out that this conversion involves a penalty, but it is only $O\left(\frac{\log\log N_0}{\ell}\right)$. Claim a) serves mainly as a tool for proving claims b)–d). It is interesting in its own right, however. We point out that it follows from claim a) that both definitions of the expected compression ratio (as defined earlier) yield the same value.

Claim b) establishes a lower bound on the achievable compression for at least some stationary ergodic sources. Furthermore, in contrast to the lower bounds of [14], [18], and [20] this lower bound is nonasymptotic in character. Since for any size training set the compression will be near the constrained conditional entropy to within terms that are $O\left(\frac{\log\log N_0}{\log N_0}\right)$. We know that the constrained conditional entropy converges to the true entropy eventually, but possibly very slowly. Thus we get a performance bound even for training sequences of moderate size. Since the lower bound is above the entropy, the difference between the constrained conditional entropy and the actual entropy is a measure of the difference between what is realizable with a finite training set and that which is theoretically achievable with an infinite training set (which is equivalent to a perfect knowledge of the source statistics).

Claim c) establishes the lower bound for a specific class of widely used algorithms. It should be pointed out that if more is known about the source, for example, if the source is known to be a Markov source, one can get better lower bounds than that of c) ([14], [18], [29]).

Finally, claim d) establishes that the HZ context algorithm is optimal in the sense of claim b).

A final point: the constrained conditional entropy is a natural alternative to the classical Shannon conditional entropy, specifically when universal coding is on the agenda.

III. UNIVERSAL PREDICTION AND CLASSIFICATION WITH MEMORY CONSTRAINTS

Consider the following situation: A device called a "classifier" observes a probability law P_ℓ on ℓ-vectors $z \in \boldsymbol{A}^\ell$. Its task is to observe data X_1^n, from a second probability law Q_ℓ and decide whether $P_\ell = Q_\ell$ or else P_ℓ and Q_ℓ are sufficiently different according to some appropriate criterion. Specifically, the classifier must produce a function $f_c(X_1^n, P_\ell)$ which with high probability equals 0 when $P_\ell = Q_\ell$ and 1 when $D_\ell(P_\ell \| Q_\ell) \geq \Delta$, where

$$D_\ell(P_\ell \| Q_\ell) = \sum_{z \in \boldsymbol{A}^\ell} P_\ell(z) \log \frac{P_\ell(z)}{Q_\ell(z)}$$

and Δ is a fixed parameter. The divergence $D_\ell(P_\ell \| Q_\ell)$ is a positive measure of "differentness" which equals 0 only if $P_\ell = Q_\ell$. We will require nothing of the classifier if the divergence is greater than 0 but less than Δ (i.e., close enough).

Suppose that the classifier f_c has sufficient memory resources to store the statistics of the entire probability law P_ℓ. We now introduce the pattern-matching technique to provide us with a suitable estimate of Q_ℓ which we then "plug in" to the divergence formula. To this end, for any pattern $z \in \boldsymbol{A}^\ell$ let $\hat{N}(z, X_1^n)$ be the smallest integer such $N \in [1, N - \ell + 1]$ such that a copy of z is equal to $X_N^{N+\ell+1}$. If z never occurs in X_1^n then let $\hat{N}(z, X_1^n) = n + 1$. For n sufficiently large, $\hat{N}(z, X_1^n)$ is the *waiting time* until pattern z occurs in string X_1^n. For most z (those without repetitive substructure), the waiting time is nearly the recurrence time which implies that the probability of z can be estimated using

$$\hat{Q}_\ell(z) = \frac{1}{\hat{N}_\ell(z, X_1^n)}.$$

In [17] it is shown that for a finite-memory source the classification task can be completed successfully provided n is at least $2^{\ell H + o(\ell)}$, where H is the entropy of Q_ℓ. More formally, for sufficiently large ℓ and $n = 2^{(H+\epsilon)\ell}$ it can be shown that $\hat{N}(z, X_1^n) \leq n$ with high probability and that

$$\Pr\left\{ \frac{1}{\ell} \left| \log \hat{N}(z, X_1^n) - \log \frac{1}{Q_\ell(z)} \right| < \epsilon \right\} \approx 1. \qquad (18)$$

It therefore follows (informally) from (18) that

$$\hat{D}_\ell(P_\ell \| Q_\ell) = \sum_{z \in \boldsymbol{A}^\ell} P_\ell(z) \log \frac{P_\ell(z)}{\hat{Q}_\ell(z)} \approx D(P_\ell \| Q_\ell).$$

The classifier then sets $f_c(X_1^n, P_\ell) = 1$ or to 0 accordingly as $\hat{D}$ exceeds a threshold (which depends on Δ). It turns out that this technique works, but only with a slight modification. Complete details are given in [17].

The case where two unknown Markov processes, each represented solely by a sequence which is a realization of the source, is discussed in [37]. There, an efficient, asymptotically optimal estimate of the divergence between the two sources is introduced. This estimator is based on pattern-matching parsing of one sequence relative to the other.

Now consider a different situation. Suppose the training data is a prefix of the incoming ℓ letters, and Q_ℓ is some empirical measure obtained from observations X_{-n+1}^0 generated from probability law P. This is the natural setup for predicting X_1^ℓ given X_{-n+1}^0.

It is reasonable to suppose that our best efforts at predicting an incoming ℓ-vector X_1^ℓ is limited by our ability to empirically estimate $P(X_1^\ell | X_{-n+1}^0)$. Assume, for example, that the closeness between the empirical measure and the true measure is expressed by the requirement that the divergence between the true probability $P(X_1^\ell | X_{-n+1}^0)$ and its empirical estimate $Q(X_1^\ell | X_{-n+1}^0)$ be small. Specifically, we say that Q and P are within ε if

$$D_{X_{-n+1}^0}(P \| Q) = \frac{1}{\ell} E \log \frac{P\left(X_1^\ell \mid X_{-n+1}^0\right)}{Q\left(X_1^\ell \mid X_{-n+1}^0\right)} \leq \varepsilon.$$

Intuitively, one may accept the idea that efficient universal compression algorithms efficiently squeeze out of the past history all the essential available statistics about the true probability law that governs the source. Hence, they should lead to empirical estimate Q which is "close" to P.

The next result shows that no empirical estimate Q can be too good for all stationary ergodic sources, unless the training data is long enough so as to yield efficient universal data compression (i.e., achieving a compression ratio close to the entropy of the source).

Converse Claim: At least for some stationary ergodic sources

$$D_{X_{-n+1}^0}(P \parallel Q) \geq H\big(X_1 \mid X_{-K(X_{-n}^1)}^0\big)$$
$$- H\big(X_1 \mid X_{-n+1}^0\big) - 0\left(\frac{\log \log n}{\log n}\right).$$

This follows from the fact that $-\log Q(X_1^\ell | X_{-n+1}^0)$ is a proper length-function. We can then use this length-function as the basis for a Shannon code that will achieve an expected compression equal to

$$H(X_1 | X_{-n+1}^0) + D_{X_{-n+1}^0}(P \parallel Q).$$

From claim b) of the preceding section (replacing N_0 by n) this expected compression must be lower-bounded by

$$H(X_1 | X_{-K(X_{-n}^1)}^0) - 0\left(\frac{\log \log n}{\log n}\right).$$

This proves the claim.

Indeed, for large enough n

$$H(X_1 | X_{-n+1}^0) \approx H \approx H(X_1 | X_{-K}^0)$$

for some K (the "memory" of the source). Hence, unless n is large enough so as to make, with high probability, $K(X_{-n}^1) \geq K$, the universal prediction error (as measured by $D_{X_{-n+1}^0}(P \parallel Q)$) cannot vanish.

On the other hand, we can also use the HZ data-compression scheme to construct an empirical measure that works well for values of n which are just "right," namely, for which

$$H(X_1 | X_{-n+1}^0) \approx H \approx H(X_1 | X_{-K}^0).$$

Claim: Let

$$Q\big(X_1^\ell \mid X_{-n+1}^0\big) = \frac{2^{-L_{\mathrm{HZ}}(X_1^\ell | X_{-n+1}^0)}}{\sum 2^{-L_{\mathrm{HZ}}(X_1^\ell | X_{-n+1}^0)}}$$

where $L_{\mathrm{HZ}}(X_1^\ell | X_{-n+1}^0)$ is the length function of the HZ universal encoder. Then

$$D_{X_{-n+1}^0}(P \parallel Q) \leq H\big(X_1 \mid X_{-K(X_{-n}^1)+\ell}^0\big)$$
$$- H\big(X_1 \mid X_{-n+1}^0\big) + 0\left(\frac{\log \log n}{\ell}\right)$$

for $O(\log \log n) \leq \ell \leq O(\log n)$.

Thus the empirical measure generated from the HZ length functions is close to the true measure P once n satisfies

$$H(X_1 | X_{-K(X_{-n}^1)}^0) \approx H(X_1 | X_{-n+1}^0).$$

IV. ON THE ROLE OF PATTERN MATCHING IN ENTROPY ESTIMATION

We have seen already how a pattern-matching-based approach to estimating a probability distribution has led to universal data compression algorithms and universal classifiers and predictors. In this section we demonstrate, both theoretically and with an example, how the entropy of a stochastic source can be estimated using pattern matching.

Shannon discovered that the entropy of a stochastic process has physical meanings: It measures a source's predictability as well as its uncertainty. It is also a computable measure of complexity. It even has a gambling interpretation [1]. The estimation process begins with a sequence of observations from a stochastic source. Since the entropy is a function of the probability law, estimation can always be accomplished by forming the empirical probability measure and calculating the actual entropy of the estimated probability distribution. As pointed out earlier, this "plug-in" approach is not always accurate: to be successful it usually requires model assumptions and large amounts of data. This estimate of the entropy is only as good as the estimate of the probability measure.

We have seen that compression can be accomplished using pattern matching in situations where a straightforward Shannon code is either impossible to construct or not likely to work. Thus one should expect that entropy estimation could also be accomplished by means of pattern matching in situations where the probability law cannot be accurately determined. This is indeed the case, as demonstrated below.

Let us return to the discussion of the relationship of the recurrence time of a random sequence looking backward into the past and the sequence's probability. We have seen that

$$\lim_{\ell \to \infty} \frac{\log N_\ell}{\ell} = -E\big[\log P\big(X_1^\ell\big)\big] = H, \text{ with probability 1.}$$

The recurrence-time theorem offers a reliable way to approximate the entropy which is widely applicable since it holds for all stationary, ergodic sources. On the other hand, it is quite impractical since the convergence is slow.

Stronger results are possible if P is assumed to satisfy an appropriate vanishing memory condition. For example, given any $t > 0$, it follows [31] that

$$\Pr\big\{N_\ell P\big(X_1^\ell\big) > t\big\} \approx \exp(-t). \qquad (19)$$

The result is surprisingly general: It holds for d-dimensional random fields with memory restrictions and for ℓ also random, but (almost) independent of the past. An example of such a random length is the stopping time

$$T_i(n) = \max\{k : -\log(P(X_i^{i+k}) > \log n\}.$$

Following the discussion in Section I we have (for vanishing memory sources) that $|L_i(n) - T_i(n)| = O(1)$, where $L_i(n)$ is the longest match of sequence $X_i, X_{i+1}, \cdots$ into the past n observations: X_{i-n}^{i-1}. The entropy reappears in the theory, since [14]

$$\lim_{n \to \infty} \frac{ET_i(n)}{\log n} = \frac{1}{H}.$$

8

TABLE I
Markov Model Entropy Estimates

Model Order	$\hat{H}(k)$	$\hat{H}_k^*(1)\ [E(k,1)]$	$\hat{H}_k^*(2)\ [E(k,2)]$	$\hat{H}_k^*(4)\ [E(k,4)]$
$k=1$	1.98	1.98 [0]	1.98 [0.1]	1.95 [2.1]
$k=2$	1.98	1.99 [0.15]	1.97 [0.15]	1.93 [1.7]
$k=4$	1.93	1.98 [0.64]	1.98 [0.92]	1.91 [0.285]

Thus it is true that for sources with an appropriate vanishing memory condition:

$$\frac{EL_i(n)}{\log n} = \frac{1}{H} + \frac{O(1)}{\log n}.$$

Similar results hold even for processes whose memory vanishes quite slowly [15].

We construct an entropy-estimation algorithm based on the mean convergence of $L_i(n)$ to $\frac{1}{H}$. Consider the following: Let k and n be chosen arbitrarily. Given observations X^k_{-n+1} from P with entropy H, let $L_i(n)$ be the match length function as defined above. Define

$$\hat{H}(n,k) = \frac{\log n}{\sum_{i=1}^{k} L_i(n)}.$$

Since the match lengths are calculated into a sliding window of length n, we label this the "sliding-window" entropy (SWE) estimator. In many respects, the estimate is basically an achievable compression ratio; that is, $\hat{H}$ measures the "compression" stripped of excess overhead which can be substantial [11]. Thus the advantages of pattern-matching-based coding also apply to pattern-matching-based entropy estimation. Specifically, pattern-matching-based entropy estimation is useful when one or more of the following is likely to be true.

- The model (or model class) is unspecified.
- The effect of model mis-specification is large.
- The data has more than trivial dependencies.
- The number of observations is small. (Equivalently, the source statistics change over time, even if the entropy does not.)

A single real example should make some of these issues more concrete. Since entropy is closely identified with information and complexity, there is consequently great interest in estimating the entropy of genetic sequences. The genetic code is billions of bases in length (a base is one of four letters: A, G, T or C), with a distinct time arrow and finite memory. Yet DNA is not stationary. The code is divided into distinct regions of known and unknown function. In this experiment we consider 25 460 bases [36] that comprise the coding regions (exons) of section DS02740 of the *Drosophila Melanogaster* (the fruit fly).[4] We choose to work only with the exons because the exon entropy is known to be closer to the maximum of 2. We point out that it is difficult to determine or even define stationarity in this setting. It is hoped that the sequence of concatenated exons will be more stationary than a contiguous

[4]The entire 83 527 base pair sequence is located in Genbank, accession number L49408.

stretch of DNA. We report that the marginal frequency of each base remains fairly constant over the entire sequence.

We denote our sequence by X_1^N, with $N = 25460$, and we compute the sliding-window entropy estimate for varying parameters. As a standard of comparison, we compute plug-in estimates of the entropy using different order Markov models. That is, for varying k we compute the empirical probabilities $\hat{P}_\ell(\cdot)$ for k-vectors $x \in \{A, G, C, T\}^k$. Then we let

$$\hat{H}(k) = \frac{1}{k} \sum_{x \in \{A,C,G,T\}^k} -\hat{P}_k(x) \log \hat{P}_k(x).$$

To investigate the robustness of this procedure we take a plug-in approach. We do not know the true empirical distribution $P_k(\cdot)$, for any k. We can, however, assume that $\hat{P}_k(\cdot)$ is the true distribution on k-tuples. With this assumption in place we can simulate from $\hat{P}_k(\cdot)$ to generate replicates of the original sequence, each of length 25460.

In our experiment, we generate 200 replicates for varying k: these we label $X^*_{i,k}$ for $i = 1, \cdots, 200$. We can compute, for any j the average of the jth-order entropy estimates over all 200 replicates. These we label $\hat{H}_k^*(j)$. By comparing $\hat{H}_k^*(j)$ to $\hat{H}(k)$ we can estimate bias and measure the effect of model mis-specification. To this end, we report the quantity

$$E(k,j) = \frac{\hat{H}_k^*(j) - \hat{H}(k)}{2 - \hat{H}(k)}$$

which corresponds to the relative error in redundancy incurred by specifying a jth-order model when the true model is kth-order.

The entropy estimates (see Table I) vary from 1.98 (first-order Markov) to 1.93 (fourth-order Markov). This is a three-fold increase in the redundancy . Observe that the relative error is small if model is specified correctly ($E(k,k)$ ranges from a minimum of 0 when $k = 1$ to a maximum of 0.285 for $k = 4$) Thus the plug-in approach is not too bad (especially for small k) if the model is accurately specified. On the other hand, the effect of model misspecification can be very large (as measured by $E(k,j)$ for $j \neq k$). The worst errors result from specification of a large model when in fact a small one is true. Significant errors are also observed when a small model is assumed when a larger one is in fact true.

In contrast to the uncertainty of the plug-in approach, the estimates based on pattern matching are universal and thus no model selection is required. Since the expected difference between $L_i(n)$ and $\frac{1}{H}$ tends to zero like $O\left(\frac{1}{\log n}\right)$ there is a considerable bias problem associated with the SWE for even reasonably large values of n. This problem is fixable. It is possible to estimate a model for the sequence and correct

TABLE II
Sliding-Window Entropy Estimates

Window Size	Mean Match Length	H	Bias-Corrected H
64	3.12	1.92	1.86
128	3.61	1.94	1.89
512	4.60	1.96	1.92
1024	5.07	1.97	1.94

for this bias again using the bootstrap (see [35]).[5] As before, we would generate replicates of X_1^N using a parametric approximation for the unknown "source" that generated the DNA sequence. The entropy of each replicate can then be computed using the SWE for varying window sizes. These values would then be subtracted from the known entropy of the replicate sequence, and then averaged over all replicates to estimate the bias of the SWE. Correcting for bias has the effect of restoring the natural entropy scaling (with a maximum of 2). We present in Table II the SWE estimates of the entropy, both bias-corrected and uncorrected, computed for varying choices in n (the window size). From Table II we notice that the size of the bias adjustments diminish as n increases. This follows from the theory which predicts a bias proportional to $\frac{1}{\log n}$. Observe also that the uncorrected entropy estimates increase in n, which is surprising since entropy estimates usually decrease as the window size increases (this is analogous to improvements in code performance as blocklength and delay increase). This is evidence that the substantial drop in entropy is due to local features in the genetic code. We confirm this by computing the quantities L_i equal to largest k such that a copy of the sequence x_i^{i+k-1} is contained *anywhere* in the sequence. The main difference between L_i and $L_i(n)$ is the latter only looks for matches into the past n observations but the former searches through the entire sequence, front and back. The resulting estimate was proposes by Grassberger [21]

$$\hat{H}_G = \frac{\log N}{\frac{1}{N}\sum_{i=1}^{N} L_i}$$

where N is the total number of observations. In our example $N = 25460$. For stationary sequences the Grassberger estimate behaves much like the SWE but only for large n (near N). In our example, the Grassberger estimate is 1.98. Since this estimate is so much higher than the estimates obtained with smaller windows we speculate that the statistics of higher order patterns are not consistent with an assumption of stationarity over the entire sequence (despite the approximate constancy of the marginal frequencies).

The lowest estimate (and thus the best) is 1.86 obtained from the SWE with a short window (likely necessary to account for slowly changing statistics) and then adjusted for bias. In real terms, this implies that sequence contains more than a tenth of a bit of redundancy per symbol. For the curious, a great deal more theory and application of this method can be found in [15] (as applied to the English language) and [13] (as applied to DNA).

[5] Bias correction using the bootstrap is not always possible. An accepted practice is to test the consistency of the bias-correction procedure with known models. This has been established for the sliding-window estimate of entropy.

V. CONCLUDING REMARKS

We have tried to motivate and explain applications of pattern matching to a variety of problems in information theory. Although it has been more than twenty years since the publication of [11] and ten years since [8] we are still surprised at how easily and thoroughly pattern matching is able to uncover information about a probability measure. In our paper, we chose to restrict our discussion of pattern matching to fundamental concerns and basic applications. Regrettably, we have omitted discussion of a great variety of substantial and important works. Indeed, the literature on the subject continues to grow in a variety of directions.

One area of great activity concerns the extension of pattern matching ideas to approximate string matching and "lossy" data compression. This work has led to a variety of noisy data compression algorithms based on LZ that are also characterized by small computational complexity. There are a number of publications that discuss the role pattern matching in lossy data compression [18], [22], [24]–[28], [37]. It seems, however, that low computational complexity is achievable only at the expense of yielding a nonoptimal distortion.

APPENDIX

Kac's lemma states that the average distance between occurrences of a fixed pattern is equal to the inverse of the probability of the pattern. Consider now the fixed pattern x_{-k+1}^ℓ. In any long realization the proportion of times the pattern x_1^ℓ occurs after x_{-k+1}^0 will be nearly $P(X_1^\ell = x_1^\ell | x_{-k+1}^0)$. Equivalently, we would expect

$$\frac{1}{P(X_1^\ell = x_1^\ell | x_{-k+1}^0)}$$

occurrences of x_{-k+1}^0 for every occurrence of x_1^ℓ.

Below we state the conditional version of Kac's lemma. In [7] this lemma is used to analyze the HZ context algorithm. On its own, it yields an efficient data compression scheme, although not necessarily as efficient as the "optimal" HZ algorithm.

Modified Kac's Lemma [7]: Let $N_{\ell+k}$ be the time of the first recurrence of the pattern X_{-k+1}^ℓ moving backward into the training sequence $X_{-N_0+1}^0$. If there is no recurrence then let $N_{k+\ell} = N_0$:

a)

$$E_{X_{-k+1}^\ell}\left\{\sum_{i=1}^{N_{\ell+k}} 1\left\{X_{-k+1-i}^{-i} = X_{-k+1}^0\right\}\right\}$$
$$\leq \frac{1}{P(X_1^\ell | X_{-k+1}^0)}. \quad (20)$$

(Equality is achieved for $N_0 \to \infty$.) We could then average over X_{-k+1}^ℓ to prove

b)

$$\frac{1}{\ell} E \log \sum_{i=1}^{N_{\ell+k}} 1\left\{X_{-k+1-i}^{-i} = X_{-k+1}^0\right\}$$
$$\leq H\left(X_1^\ell | X_{-k+1}^0\right).$$

The HZ Universal Coding Scheme: We shall now describe the HZ universal coding scheme which, by adaptively changing k, fully utilizes the training sequence in an appropriate way.

Consider blocks of length ℓ'. Let $H_0 \ll \log A$ and δ be some arbitrary positive numbers. Define $\ell = \frac{\ell'}{\delta}$ and $N_0 = \ell \, 2^{H_0 \ell}$. Furthermore, let

$$\hat{i} = \max_i \left\{ i : N_{\ell'+i}\left(X^{\ell'}_{-N_0+1}\right) < N_0 - i \right\} \quad (21)$$

(i.e., $X^{\ell'}_{-i+1}$ is the *longest* $X^{\ell'}_{-i+1}$ that re-occurs in $X^{\ell'-1}_{-N_0+1}$).
Let

$$K\left(X^{\ell'}_{-N_0+1}\right) = \begin{cases} \min\{\hat{i}; \ell - \ell'\} - 1, & \hat{i} \geq 1 \\ 0, & \text{otherwise.} \end{cases} \quad (22)$$

The block $X^{\ell'}_1$ is encoded into a binary string which consists of the binary expansion of $K(X^{\ell'}_{-N_0+1})$ (about $\log \ell$ bits), followed by the binary expansion of the pointer to the first occurrence of $X^{\ell'}_1$ in $X^{\ell'-1}_{-N_0+1}$ among all ℓ' vectors with a prefix that is equal to

$$X^{\ell'-l}_{K(X^{\ell'}_{-N_0+1})}.$$

(This takes about $\log N_{\ell'+\hat{i}}(X^{\ell'}_{-N_0+1}) + \log \log N_0$ bits.)

Proof of Claim a): Assume that one is given a coding procedure that parses a long block x^n_1 into variable-length phrases, using sliding-window or fixed-database training sequence, then apply the appropriate V-V code to each phrase. The goal of claim a) is to show that almost the same performance can be obtained by parsing into fixed-length ℓ phrases and using an F-V code on each ℓphrase, where the particular code used is allowed to depend on the past of the phrase.

Lemma 1: Let C be a complete and proper set of variable-length words and let $L(w)$ be the length function for the word w. For each j, each $1 \leq k \leq j$, and each x^K_1, there are prefix codes on $\boldsymbol{A}^j$ and on $\boldsymbol{A}^j_{k+1}$ with respective length functions $L_j(X^k_1)$ and $L_j(X^j_{k+1}|X^k_1)$ such that

$$L_j\left(X^k_1\right) + L_j\left(X^j_{k+1} \mid X^k_1\right) \leq L\left(X^j_1\right) + 2, \qquad X^j_1 \in \boldsymbol{A}^j.$$

Proof: Extend $L(w)$ to ALL words by defining $L(w) = \infty$ if w is not in C. Fix j and define the distribution

$$Q_j(w) = \frac{2^{-L(w)}}{\sum\limits_{z \in \boldsymbol{A}^j} 2^{-L(z)}}, \qquad w \in \boldsymbol{A}^j.$$

For each $1 \leq k \leq j$, let $Q_{j,k}(\cdot)$ be the projection of Q_j onto $\boldsymbol{A}^k$. Also, for each X^k_1, let $Q_j(\cdot|X^k_1)$ be the *conditional* distribution defined by the following two formulas:

$$Q_{j,k}\left(X^k_1\right) = \sum_{X^j_{k+1}} Q_j\left(X^j_1\right), \qquad X^j_1 \in \boldsymbol{A}^k$$

$$Q_j\left(X^j_{k+1} \mid X^k_1\right) = \frac{Q_j(X^j_1)}{\sum\limits_{Z^j_1 : Z^k_1 = X^k_1} Q_j(Z^j_1)}, \qquad X^j_{k+1} \in \boldsymbol{A}^j_{k+1}.$$

Let $L_j(X^k_1)$ be the length function for the Shannon code defined by $Q_{j,k}(\cdot)$ and let $L_j(X^j_{k+1}|X^k_1)$ be the length function for the Shannon code defined by $Q_j(\cdot|X^k_1)$. The factorization

$$Q_j\left(X^j_1\right) = Q_{j,k}\left(X^k_1\right) Q_j\left(X^j_{k+i} \mid X^k_1\right)$$

combined with the fact that, being a length function, $L(w)$ satisfies the Kraft inequality and therefore $-\log Q_j(w) \leq L(w)$, completes the proof of Lemma 1 above.

V-V to F-V Theorem: Suppose X^n_1 is coded by a V-V code with a training sequence of length N_0 and delay $\tau = O(\log N_0)$ into a binary sequence with length $L(X^n_1)$. Given $\ell \leq \tau = O(\log N_0)$, there is an F-V code with blocklength ℓ and training sequence of length N_0, that given the suffix $X^0_{-\ell+1}$ encodes X^n_1 into a binary sequence of length $L'(X^n_1)$ such that

$$L'\left(X^n_1\right) \leq L\left(X^n_1\right) + \frac{n}{\ell}O(\log \log N_0).$$

Proof: Change notation so that X^ℓ_1 is the next ℓ-block to be encoded and, for the V-V original parsing of the n-sequence, let $s(1) \leq 1 \leq e(1)$ be the left and right endpoints of the parsed phrase that includes X_1 and let $s(2) \leq \ell \leq e(2)$ be the left and right endpoints of the parsed phrase that includes X_ℓ. Assume that the encoder and decoder both know how the n-sequence was parsed by the V-V code, starting from any position $s(1)$.

Assume for the moment that the positions $s(1), e(1), s(2)$, and $e(2)$ are known to both the encoder and the decoder. The encoder first transmits these values to the decoder. This requires $4 \log \tau$ bits. The encoder next transmits the block $X^{e(1)}_1$ using the Shannon code defined by the conditional distribution $Q_{e(1)-s(1)+1}(\cdot|X^0_{S(1)})$, as defined in Lemma 1. The block $X^{s(2)-1}_{e(1)+1}$ is then transmitted using the V-V code, and finally, the block $X^\ell_{s(2)}$ is transmitted using the Shannon code defined by the projection of the distribution $Q_{e(2)-s(2)+1}(\cdot)$ onto its first $\ell - s(2) + 1$ coordinates, as defined in Lemma 1. The decoder, knowing the values of $s(1), e(1), s(2)$, and $e(2)$, as well as the V-V code and hence the codes of Lemma 1, can correctly decode.

However, the encoder need not know the values $s(1), e(1), s(2)$, and $e(2)$. The encoder can try all possible values $s(1), e(1), s(2)$, and $e(2)$ and determines the values that produce the shortest code, transmits these values, and uses the corresponding code. This can only improve code performance. This, together with Lemma 1 complete the proof of the V-V to F-V Theorem and claim a).

Proof of Claim c): We begin with the independent fixed database. Thus the training sequence is the vector of observations $Y^0_{-N_0+1}$ and the incoming data is X. We remind the reader that Y has the same distribution as X. We begin the proof by conditioning on the random event $\{S(1) = -t\}$ for any $t < \tau$. Let ℓ be the length of the fixed blocklength algorithm whose expected compression is nearly the expected

11

compression of the original variable length algorithm, by claim a). It follows that

$$\frac{1}{\ell}EL\big(X_1^\ell \,\big|\, Y_{N_0+1}^0, X_{S(1)}^0; S(1)\big)$$

$$\geq \frac{1}{\ell}H\big(X_1^\ell \,\big|\, X_{S(1)}^0, Y_{-N_0+1}^0\big) - \frac{1}{\ell}H(S(1)|X_{S(1)}^0, Y_{-N_0+1}^0)$$

$$\geq \frac{1}{\ell}H\big(X_1^\ell \,\big|\, X_{-K}^0\big) - \frac{\log \tau}{\ell}.$$

For the sake of clarity, the unnormalized form of the entropy function was used here. The last inequality follows specifically from the independence of the database $Y_{-N_0+1}^0$ and the incoming data X. Now $-S(1) \leq K$ by definition. Hence

$$\frac{1}{\ell}EL\big(X_1^\ell \,\big|\, Y_{-N_0+1}^0, X_{S(1)}^0\big) \geq \frac{1}{\ell}H\big(X_1^\ell \,\big|\, X_{-K}^0\big) - \frac{\log \tau}{\ell}.$$

This completes the proof of (c) for the independent fixed database.

The proof for the LZ sliding-windoe case [6] follows along the same lines.

ACKNOWLEDGMENT

The authors wish to thank Neri Merhav, Paul Shields, Wojciech Szpankowsky, Jack Wolf, and Frans Willems for valuable remarks. The V-V to F-V Theorem in the Appendix was greatly revised and simplified by Paul Shields.

REFERENCES

[1] M. C. Thomas and J. A. Thomas, *Elements of Information Theory.* New York: Wiley, 1991.

[2] B. M. Fitingof, "The compression of discrete information," *Probl. Inform. Transm.*, vol. 3, pp. 28–36, 1967.

[3] F. M. J. Willems, Y. M. Shtarkov, and T. J. Tjalkens, "The context-tree weighting method: Basic properties," *IEEE Trans. Inform. Theory*, vol. 41, pp. 653–664, May 1995.

[4] M. Kac, "On the notion of recurrence in discrete stochastic processes," *Bull. Amer. Math. Soc.*, vol. 53, pp. 1002–1010, Oct. 1947.

[5] F. J. Willems, "Universal compression and repetition times," *IEEE Trans. Inform. Theory*, vol. 35, pp. 54–58, Jan. 1989.

[6] A. D. Wyner and J. Ziv, "The sliding-window Lempel–Ziv algorithm is asymptotically optimal" (Invited Paper), *Proc. IEEE*, vol. 82, pp. 872–877, June 1994.

[7] Y. Hershkovits and J. Ziv, "On sliding-window universal data compression with limited memory," *IEEE Trans. Inform. Theory*, vol. 44, pp. 66–78, Jan. 1998.

[8] A. D. Wyner and J. Ziv, "Some asymptotic properties of the entropy of a stationary ergodic data source with applications to data compression," *IEEE Trans. Inform. Theory*, vol. 35, pp. 1250–1258, Nov. 1989.

[9] D. Ornstein and B. Weiss, "Entropy and data compression schemes," *IEEE Trans. Inform. Theory*, vol. 39, pp. 78–83, Jan. 1993.

[10] A. D. Wyner, "1994 Shannon lecture: Typical sequences an all that: Entropy, pattern matching and data compression," *IEEE Inform. Theory Soc. Newslett.*, vol. 45, pp. 8–14, June 1995.

[11] J. Ziv and A. Lempel, "A universal algorithm for sequential date-compression," *IEEE Trans. Inform. Theory*, vol. IT–23, pp. 337–343, May 1977.

[12] J. Rissanen, "Universal coding, information, prediction, and estimation," *IEEE Trans. Inform. Theory*, vol. IT–30, pp. 629–636, July 1984.

[13] M. Farach, M. Noordewier, S. Savari, L. Shepp, A. Wyner, and J. Ziv, "On the entropy of DNA: Algorithms and measurements based on memory and rapid convergence," presented at the Symposium on Discrete Algorithms (SODA), 1995.

[14] A. J. Wyner, "The redundancy and distribution of the phrase lengths for the fixed-database vLempel-Ziv algorithm," *IEEE Trans. Inform. Theory*, vol. 43, pp. 1452–1464, Sept. 1997.

[15] I. Kontoyiannis, P. H. Algoet, Y. M. Suhov, and A. J. Wyner, "Nonparametric entropy estimates for stationary processes and random fields with applications to English text," *IEEE Trans. Inform. Theory*, vol. 44, pp. 1319–1327, May 1998.

[16] A. D. Wyner and A. J. Wyner, "Improved redundancy of a version of the Lempel-Ziv algorithm," *IEEE Trans. Inform. Theory*, vol. 41, pp. 723–731, May 1995.

[17] A. D. Wyner and J. Ziv, "Classification with finite memory," *IEEE Trans. Inform. Theory*, vol. 42, pp. 337–347, Mar. 1996.

[18] G. Louchard and W. Szpankowski, "On the average redundancy rate of the Lempel-Ziv code," *IEEE Trans. Inform. Theory*, vol. 43, pp. 1–7, Jan. 1997.

[19] P. C. Shields, *The Ergodic Theory of Discrete Sample Paths.* American Math. Soc., 1996.

[20] A. Savari, "Redundancy of the Lempel-Ziv incremental parsing rule," *IEEE Trans. Inform. Theory*, vol. 43, pp. 9–21, Jan. 1997.

[21] P. Grassberger, "Estimating the information content of symbol sequences and efficient codes," *IEEE Trans. Inform. Theory*, vol. 35, pp. 669–675, May 1989.

[22] P. C. Shields, "Approximate-match waiting times for the substitution/deletion metric," preprint, submitted to ISIT-98.

[23] T. Łuczak and W. Szpankowski, "A lossy data compression based on string matching: Preliminary analysis and suboptimal algorithms," preprint 1997.

[24] E. H. Yang and J. C. Kieffer, "On the performance of data compression algorithms based upon string matching," *IEEE Trans. Inform. Theory*, vol. 44, pp. 47–65, Jan. 1998.

[25] Y. Steinberg and M. Gutman, "An algorithm for source coding based upon string matching," *IEEE Trans. Inform. Theory*, vol. 39, pp. 877–886, May 1993.

[26] I. Kontoyiannis, "A practical lossy version of the Lempel-Ziv algorithm that is asymptotically optimal—Part I: Memoryless sources," preprint 1998.

[27] H. Morita and K. Kobayashi, "An extension of LZW coding algorithm to source coding subject to a fidelity criterion," in *4th Joint Swedish–Soviet Int. Workshop on Information Theory* (Gotland, Sweden, 1989), pp. 105–109.

[28] E.-h. Yang and J. C. Kieffer, "Simple universal lossy data compression schemes derived from the Lempel-Ziv algorithm," *IEEE Trans. Inform. Theory*, vol. 42, pp. 239–245, Jan. 1996.

[29] _____, "On the redundancy of the Lempel-Ziv Algorithm for ψ-mixing sources," *IEEE Trans. Inform. Theory*, vol. 43, pp. 1101–1111, July 1997.

[30] P. Jaquet and W. Szpankowski, "Autocorrelation on words and its applications. Analysis of suffix trees by string-ruler approach," *J. Comb. Theory, Ser. A*, vol. 66, pp. 237–269, 1994.

[31] A. J. Wyner, "More on recurrence and waiting times," Tech. Rep. 486, Dept. Statist., Univ. Calif., Berkeley, to be published in *Ann. Appl. Prob.*, Sept. 1996.

[32] L. J. Guibas and A. M. Odlysko, " String overlaps, pattern matching, and non-transitive games," *Comb. Theory Applic.*, vol. 30, pp. 183–208, 1981.

[33] S.-Y. R. Li, "A martingale approach to the study of occurrence of sequence patterns in repeated experiments," *Ann. Prob.*, vol. 8, pp. 1171–1176, 1980.

[34] E. Plotnick, M. J. Weinberger, and J. Ziv, "Upper bounds on the probability of sequences emitted by finite-state sources and on the redundancy of the Lempel-Ziv algorithm," *IEEE Trans. Inform. Theory*, vol. 38, pp. 66–72, Jan. 1992.

[35] B. Efron and R. Tibshirani, *An Introduction to the Bootstrap.* London, U.K.: Chapman and Hall, 1993.

[36] G. Rubin, "Berkeley Drosophila Genome Project," private communication, May 1997.

[37] N. Merhav and J. Ziv, "A measure of relative entropy between individual sequences with application to universal classification," *IEEE Trans. Inform. Theory*, vol. 39, pp. 1270–1279, July 1993.

Fifty Years of Shannon Theory

Sergio Verdú, *Fellow, IEEE*

Abstract—A brief chronicle is given of the historical development of the central problems in the theory of fundamental limits of data compression and reliable communication.

Index Terms— Channel capacity, data compression, entropy, history of Information Theory, reliable communication, source coding.

CLAUDE Shannon's "A mathematical theory of communication" [1] published in July and October of 1948 is the Magna Carta of the information age. Shannon's discovery of the fundamental laws of data compression and transmission marks the birth of Information Theory. A unifying theory with profound intersections with Probability, Statistics, Computer Science, and other fields, Information Theory continues to set the stage for the development of communications, data storage and processing, and other information technologies.

This overview paper gives a brief tour of some of the main achievements in Information Theory. It confines itself to those disciplines directly spawned from [1]—now commonly referred to as Shannon theory.

Section I frames the revolutionary nature of "A mathematical theory of communication," in the context of the rudimentary understanding of the central problems of communication theory available at the time of its publication.

Section II is devoted to lossless data compression: the amount of information present in a source and the algorithms developed to achieve the optimal compression efficiency predicted by the theory.

Section III considers channel capacity: the rate at which reliable information can be transmitted through a noisy channel.

Section IV gives an overview of lossy data compression: the fundamental tradeoff of information rate and reproduction fidelity.

The paper concludes with a list of selected points of tangency of Information Theory with other fields.

I. BEFORE 1948

The major communication systems existing in 1948 were

- Telegraph (Morse, 1830's);
- Telephone (Bell, 1876);
- Wireless Telegraph (Marconi, 1887);
- AM Radio (early 1900's);
- Single-Sideband Modulation (Carson, 1922);
- Television (1925–1927);
- Teletype (1931);

Manuscript received June 9, 1998.
The author is with the Department of Electrical Engineering, Princeton University, Princeton, NJ 08544 USA.
Publisher Item Identifier S 0018-9448(98)06315-9.

- Frequency Modulation (Armstrong, 1936);
- Pulse-Code Modulation (PCM) (Reeves, 1937–1939);
- Vocoder (Dudley, 1939);
- Spread Spectrum (1940's).

In those systems we find some of the ingredients that would be key to the inception of information theory: a) the Morse code gave an efficient way to encode information taking into account the frequency of the symbols to be encoded; b) systems such as FM, PCM, and spread spectrum illustrated that transmitted bandwidth is just another degree of freedom available to the engineer in the quest for more reliable communication; c) PCM was the first digital communication system used to transmit analog continuous-time signals; d) at the expense of reduced fidelity, the bandwidth used by the Vocoder [2] was less than the message bandwidth.

In 1924, H. Nyquist [3] argued that the transmission rate is proportional to the logarithm of the number of signal levels in a unit duration. Furthermore, he posed the question of how much improvement in telegraphy transmission rate could be achieved by replacing the Morse code by an "optimum" code.

K. Küpfmüller [4] (1924), H. Nyquist [5] (1928), and V. Kotel'nikov [6] (1933) studied the maximum telegraph signaling speed sustainable by bandlimited linear systems. Unbeknownst to those authors, E. Whittaker [7] (1915) and J. Whittaker [8] (1929) had found how to interpolate losslessly the sampled values of bandlimited functions. D. Gabor [9] (1946) realized the importance of the duration–bandwidth product and proposed a time–frequency uncertainty principle.

R. Hartley's 1928 paper [10] uses terms such as "rate of communication," "intersymbol interference," and "capacity of a system to transmit information." He summarizes his main accomplishment as

> the point of view developed is useful in that it provides a ready means of checking whether or not claims made for the transmission possibilities of a complicated system lie within the range of physical possibility.

Intersymbol interference and basic observations with RLC circuits lead Hartley to conclude that the capacity is proportional to the bandwidth of the channel. But before being able to speak of "capacity," Hartley recognizes the need to introduce a "quantitative measure of information." He uses the letter H to denote the amount of information associated with n selections and states that

$$H = n \log s$$

where s is the number of symbols available in each selection. The principle that "information" is the outcome of a selection among a finite number of possibilities is firmly established in [10].

The aforementioned papers by Nyquist and Hartley had not quantified the effects of noise, nor had they modeled sources of information probabilistically. Much of the credit for importing random processes into the toolbox of the 1940's communications engineer is due to N. Wiener [11][1] and to S. Rice [12].

Probabilistic modeling of information sources has in fact a very long history as a result of its usefulness in cryptography. As early as 1380 and 1658, tables of frequencies of letters and pairs of letters, respectively, had been compiled for the purpose of decrypting secret messages [13].[2] At the conclusion of his WWII work on cryptography, Shannon prepared a classified report [14][3] where he included several of the notions (including entropy and the phrase "information theory") pioneered in [1] (cf. [16]). However, Shannon had started his work on information theory (and, in particular, on probabilistic modeling of information sources) well before his involvement with cryptography.[4] Having read Hartley's paper [10] in his undergraduate days, Shannon, as a twenty-two-year-old graduate student at MIT, came up with a ground-breaking abstraction of the communication process subject to a mean-square fidelity criterion [19]. After writing his landmark Master's thesis on the application of Boole's algebra to switching circuits [20] and his Ph.D. dissertation on population dynamics [21], Shannon returned to communication theory upon joining the Institute for Advanced Study at Princeton and, then, Bell Laboratories in 1941 [16].

By 1948 the need for a theory of communication encompassing the fundamental tradeoffs of transmission rate, reliability, bandwidth, and signal-to-noise ratio was recognized by various researchers. Several theories and principles were put forth in the space of a few months by A. Clavier [22], C. Earp [23], S. Goldman [24], J. Laplume [25], C. Shannon [1], W. Tuller [26], and N. Wiener [27]. One of those theories would prove to be everlasting.

II. LOSSLESS DATA COMPRESSION

A. The Birth of Data Compression

The viewpoint established by Hartley [10] and Wiener [11] is echoed by Shannon in the Introduction of [1]:

[The] semantic aspects of communication are irrelevant to the engineering problem. The significant aspect is that the actual message is one *selected from a set* of possible messages.

Shannon then makes the key observation that the source of information should be modeled as a random process:

---

[1] Originally a WWII classified report acknowledged in [1] to have influenced Shannon's thinking.

[2] Even higher order statistics had been envisioned. Jonathan Swift's *Gulliver's Travels* (1726) describes a machine by which "the most ignorant person may write in philosophy, poetry and politics." The machine selects words at random based on "the strictest computation of the general proportion between the numbers of particles, nouns and verbs."

[3] Later declassified and superseded by [1] and [15].

[4] According to interviews with Claude Shannon recorded in [16]–[18].

We can think of a discrete source as generating the message, symbol by symbol. It chooses successive symbols according to certain probabilities depending, in general, on preceding choices as well as the particular symbols in question. A physical system, or a mathematical model of a system which produces such a sequence of symbols governed by a set of probabilities is known as a stochastic process. Conversely, any stochastic process which produces a discrete sequence of symbols chosen from a finite set may be considered a discrete source.

Shannon recognizes that to exploit the redundancy of the source one should take into account not only the frequencies of its symbols but its memory. But before proceeding to tackle that problem, he considers a single random variable taking n values with probabilities $p_1, \cdots, p_n$ and defines its *entropy*:[5]

$$H = -\sum_{i=1}^{n} p_i \log p_i. \tag{1}$$

Shannon points out the similarity with Boltzmann's entropy in statistical mechanics [29] and gives an axiomatic rationale for this measure of information, as the only measure that is i) continuous in the probabilities, ii) increasing with n if the random variable is equiprobable, and iii) additive, in the sense that if the random value is the result of two choices, its entropy can be obtained by summing the entropy of the first choice and the entropy of the second choice given the first.

Much more important than the axiomatic justification of entropy are the fundamental theorems that it satisfies. Shannon goes on to consider memoryless sources, and proves the following result using the law of large numbers:

Shannon's Theorem 3 [1]: Given any $\epsilon > 0$ and $\delta > 0$, we can find N_0 such that the sequences of any length $N \geq N_0$ fall into two classes

1) A set whose total probability is less than ϵ.
2) The remainder, all of whose members have probabilities $[p]$ satisfying the inequality

$$\left| H - \frac{\log p^{-1}}{N} \right| < \delta. \tag{2}$$

Shannon refers to the second class as the "typical sequences." They are characterized by probabilities that decrease exponentially with blocklength, $p = a^{-N}$, with $a \approx 2^H$. Shannon's Theorem 3 states that the set of atypical sequences has vanishing probability. The relevance of this result to data compression is that for the purposes of coding we can treat the typical sequences as roughly equiprobable while disregarding the atypical sequences. The resulting code maps source strings of length N to strings of length slightly larger than HN. The decoder can recover the original source string with probability at least $1 - \epsilon$. Thus the rate of H encoded bits

---

[5] Full and sole credit is due to Shannon for the introduction of entropy in information theory. Wiener never worked with entropy; instead, he introduced, apparently at J. von Neumann's suggestion and independently of Shannon, the differential entropy [27] which he used in the context of Gaussian random variables. A distant relative of the differential entropy dating back to 1934 is Fisher's information [28], which gives a fundamental limit on the achievable mean-square error of parametric estimation.

per source symbol is *achievable* provided we are willing to tolerate a nonzero probability of failing to recover the original sequence. By increasing the blocklength, and thus the delay and complexity of encoding and decoding operations, we can make that probability as small as desired.

But, is that the best we can do? Shannon's Theorem 3 does not address that question, since it only suggests a suboptimal code. (The optimal code of rate R simply disregards all but the 2^{NR} most probable sequences of length N.) Shannon finds the answer in Theorem 4: as long as we require probability of error strictly less than 1, asymptotically, we cannot encode at rates below the entropy. This statement is commonly known as the strong *converse* source coding theorem. The converse (or weak converse) source coding theorem asserts that error probability cannot vanish if the compression rate is below the entropy.

The foregoing discussion was circumscribed to *fixed-length* codes (fixed-length source strings mapped to fixed-length encoded strings). Shannon also notices that by allowing encoded sequences of *variable* length, it is possible to actually achieve zero error probability without increasing the *average* encoding rate. For example, this can be accomplished by representing the typical sequences of length N with sequences of length roughly equal to HN, and leaving all the other sequences uncompressed—a prefix bit indicating whether the encoded sequence is typical. Many other possibilities arise in variable-length data compression. Shannon gives the example of a memoryless source whose symbol probabilities are powers of $1/2$. In this special case, it is easy to find a code that encodes the ith symbol with a string of $-\log p_i$ bits. Much less obvious is what to do with arbitrary distributions. Shannon describes an "arithmetic process," discovered contemporaneously and independently by R. Fano, that assigns to each symbol the appropriately truncated binary expansion of the cumulative distribution function evaluated at the symbol. The average rate of that scheme is not optimal but is only slightly above the entropy.

B. The Asymptotic Equipartition Property

For memoryless sources, Shannon's Theorem 3 is equivalent to the weak law of large numbers for independent and identically distributed random variables taking a finite number of positive values. Because of its relevance to data compression, it is natural to investigate whether Theorem 3 applies to sources with memory. This requires replacing the entropy of an individual random variable by the *entropy rate*, namely, the limit of the entropy of an N-block divided by N. Shannon [1] shows that the entropy rate of a stationary process is equal to the limiting conditional entropy of a single source symbol given the past symbols. Having made the case that the statistics of natural language can be approximated arbitrarily well by Markov chains of increasing order,[6] Shannon [1] notices that Theorem 3 (and, thus, the achievability part of the source coding theorem) applies to stationary Markov chain sources. In 1953, a step-by-step proof of the generalization of Shannon's

Theorem 3 to Markov chains was given by A. Khinchin in the first Russian article on information theory [31].

In 1953, B. McMillan [32] used the statistical-mechanics phrase "asymptotic equipartition property" (AEP) to describe the typicality property of Shannon's Theorem 3: the set of atypical sequences has vanishing probability. Moreover, McMillan showed a fundamental generalization of Shannon's Theorem 3 which is commonly referred to as the Shannon–McMillan theorem: the asymptotic equipartition property is satisfied by every *stationary ergodic* process with a finite alphabet. Unlike memoryless sources, for which the AEP is equivalent to the weak law of large numbers, showing that the AEP is satisfied for stationary ergodic sources requires a nontrivial use of the ergodic theorem. While the fundamental importance of ergodic theory to information theory was made evident by McMillan in 1953, the key role that entropy plays in ergodic theory was revealed by A. Kolmogorov [33] in 1958 and would eventually culminate in D. Ornstein's 1970 proof [34] of one of the pillars of modern ergodic theory: the isomorphy theorem.[7]

Shannon's Theorem 3 states that the normalized log-probability of the source string converges in probability as its length goes to infinity. Although this is enough for most lossless source coding theorems of interest, almost-sure convergence also holds as shown in [38] and (with a simpler proof) in [39]. Generalizations of the Shannon–McMillan theorem to continuous-valued random processes and to other functionals of interest in information theory have been accomplished in [40]–[45].

Sources that are either nonstationary or nonergodic need not satisfy Theorem 3[8]; that is, some sources require less than the entropy rate to be encoded, some require more. It is shown in [47] that the AEP is not only sufficient but necessary for the validity of the source coding theorem (in the general setting of finite-alphabet sources with nonzero entropy). Furthermore, [47] shows that the AEP is equivalent to the simpler statement in which the absolute value in (2) is removed.

C. Fixed-to-Variable Source Coding

As studied by Shannon, and used earlier in telegraphy, fixed-to-variable codes map individual information symbols (or, in general, fixed-length words of symbols) to unequal-length strings—with shorter strings assigned to the more likely symbols. In 1948, Shannon had left open two major problems in fixed-to-variable source coding: 1) the construction of a minimum average-length code, and 2) the converse variable-length source coding theorem.

The variable-length source code that minimizes average length was obtained by D. Huffman [48], as an outgrowth of a homework problem assigned in R. Fano's MIT information theory class [49]. The practicality of the Huffman code has withstood the test of time with a myriad applications ranging from facsimile [50] to high-definition television [51].

---

[6] A view challenged in [30] by N. Chomsky, the father of modern linguistics.

[7] Tutorials on the interplay between information theory and ergodic theory can be found in [35]–[37].

[8] General coding theorems for nonstationary/nonergodic sources can be found in [46].

No formula is known for the minimum average length in terms of the distribution of the source. In [1], Shannon showed that the minimum average length does not exceed the entropy plus one bit,[9] but he did not give a lower bound.

Before Huffman, another MIT student, L. Kraft, had attacked the construction of minimum redundancy codes unsuccessfully. However, in his 1949 Master's thesis [54], Kraft gave a basic condition (known as the Kraft inequality) that must be satisfied by the codeword lengths of a prefix code (i.e., a code where no codeword is the prefix of another).[10] Seven years later, and apparently unaware of Kraft's thesis, McMillan [56] showed that that condition must hold not just for prefix codes but for any uniquely decodable code. (A particularly simple proof was given in [57].) It is immediate to show (McMillan [56] attributes this observation to J. L. Doob) that the average length of any code that satisfies the Kraft inequality cannot be less than the source entropy. This, in turn, implies the converse variable-length source coding theorem, which had already been proven by Khinchin [31] using a method based on Shannon's Theorem 3.

The optimality of the Huffman code must have seemed at the time to leave little room for further work in fixed-to-variable source coding.[11] That, however, proved not to be the case, because of two major difficulties: 1) the distribution of the source may not be known[12] when the code is designed (Section II-E), and 2) although the Huffman algorithm need not operate symbol by symbol, its complexity grows very rapidly with the length of the source block.[13] The incentive for encoding blocks of source symbols stems from two important classes of sources for which symbol-by-symbol encoding may be decidedly suboptimal: sources with memory and binary (or other small alphabet) sources. Both difficulties encountered by the Huffman code also apply to the Shannon–Fano code mentioned in Section II-A. The second shortcoming is circumvented by the arithmetic coding method of J. Rissanen [60] (generalized in [61] and [62] and popularized in [63]), whose philosophy is related to that of the Shannon–Fano code.[14] The use of arithmetic coding is now widespread in the data-compression industry (and, in particular, in image and video applications [69]). Much of the success of arithmetic coding is due to its rational exploitation of source memory by using the conditional probability of the next symbol to be encoded given the observed past.

---

[9] Tighter distribution-dependent bounds are known [52], [53].

[10] Kraft [54] credits the derivation of the inequality to R. M. Redheffer, who would later coauthor the well-known undergraduate text [55].

[11] Minimum average-length source-coding problems have been solved with additional constraints such as unequal symbol lengths, infinite alphabets, lexicographic ordering of encoded strings, maximum codeword length, etc. See [58] for a recent survey.

[12] As a result of its emphasis on asymptotic stationary settings, Shannon theory has not been engulfed in the Bayesian/non-Bayesian schism that has plagued the field of statistics.

[13] For most Markov sources the minimum average length per letter approaches the entropy rate hyperbolically in the blocklength [59].

[14] The Shannon–Fano code is frequently referred to as the Shannon–Fano–Elias code, and the arithmetic coding methods described in [64] and [65] are attributed to P. Elias therein. Those attributions are unfounded [66]. In addition to [1], other contributions relevant to the development of modern arithmetic coding are [67] and [68].

D. Variable-to-Fixed Source Coding

So far we have considered data-compression methods whereby fixed-size blocks of source symbols are encoded into either variable-length or fixed-length strings. The variable-to-fixed source coding approach is advantageous whenever block formatting of encoded data is required. The key notion here is that of parsing (i.e., inserting commas) the source sequence into consecutive variable-length phrases. In variable-to-fixed source coding, those phrases belong to a predetermined fixed-size dictionary. Given the size of the dictionary, the Tunstall algorithm [70] selects its entries optimally under the condition that no phrase is the prefix of another and that every source sequence has a prefix in the dictionary. For memoryless sources, the Tunstall algorithm maximizes the expected length of the parsed phrases. Further results on the behavior of the Tunstall algorithm for memoryless sources have been obtained in [71] and [72]. For Markov sources, optimal variable-to-fixed codes have been found in [73] and [74].

Variable-to-fixed codes have been shown to have certain performance advantages over fixed-to-variable codes [75], [76].

Although variable-to-variable source coding has not received as much attention as the other techniques (cf. [77]), it encompasses the popular technique of runlength encoding [78], already anticipated by Shannon [1], [79], as well as several of the universal coding techniques discussed in the next subsection.

E. Universal Source Coding

A. Kolmogorov [80] coined the term "universal" to refer to data-compression algorithms that do not know a priori the distribution of the source. Since exact statistical knowledge of the source is the exception rather than the rule, universal source coding is of great practical interest.

If we apply a lossless data-compression algorithm tuned to one source to a different source we still recover the message error-free but with degraded compression efficiency. For memoryless sources, the increase in rate for compressing assuming distribution Q when the true source distribution is P is equal to the divergence[15] of P with respect to Q for both fixed-to-variable [81] and variable-to-fixed [82] coding. If the uncertainty on the source distribution can be modeled by a class of distributions, it was shown by B. Fitingof in [83] and by L. Davisson in [84] that for some uncertainty classes there is no asymptotic loss of compression efficiency if we use a source code tuned to the "center of gravity" of the uncertainty set. Constructive methods for various restricted classes of sources (such as memoryless and Markov) have been proposed by R. Krichevsky and V. Trofimov [59] and by T. Tjalkens and F. Willems [85].

In universal source coding, the encoder can exploit the fact that it observes the source output and, thus, can "learn" the source distribution and adapt to it. The same is true for the decoder because its output is a lossless reconstruction of the source sequence. Adaptive Huffman coding was initially considered in [86] and [52], and modified in [87] and [88]. For

---

[15] cf. Section III-G.

large-alphabet sources, lower encoding/decoding complexity can be achieved by the adaptive fixed-to-variable source codes of B. Ryabko [89], [90].[16] Showing experimental promise, the nonprobabilistic sorting method of [93] preprocesses sources with memory so that universal codes for memoryless sources achieve good compression efficiency.

Suppose now that we adopt a parametric description of the source uncertainty, say a family of distributions indexed by a string of parameters. In practice, it is useful to consider uncertainty classes that include distributions described by different numbers of parameters (e.g., Markov chains of various orders). We could envision a two-step universal compression procedure: first, using the source sequence, we estimate the unknown parameter string and describe it to the decoder; second, we compress the source sequence using a code tuned to the source distribution with the estimated parameters. What criterion do we adopt in order to estimate the source model? The choice of estimation criterion presents us with a tradeoff: the more finely we estimate the distribution (i.e., the more complex the model) the more efficiently we can compress the source, but also the longer it takes to describe the parameter string to the decoder. Rissanen [94] showed that there are fundamental reasons to choose the *minimum description length* (MDL) criterion for model selection. According to the MDL principle, the parameter string is chosen to minimize the compressed sequence length plus $\frac{m}{2} \log N$ if N is the length of the source sequence and m is the length of the parameter string. The relevance of the information-theoretic MDL principle transcends data compression and is now established as a major approach in statistical inference [95].

The most widely used universal source-coding method is the algorithm introduced by A. Lempel and J. Ziv in slightly different versions in 1976–1978 [96]–[98]. Unlike the methods mentioned so far in this subsection, the Lempel–Ziv algorithm is not based on approximating or estimating the source distribution. Like variable-to-fixed source coding, Lempel–Ziv coding is based on parsing the source sequence. The simple Lempel–Ziv parsing rule (the next phrase is the shortest phrase not seen previously) can be encoded and decoded very easily.[17] Remarkably, the Lempel–Ziv algorithm encodes any stationary ergodic source at its entropy rate as shown by Ziv [100] and Wyner–Ziv [101], [102]. The analysis of the statistical properties of the Lempel–Ziv algorithm has proven to be a fertile research ground [98], [103]–[108].

Despite its optimality and simplicity, the Lempel–Ziv algorithm is not the end of the story in universal source coding. Prior knowledge of general structural properties of the source can be exploited to give better transient (i.e., nonasymptotic) compression efficiency.[18] So far, the most fruitful effort in this direction has its roots in the finite-memory "context-tree" model introduced by Rissanen [109] and has led to the universal optimal method of F. Willems, Y. Starkov, and T.

Tjalkens [110]. The method of [110] is devoted to the universal estimation of the conditional probability of the next symbol given the past, which is then fed to a standard arithmetic encoder.[19] The coding rate of the method of [110] achieves the optimum speed of approach to the entropy rate (established in [94]).

Compression of memoryless sources with countably-infinite alphabets and unknown distributions has many practical applications. Several methods for universal encoding of the integers have been proposed in [112]–[115].

Germane to universal source coding is the topic of entropy estimation pioneered by Shannon [1], [116] in the framework of English texts. The empirical estimation of the entropy of natural language is surveyed in [117] and [118]. An obvious approach to entropy estimation is to apply a universal data compressor and observe the rate at which bits are generated at the output. Representative references of the state-of-the-art in entropy estimation [119]–[121], [108] illustrate the recent interest in string-matching approaches.

Nonprobabilistic measures of the compressibility of individual data strings can be defined as the length of the shortest compression achievable by a given class of compression algorithms. The methods and results are crucially dependent on the class of data compressors allowed. J. Ziv and A. Lempel [100], [98] considered the class of finite-state machines, among which the Lempel–Ziv is asymptotically optimal for all sequences. In the mid-1960's, A. Kolmogorov [80], [122], G. Chaitin [123], and R. Solomonoff [124] considered the class of compressors that output a binary program for a universal Turing machine. The resulting measure, which suffers from the shortcoming of being noncomputable, is called *Kolmogorov complexity* or *algorithmic complexity* and its methods of study lie in recursive function theory rather than Shannon theory. However, for some random sources, the expected Kolmogorov complexity rate converges to the entropy rate [101], [125].

F. Separate Compression of Correlated Sources

In the post-Shannon era, one of the most important advances in the theory of fundamental limits of data compression was achieved by D. Slepian and J. Wolf in [126]. Consider two information sources compressed by separate individual encoders that do not have access to the output of the other source. Noiseless separate decompression of the encoded streams requires that the coding rates be equal to the individual entropies. If joint decoding were allowed would it be possible to improve compression efficiency? In particular, can the sum of the rates be strictly smaller than the sum of the individual entropies? Let us assume that the sources are dependent (the answer is obviously negative otherwise) and, thus, the sum of their entropies is strictly larger than their joint entropy. Had we allowed joint source encoding, the answer would be affirmative as the required rate-sum would be equal to the joint entropy. Slepian and Wolf's surprising result was that this conclusion holds even with separate encoding. Shortly afterwards, T. Cover [127] introduced the powerful technique

---

[16]Rediscovered in [91] and [92].

[17]Practical issues on the implementation of the Lempel–Ziv algorithm are addressed in [99].

[18]Reference [77] gives a survey of the interplay between delay and redundancy for universal source coding with various knowledge of the statistics of the source.

[19]The connections between universal source coding and universal prediction are surveyed in [111].

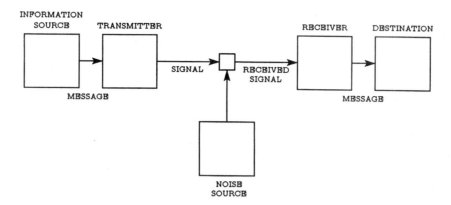

INFORMATION
SOURCE   TRANSMITTER   RECEIVER   DESTINATION

MESSAGE   SIGNAL   RECEIVED
                          SIGNAL   MESSAGE

NOISE
SOURCE

Fig. 1. Figure 1 of [1].

of random binning to generalize the Slepian–Wolf result to jointly stationary/ergodic sources.

Despite the existence of potential applications, the conceptual importance of Slepian–Wolf coding has not been mirrored in practical data compression. Not much progress on constructive Slepian–Wolf schemes has been achieved beyond the connection with error-correcting channel codes revealed in [128]. Interestingly, channel coding presents another avenue for potential applications of Slepian–Wolf coding as shown in [129].[20]

The combinatorial aspects of zero-error source coding [130] are particularly interesting in the context of separate compression of correlated sources or the more canonical setting of compression with decoder side-information. Pioneering contributions in this direction were made by H. Witsenhausen [131] and R. Ahlswede [132]. Inspired by the distributed-computing applications envisioned in the late 1970's, *interactive compression* models allow several rounds of communication between encoders so as to compute a function dependent on their individual observations [133]. The efficient exchange of remote edits to a common file is a typical application. Achievability and converse results have been obtained by A. Orlitsky *et al.* in [134]–[137].

III. RELIABLE COMMUNICATION

A. The Birth of Channel Capacity

After fifty years, it is not easy to fully grasp the revolutionary nature of Shannon's abstraction of the fundamental problem of communication depicted in [1, Fig. 1] (Fig. 1). Shannon completes the picture he initiated nine years earlier [19] by introducing a new concept: the "channel," which accounts for any deterministic or random transformation corrupting the transmitted signal. The function of the transmitter is to add "redundancy:"

The redundancy must be introduced to combat the particular noise structure involved ... a delay is generally required to approach the ideal encoding. It now has the additional function of allowing a large sample of noise to affect the signal before any judgment is made at the receiving point as to the original message.

In a world where modulation was generally thought of as an instantaneous process and no error-correcting codes had been invented[21] Shannon's formulation of the problem of reliable communication was a stroke of genius.

Shannon first develops his results on reliable communication within the context of discrete memoryless channels. He defines the channel capacity by

$$C = \mathrm{Max}\left(H(x) - H_y(x)\right) \tag{3}$$

where the maximum is with respect to all possible information sources used as input to the channel

and claims

It is possible to send information at the rate C through the channel *with as small a frequency of errors or equivocation as desired* by proper encoding. This statement is not true for any rate greater than C.

Denoting by $N(T, q)$ the maximum codebook size of duration T and error probability q, Shannon gives the stronger statement.

Shannon's Theorem 12 [1]:

$$\lim_{T \to \infty} \frac{\log N(T, q)}{T} = C \tag{4}$$

where C is the channel capacity, provided that q does not equal 0 or 1.

Shannon justifies the achievability part of this statement succinctly and intuitively, introducing the celebrated technique of random encoding. Error probability is averaged with respect to the codebook choice and shown to vanish asymptotically with T if the transmission rate is lower than C. Shannon notices that this argument leads to the conclusion that not only does there exist a capacity-achieving code, but in fact almost all codes are good. However,

no explicit description of a series of approximation[s] to the ideal has been found. Probably this is no accident but is related to the difficulty of giving an explicit construction for a good approximation to a random sequence.

[20] For example, thanks to Slepian–Wolf coding, the branch from "receiver" to "observer" in [1, Fig. 8] is redundant in order to achieve capacity.

[21] With the possible exception of the Hamming $(7, 4)$ code quoted in [1]; see also [138].

18

Although all the foregoing claims would eventually be shown to hold (Section III-D), Shannon [1] does not prove, even informally, the converse part of Theorem 12 (i.e., $\leq$ in (4)), nor the weaker statement that the error probability of codes with rate above capacity cannot vanish.[22]

B. Mutual Information

In addition to the difference between unconditional and conditional entropy maximized in (3), [1, Part IV] introduces its counterpart for continuous random variables.

$$\iint P(x,y) \log \frac{P(x,y)}{P(x)P(y)} \, dx \, dy.$$

Although no name is given in [1] for this quantity, Shannon realizes that it is "one of the central definitions in communication theory." By 1956, Shannon [140] refers to it as "mutual information," using a terminology attributed to Fano [141], which is commonly accepted today.

Shannon gives the data-processing inequality in [1], and a general approach to define mutual information encompassing the discrete and continuous definitions as special cases. This approach would be followed up by I. Gelfand, A. Yaglom, and A. Kolmogorov in [142]–[144], and by M. Pinsker (with special emphasis on Gaussian random variables and processes) in [145]. Early on, the Russian school realized the importance of the random variable whose expectation is mutual information (i.e., the log-likelihood ratio between joint and marginal-product distributions) and dubbed it *information density*.

The optimization problem posed in Shannon's formula was initially tackled in [146] and [147]. An iterative algorithm for computing the capacity of arbitrary discrete memoryless channels was given independently by S. Arimoto [148] and R. Blahut [149] in 1972.

C. Gaussian Channels

Undoubtedly, the channel that has yielded the biggest successes in information theory is the Gaussian channel.

Shannon [1] formulates the continuous-time ideal strictly bandlimited white Gaussian channel and uses the sampling theorem to show the equivalence to a discrete-time channel sampled at twice the bandwidth.[23] As a formal analog of the entropy of a discrete random variable, Shannon defines the differential entropy of a continuous random variable, and shows that it is maximized, subject to a variance constraint, by the Gaussian distribution. Taking the difference between the output differential entropy and the noise differential entropy, Shannon goes on to obtain his famous formula for the capacity of power-constrained white Gaussian channels with flat transfer function[24]

$$C = W \log \left(\frac{P+N}{N} \right) \qquad (5)$$

where W is the channel bandwidth, P is the transmitted power, and N is the noise power within the channel band. Taking the limit of (5) as the bandwidth grows without bound [154], a fundamental conclusion is reached: the minimum energy necessary to transmit one bit of information lies 1.6 dB below the noise one-sided spectral density. Expressions similar to (5) were put forth in 1948 by Wiener [27] and Tuller [26] without information-theoretic justification: Wiener simply takes the difference between Gaussian differential entropies and Tuller arrives at the formula arguing that "if N is the rms amplitude of the noise mixed with the signal, there are $1 + S/N$ significant values of signal that may be determined." By the mid-1950's, the explicit construction of channel codes with rates approaching (5) became the "holy grail" of information theory [155].

The geometric view of time-domain functions as points in a finite-dimensional space, now prevalent in communications engineering, was championed by Shannon [150] in 1949, where he justified the achievability of the rate in (5) using a sphere-hardening reasoning. Since any strictly bandlimited signal has infinite duration, the rate of information of any finite codebook of bandlimited waveforms is, strictly speaking, equal to zero. A rigorous derivation of (5) requires a careful definition of "almost-strict" bandwidth or duration (cf. [156]), and a heavy dose of functional analysis. This was accomplished by A. Wyner in [157] using the fundamental results of [158].

Referring to (5), Shannon [1] asserts that

> to approximate this limiting rate of transmission the transmitted signals must approximate in statistical properties a white noise.

A proof that capacity-achieving codes must have empirical distributions that maximize input–output mutual information was given in [159].

The generalization of (5) to dispersive/nonwhite Gaussian channels is given by the "water-filling" formula obtained by Shannon in [150] using the differential entropy of a Gaussian stationary process found in [1]. Rigorous justifications [160]–[162] of the water-filling formula for dispersive/nonwhite Gaussian channels usually appeal to the Toeplitz distribution theorem [163], [164], although it can be circumvented, as shown in [165].

Shannon [1] also studies white Gaussian channels subject to amplitude constraints, rather than power constraints. Not only does he give bounds but he notices that for low signal-to-noise ratios the capacity is essentially given by (5). A closed-form expression is not known to exist but algorithms for the computation of amplitude-constrained capacity were given in [166], and in [167] for the practically important quadrature-modulation channel. Gaussian channel capacity has been found for models that incorporate structural constraints at the receiver

---

[22] Alluding to [1], Shannon says in [139]: "I was confident I was correct, not only in an intuitive way but in a rigorous way. I knew exactly what I was doing, and it all came out exactly right."

[23] In contrast to the 1920's papers by Nyquist and Küpfmüller (Section I), Shannon's crisp statement [1] and proof [150] of the sampling theorem were instrumental in popularizing this result in engineering. Thus there is indeed some justification for the term "Shannon sampling theorem" [151], [152].

[24] Four months after the publication of [1], M. Golay [153] refers to (5) as "the now classical expression for the information reception capacity of a channel."

(e.g., quantized observations) and at the transmitter (e.g., specific modulation formats). Those results have underlied much of the development of modem technology since the early 1960's [168], [169].

The capacity of additive non-Gaussian channels is also considered in [1]. For a fixed noise power, Gaussian noise is shown to be least favorable.[25] Moreover, Shannon gives an upper bound on capacity which depends on the "non-Gaussianness" of the noise distribution through its entropy-power, i.e., the variance of a Gaussian distribution with identical entropy. An equivalent bound can be given in terms of the divergence between the actual noise distribution and a Gaussian distribution with the same variance [173]. Shannon [1] states the deceptively simple "entropy-power inequality" proved in [174]: the entropy-power of the sum of two independent random variables is lower-bounded by the sum of the individual entropy-powers. The behavior of the capacity of additive non-Gaussian noise power-constrained channels was investigated by V. Prelov for various asymptotic scenarios [175]–[178].

The development of the results on the capacity of additive Gaussian noise channels where the transmitted signals are subject to fading is surveyed in [179].

D. The Channel Coding Theorem

The major result left unproven in [1] was the converse channel coding theorem. This follows directly from Fano's inequality [180]—a fundamental result in information theory which gives a lower bound on the error probability of equiprobable hypotheses tests.

Actually, Fano's inequality leads to a more general result: if the messages to be transmitted through the channel are not equiprobable but are generated by a source with entropy $H > C$, then reliable communication (i.e., vanishing error probability) is impossible. The achievability counterpart of this *source-channel coding* setting states that if the source entropy is below channel capacity, then there exist codes that achieve vanishing error probability. This follows easily by separating the source- and channel-coding operations. At the encoder, the source is compressed to a rate equal to its entropy and fed to a channel encoder which assumes equiprobable messages; at the receiver front-end a source-independent channel decoder selects a codeword, which is then fed to a source decompressor independent of the channel statistics. Because of this structure, the source-channel coding theorem is also known as the separation theorem.[26]

The validity of the strong converse in Shannon's Theorem 12 was established by J. Wolfowitz in 1957 [182] for binary memoryless channels.

A. Feinstein [183] gave the first step-by-step proof of the achievability part of the channel coding theorem[27] in 1954. Along with a deterministic greedy method to choose the codebook, Feinstein used a suboptimal decoder that selects the message whose information density with the received signal exceeds a given threshold; an error is declared if no such message exists, and if more than one such message exists, then the message with lowest index is chosen. A combinatorial variation of Feinstein's proof was proposed by J. Wolfowitz [182] for discrete memoryless channels. This marked the first use of empirical distributions (types) in Shannon theory. Fully developed by I. Csiszár and J. Körner in [185], the method of types (surveyed in [186]), has been influential in the evolution of the Shannon theory of discrete memoryless channels and sources.

Arguably the most natural proof of the direct coding theorem follows by formalizing the intuitive argument put forth by Shannon [1] that evaluates the average probability of the ensemble of all codes. In this case, the decoder is slightly different from Feinstein's: if more than one message satisfies the threshold test, then an error is declared.[28]

Other proofs of the direct coding theorem were given by Shannon in [188] and R. Gallager in [189] by evaluating the average performance of random encoding achieved by the maximum-likelihood decoder. Popularized in [161], Gallager's simple bounding method has found widespread use.

Aside from Shannon's treatment of the nonwhite Gaussian channel [150], the first works that dealt with the capacity of channels with memory did not appear until the late 1950's: [190], [188], [191], [182], and [192]. The capacity of most channels with memory is given by the limit of maximal normalized mutual informations. R. Dobrushin [193] showed that such a limiting expression holds for a wide class of channels exhibiting a certain type of ergodic behavior. If the capacity of memoryless channels is not always computable in closed form, the limit present in the formula for channels with memory poses yet another hurdle for explicit computation, which is, nevertheless, surmountable in cases such as the stationary Gaussian channel (cf. Section III-C) and timing channels [194], [195]. A general capacity formula that does not hinge on ergodicity or stationarity restrictions was obtained in [196] by introducing a new way of proving the converse coding theorem. The approach of [196] shows a dual of Feinstein's result: the average error probability of any code is essentially lower-bounded by the cumulative distribution function of the input–output information density evaluated at the code rate.[29] In 1957, Shannon had given a precursor of this lower bound in the largely overlooked [188, Theorem 2].

---

[25] In fact, the game between signal and noise distribution with fixed variance and input–output mutual information as payoff has a saddle point achieved by Gaussian distributions. Information-theoretic games [170]–[172] are of interest in jamming problems, for example.

[26] Other than for nonstationary sources/channels the separation theorem holds in wide generality [181].

[27] Unlike other approaches, Feinstein's proof leads to a stronger notion of reliability where error probability is measured taking the worst case over all codewords—in lieu of the average. A proof of Feinstein's result in abstract measurable spaces was given in [184].

[28] The so-called "typical-sequences" proof follows this approach except that the decoder contains a superfluous (upper) threshold. Further unnecessary complication results from considering typicality with respect to individual and joint entropies rather than mutual information [187], [168], [101].

[29] Called the *information spectrum* in [46], the distribution function of the information density replaces its average (mutual information) as the fundamental information measure when dealing with nonstationary/nonergodic channels [197].

For channels with cost constraints (e.g., power limitations), capacity is given by the maximal mutual information over all input random variables that satisfy a corresponding average cost constraint. A simpler formula exists for the minimum cost per transmitted bit [198], which in the Gaussian case reduces to the -1.6 dB result quoted in Section III-C.

In a departure from the conventional discrete-time model where there as many output symbols as input symbols, R. Dobrushin [199] and S. Stambler [200] showed coding theorems for channels subject to random deletions and insertions of symbols at instants unknown to the decoder.

E. Constrained Sequences

Under the heading "Capacity of the discrete noiseless channel," [1] poses a nonprobabilistic problem quite different from those discussed in data compression/transmission. Although there is no evidence that Shannon had in mind recording applications when formulating this problem, this discipline has found a wealth of practical applications in magnetic and optical recording [201]. In those applications, certain sequences of bits are forbidden. For example, it may be required that the transmitted sequence contain at least d and at most k 0's amid 1's, or that the sequence satisfy certain spectral properties. Shannon found the fundamental asymptotic limits on the amount of information that can be encoded per symbol, when the allowable sequences are defined by a finite-state machine. In the last fifty years, considerable progress has been achieved in the design of constrained encoders that approach Shannon's bounds (cf. [201]).

F. Zero-Error Channel Capacity

Any text typed by anyone other than an infallible typist will have a nonzero probability of being erroneous, with the probability going to unity as the length increases. An information theorist can make this probability go to zero by handing the typist a redundant text derived from the original using a code that takes into account the statistics of the typist's mistakes.[30]

Imagine now that a certain typist makes mistakes but only by occasionally mistyping a neighboring letter in the keyboard—(t may become r or g, but not u). This seemingly ordinary typist opens a whole new world of information-theoretic problems. We can now encode/decode texts perfectly. For example, the typist could be given texts drawn exclusively from the alphabet {b, i, t, s}. The probability of error does not just go to zero asymptotically, it *is* zero. The rate at which information can be encoded infallibly is called the zero-error capacity. This measure no longer depends on the probabilities with which mistakes are made—all the information relevant to finding the zero-error capacity can be summarized in a graph in which pairs of letters mistakable for each other are connected by an edge. Exceedingly difficult and radically different from the nonzero error setting, the zero-error capacity problem was formulated by Shannon [140] in 1956. Once again, Shannon

created single-handedly a new research field, this time within combinatorial graph theory.

Most channels of practical interest have zero zero-error capacity. Among channels with positive zero-error capacity, the most difficult channel that has been solved corresponds to a circular typewriter with five keys. Shannon [140] showed that the zero-error capacity of this channel is no less than half of that achievable by an infallible typist ($\log_2 5 = 2.32$ bits per keystroke). In 1979, L. Lovász [202] showed that Shannon's lower bound is in fact the zero-error capacity. In 1997, N. Alon [203] disproved the conjecture in [140] that the zero-error capacity of independent channels operating in parallel is the sum of the zero-error capacities.

A tutorial survey on the results and combinatorial challenges of zero-error information theory is given in [130].

G. Error Exponent

A school of Shannon theorists has pursued a refinement of the channel coding theorem that studies the behavior of the error probability as a function of the blocklength instead of just focusing attention on the channel capacity. Rice [204] and Feinstein [205] observed the exponential decrease of error probability as a function of blocklength in Gaussian and discrete memoryless channels, respectively. The exponent of the minimum achievable probability of error is a function of the rate, which Shannon [206] christened as the *reliability function*. Upper and lower bounds on the reliability function (which coincide for all but low rates) were found in [207] for binary-symmetric channels; in [208] for symmetric discrete memoryless channels; and in [188], [209] for general discrete memoryless channels. The behavior of the reliability function of erasure channels was found in [210].

A new approach to upper-bounding the error probability averaged with respect to the choice of the encoder was found by Gallager in [189]. In addition to the proof of the direct coding theorem (Section III-D), this result led to a general lower bound on the reliability function. Lower bounds on error probability leading to improved upper bounds on the reliability function were obtained in [211] and [212].

Further improvements in bounding the reliability function were shown in [213]–[216]. The power of the method of types is illustrated by the proofs of bounds on the reliability function given in [185] and [217]. To this date, the reliability function of discrete memoryless channels (including the binary-symmetric channel) is not known for all rates.

Other than the application of Chernoff's bound, the information-theoretic work on the reliability function evolved independent of the large-deviations work initiated in the statistical literature in the 1950's. The important role played in the error exponent problem by the divergence measure introduced in statistics by S. Kullback and R. Leibler [218][31] was made evident by R. Blahut in [214]. A more fundamental information measure than either entropy or mutual information, divergence had been surprisingly slow in emerging to its rightful position in information theory, until it was popularized in the texts [185] and [168]. The vacuum left

---

[30] Alas, information theory has not made any inroads in this particular information technology, and typists continue to be rated by raw words per minute rather than by Shannon capacity.

[31] Earlier, A. Wald had used the nonnegativity of divergence in [219].

by this historical neglect has led to the overrated role played by the differential entropy measure in information theory.

Originating from the analysis of sequential decoders for convolutional codes [220], [221] and related to the reliability function, the *cutoff rate* is a measure of the "noisiness" of the channel, which has received much attention in the development of information and coding theory. Progress in coding theory has refuted the notion (e.g., [222]) that transmitting above cutoff rate requires unwieldy decoding complexity. While there are appealing heuristics on the different behavior of codes below and above cutoff rate (e.g. [168], [169]) the view that cutoff rate is a key measure of the channel transmission capabilities is not supported by the operational characterization that has been discovered so far [223].

Some applications, such as concatenated coding and transmission of sources with residual redundancy, have spurred work on a variant of Shannon's channel coding setup whereby the decoder outputs not one but a fixed-size list of messages. The problem of list decoding was introduced by P. Elias [224]. Capacity and error exponents have been studied in [225]–[228]. Zero-error list decoding (Section III-F) was investigated in [229] and [230].

H. Channels with Feedback

The first (and most widely used) feedback model in information theory was introduced by Shannon in [140]. It considers an encoder that, before sending the ith symbol, knows without error the $(i - 1)$th symbol received by the decoder. Shannon [140] shows that even this kind of ideal feedback fails to increase the capacity of the discrete memoryless channel. Because of the lack of channel memory, not only is feedback useless to predict the future behavior of the channel, but it is futile for the encoder to try to compensate for previous channel behavior, as far as channel capacity is concerned. However, feedback does increase the reliability function [231]. Moreover, a number of constructive schemes [232]–[235] made evident that the availability of feedback may simplify the coding and decoding operations. Elias and Shannon [140] showed that the zero-error capacity of discrete memoryless channels could indeed increase with feedback.

Shannon [140] anticipated that feedback would help to increase the capacity of channels with memory, at a time when the capacity of channels with memory had not yet been tackled. The ability of feedback to increase the capacity of channels with memory was studied by a number of authors in the late 1960's: [236]–[238]. In particular, P. Ebert [238] and M. Pinsker[32] independently showed that feedback may increase the capacity of a Gaussian channel by at most a factor of two—a factor that was shown to be the best possible in [239]. The additive upper bound of [240] shows that the increase afforded by feedback cannot exceed half a bit-per-channel use.

I. Channels with Unknown Parameters

In parallel with the setting discussed in Section II-E, the channel description available to the encoder/decoder may be incomplete. Suppose that the actual channel conditional

(output given input) distributions are known to belong to an uncertainty class. Depending on whether the number of parameters describing the uncertainty class remains fixed or grows with blocklength we have a *compound channel* or an *arbitrarily varying channel*, respectively. These models are relevant to practical communications systems subject to jamming, time-varying conditions, etc., and have received much attention in the Shannon theory literature [241].

The objective of the encoder/decoder is to guarantee reliable communication regardless of the actual channel in effect. This leads to a minimax problem where the probability of error is maximized over the uncertainty class and minimized over the choice of encoder/decoder.

The compound discrete memoryless channel capacity problem was posed and solved in 1959 by D. Blackwell, L. Breiman, and A. Thomasian [242] and by R. Dobrushin [243]. A year later, Wolfowitz [244] proved the strong converse (for maximal error probability) using the method of [182]. The formula for compound channel capacity is similar to (3) except that for every input distribution, the mutual information is minimized with respect to the channels in the uncertainty class, thus yielding a capacity that is less than or equal to the worst capacity of the channels in the uncertainty set.[33] The capacity of compound channels with memory was investigated in [245] and [246].

Arbitrarily varying channels[34] were introduced in [248]. The capacity was found by Ahlswede and Wolfowitz [249] in the binary output case under the pessimistic maximal error probability criterion, in which the "jammer" is allowed to know the codeword sent by the communicator. A partial generalization of the solution in [249] was obtained by Csiszár and Körner in [250]. However, a full solution of the discrete memoryless case remains elusive. In contrast, if error probability is averaged with respect to the choice of codewords, the arbitrarily varying channel capacity has been progressively solved in a series of papers [251]–[254]. Ahlswede showed in [252] that if the average-error-probability capacity is nonzero, then it does not increase further if the error probability is averaged over the choice of codebooks, i.e., if the "jammer" does not know which code is used by the communicator.

The capacity of the memoryless Gaussian arbitrarily varying channel is known both when the jammer knows the codebook [255] and when it does not [256]. In either case, the effect of the power-constrained jammer is equivalent to an additional source of Gaussian noise, except that the capacity is equal to zero if the jammer knows the codebook and has as much power as the transmitter.

Recent references on the capabilities of list decoding for arbitrarily varying channels can be found in [228] and [257].

If the receiver has incomplete knowledge of the channel or its complexity is constrained, it is of interest to investigate the capacity degradation suffered when the decoder is not maximum-likelihood. If the encoder does know both the channel distribution and the suboptimal decoding rule, then it can partially compensate for the mismatch at the receiver.

---

[32]Unpublished.

[33]Equality holds in special cases such as when the uncertainty is the crossover probability of a binary-symmetric channel.

[34]The term "arbitrarily varying" was coined in [247].

Recent results on the capacity achievable with mismatched decoding have been obtained in [258]–[262].

Channel uncertainty at the receiver need not result in loss of capacity. For example, known training sequences can be used to probe the channel. Alternatively, *universal decoding* operates in a "blind mode" and attains the same asymptotic performance as a maximum-likelihood rule tuned to the channel law. Universal decoders have been found for various uncertainty models; foremost among them are the maximum empirical mutual information decoder introduced by V. Goppa in [263] and further studied in [185], the Lempel–Ziv-based decoder introduced by J. Ziv in [264] and further studied in [265], the independence decoding rule of I. Csiszár and P. Narayan [266], and the merging decoder introduced by M. Feder and A. Lapidoth in [267].

J. Multiuser Channels

1) Two-Way Channels: Published in 1961, Shannon's last single-authored technical contribution [268] marks the foundation of the discipline of multiuser information theory. Undoubtedly inspired by telephony, [268] is devoted to the *two-way* channel subject to mutual interference between the signals transmitted in opposite directions. A new dimension arises: the tradeoff between the transmission speeds at each terminal, e.g., maximum speed in one direction is feasible when nothing is transmitted in the other direction. Thus the transmission capabilities of the two-way channel are not described by a single number (capacity) as in the conventional one-way channel but by a two-dimensional "capacity region" that specifies the set of achievable rate pairs. Shannon [268] gave a limiting expression for the capacity region of the discrete memoryless two-way channel. Unfortunately, it is not yet known how to explicitly evaluate that expression even in "toy" examples. Of more immediate use were the inner and outer bounds found in [268], and later improved in [269]–[273].

2) Multiaccess Channels: Shannon concludes [268] with

> In another paper we will discuss the case of a channel with two or more terminals having inputs only and one terminal with an output only, a case for which a complete and simple solution of the capacity region has been found.

In the terminology of [268], "inputs" and "output" are to be understood as "inputs to the channel" and "output from the channel." Thus the channel Shannon had in mind was what we now refer to as the *multiple-access channel*: several transmitters sending information to one receiver.

Multiple-access communication dates back to the systems invented in the 1870's by Thomas Edison and Alexander Graham Bell to transmit simultaneous telegraphic messages through a single wire. Time-division and frequency-division multiplexing methods were already well-known at the time of the inception of information theory. Code-division multiple access (CDMA) had also been suggested as one of the possible applications of the spread-spectrum modulation technology that sprung up from World War II. In fact, one of the early proponents of CDMA was Shannon himself [16].

Shannon wrote no further papers on multiple-access channels and it is not known what solution he had found for the multiple-access capacity region. But in a short span of time in the early 1970's several independent contributions [274]–[278] found various characterizations of the capacity region of the two-user discrete memoryless multiple-access channel. Most useful among those is the expression found by H. Liao [276] and R. Ahlswede [278] for the capacity region as the convex hull of a union of pentagons. Shortly after, Wyner [128] and Cover [279] showed (using the suboptimal successive cancellation decoder) that the memoryless Gaussian multiple-access channel admits a very simple capacity region: the pentagon defined by the single-user capacities of the channels with powers equal to the individual powers and to the sum of the powers.[35] The generalization of the capacity region to (non-Gaussian) memoryless multiple-access channels subject to power constraints did not take place until [282] (cf. [198]). The proof of the achievability part of the multiple-access coding theorem is most easily carried out by using the formalization of Shannon's approach discussed in Section III-D.

In spite (or, maybe, because) of the simplicity of these models, they lead to lessons pertinent to practical multiuser communication systems; for example, in many instances, orthogonal multiplexing strategies (such as time- or frequency-division multiplexing) incur a penalty in capacity. Thus letting transmitted signals interfere with each other (in a controlled way) increases capacity provided that the receiver takes into account the multiaccess interference.

Noiseless feedback can increase the capacity of memoryless multiple-access channels as shown in [283] and [284]. However, the capacity region with feedback is not yet known except in special cases such as the Gaussian multiple-access channel [285]. The upper bounds on the capacity of single-user non-white Gaussian channels with feedback (Section III-H) have been generalized to multiple-access channels in [286]–[288].

The capacity region of multiple-access channels with memory was given in [289]. The counterpart of the water-filling formula for the dispersive Gaussian channel was found explicitly in [290] for the two-user case and an algorithm for its computation for an arbitrary number of users was given in [291]. The practical issue of transmitter asynchronism was tackled in [292] and [293] at the frame level, and in [294] at the symbol level.

The error exponents of multiple-access channels were investigated in [295]–[297].

When the message sources are correlated it is interesting to consider the problem of joint source-channel multiuser encoding. This has been done in, among others, [298] and [299], where it is shown that the separation principle of single-user source-channel coding does not hold in the multiuser setting.

3) Interference Channels: In contrast to the multiple-access setting in which the receiver is interested in decoding the information sent by all the users, suppose now that we

---

[35] Multiaccess error-control codes derived from single-user codes have been proposed for the Gaussian multiple-access channel in [280] and for the discrete multiple-access channel in [281].

have as many receivers as transmitters and each receiver is interested in decoding only one of the sources. Think, for example, of telephone channels subject to crosstalk. We could take a multiple-access approach to this problem and use codes that ensure that each receiver can reliably decode the information sent by all the transmitters. However, higher rates are possible if we take advantage of the fact that each receiver requires reliable decoding of only one of the transmitters. In spite of many efforts surveyed in [300] and exemplified by [301]–[304], the capacity region of even the simplest two-user memoryless Gaussian interference channel remains an open problem. One of the practical lessons revealed by the study of the interference channel is the equivalence of powerful interference and no interference [301], [305]: unlike background noise, the known structure of a powerful interfering signal makes it feasible to recover it at the receiver with very high reliability and then subtract it from the received signal.

4) Broadcast Channels: In [306], Cover introduced the dual of the multiaccess channel: one sender that transmits one signal simultaneously to several receivers. If the same information is to be transmitted to each receiver, then the model reduces to a single-user (compound) channel. Otherwise, the problem becomes quite interesting and challenging. For example, in television broadcasting we may want receivers within the coverage area of a station to receive high-definition signals, while more distant (lower signal-to-noise ratio) receivers would be content to receive low-definition television. By superposition of the encoded streams it is possible to trade off the rate of information sent to different types of receivers. Although a general solution for the capacity region of the broadcast channel is not yet known, considerable progress (surveyed in [307]) has been made in exploring the fundamental limits of various classes of memoryless broadcast channels. On the practical side, superposition coding is gaining increasing attention for broadcast applications [308], [309] and other applications that require unequal error protection [310].

For certain nonergodic single-user channels, maximizing average transmission rate makes more sense than the overly conservative coding strategy that guarantees reliability in the worst case channel conditions. Those situations are another promising application of the broadcast channel approach [306], [311].

5) Wiretap Channels: The methods of multiuser information theory have been successfully applied to channels subject to eavesdropping. The basic model was introduced by Wyner [312] and generalized in [313]. The Shannon-theoretic limits of secret sharing by public discussion have been investigated by U. Maurer [314] and by Ahlswede and Csiszár [315].

K. Other Roles of Channel Capacity

Channel capacity has proven to be the key quantity, not only in reliable information transmission, but in a number of other problems.

1) Information Radius: Any parametrized family of distributions $\{P_{Y|\theta}, \theta \in \Theta\}$ can be viewed as a "channel" from the "input" space Θ to the output space where Y is defined. The maximal input–output mutual information is a measure of the dissimilarity ("information radius") of the family of distributions. More precisely, the maximal mutual information is the saddle point of a game whose payoff is the divergence measure and which is maximized over the family of distributions and minimized by a distribution that acts as the center of gravity [161], [185], [316].

2) Minimax Redundancy in Universal Lossless Coding: Consider a game between a source encoder and a source selector whose payoff is the difference between the expected codelength and the source entropy. This is a special case of the game in the previous paragraph. Thus its saddle point is the capacity of the parametrized family of source distributions [317]–[320].

3) Identification: R. Ahlswede and G. Dueck [321] introduced the following seemingly innocuous variation of Shannon's channel-coding setting. Suppose that the recipient of the message is only interested in knowing whether a certain preselected message is the true message.[36] Let us assume that the encoder and decoder ignore which message was preselected by the recipient; for, otherwise, the setting would become a standard hypothesis-testing problem. The situation is similar to the familiar one except that the decoder is free to declare a list of several messages to be simultaneously "true." The recipient simply checks whether the message of interest is in the list or not. Erroneous information is delivered whenever the preselected message is in the list but is not the true message, or if the preselected message is the true message but is not in the list. How many messages can be transmitted while guaranteeing vanishing probability of erroneous information? The surprising answer is that the number of messages grows doubly exponentially with the number of channel uses. Moreover, the second-order exponent is equal to the channel capacity. This result was shown in [321] (achievability) and [46] (converse).

4) System Simulation: Random processes with prescribed distributions can be generated by a deterministic algorithm driven by a source of random bits (independent flips of a fair coin). A key quantity that quantifies the "complexity" of the generated random process is the minimal rate of the source of bits necessary to accomplish the task. The *resolvability* of a system is defined as the minimal randomness required to generate any desired input so that the output distributions are approximated with arbitrary accuracy. Under fairly general conditions, [46] showed that the resolvability of a system is equal to its Shannon capacity.

IV. LOSSY DATA COMPRESSION

Quantization (or analog-to-digital conversion) saw its first practical applications with PCM in the 1930's (Section I) and its evolution is chronicled elsewhere in this issue [322]. The Shannon-theoretic discipline of rate-distortion theory deals with the fundamental limits of lossy data compression in the asymptotic regime of long observations. Constructive methods

---

[36]For example, the message may be header information in a communication network and the recipient is only interested in determining whether it is the addressee.

and their relationship to the development of information-theoretic data compression limits are reviewed in [323] and [324].

A. The Birth of Rate-Distortion Theory

As we mentioned, in his 1939 letter to V. Bush [19], Shannon had come up with an abstraction of the problem of waveform transmission using a mean-square fidelity criterion. The closing chapter in [1] "Part V: The rate for a continuous source" returns to source coding but now with a basic new ingredient:

> Practically, we are not interested in exact transmission when we have a continuous source, but only in transmission to within a given tolerance. The question is, can we assign a definite rate to a continuous source when we require only a certain fidelity of recovery, measured in a suitable way.

Shannon then considers an arbitrary fidelity (or distortion) criterion and states that the minimum rate at which information can be encoded within a certain tolerance is the minimum mutual information between the source and any other random variable that satisfies the average distortion constraint. Shannon also states the source/channel separation theorem with a fidelity criterion (reproduction with distortion d is possible if $R(d) < C$, and impossible if $R(d) > C$). Shannon gives a quick intuitive argument along the lines used to prove the achievability part of the channel coding theorem and accepts the converse part as a straightforward consequence of the definitions.[37]

It is not until 1959 that Shannon, already at MIT, returns to the fundamental limits of lossy data compression [325], and refers to the function he defined in [1] as the "rate-distortion function $R(d)$." He proves the rate distortion theorem for discrete memoryless sources (using the random coding approach) and evaluates the rate-distortion function in several interesting special cases.

B. Evaluation of Rate-Distortion Functions

In [1], Shannon solves the optimization problem posed by the formula for the rate-distortion function in the case of a Gaussian bandlimited continuous-time random process under the mean-square error criterion. He shows that the rate is equal to the bandwidth times the logarithm of the signal-to-reconstruction-error ratio.[38] Dealing with the discrete-time counterpart, Shannon [325] shows that the Gaussian rate-distortion function is equal to the positive part of one-half of the logarithm of the signal-to-reconstruction-error ratio. This means that every additional bit of encoded information results in an increase of 6 dB in fidelity.

But prior to 1959, the rate-distortion function had attracted the attention of Kolmogorov (and his disciples) who called

it the ϵ-entropy [327].[39] The dual to Shannon's water-filling formula for channel capacity (Section III-C) is the "flooding" formula[40] for the rate-distortion function of nonwhite Gaussian processes. It was originally given by Kolmogorov [327], with refined derivations due to Pinsker [330], [331], and B. Tsybakov [332].

When applied to Gaussian sources (with mean-square-error fidelity) and Gaussian channels (with power constraints), the separation theorem leads to particularly interesting conclusions. If the source and the channel have identical bandwidth and their spectra are flat, then the optimum encoding/decoding operations consist of simple instantaneous attenuation/amplification (or single-sideband modulation if frequency translation is required) [333], [334]. If the channel has more bandwidth than the source, then the achievable signal-to-noise ratio (in decibels) is equal to that achievable in the identical-bandwidth case times the ratio of channel-to-source bandwidth. To achieve this limit, nontrivial encoding/decoding is necessary; however, the original analog signal can still be sent uncoded through a portion of channel bandwidth without loss of optimality [335].

A very important rate-distortion function, found by Shannon [325], is that of a binary memoryless source with bit-error-rate fidelity. Ordinarily, the communication engineer specifies a certain tolerable end-to-end bit-error rate. This reliability measure is less stringent than the block-error probability used in the development of channel capacity. According to the separation theorem and Shannon's binary rate-distortion function, if the desired bit-error rate is ϵ, then the maximum transmission rate is equal to channel capacity times the factor

$$(1 + \epsilon \log \epsilon + (1 - \epsilon) \log (1 - \epsilon))^{-1}.$$

Contemporaneously with Shannon [325], Erokhin [336] found the rate-distortion function (for low distortion) of equiprobable discrete sources under bit-error-rate fidelity. Further work on the rate-distortion function in the low-distortion regime was reported by Y. Linkov [337], [338] and by F. Jelinek [339].

Iterative algorithms for the computation of the rate-distortion function of discrete sources have been proposed in [149] and [340].

A number of other sources/fidelity criteria have been shown to admit explicit rate-distortion functions: the Wiener process [341], the Poisson process and other continuous-time Markov processes [342], binary Markov chains with bit-error-rate fidelity [343], and various sources with absolute error criterion [344]–[346]. The rate-distortion function of random fields was studied in [347] and [348].

The Shannon lower bound [325] on the rate-distortion function for difference-distortion measures has played a prominent role in rate-distortion theory (cf. [323]). Other lower bounds can be constructed using Gallager's technique [161]. A formula for the minimum distortion achievable per encoded bit was found in [198].

---

[37] Such expediency is not far off the mark in contrast to the channel-coding problem with reliability measured by block error probability.

[38] In 1948, Shannon authored (with B. Oliver and J. Pierce) a tutorial [326] on the bandwidth–fidelity tradeoff in PCM.

[39] In addition to Shannon's version with an average distortion constraint, Kolmogorov [327] considered a maximum distortion constraint (cf. [328]). A nonprobabilistic gauge of the size of subsets of metric spaces is also called ϵ-entropy [329].

[40] Usually referred to as "reverse water-filling."

C. Coding Theorems

In addition to proving the lossy source coding theorem for memoryless sources, Shannon [325] sketched an approach to deal with sources with memory. A substantial class of sources was encompassed by R. Dobrushin [193] in 1963, proving a general version of the source–channel separation theorem with distortion. Several less ambitious generalizations (but with more explicit scope) were carried out in the West in the subsequent decade (cf. [323] and [322]).

By the mid-1970's, a shift in focus away from ergodic/stationary sources was spearheaded by L. Davisson, R. Gray, J. Kieffer, D. Neuhoff, D. Ornstein, and their coworkers (see [35, Part V][41]) who studied sliding-block and variable-length encoding methods in addition to the traditional fixed-length block-encoding approach used by Shannon [325]. A 1993 survey of rate-distortion coding theorems can be found in [351].

D. Universal Lossy Data Compression

Spurred by its practical importance and by the existence results [352]–[357] proved in the 1970's, the quest for universal lossy data compression algorithms that attain the rate-distortion function has attracted the efforts of many an information theorist during the 1990's. The notable advances in this topic are exemplified by [358]–[370]. In contrast to universal lossless data compression, we cannot yet state that a fully constructive optimum algorithm has been found. Moreover, while objective distortion measures may serve as useful design guidelines, the ultimate judges of the performance of most lossy data compression algorithms are the eye and the ear.

E. Multiterminal Lossy Data Compression

Consider a digital-to-analog converter operating on the compressed version of the "left" audio source and having access to the uncompressed "right" audio source. How much improvement in compression efficiency can we expect due to the auxiliary information? If the analog-to-digital converter has access to the uncompressed "right" source then the problem is fairly easy to solve using standard rate-distortion theory. Otherwise, we face a counterpart of the problem of decoding with side-information (Section II-F) in the lossy setting,[42] which was solved by Wyner and Ziv [371], [372]. In contrast to the almost-lossless setting of the Slepian–Wolf problem, in this case the absence of side-information at the encoder does incur a loss of efficiency in general. Applications and generalizations of the Wyner–Ziv rate-distortion problem have been considered in [373]–[376], [335], and [377].

The *multiple-descriptions* problem is another multiterminal lossy source-coding problem that has received much attention in the last two decades.[43] The practical relevance of this setting stems from communications systems with diversity: for increased reliability, several channels are set up to connect transmitter and receiver. If those individual channels are prone to outage, we may consider sending the same compressed version of the source through each channel in parallel. However, such a strategy is wasteful because the receiver could get a lower distortion version of the source whenever more than one channel is operational. By appropriate choice of codes it is possible to trade off the rates and distortions achievable for every subset of operational channels. Some of the more salient advances that have been reported in the two-channel case can be found in [378]–[383].

A close relative of multiple descriptions coding is the *successive refinement* problem. Sometimes, the decoder is required to provide a preliminary coarse rendition of the source before proceeding to obtain a finer version after receiving additional encoded data (e.g., a Web browser downloading an image). To that end, it would be wasteful to use codes for which the preliminary encoded data is of no use for the decompression of the higher definition version. In fact, certain sources have the property that no penalty in rate is incurred by requiring the decoding of a preliminary coarse version. The successive refinement problem was introduced by V. Koshélev [384] and by W. Equitz and T. Cover [385], and solved in more generality by B. Rimoldi in [386].

Other multiterminal lossy source-coding problems have been studied by T. Berger and coworkers [387]–[389].

V. INFORMATION THEORY AND OTHER FIELDS

To conclude, we offer some pointers to the interactions of Information Theory with various other scientific disciplines.

1) *Probability*

- Central Limit Theorem [390]
- Large Deviations [391]–[393]
- Random Processes and Divergence [394]
- Measure Concentration [395], [396]
- Queueing Theory [194], [397]

2) *Statistical Inference* [398], [399]

- Minimum Description Length [95]
- Hypothesis Testing [168]
- Decentralized Hypothesis Testing [400]
- Parameter Estimation [401]
- Density Estimation [402]
- Minimax Nonparametric Estimation [403], [404]
- Spectral Estimation [405]
- Bayesian Statistics [406]
- Inverse Problems [407]
- Prediction of Discrete Time-Series [111]
- Pattern Recognition and Learning [408]
- Neural Networks [409], [410]
- Speech Recognition [411]

---

[41] Also [349] and [350] for more recent references.

[42] A recent trend in high-fidelity audio recording is to carry out analog-to-digital conversion at the microphone. The left and right digital-to-analog converters could cooperate to lower the required rate of recorded information even if the analog-to-digital converters had no access to each other's sources. The fundamental limit for this symmetrical setup is unknown.

[43] See [378] for an account of the early history of the results on multiple descriptions.

3) *Computer Science*

- Algorithmic Complexity [412], [413]
- Data Structures: Retrieval and Hashing [59]
- Cryptology [15], [414], [314]
- Computational Complexity [415], [439]
- Quantum Computing [416]
- Random Number Generation [417]–[419]

4) *Mathematics*

- Ergodic Theory and Dynamical Systems [420], [37]
- Combinatorics and Graph Theory [130]
- Inequalities and Convex Analysis [421], [422]
- Harmonic Analysis [324]
- Differential Geometry [423], [424]
- Stochastic Combinatorial Search [425]
- Number Theory [426]
- Systems Control [427], [428]

5) *Physics* [429]

- Thermodynamics [430]
- Physics of Computation [431]
- Statistical Mechanics [432]
- Quantum Information Theory [433]
- Chaos [434]

6) *Economics*

- Portfolio Theory [101], [440]
- Econometrics [428]

7) *Biology*

- Molecular Biology [435]
- Sensory processing [436], [437]

8) *Chemistry* [438]

ACKNOWLEDGMENT

This paper has benefited from comments and suggestions by J. Abrahams, A. Barron, E. Biglieri, R. Blahut, I. Csiszár, D. Forney, A. Lapidoth, N. Merhav, A. McKellips, P. Narayan, A. Orlitsky, V. Prelov, E. Telatar, F. Willems, B. Yu, and K. Zeger.

REFERENCES

[1] C. E. Shannon, "A mathematical theory of communication," *Bell Syst. Tech. J.*, vol. 27, pp. 379–423, 623–656, July–Oct. 1948.
[2] H. Dudley, "The vocoder," *Bell Labs. Rec.*, vol. 18, pp. 122–126, Dec. 1939.
[3] H. Nyquist, "Certain factors affecting telegraph speed," *Bell Syst. Tech. J.*, vol. 3, pp. 324–352, Apr. 1924.
[4] K. Küpfmüller, "Uber Einschwingvorgange in Wellenfiltern," *Elek. Nachrichtentech.*, vol. 1, pp. 141–152, Nov. 1924.
[5] H. Nyquist, "Certain topics in telegraph transmission theory," *AIEE Trans.*, vol. 47, pp. 617–644, Apr. 1928.
[6] V. A. Kotel'nikov, "On the transmission capacity of "ether" and wire in electrocommunications," *Izd. Red. Upr. Svyazi RKKA* (Moscow, USSR) (material for the first all-union conference on questions of communications), vol. 44, 1933.
[7] E. T. Whittaker, "On the functions which are represented by the expansion of interpolating theory," in *Proc. Roy. Soc. Edinburgh*, vol. 35, pp. 181–194, 1915.
[8] J. M. Whittaker, "The Fourier theory of the cardinal functions," *Proc. Math. Soc. Edinburgh*, vol. 1, pp. 169–176, 1929.
[9] D. Gabor, "Theory of communication," *J. Inst. Elec. Eng.*, vol. 93, pp. 429–457, Sept. 1946.
[10] R. V. L. Hartley, "Transmission of information," *Bell Syst. Tech. J.*, vol. 7, pp. 535–563, July 1928.
[11] N. Wiener, *Extrapolation, Interpolation and Smoothing of Stationary Time Series*. New York: Wiley, 1949.
[12] S. O. Rice, "Mathematical analysis of random noise," *Bell Syst. Tech. J.*, vol. 23–24, pp. 282–332 and 46–156, July 1944 and Jan. 1945.
[13] F. Pratt, *Secret and Urgent*. Blue Ribbon Books, 1939.
[14] C. E. Shannon, "A mathematical theory of cryptography," Tech. Rep. MM 45-110-02, Bell Labs. Tech. Memo., Sept. 1, 1945.
[15] _____, "Communication theory of secrecy systems," *Bell Syst. Tech. J.*, vol. 28, pp. 656–715, Oct. 1949.
[16] R. Price, "A conversation with Claude Shannon," *IEEE Commun. Mag.*, vol. 22, pp. 123–126, May 1984.
[17] J. R. Pierce, "The early days of information theory," *IEEE Trans. Inform. Theory*, vol. IT-19, pp. 3–8, Jan. 1973.
[18] F. W. Hagemeyer, "Die Entstehung von Informationskonzepten in der Nachrichtentechnik: eine Fallstudie zur Theoriebildung in der Technik in Industrie- und Kriegsforschung," Ph.D. dissertation, Free University of Berlin, Berlin, Germany, 1979.
[19] C. E. Shannon, "Letter to Vannevar Bush Feb. 16, 1939," in *Claude Elwood Shannon Collected Papers*, N. J. A. Sloane and A. D. Wyner, Eds. Piscataway, NJ: IEEE Press, pp. 455–456, 1993.
[20] _____, "A symbolic analysis of relay and switching circuits," M.S. thesis, MIT, Cambridge, MA, 1938.
[21] _____, "An algebra for theoretical genetics," Ph.D. dissertation, MIT, Cambridge, MA, Apr. 15, 1940.
[22] A. G. Clavier, "Evaluation of transmission efficiency according to Hartley's expression of information content," *Elec. Commun.: ITT Tech. J.*, vol. 25, pp. 414–420, June 1948.
[23] C. W. Earp, "Relationship between rate of transmission of information, frequency bandwidth, and signal-to-noise ratio," *Elec. Commun.: ITT Tech. J.*, vol. 25, pp. 178–195, June 1948.
[24] S. Goldman, "Some fundamental considerations concerning noise reduction and range in radar and communication," *Proc. Inst. Elec. Eng.*, vol. 36, pp. 584–594, 1948,
[25] J. Laplume, "Sur le nombre de signaux discernables en présence de bruit erratique dans un système de transmission à bande passante limitée," *Comp. Rend. Acad. Sci. Paris*, pp. 1348–, 1948.
[26] W. G. Tuller, "Theoretical limitations on the rate of transmission of information," Ph.D. dissertation, MIT, Cambridge, MA, June 1948, published in *Proc. IRE*, pp. 468–478, May 1949.
[27] N. Wiener, *Cybernetics, Chaper III: Time Series, Information and Communication*. New York: Wiley, 1948.
[28] R. A. Fisher, "Probability, likelihood and quantity of information in the logic of uncertain inference," *Proc. Roy. Soc. London, A*, vol. 146, pp. 1–8, 1934.
[29] L. Boltzmann, "Beziehung zwischen dem Zweiten Hauptsatze der Mechanischen Waermertheorie und der Wahrscheilichkeitsrechnung Respektive den Saetzen uber das Waermegleichgwicht," *Wien. Ber.*, vol. 76, pp. 373–435, 1877.
[30] N. Chomsky, "Three models for the description of language," *IEEE Trans. Inform. Theory*, vol. IT-2, pp. 113–124, Sept. 1956.
[31] A. I. Khinchin, "The entropy concept in probability theory," *Usp. Mat. Nauk.*, vol. 8, pp. 3–20, 1953, English translation in *Mathematical Foundations of Information Theory*. New York: Dover, 1957.
[32] B. McMillan, "The basic theorems of information theory," *Ann. Math. Statist.*, vol. 24, pp. 196–219, June 1953.
[33] A. N. Kolmogorov, "A new metric invariant of transitive dynamical systems and automorphism in Lebesgue spaces," *Dokl. Akad. Nauk. SSSR*, vol. 119, pp. 861–864, 1958.
[34] D. S. Ornstein, "Bernoulli shifts with the same entropy are isomorphic," *Adv. Math.*, vol. 4, pp. 337–352, 1970.
[35] R. M. Gray and L. D. Davisson, Eds., *Ergodic and Information Theory*. Stroudsbourg, PA: Dowden, Hutchinson & Ross, 1977.
[36] I. Csiszár, "Information theory and ergodic theory," *Probl. Contr. Inform. Theory*, vol. 16, pp. 3–27, 1987.
[37] P. Shields, "The interactions between ergodic theory and information theory," this issue, pp. 2079–2093.
[38] L. Breiman, "The individual ergodic theorems of information theory," *Ann. Math. Statist.*, vol. 28, pp. 809–811, 1957.
[39] P. Algoet and T. M. Cover, "A sandwich proof of the Shannon–McMillan–Breiman theorem," *Ann. Probab.*, vol. 16, pp. 899–909, 1988.
[40] S. C. Moy, "Generalizations of the Shannon–McMillan theorem," *Pacific J. Math.*, vol. 11, pp. 705–714, 1961.
[41] K. Marton, "Information and information stability of ergodic sources," *Probl. Inform. Transm.*, vol. 8, pp. 179–183, 1972.

[42] J. C. Kieffer, "A simple proof of the Moy–Perez generalization of the Shannon–McMillan theorem," *Pacific J. Math.*, vol. 351, pp. 203–206, 1974.

[43] D. S. Ornstein and B. Weiss, "The Shannon–McMillan–Breiman theorem for amenable groups," *Israel J. Math.*, vol. 39, pp. 53–60, 1983.

[44] A. R. Barron, "The strong ergodic theorem for densities: Generalized Shannon–McMillan–Breiman theorem," *Ann. Probab.*, vol. 13, pp. 1292–1303, 1985.

[45] S. Orey, "On the Shannon-Perez-Moy theorem," *Contemp. Math.*, vol. 41, pp. 319–327, 1985.

[46] T. S. Han and S. Verdú, "Approximation theory of output statistics," *IEEE Trans. Inform. Theory*, vol. 39, pp. 752–772, May 1993.

[47] S. Verdú and T. S. Han, "The role of the asymptotic equipartition property in noiseless source coding," *IEEE Trans. Inform. Theory*, vol. 43, pp. 847–857, May 1997.

[48] D. Huffman, "A method for the construction of minimum redundancy codes," *Proc. IRE*, vol. 40, pp. 1098–1101, Sept. 1952.

[49] I. S. Reed, "1982 Claude Shannon lecture: Application of transforms to coding and related topics," *IEEE Inform. Theory Newslett.*, pp. 4–7, Dec. 1982.

[50] R. Hunter and A. Robinson, "International digital facsimile coding standards," *Proc. Inst. Elec. Radio Eng.*, vol. 68, pp. 854–867, July 1980.

[51] K. Challapali, X. Lebegue, J. S. Lim, W. Paik, R. Girons, E. Petajan, V. Sathe, P. Snopko, and J. Zdepski, "The grand alliance system for US HDTV," *Proc. IEEE*, vol. 83, pp. 158–174, Feb. 1995.

[52] R. G. Gallager, "Variations on a theme by Huffman," *IEEE Trans. Inform. Theory*, vol. IT-24, pp. 668–674, Nov. 1978.

[53] R. M. Capocelli and A. DeSantis, "Variations on a theme by Gallager," in *Image and Text Compression*, J. A. Storer, Ed. Boston, NA: Kluwer, pp. 181–213, 1992.

[54] L. Kraft, "A device for quantizing, grouping and coding amplitude modulated pulses," M.S. Thesis, Dept. Elec. Eng., MIT, Cambridge, MA, 1949.

[55] I. S. Sokolnikoff and R. M. Redheffer, *Mathematics of Physics and Modern Engineering*, 2d ed. New York: McGraw-Hill, 1966.

[56] B. McMillan, "Two inequalities implied by unique decipherability," *IRE Trans. Inform. Theory*, vol. IT-2, pp. 115–116, Dec. 1956.

[57] J. Karush, "A simple proof of an inequality of McMillan," *IEEE Trans. Inform. Theory*, vol. IT-7, pp. 118, Apr. 1961.

[58] J. Abrahams, "Code and parse trees for lossless source encoding," in *Proc. Compression and Complexity of Sequences 1997*, B. Carpentieri, A. De Santis, U. Vaccaro, and J. Storer, Eds. Los Alamitos, CA: IEEE Comp. Soc., 1998, pp. 145–171.

[59] R. E. Krichevsky, *Universal Compression and Retrieval*. Dordrecht, The Netherlands: Kluwer, 1994.

[60] J. Rissanen, "Generalized Kraft inequality and arithmetic coding," *IBM J. Res. Devel.*, vol. 20, pp. 198–203, 1976.

[61] R. Pasco, "Source coding algorithms for fast data compression," Ph.D. dissertation, Stanford Univ., Stanford, CA, 1976.

[62] J. Rissanen and G. G. Langdon, "Arithmetic coding," *IBM J. Res. Develop.*, vol. 23, pp. 149–162, Mar. 1979.

[63] I. H. Witten, R. M. Neal, and J. G. Cleary, "Arithmetic coding for data compression," *Commun. Assoc. Comp. Mach.*, vol. 30, pp. 520–540, June 1987.

[64] N. Abramson, *Information Theory and Coding*. New York: McGraw-Hill, 1963.

[65] F. Jelinek, *Probabilistic Information Theory*. New York: McGraw-Hill, 1968.

[66] P. Elias, personal communication, Apr. 22, 1998.

[67] E. Gilbert and E. Moore, "Variable-length binary encodings," *Bell Syst. Tech. J.*, vol. 38, pp. 933–967, 1959.

[68] T. M. Cover, "Enumerative source coding," *IEEE Trans. Inform. Theory*, vol. IT-19, pp. 73–77, 1973.

[69] R. Aravind, G. Cash, D. Duttweiler, H. Hang, B. Haskell, and A. Puri, "Image and video coding standards," *ATT Tech. J.*, vol. 72, pp. 67–89, Jan.–Feb. 1993.

[70] B. P. Tunstall, "Synthesis of noiseless compression codes," Ph.D. dissertation, Georgia Inst. Technol., Atlanta, GA, Sept. 1967.

[71] G. L. Khodak, "The estimation of redundancy for coding the messages generated by a Bernoulli source," *Probl. Inform. Transm.*, vol. 8, pp. 28–32, 1972.

[72] F. Jelinek and K. Schneider, "On variable-length to block coding," *IEEE Trans. Inform. Theory*, vol. IT-18, pp. 765–774, Nov. 1972.

[73] T. J. Tjalkens and F. M. J. Willems, "Variable to fixed-length codes for Markov sources," *IEEE Trans. Inform. Theory*, vol. IT-33, pp. 246–257, Mar. 1987.

[74] S. Savari and R. G. Gallager, "Generalized Tunstall codes for sources with memory," *IEEE Trans. Inform. Theory*, vol. 43, pp. 658–668, Mar. 1997.

[75] J. Ziv, "Variable-to-fixed length codes are better than fixed-to-variable length codes for Markov sources," *IEEE Trans. Inform. Theory*, vol. 36, pp. 861–863, July 1990.

[76] N. Merhav and D. L. Neuhoff, "Variable-to-fixed length codes provide better large deviations performance than fixed-to-variable length codes," *IEEE Trans. Inform. Theory*, vol. 38, pp. 135–140, Jan. 1992.

[77] R. E. Krichevsky and V. K. Trofimov, "The performance of universal encoding," *IEEE Trans. Inform. Theory*, vol. IT-27, pp. 199–206, Mar. 1981.

[78] S. W. Golomb, "Run length encodings," *IEEE Trans. Inform. Theory*, vol. IT-12, pp. 399–401, July 1966.

[79] C. E. Shannon, "Efficient coding of a binary source with one very infrequent symbol," Bell Labs. Memo. Jan. 29, 1954, in *Claude Elwood Shannon Collected Papers*, N. J. A. Sloane and A. D. Wyner, Eds. Piscataway, NJ: IEEE Press, 1993, pp. 455–456.

[80] A. N. Kolmogorov, "Three approaches to the quantitative definition of information," *Probl. Inform. Transm.*, vol. 1, pp. 1–7, 1965.

[81] E. Gilbert, "Codes based on inaccurate source probabilities," *IEEE Trans. Inform. Theory*, vol. IT-17, pp. 304–314, May 1971.

[82] F. Fabris, A. Sgarro, and R. Pauletti, "Tunstall adaptive coding and miscoding," *IEEE Trans. Inform. Theory*, vol. 42, pp. 2167–2180, Nov. 1996.

[83] B. M. Fitingof, "Optimal encoding with unknown and variable message statistics," *Probl. Inform. Transm.*, vol. 2, pp. 3–11, 1966.

[84] L. Davisson, "Universal noiseless coding," *IEEE Trans. Inform. Theory*, vol. IT-19, pp. 783–795, Nov. 1973.

[85] T. J. Tjalkens and F. M. J. Willems, "A universal variable-to-fixed length source code based on Lawrence's algorithm," *IEEE Trans. Inform. Theory*, vol. 38, pp. 247–253, Mar. 1992.

[86] N. Faller, "An adaptive system for data compression," in *7th Asilomar Conf. on Circuits, Systems, and Computing*, 1973, pp. 593–597.

[87] D. E. Knuth, "Dynamic Huffman coding," *J. Algorithms*, vol. 1985, pp. 163–180, 1985.

[88] J. S. Vitter, "Dynamic Huffman coding," *ACM Trans. Math. Software*, vol. 15, pp. 158–167, June 1989.

[89] B. Ryabko, "A fast on-line adaptive code," *IEEE Trans. Inform. Theory*, vol. 38, pp. 1400–1404, July 1992.

[90] _____, "Data compression by means of a book stack," *Probl. Inform. Transm.*, vol. 16, pp. 265–269, 1980.

[91] J. Bentley, D. Sleator, R. Tarjan, and V. Wei, "Locally adaptive data compression scheme," *Commun. Assoc. Comp. Mach.*, vol. 29, pp. 320–330, 1986.

[92] P. Elias, "Interval and recency rank source coding: Two on-line adaptive variable-length schemes," *IEEE Trans. Inform. Theory*, vol. IT-33, pp. 3–10, Jan. 1987.

[93] M. Burrows and D. J. Wheeler, "A block-sorting lossless data compression algorithm," Tech. Rep. 124, Digital Systems Res. Ctr., Palo Alto, CA, May 10, 1994.

[94] J. Rissanen, "Universal coding, information, prediction, and estimation," *IEEE Trans. Inform. Theory*, vol. IT-30, pp. 629–636, July 1984.

[95] A. Barron, J. Rissanen, and B. Yu, "The minimum description length principle in coding and modeling," this issue, pp. 2743–2760.

[96] A. Lempel and J. Ziv, "On the complexity of an individual sequence," *IEEE Trans. Inform. Theory*, vol. IT-22, pp. 75–81, Jan. 1976.

[97] J. Ziv and A. Lempel, "A universal algorithm for sequential data compression," *IEEE Trans. Inform. Theory*, vol. IT-24, pp. 337–343, May 1977.

[98] _____, "Compression of individual sequences via variable-rate coding," *IEEE Trans. Inform. Theory*, vol. IT-24, pp. 530–536, Sept. 1978.

[99] T. A. Welch, "A technique for high performance data compression," *Computer*, vol. 17, pp. 8–19, June 1984.

[100] J. Ziv, "Coding theorems for individual sequences," *IEEE Trans. Inform. Theory*, vol. IT-24, pp. 405–412, July 1978.

[101] T. M. Cover and J. A. Thomas, *Elements of Information Theory*. New York: Wiley, 1991.

[102] A. D. Wyner and J. Ziv, "The sliding-window Lempel-Ziv algorithm is asymptotically optimal," *Proc. IEEE*, vol. 82, pp. 872–877, June 1994.

[103] F. M. J. Willems, "Universal data compression and repetition times," *IEEE Trans. Inform. Theory*, vol. 35, pp. 54–58, Jan. 1989.

[104] A. D. Wyner and J. Ziv, "Some asymptotic properties of the entropy of a stationary ergodic data source with applications to data compression," *IEEE Trans. Inform. Theory*, vol. 35, pp. 1250–1258, Nov. 1989.

[105] D. S. Ornstein and B. Weiss, "Entropy and data compression schemes," *IEEE Trans. Inform. Theory*, vol. 39, pp. 78–83, Jan. 1993.

[106] W. Szpankowski, "Asymptotic properties of data compression and suffix trees," *IEEE Trans. Inform. Theory*, vol. 39, pp. 1647–1659, Sept. 1993.

[107] P. Jacquet and W. Szpankowski, "Asymptotic behavior of the Lempel–Ziv parsing scheme and digital search trees," *Theor. Comp. Sci.*, vol. 144, pp. 161–197, June 1995.

[108] A. D. Wyner, J. Ziv, and A. J. Wyner, "On the role of pattern matching in information theory," this issue, pp. 2045–2056.

[109] J. Rissanen, "A universal data compression system," *IEEE Trans. Inform. Theory*, vol. IT-29, pp. 656–663, Sept. 1983.

[110] F. M. J. Willems, Y. M. Shtarkov, and T. J. Tjalkens, "The context-tree weighting method: Basic properties," *IEEE Trans. Inform. Theory*, vol. IT-28, pp. 653–664, May 1995.

[111] N. Merhav and M. Feder, "Universal prediction," this issue, pp. 2124–2147.

[112] V. I. Levenshtein, "On the redundancy and delay of decodable coding of natural numbers," *Probl. Cybern.*, vol. 20, pp. 173–179, 1968.

[113] P. Elias, "Universal codeword sets and representation of the integers," *IEEE Trans. Inform. Theory*, vol. IT-21, pp. 194–203, Mar. 1975.

[114] Q. F. Stout, "Improved prefix encodings of the natural numbers," *IEEE Trans. Inform. Theory*, vol. IT-26, pp. 607–609, Sept. 1980.

[115] R. Ahlswede, T. S. Han, and K. Kobayashi, "Universal coding of integers and unbounded search trees," *IEEE Trans. Inform. Theory*, vol. 43, pp. 669–682, Mar. 1997.

[116] C. E. Shannon, "Prediction and entropy of printed English," *Bell Syst. Tech. J.*, vol. 30, pp. 47–51, Jan. 1951.

[117] T. M. Cover and R. C. King, "A convergent gambling estimate of the entropy of English," *IEEE Trans. Inform. Theory*, vol. IT-24, pp. 413–421, July 1978.

[118] L. Levitin and Z. Reingold, "Entropy of natural languages—Theory and practice," *Chaos, Solitons and Fractals*, vol. 4, pp. 709–743, May 1994.

[119] P. Grassberger, "Estimating the information content of symbol sequences and efficient codes," *IEEE Trans. Inform. Theory*, vol. 35, pp. 669–675, May 1989.

[120] P. Hall and S. Morton, "On the estimation of entropy," *Ann. Inst. Statist. Math.*, vol. 45, pp. 69–88, Mar. 1993.

[121] I. Kontoyiannis, P. Algoet, Y. Suhov, and A. J. Wyner, "Nonparametric entropy estimation for stationary processes and random fields, with applications to English text," *IEEE Trans. Inform. Theory*, vol. 44, pp. 1319–1327, May 1998.

[122] A. N. Kolmogorov, "Logical basis for information theory and probability theory," *IEEE Trans. Inform. Theory*, vol. IT-14, pp. 662–664, 1968.

[123] G. J. Chaitin, "On the length of programs for computing binary sequences," *J. Assoc. Comput. Mach.*, vol. 13, pp. 547–569, 1966.

[124] R. J. Solomonoff, "A formal theory of inductive inference," *Inform. Contr.*, vol. 7, pp. 1–22, 224–254, 1964.

[125] T. M. Cover, P. Gacs, and R. M. Gray, "Kolmogorov's contributions to information theory and algorithmic complexity," *Ann. Probab.*, vol. 17, pp. 840–865, July 1989.

[126] D. Slepian and J. K. Wolf, "Noiseless coding of correlated information sources," *IEEE Trans. Inform. Theory*, vol. IT-19, pp. 471–480, 1973.

[127] T. M. Cover, "A proof of the data compression theorem of Slepian and Wolf for ergodic sources," *IEEE Trans. Inform. Theory*, vol. IT-22, pp. 226–228, Mar. 1975.

[128] A. D. Wyner, "Recent results in the Shannon theory," *IEEE Trans. Inform. Theory*, vol. IT-20, pp. 2–9, Jan. 1974.

[129] S. Shamai (Shitz) and S. Verdú, "Capacity of channels with side information," *Euro. Trans. Telecommun.*, vol. 6, no. 5, pp. 587–600, Sept.–Oct. 1995.

[130] J. Körner and A. Orlitsky, "Zero-error information theory," this issue, pp. 2207–2229.

[131] H. S. Witsenhausen, "The zero-error side information problem and chromatic numbers," *IEEE Trans. Inform. Theory*, vol. IT-22, pp. 592–593, Sept. 1976.

[132] R. Ahlswede, "Coloring hypergraphs: A new approach to multiuser source coding," *J. Comb. Inform. Syst. Sci.*, vol. 4, pp. 76–115, 1979; Part II, vol. 5, pp. 220–268, 1980.

[133] A. C. Yao, "Some complexity questions related to distributive computing," in *Proc. 11th Assoc. Comp. Mach. Symp. Theory of Computing*, 1979, pp. 209–213.

[134] A. Orlitsky, "Worst-case interactive communication. I: Two messages are almost optimal," *IEEE Trans. Inform. Theory*, vol. 36, pp. 1534–1547, Sept. 1990.

[135] _____, "Average case interactive communication," *IEEE Trans. Inform. Theory*, vol. 38, pp. 1534–1547, Sept. 1992.

[136] M. Naor, A. Orlitsky, and P. Shor, "Three results on interactive communication," *IEEE Trans. Inform. Theory*, vol. 39, pp. 1608–1615, Sept. 1993.

[137] R. Ahlswede, N. Cai, and Z. Zhang, "On interactive communication," *IEEE Trans. Inform. Theory*, vol. 43, pp. 22–37, Jan. 1997.

[138] A. R. Calderbank, "The art of signaling: Fifty years of coding theory," this issue, pp. 2561–2595..

[139] A. Liversidge, "Profile of Claude Shannon," *Omni* magazine, Aug. 1987, in *Claude Elwood Shannon Collected Papers*, N. J. A. Sloane and A. D. Wyner, Eds. Piscataway, NJ: IEEE Press, 1993, pp. xix–xxxiii.

[140] C. E. Shannon, "The zero error capacity of a noisy channel," *IRE Trans. Inform. Theory*, vol. IT-2, pp. 112–124, Sept. 1956.

[141] J. G. Kreer, "A question of terminology," *IEEE Trans. Inform. Theory*, vol. IT-3, pp. 208, Sept. 1957.

[142] I. M. Gelfand, A. N. Kolmogorov, and A. M. Yaglom, "On the general definition of mutual information," *Repts. Acad. Sci. USSR*, vol. 3, pp. 745–748, 1956.

[143] I. M. Gelfand and A. M. Yaglom, "On the computation of the mutual information between a pair of random functions," *Adv. Math. Sci.*, vol. 12, pp. 3–52, 1957.

[144] I. M. Gelfand, A. N. Kolmogorov, and A. M. Yaglom, "Mutual information and entropy for continuous distributions," in *Proc. 3rd All Union Math. Congr.*, 1958, vol. 3, pp. 521–531.

[145] M. S. Pinsker, *Information and Information Stability of Random Variables and Processes*. San Francisco, CA: Holden-Day, 1964, originally published in Russian in 1960.

[146] S. Muroga, "On the capacity of a discrete channel," *J. Phys. Soc. Japan*, vol. 8, pp. 484–494, 1953.

[147] C. E. Shannon, "Some geometrical results in channel capacity," *Verband Deut. Elektrotechnik. Fachber.*, vol. 19, pp. 13–15, 1956.

[148] S. Arimoto, "An algorithm for computing the capacity of arbitrary discrete memoryless channels," *IEEE Trans. Inform. Theory*, vol. IT-18, pp. 14–20, Jan. 1972.

[149] R. E. Blahut, "Computation of channel capacity and rate-distortion functions," *IEEE Trans. Inform. Theory*, vol. IT-18, pp. 460–473, July 1972.

[150] C. E. Shannon, "Communication in the presence of noise," *Proc. IRE*, vol. 37, pp. 10–21, Jan. 1949.

[151] A. J. Jerri, "The Shannon sampling theorem—Its various extensions and applications: A tutorial review," *Proc. IEEE*, vol. 65, pp. 1565–1596, Nov. 1977.

[152] R. J. Marks, *Introduction to Shannon Sampling and Interpolation Theory*. New York: Springer, 1991.

[153] M. J. E. Golay, "Note on the theoretical efficiency of information reception with PPM," *Proc. IRE*, vol. 37, p. 1031, Sept. 1949.

[154] C. E. Shannon, "General treatment of the problem of coding," *IRE Trans. Inform. Theory*, vol. PGIT-1, pp. 102–104, Feb. 1953.

[155] D. Slepian, "Information theory in the fifties" (Invited Paper), *IEEE Trans. Inform. Theory*, vol. IT-19, pp. 145–147, Mar. 1973.

[156] D. Slepian, "On bandwidth," *Proc. IEEE*, vol. 64, pp. 292–300, Mar. 1976.

[157] A. D. Wyner, "The capacity of the band-limited Gaussian channel," *Bell Syst. Tech. J.*, vol. 45, pp. 359–371, Mar. 1966.

[158] H. J. Landau, D. Slepian, and H. O. Pollack, "Prolate spheroidal wave functions, Fourier analysis and uncertainty—III: The dimension of the space of essentially time- and band-limited signals," *Bell Syst. Tech. J.*, vol. 41, pp. 1295–1336, July 1962.

[159] S. Shamai (Shitz) and S. Verdú, "The empirical distribution of good codes," *IEEE Trans. Inform. Theory*, vol. 43, pp. 836–846, May 1997.

[160] J. L. Holsinger, "Digital communication over fixed time-continuous channels with memory with special application to telephone channels," Tech. Rep. 430, MIT Res. Lab. Electron., Cambridge, MA, 1964.

[161] R. G. Gallager, *Information Theory and Reliable Communication*. New York: Wiley, 1968.

[162] B. S. Tsybakov, "Capacity of a discrete-time Gaussian channel with a filter," *Probl. Inform. Transm.*, vol. 6, pp. 253–256, July–Sept. 1970.

[163] U. Grenander and G. Szegö, *Toeplitz Forms and Their Applications*. New York: Chelsea, 1958.

[164] R. M. Gray, "On the asymptotic eigenvalue distribution of toeplitz matrices," *IEEE Trans. Inform. Theory*, vol. IT-18, pp. 725–730, Nov. 1972.

[165] W. Hirt and J. L. Massey, "Capacity of the discrete-time Gaussian channel with intersymbol interference," *IEEE Trans. Inform. Theory*, vol. 34, pp. 380–388, May 1988.

[166] J. G. Smith, "The information capacity of amplitude- and variance-constrained scalar Gaussian channels," *Inform. Contr.*, vol. 18, pp. 203–219, 1971.

[167] S. Shamai (Shitz) and I. Bar-David, "The capacity of average and peak-power-limited quadrature Gaussian channels," *IEEE Trans. Inform. Theory*, vol. 41, pp. 1060–1071, July 1995.

[168] R. E. Blahut, *Principles and Practice of Information Theory*. Reading, MA: Addison-Wesley, 1987.

[169] G. D. Forney and G. Ungerboeck, "Modulation and coding for linear Gaussian channels," this issue, pp. 2384–2415.

[170] N. M. Blachman, "Communication as a game," in *IRE Wescon Rec.*, 1957, vol. 2, pp. 61–66.

[171] J. M. Borden, D. M. Mason, and R. J. McEliece, "Some information theoretic saddlepoints," *SIAM J. Contr. Optimiz.*, vol. 23, pp. 129–143, Jan. 1985.

[172] S. Shamai (Shitz) and S. Verdú, "Worst-case power constrained noise for binary-input channels," *IEEE Trans. Inform. Theory*, vol. 38, pp. 1494–1511, Sept. 1992.

[173] S. Ihara, "On the capacity of channels with additive non-Gaussian noise," *Inform. Contr.*, vol. 37, pp. 34–39, 1978.

[174] A. Stam, "Some inequalities satisfied by the quantities of information of Fisher and Shannon," *Inform. Contr.*, vol. 2, pp. 101–112, 1959.

[175] V. Prelov, "Asymptotic behavior of a continuous channel with small additive noise," *Probl. Inform. Transm.*, vol. 4, no. 2, pp. 31–37, 1968.

[176] ———, "Asymptotic behavior of the capacity of a continuous channel with large noise," *Probl. Inform. Transm.*, vol. 6 no. 2, pp. 122–135, 1970.

[177] ———, "Communication channel capacity with almost Gaussian noise," *Theory Probab. Its Applications*, vol. 33, no. 2, pp. 405–422, 1989.

[178] M. Pinsker, V. Prelov, and S. Verdú, "Sensitivity of channel capacity," *IEEE Trans. Inform. Theory*, vol. 41, pp. 1877–1888, Nov. 1995.

[179] E. Biglieri, J. Proakis, and S. Shamai, "Fading channels: Information-theoretic and communications aspects," this issue, pp. 2619–2692..

[180] R. M. Fano, "Class notes for course 6.574: Transmission of information," MIT, Cambridge, MA, 1952.

[181] S. Vembu, S. Verdú, and Y. Steinberg, "The source-channel separation theorem revisited," *IEEE Trans. Inform. Theory*, vol. 41, pp. 44–54, Jan. 1995.

[182] J. Wolfowitz, "The coding of messages subject to chance errors," *Illinois J. Math.*, vol. 1, pp. 591–606, Dec. 1957.

[183] A. Feinstein, "A new basic theorem of information theory," *IRE Trans. Inform. Theory*, vol. PGIT-4, pp. 2–22, 1954.

[184] T. T. Kadota, "Generalization of Feinstein's fundamental lemma," *IEEE Trans. Inform. Theory*, vol. IT-16, pp. 791–792, Nov. 1970.

[185] I. Csiszár and J. Körner, *Information Theory: Coding Theorems for Discrete Memoryless Systems*. New York: Academic, 1981.

[186] I. Csiszár, "The method of types," this issue, pp. 2505–2523.

[187] A. El-Gamal and T. M. Cover, "Multiple user information theory," *Proc. IEEE*, vol. 68, pp. 1466–1483, Dec. 1980.

[188] C. E. Shannon, "Certain results in coding theory for noisy channels," *Inform. Contr.*, vol. 1, pp. 6–25, Sept. 1957.

[189] R. G. Gallager, "A simple derivation of the coding theorem and some applications," *IEEE Trans. Inform. Theory*, vol. IT-11, pp. 3–18, Jan. 1965.

[190] A. I. Khinchin, "On the fundamental theorems of information theory," *Usp. Mat. Nauk.*, vol. 11, pp. 17–75, 1956, English translation in *Mathematical Foundations of Information Theory*. New York: Dover, 1957.

[191] I. P. Tsaregradsky, "On the capacity of a stationary channel with finite memory," *Theory Probab. Its Applications*, vol. 3, pp. 84–96, 1958.

[192] A. Feinstein, "On the coding theorem and its converse for finite-memory channels," *Inform. Contr.*, vol. 2, pp. 25–44, 1959.

[193] R. L. Dobrushin, "General formulation of Shannon's main theorem in information theory," *Amer. Math. Soc. Transl.*, vol. 33, pp. 323–438, 1963.

[194] V. Anantharam and S. Verdú, "Bits through queues," *IEEE Trans. Inform. Theory*, vol. 42, pp. 4–18, Jan. 1996.

[195] A. S. Bedekar and M. Azizoğlu, "The information-theoretic capacity of discrete-time queues," *IEEE Trans. Inform. Theory*, vol. 44, pp. 446–461, Mar. 1998.

[196] S. Verdú and T. S. Han, "A general formula for channel capacity," *IEEE Trans. Inform. Theory*, vol. 40, pp. 1147–1157, July 1994.

[197] T. S. Han, *Information Spectrum Methods in Information Theory*. Tokyo, Japan: Baifukan, 1998, in Japanese.

[198] S. Verdú, "On channel capacity per unit cost," *IEEE Trans. Inform. Theory*, vol. 36, pp. 1019–1030, Sept. 1990.

[199] R. L. Dobrushin, "Shannon's theorems for channels with synchronization errors," *Probl. Inform. Transm.*, vol. 3, pp. 11–26, 1967.

[200] S. Z. Stambler, "Memoryless channels with synchronization errors—General case," *Probl. Inform. Transm.*, vol. 6, no. 3, pp. 43–49, 1970.

[201] K. A. S. Immink, P. Siegel, and J. K. Wolf, "Codes for digital recorders," this issue, pp. 2260–2299.

[202] L. Lovász, "On the Shannon capacity of a graph," *IEEE Trans. Inform. Theory*, vol. IT-25, pp. 1–7, Jan. 1979.

[203] N. Alon, "The Shannon capacity of a union," *Combinatorica*, to be published.

[204] S. O. Rice, "Communication in the presence of noise—Probability of error for two encoding schemes," *Bell Syst. Tech. J.*, pp. 60–93, Jan. 1950.

[205] A. Feinstein, "Error bounds in noisy channels with memory," *IRE Trans. Inform. Theory*, vol. PGIT-1, pp. 13–14, Sept. 1955.

[206] C. E. Shannon, "Probability of error for optimal codes in a Gaussian channel," *Bell Syst. Tech. J.*, vol. 38, pp. 611–656, May 1959.

[207] P. Elias, "Coding for noisy channels," in *IRE Conv. Rec.*, Mar. 1955, vol. 4, pp. 37–46.

[208] R. L. Dobrushin, "Asymptotic bounds on error probability for transmission over DMC with symmetric transition probabilities," *Theory Probab. Applicat.*, vol. 7, pp. 283–311, 1962.

[209] R. M. Fano, *Transmission of Information*. New York: Wiley, 1961.

[210] R. L. Dobrushin, "Optimal binary codes for low rates of information transmission," *Theory of Probab. Applicat.*, vol. 7, pp. 208–213, 1962.

[211] C. E. Shannon, R. G. Gallager, and E. Berlekamp, "Lower bounds to error probability for coding on discrete memoryless channels, I," *Inform. Contr.*, vol. 10, pp. 65–103, 1967.

[212] ———, "Lower bounds to error probability for coding on discrete memoryless channels, II," *Inform. Contr.*, vol. 10, pp. 522–552, 1967.

[213] E. A. Haroutunian, "Bounds on the exponent of the error probability for a semicontinuous memoryless channel," *Probl. Inform. Transm.*, vol. 4, pp. 37–48, 1968.

[214] R. E. Blahut, "Hypothesis testing and information theory," *IEEE Trans. Inform. Theory*, vol. IT-20, pp. 405–417, July 1974.

[215] R. J. McEliece and J. K. Omura, "An improved upper bound on the block coding error exponent for binary-input discrete memoryless channels," *IEEE Trans. Inform. Theory*, vol. IT-23, pp. 611–613, Sept. 1977.

[216] S. Litsyn, "New upper bounds on error exponents," Tech. Rep. EE-S-98-01, Tel. Aviv Univ., Ramat-Aviv., Israel, 1998.

[217] I. Csiszár and J. Körner, "Graph decomposition: A new key to coding theorems," *IEEE Trans. Inform. Theory*, vol. IT-27, pp. 5–11, Jan. 1981.

[218] S. Kullback and R. A. Leibler, "On information and sufficiency," *Ann. Math. Statist.*, vol. 22, pp. 79–86, 1951.

[219] A. Wald, "Note on the consistency of the maximum likelihood estimate," *Ann. Math. Statist.*, vol. 20, pp. 595–601, 1949.

[220] I. M. Jacobs and E. R. Berlekamp, "A lower bound to the distribution of computation for sequential decoding," *IEEE Trans. Inform. Theory*, vol. IT-13, pp. 167–174, Apr. 1967.

[221] E. Arikan, "An upper bound to the cutoff rate of sequential decoding," *IEEE Trans. Inform. Theory*, vol. 34, pp. 55–63, Jan. 1988.

[222] J. L. Massey, "Coding and modulation in digital communications," in *1974 Zurich Sem. Digital Communications*, 1974, pp. E2(1)–E2(4).

[223] I. Csiszár, "Generalized cutoff rates and Rényi's information measures," *IEEE Trans. Inform. Theory*, vol. 41, pp. 26–34, Jan. 1995.

[224] P. Elias, "List decoding for noisy channels," in *IRE WESCON Conv. Rec.*, 1957, vol. 2, pp. 94–104.

[225] G. D. Forney, "Exponential error bounds for erasure list, and decision feedback schemes," *IEEE Trans. Inform. Theory*, vol. IT-14, pp. 206–220, Mar. 1968.

[226] R. Ahlswede, "Channel capacities for list codes," *J. Appl. Probab.*, vol. 10, pp. 824–836, 1973.

[227] P. Elias, "Error correcting codes for list decoding," *IEEE Trans. Inform. Theory*, vol. 37, pp. 5–12, Jan. 1991.

[228] V. Blinovsky, "List decoding," *Discr. Math.*, vol. 106, pp. 45–51, Sept. 1992.

[229] P. Elias, "Zero error capacity under list decoding," *IEEE Trans. Inform. Theory*, vol. 34, pp. 1070–1074, Sept. 1988.

[230] İ. E. Telatar, "Zero error list capacities of discrete memoryless channels," *IEEE Trans. Inform. Theory*, vol. 43, pp. 1977–1982, Nov. 1997.

[231] K. S. Zigangirov, "Upper bounds on the error probability for channels with feedback," *Probl. Inform. Transm.*, vol. 6, no. 2, pp. 87–92, 1970.

[232] J. P. M. Schalkwijk and T. Kailath, "A coding scheme for additive noise channels with feedback," *IEEE Trans. Inform. Theory*, vol. IT-12, pp. 183–189, Apr. 1966.

[233] M. S. Pinsker, "Error probability for block transmission on a Gaussian memoryless channel with feedback," *Probl. Inform. Transm.*, vol. 4, no. 4, pp. 3–19, 1968.

[234] M. S. Pinsker and A. Dyachkov, "Optimal linear transmission through a memoryless Gaussian channel with full feedback," *Probl. Inform. Transm.*, vol. 7, pp. 123–129, 1971.

[235] R. S. Liptser, "Optimal encoding and decoding for transmission of Gaussian Markov signal over a noiseless feedback channel," *Probl. Inform. Transm.*, vol. 10, no. 4, pp. 3–15, 1974.

[236] I. A. Ovseevich, "Capacity of a random channel with feedback and the matching of a source to such a channel," *Probl. Inform. Transm.*, vol. 4, pp. 52–59, 1968.

[237] M. S. Pinsker and R. L. Dobrushin, "Memory increases capacity," *Probl. Inform. Transm.*, vol. 5, pp. 94–95, Jan. 1969.

[238] P. M. Ebert, "The capacity of the Gaussian channel with feedback," *Bell Syst. Tech. J.*, vol. 49, pp. 1705–1712, Oct. 1970.

[239] S. Ihara, *Information Theory for Continuous Systems*. Singapore: World Scientific, 1993.

[240] T. M. Cover and S. Pombra, "Gaussian feedback capacity," *IEEE Trans. Inform. Theory*, vol. 35, pp. 37–43, Jan. 1989.

[241] A. Lapidoth and P. Narayan, "Reliable communication under channel uncertainty," this issue, pp. 2148–2176.

[242] D. Blackwell, L. Breiman, and A. Thomasian, "The capacity of a class of channels," *Ann. Math. Statist.*, vol. 30, pp. 1229–1241, Dec. 1959.

[243] R. L. Dobrushin, "Optimum information transmission through a channel with unknown parameters," *Radio Eng. Electron.*, vol. 4, pp. 1–8, 1959.

[244] J. Wolfowitz, "Simultaneous channels," *Arch. Rational Mech. Anal.*, vol. 4, pp. 371–386, 1960.

[245] W. L. Root and P. P. Varaiya, "Capacity of classes of Gaussian channels," *SIAM J. Appl. Math*, vol. 16, pp. 1350–1393, Nov. 1968.

[246] A. Lapidoth and İ. E. Telatar, "The compound channel capacity of a class of finite-state channels," *IEEE Trans. Inform. Theory*, vol. 44, pp. 973–983, May 1998.

[247] J. Kiefer and J. Wolfowitz, "Channels with arbitrarily varying channel probability functions," *Inform. Contr.*, vol. 5, pp. 44–54, 1962.

[248] D. Blackwell, L. Breiman, and A. Thomasian, "The capacities of certain channel classes under random coding," *Ann. Math. Statist.*, vol. 31, pp. 558–567, 1960.

[249] R. Ahlswede and J. Wolfowitz, "The capacity of a channel with arbitrarily varying cpf's and binary output alphabet," *Z. Wahrscheinlichkeitstheorie Verw. Gebiete*, vol. 15, pp. 186–194, 1970.

[250] I. Csiszár and J. Körner, "On the capacity of the arbitrarily varying channel for maximum probability of error," *Z. Wahrscheinlichkeitstheorie Verw. Gebiete*, vol. 57, pp. 87–101, 1981.

[251] R. L. Dobrushin and S. Z. Stambler, "Coding theorems for classes of arbitrarily varying discrete memoryless channels," *Probl. Inform. Transm.*, vol. 11, no. 2, pp. 3–22, 1975.

[252] R. Ahlswede, "Elimination of correlation in random codes for arbitrarily varying channels," *Z. Wahrscheinlichkeitstheorie Verw. Gebiete*, vol. 44, pp. 159–175, 1968.

[253] T. Ericson, "Exponential error bounds for random codes in the arbitrarily varying channel," *IEEE Trans. Inform. Theory*, vol. 31, pp. 42–48, Jan. 1985.

[254] I. Csiszár and P. Narayan, "The capacity of the arbitrarily varying channel revisited: Capacity, constraints," *IEEE Trans. Inform. Theory*, vol. 34, pp. 181–193, Mar. 1988.

[255] _____, "Capacity of the Gaussian arbitrarily varying channel," *IEEE Trans. Inform. Theory*, vol. 34, pp. 18–26, Jan. 1991.

[256] B. Hughes and P. Narayan, "Gaussian arbitrarily varying channels," *IEEE Trans. Inform. Theory*, vol. IT-33, pp. 267–284, Mar. 1987.

[257] B. L. Hughes, "The smallest list for the arbitrarily varying channel," *IEEE Trans. Inform. Theory*, vol. 43, pp. 803–815, May 1997.

[258] V. B. Balakirsky, "Coding theorem for discrete memoryless channels with given decision rules," in *Proc. 1st French–Soviet Work. Algebraic Coding*, July 1991, pp. 142–150.

[259] N. Merhav, G. Kaplan, A. Lapidoth, and S. Shamai, "On information rates for mismatched decoders," *IEEE Trans. Inform. Theory*, vol. 40, pp. 1953–1967, Nov. 1994.

[260] I. Csiszár and P. Narayan, "Channel decoding for a given decoding metric," *IEEE Trans. Inform. Theory*, vol. 41, pp. 35–43, Jan. 1995.

[261] A. Lapidoth, "Mismatched decoding and the multiple-access channel," *IEEE Trans. Inform. Theory*, vol. 42, pp. 1439–1452, Sept. 1996.

[262] _____, "Nearest neighbor decoding for additive non-Gaussian noise channels," *IEEE Trans. Inform. Theory*, vol. 42, pp. 1520–1528, Sept. 1996.

[263] V. D. Goppa, "Nonprobabilistic mutual information without memory," *Probl. Contr. Inform. Theory*, vol. 4, pp. 97–102, 1975.

[264] J. Ziv, "Universal decoding for finite-state channels," *IEEE Trans. Inform. Theory*, vol. IT-31, pp. 453–460, July 1985.

[265] A. Lapidoth and J. Ziv, "On the universality of the LZ-based decoding algorithm," *IEEE Trans. Inform. Theory*, vol. 44, pp. 1746–1755, Sept. 1998.

[266] I. Csiszár and P. Narayan, "Capacity and decoding rules for classes of arbitrarily varying channels," *IEEE Trans. Inform. Theory*, vol. 35, pp. 752–769, July 1989.

[267] M. Feder and A. Lapidoth, "Universal decoding for channels with memory," *IEEE Trans. Inform. Theory*, vol. 44, pp. 1726–1745, Sept. 1998.

[268] C. E. Shannon, "Two-way communication channels," in *Proc. 4th. Berkeley Symp. Mathematical Statistics and Probability* (June 20–July 30, 1960), J. Neyman, Ed. Berkeley, CA: Univ. Calif. Press, 1961, vol. 1, pp. 611–644.

[269] G. Dueck, "The capacity region of the two-way channel can exceed the inner bound," *Inform. Contr.*, vol. 40, pp. 258–266, 1979.

[270] J. P. M. Schalkwijk, "The binary multiplying channel—A coding scheme that operates beyond Shannon's inner bound," *IEEE Trans. Inform. Theory*, vol. IT-28, pp. 107–110, Jan. 1982.

[271] _____, "On an extension of an achievable rate region for the binary multiplying channel," *IEEE Trans. Inform. Theory*, vol. IT-29, pp.

445–448, May 1983.

[272] Z. Zhang, T. Berger, and J. P. M. Schwalkwijk, "New outer bounds to capacity regions of two-way channels," *IEEE Trans. Inform. Theory*, vol. IT-32, pp. 383–386, 1986.

[273] A. P. Hekstra and F. M. J. Willems, "Dependence balance bounds for single-output two-way channels," *IEEE Trans. Inform. Theory*, vol. 35, pp. 44–53, 1989.

[274] R. Ahlswede, "Multi-way communication channels," in *Proc. 2nd Int. Symp. Information Theory*, 1971, pp. 103–135.

[275] E. C. van der Meulen, "The discrete memoryless channel with two senders and one receiver," in *Proc 2nd Int. Symp. Information Theory*, 1971, pp. 103–135.

[276] H. Liao, "Multiple access channels," Ph.D. dissertation, Univ. Hawaii, Honolulu, HI, 1972.

[277] H. Liao, "A coding theorem for multiple-access communications," in *1972 Int. Symp. Information Theory*, 1972.

[278] R. Ahlswede, "The capacity region of a channel with two senders and two receivers," *Ann. Probab.*, vol. 2, pp. 805–814, Oct. 1974.

[279] T. M. Cover, "Some advances in broadcast channels," *Adv. Commun. Syst.*, vol. 4, pp. 229–260, 1975.

[280] B. Rimoldi and R. Urbanke, "A rate-splitting approach to the Gaussian multiple-access channel," *IEEE Trans. Inform. Theory*, vol. 42, pp. 364–375, Mar. 1996.

[281] A. Grant, B. Rimoldi, R. Urbanke, and P. Whiting, "Rate-splitting multiple access for discrete memoryless channels," *IEEE Trans. Inform. Theory*, to be published.

[282] R. G. Gallager, "Power limited channels: Coding, multiaccess, and spread spectrum," in *1988 Conf. Information Science and Systems*, Mar. 1988. Full version published as Rep. LIDS-P-1714, Nov. 1987.

[283] N. T. Gaarder and J. K. Wolf, "The capacity region of a multiple-access discrete memoryless channel can increase with feedback," *IEEE Trans. Inform. Theory*, vol. IT-21, pp. 100–102, Jan. 1975.

[284] T. M. Cover and S. K. Leung, "A rate region for multiple access channels with feedback," *IEEE Trans. Inform. Theory*, vol. IT-27, pp. 292–298, May 1981.

[285] L. H. Ozarow, "The capacity of the white Gaussian multiple access channel with feedback," *IEEE Trans Information Theory*, vol. IT-30, pp. 623–629, July 1984.

[286] J. A. Thomas, "Feedback can at most double Gaussian multiple access channel capacity," *IEEE Trans. Inform. Theory*, vol. IT-33, pp. 711–716, Sept. 1987.

[287] S. Pombra and T. Cover, "Nonwhite Gaussian multiple access channels with feedback," *IEEE Trans. Inform. Theory*, vol. 40, pp. 885–892, May 1994.

[288] E. Ordentlich, "On the factor of two bound for Gaussian multiple-access channels with feedback," *IEEE Trans. Inform. Theory*, vol. 42, pp. 2231–2235, Nov. 1996.

[289] S. Verdú, "Multiple-access channels with memory with and without frame-synchronism," *IEEE Trans. Inform. Theory*, vol. 35, pp. 605–619, May 1989.

[290] R. S. Cheng and S. Verdú, "Gaussian multiple-access channels with intersymbol interference: Capacity region and multiuser water-filling," *IEEE Trans. Inform. Theory*, vol. 39, pp. 773–785, May 1993.

[291] D. N. C. Tse and S. V. Hanly, "Multi-access fading channels: Part I: Polymatroid structure, optimal resource allocation and throughput capacities," *IEEE Trans. Inform. Theory*, Nov. 1998, to be published.

[292] G. S. Poltyrev, "Coding in an asynchronous multiple-access channel," *Probl. Inform. Transm.*, vol. 19, pp. 12–21, July–Sept. 1983.

[293] J. Y. N Hui and P. A. Humblet, "The capacity region of the totally asynchronous multiple-access channels," *IEEE Trans. Inform. Theory*, vol. IT-31, pp. 207–216, Mar. 1985.

[294] S. Verdú, "The capacity region of the symbol-asynchronous Gaussian multiple-access channel," *IEEE Trans. Inform. Theory*, vol. 35, pp. 733–751, July 1989.

[295] R. G. Gallager, "A perspective on multiaccess channels," *IEEE Trans. Inform. Theory*, vol. IT-31, pp. 124–142, Mar. 1985.

[296] J. Pokorny and H. M. Wallmeier, "Random coding bound and codes produced by permutations for the multiple-access channel," *IEEE Trans. Inform. Theory*, vol. 31, pp. 741–750, Nov. 1985.

[297] Y. S. Liu and B. L. Hughes, "A new universal random coding bound for the multiple-access channel," *IEEE Trans. Inform. Theory*, vol. 42, pp. 376–386, Mar. 1996.

[298] D. Slepian and J. K. Wolf, "A coding theorem for multiple-access channels with correlated sources," *Bell Syst. Tech. J.*, vol. 52, pp. 1037–1076, 1973.

[299] T. M. Cover, A. E. Gamal, and M. Salehi, "Multiple-access channels with arbitrarily correlated sources," *IEEE Trans. Inform. Theory*, vol. IT-26, pp. 648–657, Nov. 1980.

[300] E. C. van der Meulen, "Some reflections on the interference channel," in *Communications and Cryptography: Two Sides of One Tapestry*, R. E. Blahut, D. J. Costello, U. Maurer, and T. Mittelholzer, Eds. Boston, MA: Kluwer, 1994.

[301] A. B. Carleial, "A case where interference does not reduce capacity," *IEEE Trans. Inform. Theory*, vol. IT-21, pp. 569–570, Sept. 1975.

[302] T. S. Han and K. Kobayashi, "A new achievable rate region for the interference channel," *IEEE Trans. Inform. Theory*, vol. IT-27, pp. 49–60, Jan. 1981.

[303] M. H. M. Costa, "On the Gaussian interference channel," *IEEE Trans. Inform. Theory*, vol. IT-31, pp. 607–615, Sept. 1985.

[304] M. H. M. Costa and A. E. Gamal, "The capacity region of the discrete memoryless interference channel with strong interference," *IEEE Trans. Inform. Theory*, vol. IT-33, pp. 710–711, Sept. 1987.

[305] H. Sato, "The capacity of the Gaussian interference channel under strong interference," *IEEE Trans. Inform. Theory*, vol. IT-27, pp. 786–788, Nov. 1981.

[306] T. M. Cover, "Broadcast channels," *IEEE Trans. Inform. Theory*, vol. IT-18, pp. 2–4, Jan. 1972.

[307] T. M. Cover, "Comments on broadcast channels," this issue, pp. 2524–2530.

[308] M. Sablatash, "Transmission of all-digital advanced television-state-of-the-art and future directions," *IEEE Trans. Broadcast.*, vol. 40, pp. 102–121, June 1994.

[309] K. Ramchandran, A. Ortega, K. Uz, and M. Vetterli, "Multiresolution broadcast for digital HDTV using joint source channel coding," *IEEE J. Select. Areas Commun.*, vol. 11, pp. 6–23, Jan. 1993.

[310] A. R. Calderbank and N. Seshadri, "Multilevel codes for unequal error protection," *IEEE Trans. Inform. Theory*, vol. 39, pp. 1234–1248, July 1993.

[311] S. Shamai (Shitz), "A broadcast strategy for the Gaussian slowly fading channel," in *Proc. 1997 IEEE Int. Symp. Information Theory* (Ulm, Germany, July 1997), p. 150.

[312] A. D. Wyner, "The wiretap channel," *Bell Syst. Tech. J.*, vol. 54, pp. 1355–1387, 1975.

[313] I. Csiszár and J. Körner, "Broadcast channels with confidential messages," *IEEE Trans. Inform. Theory*, vol. IT-24, pp. 339–348, May 1978.

[314] U. M. Maurer, "Secret key agreement by public discussion from common information," *IEEE Trans. Inform. Theory*, vol. 39, pp. 733–742, May 1993.

[315] R. Ahlswede and I. Csiszár, "Common randomness in information theory and cryptography—Part I: Secret sharing," *IEEE Trans. Inform. Theory*, vol. IT-32, pp. 1121–1132, July 1993.

[316] D. Haussler, "A general minimax result for relative entropy," *IEEE Trans. Inform. Theory*, vol. 43, pp. 1276–1280, July 1997.

[317] B. Ryabko, "Encoding a source with unknown but ordered probabilities," *Probl. Inform. Transm.*, vol. 15, pp. 134–138, 1979.

[318] R. G. Gallager, "Source coding with side information and universal coding," Tech. Rep. LIDS-P-937, Lab. Inform. Decision Syst., MIT, Cambridge, MA, 1979.

[319] L. D. Davisson and A. Leon-Garcia, "A source matching approach to finding minimax codes," *IEEE Trans. Inform. Theory*, vol. IT-26, pp. 166–174, 1980.

[320] N. Merhav and M. Feder, "A strong version of the redundancy-capacity theorem of universal coding," *IEEE Trans. Inform. Theory*, vol. 41, pp. 714–722, May 1995.

[321] R. Ahlswede and G. Dueck, "Identification via channels," *IEEE Trans. Inform. Theory*, vol. 35, pp. 15–29, Jan. 1989.

[322] R. M. Gray and D. Neuhoff, "Quantization," *IEEE Trans. Inform. Theory*, this issue, pp. 2325–2383.

[323] T. Berger and J. Gibson, "Lossy source coding," *IEEE Trans. Inform. Theory*, this issue, pp. 2693–2723.

[324] D. L. Donoho, I. Daubechies, R. A. DeVore, and M. Vetterli, "Data compression and harmonic analysis," this issue, pp. 2435–2476.

[325] C. E. Shannon, "Coding theorems for a discrete source with a fidelity criterion," in *IRE Nat. Conv. Rec.*, Mar. 1959, pp. 142–163.

[326] B. M. Oliver, J. R. Pierce, and C. E. Shannon, "The philosophy of PCM," *Proc. IRE*, vol. 36, pp. 1324–1331, 1948.

[327] A. N. Kolmogorov, "On the Shannon theory of information transmission in the case of continuous signals," *IEEE Trans. Inform. Theory*, vol. IT-2, pp. 102–108, Sept. 1956.

[328] E. Posner and E. Rodemich, "Epsilon entropy and data compression," *Ann. Math. Statist.*, vol. 42, pp. 2079–2125, 1971.

[329] A. N. Kolmogorov and V. M. Tichomirov, "ϵ-entropy and ϵ-capacity of sets in metric spaces," *Usp. Math. Nauk.*, vol. 14, pp. 3–8o, 1959.

[330] M. S. Pinsker, "Calculation of the rate of message generation by a stationary random process and the capacity of a stationary channel," *Dokl. Akad. Nauk SSSR*, vol. 111, pp. 753–766, 1956.

[331] ——, "Gaussian sources," *Probl. Inform. Transm.*, vol. 14, pp. 59–100, 1963.

[332] B. S. Tsybakov, "Epsilon-entropy of a vector message," *Probl. Inform. Transm.*, vol. 5, pp. 96–97, 1969.

[333] T. J. Goblick, "Theoretical limitations on the transmission of data from analog sources," *IEEE Trans. Inform. Theory*, vol. IT-11, pp. 558–567, Oct. 1965.

[334] J. Ziv, "The behavior of analog communication systems," *IEEE Trans. Inform. Theory*, vol. IT-16, pp. 587–594, Sept. 1970.

[335] S. Shamai (Shitz), S. Verdú, and R. Zamir, "Systematic lossy source/channel coding," *IEEE Trans. Inform. Theory*, vol. 44, pp. 564–579, Mar. 1998.

[336] V. D. Erokhin, "The ϵ-entropy of a discrete random object," *Theory Probab. Appl.*, vol. 3, pp. 103–107, 1958.

[337] Y. N. Linkov, "Epsilon-entropy of random variables when epsilon is small," *Probl. Inform. Transm.*, vol. 1, no. 2, pp. 18–26, 1965.

[338] ——, "Epsilon-entropy of continuous random process with discrete phase space," *Probl. Inform. Transm.*, vol. 7, no. 2, pp. 16–25, 1971.

[339] F. Jelinek, "Evaluation of distortion rate functions for low distortions," *Proc. IEEE*, vol. 55, pp. 2067–2068, 1967.

[340] K. Rose, "Mapping approach to rate-distortion computation and analysis," *IEEE Trans. Inform. Theory*, vol. 40, pp. 1939–1952, Nov. 1994.

[341] T. Berger, "Information rates of Wiener processes," *IEEE Trans. Inform. Theory*, vol. IT-16, pp. 134–139, Mar. 1970.

[342] S. Verdú, "The exponential distribution in information theory," *Probl. Inform. Transm.*, vol. 32, pp. 86–95, Jan.–Mar. 1996.

[343] R. M. Gray, "Information rates of autoregressive processes," *IEEE Trans. Inform. Theory*, vol. IT-16, pp. 412–421, July 1970.

[344] T. Berger, *Rate Distortion Theory*. Englewood Cliffs, NJ: Prentice-Hall, 1971.

[345] H. H. Tan and K. Yao, "Evaluation of rate-distortion functions for a class of independent identically distributed sources under an absolute magnitude criterion," *IEEE Trans. Inform. Theory*, vol. IT-21, pp. 59–64, Jan. 1975.

[346] K. Yao and H. H. Tan, "Absolute error rate-distortion functions for sources with constrained magnitudes," *IEEE Trans. Inform. Theory*, vol. IT-24, pp. 499–503, July 1978.

[347] B. Hajek and T. Berger, "A decomposition theorem for binary Markov random fields," *Ann. Probab.*, vol. 15, pp. 1112–1125, 1987.

[348] L. A. Bassalygo and R. L. Dobrushin, "Rate-distortion function of the Gibbs field," *Probl. Inform. Transm.*, vol. 23, no. 1, pp. 3–15, 1987.

[349] M. Effros, P. A. Chou, and R. M. Gray, "Variable-rate source coding theorems for stationary nonergodic sources," *IEEE Trans. Inform. Theory*, vol. 40, pp. 1920–1925, Nov. 1994.

[350] Y. Steinberg and S. Verdú, "Simulation of random processes and rate-distortion theory," *IEEE Trans. Inform. Theory*, vol. 42, pp. 63–86, Jan. 1996.

[351] J. C. Kieffer, "A survey of the theory of source coding with a fidelity criterion," *IEEE Trans. Inform. Theory*, vol. 39, pp. 1473–1490, Sept. 1993.

[352] D. J. Sakrison, "The rate of a class of random processes," *IEEE Trans. Inform. Theory*, vol. IT-16, pp. 10–16, Jan. 1970.

[353] J. Ziv, "Coding of sources with unknown statistics—Part II: Distortion relative to a fidelity criterion," *IEEE Trans. Inform. Theory*, vol. IT-18, pp. 389–394, May 1972.

[354] D. L. Neuhoff, R. M. Gray, and L. D. Davisson, "Fixed rate universal block source coding with a fidelity criterion," *IEEE Trans. Inform. Theory*, vol. IT-21, pp. 511–523, 1975.

[355] D. L. Neuhoff and P. C. Shields, "Fixed-rate universal codes for Markov sources," *IEEE Trans. Inform. Theory*, vol. IT-24, pp. 360–367, 1978.

[356] J. Ziv, "Distortion-rate theory for individual sequences," *IEEE Trans. Inform. Theory*, vol. IT-24, pp. 137–143, Jan. 1980.

[357] R. Garcia-Muñoz and D. L. Neuhoff, "Strong universal source coding subject to a rate-distortion constraint," *IEEE Trans. Inform. Theory*, vol. IT-28, pp. 285–295, Mar. 1982.

[358] D. S. Ornstein and P. C. Shields, "Universal almost sure data compression," *Ann. Probab.*, vol. 18, pp. 441–452, 1990.

[359] Y. Steinberg and M. Gutman, "An algorithm for source coding subject to a fidelity criterion based on string matching," *IEEE Trans. Inform. Theory*, vol. 39, pp. 877–886, 1993.

[360] B. Yu and T. P. Speed, "A rate of convergence result for a universal d-semifaithful code," *IEEE Trans. Inform. Theory*, vol. 39, pp. 813–820, May 1993.

[361] T. Linder, G. Lugosi, and K. Zeger, "Rates of convergence in the source coding theorem, in empirical quantizer design, and in universal lossy source coding," *IEEE Trans. Inform. Theory*, vol. 40, pp. 1728–1740, Nov. 1994.

[362] ——, "Fixed-rate universal source coding and rates of convergence for memoryless sources," *IEEE Trans. Inform. Theory*, vol. 41, pp. 665–676,

May 1995.

[363] P. A. Chou, M. Effros, and R. M. Gray, "A vector quantization approach to universal noiseless coding and quantization," *IEEE Trans. Inform. Theory*, vol. 42, pp. 1109–1138, July 1996.

[364] Z. Zhang and E. Yang, "An on-line universal lossy data compression algorithm via continuous codebook refinement—II: Optimality for phi-mixing source models," *IEEE Trans. Inform. Theory*, vol. 42, pp. 822–836, May 1996.

[365] Z. Zhang and V. K. Wei, "An on-line universal lossy data compression algorithm via continuous codebook refinement—Part I: Basic results," *IEEE Trans. Inform. Theory*, vol. 42, pp. 803–821, May 1996.

[366] J. C. Kieffer and E. H. Yang, "Sequential codes, lossless compression of individual sequences, and Kolmogorov complexity," *IEEE Trans. Inform. Theory*, vol. 42, pp. 29–39, Jan. 1996.

[367] E. H. Yang and J. C. Kieffer, "Simple universal lossy data compression schemes derived from the Lempel-Ziv algorithm," *IEEE Trans. Inform. Theory*, vol. 42, pp. 239–245, Jan. 1996.

[368] E. H. Yang, Z. Zhang, and T. Berger, "Fixed-slope universal lossy data compression," *IEEE Trans. Inform. Theory*, vol. 43, pp. 1465–1476, Sept. 1997.

[369] T. Łuczak and W. Szpankowski, "A suboptimal lossy date compression based on approximate pattern matching," *IEEE Trans. Inform. Theory*, vol. 43, pp. 1439–1451, Sept. 1997.

[370] D. L. Neuhoff and P. C. Shields, "Simplistic universal coding," *IEEE Trans. Inform. Theory*, vol. 44, pp. 778–781, Mar. 1998.

[371] A. D. Wyner and J. Ziv, "The rate-distortion function for source coding with side information at the decoder," *IEEE Trans. Inform. Theory*, vol. IT-22, pp. 1–10, Jan. 1976.

[372] A. D. Wyner, "The rate-distortion function for source coding with side information at the decoder—II: General sources," *Inform. Contr.*, vol. 38, pp. 60–80, 1978.

[373] T. Berger, K. B. Housewright, J. K. Omura, S. Tung, and J. Wolfowitz, "An upper bound to the rate distortion function for source coding with partial side information at the decoder," *IEEE Trans. Inform. Theory*, vol. IT-25, pp. 664–666, 1979.

[374] C. Heegard and T. Berger, "Rate-distortion when side information may be absent," *IEEE Trans. Inform. Theory*, vol. IT-31, pp. 727–734, Nov. 1985.

[375] T. Berger and R. W. Yeung, "Multiterminal source encoding with one distortion criterion," *IEEE Trans. Inform. Theory*, vol. 35, pp. 228–236, Jan. 1989.

[376] R. Zamir, "The rate loss in the Wyner-Ziv problem," *IEEE Trans. Inform. Theory*, vol. 42, pp. 2073–2084, Nov. 1996.

[377] T. Linder, R. Zamir, and K. Zeger, "On source coding with side information dependent distortion measures," *IEEE Trans. Inform. Theory*, submitted for publication.

[378] Z. Zhang and T. Berger, "New results in binary multiple descriptions," *IEEE Trans. Inform. Theory*, vol. IT-33, pp. 502–521, July 1987.

[379] L. H. Ozarow, "On a source coding problem with two channels and three receivers," *Bell Syst. Tech. J.*, vol. 59, pp. 1909–1921, Dec. 1980.

[380] T. M. Cover and A. E. Gamal, "Achievable rates for multiple descriptions," *IEEE Trans. Inform. Theory*, vol. IT-28, pp. 851–857, Nov. 1982.

[381] R. Ahlswede, "The rate-distortion region for multiple descriptions without excess rate," *IEEE Trans. Inform. Theory*, vol. IT-31, pp. 721–726, Nov. 1985.

[382] V. Vaishampayan, "Design of multiple description scalar quantizers," *IEEE Trans. Inform. Theory*, vol. 39, pp. 821–834, May 1993.

[383] Z. Zhang and T. Berger, "Multiple description source coding with no excess marginal rate," *IEEE Trans. Inform. Theory*, vol. 41, pp. 349–357, Mar. 1995.

[384] V. Koshélev, "Estimation of mean error for a discrete successive approximation scheme," *Probl. Inform. Transm.*, vol. 17, pp. 20–33, July–Sept. 1981.

[385] W. H. R. Equitz and T. M. Cover, "Successive refinement of information," *IEEE Trans. Inform. Theory*, vol. 37, pp. 269–274, Mar. 1991.

[386] B. Rimoldi, "Successive refinement of information: Characterization of the achievable rates," *IEEE Trans. Inform. Theory*, vol. 40, pp. 253–259, Jan. 1994.

[387] A. H. Kaspi and T. Berger, "Rate-distortion for correlated sources and partially separated encoders," *IEEE Trans. Inform. Theory*, vol. IT-28, pp. 828–840, Nov. 1982.

[388] T. Berger, Z. Zhang, and H. Viswanathan, "The CEO problem," *IEEE Trans. Inform. Theory*, vol. 42, pp. 887–903, May 1996.

[389] H. Viswanathan and T. Berger, "The quadratic Gaussian CEO problem," *IEEE Trans. Inform. Theory*, vol. 43, pp. 1549–1561, Sept. 1997.

[390] A. R. Barron, "Entropy and the central limit theorem," *Ann. Probab.*, vol. 14, pp. 336–342, 1986.

[391] I. Csiszár, "I-divergence geometry of probability distributions and minimization problems," *Ann. Probab.*, vol. 3, pp. 146–158, Feb. 1975.

[392] _____ , "Sanov property, generalized I-projection and a conditional limit theorem," *Ann. Probab.*, vol. 12, pp. 768–793, Aug. 1984.

[393] A. Dembo and O. Zeitouni, *Large Deviations Techniques and Applications*. Boston, MA: Jones and Bartlett, 1993.

[394] S. Kullback, J. C. Keegel, and J. H. Kullback, *Topics in Statistical Information Theory*. Berlin, Germay: Springer, 1987.

[395] K. Marton, "Bounding $\bar{d}$-distance by information divergence: A method to prove concentration inequalities," *Ann. Probab.*, vol. 24, pp. 857–866, 1996.

[396] A. Dembo, "Information inequalities and concentration of measure," *Ann. Probab.*, vol. 25, pp. 927–939, 1997.

[397] A. Ephremides and B. Hajek, "Information theory and communication networks: An unconsummated union," this issue, pp. 2416–2434.

[398] S. Kullback, *Information Theory and Statistics*. New York: Dover, 1968.

[399] I. Vajda, *Theory of Statistical Inference and Information*. Dordrecht, The Netherlands: Kluwer, 1989.

[400] S. I. Amari and T. S. Han, "Statistical inference under multiterminal data compression," this issue, pp. 2300–2324.

[401] J. Ziv and M. Zakai, "Some lower bounds on signal parameter estimation," *IEEE Trans. Inform. Theory*, vol. IT-15, pp. 386–391, May 1969.

[402] L. Devroye, *A Course in Density Estimation*. Boston, MA: Birkhauser, 1987.

[403] L. Bassalygo, S. Gelfand, G. Golubev, R. Dobrushin, V. Prelov, Y. Sinai, R. Khasminskii, and A. Yaglom, "Review of scientific achievements of M. S. Pinsker," *Probl. Inform. Transm.*, vol. 32, pp. 3–14, 1996.

[404] Y. Yang and A. Barron, "Information-theoretic determination of minimax rates of convergence," *Ann. Statist.*, to be published.

[405] B. S. Choi and T. M. Cover, "An information-theoretic proof of Burg's maximum entropy spectrum," *Proc. IEEE*, vol. 72, pp. 1094–1095, 1984.

[406] A. R. Barron, "Information-theoretic characterization of Bayes performance and choice of priors in parametric and nonparametric problems," in *Bayesian Statistics 6: Proc. 6th Valencia Int. Meet.*, June 1998.

[407] I. Csiszár, "Why least squares and maximum entropy? an axiomatic approach to inference for linear inverse problems," *Ann. Statist.*, vol. 19, pp. 2032–2066, Dec. 1991.

[408] S. Kulkarni, G. Lugosi, and S. Venkatesh, "Learning pattern classification—A survey," this issue, pp. 2178–2206..

[409] A. R. Barron, "Approximation and estimation bounds for artificial neural networks," *Mach. Learn.*, vol. 14, pp. 115–133, 1994.

[410] Y. S. Abumostafa, "Information theory, complexity and neural networks," *IEEE Commun. Mag.*, vol. 27, pp. 25–30, Nov. 1989.

[411] F. Jelinek, *Statistical Methods for Speech Recognition*. Cambridge, MA: MIT Press, 1998.

[412] G. J. Chaitin, *Algorithmic Information Theory*. Cambridge, U.K.: Cambridge Univ. Press, 1987.

[413] M. Li and P. Vitányi, *An Introduction to Kolmogorov Complexity and Its Applications*. Berlin, Germany: Springer, 1993.

[414] H. Yamamoto, "Information theory in cryptology," *IEICE Trans. Commun., Electron., Inform. Syst.*, vol. 74, pp. 2456–2464, Sept. 1991.

[415] N. Pippenger, "Information theory and the complexity of Boolean functions," *Math. Syst. Theory*, vol. 10, pp. 129–167, 1977.

[416] A. Steane, "Quantum computing," *Repts. Progr. Phys.*, vol. 61, pp. 117–173, Feb. 1998.

[417] P. Elias, "The efficient construction of an unbiased random sequence," *Ann. Math. Statist.*, vol. 43, pp. 865–870, 1972.

[418] D. E. Knuth and A. C. Yao, "The complexity of random number generation," in *Algorithms and Complexity: Recent Results and New Directions*, J. F. Traub, Ed. New York: Academic, 1976.

[419] K. Visweswariah, S. Kulkarni, and S. Verdú, "Source codes as random number generators," *IEEE Trans. Inform. Theory*, vol. 44, pp. 462–471, Mar. 1998.

[420] D. Lind and B. Marcus, *Symbolic Dynamics and Coding*. Cambridge, U.K.: Cambridge Univ. Press, 1995.

[421] A. Dembo, T. M. Cover, and J. A. Thomas, "Information theoretic inequalities," *IEEE Trans. Inform. Theory*, vol. 37, pp. 1501–1518, Nov. 1991.

[422] H. S. Witsenhausen, "Some aspects of convexity useful in information theory," *IEEE Trans. Inform. Theory*, vol. IT-26, pp. 265–271, May 1980.

[423] S. I. Amari and H. Nagaoka, *Methods of Information Geometry*. Oxford, U.K,: Oxford Univ. Press, 1999.

[424] L. L. Campbell, "The relation between information theory and the differential geometry approach to statistics," *Inform. Sci.*, vol. 35, pp. 199–210, June 1985.

[425] R. Ahlswede and I. Wegener, *Search Problems*. New York: Wiley–Interscience, 1987.

[426] S. W. Golomb, "Probability, information theory and prime number theory," *Discr. Math.*, vol. 106, pp. 219–229, Sept. 1992.

[427] O. Hijab, *Stabilization of Control Systems*. New York: Springer-Verlag, 1987.

[428] J. K. Sengupta, *Econometrics of Information and Efficiency*. Dordrecht, The Netherlands: Kluwer, 1993.

[429] W. T. Grandy, "Resource letter ITP-1: Information theory in physics," *Amer. J. Phys.*, vol. 16, pp. 466–476, June 1997.

[430] H. S. Leff and A. F. Rex, Eds., *Maxwell's Demon: Entropy, Information, Computing*. Princeton, NJ: Princeton Univ. Press, 1990.

[431] R. Landauer, "Information is physical," *Phys. Today*, vol. 44, pp. 23–29, May 1991.

[432] N. Sourlas, "Statistical mechanics and error-correcting codes," in *From Statistical Physics to Statistical Inference and Back*, P. Grassberger and J. P. Nadal, Eds. Dordrecht, The Netherlands: Kluwer, 1994, pp. 195–204.

[433] C. H. Bennett and P. Shor, "Quantum information theory," this issue, pp. 2724–2742.

[434] S. Hayes, C. Grebogi, and E. Ott, "Communicating with chaos," *Phys. Rev. Lett.*, vol. 70, no. 20, pp. 3031–3034, May 17, 1993.

[435] H. P. Yockey, *Information Theory and Molecular Biology*. New York: Cambridge Univ. Press, 1992.

[436] J. J. Atick, "Could information theory provide an ecological theory of sensory processing?," *Network Comput. Neural Syst.*, vol. 3, pp. 213–251, May 1992.

[437] R. Linsker, "Sensory processing and information theory," in *From Statistical Physics to Statistical Inference and Back*, P. Grassberger and J. P. Nadal, Eds. Dordrecht, The Netherlands: Kluwer, 1994, pp. 237–248.

[438] K. Eckschlager, *Information Theory in Analytical Chemistry*. New York: Wiley, 1994.

[439] C. Papadimitriou, "Information theory and computational complexity: The expanding interface," *IEEE Inform. Theory Newslett.* (Special Golden Jubilee Issue), pp. 12–13, Summer 1998.

[440] T. M. Cover, "Shannon and investment," *IEEE Inform. Theory Newslett.* (Special Golden Jubilee Issue), pp. 10–11, Summer 1998.

The Interactions Between Ergodic Theory and Information Theory

Paul C. Shields, *Fellow, IEEE*

(Invited Paper)

Abstract— **Information theorists frequently use the ergodic theorem; likewise entropy concepts are often used in information theory. Recently, the two subjects have become partially intertwined as deeper results from each discipline find use in the other. A brief history of this interaction is presented in this paper, together with a more detailed look at three areas of connection, namely, recurrence theory, blowing-up bounds, and direct sample-path methods.**

Index Terms—**Data compression, entropy, probability, sequential coding, source coding, stochastic processes.**

I. INTRODUCTION

ERGODIC theory began at the turn of the century with the work of Boltzmann on statistical physics and Poincaré on dynamical systems, and via the later works of Birkhoff, von Neumann, Kakutani, Kolmogorov, Ornstein, and many others developed into a major field of mathematics [20], [29], [53]. Information theory grew out of Shannon's 1948 paper on communications theory and via the later work of many others, much of which is described elsewhere in this Special Issue, has become a large and flourishing branch of both engineering and mathematics.

Section II contains a short and rather personal view of the history of the interactions between the two subjects. In Section III, it is shown how the ergodic theory point of view leads to a simple, yet rigorous framework for recurrence ideas that are now widely used in information theory. Section IV is devoted to a blowing up idea that began with Ornstein's work in ergodic theory and was later recast into an information theory bound by Marton, a bound connected to a number of new and important ideas in probability theory. In Section V, the focus is on four sample path techniques that have recently been used to establish results of interest in both ergodic theory and information theory.

II. A BRIEF HISTORY

In the early days of information theory, sources were modeled as memoryless processes and analysis was based on the law of large numbers. Soon it became clear, however, that, at least for the source-coding problem, memoryless or even Markovian models did not fit real data very well, and the

Manuscript received December 5, 1997; revised May 1, 1998. This work was supported in part by NSF under Grant INT-9515485.

The author is with the Department of Mathematics, University of Toledo, Toledo, OH 43606 USA.

Publisher Item Identifier S 0018-9448(98)05711-3.

more general model of a stationary random process came into use, with the law of large numbers replaced by the ergodic theorem. A triumph of this more general point of view was the entropy-rate theorem (which information theorists call the asymptotic equipartition property or AEP), proved for ergodic finite-alphabet processes by McMillan, in the convergence-in-probability sense, and by Breiman, in the almost-sure sense [6], [39]. A proof of the entropy-rate theorem based on recent developments is given in Section V, see Theorem 6. The entropy-rate theorem was later extended to densities and to the lossy coding rate-distortion function [2], [3], see also [4], [9], and [12].

The ergodic theorem and the entropy-rate theorem suggest the concepts of frequency-typical and entropy-typical sequence, respectively, both of which have become powerful conceptual and theoretical tools in information theory; see, for example, Cover's extension of the Slepian–Wolf theorem from memoryless processes to general ergodic processes [7]. The ergodic theorem also leads to the representation of a stationary process as an average of ergodic processes, an idea put to good use by Gray and Davisson in their work on source coding [15], and for variable-rate lossy coding in [42].

These early uses of ergodic theory in information theory were confined to borrowing results, such as the ergodic theorem, to establish theorems of interest to information theorists, but there was little interaction between the ideas of the two disciplines. One reason is that, while the two disciplines share a common interest in stationary, finite-alphabet processes, they view such processes in a quite different way.[1] In a short digression from the historical discussion, the next three paragraphs summarize this difference in viewpoint.

To an information theorist, a finite-alphabet process is a sequence $\{X_n\}$ of random variables with values in some finite set A. The process is specified by its joint distributions, $\mathrm{Prob}\,(X_m^n = a_m^n)$, where a_m^n denotes the sequence $a_m, a_{m+1}, \cdots, a_n$, and the process is stationary if the joint distributions do not depend on the time origin. In many cases,

---

[1] In my first conversations with Bob Gray and Dave Neuhoff about ergodic theory and information theory in 1970, this difference in view was a source of confusion. Ergodic theorists describe a process by naming the transformation whereas to information theorists it seems much more natural to name the measure, because the transformation is usually just the canonical shift. To add to the confusion, ergodic theorists often use the word "shift" even when they focus on a variety of transformations. Other confusions are indicated in footnote 2. The effort we put into understanding each other drew me into information theory and led to ergodic theory contributions by both Bob and Dave, as well as to my more than 20 years of collaboration with Dave.

only finite sequences and joint distributions are needed. In more complicated settings, the Kolmogorov model is useful. In this model, the process is represented as the sequence of coordinate functions on the product space $A_0^\infty = \{x_0^\infty\}$, together with the measure P on A_0^∞ which is defined by requiring that

$$P(\{x \in A^\infty \colon x_m^n = a_m^n\}) = \text{Prob}\,(X_m^n = a_m^n), \quad \text{for all } a_m^n.$$

In this model, stationarity is the statement that $P(C) = P(T^{-1}C)$, for any Borel set C, where T is the shift on A_0^∞, that is, $(Tx)_n = n + 1$, $x \in A_0^\infty$, $n = 1, 2, \cdots$.

If you ask an ergodic theorist "what is a process?" the likely answer will be "a measure-preserving transformation and a partition." Ergodic theory is concerned with the orbits $x, Tx, T^2x, \cdots$ of a transformation $T \colon X \mapsto X$ on some given space X. In many interesting cases there is a natural probability measure preserved by T, relative to which information about orbit structure can be expressed in probability language. A triumph of this point of view is Birkhoff's ergodic theorem, a major generalization of the law of large numbers. To the ergodic theorist, finite measurements, which correspond to finite partitions of X, give rise to stationary processes. Suppose T preserves a probability measure P and $\Pi = \{\pi_a \colon a \in A\}$ is partition of X into measurable sets. A stationary process $\{X_n\}$, which the ergodic theorist calls the (T, Π)-process, is defined by selecting a point $x \in X$ at random according to the measure P and defining $X_n(x)$ to be the label of the member of the partition Π to which $T^n x$ belongs, that is,

$$X_n(x) = a \text{ if and only if } T^n x \in \pi_a. \tag{1}$$

The joint distribution of this process is given by the formula

$$\text{Prob}\,(X_m^n = a_m^n) = P\left(\bigcap_{i=m}^{n} T^{-i}\pi_{a_i}\right). \tag{2}$$

In particular, the mapping that sends $x \in X$ into the sequence $\{X_n(x)\}$ defined by (1) carries T onto the shift on the space A_0^∞ and the given measure P onto the Kolmogorov measure defined by (2).

In summary, for the information theorist, stationary processes serve as models for data, the emphasis is on the joint distribution, and, given the source alphabet, the shift is always the same transformation. For the ergodic theorist, on the other hand, transformations arise in many quite different settings, the focus is on properties of transformations (e.g., fixed points, chaotic orbits), and measures and processes are used as tools of analysis, in particular, the emphasis is often on the construction of partitions with nice properties, such as Markov partitions.

Remark 1: In the case when T is the shift, when P is a T-invariant probability measure on A_0^∞, and when $\Pi = \{\pi_a\}$ is the time-0 partition defined by $\pi_a = \{x \colon x_0 = a\}$, the (T, Π)-process is the same as the process defined by the coordinate functions on A_0^∞. For a more complete discussion of the transformation/partition concept of process the reader is referred to [55].

Now to return to the historical discussion. The first real interaction between information theory and ergodic theory came in the late 1950's when Kolmogorov and Sinai adapted Shannon's entropy idea, along with the entropy-rate theorem, to obtain an isomorphism invariant for measure-preserving transformations [28], [66]. Isomorphism is a natural analog of the physics idea that properties of objects should not depend on the choice of coordinates. Two measure-preserving transformations are isomorphic if there is an invertible mapping from the space of one to the space of the other that carries one measure onto the other and one transformation onto the other, see [5] for a nice discussion of isomorphism.

Kolmogorov defined the entropy of a measure-preserving transformation T as the supremum of the entropy-rates of the (T, Π)-processes as Π ranges over all the finite partitions of X. Kolmogorov's entropy is clearly an isomorphism invariant and shows, in particular, that the shifts defined by memoryless processes of different entropy are not isomorphic. Left open, however, was the question of whether equal entropy for memoryless processes implies isomorphism. Ten years later, Ornstein answered the latter question in the affirmative [45], in the course of which he introduced several new concepts that have become basic in ergodic theory. At least two of these concepts, stationary coding[2] and the $\bar{d}$-metric, are also of interest in information theory.

The stationary coding idea is best expressed in terms of doubly-infinite sequences. Let Z denote the integers and let A^Z denote the set of doubly-infinite sequences drawn from A. Given finite alphabets A and B, a Borel measurable mapping $F \colon A^Z \mapsto B^Z$ is *stationary* if it commutes with the respective shifts, that is, $F(T_A x) = T_B F(x)$, for each $x \in A^Z$. Associated with such an F is the time-0 map $f \colon A^Z \mapsto B$, defined by $f(x) = F(x)_0$, the zeroth coordinate of $F(x)$. Given a stationary mapping F with time-0 map f and a stationary A-valued process $\{X_n\}$, the stationary process $\{Y_n\}$ defined by the formula

$$y_n = f(T_A^n x), \qquad x \in A^Z, \ n \in Z$$

is said to be the *stationary coding* of $\{X_n\}$ with stationary coding function F. Note that F transports the Kolmogorov measure P for $\{X_n\}$ into the Kolmogorov measure $Q = P \circ F^{-1}$ for $\{Y_n\}$. Two stationary processes are *isomorphic* if there is an invertible stationary code taking one onto the other.

A stationary coding function F, or equivalently, its time-0 map f, is said to be a finite or sliding-window coder if there is a positive integer w such that $f(x) = f(y)$ whenever $x_{-w}^w = y_{-w}^w$; the smallest such w yields the window width, $2w + 1$. Stationary codes are a natural generalization of finite-state codes (which can be regarded as sliding-window codings of Markov chains with window width one), as well as of convolutional codes; see [13].

---

[2]Much confusion was caused in my first conversations with Gray and Neuhoff, see footnote 1, by the different meanings we attached to the word "code." To me, as an ergodic theorist, a code is just a measure-preserving mapping from one probability space to another that carries a transformation on one space to a transformation on the other, while to Bob and Dave, as information theorists, a code is a mapping from finite blocks to finite blocks, where the blocks can have fixed or variable lengths. Another confusion was that information theorists (or at least source coders) are generally trying to code to reduce entropy, while the challenge in isomorphism theory addressed by ergodic theorists is to code without reducing entropy.

A simple geometric representation, called the Rohlin–Kakutani tower, was used by Ornstein to convert block codes into stationary codes; see [46]. A sequence formulation of the technique has been very useful in information theory, for example, it can be used to show that stationary coding performs as well as block coding [41], and to build counterexamples to various string matching and redundancy questions [62], [65]. A key feature of stationary coding is that properties such as ergodicity, mixing, and trivial-tail are preserved, all of which are destroyed by the block-coding methods of information theory [56]. Stationary coding has been useful in the study of channels and channel coding, to obtain a joint source/channel coding theorem [18], to construct processes whose infinite sample paths can be fully reconstructed after passing through a noisy channel [19], and to model channels with memory [43].

A stationary coding of a memoryless process is called a B-process. An important feature of Ornstein's proof of the isomorphism of equal entropy memoryless processes was that his ideas can be extended to provide a complete theory of B-processes. This theory now includes several characterizations and a plethora of names for such processes, including finitely determined, very weak Bernoulli, almost block-independent, extremal, and almost blowing-up. The first of these, and still the most important, is the finitely determined concept, in part because it has a robustness flavor, and in part because it has statistical meaning [49], [51]. An ergodic process $\{X_n\}$ is finitely determined if any ergodic process close enough to $\{X_n\}$ in entropy-rate and joint distribution must also be $\bar{d}$-close to $\{X_n\}$.

A key step in the proof that equal entropy memoryless processes are isomorphic was the proof that memoryless processes are finitely determined; this is stated as Lemma 2 in Section IV, where its connection to recent ideas is discussed. Ornstein and others showed the quite surprising fact that many interesting processes, such as aperiodic Markov chains and aperiodic regenerative processes, are in fact B-processes, as are many of the processes studied in physics, such as geodesic flows on manifolds of negative curvature and flows defined by convex billiards, see [46], [55].

The Ornstein theory, by the way, extends to countable-alphabet and continuous-alphabet processes, as well as to continuous-time processes. A nice set of tools for doing this was provided by Feldman, see [11], particularly his concept of α-entropy, the growth rate in the minimum number of sets of n-sequences of diameter α whose union has probability $1 - \epsilon$. Thus α-entropy is a kind of operational rate-distortion function, except that it uses diameter rather than radius. Feldman establishes an equipartition theorem for α-entropy via an application of the packing and counting ideas discussed in Section V. His ideas suggested the proof in [48] that it is not possible to almost-surely compress more than the rate-distortion function allows with a sequence of codes in which most source words are within a fixed per-symbol Hamming distance of codewords; see also [25], which uses a different organization of the same proof technique.

The $\bar{d}$-distance is an extension to distributions and random processes of the Hamming distance between sequences. In the case when both processes are ergodic it is just the limiting density of changes needed to convert a typical sequence from one process into a typical sequence for the other. Its finite form defines the distance between two distributions $\bar{d}_n(P, Q)$ on n-sequences to be the minimum of per-letter expected Hamming distance over joinings of P and Q, a joining being a distribution R on $A^n \times A^n$ that has P and Q as respective marginals. For processes the $\bar{d}$-distance is defined as the limit of $\bar{d}_n(P, Q)$ as $n \to \infty$, a limit that exists if the processes are stationary; see [55, Sec. I.9] for details about the $\bar{d}$-distance. There is even an extension, called the $\bar{\rho}$-distance, to continuous alphabets, using, for example, mean-square error in place of Hamming distance [17]; see also the earlier distance concept of Vasershtein [71].

Most characterizations of B-processes are stated in terms of the $\bar{d}$-metric, e.g., the class of B-processes is $\bar{d}$-closed and a stationary process is a B-process if and only if it is the $\bar{d}$-limit as $k \to \infty$ of the k-step Markov process obtained by cutting off the memory after k steps. Its importance for information theory is due, in part, to the fact that code performance is continuous in the $\bar{d}$-metric, a fact that leads to strong universal coding theorems [40]. The $\bar{d}$-metric has also been useful in channel modeling [43], and in approximation of output statistics [21]. More will be said about $\bar{d}$-distance and its relationship to information theory and probability theory in Section IV in the context of blowing-up ideas.

Another branch of ergodic theory focuses on topological rather than probabilistic concepts. A topological version of Markov process, called a shift of finite type or constrained source, is the restriction of the shift on sequences to the set of all sequences in which some specified finite list of blocks never occur. Entropy carries over to this setting, topological entropy being the rate of growth in the number of n-length sequences compatible with the restrictions. This topological entropy is equal to the maximal entropy rate of shift-invariant measures whose support is confined to the set of compatible sequences; the maximal entropy process, in fact, turns out to be Markov. In the late 1970's, Adler developed a stronger concept of isomorphism that required some continuity properties and showed that mixing shifts of finite type with the same entropy are isomorphic in his stronger sense. A modified form of this isomorphism concept has turned out to be exactly the tool needed for studying data storage in magnetic media, see the early paper [1], the recent book [30], or other papers in this special issue for a discussion of these ideas.

In addition to the borrowing by ergodic theorists of the concept of entropy, there are several other ways in which information theory has influenced ergodic theory. Using information theory ideas, two quite different proofs have been given that the class of finitely determined processes is closed in the $\bar{d}$-metric, one viewing a joining as a channel, see [70] or [55, Lemma IV.2.11], the other using relative entropy ideas [26]. A theory of channels with memory led to the concept of almost-block-independence, which, in turn, led to a new characterization of the class of B-processes [43], [57]. Also, motivated by the need for a rigorous theory of finite-state coding and other types of coding, Gray and Kieffer developed and applied a theory of asymptotically mean stationary processes, a topic to which ergodic theorists had paid scant attention [14], [16]. Recently, by taking a more careful look at a key lemma in Ornstein's original paper, Marton produced an information-theoretic bound on $\bar{d}_n(P, Q)$ when Q is memoryless; this is discussed in more detail in Section IV.

An important information theory development in the mid-1970's was the creation by Lempel and Ziv of what are now called LZ algorithms. These are sequential coding procedures based on the idea of coding blocks by describing where they occurred earlier [75], [76]. Ziv showed in [77] that an infinite memory version of LZ is universal, that is, it compresses almost surely to entropy in the limit for any ergodic process, hence, in particular, it provides an almost surely consistent procedure for estimating entropy as sample path length goes to infinity. Ziv's proof introduced an interesting new concept of the entropy of an individual sequence, a concept to which I gave the name *Ziv entropy*.

The complexity $h(x)$ is the rate of growth in the number of n-sequences that occur anywhere in x, as $n \to \infty$; $h(x)$ is, in fact, just the topological entropy of the restriction of the shift to the smallest shift-invariant set that includes x. The Ziv entropy $H(x)$ is obtained by minimizing the topological entropy of sequences in a $\bar{d}$-neighborhood of x of radius ϵ, as $\epsilon \to 0$. Ziv showed that $H(x)$ is an upper bound on LZ compression for any sequence x, and is almost surely equal to entropy rate for ergodic processes. It amazes me that such a wonderful, simple concept as Ziv entropy has not found a use in ergodic theory, especially in its more topological branches.

LZ algorithms exploit recurrence, blocks being coded by telling where they appeared earlier. A simple coding method that focuses directly on this idea was introduced by Willems in a 1989 paper [72], a paper that was the first to use Kac's return-time theorem [23] to analyze LZ-type algorithms; see also [16], for an earlier use of Kac's theorem in information theory. Kac's theorem, in the ergodic case, asserts that the expected time between occurrences of a symbol is the reciprocal of the probability of that symbol. The Kac theorem and a related conditional form are discussed from an ergodic theory point of view in Section III.

Ornstein and Weiss developed in 1979 a remarkable new proof of the entropy-rate theorem as part of their effort to extend isomorphism theory to random fields and even more general amenable group actions, a setting in which Breiman's martingale-based proof could not be used [50]. The new proof was based on two simple combinatorial ideas, a way to extract packings from coverings and a conditional method for counting the number of sequences with given packing properties. These new techniques, which are much closer in spirit to the information theory focus on sequences, have had a significant effect on both ergodic theory and information theory. The packing part of the proof, for example, leads to a simple proof of the ergodic theorem [59], and has since been used to establish other ergodic theorems [27], [67]. The counting part of the proof is in essence a coding argument; in fact, packing and counting ideas can be used to show directly that limiting almost-sure compressibility cannot be smaller than limiting expected compressibility, from which the entropy-rate theorem follows immediately [60].

The packing and counting ideas were extended in later work by Ornstein and Weiss to obtain results about the empirical distribution of overlapping and nonoverlapping k-blocks that have applications to statistical modeling and to entropy estimation [51]. The modeling parts were sharpened in later work [49], while the entropy ideas led to new universal coding results, valid in both the lossless and lossy cases [25], [44], [48]. The empirical distribution results led to sharper connections between joint distribution estimation and entropy for processes with sufficient decay of memory [35]. Further discussion of packing and counting and some general principles for sample path analysis, as well as a proof of the entropy-rate theorem and empirical entropy results, will be given in Section V.

Motivated by the LZ algorithm, Wyner and Ziv took a careful look at recurrence and waiting time ideas. They proved a recurrence-time theorem and a waiting-time theorem. Their recurrence-time theorem asserts that, for any ergodic process, the time until the first n terms of a sample path are seen again grows exponentially at a rate asymptotically equal to entropy, in the sense of convergence in probability. Their waiting-time theorem asserts that for Markov and some related processes, the time until the first n terms of one sample path appear in an independently chosen sample path also grows at a rate asymptotically equal, in probability, to entropy [73]. Ornstein and Weiss obtained an almost-sure form of the recurrence-time theorem (again by utilizing the covering and packing ideas of their earlier work), and Marton and Shields established almost-sure forms of the waiting-time theorem for larger classes of processes and obtained an approximate-match waiting-time theorem for B-processes [36], [52].

LZ algorithms not only exploit recurrence, but focus on making the words as long as possible. In their effort to understand LZ algorithms, Ornstein and Weiss developed interesting results about the parsing of finite sample paths into distinct and repeated blocks, again by utilizing the covering and packing ideas of their earlier work [52]. They showed that, eventually almost surely, in any partition of a sample path into distinct words, wordlength must grow at least as fast as $(1/h) \log n$, while in any partition into words seen before, wordlength cannot grow faster than $(1/h) \log n$. These ideas lead to alternative proofs that infinite memory forms of LZ compress to entropy in the limit.

Some comment should also be made on the cutting and stacking method, which has recently been used to construct counterexamples for questions of interest in information theory and probability theory. The cutting and stacking method was invented by von Neumann and Kakutani around 1940 and has long since been part of the ergodic theory bag of tricks, though it is seldom used and little understood outside ergodic theory, in part because, as mentioned earlier, the ergodic theory model for a stationary process is quite different (though equivalent) to the standard Kolmogorov model used in information theory and probability theory. The cutting and stacking method produces processes by constructing transformations on the unit interval that preserve Lebesgue measure. Such constructions are done in stages, each stage specifying a collection of disjoint subintervals and linear maps, the latter being pictured by stacking intervals into columns with the linear maps being the upward maps. The next stage is obtained by cutting columns into subcolumns and restacking. The power of the method is that preservation of Lebesgue measure is automatic and hence the user is freed to focus on the properties desired. The method easily constructs any renewal or regenerative process, and in fact, can be viewed as a kind of generalized regenerative construction. For a detailed discussion of the method the reader is referred to [55, Sec. I.10] and [58].

Using cutting and stacking, an example was constructed of a binary ergodic process Q such that the limiting divergence rate

$$D_\infty(P\|Q) = \limsup_{n \to \infty} \frac{1}{n} \sum_{a_1^n} P(a_1^n) \log \frac{P(a_1^n)}{Q(a_1^n)}$$

is 0 for unbiased coin-tossing P, yet $Q \neq P$ [63]. Recently, Xu [74], used the method to show the existence of an ergodic process Q (which even can be taken to be a B-process) such that

$$D_\infty(P\|Q) = 0, \qquad \text{for every stationary } P. \qquad (3)$$

Such a Q provides an ergodic process for which the Shannon–Fano code is universal in the sense that it compresses any stationary process to entropy in the limit. (The Shannon–Fano code assigns to a_1^n a word of length $\lceil -\log Q(a_1^n) \rceil$.) It has been known since the early days of universal coding, see [54], that the mixture Q of all the processes that are Markov of any order satisfies (3), but this process is not ergodic. Xu's quite surprising result is still not well understood, though the interpretation of (3) in terms of hypothesis testing is not so surprising, namely, the process Q cannot be distinguished from any other process P with exponential decay of type II error for fixed type I error. (The type II error always goes to 0 for a fixed type I error, but, as these constructions show, it need not go to 0 exponentially fast.) Other cutting and stacking constructions produce processes with poor waiting-time behavior or explosive growth in the number of future distributions [37], [64].

Remark 2: Many interesting topics have not been included in this brief history, such as continuous-alphabet and continuous-time processes or the important subclass of Gaussian processes, the substitution/deletion metric which is used in the study of synchronization and in the branch of ergodic theory called equivalence theory [47], and to the huge and ever-growing subject of image compression, which interacts strongly with the ergodic theory of random fields. Also some topics have been treated in a too cursory manner. These omissions and too-short treatments are partly due to space considerations, but are also due to my lack of expertise in the omitted areas, which made me nervous about discussing them.

III. Ergodic Theory and Recurrence Theory

Recurrence theory for stationary finite-alphabet processes plays a central role in the analysis of LZ-type coding methods. An important tool is Kac's return-time theorem [23]; recently a conditional version of Kac's theorem has been developed and used [22, Lemma 5.1]. In this section it will be shown how such conditional versions can be reduced to the unconditioned form by using some ideas from ergodic theory. The proof is similar in spirit to the proof given in [22], the only real difference is the simplification in both concept and proof gained by focusing directly on the shift transformation and using the ergodic theory idea of induced transformation. A more detailed and more abstract version of the discussion given here can be found in [55, Sec. I.2].

Let $\{X_n\}$ be a stationary process with finite-source alphabet A. Given that $X_0 = a$, let $\tau = \tau(a)$ be the minimum $n \geq 1$ such that $X_n = a$.

Theorem 1. The Kac Return-Time Theorem [23]:

$$E(\tau(a)|X_0 = a) \leq \frac{1}{\text{Prob}(X_0 = a)}$$

with equality in the ergodic case.

The conditional theorem, in its simplest form, assumes that $X_0 = b$ and $X_1 = a$ and focuses on the expected number of b's that occur before b is again followed by a. Given that $X_0 = b$ and $X_1 = a$, let $\tau_1 = 0$ and let $\{\tau_j: j > 1\}$ be the random sequence of subsequent times when $X_n = b$, that is, τ_{j+1} is the least $n > \tau_j$ such that $X_n = b$. Let $\tau(a|b)$ be the least $n \geq 1$ such that $X_{1+\tau_n} = a$.

Theorem 2. The Conditional Return-Time Theorem:

$$E(\tau(a|b)|X_0 = b, X_1 = a) \leq \frac{1}{\text{Prob}(X_1 = a|X_0 = b)},$$

with equality in the ergodic case.

The conditional theorem follows from a general result about observing a stationary process at a subset of its possible values. The key idea is that such a contracted process *is itself a stationary process*, which, furthermore, is ergodic if the original process is ergodic. To formulate this precisely, let $\{X_n\}$ be a stationary process with source alphabet A, fix a set $B \subset A$, and assume $X_0 \in B$. Put $\sigma_0 = 0$ and let $\{\sigma_j: j \geq 1\}$ be the (random) sequence of subsequent times when $X_n \in B$, that is, σ_{j+1} is the minimum $n > \sigma_j$ such that $X_n \in B$. The process $\{Y_n\}$ defined by

$$Y_n = X_{\sigma_n}, \qquad n = 0, 1, 2, \cdots \qquad (4)$$

will be called the *contraction* of $\{X_n\}$ to the times when $X_n \in B$.

Theorem 3. The Contracted-Process Theorem: The contracted process $\{Y_n\}$ is stationary and is ergodic if $\{X_n\}$ is ergodic. Furthermore

$$\text{Prob}(Y_0 = b) = \text{Prob}(X_0 = b|X_0 \in B), \qquad b \in B. \qquad (5)$$

Before proceeding to the proof of the contracted-process theorem it will be shown how it can be used, along with Kac's theorem, to establish the conditional return-time theorem.

Proof of Theorem 2: The idea is to apply the contracted-process theorem to the overlapping-block process $\{Z_n = (X_n, X_{n+1})\}$, with A replaced by $A \times A$ and B replaced by $\{b\} \times A$. The process $\{Z_n\}$ is stationary, so that, conditioning on $Z_0 \in B$, the contracted process $\{Y_n\}$ is stationary. Furthermore

$$Y_n = (X_{\sigma_n}, X_{1+\sigma_n}) = (b, X_{1+\sigma_n})$$

records the nth return of $\{X_n\}$ to b, along with the value of the term that immediately follows that b. In particular, if $X_1 = a$, then $\tau(a|b)$ is just the time of first return of the $\{Y_n\}$ process to (b, a). An application of Kac's theorem to the $\{Y_n\}$ process produces

$$E(\tau(a|b)|X_0 = b, \; X_1 = a) \leq \frac{1}{\text{Prob}\,(Y_0 = (b, a))}$$

with equality in the case when $\{Y_n\}$ is ergodic, which holds if $\{X_n\}$ is ergodic. The proof is completed by noting that the first term of Y_n is always b, so (5) yields

$$\text{Prob}\,(Y_0 = (b, a)) = \text{Prob}\,(X_1 = a|X_0 = b)$$

establishing the conditional return-time theorem. □

Remark 3: Tjalling Tjalkens suggested to me the use of the overlapping-block process $\{Z_n\}$, thereby greatly simplifying my original argument, as well as the argument in [22]. In the latter proof, the authors put $y = x_{-j}^{-1}$ and $z = x_0^{\ell-1}$, then look at successive past occurrences of y until followed by z. Their lemma reduces to the unconditioned Kac theorem by applying the contracted-process theorem to the overlapping-block process

$$Z_n = (X_{-n-j-\ell+1}, X_{-n-j-\ell+2}, \cdots, X_{-n})$$

with $B = \{y\} \times A_0^\ell$. Other conditional return-time theorems can be obtained by using the appropriate overlapping-block process.

From the point of view of ergodic theory, the contracted-process theorem has a simple proof. The simplicity results from focusing on the shift transformation as a measure-preserving transformation. In this setting the analog of contracting a process is the transformation that only considers returns to B, the so-called induced transformation. It is not hard to show that the induced transformation preserves the conditional measure and is ergodic if the original process is ergodic. The argument is completed by noting that the transformation/partition definition of process, using the induced transformation and the partition defined by B, is just the contracted process. Details of this sketch are given in the following paragraphs.

Let $\{X_n\}$ be a stationary, ergodic process with finite-source alphabet A and Kolmogorov measure P. To simplify the discussion the two-sided Kolmogorov representation will be used, that is, P is taken to be the shift-invariant Borel probability measure on the space A^Z of doubly-infinite A-valued sequences $x_{-\infty}^\infty$ defined by requiring that

$$P(a_m^n) = \text{Prob}\,(X_i = a_i: \; m \leq i \leq n)$$

for all $m \leq n$ and all a_m^n. The (left) shift T is the mapping defined for $x \in A^Z$ by the formula $Tx = y$, where $y_n = x_{n+1}$, for all $n \in Z$. The properties of T that will be used are that it has an inverse mapping (namely, the right shift) and that it preserves the measure P, that is,

$$P(C) = P(TC) = P(T^{-1}C)$$

for any Borel set $C \subseteq A^Z$.

Fix a set $B \subset A$ such that $P(B) = \text{Prob}\,(X_0 \in B) > 0$, and let $\tilde{B}$ be the set of all sequences $x \in A^Z$ such that $x_0 \in B$ and, such that $x_n \in B$ for infinitely many positive n and infinitely many negative n. In other words, $\tilde{B}$ consists of all points that start in B at time 0 and return to B infinitely often in both the past and future directions. The set $\tilde{B}$ is a Borel set since

$$\tilde{B} = \{x: \; x_0 \in B\} - \bigcup_{k=1}^\infty \bigcap_{|n| \geq k} \{x: \; x_n \notin B\}.$$

Furthermore, it can be shown that

$$P(\tilde{B}) = P(B) \tag{6}$$

a result known as the Poincaré recurrence theorem, see [55, Theorem I.2.17]. Of course, in the ergodic case, property (6) follows from the ergodic theorem for it guarantees that for almost all x each symbol occurs in both the past and future of x with limiting relative frequency equal to its probability.

The (future) *return-time function* is the function $n(x)$ defined for $x \in \tilde{B}$ by the formula

$$n(x) = \min\{n \geq 1: \; x_n \in B\}. \tag{7}$$

Note that $n(x)$ can also be defined by the formula

$$n(x) = \min\{n \geq 1: \; T^n x \in \tilde{B}\} \tag{8}$$

that is, the time of first return to $\tilde{B}$ under the action of the shift transformation T. For $n \geq 1$, define

$$B_n = \{x \in \tilde{B}: \; n(x) = n\}.$$

The following lemma summarizes the basic properties of the sets $\{B_n\}$. The proofs use the transformation definition (8); they can also be expressed in terms of the definition (7).

Lemma 1:

a) $B_1, B_2, \cdots$, is a disjoint sequence with union $\tilde{B}$.
b) If $n > 1$, then $B_n, TB_n, T^2 B_n, \cdots, T^{n-1} B_n$ is a disjoint sequence.
c) $B_1, B_2 \cup TB_2, B_3 \cup TB_3 \cup T^2 B_3, \cdots$ is a disjoint sequence.
d) $TB_1, T^2 B_2, \cdots, T^n B_n, \cdots$ is a disjoint sequence.

Proof: Part a) follows from the definition of $n(x)$. Parts b) and c) follow from the fact that if $x \in T^i B_n$, then $x \notin T^j B_m$ for $i < j < i + n$ and any $m \geq n$. Part d) is obtained by applying the invertible transformation T to the sequence $B_1, TB_2, T^2 B_3, \cdots$, which is a disjoint sequence, by part c). □

The *induced transformation* $\tilde{T}$: $\tilde{B} \mapsto \tilde{B}$ is the mapping defined by

$$\tilde{T}x = T^{n(x)}x, \qquad x \in \tilde{B}.$$

In other words, the induced transformation just shifts the sequence x leftwards to the next place where a symbol in B occurs. The induced transformation idea is due to Kakutani [24]; see [55, Sec. I.2] for a more complete discussion of the idea.

Let $P(\cdot|B)$ denote the measure conditioned on $X_0 \in B$, that is, the measure on A^Z defined for $-\infty < m \le n < \infty$ by the formula

$$P(X_m^n = a_m^n|B) = \mathrm{Prob}\,(X_m^n = a_m^n|X_0 \in B), \quad a_m^n \in A_m^n.$$

The following theorem is the transformation form of the contracted-process theorem.

Theorem 4: The induced transformation $\tilde{T}$ preserves the conditional measure $P(\cdot|B)$, and is ergodic if $\{X_n\}$ is ergodic.

Proof: First note that $\tilde{T}^{-1}$ is also defined for all $x \in \tilde{B}$, since it was required that $x_n \in B$ for infinitely many negative n. Furthermore, $P(\tilde{B}|B) = 1$, by (6). Thus it is enough to show that $P(\tilde{T}C) = P(C)$ for any Borel subset $C \subset \tilde{B}$.

By part a) of Lemma 1, a subset $C \subset \tilde{B}$ can be expressed as the disjoint union

$$C = \bigcup_{n=1}^{\infty} (C \cap B_n)$$

so that

$$\tilde{T}C = \bigcup_{n=1}^{\infty} \tilde{T}(C \cap B_n) = \bigcup_{n=1}^{\infty} T^n(C \cap B_n)$$

since $\tilde{T}x = T^n x$, $x \in B_n$. The sequence $\{T^n(C \cap B_n)\}$ is also disjoint, by part d) of Lemma 1, hence

$$P(\tilde{T}C) = \sum_{n=1}^{\infty} P(T^n(C \cap B_n)) = \sum_{n=1}^{\infty} P(C \cap B_n) = P(C)$$

since T^n is also measure-preserving and invertible. This proves that $\tilde{T}$ preserves the conditional measure.

Now suppose $\{X_n\}$ is ergodic, that is, the only shift-invariant sets have measure 0 or 1. Suppose also that $C \subset \tilde{B}$ has positive measure and satisfies $\tilde{T}C \subseteq C$. The set

$$D = \bigcup_{n=1}^{\infty} \bigcup_{i=0}^{n-1} T^i(C \cap B_n)$$

is T-invariant, because T maps $T^i(C \cap B_n)$ into $T^{i+1}(C \cap B_n)$, if $i < n$ and

$$T^n(C \cap B_n) = \tilde{T}C \cap T^n B_n \subseteq C \cap \tilde{B}$$

since $\tilde{T}C \subseteq C$, and $T^n B_n \subseteq \tilde{B}$. The set D has positive measure and T is ergodic so $P(D) = 1$, which means that

$$P(C|B) = P(D|B) = 1.$$

This completes the proof of the induced-transformation theorem. $\square$

All that remains is to convert the induced-transformation theorem into the contracted-process theorem by using the fact that a measure-preserving transformation and partition define a stationary process, via (1). In the current setting, the transformation is $\tilde{T}$, the space is $\tilde{B}$ equipped with the measure $P(\cdot|B)$, and the partition $\Pi = \{P_b\colon b \in B\}$ is defined by the formula

$$P_b = \{x \in \tilde{B}\colon x_0 = b\}. \tag{9}$$

The $(\tilde{T}, \Pi)$-process $\{Y_n\}$ is defined by selecting $x \in \tilde{B}$ according to the $P(\cdot|B)$ measure, and, for each n, putting

$$Y_n = Y_n(x) = b, \qquad \text{if } \tilde{T}^n x \in P_b.$$

The joint distribution of $\{Y_n\}$ is defined by the formula

$$\mathrm{Prob}\,(Y_m^n = b_m^n) = P\left(\bigcap_{i=m}^{i=n} \tilde{T}^{-i}P_{b_i} \,\middle|\, B\right).$$

In other words, the $(\tilde{T}, \Pi)$-process is just the process $\{X_n\}$ observed at the times when its values belong to B. The process defined by a measure-preserving transformation and a partition is always stationary and is ergodic whenever the transformation is ergodic, hence the induced-transformation theorem implies that the contracted process is stationary, and, furthermore, is ergodic if the original process $\{X_n\}$ is ergodic. This completes the proof of the contracted-process theorem. $\square$

Remark 4: The set B in the contracted-process theorem can be replaced by any measurable subset of A^Z of positive measure, that is, the question of whether X_n is to be retained or deleted can be allowed to depend on all past and future values. This more general result reduces to Theorem 4 by considering the pair process $\{(X_n, W_n)\}$, where W_n is 1 or 0, depending on whether or not $x \in B$, and replacing A by $A \times \{0, 1\}$ and B by $A \times \{1\}$.

Remark 5: It should be noted that the Kac return-time theorem, Theorem 1, follows easily from the key Lemma 1. First note that

$$TB^* \subseteq B^*, \qquad \text{where } B^* = \bigcup_{n=1}^{\infty} \bigcup_{i=0}^{n-1} T^i B_n$$

since T maps $T^i B_n$ into $T^{i+1}B_n$ if $i < n$ and into $\tilde{B} = \cup_n B_n$ if $i = n$. Parts b) and c) of the lemma imply that

$$P(B^*) = \sum_{n=1}^{\infty} \sum_{i=0}^{n-1} P(T^i B_n) = \sum_{n=1}^{\infty} nP(B_n)$$

since $P(T^i B_n) = P(B_n)$, for all $0 \le i < n$. The theorem then follows from the fact that

$$E(n(x)|B) = (1/P(B)) \sum_{n=1}^{\infty} nP(B_n) = P(B^*)/P(B) \le 1$$

with equality in the ergodic case when the invariant set B^* has measure 1.

IV. BLOWING-UP PROPERTIES

Of interest in a wide range of settings, including combinatorics, information theory, ergodic theory, and probability theory, is the size of a Hamming neighborhood of a set B of n-sequences, given the size of B. In this discussion, size will be measured in terms of probability and per-symbol Hamming distance

$$d_n(a_1^n, b_1^n) = \frac{|\{i \in [1, n]: a_i \neq b_i\}|}{n}$$

will be used. The δ-blowup, or δ-neighborhood, of a set $B \subset A^n$ is denoted by $[B]_\delta$ and consists of all y_1^n for which there is an $x_1^n \in B$ such that $d_n(x_1^n, y_1^n) \leq \delta$. The complement of the blowup is denoted by $[B]_\delta^c$.

In a 1974 paper, Margulis gives bounds on the cardinality of the set of sequences not in B that differ in one coordinate from some member of B [31]. An extension shows that sets that are not too small must have large blowups, a fact that plays an important role in multiuser information theory, see [8, Sec. 1.5 and Ch. 3]. By now there are many different results that assert that for memoryless sources (or sources with suitable decay of memory), sets that do not have too small probability must have a large blowup, see Corollaries 2 and 3, below, for two such results.

The idea that not-too-small sets have large blowup actually appears in disguised form as a key lemma about memoryless processes in Ornstein's earlier work on the isomorphism problem, see Lemma 2 below. A careful look by Marton at the proof of that lemma led to an information-theoretic bound on the $\bar{d}_n$-distance between two distributions when one of them is memoryless [32], [33]. A special case of Marton's inequality yields basic results about small sets with large blowup, including a blowup bound obtained by other methods by Talagrand [69]. A careful statement of the original Ornstein lemma and a sketch of his proof, followed by a discussion of Marton's inequality, will be given in the following paragraphs.

Unless stated otherwise, random variables have finite-source alphabet A and random processes are assumed to be stationary. The distributional (or variational) distance between random variables X and Y with respective distributions P and Q is given by

$$|P - Q| = \frac{1}{2} \sum_{a \in A} |P(a) - Q(a)|.$$

In the random-variable context, $|P - Q|$ is often replaced in the sequel by the notation $\|X - Y\|$, a notation particularly useful when conditioning is present. For example, if Y is conditioned by the values of Z, then $\|X - Y/z\|$ denotes the distributional distance between the distribution of X and the conditional distribution of Y, given that $Z = z$, while $E_Z\|X - Y/Z\|$ denotes the expected value of this distance.

Let X_1^n and Y_1^n be random vectors with respective distributions P_n and Q_n on A^n. A joining R_n of X_1^n and Y_1^n is a distribution on $A^n \times A^n$ with marginals P_n and Q_n. The $\bar{d}_n$-distance between P_n and Q_n is defined by

$$\bar{d}_n(P_n, Q_n) = \min_{R_n} E_{R_n}(d_n(X_1^n, Y_1^n))$$

where the minimum is over all joinings R_n of P_n and Q_n. In the random vector context, the notation $\bar{d}_n(X_1^n, Y_1^n)$ is often used in the sequel in place of $\bar{d}_n(P_n, Q_n)$.

In the first-order case, the $\bar{d}$-distance is the same as distributional distance, that is,

$$\bar{d}_1(X, Y) = \|X - Y\|. \tag{10}$$

Random-variable notation is useful in the $\bar{d}$-case to keep track of the conditioning. For example, $\bar{d}_1(X_k, Y_k/Y_1^{k-1})$ is the $\bar{d}$-distance between the distribution of X_k and the distribution of Y_k, given the past Y_1^{k-1}. In particular, combining with (10) produces

$$\bar{d}_1(X_k, Y_k/Y_1^{k-1}) = \|X_k - Y_k/Y_1^{k-1}\|. \tag{11}$$

The entropy-rate of a stationary process $\{X_j\}$ is given by the limit

$$H(\{X_j\}) = \lim_{n \to \infty} \frac{1}{n} H(X_1^n) = \lim_{n \to \infty} H(X_0|X_{-n}^{-1})$$

which, in the memoryless case, is just the first-order entropy $H(X_1)$.

The following lemma is Ornstein's key lemma. It is a precise formulation of the finitely determined property for memoryless sources, namely, that an ergodic process close enough in entropy-rate and first-order distribution to a memoryless process must also be $\bar{d}$-close.

Lemma 2: Given a memoryless process $\{X_j\}$ and $\epsilon > 0$, there is a $\delta > 0$ such that

$$\bar{d}_n(X_1^n, Y_1^n) < \epsilon, \qquad n = 1, 2, \cdots$$

for any ergodic process $\{Y_j\}$ that satisfies the two conditions

    a) $\|X_1 - Y_1\| \leq \delta$

    b) $|H(\{X_j\}) - H(\{Y_j\})| \leq \delta$.

Proof: Note that a) and b) with $\delta = 0$ imply that $\{Y_j\}$ is memoryless. An approximate form is that for δ small enough, conditions a) and b) imply that $\{Y_j\}$ is so close to being an independent process that the distribution of Y_i, given $Y_1^{i-1} = y_1^{i-1}$, tends to be close to the unconditional distribution of Y_i, which is, in turn, close to the distribution of X_i. This can be expressed by saying that if δ is small enough, then a) and b) imply that

$$E_{Y_1^{i-1}}\|X_i - Y_i/Y_1^{i-1}\| \leq \epsilon, \qquad i > 1. \tag{12}$$

Ornstein proved this directly, but it is also a consequence of Pinsker's inequality

$$\|X - Y\| \leq \sqrt{D(Y\|X)/2} \tag{13}$$

see [8, Exercise 17(a), p. 58], where $D(Y\|X)$ is defined in the paragraph following (16).

Lemma 2 is now established by induction. Choose $\delta < \epsilon/2$ so small that (12) holds with $\epsilon/2$ in place of ϵ. The first-order formula (10) yields

$$\bar{d}_1(X_1, Y_1) = \|X_1 - Y_1\| < \delta < \epsilon.$$

Assume $\overline{d}_n(X_1^n, Y_1^n) < \epsilon$ and let R_n be a joining of X_1^n and Y_1^n such that

$$E_{R_n}(d_n(X_1^n, Y_1^n)) = \overline{d}_n(X_1^n, Y_1^n).$$

For each (x_1^n, y_1^n) let $R_{y_1^n}$ be a joining of X_{n+1} and Y_{n+1}, given $Y_1^n = y_1^n$, that minimizes $\overline{d}_1(X_{n+1}, Y_{n+1}/y_1^n)$, and define R_{n+1} by the product formula

$$R_{n+1}(x_1^{n+1}, y_1^{n+1}) = R_n(x_1^n, y_1^n)R_{y_1^n}(x_{n+1}, y_{n+1}). \quad (14)$$

It is easy to check that R_{n+1} is a joining of X_1^{n+1} and Y_1^{n+1} and hence, using (11) and (12), and the Hamming-distance addition formula

$$(i+1)d_{i+1}(x_1^{i+1}, y_1^{i+1}) = id_i(x_1^i, y_1^i) + d_1(x_{i+1}, y_{i+1}) \quad (15)$$

with $i = n$, it follows that

$$\overline{d}_{n+1}(X_1^{n+1}, Y_1^{n+1}) \le E_{R_{n+1}}(d_{n+1}(X_1^{n+1}, Y_1^{n+1})) < \epsilon.$$

This completes Ornstein's proof of Lemma 2. $\qquad \square$

The joining formula, (14), is a way to build joinings one step at a time. Suppose X_1^n and Y_1^n have respective distributions P_n and Q_n and X_1^n is an independent sequence. A joining of these two sequences can be obtained by first joining X_1 and Y_1, then, for each value of (x_1, y_1), joining X_2 with Y_2/y_1 to obtain a joining of X_1^2 with Y_1^2, then for each value of (x_1^2, y_1^2), joining X_3 with Y_3/y_1^2 to obtain a joining of X_1^3 with Y_1^3, continuing in this manner until a joining of X_1^n and Y_1^n is achieved. If at stage i the joining that minimizes $\overline{d}_1(X_i, Y_i/y_1^{i-1})$ is used, then the first-order formulas (10) and (11) and the Hamming distance addition formulas, (15), for $0 \le i < n$, yield the bound

$$n\overline{d}_n(X_1^n, Y_1^n) \le \|X_1 - Y_1\| + \sum_{i=2}^{n} E_{Y_1^{i-1}}\|X_i - Y_i/Y_1^{i-1}\| \quad (16)$$

a bound valid for independent sequences X_1^n and arbitrary Y_1^n.

Marton's inequality is obtained by replacing the right-hand side of the preceding bound by a relative entropy bound. The relative entropy, or informational divergence, of a random variable Y with respect to a random variable X is given by

$$D(Y\|X) = \sum_a Q(a) \ln \frac{Q(a)}{P(a)}$$

where P and Q are the respective distributions of X and Y. (Note that the natural logarithm is used here, instead of the usual base 2 logarithm.) Conditional notation extends to this setting, e.g., $D(Y/Z\|X)$ denotes the relative entropy of Y, given Z, with respect to X, with $E_Z(D(Y/Z\|X))$ denoting its expected value.

Theorem 5. Marton's Inequality: If X_1^n is memoryless and Y_1^n is arbitrary, then

$$\overline{d}_n(X_1^n, Y_1^n) \le \sqrt{\frac{D(Y_1^n\|X_1^n)}{2n}}. \quad (17)$$

Proof: Pinsker's inequality, (13), gives

$$\|X_i - Y_i/y_1^{i-1}\| \le \sqrt{D(Y_i/y_1^{i-1}\|X_i)/2}$$

so concavity of the square root together with Jensen's inequality produces

$$E_{Y_1^{i-1}}\|X_i - Y_i/Y_1^{i-1}\| \le \sqrt{E_{Y_1^{i-1}}(D(Y_i/Y_1^{i-1}\|X_i))/2}.$$

Substituting into the $\overline{d}$-bound, (16), and again using concavity of the square root then yields, after division by n

$$\overline{d}_n(X_1^n, Y_1^n)$$
$$\le \sqrt{\frac{D(Y_1\|X_1) + \sum_{i=1}^{n-1} E_{Y_1^{i-1}}(D(Y_i/Y_1^{i-1}\|X_i))}{2n}}.$$

A direct calculation of the sum on the right gives the desired bound, (17). Here, for example, is the $n = 2$ proof, which easily generalizes.

$$D(Y_1\|X_1) + E_{Y_1}(D(Y_2/Y_1\|X_2))$$
$$= \sum_{a_1} Q(a_1) \log \frac{Q(a_1)}{P(a_1)}$$
$$+ \sum_{a_1} \sum_{a_2} Q(a_1)Q(a_2|a_1) \log \frac{Q(a_2|a_1)}{P(a_2)}$$
$$= \sum_{a_1^2} Q(a_1^2) \left[\log \frac{Q(a_1)}{P(a_1)} + \log \frac{Q(a_2|a_1)}{P(a_2)} \right]$$
$$= D(Y_1^2\|X_1^2).$$

This completes the proof of Marton's inequality. $\qquad \square$

A special case of Marton's inequality that leads to blowup bounds occurs when the distribution of Y_1^n is the conditional distribution of X_1^n, given that X_1^n belongs to a subset B of A^n, that is,

$$\text{Prob}(Y_1^n = y_1^n) = P(y_1^n|B) = \begin{cases} P(y_1^n)/P(B), & y_1^n \in B \\ 0, & \text{otherwise.} \end{cases}$$

Direct calculation gives

$$D(Y_1^n\|X_1^n) = \sum_{y_1^n \in B} P(y_1^n|B) \ln \frac{P(y_1^n|B)}{P(y_1^n)} = -\ln P(B)$$

so Marton's inequality in this case takes the following set form.

Corollary 1. Set Form of Marton's Inequality:

$$\overline{d}_n(X_1^n, X_1^n/B) \le \sqrt{\frac{-\ln P(B)}{2n}}. \quad (18)$$

One consequence of the set form is that, for memoryless processes, any set of n-sequences that is not exponentially small must have a large blowup.

Corollary 2: Given a memoryless process $\{X_n\}$ and $\delta > 0$, there is a $\gamma > 0$, such that $P([B]_\delta) \ge 1 - \delta$ for any set B of n-sequences for which $P(B) \ge 2^{-n\gamma}$.

Proof: Choose $\gamma = 2\delta^4/(\ln 2)$ and suppose $P(B) \geq 2^{-n\gamma}$, so that

$$-\ln P(B) \leq n\gamma \ln 2 \leq 2n\delta^4.$$

Substitution into the set form (18) gives $\bar{d}_n(X_1^n, Y_1^n) \leq \delta^2$, and an application of the Markov inequality then yields $P([B]_\delta) \geq 1 - \delta$. $\square$

Another application of Corollary 1 leads immediately to a blowup bound due to Talagrand, stated here, as he did, in terms of Hamming distance $d(x_1^n, y_1^n) = nd_n(x_1^n, y_1^n)$, with $d(x_1^n, B)$ denoting the minimum of $d(x_1^n, y_1^n)$, $y_1^n \in B$.

Corollary 3. Talagrand: If P is the distribution of a memoryless process $\{X_i\}$ then for any n and any set $B \subset A^n$

$$P(d(X_1^n, B) \geq k) \leq \frac{1}{P(B)} \exp\left(-\frac{k^2}{n}\right). \quad (19)$$

Proof: Put $\delta = k/n$, let Y_1^n be X_1^n conditioned on B, and let Z_1^n be X_1^n conditioned on $[B]_\delta^c$, the complement of the blowup of B. These two random vectors are always at least δ apart, so that $\bar{d}_n(Y_1^n, Z_1^n) \geq \delta$, and the triangle inequality yields

$$\delta \leq \bar{d}_n(Y_1^n, X_1^n) + \bar{d}_n(X_1^n, Z_1^n).$$

An application to each term of the set form of Marton's inequality, (18), followed by a use of concavity of the square root, yields

$$\delta \leq \sqrt{\frac{-\ln P(B)}{2n}} + \sqrt{\frac{-\ln P([B]_\delta^c)}{2n}}$$
$$\leq \sqrt{\frac{-\ln P(B)P([B]_\delta^c)}{n}}, \quad (20)$$

which is equivalent to Talagrand's inequality. $\square$

Remark 6: Talagrand, in his invited paper [69], established (19) by using an exponential bounding technique related to the Chernov bounding method. He derived several other blowing-up inequalities using similar methods and showed how such bounds can be used to obtain large deviations results in a wide variety of settings. His general name for the blowing-up phenomena is "concentration of measure." By the way, the bound (20) follows from a bound obtained in [68] and earlier in [38]. Recently, Dembo has shown how to obtain many of Talagrand's bounds by an extension of Marton's technique [10].

Corollary 2 raises the question of which processes have the (asymptotic) property that any set of n-sequences that is not exponentially too small must have a large blowup? The answer is the subclass of B-processes that have large deviations bounds [34]. If it is only required that sets of "typical" n-sequences that are not exponentially too small have large blowups, the answer is precisely the class of B-processes, a result that can then be used to show that B-processes have good approximate-match waiting-time properties [36]. The basic connection between blowing-up and large deviations is sketched in the following paragraphs.

An ergodic process has the *blowing-up property* if given $\delta > 0$ there is a $\gamma > 0$ and an N such that

$$n \geq N, \; B \subset A^n, \; P_n(B) \geq 2^{-n\gamma} \Longrightarrow P_n([B]_\delta) \geq 1 - \delta. \quad (21)$$

Processes with the blowing-up property must also have large deviations properties. For example, if

$$p_k(a_1^k | x_1^n) = \frac{|\{i \in [0, n-k]: \; x_{i+1}^{i+k} = a_1^k\}|}{n - k + 1}$$

is the empirical distribution of overlapping k-blocks in x_1^n, then

$$\lim_{n \to \infty} -\frac{1}{n} \log P_n(\{x_1^n: \; |p_k(\cdot | x_1^n) - P_k| \geq \epsilon\}) > 0 \quad (22)$$

for all k and $\epsilon > 0$, for any process with the blowing-up property. The reason is simple. If k and $\epsilon > 0$ are fixed and

$$B_n = \{x_1^n: \; |p_k(\cdot | x_1^n) - P_k| \geq \epsilon\}$$

then, for δ small enough

$$[B_n]_\delta \subset \{x_1^n: \; |p_k(\cdot | x_1^n) - P_k| \geq \epsilon/2\}. \quad (23)$$

The ergodic theorem guarantees that $p_k(\cdot | x_1^n) \to P_k$, in probability, so (23) implies that $P([B_n]_\delta) \to 0$. On the other hand, if the process has the blowing-up property and $P(B_n)$ does not go to 0 exponentially fast, then $P([B_n]_\delta) \geq 1 - \delta$, for all large enough n, so the large deviations property (22) must indeed hold.

A similar argument shows that

$$\lim_{n \to \infty} -\frac{1}{n} \log P_n(\{x_1^n: \; |-\log P_n(x_1^n) - H(\{X_i\})| > \epsilon\}) > 0 \quad (24)$$

for any $\epsilon > 0$, for any process with the blowing-up property. A process satisfying the large deviations property (22) for all k and $\epsilon > 0$ is said to have exponential rates for frequencies, and a process satisfying (24) for every $\epsilon > 0$ is said to have exponential rates for entropy. The preceding argument shows that processes with the blowing-up property have exponential rates for frequencies and entropy. With somewhat more effort it can be shown that processes with the blowing-up property are B-processes, and with considerably more effort it can be shown that the processes with the blowing-up property are precisely the B-processes that have exponential rates for frequencies and entropy [34], see also [55, Sec. IV.3].

Many processes are known to have the blowing-up property. For example, it is known that mixing Markov processes are B-processes, as are mixing finite-state processes, and it is easy to see that such processes have exponential rates, see [55]. An important class of examples that can be directly shown to have the blowing-up property is the class of finitary codings of memoryless processes [34]. A stationary coding with per-symbol encoder $f: \; A^Z \mapsto B$ is called a *finitary* coding of an A-valued process $\{X_n\}$ if there is a measurable integer-valued mapping $w(x)$ such that for almost every $x, y \in A^Z$, $f(x) = f(y)$, whenever $x_{-w(x)}^{w(x)} = y_{-w(x)}^{w(x)}$. Of, course, in the case when $w(x)$ is constant such a code is called a finite code.

Not every B-process has the blowing-up property. For example, all mixing renewal processes are known to be B-processes, but it can be shown that if the distribution of the waiting time between one's is too long-tailed, then the process will not have exponential rates. Also, it can be shown that an ergodic process Q with exponential rates for frequencies and entropy must have the positive divergence property, that is, $D_\infty(P\|Q) = 0$ implies that $P = Q$, hence the B-processes constructed in [63] and [74] cannot have exponential rates.

V. DIRECT SAMPLE PATH METHODS

The ergodic theorem guarantees that for fixed k and large enough n, most n-length sample paths will be k-block frequency-typical, that is, the empirical distribution of nonoverlapping k-blocks will be close to the true distribution. Likewise, the entropy-rate theorem (AEP) guarantees that most such sample paths will be entropy-typical, that is, have probability roughly 2^{-nh}. The ideas introduced by Ornstein and Weiss in their proof of the entropy-rate theorem and in subsequent work by them and others have led to a series of finer results about "typical" sample paths. Many of these results are useful in ergodic theory and information theory.

To give the reader a taste of these developments, four of the new techniques will be described along with examples showing how they are used. The four techniques are expressed here as four lemmas, which, for want of better names, are called the packing lemma, the counting lemma, the doubling lemma, and the strong doubling lemma. The first two are strictly combinatorial results. The second two are extensions of the ergodic theorem which are used so often that it seems appropriate to give them names; the word "doubling" comes from the fact that they usually depend for their success on some other limit theorem, a convergence-in-probability theorem for doubling and an almost-sure theorem for strong doubling. Except for the counting lemma, which requires some argument, the lemmas are quite simple. A detailed discussion of most of these ideas, using somewhat different terminology, is given in [55].

A. Packing and Counting

The packing technique is a method for building "almost" packings of intervals from "almost" coverings by subintervals whose left endpoints already cover most of the interval. In this and later sections, intervals are taken to be integer intervals, that is, $[k, m]$ denotes the set of integers ℓ such that $k \le \ell \le m$. Three properties of collections $\mathcal{C}$ of subintervals of $[1, N]$ will be of interest, a strong form of "almost" covering, an "almost" packing property, and a boundedness property.

  a) $\mathcal{C}$ is called a *strong* $(1 - \delta)$-*cover* of $[1, N]$ if the set of left endpoints of its members contains at least a $(1 - \delta)$-fraction of $[1, N]$.
  b) $\mathcal{C}$ is called a $(1 - \delta)$-*packing* if it is disjoint and its union covers at least a $(1 - \delta)$-fraction of $[1, N]$.
  c) $\mathcal{C}$ is L-*bounded* if each of its members has length at most L.

For example, $\{[1, 3], [2, 3], [3, 5], [5, 6]\}$ is a 3-bounded, strong $(2/3)$-cover of $[1, 6]$, and $\{[1, 3], [5, 6]\}$ is a $(5/6)$-packing of $[1, 6]$.

Lemma 3. The Packing Lemma: If $N \ge L/\delta$, then any L-bounded, strong $(1 - \delta)$-cover $\mathcal{C}$ of $[1, N]$ contains a $(1 - 2\delta)$-packing.

Proof: A $(1 - 2\delta)$-packing is produced by proceeding sequentially from left to right, selecting the first member of $\mathcal{C}$ that is disjoint from the previous selections. This can be continued at least until within L of N. The integers not covered are either not left endpoints of members of $\mathcal{C}$ or are within L of N. $\qquad\square$

The counting lemma provides a bound on the number of sequences that are mostly packed by blocks drawn from fixed collections whose sizes are known. Positive numbers ϵ, δ, h, and M are given, along with, for each $m \ge M$, a set $B_m \subset A^m$ of cardinality at most $2^{m(h+\epsilon)}$. Let $\mathcal{B}$ be the union of the B_m, for $m \ge M$. A sequence x_1^N is said to be $(1 - \delta)$-*built-up* from $\mathcal{B}$ if it can be expressed as a concatenation of variable-length blocks

$$x_1^N = b_1 b_2 \cdots b_K$$

in which the total length of the b_i that belong to $\mathcal{B}$ is at least $(1 - \delta)N$. Let G_N be the set of x_1^N that are $(1 - \delta)$-built-up from $\mathcal{B}$. Also let

$$H_b(p) = -p \log p - (1 - p) \log(1 - p)$$

denote the binary entropy function.

Lemma 4. The Counting Lemma: If $H_b(2/M) \le \epsilon/2$ and $\delta \log |A| \le \epsilon/2$, then $|G_N| \le 2^{N(h+2\epsilon)}$.

Proof: The idea is to condition on the locations of the blocks that belong to $\mathcal{B}$ then use that fact that a location of length m can be filled in at most $2^{m(h+\epsilon)}$ ways with blocks from B_m. For a fixed set of locations this gives a bound which is only a small exponential factor more than $2^{n(h+\epsilon)}$, since each member of G_N is mostly built-up from $\mathcal{B}$. This is then multiplied by the number of possible skeletons, which is also exponentially small since M is large.

The details are as follows. A *skeleton* is a disjoint collection $\mathcal{P}$ of subintervals of $[1, N]$, each of length at least M, whose union has cardinality at least $(1 - \delta)N$. A sequence x_1^N is *compatible* with a skeleton $\mathcal{P}$ if the word x_i^j belongs to $\mathcal{B}$ whenever the interval $[i, j]$ belongs to $\mathcal{P}$. Let $G_N(\mathcal{P})$ consist of all sequences compatible with a given skeleton $\mathcal{P}$. Note that any sequence x_1^N that is $(1 - \delta)$-built-up from $\mathcal{B}$ must belong to $G_N(\mathcal{P})$ for some skeleton $\mathcal{P}$, that is, G_N is the union of $G_N(\mathcal{P})$ over all skeletons $\mathcal{P}$.

If $[i, j] \in \mathcal{P}$ and $m = j - i + 1$, there are at most $2^{m(h+\epsilon)}$ ways to fill $[i, j]$ with a member of B_m. On the other hand, there are at most $|A|^{\delta N}$ ways to fill the places that do not belong to the union of $\mathcal{P}$. Putting these two facts together yields the bound

$$|G_N(\mathcal{P})| \le 2^{N(h+\epsilon)} |A|^{\delta N}. \tag{25}$$

Each interval in a skeleton has length at least M, so at most $2N/M$ points can be endpoints of its intervals. Thus the number of possible skeletons is upper-bounded by

$$\sum_{j \le 2N/M} \binom{N}{j} \le 2^{N H_b(2/M)} \tag{26}$$

by the standard bound, see [55, Lemma I.5.4]. The set G_N is the union of the sets $G_N(\mathcal{P})$ over all skeletons $\mathcal{P}$, so the cardinality of G_N is upper-bounded by the product of the two bounds, (25) and (26), that is,

$$\log |G_N| \leq N(h + \epsilon) + \delta N \log |A| + N H_b(2/M).$$

This is bounded by $N(h + 2\epsilon)$ if $H_b(2/M) \leq \epsilon/2$ and $\delta \log |A| \leq \epsilon/2$. $\qquad\square$

B. Doubling

The simple form of doubling starts with a set $B_k \subseteq A^k$ of large probability. (In the usual applications, such a set is provided by some convergence-in-probability limit theorem.) The doubling lemma asserts that, eventually almost surely, most indices in x_1^n are starting places of k-blocks that belong to B_k.

Lemma 5. The Doubling Lemma: If $P(B_k) > 1 - \delta/2$, then, eventually almost surely as $n \to \infty$

$$x_i^{i+k-1} \in B_k \qquad (27)$$

for at least $(1 - \delta)n$ indices $i \in [1, n - k + 1]$.

Proof: If T denotes the shift and χ_{U_k} denotes the indicator function of the set $U_k = \{x: \; x_1^k \in B_k\}$ then the sum

$$\sum_{i=1}^{n-k+1} \chi_{U_k}(T^{i-1}x)$$
$$= \chi_{U_k}(x) + \chi_{U_k}(T^1 x) + \cdots + \chi_{U_k}(T^{n-k}x)$$

counts the number of indices $i \in [1, n - k + 1]$ for which $x_i^{i+k-1} \in B_k$. By the ergodic theorem

$$\lim_{n\to\infty} \frac{1}{n-k+1} \sum_{i=1}^{n-k+1} \chi_{U_k}(T^{i-1}x) = P(U_k), \text{ almost surely}$$

which establishes the lemma since

$$P(U_k) = P(B_k) > 1 - \delta/2. \qquad\square$$

Strong doubling starts with a sequence of sets $\{B_k \subseteq A^k: k = 1, 2, \cdots\}$ such that $x_1^k \in B_k$, eventually almost surely. (In applications, such a sequence is provided by some almost-sure limit theorem.) Condition (27) is replaced by the much stronger requirement that every one of the conditions

$$x_i^{i+k-1} \in B_k, \; x_i^{i+k} \in B_{k+1}, \cdots, x_i^N \in B_{N-i+1} \qquad (28)$$

holds for a large fraction of indices $i \leq n - k + 1$. Note that (28) requires that *every block in x_1^N that starts at i and has length at least k* belongs to $\cup_{j \geq k} B_j$.

Lemma 6. The Strong-Doubling Lemma: If $x_1^k \in B_k$, eventually almost surely as $k \to \infty$, then given $\delta > 0$, there is a k such that, eventually almost surely as $n \to \infty$, property (28) holds for x_1^n for at least $(1 - \delta)n$ indices $i \in [1, n - k + 1]$.

Proof: The assumption that $x_1^k \in B_k$, eventually almost surely, implies that, for k large enough, the set

$$U_k = \{x: \; x_1^j \in B_j, \text{ for all } j \geq k\}$$

has measure at least $1 - \delta/4$. The ergodic theorem implies that

$$\lim_{n\to\infty} \frac{1}{n-k+1} \sum_{i=1}^{n-k+1} \chi_{U_k}(T^{i-1}x) = P(U_k), \text{ almost surely}$$

so that, in particular

$$\frac{1}{n-k-1} \sum_{i=1}^{n-k+1} \chi_{U_k}(T^{i-1}x) \geq 1 - \delta/2 \qquad (29)$$

eventually almost surely, as $n \to \infty$.

Suppose (29) holds for a given n. This means that $T^{i-1}x \in U_k$ for at least $(1 - \delta/2)n$ indices $i \in [1, n - k + 1]$. To say that $T^{i-1}x \in U_k$, however, means that all blocks in the *infinite* sequence x that start at i and have length at least k must belong to $\cup_{j \geq k} B_k$. In particular, if $T^{i-1}x \in U_k$ and $i \leq n - k$, then all the blocks in the *finite* sequence x_1^n that start at i and have length at least k must belong to $\cup_{j \geq k} B_k$. If $n \geq 2k/\delta$ there will be at most $\delta n/2$ indices in the interval $[n - k + 1, n]$. Thus if (29) holds and $n \geq 2k/\delta$, then for x_1^n, the strong-doubling condition (28) must hold for at least $(1 - \delta)n$ indices $i \in [1, n - k + 1]$. This proves the lemma since (29) holds eventually almost surely, as $n \to \infty$. $\qquad\square$

C. An Application to Entropy

The packing, counting, and doubling lemmas lead to a proof of the entropy-rate theorem (AEP). If a process is ergodic then, except in trivial cases, the probability $P(x_1^n)$ decreases to 0 as $n \to \infty$. The entropy-rate theorem asserts that the rate of decrease is a constant h with probability 1.

Theorem 6. The Entropy-Rate Theorem (AEP): For an ergodic A-valued process there is a constant $h \geq 0$ such that

$$\lim_{n\to\infty} -\frac{1}{n} \log P(x_1^n) = h, \text{ almost surely}.$$

Proof: Define

$$h(x) = \liminf_{n\to\infty} (-1/n) \log P(x_1^n).$$

Since $h(Tx) \leq h(x)$ and the process is ergodic there is a constant h such that $h(x) = h$, with probability 1, see [55, Exercise 4, Sec. I.2]. The remaining task is to show that

$$h = \limsup_{n\to\infty} (-1/n) \log P(x_1^n).$$

Fix $\epsilon > 0$. The definition of limit inferior implies that $-(1/n) \log P(x_1^n) \geq h + \epsilon$, infinitely often, almost surely, that is,

$$P(x_1^n) \geq 2^{-n(h+\epsilon)}, \text{ infinitely often, almost surely.} \qquad (30)$$

The basic idea of the proof is to show that, eventually almost surely, as $N \to \infty$, most indices $i \in [1, N]$ are starting places of blocks in x_1^N for which $P(x_i^{i+n-1}) \geq 2^{-n(h+\epsilon)}$ for some $n \leq N - i$, then use the packing lemma to extract an almost packing and the counting lemma to show that the

46

set of N-sequences that have such an almost packing cannot have cardinality exponentially much more than $2^{N(h+\epsilon)}$. At first glance this appears to be difficult to accomplish since (30) specifies no control on the size of n. It does say, however, that, starting at i, the waiting time n until $P(x_i^{i+n-1}) \geq 2^{-n(h+\epsilon)}$ occurs is almost surely finite, and therefore is bounded except for a set of small probability; it turns out this is all that is needed to convert the basic idea into a proof.

Fix M so that $H_b(2/M) \leq \epsilon/2$, where $H_b(\cdot)$ is the binary entropy function, and fix $\delta > 0$ such that $\delta \log |A| \leq \epsilon/2$. Let $L \geq M$ be an integer to be specified later, and let $\mathcal{B}$ be the union, for $M \leq n \leq L$, of the sets

$$B_n = \{x_1^n \colon P(x_1^n) \geq 2^{-n(h+\epsilon)}\}.$$

Finally, for $N \geq L$, let G_N be the set of all sequences x_1^N that can be $(1-\delta)$-built-up from $\mathcal{B}$. Since $|B_n| \leq 2^{n(h+\epsilon)}$, the counting lemma implies that

$$|G_N| \leq 2^{N(h+2\epsilon)}. \tag{31}$$

The doubling lemma, in conjunction with the packing lemma, will be used to prove the following lemma.

Lemma 7: If L is large enough, then $x_1^N \in G_N$, eventually almost surely.

Proof: First note that the entropy-rate theorem is an immediate consequence of the lemma and the bound (31), for, if $V_n = \{x_1^n \in G_n \colon P(x_1^n) \leq 2^{-n(h+3\epsilon)}\}$, then

$$P(V_n) \leq |G_n| 2^{-n(h+3\epsilon)} \leq 2^{-\epsilon n}.$$

This is summable in n, so the Borel–Cantelli principle implies that $x_1^n \notin V_n$, eventually almost surely, which, since $x_1^n \in G_n$, eventually almost surely, implies that $P(x_1^n) \geq 2^{-n(h+3\epsilon)}$, eventually almost surely. This, however, means that

$$h = \limsup \, (-1/n) \log P(x_1^n)$$

with probability 1, from which the entropy-rate theorem follows.

To prove the lemma it must be shown how $L \geq M$ can be chosen so that $x_1^N \in G_N$, eventually almost surely. Towards this end, note that the condition (30) implies almost sure finiteness for the random variable $n(x)$ that specifies the least integer $n \geq M$ for which $x_1^n \in B_n$. Thus $L \geq M$ can be chosen such that $n(x) \leq L$, with probability at least $1 - \delta/4$. This, in turn, means that the set

$$U_L = \{x_1^L \colon x_1^j \in B_j, \text{ for some } j \in [M, L]\}$$

has measure at least $1 - \delta/4$.

The doubling lemma can now be applied to the set $U_L \subseteq A^L$. The conclusion is that for x_1^N, eventually almost surely as $N \to \infty$, there will be at least $(1-\delta/2)N$ indices $i \in [N, N-L+1]$ for which $x_i^{i+L-1} \in U_L$. But if this holds for some x_1^N then the collection $\{[i, j] \colon x_i^j \in \mathcal{B}\}$ is an L-bounded, strong $(1-\delta/2)$-cover of $[1, N]$, so that once N is large enough to satisfy $N \geq 2L/\delta$, the packing lemma implies that x_1^N is $(1-\delta)$-built-up from $\mathcal{B}$, that is, $x_1^N \in G_N$. This proves the lemma and thereby completes the proof of the entropy-rate theorem. $\square$

D. Applications to Empirical Entropy

Fix an ergodic process with *positive* entropy h. For $\epsilon > 0$ the set $B_k = \{x_1^k \colon P(x_1^k) \geq 2^{-k(h+\epsilon)}\}$ has cardinality at most $2^{k(h+\epsilon)}$. The entropy-rate theorem implies that $P(B_k) \to 1$, as $k \to \infty$, so that given $\gamma > 0$ there is a k such that $P(B_k) > 1 - \gamma$. The fact that there is a set of k-sequences that has both large probability and cardinality $\sim 2^{kh}$ is, of course, the significance of Shannon's entropy concept for communications theory. Two results of this type for the empirical distribution will be established, the first for overlapping k-block distributions using strong doubling, the second for nonoverlapping k-block distributions using doubling.

The empirical distribution of overlapping k-blocks in x_1^n is defined by the formula

$$p_k(a_1^k|x_1^n) = \frac{|\{i \in [0, n-k] \colon x_{i+1}^{i+k} = a_1^k\}|}{n-k+1}.$$

The ergodic theorem implies that $p_k(B_k|x_1^n) \to P(B_k)$, almost surely as $n \to \infty$, so that if $P(B_k) > 1 - \epsilon/2$, then $p_k(B_k|x_1^n) > 1 - \epsilon$, eventually almost surely. In other words, the set of entropy-typical sequences also has large probability with respect to the empirical measure. The surprising fact is that such a result holds even if k is allowed to grow linearly in n. The proof illustrates the use of strong doubling.

Theorem 7: Given $\epsilon > 0$, there is a K such that, eventually almost surely as $n \to \infty$

$$p_k(B_k|x_1^n) \geq 1 - \epsilon, \qquad \text{for all } k \in [K, n\epsilon/2].$$

Proof: The entropy-rate theorem implies that $x_1^k \in B_k$, eventually almost surely. The strong-doubling lemma provides a K such that for x_1^n, eventually almost surely as $n \to \infty$, there are at least $(1-\epsilon/2)n$ indices $i \in [1, n-K+1]$ such that x_i^{i+j-1} belongs to B_j for *every index* $j \in [K, n-K+1]$. But if this is so and $K \leq k \leq n\epsilon/2$, then, because there are at most $\epsilon n/2$ indices in the interval $[n-k+2, n]$, the block x_i^{i+k-1} belongs to B_k for at least $(1-\epsilon)n$ indices $i \in [1, n-k+1]$, that is, $p_k(B_k|x_1^n) \geq 1 - \epsilon$. This proves the theorem. $\square$

The nonoverlapping empirical k-block distribution $q_k(\cdot|x_1^n)$ is defined by writing $n = km + r$, $0 \leq r < k$, and using the formula

$$q_k(a_1^k|x_1^n) = \frac{|\{j \in [1, m] \colon x_{(j-1)k+1}^{jk} = a_1^k\}|}{m}, \qquad a_1^k \in A^k.$$

At first glance, a nonoverlapping result would appear to be a trivial extension of Theorem 7, but this is not the case, for the set of multiples of k is at most a $(1/m)$-fraction of $[1, n]$, so all of the indices $(j-1)k+1$ could be starting places of k-blocks that do not belong to B_k. One could argue that for some shift $s \in [0, k-1]$, the probability $q_k(B_k|x_{s+1}^n)$ is large, which is true, but this seems unsatisfactory. By allowing a somewhat weaker notion of entropy typicality, the doubling lemma produces a satisfactory result for the nonoverlapping case.

The entropy-rate theorem provides ℓ and a set $C \subset A^\ell$ of large probability and cardinality roughly $2^{\ell h}$. The doubling lemma implies that eventually almost surely, most places in an n-block are starting places of blocks that belong to C. If $k \geq \ell$, the Markov inequality implies that most of the $x_{(j-1)k+1}^{jk}$ have the property that most of their indices are starting places of blocks in C. If k is enough larger than ℓ, such k-blocks must be almost built-up from C, by the packing lemma. In other words, if "typical" now means "mostly built-up from C," then the $q_k(\cdot|x_1^n)$ probability of "typical" k-blocks must be large.

The precise formulation of this new typicality idea is as follows. The entropy-rate theorem provides an ℓ and a set $C \subset A^\ell$ such that $P(C) > 1 - \delta/2$ and $|C| \leq 2^{\ell(h+\delta)}$, where δ is a free parameter. For each k, let $\mathcal{S}_k$ be the set of x_1^k that are $(1 - \delta)$-built-up from C. The counting lemma implies that if δ is small enough then $|\mathcal{S}_k| \leq 2^{k(h+\epsilon)}$, for all k. The sets $\{\mathcal{S}_k\}$ can be regarded as typical, at least in the empirical sense stated in the following theorem, whose proof is just a matter of filling in the details of the preceding paragraph, see [55, Theorem II.3.1(a)].

Theorem 8: Given $\epsilon > 0$, there is a K such that, eventually almost surely as $n \to \infty$

$$q_k(\mathcal{S}_k|x_1^n) \geq 1 - \epsilon, \qquad \text{for all } k \in [K, n\epsilon/2].$$

Remark 7: The method used to prove Theorem 8 can be adapted to show that $p_k(\mathcal{S}_k|x_1^N) \geq 1 - \epsilon$, for $K \leq k \leq 2N/\epsilon$, which is the form of the original Ornstein–Weiss result [51, Lemma 1]. The stronger result in the overlapping case, namely, that most of the indices are starting places of k-blocks that are *actually entropy typical* is new. Ornstein and Weiss also showed, using a counting argument similar to the one used to prove the counting lemma, that for almost every x there is a $K(\epsilon, x)$ such that if $K \geq K(\epsilon, x)$ and $N \geq 2^{Kh}$, then any set $B \subset A^K$ of cardinality at most $2^{K(h-\epsilon)}$ must satisfy $p_K(B|x_1^N) < \epsilon$, (likewise, $q_K(B|x_1^N) < \epsilon$). This can also be established via a coding argument, see [55, Sec. II.3.b]. These lower bound results, in conjunction with Theorem 7 or 8, provide an entropy estimation theorem, for they show that $(1/k)H(p_{k(n)}(\cdot|x_1^n)) \to h$, almost surely, as $n \to \infty$, for any unbounded sequence $\{k(n)\}$ for which $k(n) \leq (1/h) \log n$, with comparable results for the nonoverlapping block distribution.

Remark 8: The packing lemma, along with elementary probability facts, can be used to prove ergodic theorems, yielding, in particular, an especially simple proof for the binary, ergodic form of Birkhoff's ergodic theorem that extends to the general result, see [59], as well as to a nice proof of the subadditive ergodic theorem [67]. The strong doubling idea has been used to study the growth of prefix trees, see [55], [61], and in conjunction with a martingale theorem to obtain joint distribution estimation theorems for weakly dependent processes [35]. Versions of the packing and counting lemmas, in conjunction with doubling or strong doubling, have been used in numerous recent settings, including α-entropy [11], universal coding [25], [48], [60], and more general ergodic theorems [27]. Doubling, in conjunction with the built-up set idea, was used by Ornstein and Weiss to show that, eventually almost surely, in any partition of a sample path into distinct blocks, most of the path must be covered by blocks of length

at least (roughly) $(1/h) \log n$ [52]. Finally, it should be noted that the packing lemma actually extends to random fields and some more general structures, see [50]. Of course, the simple proof given here does not extend as it uses the order structure of the natural numbers, so a more sophisticated argument is needed.

ACKNOWLEDGMENT

Bob Gray and Dave Neuhoff provided detailed reviews of an earlier draft and made many helpful suggestions for improvement. Imre Csiszár, Kati Marton, Don Ornstein, Jacek Serafin, and Sergio Verdú also contributed useful comments.

REFERENCES

[1] R. L. Adler, D. Coppersmith, and M. Hassner, "Algorithms for sliding-block codes—An application of symbolic dynamics to information theory," *IEEE Trans. Inform. Theory*, vol. IT-29, pp. 5–22, 1983.
[2] P. Algoet and T. Cover, "Asymptotic optimality and asymptotic equipartition properties of log-optimum investment," *Ann. Probab.*, vol. 16, pp. 876–898, 1988.
[3] A. Barron, "The strong ergodic theorem for densities: Generalized Shannon–McMillan–Breiman theorem," *Ann. Probab.*, vol. 13, pp. 1292–1303, 1985.
[4] T. Berger, *Rate Distortion Theory: A Mathematical Basis for Data Compression.* Englewood Cliffs, NJ: Prentice-Hall, 1971.
[5] P. Billingsley, *Ergodic Theory and Information.* New York: Wiley, 1965.
[6] L. Breiman, "The individual ergodic theorem of information theory," *Ann. Math. Statist.*, vol. 28, pp. 809–811, 1957; correction, vol. 31, pp. 809–810, 1960.
[7] T. Cover, "A proof of the data compression theorem of Slepian and Wolf for ergodic sources," *IEEE Trans. Inform. Theory*, vol. IT-21, pp. 226–228, 1975.
[8] I. Csiszár and J. Körner, *Information Theory. Coding Theorems for Discrete Memoryless Systems.* Budapest, Hungary: Akadémiai Kiadó, 1981.
[9] L. D. Davisson, "Universal noiseless coding," *IEEE Trans. Inform. Theory*, vol. IT-19, pp. 783–795, 1973.
[10] A. Dembo, "Information inequalities and concentration of measure," *Ann. Probab.*, vol. 25, pp. 927–939, 1997.
[11] J. Feldman, "r-Entropy, equipartition, and Ornstein's isomorphism theorem," *Israel J. Math.*, vol. 36, pp. 321–343, 1980.
[12] R. Gallager, *Information Theory and Reliable Communication.* New York: Wiley, 1968.
[13] R. Gray, "Sliding-block source coding," *IEEE Trans. Inform. Theory*, vol. IT-21, pp. 357–368, 1975.
[14] _____, *Entropy and Information Theory.* New York: Springer-Verlag, 1990.
[15] R. Gray and L. D. Davisson, "Source coding without the ergodic assumption," *IEEE Trans. Inform. Theory*, vol. IT-20, pp. 502–516, 1975.
[16] R. Gray and J. Kieffer, "Asymptotically mean stationary measures," *Ann. Probab.*, vol. 8, pp. 962–973, 1980.
[17] R. Gray, D. Neuhoff, and P. Shields, "A generalization of Ornstein's $\bar{d}$-distance with applications to information theory," *Ann. Probab.*, vol. 3, pp. 315–328, 1975.
[18] R. Gray and D. Ornstein, "Sliding-block joint source/noisy channel coding theorems," *IEEE Trans. Inform. Theory*, vol. IT-22, pp. 682–690, 1976.
[19] R. Gray, D. Ornstein, and R. Dobrushin, "Block synchronization, sliding-block coding, invulnerable sources and zero error codes for discrete noisy channels," *Ann. Probab.*, vol. 8, pp. 639–674, 1980.
[20] P. Halmos, *Lectures on Ergodic Theory.* New York: Chelsea, 1956.
[21] T. S. Han and S. Verdú, "Approximation theory of output statistics," *IEEE Trans. Inform. Theory*, vol. 39, pp. 752–772, 1993.
[22] Y. Hershkovits and J. Ziv, "On sliding-window universal data compression with limited memory," *IEEE Trans. Inform. Theory*, vol. 44, pp. 66–78, 1998.
[23] M. Kac, "On the notion of recurrence in discrete stochastic processes," *Ann. Math. Statist.*, vol. 53, pp. 1002–1010, 1947.
[24] S. Kakutani, "Induced measure-preserving transformations," *Proc. Japan Acad.*, vol. 19, pp. 635–641, 1943.

[25] J. C. Kieffer, "Sample converses in source coding theory," *IEEE Trans. Inform. Theory*, vol. 37, pp. 263–268, 1991.

[26] ――――, "A direct proof that VWB processes are closed in the d-bar metric," *Israel J. Math.*, vol. 41, pp. 154–160, 1982.

[27] ――――, "An ergodic theorem for constrained sequences of functions," *Bull. Amer. Math. Soc.*, vol. 21, pp. 249–254, 1989.

[28] A. N. Kolmogorov, "A new invariant for transitive dynamical systems," *Dokl. Akad. Nauk SSSR*, vol. 119, pp. 861–864, 1958.

[29] U. Krengel, *Ergodic Theorems*. Berlin, Germany: W. de Gruyter, 1985.

[30] D. Lind and B. Marcus, *An Introduction to Symbolic Dynamics and Coding*. Cambridge, U.K.: Cambridge Univ. Press, 1995.

[31] G. A. Margulis, "Probabilistic characteristics of graphs with large connectivity," *Probl. Pered. Inform.*, vol. 10, pp. 101–108, 1974.

[32] K. Marton, "A simple proof of the blowing-up lemma," *IEEE Trans. Inform. Theory*, vol. 42, pp. 445–447, 1986.

[33] ――――, "Bounding $\bar{d}$-distance by information divergence: A method to prove concentration inequalities," *Ann. Probab.*, vol. 24, pp. 857–866, 1966.

[34] K. Marton and P. Shields, "The positive-divergence and blowing-up properties," *Israel J. Math.*, vol. 86, pp. 331–348, 1994.

[35] ――――, "Entropy and the consistent estimation of joint distributions," *Ann. Probab.*, vol. 22, pp. 960–977, 1994; correction, vol. 24, pp. 541–545, 1996.

[36] ――――, "Almost sure waiting time results for weak and very weak Bernoulli processes," *Ergodic Theory and Dyn. Syst.*, vol. 15, pp. 951–960, 1995.

[37] ――――, "How many future measures can there be?," in preparation.

[38] C. McDiarmid, "On the method of bounded differences," in *Surveys in Combinatorics,* in *London Mathematical Society Lecture Notes*, vol. 141, J. Simons, Ed. Cambridge, U.K.: Cambridge Univ. Press, 1989, pp. 148–188.

[39] B. McMillan, "The basic theorems of information theory," *Ann. Math. Stat.*, vol. 24, pp. 196–216, 1953.

[40] D. Neuhoff, R. Gray, and L. D. Davisson, "Fixed rate universal block source coding with a fidelity criterion," *IEEE Trans. Inform. Theory*, vol. IT-21, pp. 511–523, 1975.

[41] D. Neuhoff and P. Shields, "Block and sliding-block source coding," *IEEE Trans. Inform. Theory*, vol. IT-23, pp. 211–215, 1977.

[42] D. Neuhoff, P. Shields, L. D. Davisson, and F. Ledrappier, "The distortion-rate function for nonergodic sources," *Ann. Probab.*, vol. 6, pp. 138–143, 1978.

[43] D. Neuhoff and P. Shields, "Channels with almost finite memory," *IEEE Trans. Inform. Theory*, vol. IT-25, pp. 440–447, 1979.

[44] ――――, "Simplistic universal coding," *IEEE Trans. Inform. Theory*, vol. 44, pp. 778–781, 1998.

[45] D. S. Ornstein, "Bernoulli shifts with the same entropy are isomorphic," *Adv. in Math.*, vol. 4, pp. 337–352, 1970.

[46] ――――, "Ergodic theory, randomness, and dynamical systems," in *Yale Mathematical Monographs 5*. New Haven, CT: Yale Univ. Press, 1974.

[47] D. Ornstein, D. Rudolph, and B. Weiss, "Equivalence of measure preserving transformations," *Memoirs AMS,* vol. 262, 1982.

[48] D. Ornstein and P. Shields, "Universal almost sure data compression," *Ann. Probab.*, vol. 18, pp. 441–452, 1990.

[49] ――――, "The $\bar{d}$-recognition of processes," *Adv. in Math.*, vol. 104, pp. 182–224, 1994.

[50] D. Ornstein and B. Weiss, "The Shannon–McMillan–Breiman theorem for amenable groups," *Israel J. Math.*, vol. 44, pp. 53–60, 1983.

[51] ――――, "How sampling reveals a process," *Ann. Probab.*, vol. 18, pp. 905–930, 1990.

[52] ――――, "Entropy and data compression," *IEEE Trans. Inform. Theory*, vol. 39, pp. 78–83, 1993.

[53] K. Petersen, *Ergodic Theory*. Cambridge, U.K.: Cambridge Univ. Press, 1983.

[54] B. Ryabko, "Twice-universal coding," *Probl. Inform. Transm.*, vol. 20, pp. 173–178, 1984.

[55] P. Shields, "The ergodic theory of discrete sample paths," *AMS Graduate Studies in Mathematics*, Amer. Math. Soc., 1996.

[56] ――――, "Stationary coding of processes," *IEEE Trans. Inform. Theory*, vol. IT-25, pp. 283–291, 1979.

[57] ――――, "Almost block independence," *Z. für Wahr.*, vol. 49, pp. 119–123, 1979.

[58] ――――, "Cutting and stacking. A method for constructing stationary processes," *IEEE Trans. Inform. Theory*, vol. 37, pp. 1605–1617, 1991.

[59] ――――, "The ergodic and entropy theorems revisited," *IEEE Trans. Inform. Theory*, vol. IT-33, pp. 263–266, 1987.

[60] ――――, "The entropy theorem via coding bounds," *IEEE Trans. Inform. Theory*, vol. 37, pp. 1645–1647, 1991.

[61] ――――, "Entropy and prefixes," *Ann. Probab.*, vol. 20, pp. 403–409, 1992.

[62] ――――, "String matching—The general ergodic case," *Ann. Probab.*, vol. 20, pp. 1199–1203, 1992.

[63] ――――, "Two divergence-rate counterexamples," *J. Theor. Prob.*, vol. 6, pp. 521–545, 1993.

[64] ――――, "Waiting times: Positive and negative results on the Wyner–Ziv problem," *J. Theor. Prob.*, vol. 6, pp. 499–519, 1993.

[65] P. Shields and B. Weiss, "Universal redundancy rates for B-processes do not exist," *IEEE Trans. Inform. Theory*, vol. 41, pp. 508–512, 1995.

[66] J. Sinai, "On the notion of entropy of a dynamical system," *Dokl. Akad. Nauk SSSR*, vol. 124, pp. 768–771, 1959.

[67] M. Steele, "Kingman's subadditive ergodic theorem," *Ann. Inst. Henri Poincaré*, vol. 25, pp. 93–98, 1989.

[68] M. Talagrand, "Concentration of measure and isoperimetric inequalities in product spaces," *Publ. of I.H.E.S.*, vol. 81, pp. 73–205, 1995.

[69] ――――, "A new look at independence," *Ann. Probab.*, vol. 24, pp. 1–34, 1996.

[70] J. Moser, E. Phillips, and S. Varadhan, *Ergodic Theory: A Seminar*, Courant Inst. Math. Sci., New York Univ., New York, 1975.

[71] L. Vasershtein, "Markov processes on countable product spaces describing large systems of automata," *Probl. Inform. Transm.*, vol. 5, pp. 64–73, 1969.

[72] F. M. J. Willems, "Universal data compression and repetition times," *IEEE Trans. Inform. Theory*, vol. 35, pp. 54–58, 1989.

[73] A. Wyner and J. Ziv, "Some asymptotic properties of the entropy of a stationary ergodic data source with applications to data compression," *IEEE Trans. Inform. Theory*, vol. 35, pp. 125–1258, 1989.

[74] S. Xu, "An ergodic process of zero divergence-distance from the class of all stationary processes," *J. Theor. Prob.*, vol. 11, pp. 181–196, 1997.

[75] J. Ziv and A. Lempel, "A universal algorithm for sequential data compression," *IEEE Trans. Inform. Theory*, vol. IT-23, pp. 337–343, 1977.

[76] ――――, "Compression of individual sequences via variable rate coding," *IEEE Trans. Inform. Theory*, vol. IT-24, pp. 530–536, 1978.

[77] J. Ziv, "Coding theorems for individual sequences," *IEEE Trans. Inform. Theory*, vol. IT-24, pp. 405–412, 1978.

Information-Theoretic Image Formation

Joseph A. O'Sullivan, *Senior Member, IEEE*, Richard E. Blahut, *Fellow, IEEE*, and Donald L. Snyder, *Fellow, IEEE*

(Invited Paper)

Abstract—The emergent role of information theory in image formation is surveyed. Unlike the subject of information-theoretic communication theory, information-theoretic imaging is far from a mature subject. The possible role of information theory in problems of image formation is to provide a rigorous framework for defining the imaging problem, for defining measures of optimality used to form estimates of images, for addressing issues associated with the development of algorithms based on these optimality criteria, and for quantifying the quality of the approximations. The definition of the imaging problem consists of an appropriate model for the data and an appropriate model for the reproduction space, which is the space within which image estimates take values. Each problem statement has an associated optimality criterion that measures the overall quality of an estimate. The optimality criteria include maximizing the likelihood function and minimizing mean squared error for stochastic problems, and minimizing squared error and discrimination for deterministic problems. The development of algorithms is closely tied to the definition of the imaging problem and the associated optimality criterion. Algorithms with a strong information-theoretic motivation are obtained by the method of expectation maximization. Related alternating minimization algorithms are discussed. In quantifying the quality of approximations, global and local measures are discussed. Global measures include the (mean) squared error and discrimination between an estimate and the truth, and probability of error for recognition or hypothesis testing problems. Local measures include Fisher information.

Index Terms—Image analysis, image formation, image processing, image reconstruction, image restoration, imaging, inverse problems, maximum-likelihood estimation, pattern recognition.

I. INTRODUCTION

IMAGE formation is the process of computing (or refining) an image both from raw sensor data that is related to that image and from prior information about that image. Information about the image is contained in the raw sensor data, and the task of image formation is to extract this information so as to compute the image. Thus it appears that information-theoretic notions can play an important role in this process. We will survey the emergent role that information theory now plays in the subject of image formation or may play in the future. This role could be to provide a rigorous framework for defining the imaging problem, for defining measures of optimality that can be used to judge estimates of images, for addressing issues associated with the development of algorithms based on these optimality criteria, and for quantifying the statistical quality of the approximations.

To this end, the domain of information theory may be divided into two parts: communication and observation. The problems of communication have been very successfully treated by information theory, in part because Shannon had the foresight to overlay the subject of communication with a clear partitioning into *sources*, *channels*, *encoders*, and *decoders*. Although Shannon's formalization seems quite obvious in our time, it was not so obvious half a century ago. In contrast, the problems of observation, including imaging, have been slower to yield to the methods of information theory, partly because the image formation problems are harder, and perhaps partly because a formal framework for the subject is still emerging. Even the terms *source*, *sensor*, and *image* can be slippery; our understanding of these terms is closely tied to and colored by our view of a particular physical problem. It is not yet common practice to study problems of image formation in terms of an abstract formalization that is not connected to a specific physical problem.

One may take the natural position that an image formation problem consists of a source to be imaged, a sensor that collects data about the source, and an algorithm that estimates the image from the data. Thus it seems that image formation closely corresponds to our commonplace notion of photography. However, upon closer examination one can find difficulties with this simple view. A physical scene has a richness and complexity well beyond what we may wish to model or can model. In some problems, the sensor data may contain very little information but the prior knowledge may be considerable. Then one uses the sensor data to supplement the prior model to produce the image. This is called *image enhancement* in some contexts and *model-based imaging* or *physics-based imaging* in others. In an extreme case of model-based imaging, the imaging task may well degenerate into the estimation of several parameters, or even a simple *yes* or *no* decision, meaning only that a previously designated object or target appears somewhere in the scene.

Similarly, the meaning of the term "sensor" can be hard to define. How much of the processing is part of the sensor and how much not? The placement or motion of a physical device does affect the data collected by the device. Is this placement or motion to be viewed as part of the sensor or as part of an encoder that prepares data for a sensor? Should one introduce the notion of an encoder into an imaging problem?

Manuscript received April 15, 1998; revised May 22, 1998. This work was supported in part by the Army Research Office under Grant ARO DAAH049510494.

J. A. O'Sullivan and D. L. Snyder are with the Department of Electrical Engineering, Washington University, St. Louis, MO 63130 USA.

R. E. Blahut is with the Coordinated Science Laboratory, University of Illinois at Urbana-Champaign, Urbana, IL 61801 USA.

Publisher Item Identifier S 0018-9448(98)06085-4.

Because we lack the greatness of Shannon, we have difficulty moving from these abstract questions to an abstract model. Instead, we tend to answer such questions only in a narrower context by relating back to specific physical situations. Nevertheless, we shall press forward in this paper to describe the emergent role of information theory in the imaging problem. Because imaging sensors of the future will provide massive amounts of data, and computers of the future will be able to process massive amounts of data, the theory that we seek is needed to guide the development of these image formation systems of the future. This implies that there is a need for a formal information-theoretic framework that can offer advice about how to process massive data sets so as to extract all of the information relevant to the task of image formation.

Many kinds of sensors passively collect data from an environment already rich with many kinds of signals, and these data sets may contain information about an object of interest. In many cases, this information is very deeply buried in the data. Powerful methods are necessary to examine the data by applying the various techniques of filtering, correlation, inference, and so forth. Seismic and acoustic systems may consist of large arrays of many small devices. Optical sensors and infrared sensors now contain very large detector arrays, such as charge-coupled device (CCD) arrays, in which individual pixels can be addressed and archived. Indeed, in a low-light environment, the time of occurrence of individual photon conversions can be reported one-by-one by each sensor pixel. Optical sensors used in imaging spectropolarimetry produce enormous quantities of data. Electromagnetic sensors in the microwave, ultra-high frequency (UHF), or very-high frequency (VHF) band can report massive amounts of data at every antenna. Lidars can now remotely probe the absorption spectrum of trace gases in the atmosphere. Even passive electromagnetic sensors at lower frequencies can report a considerable amount of useful data.

To enrich the collection of data, many sensors actively probe the environment with transmitted signals, such as radar, seismic, or lidar signals. This illumination may be necessary in order to create the necessary data-bearing reflections. It should also be noted, however, that in many cases, active probes are designed not just to increase the amount of illumination falling upon the scene, but rather to put that illumination into a form so that the received sensor data are in a convenient form. Although the environment may already contain many sources of energy that provide illumination and scattered reflections, this energy is not usually organized into waveforms that are easy to process by image formation algorithms.

To extract information from the collected data, models must be developed for the objects of interest, for the environment, and for the sensor. A system that observes a remote area must process signals that propagate long distances, and possibly through complex environments. A system that extracts information from weakly radiating objects will usually need large amounts of data and long integration times. A system that uses imaging radar for the detection of objects masked by foliage and other clutter or a system that uses acoustic sensors for the detection of underwater objects must treat the environment as a significant component of the image formation problem. Such systems may need to use prior information about the scene, or the equivalent, to augment the limitations of the sensor data.

Image formation using a prior model often can be treated as an inverse scattering problem. The measurements of the scattered signal are inverted to estimate the parameters of a model. Inverse algorithms iterate a forward algorithm, which calculates the far-field scattering of known illumination by a known object, and compares that to the measured field. The model parameters are then adjusted to reduce the discrepancy between calculations and measurements. This process is repeated until there is a satisfactory agreement.

While the task of image formation can be viewed abstractly simply as a problem of estimation, it can also be viewed as having a character and content of its own. The problems addressed, the cost functions used, and the specific models that are used for images and image sensors lead to new questions and mathematical techniques, such as the estimation of random processes on manifolds or other complex surfaces. Creating a formal information-theoretic framework forces one to think through general principles and to either justify or reject existing *ad hoc* procedures.

Thus we come to our thesis. The time is right for a far-reaching study into our notions of extracting images or other object information from very large data sets, including data sets from multiple sensors, and possibly enriched by archived models and archived data. Various communities will react to this statement differently. The information theory and statistics community will think of maximum-likelihood models, information-theoretic measures of performance, and data fusion. The statistics community will also invoke methods of correlation and statistical inference. The computer science community, under the term "data mining," will think of large archived data structures and various search engines to supplement sensor data. All, however, will agree that such methods can be very powerful, and can extract information that is very subtly and deeply buried in a massive data set. It is now timely and appropriate to attempt to survey a framework at this level for image formation. Insights will emerge from an information-theoretic framework that may not be seen when studying an individual application. This paper has been written as an early step in this direction.

This paper deals with the information-theoretic aspects of image formation. Another important area in imaging that benefits from information-theoretic methods is image compression. This is an area of active research with a large literature and is beyond the scope of this paper, which focuses on image formation. For an introduction to this literature, see for example [36], [65], and [14].

The paper is organized as follows. The problem is first structured in Sections II, III, and IV entitled "Image Space," "Sensor Data," and "Reproduction Spaces." Then performance measures are discussed in Sections V and VI, entitled "Information-Theoretic Measures," and "Performance Bounds." Sections VII and VIII, entitled "Image Formation" and "Computational Algorithms," are the core of the paper. Examples are given in Section IX, entitled "Modalites and Applications."

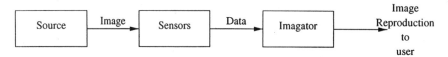

Fig. 1. Image formation model.

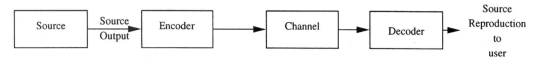

Fig. 2. Communications model.

II. IMAGE SPACE

We shall discuss the image formation problem shown in Fig. 1. This model, which can describe many estimation problems, will be interpreted herein in the context of image formation. The image formation model shown in Fig. 1 is analogous to the standard communications model shown in Fig. 2. The communications model consists of a source, a channel, and a user, and these are connected by an encoder and a decoder. Information theory studies these abstract models of communications and image formation.

The image formation problem is concerned with an underlying image or scene that is analogous to the source output in a communications problem. The source selects one image from a set called an *image space*, and the selected image—or an adequate reproduction of that image—is to be provided to the user. The images in the image space are abstractions, perhaps similar to photographs of an underlying physical scene. Just as a photograph is a compressed representation of some underlying physical reality, so too, images in the image space are abstract compressed representations of a physical reality.

The sensors in Fig. 1 play the role of the channel. The "imagator" or image-formation algorithm plays the role of the demodulator and decoder. Unlike the communication model, the ways in which the images can be encoded or otherwise modulated into sensor waveforms is quite limited by the physics of the sensor interaction with the environment. The image data are encoded by nature into radiated signals such as electromagnetic waves, diffracted X-rays, acoustic waves, or seismic waves. These signals interact with the sensors to produce the data available in imaging problems.

In some cases, only parameters of the image are of interest, and the mapping from the parameters to the image may be viewed as a modulation of the data. The parameter space may be a low-dimensional space, with dimension corresponding to the position and orientation of an object of interest, or it may be of moderate dimension, such as when it consists of the parameters in a mixture model (as in a segmentation of the image). It may be of high dimension, such as a color spectrum that varies with position.

A. Nonparametric and Parametric Models

Image space is the set of model images that represent the true, underlying physical distributions that are measured by the sensors. The image space is denoted by $\mathcal{C} = \{c : \mathcal{D}_C \to \mathcal{R}_C\}$, where c is an image, $\mathcal{D}_C$ is the domain of the image, and $\mathcal{R}_C$ is the range of the image. Models of image space that describe an image by an infinite number of parameters, typically consisting of a real function on $\mathbf{R}^2$, are known as *nonparametric models*. A traditional nonparametric imaging problem may have domain $\mathcal{D}_C$ equal to $\mathbf{R}^2$ or a compact subset of $\mathbf{R}^2$. The range of the image c is commonly $\mathbf{R}$, $\mathbf{C}$, or $\mathbf{R}_+$, but sometimes it is a vector space $\mathbf{R}^m$, $\mathbf{C}^m$, or $\mathbf{R}_+^m$ consisting of the set of elements of $\mathbf{R}^m$ with nonnegative components. For example, densities of particles, attenuation functions, intensity functions, and power spectra have nonnegative values. Radar and coherent laser signals are complex-valued and may lead to complex-valued images of target reflectivity. To give a more elaborate example of an image, we note that a real-valued three-dimensional scene may be time-varying, and so may be denoted $c(x, y, z, t)$. In this case, the domain is $\mathbf{R}^4$ and the range is $\mathbf{R}$. If viewed through a spectrally sensitive device, it may be advantageous additionally to model each point in space and time as having a spectrum associated with it. The domain is then $\mathcal{D}_C = \mathbf{R}_3 \times \mathbf{R} \times \mathbf{R}_+$, corresponding to a point in space, time, and frequency, so the domain is five-dimensional. Let $\boldsymbol{x} = [x, y, z]^T \in \mathbf{R}^3$ denote position, $t \in \mathbf{R}$ denote time, and $f \in \mathbf{R}_+$ denote frequency. Then $c(\boldsymbol{x}, t, f)$ is a point in the image, and $c(\boldsymbol{x}, t, \cdot) : \mathbf{R} \to \mathcal{D}_C$ is the frequency-dependent function associated with the point at position $\boldsymbol{x}$ at time t.

While typical scenes may be five-dimensional, or even larger if polarization effects are included, particular sensors may be insensitive to one or more of these dimensions. In that case, it is sufficient to project the five-dimensional function c onto the appropriate lower dimensional function. For example, if only a single measurement is made at a given fixed time, then the time variation may be ignored. If the measurement depends on the spectrum only through an inner product with a specified spectrum (the transfer function of the sensor), then the spectral dependence may be ignored, keeping only this projection. If the sensor is invariant to one of the three spatial dimensions, then that dimension may be ignored.

Models that describe an image by a finite number (or, rarely, by a countable number) of parameters are known as *parametric models*. Parametric models are important in model-based imaging or imaging. A *nonparametric model* for an image may consist of a restriction of the image to a function space or of a representation of the image as a countable linear combination of basis functions. The basis functions may correspond to a representation of the image in terms of pixels, in terms of a transform-domain expansion, or in terms of an orthonormal set of functions. Even when this expansion is limited to a finite number of basis functions, the terminology would still be determined by the underlying view of the image as a function on R^2, so the model could still be called a nonparametric model. An intermediate class consists of models that have a very large, but finite, number of parameters. These are called *hyperparametric models*. Most image space models, including the use of random field priors, are nonparametric descriptions. Hierarchical image models are usually hyperparametric models.

The standard imaging approach, which is to reconstruct an image as a finite array of pixels or voxels, is viewed as nonparametric. Occasionally it is desirable to combine a parametric model with a nonparametric model. This means that an expansion of an image in terms of basis functions may be found, and the coefficients in the expansion may be functions of the parameters of interest. This approach, because it relies on two steps, may not be optimal (by the data processing inequality) but may be necessary due to constraints on system implementation.

B. Priors

The observation space is denoted $\mathcal{O} = \{o : \mathcal{D}_\mathcal{O} \rightarrow \mathcal{R}_\mathcal{O}\}$ with domain $\mathcal{D}_\mathcal{O}$ and range $\mathcal{R}_\mathcal{O}$, respectively. A sensor maps the image space $\mathcal{C} = \{c : \mathcal{D}_\mathcal{C} \rightarrow \mathcal{R}_\mathcal{C}\}$ into the observation space; often this mapping is stochastic. Imaging problems are classified as either deterministic or stochastic according to whether the image and the sensor are described by deterministic or stochastic models. Typically, a deterministic model is used if little or nothing is known about the image and if the sensor noise is negligible.

Deterministic constraints are often a part of the model. These constraints will include nonnegativity constraints for functions such as intensity, attenuation, density, and scattering. The image may be known to take values in some convex subset of $\mathcal{C}$. Alternatively, the image may be parameterized in some way.

Other deterministic effects that must be captured include the projection effects of the sensor. For optical imaging, the projection onto the focal plane may be an orthographic or perspective projection; the projection onto the retina may be modeled as a spherical projection. For tomographic imaging, the data may be collected in parallel or fan beams.

In the remainder of this section, we consider the case in which something is known about the image. Prior knowledge about an image is most naturally incorporated through the use of a prior probability distribution $\mu(c)$ on the image space. Such priors may be specified directly on the image space $\mathcal{C}$, or may be specified on parameters in a parametric representation of the image space.

For some problems, the prior may be on a finite-dimensional parameter vector $\theta \in \Theta$ that characterizes the uncertainty in the image. For rigid objects, Θ may be the special Euclidean group of translations and rotations. In some passive scenarios (optical imaging, for example), there may be a scale parameter included in Θ. We assume that the set Θ is a finite-dimensional space with probability density function p_θ.

When there is such a parameter θ that characterizes the scene, it may provide a complete or a partial characterization. If it completely characterizes the scene, then c is a function of θ; that is, there is a deterministic mapping from Θ to $\mathcal{C}$ that assigns to each θ an image c. If it is a partial characterization, only part of the scene is characterized by θ. The remainder of the scene may be modeled either as an unknown deterministic function or as a stochastic process. In the latter case, a prior on the scene given the parameters is required and will be denoted by $\mu(c|\theta)$.

To recognize rigid objects in a scene automatically, the background is not directly of interest and so is regarded as a nuisance parameter. Conversely, to determine the background image in the presence of a rigid body, the rigid body may be regarded as the nuisance parameter. Alternatively, it may be of interest to estimate parameters associated with elements of the scene (such as positions and orientations of rigid bodies) and to form an image of the entire scene. This is the case in spiral tomographic imaging in the presence of high-density attenuators. Then the position and orientation of the high-density object are of interest, while simultaneously it is of interest to remove the streaking artifacts commonly seen in the images in the neighborhood of the object [103].

In object recognition problems, it may be that the image contains an object of interest, and the object is one of a finite number of object types. Further, it may be that only a determination of the object class is of interest. If the number of possible classes is fixed, then the problem of interest is one of hypothesis testing. Then the set of hypotheses will be denoted $\mathcal{H} = \{H_1, H_2, \cdots, H_m\}$. The corresponding prior probability distribution on this set of hypotheses, if there is a prior probability distribution, will be denoted $P = \{P_1, P_2, \cdots, P_m\}$.

Finally, generalizations of these problems are often of interest. For example, in automatic object recognition problems, it may be required to estimate the number of objects in a scene, perform recognition on each detected object, estimate the position and orientation of each object, and form an image of the background. In this case, inference is performed on a very complicated, high-dimensional space.

C. Mathematical Representations

Scenes may be described either nonparametrically as functions taking values in a specified function space, parametrically in terms of known functions of parameters, or as some combination of these two. For example, a three-dimensional scene may have a known rigid object embedded in an unknown background. In this case, the image has both parametric and nonparametric components. The position and orientation of the rigid object take values in the six-dimensional space corresponding to both translations and rotations; the background is an unknown function.

This example illustrates a complicating aspect of many inference problems in imaging: the parameter space need not be isomorphic to R^n. For example, the six-dimensional space of translations and rotations, denoted $SE(3)$, forms a non-Abelian group. Let $x \in R^3$ be a point on the rigid object. Let $R(\theta)$ be a 3×3 rotation matrix, and $t \in R^3$ be a translation.

Then the point x is mapped according to

$$x \mapsto R(\theta)x + t. \quad (1)$$

An $n \times n$ rotation matrix takes values in the special orthogonal group of dimension n, denoted $SO(n)$. A rotation–translation pair takes values in the special Euclidean group $SE(n)$. In many problems, $SE(2)$ and $SE(3)$ are the groups that are relevant, these corresponding to translation and rotation in R^2 and in R^3, respectively.

More generally, let Θ be a finite-dimensional parameter space. The space Θ may be a subset of R^n or it may be a group. An image c in the image space may be written as the sum of two components

$$c = c_1(\theta) + c_2 \quad (2)$$

where $c_1 : \Theta \to \mathcal{C}$ is the part of the image determined by the finite parameterization and $c_2 \in \mathcal{C}$ is the nonparametric part of the image. This may be generalized further as $c = f(\theta, c_2)$, where f is an arbitrary function of θ and c_2.

A commonly used example of a parameterization is a hierarchical parameterization. A hierarchy of parameters is an ordered set of parameters, $(\theta_1, \theta_2, \cdots, \theta_m)$ with a Markov structure. Let $\theta_k \in \Theta_k$. If θ_1 corresponds to the finest scale of the hierarchy, then there is a mapping $c_1 : \Theta_1 \to \mathcal{C}$. For other scales in the hierarchy, there are mappings $h_k : \Theta_k \to \Theta_{k-1}$. In general, the mappings $\{c_1, h_2, \cdots, h_m\}$ may be stochastic. Inference is performed on the hierarchy, with different scales providing different pieces of information about the scene and objects within the scene.

A simple example of a hierarchical model would have two scales. Let Θ_2 be a set of possible objects. Assume there is one object of interest in the scene. Selection of an element of Θ_2 corresponds to the task of object detection. Suppose further that the mapping h_2 corresponds to translation and rotation of the object in the scene. The function c_1 is the image that results, given the object position, orientation, and type.

More complicated examples of hierarchical models may involve building complex objects up from simple objects. The hierarchy may progress from pixel values to edges, from edges to boundaries, from boundaries to regions, and from regions to object types.

D. Markov Random Fields

To employ probabilistic methods, one may regard an image as a random element drawn from a prespecified set of possible images. Then one must assign a prior probability distribution to the set of images, and this assignment leads to the introduction of the notion of a random field. A random field is a generalization of a random process to two or more dimensions. Random-field models are important in image formation because of analytic tractability, because they are a very good fit for many images in applications, because these methods are robust and still give satisfactory results even when not a good fit to a particular application, and because they can convert in an orderly way an ill-posed problem into a well-posed problem.

A *random field* is a multidimensional random process. For example, a Gaussian random field is determined by a mean function $\eta(x, t, f)$ and an autocovariance function $K(x_1, t_1, f_1; x_2, t_2, f_2)$. A random field, possibly Gaussian, is an appropriate model for both real-valued images and complex-valued images. A prior that has been used successfully for imaging problems is the Markov random field.

Random variables characterized by conditional priors that account for local interactions are often used as natural and convenient priors in imaging problems. These conditional priors, placed directly on the image space $\mathcal{C}$ or on a subset or subspace of $\mathcal{C}$, are usually the most natural way to quantify our understanding of a problem. However, the fundamental probability distribution on the field is the joint probability distribution, and this is difficult or impossible to specify directly. One needs to verify that the chosen specification of conditional distributions is sufficient and consistent in the sense that a unique joint probability distribution corresponds to this set of conditional probability distributions. The simplest example is the Ising random field, which consists of a binary random variable defined at each site of the integer lattice Z^2 with each random variable conditional on the value realized at each of the four nearest neighbors. An important aid in describing such collections of conditional priors is the Hammersley–Clifford theorem which states that under certain conditions, the most natural conditional probability functions do uniquely define global probability functions.

The notion of a Markov random field extends the notion of a Markov process to multidimensional spaces by generalizing the concept of order dependence that is fundamental in the definition of a Markov process. The well-known works of Ising contain the earliest application of Markov random fields. Later, Onsager used the classic Ising random-field model to characterize magnetic domains. Important early applications to the imaging problem include the work of Besag [4], who discusses a broad variety of Markov random fields and their applications, and of Geman and Geman [34] as well as Chellappa [13].

The generalization of a one-dimensional Markov random process to a multidimensional Markov random field is not straightforward because the concepts of past and future, which are quite natural in one dimension, do not have counterparts in higher dimensional spaces. Instead, the concept of a *neighbor* is used. A random process with index set T is given by $\{x(t) \mid t \in T, \; T = \{t_1, t_2, \cdots, t_k\}\}$. The random process is called a random field if the elements of T are vectors from a multidimensional space, such as the two-dimensional plane R^2. Assume that the random variables $x(t_1), x(t_2), \cdots, x(t_k)$ are continuous random variables and that their joint probability density function $p_{x(t_1),x(t_2),\cdots,x(t_k)}(X_1, X_2, \cdots, X_k)$ exists. We shall also require for each i, $1 \le i \le k$, that the joint density of the $k-1$ random variables $\{x(t_j); j \neq i, 1 \le j \le k\}$ is strictly greater than zero

$$p_{x(t_1),\cdots,x(t_{i-1}),x(t_{i+1}),\cdots,x(t_k)}(X_1, \cdots, X_{i-1}, X_{i+1}, \cdots, X_k)$$
$$> 0. \quad (3)$$

The reason for imposing this positivity condition is to ensure the existence of the conditional densities

$$p_{x(t_i)|x(t_1),\cdots,x(t_{i-1}),x(t_{i+1}),\cdots,x(t_k)}$$
$$\times (X_i \mid X_1, \cdots, X_{i-1}, X_{i+1}, \cdots, X_k) \quad (4)$$

for $1 \leq i \leq k$. Site t_j is said to be a *neighbor* of site t_i if the above conditional density for $x(t_i)$ is dependent on X_j. Thus

$$p_{x(t_i)|x(t_1),\cdots,x(t_{i-1}),(t_{i+1}),\cdots,x(t_k)}$$
$$\times (X_i \mid X_1, \cdots, X_{i-1}, X_{i+1}, \cdots, X_k)$$
$$= p_{x(t_i)|x(t_j):t_j \in N_i}(X_i \mid \{X_j \text{ for all } j \text{ such that } t_j \in N_i\}) \quad (5)$$

where N_i is the set of neighbors of t_i. The neighbor relationship is symmetric: if $t_j \in N_i$, then $t_i \in N_j$.

A random process $\{x(t)|t \in T\}$ with a discrete index set $T = \{t_1, t_2, \cdots, t_k\}$ and a set of neighborhoods $\{N_1, N_2, \cdots, N_k\}$ and conditional densities is called a *Markov random field*. A common example of a Markov random field prior is a Gauss–Markov random field. For a Gauss–Markov random field, each of the probability density functions in (5) is Gaussian.

In any numerical implementation, the region of computation must be truncated to a region of finite size. When this happens, some assumptions about boundary conditions must be made, and these assumptions may play a crucial role in the resulting image reconstructions because the Markov random field model may exhibit phase transitions due to the boundary conditions, resulting in poor reconstructions.

The boundary conditions generally fall into three categories: periodic boundaries, random boundaries, and fixed boundaries. For periodic boundaries, the neighborhood structure is made periodic, so that every lattice site has the same neigborhood structure. For other choices, the lattice is truncated, so specific assumptions must be made about how that truncation takes place. Lattice sites whose neighborhood structure differs from others due to truncation are called boundary sites. For random boundaries, the boundary site values are chosen randomly from the marginal distribution. For fixed boundaries, the boundary values are set to specific values such as the mean of the marginal distribution.

We shall now give several examples of Markov random fields.

The simplest example of a Markov random field is one in which the neighbors of t_i for each i, are *all* the other indices $\{t_j, j \neq i, 1 \leq i \leq k\}$. For this choice,

$$N_1 = \{t_2, t_3, \cdots, t_k\}$$
$$N_k = \{t_1, t_2, \cdots, t_{k-1}\}$$
and
$$N_i = \{t_1, \cdots, t_{i-1}, t_{i+1}, \cdots, t_k\}$$

for $2 \leq i \leq k - 1$. This example, with no restrictions on the statistical dependencies between the variables, indicates that Markov random fields can be quite general.

A temporal Markov random process is another simple example of a Markov random field. Suppose that $\{x(t)|t \in T\}$ is a random process with a discrete index set $T = \{t_1, t_2, \cdots, t_k\}$ where each t_i is a real number representing time. The neighborhood structure is $N_k = \{t_{k-1}\}$, $N_1 = \{t_2\}$, and $N_i = \{t_{i-1}, t_{i+1}\}$. This is the standard definition of a first-order Markov random process.

Another simple example of a Markov random field can be constructed as follows. Define the index set to be of the form

$$T = \{t_{ij} \mid 0 \leq i \leq M_\ell - 1, 0 \leq j \leq M_j - 1\}$$

which may arise as a Markov field on the lattice points of a discrete pixelization of a finite rectangular region of the plane. Suppose that each interior point t_{ij} of a region has four neighbors defined as the four lattice points lying to the North, East, South, and West, so the neighborhood of t_{ij} is

$$N(t_{ij}) = \{t_{i,j+1}, t_{i+1,j}, t_{i,j-1}, t_{i-1,j}\}.$$

Each boundary point of a region has its neighbors defined similarly except that only lattice points within the region can be neighbors. This set of neighborhoods along with a specified conditional density for the process at each lattice point defines a two-dimensional Markov random field with nearest neighbor dependency.

It can be cumbersome to perform inference on the random field directly, so typically some discretization of the problem is required. Such a discretization may be a pixelization or an expansion in some other basis. For Gaussian random field models, the natural expansion would be in terms of the eigenfunctions of the autocovariance function. For other random field models, different expansions may be appropriate, as discussed below.

III. SENSOR DATA

The observation data are available at the output of the set of sensors. These data may be modeled either deterministically or stochastically, as appropriate for the given application.

Stochastic models arise naturally in many situations. In a radar receiver there is internal noise, and there may be external sources of noise as well. Both of these impairments of the desired signal are unrelated to the scene in question, and both are often modeled as additive Gaussian noise in the microwave frequency band or the intermediate frequency band, or as complex Gaussian noise at complex baseband. In optical bands, the data arise from photoconversions in the sensor. This situation is naturally modeled using a Poisson counting process model or, if readout noise is significant, as a Poisson–Gaussian mixture model. In positron-emission tomography, the production of annihilation photons within the patient volume is accurately modeled as a spatial point process; the resulting positron detections are well-modeled as Poisson distributed events.

In many problems, however, noise is insignificant, and stochastic models are not as well motivated, so deterministic models are used. In photographic applications, the intensity incident on the film is blurred by the lens and other known quantities in the optical path. For such optical imaging systems, the data are collected as images in a focal plane; there is also a known perspective or orthographic projection of the

55

three-dimensional scene to the focal plane. In X-ray tomographic applications, the intensity may be high enough that the Poisson statistics of the detection process can be ignored and the data reasonably modeled as being deterministic; standard analysis of computed tomography systems models the data this way, and the problem of recovery of the unknown attenuation function is treated as a deterministic inverse problem.

In general, both deterministic and stochastic effects must be taken into account. The finite size of detectors has a deterministic effect on the collected data. The bandwidth of radar signals, the motion between the antenna and the scene, and the geometry and electrical characteristics of radar antennas yield deterministic effects on radar data and any images generated from the radar data such as synthetic-aperture radar images. These may then need to be combined with stochastic models for the detection process and receiver noise. In optical systems, a deterministic model for the effects of the lens and the known geometry may need to be combined with a stochastic model for the detector and a stochastic model for turbulence in the optical path.

If the model for the available data is a deterministic one, then the observation o is a deterministic function of the image c, $o = f(c)$. Examples of such models are discussed in the applications section. A stochastic model is defined by a conditional distribution on the observation given the image. When coupled with a deterministic projection, the likelihood often can be written $L(o \mid f(c))$, where f is a known function.

There may be parameters that enter into the problem in various ways. For high-precision problems of machine vision, a known object may be viewed using a camera that has unknown parameters. In the calibration step, the focal length, the image center on the focal plane, and parameters for lens distortion and focal plane nonuniformity often need to be estimated from the data. In actual use, the position and orientation of the object must be estimated. For typical machine vision problems, a deterministic model is used and general optimization procedures are applied to find the parameters [45], [97]. In other problems, analogous parameters describing blurring functions, optical centers, and projections may need to be estimated, either in calibration steps or in every image.

Stochastic models may be combined with priors on scenes to find joint likelihoods for the data and for the underlying scenes. The joint distribution on the observations and the scene is then the product of the sensor's conditional distribution and the prior, $\pi(o \mid c)\mu(c)$.

IV. REPRODUCTION SPACES

The image space is designed to model as closely as possible an idealized representation of the physical processes that generate the data. There will always be aspects of the underlying physical situation that are not captured in the image space model. Indeed, one of the most challenging problems in information-theoretic imaging is the development of models for the underlying physical processes that are adequate for the problem at hand, but not so complicated as to present intractable mathematics. The reproduction space is the set of functions in which a computational algorithm for image formation produces its output values. The selection of a reproduction space must anticipate the needs and limitations of the computational algorithm. In the selection of the reproduction space, there is a tradeoff between its ability to represent images in C closely and the computational complexity of the resulting algorithm.

The estimated image itself is often a discrete approximation of the underlying conceptual image which usually is a continuous distribution. The discreteness could be due to quantization of values associated with the image, but usually also includes a representation of the continuous image that is sampled or pixelated in some way. For example, in astronomical imaging, there is an underlying intensity distribution corresponding to the distribution of the astronomical object being viewed. This intensity function is defined on a continuous domain. Computed images are presented as discrete values on an array of pixels, which may be considered to be an approximation of this true underlying distribution, this approximation or estimate consisting of a summation of pixel values that scale appropriate basis functions.

There is also a tradeoff between bias and variance, or a tradeoff between approximation error and estimation error. The higher the dimension of the reproduction space, the more closely the underlying image in C may be represented. That is, the discrepancy between the closest element of the reproduction space and the true image decreases as the size of the reproduction space grows (or its bias decreases). On the other hand, as the dimension of the reproduction space grows, the statistical variation in the estimate grows. That is, the discrepancy between the estimate in the reproduction space and the element of the reproduction space closest to the truth increases (or its variance increases). For any given imaging problem and some measure of the sum of these two terms, there is usually an optimal size of the reproduction space that minimizes the measure.

The reproduction space is typically a subset or a subspace of the image space. Often, the reproduction space is parameterized and the parameters may be varied as data are collected to refine existing image estimates as more data becomes available. The refinements should take values in successively higher dimensional subsets of image space. The use of sieves provides a framework for indexing the parameter in the refinements in order to achieve consistency of the image estimates as the amount of data collected increases (see Grenander [42]).

Much of the theory underlying this formulation falls within the subject of approximation theory. We will not attempt to survey the results within this broad research area, but will summarize some of the aspects that are relevant to image formation problems. In applications, computational issues may influence the choice of the reproduction space used.

Information-theoretic discrepancy measures are useful throughout this paper. For each space, we assume that there is a discrepancy measure between two elements of that space.

Definition: A discrepancy measure on a space $\mathcal{X}$ is any mapping $d : \mathcal{X} \times \mathcal{X} \to \boldsymbol{R}_+$ such that $d(x_1, x_2) \geq 0$ for all $(x_1, x_2) \in \mathcal{X} \times \mathcal{X}$ and $d(x_1, x_2) = 0$ if and only if $x_1 = x_2$ almost everywhere.

For the spaces $\mathcal{C}, \mathcal{O}, \Theta$, and $\mathcal{H}$, we will require that discrepancy measures $d_\mathcal{C}, d_\mathcal{C}, d_\Theta$, and $d_\mathcal{C}$ have been defined.

A. Regularization

In most imaging problems, the underlying image takes values in an infinite-dimensional space. The reconstruction or estimation of the image based on some given data then implies that an infinite number of variables that represent the image must be determined. Such problems are usually ill-posed, in the sense described below, and some form of regularization is required to reduce the sensitivity of the reconstruction to variations in the observed data, mismatches between the data and the model adopted for the data, and to choices made in the implementation of the reconstruction algorithm (such as the number of bits of precision and the order in which arithmetic operations are performed). One approach to regularization is the representation of an image using pixels or voxels, but this can exhibit the undesirable consequences of "dimensional instability," as described by Tapia and Thompson [55], and a tradeoff between reconstruction accuracy (when a continuous image is approximated by a piecewise-continuous one) and resolution. This necessity for making tradeoffs accompanies other forms of regularization as well; that tradeoff may be between bias and variance, or between approximation error and estimation error. Tikhonov [96], Hadamard, and Joyce and Root [53] have addressed the instability problems caused by ill-posedness and have suggested approaches for regularization to avoid such problems.

Anticipating the formal statement of an image formation problem below, suppose that the optimal image $\hat{c}(o)$ is defined as the c that achieves

$$\hat{c}(o) = \arg \min_{c \in \mathcal{C}} \psi(o, c) \qquad (6)$$

where $\psi(o, c)$ is a given objective function. The notation $\hat{c}(o)$ in (6) implies that there is a mapping from $\mathcal{O}$ to $\mathcal{C}$. If there are multiple $c \in \mathcal{C}$ that achieve the minimum, then we require that one of them is chosen arbitrarily. While typical examples of possible choices for ψ are discussed in Section VII, we introduce a few possibilities here.

For stochastic models, ψ may equal the negative of the log-likelihood function of o. If c has a deterministic model, then this is the conditional log-likelihood of o given c. If c has a stochastic model, then this is the joint log-likelihood of the pair (o, c), and the minimization is equivalent to finding the maximum a posteriori (MAP) estimate of c given o.

For deterministic models, ψ may be the discrepancy between a predicted observation $f(c)$ and the true observation o. As discussed below, additional terms may be included in ψ.

Definition: A statement posing the arg minimum is *well-posed* if for each $o \in \mathcal{O}$, there is a unique $c \in \mathcal{C}$ that achieves the minimum, and

$$\sup_{o \in \mathcal{O}} \lim_{o_1 \to o} \frac{d_\mathcal{C}(\hat{c}(o_1), \hat{c}(o))}{d_\mathcal{O}(o_1, o)} \qquad (7)$$

exists and is finite. A statement posing the arg minimum that is not well-posed is *ill-posed*.

The intention behind this definition is that, when the problem is well-posed, small changes in the data should produce small changes in the estimate. The size of a change is measured using a discrepancy measure. If a problem is well-posed, then the value of the limit in (7) is one measure of the degree to which the problem is well-posed. For deterministic inverse problems, the condition number of the mapping may be preferred as an alternative measure.

For a deterministic inverse problem, with the data modeled as $o = f(c)$, the norm of f is defined by

$$\|f\| = \sup_{c \in \mathcal{C}} \lim_{c_1 \to c} \frac{d_\mathcal{O}(f(c_1), f(c))}{d_\mathcal{C}(c_1, c)}. \qquad (8)$$

If f is invertible (that is, for each $o \in \mathcal{O}$, there is a unique $c \in \mathcal{C}$ such that $f(c) = o$), then the norm of f^{-1} is defined as in (8). The condition number of f is then

$$\chi(f) = \|f\| \, \|f^{-1}\|. \qquad (9)$$

Note that this definition is the square of the standard definition of condition number if d is squared error. This definition of condition number is suitable for our consideration because a small change in c, from c to c_1, yields a change in o that is less than $\|f\| d_\mathcal{C}(c_1, c)$. In turn, the discrepancy between the resulting estimate of c and the original value is less than

$$\|f\| \, \|f^{-1}\| d_\mathcal{C}(c_1, c) = \chi(f) d_\mathcal{C}(c_1, c). \qquad (10)$$

As discussed extensively in the literature of numerical analysis (see Golub and Van Loan [37]), the condition number quantifies the sensitivity of the problem to numerical and approximation errors.

Ill-posed problems such as the image formation problem defined in (6) using the objective function ψ may be associated with a family of well-posed problems, by defining a family of subsets of $\mathcal{C}$ that converge to $\mathcal{C}$. Suppose that a one-parameter family of sets $\{\mathcal{C}^\nu, \nu > 0\}$ is given and that the closure of this family equals $\mathcal{C}$

$$\text{Closure}[\cup_{\nu > 0} \mathcal{C}^\nu] = \mathcal{C}. \qquad (11)$$

This assumes the definition of a topology on $\mathcal{C}$. In many cases, the interest is in constructing, for each $c \in \mathcal{C}$, a sequence of functions $c^\nu \in \mathcal{C}^\nu$ such that

$$\lim_{\nu \to 0} d_\mathcal{C}(c^\nu, c) = 0. \qquad (12)$$

Definition: Suppose that the family of subsets $\mathcal{C}^\nu$ satisfies (11) and that for each $o \in \mathcal{O}$ there is a unique $\hat{c}(o)$ that achieves the minimum in (6). The family of problems

$$\hat{c}^\nu(o) = \arg \min_{c \in \mathcal{C}^\nu} \psi(o, c) \qquad (13)$$

is a *regularization* of the image formation problem defined in (6) if for each ν the problem defined by (13) is well-posed and if for almost all $o \in \mathcal{O}$

$$\lim_{\nu \to 0} \hat{c}^\nu(o) = \hat{c}(o). \qquad (14)$$

If the discrepancy measure is a distance or a squared distance, then for each ν, the mapping $\hat{c}^\nu : \mathcal{O} \to \mathcal{C}$ is continuous.

For an ill-posed problem, the function $\hat{c}$ is discontinuous, so that even small amounts of noise in the observations can lead to large changes in the estimates. For each nonzero value of ν, however, the mapping $\hat{c}^\nu$ is continuous so the regularized solution is less sensitive to noise. The functions $\hat{c}^\nu$ converge to $\hat{c}$ as ν goes to zero, so the sensitivity to noise increases as ν goes to zero. For pixelization of images, this problem is called "dimensional instability" by Tapia and Thompson [95], who observe that the estimates become increasingly ill-behaved and unstable as the discretization is refined even as more data are collected.

This definition of a regularization is a modification of the statements in Youla [106], Grenander [42, p. 358], and Kirsch [54, pp. 24–26], modified to account for the statement of the imaging problem as an inverse problem, the solution of which is defined in terms of the objective criterion ψ. Various models, including linear, nonlinear, stochastic, and deterministic models are included within this statement. A feature of this definition of regularization is that it is in terms of the reproduction space rather than the mappings $\hat{c}^\nu$. This is a departure from the statements by Youla and Kirsch who require directly that the mappings $\hat{c}^\nu$ are continuous. Grenander's definition [42, p. 358] is in terms of a one-parameter family of operators acting on $\mathcal{C}$. That is, his mapping is meant to regularize $\hat{c}(o)$, by using operations such as lowpass filtering (projections onto subspaces or subsets of $\mathcal{C}$). Later in [42], and in other settings using his method of sieves, Grenander uses a concept of regularization consistent with the definition given here.

A regularization method in general provides a framework within which the ill-posedness can be addressed quantitatively. We discuss the use of penalties, prior probability distributions, kernel sieves, and choice of reproduction space as regularization methods. The simplest and most common way to regularize a problem is by the use of pixelization. An image displayed using pixels is really a projection onto a finite-dimensional subspace. A measure of the size of a pixel is the regularization parameter ν. There are many other standard restrictions of images to subspaces, with $1/\nu$ corresponding roughly to the dimension of the subspace.

A penalty regularization alters the objective function by adding a penalty to it. Tikhonov [96] introduced a quadratic penalty. More generally, a penalty can be added to the objective function as a discrepancy between the estimate and a nominal value $d(c, c_0)$.

Given a model for the data in terms of a conditional likelihood function $L(o \mid f(c))$, and a discrepancy measure $d_\mathcal{C}$ on $\mathcal{C}$, there may be an optimal ν that minimizes a tradeoff between approximation error and estimation error, as described next.

Assume that $c^{\nu*} \in \mathcal{C}^\nu$ is the unique element of $\mathcal{C}$ that minimizes

$$c^{\nu*} = \arg\min_{c_1 \in \mathcal{C}^\nu} d_\mathcal{C}(c_1, c) \qquad (15)$$

where $c \in \mathcal{C}$ is the true image. Then the sum of the estimation error and the approximation error is

$$\delta^\nu(c, o) = d_\mathcal{C}(\hat{c}^\nu(o), c^{\nu*}) + d_\mathcal{C}(c^{\nu*}, c). \qquad (16)$$

For a stochastic problem, this error is a random variable. Typically, the first term (the estimation error) is monotonically increasing and the second term (the approximation error) is monotonically decreasing as ν decreases. For a typical problem, there is typically an optimal ν that minimizes a measure of $\delta^\nu(c, o)$ such as its expected value. The motivation for defining the sum in (16) is that for some discrepancy measures of interest, if $\mathcal{C}^\nu$ is a linear subspace

$$d_\mathcal{C}(\hat{c}^\nu(o), c) = d_\mathcal{C}(\hat{c}^\nu(o), c^{\nu*}) + d_\mathcal{C}(c^{\nu*}, c). \qquad (17)$$

This holds for discrimination and squared error as discrepancy measures. Choosing ν to minimize the expected value of $d_\mathcal{C}(\hat{c}^\nu(o), c)$ is a precise way to define an optimal regularization. If $\mathcal{C}^\nu$ is a convex set, then for these same discrepancy measures

$$d_\mathcal{C}(\hat{c}^\nu(o), c) \geq d_\mathcal{C}(\hat{c}^\nu(o), c^{\nu*}) + d_\mathcal{C}(c^{\nu*}, c). \qquad (18)$$

In this case, choosing ν to minimize the expected value of (16) corresponds to minimizing a lower bound on the mean of $d_\mathcal{C}(\hat{c}^\nu(o), c)$.

B. Pixelization

The reproduction space often can be viewed as consisting of a linear combination of basis functions. The most common example of such a representation is when the basis functions are indicator functions on some domain, and the resulting representation is referred to as a pixelization. When an image is represented as an array, the elements in the array are the coefficients in the linear combination. The basis functions need not always be viewed as indicator functions, however. If the image is assumed to have a fixed bandwidth and the representation is on a fine enough scale, the coefficients may be viewed as samples of the image. In that case, the basis functions are optimal interpolation functions. If the data are actually the result of integrating the image against a known kernel, then the coefficients may be viewed as the values used in a discrete approximation of the integral. If the integration is modeled as a Riemann sum, then the basis functions are indicator functions. If the integration is modeled as using a trapezoid rule for numerical integration, then the basis functions are first-order splines.

We shall describe some of the issues first in a one-dimensional setting and then a multidimensional setting. Let $a(t)$ be a function of time, and let a_k, for $k = 1, 2, \cdots, n$, be samples of $a(t)$ at times kT. If $a(t)$ is represented by the samples, there is an assumed nominal representation. One representation is as a linear combination of indicator functions

$$\hat{a}(t) = \sum_{k=1}^{n} a_k \Phi_T(t - kT) \qquad (19)$$

where

$$\Phi_T(t) = \begin{cases} 1, & -T/2 \leq t < T/2 \\ 0, & \text{otherwise.} \end{cases} \qquad (20)$$

Another choice, for lowpass functions, is as a linear combination of interpolation functions

$$\hat{a}(t) = \sum_{k=1}^{n} a_k p_T(t - kT) \tag{21}$$

where

$$p_T(t) = \mathrm{sinc}\,(t/T) \tag{22}$$

and $\mathrm{sinc}\,(t) = \sin(\pi t)/\pi t$. Other choices can be made for the interpolation function, and the values a_k do not necessarily correspond to samples of $a(t)$. In orthogonal representations, the values typically represent inner products of the function with basis functions.

For the multidimensional setting, let $\Phi^\nu = \{\phi_{\boldsymbol{k}}^\nu,\ \boldsymbol{k} \in \mathcal{L}\}$ be an orthonormal set of functions, where $\boldsymbol{k}$ is a discrete index taking values on the lattice $\mathcal{L}$, and where ν is a parameter roughly corresponding to the resolution of the functions. Assume that $\mathcal{C}$ consists of square integrable functions, and denote the inner product on $\mathcal{C}$ by $\langle \cdot, \cdot \rangle$. Then an ideal expansion of $c \in \mathcal{C}$ using the basis Φ^ν is obtained as

$$\hat{c}^\nu = \sum_{\boldsymbol{k} \in \mathcal{L}} c[\boldsymbol{k}] \phi_{\boldsymbol{k}}^\nu \tag{23}$$

where

$$c[\boldsymbol{k}] = \langle c, \phi_{\boldsymbol{k}}^\nu \rangle. \tag{24}$$

The expansion in (23) is a representation of $\hat{c}$ in the subspace $\mathcal{C}^\nu \subset \mathcal{C}$ consisting of all linear combinations such that

$$\sum_{\boldsymbol{k} \in \mathcal{L}} |c[\boldsymbol{k}]|^2 < \infty. \tag{25}$$

The parameter ν indexes the subspaces so that

$$\lim_{\nu \to 0} \mathcal{C}^\nu = \mathcal{C} \tag{26}$$

in the sense that for all $c \in \mathcal{C}$

$$\lim_{\nu \to 0} \langle c - \hat{c}^\nu,\ c - \hat{c}^\nu \rangle = 0. \tag{27}$$

The statement in (27) is valid for deterministic convergence. For the stochastic setting, the corresponding statement involves stochastic convergence. For convergence in a mean-square sense, given a prior on the image space $\mathcal{C}$ such that $E\{\langle c, c \rangle\} < \infty$, the sequence of functions $\hat{c}^\nu$ converges to c in a mean-square sense if

$$\lim_{\nu \to 0} E\{\langle c - \hat{c}^\nu,\ c - \hat{c}^\nu \rangle\} = 0. \tag{28}$$

A more general setting involves convergence of the mean discrepancy $E\{d_\mathcal{C}(\hat{c}^\nu, c)\}$ to zero. Other modes of convergence of $\hat{c}^\nu$ to c may also be studied.

This description can be modified to allow for $\mathcal{C}^\nu$ to consist of functions that do not form an orthonormal set. This is the typical case for polynomial splines and for some multiresolution expansions. The extension involves using a different function to extract the coefficients than is used in the expansion itself. For polynomial splines there is an additional complication that, for expansions that are not ideally chosen, the functions often are not linearly independent. There have been some descriptions of the use of "frames" to cover this situation (see [26] and [46]).

Often, the expansion functions $\phi_{\boldsymbol{k}}^\nu$ are translated versions of a single-basis function ψ^ν. Specifically, assume that $\mathcal{C} = L_2(\boldsymbol{R}^n)$, and that the sample points occur on a regular lattice in $\boldsymbol{R}^n$ with lattice basis elements $\boldsymbol{\xi}_1, \boldsymbol{\xi}_2, \cdots, \boldsymbol{\xi}_n$. Any point on the lattice is then specified by a unique integer vector $\boldsymbol{k} \in \boldsymbol{Z}$ and equals $\sum_{i=1}^{n} k_i \boldsymbol{\xi}_i$. We then have

$$\phi_{\boldsymbol{k}}^\nu(\boldsymbol{x}) = \psi^\nu \left(\boldsymbol{x} - \sum_{i=1}^{n} k_i \boldsymbol{\xi}_i \right). \tag{29}$$

The parameter ν is a measure of the size of the Voronoi cells in the lattice.

In polynomial spline expansions, the basis function ψ^ν is a polynomial in its n arguments. Clearly, there are infinitely many choices for the degree of the polynomial in its arguments. For a general discussion of splines, see the books by Chui and by Wahba [16], [102]. The simplest polynomial spline is a constant over an interval and zero outside of that interval. For the lattice described above, let

$$\psi_0^\nu(\boldsymbol{x}) = \begin{cases} \frac{1}{\sqrt{A_0}}, & \|\boldsymbol{x}\|^2 < \|\boldsymbol{x} - \sum_{i=1}^{n} k_i \boldsymbol{\xi}_i\|^2, \quad \forall \boldsymbol{k} \neq 0 \\ 0, & \text{otherwise.} \end{cases} \tag{30}$$

Note that ψ_0^ν is proportional to an indicator function on the Voronoi cell of the lattice point at the origin and that A_0 is the volume of the Voronoi cell. The reproduction space in this case consists of images that are piecewise-constant.

C. Penalty and Constraint Methods

A common method of regularization of image estimates is to use penalty or constraint methods. To motivate these methods, a specific class of examples is used.

Suppose that $\mathcal{C}^\nu = \{c \in \mathcal{C} : d_\mathcal{C}(c, c_0) \leq 1/\nu\}$, where c_0 is a nominal value. Then the regularization problem (13) is a constrained optimization problem. The constraint may be incorporated using a Lagrange multiplier, α, changing the criterion to

$$\psi(o, c) + \alpha d_\mathcal{C}(c, c_0). \tag{31}$$

For a wide class of discrepancy measures and criteria ψ, if the constraint is satisfied with equality, then there is a one-to-one correspondence between the value of α and the value of the constraint $1/\nu$. This shows an equivalence between constraint methods and penalty methods, where the additional term $\alpha d_\mathcal{C}(c, c_0)$ is viewed as a penalty.

If a squared-error discrepancy measure is used, then this yields a quadratic penalty; typically c_0 would be chosen to be zero. If discrimination is used as the discrepancy measure, then this yields entropy-type penalties. For example, if c_0 is a constant then $d_\mathcal{C}(c, c_0)$ is the Shannon entropy of the function c.

This approach also yields a method to combine positive-valued images c with real- or complex-valued data o. Then the function $\psi(o,c)$ may be a squared error, and the discrepancy measure d_C may be discrimination. Similarly, if the images are real- or complex-valued and the data are positive, ψ may be discrimination and d_C may be squared error.

Roughness penalties are often based on Good's roughness measure [38], [61], [69], [95]. When restricted to a pixelization, Good's roughness measure may be written as a sum of discriminations between the image and shifted copies of the image [69].

D. Transform-Domain Representations

A traditional engineering approach to the study of function representation is to manipulate a function in its transform-domain representation. This includes Fourier representations and wavelet representations as special cases. In Fourier-domain representations, there are several options for considering convergence of the representations. One is to assume that the image space is space-limited. The set of Fourier-series coefficients obtained by considering a periodic extension of the image space completely characterizes the image space. The parameter $1/\nu$ may correspond to the number of coefficients used in an expansion.

A second Fourier-domain option is to assume that the image is effectively bandlimited with bandwidth proportional to $1/\nu$. For each value of ν, the image is represented by its samples using the Nyquist–Shannon interpolation formula. This is equivalent to the ideal interpolation discussed in the pixelization subsection above.

There are other options for Fourier-domain representations. Typically, they correspond to expansions of the image space in the Fourier domain.

In wavelet representations, the parameter ν may correspond to the number of scaling levels considered or to sampling in the time-scale domain.

E. Sieves

A powerful method for regularization, which incorporates additional structure, is the method of sieves due to Grenander [42]. In the method of sieves, a sequence of subsets of the image space is defined and used to address issues of convergence of image estimates as the amount of data increases. For this discussion, we follow [42], assuming the underlying image c is a deterministic parameter and that there is a stochastic model for the data o given c. The conditional likelihood for the observation o given the underlying image c is denoted $\pi(o \mid c)$. In this setting, there is a true underlying image which is denoted c_0.

Definition: A one-parameter family of subsets of C, $\{C^\nu, \nu > 0\}$ is a *sieve* if the following conditions hold:

1) for almost every $o \in \mathcal{O}$, the maximum-likelihood estimate of c,

$$\hat{c}_{\mathrm{ML}}(o) = \arg\max_{c \in C} \pi(o \mid c) \qquad (32)$$

exists and is unique;

2) the closure of the union of subsets equals C

$$\text{Closure}[\cup_{\nu>0} C^\nu] = C; \qquad (33)$$

3) for each ν, the maximum-likelihood estimate restricted to C^ν

$$\hat{c}^\nu(o) = \arg\max_{c \in C^\nu} \pi(o \mid c) \qquad (34)$$

exists and is unique.

Note that this definition is essentially the same as the definition of regularization. The most visible use of sieves has been in studying the consistency of estimates. Let $o_1^n = \{o_1, o_2, \cdots, o_n\}$ be independent and identically distributed (i.i.d.) observations with distribution function $\pi(\cdot, c_0)$. Denote the maximum-likelihood estimate of c restricted to C^ν by $\hat{c}_n^\nu(o_1^n)$. Grenander [42, Ch. 9] proves that under conditions on the continuity and boundedness of the restricted log-likelihood function, and uniqueness and continuity of the discrimination function, there is a sequence of $\nu(n)$ so that $\hat{c}_n^{\nu(n)}(o_1^n)$ converges to c_0, with probability one.

The parameter ν in the definition of a sieve is referred to as the mesh size. In some instances, the sequence of spaces is nested (monotonic) in the sense that if $\nu_1 > \nu_2$, then $C^{\nu_1} \subset C^{\nu_2}$. This might appear to be a natural condition, but it is not necessary. Further details are given by Grenander [42], Chow and Grenander [15], Moulin [64], and Moulin, O'Sullivan, and Snyder [67].

Let $\mathcal{X} = \boldsymbol{R}^n$, so that $c : \boldsymbol{R}^n \to \boldsymbol{R}$. Let $k_\nu(\boldsymbol{x})$ be a function indexed by ν, referred to as the kernel. A *kernel sieve* is a set C^ν all of whose elements can be written as the result of a convolution with k_ν

$$c(\boldsymbol{x}) = \int k_\nu(\boldsymbol{x} - \boldsymbol{\xi})\gamma(\boldsymbol{\xi})\,d\boldsymbol{\xi}. \qquad (35)$$

The functions k_ν converge in distribution to a Dirac delta function as $\nu \to 0$. One choice, discussed in [89], is a circularly symmetric Gaussian kernel with space parameter ν

$$k_\nu(\boldsymbol{x}) = \frac{1}{(2\pi\nu)^{n/2}} e^{-\frac{1}{2\nu}\boldsymbol{x}^T\boldsymbol{x}}. \qquad (36)$$

F. Convergence of Sequences

The asymptotic properties of estimators are often important in estimation problems. As the amount of information increases, the estimates should converge to the truth in some sense. For regularization as described above, a setting for studying convergence is introduced.

Let $d_C(\hat{c}, c)$ be a discrepancy measure. Suppose now that the estimate $\hat{c}$ is formed from the observations. Let T be a measure of how informative the observations are. For example, T could be the time-integration interval over which data are collected or the number of independent observations in a dataset. Suppose for each T, that the estimate lies within $C^{\nu(T)}$. Then, $d_T = d_C(\hat{c}^\nu(o_T), c)$ is a random variable indexed by T. Its randomness arises due to the observations and possibly due to c being a random process. The family of estimators $\hat{c}$ is said to be consistent in the "R" sense if the random variables d_T converge to zero in the "R" sense. Here "R" may be almost everywhere, mean-square, in probability, or in distribution. That is, convergence of a discrepancy measure between the truth and the estimate in some sense.

G. Convex Constraints

The reproduction space may be constrained either by prior knowledge or by the limitations of the available sensor data. We shall be especially interested in those constraints that satisfy a convexity property because they are analytically tractable and arise frequently. In particular, the set of probability distributions on a finite set is a convex set, and information-theoretic constraints usually satisfy a convexity property. For deterministic models, the problem becomes one of finding an element of the convex set that is most consistent with the data in terms of minimizing the discrepancy between the predicted data and the available data (as discussed in Section VII). A general introduction to convex constraints is given by Combettes [17].

A set $\mathcal{A}$ is *convex* if each convex combination of two elements from $\mathcal{A}$ is also in $\mathcal{A}$. That is, for any $c_1, c_2 \in \mathcal{A}$, then for all $0 \leq \lambda \leq 1$, $\lambda c_1 + (1-\lambda)c_2 \in \mathcal{A}$. The intersection of any number of convex sets is a convex set. A *convex constraint* is a statement that the image lies in a given convex set.

Many constraints that arise very naturally are convex constraints. One example is a nonnegativity constraint. If c is real-valued, then the nonnegativity constraint that $c(\boldsymbol{x}) \geq 0$ for all $\boldsymbol{x}$ is a convex constraint. This nonnegativity constraint can also be used within the class of complex-valued functions because the set of functions $c(\boldsymbol{x})$ that are both real and nonnegative is a convex set within the set of complex functions. Thus the convex constraint can be used to enforce a very natural property of images while still allowing the larger space of complex functions to play a role in the theory.

Our second example of a convex constraint is an energy constraint for square-integrable functions. Suppose that the image space $\mathcal{C}$ is equipped with an inner product $\langle \cdot, \cdot \rangle$, and a corresponding norm

$$\|c\|^2 = \langle c, c \rangle. \tag{37}$$

Let $\mathcal{A}_B \subset \mathcal{C}$ be defined as the set of images whose norm is less than some constant B

$$\mathcal{A}_B = \{c \in \mathcal{C} : \|c\| < B\}. \tag{38}$$

By the triangle inequality on the inner product norm

$$
\begin{aligned}
\|\lambda c_1 + (1-\lambda)c_2\| &\leq \|\lambda c_1\| + \|(1-\lambda)c_2\| \\
&= \lambda^2 \|c_1\| + (1-\lambda)^2 \|c_2\|
\end{aligned} \tag{39}
$$

so we can conclude that $\mathcal{A}_B$ is a convex set. More generally, convex constraints often may be defined in terms of discrepancy measures. For this to hold, we need that for each $c_0 \in \mathcal{C}$

$$\mathcal{A}_B = \{c \in \mathcal{C} : d_\mathcal{C}(c, c_0) < B\} \tag{40}$$

is a convex set. If, in addition, the sets $\mathcal{A}_B$ in (40) are compact, then they may be used to define a regularization. Simply set $\nu = 1/B$ and $\mathcal{C}^\nu = \mathcal{A}_{1/\nu}$.

Our third example of a convex constraint is a support constraint. Let the set $\mathcal{X}_S \subset \mathcal{X}$ be the support of the function. A typical support constraint is the requirement that $c(\boldsymbol{x}) = 0$ for all $\boldsymbol{x} \notin \mathcal{X}_S$. Clearly, $\lambda c_1(\boldsymbol{x}) + (1-\lambda)c_2(\boldsymbol{x}) = 0$ for all

$\boldsymbol{x} \in \mathcal{X}_s$ if the same holds for $c_1(\boldsymbol{x})$ and $c_2(\boldsymbol{x})$ individually. Likewise, a support constraint on the Fourier transform of the function $c(\boldsymbol{x})$ is also a convex constraint.

H. Stochastic Complexity and Shrinkage Techniques

If a prior on the image is not known, the regularization approaches described above may not be desired. Alternatives to these approaches include stochastic complexity, wavelet shrinkage techniques, and complexity regularization. The goal is either to define a universal prior, the use of which will achieve asymptotically near-optimal performance for a variety of true priors, or without reference to a prior to derive a simple algorithm that achieves near-optimal performance for a variety of underlying image spaces.

To give specific examples, assume that

$$c = \sum_{\boldsymbol{k} \in \mathcal{L}} c[\boldsymbol{k}] \phi_{\boldsymbol{k}}^\nu \tag{41}$$

where $\{\phi_{\boldsymbol{k}}^\nu, \boldsymbol{k} \in \mathcal{L}\}$ is a set of basis functions such as a Fourier basis or a wavelet basis, and the coefficients $c[\boldsymbol{k}]$ are real-valued. In the image processing community, wavelet bases play an important role because of several empirically observed properties such as sparseness of significant coefficients. Suppose that we have the simple case where the observations are

$$o = c + w \tag{42}$$

where o, c, and w are real-valued, so that the coefficients of o are given by

$$o[\boldsymbol{k}] = c[\boldsymbol{k}] + w[\boldsymbol{k}]. \tag{43}$$

The specific problem addressed by these methods is to estimate the coefficients $c[\boldsymbol{k}]$. The Bayesian shrinkage, minimum description length, and complexity regularization techniques may be extended to the general case by simply adding the equivalent of a log-prior to the objective function.

Definition: A function $\hat{c} : \boldsymbol{R} \to \boldsymbol{R}$ is a called shrinkage function if

$$|\hat{c}(x)| \leq |x| \quad \text{and} \quad x\hat{c}(x) \geq 0. \tag{44}$$

Examples of shrinkage functions are the soft threshold

$$\hat{c}(x) = \min(0, x - \lambda \operatorname{sgn}(x)) \tag{45}$$

and the hard threshold

$$\hat{c}(x) = \begin{cases} 0, & |x| < \lambda \\ x, & |x| \geq \lambda. \end{cases} \tag{46}$$

These simple shrinkage functions have been shown, with proper choice of the thresholds, to provide good asymptotic performance [28]. The threshold $\sigma\sqrt{2\ln N}$, where N is the number of terms in the basis expansion and σ is the standard deviation of the additive noise, is called the universal threshold. Minimax methods may be used to determine the threshold [28].

Bayesian methods within this category define a prior on c that models the coefficients $c[\boldsymbol{k}]$ as independent and identically distributed, with common density function $p(\cdot)$. Model the noise samples $w[\mathbf{k}]$ as independent and identically distributed Gaussian random variables with zero mean and variance σ^2. The optimal estimate under this model has the form

$$\hat{c}(x) = \arg\max_c p(x \mid c)p(c)$$
$$= \arg\min_c \frac{1}{2\sigma^2}(x - c)^2 - \ln p(c) \quad (47)$$

which reflects the Gaussian assumption on $w[\mathbf{k}]$. The resulting estimated function has coefficients

$$c[\mathbf{k}] = \hat{c}(o[\mathbf{k}]). \quad (48)$$

If $p(c)$ is a Gaussian density with zero mean and variance σ_c^2, then the result is

$$\hat{c}(x) = \frac{\sigma_c^2}{\sigma^2 + \sigma_c^2} x \quad (49)$$

which is the standard Wiener filter. If $p(c)$ is a Laplacian density

$$p(c) = \frac{1}{\sigma_c \sqrt{2}} e^{\frac{-|c|\sqrt{2}}{\sigma_c}} \quad (50)$$

then the soft threshold is the optimal estimator

$$\hat{c}(x) = \begin{cases} x - \lambda \, \mathrm{sgn}\,(x), & |x| > \lambda \\ 0, & |x| \le \lambda \end{cases} \quad (51)$$

where $\lambda = \sqrt{2}\frac{\sigma^2}{\sigma_c}$. The universal threshold $\sigma\sqrt{2\ln N}$ corresponds to $\sigma_c = \sigma(\ln N)^{-1/2}$ [66].

Moulin and Liu [66] study the more general set of general Gaussian distributions whose log-priors are proportional to $-|c|^\alpha$, for $0 < \alpha \le 2$. They note that the resulting estimator has a threshold whenever the derivative of the log-prior is not continuous at $c = 0$; this is the case for $0 < \alpha \le 1$. The estimator converges to the hard threshold shrinkage function as α tends to zero.

Physics-based models provide prior information that can affect the process of image formation, and also other signal processing tasks such as detection, estimation, classification, and compression. The notion of *minimum description length*, or *Rissanen length*, plays a fundamental role in this study. The Rissanen-length estimation criterion minimizes the quantity $\log \pi(o|c) + L(c)$ over c, where $L(c)$ is a measure of complexity.

There are several closely related techniques for regularizing estimates using complexity methods and shrinkage estimators. Several of these techniques have nearly optimal performance for a variety of measures, if the true image can be assumed to belong to broad classes of signals such as Besov classes [29], [30].

V. INFORMATION-THEORETIC MEASURES

There are various measures that can be used to quantify the performance of an imaging system. The information that is available prior to acquiring data that is to be used for making inference about a scene is quantified by a prior probability distribution on the space of images. Measurements provided by the sensors add information to this prior information. The value of the new information in terms of implications on performance depends on the goal of the imaging system. The goal may be some combination of detection, recognition, parameter estimation, and scene estimation. For these goals, there are associated performance measures including probability of detection, probability of false alarm, probability of correct classification, mean-squared error, and discrepancy between the estimated image and the true image.

Each of the information measures discussed in this section is important, and each has a role in a specific class of problem. One measure is not fundamentally more important than any other. They all share an ability to quantify the information provided by a measurement, and they all depend on the likelihood of the data. In this sense, the likelihood function itself is more fundamental than any single measure of performance. Each measure reduces the likelihood function to a form that is more appropriate to a particular problem. We note, however, that for some imaging situations there is as yet no information or discrepancy measure that is entirely satisfactory. This is especially true when seeking to emulate the performance of human observers of images.

A well-known statement of information theory is the data processing theorem, which says that processing cannot increase information; processing can only refine information by presenting it in a more accessible form. The data processing theorem is an important statement whose validity is based on a formal definition of the term information. In common use, the term information is often used in a casual and imprecise way. There is always a danger of allowing the imprecision in our everyday notion of information to confuse the precision necessary in formal work.

A trivial, though perhaps not obvious, corollary of the data processing theorem is the statement that appending more data to a problem cannot decrease the amount of information and so cannot decrease the performance of an optimal algorithm.

Closely related to the data processing theorem is the concept of a sufficient statistic. The data processing theorem, and notions of uncertainty and entropy lead to the concepts of maximum entropy and minimum discrimination and thereby to the Cramer–Rao bounds, the Fisher information, least squares processing, and the maximum entropy principle.

A. Discrepancy Measures

As defined above, a discrepancy measure $d_{\mathcal{X}}$ on a space $\mathcal{X}$ is a mapping $d_{\mathcal{X}} : \mathcal{X} \times \mathcal{X} \to \mathbf{R}_+$ such that $d_{\mathcal{X}}(x_1, x_2) \ge 0$, with equality if and only if $x_1 = x_2$.

Discrepancy measures are assumed to be defined for each of the spaces in the imaging problem. Often it is natural to define discrepancy measures as sqared distances on the spaces. For example, if the space $\mathcal{X}$ has an inner product, $\langle \cdot, \cdot \rangle$, then a natural discrepancy measure is squared error

$$d_{\mathcal{X}}(x_1, x_2) = \|x_1 - x_2\|^2 = \langle x_1 - x_2, x_1 - x_2 \rangle. \quad (52)$$

If the space $\mathcal{X}$ consists of positive-valued functions, then, as discussed below, discrimination is a natural discrepancy measure. In many problems the image spaces are assumed to be linear spaces equipped with distances and norms in addition to discrepancy measures.

There have been several information-theoretic derivations of discrepancy measures presented in the literature, including [23], [51], [52], and [85]. These lead to characterizations of various discrepancy measures including squared error, discrimination, Ali–Silvey distances [1] or f-divergences [20], Bregman distances [7], and the Itakura–Saito distance [50]. From the axiomatic derivation of Csiszár [23], the discrimination for positive-valued functions and squared error for real-valued (and complex-valued) functions play unique roles in the analysis.

The discrimination function was introduced by Kullback [55], [67], under the name *information for discrimination*. Kullback took the view that the discrimination is an information measure that is more fundamental in some sense than the entropy.

1) Axiomatic Formulation Shannon [83] gave a reasonable set of axioms that a measure of information should satisfy. Shannon's approach leads to the logarithm as a measure of information. Csiszár [23], in the tradition of this approach to the entropy function and the mutual information, gives an axiomatic development for selecting discrepancy functions. Suppose a solution c to the matrix vector equation $Hc = a$ is sought. Starting with a set of reasonable axioms that a measure of discrepancy should satisfy, Csiszár concludes that if the elements of H, c, and a are required to be real-valued and are otherwise arbitrary, then the only function consistent with his axioms is the squared error $\|Hc - a\|^2$. It is well known that the choice of c that minimizes the squared error is then $\hat{c} = (H^T H)^{\#} H^T a$, where the notation $M^{\#}$ denotes the pseudoinverse of M. On the other hand, if all entries in H, c, and a are required to be both real and nonnegative, as is often the case for inverse problems in imaging, then the only discrepancy function consistent with Csiszár's axioms is the discrimination

$$
I\left(\sum_x h(\cdot, x)c(x)\|a(\cdot)\right) = \sum_y a(y) \ln\left[\frac{a(y)}{\sum_x h(y,x)c(x)}\right]
$$
$$
- \sum_y \left[a(y) - \sum_x h(y,x)c(x)\right]. \tag{53}
$$

Explicit analytical expressions for the $c = \hat{c}$ minimizing discrimination are difficult to obtain, and so numerical methods are appropriate.

2) A Discrepancy Inequality For any convex set $\mathcal{A} \subset \mathbf{R}^n$, both the discrimination

$$
d(y,x) = I(y\|x) = \sum_i \left[y_i \log \frac{y_i}{x_i} - y_i + x_i\right] \tag{54}
$$

and the squared euclidean distance $d(y,x) = \|y - x\|^2$ satisfy the inequality

$$
d(y,x) \geq d(y, y^*) + d(y^*, x), \qquad \forall x, y \in \mathcal{A} \tag{55}
$$

where

$$
y^* = \arg\min_{y \in \mathcal{A}} d(y, x). \tag{56}
$$

If $\mathcal{A}$ is further restricted to be an affine subspace, then

$$
d(y,x) = d(y, y^*) + d(y^*, x), \qquad \forall x, y \in \mathcal{A}. \tag{57}
$$

The proof of this statement for discrimination is based on the following argument [18]. Because y^* achieves the minimum, $d(y,x) \geq d(y^*, x)$ for all $y \in \mathcal{A}$; so for all $\epsilon > 0$, and $y^* + \epsilon \Delta y \in \mathcal{A}$

$$
\frac{1}{\epsilon}[d(y^* + \epsilon \Delta y, x) - d(y^*, x)] \geq 0. \tag{58}
$$

Take the limit as ϵ goes to zero to obtain

$$
\nabla_y d(y^*, x) \Delta y \geq 0. \tag{59}
$$

Now let $\Delta y = y - y^*$, and rearrange this to get

$$
\sum (y_i - y_i^*)\left(\log \frac{y_i^*}{x_i}\right)
$$
$$
= \sum_i \left[y_i \log \frac{y_i^*}{y_i} + y_i - y_i^* + y_i \log \frac{y_i}{x_i}\right.
$$
$$
\left. - y_i + x_i - y_i^* \log \frac{y_i^*}{x_i} + y_i^* - x_i\right]
$$
$$
= -d(y, y^*) + d(y, x) - d(y^*, x) \geq 0. \tag{60}
$$

In the case that $\mathcal{A}$ is an affine subspace, both Δy and $-\Delta y$ are allowable directions, yielding equality in (58).

The inequality (55) (or the equality (57) when $\mathcal{A}$ is an affine subspace) can be viewed as a statement of the tradeoff between approximation error and estimation error. The term $d(y^*, x)$ is a measure of the approximation error because it is a discrepancy between the closest element in the convex set $\mathcal{A}$ and x. The term $d(y, y^*)$ is a measure of the estimation error since it is a discrepancy between the estimated value y and the closest element in the convex set $\mathcal{A}$. The inequality says that the discrepancy between the estimate and x is bounded below by the sum of these two terms.

For the squared-error discrepancy $d(y,x) = \|y - x\|^2$, the same argument as above holds, until (59) becomes $2\langle y - y^*, y^* - x\rangle \geq 0$, which immediately implies

$$
\|y - x\|^2 = \|y - y^*\|^2 + \|y^* - x\|^2 + 2\langle y - y^*, y^* - x\rangle
$$
$$
\geq \|y - y^*\|^2 + \|y^* - x\|^2. \tag{61}
$$

The interpretation of this inequality is the same as interpretation of the discrimination criterion.

B. Mutual Information

The uncertainty associated with a random vector θ is quantified by its differential entropy (or, if θ takes on only discrete values by its entropy). Denote this differential entropy by $h(\theta)$

$$
h(\theta) = -E\{\log p(\theta)\}. \tag{62}
$$

The observations may be viewed as decreasing the uncertainty in the underlying parameters. In this view, the mutual information between the parameters and the observation quantifies the decrease in uncertainty obtained by making an observation, because

$$I(o;\theta) = h(\theta) - h(\theta|o) \qquad (63)$$

where

$$h(\theta|o) = -E\{\log p(\theta|o)\}. \qquad (64)$$

This view is helpful in coding applications. To be more precise, the rate-distortion curves for θ with the observation o lies below the rate-distortion curve for θ in the absence of observations. For any fixed distortion, the difference in the two curves is never greater than $I(o;\theta)$.

C. Fisher Information

For parameter estimation, a standard performance measure, which will be discussed in Section VI-A, is the Cramer–Rao bound and its extensions. The information provided by sensor measurements can be quantified in terms of the reduction in the variance of a parameter estimate due to the measurement. This is equivalent to looking at the increase in the Fisher information, as outlined below.

Suppose that θ, the parameters to be estimated, take values in R^n. Let the prior probability density function on θ be $p(\theta)$ and let the conditional distribution for the sensor data be $\pi(o \mid c(\theta))$. The posterior density on θ is proportional to $\pi(o \mid c(\theta))p(\theta)$; denote it by $p(\theta \mid o)$. Prior to making any measurements, the Fisher information matrix is

$$\boldsymbol{J}_\theta = E\left\{ \frac{\partial \ln p(\theta)}{\partial \theta} \frac{\partial \ln p(\theta)}{\partial \theta}^T \right\} \qquad (65)$$

where the partial derivatives are assumed to exist and yield column vectors, and T denotes transpose. After an observation, the Fisher information matrix is

$$\boldsymbol{J}_{\theta|o} = \boldsymbol{J}_{o|\theta} + \boldsymbol{J}_\theta \qquad (66)$$

where $\boldsymbol{J}_\theta$ is given above and

$$\boldsymbol{J}_{o|\theta} = E\left\{ \frac{\partial \ln \pi(o \mid c(\theta))}{\partial \theta} \frac{\partial \ln \pi(o \mid c(\theta))}{\partial \theta}^T \right\}. \qquad (67)$$

Let $\boldsymbol{R}$ be the mean-squared-error matrix for any specified estimator. Then the matrix $\boldsymbol{R} - \boldsymbol{J}_{\theta|o}^{-1}$ is nonnegative definite.

The matrix $\boldsymbol{J}_{o|\theta}$ quantifies the increase in the Fisher information obtained from the observations. For estimation problems, the relative increase in the Fisher information is one way to quantify the value of observations and the value in making additional observations.

The difference between matrices can be measured in several ways. One way is by examining the increase in the Fisher information, as in (66). Another is to examine the corresponding decrease in the inverse of the Fisher information matrix, which determines the Cramer–Rao bound on estimation (see Section VI-A)

$$\boldsymbol{J}_\theta^{-1} - \boldsymbol{J}_{\theta|o}^{-1} = \left(\boldsymbol{J}_\theta + \boldsymbol{J}_\theta \boldsymbol{J}_{o|\theta}^{-1} \boldsymbol{J}_\theta \right)^{-1}. \qquad (68)$$

A third is to measure the decrease in the inverse of the Fisher information relative to the prior

$$\boldsymbol{J}_\theta^{T/2} \left(\boldsymbol{J}_\theta^{-1} - \boldsymbol{J}_{\theta|o}^{-1} \right) \boldsymbol{J}_\theta^{1/2} = \left(\boldsymbol{I} + \boldsymbol{J}_\theta^{T/2} \boldsymbol{J}_{o|\theta}^{-1} \boldsymbol{J}_\theta^{1/2} \right)^{-1}. \qquad (69)$$

Here, $\boldsymbol{J}_\theta^{1/2} \boldsymbol{J}_\theta^{T/2} = \boldsymbol{J}_\theta$.

Other bounds for parameter estimations can be examined in a similar way.

There is a link between differential entropy and Fisher information given by de Bruijn's identity [19, pp. 494–495]. Let Z be a Gaussian random variable with mean zero and variance one. Let ϕ equal θ plus a scalar times Z

$$\phi = \theta + \sqrt{t}Z. \qquad (70)$$

Then, de Bruijn's identity says that (assuming natural logarithms)

$$2\frac{\partial h(\phi(t))}{\partial t} = J_\theta \qquad (71)$$

where $h(\phi(t))$ is the differential entropy of ϕ parameterized by t. In terms of the observation

$$2\frac{\partial h(o \mid \phi(t))}{\partial t} = J_{o|\theta} \qquad (72)$$

so

$$2\frac{\partial h(o \mid \phi(t))}{\partial t} + 2\frac{\partial h(\phi(t))}{\partial t} = J_{o|\theta} + J_\theta = J_{\theta|o}. \qquad (73)$$

Another interpretation of the Fisher-information matrix is given by Amari [2] in his discussion of the differential geometry of statistical models. Here, a parametric model $\pi(o|c(\theta))$ is interpreted as defining a manifold S in the space of all models $\pi(o)$. Amari defines an inner product between vectors in tangent planes of S as covariances, then arguing that $J_{o|\theta}$ is the metric tensor in the resulting Riemannian space. Amari uses this framework to establish general asymptotic properties of maximum-likelihood estimators of θ, such as asymptotic efficiency, consistency, and normality.

VI. PERFORMANCE BOUNDS

A goal of information-theoretic image formation is to bound achievable performance in terms of the information measures. Whenever these measures cannot be evaluated analytically, an important technique is to append information that is actually unknown so that the bounds can be evaluated analytically. The actual performance cannot be better than such a bound. An early use of this technique is in the classical book on communication theory by Wozencraft and Jacobs [104]. They introduce a "genie" in their analysis of the performance of coding systems. In a general form of the argument, the genie is assumed to provide gratuitous side information that embellishes the actual data. The performance without the genie's side information cannot be better than the performance with this extra information. The technique of introducing a genie to embellish the actual data set so that a bound on performance can be computed is quite similar to the technique of Dempster, Laird, and Rubin [27] who introduce a "complete data set" so that calculation of the maximum-likelihood solution becomes analytically tractable.

A. Cramer–Rao Bounds

The simplest problem of estimation theory involves an unknown parameter $\theta \in \mathbf{R}^n$ and a random measurement $o \in \mathcal{O}$ from which θ is to be determined. The measurement $o \in \mathcal{O}$ has probability distribution function $\pi(o \mid c(\theta))$ depending on the parameter θ. The unknown parameter θ must be estimated based upon an observation of o. The estimate of θ, given the measurement o, is a function $\hat{\theta}(o)$. This estimate $\hat{\theta}$ is itself a random variable because it is a function of the random measurement o.

The quality of an estimator is often judged by its mean value

$$E[\hat{\theta}] = E[\hat{\theta}(o)] \tag{74}$$

and by its mean-squared-error

$$\mathbf{R} = E[(\hat{\theta}(o) - \theta)(\hat{\theta}(o) - \theta)^T]. \tag{75}$$

When θ is not random, an unbiased estimator of θ is any function $\hat{\theta}(o)$ satisfying

$$E[\hat{\theta}] = \theta. \tag{76}$$

For any unbiased estimator, the matrix

$$\mathbf{R} - \mathbf{J}_{o|\theta}^{-1} \tag{77}$$

is nonnegative definite; this is the Cramer–Rao bound. When θ is random, then

$$\mathbf{R} - [\mathbf{J}_{o|\theta} + \mathbf{J}_\theta]^{-1} \tag{78}$$

is nonnegative definite.

Other bounds on the variance of an estimate can sometimes be tighter, including the Ziv–Zakai bound, the Barankin bound, and the Bhattacharyya bound. The Cramer–Rao bound when the parameters to be estimated are constrained to lie in a nonopen subset of $\mathbf{R}^n$ is developed by Gorman and Hero [41]; this bound is useful in imaging problems, for example, when the intensity has a known support or is smooth. For imaging problems, the Fisher information matrix can be, and usually is, too large to invert practically so that computing the Cramer–Rao bound on the error covariance in estimating all of the parameters that define the image is infeasible. To address this problem, Hero and Fessler [47] and Hero, Usman, Sauve, and Fessler [48] have developed a recursive procedure for computing submatrices of the inverse of the Fisher matrix; this can be especially useful for establishing Cramer–Rao bounds on subsets of the parameters (corresponding to a region in an image) that are of particular interest.

B. Bounds on Groups

If the parameters in the problem are not real-valued, then bounds other than the Cramer–Rao bound may be appropriate. A measure analogous to squared-error must be defined on the space, and bounds on errors in terms of the mean of this measure found. One approach detailed in this section is valid for group-valued parameters.

If a scene has objects of interest that are rigid bodies, the group actions consist of translation and rotation. When restricted to the plane, the group is $SO(2)$ which is isomorphic to the circle. Rotations in three dimensions take values in $SO(3)$. In either case, the group of rotations is compact, so there is a maximum distance between any two elements of the group. For small errors, as are typically encountered in high signal-to-noise-ratio problems, expansion in a local coordinate system followed by standard Cramer–Rao analysis in those coordinates is appropriate. When the estimation errors are not local, however, the curvature of the parameter space becomes important, and this local analysis does not apply. If this curvature is ignored, then it is possible to get so-called lower bounds that get arbitrarily large as a parameter (typically, signal-to-noise ratio) gets small. But this is impossible because the largest error possible on a compact set is bounded.

One approach that avoids this difficulty has been proposed by Grenander, Miller, and Srivastava [44]. It is explained here within the context of rotation groups, but can be extended to other groups.

Elements of $SO(n)$ are mapped to their $n \times n$ matrix group representative so that matrix multiplication is equivalent to the group action. For $SO(2)$, the matrices are of the form

$$\mathbf{O}(\theta) = \begin{bmatrix} \cos\theta & -\sin\theta \\ \sin\theta & \cos\theta \end{bmatrix} \tag{79}$$

where θ is the one-dimensional parameter of the group. Any norm on $n \times n$ matrices induces a norm on the group. Define the Hilbert–Schmidt norm by

$$\|A\|_{\mathrm{HS}}^2 = \sum_{i=1}^{n} \sum_{j=1}^{n} a_{ij}^2. \tag{80}$$

The squared distance between two elements of the group equals the distance between their matrix representatives

$$d_{\mathrm{HS}}(\theta_1, \theta_2) = \|\mathbf{O}(\theta_1) - \mathbf{O}(\theta_2)\|_{\mathrm{HS}}^2. \tag{81}$$

This is referred to as the Hilbert–Schmidt distance squared, and it is the natural extension of squared error in $\mathbf{R}^n$ to $SO(n)$. Note that

$$\|\mathbf{O}(\theta_1) - \mathbf{O}(\theta_2)\|_{\mathrm{HS}}^2 = \mathrm{Tr}\left[(\mathbf{O}(\theta_1) - \mathbf{O}(\theta_2))(\mathbf{O}(\theta_1) - \mathbf{O}(\theta_2))^T\right]$$
$$= 2n - 2\,\mathrm{Tr}\left[\mathbf{O}(\theta_1)\mathbf{O}(\theta_2)^T\right]. \tag{82}$$

Group-valued estimators may be evaluated in terms of this Hilbert–Schmidt distance squared. The Hilbert–Schmidt estimator is the minimum expected Hilbert–Schmidt distance-squared estimator (the extension of the minimum mean-squared-error estimator to the special orthogonal group $SO(n)$)

$$\hat{\theta}_{\mathrm{HS}} = \arg\min_{\tilde{\theta}} E[d_{\mathrm{HS}}(\theta, \tilde{\theta}) \mid o]. \tag{83}$$

That is, $\hat{\theta}$ is the orientation that minimizes the expected Hilbert–Schmidt squared error given the observations. Note that the estimator must be defined in this way because mean values are not defined on the group. There is only one operation available to combine two elements of the group; this operation is not necessarily addition.

There is a straightforward algorithm to compute the Hilbert–Schmidt estimator if the posterior is known. From (82), the optimal estimate is the one that maximizes

$E\{\text{Tr}\,[\boldsymbol{O}(\theta)\boldsymbol{O}(\tilde{\theta})^T]|o\}$. First, compute $\boldsymbol{A} = E\{\boldsymbol{O}(\theta)|o\}$, where the expectation is well-defined because this is a linear combination of $n \times n$ matrices. Next, find the singular value decomposition of $\boldsymbol{A}$ as

$$\boldsymbol{A} = \boldsymbol{U}\boldsymbol{\Sigma}\boldsymbol{V}^T. \qquad (84)$$

Assume that $\boldsymbol{\Sigma}$ is ordered so that the smallest eigenvalue is in the lower right corner. Then let $\boldsymbol{D}$ be a diagonal matrix whose diagonal entries are all one, except possibly for the lower right corner. The estimate is

$$\hat{\boldsymbol{O}}_{\text{HS}} = \boldsymbol{U}\boldsymbol{D}\boldsymbol{V}^T \qquad (85)$$

and the lower right entry of $\boldsymbol{D}$ is chosen to ensure that the determinant of $\hat{\boldsymbol{O}}_{\text{HS}}$ is equal to one. Finally, $\hat{\theta}_{\text{HS}}$ is the group element corresponding to $\hat{\boldsymbol{O}}_{\text{HS}}$. The performance of any group-valued estimator is bounded as follows [44].

Theorem: Let $\hat{\theta}(o) \in SO(n)$ be any estimator. Then

$$E[d_{\text{HS}}(\theta, \hat{\theta}(o))] \geq E[d_{\text{HS}}(\theta, \hat{\theta}_{\text{HS}}(o))]. \qquad (86)$$

It is interesting to note that for small variations, the Hilbert–Schmidt squared distance is essentially the same as would be obtained using a linearization of the space. To see this for $n = 2$, note that (82) becomes $4 - 4\cos(\theta_1 - \theta_2)$. For small differences $\theta = \theta_1 - \theta_2$, $\cos\theta \approx 1 - \theta^2/2$, and

$$4 - 4\cos(\theta_1 - \theta_2) \approx 2(\theta_1 - \theta_2)^2. \qquad (87)$$

This is twice the squared error between the angles, so for small errors this is equivalent to linearizing the space and using squared error in $\boldsymbol{R}$.

C. Resolution

The resolution achieved in image formation is an important attribute that is often cited. However, a universally acceptable definition of resolution as a performance measure is elusive. The Rayleigh criterion is often used to quantify the resolution of optical images. The width of the main lobe of the point-spread function of an imaging system is another frequently used measure of resolution. However, these measures are typically applied to image data rather than to post-processed data. Model-based processing can result in sharper image detail and, hence, improved resolution; good examples of this are the images that result from processing image data acquired in the presence of spherical aberration in the Hubble space telescope. The resolution achieved with image restoration and image estimation is more difficult to quantify. One approach is through computer simulation in which a known object is synthetically imaged and the resulting image processed for restoration. The restored imaged can be correlated against a test image formed by convolving the known object with a given point-spread function and then adjusting a "width" parameter of this function to achieve maximum correlation. An example is a circular Gaussian point spread in which the width (or spread) parameter is adjusted for maximum correlation, then used as a measure of resolution [11], [73]. The benefit of such an approach in practice depends on how well the synthetic image data matches data actually produced by the imaging system of interest.

D. Information Rate Functions

If the goal is object detection (binary hypothesis testing), then the performance may be quantified by error rates. For example, the Chernoff information determines the rate of the minimum probability of error detector, and hence can be used as a measure of information contained in a measurement. Let π_1 and π_0 be the probability distributions on the sensor data under hypotheses H_1 and H_0, respectively. Let the log-moment-generating function for the loglikelihood ratio be denoted by $\phi(s)$

$$\phi(s) = \log E_1\left\{\exp\left(s\log\frac{d\pi_1}{d\pi_0}\right)\right\} \qquad (88)$$

where E_1 denotes expectation with respect to π_1. The information rate function for the problem is given by [9], [31]

$$I(x) = \sup_{0 \geq s \geq -1}[sx - \phi(s)]. \qquad (89)$$

Then the Chernoff information equals $I(0)$ [99, p. 123].

Similarly, Stein's lemma says that fixing the probability of one type of error and minimizing the probability of the other type yields the relative entropy between the distributions under H_0 and H_1 as the measure of the information provided by a measurement. Put another way, let

$$x_1 = E_1\left\{\log\frac{d\pi_1}{d\pi_0}\right\} = D(\pi_1 \mid \pi_0) \qquad (90)$$

and

$$x_0 = E_0\left\{\log\frac{d\pi_0}{d\pi_1}\right\} = D(\pi_0 \mid \pi_1) \qquad (91)$$

then [19, pp. 309–311]

$$I(-x_0) = x_0. \qquad (92)$$

Because the Chernoff information and the rate in Stein's lemma are just samples of the information rate function $I(x)$, for $x_0 \leq x \leq x_1$, the rate function may be the proper measure of information provided by the sensor for detection problems.

The purpose of an imaging system may be to recognize, detect, or locate an object within the image; the image itself may be only of passing interest. In such a case, the performance of the imaging system is measured by the performance of the recognition or detection function. The overall performance of a system that is designed to recognize objects within an image is ultimately determined by the performance of the final decision that declares an object present. The detection algorithm may be constructed in stages where the output of one stage is fed to the next, or the detection algorithm may be designed in terms of a single, unified optimization problem. To predict the performance of an object recognition algorithm, we ask how the system would operate if the receiver knew everything except the decision.

Assume that two scenes are completely specified and that the available data are Poisson-distributed with means $T\boldsymbol{\Lambda}_1$ and $T\boldsymbol{\Lambda}_0$, where T is a measure of the signal-to-noise ratio such as the integration time. Then the log-likelihood function for the data $\boldsymbol{y}$ may be written

$$l(\boldsymbol{y}) = T[I(\boldsymbol{y}/T, \boldsymbol{\Lambda}_0) - I(\boldsymbol{y}/T, \boldsymbol{\Lambda}_1)] \qquad (93)$$

where

$$I(x, \boldsymbol{\xi}) = \sum x_i \log \frac{x_i}{\xi_i} - x_i + \xi_i$$

is discrimination. From Stein's lemma, for a fixed probability of false alarm, the probability of detection converges to one exponentially fast in T with exponent $-TI(\boldsymbol{\Lambda}_0, \boldsymbol{\Lambda}_1)$. Thus discrimination predicts asymptotic rates.

The rate depends on the clutter. If $\boldsymbol{\Lambda}_0$ has only clutter and $\boldsymbol{\Lambda}_1$ has a target and clutter, then this rate is a measure of the clutter complexity in the sense that in quantifies the clutter's ability to reduce the detection rate. For systems with small point-spread functions, the discrimination between images without and with a target is a *local* measure. This measure can be used to gain a confidence measure on the output of an object recognition system. Suboptimal algorithms may be compared on the basis of their rates. That is, a fixed algorithm will exhibit a performance that varies with signal-to-noise ratio. For large signal-to-noise ratio, the rate is all that matters.

VII. IMAGE FORMATION

We call the process of forming images from data acquired with a sensor *imagation* or *image formation*. In our use of this term, imagation includes: image reconstruction (the common term used for building a tomographic image from projection data), image restoration (a term used for correcting image data that are marred by camera defects or motion), image estimation (used for forming images from data that are stochastic), and image formation from data that indirectly depend on an image, such as in synthetic-aperture radar.

The type of models used for describing the image and data spaces, as well as the discrepancy measures that are adopted for assessing performance, influence the approaches used for imagation. Deterministic models and the use of least squares, discrimination, and maximum-entropy discrepancy-measures with and without constraints lead to one set of approaches, while stochastic models and the use of likelihood discrepancy-measures with and without priors and constraints leads to another.

A. Maximum Likelihood

The maximum-likelihood method is a long-standing method for estimating unknown, deterministic parameters that influence a set of stochastic data. The maximum-likelihood principle is a general principle of data reduction in which when reducing a set of data $\boldsymbol{x}$ described by a log-likelihood function $\Lambda(\gamma) = \log p(\boldsymbol{x} \mid \gamma)$, one chooses a γ that maximizes the log-likelihood function

$$\hat{\gamma} = \arg \max_{\gamma} \Lambda(\gamma). \qquad (94)$$

A maximum-likelihood estimate has the desired properties that it is asymptotically unbiased and efficient.

Its use for imagation follows the usual prescription of formulating a model for the data acquired with an imaging system, with this model being in the form of a probability distribution $\pi(o : c)$ that is a functional of the image c; $\pi(o : c)$ is called the *likelihood* or *data likelihood* in this context. A

maximum-likelihood estimate of the image $\hat{c}$ is an image c that maximizes the log-likelihood functional

$$\hat{c} = \arg \max_{c \in \mathcal{C}} \log \pi(o : c). \qquad (95)$$

For an image restricted to be a function of a parameter vector θ, the image estimate is $\hat{c} = c(\hat{\theta})$, where

$$\hat{\theta} = \arg \max_{\theta \in \Theta} \log \pi(o : c(\theta)). \qquad (96)$$

For example, the image could be of a known object whose position and orientation are unknown. In this instance, the likelihood can be regarded as a function of the parameters, which would be estimated by maximizing the likelihood in the usual manner.

If the image is regarded simply as an unknown function, then the problem is often ill-posed, and some regularization is required. One approach is to discretize the image, treating it as piecewise constant over pixels or by representing it as a linear combination of orthonormal functions as discussed in Section IV-B. This in effect converts the imagation problem into a parameter-estimation problem, and the maximum-likelihood method can in principle be used straightforwardly to estimate the parameterized image. For example, if the data source is modeled as a spatial Poisson process $\{N(A), A \in \sigma(\boldsymbol{R}^2)\}$ with an intensity function $\{c(x), x \in \boldsymbol{R}^2\}$, the log-likelihood functional is

$$\ln \pi(N : c) = -\int_{\boldsymbol{R}^2} c(x) \, dx + \int_{\boldsymbol{R}^2} \ln c(x) N(dx). \qquad (97)$$

This likelihood is unbounded over the space of nonnegative functions, so a maximum-likelihood estimate does not exist. Overcoming this difficulty requires the use of some form of regularization as discussed in Section IV-A, which can be in the form of imposing a discretization, imposing a prior distribution on image values, imposing a penalty functional that restricts the roughness of the estimated image values, or using Grenander's sieves [42] to restrict maximizers to a subset of the nonnegative functions.

B. Maximum a Posteriori

Maximum *a posteriori* probability (MAP) estimation is also a long-standing method of estimating parameters from observed data; it is used when the parameters to be estimated are random and have a known prior probability distribution $p(\theta)$. If the data likelihood is $\pi(r|\theta)$ for some given data r, then a MAP estimate $\hat{\theta}$ of θ is a maximizer of the posterior distribution $p(\theta|r)$. Because this conditional distribution is proportional to the product $\pi(r|\theta)p(\theta)$ of the data likelihood and the prior, this procedure is analogous to maximum-likelihood (ML) estimation of the parameters but with the likelihood scaled by the prior. MAP imagation is similar to ML imagation with a prior distribution on image values included in the functional being maximized.

C. Maximum Entropy and Minimum Discrimination

The *Jaynes maximum-entropy principle* is a principle of data reduction that says that when reducing a set of data into the form of an underlying model, one should be maximally non-committal with respect to missing data. If one must estimate a probability distribution q on the data source satisfying certain known constraints on q, such as

$$\sum_k q_k f_k = t \tag{98}$$

then, of those distributions that are consistent with the constraints, one should choose as the estimate of q the probability distribution $\hat{q}$ that has maximum entropy. A nice example can be given for a probabilistic source with a real output. Suppose the source produces a real-valued random variable X whose mean and variance are known, and otherwise the probability distribution governing the source is unknown. Then the maximum-entropy principle says that one should estimate that the probability density $q(x)$ is a Gaussian probability density with the given mean and variance. This is a consequence of the well-known fact that a Gaussian random variable has the largest differential entropy of any random variable of a given mean and variance.

The maximum-entropy and maximum-likelihood principles are equivalent when the constraint to be enforced when estimating a probability distribution is not in the form of some given moments but, rather, of some given data. When given some statistical data from which a distribution or image is to be estimated, one approach is to use those data to estimate some moments and then to use these estimated moments as if they were the exact (deterministic) moments when maximizing entropy. However, the estimated moments are exact only in the limit of a large data set and otherwise are random, resulting in a conceptual inconsistency. As discussed by Miller and Snyder [62], when entropy is maximized subject only to the constraint of some given, statistical data rather than deterministic moments, the resulting maximum-entropy estimates are also maximum-likelihood estimates.

The *Kullback minimum-discrimination principle* is an alternative principle that applies when one is given both a probability distribution p as a prior estimate of q and also a set of constraints, such as moment constraints, that the probability distribution q must satisfy. Under this principle, the optimal p is

$$\hat{p} = \arg\min_{p \in \mathcal{P}} I(p\|q) \tag{99}$$

where $\mathcal{P}$ is the set of probability distributions that satisfy the moment constraints [57], [56], and $I(\cdot\|\cdot)$ is discrimination. If the prior estimate q is a uniform distribution, then this principle yields the maximum-entropy distribution subject to the moment constraints.

D. Minimum Discrepancy: Least Squares and Discrimination

For observations in $\mathcal{O}$, assume the information-theoretic discrepancy measure $d_{\mathcal{O}}$. In deterministic problems, there is some model for the observed data o in terms of the underlying image c. Let this model be a function $f : \mathcal{C} \to \mathcal{O}$. Then the minimum-discrepancy problem is to find the $c \in \mathcal{C}$ that minimizes the predicted discrepancy from the observation

$$\hat{c}(o) = \arg\min_{c \in \mathcal{C}} d_{\mathcal{O}}(f(c), o). \tag{100}$$

This formalism includes least-squares, minimum-discrimination, and related methods.

If $\mathcal{O}$ consists of real- or complex-valued functions, then the squared error is the natural discrepancy measure. Let $\langle \cdot, \cdot \rangle$ denote an inner product on $\mathcal{O}$. The discrepancy measure is then

$$d_{\mathcal{O}}(o_1, o_2) = \langle o_1 - o_2, o_1 - o_2 \rangle. \tag{101}$$

The least-squares problem is

$$\hat{c}(o) = \arg\min_{c \in \mathcal{C}} \langle f(c) - o, f(c) - o \rangle. \tag{102}$$

If $\mathcal{O}$ consists of positive-valued functions, then discrimination is the natural discrepancy measure. Assume $o : \mathbf{R}^n \to \mathbf{R}_+$, and let $o(\mathbf{y})$ be the value of the observation at the point $\mathbf{y} \in \mathbf{R}^n$. The discrimination is defined as

$$d_{\mathcal{O}}(o_1, o_2) = \int \left[o_1(\mathbf{y}) \ln \frac{o_1(\mathbf{y})}{o_2(\mathbf{y})} - o_1(\mathbf{y}) + o_2(\mathbf{y}) \right] d\mathbf{y}$$
$$= I(o_1\|o_2). \tag{103}$$

In applications, the observations are often vectors rather than functions, in which case (103) is written as a summation as in (54) rather than an integral. For either the integral or the summation form, the optimization problem as stated in (100) becomes

$$\hat{c}(o) = \arg\min_{c \in \mathcal{C}} I(f(c)\|o). \tag{104}$$

For linear inverse problems, this formulation leads to the generalized iterative scaling or SMART (simultaneous multiplicative algebraic reconstruction technique) algorithm [12], [25].

The discrimination may be used with the arguments reversed. In this second formulation, the minimum discrepancy statement in (100) becomes

$$\hat{c}(o) = \arg\min_{c \in \mathcal{C}} I(o\|f(c)). \tag{105}$$

Since discrimination is not symmetric in its arguments, the criteria (104) and (105) can have different solutions and they lead to very different algorithms.

VIII. COMPUTATIONAL ALGORITHMS

Information-theoretic image formation yields images by the optimization of performance metrics. Analytical intractability usually accompanies any attempt to form images in this way, so numerical algorithms must be used; many algorithms used have a strong infomration-theoretic motivation. An important exception can occur with some linear problems having Gaussian statistics and quadratic metrics, but even in these cases numerical methods for performing matrix inversions or solving integral equations are often needed. For example, the original method by Rockmore and Macovski [76] for forming maximum-likelihood images for emission tomography was realized practically only when Shepp and Vardi [84] later introduced the expectation-maximization method of Dempster, Laird, and Rubin [27] as a means of constructing algorithms for computing the maximum-likelihood image. A wide variety of computational algorithms are in use for producing images numerically. Standard methods of numerical optimization, such as gradient descent, are widely used. In this section, we shall review methods based on information-theoretic concepts that have become popular and are presently finding their way into practical imaging systems. This includes the expectation-maximization method and its recent extensions introduced by Fessler and Hero [32]. Also mentioned is a similar method introduced by Snyder, Schulz, and O'Sullivan [92] for deterministic problems in which the discrepancy metric is the discrimination in the form of (105). A related algorithm originally proposed by Darroch and Ratcliff [25] for computing the distribution that maximizes entropy subject to constraints has been used to solve linear inverse problems by Byrne [12] and others. This is the generalized iterative scaling or SMART algorithm for deterministic problems in which the discrepancy metric is the discrimination in the form of (104). Stochastic search by means of the jump-diffusion algorithm of Grenander and Miller [43] is another powerful tool which we shall review briefly.

There are many other algorithms with an information-theoretic motivation that are not discussed here. Simulated annealing for imaging problems was discussed by Geman and Geman [34]; the jump-diffusion algorithm is a stochastic search without the annealing process. In addition to these stochastic search methods to combat the multimodality of optimization criteria, there are deterministic methods including the graduated nonconvexity algorithm [5] and its improvements [68]. The SMART algorithm is a descendent of ART and MART, algorithms that have been used in image reconstruction algorithms for many years (see the references in [12]). There have been many methods proposed for increasing the convergence rate of the expectation–maximization (EM) algorithm. Among the more promising techniques in the literature are those based on partitioning of the data space such as the ordered-subset EM algorithm and its variants [8], [49].

A. The Expectation–Maximization Method

The expectation–maximization method of Dempster, Laird, and Rubin [27] is a general approach for formulating recursive algorithms that can be used to determine the maximum-likelihood estimate of a parameter vector θ in terms of some measured data r. To apply the method requires judgment, and the structure of the problem must be appropriate. When successfully applied to a particular problem, the EM method yields a particular algorithm that is specific to that problem. Indeed, the EM method can even yield more than one algorithm for the same problem because there can be more than one way to apply the method. For imaging problems, θ is composed of the unknown parameters, such as pixel values, that comprise the image to be estimated, and r is composed of the data values produced by the imaging system. If some prior information regarding θ is available, this can readily be incorporated into the method by either adding the logarithm of

the prior on θ to the log-likelihood function being maximized, thereby producing MAP estimates of the parameters, or by adding a penalty function during the maximization.

The EM method begins by selecting some hypothetical data, r_{cd}, called the "complete data." There is considerable flexibility is making this selection, and making a good choice has largely been based on experience drawn from a familiarity with the physical problem at hand and its mathematical model. The choice can influence the behavior of the recursive algorithm that results, such as its rate of convergence, so careful consideration is warranted. Roughly speaking, the choice should be such that there is a function $h(\cdot)$ such that the actual data r, here termed the "incomplete data," can be recovered from the complete data, $r = h(r_{cd})$, and such that the log-likelihood function $L_{cd}(\theta)$ of the complete data can be formulated and the required analytical steps can be accomplished. At the very least, the conditional likelihood of the incomplete data given the complete data must be independent of the parameters θ. The issue of selecting complete data is discussed further in the next section.

The recursion proceeds as follows. Suppose that $\hat{\theta}^{\text{old}}$ is an estimate of θ that has been formed at some stage of the recursion. To get to the next stage, an E-step and an M-step must be performed. The E-step consists of evaluating the conditional expectation of the complete-data log-likelihood given the incomplete data and the parameter estimate available at that stage resulting in a function $Q(\theta|\hat{\theta}^{\text{old}})$, defined by

$$Q(\theta|\hat{\theta}^{\text{old}}) = E[L_{cd}(\theta)|r, \hat{\theta}^{\text{old}}].$$

The M-step is then performed to obtain an updated and possibly improved parameter estimate, $\hat{\theta}^{\text{new}}$ according to

$$\hat{\theta}^{\text{new}} = \arg\max_{\theta} Q(\theta|\hat{\theta}^{\text{old}}).$$

In many interesting situations, this maximization can be performed analytically, but in others numerical optimization is required, resulting in an iteration nested within the EM recursions.

Following Dempster, Laird, and Rubin [27], it is straightforward to demonstrate that the recursion produces a nondecreasing sequence

$$L_{id}(\hat{\theta}^{(0)}) \leq L_{id}(\hat{\theta}^{(1)}) \leq \cdots \leq L_{id}(\hat{\theta}^{(k)}) \leq \cdots$$

of log-likelihoods $L_{id}(\theta)$, of the incomplete data r. The limit, $\hat{\theta}^{(\infty)}$, if it exists, satisfies the necessary conditions for a maximizer of $L_{id}(\theta)$. To see this, let $p_{id}(r : \theta)$ and $p_{cd}(r_{cd} : \theta)$ denote the likelihood functions for the incomplete and complete data, respectively. These are related according to

$$p_{id}(r : \theta) = \int p(r|r_{cd})p_{cd}(r_{cd} : \theta)\, dr_{cd}. \tag{106}$$

Also, define the conditional likelihood $p(r_{cd}|r : \theta)$ according to Bayes rule

$$p(r_{cd} \mid r : \theta) = \frac{p(r \mid r_{cd})p_{cd}(r_{cd} : \theta)}{p_{id}(r : \theta)}. \tag{107}$$

Then

$$L_{id}(\theta) = L_{cd}(\theta) - \log p\,(r_{cd} \mid r : \theta) + \log p\,(r \mid r_{cd}) \tag{108}$$

where

$$L_{id}(\theta) = \log p_{id}(r : \theta)$$

and

$$L_{cd}(\theta) = \log p_{cd}(r_{rd} : \theta).$$

Multiplying both sides of this equation by $p(r_{cd}|r : \theta')$ and integrating over r_{cd} then yields

$$L_{id}(\theta) = Q(\theta \mid \theta') - \int p\left(r_{cd} \mid r : \theta'\right) \log p\left(r_{cd} \mid r : \theta\right) dr_{cd}$$
$$+ \int p\left(r_{cd} \mid r : \theta'\right) \log p\left(r \mid r_{cd}\right) dr_{cd}. \tag{109}$$

It follows from this expression that

$$L_{id}(\hat{\theta}^{\text{new}}) - L_{id}(\hat{\theta}^{\text{old}})$$
$$= Q(\hat{\theta}^{\text{new}} \mid \hat{\theta}^{\text{old}}) - Q(\hat{\theta}^{\text{old}} \mid \hat{\theta}^{\text{old}}) - \int p(r_{cd} \mid r : \theta^{\text{old}})$$
$$\times \log \left[\frac{p(r_{cd} \mid r : \theta^{\text{new}})}{p(r_{cd} \mid r : \theta^{\text{old}})}\right] dr_{cd}. \tag{110}$$

The entropy (discrimination) inequality, $-\int p \log q/p \geq 0$, then yields

$$L_{id}(\hat{\theta}^{\text{new}}) - L_{id}(\hat{\theta}^{\text{old}}) \geq Q(\hat{\theta}^{\text{new}} \mid \hat{\theta}^{\text{old}}) - Q(\hat{\theta}^{\text{old}} \mid \hat{\theta}^{\text{old}}). \tag{111}$$

Noting that the maximization step in the expectation–maximization method implies that

$$Q(\hat{\theta}^{\text{new}} \mid \hat{\theta}^{\text{old}}) \geq Q(\hat{\theta}^{\text{old}} \mid \hat{\theta}^{\text{old}}) \tag{112}$$

then establishes that $L_{id}(\hat{\theta}^{\text{new}}) \geq L_{id}(\hat{\theta}^{\text{old}})$ and, hence, that the sequence produced recursively via the expectation–maximization method does not reduce the incomplete-data log-likelihood at any stage.

If an estimate of θ is sought that maximizes $L_{id}(\theta) + \alpha\Phi(\theta)$, corresponding to estimating θ subject to a penalty constraint with penalty function $\Phi(\theta)$ or to estimating θ with a log-prior $\log p(\theta) = \alpha\Phi(\theta)$, then the expectation–maximization method can be used with the maximization step becoming

$$\hat{\theta}^{\text{new}} = \arg \max_{\theta}[Q(\theta \mid \hat{\theta}^{\text{old}}) + \alpha\Phi(\theta)].$$

Wu [105], Shepp and Vardi [84], and Csiszár and Tusnady [24] address the convergence properties of the sequence of parameter estimates and corresponding sequence of incomplete-data log-likelihoods towards local and global maximizers of the incomplete-data log-likelihood.

B. Space-Alternating Generalized Expectation–Maximization

The expectation–maximization method as originally formulated maximizes a conditional expectation $Q(\theta|\hat{\theta}^{\text{old}})$ of a single complete-data log-likelihood function $L_{cd}(r_{cd})$ and simultaneously updates estimates of all the parameters comprising the parameter vector θ. While this method does permit maximum-likelihood estimates of images to be obtained numerically, it is slow in convergence, and penalty functions to enforce regularization and priors can make the maximization step difficult. Fessler and Hero [32] address these deficiencies in a method they term "space-alternating generalized expectation–maximization," or SAGE. In their SAGE method, parameters in θ are grouped into subsets that are sequentially updated by alternating between multiple, small, hidden-data spaces rather than a single, large complete-data space. The result is a numerical approach that, in comparison to the usual expectation–maximization method, produces maximum-likelihood estimates of an image with a convergence rate that is potentially greater and with a complexity that may be less in the presence of constraints.

The SAGE method can be summarized as follows. Let θ be a p-dimensional vector of parameters to be estimated, and index these parameters using the set of integers $\{1, 2, \cdots, p\}$. Let S and $\tilde{S}$ be subsets of these indices such that $S \cup \tilde{S} = \{1, 2, \cdots, p\}$ and $S \cap \tilde{S} = \emptyset$. Denote by θ_S the m-dimensional vector of elements of θ having indices in S, where m is the number of indices in S. Similarly, define $\theta_{\tilde{S}}$ to be the vector of dimension $p - m$ formed from the remaining elements of θ. In general, θ may be partitioned into more than just two subvectors in this way using multiple disjoint index sets S^i, $i = 1, 2, \cdots$ whose union covers $\{1, 2, \cdots, p\}$. Functions $f(\theta_S, \theta_{\tilde{S}})$ of the m- and $p - m$-dimensional vectors θ_S and $\theta_{\tilde{S}}$ are interpreted as equal to the function $f(\theta)$ of the p-dimensional vector θ. In the SAGE method, updates are performed by sequencing through the different index sets $S = S^i$ and updating only those parameters in θ_S while holding the other parameters $\theta_{\tilde{S}}$ fixed.

Hidden-data spaces must also be defined and selected; doing so requires that complete data r_{cd}^S be selected in the usual way for estimating θ_S but now assuming that $\theta_{\tilde{S}}$ is known. Let $\hat{\theta}^{(0)}$ be an initial estimate of θ. A sequence of estimates that results in a nondecreasing sequence of incomplete-data log-likelihoods is produced by the Fessler–Hero SAGE algorithm [32], which repeats the following iteration:

Step 1. Choose an index set $S = S^i$;
Step 2. Choose complete data $r_{cd}^{S^i}$ for θ_{S^i};
Step 3. (E-step) Compute $Q_i(\theta_{S^i}|\hat{\theta}^{(i)})$;
Step 4. (M-step)

$$\hat{\theta}_{S^i}^{(i+1)} = \arg \max_{\theta_{S^i}} Q_i(\theta_{S^i} \mid \hat{\theta}^{(i)}) \tag{113}$$

$$\hat{\theta}_{\tilde{S}^i}^{(i+1)} = \hat{\theta}_{\tilde{S}^i}^{(i)}; \tag{114}$$

Step 5. (optional) Repeat Step 3 and Step 4.

The ith iteration consists of this sequence of steps. The iterations are repeated for $i = 0, 1, 2, \cdots$, halting when the iterates reach an equilibrium. Thus it is necessary to prove that the iterates of the algorithm do converge to an equilibrium. The convergence properties of the SAGE algorithm and considerations to be made in selecting complete data are discussed by Fessler and Hero [32], and extensions are given in [33].

C. The Random Sampling Method

The EM and SAGE methods for numerically producing maximizers of likelihood functionals, both with and without priors, proceed deterministically: a sequence of functions or images is produced that is predetermined by the data given and the function chosen to initiate the iteration. Although also iterative, the jump-diffusion method does not proceed deterministically but, rather, via a random search for maximizers or for estimates, such as the conditional mean (i.e., minimum mean-squared-error estimate). The method as introduced by Grenander and Miller [43] and discussed by Miller, Srivastava, and Grenander [63], [94], provides a numerical method for sampling from complicated distributions when the parameter space has both discrete and continuous components. It has been used effectively in a variety of applications, including identifying the number and shape of mitochondria in electron microscope images [43], deforming a labeled anatomy in a textbook to match a patient's anatomy [98], and detecting the number and orientation of targets in infrared images [59]. These various applications share the characteristic of having quantities in an image that are both discrete, such as the number of objects or the labeling of objects by their type, and continuous, such as the position and orientation of objects or spatially varying intensities in a scene containing the objects. The "jumps" in the method provide estimates of the discrete quantities by means of a stochastic search of the Metropolis–Hastings type, and the "diffusions" yield estimates of the continuous quantities through a stochastic optimization [35].

For example, let x_N represent parameters (such as the poses) and a_N the types of N objects in a scene. Denote the logarithm of the posterior likelihood of the data by $L(x_N : N, a_N)$ for given N and a_N. The approach is to formulate a diffusion process $\{x_N(t), t \geq 0\}$ that has the property that the log-distribution of $x_N(t)$ converges with increasing t towards $L(x_N : N, a_N)$. This diffusion is produced by the stochastic differential equation

$$dx_N(t) = \nabla_x L(x_N : N, a_N)\, dt + dw_N(t)$$

where $w_N(\cdot)$ is a standard N-dimensional Wiener process. Jumps between different choices of N and a_N are performed at the times of a Poisson process, and decisions of whether to select new values for N and a_N or to retain old ones are made in a manner similar to decisions made with the Metropolis–Hastings method of stochastic search. The cited references can be consulted for further details of the jump-diffusion approach.

D. Iterative Minimization of Discrimination

An iterative method that is similar to the expectation–maximization algorithm can be used to produce minimizers of discrimination for deterministic linear inverse problems. This approach has been suggested by Snyder, Schulz, and O'Sullivan [92]. Similar approaches are given by Vardi and Lee [100] and Byrne [12].

Linear inverse problems that can be approached with this method have the form

$$a(r) = \sum_x h(r, x)c(x) \qquad (115)$$

where the three functions $a(\cdot)$, $h(\cdot, \cdot)$, and $c(\cdot)$ are nonnegative, with $a(\cdot)$ and $h(\cdot, \cdot)$ being given and $c(\cdot)$ to be determined.

Joyce and Root [53] and many others have commented on the notoriously ill-posed character of many linear inverse problems. Various approaches have been suggested for solving them while introducing regularization to stabilize solutions. Most of these approaches are based on least squares optimization with constraints to enforce regularization, such as described by Tikhonov and Arsenin [96]. Youla [107] has proposed a method for accommodating nonnegativity constraints with least squares optimization.

As already noted, Csiszár [23] identified the important role of discrimination as a discrepancy measure for optimization when comparing nonnegative functions or images. Recognizing that a solution to the linear inverse problem described by (115) will necessarily be an approximation, a function $\hat{c}(\cdot)$ is sought such that the function $b(r : \hat{c})$, defined by

$$b(r : \hat{c}) = \sum_x h(r, x)\hat{c}(x) \qquad (116)$$

is a good approximation to the given function $a(r)$ in the sense that the discrimination $I(a\|b)$ between $b(r : \hat{c})$ and $a(r)$ is minimized. Let $c^{(0)}(x) > 0$ be a nonnegative function selected as an initial guess. Then, the sequence of functions $\{c^{(k)}(x), k = 0, 1, \cdots\}$ produced by the following recursion produces a corresponding sequence of discriminations $I(a\|\hat{b}^{(k)})$ that is nonincreasing, where $\hat{b}^{(k)}(r) \equiv b(r : \hat{c}^{(k)})$

$$\hat{c}^{(k+1)}(x) = \hat{c}^{(k)}(x)\frac{1}{H_0(k)}\sum_r \left[\frac{h(r, x)}{\sum_{x'} h(r, x')\hat{c}^{(k)}(x')}\right]a(r).$$
$$(117)$$

Properties of the sequence $\{\hat{c}^{(k)}(x), k = 0, 1, \cdots\}$ and conditions for convergence are discussed by Snyder, Schulz, and O'Sullivan [92]; these are established using results from Cover [18] and Vardi, Shepp, and Kaufmann [101]; see also Vardi and Lee [100]. Applications to tomographic imaging are given by Wang, Snyder, O'Sullivan, and Vannier [103], and by Robertson, Yuan, Wang, and Vannier [75].

E. Generalized Iterative Scaling or SMART

The generalized iterative scaling algorithm was originally introduced to find the distribution that maximizes entropy subject to a set of linear (mean-value) constraints by Darroch and Ratcliff [25]. It was shown by Byrne to minimize the discrimination in the form of (104) for linear inverse problems with nonnegative data, using an alternating minimization approach [12]. Byrne referred to this algorithm as SMART for the simultaneous multiplicative algebraic reconstruction technique. Csiszár [22] showed that generalized iterative scaling can be interpreted as alternating I-projections and the convergence is thus covered by his more general results [21]. Byrne explicitly showed that this algorithm is in fact an alternating minimization algorithm whose convergence is covered by Csiszár and Tusnady [24]. O'Sullivan [70] discussed several alternating minimization algorithms including this one.

For linear inverse problems as in (115), the problem is to minimize $I(b\|a)$, where $b(r : \hat{c})$ is the estimate for a as in (116). Let $c^{(0)}(x) > 0$ be a nonnegative function selected as an initial guess. Then, the sequence of functions $\{c^{(k)}(x), k = 0, 1, \cdots\}$ produced by the following recursion produces a corresponding sequence of discriminations $I(\hat{b}^{(k)}\|a)$ that is nonincreasing, where $\hat{b}^{(k)}(r) \equiv b(r : \hat{c}^{(k)})$

$$\hat{c}^{(k+1)}(x)$$
$$= \hat{c}^{(k)}(x) \prod_r \left[\frac{a(r)}{\sum_{x'} \hat{c}^{(k)}(x')h(r,x')} \right]^{h(r,x)/\sum_{r'} h(r',x)}.$$
$$(118)$$

If there is a nonnegative solution c to (115), then the iterates $\hat{c}^{(k)}(x)$ converge to the solution of (115) that minimizes $I(c\|\hat{c}^{(0)}(x))$ [25], [12].

F. Projection onto Convex Sets

The operation of projection onto a closed convex set in a Hilbert space is an example of a nonlinear procedure that can be explained in simple abstract terms. It is not normally viewed as a statistical method. Projection onto convex sets plays a role in image formation because the constraints on the image space are often convex. Moreover, the topic of projection onto convex sets can be expanded into the study of the powerful methods of alternating maximization [24], [70], [106]. These methods of alternating maximization applied to problems of information theory appeared earlier in the literature [3], [6] in the context of computing channel capacity and rate-distortion functions.

A general discussion of the topic of projection onto convex sets can be found in the paper of Combettes [17] and the work of Youla [106], Youla and Webb [108], and Segan and Stark [82]. The projection is unique and often can be found by analytically tractable methods, including iterative methods. Because the intersection of a finite number of convex sets $\mathcal{A}_\ell$ is convex, one may wish to project onto $\mathcal{A} = \cap_\ell \mathcal{A}_\ell$ by interatively projecting onto the individual $\mathcal{A}_\ell$. This procedure need not converge in general, but will always converge if the individual $\mathcal{A}_\ell$ are affine subspaces.

IX. MODALITIES AND APPLICATIONS

Some representative applications of information-theoretic imaging are described in this section. For each, the application is reviewed briefly and a likelihood model given for the data acquired for image formation. The applications are drawn from optical imaging, tomographic imaging, and radar imaging. The models include deterministic and random data, with the random data modeled by Poisson processes, Poisson–Gaussian mixtures, and Gaussian processes.

A. Deterministic Models

Imagation in which deterministic models are used for images and sensor data is often derived as a solution to a linear inverse problem in the form of a Fredholm integral equation

$$\int_X h(y,x)c(x) \, dx = a(y), \qquad y \in Y \qquad (119)$$

where $\{a(y), y \in Y\}$ are the sensor data, $\{h(y,x), y \in Y, x \in X\}$ is a (point-spread) function characterizing the sensor, and $\{c(x), x \in X\}$ is the image to be formed. Some examples that illustrate the nature of the image and data spaces, X and Y, respectively, and functions that are encountered are given next.

Optical Imaging In optical imaging problems, $a(\cdot)$ represents the data acquired by a camera, Y is typically a two-dimensional subset of the plane $\boldsymbol{R}^2$, $h(\cdot,\cdot)$ is the point-spread function of the optical elements of the camera, such as telescope and microscope lenses, field stops, and mirrors, $c(\cdot)$ is the scene being imaged, and X is typically a subset of $\boldsymbol{R}^2$ or $\boldsymbol{R}^3$. For coherent imaging, where phase information is maintained, the functions $a(\cdot)$, $h(\cdot,\cdot)$, and $c(\cdot)$ are complex-valued functions. For incoherent imaging, these functions are real-valued and nonnegative functions. For multispectral, hyperspectral, polarimetric, or spectropolarimetric imaging, these functions are vector-valued.

Tomographic Imaging In tomographic imaging problems, $a(\cdot)$ represents the logarithm of the data acquired by the tomograph, Y is typically a subset of $\boldsymbol{R}^n$, with $n = 2$ or $n = 3$ corresponding to planar or volumetric imaging, $h(\cdot,\cdot)$ is the point-spread function of the tomograph, $c(\cdot)$ is the X-ray absorption density being imaged, and X is typically a subset of $\boldsymbol{R}^2$ or $\boldsymbol{R}^3$. For example, in helical-scan X-ray tomographic imaging in the fan-beam geometry, $y \in Y$ is three-dimensional with $y = (\beta, \gamma, z)$, where β is the angular position of the X-ray source, γ is the angle of a particular source to detector element, and z is the axial position of the source, $x \in X$ is three-dimensional with $x = (x_1, x_2, x_3 = z)$ being the coordinates of a point location in the target volume, and, for perfectly collimated source–detector combinations

$$h(y,x) \equiv h(\gamma, \beta, z; x_1 x_2, x_3)$$
$$= \delta[D \sin\gamma - x_1 \cos(\beta + \gamma) - x_2 \sin(\beta + \gamma)]$$
$$\cdot \delta(z - x_3) \qquad (120)$$

where D is the distance from the source to the axis of rotation, $z = x_3 = p\beta$, and p is the pitch of the helical scan. All functions in the linear inverse problem of tomographic imaging are constrained to be nonnegative.

Radar Imaging Complex-valued reflectance functions and real, nonnegative scattering functions are images of radar targets formed from high-resolution radar range data. If the signal transmitted by the radar is $s_T(t)$, the ideal echo-signal received from a point reflector is $cs_T(t - \tau)e^{j2\pi f(t - \tau/2)}$, where c is the strength of the reflector, τ is the two-way propagation delay of the transmitted signal to and from the point reflector, and f is the Doppler frequency shift due to relative motion between the radar transmitter and the reflector along the line of sight. For a spatially extended reflector, the received signal to a first approximation is the superposition of the signal reflected from each point; this neglects, for example, secondary reflections of the signal from one location on the reflector to another before returning to the radar receiver. The received signal is then

$$a(t) = \int_{f_{\min}}^{f_{\max}} \int_{\tau_{\min}}^{\tau_{\max}} s_T(t-\tau)e^{j2\pi f(t-\tau/2)}c(f,\tau)\,df\,d\tau$$

$$(121)$$

where $(f_{\min}, f_{\max})$ is the range of Doppler shifts, $(\tau_{\min}, \tau_{\max})$ is the range of propagation delays that cover the reflector. This is in the form of (119) with Y being the time interval of the measurement, X being the two-dimensional space of delay-Doppler shifts

$$h(y,x) \equiv h(t; f, \tau) = s_T(t-\tau)e^{j2\pi f(t-\tau/2)}$$

and $c(x) \equiv c(f,\tau)$.

The linear inverse problem described (119) is routinely discretized to facilitate numerical solutions. While this can be accomplished in various ways, the result can generally be placed in the form of an algebraic, linear inverse problem of the form

$$\sum_x h(y,x)c(x) = a(y) \qquad (122)$$

where x and y are discrete-valued or, alternatively, in matrix–vector form

$$\boldsymbol{Hc} = \boldsymbol{a} \qquad (123)$$

in which $\boldsymbol{a}$ is a vector-valued discretization of the given data, $\boldsymbol{H}$ is a discretization of the kernel of the Fredholm equation (119), and $\boldsymbol{c}$ is a discretization of the unknown function that is sought. If $\boldsymbol{H}$ is invertible, then the obvious solution is $\boldsymbol{c} = \boldsymbol{H}^{-1}\boldsymbol{a}$. However, this ideal solution is usually impractical because $\boldsymbol{H}$ often is not invertible or is poorly conditioned so that solutions are extremely sensitive to the detailed choices made in designing a numerical implementation and to the effects of finite-precision arithmetic. Joyce and Root [53] provide a good discussion of this issue.

B. Stochastic Models

Sensor noise can be significant in inverse problems encountered in imaging. A variety of noise models are useful with the most successful results in applications occurring when the noise model selected is a good representation of the data-acquisition sensor being used. For radar sensors, an additive Gaussian model is a reasonable first choice, and for focal-plane arrays, such as a CCD camera, a Poisson model or a Poisson–Gaussian-mixture model is an appropriate initial choice. In stringent applications where high performance is sought, more refined models that account for significant effects present in a sensor must be formulated and used, so that, for example, nonuniformity of response and offset in focal plane arrays usually needs to be taken into account in scientific applications.

In the presence of additive Gaussian noise, the discrete inverse problem given by (119) becomes

$$r(y) = \sum_x h(y,x)c(x) + w(y), \qquad y \in Y$$

where $w(\cdot)$ is white with mean zero and variance σ^2, and the image recovery problem is to estimate $c(\cdot)$ given a realization of $r(\cdot)$. For describing photoconversion electrons in a focal-plane array, $a(\cdot)$ in (119) becomes a Poisson process $n(\cdot)$ with mean-value function $\sum_x h(y,x)c(x)$, and the restoration problem is to estimate $c(\cdot)$ from a realization of the Poisson process. If nonuniformity of response, offset, and thermoelectrons are significant, then the Poisson process $n(\cdot)$ modeling photoconversions has intensity $\beta(y)\sum_x h(y,x)c(x) + \mu_0(y)$. Here, $\beta(\cdot)$ and $\mu_0(\cdot)$ are functions that account for nonuniformity and offset, respectively; these functions are routinely determined in calibration measurements using a flat field and a dark field exposure of the focal-plane array. If read-out noise is a significant factor in a focal-plane-array sensor, then (119) becomes

$$r(y) = n(y) + w(y), \qquad y \in Y \qquad (124)$$

where $n(\cdot)$ is a Poisson process modeling photoconversions and offset, and $w(\cdot)$ is an independent, white, Gaussian process modeling read-out noise. The mean-value function of $n(\cdot)$ is

$$E[n(y)] = \beta(y)\sum_x h(y,x)c(x) + \mu_0(y) \qquad (125)$$

and the mean and variance of $w(y)$ are m and σ^2.

The data log-likelihoods for each of these models is a functional of $c(\cdot)$ that is fundamental to the problem of estimating $c(\cdot)$ from the available data. For the additive Gaussian noise model, the data log-likelihood (when reduced to only terms that are c-dependent) is

$$L(c) = \frac{1}{N_0}\text{Re}\left[\sum_x \sum_y r^*(y)h(y,x)c(x)\right]$$
$$- \frac{1}{2N_0}\sum_y \left|\sum_x h(y,x)c(x)\right|^2. \qquad (126)$$

For the Poisson model, it is

$$L(c) = -\sum_y \sum_x \beta(y)h(y,x)c(x)$$
$$+ \sum_y \log\left[\sum_x h(y,x)c(x) + \mu_0(y)\right]n(y). \qquad (127)$$

And, for the Poisson–Gaussian-mixture model

$$L(c) = \sum_y \log\left[\sum_{n(j)} \frac{1}{n(j)!}\mu^{n(j)}(j)e^{-\mu(j)}e^{[r(j)-n(j)-m]^2/2\sigma^2}\right]$$

$$(128)$$

where

$$\mu(j) = \beta(y)\sum_x h(y,x)c(x) + \mu_0(y). \qquad (129)$$

The purpose of imagation is to recover or estimate the object $c(\cdot)$ given the data available. The method of maximum-likelihood estimation can be applied to this problem, and if there are constraints on the form of $c(\cdot)$ or if $c(\cdot)$ is a random process with a prior distribution, the method of maximum *a posteriori* probability estimation can be used. A closed-form solution is well known for the additive Gaussian model without constraints or a prior, which is $\hat{c} = (\boldsymbol{H}^T\boldsymbol{H})^{\#}\boldsymbol{H}^T\boldsymbol{a}$. However, a closed-form solution is not possible for the Poisson and Poisson–Gaussian-mixture models, and numerical solutions such as those discussed in the next section must be employed.

Regularization is often necessary in order to obtain acceptable restorations. This is because the stochastic inverse problems are usually ill-posed and numerically unstable. In some cases, discretization is imposed by the sensor used to acquire data, such as with a charge-coupled-device camera and other focal-plane arrays. Discretization of continuous data is one form of regularization, but this alone can lead to the problem of dimensional instability described by Tapia and Thompson [95]. Grenander sieves [42] can be used to introduce regularization as was done by Snyder and Miller [89]. With this method, estimates are restricted to a subset of the function space C supporting $c(\cdot)$. The size of this subset is controlled by the amount of data available to perform the estimation, such that the subset grows as the amount of data increases, but the rate of growth is controlled so that the estimate of $c(\cdot)$ converges in a stable manner. Alternatively, regularization can be introduced via a penalty function $\Phi(c)$ that enforces smoothness (see O'Sullivan [69]). With penalty methods, the estimate maximizes the penalized log-likelihood $L(c) + \alpha\Phi(c)$, where α is a Lagrange multiplier that controls the emphasis given to the data log-likelihood and the penalty function when selecting the maximizer. When $c(\cdot)$ is a random process with a prior $p(c)$, the MAP estimate of $c(\cdot)$ is obtained by maximizing $L(c) + \log p(c)$. It is evident that many penalized maximum-likelihood estimation problems are equivalent to MAP estimation problems by defining $p(c) = \frac{1}{Z}e^{\alpha\Phi(c)}$, where Z is a normalization constant; for this equivalence to hold, Z must be finite, so that the prior defined in this way is proper.

C. An Application Modeled by Gaussian Data

For sensors that exhibit additive Gaussian noise $w(\cdot)$, (119) becomes

$$\int_X h(y,x)c(x)\,dx + w(y) = a(y), \qquad y \in Y \qquad (130)$$

for which the discrete version, analogous to (130) is

$$\boldsymbol{H}\boldsymbol{c} + \boldsymbol{w} = \boldsymbol{a}. \qquad (131)$$

If $\boldsymbol{c}$ is deterministic and $\boldsymbol{w}$ has zero mean, the data log-likelihood is

$$L(\boldsymbol{c}) = 2\mathrm{Re}\,(\boldsymbol{r}^{\dagger}\boldsymbol{W}^{-1}\boldsymbol{H}\boldsymbol{c}) - \boldsymbol{c}^{\dagger}\boldsymbol{H}^{\dagger}\boldsymbol{W}^{-1}\boldsymbol{H}\boldsymbol{c} \qquad (132)$$

when terms that do not involve $\boldsymbol{c}$ are neglected, where the superscript $\dagger$ denotes the Hermitian transpose.

A model used for spectrum estimation and radar imaging arises when $\boldsymbol{c}$ has a prior distribution that is Gaussian with zero mean and diagonal covariance $\boldsymbol{\Sigma}$ [67], [71], [91]. The ij element, σ_{ij}^2, of $\boldsymbol{\Sigma}$ corresponds to the power gain of the signal reflected from the ij pixel in the pixelized representation of the object's scattering function in delay-Doppler coordinates.

In this case, the data a are Gaussian-distributed with zero mean and covariance $\boldsymbol{K}_a = \boldsymbol{H}^{\dagger}\boldsymbol{\Sigma}\boldsymbol{H} + N_0 I$, assuming that the noise $\boldsymbol{w}$ is white Gaussian with zero mean and covariance $\boldsymbol{W} = N_0 I$, so the probability density of $\boldsymbol{a}$ is

$$p(\boldsymbol{r} : \boldsymbol{\Sigma}) = \pi^{-N}(\det \boldsymbol{K}_a)^{-1}\exp\left(-\boldsymbol{a}^{\dagger}\boldsymbol{K}_a^{-1}\boldsymbol{a}\right)$$

where N is the dimension of $\boldsymbol{a}$. The problem of forming the scattering-function image is that of estimating the diagonal matrix $\boldsymbol{\Sigma}$ from some given data set $\boldsymbol{r}$. The log-likelihood function is

$$L(\boldsymbol{\Sigma}) = -\log\det\left(\boldsymbol{H}^{\dagger}\boldsymbol{\Sigma}\boldsymbol{H} + N_0 I\right) - \boldsymbol{a}^{\dagger}(\boldsymbol{H}^{\dagger}\boldsymbol{\Sigma}\boldsymbol{H} + N_0 I)^{-1}\boldsymbol{a}.$$
$$(133)$$

The maximization of $L(\boldsymbol{\Sigma})$ with respect to $\boldsymbol{\Sigma}$ is in the class of problems studied by Burg, Luenberger, and Wenger [10] for spectrum estimation and in [67], [71], [91] for radar imaging. The following algorithm, derived using the EM method, was used in the radar imaging context by Snyder, O'Sullivan, and Miller [91].

Step 0. Choose an initial estimate $\hat{\Sigma}^{(0)}$, set $k = 0$;
Step 1. Evaluate $\hat{c}^{(k)}$ and $\hat{\Sigma}^{(k+1)}$ according to

$$\hat{c}^{(k)} = \hat{\Sigma}^{(k)}\boldsymbol{H}(\boldsymbol{H}^{\dagger}\hat{\Sigma}^{(k)}\boldsymbol{H} + N_0 I)^{-1}\boldsymbol{a} \qquad (134)$$
$$\hat{\Sigma}^{(k+1)} = \hat{\Sigma}^{(k)} - \hat{\Sigma}^{(k)}\boldsymbol{H}(\boldsymbol{H}^{\dagger}\hat{\Sigma}^{(k)}\boldsymbol{H} + N_0 I)^{-1}\boldsymbol{H}^{\dagger}\hat{\Sigma}^{(k)\dagger}$$
$$+ \hat{c}^{(k)}\hat{c}^{(k)\dagger}; \qquad (135)$$

Step 2. $k \leftarrow k + 1$;
Step 3. Repeat Step 1 until done.

D. An Application Modeled by Poisson Data

Scintillation detectors are used to sense photons emanating from radioactive decays in a radionuclide. Some radionuclides emit a single photon in each decay, as occurs in SPECT (single-photon-emission computed tomography) systems used in nuclear medicine. A decay in other radionuclides results in a positron, which interacts quickly with a nearby electron, resulting in two annihilation photons that propagate in nearly opposite directions away from the annihilation site, as in PET (positron-emission tomography) systems [90, Ch. 3]. A decay or an annihilation is called an *event*. Through the measurement of single-photon events or annihilation-pair events (typically, for PET, about 10^6 events per planar section, acquired in a time interval on the order of 10 to 20 min), the objective is to form an image displaying an estimate of the spatial distribution or concentration of the radionuclide. Three-dimensional, volumetric imaging is sought. This is usually accomplished by means of a sequence of planar images spanning the volume of interest, with each planar image being treated independently of others; however, direct volumetric imaging that accounts for intravolume dependencies has been demonstrated to be more accurate [60].

To obtain estimates of radionuclide concentrations, models for scintillation data must account for the photon-fluctuation statistics of radioactive decay and for the effects that occur when photons propagate through a scattering medium to reach detectors. The models that are used account only approximately for some effects and neglect others altogether. For example, photon scattering (that is, deviation of a photon's flight path from a straight line due to Compton and photoelastic scattering) is usually only roughly accommodated using an attenuation function, an additive and independent "photon" noise in PET, and a point-response function that is broader than would be predicted by the finite size and geometry of scintillation detectors alone. Photons that are undetected due to finite recovery time in a scintillation detector are neglected. While these effects can be significant in practice, they are usually neglected to keep data models tractable.

A source-channel model for event detections is a useful conceptual framework for formulating the problem of estimating the radionuclide distribution. It can be formulated as follows. The source produces points representing random locations of radioactive decays or positron–electron annihilations in the region containing a radionuclide. Let $\mathcal{X}$ be the source-output space. This is the space where events occur; an individual event occurs as a point at position $x \in \mathcal{X}$. This source space can be a subset of $\boldsymbol{R}^2$ (planar SPECT and PET), $\boldsymbol{R}^3$ (volumetric SPECT and PET), $\boldsymbol{R}^2 \times \boldsymbol{R}_+$ (PET in which the differential time-of-flight of the annihilation photon pair is measured [93]), and perhaps other parameters, depending on the sensor configuration. The channel, representing the sensor system, produces outputs that are points in a channel-output space Y. A detected event occurs as a point at a random position $y \in \mathcal{Y}$. The elements of y depend on the sensor configuration. In SPECT, for example, $y = (p_1, p_2, \theta)$ and $Y = \boldsymbol{R}^2 \times [0, 2\pi)$, where (p_1, p_2) are the measured positions of the detection event in the scintillation crystal of the Anger camera, and θ is the angle of the camera in its orbit. In PET, y parameterizes the flight line of annihilation photons and, in time-of-flight PET, the flight-line parameters along with the differential propagation time. The channel can map a source point at x into channel-output point at y, or it can delete the source point (corresponding to an absorbed photon), and it can add extraneous points (accounting in part for photon scatter).

A reasonable model for the source, based on the physics of radioactive decay, is that the source produces points as an inhomogeneous Poisson process, denoted by $\{N(A), A \in \sigma(X)\}$, having an intensity function that is proportional to the concentration of the radionuclide. Let $\{\lambda(x), x \in \mathcal{X}\}$ denote the intensity function of the source.

We assume that the channel action on individual source points is independent from point to point. Let $\{p(y|x), x \in \mathcal{X}, y \in \mathcal{Y}\}$ denote the transition probability-density of the channel; given that the source produces a point at x and that this point is detected, this is the density of the random location of the detection in the channel-output space. This transition density of the channel is the normalized point-spread function of the sensor. Let $\beta(y|x)$ denote the probability that a source point at x that is headed towards an output location y is detected (this is the photon survival probability), and let $\alpha(y|x) = 1 - \beta(y \mid x)$ be the probability that the source point is undetected (this is the photon-absorption probability). Finally, we assume that the channel can introduce extraneous (noise) points into its output and that these occur as an independent, inhomogeneous Poisson process with intensity $\{\mu_0(y), y \in \mathcal{Y}\}$. It follows from these assumptions, as was dis-

cussed by Miller and Snyder [62], that the channel output is also an inhomogeneous Poisson process, denoted by $\{M(B), B \in \sigma(\mathcal{Y})\}$, with intensity function $\{\mu(u), y \in \mathcal{Y}\}$, where

$$\mu(y) = \int_{\mathcal{X}} \beta(y \mid x) p(y \mid x) \lambda(x) \, dx + \mu_0(y). \quad (136)$$

Thus the log-likelihood functional of the channel-output process is given by (see Snyder and Miller [90, Chs. 2 and 3] for further discussion of this point)

$$l(\lambda) = -\int_{\mathcal{Y}} \mu(y) \, dy + \int_{\mathcal{Y}} \log[\mu(y)] \, M(dy). \quad (137)$$

The problem is to estimate the source intensity given the measured channel output points and the source-channel model. This problem was first formulated for emission tomography by Rockmore and Macovski [76] in 1976 using maximum-likelihood estimation, but their direct formulation proved to be intractable for producing maximum-likelihood estimates. It was not made computationally tractable until Shepp and Vardi [84] and Lange and Carson [58] applied the EM method to this estimation problem. Following this work, many subsequent publications have extended the approach. Recognizing that the EM algorithm will be implemented computationally, the first step is to discretize the source-output space and the channel-output space into pixels or voxels, then let $\{N(x), x \in \mathcal{X}\}$ and $\{M(y), y \in \mathcal{Y}\}$ denote the source-output and channel-output Poisson processes on the discrete spaces, where $N(x)$ is the number of single or annihilation-pair photons occurring in pixel x, and $M(y)$ is the number of detection events in pixel y. The log-likelihood functional of the channel-output process becomes

$$l(\lambda) = \sum_{y \in \mathcal{Y}} \mu(y) + \sum_{y \in \mathcal{Y}} \log[\mu(y)] M(y) \quad (138)$$

where

$$\mu(y) = \sum_{x \in \mathcal{X}} \beta(y \mid x) p(y \mid x) \lambda(x) + \mu_0(y). \quad (139)$$

Depending on the choice of complete data, Politte and Snyder [74] identify the choice of two algorithms formed by the EM method. The algorithm formed by the EM method will be either

$$\hat{\lambda}^{(k+1)}(x) = \hat{\lambda}^{(k)}(x) \left\{ \bar{\alpha}(x) + \sum_{y \in \mathcal{Y}} \left[\frac{\beta(y \mid x) p(y \mid x)}{\hat{\mu}^{(k)}(y)} \right] M(y) \right\} \quad (140)$$

or

$$\hat{\lambda}^{(k+1)}(x) = \hat{\lambda}^{(k)}(x) \frac{1}{\bar{\beta}(x)} \sum_{y \in \mathcal{Y}} \left[\frac{\beta(y \mid x) p(y \mid x)}{\hat{\mu}^{(k)}(y)} \right] M(y) \quad (141)$$

depending on the choice of complete data, where

$$\bar{\beta}(x) = 1 - \bar{\alpha}(x) = \sum_{y \in Y} \beta(y \mid x) p(y \mid x)$$

and where

$$\hat{\mu}^{(k)}(y) = \int_X \beta(y \mid x) p(y \mid x) \hat{\lambda}^{(k)}(x)\, dx + \mu_0(y). \quad (142)$$

While these two EM algorithms converge towards the same limit point, their convergence rates differ, with the second one converging more rapidly [74]. This shows that the choice of complete data does influence algorithm behavior.

The SPECT and PET inverse problems are ill-posed, so that regularization to stabilize solutions is needed. Sieves and roughness penalties have been used for this purpose [61], [74], [89].

Data acquired in optical imaging systems are also often modeled as Poisson-distributed. One important area where such models along with information-based image recovery has been used effectively is in addressing the long-standing and difficult problem faced by astronomers of forming images of objects seen through clear-air atmospheric turbulence. Roggemann and Welsh [77] review the classic methods of Labeyrie (recovery from Fourier modulus), of Knox and Thompson (recovery from squared Fourier modulus or second-order correlations), and of Weigelt (recovery from third-order correlations) developed and used effectively by astronomers for this problem. A new method of recovery of an object's image from known second-order and higher order correlation functions of the image has been developed by Snyder and Schulz [79], [80], [86], based on a Poisson data model and the use of maximum-likelihood estimation. Paxman, Schulz, and Fienup [72] and Seldin and Paxman [81] have introduced a new data-collection approach in which multiple, phase-diverse snapshots of an object seen through turbulence are used with a Poisson data model and constrained maximum-likelihood estimation to produce substantially improved object images.

E. An Application Modeled by Poisson–Gaussian Data

The following source-channel model is a useful framework for characterizing a wide variety of applications when a charge-couple-device (CCD) camera is used to image scenes in the visible and infrared portions of the spectrum. A discrete model is used because a CCD camera produces data from a pixel array and, also, because an EM algorithm will be used to perform imagation. We envision a scene that emits incoherent radiation that propagates towards a CCD camera. Light falling onto the focal plane of the camera has an intensity given by

$$i(y) = \sum_{x \in \mathcal{X}} h(y \mid x)\lambda(x), \qquad y \in \mathcal{Y} \quad (143)$$

where $\{h(y|x), x \in \mathcal{X}, y \in \mathcal{Y}\}$ is the point-spread function of the camera, $\{\lambda(x), x \in \mathcal{X}\}$ is the radiance of the scene, and are the source-output and channel-output spaces, respectively. For light that propagates through free space or through short paths in the atmosphere, the point-spread function is determined by the configuration of optical elements in the camera [39], [40], including pupil shape, obscurations, and any aberrations that are present. The number $M(y)$ of photoelectron conversions occurring during a T-second exposure interval in a pixel at y in the CCD array is Poisson-distributed with mean $\mu(y) = T\beta(y)i(y)$, where $\beta(y)$ accounts for nonuniform quantum

efficiency, pattern noise, bad pixels, and charge-transfer inefficiency. By assumption, the number of photoconversions is independent from pixel to pixel. The process of reading out the pixel values results in the channel-output process

$$R(y) = M(y) + M_0(y) + G(y), \qquad y \in \mathcal{Y} \quad (144)$$

where $\{M_0(y), y \in \mathcal{Y}\}$ is a Poisson-distributed process that accounts for extraneous thermoelectrons and for offset bias in the CCD array, and $\{G(y), y \in \mathcal{Y}\}$ is a Gaussian-distributed process accounting for noise in the readout amplifier integrated into the CCD array circuit [88]. The processes $M(\cdot)$, $M_0(\cdot)$, and $G(\cdot)$ are mutually independent and independent from pixel to pixel. The mean-value function for $\{M_0(y), y \in \mathcal{Y}\}$ is assumed to be the known function $\{\mu_0(y), y \in \mathcal{Y}\}$, and $\{G(y), y \in \mathcal{Y}\}$ is assumed to have a constant mean m and variance σ^2.

For imagation, it is convenient to embed the scene in a hypothetical stochastic process, which can be regarded as the output of the source in the source-channel model. Thus we imagine a Poisson-distributed process $\{N(x), x \in \mathcal{X}\}$ having intensity $\{\lambda(x), x \in \mathcal{X}\}$; one can regard the points of this process as "photons" emanating from the scene. The source output is the set of points (or counts in the discrete model) of this hypothetical process in the source space $\mathcal{X}$. This contrived source model is legitimate because the photoconversion process $\{M(y), y \in \mathcal{Y}\}$ will be a Poisson process with mean function $\{\mu(y), y \in \mathcal{Y}\}$ when the source output $\{N(y), y \in \mathcal{Y}\}$ is a Poisson process with mean function $\{\lambda(y), y \in \mathcal{Y}\}$ and

$$\mu(y) = T\beta(y) \sum_{x \in \mathcal{X}} h(y \mid x)\lambda(x), \qquad y \in \mathcal{Y}. \quad (145)$$

The channel, representing the camera, maps the output of the source into the channel-output process $\{R(y), y \in \mathcal{Y}\}$, which is a Poisson–Gaussian mixture. The log-likelihood functional for the channel output is

$$\ell(\lambda) = \sum_{y \in \mathcal{Y}} \log\left(\frac{1}{n(y)!}[\mu(y)+\mu_0(y)]^{n(y)} \exp\{-[\mu(y)+\mu_0(y)]\} \right.$$
$$\left. \cdot \frac{1}{\sqrt{2\pi\sigma^2}} \exp\{-[R(y)-n(y)-m]^2/2\sigma^2\} \right).$$
$$(146)$$

Selecting complete data and applying the EM algorithm yields [88]

$$\hat{\lambda}^{(k+1)}(x) = \hat{\lambda}^{(k)}(x)\frac{1}{\bar{\beta}(x)}\sum_{y \in \mathcal{Y}}\left[\frac{\beta(y)p(y \mid x)}{\hat{\mu}^{(k)}(y)} \right] f[R(y), \hat{\mu}^{(k)}, \sigma]$$
$$(147)$$

where

$$f[r, \mu, \sigma] = \frac{\displaystyle\sum_{n=0}^{\infty}(n/n!)\exp[-(r-n-m)^2/2\sigma^2]}{\displaystyle\sum_{n=0}^{\infty}(1/n!)\mu^n \exp v[-(r-n-m)^2/2\sigma^2]} \quad (148)$$

and

$$\hat{\mu}^{(k)}(y) = T\beta(y) \sum_{x \in \mathcal{X}} h(y \mid x)\hat{\lambda}^{(k)}(x) + \mu_0(y), \qquad y \in \mathcal{Y}. \tag{149}$$

Evaluation of the function $f[\cdots]$ through the use of saddle-point integration and approximations, with applications to Hubble Space Telescope imagery, is discussed by Snyder, Helstrom, Lanterman, Faisal, and White [87].

X. CONCLUSIONS AND FUTURE DIRECTIONS

An information-theoretic framework for imaging is in the earliest stages of development but can already be seen as the basis for data models, performance metrics, and processing strategies for treating image formation problems. An all-encompassing model has yet to be formulated that can play as powerful a role for imaging as Shannon's source-channel model plays for communications. Nonetheless, the importance that information-theoretic concepts already play leads us to predict that such a formal model will eventually emerge.

Image formation often involves optimization of metrics rooted in information theory, such as likelihood, divergence, discrimination, and entropy. For such methods, it is not only a requirement but also a strength that accurate models must be available for scenes, for the environment between scenes and sensors, and for the image-related data produced by sensors. These models need to account generally for the way that the underlying physics governs the production of the observed data at each stage along the way. Deterministic and stochastic models may appear different on the surface, but image-formation methods based on the optimization of information-theoretic metrics of discrimination and likelihood share many common features. Scenes exhibit great complexity and variability; methods for modeling scenes are evolving rapidly and are already sophisticated mathematically, but in many respects, available models are still too limited to accommodate effects that can have a pronounced influence on the performance of imaging systems, such as clutter that surrounds and often obscures objects to be identified in a scene. Propagation effects in optical imaging applications, such as scattering in turbid media and phase and amplitude fluctuations in turbulent media cannot be easily modeled. Sensor technology is complicated and evolves rapidly so that models for sensor data often have limited accuracy. The future effectiveness of information-theoretic approaches to image formation will rely on addressing these modeling issues.

ACKNOWLEDGMENT

The authors wish to thank the editors for inviting them to participate in the fifty-year anniversary of Information Theory through this contribution. They are grateful to Dr. Pierre Moulin, to Dr. Alfred O. Hero III, to Dr. Aaron Lanterman, to Dr. G. David Forney, Jr., and to Dr. Bruce Hajek for reading drafts of the manuscript and providing many helpful comments.

REFERENCES

[1] S. M. Ali and S. D. Silvey, "A general class of coefficients of divergence of one distribution from another," *J. Roy. Statist. Soc. Ser. B*, vol. 28, pp. 131–142, 1966.

[2] S. Amari, *Differential-Geometrical Methods in Statistics* (Lecture Notes in Statistics, vol. 28). Berlin, Germany: Springer-Verlag, 1985.

[3] S. Arimoto, "An algorithm for computing the capacity of an arbitrary discrete memoryless channel," *IEEE Trans. Inform. Theory*, vol. IT-18, pp. 14–20, 1972.

[4] J. Besag, "Spatial interaction and the statistical analysis of lattice systems," *J. Roy. Statist. Soc.*, vol. 36, pp. 192–236, 1974.

[5] A. Blake and A. Zisserman, *Visual Reconstruction*. Cambridge, MA: MIT Press, 1987.

[6] R. E. Blahut, "Computation of channel capacity and rate distortion functions," *IEEE Trans. Inform. Theory*, vol. IT-18, pp. 460–473, 1972.

[7] L. M. Bregmen, "The relaxation method of finding the common point of convex sets and its application to the solution of problems in convex programming," *U.S.S.R. Comp. Math. and Math. Phys.*, vol. 7, pp. 200–217, 1967.

[8] J. Browne and A. R. De Pierro, "A row-action alternative to the EM algorithm for maximizing likelihoods in emission tomography," *IEEE Trans. Med. Imag.*, vol. 15, pp. 687–699, Oct. 1996.

[9] J. A. Bucklew, *Large Deviation Techniques in Decision, Simulation, and Estimation*. New York: Wiley, 1990.

[10] J. P. Burg, D. G. Luenberger, and D. L. Wenger, "Estimation of structured covariance matrices," *Proc. IEEE*, vol. 70, pp. 963–974, Sept. 1982.

[11] C. S. Butler and M. I. Miller, "Maximum a posteriori estimation for single photon emission computed tomography using regularization techniques on a massively parallel computer," *IEEE Trans. Med. Imag.*, vol. 12, pp. 84–89, Mar. 1993.

[12] C. L. Byrne, "Iterative image reconstruction algorithms based on cross-entropy minimization," *IEEE Trans. Image Processing*, vol. 2, pp. 96–103, Jan. 1993.

[13] R. Chellappa, *Markov Random Fields: Theory and Applications*. New York: Academic, 1993.

[14] P. A. Chou, M. Effros, and R. M. Gray, "A vector quantization approach to universal noiseless coding and quantization," *IEEE Trans. Inform. Theory*, vol. 42, pp. 1109–1138, July 1996.

[15] Y. Chow and U. Grenander, "A sieve method for the spectral density," *Ann. Stat.*, vol. 13, no. 3, pp. 998–1010, 1985.

[16] C. K. Chui, *Multivariate Splines*. Philadelphia, PA: SIAM, 1988.

[17] P. L. Combettes, "The foundation of set theoretic estimation," *Proc. IEEE*, vol. 81, pp. 182–208, 1993.

[18] T. M. Cover, "An algorithm for maximizing expected log investment return," *IEEE Trans. Inform. Theory*, vol. IT-30, pp. 369–373, 1984.

[19] T. M. Cover and J. A. Thomas, *Elements of Information Theory*. New York: Wiley, 1991.

[20] I. Csiszár, "Information-type measures of difference of probability distributions and indirect observations," *Studia Sci. Math. Hungar.*, vol. 2, pp. 299–318, 1967.

[21] _____, "I-divergence geometry of probability distributions and minimization problems," *Ann. Prob.*, vol. 3, no. 1, pp. 146–158, 1975.

[22] _____, "A geometric interpretation of Darroch and Ratcliff's generalized iterative scaling," *Ann. Stat.*, vol. 17, no. 3, pp. 1409–1413, 1989.

[23] _____, "Why least squares and maximum entropy? An axiomatic approach to inference for linear inverse problems," *Ann. Stat.*, vol. 19, pp. 2032–2066, 1991.

[24] I. Csiszár and G. Tusnady, "Information geometry and alternating decisions," *Stat. Decisions*, Suppl. issue no. 1, pp. 205–207, 1984.

[25] J. N. Darroch and D. Ratcliff, "Generalized iterative scaling for log-linear models," *Ann. Math. Stat.*, vol. 43, no. 5, pp. 1470–1480, 1972.

[26] I. Daubechies, *Ten Lectures on Wavelets*. Philadelphia, PA: SIAM, 1992.

[27] A. P. Dempster, N. M. Laird, and D. B. Rubin, "Maximum likelihood from incomplete data via the EM algorithm," *J. Roy. Stat. Soc. Ser. B*, vol. 39, pp. 1–37, 1977.

[28] D. L. Donoho and I. M. Johnstone, "Ideal spatial adaptation via wavelet shrinkage," *Biometrika*, vol. 81, pp. 425–455, 1994.

[29] D. L. Donoho, "De-noising by soft-thresholding," *IEEE Trans. Inform. Theory*, vol. 41, pp. 613–627, May 1995.

[30] D. L. Donoho *et al.* "Wavelet shrinkage: Asymptotia?" (with discussion), *J. Roy. Stat. Soc. B*, vol. 57, no. 2, pp. 301–369, 1995.

[31] R. S. Ellis, *Entropy, Large Deviations, and Statistical Mechanics*. New York: Springer-Verlag, 1985.

[32] J. A. Fessler and A. O. Hero, "Space alternating generalized expectation-maximization algorithm," *IEEE Trans. Signal Processing*, vol. 42, pp.

2664–2677, 1994.

[33] ——, "Penalized maximum likelihood image reconstruction using space alternating generalized EM algorithms," *IEEE Trans. Image Processing*, vol. 4, pp. 1417–1429, Oct. 1995.

[34] S. Geman and D. Geman, "Stochastic relaxation, Gibbs' distributions, and Bayesian restoration of images," *IEEE Trans. Pattern Anal. Mach. Intell.*, vol. PAMI-6, pp. 721–741, Nov. 1984.

[35] S. Geman and C.-R. Hwang, "Diffusions for global optimization," *SIAM J. Contr. Optimiz.*, vol. 24, pp. 1031–1043, 1987.

[36] A. Gersho and R. M. Gray, *Vector Quantization and Signal Compression*. Boston, MA: Kluwer, 1992.

[37] G. H. Golub and C. F. Van Loan, *Matrix Computations*, 3rd ed. Baltimore, MD: Johns Hopkins Univ. Press, 1996.

[38] I. J. Good and R. A. Gaskins, "Nonparametric roughness penalties for probability densities," *Biometrika*, vol. 58, pp. 255–277, 1971.

[39] J. W. Goodman, *Statistical Optics*. New York: Wiley-Interscience, 1986.

[40] ——, *Fourier Optics*. New York: McGraw-Hill, 1985.

[41] J. D. Gorman and A. O. Hero, "Lower bounds for parameter estimation with constraints," *IEEE Trans. Inform. Theory*, vol. 36, pp. 1285–1301, Nov. 1990.

[42] U. Grenander, *Abstract Inference*. New York: Wiley, 1981.

[43] U. Grenander and M. I. Miller, "Representations of knowledge in complex systems," *J. Roy. Stat. Soc., Ser. B*, vol. 56, pp. 549–603, 1994.

[44] U. Grenander, M. I. Miller, and A. Srivastava, "Hilbert–Schmidt lower bounds for estimators on matrix Lie groups," *IEEE Trans. Pattern Anal. Mach. Intell.*, to be published.

[45] R. M. Haralick and L. G. Shapiro, *Computer and Robot Vision*, vols. 1 and 2. Reading, MA: Addison-Wesley, 1993.

[46] C. Heil, "Wavelets and frames," in *Signal Processing Part I: Signal Processing Theory*, L. Auslander *et al.*, Eds. New York: Springer-Verlag, 1990.

[47] A. Hero and J. A. Fessler, "A recursive algorithm for computing Cramer–Rao type bounds on estimator covariance," *IEEE Trans. Inform. Theory*, vol. 40, pp. 1205–1210, July 1994.

[48] A. O. Hero, M. Usman, A. C. Sauve, and J. A. Fessler, "Recursive algorithms for computing the Cramer–Rao bound," *IEEE Trans. Signal Processing*, vol. 45, pp. 803–807, Mar. 1997.

[49] H. M. Hudson and R. S. Larkin, "Accelerated image reconstruction using ordered subsets of projection data," *IEEE Trans. Med. Imag.*, vol. 13, pp. 601–609, Aug. 1994.

[50] F. Itakura and S. Saito, "Analysis synthesis telephony based on the maximum likelihood method," in *Repts. 6th Int. Congr. Acoustics*, Y. Kohasi, Ed. (Tokyo, Japan, 1968), pp. 17–20.

[51] E. T. Jaynes, "On the rationale of maximum entropy methods," *Proc. IEEE*, vol. 70, pp. 939–952, 1982.

[52] L. K. Jones and C. L. Byrne, "General entropy criteria for inverse problems, with applications to data compression, pattern classification and cluster analysis," *IEEE Trans. Inform. Theory*, vol. 36, pp. 23–30, 1990.

[53] L. S. Joyce and W. L. Root, "Precision bounds in superresolution processing," *J. Opt. Soc. Amer. A*, vol. 1, pp. 149–168, 1984.

[54] A. Kirsch, "An introduction to the mathematical theory of inverse problems," *Applied Mathematical Sciences*, vol. 120. Berlin, Germany: Springer-Verlag, 1996.

[55] S. Kullback, *Information Theory and Statistics*. New York: Wiley, 1959; Dover, 1968.

[56] S. Kullback and M. A. Khairat, "A note on minimum discrimination information," *Ann. Math. Stat.*, vol. 37, pp. 279–280, 1966.

[57] S. Kullback and R. A. Leibler, "On information and sufficiency," *Ann. Math. Stat.*, vol. 22, pp. 79–86, 1951.

[58] K. Lange and R. Carson, "EM reconstruction algorithms for emission and transmission tomography," *J. Comp. Assist. Tomogr.*, vol. 8, no. 2, pp. 306–316, 1984.

[59] A. D. Lanterman, M. I. Miller, and D. L. Snyder, "General metropolis-hastings jump diffusions for automatic target recognition in infrared scenes," *Opt. Eng.*, vol. 36, pp. 1123–1137, 1997.

[60] M. I. Miller and C. S. Butler, "3-D maximum a posteriori estimation for single photon emission computed tomography on massively parallel computers," *IEEE Trans. Med. Imag.*, vol. 12, pp. 560–565, Sept. 1993.

[61] M. I. Miller and B. Roysam, "Bayesian image reconstruction for emission tomography: Implementation of the EM algorithm and good's roughness prior on massively parallel processors," *Proc. Nat. Acad. Sci.*, vol. 88, pp. 3223–3227, 1991.

[62] M. I. Miller and D. L. Snyder, "The role of likelihood and entropy in incomplete-data problems: Applications to estimating point-process intensities and toeplitz and constrained covariances," *Proc. IEEE*, vol. 75, pp. 892–907, 1987.

[63] M. I. Miller, A. Srivastava, and U. Grenander, "Conditional-mean estimation via jump-diffusion processes in multiple target tracking and recognition," *IEEE Trans. Signal Processing*, vol. 43, pp. 2678–2690, 1995.

[64] P. Moulin, "A method of sieves for radar imaging and spectrum estimation," D.Sc. dissertation, Dept. Elec. Eng. Washington Univ., St. Louis, MO, 1990.

[65] ——, "A multiscale relaxation technique for SNR maximization in nonorthogonal subband coding," *IEEE Trans. Image Processing*, vol. 4, pp. 1269–1281, Sept. 1995.

[66] P. Moulin and J. Liu, "Analysis of multiresolution image denoising schemes using generalized-gaussian and complexity priors," preprint, submitted for publication.

[67] P. Moulin, J. A. O'Sullivan, and D. L. Snyder, "A method of sieves for multiresolution spectrum estimation and radar imaging," *IEEE Trans. Inform. Theory*, vol. 38, pp. 801–813, 1992.

[68] M. Nikolova, J. Idier, and A. Mohammad-Djafari, "Inversion of large-support Ill-posed linear operators using a piecewise Gaussian MRF," *IEEE Trans. Image Processing*, vol. 7, pp. 571–585, Apr. 1998.

[69] J. A. O'Sullivan, "Roughness penalties on finite domains," *IEEE Trans. Image Processing*, vol. 4, pp. 1258–1268, Sept. 1995.

[70] ——, "Alternating minimization algorithms: From Blahut–Arimoto to expectation–maximization," in *Codes, Curves, and Signals: Common Threads in Communications*, A. Vardy, Ed. Norwell, MA: Kluwer, 1998.

[71] J. A. O'Sullivan, D. L. Snyder, D. G. Porter, and P. Moulin, "An application of splines to maximum likelihood radar imaging," *J. Imaging Syst. Technol.*, vol. 4, pp. 256–264, 1992.

[72] R. G. Paxman, T. J. Schulz, and J. R. Fienup, "Joint estimation of object and aberrations by using phase diversity," *J. Opt. Soc. Amer. A*, vol. 9, pp. 1072–11085, July 1992.

[73] D. G. Politte, "Reconstruction algorithms for time-of-flight assisted positron-emission tomography," M.S.E.E. thesis, Sch. Eng. Appl. Sci., Washington Univ., St. Louis, MO, 1983.

[74] D. G. Politte and D. L. Snyder, "Corrections for accidental coincidences in maximum-likelihood image reconstruction for position-emission tomography," *IEEE Trans. Med. Imag.*, vol. 10, pp. 82–89, 1991.

[75] D. D. Robertson, J. Yuan, G. Wang, and M. W. Vannier, "Total hip prosthesis metal-artifact suppression using iterative deblurring reconstruction," *J. Comp. Assist. Tomogr.*, vol. 21, pp. 293–298, 1997.

[76] A. Rockmore and A. Macovski, "A maximum likelihood approach to emission image reconstruction from projections," *IEEE Trans. Nucl. Sci.*, vol. NS-23, pp. 1428–1432, 1976.

[77] M. C. Roggemann and B. Welsh, *Imaging Through Turbulence*. New York: CRC Press, 1996.

[78] I. N. Sanov, "On the probability of large deviations of random variance," *Matem. Sbornik*, vol. 42, pp. 11–44, 1957.

[79] T. J. Schulz and D. L. Snyder, "Imaging a randomly moving object from quantum-limited data: Applications to image recovery from second- and third-order autocorrelations," *J. Opt. Soc. Amer. A*, vol. 8, pp. 801–807, May 1991.

[80] ——, "Image recovery from correlations," *J. Opt. Soc. Amer. A*, vol. 9, pp. 1266–1272, Aug. 1992.

[81] J. H. Seldin and R. G. Paxman, "Phase-diverse speckle reconstruction of solar data," in *Proc. SPIE Conf. 2302*, July 1994.

[82] M. I. Sezan and H. Stark, "Image restoration by the method of convex projections: Part 2—Applications and numerical results," *IEEE Trans. Med. Imag.*, vol. MI-1, pp. 95–101, 1982.

[83] C. E. Shannon, "A mathematical theory of communication," *Bell Syst. Tech. J.*, vol. 27, pp. 379–423, 1948.

[84] L. A. Shepp and Y. Vardi, "Maximum likelihood reconstruction for emission tomography," *IEEE Trans. Med. Imag.*, vol. MI-1, pp. 113–122, 1982.

[85] J. E. Shore and R. W. Johnson, "Axiomatic derivation of the principle of maximum entropy and the principle of minimum cros-entropy," *IEEE Trans, Inform. Theory*, vol. IT-26, pp. 26–37, Jan. 1980.

[86] D. L. Snyder and T. J. Schulz, "High-resolution imaging at low-light levels through weak turbulence," *J. Opt. Soc. Amer. A*, vol. 7, pp. 1251–1265, July 1990.

[87] D. L. Snyder, C. W. Helstrom, A. D. Lanterman, M. Faisal, and R. L. White, "Compensation for read-out noise in CCD images," *J. Opt. Soc. Amer. A*, vol. 12, pp. 272–283, 1995.

[88] D. L. Snyder, A. M. Hammoud, and R. L. White, "Image recovery from data acquired with a charge-coupled-device camera," *J. Opt. Soc. Amer. A*, vol. 10, pp. 1014–1023, 1993.

[89] D. L. Snyder and M. I. Miller, "The use of sieves to stabilize images produced with the EM algorithm for emission tomography," *IEEE Trans. Nucl. Sci.*, vol. NS-32, pp. 3864–3872, 1985.

[90] ——, *Random Point Processes in Time and Space*. New York: Springer-Verlag, 1991, ch. 3.

[91] D. L. Snyder, J. A. O'Sullivan, and M. I. Miller, "The use of maximum likelihood estimation for forming images of diffuse radar targets from delay-doppler data," *IEEE Trans. Inform. Theory*, vol. 35, pp. 536–548, 1989.

[92] D. L. Snyder, T. J. Schulz, and J. A. O'Sullivan, "Deblurring subject to nonnegativity constraints," *IEEE Trans. Signal Processing*, vol. 40, pp. 1143–1150, 1992.

[93] D. L. Snyder, L. J. Thomas Jr., and M. M. TerPogossian, "A mathematical model for positron-emission tomography systems having time-of-flight measurements," *IEEE Trans. Nucl. Sci.*, vol. NS-28, pp. 3575–3583, 1981.

[94] A. Srivastava, M. I. Miller, and U. Grenander, "Multiple target direction of arrival tracking," *IEEE Trans. Signal Processing*, vol. 43, pp. 1282–1285, 1995.

[95] R. A. Tapia and J. R. Thompson, *Nonparametric Probability Density Estimation*. Baltimore, MD: Johns Hopkins Univ. Press, 1978.

[96] A. N. Tikhonov and V. Y. Arsenin, *Solutions of Ill-Posed Problems*. Washington, DC: Winston, 1977.

[97] R. Y. Tsai, "A versatile camera calibration technique for high-accuracy 3D machine vision metrology using off-the-shelf TV cameras and lenses," *IEEE J. Robot. Automat.*, vol. RA-3, no. 4, pp. 323–344, 1987.

[98] M. W. Vannier, M. I. Miller, and U. Grenander, "Modeling and data structure for registration to a brain atlas of multimodality images," in *Functional Neuroimaging—Technical Foundations*, R. W. Thatcher *et al.*, Eds. New York: Academic, 1994, pp. 217–221.

[99] H. L. Van Trees, *Detection, Estimation, and Modulation Theory*, pt. I. New York: Wiley, 1968.

[100] Y. Vardi and D. Lee, "From image deblurring to optimal investments: Maximum-likelihood solutions to positive linear inverse problems," *J. Roy. Stat. Soc. Ser. B*, pp. 569–612, 1993.

[101] Y. Vardi, L. A. Shepp, and L. Kaufmann, "A statistical model for positron emission tomography," *J. Amer. Stat. Soc.*, vol. 80, pp. 8–35, 1985.

[102] G. Wahba, *Spline Models for Observational Data*. Philadelphia, PA: SIAM, 1990.

[103] G. Wang, D. L. Snyder, J. A. O'Sullivan, and M. W. Vannier, "Iterative deblurring for CT metal artifact reduction," *IEEE Trans. Med. Imag.*, vol. 15, pp. 657–664, 1996.

[104] J. M. Wozencraft and I. M. Jacobs, *Principles of Communication Engineering*. New York: Wiley, 1965.

[105] C. F. J. Wu, "On the convergence properties of the EM algorithm," *Ann. Stat.*, vol. 11, pp. 95–103, 1983.

[106] D. C. Youla, "Generalized image restoration by the method of alternating orthogonal protections," *IEEE Trans. Circuits Syst.*, vol. CAS-25, pp. 694–702, 1978.

[107] _____, "Mathematical theory of image restoration by the method of convex projections," in *Image Recovery, Theory and Applications*, H. Stark, Ed. New York: Academic, 1987, ch. 2.

[108] D. C. Youla and H. Webb, "Image restoration by the method of convex projections: Part 1—Theory," *IEEE Trans. Med. Imag.*, vol. MI-1, no. 2, pp. 81–94, 1982.

Universal Prediction

Neri Merhav, *Senior Member, IEEE*, and Meir Feder, *Senior Member, IEEE*

(Invited Paper)

Abstract— This paper consists of an overview on universal prediction from an information-theoretic perspective. Special attention is given to the notion of probability assignment under the self-information loss function, which is directly related to the theory of universal data compression. Both the probabilistic setting and the deterministic setting of the universal prediction problem are described with emphasis on the analogy and the differences between results in the two settings.

Index Terms— Bayes envelope, entropy, finite-state machine, linear prediction, loss function, probability assignment, redundancy-capacity, stochastic complexity, universal coding, universal prediction.

I. INTRODUCTION

CAN the future of a sequence be predicted based on its past? If so, how good could this prediction be? These questions are frequently encountered in many applications. Generally speaking, one may wonder why should the future be at all related to the past. Evidently, often there is such a relation, and if it is known in advance, then it might be useful for prediction. In reality, however, the knowledge of this relation or the underlying model is normally unavailable or inaccurate, and this calls for developing methods of universal prediction. Roughly speaking, a universal predictor is one that does not depend on the unknown underlying model and yet performs essentially as well as if the model were known in advance.

This is a survey that describes some of the research work on universal prediction that has been carried out throughout the years in several scientific disciplines such as information theory, statistics, machine learning, control theory, and operations research. It should be emphasized, however, that there is no attempt to cover comprehensively the entire volume of work that has been done in this problem area. Rather, the aim is to point out a few of the highlights and the principal methodologies from the authors' personal information-theoretic perspective. Also, throughout the paper there are a few new results whose derivations are given in detail.

Manuscript received December 1, 1997; revised April 8, 1998. This work was supported by the Israel Science Foundation administered by the Israeli Academy of Sciences and Humanities.

N. Merhav is with the Department of Electrical Engineering, Technion–Israel Institute of Technology, Haifa 32000, Israel (e-mail: merhav@ee.technion.ac.il).

M. Feder is with the Department of Electrical Engineering–Systems, Tel Aviv University, Tel Aviv 69978, Israel (e-mail: meir@eng.tau.ac.il).

Publisher Item Identifier S 0018-9448(98)05086-X.

Historically, the information-theoretic approach to prediction dates back to Shannon [104], who related prediction to entropy and proposed a predictive estimate of the entropy of the English language. Inspired by Haggelbarger, Shannon [105] created later a "mind-reading" machine that predicts human decisions. About that time, Kelly [59] showed the equivalence between gambling (which, in turn, is definitely a form of prediction) and information. Following Cover [17], Rissanen [89], [90], and Rissanen and Langdon [93], it is well recognized to date that universal prediction is intimately related to universal lossless source coding. In the last three decades, starting from the pioneering work of Fittingoff [42] and Davisson [27], and later Ziv [124], Lempel and Ziv [68], [125], [126], Rissanen and Langdon [93], Krichevsky and Trofimov [63], and others, the theory and practice of universal coding have been greatly advanced. The state-of-the-art knowledge in this area is sufficiently mature to shed light on the problem of universal prediction. Specifically, prediction schemes as well as fundamental performance limits (lower bounds), stemming from those of universal coding, have been derived. It is the relation between universal coding and universal prediction that is the main theme of this paper, from the point of view of both algorithms and performance bounds.

Let us now describe the prediction problem in general. An observer sequentially receives a sequence of observations $x_1, x_2, \cdots, x_t, \cdots$ over some alphabet $\mathcal{X}$. At each time instant t, after having seen $x^{t-1} = (x_1, \cdots, x_{t-1})$ but not yet x_t, the observer predicts the next outcome x_t, or more generally, makes a decision b_t based on the observed past x^{t-1}. Associated with this prediction or decision b_t, and the actual outcome x_t, there is a loss function $l(b_t, x_t)$ that measures quality. Depending on the particular setting of the prediction problem, the objective would be to minimize this instantaneous loss, or its time-average, or the expected value of either one of these quantities. Obviously, prediction in the ordinary sense is a special case of this, where $b_t = \hat{x}_t$ is an estimate of x_t based on x^{t-1} and $l(b_t, x_t) = l(\hat{x}_t, x_t)$ is some estimation performance criterion, e.g., the Hamming distance (if x_t is discrete) or the squared error $l(b_t, x_t) = (x_t - b_t)^2$ (if x_t is continuous).

Another special case, which is more general than the above examples, is based on assigning weights or probabilities to all possible values of the next outcome. For example, the weatherman may assess 70% chance of rain tomorrow, instead of making a commitment whether it will rain or not. This is clearly more informative than the ordinary prediction described above because it gives an assessment of the degree of *confidence* or *reliability* associated with the prediction. In terms of the above described prediction problem, here b_t is a conditional probability assignment of x_t given x^{t-1}, i.e., a nonnegative function $b_t(\cdot|x^{t-1})$ that integrates (or sums) to unity for every x^{t-1}. Upon observing x_t, the performance of b_t is assessed with respect to a suitable loss function l, which should decrease monotonically with the probability assigned to the actual outcome $b_t(x_t|x^{t-1})$. A very important loss function of this kind is the *self-information loss* function, which is also referred to as the *log–loss* function in the machine-learning literature. For every probability assignment $b = \{b(x),\ x \in \mathcal{X}\}$ over $\mathcal{X}$ and every $x \in \mathcal{X}$, this function is defined as

$$l(b, x) = -\log b(x) \tag{1}$$

where logarithms throughout this paper are taken to the base 2 unless otherwise specified. For reasons to be discussed in Section II, the self-information loss function plays a central role in the literature on prediction and hence also throughout this survey.

Let us now return to the prediction problem in its general form. Quite clearly, solutions to this problem are sought according to the particular assumptions on the data-generating mechanism and on the exact objectives. Classical statistical decision theory (see, e.g., [35]) assumes that a known probabilistic source P generates the data, and so, a reasonable objective is to minimize the expected loss. The optimum strategy b_t^* then minimizes the expected loss, given the past, i.e.,

$$E\{l(b, X_t)|X^{t-1} = x^{t-1}\} = \int_{\mathcal{X}} dP(x|x^{t-1})l(b, x) \tag{2}$$

where random variables are denoted by capital letters. Moreover, under suitable assumptions on stationarity and ergodicity, optimum prediction $\{b_t^*\}$ in the expected loss sense, is optimum also in the sense of minimizing the almost sure asymptotic time-average of $l(b_t, X_t)$ (see, e.g., [4]). Given $X^{t-1} = x^{t-1}$, the quantity

$$U(x^{t-1}) = \inf_b \int dP(x|x^{t-1})l(b, x)$$

is referred to as the conditional *Bayes envelope* given x^{t-1}. For example, if $\{X_t\}$ is a binary source, $b_t = \hat{x}_t$, and $l(\cdot, \cdot)$ is the Hamming distance, then

$$b_t^* = \begin{cases} 0, & \text{if } P(0|x^{t-1}) \geq P(1|x^{t-1}) \\ 1, & \text{otherwise} \end{cases} \tag{3}$$

and the conditional Bayes envelope given x^{t-1} is

$$U(x^{t-1}) = \min\{P(0|x^{t-1}), P(1|x^{t-1})\}.$$

For $l(b, x) = (b - x)^2$

$$b_t^* = E(X_t|X^{t-1} = x^{t-1})$$

and

$$U(x^{t-1}) = \text{Var}\{X_t|X^{t-1} = x^{t-1}\}.$$

If, in addition, the underlying source P is known to be Gaussian (or, if only the class of linear predictors is allowed),

then b_t^* is well-known to be a linear function of x^{t-1} given as a special case of the causal Wiener filter [119] (see also [86, Ch. 14-3]). In the self-information loss case, $b_t^*(\cdot|x^{t-1}) = P(\cdot|x^{t-1})$ minimizes $E\{-\log b(X_t|X^{t-1} = x^{t-1})\}$, namely, the best probability assignment is the true one. The conditional Bayes envelope given x^{t-1}, is the (differential) entropy of X_t given $X^{t-1} = x^{t-1}$, i.e.,

$$U(x^{t-1}) = -E \log P(X_t|X^{t-1} = x^{t-1}).$$

While classical theory (e.g., Wiener prediction theory) assumes that the source P is known, the more realistic and interesting situation occurs when P is either unknown, or nonexistent. In the second case, there is no probabilistic data-generating mechanism and the data are considered arbitrary and deterministic. Both cases fall into the category of the universal prediction problem, where the former is referred to as the *probabilistic setting* and the latter is called the *deterministic setting*. Let us now elaborate on these two settings.

A. The Probabilistic Setting

In the probabilistic setting the objective is normally to minimize the expected cumulative loss asymptotically for large n simultaneously for any source in a certain class. A universal predictor $\{b_t^u(x^{t-1})\}$ does not depend on P, and at the same time, keeps the difference between

$$E\left\{\frac{1}{n}\sum_{t=1}^n l(b_t^u, X_t)\right\}$$

and

$$\overline{U}_n(P) = \frac{1}{n}\sum_{t=1}^n EU(X^{t-1})$$
$$= \frac{1}{n}\sum_{t=1}^n E\left\{\inf_b E[l(b, X_t)|X^{t-1}]\right\} \tag{4}$$

vanishingly small for large n. The cumulative Bayes envelope of (4) represents the performance of the optimal predictor tuned to P. For a stationary and ergodic source, the sequence $\{\overline{U}_n(P)\}_{n \geq 1}$ has a limit $\overline{U}(P)$, referred to as the *asymptotic Bayes envelope*, that coincides (by the Cesaro theorem [23]) with $\lim_{t \to \infty} E\{U(X^t)\}$, which in turn exists by nonincreasing monotonicity. In the self-information loss case, $\overline{U}(P)$ is the entropy rate of P, which means that the goal of universal prediction is equivalent to that of universal coding.

There are essentially three levels of universality according to the degree of uncertainty regarding the source.

Universality with Respect to Indexed Classes of Sources: Suppose that the source is unknown except for being a member of a certain indexed class $\{P_\theta, \theta \in \Lambda\}$, where Λ is the index set. Most commonly, θ designates a parameter vector of a smooth parametric family, e.g., the families of finite-alphabet memoryless sources, kth-order Markov sources, M-state sources, AR (p) Gaussian sources, but other index sets (e.g., finite sets) are possible as well. There are two interesting issues here. The first is to devise universal prediction schemes that asymptotically attain $\overline{U}_n(P_\theta)$ in the above defined sense for every $\theta \in \Lambda$, and the second is performance bounds beyond $\overline{U}_n(P_\theta)$ that apply to any universal predictor. Analogously to the universal coding terminology, the extra loss beyond $\overline{U}_n(P)$ will be referred to as the *redundancy*. Redundancy bounds are useful to establish necessary conditions for the existence of universal schemes as well as limitations on the rate of convergence. Both are dictated by a certain measure of the *richness* of the class $\{P_\theta\}$. Furthermore, even if the redundancy bound does not vanish as $n \to \infty$, and hence universal schemes in the above defined sense do not exist, the question of universality can be extended to that of achieving this bound. For self-information loss prediction, we will explicitly characterize such bounds, and demonstrate achievability by certain universal schemes.

Universality with Respect to Very Large Classes of Sources: Suppose that all we know about the source is that it is Markov of an unknown finite order, or that it is stationary and ergodic, or mixing in a certain sense. For such large classes, quantitative characterizations of uniform redundancy rates do not exist [60], [106], [107]. Here, one cannot hope for more than *weak universality*, a term mentioned and defined in [27], which means that universality is attained at a nonuniform convergence rate. Sometimes even weak universality cannot be obtained, and in [60] there are necessary and sufficient conditions for the existence of universal schemes.

Hierarchical Universality: In this level, the goal is to devise universal schemes with respect to a sequence $\Lambda_1, \Lambda_2, \cdots$ of index sets of sources, which may (though not necessarily) have some structure like nesting, i.e., $\Lambda_k \subset \Lambda_{k+1}$ for every positive integer k. Perhaps the most common example is where for every k, Λ_k is the class of all kth-order Markov sources of a given alphabet. Here the only prior knowledge that one may have on the source is that its index θ belongs to $\Lambda = \bigcup_{k \geq 1} \Lambda_k$. The straightforward approach would be to consider Λ as one big class and to seek universal schemes with respect to Λ. The drawback of this approach, however, is that it is pessimistic in the sense that the convergence rate towards $\overline{U}(P_\theta)$, might be very slow, if at all existent, because Λ could be a very rich class. In the above Markov example, while each Λ_k falls within the category of the first level above, the union Λ falls in the second level. Nonetheless, it turns out that in certain situations it is possible to achieve redundancy rate that is essentially as small as if k were known *a priori*. This gives rise to an elegant compromise between the two former levels of universality. It keeps the fast convergence rates of the first level without sacrificing the generality of the class of sources of the second level.

B. The Deterministic Setting

In this setting, the observed sequence is not assumed to be randomly drawn by some probability law, but is rather an individual, deterministic sequence. There are two difficulties in defining the universal prediction problem in this context. The first is associated with setting the desired goal. Formally, for a given sequence $x_1, x_2, \cdots$, there is always the perfect prediction function defined as $b_t(x^{t-1}) = x_t$, and so, the prediction problem seemingly boils down to triviality. The second difficulty is in the other way around. For a given

deterministic predictor $\{b_t(\cdot)\}_{t \geq 1}$, there is always the adversary sequence where at each time instant t, x_t is chosen to maximize $l(b_t, x_t)$.

The first difficulty is fundamental because it means that without any limitations on the class of allowed predictors, there is a severe overfitting effect, which tailors a predictor to the sequence so strongly, that it becomes, in fact, anticipating and hence completely misses the essence of prediction as a causal, sequential mechanism. Therefore, one must limit the class B of allowed predictors $\{b_t(\cdot)\}_{t \geq 1}$ in some reasonable way. For example, B could be the class of predictors that are implementable by finite-state machines (FSM's) with M states, or Markov-structured predictors of the form $b_t(x^{t-1}) = b(x_{t-k}, \cdots, x_{t-1})$, and so on. Such limitations make sense not only by virtue of avoiding these trivialities, but also because they reflect real-life situations of limited resources, like memory, computational power, and so on. Stated more formally, for a given class B of predictors, we seek a sequential predictor $\{b_t^u\}_{t \geq 1}$ that is universal in the sense of being independent of the future, and at the same time, its average loss

$$\frac{1}{n} \sum_{t=1}^{n} l(b_t^u, x_t)$$

is asymptotically the same as

$$\min_B \frac{1}{n} \sum_{t=1}^{n} l(b_t, x_t)$$

for every x^n. The universal predictor need not be necessarily in B but it must be causal, whereas the reference predictor in B, that minimizes the average loss, may (by definition) depend on the entire sequence x^n.

The second difficulty mentioned above is alleviated by allowing randomization. In other words, predictions are generated at random according to a certain probability distribution that depends on the past. Note that this is different from the above discussed case where b_t was a probability assignment, because now the assigned probability distribution is actually used for randomization.

Analogously to the probabilistic case, here we also distinguish between three levels of universality, which are now in accordance to the richness of the class B. The first level corresponds to an indexed class of predictors which is dual to the above mentioned indexed class of sources. Examples of this are parametric classes of predictors, like finite-state machines with a given number of states, fixed-order Markov predictors, predictors based on neural nets with a given number of neurons, finite sets of predictors, etc. The second level corresponds to very large classes like the class of all finite-state predictors (without specifying the number of states), operating on infinitely long sequences, etc. Finally, the third level corresponds to hierarchical universality and parallels that of the probabilistic setting. The nature of the reported results is somewhat similar to that of the probabilistic approach, but there are several important differences in algorithmic aspects as well as in existence theorems and performance bounds.

The outline of the paper is as follows. Section II is devoted to the motivation and the justification for the use of the self-information loss function as a performance criterion in prediction. In Section III, the probabilistic setting will be discussed with a great emphasis on the self-information loss case which is fairly well-understood. In Section IV, the deterministic setting will be described with special attention to the similarity and the difference from the probabilistic setting. Section V is devoted to the concept of hierarchical universality in both settings. Finally, Section VI summarizes the paper along with some open problems and directions for further research.

II. THE SELF-INFORMATION LOSS FUNCTION

We mentioned earlier the self-information loss function and its central role in universal prediction. In this section, we discuss some motivations and justifications for using this loss function as a measure of prediction performance. As explained in Section I, predictive probability assignment for the next outcome is more general and more informative than estimating the value of the next outcome, and a reasonable loss function should be monotonically decreasing with the assigned probability of the actual outcome. The self-information loss function, defined in (1), clearly satisfies this requirement, but it also possesses many other desirable features of fundamental importance.

The first advantage of the self-information loss function is technical. It is convenient to work with because the logarithmic function converts joint probability functions, or equivalently, products of conditional probabilities into cumulative sums of loss terms. This suits the framework of the general prediction problem described above.

But beyond this technical convenience, there is a deeper significance. As is well known, the self-information manifests the degree of uncertainty, or the amount of information treasured in the occurrence of an event. The conditional self-information of the future given the past, therefore, reflects the ability to deduce information from the past into the future with minimum uncertainty.

Evidently, prediction under the self-information loss function and lossless source coding are intimately related. This relation stems from the fact that $l(b, x) = -\log b(x)$ is the *ideal codelength* of x with respect to a probability function $b(\cdot)$. This codelength can be implemented sequentially within any desired precision using arithmetic coding [88]. Conversely, any codelength function can be translated into a probability assignment rule [90], [93], [109], [117]. Another direct application of self-information loss minimization to the problem area of prediction, is that of gambling [17], [19], [38]. In this case, $b_t(\cdot|x^{t-1})$ represents the distribution of money invested in each one of the possible values of the next outcome. The self-information loss function then dictates the exponential growth rate of the amount of money with time.

The paradigm of predictive probability assignment is also the basis of Dawid's *prequential principle* [31]. However, the motivation of the prequential principle was not in prediction *per se*, but rather the use of probability assignment for testing the validity of statistical models. A good probability assignment is one that behaves empirically as expected from

the true probabilistic model. For example, if $\{x_t\}$ are binary, then a good sequence $\{b_t(1|x^{t-1})\}$ of probabilities assigned to $x_t = 1$ should satisfy

$$\frac{1}{n} \sum_{t=1}^{n} (x_t - b_t) \to 0$$

namely, the law of large numbers. As further discussed in [32]–[34], other requirements are based on the central limit theorem, the law of iterated logarithm, behavior of confidence intervals, and so on.

Interestingly, it turns out that predictive probability assignment under the self-information loss criterion can be useful also for the purpose of testing the validity of statistical models as described above. One reason is that when a certain source P governs the data, then it is the true conditional probability $b_t(\cdot|x^{t-1}) = P(\cdot|x^{t-1})$ that minimizes $E\{-\log b_t(X_t|X^{t-1} = x^{t-1})\}$. In simpler words, the maximum achievable assigned probability is also the true one (a property shared by very specific loss functions, see [78]). Moreover, by the Shannon–McMillan–Breiman theorem, under certain ergodicity assumptions, this is true not only in the expected value sense, but also almost surely. Thus by combining the prequential principle with the Shannon–McMillan–Breiman theorem, a good probabilistic model for the data $b_t(\cdot|x^{t-1})$ must minimize

$$\frac{1}{n} \sum_{t=1}^{n} -\log b_t(x_t|x^{t-1})$$

i.e., the average self-information loss.

From another perspective, we observe that any sequential probability assignment mechanism gives rise to a probability assignment for the entire observation vector x^n by

$$Q(x^n) = \prod_{t=1}^{n} b_t(x_t|x^{t-1}).$$

Conversely, any consistent probability assignment Q for x^n (i.e., Q that satisfies $Q(x^{t-1}) = \sum_{x_t \in \mathcal{X}} Q(x^t)$ for all t and x^{t-1}), provides a valid sequential probability assignment by

$$b_t(x_t|x^{t-1}) = \frac{Q(x^t)}{Q(x^{t-1})}. \tag{5}$$

Therefore, the choice of $\{b_t\}$ in self-information loss prediction is completely equivalent to the choice of Q that assigns maximum probability to x^n, that is, maximum-likelihood estimation.

In our discussion thus far, we focused on motivating the self-information loss function itself. Yet another motivation for studying universal prediction in the self-information loss case is that it sheds light on the universal prediction problem for other loss functions as well. Perhaps the most direct way to look at self-information loss prediction is as a mechanism that generates a probability distribution when the underlying source is unknown or nonexistent. One plausible approach to the prediction problem with a general loss function is then to generate, at each time instant, a prediction that is a functional of the self-information-loss conditional probability assignment. For example, in the squared-error loss case, a reasonable predictor would be the conditional mean associated with $b_t(\cdot|x^{t-1})$, which hopefully tends to the true conditional probability as discussed above. As will be seen in the probabilistic setting, this technique is often successful, whereas in the deterministic setting, some modification is required.

However, there is another way in which self-information loss prediction serves as a yardstick to prediction under other loss functions, and this is the notion of *exponential weighting*. In certain situations, minimization of the cumulative loss $\sum_t l(b_t, x_t)$ corresponds to maximization of the exponentiated loss $\exp(-\alpha \sum_t l(b_t, x_t))$ $(\alpha > 0)$, which in turn can be treated altogether as an auxiliary probability assignment. In certain important special cases (though not always), the solution to this probability assignment problem translates back as a solution to the original problem. We will also see the usefulness of the exponential weighting technique as a tool for deriving lower bounds that are induced from corresponding strong lower bounds of the self-information loss case.

III. THE PROBABILISTIC SETTING

We begin with the problem of probability assignment for the next outcome given the past, under the self-information loss function. As explained above, this problem is completely equivalent to that of finding a probability assignment Q for the entire data sequence.

As we mentioned earlier, if the source P were known, then clearly, the optimal Q that minimizes the above expected self-information loss would be $Q = P$, i.e., the prediction induced by the true underlying source

$$b_t(\cdot|x^{t-1}) \triangleq Q(\cdot|x^{t-1}) = P(\cdot|x^{t-1}).$$

The average cumulative loss would then be the entropy $H_n(P) = -E\{\log P(X^n)\}$. If P is unknown and we wish to assign a certain probability distribution Q that does not depend upon the unknown P, then the extra loss beyond the entropy is given by

$$E\{-\log Q(X^n) - (-\log P(X^n))\} = D_n(P\|Q) \quad (6)$$

where $D_n(P\|Q)$ is the nth-order information divergence (relative entropy) between P and Q. In the corresponding lossless compression problem, $D_n(P\|Q)/n$ is the coding redundancy, i.e., the normalized per-symbol difference between the average code length and the entropy. Of course, the minimizations of $D_n(P\|Q)$ for two or more sources $\{P\}$ at the same time might be contradictory. Thus the problem of universal probability assignment is that of finding a good compromise Q that is uniformly as "close" as possible, in the information divergence sense, to every P in a given class of sources. We shall elaborate later on this notion of simultaneous divergence minimization.

As explained in Section I, the theory of universality splits into several levels according to the degree of uncertainty regarding the source. We begin with the conceptually simplest case where the source is known to belong to a given indexed class of sources $\{P_\theta, \theta \in \Lambda\}$, where θ is the index (e.g., a parameter vector) and Λ is the index set. Since we look at prediction from the viewpoint of probability assignment and

we start from the self-information loss criterion, our survey in this part is largely taken from the theory of universal coding.

A. Indexed Classes of Sources

1) The Self-Information Loss Function: We first describe two common approaches to universal probability assignment for indexed classes of sources.

The Plug-in Approach versus the Mixture Approach: One natural approach to universal prediction with respect to an indexed class of sources $\{P_\theta, \theta \in \Lambda\}$ is the so-called *plug-in* approach. According to this approach, at every time instant t, the index (or the parameter) θ is estimated on-line from x^{t-1} (e.g., by using the maximum-likelihood estimator), and the estimate $\hat{\theta}_t = \hat{\theta}_t(x^{t-1})$ is then used for prediction as if it were the true parameter value, i.e., the conditional probability assigned to x_t is given by $P_{\hat{\theta}_t}(x_t|x^{t-1})$.

The plug-in approach may work quite well under certain regularity conditions. Intuitively, if the estimator $\hat{\theta}_t$ is statistically consistent and $P_\theta(x_t|x^{t-1})$ is continuous in θ for every x^{t-1} and x_t, then the estimated probability assignment may converge to the true conditional probability in the probabilistic sense. Nonetheless, this convergence property does not always hold (e.g., when θ is the center of a Cauchy density estimated by the sample mean), and even if it does, the rate of convergence might be of crucial importance. Moreover, it is not true, in general, that better estimation of the conditional probability necessarily yields better self-information loss performance. The plug-in approach is, in essence, a heuristic approach that lacks a well-substantiated, deep theoretical justification in general.

An alternative approach, henceforth referred to as the *mixture approach*, is based on generating convex combinations (mixtures) of all sources in the class $\{P_\theta, \theta \in \Lambda\}$. Specifically, given a certain nonnegative weight function $w(\theta)$ that integrates to unity (and hence can be thought of as a prior on Λ), we define the mixture probability mass (or density) function over n-tuples as

$$Q_w(x^n) = \int_\Lambda dw(\theta) P_\theta(x^n). \quad (7)$$

With an appropriate choice of the weight function w, the mixture Q_w, as we shall see later, turns out to possess certain desirable properties which motivate its definition as a *universal probability measure*. This universal measure then induces a conceptually simple sequential probability assignment mechanism defined by

$$b_t(x_t|x^{t-1}) = Q_w(x_t|x^{t-1}) = \frac{Q_w(x^t)}{Q_w(x^{t-1})}. \quad (8)$$

It is interesting to note [72, Theorem 2] that the above predictive probability function induced by the mixture of $\{P_\theta, \theta \in \Lambda\}$ can also be represented as a mixture of the conditional probability functions $\{P_\theta(x_t|x^{t-1}), \theta \in \Lambda\}$, where the weighting function is given by the *posterior* probability density function of θ given x^{t-1}, i.e.,

$$Q_w(x_t|x^{t-1}) = \int_\Lambda dw(\theta|x^{t-1}) P_\theta(x_t|x^{t-1}) \quad (9)$$

where

$$w(\theta|x^{t-1}) = \frac{w(\theta)P_\theta(x^{t-1})}{\int_\Lambda dw\,(\theta')P_{\theta'}(x^{t-1})} = \frac{w(\theta)2^{-\log 1/P_\theta(x^{t-1})}}{\int_\Lambda dw\,(\theta')P_{\theta'}(x^{t-1})}$$

(10)

and where the last expression manifests the interpretation of *exponential weighting* according to the probability assignment performance (given by $\log 1/P_\theta(x^{t-1})$) on data seen thus far: points in Λ that correspond to good performance in the past are rewarded exponentially higher weights in prediction of future outcomes. The exponential weighting is an important concept. We will further elaborate later on it in a broader context of lower bounds and algorithms for sequential prediction under more general loss functions in the probabilistic as well as in the deterministic setting.

For the class of binary memoryless (Bernoulli) sources with $\theta = \Pr\{x_t = 0\}$, the mixture approach, with $w(\cdot)$ being uniform over $\Lambda = [0,1]$, leads to the well-known Laplace prediction [66], [67]. Suppose that x^{t-1} contains t_0 zeros and $t_1 = t - 1 - t_0$ ones, then

$$Q_w(x_t = 0|x^{t-1}) = \frac{\int_0^1 \theta^{t_0+1}(1-\theta)^{t_1}\,d\theta}{\int_0^1 \theta^{t_0}(1-\theta)^{t_1}\,d\theta}$$

$$= \frac{t_0+1}{(t-1)+2} = \frac{t_0+1}{t+1}$$

(11)

which, in this case, can be thought of also as a plug-in algorithm because $(t_0 + 1)/(t + 1)$ can be interpreted as a biased version of the maximum-likelihood estimator of θ. Such a bias is clearly desirable in a sequential regime because the naive maximum-likelihood estimator $\hat{\theta}_t = t_0/(t-1)$ would assign zero probability to the first occurrence of "1" which, in turn, would result in infinite loss. Also, this bias gives rise to the plausible symmetry consideration that in the absence of any data (i.e., $t_0 = t - 1 = 0$) one would assign equal probabilities to "0" and "1." But this would be also the case with any estimator of the form $\hat{\theta}_t = (t_0 + \beta)/(t + 2\beta)$, $\beta > 0$. Indeed, other weight functions (from the Dirichlet family) yield different bias terms and with slight differences in performance (see also [62]). This discussion carries over to general finite-alphabet memoryless sources [63] (as will be discussed later) and to Markov chains [28], [91]. However, it should be kept in mind that for a general family of sources $\{P_\theta, \theta \in \Lambda\}$, the mixture approach does not necessarily boil down to a plug-in algorithm as above, and that the choice of the weight function might have a much more dramatic impact on performance [76]. In this case, we would like to have some theoretical guidance regarding the choice of w.

This will be accomplished in the forthcoming subsection, where we establish the theoretical justification of the mixture approach in a fairly strong sense. Interestingly, in the next section, it will be motivated also in the deterministic setting, and for loss functions other than the self-information loss function.

Minimax and Maximin Universality: We have seen (6) that the excess loss associated with a given probability assignment Q while the underlying source is P_θ is given by $D_n(P_\theta\|Q)$. The first fundamental justification of the mixture approach (presented in [76]) is the following simple fact: given an arbitrary probability assignment Q, there exists another probability assignment Q_w in the convex hull of $\{P_\theta, \theta \in \Lambda\}$, (that is, a mixture) such that $D_n(P_\theta\|Q_w) \leq D_n(P_\theta\|Q)$ simultaneously for every $\theta \in \Lambda$. This means that when seeking a universal probability assignment, there is no loss of optimality in any reasonable sense, if we confine attention merely to the convex hull of the class $\{P_\theta\}$. Nonetheless, this interesting fact does not tell us how to select the weight function $w(\cdot)$ of the mixture Q_w. To this end, we make a few additional observations.

As mentioned earlier, we wish to find a probability assignment Q that is independent of the u.known θ, and yet guarantees a certain level of excess loss beyond the minimum achievable loss had θ been known *a priori* (i.e., the nth-order entropy $H_n(P_\theta)$). Referring again to (6), this suggests to solve the following minimax problem:

$$\inf_Q \sup_{\theta \in \Lambda} D_n(P_\theta\|Q) = \inf_Q \sup_w \int_\Lambda dw\,(\theta)D_n(P_\theta\|Q).$$

(12)

The value of this quantity, after normalizing by n, is called the *minimax redundancy* and is denoted by R_n^+ in the literature of universal coding. At first glance, this approach might seem somewhat pessimistic because it is a worst case approach. Fortunately enough, in many cases of interest, $R_n^+ \to 0$ as $n \to \infty$, which means that the minimax Q asymptotically achieves the entropy rate, uniformly rapidly in Λ. Moreover, as we shall see shortly, the minimax approach, in the self-information loss case, is not at all pessimistic even if R_n^+ does not tend to zero. Again, in view of the discussion in the previous paragraph, the minimax-optimal Q is a mixture of the sources in the class.

An alternative to the minimax criterion is the maximin criterion, whose definition has a strong Bayesian flavor that gives rise to the mixture approach from a seemingly different point of view. Here is the idea: since $\theta \in \Lambda$ is unknown, let us postulate some prior probability density function $w(\theta)$ over Λ. The performance of a given probability assignment Q would be then judged with respect to the normalized weighted average redundancy $D_n(P_\theta\|Q)$, i.e.,

$$R_n(Q, w) = \frac{1}{n}\int_\Lambda dw\,(\theta)\,D_n(P_\theta\|Q).$$

(13)

It is easy to see that for a given w, the Q that minimizes $R_n(Q, w)$ is just the Q_w defined in (7), and that the resultant average redundancy $R_n(Q_w, w)$, is exactly the mutual information $I_w(\Theta; X^n)$ between random variables Θ and X^n whose joint probability density function is given by $\mu(\theta, x^n) = w(\theta)P_\theta(x^n)$. But w is arbitrary and the question that again arises is what would be an "appropriate" choice of w? Let us adopt again a worst case approach and use the "least favorable" prior that maximizes $\inf_Q R_n(Q, w)$, that is, solve the maximin problem

$$\sup_w \inf_Q R_n(Q, w)$$

(14)

85

whose value, when normalized by n, is referred to as the *maximin redundancy* and denoted by R_n^-. It is important to note that R_n^-, which is the supremum of $I_w(\Theta; X^n)/n$ over all allowable w's, is given the interpretation of the *capacity* of the "channel" from Θ to X^n, defined by the class of sources. In this definition, each source $P_\theta(x^n)$ is thought of as the conditional probability function of the "channel output" given the "channel input" Θ. We will refer to this channel capacity as the *capacity of the class* of sources $\{P_\theta, \theta \in \Lambda\}$ and will denote it by C_n. Thus C_n is identical to R_n^-.

These notions of minimax and maximin universality were first defined by Davisson [27] in the context of universal coding (see also [11], [28], [30], [37], [58], and others). Several years after Davisson's paper [27] it was observed (first by Gallager [45], and then independently by Davisson and Leon-Garcia [29], Ryabko [96], and others) that the minimax and the maximin solutions are equivalent, i.e., $R_n^+ = R_n^- = C_n$. Furthermore, the mixture Q_{w^*}, where w^* is the *capacity-achieving prior* (i.e., $I_{w^*}(\Theta; X^n)/n = C_n$), is both minimax and maximin optimal. This result is referred to as the *redundancy-capacity theorem* of universal coding.

The capacity C_n, therefore, measures the "richness" of the class of sources. It should be pointed out, though, that C_n is not very sensitive to "distances" among the sources in the class, but rather to the effective number of essentially distinct sources. For example, the source P_1 that generates 0's only with probability one is at infinite divergence-distance from the source P_2 that generates 1's only. Yet their mixture $\frac{1}{2}P_1 + \frac{1}{2}P_2$ (in the level of n-tuples) is within normalized divergence of $1/n$ from both, and so, the capacity of $\{P_1, P_2\}$ is very small. It is a remarkable fact that the theory of universal coding is so intimately related to that of channel capacity. Moreover, the importance and significance of the redundancy-capacity theorem are fairly deep also in the broader context of probability assignment and prediction.

On the face of it, at this point the problem of universal probability assignment, or equivalently, universal prediction under the self-information loss function with respect to an indexed class of sources, is fairly well addressed. Nonetheless, there are still several important issues to be considered.

The first concern comes from a practical aspect. Explicit evaluation of the proposed minimax/maximin probability assignment is not trivial. First of all, the capacity-achieving prior w^* is hard to evaluate in general. Furthermore, even when it can be computed explicitly, the corresponding mixture Q_{w^*} as well as the induced conditional probabilities $Q_{w^*}(x_t|x^{t-1})$ might still be hard to compute. This is in contrast to the plug-in approach, which is relatively easy to implement. Nevertheless, we shall return later to the earlier example of the mixtures of Bernoulli sources, or more generally, finite-alphabet memoryless sources, and see that fortunately enough, some satisfactory approximations are available.

The second technical point has to do with the evaluation of capacity, or at least, its asymptotic behavior, which is of crucial importance. As mentioned earlier, the capacity measures the "complexity" or "richness" of the class of sources, and $C_n \to 0$ if and only if uniform redundancy rates are achievable (i.e., strong universality). This means that if the class of sources is

too rich so that C_n does not vanish as n grows without bound, one can no longer hope for uniformly small redundancy rates [48], [107]. We shall see examples of this later.

Another problem that calls for attention is that the predictor, or the sequential probability assignment mechanism that we are proposing here, is not really sequential in the sense that the horizon n must be prescribed in advance. The reason is that the capacity-achieving prior w^* depends on n, in general. A possible remedy (both to this and to the problem of computability) is to seek a fixed prior w, independent of n, that achieves capacity at least asymptotically, i.e.,

$$\lim_{n \to \infty} I_w(\Theta; X^n)/(nC_n) = 1.$$

Fortunately, this is possible in some important examples.

Finally, we mentioned earlier that the minimax approach is pessimistic in essence, a fact which seems to be of special concern when $R_n^+ = C_n$ does not tend to zero as n grows. The reason is that although $D_n(P_\theta \| Q_{w^*}) \leq nC_n$ for all θ, minimaxity guarantees that the lower bound

$$D_n(P_\theta \| Q) \geq nC_n \qquad \forall Q \tag{15}$$

is valid for *one* source P_θ in the class. The maximin point of view tells us further that this holds true also in the sense of the weighted average of $D_n(P_\theta \| Q)$ over θ with respect to w^*. Still, the optimality of Q_{w^*} is on seemingly somewhat weak grounds. Nonetheless, a closer inspection reveals that the right-hand side of (15) is essentially a lower bound in a much stronger sense which will now be discussed.

A Strong Converse Theorem: It turns out that in the self-information loss case, there is a remarkable "concentration" phenomenon: It is shown in [76] that

$$D_n(P_\theta \| Q) \geq (1 - \epsilon)nC_n \qquad \forall Q \tag{16}$$

for every $\epsilon > 0$ and for w^*-*most* values of θ. Here, the term "w^*-most" means that the total probability mass of points with this property, with respect to w^* (or any asymptotically good approximation of w^*), tends to unity as $n \to \infty$. This means that if the right-hand side of (15) is slightly reduced, namely, multiplied by a factor $(1 - \epsilon)$, it becomes a lower bound for w^*-most values of θ. Referring again to the uniform upper bound, this means that w^*-most sources in the class lie near the surface of a "sphere" (in the divergence sense) of radius nC_n, centered at Q_{w^*}. Considering the fact that we have assumed virtually nothing about the structure of the class of sources, this is quite a surprising phenomenon. The roots of this are explained and discussed in detail in [39] and [76] in relation to the competitive optimality property of the self-information function [20] (see also [61]).

There is a technical concern, however: for a class of finite-alphabet sources and any finite n, the capacity-achieving prior must be discrete with support of at most A^n points in Λ [44, p. 96, Corollary 3]. Strictly speaking, the measure w^* then ignores all points outside its support, and the term "w^*-most sources" is not very meaningful. Again, fortunately enough, in most of the important examples, one can find a smooth weight function w, which is independent of n and asymptotically achieves capacity. This solves both this difficulty and the horizon-dependency problem mentioned earlier. As an alternative remedy, there is another, more general version of this strong converse result [39], which allows for an arbitrary weight function w. It tells that Q_w is optimal for w-most points in Λ. But note that $D(P_\theta \| Q_w)$ may depend on θ for a general w, and so the uniformity property might be lost.

The above result is, in fact, a stronger version of the redundancy-capacity theorem, as detailed in [76], and it generalizes the well-known strong converse to the universal coding theorem due to Rissanen [90] for a smooth parametric family $\{P_\theta\}$ whose capacity behaves like $C_n \sim (k/2n) \log n$, where k is dimension of the parameter vector. Rissanen, in his award-winning paper [90], was the first to show such a strong converse theorem that applies to most sources at the same time. The reader is referred to [76] (see also [39]) for detailed discussion on this theorem and its significance in general, as well as in the perspective of Rissanen's work in particular. Let us now examine a few examples in light of these findings.

Examples: Perhaps the simplest example is the one where $\Lambda = \{1, 2, \cdots, N\}$, namely, there are N sources $P_1, \cdots, P_N$ in the class, and the weight function w is represented by a vector $(w_1, \cdots, w_N)$ of nonnegative numbers summing to one. In this case, the above described "concentration" phenomenon becomes even sharper [44, Theorem 4.5.1], [45] than in the general case because $D(P_i \| Q_{w^*}) = nC_n$ for every i for which $w_i^* > 0$. In other words, w^*-all sources lie *exactly* on the surface of the divergence sphere around Q_{w^*}. If the sources $\{P_i\}$ are easily distinguishable in the sense that one can reliably identify which one of the sources generated a given vector X^n, then the redundancy-capacity of the class is nearly $\log N/n$, because the "channel input" i can be "decoded" from the "channel output" X^n with small error probability. In this case, w^* tends to be uniform over $\{1, 2, \cdots, N\}$ and the best mixture Q_{w^*} is essentially a uniform mixture. If the sources are not easily distinguishable, then the redundancy-capacity is smaller. This can be thought of as a situation where the "channel" is more "noisy," or alternatively, that the effective number of distinct sources is smaller than N. In the extreme case, where $P_1 = P_2 = \cdots = P_N$, we have $C_n = 0$ as expected, since we have, in fact, only one source in the class.

Let us now revisit the Bernoulli example, or more generally, the class of memoryless sources with a given finite alphabet of size A. This is obviously a parametric class whose natural parameterization by θ is given by the letter probabilities with $A - 1$ degrees of freedom. As mentioned earlier, w^* is discrete in the finite-alphabet case, it depends on the horizon n, and it is difficult to compute. It turns out that for smooth parametric families with a bounded parameter set Λ, like the one considered here, there is no much sensitivity to the exact shape of w (used for Q_w) as long as it is bounded away from zero across Λ. In fact, any such "nice" prior essentially achieves the leading term of the capacity, which is $\frac{A-1}{2n} \log n$. Differences in performance for different choices of w are reflected in higher order terms. Specifically, Clarke and Barron [15], [16] have derived a very accurate asymptotic formula for

the redundancy associated with a mixture w

$$D_n(P_\theta \| Q_w) = \frac{A-1}{2} \ln \frac{n}{2\pi e} + \ln \frac{|I(\theta)|^{1/2}}{w(\theta)} + o(1) \quad (17)$$

where $|I(\theta)|$ is the determinant of the Fisher information matrix of $\{P_\theta\}$ (see also Takeuchi and Barron [111] for extensions to more general exponential families). In the maximin setting, the weighted average of $D_n(P_\theta \| Q_w)$ is then asymptotically maximized (neglecting the $o(1)$ term) by a prior w that maximizes the second term above, which is well known as *Jeffreys' prior* [7], [16], [57], [92]

$$w_J(\theta) = \frac{|I(\theta)|^{1/2}}{\int_\Lambda |I(\theta')|^{1/2} \, d\theta'}. \quad (18)$$

In our case, $|I(\theta)|$ is inversely proportional to the square root of the product of all letter probabilities,

$$\sqrt{\prod_{i=1}^{A} \theta_i}.$$

This, in turn, is a special case of the Dirichlet prior [63], whose general form is proportional to the product of arbitrary fixed powers of $\{\theta_i\}$. Dirichlet mixtures Q_w and conditional probabilities derived from them have easy closed-form expressions as well. Generalizing the earlier Bernoulli example to the size-A alphabet parametric family, and using Jeffreys' prior, we get the universal probability assignment

$$Q_{w_J}(x_t = j | x^{t-1}) = \frac{t_j + 1/2}{(t-1) + A/2} \quad (19)$$

where t_j is the number of occurrences of $x_\tau = j$, $1 \leq \tau \leq t - 1$. The uniform prior that leads to the Laplace estimator discussed earlier, is yet another special case of the Dirichlet prior. It should be noted that Jeffreys' prior asymptotically achieves capacity and so, it induces an asymptotically maximin probability assignment. Interestingly, as observed in [122], it is not asymptotically minimax, and it should be slightly modified to obtain minimax optimality. These results extend to more general parametric families under certain regularity conditions detailed in the above cited papers.

But the main point to be remembered here is that for parametric classes, the choice of w is not crucial in terms of performance. This gives rise to the freedom of selecting a prior from implementational considerations, i.e., the availability of closed-form expressions for mixtures, namely, conjugate priors [35]. We have just seen the example of the Dirichlet prior in classes of memoryless sources. As another example, consider the case where $\{P_\theta\}$ is a family of Gaussian memoryless sources with mean θ and variance 1. Clearly, Q_w with respect to a Gaussian prior w is Gaussian itself in this case. The idea of conjugate priors carries over in a natural manner to more general exponential families.

It should be pointed out that there are other recent extensions [51], [53], [54], [74], [83] of the redundancy-capacity theory to more abstract classes of sources whose capacities are proportional to k, where the number k is attributed a more general notion of dimensionality that is induced by the Hellinger distance, the Kullback–Leibler distance, the Vapnik–Chervonenkis (VC) dimension, etc. Other extensions to wider classes of sources exhibit different behavior of the redundancy-capacity [25], [123]. Still, the general underlying information-theoretic principle remains the same; the richness of the class is measured by its Shannon capacity. Other examples of classes of sources that are not necessarily parametric, are given in [39] and [76].

2) General Loss Functions: It turns out that satisfactory solutions to the universal prediction problem under the self-information loss function, may prove useful for more general loss functions. Intuitively, under suitable continuity conditions, an optimal predictor with respect to l, based on a good estimator of $P_\theta(x_t|x^{t-1})$, should be close to optimum under the true conditional probability. Generally speaking, since minimum self-information loss probability assignments are essentially maximum-likelihood estimates (cf. Section II), which are statistically consistent in most situations, this requirement is satisfied.

Specifically, in the discrete alphabet case, let P_θ denote the underlying source and consider the universal probability assignment $Q = Q_{w^*}$ for which $D_n(P_\theta\|Q) \leq nC_n$ for all $\theta \in \Lambda$. Using Pinsker's inequality (see, e.g., [24, Ch. 3, Problem 17]) and the concavity of the square root function, we have (20) shown at the bottom of this page. Now, for a general loss function l, let

$$b_t^\theta(x^{t-1}) = \arg \min_b E_\theta\{l(b, X_t)|X^{t-1} = x^{t-1}\} \quad (21)$$

where E_θ denotes expectation with respect to P_θ, and

$$b_t^u(x^{t-1}) = \arg \min_b E_Q\{l(b, X_t)|X^{t-1} = x^{t-1}\} \quad (22)$$

where E_Q denotes expectation with respect to Q. Assume that l is nonnegative and bounded by some constant $L > 0$. Then, by the inequality above, we get

$$E_\theta\left\{\frac{1}{n}\sum_{t=1}^n l(b_t^u, X_t)\right\} - E_\theta\left\{\frac{1}{n}\sum_{t=1}^n l(b_t^\theta, X_t)\right\}$$

$$= \frac{1}{n}\sum_{t=1}^n \sum_{x^{t-1}} P_\theta(x^{t-1}) \sum_{x_t} P_\theta(x_t|x^{t-1})$$

$$\cdot [l(b_t^u, x_t) - l(b_t^\theta, x_t)]$$

$$\leq \frac{1}{n}\sum_{t=1}^n \sum_{x^{t-1}} P_\theta(x^{t-1}) \sum_{x_t}$$

$$\cdot [Q(x_t|x^{t-1}) + |P_\theta(x_t|x^{t-1}) - Q(x_t|x^{t-1})|]$$

$$\cdot [l(b_t^u, x_t) - l(b_t^\theta, x_t)]$$

$$\leq \frac{1}{n}\sum_{t=1}^n \sum_{x^{t-1}} P_\theta(x^{t-1}) \sum_{x_t} |P_\theta(x_t|x^{t-1})$$

$$- Q(x_t|x^{t-1})|[l(b_t^u, x_t) - l(b_t^\theta, x_t)]$$

$$\leq \frac{L}{n}\sum_{t=1}^n \sum_{x^{t-1}} P_\theta(x^{t-1}) \sum_{x_t} |P_\theta(x_t|x^{t-1}) - Q(x_t|x^{t-1})|$$

$$\leq L\sqrt{2C_n \ln 2}. \quad (23)$$

In words, the optimum predictor with respect to the universal probability assignment Q_{w^*} is within $L\sqrt{2C_n \ln 2}$ close to optimum simultaneously for every $\theta \in \Lambda$. The important conclusion from this result is the following: *The existence of universal predictors with uniformly rapidly decaying redundancy rates under the self-information criterion, is a sufficient condition for the existence of such predictors for general loss functions.*

At this point, two comments are in order: first, the above assumption on boundedness of l can be weakened. For example, the leftmost side of (23), which can be thought of as a generalized divergence between P_θ and Q [75], can often be upper-bounded in terms of the variational distance between P_θ and Q. We have adopted, however, the boundedness assumption to simplify the exposition. The second comment is that the upper bound of (23) might not be tight since the true redundancy rate could be faster in certain situations. For example, minimum mean-square error, fixed-order, universal linear predictors [26], [90] have redundancy rates as small as $O(\log n/n)$, whereas the above upper bound gives $O(\sqrt{\log n/n})$. The question that arises now is whether we can provide a more precise characterization of achievable redundancy rates (tight upper and lower bounds) with respect to general loss functions.

A natural way to handle this question is to take the minimax–maximin approach similarly to the self-information loss

---

$$\sqrt{C_n} \geq \sqrt{\frac{1}{n} D_n(P_\theta\|Q)}$$

$$= \sqrt{\frac{1}{n}\sum_{t=1}^n \sum_{x^{t-1}} P_\theta(x^{t-1}) \sum_{x_t} P_\theta(x_t|x^{t-1}) \log \frac{P_\theta(x_t|x^{t-1})}{Q(x_t|x^{t-1})}}$$

$$\geq \sqrt{\frac{1}{2\ln 2} \cdot \frac{1}{n}\sum_{t=1}^n \sum_{x^{t-1}} P_\theta(x^{t-1}) \left[\sum_{x_t \in \mathcal{X}} |P_\theta(x_t|x^{t-1}) - Q(x_t|x^{t-1})|\right]^2}$$

$$\geq \frac{1}{\sqrt{2\ln 2}} \cdot \frac{1}{n}\sum_{t=1}^n \sum_{x^{t-1}} P_\theta(x^{t-1}) \sum_{x_t} |P_\theta(x_t|x^{t-1}) - Q(x_t|x^{t-1})|. \quad (20)$$

case. The minimax predictor $\{b_t\}$ is the one that minimizes

$$\sup_{\theta \in \Lambda} E_\theta \left\{ \frac{1}{n} \sum_{t=1}^n [l(b_t, x_t) - l(b_t^\theta, x_t)] \right\}$$

$$= \sup_w \int_\Lambda dw(\theta) E_\theta \left\{ \frac{1}{n} \sum_{t=1}^n [l(b_t, x_t) - l(b_t^\theta, x_t)] \right\}. \quad (24)$$

Unfortunately, there is no known closed-form expression for the minimax predictor for a general loss function. Nonetheless, game-theoretic arguments tell us that sometimes the minimax problem is equivalent to the maximin problem. Analogously to the self-information loss case, the maximin problem is defined as the supremum of

$$\inf_{\{b_t\}} \int_\Lambda dw(\theta) E_\theta \left\{ \frac{1}{n} \sum_{t=1}^n [l(b_t, X_t) - l(b_t^\theta, X_t)] \right\}$$

$$= \inf_{\{b_t\}} E_{Q_w} \left\{ \frac{1}{n} \sum_{t=1}^n l(b_t, X_t) \right\} - \int_\Lambda dw(\theta) \overline{U}_n(P_\theta) \quad (25)$$

over all nonnegative weight functions $w(\cdot)$ that integrate to unity. In general, the minimax and maximin problems are well known to be equivalent for convex–concave cost functions [95]. In our case, since (25) is always affine and hence concave in w, the remaining condition is that the set of allowable predictors is convex, and that $E_\theta \{\sum_{t=1}^n l(b_t, X_t)\}$ is convex in $\{b_t\}$ for every θ. The latter condition holds, for example, if $l(b, x) = |b - x|^\alpha$, $\alpha \geq 1$.

The maximin-optimal predictor is clearly the one that minimizes $E_{Q_w} \{l(b, X_t)|X^{t-1} = x^{t-1}\}$ for the worst case choice of w, i.e., the one that maximizes

$$\overline{U}_n(Q_w) - \int_\Lambda dw(\theta) \overline{U}_n(P_\theta). \quad (26)$$

In general, the maximizing w may not agree with the capacity-achieving prior w^* that has been defined for the self-information loss case. Nonetheless, similarly as in (22), these minimax–maximin considerations again justify the approach of Bayes-optimal prediction with respect to a mixture of $\{P_\theta\}$. It should be pointed out that in certain cases (e.g., the parametric case), prediction performance is not sensitive to the exact choice of w.

By definition, vanishingly small minimax redundancy rates guarantee uniform convergence to the Bayes envelope. However, unlike the self-information loss case, for a general loss function, there is not necessarily a "concentration phenomenon" where w-most points of Λ lie at nearly the same redundancy level. For example, in the Bernoulli case with $l(b, x)$ being the Hamming distance between b and x [77] there are only two optimal predictors: one predicts always "1" and the other predicts always "0," according to whether $\Pr\{x_t = 1\}$ is smaller or larger than $1/2$. Thus it is easy to find a zero-redundancy predictor for one half of the sources in the class, and hence there cannot be a nontrivial lower bound on the redundancy that applies to most sources. Nevertheless, by using the concept of exponential weighting, in some cases it is possible to derive strong lower bounds that hold for w-most points in Λ at the same time.

Specifically, let us assume that b is an estimate of x, the subtraction operation $x - b$ is well-defined, and that the loss function is of the form $l(b, x) = \rho(x - b)$, where the function $\rho(z)$ is monotonically increasing for $z > 0$, monotonically decreasing for $z < 0$, and $\rho(0) = 0$. We next derive a lower bound on

$$E_\theta \left\{ \frac{1}{n} \sum_{t=1}^n \rho(X_t - b_t(X^{t-1})) \right\}$$

which holds for w^*-most points in Λ, and for any predictor $\{b_t\}$ that does not depend on θ. This will extend the lower bound on universal minimum mean-square error prediction of Gaussian autoregressive moving average (ARMA) processes given by Rissanen [90].

We assume that $\rho(\cdot)$ is sufficiently "steep" in the sense that $\int e^{-s\rho(z)} dz < \infty$ for every $s > 0$, and define the log-moment generating function

$$\psi(s) = -\log \left[\int e^{-s\rho(z)} dz \right], \qquad s > 0 \quad (27)$$

and

$$\phi(d) = \inf_{s>0} [sd - \psi(s)], \qquad d > 0. \quad (28)$$

The function $\phi(d)$ can be interpreted as the (differential) entropy associated with the probability function

$$q_s(z) = e^{-s\rho(z)+\psi(s)}$$

where s is tuned so that $E_s \rho(Z) = d$, E_s being the expectation operation with respect to q_s. For a given predictor $\{b_t\}$, consider the following probability assignment:

$$Q(x^n) = \int_0^\infty ds\, \nu(s) \prod_{t=1}^n q_s(x_t - b_t(x^{t-1})) \quad (29)$$

where $\nu(\cdot)$ is a locally bounded away from zero "prior" on s. According to [103], $-\log Q(x^n)$ can be approximated as follows:

$$-\log Q(x^n) = n \cdot \inf_{s>0} \left[s \cdot \frac{1}{n} \sum_{t=1}^n \rho(x_t - b_t(x^{t-1})) - \psi(s) \right]$$

$$+ \frac{1}{2} \log n + R(x^n)$$

$$= n \cdot \phi\left(\frac{1}{n} \sum_{t=1}^n \rho(x_t - b_t(x^{t-1})) \right)$$

$$+ \frac{1}{2} \log n + R(x^n) \quad (30)$$

where $R(x^n)$ is a small remainder term. If $E_\theta R(X^n) = O(1)$ for all θ, then following the strong converse of the self-information loss case (16), we have that for w^*-most points of Λ

$$\frac{1}{n} E_\theta \{-\log Q(X^n)\} = \dot{E}_\theta \phi\left(\frac{1}{n} \sum_{t=1}^n \rho(X_t - b_t(X^{t-1})) \right)$$

$$+ \frac{\log n}{2n} + O\left(\frac{1}{n} \right)$$

$$\geq \frac{H_n(P_\theta)}{n} + (1 - \epsilon) C_n \quad (31)$$

for every $\epsilon > 0$ and all sufficiently large n. Since $\phi(\cdot)$ is concave ($\cap$), interchanging the order between the expectation operator and the function ϕ would not decrease the expression on the right-hand side of the first line of (31), and so

$$\phi\left(E_\theta\left\{\frac{1}{n}\sum_{t=1}^{n}\rho(X_t-b_t(X^{t-1}))\right\}\right)$$
$$\geq \frac{H_n(P_\theta)}{n}+(1-\epsilon)C_n-\frac{\log n}{2n}-O\left(\frac{1}{n}\right) \quad (32)$$

for every $\epsilon > 0$, n sufficiently large, and w^*-most $\theta \in \Lambda$. Since ϕ is monotonically nondecreasing, this gives a lower bound on

$$E_\theta\left\{\frac{1}{n}\sum_{t=1}^{n}\rho(X_t-b_t(X^{t-1}))\right\}.$$

The above lower bound is not always tight. Evidently, tightness depends on whether the above defined Q also satisfies the reverse inequality in (31) for some predictor. This, in turn, is the case whenever the self-information lower bound is achievable by universal *predictive coding*, which models the prediction error $e_t = x_t - b_t(x^{t-1})$ as a memoryless process with q_s being the marginal for some $s > 0$. Referring to the case where $C_n \to 0$, the above bound is nontrivial if $\phi(\overline{U}(P_\theta)) = \overline{H}(P_\theta)$, the entropy rate of P_θ. When this is the case, our lower bound suggests a converse to the previous statement on conditions for uniform redundancy rates: *The existence of universal predictors with uniformly rapidly decaying redundancy rates under the self-information criterion (i.e., $C_n \to 0$), is a necessary condition for the existence of such predictors for general loss functions.* In summary, under suitable regularity conditions, there is a uniform redundancy rate for a general l, *if and only if* there is one for the self-information loss function. Furthermore, even if $\phi(\overline{U}(P_\theta)) = \overline{H}(P_\theta)$, there is another requirement for the bound to be nontrivial, which is $C_n > \frac{\log n}{2n}$. Indeed, in the Bernoulli case, where it is possible to achieve zero redundancy for half of the sources (as mentioned earlier), $C_n \sim \frac{\log n}{2n}$ and the bound becomes meaningless.

Let us consider an important example where the above bound is useful. For $\rho(z) = z^2$, q_s is the zero-mean Gaussian density function with variance $1/(2s)$. Therefore, the log-moment generating function is given by $\psi(s) = \frac{1}{2}\ln\frac{s}{\pi}$, and the differential entropy is $\phi(d) = \frac{1}{2}\ln(2\pi ed)$. Thus we have

$$E_\theta\left\{\frac{1}{n}\sum_{t=1}^{n}(X_t-b_t(X^{t-1}))^2\right\}$$
$$\geq \frac{1}{2\pi e}\exp\left\{\frac{H_n(P_\theta)}{n}+(1-\epsilon)C_n-\frac{\ln n}{2n}-O\left(\frac{1}{n}\right)\right\}.$$
$$(33)$$

If $\{P_\theta\}$ is the class of Gaussian ARMA(p, q) sources with driving noise of variance σ^2, then $H_n(P_\theta) = \frac{1}{2}\ln(2\pi e\sigma^2)$

and $C_n \sim (p+q+1)\ln n/(2n)$, and we further obtain

$$E_\theta\left\{\frac{1}{n}\sum_{t=1}^{n}(X_t-b_t(X^{t-1}))^2\right\}\geq\sigma^2\exp\left\{(1-\epsilon)(p+q)\frac{\ln n}{n}\right\}$$
$$\geq\sigma^2\left[1+(1-\epsilon)(p+q)\frac{\ln n}{n}\right].$$
$$(34)$$

This bound has been obtained by Rissanen [90], and it is known to be tight at least in the autoregressive case [26]. Another example of a class of Gaussian sources is the one where $x_t = \theta_t + v_t$, $\{v_t\}$ being zero-mean independent and identically distributed (i.i.d.) Gaussian noise with power σ^2, and $\theta = \{\theta_t\}_{t\geq 1}$ is a deterministic signal with power,

$$\limsup_{n\to\infty}\frac{1}{n}\sum_{t=1}^{n}\theta_t^2$$

limited to S and relative bandwidth (normalized by 2π) limited to $0 \leq W \leq 1$. Here again,

$$H_n(P_\theta) = \frac{1}{2}\ln(2\pi e\sigma^2)$$

for every θ, but now

$$C_n = \frac{W}{2}\ln\left(1+\frac{S}{\sigma^2 W}\right)+o(1)$$

the capacity of the band-limited Gaussian channel, which gives

$$\liminf_{n\to\infty}E_\theta\left\{\frac{1}{n}\sum_{t=1}^{n}(X_t-b_t(X^{t-1}))^2\right\}$$
$$\geq\sigma^2\exp\left\{(1-\epsilon)W\ln\left(1+\frac{S}{\sigma^2 W}\right)\right\}$$
$$=\sigma^2\left(1+\frac{S}{\sigma^2 W}\right)^{(1-\epsilon)W}$$
$$(35)$$

As for achievability of the above bound, recall that the corresponding universal probability assignment problem is solved by the mixture Q_w with respect to the capacity-achieving input which is Gaussian, and therefore Q_w itself is Gaussian. When Q_w is in turn factored to a product of $Q_w(x_t|x^{t-1})$, each one of these conditional densities is again a Gaussian density, whose exponent depends only on $(x_t - b_t(x^{t-1}))^2$, where $b_t(\cdot)$ is a linear predictor, and the asymptotic variance is given by

$$\exp\left\{\frac{1}{2\pi}\int_0^{2\pi}\ln(F(\omega)+\sigma^2)\,d\omega\right\}$$

$F(\omega)$ being the power spectral density of the capacity-achieving input process. It can be shown (using techniques similarly as in [41]) that this Bayesian linear predictor asymptotically attains the above bound.

Another approach to derivation of lower bounds on performance of universal schemes has been proposed in the broader context of the multi-armed bandit problem [1], [2], [64], [108]. In this line of work, tight upper and lower bounds on redundancy rates have been given for a class of *uniformly good* schemes in the sense of adapting to the underlying source. However, these results are confined to the case where Λ is a finite set.

B. Very Large Classes of Sources

So far we have discussed classes of sources where there exists a uniform redundancy rate, which is given in terms of the capacity C_n, at least in the self-information loss case. The capacity may or may not tend to zero as $n \to \infty$, but even if it does not, the predictive self-information performance, or the compression ratio of the corresponding universal code, $H_n(\theta)/n + C_n$, might still be less than $\log A$ (where A is the alphabet size) for all $\theta \in \Lambda$, provided that n is sufficiently large. This means that *some* degree of compression (or nonuniform probability assignment) is still achievable for all sources at the same time, although there is no longer hope to approach the entropy for every θ.

In this section, we focus on much wider classes of sources where even this property does no longer exist. These classes are so rich that, in the self-information loss case, for every finite n and every predictive probability assignment Q, there exists a source in the class such that

$$E\{-\log Q(X^n)\} \geq n \log A - o(n).$$

In other words, there is a total "breakdown" in terms of self-information loss performance, and similar behavior with other loss functions. This happens, for instance, with the class of all stationary and ergodic sources [56], [106], [107] the class of all finite-order Markov sources (without limiting the order), and many other classes that can be represented as infinite unions of nested index sets $\Lambda_1 \subset \Lambda_2 \subset \cdots$. Nonetheless, universal schemes that approach the entropy rate, or more generally, the asymptotic Bayes envelope, may still exist if we do not insist on uniform redundancy rates. In other words, *weakly universal* schemes [27] are sometimes available. For example, the Lempel–Ziv algorithm (and hence also the predictive probability assignment that it induces [65]) is weakly universal over the class of all stationary and ergodic sources with a given finite alphabet [126]. Necessary and sufficient conditions for the existence of weak universality can be found in [60].

One straightforward observation that we can now make from an analysis similar to that of (23), is that a sufficient condition for the existence of a weakly universal predictor for a general (bounded) loss function is the existence of such predictor for probability assignment in the self-information case. Thus the predictive probability assignment with respect to the self-information loss function is again of crucial importance. In view of this fact, the fundamental problem, in this context, is that of estimating conditional probabilities.

Cover [18] has raised the question whether it is possible to produce consistent estimates of conditional probabilities with $|b_t(X_t = x|X^{t-1}) - P(X_t = x|X^{t-1})| \to 0$ almost surely as $t \to \infty$. Bailey [6] gave a negative answer to this question (see also Ryabko [98, Proposition 3]), but pointed out a positive result (Orenstein [85]) to a similar question. It states that for a two-sided stationary binary process, it is possible to estimate the value of $P(X_0 = x|X_{-1}, \cdots, X_{-t})$ strongly consistently as $t \to \infty$. The proposed estimates are based on finite-order Markov approximations where the order depends on the data itself. A similar estimator for $P(X_t = x|X^{t-1})$ turns out to converge to the true value in the $L^1(P)$ sense, which is weaker than the almost sure sense. This estimator has been shown by Bailey [6] to give

$$\frac{1}{n} \sum_t \log[P(X_t|X^{t-1})/b_t(X_t|X^{t-1})] \to 0$$

almost surely as $n \to \infty$. Algoet [3] gave an extension of Orenstein's results to more general alphabets, which was later simplified by Morvai *et al.* [80]. In a more recent paper, Morvai *et al.* [81] have simplified the estimator (which is based on empirical averages) for the finite-alphabet case, at the expense of losing the strong consistency property. Their estimator is consistent in the self-information sense, i.e., for every stationary P

$$\lim_{t \to \infty} E\left\{\log \frac{P(X_0|X_{-1}, X_{-2}, \cdots)}{b_t(X_0|X_{-1}, \cdots, X_{-t})}\right\} = 0 \qquad (36)$$

which implies consistency in the $L^1(P)$ sense.

Another line of research work concentrates on the square-error loss function. Since the minimum mean-square-error predictor for a known source is the conditional mean

$$b_t(x^{t-1}) = E\{X_t|X^{t-1} = x^{t-1}\}$$

most of the work in this direction focuses on consistent estimation of the conditional mean. For Gaussian processes with unknown covariance function, Davisson [26] has shown that a kth-order linear predictor, based on empirical covariances gives asymptotic cumulative mean-square error that behaves like $\sigma^2(k)(1 + k \ln n/n)$, where $\sigma^2(k)$ is the residual error of optimal kth-order linear prediction with known covariances. Thus by letting k grow sufficiently slowly with time, the conditional mean, given the infinite past, can be eventually attained. For general stationary processes, Scarpellini [102] used sample averages with certain spacing between time instants in order to estimate $E\{X_k|X_0, X_{-1}, \cdots\}$ where $k > 0$ is a fixed time instant. Modha and Masry [79] considered mixing processes and proposed an estimator based on slow increase of the prediction memory, using complexity regularization methods. The limitation of their method is that it depends on knowledge of the mixing rate. Meir [73] proposed a complexity regularization method in the same spirit, where for a given complexity, the class of allowable predictors is limited by a finite Vapnik–Chervonenkis (VC) dimension.

Finally, for a general loss function l, Algoet [4] (see also [5] for the special case of log-optimum investment) has proved strong ergodic theorems on the cumulative loss. First, for a known stationary and ergodic source, it is shown that the strategy that minimizes the conditional mean of $l(b, X_t)$ given the past, is also optimal in the almost sure (and L^1) limit of the time-average loss. When P is unknown, empirical estimates of the conditional probability are provided. By plugging in these estimates instead of the true P, universal schemes are obtained with the same ergodic property as above.

IV. The Deterministic Setting

In the traditional, probabilistic setting of prediction, that was described in the previous section, one assumes that the data are generated by a mechanism that can be characterized in statistical terms, such as a memoryless source, Markov source, or more generally, an arbitrary stationary and ergodic source. As we have seen, the observer estimates on-line either explicitly (plug-in approach) or implicitly (mixture approach) the conditional probability of the next outcome given the past, and then uses this estimate for prediction of future outcomes.

But when it comes to the deterministic setting of individual data sequences, the underlying philosophy must be substantially different. There is no longer an assumption of an ensemble of sequences generated by an underlying probabilistic mechanism, but rather only one arbitrary, deterministic, individual sequence. What is the best prediction strategy that one can possibly use for this fixed sequence?

We realize that, as stated, this question is completely trivial and meaningless. As explained in Section I, formally, for any sequence, there is a perfect predictor that suffers zero loss along this particular sequence. But at the same time, this particular predictor might be extremely bad for many other sequences. Evidently, we are over-tailoring a predictor to one particular sequence, and there is no hope to track the strategy of this predictor in the sequential regime that is inherent to the task of prediction. The root of this "overfitting" effect lies in the fact that we allowed, in the above discussion, too much freedom in the choice of the predictor. Loosely speaking, so much freedom that the amount of information treasured in the *choice* of this predictor is as large as the amount of information conveyed by the sequence itself! Roughly speaking, in these situations the algorithm "learns the data by heart" instead of performing the task we expect. The unavoidable conclusion is that we must limit the freedom of the choice of predictors to a certain class. This limited class of allowable predictors will be henceforth referred to as the *comparison class* (or target class) and will be denoted by B.

We would like to have a *single* universal predictor b_t^* that competes with the best predictor in B, simultaneously for every x^n, in the sense that

$$\frac{1}{n} \sum_{t=1}^{n} l(b_t^*, x_t)$$

is asymptotically the same as

$$\min_{B} \frac{1}{n} \sum_{t=1}^{n} l(b_t, x_t).$$

The universal predictor need not be necessarily in B but it must be the same predictor for every x^n, whereas the choice of the reference predictor in B, that minimizes the average loss, may depend (by definition) on the entire sequence x^n. The difference between the performance of the sequential universal predictor and the best predictor in B for x^n actually manifests

our *regret*, because the choice of this optimal predictor is the best we could have done in retrospect within B had we known the entire sequence in advance.

Loosely speaking, there is a fairly strong duality between the probabilistic and the deterministic setting. While in the former, we make certain assumptions and limitations on the data sequences that we are likely to encounter, but no prior limitations on the class of prediction algorithms, in the latter, it is the other way around. Yet, the deterministic setting is frequently considered stronger and more appealing, because the underlying model seems to be better connected to practical situations: There is no (known) probabilistic mechanism that generates the data, but on the other hand, our algorithmic resources are, after all, limited.

Perhaps one of the facts that shed even more light on this duality between the probabilistic and the deterministic setting, is that quite frequently, the comparison class B is defined as a collection of predictors that are obtained as optimal solutions for a certain class of sources in the parallel probabilistic setting. For example, fixed predictors, where $b_t(x^{t-1})$ is a constant independently of x^{t-1}, are optimal for memoryless stationary sources, linear predictors are sufficient for the Gaussian case, Markov predictors are adequate for Markov processes, and so on. In these cases, there is a remarkable degree of duality and analogy between results obtained in the deterministic setting and those of the corresponding probabilistic setting, notwithstanding the considerable difference between the two concepts. Specifically, many of the results of the individual-sequence setting are completely analogous to their probabilistic counterparts, where the probabilistic source is replaced by the empirical measure extracted from the individual sequence with respect to certain sufficient statistics that are induced by B. Indeed, the structure of this section is similar to that of the previous section, so as to manifest this analogy. Nonetheless, there are still certain aspects in which the two scenarios diverge from each other, as we shall see later.

Similarly as in the previous section, our emphasis here is on the information-theoretic point of view, and as such, it again largely focuses on the self-information loss function.

A. Indexed Comparison Classes

In analogy to the indexed class of sources, that was extensively discussed in the previous section on the probabilistic setting, there has been considerable attention in the literature to the dual comparison classes in the deterministic setting. An indexed comparison class of predictors is a class B that can be represented as $\{b^\theta, \theta \in \Lambda\}$, where θ designates the index and Λ is the index set. Similarly as in Section III-A, the index set Λ could be a finite set $\{1, \cdots, N\}$ (N—positive integer), where N may or may not grow with n, a countably infinite set, a continuum, e.g., a compact subset of the real-line or a higher dimensional Euclidean space (when θ is a parameter of a smooth parametric class), or some combination of these. As was already noted above, in many cases, b^θ could be defined as the optimum predictor for a certain member P_θ of an indexed class of sources (cf. Section III-A).

1) Self-Information Loss: In analogy to Section III, let us consider first the self-information loss function, or equivalently, the probability assignment problem for individual sequences. In other words, our goal is to sequentially assign a universal probability mass function

$$Q(x^n) = \prod_{t=1}^{n} b_t(x_t|x^{t-1}) \qquad (37)$$

to the observed sequence x^n, so that $-\frac{1}{n}\log Q(x^n)$ would be essentially as small as

$$-\frac{1}{n}\log \max_{\theta} \prod_{t=1}^{n} b^{\theta}(x_t|x^{t-1})$$

for every sequence x^n, uniformly if possible.

Shtarkov [109] has demonstrated that this is indeed possible by minimizing over Q the quantity

$$\max_{x^n} \frac{1}{n}\left[-\log Q(x^n) - \left(-\log \max_{\theta} \prod_{t=1}^{n} b^{\theta}(x_t|x^{t-1})\right)\right]. \qquad (38)$$

Specifically, the minimax-optimal probability assignment is attained by the normalized maximum-likelihood function

$$Q_n^*(x^n) = \frac{1}{K_n}\max_{\theta} \prod_{t=1}^{n} b^{\theta}(x_t|x^{t-1}) \qquad (39)$$

where K_n is a normalization factor, i.e.,

$$K_n = \sum_{x^n} \max_{\theta} \prod_{t=1}^{n} b^{\theta}(x_t|x^{t-1}). \qquad (40)$$

Indeed, it is readily seen that, by definition of Q_n^*

$$-\frac{1}{n}\log Q_n^*(x^n) = -\frac{1}{n}\log \max_{\theta} \prod_{t=1}^{n} b^{\theta}(x_t|x^{t-1}) + \frac{1}{n}\log K_n \qquad (41)$$

and so, the universal probability function Q_n^* essentially assigns uniformly as high probabilities as those assigned by the best member in the comparison class, provided that K_n does not grow exponentially rapidly with n.

If, for example, $\{b^{\theta}\}$ is the class of finite-alphabet memoryless probability assignments (i.e., $b^{\theta}(x_t|x^{t-1}) = b^{\theta}(x_t)$) with θ designating the vector of $k = A - 1$ free letter probabilities, then it is easy to show (e.g., by using the method of types [24]) that K_n grows asymptotically in proportion to $n^{k/2}$ and thus (38) behaves like $\frac{k}{2n}\log n$. This in turn is the same behavior that was obtained for smooth parametric families in the probabilistic setting.

The number $\Gamma_n = n^{-1}\log K_n$ is therefore given the interpretation of the deterministic analog to the minimax redundancy-capacity C_n, where the maximization of redundancy over θ in the probabilistic setting is now replaced by maximization over all possible sequences x^n. Intuitively, Γ_n is another measure for the richness of the comparison class of predictors, in addition to the capacity C_n of the probabilistic setting. Moreover, it turns out that there are relations between these two quantities. To demonstrate this relation between Γ_n and the operational notion of capacity as the maximum reliable transmission rate, we note that when $\Lambda = \{1, \cdots, N\}$, the quantity K_n can be interpreted as $N \cdot P_c$ where P_c is the

probability of correct decision of an N-hypotheses testing problem involving the sources

$$P_i(x^n) = \prod_{t=1}^{n} b^i(x_t|x^{t-1}), \qquad 1 \le i \le N$$

that are induced by the predictors, with a uniform prior on i. This is true because

$$P_c = \frac{1}{N}\sum_{x^n}\max_i P_i(x^n) = \frac{K_n}{N}. \qquad (42)$$

This means that if the sources $\{P_i\}$ are "far apart" and distinguishable with high probability, then the minimax redundancy is essentially $\log N$ (compare with the first example in Section III). If Λ is countably infinite or a continuum, then any finite subset $\{\theta_i, i = 1, \cdots, N\}$ of Λ gives a lower bound on K_n in the above manner. As N grows, P_c normally decreases, but the product NP_c can be kept large at least as long as N is smaller than 2^{nC_n} so as to "transmit" at a rate below capacity, which allows for keeping P_c close to unity. But the maximum achievable product NP_c might be achieved at rates beyond capacity.

It is easy to show directly that Γ_n is never smaller than C_n for the same class of sources or probability assignments indexed by Λ. This implies that a necessary condition for the existence of minimax universality in the deterministic setting is the existence of the parallel property in the dual probabilistic setting. In the smooth parametric case both C_n and Γ_n behave like $\frac{k}{2n}\log n$. More precisely (see, e.g., Rissanen [92])

$$C_n = \frac{k}{2n}\log\frac{n}{2\pi e} + \frac{1}{n}\log\int_{\Lambda}|I(\theta)|^{1/2}\,d\theta + o\left(\frac{1}{n}\right) \qquad (43)$$

whereas

$$\Gamma_n = \frac{k}{2n}\log\frac{n}{2\pi} + \frac{1}{n}\log\int_{\Lambda}|I(\theta)|^{1/2}\,d\theta + o\left(\frac{1}{n}\right). \qquad (44)$$

It turns out, however, that richer indexed classes may exhibit a considerably larger gap between these two quantities (see, e.g., the example of arbitrarily varying sources in [76]).

The main drawback of the maximum-likelihood (ML) probability assignment Q_n^* is obviously on the practical side: not only Q_n^* is hard to compute in general, but more importantly, it is again horizon-dependent, i.e., the sequence length n must be prescribed. To alleviate this difficulty, the maximum-likelihood $\max_{\theta}\prod_t b_t(x_t|x^{t-1})$ can be exponentially approximated by a mixture using Laplace integration [67]. Specifically, for the case of stationary memoryless probability assignments, Shtarkov [109] proposed, following Krichevsky and Trofimov [63], the Dirichlet-$(\frac{1}{2}, \cdots, \frac{1}{2})$ (Jeffreys' prior) mixture, which leads to the purely sequential probability assignment

$$b_t(x_t = a|x^{t-1}) = \frac{t(a) + \frac{1}{2}}{(t-1) + \frac{A}{2}} \qquad (45)$$

where $t(a)$ is the number of occurrences of the letter a in x^{t-1}. We have mentioned earlier, in Section III, the family of sequential probability assignments that arise from Dirichlet weighting in general. But the interesting property of the Dirichlet-$(\frac{1}{2}, \cdots, \frac{1}{2})$ (in addition to being Jeffreys' prior for this family), is that it is asymptotically as good as the ML probability assignment. Specifically, with $b_t(\cdot|x^{t-1})$ defined as above

$$\max_{x^n}\left[-\log\prod_{t=1}^{n}b_t(x_t|x^{t-1})\right.$$
$$\left.-\left(-\log\max_{\theta}\prod_{t=1}^{n}b^{\theta}(x_t|x_{t-1})\right)\right]$$
$$\leq \frac{k}{2}\log n + \text{Const} + o(1) \qquad (46)$$

where only the constant here is larger than the one obtained by Q_n^*.

Further refinements and extensions of this result have been recently carried out, e.g., in [92] and [121]. Specifically, Xie and Barron [121] introduce also the dual notion of the maximin redundancy (or regret) whose value coincides with Γ_n as well, and show that Jeffreys' mixture is asymptotically maximin with asymptotically constant regret for sequences whose empirical pmf's are internal to the simplex. Similarly as in the probabilistic setting, it is not asymptotically minimax though because of problematic sequences on the boundary of the simplex. Nevertheless, a slight modification of Jeffreys' mixture (which again, depends on n and hence makes it again horizon-dependent), is both asymptotically minimax and maximin.

Finally, Weinberger, Merhav, and Feder [117] have studied the problem of universal probability assignment for individual sequences under the self-information loss function with respect to the comparison class of all probability assignments that are implementable by finite-state machines with a fixed number of states. There are no such accurate formulas therein regarding the higher order redundancy terms. However, it is shown that the $\frac{k}{2}\log n$ behavior is not only minimax over all sequences, but moreover, it is a tight lower bound for *most* sequences of most *types* defined with respect to those finite-state probability assignments. This result parallels the w-almost everywhere optimality of universal probability assignments in the probabilistic setting (cf. Section III). In this context, it is interesting to note, as shown in [117], that in contrast to the probabilistic setting, the plug-in approach fails, in general, when it comes to individual sequences. We will elaborate on these results further in Section V in the context of hierarchical comparison classes.

2) General Loss Functions: The problem of universal sequential prediction or decision-making for individual sequences under general loss functions, is definitely a much wider problem area than that of the special case of probability assignment under the self-information loss function that we discussed thus far in this section. In fact, most of the classical work in this problem area, in various scientific disciplines, has concentrated primarily on the case of *constant* predictors, i.e., predictors for which each b^{θ} yields a certain fixed prediction, regardless of the observed past. For example, b^{θ}, for a certain value of θ, may suggest to predict *always* "0" as the next outcome of a binary sequence, or, it may always assign a probability of 0.8 for the next outcome being "1." This is seemingly not a very interesting comparison class because past information is entirely ignored.

Nonetheless, the motivation for carefully studying this simple comparison class is that it is fundamental for examining comparison classes of more sophisticated predictors. For example, a first-order Markov predictor, characterized by $b^{\theta}(x_t|x^{t-1}) = b^{\theta}(x_t|x_{t-1})$, can be thought of (in the binary case) as a combination of two fixed predictors operating, respectively, on two subsequences of $\boldsymbol{x}^n$: the one corresponding to all time instants $\{t\}$ that follow $x_{t-1}=0$, and the other—where $x_{t-1}=1$. Having made this observation, the problem then boils down back to that of constant predictors.

One example, which is still closely related to the self-information, is that of portfolio selection for optimal investment in the stock market [3]–[5], [21]. In this model, the goal is to maximize the asymptotic exponential growth rate of the capital, where the current investment strategy depends on the past. The corresponding loss function, in our framework, is then $l(b, x) = -\log(b^T x)$, with both b and x being m-dimensional vectors of nonnegative components, where in the former these components sum to unity. The vector x represents the return per monetary unit in several investment opportunities (stocks), whereas the vector b characterizes the fraction of the current capital allocated to each stock. Cover [21] and Cover and Ordentlich [22] have used techniques similar to those of the self-information loss described above, to develop a sequential investment algorithm and related it again to universal coding with results of a similar flavor. Again, their universal sequential strategy competes with the best constant investment strategy. These results can be viewed as an extension of the self-information loss because the latter is actually a special case where the vector x is always all-zero except for one component (corresponding to the current alphabet letter), which is 1.

3) The Sequential-Compound Decision Problem: Other examples of loss functions are not so closely related to that of the self-information loss, and consequently, the techniques and the results are considerably different. The comparison class of constant strategies for more general loss functions has been studied in a somewhat more general setting, referred to as the *sequential-compound decision problem*, which was first presented by Robbins [94] and has been thoroughly investigated later by many researchers from disciplines of mathematical statistics, game theory, and control theory (see, e.g., [8], [9], [49], [50], and [112]). Perhaps the most fundamental findings of the compound sequential decision problem are summarized in the theory of Bayes decision rules, that includes the notion of *Bayes envelope* (that is, the best achievable target performance as a functional of the empirical pmf of the sequence) and an analysis of its basic properties. This in turn has been combined with approachability–excludability theory, that provides simple necessary and sufficient conditions under which one player (in our case, the predictor) of a repeated zero-sum game can reach a certain performance level (in our case, the Bayes envelope) for every strategy of the opponent player (in our case, Nature that chooses an adversary sequence x^n).

The sequential compound decision problem is more general than our setting in the sense that the observer is assumed to access only noisy versions of the sequence x^n, yet the loss function to be minimized is still associated with the clean sequence (e.g., the expected cumulative loss, or its probabilistic limit with respect to the ensemble of noise processes). Hannan [49] has taken a game-theoretic approach to develop upper bounds on the decay rate on the regret, showing a convergence rate of $O\left(n^{-1/2}\right)$ in the finite-alphabet, finite-strategy space case, and a rate of $O\left(n^{-1}\sum_{t=1}^{n}t^{-\alpha}\right)$ in the continuous case, provided that the loss-minimizing strategy b^* as a functional of the underlying empirical pmf of x^n, that is, the *Bayes response*, satisfies a Lipschitz condition of order $\alpha > 0$. Thus for $\alpha = 1$, which is normally the case, this means a convergence rate of $\log n/n$, similarly to the self-information loss case that we have seen above.

One of the essential ideas underlying the analysis techniques, is the following simple "sandwich" argument (see, e.g., [75]): It is easy to show that

$$\min_{B}\frac{1}{n}\sum_{t=1}^{n}l(b_t,\,x_t)$$

i.e., the Bayesian envelope, is upper- and lower-bounded by the average loss associated with two strategies. The current strategy for the upper bound is optimal within B for the data seen thus far x^{t-1}, and for the lower bound, it is an (imagined) strategy that is allowed to access x^t for this optimization within B. Thus the strategy of the lower bound sees merely one more outcome than that of the upper bound. When the comparison class is that of constant strategies, the Bayes envelope depends on the sequence only through its empirical pmf, and this additional observation perturbs the current empirical pmf by a term proportional to $1/t$. Therefore, under the appropriate smoothness conditions ($\alpha = 1$ above), the instantaneous losses of the upper and lower bound differ also by a quantity that scales proportionally to $1/t$, which when averaged over the integers $1, \cdots, n$, gives $O\left(\log n/n\right)$. *A fortiori*, the difference between the upper bound and the Bayes envelope, i.e., the regret, cannot exceed $O\left(\log n/n\right)$.

In some important special cases, however, the loss function and the Bayes response are discontinuous. This happens, for example, in prediction of binary sequences under the criterion of relative frequency of mispredicted outcomes, where the Bayes response with respect to the class of constant predictors is binary itself and it depends on whether the relative frequency of zeros is below or above $1/2$. In this case, randomization of the sequential prediction strategy around the discontinuity point (see, e.g., [40], [99], and [100]) is necessary in order to achieve the target performance for problematic sequences whose empirical pmf's visit infinitely often (as $n \rightarrow \infty$) these discontinuity points. The cost of this randomization, however, is a considerable slowdown in the rate of convergence towards the Bayes envelope. In the above binary case, for example, the rate of convergence is $O\left(1/\sqrt{n}\right)$, whereas in the parallel probabilistic setting, where such a randomization is not needed (cf. Section III), it is as fast as $O\left(1/n\right)$.

Van Ryzin [112] has shown that even in the former case of smooth loss functions, the convergence rate can be more tightly upper-bounded by $O\left(\log n/n\right)$ under certain regularity conditions on the channel through which the observer receives the noisy measurements. Gilliland [46] further investigated

convergence rates for the special case of the square loss function $l(b,\,x) = (x - b)^2$ under various sets of assumptions. Several later papers [82], [113] deal with the more general case where the comparison class consists of Markov strategies, whose importance will be emphasized later.

On-Line Prediction Using Expert Advice: A completely different point of view has been taken more recently, primarily by learning theorists in their studies of a paradigm referred to as *on-line prediction using expert advice* (see, e.g., [12], [13], [36], [43], [69], [84], and [115]). In the previously defined terminology, the basic assumption is that the comparison class consists of finitely many predictors $b^1, \cdots, b^N$, referred to as *experts*. There are absolutely no assumptions on any structure or relationships among these experts. The goal is to devise a sequential universal prediction algorithm that performs essentially as well as the best of these experts along every individual sequence.

We have actually examined earlier this scenario in the context of the self-information loss function and a finite index set $\Lambda = \{1, \cdots, N\}$, where our conclusion was that the necessary minimax price of universality need not exceed $\log N/n$ in the worst case, namely, when the probability assignments b^i correspond to distinguishable sources. Interestingly, this behavior essentially continues to take place for general (but sufficiently regular) loss functions. Vovk [115] and Littlestone and Warmuth [70] proposed independently a sequential prediction algorithm, whose regret with respect to the best expert never exceeds $c_l \log N$, where c_l is a constant that depends solely on the loss function l. At the heart of this algorithm, there is a remarkable similarity to the mixture approach, or, more concretely, the notion of exponential weighting that was discussed in Section III in the special case of the self-information loss.

Here is the idea: let $\eta > 0$ be a given constant (to be chosen later) and consider the weighted average of $e^{-\eta l(b_t^i,\,x_t)}$, i.e.,

$$\sum_{i=1}^{N}w_t(i)\,e^{-\eta l(b_t^i,\,x_t)} \tag{47}$$

where b_t^i is the prediction of the ith expert at time t, and $w_t(i)$ is the *weight* assigned to this expert at this time. The weights, at each time instant, are nonnegative numbers summing to unity. Intuitively, we would like to assign higher weights to experts who were proven better in the past. Therefore, a reasonable thing to do, following (10), is to assign to each expert a weight $w_t(i)$ that is proportional to

$$\exp\left(-\eta\sum_{\tau=0}^{t-1}l(b_\tau^i,\,x_\tau)\right)$$

where for $t = 0$ the summation will be defined as zero (i.e., uniform initial weighting). Now, if we are fortunate enough that there exists a strategy b such that for every x

$$e^{-\eta l(b,\,x)} \geq \sum_{i=1}^{N}w_t(i)\,e^{-\eta l(b_t^i,\,x)} \tag{48}$$

then it is easy to see that this strategy will serve our purpose. This is true because the above condition suggests the following conceptually simple algorithm:

0) **Initialization:** Set $w_0(i) = 1/N$ for $1 \leq i \leq N$ and then $t = 1$.

1) **Prediction:** Choose a prediction b_t^* at time t that satisfies (48).

2) **Update:** Upon receiving x_t, update the weight function according to

$$w_{t+1}(i) = \frac{w_t(i) \, e^{-\eta l(b_t^i, x_t)}}{\displaystyle\sum_{j=1}^{N} w_t(j) \, e^{-\eta l(b_t^j, x_t)}}. \tag{49}$$

3) **Iteration:** Increment t and go to 1).

It follows immediately from the definition of the algorithm that the exponent of the cumulative loss associated with $\{b_t^*\}$ satisfies

$$\exp\left(-\eta \sum_{t=1}^{n} l(b_t^*, x_t)\right) \geq \frac{1}{N} \sum_{i=1}^{N} \exp\left(-\eta \sum_{t=1}^{n} l(b_t^i, x_t)\right)$$
$$\geq \frac{1}{N} \max_i \exp\left(-\eta \sum_{t=1}^{n} l(b_t^i, x_t)\right) \tag{50}$$

and so

$$\sum_{t=1}^{n} l(b_t^*, x_t) \leq \min_i \sum_{t=1}^{n} l(b_t^i, x_t) + \frac{1}{\eta} \ln N. \tag{51}$$

Thus the crucial question that remains to be addressed is regarding the conditions under which (48) is satisfied. To put this question in perspective, first, observe that for the self-information loss function and $\eta = 1$, the functions

$$\exp\left(-\eta \sum_{t=1}^{n} l(b_t^i, x_t)\right)$$

are probability measures of n-tuples. Therefore, their weighted average (mixture) is itself a probability measure and as such, can be represented by

$$\exp\left(-\eta \sum_{t=1}^{n} l(b_t^*, x_t)\right)$$

for a certain $\{b_t^*\}$, which is the probability assignment corresponding to the finite mixture. However, in general, the function $e^{-\eta l(\cdot, \cdot)}$ may not be closed to convex combinations. Fortunately, it is shown that under fairly mild regularity conditions (see [52], [115], and [116] for details), it is guaranteed that (48) always holds provided that η is chosen to be at most $1/c_l$ and that $c_l < \infty$, in which case the regret can be made as small as $c_l \ln N/n$. Many of the important loss functions, like the self-information loss and the square-error loss, satisfy these conditions. For example, if the function $e^{-\eta l(b, x)}$ is concave ($\cap$) in b for every x (which is the case in linear prediction and squared-error loss under some conditions [110]), namely,

$$\exp\left[-\eta l\left(\sum_{i=1}^{N} w_t(i) b_t^i, x\right)\right] \geq \sum_{i=1}^{N} w_t(i) e^{-\eta l(b_t^i, x)} \tag{52}$$

then it is clear that the weighted average of the experts' predictions will be a suitable solution. Unfortunately, there are also other important loss functions (like the L_1 loss function, $l(b, x) = |x - b|$) for which $c_l = \infty$. This means that for these loss functions, the regret does not behave like $O(\log N/n)$, but rather decays at a slower rate with n, e.g., like $1/\sqrt{n}$. These cases should be handled separately.

What makes this algorithm even more interesting is the fact that it turns out to be minimax-optimal in the sense that $c_l \ln N/n$ is also an asymptotic lower bound on the maximum regret. Unfortunately, the weak point of this lower bound is that this maximum is taken not only over all sequences $\{x^n\}$, but also over all possible sets of N experts! The algorithm is, therefore, asymptotically optimal in an extremely pessimistic sense, which is of special concern when N is large. What is left to be desired then is a stronger bound that depends on the relationships among the experts. As an extreme example, if all experts are identical then there is in fact only one expert, not N, and we would expect to obtain zero regret. Intuitively, we would like the formal number of experts N to be replaced by some notion of an "effective" number of distinct experts, in analogy and as an extension of the role played by capacity C_n or by Γ_n in the self-information loss case. To the best of our knowledge, to date, there are no reported results of this kind in the literature except for Cesa-Bianchi and Lugosi [14] who characterized the minimax regret along with upper and lower bounds for binary sequences and the Hamming loss function, but without any constructive algorithm yet.

Another drawback is associated with the algorithm itself. To use this algorithm in practice, one should actually implement in parallel the prediction algorithms proposed by all N experts, which might be computationally demanding for large N. This is in contrast to the situation in certain special cases, e.g., when the experts correspond to all finite-state machines with a given number of states [38], [40], [75], [126]. In these cases, there is no explicit implementation of all finite-state machines in parallel.

In spite of these shortcomings, the problem of on-line prediction with expert advice has attracted fairly much attention over the last few years and there are quite a few reported extensions, modifications, and other variations on the theme (see, e.g., [10] for a summary of recent work in on-line learning). One extension that would be especially interesting is to tie it with the setting of the compound sequential decision problem in the sense that the predictor accesses only noisy observations, whereas the loss function remains in terms of the clean outcomes. Clearly, the above weighting algorithm, in its present form, is not directly implementable since there is no perfect feedback on the loss associated with past expert advice.

B. Very Large Comparison Classes

We end this section with a natural analog to the case of very large classes of sources in the probabilistic setting, namely, very large comparison classes of predictors for which there are normally no uniform redundancy rates.

In the general level, consider a nested infinite sequence of index sets $\Lambda_1 \subset \Lambda_2 \subset \cdots$, and their union $\Lambda = \cup_{k \geq 1} \Lambda_k$.

Strictly speaking, Λ is itself an index set, whose members are of the form (k, θ), where k is the smallest integer such that $\theta \in \Lambda_k$. However, the basic property that makes Λ herein different than the index sets of Section IV-A is that it is so rich, that for every finite sequence x^n, the minimum cumulative loss over all predictors indexed by Λ is zero. In other words, there is too much freedom within Λ, and we are confronting again the undesirable overfitting effect discussed earlier. This happens in many important examples, e.g., when Λ consists of the class of all finite-state predictors with an undetermined (but finite) number of states, or the class of all Markov predictors, or even more specifically, all linear predictors with an unspecified finite order, etc. Quite clearly, in all these situations, there are enough degrees of freedom to tailor a perfect predictor for any finite sequence x^n, and thus our earlier definition (cf. Section IV-A) of the target performance $\min_\Lambda \sum_t l(b_t, x_t)$ becomes meaningless.

We are lead then to the conclusion that we must modify the definition of the target performance. The key principle for doing this is to keep an asymptotic regime of $n \gg k$. To fix ideas, consider an infinite sequence $\boldsymbol{x} = (x_1, x_2, \cdots)$, where x^n always designates the first n outcomes of $\boldsymbol{x}$. First, similarly as in Section IV-A, let us define

$$u_k(x^n) = \min_{\Lambda_k} \frac{1}{n} \sum_{t=1}^{n} l(b_t, x_t) \qquad (53)$$

where it is assumed that each Λ_k is an index set of the type discussed in Section IV-A. As for asymptotics, we let first n grow without bound, and define

$$u_k(\boldsymbol{x}) = \limsup_{n \to \infty} u_k(x^n) \qquad (54)$$

where the $\limsup$ operation manifests a worst case approach: since the sequence $\boldsymbol{x}$ is not necessarily ergodic, i.e., the limit may not exist, one must worry about the worst performance level obtained infinitely often along $\boldsymbol{x}$. Finally, we define our target performance as

$$u(\boldsymbol{x}) = \lim_{k \to \infty} u_k(\boldsymbol{x}) \qquad (55)$$

where now the limit clearly exists since $\{u_k(\boldsymbol{x})\}_{k \geq 1}$ is a monotonically nonincreasing sequence whose elements are obtained from minimizations over increasing sets of predictors. Since the limit $n \to \infty$ is taken first, the asymptotic regime here indeed meets the above mentioned requirement that $n \gg k$. The problem is now to devise a universal prediction algorithm $\{b_t^*\}_{t \geq 1}$ that asymptotically achieves $u(\boldsymbol{x})$.

One of the most popular applications of this general scenario is the one where Λ consists of all strategies that are implementable by finite-state machines, which means that each Λ_S, $S = 1, 2, \cdots$, corresponds to the class of finite-state machines with no more than S states. Specifically, each member of Λ_S is defined by two functions f and g. The function g, referred to as the *next-state function*, describes the evolution of the state of the machine, $s_t \in \{1, \cdots, k\}$, according to the recursion

$$s_t = g(x_{t-1}, s_{t-1}), \qquad t = 1, 2, \cdots \qquad (56)$$

where the initial state s_0 is fixed. The function f describes the strategy b_t at time t, which depends only on s_t by

$$b_t = f(s_t). \qquad (57)$$

The idea behind this model is that the state variable s_t represents the limited information that the machine can "memorize" from the past x^{t-1} for the purpose of choosing the current strategy. An important special case of a finite-state machine with $S = A^k$ states is that of a kth-order Markov machine (also called finite-memory machine), where $s_t = (x_{t-k}, \cdots, x_{t-1})$.

Ziv and Lempel described, in their famous paper [126], a target performance in this spirit in the context of data compression of individual sequences using finite-state machines. The best $\limsup$ compression ratio obtained by finite-state encoders over infinitely long individual sequences (in the above defined sense) has been referred to as the *finite-state compressibility* of $\boldsymbol{x}$, and the well-known Lempel–Ziv algorithm (LZ'78) has been shown to achieve the finite-state compressibility for every sequence. In a later paper [127], Ziv and Lempel extended this definition to compression of two-dimensional arrays (images), where the additional ingredient is in defining also a scanning strategy.

In [38], results in the same spirit have been obtained for sequential gambling over individual sequences, where again the comparison class is that of gambling strategies that are implementable by finite-state machines. Since the gambling problem is completely analogous to that of data compression, or more precisely, probability assignment under the self-information loss function (see also [117] discussed in Section IV-A), the results therein are largely similar to those of Ziv and Lempel [126]. The formal setting of [38], however, is somewhat more compliant than [126] to our general definition of cumulative loss minimization, where each loss term depends on one outcome x_t only.

The results of [38] in turn provided the trigger to a later work [40], where the comparison class of finite-state predictors for binary sequences was studied under the Hamming loss function, defined as $l(b, x) = 0$ if $x = b$, and $l(b, x) = 1$ otherwise. In other words, in this case, $b_t = f(s_t)$ is simply an estimate of the value of the next outcome x_t, and the performance measure is the relative frequency of prediction errors. Analogously to [126], the quantity $u(\boldsymbol{x})$, in this special case, is called the *finite-state predictability* of $\boldsymbol{x}$. Similarly, when Λ_k is further confined to the class of kth-order Markov predictors, then the correspondingly defined $u(\boldsymbol{x})$ is called the *Markov predictability* of $\boldsymbol{x}$. There are two main conclusions pointed out in [40].

The first is that the finite-state predictability and the Markov predictability are always equivalent, which means that it is sufficient to confine attention to Markov predictors in order to achieve the finite-state predictability. It is worthwhile to note that in the probabilistic setting, such a result would have been expected under certain mixing conditions because the effect of the remote past fades away as time evolves, and only the immediate past (that is stored as the state of a Markov predictor) should be essential. Yet, when it comes to individual sequences this finding is not at all trivial since the sequence is arbitrary and there is no parallel assumption on mixing or fading memory. The proof of this result stems from pure information-theoretic considerations.

The second conclusion, which is largely based on the first one, is on the algorithmic side. It turns out that a prediction strategy that corresponds to probability assignments based on the incremental parsing procedure of the LZ algorithm (see also [65] and [114]) asymptotically achieves the finite-state predictability. The incremental parsing procedure sequentially parses a sequence into distinct phrases, where each new phrase is the shortest string that is not identical to any previously parsed phrase. The reason is that the incremental parsing procedure works like a Markov predictor of time-varying order $k(t)$, where in the long run, $k(t)$ is very large most of the time because the phrases become longer and longer. Consequently, the Markov predictability, and hence also the finite-state predictability, are eventually attained. But the deep point here lies in the simple fact that the incremental parsing algorithm, which was originally developed as a building block of a compression algorithm, serves also as the engine of a probability-assignment mechanism, which is useful for prediction.

This gives rise to the idea that this probability assignment induces a universal probability measure in the context of individual sequences. Loosely speaking, it means that the universal probability measure is proportional to $2^{-\text{LZ}(x^n)}$, where $\text{LZ}(x^n)$ is the LZ codeword length for x^n [38], [65]. This in turn can be thought of as an extension of Shtarkov's ML probability assignment because $2^{-\text{LZ}(x^n)}$ is well known [87] to be an upper bound (within vanishingly small terms) of $\max_P P(x^n)$, where the maximum is taken over all finite-state sources with a fixed number of states.

The problem of [40] was later extended [75] in several directions simultaneously: the alphabet of x^n and the loss function were assumed to be more general. Also, classes of predictors other than that of deterministic finite-state predictors were considered, e.g., randomized finite-state predictors (where the next-state function is randomized), families of linear predictors, etc. Many of the results of [40] turn out to carry over to this more general case.

Finally, one additional result of [75, Theorem 3] (see, also [126]) relates the individual-sequence setting back to the probabilistic setting. It tells us that under suitable regularity conditions, for a stationary and ergodic process $\cdots, X_{-1}, X_0, X_1, \cdots$, the quantity $u(X_1, X_2, \cdots)$, defined with respect to finite-state or Markov predictors, agrees almost surely with the probabilistic performance measure $\inf_b E\{l(b, X_0)|X_{-1}, X_{-2}, \cdots\}$. One special case of this result [126] is that the finite-state compressibility is almost surely equal to the entropy rate of a stationary and ergodic source. Another important example corresponds to the case where Λ_k is the class of all linear predictors of order k, and hence $u(\boldsymbol{x})$ is the *linear predictability*. In the stationary and ergodic case, the above cited result suggests that with probability one, $u(X_1, X_2, \cdots)$ coincides with the variance of the innovation process (that is, the residual linear prediction error) given by

$$\epsilon^2 = \exp\left[\frac{1}{2\pi}\int_0^{2\pi} \ln S(e^{j\omega})\,d\omega\right]$$

where $S(e^{j\omega})$ is the power spectral density of the process.

While the duality between certain classes of sources and the corresponding classes of predictors was quite straightforward

in relatively small indexed (parametric) classes, the above result establishes a parallel duality between the very large class of stationary and ergodic sources and the very large class of finite-state predictors or Markov predictors.

V. HIERARCHICAL UNIVERSALITY

So far we have focused on two substantially different situations of universal prediction, both of which take place in the probabilistic setting as well as in the deterministic setting: Universality with respect to an indexed class,[1] which is relatively "small," as opposed to universality with respect to a very large class, where no uniform redundancy rates exist. These two extreme situations reflect the interplay between two conflicting goals, namely, fast decay of redundancy rates on the one hand, and universality with respect to classes as wide and general as possible, on the other. For example, the Lempel–Ziv algorithm for data compression (or for predictive probability assignment) is universal for all stationary and ergodic sources, but when a memoryless source is encountered, this algorithm gives a redundancy rate that might be much slower than that of a universal scheme which is tailored to the class of memoryless sources; see [71], [87], and [101].

Our basic assumption throughout this section is that the large class Λ of sources (in the probabilistic setting) or predictors (in the deterministic setting) can be represented as a countable union of a sequence of index sets $\{\Lambda_k\}_{k \geq 1}$, which may, but not necessarily, have a certain structure, such as nestedness $\Lambda_1 \subset \Lambda_2 \subset \cdots$. In the probabilistic setting, perhaps the first example that naturally comes into one's mind is where each Λ_k is the class of discrete kth-order Markov sources, and hence the union Λ is the large class of all finite-order Markov sources. Furthermore, in the finite-alphabet case, if we slightly extend this class and take its "closure" with respect to the information divergence "distance" measure, it would include the class of all stationary sources. This is because every stationary source can be approximated, in the divergence sense, by a sequence of Markov sources of growing order [44, Theorem 3.5.1, p. 57], [47, Theorem 2.6.2, p. 52]. A few other examples of hierarchical probabilistic models are the following: i) finite-state sources with deterministic/randomized next-state functions, ii) tree sources (FSMX), iii) noisy versions of signals that are representable by countable families of basis functions, iv) arbitrarily varying sources [76], v) sources with countable alphabets (referred to as sequences of classes of growing alphabets), and vi) piecewise-stationary memoryless sources. Most of these examples have dual comparison classes in the deterministic setting.

In view of the discussion in the above two paragraphs, a natural question that arises, at this point, is the following: can one devise a universal predictor that enjoys both the benefits of a small indexed class and a large class? In other words, we would like to have, if possible, a universal predictor with respect to the large class, but with the additional property that it also performs essentially as well as the best universal predictor

---

[1] Since this refers to both the probabilistic and the deterministic setting, the term "class" here corresponds both to a class of sources in the probabilistic setting, and a comparison class of predictors in the deterministic setting.

within every given indexed subclass Λ_k of Λ. In the probabilistic setting, this means that if we are so fortunate that the source happens to be a member of a relatively small indexed class (e.g., a memoryless source), then the redundancy, or the regret, would be essentially the same as that of the best universal predictor for this smaller class. In the analog deterministic setting, we would like the universal predictor of this large class to behave similarly as the best universal predictor within a certain indexed comparison subclass. Note that the above question is meaningful even if Λ is merely a finite (rather than a countably infinite) union of $\{\Lambda_k\}_{k \geq 1}$. The reason is that the uniform redundancy rate of Λ, that is, the redundancy-capacity, denoted by $C_n(\Lambda)$ in the self-information loss case, might still be larger than that of any subset $C_n(\Lambda_k)$. Therefore, even in this case, treating Λ just as one big class might not be the best thing to do.

In the probabilistic setting, Ryabko [97] was the first to address this interesting question for the above described nested sequence of classes of Markov sources, and for the self-information loss (universal coding). Generally speaking, Ryabko's idea is to apply the following conceptually simple two-part code, referred to as a *twice-universal* code. The first part of the code is a codeword for an integer i whose length is $L(i) = \log i + O(\log \log i)$, and the second part is a universal code with respect to Λ_i, where i is chosen so as to minimize the total codeword length. Clearly, this code attains redundancy of

$$\min_i [C_n(\Lambda_i) + L(i)/n] \tag{58}$$

which obviously never exceeds $C_n(\Lambda_k) + L(k)/n$ for the true value of k. Since $C_n(\Lambda_k)$ behaves like $O(\log n/n)$ in the Markov case, the additional $O(1/n)$ term does not affect the rate of convergence within each Λ_k. Thus although there cannot be uniform redundancy rates simultaneously over the entire class of Markov sources Λ there is still asymptotically optimal behavior within every Λ_k.

An alternative to this two-part code, which cannot be transformed easily into a prediction scheme, is the mixture approach. Specifically, for the problem of prediction with self-information loss, the suggested solution is based on a probability assignment formed by two-stage mixture, first within each Λ_k, and then over the integers $k = 1, 2, \cdots$ [98]. The first observation is that the mixture approach, with appropriately chosen weight functions, is no worse than the above two-part scheme. To see this, let us assume that $\{L(i)\}_{i \geq 1}$ satisfy Kraft's inequality with equality (otherwise, they can be improved), and consider the two-stage mixture

$$Q(x^n) = \sum_{i \geq 1} 2^{-L(i)} \int_\Lambda dw_i^*(\theta) P_\theta(x^n)$$
$$= \sum_{i \geq 1} 2^{-L(i)} Q_{w_i^*}(x^n) \tag{59}$$

where w_i^* is the capacity-achieving prior of Λ_i. Then

$$-\log Q(x^n) \leq -\log \left[\max_{i \geq 1} (2^{-L(i)} Q_{w_i^*}(x^n)) \right]$$
$$= \min_{i \geq 1} [-\log Q_{w_i^*}(x^n) + L(i)] \tag{60}$$

where the left-most side corresponds to the performance of the mixture approach and the right-most side corresponds to the performance of the two-part scheme with an optimum mixture within each class. The message here is that for every *individual sequence*, the mixture approach is no worse than the two-part approach. In [117] this point is further explored and developed for several examples of hierarchical classes (finite-state machines and others) in view of the fact that the first term of the right-most side above is also a lower bound for "most" sequences in a fairly strong sense (cf. Section III). Of course, the last chain of inequalities continues to hold after taking expectations in the probabilistic setting.

It turns out though, that in the probabilistic setting the mixture approach is not only no worse than the two-part approach, but moreover, it is an optimal approach in a much sharper and deeper sense. As an extension to the result of w-almost everywhere optimality of Q_w (cf. Section II), the following holds for hierarchies of classes [39, Theorem 3]: the two-stage mixture with arbitrary weight functions $\{w_i(\cdot)\}_{i \geq 1}$ within the classes, and $\pi = \{\pi_i\}_{i \geq 1}$, $\pi_i = 2^{-L(i)}$, over the positive integers, simultaneously minimizes in essence redundancy for w_i-most points in Λ_i of π-most classes $\{\Lambda_i\}$. If, in addition, $w_i = w_i^*$ is the capacity-achieving prior for all i, then this minimum redundancy can be decomposed into a sum of two terms, the first of which is $C_n(\Lambda_k)$, the capacity within the underlying class Λ_k, and the second is an extra redundancy term that reflects the additional cost of universality with respect to the unknown k. The latter term is always upper-bounded by $\frac{1}{n} \log 1/\pi_k = L(k)/n$. However, if we further assume that the classes are "easily distinguishable" in the sense that there exists a good (model order) estimator for k with small average error probability [39, Theorem 4], then $L(k)/n$ is an asymptotically tight bound. This means that in the case of distinguishable classes, $C_n(\Lambda_k) + L(k)/n$ is the optimal performance even at the level of the higher order term $L(k)/n$, which might be considerably larger for large k. However, if the classes are not easily distinguishable, the mixture approach yields a smaller second-order redundancy term whereas the two-part coding approach continues to give $L(k)/n$. Some guidelines regarding the choice of π (or, equivalently, $\{L(i)\}$) are given in [39]. It should be noted that for any monotone nonincreasing sequence of probabilities, $\pi_i \leq 1/i$ for all i, namely, $L(i) \geq \log i$, and so $C_n(\Lambda_k) + (\log k)/n$ is optimum redundancy in the distinguishable case, as it can be asymptotically attained by a universal code for the integers.

From the viewpoint of sequential predictive probability assignment, however, both the two-part method and the method of mixtures are not directly implementable because in the former, the minimizing i depends on the entire x^n, and in the latter, $\{w_i^*\}$ may depend on n. A possible alternative to the nonsequential minimization over i could be on-line estimation of i and plug-in. An algorithm in this spirit has been proposed by Weinberger, Rissanen, and Feder [118] for hierarchies of tree sources in the probabilistic setting, where the estimator of i (which is associated the context, in this case) was based on algorithm Context. Fortunately, the probability of error in estimating i decays sufficiently rapidly, so as to leave the leading redundancy term unaffected. In the deterministic setting, however, it can be shown [117] that the method based on the plug-in estimate of i does not work, i.e., there are sequences for which the resulting "redundancy" is higher than achieved when the class Λ_i is known in advance.

The mixture approach, however, is useful in both the probabilistic setting and the deterministic setting, giving us yet another reason to prefer it. To overcome the problem mentioned above, namely, the fact that the weights of the mixture over the index i depend on the horizon, we use fixed-weight functions. Fortunately, as mentioned in Section II, in many cases w_i^* are replaceable by mixture weights that do not depend on n and yet asymptotically achieve capacity.

At this point it is necessary to address a major practical concern: is it computationally feasible to implement the two-stage mixture probability assignment? More specifically, we have seen (Sections III and IV) that in some important examples the mixture within a single indexed class is easily implementable, but is it still reasonably easy to implement the second-stage mixture among (possibly infinitely) many classes. Unfortunately, there is no positive answer to this question in the general level. Nonetheless, Willems, Shtarkov, and Tjalkens, in their award-winning paper [120] provided a positive answer to this question for finite hierarchies of classes of tree sources, using an efficient recursive method, referred to as *context-tree weighting*. Their method is optimal for every individual sequence in the sense of (60). For hierarchies of countably infinitely many classes, however, the implementation issue is still unresolved. In [117] several examples are demonstrated where the countably infinite mixture over i actually collapses to a finite one. This happens because the contributions of mixtures corresponding to all i beyond a certain threshold i_0 turn out to be identical and then can be merged with the combined weight $\sum_{i \geq i_0} \pi_i$. The problem is, though, that i_0 normally grows with n, and so, the computational burden of computing i_0 mixtures at every time instant becomes explosively large as time elapses.

So far, we have discussed hierarchical universal prediction solely under the self-information loss function. What can be said about other loss functions? Apparently, we can deduce from the self-information loss function to other loss functions in the same way that this has been done in Sections III and IV. Beyond that, we are not aware of much reported work on this topic. We will mention only two directions that have been pursued explicitly. The first one is by Helmbold and Schapire [55], who have combined the exponential weighting mechanism of on-line prediction using expert advice [115] (with respect to the absolute error loss function) together with the context-tree weighting algorithm of Willems, Shtarkov, and Tjalkens [120] for competing with the best pruning of a decision tree.

Other recent work is in hierarchical linear prediction for individual sequences under the square error loss function [41], [110]. In these papers, the linear prediction problem is transformed into a Gaussian sequential probability assignment problem. The universal assignment is obtained by a two-stage mixture, over the linear prediction coefficients and over the model order. For the mixture over the parameters, a Gaussian prior is used, and the mixture can be evaluated analytically.

The probability assignment attained by the mixture does not correspond directly to a universal predictor, but fortunately, such correspondence can be made for a certain range of values of the predicted sequence. Thus by a proper choice of prior, the predictor can be scaled to any finite range of the sequence values. In addition, the mixture over the model order is performed in a computationally efficient way, since using lattice filters, all possible linear predictors with model order up to some largest order M can be weighted in an efficient recursive procedure whose complexity is not larger than that for a conventional linear predictor of the model order M. It was also noted, following [75], that a plug-in estimator of the parameter (resulting from the recursive least squares (RLS) algorithm) leads to universal prediction albeit at a slower rate than the mixture approach. The resulting universal linear predictor has been implemented and tested experimentally in several practical communication and signal processing problems [110].

VI. Conclusion and Future Directions

In this paper, an attempt has been made to provide an overview on the current state-of-the-art in the problem area of universal prediction. As explained in Section I, it is definitely not, and not meant to be, a full encyclopedic survey of all scientific work that has ever been done on this topic. The aim was to mention several important concepts from the authors' point of view. Let us summarize some of these concepts very briefly.

We have seen that the problem of universal prediction has been studied extensively both in the probabilistic and the deterministic setting. There are many common features shared by these two settings. First of all, in both of them the self-information loss case plays a central role, which stems from several facts. i) It is an important loss function on its own right for reasons that were explained in Section II. One of the main reasons is that we view the prediction problem as one of probability assignment, and as such, the self-information loss function arises in a very natural manner. ii) In the self-information loss case the theory is fairly mature and well understood. iii) Results (both lower bounds and algorithms) for other loss functions can be obtained from the self-information loss function. The second common feature of the probabilistic and the deterministic settings is in the large degree of parallelism between the theories of universal prediction: universality with respect to small indexed classes, universality with respect to very large classes, and hierarchical universality, which actually bridges them. There is also a remarkable degree of analogy between the quantitative results obtained in both settings in some cases. One of the fundamental connections is that for stationary and ergodic sequences, the best attainable performance level of the deterministic definition agrees almost surely with its probabilistic counterpart.

However, there are a few differences as well: sometimes minimax redundancy rates of the deterministic setting are different from those of the probabilistic setting. The plug-in approach for predictive probability assignment works well in many instances of the probabilistic setting, but it is normally not a good approach in the deterministic setting. The minimax redundancy of the deterministic setting is different from that of the probabilistic setting. Randomization is sometimes necessary in the deterministic setting, but not in the probabilistic setting.

Perhaps one of the interesting messages is that although the term "probability assignment" originally comes from the probabilistic world, it is still meaningful in the pure deterministic setting as well. This fact is far from being trivial. Moreover, there are very efficient algorithmic tools for obtaining good probability assignments, and one of them is the incremental parsing procedure of the Lempel–Ziv algorithm.

We also see a few more theoretical problems which might be interesting to consider for future research. Some of them have been mentioned in the body of the paper.

- Develop a more solid and general theory of universal prediction for general loss functions, in parallel and extension of the theory of the self-information loss function. Derive tighter and stronger lower bounds for general loss functions both in the probabilistic setting and in the deterministic setting. For example, in the framework of prediction using expert advice, take into account relations among the experts rather than assuming the worst set of experts.
- Extend results on universal prediction with respect to the comparison class of finite-state machines to the case noisy observations.
- Impose limitations on the resources of the universal sequential predictor. For example, if the comparison class is that of finite-state predictors, how many states should the universal predictor have to guarantee redundancy below a certain level?

Some of these challenges have defied the best efforts of many researchers so far. Others are yet to be explored.

REFERENCES

[1] R. Agrawal, D. Teneketzis, and V. Anantharam, "Asymptotic adaptive allocation schemes for controlled i.i.d. processes: Finite parameter case," *IEEE Trans. Automat. Contr.*, vol. 34, pp. 258–267, Mar. 1989.
[2] ——, "Asymptotic adaptive allocation schemes for controlled Markov chains: Finite parameter case," *IEEE Trans. Automat. Contr.*, vol. 34, pp. 1249–1259, Mar. 1989.
[3] P. H. Algoet, "Universal schemes for prediction, gambling and portfolio selection," *Ann. Probab.*, vol. 20, pp. 901–941, Apr. 1992.
[4] ——, "The strong law of large numbers for sequential decision under uncertainty," *IEEE Trans. Inform. Theory*, vol. 40, pp. 609–633, May 1994.
[5] P. H. Algoet and T. M. Cover, "Asymptotic optimality and asymptotic equipartition properties of log-optimal investment," *Ann. Probab.*, vol. 16, no. 2, pp. 876–898, 1988.
[6] D. H. Bailey, "Sequential schemes for classifying and predicting ergodic processes," Ph.D. dissertation, Stanford Univ., Stanford, CA, 1976.
[7] J. M. Bernardo, "Reference posterior distributions for Bayesian inference," *J. Roy. Statist. Soc. B*, vol. 41, no. 2, pp. 113–147, 1979.
[8] D. Blackwell, "An analog to the minimax theorem for vector payoffs," *Pac. J. Math.*, vol. 6, pp. 1–8, 1956.
[9] ——, "Controlled random walks," in *Proc. Int. Congress Math.*, vol. 3. Amsterdam, The Netherlands: North Holland, 1956, pp. 336–338.
[10] A. Blum, "On-line algorithms in machine learning." [Online.] Available WWW: http://www.cs.cmu.edu/afs/cs.cmu.edu/user/ avrim/www/ Papers/pubs.html.
[11] A. C. Blumer, "Minimax universal noiseless coding for unifilar and Markov sources," *IEEE Trans. Inform. Theory*, vol. IT-33, pp. 925–930, Nov. 1987.
[12] N. Cesa-Bianchi, Y. Freund, D. P. Helmbold, D. Haussler, R. E. Schapire, and M. K. Warmuth, "How to use expert advice," in *Annu. ACM Symp. Theory of Computing*, 1993, pp. 382–391.
[13] N. Cesa-Bianchi, Y. Freund, D. P. Helmbold, and M. K. Warmuth, "On-line prediction and conversion strategies," in *Proc. EUROCOLT'93*, (Oxford, U.K., 1993), pp. 205–216.
[14] N. Cesa-Bianchi and G. Lugosi, "On sequential prediction of individual sequences relative to a set of experts," 1998, preprint.
[15] B. S. Clarke and A. R. Barron, "Information-theoretic asymptotics of Bayesian methods," *IEEE Trans. Inform. Theory*, vol. 36, pp. 453–471, May 1990.
[16] B. S. Clarke and A. R. Barron, "Jeffreys' prior is asymptotically least favorable under entropy risk," *J. Statist. Plan. Inform.*, vol. 41, pp. 37–60, Aug. 1994.
[17] T. M. Cover, "Universal gambling schemes and the complexity measures of Kolmogorov and Chaitin," Tech. Rep. 12, Dept. Statist., Stanford Univ., Stanford, CA, Oct. 1974.
[18] ——, "Open problems in information theory," in *Proc. Moscow Information Theory Workshop.* New York: IEEE Press, 1975, pp. 35–36.
[19] T. M. Cover and R. King, "A convergent gambling estimate of the entropy of English," *IEEE Trans. Inform. Theory*, vol. IT-24, pp. 413–421, July 1978.
[20] T. M. Cover, "On the competitive optimality of Huffman code," *IEEE Trans. Inform. Theory*, vol. 37, pp. 172–174, Jan. 1991.
[21] ——, "Universal portfolios," *Math. Finance*, vol. 1, no. 1, pp. 1–29, Jan. 1991.
[22] T. M. Cover and E. Ordentlich, "Universal portfolios with side information," *IEEE Trans. Inform. Theory*, vol. 42, pp. 348–363, Mar. 1996.
[23] T. M. Cover and J. A. Thomas, *Elements of Information Theory.* New York: Wiley, 1991.
[24] I. Csiszár and J. Körner, *Information Theory–Coding Theorems for Discrete Memoryless Systems.* New York: Academic, 1981.
[25] I. Csiszár and P. C. Shields, "Redundancy rates for renewal and other processes," *IEEE Trans. Inform. Theory*, vol. 42, pp. 2065–2072, Nov. 1996.
[26] L. D. Davisson, "The prediction error of stationary Gaussian time series of unknown covariance," *IEEE Trans. Inform. Theory*, vol. IT-11, pp. 527–532, Oct. 1965.
[27] ——, "Universal noiseless coding," *IEEE Trans. Inform. Theory*, vol. IT-19, pp. 783–795, Nov. 1973.
[28] ——, "Minimax noiseless universal coding for Markov sources," *IEEE Trans. Inform. Theory*, vol. IT-29, pp. 211–215, Mar. 1983.
[29] L. D. Davisson and A. L. Garcia, "A source matching approach to finding minimax codes," *IEEE Trans. Inform. Theory*, vol. IT-26, pp. 166–174, Mar. 1980.
[30] L. D. Davisson, R. J. McEliece, M. B. Pursley, and M. S. Wallace, "Efficient universal noiseless source codes," *IEEE Trans. Inform. Theory*, vol. 27, pp. 269–278, May 1981.
[31] A. P. Dawid, "Present position and potential developments: Some personal views on statistical theory the prequential approach (with discussion)," *J. Roy. Statist. Soc. A*, vol. 147, pt. 2, pp. 278–292, 1984.
[32] ——, "Fisherian inference in likelihood and prequential frames of reference (with discussion)," *J. Roy. Statist. Soc. B*, vol. 53, pp. 79–109, 1991.
[33] ——, "Prequential data analysis," in *Current Issues in Statistical Inference* (IMS Lecture Notes—Monograph Series 17), M. Ghosh and P. K. Pathak, Eds., 1992, pp. 113–126.
[34] A. P. Dawid and V. G. Vovk, "Prequential probability: Principles and properties." [Online.] Available WWW: http://www-stat.wharton.upenn. edu/Seq96/members/vovk/index. html.
[35] M. H. DeGroot, *Optimal Statistical Decisions.* New York: McGraw-Hill, 1970.
[36] A. DeSantis, G. Markowsky, and M. Wegman, "Learning probabilistic prediction functions," in *Proc. 29th IEEE Symp. Foundations of Computer Science*, 1988, pp. 110–119.
[37] P. Elias, "Minimax optimal universal codeword sets," *IEEE Trans. Inform. Theory*, vol. IT-29, pp. 491–502, July 1983.
[38] M. Feder, "Gambling using a finite state machine," *IEEE Trans. Inform. Theory*, vol. 37, pp. 1459–1465, Sept. 1991.
[39] M. Feder and N. Merhav, "Hierarchical universal coding," *IEEE Trans. Inform. Theory*, vol. 42, pp. 1354–1364, Sept. 1996.
[40] M. Feder, N. Merhav, and M. Gutman, "Universal prediction of individual sequences," *IEEE Trans. Inform. Theory*, vol. 38, pp. 1258–1270, July 1992.
[41] M. Feder and A. Singer, "Universal data compression and linear prediction," in *Proc. DCC'98*, 1998, pp. 511–520.

[42] B. Fittingoff, "Universal methods of coding for the case of unknown statistics," in *Proc. 5th Symp. Information Theory* (Moscow/Gorky, USSR, 1972), pp. 129–135.

[43] Y. Freund and R. Schapire, "Game theory, on-line prediction and boosting," in *Proc. 9th Ann. Workshop Computational Learning Theory*, 1996, pp. 89–98.

[44] R. G. Gallager, *Information Theory and Reliable Communications.* New York: Wiley, 1968.

[45] _____, "Source coding with side information and universal coding," unpublished manuscript; also presented at the *Int. Symp. Information Theory*, Oct. 1974.

[46] D. C. Gilliland, "Sequential compound estimation," *Ann. Math. Statist.*, vol. 39, no. 6, pp. 1890–1904, 1968.

[47] R. M. Gray, *Entropy and Information Theory.* New York: Springer-Verlag, 1990.

[48] L. Györfi, I. Pali, and E. C. van der Meulen, "There is no universal source code for an infinite source alphabet," *IEEE Trans. Inform. Theory*, vol. 40, pp. 267–271, Jan. 1994.

[49] J. F. Hannan, "Approximation to Bayes risk in repeated plays," in *Contributions to the Theory of Games, Ann. Math. Studies* (Princeton Univ., Princeton, NJ), vol. 3, no. 39, pp. 97–139, 1957.

[50] J. F. Hannan and H. Robbins, "Asymptotic solutions of the compound decision problem for two completely specified distributions," *Ann. Math. Statist.*, vol. 26, pp. 37–51, 1955.

[51] D. Haussler, "A general minimax result for relative entropy," *IEEE Trans. Inform. Theory*, vol. 43, pp. 1276–1280, July 1997.

[52] D. Haussler, J. Kivinen, and M. K. Warmuth, "Sequential prediction of individual sequences under general loss functions," *IEEE Trans. Inform. Theory*, to be published.

[53] D. Haussler and M. Opper, "Mutual information, metric entropy and cumulative relative entropy risk," *Ann. Statist.*, vol. 25, no. 6, Dec. 1997, to be published.

[54] _____, "General bounds on the mutual information between a parameter and n conditionally independent observations," in *Proc. 8th Annu. Workshop Computational Learning Theory (COLT'95)*, 1995, pp. 402–411.

[55] D. P. Helmbold and R. E. Schapire, "Predicting nearly as well as the best pruning of a decision tree," *Mach. Learn.*, vol. 27, pp. 51–68, 1997.

[56] Y. Hershkovitz and J. Ziv, "On fixed-database universal data compression with limited memory," *IEEE Trans. Inform. Theory*, vol. 43, pp. 1966–1976, Nov. 1997.

[57] H. Jeffreys, "An invariant form of for the prior probability in estimation problems," *Proc. Roy. Soc. London*, vol. 186, pt. A, pp. 453–461, 1946.

[58] D. Kazakos, "Robust noiseless source coding through a game theoretic approach," *IEEE Trans. Inform. Theory*, vol. IT-29, pp. 576–583, July 1983.

[59] J. L. Kelly, Jr., "A new interpretation of information rate," *Bell Syst. Tech. J.*, vol. 35, pp. 917–926, 1956.

[60] J. C. Kieffer, "A unified approach to weak universal source coding," *IEEE Trans. Inform. Theory*, vol. IT-24, pp. 674–682, Nov. 1978.

[61] _____, "An ergodic theorem for constrained sequences of functions," *Bull. Amer. Math. Soc.*, vol. 21, pp. 249–253, 1989.

[62] R. E. Krichevskiy, "Laplace's law of succession and universal encoding," *IEEE Trans. Inform. Theory*, vol. 44, pp. 296–303, Jan. 1998.

[63] R. E. Krichevski and V. E. Trofimov, "The performance of universal encoding," *IEEE Trans. Inform. Theory*, vol. IT-27, pp. 199–207, Mar. 1981.

[64] T. L. Lai and H. Robbins, "Asymptotically efficient adaptive allocation rules," *Adv. Appl. Math.*, vol. 6, pp. 4–22, 1985.

[65] G. G. Langdon, "A note on the Lempel–Ziv model for compressing individual sequences," *IEEE Trans. Inform. Theory*, vol. IT-29, pp. 284–287, 1983.

[66] P. S. Laplace, "Memoire sur la probabilite des causes par les evenemens," *Memoires de l'Academie Royale del Sciences*, no. 6, pp. 612–656, 1774, reprinted in *Laplace Complete Work*, vol. 8. Paris, France: Gauthier-Villars, pp. 27–65. English translation by S. M. Stigler, 1986.

[67] _____, "Memoire sur les approximations des formulas qui sont functions de tres grands nombres et sur leur application aux probabilies," *Memoires de l'Academie des Sciences de Paris*, pp. 353–415, 559–565, 1810; reprinted in *Laplace Complete Work*, vol. 12. Paris, France: Gauthier-Villars,, pp. 301–353; English translation by S. M. Stigler, 1986.

[68] A. Lempel and J. Ziv, "On the complexity of finite sequences," *IEEE Trans. Inform. Theory*, vol. IT-22, pp. 75–81, Jan. 1976.

[69] N. Littlestone, P. Long, and M. K. Warmuth, "On-line learning of linear functions," in *Proc. 23rd Annu. ACM Symp. Theory of Computing*, 1991, pp. 382–391.

[70] N. Littlestone and M. K. Warmuth, "The weighted majority algorithm," *Inform. Comput.*, vol. 108, no. 2, pp. 212–261, 1994.

[71] G. Louchard and W. Szpankowski, "On the average redundancy rate of the Lempel–Ziv code," *IEEE Trans. Inform. Theory*, vol. 43, pp. 2–8, Jan. 1997.

[72] T. Matsushima, H. Inazumi, and S. Hirawasa, "A class of distortionless codes designed by Bayes decision theory," *IEEE Trans. Inform. Theory*, vol. 37, pp. 1288–1293, Sept. 1991.

[73] R. Meir, "Performance bounds for nonlinear time-series prediction," 1997, preprint.

[74] R. Meir and N. Merhav, "On the stochastic complexity of learning realizable and unrealizable rules," *Mach. Learn.*, vol. 19, no. 3, pp. 241–261, 1995.

[75] N. Merhav and M. Feder, "Universal schemes for sequential decision from individual sequences," *IEEE Trans. Inform. Theory*, vol. 39, pp. 1280–1292, July 1993.

[76] _____, "A strong version of the redundancy-capacity theorem of universal coding," *IEEE Trans. Inform. Theory*, vol. 41, pp. 714–722, May 1995.

[77] N. Merhav, M. Feder, and M. Gutman, "Some properties of sequential predictors of binary Markov sources," *IEEE Trans. Inform. Theory*, vol. 39, pp. 887–892, May 1993.

[78] J. W. Miller, R. Goodman, and P. Smyth, "On loss functions which minimize to conditional expected values and posterior probabilities," *IEEE Trans. Inform. Theory*, vol. 39, pp. 1404–1408, July 1993.

[79] D. S. Modha and E. Masry, "Universal prediction of stationary random processes," 1996, preprint.

[80] G. Morvai, S. J. Yakowitz, and L. Györfi, "Nonparametric inference for ergodic, stationary time series," *Ann. Statist.*, vol. 24, pp. 370–379, 1996.

[81] G. Morvai, S. J. Yakowitz, and P. H. Algoet, "Weakly convergent nonparametric forecasting of stationary time series," *IEEE Trans. Inform. Theory*, vol. 43, pp. 483–497, Mar. 1997.

[82] Y. Nogami, "The k-extended set-compound estimation problem in nonregular family of distributions," *Ann. Inst. Stat. Math.*, vol. 31A, pp. 169–176, 1979.

[83] M. Opper and D. Haussler, "Bounds for predictive errors in the statistical mechanics of supervised learning," *Phys. Rev. Lett.*, vol. 75, pp. 3772–3775, 1995.

[84] _____, "Worst case prediction over sequences under log loss," in *The Mathematics of Information Coding, Extraction and Distribution*, G. Cybenko, D. O'Leary, and J. Rissanen, Eds. New York: Springer-Verlag, 1997.

[85] D. S. Orenstein, "Guessing the next output of a stationary process," *Israel J. Math.*, vol. 30, pp. 292–296, 1978.

[86] A. Papoulis, *Probability, Random Variables, and Stochastic Processes*, 3rd ed. (McGraw-Hill Series in Electrical Engineering). New York: McGraw-Hill, 1991.

[87] E. Plotnik, M. J. Weinberger, and J. Ziv, "Upper bounds on the probability of sequences emitted by finite-state sources and on the redundancy of the Lempel-Ziv algorithm," *IEEE Trans. Inform. Theory*, vol. 38, pp. 66–72, Jan. 1992.

[88] J. Rissanen, "Generalized Kraft's inequality and arithmetic coding," *IBM J. Res. Develop.*, vol. 20, no. 3, pp. 198–203, 1976.

[89] _____, "Modeling by shortest data description," *Automatica*, vol. 14, pp. 465–471, 1978.

[90] _____, "Universal coding, information, prediction, and estimation," *IEEE Trans. Inform. Theory*, vol. IT-30, pp. 629–636, July 1984.

[91] _____, "Complexity of strings in the class of Markov sources," *IEEE Trans. Inform. Theory*, vol. IT-32, pp. 526–532, 1986.

[92] _____, "Fisher information and stochastic complexity," *IEEE Trans. Inform. Theory*, vol. 42, pp. 40–47, Jan. 1996.

[93] J. Rissanen and G. G. Langdon, "Universal modeling and coding," *IEEE Trans. Inform. Theory*, vol. IT-27, pp. 12–23, Jan. 1984.

[94] H. Robbins, "Asymptotically subminimax solutions of compound statistical decision problems," in *Proc. 2nd Berkeley Symp. Math. Stat. Prob.*, 1951, pp. 131–148.

[95] R. T. Rockafeller, *Convex Analysis.* Princeton, NJ: Princeton Univ. Press, 1970.

[96] B. Ya. Ryabko, "Encoding a source with unknown but ordered probabilities," *Probl. Inform. Transm.*, pp. 134–138, Oct. 1979.

[97] _____, "Twice-universal coding," *Probl. Inform. Transm.*, vol. 20, no. 3, pp. 173–177, July/Sept. 1984.

[98] _____, "Prediction of random sequences and universal coding," *Probl. Inform. Transm.*, vol. 24, no. 2, pp. 87–96, Apr./June 1988.

[99] E. Samuel, "Asymptotic solution of the sequential compound decision problem," *Ann. Math. Statist.*, pp. 1079–1095, 1963.

[100] _____, "Convergence of the losses of certain decision rules for the sequential compound decision problem," *Ann. Math. Statist.*, pp. 1606–1621, 1964.

[101] S. A. Savari, "Redundancy of the Lempel–Ziv incremental parsing rule," *IEEE Trans. Inform. Theory*, vol. 43, pp. 9–21, Jan. 1997.

[102] B. Scarpellini, "Conditional expectations of stationary processes," *Z. Wahrscheinlichkeitstheorie Verw. Gebiete*, vol. 56, pp. 427–441, 1981.

[103] G. Schwarz, "Estimating the dimension of a model," *Ann. Statist.*, vol. 6, no. 2, pp. 461–464, 1978.

[104] C. E. Shannon, "Prediction and entropy of printed English," *Bell Syst. Tech. J.*, vol. 30, pp. 5–64, 1951.

[105] _____, "The mind reading machine," in *Shannon's Collected Papers*, A. D. Wyner and N. J. A. Sloane, Eds.   New York: IEEE Press, 1993, pp. 688–689.

[106] P. C. Shields, "Uniform redundancy rates do not exist," *IEEE Trans. Inform. Theory*, vol. 39, pp. 520–524, Mar. 1993.

[107] P. C. Shields and B. Weiss, "Universal redundancy rates for the class of B-processes do not exist," *IEEE Trans. Inform. Theory*, vol. 41, pp. 508–512, Mar. 1995.

[108] N. Shimkin, "Dynamic decision problems in multi-user systems," Ph.D. dissertation, Technion–Israel Inst. Technol., Haifa, Isreal, Nov. 1991.

[109] Y. M. Shtar'kov, "Universal sequential coding of single messages," *Problems of Inform. Trans.*, vol. 23, no. 3, pp. 175–186, July/Sept. 1987.

[110] A. Singer and M. Feder, "Universal linear prediction over parameters and model orders," *IEEE Trans. Signal Processing*, to be published.

[111] J.-I. Takeuchi and A. R. Barron, "Asymptotically minimax regret for exponential and curved exponential families," 1998, preprint.

[112] J. van Ryzin, "The sequential compound decision problem with $m \times n$ finite loss matrix," *Ann. Math. Statist.*, vol. 37, pp. 954–975, 1966.

[113] S. B. Vardeman, "Admissible solutions of k-extended finite state set and the sequence compound decision problems," *J. Multiv. Anal.*, vol. 10, pp. 426–441, 1980.

[114] J. S. Vitter, "Optimal prefetching via data cxompression," in *Proc. Conf. Foundations of Computer Science*, 1991, pp. 121–130.

[115] V. G. Vovk, "Aggregating strategies," in *Proc. 3rd Annu. Workshop Computational Learning Theory* (San Mateo, CA, 1990), pp. 371–383.

[116] _____, "A game of prediction with expert advice," in *Proc. 3rd Annu. Workshop Computational Learning Theory* (New York, NY, 1995), pp. 51–60.

[117] M. J. Weinberger, N. Merhav, and M. Feder, "Optimal sequential probability assignment for individual sequences," *IEEE Trans. Inform. Theory*, vol. 40, pp. 384–396, Mar. 1994.

[118] M. J. Weinberger, J. Rissanen, and M. Feder, "A universal finite memory source," *IEEE Trans. Inform. Theory*, vol. 41, pp. 643–652, May 1995.

[119] N. Wiener, *Extrapolation, Interpolation, and Smoothing of Stationary Time Series*.   Cambridge, MA: MIT Press, 1949.

[120] F. M. J. Willems, Y. M. Shtarkov, and T. Tjalkens, "The context-tree weighting method: Basic properties," *IEEE Trans. Inform. Theory*, vol. 41, pp. 653–664, May 1995.

[121] Q. Xie and A. R. Barron, "Asymptotic minimax regret for data compression, gambling, and prediction," *IEEE Trans. Inform. Theory*, 1996, submitted for publication.

[122] _____, "Minimax redundancy for the class of memoryless sources," *IEEE Trans. Inform. Theory*, vol. 43, pp. 646–657, Mar. 1997.

[123] B. Yu, "Lower bounds on expected redundancy for nonparametric classes," *IEEE Trans. Inform. Theory*, vol. 42, pp. 272–275, Jan. 1996.

[124] J. Ziv, "Coding of sources with unknown statistics—Part I: Probability of encoding error," *IEEE Trans. Inform. Theory*, vol. IT-18, pp. 384–394, May 1972.

[125] J. Ziv and A. Lempel, "A universal algorithm for sequential data compression," *IEEE Trans. Inform. Theory*, vol. IT-23, pp. 337–343, July 1977.

[126] _____, "Compression of individual sequences via variable-rate coding," *IEEE Trans. Inform. Theory*, vol. IT-24, pp. 530–536, Sept. 1978.

[127] _____, "Universal coding of two-dimensional data," *IEEE Trans. Inform. Theory*, vol. IT-32, pp. 2–8, Jan. 1986.

Reliable Communication Under Channel Uncertainty

Amos Lapidoth, *Member, IEEE*, and Prakash Narayan, *Senior Member, IEEE*

(Invited Paper)

Abstract—In many communication situations, the transmitter and the receiver must be designed without a complete knowledge of the probability law governing the channel over which transmission takes place. Various models for such channels and their corresponding capacities are surveyed. Special emphasis is placed on the encoders and decoders which enable reliable communication over these channels.

Index Terms— Arbitrarily varying channel, compound channel, deterministic code, finite-state channel, Gaussian arbitrarily varying channel, jamming, MMI decoder, multiple-access channel, randomized code, robustness, typicality decoder, universal decoder, wireless.

I. INTRODUCTION

SHANNON'S classic paper [111] treats the problem of communicating reliably over a channel when both the transmitter and the receiver are assumed to have full knowledge of the channel law so that selection of the codebook and the decoder structure can be optimized accordingly. We shall often refer to such channels, in loose terms, as known channels. However, there are a variety of situations in which either the codebook or the decoder must be selected without a complete knowledge of the law governing the channel over which transmission occurs. In subsequent work, Shannon and others have proposed several different channel models for such situations (e.g., the compound channel, the arbitrarily varying channel, etc.). Such channels will hereafter be referred to broadly as unknown channels.

Ultimate limits of communication over these channels in terms of capacities, reliability functions, and error exponents, as also the means of attaining them, have been extensively studied over the past 50 years. In this paper, we shall review some of these results, including recent unpublished work, in a unified framework, and also present directions for future research. Our emphasis is primarily on single-user channels. The important class of multiple-access channels is not treated in detail; instead, we provide a brief survey with pointers for further study.

There are, of course, a variety of situations, dual in nature to those examined in this paper, in which an information source must be compressed—losslessly or with some acceptable distortion—without a complete knowledge of the characteristics of the source. The body of literature on this subject is vast, and we refer the reader to [23], [25], [61], [71], and [128] in this issue.

In selecting a model for a communication situation, several factors must be considered. These include the physical and statistical nature of the channel disturbances, the information available to the transmitter, the information available to the receiver, the presence of any feedback link from the receiver to the transmitter, and the availability at the transmitter and receiver of a shared source of randomness (independent of the channel disturbances). The resulting capacity, reliability function, and error exponent will also rely crucially on the performance criteria adopted (e.g., average or worst case measures).

Consider, for example, a situation controlled by an adversarial jammer. Based on the physics of the channel, the received signal can often be modeled as the sum of the transmitted signal, ambient or receiver noise, and the jammer's signal. The transmitter and jammer are typically constrained in their average or peak power. The jammer's strategy can be described in terms of the probability law governing its signal. If the jammer's strategy is known to the system designer, then the resulting channel falls in the category studied by Shannon [111] and its extensions to channels with memory. The problem becomes more realistic if the jammer can select from a family of strategies, and the selected strategy, and hence the channel law, is not fully known to the system designer. Different statistical assumptions on the family of allowable jammer strategies will result in different channel models and, hence, in different capacities. Clearly, it is easier to guarantee reliable communication when the jammer's signal is independent and identically distributed (i.i.d.), albeit with unknown law, than when it is independently distributed but with arbitrarily varying and unknown distributions. The former situation leads to a "compound channel" model, and the latter to an "arbitrarily varying channel" model.

Next, various degrees of information about the jammer's strategy may be available to the transmitter or receiver, leading to yet more variations of such models. For example, if the jammer employs an i.i.d. strategy, the receiver may learn it from the signal received when the transmitter is silent, and yet be unable to convey its inference to the transmitter if the channel is one-way. The availability of a feedback link, on the other hand, may allow for suitable adaptation of the codebook, leading to an enhanced capacity value. Of course, in the extreme situation where the receiver has access to the pathwise realization of the jammer's signal and can

Manuscript received December 10, 1997; revised May 4, 1998.

A. Lapidoth is with the Department of Electrical Engineering and Computer Science, Massachusetts Institute of Technology, Cambridge, MA 02139-4307 USA.

P. Narayan is with the Electrical Engineering Department and the Institute for Systems Research, University of Maryland, College Park, MD 20742 USA.

Publisher Item Identifier S 0018-9448(98)05288-2.

subtract it from the received signal, the transmitter can ignore the jammer's presence. Another modeling issue concerns the availability of a source of common randomness which enables coordinated randomization at the encoder and decoder. For instance, such a resource allows the use of spread-spectrum techniques in combating jammer interference [117]. In fact, access to such a source of common randomness can sometimes enable reliable communication at rates that are strictly larger than those achievable without it [6], [48].

The capacity, reliability function, and error exponent for a given model will also depend on the precise notion of reliable communication adopted by the system designer with regard to the decoding error probability. For a given system the error probability will, in general, depend on the transmitted message and the jammer's strategy. The system designer may require that the error probability be small for all jammer strategies and for all messages; a less stringent requirement is that the error probability be small only as an (arithmetic) average over the message set. While these two different performance criteria yield the same capacity for a known channel, in the presence of a jammer the capacities may be different [20]. Rather than requiring the error probability to be small for every jammer strategy, we may average it over the set of all strategies with respect to a given prior. This Bayesian approach gives another notion of reliable communication, with yet another definition of capacity.

The notions of reliable communication mentioned above do not preclude the possibility that the system performance be governed by the worst (or average) jamming strategy even when a more benign strategy is employed. In some situations, such as when the jamming strategies are i.i.d., it is possible to design a decoder with error probability decaying asymptotically at a rate no worse than if the jammer strategy were known in advance. The performance of this "universal" decoder is thus governed not by the worst strategy but by the strategy that the jammer chooses to use.

Situations involving channel uncertainty are by no means limited to military applications, and arise naturally in several commercial applications as well. In mobile wireless communications, the varying locations of the mobile transmitter and receiver with respect to scatterers leads to an uncertainty in channel law. This application is discussed in the concluding section. Other situations arise in underwater acoustics, computer memories with defects, etc.

The remainder of the paper is organized as follows. Focusing on unknown channels with finite input and output alphabets, models for such channels without and with memory, as well as different performance criteria, are described in Section II. Key results on channel capacity for these models and performance criteria are presented in Section III. In Section IV, we survey some of the encoders and decoders which have been proposed for achieving reliable communication over such channels. While our primary focus is on channels with finite input and output alphabets, we shall consider in Section V the class of unknown channels whose output equals the sum of the transmitted signal, an unknown interference .and white Gaussian noise. Section VI consists of a brief review of unknown multiple-access channels. In

the concluding Section VII, we examine the potential role in mobile wireless communications of the work surveyed in this paper.

II. CHANNEL MODELS AND PRELIMINARIES

We now present a variety of mathematical models for communication under channel uncertainty. We shall assume throughout a discrete-time framework. For waveform channels with uncertainty, care must be exercised in formulating a suitable discrete-time model as it can sometimes lead to conservative designs. Throughout this paper, all logarithms and exponentiations are with respect to the base 2.

Let $\mathcal{X}$ and $\mathcal{Y}$ be finite sets denoting the channel input and output alphabets, respectively. The probability law of a (known) channel is specified by a sequence of conditional probability mass functions (pmf's)

$$\{W_n(\boldsymbol{y}|\boldsymbol{x}): \boldsymbol{x} \in \mathcal{X}^n, \boldsymbol{y} \in \mathcal{Y}^n\}_{n=1}^{\infty} \quad (1)$$

where $W_n(\cdot|\cdot)$ denotes the conditional pmf governing channel use through n units of time, i.e., "n uses of the channel." If the known channel is a discrete memoryless channel (DMC), then its law is characterized in terms of a stochastic matrix $W: \mathcal{X} \mapsto \mathcal{Y}$ according to

$$W_n(\boldsymbol{y}|\boldsymbol{x}) = \prod_{t=1}^{n} W(y_t|x_t) \quad (2)$$

where $\boldsymbol{x} = (x_1, \cdots, x_n) \in \mathcal{X}^n$ and $\boldsymbol{y} = (y_1, \cdots, y_n) \in \mathcal{Y}^n$. For notational convenience, we shall hereafter suppress the subscript n and use $W(\boldsymbol{y}|\boldsymbol{x})$ instead of $W_n(\boldsymbol{y}|\boldsymbol{x})$.

Example 1: The binary-symmetric channel (BSC) is a DMC with $\mathcal{X} = \mathcal{Y} = \{0, 1\}$, and a stochastic matrix

$$W(y|x) = \begin{cases} p, & \text{if } y \neq x \\ 1-p, & \text{if } y = x \end{cases}$$

for a "crossover probability" $p \in [0, 1]$. The BSC can also be described by writing

$$Y_t = x_t + Z_t$$

where $\{Z_t\}_{t=1}^{\infty}$ is a Bernoulli(p) process, and addition is mod 2.

A *family* of channels indexed by $\theta \in \Theta$ can be denoted by

$$\{W(\boldsymbol{y}|\boldsymbol{x}; \theta), \boldsymbol{x} \in \mathcal{X}^n, \boldsymbol{y} \in \mathcal{Y}^n, \theta \in \Theta\}_{n=1}^{\infty} \quad (3)$$

for some parameter space Θ. For example, this family would correspond to a family of DMC's if

$$W(\boldsymbol{y}|\boldsymbol{x}; \theta) = \prod_{t=1}^{n} W(y_t|x_t; \theta) \quad (4)$$

where $\{W(y|x; \theta), x \in \mathcal{X}, y \in \mathcal{Y}, \theta \in \Theta\}$ is a suitable subset of the set of all stochastic matrices $\mathcal{X} \mapsto \mathcal{Y}$. Such a family of channels, referred to as a compound DMC, is often used to model communication over a DMC whose law belongs to the family and remains unchanged during the course of a transmission, but is otherwise unknown.

Example 2: Consider a compound BSC with $\mathcal{X} = \mathcal{Y} = \{0, 1\}$ and $\Theta \subset [0, 1]$ with

$$W(y|x; \theta) = \begin{cases} \theta, & \text{if } y \neq x \\ 1 - \theta, & \text{if } y = x. \end{cases}$$

The case $\Theta = \{0.1, 0.9\}$, for instance, represents a compound BSC of unknown polarity.

A more severe situation arises when the channel parameters vary arbitrarily from symbol to symbol during the course of a transmission. This situation can sometimes be modeled by choosing $\Theta = \mathcal{S}^\infty$ where $\mathcal{S}$ is a finite set, often referred to as the state space, and by setting

$$W(\boldsymbol{y}|\boldsymbol{x}; \boldsymbol{s}) = \prod_{t=1}^{n} W(y_t|x_t; s_t) \qquad (5)$$

where $\boldsymbol{s} = (s_1, \cdots, s_n)$, and $W: \mathcal{X} \times \mathcal{S} \mapsto \mathcal{Y}$ is a given stochastic matrix. This model is called a discrete memoryless arbitrarily varying channel and will hereafter be referred to simply as an AVC.

Example 3: Consider an AVC (5) with $\mathcal{X} = \mathcal{S} = \{0, 1\}$, $\mathcal{Y} = \{0, 1, 2\}$, and

$$W(y|x; s) = \begin{cases} 1, & \text{if } y = x + s \\ 0, & \text{otherwise.} \end{cases}$$

This AVC can also be described by writing

$$y_t = x_t + s_t.$$

All additions above are arithmetic. Since the stochastic matrix $W: \mathcal{X} \times \mathcal{S} \to \mathcal{Y}$ has entries which are all $\{0, 1\}$-valued, such an AVC is sometimes called a deterministic AVC. This example is due to Blackwell *et al.* [31].

In some hybrid situations, certain channel parameters may be unknown but fixed during the course of a transmission, while other parameters may vary arbitrarily from symbol to symbol. Such a situation can often be modeled by setting $\Theta = \mathcal{S}^\infty \times \Xi$, where $\mathcal{S}$ is as above, Ξ connotes a subset of the stochastic matrices $\mathcal{X} \times \mathcal{S} \mapsto \mathcal{Y}$, and for $\xi \in \Xi$

$$W(\boldsymbol{y}|\boldsymbol{x}; \boldsymbol{s}, \xi) = \prod_{t=1}^{n} W(y_t|x_t; s_t, \xi). \qquad (6)$$

We shall refer to this model as a hybrid DMC.

In some situations in which the channel law is *fully known,* memoryless channel models are inadequate and more elaborate models are needed. In wireless applications, a finite-state channel (FSC) model [64], [123] is often used. The memory in the transmission channel is captured by the introduction of a set of states Σ, and the probability law of the channel is given by

$$W(\boldsymbol{y}|\boldsymbol{x}) = \sum_{\sigma_0 \in \Sigma} \pi(\sigma_0) \sum_{\sigma_1, \cdots, \sigma_n \in \Sigma^n} \prod_{t=1}^{n} W(y_t, \sigma_t|x_t, \sigma_{t-1}) \qquad (7)$$

where π is a pmf on Σ, and $W: \mathcal{X} \times \Sigma \mapsto \mathcal{Y} \times \Sigma$ is a stochastic matrix. Operationally, if at time $t-1$ the state of the channel is σ_{t-1} and the input to the channel at time t is

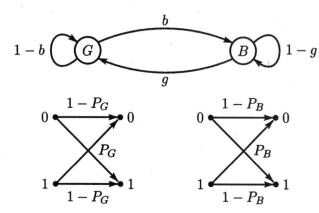

Fig. 1. Gilbert–Elliott channel model. P_G and P_B are the channel crossover probabilities in the "good" and "bad" states, and g and b are transition probabilities between states.

x_t, then the output of the channel y_t at time t and the state σ_t of the channel at time t are determined according to the conditional probability $W(y_t, \sigma_t|x_t, \sigma_{t-1})$.

In wireless applications, the states often correspond to different fading levels which the channel may experience (cf. Section VII). It should be noted that the model (7) corresponds to a *known* channel, and the set of states Σ should not be confused with the state space $\mathcal{S}$ introduced in (5) in the definition of an AVC.

Example 4: The Gilbert–Elliott channel [57], [68], [69], [101] is a finite-state channel with two states $\Sigma = \{G, B\}$, the state G corresponding to the "good" state and state B corresponding to the "bad" state (see Fig. 1). The channel has input and output alphabets $\mathcal{X} = \mathcal{Y} = \{0, 1\}$, and law

$$W(y, \sigma|x, \sigma') = q(y|x, \sigma')r(\sigma|\sigma')$$

where

$$r(G|B) = 1 - r(B|B) = g$$
$$r(B|G) = 1 - r(G|G) = b$$

and

$$q(1|0, B) = 1 - q(0|0, B) = P_B$$
$$q(0|1, B) = 1 - q(1|1, B) = P_B$$
$$q(1|0, G) = 1 - q(0|0, G) = P_G$$
$$q(0|1, G) = 1 - q(1|1, G) = P_G$$

and where π is often taken as the stationary pmf of the state process, i.e.,

$$\pi(B) = 1 - \pi(G) = \frac{b}{b + g}.$$

The channel can also be described as

$$Y_t = x_t + Z_t$$

where addition is mod 2, and where $\{Z_t\}$ is a stationary binary hidden Markov process with two internal states.

We can, of course, consider a situation which involves an unknown channel with memory. If the matrix $W: \mathcal{X} \times \Sigma \mapsto \mathcal{Y} \times \Sigma$ is unknown but remains fixed during a transmission, the channel can be modeled as a compound FSC [91] by setting Θ to be a set of pairs (π, W) of pmf's of the initial state and stochastic matrices $\mathcal{X} \times \Sigma \mapsto \mathcal{Y} \times \Sigma$ with

$$W(\boldsymbol{y}|\boldsymbol{x}; \theta) = \sum_{\sigma_0 \in \Sigma} \pi(\sigma_0; \theta)$$
$$\sum_{\sigma_1, \cdots, \sigma_n \in \Sigma^n} \prod_{t=1}^{n} W(y_t, \sigma_t | x_t, \sigma_{t-1}; \theta) \quad (8)$$

where, with an abuse of notation, $(\pi(\cdot; \theta), W(\cdot, \cdot|\cdot, \cdot; \theta))$ denotes a generic element θ of Θ.

Example 5: A compound Gilbert–Elliott channel [91] is a family of Gilbert–Elliott channels indexed by some set Θ where each channel in the family has a different set of parameters $b(\theta)$, $g(\theta)$, $P_B(\theta)$, $P_G(\theta)$.

More severe yet is a situation where the channel parameters may vary in an arbitrary manner from symbol to symbol during a transmission. This situation can be modeled in terms of an arbitrarily varying FSC, which is described by introducing a state space $\mathcal{S}$ as above, setting $\Theta = \Gamma \times \mathcal{S}^{\infty}$ where Γ is a set of pmfs on Σ, and letting

$$W(\boldsymbol{y}|\boldsymbol{x}; \gamma, \boldsymbol{s}) = \sum_{\sigma_0 \in \Sigma} \gamma(\sigma_0)$$
$$\sum_{\sigma_1, \cdots, \sigma_n \in \Sigma^n} \prod_{t=1}^{n} W(y_t, \sigma_t | x_t, \sigma_{t-1}; s_t) \quad (9)$$

where $\gamma \in \Gamma$, and

$$\{W(y, \sigma|x, \sigma'; s), x \in \mathcal{X}, y \in \mathcal{Y}, \sigma \in \Sigma, \sigma' \in \Sigma, s \in \mathcal{S}\}$$

is a family of stochastic matrices $\mathcal{X} \times \Sigma \times \mathcal{S} \mapsto \mathcal{Y} \times \Sigma$. To our knowledge, this channel model has not appeared heretofore in the literature, and is a subject of current investigation by the authors of the present paper.

The models described above for communication under channel uncertainty do not form an exhaustive list. They do, however, constitute a rich and varied class of channel descriptions.

We next provide precise descriptions of an encoder (transmitter) and a decoder (receiver). Let the set of messages be $\mathcal{M} = \{1, \cdots, M\}$. A length-$n$ block code is a pair of mappings (f, ϕ), where

$$f: \mathcal{M} \to \mathcal{X}^n \quad (10)$$

is the encoder, and

$$\phi: \mathcal{Y}^n \to \mathcal{M} \cup \{0\} \quad (11)$$

is the decoder. The rate of such a code is

$$\frac{1}{n} \log M. \quad (12)$$

Note that the encoder, as defined by (10), produces an output which is solely a function of the message. If the encoder is provided additional side information, this definition must be modified accordingly. A similar statement of appropriate nature applies to the decoder as well. Also, while 0 is allowed as a decoder output for the sake of convenience, it will signify a decoding failure and will always be taken to constitute an error.

The probability of error for the message $m \in \mathcal{M}$, when the code (f, ϕ) is used on a channel $\theta \in \Theta$ is given by

$$e(m, f, \phi, \theta) = \sum_{\boldsymbol{y}: \ \phi(\boldsymbol{y}) \neq m} W(\boldsymbol{y}|f(m); \theta). \quad (13)$$

The corresponding maximum probability of error is

$$e_{\max}(f, \phi, \theta) = \max_{m \in \mathcal{M}} e(m, f, \phi, \theta) \quad (14)$$

and the average probability of error is

$$\overline{e}(f, \phi, \theta) = \frac{1}{M} \sum_{m \in \mathcal{M}} e(m, f, \phi, \theta). \quad (15)$$

Obviously, the maximum probability of error will lead to a more stringent performance criterion than the average probability of error. In the case of known channels, both criteria result in the same capacity values. For certain unknown channels, however, these two criteria can yield different capacity results, as will be seen below [20].

For certain unknown channels, an improvement in performance can be obtained by using a *randomized code*. A randomized code constitutes a communication technique, the implementation of which requires the availability of a common source of randomness at the transmitter and receiver; the encoder and decoder outputs can now additionally depend on the outcome of a random experiment. Thus the set of allowed encoding–decoding strategies is enriched by permitting recourse to *mixed strategies*, in the parlance of game theory. The definition of a code in (10) and (11) must be suitably modified, and the potential enhancement in performance (e.g., in terms of the maximum or average probability of error in (14) and (15)) is assessed as an average with respect to the common source of randomness.

The notion of a randomized code should not be confused with the standard method of proof of coding theorems based on a *random-coding argument*. Whereas a randomized code constitutes a communication technique, a random-coding argument is a proof technique which is often used to establish the existence of a (single) deterministic code as in (10) and (11) which yields good performance on a known channel, without actually constructing the code. This is done by introducing a pmf on an ensemble of codes, computing the corresponding average performance over such an ensemble, and then invoking the argument to show that if this average performance is good, then there must exist at least one code in the ensemble with good performance. The random-coding argument is sometimes tricky to invoke when proving achievability results for families of channels. If for each channel in the family the average performance over the ensemble of codes is good, the argument cannot be used to guarantee the existence of a single code which is *simultaneously* good for all the channels in the family; for each channel, there may be a different code with performance as good as the ensemble average.

Precisely, a randomized code (F, Φ) is a random variable (rv) with values in the family of all length-n block codes (f, ϕ) defined by (10) and (11) with the same message set

$\mathcal{M} = \{1, \cdots, M\}$. While the pmf of the rv (F, Φ) may depend on a knowledge of the family of channels indexed by $\theta \in \Theta$, it is not allowed to depend on the actual value of $\theta \in \Theta$ governing a particular transmission or on the transmitted message $m \in \mathcal{M}$.

The maximum and average probabilities of error will be denoted, with an abuse of notation, by $e_{\max}(F, \Phi, \theta)$ and $\overline{e}(F, \Phi, \theta)$, respectively. These error probabilities are defined in a manner analogous to that of a deterministic code in (14) and (15), replacing $e(m, f, \phi, \theta)$ with $e(m, F, \Phi, \theta)$ given by

$$e(m, F, \Phi, \theta) = \mathbb{E}\left[\sum_{\boldsymbol{y}: \ \Phi(\boldsymbol{y}) \neq m} W(\boldsymbol{y}|F(m); \theta) \right] \quad (16)$$

where $\mathbb{E}$ denotes expectation with respect to the pmf of the rv (F, Φ). When randomized codes are allowed, the maximum and average error probability criteria lead to the same capacity value for any channel (known or unknown). This is easily seen since given a randomized code, a random permutation of the message set can be used to obtain a new randomized code of the same rate, whose maximum error probability equals the average error probability of the former (cf. e.g., [44, p. 223, Problem 5]).

While a randomized code is preferable for certain unknown channels owing to its ability to outperform deterministic codes by yielding larger capacity values, it may not be always possible to provide both the transmitter and the receiver with the needed access to a common source of randomness. In such situations, we can consider using a code in which the encoder alone can observe the outcome of a random experiment, whereas the decoder is deterministic. Such a code, referred to as a code with stochastic encoder, is defined as a pair (F, ϕ) where the encoder can be interpreted as a stochastic matrix $F: \mathcal{M} \to \mathcal{X}^n$, and the (deterministic) decoder is given by (11). In proving the achievability parts of coding theorems, the codewords $\{F(m), m \in \mathcal{M}\}$ are usually chosen independently, which completes the probabilistic description of the code (F, ϕ). The various error probabilities for such a code are defined in a manner analogous to that in (13)–(15). In comparison with deterministic codes, a code with stochastic encoder clearly cannot lead to larger capacity values for known channels (since even randomized codes cannot do so). However, for certain unknown channels, while deterministic codes may lead to a smaller capacity value for the maximum probability of error criterion than for the average probability of error criterion, codes with stochastic encoders may afford an improvement by yielding identical capacity values under both criteria.

Hereafter, a deterministic code will be termed as such in those sections in which the AVC is treated; elsewhere, it will be referred to simply as a code. On the other hand, a code with stochastic encoder or a randomized code will be explicitly termed as such.

We now define the notion of the capacity of an unknown channel which, as the foregoing discussion might suggest, is more elaborate than the capacity of a known channel. For $0 < \epsilon < 1$, a number $R \geq 0$ is an ϵ-achievable rate on (an unknown) channel for maximum (resp., average) probability of error, if for every $\delta > 0$ and every n sufficiently large, there exists a length-n block code (f, ϕ) with rate

$$\frac{1}{n} \log M > R - \delta \quad (17)$$

and maximum (resp., average) probability of error satisfying

$$\sup_{\theta \in \Theta} e_{\max}(f, \phi, \theta) \leq \epsilon \quad (18)$$

$$(\text{resp.,} \ \sup_{\theta \in \Theta} \overline{e}(f, \phi, \theta) \leq \epsilon). \quad (19)$$

A number $R \geq 0$ is an achievable rate for the maximum (resp., average) probability of error if it is ϵ-achievable for every $0 < \epsilon < 1$.

The ϵ-capacity of a channel for maximum (resp., average) probability of error is the largest ϵ-achievable rate as given by (17) and (18) (resp., (19)). It will be denoted C_ϵ^m (resp., C_ϵ^a) for those channels for which the two error probability criteria lead, in general, to different values of ϵ-capacity, in which cases, of course, $C_\epsilon^m < C_\epsilon^a$; otherwise, it will be denoted simply by C_ϵ.

The capacity of a channel for maximum or average probability of error is the largest achievable rate for that error criterion. It will be denoted by C^m or C^a for those channels for which the two error probability criteria lead, in general, to different capacity values, when, obviously, $C^m < C^a$; else, it will be denoted by C. Observe that the capacities C^m and C^a can be equivalently defined as the infima of the corresponding ϵ-capacities for $\epsilon > 0$, i.e.,

$$C^m = \lim_{\epsilon \to 0} C_\epsilon^m \quad \text{and} \quad C^a = \lim_{\epsilon \to 0} C_\epsilon^a.$$

Remark: If an ϵ-capacity of a channel (C_ϵ^m or C_ϵ^a) does not depend on ϵ, $0 < \epsilon < 1$, its value is called a strong capacity; such a result is often referred to as a strong converse. See [122] for conditions under which a strong converse holds for known channels.

When codes with stochastic encoders are allowed, analogous notions of ϵ-capacity (C_ϵ^m or C_ϵ^a) and capacity (C^m or C^a) of a channel are defined by modifying the previous definitions of these terms in an obvious way. In particular, the probabilities of error are understood in terms of expectations with respect to the probability law of the stochastic encoder. For randomized codes, too, analogous notions of ϵ-capacity and capacity are defined; note, however, that in this case the maximum and average probabilities of error will lead to the same results, as observed earlier.

While the fundamental notion of channel capacity provides the system designer with an indication of the ultimate coding rates at which reliable communication can be achieved over a channel, it is additionally very useful to assess coding performance in terms of the reductions attained in the various error probabilities by increasing the complexity and delay of a code as measured by its blocklength. This is done by determining the exponents with which the error probabilities can be made to vanish by increasing the blocklength n of the code, leading to the notions of reliability function, randomized code reliability function, and random-coding error exponent of a channel. Our survey does not address these important notions for which we direct the reader to [43], [44], [46], [64], [65], [95], [115], [116], and references therein.

In the situations considered above, quite often the selection of codes is restricted in that the transmitted codewords must satisfy appropriate input constraints. Let g be a nonnegative-valued function on $\mathcal{X}$, and let

$$g(\boldsymbol{x}) = \frac{1}{n} \sum_{t=1}^{n} g(x_t), \qquad \boldsymbol{x} \in \mathcal{X}^n \qquad (20)$$

where, for convenience, we assume that $\min_{x \in \mathcal{X}} g(x) = 0$. Given $\Gamma \geq 0$, a length-n block code (f, ϕ) given by (10) and (11), is said to satisfy input constraint Γ if the codewords $\{f(m), m \in \mathcal{M}\}$ satisfy

$$g(f(m)) \leq \Gamma, \qquad m \in \mathcal{M}. \qquad (21)$$

Similarly, a randomized code (F, Φ) or a code with stochastic encoder (F, ϕ) satisfies input constraint Γ if

$$g(F(m)) \leq \Gamma \quad \text{almost surely (a.s.)}, \qquad m \in \mathcal{M}. \qquad (22)$$

Of course, if $\Gamma \geq \max_{x \in \mathcal{X}} g(x)$, then the input constraint is inoperative.

Restrictions are often imposed also on the variations in the unknown channel parameters during the course of a transmission. For instance, in the AVC model (5), constraints can be imposed on the sequence of channel states $\boldsymbol{s} \in \mathcal{S}^n$ as follows. Let l be a nonnegative-valued function on $\mathcal{S}$, and let

$$l(\boldsymbol{s}) = \frac{1}{n} \sum_{t=1}^{n} l(s_t), \qquad \boldsymbol{s} \in \mathcal{S}^n \qquad (23)$$

where we assume that $\min_{s \in \mathcal{S}} l(s) = 0$. Given $\Lambda \geq 0$, we shall say that $\boldsymbol{s} \in \mathcal{S}^n$ satisfies state constraint Λ if

$$l(\boldsymbol{s}) \leq \Lambda. \qquad (24)$$

If $\Lambda \geq \max_{s \in \mathcal{S}} l(s)$, the state constraint is rendered inoperative.

If coding performance is to be assessed under input constraint Γ, then only such codes will be allowed as satisfy (21) or (22), as applicable. A similar consideration holds if the unknown channel parameters are subject to constraints. For instance, for the AVC model of (5) under state constraint Λ, the probabilities of error in (18) and (19) are computed with the maximization with respect to $\theta \in \Theta$ being now taken over all state sequences $\boldsymbol{s} \in \mathcal{S}^n$ which satisfy (24). Accordingly, the notion of capacity is defined.

The various notions of capacity for unknown channels described above are based on criteria involving error probabilities defined in terms of (18) and (19). The fact that these error probabilities are evaluated as being the largest with respect to the (unknown) parameter $\theta \in \Theta$ means that the resulting values of capacity can be attained when the channel uncertainty is at its severest during the course of a transmission, and, hence, in less severe instances as well. In the latter case, of course, these values may lead to a conservative assessment of coding performance.

In some situations, the system designer may have additional information concerning the vagaries of the unknown channel.

For example, in a communication situation controlled by a jammer employing i.i.d. strategies, the system designer may have prior knowledge, based on past experience, of the jammer's relative predilections for the laws (indexed by θ) governing the i.i.d. strategies. In such cases, a Bayesian approach can be adopted where the previous model of the unknown channel comprising the family of channels (3) is augmented by considering θ to be a Θ-valued rv with a known (prior) probability distribution function (pdf) μ on Θ. Thus the transmitter and receiver, while unaware of the actual channel law (indexed by θ) governing a transmission, know the pdf μ of the rv θ. The corresponding maximum and average probabilities of error are now defined by suitably modifying (18) and (19); the maximization with respect to θ in (18) and (19) is replaced by expectation with respect to the law μ of the rv θ. When dealing with randomized codes or codes with stochastic encoders, we shall assume that all the rv's in the specification of such codes are independent of the rv θ. The associated notions of capacity are defined analogously as above, with appropriate modifications. For a given channel model, their values will obviously be no smaller than their counterparts for the more stringent criteria corresponding to (18) and (19), thereby providing a more optimistic assessment of coding performance. It should be noted, however, that this approach does not assure arbitrarily small probabilities of error for every channel in the family of channels (3); rather, probabilities of error are guaranteed to be small only when they are evaluated as averages over all the channels in the family (3) with respect to the (prior) law μ of θ. For this reason, in situations where there is a prior on Θ, the notion of "capacity versus outage" is sometimes preferred to the notion of capacity (see [102]).

Other kinds of situations can arise when the transmitter or receiver are provided with side information consisting of partial or complete knowledge of the exact parameter θ dictating a transmission, i.e., the channel law governing a transmission. We consider only a few such situations below; the reader is referred to [44, pp. 220–222 and 227–230] for a wider description. Consider first the case where the receiver alone knows the exact value of θ during a transmission. This situation can sometimes be reduced to that of an unknown channel without side information at the receiver, which has been described above, and hence does not lead to a new mathematical problem. This is seen by considering a new unknown channel with input alphabet $\mathcal{X}$, and with output alphabet $\tilde{\mathcal{Y}}$ which is an expanded version of the original output alphabet $\mathcal{Y}$, viz.

$$\tilde{\mathcal{Y}} = \mathcal{Y} \times \Theta \qquad (25)$$

and specified by the family of channels

$$\{\tilde{W}(\boldsymbol{y}, \theta' | \boldsymbol{x}, \theta), \boldsymbol{x} \in \mathcal{X}^n, \boldsymbol{y} \in \mathcal{Y}^n, \theta \in \Theta, \theta' \in \Theta\}_{n=1}^{\infty} \qquad (26)$$

where

$$\tilde{W}(\boldsymbol{y}, \theta' | \boldsymbol{x}, \theta) = \begin{cases} W(\boldsymbol{y}|\boldsymbol{x}; \theta), & \text{if } \theta' = \theta, \\ 0, & \text{otherwise.} \end{cases} \qquad (27)$$

Of course, some structure may be lost in this construction (e.g., the finite cardinality of the output alphabet or the memory of the channel). A length-n block code for this channel is defined as a pair of mappings (f, ϕ), where the encoder f is defined in the usual manner by (10), while the decoder ϕ is a mapping

$$\phi: \mathcal{Y}^n \times \Theta \to \mathcal{M} \cup \{0\}. \tag{28}$$

We turn next to a case where the transmitter has partial or complete knowledge of θ prevalent during a transmission. For instance, consider communication over an AVC (5) with $\Theta = \mathcal{S}^\infty$ when the transmitter alone is provided, at each time instant $t = 1, \cdots, n$, a knowledge of all the past and present states $s_1, \cdots, s_t$ of the channel during a transmission. Then, a length-n block code is a pair of mappings (f, ϕ), where the decoder ϕ is defined as usual by (11), whereas the encoder f comprises a sequence of mappings $\{f_t\}_{t=1}^n$ with

$$f_t: \mathcal{M} \times \mathcal{S}^t \to \mathcal{X}. \tag{29}$$

This sequence of mappings determines the tth symbol of a codeword as a function of the transmitted message and the known past and present states of the channel. Significant benefits can be gained if the transmitter is provided state information in a noncausal manner (e.g., if the entire sequence of channel states $s_1, \cdots, s_n$ is known to the transmitter when transmission begins). The encoder f is then defined accordingly as a sequence of mappings $\{f_t\}_{t=1}^n$ with

$$f_t: \mathcal{M} \times \mathcal{S}^n \to \mathcal{X}. \tag{30}$$

Various combinations of the two cases just mentioned are, of course, possible with the transmitter and receiver possessing various degrees of knowledge about the exact value of θ during a transmission. In all these cases, the maximum and average probabilities of error are defined analogously as in (14) and (15), and the notion of capacity defined accordingly.

Yet another communication situation involves unknown channels with noiseless feedback from the receiver to the transmitter. At each time instant $t = 1, \cdots, n$, the transmitter knows the previous channel output symbols $y_1, \cdots, y_{t-1}$ through a noiseless feedback link. Now, in the formal definition of a length-n block code (f, ϕ), the decoder is given by (11) while the encoder f consists of a sequence of mappings $\{f_t\}_{t=1}^n$, where

$$f_t: \mathcal{M} \times \mathcal{Y}^{t-1} \mapsto \mathcal{X}. \tag{31}$$

Once again, the notion of capacity is defined accordingly.

We shall also consider the communication situation which obtains when list codes are used. Loosely speaking, in a list code, the decoder produces a list of messages, and the absence from the list of the message transmitted constitutes an error. When the size of the list is 1, the list coding problem reduces to the usual coding problem using codes as in (10) and (11). Formally, a length-n (block) list code of list size ν is a pair of mappings (f, ϕ), where the encoder f is defined by (10), while the (list) decoder ϕ is a mapping

$$\phi: \mathcal{Y}^n \to \mathcal{M}_\nu \cup \{0\} \tag{32}$$

where $\mathcal{M}_\nu$ is the set of all subsets of $\mathcal{M}$ with cardinality not exceeding ν. The rate of this list code with size ν is

$$\frac{1}{n} \log \frac{M}{\nu}. \tag{33}$$

The probability of error for the message $m \in \mathcal{M}$ when a list code (f, ϕ) with list size ν is used on a channel $\theta \in \Theta$ is defined analogously as in (13), with the modification that the sum in (13) is over those $\boldsymbol{y} \in \mathcal{Y}^n$ for which $m \notin \phi(\boldsymbol{y})$. The corresponding maximum and average probabilities of error are then defined accordingly, as is the notion of capacity.

III. CAPACITIES

We now present some key results on channel capacity for the various channel models and performance criteria described in the previous section. Our presentation of results is not exhaustive, and seldom will the presented results be discussed in detail; instead, we shall often refer the reader to the bibliography for relevant treatments.

The literature on communication under channel uncertainty is vast, and our bibliography is by no means complete. Rather than directly citing all the literature relevant to a topic, we shall when possible, refer the reader to a textbook or a recent paper which contains a survey. The citations are thus intended to serve as pointers for further study of a topic, and not as indicators of where a result was first derived or where the most significant contribution to a subject was made.

In what follows, all channels will be assumed to have finite input and output alphabets, unless stated otherwise.

A. Discrete Memoryless Channels

We begin with the model originally treated by Shannon [111] of a known memoryless channel with finite input and output alphabets $\mathcal{X}$ and $\mathcal{Y}$, respectively. The channel law is given by (2) where $W(y|x)$ is known and fixed. For this model, the capacity is given by [111]

$$C = \max_{Q \in \mathcal{P}(\mathcal{X})} I(Q, W) \tag{34}$$

where $\mathcal{P}(\mathcal{X})$ denotes the set of all (input) pmf's on $\mathcal{X}$,

$$I(Q, W) = \sum_{x \in \mathcal{X}} \sum_{y \in \mathcal{Y}} Q(x) W(y|x) \log \frac{W(y|x)}{(QW)(y)} \tag{35}$$

is the mutual information between the channel input and output, and

$$(QW)(y) = \sum_{x' \in \mathcal{X}} Q(x') W(y|x') \tag{36}$$

is the output pmf on $\mathcal{Y}$ which is induced when the channel input pmf is Q. This is the channel capacity regardless of whether the maximum or average probability of error criterion is used, and regardless of whether or not the transmitter and receiver have access to a common source of randomness. Moreover, a strong converse holds [124] so that

$$C = C_\epsilon, \qquad 0 < \epsilon < 1.$$

Upper and lower bounds on error exponents for the discrete memoryless channel can be found in [32], [44], [64], and in references therein.

Example 1 (Continued): The capacity C of a BSC with crossover probability p is given by [39], [44], [64]

$$C = 1 - h_b(p)$$

where

$$h_b(x) = -x \log x - (1-x) \log(1-x), \qquad x \in [0, 1]$$

is the binary entropy function.

In [114], Shannon considered a different model in which the channel law at time t depends on a state rv S_t, with values in a finite set $\mathcal{S}$, evolving in a memoryless (i.i.d.) fashion in accordance with a (known) pmf P_S on $\mathcal{S}$. When in state $s \in \mathcal{S}$, the channel obeys a transition law given by the stochastic matrix $\{W(y|x; s), x \in \mathcal{X}, y \in \mathcal{Y}\}$. The channel states are assumed to be known to the transmitter in a causal way, but unknown to the receiver. The symbol transmitted at time t may thus depend, not only on the message m, but also on present and past states $s_1^t = s_1, \cdots, s_t$ of the channel. A length-n block code (f, ϕ) consists of an encoder f which can be described as a sequence of mappings $\{f_t\}_{t=1}^n$ as in (29), while the decoder is defined as in (11). When such an encoding scheme is used, the probability $W(\boldsymbol{y}|f(m))$ that the channel output is $\boldsymbol{y}$ given that message m was transmitted, is

$$W(\boldsymbol{y}|f(m)) = \sum_{\boldsymbol{s} \in \mathcal{S}^n} \left(\prod_{i=1}^n P_S(s_i) \prod_{t=1}^n W(y_t|f_t(m, s_1^t); s_t) \right). \tag{37}$$

Shannon computed the capacity of this channel by observing that there is no loss in capacity if the output of the encoder is allowed to depend only on the message m and the *current* state s_t, and not on previous states s_1^{t-1}. As a consequence of this observation, we can compute channel capacity by considering a new memoryless channel $\tilde{W} \colon \mathcal{S}^{\mathcal{X}} \to \mathcal{Y}$ whose inputs are mappings from $\mathcal{S}$ to $\mathcal{X}$ and whose output is distributed for any input $\psi \colon \mathcal{S} \to \mathcal{X}$ according to

$$\tilde{W}(y|\psi) = \sum_{s \in \mathcal{S}} P_S(s) W(y|\psi(s); s). \tag{38}$$

Note that if neither transmitter nor receiver has access to state information, the channel becomes a simple memoryless one, and the results of [111] are directly applicable. Also note that in defining channel capacity, the probabilities of errors are averaged over the possible state sequences; performance is not guaranteed for every individual sequence of states. This problem is thus significantly different from the problem of computing the capacity of an AVC (5).

Regardless of whether or not the transmitter has state information, accounting for state information at the receiver poses no additional difficulty. The output alphabet can be augmented to account for this state information, e.g., by setting the new output alphabet to be

$$\tilde{\mathcal{Y}} = \mathcal{Y} \times \mathcal{S}. \tag{39}$$

For the corresponding new channel, with appropriate law, we can then use the results for the case where the receiver has no additional information. This technique also applies to situations where the receiver may have noisy observations of the channel states.

A variation of this problem was considered in [37], [67], [78], and in references therein, where state information is available to the transmitter in a *noncausal* way in that the entire realization of the i.i.d. state sequence is known when transmission begins. Such noncausal state information at the transmitter can be most beneficial (albeit rarely available) and can substantially increase capacity.

The inefficacy of feedback in increasing capacity was demonstrated by Shannon in [112]. For some of the results on list decoding, see [44], [55], [56], [62], [115], [120], and references therein.

1) The Compound Discrete Memoryless Channel: We now turn to the compound discrete memoryless channel, which models communication over a memoryless channel whose law is unknown but remains fixed throughout a transmission (see (4)). Both transmitter and receiver are assumed ignorant of the channel law governing the transmission; they only know the family Θ to which the law belongs. It should be emphasized that in this model no prior distribution on Θ is assumed, and in demonstrating the achievability of a rate R, we must therefore exhibit a code (f, ϕ) as in (10) and (11) which yields a small probability of error for *every* channel in the family.

Clearly, the highest achievable rate cannot exceed the capacity of any channel in the family, but this bound is not tight, as different channels in the family may have different capacity-achieving input pmf's. It is, however, true that the capacity of the compound channel is positive if and only if (iff) the infimum of the capacities of the channels in the family Θ is positive (see [126]).

The capacity of a compound DMC is given by the following theorem [30], [44], [52], [125], [126]:

Theorem 1: The capacity of the compound DMC (4), for both the average probability of error and the maximum probability of error, is given by

$$C = \max_{Q \in \mathcal{P}(\mathcal{X})} \inf_{\theta \in \Theta} I(Q, W(\cdot|\cdot; \theta)). \tag{40}$$

For the maximum probability of error, a strong converse holds so that

$$C = C_\epsilon^m, \qquad 0 < \epsilon < 1. \tag{41}$$

Note that the capacity value is not increased if the decoder knows the channel θ, but not the encoder. On the other hand, if the encoder knows the channel, then even if the decoder does not, the capacity is in general increased and is equal to the infimum of the capacities of the channels in the family [52], [125], [126].

Example 2 (Continued): The capacity of the compound DMC corresponding to a class of binary-symmetric channels is given by

$$C = \inf_{\theta \in \Theta} (1 - h_b(\theta)).$$

It is interesting to note that in this example the capacity of the family is the infimum of the capacities of the individual channels in the family. This always holds for memoryless families when the capacity-achieving input pmf is the same for all the channels in the family. In contrast, for families of channels with memory (Example 5), the capacity-achieving input pmf may be the same for all the channels in the family, and yet the capacity of the family can be strictly smaller than the infimum of the capacities of the individual channels.

Neither the direct part nor the converse of Theorem 1 follows immediately from the classical theorem on the capacity of a known DMC. The converse does not follow from (34) since the capacity in (40) may be strictly smaller than the capacity of any channel in the family. Nevertheless, an application of Fano's inequality and some convexity arguments [30] establishes the converse. A strong converse for the maximum probability of error criterion can be found in [44] and [126]. For the average probability of error, a strong converse need not hold [1], [44].

Proving the direct part requires showing that for any input pmf Q, any rate R, and any $\delta > 0$, there exists a sequence of encoders parametrized by the blocklength n that can be reliably decoded on any channel W that satisfies $I(Q, W) > R + \delta$. Moreover, the decoding rule must not depend on the channel. The receiver in [30] is a maximum-likelihood decoder with respect to a uniform mixture on a finite (but polynomial in the blocklength) set of DMC's which is in a sense dense in the class of all DMC's. The existence of a code is demonstrated using a random-coding argument. It is interesting to note [51], [119], that if the set of stochastic matrices $\{W(\cdot|\cdot; \theta), \theta \in \Theta\}$ is compact and convex, then the decoder can be chosen as the maximum-likelihood decoder for the DMC with stochastic matrix $W(\cdot|\cdot; \theta^*)$, where (Q^*, θ^*) is a saddle point for (40). The receiver can thus be a maximum-likelihood receiver with respect to the worst channel in the family.

Yet another decoder for the compound DMC is the maximum empirical mutual information (MMI) decoder [44]. This decoder will be discussed later in Section IV-B, when we discuss universal codes and the compound channel. The use of universal decoders for the compound channel is studied in [60] and [91], where a universal decoder for the class of finite-state channels is used to derive the capacity of a compound FSC. Another result on the compound channel capacity of a class of channels with memory can be found in [107] where the capacity of a class of Gaussian intersymbol interference channels is derived.

It should be noted that if the family of channels Θ is finite, then the problem is somewhat simplified and a Bayesian decoder [64, pp. 176–177] as well as a merged decoder, obtained by merging the maximum-likelihood decoders of each of the channels in the family [60], can be used to demonstrate achievability.

Cover [38] has shown interesting connections between communication over a compound channel and over a broadcast channel. An application of these ideas to communication over slowly varying flat-fading channels under the "capacity versus outage" criterion can be found in [109].

2) The Arbitrarily Varying Channel: The arbitrarily varying channel (AVC) was introduced by Blackwell, Breiman, and Thomasian [31] to model a memoryless channel whose law may vary with time in an arbitrary and unknown manner during the transmission of a codeword [cf. (5)]. The transmitter and receiver strive to construct codes for ensuring reliable communication, no matter which sequence of laws govern the channel during a transmission.

Formally, a discrete memoryless AVC with (finite) input alphabet $\mathcal{X}$ and (finite) output alphabet $\mathcal{Y}$ is determined by a family of channel laws $\{W(\cdot|\cdot; s), s \in \mathcal{S}\}$, each individual law in this family being identified by an index $s \in \mathcal{S}$ called the state. The state space $\mathcal{S}$, which is known to both transmitter and receiver, will be assumed to be also finite unless otherwise stated. The probability of receiving $\boldsymbol{y} \in \mathcal{Y}^n$, when $\boldsymbol{x} \in \mathcal{X}^n$ is transmitted and $\boldsymbol{s} \in \mathcal{S}^n$ is the channel state sequence, is given by (5). The standard AVC model introduced in [31], and subsequently studied by several authors (e.g., [2], [6], [10], [20], [45]), assumes that the transmitter and receiver are unaware of the actual state sequence $\boldsymbol{s} \in \mathcal{S}^n$ which governs a transmission. In the same vein, the "selector" of the state sequence $\boldsymbol{s}$, is ignorant of the actual message transmitted. However, the state "selector" is assumed to know the code when a deterministic code is used, and know the pmf generating the code when a randomized code is used (but not the actual codes chosen).[1]

There are a wide variety of challenging problems for the AVC. These depend on the nature of the performance criteria used (maximum or average probabilities of error), the permissible coding strategies (randomized codes, codes with stochastic encoders, or deterministic codes), and the degrees of knowledge of each other with which the codeword and state sequences are selected. For a summary of the work on AVC's through the late 1980's, and for basic results, we refer the reader to [6], [44], [47]–[49], and [126].

Before we turn to a presentation of key AVC results, it is useful to revisit the probability of error criteria in (18) and (19). Observe that in the definition of an ϵ-achievable rate (cf. Section II) on an AVC, the maximum (resp., average) probability of error criterion in (18) (resp., (19)) can be restated as

$$\max_{\boldsymbol{s} \in \mathcal{S}^n} e_{\max}(f, \phi, \boldsymbol{s}) \leq \epsilon \tag{42}$$

$$(\text{resp., } \max_{\boldsymbol{s} \in \mathcal{S}^n} \overline{e}(f, \phi, \boldsymbol{s}) \leq \epsilon) \tag{43}$$

with $e(m, f, \phi, \theta)$ in (13) now being replaced by

$$e(m, f, \phi, \boldsymbol{s}) = \sum_{\boldsymbol{y}: \ \phi(\boldsymbol{y}) \neq m} W(\boldsymbol{y}|f(m); \boldsymbol{s}). \tag{44}$$

In (42)–(44), recall that (f, ϕ) is a (deterministic) code of blocklength n. When a randomized code (F, Φ) is used, $e_{\max}(F, \Phi, \boldsymbol{s})$, $\overline{e}(F, \Phi, \boldsymbol{s})$, and $e(m, F, \Phi, \boldsymbol{s})$ will play the roles of $e_{\max}(f, \phi, \boldsymbol{s})$, $\overline{e}(f, \phi, \boldsymbol{s})$, and $e(m, f, \phi, \boldsymbol{s})$, respectively, in (42)–(44). Here, $e_{\max}(F, \Phi, \boldsymbol{s})$, $\overline{e}(F, \Phi, \boldsymbol{s})$, and $e(m, F, \Phi, \boldsymbol{s})$ are defined analogously as in (14)–(16), respectively.

---

[1] For the situation where a deterministic code is used and the state "selector" knows this code as well as the transmitted message, see [44, p. 233].

Given an AVC (5), let us denote by W_ζ, for any pmf ζ on $\mathcal{S}$, the "averaged" stochastic matrix $\mathcal{X} \to \mathcal{Y}$ defined by

$$W_\zeta(y|x) = \sum_{s \in \mathcal{S}} W(y|x; s)\zeta(s). \qquad (45)$$

Further, let $\mathcal{P}(\mathcal{S})$ denote the set of all pmfs on $\mathcal{S}$.

The capacity of the AVC (5) for randomized codes is, of course, the same for the maximum and average probabilities of error, and is given by the following theorem [19], [31], [119].

Theorem 2: The randomized code capacity of the AVC (5) is given by

$$C = \max_{Q \in \mathcal{P}(\mathcal{X})} \min_{\zeta \in \mathcal{P}(\mathcal{S})} I(Q, W_\zeta) = \min_{\zeta \in \mathcal{P}(\mathcal{S})} \max_{Q \in \mathcal{P}(\mathcal{X})} I(Q, W_\zeta). \qquad (46)$$

Further, a strong converse holds so that

$$C = C_\epsilon, \qquad 0 < \epsilon < 1. \qquad (47)$$

The direct part of Theorem 2 can be proved [19] using a random-coding argument to show the existence of a suitable encoder. The receiver in [19] uses a (normalized) maximum-likelihood decoder for the DMC with stochastic matrix $W_{\zeta^*}: \mathcal{X} \to \mathcal{Y}$, where (Q^*, ζ^*) is a saddle point for (46). When input or state constraints are additionally imposed, the randomized code capacity $C(\Gamma, \Lambda)$ of the AVC (5), given below (cf. (48)), is achieved by a similar code with suitable modifications to accommodate the constraints [47].

The randomized code capacity of the AVC (5) under input constraint Γ and state constraint Λ (cf. (22), (24)), denoted $C(\Gamma, \Lambda)$, is determined in [47], and is given by

$$C(\Gamma, \Lambda) = \max_{Q \in \mathcal{P}(\mathcal{X}): \ g(Q) \leq \Gamma} \min_{\zeta \in \mathcal{P}(\mathcal{S}): \ l(\zeta) \leq \Lambda} I(Q, W_\zeta)$$
$$= \min_{\zeta \in \mathcal{P}(\mathcal{S}): \ l(\zeta) \leq \Lambda} \max_{Q \in \mathcal{P}(\mathcal{X}): \ g(Q) \leq \Gamma} I(Q, W_\zeta) \qquad (48)$$

where

$$g(Q) = \sum_{x \in \mathcal{X}} Q(x)g(x) \qquad (49)$$

and

$$l(\zeta) = \sum_{s \in \mathcal{S}} \zeta(s)l(s). \qquad (50)$$

Also, a strong converse exists. In the absence of input or state constraints, the corresponding value of the randomized code capacity of the AVC (5) is obtained from (48) by setting

$$\Gamma = g_{\max} \overset{\text{def}}{=} \max_{x \in \mathcal{X}} g(x)$$

or

$$\Lambda = l_{\max} \overset{\text{def}}{=} \max_{s \in \mathcal{S}} l(s).$$

It is further demonstrated in [47] that under weaker input and state constraints—in terms of expected values, rather than on individual codewords and state sequences as in (22) and (24)—a strong converse does not exist. (Similar results had been established earlier in [80] for a Gaussian AVC; see Section V below.)

Turning next to AVC performance using deterministic codes, recall that the capacity of a DMC (cf. (34)) or a compound channel (cf. (40)) is the same for randomized codes as well as for deterministic codes. An AVC, in sharp contrast, exhibits the characteristic that its deterministic code capacity is generally smaller than its randomized code capacity. In this context, it is useful to note that unlike in the case of a DMC (2), the existence of a randomized code (F, Φ) for an AVC (5) satisfying

$$\max_{\boldsymbol{s} \in \mathcal{S}^n} e_{\max}(F, \Phi, \boldsymbol{s}) \leq \epsilon$$

or

$$\max_{\boldsymbol{s} \in \mathcal{S}^n} \bar{e}(F, \Phi, \boldsymbol{s}) \leq \epsilon$$

does not imply the existence of a deterministic code (f, ϕ) (as a realization of the rv (F, Φ)) satisfying (42) and (43), respectively. Furthermore, in contrast to a DMC (2) or a compound channel (4), the deterministic code capacities C^m and C^a of the AVC (5) for the maximum and average probabilities of error, can be different;[2] specifically, C^m can be strictly smaller than C^a. An example [6] when $C^a > 0$ but $C^m = 0$ is the "deterministic" AVC with $\mathcal{X} = \mathcal{Y} = \{0, 1, 2\}$, $\mathcal{S} = \{0, 1\}$, and $y = x + s$ modulo 3.

A computable characterization of C^m for an AVC (5) using deterministic codes, is a notoriously difficult problem which remains unsolved to date. Indeed, as observed by Ahlswede [2], it yields as a special case Shannon's famous graph-theoretic problem of determining the zero-error capacity of any DMC [96], [112], which remains a "holy grail" in information theory.

While C^m is unknown in general, a computable characterization is available in some special situations, which we next address. To this end, given an AVC (5), for any stochastic matrix $\tilde{\zeta}: \mathcal{X} \to \mathcal{S}$, we denote by $W_{\tilde{\zeta}}$ the "row-averaged" stochastic matrix $\mathcal{X} \to \mathcal{Y}$, defined by

$$W_{\tilde{\zeta}}(y|x) = \sum_{s \in \mathcal{S}} W(y|x; s) \, \tilde{\zeta}(s|x). \qquad (51)$$

Further, let $\mathcal{P}(\mathcal{X} \to \mathcal{S})$ denote the set of stochastic matrices $\mathcal{X} \to \mathcal{S}$.

The capacity C^m of an AVC with a binary output alphabet was determined in [20] and is given by the following.

Theorem 3: The deterministic code capacity C^m of the AVC (5) for the maximum probability of error, under the condition $|\mathcal{Y}| = 2$, is given by

$$C^m = \max_{Q \in \mathcal{P}(\mathcal{X})} \min_{\tilde{\zeta} \in \mathcal{P}(\mathcal{X} \to \mathcal{S})} I(Q, W_{\tilde{\zeta}})$$
$$= \min_{\tilde{\zeta} \in \mathcal{P}(\mathcal{X} \to \mathcal{S})} \max_{Q \in \mathcal{P}(\mathcal{X})} I(Q, W_{\tilde{\zeta}}). \qquad (52)$$

Further, a strong converse holds so that

$$C^m = C_\epsilon^m, \qquad 0 < \epsilon < 1. \qquad (53)$$

---

[2] As a qualification, recall from Section III-A1) that for a compound channel (4), a strong converse holds for the maximum probability of error but not for the average probability of error.

The proof in [20] of Theorem 3 considers first the AVC (5) with binary input and output alphabets. A suitable code is identified for the DMC corresponding to the "worst row-averaged" stochastic matrix from among the family of stochastic matrices $W_{\tilde{\zeta}} \colon \mathcal{X} \to \mathcal{Y}$ (cf. 51) formed by varying $\tilde{\zeta} \in \mathcal{P}(\mathcal{X} \to \mathcal{S})$; this code is seen to perform no worse on any other DMC corresponding to a "row-averaged" stochastic matrix in said family. Finally, the case of a nonbinary input alphabet is reduced to that of a binary alphabet by using a notion of two "extremal" input symbols.

Ahlswede [10] showed that the formula for C^m in Theorem 3 is valid for a larger class of AVC's than in [20]. The direct part of the assertion in [10] entails a random selection of codewords combined with an expurgation, used in conjunction with a clever decoding rule.

The sharpest results on the problem of determining C^m for the AVC (5) are due to Csiszár and Körner [45], and are obtained by a combinatorial approach developed in [44] and [46]. The characterization of C^m in [45] requires additional terminology. Specifically, we shall say that the $\mathcal{X}$-valued rv's X, X', with the same pmf Q, are connected a.s. by the stochastic matrix $W \colon \mathcal{X} \times \mathcal{S} \to \mathcal{Y}$ appearing in (5), denoted $X \overset{W}{\sim} X'$, iff there exist pmf's ζ, ζ' on $\mathcal{S}$ such that

$$\Pr \left\{ \sum_{s \in \mathcal{S}} W(y|X, s)\zeta(s) \right.$$

$$\left. = \sum_{s \in \mathcal{S}} W(y|X', s)\zeta'(s) \quad \text{for every } y \in \mathcal{Y} \right\} = 1. \quad (54)$$

Also, define

$$D(Q) = \min_{X, X' \colon P_X = P_{X'} = Q, X \overset{W}{\sim} X'} I(X \wedge X') \quad (55)$$

where P_X denotes the pmf of the rv X. The following characterization of C^m in [45] is more general than previous characterizations in [10] and [20].

Theorem 4: For the AVC (5), for every pmf $Q \in \mathcal{P}(\mathcal{X})$

$$\min \left\{ \min_{\tilde{\zeta} \in \mathcal{P}(\mathcal{X} \to \mathcal{S})} I(Q, W_{\tilde{\zeta}}), D(Q) \right\}$$

is an achievable rate for the maximum probability of error. In particular, for $(Q^*, \tilde{\zeta}^*)$, a saddle point for (52), if Q^* is such that $D(Q^*) \geq I(Q^*, W_{\tilde{\zeta}^*})$, then

$$C^m = I(Q^*, W_{\tilde{\zeta}^*}). \quad (56)$$

The direct part of Theorem 4 uses a code in which the codewords are identified by random selection from sequences of a fixed "type" (cf. e.g., [44, Sec. 1.2]), using suitable large deviation bounds. The decoder combines a "joint typicality" rule with a threshold decision rule based on empirical mutual information quantities (cf. Section IV-B6) below).

Upon easing the performance criterion to be now the average probability of error, the deterministic code capacity C^a of the AVC (5) is known. In a key paper, Ahlswede [6] observed that the AVC capacity C^a displays a dichotomy: it either equals the AVC randomized code capacity or else is zero. Ahlswede's alternatives [6] can be stated as

$$C^a = \max_{Q \in \mathcal{P}(\mathcal{X})} \min_{\zeta \in \mathcal{P}(\mathcal{S})} I(Q, W_\zeta), \qquad \text{or else } C^a = 0. \quad (57)$$

The proof of (57) in [6] used an "elimination" technique consisting of two key steps. The first step was the discovery of "random code reduction," namely, that the randomized code capacity of the AVC can be achieved by a randomized code restricted to random selections from "exponentially few" deterministic codes, e.g., from no more than n^2 deterministic codes, where n is the blocklength. Then, if $C^a > 0$, the second step entailing an "elimination of randomness," i.e., the conversion of this randomized code into a deterministic code, is performed by adding short prefixes to the original codewords so as to inform the decoder which of the n^2 deterministic codes is actually used; the overall rate of the deterministic code is, of course, only negligibly affected by the addition of the prefixes.

A necessary and sufficient computable characterization of AVC's for deciding between the alternatives in (57) was not provided in [6]. This lacuna was partially filled by Ericson [59] who gave a necessary condition for the deterministic code capacity C^a to be positive. By enlarging on an idea in [31], it was shown [59] that if the AVC state "selector" could emulate the channel input by means of a fictitious auxiliary channel (defined in terms of a suitable stochastic matrix $U \colon \mathcal{X} \to \mathcal{S}$), then the decoder fails to discern between the channel input and state, resulting in $C^a = 0$.

Formally, we say that an AVC (5) is *symmetrizable* if for some stochastic matrix $U \colon \mathcal{X} \to \mathcal{S}$

$$\sum_{s \in \mathcal{S}} W(y|x; s)U(s|x') = \sum_{s \in \mathcal{S}} W(y|x'; s)U(s|x),$$

$$x \in \mathcal{X}, x' \in \mathcal{X}, y \in \mathcal{Y}. \quad (58)$$

Let $\mathcal{U}(\mathcal{X} \to \mathcal{S})$ denote the set of all "symmetrizing" stochastic matrices $U \colon \mathcal{X} \to \mathcal{S}$ which satisfy (58). An AVC (5) for which $\mathcal{U}(\mathcal{X} \to \mathcal{S}) = \emptyset$ is termed nonsymmetrizable. Thus it is shown in [59] that if an AVC (5) is such that its deterministic code capacity C^a is positive, then the AVC (5) must be nonsymmetrizable.

A computable characterization of AVC's with positive deterministic code capacity C^a was finally completed by Csiszár and Narayan [48], who showed that nonsymmetrizability is also a sufficient condition for $C^a > 0$. The proof technique in [48] does not rely on the existence of the dichotomy as asserted by (57); nor does it rely on the fact, used materially in [6] to establish (57), that

$$\max_{Q \in \mathcal{P}(\mathcal{X})} \min_{\zeta \in \mathcal{P}(\mathcal{S})} I(Q, W_\zeta)$$

is the randomized code capacity of the AVC (5). The direct part in [48] uses a code with the codewords chosen at random from sequences of a fixed type, and selectively identified by a generalized Chernoff bounding technique due to Dobrushin and Stambler [53]. The linchpin is a subtle decoding rule which decides on the basis of a joint typicality test together with a threshold test using empirical mutual information quantities, similarly as in [45]. A key step of the proof is to show

114

that the decoding rule is unambiguous as a consequence of the nonsymmetrizability condition. An adequate bound on the average probability of error is then obtained in a standard manner using the method of types (cf. e.g., [44]).

The results in [6], [48], and [59] collectively provide the following characterization of C^a in [48].

Theorem 5: The deterministic code capacity C^a of the AVC (5) for the average probability of error is positive iff the AVC (5) is nonsymmetrizable. If $C^a > 0$, it equals the randomized code capacity of the AVC (5) given by (46), i.e.,

$$C^a = \max_{Q \in \mathcal{P}(\mathcal{X})} \min_{\zeta \in \mathcal{P}(\mathcal{S})} I(Q, W_\zeta). \qquad (59)$$

Furthermore, if the AVC (5) is nonsymmetrizable, a strong converse holds so that

$$C^a = C^a_\epsilon, \qquad 0 < \epsilon < 1. \qquad (60)$$

It should be noted that sufficient conditions for the AVC (5) to have a positive deterministic code capacity C^a had been given earlier in [6] and [53]; these conditions, however, are not necessary in general. Also, a necessary and sufficient condition for $C^a > 0$, albeit in terms of noncomputable "product space characterization" (cf. [44, p. 259]) appeared in [6]. The nonsymmetrizability condition above can be regarded as "single-letterization" of the condition in [6]. For a comparison of conditions for $C^a > 0$, we refer the reader to [49, Appendix I].

Yet another means of determining the deterministic code capacity C^a of the AVC (5) is derived as a special case of recent work by Ahlswede and Cai [15] which completely resolves the deterministic code capacity problem for a multiple-access AVC for the average probability of error. For the AVC (5), the approach in [15], in effect, consists of elements drawn from both [6] and [48]. In short, by [15], if the AVC (5) is nonsymmetrizable, then a code with the decoding rule proposed in [48] can be used to achieve "small" positive rates. Thus $C^a > 0$, whereupon the "elimination technique" of [6] is applied to yield that C^a equals the randomized code capacity given by (46).

We consider next the deterministic code capacity of the AVC (5) for the average probability of error, under input and state constraints (cf. (21) and (24)). To begin with, assume the imposition of only a state constraint but no input constraint. Let $C^a(\Lambda)$ denote the capacity of the AVC (5) under state constraint Λ (cf. (24)). If the AVC is nonsymmetrizable then, by Theorem 5, its capacity C^a without state constraint is positive and, obviously, so too is its capacity $C^a(\Lambda)$ under state constraint Λ for every $0 \leq \Lambda \leq l_{\max}$. The elimination technique in [6] can be applied to show that $C^a(\Lambda)$ equals the corresponding randomized code capacity under state constraint Λ (and no input constraint) given by

(48) as $C(g_{\max}, \Lambda)$. On the other hand, if the AVC (5) is symmetrizable, by Theorem 5, its capacity C^a without state constraint is zero. However, the capacity $C^a(\Lambda)$ under state constraint Λ may yet be positive. In order to determine $C^a(\Lambda)$, the elimination technique in [6] can no longer be applied; while the first step of "random code reduction" is valid, the second step of "elimination of randomness" cannot be performed unless the capacity without state constraint C^a is itself positive. The reason, loosely speaking, is that if C^a were zero, the state "selector" could prevent reliable communication by foiling reliable transmission of the prefix which identifies the codebook actually selected in the first step; to this end, the state "selector" could operate in an unconstrained manner during the (relatively) brief transmission of the prefix thereby denying it positive capacity, while still satisfying state constraint Λ over the entire duration of the transmission of the prefix and the codeword.

The capacity $C^a(\Lambda)$ of the AVC (5), in general, is determined in [48] by extending the approach used therein for characterizing C^a. A significant role is played by the functional $\Lambda_0(Q)$, $Q \in \mathcal{P}(\mathcal{X})$, defined by

$$\Lambda_0(Q) = \min_{U \in \mathcal{U}} \sum_{x \in \mathcal{X}, s \in \mathcal{S}} Q(x) U(s|x) l(s) \qquad (61)$$

with $\Lambda_0(Q) = \infty$ if $\mathcal{U} = \emptyset$, i.e., if the AVC (5) is nonsymmetrizable. The capacity $C^a(\Lambda)$ under state constraint Λ is shown in [48] to be zero if $\max_{Q \in \mathcal{P}(\mathcal{X})} \Lambda_0(Q)$ is smaller than Λ; on the other hand, $C^a(\Lambda)$ is positive and equals

$$C^a(\Lambda) = \max_{Q \in \mathcal{P}(\mathcal{X}):\ \Lambda_0(Q) \geq \Lambda} \min_{\zeta \in \mathcal{P}(\mathcal{S}):\ l(\zeta) \leq \Lambda} I(Q, W_\zeta)$$
$$\text{if } \max_{Q \in \mathcal{P}(\mathcal{X})} \Lambda_0(Q) > \Lambda. \qquad (62)$$

In particular, it is possible that $C^a(\Lambda)$ lies strictly between zero and the randomized code capacity under state constraint Λ which, by (48), equals $C(g_{\max}, \Lambda)$; this represents a departure from the dichotomous behavior observed in the absence of any state constraint (cf. (57)). A comparison of (48) and (62) shows that if the maximum in (48) is not achieved by an input pmf $Q \in \mathcal{P}(\mathcal{X})$ which satisfies $\Lambda_0(Q) \geq \Lambda$, then $C^a(\Lambda)$ is strictly smaller than $C(g_{\max}, \Lambda)$, while still being positive if the hypothesis in (62) holds, i.e.,

$$\max_{Q \in \mathcal{P}(\mathcal{X})} \Lambda_0(Q) > \Lambda.$$

Next, if an input constraint Γ (cf. (21)) is also imposed, the capacity $C^a(\Gamma, \Lambda)$ is given in [48] by the following.

Theorem 6: The deterministic code capacity $C^a(\Gamma, \Lambda)$ of the AVC (5) under input constraint Γ and state constraint Λ, for the average probability of error, is given by (63) at the bottom of this page. Further, in the cases considered in (63), a strong converse holds so that

$$C^a(\Gamma, \Lambda) = C^a_\epsilon(\Gamma, \Lambda), \qquad 0 < \epsilon < 1. \qquad (64)$$

$$C^a(\Gamma, \Lambda) = \begin{cases} \displaystyle\max_{Q \in \mathcal{P}(\mathcal{X}):\ \Lambda_0(Q) \geq \Lambda,\ g(Q) \leq \Gamma} \min_{\zeta \in \mathcal{P}(\mathcal{S}):\ l(\zeta) \leq \Lambda} I(Q, W_\zeta) > 0, & \text{if } \displaystyle\max_{Q \in \mathcal{P}(\mathcal{X}):\ g(Q) \leq \Gamma} \Lambda_0(Q) > \Lambda \\[4mm] 0, & \text{if } \displaystyle\max_{Q \in \mathcal{P}(\mathcal{X}):\ g(Q) \leq \Gamma} \Lambda_0(Q) < \Lambda. \end{cases} \qquad (63)$$

The case

$$\max_{Q \in \mathcal{P}(X):\ g(Q) \leq \Gamma} \Lambda_0(Q) = \Lambda$$

remains unresolved in general; for certain AVC's, $C^a(\Gamma, \Lambda)$ equals zero in this case too (cf. [48, remark following the proof of Theorem 3]). Again, it is possible that $C^a(\Gamma, \Lambda)$ lies strictly between zero and the randomized code capacity $C(\Gamma, \Lambda)$ under input constraint Γ and state constraint Λ given by (48).

The results of Theorem 6 lead to some interesting combinatorial interpretations (cf. [48, Example 1] and [49, Sec. III]).

Example 3 (Continued): We refer the reader to [48, Example 2] for a full treatment of this example. For a pmf $Q = (1 - q, q)$ on the input alphabet $\{0, 1\}$, and a pmf $\zeta = (1 - r, r)$ on the state space $\{0, 1\}$, we obtain from (35) and (45) that

$$I(Q, W_\zeta) = \tilde{I}(q, r)$$
$$= H(qr, (1 - q)(1 - r), q + r - 2qr) - h_b(r)$$

where H denotes entropy. The randomized code capacity of the AVC in Example 3 is then given by Theorem 2 as (cf. (46))

$$C = \max_q \min_r \tilde{I}(q, r) + 1/2 \tag{65}$$

where $q = r = 1/2$ is a saddle point for $\tilde{I}(q, r)$. Turning to the deterministic code capacity C^a for the average probability of error, note that the symmetrizability condition (58) is satisfied iff the stochastic matrix $U: \mathcal{X} \rightarrow \mathcal{S}$ is the identity matrix. By Theorem 5, we have $C^a = 0$; obviously, the deterministic code capacity for the maximum probability of error is then $C^m = 0$. Thus in the absence of input or state constraints, the randomized code capacity C is positive while the deterministic code capacities C^a and C^m are zero.

We now consider AVC performance under input and state constraints. Let the functions $g(x) = x$, $x \in \{0, 1\}$, and $l(s) = s$, $s \in \{0, 1\}$, be used in the input and state constraints (cf. (20)–(24)). Thus $g(\boldsymbol{x})$ in (20) and $l(\boldsymbol{s})$ in (23) are the normalized Hamming weights of the n-length binary sequences $\boldsymbol{x}$ and $\boldsymbol{s}$. Then the randomized code capacity $C(\Gamma, \Lambda)$ under the input constraint Γ and state constraint Λ, $0 \leq \Gamma, \Lambda \leq 1$, is given by (48) as

$$C(\Gamma, \Lambda) = \max_{q \leq \Gamma} \min_{r \leq \Lambda} \tilde{I}(q, r). \tag{66}$$

In particular

$$C(\Gamma, \Lambda) = C = 1/2, \qquad \text{if } \Gamma, \Lambda \geq 1/2. \tag{67}$$

Next, we turn to the deterministic code capacity $C^a(\Gamma, \Lambda)$ for the average probability of error. It is readily seen from (49), (50), and (61) that $\Lambda_0(Q) = q$, $g(Q) = q$, and $l(\zeta) = r$, respectively. It then follows from Theorem 6 that (cf. [47, Example 2])

$$C^a(\Gamma, \Lambda) = \begin{cases} 0, & \text{if } \Gamma \leq \Lambda \\ \max_{\Lambda \leq q \leq \Gamma} \min_{r \leq \Lambda} \tilde{I}(q, r), & \text{if } \Gamma > \Lambda. \end{cases} \tag{68}$$

We can conclude from (66)–(68) (cf. [48, Example 2]) that for $1/2 \leq \Gamma \leq \Lambda$, it **holds** that $C^a(\Gamma, \Lambda) = 0$ while

$C(\Gamma, \Lambda) = 1/2$. Next, if $\Gamma > \Lambda > 1/2$, we have that $C^a(\Gamma, \Lambda)$ is positive but smaller that $C(\Gamma, \Lambda)$. On the other hand, if $\Lambda \leq 1/2$, $\Gamma > \Lambda$, then $C^a(\Gamma, \Lambda) = C(\Gamma, \Lambda)$. Thus under state constraint Λ, several situations exist depending on the value of Λ, $0 \leq \Lambda \leq 1$. The deterministic code capacity for the average probability of error can be zero while the corresponding randomized code capacity is positive. Further, the former can be positive and yet smaller than the latter; or it could equal the latter.

Several of the results described above from [47]–[49] on the randomized as well as the deterministic code capacities of the AVC (5) with input constraint Γ and state constraint Λ have been extended by Csiszár to AVC's with general input and output alphabets and state space; see [41].

It remains to characterize AVC performance using codes with stochastic encoders. For the AVC (5) without input or state constraints, the following result is due to Ahlswede [6].

Theorem 7: For codes with stochastic encoders, the capacities of the AVC (5) for the maximum as well as the average probabilities of error equal its deterministic code capacity for the average probability of error.

Thus by Theorem 7, when the average probability of error criterion is used, codes with stochastic encoders offer no advantage over deterministic codes in terms of yielding a larger capacity value. However, for the maximum probability of error criterion, the former can afford an improvement over the latter, since the AVC capacity is now raised to its value under the (less stringent) average probability of error criterion. The previous assertion is proved in [6] using the "elimination technique." If state constraints (cf. (24)) are additionally imposed on the AVC (5), the previous assertion still remains true even though the "elimination technique" does not apply in the presence of state constraints (cf. [48, Sec. V]).

We next address AVC performance when the transmitter or receiver are provided with side information. Consider first the situation where this side information consists of partial or complete knowledge of the sequence of states $s_1, \cdots, s_n$ prevalent during a transmission. The reader is referred to [44, pp. 220–222 and 227–230] for a compendium of several relevant problems and results. We cite here a paper of Ahlswede [11] in which, using previous results of Gel'fand and Pinsker [67], the deterministic code capacity problem is fully solved in the case when the state sequence is known to the transmitter in a noncausal manner. Specifically, the deterministic code capacity of the AVC (5) for the maximum probability of error, when the transmitter alone is aware of the entire sequence of channel states $s_1, \cdots, s_n$ when transmission begins (cf. (30)), is characterized in terms of mutual information quantities obtained in [67]. Further, this capacity is shown to coincide with the corresponding deterministic code capacity for the average probability of error. The proof entails a combination of the aforementioned "elimination technique" with the "robustification technique" developed in [8] and [9]. The situation considered above in [11] is to be contrasted with that in [13], [67], and [78] where the channel states $s_1, \cdots, s_n$, which are known to the transmitter alone at the

116

commencement of transmission, constitute a realization of an i.i.d. sequence with (known) pmf μ on $\mathcal{S}$. The corresponding maximum probability of error is now defined by replacing the maximization with respect to $\boldsymbol{s} \in \mathcal{S}^n$ in (42) by expectation with respect to the pmf on $\mathcal{S}^n$ induced by μ.

If the state sequence $s_1, \cdots, s_n$ is known to the receiver alone, the resulting AVC performance can be readily characterized in terms of that of a new AVC with an expanded output alphabet but without any side information, and hence does not lead to a new mathematical problem as observed earlier in Section II (cf. (25)–(28)). Note that the decoder ϕ of a length-n block code (f, ϕ) is now of the form

$$\phi: \mathcal{Y}^n \times \mathcal{S}^n \to \mathcal{M} \cup \{0\} \qquad (69)$$

while the encoder f is as usually defined by (10). The deterministic code capacities of the AVC (5), with the channel states $s_1, \cdots, s_n$ known to the receiver, for the maximum and average probabilities of error, can then be seen to be the same as the corresponding capacities—without any side information at the receiver—of a new AVC with input alphabet $\mathcal{X}$, output alphabet $\mathcal{Y} \times \mathcal{S}$, and stochastic matrix $\tilde{W}: \mathcal{X} \times \mathcal{S} \to \mathcal{Y} \times \mathcal{S}$ defined by

$$\tilde{W}(y, s | x, s') = \begin{cases} W(y | x, s), & s' = s \\ 0, & s' \neq s. \end{cases} \qquad (70)$$

Using this technique, it was shown by Stambler [118] that this deterministic code capacity for the average probability of error equals

$$\max_{Q \in \mathcal{P}(\mathcal{X})} \min_{s \in \mathcal{S}} I(Q, W(\cdot | \cdot; s))$$

which is the capacity of the compound DMC (cf. (3) and (4)) corresponding to the family of DMC's with stochastic matrices $\{W(y | x; s), x \in \mathcal{X}, y \in \mathcal{Y}, s \in \mathcal{S}\}$ (cf. Theorem 1).

Other forms of side information provided to the transmitter or receiver can significantly improve AVC performance. For instance, if noiseless feedback is available from the receiver to the transmitter (cf. (31)), it can be used to establish "common randomness" between them (whereby they have access to a common source of randomness with probability close to 1), so that the deterministic code capacity C^a of the AVC (5) for the average probability of error equals its randomized code capacity given by Theorem 2. For more on this result due to Ahlswede and Csiszár, as also implications of "common randomness" for AVC capacity, see [18]. Ahlswede and Cai [17] have examined another situation in which the transmitter and receiver observe the components $U_1, \cdots, U_n$ and $V_1, \cdots, V_n$, respectively, of a memoryless correlated source $\{(U_t, V_t)\}_{t=1}^{\infty}$ (i.e., an i.i.d. process with generic rv's (U, V) which satisfy $I(U \wedge V) > 0$), and have shown that C^a equals the randomized code capacity given by Theorem 2.

The performance of an AVC (5) using deterministic list codes (cf. (32) and (33)) is examined in [5], [12], [14], [33]–[35], [82], and [83]. The value of this capacity for the maximum probability of error and vanishingly small list rate was determined by Ahlswede [5]. Lower bounds on the sizes of constant lists for a given average probability of error and an arbitrarily small maximum probability of error, respectively,

were obtained by Ahlswede [5] and Ahlswede and Cai [14]. The fact that the deterministic list code capacity of an AVC (5) for the average probability of error displays a dichotomy similar to that described by (57) was observed by Blinovsky and Pinsker [34] who also determined a threshold for the list size above which said capacity equals the randomized code capacity given by Theorem 2. A complete characterization of the deterministic list code capacity for the average probability of error, based on an extended notion of symmetrizability (cf. (58)), was obtained by Blinovsky, Narayan, and Pinsker [33] and, independently, by Hughes [82], [83].

We conclude this section by noting the role of compound DMC's and AVC's in the study of communication situations partially controlled by an adversarial jammer. For dealing with such situations, several authors (cf. e.g., [36], [79], and [97]) have proposed a game-theoretic approach which involves a two-person zero-sum game between the "communicator" and the "jammer" with mutual information as the payoff function. An analysis of the merits and limitations of this approach from the viewpoint of AVC theory is provided in [49, Sec. VI]. See also [44, pp. 219–222 and 226–233].

B. Finite-State Channels

The capacity of a finite-state channel (7) has been studied under various conditions in [29], [64], [113], and [126]. Of particular importance is [64], where error exponents for a general finite-state channel are also computed. Before stating the capacity theorem for this channel, we introduce some notation [64], [91]. A (known) finite-state channel is specified by a pmf π on the initial state[3] in Σ and a conditional pmf $\{W(y, \sigma' | x, \sigma), x \in \mathcal{X}, y \in \mathcal{Y}, \sigma, \sigma' \in \Sigma\}$ as in (7). For such a channel, the probability $W_n(\boldsymbol{y}, \sigma_n | \boldsymbol{x}, \sigma_0)$ that the channel output is $\boldsymbol{y} = (y_1, \cdots, y_n) \in \mathcal{Y}^n$ and the final channel state is σ_n, conditioned on the initial state $\sigma_0 \in \Sigma$ and the channel input $\boldsymbol{x} = (x_1, \cdots, x_n) \in \mathcal{X}^n$, is given by

$$W_n(\boldsymbol{y}, \sigma_n | \boldsymbol{x}, \sigma_0) = \sum_{\sigma_1, \cdots, \sigma_{n-1}} \prod_{i=1}^{n} W(y_i, \sigma_i | x_i, \sigma_{i-1}). \qquad (71)$$

We can sum this probability over σ_n to obtain the probability that the channel output is $\boldsymbol{y} = (y_1, \cdots, y_n) \in \mathcal{Y}^n$ conditioned on the initial state $\sigma_0 \in \Sigma$ and the channel input $\boldsymbol{x} = (x_1, \cdots, x_n) \in \mathcal{X}^n$

$$W_n(\boldsymbol{y} | \boldsymbol{x}, \sigma_0) = \sum_{\sigma_1, \cdots, \sigma_n} \prod_{i=1}^{n} W(y_i, \sigma_i | x_i, \sigma_{i-1}). \qquad (72)$$

Averaging (72) with respect to the pmf π of the initial state yields (7).

Given an initial state $\sigma_0 \in \Sigma$ and a pmf Q_n on $\mathcal{X}^n$, the joint pmf of the channel input and output is well-defined, and the mutual information between the input and the output is

---

[3] In [64], no prior pmf on the initial state is assumed and the finite-state channel is treated as a family of channels, corresponding to different initial states which may or may not be known to the transmitter or receiver.

given by

$$I(\boldsymbol{X} \wedge \boldsymbol{Y}|\sigma_0) = I(Q_n, W_n(\cdot|\cdot, \sigma_0))$$

$$= \sum_{\boldsymbol{x}, \boldsymbol{y}} Q_n(\boldsymbol{x}) W_n(\boldsymbol{y}|\boldsymbol{x}, \sigma_0)$$

$$\cdot \ln \frac{W_n(\boldsymbol{y}|\boldsymbol{x}, \sigma_0)}{\sum_{\boldsymbol{x}'} Q_n(\boldsymbol{x}') W_n(\boldsymbol{y}|\boldsymbol{x}', \sigma_0)}.$$

Similarly, a family of finite-state channels, as in (8), can be specified in terms of a family of conditional pmf's $\{W(y, \sigma'|x, \sigma; \theta), x \in \mathcal{X}, y \in \mathcal{Y}, \sigma, \sigma' \in \Sigma, \theta \in \Theta\}$, and in analogy with (71) and (72), we denote by $W_n(\boldsymbol{y}, \sigma_n|\boldsymbol{x}, \sigma_0; \theta)$ the probability that the output of channel θ is $\boldsymbol{y} \in \mathcal{Y}^n$ and the final state is $\sigma_n \in \Sigma$ conditioned on the input $\boldsymbol{x} \in \mathcal{X}^n$ and initial state $\sigma_0 \in \Sigma$, and by $W_n(\boldsymbol{y}|\boldsymbol{x}, \sigma_0; \theta)$ the probability that the output of channel θ is $\boldsymbol{y} \in \mathcal{Y}^n$ under the same conditioning. Given a channel $\theta \in \Theta$, an initial state σ_0, and a pmf Q_n on $\mathcal{X}^n$, the mutual information between the input and output of the channel θ is given by

$$I(\boldsymbol{X} \wedge \boldsymbol{Y}|\sigma_0, \theta) = I(Q_n; W_n(\cdot|\cdot, \sigma_0; \theta))$$

$$= \sum_{\boldsymbol{x}, \boldsymbol{y}} Q_n(\boldsymbol{x}) W_n(\boldsymbol{y}|\boldsymbol{x}, \sigma_0; \theta)$$

$$\cdot \ln \frac{W_n(\boldsymbol{y}|\boldsymbol{x}, \sigma_0; \theta)}{\sum_{\boldsymbol{x}'} Q_n(\boldsymbol{x}') W_n(\boldsymbol{y}|\boldsymbol{x}', \sigma_0; \theta)}.$$

The following is proved in [64].

Theorem 8: If a finite-state channel (7) is indecomposable [64] or if $\pi(\sigma_0) > 0$ for every $\sigma_0 \in \Sigma$, then its capacity C is given by

$$C = \lim_{N \to \infty} \max_{Q_N \in \mathcal{P}(\mathcal{X}^N)} \min_{\sigma_0 \in \Sigma} I(Q_N, W_N(\cdot|\cdot; \sigma_0)).$$

It should be noted that the capacity of the finite-state channel [64] can be estimated arbitrarily well, since there exist a sequence of lower bounds and a sequence of upper bounds which converge to it [64].

Example 4 (Continued): Assuming that neither b nor g takes the extreme values 0 or 1, the capacity of the Gilbert–Elliott channel [101] is given by

$$C = 1 - h(Z)$$

where $h(Z)$ is the entropy rate of the hidden Markov process $\{Z_t\}$.

Theorem 8 can also be used when the sequence of states $\sigma_0, \cdots, \sigma_n$ of the channel during a transmission is known to the receiver (but not to the transmitter). We can consider a new output alphabet $\mathcal{Y} \times \Sigma$, with corresponding transitions probabilities. The resulting channel is still a finite-state channel.

The capacity of the channel when the sequence of states is unknown to the receiver but known to the transmitter in a causal manner, was found in [86], thus extending the results of [114] to finite-state channels. Once again, knowledge at the receiver can be treated by augmenting the output alphabet. A special case of the transmitter and receiver both knowing the state sequence in a causal manner, obtains when the state is "computable at both terminals," which was studied by Shannon [113]. In this situation, given the initial state (assumed known to both transmitter and receiver), the transmitter can compute the subsequent states based on the channel input, and the receiver can compute the subsequent states based on the received signal.

1) The Compound Finite-State Channel: In computing the capacity of a class of finite-state channels (8), we shall assume that for every pair $(\pi, W) \in \Theta$ of pmf π of the initial state and conditional pmf $W(y, \sigma|x, \sigma')$, we have

$$(\pi, W) \in \Theta \quad \text{implies} \quad (\pi_u, W) \in \Theta \qquad (73)$$

where π_u is the uniform distribution on Σ. We are, thus, assuming that reliable communication must be guaranteed for every initial state and any transition law, and that neither is known to the transmitter and receiver. Under this assumption we have the following [91].

Theorem 9: Under the assumption (73), the capacity C of a family Θ of finite-state channels (8) with common (finite) input, output, and state alphabets $\mathcal{X}, \mathcal{Y}, \Sigma$, is given by

$$C = \lim_{n \to \infty} \max_{Q_n \in \mathcal{P}(\mathcal{X}^n)} \inf_{\theta, \sigma_0} \frac{1}{n} I(Q_n; W_n(\cdot|\cdot, \sigma_0, \theta)). \quad (74)$$

Example 5 (Continued): If the transition probabilities of the underlying Markov chains of the different channels are uniformly bounded away from zero, i.e.,

$$\inf_{\theta \in \Theta} \min\{g(\theta), b(\theta), 1 - g(\theta), 1 - b(\theta)\} > 0 \qquad (75)$$

then the capacity of the family is the infimum of the capacities of the individual channels in the family [91].

The following example demonstrates that if (75) is violated, the capacity of the family may be smaller than the infimum of the capacities of its members [91]. Consider a class of Gilbert–Elliott channels indexed by the positive integers. Specifically, let $P_G(k) = 0$, $P_B(k) = 1/2$, $b(k) = g(k) = 2^{-k}$ for $k \geq 1$. For any given k, we can achieve rates exceeding $1 - h_b(1/4)$ over the channel k by using a deep enough interleaver to make the channel look like a memoryless BSC with crossover probability $1/4$. Thus

$$\inf_{\theta \in \Theta} C(\theta) \geq 1 - h_b(1/4).$$

However, for any given blocklength n, the channel that corresponds to $\theta = n$, when started in the bad state, will remain in the bad state for the duration of the transmission with probability exceeding $1 - n2^{-n} \geq 1/2$. Since in the bad state the channel output is independent of the input, we conclude that reliable communication is not possible at any rate. The capacity of the family is thus zero.

The proof of Theorem 9 relies on the existence of a universal decoder for the class of finite-state channels [60], and on the fact that for rates below C the random-coding error probability (for the natural choice of codebook distribution) is bounded above *uniformly* for all the channels in Θ by an exponentially decreasing function of the blocklength.

The similarity of the expressions in (40) and (74) should not lead to a mistaken belief that the capacity of any family of channels is given by a max inf expression. A counterexample is given in [31], and [52], and is repeated in [91].

IV. ENCODERS AND DECODERS

A variety of encoders and decoders have been proposed for achieving reliable communication over the different channel models described in Section II, and, in particular, for establishing the direct parts of the results on capacities described in Section III. The choices run the gamut from standard codes with randomly selected codewords together with a "joint typicality" decoder or a maximum-likelihood decoder for known channels, to codes consisting of fairly complex decoders for certain models of unknown channels. We shall survey below some of the proposed encoders and decoders, with special emphasis on the latter. While it is customary to study the combined performance of an encoder–decoder pair in a given communication situation, we shall—for the sake of expository convenience—describe encoders and decoders separately.

A. Encoders

The encoders chosen for establishing the capacity results stated in Section III, for various models of known and unknown channels described in Section II, often use randomly selected codewords in one form or another [111]. The notion of random selection of codewords affords several uses. The classical application, of course, involves randomly selected codewords as a mathematical artifice in proving, by means of the random-coding argument technique, the existence of deterministic codes for the direct parts of capacity results for known channels and certain types of unknown channels. Second, codewords chosen by random selection afford an obvious means of constructing randomized codes or codes with stochastic encoders for enhancing reliable communication over some unknown channels (cf. Section IV-A2)), thereby serving as models of practical engineering devices. Furthermore, the notion of random selection can lead to the selective identification of deterministic codewords with refined properties which are useful for determining the deterministic code capacities of certain unknown channels (cf. Section IV-A3)).

We first present a brief description of some standard methods of picking codewords by random selection.

1) Encoding by Random Selection of Codewords: One standard method of random selection of codewords entails picking them in an i.i.d. manner according to a fixed pmf Q_n on $\mathcal{X}^n$. Specifically, let $\boldsymbol{X}_m$, $m \in \mathcal{M}$, be i.i.d. $\mathcal{X}^n$-valued rv's, each with (common) pmf Q_n. The encoder F of a (length-n block) randomized code or a code with stochastic encoder is obtained by setting

$$F(m) = \boldsymbol{X}_m, \qquad m \in \mathcal{M}. \tag{76}$$

In some situations, a random selection of codewords involves choosing them with a uniform distribution from a fixed subset of $\mathcal{X}^n$. Precisely, for a given subset $B_n \subseteq \mathcal{X}^n$, the encoder F of a randomized code or code with stochastic encoder is obtained as

$$F(m) = \boldsymbol{X}'_m, \qquad m \in \mathcal{M} \tag{77}$$

where $\boldsymbol{X}'_m$, $m \in \mathcal{M}$, are i.i.d. B_n-valued rv's, each distributed uniformly on B_n. This corresponds to Q_n being the uniform pmf on B_n. For memoryless channels (known or unknown), the random codewords in (76) are usually chosen to have a simple structure, namely, to consist of i.i.d. components, i.e., for a fixed pmf Q on $\mathcal{X}$, we set

$$F(m) = \boldsymbol{X}_m = (X_{m1}, \cdots, X_{mn}), \qquad m \in \mathcal{M} \tag{78}$$

where $X_{m1}, \cdots, X_{mn}$ are i.i.d. $\mathcal{X}$-valued rv's with (common) pmf Q on $\mathcal{X}$. This corresponds to choosing Q_n to be the n-fold product pmf on $\mathcal{X}^n$ with marginal pmf Q on $\mathcal{X}$.

In order to describe the next standard method of random selection of codewords, we now define the notions of types and typical sequences (cf. e.g., [44, Sec. 1.2]). The type of a sequence $\boldsymbol{x} = (x_1, \cdots, x_n) \in \mathcal{X}^n$ is a pmf $P_{\boldsymbol{x}}$ on $\mathcal{X}$ where $P_{\boldsymbol{x}}(x)$ is the relative frequency of x in $\boldsymbol{x}$, i.e.,

$$P_{\boldsymbol{x}}(x) = \frac{1}{n} \sum_{t=1}^{n} I\{x_t = x\} \tag{79}$$

where $I\{\cdot\}$ denotes the indicator function:

$$I\{A\} = \begin{cases} 1, & \text{if statement } A \text{ is true} \\ 0, & \text{if statement } A \text{ is false.} \end{cases}$$

For a given type P of sequences in $\mathcal{X}^n$, let $\mathcal{T}_P^n$ denote the set of all sequences $\boldsymbol{x} \in \mathcal{X}^n$ with type P, i.e.,

$$\mathcal{T}_P^n = \{\boldsymbol{x} \in \mathcal{X}^n : P_{\boldsymbol{x}}(x) = P(x), x \in \mathcal{X}\}. \tag{80}$$

Next, for a given pmf Q on X, a sequence $\boldsymbol{x} \in \mathcal{X}^n$ is Q-typical with constant $\delta > 0$, or simply Q-typical (suppressing the explicit dependence on $\delta > 0$), if

$$\max_{x \in \mathcal{X}} |P_{\boldsymbol{x}}(x) - Q(x)| \le \delta, \qquad P_{\boldsymbol{x}}(x) = 0 \text{ if } Q(x) = 0. \tag{81}$$

Let $\mathcal{T}_{[Q]}^n$ denote the set of all sequences $\boldsymbol{x} \in \mathcal{X}^n$ which are Q-typical, i.e., the union of sets $\mathcal{T}_P^n$ for those types P of sequences in $\mathcal{X}^n$ which satisfy

$$\max_{x \in \mathcal{X}} |P(x) - Q(x)| \le \delta, \qquad P(x) = 0 \text{ if } Q(x) = 0. \tag{82}$$

Similarly, for later use, joint types are pmf's on product spaces. For example, the joint type of three given sequences $\boldsymbol{x} \in \mathcal{X}^n$, $\boldsymbol{s} \in \mathcal{S}^n$, $\boldsymbol{y} \in \mathcal{Y}^n$ is a pmf $P_{\boldsymbol{xsy}}$ on $\mathcal{X} \times \mathcal{S} \times \mathcal{Y}$ where $P_{\boldsymbol{xsy}}(x, s, y)$ is the relative frequency of the triple (x, s, y) among the triples (x_t, s_t, y_t), $t = 1, \cdots, n$, i.e.,

$$P_{\boldsymbol{xsy}}(x, s, y) = \frac{1}{n} \sum_{t=1}^{n} I\{x_t = x, s_t = s, y_t = y\}. \tag{83}$$

A standard method of random selection of codewords now entails picking them from the set of sequences of a fixed type in accordance with a uniform pmf on that set. The resulting random selection is a special case of (77) with the set B_n being $\mathcal{T}_P^n$. Precisely, for a fixed type P of sequences in $\mathcal{X}^n$, the encoder F of a randomized code or a code with stochastic encoder is obtained by setting

$$F(m) = \boldsymbol{X}_m'', \qquad m \in \mathcal{M} \tag{84}$$

where $\boldsymbol{X}_m''$, $m \in \mathcal{M}$, are i.i.d. $\mathcal{T}_P^n$-valued rv's, each distributed uniformly on $\mathcal{T}_P^n$. The codewords thus obtained are often referred to as "constant-composition" codewords. This method is sometimes preferable to that given by (78). For instance, in the case of a DMC (2), it is shown in [91] that for every randomized code comprising codewords selected according to (78) used in conjunction with a maximum-likelihood decoder (cf. Section IV-A2) below), there exists another randomized code with codewords as in (84) and maximum-likelihood decoder which yields a random-coding error exponent which is at least as good.

A modification of (84) is obtained when, for a fixed pmf Q on $\mathcal{X}$, the encoder F of a randomized code or a code with stochastic encoder is obtained by setting

$$F(m) = \boldsymbol{X}_m''', \qquad m \in \mathcal{M} \tag{85}$$

where $\boldsymbol{X}_m'''$, $m \in \mathcal{M}$, are i.i.d. $\mathcal{T}_{[Q]}^n$-valued rv's, each distributed uniformly on $\mathcal{T}_{[Q]}^n$.

In the terminology of Section II, each set of randomly selected codewords $\{F(m), m \in \mathcal{M}\}$ chosen as in (76)–(85) constitutes a stochastic encoder.

Codes with randomly selected codewords as in (76)–(85), together with suitable decoders, can be used in random-coding argument techniques for establishing reliable communication over known channels. For instance, codewords for the DMC (2) can be selected according to (78) [111] or (85) [124], and for the finite-state channel (7) according to (76) [64]. In these cases, the existence of a code with deterministic encoder f, i.e., deterministic codewords $f(m)$, $m \in \mathcal{M}$, for establishing reliable communication, is obtained in terms of a realization of the random codewords $F(m)$, $m \in \mathcal{M}$, combined with a simple expurgation, to ensure a small maximum probability of error.

For certain types of unknown channels too, codewords chosen as in (76)–(85), without any additional refinement, suffice for achieving reliable communication. For instance, in the case of the AVC (5), random codewords chosen according to (5) were used [19], [119] to determine the randomized code capacity without input or state constraints in Theorem 2, and with such constraints (cf. (48)) [47].

2) Randomized Codes and Random Code Reduction: Randomly selected codewords $\{F(m), m \in \mathcal{M}\}$ as in (76)–(85), together with a decoder ϕ given by (11), obviously constitute a code with stochastic encoder (F, ϕ). They also enable the following elementary and standard construction of a (length-n block) randomized code (F, Φ). Associate with every realization $\{f(m), m \in \mathcal{M}\}$ of the randomly selected codewords $\{F(m), m \in \mathcal{M}\}$, a decoder $\phi_f \colon \mathcal{Y}^n \to \mathcal{M} \cup \{0\}$ which depends, in general, on said realization. This results in a randomized code (F, Φ), where the encoder F is as above,

and the decoder Φ is defined by

$$\Phi(\boldsymbol{y}) = \phi_F(\boldsymbol{y}), \qquad \boldsymbol{y} \in \mathcal{Y}^n. \tag{86}$$

Such a randomized code (F, Φ), in addition to serving as an artifice in random-coding arguments for proving coding theorems as mentioned earlier, can lead to larger capacity values for the AVC (5) than those achieved by codes with stochastic encoders or deterministic codes (cf. Section III-A2) above). In fact, the randomized code capacity C of the AVC (5) given by Theorem 2 is achieved [19] using a randomized code (F, Φ) as above, where the encoder F is chosen as in (78) with pmf Q^* on $\mathcal{X}$ and the decoder Φ is given by (86) with ϕ_f being the (normalized) maximum-likelihood decoder (corresponding to the codewords $\{f(m), m \in \mathcal{M}\}$) for the DMC with stochastic matrix $W_{\zeta^*} \colon \mathcal{X} \to \mathcal{Y}$, where (Q^*, ζ^*) is a saddle point for (46). When input or state constraints are additionally imposed, the randomized code capacity $C(\Gamma, \Lambda)$ of the AVC (5) given by (48) is achieved by a similar code with suitable modifications to accommodate the constraints [47].

Consequently, randomized codes become significant as models of practical engineering devices; in fact, commonly used spread-spectrum techniques such as direct sequence and frequency hopping can be interpreted as practical implementations of randomized codes [58], employing synchronized random number generators at the transmitter and receiver. From a practical standpoint, however, a (length-n block) randomized code (F, Φ) of rate R bits per channel use, such as that just described above in the context of the randomized code capacity of the AVC (5), involves making a random selection from among a prohibitively large collection—of size $|\mathcal{X}|^{nM} = |\mathcal{X}|^{n\lceil \exp(nR) \rceil}$—of sets of codewords $\{f(m), m \in \mathcal{M}\}$, where $|\cdot|$ denotes cardinality. In addition, the outcome of this random selection must be observed by the receiver; else, it must be conveyed to the receiver requiring an infeasibly large overhead transmission of $\approx n\lceil \exp(nR) \rceil \log |\mathcal{X}|$ bits in order to ensure the reliable communication of $\approx nR$ information bits.

The practical feasibility of randomized codes, in particular for the AVC (5), is supported by Ahlswede's result on "random code reduction" [6], which establishes the existence of "good" randomized codes obtained by random selection from "exponentially few" (in blocklength n) deterministic codes. This result is stated below in a version which appears in [44, Sec. 2.6], and requires the following setup. For a fixed blocklength n, consider a family of channels indexed by $\theta \in \Theta$ as in (3), where Θ is now assumed to be a finite set. Let (F, Φ) be a given randomized code which results in a maximum probability of error $e_{\max}(F, \Phi, \theta)$ (cf. (14) and (16)) when used on the channel $\theta \in \Theta$.

Theorem 10: For any ϵ and K satisfying

$$\epsilon > 2 \log \left(1 + \max_{\theta \in \Theta} e_{\max}(F, \Phi, \theta) \right), \quad K > \frac{2}{\epsilon} \left(\log M + \log |\Theta| \right) \tag{87}$$

there exists a randomized code (F', Φ') which is uniformly distributed on a family of K deterministic codes

$\{(f_k, \phi_k), k = 1, \cdots, K\}$ as in (10) and (11), and such that

$$e_{\max}(F', \Phi', \theta) < \epsilon, \qquad \theta \in \Theta. \qquad (88)$$

The assertion in (88) concerning the performance of the randomized code (F', Φ') is equivalent to

$$\frac{1}{K} \sum_{k=1}^{K} e_m(f_k, \phi_k, \theta) < \epsilon, \qquad m \in \mathcal{M}, \theta \in \Theta. \qquad (89)$$

Thus for every randomized code (F, Φ), there exists a "reduced" randomized code (F', Φ') which is uniformly distributed over K deterministic codes and has maximum probability of error on any channel not exceeding ϵ, provided the hypothesis (87) holds.

Theorem 10 above has two significant implications for AVC performance. First, for any randomized code (F, Φ) which achieves the randomized code capacity of the AVC (5) given by Theorem 2, there exists another randomized code (F', Φ') which does likewise; furthermore, (F', Φ') is obtained by random selection from no more than $K = n^2$ deterministic codes [6]. Hence, the outcome of the random selection of codewords at the transmitter can now be conveyed to the receiver using at most only $\approx 2 \log n$ bits, which represents a desirably drastic reduction in overhead transmission; the rate of this transmission, termed the "key rate" in [59], is arbitrarily small. Second, such a "reduced" randomized code (F', Φ') is amenable to conversion, by an "elimination of randomness" [6], into a deterministic code $((\hat{f}_n, f'), (\hat{\phi}_n, \phi'))$ (cf. e.g., [44, Sec. 2.6]) for the AVC (5), provided its deterministic code capacity C^a for the average probability of error is positive. Here, (f', ϕ') is as in (10) and (11), while $(\hat{f}_n, \hat{\phi}_n)$ represents a code for conveying to the receiver the outcome of the random selection at the transmitter, i.e.,

$$\hat{f}_n: \{1, \cdots, n^2\} \to \mathcal{X}^{k_n} \qquad \hat{\phi}_n: \mathcal{Y}^{k_n} \to \{1, \cdots, n^2\} \qquad (90)$$

where k_n/n tends to 0 with increasing n. As a consequence, C^a equals the randomized code capacity C of the AVC (5) given by Theorem 2. This has been discussed earlier in Section III-A2).

3) Refined Codeword Sets by Random Selection: As stated earlier, the method of random selection can sometimes be used to prove the existence of codewords with special properties which are useful for determining the deterministic code capacities of certain unknown channels.

For instance, the deterministic code capacity of the AVC (5) for the maximum or average probability of error is sometimes established by a technique relying on the method of random selection as in (78), (84), and (85), used in such a manner as to assert the existence of codewords with select properties. A deterministic code comprising such codewords together with a suitably chosen decoder then leads to acceptable bounds for the probabilities of decoding errors. This artifice is generally not needed when using randomized codes or codes with stochastic encoders. Variants of this technique have been applied, for instance, in obtaining the deterministic code capacity of the AVC (5) for the maximum probability of error in [10] and in Theorem 4 [45], as well as for the average probability of error in Theorems 5 and 6 [48].

In determining the deterministic code capacity C^m for the maximum probability of error [10], random selection as in (78), together with an expurgation argument using Bernstein's version of Markov's inequality for i.i.d. rv's, is used to show in effect the existence of a codeword set with "spread-out" codewords, namely, every two codewords are separated by at least a certain Hamming distance. A codeword set with similar properties is also shown to result from alternative random selection as in (85). Such a codeword set, in conjunction with a decoder which decides on the basis of a threshold test using (normalized) likelihood ratios, leads to a bound for the maximum probability of error. A more general characterization of C^m in [45] relies on a code with codewords from the set T_P^n of sequences in $\mathcal{X}^n$ of type P (cf. (80)) which satisfy desirable "balance" properties with probability arbitrarily close to 1, together with a suitable decoding rule (cf. Section IV-B6)). The method of random selection in (84) combined with a large-deviation argument for i.i.d. rv's as in [10], is used in proving the existence of such codewords. Loosely speaking, the codewords are "balanced" in that for a transmitted codeword $\boldsymbol{x}$ and the (unknown) state sequence $\boldsymbol{s} \in \mathcal{S}^n$ which prevails during its transmission, the proportion of other codewords $\boldsymbol{x}'$ which have a specified joint type (cf. (83)) with $\boldsymbol{x}$ and $\boldsymbol{s}$ does not greatly exceed their overall "density" in T_P^n. This limits, in effect, the number of spurious codewords which are jointly typical with $\boldsymbol{x}$, $\boldsymbol{s}$ and a received sequence $\boldsymbol{y} \in \mathcal{Y}^n$, leading to a satisfactory bound for the maximum probability of error.

The determination in [48] of the deterministic code capacity of the AVC (5) for the average probability of error, without or with input or state constraints (cf. Theorems 5 and 6) relies on codewords resulting from random selection as in (84) and a decoder described below in Section IV-B6). These codewords possess special properties in the spirit of [45], which are established using Chernoff bounding for dependent rv's as in [53].

B. Decoders

A variety of decoders have been proposed in order to achieve reliable communication in the different communication situations described in Section II. Some of these decoders will be surveyed below. We begin with decoders for known channels and describe the maximum-likelihood decoder and the various typicality decoders. We then consider the generalized likelihood-ratio test for unknown channels, the maximum-empirical mutual information (MMI) decoder, and more general universal decoders. The section ends with a discussion of decoders for the compound channel, mismatched decoders, and decoders for the arbitrarily varying channel.

1) Decoders for Known Channels: The most natural decoder for a known channel (1) is the maximum-likelihood decoder, which is optimal in the sense of minimizing the average probability of error (15). Given a set of codewords

$\{f(m), m \in \mathcal{M}\}$ in $\mathcal{X}^n$, the maximum-likelihood decoder ϕ_{ML} is defined by: $\phi_{\mathrm{ML}}(\boldsymbol{y}) = m$ only if

$$W(\boldsymbol{y}|f(m)) = \max_{m' \in \mathcal{M}} W(\boldsymbol{y}|f(m')). \qquad (91)$$

If more than one $m \in \mathcal{M}$ satisfies (91), ties are resolved arbitrarily. While the maximum-likelihood rule is indeed a natural choice for decoding over a known channel, its analysis can be quite intricate [64], and was only conducted years after Shannon's original paper [111].

Several simpler decoders have been proposed for the DMC (2), under the name of "typicality" decoders. These decoders are usually classified as "weak typicality" decoders [39] (which are sometimes referred to as "entropy typicality" decoders [44]), and "joint typicality" decoders [24], [44], [126] (which are sometimes referred to as "strong" typicality decoders). We describe below the joint-type typicality decoder as well as a more stringent version which relies on a notion of typicality in terms of the Kullback–Leibler divergence (cf. e.g., [44]).

Given a set of codewords $\{f(m), m \in \mathcal{M}\}$ in $\mathcal{T}_P^n$, where P is a fixed type of sequences in $\mathcal{X}^n$, the joint typicality decoder ϕ_T for the DMC (2) is defined as follows: $\phi_T(\boldsymbol{y}) = m$ only if

$$\max_{x \in \mathcal{X}, y \in \mathcal{Y}} |P_{f(m)\boldsymbol{y}}(x, y) - (P \circ W)(x, y)| < \eta \qquad (92)$$

where $W: \mathcal{X} \to \mathcal{Y}$ is the stochastic matrix in the definition of the DMC (2), $(P \circ W)(x, y) = P(x)W(y|x)$, and $\eta > 0$ is chosen sufficiently small. If more than one $m \in \mathcal{M}$ satisfies (92), or no $m \in \mathcal{M}$ satisfies (92), set $\phi(\boldsymbol{y}) = 0$. The capacity of a DMC (2) can be achieved by a joint typicality decoder ([111]; see also [44, Problem 7, p. 113]), but this decoder is suboptimal and does not generally achieve the channel reliability function $E(R)$.

Another version of a joint typicality decoder, which we term the divergence typicality decoder, has appeared in the literature (cf. e.g., [45] and [48]). It relies on a more stringent notion of typicality based on the Kullback–Leibler divergence (cf. e.g., [39] and [44]). Precisely, given a set of codewords $\{f(m), m \in \mathcal{M}\}$ in $\mathcal{T}_P^n$ as above, a divergence typicality decoder ϕ_{DT} for the DMC (2) is defined as follows: $\phi_{DT}(\boldsymbol{y}) = m$ only if

$$D(P_{f(m)\boldsymbol{y}} \| P \circ W) < \eta \qquad (93)$$

where $D(\cdot \| \cdot)$ denotes Kullback–Leibler divergence and $\eta > 0$ is chosen sufficiently small. If more than one $m \in \mathcal{M}$, or no $m \in \mathcal{M}$, satisfies (93), we set $\phi_{DT}(\boldsymbol{y}) = 0$. The capacity of a DMC (2) can be achieved by the divergence typicality decoder.

2) The Generalized Likelihood Ratio Test: The maximum-likelihood decoding rules for channels governed by different laws are generally different mappings, and maximum-likelihood decoding with respect to the prevailing channel cannot therefore be applied if the channel law is unknown. The same is true of joint typicality decoding. A natural candidate for a decoder for a family of channels (3) is the generalized likelihood ratio test decoder.

The generalized likelihood ratio test (GLRT) decoder ϕ_{GLRT} can be defined as follows: given a set of codewords $\{f(m), m \in \mathcal{M}\}$, $\phi_{\mathrm{GLRT}}(\boldsymbol{y}) = m$ only if

$$\sup_{\theta \in \Theta} W(\boldsymbol{y}|f(m); \theta) = \max_{m' \in \mathcal{M}} \sup_{\theta \in \Theta} W(\boldsymbol{y}|f(m'); \theta)$$

where ties can be resolved arbitrarily among all $m \in \mathcal{M}$ which achieve the maximum.

If the family of channels corresponds to the family of *all* DMC's with finite input alphabet $\mathcal{X}$ and finite output alphabet $\mathcal{Y}$, then

$$\begin{aligned} &\sup_{\theta \in \Theta} \frac{1}{n} \log W(\boldsymbol{y}|\boldsymbol{x}; \theta) \\ &= \sup_{\theta \in \Theta} \sum_{x \in \mathcal{X}} P_{\boldsymbol{x}}(x) \sum_{y \in \mathcal{Y}} P_{\boldsymbol{y}|\boldsymbol{x}}(y|x) \log W(y|x; \theta) \\ &= \sum_{x \in \mathcal{X}} P_{\boldsymbol{x}}(x) \sum_{y \in \mathcal{Y}} P_{\boldsymbol{y}|\boldsymbol{x}}(y|x) \log P_{\boldsymbol{y}|\boldsymbol{x}}(y|x) \\ &= -H(\boldsymbol{y}|\boldsymbol{x}) \\ &= I(\boldsymbol{x} \wedge \boldsymbol{y}) - H(\boldsymbol{y}) \end{aligned}$$

where the first equality follows by defining the condition empirical distribution $P_{\boldsymbol{y}|\boldsymbol{x}}(y|x)$ to satisfy

$$P_{\boldsymbol{x}\boldsymbol{y}}(x, y) = P_{\boldsymbol{x}}(x) P_{\boldsymbol{y}|\boldsymbol{x}}(y|x);$$

the second equality from the nonnegativity of relative entropy; the third equality by defining $H(\boldsymbol{y}|\boldsymbol{x})$ as the conditional entropy $H(Y|X)$, where X, Y are dummy rv's whose joint pmf on $\mathcal{X} \times \mathcal{Y}$ is the joint type $P_{\boldsymbol{x}\boldsymbol{y}}$; and the last equality by defining $I(\boldsymbol{x} \wedge \boldsymbol{y})$ as the mutual information $I(X \wedge Y)$, with X, Y as above.

Since the term $H(\boldsymbol{y})$ depends only on the output sequence $\boldsymbol{y}$, it is seen that for the family of all DMC's with input alphabet $\mathcal{X}$ and output alphabet $\mathcal{Y}$, the GLRT decoding rule is equivalent to the maximum empirical mutual information (MMI) decoder [44], which is defined by

$$\phi_{\mathrm{MMI}}(\boldsymbol{y}) = \arg \max_{m \in \mathcal{M}} I(f(m) \wedge \boldsymbol{y}). \qquad (94)$$

Note that if the family under consideration is a subset of the class of all DMC's, then the GLRT will not necessarily coincide with the MMI decoder.

The MMI decoder is a universal decoder for the family of memoryless channels, in a sense that will be made precise in the next section.

3) Universal Decoding: Loosely speaking, a sequence of codes is universal for a family of channels if it achieves the same random-coding error exponent as the maximum-likelihood decoder without requiring knowledge of the specific channel in the family over which transmission takes place [44], [60], [92], [95], [98], [103], [129]. We now make this notion precise. Let $\{B_n\}_{n=1}^{\infty}$ denote a sequence of sets, with $B_n \subseteq \mathcal{X}^n$. Consider a randomized encoder $F_n: \mathcal{M} \to B_n$ whose codewords are drawn independently and uniformly from B_n as in (77). Let $\Phi_{F_n, \theta}$ denote a maximum-likelihood receiver for the encoder F_n and the channel $\theta \in \Theta$ as in (86) and (91). As in Section II we set $\bar{e}(F_n, \Phi_{F_n, \theta}, \theta)$ to be the average probability of error corresponding to the code $(F_n, \Phi_{F_n, \theta})$ for the channel θ. Note that the average is both with respect to the messages (as in (15)) and the pmf of the randomized code (as in (16)).

A sequence of codes $\{(f_n, u_n)\}_{n=1}^\infty$, of rate R, where $f_n \colon \mathcal{M} \to B_n$ and $u_n \colon \mathcal{Y}^n \to \mathcal{M} \cup \{0\}$ is said to be universal[4] for the input sets $\{B_n\}$ and the family (3) if

$$\lim_{n \to \infty} \sup_{\theta \in \Theta} \frac{1}{n} \log \frac{\overline{e}(f_n, u_n, \theta)}{\overline{e}(F_n, \Phi_{F_n, \theta}, \theta)} = 0. \qquad (95)$$

Notice that neither encoder nor decoder is allowed to depend on the channel θ.

For families of DMC's the following result was proved by Csiszár and Körner [44].

Theorem 11: Assume that the input sets B_n correspond to type classes, i.e., $B_n = \mathcal{T}_P^n$ for some fixed type P of sequences in $\mathcal{X}^n$. Under this assumption, there exists a sequence of codes $\{(f_n, \phi_{\mathrm{MMI}, n})\}_{n=1}^\infty$ with MMI decoder which is universal for any family of discrete memoryless channels.

As we have noted above, if the family of channels (3) is a *subset* of the set of all DMC's, then the GLRT for the family may be different from the MMI decoder. In fact, in this case the GLRT may not be universal for the family [90]. It is thus seen that the GLRT may not be universal for a family even when a universal decoder for the family exists [92]. The GLRT is therefore not "canonical."

Universal codes for families of finite-state channels (8) were proposed in [129] with subsequent refinements in [60] and [92]. The decoding rule proposed in [92] and [129] is based on the joint Lempel–Ziv parsing [130] of the received sequence $\boldsymbol{y}$ with each of the possible codewords $f(m)$, $m = 1, \cdots, M$.

A different approach to universal decoding can be found in [60], where a universal decoder based on the idea of "merging" maximum-likelihood decoders is proposed. This idea leads to existence results for fairly general families of channels including some with infinite alphabets (e.g., a family of Gaussian intersymbol interference channels). To state these results, we need the notion of a "strongly separable" family. Loosely speaking, a family is strongly separable if for any blocklength n there exists a subexponential number $K(n)$ of channels such that the law of any channel in the family can be approximated by one of these latter channels. The approximation is in the sense that except for rare sequences, the normalized log likelihood of an output sequence given any input sequence is similar under the two channels. Precisely:

A family of channels (3) with common finite input and output alphabets $\mathcal{X}$, $\mathcal{Y}$ is said to be *strongly separable* for the input sets $B_n \subseteq \mathcal{X}^n$ if there exists some (finite) $L > 0$ which serves as an upper bound for all the error exponents in the family, i.e.,

$$\limsup_{n \to \infty} \sup_{\theta \in \Theta} -\frac{1}{n} \log \overline{e}(F, \Phi_{\mathrm{ML}}, \theta) < L \qquad (96)$$

such that for any $\epsilon > 0$ and blocklength n, there exists a subexponential number $K(n)$ (depending on L and ϵ) of channels $\{\theta_k^{(n)}\}_{k=1}^{K(n)} \subseteq \Theta$

$$\lim_{n \to \infty} \frac{1}{n} \log K(n) = 0 \qquad (97)$$

which can approximate any $\theta \in \Theta$ in the following sense: for any $\theta \in \Theta$, there exists a channel $\theta_{k^*}^{(n)} \in \Theta$, $1 \le k^* \le K(n)$, satisfying

$$W(\boldsymbol{y}|\boldsymbol{x}; \theta) \le 2^{n\epsilon} W(\boldsymbol{y}|\boldsymbol{x}; \theta_{k^*}^{(n)}) \qquad (98)$$

whenever $(\boldsymbol{x}, \boldsymbol{y}) \in B_n \times \mathcal{Y}^n$ is such that

$$W(\boldsymbol{y}|\boldsymbol{x}; \theta) > 2^{-n(L + \log |\mathcal{Y}|)}$$

and satisfying

$$W(\boldsymbol{y}|\boldsymbol{x}; \theta_{k^*}^{(n)}) \le 2^{n\epsilon} W(\boldsymbol{y}|\boldsymbol{x}; \theta) \qquad (99)$$

whenever $(\boldsymbol{x}, \boldsymbol{y}) \in B_n \times \mathcal{Y}^n$ is such that

$$W(\boldsymbol{y}|\boldsymbol{x}; \theta_{k^*}^{(n)}) > 2^{-n(L + \log |\mathcal{Y}|)}.$$

For example, the family of all DMC's with finite input and output alphabets $\mathcal{X}$, $\mathcal{Y}$, is strongly separable for any sequence of input sets $\{B_n\}$. Likewise, the family of all finite-state channels with finite input, output, and state alphabets $\mathcal{X}$, $\mathcal{Y}$, Σ is also strongly separable for any sequence of input sets $\{B_n\}$ [60]. For a definition of strong separability for channels with infinite alphabets see [60].

Theorem 12: If a family of channels (3) with common finite input and output alphabets $\mathcal{X}$, $\mathcal{Y}$ is strongly separable for the input sets $\{B_n\}$, then there exists a sequence of codes $\{(f_n, u_n)\}$ which is universal for the family.

Not surprisingly, in a nonparametric situation where nothing is known *a priori* about the channel statistics, universal decoding is not possible [99].

A slightly different notion of universality, referred to in [60] as "strong random-coding universality," requires that (95) hold for the "average encoder." More precisely, consider a decoding rule u which, given an encoder f, maps each possible received sequence $\boldsymbol{y}$ to some message $m \in \mathcal{M} \cup \{0\}$. We can then consider the random code (F_n, u_{F_n}) where, as before, F is a random encoder whose codewords are drawn independently and uniformly from the set B_n. The decoding rule u is strongly random coding universal for the input sets $\{B_n\}$ if

$$\lim_{n \to \infty} \sup_{\theta \in \Theta} \frac{1}{n} \log \frac{\overline{e}(F_n, u_{F_n}, \theta)}{\overline{e}(F_n, \Phi_{F_n, \theta}, \theta)} = 0. \qquad (100)$$

It is shown in [60] that the hypothesis of Theorem 12 also implies strong random-coding universality.

We next demonstrate the role played by universal decoders in communicating over a compound channel, and also discuss some alternative decoders for this situation.

4) Decoders for the Compound Channel: Consider the problem of communicating reliably over a compound channel (3). Let $\{B_n\}$ be a sequence of input sets and let F_n be a randomized rate-R encoder which chooses the codewords independently and uniformly from the set B_n as in (77). Let $\Phi_{F_n, \theta}$ denote the maximum-likelihood decoder corresponding to the encoder F_n for the channel $\theta \in \Theta$. Suppose now that the code rate R is sufficiently low so that $\overline{e}(F, \Phi_{F_n, \theta}, \theta)$

is uniformly bounded in θ by a function which decreases exponentially to zero with the blocklength n, i.e.,

$$\liminf_{n \to \infty} -\frac{1}{n} \log \sup_{\theta \in \Theta} \bar{e}(F_n, \Phi_{F_n, \theta}, \theta) > 0. \qquad (101)$$

It then follows from (95) that if $\{(f_n, u_n)\}$ is a sequence of universal codes for the family Θ and input sets $\{B_n\}$, then R is an achievable rate and can be achieved with the decoders $\{u_n\}$.

It is, thus, seen that if a family of channels admits universal decoding, then the problem of demonstrating that a rate R is achievable only requires the study of random-coding error probabilities with maximum-likelihood decoding (101).

Indeed, the capacity of the compound DMC can be attained using an MMI decoder (Theorem 11) [44], and the capacity of a compound FSC can be attained using a universal decoder for that family [91].

The original decoder proposed for the compound DMC [30] is not universal; it is based on maximum-likelihood decoding with respect to a Bayesian mixture of a finite number of "representative" channels (polynomial in the blocklength) in the family [30], [64, pp. 176–178]. Nevertheless, if the "representatives" are chosen carefully, the resulting decoder is, indeed, universal.

A completely different approach to the design of a decoder for a family of DMC's can be adopted if the family (3) and (4) is compact and convex in the sense that for every $\theta', \theta'' \in \Theta$ with corresponding stochastic matrices $W(\cdot|\cdot; \theta')$ and $W(\cdot|\cdot; \theta'')$, and for every $\alpha \in (0, 1)$, there exists $\theta^{(\alpha)} \in \Theta$ with corresponding stochastic matrix given by

$$W(y|x; \theta^{(\alpha)}) = \alpha W(y|x; \theta') + (1 - \alpha)W(y|x; \theta''),$$
$$x \in \mathcal{X}, y \in \mathcal{Y}.$$

Under these assumptions of compactness and convexity, the capacity of the family is given by

$$\max_{Q \in \mathcal{P}(\mathcal{X})} \min_{\theta \in \Theta} I(Q, W(\cdot|\cdot; \theta)) = \min_{\theta \in \Theta} \max_{Q \in \mathcal{P}(\mathcal{X})} I(Q, W(\cdot|\cdot; \theta)). \qquad (102)$$

Let (Q^*, θ^*) achieve the saddle point in (102). Then the capacity of this family of DMC's can be achieved by using a maximum-likelihood decoder for the DMC with stochastic matrix $W(\cdot|\cdot; \theta^*)$ [44], [51], [119].

The maximum-likelihood decoder with respect to $W(\cdot|\cdot; \theta^*)$ is generally much simpler to implement than a universal (e.g., MMI) decoder, particularly if the codes being used have a strong algebraic structure. A universal decoder, however, has some advantages. In particular, its performance on a channel $W(\cdot|\cdot; \tilde{\theta})$, for $\tilde{\theta} \neq \theta^*$, is generally better than the performance on the channel $W(\cdot|\cdot; \tilde{\theta})$ of the maximum-likelihood decoder for $W(\cdot|\cdot; \theta^*)$.

For example, on an average power-limited additive-noise channel with a prespecified noise variance, a Gaussian codebook and a Gaussian noise distribution form a saddle point for the mutual information functional. The maximum-likelihood decoder for the saddle-point channel is a minimum Eulidean distance decoder, which is suboptimal if the noise is not Gaussian. Indeed, if the noise is discrete rather than being Gaussian (which is worse), then a Gaussian codebook with universal decoding can achieve a positive random-coding error exponent at all positive rates; with minimum Euclidean distance decoding, however, the random-coding error exponent is positive only for rates below the saddle-point value of the mutual information [88]. In this sense, a Gaussian codebook and a minimum Euclidean distance decoder cause every noise distribution to appear as harmful as the worst (Gaussian) noise.

A situation in which transmission occurs over a channel $W(\cdot|\cdot; \theta)$, and yet decoding is performed as though the channel were $W(\cdot|\cdot; \theta')$, is sometimes referred to as "mismatched decoding." Generally, a decoder is mismatched with respect to the channel $W(\cdot|\cdot; \theta)$ if it chooses the codeword that minimizes a "metric" defined for sequences as the additive extension of a single-letter "metric" $d(\cdot, \cdot)$, where $d(\cdot, \cdot)$ is, in general, not equal to $-\log W(\cdot|\cdot; \theta)$ (see (103) below).

Mismatched decoding can arise when the receiver has a poor estimate of the channel law, or when complexity considerations restrict the metric of interest to take only a limited number of integer values. The "mismatch problem" entails determining the highest achievable rates with such a hindered decoder, and is discussed in the following subsection.

5) Mismatched Decoding: Consider a known DMC (2). Given a set of codewords $\{f(m), m \in \mathcal{M}\}$, define a decoder ϕ_d by: $\phi_d(\boldsymbol{y}) = m$ if

$$d(f(m), \boldsymbol{y}) < d(f(m'), \boldsymbol{y}), \qquad \text{for all } m' \neq m. \qquad (103)$$

If no such $m \in \mathcal{M}$ exists (owing to a tie), set $\phi_d(\boldsymbol{y}) = 0$. Here

$$d(\boldsymbol{x}, \boldsymbol{y}) = \sum_{t=1}^{n} d(x_t, y_t)$$

and $d \colon \mathcal{X} \times \mathcal{Y} \to [0, \infty]$ is a given function which is often referred to as "decoding metric" (even though it may not be a metric in the topological sense). The decoder ϕ_d thus produces that message which is "nearest" to the received sequence $\boldsymbol{y}$ according to the additive "metric" $d(\boldsymbol{x}, \boldsymbol{y})$, resolving ties by declaring an error.

Setting

$$d(x, y) = \log \tilde{W}(y|x)$$

where $\tilde{W}(\cdot|\cdot)$ is a stochastic matrix $\mathcal{X} \to \mathcal{Y}$, corresponds to the study of a situation where the true channel law is $W(\cdot|\cdot)$ but the decoder being used is a maximum-likelihood decoder tuned to the channel $\tilde{W}(\cdot|\cdot)$. This situation may arise as discussed previously when $\tilde{W}(\cdot|\cdot)$ achieves the saddle point in (102) or when maximum-likelihood decoding with respect to $\tilde{W}(\cdot|\cdot)$ is simpler to implement than maximum-likelihood decoding with respect to the true channel $W(\cdot|\cdot)$. Complexity, for example, could be reduced by using integer metrics with a relatively small range [108].

The "mismatch problem" consists of finding the set of achievable rates for this situation, i.e., the supremum $C_d(W)$ of all rates that can be achieved over the DMC $W(\cdot|\cdot)$ with the decoder ϕ_d. This problem was studied extensively in [21], [22], [43], [51], [84], [87], and [100]. A lower bound on $C_d(W)$, which can be derived using a random-coding argument, is given by the following.

Theorem 13: Consider a DMC $W(\cdot|\cdot)$ with finite input and output alphabets $\mathcal{X}$, $\mathcal{Y}$. Then the rate

$$\max_{Q \in \mathcal{P}(\mathcal{X})} \min_{PY} I(X \wedge Y)$$

is achievable with the decoder ϕ_d defined in (103). Here $I(X \wedge Y)$ denotes the mutual information between X and Y with joint pmf P_{XY} on $\mathcal{X} \times \mathcal{Y}$, and the minimization is with respect to joint pmf's P_{XY} that satisfy

$$\sum_{y \in \mathcal{Y}} P_{XY}(x, y) = Q(x)$$

$$\sum_{x \in \mathcal{X}} P_{XY}(x, y) = \sum_{x \in \mathcal{X}} Q(x)W(y|x)$$

$$\sum_{x \in \mathcal{X}} \sum_{y \in \mathcal{Y}} P_{XY}(x, y)d(x, y) \leq \sum_{x \in \mathcal{X}} \sum_{y \in \mathcal{Y}} Q(x)W(y|x)\, d(x, y).$$

It should be noted that this bound is in general not tight [51]. This is not due to a loose analysis of the random-coding performance but rather because the best code for this situation may be much better than the "average" code [100].

Improved bounds on the mismatch capacity $C_d(W)$ can be found in [51] and [87]. It appears that the problem of precisely determining the capacity of this channel is very difficult; a solution to this problem would also yield a solution to the problem of determining the zero-error capacity of a graph as a special case [51]. Nevertheless, if the input alphabet is binary, Balakirsky has shown that the lower bound of Theorem 13 is tight [22]. Several interesting open problems related to mismatched decoding are posed in [51].

Extensions of the mismatch problem to the multiple-access channel are discussed in [87], and dual problems in rate distortion theory are discussed in [89].

6) Decoders for the Arbitrarily Varying Channel: Maximum-likelihood decoders can be used to achieve the randomized code capacity of an AVC (5), without or with input or state constraints (cf. Section IV-A2), passage following (86)). On the other hand, fairly complex decoders are generally needed to achieve its deterministic code capacity for the maximum or average probability of error. In fact, the first nonstandard decoder in Shannon theory appears, to our knowledge, in [10] in the study of AVC performance for deterministic codes and the maximum probability of error.

A significantly different decoder from that proposed in [10] is used in [45] to provide the characterization in Theorem 4 of the deterministic code capacity C^m of an AVC (5) for the maximum probability of error. The decoder in [45] operates in two steps. In the first step, a decision is made on the basis of a joint typicality condition which is a modified version of that used to define the divergence typicality decoder ϕ_{DT} in Section IV-B1). Any tie is broken in a second step by a threshold test which uses empirical mutual information quantities. Precisely, given a set of codewords $\{f(m), m \in \mathcal{M}\}$ in $\mathcal{T}_P^n$, for some fixed type P of sequences in $\mathcal{X}^n$ (cf. (80)), the decoder ϕ in [45] is defined as follows: $\phi(\boldsymbol{y}) = m$ iff

$$D(P_{f(m)\boldsymbol{sy}} \| P_{f(m)\boldsymbol{s}} \circ W) < \eta, \qquad \text{for some } \boldsymbol{s} \in \mathcal{S}^n \quad (104)$$

and for every $m' \neq m$ which satisfies (104) for some $\boldsymbol{s}' \in \mathcal{S}^n$, it holds that

$$I(f(m') \wedge \boldsymbol{y}|f(m), \boldsymbol{s}) < \eta \quad (105)$$

where $W: \mathcal{X} \times \mathcal{S} \to \mathcal{Y}$ is the stochastic matrix in the definition of the AVC (5), and $\eta > 0$ is chosen sufficiently small. Here, $I(f(m') \wedge \boldsymbol{y}|f(m), \boldsymbol{s})$ is the conditional mutual information $I(X' \wedge Y|X, S)$, where X, X', S, Y are dummy rv's whose joint pmf on $\mathcal{X} \times \mathcal{X} \times \mathcal{S} \times \mathcal{Y}$ is the joint type $P_{f(m)f(m')\boldsymbol{sy}}$. In decoding for a DMC (2), a divergence typicality decoder of a simpler form than in (104) (viz. with the exclusion of the state sequence $\boldsymbol{s} \in \mathcal{S}^n$), defined by (93), suffices for achieving capacity. For an AVC (5), the additional tie-breaking step in (105) is interpreted as follows: the transmitted codeword $f(m)$, the state sequence $\boldsymbol{s} \in \mathcal{S}^n$ prevailing during its transmission, and the received sequence $\boldsymbol{y} \in \mathcal{Y}^n$, will satisfy (104) with high likelihood. If $f(m')$ is a spurious codeword which, for some $\boldsymbol{s}' \in \mathcal{S}^n$, also appears to be jointly typical with $\boldsymbol{y}$ in the sense of (104), then $f(m')$ can be expected to be only vanishingly dependent on $\boldsymbol{y}$ given $f(m)$ and $\boldsymbol{s}$, in the sense of (105). As stated in [40], the form of this decoder is, in fact, suggested by the procedure for bounding the maximum probability of error using the "method of types." An important element of the proof of Theorem 4 in [45] consists in showing that for a suitably chosen set of codewords $\{f(m), m \in \mathcal{M}\}$, the decoder in (104) and (105) for a sufficiently small $\eta > 0$ is unambiguous, i.e., it maps each received sequence into at most one message.

At this point, it is worth recalling that the joint typicality and divergence typicality decoders for known channels, described in Section IV-B1), are defined in terms of the joint types of $f(m)$ and $\boldsymbol{y}$, i.e., pairs of codewords and received sequences. Such decoders belong to the general class of α-decoders, studied in [43], which can be defined solely in terms of the joint types of pairs each consisting of a codeword and a received sequence. In contrast, for the deterministic code capacity problem for the AVC (5) under the maximum probability of error, the decoder in [45] defined by (104) and (105) involves the joint types of triples $(f(m), f(m'), \boldsymbol{y})$. This decoder, thus, belongs to a more general class of decoders, introduced in [42] under the name of β-decoders, which are based on pairwise comparisons of codewords relying on joint types of triples $(f(m), f(m'), \boldsymbol{y})$.

We turn next to decoders used for achieving the deterministic code capacity of the AVC (5) for the average probability of error, without or with input or state constraints. A comprehensive treatment is found in [49]. The decoder used in [48] to determine the AVC deterministic code capacity C^a for the average probability of error in Theorem 5 resembles that in (104) and (105), but has added complexity. It too does not belong to the class of α-decoders, but rather to the class of β-decoders. Precisely, given a set of codewords $\{f(m), m \in \mathcal{M}\}$ in $\mathcal{T}_P^n$ as above, the decoder ϕ in [48] is defined as follows: $\phi(\boldsymbol{y}) = m$ iff

$$D(P_{f(m)\boldsymbol{sy}} \| P \circ P_{\boldsymbol{s}} \circ W) < \eta, \qquad \text{for some } \boldsymbol{s} \in \mathcal{S}^n \quad (106)$$

125

and for every $m' \neq m$ which satisfies (106) for some $s' \in \mathcal{S}^n$, it holds that

$$I(f(m') \wedge f(m), \boldsymbol{y}|\boldsymbol{s}) \leq \eta \qquad (107)$$

where $\eta > 0$ is chosen sufficiently small. Here, $I(f(m') \wedge f(m), \boldsymbol{y}|\boldsymbol{s})$ is the conditional mutual information $I(X' \wedge X, Y|S)$, where X, X', S, Y are dummy rv's as arising above in (105). A main step of the proof of Theorem 5 in [48] is to show that this decoder is unambiguous if $\eta > 0$ is chosen sufficiently small. An obvious modification of the conditions in (106) and (107) by allowing only such state sequences $s \in \mathcal{S}^n$ as satisfy state constraint Λ (cf. (24)), leads to a decoder used in [48] for determining the deterministic code capacity $C^a(\Gamma, \Lambda)$ of the AVC (5) under input constraint Γ and state constraint Λ (cf. Theorem 6).

It should be noted that the divergence typicality condition in (106) is alone inadequate for the purpose of establishing the AVC capacity result in Theorem 5. Indeed, a reliance on such a limited decoder prevented a complete solution from being reached in [53], where a characterization of C^a was provided under rather restrictive conditions; for details, see [49, Remark (i), p. 756].

A comparison of the decoder in (106) and (107) with that in (104) and (105) reveals two differences. First, the divergence quantity in (104) has, as its second argument, the joint type $P_{f(m)s}$, whereas the analogous argument in (106) is the product of the associated marginal types P, P_s. Second, in (105), $I(f(m') \wedge \boldsymbol{y}|f(m), \boldsymbol{s})$ is required to be small, whereas in (107) we additionally ask that $I(f(m') \wedge f(m)|\boldsymbol{s})$ also be small.

As a practical matter, the β-decoder in (106) and (107)—although indispensable for theoretical studies—is too complex to be implementable. On the other hand, finding a good decoder in the class of less complex α-decoders for every AVC appears unlikely. Nevertheless, under certain conditions, several common α-decoders suffice for achieving the deterministic code capacity of specific classes of AVC's for the average probability of error. For instance, C^a or $C^a(\Gamma, \Lambda)$ can be achieved under suitable conditions by the joint typicality decoder, the "independence" decoder, the MMI decoder (cf. Section IV-B2)) or the minimum-distance decoder. This issue is briefly addressed below; for a comprehensive treatment, see [49].

Given a set of codewords $\{f(m), m \in \mathcal{M}\}$ in $\mathcal{T}_P^n$ as above, the joint typicality decoder ϕ in [49] is defined as follows: $\phi(\boldsymbol{y}) = m$ iff

$$\max_{x \in \mathcal{X}, y \in \mathcal{Y}} |P_{f(m)\boldsymbol{y}}(x, y) - (P \circ W_\sigma)(x, y)| < \eta,$$

$$\text{for some } \sigma \in \mathcal{P}(\mathcal{S}) \qquad (108)$$

where W_σ is defined by (45), and $\eta > 0$ is chosen suitably small. If more than one $m \in \mathcal{M}$ satisfies (108), or no $m \in \mathcal{M}$ satisfies (108), set $\phi(\boldsymbol{y}) = 0$. Observe that this decoder ϕ is akin to the joint typicality decoder in Section IV-B1), but relies on a less stringent notion of joint typicality than in (104). In a result closely related to that in [53], it is shown in [49] that for the AVC (5), if the input pmf Q^* (cf. paragraph following (47)) satisfies the rather restrictive "Condition DS" (named

after Dobrushin and Stambler [53])—which is stronger than the nonsymmetrizability condition (cf. (58) and the subsequent passage)—then C^a can be achieved by the previous joint typicality decoder. An appropriate modification of (108) leads to a joint typicality decoder which achieves $C^a(\Gamma, \Lambda)$ under an analogous "Condition DS(Λ)" [49].

For the special case of additive AVC's, the joint typicality decoder in (108) is practically equivalent to the independence decoder [49]; the latter has the merit of being universal in that it does not rely on a knowledge of the stochastic matrix $W: \mathcal{X} \times \mathcal{S} \to \mathcal{Y}$ in (5). Loosely speaking, an AVC (5) with $\mathcal{X}$ and $\mathcal{Y}$ being subsets of a commutative group is called additive if $W(y|x, s)$ depends on x and y through the difference $y - x$ only. (For a formal definition of additive AVC's, see [49, Sec. II].) For a set of codewords $\{f(m), m \in \mathcal{M}\}$ in $\mathcal{T}_P^n$ as above, the independence decoder ϕ is defined as follows: $\phi(\boldsymbol{y}) = m$ iff

$$I(f(m) \wedge \boldsymbol{y} - f(m)) < \eta \qquad (109)$$

where $I(f(m) \wedge \boldsymbol{y} - f(m))$ is the mutual information $I(X \wedge Y - X)$ involving dummy rv's X, Y with joint pmf on $\mathcal{X} \times \mathcal{Y}$ being the joint type $P_{f(m)\boldsymbol{y}}$, and $\eta > 0$ is chosen sufficiently small. If no $m \in \mathcal{M}$ or more than one $m \in \mathcal{M}$ satisfies (109), set $\phi(\boldsymbol{y}) = 0$. In effect, the independence decoder ϕ decodes a received sequence $\boldsymbol{y} \in \mathcal{Y}^n$ into a message $m \in \mathcal{M}$ whenever the codeword $f(m)$ is nearly "independent" of the "error" sequence $\boldsymbol{y} - f(m)$. This decoder is shown in [49] to achieve C^a and $C^a(\Gamma, \Lambda)$ under "Condition DS" and the analogous "Condition DS(Λ)," respectively.

The joint typicality decoder (108) reduces to an elementary form for certain subclasses of the class of deterministic AVC's, the latter class being characterized by stochastic matrices $W: \mathcal{X} \times \mathcal{S} \to \mathcal{Y}$ in (5) with $\{0, 1\}$-valued entries. This elementary decoder decodes a received sequence $\boldsymbol{y} \in \mathcal{Y}^n$ into a message $m \in \mathcal{M}$ iff the codeword $f(m)$ is "compatible" with $\boldsymbol{y}$. In this context, see [51, Theorem 4] for conditions under which the "erasures only" capacity of a deterministic AVC can be achieved by such a decoder.

The MMI decoder defined in Section IV-B2) can, under certain conditions, achieve C^a or $C^a(\Gamma, \Lambda)$. Specifically, let X, S, Y be dummy rv's with joint pmf $Q^* \circ \sigma^* \circ W$ on $\mathcal{X} \times \mathcal{S} \times \mathcal{Y}$, where (Q^*, σ^*) is a saddle point for (46). If the condition

$$I(X \wedge Y) > I(S \wedge Y) \qquad (110)$$

is satisfied, then C^a can be achieved by the MMI decoder [49]. When input or state constraints are imposed, if (Q^*, σ^*) satisfies $C^a(\Gamma, \Lambda) = I(Q^*, W_{\sigma^*}) > 0$ in Theorem 6 as well as the condition (110) above, then $C^a(\Gamma, \Lambda)$ can be achieved by the MMI decoder [49]. Next, for any channel with binary input and output alphabets, the MMI decoder is related to the simple minimum (Hamming) distance decoder [49, Lemma 2]. Thus for AVC's with binary input and output alphabets, the minimum-distance decoder often suffices to achieve C^a or $C^a(\Gamma, \Lambda)$. See [49, Theorem 5] for conditions for the efficacy of this decoder.

V. THE GAUSSIAN ARBITRARILY VARYING CHANNEL

While the discrete memoryless AVC (5) with finite input and output alphabets and finite-state space has been the beneficiary of extensive investigations, studies of AVC's with continuous alphabets and state space have been comparatively limited. In this section, we shall briefly review the special case of a Gaussian arbitrarily varying channel (Gaussian AVC). For additional results on the Gaussian AVC and generalizations, we refer the reader to [41]. (Other approaches to, and models for, the study of unknown channels with infinite alphabets can be found, for instance, in [63], [76], [106], and [107].)

A Gaussian AVC is formally defined as follows. Let the input and output alphabets, and the state space, be the real line. For any channel input sequence $\boldsymbol{x} = (x_1, \cdots, x_n)$ and state sequence $\boldsymbol{s} = (s_1, \cdots, s_n)$, the corresponding channel output sequence $\boldsymbol{Y} = (Y_1, \cdots, Y_n)$ is given by

$$Y = x + s + Z \tag{111}$$

where $\boldsymbol{Z} = (Z_1, \cdots, Z_n)$ is a sequence of i.i.d. Gaussian rv's with mean zero and variance $\sigma^2 > 0$, denoted $\mathcal{N}(0, \sigma^2)$. The state sequence $\boldsymbol{s}$ may be viewed as interference inserted by an intelligent and adversarial jammer attempting to disrupt the transmission of a codeword $\boldsymbol{x}$. As for the AVC (5), it will be understood that the transmitter and receiver are unaware of the actual state sequence $\boldsymbol{s}$. Likewise, in choosing $\boldsymbol{s}$, the jammer is assumed to be ignorant of the message actually transmitted. The jammer is , however, assumed to know the code when a deterministic code is used, and know the probability law generating the code when a randomized code is used (but not the actual codes chosen).

Power limitations of the transmitter and jammer will be described in terms of an input constraint Γ and state constraint Λ. Specifically, the codewords of a length-n deterministic code (f, ϕ) or a randomized code (F, Φ) will be required to satisfy, respectively,

$$\|f(m)\|^2 \le n\Gamma, \qquad m \in \mathcal{M} \tag{112}$$

or

$$\|F(m)\|^2 \le n\Gamma \text{ a.s.}, \qquad m \in \mathcal{M} \tag{113}$$

where $\Gamma > 0$ and $\|\cdot\|$ denotes Euclidean norm. Similarly, only those state sequences $\boldsymbol{s}$ will be permitted which satisfy

$$\|s\|^2 \le n\Lambda \tag{114}$$

where $\Lambda > 0$.

The corresponding maximum and average probabilities of error are defined as obvious analogs of (42)–(44) with appropriate modifications for randomized codes. The notions of ϵ-capacity and capacity are also defined in the obvious way.

The randomized code capacity of the Gaussian AVC (111), denoted $C_G(\Gamma, \Lambda)$, is given in [80] by the following theorem.

Theorem 14: The randomized code capacity $C_G(\Gamma, \Lambda)$ of the Gaussian AVC (111) under input constraint Γ and state constraint Λ, is given by

$$C_G(\Gamma, \Lambda) = \frac{1}{2} \log \left(1 + \frac{\Gamma}{\Lambda + \sigma^2} \right). \tag{115}$$

Further, a strong converse holds so that

$$C_G(\Gamma, \Lambda) = C_{G, \epsilon}(\Gamma, \Lambda), \qquad 0 < \epsilon < 1. \tag{116}$$

The formula in (115) appears without proof in Blachman [28, p. 58].

Observe that the value of $C_G(\Gamma, \Lambda)$ coincides with the capacity formula for the ordinary memoryless channel with additive Gaussian noise of power $\Lambda + \sigma^2$. Thus the arbitrary interference resulting from the state sequence $\boldsymbol{s}$ in (111) affects achievable rates no worse than i.i.d. Gaussian noise comprising $\mathcal{N}(0, \Lambda)$ rv's. The direct part of Theorem 14 is proved in [80] with the codewords $\{F(m), m \in \mathcal{M}\}$ being distributed independently and uniformly on an n-dimensional sphere of radius $\sqrt{n\Gamma}$. The receiver uses a minimum Euclidean distance decoder Φ_{MD}, namely $\Phi_{MD}(\boldsymbol{y}) = m$ iff

$$\|\boldsymbol{y} - F(m)\| < \|\boldsymbol{y} - F(m')\|, \qquad \text{for } m' \ne m \tag{117}$$

and we set $\Phi_{MD}(\boldsymbol{y}) = 0$ if no $m \in \mathcal{M}$ satisfies (117). The maximum probability of error is then bounded above using a geometric approach in the spirit of Shannon [116]. Theorem 14 can also be proved in an alternative manner analogous to that in [47] for determining the randomized code capacity $C(\Gamma, \Lambda)$ of the AVC (5) (cf. (48)–(50)). In particular, if (Q^*, W_{ζ^*}) is a saddle point for (48), then the counterpart of ζ^* in the present situation is a Gaussian distribution with mean zero and variance Λ; the counterpart of W_{ζ^*} is a Gaussian channel with variance $\Lambda + \sigma^2$.

If the input and state constraints in (112)–(114) on individual codewords and state sequences are weakened to restrictions on the expected values of the respective powers, the Gaussian AVC (111) ceases to have a strong converse; see [80]. The results of Theorem 14 can be extended to a "vector" Gaussian AVC [81] (see also [41]). Earlier work on the randomized code capacity of the Gaussian AVC (111) is due to Blachman [27], [28] who provided lower and upper bounds on capacity when the state sequence is allowed to depend on the actual codeword transmitted. Also, the randomized code capacity problem for the Gaussian AVC has presumably motivated the game-theoretic considerations of saddle points involving mutual information quantities in (cf. e.g., [36] and [97]).

If the state sequence $\boldsymbol{s}$ in (111) is replaced by a sequence $\boldsymbol{S} = (S_1, \cdots, S_n)$ of i.i.d. rv's with a probability distribution function which is unknown to the transmitter and receiver except that it satisfies the constraint

$$\mathbb{E}[S_i^2] \le \Lambda, \qquad i = 1, \cdots, n \tag{118}$$

the resulting channel can be termed a Gaussian compound memoryless channel (cf. Section II, (3) and (4)). The parameter space Θ (cf. (3)) now corresponds to the set of distribution functions of real-valued rv's S with $\mathbb{E}[S^2] \le \Lambda$. The capacity of this Gaussian compound channel follows from Dobrushin [52], and is given by the formula in (115). Thus ignorance of the true distribution of the i.i.d interference $\boldsymbol{S} = (S_1, \cdots, S_n)$, other than knowing that it satisfies (118), does not reduce achievable rates any more than i.i.d. Gaussian noise consisting of $\mathcal{N}(0, \Lambda)$ rv's.

We next turn to the performance of the Gaussian AVC (111) for deterministic codes and the average probability of error. Earlier work in this area is due to Ahlswede [3] who determined the capacity of an AVC comprising a Gaussian channel with noise variance arbitrarily varying but not exceeding a given bound. As for its discrete memoryless counterpart (5), the capacity $C_G^a(\Gamma, \Lambda)$ of the Gaussian AVC (111) shows a dichotomy: it either equals the randomized code capacity or else is zero, according to whether or not the transmitter power exceeds the power of the (arbitrary) interference s. This result is proved in [50] as

Theorem 15: The deterministic code capacity of the Gaussian AVC (111) under input constraint Γ and state constraint Λ, for the average probability of error, is given by

$$C_G^a(\Gamma, \Lambda) = \begin{cases} \dfrac{1}{2} \log\left(1 + \dfrac{\Gamma}{\Lambda + \sigma^2}\right), & \text{if } \Gamma > \Lambda \\ 0, & \text{if } \Gamma \leq \Lambda. \end{cases} \quad (119)$$

Furthermore, if $\Gamma > \Lambda$, a strong converse holds so that

$$C_G^a(\Gamma, \Lambda) = C_{G,\epsilon}^a(\Gamma, \Lambda), \qquad 0 < \epsilon < 1. \quad (120)$$

Although $C_G^a(\Gamma, \Lambda)$ exhibits a dichotomy similar to the capacity $C^a(\Gamma, \Lambda)$ of the AVC (5) (cf. (57)), a proof of Theorem 15 using Ahlswede's "elimination" technique [7] is not apparent. Its proof in [50] is based on a straightforward albeit more computational approach akin to that in [48]. The direct part uses a code with codewords chosen at random from an n-dimensional spheres of radius $\sqrt{n\Gamma}$ and selectively identified as in [48]. Interestingly, simple minimum Euclidean distance decoding (cf. (117)) suffices to achieve capacity, in contrast with the complex decoding rule (cf. Section IV-B6)) used for the AVC (5) in [48].

In the absence of the Gaussian noise sequence $Z = (Z_1, \cdots, Z_n)$ in (111), we obtain a noiseless additive AVC with output $y = x + s$. The deterministic code capacity of this AVC under input constraint Γ and state constraint Λ, for the average probability of error, is, as expected, the limit of the capacity of the Gaussian AVC in Theorem 15 as $\sigma^2 \to 0$ [50]. While this is not a formal consequence of Theorem 15, it can be proved by the same method. Thus the capacity of this AVC equals $1/2 \log(1 + \Gamma/\Lambda)$ if $\Gamma > \Lambda$, and zero if $\Gamma \leq \Lambda$, and can be achieved using the minimum Euclidean distance decoder (117). As noted in [50], this result provides a solution to a weakened version of an unsolved sphere-packing problem of purely combinatorial nature. This problem seeks the exponential rate of the maximum number of nonintersecting sphere of radius $\sqrt{n\Gamma}$ in n-dimensional Euclidean space with centers in a sphere of radius $\sqrt{n\Gamma}$. Consider instead a lesser problem in which the spheres are permitted to intersect, but for any given s of norm not exceeding $\sqrt{n\Gamma}$, only for a vanishingly small fraction of sphere centers x_i can $x_i + s$ be closer to another sphere center than to x_i. The exponential rate of the maximum number of spheres satisfying this condition is given by the capacity of the noiseless additive AVC above.

Multiple-access counterparts of the single-user Gaussian AVC results surveyed in this section, remain largely unresolved issues.

We note that many of the issues that were described in previous sections for DMC's have natural counterparts for Gaussian channels and for more general channels with infinite alphabets. For example, universal decoding for Gaussian channels with a deterministic but unknown parametric interference was studied in [98], and more general universal decoding for channels with infinite alphabets was studied in [60]; the mismatch problem with minimum Euclidean distance decoding was studied in [100] and [88].

VI. MULTIPLE-ACCESS CHANNELS

The study of reliable communication under channel uncertainty has not been restricted to the single-user channel; considerable attention has also been paid to the multiple-access channel (MAC). The MAC models a communication situation in which multiple users can simultaneously transmit to a single receiver, each user being ignorant of the messages of the other users [39], [44].

Many of the channel models for single-user communication under channel uncertainty have natural counterparts for the MAC. In this section, we shall briefly survey some of the studies of these models. We shall limit ourselves throughout to MAC's with two transmitters only; extensions to more users are usually straightforward.

A known discrete memoryless MAC is characterized by two finite input alphabets $\mathcal{X}_1$, $\mathcal{X}_2$, a finite output alphabet $\mathcal{Y}$, and a stochastic matrix $W: \mathcal{X}_1 \times \mathcal{X}_2 \mapsto \mathcal{Y}$. The rates R_1 and R_2 for the two users are defined analogously as in (12). The capacity region of the MAC for the average probability of error was derived independently by Ahlswede [4] and Liao [94]. A rate-pair (R_1, R_2) is achievable for the average probability of error iff

$$0 \leq R_1 \leq I(X_1 \wedge Y | X_2, V) \quad (121)$$
$$0 \leq R_2 \leq I(X_2 \wedge Y | X_1, V) \quad (122)$$

and

$$R_1 + R_2 \leq I(X_1, X_2 \wedge Y | V) \quad (123)$$

for some joint pmf $P_{VX_1X_2Y}$ on $\mathcal{V} \times \mathcal{X}_1 \times \mathcal{X}_2 \times \mathcal{Y}$ of the form

$$P_{VX_1X_2Y}(v, x_1, x_2, y)$$
$$= P_V(v) P_{X_1|V}(x_1|v) P_{X_2|V}(x_2|v) W(y|x_1, x_2)$$

where the "time-sharing" random variable V with values in the set $\mathcal{V}$ is arbitrary, but may be limited to assume two values, say $\{1, 2\}$ [44]. Extensions to account for average input constraints are discussed in [66], [121], and [127]. Low-complexity codes for the MAC are discussed in [70] and [105].

It is interesting to note that even for a *known* MAC, the average probability of error and the maximal probability of error criteria can lead to different capacity regions [54]; this is in contrast with the capacity of a known single-user channel.

The compound channel capacity region for a *finite* family of discrete memoryless MAC's has been computed by Han in [77]. In the more general case where the family is not necessarily finite, it can be shown that a rate-pair (R_1, R_2) is achievable for the family

$$\{W(y|x_1, x_2; \theta), x_1 \in \mathcal{X}_1, x_2 \in \mathcal{X}_2, y \in \mathcal{Y}, \theta \in \Theta\}$$

iff there exists a joint pmf $P_{X_1 X_2 V}$ of the form

$$P_{X_1 X_2 V}(x_1, x_2, v) = P_V(v) P_{X_1|V}(x_1|v) P_{X_2|V}(x_2|v)$$

so that (121)–(123) are satisfied for every $\theta \in \Theta$, where the mutual information quantities are computed with respect to the joint pmf

$$P_{V X_1 X_2, Y; \theta}(v, x_1, x_2, y; \theta)$$
$$= P_V(v) P_{X_1|V}(x_1|v) P_{X_2|V}(x_2|v) W(y|x_1, x_2; \theta).$$

The direct part of the proof of this claim follows from the code constructions in [95] and [103], in which neither the encoder nor the decoder depends on the channel law. The converse follows directly from [39, Sec. 14.3.4], where a converse is proved for the known MAC.

Mismatched decoding for the MAC has been studied in [87], and [88], and universal decoding in [60] and [95].

We turn next to the multiple-access AVC with stochastic matrix $W: \mathcal{X}_1 \times \mathcal{X}_2 \times \mathcal{S} \to \mathcal{Y}$ where $\mathcal{S}$ is a finite set. The deterministic code capacity region of this multiple-access AVC for the average probability of error, denoted $\mathcal{C}^a$, was determined by Jahn [85] assuming that it had a nonempty interior, i.e., $\mathrm{int}\,(\mathcal{C}^a) \neq \emptyset$. A necessary and sufficient computable characterization of multiple-access AVC's for deciding when $\mathrm{int}\,(\mathcal{C}^a) \neq \emptyset$ was not addressed in [85]. Further, assuming that $\mathrm{int}\,(\mathcal{C}^a) \neq \emptyset$, Jahn [85] characterized the randomized code capacity region, denoted $\mathcal{C}$, for the average probability of error in terms of suitable mutual information quantities, and showed that $\mathcal{C}^a = \mathcal{C}$. The validity of this characterization of $\mathcal{C}$, even without the assumption in [85] that $\mathrm{int}\,(\mathcal{C}^a) \neq \emptyset$, was demonstrated by Gubner and Hughes [75]. Observe that if $\mathrm{int}\,(\mathcal{C}^a) = \emptyset$, at least one user and perhaps both users, cannot reliably transmit information over the channel using deterministic codes.

In order to characterize multiple-access AVC's with $\mathrm{int}\,(\mathcal{C}^a) \neq \emptyset$, the notion of single-user symmetrizability (58) was extended by Gubner [72]. This extended notion of symmetrizability for the multiple-access AVC, in fact, involves three distinct conditions: symmetrizability with respect to each of the two individual users, and symmetrizability with respect to the two users jointly; these conditions are termed symmetrizability-$\mathcal{X}_1$, symmetrizability-$\mathcal{X}_2$, and symmetrizability-$\mathcal{X}_1\mathcal{X}_2$, respectively, [72]. Neither of the three conditions above need imply the others. It is readily seen in [72], by virtue of [59] and [48], that if a multiple-access AVC is such that $\mathrm{int}\,(\mathcal{C}^a) \neq \emptyset$, then it must necessarily be nonsymmetrizable-$\mathcal{X}_1$, nonsymmetrizable-$\mathcal{X}_2$, and nonsymmetrizable-$\mathcal{X}_1\mathcal{X}_2$. The sufficiency of this set of nonsymmetrizability conditions for $\mathrm{int}\,(\mathcal{C}^a) \neq \emptyset$ was conjectured in [72] and proved by Ahlswede and Cai [15], thereby completely resolving the problem of characterizing $\mathcal{C}^a$. (It was shown in [72] that $\mathrm{int}\,(\mathcal{C}^a) \neq \emptyset$ under a set of conditions which are sufficient but not necessary.)

Ahlswede and Cai [16] have further demonstrated that if the multiple-access AVC is only nonsymmetrizable-$\mathcal{X}_1\mathcal{X}_2$ (but can be symmetrizable-$\mathcal{X}_1$ or symmetrizable-$\mathcal{X}_2$), both users can still reliably transmit information over the channel using deterministic codes, if they have access to correlated side-information.

The randomized code capacity region of the multiple-access AVC under state constraint Λ (cf. (24)) for the maximum or average probability of error, denoted $\mathcal{C}(\Lambda)$, has been determined by Gubner and Hughes [75]. The presence of the state constraint renders $\mathcal{C}(\Lambda)$ nonconvex in general [75]; the corresponding capacity region $\mathcal{C}$ in the absence of any state constraint [85] is convex. Input constraints analogous to (22) are also considered in [75].

The deterministic code capacity region of the multiple-access AVC under state constraint Λ for the average probability of error remains unresolved. For preliminary results, see [73] and [74].

Indeed, multiple-access AVC counterparts of the single-user discrete memoryless AVC results of Section III-A2), which have not been mentioned above in this section, remain by and large unresolved issues.

VII. Discussion

We discuss below the potential role in mobile wireless communications of the work surveyed in this paper. Several situations in which information must be conveyed reliably under channel uncertainty are considered in light of the channel models described above. The difficulties encountered when attempting to draw practical guidelines concerning the design of transmitters and receivers for such situations are also examined. Suggested avenues for future research are indicated.

We limit our discussion to single-user channels, in which case the receiver for a given user treats all other users' signals (when present) as noise. (For some multiuser models see [26], [110], and references therein.) We do not, therefore, investigate the benefits of using the multiple-access transmitters and receivers suggested by the work mentioned in Section VI. We remark that the discrete channels surveyed above should be viewed as resulting from combinations of modulators, waveform transmission channels, and demodulators.

A few preliminary observations are in order. Considerations of delays in encoding and decoding as well as decoder complexity typically dictate the choice of blocklength n of codewords used in a given communication situation. Encoding delays result from the fact that a message must be buffered prior to transmission until an entire (block) codeword for it has been formed. Decoding delays are incurred since all the symbols in a codeword must be received before the operation of decoding can commence. Once a blocklength n has been fixed, the channel dictates a tradeoff between the transmitter power, the code rate, and the probability of decoding error. We note that if the choice of the blocklength n is determined by delay considerations rather than by those of complexity, the use of a complex decoder for enhancing channel coding performance becomes feasible. On the other hand, overriding concerns of complexity often inhibit the use of complex decoder structures. For instance, the universal MMI decoder (cf. Section III-A1)), which is known to achieve channel capacity and the random-coding error exponent in many situations, does not always afford a simple algorithmic implementation even when used in conjunction with an algebraically well-structured block code or a convolutional code on a DMC; however, see [92], [93], and [129]. Thus the task of finding universal decoders of manageable complexity constitutes a challenging research direction [93]. An alternative approach for designing receivers for use on unknown channels, which is widely used in practice, employs training sequences for estimating the parameters of the unknown channel followed by maximum-likelihood decoding (cf. Section IV-B1)) with respect to the estimated channel. In many situations, this approach leads to simple receiver designs. A drawback of this approach is that the code rate for information transmission is, in effect, reduced as the symbols of the training sequence appropriate a portion of blocklength n fixed by the considerations mentioned earlier. On the other hand, in situations where the unknown channel remains unchanged over multiple transmissions, viz. codewords, this approach is particularly attractive since channel parameters estimated with a training sequence during a transmission can be reused in subsequent transmissions.

An information signal transmitted over a mobile radio channel undergoes fading whose nature depends on the relation between the signal parameters (e.g., signal bandwidth) and the channel parameters (e.g., delay spread, Doppler spread). (For a comprehensive treatment, cf., e.g., [104, Ch. 4].) Four distinct types of fading can be experienced by an information signal, which are described next.

Doppler spread effects typically result in either "slow" fading or "fast" fading. Let T_n denote the transmission time (in seconds) of a codeword of blocklength n, and T_c the channel coherence time (in seconds). In slow fading, $T_n \ll T_c$, so that the channel remains effectively unchanged during the transmission of a codeword; hence, it can be modeled as a compound channel, without or with memory (cf. Section II). On the other hand, fast fading, when $T_n > T_c$, results in the channel undergoing changes during the transmission of a codeword, so that a compound channel model is no longer appropriate.

Independently of the previous effects, a multipath delay spread mechanism gives rise to either "flat" fading or "frequency-selective" fading. In flat fading, $T_n/n \gg \sigma_\tau$, where σ_τ is the root-mean-square (rms) delay spread (in seconds); in effect, the channel can be assumed to be memoryless from symbol to symbol of a codeword. In contrast, frequency-selective fading, when $T_n/n < \sigma_\tau$, results in intersymbol interference (ISI) which introduces memory into the channel, suggesting the use of finite-state models (cf. Section II).

The fading effects described above produce the four different combinations of slow flat fading, slow frequency-selective fading, fast flat fading and fast frequency-selective fading. It is argued below that the resulting channels can be described to various extents by the channel models of Section II; however, the work reviewed above may fail to provide satisfactory recommendations for transmitter–receiver designs which meet the delay and complexity requirements mentioned earlier.

For channels with slow flat fading, the compound DMC model (4) is an apt choice. The MMI decoder achieves the capacity of this channel (cf. Section IV-B4)); however, complexity considerations may preclude its use in practice. This situation is mitigated by the observation in [100] that a code with equi-energy codewords and minimum Euclidean distance decoder is often adequate. Alternatively, a training sequence can be used to estimate the prevailing state of the compound DMC, followed by maximum-likelihood decoding. A drawback of this approach, of course, is the effective loss of code rate alluded to earlier.

Channels characterized by slow frequency-selective fading can be described by a compound finite-state channel model (cf. Section III-A1)). The universal decoder in [60] achieves channel capacity and the random coding-error exponent. The high complexity of this decoder, however, renders it impractical if complexity is an overriding concern. In this situation, a training sequence approach as above offers a remedy, albeit at the cost of an effective reduction in code rate. A training sequence can be used to estimate the unknown ISI parameters of the compound FSC model followed by maximum-likelihood decoding; the special structure of the ISI channel renders both these operations fairly straightforward.

Channels with fast flat fading fluctuate between several different attenuation levels during the transmission of a codeword; during the period in which each such attenuation level prevails, the channels appear memoryless. A description of such a channel will depend on the severity of the fast fade. For instance, consider the case where different attenuation levels are experienced often enough during the transmission of a codeword. A compound finite-state model (cf. Section II) is a feasible candidate, where the set of states Σ corresponds to the set of attenuation levels, by dint of the fact that the "ergodicity time" T_e of the channel satisfies $T_e < T_n$. However, no encouraging options can be inferred from the work surveyed above for acceptable transmitter–receiver designs. A complex decoder [60] is generally needed to achieve channel capacity and the random-coding error exponent. Furthermore, the feasibility of the training sequence approach is also dubious owing to the inherent complexity of the estimation procedure and of the computation of the likelihood metric.[5] Next, if $T_e > T_n$, a compound FSC model is no longer appropriate, and even the task of finding an acceptable channel description from among the models surveyed appears difficult. Of course, an AVC model (5), with state space comprising the different attenuation levels, can be used provided the transitions between such levels occur in a memoryless manner; else, an arbitrarily varying FSC model (9) can be considered. When $T_e > T_n$, the choice of an arbitrarily varying channel model may, however, lead to overly conservative estimates of channel capacity. It must, however, be noted that in the former case, an AVC model does offer the feasibility of simpler transmitter and receiver designs through the use of randomized codes (with maximum-

---

[5] Even when the law of a finite-state channel is known, the maximum-likelihood decoder may be too complex to implement, since the computation of the likelihood of a received sequence given a codeword is exponential in the blocklength (7). A suboptimal decoder which does not necessarily achieve the random-coding error exponent, but does achieve capacity for some finite-state channels is discussed in [69] and [101].

likelihood decoder) for achieving channel capacity (cf. Section IV-A2)).

Finally, a channel with fast frequency-selective fading can be understood in a manner analogous to fast flat fading, with the difference that during the period of each prevalent attenuation level the channel possesses memory. Also, if $T_e < T_n$, such a channel can be similarly modeled by a compound FSC (cf. Section II), where the set of states—representing the various attenuation levels—now corresponds to a family of "smaller" FSC's with unknown parameters. Clearly, the practical feasibility of a decoder which achieves channel capacity or a receiver based on a training sequence approach appears remote. If $T_e > T_n$, similar comments apply as for the analogous situation in fast flat fading; each arbitrarily varying channel state, representing an attenuation level, will now correspond to a "smaller" FSC with unknown parameters.

Thus information-theoretic studies of unknown channels have produced classes of models which are rich enough to faithfully describe many situations arising in mobile wireless communications. There are, of course, some situations involving fast fading which yet lack satisfactory descriptions and for which new tractable channel models are needed. However, the shortcomings are acute in terms of providing acceptable guidelines for the design of transmitters and receivers which adhere to delay and complexity requirements. The feasibility of the training sequence approach is crucially reliant on the availability of good estimates of channel parameters and the ease of computation of the likelihood metric, which can pose serious difficulties especially for channels with memory. This provides an impetus for the study of efficient decoders which do not require a knowledge of the channel law and yet allow reliable communication at rates up to capacity with reasonable delay and complexity.

ACKNOWLEDGMENT

The authors are grateful to M. Pinsker for his careful reading of this paper and for his many helpful suggestions. They also thank S. Verdú and the reviewers for their useful comments.

REFERENCES

[1] R. Ahlswede, "Certain results in coding theory for compound channels," in *Proc. Coll. Inf. The. Debrecen 1967*, A. Rényi, Ed. Budapest, Hungary: J. Bolyai Math. Soc., 1968, vol. 1, pp. 35–60.

[2] _____, "A note on the existence of the weak capacity for channels with arbitrarily varying channel probability functions and its relation to Shannon's zero error capacity," *Ann. Math. Statist.*, vol. 41, pp. 1027–1033, 1970.

[3] _____, "The capacity of a channel with arbitrary varying Gaussian channel probability functions," in *Trans. 6th Prague Conf. Information Theory, Statistical Decision Functions and Random Processes*, Sept. 1971, pp. 13–21.

[4] _____, "Multi-way communication channels," in *Proc. 2nd. Int. Symp. Information Theory.* Budapest, Hungary: Hungarian Acad. Sci., 1971, pp. 23–52.

[5] _____, "Channel capacities for list codes," *J. Appl. Probab.*, vol. 10, pp. 824–836, 1973.

[6] _____, "Elimination of correlation in random codes for arbitrarily varying channels," *Z. Wahrscheinlichkeitstheorie Verw. Gebiete*, vol. 44, pp. 159–175, 1978.

[7] _____, "Elimination of correlation in random codes for arbitrarily varying channels," *Z. Wahrscheinlichkeitstheorie Verw. Gebiete*, vol. 44, pp. 159–175, 1978.

[8] _____, "Coloring hypergraphs: A new approach to multiuser source coding, Part I," *J. Combin., Inform. Syst. Sci.*, vol. 4, no. 1, pp. 76–115, 1979.

[9] _____, "Coloring hypergraphs: A new approach to multiuser source coding, Part II," *J. Combin., Inform. Syst. Sci.*, vol. 5, no. 3, pp. 220–268, 1980.

[10] _____, "A method of coding and an application to arbitrarily varying channels," *J. Comb., Inform. Syst. Sci.*, vol. 5, pp. 10–35, 1980.

[11] _____, "Arbitrarily varying channels with states sequence known to the sender," *IEEE Trans. Inform. Theory*, vol. IT-32, pp. 621–629, Sept. 1986.

[12] _____, "The maximal error capacity of arbitrarily varying channels for constant list sizes," *IEEE Trans. Inform. Theory*, vol. 39, pp. 1416–1417, July 1993.

[13] R. Ahlswede, L. A. Bassalygo, and M. S. Pinsker, "Localized random and arbitrary errors in the light of arbitrarily varying channel theory," *IEEE Trans. Inform. Theory*, vol. 41, pp. 14–25, Jan. 1995.

[14] R. Ahlswede and N. Cai, "Two proofs of Pinsker's conjecture concerning arbitrarily varying channels," *IEEE Trans. Inform. Theory*, vol. 37, pp. 1647–1649, Nov. 1991.

[15] _____, "Arbitrarily varying multiple-access channels Part I. Ericson's symmetrizability is adequate, Gubner's conjecture is true," in *Proc. IEEE Int. Symp. Information Theory* (Ulm, Germany, 1997), p. 22.

[16] _____, "Arbitrarily varying multiple-access channels, Part II: Correlated sender's side information, correlated messages, and ambiguous transmission," in *Proc. IEEE Int. Symp. Information Theory* (Ulm, Germany, 1997), p. 23.

[17] _____, "Correlated sources help transmission over an arbitrarily varying channel," *IEEE Trans. Inform. Theory*, vol. 43, pp. 1254–1255, July 1997.

[18] R. Ahlswede and I. Csiszár, "Common randomness in information theory and cryptography: Part II: CR capacity," *IEEE Trans. Inform. Theory*, vol. 44, pp. 225–240, Jan 1998.

[19] R. Ahlswede and J. Wolfowitz, "Correlated decoding for channels with arbitrarily varying channel probability functions," *Inform. Contr.*, vol. 14, pp. 457–473, 1969.

[20] _____, "The capacity of a channel with arbitrarily varying channel probability functions and binary output alphabet," *Z. Wahrscheinlichkeitstheorie Verw. Gebiete*, vol. 15, pp. 186–194, 1970.

[21] V. B. Balakirsky, "Coding theorem for discrete memoryless channels with given decision rules," in *Proc. 1st French–Soviet Workshop on Algebraic Coding* (Lecture Notes in Computer Science 573), G. Cohen, S. Litsyn, A. Lobstein, and G. Zémor, Eds. Berlin, Germany: Springer-Verlag, July 1991, pp. 142–150.

[22] _____, "A converse coding theorem for mismatched decoding at the output of binary-input memoryless channels," *IEEE Trans. Inform. Theory*, vol. 41, pp. 1889–1902, Nov. 1995.

[23] A. Barron, J. Rissanen, and B. Yu, "Minimum description length principle in modeling and coding," this issue, pp. 2743–2760.

[24] T. Berger, "Multiterminal source coding," in *The Information Theory Approach to Communications* (CISM Course and Lecture Notes, no. 229), G. Longo, Ed. Berlin, Germany: Springer-Verlag, 1977, pp. 172–231.

[25] T. Berger and J. Gibson, "Lossy data compression," this issue, pp. 2693–2723.

[26] E. Biglieri, J. Proakis, and S. Shamai, "Fading channels: Information theoretic and communications aspects," this issue, pp. 2619–2692.

[27] N. M. Blachman, "The effect of statistically dependent interference upon channel capacity," *IRE Trans. Inform. Theory*, vol. IT-8, pp. 553–557, Sept. 1962.

[28] _____, "On the capacity of a band-limited channel perturbed by statistically dependent interference," *IRE Trans. Inform. Theory*, vol. IT-8, pp. 48–55, Jan. 1962.

[29] D. Blackwell, L. Breiman, and A. J. Thomasian, "Proof of Shannon's transmission theorem for finite-state indecomposable channels," *Ann. Math. Statist.*, vol. 29, no. 4, pp. 1209–1220, 1958.

[30] _____, "The capacity of a class of channels," *Ann. Math. Statist.*, vol. 30, pp. 1229–1241, Dec. 1959.

[31] _____, "The capacities of certain channel classes under random coding," *Ann. Math. Statist.*, vol. 31, pp. 558–567, 1960.

[32] R. E. Blahut, *Principles and Practice of Information Theory.* Reading, MA: Addison-Wesley, 1987.

[33] V. Blinovsky, P. Narayan, and M. Pinsker, "Capacity of an arbitrarily varying channel under list decoding," *Probl. Pered. Inform.*, vol. 31, pp. 99–113, 1995, English translation.

[34] V. Blinovsky and M. Pinsker, "Estimation of the size of the list when decoding over an arbitrarily varying channel," in *Proc. 1st French–Israeli Workshop on Algebraic Coding*, G. Cohen et al., Eds.

(Paris, France, July 1993). Berlin, Germany: Springer, 1993, pp. 28–33.

[35] ——, "One method of the estimation of the size for list decoding in arbitrarily varying channel," in *Proc. of ISITA-94* (Sidney, Australia, 1994), pp. 607–609.

[36] J. M. Borden, D. J. Mason, and R. J. McEliece, "Some information theoretic saddlepoints," *SIAM Contr. Opt.*, vol. 23, no. 1, Jan. 1985.

[37] M. H. M. Costa, "Writing on dirty paper," *IEEE Trans. Inform. Theory*, vol. IT-29, pp. 439–441, May 1983.

[38] T. M. Cover, "Broadcast channels," *IEEE Trans. Inform. Theory*, vol. IT-18, pp. 2–14, Jan. 1972.

[39] T. M. Cover and J. A. Thomas, *Elements of Information Theory.* New York: Wiley, 1991.

[40] I. Csiszár, "The method of types," this issue, pp. 2505–2523.

[41] ——, "Arbitrarily varying channels with general alphabets and states," *IEEE Trans. Inform. Theory*, vol. 38, pp. 1725–1742, Nov. 1992.

[42] I. Csiszár and J. Körner, "Many coding theorems follow from an elementary combinatorial lemma," in *Proc. 3rd Czechoslovak–Soviet–Hungarian Sem. Information Theory* (Liblice, Czechoslovakia, 1980), pp. 25–44.

[43] ——, "Graph decomposition: A new key to coding theorems," *IEEE Trans. Inform. Theory*, vol. IT-27, pp. 5–12, Jan. 1981.

[44] ——, *Information Theory: Coding Theorems for Discrete Memoryless Systems.* New York: Academic, 1981.

[45] ——, "On the capacity of the arbitrarily varying channel for maximum probability of error," *Z. Wahrscheinlichkeitstheorie Verw. Gebiete*, vol. 57, pp. 87–101, 1981.

[46] I. Csiszár, J. Körner, and K. Marton, "A new look at the error exponent of discrete memoryless channels," in *IEEE Int. Symp. Information Theory* (Cornell Univ., Ithaca, NY, Oct. 1977), unpublished preprint.

[47] I. Csiszár and P. Narayan, "Arbitrarily varying channels with constrained inputs and states," *IEEE Trans. Inform. Theory*, vol. 34, pp. 27–34, Jan. 1988.

[48] ——, "The capacity of the arbitrarily varying channel revisited: Capacity, constraints," *IEEE Trans. Inform. Theory*, vol. 34, pp. 181–193, Jan. 1988.

[49] ——, "Capacity and decoding rules for classes of arbitrarily varying channels," *IEEE Trans. Inform. Theory*, vol. 35, pp. 752–769, July 1989.

[50] ——, "Capacity of the Gaussian arbitrarily varying channel," *IEEE Trans. Inform. Theory*, vol. 37, no. 1, pp. 18–26, Jan. 1991.

[51] ——, "Channel capacity for a given decoding metric," *IEEE Trans. Inform. Theory*, vol. 41, pp. 35–43, Jan. 1995.

[52] R. L. Dobrushin, "Optimum information transmission through a channel with unknown parameters," *Radio Eng. Electron.*, vol. 4, no. 12, pp. 1–8, 1959.

[53] R. L. Dobrushin and S. Z. Stambler, "Coding theorems for classes of arbitrarily varying discrete memoryless channels," *Probl. Pered. Inform.*, vol. 11, no. 2, pp. 3–22, 1975, English translation.

[54] G. Dueck, "Maximal error capacity regions are smaller than average error capacity regions for multi-user channels," *Probl. Contr. Inform. Theory*, vol. 7, pp. 11–19, 1978.

[55] P. Elias, "List decoding for noisy channels," in *IRE WESCON Conv. Rec.*, 1957, vol. 2, pp. 94–104.

[56] ——, "Zero error capacity under list decoding," *IEEE Trans. Infom. Theory*, vol. 34, pp. 1070–1074, Sept. 1988.

[57] E. O. Elliott, "Estimates of error rates for codes on burst-noise channels," *Bell Syst. Tech. J.*, pp. 1977–1997, Sept. 1963.

[58] T. Ericson, "A min-max theorem for antijamming group codes," *IEEE Trans. Inform. Theory*, vol. IT-30, pp. 792–799, Nov. 1984.

[59] ——, "Exponential error bounds for random codes in the arbitrarily varying channel," *IEEE Trans. Inform. Theory*, vol. IT-31, pp. 42–48, Jan. 1985.

[60] M. Feder and A. Lapidoth, "Universal decoding for channels with memory," *IEEE Trans. Inform. Theory*, vol. 44, pp. 1726–1745, Sept. 1998.

[61] N. Merhav and M. Feder, "Universal prediction," this issue, pp. 2124–2147.

[62] G. D. Forney, "Exponential error bounds for erasure, list and decision feedback systems," *IEEE Trans. Inform. Theory*, vol. IT-14, pp. 206–220, Mar. 1968.

[63] L. J. Forys and P. P. Varaiya, "The ϵ-capacity of classes of unknown channels," *Inform. Contr.*, vol. 14, pp. 376–406, 1969.

[64] R. G. Gallager, *Information Theory and Reliable Communication.* New York: Wiley, 1968.

[65] ——, "The random coding bound is tight for the average code," *IEEE Trans. Inform. Theory*, vol. IT-19, pp. 244–246, Mar. 1973.

[66] ——, "Energy limited channels: Coding, multiaccess, and spread spectrum," Tech. Rep. LIDS-P-1714, Lab. Inform. Decision Syst., Mass. Inst. Technol., Cambridge, MA, Nov. 1988.

[67] S. I. Gel'fand and M. S. Pinsker, "Coding for channel with random parameters," *Probl. Contr. Inform. Theory*, vol. 9, no. 1, pp. 19–31, 1980.

[68] E. N. Gilbert, "Capacity of burst-noise channels," *Bell Syst. Tech. J.*, vol. 39, pp. 1253–1265, Sept. 1960.

[69] A. J. Goldsmith and P. P. Varaiya, "Capacity, mutual information, and coding for finite-state Markov channels," *IEEE Trans. Inform. Theory*, vol. 42, pp. 868–886, May 1996.

[70] A. Grant, R. Rimoldi, R. Urbanke, and P. Whiting, "Rate-splitting multiple access for discrete memoryless channels," *IEEE Trans. Inform. Theory*, to be published.

[71] R. Gray and D. Neuhoff, "Quantization," this issue, pp. 2325–2383.

[72] J. A. Gubner, "On the deterministic-code capacity of the multiple-access arbitrarily varying channel," *IEEE Trans. Inform. Theory*, vol. 36, pp. 262–275, Mar. 1990.

[73] ——, "State constraints for the multiple-access arbitrarily varying channel," *IEEE Trans. Inform. Theory*, vol. 37, pp. 27–35, Jan. 1991.

[74] ——, "On the capacity region of the discrete additive multiple-access arbitrarily varying channel," *IEEE Trans. Inform. Theory*, vol. 38, pp. 1344–1346, July 1992.

[75] J. A. Gubner and B. L. Hughes, "Nonconvexity of the capacity region of the multiple-access arbitrarily varying channel subject to constraints," *IEEE Trans. Inform. Theory*, vol. 41, pp. 3–13, Jan. 1995.

[76] D. Hajela and M. Honig, "Bounds on ϵ-rate for linear, time-invariant, multi-input/multi-output channels," *IEEE Trans. Inform. Theory*, vol. 36, Sept. 1990.

[77] T. S. Han, "Information-spectrum methods in information theory," Graduate School of Inform. Syst., Univ. Electro-Communications, Chofu, Tokyo 182 Japan, Tech. Rep., 1997.

[78] C. Heegard and A. El Gamal, "On the capacity of computer memory with defects," *IEEE Trans. Inform. Theory*, vol. IT-29, pp. 731–739, Sept. 1983.

[79] M. Hegde, W. E. Stark, and D. Teneketzis, "On the capacity of channels with unknown interference," *IEEE Trans. Inform. Theory*, vol. 35, pp. 770–783, July 1989.

[80] B. Hughes and P. Narayan, "Gaussian arbitrarily varying channels," *IEEE Trans. Inform. Theory*, vol. IT-33, pp. 267–284, Mar. 1987.

[81] ——, "The capacity of a vector Gaussian arbitrarily varying channel," *IEEE Trans. Inform. Theory*, vol. 34, pp. 995–1003, Sept. 1988.

[82] B. L. Hughes, "The smallest list size for the arbitrarily varying channel," in *Proc. 1993 IEEE Int. Symp. Information Theory* (San Antonio, TX, Jan. 1993).

[83] ——, "The smallest list for the arbitrarily varying channel," *IEEE Trans. Inform. Theory*, vol. 43, pp. 803–815, May 1997.

[84] J. Y. N. Hui, "Fundamental issues of multiple accessing," Ph.D. dissertation, Mass. Inst. Technol., Cambridge, MA, 1983.

[85] J. H. Jahn, "Coding for arbitrarily varying multiuser channels," *IEEE Trans. Inform. Theory*, vol. IT-27, pp. 212–226, Mar. 1981.

[86] F. Jelinek, "Indecomposable channels with side information at the transmitter," *Inform. Contr.*, vol. 8, pp. 36–55, 1965.

[87] A. Lapidoth, "Mismatched decoding and the multiple-access channel," *IEEE Trans. Inform. Theory*, vol. 42, pp. 1439–1452, Sept. 1996.

[88] ——, "Nearest-neighbor decoding for additive non-Gaussian noise channels," *IEEE Trans. Inform. Theory*, vol. 42, pp. 1520–1529, Sept. 1996.

[89] ——, "On the role of mismatch in rate distortion theory," *IEEE Trans. Inform. Theory*, vol. 43, pp. 38–47, Jan. 1997.

[90] A. Lapidoth and İ. E. Telatar, private communication, Dec. 1997.

[91] ——, "The compound channel capacity of a class of finite-state channels," *IEEE Trans. Inform. Theory*, vol. 44, pp. 973–983, May 1998.

[92] A. Lapidoth and J. Ziv, "On the universality of the LZ-based decoding algorithm," *IEEE Trans. Inform. Theory*, vol. 44, pp. 1746–1755, Sept. 1998.

[93] ——, "Universal sequential decoding," presented at the 1998 Information Theory Workshop, Kerry, Killarney Co., Ireland.

[94] H. Liao, "Multiple access channels," Ph.D. dissertation, Dept. Elec. Eng., Univ. Hawaii, 1972.

[95] Y.-S. Liu and B. L. Hughes, "A new universal random coding bound for the multiple-access channel," *IEEE Trans. Inform. Theory*, vol. 42, pp. 376–386, Mar. 1996.

[96] L. Lovász, "On the Shannon capacity of a graph," *IEEE Trans. Inform. Theory*, vol. IT-25, pp. 1–7, Jan. 1979.

[97] R. J. McEliece, "CISM courses and lectures," in *Communication in the Presence of Jamming–An Information Theory Approach*, no. 279. New York: Springer, 1983.

[98] N. Merhav, "Universal decoding for memoryless Gaussian channels with deterministic interference," *IEEE Trans. Inform. Theory*, vol. 39, pp. 1261–1269, July 1993.

[99] ——, "How many information bits does a decoder need about the

channel statistics," *IEEE Trans. Inform. Theory*, vol. 43, pp. 1707–1714, Sept. 1997.

[100] N. Merhav, G. Kaplan, A. Lapidoth, and S. Shamai (Shitz), "On information rates for mismatched decoders," *IEEE Trans. Inform. Theory*, vol. 40, pp. 1953–1967, Nov. 1994.

[101] M. Mushkin and I. Bar-David, "Capacity and coding for the Gilbert–Elliott channel," *IEEE Trans. Inform. Theory*, vol. 35, pp. 1277–1290, Nov. 1989.

[102] L. H. Ozarow, S. Shamai, and A. D. Wyner, "Information theoretic considerations for cellular mobile radio," *IEEE Trans. Veh. Technol.*, vol. 43, pp. 359–378, May 1994.

[103] J. Pokorny and H. M. Wallmeier, "Random coding bound and codes produced by permutations for the multiple access channel," *IEEE Trans. Inform. Theory*, 1985.

[104] T. S. Rappaport, *Wireless Communications, Principles and Practice*. Englewood Cliffs, NJ: Prentice-Hall, 1996.

[105] B. Rimoldi and R. Urbanke, "A rate-splitting approach to the Gaussian multiple-access channel," *IEEE Trans. Inform. Theory*, vol. 42, pp. 364–375, Mar. 1996.

[106] W. L. Root, "Estimates of ϵ capacity for certain linear communication channels," *IEEE Trans. Inform. Theory*, vol. IT-14, pp. 361–369, May 1968.

[107] W. L. Root and P. P. Varaiya, "Capacity of classes of Gaussian channels," *SIAM J. Appl. Math.*, vol. 16, no. 6, pp. 1350–1393, Nov. 1968.

[108] J. Salz and E. Zehavi, "Decoding under integer metrics constraints," *IEEE Trans. Commun.*, vol. 43, nos. 2/3/4, pp. 307–317, Feb./Mar./Apr. 1995.

[109] S. Shamai, "A broadcast transmission strategy of the Gaussian slowly fading channel," in *Proc. Int. Symp. Information Theory ISIT'97* (Ulm, Germany, 1997), p. 150.

[110] S. Shamai (Shitz) and A. D. Wyner, "Information-theoretic considerations for systematic, cellular, multiple-access fading channels, Parts I and II," *IEEE Trans. Inform. Theory*, vol. 43, pp. 1877–1894, Nov. 1997.

[111] C. E. Shannon, "A mathematical theory of communication," *Bell Syst. Tech. J.*, vol. 27, pp. 379–423, 623–656, 1948.

[112] ——, "The zero error capacity of a noisy channel," *IRE Trans. Inform. Theory*, vol. IT-2, pp. 8–19, 1956.

[113] ——, "Certain results in coding theory for noisy channels," *Inform. Contr.*, vol. 1, pp. 6–25, 1957.

[114] ——, "Channels with side information at the transmitter," *IBM J. Res. Develop.*, vol. 2, no. 4, pp. 289–293, 1958.

[115] C. E. Shannon, R. G. Gallager, and E. R. Berlekamp, "Lower bounds to error probability for coding on discrete memoryless channels," *Inform. Contr.*, vol. 10, pp. 65–103, pt. I, pp. 522–552, pt. II, 1967.

[116] C. E. Shannon, "Probability of error for optimal codes in a Gaussian channel," *Bell Syst. Tech. J.*, vol. 38, pp. 611–656, May 1959.

[117] M. K. Simon, J. K. Omura, R. A. Scholtz, and B. K. Levitt, *Spread Spectrum Communications Handbook*. New York: McGraw-Hill, 1994, revised edition.

[118] S. Z. Stambler, "Shannon theorems for a full class of channels with state known at the output," *Probl. Pered. Inform.*, vol. 14, no. 4, pp. 3–12, 1975, English translation.

[119] I. G. Stiglitz, "Coding for a class of unknown channels," *IEEE Trans. Inform. Theory*, vol. IT-12, pp. 189–195, Apr. 1966.

[120] İ. E. Telatar, "Zero-error list capacities of discrete memoryless channels," *IEEE Trans. Inform. Theory*, vol. 43, pp. 1977–1982, Nov. 1997.

[121] S. Verdú, "On channel capacity per unit cost," *IEEE Trans. Inform. Theory*, vol. 36, pp. 1019–1030, Sept. 1990.

[122] S. Verdú and T. S. Han, "A general formula for channel capacity," *IEEE Trans. Inform. Theory*, vol. 40, pp. 1147–1157, July 1994.

[123] H. S. Wang and N. Moayeri, "Finite-state Markov channel—A useful model for radio communication channels," *IEEE Trans. Veh. Technol.*, vol. 44, pp. 163–171, Feb. 1995.

[124] J. Wolfowitz, "The coding of messages subject to chance errors," *Illinois J. Math.*, vol. 1, pp. 591–606, Dec. 1957.

[125] ——, "Simultaneous channels," *Arch. Rat. Mech. Anal.*, vol. 4, pp. 371–386, 1960.

[126] ——, *Coding Theorems of Information Theory*, 3rd ed. Berlin, Germany: Springer-Verlag, 1978.

[127] A. D. Wyner, "Shannon-theoretic approach to a Gaussian cellular multiple-access channel," *IEEE Trans. Inform. Theory*, vol. 40, pp. 1713–1727, Nov. 1994.

[128] A. D. Wyner, J. Ziv, and A. J. Wyner, "On the role of pattern matching in information theory," this issue, pp. 2045–2056.

[129] J. Ziv, "Universal decoding for finite-state channels," *IEEE Trans. Inform. Theory*, vol. IT-31, pp. 453–460, July 1985.

[130] J. Ziv and A. Lempel, "Compression of individual sequences via variable-rate coding," *IEEE Trans. Inform. Theory*, vol. IT-24, pp. 530–536, Sept. 1978.

Learning Pattern Classification—A Survey

Sanjeev R. Kulkarni, *Senior Member, IEEE*, Gábor Lugosi, and Santosh S. Venkatesh, *Member, IEEE*

(Invited Paper)

Abstract— Classical and recent results in statistical pattern recognition and learning theory are reviewed in a two-class pattern classification setting. This basic model best illustrates intuition and analysis techniques while still containing the essential features and serving as a prototype for many applications. Topics discussed include nearest neighbor, kernel, and histogram methods, Vapnik–Chervonenkis theory, and neural networks. The presentation and the large (thogh nonexhaustive) list of references is geared to provide a useful overview of this field for both specialists and nonspecialists.

Index Terms—Classification, learning, statistical pattern recognition, survey review.

I. INTRODUCTION

THE goal of learning theory is to provide answers to basic questions such as:

- What problems can and cannot be learned?
- How much data is required?
- What are good algorithms for learning from examples?

Hence, learning theory attempts to delineate the fundamental limitations on learning in much the same way as information theory does for communication, and the theory of computation does for computing.

Broadly speaking, by "learning" we think of an agent (the learner) immersed in an environment. The learner interacts with the environment, thereby gathering data. Using this data, together with any prior knowledge or assumptions about the environment, the learner forms some internal representation or model of the environment that is used for various tasks such as prediction, planning some future action, etc. Of course, to get concrete results one needs to specify in detail the different aspects of the model. Through specific choices on the prior assumptions, data, and success criterion, one can get a wide variety of topics generally associated with learning such as language identification, density and regression estimation, pat-tern classification, stochastic control, reinforcement learning, clustering, etc.

Work on these areas spans a number of fields and many years. In the last several decades, there was work in the 1940's and 1950's in areas such as statistics, information theory, cybernetics, and early work on neural networks that led to tremendous progress and, in fact, established several new fields of activity. Continued work in these areas, slightly later work on systems and control theory, pattern recognition, and optimization, and more recently the explosion of work on neural networks and other topics such as computational learning theory, are all part of this general area.

In this paper, we focus on a very specific subset of this work dealing with two-class pattern classification. This problem, defined below, serves as a prototype for many real-life learning problems, while the mathematical simplicity of the model allows us to gain insight into most of the difficulties arising in learning problems. However, this model by no means covers all aspects of learning. For example, the assumption of having only two classes hides many of the basic difficulties of some practical problems with a huge number of classes, such as continuous speech recognition. Also, by assuming independence of the training samples we exclude important applications where the dependence of the data is an essential feature. We do not discuss problems of feature selection (i.e., determining which measurements should serve as components of the feature vector), which, as anyone who has ever tried to build a pattern classifier fully appreciates, is one of the most important and difficult problem-specific elements of learning. We also do not include in this review problems of active learning and sequential learning. Still, the simple two-class classification model we review here is sufficiently rich and general so that one can gain useful intuition for other, perhaps more complex, learning problems.

The pattern classification problem is generally formulated as follows.[1] There are two classes of objects (or states of nature) of interest, which we will call class 0 and 1, respectively. Our information about an object is summarized by a finite number, say d, of real-valued measurements called *features*. Together, these measurements comprise a *feature vector* $x \in \Re^d$. To model the uncertainty about which class objects we encounter belong, we assume that there are *a priori* probabilities P_0 and P_1 for the two classes. To model the relationship between the class to which an object belongs and the feature vector (including uncertainty or noise in the measurement process),

Manuscript received January 30, 1998; revised June 2, 1998. The work of S. R. Kulkarni work was supported in part by the National Science Foundation under NYI Grant IRI-9457645. The work of G. Lugosis was supported by DGES under Grant PB96-0300. The work of S. S. Venkatesh was supported in part by the Air Force Office of Scientific Research under Grants F49620-93-1-0120 and F49620-92-J-0344.

S. R. Kulkarni is with the Department of Electrical Engineering, Princeton University, Princeton, NJ 08544 USA (e-mail: kulkarni@ee.princeton.edu).

G. Lugosi is with the Department of Economics, Pompeu Fabra University, 08005 Barcelona, Spain (e-mail: lugosi@upf.es).

S. S. Venkatesh is with the Department of Electrical Engineering, University of Pennsylvania, Philadelphia, PA 19104 USA (e-mail: venkatesh@ee.upenn.edu).

Publisher Item Identifier S 0018-9448(98)06083-0.

---

[1] Our notation is generally consistent with the mathematical statistics literature and follows [90].

we assume that an object in class $y \in \{0, 1\}$ engenders a random feature vector with class-conditional distribution function $F_y(x)$. Random feature vectors X (the "observables" in this process) are generated according to the following two-stage process: a random class $Y \in \{0, 1\}$ is first selected according to the *a priori* probabilities $\{P_0, P_1\}$; the observed feature vector X is then selected according to the class-conditional distribution F_Y. Given a realization of the measured feature vector $X = x$ the problem facing the classifier is to decide whether the unknown object engendering the feature vector x belongs to class 0 or 1. Thus a classifier or decision rule in this case is simply a map $g: \Re^d \to \{0, 1\}$ which indicates the class $g(x)$ to which an observed feature vector $X = x$ should be assigned. Given a classifier g, the performance of g can be measured by the *probability of error,* given by

$$L(g) = \boldsymbol{P}\{g(X) \neq Y\}.$$

If the *a priori* probabilities and conditional distributions are known, then it is well known that the optimal decision rule in the sense of minimum probability of error (or, more generally, minimum risk if different costs are assigned to different types of errors) is the *Bayes decision rule,* denoted g^*. This decision rule simply uses the known distributions and the observation $X = x$ to compute the *a posteriori* probabilities

$$\eta_0(x) = \boldsymbol{P}\{Y = 0 | X = x\}$$

and

$$\eta_1(x) = \boldsymbol{P}\{Y = 1 | X = x\}$$

of the two classes, and selects the class with the larger *a posteriori* probability (or smaller risk), i.e.,

$$g^*(x) = \arg \min_{y \in \{0, 1\}} \eta_y(x).$$

The performance of the Bayes decision rule, denoted L^*, is then given by

$$L^* = L(g^*) = \boldsymbol{E}\left[\min\{\eta_0(X), \eta_1(X)\}\right].$$

Of course, in many applications these distributions may be unknown or only partially known. In this case, it is generally assumed that in addition to the observed feature vector X, one has previous labeled observations

$$D_n = \{(X_1, Y_1), \cdots, (X_n, Y_n)\},$$

where $Y_k \in \{0, 1\}$ corresponds to the class of the objects and is assumed to form an independent and identically distributed (i.i.d.) sequence of labels drawn according to the unknown probability rule $\{P_0, P_1\}$, and X_k is a feature vector drawn according to the class-conditional distribution $F_{Y_k}(x)$. Thus the (X_k, Y_k) pairs are assumed to be independent and identically distributed according to the (unknown) distributions P_y and $F_y(x)$ characterizing the problem. Intuitively, the data D_n provide some partial information about the unknown distributions, and we are interested in using this data to find

good classifiers. Formally, a classifier (or classification rule) is a function $g_n(x) = g_n(x, D_n)$, which, based on the training data D_n, assigns a label (0 or 1) to any input point $X \in \Re^d$ to be classified. For fixed training data D_n, the conditional probability of error of such a classifier is

$$L(g_n) = \boldsymbol{P}\{g_n(X) \neq Y | D_n\}$$

where the pair (X, Y) is independent of D_n, and is drawn according to the same distribution as the one generating the training samples. The probability of error $L(g_n)$ is a random variable as it depends on the (random) training data D_n. The expected probability of error $\overline{L(g_n)} = \boldsymbol{E}L(g_n) = \boldsymbol{P}\{g_n(X) \neq Y\}$ tells us the average behavior of such a classifier (where the expectation is taken with respect to the random training data). In evaluating the performance of a classifier, we use as our benchmark the Bayes error rate L^* which is the best we could do even if we knew the distributions completely.

In selecting a classifier using a finite amount of random data, it is natural to expect that the error rate of our classifier can only be close to the optimal Bayes error rate in some probabilistic sense. One goal to aim for might be to design a so-called "*consistent rule*" such that as we get more and more training data ($n \to \infty$), we have $L(g_n) \to L^*$ in probability (which is equivalent to $\boldsymbol{E}L(g_n) \to L^*$ as $L(g_n)$ is dominated by 1). If, instead, we have $L(g_n) \to L^*$ with probability one then the rule is called *strongly consistent*. In general, given a rule the behavior of $L(g_n)$ will depend on the underlying (unknown) distribution of (X, Y). If a rule satisfies $\lim_{n\to\infty} L(g_n) = L^*$ in probability (respectively, with probability one) for *every* distribution of (X, Y) the rule is said to be *universally consistent* (respectively, *strongly universally consistent*). Of course, since it may be unrealistic to make assumptions or impossible to verify conditions on the distribution of (X, Y), if at all possible we would like to design universally consistent rules. A milestone in the theory of pattern recognition is the seminal paper of Stone [267] who first showed the existence of universally consistent rules. This gives the user the important guarantee that if a sufficient amount of data is collected, his classifier will perform almost as well as the optimal Bayes classifier, regardless of the underlying (unknown) distribution. However, this is not the end of the story. For all classification rules, the convergence to L^* may be arbitrarily slow, and, for any finite sample size n, the gap between L^* and the actual probability of error may be arbitrarily close to $1/2$ (see Cover [67], and Devroye [83]). These facts show that designing good classifiers is a highly nontrivial task, and many different points of view may be adopted.

An initial approach one might take in designing good rules is to assume the distributions are of some known simple form, and only a small number of parameters are unknown. Such "parametric methods" have been widely studied, and are useful when in fact the problem under consideration is sufficiently well-understood to warrant the parametric assumptions on the distributions. However, in many cases, one may have very little knowledge about the distributions and parametric assumptions may be quite unrealistic. Hence, the study of "nonparametric methods," and universally consistent rules, in particular, has also received a great deal of attention. The characterization of attainable performance, the search for good decision rules, and the analysis of their performance, for nonparametric statistical pattern classification, is the focus of this paper. Both "classical" and recent results are reviewed, with an emphasis on universally consistent rules. Several excellent books have been published containing much of the classical work and/or recent work. There are also many books focusing on various subtopics. A partial list includes Anthony and Biggs [13], Breiman, Friedman, Olshen, and Stone [50], Devijver and Kittler [78], Devroye, Györfi, and Lugosi [90], Duda and Hart [97], Fukunaga [116], Kearns and Vazirani [164], McLachlan [193], Natarajan [205], Vapnik [274], [275], Vapnik and Chervonenkis [277], and Vidyasagar [285]. A huge number of papers have also been written on the subjects discussed here. In the sections discussing the various subtopics we have cited a number of these papers, but we certainly have not attempted to provide an exhaustive bibliography, and we apologize for any omissions. Rather, our aim is to provide a presentation and some pointers to the literature that will be a useful overview or entry into this field for both specialists and nonspecialists.

In Section II, we discuss nearest neighbor classifiers, which conceptually are perhaps the simplest methods for pattern classification. The closely related kernel classifiers are presented in Section III, and histogram and classification trees are the subject of Section IV. These three techniques share many conceptual similarities, although the details in analysis and implementation are often quite distinct. A very different and more recent approach to the subject that has seen a great deal of recent activity is Vapnik–Chervonenkis theory, which is discussed in Section V. This approach has, among other things, provided a theoretical basis for the analysis of neural networks, which are discussed in Section VI. Work on neural networks has been pursued for the last several decades, but there has been an explosion of work in this area since the early 1980's. In the final two sections we discuss some recent work on improving and evaluating the performance of some of the more basic techniques. Specifically, Section VII describes large-margin classifiers and support vector machines, while Section VIII discusses automatic parameter selection and error estimation.

II. NEAREST NEIGHBOR CLASSIFIERS

In its original form (Fix and Hodges [111], [112]), the nearest neighbor classifier is perhaps the simplest pattern classification algorithm yet devised. In its classical manifestation, given a reference sample $D_n = \{(X_i, Y_i), 1 \leq i \leq n\}$, the classifier assigns any input feature vector to the class indicated by the label of the nearest vector in the reference sample. More generally, the k-nearest neighbor classifier maps any feature vector X to the pattern class that appears most frequently among the k-nearest neighbors. (If no single class appears with greatest frequency, then an auxiliary procedure can be invoked to handle ties.) Despite its simplicity, versions of this nonparametric algorithm discussed below are asymptotically consistent with a Bayes classifier, and are competitive with other popular classifiers in practical settings.

A. Formulation

Given a metric $d(X, X')$ on $\Re^d$ and a positive integer k, the k-nearest neighbor classifier generates a map from $\Re^d$ into $\{0, 1\}$ as a function of the reference sample D_n wherein each point $X \in \Re^d$ is mapped into one of the two classes according to the majority of the labels of its k-nearest neighbors in the reference sample. More particularly, fix any $X \in \Re^d$. We may suppose, without loss of generality, that the indices of the labeled feature vectors in D_n are permuted to satisfy

$$
\begin{aligned}
& d(X, X_1) \leq d(X, X_2) \leq \cdots \leq d(X, X_k), \\
& d(X, X_j) \geq d(X, X_k), \qquad \text{for } j = k+1, \cdots, n. \quad (1)
\end{aligned}
$$

The k-nearest neighbors of X are identified as the labeled subset of feature vectors

$$\{(X_1, Y_1), \cdots, (X_k, Y_k)\}$$

of the reference sample. The k-nearest neighbor classifier then assigns X to the class

$$Y' = \text{maj}\,(Y_1, \cdots, Y_k) \qquad (2)$$

viz., the most frequent class label exhibited by the k-nearest neighbors of X.

If k is even it is necessary to define an auxiliary procedure to handle ties in (2). (Although the equalities in (1) can also be problematic, they occur with zero probability if the class-conditional distributions are absolutely continuous.) A simple method is to break the tie according to a deterministic rule; for example, in the event that more than one class occurs with greatest frequency in the subset of k-nearest neighbors, then the input pattern could be assigned to the most prolific class in the subset with the smallest class label. A convenient way to describe deterministic tie-breaking rules such as this is to construct an *assignment partition* $(\mathcal{L}_0, \mathcal{L}_1)$ of the space $\{0, 1\}^k$ that describes the action of the k-nearest neighbor classifier for every possible ordered k-tuple of class labels. Here, $\mathcal{L}_i$ contains every ordered k-tuple, $\boldsymbol{Y} = (Y_1, \cdots, Y_k)$, representing the respective class labels of $X_1, \cdots, X_k$, for which an assignment to class i occurs. For example, if $k = 2$, then (2) with the smallest-class-label tie-breaking algorithm induces the assignment partition, $\mathcal{L}_0 = \{(0, 0), (0, 1), (1, 0)\}$ and $\mathcal{L}_1 = \{(1, 1)\}$. By introducing an extra element $\mathcal{L}_r$ into the partition, one can represent a k-nearest neighbor classifier that rejects certain input patterns (Hellman [146]). A k-nearest neighbor classifier that can be described by an assignment partition is called *deterministic*.

Random tie-breaking algorithms can be represented by a stochastic process in which an assignment partition is selected from an ensemble of partitions, according to a discrete probability distribution, prior to each assignment.

B. Classifier Risk

Write $L_n(k)$ for the probability of error of a k-nearest neighbor classifier conditioned on the random sample D_n, and let $\overline{L}_n(k) = \boldsymbol{E}(L_n(k))$ denote the expected risk. Let $L_\infty(k)$ and $\overline{L}_\infty(k)$ denote the corresponding values in the limit of an infinite sample. Some examples may help fix the notions.

Example 1. Nonoverlapping Distributions (Cover and Hart [69]): Consider a two-class problem in the d-dimensional feature space $\Re^d$. Suppose each class label $y \in \{0, 1\}$ comes equipped with a conditional density f_y which has probability-one support in a compact set A_y in $\Re^d$. Suppose further that the distance between the sets A_0 and A_1 is larger than the diameter of either set, i.e., $d(A_0, A_1) > \max\{\text{diam}(A_0), \text{diam}(A_1)\}$. As the two classes have nonoverlapping probability-one supports, it is clear that $\overline{L}_\infty(k) = L^* = 0$ for every positive integer k. Moreover, the finite-sample risk $\overline{L}_n(k)$ of the k-nearest neighbor classifier approaches its infinite-sample limit $\overline{L}_\infty(k)$ exponentially fast for fixed k as n increases. Indeed, for definiteness suppose that the two classes have equal *a priori* probabilities, $P_0 = P_1 = 1/2$, and that k is an odd integer. The classifier will make a mistake on a given class if, and only if, there are fewer than $k/2$ examples of that class in the reference sample, when

$$\overline{L}_n(k) = 2^{-n} \sum_{i=0}^{(k-1)/2} \binom{n}{i} = O(n^{(k-1)/2} 2^{-n}) \qquad (n \to \infty).$$

Note that the exponentially fast rate of convergence of $\overline{L}_n(k)$ to 0 is independent of the feature space dimension d.

Example 2. Normal Distributions: Consider the classification problem described by the two multivariate normal class-conditional densities

$$f_0(x) = \frac{1}{(2\pi\sigma^2)^{d/2}} \exp\left\{-\frac{1}{2\sigma^2}\left((x_1 - \mu)^2 + \sum_{j=2}^{d} x_j^2\right)\right\}$$

$$f_1(x) = \frac{1}{(2\pi\sigma^2)^{d/2}} \exp\left\{-\frac{1}{2\sigma^2}\left((x_1 + \mu)^2 + \sum_{j=2}^{d} x_j^2\right)\right\}$$

and *a priori* probabilities, $P_0 = P_1 = 1/2$. Here, again, the feature vectors $x = (x_1, \cdots, x_d)$ range over d-dimensional feature space $\Re^d$. A direct calculation now shows that the risk of the 1-nearest neighbor classifier tends to

$$\overline{L}_\infty(1) = \frac{1}{\sigma\sqrt{2\pi}} e^{-\mu^2/2\sigma^2} \int_0^\infty e^{-x^2/2\sigma^2} \text{sech}\left(\frac{\mu x}{\sigma^2}\right) dx.$$

For $\mu = \sigma = 1$, a numerical integration yields $\overline{L}_\infty(1) \approx 0.22480$, which may be compared with the Bayes risk, $L^* = (1/2)\,\text{erfc}(1/\sqrt{2}) \approx 0.15865$.

1) Limiting Results—Infinite Sample: The enduring popularity of the nearest neighbor classifier stems in part from its extreme simplicity and in part from its near-optimal asymptotic behavior.

As before, write $\eta_y(x) = \boldsymbol{P}\{Y = y | X = x\}$ for the posterior probability of class y given feature vector x. In a classical paper, Cover and Hart [69] showed that,

$$\overline{L}_n(k) \to \overline{L}_\infty(k)$$
$$= \sum_{y \in \{0, 1\}} \sum_{\boldsymbol{Y} \notin \mathcal{L}_y} \boldsymbol{E}[\eta_y(X)\eta_{y_1}(X)\cdots\eta_{y_k}(X)]$$
$$(n \to \infty)$$

for *any* choice of metric d. In particular, for k odd, they obtain

$$\overline{L}_\infty(k) = \sum_{y \in \{0, 1\}} \sum_{j=0}^{(k-1)/2} \binom{k}{j} \boldsymbol{E}[\eta_y(X)^j(1 - \eta_y(X))^{k-j}].$$
$$(3)$$

While Cover and Hart proved the above asymptotic formulas under some weak conditions on the class-conditional densities, Devroye [80] showed subsequently that in fact these results are true for *all distributions* of (X, Y). The fundamental result established by Cover and Hart now relates the infinite sample risk $\overline{L}_\infty(k)$ to the minimum achievable risk L^* of the Bayes classifier through the two-sided inequalities

$$L^* \leq \overline{L}_\infty(k) \leq \cdots \leq \overline{L}_\infty(5) \leq \overline{L}_\infty \leq \overline{L}_\infty(1) \leq 2L^*(1 - L^*)$$

where the upper and lower bounds are as tight as possible, in general. Thus when the Bayes risk is small, as is the case in several important pattern classification problems such as character recognition, the nearest neighbor classifier exhibits an asymptotically optimal character.

The first explicit bounds on $\overline{L}_\infty(k)$ in terms of L^* were established by Devijer [77] and Györfi and Györfi [138] who showed

$$\overline{L}_\infty(k) \leq L^* + \overline{L}_\infty(1)\sqrt{\frac{2}{\pi\lceil k/2 \rceil}}.$$

Consequently, the rate of convergence (in k) of $\overline{L}_\infty(k)$ to L^* is at least of the order of $k^{-1/2}$. A survey and tighter bounds may be found in [90, Ch. 5].

2) Finite Sample: These encouraging infinite sample results notwithstanding, the utility of this nonparametric approach as a *practical* classifier is, however, tempered by how rapidly the finite-sample risk $\overline{L}_n(k)$ converges to $\overline{L}_\infty(k)$. The previous examples demonstrate indeed that the rate of convergence of $\overline{L}_n(k)$ to $\overline{L}_\infty(k)$ depends critically on the underlying classification problem, and, moreover, can vary over a considerable range.

For problems with two pattern classes and a one-dimensional feature space, Cover [66] has shown that the infinite-sample limit is approached as rapidly as

$$\overline{L}_n(1) = \overline{L}_\infty(1) + O(n^{-2}) \qquad (n \to \infty)$$

if the probability distributions that define the classification problem are sufficiently smooth with densities that have compact probability-one support.

More generally, a result analogous to (3) may be obtained in the finite sample case by conditioning on the sample. Suppose the class-conditional distributions F_0 and F_1 are absolutely continuous with corresponding class-conditional densities f_0 and f_1, respectively. Let $f = P_0 f_0 + P_1 f_1$ denote the mixture density. Introduce the notation

$$B(\rho, X) \stackrel{\text{def}}{=} \{X' \in \Re^d : d(X', X) \leq \rho\}$$

for the closed ball of radius ρ at X, and write

$$S_j \stackrel{\text{def}}{=} B(d(X_j, X), X) \cap S \qquad (1 \leq j \leq k)$$

for points in the probability-one support S of the mixture density f at distance no more than $d(X_j, X)$ from X. The

137

indexing convention (1) can hence be written equivalently in the form

$$X_{j-1} \in S_j \qquad (2 \le j \le k).$$

For $\rho \ge 0$ and $x \in \Re^d$, let

$$\psi(\rho, x) \stackrel{\text{def}}{=} \int_{B(\rho, x)} f(x')\, dx'$$

represent the probability that a feature vector drawn from the mixture density f falls within the ball of radius ρ at x and introduce notation for the "falling factorial"

$$(m)_k \stackrel{\text{def}}{=} m(m-1) \cdots (m-k+1).$$

Simple conditioning arguments now show that the finite sample risk $\overline{L}_n(k)$ can be expressed in the exact integral form (cf., Snapp and Venkatesh [258])

$$\overline{L}_n(k) = (m)_k \int_S \int_S \int_{S_k} \cdots \int_{S_3} \int_{S_2} G(x, x_1, \cdots, x_k)$$
$$\cdot\, e^{-nh(d(x, x_k), x)}\, dx_1\, dx_2 \cdots dx_{k-1}\, dx_k\, dx \qquad (4)$$

where

$$G(x, x_1, \cdots, x_k) \stackrel{\text{def}}{=} \frac{\displaystyle\sum_{y \in \{0,1\}} P_y f_y(x) \sum_{Y \notin \mathcal{L}_y} \prod_{j=1}^{k} P_{y_j} f_{y_j}(x_j)}{(1 - \psi(d(x, x_k), x))^k}$$

and

$$h(\rho, x) \stackrel{\text{def}}{=} -\ln(1 - \psi(\rho, x)).$$

The form of the integral representation (4) for the finite sample risk is suggestive of a Laplace integral [108], and indeed, for sufficiently smooth class-conditional densities f_y with compact support, a complete asymptotic series expansion for the finite sample risk is obtainable in the form [119], [225], [259]

$$\overline{L}_n(k) \sim \overline{L}_\infty(k) + \sum_{j=2}^{\infty} c_j n^{-j/d} \qquad (n \to \infty).$$

The expansion coefficients c_j depend in general upon k, the choice of metric, and the chosen procedure for handling ties, in addition to the probability distributions that describe the classification problem under consideration, but are independent of the sample size n. The leading coefficient $\overline{L}_\infty(k)$ is just the infinite sample risk derived by Cover and Hart [69]; while $\overline{L}_\infty(k)$ depends on k and the underlying distributions; it is independent of the choice of metric as noted earlier. In particular, the rate of approach of $\overline{L}_n(k)$ to $\overline{L}_\infty(k)$ is given by

$$\overline{L}_n(k) = \overline{L}_\infty(k) + O(n^{-2/d}) \qquad (n \to \infty)$$

in accordance with Cover's result in one dimension. Note, however, that the result provides a vivid illustration of Bellman's curse of dimensionality: the finite-sample nearest neighbor risk $\overline{L}_n(k)$ approaches its infinite-sample limit $\overline{L}_\infty(k)$ only as slowly as the order of $n^{-2/d}$. Conversely, this indicates that the sample complexity demanded by the nearest neighbor algorithm to achieve acceptable levels of performance grows exponentially with the dimension d for a typical smooth classification problem. In particular, the sample complexity

n needed to achieve a finite sample risk which is ϵ-close to the infinite sample risk is asymptotically $n \sim (c_2/\epsilon)^{d/2}$.

The conditional risk $L_n(k)$, i.e., the probability of error of a k-nearest neighbor classifier for a given random sample D_n, has also been shown to converge *in probability* to $\overline{L}_\infty(k)$ under a variety of conditions [115], [136], [287]. Indeed, typical results for smooth distributions with compact, convex supports, for instance, show that

$$\boldsymbol{P}\{|L_n(k) - \overline{L}_\infty(k)| \ge \epsilon\} \le A e^{-Bn^\alpha}$$

where $A = A(\epsilon)$ and $B = B(\epsilon)$ are positive and depend on ϵ and $0 < \alpha < 1$ is independent of ϵ.

C. Refinements

1) Consistency and the Choice of k: All the asymptotic results mentioned so far concern the k-nearest neighbor rule with a fixed k and increasing sample size n. In such cases, the expected probability of error converges to a constant $\overline{L}_\infty(k)$. Also, as k increases, this limiting constant tends to L^*. A natural question arising immediately is if there is a way of increasing the value of k as the sample size grows such that the resulting k_n-nearest neighbor rule is consistent. This question was answered in a groundbreaking paper of Stone [267] who proved that the probability of error $L(g_n)$ of the k_n-nearest neighbor rule (with an appropriate tie-breaking strategy) satisfies

$$\lim_{n \to \infty} \boldsymbol{E}L(g_n) = L^*$$

for all distributions provided only that the sequence $\{k_n\}$ satisfies $k_n \to \infty$ and $k_n/n \to 0$ as $n \to \infty$. In other words, the k_n-nearest neighbor rule is universally consistent. Indeed, Stone's paper was the first to establish the existence of universally consistent rules—a startling result in 1977. In Devroye, Györfi, Krzyżak, and Lugosi [89] it is shown that the k_n-nearest neighbor rule is also *strongly* universally consistent under the same conditions on the sequence $\{k_n\}$. A partial list of related work includes Beck [39], Bhattacharya and Mack [41], Bickel and Breiman [42], Collomb [61]–[63], Devroye [81], [82], Devroye and Györfi [88], Györfi and Györfi [127], Mack [189], Stute [268], and Zhao [301].

Stone's consistency theorem suggests that the number of neighbors k considered in the decision should grow with the sample size n but not too rapidly. However, this theorem gives little guidance for the choice of k in a practical problem with (say) $n = 1500$. What makes the problem difficult is that it is impossible to determine k solely as a function of the sample size without erring grossly in most situations. As it turns out, the appropriate choice of k depends heavily on the actual distribution of (X, Y).

As Cover and Hart [69] observed, for some distributions $k = 1$ is optimal for all n! Thus the 1-nearest neighbor rule is *admissible*, i.e., there is no $k > 1$ for which the expected risk of the k-nearest neighbor classifier dominates that of the 1-nearest neighbor classifier for all distributions. This is seen most clearly in the case of nonoverlapping distributions as we saw earlier. Indeed, Devroye, Györfi, and Lugosi [90, Sec. 5.8]

138

argue further that, when L^* is small, there is little advantage in choosing k larger than 3.

However, in most practical problems the data-dependent choice of k is inevitable. We refer to Section VIII for a discussion and survey of such methods.

One way of smoothing the k-nearest neighbor decision rule is to introduce different weights to the different neighbors of the input point X, typically decreasing with the distance from X. For example, Royall [237] proposed the following classifier:

$$
g_n(X) = \begin{cases} 1, & \text{if } \displaystyle\sum_{i:Y_{(i)}(x)=1}^{k} w_i > \sum_{i:Y_{(i)}(x)=0}^{k} w_i \\ 0, & \text{otherwise} \end{cases}
$$

where $Y_1, \cdots, Y_k$ denote, as before, the labels of the (permuted) k-nearest neighbors of X (ordered according to their increasing distance from X) and $w_1, \cdots, w_k$ are the corresponding fixed weights. Bailey and Jain [19] proved the surprising result that if k is fixed, the asymptotic probability of error of a weighted k-nearest neighbor rule is minimal for all distributions if the weights are uniform (see [90, Sec. 5.5] for a simple proof), and therefore in this sense weighting is useless. However, weighting may be advantageous for finite sample sizes, and also if k and the weight vector are allowed to change with the sample size. Indeed, Stone [267] established conditions for the consistency of such rules. Data-dependent choices of the weights are also possible, see [90, Sec. 26.3].

2) Choice of Metric: Another parameter to be set by the user of the k-nearest neighbor rule is the metric according to which distances are measured. This is often a nontrivial task as different components of the input vector may represent quantities rather different in nature and which may indeed be given in different units. Therefore, the choice of metric plays an intimate role in the performance of the nearest neighbor classifier for a given sample size n. An optimal local linear distance measure is derived by Short and Fukunaga [253], while a corresponding optimal, global weighted Euclidean metric is derived by Fukunaga and Flick [117]. Snapp and Venkatesh [259] argue the merits of a weighted L^2 metric and show that for a family of smooth problems, the weighted Euclidean metric is optimal over all weighted L^p metrics of the form $\|A(x - x')\|_p$ where A is a nonsingular linear transformation and, for $x = (x_1, \cdots, x_d) \in \Re^d$,

$$
\|x\|_p \overset{\text{def}}{=} \begin{cases} \sqrt[p]{|x_1|^p + \cdots + |x_d|^p}, & \text{if } 1 \le p < \infty \\ \displaystyle\max_{1 \le i \le d} |x_i|, & \text{if } p = \infty \end{cases}
$$

is the usual L^p-norm. For the consistency of data-dependent choices of the transformation matrix A we refer to [90, Sec. 26.5].

A serious problem of nearest neighbor methods with the above mentioned metrics is that they are not scale-invariant, that is, the decision is sensitive to monotone transformations of the coordinate axes. Devroye [79] and Olshen [210] introduced a scale-invariant way of measuring empirical distances. Such a metric is of unquestionable importance in situations when

the different components of the input vector represent incomparable quantities. The universal consistency of the resulting k-nearest neighbor classifier is proved by Devroye [79].

A very large literature has burgeoned on the nearest neighbor classifier dealing with diverse issues ranging from algorithmic innovations, error estimation, imperfect samples, editing experiments, and computational concerns. For recent reviews the reader is directed to [75] and [90].

III. KERNEL CLASSIFIERS

Just like nearest neighbor rules, kernel rules classify an input point $X \in \Re^d$ according to a majority vote among the labels of the training points X_i in the vicinity of X. However, while the k-nearest neighbor rule bases the classification on the k training points that are closest to X, the simplest kernel rule considers all X_i's that are closer to X than some number $h > 0$. This simple rule is the so-called *moving-window* classifier, and is formally defined by

$$
g_n(X) = \begin{cases} 0, & \text{if } \displaystyle\sum_{i=1}^{n} I_{\{Y_i=0,\, X_i \in B(h,X)\}} \\ & \qquad \ge \displaystyle\sum_{i=1}^{n} I_{\{Y_i=1,\, X_i \in B(h,X)\}} \\ 1, & \text{otherwise} \end{cases}
$$

where, as before, $B(h, X)$ denotes the closed ball of radius h centered at X. In other words, the label assigned to X is 1 if and only if, among the training points within distance h to X, there are more points labeled by 1 than those labeled by 0.

Common sense suggests that training points very close to X should have a larger weight than those which are farther away. The moving-window rule gives uniform weight to all points within distance h and zero weight to all other points. Alternatively, a smoother transition might be desirable. This suggests the general definition of a *kernel classification rule*

$$
g_n(X) = \begin{cases} 0, & \text{if } \displaystyle\sum_{i=1}^{n} I_{\{Y_i=0\}} K\!\left(\frac{X - X_i}{h}\right) \\ & \qquad \ge \displaystyle\sum_{i=1}^{n} I_{\{Y_i=1\}} K\!\left(\frac{X - X_i}{h}\right) \\ 1, & \text{otherwise} \end{cases}
$$

where $K\colon \Re^d \to \Re$ is a *kernel* function which is usually nonnegative and monotonically decreasing along rays starting from the origin. The positive number h is called the *smoothing factor*, or *bandwidth*. This is the most important parameter of a kernel rule. It determines the amount of "smoothing." If h is small, the rule gives large relative weight to points near X, and the decision is very "local," while for a large h many more points are considered with fairly large weight, and the decision is more stable. In choosing a value for h, one confronts the same kind of problem as the bias/variance tradeoff in statistical estimation problems or the approximation error/estimation error conflict we see in Section V.

The kernel rule with the special choice $K(x) = I_{\{x \in B(1,0)\}}$ is just the moving-window rule. Other popular choices are listed below.

Gaussian kernel: $K(x) = e^{-\|x\|^2}$.

Cauchy kernel: $K(x) = 1/(1 + \|x\|^{d+1})$.

Epanechnikov kernel: $K(x) = (1 - \|x\|^2)I_{\{\|x\| \leq 1\}}$.

One may increase the flexibility of the kernel rule by allowing more than one adjustable parameter. For example, one may classify according to the sign of

$$\sum_{i=1}^{m} (2Y_i - 1)K_\theta(X - X_i)$$

where K_θ is a product kernel of the form

$$K_\theta(x) = \prod_{j=1}^{d} K\left(\frac{x^{(j)}}{h^{(j)}}\right)$$

where $\theta = (h^{(1)}, \cdots, h^{(d)})$ is a vector of smoothing factors, $x^{(j)}$ denotes the jth component of the vector x, and K is a fixed one-dimensional kernel. Here a different smoothing factor may be chosen along each coordinate.

The kernel classification rule has its origin in the kernel density estimates of Akaike [5], Parzen [213], and Rosenblatt [235], in the analogous regression estimators of Nadaraya [203], [204], and Watson [294], and in the *potential function rules* of Aizerman, Braverman, and Rozonoer [1]–[4], Bashkirov, Braverman, and Muchnik [33], Braverman [46], and Braverman and Pyatniskii [47]. For a more extensive bibliography we refer to Devroye, Györfi, and Lugosi [90].

Kernel rules are at the basis of many popular classifiers.

Example 3. Radial Basis Function Classifiers: These classifiers have a "neural" flavor and base their decision upon the sign of functions of the form

$$\sum_{i=1}^{k} a_i K\left(\frac{X - x_i}{h_i}\right)$$

where K is a kernel function (such as $K(u) = e^{-\|u\|^2}$ or $K(u) = 1/(1 + \|u\|^2)$), k is an integer, and the constants $a_1, \cdots, a_k$, $h_1, \cdots, h_k \in \Re$, and $x_1, \cdots, x_k \in \Re^d$ are determined based on the training data. Taking $k = n$, $a_i = 2Y_i - 1$, $h_i = h$, and $x_i = X_i$, we obtain the standard kernel classifier. However, typical radial basis function classifiers choose $k \ll n$, and tune the rest of the parameters according to some criterion. For example, the x_i's may be chosen as cluster centers after grouping the data points into k concentrated groups. These methods are closely related to *neural network classifiers* discussed in Section VI (see, for example, Broomhead and Lowe [51], Krzyżak, Linder, and Lugosi [172], Moody and Darken [201], Poggio and Girosi [220], and Powell [224]). Sometimes an even more general function is used of the form

$$\sum_{i=1}^{k} c_i K((X - x_i)^T A_i (X - x_i)) + c_0$$

where the A_i's are tunable $d \times d$ matrices, and $c_0, \cdots, c_k \in \Re$ and $x_1, \cdots, x_k \in \Re^d$ may also be set based on the data.

Example 4. Polynomial Discriminant Function Classifiers: The *polynomial discriminant functions* of Specht [261], [262] are also derived from kernel rules. Specht [261] suggests applying a polynomial expansion to the kernel $K((x-y)/h)$. This leads to a classifier based on the sign of the discriminant function

$$\sum_{i=1}^{n} (2Y_i - 1) \left(\sum_{j=1}^{k} \varphi_j(X_i)\varphi_j(X)\right)$$

where $\varphi_1, \cdots, \varphi_k$ are fixed real-valued functions on $\Re^d$. When these functions are polynomials, the corresponding classifier g_n is called a *polynomial discriminant function*. The discriminant function obtained this way may be written in the simple form

$$\sum_{j=1}^{k} w_{n,j}\varphi_j(X)$$

where the coefficients $w_{n,j}$ are given by

$$w_{n,j} = \sum_{i=1}^{n} (2Y_i - 1)\varphi_j(X_i).$$

This rule has computational advantages over the standard kernel rule as in many applications the data may be processed before seeing the observation X to be classified. The coefficients $w_{n,j}$ depend on the data D_n only, so classifying X amounts to computing the values of $\varphi_1(X), \cdots, \varphi_k(X)$, which may be done quickly since typically $k \ll n$. Specht's idea of expanding K reappeared recently in Vapnik's [275] popular *support vector machines* (see also Section VII). Such general rules are also examined in some more detail in Section VI where we revisit polynomial discriminant functions from a neural network vantage point.

The principal theoretical question of import for kernel rules is whether there is a choice of the kernel function K and the smoothing factor h that leads to a universally consistent classification rule. Indeed, such a consistency result may be deduced from Stone's [267] general theorem for local averaging regression estimates. For example, Devroye and Wagner [96] and Spiegelman and Sacks [263] prove that under certain regularity conditions on the kernel K, $\lim_{n\to\infty} \boldsymbol{E}L(g_n) = L^*$, whenever $h = h_n$ depends on the sample size n is such a way that

$$\lim_{n\to\infty} h_n = 0 \quad \text{and} \quad \lim_{n\to\infty} nh_n^d = \infty.$$

The first condition guarantees the local nature of the decision (i.e., small bias), while the second condition is necessary to control the statistical variation (small variance). For stronger versions, and related results, see Devroye and Györfi [88], Devroye, Györfi, and Lugosi [90], Devroye and Krzyżak [91], Greblicki, Krzyżak, and Pawlak [133], Greblicki and Pawlak [134], Krzyżak [170], Krzyżak and Pawlak [173], Wolverton and Wagner [299], and Zhao [302].

While the consistency of kernel rules is reassuring, for successful applications, much more is needed. For example, in high-dimensional spaces only very large values of h guarantee that sufficiently many data points are taken into account at the decision to compensate for statistical variation, but then the local nature of the decision is lost. Selecting a nearly optimal value of h in a data-dependent manner is a nontrivial task as the optimal smoothing factor is a complicated function of the unknown distribution and the sample size. This problem and its counterparts in density and regression estimation have driven much of the research in nonparametric statistics in the last two decades. (For a recent survey of the density estimation problem see Devroye [86].) Devroye, Györfi, and Lugosi [90, Ch. 25] argue that the smoothing problem of kernel classification is essentially different from its more thoroughly studied analogs in density estimation and regression, though it may be useful to adapt some heuristics from the latter problems to the classification problem. In [90, Ch. 25] the data-splitting method—discussed in Section VIII—is explored. Its success depends on the, appropriately defined, *complexity* of the kernel function. For an extensive discussion of the problem we refer to [90]. We review some general principles of automatic parameter selection in Section VIII.

IV. HISTOGRAMS AND CLASSIFICATION TREES

A. Histogram Classifiers

Histogram classifiers partition the feature space, and the classification of each point is made according to a majority vote within the cell of the partition in which the point falls. This simple idea has led to a huge variety of classification methods, depending on the way the space is partitioned.

The simplest of these methods is the *regular histogram rule*, which, independently of the data, partitions $\Re^d$ into congruent cubes of size h. In spite of its simplicity, this rule already has some nice theoretical properties: if $h = h_n$ decreases with the sample size such that

$$h_n \to 0 \quad \text{and} \quad nh_n^d \to \infty, \qquad \text{as } n \to \infty$$

then the regular histogram rule is strongly universally consistent (see [87] and [90]). The conditions on h express the simple requirements that i) each cell of the partition should be small enough so that the decision is "local," that is, the optimal decision may be well-approximated and ii) the cells should be large enough so that they contain sufficiently many points to "average out" statistical variation.

However, it is clear that even for moderately large dimensions the regular histogram rule has little practical use. For example, when $d = 10$, and X is distributed in $[0, 1]^{10}$, the choice $h = 1/4$ already generates over a million cells! Thus for "practical" sample sizes the intuitive requirements i) and ii) are far from being satisfied. This is further evidence of the *curse of dimensionality*.

To make partitioning classifiers worth considering for practical use, it is essential to let the partition depend on the data. By looking at the data, one may determine the regions where larger cells may be effective, and those where a finer partitioning is called for. Such methods have been proposed and studied from the birth of pattern recognition. For early work see, for example, Anderson [11], Anderson and Benning [12], Beakley and Tuteur [38], Friedman [114], Gessaman and Gessaman [126], Henrichon and Fu [145], Meisel and Michalopoulos [195], Morgan and Sonquist [202], Patrick [214], Patrick and Fisher [215], Quesenberry and Gessaman [226], and Sebestyen [247].

One may obtain significantly improved classifiers even by constructing partitions by looking only at the locations of the data points $X_1, \cdots, X_n$ and ignoring the labels $Y_1, \cdots, Y_n$. One such class of partitions is based on *statistically equivalent blocks*, where (about) the same number of data points are forced into each cell of the partition. See, for example, [11], [74], [90], [125], [126], [214], [215], and [226].

Universal consistency has been proved under various conditions on the partition generated by the data. The first such results were derived by Gordon and Olshen [130]–[132], followed by Breiman, Friedman, Olshen, and Stone [50], Chen and Zhao [57], Devroye, Györfi, and Lugosi [90], Lugosi and Nobel [183], Nobel [208], [209], and Zhao, Krishnaiah, and Chen [303].

B. Classification Trees

The most important family of partitioning classifiers are the so-called *binary tree classifiers*. Here the partition is built recursively, starting from $\Re^d$, splitting at each step a cell of the current partition. Such partitions may be conveniently represented by binary trees, where each node represents a set in the space $\Re^d$ and has exactly two or zero children. If a node u represents the set A and its children u', u'' represent A' and A'', then we require that $A = A' \cup A''$ and $A' \cap A'' = \emptyset$. In other words, a node A is split into the two sets A', A'' which are represented by its children in the tree. The root represents $\Re^d$, and the leaves, taken together, form a partition of $\Re^d$.

Typically, every split should represent a simple question such as: "Is the ith component of X less than a?" Trees which are entirely built from splits of this type are called *ordinary binary classification trees*. Such trees have some apparent advantages.

- Once the tree is built, the classification of an input point can be calculated easily.
- The classifier is transparent and easy to interpret.
- The trees are usually invariant under monotone transformations of the coordinate axes, that is, for any transformation $T: \Re^d \to \Re^d$ which maps every coordinate separately by a strictly increasing function, the classification remains unchanged if all data points are transformed, that is,

$$g_n(T(X); T(X_1), Y_1, \cdots, T(X_n), Y_n)$$
$$= g_n(X; X_1, Y_1, \cdots, X_n, Y_n).$$

Invariant classifiers are extremely important in practice as the user does not have to worry about measurement units: it does not make a difference whether the weight and the volume of an object are measured in kilograms and liters or in pounds and the logarithm of cubic inches.

Of course, splits perpendicular to the coordinate axes are not the only possibility. Another popular choice is to split cells by hyperplanes. Using computer science terminology, such trees may be called *binary space partition* (BSP) *trees*.

BSP trees were recommended for use in pattern recognition by Friedman [114], Henrichon and Fu [145], and Mizoguchi, Kizawa, and Shimura [199]; see also Argentiero, Chin, and Beaudet [17], Breiman, Friedman, Olshen, and Stone [50], Loh and Vanichsetakul [181], Park and Sklansky [211], Qing-Yun and Fu [227], and Sklansky and Michelotti [257]. In the sequel, we restrict our discussion to ordinary binary trees and refer the interested reader to [90] for a partial review of BSP tree classifiers.

The fundamental problem is, of course, how to "grow a tree," that is, how to determine the tree partition based on the training data. Consider partitions that depend only on the values $X_1, \cdots, X_n$, with the labels $Y_1, \cdots, Y_n$ used only to determine the majority vote in each cell. Begin with a tree in which we split every node perfectly, that is, if there are m points in a cell, we find the median according to one coordinate, and split the cell into two cells of sizes $\lfloor (m-1)/2 \rfloor$ and $\lceil (m-1)/2 \rceil$. Repeat this for k levels of nodes, at each level cutting along the next coordinate axis in a rotational manner. This leads to 2^k leaf regions, each having at least $n/2^k - k$ points and at most $n/2^k$ points. It is easy to see that the resulting tree is *balanced* in the sense that its height is k. In [90], such a tree is called a *median tree,* and its consistency is proved provided X has a density, and the number of levels $k = k_n$ satisfies $n/(k_n 2^{k_n}) \to \infty$ and $k_n \to \infty$ as $n \to \infty$.

Nobel [209] considers a tree-growing procedure, where, in each step, a cell is split such that the sum of the empirical *distortions*

$$\sum_{i: X_i \in A} \|X_i - c_A\|^2$$

is minimized, where the sum is taken over all cells A, and c_A denotes the empirical *centroid* of a cell defined by

$$c_A = \frac{\displaystyle\sum_{i: X_i \in A} X_i}{\displaystyle\sum_{i: X_i \in A} (1/n)}.$$

Nobel [209] proves that such a greedy growing procedure, equipped with an appropriate stopping rule, leads to a consistent classification rule under mild conditions. Such trees are also useful in *tree structured vector quantization* (see the references therein).

Other trees which solely depend on the X_i values include various versions of d-dimensional binary search trees. For a survey and several consistency results we refer to [90].

An obvious criticism that may be leveled against trees of the above kind is that discarding label information during the tree-building phase is inefficient. For example, there is no reason to split a large rectangle which contains only label 0 data points. In principle, one might search exhaustively among all binary trees with (say) k nodes and choose one which minimizes the empirical error. The performance of such a classifier may be estimated by bounding the VC growth function which is discussed in Section V. Indeed, such bounds are easy to prove; see [90] for examples.

C. Splitting Criteria

Unfortunately, an exhaustive search over all trees is clearly computationally prohibitive. The popularity and importance of binary tree classifiers lies precisely in the fact that one can hold out hope to obtain good classifiers by computationally inexpensive search. The basic principle is *greedy growing*, which means that the tree is built in a recursive manner, at each stage determining the next split by optimizing some criterion based on the data.

The splitting criterion that first comes into mind is splitting to minimize the number of errors on the training data. This criterion has its root in the classical work of Stoller [265] who analyzed a single-split rule in a univariate setting. Trees built based on this criterion were studied by Gordon and Olshen [131], Payne and Meisel [216], and Rounds [236]. It is pointed out in the last paper (and emphasized again in [50]) that the minimum-error criterion has serious drawbacks and cannot possibly lead to a universally consistent classifier. Nevertheless, Gordon and Olshen gave modifications with some built-in safeguards which are sufficient for consistency. (For example, they force split sets to contain a certain minimal number of data points and they also force splits along each coordinate axis.) These modifications are somewhat unnatural and many other splitting criteria have since been introduced, with a predecessor being the so-called AID criterion of Morgan and Sonquist [202].

Breiman, Friedman, Olshen, and Stone [50] consider a class of splitting criteria based on *impurity functions*. These criteria may be described as follows: let the function ϕ: $[0, 1] \to [0, \infty)$ be symmetric around $1/2$ with $\phi(0) = \phi(1) = 0$. Also, assume that ϕ is increasing in $[0, 1/2]$, and takes its maximum at $1/2$. Such a function ϕ is called an impurity function. The impurity of a cell A of a partition containing N_0 training points with label 0 and N_1 training points with label 1 is defined as

$$I_A = N\phi\left(\frac{N_0}{N}\right)$$

where $N = N_0 + N_1$ is the total number of training points in A. The total impurity of a partition is the sum of the impurities corresponding to all its cells. At every step of the tree-growing procedure, a cut is made to minimize the total impurity of the resulting partition. In other words, a cell A and its cut into A' and A'' are searched so that the difference $I_A - (I_{A'} + I_{A''})$ is maximal. Popular examples of such impurity functions include:

1) the *binary entropy function*

$$\phi(p) = -p \log p - (1-p) \log (1-p);$$

2) the *Gini function* $\phi(p) = 2p(1-p)$, leading to the Gini index of diversity advocated in [50];

3) the *probability of misclassification*

$$\phi(p, 1-p) = \min(p, 1-p).$$

In this case the splitting criterion is just the minimum-error criterion discussed earlier.

The number of different versions is endless, depending on the choice of the impurity function, and the method chosen to terminate the growing procedure.

Trees built by minimizing such criteria have been thoroughly studied, see, Breiman, Friedman, Olshen, and Stone [50], Burshtein, Della Pietra, Kanevsky, and Nádas [55], Chou [58], Ciampi [59], Gelfand and Delp [122], Gelfand, Ravishankar, and Delp [123], [124], Goodman and Smyth [129], Guo and Gelfand [135], Li and Dubes [179], Michel-Briand and Milhaud [196], Quinlan [228], Sethi [248], Sethi and Sarvarayudu [249], Talmon [270], Wang and Suen [292], among others.

To understand the danger of impurity-based growing algorithms, consider the Gini criterion, which determines a split by minimizing the sum of

$$\frac{N_0 N_1}{N_0 + N_1}$$

for every cell A. Since this quantity only depends on the *ratio* of the label 0 and label 1 points in each cell: cells containing very few points will be preferentially split as improvement is much easier to achieve there. To remedy this anomaly, in their procedure CART, Breiman, Friedman, Olshen, and Stone [50] suggest a *growing-and-pruning* algorithm, where they let the tree grow until every cell contains just a few points, and then they use a clever algorithm to "prune" it to determine the best subtree.

In Devroye, Györfi, and Lugosi [90, Ch. 20] it is shown that with an easy modification of the Gini criterion one can get good performance even without additional pruning. If, instead of the Gini criterion, the sum of the $N_0 N_1$ is minimized (i.e., the normalization by the total number of points in a cell is dropped), then all large inhomogeneous cells will be split. Indeed, they show that if the tree is based on this criterion such that splits are rotated along all coordinate axes, a simple stopping criterion suffices to achieve universal consistency of the resulting tree classifier.

Still, all the above methods are somewhat intuitively unappealing as the impurity functions (except, of course, the probability of misclassification) are not directly connected to the empirical probability of error, and artificial devices such as pruning and forced rotated splits have to be added.

There is no reason for pessimism, however. An "almost" greedy minimization of misclassification training error still leads to a good classifier. All one has to do is to "look ahead" $2d$ steps in the search (recall that d is the dimensionality of the feature space) and find, at each step, the cell with the best $2d$ splits which minimizes the training error of the resulting classifier. As shown in [90, Theorem 20.9], if tree growth is stopped after $k = k_n$ splits, then the tree classifier is universally consistent provided that $k_n \to \infty$ and $k_n = o(\sqrt{n/\log n})$.

V. VAPNIK–CHERVONENKIS THEORY

One common approach in pattern classification is to restrict the form of the classifier to belong to some class, $\mathcal{C}$, of decision rules. Such a restriction might be used as a result of prior knowledge about a problem domain, introduced for purposes

of efficiency and simplicity, or might arise implicitly as a result of the learning algorithm and architecture selected. For example, in neural networks, fixing the architecture and size of the network imposes a restriction on the class of decision rules that can be implemented by the network—namely, those rules computed by the network over all choices of the weights. A basic question of interest is to understand how learning performance depends on the class of rules $\mathcal{C}$.

Of course, with a restriction on the classifier, in general we cannot hope to perform as well as the optimal Bayes decision rule, even with a very large number of samples. Hence, we should attempt only to try to find the best rule from within the class $\mathcal{C}$. Moreover, with a finite amount of random data, we cannot hope to always find the optimal rule from $\mathcal{C}$. Therefore, for finite sample sizes it is natural to strive only to find some near-optimal classifier, and only require that we succeed in some probabilistic sense. Much early and fundamental work related to this approach to pattern classification was done in the probability and statistics literature—c.f. Dudley [99], Pollard [221], and Vapnik and Chervonenkis [274], [276], [278]. The paper of Valiant [273] spurred recent work in the computer science community in this area as well as introduced the terminology PAC learning, the acronym standing for *probably-approximately-correct learning* (cf., Haussler [140] and references, therein). Details on various aspects of this approach can be found in a number of books; cf., [13], [90], [164], [274], [275], and [285].

A. Formulation

Let $\mathcal{C}$ be a collection of mappings ϕ: $\Re^d \to \{0, 1\}$ and let $L_{\mathcal{C}}^* = \inf_{\phi \in \mathcal{C}} L(\phi)$. Then, given the data $D_n = ((X_1, Y_1), \cdots, (X_n, Y_n))$, we seek a rule $\phi \in \mathcal{C}$ such that $L(\phi) \approx L_{\mathcal{C}}^*$. Unfortunately, the performance $L(\phi)$ of a rule ϕ is unknown, in general, and the only information available to assess the performance of ϕ is the data D_n. Thus a natural approach is to select a rule from the class $\mathcal{C}$ that looks best on the data. Namely, for a given ϕ, let the *empirical error probability* of ϕ be defined as

$$\hat{L}_n(\phi) = \frac{1}{n} \sum_{i=1}^{n} I_{\{\phi(X_i) \neq Y_i\}}$$

i.e., $\hat{L}_n(\phi)$ is the fraction of examples labeled incorrectly by the *hypothesis*[2] $\phi \in \mathcal{C}$, or, more succinctly, the relative frequency of errors by ϕ on the sample D_n. Let

$$\phi_n^* = \arg \min_{\phi \in \mathcal{C}} \hat{L}_n(\phi).$$

Then ϕ_n^* is a rule in $\mathcal{C}$ that minimizes the "empirical risk," and the hope is that such a rule will in fact also be close to minimizing the actual risk.

To gain some insight into this problem, recall that the Bayes error L^* is the absolute best one could hope for, while $L_{\mathcal{C}}^*$ is the best one could hope for using rules from $\mathcal{C}$. We can write how much worse ϕ_n^* is than the Bayes classifier as follows:

$$L(\phi_n^*) - L^* = (L(\phi_n^*) - L_{\mathcal{C}}^*) + (L_{\mathcal{C}}^* - L^*). \quad (5)$$

---

[2] The terminology is from computational learning theory.

143

The second term $L_C^* - L^*$ (often called the *approximation error*) represents how much we lose in performance by restricting our classifier to come from C. That is, we have no reason to expect that C will contain the optimal Bayes classifier, and $L_C^* - L^*$ represents the closest we can possibly approximate the performance of the optimal Bayes classifier using rules from C. The first term $(L(\phi_n^*) - L_C^*)$ (often called the *estimation error*) represents how much we lose in performance by our lack of knowledge of the exact performance of the various rules from C. That is, the only way we have to judge the performance of the various rules from C is to use the data, and $(L(\phi_n^*) - L_C^*)$ is the loss we incur by estimating the actual performance by the empirical performance.

There is an inherent tradeoff in the two error terms. For a very "rich" class of rules C, we would expect the second term to be small, since we would have the representational power to closely approximate Bayes rule (whatever it might actually be). On the other hand, this approximation ability comes at the price of reducing our confidence in conclusions drawn from limited data. With a very rich collection of rules, there is a greater danger that some rule from C just happens to fit very well the particular data observed so far, but may be unlikely to fit new data.

B. VC Dimension and Empirical Risk Minimization

Vapnik and Chervonenkis [276] introduced the following combinatorial measure of the "richness" of a class C that characterizes the behavior of the estimation error. First, observe that any classifier in C can also be identified with the subset of $\Re^d$ which the classifier maps to class 1. Thus we may think of the class C as a collection of subsets of $\Re^d$. This interpretation of classifiers in C is used in the following definition.

Definition 1: Given a set of points $\Sigma = \{x_1, \cdots, x_n\} \subset \Re^d$, let $\Delta_C(\Sigma)$ denote the number of subsets of Σ generated by intersection with C, that is, the number of distinct sets of the form $\Sigma \cap \phi$ for $\phi \in C$. The nth *shatter coefficient* of C is defined as

$$s(C, n) = \max_{\Sigma = \{x_1, \cdots, x_n\} \subset \Re^d} \Delta_C(\Sigma).$$

The set $\Sigma = \{x_1, \cdots, x_n\}$ is said to be *shattered* by the class C if $\Delta_C(\Sigma) = 2^n$. The *Vapnik–Chervonenkis* (VC) *dimension* of the class C, denoted V_C, is the largest integer n such that there exists a set of cardinality n that is shattered by C. If there exist sets of arbitrarily large (integer) cardinality that are shattered by C, then C is said to have infinite VC dimension.

The main result states that as long as the classifiers in C satisfy some mild measurability conditions, empirical risk minimization works in the sense that the estimation error $(L(\phi_n^*) - L_C^*)$ (the first term in (5)) converges to zero uniformly in probability if and only if, $V_C < \infty$. Moreover, rates of convergence can be obtained thereby giving bounds on the amount of data required for a given level of performance.

The key idea behind this result is a symmetrization argument used to prove a bound on the deviations of empirical probabilities of events from their true probabilities. Namely, given a class of events $\mathcal{A}$, Vapnik and Chervonenkis [276] showed

in their landmark paper that the following explicit bound:

$$P \left\{ \sup_{A \in \mathcal{A}} |\hat{P}_n(A) - P(A)| > \epsilon \right\} \le 8s(\mathcal{A}, n) e^{-n\epsilon^2/8} \quad (6)$$

holds for *every* distribution P, where $\hat{P}_n(A)$ is the empirical probability of event A on an n-sample drawn by independent sampling from the probability measure P. This type of result is also closely related to the so-called "uniform laws of large numbers." Of course, the above inequality is useful only if the shatter coefficient grows at a subexponential rate. At first glance it is not clear how one can obtain manageable conditions for such subexponential growth. Luckily, a beautiful combinatorial result, known as the Vapnik–Chervonenkis lemma (also called Sauer's lemma in the computational learning literature), gives an easy characterization. The result, proved independently by Sauer [242] and Vapnik and Chervonenkis [276], states that for any class of sets $\mathcal{A}$

$$s(\mathcal{A}, n) \le \sum_{j=0}^{V_{\mathcal{A}}} \binom{n}{j}. \quad (7)$$

It is easy to see that the right-hand side is bounded above by $1 + n^{V_{\mathcal{A}}}$ for all n and $V_{\mathcal{A}}$, while for $n \ge V_{\mathcal{A}}$ the sharper bound $s(\mathcal{A}, n) \le (ne/V_{\mathcal{A}})^{V_{\mathcal{A}}}$ can be derived with just a modicum of effort. It follows that the nth shatter coefficient $s(\mathcal{A}, n)$ has subexponential (polynomial) growth whenever $V_{\mathcal{A}} < \infty$ (while, of course, $s(\mathcal{A}, n) = 2^n$ for all n when $V_{\mathcal{A}} = \infty$). It follows that the right-hand side of (6) tends to zero as $n \to \infty$ for all distributions provided only that $V_{\mathcal{A}} < \infty$.

This elegant "distribution-free" result can be applied directly to the pattern recognition problem to get uniform bounds on the deviations of empirical error rates of a collection of classifiers from their true error rates, that is, bounds on $\sup_{\phi \in C} |\hat{L}_n(\phi) - L(\phi)|$, which in turn imply the success of empirical risk minimization for a class C with finite VC dimension. To see how results on uniform convergence of the type (6) may be used in pattern recognition, define the *error of* ϕ to be the set $A_\phi = \{(x, y) : \phi(x) \ne y\}$, and identify the class of events $\mathcal{A}$ with the class of error events: $\mathcal{A} = \{A_\phi : \phi \in C\}$. It is easy to argue that $V_{\mathcal{A}} = V_C$ so that the Vapnik–Chervonenkis bound takes the form

$$P \left\{ \sup_{\phi \in C} |\hat{L}_n(\phi) - L(\phi)| > \epsilon \right\} \le 8 \left(\frac{ne}{V_C} \right)^{V_C} e^{-n\epsilon^2/8}$$

$$(n \ge V_C). \quad (8)$$

A little reflection now shows that

$$L(\phi_n^*) - L_C^* \le 2 \sup_{\phi \in C} |\hat{L}_n(\phi) - L(\phi)|. \quad (9)$$

This simple inequality points out that if the empirical error $\hat{L}_n(\phi)$ is a good estimate of the true probability of error $L(\phi)$ *uniformly* for every $\phi \in C$, then the probability of error of any classifier selected by minimizing the empirical error is close to the best possible error in the class. Now the Vapnik–Chervonenkis inequality (8) may be used directly to obtain upper bounds for the estimation error $L(\phi_n^*) - L_C^*$. For example, given any error parameter $\epsilon > 0$ and confidence parameter $\delta > 0$, no more than $(c'/\epsilon^2)(V_C \log(1/\epsilon) + \log(1/\delta))$

training samples are required (for some positive constant c') to ensure that with probability at least $1 - \delta$ the estimation error will be less than ϵ. This formulation is popular in the PAC learning literature.

An essentially equivalent, somewhat simpler formulation results from a consideration of the expected probability of error $EL(\phi_n^*)$ and in the sequel we focus on this measure. From (8) and (9), one may easily deduce that, for some universal constant c,

$$EL(\phi_n^*) - L_{\mathcal{C}}^* \leq c\sqrt{\frac{V_{\mathcal{C}} \log n}{n}}.$$

Thus one of the main messages of the Vapnik–Chervonenkis inequality is that if the VC dimension of the class $\mathcal{C}$ is finite, then the estimation error converges to zero at the rate $O\left(\sqrt{V_{\mathcal{C}} \log n / n}\right)$ *for all distributions* of (X, Y). The beauty and power of this result lies in its distribution-free nature and in the fact that the properties of the class are reflected through the simple combinatorial parameter $V_{\mathcal{C}}$.

A question arising immediately relates to the tightness of the inequality (6). An immediate improvement may be effected via another inequality of Vapnik and Chervonenkis [277], who improved (6) to

$$P\left\{\sup_{A \in \mathcal{A}} \frac{P(A) - \hat{P}_n(A)}{\sqrt{P(A)}} > \epsilon\right\} \leq 4s(\mathcal{A}, 2n)e^{-n\epsilon^2/4}. \quad (10)$$

(See Anthony and Shawe-Taylor [14] for a beautiful short proof.) The above inequality implies

$$EL(\phi_n^*) - L_{\mathcal{C}}^* \leq c \max\left(\sqrt{\frac{L_{\mathcal{C}}^* V_{\mathcal{C}} \log n}{n}}, \frac{V_{\mathcal{C}} \log n}{n}\right)$$

where c is a universal constant. This result points out an important phenomenon: if the smallest achievable error in the class $L_{\mathcal{C}}^*$ happens to be small, much smaller estimation errors are achievable than that predicted by the basic Vapnik–Chervonenkis inequality (6). For the special case $L_{\mathcal{C}}^* = 0$ (which is a common assumption in the PAC learning literature) one may even improve the order of magnitude of the estimate (i.e., one obtains $O(V_{\mathcal{C}} \log n / n)$ instead of $O\left(\sqrt{V_{\mathcal{C}} \log n / n}\right)$). The tightness of the above upper bound is reflected by corresponding lower bounds. For example, Devroye and Lugosi [92] prove that for *any* classification rule g_n and for any class $\mathcal{C}$ there exists a distribution of (X, Y) with $\inf_{\phi \in \mathcal{C}} L(\phi) = L_{\mathcal{C}}^*$ such that

$$EL(g_n) - L_{\mathcal{C}}^* \geq c' \max\left\{\sqrt{\frac{L_{\mathcal{C}}^* V_{\mathcal{C}}}{n}}, \frac{V_{\mathcal{C}}}{n}\right\}$$

where c' is another universal constant. For related lower bounds see also Antos and Lugosi [15], Blumer, Ehrenfeucht, Haussler, and Warmuth [44], Devroye, Györfi, and Lugosi [90], Ehrenfeucht, Haussler, Kearns, and Valiant [107], Haussler, Littlestone, and Warmuth [141], Schuurmans [246], Simon [255], [256], and Vapnik and Chervonenkis [277].

Thus the upper bound achieved by (10) is optimal up to a logarithmic factor. Quite a lot of effort has been invested in closing this gap. It follows from a now classical result of Dudley that for some constant c

$$EL(\phi_n^*) - L_{\mathcal{C}}^* \leq c\sqrt{\frac{V_{\mathcal{C}}}{n}}$$

(see, e.g., Ledoux and Talagrand [177], and Pollard [222], [223]). For the special case $L_{\mathcal{C}}^* = 0$, a beautiful result of Haussler, Littlestone, and Warmuth [141] states that, even though in this case the $\log n$ factor is necessary if one considers an arbitrary ϕ_n^* minimizing the empirical risk, there exists a classifier g_n such that

$$EL(g_n) \leq \frac{V_{\mathcal{C}}}{n}.$$

The inequalities (6) and (10) are hence extremely important from both theoretical and practical points of view. Several versions of the original inequalities have been derived since, mostly improving on the constants. For lack of space, here we only give a list of references for such improvements: Alexander [7], Devroye [84], Lugosi [182], Massart [190], Parrondo and Van den Broeck [212], Shawe-Taylor, Anthony, and Biggs [250], and Talagrand [269].

Many interesting examples of classes with finite VC dimension are known. (See, for example, [65], [95], [254], [264], [276], and [295] among others.) Below, in Section VI, we discuss some important examples. Also some general results on VC dimension bounds have been obtained. Among the most interesting of such bounds are those that relate the VC dimension of a class $\mathcal{C}$ to bounds on the covering numbers of $\mathcal{C}$ with respect to metrics induced by probability measures. Covering numbers (and the closely related notion of metric entropy) were introduced by Kolmogorov and Tihomirov [167] and arise naturally in a number of problems in approximation, statistics, and information theory. In the present context, given a probability measure P on $\Re^d$, a pseudometric on $\mathcal{C}$ (and, actually, on the set of all measurable subsets of $\Re^d$) can be defined by

$$d_P(\phi_1, \phi_2) = E|\phi_1(X) - \phi_2(X)|.$$

The covering number $N(\epsilon, \mathcal{C}, d_P)$ is defined as the smallest number of ϵ-balls required to cover $\mathcal{C}$. The known results typically provide upper and lower bounds on $\sup_P N(\epsilon, \mathcal{C}, d_P)$ in terms of the VC dimension of $\mathcal{C}$ (e.g., some known results are summarized in [174]). The upper bounds are the deeper results and the fundamental result along this line was obtained by Dudley [99], which was subsequently refined by Pollard [221] and more recently by Haussler [140]. These bounds imply that under some weak measurability conditions, $\sup_P N(\epsilon, \mathcal{C}, d_P) < \infty$ for all $\epsilon > 0$ if and only if $V_{\mathcal{C}} < \infty$ where the sup is taken over all distributions of X. Covering numbers enter naturally in learning problems when one replaces an infinite class of rules $\mathcal{C}$ by a carefully selected finite subset of rules, and then attempts to use empirical risk minimization (or other learning rule) over this finite subcollection. Work along these lines can be found in [40], [53], [102], [155], [175], [274], and [285].

C. Complexity Regularization

We end this section with a discussion of a subject that goes by various names such as structural risk minimization [274], [275] and complexity regularization [22], [185]. The basic idea is to select a classifier from a collection of classifiers (or *models*) by trading off the misfit of the classifier on the observed data with the complexity of the classifier measured in an appropriate way. Such approaches are also closely related to ideas such as Ockham's razor, Rissanen's Minimum Description Length (MDL) principle [232], Akaike's information criterion (AIC) [6], and other complexity-based methods (e.g., as studied by Barron and Cover [22], [30]). To understand the motivation of these methods, consider the approximation error/estimation error tradeoff in (5) again: as discussed earlier, a rich class $\mathcal{C}$ favors the approximation error term $L_{\mathcal{C}}^* - L^*$ at the expense of the estimation error term $L(\phi_n^*) - L_{\mathcal{C}}^*$, while for a fixed class $\mathcal{C}$, the approximation error may be unsatisfactorily large (say close to $1/2$). If we are not content with this situation, an alternative might be to consider a richer class of rules to improve the approximation error as long as the estimation error remains satisfactory.

One approach to carry out this tradeoff is to consider a hierarchy of classes $\mathcal{C}^{(1)}, \mathcal{C}^{(2)}, \cdots$ such that $V_{\mathcal{C}^{(j)}} < \infty$ for each j, but with $V_{\mathcal{C}^{(j)}} \to \infty$ as $j \to \infty$. Then we can select a rule from one of the classes $\mathcal{C}^{(j)}$ where the choice of j can, in general, depend on both how much data we have as well as the specific observations D_n. The idea is roughly that with only a small amount of data we should restrict ourselves to selecting a "simple" rule (i.e., one from a class with small j), but when there is a wealth of data we may be justified in selecting a rule from a richer class (i.e., one with large j). Now, if the classes $\mathcal{C}^{(j)}$ are chosen so that for any distribution of (X, Y), the corresponding Bayes decision rule can be approximated arbitrarily well using rules from the classes $\mathcal{C}^{(j)}$ (i.e., so that $\lim_{i \to \infty} L_{\mathcal{C}^{(i)}}^* = L^*$), then one might hope to be able to get consistency via the tradeoff discussed above.

It turns out that this can be done rather simply as follows. Assume, as before, that $V_{\mathcal{C}^{(j)}} < \infty$ for each j, and that for any distribution of (X, Y) we have $\lim_{i \to \infty} L_{\mathcal{C}^{(i)}}^* = L^*$. For each n, we select an integer k_n, and select a classifier ϕ_n^* that minimizes empirical risk over the class $\mathcal{C}^{(k_n)}$. Then, if the sequence $\{k_n\}$ satisfies the properties $k_n \to \infty$ and $V_{\mathcal{C}^{(k_n)}} \log(n)/n \to 0$ as $n \to \infty$, the classifier ϕ_n^* is strongly universally consistent.

Thus k_n selects the complexity of the class from which we select the decision rule. The conditions on k_n guarantee that both the approximation and estimation errors will converge to zero. Once the classes $\mathcal{C}^{(j)}$ are fixed (and, hence, $V_{\mathcal{C}^{(j)}}$ is known for each j) then a suitable sequence $\{k_n\}$ can be fixed independently of the data so as to guarantee strong consistency. However, as one might expect, fixing the sequence $\{k_n\}$ in advance may not give the best tradeoff of the estimation and approximation errors for all distributions. It is possible to obtain much better results in general through a data-dependent choice of k_n. Such an approach was studied by Vapnik [274] using the term "structural risk minimization." A version using the term "complexity regularization" was recently provided by Lugosi and Zeger [185] and can be summarized as follows. Given the data D_n, for each j select a decision rule $\phi_{n,j}$ from the class $\mathcal{C}^{(j)}$ that minimizes the empirical risk and define the complexity penalty

$$r(n, j) = \sqrt{\frac{32}{n} V_{\mathcal{C}^{(j)}} \log(en)}.$$

Let ϕ_n^* be that classifier among the $\phi_{n,j}$ that minimizes the sum

$$\tilde{L}_n(\phi_{n,j}) = \hat{L}_n(\phi_{n,j}) + r(n, j).$$

For this decision rule and with the previous conditions on the $\mathcal{C}^{(j)}$, it can be shown (e.g., see [185]) that for any distribution of (X, Y) we have

$$\boldsymbol{E} L(\phi_n^*) - L^* \leq \inf_{j \geq 1} \left(c\sqrt{\frac{V_{\mathcal{C}^{(j)}} \log n}{n}} + (L_{\mathcal{C}^{(j)}}^* - L^*) \right)$$

where c is some universal constant. In other words, the method of structural risk minimization automatically finds the optimal balance between the approximation error $L_{\mathcal{C}^{(j)}}^* - L^*$ and a tight upper bound of the estimation error. Thus even though the optimal value of j depends heavily on the unknown distribution, it can be learned from the data. As mentioned above, and as can be seen by the form of $\tilde{L}_n(\phi_{n,j})$, this approach is closely related to other complexity-based methods all of which utilize a misfit versus complexity tradeoff (the first term of $\tilde{L}_n(\phi_{n,j})$ is the misfit of the hypothesis with the data, while the second term is the complexity of the hypothesis). Related results and refinements may be found in the work of Barron, Birgé, and Massart [28], Kearns *et al.* [162], Krzyżak and Linder [171], Meir [194], Modha and Masry [200], Shawe-Taylor *et al.* [252], and Yang and Barron [300].

VI. NEURAL NETWORKS

The vast literature on linear discriminant functions in pattern classification begins with a classical paper of Fisher [110]. These functions have seen more attention (perhaps undeservedly) than any other largely because they are so amenable to analysis. However, they are severely limited in the class of problems to which they can be applied. The extension of the linear discriminant ideas to more flexible, complex, nonlinear "neural" forms had its antecedents in a groundbreaking article in 1943 [191] in which McCulloch and Pitts published the first mathematical codification of aspects of brain function. In their article they outlined how simple mathematical assemblies of formal neurons, modeled very crudely on biological cells and assemblies, could be used to define a basis for a logical calculus of computation. A rich variety of "neural" computational paradigms which have proved effective in a variety of computation and decision problems have evolved in the half-century following McCulloch and Pitts' paper. (For a nonexhaustive chronology and surveys see [8], [10], [16], [27], [29], [142], [147], [165], [198], [230], [231], [234], [240] and the references contained therein.) In the standard setting, an (artificial) neural network is an assembly of formal computational elements operating collectively on a

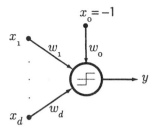

Fig. 1.   Linear threshold element.

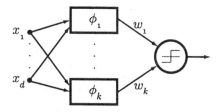

Fig. 2.   Canonical threshold element.

discrete time scale[3] and interconnected in various ways with the outputs of some elements functioning as inputs to others. If there is no feedback (i.e., the network is *acyclic*), given a set of external inputs, computation can be viewed as flowing through the network resulting ultimately in the computation of a given function of the inputs at those computational elements tagged as "output" units. The nature of the computation that is performed is dictated by the elementary computational unit that is used in the network and the graph of interconnections that describes the network architecture.

A. Neuron and Network Models

1) Formal Neurons: In the classical model of McCulloch and Pitts, a formal neuron is a *linear threshold element*, i.e., a nonlinear computational element which computes a binary decision based on the sign of a linear form of its inputs. More specifically, a generic linear threshold element accepts d real inputs $x_1, \cdots, x_d$ and produces as output a binary value (which we hereafter identify as ± 1 for definiteness) according to the threshold rule

$$y = \operatorname{sgn}\left(\sum_{i=1}^{d} w_i x_i - w_0\right) = \begin{cases} -1, & \text{if } \sum_{i=1}^{d} w_i x_i < w_0 \\ +1, & \text{if } \sum_{i=1}^{d} w_i x_i \geq w_0. \end{cases}$$

The linear threshold element is completely specified by the real parameters $w_1, \cdots, w_d$ called the *weights,* and the real value w_0 called the *threshold*. Observe that the threshold can be subsumed within the sum by the simple expedient of adding a fixed extra input, say $x_0 = -1$, as indicated schematically in Fig. 1. It will be occasionally notationally convenient to hence pretend that the threshold is identically zero, when $y = \operatorname{sgn}\left(\sum_i w_i x_i\right)$.

While this simple computational model has much to commend it, as we will see in the denouement, for the moment note just that the model incorporates a linear accumulation of inputs that allows a systematic integration of input information and a nonlinear comparison or thresholding operation which provides the critical nonlinear decision-making or logic capability. Observe that, viewed as a pattern classification device, a linear threshold element dichotomizes d-dimensional feature space $\Re^d$ into two half-spaces separated by the hyperplane

$\sum_i w_i x_i = 0$. The class of linear threshold functions (or *linear discriminant functions*) is exactly the class of decision functions from $\Re^d$ into $\{-1, +1\}$ that can be computed by such a device by varying the real weights w_i.

A natural extension of the basic linear threshold computational element computes the sign of a polynomial form of the inputs. More specifically, let

$$\mathcal{I}_D = \{I = (i_1, \cdots, i_D) \colon i_j \in \{0, 1, \cdots, d\}, j = 1, \cdots, D\}$$

denote the family of ordered multisets of cardinality D of the set $\{0, 1, \cdots, d\}$. Observe that $|\mathcal{I}_D| = (d+1)^D$. For each multiset $I = (i_1, \cdots, i_D)$ in $\mathcal{I}_D$, define the polynomial map $\varphi_I \colon \Re^d \to \Re$ by

$$\varphi_I(x) \stackrel{\text{def}}{=} x_I = \prod_{j=1}^{D} x_{i_j},$$

$$x = (x_0, x_1, \cdots, x_d) \in \{-1\} \times \Re^d.$$

A *polynomial threshold element of degree D* is specified by a set of weights w_I ($I \in \mathcal{I}_D$) and maps $\Re^d$ into $\{-1, +1\}$ according to the rule

$$y = \operatorname{sgn}\left(\sum_{I \in \mathcal{I}_D} w_I x_I\right) = \operatorname{sgn}\left(\sum_{I \in \mathcal{I}_D} w_I \varphi_I(x)\right).$$

For instance, when $D = 1$ we obtain hyperplane separating surfaces (recall $x_0 = -1$ subsumes the threshold) and when $D = 2$ we obtain quadrics (hyperhyperboloids) as separating surfaces. For general D, the separating surfaces are Dth-order rational varieties (cf. [52], [65], and [283]).

More generally, let $\varphi_1, \cdots, \varphi_k$ be a fixed set of measurement functions mapping $\Re^d$ into $\Re$ and write $\varphi = (\varphi_1, \cdots, \varphi_k)$ for the corresponding vector of measurement functions. A canonical neuron (or *canonical threshold element*) is specified by a set of k weights w_j ($1 \leq j \leq k$) and the set of measurement function φ and computes the φ-threshold function from $\Re^d$ into $\{-1, +1\}$ specified by

$$y = \operatorname{sgn}\left\{\sum_{j=1}^{k} w_j \varphi_j(x_1, \cdots, x_d)\right\}.$$

Such functions are also called φ-functions in the literature (cf. [65], [207]).

An extension of the neural model in another direction is obtained by replacing the threshold function by some fixed *activation function* $\sigma \colon \Re \to \Re$. The formal neuron thus obtained computes a mapping from $\Re^d$ into $\Re$ of the form

$$y = \sigma\left(\sum_{i=0}^{d} w_i x_i\right).$$

---

[3] Neurodynamical system models with system states evolving over continuous time have also been investigated in diverse settings where it is important to track the temporal evolution of a system. See, for instance, [9], [60], [148], [152], [217], and [218].

The most popular activation functions in practice are the *sigmoids* which are measurable functions defined most generally by the property

$$\sigma(t) \rightarrow \begin{cases} -1, & \text{if } t \rightarrow -\infty \\ +1, & \text{if } t \rightarrow +\infty. \end{cases}$$

(The limiting values ± 1 are not critical—0 and 1, for instance, would do just as well; we select these limits to keep consistency with the definition of the sgn function.) The following are admissible choices for sigmoids, encountered most frequently in practice:

Threshold activation:

$$\sigma(t) = \text{sgn}(t).$$

Piecewise-linear activation:

$$\sigma(t) = \begin{cases} -1, & \text{if } t \leq -1 \\ t, & \text{if } -1 < t < +1 \\ +1, & \text{if } t \geq +1. \end{cases} \tag{11}$$

Logistic activation:

$$\sigma(t) = \tanh\left(\frac{t}{2}\right) = \frac{1 - \exp(-t)}{1 + \exp(-t)}. \tag{12}$$

For any sigmoid σ, observe that $\sigma(t/T)$ converges pointwise to $\text{sgn}(t)$ (except possibly at $t = 0$) as the "annealing factor" $T \rightarrow 0$. Sigmoid activation functions are hence the natural generalization of the threshold activation function. While there is some biological evidence in favor of sigmoid activations (cf. [103], [104], [218]), the popularity of sigmoid neurons as the basic computational element in neural networks devolves largely upon the existence of *ad hoc* learning algorithms for training a network of sigmoid neurons from examples when σ is chosen to be sufficiently smooth.

2) Networks: A neural network is a collection of formal neurons (linear threshold elements, polynomial or canonical threshold elements, or sigmoid neurons) interconnected by having the output of each neuron function as input to any subcollection of neurons. In addition, a designated set of neurons receive external inputs, while another designated set of neurons is identified as a set of output elements. Formally, the architecture of a network is specified by a directed graph $G = \langle V, E \rangle$.

- *Vertex set V:* The set of vertices V is comprised of a set of *source nodes* (corresponding to the set of external inputs) together with a set of *computation nodes* (corresponding to the neurons in the network) some of which are designated as output nodes. For networks of sigmoid neurons, the node functionality of an output node is frequently distinguished from the rest of the network comprising, for instance, just a linear form of its inputs (in function approximation settings), or with an added threshold to produce a binary value (in pattern recognition or decision function settings).

- *Edge set E:* A directed edge (i, j) is present in the set of edges E if, and only if, i is a source node, j is a computation node, and i is connected to j, or i and j are computation nodes with the output of i serving as an input to j.

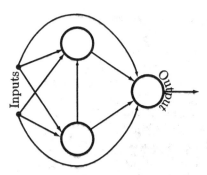

Fig. 3. Acyclic network.

Neural network architectures may be partitioned into two families based on whether the underlying graph has cycles.

A network is *acyclic* if its architectural graph has no cycles. Network functionality is not affected by the choice of a particular mode of operation[4] for an acyclic network—with external inputs fixed, the network will settle into a stable steady state (independent of the mode of operation) in a finite number of steps at which point the outputs can be read out. The number of steps needed to reach the steady state is determined by the *depth* of the network, i.e., the number of edges in its longest path. Fig. 3 shows an architectural graph of a depth-three, acyclic network.

Layered acyclic networks are of particular interest because of their very regular structure. Formally, an *L-layered feedforward* neural network is comprised of L ordered subcollections of neurons called *layers* (layers 1 through $L-1$ are sometimes called *hidden layers*); the inputs to the first layer are the network inputs; for $l = 1, \cdots, L - 1$, the inputs to layer $l + 1$ are obtained from the outputs of layer l; the outputs of the Lth layer are the network outputs. The natural graph associated with a feedforward network is an L-partite graph where the depth of the network is identically the number of layers L. In such systems, starting from the external inputs, information flows sequentially from layer to layer until the output is obtained.

For definiteness, we consider acyclic neural networks with a single output node (with an added threshold in the case of sigmoid networks) in two-class pattern recognition contexts. Any such given network dichotomizes feature space $\Re^d$ into two classes identified naturally by the binary outputs ± 1 of the network. A rich, distinct family of classifiers is engendered by each such architecture by varying the weights of the formal neurons. Thus for instance, a single linear threshold element engenders the family of hyperplane classifiers, while hyperspherical and hyperconical classifiers are obtained by suitable selection of quadric threshold element. Such facile geometrical descriptions of classifier families are unavailable, however, for even the simplest depth-two structures where we have to resort to purely abstract characterizations in terms of the underlying graph.

A neural network is said to be *recurrent* if the associated graph has cycles. In most cases in practice, for stability

---

[4]In *synchronous* operation, the network has a clock and all neurons operate on the same (synchronized) time scale. In *asynchronous* operation, all neurons operate on different time scales.

148

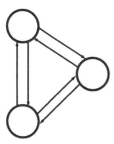

Fig. 4. Recurrent network.

reasons, the network weights are symmetric with respect to permutation of indices. In such situations, the architectural graph may be simplified to an undirected graph $G = \langle V, E \rangle$, where connections between computation nodes are assumed to be two-way.

Fig. 4 illustrates a fully recurrent network. Feedback creates potential instabilities and, indeed, the dynamics of state evolution are now strongly dependent on the mode of network operation. In the classical recurrent neural network setting it is desired to not just recognize, but retrieve prototypical patterns from distorted versions. This is the setting of associative (or content-addressable) memory (cf. [151], [165]). While the associative memory setting provides another pattern recognition (and retrieval) paradigm, the setting and issues have a somewhat different flavor from the Bayesian setting considered hitherto. We accordingly eschew considerations of recurrent networks in this paper and refer the reader to the following sampling of the more technical papers for details [10], [18], [151], [152], [165], [168], [169], [192], [206], [280], [282]–[284].

B. Universal Classification

The wide-ranging application of neural network models in pattern recognition rests upon the following fundamental result: *Formal neurons form a universal basis for computation.* The result is quite general so that virtually any kind of formal neuron is admissible as an elementary building block in a network approach to a classification problem.

1) Finite Problems: It has been long known that the working of any finite-state machine can be mimicked by a network of linear threshold elements [16], [191].

Identify the binary values -1 and $+1$ with the logical truth values 0 and 1, respectively. With this convention, a two-input NAND gate computes the truth function

$$\text{NAND}(x_1, x_2) = \begin{cases} -1, & \text{if } x_1 = x_2 = 1 \\ +1, & \text{otherwise.} \end{cases}$$

The literals x_1 and x_2 in the above expression take values ± 1 only. Observe that we may represent the logical NAND also as a linear threshold function

$$\text{NAND}(x_1, x_2) = \text{sgn}(-x_1 - x_2 + 1), \quad x_1, x_2 \in \{-1, +1\}.$$

As NAND gates form a universal basis for Boolean functions, so do linear threshold elements. In particular, any Boolean function of d literals can be computed by a depth-two network

of linear threshold elements of size no more than $2^{d-1} + 1$.[5] As a corollary, it follows immediately that the Bayes classifier can be implemented by a network of linear threshold elements if the mixture distribution of features has probability-one support over a finite set of points in feature space $\Re^d$.

2) Continuous Problems: An almost as simple Pythagorean argument shows that a corresponding universality result holds for continuous classification problems in $\Re^d$.

Let $E = [0, 1]$ denote the unit interval and consider the class $\mathcal{C} = \mathcal{C}(E^d)$ of continuous, bounded real-valued functions on the unit cube E^d. The class $\mathcal{C}$ forms a real vector space which we may equip with the natural inner product

$$\langle f, g \rangle = \int_{E^d} f(x) g(x) \, dx$$

and induced L^2-norm $\|f\|_2 = \sqrt{\langle f, f \rangle}$. Recall that the L^2-closure of $\mathcal{C}$ is just the Hilbert space $\mathcal{L}^2 = \mathcal{L}^2(E^d)$ of square-integrable functions on E^d.

Now, for any continuous sigmoid σ, let $\mathcal{N}_\sigma$ denote the family of continuous functions defined on the unit cube E^d of the form

$$g(x_1, \cdots, x_d) = \sum_{j=1}^{N} c_j \sigma \left(\sum_{i=1}^{d} w_{ij} x_i - w_{i0} \right)$$

where N runs through the positive integers and c_j and w_{ij} are real weights. Observe that $\mathcal{N}_\sigma$ is just the family of functions on E^d computable by depth-two, arbitrary-size networks of formal neurons with common activation function σ in the first layer and a linear accumulation at the output.

Let $\overline{\mathcal{N}}_\sigma$ denote the closure of $\mathcal{N}_\sigma$ under the L^2-norm. Clearly, $\overline{\mathcal{N}}_\sigma$ is a closed subspace of $\mathcal{L}^2$. Suppose $\overline{\mathcal{N}}_\sigma \neq \mathcal{L}^2$. Then there exists a nonzero $h \in \mathcal{L}^2$ which is orthogonal to the closed subspace $\overline{\mathcal{N}}_\sigma$. Now consider any function of the form

$$g(x_1, \cdots, x_d) = \sigma \left(\sum_{i=1}^{d} w_i x_i - w_0 \right).$$

As g is in $\overline{\mathcal{N}}_\sigma$, it follows that g is orthogonal to h. Consequently,

$$0 = \langle g, h \rangle$$
$$= \int_{E^d} \sigma \left(\sum_{i=1}^{d} w_i x_i - w_0 \right) h(x_1, \cdots, x_d) \, dx_1 \cdots dx_d$$

for all choices of weights w_i. It follows that $h \equiv 0$, contradicting the hypothesis. In consequence: *The subspace $\mathcal{N}_\sigma$ is dense in $\mathcal{L}^2$ (with respect to L^2-norm).*

By an elegant extension of this line of argument using the Hahn–Banach theorem, Cybenko [71] has shown the sharper result that $\mathcal{N}_\sigma$ is *uniformly dense* in $\mathcal{C}$ for a very wide range of choices for the sigmoid σ. Related approximation results and approximation error rates were derived by Barron [25], [26], Chen, Chen, and Liu [56], Darken *et al.* [73], Funahashi [120],

---

[5] Very efficient neural circuit implementations have been designed in a variety of practical computational settings by allowing unbounded fan-in to exploit more fully the computational power latent in a linear threshold element (cf. [238], for instance).

Hornik *et al.* [153], Hornik [154], Jones [157], and Leshno *et al.* [178].

The dense approximation property of depth-two networks immediately implies as a corollary the following universal approximation result: *The Bayes classifier in the feature space $\Re^d$ can be approximated arbitrarily well by networks of formal neurons.* Of course, for better approximation, more neurons are needed. This fact may tempt the unwary practitioner to increase the size of the network to be used for classification. However, one should proceed with care. A large network has many tunable parameters all of which must be learned from a fixed amount of training data. Thus one may easily run into the problem of *overfitting*, that is, the resulting classifier will perform very well on the data but no generalization will take place. As we have seen in Section V, it is the VC dimension of the class of classifiers defined by a given network architecture that determines the generalization ability. This is the same approximation/generalization tradeoff we have already encountered. Therefore, to be able to determine the size of a neural network to be used, it is important to study its VC dimension. This is precisely what we do in the next section, starting with single-neuron classifiers.

C. Acyclic Networks

Consider acyclic neural networks computing maps from $\Re^d$ into $\{-1, +1\}$. As seen earlier, the Vapnik–Chervonenkis dimension of a given network architecture (more precisely, the VC dimension of the class of decision functions computable by the architecture) is the critical parameter determining the sample complexity for learning a function in the class in a distribution-free fashion. While exact results are available only for the simplest cases of a single computational element, these results can be parlayed into fairly tight upper and lower bounds for the VC dimension of general architectures.

1) Canonical Threshold Elements: Let $\varphi_1, \cdots, \varphi_k$ be a fixed set of linearly independent measurement functions mapping $\Re^d$ into $\Re$ and suppose $\varphi = (\varphi_1, \cdots, \varphi_k)$ is the corresponding vector of functions. Recall that the canonical form for a neuron computes a φ-threshold function

$$y = \text{sgn}\left\{\sum_{j=1}^{k} w_j \varphi_j(x_1, \cdots, x_d)\right\}.$$

Let $\Sigma = \{X_i, 1 \leq i \leq n\}$ be an n-set of points in $\Re^d$ and suppose (Σ_+, Σ_-) is a dichotomy of Σ. As the entire family of φ-threshold functions may be explored by varying the weights $w_1, \cdots, w_k$, the notion of separability takes the following form: the dichotomy (Σ_+, Σ_-) is φ-*separable* (i.e., can be separated by a φ-threshold element) if, and only if, there exists a vector of weights $w = (w_1, \cdots, w_k)$ such that

$$\text{sgn}\langle w, \varphi(X)\rangle = \text{sgn}\left\{\sum_{j=1}^{k} w_j \varphi_j(X)\right\}$$
$$= \begin{cases} -1, & \text{if } X \in \Sigma_- \\ +1, & \text{if } X \in \Sigma_+ \end{cases} \quad (13)$$

where $\langle \cdot, \cdot \rangle$ denotes the usual Euclidean inner product.

Separability: Let $\Delta_\varphi(\Sigma)$ denote the number of dichotomies of Σ that are φ-separable and, as before, define the nth shatter coefficient $s_k(n) = \max \Delta_\varphi(\Sigma)$ where the maximization is over all n-sets Σ. The key to the determination of the VC dimension of a φ-threshold element is *Schläfli's recurrence* [65], [245], [295]

$$s_k(n) = s_k(n-1) + s_{k-1}(n-1) \quad (k \geq 2, n \geq 2) \quad (14)$$

with equality $\Delta_\varphi(\Sigma) = s_k(n)$ holding when Σ is in φ-general position.[6] This recurrence is fundamental to the basic Vapnik–Chervonenkis inequality and may be established in this setting by a pleasing geometrical argument: each point X_i engenders a φ-surface

$$H_i = \left\{w \in \Re^k : \sum_{j=1}^{k} w_j \varphi_j(X_i) = 0\right\}$$

which may be identified as a hyperplane in $\Re^k$. Consider the hyperplanes H_i generated by the $n-1$ points $\{X_i, 1 \leq i \leq n-1\}$. These surfaces partition $\Re^k$ into components (i.e., maximally connected regions), the number of components being exactly the number of φ-separable dichotomies of these $n-1$ points. Suppose that the first $n-1$ points X_i engender the maximum number of φ-separable dichotomies. Then the number of components in $\Re^k$ carved out by the hyperplanes $\{H_i, 1 \leq i \leq n-1\}$ is exactly $s_k(n-1)$ (by induction hypothesis). Suppose the nth point X_n is added in such a way as to retain the maximum number of φ-separable dichotomies. The $s_k(n-1)$ components may now be seen to fall into two categories: Q_1 type 1 components which are intersected by H_n, and Q_2 type 2 components which are not intersected by H_n. Observe that

$$s_k(n) = 2Q_1 + Q_2 = s_k(n-1) + Q_1.$$

To complete the argument, observe that each the projection of each type 1 component into the $(k-1)$-dimensional hyperplane H_n is itself a unique component in H_n. It follows that the number of type 1 components is exactly $s_{k-1}(n-1)$ (by induction hypothesis) completing the recurrence. It is clear that the recurrence holds for points in φ-general position as general position is preserved under projections so that the preceding induction carries through *in toto*.

The recurrence (14), together with the boundary conditions $s_k(1) = s_1(n) = 2$ immediately yield the solution

$$\Delta_\varphi(\Sigma) \leq s_k(n) = 2\sum_{j=0}^{k-1}\binom{n-1}{j} \quad (15)$$

with equality when the n-set of points Σ is in φ-general position.[7] The following fundamental result follows immediately: *The VC dimension of the class of decision functions $\mathcal{C}_\varphi$ computable by a φ-threshold element, where $\varphi = (\varphi_1, \cdots, \varphi_k)$ is any vector of linearly independent measurement functions, is given by $V(\mathcal{C}_\varphi) = k$.*

[6] A set of points $\Sigma = \{X_1, \cdots, X_n\}$ is in φ-general position if every m-element subset of the vectors $\{\varphi(X_1), \cdots, \varphi(X_n)\}$ is linearly independent for all $m \leq n$.

[7] Observe that (15) tightens the Vapnik–Chervonenkis bound (7) for the shatter coefficient in this particular case.

Example 5. Linear Threshold Function: If $k = d + 1$, $\varphi_0(x) = -1$, and $\varphi_j(x) = x_j$ $(1 \leq j \leq d)$, then φ-general position coincides with the usual notion of general position—no set of $d + 1$ points lies on a hyperplane in $\Re^d$. The separating surfaces are hyperplanes defined by equations of the form $\sum_{i=1}^{d} w_i x_i = w_0$. The VC dimension of the class of linear threshold functions is hence $V = d + 1$.

Example 6. Hyperspherical Threshold Function: A hyperspherical surface in $\Re^d$ is defined by an equation of the form $\|w - x\|^2 - r^2 = 0$, where, with

$$\langle w, x \rangle = \sum_{i=1}^{d} w_i x_i$$

denoting the usual Euclidean inner-product

$$\|w - x\| = \sqrt{\langle w - x, w - x \rangle}$$

is the usual induced metric. Now note that we can write the corresponding hyperspherical threshold function in the form

$$y = \text{sgn} \left(\|w - x\|^2 - a^2 \right)$$
$$= \text{sgn} \left((\|w\|^2 - a^2) - 2\langle w, x \rangle + \|x\|^2 \right).$$

It follows that this is a special case of a φ-threshold function with $k = d + 2$ and the mapping from $\Re^d$ into $\Re^{d+2}$ determined by $x \overset{\varphi}{\mapsto} (1, x, \|x\|^2)$. Consequently, the VC dimension is not more than $d + 2$. (Actually, in this case the VC dimension equals $d + 1$, see Dudley [100].)

Example 7. Polynomial Threshold Function: The measurement functions comprising a quadric are monomials of degree 2 or less. In general, a polynomial threshold function of degree D is generated by monomials of degree D or less. In particular, if we set $x_0 = -1$ for simplicity, the vector of measurement functions takes the form

$$\varphi(x) = \left(x_0^{i_0} x_1^{i_1} \cdots x_d^{i_d}, \; i_0, i_1, \cdots, i_d \geq 0, \; \sum_{j=0}^{d} i_j = D \right).$$

The separating surface for such a system is a Dth-order rational variety and the VC dimension is $\binom{d+D}{D}$.

A very sharp characterization of the breakdown of separability is suggested by the explicit form (15) for the growth function $s_k(n)$. Suppose Σ is a set of points in $(\varphi_1, \cdots, \varphi_k)$-general position. Then the probability that a random dichotomy (Σ_+, Σ_-) (selected uniformly from the set of 2^n possible dichotomies of Σ) is $(\varphi_1, \cdots, \varphi_k)$-separable is given by

$$P(k, n) = 2^{-n} s_k(n) = 2^{-(n-1)} \sum_{j=0}^{k-1} \binom{n-1}{j}.$$

The exponential decay of the binomial tail results in a sharp asymptotic concentration around $(n-1)/2 + O(\sqrt{n})$ and a consequent remarkable asymptotic breakdown in separability: for every $\epsilon > 0$, as $k \to \infty$

$$P(k, n) \to \begin{cases} 1, & \text{if } n = n_k \leq (1 - \epsilon)2k \\ 0, & \text{if } n = n_k \geq (1 + \epsilon)2k. \end{cases}$$

This sharp threshold property suggests that we identify $2k$ as the "capacity" of a $(\varphi_1, \cdots, \varphi_k)$-threshold element [65], [279], [283].

Learning Algorithms: A wide variety of learning algorithms are available when the data are drawn from a φ-separable class. In this case, we are assured that there exists a *solution weight vector* $w = (w_1, \cdots, w_k)$ satisfying (13). Classical off-line learning approaches for finding a solution weight vector treat the problem as an instance of linear programming which can be solved using the simplex algorithm [72], or (with guaranteed polynomial time convergence) by Karmarkar's algorithm [160]. Such off-line algebraic approaches, however, are not best suited for adaptive pattern recognition applications.

The classical on-line learning procedure for φ-separable classes is the perceptron training procedure of Rosenblatt [234]. In its simplest variant, the algorithm is provided with a sequence of training data $\{X(t), t \geq 1\}$ generated from the sample X_i $(1 \leq i \leq n)$ in such a way that each X_i recurs infinitely often in the sequence (by cyclically running through the sample, for instance). The algorithm then generates an error-driven sequence of estimates of solution weight vectors $\{w(t), t \geq 1\}$, where $w(1)$ is an arbitrary initial guess of the solution vector, and at each epoch t, the succeeding weight vector estimate $w(t + 1)$ is generated on-line as a function of the current estimate $w(t)$ and the current datum $(X(t), Y(t))$ only. To simplify presentation, observe that by the simple expedient of replacing $\varphi(X_i)$ by $-\varphi(X_i)$ whenever $Y_i = -1$, we may, without loss of generality, suppose that $Y(t) = 1$ for all t. The fixed-increment perceptron training procedure now incrementally adapts the weight vector estimate as follows:

$$w(t + 1) = \begin{cases} w(t), & \text{if } \langle w(t), \varphi(X(t)) \rangle \geq 0 \\ w(t) + \rho \varphi(X(t)), & \text{if } \langle w(t), \varphi(X(t)) \rangle < 0. \end{cases}$$

The algorithm is on-line and error-driven. Geometrically, the algorithm has the pleasing intuitive interpretation that whenever there is a misclassification, weight vector updates are in the direction of the positive half-space of the vector $\varphi(X(t))$ corresponding to the current pattern $X(t)$. The algorithm provably converges in finite time[8] whenever (13) has a solution. See [198] and [207] for proofs and considerations of algorithm behavior for nonseparable cases.

Various extensions of the basic fixed-increment perceptron training procedure exist: variable increment procedures allow a time-varying increment $\rho = \rho(t)$; relaxation procedures select $\rho = \rho(t, w(t), X(t))$ as a function of the current estimate and datum as well. See Duda and Hart [97] for the literature.

Perceptron-based procedures which focus attention on the misclassified examples have drawbacks when the sample is not separable. They are also not easily extended to general network architectures, in large part because it is not clear what classifications the intermediate (or hidden) neurons should be assigned. On the other hand, gradient-based procedures which minimize instead a continuous functional of the sample, such as the mean-squared error on the sample, are readily extendable to network situations (with the proviso that a continuously differentiable activation function is chosen) and have consequently become very popular.

---

[8] While the worst case behavior of the algorithm is not well regulated, the algorithm converges rapidly in typical situations [35], [281].

In the single element formulation, a weight vector $w = (w_1, \cdots, w_k)$ is sought which satisfies $\langle w, \varphi(X_i) \rangle = b_i$ $(1 \leq i \leq n)$ where the b_i are arbitrarily specified positive constants. (Recall that we have set $Y_i = 1$ without loss of generality.) The least mean-square approach [298] seeks to minimize the squared error

$$E(t) = [\langle w(t), \varphi(X(t)) \rangle - b(t)]^2$$

by updating the current weight vector estimate $w(t)$ in the direction of the gradient. This results in a relaxation-type update rule

$$w(t+1) = w(t) + \rho(t)[b(t) - \langle w(t), \varphi(X(t)) \rangle] \varphi(X(t)).$$

A proper choice of increment $\rho = \rho(t)$ will drive the algorithm to a limiting solution. Related procedures include stochastic approximation methods [293] and the family of Ho–Kashyap algorithms [149] which also adapt the margin vector $b = (b_1, \cdots, b_n)$. However, while computationally attractive, such relaxation approaches have the disadvantage that it is not clear how the solutions they generate are related to the best classifier in the class from the probability of error point of view.

2) General Acyclic Networks:

Computational Considerations: The results for a single computational element may be parlayed into upper bounds for general acyclic architectures by a recursive greedy use of Schläffli's counting formula (15) (cf. [37], [67]). Consider an arbitrary acyclic architecture G comprised of canonical threshold elements with d source nodes, one output node, and K programmable parameters (weights). Suppose computational node j has associated with it k_j programmable weights. Then, from (15), node j can compute at most $n^{k_j+1} + 1$ different functions from any finite n-set of points Σ in $\Re^d$ into $\{-1, +1\}$. Thus the architecture G can separate at most $\prod_j (n^{k_j+1} + 1) \leq n^{2K}$ dichotomies of Σ. As there exists a set of V points which is shattered, where $V = V(\mathcal{C}_G)$ is the VC dimension of the family of decision functions $\mathcal{C}_G$ computable in the architecture G, it follows that $2^V \leq V^{2K}$. We thus have the following upper bound on the VC dimension: *If the architecture G is comprised of canonical threshold elements with d source nodes, one output node, and K programmable parameters*

$$V(\mathcal{C}_G) \leq cK \log K \qquad (16)$$

for an absolute positive constant c.

In particular, depth-two linear threshold networks with d source nodes, k computational nodes in the first layer, and a single output node have VC dimension bounded by $V \leq c(dk + 2k + 1) \log (dk + 2k + 1)$. On the other hand, Baum [34] has shown constructively using a modified slice technique pioneered by Nilsson [207] that $V \geq 2\lfloor k/2 \rfloor d$. Thus $V = O(dk \log dk)$ and $V = \Omega(dk)$. More generally, in an L-layered, feedforward setting, the bounds suggest that the VC dimension increases faster by adding nodes to existing layers (i.e., by increasing the "width" of the network) than by adding layers (i.e., by increasing the "depth" of the network). This may be taken as a step in defense of a connectionist thesis: *shallow networks (with dense interconnectivity) are computationally more efficient than deep networks [20].*

Intuition (perhaps bolstered by (15) and Baum's lower bound for depth-two threshold networks) suggests that the VC dimension of a network of threshold elements should not exceed the sum of the VC dimensions of the individual threshold elements in the network. Surprisingly, however, constructions by Maass [187] and Sakurai [241] show that the upper bound (16) is indeed admissible (up to a multiplying constant): *there exists a sequence of linear threshold network architectures $\{G_K, K \geq 1\}$, where G_K has K free programmable parameters, for which*

$$V(\mathcal{C}_{G_K}) \geq c'K \log K \qquad (K \geq 1) \qquad (17)$$

for an absolute positive constant c'. This implies that in larger networks, an average programmable parameter can contribute more than a constant amount to the net VC dimension. In fact, an average parameter can contribute as much as the order of $\log K$, *vide* the lower bound (17), so that the contribution of a typical parameter to the VC dimension can actually *increase* with network size. This may be taken as mathematical support toward a connectionist manifesto: *a network of formal neurons is more than just the sum of its components*; (cf. [151] for another version of this sentiment—this time in a recurrent network setting).

The superlinear lower bound (17) continues to hold for networks with common logistic activation function (12) (with a threshold at the output node). However, good upper bounds are in abeyance and seem to demand a case-by-case exploitation of the specific properties of the activation function. Smoothness of the activation function is not sufficient: for instance, Sontag [260] shows that a simple depth-two network with two real-valued inputs, two first layer sigmoid elements with some common smooth sigmoid activation function, and a single linear threshold element as output in the second layer has *infinite* VC dimension. The infinite VC dimension of two-layered networks remains true even for some monotone, continuous activation functions which are convex on $(-\infty, 0)$ and concave on $(0, \infty)$ (see [90, Sec. 30.4]). For the case of acyclic networks with the popular logistic activation function, however, MacIntyre and Sontag [188] have shown that the VC dimension is finite. The explicit role played by the number of programmable parameters is open. For networks using piecewise-linear activation functions (11), real inputs and thresholded outputs, Goldberg and Jerrum [128] show an explicit upper bound $O(K^2)$ for the VC dimension of the network in terms of the number of programmable parameters (weights) K in the network. For recent work on the VC dimension of neural networks, see Bartlett, Maiorov, and Meir [32], Karpinsky and Macintyre [161], and Koiran and Sontag [166].

Learning Algorithms: In general, it is much harder to find algorithms for learning from examples with provable performance for a general network architecture. Indeed, the loading (or consistency) problem is computationally intractable[9] for all but the simplest network constructs. The first results along this direction were established by Judd (cf. [158]).

---

[9] More formally, the loading problem is NP-complete. For a reference to this and other notions of time complexity in computation, we refer the reader to Garey and Johnson [121].

Subsequently, the loading problem was shown to be intractable for several classes of neural networks of threshold elements, including: 0–1 halfspace [219]; union of two halfspaces [43]; two-layer network of linear threshold elements with two elements in the first layer and a single output element [43]; XOR of two halfspaces [43]; and two-cascade network [180]. For related results for learning models with equivalence and membership queries, see Hegedüs [144], [219]. More recently, DasGupta, Siegelmann, and Sontag [76] have shown that the loading problem remains intractable for two-layer networks with two first-layer neurons with piecewise-linear activation (and varying input dimension) and a single output threshold element. Shifting focus from the number of misclassifications as criterion function to a squared-error criterion (i.e., shifting from l^∞-norm to l^2-norm) does not improve matters: Vu [286] has shown very recently that training two-layer networks, where the first layer consists of linear threshold functions or sufficiently smooth sigmoids and the output element in the second layer simply forms a linear combination of the outputs of the first layer, so as to obtain small average squared-error is computationally infeasible.[10]

A noteworthy exception to these negative results when queries are permitted is a half-space learning algorithm due to Baum [36] which learns weights for a depth-two network of linear threshold elements via queries. The algorithm exploits the geometric interpretation of hyperplanes generated by the hidden (first) layer of linear threshold elements as partitioning input space $\Re^d$ into components (with hyperplanes as boundaries). Suppose examples are drawn at random from a function generated by a target depth-two network. Observe that all points in any given component generated by the first-layer elements of the target network will be labelled either positive or negative. The task of learning such a network can now be viewed as determining the piecewise-linear boundary between positively and negatively labeled components.

Baum's algorithm proceeds by first drawing a sufficient number of random examples and then using queries to determine the hyperplanes corresponding to the hidden first-layer elements. A boundary point between a positive and a negative example is first found by binary search following which a hyperplane containing the boundary point is identified by exploring its neighborhood randomly. Once the hyperplanes are identified, the weight vector of the output unit is determined quickly by finding a hyperplane separating positive and negative labeled components.

While geometrically appealing, the algorithm is, however, provably efficient only for relatively small networks with fewer than five first-layer elements.

For more general acyclic structures, the learning heuristic of choice is based on gradient descent ideas. Consider a sigmoid network where the activation function σ is continuously differentiable. For a given exemplar pair (X, Y), let $\hat{Y} = \hat{Y}(W) = \hat{Y}(W; X)$ denote the output of a network of given architecture with weights W. Writing $\hat{P}_n$ for the empirical probability measure which puts equal weight on each of the n examples in D_n, we can write the empirical

mean-square error on the sample in the form

$$E = E(W) = \hat{P}_n(\tilde{Y} - Y)^2.$$

The generic gradient descent algorithm modifies each weight w in the system in a natural fashion by setting

$$w \mapsto w - \rho \frac{\partial E}{\partial w}.$$

For a layered network of sigmoids, the computation of the various gradients can be recursively generated starting from the output unit and working backwards, one layer at a time, to the input layer. The procedure is sometimes hence called *back-error-propagation* or simply backpropagation [240]. Variations on this theme include conjugate gradient and sequential quadratic programming methods.

While the backpropagation heuristic is popular by virtue of its simplicity, analysis is difficult (cf. [288]–[290]) and performance guarantees hard to come by. The algorithm is beset by a variety of problems: it is notoriously inconsistent unless stringent conditions are placed upon the problem; the algorithm tends to get stuck in local minima which may abound and are very hard to characterize; algorithm convergence can be very slow; and, finally, even when it successfully attains close to a minimum of the criterion function, it is not clear how the resulting solution relates to the best classifier (in terms of the probability of error) in the class. Successful applications in practice tend to be predicated on the availability of sufficient side information to enable canny choices of network architectures and good initial conditions.

D. Performance Bounds

Equipped with the approximation-theoretic results and VC dimension bounds, it is easy to study the behavior of the probability of error of certain neural network classifiers. As always, we are interested in the performance of the classifier compared to the Bayes risk. Let g_n denote the classifier obtained by data-based tuning of the parameters of a certain neural-network architecture with (say) k neurons. Denote the class of all possible such classifiers by $\mathcal{C}_k$. Then, as before, a typical analysis splits the error into two nonnegative terms

$$L(g_n) - L^* = \left(L(g_n) - \inf_{g \in \mathcal{C}_k} L(g) \right) + \left(\inf_{g \in \mathcal{C}_k} L(g) - L^* \right).$$

Recall that the second term on the right-hand side represents the part of the error due to the limited approximation abilities of the class $\mathcal{C}_k$. The denseness results cited in Section VI-B indicate that, in most cases, as $k \to \infty$, this term converges to zero for all possible distributions. Unfortunately, the speed of convergence depends on the unknown distribution, and may be arbitrarily slow. For certain classes of smooth distributions it is possible to derive uniform upper bounds for the approximation term, as in Barron [25]. The first term on the right-hand side represents, as noted before, the estimation error which is due to the finite sample size and the limitations of the learning algorithm. In an ideal situation, when g_n minimizes the empirical error over the class $\mathcal{C}_k$, the tools of Section V may be applied to derive distribution-free upper bounds for the

---

[10]To make the statement more precise, the problem is NP-hard. See Garey and Johnson [121].

estimation error. For example, for all distributions we have

$$\boldsymbol{E}L(g_n) - \inf_{g \in \mathcal{C}_k} L(g) \leq c\sqrt{\frac{V_{\mathcal{C}_k}}{n}}$$

where $V_{\mathcal{C}_k}$ is the VC dimension of the class $\mathcal{C}_k$ and c is a universal constant. Therefore, universal consistency may be achieved simply by choosing $k = k_n$ as a function of the sample size n such that $k_n \rightarrow \infty$ and $V_{\mathcal{C}_{k_n}}/n \rightarrow 0$ as $n \rightarrow \infty$. For neural network architectures for which explicit upper bounds for $V_{\mathcal{C}_k}$ are available, this is a trivial matter.

Unfortunately, the above analysis has several weak points. First of all, the optimal network size cannot be determined solely as a function of the sample size as it heavily depends on the actual distribution of the data. Such a data-dependent choice might be based on the structural-risk-minimization ideas have discussed in Section V-C.

A more serious problem is that minimizing the empirical risk is computationally not feasible even for small toy problems. The practical learning algorithms discussed above attempt to approximate the optimal solution but without universal performance guarantees. In fact, for some malicious distributions, all practical neural network classifiers may fail miserably. Therefore, in some sense, neural networks are inferior to other, more robust classifiers such as nearest-neighbor, kernel, or decision tree-based methods.

One should also note that instead of minimizing the empirical misclassification rate, most neural network learning algorithms attempt to minimize the empirical mean-square error, which is more appropriate for regression-type problems. Even if an algorithm could minimize the empirical mean-square error, the VC dimension bounds would not be applicable anymore. Nevertheless, universal consistency of such classifiers may be achieved even for some activation functions which induce classes of infinite VC dimension (see [184], for instance). Also, in some distribution-dependent setting, neural networks trained by minimizing the empirical squared error achieve surprisingly good performance as is shown in a remarkable paper of Bartlett [31]. In fact, Bartlett points out that, as opposed to what VC-dimension bounds suggest, the total weight of the parameters is more important in a certain sense than merely the number of tunable parameters. For consistency and related results we refer to Barron [25], [26], Faragó and Lugosi [109], Haussler [140], Lugosi and Zeger [184], Mielniczuk and Tyrcha [197], Wang [288], Wang, Venkatesh, and Judd [289]–[291], and White [296], [297].

VII. LARGE-MARGIN CLASSIFIERS

Consider empirical risk minimization over the class of perceptrons (i.e., linear classifiers), and assume first, for simplicity, that the two classes are linearly separable. This means that there exists a hyperplane cutting $\Re^d$ into two halves such that it separates label 0 training points from those with label 1. Then the Vapnik–Chervonenkis bounds guarantee that the probability of error of *any* such classifier will not be more than a constant multiple of $d \log n/n$. This bound is acceptable if $d \ll n/\log n$. However, sometimes in practice, the dimensionality of the feature space is very large, making the bound unsatisfactory. A question which arises immediately is whether, among all hyperplanes separating the data, some are better than others. In other words, can we gain substantially by fine-tuning the linear classifier and, in some way, selecting a "better" separating hyperplane? We have seen that the VC bounds are basically tight in a minimax sense, that is, for any classifier there is some distribution for which the upper bound is (almost) achieved, which also indicates that it does not really matter which separating hyperplane we choose. However, one may argue that the "bad" distributions are pathological in some sense, and for distributions appearing in "real life" one may hope for much better performance. This might certainly be true, but to benefit from such "lucky" cases, one should be able to observe this from the training data at one's disposal.

The first significant step made in this direction was a beautiful observation of Vapnik and Chervonenkis [277] who proved that if one *happens* to find a separating hyperplane which separates with a *large margin* (i.e., all data points are far away from the decision surface) then one may derive a much smaller upper bound than that given by the distribution-free analysis. The reason is that the "effective" VC dimension of linear classifiers with a large margin may be much smaller than the dimensionality of the feature space, and, indeed, may only depend on the size of the margin, measured in an appropriate way. (For the precise statement and more details we refer to Vapnik [275].) Thus this bound gives a *distribution-dependent* performance guarantee, which, most importantly, can be assessed directly from the data. The same principle may be adapted to situations when the data are not necessarily separable by a hyperplane. Recently, this principle has been investigated more generally by Bartlett [31] and Shawe-Taylor, Bartlett, Williamson, and Anthony [251], [252].

The basic idea behind the *Support Vector Machines* (cf. Boser, Guyon, and Vapnik [45], Cortes and Vapnik [64], and Vapnik [275]) is to transform the data into a high-dimensional space by some transformation fixed in advance, and find a large-margin separating hyperplane in the transformed space. Clever implementational tricks make this seemingly complicated principle feasible for practical applications, and, even though very little of its theoretical properties are known, it has been reported to achieve remarkable performance for large and complex pattern classification problems (cf. [45], [64], [275]).

Closely related principles are the methods of *boosting*, developed by Freund [113] and Schapire [243], and the *bagging* and *arcing* methods of Breiman [48], [49], see also Drucker and Cortes [98], Quinlan [229]. These methods combine, by (weighted) majority voting, the decisions of several simple classifiers. For example, boosting generates a sequence of classifiers, all taken from a class of small VC dimension, in such a way that every classifier tries to classify those points well which were found to be "difficult" by the previous classifier. As argued by Schapire, Freund, Bartlett, and Lee [244], these methods attempt to maximize the "margin" in a general sense, making the decision more "stable."

VIII. AUTOMATIC PARAMETER SELECTION

In earlier sections we have seen several different principles and methods for designing classifiers. From a certain point of view all of them may look appealing. The obvious questions a practitioner facing a classification problem may ask are as follows:

1) Which of the many methods should I use?
2) Is there a classifier which is superior to all others?

The answer to the second question is "No." No single classifier is uniformly superior to all the others and, consequently, the user has to make a choice on a case-by-case basis. Since the only available information is the training data, such a selection should be based on the data. Even if one has decided to use (say) the k-nearest neighbor rule, the value of k and perhaps the metric might be selected in a data-based manner. In fact, to hope for any success in practical problems, one *must* let the data do the talking. This section deals with such data-dependent classifier selection.

The problem, in its most general form, may be formulated as follows: given a set of classifiers $\mathcal{C}_n = \{g_{n,\theta}: \theta \in \Theta\}$, choose one with a small probability of error. Here Θ is an abstract set of parameters. Interesting examples of Θ and the corresponding set of classifiers include

- $\Theta = \{1, \cdots, n\}$ and $g_{n,k}$ is the k-nearest neighbor rule with the Euclidean distance;
- Θ is a set of positive definite $d \times d$ matrices and $g_{n,\theta}$ is the 1-nearest neighbor rule based on the distance $d(x, y) = ((x - y)^t \theta (x - y))^{1/2}$;
- Θ is the set of positive integers and $g_{n,\theta}$ is the kernel rule with a fixed kernel and smoothing parameter θ;
- Θ is the set of positive integers and $g_{n,\theta}$ is a neural network classifier with a fixed architecture, trained by θ iterations of back-propagation.

Essentially, all problems of parameter selection may be cast in this general framework. In some sense, even the problem of feature extraction belongs here.

The most sensible way of making such a selection is to use the data to estimate the probability of error of each classifier $g_{n,\theta}$ in the class, and to choose a classifier minimizing the estimate. In fact, basically all methods (directly or indirectly) are based on this general principle. The basic difficulty is that the same data which defines the classifiers $g_{n,\theta}$ are to be used for estimating purposes as well, so the problem should be handled with extreme care.

The simplest case is when a separate set of labeled samples is available; call it

$$T_m = ((X_{n+1}, Y_{n+1}), \cdots, (X_{n+m}, Y_{n+m})).$$

This may be achieved by artificially holding out m samples from defining the classifiers $g_{n,\theta}$. Since in most applications data is very expensive to acquire, most designers do not like the idea of "wasting" valuable data for merely testing purposes. However, as we will see shortly, holding out just a few samples can be extremely rewarding. So, for the sake of simplicity, suppose now that a testing set T_m is available, and is independent of D_n. Then, for each classifier in $\mathcal{C}_n$, we may form the empirical error estimate

$$\hat{L}_m(g_{n,\theta}) = \frac{1}{m} \sum_{i=1}^{m} I_{\{g_{n,\theta}(X_{n+i}) \neq Y_{n+i}\}}$$

and choose a θ minimizing the estimate over all $\theta \in \Theta$. Call the obtained classifier g_{n+m}. (The subscript reflects the fact that the final classifier depends on $m + n$ samples.) Now it is easy to see that, due to the independence of the testing subsample T_m and the training sample D_m, the performance of g_{n+m} compared to the best classifier in $\mathcal{C}_n$, may be analyzed by techniques described in Section V. This simple argument is at the basis of the important paper of Devroye [85] who surveys parameter selection based on minimizing the empirical risk measured on an independent test sample. For example, it follows by a simple application of the Vapnik–Chervonenkis inequality (8) that

$$\boldsymbol{E}\left\{L(g_{n+m}) - \inf_{g_{n,\theta} \in \mathcal{C}_n} L(g_{n,\theta}) | D_n\right\} \leq c\sqrt{\frac{\log s(\mathcal{C}_n, m)}{m}} \tag{18}$$

where c is a universal constant and $s(\mathcal{C}_n, m)$ is the mth shatter coefficient of the set of classifiers $\mathcal{C}_n$ defined by a particular realization of the training data D_n. Thus the success of this parameter selection procedure is guaranteed if $\log s(\mathcal{C}_n, m)$ is small compared to the size m of the testing data. From this point on, the analysis is purely combinatorial: one has to derive upper bounds for the shatter coefficient. Since the class $\mathcal{C}_n$ is defined by the random data D_n, the shatter coefficient $s(\mathcal{C}_n, m)$ is also a random variable. However, in many interesting cases, it is possible to find upper bounds for $s(\mathcal{C}_n, m)$ that only depend on n and m, and not on the particular realization of D_n. Devroye [85] and Devroye, Györfi, and Lugosi [90] derive such bounds for several interesting classes. Here we merely mention two simple examples.

Example 8: Let $\mathcal{C}_n$ be the class of all k-nearest neighbor rules with $k = 1, 2, \cdots, n$. In this case, the value of k is to be selected by the data. Here clearly $\mathcal{C}_n$ is finite with $|\mathcal{C}_n| = n$, and (18) becomes

$$\boldsymbol{E}\left\{L(g_{n+m}) - \inf_{g_{n,\theta} \in \mathcal{C}_n} L(g_{n,\theta}) | D_n\right\} \leq c\sqrt{\frac{\log n}{m}}.$$

Therefore, in order to make sure that the probability of error of the k-nearest neighbor rule based on the selected k is close to that with the best possible k, all we have to guarantee is that $m \gg \log n$. In other words, if one is willing to "sacrifice" a tiny fraction of the training sample for testing purposes, the reward is a nearly optimal value of k. Also, the rule obtained by this procedure is consistent under very mild assumptions on m. This follows from the fact that, as we have seen before, for *some* choice of k, the k-nearest neighbor rule is consistent. This implies that

$$\boldsymbol{E}\left\{\inf_{g_{n,\theta} \in \mathcal{C}_n} L(g_{n,\theta})\right\} \to L^*, \qquad \text{as } n \to \infty,$$

and, therefore,

$$\boldsymbol{E}\{L(g_{n+m})\} \to L^*$$

whenever $n \to \infty$ and $m/\log n \to \infty$.

Example 9: Consider the class $\mathcal{C}_n$ of all moving-window classifiers (as defined in Section III) with all possible values of the smoothing parameter $h > 0$. Thus the goal is to select h in a nearly optimal way. Now $\mathcal{C}_n$ is an infinite class, so bounding $s(\mathcal{C}_n, m)$ is less trivial than in the previous example. Still, it is not difficult to find useful bounds. For example, it is easy to prove that

$$s(\mathcal{C}_n, m) \leq mn$$

(cf. [90, Ch. 25]). Substituting this bound in (18) we get

$$\boldsymbol{E}\left\{ L(g_{n+m}) - \inf_{g_{n,\theta} \in \mathcal{C}_n} L(g_{n,\theta}) | D_n \right\} \leq c\sqrt{\frac{\log n + \log m}{m}}.$$

Clearly, this bound is as useful as the one obtained in the previous example, and all conclusions mentioned there remain valid. Selection of h for more general kernels is also possible; the theory is summarized in [90, Ch. 25].

In some cases it is impossible to obtain useful bounds for $s(\mathcal{C}_n, m)$. Clearly, if the class $\mathcal{C}_n$ is too large, it may overfit the test sample T_m and minimization of the error estimate cannot work. This is the same phenomenon encountered in Section V. Many other examples are worked out in Devroye [85] and Devroye, Györfi, and Lugosi [90].

The situation is much more complicated if no independent testing data is available, and parameter selection has to be made based on error estimates calculated on the very same data from which the classifier is defined. Taking one step back, we may formulate the problem of *error estimation* as follows: given the training data $D_n = ((X_1, Y_1), \cdots, (X_n, Y_n))$ and the classifier $g_n(x) = g_n(x, D_n)$, estimate the probability of error

$$L(g_n) = \boldsymbol{P}\{g_n(X, D_n) \neq Y | D_n\}.$$

Mathematically, an error estimate $\hat{L}(g_n)$ is simply a real-valued function of the data D_n. Being able to estimate well the probability of error for each g_n in a set $\mathcal{C}_n$ of classifiers does not necessarily guarantee that the classifier minimizing the error estimate has a nearly optimal probability of error. To have such a guarantee, one needs to assure that the estimates are *uniformly* close to the true probabilities of error over the whole class $\mathcal{C}_n$. In the case of estimation using an independent test sample, we were able to derive such a guarantee using the Vapnik–Chervonenkis inequality. The absence of independent test data makes the problem significantly more difficult, so first we focus on the error estimation problem for an individual classifier g_n. Error estimation has been one of the key topics in pattern recognition. For surveys we refer to Cover and Wagner [70], Devroye, Györfi, and Lugosi [90], Glick [127], Hand [139], Jain, Dubes, and Chen [156], Kanal [159], McLachlan [193], and Toussaint [271].

Perhaps the simplest and most general method for estimating the probability of error is the *resubstitution estimate* (also called *apparent error rate*). This estimate simply counts the number of errors committed by g_n on the training sequence. Formally

$$\hat{L}^{(R)}(g_n) = \frac{1}{n} \sum_{i=1}^{n} I_{\{g_n(X_i) \neq Y_i\}}.$$

Since the estimate tests the classifier on the same data on which it was defined, there is an evident danger of being optimistically biased. In some cases this estimate is simply useless. The simplest example is the 1-nearest neighbor rule for which $\hat{L}^{(R)}(g_n) = 0$ whenever all X_i's are different, regardless of the true probability of error. Still, the resubstitution estimate has a surprisingly good performance in some cases. For example, Devroye and Wagner [93] observed that if g_n chooses a hypothesis from a fixed class of rules $\mathcal{C}$ in an arbitrary data-dependent way, then

$$\boldsymbol{E}\{|\hat{L}^{(R)}(g_n) - L(g_n)|\} \leq c\sqrt{\frac{V_\mathcal{C} \log n}{n}}$$

where c is a universal constant and $V_\mathcal{C}$ is the VC dimension of the class $\mathcal{C}$. Thus for example, for any linear classification rule, the resubstitution estimate is guaranteed to be within $O\left(\sqrt{d \log n / n}\right)$ of the true error. For additional examples, see [90].

To eliminate the bias of the resubstitution estimate, several authors have proposed the *deleted* estimate (also called the *leave-one-out* estimate or the *U-method*)—e.g., see Cover [68], Lachenbruch [176], Lunts and Brailovsky [186], and Stone [266]. In fact, the leave-one-out estimate is probably the one most frequently used among practitioners. To compute this estimate, one first deletes the first pair (X_1, Y_1) from the data, forms the classifier g_{n-1} based on the rest of the data, and tests whether g_{n-1} classifies X_1 correctly. Then the procedure is repeated n times, each time deleting a different pair (X_i, Y_i). Finally, the deleted estimate $\hat{L}^{(D)}$ is the average number of errors. Formally

$$\hat{L}^{(D)}(g_{n-1}) = \frac{1}{n} \sum_{i=1}^{n} I_{\{g_{n-1}(X_i, D_{n,i}) \neq Y_i\}}$$

where

$$D_{n,i} = \Big((X_1, Y_1), \cdots, (X_{i-1}, Y_{i-1}),$$
$$(X_{i+1}, Y_{i+1}), \cdots, (X_n, Y_n)\Big)$$

is the training set with (X_i, Y_i) deleted. Now clearly, $\hat{L}^{(D)}(g_{n-1})$ is an estimate of $L(g_{n-1})$ rather than of $L(g_n)$, but the intuition is that if n is sufficiently large and g_n is "stable" in some sense, then the difference between $L(g_{n-1})$ and $L(g_n)$ is negligible. In many cases, the analysis of the deleted estimate may be based on a general inequality of Devroye and Wagner [94] and Rogers and Wagner [233] who prove that if g_n is symmetric, then

$$\boldsymbol{E}\{(\hat{L}^{(D)}(g_{n-1}) - L(g_n))^2\}$$
$$\leq \frac{1}{n} + 6\boldsymbol{P}\{g_n(X, D_n) \neq g_{n-1}(X, D_{n-1})\}.$$

This inequality may be used to obtain useful performance bounds for the deleted estimate for nearest neighbor, kernel, and histogram rules (see [90, Ch. 24] for a survey). Recent studies by Holden [150] and Kearns and Ron [163] investigate the performance of the deleted estimate for classifiers choosing their hypotheses from fixed VC classes. In spite of the practical importance of this estimate, relatively little is known about its theoretical properties. The available theory is especially poor when it comes to analyzing parameter selection based on minimizing the deleted estimate.

The deleted estimated has been criticized for its relatively large variance and for the computational demand it imposes. Many other error estimates have been proposed and investigated in the literature and it is impossible to discuss all of them here. We merely mention some of the most popular ones:

- the smoothed error estimate of Glick [127];
- the *a posteriori* probability estimate of Fukunaga and Kessel [118];
- the rotation estimate of Toussaint and Donaldson [272];
- several versions of Efron's bootstrap estimate [105], [106];

and refer the reader to the above-mentioned survey texts on error estimation.

REFERENCES

[1] M. A. Aizerman, E. M. Braverman, and L. I. Rozonoer, "Theoretical foundations of the potential function method in pattern recognition learning," *Automat. Remote Contr.*, vol. 25, pp. 917–936, 1964.
[2] ——, "The probability problem of pattern recognition learning and the method of potential functions," *Automat. Remote Contr.*, vol. 25, pp. 1307–1323, 1964.
[3] ——, "The method of potential functions for the problem of restoring the characteristic of a function converter from randomly observed points," *Automat. Remote Contr.*, vol. 25, pp. 1546–1556, 1964.
[4] ——, "Extrapolative problems in automatic control and the method of potential functions," *Amer. Math. Soc. Transl.*, vol. 87, pp. 281–303, 1970.
[5] H. Akaike, "An approximation to the density function," *Ann. Inst. Statist. Math.*, vol. 6, pp. 127–132, 1954.
[6] ——, "A new look at the statistical model identification," *IEEE Trans. Automat. Contr.*, vol. AC-19, pp. 716–723, 1974.
[7] K. Alexander, "Probability inequalities for empirical processes and a law of the iterated logarithm," *Ann. Probab.*, vol. 4, pp. 1041–1067, 1984.
[8] I. Aleksander and H. Morton, *An Introduction to Neural Computing.* London, U.K.: Chapman & Hall, 1990.
[9] S. Amari, "Mathematical foundations of neurocomputing," *Proc. IEEE,* vol. 78, pp. 1443–1463, 1990.
[10] J. A. Anderson, *Introduction to Practical Neural Modeling.* Cambridge, MA: MIT Press, 1994.
[11] T. W. Anderson, "Some nonparametric multivariate procedures based on statistically equivalent blocks," in *Multivariate Analysis,* P. R. Krishnaiah, Ed. New York: Academic, 1966, pp. 5–27.
[12] M. W. Anderson and R. D. Benning, "A distribution-free discrimination procedure based on clustering," *IEEE Trans. Inform. Theory,* vol. IT-16, pp. 541–548, 1970.
[13] M. Anthony and N. Biggs, *Computational Learning Theory.* Cambridge, UK: Cambridge Univ. Press, 1992.
[14] M. Anthony and J. Shawe-Taylor, "A result of Vapnik with applications," *Discr. Appl. Math.,* vol. 47, pp. 207–217, 1993.
[15] A. Antos and G. Lugosi, "Strong minimax lower bounds for learning," *Machine Learn.,* 1997.
[16] M. A. Arbib, *Brains, Machines, and Mathematics.* New York: Springer-Verlag, 1987.
[17] P. Argentiero, R. Chin, and P. Beaudet, "An automated approach to the design of decision tree classifiers," *IEEE Trans. Pattern Anal. Machine Intell.,* vol. PAMI-4, pp. 51–57, 1982.
[18] A. F. Atiya and Y. S. Abu-Mostafa, "An analogue feedback associative memory," *IEEE Trans. Neural Networks,* vol. 4, pp. 117–126, 1993.
[19] T. Bailey and A. K. Jain, "A note on distance-weighted k-nearest neighbor rules," *IEEE Trans. Syst., Man, Cybern.,* vol. SMC-8, pp. 311–313, 1978.
[20] P. Baldi and S. S. Venkatesh, "On properties of networks of neuron-like elements," in *Neural Information Processing Systems,* D. Anderson, Ed. New York: Amer. Inst. Phys., 1988.
[21] A. R. Barron, "Statistical properties of artificial neural networks," in *Proc. 28th Conf. Decision and Control* (Tampa, FL, 1989), pp. 280–285.
[22] ——, "Complexity regularization with applications to artificial neural networks," in *Nonparametric Functional Estimation and Related Topics,*
G. Roussas, Ed. Dordrecht, The Netherlands: Kluwer, 1991, NATO ASI Ser., pp. 561–576.
[23] ——, "Universal approximation bounds for superpositions of a sigmoidal function," Univ. Illinois at Urbana-Champaign, Urbana, IL, Tech. Rep. 58, 1991.
[24] ——, "Complexity regularization with application to artificial neural networks," in *Nonparametric Functional Estimation and Related Topics,* G. Roussas, Ed. Dordrecht, The Netherlands: Kluwer, 1991, NATO ASI Ser., pp. 561–576.
[25] ——, "Universal approximation bounds for superpositions of a sigmoidal function," *IEEE Trans. Inform. Theory,* vol. 39, pp. 930–944, 1993.
[26] ——, "Approximation and estimation bounds for artificial neural networks," *Machine Learn.,* vol. 14, pp. 115–133, 1994.
[27] A. R. Barron and R. L. Barron, "Statistical learning networks: A unifying view," in *Proc. 20th Symp. Interface: Computing Science and Statistics,* E. J. Wegman, D. T. Gantz, and J. J. Miller, Eds. Alexandria, VA: AMS, 1988, pp. 192–203.
[28] A. R. Barron, L. Birgé, and P. Massart, "Risk bounds for model selection via penalization," *Probab. Theory Related Fields,* 1996, to be published.
[29] R. L. Barron, "Learning networks improve computer-aided prediction and control," *Comp. Des.,* vol. 75, pp. 65–70, 1975.
[30] A. R. Barron and T. Cover, "Minimum complexity density estimation," *IEEE Trans. Inform. Theory,* vol. 37, pp. 1034–1054, 1991.
[31] P. L. Bartlett, "The sample complexity of pattern classification with neural networks: The size of the weights is more important than the size of the network," *IEEE Trans. Inform. Theory,* 1997, to be published.
[32] P. Bartlett, V. Maiorov, and R. Meir, "Almost linear VC dimension bounds for piecewise polynomial networks," *Neural Comput.,* to be published.
[33] O. Bashkirov, E. M. Braverman, and I. E. Muchnik, "Potential function algorithms for pattern recognition learning machines," *Autom. Remote Contr.,* vol. 25, pp. 692–695, 1964.
[34] E. B. Baum, "On capabilities of multi-layer perceptrons," *J. Complexity,* vol. 4, pp. 193–215, 1988.
[35] ——, "The perceptron algorithm is fast for non-malicious distributions," *Neural Comput.,* vol. 2, pp. 248–260, 1990.
[36] ——, "Neural net algorithms that learn in polynomial time from examples and queries," *IEEE Trans. Neural Networks,* vol. 2, pp. 5–19, 1991.
[37] E. B. Baum and D. Haussler, "What size net gives valid generalization?," *Neural Comput.,* vol. 1, pp. 151–160, 1989.
[38] G. W. Beakley and F. B. Tuteur, "Distribution-free pattern verification using statistically equivalent blocks," *IEEE Trans. Comput.,* vol. C-21, pp. 1337–1347, 1972.
[39] J. Beck, "The exponential rate of convergence of error for $k_n - NN$ nonparametric regression and decision," *Probl. Contr. Inform. Theory,* vol. 8, pp. 303–311, 1979.
[40] G. M. Benedek and A. Itai, "Learnability with respect to fixed distributions," *Theor. Comp. Sci.,* vol. 86, no. 2, pp. 377–390, 1991.
[41] P. K. Bhattacharya and Y. P. Mack, "Weak convergence of $k - NN$ density and regression estimators with varying k and applications," *Ann. Statist.,* vol. 15, pp. 976–994, 1987.
[42] P. J. Bickel and L. Breiman, "Sums of functions of nearest neighbor distances, moment bounds, limit theorems and a goodness of fit test," *Ann. Probab.,* vol. 11, pp. 185–214, 1983.
[43] A. Blum and R. L. Rivest, "Training a 3-node neural network is NP-complete," *Neural Networks,* vol. 5, pp. 117–127, 1992.
[44] A. Blumer, A. Ehrenfeucht, D. Haussler, and M. K. Warmuth, "Learnability and the Vapnik–Chervonenkis dimension," *J. Assoc. Comput. Mach.,* vol. 36, pp. 929–965, 1989.
[45] B. Boser, I. Guyon, and V. N. Vapnik, "A training algorithm for optimal margin classifiers," in *Proc. 5th Annu. ACM Work. Computational Learning Theory.* New York: Assoc. Comput. Mach., 1992, pp. 144–152.
[46] E. M. Braverman, "The method of potential functions," *Automat. Remote Contr.,* vol. 26, pp. 2130–2138, 1965.
[47] E. M. Braverman and E. S. Pyatniskii, "Estimation of the rate of convergence of algorithms based on the potential function method," *Automat. Remote Contr.,* vol. 27, pp. 80–100, 1966.
[48] L. Breiman, "Bagging predictors," *Machine Learn.,* vol. 24, pp. 123–140, 1996.
[49] ——, "Bias, variance, and arcing classifiers," Department of Statistics, Univ. California at Berkeley, Tech. Rep. 460, 1996.
[50] L. Breiman, J. H. Friedman, R. A. Olshen, and C. J. Stone, *Classification and Regression Trees.* Pacific Grove, CA: Wadsworth & Brooks, 1984.
[51] D. S. Broomhead and D. Lowe, "Multivariable functional interpolation and adaptive networks. *Complex Syst.,* vol. 2, pp. 321–323, 1988.

[52] J. Bruck, "Harmonic analysis of polynomial threshold functions," *SIAM J. Discr. Math.*, vol. 3, no. 2, pp. 168–177, 1990.

[53] K. L. Buescher and P. R. Kumar, "Learning by canonical smooth estimation, Part I: Simultaneous estimation," *IEEE Trans. Automat. Contr.*, vol. 42, pp. 545–556, 1996.

[54] _____, "Learning by canonical smooth estimation, Part II: Learning and choice of model complexity," *IEEE Trans. Automat. Contr.*, vol. 42, pp. 557–569, 1996.

[55] D. Burshtein, V. Della Pietra, D. Kanevsky, and A. Nádas, "Minimum impurity partitions," *Ann. Statist.*, vol. 20, pp. 1637–1646, 1992.

[56] T. Chen, H. Chen, and R. Liu, "A constructive proof and an extension of Cybenko's approximation theorem," in *Proc. 22nd Symp. Interface: Computing Science and Statistics.* Alexandria, VA: Amer. Statist. Assoc., 1990, pp. 163–168.

[57] X. R. Chen and L. C. Zhao, "Almost sure L_1-norm convergence for data-based histogram density estimates," *J. Multivariate Anal.*, vol. 21, pp. 179–188, 1987.

[58] P. A. Chou, "Optimal partitioning for classification and regression trees," *IEEE Trans. Pattern Anal. Machine Intell.*, vol. 13, pp. 340–354, 1991.

[59] A. Ciampi, "Generalized regression trees," *Comput. Statisti, Data Anal.*, vol. 12, pp. 57–78, 1991.

[60] M. A. Cohen and S. Grossberg, "Absolute stability of global pattern formation and parallel memory storage by competitive neural networks," *IEEE Trans. Syst., Man, Cybern.*, vol. SMC-13, pp. 815–826, 1983.

[61] G. Collomb, "Estimation de la regression par la méthode des k points les plus proches: Propriétés de convergence ponctuelle," *C. R. l'Académie des Sciences de Paris*, vol. 289, pp. 245–247, 1979.

[62] _____, "Estimation de la regression par la méthode des k points les plus proches avec noyau," in *Lecture Notes in Mathematics.* Berlin, Germany: Springer-Verlag, 1980, vol. 821, pp. 159–175.

[63] _____, "Estimation non parametrique de la regression: Revue bibliographique," *Int. Statist. Rev.*, vol. 49, pp. 75–93, 1981.

[64] C. Cortes and V. N. Vapnik, "Support vector networks," *Machine Learn.*, vol. 20, pp. 1–25, 1995.

[65] T. M. Cover, "Geometrical and statistical properties of systems of linear inequalities with applications to pattern recognition," *IEEE Trans. Electron. Comp.* vol. EC-14, pp. 326–334, 1965.

[66] _____, "Rates of convergence of nearest neighbor decision procedures," in *Proc. 1st Annu. Hawaii Conf. Systems Theory*, 1968, pp. 413–415.

[67] _____, "Capacity problems for linear machines," in *Pattern Recognition*, L. Kanal, Ed. Thompson Book Co., 1968, pp. 283–289.

[68] _____, "Learning in pattern recognition," in *Methodologies of Pattern Recognition*, S. Watanabe, Ed. New York: Academic, 1969, pp. 111–132.

[69] T. M. Cover and P. E. Hart, "Nearest neighbor pattern classification," *IEEE Trans. Inform. Theory*, vol. IT-13, pp. 21–27, 1967.

[70] T. M. Cover and T. J. Wagner, "Topics in statistical pattern recognition," *Commun. and Cybern.*, vol. 10, pp. 15–46, 1975.

[71] G. Cybenko, "Approximation by superpositions of a sigmoidal function," *Math. Contr., Signals, Syst.*, vol. 2, pp. 303–314, 1989.

[72] G. B. Dantzig, *Linear Programming and Extensions.* Princeton, NJ: Princeton Univ. Press, 1963.

[73] C. Darken, M. Donahue, L. Gurvits, and E. Sontag, "Rate of approximation results motivated by robust neural network learning," in *Proc. 6th ACM Work. Computational Learning Theory.* New York: Assoc. Comput. Mach., 1993, pp. 303–309.

[74] S. Das Gupta, "Nonparametric classification rules," *Sankhya Ser. A*, vol. 26, pp. 25–30, 1964.

[75] B. V. Dasarathy, Ed., *Nearest Neighbor Pattern Classification Techniques.* Los Alamitos, CA: IEEE Comp. Soc. Press, 1991.

[76] B. DasGupta, H. T. Siegelmann, and E. Sontag, "On the intractability of loading neural networks," in *Theoretical Advances in Neural Computation and Learning*, V. Roychowdhury, K.-Y. Siu, and A. Orlitsky, Eds. Norwell, MA: Kluwer, 1994, pp. 357–390.

[77] P. A. Devijer, "New error bounds with the nearest neighbor rule," *IEEE Trans. Inform. Theory*, vol. IT-25, pp. 749–753, 1979.

[78] P. A. Devijver and J. Kittler, *Pattern Recognition: A Statistical Approach.* Englewood Cliffs, NJ: Prentice-Hall, 1982.

[79] L. Devroye, "A universal k-nearest neighbor procedure in discrimination," in *Proc. 1978 IEEE Computer Society Conf. Pattern Recognition and Image Processing.* Long Beach, CA: IEEE Comp. Soc., 1978, pp. 142–147.

[80] _____, "On the inequality of Cover and Hart in nearest neighbor discrimination," *IEEE Trans. Pattern Anal. Machine Intell.*, vol. 3, pp. 75–78, 1981.

[81] _____, "On the almost everywhere convergence of nonparametric regression function estimates," *Ann. Statist.*, vol. 9, pp. 1310–1309, 1981.

[82] _____, "Necessary and sufficient conditions for the almost everywhere convergence of nearest neighbor regression function estimates," *Z. für Wahrscheinlichkeitstheorie verwandte Gebiete*, vol. 61, pp. 467–481, 1982.

[83] _____, "Any discrimination rule can have an arbitrarily bad probability of error for finite sample size," *IEEE Trans. Pattern Anal. Machine Intell.*, vol. PAMI-4, pp. 154–157, 1982.

[84] _____, "Bounds for the uniform deviation of empirical measures," *J. Multivariate Anal.*, vol. 12, pp. 72–79, 1982.

[85] _____, "Automatic pattern recognition: A study of the probability of error," *IEEE Trans. Pattern Anal. Machine Intell.*, vol. 10, pp. 530–543, 1988.

[86] _____, "Universal smoothing factor selection in density estimation: Theory and practice," *Test*, vol. 6, pp. 223–320, 1997, with discussion.

[87] L. Devroye and L. Györfi, "Distribution-free exponential bound on the L_1 error of partitioning estimates of a regression function," in *Proc. 4th Pannonian Symp. Mathematical Statistics,* F. Konecny, J. Mogyoródi, and W. Wertz, Eds. Budapest, Hungary: Akadémiai Kiadó, 1983, pp. 67–76.

[88] _____, *Nonparametric Density Estimation: The L_1 View.* New York: Wiley, 1985.

[89] L. Devroye, L. Györfi, A. Krzyżak, and G. Lugosi, "On the strong universal consistency of nearest neighbor regression function estimates," *Ann. Statist.*, vol. 22, pp. 1371–1385, 1994.

[90] L. Devroye, L. Györfi, and G. Lugosi, *A Probabilistic Theory of Pattern Recognition.* New York: Springer-Verlag, 1996.

[91] L. Devroye and A. Krzyżak, "An equivalence theorem for L_1 convergence of the kernel regression estimate," *J. Statist. Planning and Infer.*, vol. 23, pp. 71–82, 1989.

[92] L. Devroye and G. Lugosi, "Lower bounds in pattern recognition and learning," *Pattern Recogn.*, vol. 28, pp. 1011–1018, 1995.

[93] L. Devroye and T. J. Wagner, "A distribution-free performance bound in error estimation," *IEEE Trans. Inform. Theory*, vol. IT-22, pp. 586–587, 1976.

[94] _____, "Nonparametric discrimination and density estimation," Electron. Res. Ctr, Univ. Texas, Tech. Rep. 183, 1976.

[95] _____, "Distribution-free inequalities for the deleted and holdout error estimates," *IEEE Trans. Inform. Theory*, vol. IT-25, pp. 202–207, 1979.

[96] _____, "Distribution-free consistency results in nonparametric discrimination and regression function estimation," *Ann. Statist.*, vol. 8, pp. 231–239, 1980.

[97] R. O. Duda and P. E. Hart, *Pattern Classification and Scene Analysis.* New York: Wiley, 1973.

[98] H. Drucker and C. Cortes, "Boosting decision trees," in *Advances in Neural Information Processing Systems 8*, 1996, pp. 148–156.

[99] R. M. Dudley, "Central limit theorems for empirical measures" *Ann. Probab.*, vol. 6, no. 6, pp. 899–929, 1978.

[100] _____, "Balls in R^k do not cut all subsets of $k+2$ points," *Adv. Math.*, vol. 31, no. 3, pp. 306–308, 1979.

[101] _____, *A Course on Empirical Processes* (Lecture Notes in Mathematics, vol. 1097). Berlin, Germany: Springer-Verlrag, 1984, pp. 1–142.

[102] R. M. Dudley, S. R. Kulkarni, T. J. Richardson, and O. Zeitouni, "A metric entropy bound is not sufficient for learnability," *IEEE Trans. Inform. Theory*, vol. 40, pp. 883–885, 1994.

[103] F. H. Eeckman, "The sigmoid nonlinearity in prepyriform cortex," in *Neural Information Processing Systems*, D. Z. Anderson, Ed. New York: Amer. Inst. Phys., 1988, pp. 242–248.

[104] F. H. Eeckman and W. J. Freeman, "The sigmoid nonlinearity in neural computation: An experimental approach," in *Neural Networks for Computing*, J. S. Denker, Ed. New York: Amer. Inst. Phys., 1986, pp. 135–145.

[105] B. Efron, "Bootstrap methods: Another look at the jackknife," *Ann. Statist.*, vol. 7, pp. 1–26, 1979.

[106] _____, "Estimating the error rate of a prediction rule: Improvement on cross validation," *J. Amer. Statist. Assoc.*, vol. 78, pp. 316–331, 1983.

[107] A. Ehrenfeucht, D. Haussler, M. Kearns, and L. Valiant, "A general lower bound on the number of examples needed for learning," *Inform. Comput.*, vol. 82, pp. 247–261, 1989.

[108] A. Erdélyi, *Asymptotic Expansions.* New York: Dover, 1956.

[109] A. Faragó and G. Lugosi, "Strong universal consistency of neural network classifiers," *IEEE Trans. Inform. Theory*, vol. 39, pp. 1146–1151, 1993.

[110] R. A. Fisher, "The use of multiple measurements in taxonomic problems," *Ann. Eugenics*, vol. 7, pt. II, pp. 179–188, 1936.

[111] E. Fix and J. L. Hodges, Jr., "Discriminatory analysis—Nonparametric discrimination: Consistency properties," USAF School of Aviation Medicine, Randolf Field, TX, Project 21-49-004, Rep. 4, pp. 261–279, 1951.

[112] ——, "Discriminatory analysis—Nonparametric discrimination: Small sample performance," *USAF School of Aviation Medicine*, Randolf Field, TX, Project 21-49-004, Rep. 11, pp. 280–322, 1952.

[113] Y. Freund, "Boosting a weak learning algorithm by majority," *Inform. Comput.*, vol. 121, pp. 256–285, 1995.

[114] J. H. Friedman, "A recursive partitioning decision rule for nonparametric classification," *IEEE Trans. Comp.*, vol. C-26, pp. 404–408, 1977.

[115] J. Fritz, "Distribution-free exponential error bound for nearest neighbor pattern classification," *IEEE Trans. Inform. Theory*, vol. IT-21, pp. 552–557, 1975.

[116] K. Fukunaga, *Introduction to Statistical Pattern Recognition*. New York: Academic, 1972.

[117] K. Fukunaga and T. E. Flick, "An optimal global nearest neighbor metric," *IEEE Trans. Pattern Anal. Machine Intell.*, vol. PAMI-6, pp. 314–318, 1984.

[118] K. Fukunaga and D. L. Kessel, "Nonparametric Bayes error estimation using unclassified samples," *IEEE Trans. Inform. Theory*, vol. IT-19, pp. 434–440, 1973.

[119] K. Fukunaga and D. M. Hummels, "Bias of nearest neighbor estimates," *IEEE Trans. Pattern Anal. Machine Intell.*, vol. PAMI-9, pp. 103–112, 1987.

[120] K. Funahashi, "On the approximate realization of continuous mappings by neural networks," *Neural Networks*, vol. 2, pp. 183–192, 1989.

[121] M. R. Garey and D. J. Johnson, *Computers and Intractability. A Guide to the Theory of NP-Completeness.* New York: Freeman, 1979.

[122] S. B. Gelfand and E. J. Delp, "On tree structured classifiers," in *Artificial Neural Networks and Statistical Pattern Recognition, Old and New Connections*, I. K. Sethi and A. K. Jain, Eds. Amsterdam, The Netherlands: Elsevier, 1991, pp. 71–88.

[123] S. B. Gelfand, C. S. Ravishankar, and E. J. Delp, "An iterative growing and pruning algorithm for classification tree design," in *Proc. 1989 IEEE Int. Conf. Systems, Man, and Cybernetics.* Piscataway, NJ: IEEE Press, 1989, pp. 818–823.

[124] ——, "An iterative growing and pruning algorithm for classification tree design," *IEEE Trans. Pattern Anal. Machine Intell.*, vol. 13, pp. 163–174, 1991.

[125] M. P. Gessaman, "A consistent nonparametric multivariate density estimator based on statistically equivalent blocks," *Ann. Math. Statist.*, vol. 41, pp. 1344–1346, 1970.

[126] M. P. Gessaman and P. H. Gessaman, "A comparison of some multivariate discrimination procedures," *J. Amer. Statist. Assoc.*, vol. 67, pp. 468–472, 1972.

[127] N. Glick, "Additive estimators for probabilities of correct classification," *Pattern Recogn.*, vol. 10, pp. 211–222, 1978.

[128] P. Goldberg and M. Jerrum, "Bounding the Vapnik–Chervonenkis dimension of concept classes parametrized by real numbers," in *Proc. 6th Annual ACM Conf. Computational Learning Theory*, 1993, pp. 361–369.

[129] R. M. Goodman and P. Smyth, "Decision tree design from a communication theory viewpoint," *IEEE Trans. Inform. Theory*, vol. 34, pp. 979–994, 1988.

[130] L. Gordon and R. Olshen, "Almost surely consistent nonparametric regression from recursive partitioning schemes," *J. Multivariate Anal.*, vol. 15, pp. 147–163, 1984.

[131] ——, "Asymptotically efficient solutions to the classification problem," *Ann. Statist.*, vol. 6, pp. 515–533, 1978.

[132] ——, "Consistent nonparametric regression from recursive partitioning schemes," *J. Multivariate Anal.*, vol. 10, pp. 611–627, 1980.

[133] W. Greblicki, A. Krzyżak, and M. Pawlak, "Distribution-free pointwise consistency of kernel regression estimate," *Ann. Statist.*, vol. 12, pp. 1570–1575, 1984.

[134] W. Greblicki and M. Pawlak, "Necessary and sufficient conditions for Bayes risk consistency of a recursive kernel classification rule," *IEEE Trans. Inform. Theory*, vol. IT-33, pp. 408–412, 1987.

[135] H. Guo and S. B. Gelfand, "Classification trees with neural network feature extraction," *IEEE Trans. Neural Networks*, vol. 3, pp. 923–933, 1992.

[136] L. Györfi, "On the rate of convergence of nearest neighbor rules," *IEEE Trans. Inform. Theory*, vol. IT-24, pp. 509–512, 1978.

[137] L. Györfi and Z. Györfi, "On the nonparametric estimate of *a posteriori* probabilities of simple statistical hypotheses," in *Colloquia Mathematica Societatis János Bolyai: Topics in Information Theory* (Keszthely, Hungary, 1975)), pp. 299–308.

[138] ——, "An upperbound on the asymptotic error probability of the *k*-nearest neighbor rule," *IEEE Trans. Inform. Theory*, vol. IT-24, pp. 512–514, 1978.

[139] D. J. Hand, "Recent advances in error rate estimation," *Pattern Recogn. Lett.*, vol. 4, pp. 335–346, 1986.

[140] D. Haussler, "Decision theoretic generalizations of the PAC model for neural net and other learning applications," *Inform. Comput.*, vol. 100, pp. 78–150, 1992.

[141] D. Haussler, N. Littlestone, and M. Warmuth, "Predicting $\{0, 1\}$ functions from randomly drawn points," in *Proc. 29th IEEE Symp. Foundations of Computer Science.* Los Alamitos, CA: IEEE Comp. Soc. Press, 1988, pp. 100–109.

[142] S. Haykin, *Neural Networks.* New York: Macmillan, 1994.

[143] D. O. Hebb, *The Organization of Behavior.* New York: Wiley, 1949.

[144] T. Hegedüs, "On training simple neural networks and small-weight neurons," in *Proc. 1st Euro. Conf. Computational Learning Theory*, 1993.

[145] E. G. Henrichon and K. S. Fu, "A nonparametric partitioning procedure for pattern classification," *IEEE Trans. Comp.*, vol. C-18, pp. 614–624, 1969.

[146] M. E. Hellman, "The nearest-neighbor classification rule with a reject option," *IEEE Trans. Syst. Sci. Cybern.*, vol. SSC-6, pp. 179–185, 1970.

[147] J. Hertz, A. Krogh, and R. G. Palmer, *Introduction to the Theory of Neural Computation.* Reading, MA: Addison-Wesley, 1991.

[148] M. W. Hirsch, "Convergent activation dynamics in continuous time networks," *Neural Networks*, vol. 2, pp. 331–349, 1989.

[149] Y.-C. Ho and R. L. Kashyap, "A class of iterative procedures for linear inequalities," *J. SIAM Contr.*, vol. 4, pp. 112–115, 1966.

[150] S. B. Holden, "PAC-like upper bounds for the sample complexity of leave-one-out cross validation," in *Proc. 9th Ann. ACM Work. Computational Learning Theory.* New York: Assoc. Comput. Mach., 1996, pp. 41–50.

[151] J. J. Hopfield, "Neural networks and physical systems with emergent collective computational capabilities," in *Proc. Nat. Acad. Sci. USA*, 1982, vol. 79, pp. 2554–2558.

[152] ——, "Neurons with graded response have collective computational properties like those of two-state neurons," in *Proc. Nat. Acad. Sci. USA*, 1984, vol. 81, pp. 3088–3092.

[153] K. Hornik, M. Stinchcombe, and H. White, "Multilayer feedforward networks are universal approximators," *Neural Networks*, vol. 2, pp. 359–366, 1989.

[154] K. Hornik, "Some new results on neural network approximation," *Neural Networks*, vol. 6, pp. 1069–1072, 1993.

[155] M. Horváth and G. Lugosi, "A data-dependent skeleton estimate and a scale-sensitive dimension for classification," *Discr. Appl. Math.* (Special Issue on the Vapnik–Chervonenkis dimension), to be published, 1997.

[156] A. K. Jain, R. C. Dubes, and C. Chen, "Bootstrap techniques for error estimation," *IEEE Trans. Pattern Anal. Machine Intell.*, vol. PAMI-9, pp. 628–633, 1987.

[157] L. Jones, "Constructive approximations for neural networks by sigmoidal functions," *Proc. IEEE*, vol. 78, pp. 1586–1589, Oct. 1990.

[158] J. S. Judd, *Neural Network Design and the Complexity of Learning.* Cambridge, MA: MIT Press, 1990.

[159] L. N. Kanal, "Patterns in pattern recognition," *IEEE Trans. Inform. Theory*, vol. IT-20, pp. 697–722, 1974.

[160] N. Karmarkar, "A new polynomial-time algorithm for linear programming," *Combinatorica*, vol. 4, no. 4, pp. 373–395, 1984.

[161] M. Karpinski and A. Macintyre, "Polynomial bounds for VC dimension of sigmoidal and general pfaffian neural networks," *J. Comp. Syst. Sci.*, vol. 54, 1997.

[162] M. Kearns, Y. Mansour, A. Y. Ng, and D. Ron, "An experimental and theoretical comparison of model selection methods," in *Proc. 8th Annu. ACM Work. Computational Learning Theory.* New York: Assoc. Comput. Mach., 1995, pp. 21–30.

[163] M. Kearns and D. Ron, "Algorithmic stability and sanity-check bounds for leave-one-out cross validation," in *Proc. 10th Annu. ACM Work. Computational Learning Theory* New York: Assoc. Comput. Mach., 1997.

[164] M. Kearns and U. Vazirani, *Introduction to Computational Learning Theory.* Cambridge, MA: MIT Press, 1994.

[165] T. Kohonen, *Self-Organization and Associative Memory.* New York: Springer-Verlag, 1984.

[166] P. Koiran and E. D. Sontag, "Neural networks with quadratic VC dimension," *J. Comp. Syst. Sci.*, vol. 54, 1997.

[167] A. N. Kolmogorov and V. M. Tihomirov, "ϵ-entropy and ϵ-capacity of sets in functional spaces," *Amer. Math. Soc. Transl.*, vol. 17, pp. 277–364, 1961.

[168] J. Komlós and R. Paturi, "Convergence results in an associative memory model," *Neural Networks*, vol. 1, pp. 239–250, 1988.

[169] ——, "Effect of connectivity in associative memory models," Univ. California, San Diego, 1988, Tech. Rep. CS88-131; to be published in *J. Comp. Syst. Sci.*

[170] A. Krzyżak, "On exponential bounds on the Bayes risk of the kernel classification rule," *IEEE Trans. Inform. Theory*, vol. 37, pp. 490–499, 1991.

[171] A. Krzyżak and T. Linder, "Radial basis function networks and complexity regularization in function learning," *IEEE Transactions on Neural Networks,* 1998, to appear.

[172] A. Krzyżak, T. Linder, and G. Lugosi, "Nonparametric estimation and classification using radial basis function nets and empirical risk minimization," *IEEE Trans. Neural Networks*, vol. 7, pp. 475–487, 1996.

[173] A. Krzyżak and M. Pawlak, "Almost everywhere convergence of recursive kernel regression function estimates," *IEEE Trans. Inform. Theory*, vol. IT-31, pp. 91–93, 1984.

[174] S. R. Kulkarni, S. K. Mitter, and J. N. Tsitsiklis, "Active learning using arbitrary binary valued queries," *Machine Learn.*, vol. 11, pp. 23–35, 1993.

[175] S. R. Kulkarni and M. Vidyasagar, "Learning classes of decision rules under a family of probability measures," *IEEE Trans. Inform. Theory*, vol. 43, pp. 154–166, 1997.

[176] P. A. Lachenbruch, "An almost unbiased method of obtaining confidence intervals for the probability of misclassification in discriminant analysis," *Biometrics*, vol. 23, pp. 639–645, 1967.

[177] M. Ledoux and M. Talagrand, *Probability in Banach Space.* New York: Springer-Verlag, 1991.

[178] M. Leshno, V. Lin, A. Pinkus, and S. Schocken, "Multilayer feedforward networks with a polynomial activation function can approximate any function," *Neural Networks*, vol. 6, pp. 861–867, 1993.

[179] X. Li and R. C. Dubes, "Tree classifier design with a permutation statistic," *Pattern Recogn.*, vol. 19, pp. 229–235, 1986.

[180] J. H. Lin and J. S. Vitter, "Complexity results on learning by neural nets," *Machine Learn.*, vol. 6, pp. 211–230, 1991.

[181] W. Y. Loh and N. Vanichsetakul, "Tree-structured classification via generalized discriminant analysis," *J. Amer. Statist. Assoc.*, vol. 83, pp. 715–728, 1988.

[182] G. Lugosi, "Improved upper bounds for probabilities of uniform deviations," *Statist. Probab. Lett.*, vol. 25, pp. 71–77, 1995.

[183] G. Lugosi and A. Nobel, "Consistency of data-driven histogram methods for density estimation and classification," *Ann. Statist.*, vol. 24, pp. 687–706, 1996.

[184] G. Lugosi and K. Zeger, "Nonparametric estimation via empirical risk minimization," *IEEE Trans. Inform. Theory*, vol. 41, pp. 677–678, 1995.

[185] ——, "Concept learning using complexity regularization," *IEEE Trans. Inform. Theory*, vol. 42, pp. 48–54, 1996.

[186] A. L. Lunts and V. L. Brailovsky, "Evaluation of attributes obtained in statistical decision rules," *Eng. Cybern.*, vol. 3, pp. 98–109, 1967.

[187] W. Maass, "Bounds for the computational power and learning complexity of analog neural nets," in *Proc. 25th Annu. ACM Symp. Theory of Computing*, 1993, pp. 335–344.

[188] M. MacIntyre and E. D. Sontag, "Finiteness results for sigmoidal neural networks," in *Proc. 25th Annu. ACM Symp. Theory of Computing*, 1993, pp. 325–334.

[189] Y. P. Mack, "Local properties of k–nearest neighbor regression estimates," *SIAM J. Algeb. Discr. Methods*, vol. 2, pp. 311–323, 1981.

[190] P. Massart, "The tight constant in the Dvoretzky–Kiefer–Wolfowitz inequality," *Ann. Probab.*, vol. 18, pp. 1269–1283, 1990.

[191] W. S. McCulloch and W. Pitts, "A logical calculus of the ideas imminent in neural activity," *Bull. Math. Biophys.*, vol. 5, pp. 115–133, 1943.

[192] R. J. McEliece, E. C. Posner, E. R. Rodemich, and S. S. Venkatesh, "The capacity of the Hopfield associative memory," *IEEE Trans. Inform. Theory*, vol. IT-33, pp. 461–482, 1987.

[193] G. J. McLachlan, *Discriminant Analysis and Statistical Pattern Recognition.* New York: Wiley, 1992.

[194] R. Meir, "Performance bounds for nonlinear time series prediction," in *Proc. 10th Annu. ACM Work. Computational Learning Theory.* New York: Assoc. Comput. Mach., 1997.

[195] W. S. Meisel and D. A. Michalopoulos, "A partitioning algorithm with application in pattern classification and the optimization of decision tree," *IEEE Trans. Comp.*, vol. C-22, pp. 93–103, 1973.

[196] C. Michel-Briand and X. Milhaud, "Asymptotic behavior of the AID method," Univ. Montpellier 2, Montpellier, France, Tech. Rep., 1994.

[197] J. Mielniczuk and J. Tyrcha, "Consistency of multilayer perceptron regression estimators," *Neural Networks*, 1993, to be published.

[198] M. L. Minsky and S. A. Papert, *Perceptrons.* Cambridge, MA: MIT Press, 1988.

[199] R. Mizoguchi, M. Kizawa, and M. Shimura, "Piecewise linear discriminant functions in pattern recognition," *Syst.-Comp.-Contr.*, vol. 8, pp. 114–121, 1977.

[200] D. S. Modha and E. Masrym "Minimum complexity regression estimation with weakly dependent observations," *IEEE Trans. Inform. Theory*, 1996, to be published.

[201] J. Moody and J. Darken, "Fast learning in networks of locally-tuned processing units," *Neural Comput.*, vol. 1, pp. 281–294, 1989.

[202] J. N. Morgan and J. A. Sonquist, "Problems in the analysis of survey data, and a proposal," *J. Amer. Statist. Assoc.*, vol. 58, pp. 415–434, 1963.

[203] E. A. Nadaraya, "On estimating regression," *Theory Probab. Applic.*, vol. 9, pp. 141–142, 1964.

[204] ——, "Remarks on nonparametric estimates for density functions and regression curves," *Theory Probab. Applic.*, vol. 15, pp. 134–137, 1970.

[205] B. K. Natarajan, *Machine Learning: A Theoretical Approach.* San Mateo, CA: Morgan Kaufmann, 1991.

[206] C. Newman, "Memory capacity in neural network models: Rigorous lower bounds," *Neural Networks*, vol. 1, pp. 223–238, 1988.

[207] N. J. Nilsson, *The Mathematical Foundations of Learning Machines.* San Mateo, CA: Morgan-Kaufmann, 1990.

[208] A. Nobel, "Histogram regression using data-dependent partitions," *Ann. Statist.*, vol. 24, pp. 1084–1105, 1996.

[209] ——, "Recursive partitioning to reduce distortion," *IEEE Trans. Inform. Theory*, vol. 43, pp. 1122–1133, 1997.

[210] R. A. Olshen, "Comments on a paper by C. J. Stone," *Ann. Statist.*, vol. 5, pp. 632–633, 1977.

[211] Y. Park and J. Sklansky, "Automated design of linear tree classifiers," *Pattern Recogn.*, vol. 23, pp. 1393–1412, 1990.

[212] J. M. Parrondo and C. Van den Broeck, "Vapnik–Chervonenkis bounds for generalization," *J. Phys. Ser. A*, vol. 26, pp. 2211–2223, 1993.

[213] E. Parzen, "On the estimation of a probability density function and the mode," *Ann. Math. Statist.*, vol. 33, pp. 1065–1076, 1962.

[214] E. A. Patrick, "Distribution-free minimum conditional risk learning systems," Purdue Univ., Lafayette, IN, Tech. Rep. TR-EE-66-18, 1966.

[215] E. A. Patrick and F. P. Fisher, "Introduction to the performance of distribution-free conditional risk learning systems," Purdue Univ., Lafayette, IN, Tech. Rep. TR-EE-67-12, 1967.

[216] H. J. Payne and W. S. Meisel, "An algorithm for constructing optimal binary decision trees," *IEEE Trans. Comput.*, vol. C-26, pp. 905–916, 1977.

[217] P. Peretto and J.-J. Niez, "Stochastic dynamics of neural networks," *IEEE Trans. Syst., Man, Cybern.*, vol. SMC-16, pp. 73–83, 1986.

[218] F. J. Pineda, "Recurrent backpropagation and the dynamical approach to adaptive neural computation," *Neural Comput.*, vol. 1, pp. 161–172, 1989.

[219] L. Pitt and L. G. Valiant, "Computational limitations of learning from examples," *J. Assoc. Comput. Mach.*, vol. 35, pp. 965–984, 1988.

[220] T. Poggio and F. Girosi, "A theory of networks for approximation and learning," *Proc. IEEE*, vol. 78, pp. 1481–1497, 1990.

[221] D. Pollard, *Convergence of Stochastic Processes.* New York: Springer-Verlag, 1984.

[222] ——, "Asymptotics via empirical processes," *Statist. Sci.*, vol. 4, pp. 341–366, 1989.

[223] ——, *Empirical Processes: Theory and Applications*, NSF-CBMS Regional Conf. Ser. Probability and Statistics, Inst. Math. Statist., Hayward, CA, 1990.

[224] M. J. D. Powell, "Radial basis functions for multivariable interpolation: A review," in *Algorithms for Approximation.* Oxford, U.K.: Clarendon, 1987.

[225] D. Psaltis, R. R. Snapp, and S. S. Venkatesh, "On the finite sample performance of the nearest neighbour classifier," *IEEE Trans. Inform. Theory*, vol. 40, pp. 820–837, 1994.

[226] C. P. Quesenberry and M. P. Gessaman, "Nonparametric discrimination using tolerance regions," *Ann. Math. Statist.*, vol. 39, pp. 664–673, 1968.

[227] S. Qing-Yun and K. S. Fu, "A method for the design of binary tree classifiers," *Pattern Recogn.*, vol. 16, pp. 593–603, 1983.

[228] J. R. Quinlan, *C4.5: Programs for Machine Learning.* San Mateo, CA: Morgan Kaufmann, 1993.

[229] ——, "Bagging, boosting, and C4.5," in *Proc. 13th Nat. Conf. Artificial Intelligence*, 1996, pp. 725–730.

[230] B. D. Ripley, "Statistical aspects of neural networks," in *Networks and Chaos—Statistical and Probabilistic Aspects*, O. E. Barndorff-Nielsen, J. L. Jensen, and W. S. Kendall, Eds. London, U.K.: Chapman and Hall, 1993, pp. 40–123.

[231] ——, "Neural networks and related methods for classification," *J. Roy. Statist. Soc.*, vol. 56, pp. 409–456, 1994.

[232] J. Rissanen, "Stochastic complexity in statistical inquiry," *World Scientific* (Series in Computer Science, vol. 15), 1989.

[233] W. H. Rogers and T. J. Wagner, "A finite sample distribution-free performance bound for local discrimination rules," *Ann. Statist.*, vol. 6, pp. 506–514, 1978.

[234] F. Rosenblatt, *Principles of Neurodynamics.* Washington, DC: Spartan, 1962.

160

[235] M. Rosenblatt, "Remarks on some nonparametric estimates of a density function," *Ann. Math. Statist.*, vol. 27, pp. 832–837, 1956.

[236] E. M. Rounds, "A combined nonparametric approach to feature selection and binary decision tree design," *Pattern Recogn.*, vol. 12, pp. 313–317, 1980.

[237] R. M. Royall, "A class of nonparametric estimators of a smooth regression function," Ph.D. dissertation, Stanford Univ., Stanford, CA, 1966.

[238] V. Roychowdhury, K.-Y. Siu, and A. Orlitsky, Eds., *Theoretical Advances in Neural Computation and Learning.* Norwell, MA: Kluwer, 1994.

[239] W. Rudin, *Real and Complex Analysis.* New York: McGraw-Hill, 1974.

[240] D. E. Rumelhart and J. L. McClelland, Eds., *Parallel Distributed Processing*, vol. 1. Cambridge, MA: MIT Press, 1986.

[241] A. Sakurai, "Tighter bounds of the VC-dimension of three-layer networks," in *Proc. WCNN*, 1993, vol. 3, pp. 540–543.

[242] N. Sauer, "On the density of families of sets," *J. Comb. Theory Ser. A*, vol. 13, pp. 145–147, 1972.

[243] R. E. Schapire, "The strength of weak learnability," *Machine Learn.*, vol. 5, pp. 197–227, 1990.

[244] R. E. Schapire, Y. Freund, P. Bartlett, and W. S. Lee, "Boosting the margin: A new explanation for the effectiveness of voting methods," 1997, unpublished.

[245] L. Schläffli, *Gesammelte Mathematische Abhandlungen I.* Basel, Switzerland: Birkhäuser, 1950, pp. 209–212.

[246] D. Schuurmans, "Characterizing rational versus exponential learning curves," in *Computational Learning Theory: Second European Conference, EuroCOLT'95.* Berlin, Germany: Springer-Verlag, 1995, pp. 272–286.

[247] G. Sebestyen, *Decision-Making Processes in Pattern Recognition.* New York: Macmillan, 1962.

[248] I. K. Sethi, "Decision tree performance enhancement using an artificial neural network interpretation," in *Artificial Neural Networks and Statistical Pattern Recognition, Old and New Connections*, I. K. Sethi and A. K. Jain, Eds. Amsterdam, the Netherlands: Elsevier, 1991, pp. 71–88.

[249] I. K. Sethi and G. P. R. Sarvarayudu, "Hierarchical classifier design using mutual information," *IEEE Trans. Pattern Anal. Machine Intell.*, vol. 4, pp. 441–445, 1982.

[250] J. Shawe-Taylor, M. Anthony, and N. L. Biggs, "Bounding sample size with the Vapnik–Chervonenkis dimension," *Discr. Appl. Math.*, vol. 42, pp. 65–73, 1993.

[251] J. Shawe-Taylor, P. L. Bartlett, R. C. Williamson, and M. Anthony, "A framework for structural risk minimization," in *Proc. 9th Annu. Conf. Computational Learning Theory.* New York: Assoc. Comput. Mach., 1996, pp. 68–76.

[252] ——, "Structural risk minimization over data-dependent hierarchies," *IEEE Trans. Inform. Theory*, vol. 44, pp. 1926–1940, Sept. 1998.

[253] R. D. Short and K. Fukunaga, "The optimal distance measure for nearest neighbor classification," *IEEE Trans. Inform. Theory*, vol. IT-27, pp. 622–627, 1981.

[254] H. U. Simon, "The Vapnik–Chervonenkis dimension of decision trees with bounded rank," *Inform. Processing Lett.*, vol. 39, pp. 137–141, 1991.

[255] ——, "General lower bounds on the number of examples needed for learning probabilistic concepts," in *Proc. 6th Annu. ACM Conf. Computational Learning Theory.* New York: Assoc. Comput. Mach., 1993, pp. 402–412.

[256] ——, "Bounds on the number of examples needed for learning functions," *SIAM J. Comput.*, vol. 26, pp. 751–763, 1997.

[257] J. Sklansky and Michelotti, "Locally trained piecewise linear classifiers," *IEEE Trans. Pattern Anal. Machine Intell.*, vol. PAMI-2, pp. 101–111, 1980.

[258] R. R. Snapp and S. S. Venkatesh, "Asymptotic derivation of the finite-sample risk of the k-nearest neighbor classifier," Dept. Comp. Sci., Univ. Vermont, Tech. Rep., TR-UVM-CS-1997-001, 1997.

[259] ——, "Asymptotic expansions of the k nearest neighbour risk," *Ann. Statist.*, 1998, to be published.

[260] E. D. Sontag, "Feedforward nets for interpolation and classification," *J. Comp. Syst. Sci.*, vol. 45, pp. 20–48, 1992.

[261] D. F. Specht, "Generation of polynomial discriminant functions for pattern classification," *IEEE Trans. Electron. Comp.*, vol. EC-15, pp. 308–319, 1967.

[262] ——, "Probabilistic neural networks and the polynomial Adaline as complementary techniques for classification," *IEEE Trans. Neural Networks*, vol. 1, pp. 111–121, 1990.

[263] C. Spiegelman and J. Sacks, "Consistent window estimation in nonparametric regression," *Ann. Statist.*, vol. 8, pp. 240–246, 1980.

[264] G. Stengle and J. Yukich, "Some new Vapnik–Chervonenkis classes," *Ann. Statist.*, vol. 17, pp. 1441–1446, 1989.

[265] D. S. Stoller, "Univariate two-population distribution-free discrimination," *J. Amer. Statist. Assoc.*, vol. 49, pp. 770–777, 1954.

[266] M. Stone, "Cross-validatory choice and assessment of statistical predictions," *J. Roy. Statist. Soc.*, vol. 36, pp. 111–147, 1974.

[267] C. J. Stone, "Consistent nonparametric regression," *Ann. Statist.*, vol. 5, 1977, pp. 595–645.

[268] W. Stute, "Asymptotic normality of nearest neighbor regression function estimates," *Ann. Statist.*, vol. 12, pp. 917–926, 1984.

[269] M. Talagrand, "Sharper bounds for Gaussian and empirical processes," *Ann. Probab.*, vol. 22, pp. 28–76, 1994.

[270] J. L. Talmon, "A multiclass nonparametric partitioning algorithm," in *Pattern Recognition in Practice II*, E. S. Gelsema and L. N. Kanal, Eds. Amsterdam, The Netherlands: Elsevier, 1986.

[271] G. T. Toussaint, "Bibliography on estimation of misclassification," *IEEE Trans. Inform. Theory*, vol. IT-20, pp. 472–479, 1974.

[272] G. T. Toussaint and R. W. Donaldson, "Algorithms for recognizing contour-traced handprinted characters," *IEEE Trans. Comput.*, vol. C-19, pp. 541–546, 1970.

[273] L. G. Valiant, "A theory of the learnable," *Comm. Asooc. Comput. Mach.*, vol. 27, no. 11, pp. 1134–1142, 1984.

[274] V. N. Vapnik, *Estimation of Dependencies Based on Empirical Data.* New York: Springer-Verlag, 1982.

[275] ——, *The Nature of Statistical Learning Theory.* New York: Springer-Verlag, 1991.

[276] V. N. Vapnik and A. Ya. Chervonenkis, "On the uniform convergence of relative frequencies of events to their probabilities," *Theory Probab. Applic.*, vol. 16, no. 2, pp. 264–280, 1971.

[277] ——, *Theory of Pattern Recognition.* Moscow, USSR: Nauka, 1974, in Russian; German translation: *Theorie der Zeichenerkennung.* Berlin, Germany: Akademie Verlag, 1979.

[278] ——, "Necessary and sufficient conditions for the uniform convergence of means to their expectations," *Theory Probab. Applic.*, vol. 26, no. 3, pp. 532–553, 1981.

[279] S. S. Venkatesh, "Computation and learning in the context of neural network capacity," in *Neural Networks for Perception*, vol. 2, H. Wechsler, Ed. San Diego, CA: Academic, 1992.

[280] ——, "Robustness in neural computation: Random graphs and sparsity," *IEEE Trans. Inform. Theory*, vol. 38, pp. 1114–1118, May 1992.

[281] ——, "Directed drift: A new linear threshold algorithm for learning binary weights on-line," *J. Comp. Syst. Sci.*, vol. 46, pp. 198–217, 1993.

[282] ——, "Connectivity versus capacity in the Hebb rule," in *Theoretical Advances in Neural Computation and Learning*, V. Roychowdhury, K.-Y. Siu, and A. Orlitsky, Eds. Norwell, MA: Kluwer, 1994.

[283] S. S. Venkatesh and P. Baldi, "Programmed interactions in higher-order neural networks: Maximal capacity," *J. Complexity*, vol. 7, no. 3, pp. 316–337, 1991.

[284] ——, "Programmed interactions in higher-order neural networks: The outer-product algorithm," *J. Complexity*, vol. 7, no. 4, pp. 443–479, 1991.

[285] M. Vidyasagar, *A Theory of Learning and Generalization.* New York: Springer-Verlag, 1997.

[286] V. H. Vu, "On the infeasibility of training neural networks with small squared error," in *Proc. Conf. Neural Information Processing Systems* (Denver, CO, 1997).

[287] T. J. Wagner, "Convergence of the nearest neighbor rule," *IEEE Trans. Inform. Theory*, vol. IT-17, pp. 566–571, 1971.

[288] C. Wang, "A theory of generalization in learning machines with neural network applications," Ph.D. dissertation, Univ. Pennsylvania, 1995.

[289] C. Wang and S. S. Venkatesh, "Machine size selection for optimal generalisation," in *Work. Applications of Descriptional Complexity to Inductive, Statistical, and Visual Inference* (New Brunswick, NJ, July 1994).

[290] C. Wang, S. S. Venkatesh, and S. J. Judd, "When to stop: On optimal stopping and effective machine size in learning," in *Conf. Neural Information Processing Systems* (Denver, CO, Nov. 1993).

[291] ——, "Optimal stopping and effective machine complexity in learning," *IEEE Trans. Inform. Theory*, to be published.

[292] Q. R. Wang and C. Y. Suen, "Analysis and design of decision tree based on entropy reduction and its application to large character set recognition," *IEEE Trans. Pattern Anal. Machine Intell.*, vol. 6, pp. 406–417, 1984.

[293] M. T. Wasan, *Stochastic Approximation.* New York: Cambridge Univ. Press, 1969.

[294] G. S. Watson, "Smooth regression analysis," *Sankhya Ser. A*, vol. 26, pp. 359–372, 1964.

[295] R. S. Wenocur and R. M. Dudley, "Some special Vapnik–Chervonenkis classes," *Discr. Math.*, vol. 33, pp. 313–318, 1981.

[296] H. White, "Connectionist nonparametric regression: Multilayer feedforward networks can learn arbitrary mappings," *Neural Networks*, vol. 3, pp. 535–549, 1990.

[297] H. White, "Nonparametric estimation of conditional quantiles using neural networks," in *Proc. 23rd Symp. Interface: Computing Science and Statistics*. Alexandria, VA: Amer. Statist. Assoc., 1991, pp. 190–199.

[298] B. Widrow and M. E. Hoff, "Adaptive switching circuits," in *IRE Wescon Conv. Rec.,* 1960, pt. 4, pp. 96–104.

[299] C. T. Wolverton and T. J. Wagner, "Recursive estimates of probability densities," *IEEE Trans. Syst., Sci. Cybern.* vol. SSC-5, p. 307, 1969.

[300] Y. Yang and A. R. Barron, "An asymptotic property of model selection criteria," *IEEE Trans. Inform. Theory*, 1998, to be published.

[301] L. C. Zhao, "Exponential bounds of mean error for the nearest neighbor estimates of regression functions," *J. Multivariate Anal.*, vol. 21, pp. 168–178, 1987.

[302] ——, "Exponential bounds of mean error for the kernel estimates of regression functions," *J. Multivariate Anal.*, vol. 29, pp. 260–273, 1989.

[303] L. C. Zhao, P. R. Krishnaiah, and X. R. Chen, "Almost sure L_r-norm convergence for data-based histogram estimates," *Theory Probab. Applic.*, vol. 35, pp. 396–403, 1990.

Zero-Error Information Theory

János Körner and Alon Orlitsky

(Invited Paper)

Abstract— The problem of error-free transmission capacity of a noisy channel was posed by Shannon in 1956 and remains unsolved. Nevertheless, partial results for this and similar channel- and source-coding problems have had a considerable impact on information theory, computer science, and mathematics. We review the techniques, results, information measures, and challenges encountered in this ongoing quest.

Index Terms— Communication complexity, data compression, extremal combinatorics, graph capacities, graph entropy, interactive communication, list codes, lossless coding, source coding, Sperner capacity.

PART I: OVERVIEW
I. INTRODUCTION

INFORMATION theory can be viewed as the study of patterns and ways to exploit them. In source coding, data patterns are used to represent a signal efficiently, while in channel coding, noise patterns are used to transmit information reliably. Typically, these objectives are achieved while tolerating a small probability of error, but there are many reasons to consider error-free, or zero-order, information theory.

- In some applications no errors can be tolerated.
- Often only a small number of channel uses or a few source instances are available. Results ensuring that the error probability decreases as the number of uses or instances increases cannot be invoked.
- Even with many uses, the rate at which the probability of erroneous transmission over a channel decreases to zero is determined by the channel's *reliability function*. Shannon, Gallager, and Berlekamp [1] showed that the reliability function also determines the channel's zero-error behavior.
- Many standard information-theoretic results can be derived using combinatorial zero-error techniques. This approach was taken in the book by Csiszár and Körner [2].
- Functionals and methods used in zero-error information theory are often applied in problems arising in mathematics and computer science.
- The problem and its simple formulation lead to many elegant results that are interesting on their own.

Manuscript received April 22, 1998; revised June 4, 1998.
J. Körner is with the Department of Computer Science, "La Sapienza" University, 00198 Rome, Italy (e-mail: korner@dsi.uniroma1.it).
A. Orlitsky is with the Department of Electrical and Computer Engineering, University of California, San Diego, CA 92093-0407 USA (e-mail: alon@ucsd.edu).
Publisher Item Identifier S 0018-9448(98)06084-2.

Shannon was the first to realize the significance of zero-error information theory. His classic paper, "The zero-error capacity of a noisy channel" [3], is a true gem in graph theory and is one of his most cited articles. The subject was subsequently studied extensively. This survey outlines some of the research in that area. For an earlier survey of zero-error channel coding results, see Körner and Lucertini [4].

II. LAYOUT

The rest of the paper is partitioned into two parts: channel and source coding.

In Part II, we consider error-free communication over a noisy channel. We are interested in the channel's *zero-error capacity*: the maximum number of bits that can be transmitted without error per channel use.

After a formal definition of the capacity we describe various techniques and results about zero-error transmission and show how different aspects of the problem are related to various areas of information theory, combinatorics, and computer science.

First we show that the number of transmitted bits can behave unexpectedly as the number of channel uses grows and that it is difficult to determine the zero-error capacity of even the simplest channels. We outline several information-theoretic and algebraic techniques for bounding the capacity and emphasize Lovász' θ function which is a polynomially computable functional "sandwiched" between the NP-hard clique and chromatic numbers of a graph.

We then consider several variations on the basic model.

- List coding: The receiver decides on a small list of messages that is guaranteed to include the transmitted message. This problem is closely related to perfect hashing.
- Compound channels: The channel is known to belong to a class of channels—but exactly which channel is used is unknown. We provide a formula for the capacity in terms of capacity-like characteristics of the individual channels in the class.
- Multiuser channels: Several senders transmit information to a number of receivers over mutually interfering channels. The problem of determining the capacity region is wide open, but we illustrate connections with extremal set theory and write-once memories.

Finally, we define two other notions of capacity.

- Sperner capacity of a directed graph which has been used to solve an open problem of Rényi on qualitative independence.

163

- Graph entropy of a graph and a probability distribution over its vertices, which has been used among other things to derive the first near-optimal polynomial-time sorting algorithm for partially ordered sets.

Part III addresses the dual problem of source coding. Two parties communicate over a noiseless channel in order to achieve a certain goal. We are interested in the minimum number of bits that must be transmitted.

In the simplest version of the problem, an informant wants to convey information to a recipient who has no related data. This version is trivial for the worst case number of bits, and has been solved by Huffman [5] for the average case. But even slight modifications of this setup prove difficult. We consider two related scenarios.

In the first scenario the recipient has some information that may be related to the informant's data. This is the case, for example, in distributed databases where closely related files are stored at different locations and occasionally a file needs to be transferred from one location to another. We consider one-way and interactive communication for a single instance and for multiple independent instances of the problem. Along with other results we show the following.

- Combined communication of multiple independent instances sometimes results in significant transmission savings: In some cases, a single instance requires a large number of bits while two independent instances require about the same number of bits as one instance and many independent instances require only one bit per instance.
- Interaction can sometimes significantly reduce communication: In some cases, interaction can reduce transmission to the logarithm of the one-way number of bits. Furthermore, for a large class of natural sources the number of bits required with interaction is about the same as that needed when the informant knows the recipient's data in advance.

In the second scenario the two communicators have unrelated information. This would render the communication problem trivial, except that instead of conveying information, they try to determine the value of a function of their combined data. The resulting *communication complexity* problem has been studied extensively in the computer science literature, both for its intrinsic interest and for its many applications to other computation models. We outline two research areas.

- Results on communication complexity *per se*, including: a) randomized protocols can significantly reduce the number of bits required; b) most functions require communication of essentially as many bits as are needed for one communicator to convey his data; c) for every integer $m > 1$ there are functions whose efficient communication requires m information exchanges while $m - 1$ or fewer exchanges require almost exponentially more bits than the minimum necessary; and d) simultaneous computation of multiple independent instances may reduce the number of bits over that required to compute each instance separately, however, one can derive a general bound on the possible savings.

- Communication complexity applications to other fields, including: a) derivation of lower bounds on the size and time of VLSI chips and b) an elegant analogy between communication complexity and circuit depth, and its implications for lower bounds on circuit complexity.

Each of the two parts is self-contained and can be read independently of the other. Throughout the paper logarithms and exponents are binary.

PART II: CHANNEL CODING

III. INTRODUCTION

A discrete memoryless (stationary) channel (DMC) W: $\mathcal{X} \to \mathcal{Y}$ is defined by a stochastic matrix whose rows are indexed by the elements of the finite set $\mathcal{X}$ while the columns are indexed by those of another finite set $\mathcal{Y}$. The (x, y)th element is the probability $W(y|x)$ that y is received when x is transmitted. If the sequence $\boldsymbol{x} = x_1 x_2 \cdots x_n \in \mathcal{X}^n$ is transmitted, the sequence $\boldsymbol{y} = y_1 y_2 \cdots y_n \in \mathcal{Y}^n$ is received with probability

$$W^n(\boldsymbol{y}|\boldsymbol{x}) = \prod_{i=1}^{n} W(y_i|x_i).$$

The product form of the distribution corresponds to the lack of memory in the channel whereas its stationarity is reflected by the fact that the factors in the product are elements of the same matrix. If two sequences $\boldsymbol{x}'$ and $\boldsymbol{x}''$ can both result in the sequence $\boldsymbol{y}$ with positive probability, then no decoder can decide with zero probability of error which of the two has been transmitted by the sender. Such sequences will be called *indistinguishable* (at the receiving end of the DMC $\{W\}$).

It is helpful to view the probability distributions $W(\cdot|x)$ and $W^n(\cdot|\boldsymbol{x})$ as vectors of dimension $|\mathcal{X}|$ and $|\mathcal{X}|^n$, respectively. Then the previous observation can be reformulated by saying that the sequences $\boldsymbol{x}' \in \mathcal{X}^n$ and $\boldsymbol{x}'' \in \mathcal{X}^n$ are distinguishable at the receiving end of the DMC $\{W\}$ if and only if the vectors $W^n(\cdot|\boldsymbol{x}')$ and $W^n(\cdot|\boldsymbol{x}'')$ are orthogonal. Hence the elements of a *codebook* $\mathcal{C} \subseteq \mathcal{X}^n$ can be transmitted without error over the DMC $\{W\}$ if and only if they are mutually orthogonal. Using the codebook $\mathcal{C}$ we can transmit on the average $(1/n) \log |\mathcal{C}|$ bits per symbol over $\{W\}$. We define $N(W, n)$ as the maximum cardinality of a set of mutually orthogonal vectors among the $W^n(\cdot|\boldsymbol{x}); \boldsymbol{x} \in X^n$. The dimension n is the *blocklength* of the code. Following Shannon [3] we call

$$C_0(W) = \limsup_{n \to \infty} \frac{1}{n} \log N(W, n)$$

the *zero-error capacity* of the DMC $\{W\}$. Intuitively, $C_0(W)$ is the theoretical limit of the bit-per-symbol error-free information transmission capability of $\{W\}$. It is easy to verify that $N(W, n)$ is *super multiplicative*

$$N(W, n + m) \geq N(W, n) \cdot N(W, m).$$

Hence an elementary lemma, usually called Fekete's lemma (cf. van Lint and Wilson [6]) shows that the limit superior is a true limit and actually coincides with the supremum of the numbers $(1/n) \log N(W, n)$.

Shannon reformulated the problem in the language of graph theory. We associate with the DMC $\{W\}$ a *characteristic graph* $G = G(W)$ as follows. Its vertex set is $V(G) = \mathcal{X}$ and its set of edges $E(G)$ consists of input pairs that cannot result in the same output, namely, pairs of orthogonal rows of the matrix W. (Notice that in the literature it is more customary to use the complement of this graph leading to an equivalent but dual formulation of the present problem.) The *clique number* $\omega(G)$ of a graph G is the largest cardinality of a set of vertices every two of which are connected in G. Then $N(W, 1) = \omega(G)$. Let $G^n = G(W^n)$. It is easy to see that G^n has the following equivalent graph-theoretic definition. $V(G^n) = (V(G))^n$, and $\{\boldsymbol{x}', \boldsymbol{x}''\} \in E(G^n)$ if for at least one $1 \le i \le n$ the ith coordinates of $\boldsymbol{x}'$ and $\boldsymbol{x}''$ satisfy $\{x_i', x_i''\} \in E(G)$. It is also easy to see that for any graph G there is a DMC $\{W\}$ such that $G = G(W)$. We can therefore redefine zero-error capacity in graph-theoretic terms as

$$C(G) = \sup_n \frac{1}{n} \log \omega(G^n).$$

Shannon [3] noticed that the zero-error capacity of the DMC $\{W\}$ is upper-bounded by the minimum of the (ordinary) capacities of all those DMC's $\{\hat{W}\}$ for which $G(\hat{W}) = G(W)$. This result is actually equivalent to a far less obvious statement in graph theory according to which

$$C(G) \le \log \chi^*(G)$$

where $\chi^*(G)$ is the fractional chromatic number of the graph G, a well-known concept of graph theory, cf. Lovász [7] or a monograph by Scheinerman and Ullman [8]. Without entering into the details, we can simply say that the fractional chromatic number is the solution of the real-valued relaxation of the integer programming problem that defines the chromatic number of G. The chromatic number of G is the smallest cardinality of a set K for which there is a function $f : V(G) \to K$ with the property that adjacent vertices (those which are the two endpoints of some edge) are mapped into different elements of K. An elementary observation shows that if $\omega(G) = \chi(G)$ then $C(G) = \log \chi(G)$. Actually, the same is true for $\chi^*(G)$ replacing the chromatic number. The smallest vertex set on which a graph exists with $C(G) \ne \chi(G)$ has five vertices and is commonly known as C_5, or the *pentagon* graph, for its edges are those pairs of vertices which are neighbors in a fixed cyclic arrangement of five vertices. Shannon was unable to determine the capacity of the pentagon but he observed that in this case even

$$\log \frac{5}{2} = \chi^*(C_5) \ge C(C_5) \ge \frac{1}{2} \log \omega(C_5^2) = \frac{1}{2} \log 5.$$

Using the interpretation of channel capacity as the divergence radius of the distributions in the rows of the channel matrix, cf. Csiszár and Körner [2, Problem 2.3.2], it is possible to interpret the Shannon upper bound as

$$C(G) \le \min_{W : G(W) = G} \min_Q \max_{x \in V(G)} D(W(\cdot|x) \| Q) \quad (1)$$

where, in the second minimization, Q is running over all probability distributions on the set of column indices of the

matrix W and $D(P\|Q)$ is the informational divergence of the distributions P and Q.

It took more than 20 years and a brilliant idea of Lovász [9] to show that for the pentagon graph, Shannon's lower bound was tight

$$C(C_5) = \frac{1}{2} \log 5.$$

Actually, the tightness of the Lovász bound is due to the very special nature of C_5, a self-complementary and rather symmetric (vertex–transitive) graph. The problem of determining zero-error capacity of an arbitrary DMC is wide open.

Lovász' upper bound introduces an important new functional in graph theory, called the *theta function*. It is defined in terms of a so-called *orthonormal representation* of the graph. Given a graph G, the representation associates with every vertex v of G a unit-norm vector $\boldsymbol{x}(v)$ from a fixed Euclidean space in such a way that if v' and v'' are adjacent vertices then the vectors $\boldsymbol{x}(v')$ and $\boldsymbol{x}(v'')$ are orthogonal. (Notice that this is remarkably similar to the orthogonal representation of G furnished by the rows of a matrix W for which $G(W) = G$. In other words, the Lovász representation goes in a direction suggested by the original channel-coding interpretation of Shannon's problem. However, Lovász' representation is more flexible since his vectors may have negative coordinates.) To an arbitrary orthonormal representation Lovász associates an additional unit-norm vector he calls the *handle of the representation*. The handle is any vector $\boldsymbol{z}$ in the same Euclidean space as the previous vectors which satisfies

$$(\boldsymbol{z}; \boldsymbol{x}(v))^{-2} = \min_{\boldsymbol{z}'} \max_{v \in V(G)} (\boldsymbol{z}'; \boldsymbol{x}(v))^{-2} \quad (2)$$

where $(\boldsymbol{z}; \boldsymbol{x}(v))$ denotes the scalar product of the vectors $\boldsymbol{z}$ and $\boldsymbol{x}(v)$. Once again, (as in (1)), the vector $\boldsymbol{z}$ is a kind of a radius of the vectors in the representation. The expression in (2) is called the *value* of the representation. Finally, $\theta(G)$ is defined as the minimum value over all orthonormal representations of G. Lovász [9] showed that

$$C(G) \le \theta(G).$$

The functional θ has many important applications in computer science. In particular, the value of $\theta(G)$ is a polynomially computable invariant of a graph "sandwiched" in between two computably hard invariants, the clique number and the chromatic number of the graph, cf. Grötschel, Lovász, and Schrijver [10] and the chapter on the "sandwich theorem" in a forthcoming book on graph algorithms by Knuth [11]. It turns out, however, that precisely because it behaves so beautifully, the value of θ is generally different from capacity. Haemers [12] derived a new bound on zero-error capacity which is sometimes better but quite often much worse than $\theta(G)$. He said that a square matrix A of $|V(G)|$ rows and columns *fits* the graph G if its diagonal entries are all nonzero and the entry $a_{v, w}$ is zero if and only if the vertices v and w form an edge in G. He then proved that the logarithm of the rank of any of these matrices upper-bounds the capacity of G and presented examples of graphs for which his bound is better than Lovász' $\theta(G)$. However, e.g., for the pentagon graph C_5 this is not true. Feige [13] and Alon and Kahale [14] studied the gap between the clique number and the function θ and explained its relevance in complexity theory.

Schrijver [8] pointed out that Lovász' bound is connected to a famous bound of Delsarte [15] for the size of cliques in association schemes. Shannon [3] formulated two conjectures about the zero-error capacity of channels whose matrix is the "product" and the "sum" of two arbitrary stochastic matrices. The product conjecture is relative to a DMC whose stochastic matrix $W: \mathcal{X}' \times \mathcal{X}'' \to \mathcal{Y}' \times \mathcal{Y}''$ is the direct product of the stochastic matrices $W': \mathcal{X}' \to \mathcal{Y}'$ and $W'': \mathcal{X}'' \to \mathcal{Y}''$. Direct product means that

$$W(y', y''|x', x'') = W'(y'|x')W''(y''|x'').$$

We can think of the DMC $\{W\}$ as of a nonstationary memoryless channel over which transmission is governed in strict alternation by the stochastic matrices W' and W''. It is easily seen from Shannon's channel coding theorem that for the ordinary capacities one has $C(W) = C(W') + C(W'')$ and Shannon conjectured the same to be true in the zero-error case. It is, however, implicit in an example of Haemers [12] that $C_0(W) > C_0(W') + C_0(W'')$ is possible. The sum conjecture is analogous. The sum channel of the DMC's $\{W'\}$ and $\{W''\}$ is a new DMC whose channel matrix has the disjoint union of $\mathcal{X}'$ and $\mathcal{X}''$ as row indices and the disjoint union of $\mathcal{Y}'$ and $\mathcal{Y}''$ as column indices. One has $W(y|x) = W'(y'|x')$ if $x = x'$, $y = y'$ and likewise, $W(y|x) = W''(y''|x'')$ if $x = x''$, $y = y''$, while all the hitherto unspecified entries of W are equal to zero. Intuitively, the DMC governed by W behaves as $\{W'\}$ if an input symbol to this channel is used, otherwise, it behaves as $\{W''\}$. Shannon [16] proved that in this case $C(W) = \log(\exp C(W') + \exp C(W''))$, and conjectured in [3] that the same holds for zero-error capacities. This was recently disproved by Alon [17]. All this amounts to saying that zero-error capacity behaves quite differently from ordinary capacity.

IV. THE GROWTH OF ZERO-ERROR CODES

Shannon's problem had a tremendous impact on graph theory. According to Claude Berge it led him to introduce the concept of a *perfect graph*. We mentioned earlier that, as is implicit in Shannon [3], if

$$\omega(G) = \chi(G) \qquad (3)$$

then its capacity is the logarithm of $\omega(G)$. In other words, for these graphs the clique number $\omega(G)$ is multiplicative over the powers G^n of G. Following Hajós [18], Berge [19], [20] noticed that this is true for so-called *interval graphs*, graphs whose vertices can be represented by closed intervals on a line, so that two vertices are adjacent if and only if the corresponding intervals are disjoint. He even interpreted these intervals as frequency ranges allotted to different symbols we intend to transmit over the channel. Naturally, by the same representation as for the whole graph, the induced subgraphs of an interval graph are also representable by intervals and hence they satisfy the same equality of clique number and chromatic number. This example, inspired by Shannon's work alongside with some others led Berge to

consider those graphs for which $\omega(G') = \chi(G')$ for every induced subgraph $G' \subseteq G$, and to call them *perfect*. We shall return to these remarkable graphs and Berge's almost 40-year-old strong *perfect-graph conjecture* later on. The interested reader might consult Berge's monograph [20]. On the other hand, (3) is just a sufficient but not a necessary condition for

$$\omega(G^n) = [\omega(G)]^n, \qquad \text{for all } n \geq 1$$

as shown by Lovász [9] for the complement of the Petersen graph, a special case of the Kneser graphs to which we shall return later. However, we still do not know whether the equality $\log \omega(G') = C(G')$ for every induced subgraph $G' \subseteq G$ implies that G is perfect. A candidate counter-example might be C_7, a minimally imperfect graph of which we ignore the Shannon capacity, cf. McEliece, Rodemich, and Rumsey [21]. The determination of the zero-error capacity of the pentagon graph C_5 was relatively simple (even if it took 20 years) because the sequence $(1/n) \log \omega(C_5^n)$ reaches its peak for $n = 2$. Alon and Orlitsky [22] showed that the jump between the values $(1/n) \log \omega(G^n)$ for $n = 1$ and $n = 2$ can be arbitrarily large by showing the existence of graphs G with $\log \omega(G) \leq \log \log |\mathcal{X}| + 2$ and $\frac{1}{2} \log \omega(G^2) \geq \frac{1}{2} \log |\mathcal{X}|$. Their results are based on Ramsey theory, a part of extremal combinatorics whose relevance for our topic was first pointed out by Erdös, McEliece, and Taylor [23].

Further information about the strange behavior of the sequence of numbers $(1/n) \log \omega(G^n)$ is provided by several authors who noticed that there exist graphs for which capacity is not attained for any finite n. The following simple example illustrating this was communicated to us by Arikan [24]. As noticed by Shannon [3], if we consider the sum of those channels whose respective graphs are a one-vertex graph and the pentagon C_5, then the resulting new graph has capacity $\log(1 + \sqrt{5})$. Since the nth power of $1 + \sqrt{5}$ is not an integer for any n, we have the desired example.

V. LIST CODES AND FEEDBACK

Since the zero-error capacity of a general DMC is unknown even for ordinary block codes, there has been an understandable reluctance to consider generalizations to more complicated code concepts. Consequently, research into such generalizations remained dormant until these mathematically natural problems re-emerged in other disciplines, e.g., in a computer-science paper of Yao [25]. It was then that several results of Elias [26], [27] (see Csiszár and Körner [2] for more details) re-emerged.

A *list code* of list size L and blocklength n for the DMC $W : \mathcal{X} \to \mathcal{Y}$ is a set $\mathcal{C} \subseteq \mathcal{X}^n$ such that for every $\boldsymbol{y} \in \mathcal{Y}^n$

$$|\{\boldsymbol{x} \in \mathcal{C}: W^n(\boldsymbol{y}|\boldsymbol{x}) > 0\}| \leq L.$$

Intuitively, for every received $\boldsymbol{y} \in \mathcal{Y}^n$, the decoder can decide on a list of at most L transmitted $\boldsymbol{x}$'s.

Let $N(W, n, L)$ denote the maximum cardinality of a list code $\mathcal{C} \subseteq \mathcal{X}^n$ with list size L and blocklength n for the DMC $\{W : \mathcal{X} \to \mathcal{Y}\}$. The list code *capacity* $C_{0,L}(W)$ of list size

L of the DMC $\{W\}$ is

$$\limsup_{n \to \infty} \frac{1}{n} \log N(W, n, L).$$

The number

$$C_{0,\infty}(W) = \sup_L C_{0,L}(W)$$

is the list code *zero-error capacity* of the channel.

Elias [27] showed that

$$C_{0,\infty}(W) = -\min_P \max_y \log \sum_{\{x: W(y|x)>0\}} P(x)$$

where the P in the minimization is running over all probability distributions over the set $\mathcal{X}$.

Since for $L = 1$ we get back precisely the zero-error capacity problem, determining the list code capacity of a DMC for list size L is hopelessly difficult. Why is it then that this problem has created so much interest in computer science even though only special cases were considered in that context? We want to give an abbreviated account on this in order to illustrate the many facets and connections of Elias' problem to a lot of beautiful mathematics.

Motivated by a paper of Yao [25], Fredman and Komlós [28] introduced the following type of constructions called *perfect hashing*. Given a finite set B of b elements and the natural numbers $k \le b$ and n we call a set $C \subseteq B^n$ *k-separated* if for every k-tuple of distinct elements of C there is a coordinate $1 \le i \le n$ in which the k values in the ith coordinates of the k sequences are all different. Let $N(n, b, k)$ denote the maximum size of a k-separated subset of B^n. Set

$$q(b, k) = \limsup_{n \to \infty} \frac{1}{n} \log N(n, b, k).$$

The following result of Körner and Marton [29] improves on earlier results of Fredman–Komlós [28] (cf. also Körner [30])

$$\frac{1}{k-1} \log \frac{1}{1-g(b,k)} \le q(b, k)$$

$$\le \min_{0 \le j \le k-2} g(b, j+1) \log \frac{b-j}{k-j-1}$$

where

$$g(b, k) = \prod_{0 \le i \le k-1} \frac{b-i}{b}.$$

The interesting part of this result is the upper bound. It improves on the Fredman–Komlós and the Elias bounds. The proof uses the subadditivity of graph (hypergraph) entropy, which will be described later in the survey. Nilli [31] gives a different proof, eliminating the use of information theory. The lower bound is by plain random selection and was improved in the case $b = k = 3$ by Körner and Marton [29] to

$$\frac{1}{4} \log \frac{9}{5}$$

showing that random choice is not the best technique to solve this kind of problem. A better upper bound than the one above was obtained by Arikan [32] in the case of $b = k = 4$.

Recently, Dyachkov [33] used ideas of Dyachkov and Rykov [34] to prove the new nonasymptotic upper bound

$$N(k-1, b, k) \le (k-1)b$$

which implies

$$q(b, k) \le \frac{\log b}{k-1}.$$

This result improves on the Körner–Marton bound for some values and is worse for others. The latter authors have noticed that perfect hashing is mathematically equivalent to the determination of the zero-error capacity of a DMC with fixed list size, cf. Körner and Marton [35]. In the same paper, they show that this problem can be viewed also as a natural generalization of Shannon's capacity problem from graphs to uniform hypergraphs. (Notice that in hypergraph language a graph is a 2-uniform hypergraph.) A highly interesting relationship between this problem and van der Waerden's permanent conjecture (now known as the Falikman–Yegoritchev theorem, cf. van Lint and Wilson [6]) is pointed out by Hajek [36]. In his paper, Hajek proposes a very bold albeit natural looking generalization of the van der Waerden conjecture which is disproved by Körner and Marton [37], even though the following very exciting open question survives.

Problem (Hajek [36]): Given the natural numbers k and n so that k^2 divides n is it true that among all pairs of k-partitions of an n-set the number of those k-tuples of elements that are completely separated (put into k different classes) by at least one of the partitions reaches its maximum if the common refinement of the two partitions is an equipartition?

An affirmative answer would immediately give a generalization of the Falikman–Yegorichev theorem which in itself is equivalent to the previous assertion limited to configurations consisting of two equipartitions.

List codes play a fundamental role in the study of feedback since we can consider a feedback code as a sequence of list codes with successively reduced list sizes. Then it is not surprising to learn that by a classical result of Elias and Shannon (published by Shannon [3]) if a DMC $\{W\}$ has a positive zero-error capacity with feedback, then its value equals $C_{0,\infty}(W)$, the list code capacity introduced by Elias.

VI. CHANNELS WITH PARTIALLY KNOWN STATISTICS

A *compound channel* (cf. Csiszár and Körner [2]) is the stochastic model of an information-transmitting device known to be a DMC except that the stochastic matrix governing transmission is not entirely specified. Abstractly, this means that a family $\mathcal{W}$ of matrices with common input alphabet $\mathcal{X}$ and input alphabet $\mathcal{Y}$ is given and the matrix of our DMC is known to belong to $\mathcal{W}$. This model has been introduced independently by Blackwell–Breiman–Thomasian [38], Dobrushin [39], and Wolfowitz [40]. A codeword set $C \subseteq \mathcal{X}^n$ determines a zero-error code for the compound channel if it defines a zero-error code for every DMC $\{W\}$ with $W \in \mathcal{W}$. If we denote by $N(\mathcal{W}, n)$ the largest cardinality of such a zero-error code, then the zero-error capacity of the compound channel can be defined as

$$C_0(\mathcal{W}) = \limsup_{n \to \infty} \frac{1}{n} \log N(\mathcal{W}, n).$$

In the graph-theory language this is equivalent to the following definition.

We are given an arbitrary family of graphs with common vertex set $\mathcal{X}$. A set $\mathcal{C} \subseteq \mathcal{X}^n$ is a clique for the graph family $\mathcal{G}$ if it induces a clique in G^n for every $G \in \mathcal{G}$. In other words, $\mathcal{C}$ must be a clique in the intersection graph $\bigcap_{G \in \mathcal{G}} G^n$. Let us denote by $N(\mathcal{G}, n)$ the largest cardinality of a clique in this intersection graph. The *capacity* of the graph family is

$$C(\mathcal{G}) = \sup_n \frac{1}{n} \log N(\mathcal{G}, n).$$

Again, it should be clear that this supremum is actually the limit of the sequence $n^{-1} \log N(\mathcal{G}, n)$. Cohen, Körner, and Simonyi [41] have observed that the problem of determining this zero-error capacity gives in special cases some very challenging combinatorial problems (to which we shall return later) and conjectured that the familiar max–min formula

$$C(\mathcal{W}) = \max_P \min_{W \in \mathcal{W}} I(P, W)$$

of Blackwell–Breiman–Thomasian might have an analog also in this case. (Here, as usual, we denote by $I(P, W)$ the mutual information between an input variable of distribution P and the corresponding output variable over the channel W.) To make the previous statement precise, we have to introduce the concept of *fixed composition codes*. We recall that a sequence $\boldsymbol{x} \in \mathcal{X}^n$ is said to have type P if for every element x of the alphabet $\mathcal{X}$ the relative frequency of x in $\boldsymbol{x}$ is $P(x)$. A set $\mathcal{C} \subseteq \mathcal{X}^n$ is said to be a code of fixed composition (or type) P if each of its elements is a sequence of type P. Following Csiszár and Körner [42], we introduce the concept of zero-error capacity of the DMC $\{W\}$ within the type P. Let $N(W, n, P)$ be the maximum cardinality of a zero-error code of blocklength n and fixed type P for the DMC $\{W\}$. If all the probabilities of P are rational numbers, then we put

$$C_0(W, P) = \sup_n \frac{1}{n} \log N(W, n, P).$$

For W fixed we extend $C_0(W, P)$ by continuity to all the distributions on the input alphabet $\mathcal{X}$ of $\{\mathcal{W}\}$.

Gargano, Körner, and Vaccaro [43] proved a general combinatorial result to which we shall return later and used it to prove

$$C_0(\mathcal{W}) = \max_P \min_{W \in \mathcal{W}} C_0(W, P). \tag{4}$$

The possibility that this relation might hold was raised (at least for certain classes of channels) by Cohen, Körner, and Simonyi [41] who proved $\leq$. The other inequality requires a novel construction.

For many channels, $C_0(W, P)$ can be determined quite easily. In the difficult cases we can use upper bounds in terms of graph entropy or the fixed-type generalization of Lovász' θ function, introduced by Marton [44].

VII. MULTIUSER PROBLEMS FOR SPECIAL CHANNELS AND COMBINATORICS

In the 1970's, the center of interest in Shannon Theory shifted to multiuser problems. Researchers soon realized that it is practically impossible to solve most of the general problems as soon as the number of users begins to grow. Nevertheless, multiuser information theory has produced a number of fascinating problems. For example, Wyner's introduction of the wire-tap channel [45] and its generalization in Csiszár and Körner [46] had a lasting impact on cryptography. In channel coding, a multiuser coding problem is a natural generalization of Shannon's original model. Several senders and receivers use, in a distributed manner, an agreed-upon communication protocol over noisy channels. The role of capacity is usually taken by a *capacity region*. While there are important and nontrivial partial results in this area, the general capacity region remains unknown for practically all models.

Highly interesting combinatorial problems appear as special cases of these models. Many of these problems arise naturally in combinatorics and are usually treated without reference to the Shannon Theory. The main purpose in emphasizing their origin in information theory is therefore to point out that while there is very little unifying framework in the theory of graphs and hypergraphs, one could be offered by information theory. We single out just one model, the *interference channel* which appears in Ahlswede [47] with a reference to Shannon.

Consider a stochastic matrix $W : \mathcal{X} \times \mathcal{Y} \to \mathcal{V} \times \mathcal{Z}$ and the corresponding DMC $\{W\}$. A quadruple $(\mathcal{C}, \mathcal{D}, \phi, \psi)$ formed by the codebooks $\mathcal{C} \subseteq \mathcal{X}^n$, $\mathcal{D} \subseteq \mathcal{Y}^n$ and the decoding functions $\phi : \mathcal{V}^n \to \mathcal{C}$, $\psi : \mathcal{Z}^n \to \mathcal{D}$ is a *zero-error coding/decoding scheme* of blocklength n for the interference channel if for every $\boldsymbol{x} \in \mathcal{C}$ and $\boldsymbol{y} \in \mathcal{D}$ the relation $\mathcal{W}^n(\boldsymbol{v}, \boldsymbol{z} | \boldsymbol{x}, \boldsymbol{y}) > 0$ implies that $\phi(\boldsymbol{v}) = \boldsymbol{x}$ and $\psi(\boldsymbol{z}) = \boldsymbol{y}$. The pair $\mathcal{C} \subseteq \mathcal{X}^n$, $\mathcal{D} \subseteq \mathcal{Y}^n$ is a *zero-error code* of blocklength n for the interference channel if there are functions ϕ and ψ so that the quadruple $(\mathcal{C}, \mathcal{D}, \phi, \psi)$ is a zero-error coding/decoding scheme. The analog of the zero-error capacity problem asks for all pairs of numbers of the form

$$\left(\frac{1}{n} \log |\mathcal{C}|, \frac{1}{n} \log |\mathcal{D}| \right)$$

for some zero-error code of blocklength n for the interference channel as n is running over the integers $n \geq 1$. Much less ambitiously, we can ask just for the determination of

$$C_{0, \text{interf}}(W) = \sup_n \frac{1}{n} \log(|\mathcal{C}| \, |\mathcal{D}|).$$

This is a hopelessly difficult problem in the general case. Consider now the special matrix

$$W : \{0, 1\} \times \{0, 1\} \to \{0, 1\} \times \{0, 1\}$$

defined by the relations

$$W(v, z | x, y) = \begin{cases} 1, & \text{if } v = \max(x, y) \text{ and } z = \min(x, y) \\ 0, & \text{otherwise.} \end{cases}$$

In a purely combinatorial reformulation, but motivated by the study of write-once memories, the problem of determining the value of $C_{0, \text{interf}}(W)$ got quite some attention in this particular case. Simonyi [48] (cf. also Ahlswede and Simonyi [49]) conjectured that

$$C_{0,\,\mathrm{interf}}(W) = 1.$$

While it is trivial that the left-hand side is at least 1, it seems very hard to establish a converse. The best upper bound, due to Holzman and Körner [50], is around 1.2118.

It is probably impossible to convince an information theorist to get to work on this problem after such an exposition. A combinatorialist would hardly be willing to listen to it at all. The irony of this is that on the one hand, as we have mentioned, excellent combinatorialists did write about it in a nice (and purely combinatorial) formulation, while, on the other hand, the converse bound quoted above was obtained using information theory. For the sake of completeness, we quote the combinatorial formulation which is easily seen to be equivalent to the above.

Let $\mathcal{C}$ and $\mathcal{D}$ be two families of subsets of an n-set. We shall say that these form a *recovering pair* if for any two ordered pairs (C, D) and (C', D') with C and C' belonging to the family $\mathcal{C}$, and D and D' coming from $\mathcal{D}$ we have the following implications:

$$C \cup D = C' \cup D' \text{ implies } C = C'$$

and, likewise,

$$C \cap D = C' \cap D' \text{ implies } D = D'.$$

We have to determine the maximum product of the cardinalities $|\mathcal{C}|\,|\mathcal{D}|$. It is easily seen that this is our previous problem in a slightly different disguise if we realize that the characteristic vectors of the set families are sets of binary vectors of length n (which justifies our use of the same notation in both cases). If we fix the size of the sets in the two families and study the asymptotics in n the question becomes much simpler and a full answer is available in a recent paper by Sali and Simonyi [51].

This problem is somewhat related to a conceptually simpler and very intriguing open question in extremal set theory. A family $\mathcal{C}$ of subsets of an n-set is said to be *cancellative* if

$$A \cup B = A' \cup B \text{ for } A \in \mathcal{C}, A' \in \mathcal{C}, B \in \mathcal{C} \text{ implies } A = A'.$$

Let us denote by $E(n)$ the maximum cardinality of a cancellative family of n-sets and, as always, consider just the number

$$\Gamma = \limsup_{n \to \infty} \frac{1}{n} \log E(n).$$

Erdös and Katona [52] have noticed that $\frac{1}{3} \log 3 \le \Gamma$ and Frankl and Füredi [53] proved the upper bound

$$\Gamma \le \log 3 - 1.$$

For a long time it has been conjectured that the lower bound is tight but this was disproved by a tricky iteration of the Erdös–Katona construction by Shearer [54]. By its very nature, Shearer's constructions can be further iterated and their main message is that we cannot even conjecture the solution at this point in time. There is no problem in the classical Shannon Theory for which a cancellative family would give a zero-error code, yet, undoubtedly, our two last problems belong together.

We hope to have convinced the reader that zero-error information theory and combinatorics are the same field and their crossfertilization is benefiting both. But there is still more to come.

VIII. CAPACITIES: FROM SHANNON TO SPERNER

Sperner's theorem [55] says that the maximum cardinality of a family of subsets of an n-set, no member of which includes another is

$$N(n) = \binom{n}{\lceil \frac{n}{2} \rceil}.$$

The theorem is a must for every introductory book on combinatorics. Its many consequences have grown into a whole subfield in extremal combinatorics, cf. a recent book by Engel [56]. At first glance, it has nothing to do with information theory. Yet, the intuitive paradigm of combinatorial search introduced by Rényi (whose lectures at the University of North Carolina at Chapel Hill were the starting point to Aigner's monograph [57] on the subject) connects variable-length codes to extremal combinatorics in a way that makes Sperner's extremal configurations emerge as the mathematical description of the optimal execution of a blood test routinely executed in the U.S. army during WW II. Rényi's students, especially Csiszár and Katona (cf. Katona [58]) continued to explore the border line between combinatorics and information theory. The mathematical equivalence between Sperner's problem and a straightforward generalization of Shannon capacity to directed graphs appears in Körner and Simonyi [59] and is fully developed in Gargano, Körner, and Vaccaro [60].

The following Sperner-type problem was posed by Rényi [61]. It was investigated primarily by the Prague school of combinatorics whose members, especially Poljak [62]–[65], also explored its connections to many parts of combinatorics.

Two partitions of a set are *qualitatively independent* if each class of one partition intersects every class of the other partition. A k-partition of a set is a partition into k classes. Let $N(n, k)$ denote the maximum number of k-partitions of an n-set with the property that any two of them are qualitatively independent.

Lower and upper bounds on this quantity were obtained by several authors but no definitive solution was known for any $k > 2$ until Gargano, Körner, and Vaccaro [66] found the following asymptotic formula:

$$\limsup_{n \to \infty} \frac{1}{n} \log N(n, k) = \frac{2}{k}. \tag{5}$$

The most surprising aspect of the solution, at least from our point of view, is that it is in terms of a generalization of Shannon capacity to directed graphs and is entirely information-theoretic. The intuitive explanation of the reasons for this is in terms of separating systems and can be found in Körner and Lucertini [4]. Here we limit ourselves to the mathematics of the new capacity concept.

A *directed graph* (digraph) is a pair $G = (V(G), E(G))$ where G is an arbitrary finite set, called the vertex set of the digraph while $E(G)$ is an arbitrary set of ordered pairs of different elements of $V(G)$, called the set of directed edges. We call a set $S \subseteq V(G)$ a *symmetric clique* in G if each of the ordered pairs of distinct elements of S is in $E(G)$. We denote by $\omega_s(G)$ the maximum cardinality of vertices inducing a symmetric clique in G, and refer to it as the symmetric clique number of the graph. Further, by analogy with the graph product used in the definition of Shannon capacity, we denote by G^n the digraph having vertex set $[V(G)]^n$ and edge set consisting of those ordered pairs of sequences $(\boldsymbol{x}, \boldsymbol{y})$ for which $(x_i, y_i) \in E(G)$ at least for one coordinate $1 \leq i \leq n$. Then the *Sperner capacity* $\Sigma(G)$ of the digraph G is defined to be

$$\Sigma(G) = \sup_n \frac{1}{n} \log \omega_s(G^n).$$

Once again, by Fekete's lemma, the supremum is attained as a limit. Körner and Simonyi [59] noticed that the number $N(n)$ in Sperner's theorem is equivalent to the symmetric clique number of S^n where S is a 2-vertex digraph with a single edge. The formal definition of Sperner capacity is exactly the same as that of Shannon's except that unordered pairs are replaced by ordered ones. In fact, Sperner capacity is the more general notion since to every undirected graph we can associate a digraph in which every formerly undirected edge is replaced by a 2-cycle, i.e., by a couple of oppositely oriented edges. Then, trivially, the Sperner capacity of the new graph equals the Shannon capacity of the old one. It is much less obvious to see what happens if we consider the digraphs corresponding to the different orientations of the edges of the same simple graph. Calderbank, Frankl, Graham, Li, and Shepp [67] proved that the Sperner capacity of the two nonisomorphic digraphs obtained from the complete graph on three vertices is actually different, thereby showing that Sperner capacity is a genuine (not just formal) generalization of Shannon's beautiful notion of capacity. Their proof relies on a generalization of the Haemers bound. It has a nice elementary version due to Blokhuis [68]. It was believed by some of us that at least for the different orientations of a complete graph, (tournament graphs) Sperner capacity would be easy to determine, but a recent paper by Alon [69] shows that not even this can be hoped for. In particular, we do not know whether the following is true.

Problem: Are there graphs G for which the maximum of the Sperner capacities of the digraphs obtained from G by replacing each of its edges by a single oriented edge is still strictly less than $C(G)$?

In a recent paper, Sali and Simonyi [70] show that the edges of a self-complementary graph and those of its complement can always be oriented in a way that preserves their isomorphy and the union of the two resulting digraphs becomes a transitive tournament. This means that self-complementary graphs have the same role in the study of Sperner capacity as they do for Shannon capacity.

Luckily, there are some "easy" graphs and this allows to use the generalization of (4) to solve many hard combinatorial problems, at least in an asymptotic sense. Analogously to the definition of fixed composition codes in Section V, let us

define, for any distribution P on $V(G)$ the quantity $\omega_s(G^n, P)$ as the maximum cardinality of a symmetric clique in G^n under the additional constraint that all vertices have to be sequences of type P. If all the probabilities of P are rational numbers, we write

$$\Sigma(G, P) = \sup_n \frac{1}{n} \log \omega(G^n, P).$$

For a fixed digraph G we extend $\Sigma(G, P)$ to all distributions on $V(G)$ by continuity. Next we define the hitherto most general notion of graph capacity in this paper.

Let $\mathcal{G}$ be an arbitrary family of digraphs with common vertex set $\mathcal{X}$. A set $\mathcal{C} \subseteq \mathcal{X}^n$ is a symmetric clique in $\mathcal{G}$ if it induces a symmetric clique in G^n for every $G \in \mathcal{G}$. In other words, $\mathcal{C}$ must be a symmetric clique in the intersection graph $\bigcap_{G \in \mathcal{G}} G^n$. Let us denote by $\omega_s(\mathcal{G}, n)$ the largest cardinality of a symmetric clique in this intersection graph. The *Sperner capacity* of the graph family is

$$\Sigma(\mathcal{G}) = \sup_n \frac{1}{n} \log \omega_s(\mathcal{G}, n).$$

Gargano, Körner, and Vaccaro [43] proved the following characterization of the Sperner capacity of a directed graph

$$\Sigma(\mathcal{G}) = \max_P \min_{G \in \mathcal{G}} \Sigma(G, P).$$

In our opinion, it would be very interesting to extend the whole range of existing results from simple graphs to the case of directed graphs. The upper bounds on capacity in terms of the chromatic number and the fractional chromatic number have a very natural extension to this more general case, cf. Fachini and Körner [71]. As we mentioned, the same is true for the Haemers bound which was generalized in [67]. On the other hand, the more powerful Lovász bound does not seem to generalize to digraphs.

An interesting application of the constructions both for perfect hashing and for qualitatively independent partitions is concerned with the Nešetřil–Pultr dimension $\dim_{\mathrm{NP}}(G)$ of a graph G [72]. This concept is much in the spirit of Shannon's functional complexity, and therefore it belongs to the general area of information theory. $\dim_{\mathrm{NP}}(G)$ is the minimum number of complete multipartite graphs whose intersection is G. In other words, $\dim_{\mathrm{NP}}(G)$ is the minimum number of vertex colorings of G for which every two nonadjacent vertices of G get the same color in at least one of the colorings.

The vertex set of the Kneser graph $G(n, k)$ is the set

$$V(G(n, k)) = \binom{[n]}{k}$$

namely, all k-subsets of a fixed n-set. Two vertices are adjacent if the corresponding sets are disjoint. Poljak, Pultr, and Rödl [62] used results for qualitative independence and perfect hashing to get bounds on the Nešetřil–Pultr dimension of Kneser graphs. Using the exact asymptotics for qualitative independence from (5), Gargano Körner, and Vaccaro [43] and Poljak, Pultr, and Rödl [62] obtained, for fixed k, asymptotically in n

$$\log \log n \leq \dim_{\mathrm{NP}}(G(n, k)) \leq \frac{k}{2} \log \log n.$$

It is unlikely that dimension should be independent from k, but we believe that the upper bound might be tight.

IX. FUNCTIONALS: GRAPH ENTROPY

The subadditivity of entropy is often used in combinatorics to get bounds in extremal set theory, within the framework of the *probabilistic method*, cf. Alon and Spencer [73]. We believe that practically all information measures could potentially be used outside information theory in a similar manner. This is one reason why the quest for new information measures should continue. We illustrate this point via graph entropy.

Graph entropy was introduced by Körner [74] in order to find a coding interpretation for all entropy-based information measures. The original definition was in terms of a source-coding problem, cf. also Körner and Longo [75]. Formally, considering graph entropy as a functional $H(G, P)$ associated with a graph G and an arbitrary probability distribution P on its vertex set, one defines it as

$$H(G, P) = \min_{X \in Y \in S(G), \, P_X = P} I(X \wedge Y)$$

where $S(G)$ denotes the family of the stable sets of vertices in G. (A subset of the vertex set is *stable* if it does not contain any edge.) Since the mutual information $I(X \wedge Y)$ measures the degree of independence between the random variables X and Y, graph entropy measures how independent a coloring (a covering by stable sets) of G can get from the vertices. (Hypergraph entropy is defined in exactly the same manner, using the stable sets of the hypergraph. Recall that a subset of the vertex set of a hypergraph is stable if it does not contain any hyperedge.) Denote by $\chi(G^n, P)$ the chromatic number of the graph induced by G^n on its vertices having type P when the latter are understood as n-length sequences of elements of $V(G)$. If the distribution P has only rational probabilities, then this induced graph G_P^n is infinitely often nonempty, and restricting the sequence $(1/n) \log \chi(G_P^n)$ to the corresponding values of n the resulting new sequence has $H(G, P)$ as its limit, as shown in Körner [74] (for this form of the statement, cf. Körner and Simonyi [76]). Hence, e.g.,

$$\limsup_{n \to \infty} \frac{1}{n} \log(\chi(G_P^n) + 1) = H(G, P).$$

As a consequence of this we obtain the formula

$$\lim_{n \to \infty} \frac{1}{n} \log \chi(G^n) = \max_P H(G, P)$$

which is an equivalent information-theoretic formulation of a well-known graph theory result of Berge and Simonovits [77] and McEliece and Posner [78] stating that the left-hand side of the last formula equals the fractional chromatic number of G (cf. also Lovász [7]).

In a closely related result, Alon and Orlitsky [79] defined the *chromatic entropy* $H_\chi(G, P)$ of a probabilistic graph G and a distribution P over the vertices to be the minimum entropy of any coloring of G (see Boppana [80] for related concepts). They showed that

$$\lim_{n \to \infty} \frac{1}{n} H_\chi(G^n, P^{(n)}) = H(G, P)$$

where $P^{(n)}$ is the probability distribution on n-tuples of graph vertices each chosen independently according to P.

The most useful property of graph entropy is its subadditivity with respect to graph union. Körner [30] showed that if F and G are two graphs on the same vertex set V and $F \cup G$ denotes the graph on V with edge set $E(F \cup G) = E(F) \cup E(G)$, then for every P

$$H(F \cup G, P) \leq H(F, P) + H(G, P). \tag{6}$$

Combined with monotonicity, meaning that if $E(F) \subseteq E(G)$, then $H(F, P) \leq H(G, P)$ the subadditivity of graph entropy becomes the basis for a very flexible bounding technique in combinatorics. If F and G are complementary graphs and thus $F \cup G$ is complete, then equality for every P above is equivalent to F and G being perfect, (cf. Csiszár, Körner, Lovász, Marton, and Simonyi [81]). This result is used in the first near-optimal polynomial-time sorting algorithm starting from an arbitrary partially ordered set, due to Kahn and Kim [82]. A further analysis of the cases of equality in (6) has led to the definition of a *perfect couple* of graphs and the analysis of the conditions guaranteeing that in a partition of the edge set of the complete graph into more than two graphs each of these be perfect, cf. Körner, Simonyi, and Tuza [83]. More general semimodularity properties of graph entropy are studied in Körner and Simonyi [76]. Graph entropy has been applied in the analysis of Boolean complexity, e.g., by Radhakhrishnan [84]. A detailed survey on the various applications of graph and hypergraph entropies was written by Simonyi [85].

PART III: SOURCE CODING

X. INTRODUCTION

The previous part mostly concerned transmission over a channel. We now consider the dual problem of describing a source output.

In the simplest version of this *source-coding* problem, $p(x)$ is a known probability distribution over a discrete set $\mathcal{X}$. In every source *instance,* a random variable X is generated according to $p(x)$, independently of all other instances. An *informant* knows the outputs and wants to convey them without error to a *recipient* who knows the encoding function but has no other information.

For a single instance, it is well known that the smallest number of bits needed in the worst case is $\lceil \log |\mathcal{X}| \rceil$, and the smallest expected number of bits, achieved by Huffman coding [5], is between $H(X)$ and $H(X) + 1$. It follows that for n independent instances, $\lceil n \log |\mathcal{X}| \rceil$ bits are needed in the worst case, and between $nH(X)$ and $nH(X) + 1$ are needed on the average. Therefore, the asymptotic, per-instance, worst case, and average number of bits are $\log |\mathcal{X}|$ and $H(X)$, respectively.

But even simple modifications are difficult to analyze. We first consider the scenario where the recipient knows some, possibly related, random variable Y, commonly called *side-information*.

A *source coding with side-information* problem $\mathcal{S}$ is defined by a joint probability distribution $p(x, y)$ over a discrete product set $\mathcal{X} \times \mathcal{Y}$. In every source *instance,* a random-variable pair (X, Y) is generated according to $p(x, y)$ independently of all other instances. The informant knows the X's and wants to convey them to the recipient who knows the Y's.

Slepian and Wolf [86] showed that if some positive error probability can be tolerated then, asymptotically, $H(X|Y)$ bits are required per-instance. Following Shannon's investigation of the zero-error capacity of a channel, Witsenhausen [87], Ferguson and Bailey [88], and Ahlswede [89] studied the zero-error rate—the number of bits required when the receiver must determine the X's with no probability of error.

It is easy to verify that the zero-error rate is determined by the *support set*

$$S \stackrel{\text{def}}{=} \{(x, y): p(x, y) > 0\}$$

the set of (XY) values occurring with positive probability. The precise (positive) values of p over the support set are irrelevant. This holds for single and multiple instances. Hence we identify a source-coding with side-information problem S with its support set S.

As in the previous section, one could try to determine the asymptotic per-instance number of bits required for specific problems, but the techniques used and results obtained would be very similar. Instead, we concentrate on other issues.

In Section XI, we address the savings afforded by simultaneous encoding of multiple instances. We show that for some sources: 1) two independent instances require about the same number of transmitted bits as one and 2) one instance requires a large number of bits but many independent instances require only one bit per instance.

In Section XII, we consider the advantages that can be derived from interaction between the communicators. Among other results, we show that interaction can reduce transmission to the logarithm of the one-way number of bits, and that for a large class of natural sources, the number of bits required with interaction is about the same as that needed if the informant had known Y in advance. For communication of multiple instances, interaction can reduce transmission by an arbitrary amount and can always achieve the number of bits needed when the informant knows Y in advance.

We then consider a different scenario where X and Y are uncorrelated, hence $S = \mathcal{X} \times \mathcal{Y}$. This would trivialize the communication problem except that instead of conveying information, the communicators try to determine the value of a function $f(X, Y)$ of their joint inputs. This *communication complexity* scenario was studied extensively in the computer-science literature.

Communication complexity is discussed in Sections XIII and XIV. In Section XIII, we introduce communication complexity via a simple example where the communicators try to decide whether $X = Y$. We use the example to illustrate some of the complexity measures involved. We then present results on the complexity of some specific functions and show that most functions require communication of essentially as many bits as needed for one communicator to convey his data. We show that for every positive integer m there is a function where exchanging at most $m - 1$ messages

requires almost exponentially more bits than needed with m messages, and describe a limit on the savings afforded by simultaneous transmission of multiple instances. In Section XIV, we mention some applications. We recount one of communication complexity's original motivations—to derive lower bounds on the size and time of VLSI chips. We also describe an elegant analogy between communication complexity and circuit depth and its implications to lower bounds on circuit complexity.

XI. ONE-WAY COMMUNICATION

We compare the number of bits required for one source instance with that needed for multiple independent instances. In Section XI-A, we formally define the problem, relate it to graph coloring, and introduce some examples. In Section XI-B1, we show that for some sources: 1) two independent instances require about the same number of transmitted bits as one instance and 2) one instance requires a large number of bits but many independent instances require roughly one bit per instance. Finally, we outline some open problems concerning high-entropy sources.

A. Single Instance

A *graph* G consists of a set V of *vertices* and a collection E of *edges,* unordered pairs of distinct vertices. If $\{x, x'\} \in E$, we say that x and x' are *connected* in G. A *coloring* of G is an assignment of colors to its vertices such that connected vertices are assigned different colors. G's *chromatic number* $\chi(G)$ is the minimum number of colors in any of its colorings.

Let S be a source with support set $S \subseteq \mathcal{X} \times \mathcal{Y}$. The *fan-out* of $x \in \mathcal{X}$ is the set $S_x \stackrel{\text{def}}{=} \{y: (x, y) \in S\}$ of y's that are *jointly possible* with x. Associated with S is a *characteristic graph* $\mathcal{G}$. Its vertex set is $\mathcal{X}$, and two (distinct) vertices x, x' are connected if their fan-out sets intersect, namely, there is a y that is jointly possible with both. Note that every graph (V, E) is the characteristic graph of some dual source: $\mathcal{X} = V$, $\mathcal{Y} = E$, and $S = \{(x, y): x \in y\}$.

The smallest number of possible messages the informant must transmit for a single instance of S is $\chi(\mathcal{G})$, the chromatic number of S's characteristic graph. Intuitively, the communicators agree in advance on a coloring of $\mathcal{G}$. Given X, the informant transmits its color. The recipient, having Y, can determine X because there is exactly one element of $\mathcal{X}$ with this color that is jointly possible with Y. Conversely, it is easy to see that if two connected vertices are assigned the same message, an error can result.

The smallest number of bits the informant must transmit in the worst case for a single instance of S is therefore $\lceil \log \chi(\mathcal{G}) \rceil$. The ceiling arises from the integral number of bits, but it detracts from the clarity of the results and changes the number of bits by at most a fraction—significantly less than the effects we consider. We therefore let

$$\sigma^{(1)} \stackrel{\text{def}}{=} \log \chi(\mathcal{G})$$

denote S's *single-instance rate.*

The next three examples illustrate various sources and their single-instance rate. We will revisit these examples later and

172

compare their single- and multiple-instance rates. We will see that each example allows for progressively more savings as we move from one to multiple independent instances.

Example 1a): In an *uncorrelated* source every two fan-out sets intersect. That is the case, for example, if $p(x, y) > 0$ for all $x \in \mathcal{X}$ and $y \in \mathcal{Y}$. $\mathcal{G}$ is the complete graph over $\mathcal{X}$, $\chi(\mathcal{G}) = |\mathcal{X}|$, and $\sigma^{(1)} = \log |\mathcal{X}|$ indicating that X has to be completely specified for the recipient to learn its value.

In a *completely correlated source* no two fan-out sets intersect. The characteristic graph $\mathcal{G}$ is the empty graph over $\mathcal{X}$, $\chi(\mathcal{G}) = 1$, and $\sigma^{(1)} = 0$ indicating that the recipient knows X and therefore no bits need be transmitted. $\square$

The *Pentagon graph*, mentioned in Section III, consists of five vertices labeled $0, \cdots, 4$. Vertex i is connected to vertices $i - 1$ and $i + 1 \, (\mathrm{mod} \, 5)$. It can be easily colored with three colors, and since no more than two vertices can be assigned the same color, its chromatic number is three.

Example 2a): The *Pentagon source* has $\mathcal{X} = \mathcal{Y} = Z_5$ and $S = \{(x, y) \colon y = x \text{ or } y = x + 1 \, (\mathrm{mod} \, 5)\}$. Figuratively, five countries are located around a lake. Occasionally, border disputes arise between two neighboring countries. The recipient knows two countries involved in a dispute and the informant knows one of them, say the one who wins the dispute. We are interested in the number of bits that the informant must transmit in the worst case for the recipient to know the winning country.

Clearly, $\mathcal{G}$ is the pentagon graph, $\chi(\mathcal{G}) = 3$, and $\sigma^{(1)} = \log 3$, indicating that $\lceil \log 3 \rceil = 2$ bits are needed for the recipient to learn the winner. $\square$

Recall from Section VIII that for integers $0 \le t \le u$, the *Kneser graph* $K = K(u, t)$ consists of all t-element subsets of $\{1, \cdots, u\}$. Two vertices are connected iff they are disjoint. Every vertex can be colored with one of its elements, say the smallest, hence $\chi(K) \le u$. But fewer colors suffice. Of every two disjoint t-element subsets of $\{1, \cdots, u\}$, at least one contains an element $\le u - 2t + 1$. Therefore, the mapping which assigns to every vertex T the smaller of $u - 2t + 2$ and $\min(T)$ also colors K. Lovász [90] showed that the number of colors cannot be further reduced:

$$\chi(K) = u - 2t + 2.$$

jjExample 3a). Neighborhood Games: u basketball players, numbered $1, \cdots, u$, meet at a neighborhood court. Two t-player teams $(t \le \lfloor u/2 \rfloor)$ soon form and play each other. The recipient knows the two teams (namely, two disjoint sets $\{i_1, \cdots, i_t\}$ and $\{j_1, \cdots, j_t\}$) while the informant knows the winning team (say $\{j_1, \cdots, j_t\}$) and would like to convey that information to the recipient.

The vertices of the characteristic graph $\mathcal{G}$ are all t-element subsets of $\{1, \cdots, u\}$. Two vertices are connected iff they are disjoint. $\mathcal{G}$ is therefore the *Kneser graph* $K(u, t)$ and

$$\sigma^{(1)} = \log(u - 2t + 2). \qquad \square$$

B. Multiple Instances

Next we determine the number of bits required for multiple independent source instances. Section XI-B1 relates the problem to that of graph products; Section XI-B2 shows that for some sources, multiple instances, even though independent, require only few additional bits; Section XI-B3 compares the number of bits needed for one instance with that required for asymptotically many.

1) Multiple Instances and Graph Products: The nth *AND* (or *normal*) *power* of a graph $G = (V, E)$ is the graph $G^{\wedge n}$ whose vertex set is V^n and where distinct vertices $(x_1, \cdots, x_n)$ and $(x'_1, \cdots, x'_n)$ are connected if $\{x_i, x'_i\} \in G$ for all $i \in \{1, \cdots, n\}$ such that $x_i \ne x'_i$.

In $n \ge 2$ instances of the source $\mathcal{S}$, the informant knows $x_1, \cdots, x_n$ while the recipient knows $y_1, \cdots, y_n$ such that each $(x_i, y_i) \in \mathcal{S}$ and wants to learn $x_1, \cdots, x_n$. Conceptually, these n instances can be viewed as a single instance of a larger source $\mathcal{S}^{(n)}$ whose support set is (equivalent to) the Cartesian power $\mathcal{S}^n \subseteq \mathcal{X}^n \times \mathcal{Y}^n$. The fan-out of $\overline{x} = (x_1, \cdots, x_n) \in \mathcal{X}^n$, is therefore

$$S_{\overline{x}}^n = \{\overline{y} \colon (\overline{x}, \overline{y}) \in S^n\} = S_{x_1} \times \cdots \times S_{x_n}.$$

Let $\mathcal{G}^{(n)}$ denote the characteristic graph of $\mathcal{S}^{(n)}$. Its vertex set is $\mathcal{X}^n$, and if $\overline{x} = (x_1, \cdots, x_n)$ and $\overline{x}' \stackrel{\text{def}}{=} (x'_1, \cdots, x'_n)$ are distinct vertices then $\{\overline{x}, \overline{x}'\} \in \mathcal{G}^{(n)}$ iff $S_{\overline{x}}$ and $S_{\overline{x}'}$ intersect iff S_{x_i} intersects $S_{x'_i}$ for all $i \in \{1, \cdots, n\}$ iff $\{x_i, x'_i\} \in \mathcal{G}$ for all $i \in \{1, \cdots, n\}$ such that $x_i \ne x'_i$ iff $\{\overline{x}, \overline{x}'\} \in \mathcal{G}^{\wedge n}$, the nth AND power of $\mathcal{G}$. Therefore,

$$\mathcal{G}^{(n)} = \mathcal{G}^{\wedge n}.$$

It follows that the number of bits the informant must transmit in the worst case to convey n instances of $\mathcal{S}$ without error is

$$\sigma^{(n)} \stackrel{\text{def}}{=} \log \chi(\mathcal{G}^{\wedge n}).$$

Therefore, to study the communication increase for multiple instances, we need to analyze the chromatic number of AND powers of graphs.

Remark: Note that in the graph power defined in Section III, distinct $(x_1, \cdots, x_n)$ and $(x'_1, \cdots, x'_n)$ are connected in G^n iff $\{x_i, x'_i\} \in G$ for some $i \in \{1, \cdots, n\}$ such that $x_i \ne x'_i$. G^n is often called the OR power of G, denoted $\mathcal{G}^{\vee n}$. It is easy to verify that $\overline{\mathcal{G}^{\vee n}} = (\overline{G})^{\vee n}$. Hence source-coding results can be described in terms of the OR powers by letting the characteristic graph be the complement of the current one. Similarly, channel-coding results could be described in terms of the AND powers. However, the OR power is traditionally used in channel coding, and the AND power is more common in source coding since, as we just saw, the chromatic number arises naturally.

2) Fixed Number of Instances: If G can be colored with χ colors, $\mathcal{G}^{\wedge 2}$ can be colored with χ^2 colors. Therefore, $\chi(G^{\wedge 2}) \le (\chi(G))^2$ for every graph G, and $\sigma^{(2)} \le 2\sigma^{(1)}$ for every source. This coincides with our intuition that encoding two instances should require at most twice as many bits as needed for one. However, since different instances of the source are completely independent of each other, it is not intuitively clear that $\sigma^{(2)}$ can be smaller than $2\sigma^{(1)}$.

Example 1b): For an uncorrelated source we saw that $\mathcal{G}$ is the complete graph over $\mathcal{X}$. Hence $\mathcal{G}^{\wedge n}$ is the complete graph over $\mathcal{X}^n$, $\chi(\mathcal{G}^{\wedge n}) = |\mathcal{X}|^n$, and $\sigma^{(n)} = n \log |\mathcal{X}|$ for all $n \geq 1$.

For a completely correlated source we saw that $\mathcal{G}$ is the empty graph over $\mathcal{X}$. Hence $\mathcal{G}^{(n)}$ is the empty graph over $\mathcal{X}^n$, $\chi(\mathcal{G}^{\wedge n}) = 1$, and $\sigma^{(n)} = 0$ for all $n \geq 1$. $\square$

Yet Witsenhausen [87] showed that for the Pentagon source, $\sigma^{(2)} < 2\sigma^{(1)}$.

Example 2b): We saw that for the Pentagon source, $\mathcal{G}$ is the Pentagon graph, whose chromatic number is 3. Using the corresponding results by Shannon and Lovász (see Section III), Witsenhausen showed that for every even n, $\chi(\mathcal{G}^{\wedge n}) = 5^{n/2}$. In particular, $\chi(\mathcal{G}^{\wedge 2}) = 5$, hence $\sigma^{(2)} < 2\sigma^{(1)}$. $\square$

But much larger savings are possible. Consider first the smallest possible increase from $\chi(G)$ to $\chi(G^{\wedge 2})$ and from $\sigma^{(1)}$ to $\sigma^{(2)}$. Clearly, $\chi(G^{\wedge 2}) \geq \chi(G)$ for every graph G. Linial and Vazirani [91] showed that for arbitrarily large values of $\chi(G)$ there are graphs such that $\chi(G^{\wedge 2}) = O(\chi(G))$. The following results use Kneser graphs to reduce the implied constant and show that for arbitrarily large values of $\chi(G)$ there are graphs such that

$$\chi(G^{\wedge 2}) \leq 34 \cdot \chi(G). \qquad (7)$$

It follows that for arbitrarily large values of $\sigma^{(1)}$ there are sources where two instances require only a few more bits than one instance

$$\sigma^{(2)} < \sigma^{(1)} + 6. \qquad (8)$$

Recall that the chromatic number of $K = K(u, t)$ is $u - 2t + 2$. Alon and Orlitsky [22] showed that AND and OR powers of Kneser graphs can be colored with relatively few colors

$$\chi(K^{\wedge n}) \leq \chi(K^{\vee n}) \leq \left\lceil \left(\frac{u}{t}\right)^n \cdot n \cdot \ln \binom{u}{t} \right\rceil. \qquad (9)$$

Setting $u = 3.25 \cdot t$, we see that

$$\chi(K) = 1.25 \cdot t + 2 \quad \text{while} \quad \chi(K^{\wedge 2}) \leq \lceil 42.4 \cdot t \rceil$$

and (7) and (8) follow. In particular, there are sources with arbitrarily high rates where two independent instances require only negligibly more bits than one instance.

3) Asymptotically Many Instances: For many instances, it is instructive to consider the *per-instance* number of bits required to convey the X's without error. The *(zero-error) n-instance rate* of a source $\mathcal{S}$ is

$$R^{(n)} = \frac{\sigma^{(n)}}{n} = \frac{\log \chi(\mathcal{G}^{\wedge n})}{n}.$$

Note that $R^{(1)} = \sigma^{(1)}$ is the number of bits required for one instance. By sub-additivity, $R^{(n)}$ tends to $R^{(\infty)}$, the *zero-error rate* of $\mathcal{S}$. $R^{(\infty)}$ is the lowest per-instance number of bits that must be transmitted in the worst case to convey the X's to recipient.

Example 1c): For an uncorrelated source $R^{(n)} = \log |\mathcal{X}|$ for all $n \in \{1, \cdots, \infty\}$. For a completely correlated source $R^{(n)} = 0$ for all $n \in \{1, \cdots, \infty\}$. $\square$

Example 2c): For the Pentagon source

$$R^{(1)} = \log 3 \approx 1.58$$

and

$$R^{(2)} = R^{(4)} = R^{(6)} = \cdots = R^{(\infty)} = \log 5/2 \approx 1.16. \quad \square$$

Inequality (9) shows that asymptotically the chromatic number of Kneser AND powers grows slower than $(u/t)^n$. The Erdös–Ko–Rado Theorem and a result of Lovász [7] on independence numbers can be combined to prove that the growth rate is at least as fast, hence

$$\lim_{n \to \infty} (\chi(K^{\wedge n}))^{1/n} = \frac{u}{t}.$$

It follows that

$$R^{(\infty)} = \lim_{n \to \infty} \log(\chi(K^{\wedge n}))^{1/n} = \log \frac{u}{t}.$$

To construct a source with a large difference between the single-instance and asymptotic zero-error rates, let $u = (2 + \epsilon)t$. Then

$$R^{(1)} = \log(\epsilon t + 2) \quad \text{but} \quad R^{(\infty)} = \log(2 + \epsilon) \leq 1 + \epsilon.$$

For small but fixed ϵ, and increasing t, a single instance requires arbitrarily many bits while multiple instances require roughly one bit per instance.

Example 3b): In a happening neighborhood, n sports are played. Each sport engages u distinct players, and a game involves two teams of t players each. On a certain day, n games take place, one in each sport. The recipient knows the $2n$ playing teams while the informant knows the n that won. How many bits must the informant transmit now?

For $n = 2$ sports, let $u = 3.25t$. Then $\sigma^{(1)} = \log(1.25t + 2)$ while (8) shows that $\sigma^{(2)} \leq \log(\lceil 42.4t \rceil) < \sigma^{(1)} + 6$. Namely, at most six additional bits are needed for two sports over the number needed for one.

For many sports, let $u = (2 + \epsilon)t$. Then $R^{(1)} = \sigma^{(1)} = \log(\epsilon t + 2)$ while $R^{(\infty)} = \log(2 + \epsilon) \leq 1 + \epsilon$. Keeping ϵ small and increasing t, we see that a single sport requires arbitrarily many bits while many sports require roughly one bit per instance. $\square$

Remark: These results can be used to derive discrepancies between the standard chromatic number $\chi(G)$ of a graph and its fractional chromatic number $\chi^*(\mathcal{G})$. McEliece and Posner [78] and Berge and Simonovits [92] showed that

$$\lim_{n \to \infty} (\chi(G^{\vee n}))^{1/n} = \chi^*(\mathcal{G})$$

where $\mathcal{G}^{\vee n}$ is the nth OR power of G. It follows from (9) that there can be an arbitrarily high discrepancy between $\chi(G)$ and $\chi^*(\mathcal{G})$. For every $\chi, \epsilon > 0$ there is a graph such that

$$\chi(G) \geq \chi \quad \text{but} \quad \chi^*(G) \leq 2 + \epsilon.$$

4) High-Rate Sources: The graphs used to derive the above results have $\chi(G)$ which is merely logarithmic in the number of vertices and therefore the implied sources have $\sigma^{(1)}$ which are only about $\log \log |\mathcal{X}|$. Sources requiring a large number of bits are of more theoretical interest.

Alon and Orlitsky [22] showed that $\chi(G^{\wedge 2})$ can be about $\chi(G)$ even when $\chi(G)$ is close to the graph's size, and therefore that $\sigma^{(2)}$ can be about $\sigma^{(1)}$ even when $\sigma^{(1)}$ is close to $\log |\mathcal{X}|$. Using probabilistic constructions of self-complementary Ramsey graphs that are also Cayley graphs they showed that for arbitrarily high values of v there are graphs G such that[1]

$$\chi(G) \geq \frac{v}{(1 + o(1))16 \log^2 v}$$

but

$$\chi(G^{\wedge 2}) \leq (1 + o(1))16\chi(G) \log^2 \chi(G).$$

Therefore, for arbitrarily high values of $|\mathcal{X}|$ there are sources such that

$$\sigma^{(1)} \geq \log |\mathcal{X}| - 2 \log \log |\mathcal{X}| - 4 - o(1) \qquad (10)$$

but

$$\sigma^{(2)} \leq \sigma^{(1)} + 2 \log \sigma^{(1)} + 4 + o(1). \qquad (11)$$

To relate the number of bits transmitted to the source's size and to account for the number of instances, we define the *(zero-error) normalized n-instance rate* of a source $\mathcal{S}$ to be

$$\tilde{R}^{(n)} = \frac{R^{(n)}}{\log |\mathcal{X}|} = \frac{\sigma^{(n)}}{n \log |\mathcal{X}|} = \frac{\log \chi(\mathcal{G}^{\wedge n})}{n \log |\mathcal{X}|}.$$

Again, by sub-additivity, the limit $\tilde{R}^{(\infty)}$ exists and reflects the normalized number of bits that must be transmitted for asymptotically many independent instances. For every $n \in \{1, \cdots, \infty\}$, $\tilde{R}^{(n)}$ ranges from 1 for sources where X and Y are unrelated, to 0 for sources where Y determines X, thereby reflecting the "difficulty" of conveying X to the recipient.

Example 1d): For an uncorrelated source $\tilde{R}^{(n)} = 1$ for all $n \in \{1, \cdots, \infty\}$. For a completely correlated source $\tilde{R}^{(n)} = 0$ for all $n \in \{1, \cdots, \infty\}$. □

Example 2d): For the Pentagon source

$$\tilde{R}^{(1)} = \log 3 / \log 5 \approx 0.683$$

and

$$\tilde{R}^{(2)} = \tilde{R}^{(4)} = \tilde{R}^{(6)} = \cdots = \tilde{R}^{(\infty)} = 0.5. \quad □$$

Inequalities (10) and (11) imply that for every $\epsilon > 0$ there is a source such that

$$\tilde{R}^{(1)} \geq 1 - \epsilon \quad \text{but} \quad \tilde{R}^{(\infty)} \leq \tilde{R}^{(2)} \leq \frac{1}{2}.$$

Note that for two instances, this difference is essentially the largest possible. Clearly, $\chi(G \wedge 2) \geq \chi(G)$ for every graph G. Hence, for all sources,

$$\tilde{R}^{(2)} - \tilde{R}^{(1)} \leq \frac{1}{2}.$$

[1] The $o(1)$ term diminishes to zero as the relevant parameters (here, v) tend to infinity.

Open Problem 1: Given an arbitrarily small $\epsilon > 0$, is there a source such that $\tilde{R}^{(1)} \geq 1 - \epsilon$ but $\tilde{R}^{(\infty)} \leq \epsilon$? Namely, a single instance requires almost complete specification of X, while multiple instances require very little information. □

XII. INTERACTIVE COMMUNICATION

Another aspect of the problem is revealed when the sender and the receiver are allowed to interact. We show that for some sources, interaction can reduce transmission to the logarithm of the one-way number of bits, and that for a large class of sources, interaction can reduce transmission to about the same number of bits required when the informant knows Y in advance.

For communication of multiple instances, interaction can reduce transmission by an arbitrary amount, and can always achieve the number of bits needed when the informant knows Y in advance.

A. The Interactive Model

$f(X, Y) = X$: We assume that the two communicators alternate in transmitting *messages*: finite sequences of bits. The messages are transmitted over an error-free channel and are determined by an agreed-upon, deterministic protocol. For every *input*—an element (x, y) of $\mathcal{S}$'s support set S—the protocol determines a finite sequence of transmitted messages. The protocol is *m-message* if, for all inputs, the number of messages transmitted is at most m.

The *worst case complexity* of a protocol is the number of bits it requires both communicators to transmit, maximized over all inputs. $\hat{C}_m$, the *m-message complexity* of $\mathcal{S}$, is the minimum complexity of an m-message protocol for $\mathcal{S}$. For example, $\hat{C}_1$, the *one-way complexity* of (X, Y), is the number of bits required in the worst case when the recipient cannot transmit to the informant, and $\hat{C}_2$ is the number of bits required in the worst case when at most two messages are permitted: the recipient transmits a message reflecting Y, then the informant responds with a message from which the recipient must infer X. Since empty messages are allowed, $\hat{C}_m$ is a nonincreasing function of m bounded below by 0. We can therefore define $\hat{C}_\infty$, the *unbounded-message complexity* of (X, Y), to be the limit of $\hat{C}_m$ as $m \to \infty$. It is the *minimum* number of bits that must be transmitted for the recipient to know X, even if no restrictions are placed on the number of messages exchanged. It follows that

$$\hat{C}_1 \geq \hat{C}_2 \geq \hat{C}_3 \geq \cdots \geq \hat{C}_\infty.$$

The next example, from Orlitsky [93], demonstrates some of these complexity measures.

Example 4: A league has t teams. The recipient knows two teams that played in a game, and the informant knows the team that won the game. They communicate in order for the recipient to learn the winning team.

If only one message is allowed, necessarily from the informant to the recipient, it must be based solely on the winner (for that is all the informant knows). If the message transmitted when team i wins is the same as (or a prefix of) the message transmitted when team j wins, then in the event of a match between teams i and j, the recipient cannot tell who the winner is (or when the message ends). Therefore, there must be t different, prefix-free, messages and at least one of them must be of length $\geq \lceil \log t \rceil$. This bound is clearly achievable, hence

$$\hat{C}_1 = \lceil \log t \rceil.$$

If two messages are allowed, the recipient considers the binary representations of the two teams that played and transmits $\lceil \log \log t \rceil$ bits describing the location of the first bit where they differ. The informant responds by transmitting a single bit describing the bit value of the winning team in that location. Therefore, $\hat{C}_2 \leq \lceil \log \log t \rceil + 1$. It can be shown (see (12)) that this protocol is optimal. For this example

$$\hat{C}_2 = \cdots = \hat{C}_\infty = \lceil \log \log t \rceil + 1. \qquad \square$$

The next two subsections address the single-instance case: Section XII-B outlines results that hold for all sources, and Section XII-C deals with a natural class of sources where stronger results hold. Finally, Section XII-D revisits the issue of multiple independent instances; this time when interaction is allowed.

Other aspects of interactive communication are not considered here. For the number of bits required when both communicators need to learn each other's information see El Gamal and Orlitsky [94] and Ahlswede, Cai, and Zhang [95]. For results on the average number of bits, see Orlitsky [96].

B. General Sources

Example 4 shows that for some sources, one message requires exponentially more bits than the minimum necessary

$$\hat{C}_1 = 2^{\hat{C}_\infty - 1}.$$

Using one-way protocols to simulate interactive ones, it is possible to show that this is the largest possible discrepancy. For all sources

$$\hat{C}_1 \leq 2^{\hat{C}_\infty - 1}. \tag{12}$$

This proves in particular that the two-message protocol described in Example 4 is optimal.

Communication with few messages is generally easier to implement, and involves less delay and overhead. It is therefore natural to ask whether a few, albeit more than one, messages can achieve the optimum number of bits. The following results address this issue.

Probabilistic arguments can be used to show that just two messages always suffice to reduce communication to almost the minimum: for all sources

$$\hat{C}_2 \leq 4\hat{C}_\infty + 3.$$

Two messages are not optimal. For arbitrarily high values of $\hat{C}_\infty$ there are sources similar to the one in Example 4 where

$$\hat{C}_2 \geq 2\hat{C}_\infty - o(\hat{C}_\infty).$$

Open Problem 2: What is the largest asymptotic ratio between $\hat{C}_2$ and $\hat{C}_\infty$? $\qquad \square$

The previous results, taken from Orlitsky [93], concern the relative optimality of one and two messages. For more than two messages, Zhang and Xia [97], and Ahlswede, Cai, and Zhang [95], showed that three messages are not optimal either. For arbitrarily high values of $\hat{C}_\infty$ there are sources where

$$\hat{C}_3 \geq 2\hat{C}_\infty - o(\hat{C}_\infty).$$

Naor, Orlitsky, and Shor [98] showed that for all sources

$$\hat{C}_4 \leq 3\hat{C}_\infty + o(\hat{C}_\infty).$$

No other results are known about the relative optimality of a given number of messages.

Open Problem 3: Is there an m such that m-message is asymptotically optimum? Namely, for all sources

$$\hat{C}_m \leq \hat{C}_\infty + o(\hat{C}_\infty). \qquad \square$$

In the next section, we consider a natural class of sources for which Open Problems 2 and 3 can be resolved.

C. Balanced Sources and Correlated Files

The recipient's *ambiguity* when he has the value y is

$$\mu(y) \stackrel{\text{def}}{=} |\{x \colon (x, y) \in S\}| \tag{13}$$

the number of possible X values when $Y = y$. The recipient's *maximum ambiguity* is

$$\hat{\mu} \stackrel{\text{def}}{=} \max_y \{\mu(y)\} \tag{14}$$

the maximum number of X values possible with any given Y value. The informant's ambiguity $\eta(x)$ when he has the value x, and his maximum ambiguity $\hat{\eta}$, are similarly defined. In the league problem of Example 4, $\hat{\mu} = 2$ as for every game known to the recipient there are two possible winners known to the informant. Similarly, $\hat{\eta} = t - 1$, corresponding to the number of possible losing teams.

Balanced sources have

$$\hat{\mu} = \hat{\eta}.$$

They arise naturally whenever there is no distinction between the two communicators, or when X and Y are known to be within some "distance" from each other. For example[2]

1) X and Y, inaccurate measurements of the same quantity, are integers within a bounded absolute difference from each other.
2) X and Y, obtained from a noisy binary transmission or from a faulty memory, are n-bit strings within a bounded Hamming distance from each other.

---

[2] The pairs below are in fact *symmetric*: $(x, y) \in S$ if and only if $(y, x) \in S$. Clearly, every symmetric pair is also balanced.

Of these and other examples of balanced pairs, the following *correlated-files*, or *edit-distance* source shows most promise of being practically useful. The *edit distance* between two binary strings x and y is the minimum number of deletions and insertions to x needed to derive y. For example, the edit distance between the empty string and any n-bit string is n, and the edit distance between 01010 and 10101 is two. In the correlated-files problem, X and Y are binary strings within a small edit distance from each other. The informant knows X while the recipient knows Y and wants to learn X.

This problem can arise in various situations: 1) The informant and the recipient write a joint book and each updates his version individually. 2) X is the new digital image taken by a satellite of the informant and Y is the previous frame, known to the recipient (successive images are assumed to be within a small edit distance). 3) X and Y are different versions of the same program or file. 4) X and Y were received from the same binary transmission with erroneous insertions, deletions, and reversal of bits.

In all those cases, the edit distance between X and Y is much smaller than the number of bits in each. We are looking for a way to communicate X to the recipient without transmitting all of it. Of course, in cases 1) and 2), if the informant keeps the original versions of the file (or image), he can efficiently transmit the locations of the insertions/deletions. But in cases 3) and 4), there is no such reference sequence. Surprisingly, there is almost no difference between the number of bits required in the two cases. We show that even when the informant knows only X (as we assume), X can be communicated to the recipient using only negligibly more bits than the number needed if the informant knew Y in advance.

Since balanced sources are a special case of general sources, stronger results hold for them. In particular, for balanced sources one can solve Open Problems 2 and 3. The following results appeared in Orlitsky [99].

For general sources, one-way communication may require exponentially more bits than the minimum necessary (e.g., $\hat{C}_1 = \lceil \log t \rceil$ versus $\hat{C}_\infty = \lceil \log \log t \rceil + 1$ for the league problem with t teams). Yet for all balanced sources, one-way communication requires at most twice the minimum necessary

$$\hat{C}_1 \leq 2\hat{C}_\infty + 1.$$

This bound is almost tight. For arbitrarily high values of $\hat{C}_\infty$ there are balanced sources where two messages require twice the minimum number of bits

$$\hat{C}_2 \geq 2\hat{C}_\infty - 6.$$

This resolves Open Problem 2 for balanced sources: The largest asymptotic ratio between $\hat{C}_1$ and $\hat{C}_\infty$ and between $\hat{C}_2$ and $\hat{C}_\infty$ is 2. In particular, two messages are not optimal.

Yet three messages are optimal. For all balanced pairs

$$\hat{C}_3 \leq \hat{C}_\infty + 3 \log \hat{C}_\infty + 11. \tag{15}$$

This follows from a stronger result showing that although the informant does not know Y, the number of bits needed to convey X to the recipient is only negligibly larger than would be required if the informant knew Y in advance.

Specifically, (13) and (14) defined the recipient's ambiguity, $\mu(y)$, when he has the value y and his maximum ambiguity $\hat{\mu}$. Clearly, at least $\lceil \log \mu(y) \rceil$ bits must be transmitted in the worst case when the recipient's value is y. Hence

$$\hat{C}_\infty \geq \lceil \log \hat{\mu} \rceil. \tag{16}$$

Had the informant known Y in advance, this bound would hold with equality. However, the informant does not know Y, hence $\lceil \log \hat{\mu} \rceil$ bits cannot be always achieved. In the league problem, for example, the maximum ambiguity, $\hat{\mu}$, is two, and if the informant knew Y (the game) he would need to transmit only one bit (say, whether the winning team is lexicographically first). Yet, the informant does not know the game and we saw that many more than $\lceil \log \hat{\mu} \rceil = 1$ bit must be transmitted: $\hat{C}_\infty = \lceil \log \log t \rceil + 1$ bits.

However, for all balanced pairs, there is almost no increase in communication when the informant does not know Y

$$\hat{C}_3 \leq \log \hat{\mu} + 3 \log \log \hat{\mu} + 11. \tag{17}$$

Inequality (15) follows as $\hat{C}_\infty \geq \log \hat{\mu}$. In particular, resolving Open Problem 3 for balanced sources showing that for all balanced sources three messages are asymptotically optimum.

To illustrate (17), consider two-million-bit files that are within edit distance of a thousand from each other. Namely, there are a thousand bit insertions and deletions that will convert one file to the other. If the informant knows the recipient's file, he needs to transmit roughly $1000 \cdot \log(1\,000\,000) \approx 20\,000$ bits. If the informant does not know the recipient's file, he needs to transmit at most $3 \cdot \log 20\,000 + 11 \leq 54$ additional bits.

D. Multiple Instances

Section XI-B considered the number of bits required for one-way transmission of multiple independent instances. We now briefly discuss multiple instances with interactive communication.

Feder, Kushilevitz, and Naor [100] compared the number of bits required in the worst case for multiple instances with that needed for a single instance. They showed that for some source-coding problems, including the league of Example 4, the per-instance number of bits is significantly lower for multiple instances than it is for one.

Recall from (13) and (14) that the recipient's maximum ambiguity $\hat{\mu}$ is the maximum number of X values possible with any given Y value. Clearly, at least $\log \hat{\mu}$ bits per instance are needed in the worst case (even if the recipient knew all the Y's in advance). Naor, Orlitsky, and Shor [98] showed that for multiple instances, this number of bits per instance is always achievable with four messages. Ahlswede, Cai, and Zheng [95] reduced the number of messages to three.

XIII. COMMUNICATION COMPLEXITY: DEFINITION AND RESULTS

Communication complexity was introduced by Abelson [101] for continuous domains, and by Yao [102] for discrete domains, considered here. It is studied intensively in the computer-science literature both for its intrinsic interest and for its applications to Turing machines, circuit complexity, distributed computing, VLSI, and other subjects.

Recall that X and Y are random variables distributed over discrete sets $\mathcal{X}$ and $\mathcal{Y}$, respectively. Communication complexity assumes that X and Y are uncorrelated, hence the support set S is $\mathcal{X} \times \mathcal{Y}$. But instead of trying to determine X, the recipient attempts to compute a known function f of X and Y. Customarily, $\mathcal{X} = \mathcal{Y} = \{0, 1\}^n$, the informant is called Alice, and the recipient is named Bob. As assumed earlier, they use an agreed-upon protocol.

In this section, we introduce the problem via an example, then describe some of the complexity measures involved, and outline a few of the many results obtained. For more results or additional details see an excellent recent book by Kushilevitz and Nisan [103] or surveys by Orlitsky and El Gamal [104], and by Lovász [105]. More specialized surveys are mentioned below.

A. Introductory Example

The following example illustrates some of the complexity measures used to characterize functions, the types of protocols used to achieve them, and the techniques used to analyze them.

Example 5: $\mathcal{X} = \mathcal{Y} = \{0, 1\}^n$ and $\mathrm{eq} : \mathcal{X} \times \mathcal{Y} \to \{0, 1\}$ is the *equality function*

$$\mathrm{eq}(x, y) \stackrel{\text{def}}{=} \begin{cases} 1, & \text{if } x = y \\ 0, & \text{if } x \neq y. \end{cases}$$

Namely, Alice has an n-bit sequence $X = (X_1, \cdots, X_n)$, Bob has an n-bit sequence $Y = (Y_1, \cdots, Y_n)$, and they are trying to determine whether $X = Y$.

Consider the following protocols.

Protocol ϕ_1:
1) Alice transmits $X_1, \cdots, X_n$.
2) Bob, who now knows both X and Y, transmits 1 if $X = Y$ and 0, otherwise.
3) They decide that $\mathrm{eq}(X, Y)$ is the bit transmitted by Bob.

Protocol ϕ_2:
1) Starting with $i = 1$, and continuing with consecutive i's, Alice and Bob exchange X_i and Y_i until $X_i \neq Y_i$ or $i = n$.
2) The computed value is 1 if the last two transmitted bits were identical and 0 otherwise.

Both protocols are *error-free*: their computed value agrees with eq for all *inputs*—elements of $\mathcal{X} \times \mathcal{Y}$. However, they differ in the number of bits transmitted. The first protocol, ϕ_1, requires a sequence of $n + 1$ transmitted bits for every input. Therefore, it requires transmission of $n + 1$ bits both in the worst case and on the average (over all 2^{2n} possible inputs, assumed equally likely). On the other hand, ϕ_2 requires $2n$ bits in the worst case (whenever $X = Y$), but only at most 4 bits on the average (for half the inputs, communication stops after exchanging the first pair of bits, for quarter, after the second, and so on).

It is therefore natural to ask whether there is an error-free protocol for the equality function that requires less than $n + 1$ bits in the worst case. The following argument, called a "crossing-sequence" argument by Lipton and Sedgewick [106], and a "fooling-set" argument by Ullman [107], provides a negative answer.

It is easy to see that if a and b are distinct sequences in $\{0, 1\}^n$, and a protocol dictates the same sequence of transmitted bits for the inputs (a, a) and (b, b), then this sequence is also transmitted for the input (a, b). But Bob's decision is based on Y and the transmitted sequence; the decision must therefore be the same for (a, b) and for (b, b). Hence the computed value will differ from $\mathrm{eq}(X, Y)$ for at least one of these inputs.

Consequently, any error-free protocol for the equality function must associate a different sequence of transmitted bits with each input in $A \stackrel{\text{def}}{=} \{(a, a) : a \in \{0, 1\}^n\}$. A more detailed treatment of the problem shows that the set of possible sequences must be prefix-free. Hence any error-free protocol must transmit at least $\lceil \log |A| \rceil = n$ bits for some input in A.

Suppose, now, that we let Alice and Bob incur some errors in deciding on the value of $\mathrm{eq}(X, Y)$. There are several ways to define the error measure. Perhaps the most natural is as the proportion of inputs for which they make the wrong decision. However, $\mathrm{eq}(X, Y) = 1$ for only 2^n of the 2^{2n} inputs. Hence, the communicators can always decide that $\mathrm{eq}(X, Y) = 0$ thereby incurring an error of $1/2^n$; as n increases, the error tends to 0.

This trivial solution leads to a different definition of the error measure which is best understood in the context of *randomized protocols*. For each input, Protocols ϕ_1 and ϕ_2 always result in the same sequence of transmitted bits and the same computed value. Such *deterministic protocols* are either always correct for a given input or always in error. *Randomized protocols*, on the other hand, allow the communicators to base their transmissions and computed value on the outcomes of random experiments. Therefore, the computed value assigned to each input is a 0–1 random variable. We define the *error a protocol incurs in computing f* to be the maximum, over all inputs, of the probability that the computed value assigned by the protocol differs from the correct value of f for that input.

Clearly, any *deterministic* protocol that computes a function with at most ϵ error ($\epsilon < 1$) under this definition must be error-free for that function. For the equality function this implies transmission of at least n bits in the worst case. The next randomized protocol, due to Rabin and Yao [108], is based on the "prime numbers algorithm" of Freivalds [109]. It incurs at most ϵ error while always transmitting only $O(\log n + \log(1/\epsilon))$ bits.

Identify $x \in \{0, 1\}^n$ with the corresponding integer $\in \{0, \cdots, 2^n - 1\}$, define

$$\sigma \stackrel{\text{def}}{=} \sqrt{2} \ln 2 \cdot \frac{n}{\epsilon}$$

and let $(x)_\alpha$ denote $x \bmod \alpha$. The protocol proceeds as follows:

1) Alice picks at random a prime α such that $\sigma \leq \alpha \leq 2\sigma$. She transmits α and $(Y)_\alpha$.

2) Bob transmits 1 if $(X)_\alpha = (Y)_\alpha$ and 0 otherwise.
3) They take the bit transmitted by Bob to be the computed value.

For all inputs (x, y) such that $x = y$, the computed value is always $1 = \text{eq}(x, y)$. For any input $x \neq y$ the computed value is wrong exactly when α divides $x - y$. The number of primes between σ and 2σ is $\geq (\sigma/\sqrt{2} \ln \sigma)$, and at most $\log_\sigma 2^n$ of them divide $x - y$. Therefore, for all inputs, the probability of a wrong decision is

$$\leq (\log_\sigma 2^n)/(\sigma/\sqrt{2} \ln \sigma) = \epsilon.$$

The number of bits transmitted for any input and any selected prime is at most

$$2(\log \ln 2^n + \log (1/\epsilon) + 1.11) = O(\log n + \log (1/\epsilon)).$$

For large values of n, this is much smaller than $n + 1$. □

B. Complexity Measures

We will outline results concerning the four most popular complexity measures. Two for deterministic protocols, and two for randomized ones.

For deterministic protocols, we consider $\hat{C}_d(f)$ and $\overline{C}_d(f)$, the number of bits required in the worst case, and on the average, respectively. Let ϕ be a deterministic protocol. For every input $(x, y) \in \{0, 1\}^n \times \{0, 1\}^n$, ϕ determines a number $L_\phi(x, y)$ of exchanged bits. The *worst case complexity* of ϕ is

$$\hat{L}_\phi \overset{\text{def}}{=} \max_{x, y \in \{0, 1\}^n} L_\phi(x, y)$$

and its *average-case complexity* is

$$\overline{L}_\phi \overset{\text{def}}{=} \frac{1}{2^{2n}} \sum_{x, y \in \{0, 1\}^n} L_\phi(x, y).$$

ϕ is *a protocol for f* if it computes the correct value of f for every input. The *worst case complexity* of f is

$$\hat{C}_d(f) \overset{\text{def}}{=} \min\{\hat{L}_\phi: \phi \text{ is a protocol for } f\}$$

and the *average-case complexity* of f is

$$\overline{C}_d(f) \overset{\text{def}}{=} \min\{\overline{L}_\phi: \phi \text{ is a protocol for } f\}.$$

$\hat{C}_d(f)$ and $\overline{C}_d(f)$ are the least number of bits required in the worst case, and on the average, by any deterministic protocol for f.

For randomized protocols, the ϵ- and zero-error complexities $\hat{C}_r(f, \epsilon)$ and $\hat{C}_r(f, 0)$ are the expected number of bits required for the worst input by an ϵ-error and error-free protocols. Specifically, if Φ is a randomized protocol, then for every input, Alice and Bob transmit a random number of bits and agree on a random value for f.

Let $\overline{L}_\Phi(x, y)$ be the expected number of transmitted bits when the input is (x, y). The *worst case complexity* of Φ is

$$\hat{L}_\Phi \overset{\text{def}}{=} \max_{x, y \in \{0, 1\}^n} \overline{L}_\Phi(x, y)$$

the expected number of bits transmitted for the worst input.

Let $\overline{E}_\Phi(x, y)$ be the probability of error when the input is (x, y). Φ is ϵ-*error* if $\overline{E}_\Phi(x, y) < \epsilon$ for all $x, y \in \{0, 1\}^n$. It is *error-free* if $\overline{E}_\Phi(x, y) = 0$ for all $x, y \in \{0, 1\}^n$.

The ϵ-*error worst case complexity* of f is

$$\hat{C}_r(f, \epsilon) \overset{\text{def}}{=} \min\{\hat{L}_\Phi: \Phi \text{ is an } \epsilon\text{-error protocol for } f\}$$

and the *zero-error worst case complexity* of f is

$$\hat{C}_r(f, 0) \overset{\text{def}}{=} \min\{\hat{L}_\Phi: \Phi \text{ is a zero-error protocol for } f\}.$$

C. Complexity of Most Functions

A well-known information-theoretic paradigm says that "most sequences are virtually incompressible." Does the same hold for communication complexity?

Let $\mathcal{F}$ be the set of functions from $\{0, 1\}^n \times \{0, 1\}^n$ to $\{0, 1\}$. When Alice and Bob compute a function in $\mathcal{F}$, each has an n-bit string and they communicate in order to evaluate a Boolean function of the combined $2n$ bits. There are $2^{2^{2n}}$ functions in $\mathcal{F}$. What is the communication complexity of most of them? Clearly, $n + 1$ bits suffice for all those functions: Alice transmits X, and Bob replies with $f(X, Y)$. But are $n + 1$ bits necessary, or will fewer bits suffice? The equality function shows that the answer may depend on the complexity measure used.

Yao [102] showed that for most functions $f \in \mathcal{F}$

$$\hat{C}_d(f) = n - o(n).$$

Orlitsky and El Gamal [104], [110] showed that most functions $f \in \mathcal{F}$ have

$$\overline{C}_d(f) = n - o(n)$$
$$\hat{C}_r(f, 0) = n - o(n)$$

and for any $0 < \epsilon < 1/2$

$$\hat{C}_r(f, \epsilon) = (1 - 2\epsilon)(n - o(n)).$$

The last result was also independently proven by Chor and Goldreich [111].

While most sequences are incompressible, a finer analysis shows that all sequences are compressible to their empirical entropy. Similarly, one can further classify functions according to the number of 0's and 1's in their function table.

Given a function $f \in \mathcal{F}$, let

$$F_0 \overset{\text{def}}{=} \{(x, y): f(x, y) = 0\}$$

and

$$F_1 \overset{\text{def}}{=} \{(x, y): f(x, y) = 1\}$$

be the subsets of inputs for which f is 0 and 1, respectively. The *density* of f is

$$\rho(f) \overset{\text{def}}{=} \min(|F_0|, |F_1|)$$

the lesser of the number of 0's and 1's in the function table. Clearly, $0 \leq \rho(f) \leq 2^{2n-1}$. For $0 \leq \rho \leq 2^{2n-1}$, let

$$\mathcal{F}_\rho \overset{\text{def}}{=} \{f \in \mathcal{F}: \rho(f) = \rho\}$$

be the set of functions in $\mathcal{F}$ with ρ 1's or ρ 0's. If $\rho(f) < 2^n$ then some "rows" and "columns" in the function table of

f are all 0 or all 1, and f can be viewed as a function with smaller domain. It, therefore, suffices to consider only $2^n \le \rho \le 2^{2n-1}$. Orlitksy and El Gamal [110] showed that for every integer $\rho \in \{2^n, \cdots, 2^{2n-1}\}$ most functions in $\mathcal{F}_\rho$ have

1) $\hat{C}_d(f), \hat{C}_r(f, 0) = n + O(1)$.
2) $\overline{C}_d(f) = \log s - n + O(\log n)$.
3) $\hat{C}_r(f, \epsilon) = (1 - 2\epsilon) \cdot (\log \rho - n + O(\log n))$ for all $0 < \epsilon < 1/2$.

Namely, the complexity measures fall into two classes: two remain hard even for sparse functions, and two are progressively easier as the density decreases.

All upper bounds hold for all functions in $\mathcal{F}_\rho$ while the lower bounds hold for most functions in $c F_\rho$. For more details, see Orlitsky and El Gamal [104].

D. Complexity of Specific Functions

The worst case deterministic complexity of the equality function, described in Example 5, is exactly $n + 1$. But typically, it is extremely difficult to determine the precise communication complexity of a given function. One is therefore often interested only in approximating the communication complexity up to a constant factor. For example, Yao [102] showed that the randomized complexity of equality is in the order of $\log n$

$$\hat{C}_r(f, \epsilon) = \Theta(\log n).$$

Namely, for every fixed $\epsilon < 0.5$, there are some constants, α_1, α_2, α_3, such that for every n

$$\alpha_1 \log n + \alpha_3 \le \hat{C}_r(f, \epsilon) \le \alpha_2 \log n + \alpha_3.$$

Since much of the interest in communication complexity stems from its applications to lower bounds in other areas, considerable effort went into proving lower bounds on communication complexity. Naturally, lower bounds on randomized complexity are more difficult, and mathematically more interesting. We mention two of them.

The first Boolean function shown to have linear randomized communication complexity was the *inner-product* function, ip : $\{0, 1\}^n \times \{0, 1\}^n \to \{0, 1\}$, defined by

$$\mathrm{ip}(x, y) = \left(\sum_{i=1}^n x_i \cdot y_i \right) \bmod 2.$$

Pang and El Gamal [112] showed that for fixed ϵ, the inner product has

$$\hat{C}_r(f, \epsilon) = \Omega(n).$$

A simpler proof was found by Chor and Goldreich [111].

Another function shown to have linear randomized communication complexity is *disjointness*, dj : $\{0, 1\}^n \times \{0, 1\}^n \to \{0, 1\}$, defined by

$$\mathrm{dj}(x, y) \overset{\text{def}}{=} \begin{cases} 0, & \text{if } x_i = y_i = 1 \text{ for some } i \in \{1, \cdots, n\} \\ 1, & \text{otherwise.} \end{cases}$$

Viewing x and y as the characteristic vectors of sets in $\{1, \cdots, n\}$, each of Alice and Bob has a set and dj is 1

iff the two sets are disjoint. Babai, Frankl, and Simon [113] showed that disjointness has $\hat{C}_r(\mathrm{dj}, \epsilon) = \Omega(\sqrt{n})$. This result was improved by Kalyanasundaram and Schnitger [114] to $\hat{C}_r(\mathrm{dj}, \epsilon) = \Omega(n)$. Razborov [115] strengthened the bound and simplified the proof.

Most lower bound proofs on randomized communication complexity consider Cartesian products in $\{0, 1\}^n \times \{0, 1\}^n$, typically called *rectangles*. The proofs show that most inputs cannot be covered by large rectangles over which the function assumes mostly one value.

E. Messages

For interactive communication, two messages suffice to get within a factor of four of the optimal number of bits and four messages always achieve at most three times that minimum. How does *communication complexity* depend on the number of messages allowed?

For concreteness, assume that only Bob needs to determine f. Let $\hat{C}_d^m(f)$ denote the total number of bits required in the worst case when at most m messages are allowed. For example, $\hat{C}_d^1(f)$ is the number of bits Alice must transmit in the worst case when Bob must determine f but cannot transmit back, and $\hat{C}_d^2(f)$ is the total number of bits required in the worst case when Bob transmits a message (based on Y), Alice replies with a message (based on X and Bob's message), and then Bob computes $f(X, Y)$.

Papadimitriou and Sipser [116], Duris, Galil, and Schnitger [117], Nisan and Wigderson [118], and Miltersen, Nisan, Safra, and Wigderson [119] successively improved and refined results on the discrepancies between $\hat{C}_d^{m-1}(f)$ and $\hat{C}_d^m(f)$. They showed that for every number m of messages there is a function f whose $(m - 1)$-message complexity is almost exponentially higher than its m-message complexity

$$\hat{C}_d^{m-1}(f) \ge \Omega\left(\frac{2^{(\hat{C}_d^m(f)/m)}}{(\hat{C}_d^m(f)/m)^{m-1}} \right).$$

One function achieving this discrepancy is defined via a complete k-ary tree of depth m. Each internal node (including the root) is labeled by a pointer to one of its k descendants, and each leaf is labeled by 0 or 1. The value of the function is determined by starting at the root and following the pointers to a leaf whose label is the function's value. If the depth m is even, Bob is given the labels of all even-depth nodes, and Alice is given the labels of all odd-depth nodes. If the depth is odd, Bob is given all odd-depth labels, and Alice is given all the even-depth ones. Note that in both cases, Bob has the labels of the leaves.

If m messages are allowed, Alice and Bob simply alternate in transmitting the pointers till they reach a leaf. The total number of bits transmitted is $m \log k$. If at most $m - 1$ messages are allowed, it can be shown that they need to exchange at least $\Omega(k / \log^{m-1} k)$ bits.

F. Multiple Instances

How does the number of bits required to solve several independent instances of a function compare with the number required for one instance?

Recall that $\mathcal{F}$ is the set of functions from $\{0, 1\}^n \times \{0, 1\}^n$ to $\{0, 1\}$. In k independent instances of $f \in \mathcal{F}$, Alice is given k arbitrary values $x^1, \cdots, x^k \in \{0, 1\}^n$ and Bob is given k arbitrary values $y^1, \cdots, y^k \in \{0, 1\}^n$. They try to evaluate

$$f^{(k)}((x^1, \cdots, x^k), (y^1, \cdots, y^k))$$
$$= f(x^1, y^1), \cdots, f(x^k, y^k).$$

Of interest is the difference between $\hat{C}_d(f^{(k)})$, the number of bits required in the worst case for simultaneous communication of all instances, and $k \cdot \hat{C}_d(f)$, the number of bits required in the worst case when the k functions are communicated independently.

Feder, Kushilevitz, and Naor [100] showed that for some functions (see Section XII-D) simultaneous communication reduces transmission. They then showed that for every function $f \in \mathcal{F}$

$$\hat{C}_d(f^{(k)}) = \Omega\left(k\sqrt{\hat{C}_d(f)} - \log n - O(1)\right).$$

Hence up to an additive $\log n$, simultaneous communication always requires at least the square root of the original number of bits.

For related results on the subject, see Ahlswede and Cai [120].

G. Additional Results

We briefly mention some of the many other communication-complexity results.

Newman [121] showed that randomized protocols require roughly the same number of bits when the communicators know each other's random source as when they do not. This frequently simplifies the construction of randomized algorithms.

Ja'Ja [122], Ahlswede and Dueck [123], [124], Verdú and Wei [125], and Han and Verdú [126] considered the minimum number of bits required to communicate the equality function over a noisy channel.

Schulman [127], [128] showed that interactive communication protocols can be simulated over certain noisy channels with only a constant factor increase in communication.

Babai, Frankl, and Simon [113] classified functions according to their communication complexity in several communication models.

Chandra, Furst, and Lipton [129], Dolev and Feder [130], Babai, Nisan, and Szegedy [131], Chung and Tetali [132], Grolmusz [133], Babai, Kimmel, and Lokam [134], Pudlák and Rödl [135], and others, considered various communication models where more than two parties interact in order to compute a function of their joint data.

XIV. COMMUNICATION COMPLEXITY: APPLICATIONS

In addition to the obvious applications to communication problems, computer-science interest in communication complexity stems from several applications. We mention two in detail, and outline several others.

A. Area–Time Bounds on VLSI

Every integrated circuit computes a function of its inputs. Therefore, information must flow between the various inputs and between the inputs and the outputs.

Consider a chip that computes a function f. Let A be the chip's area and let T be the time it takes the chip to compute f. Thompson [136] used communication complexity to derive lower bounds on the product $A \cdot T^2$. Historically, this was one of the first motivations for communication complexity.

Let $x_1, \cdots, x_n$ be the inputs of f. For a partition S_1, S_2 of $\{1, \cdots, n\}$ let $C_{S_1, S_2}(f)$ be the minimum number of bits that two communicators must exchange if one holds the inputs in S_1 and the other holds the inputs in S_2. Let

$$C(f) \stackrel{\text{def}}{=} \min\{C_{S_1, S_2}(f) : |S_1| = \lfloor n/2 \rfloor \text{ and } |S_2| = \lceil n/2 \rceil\}$$

be the minimum of C_{S_1, S_2} over all partitions of inputs into (essentially) equal-size sets. We show that

$$A \cdot T^2 \geq \Omega(C^2(f)).$$

The constant implied by Ω depends on the maximum number of bits that can be communicated along a chip wire in one time unit and the maximum number of wires that can cross side by side in one unit length.

We outline the proof for rectangular chips where each pin is fed one input. The proof generalizes easily to nonrectangular chips where certain pins are fed (necessarily sequentially) more than one input.

Without loss of generality, assume that the chip's height h is smaller than its width w. It is easy to see that there is an (almost vertical) straight line of length essentially h that partitions the chip into two parts, the left-containing $\lfloor n/2 \rfloor$ inputs and the right-containing $\lceil n/2 \rceil$ inputs. Let S_1 and S_2 be the sets of inputs to the left and right of the line, respectively.

The amount of information that has to cross this line is therefore at least C_{S_1, S_2}. But the maximum number of bits that can cross the line in any time unit is proportional to its length h, so $h \cdot T \geq C_{S_1, S_2}(f)$, hence

$$AT^2 = w \cdot h \cdot T^2 \geq (h \cdot T)^2 \geq C_{S_1, S_2}^2(f) \geq C^2(f).$$

Using this result one can derive lower bounds on $A \cdot T^2$ for circuits implementing various functions. All that needs to be done is determine $C(f)$. For multiplication of two n by n matrices over GF (2), for example, one obtains $AT^2 = \Omega(n^4)$. This bound is tight.

For other theoretical aspects of VLSI and their relationship to communication complexity, see Ullman [107], or Lengauer [137]. Note also that the same technique can be applied to distributed systems computing a function.

B. Boolean-Circuit Depth

Every Boolean function can be implemented by a Boolean circuit built of two-input AND and OR gates and single-input NOT gates. Fig. 1(a) depicts a circuit implementing the "Exclusive-Or" function

$$x_1 \oplus x_2 \stackrel{\text{def}}{=} \begin{cases} 0, & \text{if } x_1 = x_2 \\ 1, & \text{if } x_1 \neq x_2. \end{cases}$$

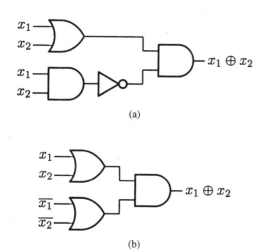

(a)

(b)

Fig. 1. Two Exclusive-Or circuits. (a) Original circuit. (b) Negations moved to inputs.

Using De Morgan's laws, we can move all the negations to the inputs and implement the circuit using only two-input AND and OR gates. Fig. 1(b) illustrates such an implementation.

The depth of a circuit is the largest number gates separating the output from any input. The circuit in Fig. 1(b) has depth two since (in this case all) the inputs are separated from the output by two gates. The depth $d(f)$ of a function is the minimum depth of a circuit implementing f. The Exclusive-Or function cannot be implemented by a single gate, hence has depth two.

A function's depth determines its computational delay and is related to the time needed to compute it on a parallel machine. It is easy to see that every n-variable function has $d(f) \leq n + o(n)$. A counting argument, as in Shannon [138], shows that most n-variable Boolean functions have depth $d(f) \geq n - o(n)$. However, no specific function is known to require linear, namely $\Omega(n)$, depth. Showing that a polynomially computable function requires linear depth would separate the computational-complexity class P of functions computable in polynomial time from the class NC of functions computable in poly-logarithmic time by polynomially many processors.

Given a function $f: \{0, 1\}^n \rightarrow \{0, 1\}$, consider the following communication problem. Let $F_0 \stackrel{\text{def}}{=} f^{-1}(0)$ and $F_1 \stackrel{\text{def}}{=} f^{-1}(1)$ be the sets of inputs for which f is 0 and 1, respectively. Alice is given an input $x = (x_1, \cdots, x_n) \in F_0$ and Bob is given an input $y = (y_1, \cdots, y_n) \in F_1$. Since F_0 and F_1 are disjoint, $x \neq y$, hence the set $T(x, y) \stackrel{\text{def}}{=} \{i: x_i \neq y_i\}$ is nonempty. Alice and Bob communicate in order to agree on one element of $T(x, y)$, namely, an integer $i \in \{1, \cdots, n\}$ such that $x_i \neq y_i$. Note that they need to find only one of the possibly many elements of $T(x, y)$ and that both must agree on the same element.

An elegant result of Karchmer and Wigderson [139] shows that the depth of f is precisely the communication complexity of the above communication problem. The proof is by a simple induction argument. For example, if f is the Exclusive-Or function then Alice has an input (x_1, x_2) such that $x_1 = x_2$ while Bob has (y_1, y_2) such that $y_1 \neq y_2$. They are looking

for an i such that $x_i \neq y_i$. In this case, $T(x, y)$ contains exactly one element. The Exclusive-Or function has depth two. Correspondingly, the shortest protocol requires 2 bits: Alice transmits x_1 ($= x_2$) and Bob lets her know whether of $x_1 \neq y_1$ or $x_2 \neq y_2$.

Unfortunately, so far no function was shown to require linear communication or (equivalently) circuit depth. Yet Karchmer and Wigderson [139] used the analogy to show that any *monotone* circuit that determines whether two points are connected requires linear depth. Gringi and Sipser [140] improved the result and simplified the proof. We note, however, that some sublinear-depth functions require linear monotone depth.

For other results on the subject, see Raz and Wigderson [141] and Razborov [142].

C. Additional Applications

In addition to the above applications, communication complexity was used in many other areas, including:

1) Decision trees; see Groger and Turan [143] and Nisan [144].
2) Turing machines; see Babai, Nisan, and Szegedy [131].
3) Threshold circuits; see Nisan [144], Roychowdhury, Orlitsky, and Siu [145], and a survey by Goldmann [146].
4) Generation of essentially random bits from slightly random sources; see Santha and Vazirani [147] and Chor and Goldreich [111].

ACKNOWLEDGMENT

The authors thank Eyal Kushilevitz, Gabor Simonyi, and Jack K. Wolf for helpful comments on an earlier version of this manuscript.

REFERENCES

[1] C. E. Shannon, R. G. Gallager, and E. R. Berlekamp, "Lower bounds to error probability for coding on discrete memoryless channels, i–ii," *Inform. Contr.*, vol. 10, pp. 65–103, 522–552, 1967.
[2] I. Csiszár and J. Körner, *Information Theory: Coding Theorems for Discrete Memoryless Systems.* New York: Academic, 1982; also published by Akadémiai Kiadó, Budapest, Hungary, 1981.
[3] C. E. Shannon, "The zero-error capacity of a noisy channel," *IRE Trans. Inform. Theory*, vol. IT-2, pp. 8–19, 1956.
[4] J. Körner and M. Lucertini, "Compressing inconsistent data," *IEEE Trans. Inform. Theory*, vol. 40, pp. 706–715, May 1994.
[5] D. A. Huffman, "A method for the construction of minimum redundancy codes," *Proc. IRE*, vol. 40, pp. 1098–1101, 1952.
[6] J. H. van Lint and R. M. Wilson, *A Course in Combinatorics.* Cambridge, U.K.: Cambridge Univ. Press, 1992.
[7] L. Lovász, "On the ratio of optimal integral and fractional covers," *Discr. Math.*, vol. 13, pp. 383–390, 1975.
[8] E. R. Scheinerman and D. H. Ullman, *Fractional Graph Theory: A Rational Approach to the Theory of Graphs.* New York: Wiley, 1997.
[9] L. Lovász, "On the Shannon capacity of a graph," *IEEE Tran. Inform. Theory*, vol. IT-25, pp. 1–7, Jan. 1979.
[10] M. Grötschel and L. Lovász, *Geometric Algorithms and Combinatorial Optimization.* Berlin, Germany: Springer, 1988.
[11] D. E. Knuth, "The art of computer programming," in preparation.
[12] W. Haemers, "On some problems of Lovász concerning the Shannon capacity of a graph," *IEEE Trans. Inform. Theory*, vol. IT-25, pp. 231–232, Mar. 1979.

[13] U. Feige, "Randomized graph products, chromatic numbers and the Lovász theta function," in *Proc. 27th ACM Symp. Theory of Computing*, 1995.

[14] N. Alon and N. Kahale, "Approximating the independence number via the θ function," *Math. Programming*, to appear.

[15] P. Delsarte, "An algebraic approach to the association schemes of coding theory," *Philips Res. Rep. Suppl.*, vol. 10, 1973.

[16] C. E. Shannon, "A texinputematical theory of communication I–II," *Bell Syst. Tech. J.*, vol. 27, pp. 379–423, 623–656, 1948.

[17] N. Alon, "The Shannon capacity of a union," unpublished manuscript.

[18] G. Hajós, "Über eine art von graphen," *Int. Math. Nachr.*, vol. 11, no. 65, 1957.

[19] C. Berge, "Sur une conjecture relative au problème des codes optimaux," in *Comm. 13ème Assemblée Générale de l'URSI, Tokyo*, 1962.

[20] C. Berge, *Graphs and Hypergraphs*. Amsterdam, The Netherlands: North Holland, 1973.

[21] R. J. McEliece, E. R. Rodemich, and H. C. Rumsey, Jr., "The Lovász bound and some generalizations," *J. Combinatorics, Inform. Syst. Sci.*, vol. 3, pp. 134–152, 1978.

[22] N. Alon and A. Orlitsky, "Repeated communication and Ramsey graphs," *IEEE Trans. Inform. Theory*, vol. 41, pp. 1276–1289, Sept. 1995.

[23] P. Erdös, R. J. McEliece, and H. Taylor, "Ramsey bounds for graph products," *Pacific J. Math.*, vol. 37, no. 1, pp. 45–46, 1971.

[24] E. Arikan, private communication, 1994.

[25] A. Yao, "Should tables be sorted?," *J. Assoc. Comput. Mach.*, vol. 28, pp. 615–628, 1981.

[26] P. Elias, "List decoding for noisy channels," in *IRE WESCON Conv. Rec.*, 1957, vol. 2.

[27] ———, "Zero error capacity under list decoding," *IEEE Trans. Inform. Theory*, vol. 34, pp. 1070–1074, Sept. 1988.

[28] M. L. Fredman and J. Komlós, "On the size of separating systems and families of perfect hash functions," *SIAM J. Alg. Discr. Methods*, vol. 5, no. 1, pp. 61–68, 1984.

[29] J. Körner and K. Marton, "New bounds for perfect hashing via information theory," *Euro. J. Comb.inatorics*, vol. 9, pp. 523–530, 1988.

[30] J. Körner, "Fredman–Komlós bounds and information theory," *SIAM J. Alg. Discr. Methods*, vol. 7, no. 4, pp. 560–570, 1986.

[31] A. Nilli, "Perfect hashing and probability," *Combinatorics, Probab. Comput.*, vol. 3, pp. 407–409, 1994.

[32] E. Arikan, "An upper bound on the zero-error list-coding capacity," *IEEE Trans. Inform. Theory*, vol. 40, pp. 1237–1240, 1994.

[33] A. G. Dyachov, "An upper bound for hash codes," in *Proc. IEEE Int. Symp. Information Theory*, 1997.

[34] A. G. Dyachkov and V. V. Rykov, "Bounds on the length of disjunctive codes," *Probl. Pered. Inform.*, vol. 18, no. 3, pp. 7–13, 1982.

[35] J. Körner and K. Marton, "On the capacity of uniform hypergraphs," *IEEE Trans. Inform. Theory*, vol. 36, pp. 153–156, 1990.

[36] B. Hajek, "A conjectured generalized permanent inequality and a multi-access problem," in *Open Problems in Communication and Computation*, T. Cover and B. Gopinath, Eds. New York: Springer, 1987.

[37] J. Körner and K. Marton, "Random access communication and graph entropy," *IEEE Trans. Inform. Theory*, vol. 34, pp. 312–314, 1988.

[38] D. Blackwell, L. Breiman, and A. J. Thomasian, "The capacity of a class of channels," *Ann. Math. Statist.*, vol. 30, pp. 1229–1241, 1959.

[39] R. L. Dobrushin, "Optimal information transfer over a channel with unknown parameters," *Radiotech. i Elektron.*, vol. 4, pp. 1951–1956, 1959.

[40] J. Wolfowitz, "Simultaneous channels," *Arch. Rat. Mech. Anal.*, vol. 4, pp. 371–386, 1960.

[41] G. Cohen, G. Simonyi, and J. Körner, "Zero-error capacities and very different sequences," in *Sequences: Combinatorics, Compression, Security and Transmission*, R. M. Capocelli, Ed. New York: Springer-Verlag, 1988, pp. 144–155.

[42] I. Csiszár and J. Körner, "On the capacity of the arbitrarily varying channel for maximum probability of error," *Z. Wahrscheinlichkeitstheorie verw. Geb.*, vol. 57, pp. 87–101, 1981.

[43] L. Gargano, J. Körner, and U. Vaccaro, "Capacities: From information theory to extremal set theory," *J. Comb. Theory*, vol. 68, no. 2, pp. 296–316, 1994.

[44] K. Marton, "On the Shannon capacity of probabilistic graphs," *J. Comb. Theory*, vol. 54, pp. 183–195, 1993.

[45] A. D. Wyner, "The wire-tap channel," *Bell Syst. Tech. J.*, Tech. Rep., Oct. 1975.

[46] I. Csiszár and J. Körner, "Broadcast channels with confidential messages," *IEEE Trans. Inform. Theory*, vol. IT-24, pp. 339–348, May 1978.

[47] R. Ahlswede, "Multi-way communication channels," in *Proc. 2nd Int. Symp. Information Theory* (Tsahkadsor, Armenia SSR). Budapest, Hungatu: Akadèmiai Kiadò, 1971.

[48] G. Simonyi, "On write uni-directional memory codes," *IEEE Trans. Inform. Theory*, vol. 35, pp. 663–669, 1989.

[49] R. Ahlswede and G. Simonyi, "On the optimal structure of recovering set pairs and the sandglass conjecture," *Discr. Math.*, vol. 128, pp. 389–394, 1994.

[50] R. Holzman and J. Körner, "Cancellative pairs of families of sets," *Euro. J. Combinatorics*, vol. 16, pp. 263–266, 1995.

[51] A. Sali and G. Simonyi, "Recovering set systems and graph entropy," *Combinatorics, Probab. Comput.*, vol. 6, pp. 481–491, 1997.

[52] G. O. H. Katona, "Extremal problems for hypergraphs," *Math. Center Tracts*, vol. 56, pp. 13–42, 1974.

[53] P. Frankl and Z. Füredi, "Union-free hypergraphs and probability," *Euro. J. Combinatorics*, vol. 5, pp. 127–131, 1984.

[54] J. B. Shearer, "On cancellative families of sets," *Electron. J. Combinatorics*, vol. 1, no. 4, 1996.

[55] E. Sperner, "Ein Satz über Untermegen einer endlichen Menge," *Math. Zeitschr.*, vol. 27, pp. 544–548, 1928.

[56] K. Engel, *Sperner Theory*. New York: Wiley, 1997.

[57] M. Aigner, *Combinatorial Search*. New York: Wiley, 1988.

[58] G. O. H. Katona, "Two applications (for search theory and truth functions) of Sperner type theorems," *Per. Math. Hung.*, vol. 3, nos. 1/2, pp. 19–26, 1973.

[59] J. Körner and G. Simonyi, "A Sperner-type theorem and qualitative independence," *J. Comb. Theory*, vol. 59, pp. 90–103, 1992.

[60] L. Gargano, J. Körner, and U. Vaccaro, "Qualitative independence and Sperner problems on directed graphs," *J. Comb. Theory*, vol. 61, pp. 173–192, 1992.

[61] A. Rényi, *Foundations of Probability*. New York: Wiley, 1971.

[62] S. Poljak, A. Pultr, and V. Rödl, "On the dimension of Kneser graphs," in *Algebraic Methods in Graph Theory, Coll. Soc. Math. J.*, pp. 631–646, 1978.

[63] ———, "On qualitatively independent partitions and related problems," *Discr. Appl. Math.*, vol. 6, pp. 193–205, 1983.

[64] S. Poljak and V. Rödl, "Orthogonal partitions and covering of graphs," *Czech Math. J.*, vol. 30, pp. 475–485, 1980.

[65] S. Poljak and Zs. Tuza, "On the maximum number of qualitatively independent partitions," *J. Comb. Theory*, vol. 51, pp. 111–116, 1989.

[66] L. Gargano, J. Körner, and U. Vaccaro, "Sperner capacities," *Graphs Combinatorics*, vol. 9, pp. 31–46, 1993.

[67] R. Calderbank, P. Frankl, R. L. Graham, W. Li, and L. Shepp, "The Sperner capacity of the cyclic triangle for linear and nonlinear codes," *J. Alg. Combinatorics*, vol. 2, pp. 31–48, 1993.

[68] A. Blokuis, "On the Sperner capacity of the cyclic triangle," *J. Alg. Combinatorics*, vol. 2, pp. 123–124, 1993.

[69] N. Alon, "On the capacity of digraphs," *Euro. J. Combinatorics*, to be published.

[70] A. Sali and G. Simonyi, "Orientations of self-complementary graphs and the relation of Sperner and Shannon capacities," unpublished manuscript.

[71] E. Fachini and J. Körner, "Chromatic number, capacity and perfectness of directed graphs," *Graphs Combinatorics*, to be published.

[72] J. Nešetřil and A. Pultr, "A Dushnik–Miller type dimension of graphs and its complexity," in *Fundamentals of Computation Theory, Proc. Conference Poznań–Kórnik (1977)* (Lecture Notes in Computer Ssience, vol. 56). Berlin, Germany: Springer, 1971, pp. 482–493.

[73] N. Alon and J. Spencer, *The Probabilistic Method*. New York: Wiley, 1992.

[74] J. Körner, "Coding of an information source having ambiguous alphabet and the entropy of graphs," in *Trans. 6th Prague Conf. Information Theory, etc., 1971*. Prague, Czechoslovakia: Academia, 1973.

[75] J. Körner and G. Longo, "Two-step encoding of finite sources," *IEEE Trans. Inform. Theory*, vol. IT-19, pp. 778–782, Nov. 1973.

[76] J. Körner and G. Simonyi, "Graph pairs and their entropies: Modularity problems," submitted for publication in *Combinatorica*.

[77] C. Berge and M. Simonovits, "Lecture notes in mathematics 411," in *Hypergraph Seminar*. Springer-Verlag, 1974, pp. 21–33.

[78] R. J. McEliece and E. C. Posner, "Hide and seek, data storage, and entropy," *Ann. Math. Statist.*, vol. 42, no. 5, pp. 1706–1716, 1971.

[79] N. Alon and A. Orlitsky, "Source coding and graphs entropies," *IEEE Trans. Inform. Theory*, vol. 42, pp. 1329–1339, Sept. 1996.

[80] R. B. Boppana, "Optimal separations between concurrent-write parallel machines," in *Proc. 21th Ann. ACM Symp. Theory of Computing*, 1989, pp. 320–326.

[81] I. Csiszár, J. Körner, L. Lovász, K. Marton, and G. Simonyi, "Entropy splitting for antiblocking pairs and perfect graphs," *Combinatorica*, vol. 10, pp. 27–40, 1990.

[82] J. Kahn and J. H. Kim, "Entropy and sorting," *J. Comp. Syst. Sci.*, vol. 51, pp. 390–399, 1995.

[83] J. Körner, G. Simonyi, and Zs. Tuza, "Perfect couples of graphs," *Combinatorica*, vol. 12, no. 2, pp. 179–172, 1992.

[84] J. Radhakrishnan, "$\sigma\pi\sigma$ threshold formulas," *Combinatorica*, vol. 14, pp. 345–374, 1994.

[85] G. Simonyi, "Graph entropy: A survey," in *Combinatorial Optimization*, W. Cook, L. Lovász, and P. Seymour, Eds. (DIMACS Series on Discrete Math and Computer Science), 1995, vol. 20, pp. 399–441.

[86] D. Slepian and J. Wolf, "Noiseless coding of correlated information sources," *IEEE Trans. Inform. Theory*, vol. IT-19, pp. 471–480, 1973.

[87] H. Witsenhausen, "The zero-error side information problem and chromatic numbers," *IEEE Trans. Inform. Theory*, vol. IT-22, pp. 592–593, Sept. 1976.

[88] M. J. Ferguson and D. W. Bailey, "Zero-error coding for correlated sources," 1975, unpublished manuscript.

[89] R. Ahlswede, "Coloring hypergraphs: A new approach to multi-user source coding-I," *J. Combinatorics, Inform. Syst. Sci.*, vol. 4, no. 1, pp. 76–115, 1979.

[90] L. Lovász, "Kneser's conjecture, chromatic number and homotopy," *J. Comb. Theory*, vol. 25, pp. 319–324, 1978.

[91] N. Linial and U. Vazirani, "Graph products and chromatic numbers," in *Proc. 30th Annu. Symp. Foundations of Computer Science*, 1989, pp. 124–128.

[92] C. Berge and M. Simonovits, "The coloring numbers of direct product of two hypergraphs," in *Hypergraph Seminar* (Lecture Notes on Mathematics, vol. 411), C. Berge and D. Ray-Chaudhuri, Eds. Berlin, Germany: Springer-Verlag, 1974.

[93] A. Orlitsky, "Worst-case interactive communication I: Two messages are almost optimal," *IEEE Trans. Inform. Theory*, vol. 36, pp. 1111–1126, Sept. 1990.

[94] A. El Gamal and A. Orlitsky, "Interactive data compression," in *Proc. 25th Annu. Symp. Foundations of Computer Science*, 1984, pp. 100–108.

[95] R. Ahlswede, N. Cai, and Z. Zhang, "On interactive communication," *IEEE Trans. Inform. Theory*, vol. 43, pp. 22–37, Jan. 1997.

[96] A. Orlitsky, "Average-case interactive communication," *IEEE Trans. Inform. Theory*, vol. 38, pp. 1534–1547, July 1992.

[97] Z. Zhang and X. G. Xia, "Three messages are not optimal in worst-case interactive communication," *IEEE Trans. Inform. Theory*, vol. 40, pp. 3–11, Jan. 1994.

[98] M. Naor, A. Orlitsky, and P. Shor, "Three results on interactive communication," *IEEE Trans. Inform. Theory*, vol. 39, pp. 1608–1615, Sept. 1993.

[99] A. Orlitsky, "Worst-case interactive communication II: Two messages are not optimal," *IEEE Trans. Inform. Theory*, vol. 37, pp. 995–1005, July 1991.

[100] T. Feder, E. Kushilevitz, and M. Naor, "Amortized communication complexity," in *Proc. 32nd Annu. Symp. Foundations of Computer Science*, 1991, pp. 239–248.

[101] H. Abelson, "Lower bounds on information transfer in distributed computations," in *Proc. 19th Annu. Symp. Foundations of Computer Science*, 1978.

[102] A. C. Yao, "Some complexity questions related to distributive computing," in *Proc. 11th Annu. ACM Symp. Theory of Computing*, 1979, pp. 209–213.

[103] E. Kushilevitz and N. Nisan, *Communication Complexity*. Cambridge, U.K.: Cambridge Univ. Press, 1997.

[104] A. Orlitsky and A. El Gamal, "Communication complexity," in *Complexity in Information Theory*, Y. Abu-Mostafa, Ed. Berlin, Germany: Springer-Verlag, 1986, pp. 16–61.

[105] L. Lovász, "Communication complexity: A survey," in *Paths, Flows, and VLSI Layout*, B. H. Korte, Ed. Berlin, Germany: Springer-Verlag, 1990.

[106] R. J. Lipton and R. Sedgewick, "Lower bounds for VLSI," in *Proc. 13th Annu. ACM Symp. Theory of Computing*, Apr. 1981, pp. 300–307.

[107] J. Ullman, *Computational Aspects of VLSI*. Computer Sci. Press, 1983.

[108] M. O. Rabin and A. C. Yao, 1979, unpublished manuscript; see also Yao [102].

[109] R. Freivalds, "Probabilistic machines can use less running time," *Information Processing, IFIP*. Amsterdam, The Netherlands: North Holland, 1977, pp. 839–842.

[110] A. Orlitsky and A. El Gamal, "Average and randomized communication complexity," *IEEE Trans. Inform. Theory*, vol. 36, pp. 3–16, Jan. 1990.

[111] B. Chor and O. Goldreich, "Unbiased bits from sources of weak randomness and probabilistic communication complexity," *SIAM J. Comput.*, vol. 17, no. 2, pp. 230–261, 1988.

[112] K. F. Pang and A. El Gamal, "Communication complexity of computing the Hamming distance," *SIAM J. Comput.*, vol. 15, no. 4, pp. 932–947, 1986.

[113] L. Babai, P. Frankl, and J. Simon, "Complexity classes in communication complexity," in *Proc. 27th Annu. Symp. Foundations of Computer Science*, 1986, pp. 337–347.

[114] B. Kalyanasundaram and G. Schnitger, "The probabilistic communication complexity of set intersection," *SIAM J. Discr. Math.*, vol. 5, no. 4, pp. 545–557, 1992.

[115] A. A. Razborov, "On the distributional complexity of disjointness," *Theor. Comp. Sci.*, vol. 106, no. 2, pp. 385–390, 1992.

[116] C. H. Papadimitriou and M. Sipser, "Communication complexity," in *Proc. 14th Annu. ACM Symp. Theory of Computing*, 1982, pp. 196–200.

[117] P. Duris, Z. Galil, and G. Schnitger, "Lower bounds on communication complexity," in *Proc. 16th Annu. ACM Symp. Theory of Computing*, 1984, pp. 81–91.

[118] N. Nisan and A. Wigderson, "Rounds in communication complexity revisited," in *Proc. 23rd Annu. ACM Symp. Theory of Computing*, 1991.

[119] P. B. Miltersen, N. Nisan, S. Safra, and A. Wigderson, "On data structures and asymmetric communication complexity," in *Proc. 27th Annu. ACM Symp. Theory of Computing*, 1995, pp. 103–111.

[120] R. Ahlswede and N. Cai, "On communication complexity of vector-valued functions," *IEEE Trans. Inform. Theory*, vol. 40, pp. 2062–2067, Nov. 1994.

[121] I. Newman, "Common random bits in communication complexity," *Inform. Processing Lett.*, vol. 39, pp. 67–71, 1991.

[122] J. Ja'Ja', "Identification is easier than decoding," in *Proc. 26th Annu. Symp. Foundations of Computer Science*, 1985.

[123] R. Ahlswede and G. Dueck, "Identification via channels," *IEEE Trans. Inform. Theory*, vol. 35, pp. 15–29, Jan. 1989.

[124] ———, "Identification in the presence of feedback—A discovery of new capacity formulas," *IEEE Trans. Inform. Theory*, vol. 35, pp. 30–36, Jan. 1989.

[125] S. Verdú and V. K. Wei, "Explicit construction of optimal constant-weight codes for identification via channels," *IEEE Trans. Inform. Theory*, vol. 39, pp. 30–36, Jan. 1993.

[126] T. S. Han and S. Verdú, "New results in the theory of identification via channels," *IEEE Trans. Inform. Theory*, vol. 38, pp. 14–25, Jan. 1992.

[127] L. J. Schulman, "Communication on noisy channels: A coding theorem for computation," in *Proc. 33rd Symp. Foundations of Computer Science*, 1992, pp. 724–733.

[128] ———, "Deterministic coding for interactive communication," in *Proc. 25th Annu. ACM Symp. Theory of Computing*, 1993, pp. 747–756.

[129] A. K. Chandra, M. L. Furst, and R. J. Lipton, "Multi-party protocols," in *Proc. 15th Annu. ACM Symp. Theory of Computing*, 1983, pp. 94–99.

[130] D. Dolev and T. Feder, "Multiparty communication complexity," in *Proc. 30th IEEE Symp. Foundations of Computer Science*, 1989, pp. 428–433.

[131] L. Babai, N. Nisan, and M. Szegedy, "Multiparty protocols, pseudorandom generators for LOGSPACE, and time-space trade-offs," *J. Comp. Syst. Sci.*, vol. 45, no. 2, pp. 204–232, 1992.

[132] Chung and Tetali, "Communication complexity and quasi randomness," *SIAM J. Discr. Math.*, vol. 6, no. 1, pp. 110–123, 1993.

[133] V. Grolmusz, "The BNS lower bound for multi-party protocols is nearly optimal," *Inform. Commut.*, vol. 112, no. 1, pp. 51–54, 1994.

[134] L. Babai, P. Kimmel, and S. V. Lokam, "Simultaneous messages vs. communication," in *Proc. 12th Symp. Aspects of Computer Science.* (Lecturen Notes in Computer Science). Berlin, Germany: Springer, 1995, pp. 361–372.

[135] Pudlák and V. Rödl, "Modified ranks of tensors and the size of circuits," in *Proc. 25th ACM Symp. Theory of Computing*, 1993, pp. 523–531.

[136] C. D. Thompson, "Area-time complexity for VLSI," in *Proc. 11th Annu. ACM Symp. Theory of Computing*, 1979.

[137] T. Lengauer, "VLSI theory," in *Handbook of Theoretical Computer Science.* Amsterdam, The Netherlands: Elsevier, 1990, vol. A, ch. 16, pp. 835–868.

[138] C. E. Shannon, "The synthesis of two-terminal switching circuits," *Bell Syst. Tech. J.*, vol. 28, pp. 59–98, 1949.

[139] M. Karchmer and A. Wigderson, "Monotone circuits for connectivity require super-logarithmic depth," *SIAM J. Discr. Math.*, vol. 3, no. 2, pp. 255–265, 1990.

[140] M. Gringi and M. Sipser, "Monotone separation of logarithmic space from logarithmic depth," *J. Comp. Syst. Sci.*, vol. 50, pp. 433–437, 1995.

[141] R. Raz and A. Wigderson, "Monotone circuits for matching require linear depth," *J. Assoc. Comput. Mach.*, vol. 39, no. 3, pp. 736–744, 1992.

[142] A. A. Razborov, "Applications of matrix methods to the theory of lower bounds in computational complexity," *Combinatorica*, vol. 10, no. 1, pp. 81–93, 1990.

[143] H. D. Groger and G. Turan, "On linear decision trees computing Boolean functions," in *Proc. 18th Int. Colloq. Automata, Languages, and Programming.* (Lecture Notes in Computer Science) Berlin, Germany:

Springer-Verlag, 1991, pp. 707–718.

[144] N. Nisan, "The communication complexity of threshold gates," in *Combinatorics, Paul Erdös is Eighty (Vol. 1)*. Budapest, Hungary: János Bolyai Math. Soc., 1993, pp. 301–315.

[145] V. P. Roychowdhury, A. Orlitsky, and K. Y. Siu, "Lower bounds on threshold and related circuits via communication complexity," *IEEE Trans. Inform. Theory*, vol. 40, pp. 467–474, Mar. 1994.

[146] M. Goldmann, "Communication complexity and lower bounds for threshold circuits," in *Theoretical Advances in Neural Computation and Learning*, V. Roychowdhury, K.-Y. Siu, and A. Orlitsky, Eds. Norwell, MA: Kluwer, 1994, ch. 3, pp. 85–125.

[147] M. Santha and U. V. Vazirani, "Generating quasi-random sequences from slightly-random sources," in *Proc. 25th IEEE Symp. Foundations of Computer Science*, 1984, pp. 434–440.

185

Detection of Stochastic Processes

Thomas Kailath, *Life Fellow, IEEE*, and H. Vincent Poor, *Fellow, IEEE*

(Invited Paper)

Abstract— **This paper reviews two streams of development, from the 1940's to the present, in signal detection theory: the structure of the likelihood ratio for detecting signals in noise and the role of dynamic optimization in detection problems involving either very large signal sets or the joint optimization of observation time and performance. This treatment deals exclusively with basic results developed for the situation in which the observations are modeled as continuous-time stochastic processes. The mathematics and intuition behind such developments as the matched filter, the RAKE receiver, the estimator–correlator, maximum-likelihood sequence detectors, multiuser detectors, sequential probability ratio tests, and cumulative-sum quickest detectors, are described.**

Index Terms— **Dynamic programming, innovations processes, likelihood ratios, martingale theory, matched filters, optimal stopping, reproducing kernel Hilbert spaces, sequence detection, sequential methods, signal detection, signal estimation.**

INTRODUCTION AND OVERVIEW

THE subject of signal detection and estimation deals with the processing of information-bearing signals in order to make inferences about the information that they contain. Although this field clearly traces its provenance to the classical work of Bayes [6], Gauss [31], Fisher [27], and Neyman and Pearson [76] on statistical inference,[1] it was not until after the mathematical stage was set in the 1930's by the pioneers of stochastic processes—Kolmogorov, Lévy, Wiener, and others—that the field took hold as a recognizable discipline. Moreover, the possibilities for implementing any more than the most basic signal processing systems did not arise until electronics reached a reasonably advanced state, also in the the same era. Add to this mix the impetus of wartime technological needs, and the result is the relatively abrupt emergence of this field in the early 1940's.

The first engineering studies in this area were perhaps those of Norbert Wiener in 1941–1942, initiated with a ($2,350!) project at MIT to design "a lead or prediction apparatus in which, when one member follows the track of an air-plane, another anticipates where the airplane is to be after a fixed lapse of time." Though the proposed solution did not perform satisfactorily, and the project was abandoned, the fundamental insights gained through the effort have had a profound influence on many later developments—a not unfamiliar story. These arose through a remarkable report [136], sweepingly titled *Extrapolation, Interpolation and Smoothing of Stationary Time Series, with Engineering Applications*, that introduced two fundamental ideas that radically changed the way engineers tackled important classes of problems. First was the emphatic assertion that communication of information is perforce a statistical problem. Second was the introduction of optimization criteria, so that performance limits could be calculated and systematic approximations sought. Here are a few relevant quotations from Wiener's 1942 report that will ring a bell with modern readers.

"Communication engineering concerns itself with the transmission of messages. For the existence of a message, it is indeed essential that variable information be transmitted. The transmission of a single fixed item of information is of no communication value. We must have a repertory of possible messages, and over this repertory a measure determining the probability of these messages."

"A message need not be the result of a conscious human effort for the transmission of ideas. For example the records of current and voltage kept on the instruments of an automatic substation are as truly messages as a telephone conversation."

"No apparatus for conveying information is useful unless it is designed to operate, not on a particular message, but on a set of messages, and its effectiveness is to be judged on the way it performs on the average on messages of this set. ... The apparatus to be used for a particular purpose is that which gives the best result 'on the average' in an appropriate sense of the word 'average'."

It took a while for Wiener's results on estimation and prediction to be fully understood, and their applications really took off only more than a decade later. However, the basic idea established in Wiener's work—namely, that mathematical models and optimization could be applied to design systems for signal processing—was the *zeitgeist* of the era, and permeated problems of more pressing interest at that time. Among these were the studies on radar detection being carried out at the MIT Radiation Laboratory and elsewhere, well summarized by Lawson and Uhlenbeck in 1948 [65]. From this, and related work, was born the field of signal detection, to which the present paper is devoted.

Manuscript received February 28, 1998; revised June 7, 1998. This work was supported in part by the Air Force Office of Scientific Research, the Army Research Office, DARPA, the National Science Foundation, and the Office of Naval Research.

T. Kailath is with the Department of Electrical Engineering, Stanford University, Stanford, CA 94305-9510 USA.

H. V. Poor is with the Department of Electrical Engineering, Princeton University, Princeton, NJ 08544 USA.

Publisher Item Identifier S 0018-9448(98)06313-5.

[1] One might trace even further back—to Leonardo Da Vinci, one of whose many remarkable insights into technological possibilities deals with the detection of distant ships by monitoring a sound tube in the ocean (see, [10]).

In particular, in this paper we review some key developments of this field from the 1940's to the present. In keeping with the tenor of these TRANSACTIONS, we focus on theoretical developments. However, the reader should not lose sight of the fact that there have been many hardware developments over these decades, without which the theoretical progress would now be of little interest. The scope of the field of signal detection is very large, with several useful textbooks available, including [39], [89], and [121]. In order to place some bounds on this treatment, we focus on some very basic principles and structures that allow us to trace the development of some interesting results, ideas, and techniques, which may also have value in various other applications. However, in so doing, we fully realize that many very interesting areas will be touched upon only lightly, or even not at all. Examples include adaptive detection, nonparametric detection, distributed detection, detection in non-Gaussian noise, quantum detection, robust detection, and detection with antenna arrays. These omissions are of course not intended to signify a lesser status in the field; indeed, much of the authors' own work lies in these areas.

The presentation is organized into two parts:

Part I deals with the most fundamental problem of signal detection—namely, the determination of the likelihood ratio for detecting signals against a noise background. This is a problem with a rich history in both electrical engineering and mathematics, and its solution has involved, over the years, a wide variety of mathematical tools and flashes of intuition. This discussion begins with the earliest "optimal" signal detection system—the matched filter—and then traces the development of many key ideas, including the RAKE receiver, the estimator–correlator, and geometric interpretations of signal detection. These developments correspond to treatment of the detection problem via various methods of probability and mathematical statistics, including stochastic calculus and the theory of reproducing-kernel Hilbert spaces.

Part II of this paper deals with a further level of complexity that arises in many detection problems after the likelihood ratio is extracted. In particular, we discuss the application of dynamic optimization—also developed in its earliest form in the 1940's (by Richard Bellman)—to two types of signal detection problems: sequence detection, and sequential detection. Sequence detection deals with the problem of testing a very large number of statistical hypotheses within signal detection models that allow for complexity reduction via dynamic programming. Basic structures such as the maximum-likelihood sequence estimator for equalizing dispersive communication channels, the maximum-likelihood multiuser detector for mitigating multiple-access interference, and the Viterbi algorithm for decoding convolutional codes on a white Gaussian channel are discussed in this context. Sequential detection deals with detection problems in which the observation time is to be optimized jointly with the error probabilities. Such problems fall within the category of optimal stopping problems. Here, we discuss two such problems: classical sequential detection, and quickest detection. Both of these can be cast as Markov optimal stopping problems, which allow them to be solved using (infinite-horizon) dynamic programming type solutions. A recent interpretation of these types of problems as "generalized parking problems" is also discussed.

Finally, we conclude the paper with brief remarks about some other aspects of the field not treated in the rest of the paper.

PART I:
THE LIKELIHOOD RATIO

In this part of the paper, we deal with the most fundamental problem in signal detection theory—namely, the determination of the likelihood ratio for detecting a signal against a noise background. This seemingly sharply defined problem is actually a very rich one, calling on many techniques of stochastic analysis. In fact, the topic is so broad that several choices have to be made to narrow the scope, for the sake of both readers and authors. In particular, we confine ourselves to problems of detecting i) known signals in noise, e.g., as in synchronous PAM and PFM communication systems, ii) signals with unknown parameters, e.g., amplitude and phase, iii) random signals in additive noise, as arise, for example, in rapidly fading channels or in radioastronomy, and iv) signals modulating jump processes.

Our review will not be strictly chronological nor will we attempt to be exhaustive in citing the literature; rather, we attempt to focus on important ideas and threads whose significance often became clear only after a considerable passage of time and effort. For example, we emphasize the physical and mathematical importance of including white noise disturbances in the received signal. The case of purely colored noise is both physically less relevant and mathematically more difficult; nevertheless, if it is to be studied, it took a long time to realize that the "best" mathematical and physical approach is via the use of reproducing kernel Hilbert spaces. It also took a while to appreciate the role of stochastic integrals and martingale theory in properly completing and reconciling the various likelihood-ratio formulas of Price [94], Stratonovich and Sosulin [116], Schweppe [101], and Shepp [105], for Gaussian signals in white Gaussian noise, and in developing their extensions to non-Gaussian processes. However, once recognized, the power of these methods became obvious. Our major aim is to give the reader some feel for the way in which these ideas evolved.

I. BEGINNINGS—THE MATCHED FILTER

As noted in the introductory section, the field of signal detection had its most recognizable beginnings in the early 1940's work on radar detection, in which the issue is one of detecting the presence or absence of a target. The original criterion for designing systems for this purpose was the maximization of the (so-called *deflection*, or) *signal-to-noise ratio*, defined as the ratio of the squared magnitude of the peak response of a linear filter to the signal, and the average noise power at the output of the filter. The solution, in the words of Lawson and Uhlenbeck [65, p. 209] was

"... *a remarkable theorem discovered by Wiener, Hansen, North, and Van Vleck independently. The theorem states that the best signal-to-noise ratio (or the lowest signal threshold) is obtained if the shape of the i–f passband is the Fourier transform of the pulse shape. Van Vleck then says that 'the i–f is matched to the pulse shape.' When 'matched' the value of the signal-to-noise ratio is independent of the pulse shape.*"

The now well-known simple proof of this result via Parseval's theorem and the Schwarz inequality is noted in [65] in a footnote. The earliest publication of the matched filter principle[2] was a classified RCA report of D. O. North [78], published in Princeton in June 1943. The term "matched filter" was first introduced by J. H. Van Vleck and D. Middleton (who independently derived the result), in a classified Harvard Radio Research Lab technical report (Report RRL no. 4111-86) of May 1944, subsequently published as [122]. North, Middleton, and Van Vleck were all trained as physicists. The prewar interests of Van Vleck (who subsequently won the Nobel Prize in physics) were in the area of spectroscopy, a background that gives some insight into his interest in the detection of signals with concentrated spectral energy [73]. North's wartime involvement in radar (and, hence signal detection) stemmed from his work on the study of noise in vacuum tubes operating in the 100-MHz band, work being conducted at RCA during its 1930's development of commercial television [79]. His 1943 report, reprinted in the PROCEEDINGS OF THE IEEE in July 1963, is also remarkable for the facility with which the author subordinates the use of sophisticated (for the time) mathematics to focus on important physical goals and insights. The matched filter itself is only a small part of this report, which introduces, *inter alia*, the Rice distribution, the concept of false alarms to set a detection threshold, studies of pre-detection and post-detection integration, etc. North clearly underestimated the significance of his contributions, because as the war was ending, "solid state physics beckoned, and I turned to it."

The matched filter is now of course a standard item in the repertoire of radar and communication engineers. A detailed survey of its many properties is given in a classic paper of Turin [120], which leads off a special June 1960 issue of these TRANSACTIONS on matched filters. However, though North and others were aware that signal-to-noise ratio was not the natural criterion for the detection problem, the connection to statistical hypothesis testing was perhaps first made by the distinguished mathematician, Mark Kac, who used to joke that his major contribution to the war effort was to provide a reference to the classic paper of Neyman and Pearson [76]. The Neyman–Pearson criterion seeks a receiver that would maximize the probability of correct detection while keeping the probability of false alarm less than a specified value, a very appropriate criterion for radar. The theory shows that the key quantity to compute is the likelihood ratio (LR), a conclusion that is also the result of applying a number of other criteria. Among those, we first mention minimizing the probability of error, which was introduced

---

independently by Siegert (see Lawson and Uhlenbeck [65], Sec. VII-C]) and in the remarkable 1947 Ph.D. dissertation of V.A. Kotel'nikov in the Soviet Union (English translation published in 1959 [62]), which we shall discuss in more detail later. P. M. Woodward [140] came to the likelihood ratio via a slightly different route (inverse probabilities), inspired by the information-theoretic result that the relevant information is all preserved in the conditional probabilities of the hypotheses given the observations. The more general formulations in the statistical literature by A. Wald of sequential hypothesis testing [132] and then of what became known as statistical decision theory [133] were first applied to signal detection problems by Middleton [72] and by Peterson, Birdsall, and Fox [86] in 1954. Again, in all cases, the basic operation is to compare a likelihood ratio with a threshold, whose value is determined by the chosen criterion.

From a purely mathematical point of view, that is almost the end of the story. The rest is apparently just detail: one needs only to compute the likelihood ratio in any particular problem and to evaluate its performance using standard numerical and statistical methods. However, from an engineering point of view, the story is usually just beginning. For one thing, mathematical models are often significant simplifications/idealizations of complex physical problems. Secondly, even if the model is reasonably good, our knowledge of the parameters in it, e.g., covariance functions, time constants, etc., may not be enough to justify a direct numerical evaluation of formulas derived from the model. The major engineering goal is to obtain *structural insights* into the mathematical solutions of classes of special problems, with the hope that these insights can then be used to intelligently modify and adapt the mathematical solution to the particular physical problem at hand; see, e.g., Siebert [110] for a nice elaboration of this philosophy.

It is the development of such insights that we hope to describe in this paper, rather than just cataloging all the important results and papers in detection theory. Of course, there are bound to be various errors of omission and commission in this process, for which we beg in advance the indulgence of authors and readers.

II. DETECTION OF SIGNALS IN WHITE GAUSSIAN NOISE

A generic problem is one in which we have to choose between two hypotheses of the form

$$H_0: y(t) = n(t), \qquad 0 \le t \le T$$

versus

$$H_1: y(t) = s(t) + n(t), \qquad 0 \le t \le T$$

where, of course, $s(\cdot)$ represents a signal of interest and $n(\cdot)$ represents random noise. Common forms of signals are

i) completely known: $s(t) = m(t)$;
ii) known except for a few parameters: e.g.,

$$s(t) = \alpha A(t) \cos(\omega_0 t + \theta)$$

where some combinations of $\{\alpha, \omega_0, \theta\}$ may be random or unknown;
iii) Purely stochastic: $s(t) = z(t)$, a stochastic process.

---

[2]In a broader sense, one can think of the matched filter as being an instance of the idea that, when averaging measurements, one should weight them according to their relative precision. This basic idea dates at least to the work of Roger Cotes [17] in the early eighteenth century, and was certainly known by the time of the development of least squares around the turn of the nineteenth century. An interesting account of the history of such methods can be found in Stigler's book [113].

Here, we will refer to the first two types of signals as *deterministic* signals, and the third type as stochastic signals. Of course, we may have combinations of these three types as well. For the noise process, the usual assumptions are that the noise has (for convenience) zero mean and that it is i) purely white and Gaussian, or ii) is colored with a white Gaussian component, or iii) is purely colored, i.e., has no white noise component at all.

The more general case of choosing between multiple hypothesis of the form

$$H_k:\ y(t) = s_k(t) + n(t), \qquad k = 1, 2 \cdots, M$$

can be handled (in most cases) by introducing a dummy hypothesis, H_0: $y(t) = n(t)$, and then using the chain rule for likelihood ratios. This situation is discussed in more detail in Section IV-A. (We may mention that certain (apparently) nonadditive noise problems will be treated in Section II-E.)

Since white noise is a physically impossible idealization of noise whose bandwidth is much larger than that of the signal, it might seem that the most important problem to study would be the case of purely colored noise. However, it turns out that this is a poor decision for both mathematical and physical reasons. Mathematically, the solution is generally much more difficult to obtain, and physically it is often unrealistic. For example, if the colored noise is twice differentiable, of course the signal must also be at least twice differentiable, and the likelihood ratio might well involve the derivatives of $y(\cdot)$. However, few engineers would attempt to implement such a scheme, at the least on the grounds that differentiation would amplify the inevitably present, but unmodeled or inadequately modeled, high-frequency components. Incorporating a white-noise component is a way of reflecting indifference to less relevant details; mathematically, it keeps the solution from requiring unrealistic operations on the data and leads to "smoother" and more robust implementations. A formal demonstration of this property is found in the robustness formulation of [88]. Finally, of course, the fact that white noise is physically impossible (it has infinite variance) is no reason why it should not be used in a *mathematical model* of the problem (all models are imperfect reflections of the real world), especially when it both simplifies the mathematical analysis and gives us reasonably implementable solutions. Moreover, infinite variance random variables are not uncommon in many useful mathematical models; in particular, likelihood ratios may often have infinite variance—see Section II-B.

So here we shall begin with the white noise assumption, as did the early engineering contributors (North [78], Kotel'nikov [62], Woodward [140]) to this field. Not unexpectedly, one of the first mathematical works in this area, that of Grenander [36], never mentions white noise.[3] (Nevertheless, we shall have to examine the treatment of white noise more closely later in Section II-B.ff. Here we remark that as long as we confine ourselves to linear operations on white noise, there is no problem in working formally with white noise. The reason is that these operations can be justified by "working under the integral sign," just as can be done to justify linear operations

with impulsive functions. As reassurance for the fainthearted, we may cite the discussion along these lines in, for example, Doob [22, Sec. IX-D], where he shows the convenience of working directly with Fourier transforms of stationary random processes, a useful method unnecessarily avoided by most engineering authors.)

A. Deterministic Signals

We shall start our discussion with the hypotheses

$$H_0:\ y(t) = v(t), \qquad 0 \le t \le T$$

versus

$$H_1:\ y(t) = m(t) + v(t), \qquad 0 \le t \le T \qquad (1)$$

with $m(\cdot)$ a known signal with finite energy,

$$E = \int_0^T m^2(t)\, dt$$

and where $v(\cdot)$ is zero-mean, unit-intensity, white Gaussian noise (WGN); i.e., $v(\cdot)$ is Gaussian with

$$E\{v(\cdot)\} \equiv 0 \quad \text{and} \quad E\{v(t)v(s)\} = \delta(t - s). \qquad (2)$$

Then, in several different ways (see, e.g., Cameron and Martin [16], Kotel'nikov [62], Woodward [140], Wozencraft and Jacobs [141]), it is shown that we can write the likelihood ratio as

$$L(T) = \exp\left\{\int_0^T m(t)y(t)\, dt - \frac{1}{2}\int_0^T m^2(t)\, dt\right\}. \qquad (3)$$

Among the approaches to deriving (3), Woodward [140] uses time-samples and then proceeds to the limit, whereas Wozencraft and Jacobs [141, Sec. IV-C] present a geometric projection argument, perhaps first used in Kotel'nikov's dissertation [62], that effectively reduces the problem to a finite-dimensional (in fact, one-dimensional) form. (Kotel'nikov's work is notable not only for being so early, but especially for its prescient emphasis on geometric formulations and interpretations; the dissertation contains several results that were often rediscovered much later, e.g., the optimality of PSK (phase-shift keying) and the maximum minimum distance property of the simplex configuration. Also, he gives a geometric interpretation of the threshold effect in frequency- and pulse-modulation systems, which is the same as the famous explanation in Shannon's 1949 Gaussian channel paper [104].)

We see from (3) that the essential data processing step is the formation of the integral $\int_0^T m(t)y(t)\, dt$, which can be implemented either by "correlating" the "stored" signal $m(\cdot)$ against the received signal $y(\cdot)$, or as is easily checked, passing $y(\cdot)$ through a filter matched to $m(\cdot)$ (i.e., one with impulse response $m(T - \cdot)$), and then sampling the output at the end $(t = T)$ of the observation interval. In other words, the matched filter of the early radar literature is in fact the optimal operation from a decision-theoretic point of view.

A generalization of the detection problem arises when the signal $m(\cdot)$ has unknown parameters. In this case, the hypotheses are

$$H_0:\ y(t) = v(t), \qquad 0 \le t \le T$$

[3]It should be noted, however, that Cameron and Martin [16] developed a version of the classic known-signal-in-white-noise likelihood ratio formula in 1944, albeit in a context different from that of signal detection.

versus

$$H_1: y(t) = m(t; \theta) + v(t), \qquad 0 \le t \le T \qquad (4)$$

where θ is a vector of unknown parameters. When an *a priori* probability distribution function is known for θ[4] then the LR is obtained by integration as

$$L(T) = \int \exp \left\{ \int_0^T m(t; \theta) y(t)\, dt - \tfrac{1}{2} \int_0^T m^2(t; \theta)\, dt \right\} \cdot p(\theta)\, d\theta. \qquad (5)$$

The best known case is that of a signal with uniformly distributed random phase

$$m(t; \theta) = A(t) \cos\left(\omega_0 t + \theta + \phi(t)\right), p(\theta) = \frac{1}{2\pi},$$
$$0 \le \theta \le 2\pi. \qquad (6)$$

with $\{A(\cdot), \phi(\cdot)\}$ slowly varying compared to $\cos \omega_0 t$. Under this "narrowband" assumption, it turns out that

$$L(T) = e^{-E/2} I_0([V_c^2(T) + V_s^2(T)]^{1/2}) \qquad (7)$$

with

$$E = \int_0^T m^2(t, \theta)\, dt = \tfrac{1}{2} \int_0^T A^2(t)\, dt$$

while I_0 denotes the zeroth-order modified Bessel function of the first kind, and where

$$V_c(T) = \int_0^T A(t) \cos\left(\omega_0 t + \phi(t)\right) y(t)\, dt$$

and

$$V_s(T) = \int_0^T A(t) \sin\left(\omega_0 t + \phi(t)\right) y(t)\, dt. \qquad (8)$$

The key operation on the received signal is the formation of the quantity $\sqrt{V_c^2(T) + V_s^2(T)}$, which is just the value at $t = T$ of the envelope of the output of a filter *matched* to the narrowband signal $A(t) \cos\left(\omega_0 + \phi(t)\right)$—see, e.g., Woodward [140, p. 78].

It should be noted that the analysis of narrowband signals is facilitated by the use of the very useful "complex envelope" representation, originally suggested by Gabor [29]; Woodward [140] was perhaps the first to exploit this description for signal detection problems and, *inter alia*, it led him to introduce the ambiguity function as a tool for understanding the resolution limits of radar (see, e.g., Siebert [110]). (As with Kotel'nikov's work, it is worthwhile to acknowledge the many early contributions of Woodward—his remarkable 1953 monograph conveys in a mere 128 pages fine introductions to probability theory, Fourier analysis, information theory, and signal detection, followed by three chapters on the radar problem that first introduced many new results such as formulas for range accuracy and the ambiguity function. Physical insight and mathematical analysis are very skillfully combined throughout the work. For example, entropy is introduced by studying how

---

[4] When $p(\theta)$ is unknown, further statistical concepts have to be introduced, e.g., the notions of *uniformly most powerful* tests, *locally optimal* tests, etc. [89].

to efficiently store binary-valued data, an operational point of view not much emphasized in 1951 when many people were more intrigued by the axiomatic aspects.)

Another special case where explicit formulas are available for the LR is when the parameters $\{A(\cdot), \phi(\cdot)\}$ are essentially constant (i.e., very slowly varying over $[0, T]$) and such that $\{A \cos \phi, A \sin \phi\}$ are independent and identically distributed (i.i.d.) zero-mean Gaussian random variables—this is the model for what is known as *Rayleigh fading*. In this case, again, the envelope of the matched filter output turns out to be the key statistic. Other distributions for $\{A(\cdot), \phi(\cdot)\}$, or the case of random ω_0, all become much more difficult and few explicit results are available.

One approach in such cases is not to focus on the parameters, but to assume that the signal is a stochastic process, a case to which we now turn. We first consider the case of a Gaussian random process, which becomes realistic, for example, in the case of communication through channels composed of many randomly moving scatterers. However, we shall find that again, as in the just-mentioned cases of signals with random parameters, the expressions for the LR will be very different from the simple known-signal formula (3). Nevertheless, it is a striking and useful fact that not only in all the above cases, but for an almost arbitrary signal process, the different likelihood ratio expressions can be rewritten to have exactly the same form as (3), except that the known signal is replaced by a least mean-squares estimate (Sections II-B and II-D). The significance of this fact is that one now has a universal "estimator–correlator" receiver structure to which one can bring all the results and all the knowledge and insight now available for the calculation and approximation of least mean-square estimators; moreover, this result also extends to an apparently quite different class of problems, as we shall see in Section II-E.

B. Gaussian Stochastic Signals

We now consider hypotheses of the form

$$H_0: y(t) = v(t), \qquad 0 \le t \le T$$

versus

$$H_1: y(t) = z(t) + v(t), \qquad 0 \le t \le T \qquad (9)$$

where, as before, $v(\cdot)$ is WGN, while the "signal" $z(\cdot)$ is now a zero-mean Gaussian process, independent of the WGN $v(\cdot)$, and with known covariance function $K(\cdot, \cdot)$, i.e.,

$$E\{z(t)v(s)\} \equiv 0 \quad \text{and} \quad E\{z(t)z(s)\} = K(t, s). \qquad (10)$$

Under the further assumptions that

i) $K(t, s)$ is continuous in t, s and ii) $\int_0^T K(t, t)\, dt < \infty$. $$\qquad (11)$$

Price [94] showed in 1956 that the likelihood ratio could be written as

$$L(T) = \frac{1}{\sqrt{B(T)}} \cdot \exp \{\Lambda(T)\} \qquad (12)$$

where $B(T)$ is a deterministic (*bias*) term, which we shall specify later (see (22) and (38)). The observations $y(\cdot)$ enter through the quadratic functional

$$\Lambda(T) = \tfrac{1}{2} \int_0^T \int_0^T H(t,s)y(t)y(s)\,dt\,ds \qquad (13)$$

where $H(\cdot,\cdot)$ is the so-called *Fredholm resolvent* of $K(\cdot,\cdot)$, defined by the integral equation

$$H(t,s) + \int_0^T H(t,\tau)K(\tau,s)\,d\tau = K(t,s), \qquad 0 \le t, s \le T. \qquad (14)$$

$H(\cdot,\cdot)$ is actually also a function of T, though for simplicity we do not show this explicitly. $\Lambda(T)$ is a weighted energy functional of $y(\cdot)$, which is reasonable since there is apparently no structure available in the random signals to allow any kind of matched filtering (or correlation) detection structure. However, Price noticed that the function

$$\hat{z}_{1,sm}(t) = \int_0^T H(t,s)y(s)\,ds, \qquad 0 \le t \le T \qquad (15)$$

had the interpretation that, when hypothesis H_1 holds (i.e., $y(\cdot) = z(\cdot) + v(\cdot)$), then $\hat{z}_{1,sm}(t)$ is the linear least mean-squares estimate of $z(t)$ given $\{y(\tau), 0 \le \tau \le T\}$; that is, $\hat{z}_{1,sm}(t)$ is the smoothed (or noncausal) estimate of $z(\cdot)$. (Notation: the caret denotes the "estimate," and the subscript the assumption that H_1 holds—such estimates are sometimes called *pseudo-estimates*.) This property follows readily from the now well-known geometric characterization of the least squares estimate as the random variable $\hat{z}_{1,sm}(t)$ such that $z(t) - \hat{z}_{1,sm}(t)$ is uncorrelated with $\{y(\tau), 0 \le \tau \le T\}$, which leads immediately to the integral equation (14). With this interpretation, $\Lambda(T)$ can indeed be expressed as a correlation integral

$$\Lambda(T) = \frac{1}{2} \int_0^T \hat{z}_{1,sm}(t)y(t)\,dt \qquad (16)$$

as in the known signal case; however, since the signal $z(\cdot)$ is random and hence unavailable, (16) says that we can replace it with the best least squares estimate of the signal $z(t)$ given $\{y(\tau) = z(\tau) + v(\tau), 0 \le \tau \le T\}$, a quite reasonable strategy.

As mentioned before, such physical interpretations of the receiver structure are useful because they allow intelligent adaptation to real-world problems. In fact, this interpretation was very effectively exploited by Price and Green in 1958 [95] to develop the anti-jamming anti-multipath communication system called RAKE, a concept now being applied again for space–time processing in mobile communication systems (see, e.g., Paulraj *et al.* [84], [85]). In the RAKE system, a narrowband filter of bandwidth approximately that of the signal process was used to provide a crude, but apparently adequate, approximation to the least squares estimate $\hat{z}_{1,m}(t)$, which was impossible to compute given the limited information available about the actual multipath channel.

However, though valuable, the formulas (13) or (16) are not always usable as they stand, because the estimate at every t, $\hat{z}_{1,sm}(t)$, depends upon "future" values of $y(\cdot)$; to compute it, therefore, we shall first have to store $\{y(s), 0 \le s \le T\}$ and then process this data to obtain $\{\hat{z}_{1,sm}(t), 0 \le t \le T\}$. Price

found a clever way around this problem, using the (evident) symmetry of the integrand in (13) to write

$$\Lambda(T) = \frac{1}{2} \cdot 2 \int_0^T y(t)\,dt \int_0^t H(t,s)y(s)\,ds \qquad (17)$$

so that now at time t we need only $\{y(s),\ s \le t\}$. Despite these nice facts, note that the LR formula (13) does not provide a true estimator–correlator interpretation: that would require that $L(T)$ be as in (3) but with $m(\cdot)$ replaced by $\hat{z}_{1,sm}(\cdot)$, which is certainly not true of (12).

However, in the early 1960's, significant progress toward a true estimator–correlator formula was made by R. L. Stratonovich and Y. G. Sosulin in 1964 [116] and F. Schweppe in 1965 [101]. Schweppe had a controls background, where recursive solutions based on state-space models had recently been made popular by the Kalman filter [55], [56]. Price's formula is not recursive, in the sense that if we had more observations, say over $[0, T_1]$, where $T_1 > T$, we would have to recompute the function $H(\cdot,\cdot)$ by resolving the integral equation (14) with upper limit T_1. On the other hand, Schweppe showed that one could rewrite Price's formula in recursive form

$$\frac{d}{dt} \ln L(t) = \hat{z}_1(t)y(t) - \frac{1}{2}\hat{z}_1^2(t), \qquad t \ge 0 \qquad (18)$$

where $\hat{z}_1(t)$ is a functional of past $y(\cdot)$, i.e., of $\{y(\tau), 0 \le \tau \le t\}$. Moreover, when H_1 holds, i.e., $y(\cdot) = z(\cdot) + v(\cdot)$, $\hat{z}_1(t)$ is the *causal* least squares estimates of $z(t)$ given $\{y(\tau), 0 \le \tau < t\}$. This causal estimate can (since $z(\cdot)$ is Gaussian) be computed by a linear operation on $y(\cdot)$

$$\hat{z}_1(t) = \int_0^t h(t,s)y(s)\,ds \qquad (19)$$

where use of the orthogonality conditions

$$E\{[z(t) - \hat{z}_1(t)]y^*(s)\} = 0, \qquad 0 \le s < t \qquad (20)$$

shows that $h(\cdot,\cdot)$ obeys, not a Fredholm equation as $H(\cdot,\cdot)$ does, but a Wiener–Hopf-type equation

$$h(t,s) + \int_0^t h(t,\tau)K(\tau,s)\,d\tau = K(t,s), \qquad 0 \le s < t \le T. \qquad (21)$$

Moreover, when the signal process has a known state-space model, $\hat{z}_1(t)$ can itself be recursively computed by using the (Stratonovich)–Kalman–Bucy filtering equations, on which there is by now a vast body of results and experience, see, e.g., [50]. In fact, Schweppe also showed that the bias term in the formula (12) could be computed as

$$B(T) = \exp\left\{-\tfrac{1}{2}\int_0^T h(t,t)\,dt\right\} \qquad (22)$$

where it turns out that

$$h(t,t) = E\{|z(t) - \hat{z}_1(t)|^2\} \triangleq E\{\tilde{z}_1^2(t)\} \qquad (23)$$

the mean-square error. The reason is that, for independent $z(\cdot)$ and $v(\cdot)$, we see using (21) that

$$E\{[z(t) - \hat{z}_1(t)]^2\} = E\{[z(t) - \hat{z}_1(t)]z(t)\}$$
$$= K(t,t) - \int_0^t h(t,s)K(s,t)\,ds$$
$$= h(t,t). \qquad (24)$$

In sum, combining (18) and (24) shows that the likelihood ratio is completely determined by knowledge of the solution to the causal filtering problem as

$$L(T) = \exp\left\{ -\frac{1}{2}\int_0^T E\{\tilde{z}_1^2(t)\}\,dt \right\}$$
$$\cdot \exp\left\{ \int_0^T \hat{z}_1(t)y(t)\,dt - \frac{1}{2}\int_0^T \hat{z}_1^2(t)\,dt \right\}. \quad (25)$$

Schweppe's formula is almost exactly the known signal formula (3), with the causal estimate $\hat{z}_1(\cdot)$ replacing the known signal $m(\cdot)$, except for the nonunity coefficient $B(T)$.

Actually, the approach and results of Schweppe and in fact of Kalman and Bucy, had been anticipated by Stratonovich, who in the late 1950's had begun to emphasize that one could go beyond Gaussian signal models to Markov (or state-space) process models. This is the program that R. E. Kalman was independently pursuing in the U.S., with greater immediate success because Kalman focused on the more elegant linear case. In 1959, Stratonovich [114] had directly attacked the nonlinear problem and showed how the Fokker–Planck partial differential equations characterizing the evolution of the transition probabilities of a Markov process could be used to obtain partial differential equations for the *conditional* probability density of the signal given observations of signal plus noise, a theme later refined by Kushner [64] and Zakai [144]. Of course, the equations are hard to solve, even numerically. Stratonovich noted that in the Gaussian case, we just need equations for the first and second moments, and for these he obtained formulas equivalent to those of Kalman and Bucy [56]. Stratonovich's work on these and related problems has not received the recognition it should.

A few years later, Stratonovich (with Sosulin) applied his approach to the detection problem. Among other results, in their first paper (in 1964) [116] they study the case of Gaussian signals that are also Markov and obtain a true estimator–correlator formula

$$L(T) = \exp\left\{ \fint_0^T \hat{z}_1(t)y(t)\,dt - \frac{1}{2}\int_0^T \hat{z}_1^2(t)\,dt \right\} \quad (26)$$

where the first integral, denoted by $\fint$, is a novel kind of object, called an *Ito stochastic integral*. However, they also noted that one could write the Ito integral as

$$\fint_0^T \hat{z}_1(t)y(t)\,dt = \oint_0^T \hat{z}_1(t)y(t)\,dt - \frac{1}{2}\int_0^T E\{\tilde{z}_1^2(t)\}\,dt \quad (27)$$

where the first integral on the right-hand side was called a *symmetric stochastic integral* (Stratonovich [116], [117]) and nowadays, the *Stratonovich integral*. Substituting (27) into (26) gives us Schweppe's formula (25), which we may recall he derived from Price's formula (12).

The uninitiated reader will wonder about the sudden emergence here of the issue of stochastic integrals. Most of us are aware that there are several definitions of ordinary (non-stochastic) integrals (Cauchy, Riemann, Lebesgue, and others), but that by and large the exact definition does not seem to

affect the final results (though it may affect the derivations). Here, however, we have a different situation—with one definition we get (25), with another (26). And as a matter of fact, other definitions than in (25) and (26), could be used, e.g., the so-called *backward* Ito integrals.

Is one definition to be preferred over the other? There was initially a lot of unnecessary controversy over this issue, sparked partly by the fact that the Stratonovich integral obeys the "usual" rules of integration, which the Ito integral does not. A classical example is the following: Let $v(\cdot)$ be unit intensity white Gaussian noise, and let $w(t) = \int_0^t v(\tau)\,d\tau$, a Wiener process. Then it can be shown

$$\oint_0^T w(t)v(t)\,dt \triangleq \oint_0^T w(t)\,dw(t) = \frac{w^2(T)}{2} \quad (28)$$

as is the case for "ordinary" integrals. However, the Ito definition gives a different answer (see, e.g. Doob [22, Sec. IX-B] or [89, Proposition VI.D.5])

$$\fint_0^T w(t)v(t)\,dt = \fint_0^T w(t)\,dw(t) = \frac{w^2(T)}{2} - \frac{T}{2}. \quad (29)$$

It was felt that since "physical" equipment for computing integrals (and other quantities) is based on the usual rules, it would always give the answer corresponding to the use of the Stratonovich integral. In this sense, the "nonstandard" Ito integral could not be computed using "ordinary," "physical" devices. However, such arguments miss the point that all mathematical models are idealizations and always imperfectly model the actual physical reality, whatever that is. This remark applies to the use in our models of pure sinewaves, step functions, impulsive functions, stationary random processes, Poisson processes, white Gaussian noise, white Poisson noise, etc., etc. We use such idealizations to get models to which we can apply consistent mathematical reasoning, to get exact results for the idealized problem. Then we have to go through the step of implementing physical approximations to these mathematical results. (We may recall some words of Nietzsche (in *Thus Spake Zarathustra*): "No more fiction for us, we calculate. But that we may calculate, we must make fiction first.")

In particular, in our detection problem we idealize a smooth random signal as a finite variance Gaussian random process, and an additive wideband noise process with an approximately flat power spectrum as a pure white Gaussian noise (a formal derivative of a Wiener process). Now we have a mathematical model and the rules we use to make calculations in this model must be mathematically consistent and as general as needed. If both the Stratonovich and Ito definitions (along with the associated rules for calculation) meet these criteria, then either one can be used. But then after the mathematical answer is obtained, we have the task of approximating these integrals with physical equipment. And it turns out that this can be done for either definition—see the discussion in [46].

However it turns out that there are detection problems where the Ito integral exists but not the Stratonovich integral; in such cases we have no choice. Fortunately, too, the Ito integral is not only more general, but it has the very useful (for further calculations—see, e.g., Section V-C below) property that as a function of its upper limit, it is a martingale process. The need for this greater generality arises when we have to go beyond the assumptions (10) and (11) that we have made so far on the Gaussian signal and noise processes. For one thing, (10) does not allow for any dependence between the signal and noise processes; secondly, the continuity assumptions (11) on the covariance function are stronger than necessary for a meaningful (i.e., nonsingular) Gaussian detection problem.

It was shown by Shepp [105] and others that the most general model that does not admit the singular[5] case of perfect discrimination between a Gaussian process and a white Gaussian noise process has the following form: under the hypothesis H_1

$$y(t) = z(t) + v(t), \qquad 0 \le t \le T < \infty \qquad (30)$$

where

$$R_y(t,s) \triangleq E\{y(t)y(s)\} = \delta(t-s) + K(t,s) \qquad (31a)$$

with

$$K(t,s) \triangleq E\{z(t)z(s)\} + E\{z(t)v(s)\} + E\{v(t)z(s)\}. \qquad (31b)$$

Note that when $z(\cdot)$ and $v(\cdot)$ are not independent, $K(\cdot, \cdot)$ is not necessarily positive definite, but, for nonsingularity, it must be such that

$$\int_0^T \int_0^T K^2(t,s)\,dt\,ds < \infty \qquad (32)$$

and

$$R_y(t,s) \text{ is } \textit{strictly} \text{ positive definite.} \qquad (33)$$

Note that the conditions (32) and (33) are always met under the earlier assumptions (10) and (11).

It is useful to recast (32) and (33) in terms of eigenvalues. To do this, we cite a famous result of Hilbert, which shows that when (32) holds, there is a countable number of solutions $\{\lambda_k, \psi_k\}_{k=1}^\infty$ to the (eigenvalue–eigenfunction) equation

$$\int_0^T K(t,s)\psi(s)\,ds = \lambda\psi(t), \qquad 0 \le t \le T. \qquad (34)$$

Since $K(\cdot, \cdot)$ is not necessarily positive definite, some of the λ_k's may be negative, but from (33) it follows that we must have $\lambda_k > -1$. The square-integrability of $K(\cdot, \cdot)$ implies that

$$\sum_{k=1}^\infty \lambda_k^2 \equiv \int_0^T \int_0^T K^2(t,s)\,dt\,ds < \infty. \qquad (35)$$

An issue here is that (35) does not imply that

$$\int_0^T K(t,t)\,dt = \sum_{k=1}^\infty \lambda_k < \infty. \qquad (36)$$

We mention this because it turns out that then the bias term $B(T)$ in Price's formula (12) becomes infinite! The reason is that $B(T)$ is actually the so-called *Fredholm determinant* of $K(\cdot, \cdot)$

$$B(T) = \lim_{N \to \infty} \prod_{k=1}^N (1 + \lambda_k) \qquad (37)$$

which diverges when $\Sigma_{k=1}^\infty \lambda_k$ diverges. However, since the LR is known to be well defined under the conditions (32) and (33), it must be true that the $\Lambda(T)$ in Price's formula (12) becomes infinite as well, but in such a way that $B^{-1/2}(T) \cdot \exp\{\Lambda(T)\}$ is finite! But how can we express the LR in this case? It turns out that to do this we must again pay attention to the definition of double stochastic integrals, such as in (13) and (17).

In [105], Shepp derived the following formula for the likelihood ratio under the general assumptions (32) and (33):

$$L(T) = \left[\frac{1}{\sqrt{C(T)}} \cdot \exp\{\text{tr}\,\{HK\}\} \right] \cdot \exp\{J(T)\}^{[6]} \qquad (38)$$

where $C(T)$ is the so-called *Fredholm–Carleman determinant* of $K(\cdot, \cdot)$

$$C(T) = \prod_{k=1}^\infty (1 + \lambda_k)e^{-\lambda_k}, \qquad (39)$$

$H(\cdot, \cdot)$ is as in (14), and

$$\text{tr}\,\{HK\} = \sum_{k=1}^\infty \frac{\lambda_k^2}{1 + \lambda_k} = \int_0^T \int_0^T H(t,s)K(s,t)\,dt\,ds. \qquad (40)$$

It can be checked that both $C(T)$ and $\text{tr}\,\{HK\}$ are well defined when $\Sigma_{k=1}^\infty \lambda_k^2 < \infty$, even if $\Sigma_{k=1}^\infty \lambda_k = \infty$. Finally, the operations on the received signal $y(\cdot)$ are given by

$$J(T) = \frac{1}{2} \int_0^T c \int_0^T H(t,s)y(t)y(s)\,dt\,ds. \qquad (41)$$

This looks just like Price's formula (13) for $\Lambda(T)$, except for the "c" between the stochastic integral signs, which Shepp uses to denote what he calls the *centered double Wiener integral*. Instead of defining such integrals (a tutorial presentation can be found in [47, Appendix II.A]), here we shall follow Ito [42] to note that we can write (cf. Price's trick (17))

$$J(T) = \fint_0^T y(t)\,dt \int_0^t H(t,s)y(s)\,ds \qquad (42)$$

where the inner integral is an ordinary white noise (Wiener) integral, but the outer integral is the previously mentioned Ito stochastic integral. In this general case, the corresponding Stratonovich integral does not exist and cannot be used. However, the Stratonovich integral can be used when the

---

[5] Any mathematical model that allows the possibility of zero error probability is clearly inadmissible, since such performance has never been observed in the real world. Nevertheless, it is important to know when an assumed mathematical model will lead to such unrealistic results, and this has been studied by several authors (see, e.g., Root [98] and the references therein). It is surprising that the assumption of additive WGN does not exclude singular cases, and this is a consequence of allowing dependence between $z(\cdot)$ and $v(\cdot)$. We shall discuss the problem of singular detection a bit further in Section III.

[6] It may be of interest to remark that though the likelihood ratio is well defined, it may have infinite variance. In fact, the variance will be infinite if $\Sigma \lambda_k^2 > 1$, whereas for nonsingularity we need only $\Sigma \lambda_k^2 < \infty$ and $\lambda_k > -1$. However, by now the reader should be well accustomed to the idea that infinite-variance random variables are just as acceptable in mathematical models as unbounded-range random variables.

stronger conditions (10) and (11) hold, which can be seen to be equivalent to having $\Sigma_{k=1}^{\infty} \lambda_k < \infty$. So the integral in the Price [94] and Schweppe [101] formulas have to be understood in retrospect as Stratonovich integrals. (This is, of course, not to detract from their work—it took many years for the significance of stochastic integrals to become clear. In fact, Stratonovich was perhaps the first engineering researcher to become aware of the difficulties lurking here, when for example, one of his first papers in this area ([115]) was prefaced by the following footnote, by the editors of the prestigous Russian journal, *Theory of Probability and its Applications:* "Part of the exposition of the problem with continuous time is not wholly convincing. In view of the great interest in the problems raised, this paper is published in the form in which it was submitted by the author." Stratonovich pondered this issue for a few years, and then submitted in January 1963 a paper [116] on stochastic integration that retrospectively clarified several of the deficiencies in his earlier work, not only on nonlinear filtering, but also other of his early work that examined the behavior of solutions of differential equations as the inputs approached pure white Gaussian noise. This latter problem was later studied by Wong and Zakai [137], who were thereby also led to the study of Ito integrals.)

It is a little less evident whether Shepp's general formula can be put into the estimator–correlator form. It turns out that this can be done, and in at least two different ways—see [47]. One is by using several operator-theoretic formulas of Gohberg and Krein [34], [35]; another is via closer analysis of stochastic processes having a white Gaussian noise component. The second route is more far-reaching since it also allows us to extend the estimator–correlator formula to non-Gaussian processes. However, to obtain the estimator–correlator interpretation, it is necessary to assume that the signal process $z(\cdot)$ is either completely independent of the noise $v(\cdot)$ or at least that future $v(\cdot)$ are independent of past $z(\cdot)$; the latter assumption allows the signal to depend upon past observations, as in feedback communications and control enviroments.

C. Innovations, Sigma Fields, and Martingales

Let us return to the Gaussian signal and white Gaussian noise model (30)–(33), recall the definitions (14) and (20) of the functions $H(\cdot, \cdot)$ and $h(\cdot, \cdot)$, and introduce the so-called *innovations* process

$$i(t) = y(t) - \int_0^t h(t,s)y(s)\,ds$$
$$= v(t) + z(t) - \int_0^t h(t,s)y(s)\,ds. \qquad (43)$$

Then some patient calculation (see [45, Appendix II]) will show that the process $i(\cdot)$ is also white with the same covariance function as $v(\cdot)$, i.e.,

$$E\{i(t)i(s)\} = \delta(t-s) = E\{v(t)v(s)\}. \qquad (44)$$

But this raises a fundamental question: $v(\cdot)$ and $i(\cdot)$ are Gaussian processes with the same mean and covariance, and so by the traditional definition of stochastic processes via a family of joint probability densities, they should be the same

stochastic process, which they are clearly not. So how we can distinguish them? For this, we need to introduce the concepts of sigma fields and martingales.

However, to first bring ourselves closer to the traditional stochastic formulations, we avoid the white noise by working with the integrated processes

$$Y(t) = \int_0^t y(s)\,ds = \int_0^t z(s)\,ds + W(t), \qquad 0 \le t \le T$$
$$(45)$$

where $W(\cdot)$ is a Wiener process, i.e., a Gaussian process such that

$$W(0) = 0, \ E\{W(t)\} \equiv 0, \ \text{and} \ E\{W(t)W(s)\} = \min\{t,s\}. \qquad (46)$$

Among the many properties of such processes we note especially that $W(\cdot)$ has independent increments, and that its sample functions are continuous but of unbounded variation. We also assume that the signal process is either completely independent of $W(\cdot)$ or at least that future increments of $W(\cdot)$ are independent of past $W(\cdot)$ and past $z(\cdot)$. Similarly, (44) means that the integrated form of (43)

$$I(t) = Y(t) - \int_0^t h(t,s)\,dY(s)$$
$$= W(t) + \int_0^t z(s)\,ds - \int_0^t h(t,s)\,dY(s) \qquad (47)$$

also defines a Wiener process with the same covariance function as $W(\cdot)$.

Now, of course, the joint density functions of the process $W(\cdot)$ and $I(\cdot)$ are all well defined, and are identical, so we are left with the same question—how can we distinguish $I(\cdot)$ from $W(\cdot)$? A clue can be obtained by noting that there is no hope of recovering the process $W(\cdot)$ knowing only $Y(\cdot)$, whereas $I(\cdot)$ is completely determined by $Y(\cdot)$. In fact, for every $t \in [0,T]$, $I(t)$ is determined by only the *past* values of $Y(\cdot)$: $\{Y(s), s \le t\}$.

The appropriate probabilistic formalism for this idea is to introduce the concept of sigma fields generated by random variables. Many readers are no doubt familiar with this concept, but for others and for convenience, we hurriedly (and somewhat imprecisely) recall the following facts and definitions; for more, see, e.g., the books of Bremaud [15], Karatzas and Shreve [57], Revuz and Yor [97], or Wong and Hajek [138]. We start, in a standard notation, with a probability space $(\Omega, \mathcal{F}, P)$, consisting of a sample space Ω, a class $\mathcal{F}$ of events, and a probability distribution P. For a real-valued function X on the sample space, the *sigma field generated by X* (denoted by $\sigma(X)$) is the collection of all subsets of Ω obtained by the standard Boolean operations on all elementary sets in Ω that are mapped by X into intervals of the real line. We are interested in the situation in which X is a random variable—that is, in which $\sigma(X)$ is a subset of $\mathcal{F}$. We extend this concept to introduce sigma fields generated by collections of random variables, e.g., for fixed $t \in [0,T]$

$$\mathcal{F}_t = \sigma\{Y(s); 0 \le s \le t\} \qquad (48)$$

194

and the "bigger" sigma field

$$\mathcal{B}_t = \sigma\{z(s), W(s); 0 \le s \le t\}. \qquad (49)$$

Increasing families of sigma fields, such as those generated by (48) and (49) as t ranges from 0 to T, are called *filtrations*. Heuristically, filtrations capture the notion of (increasing) information patterns—the filtration $\{\mathcal{F}_t\}$ describes the information available from knowledge of the process $Y(\cdot)$ as it evolves in time, while the filtration $\{\mathcal{B}_t\}$ describes the greater amount of information available from knowledge of the processes $z(\cdot)$ and $W(\cdot)$ that combine, as in (45), to give the process $Y(\cdot)$. Next, we say that a random variable, say X, is *measurable* with respect to a sigma field, such as $\mathcal{F}_t = \sigma\{Y(s), s \le t\}$, if $\sigma(X)$ is a subset of that sigma field. Heuristically, measurability of X with respect to the sigma field generated by a set of random variables means that X can be written as a (nice) function of the random variables; we indicate this by $X \in \mathcal{F}_t$, in the given situation. A stochastic process, say $\{X(t); t \ge 0\}$, is said to be *adapted* to a filtration, say $\{\mathcal{B}_t, t \ge 0\}$, if $X(t) \in \mathcal{B}_t$, for all $t \ge 0$. (As noted by Revuz and Yor [97] and others, it is the introduction of a filtration that allows for t to be thought of as time. For example, for stationary processes, where the probabilistic laws are the same for all t, it is the fact that $X(t) \in \mathcal{B}_t$ that places the event in time.)

Finally, we introduce the very fruitful notion of a *martingale* stochastic process, whose definition is linked to the specification of a filtration. Given a filtration, say $\{\mathcal{G}_t\}$, we say that $\{X(t); t \ge 0\}$ is a $\mathcal{G}_t$-martingale if $X(t) \in \mathcal{G}_t$ for all $t \ge 0$, and if $E\{X(t)|\mathcal{G}_s\} = X(s)$ for all $0 \le s \le t < \infty$. A martingale process, say $X(\cdot)$, is always a martingale with respect to its natural filtration $\sigma\{X(s); 0 \le s \le t\}$. However, if say $\mathcal{B}_t \supseteq \mathcal{G}_t$ defines a larger filtration, there is no reason that the $\mathcal{G}_t$-martingale $X(\cdot)$ should be a $\mathcal{B}_t$-martingale.

With these concepts we now return to our signal-plus-noise model (45), where we have the two natural filtrations, $\mathcal{F}_t$ and $\mathcal{B}_t$ as defined in (48) and (49). Our assumption that the Wiener process $W(\cdot)$ has independent increments and that $W(t) - W(s)$ is independent of $\{W(\tau), z(\tau); 0 \le \tau \le s < t\}$ means that $W(\cdot)$ is a $\mathcal{B}_t$-martingale, i.e., by assumption

$$E\{W(t)|\mathcal{B}_s\} = W(s), \qquad s < t. \qquad (50a)$$

However, unless $z(\cdot) \equiv 0$, $W(\cdot)$ is *not* an $\mathcal{F}_t$ martingale; i.e.,

$$E\{W(t)|\mathcal{F}_s\} \ne W(s). \qquad (50b)$$

On the other hand, we can readily check that under the assumptions on $z(\cdot)$ and $W(\cdot)$, the process $I(\cdot)$ reverses these properties

$$E\{I(t)|\mathcal{F}_s\} = I(s), \quad s < t, \quad \text{and} \quad E\{I(t)|\mathcal{B}_s\} \ne I(s). \quad (50c)$$

In other words, though $W(\cdot)$ and $I(\cdot)$ have the same mean value and covariance functions, they can have different properties with respect to different filtrations.

D. Non-Gaussian Stochastic Signals

A striking fact is that the above discussion also applies to the much more general scenario where the signal process $z(\cdot)$ is not necessarily Gaussian, but is such that

$$E\left\{\int_0^T |z(t)| \, dt\right\} < \infty \qquad (51)$$

and that[7]

$$W(t) - W(s) \text{ is independent of } \sigma\{Y(\tau), 0 \le \tau \le s\} \quad (52)$$

for all $t > s \ge 0$. In the non-Gaussian case, the estimate is taken to be the conditional expectation

$$\hat{z}(t) = E\{z(t)|\mathcal{F}_t\} \qquad (53)$$

which is well known to provide the minimum mean-square-error estimate of $z(t)$ given $\mathcal{F}_t = \sigma\{Y(s), s \le t\}$. When $\{z(\cdot), W(\cdot)\}$ are jointly Gaussian, $\hat{z}(\cdot)$ is a linear functional of past $y(\cdot)$, but in general it can be a highly nonlinear functional of the (non-Gaussian) process $Y(\cdot)$. Nevertheless, it turns out that the innovations process

$$I(t) = Y(t) - \int_0^t \hat{z}(s) \, ds \qquad (54)$$

is always a (Gaussian) Wiener process, and with the same statistics as the Wiener process $W(\cdot)$, i.e.,

$$E\{I(t)\} = 0 \quad \text{and} \quad E\{I(t)I(s)\} = \min\{t, s\}. \quad (55)$$

However, the distinction is that the process $I(\cdot)$ is an $\mathcal{F}_t$ martingale, while $W(\cdot)$ is a martingale with respect to the bigger sigma fields, $\mathcal{B}_t = \sigma\{z(s), W(s); 0 \le s \le t\}$.

The fact that though $z(\cdot)$ is non-Gaussian, $I(\cdot)$ is Gaussian is quite surprising. We can get some insight into this fact by noting that it is not hard to show by a direct calculation (see, e.g., [89, pp. 317–319]) that $E\{I(t)I(s)\} = \min\{t, s\}$, so that $I(\cdot)$ has uncorrelated increments. Since $I(\cdot)$ clearly also has continuous paths, we can write $I(t) = \Sigma \, [I(t_{i+1}^{(n)}) - I(t_i^{(n)})]$ and get many terms by refining the partition

$$0 \le t_1^{(n)} \le \cdots \le t_n^{(n)} = t.$$

So it appears that a central-limit-theorem type of argument applies to make $I(\cdot)$ Gaussian. Unfortunately, the central limit theorem does not apply to general sums of uncorrelated random variables. The fact that saves the situation is that $I(\cdot)$ is a martingale process, and the central limit theorem does apply to sums of martingale differences! This is only one of the many remarkable properties of martingales.

The original rigorous proof of the Gaussian nature of the innovations process was based (see [46]) on an early martingale theorem of Lévy (see [22, p. 384]) that needed the

---

[7]By the independence of a random variable from a sigma field, we mean that the random variable is independent of all random variables that are measurable with respect to the sigma field, or equivalently of the collection of random variables that generate the sigma field.

stronger (though still very reasonable) assumption than (51) that

$$E\left\{\int_0^T |z(t)|^2\, dt\right\} < \infty. \qquad (56)$$

However, there has been remarkable progress in martingale theory, and the closely related theory of stochastic integrals, especially since 1967, through the work of P. A. Meyer, H. Kunita, S. Watanabe, and many others, which has led to stronger and more easily proved results that enable us to use the weaker condition (51). Unfortunately, there is no elementary engineering treatment of these matters, though see Bremaud [15] and Wong and Hajek [138]; very clear but more mathematical expositions can be found in the books of Revuz and Yor [97], Dellacherie and Meyer [20], and the lecture notes of Meyer [71].

To cite the result we need for the proof, we define for any (finite-variance) process $M(\cdot)$ its *quadratic variation* as

$$[M, M]_t = \lim \sum [M(t_{i+1}^{(n)}) - M(t_i^{(n)})]^2 \qquad (57)$$

where $0 \le t_1^{(n)} \le \cdots \le t_n^{(n)} = t$ is a partition of the interval $[0, t]$. The limit is taken in probability as $\max |t_{i+1}^{(n)} - t_i^{(n)}| \to 0$. It is not hard to see that processes with continuous sample functions of bounded variation (e.g., differentiable) will have zero quadratic variation. On the other hand, the Wiener process has continuous paths, but

$$[W, W]_t = t \qquad (58)$$

from which it can be shown that its paths are not of bounded variation. To prove (58), we can check that

$$E\left\{ \left(\sum [W(t_{i+1}^{(n)}) - W(t_i^{(n)})]^2 - \sum (t_{i+1}^{(n)} - t_i^{(n)}) \right)^2 \right\}$$
$$= 2\sum [t_{i+1}^{(n)} - t_i^{(n)}]^2 \le 2t \max |t_{i+1}^{(n)} - t_i^{(n)}| \qquad (59)$$

which tends to zero as $\max |t_{i+1}^{(n)} - t_i^{(n)}| \to 0$.

(The relation (58) can be written symbolically as $dW(t) \sim O(\sqrt{dt})$ which is the reason that (Ito) stochastic integrals obey somewhat different rules than in the ordinary calculus where $df(t) \sim f'(t)\, dt \sim O(dt)$. In particular, the Taylor expansion of $W^2(t)$ has the form

$$W^2(t) = W^2(0) + 2W(t)\, dW(t) + \tfrac{1}{2} \cdot 2 \cdot (dW(t))^2 + o(dt)$$

leading to

$$2\int_0^t W(\tau)\, dW(\tau) = \int_0^t dW^2(\tau) - \int_0^t d\tau$$

which is the Ito integral formula noted earlier in (29).)

We can now state the very nice generalization of Lévy's theorem as given by Kunita and Watanabe in [63]—namely: *any continuous martingale with quadratic variation $\sigma^2 t$ must be a Wiener process with covariance function $\sigma^2 \min\{t, s\}$.* The proof of this result is also much simpler than that of the original, though we shall forego it here. Instead, we return to the innovations process

$$I(t) = Y(t) - \int_0^t \hat{z}(s)\, ds \qquad (60)$$

which, using (45), we can also rewrite as

$$I(t) = \int_0^t \tilde{z}(s)\, ds + W(t) \qquad \tilde{z}(t) = z(t) - \hat{z}(t). \qquad (61)$$

It is now easy to check that $I(\cdot)$ is an $\{\mathcal{F}_t\}$ martingale, since for $\tau < t$

$$E\{I(t)|\mathcal{F}_\tau\}$$
$$= I(\tau) + E\left\{\int_0^t [\tilde{z}(s)\, ds + dW(s)]|\mathcal{F}_\tau\right\}$$
$$= I(\tau) + \int_\tau^t E\{E\{\tilde{z}(s)|\mathcal{F}_s\}|\mathcal{F}_\tau\}\, ds$$
$$\quad + E\{W(t) - W(\tau)|\mathcal{F}_\tau\}$$
$$= I(\tau) + \int_\tau^t 0\, ds + E\{\{W(t) - W(\tau)|\mathcal{B}_\tau\}|\mathcal{F}_\tau\}$$
$$= I(\tau) + 0 + 0.$$

Moreover, the quadratic variation of $I(\cdot)$ is clearly the same as that of $Y(\cdot)$, which is the same as that of $W(\cdot)$, viz.,

$$[I, I]_t = [Y, Y]_t = [W, W]_t = t. \qquad (62)$$

Therefore, by the (generalized) Lévy theorem, $I(\cdot)$ is a Wiener process.

This result on the innovations leads us to the following generalization of the earlier estimator–correlator formulas. Consider the problem of choosing between the hypotheses (where we now return for consistency with earlier formulas to the nonintegrated form)

$$H_0: y(t) = v(t), \qquad 0 \le t \le T$$

versus

$$H_1: y(t) = z(t) + v(t), \qquad 0 \le t \le T \qquad (63)$$

where $v(\cdot)$ is zero-mean, unit intensity white *Gaussian* noise, while the signal is an arbitrary random process with almost all sample functions having finite energy, and such that the future of $v(\cdot)$ is independent of the past and present of $z(\cdot)$. Then it turns out that the likelihood ratio can be written as

$$L(T) = \exp\left\{ \fint_0^T \hat{z}_1(t) y(t)\, dt - \frac{1}{2}\int_0^T \hat{z}_1^2(t)\, dt \right\} \qquad (64)$$

where $\fint$ denotes the Ito stochastic integral and

$$\hat{z}_1(t) = E\{z(t)|y(s); 0 \le s < t, H_1\}. \qquad (65)$$

(Some technical issues have been ignored here—see [49] for a precise statement.)

This result includes as special case all the results stated earlier, e.g., the case (see (6)–(8)) of known signals with random phase

$$z(t) = A(t)\cos(\omega_0 t + \theta + \Phi(t)) \qquad p(0) = \frac{1}{2\pi} \qquad (66)$$

for which the LR was earlier expressed as (see (7) and (8))

$$L(T) = e^{-E/2} I_0([V_c^2(\tau) + V_s^2(\tau)]^{1/2}). \qquad (67)$$

The equivalence proceeds by first showing that the conditional expectation is

$$\hat{z}_1(t) = A(t) \cdot \frac{I_1(V(t))}{I_0(V(t))} \cdot \cos\left(\omega_0 t + \tan^{-1}\frac{V_s(t)}{V_c(t)}\right) \quad (68)$$

applying the rules of the Ito calculus, and then using some Bessel function identities to show the equivalence of (67) and (68). The details of the calculation and several other examples, can be found in [46].

Of course in this example, it is easier to compute $L(T)$ via the special formula (67) than via the general estimator-correlator formula; so also for several other special cases. However, we should remember that there is only a handful of cases where explicit LR formulas can be obtained; in all cases, however, the general formula suggest an implementation in the universal structure of a signal estimator followed by a correlator. This structure has other advantages. For example, if $\hat{z}_1(\cdot)$ cannot be computed, or if it is very complicated, we can use an approximation instead; this can also be done when our knowledge of $z(\cdot)$ is so limited that we cannot compute the LR via any direct formula.

A plausibility argument for the form of the result (64) can be based on the fact established above that the innovations process $I(\cdot)$ is a Wiener process, or equivalently that its derivative $i(\cdot)$ is a white Gaussian noise with the same intensity as $v(\cdot)$. Now, we first rewrite the expression

$$I(t) = Y(t) - \int_0^t \hat{z}(s)\,ds \quad (69)$$

as

$$i(t) = y(t) - \hat{z}(t) \quad (70)$$

or, equivalently,

$$y(t) = \hat{z}(t) + i(t). \quad (71)$$

Then the facts that $i(\cdot)$ is white Gaussian noise with the same intensity as $v(\cdot)$, and that future $i(\cdot)$ are independent of past $\hat{z}(\cdot)$, suggest that the original hypotheses

$$H_0: y(t) = v(t) \text{ versus } H_1: y(t) = z(t) + v(t) \quad (72)$$

can be rewritten as

$$H_0: y(t) = i(t) \text{ versus } H_1: y(t) = \hat{z}(t) + i(t). \quad (73)$$

In the latter form, though the signal $\hat{z}(\cdot)$ is random, it is a function of past $y(\cdot)$ and therefore it is known when $y(\cdot)$ is known. Therefore, the hypotheses (73) have the form of a "(conditionally) known signal in WGN" problem, for which the LR is given by the formula (64). Of course, there is much to fill in this intuitive argument, which, for instance, does not explain the need for having Ito integrals in the formula.

A rigorous (so-called 4-step) proof of (67) making much use of the then relatively new results of Kunita and Watanabe [63], as well as the innovations and the now widely used result of Girsanov [33], was given in [47]. (See, also, [89, pp. 319–322].)

Here we go briefly to a discussion of signal detection for Poisson-related processes, as encountered, for example, in optical communications. However, it will be a useful preliminary

to that discussion to note that the first estimator-correlator results for non-Gaussian signals were in fact obtained by Stratonovich and Sosulin for non-Gaussian Markov $z(\cdot)$, independent of $v(\cdot)$. The reason for this assumption is that we can then first assume that $z(\cdot)$ is known, so that the usual formula (3) applies, and then average over $z(\cdot)$, i.e.,

$$L(T) = E_{z(\cdot)}\left\{\exp\left\{\int_0^T z(t)y(t)\,dt - \tfrac{1}{2}\int_0^T z^2(t)\,dt\right\}\right\}. \quad (74)$$

Then some formal manipulation led them to the estimator-correlator formula, including a version for the Stratonovich integral. In his Ph.D. dissertation, T. E. Duncan (see, e.g., [23]) gave a more elegant derivation by applying the Ito calculus to (74). However, the point is that starting with (74) precludes the assumption of any dependence between the signal and even past noise. To handle the general case, martingale theory seems to be essential. We shall see this even more clearly in the case of Poisson-related processes.

E. Randomly Modulated Jump Processes

Processes with jumps arise when "events" occur at random times and the observation process keeps current count of the number and size of these events. An "event" can be, for example, the arrival of a charged particle at a detector, the failure of a machine, the arrival of a data packet at a node in a communication network, or a transportation accident. In most of these examples, the "signal" of interest modulates the rate and size of the occurring events. For example, in optical communications, the signal modulates the rate of arrival of photons at a photodetector. We can model this situation as follows: given a stochastic process $\lambda(\cdot)$, the observations form a counting process which is Poisson with rate (or intensity) $\lambda(\cdot)$

$$P(N(t) - N(s) = n|\lambda) = \frac{\int_s^t \lambda(\tau)\,d\tau}{n!}\exp\left\{-\int_s^t \lambda(\tau)\,d\tau\right\}. \quad (75)$$

When $\lambda(\cdot)$ is deterministic, $N(\cdot)$ is just a (nonhomogeneous) Poisson process; when $\lambda(\cdot)$ is stochastic, N is often called a "doubly stochastic" Poisson process. In this model, the signal determines the rate $\lambda(\cdot)$. For example, when there is "no signal," the rate may be constant, $\lambda(\cdot) \equiv 1$, say, while "with signal," the rate may be a stochastic process, e.g., Gaussian and diffusion processes, such as are assumed by Snyder [111]. However, this model can break down when the signal $\lambda(\cdot)$ can depend on the observations, as, for example, when the arrival of a particle at a counter blanks out the counter for a fixed or random period of time.

It appears that the most general models for counting processes, as well as for more complex processes with jumps of various sizes, are obtained via martingale theory. P. Bremaud was the pioneer in this field, followed by A. Segall, M. H. A. Davis, and then many others. A textbook by Bremaud [15] and [102] present readable accounts of those developments.

A nice consequence, as we shall see, of using the martingale approach is that the very non-Gaussian (sort of "multiplicative" noise) problems of jump processes can be made similar to the familiar "signal in additive WGN" problems. The key fact is the so-called Meyer–Doob decomposition theorem of martingale theory, which when applied to a counting process $N(\cdot)$ states that we can uniquely decompose it as

$$N(t) = A(t) + M(t) \qquad (76)$$

where $M(\cdot)$ is a martingale with respect to a filtration $\{\mathcal{B}_t\}$, and $A(\cdot)$ is an increasing, right-continuous so-called $\mathcal{B}_t$-predictable process, i.e., roughly speaking, the value $A(t)$ is completely determined from knowledge of $\{\mathcal{B}_s, s < t\}$. On the other hand, $M(\cdot)$ being a $\mathcal{B}_t$-martingale means that its future increments are completely unpredictable from past $\mathcal{B}$, i.e., $E\{M(t) - M(s)|\mathcal{B}_s\} = 0$. So what we have is a decomposition of $N(\cdot)$ into a smooth "signal" part $A(\cdot)$ and an additive noise part $M(\cdot)$. To get more insight into this decomposition, assume that (with some loss of generality—see [102]) $A(\cdot)$ can be written as

$$A(t) = \int_0^t \lambda(\tau) \, d\tau. \qquad (77)$$

Then if $\lambda(\cdot)$ is deterministic, it turns out that the counting process $N(\cdot)$ is just a Poisson process with (nonhomogenous) intensity $\lambda(\cdot)$. However, $\lambda(\cdot)$ can be stochastic, and may depend upon past $N(\cdot)$—it is called the *stochastic rate* or intensity of $N(\cdot)$, and $A(\cdot)$ is known as the integrated rate. (Reference [102] gives an example of a simple counting process for which only $A(\cdot)$ exists and not $\lambda(\cdot)$).

The martingale method can be extended to more general jump processes. But here we note only the "estimator–correlator" type of solution that it leads to for a detection problem with the hypotheses

$$H_0 : N(t) - t = M(t)$$

versus

$$H_1 : N(t) - \int_0^t \lambda(\tau) \, d\tau = M(t) \qquad (78)$$

where $M(\cdot)$ is, as above, a martingale with respect to a filtration $\{\mathcal{B}_t\}$.

When $\lambda(\cdot)$ is deterministic, we have a "Poisson" detection problem, for which the likelihood ratio is readily computed to be (see, e.g., [111], [112])

$$L(T) = \exp\left\{ \int_0^T \log \lambda(t) \, dN(t) - \int_0^T (\lambda(t) - 1) \, dt \right\}. \qquad (79)$$

But what if $\lambda(\cdot)$ is stochastic? If $\lambda(\cdot)$ is completely independent of $N(\cdot)$, then we could average the above expression over $\lambda(\cdot)$ and get explicit answers in some cases [111]. However, it turns out that in the general case, providing $\lambda(\cdot)$ is $\mathcal{B}_t$-predictable, we have the following generalized estimator-correlator formula:

$$L(T) = \exp\left\{ \int_0^T \log \hat{\lambda}_1(t^-) \, dN(t) - \int_0^T (\hat{\lambda}_1(t^-) - 1) \, dt \right\} \qquad (80)$$

where

$$\hat{\lambda}_1(t^-) = \lim_{s \to t} \hat{\lambda}_1(s) \qquad (81)$$

with

$$\hat{\lambda}_1(t) = E_1\{\lambda(t)|\mathcal{F}_t\} \quad \text{and} \quad \mathcal{F}_t = \sigma\{N(\tau), \tau \le t\}. \qquad (82)$$

(The subscript 1 denotes expectation taken under the model of hypothesis H_1.) In other words, when $\lambda(\cdot)$ is stochastic, we first determine $\hat{\lambda}_1(t^-)$, the predictable version of the optimal least squares estimate of $\lambda(\cdot)$ given past observations of $N(\cdot)$ and assuming that H_1 holds (i.e., that $N(\cdot)$ has the form (78)) and then use it in the known intensity formula (79).

The proof of this result, as well as those for more general jump processes can be obtained by using a 4-step proof along exactly the same lines as in the Gaussian noise case—using a Girsanov-type theorem, the innovations, and further results from discontinuous martingale theory—see [103].

As with the earlier formula (64), the value of this result is structural in that it suggest that one can replace the usual uncomputable $\hat{\lambda}_1(t^-)$ by the best available estimator. In fact, Davis and Andreadakis [19] were able to provide an explicit example of the value of this philosophy. They considered a so-called Poisson disorder problem where the stochastic intensity has the form

$$\lambda(t) = \lambda_0 + (\lambda_1 - \lambda_0)u(t - \theta) \qquad (83)$$

where $u(\cdot)$ denotes the unit step function and θ is a random variable (a "change point") that is zero with a fixed probability is otherwise exponentially distributed. In this problem, it turns out that the optimal least squares estimate $\hat{\lambda}_1(\cdot)$ can be found exactly, as well as the suboptimal linear least squares estimate, so that a comparison could be made using both estimates in (80). However, it turns out that there was little difference in performance between using these two different estimates; although, interestingly, it is important to use $\hat{\lambda}_1(t^-)$ rather than $\hat{\lambda}_1(t)$. For more on how these conclusions were reached, we refer to the paper [19]. (Disorder problems will be discussed further in Section V-B.)

III. DETECTION OF SIGNALS IN COLORED GAUSSIAN NOISE

In the preceeding sections, we have studied problems with additive white Gaussian noise because, in our opinion at least, this is the appropriate model for the majority of practical problems. Of course, we may have colored noise plus additive white Gaussian noise, but this case can be reduced to the earlier cases by using the chain rule for likelihood ratios [89].

However there can be problems in which likelihood ratios are used to solve other mathematical problems, e.g., evaluation of zero-crossing probabilities, stochastic integrals, etc. For this, and other reasons, in this section we briefly review problems with colored Gaussian noise. Among these other reasons we cite first of all the fact that there is a considerable engineering literature on this problem. Secondly, it turns out that many of the results of Section II can actually be extended to the colored noise case by a simple conceptual change: replacing the usual inner products by inner products in a special reproducing kernel Hilbert space (RKHS). The importance of such spaces for detection problems (and related stochastic problems) was strongly emphasized by E. Parzen ([81]–[83]; these and other papers appear in the reprint volume [135]). Because RKHS's are much less familiar than the Hilbert space $L_2(T)$ of square-integrable functions over $[0, T]$, they have often been avoided as being too abstract. However, we hope to show here how naturally they arise by introducing them via the same kind of geometric argument used in the white noise case by Kotel'nikov [62], and since then widely exposed through the textbook of Wozencraft and Jacobs [141]. We begin, however, with the traditional mathematical approach, going back to Grenander's 1950 paper [36], using the Karhunen–Loéve expansion.

A. The Integral Equation Approach

Consider the hypotheses

$$H_0: y(t) = n(t), \qquad 0 \leq t \leq T$$

versus

$$H_1: y(t) = m(t) + n(t), \qquad 0 \leq t \leq T \qquad (84)$$

where $m(\cdot)$ is a completely known signal and $n(\cdot)$ is a zero-mean Gaussian process with

$$E\{n(t)n(s)\} = R(t, s), \text{ continuous in } t, s \text{ on } [0, T] \times [0, T]. \qquad (85)$$

A natural idea for approaching this problem, especially after its successful application by Bode and Shannon [14] and Zadeh and Ragazzini [143] for linear prediction and filtering, is to use whitening filters. However, these are difficult to find for processes defined over a finite interval; satisfactory solutions were only found much later, essentially by assuming state-space structure for $n(\cdot)$ and $R(\cdot, \cdot)$ (see, e.g., Kailath, Geesey, and Weinert [52]). So, following Grenander [36], the most popular method has been to use Karhunen–Loève expansions. Briefly, one expands the signal and noise in the basis of eigenfunctions of $R(t, s)$

$$\int_0^T R(t, s)\psi_k(s)\, ds = \lambda_k \psi_k(t), \qquad t \in [0, T]. \qquad (86)$$

The corresponding Karhunen–Loève expansion

$$n(t) = \sum_{k=1}^\infty n_k \psi_k(t) \qquad n_k = \int_0^T n(t)\psi_k(t)\, dt \qquad (87)$$

is popular because of the double orthogonality

$$\int_0^T \psi_k(t)\psi_\ell(t)\, dt = \delta_{k\ell} \quad \text{and} \quad E\{n_k n_\ell\} = \lambda_k \delta_{k\ell}. \qquad (88)$$

Now, the original hypotheses can be rewritten, in an obvious notation, as

$$H_0: y_k = n_k, \qquad 1 \leq k < \infty$$

versus

$$H_1: y_k = m_k + n_k, \qquad 1 \leq k < \infty \qquad (89)$$

and we can exploit the above-noted orthogonality to obtain the likelihood ratio as

$$L(T) = \exp\left\{ \sum_{k=1}^\infty \frac{m_k y_k}{\lambda_k} - \frac{1}{2} \sum_{k=1}^\infty \frac{m_k^2}{\lambda_k} \right\}. \qquad (90)$$

The case of unit intensity white noise corresponds formally to a "limiting" case in which $\lambda_k \equiv 1$, so that

$$L(T) = \exp\left\{ \sum_{k=1}^\infty m_k y_k - \frac{1}{2} \sum_{k=1}^\infty m_k^2 \right\} \qquad (91)$$

$$= \exp\left\{ \int_0^T m(t)y(t)\, dt - \frac{1}{2} \int_0^T m^2(t)\, dt \right\} \qquad (92)$$

as expected.

In the white-noise case, the probability of correct detection depends only upon the signal energy, $\sum_{k=1}^\infty m_k^2$. However, when the noise is colored, it is the weighted energy $\sum_{k=1}^\infty m_k^2/\lambda_k$ that determines the detectability, and it was noted by Grenander that even though $\sum_{k=1}^\infty m_k^2 < \infty$, we could have $\sum_{k=1}^\infty m_k^2/\lambda_k = \infty$, in which case the decisions could be made with zero probability of error! The underlying reason is not hard to see, especially if we consider the case of very large T and stationary noise, in which case standard arguments show that, in an obvious notation,

$$\sum_{k=1}^\infty \frac{m_k^2}{\lambda_k} \equiv \int_{-\infty}^\infty \frac{|M(f)|^2}{S_n(f)}\, df. \qquad (93)$$

So divergence of $\sum_{k=1}^\infty m_k^2/\lambda_k$ means essentially that the noise spectrum falls off no slower than the signal spectrum at high frequencies—not generally a realistic assumption. The point is that, while zero error probability can never be achieved in any real problem, we may, in seeking maximum generality, set up a mathematical model that admits such singular behavior. This is one more reason for including a white-noise component to prevent the exact mathematical solution from trying to exploit the specified, but poorly known, high frequency properties of the noise. (A caution: as we noted in Section II-B, just adding white noise may not be enough when the signal is random; then more assumptions are necessary to avoid the possibility of singular detection.)

Assuming that $\sum_{k=1}^\infty m_k^2/\lambda_k < \infty$, the next step is to try to replace the difficult-to-use infinite series in (90) by integrals, as was done in going from (91) and (92). To do this we define

$$a(t) = \sum_{k=1}^\infty a_k \psi_k(t), \qquad a_k = m_k/\lambda_k \qquad (94)$$

which leads from (90) to

$$L(T) = \exp\left\{ \int_0^T a(t)y(t)\, dt - \frac{1}{2} \int_0^T m(t)a(t)\, dt \right\}. \qquad (95)$$

Moreover, note that $a(\cdot)$ also satisfies the relation

$$\int_0^T R(t, s)a(s)\, ds = \sum_{k=1}^\infty a_k \int_0^T R(t, s)\psi_k(s)\, ds$$

$$= \sum_{k=1}^\infty \frac{m_k}{\lambda_k}\lambda_k \psi_k(t) = m(t). \qquad (96)$$

As in the white noise case, the basic operation on the data is a correlation operation, but now between $y(\cdot)$ and $a(\cdot)$ rather than between $y(\cdot)$ and $m(\cdot)$; equivalently, we could use a filter matched to $a(\cdot)$. The question is: what does $a(\cdot)$ look like? For very large T, we have $\mathcal{F}\{a(\cdot)\} = A(f) \rightarrow M(f)/S_n(f)$, a reasonable expression which again shows the importance of having the signal spectrum fall off faster than the noise spectrum. Unfortunately, for finite T, the situation is much less pleasing. First is the issue of the rather cavalier way in which we went from infinite sums in (90) to the integrals in (95). If at least

$$\int_0^T a^2(t)\, dt = \sum_{k=1}^{\infty} a_k^2 = \sum_{k=1}^{\infty} \frac{m_k^2}{\lambda_k^2} < \infty \qquad (97)$$

then one might hope that the above all goes through rigorously, and in fact this is not hard to show, as was done by Grenander in [36]. Unfortunately, the condition (97) is far too restrictive. The problem is that, when $R(t,s)$ is a smooth function, the integral equation (96) can map very ill-behaved functions $a(\cdot)$ into smooth functions $m(\cdot)$. For example, when

$$R(t,s) = \frac{\alpha}{2} e^{-\alpha|t-s|} \qquad (98)$$

the solution of the integral equation (96) can be shown, with some effort, to be (the dots indicate differentiation)

$$\alpha^2 a(t) = \alpha^2 m(t) - \ddot{m}(t) + [\alpha m(0) - \dot{m}(0)]\delta(t) + [\alpha m(T) + \dot{m}(T)]\delta(t-T) \qquad (99)$$

a solution hard to obtain (or approximate) by any numerical method of solving the integral equation! On the other hand, if $R(\cdot,\cdot)$ has a delta-function component, the class of solutions $\{a(\cdot)\}$ will be the same as the class of given functions $\{m(\cdot)\}$, and much more amenable to numerical determination: this is again a major reason for the use of additive white noise in the model. For another reason, note that for large α in (99) we have $a(\cdot) \doteq m(\cdot)$, as expected; the point is not only that the answer becomes indifferent to the exact value of α (if it is large enough), but that if we are really indifferent to the details of the high frequency behavior, we should make the physically incorrect but mathematically simpler assumption that the noise is white (see also [88]).

If one, for whatever reason, really needs to work with the pure colored noise problem, then considerable effort will be required to properly define the conditions on $R(\cdot,\cdot)$ and on the family of solutions $\{a(\cdot)\}$ that allow formula (95) to be rigorously established. Kadota [43] establishes a very general result in this direction, as does Pitcher [87]. However, it turns out that an alternative way of attacking this problem avoids the above difficulties by introducing some useful new mathematical concepts that, in fact, can yield better physical implementations. This approach can be motivated by trying to extend the geometric formulation used by Kotel'nikov and others for the white noise case [44].

B. A Geometric Formulation and Reproducing Kernel Hilbert Spaces

In the geometric approach, one seeks to "project" the noise $n(\cdot)$ onto the linear space spanned by the signal $m(\cdot)$ in such a way that

$$n(\cdot) = n_1 m(\cdot) + n_{\text{rem}}(\cdot) \qquad (100)$$

where n_1 is a finite-variance random variable (r.v.) obtained by linear operations on $n(\cdot)$ that is independent of $n_{\text{rem}}(\cdot)$. That is, since the noise is Gaussian, we must have

$$0 = E\{n_1 n_{\text{rem}}(t)\} = E\{n_1[n(t) - n_1 m(t)]\} \qquad (101)$$

or

$$E\{n_1 n(t)\} = E\{n_1^2\} m(t), \qquad t \in [0, T]. \qquad (102)$$

If this can be done we can similarly decompose $m(\cdot)$ and $y(\cdot)$ as

$$m(t) = 1 \cdot m(t) + m_{\text{rem}}(t) \quad \text{and} \quad y(t) = y_1 m(t) + y_{\text{rem}}(t). \qquad (103)$$

Clearly, $m_{\text{rem}}(t) \equiv 0$, while under both hypotheses H_0 and H_1, we will have $y_{\text{rem}}(\cdot) = n_{\text{rem}}(\cdot)$. Therefore, $y_{\text{rem}}(\cdot)$ is irrelevant to the statistical problem of choosing between H_0 and H_1, leading to the one-dimensional detection problem

$$H_0: y_1 = n_1$$

versus

$$H_1: y_1 = 1 + n_1 \qquad (104)$$

with likelihood ratio

$$L(T) = \exp\left\{ -\frac{(y_1 - 1)^2 - y_1^2}{2E\{n_1^2\}} \right\} = \exp\left\{ \frac{2y_1 - 1}{2E\{n_1^2\}} \right\}. \qquad (105)$$

The only issue is how to find n_1 (and similarly y_1). One thought is to form it as the usual (L_2) projection on $m(\cdot)$

$$n_1 = \frac{\int n(t) m(t)\, dt}{\int_0^T m^2(t)\, dt}. \qquad (106)$$

But then it is easy to see that (102) will hold if and only if

$$\int_0^T R(t,s) m(s)\, ds = \left[\int_0^T m^2(t)\, dt \right] m(t), \qquad 0 \le t \le T$$

i.e., if and only if $m(\cdot)$ is an eigenfunction of $R(\cdot,\cdot)$. When the noise is white, i.e., $R(t,s) = \delta(t-s)$, then this will be true for any $m(\cdot)$ and we obtain the usual one-dimensional model (see, e.g., [141]). However, when the noise is colored, $m(\cdot)$ in general will be a combination of eigenfunctions of $R(\cdot,\cdot)$, which is one reason for using the Karhunen-Loève expansion for colored noise problems. However, we shall show below (see also [44] and [48]) that by using a less familiar form of projection than (106), we can still obtain a one-dimensional problem.

In particular, we must take

$$n_1 = \frac{\langle n(\cdot), m(\cdot) \rangle_{\mathcal{H}(R)}}{\|m(\cdot)\|_{\mathcal{H}(R)}^2} \qquad (107)$$

where $\langle\cdot,\cdot\rangle_{\mathcal{H}(R)}$ denotes the inner product and $||\cdot||^2_{\mathcal{H}(R)} = \langle\cdot,\cdot\rangle_{\mathcal{H}(R)}$ the norm in the RKHS $\mathcal{H}(R)$, associated with $R(\cdot,\cdot)$, characterized by the following properties:

i) $R(\cdot,t) \in \mathcal{H}(R), \quad \forall t \in [0,T]$ and

ii) $m(\cdot) \in \mathcal{H}(R) \Leftrightarrow \langle m(\cdot), R(\cdot,t)\rangle = m(t), \quad \forall t \in [0,T]$.

$$(108)$$

Note that the second of these properties suggests the name "reproducing kernel," since the kernel $R(\cdot,\cdot)$ reproduces the elements of $\mathcal{H}(R)$ when applied to them in the form of a linear operator. We shall show presently that

$$E\{n_1^2\} = 1/||m||^2_{\mathcal{H}(R)}. \qquad (109)$$

By definition, y_1 is obtained by applying to $y(\cdot)$ the same operations used to get n_1 from $n(\cdot)$, so that

$$y_1 = \frac{\langle y(\cdot), m(\cdot)\rangle_{\mathcal{H}(R)}}{||m(\cdot)||^2_{\mathcal{H}(R)}}. \qquad (110)$$

Substituting (109)–(110) into (105) gives the formula

$$L(T) = \exp\left\{\langle y(\cdot), m(\cdot)\rangle_{\mathcal{H}(R)} - \frac{1}{2}||m(\cdot)||^2_{\mathcal{H}(R)}\right\}. \quad (111)$$

This is a nice generalization of the white noise formula, which can be regarded as a "limiting" case in which $K(t,s) = \delta(t-s)$ and the inner product is the usual (L2) inner product. Note also that from (104) we can see that the singular case of perfect detection will arise if and only if $E\{n_1^2\} = 0$, which by (109) means $||m||^2_{\mathcal{H}(R)} = \infty$. It can be checked that $||m(\cdot)||^2_{\mathcal{H}(R)} = \sum m_k^2/\lambda_k$, which connects with the earlier discussion (below (92)). However, to see what may have been gained by this new formulation, apart from an elegant interpretation, let us reconsider the example introduced earlier of exponentially correlated noise—see (98) and (99). It can be checked that when $R(t,s) = \frac{\alpha}{2}\exp\{-\alpha|t-s|\}$, the inner product

$$\langle y(\cdot), m(\cdot)\rangle_{\mathcal{H}(R)} = \frac{1}{\alpha^2}\int_0^T [\dot{y}(t) + \alpha y(t)][\dot{m}(t) + \alpha m(t)]\,dt$$
$$+ \frac{2}{\alpha}y(0)m(0) \qquad (112)$$

has the key reproducing property (108). It follows easily from (112) that

$$||m(\cdot)||^2_{\mathcal{H}(R)} < \infty \Leftrightarrow \int_0^T \dot{m}^2(t)\,dt < \infty \text{ and } \int_0^T m^2(t)\,dt < \infty. \qquad (113)$$

It is useful to compare this result with the one from the integral equation formulation, where the quantity comparable to (112) is (cf. (95) and (99))

$$\int_0^T y(t)a(t)\,dt$$
$$= \frac{1}{\alpha^2}\left[\int_0^T [\alpha^2 m(t) - \ddot{m}(t)]y(t)\,dt + [\alpha m(0) + \dot{m}(0)]\right.$$
$$\left. \cdot y(0) + [\alpha m(T) + \dot{m}(T)]y(T)\right]. \qquad (114)$$

Note, first of all, that the integral equation approach requires a stronger assumption on $m(\cdot)$ than does the RKHS formula: viz., (114) requires the existence of the second derivative $\ddot{m}(\cdot)$, whereas nonsingularity (cf., (113) and the formula (112)) requires only the square integrability of $\dot{m}(\cdot)$. The tradeoff is that (112) requires $\dot{y}(\cdot)$, which contains white noise, whereas (114) works with $y(\cdot)$. However, as noted before, we can be quite comfortable with (especially linear) operations on white noise, so this is not a handicap. Furthermore, some thought will show that it is easier to make an electronic circuit to compute $\alpha m(\cdot) + \dot{m}(\cdot)$ than it is to make one to compute $\ddot{m}(\cdot)$. Similar statements can be made for many other examples. The point is that the supposedly more abstract RKHS formulation actually can lead to better results, both mathematically and physically. The issue of course is how to find the RKHS inner products. This can be done in a variety of ways, as discussed, e.g., in several of the papers in the reprint volume [135]; the concept of whitening and innovations representations is very helpful in this regard [52].

To justify the formulas (107)–(111), we begin by introducing the Hilbert space of random variables of the form

$$u^{(N)} = \sum_{k=1}^N c_k n(t_k), \quad N < \infty, \quad t_k \in [0,T] \qquad (115)$$

and their mean-square limits, i.e., r.v.'s u such that

$$\lim_{N\to\infty} E\{|u - u^{(N)}|^2\} = 0$$

for sequences $\{u^{(N)}\}$ of random variables of the form (115). Let us denote this Hilbert space by $LL_2(n)$. (As usual, we regard as equivalent those r.v.'s whose difference has zero variance, so that the Hilbert space $LL_2(n)$ is really a space of equivalence classes of random variables.) The inner product and norm in this Hilbert space are

$$\langle u_k, u_\ell\rangle = E\{u_k u_\ell\} \quad \text{and} \quad ||u_k||^2 = E\{u_k^2\}. \qquad (116)$$

(For simplicity, we confine ourselves to real-valued random variables.)

Our task is to find a nonzero r.v. $n_1 \in LL_2(n)$ such that

$$E\{n_1 n(t)\} = E\{n_1^2\}m(t), \qquad t \in [0,T]. \qquad (117)$$

It is useful to first consider the related problem of finding an r.v. $u \in LL^2(n)$ such that

$$E\{u n(t)\} = m(t), \qquad t \in [0,T]. \qquad (118)$$

Note that u will be the zero r.v. (i.e., one with zero variance) if and only if $m(t) \equiv 0$, which we, of course, assume not to be the case. Therefore, we can define and check that the r.v.

$$n_1 = \frac{u}{E\{u^2\}} \qquad (119)$$

will satisfy (117). Note that

$$E\{n_1^2\} = E\{u^2\}/(E\{u^2\})^2 = 1/E\{u^2\}$$

so that

$$\frac{n_1}{E\{n_1^2\}} = \frac{u}{E\{u^2\}}\cdot E\{u^2\} = u. \qquad (120)$$

So it is sufficient to consider the problem of finding $u \in LL_2(n)$ that satisfies (118) for a given function $m(\cdot)$. Clearly, a solution will be possible only if the function $m(\cdot)$ is related in some way to the noise covariance function $R(t, s)$. The striking fact is that we can set up a one-to-one relationship between the r.v. u and the function $m(\cdot)$ if and only if $m(\cdot) \in \mathcal{H}(R)$, the RKHS of $R(\cdot, \cdot)$, as previously defined by the conditions (108).

To see this we set up an isometry between the space of r.v.'s and the space of functions $m(\cdot)$ as follows: with an r.v. $u_k \in LL^2(n)$, associate a function $m_k(\cdot)$ defined as

$$m_k(\cdot) = E\{u_k n(\cdot)\}. \qquad (121a)$$

Moreover, define the norm of $m_k(\cdot)$ as equal to the norm of (its pre-image) u_k, and the inner product of $m_k(\cdot)$ and $m_\ell(\cdot)$ as the inner product of the pre-images, i.e.,

$$\langle m_k(\cdot), m_\ell(\cdot) \rangle_{\mathcal{H}(R)} = E\{u_k u_\ell\} \text{ and } \|m_k(\cdot)\|^2_{\mathcal{H}(R)} = E\{u_k^2\}. \qquad (121b)$$

With these definitions, if a sequence $u^{(N)} \in LL^2(n)$ converges to an r.v. $u \in LL^2(n)$, i.e., if $\lim_{N \to \infty} E\{|u - u^{(N)}|^2\} = 0$, then the corresponding sequence of functions $m^{(N)}(\cdot)$ in $\mathcal{H}(R)$ will converge to a function $m(\cdot)$ such that

$$\lim_{N \to \infty} \|m(\cdot) - m^{(N)}(\cdot)\|^2_{\mathcal{H}(R)} = 0.$$

In fact, this function is just $m(\cdot) = E\{un(\cdot)\}$. Therefore, since $LL^2(n)$ is a Hilbert space, so is the space of functions $m(\cdot)$, which we shall denote by $\mathcal{H}(R)$. Let us verify that $\mathcal{H}(R)$ is an RKHS.

By (108), we first have to show that the functions $R(\cdot, t) \in \mathcal{H}(R)$. But this is true since the relation $E\{n(t)n(\cdot)\} = R(\cdot, t)$ shows that their pre-images are the r.v.'s $n(t)$. Moreover, if $m(\cdot) = E\{un(\cdot)\}$, then by the isometry we must have

$$\langle m(\cdot), R(\cdot, t) \rangle_{\mathcal{H}(R)} = E\{un(t)\} = m(t). \qquad (122)$$

In other words, $\mathcal{H}(R)$ is an RKHS with reproducing kernel $R(\cdot, \cdot)$.

It is noteworthy that, unlike the space $LL^2(n)$, or the space L_2 of square-integrable functions, the elements of $\mathcal{H}(R)$ are functions and not equivalence classes of functions. In an RKHS, norm convergence implies pointwise convergence, a striking property not true in L^2. If $R(\cdot, \cdot)$ is continuous, then so are the functions $m(\cdot) \in \mathcal{H}(R)$, because

$$|m(t_1) - m(t_2)|$$
$$= |\langle m(\cdot), R(\cdot, t_1) - R(\cdot, t_2) \rangle_{\mathcal{H}(R)}| \qquad (123)$$
$$\leq \|R(\cdot, t_1) - R(\cdot, t_2)\|_{\mathcal{H}(R)} \|m(\cdot)\|_{\mathcal{H}(R)} \qquad (124)$$
$$= [R(t_1, t_1) - 2R(t_1, t_2) + R(t_2, t_2)]^{1/2} \|m(\cdot)\|_{\mathcal{H}(R)} \qquad (125)$$

Similarly, if $R(\cdot, \cdot)$ is twice differentiable, the functions in $\mathcal{H}(R)$ are once differentiable, and so on. Another useful, and easily proved, property is that the functions $\{R(\cdot, t), t \in [0, T]\}$ span $\mathcal{H}(R)$; that is,

$$m \perp R(\cdot, t) \Leftrightarrow 0 = \langle m(\cdot), R(\cdot, t) \rangle = m(t), \ \forall t \in [0, T]. \qquad (126)$$

Several other useful properties can be found in the literature; the reprint volume of Weinert [135] is a useful source for the papers up to 1982; for later work, see for example, [2]–[4].

The basic idea is that if we express $m(\cdot)$ as

$$m(\cdot) = \sum_{k=1}^{N} c_k R(\cdot, t_k), \qquad \text{then} \qquad u = \sum_{k=1}^{N} c_k n(t_k) \qquad (127)$$

and in carrying this idea to the limit. In other words, as emphasized by Parzen, if a function $m(\cdot)$ can be represented in terms of linear operations on the family $\{R(\cdot, t), t \in [0, T]\}$, including the operations of differentiation and integration, then $m(\cdot)$ belongs to $\mathcal{H}(R)$ and its preimage u may be expressed in terms of the family $\{n(t), t \in [0, T]\}$ by exactly the same linear operations as used to represent $m(\cdot)$ in terms of $\{R(\cdot, t), t \in [0, T]\}$.

So for example, if we can find, by whatever means (rigorous or not) that $m(\cdot)$ can be expressed as $m(t) = \int R(t, s)a(s)\,ds$, even with $a(s)$ a nonsquare integrable function, as in (99), then we can represent the pre-image u as $\int n(s)a(s)\,ds$. Furthermore, returning to (126) note that we can write

$$u = \sum_{k=1}^{N} c_k n(t_k) = \sum_{k=1}^{N} c_k \langle n(\cdot), R(t_k, \cdot) \rangle_{\mathcal{H}(R)}$$
$$= \left\langle n(\cdot), \sum_{k=1}^{N} c_k R(t_k, \cdot) \right\rangle_{\mathcal{H}(R)} = \langle n(\cdot), m(\cdot) \rangle_{\mathcal{H}(R)} \qquad (128)$$

which is a formal way of writing (127). (We say formal because the sample functions of a stochastic process do not belong to $\mathcal{H}(R)$. For example, for a Wiener process $y(\cdot)$ with $R(t, s) = \min\{t, s\}$, the RKHS inner product is

$$u = \langle y, m \rangle_{\mathcal{H}(R)} = \int \dot{m}(t)\dot{y}(t)\,dt + m(0)y(0).$$

But the paths of a Wiener process are not differentiable. However, the solution is clear—write the integral as $\int \dot{m}(t)\,dy(t)$ and verify that with this change the random variable u satisfies $E\{uy(t)\} = m(t)$.) With this background, we now return to the detection problem and show how to compute n_1 and y_1. We recall from (119) that $n_1 = u/E\{u^2\}$, and so the problem is that of finding (cf. (118)) u such that

$$E\{un(t)\} = m(t), \qquad t \in [0, T]. \qquad (129)$$

But as we just showed, the solution can be written as

$$u = \langle m(\cdot), n(\cdot) \rangle_{\mathcal{H}(R)} \text{ where } E\{u^2\} = \|u\|^2 = \|m(\cdot)\|^2_{\mathcal{H}(R)}. \qquad (130)$$

Therefore, as claimed at the beginning of this section in (107)

$$n_1 = \frac{u}{E\{|u|^2\}} = \frac{\langle n(\cdot), m(\cdot) \rangle_{\mathcal{H}(R)}}{\|m(\cdot)\|^2_{\mathcal{H}(R)}}$$

= the projection of $n(\cdot)$ on $m(\cdot)$ in the RKHS $\mathcal{H}(R)$.

Note also that

$$E\{|n_1|^2\} = \frac{1}{E\{|u|^2\}} = \frac{1}{\|m(\cdot)\|^2_{\mathcal{H}(R)}} \qquad (131)$$

which establishes (109). These were the underlying formulas that led to the LR formula (111). An approach similar to the above, based on (118) but not making a connection to RKHS, was used in a very rich, but little read, long paper of the late Czech statistician, J. Hajek [37]. Hajek's work is further discussed in [53].

C. Gaussian Signals in Gaussian Noise

We now turn briefly to the formulas for Gaussian signals in colored Gaussian noise, as in the problem of choosing between the hypotheses

$$H_0: y(t) \text{ has covariance function } R_0(t,s)$$

versus

$$H_1: y(t) \text{ has covariance function } R_0(t,s) + K(t,s).$$
$$(132)$$

It was shown by Parzen [83] and Kallianpur and Oodaira [54] that this problem is nonsingular if and only if $K(\cdot, \cdot)$ defines a Hilbert–Schmidt operator in the $\mathcal{H}(R_0) \otimes \mathcal{H}(R_0)$ space, and that $R_0(\cdot, \cdot) + K(\cdot, \cdot)$ defines a positive-definite operator on this space (or equivalently, that -1 is not an eigenvalue of K in this space). These conditions are a natural generalization of Shepp's conditions (32) and (33) for the white noise case, where $R_0(t,s) = \delta(t - s)$ and $\mathcal{H}(R_0)$ is $L_2[0,T]$.

Next, it is interesting to note that the computations for finding the LR for this general Gaussian detection problem can essentially be reduced to the computations of the individual RKHS norms $\langle y(\cdot), y(\cdot) \rangle_{\mathcal{H}(R_0)}$ and $\langle y(\cdot), y(\cdot) \rangle_{\mathcal{H}(R_0+K)}$. In other words, just the kinds of computations required in the *known signal* problem for noise with covariance $R_0(\cdot, \cdot)$ or $R_0(\cdot, \cdot) + K(\cdot, \cdot)$. For the details, we refer to [53].

Perhaps even more interesting is that the estimator–correlator formulas of Section II-B can be extended to this more general setting. However, now one has to re-examine and define more precisely and generally some basic notions such as causality, deterministic and stochastic integrals, etc. As just one example, a causal linear operator in $L_2(0,T)$ has an impulse response $h(\cdot, \cdot)$ with the property that $h(t,s) = 0, s > t$. However, in the RKHS defined by the exponential kernel $R(t,s) = (2\alpha)^{-1}e^{-\alpha(t-s)}$ a causal impulsive response must have the property that $h(t,s) = h(t,t)e^{-\alpha(s-t)}, s > t$! We refer the reader to the paper [51] for review of the operator theory background (drawn from the books of Gohberg and Krein [34], [35]), and for several examples showing how the generalized estimator–correlator formula reduces to the different formulas obtained in several special cases, including the very simple problem of deciding whether a single random variable is $\mathcal{N}(0,1)$ or $\mathcal{N}(0, 1 + \sigma^2)$. Once again, the point of the estimator–correlator result is that it yields a general structure that provides a basis for intelligent approximation of the likelihood ratio.

The RKHS can also be used to study detection problems with non-Gaussian signals, but this needs further generalizations of the RKHS to handle nonlinear operations of linear processes. Several new results can be obtained in this way,

but the machinery to obtain these is quite heavy, and we may refer only to [24]. Explicit RKHS results for self-similar (or *fractal*) signals and noise are found in [2].

The RKHS has several other important applications, e.g., to the study of intersymbol interference (see Messerschmidt [70]), robustness in signal estimation [3] and spline approximation (Kimeldorf and Wahba [61], Sidhu and Weinert [109]), density estimation (see Wahba [131]), performance characterization of detection systems [4], and adaptive filtering (Csibi [18]).

We now turn to Part II of the paper on sequence detection and sequential detection. Here we again focus on the additive white noise case.

PART II:
DYNAMIC OPTIMIZATION

In Part I, we traced the development of likelihood-ratio formulas, from the basic correlator for known signals in white Gaussian noise, through more general results for stochastic signals and colored noise based on stochastic calculus and reproducing kernel Hilbert space representations. Although these formulas have been discussed primarily as they apply to binary detection problems, they also form the bases for a number of other detection problems in which criteria other than the testing of simple binary hypotheses arise. In this section, we discuss fundamental results in two such problems: sequence detection, and sequential detection. In each of these problems (the characteristics of which will be elaborated below), algorithmic issues arise beyond the extraction of the likelihood ratio, and in particular dynamic optimization comes into play.

IV. SEQUENCE DETECTION

As noted in Section II, likelihood ratios for binary detection problems can be used straightforwardly to write likelihood functions for deciding among multiple signals. This is accomplished by constructing pairwise likelihoods between each of the implied multiple hypotheses and a "catalyst" hypothesis, such as that of noise only. Thus in principle, problems with multiple possible signals can be solved straightforwardly as generalizations of the single-signal-in-noise case. Typically, the complexity of such solutions grows linearly with the number of signals to be decided among.

In digital communications, problems of multihypothesis testing arise in two basic situations: the first of these is when an M-ary signaling alphabet is being used to transmit digital data. In such situations, the number of hypotheses M is often small (e.g., 8 or 16) and the complexity of M-ary hypothesis testing is manageable. The second basic situation in which multihypothesis testing problems arise is that in which signals from multiple data transmissions are received in a manner such that there is statistical dependence among them. Applications in which such problems arise include coded communications, transmission through dispersive channels, and multiple-access communications. In such situations, optimal data detection can involve the joint detection of an entire sequence or group of symbols. If the number of (binary) symbols to be jointly detected is N, then the number of possible hypotheses is 2^N, a number that can be prohibitively large for practical detection systems if linear complexity is required. So, in order for optimal detection to be practical in such situations, some form of complexity reduction is necessary. Fortunately, many applications in which such situations arise admit dynamical models for symbol dependency that allow dynamic programming to be used to provide significant reduction of the complexity of optimal detection.

This basic principle has resulted in several key results over the past three decades, including the 1960's *Viterbi algorithm* for detecting convolutionally encoded data transmitted over memoryless channels [80], [130], the 1970's *maximum-likelihood sequence estimator* (MLSE) for equalizing linearly dispersive channels [28], and the 1980's *multiuser detector* (MUD) for demodulating nonorthogonally multiplexed data [126], [127]. These three problems can all be viewed within a multihypothesis testing model, in which we have observations of the form

$$y(t) = m_{\boldsymbol{b}}(t) + v(t), \qquad -\infty < t < \infty, \ \boldsymbol{b} \in \mathcal{B} \quad (133)$$

where $m_{\boldsymbol{b}}(t)$ and $v(t)$ represent the useful signal and additive white Gaussian noise (AWGN), respectively, and where $\mathcal{B}$ is the set of all N-tuples of binary (± 1) digits

$$\mathcal{B} = \{-1, +1\}^N. \quad (134)$$

This model is straightforwardly generalized to the case of larger finite alphabets, but the binary case serves to illustrate the issues of interest here.

In the following sections, we consider optimum detection in the model of (133) when applied within the complexity-reducing structures noted above.

A. Maximum-Likelihood Detection

We begin by considering maximum-likelihood detection in the model (133). The likelihood function (i.e., the likelihood ratio with respect to a noise-only catalytic hypothesis) for this model can be written via the basic likelihood-ratio formula (3) as

$$\ell(\{y(t); -\infty < t < \infty\}|\boldsymbol{b}) = C \exp\{\Omega(\boldsymbol{b})/2\sigma^2\} \quad (135)$$

where C is a constant, σ^2 is the noise intensity, and

$$\Omega(\boldsymbol{b}) = 2 \int_{-\infty}^{\infty} m_{\boldsymbol{b}}(t)y(t)\,dt - \int_{-\infty}^{\infty} [m_{\boldsymbol{b}}(t)]^2\,dt. \quad (136)$$

Thus to make maximum-likelihood bit decisions, we need to solve the maximization problem

$$\max_{\boldsymbol{b} \in \mathcal{B}} \Omega(\boldsymbol{b}). \quad (137)$$

Since this type of problem often involves the simultaneous detection of the entire N-tuple $\boldsymbol{b}$, detectors of this type are often known as *sequence detectors*.

Note that the complexity of solving (137) by brute force (i.e., exhaustive search) is proportional to $|\mathcal{B}| = 2^N$. However, with some structural constraints on the signals $m_{\boldsymbol{b}}(t)$, this complexity can be reduced substantially. To illustrate this

issue, it is instructive to consider the case of *linear modulation*, in which the signals $m_{\boldsymbol{b}}(t)$ are of the form

$$m_{\boldsymbol{b}}(t) = \sum_{n=1}^{N} b_n s_n(t) \quad (138)$$

where b_n denotes the nth symbol in $\boldsymbol{b}$, and $s_n(t)$ is a known waveform, depending of course on n. Two key examples of channels in which this type of signals arise are linearly dispersive *intersymbol-interference channels*, and linear *multiple-access channels*. In dispersive channels, the signals $\{s_n\}$ are of the form

$$s_n(t) = Ap(t - nT) \quad (139)$$

where $p(t)$ is a basic received pulse shape, $A > 0$ is an amplitude factor, and T is the symbol interval. When the waveform $p(t)$ has duration greater than the symbol interval T, then intersymbol interference results, and sequence detection is required to optimally detect the symbols. Alternatively, in multiple-access channels, the received waveform $m_{\boldsymbol{b}}(t)$ is comprised of data signals of K active users superimposed in the channel. Such a signal can be written as

$$m_{\boldsymbol{b}}(t) = \sum_{k=1}^{K} A_k \sum_{i=-B}^{B} b_k(i)p_k(t - iT - \tau_k) \quad (140)$$

where $2B + 1$ is the number of symbols per user in the data frame of interest, T is the per-user symbol interval, and where $A_k, \tau_k, \{b_k(i)\}$, and $\{p_k(t); 0 \le t \le T\}$ denote, respectively, the received amplitude, delay, symbol stream, and normalized modulation waveform of the kth user. Here, we have a model of the form of (138) in which $N = K \times (2B + 1)$, and, with $n = (B + i) + k$, we take

$$b_n = b_k(i) \quad \text{and} \quad s_n(t) = p_k(t - iT - \tau_k). \quad (141)$$

Typically, the modulation waveforms $p_1, p_2, \cdots, p_K$ in (140) are not orthogonal (as, for example, in code-division multiple-access (CDMA) communications). So, even if these waveforms are of single-symbol duration, there will be *multiple-access interference* due to the correlation among different users' signals.

Regardless of which of the above specific models we consider, in this linear-modulation case, the objective $\Omega(\boldsymbol{b})$ becomes

$$\Omega(\boldsymbol{b}) = 2 \sum_{n=1}^{N} b_n y_n - \sum_{n=1}^{N} \sum_{m=1}^{N} b_n b_m H_{n,m} \quad (142)$$

with

$$y_n = \int_{-\infty}^{\infty} s_n(t)y(t)\,dt \quad (143)$$

and

$$H_{n,m} = \int_{-\infty}^{\infty} s_n(t)s_m(t)\,dt. \quad (144)$$

If we let $\boldsymbol{b}$ and $\boldsymbol{y}$ denote the (column) vectors with components $\{b_n\}$ and $\{y_n\}$, respectively, and $\boldsymbol{H}$ denote the matrix with elements $\{H_{n,m}\}$, then we can write (137) compactly as

$$\max_{b \in \mathcal{B}} [2b'y - b'Hb]. \qquad (145)$$

The problem (145) is an integer quadratic program, an NP-complete problem that in general offers little improvement in complexity over exhaustive search (see [125]). However, it happens in several applications of interest that H is a *banded matrix*; that is, all of H's elements greater than a certain distance from the main diagonal are zero. We can write this condition as

$$H_{m,n} = 0, \qquad |m - n| > D \qquad (146)$$

where $2D + 1$ is the number of nonzero diagonals of H. This situation arises in the linear dispersion model (138) and (139) where the product DT is the maximal *delay spread* of the channel. Similarly, in the asynchronous multiple-access model of (140), (146) is satisfied with $D = K - 1$ if each of the modulation waveforms p_k has duration T, and with a larger value of D if these waveforms have some (finite) delay spread beyond a single symbol. Note that, if $D = 0$, then (145) is solved by the conventional matched-filter detector:

$$b_n = \text{sgn}(y_n). \qquad (147)$$

In the case (146), the complexity of solving (145) can be reduced to $\mathcal{O}(N \times 2^D)$. To see this, we can use the facts that $b_n^2 = 1$ and $H_{n,m} = H_{m,n}$ to rewrite

$$
\begin{aligned}
2b'y - b'Hb &= 2\sum_{n=1}^{N} b_n y_n - 2\sum_{n=1}^{N}\sum_{m=1}^{n-1} b_n b_m H_{n,m} - \sum_{n=1}^{N} H_{n,n}^2 \\
&= 2\sum_{n=1}^{N} b_n \left[y_n - \sum_{m=n-D}^{n-1} b_m H_{n,m} \right] - \sum_{n=1}^{N} H_{n,n}^2
\end{aligned}
$$
$$\qquad (148)$$

where we take $b_n = 0$ for $n \leq 0$. From (148) we see that (137) can be written in the form

$$\max_{b \in \mathcal{B}} \sum_{n=1}^{N} f_n(b_n; x_n) \qquad (149)$$

where $\{x_n\}$ is a $D + 1$-dimensional state vector

$$x_n = \begin{pmatrix} b_n \\ b_{n-1} \\ \vdots \\ b_{n-D} \end{pmatrix}, \qquad n = 1, 2, \cdots, N \qquad (150)$$

and where

$$f_n(b_n; x_n) = b_n \left[y_n - \sum_{m=n-D}^{n-1} b_m H_{n,m} \right]. \qquad (151)$$

Note that the state sequence $\{x_n\}$ is generated by the dynamical system

$$x_n = \begin{pmatrix} 0' & 0 \\ I & 0 \end{pmatrix} x_{n-1} + \begin{pmatrix} 1 \\ 0 \end{pmatrix} b_n,$$
$$n = 1, \cdots, N, \qquad x_0 = \begin{pmatrix} 0 \\ 0 \end{pmatrix} \qquad (152)$$

where 0 denotes a D-dimensional column vector with all zero elements, and I denotes the $D \times D$-dimensional identity matrix.

From the form (149) it can be seen that (137) can be solved with a dynamic program[8] [128]. Except near the ends of the state sequence, the cardinality of the state-space of this program is 2^{D+1}, and each element of the state sequence $\{x_n\}$ is connected to exactly two successor states. Moreover, the functions f_n are odd-symmetric in b_n, which eliminates the need to evaluate them for half the states. Thus the total number of function evaluations necessary to find the solution to (149) is essentially $N \times 2^{D+1}$. Since this solution demodulates N bits (i.e., it makes N binary decisions) it follows that the time complexity per binary decision (TCB) of maximum-likelihood sequence detection with a $(2D+1)$-diagonal quadratic term is $\mathcal{O}(2^D)$. Typically, $D \ll N$, in which case this complexity is significantly lower than the exhaustive TCB, which is $\mathcal{O}(2^N/N)$.

The above linear modulation formulation applies directly to the MLSE and MUD. It should be noted, however, that the linearity of the modulation is not essential for the complexity of problem (137) to be reduced to a practical level. Such a complexity reduction will result for any signal format that admits a decomposition of the log likelihood (149) into a form amenable to dynamic programming. An example of a detector of this type is the Viterbi algorithm for detecting convolutionally encoded data transmitted over an AWGN channel. In this problem, the N-long sequence $\{b_n\}$ of binary data symbols is expanded into an N/R-long sequence $\{c_n\}$ of binary *channel* symbols by means of a *rate-R convolutional code*. In particular, for integers n and k such that $R = k/n$, the encoder produces an n-long block of channel symbol for each k-long block of the data symbol sequence. A given channel symbol block is a function of a fixed number K (the *constraint length*) of previous data symbol blocks. The channel symbols are then transmitted via linear modulation to yield a waveform

$$m_b(t) = \sum_{\ell=1}^{N/R} c_\ell \, p(t - \ell T) \qquad (153)$$

where $1/T$ is the rate at which channel symbols are transmitted, and $p(t)$ is a pulse of duration T.

Using this model, we can write (similarly to (142))

$$
\begin{aligned}
\Omega(b) &= 2\sum_{\ell=1}^{N/R} c_\ell y_\ell - \sum_{\ell=1}^{N/R}\sum_{m=1}^{N/R} c_\ell \dot{c}_m \\
&\quad \cdot \int_{-\infty}^{\infty} p(t - mT)p(t - nT) \, dt \\
&= 2\sum_{\ell=1}^{N/R} c_\ell y_\ell - \frac{N}{R} \int_{-\infty}^{\infty} p^2(t) \, dt \qquad (154)
\end{aligned}
$$

[8]Like the matched filter, dynamic programming was developed in the 1940's (by Richard Bellman, of course—see [11]). So, through sequence detection, we have the merging of these two 1940's ideas in applications, such as multiple-access communications, that are very much of the 1990's. It is noteworthy that the idea of applying dynamic programming to communications problems was considered by Bellman and Kalaba in the 1950's [12].

with

$$y_\ell = \int_{-\infty}^{\infty} y(t) p(t - \ell T)\, dt \qquad (155)$$

as before. Using (154), we can write the problem (137) as

$$\max_{\boldsymbol{b} \in \mathcal{B}} \sum_{\ell=1}^{N/k} \boldsymbol{c}_j' \boldsymbol{y}_j \qquad (156)$$

where $\boldsymbol{c}_j$ is a column vector containing the channel symbols in the jth block, and $\boldsymbol{y}_j$ is a column vector containing those elements of $\boldsymbol{y}$ having the same indices as the elements of $\boldsymbol{c}_j$. Now, ignoring end effects, the jth-channel symbol block is generated as a function of the $(j - K)$th through jth data symbol blocks. These K data symbol blocks form a state $\boldsymbol{x}_j$, which propagates forward to $\boldsymbol{x}_{j+1}$ by appending a new block on the leading edge, and deleting the oldest block on the trailing edge. This gives a representation of (156) in a form amenable to dynamic programming, the implementation of which is a form of the Viterbi algorithm. So, as in the cases of dispersive and asynchronous multiple-access channels, data detection here requires sequence detection. In this case, however, the correlation among observations in different received symbol intervals (which forces sequence detection) is due to correlation in the channel symbols introduced by the encoding of data symbols prior to their transmission, rather than by signal overlap in the physical channel.

The problem of equalizing the channel (138) and (139) can also be viewed as a problem of detecting a sequence of finite symbols that have been mixed convolutionally and then observed in additive noise. In particular, as shown by Forney in [28], the model (138) and (139) can be converted to an equivalent discrete-time model

$$y_\ell = c_\ell + n_\ell \qquad (157)$$

where the $\{c_\ell\}$ is the output of a discrete-time *linear* filter applied to the sequence $\{b_\ell\}$ of data symbols, and where $\{n_\ell\}$ is discrete-time Gaussian white noise. The sequence $\{y_\ell\}$ is obtained from $y(\cdot)$ by passing it through a time-invariant, causal, continuous-time linear filter followed by a symbol-rate sampler. The continuous-time linear filter that produces this sequence is termed a *whitened matched filter*, and it is determined by the pulse shape $p(\cdot)$ of the original channel (139). Once the observations are reduced to (157), the problem of maximum-likelihood detection of the original symbol sequence $\{b_\ell\}$ is again reducible to dynamic programming (assuming a finite-length channel) as in the Viterbi algorithm. Note that the maximum-likelihood symbol decisions obtained in this manner are identical, of course, to those obtained via (149).

B. Linear Detection

A quite different optimal detector is found in the situation in which the received amplitudes of the waveforms $\{s_n\}$ are unknown and no *a priori* distribution on them is available. In this case, we can replace s_n with, say, $a_n S_n$ where $a_n > 0$ is

the norm of $s_n(t)$

$$a_n = \sqrt{\int_{-\infty}^{\infty} |s_n(t)|^2\, dt} \qquad (158)$$

and where S_n is the corresponding normalized waveform

$$S_n(t) = s_n(t)/a_n. \qquad (159)$$

To deal with these unknown amplitudes, we can replace the problem (137) with

$$\max_{\boldsymbol{b} \in \mathcal{B}} \left\{ \max_{\boldsymbol{a} \in (\boldsymbol{R}^+)^N} [2\boldsymbol{b}' \boldsymbol{D_a} \boldsymbol{y} - \boldsymbol{b}' \boldsymbol{D_a} \boldsymbol{R} \boldsymbol{D_a} \boldsymbol{b}] \right\} \qquad (160)$$

where $\boldsymbol{a}$ denotes the N-vector with elements $\{a_n\}$, $\boldsymbol{D_a}$ denotes the diagonal matrix with $\boldsymbol{a}$ as its diagonal, and $\boldsymbol{R}$ denotes the normalized version of the matrix $\boldsymbol{H}$; i.e.,

$$R_{m,n} = \int_{-\infty}^{\infty} S_m(t) S_n(t)\, dt, \qquad m, n = 1, \cdots, N. \qquad (161)$$

It is easy to see that the solution to (160) is given by

$$b_n = \operatorname{sgn}(v_n), \qquad n = 1, 2, \cdots, N \qquad (162)$$

where $\boldsymbol{v}$ is the solution to the problem

$$\max_{\boldsymbol{v} \in \boldsymbol{R}^N} [2\boldsymbol{v}' \boldsymbol{y} - \boldsymbol{v}' \boldsymbol{R} \boldsymbol{v}]. \qquad (163)$$

Note that $\boldsymbol{R}$ is nonnegative definite, and it will be positive definite unless there is some nonzero set of amplitudes and symbols that produces an identically-zero signal $m_b(t)$. Assuming that the latter cannot happen, the maximum-likelihood sequence detector for the unknown-amplitude case is thus given by (162) with

$$\boldsymbol{v} = \boldsymbol{R}^{-1} \boldsymbol{y}. \qquad (164)$$

This detector can be interpreted as follows. Note that the vector $\boldsymbol{y}$ can be written as

$$\boldsymbol{y} = \boldsymbol{R} \boldsymbol{D_a} \boldsymbol{b} + \sigma \boldsymbol{n} \qquad (165)$$

where $\boldsymbol{n} \sim \mathcal{N}(0, \boldsymbol{R})$. So, the vector $\boldsymbol{v}$ from (164) can be written as

$$\boldsymbol{v} = \boldsymbol{D_a} \boldsymbol{b} + \sigma \boldsymbol{w} \qquad (166)$$

with $\boldsymbol{w} \sim \mathcal{N}(0, \boldsymbol{R}^{-1})$. In particular, the nth component of $\boldsymbol{v}$ is given by

$$v_n = a_n b_n + \sigma w_n \qquad (167)$$

where $w_n \sim \mathcal{N}(0, (\boldsymbol{R}^{-1})_{n,n})$. So, the transformed observable v_n contains no interference from other symbols, and the detected value $\operatorname{sgn}(v_n)$ is thus corrupted only by Gaussian noise. In the context of multiuser detection (i.e., data detection in the model (140)), this detector is known as the *decorrelating detector* [68]. In the context of the intersymbol-interference channel, it is known as the *zero-forcing equalizer*, since the output of the detector due to other symbols has been forced to zero by the transformation $\boldsymbol{R}^{-1}$ (which will, in general, represent an infinite-impulse-response filter).

Quite apart from the use of $\Omega(\boldsymbol{b})$ for extracting maximum-likelihood detected symbols, the fact that this quantity depends

206

on the received waveform $y(\cdot)$ only through the vector $\boldsymbol{y}$ of observables tells us that $\boldsymbol{y}$ is a sufficient statistic for the data symbols $\boldsymbol{b}$. Thus optimal detectors under criteria other than maximal likelihood (such as minimal error probability within a prior on $\boldsymbol{b}$) will also be functions of this vector of observables. That is, the basic structure of optimal detection in the linear modulation model (138), is a bank of filters matched to the waveforms $s_n(t)$, followed by a (software) decision algorithm. Like the maximum-likelihood problem, other criteria also lead to dynamic programming structures for this decision algorithm. For example, with a uniform prior on $\mathcal{B}$ (i.e., the symbols are independent and identically distributed (i.i.d.) and equiprobably ± 1), the detector that minimizes the probabilities that the individual b_n's are detected in error also admits a dynamic programming solution, albeit a different one from that described above. In particular, in this case the dynamic program is of the "backward–forward" type [128], similar in nature to iterative algorithms that have been applied recently to the decoding of turbo codes [69].

The detector structure (162) and (164) can also be generalized by allowing more general linear transformations of $\boldsymbol{y}$. That is, we can consider detectors of the form

$$b_n = \mathrm{sgn}\,(z_n) \tag{168}$$

where

$$\boldsymbol{z} = \boldsymbol{M}\boldsymbol{y} \tag{169}$$

and $\boldsymbol{M}$ is an arbitrary $N \times N$ matrix. Such detectors are known as *linear detectors*. Using (165), we can write

$$\begin{aligned}
\boldsymbol{z} &= \boldsymbol{M}\boldsymbol{R}\boldsymbol{D}_a\boldsymbol{b} + \sigma\boldsymbol{M}\boldsymbol{n} \\
&= \boldsymbol{D}_a\boldsymbol{b} + \sigma\boldsymbol{n} + (\boldsymbol{M}\boldsymbol{R} - \boldsymbol{I})\boldsymbol{D}_a\boldsymbol{b} + \sigma(\boldsymbol{M} - \boldsymbol{I})\boldsymbol{n}
\end{aligned} \tag{170}$$

where $\boldsymbol{I}$ denotes the $N \times N$ identity matrix. Note that this vector is comprised of the following four terms:

- the desired signal $\boldsymbol{D}_a\boldsymbol{b}$;
- the irreducible ambient noise $\sigma\boldsymbol{n}$;
- the structured interference $(\boldsymbol{M}\boldsymbol{R} - \boldsymbol{I})\boldsymbol{D}_a\boldsymbol{b}$;
- the residual noise $\sigma(\boldsymbol{M} - \boldsymbol{I})\boldsymbol{n}$.

Only the latter two terms can be controlled by choice of the matrix $\boldsymbol{M}$. If we set $\boldsymbol{M} = \boldsymbol{I}$ then the fourth term on the right-hand side of (170) is identically zero, and the linear detector (168) becomes the conventional matched filter detector of (147)

$$b_n = \mathrm{sgn}\,(y_n). \tag{171}$$

This detector is optimal when $\boldsymbol{R}$ is a diagonal matrix, but is generally susceptible to the structured interference: $(\boldsymbol{R} - \boldsymbol{I})\boldsymbol{D}_a\boldsymbol{b}$. For example, in the multiple-access signaling model (140), this detector can exhibit arbitrarily bad performance if the amplitudes of the interfering signals are not contrained. (This is the so-called "near–far" problem of multiple-access communications.) Alternatively, by choosing $\boldsymbol{M} = \boldsymbol{R}^{-1}$, we have the zero-forcing detector, which drives the third term on the right-hand side of (170) to zero. Although this detector is optimal in the maximum-likelihood sense, and

has the desirable property that its performance is invariant to the amplitudes of interfering signals, it has the undesirable potential of significantly enhancing the ambient noise.

An alternative detector to these two extremes is the linear *minimum-mean-square-error* (MMSE) detector, which uses the matrix $\boldsymbol{M}$ that minimizes the quadratic mean of the difference between the transformed vector $\boldsymbol{z}$ and the useful signal $\boldsymbol{D}_a$

$$E\{\|\boldsymbol{D}_a\boldsymbol{b} - \boldsymbol{z}\|^2\}. \tag{172}$$

This detector corresponds to (168) and (169) with [142]

$$\boldsymbol{M} = (\boldsymbol{R} + \sigma^2\boldsymbol{D}_a^{-2})^{-1}. \tag{173}$$

The MMSE detector has several favorable properties for practical data detection, among which are amenability to adaptive implementation when aspects of the channel or signaling waveforms are unknown (see, e.g., [40], [41], [134], and, more generally, [93]).

C. Performance Characteristics

The performance of the detectors discussed above can be assessed in terms of the corresponding probability of bit error under some suitable prior model on the data symbol sequence $\boldsymbol{b}$, typically that this sequence is uniformly distributed on $\mathcal{B}$. In view of (167), the error probability for the zero-forcing detector is relatively simple to compute. In particular, assuming b_n to take on the values ± 1 with equal probabilities, the probability that b_n is detected in error by the zero-forcing detector is simply

$$P_e(n) = Q\left(\frac{a_n}{\sigma\sqrt{(\boldsymbol{R}^{-1})_{n,n}}}\right) \tag{174}$$

where Q denotes the tail of the standard Gaussian distribution. Note that, if b_n were instead received in isolation of the other symbols' signals, the corresponding bit-error probability would be

$$P_e(n) = Q\left(\frac{a_n}{\sigma}\right). \tag{175}$$

So, the *efficiency* of the zero-forcing detector in the shared channel, relative to transmission in a clear channel, is $1/(\boldsymbol{R}^{-1})_{n,n} \leq 1$.

Bit-error probabilities for the other detectors described above can be considerably more difficult to compute. For example, the dynamic-programming-based MLSE and MUD typically must be evaluated in terms of error bounds. Such bounds, described in [28] and [123], involve the inclusion of the event that a given bit is received in error into the union of more elemental error events. The probability of this union is then bounded by the sum of the probabilities of the individual error events (the so-called *union bound*). By proper choice of these elemental error events, such bounds can be quite tight [124]. This is particularly true as $\sigma \to 0$, in which case the error is often dominated by a single "minimum-distance" error event. Under certain circumstances, the error probability of the linear MMSE detector of (168) and (173) is well-approximated by assuming that the error incurred by the MMSE transformation is Gaussian. This results straightforwardly in the following approximation:

$$P_e(n) \cong Q\left(\frac{a_n M_{n,n}}{\sigma\sqrt{(MRM)_{n,n}}}\right) \qquad (176)$$

where M is the MMSE transformation (173). This problem is investigated in [92]. Asympotic efficiencies (i.e., limiting efficiencies as $\sigma \to 0$) can also be determined for maximum-likelihood and MMSE detectors [126].

V. SEQUENTIAL DETECTION

In Section IV-A, we saw how dynamic programming comes into play in the optimization of detection problems with large numbers of hypotheses. The sequence detectors discussed therein are essentially discrete optimizers over large, finite, spaces. Dynamic optimization also arises in detection problems in which the observation time is not fixed, but rather can be chosen on-line as the observations are revealed. The optimization of this type of problem gives rise to so-called *optimal stopping problems*, and more specifically in the problems to be treated here, to Markov optimal stopping problems. Like the sequence detection problems of Section IV-A, such problems can be solved by dynamic programming, albeit by an infinite-interval version. In this section, we describe two such problems—classical sequential detection, and quickest detection. The former is concerned with the optimization of a hypothesis testing problem in which observations are potentially available for as long as we wish to observe. A tradeoff arises between the error probabilities (which can be made arbitrarily small by taking a sufficiently large observation interval), and the observation time. Here, we cast this problem into the framework of a Markov optimal stopping problem, and discuss its solution as the classical sequential probability ratio test of Wald. The latter problem (i.e., quickest detection) is a generalization of the classical sequential detection problem, first posed by Kolmogorov and Shiryayev in the late 1950's, in which the goal is to detect a possible change, at an unknown change point, from one statistical model to another. (The Poisson disorder problem discussed in Section II-E is an example of such a problem.) Here, in seeking to trade off detection delay with false-alarm rate, we again find a Markov optimal stopping problem, whose solution can be obtained by infinite-interval dynamic programming. Both these problems can be viewed as special cases of a more general class of optimal stopping problems known as "generalized parking" problems. As a final entry in the section, we discuss this type of problem briefly.

A. Classical Sequential Detection

Let us consider first the basic deterministic-signal detection problem

$$H_0: y(t) = v(t), \qquad t \geq 0$$

versus

$$H_1: y(t) = \mu + v(t), \qquad t \geq 0 \qquad (177)$$

where for simplicity we have assumed that the signal is the constant $\mu > 0$, and we further assume that $v(\cdot)$ is white and Gaussian with unit intensity. For the moment, we will adopt a Bayesian framework in which the prior probability that the signal is present is denoted by π.

If we observe $y(\cdot)$ over the time interval $[0, T]$, then it follows from basic detection theory that the detection strategy that minimizes the average probability of error in (177) is to decide H_1 whenever the likelihood ratio (3)

$$L(T) = \exp\left\{\mu\left(\int_0^T y(t)\,dt - \frac{\mu T}{2}\right)\right\} \qquad (178)$$

exceeds $\pi/(1-\pi)$, and to decide H_0 otherwise. The resulting probability of error can be written straightforwardly as

$$E_\pi\{\min\{\pi(T), 1 - \pi(T)\}\} \qquad (179)$$

where $\pi(T)$ denotes the posterior probability that H_1 is true, given the observations $\{y(t); 0 \leq t \leq T\}$; and where $E_\pi\{\cdot\}$ denotes expectation under the two probability models under H_0 and H_1, mixed with the prior π. The posterior probability $\pi(T)$ is given via Bayes formula as

$$\pi(T) = \frac{\pi L(T)}{1 - \pi + \pi L(T)}. \qquad (180)$$

In terms of $\pi(T)$, the optimal test is to choose H_1 whenever its posterior probability exceeds $1/2$. As $T \to \infty$, $\pi(T)$ converges almost surely to the indicator of the true hypothesis, and the quantity of (179) decreases monotonically to zero. Thus arbitrarily good performance can be obtained by increasing the length of the observation interval without bound.

In sequential detection, the length T of the observation interval is not fixed, but rather is a random variable depending on the observations. Moreover, this observation dependence must be causal, a condition that can be imposed by requiring that, for each $t \geq 0$, the event $\{T > t\}$ is a measurable function of the observations up to time t; i.e., $\{y(s); s \leq t\}$. Such a random variable is thus adapted to the observations, and is termed a *stopping time*. A *sequential decision rule* is composed of a stopping time T, which tells us when to stop observing, and a *terminal decision rule* $\delta_T \in \{0, 1\}$, which tells us which hypothesis to choose when we stop. It can be shown (see, for example, [90]) that, for a given stopping time T, the optimal terminal decision rule is the indicator of the event $\{\pi(T) \geq 1/2\}$ and the corresponding minimal error probability is given by (179). In this case, however, we must keep in mind that T is also a random variable; and so by $\pi(T)$ we mean the stochastic process $\{\pi(t); t \geq 0\}$ stopped at T, where $\pi(t)$ is the posterior probability that H_1 is true, given $\{y(s); s \leq t\}$. The expectation in (179) thus involves this additional element of randomness as well.

As noted above, we can obtain arbitrarily good performance at the expense of a long observation interval. However, in practical systems there is usually a cost of observations, either because of data acquisition costs or because of costs associated with delay. Thus a tradeoff arises between the length of the observation interval and the probability of error. A common way of optimizing this tradeoff over stopping times T is to consider the problem

$$\inf_{T \in \mathcal{T}} [E_\pi \{ \min \{ \pi(T), 1 - \pi(T) \} + cT \}] \qquad (181)$$

where $\mathcal{T}$ denotes the set of all stopping times adapted to the observations; and where $c > 0$ is the cost, per unit time, of taking observations. Since $\{\pi(t); t \geq 0\}$ is a homogeneous Markov process, the problem (181) is a Markov optimal stopping problem (see, for example, [107]), and can be solved relatively straightforwardly. In particular, the optimal stopping time is

$$T_{\text{opt}} = \inf \{ t \geq 0 | g(\pi(t)) = V(\pi(t)) \} \qquad (182)$$

where, for $\pi \in [0, 1]$,

$$g(\pi) = \min \{ \pi, 1 - \pi \} \qquad (183)$$

and

$$V(\pi) = \inf_{T \in \mathcal{T}} [E_\pi \{ \min \{ \pi(T), 1 - \pi(T) \} + cT \}]. \qquad (184)$$

It is straightforward to show that the function $V(\pi)$ is concave and is bounded as $0 \leq V(\pi) \leq g(\pi)$. From these properties it is easily seen that the optimal stopping time for (181) is the first exit time of the Markov process $\{\pi(t); t \geq 0\}$ from the interval (π_L, π_U), where π_L is the largest root of $g(\pi) = V(\pi)$ satisfying $0 \leq \pi_L \leq 1/2$, and π_U is the smallest root of $g(\pi) = V(\pi)$ satisfying $1/2 \leq \pi_U \leq 1$. That is, we have

$$T_{\text{opt}} = \inf \{ t \geq 0 | \pi(t) \notin (\pi_L, \pi_U) \}. \qquad (185)$$

So, the optimal sequential decision rule stops when $\{\pi(t); t \geq 0\}$ first exits the interval (π_L, π_U), and chooses H_1 or H_0 depending on whether the exit is at the upper or lower boundary, respectively. In view of (180), this sequential decision rule is the same as that which stops and decides at the first exit of $L(t)$ from the interval (A, B) with A and B chosen as

$$A = \frac{\pi_L (1 - \pi)}{\pi (1 - \pi_L)} \quad \text{and} \quad B = \frac{\pi_U (1 - \pi)}{\pi (1 - \pi_U)}. \qquad (186)$$

In this context, this test is known, as the *sequential probability ratio test* with boundaries (A, B) (i.e., the SPRT(A, B)).

For general A and B, the SPRT(A, B) enjoys a more general optimality property for the hypotheses of (177). In particular, it can be shown straightforwardly using Jensen's inequality (see, for example, [90]), that all sequential decision rules for (177) satisfy the following inequalities:

$$E_0 \{ T \} \geq -\frac{2}{\mu^2} \left[\alpha \log \left(\frac{1 - \gamma}{\alpha} \right) + (1 - \alpha) \log \left(\frac{\gamma}{1 - \alpha} \right) \right] \qquad (187)$$

and

$$E_1 \{ T \} \geq \frac{2}{\mu^2} \left[(1 - \gamma) \log \left(\frac{1 - \gamma}{\alpha} \right) + \gamma \log \left(\frac{\gamma}{1 - \alpha} \right) \right] \qquad (188)$$

where T is the stopping time of the rule, and where γ and α denote, respectively, the probabilities of false dismissal and

false alarm of the rule. Moreover, these inequalities become equalities for SPRT's. Thus it can be concluded that SPRT's minimize the average stopping time under both hypotheses, for fixed levels of false alarm and false dismissal, a result known as the *Wald–Wolfowitz theorem*.

The inequalities (187) and (188) allow a straightforward evaluation of the performance of the test SPRT(A, B), for which these inequalities hold with equality. In particular, since $E_0 \{T\}$ and $E_1 \{T\}$ are finite in this case, and since $\log L(t)$ is a Brownian motion under either H_0 or H_1, Wald's identity (e.g., [57]) can be used to write

$$E_0 \{ \log L(T) \} = -\frac{\mu^2}{2} E_0 \{ T \}$$

and

$$E_1 \{ \log L(T) \} = +\frac{\mu^2}{2} E_1 \{ T \}. \qquad (189)$$

Here, we have used the fact that the drift rate of $\log L(t)$ is $(-1)^{j+1} \mu^2 / 2$ under H_j. Since the sample paths of Brownian motion are almost surely continuous, $L(T)$ is a discrete random variable taking the two values A and B; that is, $L(t)$ touches the crossed boundary at the stopping time.[9] Under H_0, $L(T)$ takes the values A and B with probabilities $1 - \alpha$ and α, respectively; and under H_1, it takes the values A and B with probabilities γ and $1 - \gamma$, respectively. These distributions, together with (187)–(189), allow us to relate the performance indices $E_0\{T\}, E_1\{T\}, \gamma$, and α to the thresholds A and B and the drift parameter μ. For example, the error probabilities are related to these thresholds via the equations

$$\alpha = \frac{1 - A}{B - A} \quad \text{and} \quad \gamma = A \frac{B - 1}{B - A}. \qquad (190)$$

In the Bayesian case, $V(\pi)$ of (184) gives the minimal Bayes cost for a given prior π. This quantity can be evaluated using the relationships described in the preceding paragraph by minimizing the quantity

$$\pi \gamma + (1 - \pi) \alpha + c \pi E_1 \{ T \} + c (1 - \pi) E_0 \{ T \} \qquad (191)$$

over the region $0 < A < B < \infty$. However, a simpler way of evaluating $V(\pi)$ arises in the interpretation of Bayesian sequential detection as a generalized parking problem, as is discussed below.

B. Quickest Detection

It is of interest to generalize the simple binary model of (177) to the following composite observation model:

$$y(t) = \mu u(t - \theta) + v(t), \qquad t \geq 0 \qquad (192)$$

where μ and $v(\cdot)$ are as before, $u(\cdot)$ denotes the unit step function, and where $\theta \geq 0$ is an unknown time at which the mean of the observations shifts from zero to μ. Thus θ is an unknown change point, and we would like to detect the change at θ as quickly as possible after it occurs within some constraint on the probability of reacting too soon. This type

---

[9] Sequential tests between Poisson processes require a different treatment due to the discontinuity of sample paths. A technique based on delay-differential equations in described in [21].

of problem, and its generalizations to change points between more complicated statistical models, are known as quickest detection problems (or disorder problems—cf., Section II-E). There are many applications in which such problems arise, including remote sensing (radar, sonar, and seismography), quality control, machinery and vibration monitoring, financial decision-making, and the segmentation of data sources such as speech and video for compression. (See [5] for further discussion.)

To approach the quickest detection problem, we consider, as detectors, stopping times adapted to the observations (192). The interpretation of a stopping time T in this context is that, when $T = t$ we announce that the change has occured at or before time t. The conditional average detection delay incurred by such a detector is thus

$$E\{(T - \theta)^+|\theta\} \qquad (193)$$

where x^+ denotes $\max\{x, 0\}$; and where $E\{\cdot|\theta\}$ denotes expectation under the probability model described by (192) with θ fixed. To optimize over all possible stopping times, we would like to trade off some aggregate measure of this delay against a measure of the likelihood of reacting too early. To consider such optimization, it is useful to consider a Bayesian situation, in which the change point θ is assumed to be a random variable with a known prior distribution.[10] In this case, we can consider the overall average detection delay (i.e., the average of (193) with respect to the prior): $E\{(T-\theta)^+\}$. This quantity can be balanced with the probability of false alarm, which is $P(T < \theta)$. Analogously with the situation in (181), we can thus seek to optimize T by solving

$$\inf_{T \in \mathcal{T}} [P(T < \theta) + cE\{(T - \theta)^+\}]. \qquad (194)$$

The problem (194) can be reduced to a simpler form by defining the posterior probability

$$\pi(t) = P(\theta \leq t|y(s); s \leq t), \qquad t \geq 0 \qquad (195)$$

and rewriting (194) as

$$\inf_{T \in \mathcal{T}} \left[E \left\{ 1 - \pi(T) + c \int_0^T \pi(t)\, dt \right\} \right] \qquad (196)$$

where the second term under the expectation is derived using the (non-Gaussian) innovations theorem (cf., Section II-D) in the model (192) (see [107]). Let us now restrict attention to the *geometric prior*: $P(\theta = 0) = \pi$ and

$$P(\theta > t|\theta > s) = e^{-\lambda(t-s)}, \qquad t > s \geq 0 \qquad (197)$$

where $\lambda > 0$ is a constant. This prior is a very common one for modeling times to failure and similar phenomena. In this case, the process $\{\pi(t); t \geq 0\}$ is a homogeneous Markov process, and so (196) is a Markov optimal stopping problem. Similarly to the situation in sequential detection, the optimal stopping time is given by

$$T_{\text{opt}} = \inf\{t \geq 0|g(\pi(t)) = V(\pi(t))\} \qquad (198)$$

where now

$$g(\pi) = 1 - \pi \qquad (199)$$

and

$$V(\pi) = \inf_{T \in \mathcal{T}} \left[E_\pi \left\{ 1 - \pi(T) + c \int_0^T \pi(t)\, dt \right\} \right]. \qquad (200)$$

In (200) $E_\pi\{\cdot\}$ denotes expectation in the model of (192) with the geometric prior (197). Using analysis similar to that used in the sequential detection problem, it follows that V is concave, decreasing, and bounded as $0 \leq V(\pi) \leq g(\pi)$. From these properties, it follows that

$$T_{\text{opt}} = \inf\{t \geq 0|\pi(t) \geq \tau\} \qquad (201)$$

with $\tau = \inf\{\pi \in [0, 1]|g(\pi) = V(\pi)\}$. Thus the optimal quickest detection procedure in this model is to react when the posterior probability that the change has occurred exceeds an appropriate threshold.

In the absence of a prior on the change point θ, the above approach cannot be applied to seek an optimal detection time. An alternative formulation is to use a minimax criterion[11]

$$\inf_{T \in \mathcal{T}} \sup_{\theta \geq 0} [\text{esssup}\, E\{(T - \theta)^+|\theta; y(t), t \leq \theta\}]$$

$$\text{subject to } E\{T|\theta = \infty\} \geq \beta \qquad (202)$$

where β is a fixed lower bound. The quantity

$$\text{esssup}\, E\{(T - \theta)^+|\theta; y(t), t \leq \theta\}$$

is the worst case delay incurred by the stopping T when the change point is at θ, where the worst case is taken over all sample paths of the observations up until the change. The quantity $E\{T|\theta = \infty\}$ is the average time until a false alarm, and can equivalently be thought of as the *mean time between false alarms* if the detector is restarted after false alarms. So, the optimization criterion (202) is to choose T to have minimal maximal worst case delay, within a lower bound constraint on the mean time between false alarms. The discrete-time version of this criterion and a solution, were proposed by Lorden [67] in the 1970's, and the optimality of this solution was proved by Moustakides [75] in the 1980's. The continuous-time problem was solved recently by Beibel [8] and by Shiryaev [108] using two alternate methods of proof. This optimal solution is given by the so-called cumulative sum (CUSUM) test

$$T = \inf\{t \geq 0|X(t) \geq \tau\} \qquad (203)$$

where

$$X(t) = \sup_{\theta \leq t} \frac{L(t)}{L(\theta)} \qquad (204)$$

(as before, $L(t)$ denotes the likelihood ratio (178)), and where τ is a threshold chosen to meet the false-alarm constraint with equality. Note that

$$\log X(t) = Y(t) - \inf_{\theta \leq t} Y(\theta) \qquad (205)$$

---

[10]Note that a simple Bayesian example is given by the prior $P(\theta = 0) = \pi = 1 - P(\theta = \infty)$, in which case (192) reduces to the model of (177).

[11]The essential supremum (esssup) of a random variable is the smallest constant that dominates the random variable with probability 1.

210

where $\{Y(t); t \geq 0\}$ is the Brownian motion

$$Y(t) = \mu \int_0^t y(s)\,ds - \mu^2 t/2. \qquad (206)$$

So, the CUSUM test reacts when this Brownian motion exceeds its historical minimal value by the amount $\log \tau$. Note that $Y(t)$ drifts downward at the rate $-\mu^2/2$ before the change point, and then upward at the rate $+\mu^2/2$ after the change point.

The performance of the CUSUM test can be evaluated exactly using martingale properties of the CUSUM statistic (205) (see, for example, [66]). The minimum Bayes cost, $V(\pi)$ of (200), can also be found in closed form [107]. As in sequential detection, this quanitity can also be found from a generalized parking approach to Bayesian quickest detection, as will be discussed in the following section.

C. Generalized Parking

The above analysis of the sequential detection problem is the classical one, developed in discrete time by Wald [132] more than fifty years ago (contemporary with Shannon's fundamental work on information theory), and generalized to continuous time by several people, including Dvoretsky, Kiefer, and Wolfowitz [25] and Shiryaev [107]. Similarly, the Bayesian analysis of the quickest detection problem is the traditional one of Shiryaev from the 1960's [106]. A more recent approach to such problems is to view them as so-called *generalized parking problems* [9], and here we review this approach briefly.

In essence, a generalized parking problem (see [139]) is an optimal stopping problem of the form

$$\inf_{T \in \mathcal{T}} E\{f(X(T))\} \qquad (207)$$

where f is a function with a unique minimum, and $\{X(t); t \geq 0\}$ is a stochastic process to which the stopping times in $\mathcal{T}$ are adapted. The basic idea is that we would like to stop (i.e., "park") when $X(t)$ hits the minimizing argument of f, if possible. The Bayesian versions of both the sequential and quickest detection problems described above can be written in this way, thereby leading to an alternative solution method and interpretation of the optimal solutions. Since the observations in these problems have continuous sample paths (and can thus hit the minimum exactly), the main challenge here is to write the objectives of the optimization criteria (181) and (194) in the form (207)

Consider first the sequential detection problem (181), and denote by $R(T)$ the objective of this optimization; i.e.,

$$R(T) = E_\pi\{\min\{\pi(T), 1 - \pi(T)\} + cT\}. \qquad (208)$$

Note that, if we could write $E_\pi\{T\}$ in the form $E_\pi\{h(\pi(T))\}$ for some function h, then we we might be able to write $R(T)$ in the form (207). Let us rewrite the mixture model (177) with priors π and $1 - \pi$ as

$$y(t) = \xi\mu + v(t), \qquad t \geq 0 \qquad (209)$$

where ξ is a discrete random variable taking the values 0 and 1 with probabilities $1 - \pi$ and π, respectively. The process

$\{\pi(t); t \geq 0\}$ arising in (181) is thus given by

$$\pi(t) = E_\pi\{\xi|y(s); s \leq t\}. \qquad (210)$$

The basic theory of nonlinear filtering (see, for example, [89, Ch. VII]) then tells us that $\{\pi(t); t \geq 0\}$ is a diffusion satisfying the following Ito stochastic differential equation:

$$d\pi(t) = \mu\pi(t)[1 - \pi(t)]\,dI(t), \qquad \pi(0) = \pi \qquad (211)$$

where $\{I(t); t \geq 0\}$ denotes the innovations process

$$I(t) = \int_0^t [y(s) - \mu\pi(s)]\,ds, \qquad t \geq 0 \qquad (212)$$

which is a standard Brownian motion under the model (209), as discussed in Section II-D. Now, let us consider the function $h\colon (0, 1) \to \mathbb{R}$ given by

$$h(x) = \frac{2}{\mu^2}\left[(2x-1)\log\left(\frac{x}{1-x}\right) - (2\pi-1)\log\left(\frac{\pi}{1-\pi}\right)\right],$$
$$x \in (0, 1). \quad (213)$$

The Ito differentiation rule (e.g., [89, Proposition VII.D.1]) implies that

$$dh(\pi(t)) = h''(\pi(t))\frac{\mu^2}{2}[\pi(t)[1 - \pi(t)]]^2\,dt$$
$$+ \mu h'(\pi(t))\pi(t)[1 - \pi(t)]\,dI(t) \qquad (214)$$

which reduces to

$$dh(\pi(t)) = dt + \mu h'(\pi(t))\pi(t)[1 - \pi(t)]\,dI(t) \qquad (215)$$

or

$$h(\pi(t)) = t + \mu \int_0^t h'(\pi(s))\pi(s)[1 - \pi(s)]\,dI(s). \qquad (216)$$

The integral in (216), being the Ito integral of a bounded function with respect to Brownian motion, is a martingale under the model (209). Thus the optional sampling theorem [57] implies that, for any bounded stopping time T

$$E_\pi\{h(\pi(T))\} = E_\pi\{T\}. \qquad (217)$$

It follows that, for *bounded* stopping times T we can write $R(T)$ in the form (207) with $X(t) = \pi(t)$ and

$$f(x) = \min\{x, 1 - x\} + ch(x). \qquad (218)$$

Straightforward analysis of this function f shows that it has exactly two global minima on $(0, 1)$, at the points $x_0 \in (0, 1/2)$ and $x_1 = 1 - x_0$ solving

$$ch'(x_0) = -1 \quad \text{and} \quad ch'(x_1) = +1. \qquad (219)$$

(Note that, although h depends on π, its derivative—and thus x_0 and x_1—does not.) So, for all bounded stopping times, we have that

$$R(T) \geq f(x_0) \qquad (220)$$

a bound that can be extended via the monotone convergence theorem to all stopping times. (For analytical details of this problem, the reader is referred to [90].) Now, suppose the prior $\pi \in [x_0, x_1]$. The posterior probability $\pi(t)$ will converge almost surely to either 0 or 1 as $t \to \infty$. Since $\{\pi(t); t \geq 0\}$ has continuous sample paths, it will have to pass through one of x_0 or x_1 at some point in time. Let T_o be the first time it does so. It can be shown using the bounded convergence theorem that $R(T_o) = E_\pi\{f(\pi_{T_o})\}$. Since $\pi_{T_o} \in \{x_0, x_1\}$, it follows that $R(T_o) = f(x_0)$, and so T_o is optimal. It can also be shown (again, see, [90]) that, when $\pi \notin [x_0, x_1]$ the optimal thing to do is to stop immediately, in which case $R(T) = R(0) = \min\{\pi, 1 - \pi\}$.

In conclusion of the above, we see that the optimal stopping time for sequential detection is

$$T_{\text{opt}} = \inf\{t \geq 0 | \pi(t) \notin (x_0, x_1)\} \qquad (221)$$

and the corresponding minimal Bayes cost is

$$R(T_{\text{opt}}) = \begin{cases} f(x_0), & \text{if } \pi \in [x_0, x_1] \\ \min\{\pi, 1 - \pi\}, & \text{otherwise.} \end{cases} \qquad (222)$$

Comparing (221) with (185), we see that the thresholds π_L and π_U from (185) are just the solutions x_0 and x_1 of (219). Moreover, we conclude that the minimal Bayes cost $V(\pi) = \inf_T R(T)$ is given explicitly by (222), once x_0 is determined. (Recall that f depends on π through the dependence of h on π.)

The Bayesian quickest detection problem with geometric prior can similarly be formulated and solved as a generalized parking problem, as is shown by Beibel in [7]. Here, analogously with (210), we have the diffusion

$$\pi(t) = E_\pi\{u(t - \theta)|y(s); s \leq t\} \qquad (223)$$

which, similarly to (211), satisfies the Ito stochastic differential equation

$$d\pi(t) = \lambda[1 - \pi(t)]\,dt + \mu\pi(t)[1 - \pi(t)]\,dI(t), \pi(0) = \pi \qquad (224)$$

where λ is the parameter of the geometric prior, and $I(t)$ is the innovations process. Define the function $h\colon (0, 1) \to \mathbb{R}$ by

$$h(x) = \frac{2}{\mu^2} \int_\pi^x e^{-\Gamma H(y)} \int_0^y e^{\Gamma H(z)} \frac{1}{z(1 - z)^2}\,dz\,dy \qquad (225)$$

with $\Gamma = 2\lambda/\mu^2$ and

$$H(y) = \log\frac{y}{1 - y} - \frac{1}{y}. \qquad (226)$$

Again applying the Ito differentiation rule, we have

$$df(\pi(t)) = \pi(t)\,dt + \mu h'(\pi(t))\pi(t)[1 - \pi(t)]\,dI(t) \qquad (227)$$

which implies that

$$f(\pi(t)) = \int_0^t \pi(s)\,ds + M(t) \qquad (228)$$

where $M(t)$ is a martingale under the model (192). Thus for bounded stopping times T we can write

$$E_\pi\{(T - \theta)^+\} \equiv E_\pi\left\{\int_0^T \pi(s)\,ds\right\} = E\{h(\pi(T))\} \qquad (229)$$

and the analysis of the Bayesian quickest detection problem as a generalized parking problem follows similarly to that of the sequential detection problem outlined above.

CONCLUDING REMARKS

As noted in the introductory remarks, by necessity we have limited this review to certain subsets of the topics in this very large field, chosen to enable the authors to present a connected, and hopefully interesting, account of the evolution of the main ideas therein. There are many aspects of this problem that we have not treated here. Issues such as robustness and non-Gaussian noise have been touched upon very briefly; however, these are important issues in applications, and more detailed treatments of these issues can be found, for examples, in [1], [58], [60], and [74]. We also mentioned briefly RKHS methods for the detection of non-Gaussian signals, and for signal and noise models exhibiting fractal behavior. Further techniques for the detection of non-Gaussian signals are reviewed in [30], and methods for exploiting self-similarity are described, for examples, in [2] and [96]. Other major topics that have not been touched upon at all include distributed detection ([13], [119], [129]), nonparametric methods of detection ([32], [59], [118]), quantum detection ([38]), detection using higher-order statistics [26], [77], and detection with arrays [99], [100]. (The volume [91] contains general reviews of many developments in signal detection.) Many of these techniques are based primarily on sampled systems, and as such go beyond the basic likelihood-ratio processing described in this paper and into algorithmic issues.

Before closing, it is interesting to contemplate what may be in store for the field over the coming decades. If we examine the basic developments in likelihood-ratio-based detection of the past, we can see a clear progression from the simplest problem of detecting a single, deterministic, signal observed on a single path studied in the 1940's, through the somewhat more complex problem of detecting parametrized signals (typified by the multipath problem) studied in the 1950's, the mathematically rich problems of quickest detection and the detection of stochastic signals studied in the 1960's, into more complex algorithmic structures such as sequence detection in the 1970's and multiuser detection in 1980's and 1990's. So, we have encountered the matched filter, the RAKE receiver, the estimator–correlator, maximum-likelihood sequence detectors, and the SPRT and CUSUM detectors. Of course, in parallel with these developments in basic likelihood-ratio structures, have been other developments in detection theory and practice as noted in the preceding paragraph. In the coming years, we may expect many more applications of complex signal detection procedures (such as multiuser detection), as the relentless Moore's Law type growth in processing power permits the implementations required for such procedures.

REFERENCES

[1] C. R. Baker and A. F. Gualtierotti, "Likelihood-ratio detection of stochastic signals," in *Advances in Statistical Signal Processing—Vol. 2: Signal Detection*, H. V. Poor and J. B. Thomas, Eds. Greenwich, CT: JAI, 1993, ch. 1, pp. 1–34.

[2] R. J. Barton and H. V. Poor, "Signal detection in fractional Gaussian noise," *IEEE Trans. Inform. Theory*, vol. 34, pp. 943–959, Sept. 1988.

[3] ——, "An RKHS approach to robust L^2 estimation and signal detection," *IEEE Trans. Inform. Theory*, vol. 36, pp. 579–588, May 1990.

[4] ——, "On generalized signal-to-noise ratios in quadratic detection," *Math. Contr., Signals, Syst.*, vol. 5, no. 1, pp. 81–92, 1992.

[5] M. Basseville and I. Nikiforov, *Detection of Abrupt Changes: Theory and Applications*. Englewood Cliffs, NJ: Prentice-Hall, 1993.

[6] T. Bayes, "An essay toward solving a problem in the doctrine of chances," *Phil. Trans. Roy. Soc.*, vol. 53, pp. 370–418, 1763. (Reprinted in *Biometrika*, vol. 45, pp. 293–315, 1958.)

[7] M. Beibel, "Bayes problems in change-point models for the Wiener process," in *Change Point Problems*, Carlstein, H. G. Müller, and D. Siegmund, Eds. Hayward, CA: Inst. Math. Statist., 1994, pp. 1–6.

[8] ——, "A note on Ritov's Bayes approach to the minimax property of the CUSUM procedure," *Ann. Statist.*, vol. 24, no. 4, pp. 1804–1812, 1996.

[9] M. Beibel and H. R. Lerche, "A new look at optimal stopping problems related to mathematical finance," *Statistica Sinica*, vol. 7, pp. 93–108, 1997.

[10] T. G. Bell, "Submarine and Sonar Detection," U.S. Navy Underwater Sound Lab. Rep. 545, 1962.

[11] R. Bellman, *Dynamic Programming*. Princeton, NJ: Princeton Univ. Press, 1957.

[12] R. Bellman and R. Kalaba, "On the role of dynamic programming in statistical communication theory," *IRE Trans. Inform. Theory*, vol. IT-3, pp. 197–203, 1957. (See also: *Proc. Nat. Acad. Sci. USA*, vol. 43, no. 8, pp. 930–933, 1957.)

[13] R. S. Blum, S. A. Kassam, and H. V. Poor, "Distributed detection with multiple sensors—Part II: Advanced topics," *Proc. IEEE*, vol. 85, pp. 64–79, Jan. 1997.

[14] H. W. Bode and C. E. Shannon, "A simplified derivation of linear least squares smoothing and prediction theory," *Proc. IRE*, vol. 38, pp. 417–425, Apr. 1950.

[15] P. Bremaud, *Point Processes and Queues: Martingale Dynamics*. New York: Springer-Verlag, 1981.

[16] R. H. Cameron and W. T. Martin, "Transformation of Wiener integrals under translation," *Ann. Math.*, vol. 45, no. 3, pp. 386–396, 1944.

[17] R. Cotes, "Aestimatio errorum in mixta mathesi, per variationes partium trianguli plani et sphaerici," in *Opera Miscellanea*, published with *Harmonia Mensurarum*, R. Smith, Ed., Cambridge, England, 1722.

[18] S. Csibi, *Stochastic Processes with Learning Properties*. Berlin, Germany: Springer-Verlag, 1975.

[19] M. H. A. Davis and E. Andreadakis, "Exact and approximate filtering in signal detection: An example," *IEEE Trans. Inform. Theory*, vol. IT-23, pp. 768–772, Nov. 1977.

[20] C. Dellacherie and P. A. Meyer, *Probabilities and Potentials: Theory of Martingales*. Amsterdam, The Netherlands: North Holland, 1982.

[21] J. DeLucia and H. V. Poor, "Performance analysis of sequential tests between Poisson processes," *IEEE Trans. Inform. Theory*, vol. 41, pp. 221–238, Jan. 1997.

[22] J. L. Doob, *Stochastic Processes*. New York: Wiley, 1953.

[23] T. E. Duncan, "Evaluation of likelihood functions," *Inform. Contr.*, vol. 13, no. 1, pp. 62–74, 1968.

[24] D. L. Duttweiler and T. Kailath, "RKHS approach to detection and estimation problems—Part IV: NonGaussian detection," *IEEE Trans. Inform. Theory*, vol. IT-19, pp. 19–28, Jan. 1973.

[25] A. Dvorestsky, J. Kiefer, and J. Wolfowitz, "Sequential decision problems for processes with continuous time parameter. Testing hypotheses," *Ann. Math. Statist.*, vol. 24, pp. 254–264, 1953.

[26] R. F. Dwyer, "Broadband detection based on higher-order cumulants and spectra," in *Advances in Statistical Signal Processing—Vol. 2: Signal Detection*, H. V. Poor and J. B. Thomas, Eds. Greenwich, CT: JAI Press, 1993, ch. 2, pp. 35–60.

[27] R. A. Fisher, "On the mathematical foundations of theoretical statistics," *Phil. Trans. Roy. Soc.*, vol. A 222, pp. 309–368, 1922.

[28] G. D. Forney, Jr., "Maximum-likelihood sequence estimation of digital sequences in the presence of intersymbol interference," *IEEE Trans. Inform. Theory*, vol. IT-18, pp. 363–378, May 1972.

[29] D. Gabor, "Theory of communication," *J. Inst. Elec. Eng. (London)*, vol. 93, 1946.

[30] L. M. Garth and H. V. Poor, "The detection of non-Gaussian signals: A paradigm for modern statistical signal processing," *Proc. IEEE*, vol. 82, pp. 1061–1095, July 1994.

[31] C. F. Gauss, *Theoria Combinationis Observationum Erroribus Minimis Obnoxiae*. Göttingen, Germany: Dieterich, 1823.

[32] J. D. Gibson and J. L. Melsa, *Introduction to Nonparametric Detection with Applications*. New York: IEEE Press, 1996.

[33] I. V. Girsanov, "On transforming a certain class of stochastic processes by absolutely continuous substitution of measures," *Theory Probab. Appl.*, vol. 5, pp. 285–301, 1960.

[34] I. Gohberg and M. G. Krein, *Introduction to Linear Nonself-Adjoint Operators*. Providence, RI: Amer. Math. Soc., 1969 (English translation).

[35] I. Gohberg and M. G. Krein, *Theory and Applications of Volterra Operators in Hilbert Space*. Providence, RI: Amer. Math. Soc., 1970.

[36] U. Grenander, "Stochastic processes and statistical inference," *Arkiv für Mat.*, vol. 1, no. 17, pp. 195–277, 1950.

[37] J. Hajek, "On linear statistical problems in stochastic processes," *Czech. Math. J.*, vol. 12, pp. 404–444, 1962.

[38] C. W. Helstrom, *Quantum Detection and Estimation Theory*. New York: Academic, 1976.

[39] C. W. Helstrom, *Elements of Signal Detection and Estimation*. Englewood Cliffs, NJ: Prentice-Hall, 1995.

[40] M. L. Honig, U. Madhow, and S. Verdú, "Adaptive blind multi-user detection," *IEEE Trans. Inform. Theory*, vol. 41, pp. 944–960, July 1995.

[41] M. L. Honig and H. V. Poor, "Adaptive Interference Suppression," in *Wireless Communications: Signal Processing Perspectives*, H. V. Poor and G. W. Wornell, Eds. Upper Saddle River, NJ: Prentice-Hall, 1998, ch. 2, pp. 64–128.

[42] K. Ito, "On stochastic differential equations," *Mem. Amer. Math. Soc.*, vol. 4, 1951.

[43] T. T. Kadota, "Differentiation of Karhunen–Loève expansion and application to optimum reception of sure signals in noise," *IEEE Trans. Inform. Theory*, vol. IT-13, pp. 255–260, 1967.

[44] T. Kailath, "A projection method for signal detection in colored Gaussian noise," *IEEE Trans. Inform. Theory*, vol. IT-13, pp. 441–447, 1967.

[45] ——, "An innovations approach to least-squares estimation—Part I: Linear filtering in additive white noise," *IEEE Trans. Automat. Contr.*, vol. AC-13, pp. 646–655, 1968.

[46] ——, "A general likelihood-ratio formula for random signals in Gaussian noise," *IEEE Trans. Inform. Theory*, vol. IT-15, pp. 350–361, 1969.

[47] ——, "Likelihood ratios for Gaussian processes," *IEEE Trans. Inform. Theory*, vol. IT-16, pp. 276–287, May 1970.

[48] ——, "RKHS approach to detection and estimation problems—Part I: Determinstic signals in Gaussian noise," *IEEE Trans. Inform. Theory*, vol. IT-17, pp. 530–549, 1971.

[49] ——, "The structure of Radon–Nikodym derivatives with respect to Wiener and related measures," *Ann. Math. Statist.*, vol. 42, pp. 1054–1067, 1971.

[50] ——, *Lectures on Wiener and Kalman Filtering*. Vienna, Austria: Springer-Verlag, 1981.

[51] T. Kailath and D. Duttweiler, "An RKHS approach to detection and estimation problems—Part III: Generalized innovations representations and a likelihood-ratio formula," *IEEE Trans. Inform. Theory*, vol. IT-18, pp. 730–745, 1972.

[52] T. Kailath, R. T. Geesey, and H. L. Weinert, "Some relations among RKHS norms, Fredholm equations, and innovations representations," *IEEE Trans. Inform. Theory*, vol. IT-18, pp. 341–348, 1972.

[53] T. Kailath and H. L. Weinert, "An RKHS approach to detection and estimation problems—Part II: Gaussian signal detection," *IEEE Trans. Inform. Theory*, vol. IT-21, pp. 15–23, 1975.

[54] G. Kallianpur and H. Oodaira, "The equivalence and singularity of Gaussian measures," in *Proc. Symp. on Time Series Analysis*. New York: Wiley, 1963, pp. 279–291.

[55] R. E. Kalman, "A new approach to linear filtering and prediction problems," *J. Basic Eng.*, vol. 82, pp. 34–45, Mar. 1960.

[56] R. E. Kalman and R. S. Bucy, "New results in linear filtering and prediction theory," *Trans. ASME, Ser. D—J. Basic Eng.*, vol. 83, pp. 94–107, Dec. 1961.

[57] I. Karatzas and S. Shreve, *Brownian Motion and Stochastic Calculus—Second Edition*. New York: Springer-Verlag, 1991.

[58] S. A. Kassam, *Signal Detection in Non-Gaussian Noise*. New York: Springer-Verlag, 1988.

[59] ——, "Nonparametric signal detection," in *Advances in Statistical Signal Processing—Vol. 2: Signal Detection*, H. V. Poor and J. B. Thomas, Eds. Greenwich, CT: JAI, 1993, pp. 61–100.

[60] S. A. Kassam and H. V. Poor, "Robust techniques for signal processing: A survey," *Proc. IEEE*, vol. 73, no. 3, pp. 433–481, Mar. 1985.

[61] G. Kimeldorf and G. Wahba, "Some results on Tchebycheffian spline functions," *J. Math. Mech.*, vol. 15, pp. 953–969, 1971.

[62] V. A. Kotel'nikov, *The Theory of Optimum Noise Immunity*. New York: McGraw-Hill, 1959 (translated by R.A. Silverman).

[63] H. Kunita and S. Watanabe, "On square integrable martingales," *Nagoya Math J.*, vol. 30, pp. 209–245, 1967.

[64] H. Kushner, "On the differential equations satisfied by conditional

probability densities of Markov processes," *SIAM J. Contr.*, vol. 2, pp. 10–119, 1964.

[65] J. Lawson and G. E. Uhlenbeck, *Threshold Signals.* New York: McGraw-Hill, 1948.

[66] J. P. Lehoczky, "Formulas for stopped diffusion processes with stopping times based on the maximum," *Ann. Probab.*, vol. 5, no. 4, pp. 601–607, 1977.

[67] G. Lorden, "Procedures for reacting to a change in distribution," *Ann. Math. Statist.*, vol. 42, no. 6, pp. 1897–1908, 1971.

[68] R. Lupas and S. Verdú, "Linear multiuser detectors for synchronous code-division multiple-access channels," *IEEE Trans. Inform. Theory*, vol. 35, pp. 123–136, Jan. 1989.

[69] R. J. McEliece, D. J. C. MacKay, and J.-F. Cheng, "Turbo decoding as an instance of Pearl's 'belief propagation' algorithm," *IEEE. J. Select. Areas Commun.*, vol. 16, pp. 140–152, Feb. 1998.

[70] D. G. Messerschmitt, "A geometric theory of intersymbol interference," *Bell Syst. Tech. J.*, vol. 52, pp. 1483–1539, 1973.

[71] P. A. Meyer, "Sur les integrales stochastiques," Sem. Prob. X in *Lecture Notes in Mathematics*, vol. 511. Berlin, Germany: Springer-Verlag, 1976, pp. 246–400,

[72] D. Middleton, "Statistical theory of signal detection," *IRE Trans. Prof. Group Inform. Theory*, vol. PGIT-3, pp. 26–52, 1954.

[73] D. Middleton, personal communication, Nov. 24, 1997.

[74] D. Middleton and A. D. Spaulding, "Elements of weak-signal detection in non-Gaussian noise environments," in *Advances in Statistical Signal Processing—Vol. 2: Signal Detection*, H. V. Poor and J. B. Thomas, Eds. Greenwich, CT: JAI, 1993, ch. 6, pp. 137–216.

[75] G. V. Moustakides, "Optimal stopping times for detecting changes in distributions," *Ann. Statist.*, vol. 14, pp. 1379–1387, 1986.

[76] J. Neyman and E. Pearson, "On the problem of the most efficient tests of statistical hypotheses," *Phil. Trans. Roy. Soc.*, vol. A 231, no. 9, pp. 492–510, 1933.

[77] C. L. Nikias and A. P. Petropulu, *Higher-order Spectral Analysis: A Nonlinear Signal Processing Framework.* Englewood Cliffs, NJ: Prentice-Hall, 1993.

[78] D. O. North, "An analysis of the factors which determine signal/noise discrimination in pulsed-carrier systems," RCA Lab. Rep. PTR-6C, June 1943. (Reprinted in *Proc. IEEE*, vol. 51, pp. 1016–1027, July 1963.)

[79] D. O. North, personal communication, Apr. 15, 1998.

[80] J. K. Omura, "On the Viterbi decoding algorithm," *IEEE Trans. Inform. Theory*, vol. IT-15, pp. 177–179, Jan. 1969.

[81] E. Parzen, "An approach to time-series analysis," *Ann. Math. Stat.*, vol. 32, pp. 275–279, 1961.

[82] ——, "Extraction and detection problems and reproducing kernel Hilbert spaces," *J. SIAM Control, Ser. A*, vol. 1, no. 1, pp. 35–62, 1962.

[83] ——, "Probability density functionals and reproducing kernel Hilbert spaces," in *Proc. Symp. Time Series Analysis*. New York: Wiley, 1963, pp. 951–989.

[84] A. J. Paulraj and C. B. Papadias, "Space-time processing for wireless communications," *IEEE Signal Processing Mag.*, vol. 14, no. 6, pp. 49–83, Nov. 1997.

[85] A. J. Paulraj, C. B. Papadias, V. U. Reddy, and A. J. van der Veen, "Blind space-time signal processing," in *Wireless Communications: Signal Processing Perspectives*, H. V. Poor and G. W. Wornell, Eds. Upper Saddle River, NJ: Prentice-Hall, 1998, ch. 4, pp. 179–210.

[86] W. W. Peterson, T. G. Birdsall, and W. C. Fox, "The theory of signal detectability," *IRE Trans. Prof. Group Inform. Theory*, vol. PGIT-4, pp. 171 and ff., 1954.

[87] T. Pitcher, "Likelihood ratios of Gaussian processes," *Ark. Mat.*, vol. 4, pp. 35–44, 1959.

[88] H. V. Poor, "Robust matched filters," *IEEE Trans. Inform. Theory*, vol. IT-29, pp. 677–687, July 1983.

[89] ——, *An Introduction to Signal Detection and Estimation–Second Edition.* New York: Springer-Verlag, 1994.

[90] ——, *Quickest Detection.* Cambridge, UK: Cambridge Univ. Press, 199, to be published..

[91] H. V. Poor and J. B. Thomas, Eds., *Advances in Statistical Signal Processing—Vol. 2: Signal Detection.* Greenwich, CT: JAI, 1993.

[92] H. V. Poor and S. Verdú, "Probability of error in MMSE multiuser detection," *IEEE Trans. Inform. Theory*, vol. 43, pp. 858–871, May 1997.

[93] H. V. Poor and G. W. Wornell, Eds. *Wireless Communications: Signal Processing Perspectives.* Upper Saddle River, NJ: Prentice-Hall, 1998.

[94] R. I. Price, "Optimum detection of stochastic signals in noise with application to scatter-multipath channels," *IRE Trans. Inform. Theory*, vol. IT-2, pp. 125–135, Dec. 1956; correction, vol. IT-3, no. 4, p. 256, 1957.

[95] R. I. Price and P. E. Green, Jr., "A communication technique for multipath channels," *Proc. IRE*, vol. 46, pp. 555–570, Mar. 1958.

[96] I. S. Reed, P. C. Lee, and T. K. Truong, "Spectral representation of fractional Brownian motion in n dimensions and its properties," *IEEE Trans. Inform. Theory*, vol. 41, pp. 1493–1451, Sept. 1995.

[97] D. Revuz and M. Yor, *Continuous Martingales and Brownian Motion—Second Edition.* Berlin, Germany: Springer-Verlag, 1994.

[98] W. L. Root, "Singular Gaussian measures in detection theory," in *Proc. Symp. Time Series Analysis*, M. Rosenblatt, Ed. New York: Wiley, 1963, pp. 292–315.

[99] R. Roy and T. Kailath, "ESPRIT—Estimation of signal parameters via rotational invariance techniques," *IEEE Trans. Signal Processing*, vol. 37, pp. 984–995, 1989.

[100] R. Schmidt, "A signal subspace approach to multiple emitter location and spectral estimation," Ph.D. dissertation, Elec. Eng. Dept., Stanford Univ., Stanford, CA, 1981.

[101] F. C. Schweppe, "Evaluation of likelihood functions for Gaussian signals," *IEEE Trans. Inform. Theory*, vol. IT-11, pp. 61–70, 1965.

[102] A. Segall and T. Kailath, "The modeling of randomly modulated jump processes," *IEEE Trans. Inform. Theory*, vol. IT-21, pp. 135–143, Mar. 1975.

[103] ——, "Radon–Nikodym derivatives with respect to measures induced by discontinuous independent-increment processes," *Ann. Probab.*, vol. 3, pp. 449–464, 1975.

[104] C. E. Shannon, "Communication in the presence of noise," *Proc. IRE*, vol. 37, pp. 10–21, 1949.

[105] L. A. Shepp, "Radon–Nikodym derivatives of Gaussian measures," *Ann. Math. Statist.*, vol. 37, pp. 321–335, 1966.

[106] A. N. Shiryaev, "On optimal methods in quickest detection problems," *Theory Probab. Appl.*, vol. 8, no. 1, pp. 22–46, 1963.

[107] ——, *Optimal Stopping Rules.* New York: Springer-Verlag, 1978.

[108] ——, "Minimax optimality of the method of cumulative sums (cusum) in the case of continuous time," *Commun. Moscow Math. Soc.*, pp. 750–751, 1996.

[109] G. S. Sidhu and H. L. Weinert, "Vector-valued Lg-splines I. Interpolating splines," *J. Math. Anal. Appl.*, vol. 70, pp. 505–529, 1979.

[110] W. M. Siebert, "A radar detection philosophy," *IRE Trans. Inform. Theory*, vol. IT-6, pp. 204–211, Sept. 1956.

[111] D. L. Snyder, *Random Point Processes.* New York: Wiley, 1975.

[112] D. L. Snyder and M. I. Miller, *Random Point Processes in Time and Space—Second Edition.* New York: Springer-Verlag, 1991.

[113] S. M. Stigler, *The History of Statistics: The Measurement of Uncertainy before 1900.* Cambridge, MA: Harvard Univ. Press, 1986.

[114] R. L. Stratonovich, "Optimum nonlinear systems which bring about a separation of a signal with constant parameters from noise," *Radiofizika*, vol. 2, no. 6, pp. 892–901, 1959.

[115] ——, "Conditional Markov process theory," *Theory Probab. Appl.*, vol. 5, pp. 156–178, 1960.

[116] R. L. Stratonovich and Yu. G. Sosulin, "Optimal detection of a Markov process in noise," *Engrg. Cybernetics*, vol. 6, pp. 7–19, 1964. (See also: R. L. Stratonovich and Yu. G. Sosulin, "Optimal detection of a diffusion process in white noise," *Radio Engr. Electron. Phys.*, vol. 10, pp. 704–714, 1965.)

[117] R. L. Stratonovich, "A new form of representation of stochastic integrals and equations," *SIAM J. Contr.*, vol. 4, pp. 362–371, 1966.

[118] J. B. Thomas, "Nonparametric detection," *Proc. IEEE*, vol. 58, pp. 623–631, 1970.

[119] J. Tsitsiklis, "Decentralized detection," in *Advances in Statistical Signal Processing–Vol. 2: Signal Detection*, H. V. Poor and J. B. Thomas, Eds. Greenwich, CT: JAI, 1993, ch. 9, pp. 297–344.

[120] G. L. Turin, "An introduction to matched filters," *IRE Trans. Inform. Theory*, vol. IT-6, pp. 311–329, June 1960.

[121] H. L. Van Trees, *Detection, Estimation and Modulation Theory–Part I.* New York: Wiley, 1968.

[122] J. H. Van Vleck and D. Middleton, "A theoretical comparison of the visual, aural and meter reception of pulsed signals in the presence of noise," *J. Appl. Phys.*, vol. 17, pp. 940–971, 1946. (Originally published in May 1944, as a classified Harvard Radio Research Lab tech. rep.)

[123] S. Verdú, "Minimum probability of error for asynchronous Gaussian multiple-access channels," *IEEE Trans. Inform. Theory*, vol. IT-32, pp. 85–96, Jan. 1986.

[124] ——, "Maximum likelihood sequence detection for intersymbol interference channels: A new upper bound on error probability," *IEEE Trans. Inform. Theory*, vol. IT-33, pp. 62–68, Jan. 1987.

[125] ——, "Computational complexity of optimum multiuser detection," *Algorithmica*, vol. 4, pp. 303–312, 1989.

[126] ——, "Multiuser detection," in *Advances in Statistical Signal Processing—Vol. 2: Signal Detection*, H. V. Poor and J. B. Thomas, Eds. Greenwich, CT: JAI, 1993, ch. 11, pp. 369–409.

[127] ——, *Multiuser Detection.* Cambridge, UK: Cambridge Univ. Press, 1998.

[128] S. Verdú and H. V. Poor, "Abstract dynamic programming models under commutativity conditions," *SIAM J. Contr. Opt.*, vol. 25, no. 4, pp. 990–1006, July 1987.

[129] R. Viswanathan and P. K. Varshney, "Distributed detection with multiple sensors–Part I: Fundamentals," *Proc. IEEE*, vol. 85, pp. 54–63, Jan. 1997.

[130] A. J. Viterbi, "Error bounds for convolutional codes and an asymptotically optimum decoding algorithm," *IEEE Trans. Inform. Theory*, vol. IT-13, pp. 260–269, Apr. 1967.

[131] G. Wahba, "Interpolating spline methods for density estimation I. Equispaced knots," *Ann. Statist.*, vol. 3, pp. 30–48, 1975.

[132] A. Wald, *Sequential Analysis*. New York: Wiley, 1947.

[133] ———, *Statistical Decision Functions*. New York: Wiley, 1950.

[134] X. Wang and H. V. Poor, "Blind multiuser detection: A subspace approach," *IEEE Trans. Inform. Theory*, vol. 44, pp. 677–690, Mar. 1998.

[135] H. L. Weinert, Ed. *Reproducing Kernel Hilbert Spaces: Applications in Statistical Signal Processing*. Stroudsburg, PA: Hutchinson Ross, 1982.

[136] N. Wiener, *Extrapolation, Interpolation, and Smoothing of Stationary Time Series, with Engineering Applications*. New York: Wiley, 1949.

(Originally published in Feb. 1942, as a classified Nat. Defense Res. Council rep.)

[137] E. Wong and M. Zakai, "On the relationship between ordinary and stochastic differential equations," *Int. J. Eng. Sci.*, vol. 3, pp. 213–229, 1965.

[138] E. Wong and B. Hajek, *Stochastic Processes in Engineering Systems*. New York: Springer-Verlag, 1984.

[139] M. Woodroofe, M. Lerche, and R. Keener, "A generalized parking problem," in *Statistical Decision Theory and Related Topics V*. Berlin: Springer-Verlag, 1993, pp. 523–532.

[140] P. M. Woodward, *Probability and Information Theory with Applications to Radar*. Oxford, U.K.: Pergamon, 1953.

[141] J. M. Wozencraft and I. Jacobs, *Principles of Communication Engineering*. New York: Wiley, 1965.

[142] Z. Xie, R. T. Short, and C. K. Rushforth, "A family of suboptimum detectors for coherent multi-user communications," *IEEE J. Select. Areas Commun.*, vol. 8, pp. 683–690, May 1990.

[143] L. Zadeh and J. R. Ragazzini, "An extension of Wiener's theory of prediction," *J. Appl. Phys.*, vol. 21, pp. 645 and ff., 1950.

[144] M. Zakai, "On the optimal filtering of diffusion processes," *Z. Wahr. verw. Geb.*, vol. 11, pp. 230–243, 1969.

215

Codes for Digital Recorders

Kees A. Schouhamer Immink, *Fellow, IEEE*, Paul H. Siegel, *Fellow, IEEE*, and Jack K. Wolf, *Fellow, IEEE*

(Invited Paper)

Abstract—Constrained codes are a key component in the digital recording devices that have become ubiquitous in computer data storage and electronic entertainment applications. This paper surveys the theory and practice of constrained coding, tracing the evolution of the subject from its origins in Shannon's classic 1948 paper to present-day applications in high-density digital recorders. Open problems and future research directions are also addressed.

Index Terms—Constrained channels, modulation codes, recording codes.

I. INTRODUCTION

A S has been observed by many authors, the storage and retrieval of digital information is a special case of digital communications. To quote E. R. Berlekamp [18]:

> Communication links transmit information from here to there. Computer memories transmit information from now to then.

Thus as information theory provides the theoretical underpinnings for digital communications, it also serves as the foundation for understanding fundamental limits on reliable digital data recording, as measured in terms of data rate and storage density.

A block diagram which depicts the various steps in recording and recovering data in a storage system is shown in Fig. 1. This "Fig. 1" is essentially the same as the well-known Fig. 1 used by Shannon in his classic paper [173] to describe a general communication system, but with the configuration of codes more explicitly shown.

As in many digital communication systems, a concatenated approach to channel coding has been adopted in data recording, consisting of an algebraic error-correcting code in cascade with a modulation code. The inner modulation code, which is the focus of this paper, serves the general function of matching the recorded signals to the physical channel and to the signal-processing techniques used in data retrieval, while the outer error-correction code is designed to remove

Manuscript received December 10, 1997; revised June 5, 1998. The work of P. H. Siegel was supported in part by the National Science Foundation under Grant NCR-9612802. The work of J. K. Wolf was supported in part by the National Science Foundation under Grant NCR-9405008.

K. A. S. Immink is with the Institute of Experimental Mathematics, University of Essen, 45326 Essen, Germany.

P. H. Siegel and J. K. Wolf are with the University of California at San Diego, La Jolla, CA 92093-0407 USA.

Publisher Item Identifier S 0018-9448(98)06735-2.

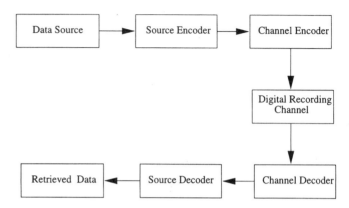

Fig. 1. Block diagram of digital recording system.

any errors remaining after the detection and demodulation process. (See [41] in this issue for a survey of applications of error-control coding.)

As we will discuss in more detail in the next section, a recording channel can be modeled, at a high level, as a linear, intersymbol-interference (ISI) channel with additive Gaussian noise, subject to a binary input constraint. The combination of the ISI and the binary input restriction has presented a challenge in the information-theoretic performance analysis of recording channels, and it has also limited the applicability of the coding and modulation techniques that have been overwhelmingly successful in communication over linear Gaussian channels. (See [56] in this issue for a comprehensive discussion of these methods.)

The development of signal processing and coding techniques for recording channels has taken place in an environment of escalating demand for higher data transfer rates and storage capacity—magnetic disk drives for personal computers today operate at astonishing data rates on the order of 240 million bits per second and store information at densities of up to 3 billion bits per square inch—coupled with increasingly severe constraints on hardware complexity and cost.

The needs of the data storage industry have not only fostered innovation in practical code design, but have also spurred the development of a rigorous mathematical foundation for the theory and implementation of constrained codes. They have also stimulated advances in the information-theoretic analysis of input-constrained, noisy channels.

In this paper, we review the progress made during the past 50 years in the theory and practical design of constrained modulation codes for digital data recording. Along the way, we will highlight the fact that, although Shannon did not mention storage in his classic two-part paper whose golden anniversary we celebrate in this issue—indeed random-access storage as we know it today did not exist at the time—a large number of fundamental results and techniques relevant to coding for storage were introduced in his seminal publication. We will also survey emerging directions in data-storage technology, and discuss new challenges in information theory that they offer.

The outline of the remainder of the paper is as follows.

In Section II, we present background on magnetic-recording channels. Section II-A gives a basic description of the physical recording process and the resulting signal and noise characteristics. In Section II-B, we discuss mathematical models that capture essential features of the recording channel and we review information-theoretic bounds on the capacity of these models. In Section II-C, we describe the signal-processing and -detection techniques that have been most widely used in commercial digital-recording systems.

In Section III-A, we introduce the input-constrained, (noiseless) recording channel model, and we examine certain time-domain and frequency-domain constraints that the channel input sequences must satisfy to ensure successful implementation of the data-detection process. In Section III-B, we review Shannon's theory of input-constrained noiseless channels, including the definition and computation of capacity, the determination of the maxentropic sequence measure, and the fundamental coding theorem for discrete noiseless channels.

In Section IV, we discuss the problem of designing efficient, invertible encoders for input-constrained channels. As in the case of coding for noisy communication channels, this is a subject about which Shannon had little to say. We will summarize the substantial theoretical and practical progress that has been made in constrained modulation code design.

In Section V, we present coded-modulation techniques that have been developed to improve the performance of noisy recording channels. In particular, we discuss families of distance-enhancing constrained codes that are intended for use with partial-response equalization and various types of sequence detection, and we compare their performance to estimates of the noisy channel capacity.

In Section VI, we give a compendium of modulation-code constraints that have been used in digital recorders, describing in more detail their time-domain, frequency-domain, and statistical properties.

In Section VII, we indicate several directions for future research in coding for digital recording. In particular, we consider the incorporation of improved channel models into the design and performance evaluation of modulation codes, as well as the invention of new coding techniques for exploratory information storage technologies, such as nonsaturation recording using multilevel signals, multitrack recording and detection, and multidimensional page-oriented storage.

Finally, in Section VIII, we close the paper with a discussion of Shannon's intriguing, though somewhat cryptic, remarks pertaining to the existence of crossword puzzles, and make some observations about their relevance to coding for multidimensional constrained recording channels.

Section IX briefly summarizes the objectives and contents of the paper.

II. BACKGROUND ON DIGITAL RECORDING

The history of signal processing in digital recording systems can be cleanly broken into two epochs. From 1956 until approximately 1990, direct-access storage devices relied upon "analog" detection methods, most notably peak detection. Beginning in 1990, the storage industry made a dramatic shift to "digital" techniques, based upon partial-response equalization and maximum-likelihood sequence detection, an approach that had been proposed 20 years earlier by Kobayashi and Tang [130], [131], [133]. To understand how these signal-processing methods arose, we review a few basic facts about the physical process underlying digital magnetic recording. (Readers interested in the corresponding background on optical recording may refer to [25], [84], [102, Ch. 2], and [163].) We distill from the physics several mathematical models of the recording channel, and describe upper and lower bounds on their capacity. We then present in more detail the analog and digital detection approaches, and we compare them to the optimal detector for the uncoded channel.

A. Digital Recording Basics

The magnetic material contained on a magnetic disk or tape can be thought of as being made up of a collection of discrete magnetic particles or domains which can be magnetized by a write head in one of two directions. In present systems, digital information is stored along paths, called tracks, in this magnetic medium. We store binary digits on a track by magnetizing these particles or domains in one of two directions. This method is known as "saturation" recording. The stored binary digits usually are referred to as "channel bits." Note that the word "bit" is used here as a contraction of the words "binary digit" and not as a measure of information. In fact, we will see that when coding is introduced, each channel bit represents only a fraction of a bit of user information. The modifier "channel" in "channel bits" emphasizes this difference. We will assume a synchronous storage system where the channel bits occur at the fixed rate of $1/T_c$ channel bits per second. Thus T_c is the duration of a channel bit. In all magnetic-storage systems used today, the magnetic medium and the read/write transducer (referred to as the read/write head) move with respect to each other. If the relative velocity of a track and the read/write head is constant, the constant time-duration of the bit translates to a constant linear channel-bit density, reflected in the length corresponding to a channel bit along the track.

The normalized input signal applied to the recording transducer (write head) in this process can be thought of as a two-level waveform which assumes the values $+1$ and -1 over consecutive time intervals of duration T_c. In the waveform, the transitions from one level to another, which effectively carry the digital information, are therefore constrained to occur at integer multiples of the time period T_c, and we can describe the waveform digitally as a sequence $\boldsymbol{w} = w_0 w_1 w_2 \cdots$ over the bipolar alphabet $\{+1, -1\}$, where w_i is the signal amplitude in the time interval $(iT_c, (i+1)T_c]$. In the simplest model, the input–output relationship of the digital magnetic recording channel can be viewed as linear. Denote by $2s(t)$

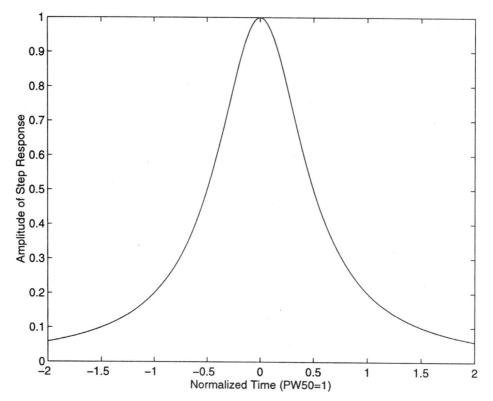

Fig. 2. Lorentzian channel step response, $PW50 = 1$.

the output signal (readback voltage), in the absence of noise, corresponding to a single transition from, say, -1 to $+1$ at time $t = 0$. Then, the output signal $y(t)$ generated by the waveform represented by the sequence w is given by

$$y(t) = \sum_{i=0}^{\infty} (w_i - w_{i-1})s(t - iT_c) \qquad (1)$$

with $w_{-1} = 1$. Note that the "derivative" sequence $\boldsymbol{w}'$ of coefficients $w'_i = w_i - w_{i-1}$ consists of elements taken from the ternary alphabet $\{0, \pm 2\}$, and the nonzero values, corresponding to the transitions in the input signal, alternate in sign.

A frequently used model for the transition response $s(t)$ is the function

$$s(t) = \frac{1}{1 + (2t/\tau)^2}$$

often referred to as the Lorentzian model for an isolated-step response. The parameter τ is sometimes denoted $PW50$, an abbreviation for "pulsewidth at 50% maximum amplitude," the width of the pulse measured at 50% of its maximum height. The Lorentzian step response with $PW50 = 1$ is shown in Fig. 2.

The output signal $y(t)$ is therefore the linear superposition of time-shifted Lorentzian pulses with coefficients of magnitude equal to 2 and alternating polarity. For this channel, sometimes called the differentiated Lorentzian channel, the frequency response is

$$H(f) = -j\pi^2 \tau f e^{-2\pi|f\tau/2|}$$

where $j = \sqrt{-1}$. The magnitude of the frequency response with $PW50 = 1$ is shown in Fig. 3.

The simplest model for channel noise $n(t)$ assumes that the noise is additive white Gaussian noise (AWGN). That is, the readback signal takes the form

$$r(t) = y(t) + n(t)$$

where

$$n(t) \sim N(0, \sigma^2)$$

and

$$E[n(t_1)n(t_2)] = 0, \qquad \text{for all } t_1 \neq t_2.$$

There are, of course, far more accurate and sophisticated models of a magnetic-recording system. These models take into account the failure of linear superposition, asymmetries in the positive and negative step responses, and other nonlinear phenomena in the readback process. There are also advanced models for media noise, incorporating the effects of material defects, thermal asperities, data dependence, and adjacent track interference. For more information on these, we direct the reader to [20], [21], [32], and [33].

B. Channel Models and Capacity

The most basic model of a saturation magnetic-recording system is a binary-input, linear, intersymbol-interference (ISI) channel with AWGN, shown in Fig. 4.

This model has been, and continues to be, widely used in comparing the theoretical performance of competing modulation, coding, and signal-processing systems. During the past

218

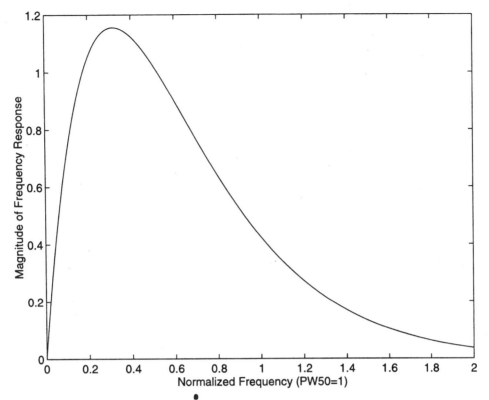

Fig. 3. Differentiated Lorentzian channel frequency response magnitude, $PW50 = 1$.

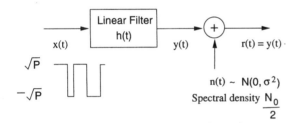

Fig. 4. Continuous-time recording channel model.

decade, there has been considerable research effort devoted to finding the capacity of this channel. Much of this work was motivated by the growing interest in digital recording among the information and communication theory communities [36], [37]. In this section, we survey some of the results pertaining to this problem. As the reader will observe, the analysis is limited to rather elementary channel models; the extension to more advanced channel models represents a major open research problem.

1) Continuous-Time Channel Models: Many of the bounds we cite were first developed for the ideal, low-pass filter channel model. These are then adapted to the more realistic differentiated Lorentzian ISI model.

For a given channel, let C_{av} denote the capacity with a constraint P on the *average* input power. Let C_p denote the capacity with a *peak* power constraint P. Finally, let C denote the capacity with *binary* input levels $\pm\sqrt{P}$. It is clear that

$$C \leq C_p \leq C_{av}.$$

The following important result, due to Ozarow, Wyner, and Ziv [159], states that the first inequality is, in fact, an equality under very general conditions on the channel ISI.

Peak-Power Achievable Rate Lemma: For the channel shown in Fig. 4, if $h(t)$ is square integrable, then any rate achievable using waveforms satifying

$$|x(t)| \leq \sqrt{P}$$

is achievable using the constrained waveforms

$$|x(t)| = \sqrt{P}.$$

We now exploit this result to develop upper and lower bounds on the capacity C. Consider, first, a continuous-time, bandlimited, additive Gaussian noise channel with transfer function

$$H(f) = \begin{cases} 1, & \text{if } |f| < W \\ 0, & \text{otherwise.} \end{cases}$$

Assume that the noise has (double-sided) spectral density $N_0/2$. Let $N = N_0 W$ be the total noise power in the channel bandwidth. Shannon established the well-known and celebrated formula for the capacity of this channel, under the assumption of an average power constraint P on the channel input signals. We quote from [173]:

Theorem 17: The capacity of a channel of band W perturbed by white thermal noise of power N when the average transmitter power is limited to P is given by

$$C_{av} = W \log \frac{P + N}{N}. \tag{2}$$

(We have substituted the notation C_{av} for Shannon's notation C to avoid confusion.)

This result is a special case of the more general "water-filling" theorem for the capacity of an average input-power constrained channel with transfer function $H(f)$ and noise power spectral density $N(f)$ [74, p. 388]

$$C_{\text{av}} = \int_{f \in F_B} \frac{1}{2} \log \left[\frac{|H(f)|^2 B}{N(f)} \right] df$$

where F_B denotes the range of frequencies in which $N(f)/|H(f)|^2 \le B$, and B satisfies the equation

$$P = \int_{f \in F_B} \log \left[B - \frac{N(f)}{|H(f)|^2} \right] df.$$

By the peak-power achievable rate lemma, this result provides an upper bound on the capacity C of the recording channel. Applications of this bound to a parameterized channel model are presented in [70].

An improved upper bound on the capacity $C = C_p$ of the low-pass AWGN channel was developed by Shamai and Bar-David [171]. This bound is a refinement of the water-filling upper bound, based upon a characterization of the power spectral density $S_x(f)$ of any *unit process*, meaning a zero-mean, stationary, two-level continuous-time random process $x(t)$ [175]. For a specified input-power spectral density $S_x(f)$, a Gaussian input distribution maximizes the capacity. Therefore, for a given channel transfer function

$$C_p \le \sup_{S_x(f)} (C_g)$$

where

$$C_g = \frac{1}{2} \int_{-\infty}^{\infty} \log \left(1 + 2 P S_x(f) |H(f)|^2 / N_0 \right) df$$

and the supremum is taken over all unit process power spectral densities. In [171], an approximate solution to this optimization problem for the ideal low-pass filter was used to prove that peak-power limiting on the bandlimited channel does indeed reduce capacity relative to the average-power constrained channel. This bounding technique was applied to the differentiated Lorentzian channel with additive colored Gaussian noise in [207].

We now consider lower bounds to the capacity $C = C_p$. Shannon [173] considered the capacity of a peak-power input constraint on the ideal bandlimited AWGN channel, noting that "a constraint of this type does not work out as well mathematically as the average power limitation." Nevertheless, he provided a lower bound, quoted below:

Theorem 20: The channel capacity C for a band W perturbed by white thermal noise of power N is bounded by

$$C_p \ge W \log \frac{2}{\pi e^3} \frac{S}{N},$$

where S is the peak allowed transmitter power ...

(We have substituted the notation C_p for Shannon's notation C to avoid confusion.)

In [159], the peak-power achievable rate lemma was used to derive a lower bound on C for the ideal, binary-input constrained, bandlimited channel

$$C \ge W \log \left[1 + \frac{2e}{\pi^3} \frac{P}{N_0 W} \right] \quad \text{nats/s.}$$

A lower bound for the more accurate channel model comprising a cascade of a differentiator and ideal low-pass filter was also determined. For this channel, it was shown that

$$C \ge W \log \left[1 + \frac{8}{\pi e} \frac{P}{N_0 W} \right] \quad \text{nats/s.}$$

In both cases, the discrepancy between the lower bounds and the water-filling upper bounds C_{av} represents an effective signal-to-noise ratio (SNR) difference of $2e/\pi^3$, or about -7.6 dB at high signal-to-noise ratios.

Heegard and Ozarow [83] incorporated the differentiated Lorentzian channel model into a similar analysis. To obtain a lower bound, they optimize, with respect to T, the inequality

$$C \ge \frac{1}{2T} \log \left(1 + \frac{4P}{\pi e N_0} 2^{\int_0^1 \log (S_{pT}(e^{j2\pi f})) df} \right)$$

where $S_{pT}(e^{j2\pi f})$ is the pulse power spectral density for the differentiated Lorentzian channel

$$S_{pT}(e^{j2\pi f}) = \frac{4\pi^2}{T \sinh \left(\dfrac{2\pi}{T} \right)} \sin^2(\pi f)$$
$$\cdot \cosh \left(\frac{4\pi}{T} \left(|f| - \frac{1}{2} \right) \right)$$

with

$$-\frac{1}{2} \le f \le \frac{1}{2}.$$

Their results indicate that, just as for the low-pass channel and the differentiated low-pass channel, the difference in effective signal-to-noise ratios between upper and lower bounds on capacity is approximately $2e/\pi^3$, for large signal-to-noise ratios. The corresponding bound for the differentiated Lorentzian channel with additive colored Gaussian noise was determined in [207].

Shamai and Bar-David [171] developed an improved lower bound on $C = C_p$ by analyzing the achievable rate of a random telegraph wave, that is, a unit process with time intervals between transitions independently governed by an exponential distribution. Again, the corresponding bound for the differentiated Lorentzian channel with additive colored Gaussian noise was discussed in [207]. Bounds on capacity for a model incorporating slope-limitations on the magnetization are addressed in [14].

Computational results for the differentiated Lorentzian channel with additive colored Gaussian noise are given in [207]. For channel densities $PW50/T_c$ in the range of 2–3.5, which corresponds to channel densities of current practical interest, the required SNR for arbitrarily low error rate was calculated. The gap between the best capacity bounds, namely, the unit process upper bound and the random telegraph wave lower bound, was found to be approximately 3 dB throughout the range.

2) Discrete-Time Channel Models The capacity of discrete-time channel models applicable to digital recording has been addressed by several authors, for example, [193], [88], [87], and [172]. The capacity of an average input-power-constrained, discrete-time, memoryless channel with additive, independent and identically distributed (i.i.d.) Gaussian noise is given by the well-known formula [74]

$$C_{\text{av}} = \frac{1}{2} \log \left(1 + \frac{P}{\sigma^2} \right)$$

where σ^2 is the noise variance and P is the average input-power constraint. This result is the discrete-time equivalent to Shannon's formula (2) via the sampling theorem. Smith [180] showed that the capacity of an amplitude-constrained, discrete-time, memoryless Gaussian channel is achieved by a finite-valued random variable, representing the input to the channel, whose distribution is uniquely determined by the input constraint. (Note that, unlike the case of an average input-power constraint, this result cannot be directly translated to the continuous-time model.)

Shamai, Ozarow, and Wyner [172] established upper and lower bounds on the capacity of the discrete-time Gaussian channel with ISI and stationary inputs. We will encounter in the next section a discrete-time ISI model of the magnetic-recording channel of the form $h(D) = (1 - D)(1 + D)^N$, for $N \geq 1$. For $N = 1$, the channel decomposes into a pair of interleaved "dicode" channels corresponding to $h(D) = 1 - D$. In [172], the capacity upper bound C_{av} was compared to upper and lower bounds on the maximum achievable information rate for the normalized dicode channel model with system polynomial $h(D) = (1/\sqrt{2})(1 - D)$, and input levels $\pm\sqrt{P}$. These upper and lower bounds are given by

$$I_u = C_b \left(\frac{P}{\sigma^2} \right) \qquad (3)$$

and

$$I_l = C_b \left(\frac{P}{2\sigma^2} \right)$$

respectively, where

$$C_b(R) = \log 2 - \int_{-\infty}^{\infty} \frac{e^{-t^2/2}}{\sqrt{2\pi}} \log \left(1 + e^{-2\sqrt{R}t - 2R} \right) dt$$

is the capacity of a binary input-constrained, memoryless Gaussian channel. Thus the upper bound on C is simply the capacity of the latter channel. These upper and lower bounds differ by 3 dB, as was the case for continuous-time channel models.

For other results on capacity estimates of recording-channel models, we refer the reader to [14] and [149]. The general problem of computing, or developing improved bounds for, the capacity of discrete-time ISI models of recording channels remains a significant challenge.

C. Detectors for Uncoded Channels

Forney [53] derived the optimal sequence detector for an uncoded, linear, intersymbol-interference channel with additive white Gaussian noise. This detection method, the well-known maximum-likelihood sequence detector (MLSD), comprises a whitened matched filter, whose output is sampled at the symbol rate, followed by a Viterbi detector whose trellis structure reflects the memory of the ISI channel. For the differentiated Lorentzian channel model, as for many communication channel models, this detector structure would be prohibitively complex to implement, requiring an unbounded number of states in the Viterbi detector. Consequently, suboptimal detection techniques have been implemented. As mentioned at the start of this section, most storage devices did not even utilize sampled detection methods until the start of this decade, relying upon equalization to mitigate effects of ISI, coupled with analog symbol-by-symbol detection of waveform features such as peak positions and amplitudes. Since the introduction of digital signal-processing techniques in recording systems, partial-response equalization and Viterbi detection have been widely adopted. They represent a practical compromise between implementability and optimality, with respect to the MLSD. We now briefly summarize the main features of these detection methods.

1) Peak Detection: The channel model described above is accurate at relatively low linear densities (say $PW50/T_c \approx 1$) and where the noise is generated primarily in the readback electronics. Provided that the density of transitions and the noise variance σ^2 are small enough, the locations of peaks in the output signal will closely correspond to the locations of the transitions in the recorded input signal. With a synchronous clock of period T_c, one could then, in principle, reconstruct the ternary sequence $\boldsymbol{w}'$ and the recorded bipolar sequence $\boldsymbol{w}$.

The detection method used to implement this process in the potentially noisy digital recording device is known as peak detection and it operates roughly as follows. The peak detector differentiates the rectified readback signal, and determines the time intervals in which zero crossings occur. In parallel, the amplitude of each corresponding extremal point in the rectified signal is compared to a prespecified threshold, and if the threshold is not exceeded, the corresponding zero crossing is ignored. This ensures that low-amplitude, spurious peaks due to noise will be excluded from consideration. Those intervals in which the threshold is exceeded are designated as having a peak. The two-level recorded sequence is then reconstructed, with a transition in polarity corresponding to each interval containing a detected peak. Clock accuracy is maintained by an adaptive timing recovery circuit—known as a phase-lock loop (PLL)—which adjusts the clock frequency and phase to ensure that the amplitude-qualified zero crossings occur, on average, in the center of their respective clock intervals.

2) PRML: Current high-density recording systems use a technique referred to as PRML, an acronym for "partial-response (PR) equalization with maximum-likelihood (ML) sequence detection." We now briefly review the essence of this technique in order to motivate the use of constrained modulation codes in PRML systems.

Kobayashi and Tang [133] proposed a digital communications approach to handling intersymbol interference in digital magnetic recording. In contrast to peak detection, their method reconstructed the recorded sequence from sample values of a suitably equalized readback signal, with the samples measured at time instants $t = nT_c, n \geq 0$. At channel bit densities corresponding to $PW50/T_c \approx 2$, the transfer characteristics of the Lorentzian model of the saturation recording channel (with a time shift of $T_c/2$) closely resemble those of a linear filter with step response $s(t)$ given by

$$s(t) = \operatorname{sinc}\left(\frac{t}{T_c}\right) + \operatorname{sinc}\left(\frac{t - T_c}{T_c}\right) \qquad (4)$$

where

$$\operatorname{sinc}(t) = \frac{\sin(\pi t)}{\pi t}.$$

Note that at the consecutive sample times $t = 0$ and $t = T_c$, the function $s(t)$ has the value 1, while at all other times which are multiples of T_c, the value is 0. Through linear superposition (1), the output signal $y(t)$ generated by the waveform represented by the bipolar sequence $\boldsymbol{w}$ is given by

$$y(t) = \sum_{i=-1}^{\infty} (w_i - w_{i-1}) s(t - iT_c)$$

which can be rewritten as

$$y(t) = \sum_{i=0}^{\infty} (w_i - w_{i-2}) \operatorname{sinc}\left(\frac{t - iT_c}{T_c}\right)$$

where we set $w_{-2} = w_{-1} = w_0$. The transition response results in controlled intersymbol interference at sample times, leading to output-signal samples $y_i = y(iT_c)$ that, in the absence of noise, assume values in the set $\{0, \pm 2\}$. Thus in the noiseless case, we can recover the recorded bipolar sequence $\boldsymbol{w}$ from the output sample values $y_i = y(iT_c)$, because the interference between adjacent transitions is prescribed. In contrast to the peak detection method, this approach does not require the separation of transitions.

Sampling provides a discrete-time version of this recording-channel model. Setting $y_i = y(iT_c)$, the input–output relationship is given by

$$y_i = w_i - w_{i-2}.$$

In D-transform notation, whereby a sequence $\boldsymbol{z}$ is represented by

$$z(D) = \sum_{i=0}^{\infty} z_i D^i$$

the input–output relationship becomes

$$y(D) = h(D)w(D)$$

where the channel transfer function $h(D)$ satisfies

$$h(D) = (1 - D)(1 + D) = 1 - D^2.$$

This representation, called a *partial-response* channel model, is among those given a designation by Kretzmer [134] and tabulated by Kabal and Pasupathy [117]. The label assigned to it—"Class-4"—continues to be used in its designation, and the model is sometimes denoted "PR4."

For higher channel bit densities, Thapar and Patel [190] introduced a general class of partial-response models, with step-response functions

$$s(t) = \sum_{k=0}^{N} \binom{N}{k} \operatorname{sinc}\left(\frac{t - kT_c}{T_c}\right). \qquad (5)$$

The corresponding input–output relationship takes the form

$$y_i = \sum_{i=0}^{N} h_{N,k} w_{i-k}$$

where the discrete-time impulse response $h_N(D) = \sum_k h_{N,k} D^k$ has the form

$$h_N(D) = (1 - D)(1 + D)^N$$

where $N \geq 1$. The frequency response corresponding to $h_N(D)$ has a first-order null at zero frequency and a null of order N at the Nyquist frequency, one-half the symbol frequency. Clearly, the PR4 model corresponds to $N = 1$. The channel models with $N \geq 2$ are usually referred to as "extended Class-4" models, and denoted by $\mathrm{E}^{N-1}\mathrm{PR4}$. The PR4, EPR4, and $\mathrm{E}^2\mathrm{PR4}$ models are used in the design of most magnetic disk drives today.

Models proposed for use in optical-recording systems have discrete-time impulse responses of the form

$$g_N(D) = (1 + D)^N$$

where $N \geq 1$. These models reflect the nonzero DC-response characteristic of some optical-recording systems, as well as their high-frequency attenuation. The models corresponding to $N = 1$ and $N = 2$ were also tabulated in [117], and are known as Class-1 (PR1) or "duobinary," and Class-2 (PR2), respectively. Recently, the models with $N \geq 3$ have been called "extended PR2" models, and denoted by $\mathrm{E}^{N-2}\mathrm{PR2}$. (See [203] for an early analysis and application of PR equalization.)

If the differentiated Lorentzian channel with AWGN is equalized to a partial-response target, the sampled channel model becomes

$$r(D) = h_N(D)w(D) + n(D)$$

where $r_i = r(iT_c)$ and $n_i = n(iT_c)$.

Under the simplifying assumption that the noise samples n_i are independent and identically distributed, and Gaussian—which is a reasonable assumption if the selected partial-response target accurately reflects the behavior of the channel at the specified channel bit density—the maximum-likelihood sequence detector determines the channel input–output pair $\hat{\boldsymbol{w}}$ and $\hat{\boldsymbol{y}}$ satisfying

$$\hat{\boldsymbol{w}} = \arg\min_{\boldsymbol{w}} \sum_{i=0}^{N} (r_i - y_i)^2$$

at each time n.

This computation can be carried out recursively, using the Viterbi algorithm. In fact, Kobayashi [130], [131] proposed the use of the Viterbi algorithm for maximum-likelihood sequence

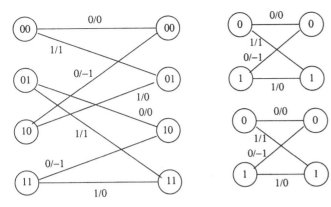

Fig. 5. Trellis diagram for PR4 channel.

detection (MLSD) on a PR4 recording channel at about the same time that Forney [53] demonstrated its applicability to MLSD on digital communication channels with intersymbol interference.

The operation of the Viterbi algorithm and its implementation complexity are often described in terms of the trellis diagram corresponding to $h(D)$ [53], [54] representing the time evolution of the channel input–output process. The trellis structure for the E^NPR4 channel has 2^{N+2} states. In the case of the PR4 channel, the input–output relationship $y_i = w_i - w_{i-2}$ permits the detector to operate independently on the output subsequences at even and odd time indices. The Viterbi algorithm can then be described in terms of a decoupled pair of 2-state trellises, as shown in Fig. 5. There has been considerable effort applied to simplifying Viterbi detector architectures for use in high data-rate, digital-recording systems. In particular, there are a number of formulations of the PR4 channel detector. See [131], [178], [206], [211], [50], and [205].

Analysis, simulation, and experimental measurements have confirmed that PRML systems provide substantial performance improvements over RLL-coded, equalized peak detection. The benefits can be realized in the form of 3–5-dB additional noise immunity at linear densities where optimized peak-detection bit-error rates are in the range of 10^{-6}–10^{-8}. Alternatively, the gains can translate into increased linear density—in that range of error rates, PR4-based PRML channels achieve 15–25% higher linear density than $(1, 7)$-coded peak detection, with EPR4-based PRML channels providing an additional improvement of approximately 15% [189], [39].

The SNR loss of several PRML systems and MLSD relative to the matched-filter bound at a bit-error rate of 10^{-6} was computed in [190]. The results show that, with the proper choice of PR target for a given density, PRML performance can achieve within 1–2 dB of the MLSD.

In [207], simulation results for MLSD and PR4-based PRML detection on a differentiated Lorentzian channel with colored Gaussian media noise were compared to some of the capacity bounds discussed in Section II-B. For $PW50/T_c$ in the range of 2–3, PR4-based PRML required approximately 2–4 dB higher SNR than MLSD to achieve a bit-error rate of 10^{-6}. The SNR gap between MLSD and the telegraph-wave information-rate lower bound [171] was approximately

4 dB, and the gap from the unit-process upper bound [171] was approximately 7 dB. These results suggest that, through suitable coupling of equalization and coding, SNR gains as large as 6 dB over PR4-based PRML should be achievable. In Section V, we will describe some of the equalization and coding techniques that have been developed in an attempt to realize this gain.

III. SHANNON THEORY OF CONSTRAINED CHANNELS

In this section, we show how the implementation of recording systems based upon peak detection and PRML introduces the need for constraints to be imposed upon channel input sequences. We then review Shannon's fundamental results on the theory of constrained channels and codes.

A. Modulation Constraints

1) Runlength Constraints: At moderate densities, peak detection errors may arise from ISI-induced shifting of peak locations and drifting of clock phase due to an inadequate number of detected peak locations.

The latter two problems are pattern-dependent, and the class of runlength-limited (RLL) (d, k) sequences are intended to address them both [132], [101]. Specifically, in order to reduce the effects of pulse interference, one can demand that the derivative sequence w' of the channel input contain some minimum number, say d, of symbols of value zero between consecutive nonzero values. Similarly, to prevent loss of clock synchronization, one can require that there be no more than some maximum number, say k, of symbols of value zero between consecutive nonzero values in w'.

In this context, we mention that two conventions are used to map a binary sequence $z = z_0 z_1 \cdots$ to the magnetization pattern along a track, or equivalently, to the two-level sequence w. In one convention, called nonreturn-to-zero (NRZ), one direction of magnetization (or $w_i = +1$) corresponds to a stored 1 and the other direction of magnetization (or $w_i = -1$) corresponds to a stored 0. In the other convention, called nonreturn-to-zero-inverse (NRZI), a reversal of the direction of magnetization (or $w'_i = \pm 2$) represents a stored 1 and a nonreversal of magnetization (or $w'_i = 0$) represents a stored 0.

The NRZI precoding convention may be interpreted as a translation of the binary information sequence z into another binary sequence $x = x_0 x_1 \cdots$ that is then mapped by the NRZ convention to the two-level sequence w. The relationship between z and x is defined by

$$x_i = x_{i-1} \oplus z_i$$

where $x_{-1} = 0$ and $\oplus$ denotes addition modulo 2.

It is easy to see that

$$w'_i = w_i - w_{i-1} = -(-1)^{x_{i-1}} \cdot 2z_i$$

and, therefore,

$$|w'_i| = 2z_i.$$

Thus under the NRZI precoding convention, the constraints on the runlengths of consecutive zero symbols in w' are reflected

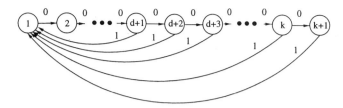

Fig. 6. Labeled directed graph for (d, k) constraint.

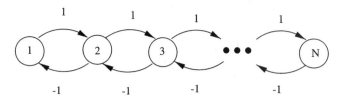

Fig. 7. DC-free constrained sequences with DSV = N.

in corresponding (d, k) constraints on the binary information sequences $\boldsymbol{z}$. The set of sequences satisfying this constraint can be generated by reading the labels off of the paths in the directed graph shown in Fig. 6.

2) Constraints for PRML Channels: Two issues arise in the implementation of PRML systems that are related to properties of the recorded sequences. The first issue is that, just as in peak detection systems, long runs of zero samples in the PR channel output can degrade the performance of the timing recovery and gain control loops. This dictates the use of a global constraint G on the number of consecutive zero samples, analogous to the k constraint described above.

The second issue arises from a property of the PR systems known as quasicatastrophic error propagation [55]. This refers to the fact that certain bi-infinite PR channel output sequences are represented by more than one path in the detector trellis. Such a sequence is produced by at least two distinct channel input sequences. For the PR channels under consideration, namely, those with transfer polynomial $h(D) = (1 - D)^M (1 - D)^N$, $M, N \geq 0$, the difference sequences $\boldsymbol{e} = \boldsymbol{x_1} - \boldsymbol{x_2}$, corresponding to pairs of such input sequences $\boldsymbol{x_1}$ and $\boldsymbol{x_2}$, are easily characterized. (For convenience, the symbols 1 and -1 are denoted by $+$ and $-$, respectively, in these difference sequences.) Specifically, if $M > 0$ and $N = 0$, then these difference sequences are $(0)^\infty, (+)^\infty$, and $(-)^\infty$. If $M = 0$ and $N > 0$, the difference sequences are of the form $(0)^\infty, (+-)^\infty$, and $(-+)^\infty$. Finally, if $M > 0$ and $N > 0$, then they are $(0)^\infty, (+)^\infty, (-)^\infty, (+-)^\infty, (-+)^\infty, (+0)^\infty$, $(0+)^\infty, (-0)^\infty$, and $(0-)^\infty$.

As a consequence of the existence of these sequences, there could be a potentially unbounded delay in the merging of survivor paths in the Viterbi detection process beyond any specified time index i, even in the absence of noise. It is therefore desirable to constrain the channel input sequences in such a way that these difference sequences are forbidden. This property makes it possible to limit the detector path memory, and therefore the decoding delay, without incurring any significant degradation in the sequence estimates produced by the detector.

In the case of PR4, this has been accomplished by limiting the length of runs of identical channel inputs in each of the even and odd interleaves, or, equivalently, the length of runs of zero samples in each interleave at the channel output, to be no more than a specified positive integer I. By incorporating interleaved NRZI (INRZI) precoding, the G and I constraints on output sequences translate into G and I constraints on binary input sequences $\boldsymbol{z}$. The resulting constraints are denoted $(0, G/I)$, where the "0" may be interpreted as a $d = 0$

constraint, emphasizing the point that intersymbol interference is acceptable in PRML systems. It should be noted that the combination of $(0, G/I)$ constraints and an INRZI precoder have been used to prevent quasicatastrophic error propagation in EPR4 channels, as well.

3) Spectral-Null Constraints: The family of (d, k) run-length-limited constraints and $(0, G/I)$ PRML constraints are representative of constraints whose description is essentially in the time domain (although the constraints certainly have implications for frequency-domain characteristics of the constrained sequences). There are other constraints whose formulation is most natural in the frequency domain. One such constraint specifies that the recorded sequences $\boldsymbol{w}$ have no spectral content at a particular frequence f; that is, the average power spectral density function of the sequences has value zero at the specified frequency. The sequences are said to have a spectral null at frequency f.

For an ensemble of sequences, with symbols drawn from the bipolar alphabet $\{+1, -1\}$ and generated by a finite labeled directed graph of the kind illustrated in Fig. 6, a necessary and sufficient condition for a spectral null at frequency $f = (m/n)(1/T_c)$, where T_c is the duration of a single recorded symbol, is that there exist a constant B such that

$$\left| \sum_{i=\ell}^{\ell'} w_i e^{-j2\pi im/n} \right| \leq B \quad (6)$$

for all recorded sequences $\boldsymbol{w} = w_0 w_1 \cdots w_{L-1}$ and $0 \leq \ell \leq \ell' < L$ [145], [162], [209].

In digital recording, the spectral null constraints of most importance have been those that prescribe a spectral null at $f = 0$ or DC. The sequences are said to be *DC-free* or *charge-constrained*. The concept of running digital sum (RDS) of a sequence plays a significant role in the description and analysis of DC-free sequences. For a bipolar sequence $\boldsymbol{w} = w_0 w_1 \cdots w_{L-1}$, the RDS of a subsequence $w_\ell \cdots w_{\ell'}$, denoted RDS $(w_\ell, \cdots, w_{\ell'})$, is defined as

$$\text{RDS}(w_\ell, \cdots, w_{\ell'}) = \sum_{i=\ell}^{\ell'} w_i.$$

From (6), we see that the spectral density of the sequences vanishes at $f = 0$ if and only if the RDS values for all sequences are bounded in magnitude by some constant integer B. For sequences that assume a range of N consecutive RDS values, we say that their *digital sum variation (DSV)* is N. Fig. 7 shows a graph describing the bipolar, DC-free system with DSV equal to N.

DC-free sequences have found widespread application in optical and magnetic recording systems. In magnetic-tape systems with rotary-type recording heads, such as the R-DAT digital audio tape system, they prevent write-signal distortion that can arise from transformer-coupling in the write electronics. In optical-recording systems, they reduce interference between data and servo signals, and also permit filtering of low-frequency noise stemming from smudges on the disk surface. It should be noted that the application of DC-free constraints has certainly not been confined to data storage. Since the early days of digital communication by means of cable, DC-free codes have been employed to counter the effects of low-frequency cutoff due to coupling components, isolating transformers, and other possible system impairments [35].

Sequences with a spectral null at $f = 1/2T_c$ also play an important role in digital recording. These sequences are often referred to as *Nyquist free*. There is in fact a close relationship between Nyquist-free and DC-free sequences. Specifically, consider sequences $\boldsymbol{w} = \{w_i\}$ over the bipolar alphabet $\{\pm 1\}$. If $\boldsymbol{w}$ is DC-free, then the sequence $\tilde{\boldsymbol{w}} = \{\tilde{w}_i\}$ defined by

$$\tilde{w}_i = (-1)^i w_i, \qquad i \geq 0$$

is Nyquist-free. *DC/Nyquist-free* sequences have spectral nulls at both $f = 0$ and $f = 1/2T_c$. Such sequences can always be decomposed into a pair of interleaved DC-free sequences. This fact is exploited in Section V-C in the design of distance-enhancing, DC/Nyquist-free codes for PRML systems.

In some recording applications, sequences satisfying both charge and runlength constraints have been used. In particular, a sequence $\boldsymbol{z}$ in the $(d, k; c)$ *charge-RLL* constraint satisfies the (d, k) runlength constraint, with the added restriction that the corresponding NRZI bipolar sequence $\boldsymbol{w}$ be DC-free with DSV no larger than $N = 2c + 1$. Codes using $(1, 3; 3)$ and $(1, 5; 3)$ constraints—known, respectively, as "zero-modulation" and "Miller-squared" codes—have found application in commercial tape-recording systems [160], [139], [150].

B. Discrete Noiseless Channels

In Section III-A, we saw that the successful implementation of analog and digital signal-processing techniques used in data recording may require that the binary channel input sequences satisfy constraints in both the time and the frequency domains.

Shannon established many of the fundamental properties of noiseless, input-constrained communication channels in Part I of his 1948 paper [173]. In that section, entitled "Discrete Noiseless Systems," Shannon considered discrete communication channels, such as the teletype or telegraph channel, where the transmitted symbols were of possibly different time duration and satisfied a set of constraints as to the order in which they could occur. We will review his key results and illustrate them using the family of runlength-limited (d, k) codes, introduced in Section III-A.

Shannon first defined the capacity C of a discrete noiseless channel as

$$C = \lim_{T \to \infty} \frac{\log N(T)}{T} \qquad (7)$$

where $N(T)$ is the number of allowed sequences of length T. The following quote, which provides a method of computing the capacity, is taken directly from Shannon's original paper (equation numbers added):

Suppose all sequences of the symbols $S_1, \cdots, S_n$ are allowed and these symbols have durations $t_1, \cdots, t_n$. What is the channel capacity? If $N(t)$ represents the number of sequences of duration t, we have

$$N(t) = N(t - t_1) + N(t - t_2) + \cdots + N(t - t_n) \qquad (8)$$

The total number is equal to the sum of the number of sequences ending in $S_1, S_2, \cdots, S_n$ and there are $N(t - t_1), N(t - t_2), \cdots, N(t - t_n)$, respectively. According to a well-known result in finite differences, $N(t)$ is then asymptotic for large t to X_0^t where X_0 is the largest real solution of the characteristic equation

$$X^{-t_1} + X^{-t_2} + \cdots + X^{-t_n} = 1 \qquad (9)$$

and, therefore,

$$C = \log X_0. \qquad (10)$$

Shannon's results can be applied directly to the case of (d, k) codes by associating the symbols $\{S_i\}$ with the $(k - d + 1)$ different allowable sequences of 0's ending in a 1. The result is

$$C = \log X_0 \qquad (11)$$

where X_0 is the largest real solution of the equation

$$X^{-(d+1)} + X^{-(d+2)} + \cdots + X^{-(k+1)} = 1. \qquad (12)$$

Shannon went on to describe constrained sequences by labeled, directed graphs, often referred to as state-transition diagrams. Again, quoting from the paper:

A very general type of restriction which may be placed on allowed sequences is the following: We imagine a number of possible states $a_1, a_2, \cdots, a_m$. For each state only certain symbols from the set $S_1, \cdots, S_n$ can be transmitted (different subsets for the different states). When one of these has been transmitted the state changes to a new state depending both on the old state and the particular symbol transmitted.

Shannon then proceeded to state the following theorem which he proved in an appendix:

Theorem 1: Let $b_{ij}^{(s)}$ be the duration of the sth symbol which is allowable in state i and leads to state j. Then the channel capacity C is equal to $\log(W)$ where W is the largest real root of the determinant equation:

$$\left| \sum_s W^{-b_{ij}^{(s)}} - \delta_{ij} \right| = 0, \qquad (13)$$

where $\delta_{ij} = 1$ if $i = j$ and is zero otherwise.

The condition that different states must correspond to different subsets of the transmission alphabet is unnecessarily restrictive. For the theorem to hold, it suffices that the state-transition diagram representation be lossless, meaning that any two distinct state sequences beginning at a common state and ending at a, possibly different, common state generate distinct symbol sequences [144].

This result can be applied to (d, k) sequences in two different ways. In the first, we let the $\{S_i\}$ be the collection of allowable runs of consecutive 0's followed by a 1, as before. With this interpretation we have only one state since any concatenation of these runs is allowable. The determinant equation then becomes the same as (12) with X replaced by W.

In the second interpretation, we let the $\{S_i\}$ be associated with the binary symbols 0 and 1 and we use the graph with $(k+1)$ states shown earlier in Fig. 6. Note now that all of the symbols are of length 1 so that the determinant equation is of the form (14), as shown at the bottom of this page.

Multiplying every element in the matrix by W, we see that this equation specifies the eigenvalues of the connection matrix, or adjacency matrix, of the graph—that is, a matrix which has i, jth entry equal to 1 if there is a symbol from state i that results in the new state j and which has i, jth entry equal to 0 otherwise. (The notion of adjacency matrix can be extended to graphs with a multiplicity of distinctly labeled edges connecting pairs of states.) Thus we see that the channel capacity C is equal to the logarithm of the largest real eigenvalue of the connection matrix of the constraint graph shown in Fig. 6.

Shannon proceeded to produce an information source by assigning nonzero probabilities to the symbols leaving each state of the graph. These probabilities can be assigned in any manner subject to the constraint that for each state, the sum of the probabilities for all symbols leaving that state is 1. Shannon gave formulas as to how to choose these probabilities such that the resulting information source had maximum entropy. He further showed that this maximum entropy is equal to the capacity C. Specifically, he proved the following theorem.

Theorem 8: Let the system of constraints considered as a channel have a capacity $C = \log W$. If we assign

$$p_{ij}^{(s)} = \frac{B_j}{B_i} W^{-l_{ij}^{(s)}}$$

where $l_{ij}^{(s)}$ is the duration of the sth symbol leading from state i to state j and the B_i satisfy

$$B_i = \sum_{s,j} B_j W^{-l_{ij}^{(s)}}$$

then H is maximized and equal to C.

It is an easy matter to apply Shannon's result to find these probabilities for (d, k) codes. The result is that the probability of a run of i 0's followed by a 1 is equal to $\lambda^{-(i+1)}$ for $i = d, \cdots, k$, and $\log(\lambda)$ is the maximum entropy. Since the sum of these probabilities (summed over all possible runlengths) must equal 1 we have

$$\lambda^{-(d+1)} + \lambda^{-(d+2)} + \cdots + \lambda^{-(k+1)} = 1. \qquad (15)$$

Note that this equation is identical to (12), except for the choice of the indeterminate. Thus the maximum entropy is achieved by choosing λ as the largest real root of this equation and the maximum entropy is equal to the capacity C. The probabilities of the symbols which result in the maximum entropy are shown in Fig. 8 (where now the branch labels are the probabilities of the binary symbols and not the symbols themselves).

The maximum-entropy solution described in the theorem dictates that any sequence $x = x_1, \cdots, x_L$ of length L, starting in state i and ending in state j, has probability

$$p(x) = P_i \lambda^{-L} \frac{B_j}{B_i}$$

where P_i denotes the probability of state i. Therefore,

$$\lim_{L \to \infty} \frac{-\log p(x)}{L} = \log(\lambda).$$

This is a special case of the notion of "typical long sequences" again introduced by Shannon in his classic paper. In this special case of maximum-entropy (d, k) sequences, for L large enough, all sequences of length L are entropy-typical in this sense. This is analogous to the case of symbols which are of fixed duration, equally probable, and statistically independent.

Shannon proved that the capacity C of a constrained channel represents an upper bound on the achievable rate of information transmission on the channel. Moreover, he defined a concept of typical sequences and, using that concept, demonstrated that transmission at rates arbitrarily close to C can in

	1	2	$\cdots$	d	$d+1$	$\cdots$	k	$k+1$
1	-1	W^{-1}		0	0		0	0
2	0	-1	$\cdots$	0	0	$\cdots$	0	0
$\vdots$								
d	0	0	$\cdots$	-1	W^{-1}	$\cdots$	0	0
$d+1$	W^{-1}	0	$\cdots$	0	-1	$\cdots$	0	0
$\vdots$								
k	W^{-1}	0	$\cdots$	0	0	$\cdots$	-1	W^{-1}
$k+1$	W^{-1}	0	$\cdots$	0	0	$\cdots$	0	-1

$$= 0. \qquad (14)$$

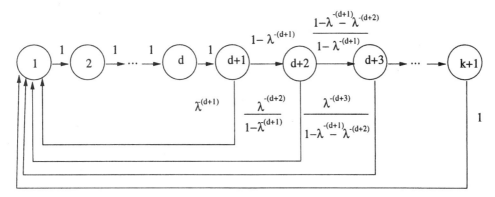

Fig. 8. Markov graph for maximum entropy (d, k) sequences.

principle be achieved. Specifically, he proved the following "fundamental theorem for a noiseless channel" governing transmission of the output of an information source over a constrained channel. We again quote from [173].

Theorem 9: Let a source have entropy H (bits per symbol) and a channel have a capacity C (bits per second). Then it is possible to encode the output of the source in such a way as to transmit at the average rate $(C/H) - \epsilon$ symbols per second over the channel where ϵ is arbitrarily small. It is not possible to transmit at an average rate greater than (C/H).

The proof technique, relying as it does upon typical long sequences, is nonconstructive. It is interesting to note, however, that Shannon formulated the operations of the source encoder (and decoder) in terms of a finite-state machine, a construct that has since been widely applied to constrained channel encoding and decoding. In the next section, we turn to the problem of designing efficient finite-state encoders.

IV. CODES FOR NOISELESS CONSTRAINED CHANNELS

For constraints described by a finite-state, directed graph with edge labels, Shannon's fundamental coding theorem guarantees the existence of codes that achieve any rate less than the capacity. Unfortunately, as mentioned above, Shannon's proof of the theorem is nonconstructive. However, during the past 40 years, substantial progress has been made in the engineering design of efficient codes for various constraints, including many of interest in digital recording. There have also been major strides in the development of general code construction techniques, and, during the past 20 years, rigorous mathematical foundations have been established that permit the resolution of questions pertaining to code existence, code construction, and code implementation complexity.

Early contributors to the theory and practical application of constrained code design include: Berkoff [19]; Cattermole [34], [35]; Cohen [40]; Freiman and Wyner [69]; Gabor [73]; Jacoby [112], [113]; Kautz [125]; Lempel [136]; Patel [160]; and Tang and Bahl [188]; and, especially, Franaszek [57]–[64].

Further advances were made by Adler, Coppersmith, and Hassner (ACH) [3]; Marcus [141]; Karabed and Marcus [120]; Ashley, Marcus, and Roth [12]; Ashley and Marcus [9], [10]; Immink [104]; and Hollmann [91]–[93].

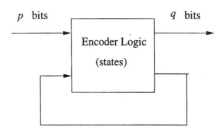

Fig. 9. Finite-state encoder schematic.

In this section, we will survey selected aspects of this theoretical and practical progress. The presentation largely follows [102], [146], and, especially, [144], where more detailed and comprehensive treatments of coding for constrained channels may be found.

A. Encoders and Decoders

Encoders have the task of translating arbitrary source information into a constrained sequence. In coding practice, typically, the source sequence is partitioned into blocks of length p, and under the code rules such blocks are mapped onto words of q channel symbols. The rate of such an encoder is $R = p/q \leq C$. To emphasize the blocklengths, we sometimes denote the rate as $p : q$.

It is most important that this mapping be done as efficiently as possible subject to certain practical considerations. Efficiency is measured by the ratio of the code rate R to the capacity C of the constrained channel. A good encoder algorithm realizes a code rate close to the capacity of the constrained sequences, uses a simple implementation, and avoids the propagation of errors in the process of decoding.

An encoder may be state-dependent, in which case the codeword used to represent a given source block is a function of the channel or encoder state, or the code may be state-independent. State-independence implies that codewords can be freely concatenated without violating the sequence constraints. A set of such codewords is called *self-concatenable*. When the encoder is state-dependent, it typically takes the form of a synchronous finite-state machine, illustrated schematically in Fig. 9.

A decoder is preferably state-independent. As a result of errors made during transmission, a state-dependent decoder could easily lose track of the encoder state, and begin to make errors, with no guarantee of recovery. In order to avoid

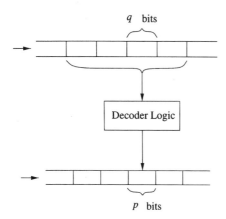

Fig. 10.   Sliding-block decoder schematic.

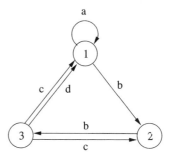

Fig. 11.   Typical labeled graph.

error propagation, therefore, a decoder should use a finite observation interval of channel bits for decoding, thus limiting the span in which errors may occur. Such a decoder is called a *sliding-block decoder*. A sliding-block decoder makes a decision on a received word on the basis of the q-bit word itself, as well as m preceding q-bit words and a upcoming q-bit words. Essentially, the decoder comprises a register of length $(m + a + 1)$ q-bit words and a logic function that translates the contents of the register into the retrieved p-bit source word. Since the constants m and a are finite, an error in the retrieved sequence can propagate in the decoded sequence only for a finite distance, at most the decoder window length. Fig. 10 shows a schematic of a sliding-block decoder. An important subclass of sliding-block decoders are the *block decoders*, which use only a single codeword for reproducing the source word, i.e., $m = a = 0$.

Generally speaking, the problem of code design is to construct practical, efficient, finite-state encoders with sliding-block decoders. There are several fundamental questions related to this problem.

   a) For a rate $R \leq C$, what encoder input and output block sizes p and q, with $R = p/q$, are realizable?

   b) Can a sliding-block decodable encoder always be found?

   c) Can 100% efficient sliding-block decodable encoders be designed when the capacity C is a rational number p/q?

   d) Are there good bounds on basic complexity measures pertaining to constrained codes for a given constraint, such as number of encoder states, encoder gate complexity, encoding delay, and sliding-block decoder window length?

Many of these questions have been answered fully or in part, as we now describe.

B. Graphs and Constraints

It is very useful and convenient, when stating code existence results and specifying code construction algorithms, to refer to labeled graph descriptions of constrained sequences. More precisely, a *labeled graph* (or a *finite labeled directed graph*) $G = (V, E, L)$ consists of a finite set of states $V = V_G$; a finite set of edges $E = E_G$, where each edge e has an initial state and a terminal state, both in V; and an edge labeling $L = L_G \colon E \to \Sigma$, where Σ is a finite alphabet. Fig. 11 shows a

"typical" labeled graph. When context makes it clear, a labeled graph may be called simply a "graph."

A labeled graph can be used to generate finite symbol sequences by reading off the labels along paths in the graph, thereby producing a *word* (also called a *string* or a *block*). For example, in Fig. 11, the word $a\ b\ b\ c\ b\ d$ can be generated by following a path along edges with state sequence 1 1 2 3 2 3 1. We will sometimes call word of length ℓ generated by G an ℓ-*block*.

The connections in the directed graph underlying a labeled graph are conveniently described by an adjacency matrix, as was mentioned in Section III. Specifically, for a graph G, we denote by $A = A_G = [(A_G)_{u,v}]_{u,v \in V_G}$ the $|V_G| \times |V_G|$ *adjacency matrix* whose entry $(A_G)_{u,v}$ is the number of edges from state u to state v in G. The adjacency matrix, of course, has nonnegative integer entries. Note that the number of paths of length q from state u to state v is simply $(A_G^q)_{u,v}$, and the number of cycles of length q is simply the trace of A_G^q.

The fundamental object considered in the theory of constrained coding is the set of words generated by a labeled graph. A *constrained system* (or *constraint*), denoted S, is the set of all words $\boldsymbol{x}$ (i.e., finite-length sequences) generated by reading the labels of paths in a labeled graph G. We will also, at times, consider *right-infinite* sequences $x_0 x_1 x_2 \cdots$ and sometimes *bi-infinite* sequences $\cdots x_{-2} x_{-1} x_0 x_1 x_2 \cdots$. The alphabet of symbols appearing in the words of S is denoted $\Sigma(S)$. We say that the graph G *presents* S or is a *presentation* of S, and we write $S = S(G)$. For a state u in G, the set of all finite words generated from u is called the *follower set* of u in G, denoted $\mathcal{F}_G(u)$.

As mentioned above, a rate $p : q$ finite-state encoder will generate a word in the constrained system S composed of a sequence of q-blocks. For a constrained system S presented by a labeled graph G, it will be very useful to have an explicit description of the words in S, decomposed into such nonoverlapping blocks of length q.

Let G be a labeled graph. The qth power of G, denoted G^q, is the labeled graph with the same set of states as G, but one edge for each path of length q in G, labeled by the q-block generated by that path. The adjacency matrix A_{G^q} of G^q satisfies

$$A_{G^q} = (A_G)^q.$$

For a constrained system S presented by a labeled graph G, the qth power of S, denoted S^q, is the constrained system presented by G^q. So, S^q is the constrained system obtained from

S by grouping the symbols in each word into nonoverlapping words of length q. Note that the definition of S^q does not depend on which presentation G of S is used.

It is important to note that a given constrained system can be presented by many different labeled graphs and, depending on the context, one presentation will have advantages relative to another. For example, one graph may present the constraint using the smallest possible number of states, while another may serve as the basis for an encoder finite-state machine.

There are important connections between the theory of constrained coding and other scientific disciplines, including symbolic dynamics, systems theory, and automata theory. Many of the objects, concepts, and results in constrained coding have counterparts in these fields. For example, the set of bi-infinite sequences derived from a constrained system is called a sofic system (or sofic shift) in symbolic dynamics. In systems theory, these sequences correspond to a discrete-time, complete, time-invariant system. Similarly, in automata theory, a constrained system is equivalent to a regular language which is recognized by a certain type of automaton [94]. The interrelationships among these various disciplines are discussed in more detail in [15], [127], and [142].

The bridge to symbolic dynamics, established in [3], has proven to be especially significant, leading to breakthroughs in both the theory and design of constrained codes. An interesting account of this development and its impact on the design of recording codes for magnetic storage is given in [2]. A very comprehensive mathematical treatment may be found in [138].

C. Properties of Graph Labelings

In order to state the coding theorems, as well as for purposes of encoder construction, it will be important to consider labelings with special properties.

We say that a labeled graph is *deterministic* if, at each state, the outgoing edges have distinct labels. In other words, at each state, any label generated from that state determines a unique outgoing edge from that state. Constrained systems that play a role in digital recording generally have natural presentations by a deterministic graph. For example, the labeled graphs in Figs. 6 and 7 are both deterministic. It can be shown that any constrained system can be presented by a deterministic graph [144]. Similarly, a graph is called *codeterministic* if, for each state, the incoming edges are distinctly labeled. Fig. 6 is not codeterministic, while Fig. 7 is.

Many algorithms for constructing constrained codes begin with a deterministic presentation of the constrained system and transform it into a presentation which satisfies a weaker version of the deterministic property called *finite anticipation*. A labeled graph is said to have finite anticipation if there is an integer N such that any two paths of length $N + 1$ with the same initial state and labeling must have the same initial edge. The *anticipation* $\mathcal{A}(G)$ of G refers to the smallest N for which this condition holds. Similarly, we define the *coanticipation* of a labeled graph G as the anticipation of the labeled graph obtained by reversing the directions of the edges in G.

A labeled graph G has *finite memory* if there is an integer N such that the paths in G of length N that generate the same word all terminate at the same state. The smallest N for which this holds is called the *memory* of G and is denoted $\mathcal{M}(G)$.

A property related to finite anticipation is that of being (m, a)-*definite*. A labeled graph has this property if, given any word $\boldsymbol{x} = x_{-m}x_{-m+1}\cdots x_0 \cdots x_a$, the set of paths $e_{-m}e_{-m+1}\cdots e_0 \cdots e_a$ that generate $\boldsymbol{x}$ all agree in the edge e_0. A graph with this property is sometimes said to have *finite memory-and-anticipation*. Note that, whereas the definition of finite anticipation involves knowledge of an initial state, the (m, a)-*definite* property replaces that with knowledge of a finite amount of memory.

Finally, as mentioned in Section III, a labeled graph is *lossless* if any two distinct paths with the same initial state and terminal state have different labelings.

The graph in Fig. 6 has finite memory k, and it is $(k, 0)$-definite because, for any given word $\boldsymbol{x}$ of length at least $k+1$, all paths that generate $\boldsymbol{x}$ end with the same edge. In contrast, the graph in Fig. 7 does not have finite memory and is not definite.

D. Finite-Type and Almost-Finite-Type Constraints

There are some special classes of constraints, called *finite-type* and *almost-finite type*, that play an important role in the theory and construction of constrained codes. A constrained system S is *finite-type* (a term derived from symbolic dynamics [138]) if it can be presented by a definite graph. Thus the (d, k)-RLL constraint is finite-type.

There is also a useful intrinsic characterization of finite-type constraints: there is an integer N such that, for any symbol $b \in \Sigma(S)$ and any word $\boldsymbol{x} \in S$ of length at least N, we have $\boldsymbol{x}b \in S$ if and only if $\boldsymbol{x}'b \in S$ where $\boldsymbol{x}'$ is the suffix of $\boldsymbol{x}$ of length N. The smallest such integer N, if any, is called the *memory* of S and is denoted by $\mathcal{M}(S)$.

Using this intrinsic characterization, we can show that not every constrained system of practical interest is finite-type. In particular, the charge-constrained system described by Fig. 7 is not. To see this, note that the symbol "+" can be appended to the word

$$-1\,1 - 1\,1 \cdots - 1\,1$$

but not to the word

$$\underbrace{1\,1 \cdots 1}_{N} - 1\,1 - 1\,1 \cdots - 1\,1.$$

Nevertheless, this constrained system falls into a natural broader class of constrained systems. These systems can be thought of as "locally finite-type." More precisely, a constrained system is *almost-finite-type* if it can be presented by a labeled graph that has both finite anticipation and finite coanticipation.

Since definiteness implies finite anticipation and finite coanticipation, every finite-type constrained system is also almost-finite-type. Therefore, the class of almost-finite-type systems does indeed include all of the finite-type systems. This inclusion is proper, as can be seen by referring to Fig. 7. There, we see that the charge-constrained systems are presented by labeled graphs with zero anticipation (i.e., deterministic) and

229

zero coanticipation (i.e., codeterministic). Thus these systems are almost-finite-type, but not finite-type. Constrained systems used in practical applications are virtually always almost-finite-type.

Another useful property of constrained systems is irreducibility. A constraint is *irreducible* if, for every pair of words $\boldsymbol{x}, \boldsymbol{x}'$ in S, there is a word $\boldsymbol{z}$ such that $\boldsymbol{x}\boldsymbol{z}\boldsymbol{x}'$ is in S. Equivalently, S is irreducible if and only if it is presented by some irreducible labeled graph. In coding, it usually suffices to consider irreducible constraints.

Irreducible constrained systems have a distinguished presentation called the *Shannon cover*, which is the unique (up to labeled graph isomorphism) deterministic presentation of S with a smallest number of states. The Shannon cover can be used to determine if the constraint is almost-finite-type or finite-type. More precisely, an irreducible constrained system is finite-type (respectively, almost-finite-type) if and only if its Shannon cover has finite memory (respectively, finite coanticipation).

Referring to Section III, recall that the (base-α) capacity of a constrained system S is given by

$$\mathsf{cap}_\alpha(S) = \lim_{\ell \to \infty} \frac{1}{\ell} \log_\alpha N(\ell; S)$$

where $N(\ell; S)$ is the number of ℓ-blocks in S. The (base-α) capacity of an irreducible system S can be obtained from the Shannon cover. In fact, as mentioned in Section III, if G is any irreducible lossless presentation of S, then

$$\mathsf{cap}_\alpha(S) = \log_\alpha \lambda(A_G).$$

E. Coding Theorems

We now state a series of coding theorems that refine and strengthen the fundamental coding theorem of Shannon, thus answering many of the questions posed above. Moreover, the proofs of these theorems are often constructive, leading to practical algorithms for code design.

First, we establish some useful notation and terminology. An encoder usually takes the form of a synchronous finite-state machine, as mentioned earlier and shown schematically in Fig. 9. More precisely, for a constrained system S and a positive integer n, an *(S, n)-encoder* is a labeled graph $\mathcal{E}$ satisfying the following properties: 1) each state of $\mathcal{E}$ has *out-degree* n, that is, n outgoing edges; 2) $S(\mathcal{E}) \subseteq S$; and 3) the presentation $\mathcal{E}$ is lossless.

A *tagged (S, n)-encoder* is an (S, n)-encoder $\mathcal{E}$ in which the outgoing edges from each state in $\mathcal{E}$ are assigned distinct words, or *input tags*, from an alphabet of size n. We will sometimes use the same symbol $\mathcal{E}$ to denote both a tagged (S, n)-encoder and the underlying (S, n)-encoder.

Finally, we define a *rate $p : q$ finite-state (S, α)-encoder* to be a tagged (S^q, α^p)-encoder where the input tags are the α-ary p-blocks. We will be primarily concerned with the binary case, $\alpha = 2$, and will call such an encoder a *rate $p : q$ finite-state encoder for S*. The encoding proceeds in the obvious fashion, given a selection of an initial state. If the current state is u and the input data is the p-block $\boldsymbol{s}$, the codeword generated is the q-block that labels the outgoing edge e from

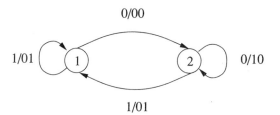

Fig. 12.   Rate 1 : 2 tagged encoder.

state u with input tag $\boldsymbol{s}$. The next encoder state is the terminal state of the edge e. A tagged encoder is illustrated in Fig. 12.

1) Block Encoders: We first consider the construction of the structurally simplest type of encoder, namely, a block encoder. A rate $p : q$ finite-state (S, α)-encoder is called a *rate $p : q$ block (S, α)-encoder* if it contains only one state. Block encoders have played an important role in digital storage systems.

The following theorem states that block encoders can be used to asymptotically approach capacity. It follows essentially from Shannon's proof of the fundamental theorem for noiseless channels.

Block-Coding Theorem: Let S be an irreducible constrained system and let α be a positive integer. There exists a sequence of rate $p_m : q_m$ block (S, α)-encoders such that

$$\lim_{m \to \infty} p_m / q_m = \mathsf{cap}_\alpha(S).$$

The next result provides a characterization of all block encoders.

Block Code Characterization: Let S be a constrained system with a deterministic presentation G and let n be a positive integer. Then there exists a block (S, n)-encoder if and only if there exists a subgraph H of G and a collection $\mathcal{L}$ of n symbols of $\Sigma(S)$, such that $\mathcal{L}$ is the set of labels of the outgoing edges from each state in H.

Freiman and Wyner [69] developed a procedure that can be used to determine whether there exists a block (S^q, α^p)-encoder for a given constrained system S with finite memory $\leq q$. Specifically, let G be a deterministic presentation of S. For every pair of states u and v in G, consider the set $\mathcal{F}_G^q(u, v)$ of all words of length q that can be generated in G by paths that start at u and terminate at v. To identify a subgraph H of G^q as in the block-code characterization, we search for a set P of states in G satisfying

$$\left| \bigcap_{u \in P} \left(\bigcup_{v \in P} \mathcal{F}_G^q(u, v) \right) \right| \geq \alpha^p.$$

Freiman and Wyner [69] simplify the search by proving that, when G has finite memory $\leq q$, it suffices to consider sets P which are *complete*; namely, if u is in P and $\mathcal{F}_G(u) \subseteq \mathcal{F}_G(v)$, then v is also in P.

Even with the restriction of the search to complete sets, this block-code design procedure is not efficient, in general. However, given α and q, for certain constrained systems S, such as the (d, k)-RLL constraints, it does allow us to effectively compute the largest p for which there exists a block

TABLE I
OPTIMAL LENGTH-5 LIST
FOR $(d, k) = (0, 2)$

Input	Output
0000	11001
0001	11011
0010	10010
0011	10011
0100	11101
0101	10101
0110	10110
0111	10111
1000	11010
1001	01001
1010	01010
1011	01011
1100	11110
1101	01101
1110	01110
1111	01111
————	11111

TABLE II
RATE 1/2 $(d, k) = (2, 7)$
VARIABLE-LENGTH BLOCK ENCODER

Input	Output
10	0100
11	1000
000	000100
010	100100
011	001000
0010	00100100
0011	00001000

(S^q, α^p)-encoder. In fact, the procedure can be used to find a largest possible set $\mathcal{L}_q$ of self-concatenable words of length q.

Block Encoder Examples: Digital magnetic-tape systems have utilized block codes satisfying $(d, k) = (0, k)$ constraints, for $k = 1, 2,$ and 3. Specifically, the codes, with rates $1/2, 4/5,$ and $8/9$, respectively, were derived from optimal lists of sizes $|\mathcal{L}_2| = 2$, $|\mathcal{L}_5| = 17$, and $|\mathcal{L}_9| = 293$, respectively. The simple rate $1 : 2$ $(d, k) = (0, 1)$ code, known as the Frequency Modulation code, consists of the two codewords 01 and 11. The 17 words of the $(d, k) = (0, 2)$ list are shown in Table I. The 16 words remaining after deletion of the all-1's word form the codebook for the rate $4/5$ Group Code Recording (GCR) code, which became the industry standard for nine-track tape drives. The input tag assignments are also shown in the table. See [146] for further details.

A rate $1/2$, $(d, k) = (2, 7)$ code, developed by Franaszek [59], [44], became an industry standard in disk drives using peak detection. It can be described as a variable-length block code, and was derived using a similar search method. The encoder table is shown in Table II.

Disk drives using PRML techniques have incorporated a block code satisfying $(0, G/I) = (0, 4/4)$ constraints [45]. The code, with rate $8/9$, was derived from the unique maximum size list of size $|\mathcal{L}_9| = 279$. The list has a very simple description. It is the set of length-9 binary words satisfying the following three conditions: 1) the maximum runlength of zeros within the word is no more than 4; 2) the maximum runlengths of zeros at the beginning and end of the word are no more than 2; and 3) the maximum runlengths

of zeros at the beginning and end of the even interleave and odd interleave of the word are no more than 2. A rate $16/17$, $(0, G/I) = (0, 6/6)$ block code, derived from an optimal list of length-17 words with an analogous definition, has also been designed for use in PRML systems [161], [1].

2) Deterministic Encoders: Block encoders, although conceptually simple, may not be suitable in many cases, since they might require a prohibitively large value of q in order to achieve the desired rate. Allowing multiple states in the encoder can reduce the required codeword length. If each state in G^q has at least α^p outgoing edges, then we can obtain a deterministic (S^q, α^p)-encoder by deleting excess edges. In fact, it is sufficient (and necessary) for G^q to have a subgraph where each state satisfies this condition. This result, characterizing deterministic encoders, is stated by Franaszek in [57].

Deterministic Encoder Characterization: Let S be a constrained system with a deterministic presentation G and let n be a positive integer. Then there exists a deterministic (S, n)-encoder if and only if there exists such an encoder which is a subgraph of G.

Let G be a deterministic presentation of a constrained system S. According to the characterization, we can derive from G a deterministic (S^q, α^p)-encoder if and only if there exists a set P of states in G, called a *set of principal states*, such that

$$\sum_{v \in P} (A_G^q)_{u,v} \geq \alpha^p, \qquad \text{for every } u \in P.$$

This inequality can be expressed in terms of the characteristic vector $\boldsymbol{x} = [x_u]_{u \in V_G}$ of the set of states P, where $x_u = 1$ if $u \in P$ and $x_u = 0$ otherwise. Then, P is a set of principal states if and only if

$$A_G^q \boldsymbol{x} \geq \alpha^p \boldsymbol{x}. \qquad (16)$$

We digress briefly to discuss the significance of this inequality. Given a nonnegative integer square $N \times N$ matrix A and an integer n, an (A, n)-*approximate eigenvector* is a nonnegative integer vector $\boldsymbol{v} \neq 0$ satisfying

$$A\boldsymbol{v} \geq n\boldsymbol{v} \qquad (17)$$

where the inequality holds componentwise. We refer to this inequality as the *approximate eigenvector inequality*, and we denote the set of all (A, n)-approximate eigenvectors by $\mathcal{X}(A, n)$. Approximate eigenvectors will play an essential role in the constructive proof of the finite-state coding theorem in the next section, as they do in many code-construction procedures.

The existence of approximate eigenvectors is guaranteed by the Perron–Frobenius theory [76], [170]. Specifically, let λ be the largest positive eigenvalue of A, and let n be a positive integers satisfying $n \leq \lambda$. Then there exists a vector $\boldsymbol{v} \neq 0$, with nonnegative integer components, satisfying (17). The following algorithm, taken from [3] and due originally to Franaszek, is an approach to finding such a vector.

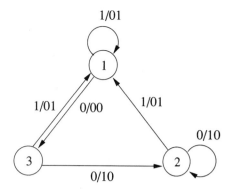

Fig. 13. Rate 1 : 2 MFM encoder.

Franaszek Algorithm for Finding an Approximate Eigenvector: Choose an initial vector $\boldsymbol{v}^{(0)}$ whose entries are $v_i^{(0)} = L$, where L is a nonnegative integer. Define inductively

$$v_i^{(m+1)} = \min\left(v_i^{(m)}, \left\lfloor\left(\frac{1}{n}\sum_{j=1}^{N} A_{ij}v_j^{(m)}\right)\right\rfloor\right).$$

Let $\boldsymbol{v} = \boldsymbol{v}^{(m)}$, where m is the first integer such that $\boldsymbol{v}^{(m+1)} = \boldsymbol{v}^{(m)}$.

There are two situations that can arise: a) $\boldsymbol{v} > 0$ and b) $\boldsymbol{v} = \boldsymbol{0}$. Case a) means that we have found an approximate eigenvector, and in case b) there is no solution, so we increase L and start from the top again. There may be multiple solutions for the vector $\boldsymbol{v}$. The choice of the vector may affect the complexity of the code constructed in this way. The components of $\boldsymbol{v}$ are often called *weights*.

From (16), it follows that P is a set of principal states if and only if the characteristic vector $\boldsymbol{x}$ is an (A_G^q, α^p)-approximate eigenvector. Hence, we can find whether there is a deterministic (S^q, α^p)-encoder by applying the Franaszek algorithm to the matrix $A = A_G^q$, the integer $n = \alpha^p$, and the all-1's vector as the initial vector $\boldsymbol{v}^{(0)}$. A nonzero output vector $\boldsymbol{v}$ is a necessary and sufficient condition for the existence of a set of principal states, for which $\boldsymbol{v}$ is then a characteristic vector.

Deterministic Encoder Example: The rate 1/2, $(d, k) = (1, 3)$ encoder—known as Modified Frequency Modulation code, Miller code, or Delay Modulation—is a deterministic encoder. The encoder is derived from the second power of the Shannon cover of the $(d, k) = (1, 3)$ constraint. A set of principal states is $P = \{1, 2, 3\}$. Fig. 13 shows a rate 1 : 2 deterministic encoder. In fact, the tagged encoder in Fig. 12 is a simpler description of the MFM tagged encoder obtained by "merging" states 2 and 3 in Fig. 13. (See Section IV-F for more on merging of states.)

3) Finite-State Coding Theorem: Although deterministic encoders can overcome some of the limitations of block encoders, further improvements may arise if we relax the deterministic property. In this section, we show that, for a desired rate $p : q$ where $p/q \leq \mathsf{cap}_\alpha(S)$, even though a deterministic encoder may not exist, a finite-state encoder always does.

If an encoder $\mathcal{E}$ has finite anticipation $\mathcal{A} = \mathcal{A}(\mathcal{E})$, then we can decode in a state-dependent manner, beginning at the initial state u_0, and retracing the path followed by the encoder, as follows. If the current state is u, then the current codeword to be decoded, together with the $\mathcal{A}$ upcoming codewords, constitute a word of length $\mathcal{A} + 1$ (measured in q-blocks) that is generated by a path that starts at u. By definition of anticipation, the initial edge e of such a path is uniquely determined; the decoded p-block is the input tag of e, and the next decoder state is the terminal state of e.

This decoding method will invert the encoder when applied to valid codeword sequences. The output of the decoder will be identical to the input to the encoder, possibly with a shift of $\mathcal{A}$ input p-blocks.

The following theorem establishes that, with finite anticipation, invertible encoders can achieve all rational rates R less than or equal to capacity, with any input and output blocklengths p and q satisfying $R = p/q$.

Finite-State Coding Theorem: Let S be a constrained system. If $p/q \leq \mathsf{cap}_\alpha(S)$ then there exists a rate $p : q$ finite-state (S, α)-encoder with finite anticipation.

The theorem improves upon Shannon's result in three important ways. First, the proof is constructive, relying upon the state-splitting algorithm, which will be discussed in Section IV-F. Next, it proves the existence of finite-state (S, α)-encoders that achieve rate equal to the capacity $\mathsf{cap}_\alpha(S)$, when $\mathsf{cap}_\alpha(S)$ is rational. Finally, for any positive integers p and q satisfying the inequality $p/q \leq \mathsf{cap}_\alpha(S)$, there is a rate $p : q$ finite-state (S, α)-encoder that operates at rate $p : q$. In particular, choosing p and q relatively prime, one can design an invertible encoder using the smallest possible codeword length q compatible with the chosen rate p/q.

For completeness, we also state the more simply proved finite-state inverse-coding theorem.

Finite-State Inverse-to-Coding Theorem: Let S be a constrained system. Then, there exists a rate $p : q$ finite-state (S, α)-encoder only if $p/q \leq \mathsf{cap}_\alpha(S)$.

4) Sliding-Block Codes and Block-Decodable Codes: As mentioned earlier, it is often desirable for finite-state encoders to have decoders that limit the extent of error propagation. The results in this section address the design of encoders with sliding-block decoders, which we now formally define.

Let m and a be integers such that $m + a \geq 0$. A *sliding-block decoder* for a rate $p : q$ finite-state (S, α)-encoder is a mapping

$$\mathcal{D} : \Sigma(S^q)^{m+a+1} \to \{0, 1, \cdots, \alpha-1\}^p$$

such that, if $\boldsymbol{x} = x_1 x_2 \cdots$ is any sequence of q-blocks generated by the encoder from the input tag sequence of p-blocks $\boldsymbol{s} = s_1 s_2 \cdots$, then, for $i > m$

$$s_i = \mathcal{D}(x_{i-m}, \cdots, x_i, \cdots, x_{i+a}).$$

We call a the *look-ahead* of $\mathcal{D}$ and m the *look-behind* of $\mathcal{D}$. The sum $m + a + 1$ is called the *decoding window length* of $\mathcal{D}$. See Fig. 10, where $m = 1$ and $a = 2$.

TABLE III
RATE 2 : 3 $(d, k) = (1, 7)$ SLIDING-BLOCK-DECODABLE ENCODER

Input \ State	1	2	3	4	5
00	101/4	100/4	001/4	010/4	000/4
01	101/3	100/3	001/3	010/3	000/3
10	101/5	100/2	001/5	010/2	000/2
11	100/5	100/1	010/5	010/1	000/1

As mentioned earlier, a single error at the input to a sliding-block decoder can only affect the decoding of q-blocks that fall in a "window" of length at most $m + a + 1$, measured in q-blocks. Thus a sliding-block decoder controls the extent of error propagation.

The following result, due to Adler, Coppersmith, and Hassner [3], improves upon the finite-state coding theorem for finite-type constrained systems.

Sliding-Block Code Theorem for Finite-Type Systems: Let S be a finite-type constrained system. If $p/q \leq \text{cap}_\alpha(S)$, then there exists a rate $p : q$ finite-state (S, α)-encoder with a sliding-block decoder.

This result, sometimes called the ACH theorem, follows readily from the proof of the finite-state coding theorem. The constructive proof technique, based upon state-splitting, is sometimes referred to as the *ACH algorithm* (see Section IV-F).

Sliding-Block Code Example: The $(d, k) = (1, 7)$ constraint has capacity $C(1, 7) \approx 0.6793$. Adler, Hassner, and Moussouris [4] used the state-splitting algorithm to construct a rate 2 : 3, $(d, k) = (1, 7)$ encoder with five states, represented in tabular form in Table III. Entries in the "state" columns indicate the output word and next encoder state. With the input tagging shown, the encoder is sliding-block decodable with $(m, a) = (0, 2)$. The decoder error propagation is limited to five input bits. The same underlying encoder graph was independently constructed by Jacoby [112] using "look-ahead" code design techniques. Weathers and Wolf [112] applied the state-splitting algorithm to design a 4-state, $(m, a) = (0, 2)$ sliding-block-decodable encoder with error propagation at most 5 input bits. This encoder has the distinction of achieving the smallest possible number of states for this constraint and rate [143].

A *block-decodable encoder* is a special case of (m, a)-sliding-block decodable encoders where both m and a are zero. Because of the favorable implications for error propagation, a block-decodable encoder is often sought in practice. The following result characterizes these encoders completely.

Block-Decodable Encoder Characterization: Let S be a constrained system with a deterministic presentation G and let n be a positive integer. Then there exists a block decodable (S, n)-encoder if and only if there exists such an encoder which is a subgraph of G.

It has been shown that the general problem of deciding whether a particular subgraph of G can be input-tagged in such a way as to produce a block-decodable encoder is NP-complete [8]. Nevertheless, for certain classes of constraints, and many other specific examples, such an input-tag assignment can be found.

Block-Decodable Code Examples: For certain irreducible constrained systems, including powers of (d, k)-RLL constrained systems, Franaszek [57], [58] showed that whenever there is a deterministic (S, n)-encoder which is a subgraph of the Shannon cover, there is also such an encoder that can be tagged so that it is block-decodable. In fact, the MFM encoder of Fig. 13 is block-decodable.

For (d, k)-RLL constrained systems, an explicit description of such a labeling was found by Gu and Fuja [79] and, independently, by Tjalkens [191]. They show that their labeling yields the largest rate attainable by any block-decodable encoder for any given (d, k)-RLL constrained system.

The Gu–Fuja construction is a generalization of a coding scheme introduced by Beenker and Immink [16]. The underlying idea, which is quite generally applicable, is to design block-decodable encoders by using *merging bits* between constrained words [16], [112], [104]. Each input p-block has a unique constrained q'-block representation, where $q' \leq q$. The encoder uses a look-up table for translating source words into constrained words of length q' plus some logic circuitry for determining the $q - q'$ merging bits. Decoding is extremely simple: discard the merging bits and translate the q'-bit word into the p-bit source word.

For (d, k) sequences, the encoder makes use of the set $\mathcal{L}(q; d, k; r)$ of all (d, k)-constrained q-blocks with at least d leading zeroes and at most r trailing zeroes. The parameters are assumed to satisfy $q > k \geq 2d, d \geq 1$, and $r = k - d$. Using a look-up table or enumeration techniques [102, p. 117], [188], [42], the encoder maps each of the 2^p p-bit input tags to a unique q-block in $\mathcal{L}(q; d, k; k - d)$, where $p = \lfloor \log_2 |\mathcal{L}(q; d, k; k-d)| \rfloor$. The codewords in $\mathcal{L}(q; d, k; k-d)$ are not necessarily freely concatenable, however. When the concatenation of the current codeword with the preceding one violates the (d, k) constraint, the encoder inverts one of the first d zeroes in the current codeword. The condition $q > k \geq 2d$ guarantees that such an inversion can always resolve the constraint violation. In this case, the first d bits of each codeword may be regarded as the merging bits.

Immink [106] gave a constructive proof that (d, k) codes with merging bits can be made for which $C(d, k) - R < 1/(2q)$. As a result, (d, k) codes with a rate only 0.1% less than Shannon's capacity can be constructed with codewords of length $q \approx 500$. Such long codewords could present an additional practical problem—beyond that of mapping the input words to the constrained words, which can be handled by enumerative coding—because a single channel bit error could corrupt the entire data in the decoded word. One proposal for resolving this difficulty is to use a special configuration of the error-correcting code and the recording code [22], [49], [106].

Another well-known application of this method is that of the Eight-to-Fourteen Modulation (EFM) code, a rate 8 : 17 code which is implemented in the compact audio disc [96], [84], [109]. A collection of 256 codewords is drawn from the set of length-14 words that satisfy the $(d, k) = (2, 10)$ constraint. With this codebook, two merging bits would suffice to achieve a rate 8 : 16 block-decodable $(d, k) = (2, 10)$ code. However, in order to induce more favorable low-frequency spectral characteristics in the recorded code sequences, the encoding algorithm introduces an additional merging bit, yielding the rate 8 : 17 block-decodable EFM encoder.

5) Extensions: In this section, we present strengthened versions of both the finite-state coding theorem and the ACH theorem.

A *noncatastrophic encoder* is a tagged (S, n)-encoder with finite anticipation and the additional property that, whenever the sequences of output labels of two right-infinite paths differ in only finitely many places, the corresponding sequences of input tags also differ in only finitely many places. A rate $p : q$ finite-state tagged (S, α)-encoder is noncatastrophic if the corresponding tagged (S^q, α^p)-encoder is noncatastrophic.

Noncatastrophic encoders restrict error propagation in the sense that they limit the number of decoded data errors spawned by an isolated channel error. They do not necessarily limit the time span in which these errors occur. The concept of noncatastrophicity appears in the theory of convolutional codes, as well, where it actually coincides with sliding-block decodability [137, Ch. 10].

The following theorem is due to Karabed and Marcus [120].

Noncatastrophic Encoder Theorem: Let S be a constrained system. If $p/q \leq \mathsf{cap}_\alpha(S)$, then there exists a noncatastrophic rate $p : q$ finite-state (S, α)-encoder.

For the noncatastrophic encoders constructed in the proof of the theorem, the decoding errors generated by a single channel error are, in fact, confined to two bursts of finite length, although these bursts may appear arbitrarily far apart.

Karabed and Marcus also extended the ACH theorem to almost-finite-type systems.

Sliding-Block Code Theorem for Almost-Finite-Type Systems: Let S be an almost-finite-type constrained system. If $p/q \leq \mathsf{cap}_\alpha(S)$, then there exists a rate $p : q$ finite-state (S, α)-encoder with a sliding-block decoder.

The proof of this result is quite complicated. Although it does not translate as readily as the proof of the ACH theorem into a practical encoder design algorithm, the proof does introduce new and powerful techniques that, in combination with the state-splitting approach, can be applied effectively in certain cases.

For example, some of these techniques were used in the design of a 100% efficient, sliding-block-decodable encoder for a $(d, k; c) = (1, 3; 3)$ combined charge-constrained runlength-limited system [8]. In fact, it was the quest for such an encoder that provided the original motivation for the theorem. Several of the ideas in the proof of this generalization of the ACH theorem from finite-type to almost-finite-type systems have also played a role in the design of coded-modulation schemes based upon spectral-null constraints, discussed in Section V-C.

F. The State-Splitting Algorithm

There are many techniques available to construct efficient finite-state encoders. The majority of these construction techniques employ approximate eigenvectors to guide the construction process. Among these code design techniques is the *state-splitting algorithm* (or *ACH algorithm*) introduced by Adler, Coppersmith, and Hassner [3]. It implements the proof of the finite-state coding theorem and provides a recipe for constructing finite-state encoders that, for finite-type constraints, are sliding-block-decodable. The state-splitting approach combines ideas found in Patel's construction of the Zero-Modulation (ZM) code [160] and earlier work of Franaszek [62]–[64] with concepts and results from the mathematical theory of symbolic dynamics [138].

The ACH algorithm proceeds roughly as follows. For a given deterministic presentation G of a constrained system S and an achievable rate $p/q \leq \mathsf{cap}_\alpha(S)$, we iteratively apply a state-splitting transformation beginning with the qth-power graph G^q. The choice of transformation at each step is guided by an approximate eigenvector, which is updated at each iteration. The procedure culminates in a new presentation of S^q with at least α^p outgoing edges at each state. After deleting edges, we are left with an (S^q, α^p)-encoder, which, when tagged, gives our desired rate $p : q$ finite-state (S, α)-encoder. (Note that, if S is finite-type, the encoder is sliding-block-decodable regardless of the assignment of input tags.)

In view of its importance in the theory and practice of code design, we now present the state-splitting algorithm in more detail. This discussion follows [144], to which we refer the reader for further details. The basic step in the procedure is an *out-splitting* of a graph, and, more specifically, an *approximate-eigenvector consistent out-splitting*, both of which we now describe.

An *out-splitting* of a labeled graph H begins with a partition of the set E_u of outgoing edges for each state u in H into $N(u)$ disjoint subsets

$$E_u = E_u^{(1)} \cup E_u^{(2)} \cup \cdots \cup E_u^{(N(u))}.$$

The partition is used to derive a new labeled graph H'. The set of states $V_{H'}$ consists of $N(u)$ descendant states $u^{(1)}, u^{(2)}, \cdots, u^{(N(u))}$ for every $u \in V_H$. Outgoing edges from state u in H are partitioned among its descendant states and replicated in H' to each of the descendant terminal states in the following manner. For each edge e from u to v in H, we determine the partition element $E_u^{(i)}$ to which e belongs, and endow H' with edges $e^{(r)}$ from $u^{(i)}$ to $v^{(r)}$ for $r = 1, 2, \cdots, N(v)$. The label on the edge $e^{(r)}$ in H' is the same as the label of the edge e in H. (Sometimes an out-splitting is called a *round* of out-splitting to indicate that several states may have been split simultaneously.) The resulting graph H' generates the same system S, and has anticipation at most $\mathcal{A}(H) + 1$. Figs. 14 and 15 illustrate an out-splitting operation on state u.

Given a labeled graph H, a positive integer n, and an (A_H, n)-approximate eigenvector $\boldsymbol{x} = [x_v]_{v \in V_H}$, an $\boldsymbol{x}$-*consistent partition* of H is defined by partitioning the set E_u of outgoing edges for each state u in H into $N(u)$ disjoint subsets

$$E_u = E_u^{(1)} \cup E_u^{(2)} \cup \cdots \cup E_u^{(N(u))}$$

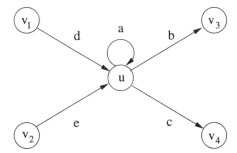

Fig. 14. Before out-splitting.

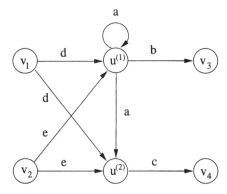

Fig. 15. After out-splitting.

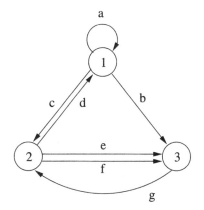

Fig. 16. Before $\boldsymbol{x}$-consistent out-splitting.

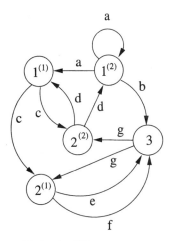

Fig. 17. After $\boldsymbol{x}$-consistent out-splitting.

with the property that

$$\sum_{e \in E_u^{(r)}} x_{\tau(e)} \geq n x_u^{(r)}, \qquad \text{for } r = 1, 2, \cdots, N(u) \quad (18)$$

where $\tau(e)$ denotes the terminal state of the edge e, $x_u^{(r)}$ are nonnegative integers, and

$$\sum_{r=1}^{N(u)} x_u^{(r)} = x_u, \qquad \text{for every } u \in V_H. \quad (19)$$

The out-splitting based upon such a partition is called an $\boldsymbol{x}$-*consistent splitting*. The vector $\boldsymbol{x}'$ indexed by the states $u^{(r)}$ of the split graph H' and defined by $x'_{u^{(r)}} = x_u^{(r)}$ is called the *induced vector*. An $\boldsymbol{x}$-consistent partition or splitting is called *nontrivial* if $N(u) \geq 2$ for at least one state u and both $x_u^{(1)}$ and $x_u^{(2)}$ are positive. Figs. 16 and 17 illustrate an $\boldsymbol{x}$-consistent splitting.

We now summarize the steps in the state-splitting algorithm for constructing a finite-state encoder with finite anticipation [144].

The State-Splitting Algorithm:

1) Select a labeled graph G and integers p and q as follows:
   a) Find a deterministic labeled graph G (or more generally a labeled graph with finite anticipation) which presents the given constrained system S (most constrained systems have a natural deterministic representation that is used to describe them in the first place).
   b) Find the adjacency matrix A_G of G.
   c) Compute the capacity $\mathsf{cap}_\alpha(S) = \log_\alpha \lambda(A_G)$.
   d) Select a desired code rate $p : q$ satisfying

   $$\mathsf{cap}_\alpha(S) \geq \frac{p}{q}.$$

   (one usually wants to keep p and q relatively small for complexity reasons).

2) Construct G^q.
3) Using the Franaszek algorithm of Section IV-E2, find an (A_G^q, α^p)-approximate eigenvector $\boldsymbol{x}$.
4) Eliminate all states u with $x_u = 0$ from G^q, and restrict to an irreducible sink H of the resulting graph, meaning a maximal irreducible subgraph with the property that all edges with initial states in H have their terminal states in H. Restrict $\boldsymbol{x}$ to be indexed by the states of H.
5) Iterate steps 5a)–5c) below until the labeled graph H has at least α^p edges outgoing from each state:
   a) Find a nontrivial $\boldsymbol{x}$-consistent partition of the edges in H. (This can be shown to be possible with a state of maximum weight.)
   b) Find the $\boldsymbol{x}$-consistent splitting corresponding to this partition, creating a labeled graph H' and an approximate eigenvector $\boldsymbol{x}'$.
   c) Replace H by H' and $\boldsymbol{x}$ by $\boldsymbol{x}'$.
6) At each state of H, delete all but α^p outgoing edges and tag the remaining edges with α-ry p-blocks, one for

235

each outgoing edge. This gives a rate $p : q$ finite-state (S, α)-encoder.

At every iteration, at least one state is split in a nontrivial way. Since a state v with weight x_v will be split into at most x_v descendant states throughout the whole iteration process, the number of iterations required to generate the encoder graph $\mathcal{E}$ is no more than $\Sigma_{v \in V_G} (x_v - 1)$. Therefore, the anticipation of $\mathcal{E}$ is at most $\Sigma_{v \in V_G} (x_v - 1)$. For the same reason, the number of states in $\mathcal{E}$ is at most $\Sigma_{v \in V_G} x_v$.

The operations of taking higher powers and out-splitting preserve definiteness (although the anticipation may increase under out-splitting). Therefore, if S is finite-type and G is a finite-memory presentation of S, any (S^q, α^p)-encoder constructed by the state-splitting algorithm will be (m, a)-definite for some m and a and, therefore, sliding-block-decodable.

The execution of the sliding-block code algorithm can be made completely systematic, in the sense that a computer program can be devised to automatically generate an encoder and decoder for any valid code rate. Nevertheless, the application of the method to just about any nontrivial code design problem will benefit from the interactive involvement of the code designers. There are some practical tools that can help the designer make "good" choices during the construction process, meaning choices that optimize certain measures of performance and complexity. Among them is state merging, a technique that can be used to simplify the encoder produced by the ACH algorithm, as we now describe.

Let G be a labeled graph and let u and u' be two states in G such that $\mathcal{F}_G(u) \subseteq \mathcal{F}_G(u')$. Suppose that $\boldsymbol{x}$ is an (A_G, n)-approximate eigenvector, and that $x_u = x_{u'}$. The (u, u')-merger of G is the labeled graph H obtained from G by: 1) eliminating all edges in $E_{u'}$; 2) redirecting into state u all remaining edges coming into state u'; and 3) eliminating the state u'. It is straightforward to show that $S(H) \subseteq S(G)$, and the vector $\boldsymbol{y}$ defined by $y_v = x_v$ for all vertices v of H is an (A_H, n)-approximate eigenvector. This operation reduces the final number of encoder states by x_u. The general problem of determining when to apply state merging during the state-splitting procedure in order to achieve the minimum number of states in the final encoder remains open.

It is also desirable to minimize the sliding-block decoder window size, in order to limit error propagation as well as decoder complexity. There are several elements of the code design that influence the window size, such as initial presentation, choice of approximate eigenvector, selection of out-splittings, excess edge elimination, and input tag assignment. There are approaches that, in some cases, can be used during the application of the state-splitting algorithm to help reduce the size of the decoder window, but the problem of minimizing the window size remains open. In this context, it should be noted that there are alternative code-design procedures that provide very useful heuristics for constructing sliding-block-decodable encoders with small decoding window. They also imply useful upper bounds on the minimum size of the decoding window and on the smallest possible anticipation (or decoding delay) [12]. In particular, Hollmann [92] has

recently developed an approach, influenced by earlier work of Immink [103], which combines the state-splitting method with a generalized look-ahead encoding technique called bounded-delay encoding, originally introduced by Franaszek [61], [63]. In a number of cases, it was found that this hybrid code design technique produced a sliding-block-decodable encoder with smaller window length than was achieved using other methods. Several examples of such codes for specific constraints of practical importance were constructed in [92].

For more extensive discussion of complexity measures and bounds, as well as brief descriptions of other general code construction methods, the reader is referred to [144].

G. Universality of State Splitting

The guarantee of a sliding-block decoder when S is finite-type, along with the explicit bound on the decoder window length, represent key strengths of the state-splitting algorithm. Another important property is its universality. In this context, we think of the state-splitting algorithm as comprising a selection of a deterministic presentation G of a constrained system S, an (A_G, n)-approximate eigenvector $\boldsymbol{x}$, a sequence of $\boldsymbol{x}$-consistent out-splittings, followed by deletion of excess edges, and finally an input-tag assignment, resulting in a tagged (S, n)-encoder.

For integers m, a, and a function $\mathcal{D}$ from $(m+a+1)$-blocks of S to the n-ary alphabet (such as a sliding-block decoder), we define $\mathcal{D}_\infty^{m,a}$ to be the induced mapping on bi-infinite sequences given by

$$\mathcal{D}_\infty^{m,a}(\cdots x_{-1}x_0x_1 \cdots) = \cdots s_{-1}s_0s_1 \cdots$$

where

$$s_i = \mathcal{D}(x_{i-m} \cdots x_{i-1}x_ix_{i+1} \cdots x_a).$$

For convenience, we use the notation $\mathcal{D}_\infty$ to denote $\mathcal{D}_\infty^{m,a}$. For a tagged (S, n)-encoder $\mathcal{E}$ with sliding-block decoder $\mathcal{D}$, we take the domain of the induced mapping $\mathcal{D}_\infty$ to be the set of all bi-infinite (output) symbol sequences obtained from $\mathcal{E}$. We say that a mapping $\mathcal{D}_\infty$ is a *sliding-block (S, n)-decoder* if $\mathcal{D}$ is a sliding-block decoder for some tagged (S, n)-encoder.

The universality of the state-splitting algorithm is summarized in the following theorem due to Ashley and Marcus [9], which we quote from [144].

Universality Theorem: Let S be an irreducible constrained system and let n be a positive integer.

a) Every sliding-block (S, n)-decoder has a unique minimal tagged (S, n)-encoder, where minimality is in terms of number of encoder states.

b) If we allow an arbitrary choice of deterministic presentation G of S and (A_G, n)-approximate eigenvector $\boldsymbol{x}$, then the state-splitting algorithm can find a tagged (S, n)-encoder for every sliding-block (S, n)-decoder. If we also allow merging of states (i.e., (u, v)-merging as described above), then it can find the minimal tagged (S, n)-encoder for every sliding-block (S, n)-decoder.

c) If we fix G to be the Shannon cover of S, but allow an arbitrary choice of (A_G, n)-approximate eigenvector

$\boldsymbol{x}$, then the state-splitting algorithm can find a tagged (S, n)-encoder for every sliding-block (S, n)-decoder $\mathcal{D}$, modulo a change in the domain of $\mathcal{D}_\infty$, possibly with a constant shift of each bi-infinite sequence prior to applying $\mathcal{D}_\infty$ (but with no change in the decoding function $\mathcal{D}$ itself). If we also allow merging of states, then, modulo the same changes, it can find the minimal tagged (S, n)-encoder for every sliding-block (S, n)-decoder. In particular, it can find a sliding-block (S, n)-decoder with minimal decoding window length.

Certain limitations on the use of the algorithm should be noted, however [9]. If we apply the state-splitting algorithm to the Shannon cover of an irreducible constrained system S, it need not be able to find a sliding-block (S, n)-decoder with smallest number of encoder states in its minimal tagged (S, n)-encoder.

Similarly, if we start with the Shannon cover of an irreducible constrained system S and, in addition, we fix $\boldsymbol{x}$ to be a minimal (A_G, n)-approximate eigenvector (i.e., with smallest eigenvector component sum), then the algorithm may fail to find a sliding-block (S, n)-decoder with minimum decoding window length [119], [103], [9].

The universality of the state-splitting algorithm is an attractive property, in that it implies that the technique can be used to produce the "best" codes. However, in order to harness the power of this design tool, strategies for making the right choices during the execution of the construction procedure are required. There is considerable room for further research in this direction, as well as in the development of other code-construction methods.

H. Practical Aspects of High-Rate Code Design

The construction of very high rate (d, k)-constrained codes and DC-balanced codes is an important practical problem [71], [102], [208]. The construction of such high-rate codes is far from obvious, as table look-up for encoding and decoding is an engineering impracticality. The usual approach is to supplement the p source bits with $m = q - p$ bits. Under certain, usually simple, rules the source word is modified in such a way that the modified word plus supplementary bits comply with the constraints. The information that certain modifications have been made is carried by the m supplementary bits. The receiver, on reception of the word, will undo the modifications. In order to reduce complexity and error propagation, the number of bits affected by a modification should be as small as possible. We now give some examples of such constructions.

A traditional example of a simple DC-free code is called the *polarity bit code* [26]. The p source symbols are supplemented by one bit called the *polarity bit*. The encoder has the option to transmit the $(p+1)$-bit word without modification or to invert all $(p+1)$ symbols. The choice of a specific translation is made in such a way that the running digital sum is as close to zero as possible. It can easily be shown that the running digital sum takes a finite number of values, so that the sequence generated is DC-balanced.

A surprisingly simple method for transforming an arbitrary word into a codeword having equal numbers of 1's and 0's—that is, a *balanced* or *zero-disparity* word—was published by Knuth [129] and Henry [85]. Let

$$d(\boldsymbol{w}) = \sum_{i=1}^{p} w_i$$

be the *disparity* of the binary source word

$$\boldsymbol{w} = (w_1, \cdots, w_p), \qquad w_i \in \{-1, 1\}.$$

Let $d_k(\boldsymbol{w})$ be the running digital sum of the first k, $k \le p$, bits of $\boldsymbol{w}$, or

$$d_k(\boldsymbol{w}) = \sum_{i=1}^{k} w_i$$

and let $\boldsymbol{w}^{(k)}$ be the word $\boldsymbol{w}$ with its first k bits inverted. For example, if

$$\boldsymbol{w} = (-1, 1, 1, 1, -1, 1, -1, 1, 1, -1)$$

we have $d(\boldsymbol{w}) = 2$ and

$$\boldsymbol{w}^{(4)} = (1, -1, -1, -1, -1, 1, -1, 1, 1, -1).$$

If $\boldsymbol{w}$ is of even length p, and if we let $\sigma_k(\boldsymbol{w})$ stand for $d(\boldsymbol{w}^{(k)})$, then the quantity $\sigma_k(\boldsymbol{w})$ is

$$\sigma_k(\boldsymbol{w}) = -\sum_{i=1}^{k} w_i + \sum_{i=k+1}^{p} w_i$$

$$= -2\sum_{i=1}^{k} w_i + d(\boldsymbol{w}).$$

It is immediate that $\sigma_0(\boldsymbol{w}) = d(\boldsymbol{w})$ (no symbols inverted), and $\sigma_p(\boldsymbol{w}) = -d(\boldsymbol{w})$ (all symbols inverted). We may, therefore, conclude that every word $\boldsymbol{w}$ can be associated with at least one k, so that $\sigma_k(\boldsymbol{w}) = 0$, or $\boldsymbol{w}^{(k)}$ is balanced. The value of k is encoded in a (preferably) zero-disparity word $\boldsymbol{u}$ of length m, m even. If m and p are both odd, we can use a similar construction. The maximum codeword length of $\boldsymbol{w}$ is governed by

$$\binom{m}{m/2}.$$

Some other modifications of the basic scheme are discussed in Knuth [129] and Alon [5].

The *sequence replacement technique* [202] converts source words of length p into $(0, k)$-constrained words of length $q = p + 1$. The control bit is set to 1 and appended at the beginning of the p-bit source word. If this $(p + 1)$-bit sequence satisfies the prescribed constraint it is transmitted. If the constraint is violated, i.e., a runlength of at least $k + 1$ 0's occur, we remove the trespassing $k + 1$ 0's. The position where the start of the violation was found is encoded in $k + 1$ bits, which are appended at the beginning of the $p+1$-bit word. Such a modification is signaled to the receiver by setting the control bit to 0. The codeword remains of length $p + 1$. The procedure above is repeated until all forbidden subsequences have been removed. The receiver can reconstruct the source word as the position information is stored at a predefined position in the codeword. In certain situations, the entire source word has to be modified which makes the procedure prone to error propagation. The class of rate $(q - 1)/q$, $(0, k)$-constrained codes, $k = 1 + \lfloor q/3 \rfloor$, $q \ge 9$, was constructed to minimize

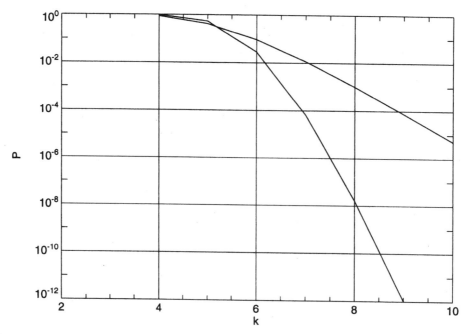

Fig. 18. Probability that no sequence of L drawings from a selection set of random sequences satisfies the $(0, k)$ constraint. Code rate $R = 0.99$. Upper curve: codeword length $q = 200$, selection set size $L = 4$; lower curve: codeword length $q = 400$, selection set size $L = 16$.

error propagation [111]. Error propagation is confined to one decoded 8-bit symbol, irrespective of the codeword length q.

Recently, the publications by Fair *et al.* [48] and Immink and Patrovics [110] on *guided scrambling* brought new insights into high-rate code design. Guided scrambling is a member of a larger class of related coding schemes called *multimode* codes. In multimode codes, the p-bit source word is mapped into $(m + p)$-bit codewords. Each source word x can be represented by a member of a *selection set* consisting of $L = 2^m$ codewords. Examples of such mappings are the guided scrambling algorithm presented by Fair *et al.* [48], the DC-free coset codes of Deng and Herro [43], and the scrambling using a Reed–Solomon code by Kunisa *et al.* [135]. A mapping is considered to be "good" if the selection set contains sufficiently distinct and random codewords.

The encoder transmits the codeword that minimizes, according to a prescribed criterion, some property of the encoded sequence, such as its low-frequency spectral content. In general, there are two key elements which need to be chosen judiciously: a) the mapping between the source words and their corresponding selection sets, and b) the criterion used to select the "best" word.

The use of multimode codes is not confined to the generation of DC-free sequences. Provided that 2^m is large enough and the selection set contains sufficiently different codewords, multimode codes can also be used to satisfy almost any channel constraint with a suitably chosen selection method. For given rate and proper selection criteria, the spectral content of multimode codes is very close to that of maxentropic RDS-constrained sequences. A clear disadvantage is that the encoder needs to generate all 2^m possible codewords, compute the criterion, and make the decision.

In the context of high-rate multimode codes, there is interest in *weakly constrained codes* [107]. Weakly constrained codes may produce sequences that violate the constraints with probability P. It is argued that if the channel is not free of errors, it is pointless to feed the channel with perfectly constrained sequences. We illustrate the effectiveness of this idea by considering the properties of two examples of weak $(0, k)$ codes. Fig. 18 shows the probability P that no sequence taken from a selection set of size L of random sequences obeys the $(0, k)$ constraint. Let the code rate $R = 99/100$, the codeword length $q = 400$, and the size of the selection set $L = 16$. Then we observe that with probability $P = 10^{-12}$ a codeword violates the $k = 9$ constraint. The alternative implementation [111] requires a rate of $R = 24/25$—four times the redundancy of the weakly constrained code—to strictly guarantee the same $(0, 9)$ constraint.

V. CONSTRAINED CODES FOR NOISY RECORDING CHANNELS

In Section III-A, we indicated how the implementation of timing recovery, gain control, and detection algorithms in recording systems created a need for suitably constrained recording codes. These codes are typically used as an inner code, in concatenation with an outer error-correcting code. The error-correcting codes improve system performance by introducing structure, usually of an algebraic nature, that increases the separation of code sequences as measured by some distance metric, such as Hamming distance.

A number of authors have addressed the problem of endowing constrained codes with advantageous distance properties. Metrics that have been considered include Hamming distance, edit (or Levenshtein) distance, and Lee distance. These metrics arise in the context of a variety of error types, including random-bit errors, insertion and deletion errors, bitshift errors, and more generally, burst errors. Code constructions, performance analyses, as well as lower and upper bounds on the achievable size of constrained codes with specified distance properties are surveyed in [144].

It is fair to say that the application of constrained codes with random or burst-error correction capabilities, proposed largely in the context of storage systems using symbol-by-symbol detection such as peak detection, has been extremely limited. However, the advent of digital signal processing techniques such as PRML has created a new role for recording codes, analogous to the role of trellis-coded modulation in digital communications. In this section, we describe how appropriately constrained code sequences can improve PRML system performance by increasing the separation between the channel output sequences with respect to Euclidean distance.

A. PRML Performance Bounds and Error Event Analysis

The design of distance-enhancing constrained codes for recording channels requires an understanding of the performance of the PRML Viterbi detector, which we now briefly review. The detector performance is best understood in terms of *error events*. For a pair of input sequences $x(D)$ and $x'(D)$, define the input error sequence $\varepsilon_x(D) = x(D) - x'(D)$ and the output error sequence $\varepsilon_y(D) = h(D)\varepsilon_x(D)$. A *closed error event* corresponds to a polynomial input error sequence

$$\varepsilon_x(D) = \sum_{k=k_1}^{k_2} \varepsilon_{x,i} D^i$$

where k_1 and k_2 are finite integers, $\varepsilon_{x,k_1} \neq 0$, and $\varepsilon_{x,k_2} \neq 0$. A closed error event is said to be *simple* if the condition $\varepsilon_{x,k} = \varepsilon_{x,k+1} = \cdots = \varepsilon_{x,k+\nu-1} = 0$ is not true for any integer $k_1 \leq k \leq k_2 - \nu$, where ν is the memory of the channel. An *open error event* corresponds to a right-infinite input error sequence of the form

$$\varepsilon_x(D) = \sum_{k=k_1}^{\infty} \varepsilon_{x,k} D^k$$

where infinitely many $\varepsilon_{x,k}$ are nonzero, but the Euclidean norm is finite

$$||\varepsilon_y(D)||^2 = \sum_i |\varepsilon_{y,i}|^2 < \infty.$$

In general, for an error event E, with corresponding input error sequence $e_x(D)$ and output error sequence $e_y(D)$, the squared-Euclidean distance is defined as

$$d^2(E) = ||\varepsilon_y(D)||^2.$$

The number of channel input-bit errors corresponding to an error event E is given by

$$w_x(E) = \sum_i |e_{x,i}|.$$

The ML detector produces an error when the selected trellis path differs from the correct path by a sequence of error events. The *union bound* provides an upper bound to the probability of an error event beginning at some time k by considering the set of all possible simple error events

$$P_e = \Pr(\text{first event at time } k) \leq \sum_{\text{events } E} \Pr(E)$$

TABLE IV
ERROR EVENT MULTIPLICITY GENERATING FUNCTIONS

Channel	$G(z)$
Dicode	$2z^2/(1 - z^4)$ $= 2z^2 + 2z^6 + 2z^{10} + O(z^{14})$
PR4	$(2z^2 + 4z^4 - 2z^6)/(1 - 2z^2 - 2z^4 - 2z^6 + z^8)$ $= 2z^2 + 8z^4 + 18z^6 + O(z^8)$
EPR4	$(5/2)z^4 + (41/8)z^6 + (417/32)z^8 + O(z^{10})$
E²PR4	$(1/4)z^6 + (9/32)z^8 + (357/256)z^{10} + O(z^{12})$
E³PR4	$(1/4)z^{12} + (1/16)z^{16} + (3/16)z^{20} + (21/128)z^{22}$ $+(11/32)z^{24} + (223/512)z^{26} + (927/512)z^{28} + O(z^{30})$
PR1	$2z^2/(1 - z^4) = 2z^2 + 2z^6 + 2z^{10} + O(z^{14})$
PR2	$z^4 + (3/2)z^6 + O(z^8)$

which in the assumed case of AWGN, yields

$$P_e \leq \sum_{\text{events } E} Q\left(\frac{d(E)}{2\sigma}\right)\left(\frac{1}{2}\right)^{w_x(E)}.$$

Reorganizing the summation according to the error event distance $d(E)$, the bound is expressed as:

$$P_e \leq \sum_{d(E)} K_{d(E)} Q\left(\frac{d(E)}{2\sigma}\right)$$

where the values $\{K_d\}$, known as the *error event distance spectrum*, are defined by

$$K_d = \sum_{E:d(E)=d} \left(\frac{1}{2}\right)^{w_x(E)}.$$

At moderate-to-high SNR, the performance of the system is largely dictated by error events with small distance $d(E)$. In particular, the events with the minimum distance $d_{\min}$ will be the dominant contributors to the union bound, leading to the frequently used approximation

$$P_e \approx K_{d_{\min}} Q\left(\frac{d_{\min}}{2\sigma}\right).$$

For a number of the PR channel models applicable to recording, the error event distance spectrum values, as well as the corresponding input error sequences, have been determined for a range of values of the distance $d(E)$ [7], [198], [6]. The calculation is made somewhat interesting by the fact, mentioned in Section II-C2, that the PR trellises support closed error events of unbounded length having certain specified, finite distances. For channels with limited ISI, analytical methods may be applied in the characterization of low distance events. However, for larger distances, and for PR channel polynomials of higher degree, computer search methods have been more effective.

Table IV gives several terms of the error event multiplicity generating functions $G(z) = \sum_d K_d z^d$ for several PR channels. Tables V and VI, respectively, list the input error sequences for simple closed events on the PR4 and EPR4 channels having squared-distance $d^2(E) \leq 6$. Table VII describes the input error sequences for simple closed events on the E²PR4 channel having squared-distance $d^2(E) \leq 10$. In the error sequence tables, the symbol "+" is used to designate "1," "−" is used to designate "−1," and a parenthesized string (s) denotes any positive number of repetitions of the string s.

239

TABLE V
CLOSED ERROR EVENTS (PER INTERLEAVE) FOR PR4 CHANNEL, $d^2 \leq 6$

d^2	e_x
2	+(0+)00
4	+(0+)+(+)0(+0)0
	+(0+)-(+-)0(-0)0
	+(0+)-(+-)+0(+0)0
6	+(0+)+(+)0(+0)++(+)0(+0)0
	+(0+)+(+)0(+0)+-(+-)0(-0)0
	+(0+)-(+-)+0(+0)+-(+-)+0(+0)0
	+(0+)-(+-)0(-0)--(-)0(-0)0
	+(0+)-(+-)0(-0)-+(-+)-0(-0)0
	+(0+)+(+)0(+0)+-(+-)+0(+0)0
	+(0+)-(+-)+0(+0)++(+)0(+0)0
	+(0+)-(+-)+0(+0)+-(+-)(+-)0(-0)0
	+(0+)-(+-)0(-0)-+(-+)0(+0)0
	+(0+)0-(0-)00

TABLE VI
CLOSED ERROR EVENTS FOR EPR4 CHANNEL, $d^2 \leq 6$

d^2	e_x
4	-+-(-+)000
	+0(+0)00
	+-+(-+)-000
6	+-000
	+-+(-+)00+-+(-+)-000
	+-+(-+)0+(0+)000
	+-+(-+)-00-+-(+-)000
	+-+(-+)-00-0(-0)00
	+0(+0)+-+(-+)-000
	+0(+0)0+-+(-+)000
	+0(+0)0+0(+0)00
	+-+(-+)00+-+(-+)000
	+-+(-+)00+0(+0)00
	+-+(-+)-00-+-(+-)+000
	+-+(-+)-0-(0-)000
	+0(+0)+-+(-+)000
	+0(+0)++0+(0+)000
	+0(+0)0+-+(-+)-000

TABLE VII
CLOSED ERROR EVENTS FOR E^{2}PR4 CHANNEL, $d^2 \leq 10$

d^2	e_x
6	+-+0000
8	+-+00+-+0000
	+-+-(+-)0000
	+-+-(+-)+0000
10	+-+0-+-0000
	+-+00+-+00+-+0000
	+-+00+00+-+0000
	+00+-+0000
	+-+00+-+-(+-)+0000
	+-+00+-+-(+-)0000
	+-+000+-+0000
	+-+00+0000
	+0000
	+-+-(+-)+00+-+0000
	+-+-(+-)00-+-0000

those that can generate the best practical distance-enhancing codes—with a specified coding gain, high-rate, simple encoder and decoder, and low-complexity sequence detector—remains open.

The code constraints $\mathcal{C}$ and the PR channel memory are then incorporated into a single detector trellis that can serve as the basis for the Viterbi detector. The final step in the design procedure is to construct an efficient code into the constraints $\mathcal{C}$. This can be accomplished using code design techniques such as those discussed in Section IV.

It is useful to distinguish between two cases in implementing this strategy for the PR channels we have discussed. The cases are determined by the relationship of the minimum distance $d_{\min}$ to the matched-filter-bound (MFB) distance, d_{MFB}, where

$$d^2_{\mathrm{MFB}} = \|h(D)\|^2,$$

the energy in the channel impulse response.

The first case pertains to those channels which are said to achieve the MFB

$$d^2_{\min} = d^2_{\mathrm{MFB}}$$

including PR4, EPR4, and PR1. For these channels, the set of minimum-distance input error sequences includes $e_x(D) = \pm 1$, and so any distance-enhancing code constraint must prevent this input error impulse from occurring.

The second case involves channels which do not achieve the MFB

$$d^2_{\min} < d^2_{\mathrm{MFB}}.$$

This case applies to E^{M}PR4, for all $M \geq 2$, as well as E^{M}PR2, for all $M \geq 0$. Note that, in this situation, a minimum-distance input error sequence—in fact, every error sequence satisfying $d^2(e_x) < d^2_{\mathrm{MFB}}$—has length strictly greater than 1, where event length refers to the span between the first and last nonzero symbols. These events can often be eliminated with constraints $\mathcal{C}$ that are quite simply specified and for which practical, efficient codes are readily constructed.

For the latter class of channels, we can determine distance-enhancing constraints that increase the minimum distance to d_{MFB}, yet are characterizable in terms of a small list $\mathcal{F}$ of

B. Code Design Strategy

The characterization of error sequences provides a basis for the design of constrained codes that eliminate events with a small Euclidean distance, thereby increasing the minimum distance and giving a performance improvement [123], [182], [122], [154]. This operation is similar in nature to expurgation in the context of algebraic codes.

More specifically, the design of distance-enhancing constrained codes for PRML systems is based upon the following strategy. First, we identify the input error sequences $e_x(D) = x_1(D) - x_2(D)$ with $d^2(e_x) < d^2_*$, where d^2_* is the target distance of the coded channel. Then, we determine a list $\mathcal{L}$ of input error strings that, if eliminated by means of a code constraint, will prevent the occurrence of error events with $d^2 < d^2_*$. We denote the set of ternary error sequences satisfying this constraint by $\mathcal{X}_{\mathcal{L}}^{\{0,\pm 1\}}$.

In order to prevent these error strings, we must next determine a code constraint $\mathcal{C}$ with the property that the corresponding set of input error sequences $\boldsymbol{E}(\mathcal{C})$ satisfies

$$\boldsymbol{E}(\mathcal{C}) \subset \mathcal{X}_{\mathcal{L}}^{\{0,\pm 1\}}. \tag{20}$$

There are many choices for the error strings $\mathcal{L}$, as well as for constraints $\mathcal{C}$ satisfying (20). The problem of identifying

240

relatively short forbidden code strings. (We will sometimes denote such constraints by $X_{\mathcal{F}}^{\{0,1\}}$.) This permits the design of high-rate codes, and also makes it possible to limit the complexity of the Viterbi detector, since the maximum length of a forbidden string may not exceed too significantly, or at all, the memory of the uncoded channel. Consequently, and perhaps surprisingly, the design of high-rate, distance-enhancing codes with acceptable encoder/decoder and Viterbi detector complexity proves to be considerably simpler for the channels in the second group, namely, the channels with relatively larger intersymbol interference.

We now turn to a discussion of some specific distance-enhancing constraints and codes for partial-response channels.

C. Matched-Spectral-Null Constraints

As mentioned above, spectral-null constraints, particularly those with DC-nulls and/or Nyquist-nulls, are well-matched to the frequency characteristics of digital recording channels, and have found application in many recording systems prior to the introduction of PRML techniques. In [121] and [46], it was shown that, in addition, constraints with spectral nulls at the frequencies where the channel frequency response has the value zero—*matched-spectral-null (MSN) constraints*—can increase the minimum distance relative to the uncoded channel. An example of this phenomenon, and one which served historically to motivate the use of matched-spectral-null codes, is the rate $1/2$ biphase code, with binary codewords 01 and 10, which, one can easily show, increases the minimum squared-Euclidean distance of the binary-input dicode channel, $h(D) = 1 - D$, from $d^2 = 2$ to $d^2 = 6$.

To state a more general bound on the distance-enhancing properties of MSN codes, we generalize the notion of a spectral null constraint to include sequences for which higher order derivatives of the power spectrum vanish at specified frequencies, as well. More precisely, we say that an ensemble of sequences has an *order-K spectral density null at f_0* if the power spectral density $S(f)$ satisfies

$$\frac{d^k}{df^k} S(f)|_{f_0} = 0, \qquad k = 0, 1, \cdots, 2K - 1.$$

We will concentrate here upon those with high-order spectral null at DC. Sequences with high-order spectral nulls can be characterized in a number of equivalent ways. The high-order running-digital-sums of a sequence $\boldsymbol{x} = \{x_i\}, 0 \leq i \leq n$, at DC can be defined recursively as

$$\text{RDS}_0^{(1)}(\boldsymbol{x}) = \text{RDS}(\boldsymbol{x}) = \sum_{i=0}^{n} x_i$$

$$\text{RDS}_0^{(k)}(\boldsymbol{x}) = \sum_{i=0}^{n} \text{RDS}_0^{(k-1)}(x_0, \cdots, x_i), \qquad k > 1.$$

Sequences with order-K spectral null at DC may be characterized in terms of properties of $\text{RDS}_0^{(k)}(\boldsymbol{x}), k = 1, \cdots, K$. Another characterization involves the related notion of high-order moments (power-sums), where the *order-k moment at*

DC of the sequence $\boldsymbol{x}$ is defined as

$$M_0^{(k)}(\boldsymbol{x}) = \sum_{i=0}^{n} i^k x_i.$$

In analogy to the characterization of (first-order) spectral null sequences, one can show that an ensemble of sequences generated by freely concatenating a set of codewords of finite length n will have an order-K spectral null at DC if and only if

$$M_0^{(k)}(\boldsymbol{c}) = 0, \qquad k = 0, \cdots, K - 1 \qquad (21)$$

for all codewords $\boldsymbol{c}$. In other words, for each codeword, the order-k moments at DC must vanish for $k = 0, \cdots, K - 1$. A sequence satisfying this condition is also said to have *zero disparity of order $K - 1$*.

Finally, we remark that a length-n sequence with D-transform

$$x(D) = x_0 + x_1 D + \cdots + x_{n-1} D^{n-1}$$

has an order-K spectral null at DC if and only if $x(D)$ is divisible by $(1 - D)^K$. This fact plays a role in bounding the distance-enhancing properties of spectral-null sequences.

For more details about high-order spectral null constraints, particularly constraints with high-order null at DC, we refer the interested reader to Immink [99], Monti and Pierobon [153], Karabed and Siegel [121], Eleftheriou and Cideciyan [46], and Roth, Siegel, and Vardy [165], as well as other references cited therein.

The original proof of the distance-enhancing properties of MSN codes was based upon a number-theoretic lower bound on the minimum Hamming distance of zero-disparity codes, due to Immink and Beenker [108]. They proved that the minimum Hamming distance (and, therefore, the minimum Euclidean distance) of a block code over the bipolar alphabet with order-K spectral-null at DC grows at least linearly in K. Specifically, they showed that, for any pair $\boldsymbol{x}, \boldsymbol{y}$ of length-n sequences in the code

$$d^H(\boldsymbol{x}, \boldsymbol{y}) \geq 2K$$

and

$$d^2(\boldsymbol{x}, \boldsymbol{y}) \geq 8K.$$

This result for block codes can be suitably generalized to any constrained system with order-K spectral null at DC. The result also extends to systems with an order-K spectral null at any rational submultiple of the symbol frequency, in particular, at the Nyquist frequency.

In [121], this result was extended to show that the Lee distance, and *a fortiori* the squared-Euclidean distance, between output sequences of a bipolar, input-constrained channel is lower-bounded by $8M$ if the input constraint and the channel, with spectral nulls at DC (or the Nyquist frequency) of orders K and L, respectively, combine to produce a spectral null at DC (or Nyquist) of order $M = K + L$. This result can be proved by applying Descartes' rule of signs to the D-transform representation of these sequences, using the divisibility conditions mentioned above [121].

This result can be applied to the PR4, EPR4, and E^2PR4 channels, which have a first-order null at DC and a Nyquist null of order $L = 1, 2,$ and 3, respectively. If the channel inputs are constrained to be bipolar sequences with an order-K Nyquist null, the channel outputs will satisfy the following lower bound on minimum squared-Euclidean distance:

$$d_{\min}^2 \geq \begin{cases} 8(K+1), & \text{for PR4} \\ 8(K+2), & \text{for EPR4} \\ 8(K+3), & \text{for } E^2\text{PR4}. \end{cases}$$

Comparing to the minimum distance of the uncoded bipolar channels, we see that the MSN constraint with $K = 1$, corresponding to a first-order Nyquist null, provides a coding gain (unnormalized for rate loss) of at least 3, 1.8, and 1.2 dB, respectively. Using the observation made in Section III-A3, one can design codes with first-order null at DC and Nyquist by twice-interleaving a DC-free code. When such a code is applied to the PR4 channel, which has an interleaved dicode decomposition, the implementation of the MSN-coded system becomes feasible. Code-design techniques such as those described in Section IV have been used to design efficient MSN codes. For analytical and experimental results pertaining to a rate $4/5$, MSN-coded PR4 system, the reader is referred to [164] and [169]. Experimental evaluation of a spectral-null coded-tape system is described in [27].

For these examples of MSN-constrained PR channels, the error event characterization discussed above provides another confirmation, and a refinement, of the coding gain bounds. The verification makes use of the moment conditions satisfied by closed input error sequences $e = e_0, \cdots, e_N$ satisfying spectral null properties, a generalization of the moment conditions in (21) above. Specifically, a first-order DC null requires that

$$\sum_{i=0}^{N} e_i = 0 \tag{22}$$

and a first-order Nyquist null requires that

$$\sum_{i=0}^{N} (-1)^i e_i = 0. \tag{23}$$

Examination of the error events for PR4 in Table V shows that each error event with $d^2 < 4$ fails to satisfy at least one of these conditions. Similarly, for EPR4, the error events in Table VI with $d^2 < 6$ are forbidden by the moment conditions. In the case of E^2PR4, the error event characterization not only confirms, but also improves, the lower bound. Table VII shows that the moment conditions cannot be satisfied by any error sequence with $d^2 < 10$, implying a nominal coding gain of 2.2 dB. MSN coding based upon Nyquist-free constraints is applicable to optical PR channels, and error-event analysis can be used to confirm the coding gain bounds in a similar manner [152].

There have been a number of extensions and variations on MSN coding techniques, most aimed at increasing code rate, improving intrinsic runlength constraints, or reducing the implementation complexity of the encoder, decoder, and detector. For further details, the reader should consult [68] and the references therein, as well as more recent results in, for example, [151] and [147].

When implementing MSN-coded PR systems, the complexity of the trellis structure that incorporates both the PR channel memory and the MSN constraints can be an issue, particularly for high-rate codes requiring larger digital sum variation. Reduced-complexity, suboptimal detection algorithms based upon a concatenation of a Viterbi detector for the PR channel and an error-event post-processor have been proposed for a DC/Nyquist-free block-coded PR4 channel [128] and EPR4 channel [184]. In both schemes, DC/Nyquist-free codewords are obtained by interleaving pairs of DC-free codewords, and discrepancies in the first-order moments of the interleaved codeword estimates produced by the PR channel detector are utilized by the post-processors to determine and correct most-probable minimum-distance error events.

It should be pointed out that aspects of the code design strategy described above were foreshadowed in an unpublished paper of Fredrickson [66] dealing with the biphase-coded dicode channel. In that paper, the observation was made that the input error sequences corresponding to the minimum squared-distance $d^2 = 6$ were of the form

$$e_x(D) = \pm 1 \, 0 \cdots$$

and those corresponding to the next-minimum distance $d^2 = 10$ were of the form

$$e_x(D) = \pm 1 - 1 \, 0 \cdots.$$

Fredrickson modified the encoding process to eliminate minimum-distance events by appending an overall "parity-check" bit to each block of k input bits, for a specified value of k. The resulting rate $k/(2k+2)$ code provided a minimum squared-Euclidean distance $d_{\min}^2 = 10$ at the output of the dicode channel, with only a modest penalty in rate for large k. The Viterbi detector for the coded channel was modified to incorporate the parity modulo-2 and to reflect the even-parity condition at the codeword boundaries. It was also shown that both the $d^2 = 6$ and the $d^2 = 10$ events can be eliminated by appending a pair of bits to each block of k input bits in order to enforce a specific parity condition modulo-3. The resulting rate $k/(2k+4)$ code yielded $d_{\min}^2 = 12$ at the dicode channel output, and the coding gain was realized with a suitably enhanced detector structure.

D. Runlength Constraints

Certain classes of runlength constraints have distance-enhancing properties when applied to the magnetic and optical PR channels. For example, the NRZI $d = 1$ constraint has been applied to the EPR4 and the E^2PR4 magnetic channels, as well as the PR1 and PR2 optical channels; see, for example [152] and the references therein. On the EPR4 and PR1 channels, the constraint does not increase minimum distance. However, it does eliminate some of the minimum distance error-events, thereby providing some performance improvement. Moreover, the incorporation of the constraint into the detector trellis for EPR4 leads to a reduction of complexity from eight states

TABLE VIII
INPUT PAIRS FOR FORBIDDEN ERROR STRINGS IN $\mathcal{L}_1$

e	+	−	+		−	+	−		+	0	+		−	0	−
x_1	1	0	1		0	1	0		1	b	1		0	b	0
x_2	0	1	0		1	0	1		0	b	0		1	b	1

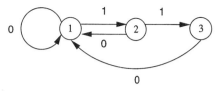

Fig. 19. Labeled graph for MTR $k_1 = 2$ constraint.

to six states, eliminating those corresponding to the NRZ channel inputs 010 and 101.

In the case of E^{2}PR4, Behrens and Armstrong [17] showed that the $d = 1$ constraint provides a 2.2-dB increase in minimum squared-Euclidean distance. To see why this is the case, observe that forbidding the input error strings $\{+ - +, - + -\}$ will prevent all closed error events with $d^2 < 10$. Forbidding, in addition, the strings $\{+0+, -0-\}$ prevents all open events with $d^2 < 10$, as well. Table VIII depicts pairs of binary input strings whose corresponding error strings belong to $\mathcal{L}_1 = \{+ - +, - + -, + 0 +, - 0 -\}$ The symbol b represents an arbitrary binary value common to both strings in a pair. Clearly, the elimination of the NRZ strings 101 and 010 precludes all of the input error strings. The precoded $d = 1$ constraint precludes the NRZ strings $\mathcal{F} = \{101, 010\}$—that is, the NRZ constraint is $X^{\{0,1\}}_{\{101, 010\}}$—confirming that the constraint prevents all events with $d^2 < 10$. When the constraint is incorporated into the detector trellis, the resulting structure has only 10 states, substantially less than the 16 states required by the uncoded channel.

The input error sequence analysis used above to confirm the distance-enhancing properties of the $d = 1$ constraint on the E^{2}PR4 channel suggests a relaxation of the constraint that nevertheless still achieves the same distance gain. Specifically, the $X^{\{0,1\}}_{\{101\}}$ constraint and the complementary $X^{\{0,1\}}_{\{010\}}$ constraint are sufficient to ensure the elimination of closed and open events with $d^2 < 10$. The capacity of this constraint satisfies $C \approx 0.8113$, and a rate 4/5, finite-state encoder with state-independent decoder is described in [122]. The corresponding detector trellis requires 12 states. Thus with a modest increase in complexity, this code achieves essentially the same performance as the rate 2/3 (1, 7) code, while increasing the rate by 20%.

This line of reasoning may be used to demonstrate the distance-enhancing properties of another class of NRZI runlength constraints, referred to as maximum-transition-run (MTR) constraints [154]. These constraints limit, sometimes in a periodically time-varying manner, the maximum number of consecutive 1's that can occur. The MTR constraints are characterized by a parameter k_1, which determined the maximum allowable runlength of 1's. These constraints can be interpreted as a generalization of the $d = 1$ constraint, which is the same as the MTR constraint with $k_1 = 1$.

The MTR constraint with $k_1 = 2$ was introduced by Moon and Brickner [154] (see also Soljanin [181]). A labeled graph representation is shown in Fig. 19. The capacity of this constraint is $C \approx 0.8791$. Imposing an additional constraint, which we now denote k_0, on the maximum runlength of 0's reduces the capacity, as shown in Table IX.

TABLE IX
CAPACITY OF MTR $k_1 = 2$
FOR SELECTED VALUES OF k_0

k_0	Capacity
4	0.8376
5	0.8579
6	0.8680
7	0.8732
8	0.8760
9	0.8774
10	0.8782
∞	0.8791

TABLE X
INPUT PAIRS FOR FORBIDDEN ERROR STRINGS IN $\mathcal{L}_2$

e	0	+	−	+		0	−	+	−
x_1	b	1	0	1		b	0	1	0
x_2	b	0	1	0		b	1	0	1

The NRZI MTR constraint with $k_1 = 2$ corresponds to an NRZ constraint $X^{\{0,1\}}_{\{0101, 1010\}}$. The error-event characterization in Table VII shows that the forbidden input error list $\mathcal{L}_2 = \{0 + - +, 0 - + -\}$ suffices to eliminate the closed error events on E^{2}PR4 with $d^2 < 10$, though not all the open events. Analysis of input pairs, shown in Table X, reveals that the MTR constraint indeed eliminates the closed error events with $d^2 < 10$. The detector trellis that incorporates the E^{2}PR4 memory with this MTR constraint requires 14 states.

A rate 4/5 block code is shown in Table XI [154]. It is interesting to observe that the MTR $k_1 = 2$ constraint is the symbol-wise complement of the $(d, k) = (0, 2)$ constraint, and the rate 4/5 MTR codebook is the symbol-wise complement of the rate 4/5 Group Code Recording code, shown in Table I. With this code, all open error events with $d^2 < 10$ are eliminated.

The MTR constraint supports codes with rates approaching its capacity, $C \approx 0.8791$ [154], [155]. However, in practical applications, a distance-enhancing code with rate 8/9 or higher is considered very desirable. It has been shown that higher rate trellis codes can be based upon time-varying MTR (TMTR) constraints [67], [23], [123], [52]. For example, the TMTR constraint defined by $k_1^{\text{even}} = 2$, which limits the maximum runlength of 1's beginning at an even time-index to at most 2, has capacity $C \approx 0.916$. The constraint has been shown to support a rate 8 : 9 block code.

Graph representations for the TMTR $k_1^{\text{even}} = 2$ constrained system are shown in Fig. 20. The states in the upper graph H are depicted as either circles or squares, corresponding to odd time indices and even time indices, respectively. The numbering of states reflects the number of 1's seen since the

TABLE XI
ENCODER TABLE FOR RATE 4/5, $k_1 = 2$
MTR BLOCK CODE

Input	Output
0000	00001
0001	00101
0010	01001
0011	01101
0100	10001
0101	10101
0110	00010
0111	00100
1000	00110
1001	01000
1010	01010
1011	01100
1100	10000
1101	10010
1110	10100
1111	10110

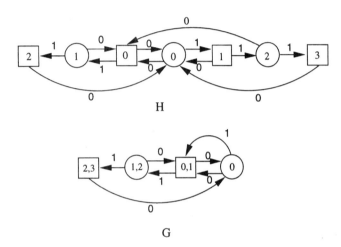

Fig. 20. Labeled graphs for TMTR $k_1^{\text{even}} = 2$ constraint.

last 0. In the upper graph H, each state represents a unique such number. The lower graph G is obtained by successively merging states with identical follower sets.

The TMTR $k_1^{\text{even}} = 2$ constraint eliminates all closed error events with $d^2 < 10$ on the E^2PR4 channel by preventing the input error sequences

$$\mathcal{L} = \{0 + - + 00, 0 - + - 00, 0 + - + -, 0 - + - +\}.$$

As with the MTR $k_1 = 2$ constraint, it can be shown that all open error events with $d^2 < 10$ can be eliminated by an appropriately designed rate 8/9, TMTR block code [123], [23], [21] [24], [52]. The time-varying trellis used by the detector for the rate 8/9 coded E^2PR4 channel requires 16 states, no more states than the uncoded system. It has been shown that these constraints and codes also may be applied to the E^3PR4 channel to increase the minimum distance to the channel MFB, that is from $d^2 = 12$ to $d^2 = 28$ [152]. Time-varying constraints for the E^2PR4 channel that support distance-enhancing codes with rates larger than 8/9 have also been found [52].

Fig. 21 shows a computer simulation of the bit-error-rate performance of four distance-enhancing constraints on the E^2PR4 channel, assuming a constant channel bit rate [152]. As a result of the favorable tradeoff between performance

and complexity offered by high-rate distance-enhancing codes for high-order PR channels, there is currently great interest in deploying them in commercial magnetic data-storage systems, and further research into the design of such codes is being actively pursued.

Finally, we remark that, for optical recording, the $d = 1$ constraint and the TMTR $k_1^{\text{even}} = 1$ constraint increase the minimum distance to d_{MFB}^2 on the PR2 and EPR2 channels, yielding nominal coding gains of 1.8 and 3 dB, respectively. A simple, rate 3/4 code for the TMTR $k_1^{\text{even}} = 1$ constraint may be used with a four-state detector to realize these coding gains [29], [152].

E. Precoded Convolutional Codes

An alternative, and in fact earlier, approach to coded-modulation for PR channels of the form $h(D) = (1 \pm D^N)$ was introduced by Wolf and Ungerboeck [204] (see also [30]). Consider first the case $N = 1$, the dicode channel. A binary input sequence $\boldsymbol{z} = z_0, z_1, \cdots$ is applied to an NRZI precoder, which implements the precoding operation characterized by the polynomial $p(D) = 1/(1 \oplus D)$. The binary precoder outputs $\boldsymbol{v} = v_0, v_1, \cdots$ are modulated to produce the bipolar channel inputs $\boldsymbol{w} = w_0, w_1, \cdots$ according to the rule $w_i = (-1)^{v_i}$. Let $\boldsymbol{z}, \boldsymbol{z}'$ be precoder inputs, with corresponding channel outputs $\boldsymbol{y}, \boldsymbol{y}'$. Then the Euclidean distance $d^2(\boldsymbol{y}, \boldsymbol{y}')$ at the output of the channel is related to the Hamming distance $d^H(\boldsymbol{z}, \boldsymbol{z}')$ at the input to the precoder by the inequality

$$d^2(\boldsymbol{y}, \boldsymbol{y}') \geq 4d^H(\boldsymbol{z}, \boldsymbol{z}'). \tag{24}$$

Now, consider as precoder inputs the set of code sequences in a convolutional code with 2^ν states in the encoder and free Hamming distance d_{free}^H. The outputs of the PR channel may be described by a trellis with $2^{\nu+1}$ or fewer states [212], which may be used as the basis for Viterbi detection. The inequality (24) leads to the following lower bound on d_{free}^2 of the coded system:

$$d_{\text{free}}^2 \geq \begin{cases} 4d_{\text{free}}^H, & \text{if } d_{\text{free}}^H \text{ is even} \\ 4(d_{\text{free}}^H + 1), & \text{if } d_{\text{free}}^H \text{ is odd.} \end{cases}$$

This coding scheme achieves coding gains on the dicode channel by the application of good convolutional codes, designed for memoryless Gaussian channels, and the use of a sequence detector trellis that reflects both the structure of the convolutional code and the memory of the channel. Using a nontrivial coset of the convolutional code ensures the satisfaction of constraints on the zero runlengths at the output of the channel.

It is clear that, by interleaving N convolutional encoders and using a precoder of the form $p(D) = 1/(1 \oplus D^N)$, this technique, and the bound on free distance, may be extended to PR channels of the form $h(D) = (1 \pm D^N)$, $N \geq 1$. In particular, it is applicable to the PR4 channel corresponding to $h(D) = 1 - D^2$. The selection of the underlying convolutional code and nontrivial coset to optimize runlength constraints, free distance, and detector trellis complexity has been investigated by several authors. See, for example, [89], [90],

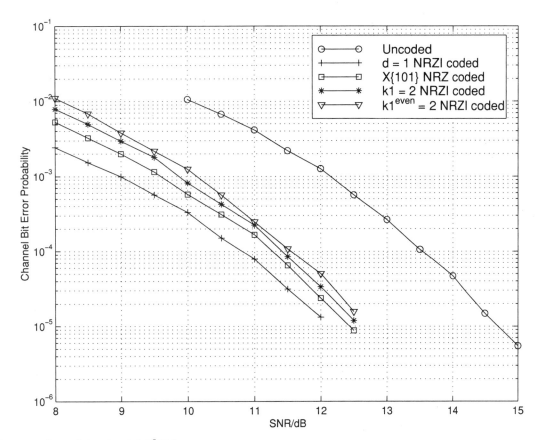

Fig. 21. Performance of uncoded and coded E^2PR4 systems.

and [212]. For the PR4 channel, and specified free Euclidean distance at the channel output, the runlength constraints and complexity of precoded convolutional codes have been found to be slightly inferior to those of matched-spectral-null (MSN) codes. For example, a rate $4/5$ precoded convolutional code was shown to achieve 3-dB gain (unnormalized for rate loss) with constraints $(0, G/I) = (0, 44/22)$ and a 16-state detector trellis with 256 branches (per interleave). The comparable MSN code with this gain achieved the equivalent of constraints $(0, G/I) = (0, 10/5)$ and used a six-state detector trellis with 24 branches (per interleave).

Recently, a modified version of this precoding approach was developed for use with a rate $4/5$ turbo code [168]. The detection procedure incorporated an *a posteriori probability* (APP) PR channel detector, combined with an iterative, turbo decoder. Performance simulations of this coding scheme on a PR4 channel with AWGN demonstrated a gain of 5.3 dB (normalized for rate loss) at a bit-error rate of 10^{-5}, relative to the uncoded PRML channel. Turbo equalization, whereby the PR detector is integrated into the iterative decoding procedure, was also considered. This increased the gain by another 0.5 dB. Thus the improvement over the previously proposed rate $4/5$ codes, which achieve 2-dB gain (normalized for rate loss) is approximately 3.3–3.8 dB. The remaining gap in E_b/N_0 between the rate $4/5$ turbo code performance at a bit-error rate of 10^{-5} and the upper bound capacity limit (3) at rate $4/5$ [172] is approximately 2.25 dB [168]. The corresponding gap to the upper bound capacity limit at rate $4/5$ for the

precoded convolutional code and the MSN code is therefore approximately 5.5–6 dB. This estimate of the SNR gap can be compared with that implied by the continuous-time channel capacity bounds, as discussed in Section II-B.

VI. COMPENDIUM OF MODULATION CONSTRAINTS

In this section, we describe in more detail selected properties of constrained systems that have played a prominent role in digital recording systems. The classes of (d, k) runlength-limited constraints and spectral-null constraints have already been introduced. In addition, there are constraints that generate spectral lines at specified frequencies, called pilot tracking tones, which can be used for servo tracking systems in videotape recorders [118], [115]. Certain channels require a combination of time and frequency constraints [128], [157], [160]; specifically DC-balanced RLL sequences have found widespread usage in recording practice. In addition, there are many other constraints that play a role in recording systems; see, for example, [102], [196], [146], [177], and [178]. Table XII gives a survey of recording constraints used in consumer electronics products.

A. Runlength-Limited Sequences

We have already encountered (d, k)-constrained binary sequences where $0 \leq d < k < \infty$. We are also interested in the case $k = \infty$. Fig. 22 illustrates a graph representing (d, ∞) constraints.

TABLE XII
SURVEY OF RECORDING CODES AND THEIR APPLICATION AREA

Device	Code	Type	Ref.
Compact Disc	EFM	RLL, DC-free	[84]
DVD	EFMPlus	RLL, DC-free	[105]
R-DAT	8-10	DC-free	[156]
floppy and hard disk	(2,7) or (1,7)	RLL	[57]
DCC	ETM	DC-free	[97]
Scoopman	LDM-2	RLL, DC-free	[86]
DVC	24 →25	DC-free with pilot tones	[118]

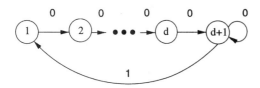

Fig. 22. Shannon cover for a (d, ∞) constraint.

TABLE XIII
CAPACITY $C(d, k)$ VERSUS RUNLENGTH PARAMETERS d AND k

k	d = 0	d = 1	d = 2	d = 3	d = 4
1	.6942				
2	.8791	.4057			
3	.9468	.5515	.2878		
4	.9752	.6174	.4057	.2232	
5	.9881	.6509	.4650	.3218	.1823
6	.9942	.6690	.4979	.3746	.2669
7	.9971	.6793	.5174	.4057	.3142
8	.9986	.6853	.5293	.4251	.3432
9	.9993	.6888	.5369	.4376	.3620
10	.9996	.6909	.5418	.4460	.3746
∞	1.000	.6942	.5515	.4650	.4057

For (d, ∞) sequences we can easily derive the characteristic equation

$$z^{-(d+1)} + z^{-1} = 1,$$

or equivalently,

$$z^{d+1} - z^d = 1.$$

Table XIII lists the capacity $C(d, k)$ for selected values of the parameters d and k.

RLL sequences are used to increase the minimum separation between recorded transitions. The quantity $T_{\min}$, called the *density ratio* or *packing density*, is defined as

$$T_{\min} = (1 + d)C(d, k).$$

It expresses the number of information bit intervals within the minimum separation between consecutive transitions of an RLL sequence. It may be shown that the density ratio $T_{\min}$ can be made arbitrarily large by choosing d sufficiently large [3]. The minimum increment within a runlength is called the timing window or detection window, denoted by T_w. Measured in units of information bit intervals, $T_w = C(d, k)$. Sequences with a larger value of d, and thus a lower capacity $C(d, k)$, are penalized by an increasingly difficult tradeoff between the detection window and the density ratio. Practical codes have typically used constraints with $d \leq 2$.

TABLE XIV
CAPACITY OF ASYMMETRICAL RUNLENGTH-LIMITED
SEQUENCES VERSUS MINIMUM RUNLENGTH

d_0	$C_a(d_0, 0)$
1	0.8114
2	0.6942
3	0.6125
4	0.5515
5	0.5037

B. Asymmetrical Runlength Constraints

Asymmetrical runlength-limited sequences [75], [194], [186] have different constraints on the runlengths of 0's and 1's. One application of these constraints has been in optical recording systems, where the minimum size of a written pit, as determined by diffraction limitations, is larger than the minimum size of the area separating two pits, a spacing determined by the mechanical positioning capabilities of the optical recording fixture.

Asymmetrical runlength-limited sequences are described by four parameters (d_0, k_0) and (d_1, k_1), $d_0, d_1 \geq 0$ and $k_0 > d_0$, $k_1 > d_1$, which describe the constraints on runlengths of 0's and 1's, respectively. An allowable sequence is composed of alternate phrases of the form $S_o = 0^i$, $i = d_0 + 1$, $d_0 + 2, \cdots, k_0 + 1$, and $S_e = 1^j$, $j = d_1 + 1$, $d_1 + 2, \cdots, k_1 + 1$. Let one sequence be composed of phrases of durations $t_m \in S_o$, and let the second sequence have phrases of durations $t_j \in S_e$. The interleaved sequence is composed of phrases taken alternately from the first, odd sequence and the second, even sequence. The interleaved sequence is composed of phrases of duration $t_i = t_j + t_m$, $t_m \in S_o$, $t_j \in S_e$, implying that the characteristic equation is

$$\left(\sum_{j \in S_e} z^{-j} \right) \left(\sum_{m \in S_o} z^{-m} \right) = 1$$

which can be rewritten as

$$\left(\sum_{i=d_0+1}^{k_0+1} z^{-i} \right) \left(\sum_{j=d_1+1}^{k_1+1} z^{-j} \right) = 1. \quad (25)$$

If we assume that $k_0 = k_1 = \infty$, then (25) can be written as

$$z^{d_0+d_1+2} - 2z^{d_0+d_1+1} + z^{d_0+d_1} - 1 = 0.$$

As an immediate implication of the symmetry in d_0 and d_1, we find for the capacity of the asymmetrical runlength-limited sequences

$$C_a(d_0, d_1) = C_a(d_0 + d_1, 0) \quad (26)$$

where $C_a(d_0, d_1)$ denotes the capacity of asymmetrical runlength-limited sequences. Thus the capacity of asymmetrical RLL sequences is a function of the sum of the two minimum runlength parameters only, and it suffices to evaluate $C_a(d_0, 0)$ by solving the characteristic equation

$$z^{d_0+2} - 2z^{d_0+1} + z^{d_0} - 1 = 0.$$

Results of computations are given in Table XIV.

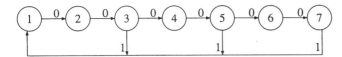

Fig. 23. Labeled graph for $(d, k, s) = (2, 6, 2)$ constraint.

We can derive another useful relation with the following observation. Let $d_0 = d_1$, i.e., the restrictions on the runlengths of 0's and 1's are again symmetric, then from (26)

$$C_a(d_0, d_0) = C_a(2d_0, 0)$$

so that we obtain the following relation between the capacity of symmetrical and asymmetrical RLL sequences:

$$C_a(2d_0, 0) = C(d_0, \infty).$$

C. RLL Sequences with Multiple Spacings

Funk [72] showed that the theory of RLL sequences is unnecessarily narrow in scope and that it precludes certain relevant coding possibilities which could prove useful in particular devices. The limitation is removed by introducing *multiple-spaced RLL sequences*, where one further restriction is imposed upon the admissible runlengths of 0's. The run-length/spacing constraints may be expressed as follows: for integers d, k, and s, where $k - d$ is a multiple of s, the number of 0's between successive 1's must be equal to $d + is$, where $0 \leq i \leq (k - d)/s$. The parameters d and k again define the minimum and maximum allowable runlength. A sequence defined in this way is called an *RLL sequence with multiple spacing* (RLL/MS). Such a sequence is characterized by the parameters (d, k, s). Note that for standard RLL sequences we have $s = 1$. Fig. 23 illustrates a state-transition diagram for the $(d, k, s) = (2, 6, 2)$ constraint.

The capacity $C(d, k, s)$ can simply be found by invoking Shannon's capacity formula

$$C(d, k, s) = \log_2 \lambda$$

where λ is the largest root of the characteristic equation

$$\sum_{i=0}^{(k-d)/s} z^{-(d+is+1)} = 1. \tag{27}$$

Note that if s and $d + 1$ have a common factor p, then $k + 1$ is also divisible by p. Therefore, a (d, k, s) sequence with the above condition on d, k, and s is equivalent to a $((d+1-p)/p, (k+1-p)/p, s/p)$ sequence. For $k = \infty$, we obtain the characteristic equation

$$z^{d+1} - z^{d+1-s} - 1 = 0.$$

Table XV shows the results of computations. Within any s adjacent bit periods, there is only one possible location for the next 1, given the location of the last 1. The detection window for an RLL/MS sequence is therefore $T_w = sC(d, k, s)$, and the minimum spacing between two transitions, $T_{\min}$, equals $(d + 1)C(d, k, s)$.

By rewriting (27) we obtain a relationship between $T_w, T_{\min}$ and $T_{\max}$, namely,

$$2^{-T_w} + 2^{-T_{\min}} - 2^{-T_{\max} - T_w} = 1.$$

TABLE XV
CAPACITY $C(d, \infty, s)$ FOR SELECTED VALUES OF d AND s

d	s	$C(d, \infty, s)$
0	2	0.6942
2	2	0.4057
3	2	0.3471
4	2	0.3063
0	3	0.5515
1	3	0.4057
2	3	0.3333

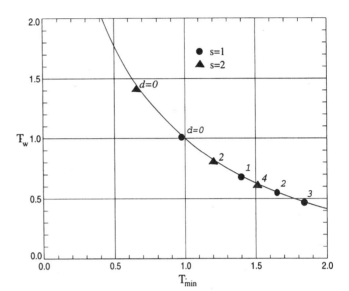

Fig. 24. Relationship between $T_{\min}$ and window T_w. The operating points of various (d, ∞, s) sequences are indicated.

This relationship is plotted, for $k = \infty$, in Fig. 24. With (d, ∞) constrained sequences, only discrete points on this curve are possible. RLL sequences with multiple spacing, however, make it possible, by a proper choice of d and s, to approximate any point on this curve.

A multiple-spaced RLL code with parameters $(2, 18, 2)$ has been designed and experimentally evaluated in exploratory magnetooptic recording systems using a resonant bias coil direct-overwrite technique [167], [200].

D. $(0, G/I)$ Sequences

The $(0, G/I)$ constraints for partial-response maximum-likelihood systems were introduced in Section II-C2. Recall that the parameter G stipulates the maximum number of allowed 0's between consecutive 1's, while the parameter I stipulates the maximum number of 0's between 1's in both the even- and odd-numbered positions of the sequence.

To describe a graph presentation of these constraints, we define three parameters. The quantity g denotes the number of 0's since the last 1. The quantities a and b denote the number of 0's since the last 1 in the even and odd subsequence, respectively. It is immediate that

$$g(a, b) = \begin{cases} 2a + 1, & \text{if } a < b \\ 2b, & \text{if } a \geq b. \end{cases}$$

Each state in the graph corresponds to a 2-tuple (a, b), with $0 \leq a, b \leq I$ and $g(a, b) \leq G$. Wherever permitted, there

TABLE XVI
CAPACITY FOR SELECTED VALUES OF G AND I

G	I	Capacity
4	4	0.9614
4	3	0.9395
3	6	0.9445
3	5	0.9415
3	4	0.9342
3	3	0.9157

TABLE XVII
CAPACITY AND SUM VARIANCE OF MAXENTROPIC RDS-CONSTRAINED
SEQUENCES VERSUS DIGITAL SUM VARIATION N

N	$C(N)$	$\sigma_z^2(N)$
3	0.5000	0.5000
4	0.6942	0.8028
5	0.7925	1.1667
6	0.8495	1.5940
7	0.8858	2.0858
8	0.9103	2.6424

is an edge from state (a, b) to state $(b, a + 1)$ with a label 0, and an edge from state (a, b) to state $(b, 0)$ with a label 1. By computing the maximum eigenvalue of the adjacency matrix corresponding to the graph, we obtain the capacity of the $(0, G/I)$ constraint. Results of computations are listed in Table XVI.

For all of these constraints, rate 8/9 codes have been constructed [146]. As mentioned earlier, a rate 8/9, $(0, 4/4)$ block code was used in early disk drives employing PRML techniques. Current disk drives make use of more relaxed constraints, such as $(0, 6/6)$ and $(0, 6/7)$, which can support codes with even higher rates, such as rate 16/17 [161], [51].

E. Spectral-Null Sequences

Frequency-domain analysis of constrained sequences is based upon the *average power spectral density*, or, as it is often called, the *power spectrum*. In order to define the power spectrum, we must endow the ensemble of constrained sequences with a probability measure. Generally, the measure chosen is the maxentropic measure determined by the transition probabilities discussed in Section III-B. The autocorrelation function is the sequence of nth-order autocorrelation coefficients $\{R(n)\}, -\infty < n < \infty$, defined by

$$R(n) = E[a_0 a_n]$$

where $\{a_i\}$ represent channel input symbols and the expectation is with respect to the given measure. According to the Wiener–Khinchin theorem, the average power spectrum is given by the discrete-time Fourier transform of the autocorrelation function

$$S(f) = \mathcal{F}[R(n)] = \sum_{n=-\infty}^{\infty} R(n)e^{-j2\pi nf}$$

where, as before, $j = \sqrt{-1}$. Alternatively, we can express $S(f)$ as

$$S(f) = \lim_{M \to \infty} E\left[\frac{1}{M}\left|\sum_{m=0}^{M} a_m e^{-j2\pi mf}\right|^2\right].$$

The computation of the power spectrum of an ensemble of Markov-chain driven sequences is well-studied and has been carried out for many families of runlength-type constraints, as well as for the subsets of constrained sequences generated by specific finite-state encoders; see [75] and references therein.

It is important to note that for a particular sequence, the average power density at a particular frequency f, if it exists at all, may differ significantly from $S(f)$ if $S(f) \neq 0$.

For spectral-null constraints with $S(f) = 0$, however, every sequence in the constraint has a well-defined average power density at f, and the magnitude is equal to zero [145]. As has already been mentioned, the spectral null frequencies of primary interest in digital recording are zero frequency (DC) and the Nyquist frequency. (Further general results on spectral-null sequences are given in [145], [100], and [102], for example.)

Chien [38] studied bipolar sequences that assume a finite range of N consecutive running-digital-sum (RDS) values, that is, sequences with digital-sum variation (DSV) N. The range of RDS values may be used, as in Fig. 7, to define a set of N allowable states. The adjacency matrix A_N for the RDS-constrained channel is given by

$$A_N(i + 1, i) = A_N(i, i + 1) = 1, \qquad i = 1, 2, \cdots, N - 1$$
$$A_N(i, j) = 0, \qquad \text{otherwise.}$$

For most constraints, it is not possible to find a simple closed-form expression for the capacity, and one has to rely on numerical methods to obtain an approximation. The RDS-constrained sequences provide a beautiful exception to the rule, as the structure of A_N allows us to provide a closed-form expression for the capacity of an RDS-constrained channel. We have [38]

$$\lambda = 2\cos\frac{\pi}{N+1}$$

and thus the capacity of the RDS-constrained channel is

$$C(N) = \log_2 \lambda = 1 + \log_2 \cos\frac{\pi}{N+1}, \qquad N \geq 3. \quad (28)$$

Table XVII lists the capacity $C(N)$, for $3 \leq N \leq 8$. It can be seen that the sum constraint is not very expensive in terms of rate loss when N is relatively large. For instance, a sequence that takes at maximum $N = 8$ sum values has a capacity $C(8) = 0.91$, which implies a rate loss of less than 10%.

Closed-form expressions for the spectra of maxentropic RDS-constrained sequences were derived by Kerpez [126]. Fig. 25 displays the power spectral density function of maxentropic RDS-constrained sequences for various values of the digital sum variation N.

Let $S(\omega)$ denote the power spectral density of a sequence with vanishing power at DC, where $\omega = 2\pi f$. The width of the spectral notch is a very important design characteristic which is usually quantified by a parameter called the *cutoff frequency*. The cutoff frequency of a DC-free constraint, denoted by ω_0,

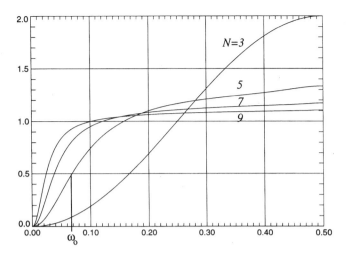

Fig. 25. Power density function $S_x(\omega)$ of maxentropic RDS-constrained sequences against frequency ω with digital sum variation N as a parameter. For the case $N = 5$, we have indicated the cutoff frequency ω_0.

is defined by [65]

$$H(\omega_0) = \frac{1}{2}.$$

It can be observed that the cutoff frequency ω_0 becomes smaller when the digital sum variation N is allowed to increase.

Let z_i denote RDS $(x_0, \cdots, x_i)$. Justesen [116] discovered a useful relation between the sum variance $s_z^2 = E\{z_i^2\}$ and the width of the spectral notch ω_0. He found the following approximation of the cutoff frequency ω_0:

$$2s_z^2\omega_0 \simeq 1. \qquad (29)$$

Extensive computations of samples of implemented channel codes, made by Justesen [116] and Immink [98] to validate the reciprocal relation (29) between ω_0 and s_z^2, have revealed that this relationship is fairly reliable. The sum variance $E\{z_i^2\}$ of a maxentropic RDS-constrained sequence, denoted by $\sigma_z^2(N)$, is given by [38]

$$\sigma_z^2(N) = \frac{2}{N+1} \sum_{k=1}^{N} \left(\frac{N+1}{2} - k \right)^2 \sin^2 \frac{\pi k}{N+1}. \qquad (30)$$

Table XVII lists the sum variance $\sigma_z^2(N)$ for $3 \leq N \leq 8$. Fig. 26, which shows a plot of the sum variance versus the redundancy $1 - C(N)$, affords more insight into the tradeoffs in the engineering of DC-balanced sequences. It presents the designer with a spectral budget, reflecting the price in terms of code redundancy for a desired spectral notch width. It also reveals that the relationship between the logarithms of the sum variance and the redundancy is approximately linear.

For large digital sum variation N, it was shown by A. Janssen [114] that

$$\sigma_z^2(N) = \left(\frac{1}{12} - \frac{1}{2\pi^2} \right) (N+1)^2 + O\left(\frac{1}{(N+1)^2} \right)$$

and similarly

$$C(N) = 1 - \frac{\pi^2}{2\ln(2)} \frac{1}{(N+1)^2} + O\left(\frac{1}{(N+1)^4} \right).$$

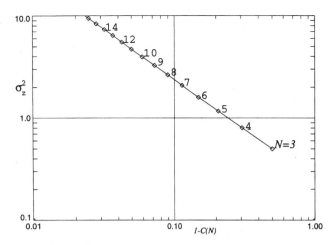

Fig. 26. Sum variance versus redundancy of maxentropic RDS-constrained sequences.

These approximations, coupled with (28) and (30), lead to a fundamental relation between the redundancy $1 - C(N)$ and the sum variance of a maxentropic RDS-constrained sequence, namely,

$$0.25 \geq (1 - C(N))\sigma_z^2(N) > \frac{\pi^2/6 - 1}{4\ln(2)} = 0.2326. \qquad (31)$$

Actually, the bound on the right is within 1% accuracy for $N > 9$. Equation (31) states that, for large enough N, the product of redundancy and sum variance of maxentropic RDS-constrained sequences is approximately constant, as was suggested by Fig. 26.

VII. FUTURE DIRECTIONS

As digital recording technology advances and changes, so does the system model that serves as the basis for information-theoretic analysis and the motivation for signal processing and coding techniques. In this section, we briefly describe several technology developments, some evolutionary and some revolutionary, that introduce new elements that can be incorporated into mathematical models for digital recording channels.

A. Improved Channel Models

Reflecting the continuing, rapid increase in areal density of conventional magnetic recording, as well as the characteristics of the component heads and disks, channel models now incorporate factors such as asymmetry in the positive and negative step responses of magnetoresistive read heads; deviations from linear superposition; spectral coloring, nonadditivity, and nonstationarity in media noise; and partial-erasure effects and other data-dependent distortions [20], [21], [32], [33].

The evaluation of the impact of these channel characteristics on the performance of the signal processing and coding techniques dicussed in this paper is an active area of research, as is the development of new approaches that take these channel properties into account. See, for example, related papers in [192].

B. Nonsaturation Multilevel Recording

At various times during the past, the possibility of abandoning saturation recording, "linearizing" the digital magnetic-recording channel, and incorporating nonbinary signaling has been examined. In all such studies, however, the potential increase in recording density that might accrue from the application or adaptation of coded-modulation techniques developed for digital communications has been outweighed by the increase in detector complexity and, more fundamentally, the cost in signal-to-noise ratio that accompanies the linearization process. However, several novel storage technologies can support multilevel alphabets, such as electron-trapping optical memories ETOM [148], [31] and optical recording with multivalued magnetooptic media [176].

C. Multitrack Recording

Another avenue toward increasing the storage capacity of disk and tape systems is to exploit their inherent two-dimensional nature. Runlength-limited codes, such as n-track (d, k) codes, that increase the per-track code rate by sharing the timing constraint k across multiple tracks have been analyzed and designed [140], [185], [47].

Using models of signal-to-noise ratio dependence upon track width, as well as intertrack interference (ITI), one can investigate information-theoretic capacity bounds as a function of track density. Multitrack recording and multihead detection techniques based upon partial-response equalization, decision-feedback-equalization, and sequence detection have been studied [13], along with coding schemes that can improve their performance. See, for example, [183] and references therein.

D. Multidimensional Recording

New, exploratory technologies, such as volume holographic data storage [80] and two-photon-based three-dimensional (3-D) optical memories [95], have generated interest in page-oriented recording and readback. Models of these processes have generated proposals for two-dimensional equalization and detection methods [82], [158], along with two-dimensional codes [81], [195].

This has generated interest in two-dimensional constrained systems and modulation codes. As an example, consider a two-dimensional binary (d, k) constrained array as an m (row) by n (column) binary array such that every 1 has no less than d 0's and no more than k 0's above it, below it, to the right of it, and to the left of it (with the exception of 1's on or near borders). The capacity of such an array is equal to the limit, as n and m approach infinity, of the ratio of the logarithm of the number of distinct arrays satisfying the constraints to the product of m times n. Little is known at this time about finding the capacity of such two-dimensional binary constrained arrays. A notable exception is that it has been proved that the two-dimensional capacity of such two-dimensional (d, k) binary arrays is equal to zero if and only if $k = d+1$ and $d > 0$ [124]. Thus the two-dimensional capacity of the $(1, 2)$ constraint is equal to 0, while the two-dimensional capacity of the $(2, 4)$ constraint is strictly greater than 0. This is in contrast to the one-dimensional case, where the capacity of both $(1, 2)$ and $(2, 4)$ constrained binary sequences are both nonzero and, in fact, are equal. Lower bounds on the capacity of some two-dimensional (d, k) constraints are presented in [124], [179], and other constraints relevant to two-dimensional recording are analyzed in [11], [187], and [199].

VIII. SHANNON'S CROSSWORD PUZZLES

A. Existence of Multidimensional Crossword Puzzles

As mentioned in the preceding section, multidimensional constrained codes represent a new challenge for information theorists, with potentially important applications to novel, high-density storage devices. We feel it is particularly fitting, then, to bring our survey to a close by returning once more to Shannon's 1948 paper [173] where, remarkably, in a short passage addressing the connection between the redundancy of a language and the existence of crossword puzzles, Shannon anticipated some of the issues that arise in multidimensional constrained coding.

Specifically, Shannon suggested that there would be cases where the capacity of a two-dimensional constraint is equal to zero, even though the capacity of the constituent one-dimensional constraint is nonzero, a situation illustrated by certain two-dimensional (d, k) constraints. We cite the following excerpt from Shannon's 1948 paper:

> The ratio of the entropy of a source to the maximum value it could have while still restricted to the same symbols will be called its *relative entropy*. ... One minus the relative entropy is the *redundancy*. ... The redundancy of a language is related to the existence of crossword puzzles. If the redundancy is zero any sequence of letters is a reasonable text in the language and any two-dimensional array of letters forms a crossword puzzle. If the redundancy is too high the language imposes too many constraints for large crossword puzzles to be possible. A more detailed analysis shows that if we assume the constraints imposed by the language are of a rather chaotic and random nature, large crossword puzzles are just possible when the redundancy is 50%. If the redundancy is 33%, three-dimensional crossword puzzles should be possible, etc.

To the best of our knowledge Shannon never published a more detailed exposition on this subject. This led us to try to construct a plausibility argument for his statement. We assume that the phrase "large crossword puzzles are just possible" should be taken to mean that the capacity of the corresponding two-dimensional constraint is nonzero.

Let A denote the number of source symbols, H denote the source binary entropy, and $H^* = H/\log_2(A)$ denote the relative entropy. We begin with all A^{mn} m by n arrays that can be formed from A symbols. We eliminate all arrays that do not have all of their rows and columns made up of a concatenation of allowable words from the language. The probability that any row of the array is made up of a concatenation of allowable words from the language is equal to the ratio of the number of allowable concatenations of words with n letters, 2^{nH}, to A^n. Thus assuming statistical independence of the rows, the probability that all m rows are concatenations of allowable words is this ratio raised to the mth power, or $(2^{nH}/A^n)^m$ or $(2^{mnH}/A^{mn})$. The identical ratio results for the probability that all n columns are made up of concatenations of allowable words. Now assuming that the rows and columns are statistically independent, we see that the probability for an array to have all of its rows and all of its columns made up of concatenations of allowable words is equal to $(2^{2mnH}/A^{2mn})$. The assumption of independence of the rows and columns is made with the sole justification that this property might be expected to be true for a language that is "of a rather chaotic and random nature." Multiplying this probability by the number of arrays A^{mn} yields the average number of surviving arrays, $2^{mn(2H-\log_2(A))}$ which grows exponentially with mn provided that $H^* > 0.5$. A similar argument for three-dimensional arrays yields the condition $H^* > 0.667$. This is Shannon's result. (The authors thank K. Shaughnessy [174] for contributions to this argument.) We remark that for ordinary English crossword puzzles, we would interpret the black square to be a 27th symbol in the alphabet. Thus to compute the "relative entropy" of English, we divide the entropy of English by $\log_2(27)$. In this context, we would propose using an unusual definition of the entropy of English, which we call H', based upon the dependencies of letters within individual words, but not across word boundaries, since the rows and columns of crossword puzzles are made up of unrelated words separated by one or more black squares. To compute H' for the English language, we can proceed as follows. Assume that a_i is the number of words in an English dictionary with i letters, for $i = 1, 2, \cdots, L$. We lengthen each word by one letter to include the black square at the end of a word and then add one more word of length 1 to represent a single black square. (This allows more than one black square between words.) Following Shannon, the number of distinct sequences of words containing exactly n symbols, $N(n)$, is given by the difference equation

$$N(n) = N(n-1) + a_1 N(n-2)$$
$$+ a_2 N(n-3) + \cdots + a_L N(n-L-1). \quad (32)$$

Then, H' is given by the logarithm of the largest real root of the equation

$$X^{-1} + a_1 X^{-2} + a_2 X^{-3} + \cdots + a_L X^{-(L+1)} = 1. \quad (33)$$

The distribution of word lengths in an English dictionary has been investigated by Lord Rothschild [166]. (See also the discussion in Section VIII-C.)

B. Connections to Two-Dimensional Constraints

Unfortunately, a direct application of Shannon's statement to the $(d, k) = (1, 2)$ and $(d, k) = (2, 4)$ constraints leads to a problem. Their one-dimensional capacities and, therefore, their relative entropies, are equal, with $H^* = H \approx 0.4057$. However, we have seen that the capacity of the two-dimensional $(1, 2)$ constraint is zero, while that of the two-dimensional $(2, 4)$ constraint is nonzero. In order to resolve this inconsistency

with Shannon's bound, we tried to modify the argument by more accurately approximating the probability of a column satisfying the specified row constraint, as follows.

Although the one-dimensional capacities of the two constraints are equal, the one-dimensional constraints have different first-order entropies H_1. In particular, $H_1 \approx 0.9777$ for the $(1, 2)$ constraint and $H_1 \approx 0.8281$ for the $(2, 4)$ constraint, since the relative frequency of 0's is higher for the $(2, 4)$ constraint than for the $(1, 2)$ constraint. In the previous plausibility argument for Shannon's result, once one chooses the rows of the array to be a concatenation of allowable words, the relative frequencies of the symbols in each column occur in accordance with the relative frequency of the symbols in the words of the language. Thus the probability that any column is a concatenation of allowable words is equal to $(2^{mH}/2^{mH_1})$. Proceeding as above, we find that the average number of surviving arrays grows exponentially with mn provided that $(H/H_1) > 0.5$ for two-dimensional arrays, or $(H/H_1) > 0.667$ for three-dimensional arrays.

However, for both the one-dimensional $(1, 2)$ and $(2, 4)$ constraints, we find $(H/H_1) < 0.5$. Therefore, this modified analysis still does not satisfactorily explain the behavior of these two constraints. A possible explanation is that a further refinement in the argument is needed. Another possibility is that these (d, k) constraints are not "chaotic and random" enough for Shannon's conclusion, and our plausibility arguments, to apply.

C. Coda

As this paper was undergoing final revisions, one of the authors (JKW) received a letter from E. Gilbert pertaining to Shannon's crossword puzzles [77]. The letter was prompted by a lecture given by JKW at the Shannon Day Symposium, held at Bell Labs on May 18, 1998, in which the connection between the capacity of two-dimensional constraints and Shannon's result on crossword puzzles was discussed. In the letter, Gilbert recalls a conversation he had with Shannon 50 years ago on this subject. Referring to Shannon's paper, he says:

> I didn't understand that crossword example and tried to reconstruct his argument. That led to a kind of handwaving "proof," which I showed to Claude. Claude's own argument turned out to have been something like mine . . . . Fortunately, I outlined my proof in the margin of my reprint of the paper (like Fermat and his copy of Diophantos). It went like this: . . . .

The argument that followed is exactly the same as the one presented in Section VIII-A above, with the small exception that arrays were assumed to be square. In fact, in a subsequent e-mail correspondence [78], Gilbert describes a calculation of the redundancy of English along the lines suggested by (32) and (33). Thus we see that the study of multidimensional constrained arrays actually dates back 50 years to the birth of information theory. A great deal remains to be learned.

IX. SUMMARY

In this paper, we have attempted to provide an overview of the theoretical foundations and practical applications of constrained coding in digital-recording systems. In keeping with the theme of this special issue, we have highlighted essential contributions to this area made by Shannon in his landmark 1948 paper. We described the basic characteristics of a digital-recording channel, and surveyed bounds on the noisy-channel capacity for several mathematical channel models. We then discussed practical equalization and detection techniques and indicated how their implementation imposes constraints on the recording-channel inputs. Following a review of Shannon's fundamental results on the capacity of discrete noiseless channels and on the existence of efficient codes, we presented a summary of key results in the theory and practice of efficient constrained code design. We then discussed the application of distance-enhancing constrained codes to improve the reliability of noisy recording channels, and compared the resulting performance to estimates of the noisy-channel capacity. Finally, we pointed out several new directions that future research in the area of recording codes might follow, and we concluded with a discussion of the connection between Shannon's remarks on crossword puzzles and the theory of multidimensional constrained codes. Through the inclusion of numerous references and indications of open research problems, we hope to have provided the reader with an introduction to this fascinating, important, and active branch of information theory, as well as with some incentive and encouragement to contribute to it.

ACKNOWLEDGMENT

The authors are grateful to Dick Blahut, Brian Marcus, Ron Roth, and Emina Soljanin for their thoughtful comments on an earlier version of this paper. They also wish to thank Bruce Moision for assistance with computer simulations and for preparation of Fig. 21.

REFERENCES

[1] K. A. S. Abdel-Ghaffar and J. H. Weber, "Constrained block codes for class–IV partial-response channels with maximum-likelihood sequence estimation," *IEEE Trans. Inform. Theory*, vol. 42, pp. 1405–1424, Sept. 1996.

[2] R. L. Adler, "The torus and the disk," *IBM J. Res. Develop.*, vol. 31, no. 2, pp. 224–234, Mar. 1987.

[3] R. L. Adler, D. Coppersmith, and M. Hassner, "Algorithms for sliding block codes: An application of symbolic dynamics to information theory," *IEEE Trans. Inform. Theory*, vol. IT-29, pp. 5–22, Jan. 1983.

[4] R. L. Adler, M. Hassner, and J. Moussouris, "Method and apparatus for generating a noiseless sliding block code for a (1, 7) channel with rate 2/3," U.S. Patent 4 413 251, June 1982.

[5] N. Alon, E. E. Bergmann, D. Coppersmith, and A. M. Odlyzko, "Balancing sets of vectors," *IEEE Trans. Inform. Theory*, vol. 34, pp. 128–130, Jan. 1988.

[6] S. Altekar, "Detection and coding techniques for magnetic recording channels," Ph.D. dissertation, Univ. Calif. San Diego, June 1997.

[7] S. A. Altekar, M. Berggren, B. E. Moision, P. H. Siegel, and J. K. Wolf, "Error-event characterization on partial-response channels," in *Proc. 1997 IEEE Int. Symp. Information Theory* (Ulm, Germany, June 29–July 4), p. 461; *IEEE Trans. Inform. Theory*, vol. 45, Jan. 1999, to be published.

[8] J. Ashley, R. Karabed, and P. H. Siegel, "Complexity and sliding-block decodability," *IEEE Trans. Inform. Theory*, vol. 42, no. 6, pt. 1, pp. 1925–1947, Nov. 1996.

[9] J. J. Ashley and B. H. Marcus, "Canonical encoders for sliding block decoders," *SIAM J. Discrete Math.*, vol. 8, pp. 555–605, 1995.

[10] _____, "A generalized state-splitting algorithm," *IEEE Trans. Inform. Theory*, vol. 43, pp. 1326–1338, July 1997.

[11] _____, "Two-dimensional low-pass filtering codes," *IEEE Trans. Commun.*, vol. 46, pp. 724–727, June 1998.

[12] J. J. Ashley, B. H. Marcus, and R. M. Roth, "Construction of encoders with small decoding look-ahead for input-constrained channels," *IEEE Trans. Inform. Theory*, vol. 41, pp. 55–76, Jan. 1995.

[13] L. C. Barbosa, "Simultaneous detection of readback signals from interfering magnetic recording tracks using array heads," *IEEE Trans. Magn.*, vol. 26, pp. 2163–2165, Sept. 1990.

[14] I. Bar-David and S. Shamai (Shitz), "Information rates for magnetic recording channels with peak- and slope-limited magnetization," *IEEE Trans. Inform. Theory*, vol. 35, pp. 956–962, Sept. 1989.

[15] M.-P. Béal, *Codage Symbolique*. Paris, France: Masson, 1993.

[16] G. F. M. Beenker and K. A. S. Immink, "A generalized method for encoding and decoding runlength-limited binary sequences," *IEEE Trans. Inform. Theory*, vol. IT-29, pp. 751–754, Sept. 1983.

[17] R. Behrens and A. Armstrong, "An advanced read/write channel for magnetic disk storage," in *Proc. 26th Asilomar Conf. Signals, Systems, and Computers* (Pacific Grove, CA, Oct. 1992), pp. 956–960.

[18] E. R. Berlekamp, "The technology of error-correcting codes," *Proc. IEEE*, vol. 68, pp. 564–593, May 1980.

[19] M. Berkoff, "Waveform compression in NRZI magnetic recording," *Proc. IEEE*, vol. 52, pp. 1271–1272, Oct. 1964.

[20] H. N. Bertram, *Theory of Magnetic Recording*. Cambridge, U.K.: Cambridge Univ. Press, 1994

[21] H. N. Bertram and X. Che, "General analysis of noise in recorded transitions in thin film recording media," *IEEE Trans. Magn.*, vol. 29, pp. 201–208, Jan. 1993.

[22] W. G. Bliss, "Circuitry for performing error correction calculations on baseband encoded data to eliminate error propagation," *IBM Tech. Discl. Bull.*, vol. 23, pp. 4633–4634, 1981.

[23] _____, "An 8/9 rate time-varying trellis code for high density magnetic recording," *IEEE Trans. Magn.*, vol. 33, pp. 2746–2748, Sept. 1997.

[24] W. G. Bliss, S. She, and L. Sundell, "The performance of generalized maximum transition run trellis codes," *IEEE Trans. Magn.*, vol. 34, no. 1, pt. 1, pp. 85–90, Jan. 1998.

[25] G. Bouwhuis, J. Braat, A. Huijser, J. Pasman, G. van Rosmalen, and K. A. S. Immink, *Principles of Optical Disc Systems*. Bristol, U.K. and Boston, MA: Adam Hilger, 1985.

[26] F. K. Bowers, U.S. Patent 2 957 947, 1960.

[27] V. Braun, K. A. S. Immink, M. A. Ribiero, and G. J. van den Enden, "On the application of sequence estimation algorithms in the Digital Compact Cassette (DCC)," *IEEE Trans. Consumer Electron.*, vol. 40, pp. 992–998, Nov. 1994.

[28] V. Braun and A. J. E. M. Janssen, "On the low-frequency suppression performance of DC-free runlength-limited modulation codes," *IEEE Trans. Consumer Electron.*, vol. 42, pp. 939–945, Nov. 1996.

[29] B. Brickner and J. Moon, "Investigation of error propagation in DFE and MTR$(1/2; k)$ coding for ultra-high density," Tech. Rep., Commun. Data Storage Lab., Univ. Minnesota, Minneapolis, July 10, 1997.

[30] A. R. Calderbank, C. Heegard, and T.-A. Lee, "Binary convolutional codes with application to magnetic recording, *IEEE Trans. Inform. Theory*, vol. IT-32, pp. 797–815, Nov. 1986.

[31] A. R. Calderbank, R. Laroia, and S. W. McLaughlin, "Coded modulation and precoding for electron-trapping optical memories," *IEEE Trans. Commun.*, vol. 46, pp. 1011–1019, Aug. 1998.

[32] J. Caroselli and J. K. Wolf, "A new model for media noise in thin film magnetic recording media," in *Proc. 1995 SPIE Int. Symp. Voice, Video, and Data Communications* (Philadelphia, PA, Oct. 1995), vol. 2605, pp. 29–38.

[33] J. Caroselli and J. K. Wolf, "Applications of a new simulation model for media noise limited magnetic recording channels," *IEEE Trans. Magn.*, vol. 32, pp. 3917–3919, Sept. 1996.

[34] K. W. Cattermole, *Principles of Pulse Code Modulation*. London, U.K.: Iliffe, 1969.

[35] _____, "Principles of digital line coding," *Int. J. Electron.*, vol. 55, pp. 3–33, July 1983.

[36] Workshop on Modulation, Coding, and Signal Processing for Magnetic Recording Channels, Center for Magnetic Recording Res., Univ. Calif. at San Diego. La Jolla, CA, May 20–22, 1985.

[37] Workshop on Modulation and Coding for Digital Recording Systems, Center for Magnetic Recording Res., Univ. Calif. at San Diego. La Jolla, CA, Jan. 8–10, 1987.

[38] T. M. Chien, "Upper bound on the efficiency of DC-constrained codes," *Bell Syst. Tech. J.*, vol. 49, pp. 2267–2287, Nov. 1970.

[39] R. Cideciyan, F. Dolivo, R. Hermann, W. Hirt, and W. Schott, "A PRML system for digital magnetic recording," *IEEE J. Select. Areas Commun.*, vol. 10, pp. 38–56, Jan. 1992.

[40] M. Cohn and G. V. Jacoby, "Run-length reduction of 3PM code via look-ahead technique," *IEEE Trans. Magn.*, vol. MAG-18, pp. 1253–1255, Nov. 1982.

[41] D. J. Costello, Jr., J. Hagenauer, H. Imai, and S. B. Wicker, "Applications of error control coding," this issue, pp. 2531–2560.

[42] T. M. Cover, "Enumerative source coding," *IEEE Trans. Inform. Theory*, vol. IT-19, pp. 73–77, Jan. 1973.

[43] R. H. Deng and M. A. Herro, "DC-free coset codes," *IEEE Trans. Inform. Theory*, vol. 34, pp. 786–792, July 1988.

[44] J. Eggenberger and P. Hodges, "Sequential encoding and decoding of variable length, fixed rate data codes," U.S. Patent 4 115 768, 1978.

[45] J. Eggenberger and A. M. Patel, "Method and apparatus for implementing optimum PRML codes," U.S. Patent 4 707 681, Nov. 17, 1987.

[46] E. Eleftheriou and R. Cideciyan, "On codes satisfying Mth order running digital sum constraints," *IEEE Trans. Inform. Theory*, vol. 37, pp. 1294–1313, Sept. 1991.

[47] T. Etzion, "Cascading methods for runlength-limited arrays," *IEEE Trans. Inform. Theory*, vol. 43, pp. 319–324, Jan. 1997.

[48] I. J. Fair, W. D. Gover, W. A. Krzymien, and R. I. MacDonald, "Guided scrambling: A new line coding technique for high bit rate fiber optic transmission systems," *IEEE Trans. Commun.*, vol. 39, pp. 289–297, Feb. 1991.

[49] J. L. Fan and A. R. Calderbank, "A modified concatenated coding scheme with applications to magnetic data storage," *IEEE Trans. Inform. Theory*, vol. 44, pp. 1565–1574, July 1998.

[50] M. J. Ferguson, "Optimal reception for binary partial response channels," *Bell Syst. Tech. J.*, vol. 51, pp. 493–505, 1972.

[51] J. Fitzpatrick and K. J. Knudson, "Rate 16/17 ($d = 0, G = 6/I = 7$) modulation code for a magnetic recording channel," U.S. Patent 5 635 933, June 3, 1997.

[52] K. K. Fitzpatrick and C. S. Modlin, "Time-varying MTR codes for high density magnetic recording," in *Proc. 1997 IEEE Global Telecommunications Conf. (GLOBECOM '97)* (Phoenix, AZ, Nov. 4–8, 1997).

[53] G. D. Forney, Jr., "Maximum likelihood sequence detection in the presence of intersymbol interference," *IEEE Trans. Inform. Theory*, vol. IT-18, pp. 363–378, May 1972.

[54] ——, "The Viterbi algorithm," *Proc. IEEE*, vol. 61, no. 3, pp. 268–278, Mar. 1973.

[55] G. D. Forney, Jr. and A. R. Calderbank, "Coset codes for partial response channels; or, cosets codes with spectral nulls," *IEEE Trans. Inform. Theory*, vol. 35, pp. 925–943, Sept. 1989.

[56] G. D. Forney, Jr. and G. Ungerboeck, "Modulation and coding for linear gaussian channels," this issue, pp. 2384–2415.

[57] P. A. Franaszek, "Sequence-state encoding for digital transmission," *Bell Syst. Tech. J.*, vol. 47, pp. 143–157, Jan. 1968.

[58] ——, "Sequence-state methods for run-length-limited coding," *IBM J. Res. Develop.*, vol. 14, pp. 376–383, July 1970.

[59] ——, "Run-length-limited variable length coding with error propagation limitation," U.S. Patent 3 689 899, Sept. 1972.

[60] ——, "On future-dependent block coding for input-restricted channels," *IBM J. Res. Develop.*, vol. 23, pp. 75–81, 1979.

[61] ——, "Synchronous bounded delay coding for input restricted channels," *IBM J. Res. Develop.*, vol. 24, pp. 43–48, 1980.

[62] ——, "A general method for channel coding," *IBM J. Res. Develop.*, vol. 24, pp. 638–641, 1980.

[63] ——, "Construction of bounded delay codes for discrete noiseless channels," *IBM J. Res. Develop.*, vol. 26, pp. 506–514, 1982.

[64] ——, "Coding for constrained channels: A comparison of two approaches," *IBM J. Res. Develop.*, vol. 33, pp. 602–607, 1989.

[65] J. N. Franklin and J. R. Pierce, "Spectra and efficiency of binary codes without DC," *IEEE Trans. Commun.*, vol. COM-20, pp. 1182–1184, Dec. 1972.

[66] L. Fredrickson, unpublished report, 1993.

[67] ——, "Time-varying modulo N trellis codes for input restricted partial response channels," U.S. Patent 5 257 272, Oct. 26, 1993.

[68] L. Fredrickson, R. Karabed, J. W. Rae, P. H. Siegel, H. Thapar, and R. Wood, "Improved trellis coding for partial response channels," *IEEE Trans. Magn.*, vol. 31, pp. 1141–1148, Mar. 1995.

[69] C. V. Freiman and A. D. Wyner, "Optimum block codes for noiseless input restricted channels," *Inform. Contr.*, vol. 7, pp. 398–415, 1964.

[70] C. A. French and J. K. Wolf, "Bounds on the capacity of a peak power constrained Gaussian channel," *IEEE Trans. Magn.*, vol. 24, pp. 2247–2262, Sept. 1988.

[71] S. Fukuda, Y. Kojima, Y. Shimpuku, and K. Odaka, "8/10 modulation codes for digital magnetic recording," *IEEE Trans. Magn.*, vol. MAG-22, pp. 1194–1196, Sept. 1986.

[72] P. Funk, "Run-length-limited codes with multiple spacing," *IEEE Trans. Magn.*, vol. MAG-18, pp. 772–775, Mar. 1982.

[73] A. Gabor, "Adaptive coding for self-clocking recording," *IEEE Trans. Electron. Comp.*, vol. EC-16, pp. 866–868, Dec. 1967.

[74] R. Gallager, *Information Theory and Reliable Communication*. New York: Wiley, 1968.

[75] A. Gallopoulos, C. Heegard, and P. H. Siegel, "The power spectrum of run-length-limited codes," *IEEE Trans. Commun.*, vol. 37, pp. 906–917, Sept. 1989.

[76] F. R. Gantmacher, *Matrix Theory, Volume II*. New York: Chelsea, 1960.

[77] E. Gilbert, private correspondence, May 1998.

[78] ——, private e-mail, June 1998.

[79] J. Gu and T. Fuja, "A new approach to constructing optimal block codes for runlength-limited channels," *IEEE Trans. Inform. Theory*, vol 40, pp. 774–785, May 1994.

[80] J. Heanue, M. Bashaw, and L. Hesselink, "Volume holographic storage and retrieval of digital data," *Science*, vol. 265, pp. 749–752, 1994.

[81] ——, "Channel codes for digital holographic data storage," *J. Opt. Soc. Amer. Ser. A*, vol. 12, pp. 2432–2439, 1995.

[82] J. Heanue, K. Gurkan, and L. Hesselink, "Signal detection for page-access optical memories with intersymbol interference," *Appl. Opt.*, vol. 35, no. 14, pp. 2431–2438, May 1996.

[83] C. Heegard and L. Ozarow, "Bounding the capacity of saturation recording: the Lorentz model and applications," *IEEE J. Select. Areas Commun.*, vol. 10, pp. 145–156, Jan. 1992.

[84] J. P. J. Heemskerk and K. A. S. Immink, "Compact disc: System aspects and modulation," *Philips Tech. Rev.*, vol. 40, no. 6, pp. 157–164, 1982.

[85] P. S. Henry, "Zero disparity coding system," U.S. Patent 4 309 694, Jan. 1982.

[86] T. Himeno, M. Tanaka, T. Katoku, K. Matsumoto, M. Tamura, and H. Min-Jae, "High-density magnetic tape recording by a nontracking method," *Electron. Commun. in Japan*, vol. 76. no. 5, pt. 2, pp. 83–93, 1993.

[87] W. Hirt, "Capacity and information rates of discrete-time channels with memory," Ph.D. dissertation (Diss. ETH no. 8671), Swiss Federal Inst. Technol. (ETH), Zurich, Switzerland, 1988.

[88] W. Hirt and J. L. Massey, "Capacity of the discrete-time Gaussian channel with intersymbol interference," *IEEE Trans. Inform. Theory*, vol. 34, pp. 380–388, May 1988.

[89] K. J. Hole, "Punctured convolutional codes for the $1 - D$ partial-response channel," *IEEE Trans. Inform. Theory*, vol. 37, pt. 2, pp. 808–817, May 1991.

[90] K. J. Hole and Ø. Ytrehus, "Improved coding techniques for partial-response channels," *IEEE Trans. Inform. Theory*, vol. 40, pp. 482–493, Mar. 1994.

[91] H. D. L. Hollmann, "Modulation codes," Ph.D. dissertation, Eindhoven Univ. Technol., Eindhoven, The Netherlands, Dec. 1996.

[92] ——, "On the construction of bounded-delay encodable codes for constrained systems," *IEEE Trans. Inform. Theory*, vol. 41, pp. 1354–1378, Sept. 1995.

[93] ——, "Bounded-delay-encodable, block-decodable codes for constrained systems," *IEEE Trans. Inform. Theory*, vol. 42, pp. 1957–1970, Nov. 1996.

[94] J. E. Hopcroft and J. D. Ullman, *Introduction to Automata Theory, Languages, and Computation*. Reading, MA: Addison-Wesley, 1979.

[95] S. Hunter, F. Kiamilev, S. Esener, D. Parthenopoulos, and P. M. Rentzepis, "Potentials of two-photon based 3D optical memories for high performance computing," *Appl. Opt.*, vol. 29, pp. 2058–2066, 1990.

[96] K. A. S. Immink, "Modulation systems for digital audio discs with optical readout," in *Proc. IEEE Int. Conf. Acoustics, Speech, and Signal Processing* (Atlanta, GA, Apr. 1981), pp. 587–590.

[97] ——, "Construction of binary DC-constrained codes," *Philips J. Res.*, vol. 40, pp. 22–39, 1985.

[98] ——, "Performance of simple binary DC-constrained codes," *Philips J. Res.*, vol. 40, pp. 1–21, 1985.

[99] ——, "Spectrum shaping with DC^2-constrained channel codes," *Philips J. Res.*, vol. 40, pp. 40–53, 1985.

[100] ——, "Spectral null codes," *IEEE Trans. Magn.*, vol. 26, pp. 1130–1135, Mar. 1990.

[101] ——, "Runlength-limited sequences," *Proc. IEEE*, vol. 78, pp. 1745–1759, Nov. 1990.

[102] ——, *Coding Techniques for Digital Recorders*. Englewood Cliffs, NJ: Prentice-Hall Int. (UK), 1991.

[103] ——, "Block-decodable runlength-limited codes via look-ahead technique," *Philips J. Res.*, vol. 46, pp. 293–310, 1992.

[104] ——, "Constructions of almost block-decodable runlength-limited codes," *IEEE Trans. Inform. Theory*, vol. 41, pp. 284–287, Jan. 1995.

[105] ——, "The Digital Versatile Disc (DVD): System requirements and channel coding," *SMPTE J.*, vol. 105, no. 8, pp. 483–489, Aug. 1996.

[106] ——, "A practical method for approaching the channel capacity

of constrained channels," *IEEE Trans. Inform. Theory*, vol. 43, pp. 1389–1399, Sept. 1997.

[107] ——, "Weakly constrained codes," *Electron. Lett.*, vol. 33, no. 23, pp. 1943–1944, Nov. 1997.

[108] K. A. S. Immink and G. F. M. Beenker, "Binary transmission codes with higher order spectral zeros at zero frequency," *IEEE Trans. Inform. Theory*, vol. IT-33, pp. 452–454, May 1987.

[109] K. A. S. Immink and H. Ogawa, "Method for encoding binary data," U.S. Patent 4 501 000, Feb. 1985.

[110] K. A. S. Immink and L. Patrovics, "Performance assessment of DC-free multimode codes," *IEEE Trans. Commun.*, vol. 45, pp. 293–299, Mar. 1997.

[111] K. A. S. Immink and A. van Wijngaarden, "Simple high-rate constrained codes," *Electron. Lett.*, vol. 32, no. 20, pp. 1877, Sept. 1996.

[112] G. V. Jacoby, "A new look-ahead code for increasing data density," *IEEE Trans. Magn.*, vol. MAG-13, pp. 1202–1204, Sept. 1977. See also U.S. Patent 4 323 931, Apr. 1982.

[113] G. V. Jacoby and R. Kost, "Binary two-thirds rate code with full word look-ahead," *IEEE Trans. Magn.*, vol. MAG-20, pp. 709–714, Sept. 1984. See also M. Cohn, G. V. Jacoby, and C. A. Bates III, U.S. Patent 4 337 458, June 1982.

[114] A. J. E. M. Janssen, private communication, 1998.

[115] A. J. E. M. Janssen and K. A. S. Immink, "Entropy and power spectrum of asymmetrically DC-constrained binary sequences', *IEEE Trans. Inform. Theory*, vol. 37, pp. 924–927, May 1991.

[116] J. Justesen, "Information rates and power spectra of digital codes," *IEEE Trans. Inform. Theory*, vol. IT-28, pp. 457–472, May 1982.

[117] P. Kabal and S. Pasupathy, "Partial-response signaling," *IEEE Trans. Commun.*, vol. COM-23, pp. 921–934, Sept. 1975.

[118] J. A. H. Kahlman and K. A. S. Immink, "Channel code with embedded pilot tracking tones for DVCR," *IEEE Trans. Consumer Electron.*, vol. 41, pp. 180–185, Feb. 1995.

[119] H. Kamabe, "Minimum scope for sliding block decoder mappings," *IEEE Trans. Inform. Theory*, vol. 35, pp. 1335–1340, Nov. 1989.

[120] R. Karabed and B. H. Marcus, "Sliding-block coding for input-restricted channels," *IEEE Trans. Inform. Theory*, vol. 34, pp. 2–26, Jan. 1988.

[121] R. Karabed and P. H. Siegel, "Matched spectral-null codes for partial response channels," *IEEE Trans. Inform. Theory*, vol. 37, no. 3, pt. II, pp. 818–855, May 1991.

[122] ——, "Coding for higher order partial response channels," in *Proc. 1995 SPIE Int. Symp. Voice, Video, and Data Communications* (Philadelphia, PA, Oct. 1995), vol. 2605, pp. 115–126.

[123] R. Karabed, P. Siegel, and E. Soljanin, "Constrained coding for channels with high intersymbol interference,"*IEEE Trans. Inform. Theory*, to be published.

[124] A. Kato and K. Zeger, "On the capacity of two-dimensional runlength-limited codes," in *Proc. 1998 IEEE Int. Symp. Information Theory* (Cambridge, MA, Aug. 16–21, 1998), p. 320; submitted for publication to *IEEE Trans. Inform. Theory*.

[125] W. H. Kautz, "Fibonacci codes for synchronization control," *IEEE Trans. Inform. Theory*, vol. IT-11, pp. 284–292, 1965.

[126] K. J. Kerpez, "The power spectral density of maximum entropy charge constrained sequences," *IEEE Trans. Inform. Theory*, vol. 35, pp. 692–695, May 1989.

[127] Z.-A. Khayrallah and D. Neuhoff, "Subshift models and finite-state codes for input-constrained noiseless channels: A tutorial," Univ. Delaware EE Tech. Rep. 90–9–1, Dover, DE, 1990.

[128] K. J. Knudson, J. K. Wolf, and L. B. Milstein, "A concatenated decoding scheme for $(1 - D)$ partial response with matched spectral–null coding," in *Proc. 1993 IEEE Global Telecommunications Conf. (GLOBECOM '93)* (Houston, TX, Nov. 1993), pp. 1960–1964.

[129] D. E. Knuth, "Efficient balanced codes," *IEEE Trans. Inform. Theory*, vol. IT-32, pp. 51–53, Jan. 1986.

[130] H. Kobayashi, "Application of probabilistic decoding to digital magnetic recording systems," *IBM J. Res. Develop.*, vol. 15, pp. 65–74, Jan. 1971.

[131] ——, "Correlative level coding and maximum-likelihood decoding," *IEEE Trans. Inform. Theory*, vol. IT-17, pp. 586–594, Sept. 1971.

[132] ——, "A survey of coding schemes for transmission or recording of digital data," *IEEE Trans. Commun.*, vol. COM-19, pp. 1087–1099, Dec. 1971.

[133] H. Kobayashi and D. T. Tang, "Appliction of partial-response channel coding to magnetic recording systems," *IBM J. Res. Develop.*, vol. 14, pp. 368–375, July 1970.

[134] E. R. Kretzmer, "Generalization of a technique for binary data transmission," *IEEE Trans. Commun. Technol.*, vol. COM-14, pp. 67–68, Feb. 1966.

[135] A. Kunisa, S. Takahashi, and N. Itoh, "Digital modulation method for recordable digital video disc," *IEEE Trans. Consumer Electron.*, vol. 42, pp. 820–825, Aug. 1996.

[136] A. Lempel and M. Cohn, "Look-ahead coding for input-restricted channels," *IEEE Trans. Inform. Theory*, vol. IT-28, pp. 933–937, Nov. 1982.

[137] S. Lin and D. J. Costello, Jr., *Error Control Coding, Fundamentals and Applications*. Englewood Cliffs, NJ: Prentice-Hall, 1983.

[138] D. Lind and B. Marcus, *Symbolic Dynamics and Coding*. Cambridge, U.K.: Cambridge Univ. Press, 1995.

[139] J. C. Mallinson and J. W. Miller, " Optimal codes for digital magnetic recording," *Radio Elec. Eng.*, vol. 47, pp. 172–176, 1977.

[140] M. W. Marcellin and H. J. Weber, "Two-dimensional modulation codes," *IEEE J. Select. Areas Commun.*, vol. 10, pp. 254–266, Jan. 1992.

[141] B. H. Marcus, "Sofic systems and encoding data," *IEEE Trans. Inform. Theory*, vol. IT-31, pp. 366–377, May 1985.

[142] ——, "Symbolic dynamics and connections to coding theory, automata theory and systems theory," in *Different Aspects of Coding Theory (Proc. Symp. Applied Matematics.)*, A. R. Calderbank, Ed., vol. 50, American Math. Soc., 1995.

[143] B. H. Marcus and R. M. Roth, "Bounds on the number of states in encoder graphs for input-constrained channels," *IEEE Trans. Inform. Theory*, vol. 37, no. 3, pt. 2, pp. 742–758, May 1991.

[144] B. H. Marcus, R. M. Roth, and P. H. Siegel, "Constrained systems and coding for recording channels," in *Handbook of Coding Theory*, R. Brualdi, C. Huffman, and V. Pless, Eds. Amsterdam, The Netherlands: Elsevier, 1998.

[145] B. H. Marcus and P. H. Siegel, "On codes with spectral nulls at rational submultiples of the symbol frequency," *IEEE Trans. Inform. Theory*, vol. IT-33, pp. 557–568, July 1987.

[146] B. H. Marcus, P. H. Siegel, and J. K. Wolf, "Finite-state modulation codes for data storage," *IEEE J. Select. Areas Commun.*, vol. 10, pp. 5–37, Jan. 1992.

[147] P. A. McEwen and J. K. Wolf, "Trellis codes for $(1, k)$ E^2PR4ML with squared-distance 18," *IEEE Trans. Magn.*, vol. 32, pp. 3995–3997, Sept. 1996.

[148] S. W. McLaughlin, "Five runlength-limited codes for M-ary recording channels, " *IEEE Trans. Magn.*, vol. 33, pp. 2442–2450, May 1997.

[149] S. W. McLaughlin and D. L. Neuhoff, "Upper bounds on the capacity of the digital magnetic recording channel," *IEEE Trans. Magn.*, vol. 29, pp. 59–66, Jan. 1993.

[150] J. W. Miller, U.S. Patent 4 027 335, 1977.

[151] T. Mittelholzer, P. A. McEwen, S. A. Altekar, and J. K. Wolf, "Finite truncation depth trellis codes for the dicode channel," *IEEE Trans. Magn.*, vol. 31, no. 6, pt. 1, pp. 3027–3029, Nov. 1995.

[152] B. E. Moision, P. H. Siegel, and E. Soljanin, "Distance-enhancing codes for digital recording," *IEEE Trans. Magn.*, vol. 34, no. 1, pt. 1, pp. 69–74, Jan. 1998.

[153] C. M. Monti and G. L. Pierobon, " Codes with a multiple spectral null at zero frequency," *IEEE Trans. Inform. Theory*, vol. 35, pp. 463–471, Mar. 1989.

[154] J. Moon and B. Brickner, " Maximum transition run codes for data storage systems," *IEEE Trans. Magn.*, vol. 32, no. 5, pt. 1, pp. 3992–3994, Sept. 1996.

[155] ——, "Design of a rate 5/6 maximum transition run code," *IEEE Trans. Magn.*, vol. 33, pp. 2749–2751, Sept. 1997.

[156] H. Nakajima and K. Odaka, "A rotary-head high-density digital audio tape recorder," *IEEE Trans. Consumer Electron.*, vol. CE-29, pp. 430–437, Aug. 1983.

[157] K. Norris and D. S. Bloomberg, "Channel capacity of charge-constrained run-length limited codes," *IEEE Trans. Magn.*, vol. MAG-17, no. 6, pp. 3452–3455, Nov. 1981.

[158] B. Olson and S. Esener,"Partial response precoding for parallel-readout optical memories," *Opt. Lett.*, vol. 19, pp. 661–663, 1993.

[159] L. H. Ozarow, A. D. Wyner, and J. Ziv, "Achievable rates for a constrained Gaussian channel," *IEEE Trans. Inform. Theory*, vol. 34, pp. 365–371, May 1988.

[160] A. M. Patel, "Zero-modulation encoding in magnetic recording," *IBM J. Res. Develop.*, vol. 19, pp. 366–378, July 1975. See also U.S. Patent 3 810 111, May 1974.

[161] ——, *IBM Tech. Discl. Bull.*, vol. 231, no. 8, pp. 4633–4634, Jan. 1989.

[162] G. L. Pierobon, "Codes for zero spectral density at zero frequency," *IEEE Trans. Inform. Theory*, vol. IT-30, pp. 435–439, Mar. 1984.

[163] K. C. Pohlmann, *The Compact Disc Handbook, 2nd ed.* Madison, WI: A–R Editions, 1992.

[164] J. Rae, G. Christiansen, S.-M. Shih, H. Thapar, R. Karabed, and P. Siegel, "Design and performance of a VLSI 120 Mb/s trellis-coded partial-response channel," *IEEE Trans. Magn.*, vol. 31, pp. 1208–1214, Mar. 1995.

[165] R. M. Roth, P. H. Siegel, and A. Vardy, "High-order spectral-null codes: Constructions and bounds," *IEEE Trans. Inform. Theory*, vol. 40, pp. 1826–1840, Nov. 1994.

[166] Lord Rothschild, "The distribution of English dictionary word lengths," *J. Statist. Planning Infer.*, vol. 14, pp. 311–322, 1986.

[167] D. Rugar and P. H. Siegel, "Recording results and coding considerations for the resonant bias coil overwrite technique," in *Optical Data Storage Topical Meet., Proc. SPIE*, G. R. Knight and C. N. Kurtz, Eds., vol. 1078, pp. 265–270, 1989.

[168] W. E. Ryan, L. L. McPheters, and S. W. McLaughlin, "Combined turbo coding and turbo equalization for PR4-equalized Lorentzian channels," in *Proc. Conf. Information Science and Systems (CISS'98)* (Princeton, NJ, Mar. 1998)..

[169] N. Sayiner, "Impact of the track density versus linear density trade–off on the read channel: TCPR4 versus EPR4," in *Proc. 1995 SPIE Int. Symp. on Voice, Video, and Data Communications* (Philadelphia, PA, Oct. 1995), vol. 2605, pp. 84–91.

[170] E. Seneta, *Non-negative Matrices and Markov Chains*, 2nd ed. New York: Springer, 1980.

[171] S. Shamai (Shitz) and I. Bar-David, "Upper bounds on the capacity for a constrained Gaussian channel," *IEEE Trans. Inform. Theory*, vol. 35, pp. 1079–1084, Sept. 1989.

[172] S. Shamai (Shitz), L. H. Ozarow, and A. D. Wyner, "Information rates for a discrete-time Gaussian channel with intersymbol interference and stationary inputs," *IEEE Trans. Inform. Theory*, vol. 37, pp. 1527–1539, Nov. 1991.

[173] C. E. Shannon, "A mathematical theory of communication," *Bell Syst. Tech. J.*, vol. 27, pp. 379–423, July 1948.

[174] K. Shaughnessy, personal communication, Dec. 1997.

[175] L. A. Shepp, "Covariance of unit processes," in *Proc. Working Conf. Stochastic Processes* (Santa Barbara, CA, 1967), pp. 205–218.

[176] K. Shimazaki, M. Yoshihiro, O. Ishizaki, S. Ohnuki, and N. Ohta, "Magnetic multi-valued magneto-optical disk," *J. Magn. Soc. Japan*, vol. 19, suppl. no. S1, p. 429–430, 1995.

[177] P. H. Siegel, "Recording codes for digital magnetic storage," *IEEE Trans. Magn.*, vol. MAG-21, pp. 1344–1349, Sept. 1985.

[178] P. H. Siegel and J. K. Wolf, "Modulation and coding for information storage," *IEEE Commun. Mag.*, vol. 29, pp. 68–86, Dec. 1991.

[179] _____, "Bit-stuffing bounds on the capacity of two-dimensional constrained arrays," in *Proc. 1998 IEEE Int. Symp. Inform. Theory* (Cambridge, MA, Aug. 16–21, 1998), p. 323.

[180] J. G. Smith, "The information capacity of amplitude and variance constrained scalar Gaussian channels," *Inform. Contr.*, vol. 18, pp. 203–219, 1971.

[181] E. Soljanin, "On–track and off–track distance properties of Class 4 partial response channels," in *Proc. 1995 SPIE Int. Symp. Voice, Video, and Data Communications* (Philadelphia, PA, Oct. 1995), vol. 2605, pp. 92–102.

[182] _____, "On coding for binary partial-response channels that don't achieve the matched-filter-bound," in *Proc. 1996 Information Theory Work.* (Haifa, Israel, June 9–13, 1996).

[183] E. Soljanin and C. N. Georghiades, "Multihead detection for multitrack recording channels," to be published in *IEEE Trans. Inform. Theory*, vol. 44, Nov. 1998.

[184] E. Soljanin and O. E. Agazzi, "An interleaved coding scheme for $(1 - D)(1 + D)^2$ partial response with concatenated decoding" in *Proc. 1993 IEEE Global Telecommunications Conf. (GLOBECOM'96)* (London, U.K., Nov. 1996).

[185] R. E. Swanson and J. K. Wolf, "A new class of two-dimensional RLL recording codes," *IEEE Trans. Magn.*, vol. 28, pp. 3407–3416, Nov. 1992.

[186] N. Swenson and J. M. Cioffi, "Sliding block line codes to increase dispersion-limited distance of optical fiber channels," *IEEE J. Select. Areas Commun.*, vol. 13, pp. 485–498, Apr. 1995.

[187] R. Talyansky, T. Etzion, and R. M. Roth, "Efficient code constructions for certain two-dimensional constraints," in *Proc. 1997 IEEE Int. Symp. Information Theory* (Ulm, Germany, June 29–July 4), p. 387.

[188] D. T. Tang and L. R. Bahl, "Block codes for a class of constrained noiseless channels," *Inform. Contr.*, vol. 17, pp. 436-461, 1970.

[189] H. K. Thapar and T. D. Howell, "On the performance of partial response maximum-likelihood and peak detection methods in digital recording," in *Tech. Dig. Magn. Rec. Conf 1991* (Hidden Valley, PA, June 1991).

[190] H. Thapar and A. Patel, "A class of partial-response systems for increasing storage density in magnetic recording," *IEEE Trans. Magn.*, vol. MAG-23, pp. 3666–3668, Sept. 1987.

[191] Tj. Tjalkens, "Runlength limited sequences," *IEEE Trans. Inform. Theory*, vol. 40, pp. 934–940, May 1994.

[192] *IEEE Trans. Magn.*, vol. 34, no. 1, pt. 1, Jan. 1998.

[193] B. S. Tsybakov, "Capacity of a discrete Gaussian channel with a filter," *Probl. Pered. Inform.*, vol. 6, pp. 78–82, 1970.

[194] C. M. J. van Uijen and C. P. M. J. Baggen, "Performance of a class of channel codes for asymmetric optical recording," in *Proc. 7th Int. Conf. Video, Audio and Data Recording*, IERE Conf. Publ. no. 79 (York, U.K., Mar. 1988), pp. 29–32.

[195] A. Vardy, M. Blaum, P. Siegel, and G. Sincerbox, "Conservative arrays: Multi-dimensional modulation codes for holographic recording," *IEEE Trans. Inform. Theory*, vol. 42, pp. 227–230, Jan. 1996.

[196] J. Watkinson, *The Art of Digital Audio*. London, U.K.: Focal, 1988.

[197] A. D. Weathers and J. K. Wolf, " A new 2/3 sliding block code for the $(1, 7)$ runlength constraint with the minimal number of encoder states," *IEEE Trans. Inform. Theory*, vol. 37, no. 3, pt. 2, pp. 908–913, May 1991.

[198] A. D. Weathers, S. A. Altekar, and J. K. Wolf, "Distance spectra for PRML channels," *IEEE Trans. Magn.*, vol. 33, pp. 2809–2811, Sept. 1997.

[199] W. Weeks IV and R. E. Blahut, "The capacity and coding gain of certain checkerboard codes," *IEEE Trans. Inform. Theory*, vol. 44, pp. 1193–1203, May 1998.

[200] T. Weigandt, "Magneto-optic recording using a (2,18,2) run-length-limited code," S.M. thesis, Mass. Inst. Technol., Cambridge, MA, 1991.

[201] A. X. Widmer and P. A. Franaszek, "A DC-balanced, partitioned-block, 8b/10b transmission code," *IBM J. Res. Develop.*, vol. 27, no. 5, pp. 440–451, Sept. 1983.

[202] A. van Wijngaarden and K. A. S. Immink, "Construction of constrained codes using sequence replacement techniques," submitted for publication to *IEEE Trans. Inform. Theory*, 1997.

[203] J. K. Wolf and W. R. Richard, "Binary to ternary conversion by linear filtering," Tech. Documentary Rep. RADC-TDR-62-230, May 1962.

[204] J. K. Wolf and G. Ungerboeck, "Trellis coding for partial-response channels," *IEEE Trans. Commun.*, vol. COM-34, pp. 765–773, Aug. 1986.

[205] R. W. Wood, "Denser magnetic memory," *IEEE Spectrum*, vol. 27, pp. 32–39, May 1990.

[206] R. W. Wood and D. A. Petersen, "Viterbi detection of class IV partial response on a magnetic recoding channel," *IEEE Trans. Commun.*, vol. COM-34, pp. 454–461, May 1986.

[207] Z.-N. Wu, S. Lin, and J. M. Cioffi, "Capacity bounds for magnetic recording channels," in *Proc. 1998 IEEE Global Telecommun. Conf. (GLOBECOM '98)* (Sydney, Australia, Nov. 8–12, 1998), to be published.

[208] H. Yoshida, T. Shimada, and Y. Hashimoto, "8-9 block code: A DC-free channel code for digital magnetic recording', *SMPTE J.*, vol. 92, pp. 918-922, Sept. 1983.

[209] S. Yoshida and S. Yajima, "On the relation between an encoding automaton and the power spectrum of its output sequence," *Trans. IECE Japan*, vol. 59, pp. 1–7, 1976.

[210] A. H. Young, "Implementation issues of 8/9 distance-enhancing constrained codes for EEPR4 channel," M.S. thesis, Univ. Calif., San Diego, June 1997.

[211] E. Zehavi, "Coding for magnetic recording," Ph.D. dissertation, Univ. Calif., San Diego, 1987.

[212] E. Zehavi and J. K. Wolf, "On saving decoder states for some trellis codes and partial response channels," *IEEE Trans. Commun.*, vol. 36, pp. 454–461, Feb. 1988.

Statistical Inference Under Multiterminal Data Compression

Te Sun Han, *Fellow, IEEE*, and Shun-ichi Amari, *Fellow, IEEE*

(Invited Paper)

Abstract— This paper presents a survey of the literature on the *information-theoretic* problems of statistical inference under multiterminal data compression with rate constraints. Significant emphasis is put on problems: 1) multiterminal hypothesis testing, 2) multiterminal parameter estimation, and 3) multiterminal pattern classification, in either case of positive rates or zero rates. In addition, the paper includes three new results, i.e., the converse theorems for all problems of multiterminal hypothesis testing, multiterminal parameter estimation, and multiterminal pattern classification at the *zero* rate.

Index Terms—Covariance, Fisher information, hypothesis testing, multiterminal data compression, parameter estimation, pattern classification, probability of error, rate constraint, statistical inference, universal coding.

I. INTRODUCTION

IN 1979, Berger [1] proposed and formulated an intriguing novel problem to put standard statistical inference problems, such as hypothesis testing and parameter estimation, in the information-theoretic framework of multiterminal data compression schemes. This was the first attempt to combine two seemingly different kinds of problems which had been separately investigated in the void between statistics and information theory. Needless to say, statistics and information theory had been separate from one another. Their fundamental approaches and methodologies were substantially different in nature, although both revealed intrinsic features of the same "information" in its wider sense. The true significance of the multiterminal statistical inference system of Berger, as well as the single-user universal coding system of Rissanen [2], is that those systems enabled us to incorporate problems of statistical inference into information theory.

The basic system that Berger has proposed is the following. Let $\mathcal{X}, \mathcal{Y}$ be any finite sets. Given a family

$$\{p_\theta = p_\theta(x, y)\}_{\theta \in \Phi}$$

of joint probability distributions on $\mathcal{X} \times \mathcal{Y}$, indexed by a parameter $\theta \in \Phi$ (Φ is a prescribed appropriate set (*finite* or *infinite*)), we may consider the following multiuser situation.

Manuscript received May 1, 1998.

T. S. Han is with the Graduate School of Information Systems, University of Electro-Communications, Chofugaoka 1-5-1, Tokyo 182-8585, Japan.

S. Amari is with the Brain-Style, Information Systems Group, RIKEN Brain Science Institute, Hirosawa, 2-1, Wako-shi, Saitama 351-0198, Japan.

Publisher Item Identifier S 0018-9448(98)05283-3.

Let data

$$\boldsymbol{x} = (x_1, x_2, \cdots, x_n) \in \mathcal{X}^n \tag{1.1}$$

$$\boldsymbol{y} = (y_1, y_2, \cdots, y_n) \in \mathcal{Y}^n \tag{1.2}$$

of blocklength n be generated at two separate remote sites A and B, respectively, where n pairs (x_i, y_i) $(i = 1, \cdots, n)$ are *independently* and *identically distributed* (i.i.d.) subject to a joint distribution $p_\theta(x, y)$ with an *unknown* parameter θ. Here, x_i and y_i are *correlated* to each other $(i = 1, 2, \cdots, n)$. In the usual situation of statistics, one makes statistical inference about the actual parameter θ under the assumption that these data $(\boldsymbol{x}, \boldsymbol{y})$ are fully available. In many practical situations, however, this is not necessarily the case, and rather, it would be usual that we impose some limitations on the capacity for transmitting the generated data $\boldsymbol{x}, \boldsymbol{y}$ from sites A and B to the statistician at another site C, or other kinds of limitations such as the precision for numerical expression of those data, and so on. It then becomes unavoidable to incorporate the operation of *compressing* the generated data $\boldsymbol{x}, \boldsymbol{y}$ into the form of $f_n(\boldsymbol{x})$ and $g_n(\boldsymbol{y})$ (f_n and g_n are called the *encoders*) at sites A and B, respectively, which are in turn transmitted to a common information-processing center at site C. It should be emphasized here that the encoders f_n, g_n can observe only $\boldsymbol{x}$ and $\boldsymbol{y}$, respectively. The center is then required to make an optimal statistical estimation of the true value θ (Fig. 1) in the form of $\hat{\theta}_n = \psi_n(f_n(\boldsymbol{x}), g_n(\boldsymbol{y}))$ (ψ_n is called the *decoder*). In many cases, the capacity restriction is expressed in the form that the sizes $\|f_n\|, \|g_n\|$ of the ranges of the encoder functions f_n, g_n are upper-bounded asymptotically as

$$\|f_n\| \leq e^{nR_1} \qquad \|g_n\| \leq e^{nR_2} \tag{1.3}$$

for sufficiently large n, where nonnegative constants R_1, R_2 are called the *rates* for the encoders f_n and g_n, respectively. Here, given rates R_1, R_2, we are allowed to choose *any* encoder functions f_n, g_n as long as rate constraint (1.3) is satisfied.

The basic question posed in the framework of such a multiuser coding system is: How should the encoders f_n, g_n be constructed under rate constraint (1.3) in order for the decoder ψ_n at the center to yield an *optimal* effective estimator

$$\hat{\theta}_n = \psi_n(f_n(\boldsymbol{x}), g_n(\boldsymbol{y})) \tag{1.4}$$

for the parameter θ ? In the present paper we shall concentrate on this basic question as well as on several related problems of statistical testing, estimation, and classification.

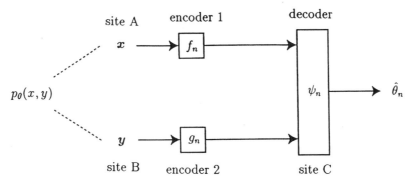

Fig. 1. Multiterminal system for statistical inference.

It should be noted here that in this system, in contrast to the case of usual data compression systems, the whole data $(\boldsymbol{x}, \boldsymbol{y})$ is *not* necessarily required to be reliably reproduced at the center C. Instead, we are concerned only with reliably reproducing the value of an unknown parameter θ governing the generation of data $(\boldsymbol{x}, \boldsymbol{y})$. If rates R_1, R_2 are large enough, the center can have access to the *full* data $\boldsymbol{x}, \boldsymbol{y}$ and then can make an optimal estimator $\hat{\theta}$ based on this full data $(\boldsymbol{x}, \boldsymbol{y})$. The problem then reduces to the well-established standard statistical inference problem. However, if rates R_1, R_2 are *not* large enough to reliably reproduce the full data $(\boldsymbol{x}, \boldsymbol{y})$ at the center, we have to construct an estimator $\hat{\theta}_n$ using only *partial* information about the data $(\boldsymbol{x}, \boldsymbol{y})$. This is the main reason why the problem of statistical inference under multiterminal data compression is made so drastically different from that of traditional multiterminal data compression. Information theory tells us that, if rates R_1, R_2 are *not* large enough (even though they are both positive), the probability of decoding error necessarily approaches one as blocklength n tends to infinity. This makes no sense from the viewpoint of traditional lossless or lossy data compression. Even in this situation, however, we can make an *effective* estimator $\hat{\theta}_n$ with high reliability.

To make the point clearer, let us consider as a special case of (1.3) the following rate constraint:

$$\lim_{n\to\infty} \frac{1}{n} \log \|f_n\| = 0 \quad \text{and/or} \quad \lim_{n\to\infty} \frac{1}{n} \log \|g_n\| = 0. \tag{1.5}$$

These rate constraints are called the *zero-rate* compression. This means that the zero-rate encoders carry asymptotically negligible informations alone, which is of *no use* in the traditional data compression but is still in general of *significant use* in constructing an effective estimator $\hat{\theta}$. Thus the zero-rate data compression becomes one of the main important subjects on statistical inference in the multiterminal framework. Therefore, in the subsequent sections we shall address also the details of the zero-rate statistical inference problem as a subject of independent interest in its own right.

The problem of statistical inference under multiterminal data compression is ramified into three main branches depending on the choice of the parameter set Φ and the manners of statistical decision.

First, we consider the case in which Φ consists of only two elements, say, $\Phi = \{H, \overline{H}\}$, where H and $\overline{H}$ are called the

null hypothesis and the *alternative hypothesis*, respectively. Then, we can write as

$$\{p_\theta\}_{\theta\in\Phi} = \{P, \overline{P}\} \tag{1.6}$$

where $P = p_H$, $\overline{P} = p_{\overline{H}}$. In this case, according to the tradition in statistics, we define two kinds of error probabilities as follows:

$$\alpha_n = \Pr\{\overline{H} = \psi_n(f_n(X^n), g_n(Y^n))\} \tag{1.7}$$
$$\beta_n = \Pr\{H = \psi_n(f_n(\overline{X}^n), g_n(\overline{Y}^n))\} \tag{1.8}$$

where (X^n, Y^n) and $(\overline{X}^n, \overline{Y}^n)$ are independent and identically distributed random variables of length n subject to the joint probability distributions $P, \overline{P}$ on $\mathcal{X} \times \mathcal{Y}$, respectively, and α_n, β_n are called the error probability of the first kind and the error probability of the second kind, respectively. Incidentally, the region defined by

$$\mathcal{A}_n \equiv \{(\boldsymbol{x}, \boldsymbol{y}) \in \mathcal{X}^n \times \mathcal{Y}^n | H = \psi_n(f_n(\boldsymbol{x}), g_n(\boldsymbol{y}))\}$$

is called the *acceptance region*. If $(\boldsymbol{x}, \boldsymbol{y}) \in \mathcal{A}_n$ then the decoder decides that H is correct; otherwise, that $\overline{H}$ is correct. In this case, our purpose is, given rate constraint (1.3), to design a statistical inference system so as to make β_n as small as possible when a prescribed upper bound on α_n is imposed. We notice here that the error probability β_n usually decays exponentially fast with blocklength n. This leads us to formulate and study the problem of *multiterminal hypothesis testing*. This is sometimes called also the problem of *distributed detection*.

The above setting is the case in which the alternative hypothesis $\overline{H}$ is *simple*. A more general case is the hypothesis testing with a *composite* alternative hypothesis $\overline{H}$ where $\overline{H}$ includes a (possibly infinite) number of distributions. Since our theory is asymptotic, composite alternative cases reduce to the simple hypothesis testing with $H : P$ and $\overline{H} : \overline{P}^{(0)}$, where

$$\overline{P}^{(0)} = \arg\inf_{Q\in\overline{H}} D(P\|Q) \tag{1.9}$$

and $D(P\|Q)$ is the Kullback–Leibler divergence defined by

$$D(P\|Q) = \sum_{x\in\mathcal{X}, y\in\mathcal{Y}} P(x,y) \log \frac{P(x,y)}{Q(x,y)}. \tag{1.10}$$

However, in the typical composite case with $H : P$ and $\overline{H} : \overline{P} \neq P$, such a reduction to the simple alternative case does not make sense. In order to treat this typical case in a reasonable way, techniques developed in the estimation problem are useful.

Another problem is the *pattern classification* or *discrimination*, where the parameter set Φ typically consists of a finite number m ($m \geq 2$) of pattern classes: $\Phi = \{C_1, \cdots, C_m\}$. Each class C_i is associated with probability distribution $P_i = \{P_i(x, y)\}$ on $\mathcal{X} \times \mathcal{Y}$. The problem here is to decide, on the basis of the encoded informations $f_n(\boldsymbol{x})$ and $g_n(\boldsymbol{y})$, which class the generated data $(\boldsymbol{x}, \boldsymbol{y})$ belongs to. The statistician tries to design the decoder ψ_n: $f_n(\mathcal{X}^n) \times g_n(\mathcal{Y}^n) \rightarrow \Phi$ so that the overall average classification error probability be minimized. This is called the problem of *multiterminal pattern classification* or the problem of *distributed pattern classification*.

On the other hand, we may consider also the case in which the parameter set Φ is an *open subset* of the r-dimensional Euclidean space and the joint distribution p_θ is a sufficiently smooth function of the parameter $\theta = (\theta_1, \cdots, \theta_r) \in \Phi$. Then, an estimator $\hat{\theta}_n$ for the parameter θ can be written as

$$\hat{\theta}_n = \psi_n(f_n(X_\theta^n), g_n(Y_\theta^n)) \qquad (1.11)$$

where

$$(X_\theta^n, Y_\theta^n) = \left(X_\theta^{(1)} Y_\theta^{(1)}, X_\theta^{(2)} Y_\theta^{(2)}, \cdots, X_\theta^{(n)} Y_\theta^{(n)} \right)$$

is an independent and identically distributed random variable of blocklength n subject to joint probability distribution p_θ on $\mathcal{X} \times \mathcal{Y}$. In this case, our purpose is, given rate constraint (1.3), to design a statistical inference system so as to make the (co)variance of $\hat{\theta}_n$ as small as possible, where $\hat{\theta}_n$ is requested in most cases to be asymptotically unbiased. Usually, the (co)variance of an effective estimator $\hat{\theta}_n$ is asymptotically proportional to the inverse of blocklength n. Thus we are lead to formulate and study another kind of problem, that is, the problem of *multiterminal parameter estimation*. This is sometimes called also the problem of *distributed estimation*.

These three areas of multiterminal hypothesis testing, multiterminal classification, and multiterminal parameter estimation are closely related to each other and they have the nice structural correspondence not only at the conceptual level but also at the technical level, where the notion of divergence (or Fisher information) plays a key role to bridge these areas. It should be kept in mind that the design of the encoders f_n, g_n and the decoder ψ_n above defined should not depend on the actual value of the parameter $\theta \in \Phi$, because the value of the actual parameter θ is *unknown* to both of encoders and decoder, which is to be evaluated at the decoder based on the encoded data. This means that only *universal codings* make sense in these multiterminal statistical inference problems.

In the present paper we deal with the problem of multiterminal statistical inference thus defined. First, in the next section, we will give a brief historical sketch of this subject, and then, in the subsequent sections, summarize several main results that had been established in this research field up to the present. It should be mentioned here that, to the best of our knowledge, until now, only very few papers have been published in this field. This would be mainly because the problem in

consideration is, in general, of formidable complexity in its own nature (cf. Ahlswede and Csiszár [3]) and so it scarcely allows us to reach the so-called *single-letter characterization* for achievable error exponents in multiterminal hypothesis testing and multiterminal pattern classification or that for achievable covariances in multiterminal parameter estimation, where the term of single-letter characterization is used to denote the *computability* of the relevant quantity. This means that this research field is not yet mature enough and it remains to be further cultivated. Thus for the sake of further possible developments of this field, it would be useful to try here to summarize several typical earlier results in as compact form as possible but not in ambiguous manner. Sections II–IX are assigned to this purpose, where Section IX includes also new results on the *optimality* concerning the *zero-rate* multiterminal pattern classification.

Finally, in Sections X and XI, we will present the solutions to two open problems on the *optimality* (i.e, the converse part) concerning both the hypothesis testing and parameter estimation under *zero-rate* multiterminal data compression. Specifically, in these sections we will prove that both the zero-rate acceptance region given by Han and Kobayashi [5] and the zero-rate parameter estimator given by Amari [13] are optimal.

The proof for the former problem is rather simple, whereas that for the latter problem is much harder and needs rather subtle large-deviation techniques as well as basic information-geometrical considerations. As a by-product, the optimality of the zero-rate pattern classifier of Amari and Han [9] is newly derived (cf. Section IX).

II. HISTORICAL SKETCH

The problem of multiterminal hypothesis testing with constant-type constraint $\alpha_n \leq \varepsilon$ has first been investigated in 1986, seven years after the original proposal of Berger [1], and Ahlswede and Csiszár [3]. They have mainly focused on the problem of hypothesis testing against independence in the case with arbitrary positive rate R_1 but with full side-information ($R_2 = +\infty$) and succeeded in establishing the single-letter characterization of the optimal exponent for the error probability of the second kind as a function of rate R_1. They have also given a single-letter lower bound (though not very tight) on the optimal exponent for the general hypothesis testing with $R_2 = +\infty$. From the technical point of view, the approach adopted by them to investigate this problem was called the *divergence characterization problem*.

Subsequently, in 1987, Han [4] has studied the problem of more general hypothesis testings with constant-type constraint $\alpha_n \leq \varepsilon$ at arbitrary positive rates R_1, R_2 and derived a single-letter lower bound on the optimal error exponent by reducing the problem to that of minimizing the relevant divergence, which with reference to the case of $R_2 = +\infty$ is much tighter than that of Ahlswede and Csiszár [3]. In particular, Han has first introduced the problem of hypothesis testing with *one-bit* data compression and established the single-letter characterization of the optimal error exponent for this one-bit compression system, where it was revealed that the exponent is still generally positive even only with one-bit information.

In 1989, Han and Kobayashi [5] have considered the same hypothesis testing problem with exponential-type constraint $\alpha_n \leq e^{-nr}$ ($r > 0$ is any constant) to obtain the results paralleling those in Han [4], including also the case of general *zero-rate* data compression in addition to the case of one-bit compression.

In 1992, Shalaby and Papamarcou [6] have refined the result of Han [4] for the one-bit compression system and extended it to the case of general zero-rate compression, where it is interesting to see that the converse part was proved by the ingenious use of "Blowing-up lemma" of Ahlswede, Gács, and Körner [7] (also, see Marton [8]). It will turn out that this lemma plays a key role also in establishing the converse part for the zero-rate hypothesis testing problem with exponential-type constraint (see Section V) as well as that for the zero-rate parameter estimation problem (see Section VII). Shalaby and Papamarcou [6] have also studied the *composite* hypothesis testing problem under zero-rate data compression.

In 1989, Amari and Han [9] have shown an information-geometrical approach to the zero-rate hypothesis testing problem to demonstrate that Pythagorean theorem on divergences plays a crucial role in formulating and studying this kind of problems. They have also studied the zero-rate multiterminal statistical classification problem.

In 1994, Shalaby and Papamarcou [10] have generalized the zero-rate hypothesis testing problem to the case where the source is a correlated Markov process to obtain several non-single-letterized results paralleling those in their previous paper [6].

In 1994, by taking into consideration also the aspect of coding error probabilities for the first time, Han, Shimokawa, and Amari [11] have established a significantly tighter single-letter lower bound on the optimal error exponent for the multiterminal hypothesis testing with full side-information ($R_2 = +\infty$) at arbitrary positive rate R_1, where they have also shown that their lower bound coincides with the optimal error exponent at higher rates R_1.

Now let us turn to the multiterminal parameter estimation problem. The first result in this area has been given in 1988 by Zhang and Berger [12] who have considered the problem of parameter estimation with one-dimensional parameter $\theta(r = 1)$ at arbitrary positive rates R_1, R_2 and demonstrated the existence of an asymptotically unbiased estimator $\hat{\theta}_{ZB}$ to establish a single-letter upper bound on the minimum variance that can be attained by the optimal estimator $\hat{\theta}_n$. Their result, however, was very restrictive, because in doing so they have imposed a stringent condition, called the *additivity* condition, on the family $\{p_\theta\}_{\theta \in \Phi}$ of joint distributions, which is the property that is *not* preserved under parameter transformations.

On the other hand, from the information-geometrical point of view, in 1989, Amari [13] has studied the parameter estimation problem under zero-rate data compression, where he has constructed a very simple asymptotically unbiased effective estimator $\hat{\theta}_A$ by using only the marginal *types*, type$(\boldsymbol{x})$ and type$(\boldsymbol{y})$ of the generated data $(\boldsymbol{x}, \boldsymbol{y})$, together with the explicit form for the covariance of $\hat{\theta}_A$. It will be shown in Section XI that the estimator $\hat{\theta}_A$ has the minimum achievable covariance under zero-rate data compression. It

should be pointed out that the estimator $\hat{\theta}_A$ of Amari has been derived by solving the maximum-likelihood equation based on the calculation of the joint probability of the statistic

$$S_A = (\text{type}(\boldsymbol{x}), \text{type}(\boldsymbol{y})) \qquad (2.1)$$

so that the covariance of $\hat{\theta}_A$ asymptotically coincides with the inverse of the Fisher information matrix of S_A.

Subsequently, in 1990, Ahlswede and Burnashev [14] have considered the minimax estimation problem for a special but important case with one-dimensional parameter $\theta(r = 1)$ and full side-information ($R_2 = +\infty$) such that the marginal $p_\theta(x)$ of the joint probability $p_\theta(x, y)$ is independent of the parameter θ. This assumption was used to avoid technical difficulties due to *universal coding* as mentioned in Section I, that is, one can dispense with universal coding techniques, owing to the assumed independence of $p_\theta(x)$ from θ. With this special multiterminal estimation system they have established a *limiting* (*not* single-letterized) formula for the optimal *minimax* variance index $V(R_1)$ as a function of rate R_1, which states that $V(R_1)$ is given by the inverse of the related maxmin Fisher information index $J(R_1)$.

In 1995, Han and Amari [15] have attempted to generalize the zero-rate estimation scheme of Amari [13] so as to make it applicable to the general multiterminal estimation system (with a multidimensional parameter $\theta \in \Phi$) working at arbitrary positive rates R_1, R_2. They, like in Zhang and Berger [12], have introduced *auxiliary* random variables U_θ, V_θ such that $U_\theta \rightarrow X_\theta \rightarrow Y_\theta \rightarrow V_\theta$ forms a Markov chain in this order and constructed an asymptotically unbiased effective estimator $\hat{\theta}_{HA}$ using only the marginal joint types type$(\hat{\boldsymbol{u}}, \boldsymbol{x})$, type$(\hat{\boldsymbol{v}}, \boldsymbol{y})$, type$(\hat{\boldsymbol{u}}, \hat{\boldsymbol{v}})$, where $\hat{\boldsymbol{u}}, \hat{\boldsymbol{v}}$ are the encoded versions of the auxiliary data generated according to conditional joint probability $P_{U_\theta V_\theta | X_\theta Y_\theta}$ given data $(\boldsymbol{x}, \boldsymbol{y})$. This estimator $\hat{\theta}_{HA}$ has been derived, like in Amari [13], by solving the maximum-likelihood equation based on the calculation of the joint probability of the statistic

$$S_{HA} = (\text{type}(\hat{\boldsymbol{u}}, \boldsymbol{x}), \text{type}(\hat{\boldsymbol{v}}, \boldsymbol{y}), \text{type}(\hat{\boldsymbol{u}}, \hat{\boldsymbol{v}})) \qquad (2.2)$$

so that the covariance matrix of $\hat{\theta}_{HA}$ asymptotically coincides with the inverse of the Fisher information matrix of S_{HA}. The form of the covariance of $\hat{\theta}_{HA}$ thus constructed is *invariant* under parameter transformations. It was also shown that the variance of the estimator $\hat{\theta}_{HA}$ specialized to the one-dimensional parameter case ($r = 1$) is in general substantially smaller than that of the estimator $\hat{\theta}_{ZB}$ of Zhang and Berger [12] when both estimation systems are working at the same rates R_1, R_2. However, the covariance matrix of $\hat{\theta}_{HA}$ does not seem to be the best possible in general at arbitrarily given rates R_1, R_2.

Thus far, we have briefly summarized "almost all" of the presently existing results in the fields of multiterminal hypothesis testing, multiterminal classification, and multiterminal parameter estimation. However, are they all? Why is it? Although we can say that the one-bit and/or zero-rate compression case has been completely solved (cf. Han [4], Shalaby and Papamarcou [6]) or is to be solved in Sections IX–XI of the present paper, problems in the general

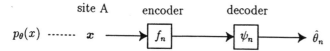

site A   encoder   decoder

$p_\theta(x)$ ······ x → f_n → ψ_n → $\hat{\theta}_n$

Fig. 2. Single-user system for statistical inference.

positive rate compression case are very intractable and many of them still remain open, except for the only special case of hypothesis testing against independence with full side-information ($R_2 = +\infty$) (cf. Ahlswede and Csiszár [3]). Does this mean that the general positive rate problem affords in its own nature no single-letter characterization at all? The approach of divergence characterization by Ahlswede and Csiszár [3] seems to be hopeless in establishing the direct part, whereas the information-geometrical approach by Han and Amari [15] seems to be insufficient in establishing the converse part.

There still exists a substantial gap between these two kinds of approaches. In this connection, we would like to remind the reader that the present problem is lying in the void between statistics and information theory and so researchers in this field need to be knowledgeable about basic elements in both of statistics and information theory. In this sense, we cannot say that enough efforts have already been devoted to investigate this subject. In addition to these difficulties, it is very likely that the subtle problem of *ancillary statistics* (cf. Rao [16]) may be one of the main obstacles to the final goal (also, cf. Körner and Marton [17], Han and Kobayashi [18]). Are these difficulties to be overcome in the near future? We believe that there exists a way of eluding the difficulties. Anyway, nobody knows about the certain future!

So far we have briefly summarized several *information-theoretic* approaches to the problem of statistical inference under multiterminal data compression. It should also be mentioned here that in the area of communication theory the bulk of related works have already been accumulated, based on various kinds of rather *non-information-theortetic* approaches. They include, for example, [25]–[47]. In the present paper, however, we have no space to review these works.

III. Single-User System for Statistical Inference

Before going into the details of the problem of multiterminal statistical inference, it would be helpful to the reader to think first about the single-user system of statistical inference in order to get some preliminary insights in this kind of problems.

The single-user statistical inference system is formulated as follows (Fig. 2). Let $\mathcal{X}$ be a finite set. Given a family $\{p_\theta = p_\theta(x)\}_{\theta \in \Phi}$ of probability distributions on $\mathcal{X}$, suppose that an i.i.d. data $\boldsymbol{x} = (x_1, x_2, \cdots, x_n) \in \mathcal{X}^n$ was generated at site A according to probability $p_\theta(x)$ with an unknown parameter θ. The encoder f_n at site A maps data $\boldsymbol{x}$ into the form $f_n(\boldsymbol{x})$ and then the decoder ψ_n at site C maps the encoded data $f_n(\boldsymbol{x})$ into the form $\hat{\theta}_n = \psi_n(f_n(\boldsymbol{x}))$.

First, let us consider the problem of hypothesis testing, i.e., the case where $\Phi = \{H, \overline{H}\}$. Then, we can write as $\{p_\theta\}_{\theta \in \Phi} = \{P, \overline{P}\}$ where $P = p_H, \overline{P} = p_{\overline{H}}$. Let $\mathcal{A}_n \subset \mathcal{X}^n$ be the Neyman–Pearson acceptance region available when data

$\boldsymbol{x}$ is fully observed by the statistician, and define the encoder f_n and the decoder ψ_n by

$$f_n(\boldsymbol{x}) = \begin{cases} 1, & \text{for } \boldsymbol{x} \in \mathcal{A}_n \\ 0, & \text{for } \boldsymbol{x} \notin \mathcal{A}_n \end{cases} \qquad (3.1)$$

$$\psi_n(1) = H \qquad \psi_n(0) = \overline{H}. \qquad (3.2)$$

With this coding scheme the center at site C can exactly recognize whether data $\boldsymbol{x}$ is in $\mathcal{A}_n$ or not. This means that one-bit information, i.e., $\|f_n\| = 2$ is enough to achieve the same optimal hypothesis testing as in the usual situation in which data $\boldsymbol{x}$ is fully available.

The pattern classification problem assumes that there are m pattern classes $C_1, \cdots, C_m$, each generating data $\boldsymbol{x}$ subject to probability distribution P_i on $\mathcal{X}$ ($i = 1, \cdots, m$). Hence, $\Phi = \{C_1, \cdots, C_m\}$, and the problem is to classify data $\boldsymbol{x}$ in one of the pattern classes so that the average classification error probability is minimized. The statistician can make the optimal Bayes classification based on $\boldsymbol{x}$. Define the encoder f_n and the decoder ψ_n by

$$f_n(\boldsymbol{x}) = i, \quad \text{when the Bayes decision is } C_i \qquad (3.3)$$

$$\psi_n(i) = C_i. \qquad (3.4)$$

This means that $\log m$ information, irrespective of n, is sufficient to achieve the optimal pattern classification. Thus the zero-rate classification achieves the same optimal performance as in the case with full data $\boldsymbol{x}$ available.

Next, consider the problem of parameter estimation. We define the encoder f_n by

$$f_n(\boldsymbol{x}) = \text{type}(\boldsymbol{x}) \qquad (3.5)$$

and the decoder ψ_n maps the encoded data $\text{type}(\boldsymbol{x})$ into the maximum-likelihood estimator $\hat{\theta}_n$. Then, the coding system thus defined achieves the same optimal parameter estimation as in the usual situation in which data $\boldsymbol{x}$ is fully available, because $\text{type}(\boldsymbol{x})$ is a sufficient statistic for the parameter θ. Since the number of different types is at most $(n+1)^{|\mathcal{X}|}$ (cf. Csiszár and Körner [19]), the rate constraint

$$\|f_n\| \le (n+1)^{|\mathcal{X}|} \quad (\forall n = 1, 2, \cdots) \qquad (3.6)$$

is enough to attain this coding scheme. Noting that (3.6) means the *zero-rate* data compression

$$\lim_{n \to \infty} \frac{1}{n} \log \|f_n\| = 0 \qquad (3.7)$$

we conclude that the zero-rate information is enough to achieve the optimal estimation with full data $\boldsymbol{x}$ available.

Thus in all these single-user cases of hypothesis testing, pattern classification, and parameter estimation, the zero-rate information always guarantees the same optimal performance as in the case with rate $R = +\infty$. As a consequence, the single-user statistical inference system is really trivial and hence entirely uninteresting to us. As will be seen in the subsequent sections, however, the situation drastically changes if we are to consider the multiterminal system; although it will turn out that even in this multiterminal case the system is immediately decomposed into two trivial single-user systems if the generation of data $\boldsymbol{x}$ and $\boldsymbol{y}$ is statistically independent.

260

IV. MULTITERMINAL HYPOTHESIS TESTING AT POSITIVE RATES

In this section we describe several but "almost all" known results in the field of multiterminal hypothesis testing with positive rates R_1, R_2.

With the multiterminal coding system, as stated in Section I, in mind, we first give the formal statement of the problem. Let us define two integer sets $\mathcal{M}_n, \mathcal{N}_n$ by

$$\mathcal{M}_n = \{1, 2, \cdots, M_n\}$$
$$\mathcal{N}_n = \{1, 2, \cdots, N_n\}.$$

Encoder $f_n \colon \mathcal{X}^n \to \mathcal{M}_n$ at site A maps each element $\boldsymbol{x} \in \mathcal{X}^n$ to the corresponding element $f_n(\boldsymbol{x}) \in \mathcal{M}_n$. Similarly, encoder $g_n \colon \mathcal{Y}^n \to \mathcal{N}_n$ at site B maps each element $\boldsymbol{y} \in \mathcal{Y}^n$ to the corresponding element $g_n(\boldsymbol{y}) \in \mathcal{N}_n$. On the other hand, decoder $\psi_n \colon \mathcal{M}_n \times \mathcal{N}_n \to \Phi \equiv \{H, \overline{H}\}$ at site C maps each element $(s, t) \in \mathcal{M}_n \times \mathcal{N}_n$ to the corresponding element $\psi_n(s, t) \in \Phi \equiv \{H, \overline{H}\}$. The region

$$\mathcal{A}_n \equiv \{(\boldsymbol{x}, \boldsymbol{y}) \in \mathcal{X}^n \times \mathcal{Y}^n | \psi_n(f_n(\boldsymbol{x}), g_n(\boldsymbol{y})) = H\} \quad (4.1)$$

is called the *acceptance region*. Define the error probabilities α_n, β_n of the first and the second kind as in (1.7) and (1.8) of Section I. The rate constraints as in (1.3) of Section I are more formally written as

$$\limsup_{n \to \infty} \frac{1}{n} \log \|f_n\| \leq R_1 \quad (4.2)$$

$$\limsup_{n \to \infty} \frac{1}{n} \log \|g_n\| \leq R_2. \quad (4.3)$$

We first impose the *constant-type* constraint on α_n as

$$\limsup_{n \to \infty} \alpha_n \leq \varepsilon \quad (4.4)$$

where $0 \leq \varepsilon < 1$ is an arbitrarily fixed constant. Let $\beta_n^*(\varepsilon | R_1, R_2)$ denote the minimum of β_n over all possible encoders f_n, g_n and decoder ψ_n satisfying conditions (4.2)–(4.4), and define

$$\sigma(\varepsilon | R_1, R_2) \equiv \liminf_{n \to \infty} \frac{1}{n} \log \frac{1}{\beta_n^*(\varepsilon | R_1, R_2)} \quad (4.5)$$

which is called the optimal *error exponent* for the hypothesis testing. The definition (4.5) is asymptotically equivalent to

$$\beta_n^*(\varepsilon | R_1, R_2) \simeq e^{-n\sigma(\varepsilon | R_1, R_2)}.$$

The final goal of the multiterminal hypothesis testing is to completely determine the value of $\sigma(\varepsilon | R_1, R_2)$ as a function of ε, R_1 and R_2. In addition, if possible, we want to attain the single-letter characterization for $\sigma(\varepsilon | R_1, R_2)$. However, this does not hold in most cases, and so in general we cannot help to be satisfied with reasonably "good" lower (and/or upper) bounds on $\sigma(\varepsilon | R_1, R_2)$.

Throughout the present paper we use the convention that P_Z denotes the probability distribution of random variable Z and $P_{Z|W}$ denotes the conditional probability distribution of random variable Z given random variable W.

The first result concerns the *full side-information* case (indicated by $R_2 = +\infty$). This means that the decoder at site C can fully observe data $\boldsymbol{y}$ generated at site B. Let us now consider the following hypothesis testing with

$$H : P_{XY} \qquad \text{(null hypothesis)} \quad (4.6)$$
$$\overline{H} : P_{\overline{XY}} = P_X \circ P_Y \quad \text{(alternative hypothesis)} \quad (4.7)$$

where $P_{XY}, P_{\overline{XY}}$ denote joint probability distributions on $\mathcal{X} \times \mathcal{Y}$, and $P_X \circ P_Y$ denotes the product probability measure, i.e., $(P_X \circ P_Y)(x, y) = P_X(x)P_Y(y)$; and P_X and P_Y are the marginals of P_{XY}, respectively. This kind of hypothesis testing is called *testing against independence*. Let

$$\mathcal{L}(R) = \{U | R \geq I(U; X), U \to X \to Y\} \quad (4.8)$$

where $U \to X \to Y$ means that U, X, Y form a Markov chain in this order and $I(U; X)$ is the mutual information (e.g., cf. Cover and Thomas [20]).

Then, we have

Theorem 4.1 (Ahlswede and Csiszár [3]): Consider the hypothesis testing with (4.6) and (4.7). Then, for all $0 \leq \varepsilon < 1$ and all $R \geq 0$

$$\sigma(\varepsilon | R, +\infty) = \max_{\substack{U \in \mathcal{L}(R) \\ \|U\| \leq |\mathcal{X}| + 1}} I(U; Y) \quad (4.9)$$

where $\|U\|$ denotes the number of values taken by random variable U, and $I(U; Y)$ is the mutual information. $\square$

Remark 4.1: The point in the derivation of Theorem 4.1 is to reproduce at the decoder the joint type $S_{AC} = \text{type}(\hat{\boldsymbol{u}}, \boldsymbol{y})$, where $\hat{\boldsymbol{u}}$ is the encoded version of the auxiliary data generated according to the conditional probability $P_{U|X}$ given data $\boldsymbol{x}$. We would like to make the following remark. If $R \geq H(X)$ (the entropy of X), we can set $U \equiv X$ in (4.8), and hence we have

$$\sigma(\varepsilon | R, +\infty) = I(X; Y) \quad (4.10)$$

for all $R \geq H(X)$ and $0 \leq \varepsilon < 1$. The right-hand side of (4.10) is nothing but the same optimal error exponent as that in the case where data $(\boldsymbol{x}, \boldsymbol{y})$ is fully available, as is well known in the field of statistics. $\square$

Now, instead of (4.6) and (4.7), let us consider the general hypothesis testing as follows with

$$H : P_{XY} \quad \text{(null hypothesis)} \quad (4.11)$$
$$\overline{H} : P_{\overline{XY}} \quad \text{(alternative hypothesis)} \quad (4.12)$$

where $P_{XY}, P_{\overline{XY}}$ are arbitrary joint distributions on $\mathcal{X} \times \mathcal{Y}$. In this general case we cannot necessarily have the exact single-letter formula for $\sigma(\varepsilon | R_1, R_2)$. However, it is possible to derive rather reasonable lower bounds on $\sigma(\varepsilon | R_1, R_2)$.

Let

$$\mathcal{L}(R_1, R_2) = \{UV | R_1 \geq I(U; X), R_2 \geq I(V; Y),$$
$$U \to X \to Y \to V\} \quad (4.13)$$

and for each $UV \in \mathcal{L}(R_1, R_2)$ let

$$\mathcal{S}(UV) = \{P_{\tilde{U}\tilde{X}\tilde{Y}\tilde{V}} | P_{\tilde{U}\tilde{X}} = P_{UX}, P_{\tilde{V}\tilde{Y}} = P_{VY},$$
$$P_{\tilde{U}\tilde{V}} = P_{UV}\} \quad (4.14)$$

and define

$$s_L(R_1, R_2) = \max_{\substack{UV \in \mathcal{L}(R_1, R_2) \\ \|U\| \leq |\mathcal{X}|+1 \\ \|V\| \leq |\mathcal{Y}|+1}} \min_{\substack{P_{\check{U}\check{X}\check{Y}\check{V}} \\ \in \mathcal{S}(UV)}} D(P_{\check{U}\check{X}\check{Y}\check{V}} \| P_{\overline{UXYV}})$$

(4.15)

where $D(P_{\check{U}\check{X}\check{Y}\check{V}} \| P_{\overline{UXYV}})$ is the divergence and the random variables $\overline{U}, \overline{V}$ are uniquely specified by the conditions

$$\overline{U} \rightarrow \overline{X} \rightarrow \overline{Y} \rightarrow \overline{V}$$

(4.16)

$$P_{\overline{U}|\overline{X}} = P_{U|X} \qquad P_{\overline{V}|\overline{Y}} = P_{V|Y}.$$

(4.17)

Then, we have the following theorem. The point in the derivation of this theorem is to reproduce at the decoder the set of joint types

$$S_{HA} = (\text{type}(\hat{\boldsymbol{u}}, \boldsymbol{x}), \text{type}(\hat{\boldsymbol{v}}, \boldsymbol{y}), \text{type}(\hat{\boldsymbol{u}}, \hat{\boldsymbol{v}}))$$

(4.18)

where $\hat{\boldsymbol{u}}, \hat{\boldsymbol{v}}$ are the encoded versions of the auxiliary data generated according to the conditional probabilities $P_{U|X}$ (given data $\boldsymbol{x}$), $P_{V|Y}$ (given data $\boldsymbol{y}$), respectively.

Theorem 4.2 (Han [4]): For all $0 \leq \varepsilon < 1$ and all $R_1 \geq 0$, $R_2 \geq 0$

$$\sigma(\varepsilon|R_1, R_2) \geq s_L(R_1, R_2).$$

(4.19)

Corollary 4.1: For all $0 \leq \varepsilon < 1$ and all $R_1 \geq H(X)$, $R_2 \geq H(Y)$

$$\sigma(\varepsilon|R_1, R_2) = D(P_{XY} \| P_{\overline{XY}}).$$

(4.20)

Proof: If $R_1 \geq H(X), R_2 \geq H(Y)$, we can set as $U \equiv X, V \equiv Y$ because $XY \in \mathcal{L}(R_1, R_2)$. Then, from (4.15) it follows that

$$s_L(R_1, R_2) = D(P_{XY} \| P_{\overline{XY}}).$$

(4.21)

The right-hand side of (4.21) is the same optimal error exponent as that in the case where data $(\boldsymbol{x}, \boldsymbol{y})$ are fully available (Stein's lemma: e.g., cf. Cover and Thomas [20]). Hence, (4.19) yields (4.20). □

As a special case of Theorem 4.2 we may consider the full side-information case ($R_2 = +\infty$). In order to describe it, define

$$\mathcal{S}(U) = \{P_{\check{U}\check{X}\check{Y}} | P_{\check{U}\check{X}} = P_{UX}, P_{\check{U}\check{Y}} = P_{UY}\}$$

(4.22)

$$s_L(R) = \max_{\substack{U \in \mathcal{L}(R) \\ \|U\| \leq |\mathcal{X}|+1}} \min_{P_{\check{U}\check{X}\check{Y}} \in \mathcal{S}(U)} D(P_{\check{U}\check{X}\check{Y}} \| P_{\overline{UXY}})$$

(4.23)

where $\mathcal{L}(R)$ is defined in (4.8) and the random variable $\overline{U}$ is uniquely specified by the condition

$$\overline{U} \rightarrow \overline{X} \rightarrow \overline{Y}, \qquad P_{\overline{U}|\overline{X}} = P_{U|X}.$$

(4.24)

Then, Theorem 4.2 yields

Corollary 4.2: For all $0 \leq \varepsilon < 1$ and all $R \geq 0$

$$\sigma(\varepsilon|R, +\infty) \geq s_L(R).$$

(4.25)

Remark 4.2: The lower bound $s_L(R)$ in (4.25) is tighter than that of Ahlswede and Csiszár [3] with full side-information ($R_2 = +\infty$). □

Remark 4.3: In the special case of testing against independence, (4.25) reduces to

$$\sigma(\varepsilon|R, +\infty) \geq \max_{\substack{U \in \mathcal{L}(R) \\ \|U\| \leq |\mathcal{X}|+1}} I(U; Y).$$

(4.26)

In view of (4.9), this means that the lower bound $s_L(R)$ is tight in this case. □

It is obvious that if we consider the case of full side-information ($R_2 = +\infty$), then Corollary 4.1 boils down to

Corollary 4.3: For all $0 \leq \varepsilon < 1$ and all $R \geq H(X)$

$$\sigma(\varepsilon|R, +\infty) = D(P_{XY} \| P_{\overline{XY}}).$$

(4.27)

□

Corollary 4.2 can be further put forth to Theorem 4.3 below as follows. All the results stated up to now in this section have been established by using those encoding schemes such that the statistic S_{HA} as in (4.18) is exactly produced at the decoder with *zero*-error probability. It is also possible, however, to consider a wider class of encoders that afford exponentially decaying *nonzero*-error probabilities. If we would incorporate this kind of wider class of encoding schemes, we need to simultaneously take into consideration the *tradeoff* aspects between two kinds of error probabilities, i.e., one due to the encoding error in specifying an acceptance region at the decoder, and the other due to the error of hypothesis testing given an acceptance region. Then, at the expense of coding error probabilities, the rates needed for effective hypothesis testing could be reduced to a considerable extent, and so it is expected that the exponent $\sigma(\varepsilon|R_1, R_2)$ could be made significantly larger. This is the basic idea underlying Theorem 4.3 below.

In order to describe Theorem 4.3, define

$$\mathcal{L}^*(R) = \{U | R \geq I(U; X|Y), U \rightarrow X \rightarrow Y\}$$

(4.28)

$$\mathcal{T}(U) = \{P_{\check{U}\check{X}\check{Y}} | P_{\check{U}\check{X}} = P_{UX}, P_{\check{Y}} = P_Y,$$

$$H(\check{U}|\check{Y}) \geq H(U|Y)\}$$

(4.29)

where $I(U; X|Y)$ is the conditional mutual information and $H(U|Y), H(\check{U}|\check{Y})$ are the conditional entropies. Furthermore, with the definitions of $\mathcal{S}(U)$ in (4.22) and $\overline{U}$ in (4.24) in mind, we define

$$\rho_1^*(U) = \min_{P_{\check{U}\check{X}\check{Y}} \in \mathcal{S}(U)} D(P_{\check{U}\check{X}\check{Y}} \| P_{\overline{UXY}})$$

(4.30)

$$\rho_2(U) = [R - I(U; X|Y)]^+$$

$$+ \min_{P_{\check{U}\check{X}\check{Y}} \in \mathcal{T}(U)} D(P_{\check{U}\check{X}\check{Y}} \| P_{\overline{UXY}})$$

(4.31)

$$\rho_2^*(U) = \begin{cases} +\infty, & \text{if } R \geq I(U; X) \\ \rho_2(U), & \text{otherwise} \end{cases}$$

(4.32)

where $[x]^+ = \max(x, 0)$. Moreover, define

$$s_L^*(R) = \max_{\substack{U \in \mathcal{L}^*(R) \\ \|U\| \leq |\mathcal{X}|+1}} \min(\rho_1^*(U), \rho_2^*(U))$$

(4.33)

then, we have

Theorem 4.3 (Han, Shimokawa, and Amari [11]): For all $0 \leq \varepsilon < 1$ and all $R \geq 0$

$$\sigma(\varepsilon|R, +\infty) \geq s_L^*(R). \qquad (4.34)$$

Remark 4.4: The exponent $\rho_1^*(U)$ is due to the error in hypothesis testing with an acceptance region identified, whereas the exponent $\rho_2^*(U)$ is due to the error in identifying the acceptance region. It is easy to see from (4.8) and (4.28) that $\mathcal{L}(R) \subset \mathcal{L}^*(R)$, and also we see from (4.30) and (4.32) that $\rho_1^*(U) \leq \rho_2^*(U)$ if $R \geq I(U; X)$. It then follows from (4.33) that

$$
\begin{aligned}
s_L^*(R) &\geq \max_{\substack{U \in \mathcal{L}(R) \\ \|U\| \leq |\mathcal{X}|+1}} \min\left(\rho_1^*(U), \rho_2^*(U)\right) \\
&= \max_{\substack{U \in \mathcal{L}(R) \\ \|U\| \leq |\mathcal{X}|+1}} \rho_1^*(U) \\
&= s_L(R)
\end{aligned}
$$

which means that the lower bound $s_L^*(R)$ in Theorem 4.3 is significantly tighter than the lower bound $s_L(R)$ in Theorem 4.2. One reason is that the constraint $R \geq I(U; X)$ is replaced here by the weaker constraint $R \geq I(U; X|Y)$. It is possible to generalize Theorem 4.3 so as to hold also in the case with general positive rates R_1, R_2. $\square$

Remark 4.5: Consider a rate R such that

$$R \geq H(X|Y) + D(P_{XY}\|P_{\overline{XY}}). \qquad (4.35)$$

Then we can set $U \equiv X$ because $X \in \mathcal{L}^*(R)$ in this case, so that we have

$$
\begin{aligned}
\rho_1^*(U) &= D(P_{XY}\|P_{\overline{XY}}) \\
\rho_2(U) &\geq D(P_{XY}\|P_{\overline{XY}})
\end{aligned}
$$

from which it follows that $s_L^*(R) \geq D(P_{XY}\|P_{\overline{XY}})$. Hence, for rates R satisfying (4.35) it is concluded that

$$\sigma(\varepsilon|R, +\infty) = D(P_{XY}\|P_{\overline{XY}}). \qquad (4.36)$$

Since $D(P_{XY}\|P_{\overline{XY}}) \leq I(X; Y)$ implies

$$H(X) \geq H(X|Y) + D(P_{XY}\|P_{\overline{XY}}) \qquad (4.37)$$

expression (4.36), with rates R in (4.35), is an improvement of Corollary 4.3, provided that $D(P_{XY}\|P_{\overline{XY}}) \leq I(X; Y)$. This case takes place when the alternative hypothesis $P_{\overline{XY}}$ is not very far from the null hypothesis P_{XY}. $\square$

V. Zero-Rate Multiterminal Hypothesis Testing

In this section let us consider the zero-rate compression case. We define the *zero-rate compression* by

$$\lim_{n \to \infty} \frac{1}{n} \log \|f_n\| = 0 \qquad (5.1)$$

$$\lim_{n \to \infty} \frac{1}{n} \log \|g_n\| = 0. \qquad (5.2)$$

Each of (5.1) and (5.2) is indicated by $R_1 = 0$ and $R_2 = 0$, respectively.

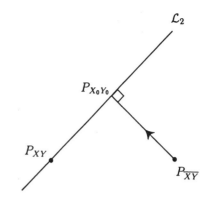

Fig. 3. Minimization: $\sigma(\varepsilon|0, R)$ for the zero-rate hypothesis testing.

First, as a special case of the zero-rate compression problem, we address the one-bit compression case. The *one-bit compression* is defined by

$$\|f_n\| = 2 \qquad (\forall n = 1, 2, \cdots) \qquad (5.3)$$

$$\|g_n\| = 2 \qquad (\forall n = 1, 2, \cdots). \qquad (5.4)$$

Each of (5.3) and (5.4) are indicated by $R_1 = 0_2$ and $R_2 = 0_2$, respectively.

Define

$$\mathcal{L}_2 = \{P_{\tilde{X}\tilde{Y}} | P_{\tilde{X}} = P_X, P_{\tilde{Y}} = P_Y\} \qquad (5.5)$$

then we have

Theorem 5.1 (Han [4]): For all $0 \leq \varepsilon < 1$

$$\sigma(\varepsilon|0_2, 0_2) \geq \min_{P_{\tilde{X}\tilde{Y}} \in \mathcal{L}_2} D(P_{\tilde{X}\tilde{Y}}\|P_{\overline{XY}}). \qquad (5.6)$$

Theorem 5.2 (Han [4]): Suppose that $D(P_{XY}\|P_{\overline{XY}}) < +\infty$ holds, then there exists some constant $0 < \varepsilon_0 \leq 1$ such that for all $0 \leq \varepsilon < \varepsilon_0$ and all $R \geq 0$

$$\sigma(\varepsilon|0_2, R) \leq \min_{P_{\tilde{X}\tilde{Y}} \in \mathcal{L}_2} D(P_{\tilde{X}\tilde{Y}}\|P_{\overline{XY}}). \qquad (5.7)$$

$\square$

Combining Theorem 5.1 with Theorem 5.2 immediately yields (Fig. 3)

Corollary 5.1: Suppose that $D(P_{XY}\|P_{\overline{XY}}) < +\infty$ holds, then there exists some constant $0 < \varepsilon_0 \leq 1$ such that for all $0 \leq \varepsilon < \varepsilon_0$ and all $R \geq 0$

$$\sigma(\varepsilon|0_2, R) = \min_{P_{\tilde{X}\tilde{Y}} \in \mathcal{L}_2} D(P_{\tilde{X}\tilde{Y}}\|P_{\overline{XY}}). \qquad (5.8)$$

Remark 5.1: Theorems 5.1 tells us that only one-bit information about the generated data $(\boldsymbol{x}, \boldsymbol{y})$ is enough to attain a positive error exponent, provided $P_X \neq P_{\overline{X}}$ or $P_Y \neq P_{\overline{Y}}$. On the other hand, Theorem 5.2 tells us that

$$\sigma(\varepsilon|0, R) = 0 \qquad (0 \leq \forall \varepsilon < \varepsilon_0, \forall R \geq 0)$$

provided that $P_X = P_{\overline{X}}$ and $P_Y = P_{\overline{Y}}$. $\square$

Shalaby and Papamarcou [6] have shown a variant with zero-rate ($R_1 = 0$) of Theorem 5.2, which is stated as follows.

Theorem 5.3 (Shalaby and Papamarcou [6]): Assume that the positivity condition

$$P_{\overline{XY}}(x, y) > 0 \quad (\forall (x, y) \in \mathcal{X} \times \mathcal{Y}) \qquad (5.9)$$

is satisfied. Then, for all $0 \le \varepsilon < 1$ and all $R \ge 0$

$$\sigma(\varepsilon|0, R) \le \min_{P_{\tilde{X}\tilde{Y}} \in \mathcal{L}_2} D(P_{\tilde{X}\tilde{Y}} \| P_{\overline{XY}}). \qquad (5.10)$$

□

Combining Theorem 5.1 with Theorem 5.3 immediately yields

Corollary 5.2: Assume that the positivity condition (5.9) is satisfied. Then, for all $0 \le \varepsilon < 1$ and all $R \ge 0$

$$\sigma(\varepsilon|0, R) = \min_{P_{\tilde{X}\tilde{Y}} \in \mathcal{L}_2} D(P_{\tilde{X}\tilde{Y}} \| P_{\overline{XY}}). \qquad (5.11)$$

Remark 5.2: The condition $D(P_{XY} \| P_{\overline{XY}}) < +\infty$ in Theorem 5.2 is replaced by the stronger condition (5.9) in Theorem 5.3, while the condition $0 \le \varepsilon < \varepsilon_0 \le 1$ in Theorem 5.2 is relaxed to $0 \le \varepsilon < 1$ in Theorem 5.3. Thus neither Theorem 5.2 nor Theorem 5.3 subsumes the other. The positivity condition (5.9) is needed in order to invoke "Blowing-up lemma" [7] in the proof of Theorem 5.3. □

We now consider the zero-rate hypothesis testing problem with the *exponential-type* constraint on the error probability α_n of the first kind as follows:

$$\liminf_{n \to \infty} \frac{1}{n} \log \frac{1}{\alpha_n} \ge r \qquad (5.12)$$

where $r > 0$ is an arbitrary fixed constant. This constraint is asymptotically equivalent to

$$\alpha_n \simeq e^{-nr}.$$

Let $\beta_n^*(r \| R_1, R_2)$ denote the minimum of the error probability β_n of the second kind over all possible encoders f_n, g_n and decoder ψ_n satisfying conditions (4.2), (4.3), and (5.12), and define the optimal *error exponent* by

$$\sigma(r \| R_1, R_2) \equiv \liminf_{n \to \infty} \frac{1}{n} \log \frac{1}{\beta_n^*(r \| R_1, R_2)}. \qquad (5.13)$$

In the sequel we will demonstrate several established results on the single-letter characterization of $\sigma(r \| R_1, R_2)$ in the zero-rate compression case. Defining

$$\mathcal{D}(r) = \{P_{\hat{X}\hat{Y}} | D(P_{\hat{X}\hat{Y}} \| P_{XY}) \le r\} \qquad (5.14)$$

$$\mathcal{H}(r) = \{P_{\tilde{X}\tilde{Y}} | P_{\tilde{X}} = P_{\hat{X}}, P_{\tilde{Y}} = P_{\hat{Y}}$$
$$\text{for some } P_{\hat{X}\hat{Y}} \in \mathcal{D}(r)\} \qquad (5.15)$$

we have the first result as follows (Fig. 4).

Theorem 5.4 (Han and Kobayashi [5]): For all $r > 0$

$$\sigma(r \| 0, 0) \ge \min_{P_{\tilde{X}\tilde{Y}} \in \mathcal{H}(r)} D(P_{\tilde{X}\tilde{Y}} \| P_{\overline{XY}}). \qquad (5.16)$$

□

The converse counterpart of Theorem 5.4 is novel, which is stated as

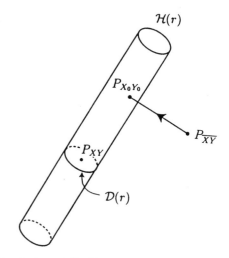

Fig. 4. Minimization: $\sigma(r \| 0, R)$ for the zero-rate hypothesis testing.

Theorem 5.5: Assume that positivity condition (5.9) is satisfied. Then, for all $r > 0$ and all $R \ge 0$

$$\sigma(r \| 0, R) \le \min_{P_{\tilde{X}\tilde{Y}} \in \mathcal{H}(r)} D(P_{\tilde{X}\tilde{Y}} \| P_{\overline{XY}}). \qquad (5.17)$$

Proof: The proof is given later in Section X. □

A consequence of Theorems 5.4 and 5.5 is

Corollary 5.3: Assume that positivity condition (5.9) is satisfied. Then, for all $r > 0$ and all $R \ge 0$

$$\sigma(r \| 0, R) = \min_{P_{\tilde{X}\tilde{Y}} \in \mathcal{H}(r)} D(P_{\tilde{X}\tilde{Y}} \| P_{\overline{XY}}). \qquad (5.18)$$

□

Let us now proceed to the one-bit compression problem. In this case, the statement of the result is a little bit complicated. Define

$$\mathcal{K}(r) = \{P_{\tilde{X}\tilde{Y}} | D(P_{\tilde{X}} \| P_X) \le r \text{ and } D(P_{\tilde{Y}} \| P_Y) \le r\} \qquad (5.19)$$

$$\mathcal{G}(\rho) = \{P_{\tilde{X}\tilde{Y}} | D(P_{\tilde{X}} \| P_{\overline{X}}) \le \rho \text{ and } D(P_{\tilde{Y}} \| P_{\overline{Y}}) \le \rho\} \qquad (5.20)$$

$$s_1(r) = \min_{P_{\tilde{X}\tilde{Y}} \in \mathcal{K}(r)} D(P_{\tilde{X}\tilde{Y}} \| P_{\overline{XY}}) \qquad (5.21)$$

$$s_2(r) = \sup \{\rho | \mathcal{G}(\rho) \cap \mathcal{D}(r) = \emptyset\} \qquad (5.22)$$

where $\mathcal{D}(r)$ is specified in (5.14). Then, we have

Theorem 5.6 (Han and Kobayashi [5]): Suppose that $D(P_{XY} \| P_{\overline{XY}}) < +\infty$ holds. Then, for all $r > 0$

$$\sigma(r \| 0_2, 0_2) = \max(s_1(r), s_2(r)). \qquad (5.23)$$

Remark 5.3: In the right-hand side of (5.23), neither

$$s_1(r) \ge s_2(r) \quad (\forall r > 0)$$

nor

$$s_1(r) \le s_2(r) \quad (\forall r > 0)$$

hold. Generally speaking, $s_1(r) > s_2(r)$ for small r and $s_1(r) < s_2(r)$ for large r (Fig. 5). □

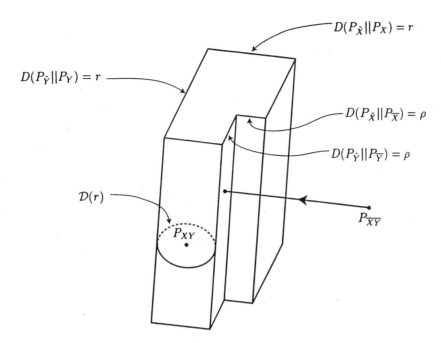

$D(P_{\tilde{Y}}\|P_Y) = r$

$D(P_{\tilde{X}}\|P_X) = r$

$D(P_{\tilde{X}}\|P_{\overline{X}}) = \rho$

$D(P_{\tilde{Y}}\|P_{\overline{Y}}) = \rho$

$\mathcal{D}(r)$

P_{XY}

$P_{\overline{XY}}$

Fig. 5. Minimization: $\sigma(r\|0_2, 0_2)$ for the one-bit hypothesis testing.

Remark 5.4: If we let $r \to 0$ in (5.23) we have

$$\lim_{r \to 0} \sigma(r\|0_2, 0_2) = \min_{P_{\tilde{X}\tilde{Y}} \in \mathcal{L}_2} D(P_{\tilde{X}\tilde{Y}}\|P_{\overline{XY}})$$

the right-hand side of which coincides with $\sigma(\varepsilon|0_2, R)$ owing to Corollary 5.1. □

VI. MULTITERMINAL PARAMETER ESTIMATION AT POSITIVE RATES

In this section we summarize some previously known results in the field of multiterminal parameter estimation with positive rates R_1, R_2.

Suppose that a family

$$\{p_\theta(x, y)\}_{\theta \in \Phi} \tag{6.1}$$

of joint distributions on $\mathcal{X} \times \mathcal{Y}$ is given, where Φ is an open subset of the r-dimensional Euclidean space and $p_\theta(x, y)$ is assumed to be a twice continuously differentiable function of $\theta = (\theta_1, \theta_2, \cdots, \theta_r) \in \Phi$.

We consider the multiterminal data compression system with universal encoders f_n, g_n and decoder ψ_n as in Section IV. As in Section I, we denote by (X_θ^n, Y_θ^n) an i.i.d. random variables of blocklength n subject to joint probability distribution p_θ $(= P_{X_\theta Y_\theta})$. Then, in general, an estimator $\hat{\theta}_n$ of the parameter θ at decoder ψ_n is written as in (1.11) of Section I, i.e.,

$$\hat{\theta}_n = \psi_n(f_n(X_\theta^n), g_n(Y_\theta^n)). \tag{6.2}$$

If the encoders f_n, g_n are satisfying rate constraints (4.2), (4.3), then the corresponding estimator $\hat{\theta}_n$ is said to be (R_1, R_2)-*achievable*. Moreover, the estimator $\hat{\theta}_n$ is said to be *asymptotically unbiased*, if

$$\lim_{n \to \infty} \mathrm{E}_\theta(\hat{\theta}_n) = \theta \qquad (\forall \theta \in \Phi). \tag{6.3}$$

The asymptotic performance of an asymptotically unbiased estimator $\hat{\theta}_n$ is measured by its covariance matrix

$$V_\theta^{(n)} \equiv \mathrm{E}_\theta[(\hat{\theta}_n - \mathrm{E}_\theta(\hat{\theta}_n))^{\mathrm{T}}(\hat{\theta}_n - \mathrm{E}_\theta(\hat{\theta}_n))] \tag{6.4}$$

where "T" denotes transpose. Since it is common that covariance $V_\theta^{(n)}$ is asymptotically proportional to the inverse of blocklength n, we define

$$V(\theta|R_1, R_2) \equiv \limsup_{n \to \infty} (nV_\theta^{(n)}) \tag{6.5}$$

which we call the *covariance index*. Any covariance index $V(\theta|R_1, R_2)$ is said to be (R_1, R_2)-*achievable* if the corresponding estimator $\hat{\theta}_n$ is asymptotically unbiased and (R_1, R_2)-achievable. It should be noted here that $V(\theta|R_1, R_2)$ depends not only on θ, R_1, R_2 but also on the sequence $\{f_n, g_n\}_{n=1}^{\infty}$ of encoders and the sequence $\{\psi_n\}_{n=1}^{\infty}$ of decoders designed so as to satisfy rate constraints (4.2) and (4.3). We want to make $V(\theta|R_1, R_2)$ as small as possible as long as rate constraints (4.2) and (4.3) are satisfied. Generally speaking, however, there does not exist a "uniformly optimal" coding scheme in the sense that $V(\theta|R_1, R_2)$ is the "minimum" for all $\theta \in \Phi$ and all $R_1 \geq 0, R_2 \geq 0$. For this reason, what matters here in general is whether a given covariance index $V(\theta|R_1, R_2)$ is (R_1, R_2)-achievable or not. This situation is in sharp contrast with that in the multiterminal hypothesis testing as treated in Sections IV and V.

Remark 6.1: If an estimator $\hat{\theta}_n$ satisfies, instead of (6.3), the stronger condition

$$\mathrm{E}_\theta(\hat{\theta}_n) = \theta + o\left(\frac{1}{\sqrt{n}}\right) \qquad (\forall \theta \in \Phi), \tag{6.6}$$

then the estimator $\hat{\theta}_n$ is said to be *strongly* asymptotically unbiased. □

265

Remark 6.2: Instead of (6.4), we may consider the mean-square error (MSE) matrix

$$\overline{V}_\theta^{(n)} \equiv \mathrm{E}_\theta[(\hat{\theta}_n - \theta)^\mathrm{T}(\hat{\theta}_n - \theta)]. \qquad (6.7)$$

It is evident that two matrices $V_\theta^{(n)}$ and $\overline{V}_\theta^{(n)}$ are connected by the relation

$$\overline{V}_\theta^{(n)} = V_\theta^{(n)} + (\theta - \mathrm{E}_\theta(\hat{\theta}_n))^\mathrm{T}(\theta - \mathrm{E}_\theta(\hat{\theta}_n)). \qquad (6.8)$$

Here, instead of (6.5), we may define the *MSE index* as follows:

$$\overline{V}(\theta|R_1, R_2) \equiv \limsup_{n \to \infty} (n\overline{V}_\theta^{(n)}). \qquad (6.9)$$

In view of (6.8), the MSE index $\overline{V}(\theta|R_1, R_2)$ is in general larger than the covariance index $V(\theta|R_1, R_2)$ in the sense $\overline{V}(\theta|R_1, R_2) - V(\theta|R_1, R_2)$ is nonnegative-definite. However, when the estimator $\hat{\theta}_n$ that we are considering is strongly asymptotically unbiased in the sense of Remark 6.1, then, by means of (6.6) and (6.8), we have

$$\overline{V}(\theta|R_1, R_2) = V(\theta|R_1, R_2) \qquad (\forall \theta \in \Phi; \forall R_1 \geq 0, R_2 \geq 0). \qquad (6.10)$$

Thus as far as we are concerned, only with strongly asymptotically unbiased estimators, we can indifferently identify $\overline{V}(\theta|R_1, R_2)$ and $V(\theta|R_1, R_2)$. □

We now state the estimator $\hat{\theta}_{ZB}$ of Zhang and Berger. They consider the one-dimensional parameter case ($r = 1$) and make a very stringent assumption that there exists a function $s: \mathcal{X} \times \mathcal{Y} \to \mathbf{R}$ (the set of real values) such that

$$\hat{s}_n(\boldsymbol{x}, \boldsymbol{y}) \equiv \frac{1}{n} \sum_{i=1}^{n} s(x_i, y_i) \qquad (6.11)$$

is an *unbiased* estimator for the parameter θ (the *additivity* condition), where $\boldsymbol{x} = (x_1, \cdots, x_n), \boldsymbol{y} = (y_1, \cdots, y_n)$. Let U_θ, V_θ be *auxiliary* random variables taking values in $\mathcal{U}, \mathcal{V}$ (arbitrary finite sets) and satisfying the following conditions:

  a) $U_\theta \to X_\theta \to Y_\theta \to V_\theta$ (Markov chain). (6.12)

  b) $P_{U_\theta|X_\theta}$ depends only on P_{X_θ} (6.13)

  $P_{V_\theta|Y_\theta}$ depends only on P_{Y_θ}. (6.14)

  c) There exists a function $t: \mathcal{U} \times \mathcal{V} \to \mathbf{R}$

  such that $E[t(U_\theta, V_\theta)|X_\theta Y_\theta] = s(X_\theta, Y_\theta)$. (6.15)

Then, we have

Theorem 6.1 (Zhang and Berger [12]): With any given rates R_1, R_2, there exists an (R_1, R_2)-achievable strongly asymptotically unbiased estimator $\hat{\theta}_{ZB}$ such that, for any $\theta \in \Phi$ satisfying the rate constraint

$$R_1 \geq I(U_\theta; X_\theta) \qquad (6.16)$$
$$R_2 \geq I(V_\theta; Y_\theta) \qquad (6.17)$$

the estimator $\hat{\theta}_{ZB}$ achieves the following variance index:

$$\begin{aligned}
V_{ZB}(\theta|R_1, R_2) = &\,\mathrm{V}(t(U_\theta, V_\theta)) + \mathrm{E}[\mathrm{E}(s(X_\theta, Y_\theta)|X_\theta)]^2 \\
&+ \mathrm{E}[\mathrm{E}(s(X_\theta, Y_\theta)|Y_\theta)]^2 \\
&- \mathrm{E}[\mathrm{E}(t(U_\theta, V_\theta)|U_\theta X_\theta)]^2 \\
&- \mathrm{E}[\mathrm{E}(t(U_\theta, V_\theta)|V_\theta Y_\theta)]^2 \qquad (6.18)
\end{aligned}$$

where "V" indicates the variance. □

Remark 6.3: Equation (6.18) can be rewritten in a more compact form (cf. Han and Amari [15]) as

$$\begin{aligned}
V_{ZB}(\theta|R_1, R_2) = &\,\mathrm{V}(t(U_\theta, V_\theta)) \\
&+ \mathrm{E}[\mathrm{E}(t(U_\theta, V_\theta)|X_\theta) - \mathrm{E}(t(U_\theta, V_\theta)|U_\theta X_\theta)]^2 \\
&+ \mathrm{E}[\mathrm{E}(t(U_\theta, V_\theta)|Y_\theta) - \mathrm{E}(t(U_\theta, V_\theta)|V_\theta Y_\theta)]^2.
\end{aligned} \qquad (6.19)$$

This expression does not contain the function $s(X_\theta, Y_\theta)$, which suggests that the role of the function $t(U_\theta, V_\theta)$ is more substantial than that of the function $s(X_\theta, Y_\theta)$. We remark that $V_{ZB}(\theta|R_1, R_2) = +\infty$ for all $\theta \in \Phi$ that does not satisfy the rate constraint (6.16) and (6.17). □

Remark 6.4: It should be noted that the stringent additivity condition (6.11) is *not* preserved under parameter transformations. Also, the right-hand side of either of (6.18) or (6.19) is of somewhat peculiar form and does not seem to provide reasonable intuitive insights into further possible developments, and so it is very likely that $V_{ZB}(\theta|R_1, R_2)$ remains to be much more improved. In fact, it is the case, as will be seen in the sequel. □

Remark 6.5: Zhang and Berger [12] have also considered the multiterminal estimation problem for correlated Gaussian sources and shown several computations of (6.18) for this case. They have also investigated, again under the additivity condition, the asymptotic performance of the modified estimator $\hat{\theta}_{ZB}^*$ that is a linear combination of the estimator $\hat{\theta}_{ZB}$ and the marginal types type$(\boldsymbol{x})$, type$(\boldsymbol{y})$. □

Next, let us proceed to the estimator of Han and Amari. We sketch a rough outline of the process to derive their estimator. First, they, like in the case of Zhang and Berger, introduce auxiliary random variables U_θ, V_θ with values in $\mathcal{U}, \mathcal{V}$, respectively, that satisfy conditions (6.12)–(6.14) alone. Then, we can write as

$$P_{U_\theta|X_\theta}(u|x) \equiv \kappa(u|x; P_{X_\theta}) \qquad (6.20)$$
$$P_{V_\theta|Y_\theta}(v|y) \equiv \omega(v|y; P_{Y_\theta}). \qquad (6.21)$$

We consider the following coding scheme. Suppose that data $(\boldsymbol{x}, \boldsymbol{y})$ was generated at sites A and B. First, denote type$(\boldsymbol{x})$, type$(\boldsymbol{y})$ by $t_{\tilde{X}}, t_{\tilde{Y}}$, respectively, and approximate $\kappa(u|x; t_{\tilde{X}}), \omega(v|y; t_{\tilde{Y}})$ by *fixed* conditional types κ_n, ω_n (cf. Csiszár and Körner [19]) so that

$$\kappa(u|x; t_{\tilde{X}}) = \kappa_n(u|x; t_{\tilde{X}}) + O\left(\frac{1}{n}\right) \qquad (6.22)$$

$$\omega(v|y; t_{\tilde{Y}}) = \omega_n(v|y; t_{\tilde{Y}}) + O\left(\frac{1}{n}\right). \qquad (6.23)$$

Let us consider a parameter $\theta \in \Phi$ that satisfies the conditions

$$R_1 \geq I(U_\theta; X_\theta|V_\theta) \qquad (6.24)$$
$$R_2 \geq I(V_\theta; Y_\theta|U_\theta) \qquad (6.25)$$
$$R_1 + R_2 \geq I(U_\theta V_\theta; X_\theta Y_\theta). \qquad (6.26)$$

Then, there exist (cf. Han and Amari [15] for the details) some *universal* encoders $f_n: \mathcal{X}^n \to \mathcal{U}^n, g_n: \mathcal{Y}^n \to \mathcal{V}^n$, under rate constraints (4.2) and (4.3), that satisfy the constraint conditions

$$\text{type}\,(\hat{\boldsymbol{u}}|\boldsymbol{x}) = \kappa_n(u|x; t_{\tilde{X}}) \qquad (6.27)$$

$$\text{type}\,(\hat{\boldsymbol{v}}|\boldsymbol{y}) = \omega_n(v|y; t_{\tilde{Y}}) \qquad (6.28)$$

with data $(\boldsymbol{x}, \boldsymbol{y})$ generated according to joint probability $p_\theta(x, y)$, where we have put $\hat{\boldsymbol{u}} = f_n(\boldsymbol{x})$, $\hat{\boldsymbol{v}} = g_n(\boldsymbol{y})$ for simplicity, and $\text{type}\,(\hat{\boldsymbol{u}}|\boldsymbol{x}), \text{type}\,(\hat{\boldsymbol{v}}|\boldsymbol{y})$ denote the conditional type of $\hat{\boldsymbol{u}}$ given $\boldsymbol{x}$ and the conditional type of $\hat{\boldsymbol{v}}$ given $\boldsymbol{y}$, respectively. In addition, the encoders f_n, g_n can also transmit to the decoder ψ_n the joint types $t_{\tilde{U}\tilde{X}} = \text{type}\,(\hat{\boldsymbol{u}}, \boldsymbol{x})$ and $t_{\tilde{V}\tilde{Y}} = \text{type}\,(\hat{\boldsymbol{v}}, \boldsymbol{y})$, respectively, with zero rates. The decoder ψ_n can compute also the joint type $t_{\tilde{U}\tilde{V}} = \text{type}\,(\hat{\boldsymbol{u}}, \hat{\boldsymbol{v}})$ in addition to $t_{\tilde{U}\tilde{X}}$ and $t_{\tilde{V}\tilde{Y}}$. Let the joint probability of the statistic $(t_{\tilde{U}\tilde{X}}, t_{\tilde{U}\tilde{V}}, t_{\tilde{V}\tilde{Y}})$ be

$$p_\theta(t_{\tilde{U}\tilde{X}}, t_{\tilde{U}\tilde{V}}, t_{\tilde{V}\tilde{Y}}) \qquad (\theta \in \Phi). \qquad (6.29)$$

The decoder can then derive the maximum-likelihood equation and thereby construct the maximum-likelihood estimator $\hat{\theta}_{HA}$ by using the formula for the probability distribution (6.29). Thus the whole problem boils down to how to compute the explicit expression for $p_\theta(t_{\tilde{U}\tilde{X}}, t_{\tilde{U}\tilde{V}}, t_{\tilde{V}\tilde{Y}})$ in (6.29), although this task is extremely complicated from the technical point of view.

In order to write down the maximum-likelihood equation, we need some preparations. First, setting

$$\mathcal{X} = \{0, 1, 2, \cdots, a\}$$
$$\mathcal{Y} = \{0, 1, 2, \cdots, b\}$$
$$\mathcal{U} = \{0, 1, 2, \cdots, c\}$$
$$\mathcal{V} = \{0, 1, 2, \cdots, d\}$$

define

$$\mathcal{X}^* = \{1, 2, \cdots, a\}$$
$$\mathcal{Y}^* = \{1, 2, \cdots, b\}$$
$$\mathcal{U}^* = \{1, 2, \cdots, c\}$$
$$\mathcal{V}^* = \{1, 2, \cdots, d\}.$$

Let us consider the joint probability distribution on $\mathcal{U} \times \mathcal{X} \times \mathcal{Y} \times \mathcal{V}$

$$p_\theta(u, x, y, v) \equiv \kappa(u|x; P_{X_\theta}) p_\theta(x, y) \omega(v|y; P_{Y_\theta}) \qquad (6.30)$$

and define its "partial" derivative $\overset{\circ}{\nabla} p_\theta$ by

$$\overset{\circ}{\nabla} p_\theta(u, x, y, v) \equiv \kappa(u|x; P_{X_\theta})(\nabla p_\theta(x, y)) \omega(v|y; P_{Y_\theta}) \qquad (6.31)$$

where "∇" denotes the derivative with respect to $\theta = (\theta_1, \cdots, \theta_r) \in \Phi$. Let the $\mathcal{X}$-marginal, the $\mathcal{Y}$-marginal, and the $(\mathcal{U} \times \mathcal{V})$-marginal of $\overset{\circ}{\nabla} p_\theta(u, x, y, v)$ be denoted by $\overset{\circ}{\nabla} p_\theta(x)$, $\overset{\circ}{\nabla} p_\theta(y)$, and $\overset{\circ}{\nabla} p_\theta(u, v)$, respectively, and put

$$\overset{\circ}{\nabla} \boldsymbol{p}_\theta = (\{\overset{\circ}{\nabla} p_\theta(x)\}_{x \in \mathcal{X}^*}, \{\overset{\circ}{\nabla} p_\theta(u, v)\}_{(u,v) \in \mathcal{U}^* \times \mathcal{V}^*},$$
$$\{\overset{\circ}{\nabla} p_\theta(y)\}_{y \in \mathcal{Y}^*}). \qquad (6.32)$$

Similarly, we define

$$\boldsymbol{p}_\theta = (\{p_\theta(x)\}_{x \in \mathcal{X}^*}, \{p_\theta(u, v)\}_{(u,v) \in \mathcal{U}^* \times \mathcal{V}^*}, \{p_\theta(y)\}_{y \in \mathcal{Y}^*}) \qquad (6.33)$$

where $p_\theta(x), p_\theta(y), p_\theta(u, v)$ are the $\mathcal{X}$-marginal, the $\mathcal{Y}$-marginal, and the $(\mathcal{U} \times \mathcal{V})$-marginal of $p_\theta(u, x, y, v)$, respectively. Furthermore, set

$$\boldsymbol{t} = (\{t_{\tilde{X}}(x)\}_{x \in \mathcal{X}^*}, \{t_{\tilde{U}\tilde{V}}(u, v)\}_{(u,v) \in \mathcal{U}^* \times \mathcal{V}^*}, \{t_{\tilde{Y}}(y)\}_{y \in \mathcal{Y}^*}). \qquad (6.34)$$

We notice that all of $\overset{\circ}{\nabla} \boldsymbol{p}_\theta, \boldsymbol{p}_\theta$, and $\boldsymbol{t}$ are $(a+b+cd)$-dimensional vectors. With these $(a+b+cd)$-dimensional (row) vectors, Han and Amari [15] have shown that the sought-after maximum-likelihood equation can be written asymptotically in the matrix form as

$$(\overset{\circ}{\nabla} \boldsymbol{p}_\theta)(H G_{\mathrm{I}} H^{\mathrm{T}})^{-1} (\boldsymbol{t} - \boldsymbol{p}_\theta)^{\mathrm{T}} = 0 \qquad (6.35)$$

where H is some (rectangular) *projection* matrix representing the structure of the asymptotic linear constraints (6.27), (6.28) due to the encoding operation (for details, see [15]); and G_{I} is a positive–definite symmetric matrix defined as follows. Set

$$\Omega_0 = \{\mathcal{X}, \mathcal{Y}, \mathcal{U}, \mathcal{V}\}. \qquad (6.36)$$

For any subset $S \subset \Omega_0$ let E_S^* denote the direct product of sets $\mathcal{X}^*, \mathcal{Y}^*, \mathcal{U}^*, \mathcal{V}^*$ over S; for example, if $S = \{\mathcal{U}, \mathcal{X}\}$ then $E_S^* = \mathcal{U}^* \times \mathcal{X}^*$, and the index $i(S)$ runs over all the elements in E_S^*. Moreover, for notational simplicity, with any subset $S \subset \Omega_0$ let us denote the E_S^*-marginal of $p_\theta(u, x, y, v)$ by $p_{S,i(S)}$. Then, for any subsets $S, T, \subset \Omega_0$, the $(i(S), j(T))$-element $g_{T,j(T)}^{S,i(S)}$ of G_{I} is defined to be

$$g_{T,j(T)}^{S,i(S)} = p_{S \cup T, i(S)j(T-S)} \delta_{i(S \cap T), j(S \cap T)} - p_{S,i(S)} p_{T,j(T)} \qquad (6.37)$$

where $\delta_{i(S \cap T), j(S \cap T)}$ is the Kronecker's delta. Here, we restrict those subsets S, T only to the elements of the index set

$$\mathcal{I}_0 \equiv \{\{\mathcal{X}\}, \{\mathcal{Y}\}, \{\mathcal{U}\}, \{\mathcal{V}\}, \{\mathcal{U}, \mathcal{X}\}, \{\mathcal{V}, \mathcal{Y}\}, \{\mathcal{U}, \mathcal{V}\}\}. \qquad (6.38)$$

Then, it can be checked that the dimension of G_{I} is

$$a + b + c + d + ac + bd + cd.$$

Finally, denoting by $\hat{\theta}_{HA}$ the estimator obtained by solving the maximum-likelihood equation (6.35), we have

Theorem 6.2 (Han and Amari [15]): With any given rates R_1, R_2, the (R_1, R_2)-achievable maximum-likelihood estimator $\hat{\theta}_{HA}$ is strongly asymptotically unbiased and, for any $\theta \in \Phi$ satisfying the rate constraint (6.24)–(6.26), the estimator $\hat{\theta}_{HA}$ achieves the following covariance index:

$$V_{HA}(\theta|R_1, R_2) = (F_\theta)^{-1} \qquad (6.39)$$

where

$$F_\theta \equiv (\overset{\circ}{\nabla} \boldsymbol{p}_\theta)(H G_{\mathrm{I}} H^{\mathrm{T}})^{-1} (\overset{\circ}{\nabla} \boldsymbol{p}_\theta)^{\mathrm{T}}. \qquad (6.40)$$

Remark 6.6: It can be checked (see [15]) that the r-dimensional matrix F_θ in (6.40) is the Fisher information index of the statistic $\boldsymbol{t}$ as defined in (6.34), where the Fisher information *index* is defined to be

$$\liminf_{n \to \infty} \frac{1}{n} F_\theta^{(n)}$$

for the Fisher information matrix $F_\theta^{(n)}$. This means that the covariance index $V_{HA}(\theta | R_1, R_2)$ is the best possible for all $\theta \in \Phi$ as far as we use only the statistic $\boldsymbol{t}$, which is guaranteed by the Cramér–Rao bound (cf. Rao [16]). □

Remark 6.7: It is obvious that the maximum-likelihood equation (6.35) has the form *invariant* under parameter transformations. Thus the form of the maximum-likelihood estimator $\hat{\theta}_{HA}$ systematically changes according to parameter transformations. □

Remark 6.8: The estimator $\hat{\theta}_{ZB}$ of Zhang and Berger [12] under the additivity condition (6.11) is constructed on the basis of partial use of the statistic $\boldsymbol{t}$, which together with Remark 6.6 ensures that the inequality

$$V_{ZB}(\theta | R_1, R_2) \geq V_{HA}(\theta | R_1, R_2)$$
$$(\forall \theta \in \Phi, \forall R_1 \geq 0, \forall R_2 \geq 0) \quad (6.41)$$

always holds when, as in [12], the dimension of the parameter θ is specialized to $r = 1$. In addition, it should be noted here that conditions (6.24)–(6.26) in the case of Han and Amari imply conditions (6.16) and (6.17) in the case of Zhang and Berger. This means that with the same rates R_1, R_2 there exists some nonempty subset Φ_0 of the parameter space Φ such that the estimator $\hat{\theta}_{HA}$ is effective (i.e., $V_{HA}(\theta | R_1, R_2) < +\infty$) for all $\theta \in \Phi_0$ while the estimator $\hat{\theta}_{ZB}$ is *not* effective (i.e., $V_{ZB}(\theta | R_1, R_2) = +\infty$) for all $\theta \in \Phi_0$. □

Remark 6.9: A geometrical interpretation of the above process of deriving the maximum-likelihood estimator $\hat{\theta}_{HA}$ is as follows (Fig. 6). Define the data space $\mathcal{L}(\boldsymbol{t})$ by

$$\mathcal{L}(\boldsymbol{t}) = \{ P_{\tilde{U} \tilde{X} \tilde{Y} \tilde{V}} | P_{\tilde{U} \tilde{X}} = t_{\tilde{U} \tilde{X}}, P_{\tilde{U} \tilde{V}} = t_{\tilde{U} \tilde{V}}, P_{\tilde{V} \tilde{Y}} = t_{\tilde{V} \tilde{Y}} \}$$
$$(6.42)$$

where $\boldsymbol{t} = (t_{\tilde{U} \tilde{X}}, t_{\tilde{U} \tilde{V}}, t_{\tilde{V} \tilde{Y}})$ is the data type observed at the decoder ψ_n. Consider to minimize the divergence $D(P_{\tilde{U} \tilde{X} \tilde{Y} \tilde{V}} \| p_\theta)$ over all $\theta \in \Phi$ and all $P_{\tilde{U} \tilde{X} \tilde{Y} \tilde{V}} \in \mathcal{L}(\boldsymbol{t})$ (*Double minimization*) and let

$$D(P_{\tilde{U}_0 \tilde{X}_0 \tilde{Y}_0 \tilde{V}_0} \| p_{\hat{\theta}}) = \min_{\theta \in \Phi} \min_{P_{\tilde{U} \tilde{X} \tilde{Y} \tilde{V}} \in \mathcal{L}(\boldsymbol{t})} D(P_{\tilde{U} \tilde{X} \tilde{Y} \tilde{V}} \| p_\theta).$$
$$(6.43)$$

Then it is possible to check by using the Taylor expansion of the divergence $D(P_{\tilde{U} \tilde{X} \tilde{Y} \tilde{V}} \| p_\theta)$ around p_θ that $\hat{\theta}_{HA} = \hat{\theta}$. This is the geometrical interpretation of the estimator $\hat{\theta}_{HA}$ (cf. Remark 8.3). □

In closing this section, we now describe the *minimax* estimator of Ahlswede and Burnashev [14]. As was mentioned

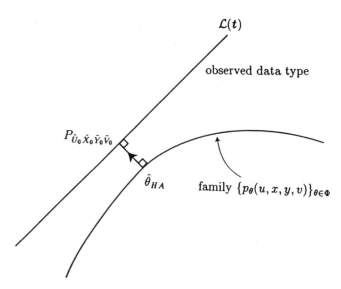

Fig. 6. Double minimization: geometrical interpretation for the estimator $\hat{\theta}_{HA}$ with positive rates.

in Section II, they have considerd the special case with one-dimensional parameter θ ($r = 1$) and full side-information ($R_1 = R, R_2 = +\infty$) such that the marginal $p_\theta(x)$ of the joint probability $p_\theta(x, y)$ is independent from the parameter θ. Here, the alphabets $\mathcal{X}$ and $\mathcal{Y}$ are not assumed to be finite. The assumption that the marginal $p_\theta(x)$ is independent from θ is made to avoid such delicate arguments on the *universal coding* as in the cases of Zhang and Berger [12] and Han and Amari [15]. Furthermore, in order to elude the subtle problem of uniform optimality, they took the minimax estimation approach. Since the marginal $p_\theta(x)$ is independent from θ, we can write XY_θ instead of $X_\theta Y_\theta$ in (6.12). Accordingly, an i.i.d. random variables (X_θ^n, Y_θ^n) of blocklength n subject to joint probability distribution p_θ ($= P_{X_\theta Y_\theta} = P_{XY_\theta}$) can be written as (X^n, Y_θ^n). Let

$$\mathcal{L}_n(R) = \{ U | nR \geq I(U; X^n), U \to X^n \to Y_\theta^n \} \quad (6.44)$$

where U denotes random variables with values in an arbitrary finite set such that the conditional distribution $P_{U|X^n}$ does *not* depend on θ. Therefore, these random variable U's do not depend on θ since X^n does not depend on θ. Denoting by $F_\theta(UY_\theta^n)$ the Fisher information of UY_θ^n, define

$$J_n(R) = \sup_{U \in \mathcal{L}_n(R)} \inf_{\theta \in \Phi} \frac{1}{n} F_\theta(UY_\theta^{n'}) \quad (6.45)$$

$$J(R) = \lim_{n \to \infty} J_n(R). \quad (6.46)$$

We call this $J(R)$ the *maxmin Fisher information index*. With these definitions, Ahlswede and Burnashev have shown the following theorem under some regularity conditions, which gives the *limiting* (*not* single-letterized) formula for the *optimal minimax variance index*.

Theorem 6.3 (Ahlswede and Burnashev [14]):

1) For any $(R, +\infty)$-achievable strongly asymptotically unbiased estimator $\hat{\theta}_n$

$$\liminf_{n \to \infty} \sup_{\theta \in \Phi} n E_\theta(\hat{\theta}_n - \theta)^2 \geq \frac{1}{J(R)} \quad (\forall R \geq 0). \quad (6.47)$$

2) There exists an $(R, +\infty)$-achievable strongly asymptotically unbiased estimator $\hat{\theta}_{AB}$ such that

$$\limsup_{n \to \infty} \sup_{\theta \in \Phi} n\mathrm{E}_\theta(\hat{\theta}_{AB} - \theta)^2 \le \frac{1}{J(R)} \quad (\forall R \ge 0). \quad (6.48)$$

Remark 6.10: Although Theorem 6.3 shows that the inverse of $J(R)$ gives the optimal minimax variance index, it is very hard to compute the values of $J(R)$ as a function of R. For this reason, Ahlswede and Burnashev [14] have defined, instead of (6.45), another type of Fisher information, say, the "minimax" Fisher information as follows:

$$J^n(R) = \inf_{\theta \in \Phi} \sup_{U \in \mathcal{L}_n(R)} \frac{1}{n} F_\theta(U Y_\theta^n) \quad (6.49)$$

and claimed the validity of the following important "local single-letterization" (cf. [14, Lemma 4]):

$$J^n(R) = J^1(R) \quad \text{for all } R \ge 0 \text{ and } n = 1, 2, \cdots. \quad (6.50)$$

This result was used by them to provide single-letterized upper bounds on $J(R)$. Unfortunately, however, the proof of (6.50) does not seem to be free of serious technical flaws. (Notice that U in $\mathcal{L}_n(R)$ must *not* depend on θ!), and so we believe that $J^n(R)$ does not single-letterize in general. $\square$

VII. Zero-Rate Multiterminal Parameter Estimation

In this section we describe the zero-rate estimator $\hat{\theta}_A$ of Amari [13]. The derivation of this estimator is along the same line as the one shown in the latter part of Section VI to derive the estimator $\hat{\theta}_{HA}$. Although the arguments adopted in Section VI were indeed involved and subtle, the arguments to be shown below are much simpler, because the auxiliary random variables U_θ, V_θ do not intervene here. We remark here that, historically, the estimator $\hat{\theta}_A$ was first derived and was then generalized to the estimator $\hat{\theta}_{HA}$.

First, consider the rate constraints

$$\|f_n\| \le (n+1)^{|\mathcal{X}|} \quad (\forall n = 1, 2, \cdots) \quad (7.1)$$
$$\|g_n\| \le (n+1)^{|\mathcal{Y}|} \quad (\forall n = 1, 2, \cdots) \quad (7.2)$$

which means the zero-rate data compression

$$\lim_{n \to \infty} \frac{1}{n} \log \|f_n\| = 0 \quad (7.3)$$

$$\lim_{n \to \infty} \frac{1}{n} \log \|g_n\| = 0. \quad (7.4)$$

Under rate constraints (7.1) and (7.2), we can define encoders f_n, g_n by

$$f_n(\boldsymbol{x}) = t_{\tilde{X}} \quad (\boldsymbol{x} \in \mathcal{X}^n) \quad (7.5)$$
$$g_n(\boldsymbol{y}) = t_{\tilde{Y}} \quad (\boldsymbol{y} \in \mathcal{Y}^n) \quad (7.6)$$

where $t_{\tilde{X}} = \text{type}\,(\boldsymbol{x})$ and $t_{\tilde{Y}} = \text{type}\,(\boldsymbol{y})$. Also, the encoding scheme given by (7.5) and (7.6) is *universal*. Let the joint probability of the statistic $(t_{\tilde{X}}, t_{\tilde{Y}})$ be denoted by

$$p_\theta(t_{\tilde{X}}, t_{\tilde{Y}}) \quad (\theta \in \Phi). \quad (7.7)$$

The decoder can then derive the maximum-likelihood equation and thereby construct the maximum-likelihood estimator $\hat{\theta}_A$

by using the formula for the probability distribution (7.7). In order to describe this maximum-likelihood equation, set, as in Section VI,

$$\mathcal{X} = \{0, 1, 2, \cdots, a\}$$
$$\mathcal{Y} = \{0, 1, 2, \cdots, b\}$$

and define

$$\mathcal{X}^* = \{1, 2, \cdots, a\}$$
$$\mathcal{Y}^* = \{1, 2, \cdots, b\}$$
$$\mathcal{I}_0 = \{\{\mathcal{X}\}, \{\mathcal{Y}\}\}. \quad (7.8)$$

Furthermore, given a family

$$\{p_\theta(x, y)\}_{\theta \in \Phi} \quad (7.9)$$

of joint distributions, we define the following $(a + b)$-dimensional (row) vectors:

$$\boldsymbol{p}_\theta = (\{p_\theta(x)\}_{x \in \mathcal{X}^*}, \{p_\theta(y)\}_{y \in \mathcal{Y}^*}) \quad (7.10)$$
$$\nabla\boldsymbol{p}_\theta = (\{\nabla p_\theta(x)\}_{x \in \mathcal{X}^*}, \{\nabla p_\theta(y)\}_{y \in \mathcal{Y}^*}) \quad (7.11)$$
$$\boldsymbol{t} = (\{t_{\tilde{X}}(x)\}_{x \in \mathcal{X}^*}, \{t_{\tilde{Y}}(y)\}_{y \in \mathcal{Y}^*}) \quad (7.12)$$

where $p_\theta(x), p_\theta(y)$ denote the $\mathcal{X}$-marginal and the $\mathcal{Y}$-marginal of $p_\theta(x, y)$, respectively, and "∇" denotes the derivative with respect to the parameter $\theta = (\theta_1, \cdots, \theta_r) \in \Phi$.

Amari [13] has shown by a simple calculation that the maximum-likelihood equation can be written asymptotically as

$$(\nabla\boldsymbol{p}_\theta) G_\mathrm{I}^{-1} (\boldsymbol{t} - \boldsymbol{p}_\theta)^\mathrm{T} = 0 \quad (7.13)$$

where G_I is the $(a + b)$-dimensional positive–definite symmetric matrix whose $(i(S), j(T))$-element $g_{T,j(T)}^{S,i(S)}$ is defined as in (6.37) with $\mathcal{I}_0$ of (7.8) in place of $\mathcal{I}_0$ of (6.38). More specifically

$$g_{\mathcal{X},x'}^{\mathcal{X},x} = p_\theta(x)\delta_{x,x'} - p_\theta(x)p_\theta(x') \quad (x, x' \in \mathcal{X}^*) \quad (7.14)$$
$$g_{\mathcal{Y},y'}^{\mathcal{Y},y} = p_\theta(y)\delta_{y,y'} - p_\theta(y)p_\theta(y') \quad (y, y' \in \mathcal{Y}^*) \quad (7.15)$$
$$g_{\mathcal{Y},y}^{\mathcal{X},x} = p_\theta(x, y) - p_\theta(x)p_\theta(y) \quad (x \in \mathcal{X}^*, y \in \mathcal{Y}^*). \quad (7.16)$$

Then, denoting by $\hat{\theta}_A$ the estimator obtained by solving the maximum-likelihood equation (7.13), we have

Theorem 7.1 (Amari [13]): The zero-rate maximum-likelihood estimator $\hat{\theta}_A$ is strongly asymptotically unbiased and for all $\theta \in \Phi$ it achieves the following covariance index:

$$V_A(\theta|0, 0) = (F_\theta)^{-1} \quad (\forall \theta \in \Phi) \quad (7.17)$$

where

$$F_\theta = (\nabla\boldsymbol{p}_\theta) G_\mathrm{I}^{-1} (\nabla\boldsymbol{p}_\theta)^\mathrm{T}. \quad (7.18)$$

Remark 7.1: It is not difficult to check (see [13]) that the r-dimensional matrix F_θ in (7.18) is the Fisher information index of the statistic $\boldsymbol{t}$ as defined in (7.12). $\square$

Remark 7.2: It is easy to check that the maximum-likelihood equation (7.13) coincides with that in (6.35) with the auxiliary random variables U_θ, V_θ set to a constant variable, i.e., $\mathcal{U}^* = \mathcal{V}^* = \emptyset$ and with the projection matrix H set to the unity. Accordingly, the estimator $\hat{\theta}_{HA}$ reduces to the estimator $\hat{\theta}_A$. It should be noticed, however, that the process of deriving $\hat{\theta}_{HA}$ with positive rates R_1, R_2 was extremely complicated (cf. Han and Amari [15]) mainly because there they had to ingeniously elaborate a *type-preserving* universal coding scheme (along with the corresponding *projection* matrix H) by introducing auxiliary random variables U_θ, V_θ, whereas here in the zero-rate case no such is needed, as may be seen from (7.5) and (7.6). $\square$

Remark 7.3: If neither $p_\theta(x)$ nor $p_\theta(y)$ depends on θ, then we have $V_A(\theta|0,0) = +\infty$ ($\forall \theta \in \Phi$). This observation corresponds to Remark 5.1 for the zero-rate hypothesis testing. $\square$

In contrast with the estimator $\hat{\theta}_{HA}$, the zero-rate estimator $\hat{\theta}_A$ can be shown to be always "optimal," although this optimality problem had been left open for a long time. This converse counterpart of Theorem 7.1 is novel, and stated as

Theorem 7.2: Suppose that the positivity condition

$$p_\theta(x,y) > 0 \qquad (\forall \theta \in \Phi, \forall (x,y) \in \mathcal{X} \times \mathcal{Y}) \qquad (7.19)$$

is satisfied. Then, any $(0,R)$-achievable covariance index $V(\theta|0,R)$ satisfies the inequality

$$V(\theta|0,R) \geq (F_\theta)^{-1} \qquad (\forall \theta \in \Phi, \forall R \geq 0) \qquad (7.20)$$

where F_θ is the Fisher information index as in (7.18) and inequality "$A \geq B$" between matrices means that $A - B$ is nonnegative–definite.

Proof: The proof, given later in Section XI, takes a large deviation approach combined with the converse theorem for the zero-rate hypothesis testing. $\square$

Remark 7.4: Inequality (7.20) is a multiterminal version of Cramér–Rao bound, and Theorem 7.1 tells us that this bound can actually be attained by the simple estimator $\hat{\theta}_A$. An immediate consequence of Theorem 7.2 is that the estimator $\hat{\theta}_A$ is "uniformly most powerful" under zero-rate data compression, because $\hat{\theta}_A$ attains the covariance index $(F_\theta)^{-1}$. $\square$

Remark 7.5: Theorems 7.1 and 7.2 for the zero-rate parameter estimation are in nice correspondence to Theorems 5.4 and 5.5 for the zero-rate hypothesis testing, respectively. $\square$

Example 7.1: Consider the zero-rate compression estimation ($R_1 = 0, R_2 = 0$) for the binary source with $\mathcal{X} = \mathcal{Y} = \{0,1\}$ where $p_\theta(x,y)(r=1)$ is given by

$$p_\theta(1,1) = \frac{1}{4} + \theta, \quad p_\theta(1,0) = \frac{1}{4} - \theta \qquad (7.21)$$

$$p_\theta(0,1) = \frac{1}{4} + 2\theta, \quad p_\theta(0,0) = \frac{1}{4} - 2\theta. \qquad (7.22)$$

Then, we have

$$p_{\mathcal{X},\theta}(0) = p_{\mathcal{X},\theta}(1) = \frac{1}{2} \qquad (7.23)$$

$$p_{\mathcal{Y},\theta}(0) = \frac{1}{2} + \theta \qquad p_{\mathcal{Y},\theta}(1) = \frac{1}{2} - \theta \qquad (7.24)$$

where $p_{\mathcal{X},\theta}(x), p_{\mathcal{Y},\theta}(y)$ denote the $\mathcal{X}$-marginal and the $\mathcal{Y}$-marginal of $p_\theta(x,y)$, respectively. Clearly, $t_{\tilde{X}} = \text{type}(\boldsymbol{x})$ alone does not provide any information about θ, because the $\mathcal{X}$-marginal $p_{\mathcal{X},\theta}$ is independent from θ. Therefore, we may think of an estimator $\hat{\theta}_{\mathcal{Y}}$ using only the $\mathcal{Y}$-marginal type $t_{\tilde{Y}} = \text{type}(\boldsymbol{y})$; for example, $\hat{\theta}_{\mathcal{Y}} = \frac{1}{2} t_{\tilde{Y}}(1)$ which is unbiased with variance

$$V(\hat{\theta}_{\mathcal{Y}}) = \frac{1}{n}\left(\frac{1}{4} - \theta^2\right). \qquad (7.25)$$

On the other hand, the maximum-likelihood estimator $\hat{\theta}_A$ using both of $t_{\tilde{X}}$ and $t_{\tilde{Y}}$ is constructed in terms of $\boldsymbol{t} = (t_{\tilde{X}}(1), t_{\tilde{Y}}(1))$ as follows. The covariance G_{I} in this case is given by

$$G_{\mathrm{I}} = \begin{array}{c} \\ \mathcal{X} \\ \mathcal{Y} \end{array} \begin{array}{c} \mathcal{X} \qquad\qquad \mathcal{Y} \\ \left[\begin{array}{c|c} 1/4 & (3/2)\theta \\ \hline (3/2)\theta & 1/4 - \theta^2 \end{array}\right] \end{array}. \qquad (7.26)$$

Hence,

$$G_{\mathrm{I}}^{-1} = \frac{1}{a}\left[\begin{array}{c|c} 1/4 - \theta^2 & -(3/2)\theta \\ \hline -(3/2)\theta & 1/4 \end{array}\right] \qquad (7.27)$$

where $a = (1/4)(1/4 - \theta^2) - (9/4)\theta^2$, which is positive for $-1/8 \leq \theta \leq 1/8$. The maximum-likelihood equation (7.13) turns out to be

$$[0,-1]G_{\mathrm{I}}^{-1}\left[\begin{array}{c} t_{\tilde{X}}(1) - 1/2 \\ t_{\tilde{Y}}(1) - (1/2 - \theta) \end{array}\right] = 0. \qquad (7.28)$$

By solving this equation, we have the estimator

$$\hat{\theta}_A = \frac{t_{\tilde{Y}}(1) - 1/2}{2(3t_{\tilde{X}}(1) - 2)}. \qquad (7.29)$$

This is nonlinear in $t_{\tilde{X}}(1)$ and $t_{\tilde{Y}}(1)$. The variance of $\hat{\theta}_A$ is

$$V(\hat{\theta}_A) \simeq \frac{1}{n}\left(\frac{1}{4} - 10\theta^2\right). \qquad (7.30)$$

Obviously, this value is smaller by $9\theta^2/n$ than the variance of $V(\hat{\theta}_{\mathcal{Y}})$ in (7.25). Therefore, $9\theta^2/n$ is the amount of statistical information contributed by the *ancillary* statistic $t_{\tilde{X}}(1)$. The variance (7.30) is optimal under the zero-rate compression, owing to Theorem 7.2. $\square$

Remark 7.6: The same geometrical observation as in Remark 6.9 for the case with positive rates R_1, R_2 continues to be valid also here in the zero-rate case only if we set $\mathcal{U} = \mathcal{V} = \{0\}$. In this case, $\mathcal{L}(\boldsymbol{t})$ in (6.42) reduces to

$$\mathcal{L}(\boldsymbol{t}) = \{P_{\tilde{X}\tilde{Y}}|P_{\tilde{X}} = t_{\tilde{X}}, P_{\tilde{Y}} = t_{\tilde{Y}}\} \qquad (7.31)$$

with $\boldsymbol{t} = (t_{\tilde{X}}, t_{\tilde{Y}})$, whereas (6.43) reduces to the double minimization

$$D(P_{\tilde{X}_0\tilde{Y}_0}||p_{\hat{\theta}}) = \min_{\theta \in \Phi} \min_{P_{\tilde{X}\tilde{Y}} \in \mathcal{L}(\boldsymbol{t})} D(P_{\tilde{X}\tilde{Y}}||p_\theta) \qquad (7.32)$$

with $\hat{\theta}_A = \hat{\theta}$ (cf. Remark 8.3). $\square$

VIII. Information-Geometrical Considerations

So far we have demonstrated that, in the multiterminal hypothesis testing, the pertinent problems of minimizing divergences under certain constraints played a key role in establishing single-letter characterizations for (lower bounds on) the optimal error exponents $\sigma(\varepsilon|R_1, R_2), \sigma(r\|R_1, R_2)$. Similarly, we have noticed in Remark 6.9 that also in the multiterminal parameter estimation the same kind of minimization problems intervene in establishing single-letter characterizations for (upper bounds on) the optimal covariance index $V(\theta|R_1, R_2)$.

In this section, we will give some information-geometrical interpretations for these minimization problems (for the general exposition, see Amari and Han [9]; for the general framework of information geometry in terms of diffential geometry, see Amari [22] and Amari and Nagaoka [23]). Let us suppose that we are given a joint probability distribution $P = (p(x, y))$ on $\mathcal{X} \times \mathcal{Y}$, where

$$\mathcal{X} = \{0, 1, 2, \cdots, a\} \tag{8.1}$$
$$\mathcal{Y} = \{0, 1, 2, \cdots, b\}. \tag{8.2}$$

The distribution P is uniquely specified by giving the values of $p(x, y)$ for all $(x, y) \in \mathcal{X} \times \mathcal{Y}$ such that $(x, y) \neq (0, 0)$. However, in the multiterminal systems it is sometimes more convenient to use other kinds of coordinate systems in order to specify these joint distributions.

We first define the *m-coordinates* η of P by

$$\eta = (\{\eta_{\mathcal{X}}(x)\}_{x \in \mathcal{X}^*}, \{\eta_{\mathcal{Y}}(y)\}_{y \in \mathcal{Y}^*}, \{\eta_{\mathcal{X}\mathcal{Y}}(x, y)\}_{x \in \mathcal{X}^*, y \in \mathcal{Y}^*}) \tag{8.3}$$

where

$$\mathcal{X}^* = \{1, 2, \cdots, a\} \tag{8.4}$$
$$\mathcal{Y}^* = \{1, 2, \cdots, b\} \tag{8.5}$$

and

$$\eta_{\mathcal{X}}(x) = \sum_{y \in \mathcal{Y}} p(x, y) \quad (x \in \mathcal{X}^*) \tag{8.6}$$

$$\eta_{\mathcal{Y}}(y) = \sum_{x \in \mathcal{X}} p(x, y) \quad (y \in \mathcal{Y}^*) \tag{8.7}$$

$$\eta_{\mathcal{X}\mathcal{Y}}(x, y) = p(x, y) \quad ((x, y) \in \mathcal{X}^* \times \mathcal{Y}^*). \tag{8.8}$$

Using these m-coordinates η we can uniquely specify the distribution $P = (p(x, y))$ as

$$p(0, 0) = 1 - \sum_{x \in \mathcal{X}^*} \eta_{\mathcal{X}}(x) - \sum_{y \in \mathcal{Y}^*} \eta_{\mathcal{Y}}(y)$$
$$+ \sum_{x \in \mathcal{X}^*, y \in \mathcal{Y}^*} \eta_{\mathcal{X}\mathcal{Y}}(x, y) \tag{8.9}$$

$$p(x, 0) = \eta_{\mathcal{X}}(x) - \sum_{y \in \mathcal{Y}^*} \eta_{\mathcal{X}\mathcal{Y}}(x, y) \quad (x \in \mathcal{X}^*) \tag{8.10}$$

$$p(0, y) = \eta_{\mathcal{Y}}(y) - \sum_{x \in \mathcal{X}^*} \eta_{\mathcal{X}\mathcal{Y}}(x, y) \quad (y \in \mathcal{Y}^*) \tag{8.11}$$

$$p(x, y) = \eta_{\mathcal{X}\mathcal{Y}}(x, y) \quad ((x, y) \in \mathcal{X}^* \times \mathcal{Y}^*). \tag{8.12}$$

Let us next define the *e-coordinates* of P by

$$\lambda = (\{\lambda_{\mathcal{X}}(x)\}_{x \in \mathcal{X}^*}, \{\lambda_{\mathcal{Y}}(y)\}_{y \in \mathcal{Y}^*}, \{\lambda_{\mathcal{X}\mathcal{Y}}(x, y)\}_{x \in \mathcal{X}^*, y \in \mathcal{Y}^*}) \tag{8.13}$$

where

$$\lambda_{\mathcal{X}}(x) = \log \frac{p(x, 0)}{p(0, 0)} \quad (x \in \mathcal{X}^*) \tag{8.14}$$

$$\lambda_{\mathcal{Y}}(y) = \log \frac{p(0, y)}{p(0, 0)} \quad (y \in \mathcal{Y}^*) \tag{8.15}$$

$$\lambda_{\mathcal{X}\mathcal{Y}}(x, y) = \log \frac{p(x, y)p(0, 0)}{p(x, 0)p(0, y)} \quad ((x, y) \in \mathcal{X}^* \times \mathcal{Y}^*). \tag{8.16}$$

Using these e-coordinates λ we can uniquely specify the distribution $P = (p(x, y))$ as

$$p(0, 0) = \left(1 + \sum_{x \in \mathcal{X}^*} \exp\left[\lambda_{\mathcal{X}}(x)\right] + \sum_{y \in \mathcal{Y}^*} \exp\left[\lambda_{\mathcal{Y}}(y)\right] \right.$$
$$+ \sum_{x \in \mathcal{X}^*, y \in \mathcal{Y}^*} \exp\left[\lambda_{\mathcal{X}}(x) + \lambda_{\mathcal{Y}}(y) \right.$$
$$\left. + \lambda_{\mathcal{X}\mathcal{Y}}(x, y)\right]\right)^{-1} \tag{8.17}$$

$$p(x, 0) = p(0, 0)\exp\left[\lambda_{\mathcal{X}}(x)\right] \quad (x \in \mathcal{X}^*) \tag{8.18}$$
$$p(0, y) = p(0, 0)\exp\left[\lambda_{\mathcal{Y}}(y)\right] \quad (y \in \mathcal{Y}^*) \tag{8.19}$$
$$p(x, y) = p(0, 0)\exp\left[\lambda_{\mathcal{X}}(x) + \lambda_{\mathcal{Y}}(y) + \lambda_{\mathcal{X}\mathcal{Y}}(x, y)\right]$$
$$((x, y) \in \mathcal{X}^* \times \mathcal{Y}^*). \tag{8.20}$$

We now consider decomposing each of these coordinates into two parts as follows:

$$\eta = (\eta_{\mathrm{I}}, \eta_{\mathrm{II}}) \tag{8.21}$$
$$\lambda = (\lambda_{\mathrm{I}}, \lambda_{\mathrm{II}}) \tag{8.22}$$

where

$$\eta_{\mathrm{I}} = (\{\eta_{\mathcal{X}}(x)\}_{x \in \mathcal{X}^*}, \{\eta_{\mathcal{Y}}(y)\}_{y \in \mathcal{Y}^*}) \tag{8.23}$$
$$\eta_{\mathrm{II}} = (\{\eta_{\mathcal{X}\mathcal{Y}}(x, y)\}_{x \in \mathcal{X}^*, y \in \mathcal{Y}^*}) \tag{8.24}$$

$$\lambda_{\mathrm{I}} = (\{\lambda_{\mathcal{X}}(x)\}_{x \in \mathcal{X}^*}, \{\lambda_{\mathcal{Y}}(y)\}_{y \in \mathcal{Y}^*}) \tag{8.25}$$
$$\lambda_{\mathrm{II}} = (\{\lambda_{\mathcal{X}\mathcal{Y}}(x, y)\}_{x \in \mathcal{X}^*, y \in \mathcal{Y}^*}). \tag{8.26}$$

With these decompostions, we can use the first part η_{I} of η and the second part λ_{II} of λ to specify P. We will call $(\eta_{\mathrm{I}}, \lambda_{\mathrm{II}})$ the *mixed coordinates* of the distribution P. A great advantage of the mixed coordinate system is the following theorem concerning the minimization of divergences under certain constraints. Denote the mixed coordinates of two joint distributions $P, \overline{P}$ on $\mathcal{X} \times \mathcal{Y}$ by $P = (\eta_{\mathrm{I}}, \lambda_{\mathrm{II}})$ and $\overline{P} = (\overline{\eta}_{\mathrm{I}}, \overline{\lambda}_{\mathrm{II}})$, respectively. Given an $\eta_{\mathrm{I}} = \eta_{\mathrm{I}}(P)$ define the set $\mathcal{L}_P$ of joint distributions on $\mathcal{X} \times \mathcal{Y}$ by

$$\mathcal{L}_P = \{\tilde{P} = (\tilde{\eta}_{\mathrm{I}}, \tilde{\lambda}_{\mathrm{II}})|\tilde{\eta}_{\mathrm{I}} = \eta_{\mathrm{I}}\}. \tag{8.27}$$

Moreover, define the joint distribution $P^{(0)}$ on $\mathcal{X} \times \mathcal{Y}$ by

$$D(P^{(0)}\|\overline{P}) = \min_{\tilde{P} \in \mathcal{L}_P} D(\tilde{P}\|\overline{P}). \tag{8.28}$$

Then we have.

271

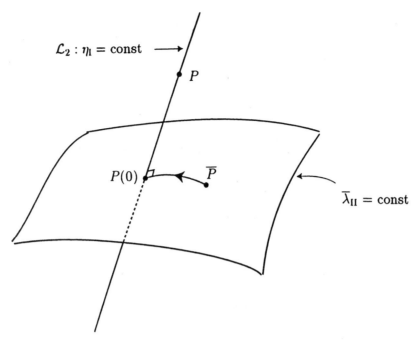

$\mathcal{L}_2 : \eta_{\mathrm{I}} = \mathrm{const} \longrightarrow$

P

$P(0)$

$\overline{P}$

$\overline{\lambda}_{\mathrm{II}} = \mathrm{const}$

Fig. 7. Pythagorean theorem: geometrical interpretation for the zero-rate hypothesis testing.

Theorem 8.1 (Pythagorean Theorem: Amari and Han [9]):

$$D(P||\overline{P}) = D(P^{(0)}||\overline{P}) + D(P||P^{(0)}) \qquad (8.29)$$

where the mixed coordinates of $P^{(0)}$ are given by $P^{(0)} = (\eta_{\mathrm{I}}, \overline{\lambda}_{\mathrm{II}})$. □

Remark 8.1: If we set $P = P_{XY}$, then the set $\mathcal{L}_P$ is actually the same one as $\mathcal{L}_2$ defined by (5.5) in Section V, and the minimization (8.28) is the same one as that on the right-hand side of (5.6) in Theorem 5.1 for the zero-rate multiterminal hypothesis testing. From the information-geometrical point of view, this set $\mathcal{L}_P$ consists of the probability distributions having the same marginals specified by $\eta_{\mathrm{I}}(P)$ and contains P. This set $\mathcal{L}_P$ is m-flat in the sense that linear mixtures of $P_1, P_2 \in \mathcal{L}_P$ again belong to $\mathcal{L}_P$. We may call $\mathcal{L}_P$ the m-fiber on P. The set $\mathcal{P}$ of all the probability distributions on $\mathcal{X} \times \mathcal{Y}$ is decomposed in the union of all m-fibers, $\cup \mathcal{L}_P$, where product distributions may be taken as representatives of $\mathcal{L}_P$. This is a foliation of $\mathcal{P}$. On the other hand, given a $\overline{P}$, we can construct the set, by using $\overline{\lambda}_{\mathrm{II}} = \lambda_{\mathrm{II}}(\overline{P})$

$$S_{\overline{P}} = \{ \tilde{P} = (\tilde{\eta}_{\mathrm{I}}, \tilde{\lambda}_{\mathrm{II}}) | \tilde{\lambda}_{\mathrm{II}} = \overline{\lambda}_{\mathrm{II}} \}. \qquad (8.30)$$

This set is *e-flat*, which contains $\overline{P}$, in the sense that $S_{\overline{P}}$ is closed under the operation of connecting its elements by an exponential family. We may call $S_{\overline{P}}$ the *e*-fiber on $\overline{P}$. The union of all *e*-fibers, $\cup S_{\overline{P}}$, define another foliation of $\mathcal{P}$. The two foliations are orthogonal to each other in the sense that two sets $\mathcal{L}_P$ and $S_{\overline{P}}$ are mutually orthogonal with the Fisher information matrix as the metric (Amari [13]; see Fig. 7). □

Let us now consider the differential counterpart of Theorem 8.1. Let $d\eta$, $d\lambda$ be the row vectors representing the differentials of the m-coordinates and the e-coordinates, respectively, and denote the differential of the joint distribution P by $dP = (d\eta) = (d\lambda)$. Then, by direct calculation, we can easily check the validity of the following Lemma.

Lemma 8.1 (Amari [13], Han and Amari [15]):

$$d\eta = (d\lambda)G \qquad (8.31)$$

$$D(P||P + dP) = \frac{1}{2}(d\lambda)G(d\lambda)^{\mathrm{T}} \qquad (8.32)$$

$$= \frac{1}{2}(d\eta)G^{-1}(d\eta)^{\mathrm{T}} \qquad (8.33)$$

where G is the $(a + b + ab)$-dimensional positive-definite symmetric matrix as specified by (6.37) with the index set

$$\mathcal{I} = \{\{\mathcal{X}\}, \{\mathcal{Y}\}, \{\mathcal{X}, \mathcal{Y}\}\} \qquad (8.34)$$

in place of the index set $\mathcal{I}_0$ of (6.38). □

It is also possible to describe Theorem 8.1 in terms of the mixed coordinates. To this end, partition the matrix G as

$$G \equiv \begin{array}{c} \\ \mathrm{I} \\ \mathrm{II} \end{array} \begin{array}{cc} \mathrm{I} & \mathrm{II} \\ \begin{bmatrix} G_{\mathrm{I}} & G_{\mathrm{III}} \\ G_{\mathrm{III}}^{\mathrm{T}} & G_{\mathrm{II}} \end{bmatrix} \end{array} \qquad (8.35)$$

then a simple direct calculation using (8.31) and (8.32) immediately yields the following lemma which demonstrates that $D(P||P + dP)$ can actually be decomposed into two parts; one is the quadratic form of $d\eta_{\mathrm{I}}$ and the other is the quadratic form of $d\lambda_{\mathrm{II}}$.

Lemma 8.2 (Differential Pythagorean Theorem: Amari [13]):

$$D(P||P + dP) = \frac{1}{2}(d\eta_{\mathrm{I}})G_{\mathrm{I}}^{-1}(d\eta_{\mathrm{I}})^{\mathrm{T}} + \frac{1}{2}(d\lambda_{\mathrm{II}})(G_{\mathrm{II}} - G_{\mathrm{III}}G_{\mathrm{I}}^{-1}G_{\mathrm{I}}^{\mathrm{T}}G_{\mathrm{III}}^{\mathrm{T}})(d\lambda_{\mathrm{II}})^{\mathrm{T}}. \qquad (8.36)$$

Remark 8.2: The two quantities on the right-hand side of (8.36) correspond to $D(P^{(0)}||\overline{P})$ and $D(P||P^{(0)})$ on the right-hand side of (8.29), respectively. The positive–definite submatrix G_{I} on the right-hand side of (8.36) is the same as

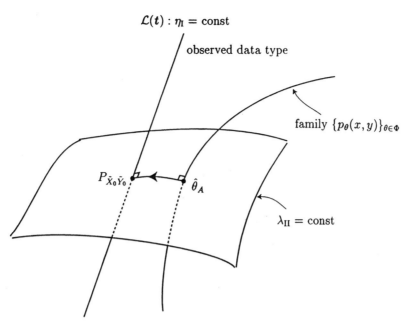

$$\mathcal{L}(t) : \eta_{\mathrm{I}} = \text{const}$$

observed data type

family $\{p_\theta(x, y)\}_{\theta \in \Phi}$

$P_{\tilde{X}_0 \tilde{Y}_0}$ $\hat{\theta}_A$

$\lambda_{\mathrm{II}} = \text{const}$

Fig. 8. Double minimization: geometrical interpretation for the zero-rate estimator $\hat{\theta}_A$.

that defined in Section VII whose dimension is $a + b$. Also, some linear algebra shows that the ab-dimensional matrix

$$D_{\mathrm{II}} \equiv G_{\mathrm{II}} - G_{\mathrm{III}} G_{\mathrm{I}}^{-1} G_{\mathrm{III}}^{\mathrm{T}} \qquad (8.37)$$

on the right-hand side of (8.36) is the inverse of the submatrix K_{II} of

$$
G^{-1} \equiv
\begin{array}{c@{}c}
 & \begin{array}{cc} \mathrm{I} & \mathrm{II} \end{array} \\
\begin{array}{c} \mathrm{I} \\ \mathrm{II} \end{array} &
\left[\begin{array}{cc} K_{\mathrm{I}} & K_{\mathrm{III}} \\ K_{\mathrm{III}}^{\mathrm{T}} & K_{\mathrm{II}} \end{array} \right]
\end{array}
\qquad (8.38)
$$

and hence it is also positive-definite. $\qquad \square$

Now, think of the case where P and $\overline{P}$ are very close to one another with

$$P = (\eta_{\mathrm{I}}, \lambda_{\mathrm{II}}), \qquad (8.39)$$

$$\overline{P} = P + dP$$

$$= (\overline{\eta}_{\mathrm{I}} = \eta_{\mathrm{I}} + d\eta_{\mathrm{I}}, \overline{\lambda}_{\mathrm{II}} = \lambda_{\mathrm{II}} + d\lambda_{\mathrm{II}}). \qquad (8.40)$$

Then, by means of Theorem 8.1, $P^{(0)}$ defined by (8.28) has the mixed coordinates

$$P^{(0)} = (\eta_{\mathrm{I}}, \lambda_{\mathrm{II}} + d\lambda_{\mathrm{II}}) \qquad (8.41)$$

which together with (8.28) and Lemma 8.2 with $P^{(0)}, \overline{P}$ in place of P and $P + dP$ yields

Theorem 8.2: Let $\mathcal{L}_P, \overline{P}$ be defined by (8.27) and (8.40), respectively. Then,

$$\min_{\tilde{P} \in \mathcal{L}_P} D(\tilde{P} \| \overline{P}) = \tfrac{1}{2} (d\eta_{\mathrm{I}}) G_{\mathrm{I}}^{-1} (d\eta_{\mathrm{I}})^{\mathrm{T}}. \qquad (8.42)$$

$\qquad \square$

Remark 8.3: Theorem 8.2 (the differential version for the minimization of divergences) provides a very powerful tool in studying the multiterminal parameter estimation problems. For example, application of Theorem 8.2 to the minimization (7.32) in Remark 7.6 immediately yields the equation (*Single minimization*)

$$D(P_{\tilde{X}_0 \tilde{Y}_0} \| p_{\hat{\theta}}) = \tfrac{1}{2} \min_{\theta \in \Phi} (\boldsymbol{t} - \boldsymbol{p}_\theta) G_{\mathrm{I}}^{-1} (\boldsymbol{t} - \boldsymbol{p}_\theta)^{\mathrm{T}} \qquad (8.43)$$

which is nothing but the maximum-likelihood equation (7.13) already driven for the multiterminal zero-rate estimation (Fig. 8). This can be easily checked by differentiating the quadratic form on the right-hand side of (8.43) with respect to θ. Also, later in Step 5 of Section XI, we effectively invoke Theorem 8.2 in order to prove Theorem 7.2 (the converse part) for the zero-rate estimation problem.

Similarly, it is technically very complicated but logically not difficult in principle to generalize the differential version in Theorem 8.2 so that its application to the minimization (6.43) in Remark 6.9 yields the maximum-likelihood equation (6.35) for the multiterminal estimation with positive rates. $\quad \square$

IX. ZERO-RATE MULTITERMINAL PATTERN CLASSIFICATION

Let us consider a finite number of pattern classes $C_1, \cdots, C_m$ which generate an i.i.d. data $(\boldsymbol{x}, \boldsymbol{y}) \in \mathcal{X}^n \times \mathcal{Y}^n$ subject to joint probability distributions

$$P_1 \equiv P_{X_1 Y_1}, \cdots, P_m \equiv P_{X_m Y_m}$$

on $\mathcal{X} \times \mathcal{Y}$, respectively. We denote by $X_i^n Y_i^n n$ independent replicas of $X_i Y_i$ $(i = 1, \cdots, m)$. The problem of statistical pattern recognition is stated as follows: Given an i.i.d. data $(\boldsymbol{x}, \boldsymbol{y})$ generated by one of P_i's, decide the true class which generated the data. In the multiterminal case, the statistician cannot have access to the original full $(\boldsymbol{x}, \boldsymbol{y})$ but uses the encoded messages $f_n(\boldsymbol{x})$ and $g_n(\boldsymbol{y})$ so that the decoder

$\psi_n: \mathcal{M}_n \times \mathcal{N}_n \to \Phi \equiv \{C_1, \cdots, C_m\}$ maps the encoded messages to a pattern class. The set

$$\mathcal{A}_n^{(i)} = \{(\boldsymbol{x}, \boldsymbol{y}) \in \mathcal{X}^n \times \mathcal{Y}^n | \psi_n(f_n(\boldsymbol{x}), g_n(\boldsymbol{y})) = C_i\} \quad (9.1)$$

is called the acceptance region of pattern C_i $(i = 1, \cdots, m)$.

In order to evaluate the performance of the above system, we use the error probability in the Bayesian framework. Let $\pi_i > 0$ be the prior probability of pattern C_i. Let $e_{ij}^{(n)}$ be the probability that pattern from C_i is classified to C_j by the system. It is written as

$$e_{ij}^{(n)} = \Pr\{X_i^n Y_i^n \in \mathcal{A}_n^{(j)}\}. \quad (9.2)$$

Hence, the average error probability is given by

$$\bar{e}_n = \sum_{i=1}^{m} \sum_{j \neq i} \pi_i e_{ij}^{(n)} = \sum_{i=1}^{m} \pi_i (1 - e_{ii}^{(n)}). \quad (9.3)$$

Let $e_n^*(R_1, R_2)$ be the minimum of $\bar{e}_n$ over all possible f_n, g_n, and ψ_n under constraints (4.2) and (4.3). It is known that in general $e_n^*(R_1, R_2)$ decreases to 0 exponentially with n, so that we put

$$\tau(R_1, R_2) = \liminf_{n \to \infty} \frac{1}{n} \log \frac{1}{e_n^*(R_1, R_2)}. \quad (9.4)$$

This is called the optimal error exponent for the multiterminal pattern classification.

In the case of the single-user system, or in the case of the multiuser system with $R_1 \geq H(X)$ and $R_2 \geq H(Y)$, the statistician at cite C can use the full data $(\boldsymbol{x}, \boldsymbol{y})$. The problem is then easily solved, where the optimal acceptance regions are given (cf. Kanaya and Han [24]) by

$$\mathcal{A}_n^{(i)} = \Big\{(\boldsymbol{x}, \boldsymbol{y}) \in \mathcal{X}^n \times \mathcal{Y}^n | \max_{1 \leq j \leq m} (\pi_j P_{X_j^n Y_j^n}(\boldsymbol{x}, \boldsymbol{y}))$$
$$= \pi_i P_{X_i^n Y_i^n}(\boldsymbol{x}, \boldsymbol{y})\Big\} \quad (i = 1, \cdots, m). \quad (9.5)$$

On the other hand, needless to say, the problem is generally nontrivial in the multiterminal case. One may say that the classification problem sits between hypothesis testing and parameter estimation. When the number of pattern classes C_i is infinite and patterns are labeled by a continuous parameter θ, it reduces to the estimation problem. Here, one of the difficulties lies in our being forced to use only *universal* coding schemes, because the encoders do not know which class the data belongs to. However, the problem is similar to hypothesis testing when one treats only a finite number of distributions. The difference is that here all the pattern classes have equal standpoints, whereas the null hypothesis H in hypothesis testing plays a special role different from the alternative $\overline{H}$.

The pattern classification is an important problem in its own right. Results from hypothesis testing and estimation may be useful for obtaining bounds of the error exponent of pattern classification. However, there have appeared no papers treating this important problem except for a preliminary study by Amari and Han [9] where the zero-rate case with $m = 2$ is treated from the information-geometrical point of view. The present paper generalizes their results to the case of an arbitrary finite number of pattern classes, and also gives the proof of the converse theorem for the first time.

In order to state the new results, we use the following concepts. In the set of all the probability distributions on $\mathcal{X} \times \mathcal{Y}$, the subset

$$\mathcal{L}_P = \{\tilde{P} = (\tilde{\eta}_{\mathrm{I}}, \tilde{\lambda}_{\mathrm{II}}) | \tilde{\eta}_{\mathrm{I}} = \eta_{\mathrm{I}}(P)\} \quad (9.6)$$

is the m-fiber on P (cf. (8.27)), where $\eta_{\mathrm{I}}(P)$ denotes the η_{I}-coordinates of distribution P on $\mathcal{X} \times \mathcal{Y}$, which specify the marginal distributions of P defined by (8.6) and (8.7).

Given a fixed distribution P on $\mathcal{X} \times \mathcal{Y}$ the divergence from the fiber $\mathcal{L}_P$ to P_i is defined by

$$D(\mathcal{L}_P || P_i) = \min_{Q \in \mathcal{L}_P} D(Q || P_i). \quad (9.7)$$

For two distributions P_i and P_j, the equi-separator $\mathcal{S}(P_i, P_j)$ of P_i and P_j is defined as the set consisting of those fibers $\mathcal{L}_P$ whose distances to P_i and to P_j are equal

$$\mathcal{S}(P_i, P_j) = \{P | D(\mathcal{L}_P || P_i) = D(\mathcal{L}_P || P_j)\}. \quad (9.8)$$

The separating divergence of P_i and P_j is defined by

$$d_S(P_i, P_j) = \min_{P \in \mathcal{S}(P_i, P_j)} D(P || P_i) \ (= \min_{P \in \mathcal{S}(P_i, P_j)} D(P || P_j)). \quad (9.9)$$

We further define

$$d_S = \min_{1 \leq i \neq j \leq m} d_S(P_i, P_j). \quad (9.10)$$

The acceptance region of P_i against P_j is defined by

$$\mathcal{R}(P_i || P_j) = \{P | D(\mathcal{L}_P || P_i) < D(\mathcal{L}_P || P_j)\} \quad (9.11)$$

and the acceptance region of P_i by

$$\mathcal{R}_i = \bigcap_{j : j \neq i} \mathcal{R}(P_i || P_j). \quad (9.12)$$

Then, we have the following generalization of Amari and Han [9]:

Theorem 9.1: The zero-rate optimal error exponent of pattern classification is lower-bounded as

$$\tau(0, 0) \geq d_S. \quad (9.13)$$

Proof: Let the encoding functions f_n and g_n map $\boldsymbol{x}$ and $\boldsymbol{y}$ to their types, $\text{type}(\boldsymbol{x})$ and $\text{type}(\boldsymbol{y})$, respectively. As in (2.1) of Section II, we set

$$S_A = (\text{type}(\boldsymbol{x}), \text{type}(\boldsymbol{y})) \equiv \eta_{\mathrm{I}}(\boldsymbol{x}, \boldsymbol{y}).$$

Based on these messages, we can construct the m-fiber $\mathcal{L}_{\tilde{P}}$ specified by the two marginal type distributions $\eta_{\mathrm{I}} = (\text{type}(\boldsymbol{x}), \text{type}(\boldsymbol{y}))$. Design the decoder ψ_n by

$$\psi_n(\eta_{\mathrm{I}}(\boldsymbol{x}, \boldsymbol{y})) = C_i, \qquad \text{where } i = \arg \min_{1 \leq j \leq m} D(\mathcal{L}_{\tilde{P}} || P_j). \quad (9.14)$$

That is, $\psi_n(\eta_{\mathrm{I}}(\boldsymbol{x}, \boldsymbol{y})) = C_i$ when P_i is the closest from $\mathcal{L}_{\tilde{P}}$ in the sense of the divergence. (When there are two or more equal minimal candidates, assign to any one of them at random.) The error probability $1 - e_{ii}^{(n)}$ for class C_i is then written as

$$1 - e_{ii}^{(n)} = \Pr\{\psi_n(\eta_{\mathrm{I}}(X_i^n Y_i^n)) \notin \mathcal{R}_i\}. \quad (9.15)$$

Then, by virtue of the Large Deviation Theorem, it follows that

$$\lim_{n \to \infty} \frac{1}{n} \log \frac{1}{1 - e_{ii}^{(n)}} = \min_{j : j \neq i} d_S(P_i, P_j). \quad (9.16)$$

By (9.3) and (9.10), we thus have

$$\lim_{n \to \infty} \frac{1}{n} \log \frac{1}{\bar{e}_n} = d_S. \quad (9.17)$$

This proves the achievability of d_S. □

Remark 9.1: The error exponent $\tau(0,0)$ does not depend on the prior distribution $\pi_i > 0$ ($i = 1, \cdots, m$) because

$$\frac{1}{n} \log \frac{1}{\pi_i (1 - e_{ii}^{(n)})} = \frac{1}{n} \log \frac{1}{1 - e_{ii}^{(n)}} - \frac{1}{n} \log \pi_i \quad (9.18)$$

where the second term on the right-hand side of (9.18) converges to 0 as n tends to $+\infty$. □

Remark 9.2: The acceptance region $\mathcal{R}_i$ defined in (9.12) is "optimal," provided that we are restricted to use the message $S_A = (\mathrm{type}\,(\boldsymbol{x}), \mathrm{type}\,(\boldsymbol{y}))$ only. □

The converse counterpart of Theorem 9.1 is novel, which is stated as follows.

Theorem 9.2: Assume that $\pi_i > 0$ and $P_i(x,y) > 0$ for all $i = 1, \cdots, m$ and all $(x,y) \in \mathcal{X} \times \mathcal{Y}$. Then, for all $R \geq 0$

$$\tau(0,R) \leq d_S. \quad (9.19)$$

Proof: Let P_k and P_l be the two distributions specified by

$$\min_{1 \leq i \neq j \leq m} d_S(P_i, P_j) = d_S(P_k, P_l) = d_S$$

and let us consider the hypothesis testing $H : P_k$ against $\overline{H} : P_l$. In order to invoke the contradiction argument, assume that there exists a zero-rate coding system $(\tilde{f}_n, \tilde{g}_n, \tilde{\psi}_n)$ with rates $R_1 = 0, R_2 = R$ for which the error exponent d_S^* of classification is larger than d_S. We use the decision rule which accepts H when the output of $\tilde{\psi}_n$ is C_k and rejects H when the output of $\tilde{\psi}_n$ is not C_k. Then, in view of (9.2), (9.3), and Remark 9.1, the error probabilities α_n, β_n of the first kind and the second kind for this hypothesis testing obviously satisfy

$$\liminf_{n \to \infty} \frac{1}{n} \log \frac{1}{\alpha_n} \geq d_S^* > d_S \equiv r \quad (9.20)$$

$$\liminf_{n \to \infty} \frac{1}{n} \log \frac{1}{\beta_n} \geq d_S^* > d_S \equiv r. \quad (9.21)$$

On the other hand, by the definition of $d_S(P_k, P_l)$ there exists a distribution P^* on $\mathcal{X} \times \mathcal{Y}$ such that

$$D(\mathcal{L}_{P^*} \| P_k) = D(\mathcal{L}_{P^*} \| P_l) = r \quad (9.22)$$

from which it follows that

$$\mathcal{H}(r) \supset \mathcal{L}_{P^*} \quad (9.23)$$

where $\mathcal{H}(r)$ is defined by (5.14) and (5.15) with P_k in place of P_{XY}. Moreover, by means of (9.20) and Theorem 5.5 with

P_l in place of $P_{\overline{XY}}$, we have

$$\begin{aligned}
\liminf_{n \to \infty} \frac{1}{n} \log \frac{1}{\beta_n} &\leq \min_{P_{\tilde{X}\tilde{Y}} \in \mathcal{H}(r)} D(P_{\tilde{X}\tilde{Y}} \| P_l) \\
&\leq \min_{P_{\tilde{X}\tilde{Y}} \in \mathcal{L}_{P^*}} D(P_{\tilde{X}\tilde{Y}} \| P_l) \\
&= D(\mathcal{L}_{P^*} \| P_l) \\
&= r \quad (9.24)
\end{aligned}$$

where we have used (9.22) and (9.23). This obviously contradicts (9.21), thus proving Theorem 9.2. □

A consequence of Theorems 9.1 and 9.2 is

Corollary 9.1: Assume that $\pi_i > 0$ and $P_i(x,y) > 0$ for all $i = 1, \cdots, m$ and all $(x,y) \in \mathcal{X} \times \mathcal{Y}$. Then, for all $R \geq 0$

$$\tau(0,R) = d_S. \quad (9.25)$$

Remark 9.3: We can generalize this result to the case where the cost of misclassifying class C_i to C_j is spefied by c_{ij}, where the target is minimizing the average cost. We have discussed only the zero-rate case. It does not seem to be so difficult to obtain some bounds in the positive rate case by combining the results of hypothesis testing and the universal coding scheme for parameter estimation. □

X. PROOF OF THEOREM 5.5

In this section, we give the proof of Theorem 5.5 stated in Section V. In order to prove it, we need the following lemma.

Lemma 10.1 (Han and Kobayashi [5]): Let $X^n Y^n$ be an i.i.d. random sequence of length n subject to probability distribution P_{XY} on $\mathcal{X} \times \mathcal{Y}$. Let $\mathcal{A}_n$ be any subset of $\mathcal{X}^n \times \mathcal{Y}^n$ such that

$$\Pr\{X^n Y^n \in \mathcal{A}_n\} \geq 1 - e^{-n\rho} \quad (10.1)$$

holds ($\rho > 0$ is a constant). If we denote by $\hat{P}_n$ any fixed joint type on $\mathcal{X}^n \times \mathcal{Y}^n$ and put

$$S_0(\hat{P}_n) = \{(\boldsymbol{x}, \boldsymbol{y}) \in \mathcal{X}^n \times \mathcal{Y}^n \,|\, \mathrm{type}\,(\boldsymbol{x}, \boldsymbol{y}) = \hat{P}_n\} \quad (10.2)$$

$$\mathcal{A}_n(\hat{P}_n) = \mathcal{A}_n \cap S_0(\hat{P}_n) \quad (10.3)$$

then we have

$$|\mathcal{A}_n(\hat{P}_n)| \geq (1 - (n+1)^{|\mathcal{X}| \cdot |\mathcal{Y}|} e^{-n(\rho - c_n)}) |S_0(\hat{P}_n)| \quad (10.4)$$

where $c_n = D(\hat{P}_n \| P_{XY})$. □

Let $\mathcal{A}_n$ be an arbitrary acceptance region for hypothesis testing (4.11) and (4.12) such that

$$\liminf_{n \to \infty} \frac{1}{n} \log \frac{1}{\alpha_n} \geq r \quad (r > 0) \quad (10.5)$$

where

$$\alpha_n = \Pr\{X^n Y^n \notin \mathcal{A}_n\}. \quad (10.6)$$

Equations (10.5) and (10.6) imply that

$$\Pr\{X^n Y^n \in \mathcal{A}_n\} \geq 1 - e^{-n(r - \gamma)} \quad (\forall n \geq n_0) \quad (10.7)$$

where $\gamma > 0$ is an arbitrarily small constant.

Next, select an arbitrary "internal point" $P_{X_0Y_0}$ of $\mathcal{D}(r)$, where $\mathcal{D}(r)$ is specified in (5.14). Then, clearly

$$D(P_{X_0Y_0}||P_{XY}) < r. \tag{10.8}$$

Define

$$\hat{\mathcal{T}}_n(\delta) = \{\text{joint types } \hat{P}_n \text{ on } \mathcal{X}^n \times \mathcal{Y}^n | D(\hat{P}_n||P_{X_0Y_0}) < \delta\} \tag{10.9}$$

where $\delta > 0$ is an arbitrary constant. Then, in view of (10.8) and the uniform continuity of the divergence, for all $\hat{P}_n \in \hat{\mathcal{T}}_n(\delta)$ it holds that

$$c_n \equiv D(\hat{P}_n||P_{XY}) < r - 2\gamma \tag{10.10}$$

provided that we take $\gamma > 0$ and $\delta > 0$ sufficiently small. Consequently, (10.4) in Lemma 10.1 with $\rho = r\gamma$ yields

$$|\mathcal{A}_n(\hat{P}_n)| \geq (1 - (n+1)^{|\mathcal{X}|\cdot|y|}e^{-n\gamma})|S_0(\hat{P}_n)| \tag{10.11}$$

for all $\hat{P}_n \in \hat{\mathcal{T}}_n(\delta)$. Now we define the set

$$\mathcal{T}_n(\delta) = \{(\boldsymbol{x}, \boldsymbol{y}) \in \mathcal{X}^n \times \mathcal{Y}^n | \text{type}\,(\boldsymbol{x}, \boldsymbol{y}) \in \hat{\mathcal{T}}_n(\delta)\} \tag{10.12}$$

and consider an i.i.d. random sequence of length n subject to probability distribution $P_{X_0Y_0}$. Then, by means of (10.11), we have

$$\begin{aligned}
\Pr\{X_0^n Y_0^n \in \mathcal{A}_n\} &\geq \Pr\{X_0^n Y_0^n \in \mathcal{A}_n \cap \mathcal{T}_n(\delta)\} \\
&= \sum_{\hat{P}_n \in \hat{\mathcal{T}}_n(\delta)} \Pr\{X_0^n Y_0^n \in \mathcal{A}_n \cap S_0(\hat{P}_n)\} \\
&= \sum_{\hat{P}_n \in \hat{\mathcal{T}}_n(\delta)} \Pr\{X_0^n Y_0^n \in \mathcal{A}_n(\hat{P}_n)\} \\
&\geq (1 - (n+1)^{|\mathcal{X}|\cdot|\mathcal{Y}|}e^{-n\gamma}) \\
&\quad \cdot \sum_{\hat{P}_n \in \hat{\mathcal{T}}_n(\delta)} \Pr\{X_0^n Y_0^n \in S_0(\hat{P}_n)\} \\
&= (1 - (n+1)^{|\mathcal{X}|\cdot|\mathcal{Y}|}e^{-n\gamma}) \\
&\quad \cdot \Pr\{\text{type}\,(X_0^n, Y_0^n) \in \hat{\mathcal{T}}_n(\delta)\} \\
&\geq (1 - (n+1)^{|\mathcal{X}|\cdot|\mathcal{Y}|}e^{-n\gamma}) \\
&\quad \cdot (1 - (n+1)^{|\mathcal{X}|\cdot|\mathcal{Y}|}e^{-n\delta}) \tag{10.13}
\end{aligned}$$

where in the last step we have used the fact (cf. [19])

$$\Pr\{\text{type}\,(X_0^n, Y_0^n) \in \hat{\mathcal{T}}_n(\delta)\} \geq 1 - (n+1)^{|\mathcal{X}|\cdot|\mathcal{Y}|}e^{-n\delta}. \tag{10.14}$$

Now consider the zero-rate $(R_1 = 0, R_2 \geq 0)$ hypothesis testing with

$$H : P_{X_0Y_0} \quad \text{(null hypothesis)} \tag{10.15}$$
$$\overline{H} : P_{\overline{XY}} \quad \text{(alternative hypothesis)} \tag{10.16}$$

and the same acceptance region $\mathcal{A}_n$ as above. Then, by virtue of (10.13), for this hypothesis testing the error probability $\alpha_n^{(0)}$ of the first kind satisfies the "constant-type" constraint

$$\limsup_{n\to\infty} \alpha_n^{(0)} \leq \varepsilon \qquad (\forall 0 \leq \varepsilon < 1) \tag{10.17}$$

which together with Theorem 5.3 yields

$$\liminf_{n\to\infty} \frac{1}{n}\log\frac{1}{\beta_n} \leq \min_{P_{\tilde{X}\tilde{Y}} \in \mathcal{L}_2^{(0)}} D(P_{\tilde{X}\tilde{Y}}||P_{\overline{XY}}) \tag{10.18}$$

where

$$\beta_n = P_n\{\overline{X}^n \overline{Y}^n \in \mathcal{A}_n\} \tag{10.19}$$
$$\mathcal{L}_2^{(0)} = \{P_{\tilde{X}\tilde{Y}}|P_{\tilde{X}} = P_{X_0}, P_{\tilde{Y}} = P_{Y_0}\}. \tag{10.20}$$

On the other hand, we notice that $P_{X_0Y_0}$ was arbitrary as far as condition (10.8) is satisfied. Therefore, in the light of the definition (5.15) of $\mathcal{H}(r)$, we see that the infimum of the right-hand side in (10.18) over all possible internal points $P_{X_0Y_0}$ satisfying (10.8) coincides with

$$\min_{P_{\tilde{X}\tilde{Y}} \in \mathcal{H}(r)} D(P_{\tilde{X}\tilde{Y}}||P_{\overline{XY}}). \tag{10.21}$$

Thus (10.18) reduces to

$$\liminf_{n\to\infty} \frac{1}{n}\log\frac{1}{\beta_n} \leq \min_{P_{\tilde{X}\tilde{Y}} \in \mathcal{H}(r)} D(P_{\tilde{X}\tilde{Y}}||P_{\overline{XY}}) \tag{10.22}$$

that is,

$$\sigma(r||0, R) \leq \min_{P_{\tilde{X}\tilde{Y}} \in \mathcal{H}(r)} D(P_{\tilde{X}\tilde{Y}}||P_{\overline{XY}}) \tag{10.23}$$

which was what to be proven. $\square$

XI. PROOF OF THEOREM 7.2

In this section we give the proof of Theorem 7.2 stated in Section VII in several steps.

Step 1:

We start with providing a lemma that plays a crucial role later in Step 5. We consider the general multiterminal hypothesis testing with (4.11) and (4.12), that is,

$$H : P_{XY} \quad \text{(null hypothesis)} \tag{11.1}$$
$$\overline{H} : P_{\overline{XY}} \quad \text{(alternative hypothesis)} \tag{11.2}$$

under zero-rate constraint $(R_1 = 0)$

$$\lim_{n\to\infty} \frac{1}{n}\log\|f_n\| = 0 \tag{11.3}$$

while $\|g_n\|$ is arbitrary $(R_2 \geq 0)$. Notice the error probabilities α_n, β_n of the first kind and the second kind as specified by (1.7) and (1.8) can be written as

$$\alpha_n = \Pr\{X^n Y^n \notin \mathcal{A}_n\} \tag{11.4}$$
$$\beta_n = \Pr\{\overline{X}^n \overline{Y}^n \in \mathcal{A}_n\} \tag{11.5}$$

where $\mathcal{A}_n$ is the acceptance region as specified by (4.1). The following lemma is a more precise restatement of Theorem 5.3 in Section V.

Lemma 11.1 (Shalaby and Papamarcou [6]): With the hypothesis testing (11.1) and (11.2), let $0 \leq \varepsilon < 1$ be any fixed constant and suppose that the positivity condition (5.9) holds. If the constraint

$$\limsup_{n \to \infty} \alpha_n \leq \varepsilon \qquad (11.6)$$

is satisfied with zero-rate $R_1 = 0$, then there exists a sequence $\{\xi_n > 0\}_{n=1}^{\infty}$ such that

$$\xi_n \to 0 \qquad (n \to \infty) \qquad (11.7)$$
$$\beta_n \geq \exp\left[-n(E_{P,\overline{P}} + \xi_n)\right] \qquad (\forall n = 1, 2, \cdots) \qquad (11.8)$$

where we have put

$$E_{P,\overline{P}} = \min_{P_{\tilde{X}\tilde{Y}} \in \mathcal{L}_2} D(P_{\tilde{X}\tilde{Y}} \| P_{\overline{XY}}) \qquad (11.9)$$

with $\mathcal{L}_2$ defined in (5.5), i.e.,

$$\mathcal{L}_2 = \{P_{\tilde{X}\tilde{Y}} | P_{\tilde{X}} = P_X, P_{\tilde{Y}} = P_Y\}. \qquad (1.10)$$

Remark 11.1: Marton [8] has shown an extended version of Blowing-up lemma [7] used to establish Lemma 11.1, which tells us that the sequence $\{\xi_n\}_{n=1}^{\infty}$ in Lemma 11.1 is independent from the hypotheses P_{XY} and $P_{\overline{XY}}$, and hence P_{XY} and $P_{\overline{XY}}$ may depend on n. This fact will be used later in Step 5.

Step 2:

Let us have a familily of joint distributions

$$\{p_\theta(x, y)\}_{\theta \in \Phi} \qquad (11.11)$$

which is continuously twice differentiable with respect to the parameter $\theta = (\theta_1, \cdots, \theta_r) \in \Phi$ and satisfies the positivity condition (7.19). Consider any asymptotically unbiased $(0, R)$-achievable estimator $\hat{\theta}_n$ for the parameter θ whose covariance index (r-dimensional matrix) is given by

$$V(\theta | 0, R). \qquad (11.12)$$

In order to prove the theorem by the contradiction argument, suppose that

$$V(\theta | 0, R) \geq (F_\theta)^{-1} \qquad (\forall \theta \in \Phi, \forall R \geq 0) \qquad (11.13)$$

does *not* hold, where F_θ is the Fisher information index specified by (7.18). Then, there exists some $\theta_0 \in \Phi$, $R_0 \geq 0$ and an r-dimensional vector $\boldsymbol{a} = (a_1, \cdots, a_r) \neq \boldsymbol{0}$ such that

$$\boldsymbol{a} V(\theta_0 | 0, R_0) \boldsymbol{a}^{\mathrm{T}} < \boldsymbol{a}(F_{\theta_0})^{-1} \boldsymbol{a}^{\mathrm{T}}. \qquad (11.14)$$

Here, we can normalize $\boldsymbol{a}$ so as to satisfy the condition

$$\boldsymbol{a}(F_{\theta_0})^{-1} \boldsymbol{a}^{\mathrm{T}} = 1. \qquad (11.15)$$

If we set $\boldsymbol{b} = \boldsymbol{a}(F_{\theta_0})^{-1}$ then (11.15) yields

$$(\boldsymbol{b} F_{\theta_0} \boldsymbol{b}^{\mathrm{T}})^{-1} = \boldsymbol{a}(F_{\theta_0})^{-1} \boldsymbol{a}^{\mathrm{T}} \qquad (11.16)$$

so that (11.14) is written as

$$\boldsymbol{a} V(\theta_0 | 0, R_0) \boldsymbol{a}^{\mathrm{T}} < (\boldsymbol{b} F_{\theta_0} \boldsymbol{b}^{\mathrm{T}})^{-1}. \qquad (11.17)$$

Let us now consider the one-dimensional parameterization of $\theta = (\theta_1, \cdots, \theta_r)$ by u such that

$$\theta = \theta(u) \equiv u\boldsymbol{b} + \theta_0 \qquad (11.18)$$

then we have

$$u = (\theta(u) - \theta_0)\boldsymbol{a}^{\mathrm{T}} \qquad (11.19)$$

because of $\boldsymbol{b}\boldsymbol{a}^{\mathrm{T}} = 1$. Clearly, $\theta(u) = \theta_0$ when $u = 0$. We define the estimator $\hat{u}_n$ for the parameter u by

$$\hat{u}_n = (\hat{\theta}_n - \theta_0)\boldsymbol{a}^{\mathrm{T}} \qquad (11.20)$$

which is easily seen to be asymptotically unbiased since $\hat{\theta}_n$ is asymptotically unbiased. Let V_u denote the variance index of the estimator $\hat{u}_n$ for the parameter value u. Then, the variance index $V_0 \equiv V_{u=0}$ of the estimator $\hat{u}_n$ at $u = 0$ coincides with the left-hand side of (11.17), i.e.,

$$V_0 = \boldsymbol{a} V(\theta_0 | 0, R_0) \boldsymbol{a}^{\mathrm{T}} \qquad (11.21)$$

so that (11.17) is rewritten as

$$\frac{1}{V_0} > \boldsymbol{b} F_{\theta_0} \boldsymbol{b}^{\mathrm{T}}. \qquad (11.22)$$

Step 3:

With any sufficiently large positive integers n, m set $N = nm$, and suppose that data $\boldsymbol{x}, \boldsymbol{y}$ of length N were generated at sites A and B, respectively. We divide these data $\boldsymbol{x}, \boldsymbol{y}$ into m subblocks of length n as

$$\boldsymbol{x} = (\boldsymbol{x}^{(1)}, \boldsymbol{x}^{(2)}, \cdots, \boldsymbol{x}^{(m)}) \qquad (11.23)$$
$$\boldsymbol{y} = (\boldsymbol{y}^{(1)}, \boldsymbol{y}^{(2)}, \cdots, \boldsymbol{y}^{(m)}) \qquad (11.24)$$

and let $\hat{u}_n^{(i)}$ be the estimator $\hat{u}_n$ using data $(\boldsymbol{x}^{(i)}, \boldsymbol{y}^{(i)})$ ($i = 1, 2, \cdots, m$), where $\hat{u}_n$ is the estimator of the parameter u defined in (11.20). Since we are considering a jointly i.i.d. data $(\boldsymbol{x}, \boldsymbol{y})$, subblocks $(\boldsymbol{x}^{(i)}, \boldsymbol{y}^{(i)})$ ($i = 1, 2, \cdots, m$) are independent from one another and hence these estimators $\hat{u}_n^{(i)}$ ($i = 1, 2, \cdots, m$) are also mutually independent. Define another estimator $\tilde{u}_{n,m}$ by

$$\tilde{u}_{n,m} = \frac{\hat{u}_n^{(1)} + \hat{u}_n^{(2)} + \cdots + \hat{u}_n^{(m)}}{m} \qquad (11.25)$$

then its variance at the parameter value u is given by

$$\mathrm{V}(\tilde{u}_{n,m}) = \frac{V_u}{nm} + o\left(\frac{1}{nm}\right). \qquad (11.26)$$

On the other hand, since we have assumed that the estimator $\hat{\theta}_n$ is asymptotically unbiased, there exists an r-dimensional sequence $\{d_n(\theta)\}_{n=1}^{\infty}$ such that for all $\theta \in \Phi$

$$\mathrm{E}_\theta(\hat{\theta}_n) = \theta + d_n(\theta) \qquad (11.27)$$
$$d_n(\theta) \to \boldsymbol{0} \qquad (n \to \infty). \qquad (11.28)$$

We now consider a sequence $\{\gamma_n > 0\}_{n=1}^{\infty}$ such that

$$\gamma_n \to 0 \qquad (n \to 0) \qquad (11.29)$$
$$\frac{\max\left(\sqrt{\xi_n}, 1/\sqrt{n}\right)}{\gamma_n} \to 0 \qquad (n \to 0) \qquad (11.30)$$

with $\{\xi_n\}_{n=1}^{\infty}$ ($\xi_n \to 0$ as $n \to +\infty$) specified in Lemma 11.1 in Step 1. Then, since it follows from (11.19), (11.20), (11.25), and (11.27) that

$$
\begin{aligned}
\mathrm{E}_u(\tilde{u}_{n,m}) &= \mathrm{E}_{\theta(u)}[(\hat{\theta}_n - \theta_0)\boldsymbol{a}^{\mathrm{T}}] \\
&= [\theta(u) + d_n(\theta(u)) - \theta_0]\boldsymbol{a}^{\mathrm{T}} \\
&= u + d_n(\theta(u))\boldsymbol{a}^{\mathrm{T}}
\end{aligned}
\tag{11.31}
$$

we have

$$
\begin{aligned}
u_0 &\equiv \mathrm{E}_{u=0}(\tilde{u}_{u,m}) \\
&= d_n(\theta(0))\boldsymbol{a}^{\mathrm{T}} = d_n(\theta_0)\boldsymbol{a}^{\mathrm{T}}
\end{aligned}
\tag{11.32}
$$

$$
\begin{aligned}
u_1 &\equiv \mathrm{E}_{u=\gamma_N}(\tilde{u}_{u,m}) \\
&= \gamma_N + d_n(\theta(\gamma_N))\boldsymbol{a}^{\mathrm{T}} \\
&= \gamma_N + d_n(\theta_0)\boldsymbol{a}^{\mathrm{T}} + o(\gamma_N)
\end{aligned}
\tag{11.33}
$$

where in the last step we have taken account of (11.29). Hence

$$
u_1 - u_0 = \gamma_N + o(\gamma_N). \tag{11.34}
$$

Step 4:
Let κ_n denote the left-hand side of (11.30), i.e.,

$$
\kappa_n = \frac{\max(\sqrt{\xi_n}, 1/\sqrt{n})}{\gamma_n}. \tag{11.35}
$$

Then (11.30) is equivalent to

$$
\kappa_n \to 0 \qquad (n \to 0) \tag{11.36}
$$

from which, together with (11.35), it follows that

$$
\frac{\max(\sqrt{\xi_n}, 1/\sqrt{n})}{\sqrt{\kappa_n}\gamma_n} = \sqrt{\kappa_n} \to 0 \qquad (n \to \infty). \tag{11.37}
$$

Let us now consider in the hypothesis testing with (11.1), (11.2) the following case using the given family (11.11) of distributions:

$$
H : P_{XY} = p_{\theta(u_0)} \quad \text{(null hypothesis)} \tag{11.38}
$$

$$
\overline{H} : P_{\overline{XY}} = p_{\theta(u_1)} \quad \text{(alternative hypothesis)}. \tag{11.39}
$$

We choose one of hypotheses H and $\overline{H}$ according to the value of the statistic $\tilde{u}_{n\cdot m}$ as follows: the null hypothesis H is adopted if $\tilde{u}_{n,m} \le \overline{u}$ and the alternative hypothesis $\overline{H}$ is adopted otherwise, where

$$
\overline{u} = u_0 + \sqrt{\kappa_N}(u_1 - u_0) \tag{11.40}
$$

with $N = nm$.
We need here the following lemma.

Lemma 11.2 (Billingsley [21]): Let

$$
S_m = \frac{Z_1 + Z_2 + \cdots + Z_m}{m} \tag{11.41}
$$

where Z_i ($i = 1, 2, \cdots, m$) are finite-valued independent and identically distributed random variables with mean μ and variance σ^2. If a sequence $\{c_m\}_{m=1}^{\infty}$ satisfies the condition

$$
c_m \to \infty, \quad \frac{c_m}{\sqrt{m}} \to 0 \qquad (m \to \infty) \tag{11.42}
$$

then

$$
\Pr\left\{S_m - \mu \ge \frac{c_m\sigma}{\sqrt{m}}\right\} = \exp\left[-\frac{c_m^2(1+\delta_m)}{2}\right] \tag{11.43}
$$

$$
\Pr\left\{S_m - \mu \le -\frac{c_m\sigma}{\sqrt{m}}\right\} = \exp\left[-\frac{c_m^2(1+\delta_m')}{2}\right] \tag{11.44}
$$

where $\delta_m \to 0, \delta_m' \to 0$ ($m \to \infty$). $\qquad\square$

Let us consider in Lemma 11.2 the case (cf. (11.25)) where

$$
Z_i = \hat{u}_n^{(i)} \qquad (i = 1, \cdots, m) \tag{11.45}
$$

$$
S_m = \tilde{u}_{n,m}. \tag{11.46}
$$

a) H: *Case of $u = 0$.*
In this case we have

$$
\mu = u_0 \qquad \sigma^2 = \frac{V_0}{n} + o\left(\frac{1}{n}\right). \tag{11.47}
$$

Put

$$
c_m = \frac{(u_1 - u_0)\sqrt{N\kappa_N}}{\sqrt{V_0}} \tag{11.48}
$$

then, from (11.34), we have

$$
c_m = \frac{\gamma_N\sqrt{N\kappa_N}}{\sqrt{V_0}} + o(\gamma_N\sqrt{N\kappa_N}). \tag{11.49}
$$

In view of (11.37) and (11.49) it is easy to check that the choice (11.48) of c_m satisfies condition (11.42). Then, taking account of (11.40), (11.48), and (11.49), application of (11.43) in Lemma 11.2 gives the evaluation for the error probability α_N of the first kind as

$$
\begin{aligned}
\alpha_N &= \Pr\{\tilde{u}_{n,m} \ge \overline{u}\} \\
&= \Pr\{\tilde{u}_{n,m} - u_0 \ge \sqrt{\kappa_N}(u_1 - u_0)\} \\
&= \Pr\left\{\tilde{u}_{n,m} - u_0 \ge \frac{c_m\sqrt{V_0}}{\sqrt{N}}\right\} \\
&= \exp\left[-\frac{c_m^2(1+\delta_m)}{2}\right] \\
&= \exp\left[-\frac{N\gamma_N^2\kappa_N(1+\rho_N+\delta_m)}{2V_0}\right]
\end{aligned}
\tag{11.50}
$$

where $\rho_N \to 0$ ($N \to \infty$). Moreover, it follows from (11.37) that

$$
N\gamma_N^2\kappa_N \to \infty \qquad (N \to \infty). \tag{11.51}
$$

On the other hand, since $N = nm$, if we set $n = m$ then $m = \sqrt{N}$. Thus (11.51) and (11.50) with $m = \sqrt{N}$ conclude that

$$
\alpha_N \to 0 \qquad (N \to \infty). \tag{11.52}
$$

b) $\overline{H}$: *Case of $u = \gamma_N$.*
In this case, by means of (11.29) with N instead of n we have

$$
\begin{aligned}
\mu &= u_1 \\
\sigma^2 &= \frac{V_{\gamma_N}}{n} + o\left(\frac{1}{n}\right) \\
&= \frac{V_0}{n} + o\left(\frac{1}{n}\right).
\end{aligned}
\tag{11.53}
$$

Put

$$c_m = \frac{(u_1 - u_0)(1 - \sqrt{\kappa_N})\sqrt{N}}{\sqrt{V_0}} \qquad (11.54)$$

then, from (11.34) we have

$$c_m = \frac{\gamma_N(1 - \sqrt{\kappa_N})\sqrt{N}}{\sqrt{V_0}} + o(\gamma_N \sqrt{N}). \qquad (11.55)$$

In view of (11.29), (11.30) with N instead of n, and (11.55) it is easy to check that the choice (11.54) of c_m satisfies condition (11.42). Then, taking account of (11.40), (11.54), and (11.55), application of (11.44) in Lemma 11.2 gives the evaluation for the error probability β_N of the second kind as

$$\begin{aligned} \beta_N &= \Pr\{\tilde{u}_{n,m} \leq \overline{u}\} \\ &= \Pr\{\tilde{u}_{n,m} - u_1 \leq -(1 - \sqrt{\kappa_N})(u_1 - u_0)\} \\ &= \Pr\left\{\tilde{u}_{n,m} - u_1 \leq -\frac{c_m\sqrt{V_0}}{\sqrt{N}}\right\} \\ &= \exp\left[-\frac{c_m^2(1 + \delta_m')}{2}\right] \\ &= \exp\left[-\frac{N\gamma_N^2(1 - \sqrt{\kappa_N})^2(1 + \epsilon_N + \delta_m')}{2V_0}\right] \qquad (11.56) \end{aligned}$$

where $\epsilon_N \to 0$ as $N \to +\infty$. Let us here also set $m = n$, then $m = \sqrt{N}$ since $N = nm$. Thus in view of $\delta_m' = \delta'_{\sqrt{N}} \to 0$ ($N \to +\infty$) and (11.36) with N in place of n, β_N can be written as

$$\beta_N = \exp\left[-\frac{N\gamma_N^2(1 + \epsilon_N')}{2V_0}\right] \qquad (11.57)$$

where $\epsilon_N' \to 0$ ($N \to \infty$).

Summarizing, it is concluded that the zero-rate ($R_1 = 0, R_2 = R_0$) hypothesis testing with (11.38) and (11.39) has the error probabilities α_N, β_N specified by (11.52) and (11.57), respectively.

Step 5:

We now think of an application of Lemma 11.1 in Step 1 to the hypothesis testing with (11.38) and (11.39) (cf. Remark 11.1) using the same decision rule as described in Step 4. This is to derive a contradiction with the fact shown in Step 4.

We first observe that, in the light of (11.29) and (11.34), the hypotheses $P_{XY} = p_{\theta(u_0)}$ and $P_{\overline{XY}} = p_{\theta(u_1)}$ asymptotically coincide with one another when N tends to infinity. It is also easy to check that $\mathcal{L}_P$ (defined by (8.27)) in Theorem 8.2 coincides with $\mathcal{L}_2$ (defined by (11.10)) in Lemma 11.1 if we set $P = p_{\theta(u_0)}$ and $\overline{P} = p_{\theta(u_1)}$ in Theorem 8.2, so that the left-hand side of (8.42) coincides with $E_{P,\overline{P}}$ in (11.9). As a consequence, by virtue of Theorem 8.2, we can write

$$E_{P,\overline{P}} = \tfrac{1}{2}(d\eta_{\mathrm{I}})G_{\mathrm{I}}^{-1}(d\eta_{\mathrm{I}})^{\mathrm{T}} \qquad (11.58)$$

where, denoting the mixed coordinates (cf. Section VIII) of $P_{XY} = p_{\theta(u_0)}, P_{\overline{XY}} = p_{\theta(u_1)}$ by $(\eta_{\mathrm{I}}^{(0)}, \lambda_{\mathrm{II}}^{(0)})$ and $(\eta_{\mathrm{I}}^{(1)}, \lambda_{\mathrm{II}}^{(1)})$, respectively, we have set

$$d\eta_{\mathrm{I}} = \eta_{\mathrm{I}}^{(1)} - \eta_{\mathrm{I}}^{(0)}. \qquad (11.59)$$

On the other hand, with the notation in Section VII (cf. (7.10)) we see that

$$\eta_{\mathrm{I}}^{(1)} = \boldsymbol{p}_{\theta(u_1)} \qquad \eta_{\mathrm{I}}^{(0)} = \boldsymbol{p}_{\theta(u_0)}, \qquad (11.60)$$

which together with (11.18), (11.34), and (11.59) yields

$$d\eta_{\mathrm{I}} = \gamma_N \boldsymbol{b}\nabla\boldsymbol{p}_{\theta_0} + o(\gamma_N), \qquad (11.61)$$

where "∇" denotes the derivative with respect to the parameter $\theta = (\theta_1, \cdots, \theta_r)$. Then, substitution of (11.61) into (11.58) gives

$$\begin{aligned} E_{P,\overline{P}} &= \frac{1}{2}\gamma_N^2 \boldsymbol{b}(\nabla\boldsymbol{p}_{\theta_0})G_{\mathrm{I}}^{-1}(\nabla\boldsymbol{p}_{\theta_0})^{\mathrm{T}}\boldsymbol{b}^{\mathrm{T}} + o(\gamma_N^2) \\ &= \frac{1}{2}\gamma_N^2 \boldsymbol{b}F_{\theta_0}\boldsymbol{b}^{\mathrm{T}} + o(\gamma_N^2) \qquad (11.62) \end{aligned}$$

where we have taken account of the definition (7.18) of the Fisher information index F_θ. Since $\alpha_N \to 0$ ($N \to \infty$) by (11.52), the assumption (11.6) in Lemma 11.1 with N instead of n is satisfied. Hence, by virtue of Lemma 11.1, the inequality

$$\beta_N \geq \exp[-N(E_{P,\overline{P}} + \xi_N)] \qquad (11.63)$$

must hold. Substitution of (11.57) and (11.62) into (11.63) leads us to

$$\begin{aligned} &\exp\left[-\frac{N\gamma_N^2(1 + \epsilon_N')}{2V_0}\right] \\ &\geq \exp\left[-\frac{N(\gamma_N^2\boldsymbol{b}F_{\theta_0}\boldsymbol{b}^{\mathrm{T}} + o(\gamma_N^2) + 2\xi_N)}{2}\right]. \qquad (11.64) \end{aligned}$$

Taking the logarithm of both sides in (11.64) and dividing them by $N\gamma_N^2/2$, we obtain

$$-\frac{1 + \epsilon_N'}{V_0} \geq -\boldsymbol{b}F_{\theta_0}\boldsymbol{b}^{\mathrm{T}} - \frac{o(\gamma_N^2)}{\gamma_N^2} - \frac{2\xi_N}{\gamma_N^2}. \qquad (11.65)$$

On the other hand, it follows from (11.30) with N in place of n that

$$\frac{\xi_N}{\gamma_N^2} \to 0 \qquad (N \to \infty). \qquad (11.66)$$

Thus noting that $\epsilon_N' \to 0$ ($N \to \infty$) and letting $N \to \infty$ in (11.65), it is concluded that

$$\frac{1}{V_0} \leq \boldsymbol{b}F_{\theta_0}\boldsymbol{b}^{\mathrm{T}} \qquad (11.67)$$

which obviously contradicts (11.22), thereby proving Theorem 7.2. $\qquad \square$

REFERENCES

[1] T. Berger, "Decentralized estimation and decision theory," presented at the IEEE 7th Spring Workshop on Information Theory, Mt. Kisco, NY, Sept. 1979.
[2] J. Rissanen, "Universal coding, information, prediction and estimation," *IEEE Trans. Inform. Theory*, vol. IT-30, pp. 629–636, 1984.
[3] R. Ahlswede and I. Csiszár, "Hypothesis testing with communication constraints," *IEEE Trans. Inform. Theory*, vol. IT-32, pp. 533–542, July 1986.
[4] T. S. Han, "Hypothesis testing with multiterminal data compression," *IEEE Trans. Inform. Theory*, vol. IT-33, pp. 759–772, Nov. 1987.

[5] T. S. Han and K. Kobayashi, "Exponential-type error probabilities for multiterminal hypothesis testing," *IEEE Trans. Inform. Theory*, vol. 35, pp. 2–14, Jan. 1989.

[6] H. M. H. Shalaby and A. Papamarcou, "Multiterminal detection with zero-rate data compression," *IEEE Trans. Inform. Theory*, vol. 38, pp. 254–267, Mar. 1992.

[7] R. Ahlswede, P. Gács, and J. Körner, "Bounds on conditional probabilities with applications in mult-user communication," *Z. für Wahrscheinlichkeitstheorie und ver wandte Gebiete*, vol. 34, pp. 157–177, 1976; correction, *ibid.* vol. 39, pp. 353–354, 1977.

[8] K. Marton, "A simple proof of the blowing-up lemma," *IEEE Trans. Inform. Theory*, vol. IT-32, pp. 445–446, May 1986.

[9] S. Amari and T. S. Han, "Statistical inference under multiterminal rate restrictions: A differential geometric approach," *IEEE Trans. Inform. Theory*, vol. 35, pp. 217–227, Mar. 1989.

[10] H. M. H. Shalaby and A. Papamarcou, "Error exponent for distributed detection of Markov sources," *IEEE Trans. Inform. Theory*, vol. 40, pp. 397–408, Mar. 1994.

[11] T. S. Han, H. Shimokawa, and S. Amari, "Error bound of hypothesis testing with data compression," in *Proc. IEEE Int. Symp. Information Theory* (Trondheim, Norway, 1994), p. 29.

[12] Z. Zhang and T. Berger, "Estimation via compressed information," *IEEE Trans. Inform. Theory*, vol. 34, pp. 198–211, Mar. 1988.

[13] S. Amari, "Fisher information under restriction of Shannon information in multi-terminal situations," *Ann. Inst. Statist. Math.*, vol. 41, no. 4, pp. 623–648, 1989.

[14] R. Ahlswede and M. Burnashev, "On minimax estimation in the presence of side information about remote data," *Ann. Statist.*, vol. 18, no. 1, pp. 141–171, 1990.

[15] T. S. Han and S. Amari, "Parameter estimation with multiterminal data compression," *IEEE Trans. Inform. Theory*, vol. 41, pp. 1802–1833, Nov. 1995.

[16] C. R. Rao, *Linear Statistical Inference and its Applications*, 2nd ed. New York: Wiley, 1973.

[17] J. Körner and K. Marton, "How to encode the modulo 2 sum of two binary sources," *IEEE Trans. Inform. Theory*, vol. IT-25, pp. 219–221, 1979.

[18] T. S. Han and K. Kobayashi, "A dichotomy of functions $F(X,Y)$ of correlated sources (X,Y) from the viewpoint of the achievable rate region," *IEEE Trans. Inform. Theory*, vol. IT-33, pp. 69–76, Jan. 1987.

[19] I. Csiszár and J. Körner, *Information Theory: Coding Theorems for Discrete Memoryless Systems*. New York: Academic, 1981.

[20] T. M. Cover and J. Thomas, *Elements of Information Theory*. New York: Wiley, 1991.

[21] P. Billingsley, *Probability and Measure*, 3rd ed. New York: Wiley, 1995.

[22] S. Amari, *Differential Geometrical Methods in Statistics* (Lecture Notes in Statistics, no. 28). Berlin-Heidelberg: Springer, 1985.

[23] S. Amari and H. Nagaoka, *Introduction to Information Geometry*, Iwanami Press, Applied Mathematics Series (in Japanese), 1995; English translation to be published by Amer. Math. Soc. and Oxford Univ. Press, 1998.

[24] F. Kanaya and T. S. Han, "The asymptotics of posterior entropy and error probability for Bayesian estimation," *IEEE Trans. Inform. Theory*, vol. 41, pp. 1988–1995, Nov. 1995.

[25] R. A. Wiggins and E. A. Robinson, "Recursive solution to the multichannel filtering problem," *J. Geo-Phys. Res.*, vol. 70, no. 8, pp. 1885–1891, 1965.

[26] R. R. Tenney and N. R. Sandell, Jr.,"Detection with distributed sensors," *IEEE Trans. Aerosp. Electron. Syst.*, vol. AES-17, pp. 501–510, 1981.

[27] S. D. Stearns, "Optimal detection using multiple sensors," in *Proc. 1982 Carnahan Conf. Crime Countermeasures*, 1982.

[28] L. K. Ekchian and R. R. Tenny, " Detection networks," in *Proc. 21th IEEE Conf. Decision and Control* (Orlando, FL, 1982), pp. 686–691.

[29] H. J. Kushner and A. Pacut, "A simulation study of a decentralized detection problem," *IEEE Trans. Autonmat. Contr.*, vol. AC-27, pp. 1116–1119, 1982.

[30] D. Teneketzis, "The debentralized Wald problem," in *IEEE 1982 Int. Large-Scale Systems Symp.* (Virginia Beach, 1982), pp. 423–430.

[31] D. Teneketzis and P. Varaiya, "The decentralized quickest detection problem," *IEEE Trans. Automat. Contr.*, vol. AC-29, no. 7, pp. 641–64, 1984.

[32] J. Tsitsiklis and M. Athins, "On the complexity of distributed decision problems," *IEEE Trans. Automat. Contr.*, vol. AC-30, no. 5, pp. 440–446, 1985.

[33] Z. Chair and P. K. Varshney, "Optimal data fusion in multiple sensor detection systems," *IEEE Trans. Aerosp. Electron. Syst.*, vol. AES-22, pp. 98–101, 1986.

[34] R. Srinivasan, "Distributed radar detection theory," *Proc. Inst. Elec. Eng.*, vol. 133, pt. F, no. 1, pp. 55–60, 1986.

[35] F. A. Sadjadi, "Hypothesis testing in a distributed environment," *IEEE Trans. Aerosp. Electron. Syst.*, vol. AES-22, pp. 134–137, 1986.

[36] J. J. Chao and C. C. Lee, "A distributed detection scheme based on soft local decisions," in *Proc. 24th Annu. Allerton Conf. Communicayion, Control and Computing*, 1986, pp. 974–983.

[37] S. C. A. Thomopoulos, R. Viswanathan, and D. P. Bougoulias, "Optimal decision fusion in multiple sensor systems," *IEEE Trans. Aerosp. Electron Syst.*, vol. AES-23, pp. 644–653, 1987.

[38] V. Alalo, R. Viswanathan, and S. C. A. Thomopoulos, "A study of distributed detection with correlated sensor noise," presented at Globecom 87, 1987.

[39] T. J. Flynn and R. M. Gray, "Encoding of correlated observations," *IEEE Trans. Inform. Theory*, vol. IT-33, pp. 773–787, Nov. 1987.

[40] B. Picinbono and P. Duvaut, " Optimal quantization for detection," *IEEE Trans. Commun.*, vol. 36, pp. 1254–1258, Nov. 1988.

[41] M. M. Al-Ibrahim and P. K. Varshney, "Non-parametric sequential detection for multi sensor data," in *Proc. 1989 Johns Hopkins Conf. Information Sciences and Systems*, 1989, pp. 157–162.

[42] N. Sayiner and R. Viswanathan, "Distributed detection in jamming environment," *IEEE Trans.Aerosp. Electron Syst.*, 1990.

[43] D. Kazakos, V. Vannicola, and M. C. Wicks, "Signal detection," in *Proc. 1989 Johns Hopkins Conf. Information Sciences and Systems*, 1989, pp. 180–185.

[44] H. R. Hashemi and I. B. Rhodes, "Decentralized sequential detection," *IEEE Trans. Inform. Theory*, vol. IT-35, pp. 509–520, May 1989.

[45] I. Y. Hoballah and P. K. Varshney, "An information theoretic approach to the distributed detection problem," *IEEE Trans. Inform. Theory*, vol. 35, pp. 988–994, 1989.

[46] ———, "Distributed Bayesian signal detection," *IEEE Trans. Inform. Theory*, vol. 35, pp. 995–1000, 1989.

[47] T. S. Han and K. Kobayashi, "Multiterminal filtering for decentralized detection systems," *IEICE Trans. Commun.*, vol. E75-B, no. 6, pp. 437–444, 1992.

280

Quantization

Robert M. Gray, *Fellow, IEEE*, and David L. Neuhoff, *Fellow, IEEE*

(Invited Paper)

Abstract— The history of the theory and practice of quantization dates to 1948, although similar ideas had appeared in the literature as long ago as 1898. The fundamental role of quantization in modulation and analog-to-digital conversion was first recognized during the early development of pulse-code modulation systems, especially in the 1948 paper of Oliver, Pierce, and Shannon. Also in 1948, Bennett published the first high-resolution analysis of quantization and an exact analysis of quantization noise for Gaussian processes, and Shannon published the beginnings of rate distortion theory, which would provide a theory for quantization as analog-to-digital conversion and as data compression. Beginning with these three papers of fifty years ago, we trace the history of quantization from its origins through this decade, and we survey the fundamentals of the theory and many of the popular and promising techniques for quantization.

Index Terms— High resolution theory, rate distortion theory, source coding, quantization.

I. INTRODUCTION

THE dictionary (*Random House*) definition of quantization is the division of a quantity into a discrete number of small parts, often assumed to be integral multiples of a common quantity. The oldest example of quantization is rounding off, which was first analyzed by Sheppard [468] for the application of estimating densities by histograms. Any real number x can be rounded off to the nearest integer, say $q(x)$, with a resulting quantization error $e = q(x) - x$ so that $q(x) = x + e$. More generally, we can define a quantizer as consisting of a set of intervals or *cells* $\mathcal{S} = \{S_i; i \in \mathcal{I}\}$, where the index set $\mathcal{I}$ is ordinarily a collection of consecutive integers beginning with 0 or 1, together with a set of *reproduction values* or *points* or *levels* $\mathcal{C} = \{y_i; i \in \mathcal{I}\}$, so that the overall quantizer q is defined by $q(x) = y_i$ for $x \in S_i$, which can be expressed concisely as

$$q(x) = \sum_i y_i 1_{S_i}(x) \qquad (1)$$

where the indicator function $1_S(x)$ is 1 if $x \in S$ and 0 otherwise. For this definition to make sense we assume that $\mathcal{S}$ is a partition of the real line. That is, the cells are disjoint and exhaustive. The general definition reduces to the rounding off

Manuscript received January 7, 1998; revised June 6, 1998. This work was supported in part by the National Science Foundation under Grants NCR-941574 and MIP-931190.

R. M. Gray is with the Department of Electrical Engineering, Stanford University, Stanford, CA 94305 USA.

D. L. Neuhoff is with the Electrical Engineering and Computer Science Department, University of Michigan, Ann Arbor, MI 48109 USA.

Publisher Item Identifier S 0018-9448(98)06317-2.

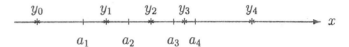

Fig. 1. A nonuniform quantizer: $a_0 = \infty$, $a_5 = \infty$.

example if $S_i = (i - 1/2, i + 1/2]$ and $y_i = i$ for all integers i. More generally, the cells might take the form $S_i = (a_{i-1}, a_i]$ where the a_i's, which are called *thresholds*, form an increasing sequence. The width of a cell S_i is its length $a_i - a_{i-1}$. The function $q(x)$ is often called the *quantization rule*. A simple quantizer with five reproduction levels is depicted in Fig. 1 as a collection of intervals bordered by thresholds along with the levels for each interval.

A quantizer is said to be *uniform* if, as in the roundoff case, the levels y_i are equispaced, say Δ apart, and the thresholds a_i are midway between adjacent levels. If an infinite number of levels are allowed, then all cells S_i will have width equal to Δ, the separation between levels. If only a finite number of levels are allowed, then all but two cells will have width Δ and the outermost cells will be semi-infinite. An example of a uniform quantizer with cell width Δ and $N = 8$ levels is given in Fig. 2. Given a uniform quantizer with cell width Δ, the region of the input space within $\Delta/2$ of some quantizer level is called the *granular region* or simply the *support* and that outside (where the quantizer error is unbounded) is called the *overload* or *saturation* region. More generally, the support or granular region of a nonuniform quantizer is the region of the input space within a relatively small distance of some level, and the overload region is the complement of the granular region. To be concrete, "small" might be defined as half the width of the largest cell of finite width.

The quality of a quantizer can be measured by the goodness of the resulting reproduction in comparison to the original. One way of accomplishing this is to define a distortion measure $d(x, \hat{x})$ that quantifies cost or distortion resulting from reproducing x as $\hat{x}$ and to consider the average distortion as a measure of the quality of a system, with smaller average distortion meaning higher quality. The most common distortion measure is the squared error $d(x, \hat{x}) = |x - \hat{x}|^2$, but we shall encounter others later. In practice, the average will be a sample average when the quantizer is applied to a sequence of real data, but the theory views the data as sharing a common probability density function (pdf) $f(x)$ corresponding to a generic random variable X and the average distortion becomes an expectation

$$D(q) = E[d(X, q(X))] = \sum_i \int_{S_i} d(x, y_i) f(x)\, dx. \qquad (2)$$

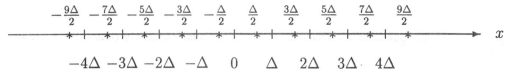

Fig. 2. A uniform quantizer.

If the distortion is measured by squared error, $D(q)$ becomes the mean squared error (MSE), a special case on which we shall mostly focus.

It is desirable to have the average distortion as small as possible, and in fact negligible average distortion is achievable by letting the cells become numerous and tiny. There is a cost in terms of the number of bits required to describe the quantizer output to a decoder, however, and arbitrarily reliable reproduction will not be possible for digital storage and communication media with finite capacity. A simple method for quantifying the cost for communications or storage is to assume that the quantizer "codes" an input x into a binary representation or channel codeword of the quantizer index i specifying which reproduction level should be used in the reconstruction. If there are N possible levels and all of the binary representations or binary codewords have equal length (a temporary assumption), the binary vectors will need $\log N$ (or the next larger integer, $\lceil \log N \rceil$, if $\log N$ is not an integer) components or bits. Thus one definition of the *rate* of the code in bits per input sample is

$$R(q) = \log N. \tag{3}$$

A quantizer with fixed-length binary codewords is said to have *fixed rate* because all quantizer levels are assumed to have binary codewords of equal length. Later this restriction will be weakened. Note that all logarithms in this paper will have base 2, unless explicitly specified otherwise.

In summary, the goal of quantization is to encode the data from a source, characterized by its probability density function, into as few bits as possible (i.e., with low rate) in such a way that a reproduction may be recovered from the bits with as high quality as possible (i.e., with small average distortion). Clearly, there is a tradeoff between the two primary performance measures: average distortion (or simply *distortion*, as we will often abbreviate) and rate. This tradeoff may be quantified as the *operational distortion-rate function* $\delta(R)$, which is defined to be the least distortion of any scalar quantizer with rate R or less. That is,

$$\delta(R) \equiv \inf_{q:\, R(q) \leq R} D(q). \tag{4}$$

Alternatively, one can define the operational *rate-distortion function* $r(D)$ as the least rate of any fixed-rate scalar quantizer with distortion D or less, which is the inverse of $\delta(R)$.

We have so far described *scalar quantization with fixed-rate coding*, a technique whereby each data sample is independently encoded into a fixed number of bits and decoded into a reproduction. As we shall see, there are many alternative quantization techniques that permit a better tradeoff of distortion and rate; e.g., less distortion for the same rate, or vice versa. The purpose of this paper is to review the development of such

techniques, and the theory of their design and performance. For example, for each type of technique we will be interested in its operational distortion-rate function, which is defined to be the least distortion of any quantizer of the given type with rate R or less. We will also be interested in the best possible performance among *all* quantizers. Both as a preview and as an occasional benchmark for comparison, we informally define the class of all quantizers as the class of quantizers that can 1) operate on scalars or vectors instead of only on scalars (vector quantizers), 2) have fixed or variable rate in the sense that the binary codeword describing the quantizer output can have length depending on the input, and 3) be memoryless or have memory, for example, using different sets of reproduction levels, depending on the past. In addition, we restrict attention to quantizers that do not change with time. That is, when confronted with the same input and the same past history, a quantizer will produce the same output regardless of the time. We occasionally use the term *lossy source code* or simply *code* as alternatives to *quantizer*. The rate is now defined as the average number of bits per source symbol required to describe the corresponding reproduction symbol. We informally generalize the operational distortion-rate function $\delta(R)$ providing the best performance for scalar quantizers, to $\bar{\delta}(R)$, which is defined as the infimum of the average distortion over all quantization techniques with rate R or less. Thus $\bar{\delta}(R)$ can be viewed as the best possible performance over all quantizers with no constraints on dimension, structure, or complexity.

Section II begins with a historical tour of the development of the theory and practice of quantization over the past fifty years, a period encompassing almost the entire literature on the subject. Two complementary approaches dominate the history and present state of the theory, and three of the key papers appeared in 1948, two of them in Volume 27 (1948) of the *Bell Systems Technical Journal*. Likely the approach best known to the readers of these TRANSACTIONS is that of rate-distortion theory or source coding with a fidelity criterion—Shannon's information-theoretic approach to source coding—which was first suggested in his 1948 paper [464] providing the foundations of information theory, but which was not fully developed until his 1959 source coding paper [465]. The second approach is that of high resolution (or high-rate or asymptotic) quantization theory, which had its origins in the 1948 paper on PCM by Oliver, Pierce, and Shannon [394], the 1948 paper on quantization error spectra by Bennett [43], and the 1951 paper by Panter and Dite [405]. Much of the history and state of the art of quantization derives from these seminal works.

In contrast to these two asymptotic theories, there is also a small but important collection of results that are not asymptotic in nature. The oldest such results are the exact analyses for special nonasymptotic cases, such as Clavier, Panter, and Grieg's 1947 analysis of the spectra of the quantization error for uniformly quantized sinusoidal signals [99], [100], and Bennett's 1948 derivation of the power spectral density of a uniformly quantized Gaussian random process [43]. The most important nonasymptotic results, however, are the basic optimality conditions and iterative-descent algorithms for quantizer design, such as first developed by Steinhaus (1956) [480] and Lloyd (1957) [330], and later popularized by Max (1960) [349].

Our goal in the next section is to introduce in historical context many of the key ideas of quantization that originated in classical works and evolved over the past 50 years, and in the remaining sections to survey selectively and in more detail a variety of results which illustrate both the historical development and the state of the field. Section III will present basic background material that will be needed in the remainder of the paper, including the general definition of a quantizer and the basic forms of optimality criteria and descent algorithms. Some such material has already been introduced and more will be introduced in Section II. However, for completeness, Section III will be largely self-contained. Section IV reviews the development of quantization theories and compares the approaches. Finally, Section V describes a number of specific quantization techniques.

In any review of a large subject such as quantization there is no space to discuss or even mention all work on the subject. Though we have made an effort to select the most important work, no doubt we have missed some important work due to bias, misunderstanding, or ignorance. For this we apologize, both to the reader and to the researchers whose work we may have neglected.

II. HISTORY

The history of quantization often takes on several parallel paths, which causes some problems in our clustering of topics. We follow roughly a chronological order within each and order the paths as best we can. Specifically, we will first track the design and analysis of practical quantization techniques in three paths: fixed-rate scalar quantization, which leads directly from the discussion of Section I, predictive and transform coding, which adds linear processing to scalar quantization in order to exploit source redundancy, and variable-rate quantization, which uses Shannon's lossless source coding techniques [464] to reduce rate. (Lossless codes were originally called *noiseless*.) Next we follow early forward-looking work on vector quantization, including the seminal work of Shannon and Zador, in which vector quantization appears more to be a paradigm for analyzing the fundamental limits of quantizer performance than a practical coding technique. A surprising amount of such vector quantization theory was developed outside the conventional communications and signal processing literature. Subsequently, we review briefly the developments from the mid-1970's to the mid-1980's which mainly concern the emergence of vector quantization as a practical technique. Finally, we sketch briefly developments from the mid-1980's to the present. Except where stated otherwise, we presume squared error as the distortion measure.

A. Fixed-Rate Scalar Quantization: PCM and the Origins of Quantization Theory

Both quantization and source coding with a fidelity criterion have their origins in pulse-code modulation (PCM), a technique patented in 1938 by Reeves [432], who 25 years later wrote a historical perspective on and an appraisal of the future of PCM with Deloraine [120]. The predictions were surprisingly accurate as to the eventual ubiquity of digital speech and video. The technique was first successfully implemented in hardware by Black, who reported the principles and implementation in 1947 [51], as did another Bell Labs paper by Goodall [209]. PCM was subsequently analyzed in detail and popularized by Oliver, Pierce, and Shannon in 1948 [394]. PCM was the first *digital* technique for conveying an analog information signal (principally telephone speech) over an analog channel (typically, a wire or the atmosphere). In other words, it is a modulation technique, i.e., an alternative to AM, FM, and various other types of pulse modulation. It consists of three main components: a sampler (including a prefilter), a quantizer (with a fixed-rate binary encoder), and a binary pulse modulator. The sampler converts a continuous-time waveform $x(t)$ into a sequence of samples $x_n = x(n/f_s)$, where f_s is the sampling frequency. The sampler is ordinarily preceded by a lowpass filter with cutoff frequency $f_s/2$. If the filter is ideal, then the Shannon–Nyquist or Shannon–Whittaker–Kotelnikov sampling theorem ensures that the lowpass filtered signal can, in principle, be perfectly recovered by appropriately filtering the samples. Quantization of the samples renders this an approximation, with the MSE of the recovered waveform being, approximately, the sum of the MSE of the quantizer $D(q)$ and the high-frequency power removed by the lowpass filter. The binary pulse modulator typically uses the bits produced by the quantizer to determine the amplitude, frequency, or phase of a sinusoidal carrier waveform. In the evolutionary development of modulation techniques it was found that the performance of pulse-amplitude modulation in the presence of noise could be improved if the samples were quantized to the nearest of a set of N levels before modulating the carrier (64 equally spaced levels was typical). Though this introduces quantization error, deciding which of the N levels had been transmitted in the presence of noise could be done with such reliability that the overall MSE was substantially reduced. Reducing the number of quantization levels N made it even easier to decide which level had been transmitted, but came at the cost of a considerable increase in the MSE of the quantizer. A solution was to fix N at a value giving acceptably small quantizer MSE and to binary encode the levels, so that the receiver had only to make binary decisions, something it can do with great reliability. The resulting system, PCM, had the best resistance to noise of all modulations of the time.

As the digital era emerged, it was recognized that the sampling, quantizing, and encoding part of PCM performs an analog-to-digital (A/D) conversion, with uses extending much beyond communication over analog channels. Even in the communications field, it was recognized that the task of analog-to-digital conversion (and source coding) should be factored out of binary modulation as a separate task. Thus

PCM is now generally considered to just consist of sampling, quantizing, and encoding; i.e., it no longer includes the binary pulse modulation.

Although quantization in the information theory literature is generally considered as a form of data compression, its use for modulation or A/D conversion was originally viewed as data expansion or, more accurately, bandwidth expansion. For example, a speech waveform occupying roughly 4 kHz would have a Nyquist rate of 8 kHz. Sampling at the Nyquist rate and quantizing at 8 bits per sample and then modulating the resulting binary pulses using amplitude- or frequency-shift keying would yield a signal occupying roughly 64 kHz, a 16–fold increase in bandwidth! Mathematically this constitutes compression in the sense that a continuous waveform requiring an infinite number of bits is reduced to a finite number of bits, but for practical purposes PCM is not well interpreted as a compression scheme.

In an early contribution to the theory of quantization, Clavier, Panter, and Grieg (1947) [99], [100] applied Rice's characteristic function or transform method [434] to provide exact expressions for the quantization error and its moments resulting from uniform quantization for certain specific inputs, including constants and sinusoids. The complicated sums of Bessel functions resembled the early analyses of another nonlinear modulation technique, FM, and left little hope for general closed-form solutions for interesting signals.

The first general contributions to quantization theory came in 1948 with the papers of Oliver, Pierce, and Shannon [394] and Bennett [43]. As part of their analysis of PCM for communications, they developed the oft-quoted result that for large rate or resolution, a uniform quantizer with cell width Δ yields average distortion $D(q) \cong \Delta^2/12$. If the quantizer has N levels and rate $R = \log N$, and the source has input range (or *support*) of width A, so that $\Delta = A/N$ is the natural choice, then the $\Delta^2/12$ approximation yields the familiar form for the signal-to-noise ratio (SNR) of

$$10 \log_{10} \frac{\operatorname{var}(X)}{E[(q(X) - X)^2]} = c + 20R \log_{10} 2$$
$$\cong c + 6R \text{ dB}$$

showing that for large rate, the SNR of uniform quantization increases 6 dB for each one-bit increase of rate, which is often referred to as the "6-dB-per-bit rule." The $\Delta^2/12$ formula is considered a *high-resolution* formula; indeed, the first such formula, in that it applies to the situation where the cells and average distortion are small, and the rate is large, so that the reproduction produced by the quantizer is quite accurate. The $\Delta^2/12$ result also appeared many years earlier (albeit in somewhat disguised form) in Sheppard's 1898 treatment [468].

Bennett also developed several other fundamental results in quantization theory. He generalized the high-resolution approximation for uniform quantization to provide an approximation to $D(q)$ for companders, systems that preceded a uniform quantizer by a monotonic smooth nonlinearity called a "compressor," say G, and used the inverse nonlinearity when reconstructing the signal. Thus the output reproduction $\hat{x}$ given an input x was given by $\hat{x} = G^{-1}(q(G(x)))$, where q is a uniform quantizer. Bennett showed that in this case

$$D(q) \cong \frac{\Delta^2}{12} \int \frac{f(x)}{g^2(x)} dx \qquad (5)$$

where $g(x) = dG(x)/dx$, Δ is the cellwidth of the uniform quantizer, and the integral is taken over the granular range of the input. (The constant $1/12$ in the above assumes that G maps to the unit interval $[0, 1]$.) Since, as Bennett pointed out, any nonuniform quantizer can be implemented as a compander, this result, often referred to as "Bennett's integral," provides an asymptotic approximation for any quantizer. It is useful to jump ahead and point out that g can be interpreted, as Lloyd would explicitly point out in 1957 [330], as a constant times a "quantizer point-density function $\lambda(x)$," that is, a function with the property that for any region S

$$\text{number of quantizer levels in } S \approx N \int_S \lambda(x) dx. \qquad (6)$$

Since integrating $\lambda(x)$ over a region gives the fraction of quantizer reproduction levels in the region, it is evident that $\lambda(x)$ is normalized so that $\int_\Re \lambda(x) dx = 1$. It will also prove useful to consider the unnormalized quantizer point density $\Lambda(x)$, which when integrated over S gives the total number of levels within S rather than the fraction. In the current situation $\Lambda(x) = N\lambda(x)$, but the unnormalized density will generalize to the case where N is infinite.

Rewriting Bennett's integral in terms of the point-density function yields its more common form

$$D(q) \cong \frac{1}{12} \frac{1}{N^2} \int \frac{f(x)}{\lambda^2(x)} dx. \qquad (7)$$

The idea of a quantizer point-density function will generalize to vectors, while the compander approach will not in the sense that not all vector quantizers can be represented as companders [192].

Bennett also demonstrated that, under assumptions of high resolution and smooth densities, the quantization error behaved much like random "noise": it had small correlation with the signal and had approximately a flat ("white") spectrum. This led to an "additive-noise" model of quantizer error, since with these properties the formula $q(X) = X + [q(X) - X]$ could be interpreted as representing the quantizer output as the sum of a signal and white noise. This model was later popularized by Widrow [528], [529], but the viewpoint avoids the fact that the "noise" is in fact dependent on the signal and the approximations are valid only under certain conditions. Signal-independent quantization noise has generally been found to be perceptually desirable. This was the motivation for randomizing the action of quantization by the addition of a dither signal, a method introduced by Roberts [442] as a means of making quantized images look better by replacing the artifacts resulting from deterministic errors by random noise. We shall return to dithering in Section V, where it will be seen that suitable dithering can indeed make exact the Bennett approximations of uniform distribution and signal independence of the overall quantizer noise. Bennett also used a variation of Rice's method to derive an exact computation of the spectrum of quantizer noise when a Gaussian process is uniformly quantized, providing one of the very few exact computations of quantization error spectra.

In 1951 Panter and Dite [405] developed a high-resolution formula for the distortion of a fixed-rate scalar quantizer using approximations similar to Bennett's, but without reference to Bennett. They then used variational techniques to minimize their formula and found the following formula for the operational distortion-rate function of fixed-rate scalar quantization: for large values of R

$$\delta(R) \cong \frac{1}{12} \left(\int f^{1/3}(x) \, dx \right)^3 2^{-2R} \qquad (8)$$

which is now called the Panter and Dite formula.[1] As part of their derivation, they demonstrated that an optimal quantizer resulted in roughly equal contributions to total average distortion from each quantization cell, a result later called the "partial distortion theorem." Though they did not rederive Bennett's integral, they had in effect derived the optimal compressor function for a compander, or, equivalently, the optimal quantizer point density

$$\lambda(x) = \frac{f^{1/3}(x)}{\int f^{1/3}(x') \, dx'}. \qquad (9)$$

Indeed, substituting this point density into Bennett's integral and using the fact that $R = \log N$ yields (8). As an example, if the input density is Gaussian with variance σ^2, then

$$\delta(R) \cong \frac{1}{12} 6\pi\sqrt{3}\sigma^2 2^{-2R}. \qquad (10)$$

The fact that for large rates $\delta(R)$ decreases with R as 2^{-2R} implies that the signal-to-noise ratio increases according to the 6-dB-per-bit rule. Virtually all other high resolution formulas to be given later will also obey this rule. However, the constant that adds to $6R$ will vary with the source and quantizer being considered.

The Panter–Dite formula for $\delta(R)$ can also be derived directly from Bennett's integral using variational methods, as did Lloyd (1957) [330], Smith (1957) [474], and, much later without apparent knowledge of earlier work, Roe (1964) [443]. It can also be derived without using variational methods by application of Hölder's inequality to Bennett's integral [222], with the additional benefit of demonstrating that the claimed minimum is indeed global. Though not known at the time, it turns out that for a Gaussian source with independent and identically distributed (i.i.d.) samples, the operational distortion-rate function given above is $\pi\sqrt{3}/2 = 2.72$ times larger than $\overline{\delta}(R)$, the least distortion achievable by any quantization technique with rate R or less. (It was not until Shannon's 1959 paper [465] that $\overline{\delta}(R)$ was known.) Equivalently, the induced signal-to-noise ratio is 4.35 dB less than the best possible, or for a fixed distortion D the rate is 0.72 bits/sample larger than that achievable by the best quantizers.

In 1957, Smith [474] re-examined companding and PCM. Among other things, he gave somewhat cleaner derivations of

Bennett's integral, the optimal compressor function, and the Panter–Dite formula.

Also in 1957, Lloyd [330] made an important study of quantization with three main contributions. First, he found necessary and sufficient conditions for a fixed-rate quantizer to be locally optimal; i.e., conditions that if satisfied implied that small perturbations to the levels or thresholds would increase distortion. Any optimal quantizer (one with smallest distortion) will necessarily satisfy these conditions, and so they are often called the *optimality conditions* or the *necessary conditions*. Simply stated, Lloyd's optimality conditions are that for a fixed-rate quantizer to be optimal, the quantizer partition must be optimal for the set of reproduction levels, and the set of reproduction levels must be optimal for the partition. Lloyd derived these conditions straightforwardly from first principles, without recourse to variational concepts such as derivatives. For the case of mean-squared error, the first condition implies a minimum distance or nearest neighbor quantization rule, choosing the closest available reproduction level to the source sample being quantized, and the second condition implies that the reproduction level corresponding to a given cell is the conditional expectation or *centroid* of the source value given that it lies in the specified cell; i.e., it is the minimum mean-squared error estimate of the source sample. For some sources there are multiple locally optimal quantizers, not all of which are globally optimal.

Second, based on his optimality conditions, Lloyd developed an iterative descent algorithm for designing quantizers for a given source distribution: begin with an initial collection of reproduction levels; optimize the partition for these levels by using a minimum distortion mapping, which gives a partition of the real line into intervals; then optimize the set of levels for the partition by replacing the old levels by the centroids of the partition cells. The alternation is continued until convergence to a local, if not global, optimum. Lloyd referred to this design algorithm as "Method I." He also developed a Method II based on the optimality properties. First choose an initial smallest reproduction level. This determines the cell threshold to the right, which in turn implies the next larger reproduction level, and so on. This approach alternately produces a level and a threshold. Once the last level has been chosen, the initial level can then be rechosen to reduce distortion and the algorithm continues. Lloyd provided design examples for uniform, Gaussian, and Laplacian random variables and showed that the results were consistent with the high resolution approximations. Although Method II would initially gain more popularity when rediscovered in 1960 by Max [349], it is Method I that easily extends to vector quantizers and many types of quantizers with structural constraints.

Third, motivated by the work of Panter and Dite but apparently unaware of that of Bennett or Smith, Lloyd rederived Bennett's integral and the Panter–Dite formula based on the concept of point-density function. This was a critically important step for subsequent generalizations of Bennett's integral to vector quantizers. He also showed directly that in situations where the global optimum is the only local optimum, quantizers that satisfy the optimality conditions have, asymptotically, the optimal point density given by (9).

---

[1] They also indicated that it had been derived earlier by P. R. Aigrain.

Unfortunately, Lloyd's work was not published in an archival journal at the time. Instead, it was presented at the 1957 Institute of Mathematical Statistics (IMS) meeting and appeared in print only as a Bell Laboratories Technical Memorandum. As a result, its results were not widely known in the engineering literature for many years, and many were independently rediscovered. All of the independent rediscoveries, however, used variational derivations, rather than Lloyd's simple derivations. The latter were essential for later extensions to vector quantizers and to the development of many quantizer optimization procedures. To our knowledge, the first mention of Lloyd's work in the IEEE literature came in 1964 with Fleischer's [170] derivation of a sufficient condition (namely, that the log of the source density be concave) in order that the optimal quantizer be the only locally optimal quantizer, and consequently, that Lloyd's Method I yields a globally optimal quantizer. (The condition is satisfied for common densities such as Gaussian and Laplacian.) Zador [561] had referred to Lloyd a year earlier in his Ph.D. dissertation, to be discussed later.

Later in the same year in another Bell Telephone Laboratories Technical Memorandum, Goldstein [207] used variational methods to derive conditions for global optimality of a scalar quantizer in terms of second-order partial derivatives with respect to the quantizer levels and thresholds. He also provided a simple counterintuitive example of a symmetric density for which the optimal quantizer was asymmetric.

In 1959, Shtein [471] added terms representing overload distortion to the $\Delta^2/12$ formula and to Bennett's integral and used them to optimize uniform and nonuniform quantizers. Unaware of prior work, except for Bennett's, he rederived the optimal compressor characteristic and the Panter–Dite formula.

In 1960, Max [349] published a variational proof of the Lloyd optimality properties for rth-power distortion measures, rediscovered Lloyd's Method II, and numerically investigated the design of fixed-rate quantizers for a variety of input densities.

Also in 1960, Widrow [529] derived an exact formula for the characteristic function of a uniformly quantized signal when the quantizer has an infinite number of levels. His results showed that under the condition that the characteristic function of the input signal be zero when its argument is greater than π/Δ, the moments of the quantized random variable are the same as the moments of the signal plus an additive signal-independent random variable uniformly distributed on $(-\Delta/2, \Delta/2)$. This has often been misinterpreted as saying that the quantized random variable can be approximated as being the input plus signal-independent uniform noise, a clearly false statement since the quantizer error $q(X) - X$ is a deterministic function of the signal. The "bandlimited" property of the characteristic function implies from Fourier transform theory that the probability density function must have infinite support since a signal and its transform cannot both be perfectly bandlimited.

We conclude this subsection by mentioning early work that appeared in the mathematical and statistical literature and which, in hindsight, can be viewed as related to scalar quantization. Specifically, in 1950–1951 Dalenius *et al.* [118],

[119] used variational techniques to consider optimal grouping of Gaussian data with respect to average squared error. Lukaszewicz and H. Steinhaus [336] (1955) developed what we now consider to be the Lloyd optimality conditions using variational techniques in a study of optimum go/no-go gauge sets (as acknowledged by Lloyd). Cox in 1957 [111] also derived similar conditions. Some additional early work, which can now be seen as relating to vector quantization, will be reviewed later [480], [159], [561].

B. Scalar Quantization with Memory

It was recognized early that common sources such as speech and images had considerable "redundancy" that scalar quantization could not exploit. The term "redundancy" was commonly used in the early days and is still popular in some of the quantization literature. Strictly speaking, it refers to the statistical correlation or dependence between the samples of such sources and is usually referred to as *memory* in the information theory literature. As our current emphasis is historical, we follow the traditional language. While not disrupting the performance of scalar quantizers, such redundancy could be exploited to attain substantially better rate-distortion performance. The early approaches toward this end combined linear processing with scalar quantization, thereby preserving the simplicity of scalar quantization while using intuition-based arguments and insights to improve performance by incorporating memory into the overall code. The two most important approaches of this variety were predictive coding and transform coding. A shared intuition was that a preprocessing operation intended to make scalar quantization more efficient should "remove the redundancy" in the data. Indeed, to this day there is a common belief that data compression is equivalent to redundancy removal and that data without redundancy cannot be further compressed. As will be discussed later, this belief is contradicted both by Shannon's work, which demonstrated strictly improved performance using vector quantizers even for memoryless sources, and by the early work of Fejes Toth (1959) [159]. Nevertheless, removing redundancy leads to much improved codes.

Predictive quantization appears to originate in the 1946 delta modulation patent of Derjavitch, Deloraine, and Van Mierlo [129], but the most commonly cited early references are Cutler's patent [117] 2 605 361 on "Differential quantization of communication signals" and on DeJager's Philips technical report on delta modulation [128]. Cutler stated in his patent that it "is the object of the present invention to improve the efficiency of communication systems by taking advantage of correlation in the signals of these systems" and Derjavitch *et al.* also cited the reduction of redundancy as the key to the reduction of quantization noise. In 1950, Elias [141] provided an information-theoretic development of the benefits of predictive coding, but the work was not published until 1955 [142]. Other early references include [395], [300], [237], [511], and [572]. In particular, [511] claims Bennett-style asymptotics for high-resolution quantization error, but as will be discussed later, such approximations have yet to be rigorously derived.

From the point of view of least squares estimation theory, if one were to optimally predict a data sequence based on its past

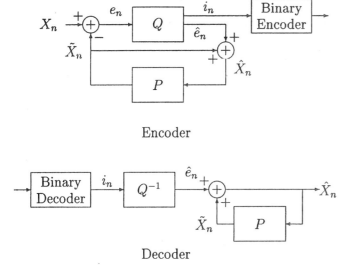

Encoder

Decoder

Fig. 3. Predictive quantizer encoder/decoder.

in the sense of minimizing the mean-squared error, then the resulting error or residual or innovations sequence would be uncorrelated and it would have the minimum possible variance. To permit reconstruction in a coded system, however, the prediction must be based on past reconstructed samples and not true samples. This is accomplished by placing a quantizer inside a prediction loop and using the same predictor to decode the signal. A simple predictive quantizer or differential pulse-coded modulator (DPCM) is depicted in Fig. 3. If the predictor is simply the last sample and the quantizer has only one bit, the system becomes a delta-modulator. Predictive quantizers are considered to have *memory* in that the quantization of a sample depends on previous samples, via the feedback loop.

Predictive quantizers have been extensively developed, for example there are many adaptive versions, and are widely used in speech and video coding, where a number of standards are based on them. In speech coding they form the basis of ITU-G.721, 722, 723, and 726, and in video coding they form the basis of the interframe coding schemes standardized in the MPEG and H.26X series. Comprehensive discussions may be found in books [265], [374], [196], [424], [50], and [458], as well as survey papers [264] and [198].

Though decorrelation was an early motivation for predictive quantization, the most common view at present is that the primary role of the predictor is to reduce the variance of the variable to be scalar-quantized. This view stems from the facts that a) it is the prediction errors rather than the source samples that are quantized, b) the overall quantization error precisely equals that of the scalar quantizer operating on the prediction errors, c) the operational distortion-rate function $\delta(R)$ for scalar quantization is proportional to variance (more precisely, a scaling of the random variable being quantized by a factor a results in a scaling of $\delta(R)$ by a^2), and d) the density of the prediction error is usually sufficiently similar in form to that of the source that its operational distortion-rate function is smaller than that of the original source by, approximately, the ratio of the variance of the source to that of the prediction error, a quantity that is often

called a *prediction gain* [350], [396], [482], [397], [265]. Analyses of this form usually claim that under high-resolution conditions the distribution of the prediction error approaches that of the error when predictions are based on past source samples rather than past reproductions. However, it is not clear that the accuracy of this approximation increases sufficiently rapidly with finer resolution to ensure that the difference between the operational distortion-rate functions of the two types of prediction errors is small relative to their values, which are themselves decreasing as the resolution becomes finer. Indeed, it is still an open question whether this type of analysis, which typically uses Bennett and Panter–Dite formulas, is asymptotically correct. Nevertheless, the results of such high resolution approximations are widely accepted and often compare well with experimental results [156], [265]. Assuming that they give the correct answer, then for large rates and a stationary, Gaussian source with memory, the distortion of an optimized DPCM quantizer is less than that of a scalar quantizer by the factor σ_1^2/σ^2, where σ^2 is the variance of the source and σ_1^2 is the one-step prediction error; i.e., the smallest MSE of any prediction of one sample based on previous samples. It turns out that this exceeds $\overline{\delta}(R)$ by the same factor by which the distortion of optimal fixed-rate scalar quantization exceeds $\overline{\delta}(R)$ for a memoryless Gaussian source. Hence, it appears that DPCM does a good job of exploiting source memory given that it is based on scalar quantization, at least under the high-resolution assumption.

Because it has not been rigorously shown that one may apply Bennett's integral or the Panter–Dite formula directly to the prediction error, the analysis of such feedback quantization systems has proved to be notoriously difficult, with results limited to proofs of stability [191], [281], [284], i.e., asymptotic stationarity, to analyses of distortion via Hermite polynomial expansions for Gaussian processes [124], [473], [17], [346], [241], [262], [156], [189], [190], [367]–[369], [293], to analyses of distortion when the source is a Wiener process [163], [346], [240], and to exact solutions of the nonlinear difference equations describing the system and hence to descriptions of the output sequences and their moments, including power spectral densities, for constant and sinusoidal signals and finite sums of sinusoids using Rice's method, results which extend the work of Panter, Clavier, and Grieg to quantizers inside a feedback loop [260], [71], [215], [216], [72]. Conditions for use in code design resembling the Lloyd optimality conditions have been studied for feedback quantization [161], [203], [41], but the conditions are not optimality conditions in the Lloyd sense, i.e., they are not necessary conditions for a quantizer within a feedback loop to yield the minimum average distortion subject to a rate constraint. We will return to this issue when we consider finite-state vector quantizers. There has also been work on the optimality of certain causal coding structures somewhat akin to predictive or feedback quantization [331], [414], [148], [534], [178], [381], [521].

Transform coding is the second approach to exploiting redundancy by using scalar quantization with linear preprocessing. Here, the source samples are collected into a vector of, say, dimension k that is multiplied by an orthogonal matrix (an

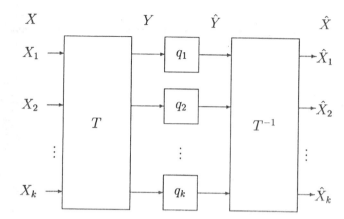

Fig. 4. Transform code.

orthogonal transform) and the resulting transform coefficients are scalar quantized, usually with a different quantizer for each coefficient. The operation is depicted in Fig. 4. This style of code was introduced in 1956 by Kramer and Mathews [299] and analyzed and popularized in 1962–1963 by Huang and Schultheiss [247], [248]. Kramer and Mathews simply assumed that the goal of the transform was to decorrelate the symbols, but Huang and Schultheiss proved that decorrelating does indeed lead to optimal transform code design, at least in the case of Gaussian sources and high resolution. Transform coding has been extensively developed for coding images and video, where the discrete cosine transform (DCT) [7], [429] is most commonly used because of its computational simplicity and its good performance. Indeed, DCT coding is the basic approach dominating current image and video coding standards, including H.261, H.263, JPEG, and MPEG. These codes combine uniform scalar quantization of the transform coefficients with an efficient lossless coding of the quantizer indices, as will be considered in the next section as a variable-rate quantizer. For discussions of transform coding for images see [533], [422], [375], [265], [98], [374], [261], [424], [196], [208], [408], [50], [458], and More recently, transform coding has also been widely used in high-fidelity audio coding [272], [200].

Unlike predictive quantizers, the transform coding approach lent itself quite well to the Bennett high-resolution approximations, the classical analysis being that of Huang and Schultheiss [247], [248] of the performance of optimized transform codes for fixed-rate scalar quantizers for Gaussian sources, a result which demonstrated that the Karhunen–Loève decorrelating transform was optimum for this application for the given assumptions. If the transform is the Karhunen–Loève transform, then the coefficients will be uncorrelated (and hence independent if the input vector is also Gaussian). The seminal work of Huang and Schultheiss showed that high-resolution approximation theory could provide analytical descriptions of optimal performance and design algorithms for optimizing codes of a given structure. In particular, they showed that under the high-resolution assumptions with Gaussian sources, the average distortion of the best transform code with a given rate is less than that of optimal scalar quantization by the factor $(\det K_k)^{1/k}/\sigma^2$, where σ^2 is the average of the

variances of the components of the source vector and K_k is its $k \times k$ covariance matrix. Note that this reduction in distortion becomes larger for sources with more memory (more correlation) because the covariance matrices of such sources have smaller determinants. When k is large, it turns out that the distortion of optimized transform coding with a given rate exceeds $\bar{\delta}(R)$ by the same factor by which the distortion of optimal fixed-rate scalar quantization exceeds $\bar{\delta}(R)$ for a memoryless Gaussian source. Hence, like DPCM, transform coding does a good job of exploiting source memory given that it is a system based on scalar quantization.

C. Variable-Rate Quantization

Shannon's lossless source coding theory (1948) [464] made it clear that assigning equal numbers of bits to all quantization cells is wasteful if the cells have unequal probabilities. Instead, the number of bits produced by the quantizer will, on the average, be reduced if shorter binary codewords are assigned to higher probability cells. Of course, this means that longer codewords will need to be assigned to the less probable cells, but Shannon's theory shows that, in general, there is a net gain. This leads directly to *variable-rate quantization*, which has the partition into cells and codebook of levels as before, but now has binary codewords of varying lengths assigned to the cells (alternatively, the levels). Ordinarily, the set of binary codewords is chosen to satisfy the prefix condition that no member is a prefix of another member, in order to insure unique decodability. As will be made precise in the next section, one may view a variable-rate quantizer as consisting of a partition, a codebook, and a lossless binary code, i.e., an assignment of binary codewords.

For variable-rate quantizers the rate is no longer defined as the logarithm of the codebook size. Rather, the instantaneous rate for a given input is the number of binary symbols in the binary codeword (the length of the binary codeword) and the rate is the average length of the binary codewords, where the average is taken over the probability distribution of the source samples. The operational distortion-rate function $\delta(R)$ using this definition is the smallest average distortion over all (variable-rate) quantizers having rate R or less. Since we have weakened the constraint by expanding the allowed set of quantizers, this operational distortion-rate function will ordinarily be smaller than the fixed-rate optimum.

Huffman's algorithm [251] provides a systematic method of designing binary codes with the smallest possible average length for a given set of probabilities, such as those of the cells. Codes designed in this way are typically called Huffman codes. Unfortunately, there is no known expression for the resulting minimum average length in terms of the probabilities. However, Shannon's lossless source coding theorem implies that given a source and a quantizer partition, one can always find an assignment of binary codewords (indeed, a prefix set) with average length not more than $H(q(X)) + 1$, and that no uniquely decodable set of binary codewords can have average length less than $H(q(X))$, where

$$H(q(X)) = -\sum_i P_i \log P_i$$

is the Shannon *entropy* of the quantizer output and $P_i = \Pr(X \in S_i)$ is the probability that the source sample X lies in the ith cell S_i. Shannon also provided a simple way of attaining performance within the upper bound: if the quantizer index is i, then assign it a binary codeword with length $\lceil -\log P_i \rceil$ (the Kraft inequality ensures that this is always possible by simply choosing paths in a binary tree). Moreover, tighter bounds have been developed. For example, Gallager [181] has shown that the entropy can be at most $P_{\max} + 0.0861$ smaller than the average length of the Huffman code, when $P_{\max}$, the largest of the P_i's, is less than $1/2$. See [73] for discussion of this and other bounds. Since $P_{\max}$ is ordinarily much smaller than $1/2$, this shows that $H(q(X))$ is generally a fairly accurate estimate of the average rate, especially in the high-resolution case.

Since there is no simple formula determining the rate of the Huffman code, but entropy provides a useful estimate, it is reasonable to simplify the variable-length quantizer design problem a little by redefining the instantaneous rate of a variable-rate quantizer as $-\log P_i$ for the ith quantizer level and hence to define the average rate as $H(q(X))$, the entropy of its output. As mentioned above, this underestimates the true rate by a small amount that in no case exceeds one. We could again define an operational distortion-rate function as the minimum average distortion over all variable-rate quantizers with output entropy $H(q(X)) \leq R$. Since the quantizer output entropy is a lower bound to actual rate, this operational distortion-rate function may be optimistic; i.e., it falls below $\delta(R)$ defined using average length as rate. A quantizer designed to provide the smallest average distortion subject to an entropy constraint is called an *entropy-constrained scalar quantizer*.

Variable-rate quantization is also called *variable-length quantization* or *quantization with entropy coding*. We will not, except where critical, take pains to distinguish entropy-constrained quantizers and entropy-coded quantizers. And we will usually blur the distinction between average length and entropy as measures of the rate of such quantizers unless, again, it is important in some particular discussion. This is much the same sort of blurring as using $\log N$ instead of $\lceil \log N \rceil$ as the measure of rate in fixed-rate quantization.

It is important to note that the number of quantization cells or levels does not play a primary role in variable-rate quantization because, for example, there can be many levels in places where the source density is small with little effect on either distortion or rate. Indeed, the number of levels can be infinite, which has the advantage of eliminating the overload region and resulting overload distortion.

A potential drawback of variable-rate quantization is the necessity of dealing with the variable numbers of bits that it produces. For example, if the bits are to be communicated through a fixed-rate digital channel, one will have to use buffering and to take buffer overflows and underflows into account. Another drawback is the potential for error propagation when bits are received by the decoder in error.

The most basic and simple example of a variable-rate quantizer, and one which plays a fundamental role as a benchmark for comparison, is a uniform scalar quantizer with a variable-length binary lossless code.

The possibility of applying variable-length coding to quantization may well have occurred to any number of people who were familiar with both quantization and Shannon's 1948 paper. The earliest references to such that we have found are in the 1952 papers by Kretzmer [300] and Oliver [395]. In 1960, Max [349] had such in mind when he computed the entropy of nonuniform and uniform quantizers that had been designed to minimize distortion for a given number of levels. For a Gaussian source, his results showed that variable-length coding would yield rate reductions of about 0.5 bit/sample.

High-resolution analysis of variable-rate quantization developed in a handful of papers from 1958 to 1968. However, since these papers were widely scattered or unpublished, it was not until 1968 that the situation was well understood in the IEEE community.

The first high-resolution analysis was that of Schutzenberger (1958) [462] who showed that the distortion of optimized variable-rate quantization (both scalar and vector) decreases with rate as 2^{-2R}, just as with fixed-rate quantization. But he did not find the multiplicative factors, nor did he describe the nature of the partitions and codebooks that are best for variable-rate quantization.

In 1959, Renyi [433] showed that a uniform scalar quantizer with infinitely many levels and small cell width Δ has output entropy given approximately by

$$H(q(X)) \cong h(X) - \log \Delta \qquad (11)$$

where

$$h(X) = -\int f(x) \log f(x)\, dx$$

is the *differential entropy* of the source variable X.

In 1963, Koshelev [579] discovered the very interesting fact that in the high-resolution case, the mean-squared error of uniform scalar quantization exceeds that of the least distortion achievable by any quantization scheme whatsoever, i.e., $\bar{\delta}(R)$, by a factor of only $\pi e/6 = 1.42$. Equivalently, the induced signal-to-noise ratio is only 1.53 dB less than the best possible, or for a fixed distortion D, the rate is only 0.255 bit/sample larger than that achievable by the best quantizers. (For the Gaussian source, it gains 2.82 dB or 0.47 bit/sample over the best fixed-rate scalar quantizer.) It is also of interest to note that this was the first paper to compare the performance of a specific quantization scheme to $\bar{\delta}(R)$. Unfortunately, Koshelev's paper was published in a journal that was not widely circulated.

In an unpublished 1966 Bell Telephone Laboratories Technical Memo [562], Zador also studied variable-rate (as well as fixed-rate) quantization. As his focus was on vector quantization, his work will be described later. Here we only point out that for variable-rate scalar quantization with large rate, his results showed that the operational distortion-rate function (i.e., the least distortion of such codes with a given rate) is

$$\delta(R) \cong \frac{1}{12} 2^{2h(X)} 2^{-2R}. \qquad (12)$$

Though he was not aware of it, this turns out to be the formula found by Koshelev, therby demonstrating that in the high-resolution case, uniform is the best type of scalar quantizer when variable-rate coding is applied.

Finally, in 1967 and 1968 two papers appeared in the IEEE literature (in fact in these TRANSACTIONS) on variable-rate quantization, without reference to any of the aforementioned work. The first, by Goblick and Holsinger [205], showed by numerical evaluation that uniform scalar quantization with variable-rate coding attains performance within about 1.5 dB (or 0.25 bit/sample) of the best possible for an i.i.d. Gaussian source. The second, by Gish and Pierce [204], demonstrated analytically what the first paper had found empirically. Specifically, it derived (11), and more generally, the fact that a high-resolution nonuniform scalar quantizer has output entropy

$$H(q(X)) \cong h(X) + \int f(x) \log \Lambda(x) \, dx \quad (13)$$

where $\Lambda(x)$ is the unnormalized point density of the quantizer. They then used these approximations along with Bennett's integral to rederive (12) and to show that in the high-resolution case, uniform scalar quantizers achieve the operational distortion-rate function of variable-rate quantization. Next, by comparing to what is called the *Shannon lower bound* to $\bar{\delta}(R)$, they showed that for i.i.d. sources, the latter is only 1.53 dB (0.255 bit/sample) from the best possible performance $\bar{\delta}(R)$ of any quantization system whatsoever, which is what Koshelev [579] found earlier. Their results showed that such good performance was attainable for any source distribution, not just the Gaussian case checked by Goblick and Holsinger. They also generalized the results from squared-error distortion to nondecreasing functions of magnitude error.

Less well known is their proof of the fact that in the high resolution case, the entropy of k successive outputs of a uniformly scalar quantized stationary source, e.g., with memory, is

$$H(q(X_1), \cdots, q(X_k)) \cong h(X_1, \cdots, X_k) - \log \Delta. \quad (14)$$

They used this, and the generalization of (13) to vectors, to show that when rate and k are large, uniform scalar quantization with variable-length coding of k successive quantizer outputs (*block entropy coding*) achieves performance that is 1.53 dB (0.255 bit/sample) from $\bar{\delta}(R)$, even for sources with memory. (They accomplished this by comparing to Shannon lower bounds.) This important result was not widely appreciated until rediscovered by Ziv (1985) [578], who also showed that a similar result holds for small rates. Note that although uniform scalar quantizers are quite simple, the lossless code capable of approaching the kth-order entropy of the quantized source can be quite complicated. In addition, Gish and Pierce observed that when coding vectors, performance could be improved by using quantizer cells other than the cube implicitly used by uniform scalar quantizers and noted that the hexagonal cell was superior in two dimensions, as originally demonstrated by Fejes Toth [159] and Newman [385].

Though uniform quantization is asymptotically best for entropy-constrained quantization, at lower rates nonuniform quantization can do better, and a series of papers explored algorithms for designing them. In 1969, Wood [539] provided a numerical descent algorithm for designing an entropy-constrained scalar quantizer, and showed, as predicted by Gish and Pierce, that the performance was only slightly superior to a uniform scalar quantizer followed by a lossless code.

In a 1972 paper dealing with a vector quantization technique to be discussed later, Berger [47] described Lloyd-like conditions for optimality of an entropy-constrained scalar quantizer for squared-error distortion. He formulated the optimization as an unconstrained Lagrangian minimization and developed an iterative algorithm for the design of entropy-constrained scalar quantizers. He showed that Gish and Pierce's demonstration of approximate optimality of uniform scalar quantization for variable-rate quantization holds approximately even when the rate is not large and holds exactly for exponential densities, provided the levels are placed at the centroids. In 1976, Netravali and Saigal introduced a fixed-point algorithm with the same goal of minimizing average distortion for a scalar quantizer with an entropy constraint [376]. Yet another approach was taken by Noll and Zelinski (1978) [391]. Berger refined his approach to entropy-constrained quantizer design in [48].

Variable-rate quantization was also extended to DPCM and transform coding, where high-resolution analysis shows that it gains the same relative to fixed-rate quantization as it does when applied to direct scalar quantizing [154], [398]. We note, however, that the variable-rate quantization analysis for DPCM suffers from the same flaws as the fixed-rate quantization analysis for DPCM.

Numerous extensions of the Bennett-style asymptotic approximations and the approximation of $r(D)$ or $\delta(R)$ and the characterizations of properties of optimal high-resolution quantization for both fixed- and variable-rate quantization for squared error and other error moments appeared during the 1960's, e.g., [497], [498], [55], [467], [8]. An excellent summary of the early work is contained in a 1970 paper by Elias [143].

We close this section with an important practical observation. The current JPEG and related standards can be viewed as a combination of transform coding and variable-length quantization. It is worth pointing out how the standard resembles and differs from the models considered thus far. As previously stated, the transform coefficients are separately quantized by possibly different uniform quantizers, the bin lengths of the quantizers being determined by a customizable quantization table. This typically produces a quantized transformed image with many zeros. The lossless, variable-length code then scans the image in a zig-zag (or Peano) fashion, producing a sequence of runlengths of the zeros and indices corresponding to nonzero values, which are then Huffman-coded (or arithmetic-coded). This procedure has the effect of coding only the transform coefficients with the largest magnitude, which are the ones most important for reconstruction. The early transform coders typically coded the first, say, K coefficients, and ignored the rest. In essence, the method adopted for the standards selectively coded the most important coefficients, i.e., those having the largest magnitude, rather than simply the lowest frequency coefficients. The runlength coding step can in hindsight be viewed as a simple way of locating the most significant coefficients, which in turn are described the most accurately. This implicit "significance" map was an early version of an idea that would later be essential to wavelet coders.

D. The Beginnings of Vector Quantization

As described in the three previous subsections, the 1940's through the early 1970's produced a steady stream of advances in the design and analysis of practical quantization techniques, principally scalar, predictive, transform, and variable-rate quantization, with quantizer performance improving as these decades progressed. On the other hand, at roughly the same time there was a parallel series of developments that were more concerned with the fundamental limits of quantization than with practical quantization issues. We speak primarily of the remarkable work of Shannon and the very important work of Zador, though there were other important contributors as well. This work dealt with what is now called *vector quantization* (VQ) (or *block* or *multidimensional quantization*), which is just like scalar quantization except that all components of a vector, of say k successive source samples, are quantized simultaneously. As such they are characterized by a k-dimensional partition, a k-dimensional codebook (containing k-dimensional *points*, *reproduction codewords* or *codevectors*), and an assignment of binary codewords to the cells of the partition (equivalently, to the codevectors).

An immediate advantage of vector quantization is that it provides a model of a general quantization scheme operating on vectors without any structural constraints. It clearly includes transform coding as a special case and can also be considered to include predictive quantization operating locally within the vector. This lack of structural constraints makes the general model more amenable to analysis and optimization. In these early decades, vector quantization served primarily as a paradigm for exploring fundamental performance limits; it was not yet evident whether it would become a practical coding technique.

Shannon's Source Coding Theory: In his classic 1948 paper, Shannon [464] sketched the idea of the rate of a source as the minimum bit rate required to reconstruct the source to some degree of accuracy as measured by a fidelity criterion such as mean-squared error. The sketch was fully developed in his 1959 paper [465] for i.i.d. sources, additive measures of distortion, and block source codes, now called vector quantizers. In this later paper, Shannon showed that when coding at some rate R, the least distortion achievable by vector quantizers of any kind is equal to a function $D(R)$, subsequently called the *Shannon distortion-rate function*, that is determined by the statistics of the source and the measure of distortion.[2]

To elaborate on Shannon's theory, we note that one can immediately extend the quantizer notation of (1), the distortion and rate definitions of (2) and (3), and the operational distortion-rate functions to define the smallest distortion $\delta_k(R)$ possible for a k-dimensional fixed-rate vector quantizer that achieves rate R or less. (The distortion between two k-dimensional vectors is defined to be the numerical average of the distortions between their respective components. The rate is $1/k$ times the (average) number of bits to describe a k-dimensional source vector.) We will make the dimension k explicit in the notation when we are allowing it to vary and omit it when not. Furthermore, as with Shannon's channel coding and lossless source coding theories, one can consider the best possible performance over codes of *all* dimensions (assuming the data can be blocked into vectors of arbitrary size) and define an operational distortion-rate function

$$\overline{\delta}(R) = \inf_k \delta_k(R). \qquad (15)$$

The operational rate-distortion functions $r_k(D)$ and $\overline{r}(D)$ are defined similarly. For finite dimension k, the function $\delta_k(R)$ will depend on the definition of rate, i.e., whether it is the log of the reproduction size, the average binary codeword length, or the quantizer output entropy. It turns out, however, that $\overline{\delta}(R)$ is not affected by this choice. That is, it is the same for all definitions of rate.

For an i.i.d. source $\{X_n\}$, the *Shannon distortion-rate function* $D(R)$ is defined as the minimum average distortion $E[\dot{d}(X, Y)]$ over all conditional distributions of Y given X for which the mutual information $I(X; Y)$ is at most R, where we emphasize that X and Y are scalar variables here. In his principal result, the coding theorem for source coding with a fidelity criterion, Shannon showed that for every R, $\overline{\delta}(R) = D(R)$. That is, no VQ of any dimension k with rate R could yield smaller average distortion than $D(R)$, and that for some dimension—possibly very large—there exists a VQ with rate no greater than R and distortion very nearly $D(R)$. As an illustrative example, the Shannon distortion-rate function of an i.i.d. Gaussian source with variance σ^2 is

$$D(R) = \sigma^2 2^{-2R} \qquad (16)$$

where σ^2 is the variance of the source. Equivalently, the Shannon rate-distortion function is $R(D) = \frac{1}{2} \log(\sigma^2/D)$, $0 \leq D \leq \sigma^2$. Since it is also known that this represents the best possible performance of any quantization scheme whatsoever, it is these formulas that we used previously when comparing the performance of scalar quantizers to that of the best quantization schemes. For example, comparing (10) and (16), one sees why we made earlier the statement that the operational distortion-rate function of scalar quantization is $\pi\sqrt{3}/2$ times larger than $\overline{\delta}(R)$. Notice that (16) shows that for this source the 2^{-2R} exponential rate of decay of distortion with rate, demonstrated by high resolution arguments for high rates, extends to all rates. This is not usually the case for other sources.

Shannon's approach was subsequently generalized to sources with memory, cf. [180], [45], [46], [218], [549], [127], [126], [282], [283], [138], and [479]. The general

---

[2] Actually, Shannon described the solution to the equivalent problem of minimizing rate subject to a distortion constraint and found that the answer was given by a function $R(D)$, subsequently called the *Shannon rate-distortion function*, which is the inverse of $D(R)$. Accordingly, the theory is often called *rate-distortion theory*, cf. [46].

definitions of distortion-rate and rate-distortion functions resemble those for operational distortion-rate and rate-distortion functions in that they are infima of kth-order functions. For example, the kth-order distortion-rate function $D_k(R)$ of a stationary random process $\{X_n\}$ is defined as an infimum of the average distortion $E[d(X, Y)]$ over all conditional probability distributions of $Y = (Y_1, Y_2, \cdots, Y_k)$ given $X = (X_1, X_2, \cdots, X_k)$ for which average mutual information $(1/k)I(X, Y) \leq R$. The distortion-rate function for the process is then given by $\overline{D}(R) = \inf_k D_k(R)$. For i.i.d. sources $\overline{D}(R) = D_1(R)$, where $D_1(R)$ is what we previously called $D(R)$ for i.i.d. sources. (The rate-distortion functions $R_k(D)$ and $\overline{R}(D)$ are defined similarly.) A source coding theorem then shows under appropriate conditions that, for sources with memory, $\overline{\delta}(R) = \overline{D}(R)$ for all rates R. In other words, Shannon's distortion-rate function represents an asymptotically achievable, but never beatable, lower bound to the performance of any VQ of any dimension. The *positive coding theorem* demonstrating that the Shannon distortion-rate function is in fact achievable if one allows codes of arbitrarily large dimension and complexity is difficult to prove, but the existence of good codes rests on the law of large numbers, suggesting that large dimensions might indeed be required for good codes, with consequently large demands on complexity, memory, and delay.

Shannon's results, like those of Panter and Dite, Zador, and Gish and Pierce provide benchmarks for comparison for quantizers. However, Shannon's results provide an interesting contrast with these early results on quantizer performance. Specifically, the early quantization theory had derived the limits of scalar quantizer performance based on the assumption of high resolution and showed that these bounds were achievable by a suitable choice of quantizer. Shannon, on the other hand, had fixed a finite, nonasymptotic rate, but had considered asymptotic limits as the dimension k of a vector quantizer was allowed to become arbitrarily large. The former asymptotics, high resolution for fixed dimension, are generally viewed as quantization theory, while the latter, fixed-rate and high dimension, are generally considered to be source coding theory or information theory. Prior to 1960, quantization had been viewed primarily as PCM, a form of analog-to-digital conversion or digital modulation, while Shannon's source coding theory was generally viewed as a mathematical approach to data compression. The first to explicitly apply Shannon's source coding theory to the problem of analog-to-digital conversion combined with digital transmission appear to be Goblick and Holsinger [205] in 1967, and the first to make explicit comparisons of quantizer performance to Shannon's rate-distortion function was Koshelev [579] in 1963.

A distinct variation on the Shannon approach was introduced to the English literature in 1956 by Kolmogorov [288], who described several results by Russian information theorists inspired by Shannon's 1948 treatment of coding with respect to a fidelity criterion. Kolmogorov considered two notions of the rate with respect to a fidelity criterion: His second notion was the same as Shannon's, where a mutual information was minimized subject to a constraint on the average distortion, in this case measured by squared error. The first peformed a similar minimization of mutual information, but with the requirement that maximum distortion between the input and reproduction did not exceed a specified level ϵ. Kolmogorov referred to both functions as the "ϵ-entropy" $H_\epsilon(X)$ of a random object X, but the name has subsequently been considered to apply to the maximum distortion being constrained to be less than ϵ, rather than the Shannon function, later called the rate-distortion function, which constrained the average distortion. Note that the maximum distortion with respect to a distortion measure d can be incorporated in the average distortion formulation if one considers a new distortion measure ρ defined by

$$\rho(x, \hat{x}) = \begin{cases} 0, & \text{if } d(x, y) \leq \epsilon \\ \infty, & \text{otherwise.} \end{cases} \tag{17}$$

As with Shannon's rate-distortion function, this was an information-theoretic definition. As with quantization, there are corresponding operational definitions. The operational epsilon entropy (ϵ-entropy) of a random variable X can be defined as the smallest entropy of a quantized output such that the reproduction is no further from the input than ϵ (at least with probability 1):

$$\mathcal{H}_\epsilon(X) = \inf_{q:\, \sup_x d(x, q(x)) \leq \epsilon} H(q(X)). \tag{18}$$

This is effectively a variable-rate definition since lossless coding would be required to achieve a bit rate near the entropy. Alternatively, one could define the operational epsilon entropy as $\log N_\epsilon$, where N_ϵ is the smallest number of reproduction codevectors for which all inputs are (with probability 1) within ϵ of a codevector. This quantity is clearly infinite if the random object X does not have finite support. As in the Shannon case, all these definitions can be made for k-dimensional vectors X^k and the limiting behavior can be studied. Results regarding the convergence of such limits and the equality of the information-theoretic and operational notions of epsilon entropy can be found, e.g., in [421], [420], [278], and [59]. Much of the theory is concerned with approximating epsilon entropy for small ϵ.

Epsilon entropy extends to function approximation theory with a slight change by removing the notion of probability. Here the epsilon entropy becomes the log of the smallest number of balls of radius ϵ required to cover a compact metric space (e.g., a function space—see, e.g., [520] and [420] for a discussion of various notions of epsilon entropy).

We mention epsilon entropy because of its close mathematical connection to rate-distortion theory. Our emphasis, however, is on codes that minimize average, not maximum, distortion.

The Earliest Vector Quantization Work: Outside of Shannon's sketch of rate-distortion theory in 1948, the earliest work with a definite vector quantization flavor appeared in the mathematical and statistical literature. Most important was the remarkable work of Steinhaus in 1956 [480], who considered a problem equivalent to a three-dimensional generalization of scalar quantization with a squared-error distortion measure.

Suppose that a mass density $m(x)$ is defined on Euclidean space. For any finite N, let $\mathcal{S} = \{S_i;\ i = 1, \cdots, N\}$ be a partition of Euclidean space into N disjoint bodies (cells) and let $\mathcal{C} = \{y_i;\ i = 1, \cdots, N\}$ be a collection of N vectors, one associated with each cell of the partition. What partition $\mathcal{S}$ and collection of vectors $\mathcal{C}$ minimizes

$$\sum_{i=1}^{N} \int_{S_i} m(x)\|x - y_i\|^2 \, dx$$

the sum of the moments of inertia of the cells about the associated vectors? This problem is formally equivalent to a fixed-rate three-dimensional vector quantizer with a squared-error distortion measure and a probability density $m(x)/\int m(x')\,dx'$. Steinhaus derived what we now consider to be the Lloyd optimality conditions (centroid and nearest neighbor mapping from fundamental principles (without variational techniques), proved the existence of a solution, and described the iterative descent algorithm for finding a good partition and vector collection. His derivation applies immediately to any finite-dimensional space and hence, like Lloyd's, extends immediately to vector quantization of any dimension. Steinhaus was aware of the problems with local optima, but stated that "generally" there would be a unique solution. No mention is made of "quantization," but this appears to be the first paper to both state the vector quantization problem and to provide necessary conditions for a solution, which yield a design algorithm.

In 1959, Fejes Toth described the specific application of Steinhaus' problem in two dimensions to a source with a uniform density on a bounded support region and to quantization with an asymptotically large number of points [159]. Using an earlier inequality of his [158], he showed that the optimal two-dimensional quantizer under these assumptions tessellated the support region with hexagons. This was the first evaluation of the performance of a genuinely multidimensional quantizer. It was rederived in a 1964 Bell Laboratories Technical Memorandum by Newman [385]; its first appearance in English. It made a particularly important point: even in the simple case of two independent uniform random variables, with no redundancy to remove, the performance achievable by quantizing vectors using a hexagonal-lattice encoding partition is strictly better than that achievable by uniform scalar quantization, which can be viewed as a two-dimensional quantizer with a square encoding lattice.

The first high-resolution approximations for vector quantization were published by Schutzenberger in 1958 [462], who found upper and lower bounds to the least distortion of k-dimensional variable-rate vector quantizers, both of the form $K2^{-2R}$. Unfortunately, the upper and lower bounds diverge as k increases.

In 1963, Zador [561] made a very large advance by using high-resolution methods to show that for large rates, the operational distortion-rate function of fixed-rate quantization has the form

$$\delta_k(R) \cong b_k \|f\|_{k/(k+2)} 2^{-2R} \tag{19}$$

where b_k is a term that is independent of the source, $f(x)$ is the k-dimensional source density, and

$$\|f\|_{k/(k+2)} = \left(\int f^{k/(k+2)}(x) \, dx \right)^{(k+2)/k}$$

is the term that depends on the source. This generalized the Panter–Dite formula to the vector case. While the formula for $\delta_k(R)$ obviously matches the Shannon distortion-rate function $D(R)$ when both dimension and rate are large (because in this case both are approximations to $\delta_k(R) \cong \overline{\delta}(R)$), Zador's formula has the advantage of being applicable for any dimension k while the Shannon theory is applicable only for large k. On the other hand, Shannon theory is applicable for any rate R while high resolution theory is applicable only for large rates. Thus the two theories are complementary. Zador also explicitly extended Lloyd's optimality properties to vectors with distortion measures that were integer powers of the Euclidean norm, thereby also generalizing Steinhaus' results to dimensions higher than three, but he did not specifically consider descent design algorithms. Unfortunately, the results of Zador's thesis were not published until 1982 [563] and were little known outside of Bell Laboratories until Gersho's important paper of 1979 [193], to be described later.

Zador's dissertation also dealt with the analysis of variable-rate vector quantization, but the asymptotic formula given there is not the correct one. Rather it was left to his subsequent unpublished 1966 memo [562] to derive the correct formula. (Curiously, his 1982 paper [563] reports the formula from the thesis rather than the memo.) Again using high-resolution methods, he showed that for large rates, the operational distortion-rate function of variable-rate vector quantization has the form

$$\delta_k(R) \cong c_k 2^{2h_k(X)} 2^{-2R} \tag{20}$$

where c_k is a term that is independent of the source and $h_k = (1/k)h(X_1, \cdots, X_k)$ is the dimension-normalized differential entropy of the source. This completed what he and Schutzenberger had begun.

In the mid-1960's, the optimality properties described by Steinhaus, Lloyd, and Zador and the design algorithm of Steinhaus and Lloyd were rediscovered in the statistical clustering literature. Similar algorithms were introduced in 1965 by Forgey [172], Ball and Hall [29], [230], Jancey [263], and in 1969 by MacQueen [341] (the "k-means" algorithm). These algorithms were developed for statistical clustering applications, the selection of a finite collection of templates that well represent a large collection of data in the MSE sense, i.e., a fixed-rate VQ with an MSE distortion measure in quantization terminology, cf. Anderberg [9], Diday and Simon [133], or Hartigan [238]. MacQueen used an incremental incorporation of successive samples of a training set to design the codes, each vector being first mapped into a minimum-distortion reproduction level representing a cluster, and then the level for that cluster being replaced by an adjusted centroid. Forgey and Jancey used simultaneous updates of all centroids, as did Steinhaus and Lloyd.

Unfortunately, many of these early results did not propagate among the diverse groups working on similar problems. Zador's extensions of Lloyd's results were little known outside of Bell Laboratories. The work of Steinhaus has been virtually unknown in the quantization community until recently. The work in the clustering community on what were effectively vector quantizer design algorithms in the context of statistical clustering was little known at the time in the quantization community, and it was not generally appreciated that Lloyd's algorithm was in fact a clustering algorithm. Part of the lack of interest through the 1950's was likely due to the fact that there had not yet appeared any strong motivation to consider the quantization of vectors instead of scalars. This motivation came as a result of Shannon's landmark 1959 paper on source coding with a fidelity criterion.

E. Implementable Vector Quantizers

As mentioned before, it was not evident from the earliest studies that vector quantization could be a practical technique. The only obvious encoding procedure is brute-force nearest neighbor encoding: compare the source vector to be quantized with all reproduction vectors in the codebook. Since a (fixed-rate) VQ with dimension k and rate R has 2^{kR} codevectors, the number of computations required to do this grows exponentially with the dimension-rate product kR, and gets quickly out of hand. For example, if $k = 10$ and $R = 2$, there are roughly one million codevectors. Moreover, these codevectors need to be stored, which also consumes costly resources. Finally, the proof of Shannon's source coding theorem relies on the dimension becoming large, suggesting that large dimension might be needed to attain good performance. As a point of reference, we note that in the development of channel codes, for which Shannon's theory had also suggested large dimension, it was common circa 1970 to consider channel codes with dimensions on the order of 100 or more. Thus it no doubt appeared to many that similarly large dimensions might be needed for effective quantization. Clearly, a brute-force implementation of VQ with such dimensions would be out of the question. On the other hand, the channel codes of this era with large dimension and good performance, e.g., BCH codes, were highly *structured* so that encoding and decoding need not be done by brute force.

From the above discussion, it should not be surprising that the first VQ intended as a practical technique had a reproduction codebook that was highly structured in order to reduce the complexity of encoding and decoding. Specifically, we speak of the fixed-rate vector quantizer introduced in 1965 by Dunn [137] for multidimensional i.i.d. Gaussian vectors. He argued that his code was effectively a permutation code as earlier used by Slepian [472] for channel coding, in that the reproduction codebook contains only codevectors that are permutations of each other. This leads to a quantizer with reduced (but still fairly large) complexity. Dunn compared numerical computations of the performance of this scheme to the Shannon rate-distortion function. As mentioned earlier, this was the first such comparison. In 1972, Berger, Jelinek, and Wolf [49], and Berger [47] introduced lower complexity

encoding algorithms for permutation codes, and Berger [47] showed that for large dimensions, the operational distortion-rate function of permutation codes is approximately equal to that of optimal variable-rate scalar quantizers. While they do not attain performance beyond that of scalar quantization, permutation codes have the advantage of avoiding the buffering and error propagation problems of variable-rate quantization.

Notwithstanding the skepticism of some about the feasibility of brute-force unstructured vector quantization, serious studies of such began to appear in the mid-1970's, when several independent results were reported describing applications of clustering algorithms, usually k-means, to problems of vector quantization. In 1974–1975, Chaffee [76] and Chaffee and Omura [77] used clustering ideas to design a vector quantizer for very low rate speech vocoding. In 1977, Hilbert used clustering algorithms for joint image compression and image classification [242]. These papers appear to be the first applications of direct vector quantization for speech and image coding applications. Also in 1977, Chen used an algorithm equivalent to a two-dimensional Lloyd algorithm to design two-dimensional vector quantizers [87].

In 1978 and 1979, a vector extension of Lloyd's Method I was applied to linear predictive coded (LPC) speech parameters by Buzo and others [220],[67], [68], [223] with a weighted quadratic distortion measure on parameter vectors closely related to the Itakura–Saito spectral distortion measure [258], [259], [257]. Also in 1978, Adoul, Collin, and Dalle [3] used clustering ideas to design two-dimensional vector quantizers for speech coding. Caprio, Westin, and Esposito in 1978 [74] and Menez, Boeri, and Esteban in 1979 [353] also considered clustering algorithms for the design of vector quantizers with squared error and magnitude error distortion measures.

The most important paper on quantization during the 1970's was without a doubt Gersho's paper on "Asymptotically optimal block quantization" [193]. The paper popularized high resolution theory and the potential performance gains of vector quantization, provided new, simplified variations and proofs of Zador's results and vector extensions of Gish and Pierce's results with squared-error distortion, and introduced lattice vector quantization as a means of achieving the asymptotically optimal quantizer point density for entropy-constrained vector quantization for a random vector with bounded support. The simple derivations combined the vector quantizer point-density approximations with the use of Hölder's and Jensen's inequalities, generalizing a scalar quantizer technique introduced in 1977 [222]. One step of the development rested on a still unproved conjecture regarding the asymptotically optimal quantizer cell shapes and Zador's constants, a conjecture which since has borne Gersho's name and which will be considered at some length in Section IV. Portions of this work were extended to nondecreasing functions of norms in [554].

Gersho's work stimulated renewed interest in the theory and design of direct vector quantizers and demonstrated that, contrary to the common impression that very large dimensions were required, significant gains could be achieved over scalar quantization by quantizing vectors of modest dimension and, as a result, such codes might be competitive with predictive and transform codes in some applications.

In 1980, Linde, Buzo, and Gray explicitly extended Lloyd's algorithm to vector quantizer design [318]. As we have seen, the clustering approach to vector quantizer design originated years earlier, but the Linde *et al.* paper introduced it as a direct extension to the original Lloyd optimal PCM design algorithm, extended it to more general distortion measures than had been previously considered (including an input-weighted quadratic distortion useful in speech coding), and succeeded in popularizing the algorithm to the point that it is often referred to as the "LBG algorithm." A "splitting" method for designing the quantizer from scratch was developed, wherein one first designs a quantizer with two words (2-means), then doubles the codebook size by adding a new codevector near each existing codevector, then runs Lloyd's algorithm again, and so on. The numerical examples of quantizer design complemented Gersho's high-resolution results much as Lloyd's had complemented Panter and Dite: it was shown that even with modest dimensions and modest rates, significant gains over scalar quantization could be achieved by direct vector quantization of modest complexity. Later in the same year, Buzo *et al.* [69] developed a tree-structured vector quantizer (TSVQ) for ten-dimensional LPC vectors that greatly reduced the encoder complexity from exponential growth with codebook size to linear growth by searching a sequence of small codebooks instead of a single large codebook. The result was an 800-bits/s LPC speech coder with intelligible quality comparable to that of scalar-quantized LPC speech coders of four times the rate. (See also [538].) In the same year, Adoul, Debray, and Dalle [4] also used a spectral distance measure to optimize predictors for DPCM and the first thorough study of vector quantization for image compression was published by Yamada, Fujita, and Tazaki [551].

In hindsight, the surprising effectiveness of low-dimensional VQ, e.g., $k = 2$ to 10, can be explained by the fact that in Shannon's theory large dimension is needed to attain performance arbitrarily close to the ideal. In channel coding at rates less than capacity, ideal performance means zero error probability, and large dimension is needed for codes to approach this. However, when quantizing at a given rate R, ideal performance means distortion equal to $\bar{\delta}(R)$. Since this is not zero, there is really no point to making the difference between actual and ideal performance arbitrarily small. For example, it might be enough to come within 5% to 20% (0.2 to 0.8 dB) of $\bar{\delta}(R)$, which does not require terribly large dimension. We will return to this in Section IV with estimates of the required dimension.

There followed an active period for all facets of quantization theory and design. Many of these results developed early in the decade were fortuitously grouped in the March 1982 special issue on Quantization of these TRANSACTIONS, which published the Bell Laboratories Technical Memos of Lloyd, Newman, and Zador along with Berger's extension of the optimality properties of entropy-constrained scalar quantization to rth-power distortion measures and his extensive comparison of minimum-entropy quantizers and fixed-rate permutation codes [48], generalizations by Trushkin of Fleischer's conditions for

uniqueness of local optima [503], results on the asymptotic behavior of Lloyd's algorithm with training-sequence size based on the theory of k-means consistency by Pollard [418], two seminal papers on lattice quantization by Conway and Sloane [103], [104], rigorous developments of the Bennett theory for vector quantizers and rth-power distortion measures by Bucklew and Wise [64], Kieffer's demonstration of stochastic stability for a general class of feedback quantizers including the historic class of predictive quantizers and delta modulators along with adaptive generalizations [281], Kieffer's study of the convergence rate of Lloyd's algorithm [280], and the demonstration by Garey, Johnson, and Witsenhausen that the Lloyd–Max optimization was NP-hard [187].

Toward the middle of the 1980's, several tutorial articles on vector quantization appeared, which greatly increased the accessibility of the subject [195], [214], [342], [372].

F. The Mid-1980's to the Present

In the middle to late 1980's, a wide variety of vector quantizer design algorithms were developed and tested for speech, images, video, and other signal sources. Some of the quantizer design algorithms developed as alternatives to Lloyd's algorithm include simulated annealing [140], [507], [169], [289], deterministic annealing [445]–[447], pairwise nearest neighbor [146] (which had its origins in earlier clustering techniques [524]), stochastic relaxation [567], [571], self-organizing feature maps [290], [544], [545], and other neural nets [495], [301], [492], [337], [65]. A variety of quantization techniques were introduced by constraining the structure of the vector quantization to better balance complexity with performance and these methods were applied to real signals (especially speech and images) as well as to random sources, which permitted comparison to the theoretical high-resolution and Shannon bounds. The literature begins to grow too large to cite all works of possible interest, but several of the techniques will be considered in Section V. Here, we only mention several examples with references and leave further discussion to Section V.

As will be discussed in some depth in Section V, fast search algorithms were developed for unstructured reproduction codebooks, and even faster searches for reproduction codebooks constrained to have a simple structure, for example to be a subset of points of a regular lattice as in a lattice vector quantizer. Additional structure can be imposed for faster searches with virtually no loss of performance, as in Fisher's pyramid VQ [164], which takes advantage of the asymptotic equipartition property to choose a structured support region for the quantizer. Tree-structured VQ uses a tree-structured reproduction codebook with a matched tree-structured search algorithm. A tree-structured VQ with far less memory is provided by a multistage or residual VQ. A variety of product vector quantizers use a Cartesian product reproduction codebook, which often can be rapidly searched. Examples include polar vector quantizers, mean-removed vector quantizers, and shape-gain vector quantizers. Trellis encoders and trellis-coded quantizers use a Viterbi algorithm encoder matched to a reproduction codebook with a trellis structure. Hierarchical table-lookup vector quantizers provide fixed-rate vector quantizers with minimal computational complexity. Many of the early quantization techniques, results, and applications can be found in original form in Swaszek's 1985 reprint collection on quantization [484] and Abut's 1990 IEEE Reprint Collection on Vector Quantization [2].

We close this section with a brief discussion of two specific works which deal with optimizing variable-rate scalar quantizers without additional structure, the problem that leads to the general formulation of optimal quantization in the next section. In 1984 Farvardin and Modestino [155] extended Berger's [47] necessary conditions for optimality of an entropy-constrained scalar quantizer to more general distortion measures and described two design algorithms: the first is similar to Berger's iterative algorithm, but the second was a fixed-point algorithm which can be considered as a natural extension of Lloyd's Method I from fixed-rate to variable-rate vector quantization. In 1989, Chou et al. [93] developed a generalized Lloyd algorithm for entropy-constrained vector quantization that generalized Berger's [47], [48] Lagrangian formulation for scalar quantization and Farvardin and Modestino's fixed-point design algorithm [155] to vectors. Optimality properties for minimizing a Lagrangian distortion $D(q) + \lambda R(q)$ were derived, where rate could be either average length or entropy. Lloyd's optimal decoder remained unchanged and the lossless code is easily seen to be an optimal lossless code for the encoded vectors, but this formulation shows that the optimal encoder must simultaneously consider both the distortion and rate resulting from the encoder. In other words, quantizers with variable rate should use an encoder that minimizes a sum of squared error and weighted bit rate, and not only the squared error. Another approach to entropy-constrained scalar quantization is described in [285].

This is a good place to again mention Gish and Pierce's result that if the rate is high, optimal entropy-constrained scalar or vector quantization can provide no more than roughly 1/4-bit improvement over uniform scalar quantization with block entropy coding. Berger [47] showed that permutation codes achieved roughly the same performance with a fixed-rate vector quantizer. Ziv [578] showed in 1985 that if subtractive dithering is allowed, dithered uniform quantization followed by block lossless encoding will be at most 0.754 bit worse than the optimal entropy-constrained vector quantizer with the same block size, even if the rate is not high. (Subtractive dithering, as will be discussed later, adds a random dither signal to the input and removes it from the decompressed output.) As previously discussed, these results do not eliminate the usefulness of fixed-rate quantizers, because they may be simpler and avoid the difficulties associated with variable-rate codes. These results do suggest, however, that uniform quantization and lossless coding is always a candidate and a benchmark for performance comparison. It is not known if the operational distortion-rate function of variable-rate quantization with dithering is better than that without dithering.

The present decade has seen continuing activity in developing high resolution theory and design algorithms for a variety of quantization structures, and in applying many of the principles of the theory to optimizing signal processing

and communication systems incorporating quantizers. As the arrival of the present is a good place to close our historical tour, many results of the current decade will be sketched through the remaining sections. It is difficult to resist pointing out, however, that in 1990 Lloyd's algorithm was rediscovered in the statistical literature under the name of "principal points," which are distinguished from traditional k-means by the assumption of an absolutely continuous distribution instead of an empirical distribution [171], [496], a formulation included in the VQ formulation for a general distribution. Unfortunately, these works reflect no awareness of the rich quantization literature.

Most quantizers today are indeed uniform and scalar, but are combined with prediction or transforms. In many niche applications, however, the true vector quantizers, including lattices and other constrained code structures, exhibit advantages, including the coding of speech residuals in code excited linear predictive (CELP) speech coding systems and VXTreme/Microsoft streaming video in WebTheater. Vector quantization, unlike scalar quantization, is usually applied to digital signals, e.g., signals that have already been "finely" quantized by an A/D converter. In this case, quantization (vector or scalar) truly represents compression since it reduces the number of bits required to describe a signal and it reduces the bandwidth required to transmit the signal description if an analog link is used.

Modern video coding schemes often incorporate the Lagrangian distortion viewpoint for accomplishing rate control, while using predictive quantization in a general sense through motion compensation and uniform quantizers with optimized lossless coding of transform coefficients for the intraframe coding (cf. [201], [202]).

III. QUANTIZATION BASICS: ENCODING, RATE, DISTORTION, AND OPTIMALITY

This section presents, in a self-contained manner, the basics of memoryless quantization, that is, vector quantizers which operate independently on successive vectors. For brevity, we omit the "memoryless" qualifier for most of the rest of this section. A key characteristic of any quantizer is its *dimension* k, a positive integer. Its input is a k-dimensional vector $x = (x_1, \cdots, x_k)$ from some alphabet $A \subset \Re^k$. (Abstract alphabets are also of interest in rate-distortion theory, but virtually all alphabets encountered in quantization are real-valued vector spaces, in which case the alphabet is often called the *support* of the source distribution.) If $k = 1$ the quantizer is *scalar*; otherwise, it is *vector*. In any case, the quantizer consists of three components—a *lossy encoder* $\alpha: A \to \mathcal{I}$, where the index set $\mathcal{I}$ is an arbitrary countable set, usually taken as a collection of consecutive integers, a *reproduction decoder* $\beta: \mathcal{I} \to \hat{A}$, where $\hat{A} \subset \Re^k$ is the *reproduction alphabet*, and a *lossless encoder* $\gamma: \mathcal{I} \to \mathcal{J}$, an invertible mapping (at least with probability 1) into a collection $\mathcal{J}$ of variable-length binary vectors that satisfies the prefix condition. Alternatively, a lossy encoder is specified by a partition $\mathcal{S} = \{S_i; i \in \mathcal{I}\}$ of A, where $S_i = \{x: \alpha(x) = i\}$; a reproduction decoder is specified by a *(reproduction) codebook*

$\mathcal{C} = \{\beta(i); \ i \in \mathcal{I}\}$ of *points, codevectors,* or *reproduction codewords*; and the lossless encoder γ can be described by its *binary codebook* $\mathcal{J} = \{\gamma(i); \ i \in \mathcal{I}\}$ containing *binary* or *channel codewords*. The *quantization rule* is the function $q(x) = \beta(\alpha(x))$ or, equivalently, $q(x) = \beta(i)$ whenever $x \in S_i$.

A k-dimensional quantizer is used by applying its lossy and lossless encoders, followed by the corresponding decoders, to a sequence of k-dimensional input vectors $\{\underline{x}_n; \ n = 1, 2, \cdots\}$ extracted from the data being encoded. There is not a unique way to do such vector extraction; and the design and performance of the quantizer usually depend significantly on the specific method that is used. For data that naturally forms a sequence $x_1, x_2, \cdots$ of scalar-valued samples, e.g., speech, vector extraction is almost always done by parsing the data into successive k-tuples of adjacent samples, i.e., $\underline{x}_n = (x_{(n-1)k+1}, \cdots, x_{nk})$. As an example of other possibilities, one could also extract the first k even samples, followed by the first k odd samples, the next k even samples, and so on. This subsampling could be useful for a multiresolution reconstruction, as in interpolative vector quantization [234], [194]. For other types of data there may be no canonical extraction method. For example, in stereo speech the k-dimensional vectors might consist just of left samples, or just of right samples, or half from each, or k from the left followed by k from the right, etc. Another example is grayscale imagery where the k-dimensional vectors might come from parsing the image into rectangular m-by-n blocks of pixels, where $mn = k$, or into other tiling polytopes, such as hexagons and other shapes aimed at taking advantage of the eye's insensitivity to noise along diagonals in comparison with along horizontal and vertical lines [226]. Or the vectors might come from some less regular parsing. If the image has color, with each pixel value represented by some three-dimensional vector, then k-dimensional vectors can be extracted in even more ways. And if the data is a sequence of color of images, e.g., digital video, the extraction possibilities increase immensely.[3]

There are two generic domains in which (memoryless) quantization theory, both analysis and design, can proceed. In the first, which we call the *random vector domain*, the input data, i.e., source, to be quantized is described by a fixed value of k, an alphabet $A \subset \Re^k$, and a probability distribution on A; and the quantizer must be k-dimensional. This is the case when the specific vector dimension and contents are not allowed to vary, e.g., when ten-dimensional speech parameter vectors of line spectral pairs or reflection coefficients are coded together. In the second, which we call the *random process domain*, the input data is characterized as a discrete parameter random process, i.e., a countable collection (usually infinite) of random variables; and different ways of extracting vectors from its component variables may be considered and compared, including different choices of the dimension k. As indicated above, there are in general many ways to do this. However, for concreteness and because it provides the opportunity to make some key points, whenever the random process domain is of interest in this and the next section, we focus exclusively

on the canonical case where the data naturally forms a one-dimensional, scalar-valued sequence, and successive k-tuples of adjacent samples are extracted for quantization. We will also assume that the random process is stationary, unless a specific exception is made. Stationary models can easily be defined to include processes that exhibit distinct local and global stationarity properties (such as speech and images) by the use of models such as composite, hidden Markov, and mixture sources. In the random vector domain, there is no first-order stationarity assumption; e.g., the individual components within each vector need not be identically distributed. In either domain we presume that the quantizer operates on a k-dimensional random vector $X = (X_1, \cdots, X_k)$, usually assumed to be absolutely continuous so that it is described by a probability density function (pdf) $f(x)$. Densities are usually assumed to have finite variance in order to avoid technical difficulties.

Memoryless quantizers, as described here, are also referred to as "vanilla" vector quantizers or block-source codes. The alternative is a quantizer with *memory*. Memory can be incorporated in a variety of ways; it can be used separately for the lossy encoder (for example, different mappings can be used, conditional on the past) or for the lossless encoder (the index produced by a quantizer can be coded conditionally based on previous indices). We shall return to vector quantizers with memory in Section V, but our primary emphasis will remain on memoryless quantizers. We will occasionally use the term *code* as a generic substitute for *quantizer*.

The instantaneous rate of the quantizer applied to a particular input is the normalized length $r(x) = (1/k)l(\gamma(\alpha(x)))$ of the channel codeword, the number of bits per source symbol that must be sent to describe the reproduction. An important special case is when all binary codewords have the same length r, in which case the quantizer is referred to as *fixed-length* or *fixed-rate*.

To measure the quality of the reproduction, we assume the existence of a nonnegative distortion measure $d(x, \hat{x})$ which assigns a distortion or cost to the reproduction of input x by $\hat{x}$. Ideally, one would like a distortion measure that is easy to compute, useful in analysis, and perceptually meaningful in the sense that small (large) distortion means good (poor) perceived quality. No single distortion measure accomplishes all three goals, but the common squared-error distortion

$$d(x, \hat{x}) = \|x - \hat{x}\|^2 = (x - \hat{x})^t (x - \hat{x}) = \sum_{i=1}^{k} |x_i - \hat{x}_i|^2$$

satisfies the first two. Although much maligned for lack of perceptual meaningfulness, it often is a useful indicator of perceptual quality and, perhaps more importantly, it can be generalized to a class of distortion measures that have proved useful in perceptual coding, the input-weighted quadratic distortion measures of the form

$$d(x, \hat{x}) = (x - \hat{x})^t W_x (x - \hat{x}) \tag{21}$$

where W_x is a positive-definite matrix that depends on the input, cf. [258], [259], [257], [224], [387], [386], [150], [186], [316], [323], [325]. Most of the theory and design techniques

---

[3] For example, the video community has had a longstanding debate between progressive versus interlaced scanning—two different extraction methods.

considered here extend to such measures, as will be discussed later. We also assume that $d(x, \hat{x}) = 0$ if and only if $x = \hat{x}$, an assumption that involves no genuine loss of generality and allows us to consider a lossless code as a code for which $d(x, \beta(\alpha(x))) = 0$ for all inputs x.

There exists a considerable literature for various other distortion measures, including l_p and other norms of differences and convex or nondecreasing functions of norms of differences. These have rarely found application in real systems, however, so our emphasis will be on the MSE with comments on generalizations to input-weighted quadratic distortion measures.

The overall performance of a quantizer applied to a source is characterized by the normalized rate

$$R(\alpha, \gamma) = E[r(X)] = \frac{1}{k} E[l(\gamma(\alpha(X)))]$$
$$= \frac{1}{k} \sum_i l(\gamma(i)) \int_{S_i} f(x)\, dx$$

and the normalized average distortion

$$D(\alpha, \beta) = \frac{1}{k} E[d(X, \beta(\alpha(X)))]$$
$$= \frac{1}{k} \sum_i \int_{S_i} d(x, y_i) f(x)\, dx.$$

Every quantizer (α, γ, β) is thus described by a rate-distortion pair $(R(\alpha, \gamma),\ D(\alpha, \beta))$. The goal of compression system design is to optimize the rate-distortion tradeoff. Fixed-rate quantizers constrain this optimization by not allowing a code to assign fewer bits to inputs that might benefit from such, but they provide simpler codes that avoid the necessity of buffering in order to match variable-rate codewords to a possibly fixed-rate digital channel.

The optimal rate-distortion tradeoff for a fixed dimension k can be formalized in several ways: by optimizing distortion for a constrained rate, by optimizing rate for a constrained distortion, or by an unconstrained optimization using a Lagrange approach. These approaches lead, respectively, to the operational distortion-rate function

$$\delta(R) = \inf_{(\alpha, \gamma, \beta):\, R(\alpha, \gamma) \le R} D(\alpha, \beta)$$

the operational rate-distortion function

$$r(D) = \inf_{(\alpha, \gamma, \beta):\, D(\alpha, \beta) \le D} R(\alpha, \gamma)$$

and the operational Lagrangian or weighted distortion-rate function

$$L(\lambda) = \inf_{(\alpha, \gamma, \beta)} D(\alpha, \beta) + \lambda R(\alpha, \gamma)$$

where λ is a nonnegative number. A small value of λ leads to a low-distortion, high-rate solution and a large value leads to a low-rate, high-distortion solution. Note that

$$D(\alpha, \beta) + \lambda R(\alpha, \gamma) = E[d(X, \beta(\alpha(X)) + \lambda l(\gamma(\alpha(X))))]$$

so that the bracketed term can be considered to be a modified or Lagrangian distortion, and that $L(\lambda)$ is the smallest average

Lagrangian distortion. All of these formalizations of optimal performance have their uses, and all are essentially equivalent: the distortion-rate and rate-distortion functions are duals and every distortion-rate pair on the convex hull of these curves corresponds to the Lagrangian for some value of λ. Note that if one constrains the problem to fixed-rate codes, then the Lagrangian approach reduces to the distortion-rate approach since $R(\alpha, \gamma)$ no longer depends on the code and γ can be considered as just a binary indexing of $\mathcal{I}$.

Formal definitions of quantizer optimality easily yield optimality conditions as direct vector extensions and variations on Lloyd's conditions. The conditions all have a common flavor: if two components of the code (α, γ, β) are fixed, then the third component must have a specific form for the code to be optimal. The resulting optimality properties are summarized below. The proofs are simple and require no calculus of variations or differentiation. Proofs may be found, e.g., in [94] and [196].

- For a fixed lossy encoder α, regardless of the lossless encoder γ, the optimal reproduction decoder β is given by

$$\beta(i) = \underset{y}{\arg\min}\ E[d(X, y)|\alpha(X) = i]$$

the output minimizing the conditional expectation of the distortion between the output and the input given that the encoder produced index i. These vectors are called the Lloyd centroids. Note that the optimal decoder output for a given encoder output i is simply the optimal estimate of the input vector X given $\alpha(X) = i$ in the sense of minimizing the conditional average distortion. If the distortion is squared-error, the reproduction decoder is simply the conditional expectation of X given it was encoded into i

$$\text{centroid}\,(S_i) = E[X|X \in S_i].$$

If the distortion measure is the input-weighted squared error of (21), then [318], [224]

$$\text{centroid}\,(S_i) = E[W_X|X \in S_i]^{-1} E[W_X X|X \in S_i].$$

- For a fixed lossy encoder α, regardless of the reproduction decoder β, the optimal lossless encoder γ is the optimal lossless code for the discrete source $\alpha(X)$, e.g., a Huffman code for the lossy encoded source.

- For a fixed reproduction decoder β, lossless code γ, and Lagrangian parameter λ, the optimal lossy encoder is a minimum-distortion (nearest neighbor) encoder for the modified Lagrangian distortion measure

$$\alpha(x) = \underset{i \in \mathcal{I}}{\arg\min}\ (d(x, \beta(i)) + \lambda l(\gamma(i))).$$

If the code is constrained to be fixed-rate, then the second property is irrelevant and the third property reduces to the familiar minimum distortion encoding with respect to d, as in the original formulation of Lloyd (and implicit in Shannon). (The resulting partition is often called a *Voronoi* partition.) In the general variable-rate case, the minimum distance (with respect to the distortion measure d) encoder is suboptimal;

the optimal rule takes into account both distortion and code-word length. Thus simply cascading a minimum MSE vector quantizer with a lossless code is suboptimal. Instead, in the general case, instantaneous rate should be considered in an optimal encoding, as the goal is to trade off distortion and rate in an optimal fashion. In all of these cases, the encoder can be viewed as a mechanism for controlling the output of the decoder so as to minimize the total Lagrangian distortion.

The optimality conditions imply a descent algorithm for code design: Given some λ, begin with an initial code (α, β, γ). Optimize the encoder α for the other two components, then optimize the reproduction decoder β for the remaining components, then optimize the lossless coder γ for the remaining components. Let T denote the overall transformation resulting from these three operations. One such iteration of T must decrease or leave unchanged the average Lagrangian distortion. Iterate until convergence or the improvement falls beneath some threshold. This algorithm is an extension and variation on the algorithm for optimal scalar quantizer design introduced for fixed-rate scalar quantization by Lloyd [330]. The algorithm is a fixed-point algorithm since if it converges to a code, the code must be a fixed point with respect to T. This generalized Lloyd algorithm applies to any distribution, including parametric models and empirical distributions formed from training sets of real data. There is no obvious means of choosing the "best" λ, so the design algorithm might sweep through several values to provide a choice of rate-distortion pairs. We also mention that Lloyd-style iterative algorithms have been used to design many structured forms of quantization. For example, when the codes are constrained to have fixed rate, the algorithm becomes k-means clustering, finding a fixed number of representative points that yield the minimum average distortion when a minimum distortion mapping is assumed.

As mentioned in Section I, a variety of other clustering algorithms exist that can be used to design vector quantizers (or solve any other clustering problems). Although each has found its adherents, none has convincingly yielded significant benefits over the Lloyd algorithm and its variations in terms of trading off rate and distortion, although some have proved much faster (and others much slower). Some algorithms such as simulated and deterministic annealing have been found experimentally to do a better job of avoiding local optima and finding globally optimal distortion-rate pairs than has the basic Lloyd algorithm, but repeated applications of the Lloyd algorithm with different initial conditions has also proved effective in avoiding local optima. We focus on the Lloyd algorithm because of its simplicity, its proven merit at designing codes, and because of the wealth of results regarding its convergence properties [451], [418], [108], [91], [101], [321], [335], [131], [36].

The centroid property of optimal reproduction decoders has interesting implications in the special case of a squared-error distortion measure, where it follows easily [137], [60], [193], [184], [196] that

- $E[q(X)] = E[X]$, so that the quantizer output can be considered as an unbiased estimator of the input.

- $E[q_i(X)(q_j(X) - X_j)] = 0$, for all i, j so that each component of the quantizer output is orthogonal to each component of the quantizer error. This is an example of the well-known fact that the minimum mean-squared error estimate of an unknown, X, given an observation, $\alpha(X)$, causes the estimate to be orthogonal to the error. In view of the previous property, this implies that the quantizer error is uncorrelated with the quantizer output rather than, as is often assumed, with the quantizer input.

- $E[||q(X) - X||^2] = E[||X||^2] - E[||q(X)||^2]$, which implies that the energy (or variance) of the quantized signal must be less than that in the original signal.

- $E[X^t(q(X) - X)] = -E[||q(X) - X||^2]$, which shows that the quantizer error is *not* uncorrelated with the input. In fact, the correlation is minus the mean-squared error.

It is instructive to consider the extreme points of the rate-distortion tradeoff, when the distortion is zero (or $\lambda = 0$) and the rate is 0 (when $\lambda = \infty$). First suppose that $\lambda = 0$. In this case, the rate does not affect the Lagrangian distortion at all, but MSE counts. If the source is discrete, then one can optimize this case by forcing zero distortion, that is, using a lossless code. In this case, Shannon's lossless coding theorem implies that for rate measured by average instantaneous codelength

$$H(X) \leq r(0) < H(X) + 1$$

or, if rate is measured by entropy, then simply $r(0) = H(X)$, the entropy of the vector. In terms of the Lagrangian formulation, $L(0) = 0$. Conversely, suppose that $\lambda \to \infty$. In this case distortion costs a negligible amount and rate costs an enormous amount, so here the optimal is attained by using zero rate and simply tolerating whatever distortion one must suffer. The distortion for a zero-rate code is minimized by the centroid of the unconditional distribution,

$$D(0) = \min_y E[d(X, y)]$$

which is simply the mean $E[X]$ in the MSE case. Here the Lagrangian formulation becomes $L(\infty) = \min_y E[d(X, y)]$. Both of these extreme points are global optima, albeit the second is useless in practice.

So far, we have focused on the random vector domain and considered optimality for quantizers of a fixed dimension. In practice, however, and in source coding theory, the dimension k may be a parameter of choice, and it is of interest to consider how the optima depend on it. Accordingly, we now focus on the random process domain, assuming that the source is a one-dimensional, scalar-valued, stationary random process. In this situation, the various operational optima explicitly note the dimension, e.g., $\delta_k(R)$ denotes the operational distortion-rate function for dimension k and rate R and, similarly, $r_k(D)$ and $L_k(\lambda)$ denote the operational rate-distortion and Lagrange functions. Moreover, the overall optimal performance for all quantizers of rate less than or equal to R is defined by

$$\bar{\delta}(R) = \inf_k \delta_k(R). \tag{22}$$

Similar definitions hold for the rate-versus-distortion and the Lagrangian viewpoints.

Using stationarity, it can be shown (cf. [562], [577], [221], [217, Lemma 11.2.3]) that the operational distortion-rate function is *subadditive* in the sense that for any positive integers k and l

$$\delta_{k+l}(R) \leq \frac{k}{k+l} \delta_k(R) + \frac{l}{k+l} \delta_l(R) \qquad (23)$$

which shows the generally decreasing trend of the $\delta_k(R)$'s as k increases. It is not known whether or not $\delta_{k+1}(R)$ is always less than or equal to $\delta_k(R)$. However, it can be shown that subadditivity implies (cf. [180, p. 112])

$$\overline{\delta}(R) = \lim_{k \to \infty} \delta_k(R). \qquad (24)$$

Hence high-dimensional quantizers can do as well as any quantizer. Note that (23) and (24) both hold for the special cases of fixed-rate quantizers as well as for variable-rate quantizers.

It is important to point out that for squared error and most other distortion measures, the "inf" in (22) is not a "min." Specifically, $\overline{\delta}(R)$ represents performance that cannot be achieved exactly, except in degenerate situations such as when $R = 0$ or the source distribution is discrete rather than continuous. Of course, by the infimum definition of $\overline{\delta}(R)$, there are always quantizers with performance arbitrarily close to it. We conclude that no quantizers are *truly* optimal. Thus it is essential to understand that whenever the word "optimal" is used in the random process domain, it is *always* in the context of some specific constraint or class of quantizers, such as eight-dimensional fixed-rate VQ or entropy-constrained uniform scalar quantization or pyramid coding with dimension 20, to name a few at random. Indeed, though desirable, "optimality" loses a bit of its lustre when one considers the fact that an optimal code in one class might not work as well as a suboptimal code in another. It should now be evident that the importance of the Lloyd-style optimality principles lies ultimately in their ability to guide the optimization of quantizers within specific constraints or classes.

IV. HIGH RESOLUTION QUANTIZATION THEORY

This section presents an overview of high resolution theory and compares its results to those of Shannon rate-distortion theory. For simplicity, we will adopt squared error as the distortion measure until late in the section, where extensions to other distortion measures are discussed. There have been two styles of high resolution theory developments: informal, where simple approximations are made, and rigorous, where limiting formulas are rigorously derived. Here, we proceed with the informal style until later when the results of the rigorous approach are summarized. We will also presume the "random vector domain" of fixed dimension, as described in the previous section, until stated otherwise.

A. Asymptotic Distortion

As mentioned earlier, the first and most elementary result in high resolution theory is the $\Delta^2/12$ approximation to the mean-squared error of a uniform scalar quantizer with step size Δ [43], [394], [468], which we now derive. Consider an N-level uniform quantizer q whose levels are $y_1, \cdots, y_N$, with $y_i = y_{i-1} + \Delta$. When this quantizer is applied to a continuous random variable X with probability density $f(x)$, when Δ is small, and when overload distortion can be ignored, the mean-squared error (MSE) distortion may be approximated as follows:

$$
\begin{aligned}
D(q) &= E[(X - q(X))^2] \\
&\cong \sum_{i=1}^{N} \int_{y_i - \Delta/2}^{y_i + \Delta/2} (x - y_i)^2 f(x)\, dx \\
&\cong \sum_{i=1}^{N} f(y_i) \int_{y_i - \Delta/2}^{y_i + \Delta/2} (x - y_i)^2 \, dx \\
&= \frac{\Delta^2}{12} \sum_{i=1}^{N} f(y_i) \Delta \\
&\cong \frac{\Delta^2}{12} \int_{y_1 - \Delta/2}^{y_N + \Delta/2} f(x)\, dx \\
&\cong \frac{\Delta^2}{12}.
\end{aligned}
$$

The first approximation in the above derives from ignoring overload distortion. If the source density is entirely contained in the granular region of the quantizer, then this approximation is not needed. The second approximation derives from observing that the density may be approximated as a constant on a small interval. Usually, as in the mean value theorem of integration, one assumes the density is continuous, but as any measurable function is approximately continuous, when Δ is sufficiently small this approximation is valid even for discontinuous densities. The third approximation derives from recognizing that by the definition of a Riemann integral, $\sum_{i=1}^{N} f(y_i)\Delta$ is approximately equal to the integral of f. Finally, the last approximation derives from again ignoring the overload region. As mentioned in earlier sections, there are situations, such as variable-rate quantization, where an infinite number of levels are permitted. In such cases, if the support of the uniform scalar quantizer contains that of the source density, then there will be no overload distortion to ignore, and again we have $D \cong \Delta^2/12$.

It is important to mention the sense in which D is approximated by $\Delta^2/12$. After all, when Δ is small, both D and $\Delta^2/12$ will be small, so it is not saying much to assert that their difference is small. Rather, as discussed later in the context of the rigorous framework for high resolution theory, it can be shown that under ordinary conditions, the ratio of D and $\Delta^2/12$ tends to 1 as Δ decreases. Though we will not generally mention it, all future high-resolution approximations discussed in this paper will also hold in this ratio-tending-to-one sense.

Each of the assumptions and simple approximations made in deriving $\Delta^2/12$ reoccurs in some guise in the derivation of all subsequent high-resolution formulas, such as for nonuniform, vector, and variable-rate quantizers. Thus they might be said to be principal suppositions. Indeed, the small cell type of supposition is what gives the theory its "high resolution" name.

In uniform quantization, all cells have the same size and shape and the levels are in the center of each cell (except for the outermost cells which are ignored). Thus the cell size Δ is the key performance determining gross characteristic. In more advanced, e.g., vector, quantization, cells may differ in size and shape, and the codevectors need not be in the centers of the cells. Consequently, other gross characterizations are needed. These are the *point density* and the *inertial profile*.

The point density of a vector quantizer is the direct extension of the point density introduced in Section II. That is, it is a nonnegative, usually smooth function $\lambda(x)$ that, when integrated over a region, determines the approximate fraction of codevectors contained in that region. In fixed-rate coding, the point density is usually normalized by the number of codevectors so that its total integral is one. In variable-rate coding, where the number of codevectors is not a key performance-determining parameter and may even be infinite, the point density is usually left unnormalized. As we consider fixed-rate coding first, we will presume λ is normalized, until stated otherwise. There is clearly an inverse relationship between the point density and the volume of cells, namely, $\lambda(x) \cong (N \operatorname{vol}(S_x))^{-1}$, where, as before, N is the number of codevectors or cells and S_x denotes the cell containing x.

As with any density that describes a discrete set of points, there is no unique way to define it for a specific quantizer. Rather, the point density is intended as a high-level gross characterization, or a model or target to which a quantizer aspires. It describes the codevectors, in much the way that a probability density describes a set of data points—it does not say exactly where they are located, but roughly characterizes their distribution. Quantizers with different numbers of codevectors can be compared on the basis of their point density, and there is an ideal point density to which quantizers aspire—they cannot achieve it exactly, but may approximate it. Nevertheless, there are times when a concrete definition of the point density of a specific quantizer is needed. In such cases, the following is often used: the *specific point density* of a quantizer q is $\lambda_q(x) \equiv (N \operatorname{vol}(S_x))^{-1}$. This piecewise-constant function captures all the (fine) detail in the quantizer's partition, in contrast to the usual notion of a point density as a gross characterization. As an example of its use, we mention that for fixed-rate quantization, the ideal point density $\lambda(x)$ is usually a smooth function, closely related to the source density, and one may say that a quantizer has point density approximately $\lambda(x)$ if $\lambda_q(x) \cong \lambda(x)$ for all x in some set with high probability (relative to the source density). When a scalar quantizer is implemented as a compander, $\lambda(x)$ is proportional to the derivative of the compressor function applied to the input. Though the notion of point density would no doubt have been recognizable to the earliest contributors such as Bennett, Panter, and Dite, as mentioned earlier, it was not explicitly introduced until Lloyd's work [330].

In nonuniform scalar quantization and vector quantization, there is the additional issue of codevector placement within cells and, in the latter case, of cell shape. The effect of point placement and cell shape is exhibited in the following approximation to the contribution of a small cell S_i with

codevector y_i to the MSE of a k-dimensional vector quantizer

$$D_i(q) = \frac{1}{k} \int_{S_i} \|x - y_i\|^2 f(x) \, dx \tag{25}$$

$$\cong f(y_i) M(S_i, y_i) \operatorname{vol}(S_i)^{1+2/k} \tag{26}$$

where $M(S_i, y_i)$ is the normalized moment of inertia of the cell S_i about the point y_i, defined by

$$M(S_i, y_i) \equiv \frac{1}{k} \frac{1}{\operatorname{vol}(S_i)^{1+2/k}} \int_{S_i} \|x - y_i\|^2 \, dx.$$

Normalizing by volume makes M independent of the size of the cell. Normalizing by dimension yields a kind of invariance to dimension, namely, that $M(S_i \times S_i, (y_i, y_i)) = M(S_i, y_i)$. We often write $M(S_i)$ when y_i is clear from the context. The normalized moment of inertia, and the resulting contribution $D_i(q)$, is smaller for sphere-like cells with codevectors in the center than for cells that are oblong, have sharply pointed vertices, or have displaced codevectors. In the latter cases, there are more points farther from y_i that contribute substantially to normalized moment of inertia, especially when dimension is large.

In some quantizers, such as uniform scalar and lattice quantizers, all cells (with the exception of the outermost cells) have the same shape and the same placement of codevectors within cells. In other quantizers, however, cell shape or codevector placement varies with position. In such cases, it is useful to characterize the variation of cell normalized moment of inertia by a nonnegative, usually smooth function $m(x)$, called the *inertial profile*. That is, $m(x) \cong M(S_i, y_i)$ when $x \in S_i$. As with point densities, we do not define $m(x)$ to be equal to $M(S_x, q(x))$, because we want it to be a high-level gross characterization or model to which a quantizer aspires. Instead, we let $m_q(x) \equiv M(S_x, q(x))$ be called the *specific inertial profile* of the quantizer q. This is a piecewise-constant function that captures the fine details of cell normalized moment of inertia.

Returning to $D_i(q)$ expressed in (26), the effect of cell size is obviously in the term $\operatorname{vol}(S_i)$. Using the inverse relationship between point density and cell volume yields

$$D_i(q) \cong \frac{1}{N^{2/k}} f(y_i) \frac{M(S_i, y_i)}{\lambda^{2/k}(y_i)} \operatorname{vol}(S_i)$$

which shows how point density locally influences distortion. Summing the above over all cells and recognizing the sum as an approximation to an integral yields the following approximation to the distortion of a vector quantizer:

$$D(q) \cong \frac{1}{N^{2/k}} \int \frac{m(x)}{\lambda^{2/k}(x)} f(x) \, dx. \tag{27}$$

For scalar quantizers ($k = 1$) with points in the middle of the cells, $m(x) = 1/12$ and the above reduces to

$$D(q) \cong \frac{1}{12} \frac{1}{N^2} \int \frac{1}{\lambda^2(x)} f(x) \, dx \tag{28}$$

which is what Bennett [43] found for companders, as restated in terms of point densities by Lloyd [330]. Both (28) and the more general formula (27) are called *Bennett's integral*. The extension of Bennett's integral to vector quantizers was first made by Gersho (1979) [193] for quantizers with congruent cells for which the concept of inertial profile was not needed, and then to vector quantizers with varying cell shapes (and codevector placements) by Na and Neuhoff (1995) [365].

Bennett's integral (27) can be expected to be a good approximation under the following conditions: i) Most cells are small enough that $f(x)$ can be approximated as being constant over the cell. (There can be some large cells where $f(x)$ is very small.) Ordinarily, this requires N to be large. ii) The specific point density of the quantizer approximately equals $\lambda(x)$ on a high probability set of x's. iii) The specific inertial profile approximately equals $m(x)$ on a high probability set of x's. iv) Adjacent cells have similar volumes. The last condition rules out quantizers such as a scalar one whose cells have alternating lengths such as $\Delta, \frac{1}{2}\Delta, \frac{1}{2}\Delta, \Delta, \frac{1}{2}\Delta, \frac{1}{2}\Delta, \Delta, \cdots$. The point density of such a quantizer is $\lambda(x) = 3/(2\Delta N)$, because there are three points in an interval of width 2Δ. Assuming, for simplicity, that the source density is uniform on $[0, 1]$, it is easy to compute $D = (5/96)\Delta^2$, whereas Bennett's integral equals $(1/27)\Delta^2$. One may obtain the correct distortion by separately applying Bennett's integral to the union of intervals of length Δ and to the union of intervals of length $\frac{1}{2}\Delta$. The problem is that Bennett's integral is not linear in the point density. So for it to be accurate, cell size must change slowly or only occasionally. Since Bennett's integral is linear in the inertial profile, it is not necessary to assume that adjacent cells have similar shapes, although one would normally expect this to be the case in situations where Bennett's integral is applied. Examples of the use of the vector extension of Bennett's integral will be given later.

Approximating the source density as a constant over each quantization cell, which is a key step in the derivations of (26) and (28), is like assuming that the effect of quantization is to add noise that is uniformly distributed. However, the range of noise values must match the size and shape of the cell. And so when the cells are not all of the same size and shape, such quantization noise is obviously correlated with the vector X being quantized. On the other hand, for uniform scalar and lattice vector quantizers, the error and X are approximately uncorrelated. A more general result, mentioned in Section III, is that the correlation between the input and the quantization error is approximately equal to the MSE of the quantizer when the codevectors are approximately centroids.

B. Performance of the Best k-Dimensional, Fixed-Rate Quantizers

Having Bennett's integral for distortion, one can hope to find a formula for $\delta_k(R)$, the operational distortion-rate function for k-dimensional, fixed-rate vector quantization, by choosing the key characteristics, point density and inertial profile, to minimize (27). Unfortunately, it is not known how to find the best inertial profile. Indeed, it is not even known what functions are allowable as inertial profiles. However, Gersho (1979) [193] made the now widely accepted conjecture that when rate is large, most cells of a k-dimensional quantizer with rate R and minimum or nearly minimum MSE are approximately

congruent to some basic tessellating[4] k-dimensional cell shape T_k. In this case, the optimum inertial profile is a constant and Bennett's integral can be minimized by variational techniques or Hölder's inequality [193], [222], resulting in the optimal point density

$$\lambda_k^*(x) = \frac{f^{k/(k+2)}(x)}{\int f^{k/(k+2)}(x')\, dx'} \tag{29}$$

and the following approximation to the operational distortion-rate function: for large R

$$\delta_k(R) \cong M_k \beta_k \sigma^2 2^{-2R} \equiv Z_k(R) \tag{30}$$

where $M_k \equiv M(T_k)$, which is the least normalized moment of inertia of k-dimensional tessellating polytopes, and

$$\beta_k \equiv \frac{1}{\sigma^2} \left(\int f^{k/(k+2)}(x)\, dx \right)^{(k+2)/k}$$

is the term depending on the source distribution. Dividing by variance makes β_k invariant to a scaling of the source. We will refer to M_k, β_k, and $Z_k(R)$ as, respectively, Gersho's constant (in dimension k), Zador's factor (for k-dimensional, fixed-rate quantization), and the Zador–Gersho function (for k-dimensional, fixed-rate quantization). (Zador's role will be described later.) When $k = 1$, $Z_1(R)$ reduces to the Panter–Dite formula (8).

From the form of $\lambda_k^*(x)$ one may straightforwardly deduce that cells are smaller and have higher probability where $f(x)$ is larger, and that all cells contribute roughly the same to the distortion; i.e., $D_i(q)$ in (26) is approximately the same for all i, which is the "partial distortion theorem" first deduced for scalar quantization by Panter and Dite.

A number of properties of M_k and β_k are known; here, we mention just a few. Gersho's constant M_k is known only for $k = 1$ and 2, where T_k is, respectively, an interval and a regular hexagon. It is not known whether the M_k's are monotonically nonincreasing for all k, but it can be shown that they form a subadditive sequence, which is a property strong enough to imply that the infimum over k equals the limit as k tends to infinity. Though it has long been presumed, only recently has it been directly shown that the M_k's tend to $1/2\pi e$ as k increases (Zamir and Feder [564]), which is the limit of the normalized moment of inertia of k-dimensional spheres as k tends to infinity. Previously, the assertion that the M_k's tend to $1/2\pi e$ depended on Gersho's conjecture. Zador's factor β_k tends to be smaller for source densities that are more "compact" (lighter tails and more uniform) and have more dependence among the source variables.

Fortunately, high resolution theory need not rely solely on Gersho's conjecture, because Zador's dissertation [561] and subsequent memo [562] showed that for large rate $\delta(R)$ has the form $b_k \beta_k \sigma^2 2^{-2R}$, where b_k is independent of the

---

[4] A cell T "tessellates" if there exists a partition of $\Re^k$ whose cells are, entirely, translations and rotations of T. The Voronoi cell of any lattice tessellates, but not all tessellations are generated by lattices. Gersho also conjectured that T_k would be *admissible* in the sense that the Voronoi partition for the centroids of the tessellation would coincide with the tessellation. But this is not essential.

source distribution. Thus Gersho's conjecture is really just a conjecture about b_k.

In deriving the key result, Zador first showed that for a random vector that is uniformly distributed on the unit cube, $\delta(R)$ has the form $b_k 2^{-2R}$ when R is large, which effectively defines b_k. (In this case, $\beta_k \sigma^2 = 1$.) He then used this to prove the general result by showing that no quantizer with high rate could do better than one whose partition is hierarchically constructed by partitioning $\Re^k$ into small equally sized cubes and then subdividing each with the partition of the quantizer that is best for a uniform distribution on that cube, where the number of cells within each cube depends on the source density in that cube. In other words, the local structure of an asymptotically optimal quantizer can be that of the optimum quantizer for a uniform distribution.

In this light, Gersho's conjecture is true if and only if. at high rates. one may obtain an asymptotically optimal quantizer for a uniform distribution by tessellating with T_k. The latter statement has been proven for $k = 1$ (cf. [106, p. 59]) and for $k = 2$ by Fejes Toth (1959) [159]; see also [385]. For $k = 3$, it is known that the best lattice tessellation is the body-centered cubic lattice, which is generated by a truncated octahedron [35]. It has not been proven that this is the best tessellation, though one would suspect that it is. In summary, Gersho's conjecture is known to be true only for $k = 1$ and 2. Might it be false for $k \geq 3$? If it is, it might be that the best quantizers for a uniform source have a *periodic* tessellation in which two or more cell shapes alternate in a periodic fashion, like the hexagons and pentagons on the surface of a soccer ball. If the cells in one period of the tessellation have the same volumes, then one may apply Bennett's integral, and (30) holds with M_k replaced by the average of the normalized moment of inertia of the cells in one period. However, if the cells have unequal volumes, then as in the example given while discussing Condition iv) of Bennett's integral, the MSE will be the average of distortions computed by using Bennett's integral separately on the union of cells of each type, and a macrolevel definition of M_k will be needed. It might also be that the structure of optimal quantizers is aperiodic. However, it seems likely to us that, asymptotically, one could always find a quantizer with a periodic structure that is essentially as good as any aperiodic one.

It is an open question in dimensions three and above whether the best tessellation is a lattice. In most dimensions, the best known tessellation is a lattice. However, tessellations that are better than the best known lattices have recently been found for dimensions seven and nine by Agrell and Eriksson [149].

From now on, we shall proceed assuming Gersho's conjecture is correct, with the knowledge that if this is not the case, then analyses based on M_k will be wrong (for $k \geq 3$) by the factor M_k/b_k, which will be larger than 1 (but probably not much larger), and which in any case will converge to one as $k \to \infty$, as discussed later.

C. Performance of the Best k-Dimensional, Variable-Rate Quantizers

Extensions of high resolution theory to variable-rate quantization can also be based on Bennett's integral, as well as approximations, originally due to Gish and Pierce [204], to the entropy of the output of a quantizer. Two such approximations, which can be derived using approximations much like those used to derive Bennett's integral, were stated earlier for scalar quantizers in (11) and (13). However, the approximation (13), which says that for quantizers with mostly small cells $H(q) \cong h(X) + E[\log \Lambda(X)]$, where $\Lambda(x)$ is the unnormalized point density, holds equally well for vector quantizers, when X is interpreted as a vector rather than a scalar variable. As mentioned before, unnormalized point density is used because with variable-rate quantization, the number of codevectors is not a primary characteristic and may even be infinite. For example, one can always add levels in a way that has negligible impact on the distortion and entropy.

We could now proceed to use Bennett's integral and the entropy approximation to find the operational distortion-rate function for variable-rate, k-dimensional, memoryless VQ. However, we wish to consider a somewhat more general case. Just as Gish and Pierce found something quite interesting by examining the best possible performance of scalar quantization with *block* entropy coding, we will now consider the operational distortion-rate function for vector quantization with block entropy coding. Specifically, we seek $\delta_{k,L}(R)$, which is defined to be the infimum of the distortions of any quantizer with rate R or less, whose lossy encoder is k-dimensional and memoryless, and whose lossless encoder simultaneously codes a block of L successive quantization indices with a variable-length prefix code. In effect, the overall code is a kL-dimensional, memoryless VQ. However, we will refer to it as a k-dimensional (memoryless) quantizer with Lth-order variable-length coding (or Lth-order entropy coding). When $L = 1$, the code becomes a conventional memoryless, variable-rate vector quantizer. It is convenient to let $L = 0$ connote fixed-length coding, so that $\delta_{k,0}(R)$ means the same as $\delta_k(R)$ of the previous section. By finding high-resolution approximations to $\delta_{k,L}(R)$ for all values of $k \geq 1$ and $L \geq 0$, we will be able to compare the advantages of increasing the dimension k of the quantizer to those of increasing the order L of the entropy coder.

To find $\delta_{k,L}(R)$ we assume that the source produces a sequence $(\underline{X}_1, \cdots, \underline{X}_L)$ of identical, but not necessarily independent, k-dimensional random vectors, each with density $f(x)$. A straightforward generalization of (13) shows that under high-resolution conditions, the rate is given by

$$R \cong \frac{1}{kL} h(X_1, \cdots, X_{kL}) + \frac{1}{k} \int f(x) \log \Lambda(x) \, dx. \quad (31)$$

On the other hand, the distortion of such a code may be approximated using Bennett's integral (27), with $\Lambda(x)/N^{2/k}$ substituted for the normalized point density $\lambda(x)$. Then, as with fixed-rate vector quantization, one would like to find $\delta_{k,L}(R)$ by choosing the inertial profile m and the point density Λ to minimize Bennett's integral subject to a constraint on the rate that the right-hand side of (31) be at most R.

Once again, though it is not known how to find the best inertial profile, Gersho's conjecture suggests that when rate is large, the cells of the best rate-constrained quantizers are, mostly, congruent to T_k. Hence, from now on we shall assume

303

that the inertial profile of the best variable-rate quantizers is, approximately, $m(x) = M_k$. In this case, using variational techniques or simply Jensen's inequality, one can show that the best point density is uniform on all of $\Re^k$ (or at least over the support of the source density). In other words, all quantizer cells have the same size, as in a tessellation. Using this fact along with (27) and (31) yields

$$\delta_{k,L}(R) \cong M_k \gamma_{kL} \sigma^2 2^{-2R} \equiv Z_{k,L}(R) \qquad (32)$$

where

$$\gamma_k \equiv \frac{1}{\sigma^2} 2^{2(1/k)h(X_1,\cdots,X_k)}$$

is the term depending on the source distribution. Dividing by variance makes it invariant to scale. We call γ_k the (kth-order) Zador entropy factor and $Z_{k,L}(R)$ a Zador–Gersho function for variable-rate coding. Since fixed-rate coding is a special case of variable-length coding, it must be that γ_k is less than or equal to β_k in (30). This can be directly verified using Jensen's inequality [193].

In the case of scalar quantization ($k = 1$), the optimality of the uniform point density and the operational distortion-rate function $\delta_{1,L}(R)$ were found by Gish and Pierce (1968) [204]. Zador (1966) [562] considered the $L = 1$ case and showed that $\delta_{k,1}(R)$ has the form $c_k \gamma_k \sigma^2 2^{-2R}$ when R is large, where c_k is a constant that is independent of the source density and no larger than the constant b_k that he found for fixed-rate quantization. Gersho [193] used the argument given above to find the form of $\delta_{k,1}(R)$ given in (32).

As with fixed-rate quantization, we shall proceed under the assumption that Gersho's conjecture is correct, in which case $c_k = b_k = M_k$. If it is wrong, then our analyses will be off by the factor M_k/c_k, which, as before, will probably be just a little larger than one, and which in any case will converge to one as $k \to \infty$.

D. Fixed-Rate Quantization with Arbitrary Dimension

We now restrict attention to the random process domain wherein the source is assumed to be a one-dimensional, scalar-valued, stationary random process. We seek a high-resolution approximation to the operational distortion-rate function $\overline{\delta}(R) \equiv \inf_k \delta_k(R)$, which represents the best possible performance of any fixed-rate (memoryless) quantizer. As mentioned in Section III, for stationary sources $\overline{\delta}(R) = \lim_{k \to \infty} \delta_k(R)$. Therefore, taking the limit of the high-resolution approximation (30) for $\delta_k(R)$ yields the fact that for large R

$$\overline{\delta}(R) \cong \overline{M}\,\overline{\beta}\sigma^2 2^{-2R} \equiv \overline{Z}(R) \qquad (33)$$

where

$$\overline{M} = \lim_{k \to \infty} M_k = \frac{1}{2}\pi e$$
$$\overline{\beta} = \lim_{k \to \infty} \beta_k$$

and

$$\overline{Z}(R) \equiv \lim_{k \to \infty} Z_k(R)$$

is another Zador–Gersho function. This operational distortion-rate function was also derived by Zador [561], who showed that his unknown factors b_k and c_k converged to $1/2\pi e$. The derivation given here is due to Gersho [193]. Notice that in this limiting case, there is no doubt about the constant $\overline{M}$.

As previously mentioned, the M_k's are subadditive, so that they are smallest when k is large. Similarly, for stationary sources it can be shown that the sequence $\{\log \beta_k\}$ is also subadditive [193], so that they too are smallest when k is large. Therefore, another expression for the above Zador–Gersho function is $\overline{Z}(R) = \inf_k Z_k(R)$.

E. The Benefits of Increasing Dimension in Fixed-Rate Quantization

Continuing in the random process domain (stationary sources), the generally decreasing natures of M_k and β_k directly quantify the benefits of increasing dimension in fixed-rate quantization. (Of course, there is also a cost to increasing dimension, namely, the increase in complexity.) For example, M_k decreases from $1/12 = 0.0833$ for $k = 1$ to the limit $1/2\pi e = 0.0586$. In decibels, this represents a 1.53-dB decrease in MSE. For an i.i.d. Gaussian source, β_k decreases from $6\sqrt{3}\pi = 32.6$ for $k = 1$ to the limit $2\pi e = 17.1$, which represents an additional 2.81-dB gain. In total, high-dimensional quantization gains 4.35 dB over scalar quantization for the i.i.d. Gaussian source. For a Gauss–Markov source with correlation coefficient $\rho = 0.9$, β_k decreases from $6\sqrt{3}\pi = 32.6$ for $k = 1$ to the limit $2\pi e(1 - \rho^2) = 3.25$ or a gain of 10.0 dB, yielding a total high-dimensional VQ gain of 11.5 dB over scalar quantization. Because of the 6-dB-per-bit rule, any gain stated in decibels can be translated to a reduction in rate (bits per sample) by dividing by 6.02.

On the other hand, it is also important to understand what specific characteristics of vector quantizers improve with dimension and by how much. Motivated by several prior explanations [342], [333], [365], we offer the following. We wish to compare an optimal quantizer q_k with dimension k to an optimal k'-dimensional quantizer $q_{k'}$ with $k' \gg k$. To simplify the discussion, assume k' is a multiple of k. Though these two quantizers have differing dimensions, their characteristics can be fairly compared by comparing $q_{k'}$ to the "product" VQ $q_{\mathrm{pr},k'}$ that is implicitly formed when q_k is used k'/k times in succession. Specifically, the product quantizer has quantization rule

$$q_{\mathrm{pr},k'}(x) = (q_k(\underline{x}_1), \cdots, q_k(\underline{x}_{k'/k}))$$

where $\underline{x}_1, \cdots, \underline{x}_{k'/k}$ are the successive k-tuples of x, and reproduction codebook $\mathcal{C}_{\mathrm{pr},k'}$ consisting of the concatenations of all possible sequences of k'/k codevectors from q_k's reproduction codebook $\mathcal{C}_k$. The subscripts "k" and "pr,k'" will be attached as needed to associate the appropriate features with the appropriate quantizer. The distortion and rate of the product quantizer are easily seen to be those of the k-dimensional VQ. Thus the shortcomings of an optimal k-dimensional quantizer relative to an optimal high-dimensional quantizer may be identified with those of the product quantizer—in particular, with the latter's suboptimal point density and inertial profile, which we now find.

To simplify discussion, assume for now that $k = 1$, and let q_1 be a fixed-rate scalar quantizer, with large rate, levels in the middle of the cells, and point density $\lambda_{\mathrm{sq}}(x_1)$. The cells of the product quantizer $q_{\mathrm{pr}, k'}$ are k'-dimensional rectangles formed by Cartesian products of cells from the scalar quantizer. When the scalar cells have the same width, a k'-dimensional cube is formed; otherwise, a rectangle is formed, i.e., an "oblong" cube. Since the widths of the cells are, approximately, determined by $\lambda_{\mathrm{sq}}(x_1)$, the point density and inertial profile of $q_{\mathrm{pr}, k'}$ are determined by λ_{sq}. Specifically, from the rectangular nature of the product cells one obtains [365], [378]

$$\lambda_{\mathrm{pr}, k'}(x) = \prod_{i=1}^{k'} \lambda_{\mathrm{sq}}(x_i) \tag{34}$$

and

$$m_{\mathrm{pr}, k'}(x) = \frac{1}{12} \frac{\dfrac{1}{k'} \displaystyle\sum_{i=1}^{k'} \dfrac{1}{\lambda_{\mathrm{sq}}^2(x_i)}}{\left(\displaystyle\prod_{i=1}^{k'} \dfrac{1}{\lambda_{\mathrm{sq}}^2(x_i)}\right)^{1/k'}} \tag{35}$$

which derive, respectively, from the facts that the volume of a rectangle is the product of its side lengths, that the normalized moment of inertia of a rectangle is that of a cube ($1/12$) times the ratio of the arithmetic mean of the square of the side lengths to their geometric mean, and that the side lengths are determined by the scalar point density. Note that along the diagonal of the first "quadrant" (where $x_1 = x_2 = \cdots = x_{k'}$), the product cells are cubes and $m_{\mathrm{pr}, k'}(x) = 1/12$, the minimum value. Off the diagonal, the cells are usually rectangular and, consequently, $m_{\mathrm{pr}, k'}(x)$ is larger.

To quantify the suboptimality of the product quantizer's principal feature, we factor the ratio of the distortions of $q_{\mathrm{pr}, k'}(x)$ and $q_{k'}$, which is a kind of loss, into terms that reflect the loss due to the inertial profile and point density [365], [378][5]

$$
\begin{aligned}
L &= \frac{D(q_{\mathrm{pr}, k'})}{\delta_{k'}(R)} \cong \frac{B(k', m_{\mathrm{pr}, k'}, \lambda_{\mathrm{pr}, k'}, f)}{B(k', M_{k'}, \lambda_{k'}^*, f)} \\
&= \underbrace{\frac{B(k', m_{\mathrm{pr}, k'}, \lambda_{\mathrm{pr}, k'}, f)}{B(k', M_{k'}, \lambda_{\mathrm{pr}, k'}, f)}}_{L_{\mathrm{ce}}} \times \underbrace{\frac{B(k', M_{k'}, \lambda_{\mathrm{pr}, k'}, f)}{B(k', M_{k'}, \lambda_{k'}^*, f)}}_{L_{\mathrm{pt}}} \\
&= L_{\mathrm{ce}} \times L_{\mathrm{pt}} \tag{36}
\end{aligned}
$$

where

$$B(k, m, \lambda, f) \equiv \int \frac{m(x)}{\lambda^{2/k}(x)} f(x)\, dx$$

is the part of Bennett's integral that does not depend on N, where the *cell-shape loss*, L_{ce}, is the ratio of the distortion of the product quantizer to that of a hypothetical quantizer with same point density and an optimal inertial profile, and where

[5] Na and Neuhoff considered the ratio of the product code distortion to that of an optimal k-dimensional VQ for arbitrary k, not just for large k.

the *point-density loss*, L_{pt}, is the ratio of the distortion of a hypothetical quantizer with the point density of the product quantizer and a constant (e.g., optimal) inertial profile to that of a hypothetical quantizer with an optimal point density and the same (constant) inertial profile. Substituting (35) into (36) and using the fact that for large k', $M_{k'} \cong 1/2\pi e$, one finds

$$
\begin{aligned}
L &= \frac{\pi e}{6} \times \frac{\displaystyle\int \frac{1}{k'} \sum_{i=1}^{k'} \frac{1}{\lambda_{\mathrm{sq}}^2(x_i)} f_{k'}(x)\, dx}{\displaystyle\int \frac{1}{\left(\displaystyle\prod_{i=1}^{k'} \lambda_{\mathrm{sq}}^2(x_i)\right)^{1/k'}} f_{k'}(x)\, dx} \\
&\quad \times \frac{\displaystyle\int \frac{1}{\displaystyle\prod_{i=1}^{k'} \lambda_{\mathrm{sq}}^{2/k'}(x_i)} f_{k'}(x)\, dx}{\displaystyle\int \frac{1}{\lambda_{k'}^{*2/k'}(x)} f_{k'}(x)\, dx} \\
&= L_{\mathrm{sp}} \times L_{\mathrm{ob}} \times L_{\mathrm{pt}} \tag{37}
\end{aligned}
$$

where the cell shape loss has been factored into the product of a *space-filling loss* [333],[6] L_{sp}, which is the ratio of the normalized moment of inertia of a cube to that of a high-dimensional sphere, and an *oblongitis* loss, L_{ob}, which is the factor by which the rectangularity of the cells makes the cell shape loss larger than the space-filling loss.

To proceed further, consider first an i.i.d. source (stationary and memoryless) and consider how to choose the scalar point density $\lambda_{\mathrm{sq}}(x_1)$ in order to minimize L. On the one hand, choosing $\lambda_{\mathrm{sq}}(x_1)$ to be uniform on the set where the one-dimensional density[7] $f_1(x_1)$ is not small causes the product cells in the region where the k'-dimensional density $f_{k'}(x)$ is not small to be cubes and, consequently, makes $L_{\mathrm{ob}} \cong 1$, which is the smallest possible value. However, it causes the product point density to be poorly matched to the source density and, as a result, L_{pt} is large. On the other hand, choosing $\lambda_{\mathrm{sq}}(x_1) \cong f_1(x_1)$ causes the product quantizer to have, approximately, the optimal point density[8]

$$\lambda_{\mathrm{pr}, k'}(x) \cong \prod_{i=1}^{k'} f_1(x_i) = f_{k'}(x) \cong \lambda_{k'}^*(x)$$

where the last step uses the fact that k' is large. However, this choice causes L_{ob} to be infinite.[9] The best point density, as implicitly found by Panter and Dite, is the compromise

$$\lambda_1^*(x_1) = \frac{f_1^{1/3}(x_1)}{\int f_1^{1/3}(u)\, du}$$

as given in (29). In the region where $f_1(x_1)$ is not small, $\lambda_1^*(x_1)$ is "more uniform" than $\lambda_1(x_1) = f_1(x_1)$ that causes

[6] Actually, Lookabaugh and Gray defined the inverse as a vector quantizer *advantage*. The space-filling loss was called a *cubic* loss in [365].

[7] Dimension will be added as a subscript to f in places where the dimension of X needs to be emphasized.

[8] The fact that product quantizers can have the optimal point density is often overlooked.

[9] This implies that distortion will not decrease as 2^{-2R}.

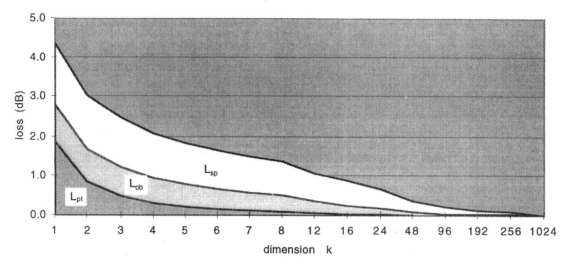

Fig. 5. Losses of optimal k-dimensional quantization relative to optimal high-dimensional quantization for an i.i.d. Gaussian source. The bottom curve is point-density loss; above that is point-density loss plus oblongitis loss; and the top curve is the total loss. For $k \geq 4$, the space-filling losses are estimates.

the product quantizer to have the optimum point density. Therefore, it generates a product quantizer whose cells in the region where $f_{k'}(x)$ is largest are more cubic, which explains why it has less oblongitis loss.

As an example, for an i.i.d. Gaussian source, the optimal choice of scalar quantizer causes the product quantizer to have 0.94-dB oblongitis loss and 1.88-dB point-density loss. The sum of these, 2.81 dB, which equals $10 \log_{10} \beta_1/\overline{\beta}$, has been called the "shape loss" [333] because it is determined by the shape of the density—the more uniform the density the less need for compromise because the scalar point densities leading to best product cell shapes and best point density are more similar. Indeed, for a uniform source density, there is no shape loss. In summary, for an i.i.d. source, in comparison to high-dimensional quantization, the shortcomings of scalar quantization with fixed-rate coding are 1) the $L_{\mathrm{sp}} = 1.53$-dB space-filling loss and 2) the lack of sufficient degrees of freedom to simultaneously attain good inertial profile (small L_{ob}) and good point density (small L_{pt}). On the other hand, it is often surprising to newcomers that vector quantization gains anything at all over scalar quantizers for i.i.d. sources, and secondly, that the gain is more than just the recovery of the space-filling loss.

A similar comparison can be made between k-dimensional $(k \geq 2)$ and high-dimensional VQ, by comparing the product quantizer formed by k'/k uses of a k-dimensional VQ to an optimal k'-dimensional quantizer, for large k'. The results are that as k increases 1) the space-filling loss $L_{\mathrm{sp}} = M_k/(1/2\pi e)$ decreases, and 2) there are more degrees of freedom so that less compromise is needed between the k-dimensional point density that minimizes oblongitis and the one that gives the optimal point density. As a result, the oblongitis, point density, and shape losses decrease to zero, along with the space-filling loss. For the i.i.d. Gaussian source, these losses are plotted in Fig. 5.

For sources with memory, scalar quantization $(k = 1)$ engenders an additional loss due to its inability to exploit the dependence between source samples. Specifically, when there is dependence/correlation between source samples, the

product point density cannot match the ideal point density, not even approximately. See [333] and [365] for a definition of memory loss. (One can factor both the point density and oblongitis losses into two terms, one of which is due to the quantizer's inability to exploit memory.) There is also a memory loss for k-dimensional quantization, which decreases to 1 as k increases. The value of k for which the memory loss becomes close to unity (i.e., negligible) can be viewed as kind of "effective memory or correlation length" of the source. It is closely related to the decorrelation/independence length of the process, i.e., the smallest value of k such that source samples are approximately uncorrelated when separated by more than k.

F. Variable-Rate Quantization with Arbitrary Quantizer Dimension and Entropy Coding Order

We continue in the random process domain (stationary sources). To find the best possible performance of vector quantizers with block entropy coding over all possible choices of the dimension k of the lossy encoder and the order L of the entropy coder, we examine the high-resolution approximation (32), which shows that $\delta_{k,L}(R) \cong M_k \gamma_{kL} \sigma^2 2^{-2R}$. As mentioned previously, the M_k's are subadditive, so choosing k large makes M_k as small as possible, namely, as small as $\overline{M}$. Next, for stationary sources, it is well known that kth-order differential entropy $h_k \equiv (1/k)h(X_1, \cdots, X_k)$ is monotonically nonincreasing in k. Therefore, choosing either k or L large makes $\gamma_{kL} = 2^{2h_{kL}}$ as small as possible, namely, as small as $\overline{\gamma} \equiv \lim_{k\to\infty} \gamma_k$. Interestingly, $\overline{\gamma} = \overline{\beta} \equiv \lim_{k\to\infty} \beta_k$, as shown by Gersho [193], who credits Thomas Liggett. It follows immediately that the best possible performance of vector quantizers with block entropy coding is given by $\overline{\delta}(R) = \overline{M}\,\overline{\beta}\sigma^2 2^{-2R}$, which is the operational distortion-rate function of fixed-rate quantizers. In other words, entropy coding does not permit performance better than high-dimensional fixed-rate quantization.

Let us now re-examine the situation a bit more carefully. We may summarize the various high-resolution approximations to

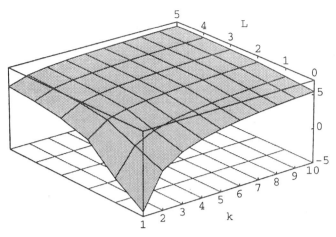

Fig. 6. $10 \log_{10} \alpha_{k, L}$ for a Gauss–Markov source with correlation coefficient 0.9.

operational distortion-rate functions as

$$\delta_{k, L}(R) \cong M_k \alpha_{k, L} \sigma^2 2^{-2R}, \qquad k \geq 1, L \geq 0 \qquad (38)$$

where by convention $L = 0$ refers to fixed-rate coding, $L \geq 1$ refers to Lth-order entropy coding, and

$$\alpha_{k, L} \equiv \begin{cases} \beta_k, & L = 0 \\ \gamma_{kL}, & L \geq 1. \end{cases}$$

Note that both M_k's and $\alpha_{k, L}$'s tend to decrease as k or L increase. (The M_k's and the $\log \beta_k$'s are subadditive. The γ_k's are nonincreasing.) As an illustration, Fig. 6 plots $10 \log_{10} \alpha_{k, L}$ (in decibels) versus k and L for a Gauss–Markov source with correlation coefficient $\rho = 0.9$.

Consider how $\delta_{k, L}(R)$ decreases, i.e., improves, with k and L increasing. On the one hand, for fixed k, it decreases with increasing L (actually, it is monotonically nonincreasing) to

$$\delta_{k, \infty}(R) = M_k \overline{\beta} \sigma^2 2^{-2R} = \frac{M_k}{\overline{M}} \overline{\delta}(R). \qquad (39)$$

Thus k-dimensional quantization with high-order entropy coding suffers only the k-dimensional space-filling loss. On the other hand, for fixed L, $\delta_{k, L}(R)$ decreases with k (actually it is subadditive) to

$$\delta_{\infty, L}(R) = \overline{M} \overline{\beta} \sigma^2 2^{-2R} = \overline{\delta}(R). \qquad (40)$$

Hence, high-dimensional quantization suffers no loss relative to the best possible performance, no matter the order or absence of an entropy coder.

From the above, we see that to attain performance close to $\overline{\delta}(R)$, k must be large enough that the space-filling loss $M_k/\overline{M}$ is approximately one, and the combination of k and L must be large enough that $\alpha_{k, L}/\overline{\beta}$ is also approximately one. Regarding the first of these, even $k = 1$ (scalar quantization) yields $M_1/\overline{M} = \pi e/6 = 1.42$, representing only a 1.53-dB loss, which may be acceptable in many situations. When it is not acceptable, k needs to be increased. Unfortunately, as evident in Fig. 5, the space-filling loss decreases slowly with increasing k. Regarding the second, we note that one has considerable freedom. There are two extreme cases: 1) k large and $L = 0$, i.e., fixed-rate high-dimensional quantization,

or 2) L large and $k = 1$, i.e., scalar quantization with high-order entropy coding. In fact, uniform scalar quantization will suffice in the second case. Alternatively, one may choose moderate values for both k and L. Roughly speaking, kL must be approximately equal to the effective memory length of the source plus the value needed for a memoryless source. In effect, if the source has considerable memory, such memory can be exploited either by the lossy encoder (k large), or the lossless encoder (L large), or both (moderate values of k and L). Moreover, in such cases the potential reductions in $\alpha_{k, L}$ due to increasing k or L tend to be much larger than the potential reductions in the space-filling loss. For example, for the Gauss–Markov source of Fig. 6, $\alpha_{k, 0} = \beta_k$ decreases 10.0 dB as k increases from one to infinity, and has already decreased 8.1 dB when $k = 6$.

From the point of view of the lossy encoder, the benefit of entropy coding is that it reduces the dimension required of the lossy encoder. Similarly, from the point of view of the lossless encoder, the benefit of increasing the dimension of the vector quantizer is that it decreases the order required of the lossless encoder. Stated another way, the benefits of entropy coding decrease with increasing quantizer dimension, and the benefits of increasing quantizer dimension decrease with increasing entropy coding order. In summary (cf. [377]), optimal performance is attainable with and only with a high-dimensional lossy encoder, and with or without entropy coding. However, good performance (within 1.53 dB of the best) is attainable with uniform scalar quantizer and high-order entropy coding. Both of these extreme approaches are quite complex, and so practical systems tend to be compromises with moderate quantizer dimension and entropy coding order.

As with fixed-rate quantization, it is important to understand what specific characteristics of variable-rate quantizers cause them to perform the way they do. Consequently, we will take another look at variable-rate quantization, this time from the point of view of the point density and inertial profile of the high-dimensional product quantizer induced by an optimal low-dimensional variable-rate quantizer. The situation is simpler than it was for fixed-rate quantization. As mentioned earlier, when rate is large, an optimal k-dimensional variable-rate quantizer has a uniform point density and a partition and codebook formed by tessellating T_k. Suppose k is small and k' is a large multiple of k. From the structure of optimal variable-rate quantizers, one sees that using an optimal k-dimensional quantizer k'/k times yields a k'-dimensional quantizer having the same (uniform) point density as the optimal k'-dimensional quantizer and differing, mainly, in that its inertial profile equals the constant M_k, whereas that of the optimal k'-dimensional quantizer equals $M_{k'} \cong \overline{M}$. Thus the loss due to k-dimensional quantization is only the space-filling loss $M_k/\overline{M}$, which explains what Gish and Pierce found for scalar quantizers in 1968 [204]. We emphasize that there is no point density, oblongitis, or memory loss, even for sources with memory. In effect, the entropy code has eliminated the need to shape the point density, and as a result, there is no need to compromise cell shapes.

Finally, let us compare the structure of the fixed-rate and variable-rate approaches when dimension is large. On the one hand, optimal quantizers of each type have the same constant inertial profile, namely, $m(x) \cong M_k$. On the other hand, they have markedly different point densities: an optimal fixed-rate quantizer has point density $\lambda_k^*(x) \cong f_k(x)$, whereas an optimal variable-rate quantizer has point density that is uniform over all of $\Re^k$. How is it that two such disparate point densities do in fact yield the same distortion? The answer is provided by the asymptotic equipartition property (AEP) [110], which is the key fact upon which most of information theory rests. For a stationary, ergodic source with continuous random variables, the AEP says that when dimension k is large, the k-dimensional probability density is approximately constant, except on a set with small probability. More specifically, it shows $\Pr(X \in \mathcal{T}_k) \cong 1$, where

$$\mathcal{T}_k \equiv \left\{ x \in \Re^k \colon -\frac{1}{k} \log f_k(x) \cong h_\infty \right\}$$

is a set of *typical sequences*, where $h_\infty \equiv \lim_{k \to \infty} h_k$ is the *differential entropy rate* of the source. It follows immediately from the AEP and the fact that $\lambda_k^*(x) \cong f_k(x)$ that the point density of an optimal fixed-rate quantizer is approximately uniform on $\mathcal{T}_k$ and zero elsewhere. Moreover, for an optimal variable-rate quantizer, whose point density is uniform over all of $\Re^k$, we see that the cells not in $\mathcal{T}_k$ can be ignored, because they have negligible probability, and that the cells in $\mathcal{T}_k$ all have the same probability and, consequently, can be assigned codewords of equal length. Thus both approaches lead to quantizers that are identical on $\mathcal{T}_k$ (uniform point density and fixed-length codewords) and differ only in what they do on the complement of $\mathcal{T}_k$, a set of negligible probability.

It is worthwhile emphasizing that in all of the discussion in this section we have restricted attention to quantizers with memoryless lossy encoders and either fixed-rate, memoryless or block lossless encoders. Though there are many lossy and lossless encoders that are not of this form, such as DPCM or finite-state, predictive or address vector VQ, and Lempel–Ziv or arithmetic lossless coding, we believe that the easily analyzed case studied here shows, representatively, the effects of increasing memory in the lossy and lossless encoders.

G. Other Distortion Measures

By far the most commonly assumed distortion measure is squared error, which for scalars is defined by $d(x, y) = |x - y|^2$ and for vectors is defined by

$$d_k(x, y) = \sum_{i=1}^{k} |x_i - y_i|^2, \qquad \text{where } x = (x_1, \cdots, x_k).$$

Often the distortion is normalized by $1/k$. A variety of more general distortion measures have been considered in the literature, but the simplicity and tractability of squared error has long given it a central role. Intuitively, the average squared error is the average energy or power in the quantization noise. The most common extension of distortion measures for scalars is the rth-power distortion $d(x, y) = |x - y|^r$. For example, Roe [443] generalized Max's formulation to distortion measures of this form. Gish and Pierce [204] considered a more general distortion measure of the form $d(x, y) =$

$L(x - y)$, where L is a monotone increasing function of the magnitude of its argument and $L(0) = 0$ with the added property that

$$M(v) \equiv \frac{1}{v} \int_{-v/2}^{v/2} L(u) \, du$$

has the property that $vM'(v)$ is monotone. None of these distortion measures has been widely used, although the magnitude error (rth power with $r = 1$) has been used in some studies, primarily because of its simple computation in comparison with the squared error (no multiplications).

The scalar distortion measures have various generalizations to vectors. If the dimension is fixed, then one needs only a distortion measure, say $d_k(x, y)$, defined for all $x, y \in \Re^k$. If the dimension is allowed to vary, however, then one requires a family of distortion measures $d_k(x, y)$, $k = 1, 2, \cdots$, which collection is called a *fidelity criterion* in source coding theory. Most commonly it is assumed that the fidelity criterion is *additive* or *single letter* in the sense that

$$
\begin{aligned}
d_k&((x_1, \cdots, x_k), (y_1, \cdots, y_k)) \\
&= d_l((x_1, \cdots, x_l), (y_1, \cdots, y_l)) \\
&\quad + d_{k-l}((x_{l+1}, \cdots, x_k), (y_{l+1}, \cdots, y_k))
\end{aligned}
\tag{41}
$$

for $l = 1, 2, \cdots, k - 1$, or, equivalently,

$$d_k((x_1, \cdots, x_k), (y_1, \cdots, y_k)) = \sum_{i=1}^{k} d_1(x_i, y_i). \tag{42}$$

Additive distortion measures are particularly useful for proving source coding theorems since the normalized distortion will converge under appropriate conditions as the dimension grows large, thanks to the ergodic theorem. One can also assume more generally that the distortion measure is subbadditive in the sense that

$$
\begin{aligned}
d_k&((x_1, \cdots, x_k), (y_1, \cdots, y_k)) \\
&\leq d_l((x_1, \cdots, x_l), (y_1, \cdots, y_l)) \\
&\quad + d_{k-l}((x_{l+1}, \cdots, x_k), (y_{l+1}, \cdots, y_k))
\end{aligned}
\tag{43}
$$

and the subadditive ergodic theorem will still lead to positive and negative coding theorems [218], [340].[10] An example of a subadditive distortion measure is the Levenshtein distance [314] which counts the number of insertions and deletions along with the number of changes that it takes to convert one sequence into another. Originally developed for studying error-correcting codes, the Levenshtein distance was rediscovered in the computer science community as the "edit distance."

For a fixed dimension k one can observe that the squared-error distortion measure can be written as $\|x - y\|^2$, where $\|x - y\|$ is the l_2 norm

$$\|x - y\| = \left(\sum_{i=1}^{k} |x_i - y_i|^2 \right)^{1/2}.$$

---

[10]This differs slightly from the previous definition of subadditive because the d_k are not assumed to be normalized. The previous definition applied to d_k/k is equivalent to this definition.

This idea can be extended by using any power of any l_p norm, e.g.,

$$d(x, y) = \|x - y\|_p^r$$

where

$$\|x - y\|_p = \left(\sum_{i=1}^{k} |x_i - y_i|^p \right)^{1/p}.$$

(In this notation the l_2 norm is $\|\cdot\|_2$.) If we choose $p = r$, then this distortion measure (sometimes referred to simply as the rth-power distortion) is additive. Zador [562] defined a very general *rth-power distortion measure* as any distortion measure of the form $d(x, y) = \rho(x - y)$ where for any $a > 0$, $\rho(ax) = a^r \rho(|x_1|, \cdots, |x_k|)$, for some $r > 0$. This includes rth-power distortion in the narrow sense $\|x - y\|_2^r$, as well as the additive distortion measures of the form

$$\|x - y\|_r^r = \sum_{i=1}^{k} |x_i - y_i|^r$$

and even weighted average distortions such as

$$\left(\sum_{i=1}^{k} w_i |x_i - y_i|^2 \right)^r$$

and

$$\sum_{i=1}^{k} w_i |x_i - y_i|^r$$

where the w_i's are nonnegative.

A variation on the l_p norm is the l_∞ norm defined by $\|x - y\|_\infty = \max_i |x_i - y_i|$, which has been proposed as a candidate for a perceptually meaningful norm. Quantizer design algorithms exist for this case, but to date no high-resolution quantization theory or rate-distortion theory has been developed for this distortion measure (cf. [347], [231], and [348]).

High resolution theory usually considers a fixed dimension k, so neither additivity nor a family of distortion measures is required. However, high resolution theory has tended to concentrate on difference distortion measures, i.e., distortion measures that have the form $d(x, y) = L(x - y)$, where $x - y$ is the usual Euclidean difference and L is usually assumed to have nice properties, such as being monotonic in some norm of its argument. The rth-power distortion measures (of all types) fall into this category.

Recently, the basic results of high resolution theory have been extended to a family of nondifference distortion measures that are locally quadratic in the sense that provided $x \cong y$, the distortion measure is given approximately by a Taylor series expansion as $(x - y)^t B(y)(x - y)$, where $B(y)$ is a positive definite weighting matrix that depends on the output. This form is ensured by assuming that the distortion measure $d(x, y)$ has continuous partial derivatives of third order almost everywhere and that the matrix $B(y)$ defined as a k by k dimensional matrix with the $)j, n)$th element

$$B_{j,n}(y) = \frac{1}{2} \left. \frac{\partial^2 d(x, y)}{\partial x_j \, \partial x_n} \right|_{x=y} \quad (44)$$

is positive definite almost everywhere. The basic idea for this distortion measure was introduced by Gardner and Rao [186] to model a perceptual distortion measure for speech, where the matrix $B(y)$ is referred to as the "sensitivity matrix." The requirement for the existence of the derivatives of third order and for the $B(y)$ to be positive definite were added in [316] as necessary for the analysis. Examples of distortion measures meeting these conditions are the time-domain form of the Itakura–Saito distortion [258], [259], [257], [224], which has the form of an input-weighted quadratic distortion measure of the form of (21). For this case, the input weighting matrix W_x is related to the partial derivative matrix by $B(x) = \frac{1}{2}(W_x + W_x^t)$, so that positive definiteness of W_x assures that of $B(x)$ and the derivative conditions are transferred to W_x. Other distortion measures satisfying the assumptions are the image distortion measures of Eskicioglu and Fisher [150] and Nill [386], [387]. The Bennett integral has been extended to this type of distortion, and approximations for both fixed-rate and variable-rate operational distortion-rate functions have been developed [186], [316]. For the fixed-rate case, the result is that

$$D(q) \cong \frac{1}{N^{2/k}} \int f(x)(\det(B(x)))^{1/k} \frac{m(x)}{\lambda^{2/k}(x)} \, dx \quad (45)$$

where the modified inertial profile $m(x)$ is assumed to be the limit of

$$M(S_i, y_i) = (\det(B(y_i)))^{-(1/k)}$$
$$\cdot \frac{\int_{S_i} (x_i - y_i)^t B(y_i)(x_i - y_i) \, dx}{[V(S_i)]^{(k+2)/k}}.$$

A natural extension of Gersho's conjecture to the nondifference distortion measures under consideration implies that, as in the squared-error case, the optimal inertial profile is assumed to be constant (which in any case will yield a bound) and minimizing the above (for example, using Hölder's inequality) yields the optimal point density

$$\lambda(x) = \frac{(f(x)(\det(B(x)))^{1/k})^{k/(k+2)}}{\int (f(x')(\det(B(x')))^{1/k})^{k/(k+2)} \, dx'} \quad (46)$$

and the operational distortion-rate function (analogous to (30))

$$\delta(R) \cong M_k \beta_k \sigma^2 2^{-2R} \quad (47)$$

where now

$$\beta_k = \frac{1}{\sigma^2} \left\{ \int (f(x)(\det(B(x)))^{1/k})^{k/(k+2)} \, dx \right\}^{(k+2)/k} \quad (48)$$

generalizes Zador's factor to the given distortion measure. As shown later in (58), M_k can be bounded below by the moment of inertia of a sphere. Similarly, in the variable-rate case

$$\delta(R) \cong M_k 2^{(2/k)(h(X)+(1/2) \int \log(\det(B(x)))f(x) \, dx)} 2^{-2R} \quad (49)$$

with optimal inertial profile $m(x) = M_k$ and optimal point density

$$\lambda(x) = \frac{(\det(B(x)))^{1/2}}{\int (\det(B(x')))^{1/2}\,dx'}. \qquad (50)$$

Both results reduce to the previous results for the special case of a squared-error distortion measure since then $\det(B(x)) = 1$. Note in particular that the optimal point density for the entropy-constrained case is not in general a uniform density.

Parallel results for Shannon lower bounds to the rate-distortion function have been developed for this family of distortion measures by Linder and Zamir [323] and results for multidimensional companding with lattice codes for similar distortion measures have been developed by Linder, Zamir, and Zeger [325].

H. Rigorous Approaches to High Resolution Theory

Over the years, high-resolution analyses have been presented in several styles. Informal analyses of distortion, such as those used in this paper to obtain $\Delta^2/12$ and Bennett's integral (25), generally ignore overload distortion and estimate granular distortion by approximating the density as being constant within each quantization cell. In contrast, rigorous analyses generally focus on sequences of ever finer quantizers, for which they demonstrate that, in the limit, overload distortion becomes negligible in comparison to granular distortion and the ratio of granular distortion to some function of the fineness parameter tends to a constant. Though informal analyses generally lead to the same basic results as rigorous ones, the latter make it clear that the approximations are good enough that their percentage errors decrease to zero as the quantizers become finer, whereas the former do not. Moreover, the rigorous derivations provide explicit conditions under which the assumption of negligible overload distortion is valid. Some analyses (informal and rigorous) provide corrections for overload distortion, and some even give examples where the overload distortion cannot be asymptotically ignored but can be estimated nevertheless. Similar comments apply to informal versus rigorous analyses of asymptotic entropy. In the following we review the development of rigorous theory.

Many analyses—informal and rigorous—explicitly assume the source has finite range (i.e., a probability distribution with bounded support); so there is no overload distortion to be ignored [43], [405], [474]. In some cases, the source really does have finite range. In others, for example speech and images, the source samples have infinite range, but the measurement device has finite range. In such cases, the truncation by the measurement device creates an implicit overload distortion that is not affected by the design of the quantizer. It makes little sense, then, to choose a quantizer so fine that its (granular) distortion is significantly less than this implicit overload distortion. This means there is an upper limit to the fineness of quantizers that need be considered, and consequently, one must question whether such fineness is small enough that the source density can be approximated as constant within cells. Some analyses do not explicitly

assume the source density has finite support, but merely assert that overload distortion can be ignored. We view that this differs only stylistically from an explicit assumption of finite support, for both approaches ignore overload distortion. However, assuming finite support is, arguably, humbler and mathematically more honest.

The earliest quantizer distortion analyses to appear in the open literature [43], [405], [474] assumed finite range and used the density-approximately-constant-in-cells assumption. Several papers avoided the latter by using a Taylor series expansion of the source density. For example, Lloyd [330] used this approach to show that, ignoring overload distortion, the approximation error in the Panter–Dite formula is $o(1/N^2)$, which means that it tends to zero, even when multiplied by N^2. Algazi [8], Roe [443], and Wood [539] also used Taylor series.

Overload distortion was first explicitly considered in the work of Shtein (1959) [471], who optimized the cell size of uniform scalar quantization using an explicit formula for the overload distortion (as well as $\Delta^2/12$ for the granular distortion) and while rederiving the Panter–Dite formula, added an overload distortion term.

The earliest rigorous analysis[11] is contained in Schutzenberger's 1958 paper [462], which showed that for k-dimensional variable-rate quantization ($L = 1$), rth-power distortion ($\|x - y\|^r$), and a source with finite differential entropy and $E[\|X\|^{r'}] < \infty$ for some $r' > r$, there is a $K_{k,r} > 0$, depending on the source and the dimension, such that any k-dimensional quantizer with finitely or infinitely many cells, and output entropy H, has distortion at least $K_{k,r}2^{-(r/k)H}$. Moreover, there exists $K'_{k,r} > K_{k,r}$ and a sequence of quantizers with increasing output entropies H and distortion no more than $K'_{k,r}2^{-(r/k)H}$. In essence, these results show that

$$K_{k,r}2^{(-r/k)R} \le \delta_{k,1}(R) \le K'_{k,r}2^{(-r/k)R}, \qquad \text{for all } R.$$

Unfortunately, as Schutzenberger notes, the ratio of $K'_{k,r}$ to $K_{k,r}$ tends to infinity as dimension increases. As he indicates, the problem is that in demonstrating the upper bound, he constructs a sequence of quantizers with cubic cells of equal size and then bounds from above the distortion in each cell by something proportional to its diameter to the rth power. If instead one were to bound the distortion by the moment of inertia of the cell times the maximum value of the density within it, then $K'_{k,r}/K_{k,r}$ would not tend to infinity.

Next, two papers appeared in the same issue of *Acta Math. Acad. Sci. Hungar.* in 1959. The paper by Renyi [433] gave, in effect, a rigorous derivation of (11) for a uniform quantizer with infinitely many levels. Specifically, it showed that $H(q_n(X)) = h(X) + \log n + o(1)$, provided that the source distribution is absolutely continuous and that $H(q_n(X))$ and $h(X)$ are finite, where q_n denotes a uniform quantizer with step size $1/n$ and $o(1)$ denotes a quantity that approaches zero as n goes to ∞. They paper also explores what happens when the distribution is not absolutely continuous.

---

[11] Though Lloyd [330] gave a fairly rigorous analysis of distortion, we do not include his paper in this category because it ignored overload distortion.

In the second paper, Fejes Toth [159] showed that for a two-dimensional random vector that is uniformly distributed on the unit square, the mean-squared error of any N-point quantizer is bounded from below by $M(\text{hexagon})/N$. This result was independently rederived in a simpler fashion by Newman (1964) [385]. Clearly, the lower bound is asymptotically achievable by a lattice with hexagonal cells. It follows then that the ratio of $\delta_2(R)$ to $M(\text{hexagon})\sigma^2 2^{-2R}$ tends to one, and also, that Gersho's conjecture holds for dimension two.

Zador's thesis (1963) [561] was the next rigorous work. As mentioned earlier, it contains two principal results. For fixed-rate quantization, rth-power distortion measures of the form $\|x - y\|^r$ and a source that is uniformly distributed on the unit cube, it first shows ([561, Lemma 2.3]) that the operational distortion-rate function[12] $\delta_k(N)$ multiplied by $N^{r/k}$ approaches a limit $b_{k,r}$ as $N \to \infty$. The basic idea, which Zador attributes to J. M. Hammersley, is the following: For any positive integers N and n, divide the unit cube into n^k subcubes, each with sides of length $1/n$. Clearly, the best code with $\tilde{N} = n^k N$ codevectors is at least as good as the code constructed by using the best code with N points for each subcube. It follows then that $\delta_k(\tilde{N}) \leq \delta_k(n, N) = (1/n^r)\delta_k(N)$, where $\delta_k(n, N)$ is the operational distortion-rate function of a source that is uniformly distributed on a subcube and where the second relation follows from the fact that this "sub" source is just a scaling of the original source. Multiplying both sides by $\tilde{N}^{r/k}$ yields

$$\tilde{N}^{r/k}\delta_k(\tilde{N}) \leq N^{r/k}\delta_k(N).$$

Thus we see that increasing the number of codevectors from N to $\tilde{N} = n^k N$ does not increase $N^{r/k}\delta_k(N)$. A somewhat more elaborate argument shows that this is approximately true for any sufficiently large $\tilde{N}$ and, as a result, that

$$\limsup_{N\to\infty} N^{r/k}\delta_k(N) \leq \liminf_{N\to\infty} N^{r/k}\delta_k(N)$$

i.e., $N^{r/k}\delta_k(N)$ has a limit. One can see how the selfsimilarity of the uniform density (it is divisible into similar subdensities) plays a key role in this argument. Notice also that nowhere do the shapes of the cells or the point density enter into it.

Zador next addresses nonuniform densities. With $\|f\|_s$ denoting $(\int f^s(x)\,dx)^{1/s}$, his Theorem 2.2 shows that if the k-dimensional source density satisfies $\|f\|_{k/(k+r)} < \infty$ and $E[\|X\|^{k-1+r+\epsilon}] < \infty$ for some $\epsilon > 0$, then

$$N^{r/k}\delta_k(N) \to b_{k,r}\|f\|_{k/(k+r)}$$

as $N \to \infty$. The positive part, namely, that

$$\limsup_{N\to\infty} N^{r/k}\delta_k(N) \leq b_{k,r}\|f\|_{k/(k+r)}$$

is established by constructing codes in, approximately, the following manner: Given N, one chooses a sufficiently large support cube (large enough that overload distortion contributes little), subdivides the cube into n^k equally sized subcubes, and places within each subcube a set of codevectors that are optimal for the uniform distribution on that subcube, where

the number of codevectors in a subcube is carefully chosen so that the point density in that subcube approximates the optimal point density for the original source distribution. One then shows that the distortion of this code, multiplied by $N^{r/k}$, is approximately $b_{k,r}\|f\|_{k/(k+r)}$. The best codes are at least this good and it follows that

$$\limsup_{k\to\infty} N^{r/k}\delta_k(N) \leq b_{k,r}\|f\|_{k/(k+r)}.$$

One can easily see how this construction creates codes with essentially optimal point density and cell shape. We will not describe the converse.

Zador's 1966 Bell Labs Memorandum [562] reproves these two main results under weaker conditions. The distortion measure is rth power in the general sense, which includes as special cases the narrow sense of the rth power of the Euclidean norm considered by Schutzenberger [462]. The requirement on the source density is only that each of its marginals has the property that it is bounded from above by $|x|^{r+\epsilon}$, for some $\epsilon > 0$ and all x of sufficiently large magnitude. This is a pure tail condition, as opposed to the finite moment condition of the thesis, which constrains both the tail and the peak of the density. Note also that it no longer requires that $\|f\|_{k/(k+r)}$ be finite.

As indicated earlier, Zador's memorandum also derives the asymptotic form of the operational distortion-rate function of variable-rate quantization. In other words, it finishes what his thesis and Schutzenberger [462] started, though he was apparently unaware of the latter. Specifically, it shows that

$$2^{rR}\delta_{k,1}(R) \to c_{k,r}2^{r(1/k)h(X_1,\cdots,X_k)} \text{ as } R \to \infty$$

where $c_{k,r}$ is some constant no larger than $b_{k,r}$, assuming the same conditions as the fixed-rate result, plus the additional requirement that for any $\epsilon > 0$ there is a bounded set containing all points x such that $f(x) \geq \epsilon$.

Gish and Pierce (1968) [204], who discovered that uniform is the asymptotically best type of scalar quantizer for variable-rate coding, presented both informal and rigorous derivations—the latter being the first to appear in these TRANSACTIONS. Specifically, they showed rigorously that for uniform scalar quantization with infinitely many cells of width Δ, the distortion D_Δ and the output entropy H_Δ behave as follows:

$$\lim_{\Delta\to 0} \frac{D_\Delta}{\Delta^2/12} = 1 \tag{51}$$

$$\lim_{\Delta\to 0} (H_\Delta + \log \Delta) = h(X) \tag{52}$$

which makes rigorous the $\Delta^2/12$ formula and (11), respectively. For this result, they required the density to be continuous except at finitely many points, and to satisfy a tail condition similar to Zador's and another condition about the behavior at points of discontinuity. The paper also outlined a rigorous proof of (32) in the scalar case, i.e., that $\delta_{1,1}(R)/Z_{1,1}(R) \to 1$ as $R \to \infty$. But as to the details it offered only that: "The complete proof is surprisingly long and will not be given here." Though Gish and Pierce were the first to informally derive (13), neither this paper nor any paper to date has provided a rigorous derivation.

---

[12] We abuse notation slightly and let $\delta_k(N)$ denote the least distortion of k-dimensional quantizers with N codevectors.

Elias (1970) [143] also made a rigorous analysis of scalar quantization, giving asymptotic bounds to the distortion of scalar quantizers with a rather singularly defined measure of distortion, namely, the rth root of the average of the rth power of the cell widths. A companion paper [144] considers similar bounds to the performance of vector quantizers with an analogous average-cell-size distortion measure.

In 1973, Csiszàr [114] presented a rigorous generalization of (52) to higher dimensional quantizers. Of most interest here is the following special case of his principal result ([114, Theorem 1]): Consider a k-dimensional source and a sequence of k-dimensional quantizers $q_1, q_2, \cdots$, where q_n has a countably infinite number of cells, each with volume v_n, where the v_n's and also the maximum of the cell diameters tends to zero. Then under certain conditions, including the condition that there be at least some quantizer with finite output entropy, the output entropy H_n satisfies

$$\lim_{n \to \infty} (H_n + \log v_n) = h(X). \qquad (53)$$

Clearly, this result applies to quantizers generated by lattices and, more generally, tessellations. It also applies to quantizers with finitely many cells for sources with compact support. But it does not apply to quantizers with finitely many cells and sources with infinite support, because it does not deal with the overload region of such quantizers.

In 1977, Babkin et $al.$ [580] obtained results indicating how rapidly the distortion of fixed-rate lattice quantizers approach $\bar{\delta}(R)$ as rate R and dimension k increase, for difference distortion measures. In 1978, these same authors [581] studied uniform scalar quantization with variable-rate coding, and extended Koshelev's results to rth power distortion measures.

The next contribution is that of Bucklew and Gallagher (1980) [63], who studied asymptotic properties of fixed-rate uniform scalar quantization. With Δ_N denoting the cell width that minimizes distortion among N cell uniform scalar quantizers and D_N denoting the resulting minimum mean-squared error, they showed that for a source with a Riemann integrable density $f(x)$

$$\lim_{N \to \infty} N\Delta_N = \text{supp}\,(f)$$

and

$$\lim_{N \to \infty} N^2 D_N = \frac{\text{supp}\,(f)^2}{12}$$

where $\text{supp}\,(f)$ is the length of the shortest interval (a, b) with probability one. When the support is finite, i.e., a and b are finite, the above implies $D_N/(\Delta_N^2/12) \to 1$ as $N \to \infty$, and so D_N decreases as $1/N^2$. This makes the $\Delta^2/12$ formula rigorous in the finite N case, at least when Δ is chosen optimally. However, when the support is infinite, e.g., a Gaussian density, D_N decreases at a rate slower than $1/N^2$, and the resulting signal-to-noise ratio versus rate curve separates from any line of slope 6 dB/bit. Consequently, the ratio of the operational distortion-rate functions of uniform and nonuniform scalar quantizers increases without bound as the rate increases; i.e., uniform quantization is asymptotically bad. Moreover, they showed that $D_N/(\Delta_N^2/12)$ does not always converge to 1. Instead, $\liminf_{N \to \infty} D_N/(\Delta_N^2/12) \geq 1$, and

they exhibited densities where the inequality is strict. In such cases, the $\Delta^2/12$ formula is invalidated by the heavy tails of the density. It was not until much later that the asymptotic form of Δ_N and D_N were found, as will be described later.

Formal theory advanced further in papers by Bucklew and Wise, Cambanis and Gerr, and Bucklew. The first of these (1982) [64] demonstrated Zador's fixed-rate result for rth-power distortion $\|x-y\|^r$, assuming only that $E[\|X\|^{r+\delta}] < \infty$ for some $\delta > 0$. It also contained a generalization to random vectors without probability densities, i.e., with distributions that are not absolutely continuous or even continuous. The paper also gave the first rigorous approach to the derivation of Bennett's integral for scalar quantization via companding. However, as pointed out by Linder (1991) [320], there was "a gap in the proof concerning the convergence of Riemann sums with increasing support to a Riemann integral." Linder fixed this and presented a correct derivation with weaker assumptions. Cambanis and Gerr (1983) [70] claimed a similar result, but it had more restrictive conditions and suffered from the same sort of problems as [64]. A subsequent paper by Bucklew (1984) [58] derived a result for vector quantizers that lies between Bennett's integral and Zador's formula. Specifically, it showed that when a sequence of quantizers is asymptotically optimal for one probability density $f^{(1)}(x)$, then its rth-power distortion on a source with density $f^{(2)}(x)$ is asymptotically given by $N^{-r/k} b_{k,r} \int \lambda^{-r/k}(x) f^{(2)}(x)\, dx$, where $\lambda(x)$ is the optimal point density for $f^{(1)}(x)$. On the one hand, this is like Bennett's integral in that $f^{(1)}(x)$, and consequently $\lambda(x)$, can be arbitrary. On the other hand, it is like Zador's result (or Gersho's generalization of Bennett's integral [193]) in that, in essence, it is assumed that the quantizers have optimal cell shapes.

In 1994, Linder and Zeger [326] rigorously derived the asymptotic distortion of quantizers generated by tessellations by showing that the quantizer q_α formed by tessellating with some basic cell shape S scaled by a positive number α has average (narrow-sense) rth-power distortion D_α satisfying

$$\lim_{\alpha \to 0} \frac{D_\alpha}{\alpha^r \text{vol}\,(S)^{r/k} M(S)} = 1.$$

They then combined the above with Csiszàr's result (53) to show that under fairly weak conditions (finite differential entropy and finite output entropy for some $\alpha > 0$) the output entropy H_α and the distortion D_α are asymptotically related via

$$\lim_{\alpha \to 0} \frac{D_\alpha}{M(S) 2^{(r/k)(h(X) - H_\alpha)}} = 1$$

which is what Gersho derived informally [193].

The generalization of Bennett's integral to fixed-rate vector quantizers with rather arbitrary cell shapes was accomplished by Na and Neuhoff (1995) [365], who presented both informal and rigorous derivations. In the rigorous derivations, it was shown that if a sequence of quantizers $\{q_N\}$, parameterized by the number of codevectors, has specific point density and specific inertial profile converging in probability to a model point density and a model inertial profile, respectively, then $N^{r/k}D(q_N)$ converges to Bennett's integral $\int m(x)\lambda^{-r/k}(x)f(x)\,dx$, where distortion is rth power $\|x-y\|^r$. A couple of additional conditions were also required, including one that is, implicitly, a tail condition.

Though uniform scalar quantization with finitely many levels is the oldest and most elementary form of quantization, the asymptotic form of the optimal step size Δ_N and resulting mean-squared error D_N has only recently been found for Gaussian and other densities with infinite support. Specifically, Hui and Neuhoff [253]–[255] have found that for a Gaussian density with variance σ^2

$$\lim_{N\to\infty}\frac{\Delta_N}{4\sigma\frac{1}{N}\sqrt{\ln N}}=1 \text{ and } \lim_{N\to\infty}\frac{D_N}{\frac{4}{3}\sigma^2\frac{1}{N^2}\ln N}=1.$$

This result was independently found by Eriksson and Agrell [149]. Moreover, it was shown that overload distortion is asymptotically negligible and that $D_N/(\Delta_N^2/12)\to 1$, which is the first time this has been proved for a source with infinite support. It follows from the above that the signal-to-noise ratio increases as $6.02R-10\log_{10}R$, which shows concretely how uniform scalar quantization is asymptotically bad. Hui and Neuhoff also considered non-Gaussian sources and provided a fairly general characterization of the asymptotic form of Δ_N and D_N. It turned out that the overload distortion is asymptotically negligible when and only when the tail parameter $\tau\equiv\lim_{y\to\infty}(E[X|X>y])/y$ equals one, which is the case for all generalized Gaussian densities. For such cases, more accurate approximations to Δ_N and D_N can be given. For densities with $\tau>1$, the ratio of overload to granular distortion is $(2\tau-2)/(2-\tau)$, and $D_N/(\Delta_N^2/12)\to\tau/(2-\tau)$. There are even densities with tails so heavy that $\tau=2$ and the granular distortion becomes negligible in comparison to the overload distortion. In a related result, the asymptotic form of the optimal scaling factor for lattice quantizers has also been found recently for an i.i.d. Gaussian source [359], [149].

We conclude this subsection by mentioning some gaps in rigorous high resolution theory. One, of course, is a proof or counterproof of Gersho's conjecture in dimensions three and higher. Another is the open question of whether the best tessellation in three or more dimensions is a lattice. Both of these are apparently difficult questions. There have been no rigorous derivations of (11), or its extension to higher dimensional tesselations, where the quantizers have finitely many levels, and overload distortion must be dealt with. Likewise, there have been no rigorous derivations of (13), or its higher dimensional generalization, except in the case where the point density is constant. Even assuming Gersho's conjecture is correct, there is no rigorous derivation of the Zador–Gersho formulas (30) and (32) along the lines of the informal derivations that start with Bennett's integral. We also mention that the tail conditions given in some of the rigorous results (e.g., [58], [365]) are very difficult to check. Simpler ones are needed. Finally, as discussed in Section II there are no convincing (let alone rigorous) asymptotic analyses of the operational distortion-rate function of DPCM.

I. Comparing High Resolution Theory and Shannon Rate Distortion Theory

It is interesting to compare and contrast the two principal theories of quantization, and we shall do so in a number of different domains.

Applicability: Sources—Shannon rate-distortion theory applies, fundamentally, to infinite sequences of random variables, i.e., to sources modeled as random processes. Its results derive from the frequencies with which events repeat, as expressed in a law of large numbers, such as the weak law or an ergodic theorem. As such, it applies to sources that are stationary in either the strict sense or some weaker sense, such as asymptotic mean stationarity (cf. [218, p. 16]). Though originally derived for ergodic sources, it has been extended to nonergodic sources [221], [469], [126], [138], [479]. In contrast, high resolution theory applies, fundamentally, to finite-dimensional random vectors. However, for stationary (or asymptotically stationary) sources, taking limits yields results for random processes. For example, the operational distortion-rate function $\bar{\delta}(R)$ was found to equal $\overline{Z}(R)$ in this way; see (33). Rate distortion theory also has one result relevant to finite-dimensional random vectors, namely, that the operational distortion-rate functions for fixed- and variable-rate quantization, $\delta_k(R)$ and $\delta_{k,1}(R)$, are (strictly) bounded from below by the kth-order Shannon distortion-rate function.

Both theories have been extended to continuous-time random processes. However, the high-resolution results are somewhat sketchy [43], [330], [204]. Both can be applied to two- or higher dimensional sources such as images or video. Both have been developed the most for Gaussian sources in the context of squared-error distortion, which is not surprising in view of the tractability of squared error and Gaussianity.

Applicability: Distortion Measures—Shannon rate distortion theory applies primarily to additive distortion measures; i.e., distortion measures of the form

$$d(x,y)=\sum_{i=1}^{k}d_1(x_i,y_i)$$

(or a normalized version), though there are some results for subadditive distortion measures [218], [340] and some for distortion measures such as $(x-y)^t B_x(x-y)$ [323]. High resolution theory has the most results for rth-power difference distortion measures, and as mentioned previously, some of its results have recently been extended to nondifference distortion measures such as $(x-y)^t B_x(x-y)$ [186], [316], [325]. In any event, both theories are the most fully developed for the squared-error distortion measure, especially for Gaussian sources. In addition, both theories require a finite moment condition, specific to the distortion measure. For squared-error distortion, it is simply that the variance of the source be finite. More generally, it is that $E[d(X,y)]<\infty$ for some y. In addition, as discussed previously, rigorous high resolution theory results require tail conditions on the source density, for example, $E[X^{2+\delta}]<\infty$ for some $\delta>0$.

Complementarity—The two theories are complementary in the sense that Shannon rate distortion theory prescribes the best possible performance of quantizers with a given rate and asymptotically large dimension, while high resolution theory prescribes the best possible performance of codes with a given dimension and asymptotically large rate. That is, for fixed-rate codes

$$\delta_k(R) \cong \overline{D}(R), \qquad \text{for large } k \text{ and any } R \qquad (54)$$

$$\delta_k(R) \cong Z_k(R), \qquad \text{for large } R \text{ and any } k \qquad (55)$$

and, similarly, for variable-rate codes

$$\delta_{k,L}(R) \cong \overline{D}(R), \qquad \text{for large } k \text{ and any } L, R \qquad (56)$$

$$\delta_{k,L}(R) \cong Z_{k,L}(R), \qquad \text{for large } R \text{ and any } k, L. \qquad (57)$$

When both dimension and rate are large, they all give the same result, i.e.,

$$\delta_k(R) \cong \delta_{k,L}(R) \cong \overline{\delta}(R) \cong \overline{D}(R).$$

Rates of Convergence—It is useful to know how large R and k must be, respectively, for high resolution and rate distortion theory formulas to be accurate. As a rule of thumb, high resolution theory is fairly accurate for rates greater than or equal to about 3. And it is sufficiently accurate at rates about 2 for it to be useful when comparing different sources and codes. For example, Fig. 7 shows signal-to-noise ratios for fixed-rate quantizers produced by conventional design algorithms and predictions thereof based on the Zador–Gersho function $Z_k(R)$, for two Gaussian sources: i.i.d. and Markov with correlation coefficient 0.9. It is apparent from data such as this that the accuracy of the Zador–Gersho function approximation to $\delta_k(R)$ increases with dimension.

The convergence rate of $\delta_k(R)$ to $\overline{\delta}(R)$ as k tends to infinity has also been studied [413], [548], [321], [576]. Roughly speaking these results show that for memoryless sources, the convergence rate is between $\sqrt{(\log k)/k}$ and $(\log k)/k$. Unfortunately, this theory does not enable one to actually predict how large the dimension must be in order that $\delta_k(R)$ is within some specified percentage, e.g., 10%, of $\overline{\delta}(R)$. However, one may use high resolution theory to do this, by comparing $M_k\beta_k$ (or $M_k\gamma_{kL}$ in the variable-rate case) to $\overline{M}\beta$. For example, for the i.i.d. Gaussian source Fig. 5 shows that $\delta_k(R)$ yields distortions within 1 and 0.2 dB of that predicted by $\overline{\delta}(R)$ at dimensions 12 and 100, respectively. For sources with memory, the dimension needs to be larger, by roughly the effective memory length. One may conclude that the Shannon distortion-rate function approximation to $\delta_k(R)$ is applicable for moderate to large dimensions k.

Quantitative Relationships—For squared-error distortion, the Zador–Gersho function $\overline{Z}(R)$ is precisely equal to the well-known Shannon lower bound $\overline{D}_{\text{slb}}(R)$ to the Shannon distortion-rate function. It follows that when rate is not large, $\overline{Z}(R)$ is, at least, a lower bound to $\overline{\delta}(R)$. Similarly, the Shannon lower bound $D_{\text{slb},k}(R)$ to the kth-order Shannon distortion-rate function equals $Z_{k,1}(R)(\overline{M}/M_k)$, from which it follows that $D_{\text{slb},k}(R)$ may be thought of as the distortion of a fictional quantizer having the distortion of an optimal k-dimensional variable-rate quantizer with first-order entropy coding, except that its cells have the normalized moment of inertia of a high-dimensional sphere instead of M_k. It is well known that $\overline{D}_{\text{slb}}(R)/\overline{D}(R)$ approaches one as R increases

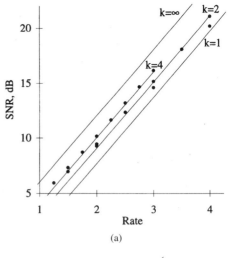

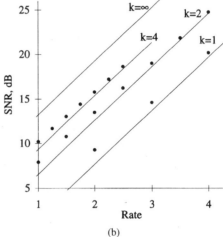

Fig. 7. Signal-to-noise ratios for optimal VQ's (dots) and predictions thereof based on the Zador–Gersho formula (straight lines). (a) i.i.d. Gaussian. (b) Gauss–Markov, correlation coefficient 0.9.

[327], [267], [46], [322], which is entirely consistent with the fact that $\overline{Z}(R)/\overline{\delta}(R)$ approaches one as R increases. The relationships among the various distortion-rate functions are summarized below. Inequalities marked with a "•" become tight as dimension k increases, and those marked with a "+" become tight as R increases.

$$
\begin{array}{ccccccc}
\overline{D}(R) & \overset{+}{\geq} & & \overline{D}_{\text{slb}}(R) & & = & \overline{Z}(R) \\
\wedge\vert\bullet & & & \wedge\vert\bullet & & & \wedge\vert\bullet \\
D_k(R) & \overset{+}{\geq} & D_{\text{slb},k}(R) & = & Z_{k,1}(R)\dfrac{\overline{M}}{M_k} & \overset{\bullet}{<} & Z_k(R).
\end{array}
$$

Applicability: Quantizer Types—Rate distortion theory finds the performance of the best quantizers of any type for stationary sources. It has nothing to say about suboptimal, structured or dimension-constrained quantizers except, as mentioned earlier, that quantizers of dimension k have distortion bounded from below by the kth-order Shannon distortion-rate function. In contrast, high resolution theory can be used to analyze and optimize the performance of a number of families of structured quantizers, such as transform, lattice, product, polar, two-stage, and, most directly, dimension-constrained quantizers. Such analyses are typically based on Bennett's integral. Indeed, the ability to analyze structured or dimension-constrained quantizers is the true forte of high resolution theory.

Performance versus Complexity: Assessing performance versus complexity should be a major goal of quantization theory. On the one hand, rate distortion theory specifies the fundamental limits to performance without regard to complexity. On the other hand, because high resolution theory can analyze the performance of families of quantizers with complexity-reducing structure, one can learn much from it about how complexity relates to performance. In recent work, Hui and Neuhoff [256] have combined high resolution theory and Turing complexity theory to show that asymptotically optimal quantization can be implemented with complexity increasing at most polynomially with the rate.

Computability: First-order Shannon distortion-rate functions can be computed analytically for squared error and magnitude error and several source densites, such as Gaussian and Laplacian, and for some discrete sources, cf. [46], [494], [560], [217]. For other sources it can be computed with Blahut's algorithm [52]. And in the case of squared error, it can be computed with simpler algorithms [168], [444]. For sources with memory, complete analytical formulas for kth-order distortion-rate functions are known only for Gaussian sources. For other cases, the Blahut algorithm [52] can be used to compute $D_k(R)$, though its computational complexity becomes overwhelming unless k is small. Due to the difficulty of computing it, many (mostly lower) bounds to the Shannon distortion-rate function have been developed which for reasonably general cases yield the distortion-rate function exactly for a region of small distortion (cf. [465], [327], [267], [239], [46], [212], [550], [559], [217]). An important upper bound derives from the fact that with respect to squared error, the Gaussian source has the largest Shannon distortion-rate function (kth-order or in the limit) of any source with the same covariance function.

To compute a Zador–Gersho function, one needs to find M_k and either β_k or γ_k in the fixed- and variable-rate cases, respectively. Though M_k is known only for $k \leq 2$, there are bounds for other values of k. One lower bound is the normalized moment of inertia of a sphere of the same dimension

$$M_k \geq \frac{k}{k+2}\left(\frac{2\pi^{k/2}}{k\Gamma(k/2)}\right)^{-(2/k)}. \tag{58}$$

Another bound is given in [106]. One upper bound was developed by Zador; others derive from the currently best known tessellations (cf. [5] and [106]). The Zador factors β_k and γ_k can be computed straightforwardly for $k = 1$ and, also, for $k \geq 2$ for i.i.d. sources. In some cases, simple closed-form expressions can be found, e.g., for Gaussian, Laplacian, gamma densities. In other cases, numerical integration can be used. Upper bounds to β_1 are given in [294]. To the authors' knowledge, for sources with memory, simple expressions for the Zador factors have been found only for Gaussian sources; they depend on the covariance matrix.

Underlying Principles: Rate distortion theory is a deep and elegant theory based on the law of large numbers and the key information-theoretic property that derives from it, namely, the AEP. High resolution theory is a simpler, less elegant theory based on geometric characterizations and integral approximations over fine partitions.

Siblings: Lossless source coding and channel coding are sibling branches of information theory, also based on the law of large numbers and the asymptotic equipartition property. Siblings of high resolution theory include error probability analyses in digital modulation and channel coding based on minimum distance and a high signal-to-noise ratio assumption, and the average power analyses for the additive Gaussian channel based on the continuous approximation.

Code Design Philosophy: Neither theory is ordinarily considered to be constructive, yet each leads to its own design philosophy. Rate distortion theory shows that, with high probability, a good high-dimensional quantizer can be constructed by randomly choosing codevectors according to the output distribution of the test channel that achieves the Shannon rate-distortion function. As a construction technique, this leaves much to be desired because the dimension of such codes is large enough that the codes so constructed are completely impractical. On the other hand, the AEP indicates that such codevectors will be roughly uniformly distributed over a "typical" set, and this leads to the design philosophy that a good code has its codevectors uniformly distributed throughout this set. In the special case of squared-error distortion and an i.i.d. Gaussian source with variance σ^2, the output distribution is i.i.d. Gaussian with variance $\sigma^2 - D(R)$; the typical set is a thin shell near the surface of a sphere of radius $\sqrt{k(\sigma^2 - D(R))}$; and a good code has its codevectors uniformly distributed on this shell. Since the interior volume of such a (high-dimensional) sphere is negligible, it is equally valid for the codevectors to be uniformly distributed throughout the sphere. For other sources, the codevectors will be uniformly distributed over some subset of the shell.

High resolution theory indicates that for large rate and arbitrary dimension k, the quantization cells should be as spherical as possible—preferably shaped like T_k, with normalized moment of inertia M_k. Moreover, the codevectors should be distributed according to the optimal point density λ_k^*. Thus high resolution theory yields a very clear design philosophy. In the scalar case, one can use this philosophy directly to construct a good quantizer, by designing a compander whose nonlinearity $c(x)$ has derivative $\lambda_1^*(x)$, and extracting the resulting reconstruction levels and thresholds to obtain an approximately optimal point quantizer. This was first mentioned in Panter–Dite [405] and rediscovered several times. Unfortunately, at higher dimensions, companders cannot implement an optimal point density without creating large oblongitis [193], [56], [57]. So there is no direct way to construct optimal vector quantizers with the high resolution philosophy.

When dimension as well as rate is large, the two philosophies merge because the output distribution that achieves the Shannon distortion-rate function converges to the source density itself, as does the optimal point density. However, for small to moderate values of k, λ_k^* specifies a better distribution of points than the rate distortion philosophy of uniformly distributing codevectors over the typical set. For example, in the i.i.d. Gaussian case it indicates that the point density should be a Gaussian hill with somewhat larger variance than that of the source density. Which design philosophy is more useful? At low rates (say 1 bit per sample or less), one has no choice but to look to rate distortion theory. But at moderate to high rates, it appears that the high-resolution design philosophy is the better choice. To see this consider an i.i.d. Gaussian source, a target rate R, and a k-dimensional quantizer with 2^{kR} points uniformly distributed throughout a spherical support region. This is the ideal code suggested by rate distortion theory. One obtains a lower bound to its distortion by assuming that source vectors outside the support region are quantized to the closest point on the surface of the sphere, and by assuming that the cells within the support region are k-dimensional spheres. In this case, at moderate to large rates (say rate ten), after choosing the diameter of the support region to minimize this lower bound, it has been found that the dimension k must be larger than 250 in order that the resulting signal-to-noise ratio be within 1 dB of that predicted by the Shannon distortion-rate function [25]. Similar results were reported by Pepin *et al.* [409]. On the other hand, as mentioned earlier, a quantizer with dimension 12 can achieve this same distortion. It is clear then that the ability to come fairly close to $\overline{\delta}(R)$ with moderately large dimension is not due to the rate distortion theory design philosophy, the AEP, nor the use of spherical codes. Rather, it is due to the fact that good codes with small to moderate dimension have appropriately tapered point densities, as suggested by high resolution theory.

Finally, it is interesting to note that high resolution theory actually contains some analyses of the Shannon random coding approach. For example, Zador's thesis [561] gives an upper bound on the distortion of a randomly generated vector quantizer.

Nature of the Error Process: Both theories have something to say about the distribution of quantization errors. Generally speaking, what rate distortion theory has to say comes from assuming that the error distribution caused by a quantizer whose performance is close to $\overline{\delta}(R)$ is similar to that caused by a test channel that comes close to achieving the Shannon distortion-rate function. This is reasonable because Shannon's random coding argument shows that using such a test channel to randomly generate high-dimensional codevectors leads, with very high probability, to a code whose distortion is close to $\overline{\delta}(R)$. For example, one may use this sort of argument to deduce that the quantization error of a good high-dimensional quantizer is approximately white and Gaussian when the source is memoryless, the distortion is squared error, and the rate is large, cf. [404], which shows Gaussian-like histograms for the quantization error of VQ's with dimensions 8 to 32. As another example, for a Gaussian source with memory and squared-error distortion, rate distortion theory shows there is a simple relation between the spectra of the source and the spectra of the error produced by an optimal high-dimensional quantizer, cf. [46].

High resolution theory also has a long tradition of analyzing the error process, beginning with Clavier *et al.* [95], [100], and Bennett [43], and focusing on the distribution of the error, its spectrum, and its correlation with the input. Bennett showed

that in the high-resolution case, the power spectral density of the quantizer error with uniform quantization is approximately white (and uniformly distributed) provided the assumptions of the high resolution theory are met and the joint density of sample pairs is smooth. (See also [196, Sec. 5.6].) Bennett also found exact expressions for the power spectral density of a uniformly quantized Gaussian process. Sripad and Snyder [477] and Claasen and Jongepier [97] derived conditions under which the quantization error is white in terms of the joint characteristic functions of pairs of samples, two-dimensional analogs of Widrow's [529] condition. Zador [562] found high-resolution expressions for the characteristic function of the error produced by randomly chosen vector quantizers. Lee and Neuhoff [312], [379] found high-resolution expressions for the density of the error produced by fairly general (deterministic) scalar and vector quantizers in terms of their point density and their *shape profile*, which is a function that conveys more cell shape information than the inertial profile. As a side benefit, these expressions indicate that much can be deduced about the point density and cell shapes of a quantizer from a histogram of the lengths of the errors. Zamir and Feder [564] showed that the error produced by an optimal lattice quantizer with infinitely many small cells is asymptotically white in the sense that its components are uncorrelated with zero means and identical variances. Moreover, they showed that it becomes Gaussian as the dimension increases. The basic ideas are that as dimension increases good lattices have nearly spherical cells and that a uniform distribution over a high-dimensional sphere is approximately Gaussian, cf. [525]. Since optimal high-dimensional, high-rate VQ's can also be expected to have nearly spherical cells and since the AEP implies that most cells will have the same size, we reach the same conclusion as from rate distortion theory, namely, that good high-rate high-dimensional codes cause the quantization error to be approximately white and Gaussian.

Successive Approximation: Many vector quantizers operate in a successive approximation or progressive fashion, whereby a low-rate coarse quantization is followed by a sequence of finer and finer quantizations, which add to the rate. Tree-structured, multistage and hierarchical quantizers, to be discussed in the next section, are examples of such. Other methods can be used to design progressive indexing into given codebooks, as in Yamada and Tazaki (1991) [553] and Riskin *et al.* (1994) [440].

Successive approximation is useful in situations where the decoder needs to produce rough approximations of the data from the first bits it receives and, subsequently, to refine the approximation as more bits are received. Moreover, successive approximation quantizers are often structured in a way that makes them simpler than unstructured ones. Indeed, the three examples just cited are known more for their good performance with low complexity than for their progressive nature. An important question is whether the performance of a successive refinement quantizer will be better than one that does quantization in one step. On the one hand, rate distortion theory analysis [228], [291], [292], [557], [147], [437], [96] has shown that there are situations where successive approximation can be done without loss of optimality. On the other hand, high-resolution analyses of TSVQ [383] and two-stage VQ [311] have quantified the loss of these particular codes, and in the latter case shown ways of modifying the quantizer to eliminate the loss. Thus both theories have something to say about successive refinement.

V. QUANTIZATION TECHNIQUES

This section presents an overview of quantization techniques (mainly vector) that have been introduced, beginning in the 1980's, with the goal of attaining rate/distortion performance better than that attainable by scalar-based techniques such as direct scalar quantization, DPCM, and transform coding, but without the inordinately large complexity of brute-force vector quantization methods. Recall that if the dimension of the source vector is fixed, say at k, then the goal is to attain performance close to the optimal performance as expressed by $\delta_k(R)$ in the fixed-rate case, or $\delta_{k,L}(R)$ (usually $\delta_{k,1}(R)$) in the general case where variable-rate codes are permitted. However, if, as in the case of a stationary source, the dimension k can be chosen arbitrarily, then in both the fixed- and variable-rate cases, the goal is to attain performance close to $\bar{\delta}(R)$. In this case, all quantizers with $R > 0$ are suboptimal, and quantizers with various dimensions and even memory (which blurs the notion of dimension) can be considered.

We would have liked to make a carefully categorized, ordered, and ranked presentation of the various methods. However, the literature and variety of such techniques is quite large; there are a number of competing ways in which to categorize the techniques; complexity is itself a difficult thing to quantify; there are several special cases (e.g., fixed or variable rate, and fixed or choosable dimension); and there has not been much theoretical or even quantitative comparison among them. Consequently, much work is still needed in sorting the wheat from the chaff, i.e., determining which methods give the best performance versus complexity tradeoff in which situations, and in gaining an understanding of why certain complexity-reducing approaches are better than others. Nevertheless, we have attempted to choose a reasonable set of techniques and an ordering of them for discussion. Where possible we will make comments about the efficacies of the techniques. In all cases, we include references.

We begin with a brief discussion of complexity. Roughly speaking, it has two aspects: arithmetic (or computational) complexity, which is the number of arithmetic operations per sample that must be performed when encoding or decoding, and storage (or memory or space) complexity, which is the amount of auxiliary storage (for example, of codebooks) that is required for encoding or decoding. Rather than trying to combine them, it makes sense to keep separate track, because their associated costs vary with implementation venue, e.g., a PC, UNIX platform, generic DSP chip, specially designed VLSI chip, etc. In some venues, storage is of such low cost that one is tempted to ignore it. However, there are techniques that benefit sufficiently from increased memory that even though the per-unit cost is trivial, to obtain the best performance–complexity tradeoff, memory usage should be increased until the marginal gain-to-cost ratio of further increases is small, at which point the total cost of memory

may be signficant. As a result, one might think of a quantizer as being characterized by a four-tuple (R, D, A, M); i.e., arithmetic complexity A and storage complexity M have been added to the usual rate R and distortion D.

As a reminder, given a k-dimensional fixed-rate VQ with codebook $\mathcal{C}$ containing 2^{kR} codevectors, brute-force *full-search encoding* finds the closest codevector in $\mathcal{C}$ by computing the distortion between x and each codevector. In other words, it uses the optimal lossy encoder for the given codebook, creating the Voronoi partition. In the case of squared error, this requires computing approximately $A = 3 \times 2^{kR}$ operations per sample and storing approximately $M = k \times 2^{kR}$ vector components. For example, a codebook with rate 0.25 bits per pixel (bpp) and vector dimension $8 \times 8 = 64$ has $2^{kR} = 2^{16}$ codevectors, an impractical number for, say, real-time video coding. This exponential explosion of complexity and memory can cause serious problems even for modest dimension and rate, but it can in general make codes completely impractical in either the high-resolution or high-dimension extremes. A brute-force variable-rate scheme of the same rate will be even more complex—typically involving a much greater number of codevectors, a Lagrangian distortion computation, and an entropy coding scheme as well. It is the high complexity of such brute-force techniques that motivates the reduced complexity techniques to be discussed later in this section.

Simple measures such as arithmetic complexity and storage need a number of qualifications. One must decide whether encoding and decoding complexities need to be counted separately or summed, or, indeed, whether only one of them is important. For example, in record-once-play-many situations, it is the decoder that must have low complexity. Having no particular application in mind, we will focus on the sum of encoder and decoder complexities. For some techniques (perhaps most) it is possible to trade computations for storage by the use of precomputed tables. In such cases a quantizer is characterized, not by a single A and M but by a curve of such. In some cases, a given set of precomputed tables is the heart of the method. Another issue is the cost of memory accesses. Such operations are usually signficantly less expensive than arithmetic operations. However, some methods do such a good job of reducing arithmetic operations that the cost of memory accesses becomes significant. Techniques that attain smaller values of distortion need higher precision in their arithmetic and storage, which though not usually accounted for in assessments of complexity may sometimes be of significance. For example, a recent study of VQ codebook storage has shown that in routine cases one needs to store codevector components with only about $R + 4$ bits per component, where R is the rate of the quantizer [252]. Though this study did not assess the required arithmetic precision, one would guess that it need not be more than a little larger than that of the storage; e.g., R plus 5- or 6-bit arithmetic should suffice. Finally, variable-rate coding raises additional issues such as the costs associated with buffering, with storing and accessing variable-length codewords, and with the decoder having to parse binary sequences into variable-length codewords.

When assessing complexity of a quantization technique, it is interesting to compare the complexity invested in the lossy encoder/decoder versus that in the lossless encoder/decoder. (Recall that good performance can theoretically be attained with either a simple lossy encoder, such as a uniform scalar quantizer, and a sophisticated lossless encoder or, vice versa, as in high-dimensional fixed-rate VQ.) A quantizer is considered to have low complexity only when both encoders have low complexity. In the discussion that follows we focus mainly on quantization techniques where the lossless encoder is conceptually if not quantitatively simple. We wish, however, to mention the indexing problem, which may be considered to lie between the lossless and the lossy encoder. There are certain fixed-rate techniques, such as lattice quantization, pyramid VQ, and scalar-vector quantization, where it is fairly easy to find the cell in which the source vector lies, but the cells are associated with some set of N indices that are not simply the integers from 1 to N, where N is the number of cells, and converting the identity of the cell into a sequence of $\log N$ bits is nontrivial. This is referred to as an *indexing* problem.

Finally, we mention two additional issues. The first is that there are some VQ techniques whose implementation complexities are not prohibitive, but which have sufficiently many codevectors that designing them is inordinately complex or requires an inordinate amount of training data. A second issue is that in some applications it is desirable that the output of the encoder be progressively decodable in the sense that a rough reproduction can be made from the first bits that it receives, and improved reproductions are made as more bits are received. Such quantizers are said to be *progressive* or embedded. Now it is true that a progressive decoder can be designed for any encoder (for example, it can compute the expected value of the source vector given whatever bits it has received so far). However, a "good" progressive code is one for which the intermediate distortions achieved at the intermediate rates are relatively good (though not usually as good as those of quantizers designed for one specific rate) and that rather than restarting from scratch every time the decoder receives a new bit (or group of bits), it uses some simple method to update the current reproduction. It is also desirable in some applications for the encoding to be progressive, as well. Though not designed with them in mind, it turns out that a number of reduced-complexity VQ approaches also address these last two issues. That is, they are easier to design, as well as progressive.

A. Fast Searches of Unstructured Codebooks

Many techniques have been developed for speeding the full (minimum-distortion) search of an arbitrary codebook C containing N k-dimensional codevectors, for example, one generated by a Lloyd algorithm. In contrast to codebooks to be considered later these will be called *unstructured*. As a group these techniques use substantial amounts of additional memory in order to significantly reduce arithmetic complexity. A variety of such techniques are mentioned in [196, Sec. 12.16].

A number of fast-search techniques are similar in spirit to the following: the Euclidean distances between all pairs of codevectors are precomputed and stored in a table. Now,

given a source vector x to quantize, some initial codevector $\tilde{y}$ is chosen. Then all codevectors y_i whose distance from $\tilde{y}$ is greater than $2\|x-\tilde{y}\|$ are eliminated from further consideration because they cannot be closer than $\tilde{y}$. Those not eliminated are successively compared to x until one that is closer than $\tilde{y}$ is found, which then replaces $\tilde{y}$, and the process continues. In this way, the set of potential codevectors is gradually narrowed. Techniques in this category, with different ways of narrowing the search, may be found in [362], [517], [475], [476], [363], [426], [249], [399], [273], [245], [229], [332], [307], [547], [308], and [493].

A number of other fast-search techniques begin with a "coarse" prequantization with some very low-complexity technique. It is called "coarse" because it typically has larger cells than the Voronoi regions of the codebook C that is being searched. The coarse prequantization often involves scalar quantization of some type or a tree-structuring of binary quantizers, such as what are called K-d trees. Associated with each coarse cell is a *bucket* containing the indices of each codevector that is the nearest codevector to some source vector in the cell. These buckets are determined in advance and saved as tables. Then to encode a source vector x, one applies the prequantization, finds the index of the prequantization cell in which x is contained, and performs a full search on the corresponding bucket for the closest codevector to x. Techniques of this type may be found in [44], [176], [88], [89], [334], [146], [532], [423], [415], [500], and [84]. In some of these, the coarse prequantization is one-dimensional; for example, the length of the source vector may be quantized, and then the bucket of all codevectors having similar lengths is searched for the closest codevector.

Another class of techniques is like the previous except that the low-complexity prequantization has much smaller cells than the Voronoi cells of C, i.e., it is finer. In this case, the buckets associated with most "fine" prequantization cells contain just one codevector, i.e., the same codevector in C is the closest codevector to each point in the fine cell. The indices of these codevectors, one for each fine cell, are stored in a precomputed table. For each of those relatively few fine cells that have buckets containing more than one codevector, one member of the bucket is chosen and its index is placed in the table as the entry for that fine cell. Quantization of x then proceeds by applying the fine prequantizer and then using the index of the fine cell in which x lies to address the table containing codevectors from C, which then outputs the index of a codeword in C. Due to the fact that not every bucket contains only one codevector, such techniques, which may be found in [86], [358], [357], [518], [75], and [219], do not do a perfect full search. Some quantitative analysis of the increased distortion is given in [356] for a case where the prequantization is a lattice quantizer. Other fast-search methods include the *partial distortion* method of [88], [39], [402] and the transform subspace-domain approach of [78].

Consideration of methods based on prequantization leads to the question of how fine the prequantization cells should be. Our experience is that the best tradeoffs come when the prequantization cells are finer rather than coarser, the explanation being that if one has prequantized coarsely and now has to determine which codevector in a bucket is closest to x, it is more efficient to use some fast search method than to do full search. Dividing the coarse cells into finer ones is a way of doing just this. Another question that arises for all fast search techniques is whether it is worth the effort to perform a full search or whether one should instead stop short of this, as in the methods with fine prequantization cells. Our experience is that it is usually not worth the effort to do a full search, because by suffering only a very small increase in MSE one can achieve a significant reduction in arithmetic complexity and storage. Moreover, in the case of stationary sources where the dimension is subject to choice, for a given amount of arithmetic complexity and storage, one almost always gets better performance by doing a suboptimal search of a higher dimensional codebook than a full search of a lower dimensional one.

Fast search methods based on fine prequantization can be improved by optimizing the codebook for the given prequantizer. Each cell of the partition corresponding to C induced by prequantization followed by table lookup is the union of some number of fine cells of the prequantizer. Thus the question becomes: what is the best partition into N cells, each of which is the union of some number of fine cells. The codevectors in C should then be the centroids of these cells. Such techniques have been exploited in [86] and [358]. One technique worth particular mention is called *hierarchical table lookup* VQ [86], [518], [75], [219]. In this case, the prequantizer is itself an unstructured codebook that is searched with a fine prequantizer that is in turn searched with an even finer prequantizer, and so on. Specifically, the first prequantizer uses a high-rate scalar quantizer k times. The next level of prequantization applies a two-dimensional VQ to each of $k/2$ pairs of scalar quantizer outputs. The next level applies a four-dimensional VQ to each of $k/4$ pairs of outputs from the two-dimensional quantizers, and so on. Hence the method is hierarchical. Because each of the quantizers can be implemented entirely with table lookup, this method eliminates all arithmetic complexity except memory accesses. It has been successfully used for video coding [518], [75].

B. Structured Quantizers

We now turn to quantizers with structured partitions or reproduction codebooks, which in turn lend themselves to fast searching techniques and, in some cases, to greatly reduced storage. Many of these are discussed in [196] and [458].

Lattice Quantizers: Lattice quantization can be viewed as a vector generalization of uniform scalar quantization. It constrains the reproduction codebook to be a subset of a regular lattice, where a lattice is the set of all vectors of the form $\sum_{i=1}^{n} m_i u_i$, where m_i are integers and the u_i are linearly independent (usually nondegenerate, i.e., $n = k$). The resulting Voronoi partition is a tessellation with all cells (except for those overlapping the overload region) having the same shape, size, and orientation. Lattice quantization was proposed by Gersho [193] because of its near optimality for high-resolution variable-rate quantization and, also, its near optimality for high-resolution fixed-rate quantization of uniformly distributed

sources. (These assume that Gersho's conjecture holds and that the best lattice quantizer is approximately as good as the best tessellation.) Especially important is the fact that their highly structured nature has led to algorithms for implementing their lossy encoders with very low arithmetic and storage complexity [103]–[105], [459], [106], [199]. These find the integers m_i associated with the closest lattice point. Conway and Sloane [104], [106] have reported the best known lattices for several dimensions, as well as fast quantizing and decoding algorithms. Some important n-dimensional lattices are the root lattices $A_n(n \geq 1)$, $D_n(n \geq 2)$, and $E_n(n = 6, 7, 8)$, the Barnes–Wall lattice Λ_{16} in dimension 16, and the Leech lattice Λ_{24} in 24 dimensions. These latter give the best sphere packings and coverings in their respective dimensions. Recently, Agrell and Eriksson [5] have found improved lattices in dimensions 9 and 10.

Though low complexity algorithms have been found for the lossy encoder, there are other issues that affect the performance and complexity of lattice quantizers. For variable-rate coding, one must scale the lattice to obtain the desired distortion and rate, and one must implement an algorithm for mapping the m_i's to the variable-length binary codewords. The latter could potentially add much complexity. For fixed-rate coding with rate R, the lattice must be scaled and a subset 2^{kR} lattice points must be identified as the codevectors. This induces a support region. If the source has finite support, the lattice quantizer will ordinarily be chosen to have the same support. If not, then the scaling factor and lattice subset are usually chosen so that the resulting quantizer support region has large probability. In either case, a low complexity method is needed for assigning binary sequences to the chosen codevectors; i.e., for indexing. Conway and Sloane [105] found such a method for the important case that the support has the shape of an enlarged cell. For sources with infinite support, such as i.i.d. Gaussian, there is also the difficult question of how to quantize a source vector x lying outside the support region. For example, one might scale x so that it lies on or just inside the boundary of the support region, and then quantize the scaled vector in the usual way. Unfortunately, this simple method does not always find the closest codevector to x. Indeed, it often increases overload distortion substantially over that of the minimum-distance quantization rule. To date, there is apparently no low complexity method that does not substantially increase overload distortion.

High resolution theory applies immediately to lattice VQ when the entire lattice is considered to be the codebook. The theory becomes more difficult if, as is usually the case, only a bounded portion of the lattice is used as the codebook and one must separately consider granular and overload distortion. There are a variety of ways of considering the tradeoffs involved, cf. [580], [151], [359], [149], [409]. In any case, the essence of a lattice code is its uniform point density and nicely shaped cells with low normalized moment of inertia. For fixed-rate coding, they work well for uniform sources or other sources with bounded support. But as discussed earlier, for sources with unbounded support such as i.i.d. Gaussian, they require very large dimensions to achieve performance close to $\bar{\delta}(R)$.

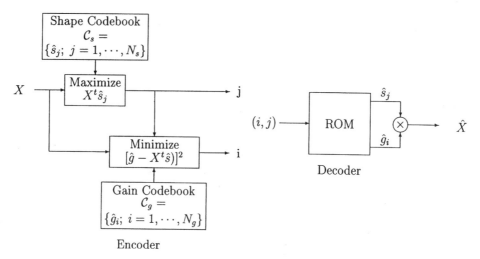

Fig. 8. Shape-gain VQ.

Product Quantizers: A product quantizer uses a reproduction codebook that is the Cartesian product of lower dimensional reproduction codebooks. For example, the application of a scalar quantizer to k successive samples $X_1, X_2, \cdots, X_k$ can be viewed as a product quantizer operating on the k-dimensional vector $X = (X_1, X_2, \cdots, X_k)$. The product structure makes searching easier and, unlike the special case of a sequence of scalar quantizers, the search need not be comprised of k independent searches. Products of vector quantizers are also possible. Typically, the product quantizer is applied, not to the original vector of samples, but to some functions or features extracted from the vector. The complexities of a product quantizer (arithmetic and storage, encoding and decoding) are the sums of those of the component quantizers. As such, they are ordinarily much less than the complexities of an unstructured quantizer with the same number of codevectors, whose complexities equal the product of those of the components of a product quantizer.

A *shape-gain* vector quantizer [449], [450] is an example of a product quantizer. It uses a product reproduction codebook consisting of a gain codebook $\mathcal{C}_g = \{\hat{g}_i; i = 1, \cdots, N_g\}$ of positive scalars and a shape codebook $\mathcal{C}_s = \{\hat{s}_j; j = 1, \cdots, N_s\}$ of unit norm k-dimensional vectors, and the overall reproduction vector is defined by $\hat{x} = \hat{g}\hat{s}$. It is easy to see the minimum-squared-error reproduction codeword $\hat{g}_i\hat{s}_j$ for an input vector x is found by the following encoding algorithm: First choose the index j that maximizes the correlation $x^t\hat{s}_j$, then for this chosen j choose the index i minimizing $|\hat{g}_i - x^t\hat{s}_j|$. This sequential rule gives the minimum-squared-error reproduction codeword without explicitly normalizing the input vector (which would be computationally expensive). The encoder and decoder are depicted in Fig. 8.

A potential advantage of such a system is that by separating these two "features," one is able to use a scalar quantizer for the gain feature and a lower rate codebook for the shape feature, which can then have a higher dimension, for the same search complexity. A major issue arises here: given a total rate constraint, how does one best divide the bits between the two codebooks? This is an example of a rate-allocation problem

that arises in all product codebooks and about which more will be said shortly.

It is important to notice that the use of a product quantizer does not mean the use of independent quantizers for each component. As with shape-gain VQ, the optimal lossy encoder will in general not view only one coordinate at a time. Separate and independent quantization of the components provides a low-complexity but generally suboptimal encoder. In the case of the shape-gain VQ, the optimal lossy encoder is happily a simple sequential operation, where the gain quantizer is scalar, but the selection of one of its quantization levels depends on the result of another quantizer, the shape quantizer. Similar ideas can be used for mean-removed VQ [20], [21] and mean/gain/shape VQ [392]. The most general formulation of product codes has been given by Chan and Gersho [82]. It includes a number of schemes with dependent quantization, even tree-structured and multistage quantization, to be discussed later.

Fischer's *pyramid VQ* [164] is also a kind of shape-gain VQ. In this case, the codevectors of the shape codebook are constrained to lie on the surface of a k-dimensional pyramid, namely, the set of all vectors whose components have magnitudes summing to one. Pyramid VQ's are very well suited to i.i.d. Laplacian sources. An efficient method for indexing the shape codevectors is needed and a suitable method is included in pyramid VQ.

Two-dimensional shape-gain product quantizers, usually called *polar quantizers*, have been extensively developed [182], [183], [407], [406], [61], [62], [530], [489], [490], [483], [485], [488], [360]. Here, a two-dimensional source vector is represented in polar coordinates and, in the basic scheme, the codebook consists of the Cartesian product of a nonuniform scalar codebook for the magnitude and a uniform scalar codebook for the phase. Early versions of polar quantization used independent quantization of the magnitude and phase information, but later versions used the better method described above, and some even allowed the phase quantizers to have a resolution that depends on the outcome of the magnitude quantizer. Such polar quantizers are called "unrestricted" [488], [530]. High-resolution analysis can be used to study the rate-distortion performance of these quantizers [61], [62], [483], [485], [488], [360]. Among other things, such analyses find the optimal point density for the magnitude quantizer and the optimal bit allocation between magnitude and phase. Originally, methods were developed specifically for polar quantizers. However, recently it has been shown that Bennett's integral can be applied to analyze polar quantization in a straightforward way [380]. It turns out that for an i.i.d. Gaussian source, optimized conventional polar quantization gains about 0.41 dB over direct scalar quantization, and optimized unrestricted polar quantization gains another 0.73 dB. Indeed, the latter has, asymptotically, square cells and the optimal two-dimensional point density, and loses only 0.17 dB relative to optimal two-dimensional vector quantization, but is still 3.11 dB from $\overline{\delta}(R)$.

Product quantizers can be used for any set of features deemed natural for decomposing a vector. Perhaps the most famous example is one we have seen already and now revisit: transform coding.

Transform Coding: Though the goal of this section is mainly to discuss techniques beyond scalar quantization, DPCM and transform coding, we discuss the latter here because of its relationships to other techniques and because we wish to discuss work on the bit-allocation problem.

Traditional transform coding can be viewed as a product quantizer operating on the transform coefficients resulting from a linear transform on the original vector. We have already mentioned the traditional high-resolution fixed-rate analysis and the more recent high-resolution entropy-constrained analysis for separate lossless coding of each quantized transform coefficient. An asymptotic low-resolution analysis [338], [339] has also been performed. In almost all actual implementations, however, scalar quantizers are combined with a block lossless code, where the lossless code is allowed to effectively operate on an entire block of quantized coefficients at once, usually by combining run-length coding with Huffman or arithmetic coding. As a result, the usual high-resolution analyses are not directly applicable.

Although high resolution theory shows that the Karhunen–Loève transform is optimal for Gaussian sources, and the asymptotic low-resolution analysis does likewise, the dominant transform for many years has been the discrete cosine transform (DCT) used in most current image and video coding standards. The primary competition for future standards comes from discrete wavelet transforms, which will be considered shortly. One reason for the use of the DCT is its lower complexity. An "unstructured" transform like the Karhunen–Loève requires approximately $2k$ operations per sample, which is small compared to the arithmetic complexity of unstructured VQ, but large compared to the approximately $\log k$ operations per sample for a DCT. Another motivation for the DCT is that in some sense it approximates the behavior of the Karhunen–Loève transform for certain sources. And a final motivation is that the frequency decomposition done by the DCT mimics, to some extent, that done by the human visual system and so one may quantize the DCT coefficients taking perception into account. We will not delve into the large

literature of transforms, but will observe that bit allocation becomes an important issue, and one can either use the high-resolution approximations or a variety of nonasymptotic allocation algorithms such as the "fixed-slope" or Pareto-optimality considered in [526], [470], [94], [439], [438], and [463]. The method involves operating all quantizers at points on their operational distortion-rate curves of equal slopes. For a survey of some of these methods, see [107] or [196, Ch. 10]. A combinatorial optimization method is given in [546].

As a final comment on traditional transform coding, the code can be considered as being suboptimal as a k-dimensional quantizer because of the constrained structure (transform and product code). It gains, however, in having a low complexity, and transform codes remain among the most popular compression systems because of their balance of performance and complexity.

Subband/Wavelet/Pyramid Quantization: Subband codes, wavelet codes, and pyramid codes are intimately related and all are cousins of a transform code. The oldest of these methods (so far as quantization is concerned) is the pyramid code of Burt and Adelsen [66] (which is quite different from Fischer's pyramid VQ). The Burt and Adelsen pyramid is constructed from an image first by forming a Gaussian pyramid by successively lowpass filtering and downsampling, and then by forming a Laplacian pyramid which replaces each layer of the Gaussian pyramid by a residual image formed by subtracting a prediction of that layer based on the lower resolution layers. The resulting pyramid of images can then be quantized, e.g., by scalar quantizers. The approximation for any layer can be reconstructed by using the inverse quantizers (reproduction decoders) and upsampling and combining the reconstructed layer and all lower resolution reconstructed layers. Note that as one descends the pyramid, one easily combines the new bits for that layer with the bits already used to produce a higher resolution spatially and in amplitude. The pyramid code can be viewed as one of the original multiresolution codes. It can be viewed as a transform code because the entire original structure can be viewed as a linear transform of the original image, but observe that the number of pixels has been roughly doubled.

Subband codes decompose an image into separate images by using a bank of linear filters, hence once again performing a linear transformation on the data prior to quantizing it. Traditional subband coding used filters of equal or roughly equal bandwidth. Wavelet codes can be viewed as subband codes of logarithmically varying bandwidths instead of equal bandwidths, where the filters used satisfy certain properties. Since the introduction of subband codes in the late 1980's and wavelet codes in the early 1990's, the field has blossomed and produced several of the major contenders for the best speech and image compression systems. The literature is beyond the scope of this article to survey, and much is far more concerned with the transforms, filters, or basis functions used and the lossless coding used following quantization than with the quantization itself. Hence we content ourselves with the mention of a few highlights. The interested reader is referred to the book by Vetterli and Kovačević on wavelets and subband coding [516].

Subband coding was introduced in the context of speech coding in 1976 by Crochiere *et al.* [113]. The extension of subband filtering from 1-D to 2-D was made by Vetterli [515] and 2-D subband filtering was first applied to image coding by Woods *et al.* [541], [527], [540]. Early wavelet-coding techniques emphasized scalar or lattice vector quantization [12], [13], [130], [463], [14], [30], [185], and other vector quantization techniques have also been applied to wavelet coefficients, including tree encoding [366], residual vector quantization [295], and other methods [107]. A major breakthrough in performance and complexity came with the introduction of zerotrees [315], [466], [457], which provided an extremely efficient embedded representation of scalar quantized wavelet coefficients, called *embedded zerotree wavelet* (EZW) coding. As done by JPEG in a primitive way, the zerotree approach led to a code which first sent bits about the transform coefficients with the largest magnitude, and then sent subsequent bits describing these significant coefficients to greater accuracy as well as bits about originally less significant coefficients that became significant as the accuracy improved. The zerotree approach has been extended to vector quantization (e.g., [109]), but the slight improvement comes at a significant cost in added complexity. Rate-distortion ideas have been used to optimize the rate-distortion tradeoffs using wavelet packets by minimizing a Lagrangian distortion over code trees and bit assignments [427]. Recently, competitive schemes have demonstrated that separate scalar quantization of individual subbands coupled with a sophisticated but low-complexity lossless coding algorithm called stack-run coding can provide performance nearly as good as EZW [504].

The best wavelet codes tend to use very smart lossless codes, lossless codes which effectively code very large vectors. While wavelet advocates may credit the decomposition itself for the gains in compression, the theory suggests that rather it is the fact that vector entropy coding for very large vectors is feasible.

Scalar-Vector Quantization: Like permutation vector quantization and Fischer's pyramid vector quantizer, Laroia and Farvardin's [305] *scalar-vector quantization* attempts to match the performance of an optimal entropy-constrained scalar quantizer with a low-complexity fixed-rate structured vector quantizer. A derivative technique called *block-constrained quantization* [24], [27], [23], [28] is simpler and easier to describe. Here the reproduction codebook is a subset of the k-fold product of some scalar codebook. Variable-length binary codewords are associated with the scalar levels, and given some target rate R, the k-dimensional codebook contains only those sequences of k quantization levels for which the sum of the lengths of the binary codewords associated with the levels is at most kR. The minimum distortion codevector can be found using dynamic programming. Alternatively, an essentially optimal search can be performed with very low complexity using a knapsack packing or Lagrangian approach. The output of the encoder is the sequence of binary codewords corresponding to the codevector that was found, plus some padded bits if the total does not equal kR. The simplest method requires approximately $20N^2/k + 20$ operations per sample and storage for approximately N^2 numbers, where

N is the number of scalar quantization levels. The original scalar-vector method differs in that rational lengths rather than binary codewords are assigned to the scalar quantizer levels, dynamic programming is used to find the best codevector, and the resulting codevectors are losslessly encoded with a kind of lexicographic encoding. For i.i.d. Gaussian sources these methods attain SNR within about 2 dB of $\bar{\delta}(R)$ with k on the order of 100, which is about 0.5 dB from the goal of 1.53 dB larger than $\bar{\delta}(R)$. A high-resolution analysis is given in [26] and [23]. The scalar-vector method extends to sources with memory by combining it with transform coding using a decorrelating or approximately decorrelating transform [305].

Tree-Structured Quantization: In its original and simplest form, a k-dimensional tree-structured vector quantizer (TSVQ) [69] is a fixed-rate quantizer with, say, rate R whose encoding is guided by a balanced (fixed-depth) binary tree of depth kR. There is a codevector associated with each of its 2^{kR} terminal nodes (leaves), and a k-dimensional testvector associated with each of its $2^{kR} - 1$ internal nodes. Quantization of a source vector x proceeds in a tree-structured search by finding which of the two nodes stemming from the root node has the closer testvector to x, then finding which of the two nodes stemming from this node has the closer testvector, and so on, until a terminal node and codevector are found. The binary encoding of this codevector consists of the sequence of kR binary decisions that lead to it. Decoding is done by table lookup as in unstructured VQ. As in successive approximation scalar quantization, TSVQ yields an embedded code with a naturally progressive structure.

With this method, encoding requires storing the tree of testvectors and codevectors, demanding approximately twice the storage of an unstructured codebook. However, encoding requires only $2kR$ distortion calculations, which is a tremendous decrease over the 2^{kR} required by full search of an unstructured codebook. In the case of squared-error distortion, instead of storing testvectors and computing the distortion between x and each of them, at each internal node one may store the normal to the hyperplane bisecting the testvectors at the two nodes stemming from it, and determine on which side of the hyperplane x lies by comparing an inner product of x with the normal to a threshold that is also stored. This reduces the arithmetic complexity and storage roughly in half to approximately kR operations per sample and 2^{kR} vectors. Further reductions in storage are possible, as described in [252].

The usual (but not necessarily optimal) *greedy* method for designing a balanced TSVQ [69], [225] is first to design the testvectors stemming from the root node using the Lloyd algorithm on a training set. Then design the two testvectors stemming from, say, the left one of these by running the Lloyd algorithm on the training vectors that were mapped to the left one, and so on.

In the scalar case, a tree can be found that implements any quantizer, indeed, the optimal quantizer. So tree-structuring loses nothing, though the above design algorithm does not necessarily generate the best possible quantizers. In the multidimensional case, one cannot expect that the greedy algorithm will produce a TSVQ that is as good as the best unstructured

VQ or even the best possible TSVQ. Nevertheless, it seems to work pretty well. It has been observed that in the high-resolution case, the cells of the resulting TSVQ's are mostly a mixture of cubes, cubes cut in half, the latter cut in half again, and so on until smaller cubes are formed. And it has been found for i.i.d. Gauss and Gauss–Markov sources that the performances of TSVQ's with moderate to high rates designed by the greedy algorithm are fairly well predicted by Bennett's integral, assuming the point density is optimum and the cells are an equal mixture of cubes, cubes cut in half, and so on. This sort of analysis indicates that the primary weakness of TSVQ is in the shapes of the cells that it produces. Specifically, its loss relative to optimal k-dimensional fixed-rate VQ ranges from 0.7 dB for $k = 2$ to 2.2 dB for very large dimensions. Part of the loss is $(1/12)/M_k$, the ratio of the normalized moment of inertia of a cube to that of the best k-dimensional cell shape, which approaches 1.53 dB for large k, and the remainder, about 0.5 to 0.7 dB, is due to the oblongitis caused by the cubes being cut into pieces [383]. A paper investigating the nature of TSVQ cells is [569].

Our experience has been that when taking both performance and complexity into account, TSVQ is a very competitive VQ method. For example, we assert that for most of the fast search methods, one can find a TSVQ (with quite possibly a different dimension) that dominates it in the sense that D, R, A, and M are all at least as good. Indeed, many of the fast-search approaches use a tree-structured prequantization. However, in TSVQ the searching tree and codebook are matched in size and character in a way that makes them work well together. A notable exception is the hierarchical table lookup VQ which attains a considerably smaller arithmetic complexity than attainable with TSVQ, at the expense of higher storage. The TSVQ will still be competitive in terms of throughput, however, as the tree-structured search is amenable to pipelining.

TSVQ's can be generalized to unbalanced trees (with variable depth as opposed to the fixed depth discussed above) [342], [94], [439], [196] and with larger branching factors than two or even variable branching factors [460]. However, it should be recalled that the goodness of the original TSVQ means that the gains of such are not likely to be substantial except in the low-resolution case or if variable-rate coding is used or if the source has some complex structure that the usual greedy algorithm cannot exploit.

A tree-structured quantizer is analogous to a classification or regression tree, and as such unbalanced TSVQ's can be designed by algorithms based on a gardening metaphor of *growing* and *pruning*. The most well known is the CART algorithm of Breiman, Friedman, Olshen, and Stone [53], and the variation of CART for designing TSVQ's bears their initials: the BFOS algorithm [94], [439], [196]. In this method, a balanced or unbalanced tree with more leaves than needed is first grown and then pruned. One can grow a balanced tree by splitting all nodes in each level of the tree, or by splitting one node at a time, e.g., by splitting the node with the largest contribution to the distortion [342] or in a greedy fashion to maximize the decrease in distortion for the increase in rate [439]. Once grown, the tree can be pruned by removing all

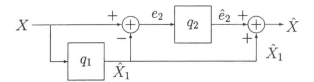

Fig. 9. Two-stage VQ.

descendants of any internal node, thereby making it a leaf. This will increase average distortion, but will also decrease the rate. Once again, one can select for pruning the node that offers the best tradeoff in terms of the least increase in distortion per decrease in bits. It can be shown that, for quite general measures of distortion, pruning can be done in an optimal fashion and the optimal subtrees of decreasing rate are nested [94] (see also [355]). It seems likely that in the moderate-to high-rate case, pruning removes leaves corresponding to cells that are oblong such as cubes cut in half, leaving mainly cubic cells. We also wish to emphasize that if variable-rate quantization is desired, the pruning can be done so as to optimize the tradeoff between distortion and leaf entropy.

There has been a flurry of recent work on the theory of tree-growing algorithms for vector quantizers, which are a form of recursive partitioning. See, for example, the work of Nobel and Olshen [390], [388], [389]. For other work on tree growing and pruning see [393], [439], [276], [22], and [355].

Multistage Vector Quantization: Multistage (or multistep, or cascade, or residual) vector quantization was introduced by Juang and Gray [274] as a form of tree-structured quantization with much reduced arithmetic complexity and storage. Instead of having a separate reproduction codebook for each branch in the tree, a single codebook could be used for all branches of a common length by coding the residual error accumulated to that point instead of coding the input vector directly. In other words, the quantization error (or residual) from the previous stage is quantized in the usual way by the following stage, and a reproduction is formed by summing the previous reproduction and the newly quantized residual. An example of a two-stage quantizer is depicted in Fig. 9. The rate of the multistage quantizer is the sum of the rates of the stages, and the distortion is simply that of the last stage. (It is easily seen that the overall error is just that of the last stage.) A multistage quantizer has a *direct sum* reproduction codebook in the sense that it contains all codevectors formed by summing codevectors from the reproduction codebooks used at each stage. One may also view it as a kind of product code in the sense that the reproduction codebook is determined by the Cartesian product of the stage codebooks. And like product quantization, its complexities (arithmetic and storage, encoding and decoding) are the sum of those of the stage quantizers plus a small amount for computing the residuals at the encoder or the sums at the decoder. In contrast, a conventional single-stage quantizer with the same rate and dimension has complexities equal to the product of those of the stage quantizers.

Since the total rate is the sum of the stage rates, a bit-allocation problem arises. In two-stage quantization using fixed-rate, unstructured, k-dimensional VQ's in both stages, it usually happens that choosing both stages to have the same rate leads to the best performance versus complexity tradeoff. In this case, the complexities are approximately the square root of what they would be for a single-stage quantizer.

Though we restrict attention here to the case where all stages are fixed-rate vector quantizers with the same dimension, there is no reason why they need have the same dimension, have fixed rate, or have any similarity whatsoever. In other words, multistage quantization can be used (and often is) with very different kinds of quantizers in its stages (different dimensions and much different structures, e.g., DPCM or wavelet coding). For example, structuring the stage quantizers leads to good performance and further substantial reductions in complexity, e.g., [243], [79].

Of course, the multistage structuring leads to a suboptimal VQ for its given dimension. In particular, the direct-sum form of the codebook is not usually optimal, and the greedy-search algorithm described above, in which the residual from one stage is quantized by the next, does not find the closest codevector in the direct-sum codebook. Moreover, the usual greedy design method, which uses a Lloyd algorithm to design the first stage in the usual way and then to design the second stage to minimize distortion when operating on the errors of the first, and so on, does not, in general, design an optimal multistage VQ, even for greedy search. However, two-stage VQ's designed in this way work fairly well.

A high-resolution analysis of two-stage VQ using Bennett's integral on the second stage can be found in [311] and [309]. In order to apply Bennett's integral, it was necessary to find the form of the probability density of the quantization error produced by the first stage. This motivated the asymptotic error-density analysis of vector quantization in [312] and [379].

Multistage quantizers have been improved in a number of ways. More sophisticated (than greedy) encoding algorithms can take advantage of the direct sum nature of the codebook to make optimal or nearly optimal searches, though with some (and sometimes a great deal of) increased complexity. And more sophisticated design algorithms (than the greedy one) can also have benefits [32], [177], [81], [31], [33]. Variable-rate multistage quantizers have been developed [243], [297], [298], [441], [296].

Another way of improving multistage VQ is to adapt each stage to the outcome of the previous. One such scheme, introduced by Lee and Neuhoff [310], [309], was motivated by the observation that if the first stage quantizer has high rate, say R_1, then by Gersho's conjecture, the first stage cells all have approximately the shape of T_k, the tesselating polytope with least normalized moment of inertia, and the source density is approximately constant on them. This implies that the conditional distribution of the residual given that the source vector lies in the ith cell differs from that for the jth only by a scaling and rotation, because cell S_j differs from S_i by just a scaling and rotation. Therefore, if first-stage-dependent scaling and rotation are done prior to second-stage quantization, the conditional distribution of the residual will be the same for all cells, and the second stage can be designed for this distribution, rather than having to be a compromise, as is otherwise the case in two-stage VQ. Moreover, since this distribution is essentially uniform on a support region shaped like T_k, the second stage can itself be a uniform tesselation. The net effect is a quantizer that inherits the optimal point density of the first stage[13] and the optimal cell shapes of the second. Therefore, in the high-resolution case, this *cell-conditioned* two-stage VQ works essentially as well as an optimal (single-stage) VQ, but with much less complexity.

Direct implementation of cell-conditioned two-stage VQ, requires the storing of a scale factor and a rotation for each first stage cell, which operate on the first stage residual before quantization by the second stage. Their inverses are applied subsequently. However, since the first stage cells are so nearly spherical, the rotations gain only a small amount, typically about 0.1 dB, and may be omitted. Moreover, since the best known lattice tesselations are so close to the best known tesselations, one may use lattice VQ as the second stage, which further reduces complexity. Good schemes of this sort have even been developed for low to moderate rates by Gibson [270], [271] and Pan and Fischer [403], [404].

Cell-conditioned two-stage quantizers can be viewed as having a piecewise-constant point density of the sort proposed earlier by Kuhlmann and Bucklew [302] as a means of circumventing the fact that optimal vector quantizers cannot be implemented with companders. This approach was further developed by Swaszek in [487].

Another scheme for adapting each stage to the previous is called codebook sharing, as introduced by Chan and Gersho [80], [82]. With this approach, each stage has a finite set of reproduction codebooks, one of which is used to quantize the residual, depending on the sequence of outcomes from the previous stages. Thus each codebook is shared among some subset of the possible sequences of outcomes from the previous stages. This method lies between conventional multistage VQ in which each stage has one codebook that is shared among all sequences of outcomes from previous stages, and TSVQ in which, in effect, a different codebook is used for each sequence of outcomes from the previous stages. Chan and Gersho introduced a Lloyd-style iterative design algorithm for designing shared codebooks; they showed that by controlling the number and rate of the codebooks one could optimize multistage VQ with a constraint on storage; and they used this method to good effect in audio coding [80]. In the larger scheme of things, TSVQ, multistage VQ, and codebook sharing all fit within the broad family of generalized product codes that they introduced in [82].

Feedback Vector Quantization: Just as with scalar quantizers, a vector quantizer can be predictive; simply replace scalars with vectors in the predictive quantization structure depicted in Fig. 3 [235], [116], [85], [417]. Alternatively, the encoder and decoder can share a finite set of states and a quantizer custom designed for each state. Both encoder and decoder must be able to track the state in the absence of channel errors, so that the state must be determinable from knowledge of an initial state combined with the binary codewords transmitted to the decoder. The result is a finite-state version of a predictive

---

[13] Since the second stage uniformly refines the first stage cells, the overall point density is approximately that of the first stage.

324

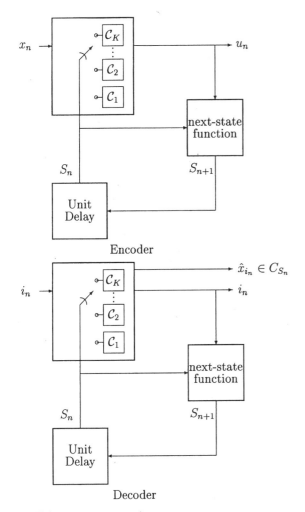

Encoder

Decoder

Fig. 10. Finite-state vector quantizer.

quantizer, referred to as a finite-state vector quantizer and depicted in Fig. 10. Although little theory has been developed for finite-state quantizers [161], [178], [179], a variety of design methods exist [174], [175], [136], [236], [15], [16], [286], [196], Lloyd's optimal decoder extends in a natural way to finite-state vector quantizers, the optimal reproduction decoder is a conditional expectation of the input vector given the binary codeword *and* the state. The optimal lossy encoder is not easily described, however, as the next state must be chosen in a way that ensures good future behavior, and not just in a greedy fashion that minimizes the current squared error. If look-ahead is allowed, however, then a tree or trellis search can be used to pick a long-term minimum distortion path, as will be considered in the next subsection.

Both predictive and finite-state vector quantizers typically use memory in the lossy encoder, but use a memoryless lossless code independently applied to each successive binary codeword. One can, of course, also make the lossless code depend on the state, or be conditional on the previous binary codeword. One can also use a memoryless VQ combined with a conditional lossless code (conditioned on the previous binary codeword) designed with a conditional entropy constraint [95], [188]. A simple approach that works for TSVQ is to code the binary path to the codevector for the present source vector relative to the binary path to that of the previous source vector,

which is usually very similar. This is a kind of interblock lossless coding [384], [410], [428].

Address-vector quantization, introduced by Nasrabadi and Feng [371] (see also [160] and [373]), is another way to introduce memory into the lossy encoder of a vector quantizer with the goal of attaining higher dimensional performance with lower dimensional complexity. With this approach, in addition to the usual reproduction codebook C, there is an address codebook C_a containing permissible sequences of indices of codevectors in C. The address codebook plays the same role as the outer code in a concatenated channel code (or the trellis in trellis-encoded quantization discussed below), namely, it limits the allowable sequences of codewords from the inner code, which in this case is C. In this way, address-vector quantization can exploit the property that certain sequences of codevectors are much more probable than others; these will be the ones contained in C_a.

As with DPCM, the introduction of memory into the lossy encoder seriously complicates the theory of such codes, which likely explains why there is so little.

Tree/Trellis-Encoded Quantization: Channel coding has often inspired source coding or quantization structures. Channel coding matured much earlier and the dual nature of channel and source coding suggests that a good channel code can be turned into a good source code by reversing the order of encoder and decoder. This role reversal was natural for the codes which eased search requirements by imposition of a tree or trellis structure. Unlike the tree-structured vector quantizers, these earlier systems imposed the tree structure on the sequence of symbols instead of on a single vector of symbols. For the channel coding case, the encoder was a convolutional code, input symbols shifted into a shift register as output symbols, formed by linear combinations (in some field) of the shift-register contents, shifted out. Sequences of output symbols produced in this fashion could be depicted with a tree structure, where each node of the tree corresponded to the state of the shift register (all but the final or oldest symbol) and the branches connecting nodes were determined by the most recent symbol to enter the shift register and were labeled by the corresponding output, the output symbol resulting if that branch is taken. The goal of a channel decoder is to take such a sequence of tree branch labels that has been corrupted by noise, and find a minimum-distance valid sequence of branch labels. This could be accomplished by a tree-search algorithm such as the Fano, stack, or M-algorithm. Since the shift register is finite, the tree becomes redundant and new nodes will correspond to previously seen states so that the tree diagram. becomes a merged tree or trellis, which can be searched by a dynamic programming algorithm, the Viterbi algorithm, cf. [173]. In the early 1970's, the algorithms for tree-decoding channel codes were inverted to form tree-encoding algorithms for sources by Jelinek, Anderson, and others [268], [269], [11], [132], [123], [10]. Later, trellis channel-decoding algorithms were modified to trellis-encoding algorithms for sources by Viterbi and Omura [519]. While linear encoders sufficed for channel coding, nonlinear decoders were required for the source coding application, and a variety of design algorithms were developed for designing the decoder to populate the trellis searched by the encoder [319], [531], [481], [18], [40]. Observe that the reproduction decoder of a finite-state VQ can be used as the decoder in a trellis-encoding system, where the finite-state encoder is replaced by a minimum-distortion search of the decoder trellis implied by the finite-state VQ decoder, which is an optimal encoding for a sequence of inputs.

Tree- and trellis-encoded quantizers can both be considered as a VQ with large blocklength and a reproduction codebook constrained to be the possible outputs of a nonlinear filter or a finite-state quantizer or vector quantizer of smaller dimension. Both structures produce long codewords with a trellis structure, i.e., successive reproduction symbols label the branches of a trellis and the encoder is just a minimum-distortion trellis search algorithm such as the Viterbi algorithm.

Trellis-Coded Quantization: Trellis-coded quantization, both scalar and vector, improves upon traditional trellis-encoded systems by labeling the trellis branches with entire subcodebooks (or "subsets") rather than with individual reproduction levels [345], [344], [166], [167], [522], [343], [478], [514]. The primary gain resulting is a reduction in encoder complexity for a given level of performance. As the original trellis encoding systems were motivated by convolutional channel codes with Viterbi decoders, trellis-coded quantization was motivated by Ungerboeck's enormously successful coded-modulation approach to channel coding for narrowband channels [505], [506].

Recent combinations of TCQ to coding wavelet coefficients [478] have yielded excellent performance in image coding applications, winning the JPEG 2000 contest of 1997 and thereby a position as a serious contender for the new standard.

Gaussian Quantizers: Shannon [465] showed that a Gaussian i.i.d. source had the worst rate-distortion function of any i.i.d. source with the same variance, thereby showing that the Gaussian source was an extremum in a source coding sense. It was long assumed and eventually proved by Sakrison in 1975 [456] that this provided a robust approach to quantization in the sense there exist vector quantizers designed for the i.i.d. Gaussian source with a given average distortion which will provide no worse distortion when applied to any i.i.d. source with the same variance. This provided an approach to *robust* vector quantization, having a code that might not be optimal for the actual source, but which would perform no worse than it would on the Gaussian source for which it was designed.

Sakrison extended the extremal properties of the rate distortion functions to sources with memory [453]–[455] and Lapidoth [306] (1997) showed that a code designed for a Gaussian source would yield essentially the same performance when applied to another process with the same covariance structure.

These results are essentially Shannon theory and hence should be viewed as primarily of interest for high-dimensional quantizers.

In a different approach toward using a Gaussian quantizer on an arbitrary source, Popat and Zeger (1992) took advantage of the central limit theorem and the known structure of an optimal scalar quantizer for a Gaussian random variable to code a general process by first filtering it to produce an approximately Gaussian density, scalar-quantizing the result, and then inverse-filtering to recover the original [419].

C. Robust Quantization

The Gaussian quantizers were described as being *robust* in a minimax average sense: a vector quantizer suitably designed for a Gaussian source will yield no worse average distortion for any source in the class of all sources with the same second-order properties. An alternative formulation of robust quantization is obtained if instead of dealing with average distortion, as is done in most of this paper, one places a maximum distortion requirement on quantizer design. Here a quantizer is considered to be robust if it bounds the maximum distortion for a class of sources. Morris and Vandelinde (1974) [361] developed the theory of robust quantization and provide conditions under which the uniform quantizer is optimum in this minimax sense. This can be viewed as a variation on epsilon entropy since the goal is to minimize the maximum distortion. Further results along this line may be found in [37], [275], [491]. Because these are minimax results aimed at scalar quantization, these results apply to any rate or dimension.

D. Universal Quantization

The minimax approaches provide one means of designing a fixed-rate quantizer for a source with unknown or partially known statistics: a quantizer can be designed that will perform no worse than a fixed value of distortion for all sources in some collection. An alternative approach is to be more greedy and try to design a code that yields nearly optimal performance regardless of which source within some collection is actually coded. This is the idea behind universal quantization.

Universal quantization or universal source coding had its origins in an approach to universal lossless compression developed by Rice and Plaunt [435], [436] and dubbed the "Rice machine." Their idea was to have a lossless coder that would work well for distinct sources by running multiple lossless codes in parallel and choosing the one producing the fewest bits for a period of time, sending a small amount of overhead to inform the decoder which code the encoder was using. The classic work on lossy universal source codes was Ziv's 1972 paper [577], which proved the existence of fixed-rate universal lossy codes under certain assumptions on the source statistics and the source and codebook alphabets. The multiple codebook idea was also used in 1974 [221] to extend the Shannon source coding theorem to nonergodic stationary sources by using the ergodic decomposition to interpret a nonergodic source as a universal coding problem for a family of ergodic sources. The idea is easily described and provides one means of constructing universal codes. Suppose that one has a collection of k-dimensional codebooks $\mathcal{C}_k$ with 2^{kR_k} codevectors, $k = 1, \cdots, K$, each designed for a different type of local behavior. For example, one might have different codebooks in an image coder for edges, textures, and gradients. The union codebook $\bigcup_{k=1}^{K} \mathcal{C}_k$ then contains all the codevectors in all of the codes, for a total of $\sum_{k=1}^{K} 2^{kR_k}$ codevectors. Thus for example, if all of the subcodebooks $\mathcal{C}_k$ have equal rate $R_k = R$, then the rate of the universal code is $R + k^{-1} \log K$

bits per symbol, which can be small if the dimension k is moderately large. This does not mean that it is necessary to use a large-dimensional VQ, since the VQ can be a product VQ, e.g., for an image one could have $k = 64$ by coding each square of dimension $8 \times 8 = 64$ using four applications of a VQ of dimension $4 \times 4 = 16$. If one had, say, four different codes, the resulting rate would be $R + 2/64 = R + 0.031$, which would be a small increase over the original rate if the original rate is, say, 0.25.

A universal code is in theory more complicated than an ordinary code, but in practice it can mean codes with smaller dimension might be more efficient since separate codebooks can be used for distinct short-term behavior.

Subsequently, a variety of notions of fixed-rate universal codes were considered and compared [382], and fixed-distortion codes with variable rate were developed by Mackenthun and Pursley [340] and Kieffer [277], [279].

As with the early development of block source codes, universal quantization during its early days in the 1970's was viewed as more of a method for developing the theory than as a practical code-design algorithm. The Rice machine, however, proved the practicality and importance of a simple multiple codebook scheme for handling composite sources.

These works all assumed the encoder and decoder to possess copies of the codebooks being used. Zeger, Bist, and Linder [566] considered systems where the codebooks are designed at the encoder, but must be also coded and transmitted to the decoder, as is commonly done in codebook replenishment [206].

A good review of the history of universal source coding through the early 1990's may be found in Kieffer (1993) [283].

Better performance tradeoffs can be achieved by allowing both rate and distortion to vary, and in 1996, Chou *et al.* [92] formulated the universal coding problem as an entropy-constrained vector quantization problem for a family of sources and provided existence proofs and Lloyd-style design algorithms for the collection of codebooks subject to a Lagrangian distortion measure, yielding a fixed rate-distortion slope optimization rather than fixed distortion or fixed rate. The clustering of codebooks was originally due to Chou [90] in 1991. High-resolution quantization theory was used to study rates of convergence with blocklength to the optimal performance, yielding results consistent with earlier convergence results developed by other means, e.g., Linder *et al.* [321]. The fixed-slope universal quantizer approach was further developed with other code structures and design algorithms by Yang *et al.* [558].

A different approach which more closely resembles traditional adaptive and codebook replenishment was developed by Zhang, Yang, Wei, and Liu [329], [575], [574]. Their approach, dubbed "gold washing," did not involve training, but rather created and removed codevectors according to the data received and an auxiliary random process in a way that could be tracked by a decoder without side information.

E. Dithering

Dithered quantization was introduced by Roberts [442] in 1962 as a means of randomizing the effects of uniform quantization so as to minimize visual artifacts. It was further developed for images by Limb (1969) [317] and for speech by Jayant and Rabiner (1972) [266]. Intuitively, the goal was to cause the reconstruction error to look more like signal-independent additive white noise. It turns out that for one type of dithering, this intuition is true. In a dithered quantizer, instead of quantizing an input signal X_n directly, one quantizes a signal $U_n = X_n + W_n$, where W_n is a random process, independent of the signal X_n, called a *dither* process. The dither process is usually assumed to be i.i.d.. There are two approaches to dithering. Roberts considered subtractive dithering, where the final reconstruction is formed as $\tilde{X} = q(X_n + W_n) - W_n$. An obvious problem is the need for the decoder to possess a copy of the dither signal. Nonsubtractive dithering forms the reproduction as $\hat{X} = q(X_n + W_n)$.

The principal theoretical property of nonsubtractive dithering was developed by Schuchman [461], who showed that the quantizer error

$$e_n = X_n - \tilde{X}_n = X_n - q(X_n + W_n) + W_n$$

is uniformly distributed on $(-\Delta/2, \Delta/2]$ and is independent of the original input signal X_n if and only if the quantizer does not overload and the characteristic function $M_W(ju) = E[e^{juW}]$ satisfies $M_W(j2\pi l/\Delta) = 0$; $l \neq 0$. Schuchman's conditions are satisfied, for example, if the dither signal has a uniform probability density function on $(-\Delta/2, \Delta/2]$. It follows from the work of Jayant and Rabiner [266] and Sripad and Snyder [477] (see also [216]) that Schuchman's condition implies that the sequence of quantization errors $\{e_n\}$ is independent. The case of uniform dither remains by far the most widely studied in the literature.

The subtractive dither result is nice mathematically because it promises a well-behaved quantization noise as well as quantization error. It is impractical in many applications, however, for two reasons. First, the receiver will usually not have a perfect analog link to the transmitter (or else the original signal could be sent in analog form) and hence a pseudorandom deterministic sequence must be used at both transmitter and receiver as proposed by Roberts. In this case, however, there will be no mathematical guarantee that the quantization error and noise have the properties which hold for genuinely random i.i.d. dither. Second, subtractive dither of a signal that indeed resembles a sample function of a memoryless random process is complicated to implement, requiring storage of the dither signal, high-precision arithmetic, and perfect synchronization. As a result, it is of interest to study the behavior of the quantization noise in a simple nonsubtractive dithered quantizer. Unlike subtractive dither, nonsubtractive dither is not capable of making the reconstruction error independent of the input signal (although claims to the contrary have been made in the literature). Proper choice of dithering function can, however, make the conditional moments of the reproduction error independent of the input signal. This can be practically important. For example, it can make the perceived quantization noise energy constant as an input signal fades from high intensity to low intensity, where otherwise it can (and does) exhibit strongly signal-dependent behavior. The properties of nonsubtractive dither were originally developed in unpublished work by Wright [542] in 1979 and Brinton [54] in 1984, and subsequently extended and refined with a variety of proofs [513], [512], [328], [227]. For any $k = 1, 2, \cdots$ necessary and sufficient conditions on the characteristic function M_W are known which ensure that the kth moment of the quantization noise $\epsilon_n = q(X_n + W_n) - X_n$ conditional on X_n does not depend on X_n. A sufficient condition is that the dither signal consists of the sum of k independent uniformly distributed random variables on $[-\Delta/2, \Delta/2]$. Unfortunately, this conditional independence of moments comes at the expense of a loss of fidelity. For example, if $k = 2$ then the quantizer noise power (the mean-squared error) will be

$$E[\epsilon^2|X] = E[\epsilon^2] = E[W^2] + \frac{\Delta^2}{12}.$$

This means that the power in the dither signal is directly added to that of the quantizer error in order to form the overall mean-squared error.

In addition to its role in whitening quantization noise and making the noise or its moments independent of the input, dithering has played a role in proofs of "universal quantization" results in information theory. For example, Ziv [578] showed that even without high resolution theory, uniform scalar quantization combined with dithering and vector lossless coding could yield performance within 0.75 bit/symbol of the rate-distortion function. Extensions to lattice quantization and variations of this result have been developed by Zamir and Feder [565].

F. Quantization for Noisy Channels

The separation theorem of information theory [464], [180] states that nearly optimal communication of an information source over a noisy channel can be accomplished by separately quantizing or source coding the source and channel coding or error-control coding the resulting encoded source for reliable transmission over a noisy channel. Moreover, these two coding functions can be designed separately, without knowledge of each other. The result is only for point-to-point communications, however, and it is a limiting result in the sense that large blocklengths and hence large complexity must be permitted. If one wishes to perform near the Shannon limit for moderate delay or blocklengths, or in multiuser situations, it is necessary to consider joint source and channel codes, codes which jointly consider quantization and reliable communication. It may not actually be necessary to combine the source and channel codes, but simply to jointly design them. There are a variety of code structures and design methods that have been considered for this purpose, many of which involve issues of channel coding which are well beyond the focus of this paper. Here we mention only schemes which can be viewed as quantizers which are modified for use on a noisy channel and not those schemes which involve explicit channel codes. More general discussions can be found, e.g., in [122].

One approach to designing quantizers for use on noisy channels is to replace the distortion measure with respect to which a quantizer is optimized by the expected distortion over the noisy channel. This simple modification of the distortion measure allows the channel statistics to be included in an optimal quantizer design formulation. Recently, the method has been referred to as "channel-optimized quantization," where the quantization might be scalar, vector, or trellis.

This approach was introduced in 1969 by Kurtenbach and Wintz [304] for scalar quantizers. A Shannon source coding theorem for trellis encoders using this distortion measure was proved in 1981 [135] and a Lloyd-style design algorithm for such encoders provided in 1987 [19]. A Lloyd algorithm for vector quantizers using the modified distortion measure was introduced in 1984 by Kumazawa, Kasahara, and Namekawa [303] and further studied in [157], [152], and [153]. The method has also been applied to tree-structured VQ [412]. It can be combined with a maximum-likelihood detector to further improve performance and permit progressive transmission over a noisy channel [411], [523]. Simulated annealing has also been used to design such quantizers [140], [152], [354].

Another approach to joint source and channel coding based on a quantizer structure and not explicitly involving typical channel-coding techniques is to design a scalar or vector quantizer for the source without regard to the channel, but then code the resulting indices in a way that ensures that small (large) Hamming distance of the channel codewords corresponds to small (large) distortion between the resulting reproduction codewords, essentially forcing the topology on the channel codewords to correspond to that of the resulting reproduction codewords. The codes that do this are often called index assignments. Several specific index assignment methods were considered by Rydbeck and Sundberg [448]. DeMarca and Jayant in 1987 [121] introduced an iterative search algorithm for designing index assignments for scalar quantizers, which was extended to vector quantization by Zeger and Gersho [568], who dubbed the approach "pseudo-Gray" coding. Other index assignment algorithms include [210], [543], [287]. For binary-symmetric channels and certain special sources and quantizers, analytical results have been obtained [555], [556], [250], [501], [112], [351], [42], [232], [233], [352]. For example, it was shown by Crimmins et al. in 1969 [112] that the index assignment that minimizes mean-squared error for a uniform scalar quantizer used on a binary-symmetric channel is the natural binary assignment. However, this result remained relatively unknown until rederived and generalized in [351].

When source and channel codes are considered together, a key issue is the determination of the quantization rate to be used when the total of number of channel symbols per source symbol is held fixed. For example, as quantization rate is increased, the quantization noise decreases, but channel-induced noise increases because the ability of the channel code to protect the bits is reduced. Clearly, there is an optimal choice of quantization rate. Another issue is the determination of the rate at which overall distortion decreases in an optimal system as the total number of channel uses per source symbol increases. These issues have been addressed in recent papers by Zeger and Manzella [570] and Hochwald and Zeger [244], which use both exponential formulas produced by high resolution quantization theory and exponential bounds to channel coding error probability.

There are a variety of other approaches to joint source and channel coding, including the use of codes with a channel encoder structure optimized for the source or with a special decoder matched to the source, using unequal error protection to better protect more important (lower resolution) reproduction indices, jointly optimized combinations of source and channel codes, and combinations of channel-optimized quantizers with source-optimized channel codes, but we leave these to the literature as they involve a heavy dose of channel coding ideas.

G. Quantizing Noisy Sources

A parallel problem to quantizing for a noisy channel is quantizing for a noisy source. The problem can be seen as trying to compress a dirty source into a clean reproduction, or as doing estimation of the original source based on a quantized version of a noise-corrupted version. If the underlying statistics are known or can be estimated by a training sequence, then this can be treated as a quantization problem with a modified distortion measure, where now the distortion between a noise-corrupted observation $Y = y$ of an unseen original X and a reconstruction $\hat{x}$ based on the encoded and decoded y is given as the conditional expectation $E[d(X, \hat{x})|Y = y]$. The usefulness of this modified distortion for source-coding noisy sources was first seen by Dobrushin and Tsybakov (1962) [134] and was used by Fine (1965) [162] and Sakrison (1968) [452] to obtain information-theoretic bounds an quantization and source coding for noisy sources. Berger (1971) [46] explicitly used the modified distortion in his study of Shannon source coding theorems for noise-corrupted sources.

In 1970, Wolf and Ziv [537] used the modified distortion measure for a squared-error distortion to prove that the optimal quantizer for the modified distortion could be decomposed into the cascade of a minimum mean-squared error estimator followed by an optimal quantizer for the estimated original source. This result was subsequently extended to a more general class of distortion measures include the input-weighted quadratic distortion of Ephraim and Gray [145], where a generalized Lloyd algorithm for design was presented.

Related results and approaches can be found in Witsenhausen's (1980) [535] treatment of rate-distortion theory with modified (or "indirect") distortion measures, and in the Occam filters of Natarajan (1995) [370].

H. Multiple Description Quantization

A topic closely related to quantization for noisy channels is multiple description quantization. The problem is usually formulated as a source-coding or quantization problem over a network, but it is most easily described in terms of packet communications. In the simplest case, suppose that two packets of information, each of rate R, are transmitted to describe a reproduction of a single random vector X. The encoder might receive one or the other packet or the two together and wishes to provide the best reconstruction possible for the bit rate it receives. This can be viewed as a network problem with one receiver seeing only one channel, another receiver seeing the second channel, and a third reciever seeing both channels, and the goal is that each have an optimal reconstruction for the total received bitrate. Clearly, one can do no better than having each packet alone result in in a reproduction with distortion near the Shannon distortion-rate function $D(R)$ while simultaneously having the two packets together yield a reproduction with distortion near $D(2R)$, but this optimistic performance is in general not possible. This problem was first tackled in the information theory community in 1980 by Wolf, Wyner, and Ziv [536] and Ozarow [401] who developed achievable rate regions and lower bounds to performance. The results were extended by Ahlswede (1985) [6], El Gamal and Cover (1982) [139], and Zhang and Berger (1987) [573].

In 1993, Vaishampayan et al. used a Lloyd algorithm to actually design fixed-rate [508] and entropy-constrained [509] scalar quantizers for the multiple description problem. High-resolution quantization ideas were used to evaluate achievable performance in 1998 by Vaishampayan and Batllo [510] and Linder, Zamir, and Zeger [324]. An alternative approach to multiple-description quantization using transform coding has also been considered, e.g., in [38] and [211].

I. Other Applications

We have not treated many interesting variations and applications of quantization, several of which have been successfully analyzed or designed using the tools described here. Examples which we would have included had time, space, and patience been more plentiful include mismatch results for quantizers designed for one distribution and applied to another, quantizers designed to provide inputs to classification, detection, or estimation systems, quantizers in multiuser systems such as simple networks, quantizers implicit in finite-precision arithmetic (the modern form of roundoff error), and quantization in noise-shaping analog-to-digital and digital-to-analog converters such as $\Delta\Sigma$-modulators. Doubtless we have failed to mention a few, but this list suffices to demonstrate how rich the theoretical and applied fields of quantization have become in their half century of active development.

ACKNOWLEDGMENT

The authors gratefully acknowledge the many helpful comments, corrections, and suggestions from colleagues, students, and reviewers. Of particular assistance were A. Gersho, B. Girod, N. Kashyap, T. Linder, N. Moayeri, P. Moo, Y. Shtarkov, S. Verdú, M. Vetterli, and K. Zeger.

REFERENCES

[1] E. Abaya and G. L. Wise, "Some notes on optimal quantization," in *Proc. Int. Conf. Communications,* June 1981, vol. 2, pp. 30.7.1–30.7.5.
[2] H. Abut, *Vector Quantization* (IEEE Reprint Collection). Piscataway, NJ: IEEE Press, 1990.
[3] J. P. Adoul, C. Collin, and D. Dalle, "Block encoding and its application to data compression of PCM speech," in *Proc. Canadian Communications and EHV Conf.* (Montreal, Que., Canada, 1978), pp. 145–148.
[4] J.-P. Adoul, J.-L. Debray, and D. Dalle, "Spectral distance measure applied to the optimum design of DPCM coders with L predictors," in *Proc. IEEE Int. Conf. Acoustics, Speech and Signal Processing (ICASSP)* (Denver, CO, 1980), pp. 512–515.
[5] E. Agrell and T. Eriksson, "Optimization of lattices for quantization," *IEEE Trans. Inform. Theory,* vol. 44, pp. 1814–1828, Sept. 1998. This work also appears in "Lattice-based quantization, Part I" Dept. Inform.

Theory, Chalmers Univ. Technol., Goteborg, Sweden, Rep. 17, Oct. 1996.

[6] R. Ahlswede, "The rate-distortion region for multiple descriptions without excess rate," *IEEE Trans. Inform. Theory*, vol. IT-31, pp. 721–726, Nov. 1985.

[7] N. Ahmed, T. Natarajan, and K. Rao, "Discrete cosine transform," *IEEE Trans. Comput.*, vol. C-23, pp. 90–93, 1974.

[8] V. R. Algazi, "Useful approximation to optimum quantization," *IEEE Trans. Commun.*, vol. COM-14, pp. 297–301, June 1966.

[9] M. R. Anderberg, *Cluster Analysis for Applications.* San Diego, CA: Academic, 1973.

[10] J. B. Anderson and J. B. Bodie, "Tree encoding of speech," *IEEE Trans. Inform. Theory*, vol. IT-20, pp. 379–387, 1975.

[11] J. B. Anderson and F. Jelinek, "A 2-cycle algorithm for source coding with a fidelity criterion," *IEEE Trans. Inform. Theory*, vol. IT-19, pp. 77–92, Jan. 1973.

[12] M. Antonini, M. Barlaud, P. Mathieu, and I. Daubechies, "Image coding using vector quantization in the wavelet transform domain," in *Proc. IEEE Int. Conf. Acoustics, Speech and Signal Processing (ICASSP)* (Albuquerque, NM, Apr. 1990), pp. 2297–2300.

[13] M. Antonini, M. Barlaud, and P. Mathieu, "Image coding using lattice vector quantization of wavelet coefficients," in *Proc. IEEE Int. Conf. Acoustics, Speech and Signal Processing (ICASSP)* (Toronto, Ont., Canada, May 1991), vol. 4, pp. 2273–2276.

[14] M. Antonini, M. Barlaud, P. Mathieu, and I. Daubechies, "Image coding using wavelet transform," *IEEE Trans. Image Processing*, vol. 1, pp. 205–220, Apr. 1992.

[15] R. Aravind and A. Gersho, "Low-rate image coding with finite-state vector quantization," in *Proc. Int. Conf. Acoustics, Speech and Signal Processing (ICASSP)*, (Tokyo, Japan, 1986), pp. 137–140.

[16] ——, "Image compression based on vector quantization with finite memory," *Opt. Eng.*, vol. 26, pp. 570–580, July 1987.

[17] D. S. Arnstein, "Quantization error in predictive coders," *IEEE Trans. Commun.*, vol. COM-23, pp. 423–429, Apr. 1975.

[18] E. Ayanoğlu and R. M. Gray, "The design of predictive trellis waveform coders using the generalized Lloyd algorithm," *IEEE Trans. Commun.*, vol. COM-34, pp. 1073–1080, Nov. 1986.

[19] ——, "The design of joint source and channel trellis waveform coders," *IEEE Trans. Inform. Theory*, vol. IT-33, pp. 855–865, Nov. 1987.

[20] R. L. Baker and R. M. Gray, "Image compression using nonadaptive spatial vector quantization," in *Conf. Rec. 16th Asilomar Conf. Circuits Systems and Computers* (Asilomar, CA, Nov. 1982), pp. 55–61.

[21] ——, "Differential vector quantization of achromatic imagery," in *Proc. Int. Picture Coding Symp.*, Mar. 1983, pp. 105–106.

[22] M. Balakrishnan, W. A. Pearlman, and L. Lu, "Variable-rate tree-structured vector quantizers," *IEEE Trans. Inform. Theory*, vol. 41, pp. 917–930, July 1995.

[23] A. S. Balamesh, "Block-constrained methods of fixed-rate entropy constrained quantization," Ph.D. dissertation, Univ. Michigan, Ann Arbor, Jan. 1993.

[24] A. S. Balamesh and D. L. Neuhoff, "New methods of fixed-rate entropy-coded quantization," in *Proc. 1992 Conf. Information Sciences and Systems* (Princeton, NJ, Mar. 1992), pp. 665–670.

[25] ——, Unpublished notes, 1992.

[26] ——, "Block-constrained quantization: Asymptotic analysis," *DI-MACS Ser. Discr. Math. and Theoretical Comput. Sci.*, vol. 14, pp. 67–74, 1993.

[27] ——, "A new fixed-rate quantization scheme based on arithmetic coding," in *Proc. IEEE Int. Symp. Information Theory* (San Antonio, TX, Jan. 1993), p. 435.

[28] ——, "Block-constrained methods of fixed-rate entropy-coded, scalar quantization," *IEEE Trans. Inform. Theory*, submitted for publication.

[29] G. B. Ball, "Data analysis in the social sciences: What about the details?," in *Proc. Fall Joint Computing Conf.* Washington, DC: Spartan, 1965, pp. 533–559.

[30] M. Barlaud, P. Solé, T. Gaidon, M. Antonini, and P. Mathieu, "Pyramidal lattice vector quantization for multiscale image coding," *IEEE Trans. Image Processing*, vol. 3, pp. 367–381, July 1994.

[31] C. F. Barnes, "New multiple path search technique for residual vector quantizers," in *Proc. Data Compression Conf.* (Snowbird, UT, 1994), pp. 42–51.

[32] C. F. Barnes and R. L. Frost, "Vector quantizers with direct sum codebooks," *IEEE Trans. Inform. Theory*, vol. 39, pp. 565–580, Mar. 1993.

[33] C. F. Barnes, S. A. Rizvi, and N. M. Nasrabadi, "Advances in residual vector quantization: A review," *IEEE Trans. Image Processing*, vol. 5, pp. 226–262, Feb. 1996.

[34] C. W. Barnes, B. N. Tran, and S. H. Leung, "On the statistics of fixed-point roundoff error," *IEEE Trans. Acoust., Speech, Signal Processing*, vol. ASSP-3, pp. 595–606, June 1985.

[35] E. S. Barnes and N. J. A. Sloane, "The optimal lattice quantizer in three dimensions," *SIAM J. Alg. Discr. Methods*, vol. 4, pp. 30–41, Mar. 1983.

[36] P. Bartlett, T. Linder, and G. Lugosi, "The minimax distortion redundancy in empirical quantizer design," *IEEE Trans. Inform. Theory*, vol. 44, pp. 1802–1813, Sept. 1998.

[37] W. G. Bath and V. D. Vandelinde, "Robust memoryless quantization for minimum signal distortion," *IEEE Trans. Inform. Theory*, vol. IT-28, pp. 296–306, 1982.

[38] J.-C. Batllo and V. A. Vaishampayan, "Asymptotic performance of multiple description codes," *IEEE Trans. Inform. Theory*, vol. 43, pp. 703–707, Mar. 1997.

[39] C. D. Bei and R. M. Gray, "An improvement of the minimum distortion encoding algorithm for vector quantization," *IEEE Trans. Commun.*, vol. COM-33, pp. 1132–1133, Oct. 1985.

[40] ——, "Simulation of vector trellis encoding systems," *IEEE Trans. Commun.*, vol. COM-34, pp. 214–218, Mar. 1986.

[41] P. Bello, R. Lincoln, and H. Gish, "Statistical delta modulation," *Proc. IEEE*, vol. 55, pp. 308–319, Mar. 1967.

[42] G. Ben-David and D. Malah, "On the performance of a vector quantizer under channel errors," in *Signal Proc. VI: Theories and Applications, Proc. EUSIPCO'92*, 1992, pp. 1685–1688.

[43] W. R. Bennett, "Spectra of quantized signals," *Bell Syst. Tech. J.*, vol. 27, pp. 446–472, July 1948.

[44] J. L. Bentley, "Multidimensional binary search trees used for associative searching," *Commun. Assoc. Comput. Mach.*, pp. 209–226, Sept. 1975.

[45] T. Berger, "Rate distortion theory for sources with abstract alphabet and memory," *Inform. Contr.*, vol. 13, pp. 254–273, 1968.

[46] ——, *Rate Distortion Theory.* Englewood Cliffs, NJ: Prentice-Hall, 1971.

[47] ——, "Optimum quantizers and permutation codes," *IEEE Trans. Inform. Theory*, vol. IT-18, pp. 759–765, Nov. 1972.

[48] ——, "Minimum entropy quantizers and permutation codes," *IEEE Trans. Inform. Theory*, vol. IT-28, pp. 149–157, Mar. 1982.

[49] T. Berger, F. Jelinek, and J. K. Wolf, "Permutation codes for sources," *IEEE Trans. Inform. Theory*, vol. IT-18, pp. 160–169, Jan. 1972.

[50] V. Bhaskaran and K. Konstantinides, *Image and Video Compression Standards.* Boston, MA: Kluwer, 1995.

[51] H. S. Black, "Pulse code modulation," *Bell Lab. Rec.*, vol. 25, pp. 265–269, July 1947.

[52] R. E. Blahut, "Computation of channel capacity and rate-distortion functions," *IEEE Trans. Inform. Theory*, vol. IT-18, pp. 460–473, July 1972.

[53] L. Breiman, J. H. Friedman, R. A. Olshen, and C. J. Stone, *Classification and Regression Trees.* Belmont, CA: Wadsworth, 1984.

[54] L. K. Brinton, "Nonsubtractive dither," M.S. thesis, Elec. Eng. Dept., Univ. Utah, Salt Lake City, UT, Aug. 1984.

[55] J. D. Bruce, "On the optimum quantization of stationary signals," in *1964 IEEE Int. Conv. Rec.*, 1964, pt. 1, pp. 118–124.

[56] J. A. Bucklew, "Companding and random quantization in several dimensions," *IEEE Trans. Inform. Theory*, vol. IT-27, pp. 207–211, Mar. 1981.

[57] ——, "A note on optimal multidimensional companders," *IEEE Trans. Inform. Theory*, vol. IT-29, p. 279, Mar. 1983.

[58] ——, "Two results on the asymptotic performance of quantizers," *IEEE Trans. Inform. Theory*, vol. IT-30, pp. 341–348, Mar. 1984.

[59] ——, "A note on the absolute epsilon entropy," *IEEE Trans. Inform. Theory*, vol. 37, pp. 142–144, Jan. 1991.

[60] J. A. Bucklew and N. C. Gallagher, Jr., "A note on optimum quantization," *IEEE Trans. Inform. Theory*, vol. IT-25, pp. 365–366, May 1979.

[61] ——, "Quantization schemes for bivariate Gaussian random variables," *IEEE Trans. Inform. Theory*, vol. IT-25, pp. 537–543, Sept. 1979.

[62] ——, "Two-dimensional quantization of bivariate circularly symmetric densities," *IEEE Trans. Inform. Theory*, vol. IT-25, pp. 667–671, Nov. 1979.

[63] ——, "Some properties of uniform step size quantizers," *IEEE Trans. Inform. Theory*, vol. IT-26, pp. 610–613, Sept. 1980.

[64] J. A. Bucklew and G. L. Wise, "Multidimensional asymptotic quantization theory with rth power distortion measures, *IEEE Trans. Inform. Theory*, vol. IT-28, pp. 239–247, Mar. 1982.

[65] J. Buhmann and H. Kühnel, "Vector quantization with complexity costs," *IEEE Trans. Inform. Theory*, vol. 39, pp. 1133–1145, July 1988.

[66] P. J. Burt and E. H. Adelson, "The Laplacian pyramid as a compact image code," *IEEE Trans. Commun.*, vol. COM-31, pp. 532–540, Apr. 1983.

[67] A. Buzo, R. M. Gray, A. H. Gray, Jr., and J. D. Markel, "Optimal quantizations of coefficient vectors in LPC speech," in *1978 Joint Meet. Acoustical Society of America and the Acoustical Society of Japan* (Honolulu, HI, Dec. 1978).

[68] A. Buzo, A. H. Gray, Jr., R. M. Gray, and J. D. Markel, "Optimal quantizations of coefficient vectors in LPC, speech," in *Proc. IEEE Int. Conf. Acoustics, Speech, and Signal Processing (ICASSP)* (Washington, DC, Apr. 1979), pp. 52–55.

[69] ——, "Speech coding based upon vector quantization," *IEEE Trans. Acoust., Speech, Signal Processing*, vol. ASSP-28, pp. 562–574, Oct. 1980.

[70] S. Cambanis and N. Gerr, "A simple class of asymptotically optimal quantizers," *IEEE Trans. Inform. Theory*, vol. IT-29, pp. 664–676, Sept. 1983.

[71] J. C. Candy and O. J. Benjamin, "The structure of quantization noise from Sigma-Delta modulation," *IEEE Trans. Commun.*, vol. COM-29, pp. 1316–1323, Sept. 1981.

[72] J. Candy and G. Temes, Eds. *Oversampling Delta-Sigma Data Converters.* New York: IEEE Press, 1991.

[73] R. M. Capocelli and A. DeSantis, "Variations on a theme by Gallager," in *Image and Text Compression*, J. A. Storer, Ed. Boston, MA: Kluwer, 1992, pp. 181–213.

[74] J. R. Caprio, N. Westin, and J. Esposito, "Optimum quantization for minimum distortion," in *Proc. Int Telemetering Conf.*, 1978, pp. 315–323.

[75] N. Chaddha, M. Vishwanath, and P. A. Chou, "Hierarchical vector quantization of perceptually weighted block transforms," in *Proc. Compression Conf.* (Snowbird, UT). Los Alamitos, CA: IEEE Comp. Soc. Press, 1995, pp. 3–12.

[76] D. L. Chaffee, "Applications of rate distortion theory to the bandwidth compression," Ph.D. dissertation, Elec. Eng. Dept., Univ. California, Los Angeles, 1975.

[77] D. L. Chaffee and J. K. Omura, "A very low rate voice compression system," in *Abstracts of Papers IEEE Int. Symp. Information Theory*, Oct. 1974.

[78] C.-K. Chan and L.-M. Po, "A complexity reduction technique for image vector quantization," *IEEE Trans. Image Processing*, vol. 1, pp. 312–321, July 1992.

[79] W.-Y. Chan and A. Gersho, "High fidelity audio transform coding with vector quantization," in *Proc. IEEE Int. Conf. Acoustics, Speech, and Signal Processing (ICASSP)* (Albuquerque, NM, Apr. 1990), vol. 2, pp. 1109–1112.

[80] ——, "Constrained-storage vector quantization in high fidelity audio transform coding," in *Proc. IEEE Int. Conf. Acoustiics, Speech, and Signal Processing (ICASSP)* (Toronto, Ont., Canada, May 1991), pp. 3597–3600.

[81] ——, "Enhanced multistage vector quantization by joint codebook design," *IEEE Trans. Commun.*, vol. 40, pp. 1693–1697, Nov. 1992.

[82] ——, "Generalized product code vector quantization: a family of efficient techniques for signal compression," *Digital Signal Processing*, vol. 4, pp. 95–126, 1994.

[83] W.-Y. Chan, S. Gupta, and A. Gersho, "Enhanced multistage vector quantization by joint codebook design," *IEEE Trans. Commun.*, vol. 40, pp. 1693–1697, Nov. 1992.

[84] Y.-H. Chan and W. Siu, "In search of the optimal searching sequence for VQ encoding," *IEEE Trans. Commun.*, vol. 43, pp. 2891–2893, Dec. 1995.

[85] P. C. Chang and R. M. Gray, "Gradient algorithms for designing predictive vector quantizers," *IEEE Trans. Acoust., Speech, Signal Processing*, vol. ASSP-34, pp. 679–690, Aug. 1986.

[86] P. C. Chang, J. May, and R. M. Gray, "Hierarchical vector quantizers with table-lookup encoders," in *Proc. 1985 IEEE Int. Conf. Communications*, June 1985, vol. 3, pp. 1452–1455.

[87] D. T. S. Chen, "On two or more dimensional optimum quantizers," in *Proc. IEEE Int. Conf. Acoustics, Speech, and Signal Processing (ICASSP)* (Hartford, CT, 1977), pp. 640–643.

[88] D.-Y. Cheng, A. Gersho, B. Ramamurthi, and Y. Shoham, "Fast search algorithms for vector quantization and pattern matching," in *Proc. IEEE Int. Conf. Acoust.ics, Speech, and Signal Processing (ICASSP)* (San Diego, CA, Mar. 1984), pp. 911.1–911.4.

[89] D.-Y. Cheng and A. Gersho, "A fast codebook search algorithm for nearest-neighbor pattern matching," in *Proc. IEEE Int. Conf. Acoustics, Speech, and Signal Processing (ICASSP)* (Tokyo, Japan, Apr. 1986), vol. 1, pp. 265–268.

[90] P. A. Chou, "Code clustering for weighted universal VQ and other applications," in *Proc. IEEE Int. Symp. Information Theory* (Budapest, Hungary, 1991), p. 253.

[91] ——, "The distortion of vector quantizers trained on n vectors decreases to the optimum as $O_p(1/n)$," in *Proc. IEEE Int. Symp. Information Theory* (Trondheim, Norway, 1994).

[92] P. A. Chou, M. Effros, and R. M. Gray, "A vector quantization approach to universal noiseless coding and quantization," *IEEE Trans. Inform. Theory*, vol. 42, pp. 1109–1138, July 1996.

[93] P. A. Chou, T. Lookabaugh, and R. M. Gray, "Entropy-constrained vector quantization," *IEEE Trans. Acoust., Speech, Signal Processing*, vol. 37, pp. 31–42, Jan. 1989.

[94] ——, "Optimal pruning with applications to tree-structured source coding and modeling," *IEEE Trans. Inform. Theory*, vol. 35, pp. 299–315, Mar. 1989

[95] P. A. Chou and T. Lookabaugh, "Conditional entropy-constrained vector quantization of linear predictive coefficients," in *Proc. Int. Conf. Acoustics, Speech, and Signal Processing*, 1990, pp. 187–200.

[96] J. Chow and T. Berger, "Failure of successive refinement for symmetric Gaussian mixtures," *IEEE Trans. Inform. Theory*, vol. 43, pp. 350–352, Jan. 1957.

[97] T. A. C. M. Claasen and A. Jongepier, "Model for the power spectral density of quantization noise," *IEEE Trans. Acoust., Speech, Signal Processing*, vol. ASSP-29, pp. 914–917, Aug. 1981.

[98] R. J. Clarke, *Transform Coding of Images.* Orlando, FL: Academic, 1985.

[99] A. G. Clavier, P. F. Panter, and D. D. Grieg, "Distortion in a pulse count modulation system," *AIEE Trans.*, vol. 66, pp. 989–1005, 1947.

[100] ——, "PCM, distortion analysis," *Elec. Eng.*, pp. 1110–1122, Nov. 1947.

[101] D. Cohn, E. Riskin, and R. Ladner, "Theory and practice of vector quantizers trained on small training sets," *IEEE Trans. Pattern Anal. Machine Intell.*, vol. 16, pp. 54–65, Jan. 1994.

[102] R. R. Coifman and M. V. Wickerhauser. "Entropy-based algorithms for best basis selection," *IEEE Trans. Inform. Theory*, vol. 38, pp. 713–718, Mar. 1992.

[103] J. H. Conway and N. J. A. Sloane, "Voronoi regions of lattices, second moments of polytopes, and quantization," *IEEE Trans. Inform. Theory*, vol. IT-28, pp. 211–226, Mar. 1982.

[104] ——, "Fast quantizing and decoding algorithms for lattice quantizers and codes," *IEEE Trans. Inform. Theory*, vol. IT-28, pp. 227–232, Mar. 1982.

[105] ——, "A fast encoding method for lattice codes and quantizers, *IEEE Trans. Inform. Theory*, vol. IT-29, pp. 820–824, Nov. 1983.

[106] ——, *Sphere Packings,Lattices and Groups.* New York: Springer-Verlag, 1988.

[107] P. C. Cosman, R. M. Gray, and M. Vetterli, "Vector quantization of image subbands: A survey," *IEEE Trans. Image Processing*, vol. 5, pp. 202–225, Feb. 1996.

[108] P. C. Cosman, K. O. Perlmutter, S. M. Perlmutter, R. M. Gray, and R. A. Olshen, "Training sequence size and vector quantizer performance," in *Proc. 25th Annu. Asilomar Conf. Signals, Systems, and Computers* (Pacific Grove, CA, Nov. 1991), pp. 434–438.

[109] P. C. Cosman, S. M. Perlmutter, and K. O. Perlmutter, "Tree-structured vector quantization with significance map for wavelet image coding," in *Proc. 1995 IEEE Data Compression Conf. (DCC)*, J. A. Storer and M. Cohn, Eds. Los Alamitos, CA: IEEE Comp. Soc. Press, Mar. 1995.

[110] T. M. Cover and J. A. Thomas, *Elements of Information Theory.* Chichester, U.K.: Wiley, 1991.

[111] D. R. Cox, "Note on grouping," *J. Amer. Statist. Assoc.*, vol. 52, 543–547, 1957.

[112] T. R. Crimmins, H. M. Horwitz, C. J. Palermo, and R. V. Palermo, "Minimization of mean-squared error for data transmitted via group codes," *IEEE Trans. Inform. Theory*, vol. IT-15, pp. 72–78, Jan. 1969.

[113] R. E. Crochiere, S. M. Webber, and J. K. L. Flanagan, "Digital coding of speech in sub-bands," *Bell Syst. Tech. J.*, vol. 55, pp. 1069–1086, Oct. 1976.

[114] I. Csiszár, "Generalized entropy and quantization problems," in *Proc. 6th Prague Conf.*, 1973, pp. 159–174.

[115] I. Csiszár and J. Körner, *Information Theory: Coding Theorems for Discrete Memoryless Systems.* New York: Academic, 1981.

[116] V. Cuperman and A. Gersho, "Vector predictive coding of speech at 16 Kb/s," *IEEE Trans. Commun.*, vol. COM-33, pp. 685–696, July 1985.

[117] C. C. Cutler, "Differential quantization of communication signals," U.S. Patent 2 605 361, July 29, 1952.

[118] T. Dalenius, "The problem of optimum stratification," *Skand. Aktuarietidskrift*, vol. 33, pp. 201–213, 1950.

[119] T. Dalenius and M. Gurney, "The problem of optimum stratification II," *Skand. Aktuarietidskrift*, vol. 34, pp. 203–213, 1951.

[120] E. M. Deloraine and A. H. Reeves, "The 25th anniversary of pulse code modulation," *IEEE Spectrum*, pp. 56–64, May 1965.

[121] J. R. B. DeMarca and N. S. Jayant, "An algorithm for assigning binary indices to the codevectors of multidimensional quantizers," in *Proc.*

IEEE Int. Conf. Communications, June 1987, pp. 1128–1132.

[122] N. Demir and K. Sayood "Joint source/channel coding for variable length codes," in *Proc. 1998 IEEE Data Compression Conf.*, J. A. Storer and M. Cohn, Eds. Los Alamitos, CA: Computer Soc. Press, Mar. 1998, pp. 139–148.

[123] C. R. Davis and M. E. Hellman, "On tree coding with a fidelity criterion," *IEEE Trans. Inform. Theory*, vol. IT-21, pp. 373–378, July 1975.

[124] L. D. Davisson, "Information rates for data compression," in *IEEE WESCON*, Session 8, Paper 1, 1968.

[125] L. D. Davisson and R. M. Gray, Eds., *Data Compression, vol. 14*, in *Benchmark Papers in Electrical Engineering and Computer Science.* Stroudsburg, PA: Dowden, Hutchinson, and Ross, 1976.

[126] L. D. Davisson, A. Leon-Garcia, and D. L. Neuhoff, "New results on coding of stationary nonergodic sources," *IEEE Trans. Inform. Theory*, vol. IT-25, pp. 137–144, Mar. 1979.

[127] L. D. Davisson and M. B. Pursley, "A direct proof of the coding theorem for discrete sources with memory," *IEEE Trans. Inform. Theory*, vol. IT-21, pp. 301–310, May 1975.

[128] F. DeJager, "Delta modulation, a method of PCM transmission using a one-unit code," *Philips Res. Repts.*, vol. 7, 1952.

[129] B. Derjavitch, E. M. Deloraine, and V. Mierlo, French Patent 932 140, Aug. 1946.

[130] R. A. DeVore, B. Jawerth, and B. Lucier, "Image compression through wavelet transform coding," *IEEE Trans. Inform. Theory*, vol. 38, pp. 719–746, Mar. 1992.

[131] L. Devroye, L. Györfi, and G. Lugosi, *A Probabilistic Theory of Pattern Recognition.* New York: Springer, 1996.

[132] R. J. Dick, T. Berger, and F. Jelinek, "Tree encoding of Gaussian sources," *IEEE Trans. Inform. Theory*, vol. IT-20, pp. 332–336, May 1974.

[133] E. Diday and J. C. Simon, "Clustering analysis," in *Digital Pattern Recognition*, K. S. Fu, Ed. New York: Springer-Verlag, 1976.

[134] R. L. Dobrushin and B. S. Tsybakov, "Information transmission with additional noise," *IRE Trans. Inform. Theory*, vol. IT-8, pp. S293–S304, 1962.

[135] J. G. Dunham and R. M. Gray, "Joint source and noisy channel trellis encoding," *IEEE Trans. Inform. Theory*, vol. IT-27, pp. 516–519, July 1981.

[136] M. Ostendorf Dunham and R. M. Gray, "An algorithm for the design of labeled-transition finite-state vector quantizers," *IEEE Trans. Commun.*, vol. COM-33, pp. 83–89, Jan. 1985.

[137] J. G. Dunn, "The performance of a class of n dimensional quantizers for a Gaussian source," in *Proc. Columbia Symp. Signal Transmission Processing* (Columbia Univ., New York, 1965), pp. 76–81; reprinted in *Data Compression* (Benchmark Papers in Electrical Engineering and Computer Science, vol. 14), L. D. Davisson and R. M. Gray, Eds. Stroudsberg, PA: Dowden, Hutchinson and Ross, 1975.

[138] M. Effros, P. A. Chou, and R. M. Gray, "Variable-rate source coding theorems for stationary nonergodic sources," *IEEE Trans. Inform. Theory*, vol. 40, pp. 1920–1925, Nov. 1994.

[139] A. E. El Gamal and T. M. Cover, "Achievable rates for multiple descriptions," *IEEE Trans. Inform. Theory*, vol. IT-28, pp. 851–857, Nov. 1982.

[140] A. E. El Gamal, L. A. Hemachandra, I. Shperling, and V. K. Wei, "Using simulated annealing to design good codes," *IEEE Trans. Inform. Theory*, vol. IT-33, pp. 116–123, Jan. 1987.

[141] P. Elias, "Predictive coding," Ph.D. dissertation, Harvard Univ., Cambridge, MA, 1950.

[142] ——, "Predictive coding I, and II," *IRE Trans. Inform. Theory*, vol. IT-1, pp. 16–33, Mar. 1955.

[143] ——, "Bounds on performance of optimum quantizers," *IEEE Trans. Inform. Theory*, vol. IT-16, pp. 172–184, Mar. 1970.

[144] ——, "Bounds and asymptotes for the performance of multivariate quantizers," *Ann. Math. Statist.*, vol. 41, no. 4, pp. 1249–1259, 1970.

[145] Y. Ephraim and R. M. Gray, "A unified approach for encoding clean and noisy sources by means of waveform and autoregressive vector quantization," *IEEE Trans. Inform. Theory*, vol. 34, pp. 826–834, July 1988.

[146] W. H. Equitz, "A new vector quantization clustering algorithm," *IEEE Trans. Acoust., Speech, Signal Processing*, vol. 37, pp. 1568–1575, Oct. 1989.

[147] W. Equitz and T. Cover, "Successive refinement of information," *IEEE Trans. Inform. Theory*, vol. 37, pp. 269–275, Mar. 1991.

[148] T. Ericson, "A result on delay-less information transmission," in *Abstracts IEEE Int. Symp. Information Theory* (Grignano, Italy, June, 1979).

[149] T. Eriksson and E. Agrell, "Lattice-based quantization, Part II," Rep. 18, Dept. Inform. Theory, Chalmers Univ. Technol., Goteborg, Sweden,

Oct. 1996.

[150] A. M. Eskicioğlu and P. S. Fisher, "Image quality measures and their performance," *IEEE Trans. Commun.*, vol. 43, pp. 2959–2965, Dec. 1995.

[151] M. Vedat Eyuboğlu and G. D. Forney, Jr., "Lattice and trellis quantization with lattice- and trellis-bounded codebooks-high-rate theory for memoryless sources," *IEEE Trans. Inform. Theory*, vol. 39, pp. 46–59, Jan. 1993.

[152] N. Farvardin, "A study of vector quantization for noisy channels," *IEEE Trans. Inform. Theory*, vol. 36, pp. 799–809, July 1990.

[153] ——, "On the performance and complexity of channel optimized vector quantizers," in *Speech Recognition and Coding: New Advances and Trends,* Berlin, Germany: Springer, 1995, pp. 699–704.

[154] N. Farvardin and F. Y. Lin, "Performance of entropy-constrained block transform quantizers," *IEEE Trans. Inform. Theory*, vol. 37, pp. 1433–1439, Sept. 1991.

[155] N. Farvardin and J. W. Modestino, "Optimal quantizer performance for a class of non-Gaussian memoryless sources," *IEEE Trans. Inform. Theory*, vol. IT-30, pp. 485–497, May 1984.

[156] ——, "Rate-distortion performance of DPCM schemes," *IEEE Trans. Inform. Theory*, vol. IT-31, pp. 402–418, May 1985.

[157] N. Farvardin and V. Vaishampayan, "Optimal quantizer design for noisy channels: An approach to combined source-channel coding," *IEEE Trans. Inform. Theory*, vol. IT-33, pp. 827–838, Nov. 1987.

[158] L. Fejes Toth, *Lagerungen in der Ebene, auf der Kugel und im Raum.* Berlin, Germany: Springer Verlag, 1953.

[159] ——, "Sur la representation d'une population infinie par un nombre fini d'elements," *Acta Math. Acad. Sci. Hung.*, vol. 10, pp. 76–81, 1959.

[160] Y. S. Feng and N. M. Nasrabadi, "Dynamic address-vector quantization of RGB color images," *Proc. Inst. Elec. Eng., Part I, Commun. Speech Vision*, vol. 138, pp. 225–231, Aug. 1991.

[161] T. L. Fine, "Properties of an optimal digital system and applications," *IEEE Trans. Inform. Theory*, vol. IT-10, pp. 287–296, Oct. 1964.

[162] ——, "Optimum mean-square quantization of a noisy input," *IEEE Trans. Inform. Theory*, vol. IT-11, pp. 293–294, Apr. 1965.

[163] ——, "The response of a particular nonlinear system with feedback to each of two random processes," *IEEE Trans. Inform. Theory*, vol. IT-14, pp. 255–264, Mar. 1968.

[164] T. R. Fischer "A pyramid vector quantizer," *IEEE Trans. Inform. Theory*, vol. IT-32, pp. 568–583, July 1986.

[165] ——, "Geometric source coding and vector quantization," *IEEE Trans. Inform. Theory*, vol. 35, pp. 137–145, July 1989.

[166] T. R. Fischer, M. W. Marcellin, and M. Wang, "Trellis-coded vector quantization," *IEEE Trans. Inform. Theory*, vol. 37, pp. 1551–1566, Nov. 1991.

[167] T. R. Fischer and M. Wang, "Entropy-constrained trellis-coded quantization," *IEEE Trans. Inform. Theory*, vol. 38, pp. 415–426, Mar. 1992.

[168] S. Fix, "Rate distortion functions for continuous alphabet memoryless sources," Ph.D. dissertation, Univ. Michigan, Ann Arbor, 1977.

[169] J. K. Flanagan, D. R. Morrell, R. L. Frost, C.J. Read, and B. E. Nelson, "Vector quantization codebook generation using simulated annealing," in *Proc. Int. Conf. Acoustics, Speech, and Signal Processing* (Glasgow, Scotland, May 1989), pp. 1759–1762.

[170] P. Fleischer, "Sufficient conditions for achieving minimum distortion in a quantizer," in *IEEE Int. Conv. Rec.*, 1964, pp. 104–111.

[171] B. A. Flury "Principal points," *Biometrika*, vol. 77, no. 1, pp. 31–41, 1990.

[172] E. Forgey, "Cluster analysis of multivariate data: Efficiency vs. interpretability of classification," *Biometrics*, vol. 21, p. 768, 1965 (abstract).

[173] G. D. Forney, Jr., "The Viterbi algorithm," *Proc. IEEE*, vol. 61, pp. 268–278, Mar. 1973.

[174] J. Foster and R. M. Gray, "Finite-state vector quantization," in *Abstracts 1982 IEEE Int. Symp. Information Theory* (Les Arcs France, June 1982).

[175] J. Foster, R. M. Gray, and M. Ostendorf Dunham, "Finite-state vector quantization for waveform coding," *IEEE Trans. Inform. Theory*, vol. IT-31, pp. 348–359, May 1985.

[176] J. H. Friedman, F. Baskett, and L. J. Shustek, "An algorithm for finding nearest neighbors," *IEEE Trans. Comput.*, vol. C-24, pp. 1000–1006, Oct. 1975.

[177] R. L. Frost, C. F. Barnes, and F. Xu, "Design and performance of residual quantizers," in *Proc. Data Compression Conf.*, J. A. Storer and J. H. Reif, Eds. Los Alamitos, CA: IEEE Comp. Soc. Press, Apr. 1991, pp. 129–138.

[178] N. T. Gaarder and D. Slepian, "On optimal finite-state digital transmission systems," *IEEE Trans. Inform. Theory*, vol. IT-28, pp. 167–186, Mar. 1982.

[179] G. Gabor and Z. Gyorfi, *Recursive Source Coding.* New York: Springer-Verlag, 1986.

[180] R. G. Gallager, *Information Theory and Reliable Communication*. New York: Wiley, 1968.

[181] ———, "Variations on a theme by Huffman," *IEEE Trans. Inform. Theory*, vol. IT-24, pp. 668–674, Nov. 1978.

[182] N. C. Gallager, Jr., "Discrete spectral phase coding," *IEEE Trans. Inform. Theory*, vol. IT-22, pp. 622–624, Sept. 1976.

[183] ———, "Quantizing schemes for the discrete Fourier transform of a random time-series," *IEEE Trans. Inform. Theory*, vol. IT-24, pp. 156–163, Mar. 1978.

[184] N. C. Gallagher and J. A. Bucklew, "Properties of minimum mean squared error block quantizers," *IEEE Trans. Inform. Theory*, vol. IT-28, pp. 105–107, Jan. 1982.

[185] Z. Gao, F. Chen, B. Belzer, and J. Villasenor, "A comparison of the Z, E_8, and Leech lattices for image subband quantization," in *Proc. 1995 IEEE Data Compression Conf.*, J. A. Storer and M. Cohn, Eds. Los Alamitos, CA: IEEE Comp. Soc. Press, Mar. 1995, pp. 312–321.

[186] W. R. Gardner and B. D. Rao, "Theoretical analysis of the high-rate vector quantization of LPC parameters," *IEEE Trans. Speech Audio Processing*, vol. 3, pp. 367–381, Sept. 1995.

[187] M. Garey, D. S. Johnson, and H. S. Witsenhausen, "The complexity of the generalized Lloyd–Max problem," *IEEE Trans. Inform. Theory*, vol. IT-28, pp. 255–266, Mar. 1982.

[188] D. P. de Garrido, L. Lu, and W. A. Pearlman, "Conditional entropy-constrained vector quantization of frame difference subband signals," in *Proc. IEEE Int. Conf. Image Processing* (Austin, TX, 1994), pt. 1 (of 3), pp. 745–749.

[189] N. L. Gerr and S. Cambanis, "Analysis of delayed delta modulation," *IEEE Trans. Inform. Theory*, vol. IT-32, pp. 496–512, July 1986.

[190] ———, "Analysis of adaptive differential PCM of a stationary Gauss–Markov input," *IEEE Trans. Inform. Theory*, vol. 35, pp. 350–359, May 1987.

[191] A. Gersho, "Stochastic stability of delta modulation," *Bell Syst. Tech. J.*, vol. 51, pp. 821–841, Apr. 1972.

[192] ———, "Principles of quantization," *IEEE Trans. Circuits Syst.*, vol. CAS-25, pp. 427–436, July 1978.

[193] ———, "Asymptotically optimal block quantization," *IEEE Trans. Inform. Theory*, vol. IT-25, pp. 373–380, July 1979.

[194] ———, "Optimal nonlinear interpolative vector quantization," *IEEE Trans. Commun.*, vol. 38, pp. 1285–1287, Sept. 1990.

[195] A. Gersho and V. Cuperman, "Vector quantization: A pattern-matching technique for speech coding," *IEEE Commun. Mag.*, vol. 21, pp. 15–21, Dec. 1983.

[196] A. Gersho and R. M. Gray, *Vector Quantization and Signal Compression*. Boston, MA: Kluwer, 1992.

[197] A. Gersho and B. Ramamurthi, "Image coding using vector quantization," in *Proc. Int. Conf. Acoustics, Speech, and Signal Processing* (Paris, France, Apr. 1982), vol. 1, pp. 428–431.

[198] J. D. Gibson, "Adaptive prediction in speech differential encoding systems," *Proc. IEEE*, vol. 68, pp. 488–525, Apr. 1980.

[199] J. D. Gibson and K. Sayood, "Lattice quantization," *Adv. Electron. Electron Phys.*, vol. 72, pp. 259–330, 1988.

[200] N. Gilchrist and C. Grewin, *Collected Papers on Digital Audio Bit-Rate Reduction*. New York: Audio Eng. Soc., 1996.

[201] B. Girod, "Rate-constrained motion estimation," in *Visual Communication and Image Processing VCIP'94, Proc. SPIE*, A. K. Katsaggelos, Ed., Sept. 1994, vol. 2308, pp. 1026–1034.

[202] B. Girod, R. M. Gray, J. Kovačević, and M. Vetterli, "Image and video coding," part of "The past, present, and future of image and multidimensional signal processing," in *Signal Proc. Mag.*, R. Chellappa, B. Girod, D. C. Munson, Jr., A. M. Telkap, and M. Vetterli, Eds., Mar. 1998, pp. 40–46.

[203] H. Gish, "Optimum quantization of random sequences," Ph.D. dissertation, Harvard Univ., Cambridge, MA, Mar. 1967.

[204] H. Gish and J. N. Pierce, "Asymptotically efficient quantizing," *IEEE Trans. Inform. Theory*, vol. IT-14, pp. 676–683, Sept. 1968.

[205] T. J. Goblick and J. L. Holsinger, "Analog source digitization: A comparison of theory and practice," *IEEE Trans. Inform. Theory*, vol. IT-13, pp. 323–326, Apr. 1967.

[206] M. Goldberg and H. Sun, "Image sequence coding using vector quantization," *IEEE Trans. Commun.*, vol. COM-34, pp. 703–710, July 1986.

[207] A. J. Goldstein, "Quantization noise in P.C.M.," Bell Telephone Lab. Tech. Memo., Oct. 18, 1957.

[208] R. C. Gonzales and R. C. Woods, *Digital Image Processing*. Reading, MA: Addison-Wesley, 1992.

[209] W. M. Goodall, "Telephony by pulse code modulation," *Bell Syst. Tech. J.*, vol. 26, pp. 395–409, July 1947.

[210] D. J. Goodman and T. J. Moulsley "Using simulated annealing to design transmission codes for analogue sources," *Electron. Lett.*, vol. 24, pp. 617–618, May 1988.

[211] V. K. Goyal and J. Kovačević, "Optimal multiple description transform coding of Gaussian vectors," in *Proc. Data Compression Conf.*, J. A. Storer and M. Cohn, Eds. Los Alamitos, CA: Comp. Soc. Press, Mar./Apr. 1998, pp. 388–397.

[212] R. M. Gray, "Information rates of autoregressive processes," *IEEE Trans. Inform. Theory*, vol. IT-16, pp. 516–523, Mar. 1971.

[213] ———, "A new class of lower bounds to information rates of stationary sources via conditional rate-distortion functions," *IEEE Trans. Inform. Theory*, vol. IT-19, pp. 480–489, July 1973.

[214] ———, "Vector quantization," *IEEE ASSP Mag.*, vol. 1, pp. 4–29, Apr. 1984.

[215] ———, "Oversampled sigma–delta modulation," *IEEE Trans. Commun.*, vol. COM-35, pp. 481–489, Apr. 1987.

[216] ———, "Quantization noise spectra," *IEEE Trans. Inform. Theory*, vol. 36, pp. 1220–1244, Nov. 1990.

[217] ———, *Source Coding Theory*. Boston, MA: Kluwer, 1990.

[218] ———, *Entropy and Information Theory*. New York: Springer-Verlag, 1990.

[219] ———, "Combined compression and segmentation of images," in *Proc. 1997 Int. Workshop Mobile Multimedia Communication (MoMuC97)* (Seoul, Korea, Sept./Oct. 1997).

[220] R. M. Gray, A. Buzo, Y. Matsuyama, A. H. Gray, Jr., and J. D. Markel, "Source coding and speech compression," in *Proc. Int. Telemetering Conf.* (Los Angeles, CA, Nov. 1978), vol. XIV, pp. 871–878.

[221] R. M. Gray and L. D. Davisson, "Source coding theorems without the ergodic assumption," *IEEE Trans. Inform. Theory*, vol. IT-20, pp. 502–516, July 1974.

[222] R. M. Gray and A. H. Gray, Jr., "Asymptotically optimal quantizers," *IEEE Trans. Inform. Theory*, vol. IT-23, pp. 143–144, Feb. 1977.

[223] R. M. Gray, A. H. Gray, Jr., and G. Rebolledo, "Optimal speech compression," in *Proc. 13th Asilomar Conf. Circuits Systems and Computers* (Pacific Grove, CA, 1979).

[224] R. M. Gray and E. Karnin, "Multiple local optima in vector quantizers," *IEEE Trans. Inform. Theory*, vol. IT-28, pp. 708–721, Nov. 1981.

[225] R. M. Gray and Y. Linde, "Vector quantizers and predictive quantizers for Gauss-Markov sources," *IEEE Trans. Commun.*, vol. COM-30, pp. 381–389, Feb. 1982.

[226] R. M. Gray, S. J. Park, and B. Andrews, "Tiling shapes for image vector quantization," in *Proc. 3rd Int. Conf. Advances in Commun. and Control Systems (COMCON III)* (Victoria, BC, Canada, Sept. 1991).

[227] R. M. Gray and T. G. Stockham, Jr. "Dithered quantizers," *IEEE Trans. Inform. Theory*, vol. 39, pp. 805–812, May 1993.

[228] R. M. Gray and A. D. Wyner, "Source coding over simple networks," *Bell Syst. Tech. J.*, vol. 53, pp. 1681–1721, Nov. 1974.

[229] L. Guan and M. Kamel, "Equal-average hyperplane partitioning method for vector quantization of image data," *Patt. Recogn. Lett.*, vol. 13, pp. 605–609, Oct. 1992.

[230] D. J. Hall and G. B. Ball, "ISODATA: A novel method of data analysis and pattern classification," Stanford Res. Inst., Menlo Park, CA, Tech. Rep., 1965.

[231] P. J. Hahn and V. J. Mathews, "Distortion-limited vector quantization," in *Proc. Data Compression Conf.—DCC'96*. Los Alamitos, CA: IEEE Comp. Soc. Press, 1996, pp. 340–348.

[232] R. Hagen and P. Hedelin, "Robust vector quantization by linear mappings of block-codes," in *Proc. IEEE Int. Symp. Information Theory* (San Antonio, TX, Jan. 1993), p. 171.

[233] ———, "Design methods for VQ by linear mappings of block codes," in *Proc. IEEE Int. Symp. Information Theory* (Trondheim, Norway, June 1994), p. 241.

[234] H. Hang and B. Haskell, "Interpolative vector quantization of color images," *IEEE Trans. Commun.*, vol. 36, pp. 465–470, 1988.

[235] H.-M. Hang and J. W. Woods, "Predictive vector quantization of images," *IEEE Trans. Commun.*, vol. COM-33, pp. 1208–1219, Nov. 1985.

[236] A. Haoui and D. G. Messerschmitt, "Predictive vector quantization," in *Proc. Int. Conf. Acoustics, Speech, and Signal Processing* (San Diego, CA, Mar. 1984), vol. 1, pp. 10.10.1–10.10.4.

[237] C. W. Harrison, "Experiments with linear prediction in television," *Bell Syst. Tech. J.*, vol. 31, pp. 764–783, July 1952.

[238] J. A. Hartigan, *Clustering Algorithms*. New York: Wiley, 1975.

[239] B. Haskell, "The computation and bounding of rate-distortion functions," *IEEE Trans. Inform. Theory*, vol. IT-15, pp. 525–531, Sept. 1969.

[240] A. Hayashi, "Differential pulse code modulation of the Wiener process," *IEEE Trans. Commun.*, vol. COM-26, pp. 881–887, June 1978.

[241] ———, "Differential pulse code modulation of stationary Gaussian inputs," *IEEE Trans. Commun.*, vol. COM-26, pp. 1137–1147, Aug. 1978.

[242] E. E. Hilbert, "Cluster compression algorithm: a joint clustering/data

compression concept," Jet Propulsion Lab., Pasadena, CA, Publication 77-43, Dec. 1977.

[243] Y.-S. Ho and A. Gersho, "Variable-rate multi-stage vector quantization for image coding," in *Proc. IEEE Int. Conf. Acoustics, Speech and Signal Processing (ICASSP)*, 1988, pp. 1156–1159.

[244] B. Hochwald and K. Zeger, "Tradeoff between source and channel coding," *IEEE Trans. Inform. Theory*, vol. 43, pp. 1412–1424, Sept. 1997.

[245] C. H. Hsieh, P. C. Lu, and J. C. Chang, "Fast codebook generation algorithm for vector quantization of images," *Patt. Recogn. Lett.*, vol. 12, pp. 605–609, 1991.

[246] C. H. Hsieh and J. C. Chang, "Lossless compression of VQ index with search-order coding," *IEEE Trans. Image Processing*, vol. 5, pp. 1579–1582, Nov. 1996.

[247] J. Huang, "Quantization of correlated random variables," Ph.D. dissertation, School of Engi., Yale Univ., New Haven, CT, 1962.

[248] J.-Y. Huang and P. M. Schultheiss, "Block quantization of correlated Gaussian random variables," *IEEE Trans. Commun.*, vol. COM-11, pp. 289–296, Sept. 1963.

[249] S. H. Huang and S. H. Chen, "Fast encoding algorithm for VQ-based encoding," *Electron. Lett.*, vol. 26, pp. 1618–1619, Sept. 1990.

[250] T. S. Huang, "Optimum binary code," MIT Res. Lab. Electron., Quart. Progr. Rep. 82, pp. 223–225, July 15, 1966.

[251] D. A. Huffman, "A method for the construction of minimum redundancy codes," *Proc. IRE*, vol. 40, pp. 1098–1101, Sept. 1952.

[252] D. Hui, D. F. Lyons, and D. L. Neuhoff, "Reduced storage VQ via secondary quantization," *IEEE Trans. Image Processing*, vol. 7, pp. 477–495, Apr. 1998.

[253] D. Hui and D. L. Neuhoff, "Asymptotic analysis of optimum uniform scalar quantizers for generalized Gaussian distributions," in *Proc. 1994 IEEE Int. Symp. Information Theory* (Trondheim, Norway, June 1994), p. 461.

[254] ———, "When is overload distortion negligible in uniform scalar quantization," in *Proc. 1997 IEEE Int. Symp. Information Theory* (Ulm, Germany, July 1997), p. 517.

[255] ———, "Asymptotic analysis of optimal fixed-rate uniform scalar quantization," *IEEE Trans. Inform. Theory*, submitted for publication.

[256] ———, "On the complexity of scalar quantization," in *Proc. 1995 IEEE Int. Symp. Information Theory* (Whistler, BC, Canada, Sept. 1995), p. 372.

[257] F. Itakura, "Maximum prediction residual principle applied to speech recognition," *IEEE Trans. Acoust., Speech, Signal Processing*, vol. ASSP-23, pp. 67–72, Feb. 1975.

[258] F. Itakura and S. Saito, "Analysis synthesis telephony based on the maximum likelihood method," in *Proc. 6th Int. Congr. Acoustics* (Tokyo, Japan, Aug. 1968), pp. C-17–C-20.

[259] ———, "A statistical method for estimation of speech spectral density and formant frequencies," *Electron. Commun. Japan*, vol. 53-A, pp. 36–43, 1970.

[260] J. E. Iwersen, "Calculated quantizing noise of single-integration delta-modulation coders," *Bell Syst. Tech. J.*, vol. 48, pp. 2359–2389, Sept. 1969.

[261] A. K. Jain, *Fundamentals of Digital Image Processing*. Englewood Cliffs, NJ: Prentice-Hall, 1989.

[262] E. Janardhanan, "Differential PCM systems," *IEEE Trans. Commun.*, vol. COM-27, pp. 82–93, Jan. 1979.

[263] R. C. Jancey, "Multidimensional group analysis," *Australian J. Botany*, vol. 14, pp. 127–130, 1966.

[264] N. S. Jayant, "Digital coding of speech waveforms: PCM, DPCM, and DM quantizers," *Proc. IEEE*, vol. 62, pp. 611–632, May 1974

[265] N. S. Jayant and P. Noll, *Digital Coding of Waveforms: Principles and Applications to Speech and Video*. Englewood Cliffs, NJ: Prentice-Hall, 1984.

[266] N. S. Jayant and L. R. Rabiner, "The application of dither to the quantization of speech signals," *Bell Syst. Tech. J.*, vol. 51, pp. 1293–1304, July/Aug. 1972.

[267] F. Jelinek, "Evaluation of rate distortion functions for low distortions," *Proc. IEEE* (Lett.), vol. 55, pp. 2067–2068, Nov. 1967.

[268] ———, "Tree encoding of memoryless time-discrete sources with a fidelity criterion," *IEEE Trans. Inform. Theory*, vol. IT-15, pp. 584–590, Sept. 1969.

[269] F. Jelinek and J. B. Anderson, "Instrumentable tree encoding of information sources," *IEEE Trans. Inform. Theory*, vol. IT-17, pp. 118–119, Jan. 1971.

[270] D. G. Jeong and J. D. Gibson, "Uniform and piecewise uniform lattice vector quantization for memoryless Gaussian and Laplacian sources," *IEEE Trans. Inform. Theory*, vol. 39, pp. 786–804, May 1993.

[271] ———, "Image coding with uniform and piecewise-uniform vector quantizers," *IEEE Trans. Inform. Theory*, vol. 39, pp. 786–804, May.

1993.

[272] J. D. Johnston, "Transform coding of audio signals using perceptual noise criteria," *IEEE J. Select. Areas Commun.*, vol. 6, pp. 314–323, Feb. 1988.

[273] R. L. Joshi and P. G. Poonacha, "A new MMSE encoding algorithm for vector quantization," in *Proc. IEEE Int. Conf. Acoust. Speech, and Signal Processing (ICASSP)* (Toronto, Ont., Canada, 1991), pp. 645–648.

[274] B.-H. Juang and A. H. Gray, Jr., "Multiple stage vector quantization for speech coding," in *Proc. Int. Conf. Acouststics, Speech, and Signal Processing (ICASSP)* (Paris, France, Apr. 1982), vol. 1, pp. 597–600.

[275] D. Kazakos, "New results on robust quantization," *IEEE Trans. Commun.*, pp. 965–974, Aug. 1983.

[276] S.-Z. Kiang, R. L. Baker, G. J. Sullivan, and C.-Y. Chiu, "Recursive optimal pruning with applications to tree structured vector quantizers," *IEEE Trans. Image Processing*, vol. 1, pp. 162–169, Apr. 1992.

[277] J. C. Kieffer, "A generalization of the Pursley–Davisson–Mackenthun universal variable-rate coding theorem," *IEEE Trans. Inform. Theory*, vol. IT-23, pp. 694–697, Nov. 1977.

[278] ———, "Block coding for an ergodic source relative to a zero-one valued fidelity criterion," *IEEE Trans. Inform. Theory*, vol. IT-24, pp. 422–437, July 1978.

[279] ———, "A unified approach to weak universal source coding," *IEEE Trans. Inform. Theory*, vol. IT-24, pp. 674–682, Nov. 1978.

[280] ———, "Exponential rate of convergence for Lloyd's method I," *IEEE Trans. Inform. Theory*, vol. IT-28, pp. 205–210, Mar. 1982.

[281] ———, "Stochastic stability for feedback quantization schemes," *IEEE Trans. Inform. Theory*, vol. IT-28, pp. 248–254, Mar. 1982.

[282] ———, "History of source coding," *Inform. Theory Soc. Newslett.*, vol. 43, pp. 1–5, 1993.

[283] ———, "A survey of the theory of source coding with a fidelity criterion," *IEEE Trans. Inform. Theory*, vol. 39, pp. 1473–1490, Sept. 1993.

[284] J. C. Kieffer and J. G. Dunham, "On a type of stochastic stability for a class of encoding schemes," *IEEE Trans. Inform. Theory*, vol. IT-29, pp. 703–797, Nov. 1983.

[285] J. C. Kieffer, T. M. Jahns, and V. A. Obuljen, "New results on optimal entropy-constrained quantization," *IEEE Trans. Inform. Theory*, vol. 34, pp. 1250–1258, Sept. 1988.

[286] T. Kim, "Side match and overlap match vector quantizers for images," *IEEE Trans. Image Processing*, vol. 1, pp. 170–185, Apr. 1992.

[287] P. Knagenhjelm and E. Agrell, "The Hadamard transform—A tool for index assignment," *IEEE Trans. Inform. Theory*, vol. 42, pp. 1139–1151, July 1996.

[288] A. N. Kolmogorov, "On the Shannon theory of information transmission in the case of continuous signals," *IEEE Trans. Inform. Theory*, vol. IT-2, pp. 102–108, Sept. 1956.

[289] H. Kodama, K. Wakasugi, and M. Kasahara, "A construction of optimum vector quantizers by simulated annealing," *Trans. Inst. Electron., Inform. Commun. Eng. B-I*, vol. J74B-I, pp. 58–65, Jan. 1991.

[290] T. Kohonen, *Self-Organization and Associative Memory*, 3rd ed. Berlin Germany: Springer-Verlag, 1989.

[291] V. Koshélev, "Hierarchical coding of discrete sources," *Probl. Pered. Inform.*, vol. 16, no. 3, pp. 31–49, July–Sept. 1980.

[292] ———, "Estimation of mean error for a discrete successive-approximation scheme," *Probl. Pered. Inform.*, vol. 17, no. 3, pp. 20–33, July–Sept. 1981.

[293] T. Koski and S. Cambanis, "On the statistics of the error in predictive coding for stationary Ornstein-Uhlenbeck processes," *IEEE Trans. Inform. Theory*, vol. 38, pp. 1029–40, May 1992.

[294] T. Koski and L.-E. Persson, "On quantizer distortion and the upper bound for exponential entropy," *IEEE Trans. Inform. Theory*, vol. 37, pp. 1168–1172, July 1991.

[295] F. Kossentini, W. C. Chung, and M. J. T. Smith, "Subband image coding using entropy-constrained residual vector quantization," *Inform. Processing and Manag.*, vol. 30, no. 6, pp. 887–896, 1994.

[296] ———, "Conditional entropy-constrained residual VQ with application to image coding," *IEEE Trans. Image Processing*, vol. 5, pp. 311–320, Feb. 1996.

[297] F. Kossentini, M. J. T. Smith, and C. F. Barnes, "Image coding using entropy-constrained residual vector quantization" *IEEE Trans. Image Processing*, vol. 4, pp. 1349–1357, Oct. 1995.

[298] ———, "Necessary conditions for the optimality of variable-rate residual vector quantizers," *IEEE Trans. Inform. Theory*, vol. 41, pp. 1903–1914, Nov. 1995.

[299] H. P. Kramer and M. V. Mathews, "A linear coding for transmitting a set of correlated signals," *IRE Trans. Inform. Theory*, vol. IT-2, pp. 41–46, Sept. 1956.

[300] E. R. Kretzmer, "Statistics of television signals," *Bell Syst. Tech. J.*, vol. 31, pp. 751–763, July 1952.

334

[301] A. K. Krishnamurthy, S. C. Ahalt, D. E. Melton, and P. Chen, "Neural networks for vector quantization of speech and images," *IEEE J. Select. Areas Commun.*, vol. 8, pp. 1449–1457, Oct. 1990.

[302] F. Kuhlmann and J. A. Bucklew, "Piecewise uniform vector quantizers," *IEEE Trans. Inform. Theory*, vol. 34, pp. 1259–1263, Sept. 1988.

[303] H. Kumazawa, M. Kasahara, and T. Namekawa, "A construction of vector quantizers for noisy channels," *Electron. and Eng. Japan*, vol. 67-B, pp. 39–47, 1984, translated from *Denshi Tsushin Gakkai Ronbunshi*, vol. 67-B, pp. 1–8, Jan. 1984.

[304] A. J. Kurtenbach and P. A. Wintz, *IEEE Trans. Commun. Technol.*, vol. COM-17, pp. 291–302, Apr. 1969.

[305] R. Laroia and N. Farvardin, " A structured fixed-rate vector quantizer derived from a variable-length scalar quantizer. I. Memoryless sources. II. Vector sources," *IEEE Trans. Inform. Theory*, vol. 39, pp. 851–876, May 1993.

[306] A. Lapidoth, "On the role of mismatch in rate distortion theory," *IEEE Trans. Inform. Theory*, vol. 43, pp. 38–47, Jan. 1997.

[307] C.-H. Lee and L.-H. Chen, "Fast closest codeword search algorithm for vector quantization," *Proc. Inst. Elec. Eng.—Vis. Image Signal Processing* vol. 141, pp. 143–148, June 1994.

[308] _____, "A fast search algorithm for vector quantization using mean pyramids of codewords," *IEEE Trans. Commun.*, vol. 43, pp. 1697–1702, Feb.–Apr. 1995.

[309] D. H. Lee, "Asymptotic quantization error and cell-conditioned two-stage vector quantization," Ph.D. dissertation, Univ. Michigan, Ann Arbor, Dec. 1990.

[310] D. H. Lee and D. L. Neuhoff, "Conditionally corrected two-stage vector quantization," in *Conf. Information Sciences and Systems* (Princeton, NJ, Mar. 1990), pp. 802–806.

[311] _____, "An asymptotic analysis of two-stage vector quantization," in *1991 IEEE Int. Symp. Information Theory* (Budapest, Hungary, June 1991), p. 316.

[312] _____, "Asymptotic distribution of the errors in scalar and vector quantizers," *IEEE Trans. Inform. Theory*, vol. 42, pp. 446–460, Mar. 1996.

[313] D. H. Lee, D. L. Neuhoff, and K. K. Paliwal, "Cell-conditioned two-stage vector quantization of speech," in *Proc. IEEE Int. Conf. Acoustics, Speech, and Signal Processing (ICASSP)* (Toronto, Ont., May 1991), vol. 4, pp. 653–656.

[314] V. I. Levenshtein, "Binary codes capable of correcting deletions, insertions, and reversals," *Sov. Phys.—Dokl.*, vol. 10, pp. 707–710, 1966.

[315] A. S. Lewis and G. Knowles, "Image compression using the 2-D, wavelet transform," *IEEE Trans. Image Processing*, vol. 1, pp. 244–250, Apr. 1992.

[316] J. Li, N. Chaddha, and R. M. Gray, "Asymptotic performance of vector quantizers with a perceptual distortion measure," in *1997 IEEE Int. Symp. Information Theory* (Ulm, Germany, June 1997); full paper submitted for publication. Preprint available online at http://www-isl.stanford.edu/gray/compression.html.

[317] J. O. Limb, "Design of dithered waveforms for quantized visual signals," *Bell Syst. Tech. J.*, vol. 48, pp. 2555–2582, Sept. 1968.

[318] Y. Linde, A. Buzo, and R. M. Gray, "An algorithm for vector quantizer design," *IEEE Trans. Commun.*, vol. COM-28, pp. 84–95, Jan. 1980.

[319] Y. Linde and R. M. Gray, "A fake process approach to data compression," *IEEE Trans. Commun.*, vol. COM-26, pp. 840–847, June 1978.

[320] T. Linder, "On asymptotically optimal companding quantization," *Probl. Contr. Inform. Theory*, vol. 20, no. 6, pp. 465–484, 1991.

[321] T. Linder, T. Lugosi, and K. Zeger, "Rates of convergence in the source coding theorem, in empirical quantizer design, and in universal lossy source coding," *IEEE Trans. Inform. Theory*, vol. 40, pp. 1728–1740, Nov. 1994.

[322] T. Linder and R. Zamir, "On the asymptotic tightness of the Shannon lower bound," *IEEE Trans. Inform. Theory*, vol. 40, pp. 2026–2031, Nov. 1994.

[323] _____, "High-resolution source coding for nondifference distortion measures: The rate distortion function," in *Proc. 1997 IEEE Int. Symp. Information Theory* (Ulm, Germany, June 1997), p. 187. Also, submitted for publication to *IEEE Trans. Inform. Theory*.

[324] T. Linder, R. Zamir, and K. Zeger, "The multiple description rate region for high resolution source coding," in *Proc. Data Compression Conf.*, J. A. Storer and M. Cohn, Eds. Los Alamitos, CA: Comp. Soc. Press, Mar./Apr. 1998.

[325] _____, "High resolution source coding for nondifference distortion measures: multidimensional companding," *IEEE Trans. Inform. Theory*, submitted for publication.

[326] T. Linder and K. Zeger, "Asymptotic entropy-constrained performance of tessellating and universal randomized lattice quantization," *IEEE Trans. Inform. Theory*, vol. 40, pp. 575–579, Mar. 1994.

[327] Y. N. Linkov, "Evaluation of epsilon entropy of random variables for small epsilon," *Probl. Inform. Transm.*, vol. 1, pp. 12–18, 1965; translated from *Probl. Pered. Inform.*, vol. 1, pp. 18–26.

[328] S. P. Lipshitz, R. A. Wannamaker, and J. Vanderkooy, "Quantization and dither: A theoretical survey," *J. Audio Eng. Soc.*, vol. 40, no. 5, pp. 355–75, May 1992.

[329] Q. Liu, E. Yang, and Z. Zhang, "A fixed-slope universal sequential algorithm for lossy source coding based on Gold–Washing mechanism," in *Proc. 33rd Annu. Allerton Conf. Communication, Control, and Computing* (Monticello, IL, Urbana-Champaign, IL, Oct. 1995), pp. 466–474.

[330] S. P. Lloyd, "Least squares quantization in PCM," unpublished Bell Lab. Tech. Note, portions presented at the Institute of Mathematical Statistics Meet., Atlantic City, NJ, Sept. 1957. Also, *IEEE Trans. Inform. Theory* (Special Issue on Quantization), vol. IT-28, pp. 129–137, Mar. 1982.

[331] _____, "Rate versus fidelity for the binary source," *Bell Syst. Tech. J.*, vol. 56, pp. 427–437, Mar. 1977.

[332] K. T. Lo and W. K. Cham, "Subcodebook searching algorithm for efficient VQ encoding of images," *Proc. Inst. Elec. Eng.–Vis. Image Signal Processing*, vol. 140, pp. 327–330, Oct. 1993.

[333] T. D. Lookabaugh and R. M. Gray, "High-resolution quantization theory and the vector quantizer advantage," *IEEE Trans. Inform. Theory*, vol. 35, pp. 1020–1033, Sept. 1989.

[334] A. Lowry, S. Hossain, and W. Millar, "Binary search trees for vector quantization," in *Proc. IEEE Int. Conf. Acoustics, Speech, and Signal Processing* (Dallas, TX, 1987), pp. 2206–2208.

[335] G. Lugosi and A. Nobel, "Consistency of data-driven histogram methods for density estimation and classification," *Ann. Statist.*, vol. 24, pp. 687–706, 1996.

[336] J. Łukaszewicz and H. Steinhaus, "On measuring by comparison," *Zastosowania Matematyki*, vol. 2, pp. 225–231, 1955, in Polish.

[337] S. P. Luttrell, "Self-supervised training of hierarchical vector quantizers," in *II Int. Conf. Artificial Neural Networks* (London, U.K., IEE, 1991), Conf. Publ. 349, pp. 5–9.

[338] D. F. Lyons, "Fundamental limits of low-rate transform codes," Ph.D. dissertation, Univ. Michigan, Ann Arbor, 1992.

[339] D. F. Lyons and D. L. Neuhoff, "A coding theorem for low-rate transform codes," in *Proc. IEEE Int. Symp. Information Theory* (San Antonio, TX, Jan. 1993), p. 333.

[340] K. M. Mackenthun and M. B. Pursley, "Strongly and weakly universal source coding," in *Proc. 1977 Conf. Information Science and Systems* (Baltimore, MD, The Johns Hopkins Univ., 1977), pp. 286–291.

[341] J. MacQueen, "Some methods for classification and analysis of multivariate observations," in *Proc. 5th Berkeley Symp. on Mathematical Statistics and Probability* 1967, vol. 1, pp. 281–296.

[342] J. Makhoul, S. Roucos, and H. Gish, "Vector quantization in speech coding," *Proc. IEEE*, vol. 73, pp. 1551–1588, Nov. 1985.

[343] M. W. Marcellin, "On entropy-constrained trellis-coded quantization," *IEEE Trans. Commun.*, vol. 42, pp. 14–16, Jan. 1994.

[344] M. W. Marcellin and T. R. Fischer, "Trellis coded quantization of memoryless and Gauss–Markov sources," *IEEE Trans. Commun*, vol. 38, pp. 82–93, Jan. 1990.

[345] M. W. Marcellin, T. R. Fischer, and J. D. Gibson, "Predictive trellis coded quantization of speech," *IEEE Trans. Acoust., Speech, Signal Processing*, vol. 38, pp. 46–55, Jan. 1990.

[346] E. Masry and S. Cambanis, "Delta modulation of the Wiener process," *IEEE Trans. Commun.*, vol. COM-23, pp. 1297–1300 Nov. 1975.

[347] V. J. Mathews, "Vector quantization of images using the L_∞ distortion measure," in *Proc. Int. Conf. Image Processing* (Washington, DC, Oct. 1995), vol. 1, pp. 109–112.

[348] _____, "Vector quantization using the L_∞ distortion measure," *IEEE Signal Processing Lett.*, vol. 4, pp. 33–35, 1997.

[349] J. Max, "Quantizing for minimum distortion," *IRE Trans. Inform. Theory*, vol. IT-6, pp. 7–12, Mar. 1960.

[350] R. A. McDonald, "Signal-to-noise and idle channel performance of DPCM systems with particular application to voice signals," *Bell Syst. Tech. J.*, vol. 45, pp. 1123–1151, Sept. 1966.

[351] S. W. McLaughlin, D. L. Neuhoff, and J. K. Ashley, "Optimal binary index assignments for a class of equiprobable scalar and vector quantizers," *IEEE Trans. Inform. Theory*, vol. 41, pp. 2031–2037, Nov. 1995.

[352] A. Méhes and K. Zeger, "Binary lattice vector quantization with linear block codes and affine index assignments," *IEEE Trans. Inform. Theory*, vol. 44, pp. 79–94, Jan. 1998.

[353] J. Menez, F. Boeri, and D. J. Esteban, "Optimum quantizer algorithm for real-time block quantizing," in *Proc. 1979 IEEE Int. Conf. Acoustics, Speech, and Signal Processin*, 1979, pp. 980–984.

335

[354] D. Miller and K. Rose, "Combined source-channel vector quantization using deterministic annealing," *IEEE Trans. Commun.*, vol. 42, pp. 347–356, Feb.–Apr. 1994.

[355] N. Moayeri, "Some issues related to fixed-rate pruned tree-structured vector quantizers," *IEEE Trans. Inform. Theory*, vol. 41, pp. 1523–1531, 1995.

[356] N. Moayeri and D. L. Neuhoff, "Theory of lattice-based fine-coarse vector quantization," *IEEE Trans. Inform. Theory*, vol. 37, pp. 1072–1084, July 1991.

[357] ——, "Time-memory tradeoffs in vector quantizer codebook searching based on decision trees," *IEEE Trans. Speech Audio Processing*, vol. 2, pp. 490–506, Oct. 1994.

[358] N. Moayeri, D. L. Neuhoff, and W. E. Stark, "Fine-coarse vector quantization," *IEEE Trans. Signal Processing*, vol. 39, pp. 1503–1515, July 1991.

[359] P. W. Moo and D. L. Neuhoff, "An asymptotic analysis of fixed-rate lattice vector quantization," in *Proc. Int. Symp. Information Theory and Its Applications* (Victoria, BC, Canada, Sept. 1996), pp. 409–412.

[360] ——, "Uniform polar quantization revisited," to be published in *Proc. IEEE Int. Symp. Information Theory* (Cambridge, MA, Aug. 17–21, 1998).

[361] J. M. Morris and V. D. Vandelinde, "Robust quantization of discrete-time signals with independent samples," *IEEE Trans. Commun.*, vol. COM-22, pp. 1897–1901, 1974.

[362] K. Motoishi and T. Misumi, "On a fast vector quantization algorithm," in *Proc. VIIth Symp. Information Theory and Its Applications*, 1984, not in INSPEC.

[363] ——, "Fast vector quantization algorithm by using an adaptive searching technique," in *Abstracts IEEE Int. Symp. Information Theory* (San Diego, CA, Jan. 1990).

[364] T. Murakami, K. Asai, and E. Yamazaki, "Vector quantizer of video signals," *Electron. Lett.*, vol. 7, pp. 1005–1006, Nov. 1982.

[365] S. Na and D. L. Neuhoff, " Bennett's integral for vector quantizers," *IEEE Trans. Inform. Theory*, vol. 41, pp. 886–900, July 1995.

[366] S. Nanda and W. A. Pearlman, "Tree coding of image subbands," *IEEE Trans. Image Processing*, vol. 1, pp. 133–147, Apr. 1992.

[367] M. Naraghi-Pour and D. L. Neuhoff, "Mismatched DPCM encoding of autoregressive processes," *IEEE Trans. Inform. Theory*, vol. 36, pp. 296–304, Mar. 1990.

[368] ——, "On the continuity of the stationary state distribution of DPCM," *IEEE Trans. Inform. Theory*, vol. 36, pp. 305–311, Mar. 1990.

[369] ——, "Convergence of the projection method for an autoregressive process and a matched DPCM code," *IEEE Trans. Inform. Theory*, vol. 36, pp. 1255–1264, Nov. 1990.

[370] B. K. Natarajan, "Filtering random noise from deterministic signals via data compression," *IEEE Trans. Signal Processing*, vol. 43, Nov. 1995.

[371] N. M. Nasrabadi and Y. Feng, "Image compression using address-vector quantization," *IEEE Trans. Commun.*, vol. 38, pp. 2166–2173 Dec. 1990.

[372] N. M. Nasrabadi and R. A. King, "Image coding using vector quantization: A review," *IEEE Trans. Commun.*, vol. 36, pp. 957–971, Aug. 1988.

[373] N. M. Nasrabadi, J. U. Roy, and C. Y. Choo, "An interframe hierarchical address-vector quantization," *IEEE Trans. Select. Areas Commun.*, vol. 10, pp. 960–967, June 1992.

[374] A. N. Netravali and B. G. Haskell, *Digital Pictures: Representation and Compression.* New York: Plenum, 1988, 2nd ed. 1995.

[375] A. N. Netravali and J. O. Limb, "Picture coding: A review," *Proc. IEEE*, vol. 68, pp. 366–406, Mar. 1980.

[376] A. N. Netravali and R. Saigal, "Optimal quantizer design using a fixed-point algorithm," *Bell Syst. Tech. J.*, vol. 55, pp. 1423–1435, Nov. 1976.

[377] D. L. Neuhoff, "Source coding strategies: Simple quantizers vs. simple noiseless codes," in *Proc. 1986 Conf. Information Sciences and Systems*, Mar. 1986, vol. 1, pp. 267–271.

[378] ——, "Why vector quantizers outperform scalar quantizers on stationary memoryless sources," in *IEEE Int. Symp. Information Theory* (Whistler, BC, Canada, Sept. 1995), p. 438.

[379] ——, "On the asymptotic distribution of the errors in vector quantization," *IEEE Trans. Inform. Theory*, vol. 42, pp. 461–468, Mar. 1996.

[380] ——, "Polar quantization revisited," in *Proc. IEEE Int. Symp. Information Theory* (Ulm, Germany, July 1997), p. 60.

[381] D. L. Neuhoff and R. K. Gilbert, "Causal source codes," *IEEE Trans. Inform. Theory*, vol. IT-28, pp. 701–713, Sept. 1982.

[382] D. L. Neuhoff, R. M. Gray, and L. D. Davisson, "Fixed rate universal block source coding with a fidelity criterion," *IEEE Trans. Inform. Theory*, vol. IT-21, pp. 511–523, Sept. 1975.

[383] D. L. Neuhoff and D. H. Lee, "On the performance of tree-structured vector quantization," in *Proc. IEEE Int. Conf. Acoustics, Speech, and Signal Processing (ICASSP)* (Toronto, Ont., Canada, May 1991), vol. 4, pp. 2277–2280.

[384] D. L. Neuhoff and N. Moayeri, "Tree searched vector quantization with interblock noiseless coding," in *Proc. Conf. Information Science and Systems* (Princeton, NJ, Mar. 1988), pp. 781–783.

[385] D. J. Newman, "The hexagon theorem," Bell Lab. Tech. Memo., 1964, published in the special issue on quantization of the *IEEE Trans. Inform. Theory*, vol. IT-28, pp. 137–139, Mar. 1982.

[386] N. B. Nill, "A visual model weighted cosine transform for image compression and quality assessment," *IEEE Trans. Commun.*, vol. COM-33, pp. 551–557, June 1985.

[387] N. B. Nill and B. H. Bouxas, "Objective image quality measure derived from digital image power spectra," *Opt. Eng.*, vol. 31, pp. 813–825, Apr. 1992.

[388] A. B. Nobel, "Vanishing distortion and shrinking cells," *IEEE Trans. Inform. Theory*, vol. 42, pp. 1303–1305, July 1996.

[389] ——, "Recursive partitioning to reduce distortion," *IEEE Trans. Inform. Theory*, vol. 43, pp. 1122–1133, July 1997.

[390] A. B. Nobel and R. A. Olshen, "Termination and continuity of greedy growing for tree-structured vector quantizers," *IEEE Trans. Inform. Theory*, vol. 42, pp. 191–205, Jan. 1996.

[391] P. Noll and R. Zelinski, "Bounds on quantizer performance in the low bit-rate region," *IEEE Trans. Commun.*, vol. COM-26, pp. 300–305, Feb. 1978.

[392] K. L. Oehler and R. M. Gray, "Mean-gain-shape vector quantization," in *Proc. IEEE Int. Conf. Acoustics, Speech, and Signal Processing* (Minneapolis, MN, Apr. 1993), pp. 241–244.

[393] K. L. Oehler, E. A. Riskin, and R. M.Gray, "Unbalanced tree-growing algorithms for practical image compression," in *Proc. IEEE Int. Conf. Acoustics, Speech, and Signal Processing (ICASSP)* (Toronto, Ont., Canada, 1991), pp. 2293–2296.

[394] B. M. Oliver, J. Pierce, and C. E. Shannon, "The philosophy of PCM," *Proc. IRE*, vol. 36, pp. 1324–1331, Nov. 1948.

[395] ——, "Efficient coding," *Bell Syst. Tech. J.*, vol. 31, pp. 724–750, July 1952.

[396] J. B. O'Neal, Jr., "A bound on signal-to-quantizing noise ratios for digital encoding systems," *Proc. IEEE*, vol. 55, pp. 287–292, Mar. 1967.

[397] ——, "Signal to quantization noise ratio for differential PCM," *IEEE Trans. Commun.*, vol. COM-19, pp. 568–569, Aug. 1971.

[398] ——, "Entropy coding in speech and television differential PCM systems," *IEEE Trans. Inform. Theory*, vol. IT-17, pp. 758–761, Nov. 1971.

[399] M. T. Orchard, "A fast nearest neighbor search algorithm," in *Proc. IEEE Int. Conf. on Acoustics, Speech, and Signal Processing (ICASSP)* (Toronto, Ont., Canada, 1991), pp. 2297–2300.

[400] M. T. Orchard and C. A. Bouman, "Color quantization of images," *IEEE Trans. Signal Processing*, vol. 39, pp. 2677–2690, Dec. 1991.

[401] L. Ozarow, "On a source-coding problem with two channels and three receivers," *Bell Syst. Tech. J.*, vol. 59, pp. 1909–1921, Dec. 1980.

[402] K. K. Paliwal and V. Ramasubramanian, "Effect of ordering the codebook on the efficiency of the partial distance search algorithm for vector quantization," *IEEE Trans. Commun.*, vol. 37, pp. 538–540, May 1989.

[403] J. Pan and T. R. Fischer, "Vector quantization-lattice vector quantization of speech LPC coefficients," in *Proc. IEEE Int. Conf. Acoust.ics, Speech, and Signal Processing (ICASSP)* (Adelaide, Australia, 1994), pt. 1.

[404] ——, "Two-stage vector quantization-lattice vector quantization," *IEEE Trans. Inform. Theory*, vol. 41, pp. 155–163, Jan. 1995.

[405] P. F. Panter and W. Dite, "Quantizing distortion in pulse-count modulation with nonuniform spacing of levels," *Proc. IRE*, vol. 39, pp. 44–48, Jan. 1951.

[406] W. A. Pearlman, "Polar quantization of a complex Gaussian random variable," *IEEE Trans. Commun.*, vol. COM-27, pp. 892–899, June 1979.

[407] W. A. Pearlman and R. M. Gray, "Source coding of the discrete Fourier transform," *IEEE Trans. Inform. Theory*, vol. IT-24, pp. 683–692, Nov. 1978.

[408] W. B. Pennebaker and J. L. Mitchell, *JPEG Still Image Compression Standard.* New York: Van Nostrand Reinhold, 1993.

[409] C. Pépin, J.-C. Belfiore, and J. Boutros, "Quantization of both stationary and nonstationary Gaussian sources with Voronoi constellations," in *Proc. IEEE Int. Symp. Information Theory* (Ulm, Germany, July 1997), p. 59.

[410] N. Phamdo and N. Farvardin, "Coding of speech LSP parameters using TSVQ with interblock noiseless coding," in *Proc. IEEE Int. Conf. Acoustics, Speech, and Signal Processing (ICASSP)* (Albuquerque, NM, 1990), pp. 193–196.

[411] ——, "Optimal detection of discrete Markov sources over discrete memoryless channels—Applications to combined source-channel coding," *IEEE Trans. Inform. Theory*, vol. 40, pp. 186–193, Jan. 1994.

[412] N. Phamdo, N. Farvardin, and T. Moriya, "A unified approach to tree-structured and multistage vector quantization for noisy channels," *IEEE Trans. Inform. Theory*, vol. 39, pp. 835–850, May 1993.

[413] R. Pilc, "The transmission distortion of a source as a function of the encoding block length," *Bell Syst. Tech. J.*, vol. 47, pp. 827–885, 1968.

[414] P. Piret, "Causal sliding block encoders with feedback," *IEEE Trans. Inform. Theory*, vol. IT-25, pp. 237–240, Mar. 1979.

[415] G. Poggi, "Fast algorithm for full-search VQ encoding," *Electron. Lett.*, vol. 29, pp. 1141–1142, June 1993.

[416] ———, "Generalized-cost-measure-based address-predictive vector quantization," *IEEE Trans. Image Processing*, vol. 5, pp. 49–55, Jan. 1996.

[417] G. Poggi and R. A. Olshen, "Pruned tree-structured vector quantization of medical images with segmentation and improved prediction," *IEEE Trans. Image Processing*, vol. 4, pp. 734–742, Jan. 1995.

[418] D. Pollard, "Quantization and the method of k-means," *IEEE Trans. Inform. Theory*, vol. IT-28, pp. 199–205, Mar. 1982.

[419] K. Popat and K. Zeger, "Robust quantization of memoryless sources using dispersive FIR filters," *IEEE Trans. Commun.*, vol. 40, pp. 1670–1674, Nov. 1992.

[420] E. Posner and E. Rodemich, "Epsilon entropy and data compression," *Ann. Math. Statist.*, vol. 42, pp. 2079–2125, 1971.

[421] E. Posner, E. Rodemich, and H. Rumsey, Jr., "Epsilon entropy of stochastic processes," *Ann. Math. Statist.*, vol. 38, pp. 1000–1020, 1967.

[422] W. K. Pratt, *Image Transmission Techniques*. New York: Academic, 1979.

[423] S. W. Ra and J. K. Kim, "A fast mean-distance-ordered partial codebook search algorithm for image vector quantization," *IEEE Trans. Circuits Syst. II*, vol. 40, pp. 576–579, Sept. 1993.

[424] M. Rabbani and P. W. Jones, *Digital Image Compression Techniques*, vol. TT7 of *Tutorial Texts in Optical Engineering*. Bellingham, WA: SPIE Opt. Eng. Press, 1991.

[425] V. Ramasubramanian and K. K. Paliwal, "An optimized k-d tree algorithm for fast vector quantization of speech," in *Proc. Euro. Signal Processing Conf.* (Grenoble, France, 1988), pp. 875–878.

[426] ———, "An efficient approximation-elimination algorithm for fast nearest-neighbor search based on a spherical distance coordinate formulation," in *Proc. Euro. Signal Processing Conf.* (Barcelona, Spain, Sept. 1990).

[427] K. Ramchandran and M. Vetterli, "Best wavelet packet bases in a rate-distortion sense," *IEEE Trans. Image Processing*, vol. 2, pp. 160–176, Apr. 1993.

[428] X. Ran and N. Farvardin, "Combined VQ-DCT coding of images using interblock noiseless coding," in *Proc. IEEE Int. Conf. Acoustics, Speech, and Signal Processing* (Albuquerque, NM, 1990), pp. 2281–2284.

[429] D. R. Rao and P. Yip, *Discrete Cosine Transform*. San Diego, CA: Academic, 1990.

[430] C. J. Read, D. M. Chabries, R. W. Christiansen, and J. K. Flanagan, "A method for computing the DFT of vector quantized data," in *Proc. IEEE Int. Conf. Acoustics, Speech, and Signal Processing (ICASSP)* (Glasgow, Scotland, May 1989), pp. 1015–1018.

[431] G. Rebolledo, R. M. Gray, and J. P. Burg, "A multirate voice digitizer based upon vector quantization," *IEEE Trans. Commun.*, vol. COM-30, pp. 721–727, Apr. 1982.

[432] A. H. Reeves, French Patent 852 183, Oct. 3, 1938.

[433] A. Rényi, "On the dimension and entropy of probability distributions," *Acta Math. Acad. Sci. Hungar.*, vol. 10, pp. 193–215, 1959.

[434] S. O. Rice, "Mathematical analysis of random noise," *Bell Syst. Tech. J.*, vol. 23, pp. 282–332, 1944, and vol. 24, pp. 46–156, 1945, reprinted in *Selected Papers on Noise and Stochastic Processes*, N. Wax and N. Wax, Eds. New York: Dover, 1954, pp. 133–294.

[435] R. F. Rice and J. R. Plaunt, "The Rice machine: Television data compression," Jet Propulsion Lab., Pasadena, CA, Tech. Rep. 900-408, Sept. 1970.

[436] ———, "Adaptive variable-length coding for efficient compression of spacecraft television data," *IEEE Trans. Commun.*, vol. COM-19, pp. 889–897, Dec. 1971.

[437] B. Rimoldi, "Successive refinement of information: Characterization of the achievable rates," *IEEE Trans. Inform. Theory*, vol. 40, pp. 253–259, Jan. 1994.

[438] E. A. Riskin, "Optimal bit allocation via the generalized BFOS algorithm," *IEEE Trans. Inform. Theory*, vol. 37, pp. 400–402, Mar. 1991.

[439] E. A. Riskin and R. M. Gray, "A greedy tree growing algorithm for the design of variable rate vector quantizers," *IEEE Trans. Signal Processing*, vol. 39, pp. 2500–2507, Nov. 1991.

[440] E. A. Riskin, R. Ladner, R. Wang, and L. E. Atlas, "Index assignment for progressive transmission of full-search vector quantization," *IEEE Trans. Image Processing*, vol. 3, pp. 307–312, May 1994.

[441] S. A. Rizvi, N. M. Nasrabadi, and W. L. Cheng, "Entropy-constrained predictive residual vector quantization," *Opt. Eng.*, vol. 35, pp. 187–197, Jan. 1996.

[442] L. G. Roberts, "Picture coding using pseudo-random noise," *IRE Trans. Inform. Theory*, vol. IT-8, pp. 145–154, Feb. 1962.

[443] G. M. Roe, "Quantizing for minimum distortion," *IEEE Trans. Inform. Theory*, vol. IT-10, pp. 384–385, Oct. 1964.

[444] K. Rose, "Mapping approach to rate-distortion computation and analysis," *IEEE Trans. Inform. Theory*, vol. 40, pp. 1939–1952, Nov. 1994.

[445] K. Rose, E. Gurewitz, and G. C. Fox, "A deterministic annealing approach to clustering," *Pattern Recogn. Lett.*, vol. 11, pp. 589–594, Sept. 1990.

[446] ———, "Vector quantization by deterministic annealing," *IEEE Trans. Inform. Theory*, vol. 38, pp. 1249–1257, July 1992.

[447] ———, "Constrained clustering as an optimization method," *IEEE Trans. Pattern Anal. Machine Intell.*, vol. 15, pp. 785–794, Aug. 1993.

[448] N. Rydbeck and C.-E. W. Sundberg, "Analysis of digital errors in nonlinear PCM systems," *IEEE Trans. Commun.*, vol. COM-24, pp. 59–65, Jan. 1976.

[449] M. J. Sabin and R. M. Gray, "Product code vector quantizers for speech waveform coding," in *Conf. Rec. GLOBECOM*, Dec. 1982, pp. 1087–1091.

[450] M. J. Sabin and R. M. Gray, "Product code vector quantizers for waveform and voice coding," *IEEE Trans. Acoust., Speech, Signal Processing*, vol. ASSP-32, pp. 474–488, June 1984.

[451] ———, "Global convergence and empirical consistency of the generalized Lloyd algorithm," *IEEE Trans. Inform. Theory*, vol. IT-32, pp. 148–155, Mar. 1986.

[452] D. J. Sakrison, "Source encoding in the presence of random disturbance," *IEEE Trans. Inform. Theory*, vol. IT-14, pp. 165–167, Jan. 1968.

[453] ———, "The rate distortion function of a Gaussian process with a weighted square error criterion," *IEEE Trans. Inform. Theory*, vol. IT-14, pp. 506–508, May 1968.

[454] ———, "The rate distortion function for a class of sources," *Inform. Contr.*, vol. 15, pp. 165–195, Aug. 1969.

[455] ———, "Addendum to 'The rate distortion function of a Gaussian process with a weighted-square error criterion'," *IEEE Trans. Inform. Theory*, vol. IT-15, pp. 610–611, Sept. 1969.

[456] ———, "Worst sources and robust codes for difference distortion measures," *IEEE Trans. Inform. Theory*, vol. IT-21, pp. 301–309, May 1975.

[457] A. Said and W. Pearlman, "A new, fast, and efficient image codec based on set partitioning in hierarchical trees," *IEEE Trans. Circuits Syst. for Video Technol.*, vol. 6, pp. 243–50, June 1996.

[458] K. Sayood, *Introduction to Data Compression*. San Francisco, CA: Morgan Kaufmann, 1996.

[459] K. Sayood, J. D. Gibson, and M. C. Rost, "An algorithm for uniform vector quantizer design," *IEEE Trans. Inform. Theory*, vol. IT-30, pp. 805–814, Nov. 1984.

[460] T. Schmidl, P. C. Cosman, and R. M. Gray, "Unbalanced nonbinary tree-structured vector quantization," in *Proc. 27th Asilomar Conf. on Signals, Systems, and Computers* (Pacific Grove, CA, Oct./Nov. 1993), pp. 1519–1523.

[461] L. Schuchman, "Dither signals and their effects on quantization noise," *IEEE Trans. Commun.*, vol. COM-12, pp. 162–165, Dec. 1964.

[462] M. P. Schutzenberger, "On the quantization of finite dimensional messages," *Inform. Contr.*, vol. 1, pp. 153–158, 1958.

[463] T. Senoo and B. Girod, "Vector quantization for entropy coding of image subbands," *IEEE Trans. Image Processing*, vol. 1, pp. 526–532, Oct. 1992.

[464] C. E. Shannon, "A mathematical theory of communication," *Bell Syst. Tech. J.*, vol. 27, pp. 379–423, 623–656, 1948.

[465] ———, "Coding theorems for a discrete source with a fidelity criterion," in *IRE Nat. Conv. Rec.*, Pt. 4, 1959, pp. 142–163.

[466] J. Shapiro, "Embedded image coding using zerotrees of wavelet coefficients," *IEEE Trans. Signal Processing*, vol. 41, pp. 3445–3462, Dec. 1993.

[467] H. N. Shaver, "Topics in statistical quantization," Syst. Theory Lab., Stanford Electron. Lab., Stanford Univ., Stanford, CA, Tech. Rep. 7050-5, May 1965.

[468] W. F. Sheppard, "On the calculation of the most probable values of frequency constants for data arranged according to equidistant divisions of a scale," *Proc. London Math. Soc.*, vol. 24, pt. 2, pp. 353–380, 1898.

[469] P. C. Shields, D. L. Neuhoff, L. D. Davisson, and F. Ledrappier, "The distortion-rate function for nonergodic sources," *Ann. Probab.*, vol. 6, no. 1, pp. 138–143, 1978.

[470] Y. Shoham and A. Gersho, "Efficient bit allocation for an arbitrary set of quantizers," *IEEE Trans. Acoust., Speech Signal Processing*, vol. 36,

337

pp. 1445–1453, Sept. 1988.

[471] V. M. Shtein, "On group transmission with frequency division of channels by the pulse-code modulation method," *Telecommun.*, pp. 169–184, 1959, a translation from *Elektrosvyaz*, no. 2, pp 43–54, 1959.

[472] D. Slepian, "A class of binary signaling alphabets," *Bell Syst. Tech. J.*, vol. 35, pp. 203–234, 1956.

[473] ———, "On delta modulation," *Bell Syst. Tech. J.*, vol. 51, pp. 2101–2136, 1972.

[474] B. Smith, "Instantaneous companding of quantized signals," *Bell Syst. Tech. J.*, vol. 36, pp. 653–709, 1957.

[475] M. R. Soleymani and S. D. Morgera, "An efficient nearest neighbor search method," *IEEE Trans. Commun.*, vol. COM-35, pp. 677–679, July 1987.

[476] ———, "A fast MMSE encoding algorithm for vector quantization," *IEEE Trans. Commun.*, vol. 37, pp. 656–659, June 1989.

[477] A. B. Sripad and D. L. Snyder, "A necessary and sufficient condition for quantization errors to be uniform and white," *IEEE Trans. Acoust., Speech, Signal Processing*, vol. ASSP-25, pp. 442–448, Oct. 1977.

[478] P. Sriram and M. Marcellin, "Image coding using wavelet transforms and entropy-constrained trellis-coded quantization," *IEEE Trans. Image Processing*, vol. 4, pp. 725–733, June 1995.

[479] Y. Steinberg and S. Verdú, "Simulation of random processes and rate-distortion theory," *IEEE Trans. Inform. Theory*, vol. 42, pp. 63–86, Jan. 1996.

[480] H. Steinhaus, "Sur la division des corp materiels en parties," *Bull. Acad. Polon. Sci.*, C1. III, vol. IV, pp. 801–804, 1956.

[481] L. C. Stewart, R. M. Gray, and Y. Linde, "The design of trellis waveform coders," *IEEE Trans. Commun.*, vol. 30, pp. 702–710, Apr. 1982.

[482] R. W. Stroh, "Optimum and adaptive differential pulse code modulation," Ph.D. dissertation, Polytech. Inst. Brooklyn, Brooklyn, NY, 1970.

[483] P. F. Swaszek, "Uniform spherical coordinate quantization of spherically symmetric sources," *IEEE Trans. Commun.*, vol. COM-33, pp. 518–521, June 1985.

[484] P. F. Swaszek, Ed., *Quantization* (Benchmark Papers in Electrical Engineering and Computer Science), vol. 29. New York: Van Nostrand Reinhold, 1985.

[485] P. Swaszek, "Asymptotic performance of Dirichlet rotated polar quantizers," *IEEE Trans. Inform. Theory*, vol. IT-31, pp. 537–540, July 1985.

[486] ———, "A vector quantizer for the Laplace source," *IEEE Trans. Inform. Theory*, vol. 37, pp. 1355–1365, Sept. 1991.

[487] ———, "Unrestricted multistage vector quantizers," *IEEE Trans. Inform. Theory*, vol. 38, pp. 1169–1174, May 1992.

[488] P. F. Swaszek and T. W. Ku, "Asymptotic performance of unrestricted polar quantizers," *IEEE Trans. Inform. Theory*, vol. IT-32, pp. 330–333, Mar. 1986.

[489] P. F. Swaszek and J. B. Thomas, "Optimal circularly symmetric quantizers," *Franklin Inst. J.*, vol. 313, no. 6, pp. 373–384, 1982.

[490] ———, "Multidimensional spherical coordinates quantization," *IEEE Trans. Inform. Theory*, vol. IT-29, pp. 570–576, July 1983.

[491] ———, "Design of quantizers from histograms," *IEEE Trans. Commun.*, vol. COM-32, pp. 240–245, 1984.

[492] N. Ta, Y. Attikiouzel, and C. Crebbin, "Vector quantization of images using the competitive networks," in *Proc. 2nd Austrailian Conf. Neural Networks, ACNN'91*, 1991, pp. 258–262.

[493] S. C. Tai, C. C. Lai, and Y. C. Lin, "Two fast nearest neighbor searching algorithms for image vector quantization," *IEEE Trans. Commun.*, vol. 44, pp. 1623–1628, Dec. 1996.

[494] H. H. Tan and K. Yao, "Evaluation of rate-distortion functions for a class of independent identically distributed sources under an absolute magnitude criterion," *IEEE Trans. Inform. Theory*, vol. IT-21, pp. 59–64, Jan. 1975.

[495] D. W. Tank and J. J. Hopfield, "Simple 'neural' optimization networks: An A/D converter, signal decision circuit, and a linear programming circuit," *IEEE Trans. Circuits Syst.*, vol. CAS-33, pp. 533–541, May 1986.

[496] T. Tarpey, L. Li, and B. D. Flury, "Principal points and self-consistent points of elliptical distributions," *Ann. Statist.*, vol. 23, no. 1, pp. 103–112, 1995.

[497] R. C. Titsworth, "Optimal threshold and level selection for quantizing data," JPL Space Programs Summary 37-23, vol. IV, pp. 196–200, Calif. Inst. Technol., Pasadena, CA, Oct. 1963.

[498] ———, "Asymptotic results for optimum equally spaced quantization of Gaussian data," JPL Space Programs Summary 37-29, vol. IV, pp. 242–244, Calif. Inst. Technol., Pasadena, CA, Oct. 1964.

[499] I. Tokaji and C. W. Barnes, "Roundoff error statistics for a continuous range of multiplier coefficients," *IEEE Trans. Circuits Syst.*, vol. CAS-34, pp. 52–59, Jan. 1987.

[500] L. Torres and J. Huhuet, "An improvement on codebook search for vector quantization" *IEEE Trans. Commun.*, vol. 42, pp. 208–210, Feb.–Apr. 1994.

[501] R. E. Totty and G. C. Clark, "Reconstruction error in waveform transmission," *IEEE Trans. Inform. Theory*, vol. IT-13, pp. 336–338, Apr. 1967.

[502] A. V. Trushkin, "Optimal bit allocation algorithm for quantizing a random vector," *Probl. Inform. Transm.*, vol. 17, no. 3, pp. 156–161, July–Sept. 1981; translated from Russian.

[503] ———, "Sufficient conditions for uniqueness of a locally optimal quantizer for a class of convex error weighting functions," *IEEE Trans. Inform. Theory*, vol. IT-28, pp. 187–198, Mar. 1982.

[504] M. J. Tsai, J. D. Villasenor, and F. Chen, "Stack-run image coding," *IEEE Trans. Circuits Syst. Video Technol.*, vol. 6, pp. 519–521, Oct. 1996.

[505] G. Ungerboeck, "Channel coding with multilevel/phase signals," *IEEE Trans. Inform. Theory*, vol. IT-28, pp. 55–67, Jan. 1982.

[506] ———, "Trellis-coded modulation with redundant signal sets, Parts I and II," *IEEE Commun. Mag.*, vol. 25, pp. 5–21, Feb. 1987.

[507] J. Vaisey and A. Gersho, "Simulated annealing and codebook design," in *Proc. IEEE Int. Conf. Acoustics, Speech, and Signal Processing (ICASSP)* (New York, Apr. 1988), pp. 1176–1179.

[508] V. A. Vaishampayan, "Design of multiple description scalar quantizers," *IEEE Trans. Inform. Theory*, vol. 39, pp. 821–824, May 1993.

[509] ———, "Design of entropy-constrained multiple-description scalar quantizers," *IEEE Trans. Inform. Theory*, vol. 40, pp. 245–250, Jan. 1994.

[510] V. A. Vaishampayan and J.-C. Batllo "Asymptotic analysis of multiple description quantizers," *IEEE Trans. Inform. Theory*, vol. 44, pp. 278–284, Jan. 1998.

[511] H. Van de Weg, "Quantization noise of a single integration delta modulation system with an N-digit code," *Phillips Res. Rep.*, vol. 8, pp. 568–569, Aug. 1971.

[512] J. Vanderkooy and S. P. Lipshitz, "Dither in digital audio," *J. Audio Eng. Soc.*, vol. 35, pp. 966–975, Dec. 1987.

[513] ———, "Resolution below the least significant bit in digital systems with dither," *J. Audio Eng. Soc.*, vol. 32, pp. 106–113, Nov. 1984, correction *Ibid.*, p. 889.

[514] R. J. van der Vleuten and J. H. Weber, "Construction and evaluation of Trellis-coded quantizers for memoryless sources," *IEEE Trans. Inform. Theory*, vol. 41, pp. 853–859, May 1995.

[515] M. Vetterli, "Multi-dimensional sub-band coding: Some theory and algorithms," *Signal Processing*, vol. 6, pp. 97–112, Apr. 1984.

[516] M. Vetterli and J. Kovačević, *Wavelets and Subband Coding*. Englewood Cliffs, NJ: Prentice-Hall, 1995.

[517] E. Vidal, "An algorithm for finding nearest neighbors in (approximately) constant average time complexity," *Patt. Recogn. Lett.*, vol. 4, pp. 145–157, 1986.

[518] M. Vishwanath and P. Chou, "Efficient algorithm for hierarchical compression of video," in *Proc. Int. Conf. Image Processing* (Austin, TX, Nov. 1994). Los Alamitos, CA: IEEE Comp. Soc. Press, 1994, vol. III, pp. 275–279.

[519] A. J. Viterbi and J. K. Omura, "Trellis encoding of memoryless discrete-time sources with a fidelity criterion," *IEEE Trans. Inform. Theory*, vol. IT-20, pp. 325–332, May 1974.

[520] A. G. Vitushkin, *Theory of the Transmission and Processing of Information*. New York: Pergaman, 1961. (Translation by R. Feinstein of *Otsenka Slozhnosti Zadachi Tabulirovaniya*. Moscow, USSR: Fizmatgiz., 1959.)

[521] J. C. Walrand and P. Varaiya, "Optimal causal coding-decoding problems," *IEEE Trans. Inform. Theory*, vol. IT-19, pp. 814–820, Nov. 1983.

[522] H. S. Wang and N. Moayeri, "Trellis coded vector quantization," *IEEE Trans. Commun.*, vol. 40, pp. 1273–1276, Aug. 1992.

[523] R. Wang, E. A. Riskin, and R. Ladner, "Codebook organization to enhance maximum a posteriori detection of progressive transmission of vector quantized images over noisy channels," *IEEE Trans. Image Processing*, vol. 5, pp. 37–48, Jan. 1996.

[524] J. Ward, "Hierarchical grouping to optimize an objective function," *J. Amer. Statist. Assoc.*, vol. 37, pp. 236–244, Mar. 1963.

[525] G. S. Watson, *Statistics on Spheres*. New York: Wiley, 1983.

[526] P. H. Westerink, J. Biemond, and D. E. Boekee, "An optimal bit allocation algorithm for sub-band coding," in *Proc. IEEE Int. Conf. Acoustics, Speech, and Signal Processing (ICASSP)*, 1988, pp. 757–760.

[527] P. H. Westerink, D. E. Boekee, J. Biemond, and J. W. Woods, "Subband coding of images using vector quantization," *IEEE Trans. Commun.*, vol. 36, pp. 713–719, June 1988.

[528] B. Widrow, "A study of rough amplitude quantization by means of Nyquist sampling theory," *IRE Trans. Circuit Theory*, vol. CT-3, pp. 266–276, 1956.

[529] ——, "Statistical analysis of amplitude quantized sampled data systems," *Trans. AIEE, Pt. II: Appl. Ind.*, vol. 79, pp. 555–568, 1960.

[530] S. G. Wilson, "Magnitude/phase quantization of independent Gaussian variates," *IEEE Trans. Commun.*, vol. COM-28, pp. 1924–1929, Nov. 1990.

[531] S. G. Wilson and D. W. Lytle, "Trellis encoding of continuous-amplitude memoryless sources," *IEEE Trans. Inform. Theory*, vol. IT-28, pp. 211–226, Mar. 1982.

[532] A. P. Wilton and G. F. Carpenter, "Fast search methods for vector lookup in vector quantization," *Electron. Lett.*, vol. 28, pp. 2311–2312, Dec. 1992.

[533] P. A. Wintz, "Transform picture coding," *Proc. IEEE*, vol. 60, pp. 809–820, July 1972.

[534] H. S. Witsenhausen, "On the structure of real-time source coders," *Bell Syst. Tech. J.*, vol. 58, pp. 1437–1451, Jul./Aug. 1979

[535] ——, "Indirect rate-distortion problems," *IEEE Trans. Inform. Theory*, vol. IT-26, pp. 518–521, Sept. 1980.

[536] J. K. Wolf, A. D. Wyner, and J. Ziv, "Source coding for multiple descriptions," *Bell Syst. Tech. J.*, vol. 59, pp. 1417–1426, Oct. 1980.

[537] J. K. Wolf and J. Ziv, "Transmission of noisy information to a noisy receiver with minimum distortion," *IEEE Trans. Inform. Theory*, vol. IT-16, pp. 406–411, July 1970.

[538] D. Wong, B.-H. Juang, and A. H. Gray, Jr., "An 800 bit/s vector quantization LPC vocoder," *IEEE Trans. Acoust., Speech, Signal Processing*, vol. ASSP-30, pp. 770–779, Oct. 1982.

[539] R. C. Wood, "On optimal quantization," *IEEE Trans. Inform. Theory*, vol. IT-5, pp. 248–252, Mar. 1969.

[540] J. W. Woods, Ed., *Subband Image Coding*. Boston, MA: Kluwer, 1991.

[541] J. W. Woods and S. D. O'Neil, "Subband coding of images," *IEEE Trans. Acoust., Speech, Signal Processing*, vol. ASSP-34, pp. 1278–1288, Oct. 1986.

[542] N. Wright, unpublished work.

[543] H.-S. Wu and J. Barba, "Index allocation in vector quantization for noisy channels," *Electron. Lett.*, vol. 29, pp. 1318–1320, July 1993.

[544] L. Wu and F. Fallside, "On the design of connectionist vector quantizers," *Comp. Speech Language*, vol. 5, pp. 207–229, 1991.

[545] ——, "Source coding and vector quantization with codebook-excited neural networks," *Comp. Speech Language*, vol. 6, pp. 43–276, 1992.

[546] X. Wu, "Globally optimum bit allocation," in *Proc. Data Compression Conf.* (Snowbird, UT, 1993), pp. 22–31.

[547] X. Wu and L. Guan, "Acceleration of the LBG algorithm," *IEEE Trans. Commun.*, vol. 42, pp. 1518–1523, Feb.–Apr. 1994.

[548] A. D. Wyner, "Communication of analog data from a Gaussian source over a noisy channel," *Bell Syst. Tech. J.*, vol. 47, pp. 801–812, May/June 1968.

[549] ——, "Recent results in the Shannon theory," *IEEE Trans. Inform. Theory*, vol. IT-20, pp. 2–10, Jan. 1994.

[550] A. D. Wyner and J. Ziv, "Bounds on the rate-distortion function for stationary sources with memory," *IEEE Trans. Inform. Theory*, vol. IT-17, pp. 508–513, Sept. 1971.

[551] Y. Yamada, K. Fujita, and S. Tazaki, "Vector quantization of video signals," in *Proc. Annu. Conf. IECE*, 1980, p. 1031.

[552] Y. Yamada and S. Tazaki, "Vector quantizer design for video signals," *IECE Trans.*, vol. J66-B, pp. 965–972, 1983.

[553] ——, "Recursive vector quantization for monochrome video signals," *IEICE Trans.*, vol. E74, pp. 399–405, Feb. 1991.

[554] Y. Yamada, S. Tazaki, and R. M. Gray, "Asymptotic performance of block quantizers with a difference distortion measure," *IEEE Trans. Inform. Theory*, vol. IT-26, pp. 6–14, Jan. 1980.

[555] Y. Yamaguchi and T. S. Huang, "Optimum fixed-length binary code," MIT Res. Lab. Electron., Quart. Progr. Rep. 78, pp. 231–233, July 15, 1965.

[556] ——, "Optimum binary code," MIT Res. Lab. Electron., Quart. Progr. Rep. 78, pp. 214–217, July 25, 1965.

[557] H. Yamamoto, "Source coding theory for cascade and branching communication systems," *IEEE Trans. Inform. Theory*, vol. IT-27, pp. 299–308, May 1981.

[558] E. Yang, Z. Zhang, and T. Berger, "Fixed-slope universal lossy data compression," *IEEE Trans. Inform. Theory*, vol. 43, pp. 1465–1476, Sept. 1997.

[559] K. Yao and H. H. Tan, "Some comments on the generalized Shannon lower bound for stationary finite-alphabet sources with memory," *IEEE Trans. Inform. Theory*, vol. IT-19, pp. 815–817, Nov. 1973.

[560] ——, "Absolute error rate-distortion functions for sources with constrained magnitudes," *IEEE Trans. Inform. Theory*, vol. IT-24, pp. 499–503, July 1978.

[561] P. L. Zador, "Development and evaluation of procedures for quantizing multivariate distributions," Ph.D. dissertation, Stanford Univ., 1963, also Stanford Univ. Dept. Statist. Tech. Rep.

[562] ——, "Topics in the asymptotic quantization of continuous random variables," Bell Lab. Tech. Memo., 1966.

[563] ——, "Asymptotic quantization error of continuous signals and the quantization dimension," *IEEE Trans. Inform. Theory*, vol. IT-28, pp. 139–148, Mar. 1982, revised version of [562].

[564] R. Zamir and M. Feder, "On lattice quantization noise," *IEEE Trans. Inform. Theory*, vol. 42, pp. 1152–1159, July 1996.

[565] ——, "Information rates of pre/post-filtered dithered quantizers," *IEEE Trans. Inform. Theory*, vol. 42, pp. 1340–1353, Sept. 1996.

[566] K. Zeger, A. Bist, and T. Linder, "Universal source coding with codebook transmission," *IEEE Trans. Commun.*, vol. 42, pp. 336–346, Feb. 1994.

[567] K. Zeger and A. Gersho, "A stochastic relaxation algorithm for improved vector quantiser design," *Electron. Lett.*, vol. 25, pp. 896–898, July 1989.

[568] ——, "Pseudo-Gray coding," *IEEE Trans. Commun.*, vol. 38, pp. 2147–2156, May 1990.

[569] K. Zeger and M. R. Kantorovitz, "Average number of facets per cell in tree-structured vector quantizer partitions," *IEEE Trans. Inform. Theory*, vol. 39, pp. 1053–1055, Sept. 1993.

[570] K. Zeger and V. Manzella, "Asymptotic bounds on optimal noisy channel quantization via random coding," *IEEE Trans. Inform. Theory*, vol. 40, pp. 1926–1938, Nov. 1994.

[571] K. Zeger, J. Vaisey, and A. Gersho, "Globally optimal vector quantizer design by stochastic relaxation," *IEEE Trans. Signal Processing*, vol. 40, pp. 310–322, Feb. 1992.

[572] L. H. Zetterberg, "A comparison between delta and pulse code modulation," *Ericsson Technics*, vol. 11, no. 1, pp. 95–154, 1955.

[573] Z. Zhang and T. Berger, "New results in binary multiple descriptions," *IEEE Trans. Inform. Theory*, vol. IT-33, pp. 502–521, July 1987.

[574] Z. Zhang and V. K. Wei, "An on-line universal lossy data compression algorithm via continuous codebook refinement. I. Basic results," *IEEE Trans. Inform. Theory*, vol. 42, pp. 803–821, May 1996.

[575] Z. Zhang and E. Yang, "An on-line universal lossy data compression algorithm via continuous codebook refinement. II. Optimality for phi-mixing source models," *IEEE Trans. Inform. Theory*, vol. 42, pp. 822–836, May 1996.

[576] Z. Zhang, E.-H. Yang, and V. K. Wei, "The redundancy of source coding with a fidelity criterion—Part One: Known statistics," *IEEE Trans. Inform. Theory*, vol. 43, pp. 71–91, Jan. 1997.

[577] J. Ziv, "Coding sources with unknown statistics—Part II: Distortion relative to a fidelity criterion," *IEEE Trans. Inform. Theory*, vol. IT-18, pp. 389–394, May 1972.

[578] ——, "Universal quantization," *IEEE Trans. Inform. Theory*, vol. IT-31, pp. 344–347, May 1985.

[579] V. N. Koshelev, "Quantizataion with minimal entropy," *Probl. Pered. Inform.*, no. 14, pp. 151–156, 1993.

[580] V. F. Babkin, M. M. Lange, and Yu. M. Shtarkov, "About fixed rate lattice coding of sources with difference fidelity criterion," *Voprosi Kibernetikia, Probl. Redundancy in Inform Syst.*, vol. 34, pp. 10–30, 1977.

[581] ——, "About coding of sequence of independent continuously distributed random values after quantizing," *Voprosi Kibernetikia, Probl. Redundancy in Comp. Networks*, vol. 35, pp. 132–137, 1978.

Modulation and Coding for Linear Gaussian Channels

G. David Forney, Jr., *Fellow, IEEE*, and Gottfried Ungerboeck, *Fellow, IEEE*

(Invited Paper)

Abstract—Shannon's determination of the capacity of the linear Gaussian channel has posed a magnificent challenge to succeeding generations of researchers. This paper surveys how this challenge has been met during the past half century. Orthogonal minimum-bandwidth modulation techniques and channel capacity are discussed. Binary coding techniques for low-signal-to-noise ratio (SNR) channels and nonbinary coding techniques for high-SNR channels are reviewed. Recent developments, which now allow capacity to be approached on any linear Gaussian channel, are surveyed. These new capacity-approaching techniques include turbo coding and decoding, multilevel coding, and combined coding/precoding for intersymbol-interference channels.

Index Terms—Binary coding, block codes, canonical channel, capacity, coding gain, convolutional codes, lattice codes, multicarrier modulation, nonbinary coding, orthogonal modulation, precoding, shaping gain, single-carrier modulation, trellis codes.

I. INTRODUCTION

THE problem of efficient data communication over linear Gaussian channels has driven much of communication and coding research in the half century since Shannon's original work [93], [94], where this problem was central. Shannon's most celebrated result was the explicit computation of the capacity of the additive Gaussian noise channel. His result has posed a magnificent challenge to succeeding generations of researchers. Only in the past decade can we say that methods of approaching capacity have been found for practically all linear Gaussian channels. This paper focuses on the modulation, coding, and equalization techniques that have proved to be most effective in meeting Shannon's challenge.

Approaching channel capacity takes different forms in different domains. There is a fundamental difference between the power-limited regime with low signal-to-noise ratio (SNR) and the high-SNR bandwidth-limited regime.

Early work focused on the power-limited regime. In this domain, binary codes suffice, and intersymbol interference (ISI) due to nonflat channel responses is rarely a serious problem. As early as the 1960's, sequential decoding [119] of binary convolutional codes [31] was shown to be an implementable method for achieving the cutoff rate R_0, which at low SNR is 3 dB away from the Shannon limit. Many

Manuscript received February 9, 1998; revised June 5, 1998.

G. D. Forney, Jr. is with Motorola, Information Systems Group, Mansfield, MA 02048-1193 USA (e-mail: LUSE27@email.mot.com).

G. Ungerboeck was with IBM Research Division, Zurich Research Laboratory, CH-8803 Rueschlikon, Switzerland (e-mail: g.ungerboeck@bluewin.ch).

Publisher Item Identifier S 0018-9448(98)06314-7.

leading communications engineers took R_0 [78], [118] to be the "practical capacity," and concluded that the problem of reaching capacity had effectively been solved. Nonetheless, only in the 1990's have coding schemes that reach or exceed R_0 actually been implemented, even for such important and effectively ideal additive white Gaussian noise (AWGN) channels as deep-space communication channels.

Meanwhile, in the bandwidth-limited regime there was essentially no practical progress beyond uncoded multilevel modulation until the invention of trellis-coded modulation in the mid-1970's and its widespread implementation in the 1980's [104]. An alternative route to capacity in this regime is via multilevel coding, which was also introduced during the 1970's [60], [75]. Trellis-coded modulation and multilevel coding are both based on the concept of set partitioning. In the late 1980's, constellation shaping was recognized as a separable part of the high-SNR coding problem, which yields a small but essential contribution to approaching capacity [48].

For channels with strongly frequency-dependent attenuation or noise characteristics, it had long been known that multicarrier modulation could in principle be used to achieve the power and rate allocations prescribed by "water pouring" (see, e.g., [51]). However, practical realizations of multicarrier modulation in combination with powerful codes have been achieved only in recent years [90]. Multicarrier techniques are particularly attractive for channels for which the capacity-achieving band consists of multiple disconnected frequency intervals, as may happen with narrowband interference.

When the capacity-achieving band is a single interval, methods for approaching capacity using serial transmission and nonlinear transmitter pre-equalization ("precoding") have been developed in the past decade [34]. With these methods, the received signal is apparently ISI-free, so ideal-channel decoding can be performed at the channel output. In addition, signal redundancy at the channel output is exploited for constellation shaping at the channel input. The performance achieved is equivalent to the performance that would be obtained if ISI could be perfectly canceled in the receiver with decision-feedback equalization (DFE). At high SNR, the effective SNR is approximately equal to the optimal effective SNR achieved by water pouring. The capacity of an ISI channel can therefore be approached as closely as the capacity of an ideal ISI-free channel.

Currently, the invention of turbo codes [13] and the rediscovery of low-density parity-check (LDPC) codes [50] have created tremendous excitement. These schemes operate successfully at rates well beyond the cutoff rate R_0, within tenths of a decibel of the Shannon limit, in both the low-SNR and high-SNR regimes. Whereas coding for rates below R_0 is a rather mature field, coding in the beyond-R_0 regime is in its early stages, and theoretical understanding is still weak. At R_0, it seems that a "phase transition" occurs from a static regime of regular code structures to a statistical regime of quasirandom codes, comparable to a phase transition between a solid and a liquid or gas.

In Section II, we define the general linear Gaussian channel and the ideal band-limited additive white Gaussian noise (AWGN) channel. We review how orthogonal modulation techniques convert a waveform channel to an equivalent ideal discrete-time AWGN channel. We discuss the Shannon limit for such channels, and emphasize the difference between the low-SNR and high-SNR regimes. We give baseline performance curves of uncoded M-ary PAM modulation, and evaluate the error probability as a function of the gap to capacity. We review union-bound performance analysis, which is a useful tool below R_0, but useless beyond R_0.

In Section III, we discuss the performance and complexity of binary block codes and convolutional codes for the low-SNR regime at rates below R_0. We also examine more powerful binary coding and decoding techniques such as sequential decoding, code concatenation with outer Reed–Solomon codes, turbo codes, and low-density parity-check codes.

In Section IV, we do the same for lattice and nonbinary trellis codes, which are the high-SNR analogs of binary block and convolutional codes, respectively. We also discuss more powerful schemes, such as multilevel coding with binary turbo codes [109].

Finally, in Section V, we consider the general linear Gaussian channel. We review water pouring and discuss approaching capacity with multicarrier modulation. For serial single-carrier transmission, we explain how to reduce the channel to an equivalent discrete-time channel without loss of optimality. We show that capacity can be approached if the intersymbol interference in this channel can be eliminated, and discuss various transmitter precoding techniques that have been developed to achieve this objective.

Appendix I discusses various forms of multicarrier modulation. In Appendix II, several uniformity properties that have proved to be helpful in the design and analysis of Euclidean-space codes are reviewed. Appendix III addresses discrete-time spectral factorization.

II. Modulation and Coding for the Ideal AWGN Channel

In this section, we first define the general linear Gaussian channel and the ideal band-limited AWGN channel. We then review minimum-bandwidth orthogonal pulse amplitude modulation (PAM) for serial transmission of real and complex symbol sequences over the ideal AWGN channel. As is well known, orthogonal transmission at a rate of $1/T$ real (respectively, complex) symbols per second requires a minimum one-sided bandwidth of $1/2T$ Hz (respectively, $1/T$ Hz).

This can be accomplished in a variety of ways. Any such modulation technique converts the continuous-time AWGN channel without loss of optimality to an ideal discrete-time AWGN channel.

We then review the channel capacity of the ideal AWGN channel, and give capacity curves for equiprobable M-ary PAM (M-PAM) inputs. We emphasize the significant differences between the low-SNR and high-SNR regimes. As a fundamental figure of merit for coding, we use the normalized signal-to-noise ratio SNR_{norm} defined in Section II-E, and compare it with the traditional figure of merit E_b/N_0. We propose that E_b/N_0 should be used only in the low-SNR regime. We give baseline performance curves for uncoded 2-PAM modulation as a function of SNR_{norm} and E_b/N_0, and for M-PAM as a function of SNR_{norm}. Finally, we discuss union-bound performance analysis.

A. General Linear Gaussian Channel and Ideal AWGN Channel

The general *linear Gaussian channel* is a real waveform channel with input signal $s(t)$, a channel impulse response $g(t)$, and additive Gaussian noise $n(t)$. The received signal is

$$r(t) = s(t) * g(t) + n(t) \tag{2.1}$$

where "$*$" denotes convolution. The Fourier transform (spectral response) of $g(t)$ will be denoted by $G(f)$. The input signal is subject to a power constraint P, and the noise has one-sided power spectral density (p.s.d.) $N(f)$.

Since all waveforms are real and thus have Hermitian-symmetric spectra about $f = 0$, only positive frequencies need to be considered. We will follow this long-established tradition, although for analytic purposes it is often preferable to consider both positive and negative frequencies. All bandwidths and power spectral densities in this paper will therefore be "one-sided."

The *ideal band-limited additive white Gaussian noise (AWGN) channel* (for short, the *ideal AWGN channel*) is a linear Gaussian channel with flat (constant) $G(f)$ and $N(f)$ over a frequency band B of one-sided bandwidth $W = \int_B df$. Signals can be transmitted only in the band B, which is not necessarily one continuous interval. The restriction to B may be due either to the channel ($G(f) = 0$ for $f \notin B$) or to system constraints.

Without loss of generality, we may normalize $G(f)$ to 1 within B, so that

$$r(t) = s(t) + n(t) \tag{2.2}$$

where $n(t)$ is AWGN with one-sided p.s.d. $N(f) = N_0$. The signal-to-noise ratio is then

$$\text{SNR} = P/N_0 W. \tag{2.3}$$

B. Real and Complex Pulse Amplitude Modulation

Let $\{a_i\}$ be a sequence of real modulation symbols representing digital data. Assume that $\{\phi_i(t)\}$ represents a set of real orthonormal waveforms; i.e., $\int \phi_i(t)\phi_{i'}(t)\,dt = \delta_{i-i'}$, where the integral is over all time, and δ_ℓ denotes the Kronecker delta function: $\delta_\ell = 1$ if $\ell = 0$, else 0. A PAM modulator transmits the continuous-time signal

$$s(t) = \sum_i a_i \phi_i(t) \qquad (2.4)$$

over an ideal AWGN channel. An optimal demodulator recovers a sequence $\{z_i\}$ of noisy estimates of the transmitted symbols $\{a_i\}$ by correlating the received signal $r(t) = s(t) + n(t)$ with the waveforms $\{\phi_i(t)\}$ (matched filtering)

$$z_i = \int r(t) \phi_i(t)\, dt = a_i + w_i. \qquad (2.5)$$

By optimum detection theory [118], the sequence $\{z_i\}$ is a set of sufficient statistics about the sequence $\{a_i\}$; i.e., all information about $\{a_i\}$ that is contained in the continuous-time received signal $r(t)$ is condensed into the discrete-time sequence $\{z_i\}$. Moreover, the orthonormality of the $\{\phi_i(t)\}$ ensures that there is no intersymbol interference (ISI), and that the sequence $\{w_i\}$ is a set of independent and identically distributed (i.i.d.) Gaussian random noise variables with mean zero and variance $\sigma_w^2 = N_0/2$. The waveform channel is thus reduced to an equivalent *discrete-time ideal AWGN channel*.

For serial PAM transmission, the orthogonal waveforms are chosen to be time shifts of a pulse $p(t)$ by integer multiples of the modulation interval T; i.e., $\{\phi_i(t)\} = \{p(t - iT)\}$, so that the transmitted signal becomes

$$s(t) = \sum_i a_i p(t - iT). \qquad (2.6)$$

The orthonormality condition requires that

$$\int p(t - iT) p(t - i'T)\, dt = \delta_{i - i'}$$

which is equivalent to

$$p(t) * p(-t)\big|_{t = \ell T} = h(\ell T) = \delta_\ell. \qquad (2.7)$$

The frequency-domain equivalent to (2.7) is known as the *Nyquist criterion* for zero ISI, namely,

$$\tilde{H}(f) = \frac{1}{T} \sum_{m \in \mathbf{Z}} H(f + m/T)$$

$$= \frac{1}{T} \sum_{m \in \mathbf{Z}} |P(f + m/T)|^2 = 1, \qquad \text{for all } f \qquad (2.8)$$

where $H(f) = |P(f)|^2$ is the Fourier transform of $h(t) = p(t) * p(-t)$ and $\tilde{H}(f)$ is the $(1/T)$-aliased spectrum of $H(f)$. The Nyquist criterion imposes no restriction on the phase of $P(f)$. Because $\tilde{H}(f)$ is periodic with period $1/T$, and for real signals $H(f)$ and thus $\tilde{H}(f)$ are symmetric around $f = 0$, it suffices that $\tilde{H}(f) = 1$ for the frequency interval $B_N = \{f: 0 \le f \le 1/2T\}$. This implies that for each $f \in B_N$, $H(f + m/T) > 0$ for at least one $m \in \mathbf{Z}$. It follows that serial ISI-free transmission of $1/T$ real symbols per second over a real channel requires a minimum one-sided bandwidth of $W = 1/2T$ Hz, or 1/2 Hz per symbol dimension transmitted per second (1/2 Hz/dim/s).

For *serial baseband transmission*, the Nyquist criterion is met with minimum bandwidth by the brick-wall spectrum

$$|P_b(f)|^2 = H_b(f) = \begin{cases} T, & |f| \le 1/2T \\ 0, & \text{elsewhere} \end{cases}$$

$$\Leftrightarrow p_b(t) * p_b(-t) = h_b(t) = \frac{\sin(\pi t/T)}{\pi t/T}. \qquad (2.9)$$

Solutions requiring more bandwidth include spectra with symmetric finite rolloffs at the band-edge frequencies $\pm 1/2T$, e.g., the well-known family of *raised-cosine* spectra [74]. Of course, the Nyquist criterion is also satisfied by the spectrum $|P(f)|^2 = T \sin(\pi f T)/(\pi f T)$, which corresponds to "unfiltered" modulation with the rectangular pulse $p(t) = 1/\sqrt{T}$ for $0 \le t \le T$ (0 elsewhere).

Serial passband transmission of real modulation symbols can be achieved with minimum bandwidth by $|P(f)|^2 = T$ for $\ell/2T \le |f| \le (\ell + 1)/2T$, $\ell \ge 1$, and zero elsewhere. This type of modulation may be referred to as *carrierless single-sideband* (CSSB) modulation; it is not often used. Serial passband transmission of complex modulation symbols $a_i = a_i^R + ja_i^I$ by *carrierless amplitude-phase* (CAP) modulation or *quadrature amplitude modulation* (QAM) is usually preferred.

To transmit a complex signal over a real passband channel, one may use a complex signal with only positive-frequency components. Sending the real part thereof creates a negative-frequency image spectrum. In the receiver, the complex signal is recovered by suppressing the negative-frequency spectrum. Let $p_b(t)$ be as defined in (2.9), and let

$$p_c(t) = p_b(t) \exp(j2\pi f_c t) = p_c^R(t) + jp_c^I(t)$$

where $f_c > T/2$ so that the Fourier transform of $p_c(t)$ is *analytic*, i.e., $P_c(f) = 0$ for $f < 0$. Then $p_c^I(t)$ is the Hilbert transform of $p_c^R(t)$, and the two pulses are said to form a *Hilbert pair*. The two pulses are orthogonal with energy $1/2$, and both have one-sided bandwidth $1/T$ Hz centered at f_c.

The transmit signals for minimum-bandwidth CAP and QAM are, respectively,

$$s_{\mathrm{CAP}}(t) = \mathrm{Re}\left\{ \sum_i a_i p_c(t - iT) \right\}$$

$$= \sum_i a_i^R p_c^R(t - iT) - a_i^I p_c^I(t - iT) \qquad (2.10)$$

and

$$s_{\mathrm{QAM}}(t) = \mathrm{Re}\left\{ \sum_i a_i p_b(t - iT) \exp(j2\pi f_c t) \right\}$$

$$= \sum_i b_i^R p_c^R(t - iT) - b_i^I p_c^I(t - iT),$$

$$b_i = a_i \exp(j2\pi f_c iT). \qquad (2.11)$$

Notice that QAM is equivalent to CAP with the symbols a_i replaced by the rotated symbols b_i. If f_c is an integer multiple of $1/T$, then there is no difference between CAP and QAM.

An advantage of CAP over CSSB is that the CAP spectrum does not need to be aligned with integer multiples of $1/2T$, as is the case for CSSB. CAP may be preferred over QAM when f_c does not substantially exceed $1/2T$. On the other hand, QAM is the modulation of choice when $f_c \gg 1/2T$. For ISI-free transmission of $1/T$ complex (two-dimensional) signals

CAP and QAM require a minimum one-sided bandwidth of $W = 1/T$ Hz, which again is 1/2 Hz/dim/s.

There exists literally an infinite variety of orthonormal modulation schemes with the same bandwidth efficiency. Consider general serial/parallel PAM modulation in which real N-vectors $\boldsymbol{a}_i = [a_i^0, a_i^1, \cdots, a_i^{N-1}]$ are transmitted at a rate of $1/T$ vectors per second over an ideal AWGN channel. Let $\boldsymbol{p}(t) = [p^0(t), p^1(t), \cdots, p^{N-1}(t)]$ be an N-vector of real pulses. A general PAM modulator transmits

$$s(t) = \sum_i \langle \boldsymbol{a}_i, \boldsymbol{p}(t - iT) \rangle \qquad (2.12)$$

where $\langle \, , \, \rangle$ denotes the inner product. If $\{p^n(t - iT)\}$ is a set of orthonormal functions, an optimum demodulator may recover noisy estimates of $\boldsymbol{z}_i$ of $\boldsymbol{a}_i$ from $r(t)$ by matched filtering

$$\boldsymbol{z}_i = \int r(t)\boldsymbol{p}(t - iT)\,dt = \boldsymbol{a}_i + \boldsymbol{w}_i. \qquad (2.13)$$

The sequence $\{\boldsymbol{w}_i\}$ is a sequence of i.i.d. Gaussian N-vectors, whose elements have variance σ_w^2. Thus the AWGN waveform channel is converted to a discrete-time vector AWGN channel, which is equivalent to N real discrete-time AWGN channels operating in parallel.

Let $\boldsymbol{P}(f) = [P^0(f), P^1(f), \cdots, P^{N-1}(f)]$ be the vector of the Fourier transforms of the elements of $\boldsymbol{p}(t)$. The frequency-domain condition for orthonormality is the *generalized Nyquist criterion* [74]

$$\begin{aligned}
\tilde{\boldsymbol{H}}(f) &= \frac{1}{T} \sum_{m \in \boldsymbol{Z}} \boldsymbol{H}(f + m/T) \\
&= \frac{1}{T} \sum_{m \in \boldsymbol{Z}} \boldsymbol{P}^*(f + m/T)\boldsymbol{P}(f + m/T) \\
&= \boldsymbol{I}_N, \qquad \text{for all } f. \qquad (2.14)
\end{aligned}$$

In (2.14), $\boldsymbol{P}^*(f)$ denotes the conjugate transpose of $\boldsymbol{P}(f)$, $\boldsymbol{H}(f)$ is the $N \times N$ matrix $\boldsymbol{H}(f) = \{[P^n(f)]^* P^{n'}(f), 0 \leq n, n' \leq N-1\}$, $\tilde{\boldsymbol{H}}(f)$ denotes the $(1/T)$-aliased spectrum of $\boldsymbol{H}(f)$, and $\boldsymbol{I}_N$ is the $N \times N$ identity matrix. As with (2.8), it suffices that $\tilde{\boldsymbol{H}}(f) = \boldsymbol{I}_N$ for the frequency interval $B_N = \{f : 0 \leq f \leq 1/2T\}$. Now consider the $\infty \times N$ matrix

$$\boldsymbol{U}(f) = T^{-1/2} \times \{P^n(f + m/T), m \in \boldsymbol{Z}, 0 \leq n \leq N - 1\}. \qquad (2.15)$$

Then (2.14) can be written as $\tilde{\boldsymbol{H}}(f) = \boldsymbol{U}^*(f)\boldsymbol{U}(f) = \boldsymbol{I}_N$, which implies that $\boldsymbol{U}(f)$ must have rank N for all f. It follows that the total one-sided bandwidth for which some $P^n(f)$, $0 \leq n \leq N-1$, $f \geq 0$ is nonzero must be at least $N/(2T)$ Hz. Because N/T symbol dimensions are transmitted per second, again a minimum one-sided bandwidth of 1/2 Hz/dim/s is needed.

If $\boldsymbol{U}(f)$ meets the minimum-bandwidth condition, then the N nonzero rows of $\boldsymbol{U}(f)$ must form an $N \times N$ unitary matrix in order that $\boldsymbol{U}^*(f)\boldsymbol{U}(f) = \boldsymbol{I}_N$. Conversely, any set of unitary matrices $\{\boldsymbol{U}(f), f \in B_N\}$ defines a minimum-bandwidth orthonormal transmission scheme. The number of such schemes is therefore uncountably infinite.

Appendix I describes two currently popular multicarrier modulation schemes, namely, discrete multitone (DMT) and discrete wavelet multitone (DWMT) modulation.

The optimum design of transmitter and receiver filters for serial/parallel transmission over general noisy linear channels has been discussed in [28].

C. Capacity of the Ideal AWGN Channel

We have seen that all orthonormal modulation schemes with optimum matched-filter detection are equivalent to an ideal discrete-time AWGN channel with real input symbols a_i and real output signals z_i, where $z_i = a_i + w_i$. The i.i.d. Gaussian noise variables w_i have zero mean and variance $\sigma_w^2 = N_0/2$.

Let the average input-symbol energy per dimension be $E_s = E\{a_i^2\}$, and let the average energy per information bit be $E_b = E_s/R$, where R is the code rate in bits per dimension (b/dim). Because $P = E_s/T$ and $W = 1/2T$, the signal-to-noise ratio (SNR) of the AWGN waveform channel and the discrete-time AWGN channel are identical:

$$\text{SNR} = \frac{P}{N_0 W} = \frac{E_s}{\sigma_w^2} = 2R \frac{E_b}{N_0}. \qquad (2.16)$$

The channel capacity is the maximum mutual information between channel input and output, which is obtained with a Gaussian distribution over the symbols a_i with average power E_s. Shannon's most famous result states the capacity in bits per second as

$$C_{[\text{b/s}]} = W \log_2(1 + \text{SNR}). \qquad (2.17)$$

Equivalently, the capacity in bits per dimension is given by

$$C = \tfrac{1}{2} \log_2(1 + \text{SNR}) \; [\text{b/dim}]. \qquad (2.18)$$

Shannon [93], [94] showed that reliable transmission is possible for any rate $R < C$, and impossible if $R > C$. (Unless stated otherwise, in this paper capacity C and code rates R are given in bits per dimension.)

The capacity can be upper-bounded and approximated for low SNR by a linear function in SNR, and lower-bounded and approximated for high SNR by a logarithmic function in SNR, as follows:

$$\text{SNR} \ll 1: \quad C \underset{(\geq)}{\cong} \tfrac{1}{2} \text{SNR} \log_2(e) \qquad (2.19)$$

$$\text{SNR} \gg 1: \quad C \underset{(\leq)}{\cong} \tfrac{1}{2} \log_2(\text{SNR}). \qquad (2.20)$$

A finite set A from which modulation symbols a_i can be chosen is called a *signal alphabet* or *signal constellation*. An M-PAM constellation contains $M \geq 2$ equidistant real symbols centered on the origin; i.e., $A = (d_0/2)\{-M + 1, -M + 3, \cdots, M - 1\}$, where d_0 is the minimum distance between symbols. For example, $A = \{-3, -1, +1, +3\}$ is a 4-PAM constellation with $d_0 = 2$. If the symbols are equiprobable, then the average symbol energy is

$$E_s = (M^2 - 1) d_0/12. \qquad (2.21)$$

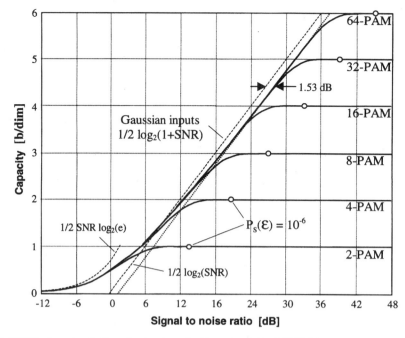

Fig. 1. Capacity of the ideal AWGN channel with Gaussian inputs and with equiprobable M-PAM inputs.

Fig. 1 shows the capacity and the mutual information achieved with equiprobable M-PAM ("equiprobable M-PAM capacity"), for $M = 2, 4, \cdots, 64$, as a function of SNR. The M-PAM curves saturate because information cannot be sent at a rate higher than $R = \log_2 M$.

D. Low-SNR and High-SNR Regimes

We see from Fig. 1 that in the low-SNR regime an equiprobable binary alphabet is nearly optimal. For SNR < 1 (0 dB), the reduction in capacity is negligible.

In the high-SNR regime, the capacity of equiprobable M-PAM constellations asymptotically approaches a straight line parallel to the capacity of the AWGN channel. The asymptotic loss of $\pi e/6$ (1.53 dB) is due to using a uniform rather than a Gaussian distribution over the signal set. To achieve capacity, the use of powerful coding with equiprobable M-PAM signals is not enough. To obtain the remaining 1.53 dB, constellation-shaping techniques that produce a Gaussian-like distribution over an M-PAM constellation are required (see Section IV-B).

Thus coding techniques for the low-SNR and high-SNR regimes are quite different. In the low-SNR regime, binary codes are nearly optimal, and no constellation shaping is required. Good binary coding and decoding techniques have been known since the 1960's.

On the other hand, in the high-SNR regime, nonbinary signal constellations must be used. Very little progress in developing practical codes for this regime was made until the advent of trellis-coded modulation in the late 1970's and 1980's. To approach capacity, coding techniques must be supplemented with constellation-shaping techniques. Moreover, on bandwidth-limited channels, ISI is often a dominant impairment, and practical techniques for combined coding, shaping, and equalization are required to approach capacity. Most of the progress in these areas has been made only in the past decade.

For these reasons, we discuss coding for the low-SNR and high-SNR regimes separately in Sections III and IV, and coding for the general linear Gaussian channel in Section V.

E. Baseline Performance of Uncoded M-PAM and Normalized SNR

In an uncoded M-PAM system, $R = \log_2 M$ information bits are independently encoded into each M-PAM symbol transmitted. In the receiver, the optimum decoding rule is then to make independent symbol-by-symbol decisions. The probability that a Gaussian noise variable w_i exceeds half of the distance d_0 between adjacent M-PAM symbols is $Q(d_0/2\sigma_w)$, where [74]

$$Q(x) = \frac{1}{\sqrt{2\pi}} \int_x^\infty \exp\left(-y^2/2\right) dy < \exp\left(-x^2/2\right). \quad (2.22)$$

The error probability per symbol is given by $P_s(\mathcal{E}\,|\,\text{outer}) = Q(d_0/2\sigma_w)$ for the two outer points, and by $P_s(\mathcal{E}\,|\,\text{inner}) = 2Q(d_0/2\sigma_w)$ for the $M-2$ inner points, so the average error probability per symbol is

$$\begin{aligned} P_s(\mathcal{E}) &= \frac{2(M-1)}{M} Q(d_0/2\sigma_w) \\ &= \frac{2(M-1)}{M} Q\left(\sqrt{\frac{3\,\text{SNR}}{M^2-1}}\right) \end{aligned} \quad (2.23)$$

where $(d_0/2\sigma_w)^2 = 3\,\text{SNR}/(M^2-1)$ follows from (2.16) and (2.21). Thus $P_s(\mathcal{E})$ is a function only of M and SNR. The circles in Fig. 1 indicate the values of SNR for which $P_s(\mathcal{E}) = 10^{-6}$ is achieved.

The capacity formula (2.18) can be rewritten as $\text{SNR}/(2^{2C} - 1) = 1$. This suggests defining the *normalized SNR*

$$\text{SNR}_{\text{norm}} = \text{SNR}/(2^{2R} - 1) \quad (2.24)$$

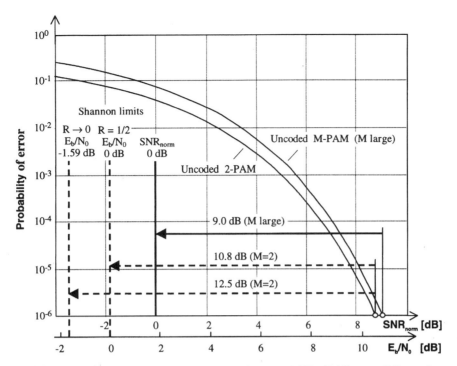

Fig. 2. Bit-error probability $P_b(\mathcal{E})$ versus E_b/N_0 for uncoded 2-PAM, and symbol-error probability $P_s(\mathcal{E})$ versus SNR_{norm} for uncoded M-PAM (M large).

where R is the actual data rate of a given modulation and coding scheme. For a capacity-achieving scheme, R equals the channel capacity C and $\text{SNR}_{\text{norm}} = 1$ (0 dB). If $R < C$, as will always be the case in practice, then $\text{SNR}_{\text{norm}} > 1$. The value of SNR_{norm} thus signifies how far a system is operating from the Shannon limit (the "gap to capacity").

For uncoded M-PAM, from $R = \log_2 M$ and (2.24) one obtains

$$\text{SNR}/(M^2 - 1) = \text{SNR}/(2^{2R} - 1) = \text{SNR}_{\text{norm}}.$$

Therefore, the average error probability per symbol of uncoded M-PAM can be written as

$$P_s(\mathcal{E}) = \frac{2(M-1)}{M} Q(\sqrt{3\,\text{SNR}_{\text{norm}}})$$
$$\cong 2\,Q(\sqrt{3\,\text{SNR}_{\text{norm}}})\ (M\ \text{large}). \qquad (2.25)$$

Note that the baseline M-PAM performance curve of $P_s(\mathcal{E})$ versus SNR_{norm} is nearly independent of M, if M is large. This shows that SNR_{norm} is appropriately normalized for rate in the high-SNR regime.

Because $E_b/N_0 = \text{SNR}/2R$ by (2.16), the general relation between SNR_{norm} and E_b/N_0 at a given rate R (in bits per dimension) is given by

$$\frac{E_b}{N_0} = \frac{2^{2R} - 1}{2R}\,\text{SNR}_{\text{norm}}. \qquad (2.26)$$

If $R \ll 1$, then $E_b/N_0 \cong (\ln 2)\,\text{SNR}_{\text{norm}}$, so the two figures of merit are equivalent. If $R = 1/2$, then $E_b/N_0 = \text{SNR}_{\text{norm}}$; if $R = 1$, then $E_b/N_0 = (3/2)\,\text{SNR}_{\text{norm}}$.

In the low-SNR regime, if bandwidth is truly unconstrained, then as bandwidth is increased to permit usage of powerful low-rate binary codes, both SNR and R tend toward zero. In

this power-limited regime, it is appropriate to use as a figure of merit the traditional ratio E_b/N_0.

From the general Shannon limit $\text{SNR}_{\text{norm}} > 1$, we obtain the Shannon limit on E_b/N_0 for a given rate R

$$E_b/N_0 > (2^{2R} - 1)/2R. \qquad (2.27)$$

This lower bound decreases monotonically with R, and as R approaches 0, it approaches the *ultimate Shannon limit*

$$E_b/N_0 > \ln 2\ (-1.59\ \text{dB}). \qquad (2.28)$$

However, if bandwidth is limited, then the Shannon limit on E_b/N_0 is higher. For example, if $R = 1/2$, then $E_b/N_0 > 1$ (0 dB).

Because $E_b/N_0 = (3/2)\,\text{SNR}_{\text{norm}}$ at $R = 1$, the error probability per symbol (or per bit) of uncoded 2-PAM may be expressed in two equivalent ways

$$P_b(E) = Q(\sqrt{3\,\text{SNR}_{\text{norm}}}) = Q\left(\sqrt{\frac{2E_b}{N_0}}\right). \qquad (2.29)$$

In this paper we will use E_b/N_0 in the low-SNR regime and SNR_{norm} in the high-SNR regime as the fundamental figures of merit of uncoded and coded modulation schemes. This practice appears to be on its way to general adoption.

The "effective coding gain" of a coded modulation scheme is measured by the reduction in required E_b/N_0 or SNR_{norm} to achieve a certain target error probability relative to a baseline uncoded scheme. In the low-SNR regime, the baseline will be taken as 2-PAM; in the high-SNR regime, the baseline will be taken as M-PAM (M large).

Fig. 2 gives the probability of bit error $P_b(\mathcal{E})$ for uncoded 2-PAM as a function of both SNR_{norm} and E_b/N_0. Note that the axis for E_b/N_0 is shifted by a factor of $3/2$ (1.76 dB) relative to the axis for SNR_{norm}. At $P_b(\mathcal{E}) = 10^{-6}$, the baseline uncoded binary modulation scheme operates about 12.5 dB away from the Shannon limit. Therefore, a coding gain of up to 12.5 dB in E_b/N_0 is in principle possible at this $P_b(\mathcal{E})$, provided that bandwidth can be expanded sufficiently to permit the use of powerful very-low-rate binary codes ($R \ll 1$). If bandwidth can be expanded by a factor of only 2, then with binary codes of rate $R = 1/2$ a coding gain of up to about 10.8 dB can in principle be achieved.

Fig. 2 also depicts the probability of symbol error $P_s(\mathcal{E})$ for uncoded M-PAM as a function of SNR_{norm} for large M (in this case, the E_b/N_0 axis should be ignored). At $P_s(\mathcal{E}) = 10^{-6}$, a baseline uncoded M-PAM modulation scheme operates about 9 dB away from the Shannon limit in the bandwidth-limited regime. Thus if bandwidth is a fixed, nonexpandable resource, a coding gain of up to about 9 dB in SNR_{norm} is in principle possible at $P_s(\mathcal{E}) = 10^{-6}$. This conclusion holds even at $R = 1$.

F. The Union Bound

The union bound is a useful tool for evaluating the performance of moderately powerful codes, although it breaks down for rates beyond the cutoff rate R_0.

The union bound is based on evaluating pairwise error probabilities between pairs of coded sequences. On an ideal real discrete-time AWGN channel, the received sequence $\boldsymbol{z} = \boldsymbol{a} + \boldsymbol{w}$ is the sum of the transmitted coded sequence $\boldsymbol{a}$ and an i.i.d. Gaussian sequence $\boldsymbol{w}$ with mean 0 and variance σ_w^2 per symbol. Because $p(\boldsymbol{z}|\boldsymbol{a}) \propto \exp\left(-\|\boldsymbol{z} - \boldsymbol{a}\|^2/2\sigma_w^2\right)$, maximum-likelihood (ML) decoding is equivalent to minimum-distance decoding.

Given two coded sequences $\boldsymbol{a}$ and $\boldsymbol{a}'$ that differ by the Euclidean distance $d(\boldsymbol{a}, \boldsymbol{a}')$, the probability that the received sequence $\boldsymbol{z} = \boldsymbol{a} + \boldsymbol{w}$ will be closer to $\boldsymbol{a}'$ than to $\boldsymbol{a}$ is given by

$$\Pr(\boldsymbol{a}'|\boldsymbol{a}) = Q(d(\boldsymbol{a}, \boldsymbol{a}')/2\sigma_w). \tag{2.30}$$

The probability that $\boldsymbol{z}$ will be closer to $\boldsymbol{a}'$ than to $\boldsymbol{a}$ for any $\boldsymbol{a}' \neq \boldsymbol{a}$, which is precisely the probability of error with ML decoding, is thus upperbounded by

$$P(\mathcal{E}|\boldsymbol{a}) \leq \sum_{\boldsymbol{a}' \neq \boldsymbol{a}} Q(d(\boldsymbol{a}', \boldsymbol{a})/2\sigma_w). \tag{2.31}$$

The average probability of error over all coded sequences $\boldsymbol{a}$ is upperbounded by the *union bound*

$$P(\mathcal{E}) \leq \sum_d K_d Q(d/2\sigma_w) \tag{2.32}$$

where K_d is the average number of coded sequences $\boldsymbol{a}' \neq \boldsymbol{a}$ at distance d from $\boldsymbol{a}$.

The Gaussian error probability function $Q(x)$ decays exponentially as $\exp\left(-x^2/2\right)$. Therefore, if K_d does not rise too rapidly with d, the union bound is dominated by its first term, which is called the *union bound estimate* (UBE)

$$P(\mathcal{E}) \cong K_{\min} Q(d_{\min}/2\sigma_w) \tag{2.33}$$

where $d_{\min}$ is the minimum distance between coded sequences, and $K_{\min}$ is the average number of sequences at minimum distance $d_{\min}$ from a given coded sequence. The squared

argument of the $Q(\bullet)$ function in the union bound estimate yields a first-order estimate of performance, namely,

$$
\begin{aligned}
\frac{d_{\min}^2}{4\sigma_w^2} &= \frac{d_{\min}^2}{d_0^2} \frac{2^{2R} - 1}{2^{2R_b} - 1} 3\,\text{SNR}_{\text{norm}} \\
&= \frac{d_{\min}^2}{d_0^2} \frac{R}{R_b} \frac{2E_b}{N_0}
\end{aligned}
\tag{2.34}
$$

where d_0^2 is the squared baseline distance, $R_b = \log_2 M$ is the baseline rate, and $R < R_b$ is the actual rate.

In comparison to the baseline squared distance, there is a *distance gain* of a factor of $d_{\min}^2/d_0^2$. However, in comparison to the baseline rate R_b there is also a *redundancy loss*. In the high-SNR regime, the redundancy loss is approximately $2^{-2r} = 2^{2(R-R_b)}$, where $r = R_b - R$ is the redundancy of the code in b/dim. In the low-SNR regime, with 2-PAM signaling ($R_b = 1$), the redundancy loss is simply a factor of $R/R_b = R$. The product of these factors gives the *nominal* (or asymptotic) *coding gain*, which is based solely on the argument of the $Q(\bullet)$ function in the UBE.

The *effective coding gain* is the difference between the signal-to-noise ratios required to achieve a certain target error rate with a coded modulation scheme and to obtain the same error rate with an uncoded scheme of the same rate R. The effective coding gain is typically less than the nominal coding gain, because the *error coefficient* $K_{\min}$ is typically larger than the baseline error coefficient. Note that $K_{\min}$ depends on exactly what is being estimated, e.g., bit-error probability, block-error probability, etc., over which interval, per bit, per dimension, per block, etc. A rule of thumb based on the slope of the $Q(\bullet)$ curve in the 10^{-5}–10^{-6} region is that every increase of a factor of two in the error coefficient $K_{\min}$ costs about 0.2 dB in effective coding gain, provided that $K_{\min}$ is not too large.

The union bound blows up even for optimal codes at the cutoff rate R_0, i.e., the corresponding error exponent goes to zero [51]. For low-SNR channels, the cutoff rate is 3 dB away from the Shannon limit; i.e., the cutoff rate limit is $E_b/N_0 = 2\ln 2$ (1.42 dB). For high-SNR channels, the cutoff rate corresponds to an SNR_{norm} which is a factor of $4/e$ away from the Shannon limit [95]; i.e., the cutoff rate limit is $\text{SNR}_{\text{norm}} = 4/e$ (1.68 dB).

Beyond R_0, codes cannot be analyzed by using the union bound estimate. Any apparent agreement between a union bound estimate and actual performance in the region between R_0 and C must be regarded as fortuitous. Because the operational significance of minimum distance or nominal coding gain is that they give a good estimate of performance via the union bound, their significance in the beyond-R_0 regime is questionable.

III. BINARY CODES FOR POWER-LIMITED CHANNELS

In this section we discuss coding techniques for power-limited (low-SNR) ideal AWGN channels. As we have seen, low-rate binary codes are near-optimal in this regime, as long as soft decisions are used at the output. We develop a union bound estimate of probability of error per bit with maximum-likelihood (ML) decoding. We also show that the nominal coding gain of a rate-k/n binary code C with minimum Hamming distance d over baseline 2-PAM is simply $\gamma_c(C) = (k/n)d$.

Then we give the effective coding gains of known moderate-complexity block and convolutional codes versus the branch complexity of their minimal trellises, assuming ML decoding at rates below R_0. Convolutional codes are clearly superior in terms of coding gain versus trellis complexity.

Finally, we briefly discuss higher-performance codes, including convolutional codes with sequential decoding, concatenated codes with outer Reed–Solomon codes, and turbo codes and other capacity-approaching codes.

A. Optimality of Low-Rate Binary Linear Codes with Soft Decisions

We have seen in Fig. 1 that on an AWGN channel with SNR < 1, the capacity with equiprobable binary signaling is negligibly less than the true capacity. Moreover, on symmetric channels such as the ideal AWGN channel, it has long been known that there is no reduction in capacity if one restricts one's attention to *linear* binary codes [31], [51].

As shown by (2.26), if the code rate $R = k/n$ is greater than zero, the figure of merit E_b/N_0 is lower-bounded by $(2^{2R} - 1)/2R$, which exceeds the ultimate Shannon limit of $\ln 2$ (−1.59 dB). If R is small, then

$$(2^{2R} - 1)/2R \cong (\ln 2)(1 + R \ln 2) \cong (\ln 2)2^R \quad (3.1)$$

so the lower bound is approximately

$$E_b/N_0 > (\ln 2)2^R \quad (-1.59 + 3.01R \text{ decibels}). \quad (3.2)$$

For example, the penalty to operate at rate $R = 1/4$ is about 0.77 dB, which is not insignificant. However, there may be a limit on bandwidth, which scales as $1/R$. Moreover, even if bandwidth is unlimited, there is usually a technology-dependent lower limit on the energy $E_s = RE_b$ per transmitted symbol below which the performance of other system elements (e.g., tracking loops) degrades significantly.

On the other hand, whereas two-level quantization of the channel input costs little, two-level quantization of the channel output (hard decisions) costs of the order of 2–3 dB [118]. Optimized three-level quantization (hard decisions with erasures) costs only about half as much (1–1.5 dB) [39]. However, optimized uniform eight-level (3-bit) quantization (quantized soft decisions) costs only about 0.2 dB, and has often been used in practice [55].

B. The Union Bound and Nominal Coding Gain

An (n, k, d) binary linear block code C is a k-dimensional subspace of the n-dimensional binary vector space $(\boldsymbol{F}_2)^n$ such that the minimum Hamming distance between any two code n-tuples is d. Its size is $|C| = 2^k$.

For use on the Gaussian channel, code bits are usually mapped to real numbers via the standard 2-PAM map $m : \{0, 1\} \to \{\pm d_0/2\}$. The Euclidean image $m(C)$ is then a subset of 2^k vertices of the 2^n vertices $m((\boldsymbol{F}_2)^n) \subseteq \boldsymbol{R}^n$ of an n-cube of side d_0 centered on the origin. If two code n-tuples $\boldsymbol{c}, \boldsymbol{c}' \in C$ differ in d_H places, then the squared

distance between their Euclidean images $m(\boldsymbol{c})$ and $m(\boldsymbol{c}')$ is $d_0^2 d_H$. Consequently, the minimum squared Euclidean distance between any two vectors in $m(C)$ is

$$d_{\min}^2(C) = d_0^2 d. \quad (3.3)$$

Moreover, if C has K_d words of minimum weight d, then by linearity there are K_d vectors $m(\boldsymbol{c}')$ at minimum squared distance $d_{\min}^2(C)$ from every vector $m(\boldsymbol{a})$ in $m(C)$.

The union bound estimate (UBE) of the probability of a block decoding error $P(\mathcal{E})$ is then

$$P(\mathcal{E}) \cong K_d Q(d_{\min}(C)/2\sigma_w) = K_d Q(\sqrt{d}\, d_0/2\sigma_w). \quad (3.4)$$

Because $E_b = (n/k)\, d_0^2/4$ and $\sigma_w^2 = N_0/2$, we may write the UBE as

$$P(\mathcal{E}) \cong K_d Q(\sqrt{\gamma_c(C)2E_b/N_0}) \quad (3.5)$$

where the *nominal coding gain* of an (n, k, d) binary linear code C is defined as

$$\gamma_c(C) = (k/n)\, d. \quad (3.6)$$

This is the product of a distance gain of a factor of d with a redundancy loss of a factor of $R = k/n$. The uncoded 2-PAM baseline corresponds to a $(1, 1, 1)$ code, for which $\gamma_c(C) = 1$ and $K_d = 1$.

For comparability with the uncoded baseline, it is appropriate to normalize $P(\mathcal{E})$ by k to obtain the probability of block decoding error per information bit (not the bit-error probability)

$$P_b(\mathcal{E}) \cong K(C)Q(\sqrt{\gamma_c(C)2E_b/N_0}) \quad (3.7)$$

in which the normalized error coefficient is $K(C) = K_d/k$.

Graphically, a curve of the form of (3.7) may be obtained simply by moving the baseline curve $P_b(\mathcal{E}) = Q(\sqrt{2E_b/N_0})$ of Fig. 2 to the left by $\gamma_c(C)$ (in decibels), and upward by a factor of $K(C)$.

C. Biorthogonal Codes

Biorthogonal codes are asymptotically optimal codes for the ideal AWGN channel, provided that bandwidth is unlimited. They illustrate both the usefulness and the limitations of union bound estimates.

For any integer $k > 1$ there exists a $(2^{k-1}, k, 2^{k-2})$ binary linear code C, e.g., a first-order Reed–Muller code, such that its Euclidean image $m(C)$ is a biorthogonal signal set in 2^{k-1}-space (i.e., a set of 2^{k-1} orthogonal vectors and their negatives). Its nominal coding gain is

$$\gamma_c(C) = k/2 \quad (3.8)$$

which goes to infinity as k goes to infinity.

Such a code consists of the all-zero word, the all-one word, and $K_d = 2^k - 2$ codewords of weight $d = 2^{k-2}$. The union bound on block error probability thus becomes

$$P(\mathcal{E}) \leq (2^k - 2)Q(\sqrt{kE_b/N_0}) + Q(\sqrt{2kE_b/N_0})$$
$$< 2^k Q(\sqrt{kE_b/N_0})$$
$$< \exp(-k(E_b/2N_0 - \ln 2)) \quad (3.9)$$

347

TABLE I
PARAMETERS AND CODING GAINS OF REED–MULLER CODES AND THE GOLAY CODE

(n, k, d)	$\gamma_c(C)$	(dB)	N_d	$K(C)$	$\gamma_{\text{eff}}(C)$ (dB)	s
(8, 4, 4)	2	3.01	14	3.5	2.6	3
(16, 5, 8)	2.5	3.98	30	6	3.5	4
(24, 12, 8)	4	6.02	759	63.2	4.8	9
(32, 6, 16)	3	4.77	62	10.3	4.1	5
(32, 16, 8)	4	6.02	620	38.8	5.0	9
(64, 7, 32)	3.5	5.44	126	18	4.6	6
(64, 22, 16)	5.5	7.40	2604	118.4	6.0	14
(128, 8, 64)	4	6.02	254	31.8	5.0	7
(128, 29, 32)	7.25	8.60	10668	367.9	6.9	20
(128, 64, 16)	8	9.03	94488	1476.4	6.9	30
(256, 9, 128)	4.5	6.53	510	56.7	5.4	8
(256, 37, 64)	9.25	9.66	43180	1167.0	7.6	27
(256, 93, 32)	11.625	10.65	777240	8357.4	8.0	50

where we have used the upper bound $Q(x) < \exp(-x^2/2)$. Thus if $E_b/N_0 > 2\ln 2$ (1.42 dB), or if $\text{SNR}_{\text{norm}} > 2$, then the union bound approaches zero exponentially with k. Thus the union bound shows that with biorthogonal codes it is possible to approach within 3 dB of the Shannon limit, which corresponds to the cutoff rate R_0 of the low-SNR AWGN channel.

A more refined upper bound [118] shows that for $\ln 2 < E_b/N_0 \le 4\ln 2$

$$P(\mathcal{E}) < \exp\left(-k(\sqrt{E_b/N_0} - \sqrt{\ln 2})^2\right) \qquad (3.10)$$

which approaches zero exponentially with k if $E_b/N_0 > \ln 2$ (−1.59 dB), or if $\text{SNR}_{\text{norm}} > 1$. In other words, this bound shows that biorthogonal codes can achieve an arbitrarily small error probability for any E_b/N_0 above the ultimate Shannon limit. It also illustrates the limitations of the union bound, which blows up 3 dB away.

Of course, the code rate $R = k2^{-k+1}$ approaches zero rapidly as k becomes large, so long biorthogonal codes can be used only if bandwidth is effectively unlimited. They can be decoded efficiently by fast Hadamard transform techniques [43], but even so the decoding complexity is proportional to $k2^k$, which increases exponentially with k.

A (32, 6, 16) biorthogonal code decoded by a fast Hadamard transform ("Green machine") was used for an early deep-space mission (Mariner, 1969) [79].

D. Effective Coding Gains of Known Codes

For moderate codelengths, Bose–Chaudhuri–Hocquenghem (BCH) codes form a large and well-known class of binary linear block codes that often are the best known codes in terms of their parameters (n, k, d). Unfortunately, not much is known about soft-decision ML decoding algorithms for such codes. The most efficient general methods are trellis-based methods—i.e., the code is represented by a trellis, and the Viterbi algorithm (VA) is used for ML decoding.

There has been considerable recent work on efficient trellis representations of binary linear block codes, including BCH codes [107].

Reed–Muller (RM) codes are as good as BCH codes for $n \le 32$, and almost as good for $n \le 128$ in terms of the parameters (n, k, d). Efficient trellis representations are known for all RM codes [43]. In fact, in terms of nominal coding gain $(k/n)d$ or effective coding gain versus trellis complexity, RM codes are often better than BCH codes [107]. Moreover, the number K_d of minimum-weight codewords is known for all RM codes, but not for all BCH codes [77].

In Table I we give the parameters n, k, d, N_d, $\gamma_c(C)$, and $\gamma_{\text{eff}}(C)$ for all RM codes with lengths n up to 256 and code rates $R = k/n$ up to 1/2, including biorthogonal codes, and also for the (24, 12, 8) Golay code. We also give a parameter s that measures trellis complexity (the log branch complexity). To estimate from $\gamma_c(C)$ the effective coding gain $\gamma_{\text{eff}}(C)$, we use the normalized error coefficient $K(C) = K_d/k$, and apply the "0.2-dB loss per factor of 2" rule, which is not very accurate for large K_d. We remind the reader that these estimated effective coding gains assume soft decisions, ML decoding, and the accuracy of the union bound estimate, and that the complexity parameter assumes trellis-based decoding. Moreover, complexity comparisons are always technology-dependent.

There also exist algebraic decoding algorithms for all of these codes, as well as for BCH codes. Algebraic error-correcting decoders that are based on hard decisions are not appropriate for the AWGN channel, since hard decisions cost 2 to 3 dB. For BCH and other algebraic block codes, there do exist efficient soft-decision decoding algorithms such as generalized minimum distance (GMD) decoding [39] and the Chase algorithms [19] that are capable of approaching ML performance; furthermore, the complexity of "one-pass" GMD decoding [12] is not much greater than that of error-correction only. However, we know of no published results showing that

TABLE II
PARAMETERS AND CODING GAINS OF SELECTED LOW-RATE COVOLUTIONAL CODES

(n, k, ν, d)	$\gamma_c(C)$	(dB)	$K_d = K(C)$	$\gamma_{\text{eff}}(C)$ (dB)	s
(2, 1, 1, 3)	1.5	1.76	1	1.8	2
(2, 1, 2, 5)	2.5	3.98	1	4.0	3
(2, 1, 3, 6)	3	4.77	1	4.8	4
(2, 1, 4, 7)	3.5	5.44	2	5.2	5
(2, 1, 5, 8)	4	6.02	2	5.8	6
(2, 1, 6, 10)	5	6.99	12	6.3	7
(2, 1, 7, 10)	5	6.99	1	7.0	8
(2, 1, 8, 12)	6	7.78	10	7.1	9
(3, 1, 1, 5)	1.67	2.22	1	2.2	2
(3, 1, 2, 8)	2.67	4.26	2	4.1	3
(3, 1, 3, 10)	3.33	5.23	3	4.9	4
(3, 1, 4, 12)	4	6.02	5	5.6	5
(3, 1, 5, 13)	4.33	6.37	1	6.4	6
(3, 1, 6, 15)	5	6.99	3	6.7	7
(3, 1, 7, 16)	5.33	7.27	1	7.3	8
(3, 1, 8, 18)	6	7.78	5	7.4	9
(4, 1, 1, 7)	1.75	2.43	1	2.4	2
(4, 1, 2, 10)	2.5	3.98	1	4.0	3
(4, 1, 3, 13)	3.25	5.12	2	4.9	4
(4, 1, 4, 16)	4	6.02	4	5.6	5
(4, 1, 5, 18)	4.5	6.53	3	6.2	6
(4, 1, 6, 20)	5	6.99	10	6.4	7
(4, 1, 7, 22)	5.5	7.40	1	7.4	8
(4, 1, 8, 24)	6	7.78	2	7.6	9

the performance–complexity tradeoff for moderate-complexity binary block codes with soft-decision algebraic decoding can be better than that of moderate-complexity binary convolutional codes with trellis-based decoding on AWGN channels.

From this table it appears that the best tradeoff between effective coding gain and trellis complexity is obtained with low-rate biorthogonal codes, if bandwidth is not an issue. An effective coding gain of about 5 dB can be obtained with the (128, 8, 64) code, whose code rate is $R = 1/16$, with a trellis branch complexity of only $2^7 = 128$. The (24, 12, 8) and (32, 16, 8) codes, which are close cousins, can also obtain an effective coding gain of about 5 dB, with a somewhat greater branch complexity of $2^9 = 512$, but with a more comfortable code rate of $R = 1/2$. Beyond these codes, complexity increases rapidly.

A similar analysis can be performed for binary linear convolutional codes. For a rate-k/n binary linear convolutional code C with free distance d, the nominal coding gain is again $\gamma_c(C) = (k/n)d$. If K_d is the number of weight-d code sequences that start in a given k-input, n-output block, then the appropriate error coefficient to measure the probability of error event per information bit is again K_d/k.

Table II gives the parameters of the best known rate-$1/n$ time-invariant binary linear convolutional codes for $n = 2, 3$, 4 with constraint lengths $\nu \leq 7$ [18]. The log branch complexity parameter s equals $\nu + 1$. (For some combinations of parameters (n, k, ν), superior time-varying codes are known [70].)

It is apparent from a comparison of Tables I and II that convolutional codes offer a much better performance/complexity tradeoff than block codes. It is possible to obtain more than 6 dB of effective coding gain with a 32-state or 64-state rate-1/2 or rate-1/3 convolutional code with a simple, regular trellis (VA) decoder. No block code approaches such performance with such modest complexity.

Consequently, for power-limited channels such as the deep-space channel, convolutional codes rather than block codes have been used almost from the earliest days [26]. Although this is due in part to the historical fact that efficient maximum-likelihood (ML) or near-ML soft-decision decoding algorithms were invented much earlier for convolutional codes, Tables I and II show that convolutional codes have an inherent performance/complexity advantage.

E. Sequential Decoding

Sequential decoding of convolutional codes was perhaps the earliest near-ML decoding algorithm, and is still one of the few that can operate at the cutoff rate R_0. For this reason, sequential decoding was the first coding scheme used for the deep-space application (Pioneer, 1968) [26].

Although there exist many variants of sequential decoding, they have in common a sequential search through a code tree (not a trellis) for the ML code sequence. The code constraint length ν can be infinite in principle, although for synchronization purposes (whether via zero-tail termination, tail-biting, or self-resynchronization) it is usually chosen to be not too large (of the order of 15–30).

The amount of computation to decode a given number of information bits is (highly) variable in sequential decoding, but is more or less independent of ν. The distribution of computation N follows a Pareto distribution, $\Pr(N \geq x) \cong x^{-\alpha}$, where α is the Pareto exponent [63]. The Pareto exponent is equal to 1 at the cutoff rate R_0, which is usually considered to be the practical limit of sequential decoding (because a Pareto distribution has a finite mean only if $\alpha > 1$). Thus on the low-SNR ideal AWGN channel, sequential decoding of low-rate binary linear convolutional codes can approach the Shannon limit within a factor of about 3 dB.

If ν is large enough, then sequential decoders rarely make errors; rather, they fail to decode due to excessive computation. This error-detection property is useful in many applications, such as deep-space telemetry.

Moreover, experiments have shown that bidirectional sequential decoding of moderate-length blocks can approximately double the Pareto exponent and thus significantly reduce the gap to capacity, even after giving effect to the rate loss due to zero-tail termination [65].

In view of these desirable properties, it is something of a mystery why sequential decoding has received so little practical attention during the past 30 years.

F. Concatenated Codes and RS Codes

Like the Viterbi algorithm and the Lempel–Ziv algorithm, concatenated codes were originally introduced to solve a theoretical problem [39], but have turned out to be useful for a variety of practical applications.

The basic idea is to use a moderate-strength "inner code" with an ML or near-ML decoding algorithm to achieve a moderate error rate like 10^{-2}–10^{-3} at a code rate as close to capacity as possible. Then a powerful algebraic "outer code" capable of correcting many errors with low redundancy is used to drive the error rate down to as low an error rate as may be desired. It was shown in [39] that the error rate could be made to decrease exponentially with blocklength at any rate less than capacity, while decoding complexity increases only polynomially.

Reed–Solomon (RS) codes are ideal for use as outer codes. (They are not suitable for use as inner codes because they are nonbinary.) RS codes are defined over finite fields $\boldsymbol{F}_q$ whose order q is typically large (e.g., $q = 256$). An $(n, k, n-k+1)$ RS code over $\boldsymbol{F}_q$ exists for every $n \leq q+1$ and $1 \leq k \leq n$ [77]. The minimum distance $n-k+1$ is as large as possible, in view of the Singleton bound [77].

Very efficient polynomial-time algebraic decoding algorithms are known, not just for error correction but also for erasure-and-error correction and even for near-ML soft-decision decoding (i.e., generalized minimum-distance decoding [39]). RS error-correction algorithms are standard in VLSI libraries, and today are typically capable of decoding dozens of errors per block over $\boldsymbol{F}_{256}$ at data rates of tens of megabits per second (Mb/s) [98].

When used with interleaving, RS codes are also ideal burst-error correctors in the sense of requiring the least possible guard space [40].

For these reasons RS codes are used in a large variety of applications, including the NASA deep-space standard adopted in the 1970's [24]. RS codes are clearly the outstanding practical success story of the field of algebraic block coding.

G. Turbo Codes and Other Capacity-Approaching Codes

The invention of "turbo codes" [13] put a decisive end to the long-standing conjecture that the cutoff rate R_0 might represent the "practical capacity." Performance within tenths of a decibel of the Shannon limit is now routinely demonstrated with reasonable decoding complexity, albeit with large delay [61].

The original turbo code operates as follows. An information bit sequence is encoded in a simple (e.g., 16-state) recursive systematic rate-1/2 convolutional encoder to produce one check bit sequence. The same information bit sequence is permuted in a very long (e.g., 10^4–10^5 bits) interleaver and then encoded in a second recursive systematic rate-1/2 convolutional encoder to produce a second check bit sequence. The information bit sequence and both check bit sequences are transmitted, so the code rate is 1/3. (Puncturing can be used to raise the rate.)

Decoding is performed in an iterative fashion as follows. The received sequences corresponding to the information bit sequence and the first check bit sequence are decoded by a soft-decision decoder for the first convolutional code. The outputs of this decoder are a sequence of soft decisions for each bit of the information sequence. (This is done by some version of the forward–backward algorithm [5], [6].) These soft decisions are then used by a similar decoder for the second convolutional code, which hopefully produces still better soft decisions that can then be used by the first decoder for a new iteration. Decoding iterates in this way for 10 to 20 cycles, before hard decisions are finally made on the information bits.

Empirically, operation within 0.3–0.7 dB of the Shannon limit can be achieved at moderate error rates. Theoretical understanding of turbo codes is still weak. At low E_b/N_0, turbo codes appear to behave like random codes whose blocklength is comparable to the interleaver length [84]. At higher E_b/N_0, the performance of a turbo decoder is dominated by certain low-weight codewords, whose multiplicity is inversely proportional to the interleaver length (the so-called "error floor" effect) [11].

The turbo decoding algorithm is now understood to be the general sum-product (APP) decoding algorithm, with a particular update schedule that is well matched to the turbo-code structure [116]. However, little is known about the theoretical performance and convergence properties of this algorithm applied to turbo codes, or more generally to codes defined on graphs with cycles.

Many variants of the turbo coding idea have been studied. Different arrangements of compound codes have been investigated, including "serially concatenated" codes like those of [39], which mitigate the error floor effect [9]. The decoding algorithm has been refined in various ways. Overall, however, improvements have been minor.

A turbo coding scheme is now being standardized for future deep-space missions [29].

Even more recently, codes and decoding algorithms that approach turbo coding performance have been devised according to quite different principles. With these methods turbo-code performance has been approached and even exceeded. Notable among these are low-density parity-check (LDPC) codes, originally proposed by Gallager in the early 1960's [50], subsequently almost forgotten, and recently rediscovered by various authors [76], [96], [116]. Like turbo codes, these codes may be viewed as "codes defined on graphs" and may be decoded by similar iterative APP decoding algorithms [116]. Long LDPC codes can operate well beyond R_0; furthermore, they have no error floor and rarely make decoding errors, but rather simply fail to decode [76]. Theoretically, it has been shown that long LDPC codes can achieve rates up to capacity with ML decoding [50], [76]. Very recently, nonbinary LDPC codes have been devised that outperform turbo codes [27]. However, the parallel ("flooding") version of the iterative decoding algorithm that is usually used with these codes is computationally expensive, and their lengths are comparable to those of turbo codes.

IV. NONBINARY CODES FOR BANDWIDTH-LIMITED CHANNELS

In this section we discuss coding techniques for high-SNR ideal bandwidth-limited AWGN channels. In this regime nonbinary signal alphabets such as M-PAM must be used to approach capacity. Using large-alphabet approximations, we show that the total coding gain of a coded-modulation scheme for the high-SNR ideal AWGN channel is the sum of a coding gain and a shaping gain. At high SNR's, the coding and shaping problems are separable.

Shaping gains are obtained by using signal constellations in high-dimensional spaces that are bounded by a quasispherical region, rather than the cubical region that results from independent M-PAM signaling; or, alternatively, by using points in a low-dimensional constellation with a Gaussian-like probability distribution rather than equiprobably. The maximum possible shaping gain is a factor of $\pi e/6$ (1.53 dB). We briefly mention several shaping methods that can easily obtain about 1 dB of shaping gain.

In the high-SNR regime, the SNR gap between uncoded baseline performance at $P_s(\mathcal{E}) \cong 10^{-6}$ and the cutoff limit without shaping is about 5.8 dB. This gap arises as follows: the gap to the Shannon limit is 9 dB; with shaping the cutoff limit is 1.7 dB below the Shannon limit; and without shaping the cutoff limit is 1.5 dB lower than with shaping. Coding gains of the order of 3–5 dB at error probabilities of 10^{-5}–10^{-6} can be obtained with moderate complexity.

The two principal classes of high-SNR codes are lattices and trellis codes, which are analogous to binary block and convolutional codes, respectively. By now the principles of construction of such codes are well understood, and it seems likely that the best codes have been found. We plot the effective coding gains of these known moderate-complexity lattices and trellis codes versus the branch complexity of their minimal trellises, assuming maximum-likelihood decoding. Trellis codes are somewhat superior, due mainly to their lower error coefficients.

We briefly discuss coding schemes that can achieve coding gains beyond R_0, of the order of 5 to 7 dB, at error probabilities of 10^{-5}–10^{-6}. Multilevel schemes with multistage decoding allow the use of high-performance binary codes such as those described in the previous section to be used to approach the Shannon limit of high-SNR channels. Such high-performance schemes naturally involve greater decoding complexity and large delays.

We particularly note techniques that have been used in telephone-line modem standards, which have generally reflected the state of the art for high-SNR channels.

A. Lattice Constellations

It is clear from the proof of Shannon's capacity theorem that an optimal block code for a high-SNR ideal band-limited AWGN channel consists of a dense packing of signal points within a sphere in a high-dimensional Euclidean space. Most of the known densest packings are lattices [25]. In this section we briefly describe lattice constellations, and analyze their performance using the union bound estimate and large-constellation approximations.

An N-dimensional *lattice* Λ is a discrete subgroup of N-space $\boldsymbol{R}^N$, which without essential loss of generality may be assumed to span $\boldsymbol{R}^N$. The points of the lattice form a uniform infinite packing of $\boldsymbol{R}^N$. By the group property, each point of the lattice has the same number of neighbors at each distance, and all decision regions of a minimum-distance decoder (Voronoi regions) are congruent and tessellate $\boldsymbol{R}^N$. These properties hold for any lattice translate $\Lambda + t$.

The key geometrical parameters of a lattice are the *minimum squared distance* $d_{\min}^2(\Lambda)$ between lattice points, the *kissing number* $K_{\min}(\Lambda)$ of nearest neighbors to any lattice point, and the *volume* $V(\Lambda)$ of N-space per lattice point, which is equal to the volume of any Voronoi region [25]. The *Hermite parameter* is the normalized parameter $\gamma_c(\Lambda) = d_{\min}^2(\Lambda)/V(\Lambda)^{2/N}$, which we will soon identify as the nominal coding gain of Λ.

A *lattice constellation* $C(\Lambda, \mathbb{R}) = (\Lambda + t) \cap \mathbb{R}$ is the finite set of points in a lattice translate $\Lambda + t$ that lie within a compact bounding region $\mathbb{R}$ of N-space. The key geometric properties of the region $\mathbb{R}$ are its *volume* $V(\mathbb{R})$ and the *average energy* $P(\mathbb{R})$ per dimension of a uniform probability density function over $\mathbb{R}$:

$$P(\mathbb{R}) = \int_{\mathbb{R}} (\|\boldsymbol{x}\|^2/N) \, d\boldsymbol{x}/V(\mathbb{R}). \quad (4.1)$$

The *normalized second moment* of $\mathbb{R}$ is defined as $G(\mathbb{R}) = P(\mathbb{R})/V(\mathbb{R})^{2/N}$ [25].

For example, an M-PAM constellation with M even

$$(d_0/2)\{\pm 1, \pm 3, \cdots, \pm(M-1)\}$$

is a one-dimensional lattice constellation $C(\mathbf{Z}, \mathbb{R})$ with $\Lambda + t = d_0(\mathbf{Z} + 1/2)$ and $\mathbb{R} = (d_0/2)[-M, M]$. The key geometrical parameters of $\Lambda = d_0\mathbf{Z}$ are

$$d_{\min}^2(d_0\mathbf{Z}) = d_0^2$$
$$K_{\min}(d_0\mathbf{Z}) = 2$$
$$V(d_0\mathbf{Z}) = d_0$$
$$\gamma_c(d_0\mathbf{Z}) = 1. \qquad (4.2)$$

The key parameters of $\mathbb{R} = (d_0/2)[-M, M]$ are

$$V(\mathbb{R}) = d_0 M$$
$$P(\mathbb{R}) = (d_0 M)^2/12$$
$$G(\mathbb{R}) = 1/12. \qquad (4.3)$$

Both $\gamma_c(\Lambda)$ and $G(\mathbb{R})$ are invariant under scaling, orthogonal transformations, and Cartesian products; i.e., $\gamma_c(\alpha U \Lambda^N) = \gamma_c(\Lambda)$ and $G(\alpha U \mathbb{R}^N) = G(\mathbb{R})$, where $\alpha > 0$ is any scale factor, U is any orthogonal matrix, and $N \geq 1$ is any positive integer. In particular, this implies that $\gamma_c(\alpha U \mathbf{Z}^N) = 1$ for any version of an integer lattice $\mathbf{Z}^N$, and that the normalized second moment of any N-cube centered at the origin is $1/12$.

For large lattice constellations, one may use the following approximations, the first two of which are collectively known as the *continuous approximation* [48]:

- the size of the constellation is $|C(\Lambda, \mathbb{R})| \cong V(\mathbb{R})/V(\Lambda)$;
- the average energy per dimension of an equiprobable distribution over $C(\Lambda, \mathbb{R})$ is $P(C(\Lambda, \mathbb{R})) \cong P(\mathbb{R})$;
- for large rates $R = (1/N) \log_2 |C(\Lambda, \mathbb{R})|$, we have $2^{2R} - 1 \cong 2^{2R}$;
- the average number of nearest neighbors to any point in $C(\Lambda, \mathbb{R})$ is approximately $K_{\min}(\Lambda)$.

The union bound estimate on probability of block decoding error is

$$P(\mathcal{E}) \cong K_{\min}(\Lambda)Q(d_{\min}(\Lambda)/2\sigma_w). \qquad (4.4)$$

Because

$$R = (1/N)\log_2|C(\Lambda, \mathbb{R})| \cong (1/N)\log_2 V(\mathbb{R})/V(\Lambda) \quad (4.5)$$
$$\mathrm{SNR} = P(C(\Lambda, \mathbb{R}))/\sigma_w^2 \cong P(\mathbb{R})/\sigma_w^2 \qquad (4.6)$$
$$\mathrm{SNR}_{\mathrm{norm}} \cong \mathrm{SNR}/2^{2R} = (V(\Lambda)^{2/N}/V(\mathbb{R})^{2/N})(P(\mathbb{R})/\sigma_w^2) \qquad (4.7)$$

we may write the union bound estimate as

$$P(\mathcal{E}) \cong K_{\min}(\Lambda)Q\left(\sqrt{\gamma_c(\Lambda)\gamma_s(\mathbb{R})3\,\mathrm{SNR}_{\mathrm{norm}}}\right) \qquad (4.8)$$

where the *nominal coding gain* of Λ and the *shaping gain* of $\mathbb{R}$ are defined, respectively, as

$$\gamma_c(\Lambda) = d_{\min}^2(\Lambda)/V(\Lambda)^{2/N} \qquad (4.9)$$
$$\gamma_s(\mathbb{R}) = V(\mathbb{R})^{2/N}/(12P(\mathbb{R})) = (1/12)/G(\mathbb{R}). \quad (4.10)$$

For a baseline M-PAM constellation, we have $\gamma_c(\Lambda) = \gamma_s(\mathbb{R}) = 1$, and the UBE reduces to

$$P(\mathcal{E}) \cong 2Q(\sqrt{3\,\mathrm{SNR}_{\mathrm{norm}}}).$$

The nominal coding gain $\gamma_c(\Lambda)$ measures the increase in density of Λ over a baseline lattice, $\mathbf{Z}$ or $\mathbf{Z}^N$. The shaping gain $\gamma_s(\mathbb{R})$ measures the decrease in average energy of $\mathbb{R}$ relative to a baseline region, namely, an interval $[-d_0/2, d_0/2]$ or an N-cube $[-d_0/2, d_0/2]^N$. Both contribute a multiplicative factor of gain to the argument of the $Q(\sqrt{\bullet})$ function.

As before, the effective coding gain is reduced by the error coefficient $K_{\min}(\Lambda)$. For comparability with the M-PAM uncoded baseline, it is appropriate to normalize $P(\mathcal{E})$ by the dimension N to obtain the probability of block decoding error per symbol

$$P_s(\mathcal{E}) = P(\mathcal{E})/N \cong K(\Lambda)Q\left(\sqrt{\gamma_c(\Lambda)\gamma_s(\mathbb{R})3\,\mathrm{SNR}_{\mathrm{norm}}}\right) \qquad (4.11)$$

in which the normalized error coefficient is $K(\Lambda) = K_{\min}(\Lambda)/N$.

Graphically, a curve of the form of (4.11) may be obtained simply by moving the baseline curve $P_s(\mathcal{E}) = 2Q(\sqrt{3\,\mathrm{SNR}_{\mathrm{norm}}})$ of Fig. 2 to the left by $\gamma_c(\Lambda)$ and $\gamma_s(\mathbb{R})$ (in decibels), and upward by a factor of $K(\Lambda)/2$.

B. Shaping Gain and Shaping Techniques

Although shaping is a newer and less important topic than coding, we discuss it first because its story is quite simple.

The optimum N-dimensional shaping region is an N-sphere. The key geometrical parameters of an N-sphere ($= \otimes$) of radius r for N even are [25]

$$V(\otimes) = \frac{(\pi r^2)^{N/2}}{(N/2)!}$$
$$P(\otimes) = \frac{r^2}{N+2}$$
$$G(\otimes) = P(\otimes)V(\otimes)^{2/N} = \frac{((N/2)!)^{2/N}}{\pi(N+2)}. \qquad (4.12)$$

By Stirling's approximation, namely $m! \cong (m/e)^m$ as m goes to infinity [51], we have

$$G(\otimes) \overset{N\to\infty}{\to} 1/2\pi e$$
$$\gamma_s(\otimes) = (1/12)/G(\otimes) \overset{N\to\infty}{\to} \pi e/6. \qquad (4.13)$$

The shaping gain of an N-sphere is plotted for dimensions $N = 1, 2, 4, 8, \cdots, 512$ in Fig. 3. Note that the shaping gain of a 16-sphere is approximately 1 dB. However, for larger dimensions, we see from Fig. 3 that the shaping gain approaches the *ultimate shaping gain* $\pi e/6$ (1.53 dB) rather slowly.

The projection of a uniform probability distribution over an N-sphere onto one or two dimensions is a nonuniform probability distribution that approaches a Gaussian density as $N \to \infty$. The ultimate shaping gain of $\pi e/6$ (1.53 dB) may be derived alternatively as the difference between the average power of a uniform density over an interval and that of a Gaussian density with the same differential entropy [48].

Shaping therefore induces a Gaussian-like probability distribution on a one-dimensional PAM (or two-dimensional QAM) constellation, rather than an equiprobable distribution.

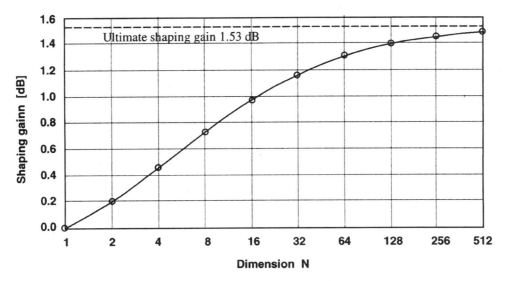

Fig. 3. Shaping gains of N-spheres over N-cubes for $N = 1, 2, 4, \cdots, 512$.

In principle, with spherical shaping, the lower dimensional constellation will become arbitrarily large, even with fixed average power. In practice, the lower dimensional "shaping constellation expansion" is constrained by design to a permitted peak amplitude. If the N-dimensional shape approximates spherical shaping subject to this constraint, then the lower dimensional probability distribution approaches a truncated Gaussian distribution [48].

A nonuniform distribution over a low-dimensional constellation may alternatively be obtained by codes over bits that specify regions of the constellation [16].

With large constellations, shaping can be implemented more or less independently of coding by operations on the "most significant bits" of PAM or QAM constellation labels, which affect the large-scale shape of the N-dimensional constellation. In contrast, coding affects the "least significant bits" and determines small-scale structure.

Two practical schemes that can easily obtain shaping gains of 1 dB or more while limiting two-dimensional (2-D) shaping constellation expansion to a factor of 1.5 or less are "trellis shaping" and "shell mapping."

Trellis shaping [45] is a kind of dual to trellis coding. Using a trellis, one defines a set of equivalence classes of coded sequences. The shaping operation consists of determining among equivalent sequences in the trellis the minimum-energy sequence. Shaping gains of the order of 1 dB are easily obtained.

In shell mapping [49], [66], [68], [69], [72] the signals in an N-dimensional lattice constellation are in principle labeled in order of increasing signal energy, and a one-to-one map is defined between possible input data sequences and an equal number of least energy constellation points. In practice, generating-function methods are used to label points in Cartesian-product constellations in approximate increasing order of energy based on shell-mapping labelings of lower dimensional constituent constellations. The V.34 modem uses 16-dimensional shell mapping, and obtains shaping gains of the order of 0.8 dB with 2-D shaping constellation expansion limited to 25% [47]. These shaping methods are also useful for accommodating noninteger numbers of bits per symbol. The latter objective is also achieved by a mapping technique known as "modulus conversion" [3], which is an enumerative encoding technique for mapping large integers into blocks ("mapping frames") of signals in lexicographical order, where the sizes of the signal constellations do not need to be powers of 2.

C. Coding Gains of Dense Lattices

Finding the densest lattice packings in a given number of dimensions is a mathematical problem of long standing. A summary of the densest known packings is given in [25]. The nominal coding gains of these lattices in up to 24 dimensions is plotted in Fig. 4. Notable lattices include the eight-dimensional Gosset lattice E_8, whose nominal coding gain is 2 (3 dB), and the 24-dimensional Leech lattice L_{24}, whose nominal coding gain is 4 (6 dB).

In contrast to shaping gain, the nominal coding gains of dense N-dimensional lattices become infinite as $N \to \infty$. For example, for any integer $m \geq 0$, there exists a 2^{m+1}-dimensional Barnes–Wall lattice whose nominal coding gain is $2^{m/2}$ (which is by no means the densest possible for large m) [25].

However, effective coding gains cannot become infinite. Indeed, the Shannon limit shows that no lattice can have a combined effective coding gain and shaping gain greater than 9 dB at $P(\mathcal{E}) \cong 10^{-6}$. This limits the maximum possible effective coding gain to 7.5 dB, because shaping gain can contribute up to 1.53 dB.

What limits effective coding gain is the number of near neighbors, which becomes very large for high-dimensional dense lattices. For example, the kissing number of the 2^{m+1}-dimensional Barnes–Wall (BW) lattice is [25]

$$K_{\min}(\text{BW}_{2^{m+1}}) = \prod_{1 \leq i \leq m} (2^i + 2) \qquad (4.14)$$

which yields, for example, $K_{\min}(\text{BW}_{32}) = 146880$ and $K_{\min}(\text{BW}_{128}) = 1260230400$.

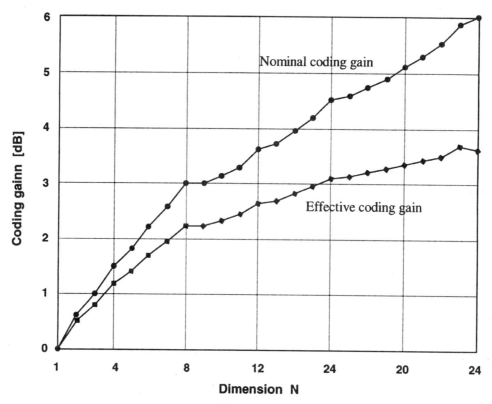

Coding gainn [dB] (y-axis)

Dimension N (x-axis)

Fig. 4. Nominal and effective coding gains of densest known lattices in dimensions $N \leq 24$.

D. Trellis Codes

Trellis codes are dense packings in infinite-dimensional Euclidean sequence space. Trellis codes are to lattices as binary convolutional codes are to block codes. We will see that trellis codes give a better performance/complexity tradeoff than lattices in the high-SNR regime, just as convolutional codes give a better performance/complexity tradeoff than block codes in the low-SNR regime, although the difference is not as dramatic.

The key ideas in the invention of trellis codes [104] were

- use of minimum squared Euclidean distance as the design criterion;
- set partitioning of a constellation A into 2^n subsets;
- maximizing intrasubset minimum squared distances;
- rate-k/n convolutional coding over the subsets;
- selection of signals within subsets by further uncoded bits (if necessary).

Most practical trellis codes have used either N-dimensional lattice constellations based on versions of $\boldsymbol{Z}^N$ with $N = 1$, 2, 4, or 8, or $2K$-dimensional $K \times M$-PSK constellations with $K = 1, 2, 3$, or 4 and $M = 8$. We will focus on lattice-type trellis codes in this section.

Set partitioning of an N-dimensional constellation A into 2^n subsets is usually performed by n partitioning steps, with each two-way selection being identified by a label bit $c^j \in \{0, 1\}$, $1 \leq j \leq n$ [104], [105]

$$A \xrightarrow{c^1} B(c_1) \xrightarrow{c^2} C(c_2, c_1) \xrightarrow{c^3} \cdots \xrightarrow{c^n} S(\boldsymbol{c})$$
$$\Delta_0^2 \leq \quad \Delta_1^2 \quad \leq \quad \Delta_2^2 \quad \leq \cdots \leq \quad \Delta_n^2. \quad (4.15)$$

The quantities Δ_j^2, $j = 0, \cdots, n$, are the intrasubset minimum squared distances of the jth-level (sub)sets A, $B(c^1)$, $C(c^2, c^1)$, $\cdots$. The objective of set partitioning is to increase these distances as much as possible at every subset level. Set partitioning is continued until Δ_n^2 is at least as large as the desired minimum squared distance $d_{\min}^2(C)$ between trellis code sequences. The binary n-tuples $\boldsymbol{c} = [c^n \cdots c^1]$ are called the subset labels of the final subsets $S(\boldsymbol{c})$.

Partitioning one- or two-dimensional constellations in this way is trivial [104]. Partitioning of higher dimensional constellations was first performed starting from lower dimensional partitions [113]. Subsequently, partitioning of lattice constellations was introduced using lattice partitions [17], [42], [43] (or, more generally, group-theoretic partitions [44]), as we will discuss below.

In almost all cases of practical interest, the two first-level subsets $B(0)$ and $B(1)$ will be geometrically congruent to each other (see Appendix II-B); i.e., they will differ only by translation, rotation, and/or reflection.

An encoder for a trellis code C then operates as shown in Fig. 5 [105]. Given m input bits per N-dimensional symbol, k input bits are encoded by a rate-k/n binary convolutional encoder with 2^ν states into a coded sequence of subset labels $\boldsymbol{c}_i$. At time i, the label $\boldsymbol{c}_i$ is used to select subset $S(\boldsymbol{c}_i)$. The remaining $m - k$ input bits are used to choose one signal a_i from 2^{m-k} signals in the selected subset $S(\boldsymbol{c}_i)$. The size of A must therefore be $2^{m+(n-k)}$, or a factor of 2^{n-k} (the "coding constellation expansion" factor per N dimensions) larger than needed to send m uncoded bits per symbol. (If there is any shaping, it is performed on the uncoded bits and results in further "shaping constellation expansion.")

354

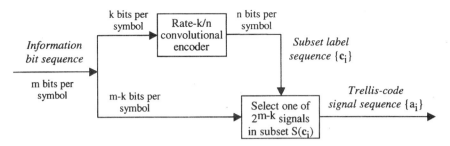

k bits per symbol → Rate-k/n convolutional encoder → n bits per symbol

Information bit sequence

m bits per symbol

m-k bits per symbol

Subset label sequence {c_i}

Select one of 2^{m-k} signals in subset $S(c_i)$

Trellis-code signal sequence {a_i}

Fig. 5. Trellis-code encoder.

A trellis code may be maximum-likelihood decoded by a Viterbi algorithm (VA) decoder as follows. Given a received point $z_i \in \mathbf{R}^N$, the receiver first finds the closest signal point $\hat{a}_i(c)$ in each subset $S(c)$. This is called subset decoding. A VA decoder then finds the code sequence $\{\hat{c}_i\}$ for which the signals chosen in the subsets are closest to the entire received sequence $\{z_i\}$. The decoding complexity is dominated by the complexity of the VA decoder, which is approximately given by the branch complexity $2^{\nu+k}$ of the convolutional code, normalized by the dimension N.

In practice, the redundancy of the convolutional code is almost always one bit per N-dimensional symbol ($k = n - 1$), so that the coding constellation expansion factor is 2 per N dimensions. The lowest level ("least significant") label bit c^1 is then the sole parity-check bit. If the convolutional code is linear, then in D-transform notation the check sequence $c^1(D)$ is determined from the information bit sequences $c^2(D), \cdots, c^n(D)$ by a linear parity-check equation of the form

$$h^n(D)c^n(D) \oplus \cdots h^2(D)c^2(D) \oplus h^1(D)c^1(D) = 0 \quad (4.16)$$

where

$$\{h^j(D) = h^j_{\nu_j}D^{\nu_j} + \cdots + h^j_2 D^2 + h^j_1 D + h^j_0, \ 1 \le j \le n\}$$

is a set of n relatively-prime parity-check polynomials. If the greatest degree of any of these polynomials is ν, then a minimal encoder for the code has 2^ν states.

The convolutional code is chosen primarily to maximize the minimum squared distance $d^2_{\min}(C)$ between trellis-code sequences. If the redundancy is one bit per symbol, then a good first step is to ensure that in any encoder state s_i the set of possible next outputs is either $B(0)$ or $B(1)$, so that a squared distance contribution of Δ^2_1 is immediately obtained when code sequences diverge from a common state. With a linear convolutional code, this is achieved by choosing the low-order coefficients h^j_0 of the parity-check polynomials $h^j(D)$ such that $h^1_0 = 1$ and $h^j_0 = 0$, $2 \le j \le n$. The same argument applies in the reverse time direction to the high-order coefficients h^j_ν. This design rule guarantees that $d^2_{\min}(C) \ge 2\Delta^2_1$ [104].

An important consequence of such a choice is that at time i the lowest level label bit c^1_i, which selects $B(0)$ or $B(1)$, depends only on the encoder state s_i. This observation leads to the idea of *feedback trellis encoding* [71], which was proposed during the development of the V.34 modem standard to permit an improved type of precoding (see Section V). With this

technique, the sequence of encoding operations at time i is as follows:

a) the check bit c^1_i is determined from the encoder state s_i;
b) the m input bits at time i select a signal a_i from $B(c^1_i)$;
c) the remaining label bits $[c^n_i, \cdots, c^2_i]$ are determined from a_i;
d) the next encoder state s_{i+1} is determined from s_i and c_i.

E. Lattice Constellation Partitioning

Partitioning of lattice constellations by means of lattice partitions is done as follows [17], [43]. One starts with an N-dimensional lattice constellation $C(\Lambda, \mathbb{R})$, where Λ is almost always a version of an N-dimensional integer lattice $\mathbf{Z}^N$. The constellation $C(\Lambda, \mathbb{R})$ is partitioned into 2^n subsets of equal size that are congruent to a sublattice Λ' of index $|\Lambda/\Lambda'| = 2^n$ in Λ, so that Λ is the union of 2^n cosets (translates) of Λ'. The 2^n subsets are then the points of $C(\Lambda, \mathbb{R})$ that lie in each such subset, which form sublattice constellations of the form $C(\Lambda', \mathbb{R})$. The region $\mathbb{R}$ must be chosen so that there are an equal number of points in each subset. The sublattice Λ' is usually chosen to be as dense as possible.

Codes based on lattice partitions Λ/Λ' are called *coset codes*. The nominal coding gain of a coset code based on a lattice $\Lambda = \mathbf{Z}^N$ is [42]

$$\gamma_c(C) = d^2_{\min}(C)2^{-2\rho(C)} \quad (4.17)$$

where $\rho(C) = 1/N$ is the redundancy of the convolutional encoder in bits per dimension. Again, this coding gain is the product of a distance gain of $d^2_{\min}(C)$ over $d^2_{\min}(\mathbf{Z}^N) = 1$, and a redundancy loss $2^{-2\rho(C)}$. The effective coding gain is reduced by the amount that the error coefficient $K_{\min}(C)/N$ per dimension exceeds the baseline M-PAM error coefficient of 2 per dimension. Again, the rule of thumb that an increase of a factor of two costs 0.2 dB may be used.

The encoder redundancy $\rho(C)$ also leads to a "coding constellation expansion ratio" of a factor of $2^{2\rho(C)}$ per two dimensions [42]—i.e., a factor of 4, 2, $\sqrt{2}, \cdots$ for 1D, 2D, 4D, $\cdots$, codes, respectively. Minimization of coding constellation expansion has motivated the use of higher dimensional trellis codes.

F. Coding Gains of Known Trellis Codes

Fig. 6 shows the effective coding gains of important families of trellis codes for lattice-type signal constellations. The effective coding gains are plotted versus their VA decoding

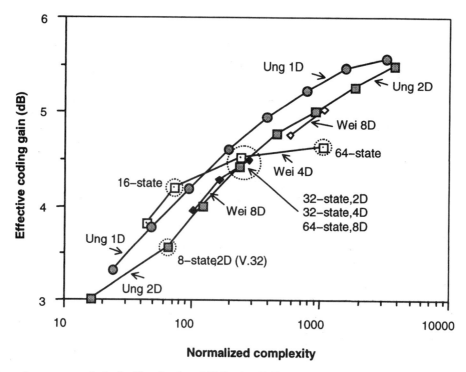

Fig. 6. Effective coding gain versus complexity for Ungerboeck and Wei codes; V.32 and V.34 codes circled.

complexity, measured by a detailed operation count. The codes considered are as follows:

1) The original 1D (PAM) trellis codes with $\rho(C) = 1$ of Ungerboeck [104], based on rate-1/2 convolutional codes with $2 \leq \nu \leq 9$ and the four-way partition $\boldsymbol{Z}/4\boldsymbol{Z}$.

2) The 2D (QAM) trellis codes with $\rho(C) = 1/2$ of Ungerboeck [104], based on (except for the simplest code with $\nu = 2$) rate-2/3 convolutional codes with $3 \leq \nu \leq 9$ and the eight-way partition $\boldsymbol{Z}^2/2R\boldsymbol{Z}^2$ (where R is a 2×2 Hadamard matrix).

3) The 4D trellis codes with $\rho(C) = 1/4$ of Wei [113], based on

   a) rate-2/3 8- and 16-state convolutional codes and the eight-way partition $\boldsymbol{Z}^4/R D_4$;

   b) a rate-3/4 32-state convolutional code and the 16-way partition $\boldsymbol{Z}^4/2\boldsymbol{Z}^4$;

   c) a rate-4/5 64-state convolutional code and the 32-way partition $\boldsymbol{Z}^4/2D_4$;

4) Two families of 8D trellis codes of Wei [113].

The V.32 modem (1984) uses an eight-state 2D trellis code, also due to Wei [112]. The performance/complexity tradeoff is the same as that of the original eight-state 2D Ungerboeck code. However, the Wei code uses a nonlinear convolutional encoder to achieve 90° rotational invariance. This code has an effective coding gain of about 3.6 dB, a branch complexity of 2^5 per two dimensions, and a coding constellation expansion ratio of 2.

The V.34 modem (1994) specifies three 4D trellis codes, with performance and complexity equivalent to the 4D Wei codes circled on Fig. 6 [47]. All have a coding constellation expansion ratio of $\sqrt{2}$. The 16-state code, which is the only code implemented by most manufacturers, is the original 16-

state 4D Wei code, which has an effective coding gain of about 4.2 dB and a branch complexity of 2^6 per four dimensions. The 32-state code is due to Williams [117] and is based on a 16-way partition of $\boldsymbol{Z}^4$ into 16 subsets congruent to $H\boldsymbol{Z}^4$, where H is a 4×4 Hadamard matrix, to ensure that there are no minimum-distance error events whose length is only two dimensions; it has an effective coding gain of about 4.5 dB and a branch complexity of 2^8 per four dimensions. The 64-state code is a modification of the original 4D Wei code, modified to prevent quasicatastrophic error propagation; it has an effective coding gain of about 4.7 dB and a branch complexity of 2^{10} per four dimensions.

It is noteworthy that no one has improved on the performance/complexity tradeoff of the original 1D and 2D trellis codes of Ungerboeck or the subsequent multidimensional codes of Wei. By this time it seems safe to predict that no one will ever do so. There have, however, been new trellis codes that feature other properties and have about the same performance and complexity, as described in the previous two paragraphs, and there may still be room for further improvements of this kind.

Finally, we see that trellis codes have a performance/complexity advantage over lattice codes, when used with maximum-likelihood decoding. Effective coding gains of 4.2–4.7 dB, better than that of the Leech lattice or of BW_{32}, are attainable with less complexity and much less constellation expansion. With the 512-state 1D or 2D trellis codes, effective coding gains of the order of 5.5 dB can be achieved. These gains are larger than the gains that can be obtained with lattice codes of far greater complexity.

On the other hand, it seems very difficult to obtain effective coding gains approaching 6 dB. This is not surprising, because at $P(\mathcal{E}) \cong 10^{-6}$ the effective coding gain at the Shannon limit

356

is about 7.5 dB, and at the cutoff rate limit it is about 5.8 dB. To approach the Shannon limit, codes and decoding methods of higher complexity are necessary.

So far in this section we have only discussed trellis codes for lattice-type signals. However, the principle of set partitioning and the general encoder structure of Fig. 5 are also valid for trellis codes with signals from constellations which are not of lattice type, such as 8-PSK and 16-PSK constellations. Code tables for 8-PSK and 16-PSK trellis codes are given in [104] and [105]. A number of multidimensional linear PSK-type trellis codes are described in [114], all fully rotationally invariant. In [87], principles of set partitioning of multidimensional $K \times M$-PSK constellations are given, based on concepts of multilevel block coding; tables of linear $K \times M$-PSK trellis codes are presented for $M = 4, 8, 16$ and $K = 1, 2, 3, 4$, with the largest degree of rotational invariance given for each code; and figures similar to Fig. 6 that summarize effective coding gains versus decoding complexity are shown.

G. Sequential Decoding in the High-SNR Regime

In the high-SNR regime, the cutoff rate is a factor of $4/e$ (1.68 dB) away from capacity [95]. Therefore, sequential decoders should be able to achieve an effective coding gain of about 5.8 dB at $P(\mathcal{E}) \cong 10^{-6}$. Experiments have confirmed that sequential decoders can indeed achieve such performance [111].

H. Multilevel Codes and Multistage Decoding

To approach the Shannon limit even more closely, it is clear that much more powerful codes must be used, together with decoding methods that are simpler than optimal maximum-likelihood (ML) decoding, but with near-ML performance. Multilevel codes and multistage decoding may be used for this purpose [60], [75]. Multilevel coding may be based on a chain of sublattices of $\mathbf{Z}^N$

$$\Lambda_n \subset \Lambda_{n-1} \subset \cdots \subset \Lambda_1 \subset \Lambda_0 = \mathbf{Z}^N \qquad (4.18)$$

which lead to a chain of lattice partitions Λ_{j-1}/Λ_j, $1 \leq j \leq n$. A different trellis encoder as in Fig. 5 may be used independently on each such lattice partition.

Remarkably, it follows from the chain rule of mutual information that the capacity $C(\Lambda_0/\Lambda_n)$ that can be obtained by coding over the lattice partition Λ_0/Λ_n is equal to the sum of the capacities $C(\Lambda_{j-1}/\Lambda_j)$ that can be obtained by independent coding and decoding at each level [46], [58], [67], [110]. With multistage decoding, decoding is performed separately at each level; at the jth level the decisions at lower levels $(0, 1, \cdots, j-1)$ are taken into account, whereas no coding is assumed for the higher levels $(j+1, \cdots, n)$. If the partition Λ_0/Λ_n is "large enough" and appropriately scaled, then $C(\Lambda_0/\Lambda_n)$ approaches the capacity of the ideal AWGN channel.

The lattices may be the one- or two-dimensional integer lattices $\mathbf{Z}$ or $\mathbf{Z}^2$, and the standard binary partition chains

$$\cdots \subset 8\mathbf{Z} \subset 4\mathbf{Z} \subset 2\mathbf{Z} \subset \mathbf{Z};$$
$$\cdots \subset 4\mathbf{Z}^2 \subset 2R\mathbf{Z}^2 \subset 2\mathbf{Z}^2 \subset R\mathbf{Z}^2 \subset \mathbf{Z}^2 \qquad (4.19)$$

may be used. Then a powerful binary code with rate close to $C(\Lambda_{j-1}/\Lambda_j)$ can be used at each level to approach the Shannon limit. In particular, by using turbo codes of appropriate rate at each level, it has been shown that reliable transmission can be achieved within 1 dB of the Shannon limit [109].

Powerful probabilistic coding methods such as turbo codes are really needed only at the lower levels. At the higher levels, the channels become quite clean and the capacity $C(\Lambda_{j-1}/\Lambda_j)$ approaches $\log_2 |\Lambda_{j-1}/\Lambda_j|$, so that the desired redundancy approaches zero. For these levels, algebraic codes and decoding methods may be more appropriate [46], [110].

In summary, multilevel codes and multistage decoding allow the Shannon limit to be approached as closely in the high-SNR regime as it can be approached in the low-SNR regime with binary codes. The state of the art in multilevel coding is reviewed in [110].

I. Other Capacity-Approaching Nonbinary Coded-Modulation Schemes

Various capacity-approaching alternative schemes to multilevel coding have been proposed.

One scheme, called *bit-interleaved coded modulation* (BICM) [15], has been developed primarily for fading channels, but has turned out to be capable of approaching the capacity of high-SNR AWGN channels as well. A BICM transmitter comprises an encoder for a binary code C, a "bit interleaver," and a signal mapper. The output sequence of the bit interleaver is segmented into m-bit blocks, which are mapped into a 2^m-point signal constellation using Gray coding. Although BICM cannot operate arbitrarily closely to capacity, good performance close to capacity can be obtained if C is a long parallel or serially concatenated turbo code, and the decoder is an iterative turbo decoder.

Other schemes that are more straightforward extensions of standard binary turbo codes are called *turbo trellis-coded modulation* (TTCM) [89] and *parallel concatenated trellis-coded modulation* (PCTCM) [8]. Instead of two binary systematic convolutional encoders, two rate-$k/(k+1)$ trellis encoders are used. The interleaver is arranged so that the two encoded output bits of the two encoders are aligned with the same k information bits. To avoid excessive rate loss, a special puncturing technique is used in TTCM: only one of the two coded bits is transmitted with each symbol, and the two encoder outputs are chosen alternately.

V. CODING AND EQUALIZATION FOR LINEAR GAUSSIAN CHANNELS

In this section we discuss coding and equalization methods for a general linear Gaussian channel. We first present the "water-pouring" solution for the capacity-achieving transmit spectrum. Then we describe the multicarrier approach to approaching capacity. The remaining parts of the section are devoted to serial transmission. We show how the linear Gaussian channel may be converted, without loss of optimality, to a discrete-time AWGN channel with intersymbol interference. We then give a pictorial illustration of the coding principles required to approach capacity. Finally, we review practical

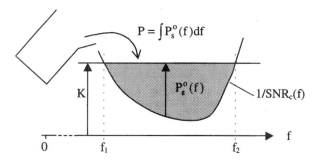

Fig. 7. Optimization of transmit p.s.d. $P(f)$ by "water pouring."

precoding methods that have been developed to implement these principles.

A. Water Pouring

The general linear Gaussian channel was characterized in Section II as a real channel with input signal $s(t)$, impulse response $g(t)$, and additive Gaussian noise $n(t)$ with one-sided p.s.d. $N(f)$. The channel output signal is $r(t) = s(t)*g(t)+n(t)$ (see Fig. 8 below). In addition, the transmit signal $s(t)$ has to satisfy a power constraint of the form

$$\int_{f \geq 0} P_s(f) \, df \leq P \qquad (5.1)$$

where $P_s(f)$ is the one-sided p.s.d. of $s(t)$. The *channel SNR function* for this channel is defined as

$$\mathrm{SNR}_c(f) = |G(f)|^2/N(f). \qquad (5.2)$$

Intuitively, the preferred transmission band is where $\mathrm{SNR}_c(f)$ is largest.

The optimum $P_s(f)$ maximizes the mutual information between channel input and output subject to the power constraint (5.1) and $P_s(f) \geq 0$. A Lagrange multiplier argument shows that the largest mutual information is achieved by the "water-pouring" solution [94], illustrated in Fig. 7 for a typical $\mathrm{SNR}_c(f)$

$$P_s^o(f) = \begin{cases} K - 1/\mathrm{SNR}_c(f), & f \in B \\ 0, & f \notin B \end{cases} \qquad (5.3)$$

where $B = \{f : P_s^o(f) > 0\}$ is called the capacity-achieving band, and K is a constant chosen such that (5.1) is satisfied with equality. Capacity is achieved if $s(t)$ is a Gaussian process with p.s.d. $P_s^o(f)$, and in bits per second is equal to

$$C_{[b/s]} = \int_B \log_2(1 + P_s^o(f) \, \mathrm{SNR}_c(f)) \, df. \qquad (5.4)$$

In analogy to an ideal AWGN channel, a linear Gaussian channel may be roughly characterized by two parameters, its one-sided bandwidth $W = \int_B df$, and its *effective signal-to-noise ratio* $\mathrm{SNR}_{\mathrm{eff}}$, defined implicitly such that

$$C_{[b/s]} = W \log_2(1 + \mathrm{SNR}_{\mathrm{eff}}). \qquad (5.5)$$

Comparison with (5.4) yields

$$\mathrm{SNR}_{\mathrm{eff}} = \exp\left(\int_B \ln(1 + P_s^o(f) \, \mathrm{SNR}_c(f)) \, df/W\right) - 1. \qquad (5.6)$$

In other words, $1 + \mathrm{SNR}_{\mathrm{eff}}$ is the geometric mean of $1 + P_s^o(f) \, \mathrm{SNR}_c(f)$ over B. In further analogy to an ideal AWGN

channel, it is then also appropriate to define the normalized signal-to-noise ratio for a system operating at rate R (in b/dim) on a general linear Gaussian channel as

$$\mathrm{SNR}_{\mathrm{norm}} = \mathrm{SNR}_{\mathrm{eff}}/(2^{2R} - 1) \qquad (5.7)$$

where $\mathrm{SNR}_{\mathrm{norm}} > 1$ again measures the "gap to capacity."

The capacity-achieving band B is the most important feature of the water-pouring spectrum. For many practical channels, B will be a single frequency interval $[f_1, f_2]$, as illustrated in Fig. 7. However, in other cases, e.g., in the presence of severe narrow-band interference, B may consist of multiple frequency intervals. The dependency of mutual information on the exact choice of $P_s(f)$ is not as critical as its dependency on B. Mutual information achieved with a flat spectrum over B is often nearly equal to capacity [64], [90].

B. Approaching Capacity with Multicarrier Transmission

One way of approaching capacity is suggested directly by the water-pouring argument. The capacity-achieving band B may be divided into disjoint subbands of small enough width Δf that $\mathrm{SNR}_c(f)$ and thus $P_s^o(f)$ are nearly constant over each subband. Each subband can then be treated as an ideal AWGN channel with bandwidth Δf. Multicarrier transmission methods that can be used for this purpose are discussed in Appendix I.

The transmit power allocated to a subband centered at f should be approximately $P_s^o(f) \Delta f$. Then the signal-to-noise ratio in that subband will be approximately $P_s^o(f) \mathrm{SNR}_c(f)$, and the subband capacity will be approximately

$$C_{[b/s]}(f) = \log_2(1 + P_s^o(f) \, \mathrm{SNR}_c(f)) \Delta f. \qquad (5.8)$$

As Δf is made sufficiently small, the aggregate power in all subbands approaches P and the aggregate capacity approaches $C_{[b/s]}$ as given in (5.4). To approach this capacity, powerful coding in each subband at a rate $R_{[b/s]}(f)$ near the subband capacity $C_{[b/s]}(f)$ is needed. To minimize delay, coding should be applied "across subbands" with variable numbers of bits per symbol in each subband [14], [90].

Multicarrier transmission is inherently well suited for channels with a highly frequency-dependent channel SNR function, particularly for channels whose capacity-achieving band B consists of multiple intervals. The symbol length in each subchannel is of the order of $1/\Delta f$, so that symbols become long, generally much longer than the response $g(t)$ of the channel. This makes multicarrier transmission less sensitive to moderate impulsive noise than serial transmission, and simplifies equalization. However, the resulting delay is undesirable for some applications.

As the transmitted signal is the sum of many independent components, its distribution tends to be Gaussian. The resulting large peak-to-average ratio (PAR) is a potential disadvantage of multicarrier transmission. However, recently several methods of controlling the PAR of multicarrier signals have been developed [81], [82].

C. Approaching Capacity with Serial Transmission

Alternatively, the capacity of a linear Gaussian channel may be approached by serial transmission. In this subsection, we

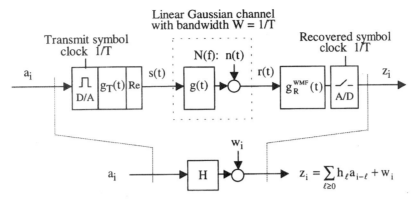

Fig. 8. Conversion of a continuous-time linear Gaussian channel to an equivalent canonical discrete-time linear Gaussian channel.

first examine the conversion of the waveform channel to an equivalent discrete-time channel with intersymbol interference. This is achieved by using a transmit filter that shapes the transmit spectrum to the optimal water-pouring form, and employing a sampled matched filter (MF) or whitened matched filter (WMF) in the receiver. With the WMF, a canonical discrete-time channel with trailing intersymbol interference (ISI) and i.i.d. Gaussian noise is obtained, as depicted in Fig. 8. We show that the contribution of ISI to channel capacity vanishes at high SNR. This suggests that combining an ISI-canceling equalization technique with ideal-channel coding and shaping will suffice to approach capacity. In the following two subsections, we will then discuss the implementation of this approach.

We assume that the capacity-achieving band B is a single positive-frequency interval $[f_1, f_2]$ of width $W = f_2 - f_1$. If B consists of several frequency intervals, then the same approach may be used over each interval separately, although the practical attractiveness of this approach diminishes with multiple intervals. We concentrate on minimum-bandwidth passband transmission of complex symbols at modulation rate $1/T = W$. The transmission of complex signals over a real channel has been discussed in Section II.

In Fig. 8, the transmitted real signal is

$$s(t) = \mathrm{Re}\left(\sum_i a_i g_T(t - iT)\right) \quad (5.9)$$

where ideally $\{a_i\}$ should be a sequence of i.i.d. complex Gaussian symbols with variance (average energy) σ_a^2 per symbol, and $g_T(t)$ is a positive-frequency transmit symbol response with Fourier transform $G_T(f)$. The transmit filter is chosen so that the p.s.d. of $s(t)$ is the water-pouring p.s.d. $P_s^0(f)$; i.e.,

$$\frac{\sigma_a^2}{T}|G_T(f)|^2 = P_s^o(f). \quad (5.10)$$

In the receiver, the received real signal $r(t)$ is first passed through a filter which suppresses negative-frequency components and whitens the noise in the positive-frequency band. This filter may be called a noise-whitening *Hilbert splitter*, because in terms of one-dimensional signals it "splits" the positive-frequency component of a real signal into its real and imaginary parts. The transfer function $G_w(f)$ of this filter is

chosen such that $|G_w(f)|^2 = 1/N(f)$ at least over the band B, and $G_w(f) = 0$ for $f < 0$. The resulting complex signal is then

$$r'(t) = \sum_i a_i v(t - iT) + w(t) \quad (5.11)$$

where $v(t)$ is a symbol response with Fourier transform $V(f) = G_T(f)G(f)G_w(f)$, and $w(t)$ is normalized AWGN with p.s.d. 1 over the signal band B.

Because the set of responses $\{v(t - iT)\}$ represents a basis for the signal space, by the principles of optimum detection theory [118] the set $\{\check{z}_i\}$ of T-sampled matched-filter outputs

$$\check{z}_i = \int r'(t)v * (t - iT)\, dt \quad (5.12)$$

of a matched filter (MF) with response $v^*(-t)$ is a set of sufficient statistics for the detection of the symbol sequence $\{a_i\}$. Thus no loss of mutual information or optimality occurs in the course of reducing $r(t)$ to the sequence $\{\check{z}_i\}$. The composite receive filter consisting of the noise-whitening filter and the MF has the transfer function

$$G_R^{\mathrm{MF}}(f) = G_w(f)V^*(f) = G_T^*(f)G^*(f)/N(f). \quad (5.13)$$

The Fourier transform of the end-to-end symbol response

$$Q(f) = G_T(f)G(f)G_R^{\mathrm{MF}}(f) = |G_T(f)G(f)|^2/N(f) \quad (5.14)$$

has the properties of a real nonnegative power spectrum that is band-limited to B. Moreover, $Q(f)$ is equal to the noise p.s.d. $P_n(f)$ at the MF output, because

$$P_n(f) = N(f)|G_R^{\mathrm{MF}}|^2 = |G_T(f)G(f)|^2/N(f) = Q(f). \quad (5.15)$$

The sampled output sequence of the MF is given by

$$\check{z}_i = \sum_\ell q_\ell a_{i-\ell} + n_i \quad (5.16)$$

where the coefficients $q_\ell = q(\ell T)$ are the sample values of the end-to-end symbol response $q(t)$. In general, the discrete-time Fourier transform of the sequence $\{q_\ell\}$ is the $1/T$-aliased spectrum

$$\tilde{Q}(f) = \frac{1}{T}\sum_{m \in \mathbf{Z}} Q(f + m/T). \quad (5.17)$$

359

In our case, because $Q(f)$ is limited to a positive-frequency band B of width $W = 1/T$, there is no aliasing; i.e., the $1/T$-periodic function $\tilde{Q}(f)$ is equal to $(1/T)\,Q(f)$ within B. Because $P_n(f) = Q(f)$, $\{n_i\}$ is a Gaussian noise sequence with autocorrelation sequence $\{R_{nn,\ell}\} = \{q_\ell\}$. Note that $\{q_\ell\}$ is Hermitian-symmetric, because $Q(f)$ is real.

So far, we have obtained without loss of optimality an equivalent discrete-time channel model which can be written in D-transform notation as

$$\breve{z}(D) = a(D)q(D) + n(D) \qquad (5.18)$$

where $q(D)$ is Hermitian-symmetric. We now proceed to develop an alternative, equivalent discrete-time channel model with a causal, monic, minimum-phase ("canonical") response $h(D)$ and white Gaussian noise $w(D)$. For this purpose, we appeal to the discrete-time spectral factorization theorem:

Spectral Factorization Theorem (Discrete-Time) [83]: Let $\{q_\ell\}$ be an autocorrelation sequence with D-transform $q(D) = \sum_\ell q_\ell D^\ell$, and assume its discrete-time Fourier transform $\tilde{Q}(f) = q(e^{-j2\pi fT})$ satisfies the discrete-time Paley–Wiener condition

$$\int_{1/T} |\log \tilde{Q}(f)|\, df < \infty$$

where $\int_{1/T}$ denotes integration over any interval of width $1/T$. Then $q(D)$ can be factored as follows:

$$q(D) = h^*(D^{-1}) A^2 h(D)$$
$$\tilde{Q}(f) = \tilde{H}^*(f) A^2 \tilde{H}(f) \qquad (5.19)$$

where $h(D) = 1 + h_1 D + \cdots$ is causal ($h_\ell = 0$ for $\ell < 0$), monic ($h_0 = 1$), and minimum-phase, and $\tilde{H}(f) = h(e^{-j2\pi fT})$ is the discrete-time Fourier transform of $h(D)$. The factor A^2 is the geometric mean of $\tilde{Q}(f)$ over a band of width $1/T$; i.e.,

$$\log A^2 = T \int_{1/T} \log \tilde{Q}(f)\, df \qquad (5.20)$$

where the logarithms may have any common base.

The discrete-time Paley–Wiener criterion implies that $\tilde{Q}(f)$ can have only a discrete set of algebraic zeroes. Spectral factorization is further explained in Appendix III.

A causal, monic, minimum-phase response $h(D)$ is called canonical. The spectral factorization above is unique under the constraint that $h(D)$ be canonical.

If $\tilde{Q}(f)$ satisfies the Paley–Wiener condition, then (5.18) can be written in the form

$$\breve{z}(D) = a(D)A^2 h(D)h^*(D^{-1}) + w(D)Ah^*(D^{-1}) \quad (5.21)$$

in which $w'(D)$ is an i.i.d. Gaussian noise sequence with symbol variance 1. Filtering $\breve{z}(D)$ by $1/A^2 h^*(D^{-1})$ yields the channel model of the *equivalent canonical discrete-time Gaussian channel*

$$z(D) = a(D)h(D) + w(D) \qquad (5.22)$$

where $w(D)$ is an i.i.d. Gaussian noise sequence with variance $1/A^2$. This requires that $h(D)$ has a stable inverse, and hence $h^*(D^{-1})$ has a stable anti-causal inverse, which is true if $q(D)$ has no spectral zeroes.

However, the invertibility of $h(D)$ is not a serious issue because $z(D)$ can be obtained directly as the sequence of sampled outputs of a *whitened matched filter* (WMF) [41]. The transfer function of the composite receive filter consisting of the noise-whitening filter and the WMF is given by

$$G_R^{\mathrm{WMF}}(f) = \frac{G_R^{\mathrm{MF}}(f)}{A^2 \tilde{H}^*(f)} = \frac{G_T^*(f)G^*(f)}{N(f)} \frac{\tilde{H}(f)}{\tilde{Q}(f)}. \quad (5.23)$$

The only condition for the stability of this filter is the Paley–Wiener criterion. It is shown in [41] that the time response of this filter is always well defined.

(The channel model $z(D) = a(D)h(D) + w(D)$ expresses the output sequence $z(D)$ as the sum of a noise-free sequence $y(D) = a(D)h(D)$ and additive white Gaussian noise. If $a(D)$ is an uncoded sequence of symbols from a finite signal constellation, and $h(D)$ is of finite length, then the noise-free received signal $y(D) = a(D)h(D)$ is the output of a finite-state machine, and the sequence $a(D)$ may be optimally detected by maximum-likelihood sequence detection (MLSD)—i.e., by the Viterbi algorithm [41]. Alternatively, as shown in [103], MLSD may be performed directly on the MF output sequence $\breve{z}(D)$, using a trellis of the same complexity. However, the main point of the development of this section is that MLSD is not necessary to approach capacity; powerful coding of $a(D)$ plus tail-canceling equalization suffices!)

From the sequence $z(D)$ of sampled WMF outputs the sequence $\breve{z}(D)$ of sampled MF outputs can always be obtained by filtering $z(D)$ with the stable filter response $A^2 h^*(D^{-1})$. Because $\breve{z}(D)$ is a set of sufficient statistics for the estimation of $a(D)$, $z(D)$ must equally be a set of sufficient statistics. The mutual information between the channel input and the MF or WMF output sequence is therefore equal to the capacity $C_{[\mathrm{b/s}]}$ as given in (5.4). Because

$$Q(f) = \frac{|G_T(f)G(f)|}{N(f)} = \frac{T}{\sigma_a^2} P_s^o(f)\,\mathrm{SNR}_c(f) \quad (5.24)$$

and $\tilde{Q}(f) = (1/T)Q(f)$, the capacity $C_{[\mathrm{b/s}]}$ and its high-SNR approximation can be written as

$$C_{[\mathrm{b/s}]} = \int_B \log_2(1 + \sigma_a^2 \tilde{Q}(f))\, df \cong \int_B \log_2(\sigma_a^2 \tilde{Q}(f))\, df.$$
$$(5.25)$$

We now show that at high SNR the capacity $C_{[\mathrm{b/s}]}$ of the linear Gaussian channel is approximately equal to the capacity of the ideal ISI-free channel that would be obtained if somehow ISI could be eliminated from the sequence $z(D)$. In other words, ISI does not contribute significantly to capacity. This observation was first made by Price [85].

Suppose that somehow the ISI-causing "tail" of the response $h(D)$ could be eliminated, so that in the receiver $z'(D) = a(D) + w(D)$ rather than $z(D) = a(D)h(D) + w(D)$ could be observed. The signal-to-noise ratio of the resulting ideal AWGN channel would be $\mathrm{SNR}_{\mathrm{ISI\text{-}free}} = \sigma_a^2 A^2$. Thus the capacity of the ISI-free channel, and its high-SNR approximation, would be

$$C_{\mathrm{ISI\text{-}free}\,[\mathrm{b/s}]} = W \log_2(1 + \sigma_a^2 A^2) \cong W \log_2(\sigma_a^2 A^2). \quad (5.26)$$

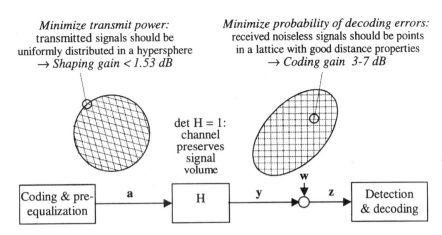

Fig. 9. Coding objectives for a linear Gaussian channel with a known channel response H.

Price observed that at high SNR $C_{[b/s]} \cong C_{\text{ISI-free}[b/s]}$, i.e.,

$$C_{[b/s]} \cong \int_B \log_2 \sigma_a^2 \tilde{Q}(f) \, df = W \log_2 \sigma_a^2 A^2 \cong C_{\text{ISI-free}[b/s]}$$

$$(5.27)$$

where the equality in (5.27) follows from (5.20).

An alternative "minimum-mean-squared error" (MMSE) form of this result has been obtained in [22] and [23]. This result shows that if both ISI and bias are eliminated in an MMSE-optimized receiver, then the resulting signal-to-noise ratio $\text{SNR}_{\text{ISI-free, MMSE}}$ is equal to SNR_{eff} for any linear Gaussian channel at any signal-to-noise ratio. If the interference in the MMSE-optimized unbiased receiver were Gaussian and uncorrelated with the signal, then this would imply $C_{[b/s]} = C_{\text{ISI-free}[b/s]}$ with equality at all SNR's; however, in general, this relation is again only approximate.

Price's result and the alternative MMSE result suggest strongly that the combination of ISI-canceling equalization method and powerful ideal-channel coding and shaping will suffice to approach channel capacity on any linear Gaussian channel, particularly in the high-SNR regime.

D. Coding Objectives for Linear ISI-AWGN Channels

An intuitive explanation of the coding objectives for linear Gaussian channels is presented in Fig. 9.

Signal sequences are shown here as finite-dimensional vectors $\boldsymbol{a}$, $\boldsymbol{y}$, $\boldsymbol{w}$, and $\boldsymbol{z}$. The convolution $y(D) = a(D)h(D)$ that determines the noise-free output sequence becomes a vector transformation $\boldsymbol{y} = \boldsymbol{a}H$ by a channel matrix H. Because the canonical response $h(D)$ is causal and monic ($h_0 = 1$), the matrix H is triangular with an all-ones diagonal, so it has unit determinant: $\det H = 1$. It follows that the linear transformation from $\boldsymbol{a}$ to $\boldsymbol{y}$ is *volume-preserving* [23].

To achieve shaping gain (minimize transmit power for a given volume), at the channel input the constellation points $\boldsymbol{a}$ should be uniformly distributed within a hypersphere. The channel matrix H transforms the hypersphere into a hyperellipse of equal volume containing an equal number of constellation points $\boldsymbol{y}$.

To achieve coding gain, the noise-free channel output vectors $\boldsymbol{y}$ should be points in an infinite signal set Λ with good distance properties (figuratively shown as an integer lattice). If

the transmitter knows the channel matrix H, it can predistort the input vectors $\boldsymbol{a}$ to be points in an appropriately predistorted signal set ΛH^{-1} (figuratively shown as a skewed integer lattice). The volumes $V(\Lambda)$ and $V(\Lambda H^{-1})$ per point in the two signal sets are equal.

The noise-free output vectors are observed in the presence of i.i.d. Gaussian noise $\boldsymbol{w}$. A minimum-distance detector for the infinite signal set Λ can therefore obtain the coding gain of Λ on an ideal AWGN channel.

In summary, coding and shaping take place in two different Euclidean spaces, which are connected by a known volume-preserving linear transformation. Coding and shaping may be separately optimized, by choosing an infinite signal set with a large coding gain (density) for an ideal AWGN channel in the coding space, and by choosing a shaping scheme with a large shaping gain (small normalized second moment) in the shaping space. The channel intersymbol interference may be eliminated at the channel output by predistortion of the infinite signal set at the input, based on the known channel response.

E. Precoding and Trellis Coding for Linear Gaussian Channels

Precoding is a pre-equalization method that achieves the coding objectives set out in Section V-D, assuming that the canonical channel response $h(D)$ is known at the transmitter. A pre-equalized sequence $a(D) = y(D)/h(D)$ is transmitted such that

a) the output sequence $z(D) = y(D) + w(D)$ is the output of an apparently ISI-free ideal channel with input sequence $y(D)$;

b) the noise-free output sequence $y(D)$ may therefore be a coded sequence from a code designed for the ideal AWGN channel, and may be decoded by an ideal-channel decoder;

c) redundancy in $y(D)$ may be used to minimize the average power of the input sequence $a(D) = y(D)/h(D)$, or to achieve other desirable characteristics for $a(D)$.

Precoding was first developed for uncoded M-PAM transmission in two independent masters' theses by Tomlinson [97] and Harashima [54]. Its application was not pursued at that time because decision-feedback equalization was, and still is, the preferred ISI-canceling method for uncoded transmission.

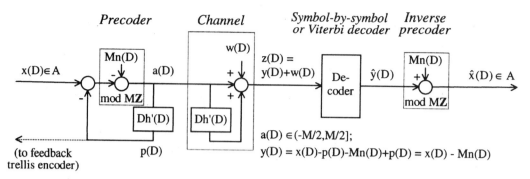

Fig. 10. Tomlinson–Harashima precoding for one-dimensional M-PAM transmission, with or without trellis coding.

With trellis coding, however, decision-feedback equalization is no longer attractive, because reliable decisions are not available from a Viterbi decoder without significant delay. As we shall see, Tomlinson–Harashima precoding can be combined with trellis coding, but not with shaping.

Trellis precoding [35] was the first technique that allowed combining trellis coding, precoding, and shaping. However, in trellis precoding, coding and shaping are coupled, which to some degree inhibits control of constellation characteristics such as peak-to-average ratio (PAR). Therefore, during the development of the V.34 modem standard techniques called "flexible precoding" were proposed independently by Eyuboglu [80], Cole and Goldstein [52], and Laroia et al. [73]. In flexible precoding, coding and shaping are decoupled. Later, Laroia [71] proposed an "ISI precoding" technique that used feedback trellis coding (see Section IV-D) to reduce "dither power." Further improvements were made by Cole and Eyuboglu [53] and by Betts [4], and the [53] scheme was ultimately adopted for the V.34 standard [62]. Recently, feedback trellis coding has been combined with Tomlinson–Harashima precoding [20].

We will describe Tomlinson–Harashima precoding and flexible precoding, with and without trellis coding. The general principle applied in these schemes is as follows. Let the canonical channel response $h(D) = 1 + h_1 D + h_2 D^2 \cdots$ be written as $h(D) = 1 + Dh'(D)$. Then the noise-free output sequence of the channel is given by

$$y(D) = a(D) + a(D)Dh'(D) = a(D) + p(D) \quad (5.28)$$

where $p(D)$ is the sequence of trailing intersymbol interference. In all types of precoding, the precoder determines $p_i = \sum_{\ell>0} h_\ell a_{i-\ell}$ from past signals and sends $a_i = y_i - p_i$ so that the channel output will be a desired signal y_i.

Tomlinson–Harashima (TH) precoding is illustrated in Fig. 10 for one-dimensional transmission with M-PAM signal constellations as defined in Section II-C. In the language of lattice constellations introduced in Section IV-A, an M-PAM signal constellation with a signal spacing of $d_0 = 1$ is defined as

$$A = C(\mathbf{Z}, \mathbb{R}(M\mathbf{Z})) = (\mathbf{Z} + t) \cap \mathbb{R}(M\mathbf{Z})$$

where $t = 1/2$ for M even and $t = 0$ for M odd, and $\mathbb{R}(M\mathbf{Z}) = (-M/2, M/2]$ is the fundamental Voronoi region of the sublattice $M\mathbf{Z}$. The translates of $\mathbb{R}(M\mathbf{Z})$ by integer

multiples of M then cover ("tile") all of real signal space, so every real signal may be expressed uniquely as $r = a + Mn$ for $a \in \mathbb{R}(M\mathbf{Z})$ and some integer $n \in Z$. The unique $a \in \mathbb{R}(M\mathbf{Z})$ so determined is called "r mod $M\mathbf{Z}$."

Fig. 10 is drawn such that one can easily see that the noiseless channel-output sequence is $y(D) = x(D) - Mn(D)$, where $x(D) \in A$ is the sequence of PAM signals to be transmitted, and $n(D)$ is an integer sequence generated by the "r mod $M\mathbf{Z}$" unit in the precoder so that the elements of the transmitted sequence $a(D)$ are contained in $(-M/2, M/2]$, and the elements of $y(D)$ are in $Z + t$. The decoder operates on the noisy sequence $z(D) = y(D) + w(D)$ and outputs the sequence $\hat{y}(D)$, which is then reduced by the "mod $M\mathbf{Z}$" unit to the sequence $\hat{x}(D) = \hat{y}(D) + M\hat{n}(D) \in A$. In the absence of decoding errors, $\hat{y}(D) = y(D)$ and therefore $\hat{x}(D) = x(D)$. Note that "inverse precoding" is memoryless, so no error propagation can occur. Because the channel response $h(D)$ does not need to be inverted in the receiver, $h(D)$ may exhibit spectral nulls, e.g., contain factors of the form $(1 \pm D)$.

The combination of trellis coding with TH precoding requires that $y(D) = x(D) - Mn(D)$ is a valid code sequence. For practically all trellis codes, when M is a multiple of 4 and $x(D)$ is a code sequence, then $y(D)$ is also a code sequence (in particular, this holds for "mod 2" or "mod 4" coset codes [42], [43]). Thus trellis coding and Tomlinson–Harashima precoding are easily combined.

With a more complicated constellation A, trellis coding can be combined with TH precoding by using the idea of feedback trellis coding [20], provided that a) the first-level subsets $B(0)$ and $B(1)$ of A are congruent; b) the constellation shape region $\mathbb{R}(A)$, namely, the union of the Voronoi regions of the signals in A, is a space-filling region (has the "tiling" property). Condition b) obviously holds for M-PAM and square $M \times M$-QAM constellations. It also holds for a 12-QAM "cross" constellation, for example, but not for a 32-QAM cross constellation. We note that signal constellations whose sizes are not powers of two have become practically important in connection with mapping techniques such as shell mapping and modulus conversion (see Section IV-B).

In summary, Tomlinson–Harashima precoding permits the combination of trellis coding with ISI-canceling (DFE-equivalent) equalization. Its main problem is the requirement that the signal space can be "tiled" with translates of the

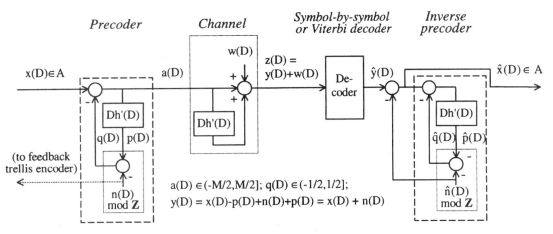

Fig. 11. Flexible precoding for one-dimensional M-PAM transmission, with or without trellis coding.

constellation shape region. Tomlinson–Harashima precoding results in a small increase in transmit signal power, equal to the average energy of a random "dither variable" uniformly distributed over the Voronoi region around the constellation signals. If the Voronoi region is $\mathbb{R}(Z)$, then the increase in signal power is $1/12$, which is negligible for large constellations.

Flexible (FL) precoding is illustrated in Fig. 11, again for one-dimensional M-PAM transmission. The general concept of FL precoding is to subtract from a sequence $x(D)$ of M-PAM signals a sequence of smallest "dither" variables $q(D)$ such that the channel-output sequence $y(D)$ is a valid uncoded or coded sequence with elements in $Z + t$. The constellation shape region of the signal constellation A can be arbitrary, so any shaping scheme can be used. At time i, given the ISI term p_i, the "mod Z" unit in the precoder determines the integer $n_i \in Z$ that is closest to p_i. The dither variable is the difference $q_i = p_i - n_i$. Clearly, q_i lies in the Voronoi interval $\mathbb{R}(Z) = (-1/2, 1/2]$. It will typically be uniformly distributed over $\mathbb{R}(Z)$, and thus increases the average energy of the transmit signal $a_i = x_i - q_i$ by $1/12$.

As can be seen from Fig. 11, the sequence of noiseless channel-output signals becomes

$$y(D) = x(D) - q(D) + p(D) = x(D) + n(D).$$

The decoder operates on the noisy sequence $z(D) = y(D) + w(D)$ and produces the sequence $\hat{y}(D)$. To obtain the sequence $\hat{x}(D) = \hat{y}(D) - \hat{n}(D)$, the sequence $\hat{n}(D)$ is recovered by channel inversion as shown in Fig. 11. A "bit-identical" realization of the two functional blocks shown in dashed blocks in Fig. 11 is absolutely essential.

The combination of flexible precoding with feedback trellis coding works as follows. At time i, the transmitter knows the integer n_i and the current trellis-code state s_i. To continue a valid code sequence $y(D)$ at the noiseless channel output, the transmitter selects a data symbol x_i such that $y_i = x_i + n_i$ is in the first-level infinite subset $B(0)$ or $B(1)$ determined by s_i. The symbol x_i is chosen to lie in a desired constellation shape region $\mathbb{R}(A)$, or according to some other shaping scheme. The symbol y_i then determines the next state s_{i+1}, as explained in Section IV-D.

The main advantage of flexible precoding is that any constellation-shaping method can be used, whereas with Tomlinson–Harashima precoding or trellis precoding, shaping is connected with coding. The main disadvantage is that decoding errors tend to propagate due to the channel inversion in the receiver, which is particularly troublesome on channels with spectral nulls. A technique to mitigate error propagation in the inverse precoder is described in [37]. The main application of flexible precoding so far has been in V.34 modems. The application of precoding in digital subscriber lines has been studied in [38].

In conclusion, at high SNR's, precoding in combination with powerful trellis codes and shaping schemes allows the capacity of an arbitrary linear Gaussian channel to be approached as closely as capacity can be approached on an ideal ISI-free AWGN channel, with about the same coding and shaping complexity.

VI. FINAL REMARKS

Shannon's papers established ultimate limits, but gave no constructive methods to achieve them. They thereby threw down the gauntlet for the new field of coding. In particular, they established fundamental benchmarks for linear Gaussian channels that have posed tough challenges for subsequent code inventors.

The discouraging initial progress in developing good constructive codes was captured by the folk theorem [119]: "All codes are good, except those that we know of." However, by the early 1970's, good practical codes had been developed for the low-SNR regime:

- moderate-constraint-length binary convolutional codes with Viterbi decoding for 3–6-dB coding gain with moderate complexity;
- long-constraint length convolutional codes with sequential decoding to reach R_0;
- oncatenation of RS outer codes with algebraic decoding and moderate-complexity inner codes to achieve very low error rates near R_0.

By the 1980's, the invention of trellis codes enabled similar progress to be made in the high-SNR regime, at least for the ideal band-limited AWGN channel. In the 1990's, these gains were extended to general linear Gaussian channels by use of multicarrier modulation, or alternatively by use of single-carrier modulation with transmitter precoding.

Notably, many of these techniques were developed by practically oriented engineers in standards-setting groups and in industrial R&D environments. Moreover, as a consequence of advances in VLSI design and technology, the lag between invention and appearance in commercial products has often been very short.

By now, it certainly appears that the field of modulation and coding for Gaussian channels has reached a mature state, at least below the cutoff rate R_0, even though very few systems reaching R_0 have ever actually been implemented. In the beyond-R_0 regime, however, the invention of turbo codes has touched off intense activity that seems likely to continue well into the next half-century.

APPENDIX I
MULTICARRIER MODULATION

The history of multicarrier modulation began more than 40 years ago with an early system called Kineplex [30] designed for digital transmission in the HF band. Work by Holsinger [57] and others followed.

The use of the discrete Fourier transform (DFT) for modulation and demodulation was proposed in [115]. DFT-based multicarrier systems are now referred to as *orthogonal frequency-division multiplexing* (OFDM) or *discrete multitone* (DMT) systems [2], [14], [56], [90]. Basically, OFDM/DMT is a form of frequency-division multiplexing (FDM) in which modulation symbols are transmitted in individual subchannels using QAM or CAP modulation (see Section II-B). Current applications of OFDM/DMT include digital audio broadcasting (DAB) [33] and asynchronous digital subscriber lines (ADSL) [1].

Another multicarrier transmission technique of the FDM type became more recently known as *discrete wavelet multitone* (DWMT) modulation [91], [102]. DWMT modulation has its origin in filter banks for subband source coding. Efficient implementations of DWMT modulation and demodulation employ the discrete cosine transform (DCT).

A comprehensive treatment of multirate systems and filter banks is given in [106]. Recent reviews of theory and applications of filter banks and wavelet transforms are presented in [99].

The coding aspects of multicarrier systems have been discussed in Section IV-B. In this appendix, we give brief descriptions of DMT and DWMT modulation (together with some background information). For the purposes of this appendix, we assume transmission over a noise-free discrete-time real linear channel which is modeled by $y(D) = x(D)h(D)$, where $h(D)$ is the channel response.

A. DFT-Based Filter Banks and Discrete Multitone (DMT) Modulation

Before specifically addressing DMT modulation, we examine the general concept of DFT-based multicarrier modulation. These systems subdivide the channel into N narrowband subchannels whose center frequencies are spaced by integer multiples of the subchannel modulation rate $1/T$. Let $\{A_\ell(k)\}$ be the sequence of generally complex data symbols transmitted in the kth subchannel, and let $\boldsymbol{A}_\ell = [A_\ell(k), 0 \leq k \leq N-1]$ denote the N-vector transmitted over these channels at time ℓT.

A DFT-based "synthesis" filter bank generates at rate N/T the transmit signals

$$x_i = \sum_{k=0}^{N-1} \sum_\ell A_\ell(k) v_{i-\ell N} \exp(j2\pi ki/N) \qquad \text{(AI.1)}$$

where $\{v_i, \; i \geq 0\}$ is a real causal symbol response with a baseband spectrum $V(f)$. This N/T-sampled response is sometimes called the "prototype response." The least integer $\gamma \geq 0$ such that $v_i = 0$ for all $i \geq (\gamma + 1)N$ is called the "overlap factor." Note that the sequence $\{x_i\}$ has an N/T-periodic spectrum and is composed of subchannels whose center frequencies are located at integer multiples of $1/T$, as illustrated in Fig. 12.

If we express the time index as $i = mN + n$, with $m \in \boldsymbol{Z}$ and $0 \leq n \leq N-1$, then (AI.1) becomes

$$
\begin{aligned}
x_{mN+n} &= \sum_\ell \left(\sum_{k=0}^{N-1} A_\ell(k) \exp(j2\pi kn/N) \right) v_{(m-\ell)N+n} \\
&= \sum_\ell a_\ell(n) v_{(m-\ell)N+n} \\
&= \sum_{\ell=0}^{\gamma} p_\ell(n) a_{m-\ell}(n), \qquad 0 \leq n \leq N-1 \quad \text{(AI.2)}
\end{aligned}
$$

where $\boldsymbol{a}_\ell = [a_\ell(n), 0 \leq n \leq N-1]$ is the inverse discrete Fourier transform (IDFT) of $\boldsymbol{A}_\ell = [A_\ell(k), 0 \leq k \leq N-1]$, and $\{p_\ell(n) = v_{\ell N+n}, 0 \leq \ell \leq \gamma\}$, for $0 \leq n \leq N-1$, is the $1/T$-sampled nth-phase component of the prototype response. Thus (AI.2) shows that the signals of $\{x_i\}$ may be generated by N independent convolutions of sequences of the time-domain symbols $\{a_\ell(n)\}$ with the corresponding phase components $\{p_\ell(n)\}$ of the prototype response. Such a system is called a DFT-based polyphase filter bank [7], [106].

To obtain real transmit signals, the frequency-domain modulation symbols must exhibit Hermitian symmetry; i.e., $A_\ell(k) = A_\ell^*(N-k)$. Then the IDFT coefficients $a_\ell(n)$ are real and hence the signals $x_i = x_{mN+n}$ are real. The restriction to Hermitian symmetry allows for N real-signal degrees of freedom, i.e., it permits mappings of N real data symbols $\{\overline{a}_\ell(k), 0 \leq k \leq N-1\}$ into N complex symbols $\{A_\ell(k), 0 \leq k \leq N-1\}$. For N even, one possible mapping is

$$
\begin{aligned}
A_\ell(0) &= \overline{a}_\ell(0) \\
A_\ell(N/2) &= \overline{a}_\ell(N-1) \\
A_\ell(k) &= \overline{a}_\ell(2k-1) + j\overline{a}_\ell(2k) = A_\ell^*(N-k), \\
& \qquad\qquad 1 \leq k \leq N/2 - 1. \quad \text{(AI.3)}
\end{aligned}
$$

In the absence of distortion, the IDFT coefficients can be recovered from $\{y_i\} = \{x_i\}$ by a polyphase "analysis" filter bank, which performs the matched filter operations

$$\sum_m x_{mN+n} p_{m-\ell}(n) = \hat{a}_\ell(n). \qquad \text{(AI.4)}$$

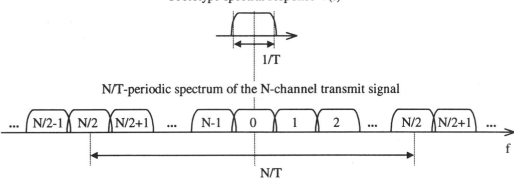

Prototype spectral response V(f)

N/T-periodic spectrum of the N-channel transmit signal

Fig. 12. Spectrum of DFT-based multicarrier modulation (N even).

If the orthogonality conditions

$$\sum_m p_m(n)p_{m-\ell}(n) = \delta_\ell \qquad \text{(AI.5)}$$

are satisfied for all $\ell \in \mathbf{Z}$ and $0 \le n \le N-1$, then $\hat{a}_\ell(n) = a_\ell(n)$. Finally, the N-vector $\boldsymbol{A}_\ell = [A_\ell(k), 0 \le k \le N-1]$ is obtained as the DFT of $\boldsymbol{a}_\ell = [a_\ell(n), 0 \le n \le N-1]$.

We note from (AI.5) that in an ideal system each of the N phase components of the prototype response must individually satisfy the Nyquist condition for zero-ISI transmission in that subchannel. Then, summing (A1.4) over $n = 0, 1, \cdots, N-1$ shows that also the prototype response satisfies the orthogonality condition for transmission at rate $1/T$.

The orthogonality conditions are trivially satisfied if the prototype response is a sampled rectangular pulse of length T, i.e., $\{v_i = \text{const.}, 0 \le i \le N-1\}$ ($\gamma = 0$). In this case, no polyphase filtering is required. However, because the spectra of the subchannels will then overlap according to the $\sin(x)/x$ shape of the prototype response spectrum, small amounts of channel distortion can be sufficient to destroy orthogonality and cause severe interchannel interference (ICI). For some applications, a higher spectral concentration of the subchannel spectra will therefore be desirable. This leads to a filter design problem, which consists in minimizing for given filter length, i.e., for given overlap factor $\gamma > 0$, the spectral energy of the prototype response outside of the band $|f| < 1/2T$ while approximately maintaining orthogonality.

For DMT modulation, $v_i = 1$ for $0 \le i \le N-1$ is used, and the transmitted signals could simply be the unfiltered IDFT coefficients:

$$x_i = x_{mN+n} = a_m(n). \qquad \text{(AI.6)}$$

In the absence of channel distortion, this simple scheme would be sufficient. However, if the channel response $\{h_i\}$ has length L' (i.e., $h_0 \ne 0, \cdots h_L \ne 0$), then the L' last IDFT coefficients of every transmitted block of N IDFT coefficients would interfere with the first L' coefficients of the next block (assuming $L' \le N$). In principle, combinations of pre-equalization and post-equalization (before and after the DFT operation in the receiver) could be used to mitigate the effects of this interference.

Practical DMT systems employ the simpler method of "cyclic extension," originally suggested in [86], to cope with distortion. If the channel response has at most length L, then every block of IDFT coefficients is cyclically extended by L coefficients. For example, with "cyclic prefix extension" the mth block is extended from length N to length $L+N$ as follows:

$$\{a_m(N-L), \cdots, a_m(N-1);$$
$$a_m(0), a_m(1), \cdots, a_m(N-1), a_m(N-1)\}. \qquad \text{(AI.7)}$$

Assume the actual length of the channel response is $L' < L$. Then the received sequence $\{y_i\}$ contains cyclic signal repetitions within windows of length $L - L'$ for every received block of extended length $L + N$. The receiver selects blocks of signals of length N such that the received signals at the beginning and end of these blocks are cyclically repeating. The DFT of these blocks is then

$$\{A_m(n)H(n/T), 0 \le n \le N-1\} \qquad \text{(AI.8)}$$

where $H(n/T)$ is the Fourier transform of the channel response at $f = n/T$. Multiplication with the estimated inverse spectral channel response yields the desired symbols $A_m(n)$. With this "one tap per symbol" equalization method, distortion is dealt with in a simple manner at the expense of a rate loss by the factor of $L/(L+N)$. For example, the ADSL standard [1] specifies $N = 512$ and $L = 32$, which results in a loss of 5.8%.

In practical DMT systems, one may not rely entirely on the cyclic-extension method to cope with distortion. An adaptive pre-equalizer may be employed to minimize the channel-response length prior to the DFT-based receiver operations described above. The problem is essentially similar to adjusting the forward filter in a decision-feedback equalizer or an MLSD receiver such that the channel memory is truncated to a given length [21], [36].

B. Cosine-Modulated Filter Banks and Discrete Wavelet Multitone (DWMT) Modulation

Cosine-modulated filter banks were first introduced for subband speech coding. The related concept of quadrature mirror filters (QMF) was probably first mentioned in [32]. In the field of digital communications, multicarrier modulation by means of cosine-modulated filter banks is referred to as DWMT modulation [91], [102]. The main feature of DWMT is that all signal processing is performed on real signals.

Prototype spectral response V(f)

1/2T

N/T-periodic spectrum of the N-channel transmit signal

The phase of adjacent subchannel responses differs by ±π/2

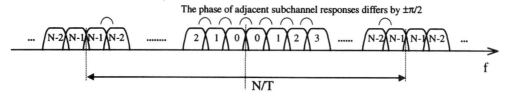

f

N/T

Fig. 13. Spectrum of cosine-modulated multicarrier modulation.

DWMT can be understood as a form of multiple carrierless single-sideband modulation (CSSB, see Section II-B).

The sequences $\{A_\ell(k)\}$, $0 \le k \le N-1$, are now sequences of real modulation symbols. DWMT employs a real prototype response $\{v_i\}$ with a baseband spectrum $V(f)$ that satisfies the Nyquist criterion for ISI-free transmission at symbol rate $1/2T$. Also, $V(f)$ has no more than 100% spectral roll-off (i.e., $V(f) = 0$ for $|f| > 1/2T$). Furthermore, it is convenient to assume that $V(f)$ has zero phase.

A cosine-modulated "synthesis" filter bank generates at rate N/T the transmit signals

$$x_i = \sum_{k=0}^{N-1} \sum_{\ell} A_\ell(k) p_{i-\ell N}(k) \qquad (AI.9)$$

where the samples of the symbol response for the kth subchannel are given by

$$p_i(k) = 2v_i \cos(\pi(k + 0.5)i/N + \varphi_k)$$
$$\varphi_k = (-1)^k \pi/4. \qquad (AI.10)$$

The corresponding spectral symbol response is then

$$P^k(f) = e^{-j\varphi_k} V\left(f + \frac{k + 0.5}{2T}\right) + e^{j\varphi_k} V\left(f - \frac{k + 0.5}{2T}\right).$$
$$(AI.11)$$

The spectrum of the transmitted signal is shown in Fig. 13. One can verify that any two overlapping frequency-shifted prototype spectra differ in phase by $\pm\pi/2$. This is the so-called QMF condition, which ensures orthogonality [106].

For a DCT-based polyphase realization of cosine-modulated filter banks, see [106].

APPENDIX II
UNIFORMITY PROPERTIES OF EUCLIDEAN-SPACE CODES

A binary linear code has a useful and fundamental uniformity property: the code "looks the same" from the viewpoint of any of its sequences. The number of neighbors at each distance is the same for all code sequences, and, provided the channel has appropriate symmetry, the error probability is independent of which code sequence is transmitted. If this uniformity property holds, then one has to consider only the set of code distances from the all-zero sequence (i.e., the set of

code weights), and in performance analysis one may assume that the all-zero sequence was transmitted.

Similar uniformity properties are helpful in the design and analysis of Euclidean-space codes. A variety of such properties have been introduced, from the original "quasilinearity" property of Ungerboeck [104] to geometric uniformity [44] (a property that generalizes the group property of binary linear codes), and finally rotational invariance. In this section we briefly review these properties.

A. Geometrical Uniformity

As we have seen in Section IV, for coding purposes it is useful to regard a large constellation based on a dense packing such as a lattice translate $\Lambda + t$ as an effectively infinite constellation consisting of the entire packing. This approximation eliminates boundary effects, and the resulting infinite constellation usually has greater symmetry. As we have seen, shaping methods (selection of a finite subconstellation) may be designed and analyzed separately in the high-SNR regime.

The symmetry group of a constellation is the set of isometries of Euclidean n-space $\boldsymbol{R}^n$ (i.e., rotations, reflections, translations) that map the constellation to itself. For a lattice translate $\Lambda + t$, the symmetry group includes the infinite set $\{t_\lambda, \lambda \in \Lambda\}$ of all translations t_λ by lattice elements $\lambda \in \Lambda$. It will also generally include a finite set of orthogonal transformations; e.g., the symmetry group of the QAM lattice translate $\boldsymbol{Z}^2 + (1/2, 1/2)$ includes the eight symmetries of the square (the dihedral group D_8). A constellation is geometrically uniform if it is the orbit of any of its points under its symmetry group. A lattice translate $\Lambda + t$ is necessarily geometrically uniform, because it can be generated by the translation group $\{t_\lambda, \lambda \in \Lambda\}$. An M-PSK constellation is geometrically uniform, because it can be generated by rotations of multiples of $2\pi/M$.

A fundamental region $R(\Lambda)$ of a lattice Λ is a compact region that contains precisely one point from each translate (coset) $\Lambda + t$ of Λ. For example, any Voronoi region of Λ is a fundamental region if boundary points are appropriately divided between neighboring regions. The translates $\{R(\Lambda) + \lambda, \lambda \in \Lambda\}$ of any fundamental region $R(\Lambda)$ tile n-space

$\boldsymbol{R}^n$ without overlap, so that every $x \in \boldsymbol{R}^n$ can be uniquely expressed as $x = r + \lambda$ for some $r \in R(\Lambda)$ and $\lambda \in \Lambda$, where r is the unique element of $R(\Lambda)$ in the coset $\Lambda + x$. The volume of any fundamental region is $V(\Lambda)$.

As discussed in Section IV, trellis codes are often based on lattice partitions Λ/Λ'. A useful viewpoint that has emerged from multilevel coding is to regard such codes as being defined on a fundamental region $R(\Lambda')$ of the sublattice Λ'. The $|\Lambda/\Lambda'|$ cosets of Λ' in $\Lambda + t$ are represented by their unique representatives in $R(\Lambda')$. At the front end of the receiver, each received point $x \in \boldsymbol{R}^n$ is mapped to the unique point of $\Lambda' + x$ in $R(\Lambda')$. Although such a "mod-Λ' map" is not information-lossless, it has been shown that it does not reduce capacity [46]. Moreover, it decouples coding and decoding implementation and performance from any coding that may occur at other levels. Conceptually, this viewpoint reduces infinite-constellation coding and decoding to coding and decoding using a finite constellation of $|\Lambda/\Lambda'|$ points on the compact region $R(\Lambda')$.

A *geometrically uniform code* based on a lattice partition Λ/Λ' may be constructed as follows. Let G be a label group that is isomorphic to the quotient group Λ/Λ'; or, more generally, let G be a group of $|\Lambda/\Lambda'|$ symmetries that can generate a set of $|\Lambda/\Lambda'|$ subsets congruent to Λ' whose union is $\Lambda + t$. Let T be a time axis (e.g., $T = \{1, \cdots, n\}$ for block codes, or $T = \boldsymbol{Z}$ for convolutional codes), let G^T be the set of all sequences $(g_t, t \in T)$ of elements of G defined on T, which form a group under the componentwise group operation of G, and let $C \subset G^T$ be any subgroup of G^T. Then the orbit of any sequence of subsets of $\Lambda + t$ under C is a geometrically uniform Euclidean-space code. In particular, for any geometrically uniform code, the set of distances from any code sequence to all other code sequences is the same for all code sequences, and the probability of error on an ideal AWGN channel does not depend on which sequence was sent.

This observation has stimulated research into *group codes*, namely codes C that are subgroups of sequence groups G^T, and their geometrically uniform Euclidean-space images. Although the ultimate goal of this research has been to construct new classes of good codes, the main results so far have been to show that most known good codes constructed by other methods are geometrically uniform. Ungerboeck's original 1D and 2D codes are easily shown to be geometrically uniform. Trott showed that the nonlinear Wei 4D 8-state trellis code used in the V.32 modem standard may be represented as a group code whose state space is the non-Abelian dihedral group D_8 [100]. The 4D 16-state Wei code and the 32-state Williams code used in the V.34 modem standard are both geometrically uniform; however, Sarvis and Trott have shown that there is no geometrically uniform code with the same parameters as the 4D 64-state Wei V.34 code [92].

B. Quasilinearity

A weaker uniformity property introduced in [104] is quasilinearity. This property permits the minimum squared distance $d_{\min}^2(C)$ of a trellis code C to be found by simply computing the weights of a set of error sequences, rather than by pairwise comparison of all pairs of possible code sequences.

Quasilinearity depends only on the use of a rate-$(n-1)/n$ binary linear convolutional code in an encoder like that in Fig. 5, and the fact that the subsets $B(0)$ and $B(1)$ associated with the first-level partition are geometrically congruent to each other.

Let $\{\boldsymbol{c}_i\}$ and $\{\boldsymbol{c}_i'\}$ be any two binary convolutional code sequences, and let their difference be the error sequence $\{\boldsymbol{e}_i\} = \{\boldsymbol{c}_i + \boldsymbol{c}_i'\}$, which by linearity is also a code sequence. For each error term $\boldsymbol{e}_i$, define the squared Euclidean weight

$$w^2(\boldsymbol{e}_i | c_i^1) = \min \| a(\boldsymbol{c}_i) - a(\boldsymbol{c}_i + \boldsymbol{e}_i) \|^2 \qquad (\text{AII.1})$$

where $\boldsymbol{c}_i$ ranges over all binary n-tuples $\boldsymbol{c}_i = [c_i^n \cdots c_i^2]$ with the given bit c_i^1, and $a(\boldsymbol{c}_i)$ and $a(\boldsymbol{c}_i + \boldsymbol{e}_i)$ range over all signals in the subsets labeled by $\boldsymbol{c}_i$ and $\boldsymbol{c}_i + \boldsymbol{e}_i$, respectively.

If $B(0)$ and $B(1)$ are congruent, then it is easy to see that $w^2(\boldsymbol{e}_i | 0) = w^2(\boldsymbol{e}_i | 1)$. We may then simply write $w^2(\boldsymbol{e}_i)$ for this common minimum.

It then follows that the minimum squared distance $d_{\min}^2(C)$ between any two trellis-code sequences that correspond to different convolutional-code sequences $\{\boldsymbol{c}_i\}$ and $\{\boldsymbol{c}_i'\}$ is

$$d_{\min}^2(C) = \min_{\{\boldsymbol{e}_i\} \neq \{0\}} \sum_i w^2(\boldsymbol{e}_i). \qquad (\text{AII.2})$$

The proof is that $\{\boldsymbol{c}_i\}$ and $\{\boldsymbol{c}_i'\}$ may differ arbitrarily in the $n - 1$ label bits $[c_i^n \cdots c_i^2]$ and $[c_i'^n \cdots c_i'^2]$, to which the encoder adds appropriate parity-check bits c_i^1 and $c_i'^1$, and for any $\boldsymbol{e}_i$ the minimum $\| a(\boldsymbol{c}_i) - a(\boldsymbol{c}_i + \boldsymbol{e}_i) \|^2$ is achievable with either choice of c_i^1.

Thus quasilinearity permits $d_{\min}^2(C)$ to be computed just as the minimum Hamming distance of binary linear convolutional codes is computed; one simply replaces Hamming weights $w_H(\boldsymbol{e}_i)$ by the squared Euclidean weights $w^2(\boldsymbol{e}_i)$ [104], [120] in trellis searches. This property has been used extensively in searches for the trellis codes reported in [104] and by subsequent authors.

The number of codes to be searched for a code with the highest value of $d_{\min}^2(C)$ can be further reduced significantly if $w^2(\boldsymbol{e}_i)$ attains for all $\boldsymbol{e}_i$ the set-partitioning lower bound $\Delta_{q(e_i)}^2$, where $\Delta_{q(e_i)}^2$ is the minimum intrasubset squared distance at the first partitioning level q for which $e_i^q \neq 0$ [104]. This property usually holds for large geometrically uniform constellations.

C. Rotational Invariance

In carrier-modulated complex-signal transmission systems, the absolute carrier phase of the received waveform signal is generally not known. The receiver may demodulate the received signal with a constant carrier-phase offset $\Delta\varphi \in \Phi$, where Φ is the group of phase rotations that leave the two-dimensional signal constellation invariant. Then, if a signal sequence $\{a_i\}$ was transmitted, the decoder operates on the sequence of rotated signals $\{a_i \exp(\Delta\varphi)\}$. For example, for M-QAM we have $\Phi = \{0°, 90°, 180°, 270°\}$. Rotational invariance is the property that rotated code sequences are also valid code sequences. This is obviously the case for uncoded modulation with signal constellations that exhibit rotational symmetries. To achieve transparency of the transmitted information under phase offsets, phase-differential encoding and decoding may be employed.

A trellis code C is *fully rotationally invariant* if for all coded signal sequences $\{a_i\} \in C$ and all phase offsets $\Delta\varphi \in \Phi$ the rotated sequences are code sequences, i.e., $\{a_i \exp(\Delta\varphi)\} \in C$. Note that signals a_i here always denote two-dimensional signals, which may be component signals of a higher dimensional signal constellation.

Trellis codes are not necessarily rotationally invariant under the same set of symmetries Φ as their two-dimensional signal constellations. It has been shown that trellis codes based on linear binary convolutional codes with mapping into two-dimensional M-PSK or M-QAM ($M > 2$) signals can at most be invariant under $180°$ rotation. Fully rotationally invariant linear trellis codes exist only for higher dimensional constellations. Such codes are given for $K \times$ QAM in [105], [113], ($K = 2, 4$), and for $K \times M$-PSK in [87], [114], ($M = 8, 16$; $K = 2, 3, 4$).

Fully rotationally invariant trellis codes over two-dimensional PSK or QAM constellations must be nonlinear [88], [112]. We briefly describe the analytic approach presented in [88] for the design of nonlinear two-dimensional PSK and QAM trellis codes by an example. Let a QAM signal constellation be partitioned into eight subsets with subset labels $\boldsymbol{c} = [c^3, c^2, c^1] = [c^3, c^r]$, where $c^r = 2c^2 + c^1 \in \boldsymbol{Z}_4$ (ring of integers modulo 4). The labeling is chosen such that under $90°$ rotation the labels are transformed into $\boldsymbol{c}' = [c^3, (c^r + 1) \bmod 4]$. A fully rotationally invariant trellis code can then be found by requiring that for all label sequences $\{\boldsymbol{c}_i\} = \{[c_i^3, c_i^r]\}$ that satisfy a given parity-check equation, the sequences $\{\boldsymbol{c}_i'\} = \{[c_i^3, (c_i^r + 1) \bmod 4]\}$ also satisfy this equation. This is achieved by a binary nonlinear parity-check equation of the form

$$h^3(D)c^3(D) \oplus [h^r(D)c^r(D) \bmod 4]^1 = 0(D) \qquad \text{(AII.3)}$$

where the coefficients of $h^3(D)$ are binary, and the coefficients of $h^r(D)$ and the elements of $c^r(D)$ are elements of $\boldsymbol{Z}_4$. The notation $[\alpha(D)]^1$ means that from the binary representation of every element $\alpha_i = 2\alpha_i^1 + \alpha_i^0 \in \boldsymbol{Z}_4$ in $\alpha(D)$ the most significant bit $\alpha_i^1 \in \{0, 1\}$ is chosen. Let $1(D)$ denote the all-ones sequence. The codes defined by the parity-check equation are rotationally invariant if $h^r(D)[c^r(D) + 1(D)] \equiv h^r(D)c^r(D) \bmod 4$ for all $c^r(D)$, which requires that the coefficient sum of $h^r(D)$ must be $0 \bmod 4$.

Code tables for fully rotationally invariant nonlinear trellis codes over two-dimensional QAM and M-PSK ($M = 4, 8, 16$) signal constellations are given in [88].

Alternative methods for the construction of rotationally invariant trellis codes are discussed in [10] and [101].

APPENDIX III
DISCRETE-TIME SPECTRAL FACTORIZATION

The spectral factorization $\tilde{Q}(f) = \tilde{H}^*(f)A^2\tilde{H}(f)$ given by (5.19) may be obtained by expressing $\log \tilde{Q}(f)$ as a Fourier series

$$\log \tilde{Q}(f) = \sum_{\ell} \alpha_\ell e^{-j2\pi f\ell T} \qquad \text{(AIII.1)}$$

whose coefficients are given by

$$\alpha_\ell = T \int_{1/T} \log \tilde{Q}(f)e^{j2\pi f\ell T}\, df. \qquad \text{(AIII.2)}$$

The Paley–Wiener condition ensures that this Fourier series exists. Grouping the terms with negative, zero, and positive indices of this Fourier series yields the desired factorization

$$\log \tilde{H}^*(f) = \sum_{\ell < 0} \alpha_\ell e^{-j2\pi f\ell T}$$
$$\log A^2 = \alpha_0 = T \int_{1/T} \log \tilde{Q}(f)\, df$$
$$\log \tilde{H}(f) = \sum_{\ell > 0} \alpha_\ell e^{-j2\pi f\ell T}. \qquad \text{(AIII.3)}$$

In particular, this yields (5.20).

To obtain an explicit expression for the coefficients of $h(D)$, define the formal power series

$$\psi(D) = \sum_{\ell > 0} \alpha_\ell D^\ell \qquad \text{(AIII.4)}$$

where D is an indeterminate. Because $\tilde{H}(f) = h(e^{-j2\pi fT})$, we have

$$\psi(D) = \log h(D). \qquad \text{(AIII.5)}$$

Taking formal derivatives yields

$$\psi^{(1)}(D) = h^{(1)}(D)/h(D) \qquad \text{(AIII.6)}$$

or, equivalently,

$$h^{(1)}(D) = \psi^{(1)}(D)h(D). \qquad \text{(AIII.7)}$$

Repeated formal differentiation of (AIII.7) yields the recursive relation for $k \geq 1$

$$h^{(k)}(D) = \sum_{i=0}^{k-1} \binom{k-1}{i} \psi^{(k-i)}(D)h^{(i)}(D), \qquad k \geq 1. \qquad \text{(AIII.8)}$$

Finally, noting that

$$h^{(k)}(0) = (k!)h_k$$
$$\psi^{(k-i)}(0) = ((k-i)!)\alpha_{k-i} \qquad \text{(AIII.9)}$$

we obtain the explicit expressions

$$h_0 = 1$$
$$h_k = \sum_{i=0}^{k-1} \frac{k-i}{k} h_i\alpha_{k-i}, \qquad k \geq 1. \qquad \text{(AIII.10)}$$

This shows that $h(D)$ is causal and monic, and that $h(D)$ is uniquely determined by $q(D)$. For a proof that $h(D)$ is minimum-phase, see [83].

ACKNOWLEDGMENT

G. D. Forney wishes to acknowledge the education, stimulation, and support offered by many mentors and colleagues over the past 35 years, particularly R. G. Gallager, J. L. Massey, J. M. Wozencraft, A. Kohlenberg, S. U. Qureshi, G. R. Lang, F. M. Longstaff, L.-F. Wei, and M. V. Eyuboglu.

G. Ungerboeck wishes to thank K. E. Drangeid, Director of the IBM Zurich Research Laboratory, for his essential support of this author's early work on new modem concepts and their implementation. He also gratefully acknowledges the stimulation and encouragement that he has received throughout his career from numerous colleagues, in particular R. E. Blahut, G. D. Forney, J. L. Massey, and A. J. Viterbi.

REFERENCES

[1] American National Standards Institute, "Network and customer installation interfaces—Asymmetrical digital subscriber line (ADSL) metallic interface," ANSI Std. T1E1, pp. 413–1995, Aug. 18, 1995.

[2] A. N. Akansu, P. Duhamel, X. Lin, and M. de Courville, "Orthogonal transmultiplexers in communications: A review," *IEEE Trans. Signal Processing*, vol. 46, pp. 979–995, Apr. 1998.

[3] AT&T (B. Betts), "Additional details on AT&T's candidate modem for V.fast," Contribution D157, ITU Study Group XVII, Geneva, Switzerland, Oct. 1991.

[4] AT&T (B. Betts), "Trellis-enhanced precoder—Combined coding and precoding," TIA TR30.1 contribution, Boston, MA, July 1993.

[5] L. R. Bahl, J. Cocke, F. Jelinek, and J. Raviv, "Optimal decoding of linear codes for minimizing symbol error rate," *IEEE Trans. Inform. Theory*, vol. IT-20, pp. 284–287, Mar. 1974.

[6] L. E. Baum and T. Petrie, "Statistical inference for probabilistic functions of finite-state Markov chains," *Ann. Math. Statist.*, vol. 37, pp. 1554–1563, 1966.

[7] M. Bellanger, G. Bonnerot, and M. Coudreuse, "Digital filtering by polyphase network: Application to the sample rate alteration and filter banks," *IEEE Trans. Acoust., Speech, Signal Processing*, vol. ASSP-24, pp. 109–114, Apr. 1976.

[8] S. Benedetto, D. Divsalar, G. Montorsi, and F. Pollara, "Bandwidth efficient parallel concatenated coding schemes," *Electron. Lett.*, vol. 31, pp. 2067–2069, 1995.

[9] _____, "Serial concatenation of interleaved codes: Performance analysis, design, and iterative decoding," *IEEE Trans. Inform. Theory*, vol. 44, pp. 909–926, May 1998.

[10] S. Benedetto, R. Garello, M. Mondin, and M. D. Trott, "Rotational invariance of trellis codes—Part II: Group codes and decoders," *IEEE Trans. Inform. Theory*, vol. 42, pp. 766–778, May 1996.

[11] S. Benedetto and G. Montorsi, "Unveiling turbo codes: Some results on parallel concatenated coding schemes," *IEEE Trans. Inform. Theory*, vol. 42, pp. 409–428, Mar. 1996.

[12] E. R. Berlekamp, "Bounded distance +1 soft-decision Reed–Solomon decoding," *IEEE Trans. Inform. Theory*, vol. 42, pp. 704–720, May 1996.

[13] C. Berrou, A. Glavieux, and P. Thitimajshima, "Near Shannon limit error-correcting coding and decoding: Turbo codes," in *Proc. 1993 Int. Conf. Communication* (Geneva, Switzerland, May 1993), pp. 1064–1070.

[14] J. A. Bingham, "Multicarrier modulation for data transmission: An idea whose time has come," *IEEE Commun. Mag.*, vol. 28, pp. 5–14, May 1990.

[15] G. Caire, G. Taricco, and E. Biglieri, "Bit-interleaved coded modulation," *IEEE Trans. Inform. Theory*, vol. 44, pp. 927–946, May 1998.

[16] A. R. Calderbank and L. H. Ozarow, "Nonequiprobable signaling on the Gaussian channel," *IEEE Trans. Inform. Theory*, vol. 36, pp. 726–740, July 1990.

[17] A. R. Calderbank and N. J. A. Sloane, "New trellis codes based on lattices and cosets," *IEEE Trans. Inform. Theory*, vol. IT-33, pp. 177–195, Mar. 1987.

[18] M. Cedervall and R. Johannesson, "A fast algorithm for computing the distance spectrum of convolutional codes," *IEEE Trans. Inform. Theory*, vol. 35, pp. 1146–1159, Nov. 1989.

[19] D. A. Chase, "A class of algorithms for decoding block codes with channel measurement information," *IEEE Trans. Inform. Theory*, vol. IT-18, pp. 170–182, Jan. 1972.

[20] G. Cherubini, S. Oelcer, and G. Ungerboeck, "Trellis precoding for channels with spectral nulls," in *Proc. 1997 IEEE Int. Symp. Information Theory* (Ulm, Germany, June 1997), p. 464.

[21] J. S. Chow, J. M. Cioffi, and J. A. Bingham, "Equalizer training algorithms for multicarrier modulation systems," in *Proc. 1993 Int. Conf. Communication* (Geneva, Switzerland, May 1993), pp. 761–765.

[22] J. M. Cioffi, G. P. Dudevoir, M. V. Eyuboglu, and G. D. Forney, Jr., "MMSE decision-feedback equalizers and coding—Parts I and II," *IEEE Trans. Commun.*, vol. 43, pp. 2582–2604, Oct. 1995.

[23] J. M. Cioffi and G. D. Forney, Jr., "Generalized decision-feedback equalization for packet transmission with ISI and Gaussian noise," in *Communications, Computation, Control and Signal Processing*, A. Paulraj *et al.*, Eds. Boston, MA: Kluwer, 1997, pp. 79–127.

[24] Consultative Committee for Space Data Standards, "Recommendations for space data standard: Telemetry channel coding," *Blue Book* Issue 2, CCSDS 101.0-B2, Jan. 1987.

[25] J. H. Conway and N. J. A. Sloane, *Sphere Packings, Lattices and Groups*. New York: Springer, 1988.

[26] D. J. Costello, Jr., J. Hagenauer, H. Imai, and S. B. Wicker, "Applications of error control coding," this issue, pp. 0000–0000.

[27] M. C. Davey and D. J. C. MacKay, "Low-density parity-check codes over GF(q)," in *Proc. 1998 Information Theory Workshop* (Killarney, Ireland, June 1998).

[28] B. Dejon and E. Hämsler, "Optimum multiplexing of sampled signals on noisy channels," *IEEE Trans. Inform. Theory*, vol. IT-17, pp. 257–262, May 1971.

[29] D. Divsalar, S. Dolinar, and F. Pollara, "Draft CCDS recommendation for telemetry channel coding (updated to include turbo codes)," Consultative Committee for Space Data Systems, *White Book*, Jan. 1997.

[30] M. L. Doeltz, E. T. Heald, and D. L. Martin, "Binary data transmission techniques for linear systems," *Proc. IRE*, vol. 45, pp. 656–661, May 1957.

[31] P. Elias, "Coding for noisy channels," in *IRE Conv. Rec.*, Mar. 1955, vol. 3, pt. 4, pp. 37–46.

[32] D. Esteban and C. Galand, "Application of quadrature mirror filters to splitband voice coding schemes," in *Proc. IEEE Int. Conf. Acoustics, Speech, and Signal Processing*, May 1977, pp. 191–195.

[33] European Telecommunication Standards Institute, "Radio broadcasting systems; digital audio broadcasting (DAB) to mobile, portable and fixed receivers," ETSI Std. ETS 300 401, Feb. 1995.

[34] M. V. Eyuboglu and G. D. Forney, Jr., "Combined equalization and coding using precoding," *IEEE Commun. Mag.*, vol. 29, no. 12, pp. 25–34, Dec. 1991.

[35] _____, "Trellis precoding: Combined coding, precoding and shaping for intersymbol interference channels," *IEEE Trans. Inform. Theory*, vol. 38, pp. 301–314, Mar. 1992.

[36] D. D. Falconer and F. R. Magee, "Adaptive channel memory truncation for maximum likelihood sequence estimation," *Bell Syst. Tech. J.*, vol. 52, pp. 1541–1562, Nov. 1973.

[37] R. F. H. Fischer, "Using flexible precoding for channels with spectral nulls," *Electron. Lett.*, vol. 31, pp. 356–358, Mar. 1995.

[38] R. F. H. Fischer and J. B. Huber, "Comparison of precoding schemes for digital subscriber lines," *IEEE Trans. Commun.*, vol. 45, pp. 334–343, Mar. 1997.

[39] G. D. Forney, Jr., *Concatenated Codes*. Cambridge, MA: MIT Press, 1966.

[40] _____, "Burst-correcting codes for the classic bursty channel," *IEEE Trans. Commun. Technol.*, vol. COM-19, pp. 772–781, Oct. 1971.

[41] _____, "Maximum-likelihood sequence estimation of digital sequences in the presence of intersymbol interference," *IEEE Trans. Inform. Theory*, vol. IT-18, pp. 363–378, May 1972.

[42] _____, "Coset codes—Part I: Introduction and geometrical classification," *IEEE Trans. Inform. Theory*, vol. 34, pp. 1123–1151, Sept. 1988.

[43] _____, "Coset codes—Part II: Binary lattices and related codes," *IEEE Trans. Inform. Theory*, vol. 34, pp. 1152–1187, Sept. 1988.

[44] _____, "Geometrically uniform codes," *IEEE Trans. Inform. Theory*, vol. 37, pp. 1241–1260, Sept. 1991.

[45] _____, "Trellis shaping," *IEEE Trans. Inform. Theory*, vol. 38, pp. 281–300, Mar. 1992.

[46] _____, "Approaching the channel capacity of the AWGN channel with coset codes and multilevel coset codes," Aug. 1997, submitted to *IEEE Trans. Inform. Theory*.

[47] G. D. Forney, Jr., L. Brown, M. V. Eyuboglu, and J. L. Moran, III, "The V.34 high-speed modem standard," *IEEE Commun. Mag.*, vol. 34, pp. 28–33, Dec. 1996.

[48] G. D. Forney, Jr. and L.-F. Wei, "Multidimensional constellations–Part I: Introduction, figures of merit, and generalized cross constellations," *IEEE J. Select. Areas Commun.*, vol. 7, pp. 877–892, Aug. 1989.

[49] P. Fortier, A. Ruiz, and J. M. Cioffi, "Multidimensional signal sets through the shell construction for parallel channels," *IEEE Trans. Commun.*, vol. 40, pp. 500–512, Mar. 1992.

[50] R. G. Gallager, *Low-Density Parity-Check Codes*. Cambridge, MA: MIT Press, 1962.

[51] ——, *Information Theory and Reliable Communication*. New York: Wiley, 1968.

[52] General Datacomm (P. Cole and Y. Goldstein), "Distribution-preserving Tomlinson algorithm," contribution D189 to CCITT Study Group XVII, Geneva, Switzerland, June 1992.

[53] General Datacomm (Y. Goldstein), Motorola (M. V. Eyuboglu), and Rockwell (S. Olafsson), "Precoding for V.fast," TIA TR30.1 contribution, Boston, MA, July 1993.

[54] H. Harashima and H. Miyakawa, "A method of code conversion for a digital communication channel with intersymbol interference," *IEEE Trans. Commun.*, vol. COM-20, pp. 774–780, Aug. 1972.

[55] J. A. Heller and I. M. Jacobs, "Viterbi decoding for satellite and space communication," *IEEE Trans. Commun. Technol.*, vol. COM-19, pp. 835–848, Oct. 1971.

[56] B. Hirosaki, "An orthogonally multiplexed QAM system using the discrete Fourier transform," *IEEE Trans. Commun.*, vol. COM-29, pp. 982–989, July 1981.

[57] J. L. Holsinger, "Digital communication over fixed time-continuous channels with memory, with special application to telephone channels," MIT Res. Lab. Electron., Tech. Rep. 430, 1964.

[58] J. Huber and U. Wachsmann, "Capacities of equivalent channels in multilevel coding schemes," *Electron. Lett.*, vol. 30, pp. 557–558, Mar. 1994.

[59] J. Huber, U. Wachsmann, and R. Fischer, "Coded modulation by multilevel codes: Overview and state of the art," in *Proc. ITG Fachtagung "Codierung fuer Quelle, Kanal und Uebertragung"* (Aachen, Germany, Mar. 1998), pp. 255–266.

[60] H. Imai and S. Hirakawa, "A new multilevel coding method using error correcting codes," *IEEE Trans. Inform. Theory*, vol. 23, pp. 371–377, May 1977.

[61] *Proc. Int. Symp. Turbo Codes* (Brest, France, Sept. 1997).

[62] ITU-T Recommendation V.34, "A modem operating at data signalling rates of up to 33 600 bit/s for use on the general switched telephone network and on leased point-to-point 2-wire telephone-type circuits," Oct. 1996, replaces first version of Sept. 1994.

[63] I. M. Jacobs and E. R. Berlekamp, "A lower bound to the distribution of computation for sequential decoding," *IEEE Trans. Inform. Theory*, vol. IT-13, pp. 167–174, 1967.

[64] I. Kalet, "The multitone channel," *IEEE Trans. Commun.*, vol. 37, pp. 119–124, Feb. 1989.

[65] S. Kallel and K. Li, "Bidirectional sequential decoding," *IEEE Trans. Inform. Theory*, vol. 43, pp. 1319–1326, July 1997.

[66] A. K. Khandani and P. Kabal, "Shaping multidimensional signal spaces—Part I: Optimum shaping, shell mapping," *IEEE Trans. Inform. Theory*, vol. 39, pp. 1799–1808, Nov. 1993.

[67] Y. Kofman, E. Zehavi, and S. Shamai (Shitz), "Performance analysis of a multilevel coded modulation system," *IEEE Trans. Commun.*, vol. 42, pp. 299–312, Feb. 1994.

[68] F. R. Kschischang and S. Pasupathy, "Optimal nonuniform signaling for Gaussian channels," *IEEE Trans. Inform. Theory*, vol. 39, pp. 913–929, May 1993.

[69] G. R. Lang and F. M. Longstaff, "A Leech lattice modem," *IEEE J. Select. Areas Commun.*, vol. 7, pp. 968–973, Aug. 1989.

[70] P. J. Lee, "There are many good periodically-time-varying convolutional codes," *IEEE Trans. Inform. Theory*, vol. 35, pp. 460–463, Mar. 1989.

[71] R. Laroia, "Coding for intersymbol interference channels—Combined coding and precoding," *IEEE Trans. Inform. Theory*, vol. 42, pp. 1053–1061, July 1996.

[72] R. Laroia, N. Farvardin, and S. Tretter, "On optimal shaping of multidimensional constellations," *IEEE Trans. Inform. Theory*, vol. 40, pp. 1044–1056, July 1994.

[73] R. Laroia, S. Tretter, and N. Farvardin, "A simple and effective precoding scheme for noise whitening on intersymbol interference channels," *IEEE Trans. Commun.*, vol. 41, pp. 1460–1463, Oct. 1993.

[74] E. A. Lee and D. G. Messerschmitt, *Digital Communication*, 2nd ed. Boston, MA: Kluwer, 1994.

[75] J. Leech and N. J. A. Sloane, "Sphere packing and error-correcting codes," *Canad. J. Math.*, vol. 23, pp. 718–745, 1971.

[76] D. J. C. MacKay and R. M. Neal, "Near Shannon limit performance of low-density parity-check codes," *Electron. Lett.*, vol. 32, pp. 1645–1646, Aug. 1996, reprinted in vol. 33, pp. 457–458, Mar. 1997.

[77] F. J. MacWilliams and N. J. A. Sloane, *The Theory of Error-Correcting Codes*. Amsterdam, The Netherlands: North-Holland, 1977.

[78] J. L. Massey, "Coding and modulation in digital communications," in *Proc. 1974 Int. Zurich Seminar on Digital Communication* (Zurich, Switzerland, Mar. 1974), pp. E2(1)–(4).

[79] R. J. McEliece and L. Swanson, "Reed–Solomon codes and the exploration of the solar system," in *Reed–Solomon Codes and Their Applications*, S. B. Wicker and V. K. Bhargava, Eds. Piscataway, NJ: IEEE Press, 1994, pp. 25–40.

[80] Motorola Information Systems Group (M. V. Eyuboglu), "A flexible form of precoding for V.fast," Contribution D194, CCITT Study Group XVII, Geneva, Switzerland, June 1992.

[81] S. H. Mueller and J. B. Huber, "A comparison of peak power reduction schemes for OFDM," in *Proc. 1997 IEEE Global Telecomm. Conf. (Globecom'97)* (Phoenix, AZ, Nov. 1997), pp. 1–5.

[82] A. Narula and F. R. Kschischang, "Unified framework for PAR control in multitone systems," ANSI T1E1.4 contribution 98-183, Huntsville, AL, June 1998.

[83] A. Papoulis, *Signal Analysis*. New York: McGraw-Hill, 1984.

[84] L. C. Perez, J. Seghers, and D. J. Costello, Jr., "A distance spectrum interpretation of turbo codes," *IEEE Trans. Inform. Theory*, vol. 42, pp. 1698–1709, Nov. 1996.

[85] R. Price, "Nonlinearly feedback-equalized PAM versus capacity for noisy filter channels," in *Proc. 1972 Int. Conf. Communication*, June 1972, pp. 22.12–22.17.

[86] A. Peled and A. Ruiz, "Frequency domain data transmission using reduced computational complexity algorithms," in *Proc. IEEE Int. Conf. Acoustics, Speech, and Signal Processing*, Apr. 1980, pp. 964–967.

[87] S. S. Pietrobon, R. H. Deng, A. Lafanechere, G. Ungerboeck, and D. J. Costello, Jr., "Trellis-coded multidimensional phase modulation," *IEEE Trans. Inform. Theory*, vol. 36, pp. 63–89, Jan. 1990.

[88] S. S. Pietrobon, G. Ungerboeck, L. C. Perez, and D. J. Costello, Jr., "Rotationally invariant nonlinear trellis codes for two-dimensional modulation," *IEEE Trans. Inform. Theory*, vol. 40, pp. 1773–1791, Nov. 1994.

[89] P. Robertson and T. Woerz, "Coded modulation scheme employing turbo codes," *Electron. Lett.,* vol. 31, pp. 1546–1547, Aug. 1995.

[90] A. Ruiz, J. M. Cioffi, and S. Kasturia, "Discrete multiple tone modulation with coset coding for the spectrally shaped channel," *IEEE Trans. Commun.*, vol. 40, pp. 1012–1029, June 1992.

[91] S. D. Sandberg and M. A. Tzannes, "Overlapped discrete multitone modulation for high speed copper wire commmunications," *IEEE J. Select. Areas Commun.*, vol. 13, pp. 1570–1585, Dec. 1995.

[92] J. P. Sarvis, "Symmetries of trellis codes," M. Eng. thesis, Dept. Elec. Eng. and Comp. Sci., MIT, Cambridge, MA, June 1995.

[93] C. E. Shannon, "A mathematical theory of communication," *Bell Syst. Tech. J.*, vol. 27, pp. 379–423 and pp. 623–656, July and Oct. 1948.

[94] ——, "Communication in the presence of noise," *Proc. IRE*, vol. 37, pp. 10–21, 1949.

[95] ——, "Probability of error for optimal codes in a Gaussian channel," *Bell Syst. Tech. J.*, vol. 38, pp. 611–656, May 1959.

[96] M. Sipser and D. A. Spielman, "Expander codes," *IEEE Trans. Inform. Theory*, vol. 42, pp. 1710–1722, Nov. 1996.

[97] M. Tomlinson, "New automatic equalizer employing modulo arithmetic," *Electron. Lett.*, vol. 7, pp. 138–139, Mar. 1971.

[98] P. Tong, "A 40 MHz encoder-decoder chip generated by a Reed–Solomon compiler," in *Proc. Cust. Int. Circuits Conf.* (Boston, MA, May 1990), pp. 13.5.1–13.5.4.

[99] *IEEE Trans. Signal Processing* (Special Issue on Theory and Applications of Filter Banks and Wavelet Transforms), vol. 46, Apr. 1998.

[100] M. D. Trott, "The algebraic structure of trellis codes," Ph.D. dissertation, Dept. Elec. Eng., Stanford Univ., Stanford, CA, Aug. 1992.

[101] M. D. Trott, S. Benedetto, R. Garello, and M. Mondin, "Rotational invariance of trellis codes—Part I: Encoders and precoders," *IEEE Trans. Inform. Theory*, vol. 42, pp. 751–765, May 1996.

[102] M. A. Tzannes, M. C. Tzannes, J. Proakis, and P. N. Heller, "DMT systems, DWMT systems, and filter banks," in *Proc. Int. Communication Conf.*, 1994.

[103] G. Ungerboeck, "Adaptive maximum-likelihood receiver for carrier-modulated data-transmission systems," *IEEE Trans. Commun.*, vol. COM-22, pp. 1124–1136, May 1974.

[104] ——, "Channel coding with multilevel/phase signals," *IEEE Trans. Inform. Theory*, vol. IT-28, pp. 55–67, Jan. 1982.

[105] ——, "Trellis-coded modulation with redundant signal sets: Part II," *IEEE Commun. Mag.*, vol. 25, pp. 12–21, Feb. 1987.

[106] P. P. Vaidyanathan, *Multirate Systems and Filter Banks*. Englewood Cliffs, NJ: Prentice-Hall, 1993.

[107] A. Vardy, "Trellis structure of codes," in *Handbook of Coding Theory* V. S. Pless *et al.*, Eds. Amsterdam, The Netherlands: Elsevier, 1998.

[108] A. J. Viterbi and J. K. Omura, *Principles of Digital Communication and Coding*. New York: McGraw-Hill, 1979.

370

[109] U. Wachsmann and J. Huber, "Power and bandwidth efficient digital communication using turbo codes in multilevel codes," *Euro. Trans. Telecommun.*, vol. 6, pp. 557–567, Sept. 1995.

[110] U. Wachsmann, R. Fischer, and J. Huber, "Multilevel codes: Parts 1–3," June 1997, submitted to *IEEE Trans. Inform. Theory*.

[111] F.-Q. Wang and D. J. Costello, Jr., "Sequential decoding of trellis codes at high spectral efficiencies," *IEEE Trans. Inform. Theory*, vol. 43, pp. 2013–2019, Nov. 1997.

[112] L.-F. Wei, "Rotationally invariant convolutional channel encoding with expanded signal space, Part II: Nonlinear codes," *IEEE J. Select. Areas Commun.*, vol. 2, pp. 672–686, Sept. 1984.

[113] _____, "Trellis-coded modulation using multidimensional constellations," *IEEE Trans. Inform. Theory*, vol. IT-33, pp. 483–501, July 1987.

[114] _____, "Rotationally invariant trellis-coded modulations with multidimensional M-PSK," *IEEE J. Select. Areas Commun.*, vol. 7, pp. 1281–1295, Dec. 1989.

[115] S. B. Weinstein and P. M. Ebert, "Data transmission by frequency-division multiplexing," *IEEE Trans. Commun.*, vol. COM-19, pp. 628–634, Oct. 1971.

[116] N. Wiberg, H.-A. Loeliger, and R. Kötter, "Codes and iterative decoding on general graphs," *Euro. Trans. Telecommun.*, vol. 6, pp. 513–526, Sept. 1995.

[117] R. G. C. Williams, "A trellis code for V.fast," CCITT V.fast rapporteur meeting, Bath, U.K., Sept. 1992.

[118] J. M. Wozencraft and I. M. Jacobs, *Principles of Communication Engineering*. New York: Wiley, 1965.

[119] J. M. Wozencraft and B. Reiffen, *Sequential Decoding*. Cambridge, MA: MIT Press, 1961.

[120] E. Zehavi and J. K. Wolf, "On the performance evaluation of trellis codes," *IEEE Trans. Inform. Theory*, vol. IT-33, pp. 192–201, Jan. 1987.

Information Theory and Communication Networks: An Unconsummated Union

Anthony Ephremides, *Fellow, IEEE*, and Bruce Hajek, *Fellow, IEEE*

(Invited Paper)

Abstract—Information theory has not yet had a direct impact on networking, although there are similarities in concepts and methodologies that have consistently attracted the attention of researchers from both fields. In this paper, we review several topics that are related to communication networks and that have an information-theoretic flavor, including multiaccess protocols, timing channels, effective bandwidth of bursty data sources, deterministic constraints on datastreams, queuing theory, and switching networks.

Index Terms—Communication networks, effective bandwidth, multiaccess, switching.

I. INTRODUCTION

INFORMATION theory is the conscience of the theory of communication; it has defined the "playing field" within which communication systems can be studied and understood. It has provided the spawning grounds for the fields of coding, compression, encryption, detection, and modulation, and it has enabled the design and evaluation of systems whose performance is pushing the limits of what can be achieved. Thus it constitutes a scientific success story of almost unparalleled proportions to which we pay tribute during this golden anniversary year of its birth.

However, information theory has not yet made a comparable mark in the field of communication networks, the sister field and natural extension of communication theory, that is today, and is likely to remain for many years, the center of activity and attention in most information technology areas. The principal reason for this failure is twofold. First, by focusing on the classical point-to-point, source–channel–destination model of communication, information theory has ignored the bursty nature of real sources. Early on there seemed to be no point in considering the idle periods of source silence or inactivity. However, in networks, source burstiness is the central phenomenon that underlies the process of resource sharing for communication. Secondly, by focusing on the asymptotic limits of the tradeoff between accuracy and rate of communication, information theory ignored the role of delay as a parameter that may affect this tradeoff. In networking, delay is a fundamental quantity, not only as a performance measure, but also as a parameter that may control and affect the fundamental limits of the rate–accuracy tradeoff.

In fact, part of the reason why information theory did not go far enough in providing a solid theoretical foundation for networking is the urgency for rapid resolution of practical network design problems that has contributed to the creation of an anti-intellectual bias in parts of the networking community. At the same time, information theory has not done much to dispel that bias.

During its early development, information theory did consider multiuser systems [1], [2] and much of the subsequent work on such systems tried to capture (and did) many of the fundamental differences between the classical, stand-alone, single-channel case and that of the shared channel in multiuser systems. For example, it was realized that although feedback from the receiver to the source did not have an effect on channel capacity in single-user memoryless systems, it did have an effect in the case of multiuser systems [3]. But, still, the study of these systems has continued to be conducted in the restricted framework of nonbursty and delay-insensitive sources.

In this paper we will not address multiuser information theory, which is reviewed elsewhere in this issue [4]. Yet, there is a major need for a better synthesis between multiuser information theory and the networking topics discussed in the sequel.

In the past few years, the impact of the development of wireless systems, such as cellular networks, on information theory has been to steer the attention of its powerful principles and techniques toward the deeper significance of feedback information, in the form of channel measurement, and its effect on the choice of adjustable parameters such as transmission power and rate. But even in this case, the main thrust of the work continues to ignore the intrinsic role of delay and burstiness. Nonetheless, it has spawned the rapid development of the field of multiuser detection (see [5] in this issue and, for a more thorough account, [6]). In a sense, both multiuser information theory and multiuser detection theory represent major forays of information theory toward the field of networks that, so far, have revealed insights but have not yet produced the deep breakthrough that will have the same definitive impact on networking as it did on single point-to-point communication. We will not be addressing multiuser detection theory here either. It represents a distinct, self-sufficient field that, nonetheless, has intrinsic connections to both multiuser information theory and networking.

Manuscript received December 9, 1997; revised May 4, 1998.

A. Ephremides is with the Department of Electrical Engineering and the Institute for Systems Research, University of Maryland, College Park, MD 20742 USA (e-mail: tony@eng.umd.edu).

B. Hajek is with the Department of Electrical and Computer Engineering and the Coordinated Science Laboratory, University of Illinois at Urbana-Champaign, Urbana, IL 61801 USA (e-mail: b-hajek@uiuc.edu).

Publisher Item Identifier S 0018-9448(98)05286-9.

Just as communication systems were designed and built during the pre-Shannon years based mostly on heuristics, empirical knowledge, and partial dependence on theories of related fields (such as propagation, filtering, etc.), it is fair to say that today communication networks are designed and built based on similarly inadequate principles and techniques. And, yet, there is increasing evidence that the catalytic (almost messianic) effect of Shannon's work on point-to-point communication may be brought about on the field of networks as well, either by the elaboration and enhancement of the same fundamental ideas of information theory that caused the revolution that started in 1948, or by some novel and revealing breakthroughs of a different kind that are, however, just as likely to come from information theorists or people with information-theoretic training and background.

This assertion is based on the fact that some of the most influential and far-reaching advances in the field of networking, as well as some of the most intriguing observations about network behavior, originated from information theory scientists. It should be remembered that for the first twenty years, or so, of information theory, very little was actually accomplished in bridging the gap between theory and practice in point-to-point communication.

It is the intention of this paper to document this assertion and to describe in more detail the relationship between information-theoretic ideas and networking. Thus although the final chapters of the impact of information theory on networking have not been written yet, we intend to review what has been achieved so far, inadequate and incomplete thought it may be, but to also speculate about the powerful potential of information theory to shape the future of communication networks.

The paper is organized as follows. The next section reviews early work. Section III discusses timing channels and related topics, that include the protocol information needed to properly identify packets, and the existence of covert channels associated with the timing of signals or packets. Section IV reviews two methods for quantifying the effective data rate of a bursty source, that are similar to the use of entropy and rate-distortion functions as measures of effective data rates. One method is based on the theory of large deviations in queues, and the other on a calculus of deterministic constraints. Section V discusses the problem of random multiaccess communication, in which information plays a key role in a distributed setting. Two works combining aspects of multiaccess and information theory are discussed. Section VI briefly discusses queuing theory and its relation to information theory. Section VII discusses switching networks. The theory of basic switching network design is intertwined with information theory, and switching networks form the heart of the nodes within large communication networks. Section VII concludes the paper with a look to the future.

II. Early Work

A. Network Layers

The principal communication network that existed during the formative years of information theory was the circuit-switched telephone network that was, by and large, conceived of, and operated as, a conglomeration of individual point-to-point links. The origins of the ideas of message and packet switching that have transformed the way communication networks are thought of, can be found in the emergence of computer communication and the interconnection of the, then, so-called, interface message processors. Among the first who formulated the backbone elements of packet-switched networking was Kleinrock who, first, in his original work [7] that was based on his Ph.D. dissertation and, subsequently, in his two-volume book [8] on queuing systems, popularized many of the innovative intricacies and challenges of communication networks.[1] A substantial volume of other work in the late 1960's and early 1970's [9]–[15], mostly by computer scientists and engineers, and the global interest on the still embryonic, but rapidly growing, field led to the formulation of the seven-layer Open System Interconnection (OSI) framework and to the useful, at the time, separation between the physical, the link, and the higher layers.

There is a strong revisionist feeling today with respect to the notion of layering. It is increasingly realized that the original convenience and structure provided by the layering concept is superseded by the inherent coupling between the layers in almost every aspect of network operation. The artificiality of layer definition is apparent in some cases and concealed in some others. A case in point is that the original seven-layer OSI model left no natural place for multiaccess mechanisms, which parallel certain physical, link, and network layer mechanisms in the OSI model.

Nonetheless, the layered framework of network study has helped considerably in isolating individual networking problems that have been successfully attacked. Interestingly, in a way, the layering idea is first found in Shannon's work. Shannon clearly conveyed that the discrete, digital channel that he studied is a layer above the underlying physical, analog channel and the process of channel coding is a layer below the process of data compression. It is a pity that, in his work, Shannon did not expand on this concept. It might have saved a lot of time for networking researchers who, in a sense, reinvented the concept and first implemented it in an awkward framework.

B. Protocol Overhead

The first to recognize the significance of networking to information theory, both in terms of the challenges as well as the opportunities it presented, was Gallager who in 1973 [16] offered a clear vision of the natural connection between the two areas.[2] And he was the first to point out the fundamental signif-

[1] The serendipitous presence of Claude Shannon in Kleinrock's Ph.D. defense committee may have been the forecaster of the bond between the two fields.

[2] We do not consider Shannon's work on the two-way channel [17] to be a genuine grasp of networking; this may be a debatable point, however. If we do accept that it does, then, again, Shannon must be credited with the prophesy of almost all aspects of the field of communication. It is also interesting to note that in [18] (as well as in [19] and [20]), a first look at max-flow min-cut relationships is provided; thus the notion of flow approximations, widely used in network studies, was again, first noted by Shannon (among others). This notion was pursued further by Elias in [21].

icance of source burstiness and its relationship to information rate. In his landmark paper [22] on the subject, he considered a simple multiplexer of a finite number of sources, each of which was transmitting symbols from a ternary alphabet $(0, 1, i)$, where i indicated idleness and, therefore, did not carry message information. The critical observation was that, nonetheless, i did carry information. It carried the "message-start" or "message-end" information and was, therefore, an important participant in the information output of the source. By assuming geometrically distributed message-lengths and idle-period-lengths and independence among the sources, he computed the entropy of the sources, and hence the channel capacity needed to transmit the generated information with constant delay. The surplus (over the mean rate of data bits) was due to the "start" and "end" information inherently generated by the transitions between the "on" state and the "off" state. Gallager called this surplus the "protocol" information, since it represented the overhead price that had to be paid to accommodate the multiplexing of the bursty sources. The remarkable result is that this information can dominate the total transmitted amount of information. This work is discussed in more detail in Section III.

The key contribution of that early work was to show that even in the simplest of networks the need of overhead protocol information can expand significantly the amount of needed resources. This observation provided crucial conceptual and quantitative explanation to the alarming experience of early network engineers who found that their designs sometimes required that each packet carry a substantial amount of overhead bits, and so appeared to be very inefficient.

However, there has been almost no impact of this work on the design of practical systems. The reason is that the actual overhead inefficiency of most currently used network protocols is so large that the portion of overhead that handles burstiness is relatively limited and thus tolerable. This is not to say, however, that the timing overhead idea will not find application at some point in the future.

C. ALOHA and Multiaccess Protocols

At about the same time another early contributor to information theory, Abramson, proposed a simple idea that, perhaps because of its simplicity and its potency, had a major impact on the entire field of multiaccess communication [23]. Confronted with the practical difficulty of ensuring access to the mainframe computers of the University of Hawaii by terminals located in the outer islands of the state, Abramson proposed the simplest of ideas—pure random access. Eventually known as the ALOHA protocol, the simple scheme of attempting transmission randomly, independently, distributively, and based on simple quantized feedback from the receiver, fertilized (if not created) the field of local-area networks (whether radio-based or cable-based) and triggered an avalanche of work on what came to be known as the multiaccess problem. Subsequently, sophisticated schemes were proposed that combined ideas of fixed allocation (such as TDMA or FDMA), with reservations and contention to create the familiar protocols of Carrier Sense Multiple Access (CSMA) and CSMA-CD (CSMA with collision detection). To this day, the basic problem of access, that was so brilliantly illuminated by Abramson's ALOHA ideas, remains generally unresolved although quite thoroughly understood. The beauty of the ALOHA protocol was enhanced by Abramson's method of analysis, described in Section V.

It should be noted that there is no aspect of information theory that is directly involved in the entire story of ALOHA and random access. Still there is a flavor that is unmistakably information-theoretic in the formulation, exposition, and interpretation of this simple protocol. The ability of the model to capture what is essential in the contention process brings to mind the familiar models of the binary-symmetric channel (BSC) or the additive white Gaussian channel (AWGN), or, later, the multiaccess adder channel, all of which share with ALOHA the same simplicity and predictive power.

The explosive spread of interest in the collision channel model and the problem of multiaccess communication that Abramson's work generated, led naturally to sophisticated and detailed analyses of modifications that would guarantee stability, and to an eventual refinement and redefinition of the problem that identified its connection to the problem of group testing or collision resolution. The area is briefly reviewed in Section V of this paper.

D. Routing

Another early landmark in the history of contributions to the field of networks by information theory (or information theorists) is the resolution of the question of minimum-delay routing in packet-switched, store-and-forward networks. In a network of fixed topology and given source–destination node pairs with associated input traffic levels, the (very practical and important) question was to determine the optimal routing paths that yield minimum weighted total average delay. For clear implementation reasons (to reduce state-information latency and overhead and to ensure improved survivability and robustness) dynamic and distributed solutions were preferable. In [24], Gallager presented a concise and direct formulation of the problem accompanied by an elegant solution that permitted each node, based on simple periodic information exchanges with its neighbors, to determine the best next step in the path of each "commodity" (i.e., source–destination pair). The proposed algorithm yields convergence to the optimum and is even able to successfully "chase" a shifting optimum provided that conditions in the network (such as input traffic and topology) change at a rate less than the convergence rate of the algorithm.

It was realized soon after the publication of [24] that Gallager's algorithm is an independently derived solution to a special case of convex optimization problems eminently studied and analyzed by Bertsekas [25]. This realization led to the collaboration between these two authors that produced the classic text on networking [26] that summarizes the field in the most complete and scientifically sound fashion. The algorithm originally proposed in [24] and modified accordingly in [25] is compatible with the class of distributed Bellman–Ford-type algorithms [27] and charts a journey in the connection between networking and distributed algorithms, graph theory, and optimization. It is ironic that the relationship between communication networks and control system methodology (another, not fully explored and exploited relationship) that has been identified in [28] as well as in several subsequent publications and forums [29], was actually first pointed out, through [24], by information theorists.

Information theorists played a part in the origins of the field of distributed network protocols. Early in the implementation of packet switching networks it became clear that protocols are needed to coordinate a network. For example, upon startup, each node in a network might first learn the identity of its neighbors. Then through message passing, a spanning tree might be discovered by the nodes in order to serve as a backbone for the passing of control information. One basic question, quite natural for an information theorist, is what sorts of things are possible. For example, if nodes can enter and exit a network, and if routing tables are to be maintained, is it necessary to use sequence numbers? (The answer is no [30].) Another basic question, quite natural for an information theorist to ask, is, "How many messages must be passed to accomplish a task." This is known as the communication complexity. For example, the paper by Gallager *et al.* [31] gives an efficient distributed algorithm for finding a minimum-weight spanning tree given weights on the edges-connecting nodes.

There has been much more in the brief history of networking that can be attributed to information-theoretic thinking. Much of it is reviewed in this paper. What is even more interesting is what has not yet been done that can be done by information-theoretic methods. We attempt to provide some glimpses to some of these opportunities as well.

III. TIMING CHANNELS

There are interesting connections between information theory and the timing of packets in a communication network. We first mention a source-coding problem and then some channel-coding problems that arise in connection with timing. Early in the development of computer communication, asynchronous communication emerged in which data is sent in packets. A packet is a finite sequence of bits. Typically, packets generated by a source in a communication network are to be reproduced at a destination. This necessitates the use of some mechanism such as start or stop flags, or headers indicating packet length, or synchronization and fixed packet lengths. In a pioneering paper, Gallager [22] quantified the amount of protocol information per packet that is needed for reconstruction of the packets at the destination with a specified mean delay. Gallager took the interesting stance that, "to an information theorist, a protocol is a source code for representing control information." For example, if the delay per packet is to be identically constant, then the protocol must convey not only the values of the bits within the packets, but it must also convey the generation time of the packets and the packet lengths. As pointed out in [22], if the packet lengths are small compared to the random interarrival times, then the protocol information required per packet can far exceed the mean number of data bits in a packet.

For example, a datastream generated by a bursty source could consist of data bits (0's and 1's), interspersed with strings of i's representing idle time slots. The information rate required to reconstruct the source exactly is not just the mean arrival rate of data bits, but is equal to the entropy rate of the source viewed as one with the ternary alphabet $\{0, 1, i\}$.

Gallager realized that constant delay reproduction of packets is too strong of a requirement, so he explored the protocol information required to reconstruct a sequence of packets within a certain mean delay. This gives rise to the formulation of a rate-distortion problem, where the distortion measure is mean delay, and the rate is the protocol information per packet. The source generates packets according to a Poisson point process of specified rate, and the protocol must convey sufficient information per packet to enable reconstruction of the packets with specified mean delay. It is also assumed that packets are presented at the destination in order, and that each packet is presented at the destination only after it is generated by the source. For example, the time axis could be divided into intervals of length $2D$, and all packets arriving during each such interval could be delivered at the destination at the end of the interval. Then the required protocol information per packet related to arrival times would simply be the entropy of the number of arrivals per period divided by the mean number of arrivals per period. Note that the output would not determine the exact arrival times. A different rate-distortion function for Poisson processes was defined and identified by Verdú [32].

Even if enough protocol information is provided to identify the packets at the destination within a specified delay, such delay may be unobtainable due to the possible queuing delay experienced by bursty datastreams transmitted by constant-rate transmitters. This issue is addressed in Sections IV and VI.

The flip side of the coin is that timing can be used to convey information. For example, if a source can make use of the three symbols $\{0, 1, i\}$, then through coding it could send information at rate $\log_2 3 \approx 1.585$ bits per channel use. The actual capacity of this channel is thus higher than the naive thought that at most one bit per channel use can be conveyed. In some situations, the information-carrying capacity hidden in packet timing can be undesirable. For example, suppose that an agent is only authorized to send (or only pays for sending) particular types or amounts of information. The packets sent by the agent might be monitored. However, the agent could transmit additional information covertly by encoding it into the timing of packets.

Another example of a timing channel is the phone-ringing channel. One party can convey information to a second party at no charge. The second party never answers the phone but only observes the times that it rings, that are controlled by the first party so as to convey a message (see [33] for a mathematical formulation and capacity result). A so-called two-ring, four-ring answering machine conveys information in the reverse direction as follows. It answers after four rings if it contains any unplayed messages, and after two rings otherwise. When picking up messages remotely, the owner hangs up after three rings, knowing there are no unplayed messages.

One countermeasure for covert communication is to introduce "timing noise" into the communication channel. A device that randomly delays packets could be inserted on all output lines in an effort to mask timing information. One possible device is a simple single-server queue with random service times. In fact, the Shannon capacity of the single-server queue with service times that are independent, identically distributed random variables with some fixed mean μ was recently identified by Anantharam and Verdú [33]. They found that the capacity of such a queue, when over the long run packets transit the queue at rate λ, is given by the surprisingly simple formula $C(\lambda) = \lambda \log(\mu/\lambda)$ for $0 \leq \lambda \leq \mu$. This capacity tends to zero as either λ tends to zero (since then there are few packets to convey information) or λ tends to μ, since then the queue is nearly always full of packets so that the time between outputs is often just that of the service time distribution. Remarkably, the capacity of the $\cdot/M/1$ queue does not increase with feedback information. In addition, if the exponential service time distribution is replaced by another with the same mean, then the capacity cannot decrease [33]. The Shannon capacity of a discrete-time queue is addressed in [34] and [35].

As an aside, we briefly note an application of [33] to the source-coding problem of [22]. Given a rate λ Poisson process of packet arrivals and a mean delay constraint D, the rate-distortion problem of [22] involves randomly delaying the points by at most D on average, in such a way as to minimize the mutual information per packet between the input and output streams. One could simply try taking the single-server exponential queue as the delaying mechanism. The service rate μ should be selected to be $\mu = \lambda + 1/D$, so that the mean delay induced by the queue is D. The mutual information between input and output, divided by the input rate, is thus $R_\lambda(D) = \log(1 + 1/\lambda D)$. This is an upper bound on the rate-distortion (where distortion is delay) function of [22]. For small λD this bound asymptotically coincides with the lower bound on the distortion rate-distortion function given by Gallager, therefore eliminating a small gap left in his paper. However, for large λD a bound in [22] is smaller, indicating that the single-server exponential server queue is not a mutual-information minimizing delay mechanism for a Poisson input source.

There are many less obvious examples of covert communication channels within distributed computing systems and computer networks. For example, a multiple-level security system is to offer services to clients with different levels of security. There may be two clients, one low and one high, and the system should restrict, and ideally completely prevent, the flow of information from high to low. One scenario is known as the computer processing unit (CPU) scheduling channel, and dates back to [36] and [37]. (See [38] for more background and citations.) Both clients submit tasks to their respective queues, one low queue and one high queue. The tasks are served by a single processor, that divides its service among the two queues in a round-robin fashion. Each client observes the completion times of the jobs that it submits to the queues. The question is, can the high client send information to the low client? The answer is clearly yes. The high client, depending on what message it wants to send to the server, carefully controls the times that it places jobs in its own queue. For its part, the

low client carefully submits jobs to the queue and observes the sequence of response times. From the response times, the low client can learn the message that the high client intended to covertly send.

In another scenario, the low client sends a datastream to the high client. (The data sent need not be covert—the point of the multiple-level security is to prevent information exchange in the reverse direction.) On the high side of the system there is a finite buffer into which the data is first placed, and later it is taken up by the high client. Suppose there is some protocol that gives feedback from the high side to the low side in order to acknowledge receipt of the data, or to warn the low side client to slow down because the buffer is nearly full, or to notify the low side client that the buffer did overflow and drop packets that must be retransmitted. Again, the question is, can the high client send information to the low client? Yes, the high client can carefully choose when to read data from the buffer, which influences the feedback messages from the high side buffer to the low side client. In this way the high side client can convey messages to the low side client.

In either of the above scenarios, the existence of other clients that are not participating in the covert communication could be considered to cause noise on the covert channel, giving rise to subtle and complex multiuser communication channels [39].

To summarize this section we note that there is much to the theory and practice of timing information and timing channels which remains to be understood, especially in network scenarios. Additionally, information-theoretic ideas can play an important role in providing such understanding.

IV. Traffic Modeling

There has been an extensive effort since the inception of packet-switched communication networks to characterize the traffic carried by networks. The work aims to account for the bursty nature of many data sources. In this section, two concepts arising in this work that strike us to be particularly close to the ideas and principles of information theory are reviewed: the effective bandwidth of datastreams, and deterministic traffic constraints.

Recently, there has been a keen interest in accounting for the observations of many studies of traffic in real networks, that indicate that datastreams exhibit self-similar behavior. That is, the random fluctuations in the arrival rate of packets appears to be nearly statistically the same on different time scales, ranging over several orders of magnitude. We touch on this development briefly in the context of the effective bandwidth of a self-similar Gaussian source. An extensive annotated bibliography on the subject is given in [40].

A. Effective Bandwidth of a Datastream

One of the primary goals of information theory is to identify the effective information rate of a data source. The entropy or the rate-distortion function of a data source may be thought of as such. The theory of effective bandwidth, described in this section, has a similar goal. The word "bandwidth" is in this context an entrenched misnomer for data rate. Another connection between the theory of effective bandwidth of datastreams and information theory is that much of the theory of effective bandwidth is based on large deviations theory, which intersects Shannon's theory of information. Moreover, more direct connections between the theory of effective bandwidth and Shannon's theory of information are possible. For example, perhaps an "effective-bandwidth versus distortion" function can be computed for some nontrivial sources.

A major way that the theory of effective bandwidth differs from the Shannon theory is that it treats the flow of data bits as it would the flow of a fluid. The values of the bits are not especially relevant. The idea is that individual connections or datastreams carried by a network may be variable in nature. The data rate of each source may be constant in time, but *a priori* unknown, in which case we suppose the rate of such a source to be random. Or the sources can have time-varying rates. Suppose many variable datastreams are multiplexed together onto a line with a fixed capacity (measured in bits per second). Because of statistical multiplexing, the multiplexer has less work to do than if all the datastreams were sending data at the peak rate all the time. Therefore, a given datastream has an effective bandwidth (that depends on the context) somewhere between the mean and peak rate of the stream.

To illustrate the ideas in the simplest setting first, we begin by considering a bufferless communication link, following Hui [41], [42]. The total offered load (measured in bits per second, for example) is given by

$$X = \sum_{j=1}^{J} \sum_{i=1}^{n_j} X_{ji}$$

where J is the number of connection types, n_j is the number of connections of type j, and X_{ji} is the data rate required by the ith connection of type j. Assume that the variables X_{ji} are independent, with the distribution of each depending only on the index j. If the link capacity is C then the probability of overload, $P[X > C]$, can be bounded by Chernoff's inequality

$$\log P[X \geq C] \leq \log E[e^{s(X-C)}] = s\left(\sum_{j=1}^{J} n_j \alpha_j(s) - C\right) \tag{1}$$

where $\alpha_j(s)$ is given by

$$\alpha_j(s) = \frac{1}{s} \log E[e^{sX_{ji}}]. \tag{2}$$

(The bound (1) is trivial in case $\alpha_j(s) = +\infty$ for some j.) Thus for a given value of γ, the quality of service constraint $\log P[X > C] \leq -\gamma$ is satisfied if the vector $n = (n_1, \cdots, n_J)$ lies in the region

$$\mathcal{A} = \left\{ n \in R_+^J : \min_{s>0} \left[s\left(\sum_{j=1}^{J} n_j \alpha_j(s) - C\right) \right] \leq -\gamma \right\}$$
$$= \cup_s \mathcal{A}(s) \tag{3}$$

where

$$\mathcal{A}(s) = \left\{ n \in R_+^J : \sum_{j=1}^{J} n_j \alpha_j(s) \leq C - \frac{\gamma}{s} \right\}. \tag{4}$$

The *complement* of $\mathcal{A}$ relative to R_+^J is convex. Let n^* be on the boundary of $\mathcal{A}$ (think of n^* as a "nominal" value of the vector n). A polyhedral subset of $\mathcal{A}$, delineated by a hyperplane tangent to the boundary of $\mathcal{A}$ at n^*, is given by $\mathcal{A}(s^*)$, where s^* achieves the minimum in (3). Thus any vector $n \in Z_+^J$ satisfying

$$\sum_{j=1}^{J} n_j \alpha_j(s^*) \leq C - \frac{\gamma}{s^*} \tag{5}$$

satisfies the quality-of-service constraint. Once C, γ, and s^* are fixed, the sufficient condition (5) is rather simple. The number $\alpha_j(s^*)$ is the effective bandwidth of a type j connection, and $C - \gamma/s^*$ is the effective capacity. Condition (5) is analogous to the condition in classical information theory that ensures that a particular channel is capable of conveying several independent data sources within specified average distortions, namely, that the sum of the rate distortion functions evaluated at the targeted distortions should be less than or equal to the channel capacity.

A caveat regarding the use of (5) is in order: for large values of s^* the value of $\alpha_j(s^*)$ can be very sensitive to variations in the upper tail of the distribution of X_{ji}.

As long as the random variables X_{ji} are not constant, the function α_j is strictly increasing, and ranging from the mean, $E[X_{ji}]$ as $s \to 0$, to the peak (actually the essential supremum, $\sup\{c: P[X_{ji} > c] > 0\}$) of X_{ji}. Note that the effective bandwidth used depends on the variable s^*. Such dependence is natural, for there is a tradeoff between the degree of statistical multiplexing and the probability of overload, and the choice of the parameter s^* corresponds to selecting a point along that tradeoff curve. As the constraint on the overflow probability becomes more severe, a larger value of s^* is appropriate. For example, if γ is very large, then the sets $\mathcal{A}(s)$ are nonempty only for large s, so that the choice of s^* is also large, meaning that the effective bandwidths will be near the peak values.

The set $\mathcal{A} \cap Z_+^J$, where $\mathcal{A}$ is defined in (3), is only a subset of the true acceptance region $\mathcal{A}_o$, defined by

$$\mathcal{A}_o = \{n \in Z_+^J : \log P[X > C] \leq -\gamma\}.$$

However, the sets $\mathcal{A}$ and $\mathcal{A}_o$ are asymptotically equivalent in the following sense. Let $\mathcal{A}/C$ (respectively, $\mathcal{A}_o/C$) denote the set $\mathcal{A}$ (respectively, $\mathcal{A}_o$) scaled down by a factor C. Note that $\mathcal{A}/C$ depends on C and γ only through the ratio C/γ. Then the Hausdorff distance between the sets $\mathcal{A}/C$ and $\mathcal{A}_o/C$ tends to zero as C and γ tend to infinity with C/γ fixed [43]. This follows from Cramér's theorem (see [44]), to the effect that Chernoff's bound gives the correct exponent.

So far, only a bufferless link confronted with demand that is constant over all time has been considered. The notion of effective bandwidth can be extended to cover sources of data that vary in time, but that are statistically stationary and mutually independent [45]–[47]. Let $X_{ji}[a, b]$ denote the amount of data generated by the ith connection of type j during an interval $[a, b]$. We assume that the process X is stationary in time. Set

$$\alpha_j(s, t) = \frac{1}{st} \log E[e^{sX_{ij}[0,t]}]. \tag{6}$$

For t fixed, the function α_j is the same as the one-parameter version of α_j considered above, applied to the amount of work generated in an interval of length t. Beginning with the well-known representation of Loynes for the stationary queue length

$$Q(0) = \sup_{t \geq 0} X[-t, 0] - tC$$

we write

$$\log P[Q(0) > B]$$

$$= \log P[\sup_{t \geq 0}\{X[-t, 0] - tC\} > B] \tag{7}$$

$$\sim \sup_{t \geq 0} \log P[X[-t, 0] - tC > B] \tag{8}$$

$$\sim \sup_{t \geq 0} \min_{s \geq 0} \left[st \sum_{j=1}^{J} n_j \alpha_j(s, t) - s(B + tC) \right]. \tag{9}$$

The symbol "$\sim$" used in (8) and (9) denotes that the ratio between the quantities on either side of it tend to one. This asymptotic equivalence is justified by limit theorems in at least two distinct regimes: 1) the buffer size B tends to infinity with n and C fixed and 2) the elements of the vector n, the capacity C, and the buffer space B all tend to infinity with the ratios among them fixed. Under either limiting regime, the line (8) is justified by the fact that the probability of the union of many rare events (with probabilities tending to zero at various exponential rates) is dominated by the probability of the most probable of those events. The line (9), which represents the use of the Chernoff bound as in (1), relies on the asymptotic exactness of the Chernoff bound (Cramér's theorem or more general large deviations principles such as the Gärtner–Ellis theorem [44]).

Equations (7)–(9) suggest that the effective bandwidth to be associated with a connection of type j is $\alpha_j(s^*, t^*)$, where t^* achieves the supremum in (9), and s^* achieves the minimum in (9) for a nominal value n^* of n. The approximate condition for meeting the quality-of-service requirement $\log P[Q(0) > B] \leq -\gamma$ for n near n^* is then

$$\sum_{j=1}^{J} n_j \alpha_j(s^*, t^*) \leq C + \frac{B}{t^*} - \frac{\gamma}{s^* t^*}.$$

This region scales linearly in γ if n^*, B, and C scale linearly in γ, and asymptotically becomes a tight constraint as $\gamma \to \infty$. The value t^* is the amount of time that the system behaves in an unusual way to build up the queue length just before the queue length exceeds B. The quantity $C + B/t^* - \gamma/s^* t^*$ is the effective capacity of the link. Following [48], we call t^* the critical time scale. In the first limiting regime, described above, t^* tends to infinity, so the effective bandwidth becomes $\alpha_j(\infty, s^*)$. Use of the Gärtner–Ellis theorem of large deviations theory allows the limit theorems in the first limiting regime to be carried out for a wide class of datastreams with memory.

The above approximation simplifies considerably in the case that the datastream rate is Gaussian. In particular, suppose also that there is only one class of customers (so we drop the index j and let n denote the number of connections) and that for each i, $X_i(0, t]$ is a Gaussian random variable with mean λt and variance $V(t)$. The corresponding effective bandwidth function is $\alpha(s, t) = \lambda + sV(t)/2t$. Inserting this into (9) and then performing the minimization over s yields that

$$\log P[Q(0) > B] \sim -n \inf_t \frac{((c - \lambda)t + b)^2}{2V(t)} \tag{10}$$

where b is the buffer space per connection (so $B = nb$) and c is the capacity per connection ($C = nc$).

Suppose $V(t)/t^{2H}$ converges to a finite constant σ^2 as t tends to infinity, where H, known as the Hurst parameter, typically satisfies $\frac{1}{2} \leq H < 1$. If $H = \frac{1}{2}$, we see the process does not exhibit long-range dependence. In particular, if X has independent increments (therefore the increments of a Brownian motion with drift λ and diffusion parameter σ^2), then $V(t) = \sigma^2 t$ and moreover (10) holds with exact equality.

If $H > \frac{1}{2}$ (but still $H < 1$) then the critical time scale t^* is still finite. That is, even in the presence of long-range dependence, the critical time scale is still finite in the limiting regime of C, B, and n tending to infinity with fixed ratios among them [48]. The value of $V(t)$ for t larger than t^* therefore does not influence the approximation.

See [43] and [49] for extensive surveys on effective bandwidth, and [40] for a very extensive bibliographic guide to self-similar datastream models and their use. The paper [50] presents significant bounds and analysis related to notions of equivalent bandwidth with a different terminology. Finally, the paper [51] connects the theory of effective bandwidths to thermodynamics and statistical mechanics.

B. Network Engineering Through Traffic Constraints

An alternative to treating datastreams with statistical methods is to impose deterministic constraints on the data admitted into the network. The responsibility for respecting the constraints might lie with the end user, or it could be policed at the network entry points. The selection of which constraints would be imposed on a particular datastream would be done at the time a connection is requested, possibly in conjunction with a pricing mechanism. In return, the network should be able to provide a guaranteed quality of service (such as specified maximum transit time) for a particular connection. The type of constraints used should satisfy the following requirements.

Flexibility: The constraints should allow for a controlled degree of burstiness on the part of data sources.

Easy to Enforce or Monitor: Should be easy to police a datastream (through dropping or delaying part of the stream) to produce an output stream satisfying the constraints. Also, it should be easy to determine whether a datastream is meeting a particular declared set of constraints.

Operational Significance to the Network: It should be possible for the network to exploit the constraints on admitted datastreams in order to deliver performance guarantees.

378

This may entail, for example, providing end-to-end delay guarantees by bounding the delay for each device or link transmitted.

A popular datastream constraint, introduced by Cruz in [52] and [53] is the (σ, ρ) constraint, defined as follows. Consider a datastream described by a function $(R(t): t \geq 0)$, where $R(t)$ denotes the amount of data generated up to time t. Assume that $R(0) = 0$, and that R is right-continuous. Clearly, R is nondecreasing. Let $\sigma \geq 0$ and $\rho > 0$. The stream R is said to satisfy the (σ, ρ) constraint if

$$R(t) - R(s) \leq \sigma + \rho(t - s) \text{ whenever } s < t.$$

We discuss briefly why this particular constraint satisfies the requirements above.

First, regarding flexibility, the constraint allows a stream to contain an occasional burst of size σ, as long as in between the bursts the data rate falls below ρ enough. Secondly, in order to enforce a (σ, ρ) constraint, or to monitor a datastream to see whether it is in compliance with the constraint, a so-called "leaky bucket" regulator can be used. A leaky bucket regulator operates as follows. Imagine a bucket that holds tokens, such that tokens arrive at rate ρ. Tokens that arrive to find the bucket full are lost (this represents the leaking from the bucket). Data packets that arrive at the input of the regulator instantaneously take a token from the bucket with them and then pass through the network. However, if no tokens are available in the bucket for a given data packet, then the packet may be queued until a token becomes available, or the packet may be simply dropped. In practice, the scheme can be implemented by using a single counter, that is incremented at rate ρ and is decremented whenever a packet passes through (as long as the counter is not already at zero).

Finally, the (σ, ρ) constraint has operational significance for a network. For example, if a (σ, ρ) stream passes through a buffered link with a constant service rate C, then the delay at the buffer will never exceed $D = \sigma/(C - \rho)$, and the output stream satisfies the (σ', ρ) constraint for $\sigma' = \sigma + \rho D$. The basic approach taken by Cruz [52], [53] allowed arbitrary or first-come, first-served order-of-service when multiple datastreams arrive at a link. Bounds on network transit delay were derived. Parekh and Gallager [54], [55] showed how tighter bounds on network transit delay can be obtained in a network through the use of datastream constraints and generalized processor sharing (weighted round-robin) scheduling disciplines at network nodes. The paper [54] also introduced the important concept of a service curve, that summarizes the performance of a server using the generalized processor sharing discipline. The notion of service curves has been refined, beginning with [56], in order to provide a calculus characterizing both sources and servers in a unified framework with an appealing algebraic structure. Additionally, [57] indicates how to provide transit-delay guarantees through the use of deadlines at intermediate nodes and earliest-deadline-first scheduling. Many concepts can be formulated in both a stochastic framework and in a deterministically constrained framework. For example, delay bounds in a switch under deterministic constraints at the input and output ports

are given in [58], and a notion of equivalent bandwidth for datastreams satisfying (σ, ρ) (and peak) constraints is given in [59].

V. MULTIACCESS COMMUNICATION

The problem of multiaccess communication arises in the consideration of the simplest possible, nontrivial multiuser system. A common receiver is accessed by N sources through a common channel. The principal motivating practical applications are i) "cable" local-area networks and ii) "radio" local-area networks. In either case, the main ingredient of the problem is the contention among the sources and the need to share the channel resource.

The approach taken by multiuser information theory is to consider the N sources as abstract digital emitters that produce bits at constant rates $R_1, R_2, \cdots, R_N$, and to aim at characterizing the region of values of the R_i's that (with appropriate encoding) permit error-free communication to the receiver. This approach is amply explored elsewhere in this issue [4].

An intermediate approach, taken rather recently by researchers who are motivated by the cellular communication paradigm, continues to consider nonbursty, continuously transmitting sources, but it gives up the asymptotic approach of multiuser information theory. It focuses on finite performance criteria and goals. This approach has become known as the multiuser detection theory approach to multiaccess communication. It is also explored elsewhere in this issue [5]. The key notion is that, in principle, it is possible to improve upon the performance of the traditional matched-filter-based receivers that are optimal in single-user, AWGN channel environments. The details of implementation become especially interesting when code-division multiple-access (CDMA) signals are used, when adaptive antenna arrays are used to provide diversity transmission or reception, and when fading channels are encountered.

Coding, detection, good channel modeling, source burstiness, and delay are all important issues. The canonical multiaccess network model described below focuses on the later two, whereas multiuser information theory and multiuser detection theory focus on the first three. In the terminology of layers, the topics of this paper are more at a multiaccess (MAC) layer or network layer, and the other topics are more at the physical layer. Research on the canonical multiaccess network model, in which data packets are dealt with as "black boxes" whose internal structure is irrelevant, helped to crystallize some basic concepts of multiaccess communication, especially regarding bursty sources and delay. However, the physical and MAC cannot be cleanly separated (see discussion in Section II-A), so that the areas of multiuser information theory, multiuser detection, and multiaccess networking issues are best understood or developed in concert.

The canonical networking model of multiaccess, considers the so-called collision channel as its basic resource model. This channel is time-slotted (the non-time-slotted version introduces nonessential variations that are nowhere as significant as the differences between synchronism and lack thereof in single-user channels or in channels in which the "bit-structure" of the packets is not ignored). The signals transmitted by the sources are modeled by fixed-length packets (the bit-content of which are irrelevant), each of which fits snugly within one channel time slot. If two or more users transmit their packets in the same slot, none of the packets are correctly received (i.e., a collision is said to occur). The users are informed about the outcome of events in each slot by a variety of feedback structures. The simplest assumes instantaneous ternary feedback (denoted by 0, 1, or e) that indicates to all sources whether the slot was unutilized or idle (denoted by "0"), was utilized successfully through a single, and hence successful, transmission (denoted by "1"), or was wasted through a collision (denoted by "e"). There have been many variations of this structure (binary feedback; M-ary feedback, in which the number of colliding packets is known; delayed feedback; etc.). They are adequately reviewed in [26] and [60]. The fundamental behavior exhibited in this model is impervious to these perturbations. So, we focus here on the simple, ternary, instantaneous feedback, even though this particular model is (at least almost) never encountered in practice.

The basic question was to determine allowable transmission strategies of the N sources that can achieve high aggregate "throughput" with small access delay. If a magic genie could coordinate the transmissions, then the channel would act like a multiplexer with throughput one packet per slot, and the resulting delay would be caused only by congestion due to possibly bursty arrival streams, rather than by the access problem *per se*. Without such a genie, throughput near one can still be obtained by the use of a sophisticated distributed algorithm such as an adaptive version of time-division multiplexing. However, it is believed that to achieve throughput near one for very large N, the mean delay must also be large.

The first consideration of this model by Abramson [23] made the additional natural simplification that the number of sources N is infinite. Such an assumption, unnatural though it may appear at first, is a clever and useful one in that, first of all, it lower-bounds the performance of a finite-user system (since it amounts to a pessimistic assumption that each user's packets may compete against each other). In particular, if for a given throughput rate the mean average packet delay is finite for the infinite N model, then bounded delay can be achieved uniformly over all large finite N. (Researchers believe that the converse is true as well, but we know of no proof of such a converse.) More importantly, the infinite N assumption permits the decoupling of the analysis from the nonessential details of each source's storage of incoming packets. With an infinite number of users and a finite combined offered data rate of λ packets per slot, each source will only generate a single packet in its lifetime and thus there is no need to track queuing delays at each terminal. Thus the multiaccess channel model was coupled from the outset with the assumption of aggregate input data that was generated by a Poisson process of rate λ.

A. The ALOHA Multiaccess Protocol

The next question was, of course, to determine the protocol for packet transmission and retransmission. As mentioned earlier, Abramson proposed the original, simple, random access in which a terminal attempts transmission as soon as its packet is generated and, if unsuccessful, continues to attempt transmission after a random waiting period. This is the ALOHA protocol. By assuming (incorrectly) that the aggregate data process (that includes new and retransmitted data) is also Poisson of rate G and by assuming (incorrectly) that this protocol yields a steady-state equilibrium, it is a trivial exercise to determine that $\lambda = Ge^{-G}$. This equation captures the essence of ALOHA. It implies that the maximum achievable throughput is equal to $e^{-1} \sim 0.36$ and occurs at $G = 1$. It further implies that there is a bistable behavior (i.e., for the same value of λ there are two possible corresponding values, G_1 and G_2, of the total data rate). By turning the situation around and abandoning the stability assumption, one can still use this equation to see that the actual ALOHA behavior (as confirmed by experiments) will produce a deteriorating throughput $(\lambda \to 0)$ and an increasing total transmission intensity $(G \to \infty)$ as more and more terminals get "blocked" and thus slide into the retransmission mode.

The bottom line of the ALOHA analysis is that uncontrolled random access, in both theory and practice, is a poor performer (no surprise). Left alone under pure ALOHA, the system disintegrates. With appropriate controls that steer G around its optimal values of 1, only 36% of the "capacity"[3] of the collision channel is utilized. Clearly there should be better ways of legislating transmission and retransmission rights to improve performance. Indeed, for almost two decades after the introduction of the ALOHA concept, massive research (much of which is accounted and summarized in [60]) ensued, with the goal of determining the ultimate capabilities of random access; that is, determining the maximum stable throughput over the collision channel. And, yet, the simple ideas of the ALOHA protocol galvanized everyone's thinking about channel access in general. And, eventually, practical and well-performing protocols were developed, that actually mix the random-access element with ingredients of reservation and the concept of fixed access (like the standard carrier-sensing-multiple-access with collision-detection (CSMA-CD)). Such protocols might not have been invented without the catalytic effects of ALOHA, even though many of the assumptions in the ALOHA model are far from being practical.

Naturally, the first subsequent attempts centered around the modification and stabilization of ALOHA. Metcalfe [61] and Lam and Kleinrock [62] were the first to suggest control mechanisms that reduce the retransmission rates of individual sources when the transmission intensity increases. Based on the observed ternary feedback, it is possible to adjust the packet retransmission probability so as to keep G close to 1. The papers [63] and [64] independently gave the first proofs that finite mean delay can be achieved for the canonical model (with Poisson arrivals, corresponding to infinite N). Several other stabilization algorithms were given, including an interesting one of Rivest [65] based on Bayesian estimation.

---

[3]The term "capacity" is used here in the sense of maximum achievable throughput and has nothing to do with the concept of Shannon channel capacity.

380

The famous exponential "backoff" algorithm, that basically reduces the retransmission probability of a packet by a factor of 2 every time the packet experiences a collision, preoccupied the minds of many researchers for a while. It was initially conjectured that this algorithm would stabilize ALOHA's behavior but it was eventually shown that (somewhat surprisingly) it did not for the case of $N = \infty$. For the values of N encounted in practice, the exponential backoff protocol and many other protocols are adequate, even though they would lead to instability for $N = \infty$, or to bistability or large mean delay for very large finite N.

In parallel, practically oriented engineers started incorporating elements of the real environment in the ALOHA protocol. For example, the ability to "listen" to the channel, and determine whether it is in use or not, should be used to avoid unnecessary collisions. Thus CSMA was born, and its variants, based on the values of its various parameters (like persistence in transmission or propagation delay) and on whether a packet is divisible or not (i.e., whether a detected collision can be aborted before the full length of a slot is wasted), were painstakingly analyzed [66] and were shown to yield throughput performance that did approach the limit of 1 packet per slot.

B. Conflict Resolution

To information theorists, however, this thinking was unsatisfying. Before understanding and exhausting the possibilities of what is achievable with the basic model, the rush to explore its modifications (useful in practice, though the latter may be) suggested lack of intellectual tenaciousness. So, it was not surprising that, as a segment of the community pursued the development of practical protocols that depended on ALOHA to variable extents, information theorists relentlessly continued to pursue the basic collision channel model.

The major thrust began when Capetanakis [67] and Tsybakov and Mikhailov [68] adopted a radically different approach to the problem of retransmission, that was also suggested by Hayes [69] in a somewhat different context. Capetanakis and Tsybakov and Mikhailov explored the simple idea that every collision should be resolved before additional transmissions could be permitted. What better way to resolve a collision than subdivide the sources of the collided packets into groups and permit those groups to transmit one at a time in a TDMA fashion? Thus the connection of conflict resolution to group testing was identified.

It may be argued that, in so doing, one mixes pure random access with fixed sharing and/or reservations, depending on how one views the allocation of the slots to the subgroups of the collided users. This is true; however, this is done in response to the channel feedback, without violating the basic assumptions of "indivisible" packets, and without introducing additional features of the environment into the model. Thus it penetrates the essence of the conflict-resolution process.

Capetanakis started by considering a finite number of users (2^n), with known binary identities of length n. Each user could be thought of as a leaf of a binary tree of depth n. After a collision, one half of the users were allowed to attempt

retransmission in the next slot (say, the half that corresponded to the upper half of the tree); if a success or an idle occurred, the users in the bottom half of the tree were enabled next. If a collision occurred, the subgroup was subdivided again into two subgroups and the process was repeated. The end of such a search through a given subset of the tree could be detected by the occurrence of two successive slots with successful transmissions and thus, one by one, all subgroups would be explored (with the size of each subgroup being as large as the feedback information would permit).

Such a search was, indeed, similar to that of statistical group testing methods that were introduced in the first half of this century. Soon, the partitioning method that was based on user-ID was replaced by an equivalent random experiment with binary outcomes, performed independently by each user involved in the collision. In this way, the method of Capetanakis could be performed on the canonical, infinite-user ALOHA model. The first results were not spectacular. The basic tree-algorithm (as it came to be known) was achieving a maximum throughput that was slightly higher than that of ALOHA (it was, in fact, 0.43). The big difference, however, was that the protocol was stable. So long as the input data rate was less than 0.43, the successful throughput rate was equal to the input rate.

One difficulty with the tree algorithm (as well as with all subsequent variations) was that it did not offer itself to an elegant analysis. To track (and prove) the stability and to calculate the length of the conflict-resolution period (which is a measure of packet delay and another quantity of fundamental interest in the networking view of multiaccess communication), one had to resort to rather abstruse and lengthy derivations, the likes of which have been referred to at times as "brute-force" methods, or as "19th century mathematics."

The ideas of Capetanakis and Tsybakov and Mikhailov excited the community (more so its information-theoretically inclined members). Several people on both sides of the Iron Curtain started thinking seriously about this new view of conflict resolution. Among others, Gallager, Massey, Berger, Humblet, Mikhailov, Moseley, Tsybakov, all contributed insights and suggestions that led to a series of improvements to the basic tree algorithm that gradually yielded higher values of maximum stable throughput. There is little value in recounting them here; in detail they were reviewed in [60], and most of them were building blocks that helped clarify the essence of the splitting process.

Eventually, the most natural formulation that emerged parsed the packets of the different users on the basis of time of arrival [70], [71]. So, in slot t (just after having resolved all collisions that were caused by packets that were generated prior to an earlier time slot t'), two parameters needed to be chosen: i) the length Δ of the next interval to be resolved, i.e., the interval from t' to $t' + \Delta$, so that all packets that arrived at instants within that interval would form the next group that would be "searched" and ii) the fraction α of that interval that would be searched next if a collision occurred when all arrivals in interval $(t', t' + \Delta)$ were enabled. The search was to proceed pretty much as in the basic tree algorithm of Capetanakis. That is, if the channel feedback was 0 or 1, this marked the end of the (in this case, very brief) current conflict resolution period. If the feedback was e (collision), the users in the first fraction α of the original interval would be enabled next. In case of collision that fraction would be subdivided anew (by the same fraction α); in case of success, the "enabled" interval would shift starting from $t' + \alpha\Delta$ and extending to $t' + \Delta$; and in case of an idle slot, the enabled interval would start from $t' + \alpha\Delta$ but would only extend to the fraction α of the interval $(t' + \alpha\Delta, t' + \Delta)$. The reason for the last choice resulted from the crucial observation, that was first made on Capetanakis's algorithm, that if a collision is followed by an idle, another collision is certain to occur if the entire balance of the originally enabled subgroup, that produced the collision in the first place, is enabled again. Thus it is important to anticipate this occurrence and explore only a subset of that balance.

Another important observation is that if a collision follows upon the heels of another, there is no information about the contents of the unexplored portion of the first interval that yielded the first collision. Thus instead of, when its time comes, visiting the unexplored portion alone, (of length $(1-\alpha)\Delta$), it is preferable to enable a full-length interval from $t' + \alpha\Delta$ to $t' + \alpha\Delta + \Delta$ (or to the current slot t, whichever is less).

These intricacies of the algorithm are clearly explained in [26]. The analysis of it, however, has been similarly plagued by the need for inelegant, computationally intensive methods that have aimed at establishing the same two performance indices of interest, i.e., the maximum stable throughput and the average packet latency. Clearly, though, by mapping the entire process of splitting into the time axis, based on time of arrival, one can see that both quantities (i.e., stability and delay) are captured by the "lag" between the current time t and the time of completed resolutions t'. Thus the difference $t - t'$ is closely related to the duration of the conflict resolution period (and hence the packet delay) as well as to the "drift" of the resolution process. Unless $t - t'$ approaches a limiting distribution, the process is unstable.

The precise calculation of the maximum stable throughput of the FCFS (first-come, first-served) splitting algorithm (as it was eventually known) was accomplished in [72] through the policy iteration method of dynamic programming (where the problem was posed as one of optimization, i.e., maximization of the stable throughput, with respect to the choices of Δ and α). The precise calculation relies on extensive computations and thus the numerical accuracy of the results has been a question of some dispute. If α is decided to be chosen as $1/2$ and the optimization is carried out only with respect to Δ, it was determined that $\Delta \cong 2.6$ slots and the corresponding maximum stable throughput should be 0.4871 packets per slot (a significant improvement over ALOHA and the basic tree algorithm). However, the optimal value of α is not $1/2$, but, rather, very slightly less than $1/2$. There is no easy explanation for this but it does yield slightly higher throughput (0.487117 as claimed by Moseley and Humblet in [72]). Even more puzzling is an observation by Vvedenskaya and Pinsker [73] that the throughput can gain another small increment by somewhat modifying the lengths of the intervals after a large

number of collisions. A possible resolution of these somewhat variable numerical values is offered by Verdú in an over-looked technical note [74], where the maximization problem is formulated in an elegant, iterative fashion that bypasses the need for complicated dynamic-programming-based reasoning. The result is that the FCFS algorithm with $\alpha = \frac{1}{2}$ yields a throughput of 0.487117, the Tsybakov–Mikhailov version with $\alpha = 0.485$ yields 0.487694, and the precise calculation by Verdú yields 0.487760.

It should be mentioned that the value of 0.4871 obtained by Gallager follows from a very elegant and simple argument based on the drift of the quantity $t - t'$ and also bypasses the obscuring mathematical details.

At the same time, a great deal of effort had been focused on looking at the problem from the other end. That is, by assuming that additional information is available and by determining the corresponding maximal throughput, one can obtain upper bounds on the throughput in the original problem. The first to obtain such a bound was Pippenger [75] who showed that the maximum stable throughput cannot exceed ~ 0.73. A series of similar efforts followed and the currently known least upper bound [76] is 0.587. Some researchers conjectured that the optimal value might be 0.5, but this claim was quickly abandoned as baseless.

In this brief (about five-year), but intense, saga about zeroing-in on the maximum stable throughput of random access over the collision channel, there was a modest degree of similarity to the quest for establishing the true capacity of a channel in the usual Shannon-theoretic sense. The problem here had nothing to do with Shannon capacity and it was mostly an academic exercise of limited practical value.

The study of the collision-resolution problem did not stop after the derivation of the results quoted above. A myriad of possible extensions and modifications were possible and many of them were pursued in considerable depth. For example, the issue of feedback delay or feedback errors, the issue of new users coming into the system (or old users dropping out) in the middle of a resolution period, the issue of multiple levels of feedback, and many other variations have been looked at over the years and continue to be looked at today, albeit with somewhat diminished interest. Again, many of these variations are reviewed in [26].

C. Finite-User ALOHA

Useful though the infinite-user model is, it is also worthwhile to examine systems with a finite number of users, in which, or course, a user's own packets do not collide with each other on the channel. In this case, each user generates a finite percentage of the total input data and, thus it is necessary to queue up the arriving packets. Even if the other features of the collision channel model remain the same, the problem is now transformed in a significant way. It becomes a problem of nonstandard queuing theory (i.e., one in which successive service times in each queue are not independent and/or in which service time durations are not independent of the arrival processes), known also as a problem of interacting, or coupled, queues.

Consider N users, each with an infinite buffer and receiving packets independently at a rate λ_i. Thus the total input rate is $\sum_{i=1}^{N} \lambda_i$. Each user attempts to transmit the packet at the head-of-the-line position in the queue in each slot with probability p_i (irrespectively of whether this is the first attempted transmission or a retransmission). The feedback from the collision channel is as before (0, 1, or e). This model encapsulates the ALOHA protocol in a queuing environment. A central question is to determine the values of the rates λ_i, $i = 1, \cdots, N$, for which the average delay in all of the queues is finite.

With Bernoulli arrivals (or any other independent, identically distributed arrivals) this problem can be accurately modeled in a straightforward way as an N-dimensional random walk. From the early work by Fayolle and Iasnogorodski [77] to more recent works by Szpankowski [78], Sidi and Segall [79], Rao and Ephremides [80], Anantharam [81], and others, it has become well known that such chains cannot be easily solved. Thus much of the work has concentrated on obtaining outer and inner bounds to the region of stability. A key idea that has yielded some of these bounds relies on partially decoupling the queues by considering as "bounding" systems those in which some of the queues stochastically dominate their counterparts in the original one and, hence, their stability implies the stability of the original system. Note, also, that in the N-user model, it is possible that some of the queues may be stable and others unstable. Recently, an index of "potential instability" for each queue was obtained [82], given by $\lambda_i(1 - p_i)/p_i$. The meaning of this index is that if the queues are ranked on the basis of this index, that is, if queue i is stable, all queues j ($j < i$) are also stable and if queue i is unstable, all queues j ($j > i$) are also unstable.

If the transmission probability vector p can be adjusted as a function of the arrival rates (but not as a function of backlogs and feedback), we are led to consider a capacity region that is the union of arrival rate regions over all vectors p. Before examining such capacity region for the queuing model, we shall discuss the capacity region defined by Abramson [83] (and summarized in [8, vol. II]). The definition corresponds to the throughput vectors achieved by a saturated ALOHA system in which all users always have packets to send, so considerations of queuing and delay are avoided. Suppose that user i transmits in each slot with probability p_i, independently from slot to slot, and independently of other users. The success probability for user i is then

$$\lambda_i = p_i \prod_{j:\, j \neq i} (1 - p_j).$$

Abramson's capacity region, that we write as $\mathcal{C}_A$, is given as the set of all vectors $\lambda = (\lambda_1, \cdots, \lambda_N)$ obtained in this way, as the vector $p = (p_1, \cdots, p_N)$ varies. Abramson showed that the upper boundary of $\mathcal{C}_A$ is the set of those vectors λ obtained when p is a probability vector, meaning that it is desirable for the mean number of transmissions per slot to be one. In the special case of two users, Abramson showed the region reduces to

$$\mathcal{C}_A = \left\{ (\lambda_1, \lambda_2) : \sqrt{\lambda_1} + \sqrt{\lambda_2} \leq 1 \right\}. \tag{11}$$

Now we return to the queuing model. From the perspective of a given user i, the assumption that all the other users are busy is a pessimistic one. Therefore, the buffered ALOHA network is ergodic if the vector of arrival rates falls within $\mathcal{C}_A^o$, where $\mathcal{C}_A^o$ is the set of all $\lambda \in R_+^N$ such that for some p (depending on λ)

$$\lambda_i < p_i \prod_{j:\, j \neq i} (1 - p_j).$$

Equivalently, $\mathcal{C}_A^o$ is $\mathcal{C}_A$ with all points on the upper boundary deleted, and for the case of $N = 2$ users

$$\mathcal{C}_A^o = \left\{ (\lambda_1, \lambda_2) : \sqrt{\lambda_1} + \sqrt{\lambda_2} < 1 \right\}. \tag{12}$$

Tsybakov and Mikhailov [84] first published this result, and moreover they showed for the case $N = 2$ that the region $\mathcal{C}_A^o$ is the *complete* stability region for the ALOHA network, rather than a proper subset of it. Specifically, with $N = 2$ and independent, identically distributed arrivals at each of the two users with means λ_i (and finite variance) per slot, the buffered ALOHA network is ergodic if and only if $\lambda \in \mathcal{C}_A^o$. Anantharam [81] showed that $\mathcal{C}_A^o$ is also the entire stability region for any N, but only for particular (unrealistic) arrival sequences that for different users are weakly statistically dependent. Anantharam's result suggests that $\mathcal{C}_A^o$ may well be equal to the stability region for any N and independent arrivals, but it also shows that the issue depends on subtle details about the interactions of the queues that are probably unimportant in applications.

D. Models with Elements of Multiuser Information Theory

Two noteworthy models that involve elements of multiuser information theory, and either queuing or collision access (but not both at once) are discussed in this section. One is the model of a collision channel without feedback, introduced by Massey and Mathys [85]. It is assumed that there is no feedback, and moreover there is not even a way for the users to synchronize their transmissions. Forward error correction, rather than a retransmission protocol, is thus needed to achieve reliability. In this sense, the model is similar to the models used in the multiuser information theory literature, initiated by Shannon. On the other hand, the model differs from the usual models of multiuser information theory in that, to quote [85], "information is transmitted only in the contents of packets and not also in the timing of access attempts."

Massey and Mathys identify the capacity region, and show that it does not depend on whether the system is slot-synchronized or whether zero-error (rather than arbitrarily small error) probability is required. The capacity (= zero-error capacity) region they obtained is precisely the region $\mathcal{C}_A$ obtained by Abramson [83]. Massey and Mathys noted in [85] that it "seems somewhat surprising" that precisely the same set of rates can be achieved error-free without feedback as can be achieved under the slotted ALOHA system with feedback. See [80] for further elaboration. Is it a meaningless coincidence? Perhaps, but not likely. If not, then, what is the significance of it and in what way do the two very different notions relate to each other? To this day, there is no answer.

The other model we mention, proposed by Teletar and Gallager [86], combines elements of queuing theory and information theory for multiaccess communication. As in the buffered ALOHA model discussed above, a finite number of users accumulate randomly arriving packets to be transmitted. The packets are sent using forward error correction, and a small amount of feedback is available from the receiver to the users. Teletar and Gallager investigate the use of optimal codes (known to exist by random coding arguments, and hence the connection to information theory) for the forward error correction. The time needed to send a packet is variable in length, since the number of active users fluctuates. The feedback allows the receiver to notify the transmitter as soon as the receiver is able to decode a packet, for otherwise the transmitter would not know when to cease transmitting (redundant) bits pertaining to the packet. The resulting dynamics of the queuing process are much like processor sharing, in which the service rate experienced by a user is roughly inversely proportional to the number of active users.

The scheme of Teletar and Gallager is similar to IS-99 [87], the link-level data protocol recently designed for use with the IS-95 CDMA cellular standard. Under the IS-99 link protocol, a standard Transport Control Protocol packet is divided into 32 frames, that are each transmitted using CDMA. Negative selective acknowledgments are sent by the receiver to a user to compensate for frame errors, that typically occur in 1 or 2% of the frames. A user with data sends a frame each 20 ms with a probability p, where p is varied dynamically based on feedback from the base station, that is monitoring the signal-to-interference level. Thus the transfer speed per user tends to diminish with the number of users.

E. Interaction Between Physical and Higher Network Layers

Another direction in which network multiaccess communication has become intriguing is that of spatial diversity. With the increasing importance of sectorized and directional antennas, let alone adaptive antenna arrays, the possibility of space-division multiple access (SDMA) has becomes a reality. In the field of multiuser detection theory, which represents an intermediate stage between multiaccess information theory and network multiaccess, there has been considerable activity centered on detailed signal modeling, power-control, antenna patterns, channel interference models, and receiver structures that yield "throughput" results indirectly as functions of the required quality-of-service. That is, bit-error rates are calculated as functions of the transmission rates, the transmission powers, the channel bandwidth, and the other design parameters.

At the networking level, it is of interest again (at least as a first approach) to suppress the system details into rigid "black boxes" and to attempt to capture the effect of directionality as a means of aiding in the resource allocation. It should be mentioned, as an additional example of the different viewpoints of multiuser detection theory and networking, that the phenomenon of "capture" (meaning that one of many competing simultaneously transmitted signals may be correctly received by a single receiver) can be modeled in very different

ways. At one end, by taking into account the synchronization preambles of the signals (especially in the case of CDMA), the received powers, and the exact times of arrival, it is possible to get a detailed and accurate micromodel of how capture occurs and to then analyze its effects. At the other end, the networking view of capture has simply assumed that if multiple packets are simultaneously received, then either one packet can be successfully received with some probability p, or the packet with the highest received power is correctly received. Based on such simple modeling, one can derive the effect of capture on the throughput of the otherwise classical collision channel with the associated random-access protocol. This was, in fact, done since the very early days of the history of multiaccess communication [88].

Recently [89], some attempts have been made to combine (up to a certain extent) the "black-box" mentality on capture with the detection-theoretic needs for more detailed modeling. The motivation for some of this work has been to study the role of energy conservation in wireless networks as a means of network control. Thus the model in [82] assumes that the length of the packet is not constant anymore. Rather, for a fixed number of symbols per packet, it is possible to adjust its length (i.e., the rate of transmission) and keep the detectability criterion of the signal-to-interference ratio unaffected, provided that the transmission power is adjusted simultaneously. The effect on throughput performance is clear. If the packets shrink in length, and if the packet input rate stays constant, the overlaps that cause collisions become less likely. At the same time increasing the transmission power depletes battery energy faster, unless the energy savings, from having less wasteful transmissions due to reduced packet overlaps, prevail. At the same time, keeping several distinct power levels among the users facilitates capture (which enhances throughput). A first study of this elaborate tradeoff shows that the throughput (as well as the normalized throughput per energy unit) is maximized if all users transmit at peak power [82].

The problem becomes more intriguing when the coupling to the physical layer is permitted to strengthen. For example, if the modulation choice is not fixed, then the value of the threshold for the signal-to-interference ratio to ensure detectability at the desired bit-error rate changes nonlinearly and the effect of the transmission power (vis-a-vis the transmission rate and the associate packet length) is unclear; furthermore, the vertical interlayer coupling can also be strengthened if a multiuser detector is assumed at the receiver. These ideas are still premature, and they represent only initial thoughts of current concern in the field of multiaccess communication.

But let us return to the issue of spatial diversity. The networking view is to simply consider the packets of the different users as having not only a "time-of-arrival" coordinate but also a "space-location" coordinate (limited for the moment to the single dimension of planar angle-of-arrival). Thus the collision channel can now be studied as before with the simple additional feature that the receiver is able to focus an ideal beam onto the location that it chooses, along with a chosen value of beamwidth angle. This is simply equivalent to enabling the transmissions of subgroups of users not only by sorting out their time-of-arrival, but also their location. At first glance, it might appear that this increased capability can produce an increase in the value of the maximum stable throughput. After some thinking, however, it is not surprising to see that, as shown in [90], this additional degree of freedom cannot increase the throughput.

Of course, the interesting case is the one that involves more than a single beam; in that case it is clear that throughput gains can be indeed realized. This is another case for which work is just beginning and it is premature to report any definitive ideas or progress.

F. Wireless Networks

The rapid growth of wireless networking today is causing continued interest in a variety of multiaccess communication problems. The most prominent type of a wireless network today is the one based on the cellular model. In that model, the base nodes are accessed by mobile nodes, but are inter-connected among themselves via a wired infrastructure that is part of the telephone switched network. The principal issues that need to be addressed in such networks include spectral efficiency (in terms of spatial frequency reuse), power control (for combatting the near–far problem of CDMA signals), handoffs among base-stations nodes, and mobile tracking as nodes move from cell to cell. Additional issues that deal with specialized applications (like mobile computing, multicasting, or information distribution) have to do with database structures and signal compression. All these together transcend the confines of the subject of multiaccess communication. They have captivated the interest of the networking community (and the dollars of the community at large), and it is not clear what role information theory can play in it. However, multiuser detection theory and some recent work by Tse [91], Hanly [92], Knopp and Humblet [93], and Gallager and Medard [94], that study a variety of subjects associated with cellular models (such as effective wireless bandwidth, power-rate control, etc.) have a strong information-theoretic flavor. In addition, the theory of compression and multiple descriptions will undoubtedly play a key role in those wireless applications that deal with information distribution and database access.

But there is another form of wireless network that has emerged recently as a subject of great interest (especially in military applications) called all-mobile networks. They are described by a variety of other names like peer-to-peer, flat, multihop, *ad hoc*, and others. All-mobile networks have a large number of nodes with no hierarchy (no base-station nodes) and no fixed infrastructure. All nodes may move and constantly change their neighbor sets. They all share the same frequency band and must communicate with each other in a flexible fashion that permits all kinds of services (data, voice, video, etc.). Clearly, they involve all the problems encountered in cellular networks plus many more. Early work on such networks [95] identified the need for, and methods to achieve, distributed self-reconfiguration and has established some principles (or more accurately, problem areas) that govern their design and operation. An increasing segment of the networking community is zeroing-in on them and it is too

soon to tell how information-theoretic ideas may contribute to their study. Multiaccess communication, however, is a central issue for these networks and we would be remiss if we did not identify these networks in this section.

In conclusion, the burgeoning field of channel access, from its early modest phases to its current complex and multifaceted profile, has been one of the principal areas in which information theory has played, and will likely continue to play, a major role. The complexity and multitude of multiaccess-related issues that arise today (especially in the area of wireless networks) has led much of the networking community to a state of mild confusion. We believe that the simplicity and sharpness of information-theoretic ideas may yet penetrate the field further and illuminate those issues that are basic and fundamental.

VI. QUEUEING THEORY

Queuing theory has provided the most useful analytical tools in the study of communication and computer networks. It has offered a natural foundation for delay analysis and has also been the source of sophistication for the description of complex interplay among network parameters.

Despite its central role in the theoretical side of networking, queuing theory remains, for the most part, uncoupled to information theory. It is, of course, closely connected to the theory of stochastic processes and, to the extent that the latter is related to information theory, one may claim that there is a certain connection between the two fields. But beyond the limited similarity in terms of asymptotics and stochastic analysis, there is no fundamental bond between the two disciplines. In fact, if there was such a bond, the missing link between delay and information theory would have been uncovered by now as well.

Actually, queuing theory has displayed much more affinity to control theory. Stochastic control of simple queuing models [96], dynamic adjustment of retransmission probabilities in random-access systems [63], optimal routing [26], flow control, and many other networking problems have been fruitfully cast in the framework of control and optimization theory. A thorough survey of that connection can be found in [28], where it is shown how the methodology of system theory applies naturally to networking. Furthermore, the theory of discrete-event systems [29] has also found applicability to problem of network design and operation [97].

Yet, there have been some hopeful, albeit feeble, signs that the right way of combining information theory and queuing theory may, indeed, be taking shape. In Section III of this paper we mentioned the pioneering work of Anantharam and Verdú [33] on the Shannon capacity of a queue. In addition to determining the capacity of the simple queue channel, this work sets a landmark in the study of the two fields. Viewing a service system as a channel may prove to be nothing more than a whimsical, cute exercise; yet, it may prove to have a catalytical role in creating a common platform for the joint study of information-theoretic and queuing-theoretic systems. It may represent a pivotal moment in the history of the two fields. The interesting (common) part of that history has yet to be written, however. The enthusiasm of those who saw in this work an opportunity to advance the coupling of the two disciplines was quickly tempered by the difficulty of extending the approach to even the slightest perturbation of the plain $M/M/1$ system. For example, simply adding one more server (i.e., considering an $M/M/2$ system) complicates the analysis considerably. And yet, the two-server model would be invaluable in shedding more light on the interplay between information and waiting, since it captures the notion of increased bandwidth and parallel service.

The fact, discussed in Section V-D, that the queuing-theoretic capacity region for multiaccess communication coincides (at least for $N = 2$ stations) with the capacity region of the collision channel without feedback of Massey and Mathys [85] **may** (just may) be something fundamental tying queuing theory to information theory. The identity of the regions may be an instance of a yet undiscovered broader principle. The work of Teletar and Gallager [86], also discussed in Section V-D, illustrates some of the significant interactions between queuing and physical-layer considerations, many of which involve elements of information theory. The notion of effective bandwidth, described in Section IV-A, is grounded in queuing theory, and as we mentioned it has some natural compatibility with information theory.

There have been other approaches recently that also attempt a joint study of information-theoretic and queuing-theoretic system aspects. For example, the use of variable-rate source coding in conjunction with congestion control combines rate distortion theory with buffer management. It does not reach into any level of profundity, but it does permit (at least) a phenomenological coupling. In [98], Tse considered a version of this problem that can be thought of not only as a study of the tradeoff between information fidelity and congestion, but, also as a means of coupling among the OSI networking layers, at least as far as quality of service is concerned.

VII. SWITCHING NETWORKS

There is a natural interplay between Shannon information theory and the theory of switching, routing, and sorting in interconnection networks. The classical example is a circuit switch with n inputs and n outputs, interconnected by wires and relays (or crosspoints). Each relay has two states: open or closed, so that the number of internal states of the network is 2^R, where R is the number of relays. Suppose the switch is to be capable of connecting the n inputs to the n outputs according to any permutation. Because different permutations require different network states, the network must have at least $n!$ network states. This requires that $2^R \geq n!$ or that $R \geq \log_2 n! \sim n \log n$. The earliest published account of this idea is that of Shannon [99]. Similarly, if the network is constructed of component switches of fixed in-degree and out-degree s and links between them, with each component switch capable of handing any of the $s!$ possible permutations of input-to-output connections, at least a constant times $n \log n$ such switches (for fixed s) are needed to connect any input to any output.

A simple, elegant construction of switching networks with the minimum number of two-by-two switches (within a factor of two) is the Beneš network, attributed by Beneš [100] to Slepian, Duguid, and Le Core. A simple algorithm, now known as the "looping algorithm," was given for the determination of routes. The Beneš network is not well-suited to dynamic operation in that if a set of routes are in progress and a new route between an idle input and idle output is requested, then rerouting of existing connections is sometimes required.

Thus in addition to being able to route any permutation, it is also desirable that a switch be able to emulate a full crossbar switch in a *dynamic* fashion. The strongest form of this property, termed *strict sense nonblocking*, is the following: whenever a set of compatible routes are already carried by the network, and an idle input and an idle output are identified, it is possible to assign a route to the new input–output pair that is compatible with the routes already given. There is no information-theoretic argument that rules out the existence of strict-sense nonblocking switches with complexity $O(n \log n)$, and indeed they were shown to exist by Pinsker and Bassalygo [101]. Pinsker and Bassalygo first showed the existence of bipartite graphs with certain expansion properties. Several stages of switches were then interconnected using such graphs at each step, so that from any idle input, or any idle output, strictly more than half the idle center-state lines can be reached, so that there exist an end-to-end connection between the idle input and idle output. The construction of Pinsker and Bassalygo was nonexplicit, because the existence of the expanders was only shown by a random construction. That is, it was shown that with nonzero probability (in fact, with probability tending to one as the size tends to infinity) a randomly constructed regular bipartite graph has the desired expansion property.

Just as algebraic coding theory seeks to find explicit and structured solutions to replace the nonexplicit constructions in Shannon's coding theorems, so too have researchers worked to find explicit and structured solutions for the construction of strict-sense nonblocking networks. A breakthrough came in the paper of Margulis [102], who proposed a construction of related graphs with an expansion property, and used deep theorems from the theory of group representations to prove the expansion property. Gabbar and Galil [103], using relatively elementary methods of harmonic analysis, provided explicit constructions of expanders with explicit (though large) bounds on the required size. See [104] for a more detailed account of the chronology given here, including an exposition of the construction and proof of [103]. Of many notable improvements in explicit constructions of expanders that followed, we mention the work of [105].

In addition, with the growth of data over networks in packetized form, circuit-switched connections have evolved to packet-oriented connections such as virtual circuit connections or pure one-at-a-time datagram packet routing. Packet routing is closely connected to the theory of sorting networks. For example, if a batch of input packets are addressed to the outputs in a one-to-one fashion, then routing the packets may be done exactly by a sorting network. The story regarding existence and explicit constructions for sorting networks somewhat parallels that for circuit-switching networks. The explicit constructions of sorting networks with the minimum required order of complexity $O(n \log n)$, starting with [106], are much too large for currently practical implementation, whereas the sorting network of Batcher, with complexity $n \log n^2$, is quite effective for small networks.

The above story of probabilistic constructions followed later by explicit constructions parallels the development of channel codes. Recently, a more concrete connection between the topics was made by Sipser and Spielman [107], who used expander graphs to construct a new family of asymptotically good, linear error-correcting codes with linear time-sequential decoding algorithms.

The search for asymptotically optimal complexity strict-sense expanders and sorting networks has so far been primarily one of theoretical consequence. In practical networks, switches are engineered only to have a small probability of internal blocking. This is akin to using codes, such as turbo-codes, that have small minimum distance but still have a small error probability.

Information-theoretic ideas are applied in [108] in the context of switching networks using deflection routing of packets. Deflection routing implies that all packets entering a node in one time slot exit the node in the next time slot. While the transit delay in a node is thus minimized, the drawback is that sometimes a packet exits a node on a link that does not help the packet progress towards its destination, in which case we say the packet is deflected. A lower bound on the mean number of hops a packet needs to travel is given in [108], assuming there are two outgoing links per node and that a packet is independently deflected with probability q in each slot. The lower bound is roughly the entropy of the probability distribution of the packet destination divided by the Shannon capacity of a binary-symmetric channel with crossover probability q. The idea is that by observing the progress of a packet, an observer learns the destination of the packet, and such information is conveyed in spite of the deflections, that are essentially noise. If there is only a single source node, the lower bound can be asymptotically achieved through the use of a graph based on good channel codes for the binary-symmetric channel [108]. For the more natural case in which any node can be a source or destination node, there is a gap between the lower bound and the mean number of hops needed for packets in the graph constructed in [108].

VIII. FUTURE WORK

Several problem areas from networking may hold considerable potential for information-theoretic analysis, and the opportunities to impact actual system implementation abound. The development of communication networks to support heterogeneous datastreams in heterogeneous networks promises to continue at a torrid pace for the next decade and beyond. This trend is fueled by the demand for higher speed, lower delay communication, anywhere, anytime. The distinction between computing and communication will increasingly blur, as network resource allocation involves interactions among fluctuations in datastreams (due to bursty sources), fluctu-

ations in link capacities (due to fading channels and node mobility), and fluctuations of demand for computer cycles in multiprocessor environments. As the feature sizes of very large scale integrated (VLSI) chips decrease, the performance of the interconnects suffers relatively more than the performance of the devices [109]. Thus VLSI designers will have to confront increasingly slow and unreliable data links within a chip. Massive network communication problems emerge, and information theory should have a role to play in it.

The use of sophisticated antenna arrays for communication in fading-channel environments is not well understood, though it seems that feedback provided by protocols can play an important role. Much more development in multiuser detection theory, including better channel modeling, will be needed, and much of that may be difficult to cleanly separate from network issues. Information theory could play a significant role in the mix.

While information theorists have made important contributions to the theory of automatic repeat request protocols [110], for the most part information theorists have invested much more effort in forward error control. Still, the use of feedback and automatic repeat request is sometimes clearly preferable to forward error correction. Consider, for example, a synchronous binary erasure channel in which each transmitted bit reaches the receiver with probability p, and is replaced by a null symbol otherwise, and the outcomes of different transmissions are mutually independent. The Shannon capacity of this channel is p bits per second, and if immediate error-free feedback is available, then simply repeating each bit until it is successfully received achieves the capacity and at the same time minimizes the delay. The scheme is essentially unaffected if p is unknown or even time-varying in an arbitrary way. In contrast, a forward error-correcting scheme is almost unworkable in this circumstance. On the other hand, forward error control is typically better when feedback is not available or comes with long delay, and when the channel is well modeled. Better error-control mechanisms, integrating both forward error correction and automatic repeat protocols, are needed in the context of networks. Feedback and delay considerations, as well as bit-error probabilities, are important.

The interaction of source coding with network-induced delay cuts across the classical network layers and has to be better understood. The interplay between the distortion of the source output and the delay distortion induced on the queue that this source output feeds into may hold the secret of a deeper connection between information theory. Again, feedback and delay considerations are important.

But information theory has not paid full attention to the subtleties of feedback. Even though it was Shannon himself who chose to speak on the notion of feedback [111] in his speech that inaugurated the Shannon Lecture series, the important result [112] that feedback does not improve single-user memoryless-channel capacity stymied somewhat the growth of interest on the issue of feedback. Even when it was shown that [3] feedback may increase multiuser capacity, the main action continued to be based on constant-rate transmission. Thus feedback was incorporated only in the form of (to use a uniquely information-theoretic term for feedback) side-information at the transmitter. It was not considered in the networking context of timing, delay, and sporadic transmission.

A recent trend to replace circuits on long-haul backbone networks with packet-switched data, and the evolution of the Internet, raises numerous challenges regarding fault-tolerance and security. We touched on the problem of covert channels, but many other security issues would seem amenable to information-theoretic style approaches.

Our review of the topics in which information theory and networking seem to make contact suggest that the union between the two fields remains unconsummated. Yet, information theorists have maintained active attention to several problems of communication networks and several of their contributions strongly suggest a deeper relationship. In addition, many of the theoretical techniques used in network modeling and analysis are similar to those used in information theory. Finally, there are several aspects of networking, some old (like error control), some new (like uses of antenna diversity), and some spawned by recent observations (like timing in channels and queues) that hold promise for the eventual establishment of a firm and clear relationship between the two fields.

ACKNOWLEDGMENT

The authors wish to acknowledge very helpful comments from an anonymous reviewer and from Dr. Richard Blahut.

REFERENCES

[1] R. Ahlswede, "Multiway communication channels," in *Proc. 2nd Int. Symp. Information Theory* (Tsahkadsor, Armenia, 1971).

[2] A. El Gamal and T. M. Cover, "Multiple user information theory," *Proc. IEEE*, vol. 68, pp. 1466–1483, 1980.

[3] N. T. Gaarder and J. K. Wolf, "The capacity region of a multiple access discrete memory less channel can increase with feedback," *IEEE Trans. Inform. Theory*, vol. IT-21, pp. 100–102, 1975.

[4] S. Verdú, "Fifty years of Shannon Theory," this issue, pp. 2057–2078. T. Cover, "Comments on broadcast channels," this issue, pp. 2524–2530.

[5] T. Kailath and H. V. Poor, "Detection of stochastic processes," this issue, pp. 2230–2259.

[6] S. Verdú, *Multiuser Detection*. New York: Cambridge Univ. Press, 1998.

[7] L. Kleinrock, *Communication Nets*. New York: Dover, 1964.

[8] ———, *Queuing Systems, Vols. 1 & 2*. New York: Wiley, 1975.

[9] V. G. Cerf and R. E. Kahn, "A protocol for packet network communication," *IEEE Trans. Commun.*, vol. COM-22, pp. 637–648, 1974.

[10] H. Frank and W. Chou, "Topological optimization of computer networks," *Proc. IEEE*, vol. 60, pp. 1385–1397, 1972.

[11] I. Rubin, "Communication networks: Message path delays," *IEEE Trans. Inform. Theory*, vol. IT-20, pp. 738–745, 1974.

[12] B. Meister, H. Muller, and H. Rudin, "New optimization criteria for message switching networks," *IEEE Trans. Commun.*, vol. COM-19, pp. 256–260, 1971.

[13] F. W. Heart, R. E. Kahn, S. M. Ornstein, W. R. Crowther, and D. C. Walden, "The interface message processor for the ARPA computer network," in *AFIPS Conf. Proc.*, 1970, vol. 36, pp. 551–567.

[14] H. Frank and I. T. Frisch, *Communication, Transmission, and Transportation Networks*. Reading, MA: Addison-Wesley, 1971.

[15] S. D. Crocker, J. F. Heafner, R. M. Metcalfe, and J. R. Postel, "Function-oriented protocols for the ARPA computer network," in *AFIPS Conf. Proc.*, 1972, vol. 40, pp. 271–279.

[16] R. G. Gallager, "Information theory—The first 25 years," in *IEEE Int. Symp. Information Theory* (Ashkelon, Israel, June 1973), Keynote Address.

[17] C. E. Shannon, "Two-way communication channels," in *Proc. 4th Berkeley Symp. Probability and Statistics*, 1960. D. Slepian, Ed., *Key Papers in the Development of Information Theory*. New York: IEEE Press, 1974, pp. 611–644, reprint.

N. Sloane and A. Wyner, Eds., *Collected Papers of C. E. Shannon*. Piscataway, NJ: IEEE Press, 1993.

[18] P. Elias, A. Feinstein, and C. E. Shannon, "A note on the maximal flow through a network," *IRE Trans. Inform. Theory*, vol. IT-2, Dec. 1956.

[19] G. B. Dantzig and D. R. Fulkerson, "On the max-flow min-cut theorem of networks," in *Linear Inequalities*. (Ann. Math. Studies, vol. 38, 1956).

[20] L. R. Ford and D. R. Fulkerson, "Maximal flow through a network," *Can. J. Math.*, vol. 8, pp. 399–404, 1956.

[21] P. Elias, "Networks of Gaussian channels with applications to feedback systems," *IEEE Trans. Inform. Theory*, vol. IT-13, pp. 493–501, July 1967.

[22] R. G. Gallager, "Basic limits on protocol information in data communication networks," *IEEE Trans. Inform. Theory*, vol. IT-22, pp. 385–399, 1976.

[23] N. Abramson, "The ALOHA system—Another alternative for computer communications," in *AFIPS Conf. Proc.*, 1970, vol. 37, pp. 281–285.

[24] R. G. Gallager, "A minimum delay routing algorithm using distributed computation," *IEEE Trans. Commun.*, vol. COM-23, pp. 73–85, 1977.

[25] D. P. Bertsekas, "Dynamic models of shortest path routing algorithms for communication networks with multiple destinations," in *Proc. IEEE Conf. Decision and Control* (Ft. Lauderdale, FL, 1979), pp. 127–133.

[26] D. Bertsekas and R. Gallager, *Data Networks*. Englewood Cliffs, NJ: Prentice-Hall, 1st ed., 1987; 2nd ed., 1992.

[27] L. Ford, Jr., and D. Fulkerson, *Flows in Networks*. Princeton, NJ: Princeton Univ. Press, 1962.

[28] A. Ephremides and S. Verdú, "Control and optimization methods in communication network problems," *IEEE Trans. Automat. Contr.*, vol. 34, pp. 930–942, 1989.

[29] C. Cassandras, *Discrete-Event Systems: Modeling and Performance Analysis*. Homewood, IL: Irwin, 1993.

[30] J. M. Spinelli and R. G. Gallager, "Event driven topology broadcast without sequence numbers," *IEEE Trans. Commun.*, vol. 37, pp. 468–474, 1989.

[31] R. G. Gallager, P. A. Humblet, and P. M. Spira, "A distributed algorithm for minimum-weight spanning trees," *ACM Trans. Programming Language Syst.*, vol. 5, pp. 66–77, 1983.

[32] S. Verdú, "The exponential distribution in information theory," *Probl. Pered. Inform.*, vol. 32, no. 1, pp. 100–111, Jan./Mar. 1996; English version in *Probl. Inform. Transm.*, vol. 32, no. 1, pp. 86–95, Jan./Mar. 1996.

[33] V. Anantharam and S. Verdú, "Bits through queues," *IEEE Trans. Inform. Theory*, vol. 42, pp. 4–18, Jan. 1996.

[34] A. S. Bedekar and M. Azizoğlu, "The information-theoretic capacity of discrete-time queues," *IEEE Trans. Inform. Theory*, vol. 44, pp. 446–461, Mar. 1998.

[35] J. A. Thomas, "On the Shannon capacity of discrete time queues," in *IEEE Int. Symp. Information Theory* (Ulm, Germany, June 1997).

[36] S. B. Lipner "A comment on the confinement problem," in *Proc. 5th Symp. Operating System Principles* (Univ. Texas at Austin, Nov. 1975), pp. 192–196.

[37] M. Schaefer, B. Gold, R. Linde, and J. Scheid, "Program confinement in KVM/370," in *Proc. Annu. Conf.* ACM (Seattle, WA, Oct. 1977), pp. 404–410.

[38] I. S. Moskowitz, S. J. Greenwald, and M. H. Kang, "An analysis of the timed Z-channel," in *Proc. IEEE Symp. Security and Privacy* (Oakland, CA, May 6–8, 1996), pp. 2–11.

[39] M. H. Kang, I. S. Moskowitz, and D. C. Lee, "A network pump," *IEEE Trans. Software Eng.*, vol. 22, pp. 329–337, May 1996.

[40] W. Willinger, M. S. Taqqu, and A. Erramilli, "A bibliographical guide to self-similar traffic and performance modeling for modern high-speed networks," in *Stochastic Networks Theory and Applications*, F. P. Kelly, S. Zachary, and I. Ziedins, Eds. Oxford, U.K.: Science, 1996, pp. 339–366.

[41] J. Y. Hui, "Resource allocation for broadband networks," *IEEE J. Select. Areas Commun.*, vol. 6, pp. 1598–1608, 1988.

[42] ———, *Switching an Traffic Theory for Integrated Broadband Networks*. Boston, MA: Kluwer, 1990.

[43] F. P. Kelly, "Notes on effective bandwidth," in *Stochastic Networks Theory and Applications*, F. P. Kelly, S. Zachary, and I. Ziedins, Eds. Oxford, U.K.: Science, 1996, pp. 141–168.

[44] A. Shwartz and A. Weiss, *Large Deviations for Performance Analysis, Queues, Communication and Computing*. London, U.K.: Chapman & Hall, 1995.

[45] D. D. Botvich and N. Duffield, "Large deviations, the shape of the loss curve, and economies of scale in large multiplexers," *Queuing Syst.*, vol. 20, pp. 293–320, 1995.

[46] A. Simonian and J. Guibert, "Large deviations approximations for fluid queues fed by a large number of on/off sources," *IEEE J. Select. Areas Commun.*, vol. 13, pp. 1017–1027, Aug. 1995

[47] C. Courcoubetis and R. Weber, "Buffer overflow asymptotics for a switch handling many traffic sources," *J. Appl. Prob.*, vol. 33, no. 3, pp. 886–903, 1996.

[48] B. K. Ryu and A. Elwalid, "The importance of long-range dependence of VBR traffic engineering: Myths and realities," in *Proc. ACM SIGCOMM*, Aug. 1996, pp. 3–14.

[49] G. de Veciana, G. Kesidis, and J. Walrand, "Resource management in wide-area ATM networks using effective bandwidths," *IEEE J. Select. Areas Commun.*, vol. 13, pp. 1081–1090, Aug. 1995.

[50] C. S. Chang, "Stability, queue length, and delay of deterministic and stochastic queuing networks," *IEEE Trans. Automat. Contr.*, vol. 39, pp. 913–931, May 1994.

[51] J. Y. Hui and E. Karasan, "A thermodynamic theory of broadband networks with application to dynamic routing," *IEEE J. Select. Areas Commun.*, vol. 13, pp. 991–1003, Aug. 1995.

[52] R. L. Cruz, "A calculus for network delay, part I: Network elements in isolation," *IEEE Trans. Inform. Theory,* vol. 37, pp. 114–131, Jan. 1991.

[53] ———, "A calculus for network delay, part II: Network analysis," *IEEE Trans. Inform. Theory*, vol. 37, pp. 132–141, Jan. 1991.

[54] A. K. Parekh and R. G. Gallager, "A generalized processor sharing approach to flow control in integrated services networks: The single node case," *IEEE/ACM Trans. Networking*, vol. 1, pp. 344–357, June 1993.

[55] ———, "A generalized processor sharing approach to flow control in integrated services networks: The multiple-node case," in *IEEE INFOCOM'93* (San Francisco, CA, Mar. 1993), pp. 521–530.

[56] R. L. Cruz, "Service burstiness and dynamic burstiness measures: A framework," *J. High Speed Networks*, vol. 1, no. 2, pp. 105–127, 1992.

[57] G. L. Georgiadis, R. Guérin, V. Peris, and K. N. Sivrajan, "Efficient network QOS provisioning based on per node traffic shaping," *IEEE/ACM Trans. Networking*, vol. 4, pp. 482–501, Aug. 1996.

[58] T. Weller and B. Hajek, "Scheduling nonuniform traffic in a packet switching system with small propagation delay," *IEEE/ACM Trans. Networking*, vol. 5, pp. 813–823, Dec. 1997.

[59] A. Elwalid, D. Mitra, and R. H. Wentworth, "A new approach for allocating buffers and bandwidth to heterogeneous, regulated traffic in an ATM node," *IEEE J. Select. Areas Commun.*, vol. 13, pp. 1115–1127, Aug. 1995.

[60] *IEEE Trans. Information Theory* (Special Issue on Random-Access Communications), vol. IT-31, Mar. 1985.

[61] R. Metcalfe, "Steady state analysis of a slotted and controlled Aloha system with blocking," in *Proc. 6th Hawaii Conf. System Science* (Honolulu, HI, 1973).

[62] S. Lam and L. Kleinrock, "Packet switching in a multi access broadcast channel: Dynamic control procedures," *IEEE Trans. Commun.*, vol. COM-23, pp. 891–904, 1975.

[63] B. Hajek and T. Van Loon, "Decentralized dynamic control of a multi access broadcast channel," *IEEE Trans. Automat. Contr.*, vol. AC-27, pp. 559–569, 1982.

[64] V. A. Mikhailov, "Geometrical analysis of the stability of Markov chains in R^n and its application to throughput evaluation of the adaptive random multiple access algorithm," *Probl. Inform. Transm.*, vol. 24, pp. 47–56, Jan.–Mar. 1988.

[65] R. Rivest, "Network control by Bayesian broadcast," *IEEE Trans. Inform. Theory*, vol. IT-33, pp. 323–328, May 1987.

[66] L. Kleinrock and F. A. Tobagi, "Packet switching in radio channels: Part 1: CSMA mode and their throughput-delay characteristics," *IEEE Trans. Commun.*, vol. COM-23, pp. 1400–1416, 1975.

[67] J. I. Capetanakis, "The multiple access broadcast channel: Protocol and capacity considerations," Ph.D. dissertation, Dept. Elec. Eng. Comp. Sci., MIT, Cambridge, MA, 1977; also *IEEE Trans. Inform. Theory*, vol. IT-25, pp. 505–515, Sept. 1979.

[68] B. S. Tsybakov and V. A. Mikhailov, "Free synchronous packet access in a broadcast channel with feedback," *Probl. Pered. Inform.*, vol. 14, no. 4, pp. 32–59, 1978.

[69] J. Hayes, "An adaptive technique for local distribution," *IEEE Trans. Commun.*, vol. COM-26, pp. 1178–1186, 1978; also Bell Telephone Lab. Memo TM-76-3116-1, 1976.

[70] R. G. Gallager, "Conflict resolution in random access broadcast networks," in *Proc. AFOSR Workshop Communication Theory and Applications* (Provincetown, MA, 1978), pp. 74–76.

[71] B. S. Tsybakov and V. A. Mikhailov, "Random multiple access of packets: Part and try algorithms," *Probl. Pered. Inform.*, vol. 16, pp. 65–79, 1980.

[72] J. Moseley and P. Humblet, "A class of efficient contention resolution algorithms for multiple access channels," *IEEE Trans. Commun.*, vol. COM-33, pp. 145–151, 1985.

[73] N. Vvedenskaya and M. S. Pinsker, "Non-optimality of the part-and-try algorithm," in *Abstracts Int. Workshop Convolutional Codes & Multiuser Communication* (Sochi, USSR, 1983), pp. 141–148.

[74] S. Verdú, "Computation of the efficiency of the Moseley Humblet contention resolution algorithm: A simple method," *Proc. IEEE*, vol. 74, pp. 613–614, 1986.

[75] N. Pippenger, "Bounds on the performance of protocols for a multiple access broadcast channel," *IEEE Trans. Inform. Theory*, vol. IT-27, pp. 145–151, Jan. 1981.

[76] V. A. Mikhailov and B. S. Tsybakov, "Upper bound for the capacity of a random multiple access system," *Probl. Pered. Inform.*, vol. 17, pp. 90–95, 1981.

[77] G. Fayolle and R. Iasnogorodski, "Two coupled processors: The reduction to a Riemann–Hilbert problem," *Wahrscheinlichkeitstheorie*, pp. 1–27, 1979.

[78] W. Szpankowski, "Stability conditions for some multiqueue distributed systems: Buffered random access systems," *Adv. Appl. Prob.*, vol. 26, pp. 498–515, 1994.

[79] M. Sidi and A. Segall, "Two interacting queues in packet-radio networks," *IEEE Trans. Commun.*, vol. COM-31, pp. 123–129, 1983.

[80] R. Rao and A. Ephremides, "On the stability of interacting queues in a multiple-access system," *IEEE Trans. Inform. Theory*, vol. 34, pp. 918–930, 1988.

[81] V. Anantharam, "The stability region of the finite-user slotted ALOHA protocol," *IEEE Trans. Inform. Theory*, vol. 37, pp. 535–540, 1991.

[82] W. Luo and A. Ephremides, "Effect of packet lengths and power levels on random access systems," in *Proc. 35th Allerton Conf. Communication, Control, and Computation* (Allerton, IL, 1997).

[83] N. Abramson, "Packet switching with satellites," in *AFIPS Conf. Proc.*, 1973, vol. 42, pp. 695–702.

[84] B. S. Tsybakov and V. A. Mikhailov, "Ergodicity of a slotted ALOHA system," *Probl. Pered. Inform.*, vol. 15, no. 4, pp. 73–87, Oct./Dec. 1979; English translation, *Probl. Inform. Transm.*, vol. 15, no. 4, pp. 301–312, Oct./Dec. 1979.

[85] J. L. Massey and P. Mathys, "The collision channel without feedback," *IEEE Trans. Inform. Theory*, vol. IT-31, pp. 192–204, 1985.

[86] I. E. Teletar and R. G. Gallager, "Combining queuing theory and information theory for multiaccess," *IEEE J. Select. Areas Commun.*, vol. 13, pp. 963–969, Aug. 1995.

[87] Electronic Industries Alliance Std. TIA/EIA/IS-99, "Data service option standard for wideband spread spectrum digital cellular system," July 1995.

[88] L. Roberts, "Aloha packet system with and without slots and capture," ASS Note 8, ARPA, Stanford Res. Inst., June 1972.

[89] R. O. LaMaire, A. Krishna, and M. Zorzi, "Optimization of capture in multiple access radio systems with Rayleigh fading and random power levels," in *Multiaccess, Mobility, and Teletraffic for Personal Communications*, B. Jabbari, P. Godlewski, and X. Lagrange, Eds. Boston, MA: Kluwer, 1996, pp. 321–336.

[90] K. Sayrafianpour and A. Ephremides, "Can spatial separation increase throughput of conflict resolution algorithms?" in *IEEE Int. Symp. Information Theory* (Ulm, Germany, June 1997).

[91] D. N. Tse and S. V. Hanly, "Multiuser demodulation: Effective interference, effective bandwidth, and capacity," in *Proc. 35th Allerton Conf. Communication, Control, and Computing* (Allerton, IL, 1997).

[92] S. V. Hanly, "Congestion measures and capacity constraints in spread spectrum networks," in *Multiaccess, Mobility and Teletraffic for Personal Communications*, B. Jabbari, P. Godlewski, and X. Lagrange, Eds. Boston, MA: Kluwer, 1996, pp. 15–28.

[93] R. Knopp and P. Humblet, "Channel control and multiple access," in *Multiaccess, Mobility, and Teletraffic for Personal Communications*, B. Jabbbari, P. Godlewski, and X. Lagrange, Eds. Boston, MA: Kluwer, 1996, pp. 29–42.

[94] R. G. Gallager and M. Medard, "Bandwidth scaling for fading channels," in *IEEE Int. Symp. Inform. Theory* (Ulm, Germany, June 1997).

[95] A. Ephremides, J. Wieselthier, and D. Baker, "A design concept for reliable mobile radio networks with frequency hopping signaling," *Proc. IEEE*, vol. 75, pp. 56–73, 1987.

[96] A. Ephremides, P. Varaiya, and J. Walrand, "A simple dynamic routing problem," *IEEE Trans. Automat. Contr.*, vol. AC-25, pp. 690–693, 1980.

[97] J. Wieselthier, C. Barnhart, and A. Ephremides, "Ordinal optimization of admission control in wireless multihop integrated networks via standard clock simulation," NRL Tech. Rep. 5521-95-9781, Aug. 1995.

[98] D. N. Tse, "Variable-rate lossy compression and its effects on communication networks," Ph.D. dissertation, LIDS-TH: 2269, MIT, Cambridge, MA, Sept. 1994.

[99] C. E. Shannon, "Memory requirements in a telephone exchange," *Bell Syst. Tech. J.*, vol. 29, pp. 343–349, 1950.

[100] V. E. Beněs, "On rearrangeable three-stage connecting networks," *Bell Syst. Tech. J.*, vol. 41, pp. 1481–1492, 1962.

389

[101] L. A. Bassalygo and M. S. Pinsker, "Complexity of an optimum nonblocking switching network without reconnections," *Probl. Pered. Inform.*; English translation, *Probl. Inform. Transm.*, vol. 9, no. 1, pp. 84–87, 1973.

[102] G. A. Margulis, "Explicit constructions of expanders," *Probl. Pered. Inform.*; English translation, *Probl. Inform. Transm.*, vol. 9, no. 4, pp. 71–80, 1973.

[103] O. Gabber and Z. Galil, "Explicit constructions of linear-sized super-concentrators," *J. Comp. Syst. Sci.*, vol. 22, pp. 407–420, 1981.

[104] N. Pippenger, "Telephone switching networks," in *The Mathematics of Networks*, Stefan A. Burr, Ed., *Proc. Symp. Applied Mathematics*, Amer. Math. Soc., 1982, vol. 25, pp. 101–134.

[105] A. Lubotzky, R. Phillips, and P. Sarnak, "Ramanujan graphs," *Combinatroica*, vol. 8, no. 3, pp. 261–277, 1988.

[106] M. Ajtai, J. Komlos, and E. Szemeredi, "An $O(N \log N)$ sorting network," in *Proc. 15th Annu. ACM Symp. Theory of Computing*, ACM, 1983, pp. 1–9.

[107] M. Sipser and D. A. Spielman, "Expander codes," *IEEE Trans. Inform. Theory*, vol. 42, pp. 1710–1722, 1996

[108] B. Hajek and R. L. Cruz, "On the average delay for routing subject to independent deflections," *IEEE Trans. Inform. Theory*, vol. 39, pp. 84–91, Jan. 1993.

[109] *National Technology Roadmap for Semiconductors*, Semiconductor Industry Association. [Online.] Available URL: www.sematech.org, 1997.

[110] S. Lin and D. J. Costello, *Error Control Coding: Fundamentals and Applications.* Englewood Cliffs, NJ: Prentice-Hall, 1983.

[111] C. E. Shannon, "The wonderful world of feedback," First Shannon Lecture in *IEEE Int. Symp. Information Theory* (Ashkelon, Israel, 1973).

[112] R. G. Gallager, *Information Theory and Reliable Communication.* New York: Wiley, 1968.

Data Compression and Harmonic Analysis

David L. Donoho, Martin Vetterli, *Fellow, IEEE*, R. A. DeVore, and Ingrid Daubechies, *Senior Member, IEEE*

(Invited Paper)

Abstract— In this paper we review some recent interactions between harmonic analysis and data compression. The story goes back of course to Shannon's $R(D)$ theory in the case of Gaussian stationary processes, which says that transforming into a Fourier basis followed by block coding gives an optimal lossy compression technique; practical developments like transform-based image compression have been inspired by this result. In this paper we also discuss connections perhaps less familiar to the Information Theory community, growing out of the field of harmonic analysis. Recent harmonic analysis constructions, such as wavelet transforms and Gabor transforms, are essentially optimal transforms for transform coding in certain settings. Some of these transforms are under consideration for future compression standards.

We discuss some of the lessons of harmonic analysis in this century. Typically, the problems and achievements of this field have involved goals that were not obviously related to practical data compression, and have used a language not immediately accessible to outsiders. Nevertheless, through an extensive generalization of what Shannon called the "sampling theorem," harmonic analysis has succeeded in developing new forms of functional representation which turn out to have significant data compression interpretations. We explain why harmonic analysis has interacted with data compression, and we describe some interesting recent ideas in the field that may affect data compression in the future.

Index Terms— Besov spaces, block coding, cosine packets, ϵ-entropy, Fourier transform, Gabor transform, Gaussian process, Karhunen–Loève transform, Littlewood–Paley theory, non-Gaussian process, n-widths, rate-distortion, sampling theorem, scalar quantization, second-order statistics, Sobolev spaces, subband coding, transform coding, wavelet packets, wavelet transform, Wilson bases.

"Like the vague sighings of a wind at even
That wakes the wavelets of the slumbering sea."

Shelley, 1813

Manuscript received June 1, 1998; revised July 6, 1998. The work of D. L. Donoho was supported in part by NSF under Grant DMS-95-05151, by AFOSR under Grant MURI-95-F49620-96-1-0028, and by other sponsors. The work of M. Vetterli was supported in part by NSF under Grant MIP-93-213002 and by the Swiss NSF under Grant 20-52347.97. The work of R. A. DeVore was supported by ONR under Contract N0014-91-J1343 and by Army Research Office under Contract N00014-97-0806. The work of I. Daubechies was supported in part by NSF under Grant DMS-9706753, by AFOSR under Grant F49620-98-1-0044, and by ONR under Contract N00014-96-1-0367.

D. L. Donoho is with Stanford University, Stanford, CA USA 94205.

M. Vetterli is with the Communication Systems Division, the Swiss Federal Institute of Technology, CH-1015 Lausanne, Switzerland, and with the Department of Electrical Engineering and Computer Science, University of California, Berkeley, CA 94720 USA.

R. A. DeVore is with the Department of Mathematics, University of South Carolina, Columbia, SC 29208 USA.

I. Daubechies is with the Department of Mathematics, Princeton University, Princeton, NJ 08544 USA.

Publisher Item Identifier S 0018-9448(98)07005-9.

"ASBOKQTJEL"

Postcard from J. E. Littlewood to A. S. Besicovich, announcing A. S. B.'s election to fellowship at Trinity

"... the 20 bits per second which, the psychologists assure us, the human eye is capable of taking in, ..."

D. Gabor, Guest Editorial, *IRE Trans. Inform Theory*, Sept. 1959.

I. INTRODUCTION

DATA compression is an ancient activity; abbreviation and other devices for shortening the length of transmitted messages have no doubt been used in every human society. Language itself is organized to minimize message length, short words being more frequently used than long ones, according to Zipf's empirical distribution.

Before Shannon, however, the activity of data compression was informal and *ad hoc*; Shannon created a formal intellectual discipline for both lossless and lossy compression, whose 50th anniversary we now celebrate.

A remarkable outcome of Shannon's formalization of problems of data compression has been the intrusion of sophisticated theoretical ideas into widespread use. The JPEG standard, set in the 1980's and now in use for transmitting and storing images worldwide, makes use of quantization, run-length coding, entropy coding, and fast cosine transformation. In the meantime, software and hardware capabilities have developed rapidly, so that standards currently in process of development are even more ambitious. The proposed standard for still image compression—JPEG-2000—contains the possibility for conforming codecs to use trellis-coded quantizers, arithmetic coders, and fast wavelet transforms.

For the authors of this paper, one of the very striking features of recent developments in data compression has been the applicability of ideas taken from the field of harmonic analysis to both the theory and practice of data compression. Examples of this applicability include the appearance of the fast cosine transform in the JPEG standard and the consideration of the fast wavelet transform for the JPEG-2000 standard. These fast transforms were originally developed in applied mathematics for reasons completely unrelated to the demands of data compression; only later were applications in compression proposed.

John Tukey became interested in the possibility of accelerating Fourier transforms in the early 1960's in order to enable spectral analysis of long time series; in spite of the fact that Tukey coined the word "bit," there was no idea in his mind at the time of applications to data compression. Similarly, the construction of smooth wavelets of compact support was prompted by questions posed implicitly or explicitly by the multiresolution analysis concept of Mallat and Meyer, and not, at that time, by direct applications to compression.

In asking about this phenomenon—the applicability of computational harmonic analysis to data compression—there are, broadly speaking, two extreme positions to take.

The first, *maximalist* position holds that there is a deep reason for the interaction of these disciplines, which can be explained by appeal to information theory itself. This point of view holds that sinusoids and wavelets will necessarily be of interest in data compression because they have a special "optimal" role in the representation of certain stochastic processes.

The second, *minimalist* position holds that, in fact, computational harmonic analysis has exerted an influence on data compression merely by happenstance. This point of view holds that there is no fundamental connection between, say, wavelets and sinusoids, and the structure of digitally acquired data to be compressed. Instead, such schemes of representation are privileged to have fast transforms, and to be well known, to have been well studied and widely implemented at the moment that standards were being framed.

When one considers possible directions that data compression might take over the next fifty years, the two points of view lead to very different predictions. The maximalist position would predict that there will be continuing interactions between ideas in harmonic analysis and data compression; that as new representations are developed in computational harmonic analysis, these will typically have applications to data compression practice. The minimalist position would predict that there will probably be little interaction between the two areas in the future, or that what interaction does take place will be sporadic and opportunistic.

In this paper, we would like to give the reader the background to appreciate the issues involved in evaluating the two positions, and to enable the reader to form his/her own evaluation. We will review some of the connections that have existed classically between methods of harmonic analysis and data compression, we will describe the disciplines of theoretical and computational harmonic analysis, and we will describe some of the questions that drive those fields.

We think there is a "Grand Challenge" facing the disciplines of both theoretical and practical data compression in the future: the challenge of dealing with the particularity of naturally occurring phenomena. This challenge has three facets:

GC1 Obtaining accurate models of naturally occurring sources of data.

GC2 Obtaining "optimal representations" of such models.

GC3 Rapidly computing such "optimal representations."

We argue below that current compression methods might be far away from the ultimate limits imposed by the underlying structure of specific data sources, such as images or acoustic phenomena, and that efforts to do better than what is done today—particularly in specific applications areas—are likely to pay off.

Moreover, parsimonious representation of data is a fundamental problem with implications reaching well beyond compression. Understanding the compression problem for a given data type means an intimate knowledge of the modeling and approximation of that data type. This in turn can be useful for many other important tasks, including classification, denoising, interpolation, and segmentation.

The discipline of harmonic analysis can provide interesting insights in connection with the Grand Challenge.

The history of theoretical harmonic analysis in this century repeatedly provides evidence that in attacking certain challenging and important problems involving characterization of infinite-dimensional classes of functions, one can make progress by developing new functional representations based on certain geometric analogies, and by validating that those analogies hold in a quantitative sense, through a norm equivalence result. Also, the history of computational harmonic analysis has repeatedly been that geometrically motivated analogies constructed in theoretical harmonic analysis have often led to fast concrete computational algorithms.

The successes of theoretical harmonic analysis are interesting from a data compression perspective. What the harmonic analysts have been doing—showing that certain orthobases afford certain norm equivalences—is analogous to the classical activity of showing that a certain orthobasis diagonalizes a quadratic form. Of course, the diagonalization of quadratic forms is of lasting significance for data compression in connection with transform coding of Gaussian processes. So one could expect the new concept to be interesting *a priori*. In fact, the new concept of "diagonalization" obtained by harmonic analysts really does correspond to transform coders—for example, wavelet coders and Gabor coders.

The question of whether the next 50 years will display interactions between data compression and harmonic analysis more like a maximalist or a minimalist profile is, of course, anyone's guess. This paper provides encouragement to those taking the maximalist position.

The paper is organized as follows. At first, classical results from rate-distortion theory of Gaussian processes are reviewed and interpreted (Sections II and III). In Section IV, we develop the functional point of view, which is the setting for harmonic analysis results relevant to compression, but which is somewhat at variance with the digital signal processing viewpoint. In Section V, the important concept of Kolmogorov ϵ-entropy of function classes is reviewed, as an alternate approach to a theory of compression. In Section VI, practical transform coding as used in image compression standards is described. We are now in a position to show commonalities between the approaches seen so far (Section VII), and then to discuss limitations of classical models (Section VIII) and propose some variants by way of simple examples. This leads to pose the "Grand Challenges" to data compression as seen from our perspective (Section IX), and to overview how Harmonic Analysis might participate in their solutions. This leads to a survey of Harmonic Analysis results, in particular on norm equivalences (Sections XI–XIII) and nonlinear approximation (Section XIV). In effect, one can show that harmonic analysis, which is effective at establishing norm

392

equivalences, leads to coders which achieve the ϵ-entropy of functional classes (Section XV). This has a transform coding interpretation (Section XVI), showing a broad analogy between the deterministic concept of unconditional basis and the stochastic concept of Karhunen–Loève expansion. In Section XVII, we discuss the role of tree-based ideas in harmonic analysis, and the relevance for data compression. Section XVIII briefly surveys some harmonic analysis results on time–frequency-based methods of data compression. The fact that many recent results from theoretical harmonic analysis have computationally effective counterparts is described in Section XIX. Practical coding schemes using or having led to some of the ideas described thus far are described in Section XX, including current advanced image compression algorithms based on fast wavelet transforms. As a conclusion, a few key contributors in harmonic analysis are used to iconify certain key themes of this paper.

II. $R(D)$ for Gaussian Processes

Fifty years ago, Claude Shannon launched the subject of lossy data compression of continuous-valued stochastic processes [83]. He proposed a general idea, the rate-distortion function, which in concrete cases (Gaussian processes) leads to a beautifully intuitive method to determine the number of bits required to approximately represent sample paths of a stochastic process.

Here is a simple outgrowth of the Shannon theory, important for comparison with what follows. Suppose $X(t)$ is a Gaussian zero-mean stochastic process on an interval T and let $N(D, X)$ denote the minimal number of codewords needed in a codebook $\mathcal{C} = \{X'\}$ so that

$$E \min_{X' \in \mathcal{C}} \|X - X'\|^2_{L^2(T)} \leq D. \tag{2.1}$$

Then Shannon proposed that in an asymptotic sense

$$\log N(D, X) \approx R(D, X) \tag{2.2}$$

where $R(D, X)$ is the rate-distortion function for X

$$R(D, X) = \inf \{I(X, Y) \colon E\|X - Y\|^2_{L^2(T)} \leq D\} \tag{2.3}$$

with $I(X, Y)$ the usual mutual information, given formally by

$$I(X, Y) = \int p(x, y) \log \frac{p(x, y)}{p(x)p(y)} \, dx \, dy. \tag{2.4}$$

Here $R(D, X)$ can be obtained in parametric form from a formula which involves functionals of the covariance kernel $K(s, t) = \text{Cov}(X(t), X(s))$; more specifically of the eigenvalues (λ_k). In the form first published by Kolmogorov (1956), but probably known earlier to Shannon, for $\theta > 0$ we have

$$R(D_\theta) = \sum_{k, \lambda_k > \theta} \log(\lambda_k / \theta) \tag{2.5}$$

where

$$D_\theta = \sum_k \min(\theta, \lambda_k). \tag{2.6}$$

The random process Y^* achieving the minimum of the mutual information problem can be described as follows. It has a covariance with the same eigenfunctions as that of X, but the eigenvalues are reduced in size:

$$\mu_k = (\lambda_k - \theta)_+.$$

To obtain a codebook achieving the value predicted by $R(D, X)$, Shannon's suggestion would be to sample realizations from the reproducing process Y^* realizing the minimum of the least mutual information problem.

Formally, then, the structure of the optimal data compression problem is understood by passing to the Karhunen–Loève expansion

$$X(t) = \sum_k \sqrt{\lambda_k} Z_k \phi_k(t).$$

In this expansion, the coefficients are independent zero-mean Gaussian random variables. We have a similar expansion for the reproducing distribution

$$Y^*(t) = \sum_k \sqrt{\mu_k} \tilde{Z}_k \phi_k(t).$$

The process Y^* has only finitely many nonzero coefficients, namely, those coefficients at indices k where $\lambda_k > \theta$; let $K(D)$ denote the indicated subset of coefficients. Random codebook compression is effected by comparing the vector of coefficients $(\langle X, \phi_k \rangle \colon k \in K(D))$ with a sequence of codewords $(\sqrt{\mu_k} \tilde{Z}_{k,i} \colon k \in K(D))$, for $i = 1, \cdots, N$, looking for a closest match in Euclidean distance. The approach just outlined is often called "reverse waterfilling," since only coefficients above a certain water level are described in the coding process.

As an example, let $T = [0, 1)$ and let $X(t)$ be the Brownian Bridge, i.e., the continuous Gaussian process with covariance $K(s, t) = \min(s, t) - st$. This Gaussian process has $X(0) = X(1) = 0$ and can be obtained by taking a Brownian motion $B(t)$ and "pinning" it down at 1: $X(t) = B(t) - tB(1)$. The covariance kernel has sinusoids for eigenvectors: $\phi_k(t) = \sin(2\pi kt)$, and has eigenvalues $\lambda_k = (4\pi^2 k^2)^{-1}$. The subset $K(D)$ amounts to a frequency band of the first $\#K(D) \asymp D^{-1}$ frequencies as $D \to 0$. (Here and below, we use $A \asymp B$ to mean that the two expressions are equivalent to within multiplicative constants, at least as the underlying argument tends to its limit.) Hence the compression scheme amounts to "going into the frequency domain," "extracting the low frequency coefficients," and "comparing with codebook entries." The number of low frequency coefficients to keep is directly related to the desired distortion level. The achieved $R(D, X)$ in this case scales as $R(D, X) \asymp D^{-1}$.

Another important family of examples is given by stationary processes. In this case, the eigenfunctions of the covariance are essentially sinusoids, and the Karhunen–Loève expansion has a more concrete interpretation. To make things simple and analytically exact, suppose we are dealing with the circle $T = [0, 2\pi)$, and considering stationarity with respect to circular shifts. The stationarity condition is $K(s, t) = \gamma(s -_\circ t)$, where $s -_\circ t$ denotes circular (clock) arithmetic. The eigenfunctions of K are the sinusoids

$$\phi_1(t) = 1/\sqrt{2\pi}$$
$$\phi_{2k}(t) = \cos(kt)/\sqrt{\pi}$$
$$\phi_{2k+1}(t) = \sin(kt)/\sqrt{\pi}$$

and the eigenvalues λ_k are the Fourier coefficients of γ

$$\lambda_k = \int_0^{2\pi} \gamma(t)\phi_k(t)\,dt.$$

We can now identify the index k with frequency, and the Karhunen–Loève representation effectively says that the Fourier coefficients of X are independently zero-mean Gaussian, with variances λ_k, and that the reproducing process Y^* has Fourier coefficients which are independent Gaussian coefficients with variances μ_k. For instance, consider the case $\lambda_k \sim Ck^{-2m}$ as $k \to \infty$; then the stationary process has nearly $(m - 1/2)$-derivatives in a mean-square sense. For this example, the band $K(D)$ amounts to the first $\#K(D) \asymp D^{-1/(2m-1)}$ frequencies. Hence once again the compression scheme amounts to "going into the frequency domain," "extracting the low frequency coefficients," and "comparing with codebook entries," and the number of low frequency coefficients retained is given by the desired distortion level. The achieved $R(D, X)$ in this case scales as $R(D, X) \asymp D^{-1/(2m-1)}$.

III. Interpretations of $R(D)$

The compression scheme described by the solution of $R(D)$ in the Gaussian case has several distinguishing features.

- *Transform Coding Interpretation:* Undoubtedly the most important thing to read off from the solution is that *data compression can be factored into two components: a transform step followed by a coding step*. The transform step takes continuous data and yields discrete sequence data; the coding step takes an initial segment of this sequence and compares it with a codebook, storing the binary representation of the best matching codeword.

- *Independence of the Transformed Data:* The transform step yields uncorrelated Gaussian data, hence *stochastically independent* data, which are, after normalization by factors $1/\sqrt{\lambda_k}$, identically distributed. Hence, the apparently abstract problem of coding a process $X(t)$ becomes closely related to the concrete problem of coding a Gaussian memoryless source, under weighted distortion measure.

- *Manageable Structure of the Transform:* The transform itself is mathematically well-structured. It amounts to expanding the object X in the orthogonal eigenbasis associated with a self-adjoint operator, which at the abstract level is a well-understood notion. In certain important concrete cases, such as the examples we have given above, the basis even reduces to a well-known Fourier basis, and so optimal coding involves explicitly *harmonic analysis* of the data to be encoded.

There are two universality aspects we also find remarkable:

- *Universality Across Distortion Level:* The structure of the ideal compression system does not depend on the distortion level; the same transform and coder structure are employed, but details of the "useful components" $K(D)$ change.

- *Universality Across Stationary Processes:* Large classes of Gaussian processes will share approximately the same coder structure, since there are large classes of covariance kernels with the same eigenstructure. For example, all stationary covariances on the circle have the same eigenfunctions, and so, there is a single "universal" transform that is appropriate for transform coding of all such processes—the Fourier transform.

At a higher level of abstraction, we remark on two further aspects of the solution.

- *Dependence on Statistical Characterization:* To the extent that the orthogonal transform is not universal, it nevertheless depends on the statistical characterization of the process in an easily understandable way—via the eigenstructure of the covariance kernel of the process.

- *Optimality of the Basis:* Since the orthobasis underlying the transform step is the Karhunen–Loève expansion, it has an optimality interpretation independently from its coding interpretation; in an appropriate ordering of the basis elements, partial reconstruction from the first K components gives the best mean-squared approximation to the process available from any orthobasis.

These features of the $R(D)$ solution are so striking and so memorable, that it is unavoidable to incorporate these interpretations as deep "lessons" imparted by the $R(D)$ calculation. These "lessons," reinforced by examples such as those we describe later, can harden into a "world view," creating expectations affecting data compression work in practical coding.

- *Factorization:* One expects to approach coding problems by compartmentalization: attempting to design a two-step system, with the first step a transform, and the second step a well-understood coder.

- *Optimal Representation:* One expects that the transform associated with an optimal coder will be an expansion in a kind of "optimal basis."

- *Empiricism:* One expects that this basis is associated with the statistical properties of the process and so, in a concrete application, one could approach coding problems empirically. The idea would be to obtain empirical instances of process data, and to accurately model the covariance kernel (dependence structure) of those instances; then one would obtain the corresponding eigenfunctions and eigenvalues, and design an empirically derived near-ideal coding system.

These expectations are inspiring and motivating. Unfortunately, there is really nothing in the Shannon theory which supports the idea that such "naive" expectations will apply outside the narrow setting in which the expectations were formed. If the process data to be compressed are not Gaussian, the $R(D)$ derivation mentioned above does not apply, and one has no right to expect these interpretations to apply.

In fact, depending on one's attraction to pessimism, it would also be possible to entertain completely opposite expectations when venturing outside the Gaussian domain. If we consider the problem of data compression of arbitrary stochastic processes, the following expectations are essentially all that one can apply.

- *Lack of Factorization:* One does not expect to find an ideal coding system for an arbitrary non-Gaussian process that involves transform coding, i.e., a two-part factorization into a transform step followed by a step of coding an independent sequence.

- *Lack of Useful Structure:* In fact, one does not expect to find any intelligible structure whatsoever, in an ideal coding system for an arbitrary non-Gaussian process—beyond the minimal structure on the random codebook imposed by the $R(D)$ problem.

For purely human reasons, it is doubtful, however, that this set of "pessimistic" expectations is very useful as a working hypothesis. The more "naive" picture, taking the $R(D)$ story for Gaussian processes as paradigmatic, leads to the following possibility: *as we consider data compression in a variety of settings outside the strict confines of the original Gaussian $R(D)$ setting, we will discover that many of the expectations formed in that setting still apply and are useful, though perhaps in a form modified to take account of the broader setting.* Thus for example, we might find that factorization of data compression into two steps, one of them an orthogonal transform into a kind of optimal basis, is a property of near-ideal coders that we see outside the Gaussian case; although we might also find that the notion of optimality of the basis and the specific details of the types of bases found would have to change. We might even find that we have to replace "expansion in an optimal basis" by "expansion in an optimal decomposition," moving to a system more general than a basis.

We will see several instances below where the lessons of Gaussian $R(D)$ agree with ideal coders under this type of extended interpretation.

IV. FUNCTIONAL VIEWPOINT

In this paper we have adopted a point of view we call the *functional viewpoint.* Rather than thinking of data to be compressed as numerical arrays x_u with integer index u, we think of the objects of interest as functions—functions $f(t)$ of time or functions of space $f(x, y)$. To use terminology that Shannon would have found natural, we are considering compression of analog signals. This point of view is clearly the one in Shannon's 1948 introduction of the optimization problem underlying $R(D)$ theory, but it is less frequently seen today, since many practical compression systems start with sampled data. Practiced IT researchers will find one aspect of our discussion unnatural: we study the case where the index set T stays fixed. This seems at variance even

with Shannon, who often let the domain of observation grow without bound. The fixed-domain functional viewpoint is essential for developing the themes and theoretical connections we seek to expose in this paper—it is only through this viewpoint that the connections with modern Harmonic analysis become clear. Hence, we pause to explain how this viewpoint can be related to standard information theory and to practical data compression.

A practical motivation for this viewpoint can easily be proposed. In effect, when we are compressing acoustic or image phenomena, there is truly an underlying analog representation of the object, and a digitally sampled object is an approximation to it. Consider the question of an appropriate model for data compression of still-photo images. Over time, consumer camera technology will develop so that standard cameras will routinely be able to take photos with several megapixels per image. By and large, consumers using such cameras will not be changing their photographic compositions in response to the increasing quality of their equipment; they will not be expanding their field of view in picture taking, but rather, they will instead keep the field of view constant, and so as cameras improve they will get finer and finer resolution on the same photos they would have taken anyway. So what is increasing asymptotically in this setting is the resolution of the object rather than the field of view. In such a setting, the functional point of view is sensible. There is a continuum image, and our digital data will sooner or later represent a very good approximation to such a continuum observation. Ultimately, cameras will reach a point where the question of how to compress such digital data will best be answered by knowing about the properties of an ideal system derived for continuum data.

The real reason for growing-domain assumptions in information theory is a technical one: it allows in many cases for the proof of source coding theorems, establishing the asymptotic equivalence between the "formal bit rate" $R(D, X)$ and the "rigorous bit rate" $N(D, X)$. In our setting, this connection is obtained by considering asymptotics of both quantities as $D \to 0$. In fact, it is the $D \to 0$ setting that we focus on here, and it is under this assumption that we can show the usefulness of harmonic analysis techniques to data compression.[1] This may seem at first again at variance with Shannon, who considered the distortion fixed (on a per-unit basis) and let the domain of observation grow without bound.

We have two nontechnical responses.

- *The Future:* With the consumer camera example in mind, high-quality compression of very large data sets may soon be of interest. So the functional viewpoint, and low-distortion coding of the data, may be very interesting settings in the near future.

- *Scaling:* In important situations there is a near equivalence between the "growing domain" viewpoint and the "functional viewpoint." We are thinking here of phenomena like natural images which have scaling properties: if we dilate an image, "stretching it out" to live on a growing

---

[1] The $D \to 0$ case is usually called the fine quantization or high-resolution limit in quantization theory; see [48].

domain, then after appropriate rescaling, we get statistical properties that are the same as the original image [37], [81]. The relevance to coding is evident, for example, in the stationary Gaussian $R(D)$ case for the process defined in Section II, which has eigenvalues obeying an asymptotic power law, and hence which asymptotically obeys scale invariance at fine scales. Associated to a given distortion level is a characteristic "cutoff frequency" $\#K(D)$; dually this defines a scale of approximation; to achieve that distortion level it is necessary only to know the Fourier coefficients out to frequency $\#K(D)$, or to know the samples of a bandlimited version of the object out to scale $\approx 2\pi/\#K(D)$. This characteristic scale defines a kind of effective pixel size. As the distortion level decreases, this scale decreases, and one has many more "effective pixels." Equivalently, one could rescale the object as a function of D so that the characteristic scale stays fixed, and then the effective domain of observation would grow.

In addition to these relatively general responses, we have a precise response: $D \to 0$ *allows Source Coding Theorems.* To see this, return to the $R(D)$ setting of Section II, and the stochastic process with asymptotic power law eigenvalues given there. We propose grouping frequencies into subbands $K_b = \{k_b, k_b + 1, \cdots, k_{b+1} - 1\}$. The subband boundaries k_b should be chosen in such a way that they get increasingly long with increasing k but that in a relative sense, measured with respect to distance from the origin, they get increasingly narrow

$$k_{b+1} - k_b \to \infty, \qquad b \to \infty$$
$$(k_{b+1} - k_b)/k_b \to 1, \qquad b \to \infty. \qquad (4.1)$$

The Gaussian $R(D)$ problem of Section II has the structure suggesting that one needs to code the first $K(D)$ coefficients in order to get a near-ideal system. Suppose we do this by dividing the first $K(D)$ Fourier coefficients of X into subband blocks and then code the subband blocks using the appropriate coder for a block from a Gaussian independent and identically distributed (i.i.d.) source.

This makes sense. For the process we are studying, the eigenvalues λ_k decay smoothly according to a power law. The subbands are chosen so that the variances λ_k are roughly constant in subbands

$$\max\{\lambda_k : k \in K_b\}/\min\{\lambda_k : k \in K_b\} \to 1, \qquad b \to \infty. \qquad (4.2)$$

Within subband blocks, we may then reasonably regard the coefficients as independent Gaussian random variables with a common variance. It is this property that would suggest to encode the coefficients in a subband using a coder for an i.i.d. Gaussian source. The problem of coding Gaussian i.i.d. data is among the most well-studied problems in information theory, and so this subband partitioning reduces the abstract problem of coding the process to a very familiar one.

As the distortion D tends to zero, the frequency cutoff $K(D)$ in the underlying $R(D)$ problem tends to infinity,

and so the subband blocks we must code include longer and longer blocks farther and farther out in the frequency domain. These blocks behave more and more nearly like long blocks of Gaussian i.i.d. samples, and can be coded more and more precisely at the rate for a Gaussian source, for example using a random codebook. An increasing fraction of all the bits allocated comes from the long blocks, where the coding is increasingly close to the rate. Hence we get the asymptotic equality of "formal bits" and "rigorous bits" as $D \to 0$.

(Of course in a practical setting, as we will discuss farther below, block coding of i.i.d. Gaussian data, is impractical to "instrument;" there is no known computationally efficient way to code a block of i.i.d. Gaussians approaching the $R(D)$ limit. But in a practical case one can use known suboptimal coders for the i.i.d. problem to code the subband blocks. Note also that such suboptimal coders can perform rather well, especially in the high-rate case, since an entropy-coded uniform scalar quantizer performs within 0.255 bit/sample of the optimum.)

With the above discussion, we hope to have convinced the reader that our functional point of view, although unconventional, will shed some interesting light on at least the high-rate, low-distortion case.

V. THE ϵ-ENTROPY SETTING

In the mid-1950's, A. N. Kolmogorov, who had been recently exposed to Shannon's work, introduced the notion of the ϵ-entropy of a functional class, defined as follows. Let T be a domain, and let $\mathcal{F}$ be a class of functions $(f(t): t \in T)$ on that domain; suppose $\mathcal{F}$ is compact for the norm $|| \cdot ||$, so that there exists an ϵ-net, i.e., a system $\mathcal{N}_\epsilon = \{f'\}$ such that

$$\sup_{f \in \mathcal{F}} \inf_{f' \in \mathcal{N}_\epsilon} ||f - f'|| \le \epsilon. \qquad (5.1)$$

Let $N(\epsilon, \mathcal{F}, || \cdot ||)$ denote the minimal cardinality of all such ϵ-nets. The Kolmogorov ϵ-entropy for $(\mathcal{F}, || \cdot ||)$ is then

$$H_\epsilon(\mathcal{F}, || \cdot ||) = \log_2 N(\epsilon, \mathcal{F}, || \cdot ||). \qquad (5.2)$$

It is the least number of bits required to specify any arbitrary member of $\mathcal{F}$ to within accuracy ϵ. In essence, Kolmogorov proposed a notion of data compression for *classes of functions* while Shannon's theory concerned compression for *stochastic processes*.

There are some formal similarities between the problems addressed by Shannon's $R(D)$ and Kolmogorov's H_ϵ. To make these clear, notice that in each case, we consider a "library of instances"—either a function class $\mathcal{F}$ or a stochastic process X, each case yielding as typical elements functions defined on a common domain T—and we measure approximation error by the same norm $|| \cdot ||$.

In both the Shannon and Kolmogorov theories we encode by first constructing finite lists of representative elements—in one case, the list is called a codebook; in the other case, a net. We represent an object of interest by its closest representative in the list, and we may record simply the index into our list. The length in bits of such a recording is called in the Shannon case the rate of the codebook; in the Kolmogorov case, the entropy of the net. Our goal is to minimize the number of bits while

	Shannon Theory	Kolmogorov Theory
Library	X Stochastic	$f \in \mathcal{F}$
Representers	Codebook $\mathcal{C}$	Net $\mathcal{N}$
Fidelity	$E \min_{X' \in \mathcal{C}} \|X - X'\|^2$	$\max_{f \in \mathcal{F}} \min_{f' \in \mathcal{N}} \|f - f'\|^2$
Complexity	$\log \#\mathcal{C}$	$\log \#\mathcal{N}$

achieving sufficient fidelity of reproduction. In the Shannon theory this is measured by mean discrepancy across random realizations; in the Kolmogorov theory this is measured by the maximum discrepancy across arbitrary members of $\mathcal{F}$. These comparisons may be summarized in the table at the top of this page.

In short, the two theories are parallel—except that one of the theories postulates a library of samples arrived at by sampling a stochastic process, while the other selects arbitrary elements of a functional class.

While there are intriguing parallels between the $R(D)$ and H_ϵ concepts, the two approaches have developed separately, in very different contexts. Work on $R(D)$ has mostly stayed in the original context of communication/storage of random process data, while work with H_ϵ has mostly stayed in the context of questions in mathematical analysis: the Kolmogorov entropy numbers control the boundedness of Gaussian processes [35] and the properties of certain operators [10], [36], of convex sets [78], and of statistical estimators [6], [67].

At the general level which Kolmogorov proposed, almost nothing useful can be said about the structure of an optimal ϵ-net, nor is there any principle like mutual information which could be used to derive a formal expression for the cardinality of the ϵ-net.

However, there is a particularly interesting case in which we can say more. Consider the following typical setting for ϵ-entropy. Let T be the circle $T = [0, 2\pi)$ and let $W_{2,0}^m(\gamma)$ denote the collection of all functions $f = (f(t): t \in T)$ such that $\|f\|_{L^2(T)}^2 + \|f^{(m)}\|_{L^2(T)}^2 \leq \gamma^2$. Such functions are called "differentiable in quadratic mean" or "differentiable in the sense of H. Weyl." For approximating functions of this class in L^2-norm, we have the precise asymptotics of the Kolmogorov ϵ-entropy [34]

$$H_\epsilon(W_{2,0}^m(\gamma)) \sim 2m(\log_2 e)(\gamma/2\epsilon)^{1/m}, \qquad \epsilon \to 0. \quad (5.3)$$

A transform-domain coder can achieve this H_ϵ asymptotic. One divides the frequency domain into subbands K_b, defined exactly as in (4.1) and (4.2). Then one takes the Fourier coefficients θ_k of the object f, obtaining blocks of coefficients $\theta^{(b)}$. Treating these coefficients now as if they were arbitrary members of spheres of radius $\rho_b = \|\theta^{(b)}\|$, one encodes the coefficients using an ϵ_b-net for the sphere of radius ρ_b. One represents the object θ by concatenating a prefix code together with the code for the individual subbands. The prefix code records digital approximations to the (ϵ_b, ρ_b) pairs for subbands, and requires asymptotically a small number of bits. The body code simply concatenates the codes for each of the individual subbands. With the right fidelity allocation—i.e.,

choice of ϵ_b—the resulting code has a length described by the right side of (5.3).

VI. THE JPEG SETTING

We now discuss the emergence of transform coding ideas in practical coders. The discrete-time setting of practical coders makes it expedient to abandon the functional point of view throughout this section, in favor of a viewpoint based on sampled data.

A. History

Transform coding plays an important role for images and audio compression where several successful standards incorporate linear transforms. The success and wide acceptance of transform coding in practice is due to a combination of factors. The Karhunen–Loève transform and its optimality under some (restrictive) conditions form a theoretical basis for transform coding. The wide use of particular transforms like the discrete cosine transform (DCT) led to a large body of experience, including design of quantizers with human perceptual criteria. But most importantly, transform coding using a unitary matrix having a fast algorithm represents an excellent compromise in terms of computational complexity versus coding performance. That is, for a given cost (number of operations, run time, silicon area), transform coding outperforms more sophisticated schemes by a margin.

The idea of compressing stochastic processes using a linear transformation dates back to the 1950's [63], when signals originating from a vocoder were shown to be compressible by a transformation made up of the eigenvectors of the correlation matrix. This is probably the earliest use of the Karhunen–Loève transform (KLT) in data compression. Then, in 1963, Huang and Schultheiss [55] did a detailed analysis of block quantization of random variables, including bit allocation. This forms the foundation of transform coding as used in signal compression practice. The approximation of the KLT by trigonometric transforms, especially structured transforms allowing a fast algorithm, was done by a number of authors, leading to the proposal of the discrete cosine transform in 1974 [1]. The combination of discrete cosine transform, scalar quantization, and entropy coding was studied in detail for image compression, and then standardized in the late 1980's by the joint picture experts group (JPEG), leading to the JPEG image compression standard that is now widely used. In the meantime, another generation of image coders, mostly based on wavelet decompositions and elaborate quantization and entropy coding, are being considered for the next standard, called JPEG-2000.

B. The Standard Model and the Karhunen–Loève Transform

The structural facts described in Section II, concerning $R(D)$ for Gaussian random processes, become very simple in the case of Gaussian random vectors. Compression of a vector of correlated Gaussian random variables factors into a linear transform followed by independent compression of the transform coefficients.

Consider $\boldsymbol{X} = [X_0 X_1 \cdots X_{N-1}]^T$, a size N vector of zero mean random variables and $\boldsymbol{Y} = [Y_0 Y_1 \cdots Y_{N-1}]^T$ the vector of random variables after transformation by $\boldsymbol{T}$, or $\boldsymbol{Y} = \boldsymbol{T} \cdot \boldsymbol{X}$. Define $\boldsymbol{R_X} = E[\boldsymbol{XX}^T]$ and $\boldsymbol{R_Y} = E[\boldsymbol{YY}^T]$ as autocovariance matrices of $\boldsymbol{X}$ and $\boldsymbol{Y}$, respectively. Since $\boldsymbol{R_X}$ is symmetric and positive-semidefinite, there is a full set of orthogonal eigenvectors with nonnegative eigenvalues. The Karhunen–Loève transform matrix $\boldsymbol{T}_{\mathrm{KL}}$ is defined as the matrix of unit-norm eigenvectors of $\boldsymbol{R_X}$ ordered in terms of decreasing eigenvalues, that is,

$$\boldsymbol{R_X}\boldsymbol{T}_{\mathrm{KL}} = \boldsymbol{T}_{\mathrm{KL}}\boldsymbol{\Lambda}, \qquad \boldsymbol{\Lambda} = \mathrm{diag}\,(\lambda_0, \lambda_1, \cdots, \lambda_{N-1})$$

where $\lambda_i \geq \lambda_j \geq 0, i < j$ (for simplicity, we will assume that $\lambda_i > 0$). Clearly, transforming X with $\boldsymbol{T}_{\mathrm{KL}}^T$ will diagonalize $\boldsymbol{R_Y}$

$$\boldsymbol{R_Y} = E[\boldsymbol{T}_{\mathrm{KL}}^T \boldsymbol{XX}^T \boldsymbol{T}_{\mathrm{KL}}] = \boldsymbol{T}_{\mathrm{KL}}^T \boldsymbol{R_X} \boldsymbol{T}_{\mathrm{KL}} = \boldsymbol{\Lambda}.$$

The KLT satisfies a best linear approximation property in the mean-squared error sense which follows from the eigenvector choices in the transform. That is, if only a fixed subset of the transform coefficients are kept, then the best transform is the KLT.

The importance of the KLT for compression comes from the following standard result from source coding [46]. A size-N Gaussian vector source $\boldsymbol{X}$ with correlation matrix $\boldsymbol{R_X}$ and mean zero is to be coded with a linear transform. Bits are allocated optimally to the transform coefficients (using reverse waterfilling). Then the transform that minimizes the MSE in the limit of fine quantization of the transform coefficients is the Karhunen–Loève transform $\boldsymbol{T}_{\mathrm{KL}}$. The coding gain due to optimal transform coding over straight PCM coding is

$$\frac{D_{\mathrm{PCM}}}{D_{\mathrm{KLT}}} = \frac{\sigma_x^2}{\left(\prod_{i=0}^{N-1}\sigma_i^2\right)^{1/N}} = \frac{1/N\sum_{i=0}^{N-1}\sigma_i^2}{\left(\prod_{i=0}^{N-1}\sigma_i^2\right)^{1/N}} \qquad (6.1)$$

where we used $N \cdot \sigma_x^2 = \Sigma \sigma_i^2$. Recalling that the variances σ_i^2 are the eigenvalues of $\boldsymbol{R_X}$, it follows that the coding gain is the ratio of the arithmetic and geometric means of the eigenvalues of the autocorrelation matrix.

Using reverse waterfilling, the above construction can be used to derive the $R(D)$ function of i.i.d. Gaussian vectors [19]. However, an important point is that in a practical setting and for complexity reasons, only scalar quantization is used on the transform coefficients (see Fig. 1). The high rate scalar distortion rate function (with entropy coding) for i.i.d. Gaussian samples of variance σ^2 is given by $D_s(R) = (\pi e)/6 \cdot \sigma^2 \cdot 2^{-2R}$ while the Shannon distortion rate function

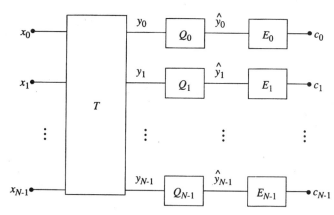

Fig. 1.   Transform coding system, where T is a unitary transform, Q_i are scalar quantizers, and E_i are entropy coders.

is $D(R) = \sigma^2 \cdot 2^{-2R}$ (using block coding). This means that a penalty of about a quarter bit per sample is paid, a small price at high rates or small distortions.

C. The Discrete Cosine Transform

To make the KLT approach to block coding operational requires additional steps. Two problems need to be addressed: the signal dependence of the KLT (finding eigenvectors of the correlation matrix), and the complexity of computing the KLT (N^2 operations). Thus fast fixed transforms (with about $N \log N$ operations) leading to approximate diagonalization of correlation matrices are used. The most popular among these transforms is the discrete cosine transform, which has the property that it diagonalizes approximately the correlation matrix of a first-order Gauss–Markov process with high correlation ($\rho \rightarrow 1$), and also the correlation matrix of an arbitrary Gauss–Markov process (with correlation of sufficient decay, $\Sigma_{k=0}^{\infty} kr^2(k) < \infty$) and block sizes $N \rightarrow \infty$. The DCT is closely related to the discrete Fourier transform, and thus can be computed with a fast Fourier transform like algorithm in $N \log N$ operations. This is a key issue: the DCT achieves a good compromise between coding gain or compression, and computational complexity. Therefore, for a given computational budget, it can actually outperform the KLT [49].

VII. THE COMMON GAUSSIAN MODEL

At this point we have looked at three different settings in which we can interpret the phrase "data compression." In each case *we have available a library of instances which we would like to represent with few bits.*

- a) In Section II (on $R(D)$ theory) we are considering the instances to be realizations of Gaussian processes. The library is the collection of all such realizations.

- b) In Section V (on ϵ-entropy) we are considering the instances to be smooth functions. The library $\mathcal{F}$ is the collection of such smooth functions obeying the constraint $\|f\|_{L^2(T)}^2 + \|f^{(m)}\|_{L^2(T)}^2 \leq \gamma^2$.

398

c) In Section VI (on JPEG), we are considering the instances to be existing or future digital images. The library is implicitly the collection of all images of potential interest to the JPEG user population.

We can see a clear similarity in the coding strategy used in each setting.

- Transform into the frequency domain.
- Break the transform into homogeneous subbands.
- Apply simple coding schemes to the subbands.

Why the common strategy of transform coding?

The theoretically tightest motivation for transform coding comes from Shannon's $R(D)$ theory, which tells us that in order to best encode a Gaussian process, one should transform the process realization to the Karhunen–Loève domain, where the resulting coordinates are independent random variables. This sequence of independent Gaussian variables can be coded by traditional schemes for coding discrete memoryless sources.

So when we use transform coding in another setting—ϵ-entropy or JPEG—it appears that we are *behaving as if that setting could be modeled by a Gaussian process.*

In fact, it is sometimes said that the JPEG scheme is appropriate for real image data because if image data were first-order Gauss–Markov, then the DCT would be approximately the Karhunen–Loève transform, and so JPEG would be approximately following the script of the $R(D)$ story. Implicitly, the next statement is "and real image data behave something like first-order Gauss–Markov."

What about ϵ-entropy? In that setting there is no obvious "randomness," so it would seem unclear how a connection with Gaussian processes could arise. In fact, a proof of (5.3) can be developed by exhibiting just such a connection [34]; one can show that there are Gaussian random functions whose sample realizations obey, with high probability, the constraint $\|f\|^2_{L^2(T)} + \|f^{(m)}\|^2_{L^2(T)} \leq \gamma^2$ and for which the $R(D)$ theory of Shannon accurately matches the number of bits required, in the Kolmogorov theory, to represent f within a distortion level ϵ^2 (i.e., the right side of (5.3)). The Gaussian process with this property is a process naturally associated with the class $\mathcal{F}$ obeying the indicated smoothness constraint—the least favorable process for Shannon data-compression; a successful Kolmogorov-net for the process $\mathcal{F}$ will be effectively a successful Shannon codebook for the least favorable process. So even in the Kolmogorov case, transform coding can be motivated by recourse to $R(D)$ theory for Gaussian processes, and to the idea that the situation can be modeled as a Gaussian one. (That a method derived from Gaussian assumptions helps us in other cases may seem curious. This is linked to the fact that the Gaussian appears as a worst case scenario. Handling the worst case well will often lead to adequate if not optimal performance for more favorable cases.)

VIII. GETTING THE MODEL RIGHT

We have so far considered only a few settings in which data compression could be of interest. In the context of $R(D)$ theory, we could be interested in complex non-Gaussian processes; in H_ϵ theory we could be interested in functional classes defined by norms other than those based on L^2; in image coding we could be interested in particular image compression tasks, say specialized to medical imagery, or to satellite imagery.

Certainly, the simple idea of Fourier transform followed by block i.i.d. Gaussian coding cannot be universally appropriate. *As the assumptions about the collection of instances to be represented change,* presumably the corresponding *optimal representation will change.* Hence it is important to explore a range of modeling assumptions and to attempt to get the assumptions right! Although Shannon's ideas have been very important in supporting diffusion of frequency-domain coding in practical lossy compression, we feel that he himself would have been the first to suggest a careful examination of the underlying assumptions, and to urge the formulation of better assumptions. (See, for instance, his adhortations in [85].)

In this section we consider a wider range of models for the libraries of instances to be compressed, and see how alternative representations emerge as useful.

A. Some Non-Gaussian Models

Over the last decade, studies of the statistics of natural images have repeatedly shown the non-Gaussian character of image data. While images make up only one application area for data compression, the evidence is quite interesting.

Empirical studies of wavelet transforms of images, considering histograms of coefficients falling in a common subband, have uncovered markedly non-Gaussian structure. As noted by many people, subband histograms are consistent with probability densities having the form $C \cdot \exp\{-|u|^\mu\}$, where the exponent "μ" would be "2" if the Gaussian case applied, but where one finds radically different values of "μ" in practice; e.g., Simoncelli [87] reports evidence for $\mu = 0.7$. In fact, such generalized Gaussian models have been long used to model subband coefficients in the compression literature (e.g., [101]). Field [37] investigated the fourth-order cumulant structure of images and showed that it was significantly nonzero. This is far out of line with the Gaussian model, in which all cumulants of order three and higher vanish.

In later work, Field [38] proposed that wavelet transforms of images offered probability distributions which were "sparse." A simple probability density with such a sparse character is the Gaussian scale mixture $(1 - \epsilon)\phi(x/\delta)/\delta + \epsilon\phi(x)$, where ϵ and δ are both small positive numbers; this corresponds to data being of one of two "types:" "small," the vast majority, and "large," the remaining few. It is not hard to understand where the two types come from: a wavelet coefficient can be localized to a small region which contains an edge, or which does not contain an edge. If there is no edge in the region, it will be "small;" if there is an edge, it will be "large."

Stationary Gaussian models are very limited and are unable to duplicate these empirical phenomena. Images are best thought of as spatially stationary stochastic processes, since logically the position of an object in an image is rather arbitrary, and a shift of that object to another position would produce another equally valid image. But if we impose stationarity on a Gaussian process we cannot really exhibit both edges and smooth areas. A stationary Gaussian process must exhibit a great deal of spatial homogeneity. From results in the mean-square calculus we know that if such a process is mean-square-continuous at a point, it is mean-square-continuous at every point. Clearly, most images will not fit this model adequately.

Conditionally Gaussian models offer an attractive way to maintain ties with the Gaussian case while exhibiting globally non-Gaussian behavior. In such models, image formation takes place in two stages. An initial random experiment lays down regions separated by edges, and then in a subsequent stage each region is assigned a Gaussian random field.

Consider a simple model of random piecewise-smooth functions in dimension one, where the piece boundaries are thrown down at random, say by a Poisson process, the pieces are realizations of (different) Gaussian processes (possibly stationary), and discontinuities are allowed across the boundaries of the pieces [12]. This simple one-dimensional model can replicate some of the known empirical structure of images, particularly the sparse histogram structure of wavelet subbands and the nonzero fourth-order cumulant structure.

B. Adaptation, Resource Allocation, and Nonlinearity

Unfortunately, when we leave the domain of Gaussian models, we lose the ability to compute $R(D)$ in such great generality. Instead, we begin to operate heuristically. Suppose, for example, we employ a conditionally Gaussian model. There is no general solution for $R(D)$ for such a class; but it seems reasonable that the two-stage structure of the model gives clues about optimal coding; accordingly, one might suppose that an effective coder should factor into a part that adapts to the apparent segmentation structure of the image and a part that acts in a traditional way conditional on that structure. In the simple model of piecewise-smooth functions in dimension one, it is clear that coding in long blocks is useful for the pieces, and that the coding must be adapted to the characteristics of the pieces. However, discontinuities must be well-represented also. So it seems natural that one attempts to identify an empirically accurate segmentation and then adaptively code the pieces. If transform coding ideas are useful in this setting, it might seem that they would play a role subordinate to the partitioning—i.e., appearing only in the coding of individual pieces. It might seem that applying a single global orthogonal transform to the data is simply not compatible with the assumed two-stage structure.

Actually, transform coding *is* able to offer a degree of adaptation to the presence of a segmentation. The wavelet transform of an object with discontinuities will exhibit large coefficients in the neighborhood of discontinuities, and, at finer scales, will exhibit small coefficients away from discontinuities. If one designs a coder which does well in representing such "sparse" coefficient sequences, it will attempt to represent all the coefficients at coarser scales, while allocating bits to represent only those few big coefficients at finer scales. Implicitly, coefficients at coarser scales represent the structure of pieces, and coefficients at finer scales represent discontinu-

ities between the pieces. The resource allocation is therefore achieving some of the same effect as an explicit two-stage approach.

Hence, adaptivity to the segmentation can come from applying a fixed orthogonal transform together with adaptive resource allocation of the coder. Practical coding experience supports this. Traditional transform coding of i.i.d. Gaussian random vectors at high rate assumes a fixed rate allocation per symbol, but practical coders, because they work at low rate and use entropy coding, typically adapt the coding rate to the characteristics of each block. Specific adaptation mechanisms, using context modeling and implicit or explicit side-information are also possible.

Adaptive resource allocation with a fixed orthogonal transform is closely connected with a mathematical procedure which we will explore at length in Sections XIV and XV: nonlinear approximation using a fixed orthogonal basis. Suppose that we have an orthogonal basis and we wish to approximate an object using only n basis functions. In traditional linear approximation, we would consider using the first-n basis functions to form such an approximation. In nonlinear approximation, we would consider using the best-n basis functions, i.e., to adaptively select the n terms which offer the best approximation to the particular object being considered. This adaptation is a form of resource allocation, where the resources are the n terms to be used. Because of this connection, we will begin to refer to "the nonlinear nature of the approximation process" offered by practical coders.

C. Variations on Stochastic Process Models

To bring home the remarks of the last two subsections, we consider some specific variations on the stochastic process models of Section II. In these variations, we will consider processes that are non-Gaussian; and we will compare useful coding strategies for those processes with the coding strategies for the Gaussian processes having the same second-order statistics.

- *Spike Process.* For this example, we briefly leave the functional viewpoint.

  Consider the following simple discrete-time random process, generating a single "spike." Let $x(n) = \alpha \cdot \delta(n-k)$ where $n, k \in [0, \cdots, N-1]$, k is uniformly distributed between 0 and $N-1$ and α is $N(0, \sigma^2)$. That is, after picking a random location k, one puts a Gaussian random variable at that location. The autocorrelation $\boldsymbol{R_X}$ is equal to $(\sigma^2/N) \cdot \boldsymbol{I}$, thus the KLT is the identity transformation. Allocating R/N bits to each coefficient leads to a distortion of order $2^{-2(R/N)}$ for the single nonzero coefficient. Hence the distortion-rate function describing the operational performance of the Gaussian codebook coder in the KLT domain has

  $$D_{\mathrm{KL}}(R) \approx c \cdot \sigma^2 \cdot 2^{-2(R/N)}.$$

  Here the constant c depends on the quantization and coding of the transform coefficients.

  An obvious alternate scheme at high rates is to spend $\log_2(N)$ bits to address the nonzero coefficient, and use

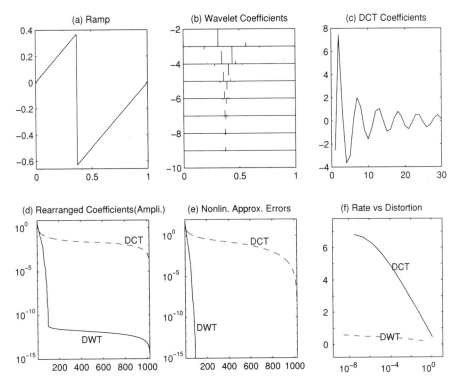

Fig. 2. (a) Realization of *Ramp*. (b) Wavelet and (c) DCT coefficients. (d) Rearranged coefficients. (e) Nonlinear approximation errors (14.2). (f) Operating performance curves of scalar quantization coding.

the remaining $R - \log_2(N)$ bits to represent the Gaussian variable. This *position-indexing* method leads to

$$D_p(R) \approx c \cdot \sigma^2 \cdot 2^{-2(R - \log_2(N))}.$$

This coder relies heavily on the non-Gaussian character of the joint distribution of the entries in $x(n)$, and for $R \gg \log_2(N)$ this non-Gaussian coding clearly outperforms the former, Gaussian approximation method. While this is clearly a very artificial example, it makes the point that if location (or phase) is critical, then time-invariant, linear methods like the KLT followed by independent coding of the transform coefficients are suboptimal.

Images are very phase critical: edges are among the most visually significant features of images, and thus efficient position coding is of essence. So it comes as no surprise that some nonlinear approximation ideas made it into standards, namely, ideas where addressing of large coefficients is efficiently solved.

- *Ramp Process.* Yves Meyer [75] proposed the following model. We have a process $X(t)$ defined on $[0, 1]$ through a single random variable τ uniformly distributed on $[0, 1]$ by

$$X(t) = t - 1_{\{t \geq \tau\}}.$$

This is a very simple process, and very easy to code accurately. A reasonable coding scheme would be to extract τ by locating the jump of the process and then quantizing it to the required fidelity.

On the other hand, *Ramp* is covariance equivalent to the Brownian Bridge process $B_0(t)$ which we mentioned already in Section II, the Gaussian zero-mean process on $[0, 1]$ with covariance $\text{Cov}(B_0(t), B_0(s)) = \min(t, s) - st$.

An asymptotically $R(D)$-optimal approach to coding Brownian Bridge can be based on the Karhunen–Loève transform; as we have seen, in this case the sine transform. One takes the sine transform of the realization, breaks the sequence of coefficients into subbands obeying (4.1) and (4.2) and then treats the coefficients, in subbands, exactly as in discrete memoryless source compression.

Suppose we ignored the non-Gaussian character of the *Ramp* process and simply applied the same coder we would use for Brownian Bridge. After all, the two are covariance-equivalent. This would result in orders of magnitude more bits than necessary. The coefficients in the sine transform of *Ramp* are random; their typical size is measured in mean square by the eigenvalues of the covariance—namely, $\lambda_k = (4\pi^2 k^2)^{-1}$. In order to accurately represent the Ramp process with distortion D, we must code the first $\#K(D) \asymp D^{-1}$ coefficients, at rates exceeding 1 bit per coefficient. How many coefficients does it take to represent a typical realization of *Ramp* with a relative error of 1%? About 10^5.

On the other hand, as Meyer pointed out, the wavelet coefficients of *Ramp* decay very rapidly, essentially exponentially. As a result, very simple scalar quantization schemes based on wavelet coefficients can capture realizations of *Ramp* with 1% accuracy using a few dozens rather than tens of thousands of coefficients, and with a corresponding advantage at the level of bits; this is illustrated in Fig. 2.

The point here is that if we pay attention to second-order statistics only, and adopt an approach that would be good under a Gaussian model, we may pay orders of magnitude more bits than would be necessary for

401

coding the process under a more appropriate model. By abandoning the Karhunen–Loève transform in this non-Gaussian case, we get a transform in which very simple scalar quantization works very well.

Note that we could in principle build a near-optimal scheme by transform coding with a coder based on Fourier coefficients, but we would have to apply a much more complex quantizer; it would have to be a vector quantizer. (Owing to Littlewood–Paley theory described later, it is possible to say what the quantizer would look like; it would involve quantizing coefficients near wavenumber k in blocks of size roughly $k/2$. This is computationally impractical.)

D. Variations on Function Class Models

In Section V, we saw that subband coding of Fourier coefficients offered an essentially optimal method, under the Kolmogorov ϵ-entropy model, of coding objects f known a priori to obey L^2 smoothness constraints $||f||^2_{L^2(T)} + ||f^{(m)}||^2_{L^2(T)} \leq \gamma^2$.

While this may not be apparent to outsiders, there are major differences in the implications of various smoothness constraints. Suppose we maintain the L^2 distortion measure, but make the seemingly minor change from the L^2 form of constraint to an L^p form, $||f||^p_{L^p(T)} + ||f^{(m)}||^p_{L^p(T)} \leq \gamma^p$ with $p < 2$. This can cause major changes in what constitutes an underlying optimal strategy. Rather than transform coding in the frequency domain, we can find that transform coding in the wavelet domain is appropriate.

Bounded Variation Model: As a simple example, consider the model that the object under consideration is a function $f(t)$ of a single variable that is of bounded variation. Such functions f can be interpreted as having derivatives which are signed measures, and then we measure the norm by

$$||f||_{\mathrm{BV}} = \int |df|.$$

The important point is such f can have jump discontinuities, as long as the sum of the jumps is finite. Hence, the class of functions of bounded variation can be viewed as a model for functions which have discontinuities; for example, a scan line in a digital image can be modeled as a typical BV function.

An interesting fact about BV functions is that they can be essentially characterized by their Haar coefficients. The BV functions with norm $\leq \gamma$ obey an inequality

$$\sup_j \sum_k |\alpha_{j,k}| 2^{j/2} \leq 4\gamma$$

where $\alpha_{j,k}$ are the Haar wavelet expansion coefficients. It is almost the case that every function that obeys this constraint is a BV function. This says that geometrically, the class of BV functions with norm $\leq \gamma$ is a convex set inscribed in a family of ℓ^1 balls.

An easy coder for functions of Bounded Variation can be based on scalar quantization of Haar coefficients. However,

scalar quantization of the Fourier coefficients would not work nearly as well; as the desired distortion $\epsilon \to 0$, the number of bits for Fourier/scalar quantization coding can be orders of magnitude worse than the number of bits for wavelet/scalar quantization coding. This follows from results in Sections XV and XVI below.

E. Variations on Transform Coding and JPEG

When we consider transform coding as applied to empirical data, we typically find that a number of simple variations can lead to significant improvements over what the strict Gaussian $R(D)$ theory would predict. In particular, we see that when going from theory to practice, KLT as implemented in JPEG becomes nonlinear approximation!

The image is first subdivided into blocks of size N by N (N is typically equal to 8 or 16) and these blocks are treated independently. Note that blocking the image into independent pieces allows to adapt the compression to each block individually. An orthonormal basis for the two-dimensional blocks is derived as a product basis from the one-dimensional DCT. While not necessarily best, this is an efficient way to generate a two-dimensional basis.

Now, quantization and entropy coding is done in a manner that is quite at variance with the classical setup. First, based on perceptual criteria, the transform coefficient $y(k, l)$ is quantized with a uniform quantizer of stepsize $\Delta_{k,l}$. Typically, $\Delta_{k,l}$ is small for low frequencies, and large for high ones, and these stepsizes are stored in a quantization matrix $\boldsymbol{M}_Q$. Technically, one could pick different quantization matrices for different blocks in order to adapt, but usually, only a single scale factor α is used to multiply $\boldsymbol{M}_Q$, and this scale factor can be adapted depending on the statistics in the block. Thus the approximate representation of the (k, l)th coefficient is $\hat{y}(k, l) = Q[y(k, l), \alpha\Delta_{k,l}]$ where $Q[y, \Delta] = \Delta \cdot \lfloor y/\Delta \rfloor + \Delta/2$. The quantized variable $\hat{y}(k, l)$ is discrete with a finite number of possible values ($y(k, l)$ is bounded) and is entropy-coded.

Since there is no natural ordering of the two-dimensional DCT plane, yet known efficient entropy coding techniques work on one-dimensional sequences of coefficients, a prescribed 2D to 1D scanning is used. This so-called "zig-zag" scan traverses the DCT frequency plane diagonally from low to high frequencies. For this resulting one-dimensional length-N^2 sequence, nonzero coefficients are entropy-coded, and stretches of zero coefficients are encoded using entropy coding of run lengths. An *end-of-block* (EOB) symbol terminates a sequence of DCT coefficients when only zeros are left (which is likely to arrive early in the sequence when coarse quantization is used).

Let us consider two extreme modes of operation: In the first case, assume very fine quantization. Then, many coefficients will be nonzero, and the behavior of the rate–distortion tradeoff is dominated by the quantization and entropy coding of the individual coefficients, that is, $D(R) \sim 2^{-2R}$. This mode is also typical for high variance regions, like textures.

In the second case, assume very coarse quantization. Then, many coefficients will be zero, and the run-length coding is an efficient indexing of the few nonzero coefficients. We are

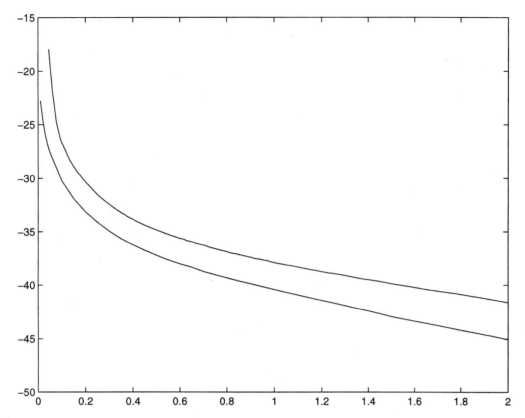

Fig. 3. Performance of real transform coding systems. The logarithm of the MSE is shown for JPEG (top) and SPIHT (bottom). Above about 0.5 bit/pixel, there is the typical −6 dB per bit slope, while at very low bit rate, a much steeper slope is achieved.

in a nonlinear approximation case, since the image block is approximated with a few basis vectors corresponding to large inner products. Then, the $D(R)$ behavior is very different, dominated by the faster decay of ordered transform coefficients, which in turn is related to the smoothness class of the images. Such a behavior is also typical for structured regions, like smooth surfaces cut by edges, since the DCT coefficients will be sparse.

These two different behaviors can be seen in Fig. 3, where the logarithm of the distortion versus the bit rate per pixel is shown. The $-2R$ slope above about 0.5 bit/pixel is clear, as is the steeper slope below. An analysis of the low-rate behavior of transform codes has been done recently by Mallat and Falzon [70]; see also related work in Cohen, Daubechies, Guleryuz, and Orchard [14].

IX. GOOD MODELS FOR NATURAL DATA?

We have now seen, by considering a range of different intellectual models for the class of objects of interest to us, that depending on the model we adopt, we can arrive at very different conclusions about the "best" way to represent or compress those objects. We have also seen that what seems like a good method in one model can be a relatively poor method according to another model. We have also seen that existing models used in data compression are relatively poor descriptions of the phenomena we see in natural data. We think that we may still be far away from achieving an optimal representation of such data.

A. How Many Bits for Mona Lisa?

A classic question, somewhat tongue in cheek, is: how many bits do we need to describe Mona Lisa? JPEG uses 187 Kbytes in one version. From many points of view, this is far more than the number intrinsically required.

Humans will recognize a version based on a few hundred bits. An early experiment by L. Harmon of Bell Laboratories shows a recognizable Abraham Lincoln at 756 bits, a trick also used by S. Dali in his painting "*Slave Market with Invisible Bust of Voltaire.*"

Another way to estimate the number of bits in a representation is to consider an index of every photograph ever taken in the history of mankind. With a generous estimate of 100 billion pictures a year, the 100 years of photography need an index of about 44 bits. Another possibility yet is to index all pictures that can possibly be viewed by all humans. Given the world population, and the fact that at most 25 pictures a second are recognizable, a hundred years of viewing is indexed in about 69 bits.

Given that the Mona Lisa is a very famous painting, it is clear that probably a few bits will be enough (with the obvious variable length code: [is it Lena?, is it Mona Lisa?, etc. . . .]). Another approach is the interactive search of the image, for example, on the Web. A search engine prompted with a few key words will quickly come back with the answer at the top of the following page, and just a few bytes have been exchanged.

These numbers are all very suggestive when we consider estimates of the information rate of the human visual system.

Barlow [4] summarizes evidence that the many layers of processing in the human visual system reduce the information flow from several megabits per second at the retina to about 40 bits per second deep in the visual pathway.

From all points of view, *images ought to be far more compressible than current compression standards allow.*

B. The Grand Challenge

An effort to do far better compression leads to the Grand Challenge, items GC1–GC3 of Section I. However, to address this challenge by orthodox application of the Shannon theory seems to us hopeless. To understand why, we make three observations.

- *Intrinsic Complexity of Natural Data Sources:* An accurate model for empirical phenomena would be of potentially overwhelming complexity. In effect, images, or sounds, even in a restricted area of application like medical imagery, are naturally infinite-dimensional phenomena. They take place in a continuum, and in principle the recording of a sound or image cannot be constrained in advance by a finite number of parameters. The true underlying mechanism is in many cases markedly non-Gaussian, and highly nonstationary.

- *Difficulty of Characterization:* There exists at the moment no reasonable "mechanical" way to characterize the structure of such complex phenomena. In the zero-mean Gaussian case, all behavior can be deduced from properties of the countable sequence of eigenvalues of the covariance kernel. Outside of the Gaussian case, very little is known about characterizing infinite-dimensional probability distributions which would be immediately helpful in modeling real-world phenomena such as images and sounds. Instead, we must live by our wits.

- *Complexity of Optimization Problem:* If we take Shannon literally, and apply the abstract $R(D)$ principle, determining the best way to code a naturally occurring source of data would require to solve a mutual information problem involving probability distributions defined on an infinite-dimensional space. Unfortunately, it is not clear that one can obtain a clear intellectual description of such probability distributions in a form which would be manageable for actually stating the problem coherently, much less solving it.

In effect, uncovering the optimal codebook structure of naturally occurring data involves more challenging empirical questions than any that have ever been solved in empirical work in the mathematical sciences. Typical empirical questions that have been adequately solved in scientific work to date involve finding structure of very simple low-dimensional, well-constrained probability distributions.

The problem of determining the solution of the $R(D, X)$-problem, given a limited number of realizations of X, could be considered a branch of what is becoming known in statistics as "functional data analysis"—the analysis of data when the observations are images, sounds, or other functions, and so naturally viewed as infinite-dimensional. Work in that field aims to determine structural properties of the probability distribution of functional data—for example, the covariance and/or its eigenfunctions, or the discriminant function for testing between two populations. Functional data analysis has shown that many challenging issues impede the extension of simple multivariate statistical methods to the functional case [79]. Certain simple multivariate procedures have been extended to the functional case: principal components, discriminant analysis, canonical correlations being carefully studied examples. The problem that must be faced in such work is that one has always a finite number of realizations from which one is to infer aspects of the infinite-dimensional probabilistic generating mechanism. This is a kind of rank deficiency of the data set which means that, for example, one cannot hope to get quantitatively accurate estimates of eigenfunctions of the covariance.

The mutual information optimization problem in Shannon's $R(D)$ in the general non-Gaussian case requires far more than just knowledge of a covariance or its eigenfunctions; it involves in principle all the joint distributional structure of the process. It is totally unclear how to deal with the issues that would crop up in such a generalization.

X. A ROLE FOR HARMONIC ANALYSIS

In this section, we comment on some interesting insights that harmonic analysis has to offer against the background of this "Grand Challenge."

A. Terminology

The phrase "harmonic analysis" means many things to many different people. To some, it is associated with an abstract procedure in group theory—unitary group representations [54]; to others it is associated with classical mathematical physics—expansions in special functions related to certain differential operators; to others it is associated with "hard" analysis in its modern form [90].

The usual senses of the phrase all have roots in the bold assertions of Fourier that a) "any" function can be expanded in a series of sines and cosines and that, b) one could understand the complex operator of heat propagation by understanding merely its action on certain "elementary" initial distributions—namely, initial temperature distributions following sinusoidal profiles. As is now well known, making sense in one way or another of Fourier's assertions has spawned an amazing array of concepts over the last two centuries; the theories of the Lebesgue integral, of Hilbert spaces, of L^p

spaces, of generalized functions, of differential equations, are all bound up in some way in the development, justification, and refinement of Fourier's initial ideas. So no single writer can possibly mean "*all* of harmonic analysis" when using the term "harmonic analysis."

For the purposes of this paper, harmonic analysis refers instead to a series of ideas that have evolved throughout this century, a set of ideas involving two streams of thought.

On the one hand, to develop ways to analyze functions using decompositions built through a geometrically motivated "cutting and pasting" of time, frequency, and related domains into "cells" and the construction of systems of "atoms" "associated naturally" to those "cells."

On the other hand, to use these decompositions to find characterizations, to within notions of equivalence, of interesting function classes.

It is perhaps surprising that one can combine these two ideas. *A priori* difficult to understand classes of functions in a functional space turn out to have a characterization as a superposition of "atoms" of a more or less concrete form. Of course, the functional spaces where this can be true are quite special; the miracle is that it can be done at all.

This is a body of work that has grown up slowly over the last ninety years, by patient accumulation of a set of tools and cultural attitudes little known to outsiders. As we stand at the end of the century, we can say that this body of work shows that there are many interesting questions about infinite-dimensional function classes where experience has shown that it is often difficult or impossible to obtain exact results, but where fruitful analogies do suggest similar problems which are "good enough" to enable approximate, or asymptotic solutions.

In a brief survey paper, we can only superficially mention a few of the decomposition ideas that have been proposed and a few of the achievements and cultural attitudes that have resulted; we will do so in Sections XII, XVII, and XVIII below. The reader will find that [58] provides a wealth of helpful background material complementing the present paper.

B. Relevance to the Grand Challenge

Much of harmonic analysis in this century can be characterized as carrying out a three-part program

HA1 Identify an interesting class of mathematically defined objects (functions, operators, etc.).

HA2 Develop tools to characterize the class of objects in terms of functionals derivable from an analysis of the objects themselves.

HA3 Improve the characterization tools themselves, refining and streamlining them.

This program, while perhaps obscure to outsiders, has borne interesting fruit. As we will describe below, wavelet transforms arose from a long series of investigations into the structure of classes of functions defined by L^p constraints, $p \neq 2$. The original question was to characterize function classes $\{f : \int |f|^p < \infty\}$ by analytic means, such as by the properties of the coefficients of the considered functions in an orthogonal expansion. It was found that the obvious

first choice—Fourier coefficients—could not offer such a characterization when $p \neq 2$, and eventually, after a long series of alternate characterizations were discovered, it was proved that wavelet expansions offered such characterizations—i.e., that by looking at the wavelet coefficients of a function, one could learn the L^p-norm to within constants of equivalence, $1 < p < \infty$. It was also learned that for $p \in \{1, \infty\}$ no norm characterization was possible, but after replacing L^1 by the closely related space H^1 and L^∞ by the closely related space BMO (the space of functions of Bounded Mean Oscillation), the wavelet coefficients again contained the required information for knowing the norm to within constants of equivalence.

The three parts HA1–HA3 of the harmonic analysis program are entirely analogous to the three steps GC1–GC3 in the Grand Challenge for data compression—except that for data compression, the challenge is to deal with *naturally occurring data sources* while for harmonic analysis the challenge is to deal with *mathematically interesting classes of objects*.

It is very striking to us that the natural development of harmonic analysis in this century, while in intention completely unrelated to problems of data compression, has borne fruit which seems very relevant to the needs of the data compression community. Typical byproducts of this effort so far include the fast wavelet transform, and lossy wavelet domain coders which exploit the "tree" organization of the wavelet transform. Furthermore, we are aware of many other developments in harmonic analysis which have not yet borne fruit of direct impact on data compression, but seem likely to have an impact in the future.

There are other insights available from developments in harmonic analysis. In the comparison between the three-part challenge facing data compression and the three-part program of harmonic analysis, the messiness of understanding a natural data source—which requires dealing with specific phenomena in all their particularity—is replaced by the precision of understanding a class with a formal mathematical definition. Thus harmonic analysis operates in a more ideal setting for making intellectual progress; but sometimes progress is not as complete as one would like. It is accepted by now that many characterization problems of function classes cannot be exactly solved. Harmonic analysis has shown that often one can make substantial progress by replacing hard characterization problems with less demanding problems where answers can be obtained explicitly. It has also shown that such cruder approximations are still quite useful and important.

A typical example is the study of operators. The eigenfunctions of an operator are fragile, and can change radically if the operator is only slightly perturbed in certain ways. It is in general difficult to get explicit representations of the eigenfunctions, and to compute them. Harmonic analysis, however, shows that for certain problems, we can work with "almost eigenfunctions" that "almost diagonalize" operators. For example, wavelets work well on a broad range of operators, and moreover, they lend themselves to concrete fast computational algorithms. That is, the exact problem, which is potentially intractable, is replaced by an approximate problem for which computational solutions exist.

C. Survey of the Field

In the remainder of this paper we will discuss a set of developments in the harmonic analysis community and how they can be connected to results about data compression. We think it will become clear to the reader that in fact the lessons that have been learned from the activity of harmonic analysis are very relevant to facing the Grand Challenge for data compression.

XI. NORM EQUIVALENCE PROBLEMS

The problem of characterizing a class of functions $F = \{f : \|f\|_F < \infty\}$, where $\|\cdot\|_F$ is a norm of interest, has occupied a great deal of attention of harmonic analysts in this century. The basic idea is to relate the norm, defined in say continuum form by an integral, to an equivalent norm defined in discrete form

$$\|f\|_F \asymp \|\theta(f)\|_{\boldsymbol{f}}. \qquad (11.1)$$

Here $\theta = \theta(f)$ denotes a collection of coefficients arising in a decomposition of f; for example, these coefficients would be obtained by

$$\theta_k = \langle f, \phi_k \rangle$$

if the (ϕ_k) made up an orthonormal basis. The norm $\|\cdot\|_F$ is a norm defined on the continuum object f and the norm $\|\cdot\|_{\boldsymbol{f}}$ is a norm defined on the corresponding discrete object $\theta(f)$. The equivalence symbol $\asymp$ in (11.1) means that there are constants A and B, not depending on f, so that

$$A\|f\|_F \leq \|\theta(f)\|_{\boldsymbol{f}} \leq B\|f\|_F. \qquad (11.2)$$

The significance is that the coefficients θ contain within them the information needed to approximately infer the size of f in the norm $\|\cdot\|_F$. One would of course usually prefer to have $A = B$, in which case the coefficients characterize the size of f precisely, but often this kind of *tight* characterization is beyond reach.

The most well-known and also tightest form of such a relationship is the Parseval formula, valid for the continuum norm of L^2: $\|f\|_{L^2} = (\int_T |f(t)|^2 \, dt)^{1/2}$. If the $(\phi_k)_k$ constitute a complete orthonormal system for $L^2(T)$, then we have

$$\|f\|_{L^2(T)} = \left(\sum_k |\theta_k|^2\right)^{1/2}. \qquad (11.3)$$

Another frequently encountered relationship of this kind is valid for functions on the circle $T = [0, 2\pi)$, with (ϕ_k) the Fourier basis of Section II. Then we have a norm equivalence for a norm defined on the mth derivative

$$\|f^{(m)}\|_{L^2(T)} = \left(\sum_k k^{2m}(|\theta_{2k}|^2 + |\theta_{2k+1}|^2)\right)^{1/2}. \qquad (11.4)$$

These two equivalences are, of course, widely used in the mathematical sciences. They are beautiful, but also potentially misleading. A naive reading of these results might promote the expectation that one can frequently have tightness $A = B = 1$

in characterization results, or that the Fourier basis works in other settings as well.

We mention now five kinds of norms for which we might like to solve norm-equivalence, and for which the answers to all these norm-equivalence problems are by now well-understood.

- *L^p-norms:* Let $1 \leq p < \infty$. The L^p-norm is, as usual, just

  $$\|f\|_{L^p(T)} = \left(\int_T |f(t)|^p \, dt\right)^{1/p}.$$

  We can extend this scale of norms to $p = \infty$ by taking

  $$\|f\|_{L^\infty} = \sup_{t \in T} |f(t)|.$$

- *Sobolev-norms:* Let $1 \leq p < \infty$. The L^p-Sobolev norm is

  $$\|f\|_{W_p^m(T)} = \|f\|_{L^p} + \|f^{(m)}\|_{L^p}.$$

- *Hölder classes:* Let $0 < \alpha < 1$. The Hölder class $C^\alpha(T)$ is the collection of continuous functions f on the domain T with $|f(t) - f(t')| \leq C|t - t'|^\alpha$ and $\|f\|_{L^\infty} < C$, for some $C > 0$; the smallest such C is the norm. Let $m < \alpha < m + 1$, for integer $m \geq 1$; the Hölder class $C^\alpha(T)$ is the collection of continuous functions f on the domain T with

  $$|f^{(m)}(t) - f^{(m)}(t')| \leq C|t - t'|^\delta$$

  for $\delta = \alpha - m$.

- *Bump Algebra:* Suppose that f is a continuous function on the line $T = (-\infty, \infty)$. Let $g(t) = e^{-t^2}$ be a Gaussian normalized to height one rather than area one. Suppose that f can be represented as $\Sigma_i a_i g((t - t_i)/s_i)$ for a countable sequence of triples (a_i, t_i, s_i) with $s_i > 0$, $t_i \in T$, and $\Sigma_i |a_i| = C < \infty$. Then f is said to belong to the Bump Algebra, and its Bump norm $|f|_B$ is the smallest value of C for which such a decomposition exists. Evidently, a function in the Bump Algebra is a superposition of Gaussians, with various polarities, locations, and scales.

- *Bounded Variation:* Suppose that f is a function on the interval $T = [0, 1]$ that is integrable and such that the increment obeys

  $$\|f(\cdot + h) - f(\cdot)\|_{L^1[0, 1-h]} \leq C|h|$$

  for $0 < h < 1$. The BV seminorm of f is the smallest C for which this is true.

In each case, the norm equivalence problem is: *Find an orthobasis (ϕ_k) and a discrete norm $\|\theta\|_{\boldsymbol{f}}$ so that the F norm $\|f\|_F$ is equivalent to the discrete norm $\|\theta(f)\|_{\boldsymbol{f}}$.* In-depth discussions of these spaces and their norm-equivalence problems can be found in [103], [89], [90], [96], [43], and [74]. In some cases, as we explain in Section XII below, the norm equivalence has been solved; in other cases, it has been proven that there can never be a norm equivalence, but a closely related space has been discovered for which a norm equivalence is available.

In these five problems, Fourier analysis does not work; that is, one cannot find a "simple" and "natural" norm on the Fourier coefficients which provides an equivalent norm to the considered continuous norm. It is also true that tight equivalence results, with $A = B = 1$, seem out of reach in these cases.

The key point in seeking a norm equivalence is that the discrete norm must be "simple" and "natural." By this we really mean that the discrete norm *should depend only on the size of the coefficients* and not on the signs or phases of the coefficients. We will say that the discrete norm is *unconditional* if it obeys the relationship

$$||\theta'||_f \leq ||\theta||_f$$

whenever $\theta'_k = s_k \theta_k$ with s_k any sequence of weights $|s_k| \leq 1$. The idea is that "shrinking the coefficients in size" should "shrink" the norm.

A norm equivalence result therefore requires discovering both a representing system (ϕ_k) and a special norm on a sequence space, one which is equivalent to the considered continuum norm and also has the unconditionality property. For future reference, we call a basis yielding a norm equivalence between a norm on function space and such an unconditional norm on sequence space an *unconditional basis*. It has the property that for any object in a function class F, and any set of coefficients θ'_k obeying

$$|\theta'_k| \leq |\theta_k(f)|, \qquad \forall k$$

the newly constructed object

$$f' = \sum_k \theta'_k \phi_k$$

belongs to F as well.

There is a famous result dramatizing the fact that the Fourier basis is not an unconditional basis for classes of continuous functions, due to DeLeeuw, Kahane, and Katznelson [25]. Their results allows us to construct pairs of functions: one, g, say, which is uniformly continuous on the circle; and the other, h, say, very wild, having square integrable singularities on a dense subset of the circle. The respective Fourier coefficients obey

$$|\theta_k(g)| > |\theta_k(h)| \qquad \forall k.$$

In short, the ugly and bizarre object h has the *smaller* Fourier coefficients. Another way of putting this is that an extremely delicate pattern in the phases of the coefficients, rather than the size of the coefficients, control the regularity of the function. The fact that special "conditions" on the coefficients, unrelated to their size, are needed to impose regularity may help to explain the term "unconditional" and the preference for unconditional structure.

XII. HARMONIC ANALYSIS AND NORM EQUIVALENCE

We now describe a variety of tools that were developed in harmonic analysis over the years in order to understand norm equivalence problems, and some of the norm equivalence problems that were solved.

A. Warmup: The Sampling Theorem

A standard procedure by which interesting orthobases have been constructed by harmonic analysts is to first develop a kind of "overcomplete" continuous representation, and later develop a discretized variant based on a geometric model.

An elementary example of this procedure will be familiar to readers in the information theory community, as Shannon's Sampling Theorem [84] in signal analysis. Let $\hat{f}(\omega)$ be an L^2 function supported in a finite frequency interval $[-\pi\Omega, \pi\Omega]$; and let $f(t) = (1/2\pi) \int \hat{f}(\omega) \exp\{i\omega t\} \, d\omega$ be the time-domain representation. This representation is an L^2-isometry, so that

$$\frac{1}{2\pi} \int_{-\pi\Omega}^{\pi\Omega} |\hat{f}(\omega)|^2 = \int_T |f(t)|^2 \, dt.$$

The size of the function on the frequency side and on the time side are the same, up to normalization. By our assumptions, the time-domain representation $f(t)$ is a bandlimited function, which is very smooth, and so the representation of f in the time domain is very redundant. A nonredundant representation is obtained by sampling, and retaining only the $f(k/\Omega)$. The mathematical expression of the perfect nonredundancy of this representation is the fact that we have the norm equivalence

$$||f||_{L^2(\boldsymbol{R})} = \left(\frac{1}{\Omega} \sum_k |f(k/\Omega)|^2 \right)^{1/2} \qquad (12.1)$$

and that there is an orthobasis of sampling functions $\varphi_k(t) = \Omega^{1/2} \operatorname{sinc}(\Omega t - k)$ so that $f(k/\Omega) = \langle \varphi_k, f \rangle \cdot \Omega^{1/2}$ and

$$f(t) = \sum_k f(k/\Omega)\varphi_k(t).$$

This time-domain representation has the following geometric interpretation: there is a sequence of disjoint "cells" of length $1/\Omega$, indexed by k; the samples summarize the behavior in those cells; and the sampling functions provide the details of that behavior. While this circle of ideas was known to Shannon and was very influential for signal analysis, we should point out that harmonic analysts developed ideas such as this somewhat earlier, under more general conditions, and based on an exploration of a geometric model explaining the phenomenon. For example, work of Paley and Wiener in the early 1930's and of Plancherel and Polya in the mid 1930's concerned norm equivalence in the more general case when the points of sampling were not equispaced, and obtained methods giving equivalence for all L^p norms, $p > 0$

$$||f||_{L^p(\boldsymbol{R})} \asymp \left(\frac{1}{\Omega} \sum_k |f(t_k)|^p \right)^{1/p} \qquad (12.2)$$

provided the points t_k are approximately equispaced at density $1/\Omega$.

The results that the harmonic analysts obtained can be interpreted as saying that the geometric model of the sampling theorem has a very wide range of validity. For this geometric model, we define a collection of "cells" I_k, namely, intervals of length $1/\Omega$ centered at the sampling points t_k, and construct the piecewise-constant object $\tilde{f} = \Sigma_k f(t_k)1_{I_k}(t)$. The norm equivalence (12.2) says, in fact, that

$$||f||_{L^p(\mathbf{R})} \asymp ||\tilde{f}||_{L^p(\mathbf{R})} \qquad (12.3)$$

for a wide range of p.

This pattern—continuous representation, discretization, geometric model—has been of tremendous significance in harmonic analysis.

B. Continuous Time-Scale Representations

At the beginning of this century, a number of interesting relationships between Fourier series and harmonic function theory were discovered, which showed that valuable information about a function f defined on the circle T or the line $\mathbf{R}$ can be garnered from its harmonic extension into the interior of the circle, respectively the upper half plane; in other words, by viewing f as the boundary values of a harmonic function U. This theory also benefits from an interplay with complex analysis, since a harmonic function U is the real part of an analytic function $F = U + i\tilde{U}$. The imaginary part $\tilde{U}$ is called the conjugate function of U. The harmonic function U and the associated analytic function F give much important information about f. We want to point out how capturing this information on f through the functions $U(\cdot, y)$ ultimately leads to favorable decompositions of f into fundamental building blocks called "atoms." These decompositions can be viewed as a precursor to wavelet decompositions. For expository reasons we streamline the story and follow [89, Chs. III, IV], [43, Ch. 1], and [45]. Let f be any "reasonable" function on the line. It has a harmonic extension U into the upper half plane given by the Poisson integral

$$U(t, y) = \int_{\mathbf{R}} P_y(u)f(t - u) \, du, \qquad y > 0, \qquad (12.4)$$

where $P_y(t) = \pi^{-1}y/(y^2 + t^2)$ is the Poisson kernel. This associates to a function f of one variable the harmonic function U of two variables, where the argument t again ranges over the line and y ranges over the positive reals. The physical interpretation of this integral is that f is the boundary value of U and $U(t, y)$ is what can be sensed at some "depth" y. Each of the functions $U(\cdot, y)$ is infinitely differentiable. Whenever $f \in L^p(\mathbf{R})$, $1 \le p \le \infty$, the equal-depth sections $U(\cdot, y)$ converge to f as $y \to 0$ and, therefore, the norms converge as well: $||U(\cdot, y)||_{L^p} \to ||f||_{L^p}$. We shall see next another way to capture $||f||_{L^p}$ through the function $U(\cdot, y)$. Hardy in 1914 developed an identity in the closely related setting where one has a function defined on the unit circle, and one uses the harmonic extension into the interior of the unit disk [53]; he noticed a way to recover the norm of the boundary values from the norm of the values on the interior of the disk. By conformal mapping and some simple identities based on Green's theorem, this is recognized today as equivalent to the statement that in the setting (12.4) the L^2 norm of the "boundary values" $f(t)$ can be recovered from the behavior of the whole function $U(t, y)$

$$\int |f(t)|^2 \, dt = 8\pi \iint \left| \frac{\partial}{\partial y} U(t, y) \right|^2 y \, dy \, dt. \qquad (12.5)$$

Defining $V(t, y) = 2\sqrt{2\pi} \cdot y \cdot (\partial/\partial y)U(t, y)$, this formula says

$$\int_{\mathbf{R}} |f(t)|^2 \, dt = \int_{\mathbf{R}} \int_0^\infty |V(t, y)|^2 \frac{dy}{y} \, dt. \qquad (12.6)$$

Now the object $V(t, y)$ is itself an integral transform

$$V(t, y) = \int Q_y(u)f(t - u) \, du$$

where the kernel $Q_y(u) = 2\sqrt{2\pi} \cdot y \cdot (\partial/\partial y)P_y(u)$ results from differentiating the Poisson kernel. This gives a method of assigning, to a function of a single real variable, a function of two variables, in an L^2 norm-preserving way. In addition, this association is invertible since, formally,

$$f(t) = \lim_{y' \to 0} U(t, y') = \lim_{y' \to 0} \frac{1}{2\sqrt{2\pi}} \int_{y'}^\infty V(t, y) \frac{dy}{y}$$
$$= \frac{1}{2\sqrt{2\pi}} \int_0^\infty V(t, y) \frac{dy}{y}$$

when f is a "nice" function. In the 1930's, Littlewood and Paley, working again in the closely related setting of functions defined on the circle, found a way to obtain information on the L^p norms of a function defined on the circle, from an appropriate analysis of its values inside the circle. This is now understood as implying that V contains not just information about the L^2 norm as in (12.6), but also on L^p norms, $p \ne 2$. Defining $g_2(t) = (\int_0^\infty |V(t, y)|^2 (dy/y)^{1/2}$, Littlewood–Paley theory in its modern formulation says that

$$||f||_{L^p} \asymp ||g_2||_{L^p} \qquad (12.7)$$

for $1 < p < \infty$. The equivalence (12.7) breaks down when $p \to 1$. (We shall not discuss the other problem point $p = \infty$ here since these L^∞-spaces are not separable and therefore do not have the series representations we seek.) To understand the reason for this breakdown one needs to examine the conjugate function $\tilde{U}$ of U mentioned above. It enjoys the same properties of U provided $1 < p < \infty$. It has boundary values $\tilde{f}$ and the function $\tilde{f}$ (called the conjugate function of f) is also in $L^p(\mathbf{R})$. But the story takes a turn for the worse when $p = 1$: for a function $f \in L^1(\mathbf{R})$, its conjugate function $\tilde{f}$ need not be in $L^1(\mathbf{R})$. The theory of the real Hardy spaces H^p is a way to repair the situation and better understand the norm equivalences (12.7). A function f is said to be in real H^p, $1 \le p < \infty$, if and only if both f and its conjugate function $\tilde{f}$ are in L^p; the norm of f in H^p is the sum of the L^p norms of f and $\tilde{f}$. Replacing $||f||_{L^p}$ by $||f||_{H^p}$ on the left side of (12.7), we obtain equivalences with absolute constants that hold even for $p = 1$. In summary, the spaces H^p are a natural replacement for L^p when discussing representations and norm equivalences.

In modern parlance, the object V would be called an instance of *continuous wavelet transform*. This terminology was used for the first time in the 1980's by Grossmann and Morlet [52], who proposed the study of the integral transform

$$Wf(a, b) = \int_{-\infty}^\infty f(t)\overline{\psi}_{a,b}(t) \, dt \qquad (12.8)$$

where

$$\psi_{a,b}(t) = |a|^{-1/2}\psi((t-b)/a)$$

and ψ is a so-called "wavelet," which must be chosen to obey an *admissibility condition*; for convenience, we shall require here a special form of this condition

$$2\pi = \int_0^\infty |\hat{\psi}(\xi)|^2 |\xi|^{-1}\, d\xi = \int_{-\infty}^0 |\hat{\psi}(\xi)|^2 |\xi|^{-1}\, d\xi. \quad (12.9)$$

Here b is a location parameter and a is a scale parameter, and the transform maps f into a time-scale domain. (Under a different terminology, a transform and admissibility condition of the same type can also be found in [2].) The wavelet transform with respect to an admissible wavelet is invertible

$$f(t) = \iint Wf(a,b)\psi_{a,b}(t)\frac{da}{a^2}\, db \quad (12.10)$$

and also an isometry

$$\|f\|_{L^2}^2 = \iint |Wf(a,b)|^2 \frac{da}{a^2}\, db. \quad (12.11)$$

One sees by simple comparison of terms that the choice $\psi(t) = Q_1(t)$ yields $V(t,y) = W(a,b)$ under the calibration $a = y$ and $t = b$. We thus gain a new interpretation of V: the function Q_y has "scale" y and so we can interpret $V(t,y)$ as providing an association of the object f with a certain "time-scale" portrait.

The continuous wavelet transform is highly redundant, as the particular instance V shows: it is harmonic in the upper half-plane. Insights into the redundancy of the continuous wavelet transform are provided (for example) in [23]. Suppose we associate to the point (b,a) the rectangle

$$\rho(a,b) = [b-a, b+a] \times [a/2, 2a]$$

then the information "near (b,a)" in the wavelet transform is weakly related to information near (b',a') if the corresponding rectangles are well-separated.

C. Atomic Decomposition

As pointed out earlier, it is natural to replace the study of the spaces L^p with that of the spaces H^p; in particular, we avoid certain unsatisfactory aspects of L^1, which does not have any unconditional basis, and which behaves quite unlike its logically neighboring spaces L^p for $p > 1$. The norm equivalence (12.7), which does not work at $p = 1$, is then replaced by

$$\|f\|_{H^p} \asymp \|g_2\|_{L^p}$$

valid for all $1 \leq p < \infty$.

In the late 1960's and early 1970's, one of the most successful areas of research in harmonic analysis concerned H^1 and associated spaces. At that time, the concept of "atomic decomposition" arose, the key point was the discovery by Fefferman that one can characterize membership in the space H^1 precisely by the properties of its atomic decomposition

into atoms obeying various size, oscillation, and support constraints. Since then "atomic decomposition" has come to mean a decomposition of a function f into a discrete superposition of nonrigidly specified pieces, where the pieces obey various analytic constraints (size, support, smoothness, moments) determined by a space of interest, with the size properties of those pieces providing the characterization of the norm of the function [16], [29], [42], [43].

The continuous wavelet transform gives a natural tool to build atomic decompositions for various spaces. Actually, the tool predates the wavelet transform, since already in the 1960's Calderón [9] established a general decomposition, a "resolution of identity operator" which in wavelet terms can be written

$$\int_{-\infty}^\infty \int_0^\infty \langle \cdot, \psi_{a,b}\rangle \psi_{a,b}\frac{da}{a^2}\, db = Id.$$

The goal is not just to write the identity operator in a more complicated form; by decomposing the integration domain using a partition into disjoint sets, one obtains a family of nontrivial operators, corresponding to different time-scale regions, which sum to the identity operator.

Let now I denote a *dyadic interval*, i.e., an interval of the form $I = I_{j,k} = [k/2^j, (k+1)/2^j)$ with j and k integers, and let $R(I)$ denote a time-scale (b,a)-rectangle sitting "above" I

$$R(I) = I \times (2^{-j-1}, 2^{-j}].$$

The collection $\mathcal{I}$ of all dyadic intervals I is obtained as the scale index j runs through the integers (both positive and negative) and the position index k runs through the integers as well. The corresponding collection $\mathcal{R}$ of all rectangles $R(I)$ forms a disjoint cover of the whole (a,b) plane; compare Fig. 4. If we now take the Calderón reproducing formula and partition the range of integration using this family of rectangles we have formally that $Id = \Sigma_I A_I$, where

$$A_I f = \iint_{R(I)} \langle f, \psi_{a,b}\rangle \psi_{a,b}\frac{da}{a^2}\, db.$$

Here A_I is an operator formally associating to f that "piece" coming from time-scale region $R(I)$. In fact, it makes sense to call $A_I f$ a time-scale atom [43]. The region $R(I)$ of the wavelet transform, owing to the redundancy properties, constitutes in some sense a minimal coherent piece of the wavelet transform. The corresponding atom summarizes the contributions of this coherent region to the reconstruction, and has properties one would consider natural for such a summary. If ψ is supported in $[-1, 1]$, then $A_I f$ will be supported in $3 \cdot I$, the interval with same center as I but three times its width. Also, if ψ is smooth and admissible then $A_I f$ will be smooth, oscillating only as much as required to be supported in $3 \cdot I$. For example, if f is m-times differentiable, and the wavelet ψ is chosen appropriately,

$$\left|\frac{\partial^m}{\partial t^m}(A_I f)(t)\right| \leq C(\psi) \cdot |I|^{-m+1/2} \cdot \|f\|_{C^m(5 \cdot I)} \quad (12.12)$$

and we cannot expect a better dependence of the properties of an atom on f in general. So the formula $f = \Sigma_I A_I f$ decomposes f into a countable sequence of time-scale atoms.

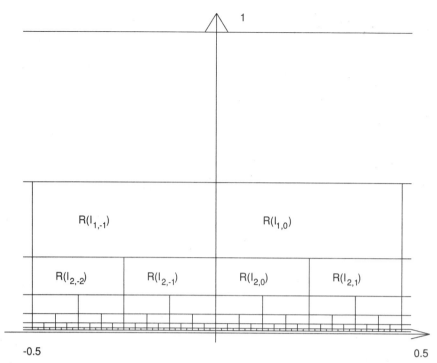

Fig. 4. A tiling of the time-scale plane by rectangles.

This analysis into atoms is informative about the properties of f; for example, suppose that f "is built from many large atoms at fine scales" then from (12.12) f cannot be very smooth. As shown in [43], one can express a variety of function space norms in terms of the size properties of the atoms; or, more properly, of the continuous wavelet transform associated to the "cells" $R(I)$. For example, if our measure of the "size" of the atom $A_I f$ is the "energy" of the "associated time-scale cell"

$$s_I(f) = \left(\iint_{R(I)} |Wf(a,b)|^2 (da/a^2)\, db \right)^{1/2}$$

then $\Sigma_I\, s_I^2 = \|f\|_{L^2}^2$.

D. Unconditional Basis

By the end of the 1970's, atomic decomposition methods gave a satisfactory understanding of H^p spaces; but in the early 1980's, the direction of research turned toward establishing a basis for these spaces. B. Maurey had shown by abstract analysis that an unconditional basis of H^1 must exist, and Carleson had shown a way to construct such a basis by. in a sense. repairing the lack of smoothness of the Haar basis.

Let $h(t) = 1_{[1/2,1)}(t) - 1_{[0,1/2)}(t)$ denote the Haar function; associate a scaled and translated version of h to each dyadic interval $I = 2^{-j}[k, k, +1]$ according to $h_I(t) = 2^{j/2}h(2^j t - k)$. This collection of functions makes a complete orthonormal system for $L^2(R)$. In particular, $f = \Sigma_I \langle f, h_I \rangle h_I$. This is similar in some ways to the atomic decomposition idea of the last section—it is indexed by dyadic intervals and associates a decomposition to a family of dyadic intervals. However, it is better in other ways, since the h_I are fixed functions rather

than atoms. Unfortunately, while it gives an unconditional basis for L^2, it does not give an unconditional basis for most of the spaces where Littlewood–Paley theory applies; the discontinuities in the h_I are problematic.

Carleson's attempt at 'repairing the Haar basis' stimulated Stromberg (1982), who succeeded in constructing an orthogonal unconditional basis for H^p spaces with $0 < p \leq 1$. In effect, he showed how, for any $p \leq 1$, to construct a function ψ so that the functions $\psi_I(t) = 2^{j/2}\psi(2^j t - k)$ were orthogonal and constituted an unconditional basis for H^p. Today we would call such a ψ a wavelet; in fact, Stromberg's ψ is a spline wavelet—a piecewise polynomial—and (ψ_I) constituted the first orthonormal wavelet basis with smooth elements. In [92], Stromberg testifies that at the time that he developed this basis he was not aware of, or interested in, applications outside of harmonic analysis. Stromberg's work was published in a conference proceedings volume and was not widely noticed at the time.

In the mid-1980's, Yves Meyer and collaborators became very interested in the continuous wavelet transform as developed by Grossmann and Morlet. They first built frame expansions, which are more discrete than the continuous wavelet transform and more rigid than the atomic decomposition. Then, Meyer developed a bandlimited function ψ—the Meyer wavelet—which generated an orthonormal basis for L^2 having elements ψ_I which were infinitely differentiable and decayed rapidly at $\pm\infty$. Lemarié and Meyer [64] then showed that this offered an unconditional basis for a very wide range of spaces: all the L^p-Sobolev, $1 < p < \infty$, of all orders $m = 0, 1, 2, \cdots$; all the Hölder H^1, and more generally, all Besov spaces. Frazier and Jawerth have shown that the Meyer basis offers unconditional bases for all the spaces in the Triebel scale; see [43].

410

E. Equivalent Norms

The solution of these norm-equivalence problems required the introduction of two new families of norms on sequence space; the general picture is due to Frazier and Jawerth [42], [43].

The first family is the (homogeneous) *Besov sequence norms*. With $\theta_{j,k}$ a shorthand for the coefficient θ_I arising from the dyadic interval $I = I_{j,k} = [k/2^j, (k+1)/2^j)$,

$$||\theta||_{\dot{b}^\alpha_{p,q}} = \left(\sum_j 2^{j(\alpha+1/2-1/p)q} \left(\sum_k |\theta_{j,k}|^p \right)^{q/p} \right)^{1/q},$$

with an obvious modification if either p or $q = \infty$. These norms first summarize the sizes of the coefficients at all positions k with a single scale j using an ℓ^p norm and then summarize across scales, with an exponential weighting.

The second family involves the (homogeneous) *Triebel sequence norms*. With χ_I the indicator of $I = I_{j,k}$,

$$||\theta||_{\dot{f}^\alpha_{pq}} = \left\| \left(\sum_I (2^{j(\alpha+1/2)} \chi_I(t) |\theta_I|)^q \right)^{1/q} \right\|_{L^p},$$

with an obvious modification if $p = \infty$ and a special modification if $q = \infty$ (which we do not describe here; this has to do with the space BMO). These norms first summarize the sizes of the coefficients across scales, and then summarize across positions.

The reader should note that the sequence space norm expressions have the unconditionality property: they only involve the sizes of the coefficients. If one shrinks the coefficients in such a way that they become term-wise smaller in absolute values, then these norms must decrease.

We give some brief examples of norm equivalences using these families. Recall the list of norm equivalence problems listed in Section XI. Our first two examples use the Besov sequence norms.

- (Homogeneous) Hölder Space $\dot{C}^\alpha(\mathbf{R})$: For $0 < \alpha < 1$, the norm $||f||_{\dot{C}^\alpha}$ is the smallest constant C so that

$$|f(t) - f(t')| \leq C |t - t'|^\alpha.$$

To get an equivalent norm, use an orthobasis built from (say) Meyer wavelets, and measure the norm of the wavelet coefficients by the Besov norm with α, $p = q = \infty$. This reduces to a very simple expression, namely,

$$||\theta||_{\dot{b}^\alpha_{\infty,\infty}} = \sup_I |\theta_I| 2^{j(\alpha+1/2)}. \qquad (12.13)$$

In short, membership in $\dot{C}^\alpha$ requires that the wavelet coefficients *all* decay like an appropriate power of the associated scale: $|\theta_I| \leq C' \cdot 2^{-j(\alpha+1/2)}$.

- *Bump Algebra:* Use an orthobasis built from the Meyer wavelets, and measure the norm of the wavelet coefficients by the Besov norm with $\alpha = 1, p = q = 1$. This reduces to a very simple expression, namely,

$$||\theta||_{\dot{b}^1_{1,1}} = \sum_I |\theta_I| 2^{j/2}. \qquad (12.14)$$

Membership in the Bump Algebra thus requires that the sum of the wavelet coefficients decay like an appropriate power of scale. Note, however, that some coefficients could be large, at the expense of others being correspondingly small in order to preserve the size of the sum.

We can also give examples using the Triebel sequence norms.

- L^p: For $1 < p < \infty$, use an orthobasis built from, e.g., the Meyer wavelets, and measure the norm of the wavelet coefficients by the Triebel sequence norm with $\alpha = 0$, $q = 2$, and p precisely the same as the p in L^p.

- L^p-*Sobolev spaces* W^m_p: For $1 < p < \infty$, use an orthobasis built from, e.g., the Meyer wavelets, and measure the norm of the wavelet coefficients by a superposition of two Triebel sequence norms, one with $\alpha = 0$, $q = 2$, and p precisely the same as the p in L^p; the other with $\alpha = m$, $q = 2$, and p precisely the same as the p in L^p.

F. Norm Equivalence as a Sampling Theorem

The Besov and Triebel sequence norms have an initially opaque appearance. A solid understanding of their structure comes from a view of norm equivalence as establishing a sampling theorem for the upper half-plane, in a manner reminiscent of the Shannon sampling theorem and its elaborations (12.1) and (12.2).

Recall the Littlewood–Paley theory of the upper half plane of Section XII-A and the use of dyadic rectangles $R(I)$ built "above" dyadic intervals from Section XII-B. Partition the upper half-plane according to the family $R(I)$ of rectangles. Given a collection of wavelet coefficients $\theta = (\theta_I)$, assign to rectangle $R(I)$ the value $|\theta_I|$. One obtains in this way a pseudo-V-function

$$\tilde{V}(t,y) = \sum_I |\theta_I| 1_{R(I)}(t,y).$$

This is a kind of caricature of the Poisson integral V. Using this function as if it were a true Poisson integral suggests to calculate, for $q < \infty$,

$$\tilde{g}_q(t) = \left(\int_0^\infty |\tilde{V}(t,y)|^q \frac{dy}{y} \right)^{1/q}.$$

As it turns out, the Triebel sequence norm is *precisely* a simple continuum norm of the object g_q

$$||\theta||_{\dot{f}^0_{p,q}} = ||\tilde{g}_q||_{L^p}.$$

In short, the Triebel sequence norm expresses the geometric analogy that the piecewise-constant object $\tilde{V}$ may be treated as if it were a Poisson integral. Why is this reasonable?

Observe that the wavelet coefficient θ_I is *precisely* a sample of the continuous wavelet transform with respect to the wavelet ψ generating the orthobasis ψ_I

$$\theta_I = \langle f, \psi_I \rangle = (W_\psi f)(2^{-j}, k2^{-j}).$$

The sampling point is $(a_j, b_{j,k})$, where $a_j = 2^{-j}, b_{j,k} = k/2^j$; these are the coordinates of the lower left corner of the rectangle $R(I_{j,k})$. In the $\alpha = 0$ case, we have

$$\tilde{V}(t,y) = \sum_{j,k} |W_\psi f(2^{-j}, k2^{-j})| 1_{R(I_{j,k})}(t,y).$$

That is, $\tilde{V}$ is a pseudo-continuous wavelet transform, gotten by replacing the true continuous wavelet transform on each cell by a cell-wise constant function with the same value in the lower left corner of each cell.

The equivalence of the true L^p norm with the Triebel sequence norm of the wavelet coefficients expresses the fact that the piecewise-constant function $\tilde{V}$, built from time-scale samples of Wf has a norm—defined on the whole time-scale plane—which is equivalent to Wf. Indeed, define a norm on the time-scale plane by

$$\|U\|_{T_{p,q}} = \left(\int_{-\infty}^{\infty} \left(\int_0^{\infty} |U(t,y)|^q \frac{dy}{y} \right)^{p/q} dt \right)^{1/p}$$

summarizing first across scales and then across positions. We have the identity $\|\tilde{g}_q\|_{L_p} = \|\tilde{V}\|_{T_{p,q}}$. The equivalence of norms $\|f\|_{L^p} \asymp \|\theta(f)\|_{f^0_{p,2}}$ can be broken into the following stages:

$$\|f\|_{L^p} \asymp \|V\|_{T_{p,2}}$$

which follows from Littlewood–Paley theory,

$$\|V\|_{T_{p,2}} \asymp \|Wf\|_{T_{p,2}}$$

which says that the "Poisson wavelet" Q_1, and some other nice wavelet ψ obtain equivalent information, and finally

$$\|Wf\|_{T_{p,2}} \asymp \|\tilde{V}\|_{T_{p,2}}.$$

This is a sampling theorem for the upper half-plane, showing that an object Wf and its piecewise-constant approximation $\tilde{V}$ have equivalent norms. It is exactly analogous to the equivalence (12.3) that we discussed in the context of the Shannon sampling theorem. Similar interpretations can be given for the Besov sequence norm as *precisely* a simple continuum norm of the object $\tilde{V}$. In the case $p, q < \infty$

$$\|\theta\|_{b^0_{p,q}} = \left(\int_0^{\infty} \left(\int_{-\infty}^{\infty} |\tilde{V}(t,y)|^p \, dt \right)^{q/p} \frac{dy}{y} \right)^{1/q}.$$

The difference is that the Besov norm involves first a summarization in position t and then a summarization in scale y; this is the opposite order from the Triebel case.

XIII. NORM EQUIVALENCE AND AXES OF ORTHOSYMMETRY

There is a striking geometric significance to the unconditional basis property.

Consider a classical example using the exact norm equivalence properties (11.3) and (11.4) from Fourier analysis. Suppose we consider the class $W^m_{2,0}(\gamma)$ consisting of all functions f obeying

$$\|f\|_{W^m_{2,0}} \leq \gamma$$

with

$$\|f\|^2_{W^m_{2,0}} = \|f\|^2_{L^2} + \|f^{(m)}\|^2_{L^2}.$$

This is a body in infinite-dimensional space; defined as it is by quadratic constraints, we call it an ellipsoid. Owing to the exact norm equivalence properties (11.3), (11.4), the axes of symmetry of the ellipsoid are precisely the sinusoids (ϕ_k).

Something similar occurs in the nonclassical cases. Consider, for example, the Hölder norm equivalence (12.13). This says that, up to an equivalent re-norming, the Hölder class is a kind of hyperrectangle in infinite-dimensional space. This hyperrectangle has axes of symmetry; the directions of these axes are given by the members of the wavelet basis.

Consider now the Bump Algebra norm equivalence (12.14). This says that, up to an equivalent re-norming, the Bump Algebra is a kind of octahedron in infinite-dimensional space. This octahedron has axes of symmetry, and these are again given by the members of the wavelet basis.

So the *unconditional basis property* means that the *basis functions serve as axes of symmetry* for the corresponding function ball. This is analogous to the existence of axes of symmetry for an ellipsoid, but is more general: it applies in the case of function balls which are not ellipsoidal, i.e., not defined by quadratic constraints.

There is another way to put this that might also be useful. The axes of orthosymmetry of an ellipsoid can be derived as eigenfunctions of the quadratic form defining the ellipsoid. The axes of orthosymmetry solve the problem of "rotating the space" into a frame where the quadratic form becomes diagonal. In the more general setting, where the norm balls are not ellipsoidal, we can say that an unconditional basis solves the problem of "rotating the space" into a frame where the norm, although not involving a quadratic functional, is "diagonalized."

XIV. BEST ORTHOBASIS FOR NONLINEAR APPROXIMATION

The unconditional basis property has important implications for schemes of nonlinear approximation which use the best n-terms in an orthonormal basis. In effect, the unconditional basis of a class F will be, in a certain asymptotic sense, the best orthonormal basis for n-term approximation of members of the associated function ball $\mathcal{F}$. We highlight these results and refer the reader to [26] and [30] for more details on nonlinear approximation.

A. n-Term Approximations: Linear and Nonlinear

Suppose one is equipped with an orthobasis (ϕ_k), and that one wishes to approximate a function f using n-term expansions

$$f \approx P_n(f; (\phi_k), (k_i)) \equiv \sum_{i=1}^{n} a_i \phi_{k_i}.$$

If the k_i are fixed—for example as the first n-basis elements in the assumed ordering—this is a problem of linear approximation, which can be solved (owing to the assumed orthogonality of the ϕ_k) by taking $a_i = \langle f, \phi_{k_i} \rangle$. Supposing that the $(k_i: i = 1, 2, \cdots)$ is an enumeration of the integers, the approximation error in such an orthogonal system is $\Sigma_{i>n} a_i^2$, which means that the error is small if the important coefficients occur in the leading n-terms rather than in tail of the sequence.

412

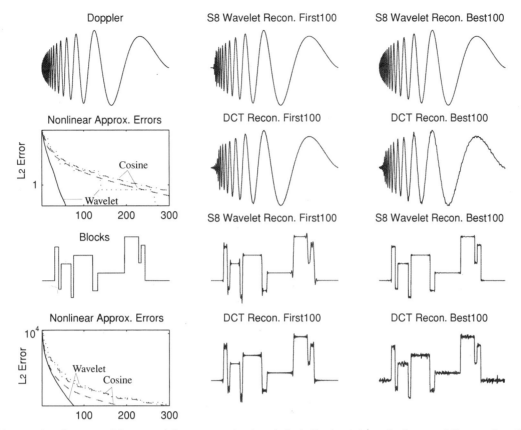

Fig. 5. Two objects, and performance of best-n and first-n approximations in both Fourier and wavelet bases, and linear and nonlinear approximation numbers (14.2).

Such linear schemes of approximation seem very natural when the orthobasis is either the classical Fourier basis or else a classical orthogonal polynomial basis, and we think in terms of the "first n-terms" as the "n lowest frequencies." Indeed, several results on harmonic analysis of smooth functions promote the expectation that the coefficients $\langle f, \phi_k \rangle$ decay with increasing frequency index k. It therefore seems natural in such a setting to adopt once and for all the standard ordering $k_i = i$, to expect that the a_i decay with i, or in other words, that the important terms in the expansion occur at the early indices in the sequence. There are many examples in both practical and theoretical approximation theory showing the essential validity of this type of linear approximation.

In general, orthobases besides the classical Fourier/orthogonal polynomial sets (and close relatives) cannot be expected to display such a fixed one-dimensional ordering of coefficient amplitudes. For example, the wavelet basis has two indices, one for scale and one for position, and it can easily happen that the "important terms" in an expansion cluster at coefficients corresponding to the same position but at many different scales. This happens, for example, when we consider the coefficients of a function with punctuated smoothness, i.e., a function which is piecewise-smooth away from discontinuities. Since, in general, the position of such singularities varies from one function to the next, in such settings, one cannot expect the "n-most important coefficients" to occur in indices chosen in a fixed nonadaptive fashion. It makes more sense to consider approximation schemes using n-term approximations where the n-included terms are the *biggest-n-terms* rather then the

first-n-terms in a fixed ordering; compare Fig. 5. Equivalently, we consider the ordering $k_i^* \equiv k_i^*(f)$ defined by coefficient amplitudes

$$|a_{k_1^*}| \geq |a_{k_2^*}| \geq \cdots \geq |a_{k_i^*}| \geq |a_{k_{i+1}^*}| \geq \cdots \qquad (14.1)$$

and define

$$Q_n(f; (\phi_k)) = \sum_{i=1}^{n} a_i \phi_{k_i^*(f)}$$

where again $a_i = \langle f, \phi_{k_i^*(f)} \rangle$. This operator at first glance seems linear, because the functionals $a_i(f)$ derive from inner products of f with basis functions $\phi_{k_i^*}$; however, in fact it is nonlinear, because the functionals $k_i^*(f)$ depend on f.

This nonlinear approximation operator conforms in the best possible fashion with the idea that the n-most-important coefficients should appear in the approximation, while the less important coefficients should not. It is also quantitatively better than any fixed linear approximation operator built from the basis (ϕ_k)

$$\|f - Q_n(f; (\phi_k))\|_{L^2} = \min_{(k_i)} \|f - P_n(f; (\phi_k), (k_i))\|_{L^2}$$

because the square of the left-hand side is $\Sigma_{i > n} \langle f, \phi_{k_i^*(f)} \rangle^2$, which by the rearrangement relation (14.1) is not larger than any sum $\Sigma_{i > n} \langle f, \phi_{k_i} \rangle^2$.

413

B. Best Orthobasis for n-Term Approximation

In general, it is not possible to say much interesting about the error in n-term approximation for a fixed function f. We therefore consider the approximation for a function class $\mathcal{F}$ which is a ball $\{f: \|f\|_F \le \gamma\}$ of a normed (or quasinormed) linear space F of functions. Given such a class $\mathcal{F}$ and an orthogonal basis Φ, the error of best n-term approximation is defined by

$$d_n(\Phi, \mathcal{F}) = \sup_{f \in \mathcal{F}} \|f - Q_n(f; \Phi)\|_{L^2}. \qquad (14.2)$$

We call the sequence $(d_n(\mathcal{F}))_{n=1}^{\infty}$ the Stechkin numbers of $\mathcal{F}$, honoring the work of Russian mathematician S. B. Stechkin, who worked with a similar quantity in the Fourier basis. The Stechkin numbers give a measure of the quality of representation of $\mathcal{F}$ from the basis Φ. If $d_n(\mathcal{F}, \Phi)$ is small, this means that every element of $\mathcal{F}$ is well-approximated by n-terms chosen from the basis, with the possibility that different sets of n-terms are needed for different $f \in \mathcal{F}$.

Different orthonormal bases can have very different approximation characteristics for a given function class. Suppose we consider the class $BV(1)$ of all functions on $T = [0, 2\pi)$, with bounded variation ≤ 1 as in [31]. For the Fourier system, $d_n(BV(1), \text{FOURIER}) \asymp n^{-1/2}$, owing to the fact that BV contains objects with discontinuities, and sinusoids have difficulty representing such discontinuities, while for the Haar-wavelet system $d_n(BV(1), \text{HAAR}) \asymp n^{-1}$, intuitively because the operator Q_n in the Haar expansion can easily adapt to the presence of discontinuities by including terms in the expansion at fine scales in the vicinity of such singularities and using only terms at coarse scales far away from singularities.

Consider now the problem of finding a best orthonormal basis—i.e., of solving

$$d_n^*(\mathcal{F}) = \inf_{\Phi} d_n(\Phi, \mathcal{F}).$$

We call $d_n^*(\mathcal{F})$ the nonlinear orthowidth of $\mathcal{F}$; this is not one of the usual definitions of nonlinear widths (see [77]) but is well suited for our purposes. This width seeks a basis, in some sense, ideally adapted to $\mathcal{F}$, getting the best guarantee of performance in approximation of members of $\mathcal{F}$ by the use of n adaptively chosen terms. As it turns out, it seems out of reach to solve this problem exactly in many interesting cases; and any solution might be very complex, for example, depending delicately on the choice of n. However, it is possible, for balls $\mathcal{F}$ arising from classes F which have an unconditional orthobasis and sufficient additional structure,

to obtain asymptotic results. Thus for function balls $W_2^m(\gamma)$ defined by quadratic constraints on the function and its mth derivative, we have

$$\begin{aligned} d_n^*(W_2^m(\gamma)) \\ &\asymp d_n(\text{FOURIER}, W_2^m(\gamma)) \\ &\asymp d_n(\text{PERIODIC WAVELETS}, W_2^m(\gamma)) \asymp n^{-m}, \quad n \to \infty \end{aligned}$$

saying that either the standard Fourier basis, or else a smooth periodic wavelet basis, is a kind of best orthobasis for such a class. For the function balls $BV(\gamma)$ consisting of functions on the interval with bounded variation $\le \gamma$

$$d_n^*(BV(\gamma)) \asymp d_n(\text{HAAR}, BV(\gamma)) \asymp n^{-1}, \qquad n \to \infty$$

so that the Haar basis is a kind of best orthobasis for such a class. For comparison, a smooth wavelet basis is also a kind of best basis, $d_n(\text{WAVELETS}, BV(\gamma)) \asymp n^{-1}$, while a Fourier basis is not: $d_n(\text{FOURIER}, BV(\gamma)) \asymp n^{-1/2} \ne O(n^{-1})$. A summary is given in the table at the bottom of this page.

Results on rates of nonlinear approximation by wavelet series for an interesting range Besov classes were obtained in [29].

C. Geometry of Best Orthobasis

There is a nice geometric picture which underlies these results about best orthobases; essentially, *an orthobasis unconditional for a function class F is asymptotically a best orthobasis for that class*. Thus the extensive work of harmonic analysts to build unconditional bases—a demanding enterprise whose significance was largely closed to outsiders for many years—can be seen as an effort which, when successful, has as a byproduct the construction of best orthobases for nonlinear approximation.

To see this essential point requires one extra element. Let $0 < p < 2$, and note especially that we include the possibility that $0 < p < 1$. Let $|\theta|_{(k)}$ denote the kth element in the decreasing rearrangement of magnitudes of entries in θ, so that $|\theta|_{(1)} \ge |\theta|_{(2)} \ge \cdots$. The weak-$\ell^p$-norm is

$$\|\theta\|_{w\ell^p} = \sup_{k > 0} k^{1/p} |\theta|_{(k)}.$$

This is really only a quasinorm; it does not in general obey the triangle inequality. This norm is of interest because of the way it expresses the rate of approximation of operators Q_n in a given basis. Indeed, if $p = 2/(2m+1)$ then

$$\|f - Q_n f\|_2 \le C_1(p) \|\theta\|_{w\ell^p} \cdot (n+1)^{-m}, \qquad n \ge 0.$$

Name	F	Best Basis	$d_n^*(\mathcal{F}) \asymp$	$\alpha_n^*(\mathcal{F})$
L^2-Sobolev	W_2^m	Fourier or Wavelet	n^{-m}	m
L^p-Sobolev	W_p^m	Wavelet	n^{-m}	m
Hölder	$\dot{C}^\alpha$	Wavelet	$n^{-\alpha}$	α
Bump Algebra	$\dot{B}_{1,1}^1$	Wavelet	n^{-1}	1
Bounded Variation	BV	Haar	n^{-1}	1
Segal Algebra	S	Wilson	$n^{-1/2}$	$1/2$

414

The result has a converse

$$\sup_{n \geq 0} (n+1)^m \cdot ||f - Q_n f||_2 \geq C_0(p) ||\theta||_{w\ell^p}.$$

A given function f can be approximated by Q_n with error $\leq C_1(n+1)^{-m}$ for all n if $||\theta||_{w\ell^p} \leq 1$; it can only be approximated with error $\leq C_0(n+1)^{-m}$ if $||\theta||_{w\ell^p} \leq 1$. A given function ball $\mathcal{F}(\gamma)$ has functions f all of which can be approximated by $Q_n(f; (\phi_k))$ at error $\leq C \cdot (n+1)^{-m}$ for all n and for some C fixed independently of f if and only if for some C'

$$\sup \{||\theta(f)||_{w\ell^p} \colon f \in \mathcal{F}(\gamma)\} < C'.$$

Suppose we have a ball $\mathcal{F}$ arising from a class F with an unconditional basis (ϕ_k) and we consider using a possibly different orthobasis (φ_k) to do the nonlinear approximation: $Q_n(\cdot; (\varphi_k))$. The coefficient sequence $\omega = (\langle \varphi_k, f \rangle)$ obeys $\omega = U\theta$ where U is an orthogonal transformation of ℓ^2. Define then $\Theta = \{\theta(f) \colon f \in \mathcal{F}(\gamma)\}$. The rate of convergence of nonlinear approximation with respect to the new system is constrained by the relation

$$\sup \{||\omega(f)||_{w\ell^p} \colon f \in \mathcal{F}(\gamma)\}$$
$$= \sup \{||U\theta(f)||_{w\ell^p} \colon f \in \mathcal{F}(\gamma)\}$$
$$\geq \sup \{||U\theta||_{w\ell^p} \colon \theta \in \Theta\}.$$

By the unconditional basis property, there is an orthosymmetric set Θ^0 and constants A and B such that $A \cdot \Theta^0 \subset \Theta \subset B \cdot \Theta^0$. Hence, up to homothetic multiples, Θ is orthosymmetric.

Now the fact that Θ^0 is orthosymmetric means that it is in some sense "optimally positioned" about its axes; hence it is intuitive that rotating by U cannot improve its position. Thus [31]

$$\sup \{||U\theta||_{w\ell^p} \colon \theta \in \Theta^0\} \geq c(p) \sup \{||\theta||_{w\ell^p} \colon \theta \in \Theta^0\}.$$

We conclude that if (ϕ_k) is an orthogonal unconditional basis for F and if $d_n(\mathcal{F}(\gamma); (\phi_k)) \asymp n^{-m}$, then it is impossible that $d_n^*(\mathcal{F}(\gamma)) \leq C \cdot n^{-m'}$ for any $m' > m$. Indeed, if it were so, then we would have some basis (φ_k) achieving $d_n(\mathcal{F}(\gamma); (\varphi_k)) \leq C \cdot n^{-m'}$, which would imply that also the unconditional basis achieves $d_n(\mathcal{F}(\gamma); (\phi_k)) \leq C' \cdot n^{-m'}, m' > m$, contradicting the assumption that merely $d_n(\mathcal{F}(\gamma); (\phi_k)) \asymp n^{-m}$. In a sense, up to a constant factor improvement, the axes of symmetry make a best orthogonal basis.

XV. ϵ-ENTROPY OF FUNCTIONAL CLASSES

We now show that nonlinear approximation in an orthogonal unconditional basis of a class F can be used, quite generally, to obtain asymptotically, as $\epsilon \to 0$, the optimal degree of data compression for a corresponding ball $\mathcal{F}$. This completes the development of the last few sections.

A. State of the Art

Consider the problem of determining the Kolmogorov ϵ-entropy for a function ball $\mathcal{F}$; this gives the minimal number of bits needed to describe an arbitrary member of $\mathcal{F}$ to within accuracy ϵ.

This is a hard problem, with very few sharp results. Underscoring the difficulty of obtaining results in this area is the commentary of V. M. Tikhomirov in Kolmogorov's *Selected Works* [94]

> The question of finding the exact value of the ϵ-entropy ... is a very difficult one .... Besides [one specific example] ... the author of this commentary knows no meaningful examples of infinite-dimensional compact sets for which the problem of ϵ-entropy ... is solved exactly.

This summarizes the state of work in 1992, more than 35 years after the initial concept was coined by Kolmogorov. In fact, outside of the case alluded to by Tikhomirov, of ϵ-entropy of Lipschitz functions measured in L^∞ metric, and the case which has emerged since then, of smooth functions in L^2 norm as mentioned above, there are no asymptotically exact results. The typical state of the art for research in this area is that within usual scales of function classes having finitely many derivatives, one gets order bounds: finite positive constants A_0 and A_1, and an exponent m depending on $\mathcal{F}$ but not on $\epsilon < \epsilon_0$, such that

$$A_0 \epsilon^{-1/m} \leq H_\epsilon(\mathcal{F}) \leq A_1 \epsilon^{-1/m}, \qquad \epsilon \to 0. \quad (15.1)$$

Such order bounds display some paradigmatic features of the state of the art of ϵ-entropy research. First, such a result *does* tie down the precise rate involved in the growth of the net (i.e., $H_\epsilon = O(\epsilon^{-1/m})$ as $\epsilon \to 0$). Second, it *does not* tie down the precise constants involved in the decay (i.e., $A_0 \neq A_1$). Third, the result (and its proof) does not directly exhibit information about the properties of an optimal ϵ-net. For a review of the theory see [66].

In this section we consider only the rough asymptotics of the ϵ-entropy via the critical exponent

$$\alpha^*(\mathcal{F}) = \sup \{\alpha \colon H_\epsilon(\mathcal{F}) = O(\epsilon^{-1/\alpha})\}.$$

If $H_\epsilon(\mathcal{F}) = \epsilon^{-1/\alpha}$ then $\alpha^*(\mathcal{F}) = \alpha$; but it is also true that if $H_\epsilon(\mathcal{F}) = \log(\epsilon^{-1})^\beta \cdot \epsilon^{-1/\alpha}$ then $\alpha^*(\mathcal{F}) = \alpha$. We should think of α^* as capturing only crude aspects of the asymptotics of ϵ-entropy, since it ignores "log terms" and related phenomena. We will show how to code in a way which achieves the rough asymptotic behavior.

B. Achieving the Exponent of ϵ-Entropy

Suppose we have a function ball $\mathcal{F}(\gamma)$ of a class F with unconditional basis (ϕ_k), and that, in addition, $\mathcal{F}(\gamma)$ has a certain tail compactness for the L^2 norm. In particular, suppose that in some fixed arrangement (k_i) of coordinates

$$\sup_{f \in \mathcal{F}(\gamma)} ||f - P_n(f; (\phi_k), (k_i))||_{L^2}^2 \leq C \cdot n^{-\mu} \quad (15.2)$$

for some $\mu > 0$.

415

We use nonlinear approximation in the basis (ϕ_k) to construct a binary coder giving an ϵ-description for all members f of $\mathcal{F}(\gamma)$. The idea: for an appropriate squared-L^2 distortion level ϵ^2, there is an $n = n(\epsilon, \mathcal{F})$ so that the best n-term approximation $Q_n(f; (\phi_k))$ achieves an approximation error $\leq \epsilon/2$. We then approximately represent f by digitally encoding the approximant. A reasonable way to do this is to concatenate a lossless binary code for the positions $k_1^*, \cdots, k_n^*$ of the important coefficients with a lossy binary code for quantized values $\tilde{a}_i$ of the coefficients a_i, taking care that the coefficients are encoded with an accuracy enabling accurate reconstruction of the approximant

$$\|Q_n(f; (\phi_k)) - \sum_{i=1}^{n} \tilde{a}_i \phi_{k_i^*}\|_2 \leq \epsilon/2. \qquad (15.3)$$

Such a two-part code will produce a decodable binary representation having distortion $\leq \epsilon$ for every element of $\mathcal{F}(\gamma)$.

Here is a very crude procedure for choosing the quantization of the coefficients: there are n coefficients to be encoded; the coefficients can all be encoded with accuracy δ using a total of $\log(4/\delta)n$ bits. If we choose δ so that $n\delta^2 = \epsilon^2/4$, then we achieve (15.3).

To encode the positional information giving the locations $k_1^*, \cdots, k_n^*$ of the coefficients used in the approximant, use (15.2). This implies that there are C and ν so that, with $K_n = Cn^\nu$, for a given n, we can ignore coefficients outside the range $1 \leq k \leq K_n$. Hence, the positions can be encoded using at most $n \cdot \log_2(Cn^\nu)$ bits.

This gives a total codelength of $(C_1 + C_2 \log(n)) \cdot n$ bits. Now if $d_n^*(\mathcal{F}) \asymp n^{-m}$ then $n(\epsilon) \asymp \epsilon^{-1/m}$. Hence, assuming only that $d_n^*(\mathcal{F}) \asymp n^{-m}$ and that $\mathcal{F}$ is minimally tail compact, we conclude that

$$\alpha^*(\mathcal{F}) \leq m \qquad (15.4)$$

and that a nonlinear approximation-based coder achieves this upper bound.

C. Lower Bound via $R(D)$

The upper bound realized through nonlinear approximation is sharp, as shown by the following argument [32]. Assume that $\mathcal{F}$ is a ball in a function class F that admits (ϕ_k) as an unconditional basis. The unconditional basis property means, roughly speaking, that $\mathcal{F}$ contains many very-high-dimensional hypercubes of appreciable sidelength. As we will see, $R(D)$ theory tells us precisely how many bits are required to D-faithfully represent objects in such hypercubes *chosen on average*. Obviously, one cannot faithfully represent *every object* in such hypercubes with fewer than the indicated number of bits.

Suppose now that (15.2) holds. We shall assume also that m is the best possible exponent; more precisely, we assume that, for some $A, B > 0$

$$A \cdot n^{-m} \leq d_n^*(\mathcal{F}, (\phi_k)) \leq B \cdot n^{-m}. \qquad (15.5)$$

For fixed n, take f_n such that it attains the nonlinear n-width

$$\|f_n - Q_n(f_n; (\phi_k))\|_{L^2} = d_n^*(\mathcal{F}, (\phi_k)).$$

Let $\eta = \min_{1 \leq i \leq n} |a_i|$. By the unconditionality of the norm $\|\theta\|$, for every sequence of signs ($\pm_i : 1 \leq i \leq n$) the object $g = \Sigma_i \pm_i \eta \phi_{k_i^*}$ belongs to $\mathcal{F}$. Hence we have constructed an orthogonal hypercube $\mathcal{H}$ of dimension n and sidelength η with $\mathcal{H} \subset \mathcal{F}$. Consider now h a random vertex of the hypercube $\mathcal{H}$. Representing this vertex with L^2 error $\leq n^{1/2} \cdot \eta \cdot \gamma$ is, owing to the orthogonality of the hypercube, the same as representing the sequence of signs with ℓ^2 error $\leq n^{1/2} \cdot \gamma$. Fix $\gamma < 1$; now use rate-distortion theory to obtain the rate-distortion curve for a binary discrete memoryless source with mean-squared error for single-letter difference distortion measure. No γ-faithful code for this source can use essentially fewer than $R(\gamma) \cdot n$ bits, where $R(\gamma) > 0$. Hence setting $\epsilon = n^{1/2} \cdot \eta \cdot \gamma$, we have

$$H_\epsilon(\mathcal{F}) \geq R(\gamma) \cdot n. \qquad (15.6)$$

Since, for sufficiently large C, $d_{Cn}^*(\mathcal{F}, (\phi_k)) \leq A/2 \cdot n^{-m}$, we find that

$$\|Q_n(f_n; (\phi_k)) - Q_{Cn}(f_n; (\phi_k))\|_{L^2} \geq A/2 \cdot n^{-m}$$

which implies that $\eta^2(C - 1)n \geq [A/2 \cdot n^{-m}]^2$, or $\eta \geq C'n^{-1/p}$. In other words,

$$\epsilon \geq \text{const } n^{1/2-1/p} = \text{const } n^{-m}.$$

We then conclude from (15.6) that

$$\alpha^*(\mathcal{F}) \geq m.$$

D. Order Asymptotics of ϵ-Entropy

The notion of achieving the exponent of the ϵ-entropy, while leading to very general results, is less precise than we would like. We now know that for a wide variety of classes of smooth functions, not only can the exponent be achieved, but also the correct order asymptotics (15.1) can be obtained by coders based on scalar quantization of the coefficients in a wavelet basis, followed by appropriate positional coding [14], [7], [15].

An important ingredient of nonlinear approximation results is the ability of the selected n-terms to occur at variable positions in the expansion. However, provision for the selected terms to occur in *completely arbitrary* arrangements of time-scale positions is actually not necessary, and we can obtain bit savings by exploiting the more limited range of possible positional combinations. A second factor is that most of the coefficients occurring in the quantized approximant involve small integer multiples of the quantum, and it can be known in advance that this is typically so at finer scales; provision for the "big coefficients" to occur in completely arbitrary orders among the significant ones is also not necessary. Consequently, there are further bit savings available there as well. By exploiting these two facts, one can develop coders which are within constant factors of the ϵ-entropy. We will explain this further in Section XVII below.

XVI. COMPARISON TO TRADITIONAL TRANSFORM CODING

The results of the last few section offer an interesting comparison with traditional ideas of transform coding theory, for example the $R(D)$ theory of Section II.

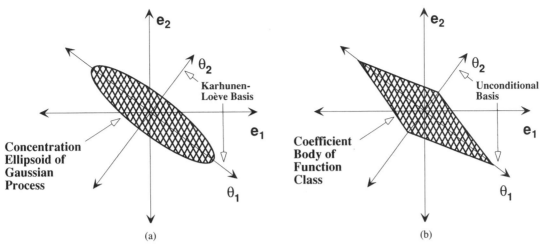

Fig. 6. A comparison of "diagonalization" problems. (a) Karhunen–Loève finds axes of symmetry of concentration ellipsoid. (b) Unconditional basis finds axes of symmetry of function class.

A. Nonlinear Approximation as Transform Coding

Effectively, the above results on nonlinear approximation can be interpreted as describing a very simple transform coding scheme. Accordingly, the results show that *transform coding in an unconditional basis for a class F* provides a near-optimal coding scheme for corresponding function balls $\mathcal{F}$.

Consider the following very simple transform coding idea. It has the following steps.

- We assume that we are given a certain *quantization step* q and a certain *bandlimit* K.
- Given an f to be compressed, we obtain the first K coefficients of f according to the system (ϕ_k): $(a_k: 1 \leq k \leq K)$.
- We then apply simple scalar quantization to those coefficients, with stepsize q.

$$\tilde{a}_k = \mathrm{sgn}\,(a_k) \cdot q \cdot \mathrm{Floor}\,(|a_k|/q).$$

- Anticipating that the vast majority of these K quantized coefficients will turn out to be zero, we apply run-length coding to the quantized coefficients to efficiently code long runs of zeros.

This is a very simple coding procedure, perhaps even naive. But it turns out that

- if we apply this procedure to functions in the ball $\mathcal{F}(\gamma)$;
- if this ball arises from a function class F for which (ϕ_k) is an unconditional basis;
- if this ball obeys the minimal tail compactness condition (15.2), and the Stechkin numbers obey (15.5);
- if the coding parameters are appropriately calibrated;

the coder can achieve ϵ-descriptions of every $f \in \mathcal{F}(\gamma)$ achieving the rough asymptotics for the ϵ-entropy as described by $\alpha^*(\mathcal{F})$.

Essentially, the idea is that the behavior of the "nonlinear approximation" coder of Section XV can be realized by the "scalar quantization" coder, when calibrated with the right parameters. Indeed, it is obvious that the parameter K of the scalar quantizer and the parameter K_n of the nonlinear approximation coder play the same role; to calibrate the two coders they should simply be made equal. It then seems natural

to calibrate q with n via

$$n(q) = \sum_k 1_{\{|\theta_k(f)| > q\}}.$$

After this calibration the two coders are roughly equivalent: they select approximants with precisely the same nonzero coefficients. The nonzero coefficients might be quantized slightly differently ($q \neq \delta$), but using a few simple estimates deriving from the assumption $d_n^*(\mathcal{F}(\gamma)) \asymp n^{-m}$, one can see that they give comparable performance both in bits used and distortion achieved.

B. Comparison of Diagonalization Problems

Now we are in a position to compare the theory of Sections XI–XV with the Shannon $R(D)$ story of Section II. The $R(D)$ story of Section II says: to optimally compress a Gaussian stochastic process, transform the data into the Karhunen–Loève domain, and then quantize. The ϵ-entropy story of Sections XI–XV says: to (roughly) optimally compress a function ball $\mathcal{F}$, transform into the unconditional basis, and quantize.

In short, an orthogonal unconditional basis of a normed space plays the same role for function classes as the eigenbasis of the covariance plays for stochastic processes.

We have pointed out that an unconditional basis furnishes a generalization to nonquadratic forms of the concept of diagonalization of quadratic form. The Hölder class has, after an equivalent renorming, the shape of a hyperrectangle. The Bump Algebra has, after an equivalent renorming, the shape of an octahedron. A wavelet basis serves as axes of symmetry of these balls, just as an eigenbasis of a quadratic form serves as axes of symmetry of the corresponding ellipsoid.

For Gaussian random vectors, there is the concept of "ellipsoid of concentration;" this is an ellipsoidal solid which contains the bulk of the realizations of the Gaussian distribution. In effect, the Gaussian-$R(D)$ coding procedure identifies the problem of coding with one of transforming into the basis serving as axes of symmetry of the concentration ellipsoid. In comparison, our interpretation of the Kolmogorov-H_ϵ theory is that one should transform into the basis serving as axes of symmetry of the function ball, as illustrated by Fig. 6.

	Class	Process	Basis
L^2	Ellipsoid	Gaussian	Eigenbasis
non-L^2	Body	non-Gaussian	Unconditional Orthobasis

In effect, the function balls that we can describe by wavelet bases through norm equivalence, are often nonellipsoidal and in such cases do not correspond to the concentration ellipsoids of Gaussian phenomena. There is in some sense an analogy here to finding an *appropriate orthogonal transform for non-Gaussian data*. In the table at the top of this page, we record some aspects of this analogy without taking space to fully explain it. See also [34].

The article [27] explored using functional balls as models for real image data. The "Gaussian model" of data is an ellipsoid; but empirical work shows that, within the Besov and related scales, the nonellipsoidal cases provide a better fit to real image data. So the "better" diagonalization theory may well be the nontraditional one.

XVII. Beyond Orthogonal Bases: Trees

The effort of the harmonic analysis community to develop unconditional orthogonal bases can now be seen to have relevance to data compression and transform coding.

Unconditional bases exist only in very special settings, and the harmonic analysis community has developed many other interesting structures over the years—structures which go far beyond the concept of orthogonal basis.

We expect these broader notions of representation also to have significant data compression implications. In this section, we discuss representations based on the notion of dyadic tree and some data compression interpretations.

A. Recursive Dyadic Partitioning

A *recursive dyadic partition* (RDP) of a dyadic interval I_0 is any partition reachable by applying two rules.

- *Starting Rule:* $\{I_0\}$ itself is an RDP.
- *Dyadic Refinement:* If $\{I_1, \cdots, I_m\}$ is an RDP, and $I_j = I_{j,1} \cup I_{j,2}$ is a partition of the dyadic interval I_j into its left and right dyadic subintervals, then $\{I_1, \cdots, I_{j-1}, I_{j,1}, I_{j,2}, I_{j+1}, \cdots, I_m\}$ is a new RDP.

RDP's are also naturally associated to binary trees; if we label the root node of a binary tree by I_0 and let the two children of the node correspond to the two dyadic subintervals of I_0, we associate with each RDP a tree whose terminal nodes are subintervals comprising members of the partition. This correspondence allows us to speak of methods exploiting RDP's as "tree-structured methods."

Recursive dyadic partitioning has played an important role throughout the subject of harmonic analysis, as one can see from many examples in [89] and [45]. It is associated with ideas like the Whitney decomposition of the 1930's, and the Calderón–Zygmund Lemma in the 1950's.

A powerful strategy in harmonic analysis is to construct RDP's according to "stopping time rules" which describe when to stop refining. This gives rise to data structures that are highly adapted to the underlying objects driving the construction. One then obtains analytic information about the objects of interest by combining information about the structure of the constructed partition and the rule which generated it. In short, recursive dyadic partitioning is a flexible general strategy for certain kinds of delicate nonlinear analysis.

The RDP concept allows a useful decoration of the time-scale plane, based on the family of time-scale rectangles $R(I)$ which we introduced in Section XII-B. If we think of all the intervals visited in the sequential construction of an RDP starting from the root I_0 as intervals where something "important is happening" and the ones not visited, i.e., those occurring at finer scales than intervals in the partition, as ones where "not much is happening," we thereby obtain an adaptive labeling of the time-scale plane by "importance."

Here is a simple example, useful below. Suppose we construct an RDP using the rule "stop when no subinterval of the current interval has a wavelet coefficient $|\theta_I| > \epsilon$;" the corresponding labeling of the time-scale plane shows a "stopping time region" outside of which all intervals are unimportant, i.e., are associated to wavelet coefficients $\leq \epsilon$. For later use, we call this stopping-time region the *hereditary cover of the set of wavelet coefficients larger than ϵ*; it includes not only the cells $R(I)$ associated to "big" wavelet coefficients, but also the ancestors of those cells. The typical appearance of such a region, in analyzing an object with discontinuities, is that of a region with very fine "tendrils" reaching down to fine scales in the vicinity of the discontinuities; the visual appearance can be quite striking; see Fig. 7.

Often, as in the Whitney and Calderón–Zygmund constructions, one runs the "stopping time" construction only once, but there are occasions where running it repeatedly is important. Doing so will produce a sequence of nested sets; in the hereditary cover example, one can see that running the stopping time argument for $\epsilon = 2^{-k}$ will give a sequence of regions; outside of the kth one, no coefficient can be larger than 2^{-k}.

In the 1950's and early 1960's, Carleson studied problems of interpolation in the upper half-plane. In this problem, we suppose we are given prescribed values u_k at an irregular set of points (t_k, y_k) in the upper half-plane

$$U(t_k, y_k) = u_k, \qquad k = 1, 2, \cdots$$

and we ask whether there is a bounded function f on the line whose Poisson integral U obeys the stated conditions. Owing to the connection with wavelet transforms, this is much like asking whether, from a given scattered collection of data

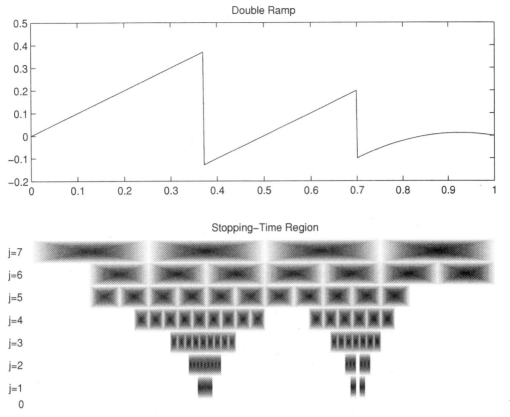

Fig. 7. An object, and the stopping-time region for the q-big coefficients.

about the wavelet transform (b_k, a_k) we can reconstruct the underlying function. Carleson developed complete answers to this problem, through a method now called the "Corona Construction," based on running stopping time estimates repeatedly. Recently P. Jones [57] discussed a few far-reaching applications of this idea in various branches of analysis, reaching the conclusion that it ". . . is one of the most malleable tools available."

B. Trees and Data Compression

In the 1960's, Birman and Solomjak [8] showed how to use recursive dyadic partitions to develop coders achieving the correct order of Kolmogorov ϵ-entropy for L^p-Sobolev function classes.

The Birman–Solomjak procedure starts from a function f of interest, and constructs a partition based on a parameter δ. Beginning with I_0 the whole domain of interest, the stopping rule refines the dyadic interval I only if approximating the function f on I by a polynomial of degree m gives an error exceeding δ. Call the resulting RDP a δ-partition. The coding method is to construct a δ-partition, where the parameter δ is chosen to give a certain desired global accuracy of approximation, and to represent the underlying function by digitizing the approximating polynomials associated with the δ-partition. By analyzing the number of pieces of an ϵ-partition, and the total approximation error of a δ-partition, and by studying the required number of bits to code for the approximating polynomials on each individual, they showed that their method gave optimal order bounds on the number of bits required to ϵ-approximate a function in a $W_p^m(\gamma)$ ball.

This type of result works in a broader scale of settings than just the L^p-Sobolev balls. A modern understanding of the underlying nonlinear approximation properties of this approach is developed in [28].

This approximation scheme is highly adaptive, with the partition adapting spatially to the structure of the underlying object. The ability of the scheme to refine more aggressively in certain parts of the domain than in others is actually necessary to obtaining optimal order bounds for certain choices of the index p defining the Sobolev norm; if we use L^2 norm for measuring approximation error, the adaptive refinement is necessary whenever $p < 2$. Such spatially inhomogeneous refinement allows to use fewer bits to code in areas of unremarkable behavior and more bits in areas of rapid change.

RDP ideas can also be used to develop wavelet-domain transform coders that achieve the optimal order ϵ-entropy bounds over L^p-Sobolev balls $W_p^m(\gamma)$, with $m+1/2-1/p > 0$. Recall that the argument of Section XV showed that any coding of such a space must require $\geq C\epsilon^{-1/m}$ bits, while a very crude transform coding was offered that required order $\log(\epsilon^{-1})\epsilon^{-1/m}$ bits. We are claiming that RDP ideas can be used to eliminate the log term in this estimate [14]. In effect, we are saying that by exploiting trees, we can make the cost of coding the position of the big wavelet coefficients at worst comparable to the ϵ-entropy.

The key point about a function in L^p-Sobolev space is that, on average, the coefficients $\theta_{j,k}$ decay with decreasing scale 2^{-j}. Indeed, from the g-function representation described in Section XII-D, we can see that the wavelet coefficients of such a function obey, at level j

$$\left(\sum_k |\theta_{j,k}|^p\right)^{1/p} \leq \text{Const} \cdot 2^{-j(m+1/2-1/p)}. \quad (17.1)$$

In the range $m + 1/2 - 1/p > 0$, this inequality controls rather powerfully the number and position of nonzero coefficients in a scalar quantization of the wavelet coefficients. Using it in conjunction with RDP ideas allows to code the position of the nonzero wavelet coefficients with far fewer bits than we have employed in the run-length coding ideas of Section XV.

After running a scalar quantizer on the wavelet coefficients, we are left with a scattered collection of nonzero quantizer outputs; these correspond to coefficients exceeding the quantizer interval q. Now form the hereditary cover of the set of all coefficients exceeding q, using the stopping time argument described in Section XVII-A. The coder will consist of two pieces: a lossless code describing this stopping time region (also the positions within the region containing nonzero quantizer outputs), and a linear array giving the quantizer outputs associated with nonzero cells in the region.

This coder allows the exact same reconstruction that was employed using the much cruder coder of Section XV. We now turn to estimates of the number of bits required.

A stopping-time region can be easily coded by recording the bits of the individual refine/don't refine decisions; we should record also the presence/absence of a "big" coefficient at each nonterminal cell in the region, which involves a second array of bits.

The number of bits required to code for a stopping-time region is, of course, proportional to the number of cells in the region itself. We will use in a moment the inequality (17.1) to argue that in a certain maximal sense the number of cells in a hereditary cover is not essentially larger than the original number of entries generating the cover. It will follow from this that the number of bits required to code the positions of the nonzero quantizer outputs is in a maximal sense proportional to the number n of nonzero quantizer outputs. This, in turn, is the desired estimate; the cruder approach of Section XV gave only the estimate $n \log(n)$, where n is the number of quantizer outputs. For a careful spelling-out of the kind of argument we are about to give, see [33, Lemma 10.3].

We now estimate the maximal number of cells in the stopping-time region, making some remarks about the kind of control exerted by (17.1) on the arrangement and sizes of the wavelet coefficients; compare Fig. 7. The wavelet coefficients of functions in an L^p-Sobolev ball associated to I_0 have a "Last Full Level" J_0: this is the finest level j for which one can find some f in the ball such that for all $I \subset I_0$ of length 2^{-j}, the associated wavelet coefficient exceeds q in absolute value. By (17.1), any such j obeys $j \leq j_0$, where j_0 is the real solution of

$$2^{j_0/p} q = C \cdot 2^{-j_0(\alpha+1/2-1/p)}.$$

The wavelet coefficients also have a "First Empty Level" J_1, i.e., a coarsest level beyond which all wavelet coefficients are bounded above in absolute value by q. By (17.1), any

nonzero quantizer output occurs at $j \leq j_1$, where

$$q = C \cdot 2^{-j_1(\alpha+1/2-1/p)}.$$

At scales intermediate between the two special values, $j_0 < j < j_1$, there are possibly "sparse levels" which can contain wavelet coefficients exceeding q, in a subset of the positions. However, the maximum possible number n_j of such nonzero quantizer outputs at level j thins out rapidly, in fact exponentially, with increasing $j - j_0$. Indeed, we must have

$$n_j^{1/p} q \leq C \cdot 2^{-j(\alpha+1/2-1/p)}$$

and from $n_{\lfloor j_0 \rfloor} \leq 2^{j_0}$ we get

$$n_j \leq \text{Const} \cdot 2^{j_0} \cdot 2^{-\beta(j-j_0)}$$

with $\beta > 0$.

In short, there are about 2^{j_0} possible "big" coefficients at the level nearest j_0, but the maximal number of nonzero coefficients decays exponentially fast at scales away from j_0. In an obvious probabilistic interpretation of these facts the "expected distance" of a nonzero coefficient below j_0 is $O(1)$.

Now obviously, in forming the hereditary cover of the positions of nonzero quantizer outputs, we will not obtain a set larger than the set we would get by including all positions through level j_0, and also including all "tendrils" reaching down to positions of the nonzeros at finer scales than this. The expected number of cells in a tendril is $O(1)$ and the number of tendrils is $O(2^{j_0})$. Therefore, the maximal number of cells in the q-big region is not more than $C2^{j_0(q)}$. The maximal number of nonzeros is of size $C2^{j_0(q)}$.

These bounds imply the required estimates on the number of bits to code for positional information.

One needs to spend a little care also on the encoding of the coefficients themselves. A naive procedure would spend $O\left(\log\left(\epsilon^{-1}\right)\right)$ on each of $O\left(\epsilon^{-1/m}\right)$ coefficients, leading to a crude estimate requiring $\log\left(\epsilon^{-1}\right)\epsilon^{-1/m}$ bits, now to encode the coefficient information. By making use of the nested sets in the hereditary cover described earlier, one can structure the coefficients to be retained into layers, in which the label of the layer indicates how many (or few) bits need to be spent on coefficients in that layer. One can estimate, similarly to what was done above, that the layers with large coefficients, for which more bits are required, contain few elements; layers corresponding to much smaller coefficients have many more elements, but because their label already restricted their size, we spend fewer bits on them to specify them with the same precision. Accounting for the cost in bits of this procedure, one finds that encoding the coefficients also requires $O\left(\epsilon^{-1/m}\right)$ bits only.

This encoding strategy can be modified so as to be progressive and universal. By adding one bit for each existing coefficient and new bits to specify the new coefficients and their position, it becomes progressive. Each additional stream of bits serves to add new detail to the existing approximation in a nonredundant way. The encoding is also universal in the sense that the encoder does not need to know the characteristics of the class $\mathcal{F}$: the encoder is defined once and for all and enjoys the property that each class $\mathcal{F}$ which has Φ as an unconditional basis will be optimally encoded with respect to Kolmogorov entropy. It is interesting to note that practical wavelet-based encoders, such as those introduced for images in [86] and [82], carry out a similar procedure.

XVIII. Beyond Time Scale: Time Frequency

The analysis methods described so far—wavelets or trees—were *Time-Scale* methods. These methods associate, to a simple function of time only, an object extending over both time and scale, and they extract analytic information from that two-variable object.

An important complement to this is the family of *Time-Frequency* methods. Broadly speaking, these methods try to identify the different frequencies present in an object at time t.

In a sense, time-scale methods are useful for compressing objects which display punctuated smoothness—e.g., which are typically smooth away from singularities. Time-frequency methods work for oscillatory objects where the frequency content changes gradually in time.

One thinks of time-scale methods as more naturally adapted to image data, while time-frequency methods seem more suited for acoustic phenomena. For some viewpoints on mathematical time-frequency analysis, see [21], [23], and [39].

In this section we very briefly cover time-frequency ideas, to illustrate some of the potential of harmonic analysis in this setting.

A. Modulation Spaces

Let $g(t) = \sqrt{2} \cdot \pi^{1/2} \cdot e^{-t^2/2}$ be a Gaussian window. Let $g_{u,\omega}(t) = \exp\{-i\omega t\} g(t - u)$ denote the *Gabor function* localized near time u and frequency ω. The family of all Gabor functions provides a range of oscillatory behavior associated with a range of different intervals in time. These could either be called "time-frequency atoms" or, more provocatively, "musical notes."

Let S denote the collection of all functions $f(t)$ which can be decomposed as

$$f = \sum_{i=1}^{\infty} a_i g_{u_i, \omega_i}(t)$$

where $\Sigma_i |a_i| < \infty$. Let $\|f\|_S$ denote the smallest value $\Sigma_i |a_i|$ occurring in any such decomposition. This provides a normed linear space of functions, which Feichtinger calls the *Segal algebra* [40]. For a given amplitude A, the norm constraint $\|f\|_S \leq \gamma$ controls the number of "musical notes" of strength A which f can contain: $n \cdot A \leq \gamma$. So such a norm controls in a way the complexity of the harmonic structure of f.

A special feature of the above class is that there is no unique way to obtain a decomposition of the desired type, and no procedure is specified for doing so. As with our earlier analyses, it would seem natural to seek a basis for this class; one could even ask for an unconditional basis.

This Segal algebra is an instance of Feichtinger's general family *modulation spaces* $M_{p,q}^{\alpha}(\boldsymbol{R})$ and we could more generally ask for unconditional bases for any of these spaces. The modulation spaces offer an interesting scale of spaces in

certain respects analogous to L^p-Sobolev and related Besov and Triebel scales; in this brief survey, we are unable to describe them in detail.

B. Continuous Gabor Transform

Even older than the wavelet transform is the continuous Gabor transform (CGT). The Gabor transform can be written in a form analogous to (12.8) and (12.10)

$$(Gf)(u, \omega) = \langle f, g_{u,\omega} \rangle \tag{18.1}$$

$$f(t) = \iint (Gf)(u, \omega) g_{u,\omega} \, du \, d\omega. \tag{18.2}$$

Here $g_{u,\omega}$ can be a Gabor function as introduced above; it can also be a "Gabor-like" function generated from a non-Gaussian window function g.

If both g and its Fourier transform $\hat{g}$ are "concentrated" around 0 (which is true for the Gaussian), then (18.1) captures information in f that is localized in time (around u) and frequency (around ω); (18.2) writes f as a superposition of all the different time-frequency pieces.

Paternity of this transform is not uniquely assignable; it may be viewed as a special case in the theory of square-integrable group representations, a branch of abstract harmonic analysis [47]; it may be viewed as a special case of decomposition into canonical coherent states, a branch of mathematical physics [59]. In the signal analysis literature it is generally called the CGT to honor Gabor [44], and that appellation is very fitting on this occasion. Gabor proposed a "theory of communication" in 1946, two years before Shannon's work, that introduced the concept of logons—information carrying "cells"—highly relevant to the present occasion, and to Shannon's sampling theory.

The information in G is highly redundant. For instance, $Gf(u, \omega)$ captures what happens in f not only at time $t = u$, but also t near u and similarly in frequency. The degree to which this "spreading" occurs is determined by the choice of the window function g: if g is very narrowly concentrated around $t = 0$, then the sensitivity of $Gf(u, \omega)$ to the behavior of $f(t)$ is concentrated to the vicinity of $t = u$. The Heisenberg Uncertainty Principle links the concentration of g with that of the Fourier transform $\hat{g}$. If we define

$$\Delta_t^2(g) = \int t^2 |g|^2(t) \, dt$$

and

$$\Delta_\omega^2(g) = \int \omega^2 |\hat{g}|^2(\omega) \, d\omega$$

then $\Delta_t \cdot \Delta_\omega \geq \sqrt{\frac{\pi}{2}} \|g\|_{L^2}^2$, so that as g becomes more concentrated, $\hat{g}$ becomes less so, implying that the frequency sensitivity of $Gf(u, \omega)$ becomes more diffuse when we improve the time localization of g. Formalizing this, let $\rho_g(u, \omega)$ denote the rectangle of dimensions $\Delta_t(g) \times \Delta_\omega(g)$ centered at (u, ω). The choice of g influences the shape of the region (more narrow in time, but elongated in frequency if we choose g very concentrated around 0); the area of the cell is bounded below by the Uncertainty Principle. We think of each point $Gf(u, \omega)$ as measuring properties of a "cell" in the time-frequency domain, indicating the region that is "captured" in

$Gf(u, \omega)$. For example, if $\rho_g(u, \omega)$ and $\rho_g(u', \omega')$ are disjoint, we think of the corresponding Gf values as measuring disjoint properties of f.

C. Atomic Decomposition

Together, (18.1) and (18.2) can be written as

$$\iint \langle \cdot, g_{u,\omega} \rangle g_{u,\omega} \, du \, d\omega = Id, \qquad (18.3)$$

another resolution of the identity operator.

For parameters δ_t, δ_ω to be chosen, define equispaced time points $u_k = k\delta_t$ and frequency points $\omega_\ell = \ell\delta_\omega$. Consider now a family of time-frequency rectangles

$$R_{k,\ell} = \{(u, \omega) : |u - u_k| \leq \delta_t/2; |\omega - \omega_\ell| \leq \delta_\omega/2\}.$$

Evidently, these rectangles are disjoint and tile the time-frequency plane.

Proceeding purely formally, we can partition the integral in the resolution of the identity to get a decomposition $Id = \Sigma_{k,\ell} A_{k,\ell}$ with individual operators

$$A_{k,\ell} = \iint_{R_{k,\ell}} \langle \cdot, g_{u,\omega} \rangle g_{u,\omega} \, du \, d\omega.$$

This provides formally an atomic decomposition

$$f = \sum_{k,\ell} A_{k,\ell} f. \qquad (18.4)$$

In order to justify this approach, we would have to justify treating a rectangle $R_{k,\ell}$ as a single coherent region of the time-frequency plane. Heuristically, this coherence will apply if δ_t is smaller than the spread $\Delta_t(g)$ and if δ_ω is smaller than the spread $\Delta_\omega(g)$ of $\hat{g}$. In short, if the rectangle $R_{k,l}$ has the geometry of a Heisenberg cell, or smaller, then the above approach makes logical sense.

One application for atomic decomposition would be to characterize membership in the Segal Algebra S. Feichtinger has proved that, with g a sufficiently nice window, like the Gaussian, if we pick δ_t and δ_ω sufficiently small, atomic decomposition allows to measure the norm of S. Let $s_{k,l} = \int_{R_{k,\ell}} |G(u, \omega)|$ measure the size of the atom $A_{k,l}f$; then a function f is in S if and only if $\Sigma_{k,l} s_{k,l} < \infty$. Moreover, $\|A_{k,\ell}f\|_S \leq \text{Const} \cdot s_{k,l}$ so the series $f = \Sigma_{k,\ell} A_{k,\ell} f$ represents a decomposition of f into elements of S, and

$$\|f\|_S \asymp \sum_{k,l} s_{k,l}.$$

So we have an equivalent norm for the S-norm. This in some sense justifies the Gabor "logon" picture, as it shows that an object can really be represented in terms of elementary pieces, those pieces being associated with rectangular time-frequency cells, and each piece uniformly in S.

D. Orthobasis

Naturally, one expects to obtain not just an atomic decomposition, but actually an orthobasis. In fact, Gabor believed that one could do so. One approach is to search for a window g, not necessarily the Gaussian, and a precise choice of δ_u and δ_ω so that the samples $Gf(u_k, \omega_l)$ at equispaced points $u_k = k\delta_t \omega_\ell = \ell\delta_\omega$ provide an exact norm equivalence

$$\sum_{k,\ell} |Gf(u_k, \omega_l)|^2 = \int |f(t)|^2 \, dt.$$

While this is indeed possible, a famous result due to Balian and Low shows that it is not possible to achieve orthogonality using a g which is nicely concentrated in both time and frequency; to get an orthogonal basis from Gabor functions requires to have $\Delta_t(g) \cdot \Delta_\omega(g) = +\infty$. Hence the geometric picture of localized contributions from rectangular regions is not compatible with an orthogonal decomposition. A related effect is that the resulting Gabor orthogonal basis would not provide an unconditional bases for a wide range of modulation spaces. In fact, for certain modulation spaces, nonlinear approximation in such a basis would not behave optimally; e.g., we have examples of function balls $\mathcal{F}$ in modulation spaces where $d_n^*(\mathcal{F}) \ll d_n(\mathcal{F}, \text{GABOR ORTHOBASIS})$.

A way out was discovered with the construction of so-called *Wilson* orthobases for L^2 [22]. These are Gabor-like bases, built using a special smooth window $g(t)$ of rapid decay, and consist of basis elements $\phi_{k,\ell}$, where k is a position index and ℓ is a frequency index. k runs through the integers, and ℓ runs through the nonnegative integers; the two parameters vary independently, except that $\ell = 0$ is allowed in conjunction only with even k. In detail

$$\phi_{k,l}(t) = \begin{cases} \sqrt{2}g(t - k2\pi)\cos\left(\frac{\ell}{2}t\right), & k = 0, \pm 2, \pm 4, \cdots \\ & \ell = 1, 2, 3, \cdots \\ g(t - k2\pi), & k = 0, \pm 2, \pm 4, \cdots \\ & \ell = 0 \\ \sqrt{2}g(t - k2\pi)\sin\left(\frac{\ell}{2}t\right), & k = \pm 1, \pm 3, \cdots \\ & \ell = 1, 2, 3, \cdots. \end{cases}$$

Owing to the presence of the cosine and sine terms, as opposed to complex exponentials, the $\phi_{k,\ell}$ are not truly Gabor functions; but they can be viewed as superpositions of certain pairs of Gabor functions. The Gabor functions used in those pairs do not fill out the vertices of a single rectangular lattice, but instead they use a subset of the vertices of two distinct lattices. Hence the information in the Wilson coefficients derives indeed from sampling of the CGT with special generating window $g(t)$, only the samples must be taken on two interleaved Cartesian grids; and the samples must be combined in pairs in order to create the Wilson coefficients, as shown in Fig. 8.

The resulting orthobasis has good analytic properties. Grochenig and Walnut [51] have proved that it offers an unconditional basis for all the modulation spaces; in particular, it is an unconditional basis for S. As a result, Wilson bases are best orthobases for nonlinear approximation; for function balls $\mathcal{F}$ arising from a wide range of modulation spaces

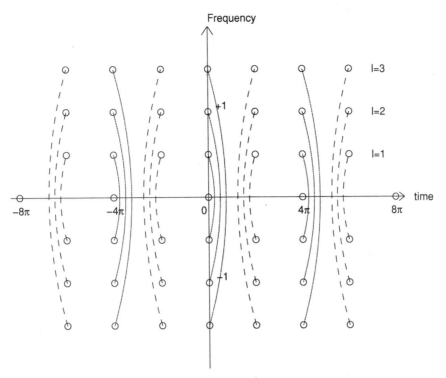

Fig. 8. The sampling set associated with the Wilson basis. Sampling points linked by solid lines are combined by addition. Sampling points linked by dashed lines are combined by subtraction.

$d_n^*(\mathcal{F}) \asymp d_n(\mathcal{F},$ WILSON ORTHOBASIS$)$. See also [50]. There are related data compression implications, although to state them requires some technicalities, for example, imposing on the objects to be compressed some additional decay conditions in both the time and frequency domains.

E. Adaptive Time-Frequency Decompositions

In a sense, CGT analysis/Gabor Atomic Decomposition/ Wilson bases merely scratch the surface of what one hopes to achieve in the time-frequency domain. The essential limitation of these tools is that they are *monoresolution*. They derive from a uniform rectangular sampling of time and frequency which is suitable for some phenomena; but it is easy to come up with models requiring highly nonuniform approaches.

Define the multiscale Gabor dictionary, consisting of Gabor functions with an additional scale parameter δ

$$g_{(u,\omega,\delta)}(t) = \exp\{i\omega(t-u)\}\exp\{(t-u)^2/\delta^2\}.$$

For $0 < p \leq 1$, consider the class MS^p of objects f having a multiscale decomposition

$$f = \sum_i a_i g_{(u_i,\omega_i,\delta_i)} \qquad (18.5)$$

with $\Sigma |a_i|^p < C^p$. In a sense, this class is obtained by combining features of the Bump Algebra—multiscale decomposition—and the Segal Algebra—time-frequency decomposition. This innocent-looking combination of features responds to a simple urge for common-sense generalization, but it gets us immediately into mathematical hot water. Indeed, one cannot use a simple monoscale atomic decomposition based on the CGT to effectively decompose such an f into its

pieces at different scales; one cannot from the monoscale analysis infer the size of the minimal C appearing in such a decomposition. Moreover, we are unaware of any effective means of decomposing members of this class in a way which achieves a near-optimal representation, i.e., a representation (18.5) with near-minimal C.

One might imagine performing a kind of "multiscale Gabor transform"—with parameters time, scale, and frequency, and developing an atomic decomposition or even a basis based on a three-dimensional rectangular partitioning of this time-scale-frequency domain, but this cannot work without extra precautions [95]. The kind of sampling theorem and norm equivalence result one might hope for has been proven impossible in that setting.

An important organizational tool in getting an understanding of the situation is to consider dyadic Heisenberg cells only, and to understand the decompositions of time and frequency which can be based upon them. These dyadic Heisenberg cells $H(j, k_1, k_2)$ are of side $2^{-j} \times 2^j$ and volume 1, with lower left corner at $k_1/2^j, k_2 2^j$ in the time-frequency plane. The difficulty of the time-frequency-scale decomposition problem is expressed by the fact that each Heisenberg cell overlaps with infinitely many others, corresponding to different aspect ratios at the same location. This means that even in a natural discretization of the underlying parameter space, there are a wide range of multiscale Gabor functions interacting with each other at each point (u, ω) of the time-frequency domain.

This kind of dyadic structuring has been basic to the architecture of some key results in classical analysis, namely, Carleson's proof of the a.e. convergence of Fourier series, and also Fefferman's alternate proof of the Carleson theorem. Both of those proofs were based on dyadic decomposition of time and frequency, and the driving idea in those proofs is to find ingenious ways to effectively combine estimates from all different Heisenberg cells despite the rather massive degree of overlap present in the family of all these cells. For example, Fefferman introduced a tree-ordering of dyadic Heisenberg cells, and was able to get effective estimates by constructing many partitions of the time-frequency domain according to the properties of the Fourier partial sums he was studying, obtaining a decomposition of the sums into operators associated with special time-frequency regions called trees, and combining estimates across trees into forests.

Inspired by their success, one might imagine that there is some way to untangle all the overlap in the dyadic Heisenberg cells and develop an effective multiscale time-frequency analysis. The goal would be to somehow organize the information coming from dyadic Heisenberg cells to iteratively extract from this time-scale-frequency space various "layers" of information. As we have put it this program is, of course, rather vague.

More concrete is the idea of *nonuniform tiling of the time-frequency plane*. Instead of decomposing the plane by a sequence of disjoint congruent rectangles, one uses rectangles of various shapes and sizes, where the cells have been chosen specially to adapt to the underlying features of the object being considered.

The idea of adaptive tiling is quite natural in connection with the problem of multiscale time-frequency decomposition, though it originally arose in other areas of analysis. Fefferman's survey [41] gives examples of this idea in action in the study of partial differential equations, where an adaptive time-frequency tiling is used to decompose operator kernels for the purpose of estimating eigenvalues.

Here is how one might expect adaptive tiling to work in a multiscale time-frequency setting. Suppose that an object had a representation (18.5) where the fine-scale atoms occurred at particular time locations well separated from the coarse-scale atoms. Then one could imagine constructing a time-frequency tiling that had homologous structure: rectangles with finer time scales where the underlying atoms in the optimal decomposition needed to be fine-scale; rectangles with coarser time-scale elsewhere. The idea requires more thought than it might at first seem, since the rectangles cannot be chosen freely; they must obey the Heisenberg constraint. The dyadic Heisenberg system provides a constrained set of building blocks which often can be fit together quite easily to create rather inhomogeneous tilings. Also, the rectangles must correspond rigorously to an analyzing tool: there must be an underlying time-frequency analysis with a width that is changing with spatial location. It would be especially nice if one could do this in a way providing true orthogonality.

In any event, it is clear that an appropriate multiscale time-frequency analysis in the setting of MS^p or related classes cannot be constructed within a single orthobasis. At the very least, one would expect to consider large families of orthobases, and select from such a family an individual basis best adapted for each individual object of interest. However, even there it is quite unlikely that one could obtain true characterization of a space like MS^p; i.e., it is unlikely that even within

the broader situation of adaptively chosen orthobases, the decompositions one could obtain would rival an optimal decomposition of the form (18.5), i.e., a decomposition with minimal C. A corollary to this is that we really know of no effective method for data compression for this class: *there is no effective transform coding for multiscale time-frequency classes*.

XIX. COMPUTATIONAL HARMONIC ANALYSIS

The theoretical constructions of harmonic analysts correspond with practical signal-processing tools to a remarkable degree. The ideas which are so useful in the functional viewpoint, where one is analyzing functions $f(t)$ of a continuous argument, correspond to completely analogous tools for the analysis of discrete-time signals $x(n)$. Moreover, the tools can be realized as fast algorithms, so that on signals of length N they take order N or $N \log(N)$ operations to complete. Thus corresponding to the theoretical developments traced above, we have today fast wavelet transforms, fast Gabor transforms, fast tree approximation algorithms, and even fast algorithms for adapted multiscale time-frequency analysis.

The correspondence between theoretical harmonic analysis and effective signal processing algorithms has its roots in two specific facts which imply a rather exact connection between the functional viewpoint of this paper and the digital viewpoint common in signal processing.

- *Fast Fourier Transform:* The finite Fourier transform provides an orthogonal transform for discrete-time sequences which, in a certain sense, matches perfectly with the classical Fourier series for functions on the circle. For example, on appropriate trigonometric polynomials, the first N Fourier series coefficients are (after normalization) precisely the N finite Fourier coefficients of the digital signal obtained by sampling the trigonometric polynomial. This fact provides a powerful tool to connect concepts from the functional setting with the discrete-time signal setting. The availability of fast algorithms has made this correspondence a computationally effective matter. It is an eerie coincidence that the most popular form of the FFT algorithm prefers to operate on signals of dyadic length; for connecting theoretical harmonic analysis with the digital signal processing domain, the dyadic length is also the most natural.

- *Sampling Theorem:* The classical Shannon sampling theorem for bandlimited functions on the line has a perfect analog for digital signals obeying discrete-time bandlimiting relations. This is usually interpreted as saying that one can simply subsample a data series and extract the minimal nonredundant subset. A different way to put it is that there is an orthonormal basis for the bandlimited signals and that sampling provides a fast algorithm for obtaining the coefficients of a signal in that basis.

There are, in addition, two particular tools for partitioning signal domains which allow effective digital implementation of breaking a signal into time-scale or time-frequency pieces.

- *Smooth Orthonormal Localization:* Suppose one takes a discrete-time signal of length $2N$ and breaks it into two subsignals of length N, corresponding to the first half and the second half. Now subject those two halves to further processing, expanding each half into an orthonormal basis for digital signals of length N. In effect, one is expanding the original length $2N$ signal into an orthonormal basis for length $2N$. The implicit basis functions may not be well-behaved near the midpoint. For example, if the length N basis is the finite Fourier basis, then the length $2N$ basis functions will be discontinuous at the segmentation point. This discontinuity can be avoided by changing the original "splitting into two pieces" into a more sophisticated partitioning operator based on a kind of smooth orthonormal windowing. This involves treating the data near the segmentation point specially, taking pairs of values located equal distances from the segmentation point and on opposite sides and, instead of simply putting one value in one segment and the other value in the other segment, one puts special pairs of linear combinations of the two values in the two halves; see for example [71], [72], and [3].

- *Subband Partitioning:* Suppose we take a discrete-time signal, transform it into the frequency domain, and break the Fourier transform into two pieces, the high and low frequencies. Now transform the pieces back into the time domain. As the pieces are now bandlimited/bandpass, they can be subsampled, creating two new vectors consisting of the 'high frequency' and 'low frequency' operations. The two new vectors are related to the original signal by orthogonal transformation, so the process is in some sense exact. Unfortunately, the brutal separation into high and low frequencies has many undesirable effects. One solution to this problem would have been to apply smooth orthonormal localization in the frequency domain. A different approach, with many advantages, is based on the time domain method of *conjugate quadrature filters.*

  In this approach, one applies a special pair of digital filters, high- and lowpass, to a digital signal of length $2N$, and then subsamples each of the two results by a factor two [88], [76], [97], [99]. The result is two signals of length N, so that the original cardinality of $2N$ is preserved, and *if the filters are very specially chosen*, the transform can be made orthogonal. The key point is that the filters can be short. The most elementary example is to use a highpass filter with coefficients $(1/\sqrt{2}, -1/\sqrt{2})$ and a lowpass filter with coefficients $(1/\sqrt{2}, 1/\sqrt{2})$. The shortness of this filter means that the operator does not have the time-localization problems of the frequency-domain algorithm, but unfortunately this filter pair will not have very good frequency-domain selectivity. More sophisticated filter pairs, with lengths >2, have been developed; these are designed to maintain the orthogonality and to impose additional conditions which ensure both time- and frequency-domain localization.

This set of tools can lead to fast algorithms for digital implementation of the central ideas in theoretical harmonic analysis.

A key point is that one can cascade the above operations. For example, if one can split a signal domain into two pieces, then one can split it into four pieces, by applying the same type of operation again to each piece. In this way, the dyadic structuring ideas that were so useful in harmonic analysis—dyadic partitioning of time-scale and time-frequency—correspond directly to dyadic structuring in the digital setting.

We give a few examples of this, stressing the role of combining elementary dyadic operations.

- *Fast Meyer Wavelet Transform:* The Meyer wavelet basis for $L^2(\boldsymbol{R})$ was originally defined by its frequency-domain properties, and so it is most natural to construct a digital variant using the Fourier domain. The forward transform algorithm goes as follows. Transform into the frequency domain. Apply smooth orthonormal windowing, breaking up the frequency domain into subbands of pairs of intervals of width 2^{j-1} samples, located symmetrically about zero frequency. Apply to each subband a Fourier analysis (actually either a sine or cosine transform) of length adapted to the length of the subband. The cost of applying this algorithm is dominated by the initial passage to the Frequency domain, which is order $O(N \log(N))$. The inverse transform systematically reverses these operations.

  The point of the fast algorithm is, of course, that one does not literally construct the basis functions, and one does not literally take the inner product of the digital signal with the basis function. This is all done implicitly. However, it is easy enough to use the algorithm to display the basis functions. When one does so, one sees that they are trigonometric polynomials which are periodic and effectively localized near the dyadic interval they should be associated with.

- *Mallat Algorithm:* Improving in several respects on the frequency-domain digital Meyer wavelet basis is a family of orthonormal wavelet bases based on time-domain filtering [69]. The central idea here is by now very well known: it involves taking the signal, applying subband partitioning with specially chosen digital highpass and lowpass filters, subsampling the two pieces by dyadic decimation, and then recursively applying the same procedure on the lowpass piece only. When the filters are appropriately specified, the result is an orthonormal transform on N-space.

  The resulting transform on digital signals takes only order N arithmetic operations, so it has a speed advantage over the fast Meyer wavelet transform, which requires order $N \log(N)$ operations. Although we do not describe it here, there is an important modification of the filtering operators at the ends of the sequence which allows the wavelet basis functions to adapt to the boundary of the signal, i.e., we avoid the periodization of the fast Meyer transform [13]. Finally, the wavelet basis functions are compactly supported, with basis element $\psi_{j,k}$ vanishing in the time domain outside an interval homothetic to $I_{j,k}$. This means that they have the correct structure to be called a wavelet transform. The support property also means that a small number of wavelet coefficients at a given scale are affected by singularities, or to put it another way, the effect of a singularity is compressed into a small number of coefficients.

- *Fast Wilson Basis Transform* is a digital version of the Wilson basis; the fast transform works as follows. First, one applies a smooth orthonormal partitioning to break up the time domain into equal-length segments. (It is most convenient if the segments have dyadic lengths.) Then one applies Fourier analysis, in the form of a sine or cosine transform, to each segment. The whole algorithm is order $N \log(M)$, where M is the length of a segment. The implicitly defined basis functions look like windowed sinusoids with the same arrangement of sine and cosine terms as in the continuum Wilson basis.

We should now stress that for the correspondence between a theoretical harmonic analysis concept and a computational harmonic analysis tool, dyadic structuring operators should not be performed in a cavalier fashion. For example, if one is going to cascade subband partitioning operations many times, as in the Mallat algorithm, it is important that the underlying filters be rather specially chosen to be compatible with this repetitive cascade.

When this is done appropriately, one can arrive at digital implementations that are not vague analogies of the corresponding theoretical concepts, but can actually be viewed as "correct" digital realizations. As the reader expects by now, the mathematical expression that one has a "correct" realization is achieved by establishing a norm equivalence result. For example, if in the Mallat algorithm one cascades the subband partitioning operator using appropriate finite-length digital filters, one can construct a discrete wavelet transform for digital signals. This discrete transform is "correctly related" to a corresponding theoretical wavelet transform on the continuum because of a norm equivalence: if $f(t)$ is a function on the interval $[0,1]$, and if $(\tilde{\theta}_I)$ is a set of digital wavelet coefficients for the digitally sampled object $(f(n/N))$, then the appropriate Triebel and Besov norms of the digital wavelet coefficients behave quite precisely like the same norms of the corresponding initial segments of the theoretical wavelet coefficients (θ_I) of the continuum f. This is again a form of sampling theorem, showing that an ℓ^2 equality of norms (which follows simply from orthogonality) is accompanied by an equivalence in many other norms (which follows from much more delicate facts about the construction). A consequence, and of particular relevance for this paper, is that under simple assumptions, one can use the digital wavelet transform coefficients for nonlinear approximation and expect the same bounds on approximation measures to apply; *hence digital wavelet-based transform coding of function classes obeys the same types of estimates as theoretical wavelet-based transform coding.*

The "appropriate finite-length filters" referred to in the last paragraph are in fact arrived at by a delicate process of design. In [20], a collection of finite-length filters was constructed that gave orthonormal digital wavelet transforms.

For the constructed transforms, if one views the N digital samples as occurring at points n/N for $0 \leq n < N$, and takes individual digital basis elements corresponding to the "same" location and scale at different dyadic N, appropriately normalized and interpolated to create functions of a continuous variable, one obtains a sequence of functions which tends to a limit. Moreover, the limit must be a translate and dilate of a single smooth function of compact support. In short, the digital wavelet transform is truly a digital realization of the theoretical wavelet transform. The norm equivalence statement of the previous paragraph is a way of mathematically completing this fundamental insight. In the last ten years, a large number of interesting constructions of "appropriate finite-length filters" have appeared, which we cannot summarize here. For more complete information on the properties of wavelet transforms and the associated filters, see for example, [100] and [23].

The success in developing ways to translate theoretical wavelet transforms and Gabor transforms into computationally effective methods naturally breeds the ambition to do the same in other cases. Consider the dyadic Heisenberg cells of Section XVIII-E, and the resulting concept of nonuniform tiling of the time-frequency plane. It turns out that for a large collection of nonuniform tilings, one can realize—in a computationally effective manner—a corresponding orthonormal basis [18]; see Fig. 9.

Here are two examples:

- *Cosine Packets:* Take a recursive dyadic partition of the time interval into dyadic segments. Apply smooth orthonormal partitioning to separate out the original signal into a collection of corresponding segments. Take appropriate finite Fourier transforms of each segment. The result is an orthogonal transform which is associated with a specific tiling of the time-frequency domain. That tiling has, for its projection on the time axis, simply the original partition of the time domain; over the whole time-frequency domain, it consists of columns whose widths are defined by intervals of the time-partition; within a column, the tiling simply involves congruent dyadic Heisenberg cells with specified width.

- *Wavelet Packets:* Take a recursive dyadic partition of the frequency interval into dyadic segments. Apply subband partitioning to separate out the original signal into a collection of corresponding frequency bands. The result is an orthogonal transform which costs at most $O(N)$ operations. It is associated with a specific tiling of the time-frequency domain. That tiling has, for its projection on the frequency axis, simply the original partition of the frequency domain; over the whole time-frequency domain, it consists of rows whose widths are defined by intervals of the frequency-partition; within a row, the tiling simply involves congruent dyadic Heisenberg cells with specified height.

Do these bases correspond to "correct" digital implementation of the theoretical partitioning? While they are orthogonal, we are not aware of results showing that they obey a wide range of other norm equivalences. It would be interesting to

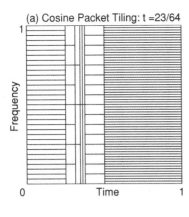

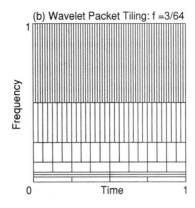

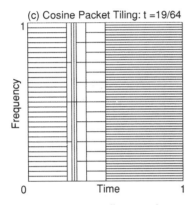

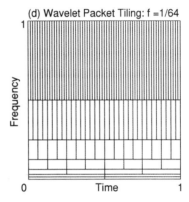

Fig. 9. Some time-frequency tilings corresponding to orthonormal bases.

know if they obey *sufficiently strong equivalences to imply that transform coding in an adaptively constructed basis can provide near-optimal coding* for an interesting class of objects. At the very least, results of this kind would require detailed assumptions, allowing the partitioning to be inhomogeneous in interesting ways and yet not very wild, and also supposing that the details of window lengths in the smooth orthonormal windowing or the filter choice in the subband partitioning are chosen appropriately.

The time-frequency tiling ideas raise interesting possibilities. In effect, the wavelet packet and cosine packet libraries create large libraries of orthogonal bases, all of which have fast algorithms. The Fourier and Wavelet bases are just two examples in this library; Gabor/Wilson-like bases provide other examples. These two collections have been studied by Coifman and Wickerhauser [17], who have shown that for certain "additive" objective functions the search through the library of all cosine packet or wavelet packet bases can be performed in $O(N \log(N))$ operations. This search is dependent on the function to be analyzed, so it is an instance of nonlinear approximation. In the case when this search is done for compression purposes, an operational rate-distortion-based version was presented in [80].

XX. PRACTICAL CODING

How do the ideas from harmonic analysis work on *real data*?

Actually, many of these ideas have been in use for some time in the practical data compression community, though discovered independently and studied under other names.

This is an example of a curious phenomenon commented on by Yves Meyer [73]: some of the really important ideas of harmonic analysis have been discovered, in some cognate or approximate form, in a wide range of practical settings, ranging from signal processing to mathematical physics, to computer-aided design. Often the basic tools are the same, but harmonic analysis imposes a different set of requirements on those tools.

To emphasize the relationship of the theory of this paper to practical coders, we briefly comment on some developments.

DCT coding of the type used in JPEG is based on a partitioning of the image domain into blocks, followed by DCT transform coding. The partitioning is done brutally, with the obvious drawback of DCT coding, which is the blocking effect at high compression ratios. Subband coding of images was proposed in the early 1980's [98], [102]. Instead of using rectangular windows as the DCT does, the subband approach effectively uses longer, smooth windows, and thus achieves a smooth reconstruction even at low bit rates. Note that early subband coding schemes were trying to approximate decorrelating transforms like the KLT, while avoiding some of the pitfalls of the DCT. Coding gains of filter banks were used as a performance measure. Underlying such investigations was a Gaussian model for signals, or a Markov random field (MRF) model for images.

Among possible subband coding schemes for images, a specific structure enjoyed particular popularity, namely, the scheme where the decomposition of the lower frequency band is iterated. This was due to several factors:

1) Its relationship with pyramid coding.

2) The fact that most of the energy remains concentrated in the lowpass version.
3) Its computational efficiency and simplicity.

Of course, this computational structure is equivalent to the discrete wavelet transform, and, as we have described, with appropriately designed digital filters, it can be related to the continuous wavelet series expansion.

Because of the concentrated efforts on subband coding schemes related to discrete wavelet transforms, interesting advances were achieved leading to improved image compression. The key insight derived from thinking in scale-location terms, and realizing that edges caused an interesting clustering effect across scales: the positions of "big" coefficients would remain localized in the various frequency bands, and could therefore be efficiently indexed using a linking across frequencies [68]. This idea was perfected by J. Shapiro into a data structure called an embedded zero tree [86]. Together with a successive approximation quantization, this coder achieves high-quality, successive approximation compression over a large range of bit rates, outperforming JPEG at any given bit rate by several decibels in signal-to-noise ratio. Many generalizations of Shapiro's algorithm have been proposed, and we will briefly outline the basic scheme to indicate its relation to nonlinear approximation in wavelet decompositions.

A key idea is that the significant wavelet coefficients are well-localized around points of discontinuity at small scales (or high frequency), see Fig. 10(a). This is unlike local cosine or DCT bases. Therefore, an edge of a given orientation will appear roughly as an edge in the respective orientation subband, and this at all scales. Conversely, smooth areas will be nulled out in passbands, since the wavelet has typically several zero moments. Therefore, a conditional entropy coder can take advantage of this "dependence across scales." In particular, the zero tree structure gathers regions of low energy across scales, by simply predicting that if a passband is zero at a given scale, its four children at the next finer scale (and similar orientation) are most likely to be zero as well (see Fig. 10(b)). This scheme can be iterated across scales. In some sense, it is a generalization of the end of block symbol used in DCT coding. (Note that such a prediction across scales would be fruitless in a Gaussian setting, because of independence of different bands.) Also, note that the actual values of the coefficients are *not* predicted, but only the "insignificance" or absence of energy; i.e., the idea is one of positional coding. Usually, the method is combined with successive approximation quantization, leading to an embedded bit stream, where successive approximation decoding is possible. An improved version, where larger blocks of samples are used together in a technique called set partitioning, lead to the SPIHT algorithm [82] with improved performance and lower computational complexity. Other variations include context modeling in the various bands [65]. Comparing these ideas with the present paper, we see a great commonality of approach to the use of trees for positional coding of the "big" wavelet coefficients as we have discussed in Section XVII-B.

At a more abstract level, such an approach to wavelet image coding consists in picking a subset of the largest coefficients of the wavelet transform, and making sure that the cost of

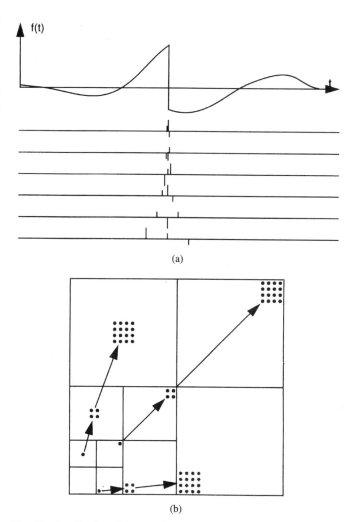

Fig. 10. Localization of the wavelet transform. (a) One-dimensional signal with discontinuity. (b) Two-dimensional signal and linking of scale-space points used in wavelet image coding (EZW and SPIHT).

addressing these largest coefficients is kept down by a smart conditional entropy code. That is, the localization property of the wavelet transform is used to perform efficient addressing of singularities, while the polynomial reproduction property of scaling functions allows a compact representation of smooth surfaces.

How about the performance of this coder and its related cousins? In Fig. 3, we see that a substantial improvement is achieved over JPEG (the actual coder is from [82]). However, the basic behavior is the same, that is, at fine quantization, we find again the typical $D(R) \sim 2^{-2R}$ slope predicted by classical high rate-distortion theory. Instead, we would hope for a decay related to the smoothness class. At low bit rate, a recent analysis by Mallat and Falzon [70] shows $D(R) \sim R^{-1}$ by modeling the nonlinear approximation features of such a wavelet coder.

The next generation image coding standard, JPEG-2000, is considering schemes similar to what was outlined above. That is, it has been proposed to exploit properties of the wavelet transform and of the structure of wavelet coefficients across scales, together with state-of-the-art quantization (using, for example, trellis-coded quantizers) and adaptive entropy coders.

In short, there are a variety of interesting parallels between practical coding work and the work in harmonic analysis. We are aware of other areas where interesting comparisons can be made, for example, in speech coding, but omit a full comparison of literatures for reasons of space.

XXI. SUMMARY AND PROGNOSIS

In composing this survey, we have been inspired by an attractive mixture of ideas. To help the reader, we find it helpful to summarize these ideas, and to make them memorable by associating them with prominent figures of this century.

A. Pure Mathematics Disdaining Usefulness

G. H. Hardy is a good example for this position. In *A Mathematician's Apology*, he gave a famous evaluation of his life's work:

"I have never done anything 'useful.' No discovery of mine has made, or is likely to make, directly or indirectly, for good or for ill, the least difference to the world."

In the same essay, he argued strenuously against the proposition that pure mathematics could ever have "utility."

The irony is, of course, that, as discussed above, the purely mathematical impulse to understand Hardy H^p spaces gave rise to the first orthonormal basis of smooth wavelets.

In this century, harmonic analysis has followed its own agenda of research, involving among other things the understanding of equivalent norms in functional spaces. It has developed its own structures and techniques for addressing problems of its own devising; and if one studies the literature of harmonic analysis one is struck by the way the problems—e.g., finding equivalent norms for H^p spaces—seem unrelated to any practical needs in science or engineering—e.g., H^p spaces do not consist of "objects" which could be understood as modeling a collection of "naturally occurring objects" of "practical interest." Nor should this be surprising; David Hilbert once said that "the essence of mathematics is its freedom" and we suspect he means "freedom from any demands of the outside world to be other than what its own internal logic demands."

Despite the freedom and in some sense "unreality" of its orientation, the structures and techniques that harmonic analysis has developed in pursuing its agenda have turned out to be significant for practical purposes—in particular, as mentioned above, discrete wavelet transforms are being considered for inclusion in future standards like JPEG-2000.

In this paper we have attempted to "explain" how an abstractly oriented endeavor could end up interacting with practical developments in this way. In a sense, harmonic analysts, by carrying out their discipline's internal agenda, discovered a way to "diagonalize" the structure of certain functional classes outside of the L^2 cases where this concept arose. This "diagonalization" carries a data compression interpretation, and leads to algorithmic ideas for dealing with other kinds of data than traditional Gaussian data compression theory allows.

B. Stochastic versus Deterministic Viewpoints

Even if one accepts that pure mathematics can have unexpected outcomes of relevance to practical problems, it may seem unusual that analysis *per se*—which concerns deterministic objects—could be connected with the compression of real data, which concerns random objects. To symbolize this possibility, we make recourse to one of the great mathematicians of this century, A. N. Kolmogorov. V. M. Tikhomirov, in an appreciation of Kolmogorov, said [93]

... "our vast mathematical world" is itself divided into two parts, as into two kingdoms. Deterministic phenomena are investigated in one part, and random phenomena in the other.

To Kolmogorov fell the lot of being a trailblazer in both kingdoms, a discoverer in their many unexplored regions ... he put forth a grandiose programme for a simultaneous and parallel study of the complexity of deterministic phenomena and the uncertainty of random phenomena, and the experience of practically all his creative biography was concentrated in this programme.

From the beginning of this programme, the illusory nature of setting limits between the world of order and the world of chance revealed itself.

The scholarly record makes the same point. In his paper at the 1956 IRE Conference on Information Theory, held at MIT, Kolmogorov [60] published the "reverse water-filling formula" giving $R(D)$ for Gaussian processes (2.5), (2.6), which as we have seen is the formal basis for transform coding. He also described work with Gel'fand and Yaglom rigorously extending the sense of the mutual information formula (2.4) from finite-dimensional vectors X and Y to functional data. These indicate that the functional viewpoint was very much on his mind in connection with the Shannon theory. In that same paper he also chose to mention the ϵ-entropy concept which he had recently defined [61], and he chose a notation which allowed him to make the point that ϵ-entropy is formally similar to Shannon's $R(D)$. One gets the sense that Kolmogorov thought the two theories might be closely related at some level, even though one concerns deterministic objects and the other concerns random objects; see also his return to this theme in more depth in the appendix in the monograph [62].

C. Analysts Return to Concrete Arguments

Shannon's key discoveries in lossy data compression are summarized in (2.2)–(2.4). These are highly abstract and in fact can be proved in an abstract setting; compare the abstract alphabet source coding theorem and converse in Berger (1971). In this sense, Shannon was a man of his time. During the 1930's–1950's, abstraction in mathematical science was in full bloom; it was the era that produced the formalist mathematical school of Bourbaki and fields like "abstract harmonic analysis."

Kolmogorov's work in lossy data compression also was a product of this era; the concept of ϵ-entropy is, to many newcomers' tastes, abstraction itself.

Eventually the pendulum swung back, in a return to more concrete arguments and constructions, as illustrated by the work of the Swedish mathematician Lennart Carleson. In a very distinguished research career spanning the entire period from 1950 to the present, Carleson obtained definitive results of lasting value in harmonic analysis, the best known of which is the almost everywhere convergence of Fourier series, an issue essentially open since the 19th century, and requiring a proof which has been described by P. Jones as "one of the most complicated to be found in modern analysis" [57]. Throughout his career, Carleson created new concepts and techniques as part of resolving very hard problems; including a variety of dyadic decomposition ideas and the concept of Carleson measures. It is interesting to read Carleson's own words [11].

> There was a period, in the 1940's and 1950's, when classical analysis was considered dead and the hope for the future of analysis was considered to be in the abstract branches, specializing in generalization. As is now apparent, the death of classical analysis was greatly exaggerated and during the 1960's and 1970's the field has been one of the most successful in all of mathematics. . . . the reasons for this . . . [include] . . . the realization that in many problems complications cannot be avoided, and that intricate combinatorial arguments rather than polished theories are in the center.

Carleson "grew up" as a young mathematician in the early 1950's, and so it is natural that he would react against the prevailing belief system at the time of his intellectual formation. That system placed great weight on abstraction and generality; Carleson's work, in contrast, placed heavy emphasis on creating useful tools for certain problems which by the standards of abstract analysts of the day, were decidedly concrete.

Carleson can be taken as symbolic of the position that a concrete problem, though limited in scope, can be very fertile.

D. The Future?

So far, we have used important personalities to symbolize progress to date. What about the future?

One of the themes of this paper is that harmonic analysts, while knowingly working on hard problems in analysis, and discovering tools to prove fundamental results, have actually been developing tools with a broad range of applications, including data compression. Among harmonic analysts, this position is championed by R. R. Coifman. His early work included the development of atomic decompositions for H^p spaces, $p \leq 1$. Today, his focus is in another direction entirely, as he develops ways to accelerate fundamental mathematical algorithms and to implement new types of image compression. This leads him to reinterpret standard harmonic analysis results in a different light.

For example, consider his attitude toward a milestone of classical analysis: L. Carleson's proof of the almost-everywhere convergence of Fourier series, which is generally thought of as a beautiful and extremely complex pure analysis argument. But apparently Coifman sees here a serious effort

to understand the underlying "combinatorics" of time and frequency bases, a "combinatorics" potentially also useful (say) for "time-frequency-based signal compression."

In another direction, consider the work of P. Jones [56] who established a beautiful result showing that one can approximately measure the length of the traveling salesman tour of a set of points in the plane by a kind of nonlinear Littlewood–Paley analysis. (This has far-reaching extensions by David and Semmes [24].) Others may see here the beginnings of a theory of quantitative geometric measure theory. Coifman apparently sees a serious effort to understand the underlying combinatorics of curves in the plane (and in David–Semmes, hypersurfaces in higher dimensional spaces), a "combinatorics" which is potentially also useful (say) for compressing two- and higher dimensional data containing curvilinear structure.

The position underlying these interpretations is exactly the opposite of Hardy: Hardy believed that his research would not be "useful" because he did not *intend* it to be; yet, it turns out that research in harmonic analysis has been and may well continue to be "useful" even when researchers, like Hardy, have no conscious desire to be useful.

How far can the connection of Harmonic Analysis and Data Compression go? We are sure it will be fun to find out.

ACKNOWLEDGMENT

The authors would like to thank R. R. Coifman for exposing us to many iconoclastic statements which were provocative, initially mysterious, and ultimately very fruitful. They would also like to thank the editors of this special issue. Sergio Verdú had the idea for assembling this team for this project; both he and Stephen McLaughlin displayed great patience with us in the stages near completion.

D. L. Donoho would like to thank Miriam Donoho for vigorously supporting the effort to make this paper appear. He would also like to thank Xiaoming Huo for extensive effort in preparing several figures for this paper.

M. Vetterli would like to thank Robert M. Gray, Vivek Goyal, Jelena Kovačević, Jérôme Lebrun, Claudio Weidmann, and Bin Yu for interactions and help.

I. Daubechies would like to thank Nela Rybowicz for her extraordinary helpfulness in correcting the page proofs.

REFERENCES

[1] N. Ahmed, T. Natarajan, and K. R. Rao, "Discrete cosine transform," *IEEE Trans. Comput.*, vol. C-23, pp. 88–93, Jan. 1974.
[2] E. W. Aslaksen and J. R. Klauder, "Unitary representations of the affine group," *J. Math. Phys.*, vol. 9, pp. 206–211, 1968.
[3] P. Auscher, G. Weiss, and G. Wickerhauser, "Local sine and cosine bases of Coifman and Meyer and the construction of smooth wavelets," in *Wavelets: A Tutorial in Theory and Applications*, C. K. Chui, Ed. New York: Academic, 1992.
[4] H. B. Barlow, "Possible principles underlying the transformation of sensory messages," in *Sensory Communication*, W. A. Rosenbluth, Ed. Cambrige, MA: MIT Press, 1961, pp. 217–234.
[5] T. Berger, *Rate Distortion Theory: A Mathematical Basis for Data Compression.* Englewood Cliffs, NJ: Prentice Hall, 1971.
[6] L. Birgé, "Approximation dans les espaces métriques et théorie de l'estimation," (in French), ("Approximation in metric spaces and the theory of estimation"), *Z. Wahrsch. Verw. Gebiete*, vol. 65, no. 2, pp. 181–237, 1983.

[7] L. Birgé and P. Massart, "An adaptive compression algorithm in Besov spaces," *Constr. Approx.*, to be published.

[8] M. S. Birman and M. Z. Solomjak, "Piecewise-polynomial approximations of functions of the classes W_p^α," *Mat. Sbornik*, vol. 73, pp. 295–317, 1967.

[9] A. P. Calderón, "Intermediate spaces and interpolation, the complex method," *Studia Math.*, vol. 24, pp. 113–190, 1964.

[10] B. Carl and I. Stephani, *Entropy, Compactness, and the Approximation of Operators.* Cambridge, U.K.: Cambridge Univ. Press, 1990.

[11] L. Carleson, "The work of Charles Fefferman," in *Proc. Int. Congr. Mathematics* (Helsinki, Finland, 1978). Helsinki, Finland: Acad. Sci. Fennica, 1980, pp. 53–56.

[12] A. Cohen and J. P. D'Ales, "Non-linear approximation of random functions," *SIAM J. Appl. Math.*, vol. 57, pp. 518–540, 1997.

[13] A. Cohen, I. Daubechies, and P. Vial, "Orthonormal wavelets for the interval," *Appl. Comput. Harmonic Anal.*, vol. 1, no. 1, 1993.

[14] A. Cohen, I. Daubechies, O. Guleryuz, and M. Orchard, "On the importance of combining wavelet-based nonlinear approximation in coding strategies," unpublished manuscript, 1997.

[15] A. Cohen, W. Dahmen, I. Daubechies, and R. A. DeVore, "Tree, Approximation and Encoding," preprint, 1998..

[16] R. R. Coifman, "A real-variable characterization of H^p," *Studia Math.*, vol. 51, pp. 269–274, 1974.

[17] R. R. Coifman and M. V. Wickerhauser, "Entropy-based algorithms for best basis selection," vol. 38, no. 2, pp. 713–718, Mar. 1992.

[18] R. R. Coifman and Y. Meyer, "Remarques sur l'analyze de Fourier à fenêtre, *C. R. Acad Sci. Paris*, vol. 312, pp. 259–261, 1991.

[19] T. M. Cover and J. A. Thomas, *Elements of Information Theory.* New York: Wiley, 1991.

[20] I. Daubechies, "Orthonormal bases of compactly supported wavelets," *Commun. Pure Appl. Math.*, vol. 41, pp. 909–996, 1988.

[21] ——, "The wavelet transform, time-frequency localization, and signal analysis," *IEEE Trans. Inform. Theory*, vol. 36, pp. 961–1005, 1990.

[22] I. Daubechies, S. Jaffard, and J. L. Journé, "A simple Wilson orthonormal basis with exponential decay," *SIAM J. Math. Anal.*, vol. 24, pp. 520–527, 1990.

[23] I. Daubechies, *Ten Lectures on Wavelets.* Philadelphia, PA: SIAM, 1992.

[24] G. David and S. Semmes, *Analysis of and on Uniformly Rectifiable Sets.* (Amer. Math. Soc., Mathematical Surveys and Monographs, vol. 38), 1993.

[25] K. DeLeeuw, J. P. Kahane, and Y. Katznelson, "Sur les coefficients de Fourier des fonctions continues," *C. R. Acad. Sci. Paris*, vol. 285, pp. 1001–1003, 1978.

[26] R. A. DeVore, "Nonlinear approximation," *Acta Numer.*, vol. 7, pp. 51–150, 1998.

[27] R. A. DeVore, B. Jawerth, and B. Lucier, "Image compression through wavelet transform coding," *IEEE Trans. Inform. Theory*, vol. 38, pp. 719–746, 1992.

[28] R. DeVore and X. M. Yu, "Degree of adaptive approximation," *Math. Comput.*, vol. 55, pp. 625–635, 1990.

[29] R. DeVore, B. Jawerth, and V. A. Popov, "Compression of wavelet decompositions," *Amer. J. Math.*, vol. 114, pp. 737–785, 1992.

[30] R. A. DeVore and G. G. Lorentz, *Constructive Approximation.* New York: Springer, 1993.

[31] D. L. Donoho, "Unconditional bases are optimal bases for data compression and statistical estimation," *Appl. Comput. Harmonic Anal.*, vol. 1, no. 1. pp. 100–105, 1993.

[32] ——, "Unconditional bases and bit-level compression," *Appl. Comput. Harmonic Anal.*, vol. 3, no. 4, pp. 388–392, 1996.

[33] ——, "CART and best-ortho-basis: A connection," *Ann. Statist.*, vol. 25, no. 5, pp. 1870–1911, 1997.

[34] ——, "Counting bits with Kolmogorov and Shannon," manuscript, 1998.

[35] R. M. Dudley, "The sizes of compact subsets of Hilbert spaces and continuity of Gaussian processes," *J. Funct. Anal.*, vol. 1, pp. 290–330, 1967.

[36] D. E. Edmunds and H. Triebel, *Function Spaces, Entropy Numbers, and Differential Operators.* Cambridge, U.K.: Cambridge Univ. Press, 1996.

[37] D. J. Field, "The analysis of natural images and the response properties of cortical cells," *J. Opt. Soc. Amer.*, 1987.

[38] ——, "What is the goal of sensory coding?" *Neural Comput.*, vol. 6, no. 4, pp. 559–601, 1994.

[39] G. Folland, *Harmonic Analysis in Phase Space.* Princeton, NJ: Princeton Univ. Press, 1989.

[40] H. G. Feichtinger, "Atomic characterizations of modulation spaces through Gabor-type representations," *Rocky Mount. J. Math.*, vol. 19, pp. 113–126, 1989.

[41] C. Fefferman, "The uncertainty principle," *Bull. Amer. Math. Soc.*, vol. 9, pp. 129–206, 1983.

[42] M. Frazier and B. Jawerth, "The ϕ-transform and applications to distribution spaces," in *Function Spaces and Applications* (Lecture Notes in Mathematics, vol. 1302), M. Cwikel, *et al.*, Eds. Berlin, Germany: Springer-Verlag, 1988, pp. 223–246.

[43] M. Frazier, B. Jawerth, and G. Weiss, *Littlewood–Paley Theory and the Study of Function Spaces* (CBMS Reg. Conf. Ser. in Mathematics, no. 79). Amer. Math. Soc., 1991.

[44] D. Gabor, "Theory of communication," *J. Inst. Elect. Eng.*, vol. 93, pp. 429–457, 1946.

[45] J. Garnett, *Bounded Analytic Functions.* New York: Academic, 1981.

[46] A. Gersho and R. M. Gray, *Vector Quantization and Signal Compression.* Boston, MA: Kluwer, 1992.

[47] R. Godement, "Sur les relations d'orthogonalité de V. Bargmann," *C. R. Acad. Sci. Paris*, vol. 255, pp. 521–523, 657–659, 1947.

[48] R. M. Gray and D. L. Neuhoff, "Quantization," *IEEE Trans. Inform. Theory*, this issue, pp. 2325–2383.

[49] V. Goyal and M. Vetterli "Computation-distortion characteristics of block transform coding," in *ICASSP-97* (Munich, Germay, Apr. 1997), vol. 4, pp. 2729–2732.

[50] K. Gröchenig and S. Samarah, "Nonlinear approximation with local Fourier bases," unpublished manuscript, 1998.

[51] K. Gröchenig and D. Walnut, "Wilson bases are unconditional bases for modulation spaces," unpublished manuscript, 1998.

[52] A. Grossmann and J. Morlet, "Decomposition of Hardy functions into square-integrable wavelets of constant shape," *SIAM J. Appl. Math.*, vol. 15, pp. 723–736, 1984.

[53] G. H. Hardy, *A Mathematician's Apology.* Cambridge, U.K.: Cambridge Univ. Press, 1940.

[54] R. Howe, "On the role of the Heisenberg group in hran.onic analysis." *Bull Amer. Math. Soc.*, vol. 3, pp. 821–843, 1980.

[55] J. J. Y. Huang and P. M. Schultheiss, "Block quantization of correlated Gaussian random variables," *IEEE Trans. Commun.*, vol. CUM-11, pp. 289–296, Sept. 1963.

[56] P. Jones, "Rectifiable sets and the travelling salesman problem," *Inventiones Mathematicae*, vol. 102, pp. 1–15, 1990.

[57] ——, "Lennart Carleson's work in analysis," in *Festschrift in Honor of Lennart Carleson and Yngve Domar*, (Acta Universitatis Upsaliensis, vol. 58). Stockholm, Sweden: Almquist and Wiksell Int., 1994.

[58] J. P. Kahane and P. G. Lemarié-Rieusset, *Fourier Series and Wavelets.* Luxemburg: Gordon and Breach, 1995.

[59] J. Klauder and B. Skagerstam *Coherent States, Applications in Physics and Mathematical Physics.* Singapore: World Scientific, 1985.

[60] A. N. Kolmogorov, "On the Shannon theory of information transmission in the case of continuous signals," *IRE Trans. Inform. Theory*, vol. IT-2, pp. 102–108, 1956.

[61] ——, "Some fundamental problems in the approximate and exact representation of functions of one or several variables," in *Proc III. Math Congress USSR*, vol. 2. Moscow, USSR: MCU Press, 1956, pp. 28–29. Reprinted in Komogorov's *Selected Works*, vol. I.

[62] A. N. Kolmogorov and V. M. Tikhomirov, ϵ-entropy and ϵ-capacity. *Usp. Mat. Nauk*, vol. 14, pp: 3–86, 1959. (English transl. *Amer. Math. Soc. Transl.*, ser. 2, vol 17, pp. 277–364.)

[63] H. P. Kramer and M. V. Mathews, "A linear coding for transmitting a set of correlated signals," *IRE Trans. Inform. Theory*, vol. IT-23, pp. 41–46, Sept. 1956.

[64] P. G. Lemarié and Y. Meyer, "Ondelettes et Bases Hilbertiennes," *Revista Mat. Iberomamericana*, vol. 2, pp. 1–18, 1986.

[65] S. LoPresto, K. Ramchandran, and M. T. Orchard, "Image coding based on mixture modeling of wavelet coefficients and a fast estimation-quantization framework," in *Data Compression Conf. '97* (Snowbird, UT, 1997), pp. 221–230.

[66] G. G. Lorentz, "Metric entropy and approximation," *Bull. Amer. Math. Soc.*, vol. 72, pp. 903–937, Nov. 1966.

[67] L. Le Cam, "Convergence of estimates under dimensionality restrictions," *Ann. Statist.*, vol. 1, pp. 38–53, 1973.

[68] A. S. Lewis and G. Knowles, "Image compression using the 2-D wavelet transform," *IEEE Trans. Image Processing*, vol. 1, pp. 244–250, Apr. 1992.

[69] S. Mallat, "A theory for multiresolution signal decomposition: The wavelet representation," *IEEE Trans. Pattern Anal. Machine Intell.*, vol. 11, pp. 674–693, July 1989.

[70] S. Mallat and F. Falzon, "Analysis of low bit rate image transform coding," *IEEE Trans. Signal Processing*, vol. 46, pp. 1027–1042, Apr. 1998.

[71] H. S. Malvar and D. H. Staelin, "The LOT: Transform coding without blocking effects," *IEEE Trans. Acoust., Speech, Signal Processing*, vol. 37, no. 4, pp. 553–559, 1989.

[72] H. S. Malvar, "Extended lapped transforms: Properties, applications, and fast algorithms," *IEEE Trans. Signal Processing*, vol. 40, pp. 2703–2714, 1992.

[73] Y. Meyer, "Review of 'An Introduction to Wavelets' and 'Ten Lectures on Wavelets'," *Bull. Amer. Math. Soc.*, vol. 28, pp. 350–359, 1993.

[74] ——, *Ondelettes et Operateurs.* Paris, France: Hermann, 1990.

[75] ——, "Wavelets and applications" (Lecture at CIRM Luminy meeting, Luminy, France, Mar. 1992).

[76] F. Mintzer, "Filters for distortion-free two-band multirate filter banks," *IEEE Trans. Acoust., Speech, Signal Processing*, vol. 33, pp. 626–630, June 1985.

[77] A. Pinkus, *n-Widths in Approximation Theory.* New York: Springer, 1983.

[78] G. Pisier, *The Volume of Convex Bodies and Banach Space Geometry.* Cambridge, U.K.: Cambridge Univ.Press, 1989.

[79] J. O. Ramsay and B. W. Silverman, *Functional Data Analysis.* New York: Springer, 1997.

[80] K. Ramchandran and M. Vetterli, "Best wavelet packet bases in a rate-distortion sense," *IEEE Trans. Image Processing*, vol. 2, pp. 160–175, Apr. 1993.

[81] D. L. Ruderman, "Origins of scaling in natural images" *VISION RES.*, vol. 37, no. 23, pp. 3385–3398, Dec. 1997.

[82] A. Said and W. A. Pearlman, "A new, fast, and efficient image codec based on set partitioning in hierachical trees," *IEEE Trans. Circuits Syst. Video Technol.*, vol. 6, pp. 243–250, June 1996.

[83] C. E. Shannon, "A mathematical theory of communication," *Bell Syst. Tech. J.*, vol. 27, pp. 379–423, 623–656, 1948.

[84] ——, "Communication in the presence of noise," *Proc. IRE*, vol. 37, pp. 10–21, 1949.

[85] ——, "The bandwagon" (1956), in *Claude Elwood Shannon: Collected Papers*, N. J. A. Sloane and A. D. Wyner, Eds. Piscataway, NJ: IEEE Press, 1993.

[86] J. M. Shapiro, "Embedded image coding using zerotrees of wavelet coefficients," *IEEE Trans. Signal Processing*, vol. 41, pp. 3445–3462, Dec. 1993.

[87] E. Simoncelli, "Statistical models for images: Compression, restoration and synthesis,"presented at the IEEE 31st Asilomar Conf. Signals, Systems, and Computers, Pacific Grove, CA, 1997.

[88] M. J. T. Smith and T. P. Barnwell, III, "Exact reconstruction for tree-structured subband coders," *IEEE Trans. Acoust., Speech, Signal Processing*, vol. 35, pp. 431–441, 1986.

[89] E. Stein, *Singular Integrals and Differentiability Properties of Functions.* Princeton, NJ: Princeton Univ. Press, 1970.

[90] ——, *Harmonic Analysis: Real Variable Methods, Orthogonality, and Oscillatory Integrals.* Princeton, NJ: Princeton Univ. Press, 1993.

[91] J. O. Stromberg, *Festschrift in Honor of Antoni Zygmund.* Monterey, CA: Wadsworth, 1982.

[92] ——, "Maximal functions, Hardy Spaces, BMO, and Wavelets, from my point of view," in *Festschrift in Honor of Lennart Carleson and Yngve Domar*, (Acta Universitatis Upsaliensis vol. 58). Stockholm, Sweden: Almquist and Wiksell Int., 1994.

[93] V. M. Tikhomirov, "Widths and entropy," *Usp. Mat. Nauk*, vol. 38, pp. 91–99, 1983 (in Russian). English transl. in *Russian Math Surveys*, vol. 38, pp. 101–111.

[94] ——, "Commentary: ϵ-entropy and ϵ-capacity," in *A. N. Kolmogorov: Selected Works. III. Information Theory and Theory of Algorithms*, A. N. Shiryaev, Ed. Boston, MA: Kluwer, 1992.

[95] B. Torrésani, "Time-frequency representations: Wavelet packets and optimal decomposition," *Ann. l'Institut Henri Poincare (Physique Théorique)*, vol. 56, no. 2, pp. 215–34, 1992.

[96] H. Triebel, *Theory of Function Spaces.* Basel, Switzerland: Birkhauser, 1983.

[97] P. P. Vaidyanathan, "Quadrature mirror filter banks, M-band extensions and perfect reconstruction techniques," *IEEE ASSP Mag.*, vol. 4, pp. 4–20, July 1987.

[98] M. Vetterli, "Multi-dimensional subband coding: Some theory and algorithms," *Signal Processing*, vol. 6, no. 2, pp. 97–112, Apr. 1984.

[99] ——, "Filter banks allowing perfect reconstruction," *Signal Processing*, vol. 10, no. 3, pp. 219–244, Apr. 1986.

[100] M. Vetterli and J. Kovačević, *Wavelets and Subband Coding.* Englewood Cliffs, NJ: Prentice-Hall, 1995.

[101] P. H. Westerink, J. Biemond, D. E. Boekee, and J. W. Woods, "Subband coding of images using vector quantization," *IEEE Trans. Commun.*, vol. 36, pp. 713–719, June 1988.

[102] J. W. Woods and S. D. O'Neil, "Sub-band coding of images," *IEEE Trans. Acoust., Speech Siganl Processing*, vol. 34, pp. 1278–1288, Oct. 1986.

[103] A. Zygmund, *Trigonometric Series*, vols. I & II. Cambridge, U.K.: Cambridge Univ. Press, 1959.

Association Schemes and Coding Theory

Philippe Delsarte and Vladimir I. Levenshtein, *Associate Member, IEEE*

(Invited Paper)

Abstract—This paper contains a survey of association scheme theory (with its algebraic and analytical aspects) and of its applications to coding theory (in a wide sense). It is mainly concerned with a class of subjects that involve the central notion of the distance distribution of a code. Special emphasis is put on the linear programming method, inspired by the MacWilliams transform. This produces upper bounds for the size of a code with a given minimum distance, and lower bounds for the size of a design with a given strength. The most specific results are obtained in the case where the underlying association scheme satisfies certain well-defined "polynomial properties;" this leads one into the realm of orthogonal polynomial theory. In particular, some "universal bounds" are derived for codes and designs in polynomial type association schemes. Throughout the paper, the main concepts, methods, and results are illustrated by two examples that are of major significance in classical coding theory, namely, the Hamming scheme and the Johnson scheme. Other topics that receive special attention are spherical codes and designs, and additive codes in translation schemes, including $\mathbb{Z}_4$-additive binary codes.

Index Terms— Association schemes, codes and designs, duality, linear programming, orthogonal polynomials, polynomial schemes, translation schemes, universal bounds.

I. INTRODUCTION

ASSOCIATION scheme theory is part of what is now called algebraic combinatorics [10], [54]. It has two main origins. *Association schemes* were introduced in statistical (combinatorial) design theory by Bose and Shimamoto [23], and the appropriate algebraic setting was given by Bose and Mesner [21]. In fact, the subject can be traced back to a paper by Bose and Nair in 1939 [22].

The second origin is group theory and, more precisely, *character theory of finite groups*, developed by Frobenius, Schur, and Burnside. For example, as pointed out by Bannai and Ito [10], a paper by Hoheisel in 1939 derives the orthogonality relations for group characters by a method belonging to "association scheme theory" (before the appearance of association schemes in combinatorics) [61]. Another pioneering contribution in this area is a paper by Kawada on character algebras [67] (see [10]). In fact, one may even say that association scheme theory is as old as Frobenius' representation theory of finite groups (see [11]).

In combinatorics, an association scheme is defined in terms of certain *regularity properties*. In the "group case," the association scheme structure arises from certain *symmetry properties*, which directly induce the desired regularity properties. Thus following Bannai and Ito, we may say that association scheme theory is a "group theory without groups" [10]. Such a distinction between regularity and symmetry can be found in several subjects. An important example, which belongs to association scheme theory, is the distinction between distance-regular graphs and distance-transitive graphs [26].

The association scheme approach was introduced in *coding theory* in 1973 [37] to deal with a collection of topics involving the notion of the "distance distribution" of a code (see [35] and [36]). One of the main subjects is the general concept of a τ-design or a code with "dual distance" $\tau + 1$ and a universal (lower) bound on the size of τ-designs. (Term "universal" means here that the bound is valid for all τ-designs in all association schemes under consideration.) This allows one to explain the unified nature of different combinatorial objects and bounds. If a covering radius of a code Y in a metric space X characterizes a degree of the approximation of *any* element of X by elements of Y, then the "dual distance" of Y characterizes an approximation degree of X by Y "at the whole." This idea turned out to be very useful for some problems of numerical analysis [45] and cryptography [122] and was extended to any finite and compact infinite metric spaces in [81]. Another important topic is the problem of finding a universal (upper) bound on the size of a code with minimum distance $\geq d$ or, briefly, a d-code (see [82] and [88]). Short introductions to "association schemes and coding theory" were given by Sloane [155] and by Goethals [55]. The same subject is treated in detail in a recent paper by Camion [32].

One of the most significant (although elementary) discoveries was the fact that the MacWilliams transform[1] of the distance distribution of *any* code is nonnegative as the mean value of nonnegative definite functions (matrices) over the code [35], [37]. This "innocent appearing result" (to quote Welch, McEliece, and Rumsey [131]) has far-reaching consequences. The method of obtaining bounds for d-codes based on nonnegative definite functions $F(x,y)$ depending on distance $d(x,y)$, i.e., $F(x,y) = f(d(x,y))$, has been

Manuscript received December 2, 1997; revised March 6, 1998. The work of V. I. Levenshtein was supported by the Russian Foundation for Basic Research under Grant 98-01-00146 and by the Civilian Research and Development Foundation under Grant RM1-346.

P. Delsarte is with the Department of Computing Science and Engineering, Catholic University of Louvain, Louvain-la-Neuve, Belgium.

V. I. Levenshtein is with the Keldysh Institute for Applied Mathematics, Russian Academy of Science, 125047 Moscow, Russia.

Publisher Item Identifier S 0018-9448(98)05287-0.

[1] Recall that the *MacWilliams identities* relate the weight distribution of a linear code (over a finite field) with that of its orthogonal code by a well-defined linear transform (over the reals) [86], [87].

applied by Blichfeldt [19], Rankin [97], and Sidelnikov [110], [111]. However, for association schemes (and some of their generalizations) there is a description of all such functions. This makes it possible to apply a linear programming method for finding the best universal bound for d-codes (and τ-designs as well) [35], [37]. For a class of association schemes of important interest for coding theory, the corresponding linear programs can be treated as extremum problems for systems of orthogonal polynomials. Thus any choice of a permissible polynomial gives rise to a universal bound for d-codes. In 1977, McEliece, Rodemich, Rumsey, and Welch (MRRW) [90] proposed a polynomial which gives an improvement of the best asymptotic bound obtained before in [111]. One year later, another polynomial was proposed [73]; it gives rise to a universal bound for d-codes that improves upon the MRRW bound and is attained for many cases in different spaces although it gives the same asymptotic result. It turned out [77], [112] that this polynomial is an optimal solution of the corresponding extremum problem in the class of polynomials of a restricted degree. This progress in bounding d-codes allowed one to improve bounds on the *Shannon reliability function* [107] for some probabilistic channels (see [65]).

In classical coding theory, dealing with codes in a *Hamming scheme*, the MacWilliams transform involves a family of orthogonal polynomials [121] known as the *Krawtchouk polynomials* [68]. Surprisingly enough, this fact was not uncovered before 1972 [35], although the "polynomial property" of the MacWilliams transform was pointed out by MacWilliams herself in 1963 [86]. The importance of the role played by Krawtchouk polynomials in coding theory is well recognized nowadays [78], [82], [88]. It can be explained by the fact that these polynomials give the *eigenvalues of the distance relation matrices of the Hamming scheme* [37]. This was first proved implicitly by Vere-Jones in the binary case [128]. A thorough investigation of the group-theoretic significance of the Krawtchouk polynomials was given by Dunkl [46].

The familiar "block codes of length n over a q-ary alphabet," which belong to classical coding theory, can be called "codes in the Hamming (association) scheme H_q^n." The general association scheme approach provides us naturally with a considerable extension of the theory in that it applies to "*codes*" and "*designs*" in *any association scheme* [37], [39]. This combinatorial structure consists of a nonempty finite set X endowed with a collection of binary relations $R_0, R_1, \cdots, R_n$ having strong regularity properties. The adjacency matrices of the graphs (X, R_i) generate a commutative and associative algebra (over the complex numbers) both for the matrix product and the pointwise product. This is called the *Bose–Mesner algebra* of the association scheme. It has two distinguished bases: the basis consisting of the *adjacency matrices* D_i, and the basis consisting of the *irreducible idempotent matrices* E_k. By definition, there exist well-defined complex numbers $p_i(k)$ and $q_k(i)$ such that

$$D_i = \sum_{k=0}^{n} p_i(k) E_k \qquad |X| E_k = \sum_{i=0}^{n} q_k(i) D_i.$$

The p-numbers $p_i(k)$ and the q-numbers $q_k(i)$ play a prominent role in the theory. They satisfy some well-defined *orthog-*

onality relations. (In the case of the Hamming scheme, we have $p_i(k) = q_i(k) = K_i(k)$, where $K_i(z)$ is the Krawtchouk polynomial of degree i.) It appears that the p-numbers $p_i(k)$ are the eigenvalues of the adjacency matrix D_i.

There is an important *formal duality* in the theory, called the Krein duality, which permutes the roles of the matrix and pointwise products in the Bose–Mesner algebra [8], [42], [95]. This duality is a rich source of research ideas: "trying to make the theory closed under duality."

A *code* Y in an association scheme is a nonempty subset of the point set X (with the inherited relations $R_i|Y$). The *inner distribution*[2] of Y is the $(n + 1)$-tuple $(a_i)_{i=0}^n$ where $|Y| a_i$ counts the ordered pairs of code points $y, y' \in Y$ with $(y, y') \in R_i$. In this general context, the "innocent appearing result" alluded to above is the fact that *the Q-transform of the inner distribution is nonnegative*, in the sense that $\Sigma_{i=0}^n a_i q_k(i)$ is a nonnegative real number (for $k = 0, 1, \cdots, n$). This is the basis of the *linear programming method* to find upper bounds for D-codes and lower bounds for D-designs in an association scheme [37]. "Duality" between D-codes and D-designs manifests itself in the fact that any linear programming bound for D-codes gives a linear programming bound for D-designs and conversely [80]. Explicit universal bounds for codes and designs in some classes of association schemes have been obtained by use of this approach [37], [73], [76], [77], [81].

Certain parts of the theory can be developed further, when appropriate restrictive assumptions are imposed on the p- or q-numbers. An association scheme is said to be a *P-polynomial scheme* if the p-numbers can be represented in the form $p_i(k) = P_i(\xi_k)$ where $P_i(t)$ is a real polynomial of degree i in t and $\xi_0, \cdots, \xi_n$ are distinct real numbers. The orthogonality relations on the p-numbers show that $(P_i(t))_{i=0}^n$ is a system of *orthogonal polynomials*. There is a similar (dual) definition and a similar result for a *Q-polynomial scheme* (involving the q-numbers instead of the p-numbers) [37].

The P-polynomial property has a clear interpretation: R_i contains the pairs of points that are at distance i apart in the "generator graph" (X, R_1). In other words, (X, R_1) is a *distance-regular graph*. This subject was introduced by Biggs in 1969 (see [18]); it is treated in great detail by Brouwer, Cohen, and Neumaier [26]. The dual notion of a Q-polynomial scheme is equally interesting and has been investigated by several authors [10], [54], [71], [72], [77], [81], [93], [94], [126]. It should be noted, however, that this notion does not have a simple "combinatorial meaning."

The theory of Q-polynomial schemes can be extended so as to include "continuous analogs" such as the *Euclidean sphere* and the *projective space* in a unified framework [48], [54], [65], [77], [81], [93], [116], [119]. In particular, the linear programming method can be applied to derive upper bounds for spherical codes with a given minimum distance and lower bounds for spherical designs with a given strength (see [45], [77], [81], [116], and [135]).

If the point set X is endowed with the structure of an Abelian group and if the relations R_i are "translation-

---

[2] A related notion is the *outer distribution*, which enumerates the R_i-associates of each point $x \in X$ in the code Y.

invariant" with respect to that group, then the association scheme is said to be a *translation scheme* (with respect to the given group). This notion is equivalent to that of a commutative Schur ring, investigated in detail by Tamaschke [123]. There exists a *dual* translation scheme (with respect to the dual group of X). If Y is an additive code in X, i.e., a subgroup of X, then there is a natural definition of an *annihilator code* Y° in the dual scheme. (The relation between Y and Y° generalizes the relation between a linear code Y in Hamming scheme and its orthogonal code $Y^\perp$.) The inner distributions of the codes Y and Y° are related by *generalized MacWilliams identities*, in the sense that they are the P-transform and Q-transform of each other (within scaling) [32], [37], [42].

Thus the theory of translation schemes is quite interesting in that it provides the formal Krein duality with an actual duality interpretation. Furthermore, in this restricted context, there is a simple criterion to check whether a given additive code Y carries a "subscheme" of the translation scheme X, and to characterize the dual scheme of Y (see [37] in the case of the Hamming scheme).

This paper aims at giving a self-contained account of those parts of association scheme theory that are especially relevant to coding theory (in a wide sense), along the lines of the present introduction.

Section II contains the basic definitions; it is focused on the Bose–Mesner algebra and its formal duality. Section III introduces the subject of codes (and designs) in an association scheme, with special emphasis on the notions of the inner and outer distributions. This also includes the linear programming approach and a duality in bounding the sizes of codes and designs based on the existence of two orthogonality conditions. Section IV gives up-to-date bounds on fundamental parameters of codes and designs in P- and/or Q-polynomial schemes. Two extremum problems for systems of orthogonal polynomials are considered and their optimal solutions are used to describe the best known linear programming bounds. The results for Q-polynomials schemes are extended to the case of the unit Euclidean sphere. For P- and Q-polynomial schemes, three pairs of universal bounds and main asymptotic results are presented. Section V deals with translation schemes and their additive codes; it includes an introduction to $\mathbb{Z}_4$-additive binary codes.

II. BASIC NOTIONS

A. Definitions and Examples

Let X be a finite set of "points," with $|X| \geq 2$. For an integer $n \geq 1$, consider a set $R = \{R_0, R_1, \cdots, R_n\}$ of $n+1$ nonempty *binary relations* R_i on X (i.e., $R_i \subseteq X^2$), forming a *partition* of the Cartesian square X^2 of X.

For integers a and b with $a \leq b$, we shall use the notation N_b^a for the integer interval $\{a, a+1, \cdots, b\}$ and put $N_n := N_n^0 = \{0, 1, \cdots, n\}$.

Definition 1: The pair (X, R) is said to be an *n-class association scheme* if

a) R_0 is the diagonal, i.e., $R_0 = \{(x, x) \in X^2 : x \in X\}$.

b) For $i \in N_n$, the converse

$$R_i^\cup := \{(x, y) \in X^2 : (y, x) \in R_i\}$$

of R_i belongs to R.

c) There exist integer numbers $p_{i,j}^k$, called *intersection numbers*, with $p_{i,j}^k = p_{j,i}^k$, such that, for each pair $(x, y) \in R_k$, the number of points $z \in X$ with $(x, z) \in R_i$ and $(z, y) \in R_j$ is equal to the constant $p_{i,j}^k$ (for $i, j, k \in N_n$).

Condition b) induces a *pairing* $i \mapsto i^\sigma$ over N_n, defined by $R_{i^\sigma} = R_i^\cup$. The number p_{i,i^σ}^0 is denoted by v_i and is called the *valency* (or the *degree*) of the directed graph (X, R_i); it counts the points $z \in X$ with $(x, z) \in R_i$, for any fixed $x \in X$. Clearly, $v_{i^\sigma} = v_i$ and $\Sigma_{i=0}^n v_i = |X|$.

In most coding-theoretic applications, the definition above can be made more restrictive. The association scheme (X, R) is said to be *symmetric* if all its relations R_i are symmetric. Thus condition b) is replaced by

b)* $R_i = R_i^\cup$, for each $i \in N_n$.

In other words, a symmetric association scheme has a *trivial pairing*, i.e., $i = i^\sigma$ for all i. (Notice that the identity $p_{i,j}^k = p_{j,i}^k$ in c) can be omitted in the symmetric case, since it becomes a consequence of the other requirements.)

In particular, a 2-class association scheme ($n = 2$) is equivalent to a *strongly regular graph* [20], [105] in the symmetric case, and to a *skew conference matrix* in the nonsymmetric case [13], [56].

Note that we can consider an association scheme (X, R) with an ordering of R_i, $i = 0, 1, \cdots, n$, as a space X with the function $\partial_R : X^2 \to N_n$ which is defined as follows:

$$\partial_R(x, y) = i \text{ if and only if } (x, y) \in R_i. \quad (1)$$

In the symmetric case this function has, in particular, the properties $\partial_R(x, y) = 0$ if and only if $x = y$ and $\partial_R(x, y) = \partial_R(y, x)$, but, in general, does not satisfy the triangle inequality and hence is not a distance function. On the other hand, a metric space X with a distance function $\partial(x, y)$ which takes values from N_n is a symmetric n-class association scheme (X, R) with $\partial_R(x, y) = \partial(x, y)$ if and only if for any $i, j \in N_n$ and $x, y \in X$, the number

$$\lambda_{i,j}(x, y) := |\{z \in X : \partial(x, z) = i, \partial(z, y) = j\}| \quad (2)$$

depends only on i, j, and $\partial(x, y)$. In fact, we state that this is true for the first two examples below.

Example 1: Let $X = \mathbf{F}^n$ be the nth Cartesian power of a finite *alphabet* $\mathbf{F}$, with $|\mathbf{F}| = q \geq 2$. Let $\partial_H : X^2 \to N_n$ denote the *Hamming distance function*

$$\partial_H(x, y) := |\{j \in N_n^1 : x_j \neq y_j\}|.$$

Then (X, R) with $\partial_R(x, y) = \partial_H(x, y)$ is a symmetric n-class association scheme, called the *Hamming scheme* and denoted by H_q^n. It appears as the natural framework of the classical theory of "block codes" [82], [88]. When q is a prime power, $\mathbf{F}$ can be endowed with the structure of the *finite field* $\mathbb{F}_q$. In this case, $\partial_H(x, y) = w_H(x - y)$, where $w_H : X \to N_n$ is the *Hamming weight function*, given by $w_H(x) := |\{j \in N_n^1 : x_j \neq 0\}|$. More generally, this applies to the case where $\mathbf{F}$ has the structure of an *additive Abelian group*. (No multiplicative operation is required here.)

Example 2: Let X be the set of binary v-tuples of a fixed weight n, with $1 \leq n \leq \lfloor v/2 \rfloor$. Thus

$$X := \{x \in \{0,1\}^v \colon w_H(x) = n\}.$$

For $i \in N_n$, define

$$R_i := \{(x,y) \in X^2 \colon \partial_H(x,y) = 2i\}$$

and

$$R := \{R_0, R_1, \cdots, R_n\}.$$

Then (X,R) is a symmetric n-class association scheme, called the *Johnson scheme* and denoted by J_n^v. It is a "subscheme" of the binary Hamming scheme H_2^v with $\partial_R(x,y) = \frac{1}{2}\partial_H(x,y)$. The Johnson scheme plays a useful role in combinatorial coding theory.

Example 3: Let $\boldsymbol{F} = \{\alpha_0, \alpha_1, \cdots, \alpha_{q-1}\}$, and $X := \boldsymbol{F}^v$. The *composition* of a point x in X is the integer q-tuple $(s_0(x), s_1(x), \cdots, s_{q-1}(x))$ defined by

$$s_l(x) := |\{j \in N_v^1 \colon x_j = \alpha_l\}|.$$

Assume that $\boldsymbol{F}$ is an Abelian group. Define a set R of binary relations R_i on X as follows. A pair (x,y) in X^2 belongs to a certain relation R_i if and only if the difference $x - y$ has a specified composition. Then (X,R) is an n-class association scheme, with $n = \binom{v+q-1}{q-1} - 1$, called the *composition scheme*. It is symmetric when $x = -x$ for all $x \in X$, i.e., when $\boldsymbol{F}$ is an elementary Abelian 2-group (of order $q = 2^m$). In particular, the composition scheme with $q = 2$ reduces to the binary Hamming scheme H_2^n.

There are several other families of association schemes that have interesting applications in coding theory. Let us mention five of them: i) the association scheme relative to the *split weight enumerator* [42], [88]; ii) the *Lee scheme* [124]; iii) the *nonbinary Johnson scheme* [1], [124], [125]; iv) the association scheme of $m \times n$ *matrices over a finite field* [41] (which has applications in crisscross error correcting codes [52], [102]); v) the association scheme of $n \times n$ *skew-symmetric matrices over a finite field* [43]. In the last two cases, the relations R_i are defined from the *rank metric* over the matrix set X.

Of course, there exist applications of association schemes outside the area of coding theory (in a wide sense). It is especially worth saying that association schemes have recently found considerable interest in *spin model theory* (a branch of mechanical statistics). The idea is due to Jaeger (see [63] and the references therein).

Finally, let us mention some constructions that produce association schemes from other association schemes. In particular, there is the notion of the *extension* [37], *product* [54], and *merging* [32] of association schemes.

B. The Bose–Mesner Algebra

It proves very useful to investigate a combinatorial structure such as an association scheme (X,R) by matrix algebra methods. Let $\mathbb{C}(X^2)$ denote the set of square complex matrices M of order $|X|$, where rows and columns are labeled with the points $x \in X$, and the (x,y) entry of M is denoted

by $M(x,y)$. The directed graph (X,R_i) is represented by its *adjacency matrix* $D_i \in \mathbb{C}(X^2)$, defined by

$$D_i(x,y) := \begin{cases} 1, & \text{for } (x,y) \in R_i \\ 0, & \text{for } (x,y) \notin R_i. \end{cases} \tag{3}$$

Definition 2: Let (X,R) be an n-class association scheme (see Definition 1). The *Bose–Mesner algebra* of (X,R), denoted by $\mathcal{A}$, is the complex vector space generated by the adjacency matrices D_i, that is,

$$\mathcal{A} := \{c_0 D_0 + c_1 D_1 + \cdots + c_n D_n \colon c_0, c_1, \cdots, c_n \in \mathbb{C}\}. \tag{4}$$

From the fact that R is a partition of X^2 and from condition a), it follows that $\mathcal{A}$ *contains the all-one matrix J and the unit matrix I*, since

$$D_0 + D_1 + \cdots + D_n = J \qquad D_0 = I. \tag{5}$$

Condition b) says that $\mathcal{A}$ is *closed under conjugation* ($M \mapsto \overline{M}$) *and under transposition* ($M \mapsto M^T$), whence under conjugate transposition ($M \mapsto M^* := \overline{M}^T$), since

$$\overline{D_i} = D_i \qquad D_i^T = D_{i^\sigma}. \tag{6}$$

Condition c) says that $\mathcal{A}$ is *closed under matrix multiplication*, and that multiplication in $\mathcal{A}$ is *commutative*, since

$$D_i D_j = \sum_{k=0}^{n} p_{i,j}^k D_k = D_j D_i. \tag{7}$$

This shows that the $(n+1)$-dimensional vector space $\mathcal{A}$ defined by (4) has the structure of a *commutative algebra* (over $\mathbb{C}$). As indicated in Definition 2 (with some anticipation in the use of the term "algebra"), $\mathcal{A}$ is usually referred to as the *Bose–Mesner algebra* (or *adjacency algebra*) of the association scheme (X,R) (see [21]).

For a symmetric association scheme, we have $D_i^T = D_i$ for all i. In this case, we can define the Bose–Mesner algebra over the *reals*, i.e., replace $\mathbb{C}$ by $\mathbb{R}$ in (4).

The adjacency algebra $\mathcal{A}$ is known to be *semi-simple*. This means that there exists a unitary matrix U of order $|X|$ that reduces each matrix $M \in \mathcal{A}$ to a diagonal form $\Delta_M = U^{-1}MU$. As a consequence, $\mathcal{A}$ possesses a unique basis of *irreducible idempotent matrices* $E_0, E_1, \cdots, E_n$, which are mutually orthogonal

$$E_k E_l = \delta_{k,l} E_k, \qquad \text{for } k, l \in N_n. \tag{8}$$

In particular, $E_0 = |X|^{-1}J$. The rank of E_k will be denoted by m_k, and the numbers $m_0, m_1, \cdots, m_n$ will be referred to as the *multiplicities* of the association scheme (X,R). By definition, E_k has eigenvalues 1 and 0 with multiplicities m_k and $|X| - m_k$. Notice that $m_0 = 1$ and $\sum_{k=0}^{n} m_k = |X|$. Considering the inner product

$$\langle v, w \rangle = \frac{1}{|X|} \sum_{x \in X} v(x)\overline{w(x)} \tag{9}$$

for complex functions v, w defined on X, one can represent the matrix E_k in the form

$$E_k(x,y) = \frac{1}{|X|} \sum_{j=1}^{m_k} v_{k,j}(x)\overline{v_{k,j}(y)} \tag{10}$$

where $\{v_{k,j} \colon j = 1, \cdots, m_k\}$ is an arbitrary orthonormal basis of the linear space V_k generated by the columns of E_k. (It is orthonormal with respect to (9).)

Definition 3: The *p-numbers* of an *n*-class association scheme (X, R) are the complex numbers $p_i(k)$, with $k, i \in N_n$, defined from the expansion of the adjacency matrices D_i in the basis of the irreducible idempotent matrices E_k of the algebra $\mathcal{A}$, i.e.,

$$D_i = \sum_{k=0}^{n} p_i(k) E_k, \qquad \text{for } i \in N_n. \tag{11}$$

Analogously, the *q-numbers* of (X, R) are the complex numbers $q_k(i)$, with $i, k \in N_n$, defined from the inverse expansion, within the normalizing factor $|X|$, i.e.,

$$|X| E_k = \sum_{i=0}^{n} q_k(i) D_i, \qquad \text{for } k \in N_n. \tag{12}$$

These numbers play a major role in the theory. It follows from (11) that the *p*-number $p_i(k)$ is the *eigenvalue* of D_i relative to the m_k-dimensional space V_k spanned by the columns of E_k. In particular, $p_i(0) = v_i$ (valency of R_i). Notice that $q_k(0) = m_k$ (rank of E_k). In view to (3) and (1), (12) can be written in the form

$$|X| E_k(x, y) = q_k(\partial_R(x, y)). \tag{13}$$

If the association scheme (X, R) is *symmetric*, then its *p*-numbers and *q*-numbers are *real*.

Let $F(N_n)$ denote the linear space of complex (or real in the symmetric case) functions defined on N_n. In particular, the *p*-numbers $p_i(k)$ and the *q*-numbers $q_k(i)$ are values of the *p-functions* $p_i \in F(N_n)$ and *q-functions* $q_k \in F(N_n)$ which form two bases of $F(N_n)$. This implies that any function $h \in F(N_n)$ has a unique expansion over either of these bases

$$h = \sum_{i=0}^{n} h_i(p) p_i \qquad h = \sum_{k=0}^{n} h_k(q) q_k. \tag{14}$$

The following result expresses the well-known *orthogonality relations* for the *p*-functions and *q*-functions. It appears as a consequence of (8), basically.

Theorem 1: The *p-functions* $p_i \in F(N_n)$ $(i = 0, 1, \cdots, n)$ are pairwise-orthogonal on N_n with respect to the multiplicities m_k and the *q-functions* $q_k \in F(N_n)$ $(k = 0, 1, \cdots, n)$ are pairwise-orthogonal on N_n with respect to the valencies v_i. More precisely

$$\sum_{k=0}^{n} m_k \overline{p_i(k)} p_j(k) = |X| v_i \delta_{i,j}$$

$$\sum_{i=0}^{n} v_i \overline{q_k(i)} q_l(i) = |X| m_k \delta_{k,l}.$$

In view of the fact that the relations (11) and (12) are inverse of each other, the *p*-numbers and the *q*-numbers are related by

$$m_k \overline{p_i(k)} = v_i q_k(i). \tag{15}$$

Example 1 (continued): For given values of n (the "length") and q (the "alphabet size"), and for $k \in N_n$, we define the *Krawtchouk polynomial* $K_k^n(z)$ as follows [68]:

$$K_k^n(z) := \sum_{j=0}^{k} (-1)^j (q-1)^{k-j} \binom{z}{j} \binom{n-z}{k-j}. \tag{16}$$

Clearly, $K_k^n(z)$ is a polynomial of degree k in z. The *p*-numbers and the *q*-numbers of H_q^n are the values assumed by the Krawtchouk polynomials at the integer points $0, 1, \cdots, n$. More precisely

$$p_i(k) = K_i^n(k) \qquad q_k(i) = K_k^n(i). \tag{17}$$

The valencies and multiplicities are $v_k = m_k = \binom{n}{k}(q-1)^k$.

Example 2 (continued): For given values of v (the "length") and n (the "weight"), the valencies and multiplicities of the Johnson scheme J_n^v are given by

$$v_i = \binom{n}{i}\binom{v-n}{i} \qquad m_k = \binom{v}{k} - \binom{v}{k-1}.$$

For $k, i \in N_n$, we define the *Hahn polynomial*[3] $H_k(z)$ and the *dual Hahn polynomial* $\tilde{H}_i(z)$ as follows [66]:

$$H_k(z) = m_k \sum_{j=0}^{k} (-1)^j \frac{\binom{k}{j}\binom{v+1-k}{j}}{\binom{n}{j}\binom{v-n}{j}} \binom{z}{j} \tag{18}$$

$$\tilde{H}_i(z) = \sum_{j=0}^{i} (-1)^{i-j} \binom{n-j}{i-j}\binom{n-z}{j}\binom{v-n+j-z}{j}. \tag{19}$$

Clearly, $H_k(z)$ is a polynomial of degree k in z. It is easily seen that $\tilde{H}_i(z)$ is a polynomial of degree i in $z(v+1-z)$. The *p*-numbers and the *q*-numbers of J_n^v can be determined (see [37]) from these polynomials by

$$p_i(k) = \tilde{H}_i(k) \qquad q_k(i) = H_k(i). \tag{20}$$

C. Formal Duality

The adjacency matrices D_i and the idempotent matrices E_k play *dual roles* in the theory. This formal duality, which interchanges the *p*-numbers and the *q*-numbers, will be referred to as the *Krein duality* [8]. Let us examine this subject in some detail. The Bose–Mesner algebra $\mathcal{A}$ is closed not only under ordinary matrix multiplication $(M, N) \mapsto MN$, but also under *pointwise* (or *Hadamard*) *multiplication* $(M, N) \mapsto M \circ N$, defined by $(M \circ N)(x, y) := M(x, y) N(x, y)$. This stems from the fact that the adjacency matrices D_i are "idempotent" and "mutually orthogonal" with respect to the pointwise product

$$D_i \circ D_j = \delta_{i,j} D_i, \qquad \text{for } i, j \in N_n. \tag{21}$$

The formal Krein duality under discussion *permutes the roles of the matrix product and the pointwise product.* Thus

---

[3] In fact, these are the Hahn polynomials of *spherical type*.

the identities (8) and (21) are dual of each other. As duals of (5) and (6), we have

$$E_0 + E_1 + \cdots + E_n = I \qquad E_0 = |X|^{-1}J$$
$$E_k^* = E_k \qquad E_k^T = E_{k^\tau}$$

where $k \mapsto k^\tau$ is a well-defined pairing over N_n. For a symmetric association scheme, this pairing is trivial: $E_k^T = E_k$ for all k.

Let us stress the fact that the idempotent matrices E_k are *Hermitian* and *nonnegative definite*, since their eigenvalues are 0 and 1. (It can be viewed as a dual of the property of adjacency matrices, having entries 0 and 1.)

The following property is essential for the linear programming method introduced in Section III below.

Theorem 2: For any function $h \in F(N_n)$ the matrix $h(\partial_R(x,y))$ is Hermitian and nonnegative definite if and only if $h_k(q) \geq 0, k = 0, 1, \cdots, n$.

Next, we examine the dual of identity (7), that is,

$$|X|(E_k \circ E_l) = \sum_{m=0}^{n} q_{k,l}^m E_m. \qquad (22)$$

The numbers $q_{k,l}^m$ defined from (22) are usually called the *Krein parameters;* they are the duals of the intersection numbers $p_{i,j}^k$. In particular, $q_{k,k^\tau}^0 = m_k$ and $q_{k,l}^0 = 0$ when $l \neq k^\tau$. Thus the multiplicities m_k are the duals of the valencies v_i. Notice that $E_k \circ E_l$ is a Hermitian nonnegative definite matrix according to (10). Hence, by (13) and Theorem 2 the Krein parameters satisfy $q_{k,l}^m \geq 0$ (see [55] and [101]).

By use of (7) and (22) we deduce that the intersection numbers $p_{i,j}^s$ and the Krein parameters $q_{k,l}^t$ are the *linearization factors* relative to the p-numbers $p_i(k)$ and to the q-numbers $q_k(i)$, respectively, in the sense that

$$p_i(k)p_j(k) = \sum_{s=0}^{n} p_{i,j}^s p_s(k) \qquad (23)$$

$$q_k(i)q_l(i) = \sum_{m=0}^{n} q_{k,l}^m q_m(i). \qquad (24)$$

Two n-class association schemes (X, R) and (X', R'), with $|X| = |X'|$, are *formal dual* of each other if the p-numbers of (X, R) are the q-numbers of (X', R'), and conversely, i.e.,

$$p_k'(i) = q_k(i) \qquad q_i'(k) = p_i(k). \qquad (25)$$

A necessary condition for an association scheme to have a formal dual is that its Krein parameters be integers (since they are the intersection numbers of the dual).

Example 1 (continued): In view of (17), the Hamming scheme H_q^n is formally self-dual. In fact, it is actually self-dual in the strong sense of "duality in translation schemes" (see Section V below).

Example 2 (continued): The Johnson scheme J_n^v has no formal dual. However, the general Krein duality applies; it permutes the Hahn and dual Hahn polynomials.

D. The Group Case and Generalizations

In Examples 1–3 of Section II-A, the *regularity properties* defining the association scheme structure are induced by some *symmetry properties*, i.e., by a certain "group of automorphisms." We now say a few words on this subject (see [10], [58], and [132]). Let G be a transitive permutation group acting on the point set X. It induces a partition of X^2 into a well-defined set $R = \{R_0, R_1, \cdots, R_n\}$ of *orbits* R_i. (By definition, such an orbit R_i contains the images $(x_i^g, y_i^g) \in X^2$ of a fixed pair $(x_i, y_i) \in X^2$ under all mappings $g \in G$.). The resulting structure (X, R) satisfies conditions a)– c) of an association scheme, except possibly the "commutativity condition" $p_{i,j}^k = p_{j,i}^k$. In any case, the adjacency matrices D_i form the basis of a subalgebra of $\mathbb{C}(X^2)$. (It is called the *Hecke algebra*.) This algebra is commutative if and only if $p_{i,j}^k = p_{j,i}^k$ (for all i, j, k).

Example 1 (continued): Let G be the permutation group on $X := \boldsymbol{F}^n$ generated by two types of mappings:

i) a permutation on the n coordinates;
ii) in each coordinate position, a permutation on the q alphabet symbols.

This group has order $n!(q!)^n$, and it is transitive on X. The corresponding structure (X, R) is the Hamming scheme H_q^n. In particular, the binary Hamming scheme H_2^n arises from the (complete) *monomial group* $G = M_n$ of degree n, containing the matrices of order n that have one nonzero element, equal to ± 1, in each row and each column.

Example 2 (continued): Let G be the *symmetric group* S_v of degree v, containing the $v!$ permutations on v coordinates. It acts in a natural way on the set X of binary v-tuples of weight n. The corresponding structure (X, R) is the Johnson scheme J_n^v.

The notion of an association scheme (X, R) can be generalized, by omitting the commutativity requirement $p_{i,j}^k = p_{j,i}^k$. A further extension is obtained by relaxing the "homogeneity condition" a) in Definition 1. In general, it is only required that the diagonal relation $\{(x, x): x \in X\}$ be a *union* of some relations belonging to the set R. Thus we arrive at a combinatorial structure (X, R) called a *coherent configuration* [59] (equivalent to a *cellular ring* [50]). The group theoretic counterpart of this general structure is obtained by leaving out the transitivity assumption.

Certain infinite metric spaces occur as analogs of association schemes that are important in coding theoretic applications. We call *distance-transitive* (or two-point homogeneous [130]) a connected compact metric space X with the distance function $\partial(\cdot, \cdot)$ and the isometry group G, if for any $x_1, x_2, y_1, y_2 \in X$ the equality $\partial(x_1, y_1) = \partial(x_2, y_2)$ implies the existence of some $g \in G$ such that $x_2 = x_1^g$ and $y_2 = y_1^g$. As an example of a distance-transitive space we mention the unit Euclidean sphere S^{n-1} in $\mathbb{R}^n$ (considered in more detail in Section IV-E) whose isometry group consists of all orthogonal matrices of order n. A distance-transitive space X has many strong properties [9], [53], [65], [120], [129]. The isometry group G of X acts *transitively* on X and hence there exists a unique *normalized invariant measure* μ ($\mu(X) = 1$ and $\mu(A^g) = \mu(A)$ for any measurable $A \subseteq X$ and $g \in G$). If n_X is the *diameter* of X, then for any (real) $i, j \in [0, n_X]$ and $x, y \in X, \mu\{z \in X: \partial(x, z) \leq i, \partial(z, y) \leq j\}$ (cf. (2)) depends only on i, j, and $\partial(x, y)$. For any *invariant* function $H(x, y)$ on X^2 (this means that $H(x^g, y^g) = H(x, y)$ for any $g \in G$) there exists a function h on $[0, n_X]$ such that $H(x, y) = h(\partial(x, y))$. Continuous invariant functions $H(x, y)$ on X^2 form a commutative algebra $\mathcal{A}$ with respect to the operations of addition and *convolution*

$$F * H(x, z) = \int_X F(x, y) H(y, z) \, d\mu(y).$$

In the linear space V of continuous functions $v(x)$ on X with the inner product

$$\langle v, w \rangle = \int_X v(x) \overline{w(x)} \, d\mu(x) \qquad (26)$$

(cf. (9)), the unitary representation $L(g)$ of G defined as follows: $L(g)v(x) = v(x^{g^{-1}})$, decomposes into a countable direct sum of pairwise inequivalent irreducible representations $L_k(g)$ acting on (mutually orthogonal) subspaces $V_k, k = 0, 1, \cdots$, of continuous functions. Each subspace V_k has a finite dimension m_k (V_0 consists of constants and $m_0 = 1$) and is *invariant* (i.e., if $v(x) \in V_k$, then $v(x^g) \in V_k$ for any $g \in G$). The invariant functions (cf. (10))

$$\tilde{E}_k(x, y) = \sum_{j=1}^{m_k} v_{k,j}(x) \overline{v_{k,j}(y)}, \qquad k = 0, 1, \cdots \qquad (27)$$

where $\{v_{k,j}(x): j = 1, \cdots, m_k\}$ is an arbitrary orthonormal (with respect to (26)) basis of V_k, form a basis of $\mathcal{A}$ consisting of irreducible idempotents, which are mutually orthogonal

$$\tilde{E}_k * \tilde{E}_l = \delta_{k,l} \tilde{E}_k, \qquad k, l = 0, 1, \cdots.$$

The corresponding "q-functions" q_k on $[0, n_X]$ such that $\tilde{E}_k(x, y) = q_k(\partial(x, y))$ are real and satisfy the following orthogonality and normalization conditions:

$$\int_0^{n_X} q_k(z) q_l(z) d\tilde{\mu}(z) = m_k \delta_{k,l}, \qquad q_k(0) = m_k \qquad (28)$$

where $\tilde{\mu}$ is the measure on $[0, n_X]$ such that $\tilde{\mu}(A) = \mu\{y \in X: \partial(x_0, y) \in A\}$ (this does not depend on $x_0 \in X$). For any element $H(x, y) = h(\partial(x, y))$ of $\mathcal{A}$, the series

$$\sum_{k=0}^{\infty} h_k q_k(z)$$

with

$$h_k = (m_k)^{-1} \int_0^{n_X} h(z) q_k(z) \, d\tilde{\mu}(z)$$

converges to $h(z)$ on $[0, n_X]$. Moreover, for these functions $q_k, k = 0, 1, \cdots$, an analog of Theorem 2 is valid and the linearization factors $q_{k,l}^m$ are nonnegative. All (infinite) compact distance transitive spaces have been classified in [130] as the unit Euclidean spheres S^{n-1}, the projective spaces in n dimensions over $\mathbb{R}, \mathbb{C}$, and quaternions $\mathbb{H}$ ($n = 2, 3, \cdots$), and the Cayley projective plane.

Note that the definition and all properties of distance-transitive spaces are also correct for finite metric spaces, and any finite distance-transitive metric space X is an n-class symmetric association scheme (X, R) with $\partial_R(x, y) = \partial(x, y)$ and n equal to the number of nonzero values of $\partial(x, y)$. In particular, the Hamming and Jonhson spaces are distance-transitive. The fact that in the case of finite spaces $\tilde{E}_k(x, y) = |X| E_k(x, y)$ (compare (10) with (27)) is explained by the distinctness between the product and convolution of matrices.

III. CODES AND DESIGNS

In coding theory and related subjects, an association scheme (such as the Hamming scheme) should mainly be viewed as a "structured space" in which the objects of interest (such as codes, or designs) are living.

Let Y be a nonempty subset of the point set X of an association scheme (X, R). Then Y will be called a *code* in (X, R). (In certain contexts, Y is preferably called a *design*.) We now introduce the important concept of the inner distribution of a code.

A. Inner Distribution

Definition 4: The *inner distribution* of a code Y in an n-class association scheme (X, R) is the rational $(n + 1)$-tuple $(a_0, a_1, \cdots, a_n)$ where $|Y| a_i$ counts the pairs of points in Y that belong to the relation R_i. Formally

$$a_i = a_i(Y) := \frac{1}{|Y|} |Y^2 \cap R_i|, \qquad \text{for } i \in N_n. \qquad (29)$$

A code Y in the Hamming scheme H_q^n is nothing but a *q-ary code of length n*. The inner distribution of Y is its *(Hamming) distance distribution*. In effect, $|Y| a_i$ counts the pairs of codewords $y, y' \in Y$ with $\partial_H(y, y') = i$.

Coding theorists are often interested in a code having a specified set of admissible distances (in particular: a specified minimum distance). In the general framework of association schemes, this notion extends as follows.

Definition 5: Let D be a subset of N_n^1. A code Y in (X, R) is called a *D-code* if all pairs of distinct points in Y belong to the admissible relation $\cup_{i \in D} R_i$. In terms of the inner distribution, this becomes $a_i(Y) = 0$ for each $i \in N_n^1 \backslash D$.

Consider, for a while, the familiar situation where Y is a *linear code of length n over the field* $\mathbb{F}_q$ (in the Hamming scheme). Then the distance distribution of Y reduces to its *weight distribution:* $a_i(Y)$ counts the codewords $y \in Y$ with $w_H(y) = i$. From the linear code Y we can define its *orthogonal code* (often called the dual code), that is,

$$Y^\perp := \{x \in \mathbb{F}_q^n: xy^T = 0 \text{ for all } y \in Y\}.$$

The weight distributions of Y and $Y^\perp$ are related by the *MacWilliams identities* [86], [87]. These are well-defined linear relations involving the Krawtchouk polynomials (16). (We shall go back to this subject in Section V.)

As a result, the "Krawtchouk–MacWilliams transform" of the distance (or weight) distribution of a linear code Y yields *nonnegative real numbers*, which can be interpreted as the components $a_k(Y^\perp)$ of the distance distribution of the orthogonal code $Y^\perp$. It turns out that this nonnegativity result can be extended to *arbitrary codes* (in a Hamming scheme), even though the orthogonal code notion is lost. Moreover, as shown below, the result extends to codes in *any* association scheme.

Definition 6: Let $q_k(i)$ denote the q-numbers of an n-class association scheme (with $i, k \in N_n$). The *Q-transform* of a complex $(n+1)$-tuple $(a_i)_{i=0}^n$ is the complex $(n+1)$-tuple $(a_k')_{k=0}^n$ given by

$$a_k' := \sum_{i=0}^n a_i q_k(i), \qquad \text{for } k \in N_n. \tag{30}$$

Note that this definition of the Q-transform in fact depends on the choice of an ordering of the functions q_k (or the matrices E_k), $k = 0, 1, \cdots, n$. From Theorem 1 and (15) it follows that

$$|X| a_i = \sum_{k=0}^n a_k' p_i(k). \tag{31}$$

Moreover (see (14)), for any $h \in F(N_n)$

$$\sum_{i=0}^n a_i h(i) = \sum_{k=0}^n a_k' h_k(q) \tag{32}$$

$$\sum_{k=0}^n a_k' h(k) = |X| \sum_{i=0}^n a_i h_i(p). \tag{33}$$

Theorem 3 (Generalized MacWilliams Inequalities [37]): Let $(a_i(Y))_{i=0}^n$ be the inner distribution of a code Y in (X, R), and let $(a_k'(Y))_{k=0}^n$ be its Q-transform. Then $a_k'(Y) \geq 0$ (i.e., $a_k'(Y) \in \mathbb{R}_+$) for each $k \in N_n$.

The proof is quite easy since, in view of (13) and (10),

$$|Y| a_k'(Y) = \sum_{x,y \in Y} q_k(\partial_R(x,y)) = \sum_{j=1}^{m_k} \left| \sum_{x \in Y} v_{k,j}(x) \right|^2 \geq 0. \tag{34}$$

This also shows that $a_k'(Y)$ is an *averaging* parameter of a code Y. In this connection note that $a_k'(X) = 0$ for all $k = 1, \cdots, n$.

The Q-transform of the inner distribution of a code Y will sometimes be referred to as the "dual (inner) distribution" of Y.

Definition 7: Let D be a subset of N_n^1. A code Y in (X, R) is called a *D-design* if the Q-transform of its inner distribution satisfies $a_k'(Y) = 0$ for each $k \in N_n^1 \backslash D$.

Example 1 (continued): In H_q^n, an $N_n^{\tau+1}$-design Y is an *orthogonal array of strength τ* (see [37] and [40]). This means that the restriction of Y to any set of τ coordinates shows all τ-tuples of alphabet symbols appearing the same number of times [98]. Orthogonal arrays are closely related to "resilient functions" and to "correlation-immune functions" which occur in some cryptography applications [16], [33], [79], [113], [122].

Example 2 (continued): In J_n^v, an $N_n^{\tau+1}$-design Y is a *combinatorial τ-design* (see [37]). This is a collection of blocks of size n, out of a point set of size v, such that all τ-subsets of the v-set are contained in the same number of blocks [15], [62]. There is a close connection between coding theory and design theory [3], [5]. It is interesting to point out that a three-parameter class of Hahn polynomials (larger than the "spherical class" involved in the q-numbers) plays a significant role in the theory of combinatorial τ-designs [133], [134] and in an extension thereof [28].

B. The Linear Programming Method

Theorem 3 strongly suggests using linear programming to find bounds on the size of a code Y characterized by some linear constraints on its inner distribution $(a_i(Y))_{i=0}^n$. In particular, this method leads to upper bounds for D-codes and to lower bounds for D-designs. We shall use the "nonstandard forms" of the linear programming problem. For simplicity we assume, in this subsection, that (X, R) is a *symmetric* association scheme, which implies that the p- and q-numbers are *real*. For the problems that we are considering here, this entails no loss of generality. While simultaneously considering p-functions and q-functions it is convenient to use the letter u instead of either p or q, and use $\overline{u}$ for the other one. For any $h \in F(N_n)$ with the expansion $h = \Sigma_{k=0}^n h_k(u) u_k$ we put

$$\Omega_u(h) = h(0)/h_0(u) \text{ if } h_0(u) \neq 0.$$

For any $D \subseteq N_n^1$, we say that $h \in F(N_n)$ has the property $\mathfrak{A}_u(D)$ if

$$h_0(u) > 0 \qquad h_i(u) \geq 0, \qquad \text{for } i \in N_n^1$$
$$h(0) > 0 \qquad h(i) \leq 0, \qquad \text{for } i \in D$$

and has the property $\mathfrak{B}_u(D)$ if

$$h_0(u) > 0 \qquad h_i(u) \leq 0, \qquad \text{for } i \in D$$
$$h(0) > 0 \qquad h(i) \geq 0, \qquad \text{for } i \in N_n^1.$$

Let

$$A_u(X, D) = \min \Omega_u(h)$$

where the minimum is taken over all functions $h \in F(N_n)$ with the property $\mathfrak{A}_u(D)$ and

$$B_u(X, D) = \max \Omega_u(h)$$

where the maximum is taken over all functions $h \in F(N_n)$ with the property $\mathfrak{B}_u(D)$. It should be noted that both extremum problems are linear programming problems, because without loss of generality one can assume that $h_0(u) = 1$ and then

$$\Omega_u(h) = h(0) = \sum_{j=0}^n h_j(u) u_j(0).$$

The following two results are obtained, respectively, with the help of (32) and (33) with $a_i = a_i(Y)$ and $a_i' = a_i'(Y)$. One also makes use of $a_0(Y) = 1, a_0'(Y) = \Sigma_{i=0}^n a_i(Y) = |Y|$, $a_i(Y) \geq 0, a_i'(Y) \geq 0$ (by Theorem 3), $a_i(Y) = 0$ if $i \in N_n^1 \backslash D$ when Y is a D-code, and $a_i'(Y) = 0$ if $i \in N_n^1 \backslash D$ when Y is a D-design.

Theorem 4 [37]: If Y is a D-code and $h \in F(N_n)$ has the property $\mathfrak{A}_q(D)$, then

$$|Y| \le A_q(X, D) \le \Omega_q(h). \qquad (35)$$

If Y is a D-design and $h \in F(N_n)$ has the property $\mathfrak{B}_q(D)$, then

$$|Y| \ge B_q(X, D) \ge \Omega_q(h). \qquad (36)$$

In each case, equality $|Y| = \Omega_q(h)$ holds if and only if

$$a_i(Y)h(i) = a_i'(Y)h_i(q) = 0, \qquad i \in N_n^1.$$

Theorem 5 [37]: If Y is a D-code and $h \in F(N_n)$ has the property $\mathfrak{B}_p(D)$, then

$$|Y| \le |X|/B_p(X, D) \le |X|/\Omega_p(h). \qquad (37)$$

If Y is a D-design and $h \in F(N_n)$ has the property $\mathfrak{A}_p(D)$, then

$$|Y| \ge |X|/A_p(X, D) \ge |X|/\Omega_p(h). \qquad (38)$$

In each case, equality $|Y| = |X|/\Omega_p(h)$ holds if and only if

$$a_i(Y)h_i(p) = a_i'(Y)h(i) = 0, \qquad i \in N_n^1.$$

The necessary and sufficient conditions for these bounds to be sharp have many useful consequences, a nice example being the (generalized) *Lloyd condition* for perfect codes [17], [37], [70], [84], [101], [117]. Note that Theorems 4 and 5 imply that the functions h for which $|Y| = \Omega_q(h)$ or $|Y| = |X|/\Omega_p(h)$ holds are *optimal* solutions of the corresponding extremum problems.

Coding theorists are especially interested in applying Theorems 4 and 5 to the class of codes with a *specified minimum distance* d, which are N_n^d-codes in H_q^n and J_n^v. It was shown in [35] that the classical "elementary bounds" such as the *Hamming*, *Plotkin*, and *Singleton* bounds occur as simple cases of these theorems. In the next section we give bounds which are obtained with the help of *optimal solutions of some extremum problems for systems of orthogonal polynomials*. Combinatorial proofs of some of these bounds are unknown. It should be noted that the bounds of Theorems 4 and 5 can be improved by the same linear programming method if one knows an additional information about $a_i(Y)$ and $a_i'(Y), i \in N_n$ (not only their nonnegativity). It was successfully used in the analysis of concrete codes (see [14], [27], and [88]).

In conclusion of this subsection we verify that there exists a duality in bounding the sizes of D-codes and D-designs [78], [80]. For any $h \in F(N_n)$ and u (which is again either p or q), we define an u-dual function $h^{(u)}$ to h as follows:

$$h^{(u)} := |X|^{-(1/2)} \sum_{i=0}^{n} h(i)u_i. \qquad (39)$$

Using Theorem 1 and (15) one can show that $h^{(u)}(i) = |X|^{1/2}h_i(\overline{u})$ and hence $h = (h^{(u)})^{(\overline{u})}, \Omega_{\overline{u}}(h)\Omega_u(h^{(u)}) = |X|$, and h has the property $\mathfrak{A}_{\overline{u}}(D)$ or $\mathfrak{B}_{\overline{u}}(D)$ if and only if $h^{(u)}$ has, respectively, the property $\mathfrak{B}_u(D)$ or $\mathfrak{A}_u(D)$. In particular, this implies the equivalence of the bounds (35) and (37) and also (36) and (38).

Theorem 6 [80]: For any symmetric association scheme X and any $D \subseteq N_n^1$

$$A_q(X, D)B_p(X, D) = B_q(X, D)A_p(X, D) = |X|.$$

C. Outer Distribution and Fundamental Parameters of Codes

The inner distribution of a code Y is concerned with the mutual relations or "distances" between the code points which are values of the function $\partial_R(x, y)$. We shall omit the quotes when, for a symmetric association scheme (X, R), $\partial_R(x, y)$ satisfies the triangle inequality and hence is a distance function. Let $D(Y)$ denote the set of distinct values of the function $\partial_R(x, y)$ when $x, y \in Y, x \ne y$. Note that

$$D(Y) = \{i \in N_n^1 : a_i(Y) \ne 0\}$$

and define

$$D'(Y) := \{i \in N_n^1 : a_i'(Y) \ne 0\}.$$

For simplicity, we shall consider codes Y in an n-class association scheme (X, R), such that $1 < |Y| < |X|$. Then we can state that both $D(Y)$ and $D'(Y)$ are not empty. Define the following fundamental parameters of a code Y [36]:

- *the minimum "distance"* $d(Y) := \min D(Y)$;
- *the (minimum) dual "distance"* $d'(Y) := \min D'(Y)$;
- *the degree* $s(Y) := |D(Y)|$;
- *the dual degree* $s'(Y) := |D'(Y)|$.

Together with $d'(Y)$ we will also consider

- *the (maximum) strength* $\tau(Y) := d'(Y) - 1$.

Moreover, we consider two auxiliary parameters

$$\gamma(Y) = \begin{cases} 1, & \text{if } n \in D(Y) \\ 0, & \text{otherwise,} \end{cases}$$

and

$$\gamma'(Y) = \begin{cases} 1, & \text{if } n \in D'(Y) \\ 0, & \text{otherwise.} \end{cases}$$

For given integers d and τ (with $1 \le d \le n$ and $0 \le \tau \le n-1$), a code Y is called a *d-code* if $d(Y) \ge d$ and a *τ-design* if $\tau(Y) \ge \tau$. These notions are special cases of a D-code and a D-design, respectively, for $D = N_n^d$ and $D = N_n^{\tau+1}$. The examples of τ-designs in the Hamming and Johnson schemes are examined in Section III-A above. The given definitions clearly show the dual character of the notions of d-codes and $(d-1)$-designs. Let $A(X, d)$ denote the maximum size of a d-code in (X, R) and let $B(X, d)$ denote the minimum size of a $(d-1)$-design in (X, R). A d-code Y in (X, R) is called *maximal* if $|Y| = A(X, d)$ and a $(d-1)$-design Y in (X, R) is called *minimal* if $|Y| = B(X, d)$.

Now we introduce a definition that involves the relations ("distances") between the code Y and the whole ambient set X.

Definition 8: The *outer distribution* of a code Y in an n-class association scheme (X, R) is the $|X| \times (n+1)$ matrix M whose (x, i) entry $M_i(x)$ equals

$$a_i(x, Y) := |\{y \in Y : (x, y) \in R_i\}|.$$

Some fundamental properties of a code Y are defined in terms of the rows $M(x) = (a_0(x, Y), \cdots, a_n(x, Y))$ of its outer distribution M. A code Y is called *distance-invariant* if $M(x) = M(y)$ for any $x, y \in Y$ and *completely distance-regular* if $M(x) = M(y)$ for any $x, y \in X$ such that $\partial_R(x, Y) = \partial_R(y, Y)$ where

$$\partial_R(x, Y) = \min \{\partial_R(x, z): z \in Y\}.$$

When Y is a *linear code over* $\mathbb{F}_q$ (in the Hamming scheme), the rows $M(x)$ of the outer distribution M are the weight distributions of the coset codes $Y + x$.

It is easily seen that $M^T M$ can be expressed linearly in terms of the inner distribution of Y. Let us give the "Q-transform version" of this expression. Consider the Q-transform of each row $M(x)$ of the outer distribution M. This produces the matrix MQ, with $Q := (q_k(i))_{i,k \in N_n}$.

Theorem 7 [37]: The Q-transform MQ of the outer distribution is related to the Q-transform $(a'_k(Y))_{k=0}^n$ of the inner distribution by

$$Q^* M^T M Q = |X||Y| \operatorname{diag}(a'_0(Y), a'_1(Y), \cdots, a'_n(Y)).$$

As an immediate consequence, the *rank of M is equal to* $s'(Y) + 1$. Furthermore, we obtain

$$\sum_{x \in X} |a'_k(x, Y)|^2 = |X||Y| a'_k(Y)$$

whence $a'_k(x, Y) = 0$ for any $k \in N_n^1 \backslash D'(Y)$. This can also be deduced from (34) as follows: If $k \in N_n^1 \backslash D'(Y)$, then

$$a'_k(x, Y) = \sum_{i=0}^n a_i(x, Y) q_k(i) = \sum_{y \in Y} q_k(\partial_R(x, y))$$
$$= \sum_{j=1}^{m_k} v_{k,j}(x) \sum_{y \in Y} v_{k,j}(y) = 0. \quad (40)$$

Some interesting problems in classical coding theory are concerned with the *covering radius* $\rho(Y)$ of a code Y (in the Hamming scheme) (see [6], [31], [34], and [64]). By definition,

$$\rho(Y) := \max \{\partial_H(x, Y): x \in X\}$$

where

$$\partial_H(x, Y) := \min \{\partial_H(x, y): y \in Y\}.$$

(Thus for a linear code, $\rho(Y)$ is the maximum weight of coset leaders.) This definition is extended to any association scheme (X, R) if one replaces $\partial_H(x, u)$ by $\partial_R(x, u)$. The covering radius $\rho(Y)$ can be found from the outer distribution M of Y, since $\partial_R(x, Y)$ is the smallest $i \in N_n$ such that $a_i(x, Y) \neq 0$. Notice that $\rho(Y)$ generally cannot be determined from the inner (distance) distribution of Y; however, some upper bounds on $\rho(Y)$ can be obtained from these data [37], [51], [118], [127]. (See also Sections IV-C and IV-D below.)

IV. POLYNOMIAL SCHEMES

A. Orthogonal Polynomials

In the examples of the Hamming and Johnson schemes (and in several other interesting cases), the p-numbers $p_i(k)$ and the q-numbers $q_k(i)$ are representable by polynomials of degree i and k, respectively, in an "appropriate variable" (see Section II-B). This leads us to investigate the class of association schemes that enjoy either of these "polynomial properties" (or both of them).

Definition 9:

i) A symmetric n-class association scheme is P-*polynomial*, with respect to a function $\sigma_P \in F(N_n)$, if there exist real polynomials $P_i(t)$ of degree $i, i = 0, 1, \cdots, n$, such that $p_i(k) = P_i(\sigma_P(k))$ for any $k \in N_n$.

ii) A symmetric n-class association scheme is Q-*polynomial*, with respect to a function $\sigma_Q \in F(N_n)$, if there exist real polynomials $Q_k(t)$ of degree $k, k = 0, 1, \cdots, n$, such that $q_k(i) = Q_k(\sigma_Q(i))$ for any $i \in N_n$.

It can be proved that these functions σ_P and σ_Q must be linear functions of the first p- and q-functions p_1 and q_1 (respectively), which take different values $p_1(j)$ and $q_1(j)$ for different $j \in N_n$ such that $|p_1(j)| \leq p_1(0) = v_1$ and $|q_1(j)| \leq q_1(0) = m_1$. We will use the following functions σ_P and σ_Q:

$$\sigma_P(d) = 1 - 2 \frac{p_1(d) - v_1}{p_1(n) - v_1}$$
$$\sigma_Q(d) = 1 - 2 \frac{q_1(d) - m_1}{q_1(n) - m_1}. \quad (41)$$

Then $\sigma_P(0) = 1, \sigma_P(n) = -1$ and $\sigma_Q(0) = 1, \sigma_Q(n) = -1$. When the function p_1 or q_1 is decreasing on N_n we will extend it to a continuous decreasing function on $[0, n]$ (usually the latter is defined by the same formula). In this case, the corresponding function given by (41) is a decreasing continuous mapping from $[0, n]$ onto $[-1, 1]$ and it is called *standard*.

It follows directly from Theorem 1 and (15) that $P = \{P_i(t): i \in N_n\}$ and $Q = \{Q_k(t): k \in N_n\}$ are *systems of orthogonal polynomials* with the following orthogonality conditions:

$$\sum_{k=0}^n P_i(\sigma_P(k)) P_j(\sigma_P(k)) m_k = v_i |X| \delta_{i,j} \quad (42)$$

$$\sum_{i=0}^n Q_k(\sigma_Q(i)) Q_l(\sigma_Q(i)) v_i = m_k |X| \delta_{k,l} \quad (43)$$

and the properties:

$$m_k P_i(\sigma_P(k)) = v_i Q_k(\sigma_Q(i)), \qquad i, k \in N_n. \quad (44)$$

These orthogonal systems P and Q are uniquely determined by *three-term recurrence relations* [49] of the form

$$p_{i,1}^{i+1} P_{i+1}(t) = (P_1(t) - p_{i,1}^i) P_i(t) - p_{i,1}^{i-1} P_{i-1}(t)$$
$$q_{k,1}^{k+1} Q_{k+1}(t) = (Q_1(t) - q_{k,1}^k) Q_k(t) - q_{k,1}^{k-1} Q_{k-1}(t)$$

where

$$P_0(t) = 1 \qquad 2P_1(t) = v_1 + p_1(n) + t(v_1 - p_1(n))$$
$$Q_0(t) = 1 \qquad 2Q_1(t) = m_1 + q_1(n) + t(m_1 - q_1(n)).$$

Definition 9 depends on the ordering of the relations R_i and of the idempotents E_k, respectively. For this reason, a given association scheme may possess more than one P-polynomial structure and more than one Q-polynomial structure (see [10]).

The algebraic notion of a P-polynomial scheme is equivalent [37] to the combinatorial notion of a distance-regular graph, defined as follows. Let (X, R_1) be a simple connected finite graph of diameter n. For $i \in N_n$, define R_i as the set of pairs $(x, y) \in X^2$ such that x and y are at distance i apart in (X, R_1), and let $R := \{R_0, R_1, \cdots, R_n\}$. If (X, R) is an association scheme, then (X, R_1) is said to be *distance-regular* [26]. Thus if (X, R) is a P-polynomial scheme, then ∂_R (see (1)) is a distance function. Note that a symmetric association scheme (X, R) with a distance function ∂_R need not be P-polynomial. (An example is provided by the "ordered Hamming scheme" [89].) On the other hand, the algebraic notion of a Q-polynomial scheme has no simple combinatorial interpretation, except in some important special cases where (X, R) can be embedded in a certain "lattice-type structure" [38], [39], [94]. Nevertheless, there exist some useful general characterizations of Q-polynomial schemes [54], [126]. There is an elementary criterion for the P-polynomial property in terms of the intersection numbers, namely, $p_{i,1}^{i+1} \neq 0$ and $p_{i,1}^k = 0$ for $k > i + 1$. This characterizes the "distance structure" in a clear manner. Similarly, a criterion for the Q-polynomial property is $q_{k,1}^{k+1} \neq 0$ and $q_{k,1}^t = 0$ for $t > k + 1$.

Example 1 (continued): For the Hamming scheme H_q^n, (17) holds and

$$p_1(d) = q_1(d) = n(q - 1) - dq.$$

Hence, H_q^n is P- and Q-polynomial with respect to the standard function $\sigma(d) = 1 - 2d/n$, systems P and Q coincide and consist of the polynomials

$$P_i(t) = K_i^n((1 - t)n/2), \qquad i = 0, 1, \cdots, n.$$

Example 2 (continued): For the Johnson scheme J_n^v, (17) holds and

$$p_1(d) = v_1 - d(v + 1 - d), q_1(d) = m_1(1 - (dv/n(v - n))).$$

Hence, J_n^v is P-polynomial with respect to the standard function

$$\sigma_P(d) = 1 - 2(d(v + 1 - d)/n(v + 1 - n))$$

and Q-polynomial with respect to the standard function $\sigma_Q(d) = 1 - 2d/n$. Systems P and Q are defined by means of $P_i(\sigma_P(z)) = \tilde{H}_i(z)$ and

$$Q_i(\sigma_Q(z)) = H_i(z), \qquad i = 0, 1, \cdots, n.$$

The number of independent parameters of an n-class P-polynomial or Q-polynomial scheme is equal to $2n - 1$. In contrast with this observation, Leonard has proved that all parameters of a P- *and* Q-polynomial scheme can be

determined from only *five* independent numbers [72]. The same author [71] has shown that the polynomials $P_i(t)$ and $Q_k(t)$ relative to P- and Q-polynomial schemes belong to a well-defined five-parameter class of orthogonal polynomials of the generalized hypergeometric type [114], known as the *Askey–Wilson polynomials* [2]. His result produces closed-form expressions for the p-numbers and the q-numbers. Furthermore, it characterizes the Askey–Wilson polynomials as those orthogonal polynomials having "duals."

For a code Y in a Q-polynomial scheme, a polynomial f is called an *annihilator* for Y if $f(\sigma_Q(i)) = 0$ for all $i \in D(Y)$. An annihilator f of minimal degree (i.e., degree $s(Y)$) is called *minimal* and denoted by $f^{Y,Q}$ if $f(\sigma_Q(0)) = f(1) = 1$. For a code Y in a P-polynomial scheme, a polynomial f is called a *dual annihilator* for Y if $f(\sigma_P(i)) = 0$ for all $i \in D'(Y)$. A dual annihilator f of minimal degree (i.e., degree $s'(Y)$) is called *dual minimal* and denoted by $f^{Y,P}$ if $f(\sigma_P(0)) = f(1) = 1$. In particular, if for $d \in N_n$ and $U = P$ or $U = Q$

$$g^{d,U}(t) = \prod_{j=d}^n \frac{t - \sigma_U(j)}{1 - \sigma_U(j)} \qquad (45)$$

then $f^{X,Q} = g^{0,Q}$ and $f^{X,P} = g^{0,P}$. For any nonempty $D \subseteq N_n$ and any $i \in D$ denote by $g^{D,i,U}$ the polynomial of degree $|D| - 1$ uniquely defined by the conditions: $g^{D,i,U}(\sigma_U(j)) = \delta_{i,j}$ for any $j \in D$. Any function h on D can be represented by the *interpolation* polynomial $\Sigma_{i=0}^n h(i) g^{D,i,U}$ of degree $|D| - 1$. In particular, for any $h \in F(N_n)$ we have

$$h(j) = \sum_{i=0}^n h(i) g^{N_n,i,U}(\sigma_U(j)).$$

In the case of a U-polynomial association scheme (X, R) (where U is either P or Q), we can rephrase the linear programming bounds of Theorems 4 and 5 in terms of extremum problems for the system U of orthogonal polynomials. Denote by $F_n[t]$ the set of real polynomials of degree at most n in t. For any $f \in F_n[t]$, let $f_j(U), j \in N_n$, be the coefficients of the (unique) expansion of f over the system U, i.e., $f = \Sigma_{j=0}^n f_j(U) U_j$. Put $\Omega_U(f) = f(1)/f_0(U)$ if $f_0(U) \neq 0$. Note that $f \mapsto h := f(\sigma_U)$ gives a one-to-one mapping of $F_n[t]$ onto $F(N_n)$ with $h(j) = f(\sigma_U(j))$ and $h_j(u) = f_j(U)$ for any $j \in N_n$ (see (14) and Definition 9). We restrict our attention to the case of d-codes and $(d-1)$-designs (i.e., codes with dual "distance" d or more), which corresponds to the case of D-codes and D-designs for $D = N_n^d$. We say that $f \in F_n[t]$ has the *property* $\mathfrak{A}_U(d)$ ($\mathfrak{B}_U(d)$) if $h = f(\sigma_U) \in F(N_n)$ has the property $\mathfrak{A}_u(N_n^d)$ (respectively, $\mathfrak{B}_u(N_n^d)$). Let $A_U(X, d) = \min \Omega_U(f)$ where the minimum is taken over all polynomials $f \in F_n[t]$ with the property $\mathfrak{A}_U(d)$. Similarly, let $B_U(X, d) = \max \Omega_U(f)$ where the maximum is taken over all polynomials $f \in F_n[t]$ with the property $\mathfrak{B}_U(d)$. Since $\Omega_U(f) = \Omega_u(h)$ for $h = f(\sigma_U)$, we have

$$A_U(X, d) = A_u(X, N_n^d) \qquad B_U(X, d) = B_u(X, N_n^d) \quad (46)$$

and we can use Theorems 4–6 to estimate the size of d-codes and $(d-1)$-designs with the help of the above extremum problems for the system U.

Without going into any detail, let us finally point out that the classical examples of P- and Q-polynomial schemes are induced by some classical *permutation groups* (see Section II-D). Extensive research work has been devoted, in this context, to the subject of "orthogonal polynomials and permutation groups" [48], [119].

B. Adjacent Systems of Orthogonal Polynomials and Two Extremum Problems

Some important estimates on fundamental parameters of codes are expressed in terms of values connected with systems of orthogonal polynomials which are *adjacent* to the systems P and Q. Consider two functions σ and w on N_n. We assume that the first function (*change of variable*) σ takes the values $\sigma(n) = -1, \sigma(0) = 1$, and maps N_n into the interval $[-1, 1]$, and the second (*weight*) function w has the properties $w(i) > 0$ and $\Sigma_{i=0}^{n} w(i) = 1$. We call the change of variable σ *standard* if it can be represented as a continuous decreasing function on the whole interval $[0, n]$. It is known [49], [121] that the orthogonality conditions

$$\sum_{d=0}^{n} U_i(\sigma(d)) U_j(\sigma(d)) w(d) = U_i(1) \delta_{i,j} \qquad (47)$$

uniquely define a system $U = \{U_i(t) : i \in N_n\}$ of polynomials $U_i(t)$ of degree i with some positive values $U_i(1)$. We denote by σ_U and w_U the functions σ and w for the system U. In particular, for the systems P and Q we have (see (42) and (43)) $w_P(i) = |X|^{-1} m_i, P_i(1) = v_i, w_Q(i) = |X|^{-1} v_i, Q_i(1) = m_i$. We assume that U satisfies the *Krein condition*: for any $i, j, k \in N_n$ there exist nonnegative real numbers $u_{i,j}^k$ such that

$$U_i(t) U_j(t) = \sum_{k=0}^{n} u_{i,j}^k U_k(t) \pmod{g^{0,U}(t)}.$$

By (23) and (24) this is fulfilled for the systems P and Q. For the system U and any $k \in N_n$ we define the *kernel* function

$$T_k(t_1, t_2; U) = \sum_{i=0}^{k} U_i(t_1) U_i(t_2) / U_i(1).$$

For any $a, b \in \{0, 1\}$ we consider a weight function $w_U^{a,b}$ on N_n such that

$$w_U^{a,b}(i) = c^{a,b} (1 - \sigma_U(i))^a (1 + \sigma_U(i))^b w_U(i) \qquad (48)$$

where the constant $c^{a,b}$ is chosen so that

$$\sum_{i=0}^{n} w_U^{a,b}(i) = 1.$$

The initial change of variable σ_U and the new weight function $w_U^{a,b}$ uniquely define a system $U^{a,b} = \{U_i^{a,b}(t) : i \in N_{n-a-b}\}$ of polynomials $U_i^{a,b}(t)$ of degree i by means of the following conditions:

$$\sum_{d=0}^{n-a-b} U_i^{a,b}(\sigma_U(d)) U_j^{a,b}(\sigma_U(d)) w_U^{a,b}(d) = U_i^{a,b}(1) \delta_{i,j}. \qquad (49)$$

(The system $U^{a,b}$ consists of $n + 1 - a - b$ polynomials since $a + b$ weights become zero.) We put

$$T_k^{a,b}(t_1, t_2; U) := T_k(t_1, t_2; U^{a,b}).$$

Let $t_k^{a,b}(U)$ be the largest zero of the polynomial $U_k^{a,b}$. If σ_U is standard we can uniquely define the numbers $d_k^{a,b}(U)$ by $\sigma_U(d_k^{a,b}(U)) = t_k^{a,b}(U)$. We will omit the indices a, b in the notations $U_k^{a,b}, t_k^{a,b}(U), d_k^{a,b}(U)$ when $a = b = 0$.

Example 1 (continued): Let $K_k^n(z)$ be the Krawtchouk polynomial of degree k defined by (16) and let $d_k(n)$ be its smallest zero. For the Hamming scheme H_q^n

$$P_k^{a,b}(1 - 2z/n) = C_k^{a,b} K_k^{n-a-b}(z - a)$$

where

$$C_k^{1,b} = \sum_{i=0}^{k} \binom{n-b}{i} (q-1)^{i-k} \Bigg/ \binom{n-1-b}{k}$$

and $C_k^{0,b} = 1$, and hence

$$d_k^{a,b}(Q) = d_k^{a,b}(P) = d_k(n - a - b) + a. \qquad (50)$$

In particular,

$$Q_k^{0,1}(1) = \binom{n-1}{k} (q-1)^k.$$

Example 2 (continued): Let $H_k^{v,n}(z)$ and $\tilde{H}_k^{v,n}(z)$ be the polynomials of degree k defined, respectively, by (18) and (19), and let $d_k(v, n)$ and $\tilde{d}_k(v, n)$ be their smallest zeros. For the Johnson scheme J_n^v

$$Q_k^{0,1}(\sigma_Q(z)) = H_k^{v-1,n-1}(z)$$

and $P_k^{1,0}(\sigma_P(z))$ is proportional to $\tilde{H}_k^{v-2,n-1}(z - 1)$. Hence

$$d_k^{0,1}(Q) = d_k(v - 1, n - 1)$$
$$d_k^{1,0}(P) = \tilde{d}_k(v - 2, n - 1) + 1$$

and

$$Q_k^{0,1}(1) = \binom{v-1}{k} - \binom{v-1}{k-1}.$$

Now we consider two extremum problems for the system U of orthogonal polynomials under consideration. For any $d \in N_n^2$, the $K_U(d)$-*problem* consists in finding

$$K_U(d) := \max \Omega_U(f)$$

where the maximum is taken over all polynomials $f \in F_{d-1}[t]$ such that $f_0(U) > 0$ and $f(t) \geq 0$ for $-1 \leq t \leq 1$. A polynomial f having these properties for which $\Omega_U(f) = f(1)/f_0(U) = K_U(d)$ is called an *optimal solution* of the $K_U(d)$-problem. These properties are in general stronger than $\mathfrak{B}_U(d)$ since they include nonnegativity of f on the whole interval $[-1, 1]$ (not only at points $\sigma_U(i), i \in N_n$) and a restriction on its degree. This implies that for any U-polynomial (U is either P or Q) association scheme X

$$B_U(X, d) \geq K_U(d). \qquad (51)$$

From now on we assume that l and θ denote arbitrary numbers such that $l \in N_n^1$ and $\theta \in \{0, 1\}$.

Theorem 8 [103]: For any $d = 2l + 1 - \theta \in N_n^2$ the polynomial

$$g^{(d)}(t) = (t+1)^\theta (U_{l-\theta}^{1,\theta}(t))^2$$

of degree $d - 1$ is the unique (up to a constant factor) optimal solution of the $K_U(d)$-problem and

$$K_U(d) = \left(1 - \frac{U_1(1)}{U_1(-1)}\right)^\theta \sum_{i=0}^{l-\theta} U_i^{0,\theta}(1).$$

One can show that $K_U(d)$ is a positive-valued increasing function in $d \in N_n$ and admits another expression

$$K_U(2l + 1 - \theta) = \left(1 - \frac{U_l(1)U_{l-1}^{1,0}(-1)}{U_l(-1)U_{l-1}^{1,0}(1)}\right)^\theta \sum_{i=0}^{l-\theta} U_i(1).$$

For odd d and $U = Q$ the polynomials

$$g^{(2l+1)}(t) = \left(\sum_{i=0}^{l} U_i(t)\right)^2$$

were first used in 1973 in [37] to obtain a lower bound on the size of $(d-1)$-designs (see Theorem 19 below). In the general case Theorem 8 was applied to this end in [47].

Example 1 (continued): For the Hamming scheme H_q^n and $d = 2l + 1 - \theta$

$$K_P(d) = K_Q(d) = q^\theta \sum_{i=0}^{l-\theta} \binom{n-\theta}{i}(q-1)^i. \quad (52)$$

Example 2 (continued): For the Johnson scheme J_n^v and $d = 2l + 1 - \theta$

$$K_P(d) = \sum_{i=0}^{l-\theta} \binom{n-\theta}{i}\binom{v-n+\theta}{i+\theta} \quad (53)$$

$$K_Q(d) = \left(\frac{v}{n}\right)^\theta \binom{v-\theta}{l-\theta}. \quad (54)$$

Now we formulate the second extremum problem for the system U with a standard function σ_U. It is known [103] that the largest zeros $t_k^{a,b} = t_k^{a,b}(U)$ of the polynomials $U_k^{a,b}$ satisfy the following inequalities:

$$t_{k-1}^{1,1} < t_k^{1,0} < t_k^{1,1}, \qquad k = 1, \cdots, n-1$$

where it is assumed that $t_0^{1,1} = -1 = \sigma_U(n)$ and $t_{n-1}^{1,1} = \sigma_U(1)$. This means that the half-open interval $[-1, \sigma_U(1))$ is partitioned into the half-open intervals $[t_{k-1}^{1,1}, t_k^{1,0})$ and $[t_k^{1,0}, t_k^{1,1})$, $k = 1, \cdots, n-1$. Enumerate in succession all these half-open intervals from the left to the right by positive integers. For any real number $\sigma, -1 \leq \sigma < \sigma_U(1)$, denote by $h(\sigma)$ *the number* of the (unique) half-open interval containing σ. Let $k(\sigma) = k$ when $\sigma \in [t_{k-1}^{1,1}, t_k^{1,0})$ or $\sigma \in [t_k^{1,0}, t_k^{1,1})$, and let $\varepsilon(\sigma) = 0$ if $\sigma \in [t_{k(\sigma)-1}^{1,1}, t_{k(\sigma)}^{1,0})$ and $\varepsilon(\sigma) = 1$ if $\sigma \in [t_{k(\sigma)}^{1,0}, t_{k(\sigma)}^{1,1})$. Then it is clear that $h(\sigma) = 2k(\sigma) - 1 + \varepsilon(\sigma)$. For any number $\sigma, -1 \leq \sigma < \sigma_U(1)$, the $L_U(\sigma)$-*problem* consists in finding

$$L_U(\sigma) := \min \Omega_U(f)$$

where the minimum is taken over all polynomials $f \in F_{h(\sigma)}[t]$ such that $f_0(U) > 0$ and $f(t) \leq 0$ for $-1 \leq t \leq \sigma$. A polynomial f having these properties for which $\Omega_U(f) = f(1)/f_0(U) = L_U(\sigma)$ is called an *optimal solution* of the $L_U(\sigma)$-problem. Note that for $\sigma = \sigma_U(d)$ these properties as compared to $\mathfrak{A}_U(d)$ say nothing about nonnegativity of $f_i(U)$ for $i \in N_n^1$, include a stronger condition than $f(\sigma_U(i)) \leq 0$ for $i \in N_n^d$, and introduce a restriction to the degree of the polynomials. Note that this restriction means that, in the $L_U(\sigma)$-problem, polynomials whose degree does not exceed the number of the half-open interval containing σ are considered. This also holds in the case of the $K_U(d)$-problem since $(1, n]$ is partitioned into the half-open intervals $(i, i+1]$, $i \in N_{n-1}^1$, and $d - 1$ is the number of the half-open interval containing $d \in N_n^2$.

Theorem 9 [77], [81]: For any real number $\sigma, -1 \leq \sigma < \sigma_U(1)$, let $\varepsilon = \varepsilon(\sigma)$ and $k = k(\sigma)$. Then the polynomial

$$f^{(\sigma)}(t) = (t - \sigma)(t+1)^\varepsilon (T_{k-1}^{1,\varepsilon}(t, \sigma; U))^2 \quad (55)$$

of degree $h(\sigma) = 2k - 1 + \varepsilon$ is an optimal solution of the $L_U(\sigma)$-problem. The function $L_U(\sigma)$ is equal to

$$\left(1 - \frac{U_1(1)}{U_1(-1)}\right)^\varepsilon \left(1 - \frac{U_k^{0,\varepsilon}(1)U_{k-1}^{1,\varepsilon}(\sigma)}{U_k^{0,\varepsilon}(\sigma)U_{k-1}^{1,\varepsilon}(1)}\right) \sum_{i=0}^{k-1} U_i^{0,\varepsilon}(1),$$

positive-valued and continuous, grows with σ, and takes the following values at the left ends of these half-open intervals:

$$L_U(t_{l-\theta}^{1,\theta}) = K_U(2l + 1 - \theta). \quad (56)$$

We give some additional facts on the polynomials $f^{(\sigma)}(t)$. For $\sigma \neq t_{l-\theta}^{1,\theta}$ the polynomial $f^{(\sigma)}(t)$ is the unique (up to a constant factor) optimal solution of the $L_U(\sigma)$-problem. For $\sigma = t_l^{1,0}$ we have $k(\sigma) = l, \varepsilon(\sigma) = 1$, and the polynomial $f^{(\sigma)}(t)$ has factor $t + 1$. For $\sigma = t_{l-1}^{1,1}$ we have $k(\sigma) = l, \varepsilon(\sigma) = 0$, and $f^{(\sigma)}(t)$ is also divisible by $t + 1$. In both cases the polynomial $f(t) = f^{(\sigma)}(t)/(t+1)$ is an optimal polynomial for the $L_U(\sigma)$-problem as well. Moreover, for $\sigma = t_{l-\theta}^{1,\theta}$ the polynomial $(t - \sigma)f^{(\sigma)}(t)/(t+1)$ is proportional to the optimal solution $g^{(2l+1-\theta)}(t)$ of the $K_U(2l + 1 - \theta)$-problem. These facts and Theorems 8 and 9 follow from the following main theorem which (as we shall see below) also determines the inner distribution of optimal codes and designs.

Theorem 10 [77], [81]: For any $\sigma, -1 \leq \sigma < \sigma(1)$, the polynomial

$$(t - \sigma)(t+1)^\varepsilon T_{k-1}^{1,\varepsilon}(t, \sigma; U) \quad (57)$$

with $k = k(\sigma)$ and $\varepsilon = \varepsilon(\sigma)$ has $k + \varepsilon$ simple zeros

$$\alpha_0, \alpha_1, \cdots, \alpha_{k+\varepsilon-1} \quad (\alpha_0 < \alpha_1 < \cdots < \alpha_{k+\varepsilon-1})$$

where $\alpha_{k+\varepsilon-1} = \sigma$ and $\alpha_0 \geq -1$ with equality holding if and only if $\varepsilon = 1$ or $\varepsilon = 0$ and $\sigma = t_{k-1}^{1,1}$. Moreover, for any polynomial $f(t)$ of degree at most $h(\sigma) = 2k - 1 + \varepsilon$ the following equality holds:

$$f_0(U) = (L_U(\sigma))^{-1}f(1) + \sum_{j=0}^{k+\varepsilon-1} \rho_j^{(\sigma)}(U)f(\alpha_j) \quad (58)$$

where for $i = 0, \cdots, k - 1$

$$\rho_{i+\varepsilon}^{(\sigma)}(U) = \frac{1}{c^{1,\varepsilon}(1 + \alpha_{i+\varepsilon})^\varepsilon(1 - \alpha_{i+\varepsilon})T_{k-1}^{1,\varepsilon}(\alpha_{i+\varepsilon}, \alpha_{i+\varepsilon}; U)}$$

are positive, and in the case $\varepsilon = 1$

$$\rho_0^{(\sigma)}(U) = \frac{T_k(\sigma, 1)}{T_k(-1, -1)T_k(\sigma, 1) - T_k(-1, 1)T_k(\sigma, -1)} \geq 0$$

with equality holding if and only if $\sigma = t_k^{1,0}$ (here U is omitted in the notation $T_k(t_1, t_2; U)$).

Example 1 (continued): In the case of the Hamming scheme H_q^n for any $d \in N_n^2$ there exist $k \in N_{n-1}^1$ and $\varepsilon \in \{0, 1\}$ such that

$$d_k(n - 1 - \varepsilon) < d - 1 \leq d_{k-1+\varepsilon}(n - 2 + \varepsilon).$$

Then $L_Q(\sigma) = L_P(\sigma)$ for $\sigma = \sigma(d) = 1 - 2d/n$ can be expressed by the following formula:

$$q^\varepsilon \left(\sum_{i=0}^{k-1} \binom{n'}{i}(q-1)^i - \binom{n'}{k}(q-1)^k \frac{K_{k-1}^{n'-1}(d-1)}{K_k^{n'}(d)} \right)$$

where $n' = n - \varepsilon$. In particular, when the number d belongs to the half-open intervals

$$\left(\frac{(q-1)n + 1}{q}, n \right]$$
$$\left(\frac{(q-1)(n-1) + 1}{q}, \frac{(q-1)n + 1}{q} \right]$$
$$\left(d_2(n-1) + 1, \frac{(q-1)(n-1) + 1}{q} \right]$$

this, respectively, gives the values

$$\frac{qd}{qd - (q-1)n}$$
$$\frac{q^2 d}{qd - (q-1)(n-1)}$$
$$\frac{qd((n(q-1) + 1)(n(q-1) - qd + 2) - q)}{qd(2n(q-1) - q + 2 - qd) - n(n-1)(q-1)^2}$$

which are obtained with the help of the optimal polynomials $f^{(\sigma)}(t)$ of the first, second, and third degree.

Example 2 (continued): In the case of the Johnson scheme J_n^v, when d belongs to the half-open intervals

$$\left(\frac{n(v-n)}{v-1}, n \right]$$
$$\left(\frac{(n-1)(v-n)}{v-2}, \frac{n(v-n)}{v-1} \right]$$
$$\left(d_2^{1,0}(Q) + 1, \frac{(n-1)(v-n)}{v-2} \right]$$

the function $L_Q(\sigma)$ for $\sigma = \sigma_Q(d) = 1 - 2d/n$, respectively, equals the expression given at the bottom of this page. This is obtained with the help of the optimal polynomial $f^{(\sigma)}(t)$ for the $L_Q(\sigma)$-problem of the first, second, and third degree (see [76]).

In order to prove that for $\sigma = \sigma_U(d)$ the optimal polynomial $f^{(\sigma)}(t)$ for the $L_U(\sigma)$-problem has the property $\mathfrak{A}_U(d)$ and hence the inequality $A_U(X, d) \leq L_U(\sigma_U(d))$ holds, one must check that all coefficients $f_i^{(\sigma)}(U)$ of its expansion over system U are nonnegative. Note that in the case $U = Q$ by Theorem 2 the latter means that the symmetric matrix $f^{(\sigma)}(\sigma_Q(\partial_R(x, y)))$ for Q-polynomial association scheme (X, R) is nonnegative definite. Now it is known [77], [81] that all coefficients $f_i^{(\sigma)}(U), i \in N_{h(\sigma)}$, are positive when $\varepsilon(\sigma) = 0$ (or $f^{(\sigma)}$ has odd degree $2k(\sigma) - 1$), in particular, for $\sigma = t_{l-1}^{1,1}$, and also when $\sigma = t_l^{1,0}, l \in N_n^1$. Moreover, the same is true for all σ if the system U satisfies the *strengthened Krein condition*: for any $i, j \in N_{n-2}$ the coefficients of the expansion of $(1 + t)U_i^{1,1}(t)U_j^{1,1}(t) \pmod{g^{0,U}(t)}$ over the system U are positive. It is known that the system Q satisfies the strengthened Krein condition for *decomposable Q-polynomial schemes* [77]. The class of decomposable schemes contains some known infinite families of P- and Q-polynomial association schemes, in particular, H_q^n and J_n^v. It seems to be true that all coefficients $f_i^{(\sigma)}(U), i \in N_{h(\sigma)}$, are also positive when σ belongs to the open interval $(t_{k(\sigma)}^{1,0}, t_{k(\sigma)}^{1,1})$. Unfortunately, this question is still open for $k(\sigma) \geq 2$. Thus for any system U under consideration

$$A_U(X, d) \leq L_U(t_{l-\theta}^{1,\theta}) = K_U(2l + 1 - \theta) \tag{59}$$

if $d \geq d_{l-\theta}^{1,\theta}(U)$ (see (56)), and for any d

$$A_U(X, d) \leq L_U(\sigma_U(d)) \tag{60}$$

if U satisfies the strengthened Krein condition.

The known earlier bounds for a d-code Y can be described in terms of polynomials $f(t)$ which have the $\mathfrak{A}_Q(d)$-property $(f_0(Q) > 0, f_i(Q) \geq 0$ for $i = 1, \cdots, n, f(1) > 0, f(t) \leq 0$

$$\frac{vd}{vd - n(v-n)}$$
$$\frac{v(v-1)d}{n(d(v-1) - (n-1)(v-n))}$$
$$\frac{v(v-1)\, d(n(v-n) - 1 - d(v-2))}{d(v-1)(2n(v-n) - v - d(v-2)) - n(n-1)(v-n)(v-n-1)}.$$

for $-1 \leq t \leq \sigma = \sigma_Q(d)$) and hence imply $|Y| \leq \Omega(f)$. In particular, the bounds due to Blichfeldt [19], Rankin [97], Plotkin and Johnson (see [88]) are in fact based on the polynomial $f(t) = t - \sigma$ with $\sigma = \sigma_Q(d) \leq t_1(Q)$ which provides $f_0(Q) > 0, f_1(Q) \geq 0$. The Sidelnikov results [110], [111] are obtained with the help of polynomials $f(t) = t^{2l} - \sigma^{2l}$ for a suitable choice of an integer l. In [90] (and later in [65] for the Euclidean sphere) the polynomials

$$f(t) = (t - \sigma)(T_{k-1}(t, \sigma; Q))^2 \qquad (61)$$

were used, where the integer k is defined by $t_{k-1} < \sigma = \sigma_Q(d) < t_k$. The polynomials (55) were found with the help of the Lagrange method and presented in [73]. Some extremum properties of these polynomials were found in [112] and they were essentially used to prove the optimality of (55) for the $L_U(\sigma)$-problem (see Theorems 10 and 9).

The solutions of the $K_U(d)$- and $L_U(\sigma)$-problems can also be applied to codes and designs in the Cartesian product X^m of m copies of a P-polynomial association scheme (X, R) with the distance $\max_{1 \leq i \leq m} \partial_R(x_i, y_i)$ or $\Sigma_{i=1}^m \partial_R(x_i, y_i)$ on X^m. In particular, for the case of the distance $\max_{1 \leq i \leq m} \partial_R(x_i, y_i)$ on X^m, this allows one to estimate the Shannon capacity [106] $\lim_{m \to \infty} (A(X^m, 2))^{1/m}$ of a graph (X, R_1) (see [85], [91], [104], and also [79]).

In the remainder of this section, considering a code Y in an n-class P- and/or Q-polynomial scheme we shall assume for simplicity that $n \geq 2, d(Y) \geq 2, d'(Y) \geq 2$.

C. Codes and Designs in P-Polynomial Schemes

Throughout this subsection, we consider an n-class P-polynomial scheme (X, R). In this case $\partial_R(x, y)$ (see (1)) is a distance function and (X, R) can be considered as a metric space X with the metric $\partial(x, y) = \partial_R(x, y)$. It follows that for any code $Y \subseteq X$, the metric spheres (balls)

$$S_r(y) := \{x \in X : 0 \leq \partial(x, y) \leq r\}$$

of radius r centered at the code points $y \in Y$ do not intersect when r is equal to the packing radius $e(Y) = \lfloor (d(Y) - 1)/2 \rfloor$ and cover X when r is equal to the covering radius $\rho(Y)$. This gives the following sphere-packing and sphere-covering bounds for any code Y in (X, R):

$$|Y| \sum_{i=0}^{e(Y)} v_i \leq |X| \leq |Y| \sum_{i=0}^{\rho(Y)} v_i. \qquad (62)$$

Thus we have $e(Y) \leq \rho(Y)$. A code Y for which $e(Y) = \rho(Y)$ is called perfect. A code Y is perfect if and only if $d(Y) = 2\rho(Y) + 1$ or, equivalently, the spheres $S_{\rho(Y)}(y), y \in Y$, form a partition of X.

From the existence of polynomials which are dual annihilators for codes we can derive some inequalities between their fundamental parameters.

Theorem 11: For any code Y in an n-class P-polynomial scheme X
1) $d(Y) + d'(Y) \leq n + 2$.
2) $d(Y) \leq 2s'(Y) - \gamma'(Y) + 1$; equality implies $|Y|\Omega_P(f) = |X|$ where $f(t) = (1+t)^{-\gamma'(Y)}(f^{Y,P}(t))^2$.

3) If $d(Y) \geq s'(Y)$, then Y is distance-invariant and

$$a_i'(x, Y) = |X|g_0^{D'(Y),i,P}(P) - |Y|g^{D'(Y),i,P}(1)$$

for any $x \in Y$ and $i \in D'(Y)$.
4) If σ_P is standard and $d(Y) \geq 2l - \theta + 1$, then

$$d'(Y) \leq d_{l-\theta}^{1,\theta}(P)$$

with equality if and only if $l = s'(Y), \theta = \gamma'(Y)$, and $(1 + t)^\theta P_{l-\theta}^{1,\theta}(t)$ is dual-minimal for Y.

A simple proof of Theorem 11 is based on the fact that for any $f \in F_n[t]$, (33) with $h = f(\sigma_P)$ and $a_i = a_i(x, Y), x \in Y$, gives

$$|X|f_0(P) + |X| \sum_{i=d(Y)}^{n} a_i(x, Y)f_i(P)$$

$$= |Y|f(1) + \sum_{k=d'(Y)}^{n} a_k'(x, Y)f(\sigma_P(k)). \qquad (63)$$

Therefore, if f is a dual annihilator for Y such that $f(1) = 0$ and $f_0(P) > 0$, then $d(Y) \leq \deg f$. The polynomials

$$f(t) = (1 - t)g^{d'(Y),P}(t)$$

and

$$f(t) = (1 - t)(f^{Y,P}(t))^2/(1 + t)^{\gamma'(Y)}$$

(see (45)) have these properties and give rise to the first and second statements. The third statement is obtained if one uses the polynomial $g^{D'(Y),i,U}$ of degree $s'(Y) - 1$ in (63) and takes (31) into account. To prove the last statement note that the left-hand side of (63) equals zero for

$$f(t) = (1 - t)(1 + t)^\theta (P_{l-\theta}^{1,\theta}(t))^2/(t_{l-\theta}^{1,\theta}(P) - t)$$

since $f_0(P) = 0$ (see (48) and (49) for $a = 1, b = \theta$) and $d(Y) > \deg f$. Moreover, $s'(Y) \geq l$ by the second statement and $f(\sigma_P(k)) \geq 0$ if $k \geq d_{l-\theta}^{1,\theta}(P)$.

We can apply similar arguments to the rows of the outer distribution M which has rank $s'(Y) + 1$ by Theorem 7. Considering in (33) $a_i = a_i(x, Y), x \in X$, and $h = f(\sigma_P)$ with a dual annihilator $f \in F_n[t]$ for Y we find that

$$|X| \sum_{i=0}^{n} a_i(x, Y)f_i(P) = |Y|f(1). \qquad (64)$$

In particular, for the dual minimal polynomial $f = f^{Y,P}$ we have

$$|X| \sum_{i=0}^{s'(Y)} a_i(x, Y)f_i(P) = |Y|$$

and for any integer $k, s'(Y) < k \leq n$, and

$$f(t) = (1 - t)^{k-s'(Y)} f^{Y,P}(t)$$

we have

$$\sum_{i=0}^{k} a_i(x, Y)f_i(P) = 0$$

with $f_k(P) \neq 0$. Since in both cases $f_i(P)$ depends only on $D'(Y)$, this allows one to compute the outer distribution of a code Y from a "small set of data."

Theorem 12 [37]: Each column M_i of the outer distribution $M = [M_0, \cdots, M_n]$ of Y is a linear combination of the all-one vector and the first $s'(Y)$ columns $M_0, \cdots, M_{s'(Y)-1}$, the coefficients of which are determined by the inner distribution.

Thus the first $s'(Y) + 1$ entries of any row $M(x), x \in X$, of the outer distribution of a code Y are not all equal to zero and they uniquely determine the remaining entries of the row. This has some interesting consequences presented in [37]. In particular

$$\rho(Y) \leq s'(Y)$$

and, hence, for any Y

$$|Y| \sum_{i=0}^{s'(Y)} v_i \geq |X|. \tag{65}$$

Moreover, if $d(Y) \geq 2s'(Y) - 1$, then the first $s'(Y)$ entries of any row $M(x), x \in X$, are all zero except for $a_i(x, Y) = 1$ when $i = \partial(x, Y)$. For $i = s'(Y)$, the entry $a_i(x, Y)$ is uniquely determined from (64). In particular, this gives $a_i(x, Y) = |Y|/(|X|f_i^{Y,P}(P))$ when $i = s'(Y) = \partial(x, Y)$ (see Example 1 below). Therefore, Y is completely regular if $d(Y) \geq 2s'(Y) - 1$.

Note that from (33) it also follows that for any $f \in F_{\rho(Y)-1}[t]$ there exists $x \in X$ such that

$$|Y|f(1) + \sum_{k=d'(Y)}^{n} a'_k(x, Y)f(\sigma_P(k)) = 0.$$

This fact was used in [69], [83], and [118] for obtaining asymptotic upper bounds for the covering radius $\rho(Y)$ of linear codes $Y \subseteq H_q^n$ when the dual distance $d'(Y)$ grows linearly with n. This approach is based on the inequalities

$$|a'_i(x, Y)| \leq a'_i(Y), \qquad i \in N_n, \; x \in X$$

which are satisfied by all linear codes $Y \subseteq H_q^n$; it makes use of the Chebyshev polynomials, characterized by the fact that they exhibit the smallest deviation from zero.

We now give the linear programming bounds which follow from solutions of the above extremum problems for the system P (see (46), (51), (59), and (60)).

Theorem 13: Let Y be any code in a P-polynomial scheme X. Then

$$|Y|K_P(d(Y)) \leq |X| \tag{66}$$

with equality if and only if $d(Y) = 2s'(Y) - \gamma'(Y) + 1$ and $(t + 1)^\theta P_{l-\theta}^{1,\theta}(t)$ is a dual minimal polynomial for Y where $l = s'(Y)$ and $\theta = \gamma'(Y)$.

In particular, for odd $d(Y) = 2l + 1$ Theorem 13 gives the sphere-packing bound (left-hand side of (62)) and implies that $P_l^{1,0}(t) = \Sigma_{i=0}^{l} P_i(t)$ is dual minimal for any perfect code Y. The latter is the (generalized) *Lloyd theorem* for perfect codes [17], [37].

Theorem 14 [80], [81]: Let Y be a code in a P-polynomial scheme X with the standard function σ_P. If $d'(Y) \geq d_{l-\theta}^{1,\theta}(P)$, then

$$|Y|K_P(2l + 1 - \theta) \geq |X| \tag{67}$$

with equality if and only if $d(Y) = 2s'(Y) - \gamma'(Y) + 1$ and $(t + 1)^\theta P_{l-\theta}^{1,\theta}(t)$ is a dual minimal polynomial for Y where $l = s'(Y)$ and $\theta = \gamma'(Y)$.

Thus the bounds (66) and (67) can be attained only simultaneously and in this case Y is a maximal d-code for $d = d(Y)$ and a minimal τ-design for $\tau = d'(Y) - 1$. Note that (65) gives a lower bound on the size of a code with a given number of dual "distances." Probably a stronger inequality

$$|Y|K_P(2s'(Y) - \gamma'(Y) + 1) \geq |X| \tag{68}$$

holds which (together with (66)) would imply statement 2) of Theorem 11. Then all bounds (66)–(68) can be attained only simultaneously. In any case, this is true for perfect codes (odd $d(Y)$). The inequality (68) was proved for the Hamming scheme in [78] but it is an open problem in the general case.

The following statement extends Theorem 14 from the case $d'(Y) = d_{l-\theta}^{1,\theta}(P)$ (see (56)) to the general case under the additional restriction that P satisfies the strengthened Krein condition. Therefore, we do not repeat the necessary and sufficient conditions for this special case.

Theorem 15 [80], [81]: Let X be a P-polynomial scheme with standard σ_P and assume that P satisfies the strengthened Krein condition. Then for any code $Y \subset X$

$$|Y|L_P(\sigma_P(d'(Y))) \geq |X| \tag{69}$$

with equality in the case $d'(Y) \neq d_{l-\theta}^{1,\theta}(P)$ if and only if $d(Y) = 2s'(Y) - \gamma'(Y)$ and the polynomial (57) with $U = P$ is dual minimal for Y where $\sigma = \sigma_P(d'(Y)), k = k_P(\sigma)$, $\varepsilon = \varepsilon_P(\sigma), \gamma'(Y) = \varepsilon, s'(Y) = k + \varepsilon$.

Note that codes Y for which the bounds of Theorems 13–15 are attained belong to the class of codes satisfying $d(Y) \geq 2s'(Y) - \gamma'(Y)$ (cf. statement 2) of Theorem 11). There exists the following characterization of codes in this class.

Theorem 16 [77]: Let Y be a code in a P-polynomial scheme X with the standard function σ_P such that $d = d(Y) \geq 2, s' = s'(Y) \geq 1, \gamma' = \gamma'(Y), \sigma = \sigma_P(d'(Y))$, $k = k_P(\sigma), \varepsilon = \varepsilon_P(\sigma)$, and hence $t_{k-1+\varepsilon}^{1,1-\varepsilon}(P) \leq \sigma < t_k^{1,\varepsilon}(P)$. Then $d = 2s' - \gamma' + 1$ if and only if $s' = k, \gamma' = 1 - \varepsilon, \sigma = t_{k-1+\varepsilon}^{1,1-\varepsilon}(P), |Y|K_P(d'(Y)) = |X|$, and $(t + 1)^{1-\varepsilon} P_{k-1+\varepsilon}^{1,1-\varepsilon}(t)$ is dual minimal for Y; and $d = 2s' - \gamma'$ if and only if $s' = k + \varepsilon, \gamma' = \varepsilon, \sigma \neq t_{k-1+\varepsilon}^{1,1-\varepsilon}(P), |Y|L_P(\sigma) = |X|$, and the polynomial (57) with $U = P$ is dual minimal for Y.

Note that for the class of codes Y in a P-polynomial scheme X defined by the condition $d(Y) \geq 2s'(Y) - \gamma'(Y) \geq 2$, the only parameter $|Y|$ (or $d'(Y)$) uniquely determines all fundamental parameters, the inner distribution, its Q-transform (or "dual distribution"), and the outer distribution of the code Y. Indeed, by Theorem 16 we know the dual minimal polynomial $f^{Y,P}(t)$ and hence the set $D'(Y) = \{i_1, \cdots, i_{s'(Y)}\}$ of integers which are dual distances, $d(Y), s'(Y), \gamma'(Y)$. From Theorem

10 and statement 3) of Theorem 11 it follows (by use of the polynomial $g^{D'(Y),i_j,P}(t)$ in (58)) that for any code Y in the class

$$a'_{i_j}(Y) = |X|\rho^{(\sigma)}_{k+\varepsilon-j}(P), \qquad j = 1, \cdots, s'(Y) \quad (70)$$

where $\sigma = \sigma_P(d'(Y)), k = k_P(\sigma), \varepsilon = \varepsilon_P(\sigma)$. The inner distribution of Y and, in particular, the parameters $s(Y), \gamma(Y)$ can be found with the help of (31). Moreover, all codes Y in this class are distance-invariant and completely distance-regular. This allows us to compute the outer distribution of Y with the help of (64) as was explained above. Note that from Theorem 16 it follows that the condition on a dual minimal polynomial in Theorems 13–15 is a consequence of the first condition and can be omitted.

Example 1 (continued): Apply these results to a code Y in the Hamming scheme H_2^{24} for which $d(Y) = 8$ or $d'(Y) = 8$. Since

$$d_3^{1,1}(P) = d_3(22) + 1 = 8$$

and

$$K_P(8) = 2 \sum_{i=0}^{3} \binom{23}{i} = 2^{12}$$

(see (50) and (52)), we have $|Y| \le 2^{12}$ or $|Y| \ge 2^{12}$, respectively, by (66) and (67). Consider a code Y for which either of these bounds is attained. Any such Y is a maximal 8-code and a minimal 7-design, and must have the following properties: $d(Y) = 8, d'(Y) = 8, s'(Y) = 4, \gamma'(Y) = 1$, and

$$2^{12} f^{Y,P}(t) = \frac{385}{512}(t+1)P_3^{1,1}(t)$$
$$= 2^8 t(t+1)(9t^2 - 1)$$
$$= \sum_{i=0}^{3} P_i(t) + \frac{1}{6} P_4(t).$$

Since $\sigma_P(d) = 1 - 2d/n$, $D'(Y) = \{8, 12, 16, 24\}$. Using statement 3) of Theorem 11 (or (70)) and (31) we can find that $D(Y) = D'(Y), a_8(Y) = a_{16}(Y) = 759$, $a_{12}(Y) = 2576, a_0(Y) = a_{24}(Y) = 1$, and $a'_i(Y) = 2^{12} a_i(Y)$ for all $i \in N_n$. (This means that Y must be *formally self-dual*.) Finally, $d(Y) \ge 2s'(Y) - 1$ and hence Y is completely distance-regular. By use of the method explained above, we can mechanically compute the outer distribution M of the code Y. The following table gives the entries $M_i(x)$ for $0 \le i \le 8$, and for all $x \in \mathbb{F}_2^{24}$.

dist	0	1	2	3	4	5	6	7	8	#
0	1								759	1
1		1						253		24
2			1				77		352	276
3				1	21		168			2024
4					6		64		360	1771

In fact, a code Y having the above properties exists and is unique (within equivalence); it is the *extended binary Golay code* $Y = G_2(24, 12)$ (see [88]). Thus our table gives the *weight distribution of all cosets* of $G_2(24, 12)$.

Example 2 (continued): Apply (66) and (67) to a code Y in the Johnson scheme J_8^{24} for which $d(Y) = 4$ or $d'(Y) = 6$. Since $d_1^{1,1}(P) = 6$ and

$$K_P(4) = \sum_{i=0}^{1} \binom{7}{i}\binom{17}{i+1} = 969$$

(see (53)), we have $|Y| \le 759$ or $|Y| \ge 759$, respectively. Consider a code Y for which either of these bounds is attained. It must have the following properties: $d(Y) = 4$, $d'(Y) = 6, s'(Y) = 2, \gamma'(Y) = 1$, and

$$114 f^{Y,P}(t) = \frac{15}{19}(t+1)P_1^{1,1}(t) = (t+1)(23+34t)$$
$$= \frac{2}{17}\left(P_0(t) + P_1(t) + \frac{1}{4}P_2(t)\right).$$

Because

$$\sigma_P(d) = 1 - 2\frac{d(v+1-d)}{n(v+1-n)}$$

$D'(Y) = \{6, 8\}$. Using statement 3) of Theorem 11 and (31) we can find that $a'_6(Y) = 262752, a'_8(Y) = 471960$, $D(Y) = \{4, 6, 8\}$, and $a_4(Y) = 280, a_6(Y) = 448$, $a_8(Y) = 30$. Again in this case Y is completely distance-regular, since $d(Y) \ge 2s'(Y) - 1$, and one can compute the outer distribution M of the code Y. In fact, a code Y having the above properties exists and is unique; it is the "octade code" formed by all vectors of Hamming weight 8 in the extended Golay code $G_2(24, 8)$ (see [88]).

More sophisticated applications can be found in [6], [36], [37], and [76].

D. Codes and Designs in Q-Polynomial Schemes

Let us consider codes in an n-class Q-polynomial scheme (X, R). Using (32) with $h = f(\sigma_Q)$ where $f \in F_n[t]$ are some annihilators for a code Y one can obtain the following dual analog of Theorem 11.

Theorem 17: For any code Y in an n-class Q-polynomial scheme (X, R)

1) $d(Y) + d'(Y) \le n + 2$.
2) $d'(Y) \le 2s(Y) - \gamma(Y) + 1$; equality implies $|Y| = \Omega_Q(f)$ where

$$f(t) = (1+t)^{-\gamma(Y)}(f^{Y,Q}(t))^2.$$

3) If $d'(Y) \ge s(Y)$, then Y is distance-invariant and

$$a_i(x, Y) = |Y| g_0^{D(Y),i,Q}(Q) - g^{D(Y),i,Q}(1)$$

for any $x \in Y$ and $i \in D(Y)$.
4) If σ_Q is standard and $d'(Y) \ge 2l - \theta + 1$, then

$$d(Y) \le d_{l-\theta}^{1,\theta}(Q) \quad (71)$$

with equality if and only if $l = s(Y), \theta = \gamma(Y)$, and $(1+t)^\theta Q_{l-\theta}^{1,\theta}(t)$ is minimal for Y.

449

Many results concerning codes Y in Q-polynomial schemes are based on the existence of the representation

$$Q_k(\sigma_Q(\partial_R(x,y))) = \sum_{j=1}^{m_k} v_{k,j}(x)\overline{v_{k,j}(y)}, \qquad k \in N_n \quad (72)$$

(see (10) and (13)). In particular, let us emphasize the following important "dual" analog of (65).

Theorem 18 (The Absolute Bound [37]): For any code Y in a Q-polynomial scheme

$$|Y| \le \sum_{j=0}^{s(Y)} m_j. \quad (73)$$

The proof of Theorem 18 is based on the fact that the $|Y|$ functions $f^{Y,Q}(\sigma_Q(\partial_R(x,y))), y \in Y$, belong to the space generated by the functions $v_{k,j}(x), k \in N_{s(Y)}, j \in N^1_{m_k}$, equal to $\delta_{x,y}$ when $x \in Y$, and hence are linearly independent functions in $x \in X$.

In fact, the fundamental parameters of a code Y are determined from the sequence $a_i = a_i(Y), i \in N_n$, and its Q-transform (see Section III-C). Analogously, for any $x \in X$, we can consider the sequence $a_i = a_i(x,Y), i \in N_n$, and define the corresponding parameters; in particular, $d'(x,Y), s(x,Y), \gamma(x,Y)$. Note that, by (40), $d'(Y) \le d'(x,Y)$ for any $x \in X$, and, similarly to statement 2) of Theorem 17, $d'(x,Y) \le 2s(x,Y) - \gamma(x,Y)$ for any $x \in X \backslash Y$. Therefore, if we assume that $d'(Y) \ge 2l - \theta$ and $x \in X \backslash Y$, then $s(x,Y) \ge l$. For the polynomial

$$f(t) = (1+t)^\theta (Q^{0,\theta}_{l-\theta}(t))^2 / (t^{0,\theta}_{l-\theta}(Q) - t)$$

of degree $2l - \theta - 1$ we have $f_0(Q) = 0$ (see (48) and (49) for $a = 0, b = \theta$), and the use of $h = f(\sigma_Q)$ and $a_i = a_i(x,Y)$ in (32) shows that

$$\sum_{k=1}^n a_k(x,Y)f(\sigma_Q(k)) = 0$$

under our assumption. If σ_Q is standard, then $f(\sigma_Q(k)) \ge 0$ if $d = d^{0,\theta}_{l-\theta}(Q) \le k \le n$ with equality in at most l points $k \in N^d_n$ while

$$s(x,Y) = |\{k \in N^1_n \colon a_k(x,Y) > 0\}| \ge l.$$

This implies that for any code Y in a Q-polynomial scheme (X, R) with standard σ_Q such that $d'(Y) \ge 2l - \theta$

$$\rho(Y) \le d^{0,\theta}_{l-\theta}(Q) \quad (74)$$

with equality if and only if there exists a point $x \in X \backslash Y$ such that $(1+t)^\theta Q^{0,\theta}_{l-\theta}(t)$ is a polynomial of minimal degree which equals zero at $t = \sigma_Q(\partial_R(x,y))$ for each $y \in Y$.

The inequality (74) for the Hamming scheme is due to Tietäväinen [127]. For the general case it was given together with the necessary and sufficient condition for its attainability in [51]. Note that (71) and (74) give the following upper bounds on the minimum distance and covering radius of a $(2l - \theta)$-design Y:

$$d(Y) \le d^{1,\theta}_{l-\theta}(Q) \qquad \rho(Y) \le d^{0,1-\theta}_l(Q).$$

Let $R|Y$ be the set consisting of the $s(Y) + 1$ nonempty relations $R_i \cap Y^2$ (those with $a_i(Y) \ne 0$). Then $(Y, R|Y)$ is called the *restriction of (X,R) to Y*. It can be shown that if $d'(Y) \ge 2s(Y) - 1$, then $(Y, R|Y)$ is an $s(Y)$-class Q-polynomial scheme [37]. This theorem is a kind of "dual" of the result mentioned in Section IV-C about completely distance-regular codes. The intersection numbers of this scheme can be computed with the help of the polynomials $f^{Y,Q}$ and $g^{D(Y),i,Q}$.

Next, we give linear programming bounds which follow from solutions of the above extremum problems for the system Q (see (46), (51), (59), and (60)). Recall that the representation (72) was used to prove that for the decomposable Q-polynomial schemes (in particular, for the Hamming and Johnson schemes) the system Q satisfies the strengthened Krein condition [77].

Theorem 19 [37], [47]: For any code Y in a Q-polynomial scheme (X, R)

$$|Y| \ge K_Q(d'(Y)) \quad (75)$$

with equality if and only if $d'(Y) = 2s(Y) - \gamma(Y) + 1$ and $(t+1)^\theta Q^{1,\theta}_{l-\theta}(t)$ is a minimal polynomial for Y where $l = s(Y)$ and $\theta = \gamma(Y)$.

The well-known Rao bound [98] for τ-designs (orthogonal arrays) in the Hamming scheme and the Ray-Chaudhuri–Wilson bound [99] for τ-designs (block designs) in the Johnson scheme are special cases of (75) for these schemes (see (52) and (54)). A design which satisfies equality in (75) is called a *tight τ-design* where $\tau = d'(Y) - 1$. The subject of tight τ-designs in the Johnson scheme has been introduced by Ray-Chaudhuri and Wilson [99] and has been investigated by several authors (see especially [7], [134], and the references therein). In particular, the polynomial $Q^{1,0}_l(t) = \Sigma^l_{i=0} Q_i(t)$ is minimal for any tight $2l$-design. This is (a generalized version of) the *Ray-Chaudhuri–Wilson theorem* for tight designs [99]; it is a "dual" of the Lloyd theorem for perfect codes [37], [101].

Theorem 20 [73], [77]: Let Y be a code in a Q-polynomial scheme (X, R) with the standard function σ_Q. If $d(Y) \ge d^{1,\theta}_{l-\theta}(Q)$, then

$$|Y| \le K_Q(2l + 1 - \theta) \quad (76)$$

with equality if and only if $d'(Y) = 2s(Y) - \gamma(Y) + 1$ and $(t+1)^\theta Q^{1,\theta}_{l-\theta}(t)$ is a minimal polynomial for Y where $l = s(Y)$ and $\theta = \gamma(Y)$.

Analogously, the bounds (75) and (76) can be attained only simultaneously and in this case Y is a minimal τ-design for $\tau = d'(Y) - 1$ and a maximal d-code for $d = d(Y)$. Note that the absolute bound (73) gives an upper bound on the size of a code with a given number of "distances." Probably a stronger inequality

$$|Y| \le K_Q(2s(Y) - \gamma(Y) + 1) \quad (77)$$

holds which (together with (75)) would imply statement 2) of Theorem 17. Then all bounds (75)–(77) can be attained only simultaneously. In any case, this is true for tight τ-designs with

450

even τ (odd $d'(Y)$). The inequality (77) was proved in [77] for all decomposable Q-polynomial schemes (in particular, for the Hamming and Johnson schemes), but it is an open problem in the general case.

The following statement extends Theorem 20 from the case $d(Y) = d^{1,\theta}_{l-\theta}(Q)$ (see (56)) to the general case under the additional restriction that Q satisfies the strengthened Krein condition. Therefore, we do not repeat the necessary and sufficient conditions for this special case.

Theorem 21 [73], [77]: Let (X, R) be a Q-polynomial scheme with standard σ_Q and assume that Q satisfies the strengthened Krein condition. Then for any code Y in (X, R)

$$|Y| \leq L_Q(\sigma_Q(d(Y))) \tag{78}$$

with equality in the case $d(Y) \neq d^{1,\theta}_{l-\theta}(Q)$ if and only if $d'(Y) = 2s(Y) - \gamma(Y)$ and the polynomial (57) with $U = Q$ is minimal for Y where $\sigma = \sigma_Q(d(Y)), k = k_Q(\sigma)$, $\varepsilon = \varepsilon_Q(\sigma), \gamma(Y) = \varepsilon, s(Y) = k + \varepsilon$.

For the Hamming and Johnson schemes the bound (78) in the first interval when $d^{1,0}_1(Q) \leq d(Y) \leq n$ coincides with the well-known Plotkin and Johnson bounds, respectively (see [88] and the calculation of $L_Q(\sigma)$ in Section IV-B). For $d(Y) < d^{1,0}_1(Q)$, (78) improves upon these bounds. (We remind that (78) is true in the second interval and in all odd intervals without the restriction of the strengthened Krein condition.)

Note that codes Y for which the bounds of Theorems 19–21 are attained belong to the class of codes satisfying $d'(Y) \geq 2s(Y) - \gamma(Y)$ (cf. statement 2) of Theorem 17) and forming $s(Y)$-class Q-polynomial schemes. There exists the following characterization of codes in this class.

Theorem 22 [77]: Let Y be a code in a Q-polynomial scheme (X, R) with the standard function σ_Q such that $d' = d'(Y) \geq 2, s = s(Y) \geq 1, \gamma = \gamma(Y), \sigma = \sigma_Q(d(Y))$, $k = k_Q(\sigma), \varepsilon = \varepsilon_Q(\sigma)$, and hence

$$t^{1,1-\varepsilon}_{k-1+\varepsilon}(Q) \leq \sigma < t^{1,\varepsilon}_k(Q).$$

Then $d' = 2s - \gamma + 1$ if and only if $s = k, \gamma = 1 - \varepsilon$, $\sigma = t^{1,1-\varepsilon}_{k-1+\varepsilon}(Q), |Y| = K_Q(d(Y))$, and $(t+1)^{1-\varepsilon} Q^{1,1-\varepsilon}_{k-1+\varepsilon}(t)$ is a minimal polynomial for Y; and $d' = 2s - \gamma$ if and only if $s = k + \varepsilon, \gamma = \varepsilon, \sigma \neq t^{1,1-\varepsilon}_{k-1+\varepsilon}(Q), |Y| = L_Q(\sigma)$, and the polynomial (57) with $U = Q$ is minimal for Y.

For the class of codes Y in a Q-polynomial scheme (X, R) defined by the condition $d'(Y) \geq 2s(Y) - \gamma(Y) \geq 2$, the only parameter $|Y|$ (or $d(Y)$) uniquely determines all fundamental parameters, the inner and dual distributions of the code Y, and also the intersection numbers of the Q-polynomial scheme formed by Y. Indeed, by Theorem 22 we know the minimal polynomial $f^{Y,Q}(t)$ and hence the set $D(Y) = \{i_1, \cdots, i_{s(Y)}\}$ of integers which are "distances," $d'(Y), s(Y), \gamma(Y)$. From Theorem 10 and statement 3) of Theorem 17 it follows (by use of the polynomial $g^{D(Y),i_j,Q}(t)$ in (58)) that for any code Y in the class

$$a_{i_j}(Y) = |Y|\rho^{(\sigma)}_{k+\varepsilon-j}(Q), \qquad j = 1, \cdots, s(Y)$$

where $\sigma = \sigma_Q(d(Y))$, $k = k_Q(\sigma)$, $\varepsilon = \varepsilon_Q(\sigma)$. The dual distribution of Y is computed by (30). Codes Y in the class are

distance-invariant and form $s(Y)$-class Q-polynomial schemes whose intersection numbers are determined with the help of the polynomials $f^{Y,Q}$ and $g^{D(Y),i,Q}$ (see [37, Theorem 5.25] or [81, Theorem 3.21]). Note that from Theorem 22 it follows that the condition on a minimal polynomial in Theorems 19–21 is a consequence of the first condition and can be omitted.

E. Bounds for Spherical Codes and Designs

The results of Section IV-D are applicable to infinite distance-transitive spaces (see Section II-D). The unit sphere

$$S^{n-1} = \left\{ x = (x_1, \cdots, x_n) \in \mathbb{R}^n \colon \sum_{i=1}^n x_i^2 = 1 \right\}$$

is a distance-transitive space with the Euclidean distance

$$d(x, y) = \sqrt{\sum_{i=1}^n (x_i - y_i)^2}$$

and the isometry group $G = O(n)$ consisting of all orthogonal matrices of order n. Any finite set $Y \subset S^{n-1}$ (called a *spherical code*) is characterized by the finite set $D(Y)$ of distinct nonzero values of $d(x, y)$ when $x, y \in Y$. It allows us to define for any spherical code Y the *minimum distance* $d(Y) := \min D(Y)$ and the *degree* $s(Y) := |D(Y)|$, and also the parameter $\gamma(Y)$ which equals 1 if the diameter 2 of S^{n-1} belongs to $D(Y)$, and equals zero otherwise. We can also measure the distance between $x, y \in S^{n-1}$ by the angle $\varphi = \varphi(x, y), 0 \leq \varphi \leq \pi$, where

$$\cos \varphi(x, y) = \sum_{i=1}^n x_i y_i = 1 - \tfrac{1}{2} d^2(x, y)$$

and denote by $\varphi(Y)$ the *minimum angular distance* between distinct points of Y. It is clear that $d(Y) = 2 \sin(\varphi(Y)/2)$. The normalized invariant measure μ on S^{n-1} is the normalized surface area of S^{n-1}. Let $\sigma_{n-1}(\varphi)$ be the surface area of

$$S^{n-1}(x, \varphi) = \{y \colon y \in S^{n-1}, \varphi(x, y) \leq \varphi\}$$

and let $\sigma_{n-1} = 2\sigma_{n-1}(\pi/2)$ be the surface area of S^{n-1}. It is well known that $\sigma_{n-1} = 2\pi^{n/2}/\Gamma(n/2)$ and

$$\mu(S^{n-1}(x, \varphi)) = \frac{\sigma_{n-1}(\varphi)}{\sigma_{n-1}} = c_n \int_{\cos \varphi}^1 (1 - z^2)^{(n-3)/2} \, dz \tag{79}$$

where $c_n = \Gamma(\frac{n}{2})/(\Gamma(\frac{n-1}{2})\Gamma(\frac{1}{2}))$ and $\Gamma(x)$ is the gamma function. The inner and outer distributions of a spherical code Y are given by the values

$$a_d(Y) := \frac{1}{|Y|}|\{(x, y) \colon x, y \in Y, d(x, y) = d\}|, \quad d \in [0, 2]$$

and, for any $x \in S^{n-1}$

$$a_d(x, Y) := |\{(x, y) \colon y \in Y, d(x, y) = d\}|, \qquad d \in [0, 2].$$

Note that $a_d(Y)$ and $a_d(x, Y)$, considered as functions of $d \in [0, 2]$, differ from zero only at a finite set of points d. For any function a_d which has this property (in particular, for

$a_d(Y)$ and $a_d(x,Y))$ we can define its *Q-transform* as the infinite sequence $(a_i')_{i=0}^{\infty}$ where

$$a_i' := \sum_{d \in [0,2]} a_d q_i(d), \qquad i = 0, 1, \cdots.$$

As in the case of association schemes we can define (see Section III-C) the set $D'(Y)$, the *dual distance* $d'(Y)$ of Y and its *strength* $\tau(Y) = d'(Y) - 1$. Spherical τ-designs Y (i.e., $\tau(Y) \geq \tau$) were introduced in [45], in connection with an approximation formula for the evaluation of multidimensional integrals over S^{n-1} of the following form:

$$\int_{S^{n-1}} u(x)\, d\mu(x) \approx \frac{1}{|Y|} \sum_{x \in Y} u(x). \qquad (80)$$

The code $Y \subset S^{n-1}$ is a τ-*design* if and only if the approximation formula (80) becomes equality for all functions $u(x)$ which are polynomials in coordinates of $x = (x_1, \cdots, x_n) \in S^{n-1}$ of degree at most τ. Thus $B(S^{n-1}, \tau + 1)$ is the minimum number of nodes in the approximation formula under consideration.

Now we verify that S^{n-1} is "Q-polynomial" with respect to the standard change of variable $\sigma(d) = 1 - d^2/2$ (this means that $\sigma(d)$ is a decreasing continuous function such that $\sigma(0) = 1, \sigma(2) = -1$). Indeed, from (28) and (79) it follows that the orthogonality and normalization conditions

$$c_n \int_{-1}^1 Q_i(t) Q_j(t)(1-t^2)^{(n-3)/2}\, dt = m_i \delta_{i,j}, \quad Q_k(1) = m_k \qquad (81)$$

uniquely define polynomials $Q_k(t)$ of degree k such that $q_k(z) = Q_k(\sigma(z))$ $(k = 0, 1, \cdots)$ and hence

$$\tilde{E}_k(x,y) = q_k(\partial(x,y)) = Q_k(\sigma(d(x,y))).$$

In the case of S^{n-1} the subspace V_k consists of all homogeneous harmonic polynomials in $x = (x_1, \cdots, x_n) \in S^{n-1}$ of degree k and has the dimension

$$m_k = \binom{n+k-1}{n-1} - \binom{n+k-3}{n-1}, \qquad k = 0, 1, \cdots.$$

Thus

$$Q_i(t) = m_i P_i^{(n-3)/2, (n-3)/2}(t)$$

where

$$P_i^{\alpha, \beta}(t) = \frac{1}{2^i \binom{i+\alpha}{\alpha}} \sum_{j=0}^{i} \binom{i+\alpha}{j}\binom{i+\beta}{i-j}$$
$$\cdot (t-1)^{i-j}(t+1)^j$$

are the *Jacobi polynomials* normalized by $P_i^{\alpha,\beta}(1) = 1$. (The Jacobi polynomials $P_i^{\alpha,\beta}(t)$ with $\alpha = \beta$ are called the *Gegenbauer polynomials*.) All results of Section IV-D are valid for spherical codes except for statement 1) of Theorem 17 whose proof uses the finiteness of association schemes. (The absolute bound for S^{n-1} was proved in [45] in the strong form (77).) In particular, the $K_Q(d)$- and $L_Q(\sigma)$-problems and their solutions are valid for countable systems Q (compare (47) with (81)) and give rise to the following two results.

Theorem 23 (The DGS Bound [45]): For a code $Y \subset S^{n-1}$, let $\tau(Y) = 2l - \theta$. Then

$$|Y| \geq \binom{l+n-2}{n-1} + \binom{l+n-1-\theta}{n-1} \qquad (82)$$

with equality if and only if $\tau(Y) = 2s(Y) - \gamma(Y)$.

Note that if $p_i^{\alpha,\beta}$ is the largest zero of $P_i^{\alpha,\beta}(t)$ and $t_i^{a,b}$ is the largest zero of $Q_i^{a,b}(t)$, then $t_i^{a,b} = p_i^{(n-3)/2+a, (n-3)/2+b}$ and that Q satisfies the strengthened Krein condition.

Theorem 24 [73], [74]: For a code $Y \subset S^{n-1}$, let $\sigma = \cos\varphi(Y), \alpha = (n-3)/2$, and $k = k_Q(\sigma), \varepsilon = \varepsilon_Q(\sigma)$. Then $|Y|$ does not exceed

$$\left(\binom{n+k-2}{n-1} + \binom{n+k-3+\varepsilon}{n-1}\right)\left(1 - \frac{P_{k-1}^{\alpha+1,\alpha+\varepsilon}(\sigma)}{P_k^{\alpha,\alpha+\varepsilon}(\sigma)}\right) \qquad (83)$$

and, in particular, if $\sigma \leq p_{l-\theta}^{\alpha+1,\alpha+\theta}$, then

$$|Y| \leq \binom{l+n-2}{n-1} + \binom{l+n-1-\theta}{n-1}. \qquad (84)$$

The bound (83) is attained if and only if

$$\tau(Y) \geq 2s(Y) - \gamma(Y) - 1 \geq 1.$$

The class of spherical codes for which the bounds of Theorems 23 and 24 are attained is described by Theorem 22; these codes carry Q-polynomial subschemes. Many examples can be found in [45], [74], and [77]. In particular, the tight 7-design in S^7 containing 240 points and the tight 11-design in S^{23} containing 196 560 points are the maximal codes with the angular distance 60°; they allow one to determine the *kissing numbers* in dimensions 8 and 24 [74], [96].

The following asymptotic bound follows from (84). However, it was obtained earlier with the help of the MRRW polynomials (61).

Theorem 25 (The KL Bound [65]): For any fixed φ, $0 < \varphi < \frac{\pi}{2}$, and $n \to \infty$

$$\frac{1}{n} \log A\left(S^{n-1}, 2\sin\frac{\varphi}{2}\right)$$
$$\lesssim \frac{1+\sin\varphi}{2\sin\varphi} \log \frac{1+\sin\varphi}{2\sin\varphi} - \frac{1-\sin\varphi}{2\sin\varphi} \log \frac{1-\sin\varphi}{2\sin\varphi}.$$

It should be noted that Theorems 23 and 24 give the best linear programming bounds in the class of polynomials of restricted degree. The necessary and sufficient conditions for optimality of $f^{(\sigma)}(t)$ for the $L_Q(\sigma)$-problem without this restriction were found in [24] and [25], together with an improvement of (83) in some range when these conditions are not fulfilled. On the other hand, in [135] there was found a continuous function $f(t)$ having the properties $f(t) \geq 0$ for $-1 \leq t \leq 1$ and $f_i(Q) \leq 0, i = \tau, \tau + 1, \cdots$; this yields an improvement of the DGS bound (82) for τ-designs if τ is sufficiency large.

Theorem 26 [135]: For any spherical design $Y \subset S^{n-1}$

$$|Y|\sigma_{n-1}(\arccos p_{\tau(Y)}^{(n-1)/2,(n-1)/2}) \geq \sigma_{n-1}. \quad (85)$$

In a certain sense, the sphere-packing bound

$$|Y|\sigma_{n-1}(\varphi(Y)/2) \leq \sigma_{n-1}$$

and the bound (85) are analogs of the bounds (62) and (69) for P-polynomial schemes.

The projective spaces in n dimensions over $\mathbb{R}, \mathbb{C}$, and quaternions $\mathbb{H}$ ($n = 2, 3, \cdots$) also are Q-polynomial; the corresponding systems Q are systems of Jacobi polynomials and satisfy the strengthened Krein condition. Elements of these spaces can be considered as lines going through the origin. The results of Section IV-D are applicable to codes and designs in the projective spaces which were studied earlier in [44], [60], [65], and [77]. The bounds for codes in the projective spaces have been successfully used to estimate "crosscorrelation" of codes [65], [75], [76], [109].

F. Universal Bounds for Codes and Designs in P- and Q-Polynomial Schemes—Asymptotic Results

In this subsection we consider a code Y in an n-class P- and Q-polynomial scheme X and tacitly suppose that the functions σ_P and σ_Q are standard. Of course, all results of Sections IV-C and IV-D are applicable. We give three pairs of *universal* bounds for codes and designs in such schemes. The term "universal" reflects the fact that these bounds are valid for all codes in all schemes under consideration.

First, for a P- and Q-polynomial association scheme X we extend the duality in bounding the optimal sizes of d-codes and $(d-1)$-designs to the polynomial case. For any $f \in F_n[t]$ and U (we use U for either P or Q, and use $\overline{U}$ for the other one), we define an U-dual polynomial $f^{(U)}$ to f as follows:

$$f^{(U)} := |X|^{-(1/2)} \sum_{i=0}^{n} f(\sigma_{\overline{U}}(i))U_i$$

(cf. (39)). Analogously, using (42)–(44) one can show that

$$f^{(U)}(\sigma_U(i)) = |X|^{1/2} f_i(\overline{U})$$

and hence

$$f = (f^{(U)})^{(\overline{U})} \qquad \Omega_{\overline{U}}(f)\Omega_U(f^{(U)}) = |X|$$

and f has the property $\mathfrak{A}_{\overline{U}}(d)$ or $\mathfrak{B}_{\overline{U}}(d)$ if and only if $f^{(U)}$ has the property $\mathfrak{B}_U(d)$ or $\mathfrak{A}_U(d)$, respectively. In particular, for any $d \in N_n^1$, the following equalities hold [80]:

$$A_P(X,d)B_Q(X,d) = B_P(X,d)A_Q(X,d) = |X|. \quad (86)$$

As an example, consider the polynomial $g^{d,U}(t)$ defined by (45) and note that $g^{d,U}(\sigma_U(j)) \geq 0$ for $j \in N_n$ according to the assumption that σ_U is standard. Using the orthogonality condition and the property

$$U_k(1)\overline{U}_i(\sigma_{\overline{U}}(k)) = \overline{U}_i(1)U_k(\sigma_U(i))$$

(see (42)–(44)) one can check that the $\overline{U}$-dual of $g^{d,U}(t)$ is the polynomial $|X|^{1/2}g^{n-d+2,\overline{U}}(t)/g_0^{d,U}(U)$ and hence $g^{d,U}(t)$ has the properties $\mathfrak{A}_U(d)$ and $\mathfrak{B}_U(n-d+2)$. This shows that

$$A_U(X,d) \leq 1/g_0^{d,U}(U) = |X|g_0^{n-d+2,\overline{U}}(\overline{U})$$
$$B_U(X,d) \geq 1/g_0^{n-d+2,U}(U) = |X|g_0^{d,\overline{U}}(\overline{U})$$

and implies the *first pair of universal bounds* [81]

$$|X|g_0^{d'(Y),P}(P) \leq |Y| \leq 1/g_0^{d(Y),Q}(Q).$$

Each of these bounds is attained if and only if $d(Y)+d'(Y) = n + 2$. In this case, $g^{d(Y),Q}$ is an annihilator and $g^{d'(Y),P}$ is a dual annihilator for Y.

For the Hamming scheme H_q^n and the Johnson scheme J_n^v, the first pair of universal bounds takes the following forms:

$$q^{d'(Y)-1} \leq |Y| \leq q^{n-d(Y)+1} \quad (87)$$

$$\frac{\binom{v}{d'(Y)-1}}{\binom{n}{d'(Y)-1}} \leq |Y| \leq \frac{\binom{v}{n-d(Y)+1}}{\binom{n}{n-d(Y)+1}} \quad (88)$$

respectively. These bounds for codes are called the Singleton and Johnson bounds [88], and codes satisfying equality in (87) or (88) are called MDS-codes and Steiner systems, respectively [88], [15]. In particular, (87) is attained for the Reed–Solomon codes and (88) is attained for the "octade" code (together with the four other bounds (66), (67), (75), and (76)).

From the results of Sections IV-C and IV-D we deduce the *second pair of universal bounds* [37]

$$K_Q(d'(Y)) \leq |Y| \leq \frac{|X|}{K_P(d(Y))} \quad (89)$$

with equality in the left- and right-hand side if and only if $d'(Y) = 2s(Y) - \gamma(Y) + 1$ and $d(Y) = 2s'(Y) - \gamma'(Y) + 1$, respectively.

Finally, if the systems Q and P satisfy the strengthened Krein condition, the results of Sections IV-C and IV-D imply the *third pair of universal bounds* [78], [81]

$$\frac{|X|}{L_P(\sigma_P(d'(Y)))} \leq |Y| \leq L_Q(\sigma_Q(d(Y))) \quad (90)$$

with equality (when $d(Y) > 1$ and $d'(Y) > 1$) in the left- and right-hand side if and only if $d(Y) \geq 2s'(Y) - \gamma'(Y)$ and $d'(Y) \geq 2s(Y) - \gamma(Y)$, respectively.

The characterization of the codes for which the bounds in (89) and (90) are attained is given by Theorems 16 and 22. A list of the known codes in the Hamming and Johnson schemes for which (90) is attained can be found in [77] and [78].

For finding asymptotic results the following special cases of bounds (89) and (90) are useful:

$$A_Q(X,d) \leq \begin{cases} |X| \Big/ \sum_{i=0}^{k} v_i, & \text{if } d \geq 2k+1 \\ \sum_{i=0}^{k} m_i, & \text{if } d \geq d_k^{1,0}(Q) \end{cases} \quad (91)$$

$$B_Q(X,d) \geq \begin{cases} \sum_{i=0}^{k} m_i, & \text{if } d \geq 2k+1 \\ |X| \Big/ \sum_{i=0}^{k} v_i, & \text{if } d \geq d_k^{1,0}(P). \end{cases} \quad (92)$$

In particular, in the case of the Hamming scheme H_q^n, if $1 \leq k = k(n) \leq n(q-1)/q$ and $n \to \infty$, then

$$d_k^{1,0}(Q)/n = \gamma_q(k/n) + o(1)$$

where

$$\gamma_q(x) = \frac{1}{q}\Big(q - 1 - (q-2)x - 2\sqrt{(q-1)x(1-x)}\Big)$$

(see [90] and [78]). Notice that $\gamma_q(x)$ is a decreasing continuous function on $[0, (q-1)/q]$ which coincides with its inverse function, that is, $\gamma_q(\gamma_q(x)) = x$. Therefore, if q is fixed and

$$\lim_{n \to \infty} \frac{d}{n} = \delta, \qquad 0 \leq \delta \leq (q-1)/q$$

then the second bounds in (91) and (92) give rise to the *first form of the MRRW bound for codes* [90]

$$\frac{1}{n} \log_q A(H_q^n, d) \lesssim H(\gamma_q(\delta), q) \quad (93)$$

and the following asymptotic bound for designs [78]:

$$\frac{1}{n} \log_q B(H_q^n, d) \gtrsim 1 - H(\gamma_q(\delta), q) \quad (94)$$

where

$$H(x, q) = -x \log_q x - (1-x) \log_q (1-x) + \log_q (q-1)$$

is the *Shannon entropy*. In the case of the Johnson scheme J_n^v, if $\lim_{n \to \infty} \frac{k}{v} = \zeta$ and $\lim_{v \to \infty} \frac{n}{v} = \eta$, where $0 \leq \zeta \leq \eta$ and $0 < \eta \leq \frac{1}{2}$, then

$$d_k^{1,0}(Q)/v = \xi_\eta(\zeta) + o(1)$$

where, for any $\eta, 0 \leq \eta \leq \frac{1}{2}$

$$\xi_\eta(x) = \frac{\eta(1-\eta) - x(1-x)}{1 + 2\sqrt{x(1-x)}}$$

is a decreasing continuous function which maps the interval $[0, \eta]$ onto $[0, \eta(1-\eta)]$ (see [90] and [81]). The inverse function $\xi_\eta^{-1}(x)$ can be expressed in the following explicit form:

$$\xi_\eta^{-1}(x) = \frac{1}{2}\left(1 - \sqrt{1 - 4\Big(\sqrt{\eta(1-\eta) - x(1-x)} - x\Big)^2}\right).$$

Therefore, if $\lim_{v \to \infty} \frac{n}{v} = \eta$ and $\lim_{v \to \infty} \frac{d}{v} = \delta$, where $0 < \eta \leq \frac{1}{2}$ and $0 \leq \delta \leq \eta(1-\eta)$, then the second bound in (91) gives rise to the asymptotic bound [90]

$$\frac{1}{v} \log_2 A(J_n^v, d) \lesssim H(\xi_\eta^{-1}(\delta)) \quad (95)$$

where $H(x) = H(x, 2)$. On the other hand, as was shown in [81], if $\lim_{v \to \infty} \frac{n}{v} = \eta$ and $\lim_{v \to \infty} \frac{k}{v} = \zeta$, where $0 \leq \zeta \leq \eta(1-\eta)$ and $0 < \eta \leq \frac{1}{2}$, then

$$d_k^{1,0}(P)/v = \xi_\eta^{-1}(\zeta) + o(1)$$

and hence, for $\lim_{v \to \infty} \frac{n}{v} = \eta$ and $\lim_{v \to \infty} \frac{d}{v} = \delta$, where $0 < \eta \leq \frac{1}{2}$ and $0 \leq \delta \leq \eta$, the second bound in (92) gives rise to the asymptotic bound

$$\frac{1}{n} \log_2 B(J_n^v, d) \gtrsim H(\eta) - \eta H\left(\frac{\xi_\eta(\delta)}{\eta}\right) - (1-\eta) H\left(\frac{\xi_\eta(\delta)}{1-\eta}\right).$$

In the typical situation the second bounds in (91) and (92) (which follow from the third pair of universal bounds) are better than the first ones when the parameter d is sufficiently large and become worse when d is small. In particular, this is true for the bound (93) which for sufficiently small d is worse than the Hamming asymptotic bound

$$\frac{1}{n} \log_q A(H_q^n, d) \lesssim 1 - H(\delta, q).$$

This raises the problem of "smoothing" these bounds. A similar problem of bounding the *Shannon reliability function* for probabilistic channels was considered in [108] where the *straight-line bound* was found. The *principle of the multiple packing* (applicable to the translation schemes, see Section V) gives the Bassalygo–Elias inequality [12]

$$\binom{n}{w} A(H_2^n, 2d) \leq 2^n A(J_w^n, d) \quad (96)$$

where $1 \leq w \leq n/2$, and the straight-line bound for H_q^n [69]

$$A(H_q^n, d) \sum_{i=0}^{r} \binom{l}{i} (q-1)^i \leq q^l A(H_q^{n-l}, d - 2r)$$

where $r \leq l, 2r \leq d$. A consequence of (95) and (96) for

$$\lim_{n \to \infty} \frac{d}{n} = \delta, \qquad 0 \leq \delta \leq \frac{1}{2}$$

is the *second form of the MRRW bound for codes* [90]

$$\frac{1}{n} \log_2 A(H_2^n, d) \lesssim 1 - \max_\eta \left(H(\eta) - H\left(\xi_\eta^{-1}\left(\frac{\delta}{2}\right)\right)\right)$$

where $\eta \in [\frac{1}{2}(1 - \sqrt{1 - 2\delta}), \frac{1}{2}]$ and $\xi_\eta^{-1}(x)$ is defined above. This becomes better than (95) with $q = 2$ when $\delta < 0.272$.

The argument that leads to (96) does not apply to the minimal design problem. However, a similar result is valid in terms of the linear programming bounds. Rodemich (see [100], [42]) used the fact that any nonnegative-definite function $h(\partial_H(x, y))$ on H_2^n is nonnegative-definite on (subset) J_w^n as well and proved the following analog of (96) for objective functions of linear programming bounds:

$$\binom{n}{w} A_Q(H_2^n, 2d) \leq 2^n A_Q(J_w^n, d). \quad (97)$$

Combination of (97) with (86) for $X = H_2^n$ and $X = J_w^n$ gives the following results [80]:

$$B_P(H_2^n, 2d) \geq B_P(J_w^n, d) \quad (98)$$

$$B(H_2^n, 2d) \geq B_P(J_w^n, d) = \frac{\binom{n}{w}}{A_Q(J_w^n, d)}. \quad (99)$$

In particular, (99) and (95) (considered as a bound on $A_Q(J_w^n, d)$) for

$$\lim_{n \to \infty} \frac{d}{n} = \delta, \qquad 0 \le \delta \le \frac{1}{2}$$

give the following asymptotic bound [80]:

$$\frac{1}{n} \log_2 B(H_2^n, d) \gtrsim \max_\eta \left(H(\eta) - H\left(\xi_\eta^{-1}\left(\frac{\delta}{2} \right) \right) \right) \quad (100)$$

where $\eta \in [\frac{1}{2}(1 - \sqrt{1 - 2\delta}), \frac{1}{2}]$.

The essential difficulty in extending the second form of the MRRW bound to the case $q \ge 3$ is caused by the fact that the natural generalization of (96) connects H_q^n with subschemes of the association scheme considered in Example 3 which are not Q-polynomial. Some results in this direction were obtained in [1] and [125].

Finally, in addition to the (nonconstructive) results (96)–(99) which give bounds for the Hamming space from bounds for the Johnson space, let us point out a "constructive" relationship between codes and designs in the Hamming and Johnson schemes. It is the celebrated *Assmus–Mattson theorem* [4], which allows one to obtain good combinatorial designs and constant-weight codes from certain codes in the binary Hamming scheme. A strengthening of this result can be found in [29].

V. Translation Schemes

A. Definitions and Preliminaries

Certain association schemes are invariant under "translations," of the form $(x, y) \mapsto (x + z, y + z)$. Examples are the Hamming scheme and the composition scheme, described in Section II-A (Examples 1 and 3). We shall examine the appropriate generalization, under the name of "translation schemes," borrowed from [26]. A comprehensive treatment of that subject is given by Camion [32]. The material of this section is mainly taken from [42].

Definition 10: Let $(X, +)$ be a finite Abelian group, and let (X, R) be an n-class association scheme. Assume that (X, R) is $(X, +)$-*invariant*, i.e.,

$$\text{if } (x, y) \in R_i, \text{ then } (x + z, y + z) \in R_i$$

for all $z \in X, i \in N_n$. Then (X, R) is said to be a *translation scheme with respect to the group* $(X, +)$.

We briefly examine the Hamming scheme H_q^n from this viewpoint. Let $H_1, \cdots, H_n$ be n Abelian groups of order q, and consider their direct product $X := H_1 \times \cdots \times H_n$. It is clear that H_q^n is a translation scheme with respect to *any* of these group structures.

This simple example shows that a given association scheme (X, R) may be a translation scheme with respect to several group structures. Further explanation of the phenomenon will be given in Section V-C.

For a translation scheme, the p-numbers and the q-numbers (Definition 3) can be determined as follows.

The homomorphisms of the group $(X, +)$ to the group $(\mathbb{C}^*, \cdot)$ are referred to as the (irreducible) *characters* of X. (Henceforth we often write X instead of $(X, +)$.) The set of characters of X has the structure of an Abelian group, isomorphic to X itself; this character group is called the *dual* of X and is denoted by X'. We shall use a bracket notation for characters, that is, $\langle x, x' \rangle := x'(x)$, for $x \in X$ and $x' \in X'$. The group characters satisfy the *orthogonality relations*

$$\sum_{x \in X} \langle x, x' \rangle = |X| \delta_{0, x'} \qquad \sum_{x' \in X'} \langle x, x' \rangle = |X| \delta_{0, x}.$$

It is possible to identify X' with X so as to have the symmetry property $\langle x, x' \rangle = \langle x', x \rangle$ for all $x \in X, x' \in X$.

From the n-class translation scheme (X, R) we define a partition $\Pi := \{X_0, X_1, \cdots, X_n\}$ of the group X into $n + 1$ blocks $X_i := \{x \in X: (x, 0) \in R_i\}$. This implies $X_0 = \{0\}$ and $X_{i^\sigma} = -X_i$ (for the pairing $i \mapsto i^\sigma$). The relation R_i can be recovered from the block X_i as follows:

$$R_i = \{(x, y) \in X^2: x - y \in X_i\}. \quad (101)$$

It can be shown that there exists a unique partition $\Pi' = \{X_0', X_1', \cdots, X_n'\}$ of the dual group X' into $n + 1$ blocks X_k', with $X_0' = \{0\}$ and with the following property. For $i, k \in N_n$, define $\phi_i: X' \to \mathbb{C}$ and $\psi_k: X \to \mathbb{C}$ by

$$\phi_i(x') := \sum_{x \in X_i} \langle x, x' \rangle \qquad \psi_k(x) := \sum_{x' \in X_k'} \langle x, x' \rangle. \quad (102)$$

Then ϕ_i is constant over each block X_k' and ψ_k is constant over each block X_i. More precisely

$$\phi_i(x') = \overline{p_i(k)} \text{ for } x' \in X_k', \qquad k, i \in N_n \quad (103)$$

$$\psi_k(x) = q_k(i) \text{ for } x \in X_i, \qquad i, k \in N_n \quad (104)$$

where the numbers $p_i(k)$ and $q_k(i)$ are the p-numbers and the q-numbers of (X, R).

The partition Π' (of X') will be called the *dual* of the partition Π (of X). From Π' we define a partition R' of X'^2 like in (101). More precisely, $R' := \{R_0', R_1', \cdots, R_n'\}$ with

$$R_k' := \{(x', y') \in X'^2: y' - x' \in X_k'\}.$$

It can be shown that (X', R') is a translation scheme with respect to the dual group $(X', +)$. From (102) it follows that *the p-numbers of (X', R') are the q-numbers of (X, R) and conversely.* Thus with an obvious notation, we have the duality relations $p_k'(i) = q_k(i)$ and $q_i'(k) = p_i(k)$, given in (25). In particular, $v_k' = m_k$ and $m_i' = v_i$.

In the context of the Krein duality (Section II-C), this leads us to introduce the following definition of duality for translation schemes. It is equivalent to a concept introduced by Tamaschke for commutative Schur rings [123].

Definition 11: Let (X, R) be a translation scheme, with respect to a given Abelian group $(X, +)$, and let $\Pi = \{X_i: i \in N_n\}$ be the corresponding partition of X. The translation scheme (X', R'), with respect to the dual group $(X', +)$ and corresponding to the dual partition $\Pi' = \{X_k': k \in N_n\}$ of X', is called the *dual* of the translation scheme (X, R).

An interesting treatment of duality in translation schemes is given by Godsil, in relation with the theory of *equitable partitions* [54].

As an example, consider once again the Hamming scheme (X, R), together with the Abelian group structure $X = H_1 \times \cdots \times H_n$. In this case, the block X_i in Π consists of the q-ary n-tuples of weight i (i.e., those having i nonzero components). Let us identify the dual group X' with X. It turns out that the dual partition Π' coincides with the weight partition Π. Thus for a suitable ordering, we have $X_i' = X_i$ for all $i \in N_n$, which shows that the Hamming scheme is *self-dual*. The formulas (103) and (104) lead to the expressions (17) of the p- and q-numbers in terms of the Krawtchouk polynomials.

Similarly, the composition scheme (Example 3 in Section II-A) is a self-dual translation scheme. There are other interesting families of that type [41], [43], [89]. Some examples of translation schemes that are *not* self-dual can be found in [30] and [37].

B. Additive Codes in a Translation Scheme

As a generalization of the classical notion of a *linear code* over a field alphabet (in Hamming scheme), we shall examine additive codes in a translation scheme.

Definition 12: A code Y in a translation scheme (X, R) is said to be *additive* if Y is a subgroup of the underlying Abelian group $(X, +)$.

Consider the inner distribution $(a_0, a_1, \cdots, a_n)$ of an additive code Y (see Definition 5). It follows from (101) that a_i counts the code points belonging to the block X_i in the partition Π, that is,

$$a_i = a_i(Y) = |Y \cap X_i|, \qquad \text{for } i \in N_n.$$

Next, we define the "annihilator code" of an additive code Y by generalizing the usual notion of the orthogonal code of a linear code in Hamming scheme. (The terminology is not standard, but "annihilator" seems preferable to "orthogonal," in the general setting.)

Definition 13: Let Y be an additive code in a translation scheme (X, R). The *annihilator code* of Y (with respect to the given group $(X, +)$) is the code Y° in the dual translation scheme (X', R') defined by

$$Y^\circ := \{x' \in X' : \langle x, x' \rangle = 1 \text{ for all } x \in Y\}.$$

It is clear that Y° is an additive code in (X', R'). Similarly, for an additive code V in (X', R'), we define its annihilator code to be

$$^\circ V := \{x \in X : \langle x, x' \rangle = 1 \text{ for all } x' \in V\}.$$

This is an additive code in (X, R). For double annihilators, we simply have

$$Y = {}^\circ(Y^\circ) \qquad V = ({}^\circ V)^\circ.$$

The character group Y' of Y is related to Y° by $Y' = X'/Y^\circ$ (the group of coset codes $x' + Y^\circ$ with $x' \in X'$). This

implies $|Y||Y^\circ| = |X|$. As a consequence of the orthogonality relations on group characters, we obtain

$$\sum_{x \in Y} \langle x, x' \rangle = \begin{cases} |Y|, & \text{if } x' \in Y^\circ \\ 0, & \text{if } x' \notin Y^\circ. \end{cases} \tag{105}$$

If Y is a linear code of length n over $\mathbb{F}_q$ (in the usual sense), then $Y^\circ = Y^\perp$, the orthogonal of Y. This stems from the fact that the characters of $(\mathbb{F}_q^n, +)$ are given by

$$\langle x, x' \rangle = \exp\left(\frac{2\pi i}{p} \operatorname{Tr}(x' x^T)\right)$$

for all $x, x' \in \mathbb{F}_q^n$. Here, Tr denotes the *trace* from the field $\mathbb{F}_q$ to its prime subfield $\mathbb{F}_p$. In the binary case, $q = p = 2$, this reduces to $\langle x, x' \rangle = (-1)^{x' x^T}$.

The next result is a generalization of the MacWilliams identities on the weight distributions of a linear code and its orthogonal. It produces a clear interpretation of Theorem 3 in the restricted framework of additive codes in translation schemes. The proof is based on (103)–(105).

Theorem 27 (Generalized MacWilliams Identities [37], [42]): The inner distribution $(a_k(Y^\circ) = |Y^\circ \cap X_k'|)_{k=0}^n$ of Y° is proportional to the Q-transform of the inner distribution $(a_i(Y) = |Y \cap X_i|)_{i=0}^n$ of Y. More precisely

$$a_k(Y^\circ) = |Y|^{-1} a_k'(Y) \qquad a_i(Y) = |Y^\circ|^{-1} a_i'(Y^\circ).$$

As a consequence, the fundamental parameters (see Section III-C) of a code Y in a translation scheme are related to those of its annihilator code Y° by $d(Y) = d'(Y^\circ)$, $d'(Y) = d(Y^\circ)$, $s(Y) = s'(Y^\circ)$, $s'(Y) = s(Y^\circ)$, $\gamma(Y) = \gamma'(Y^\circ)$, $\gamma'(Y) = \gamma(Y^\circ)$.

Finally, let us examine the outer distribution M of an additive code Y (see Definition 8). In view of (101), noting that $Y = -Y$, we obtain

$$M_i(x) = |(x + Y) \cap X_i|, \qquad \text{for } i \in N_n, x \in X.$$

This means that the x-row $M(x)$ of M is the distribution of the *coset code* $x + Y$ with respect to the partition Π.

For the outer distribution M' of the annihilator code Y°, we similarly have $M_k'(x') = |(-x' + Y^\circ) \cap X_k'|$, with $k \in N_n$ and $x' \in X'$. As an extension of Theorem 27 we obtain the following expression for the Q-transform of the outer distribution rows:

$$\sum_{k=0}^n M_k'(x') p_i(k) = |Y^\circ| \sum_{y \in Y \cap X_i} \langle y, x' \rangle. \tag{106}$$

By use of (106) we can derive a remarkable result (Theorem 28 below) that allows us to decide whether a given additive code Y carries a (translation) subscheme of (X, R), and to characterize the dual of this subscheme. Note that by Theorems 7 and 27 the rank of the outer distribution M' of Y° is equal to $s(Y) + 1$.

Definition 14: Let Y be an additive code of degree $s = s(Y)$ in a translation scheme (X, R). If the restriction $(Y, R|Y)$ is an association scheme (with s classes), then it is called a *subscheme* of (X, R).

Theorem 28 [37]: Given an additive code Y of degree s, the restriction $(Y, R|Y)$ is a subscheme of (X, R) if and only if the outer distribution M' of the annihilator code Y° has $s + 1$ distinct rows.

In this case, the dual scheme of the translation scheme $(Y, R|Y)$ is (Y', R^*) where $R^* = \{R_0^*, \cdots, R_s^*\}$ consists of the $s + 1$ relations on $Y' := X'/Y^\circ$ defined as follows: a pair of coset codes $(x_1' + Y^\circ, x_2' + Y^\circ)$ belongs to a given relation R_k^* if and only if the outer distribution row $M'(x_1' - x_2')$ is a fixed $(n + 1)$-tuple (among the $s + 1$ possibilities).

For example, Theorem 28 applies to the extended binary Golay code Y examined in Section IV-C. Recall that Y is self-orthogonal: $Y = Y^\perp = Y^\circ$. The code Y has degree $s = 4$, and the outer distribution $M' = M$ of its orthogonal Y° has five $(= s + 1)$ distinct rows. The 4-class association scheme carried by Y is mentioned at the end of Section IV-D. Since $(Y, R|Y)$ is Q-polynomial, its dual scheme (Y', R^*), carried by the factor group $Y' = X'/Y^\circ$, is P-polynomial. It is the "distance scheme" for the cosets of the extended binary Golay code (see [26, p. 361]).

The reader familiar with the Golay code may be interested in a more sophisticated example. Take Y to be the perfect binary Golay code of length 23 (and dimension 12). This code has degree $s = 7$. The orthogonal code $Y^\perp$ can be shown to be completely regular; its outer distribution M' has eight distinct rows $M'(x)$, corresponding to the eight values $\partial_H(x, Y^\perp) = 0, 1, \cdots, 6, 7$ (see [26, p. 362]).

C. $\mathbb{Z}_4$-Additive Binary Codes

Important research work has been devoted recently to the class of binary codes that are additive over $\mathbb{Z}_4$, the cyclic group of order 4 (see especially [57] and [92]). This subsection aims at showing how that subject fits into the framework of association scheme theory.

From a group-theoretic viewpoint, translation schemes can be presented as follows. Let $\mathrm{Aut}\,(X, R)$ denote the automorphism group of a given association scheme (X, R). Assume that $\mathrm{Aut}\,(X, R)$ contains an Abelian subgroup G which is *regular* on X, in the sense that G is transitive on X and has order $|X|$. This provides the point set X with the structure of an Abelian group $(X, +)$, isomorphic to G, through the definition

$$x_0^g + x_0^h := x_0^{gh}, \qquad \text{for all } g, h \in G$$

where x_0 is a fixed point in X. It is clear that (X, R) is a translation scheme with respect to $(X, +)$ (see Definition 10). In fact, the "translation structures" of (X, R) correspond exactly to the regular Abelian subgroups of $\mathrm{Aut}\,(X, R)$.

Consider the binary Hamming scheme H_2^n (see Example 2 in Section II-D). Its automorphism group is the monomial group (or hyperoctahedral group) M_n of degree n (and order $n!2^n$). As we shall see, M_n contains several regular Abelian subgroups.

For $n = 2$, the monomial group M_2 (of order 8), is the symmetry group of the square $\{1, -1\}^2$. It contains an element g of order 4 that cyclically permutes the four vertices

$(\pm 1, \pm 1)$, namely,

$$g := \begin{bmatrix} 0 & -1 \\ 1 & 0 \end{bmatrix}.$$

In effect, for $p_0 := (1, 1)$ we obtain

$$p_1 := p_0 g = (1, -1)$$
$$p_2 := p_1 g = (-1, -1)$$
$$p_3 := p_2 g = (-1, 1)$$
$$p_0 = p_3 g.$$

In terms of the usual binary alphabet $\{0, 1\}$, this induces the cyclic permutation (x_0, x_1, x_2, x_3) of the binary ordered pairs, with

$$x_0 := (0, 0) \qquad x_1 := (0, 1) \qquad x_2 := (1, 1) \qquad x_3 := (1, 0). \tag{107}$$

As a conclusion, M_2 contains *two* regular Abelian subgroups: not only the elementary Abelian group $\mathbb{Z}_2 \times \mathbb{Z}_2$ (consisting of the diagonal matrices), but also the cyclic group $\mathbb{Z}_4$ generated by g.

Note that the cyclic permutation in (107) corresponds to the *Gray map* between $\mathbb{Z}_2 \times \mathbb{Z}_2$ and $\mathbb{Z}_4$, that is, $(0, 0) \mapsto 0, (0, 1) \mapsto 1, (1, 1) \mapsto 2, (1, 0) \mapsto 3$. This map underlies the "concrete approach" to $\mathbb{Z}_4$-additive binary codes [57].

Let us now turn to the general case of H_2^n with $n \geq 2$. By considering partitions of the n coordinate positions in blocks of size 1 or 2, we obtain a whole class of regular Abelian subgroups of M_n of the form

$$G = \mathbb{Z}_2^k \times \mathbb{Z}_4^m, \qquad \text{with } k + 2m = n.$$

Each of the groups G (together with a corresponding co-ordinate partition) provides H_2^n with a translation scheme structure, and gives rise to a well-defined class of additive (binary) codes (see Definition 12).

Let Y be an additive code with respect to G, and let Y° be the annihilator code of Y (see Definition 13). In view of Theorem 27, the inner distributions of Y and Y° (which are their ordinary weight distributions) are related to each other by the MacWilliams identities in the *usual sense*.

The "homogeneous cases" are $G = \mathbb{Z}_2^n$, which yields the class of linear binary codes, and $G = \mathbb{Z}_4^{n/2}$ (for even n), which yields the class of $\mathbb{Z}_4$-*additive binary codes* [57]. In the latter case, the annihilator code Y° of Y is the natural orthogonal code $Y^\perp$ over the cyclic group $\mathbb{Z}_4$.

A very interesting example is provided by the *Kerdock codes* $\mathcal{K}$ and their $\mathbb{Z}_4$-orthogonals $\mathcal{K}^\perp$ which are the "Preparata codes" $\mathcal{P}$ (see [57]). Quotes are used here because $\mathcal{P}$ is not exactly the same as the official Preparata code, although they both have the same essential properties and, in particular, the same distance distribution. This example is quite remarkable for the following reason. It has been known for a long time that the weight distributions of the Kerdock and Preparata codes are the MacWilliams transform of each other, although these codes are *nonlinear* (over $\mathbb{F}_2$). The result in [57] alluded to above says that $\mathcal{K}$ is $\mathbb{Z}_4$-additive, and it identifies the $\mathbb{Z}_4$-orthogonal $\mathcal{K}^\perp$ of $\mathcal{K}$ as a certain "Preparata code" $\mathcal{P}$.

REFERENCES

[1] M. Aaltonen, "A new upper bound on nonbinary block codes," *Discr. Math.*, vol. 83, pp. 139–160, 1990.

[2] R. Askey and J. Wilson, "A set of orthogonal polynomials that generalize the Racah coefficients or $6 - j$ symbols," *SIAM J. Math. Anal.*, vol. 10, pp. 1008–1016, 1979.

[3] E. F. Assmus, Jr., and J. D. Key, *Designs and Their Codes.* Cambridge, U.K.: Cambridge Univ. Press, 1992.

[4] E. F. Assmus, Jr., and H. F. Mattson, Jr., "New 5-designs," *J. Combin. Theory*, vol. 6, pp. 122–151, 1969.

[5] ——, "Coding and combinatorics," *SIAM Rev.*, vol. 16, pp. 349–388, 1974.

[6] E. F. Assmus, Jr., and V. Pless, "On the covering radius of extremal self-dual codes," *IEEE Trans. Inform. Theory*, vol. IT-29, pp. 359–363, 1983.

[7] E. Bannai, "On tight designs," *Quart. J. Math. Oxford*, vol. 28, pp. 433–448, 1977.

[8] ——, "Tannaka–Krein duality for association schemes," *Linear Algebra Appl.*, vol. 46, pp. 83–90, 1982.

[9] ——, "Orthogonal polynomials in coding theory and algebraic combinatorics," in *Orthogonal Polynomials*, P. Nevai, Ed. Norwell, MA: Kluwer, 1990, pp. 25–53.

[10] E. Bannai and T. Ito, *Algebraic Combinatorics I. Association Schemes.* Menlo Park, CA: Benjamin/Cummings, 1984.

[11] ——, "Current research on algebraic combinatorics," *Graphs Combin.*, vol. 2, pp. 287–308, 1986.

[12] L. A. Bassalygo, "New upper bounds for error correcting codes," *Probl. Inform. Transm.*, vol. 1, no. 4, pp. 32–35, 1965.

[13] V. Belevitch, "Conference networks and Hadamard matrices," *Ann. Soc. Scient. Bruxelles*, vol. 82, pp. 13–32, 1968.

[14] M. R. Best and A. E. Brouwer, "The triply shortened binary Hamming code is optimal," *Discr. Math.*, vol. 17, pp. 235–245, 1977.

[15] T. Beth, D. Jungnickel, and H. Lenz, *Design Theory.* Manheim, Germany: Bibl. Institut-Wissenschaftsverlag, 1985.

[16] J. Bierbrauer, K. Gopalakrishnan, and D. R. Stinson, "Bounds for resilient functions and orthogonal arrays," in *Advances in Cryptology–CRYPTO'94, Lecture Notes in Computer Science No. 839*, Y. G. Desmedt, Ed. New York: Springer-Verlag, 1994, pp. 247–256.

[17] N. L. Biggs, "Perfect codes in graphs," *J. Combin. Theory Ser. B*, vol. 15, pp. 289–296, 1973.

[18] ——, *Algebraic Graph Theory.* Cambridge, U.K.: Cambridge Univ. Press, 1974.

[19] H. F. Blichfeldt, "The minimum value of quadratic forms and the closest packing of spheres," *Math. Ann.*, vol. 101, pp. 605–608, 1929.

[20] R. C. Bose, "Strongly regular graphs, partial geometries and partially balanced designs," *Pacific J. Math.*, vol. 13, pp. 389–419, 1963.

[21] R. C. Bose and D. M. Mesner, "On linear associative algebras corresponding to association schemes of partially balanced designs," *Ann. Math. Statist.*, vol. 30, pp. 21–38, 1959.

[22] R. C. Bose and K. R. Nair, "Partially balanced incomplete block designs," *Sankhyā*, vol. 4, pp. 337–372, 1939.

[23] R. C. Bose and T. Shimamoto, "Classification and analysis of partially balanced incomplete block designs with two associate classes," *J. Amer. Statist. Assoc.*, vol. 47, pp. 151–184, 1952.

[24] P. G. Boyvalenkov, D. P. Danev, and S. P. Bumova, "Upper bounds on the minimum distance of spherical codes," *IEEE Trans. Inform. Theory*, vol. 42, pp. 1576–1581, 1996.

[25] P. Boyvalenkov and D. Danev, "On linear programming bounds for codes in polynomial metric spaces," to be published in *Probl. Inform. Transm.*

[26] A. E. Brouwer, A. M. Cohen, and A. Neumaier, *Distance-Regular Graphs.* Berlin, Germany: Springer-Verlag, 1989.

[27] A. E. Brouwer and T. Verhoeff, "An updated table of minimum-distance bounds for binary linear codes," *IEEE Trans. Inform. Theory*, vol. 39, pp. 662–675, 1993.

[28] A. R. Calderbank and P. Delsarte, "Extending the t-design concept," *Trans. Amer. Math. Soc.*, vol. 338, pp. 941–952, 1993.

[29] A. R. Calderbank, P. Delsarte, and N. J. A. Sloane, "A strengthening of the Assmus–Mattson theorem," *IEEE Trans. Inform. Theory*, vol. 37, pp. 1261–1268, 1991.

[30] A. R. Calderbank and J.-M. Goethals, "On a pair of dual subschemes of the Hamming scheme $H_n(q)$," *Europ. J. Comb.*, vol. 6, pp. 133–147, 1985.

[31] A. R. Calderbank and N. J. A. Sloane, "Inequalities for covering codes," *IEEE Trans. Inform. Theory*, vol. 34, pp. 1276–1280, 1988.

[32] P. Camion, "Codes and association schemes," in *Handbook of Coding Theory*, V. S. Pless and W. C. Huffman, Eds. Amsterdam, The Netherlands: Elsevier, 1998.

[33] P. Camion, C. Carlet, P. Charpin, and N. Sendrier, "On correlation-immune functions," in *Advances in Cryptology–CRYPTO'91, Lecture Notes in Computer Science No. 676*, J. Feigenbaum, Ed. New York: Springer-Verlag, 1991, pp. 86-100.

[34] G. D. Cohen, M. G. Karpovsky, H. F. Mattson, Jr., and J. R. Schatz, "Covering radius—Survey and recent results," *IEEE Trans. Inform. Theory*, vol. IT-31, pp. 328–343, 1985.

[35] P. Delsarte, "Bounds for unrestricted codes, by linear programming," *Philips Res. Repts.*, vol. 27, pp. 272–289, 1972.

[36] ——, "Four fundamental parameters of a code and their combinatorial significance," *Inform. Contr.*, vol. 23, pp. 407–438, 1973.

[37] ——, "An algebraic approach to the association schemes of coding theory," *Philips Res. Repts. Suppl.*, vol. 10, 1973.

[38] ——, "Association schemes and t-designs in regular semilattices," *J. Combin. Theory Ser. A*, vol. 20, pp. 230–243, 1976.

[39] ——, "Pairs of vectors in the space of an association scheme," *Philips Res. Repts.*, vol. 32, pp. 373–411, 1977.

[40] ——, "Hahn polynomials, discrete harmonics, and t-designs," *SIAM J. Appl. Math.*, vol. 34, pp. 157–166, 1978.

[41] ——, "Bilinear forms over a finite field, with applications to coding theory," *J. Combin. Theory Ser. A*, vol. 25, pp. 226–241, 1978.

[42] ——, "Application and generalization of the MacWilliams transform in coding theory," in *Proc. 15th Symp. Information Theory in the Benelux* (Louvain-la-Neuve, Belgium, 1994), pp. 9–44.

[43] P. Delsarte and J.-M. Goethals, "Alternating bilinear forms over GF(q)," *J. Combin. Theory Ser. A*, vol. 19, pp. 26–50, 1975.

[44] P. Delsarte, J.-M. Goethals, and J. J. Seidel, "Bounds for systems of lines, and Jacobi polynomials," *Philips Res. Repts.*, vol. 30, pp. 91*–105*, 1975.

[45] ——, "Spherical codes and designs," *Geom. Dedicata*, vol. 6, pp. 363–388, 1977.

[46] C. F. Dunkl, "A Krawtchouk polynomial addition theorem and wreath products of symmetric groups," *Indiana Univ. Math. J.*, vol. 25, pp. 335–358, 1976.

[47] ——, "Discrete quadrature and bounds on t-design," *Mich. Math. J.*, vol. 26, pp. 81–102, 1979.

[48] ——, "Orthogonal functions on some permutation groups," in *Proc. Symp. Pure Math. 34* (Providence, RI: Amer. Math. Soc., 1979), pp. 129–147.

[49] A. Erdélyi, W. Magnus, F. Oberhettinger, and F. G. Tricomi, *Higher Transcendental Functions*, vol. 2. New York: McGraw-Hill, 1953.

[50] I. A. Faradžev, A. A. Ivanov, and M. H. Klin, "Galois correspondence between permutation groups and cellular rings (association schemes)," *Graphs Combin.*, vol. 6, pp. 303–332, 1990.

[51] G. Fazekas and V. I. Levenshtein, "On upper bounds for code distance and covering radius of designs in polynomial metric spaces," *J. Combin. Theory Ser. A*, vol. 70, pp. 267–288, 1995.

[52] E. M. Gabidulin, "Theory of codes with maximum rank distance," *Probl. Inform. Transm.*, vol. 21, no. 1, pp. 1–12, 1985.

[53] R. Gangolli, "Positive definite kernels on homogeneous spaces and certain stochastic processes related to Levy's Brownian motion of several parameters," *Ann. Inst. Henri Poincaré*, vol. 3, pp. 121–226, 1967.

[54] C. D. Godsil, *Algebraic Combinatorics.* New York: Chapman & Hall, 1993.

[55] J.-M. Goethals, "Association schemes," in *Algebraic Coding Theory and Applications, CISM Courses and Lectures No. 258*, G. Longo, Ed. New York: Springer-Verlag, 1979, pp. 243–283.

[56] J.-M. Goethals and J. J. Seidel, "Orthogonal matrices with zero diagonal," *Canad. J. Math.*, vol. 19, pp. 1001–1010, 1967.

[57] A. R. Hammons, Jr., P. V. Kumar, A. R. Calderbank, N. J. A. Sloane, and P. Solé, "The $\mathbf{Z}_4$-linearity of Kerdock, Preparata, Goethals, and related codes," *IEEE Trans. Inform. Theory*, vol. 40, pp. 301–319, 1994.

[58] D. G. Higman, "Intersection matrices for finite permutation groups," *J. Algebra*, vol. 6, pp. 22–42, 1967.

[59] ——, "Coherent configurations. Part I: Ordinary representation theory," *Geom. Dedicata*, vol. 4, pp. 1–32, 1975.

[60] S. G. Hoggar, "t-designs in projective spaces," *Europ. J. Combin.*, vol. 3, pp. 233–254, 1982.

[61] G. Hoheisel, "Über Charaktere," *Monatsch. Math. Phys.*, vol. 48, pp. 448–456, 1939.

[62] D. R. Hughes and F. C. Piper, *Design Theory*. Cambridge, U.K.: Cambridge Univ. Press, 1985.

[63] F. Jaeger, "On spin models, triply regular association schemes, and duality," *J. Algebraic Combin.*, vol. 4, pp. 103–144, 1995.

[64] H. Janwa, "Some new upper bounds on the covering radius of binary linear codes," *IEEE Trans. Inform. Theory*, vol. 35, pp. 110–122, 1989.

[65] G. A. Kabatyanskii and V. I. Levenshtein, "Bounds for packings on a sphere and in space," *Probl. Inform. Transm.*, vol. 14, no. 1, pp. 1–17, 1978.

[66] S. Karlin and J. L. McGregor, "The Hahn polynomials, formulas and an application," *Scripta Math.*, vol. 26, pp. 33–46, 1961.

[67] Y. Kawada, "Über den Dualitätssatz der Charaktere nichtcommutativer Gruppen," *Proc. Phys. Math. Soc. Japan (3)*, vol. 24, pp. 97–109, 1942.

[68] M. Krawtchouk, "Sur une généralisation des polynômes d'Hermite," *C. R. Acad. Sci. Paris*, vol. 189, pp. 620–622, 1929.

[69] T. Laihonen and S. Litsyn, "On upper bounds for minimum distance and covering radius of non-binary codes," *Des., Codes Cryptogr.*, vol. 14, pp. 71–80, 1998.

[70] H. W. Lenstra, Jr., "Two theorems on perfect codes," *Discr. Math.*, vol. 3, pp. 125–132, 1972.

[71] D. A. Leonard, "Orthogonal polynomials, duality, and association schemes," *SIAM J. Math. Anal.*, vol. 13, pp. 656–663, 1982.

[72] ——, "Metric, co-metric association schemes," in *Combinatorics, Graph Theory and Computing, Proc. 15th Southeast. Conf.* (Louisiana State Univ., Congr. Numerantium 44, 1984), pp. 277–282.

[73] V. I. Levenshtein, "On choosing polynomials to obtain bounds in packing problems," in *Proc. 7th All-Union Conf. Coding Theory and Information Transmission*, Part II (Moscow, Vilnius, 1978), pp. 103–108 (in Russian).

[74] ——, "On bounds for packings in n-dimensional Euclidean space," *Sov. Math.–Dokl.*, vol. 20, no. 2, pp. 417–421, 1979.

[75] ——, "Bounds on the maximal cardinality of a code with bounded modulus of the inner product," *Sov. Math.–Dokl.*, vol. 25, no. 2, pp. 526–531, 1982.

[76] ——, "Bounds for packings of metric spaces and some of their applications," *Probl. Cybern.*, vol. 40. Moscow, USSR: Nauka, 1983, pp. 43–110 (in Russian).

[77] ——, "Designs as maximum codes in polynomial metric spaces," *Acta Applic. Math.*, vol. 29, pp. 1–82, 1992.

[78] ——, "Krawtchouk polynomials and universal bounds for codes and designs in Hamming spaces," *IEEE Trans. Inform. Theory*, vol. 41, pp. 1303–1321, 1995.

[79] ——, "Split orthogonal arrays and maximum independent resilient systems of functions," *Des., Codes Cryptogr.*, vol. 12, pp. 131–160, 1997.

[80] ——, "Equivalence of Delsarte's bounds for codes and designs in symmetric association schemes, and some applications," *Discr. Math*, to be published.

[81] ——, "Universal bounds for codes and designs," in *Handbook of Coding Theory*, V. S. Pless and W. C. Huffman, Eds. Amsterdam, The Netherlands: Elsevier, 1998.

[82] J. H. van Lint, *Coding Theory*. Berlin, Germany: Springer-Verlag, 1982.

[83] S. Litsyn and A. Tietäväinen, "Upper bounds on the covering radius of a code with a given dual distance," *Europ. J. Combin.*, vol. 173, pp. 265–270, 1996.

[84] S. P. Lloyd, "Binary block coding," *Bell Syst. Tech. J.*, vol. 36, pp. 517–535, 1957.

[85] L. Lovász, "On the Shannon capacity of a graph," *IEEE Trans. Inform. Theory*, vol. IT-25, pp. 1–7, 1979.

[86] F. J. MacWilliams, "Combinatorial problems of elementary group theory," Ph.D. dissertation, Dept. Math., Harvard Univ., Cambridge, MA, 1962.

[87] ——, "A theorem on the distribution of weights in a systematic code," *Bell Syst. Tech. J.*, vol. 42, pp. 79–94, 1963.

[88] F. J. MacWilliams and N. J. A. Sloane, *The Theory of Error-Correcting Codes*. New York: North-Holland, 1977.

[89] W. J. Martin and D. R Stinson, "Association schemes for ordered orthogonal arrays and (T, M, S)-nets," preprint.

[90] R. J. McEliece, E. R. Rodemich, H. Rumsey, Jr., and L. R. Welch, "New upper bounds on the rate of a code via the Delsarte–MacWilliams inequalities," *IEEE Trans. Inform. Theory*, vol. IT-23, pp. 157–166, 1977.

[91] R. J. McEliece, E. R. Rodemich, and H. C. Rumsey, Jr., "The Lovász bound and some generalizations," *J. Comb., Inform. Syst. Sci.*, vol. 3, pp. 134–152, 1978.

[92] A. A. Nechaev, "The Kerdock code in a cyclic form" *Diskret. Math.*, vol. 1, no. 4, pp. 123–139, 1989 (in Russian). English translation in *Discr. Math. Appl.*, vol. 1, pp. 365–384, 1991.

[93] A. Neumaier, "Distances, graphs and designs," *Europ. J. Combin.*, vol. 1, pp. 163–174, 1980.

[94] ——, "Combinatorial configurations in terms of distances," Memorandum 81-09 (Wiskunde), Eindhoven Univ. Technol., Eindhoven, The Netherlands, 1980.

[95] ——, "Duality in coherent configurations," *Combinatorica*, vol. 9, pp. 59–67, 1989.

[96] A. M. Odlyzko and N. J. A. Sloane, "New bounds on the number of unit spheres that can touch a unit sphere in n dimensions," *J. Combin. Theory Ser. A*, vol. 26, pp. 210–214, 1979.

[97] R. A. Rankin, "The closest packing of spherical caps in n dimensions," *Proc. Glasgow Math. Assoc.*, vol. 2, pp. 139–144, 1955.

[98] C. R. Rao, "Factorial experiments derivable from combinatorial arrangements of arrays," *J. Roy. Statist. Soc.*, vol. 9, pp. 128–139, 1947.

[99] D. K. Ray-Chaudhuri and R. M. Wilson, "On t-designs," *Osaka J. Math.*, vol. 12, pp. 737–744, 1975.

[100] E. R. Rodemich, "An inequality in coding theory," presented at the Annu. Amer. Math. Soc. Meet., San Antonio, TX, Jan. 1980.

[101] C. Roos, "On metric and cometric association schemes," *Delft Progr. Rep.*, vol. 4, pp. 191–220, 1979.

[102] R. M. Roth, "Maximum-rank array codes and their application to crisscross error correction," *IEEE Trans. Inform. Theory*, vol. 37, pp. 328–336, 1991.

[103] I. Schoenberg and G. Szegö, "An extremum problem for polynomials," *Composito Math.*, vol. 14, pp. 260–268, 1960.

[104] A. A. Schrijver, "A comparison of the bounds of Delsarte and Lovász," *IEEE Trans. Inform. Theory*, vol. IT-25, pp. 425–429, 1979.

[105] J. J. Seidel, "Strongly regular graphs," in *Surveys in Combinatorics, London Math. Soc. Lecture Notes Series No. 38*, B. Bollobàs, Ed. Cambridge, U.K.: Cambridge Univ. Press, 1979, pp. 157–180.

[106] C. Shannon, "The zero error capacity of a noisy channel," *IRE Trans. Inform. Theory*, vol. 2, pp. 8–19, 1956.

[107] ——, "Probability of error for optimal codes in Gaussian channel," *Bell Syst. Tech. J.*, vol. 38, pp. 611–656, 1959.

[108] C. Shannon, R. G. Gallager, and E. R. Berlekamp, "Lower bounds to error probability for coding on discrete memoryless channels," *Inform. Contr.*, vol. 10, pp. 65–103 and 522–552, 1967.

[109] V. M. Sidelnikov, "On mutual correlation of sequences," *Sov. Math.–Dokl.*, vol. 12, no. 1, pp. 197–201, 1971.

[110] ——, "New bounds for densest packings of spheres in n-dimensional Euclidean space," *Math. USSR Sbornik*, vol. 24, pp. 147–157, 1974.

[111] ——, "Upper bounds on the number of points of a binary code with a specified code distance," *Probl. Inform. Transm.*, vol. 10, no. 2, pp. 124–131, 1974.

[112] ——, "Extremal polynomials used in bounds of code volume," *Probl. Inform. Transm.*, vol. 16, no. 3, pp. 174–186, 1980.

[113] T. Siegenthaler, "Correlation immunity of nonlinear combining function for cryptographic applications," *IEEE Trans. Inform. Theory*, vol. IT-30, pp. 776–780, 1984.

[114] L. J. Slater, *Generalized Hypergeometric Functions*. Cambridge, U.K.: Cambridge Univ. Press, 1966.

[115] N. J. A. Sloane, "An introduction to association schemes and coding theory," in *Theory and Application of Special Functions*, R. A. Askey, Ed. New York: Academic, 1975, pp. 225–260.

[116] ——, "Recent bounds for codes, sphere packings and related problems obtained by linear programming and other methods," *Contemp. Math.*, vol. 9, pp. 153–185, 1982.

[117] P. Solé, "A Lloyd theorem in weakly metric association schemes," *Europ. J. Combin.*, vol. 10, pp. 189–196, 1989.

[118] P. Solé and P. Stokes, "Covering radius, codimension, and dual distance width," *IEEE Trans. Inform. Theory*, vol. 39, pp. 1195–1203, 1993.

[119] D. Stanton, "Orthogonal polynomials and Chevalley groups," in *Special Functions: Group Theoretical Aspects and Applications*, R. A. Askey, Ed. Dordrecht, The Netherlands: Reidel, 1984, pp. 87–128.

[120] ——, "An introduction to group representations and orthogonal polynomials" in *Orthogonal Polynomials*, P. Nevai, Ed. Norwell, MA: Kluwer, 1990, pp. 419–433.

[121] G. Szegö, *Orthogonal Polynomials*. New York: Amer. Math. Soc., 1959.

[122] D. R. Stinson, "Combinatorial designs and cryptography" in *Surveys in Combinatorics, 1993*, K. Walter, Ed. Cambridge, U.K.: Cambridge Univ. Press, 1993, pp. 257–287.

[123] O. Tamaschke, "Zur Theorie der Permutationsgruppen mit regulärer Untergruppe I," *Math. Z.*, vol. 80, pp. 328–354, 1963.

[124] H. Tarnanen, "An approach to construct constant weight and Lee codes by using the method of association schemes," *Ann. Univ. Turku Ser. A I*, vol. 182, 1982.

[125] H. Tarnanen, M. J. Aaltonen, and J.-M. Goethals, "On the nonbinary Johnson scheme," *Europ. J. Combin.*, vol. 6, pp. 279–285, 1985.

[126] P. Terwilliger, "A characterization of P- and Q-polynomial association schemes," *J. Combin. Theory Ser. A*, vol. 45, pp. 8–26, 1987.

[127] A. A. Tietäväinen, "An upper bound on the covering radius as a function of the dual distance," *IEEE Trans. Inform. Theory*, vol. 36, pp. 1472–1474, 1990.

[128] D. Vere-Jones, "Finite bivariate distributions and semigroups of non-negative matrices," *Quart. J. Math. Oxford (2)*, vol. 22, pp. 247–270, 1971.

[129] N. Vilenkin, *Special Functions and the Theory of Group Representation*. Providence, RI: Amer. Math. Soc., 1968.

[130] H. Wang, "Two-point homogeneous spaces," *Ann. Math.*, vol. 55, pp. 177–191, 1952.

[131] L. R. Welch, R. J. McEliece, and H. Rumsey, Jr., "A low-rate improvement on the Elias bound," *IEEE Trans. Inform. Theory*, vol. IT-20, pp. 676–678, 1974.

[132] H. Wielandt, *Finite Permutation Groups*. New York: Academic, 1964.

[133] R. M. Wilson, "Inequalities for t-designs," *J. Comb. Theory Ser. A*, vol. 34, pp. 313–324, 1983.

[134] _____, "On the theory of t-designs," in *Enumeration and Designs*, D. M. Jackson and S. A. Vanstone, Eds. New York: Academic, 1984, pp. 19–49.

[135] V. A. Yudin, "Lower bounds for spherical designs," *Izvestiya: Matematika*, vol. 61, no. 3, pp. 673–683, 1997.

[136] J. Rifà and J. Pujol, "Translation-invariant propelinear codes," *IEEE Trans. Inform. Theory*, vol. 43, pp. 590–598, Mar. 1997.

The Method of Types

Imre Csiszár, *Fellow, IEEE*

(*Invited Paper*)

Abstract— The method of types is one of the key technical tools in Shannon Theory, and this tool is valuable also in other fields. In this paper, some key applications will be presented in sufficient detail enabling an interested nonspecialist to gain a working knowledge of the method, and a wide selection of further applications will be surveyed. These range from hypothesis testing and large deviations theory through error exponents for discrete memoryless channels and capacity of arbitrarily varying channels to multiuser problems. While the method of types is suitable primarily for discrete memoryless models, its extensions to certain models with memory will also be discussed.

Index Terms—Arbitrarily varying channels, choice of decoder, counting approach, error exponents, extended type concepts, hypothesis testing, large deviations, multiuser problems, universal coding.

I. INTRODUCTION

ONE of Shannon's key discoveries was that—for quite general source models—the negative logarithm of the probability of a typical long sequence divided by the number of symbols is close to the source entropy H; the total probability of all n-length sequences not having this property is arbitrarily small if n is large. Thus "it is possible for most purposes to treat long sequences as though there were just 2^{Hn} of them, each with a probability 2^{-Hn}" [75, p. 24]. Shannon demonstrated the power of this idea also in the context of channels. It should be noted that Shannon [75] used the term "typical sequence" in an intuitive rather than technical sense. Formal definitions of typicality, introduced later, need not concern us here.

At the first stage of development of information theory, the main theoretical issue was to find the best rates of source or channel block codes that, assuming a known probabilistic model, guarantee arbitrarily small probability of error (or tolerable average distortion) when the blocklength n is sufficiently large. For this purpose, covered by the previous quotation from Shannon [75], typical sequences served as a very efficient and intuitive tool, as demonstrated by the book of Wolfowitz [81].

The limitations of this tool became apparent when interest shifted towards the speed of convergence to zero of the error probability as $n \to \infty$. Major achievements of the 1960's were, in the context of discrete memoryless channels (DMC's),

Manuscript received December 16, 1997; revised April 20, 1998. This work was supported by the Hungarian National Foundation for Scientific Research under Grant T016386.

The author is with the Mathematical Institute of the Hungarian Academy of Sciences, H1364 Budapest, P.O. Box 127, Hungary.

Publisher Item Identifier S 0018-9448(98)05285-7.

the "random coding" upper bound and the "sphere packing" lower bound to the error probability of the best code of a given rate less than capacity (Fano [44], Gallager [46], Shannon, Gallager, and Berlekamp [74]). These bounds exponentially coincide for rates above a "critical rate" and provide the exact error exponent of a DMC for such rates. These results could not be obtained via typical sequences, and their first proofs used analytic techniques that gave little insight.

It turned out in the 1970's that a simple refinement of the typical sequence approach is effective—at least in the discrete memoryless context—also for error exponents, as well as for situations where the probabilistic model is partially unknown. The idea of this refinement, known as the method of types, is to partition the n-length sequences into classes according to type (empirical distribution). Then the error event of interest is partitioned into its intersections with the type classes, and the error probability is obtained by summing the probabilities of these intersections. The first key fact is that the number of type classes grows subexponentially with n. This implies that the error probability has the same exponential asymptotics as the largest one among the probabilities of the above intersections. The second key fact is that sequences of the same type are equiprobable under a memoryless probabilistic model. Hence to bound the probabilities of intersections as above it suffices to bound their cardinalities, which is often quite easy. This informal description assumes models involving one set of sequences (source coding or hypothesis testing); if two or more sets of sequences are involved (as in channel coding), joint types have to be considered.

In this paper, we will illustrate the working and the power of the method of types via a sample of examples that the author considers typical and both technically and historically interesting. The simple technical background, including convenient notation, will be introduced in Section II. The first key applications, viz. universally attainable exponential error bounds for hypothesis testing and channel block-coding, will be treated in Sections III and IV, complete with proofs. The universally attainable error exponent for source block-coding arises as a special case of the hypothesis testing result. A basic result of large deviations theory is also included in Section III. Section V is devoted to the arbitrarily varying channel (AVC) capacity problem. Here proofs could not be given in full, but the key steps are reproduced in detail showing how the results were actually obtained and how naturally the method of types suggested a good decoder. Other typical applications are reviewed in Section VI, including rate-distortion theory, source-channel error exponents, and

461

multiuser problems. Although the method of types is tailored to discrete memoryless models, there exist extensions of the type concept suitable for certain models with memory. These will be discussed in Section VII.

The selection of problems and results treated in this paper has been inevitably subjective. To survey all applications of the method of types would have required a paper the size of a book. In particular, several important applications in Combinatorics are not covered, in this respect the reader should consult the paper of Körner and Orlitsky in this issue.

While historical aspects were taken seriously, and a rather large list of references has been included, no attempts were made to give a detailed account of the history of the method of types. About its origins let us just make the following brief comments.

The ingredients have been around for a long time. In probability theory, they appear in the basic papers of Sanov [72] and Hoeffding [53] on large deviations, cf. Section III below. A similar counting approach had been used in statistical physics even earlier, dating back to Boltzmann [18]. A remarkable example is the paper of Schrödinger [73] that predates modern large deviations theory but remained unknown outside the physics community until recently. Information theorists have also used ideas now considered pertinent to the method of types. Fano's [44] approach to the DMC error exponent problem was based on "constant composition codes," and Berger's [13] extension of the rate-distortion theorem to sources with partially known and variable statistics relied upon his key lemma about covering a type class. Later, in the 1970's, several authors made substantial use of the concept now called joint type, including Blahut [16], Dobrushin and Stambler [40], and Goppa [48].

While the ideas of the method of types were already around in the 1970's, this author believes that his research group is fairly credited for developing them to a general method, indeed, to a basic tool of the information theory of discrete memoryless systems. The key coworkers were János Körner and Katalin Marton. A systematic development appears in the book of Csiszár and Körner [30]. Were that book written now, both authors would prefer to rely even more extensively on types, rather than typical sequences. Indeed, while "merging nearby types, i.e., the formalism of typical sequences has the advantage of shortening computations" [30, p. 38], that advantage is relatively minor in the discrete memoryless context. On the other hand, the less delicate "typical sequence" approach is more robust, it can be extended also to those models with memory or continuous alphabets for which the type idea apparently fails.

II. Technical Background

The technical background of the method of types is very simple. In the author's information theory classes, the lemmas below are part of the introductory material.

$\mathcal{X}, \mathcal{Y}, \cdots$ will denote finite sets, unless stated otherwise; the size of $\mathcal{X}$ is denoted by $|\mathcal{X}|$. The set of all probability distributions (PD's) on $\mathcal{X}$ is denoted by $\mathcal{P}(\mathcal{X})$. For PD's P and Q, $H(P)$ denotes entropy and $D(P\|Q)$ denotes information divergence, i.e.,

$$H(P) = - \sum_{a \in \mathcal{X}} P(a) \log P(a)$$

$$D(P\|Q) = \sum_{x \in \mathcal{X}} P(a) \log \frac{P(a)}{Q(a)}$$

with the standard conventions that $0 \log 0 = 0 \log 0/0 = 0$, $p \log (p/0) = \infty$ if $p > 0$. Here and in the sequel the base of log and of exp is arbitrary but the same; the usual choices are 2 or e.

The type of a sequence $\boldsymbol{x} = x_1 \cdots x_n \in \mathcal{X}^n$ and the joint type of $\boldsymbol{x}$ and $\boldsymbol{y} = y_1 \cdots y_n \in \mathcal{Y}^n$ are the PD's $P_{\boldsymbol{x}} \in \mathcal{P}(\mathcal{X})$ and $P_{\boldsymbol{xy}} \in \mathcal{P}(\mathcal{X} \times \mathcal{Y})$ defined by letting $P_{\boldsymbol{x}}(a)$ and $P_{\boldsymbol{xy}}(a, b)$ be the relative frequency of a among $x_1, \cdots, x_n$ and of (a, b) among $(x_1, y_1), \cdots, (x_n, y_n)$, respectively, for all $a \in \mathcal{X}$, $b \in \mathcal{Y}$. Joint types of several n-length sequences are defined similarly. The subset of $\mathcal{P}(\mathcal{X})$ consisting of the possible types of sequences $\boldsymbol{x} \in \mathcal{X}^n$ is denoted by $\mathcal{P}_n(\mathcal{X})$.

Lemma II.1:

$$|\mathcal{P}_n(\mathcal{X})| = \binom{n + |\mathcal{X}| - 1}{|\mathcal{X}| - 1}.$$

Proof: Elementary combinatorics.

The probability that n independent drawings from a PD $Q \in \mathcal{P}(\mathcal{X})$ give $\boldsymbol{x} \in \mathcal{X}^n$, is denoted by $Q^n(\boldsymbol{x})$. Similarly, the probability of receiving $\boldsymbol{y} \in \mathcal{Y}^n$ when $\boldsymbol{x} \in \mathcal{X}^n$ is sent over a DMC with matrix W, is denoted by $W^n(\boldsymbol{y}|\boldsymbol{x})$. Clearly, if $\boldsymbol{x} \in \mathcal{X}^n$ have type P and $(\boldsymbol{x}, \boldsymbol{y})$ have joint type $\tilde{P}$

$$Q^n(\boldsymbol{x}) = \prod_{a \in \mathcal{X}} Q(a)^{nP(a)}$$
$$= \exp\{-n[H(P) + D(P\|Q)]\} \qquad \text{(II.1)}$$
$$W^n(\boldsymbol{y}|\boldsymbol{x}) = \prod_{a \in \mathcal{X}, b \in \mathcal{Y}} W(b|a)^{n\tilde{P}(a, b)}$$
$$= \exp\{-n[H(\tilde{P}) - H(P) + D(\tilde{P}\|W)]\}. \qquad \text{(II.2)}$$

Here $D(\tilde{P}\|W)$ is defined for any $\tilde{P} \in \mathcal{P}(\mathcal{X} \times \mathcal{Y})$ by

$$D(\tilde{P}\|W) = D(\tilde{P}\|P \times W)$$
$$(P \times W)(a, b) = P(a)W(b|a) \qquad \text{(II.3)}$$

where P denotes the $\mathcal{X}$-marginal of $\tilde{P}$.

We will write $P \ll Q$, respectively $\tilde{P} \ll W$, to denote that P or $\tilde{P}$ is 0 for each $a \in \mathcal{X}$ or $(a, b) \in \mathcal{X} \times \mathcal{Y}$ with $Q(a) = 0$ or $W(b|a) = 0$ respectively. The divergences in (II.1) and (II.2) are finite iff $P \ll Q$, respectively, $\tilde{P} \ll W$.

For $P \in \mathcal{P}_n(\mathcal{X})$, the type class $\{\boldsymbol{x} \in \mathcal{X}^n, P_{\boldsymbol{x}} = P\}$ will be denoted by $\mathcal{T}_P^n$. Similarly, for $\tilde{P} \in \mathcal{P}_n (\mathcal{X} \times \mathcal{Y})$ we write $\mathcal{T}_{\tilde{P}}^n = \{(\boldsymbol{x}, \boldsymbol{y}): \boldsymbol{x} \in \mathcal{X}^n, \boldsymbol{y} \in \mathcal{Y}^n, P_{\boldsymbol{xy}} = \tilde{P}\}$.

Lemma II.2: For any type $P \in \mathcal{P}_n(\mathcal{X})$

$$|\mathcal{P}_n(\mathcal{X})|^{-1} \exp\{nH(P)\} \leq |\mathcal{T}_P^n| \leq \exp\{nH(P)\} \qquad \text{(II.4)}$$

and for any PD $Q \in \mathcal{P}(\mathcal{X})$

$$|\mathcal{P}_n(\mathcal{X})|^{-1} \exp\{-nD(P\|Q)\} \leq Q^n(\mathcal{T}_P^n)$$
$$\leq \exp\{-nD(P\|Q)\}. \qquad \text{(II.5)}$$

Proof: Equation (II.1) with $Q = P$ gives

$$P^n(T_P^n) = |T_P^n| \exp\{-nH(P)\}.$$

Hence (II.4) follows because

$$1 \geq P^n(T_P^n) = \max_{P' \in \mathcal{P}_n(\mathcal{X})} P^n(T_{P'}^n)$$
$$\geq |\mathcal{P}_n(\mathcal{X})|^{-1} \sum_{P' \in \mathcal{P}_n(\mathcal{X})} P^n(T_{P'}^n)$$
$$= |\mathcal{P}_n(\mathcal{X})|^{-1}$$

where the first equality can be checked by simple algebra. Clearly, (II.1) and (II.4) imply (II.5).

Remark: The bounds (II.4) and (II.5) could be sharpened via Stirling approximation to factorials, but that sharpening is seldom needed.

In the sequel, we will use the convenient notations $\lesssim$ and $\approx$ for inequality and equality up to a polynomial factor, i.e., $f(n) \lesssim g(n)$ means that $f(n) \leq p(n)g(n)$ for all n, where $p(n)$ is some polynomial of n, and $f(n) \approx g(n)$ means that both $f(n) \lesssim g(n)$ and $g(n) \lesssim f(n)$. When $f(n)$ and $g(n)$ depend not only on n but on other variables as well, it is understood that the polynomial $p(n)$ can be chosen independently of those. With this notation, by Lemmas II.1 and II.2, we can write

$$|T_P^n| \approx \exp\{nH(P)\}$$
$$Q^n(T_P^n) \approx \exp\{-nD(P\|Q)\}. \quad (II.6)$$

Random variables (RV's) with values in $\mathcal{X}$, $\mathcal{Y}$, etc., will be denoted by X, Y, $\cdots$ (often with indices). Distributions, respectively, joint distributions of RV's are denoted by P_X, P_{XY}, etc. It is often convenient to represent types, particularly joint types, as (joint) distributions of dummy RV's. For dummy RV's with $P_X = P \in \mathcal{P}_n(\mathcal{X})$ or $P_{XY} = \tilde{P} \in \mathcal{P}_n(\mathcal{X}\times)$, etc., we will write T_X^n, T_{XY}^n, etc., instead of T_P^n, $T_{\tilde{P}}^n$, etc. Also, we will use notations like $T_{Y|X}^n(\boldsymbol{x}) = \{\boldsymbol{y}: (\boldsymbol{x}, \boldsymbol{y}) \in T_{XY}^n\}$.

Lemma II.3: For X, Y representing a joint type, i.e., $P_{XY} \in \mathcal{P}_n(\mathcal{X} \times \mathcal{Y})$, and any $\boldsymbol{x} \in T_X^n$ and channel W

$$|T_{Y|X}^n(\boldsymbol{x})| \approx \exp\{nH(Y|X)\}$$
$$W^n(T_{Y|X}^n(\boldsymbol{x})|\boldsymbol{x}) \approx \exp\{-nD(P_{XY}\|W)\}. \quad (II.7)$$

Proof: As $|T_{Y|X}^n(\boldsymbol{x})|$ is constant for $\boldsymbol{x} \in T_X^n$, it equals $|T_{XY}^n|/|T_X^n|$. Thus the first assertion follows from (II.4), since $H(P_{XY}) - H(P_X) = H(Y|X)$. The second assertion follows from the first one and (II.2).

The representation of types by dummy RV's suggests the introduction of "information measures" for (nonrandom) sequences. Namely, for $\boldsymbol{x} \in \mathcal{X}^n$, $\boldsymbol{y} \in \mathcal{Y}^n$, we define the (nonprobabilistic or empirical) entropy $H(\boldsymbol{x})$, conditional entropy $H(\boldsymbol{y}|\boldsymbol{x})$, and mutual information $I(\boldsymbol{x} \wedge \boldsymbol{y})$ as $H(X)$, $H(Y|X)$, $I(X \wedge Y)$ for dummy RV's X, Y whose joint distribution P_{XY} equals the joint type $P_{\boldsymbol{xy}}$. Of course, nonprobabilistic conditional mutual information like $I(\boldsymbol{x} \wedge \boldsymbol{y}|\boldsymbol{z})$ is defined similarly. Notice that on account of (II.1), for any $\boldsymbol{x} \in \mathcal{X}^n$ the probability $Q^n(\boldsymbol{x})$ is maximum if $Q = P_{\boldsymbol{x}}$. Hence the nonprobabilistic entropy $H(\boldsymbol{x}) = H(P_{\boldsymbol{x}})$ is actually the maximum-likehood estimate of the entropy $H(Q)$ based upon the observed sequence $\boldsymbol{x}$.

III. SOURCE BLOCK CODING, HYPOTHESIS TESTING, LARGE DEVIATION THEORY

The working of the method of types is particularly simple in problems that involve only one set of sequences, such as source coding and hypothesis testing. Theorems III.1 and III.2 below establish the existence of source block codes and tests of (in general, composite) hypotheses, universally optimal in the sense of error exponents. Theorem III.1 appeared as a first illustration of the method of types in Csiszár and Körner [30, p. 37], cf. also Longo and Sgarro [63]. Formally, as pointed out below, it is a special case of Theorem III.2. The latter is effectively due to Hoeffding [53].

Theorem III.1: Given $0 < R < \log|\mathcal{X}|$, the sets $A_n = \{\boldsymbol{x}: H(\boldsymbol{x}) \leq R\} \subset \mathcal{X}^n$ satisfy

$$\frac{1}{n} \log|A_n| \to R \quad (III.1)$$

and for every PD $Q \in \mathcal{P}(\mathcal{X})$

$$\frac{1}{n} \log Q^n(A_n^c) \to -e_Q(R) \quad (III.2)$$

where

$$e_Q(R) = \min_{P: H(P) \geq R} D(P\|Q)$$
$$e_Q(R) > 0, \quad \text{if } H(Q) < R. \quad (III.3)$$

Moreover, for any sequence of sets $\tilde{A}_n \subset \mathcal{X}^n$ satisfying (III.1), we have for all $Q \in \mathcal{P}(\mathcal{X})$

$$\liminf_{n \to \infty} \frac{1}{n} \log Q^n(\tilde{A}_n^c) \geq -e_Q(R). \quad (III.4)$$

Interpretation: Encoding n-length sequences $\boldsymbol{x} \in \mathcal{X}^n$ by assigning distinct codewords to sequences of empirical entropy $\leq R$, this code is universally optimal among those of (asymptotic) rate R, for the class of memoryless sources: for any source distribution Q of entropy less than R, the error probability goes to 0 exponentially, with exponent that could not be improved even if the distribution Q were known.

For a set $\Pi \subset \mathcal{P}(\mathcal{X})$ of PD's, and $Q \in \mathcal{P}(\mathcal{X})$, write

$$D(\Pi\|Q) = \inf_{P \in \Pi} D(P\|Q). \quad (III.5)$$

Further, for $P \in \mathcal{P}(\mathcal{X})$ and $\alpha > 0$, denote by $B(P, \alpha)$ the "divergence ball with center P and radius α," and for $\Pi \subset \mathcal{P}(\mathcal{X})$ denote by $B(\Pi, \alpha)$ the "divergence α-neighborhood" of Π

$$B(P, \alpha) = \{P': D(P'\|P) < \alpha\}$$
$$B(\Pi, \alpha) = \bigcup_{P \in \Pi} B(P, \alpha). \quad (III.6)$$

463

Theorem III.2: Given any set $\Pi \subset \mathcal{P}(\mathcal{X})$ of PD's and $\alpha \geq 0$, let $A_n \subset \mathcal{X}^n$ be the set of those $\boldsymbol{x} \in \mathcal{X}^n$ whose type $P_{\boldsymbol{x}}$ is in the complement of $B(\Pi, \alpha)$ if $\alpha > 0$, respectively, in the complement of $B(\Pi, \alpha_n)$ if $\alpha = 0$ where $\alpha_n \to 0$, $\alpha_n n / \log n \to \infty$. Then

$$\sup_{P \in \Pi} P^n(A_n) \to 0, \quad \limsup_{n \to \infty} \frac{1}{n} \log \sup_{P \in \Pi} P^n(A_n) \leq -\alpha$$
$$\text{(III.7)}$$

and for every $Q \in \mathcal{P}(\mathcal{X})$

$$\lim_{n \to \infty} \frac{1}{n} \log Q^n(A_n^c) = \begin{cases} -D(B(\Pi, \alpha)\|Q), & \text{if } \alpha > 0 \\ -D(\overline{\Pi}\|Q), & \text{if } \alpha = 0 \end{cases}$$
$$\text{(III.8)}$$

where $\overline{\Pi}$ denotes the closure of Π.

Moreover, for arbitrary P and Q in $\mathcal{P}(\mathcal{X})$ and any sequence of sets $\tilde{A}_n \subset \mathcal{X}^n$

$$\limsup_{n \to \infty} \frac{1}{n} \log P^n(\tilde{A}_n) \leq -\alpha < 0$$

implies

$$\liminf_{n \to \infty} \frac{1}{n} \log Q^n(\tilde{A}_n^c) \geq -D(B(P, \alpha)\|Q) \qquad \text{(III.9)}$$

and

$$\limsup_{n \to \infty} P^n(\tilde{A}_n) \leq 1$$

implies

$$\liminf_{n \to \infty} \frac{1}{n} \log Q^n(\tilde{A}_n^c) \geq -D(P\|Q). \qquad \text{(III.10)}$$

Interpretation: For testing the null-hypothesis that the true distribution belongs to Π, with type 1 error probability required to decrease with a given exponential rate or just go to zero, a universally rate optimal test is the one with critical region A_n (i.e., the test rejects the null-hypothesis iff $\boldsymbol{x} \in A_n$). Indeed, by (III.9), (III.10), no tests meeting the type 1 error requirement (III.7), even if designed against a particular alternative Q, can have type 2 error probability decreasing with a better exponential rate than that in (III.8) (when $\alpha > 0$, this follows simply because

$$D(B(\Pi, \alpha)\|Q) = \inf_{P \in \Pi} D(B(P, \alpha)\|Q)$$

by (III.5) and (III.6); in the case $\alpha = 0$, one needs the observation that

$$\sup_{P \in \Pi} P^n(A) = \sup_{P \in \overline{\Pi}} P^n(A)$$

for every $A \subset \mathcal{X}^n$). In particular, for Q such that the exponent in (III.8) is 0, the type 2 error probability cannot exponentially decrease at all. The notion that the null-hypothesis is rejected whenever the type of the observed sample $\boldsymbol{x}$ is outside a "divergence neighborhood" of Π is intuitive enough. In addition, notice that by Lemma II.1 the rejection criterion $P_{\boldsymbol{x}} \notin B(\Pi, \alpha)$ is equivalent to

$$\frac{\sup_{P \in \Pi} P^n(\boldsymbol{x})}{\sup_{P \in \mathcal{P}(\mathcal{X})} P^n(\boldsymbol{x})} = \exp\left\{-n \inf_{P \in \Pi} D(P_{\boldsymbol{x}}\|P)\right\} \leq \exp(-n\alpha).$$

Hence the above universally rate optimal tests are what statisticians call likelihood ratio tests.

Remarks:

i) One sees from (III.9) that in the case $\alpha > 0$, the type 2 error probability exponent (III.8) could not be improved even if (III.7) were replaced by the weaker requirement that

$$\limsup_{n \to \infty} \frac{1}{n} \log P^n(A_n) \leq -\alpha, \qquad \text{for each } P \in \Pi.$$

ii) In the case $\alpha = 0$, the requirement (III.7) could be relaxed to

$$\limsup_{n \to \infty} P^n(A_n) < 1, \qquad \text{for each } P \in \Pi$$

provided that $D(\overline{\Pi}\|Q) = D(\Pi\|Q)$; the latter always holds if $P \ll Q$ for each $P \in \Pi$ but not necessarily otherwise.

A particular case of this result is known as Stein's lemma, cf. Chernoff [20]: if a simple null-hypothesis P is to be tested against a simple alternative Q, with an arbitrarily fixed upper bound on the type 1 error probability, the type 2 error probability can be made to decrease with exponential rate $D(P\|Q)$ but not better.

iii) Theorem III.2 contains Theorem III.1 as the special case $\Pi = \{P_0\}$, $\alpha = \log |\mathcal{X}| - R$, where P_0 is the uniform distribution on $\mathcal{X}$.

Proof of Theorem III.2: Suppose first that $\alpha > 0$. Then A_n is the union of type classes $\mathcal{T}_{P'}^n$ for types P' not belonging to $B(P, \alpha)$ whenever $P \in \Pi$. By the definition (III.6) of $B(P, \alpha)$, for such P' we have $D(P'\|P) \geq \alpha$ and hence, by Lemma II.2, $P^n(\mathcal{T}_{P'}^n) \leq \exp(-n\alpha)$ for each $P \in \Pi$. This gives by Lemma II.1

$$P^n(A_n) \lesssim \exp(-n\alpha), \qquad \text{for } P \in \Pi \qquad \text{(III.11)}$$

establishing (III.7) (the notation $\lesssim$ has been defined in Section II). Further, A_n^c is the union of type classes $\mathcal{T}_{P'}^n$ for types P' that belong to $B(\Pi, \alpha)$, thus satisfy $D(P'\|Q) \geq D(B(\Pi, \alpha)\|Q)$. Hence we get as above

$$Q^n(A_n^c) \lesssim \exp\{-nD(B(\Pi, \alpha)\|Q)\} \qquad \text{(III.12)}$$

and this gives

$$\limsup_{n \to \infty} \frac{1}{n} \log Q_n(A_n^c) \leq -D(B(\Pi, \alpha)\|Q). \qquad \text{(III.13)}$$

To complete the proof in the case $\alpha > 0$, it suffices to prove (III.9). Given any $0 < \alpha' < \alpha$, the assumption in (III.9) implies for n sufficiently large that

$$|\mathcal{T}_{P'}^n \cap \tilde{A}_n^c| \geq \tfrac{1}{2}|\mathcal{T}_{P'}^n|, \qquad \text{for all } P' \in B(P, \alpha') \cap \mathcal{P}_n(\mathcal{X}).$$
$$\text{(III.14)}$$

Indeed, else $|\mathcal{T}_{P'}^n \cap \tilde{A}_n| > \tfrac{1}{2}|\mathcal{T}_{P'}^n|$ would hold for some $P' \in B(P, \alpha') \cap \mathcal{P}_n(\mathcal{X})$. Since sequences in the same type class are equiprobable, the latter would imply by Lemma II.2 that

$$P^n(\tilde{A}_n) \geq P^n(\mathcal{T}_{P'}^n \cap \tilde{A}_n)$$
$$\geq \tfrac{1}{2}P^n(\mathcal{T}_{P'}^n) \approx \exp\{-nD(P'\|P)\} \gtrsim \exp(-n\alpha')$$

contradicting the assumption in (III.9).

Given any $\varepsilon > 0$, take $\alpha' < \alpha$ such that

$$D(B(P, \alpha')\|Q) \leq D(B(P, \alpha)\|Q) + \varepsilon$$

and take $P' \in B(P, \alpha') \cap \mathcal{P}_n(\mathcal{X})$ such that

$$D(P'\|Q) < D(B(P, \alpha')\|Q) + \varepsilon$$

(possible for large n). Then by (III.14) and (II.6)

$$
\begin{aligned}
Q^n(A_n^c) &\geq Q^n(\mathcal{T}_{P'}^n \cap A_n^c) \geq \tfrac{1}{2} Q^n(\mathcal{T}_{P'}^n) \\
&\approx \exp\{-nD(P'\|Q)\} \\
&\geq \exp\{-n(D(B(P, \alpha)\|Q) - 2\varepsilon)\}. \quad \text{(III.15)}
\end{aligned}
$$

As $\varepsilon > 0$ was arbitrary, (III.15) establishes (III.9).

In the remaining case $\alpha = 0$, (III.11) will hold with α replaced by α_n; using the assumption $\alpha_n n / \log n \to \infty$, this yields (III.7). Also (III.12) will hold with α replaced by α_n. It is easy to see that $\alpha_n \to 0$ implies

$$D(B(\Pi, \alpha_n)\|Q) \to D(\overline{\Pi}\|Q)$$

hence we get

$$\limsup_{n \to \infty} \frac{1}{n} \log Q^n(A_n^c) \leq -D(\overline{\Pi}\|Q). \quad \text{(III.16)}$$

To complete the proof, it suffices to prove (III.10). Now, $P^n(\tilde{A}_n) < 1 - \varepsilon$ implies, for large n, that

$$|\mathcal{T}_{P'}^n \cap \tilde{A}_n^c| \geq \frac{\varepsilon}{2} |\mathcal{T}_{P'}^n|, \quad \text{for some } P' \in B(P, \alpha_n) \cap \mathcal{P}_n(\mathcal{X}). \quad \text{(III.17)}$$

Indeed, else $|\mathcal{T}_{P'}^n \cap \tilde{A}_n| > (1 - (\varepsilon/2))|\mathcal{T}_{P'}^n|$ would hold for all $P' \in B(P, \alpha_n) \cap \mathcal{P}_n(\mathcal{X})$, implying

$$
\begin{aligned}
P^n(\tilde{A}_n) &\geq \sum_{P' \in B(P, \alpha_n) \cap \mathcal{P}_n(\mathcal{X})} P^n(\tilde{A}_n \cap \mathcal{T}_{P'}^n) \\
&\geq \left(1 - \frac{\varepsilon}{2}\right) P^n \left(\bigcup_{P' \in B(P, \alpha_n) \cap \mathcal{P}_n(\mathcal{X})} \mathcal{T}_{P'}^n \right).
\end{aligned}
$$

For large n, this contradicts $P^n(\tilde{A}_n) < 1 - \varepsilon$, since $\alpha_n n / \log n \to \infty$ implies by Lemmas II.1 and II.2 that the P^n-probability of the union of type classes with $P' \notin B(P, \alpha_n)$ goes to 0 as $n \to \infty$.

Pick $P'_n \in B(P, \alpha_n) \cap \mathcal{P}_n(\mathcal{X})$ satisfying (III.17), then

$$
\begin{aligned}
Q^n(A_n^c) &\geq Q^n(\mathcal{T}_{P'_n}^n \cap A_n^c) \geq \frac{\varepsilon}{2} Q^n(\mathcal{T}_{P'_n}^n) \\
&\approx \exp\{-nD(P'_n\|Q)\}. \quad \text{(III.18)}
\end{aligned}
$$

Here $D(P'_n\|P) < \alpha_n \to 0$ by assumption, and this implies $D(P'_n\|Q) \to D(P\|Q)$. Thus (III.18) gives (III.10).

Large Deviations, Gibbs' Conditioning Principle

Large deviation theory is concerned with "small probability events," typically of probability going to zero exponentially. An important example of such events is that the type of an independent and identically distributed (i.i.d.) random sequence $X^n = (X_1, \cdots, X_n)$ belongs to a given set $\Pi \subset \mathcal{P}(\mathcal{X})$ of PD's on $\mathcal{X}$ that does not contain the distribution Q of the RV's X_i. In this context, the type of X^n is called the empirical distribution $\tilde{P}_n$. Thus

$$\Pr\{\tilde{P}_n \in \Pi\} = Q^n(\{\boldsymbol{x}: P_{\boldsymbol{x}} \in \Pi\}). \quad \text{(III.19)}$$

Theorem III.3: For any $\Pi \subset \mathcal{P}(\mathcal{X})$

$$\limsup_{n \to \infty} \frac{1}{n} \log \Pr\{\tilde{P}_n \in \Pi\} \leq -D(\Pi\|Q) \quad \text{(III.20)}$$

and if Π has the property that

$$\lim_{n \to \infty} D(\Pi \cap \mathcal{P}_n(\mathcal{X})\|Q) = D(\Pi\|Q) \quad \text{(III.21)}$$

then

$$\lim_{n \to \infty} \frac{1}{n} \log \Pr\{\tilde{P}_n \in \Pi\} = -D(\Pi\|Q). \quad \text{(III.22)}$$

Corollary: If Π satisfies (III.21) and a unique $P^* \in \overline{\Pi}$ satisfies $D(P^*\|Q) = D(\Pi\|Q)$ then for any fixed k, the conditional joint distribution of $X_1, \cdots, X_k$ on the condition $\tilde{P}_n \in \Pi$ approaches P^{*k} as $n \to \infty$.

Remarks:

i) The condition (III.21) is trivially satisfied if Π is an open subset of $\mathcal{P}(\mathcal{X})$ or, more generally, if each $P \in \Pi$ with $P \ll Q$ is contained in the closure of the set of those $\tilde{P} \ll Q$ for which all $P' \ll \tilde{P}$ sufficiently close to $\tilde{P}$ belong to Π. In particular, (III.8) for $\alpha > 0$ is an instance of (III.22). Hoeffding [53] considered sets of PD's Π such that (III.21) holds with rate of convergence $O(\log n/n)$. For such Π, (III.22) can be sharpened to

$$\Pr\{\tilde{P}_n \in \Pi\} \approx \exp\{-nD(\Pi\|Q)\}. \quad \text{(III.23)}$$

ii) The empirical distribution $\tilde{P}_n$ can be defined also for RV's $X_1, \cdots, X_n$ taking values in an arbitrary (rather than finite) set $\mathcal{X}$, cf. Section VII, (VII.21). Theorem III.3 and its extensions to arbitrary $\mathcal{X}$ are referred to as Sanov's theorem, the first general result being that of Sanov [72], cf. also Dembo and Zeitouni [39].

iii) The Corollary is an instance of "Gibbs' conditioning principle," cf. [39].

Proof: By (III.19) we have

$$\Pr\{\tilde{P}_n \in \Pi\} = \sum_{P \in \Pi \cap \mathcal{P}_n(\mathcal{X})} Q^n(\mathcal{T}_P^n). \quad \text{(III.24)}$$

By Lemma II.2 and (III.5), this gives

$$
\begin{aligned}
|\mathcal{P}_n(\mathcal{X})|^{-1} &\exp\{-nD(\Pi \cap \mathcal{P}_n(\mathcal{X})\|Q)\} \\
&\leq \Pr\{\tilde{P}_n \in \Pi\} \\
&\leq |\mathcal{P}_n(\mathcal{X})| \exp\{-nD(\Pi \cap \mathcal{P}_n(\mathcal{X})\|Q)\} \quad \text{(III.25)}
\end{aligned}
$$

whence Theorem III.3 follows.

To prove the Corollary, notice first that for any type $P \in \mathcal{P}_n(\mathcal{X})$ the conditional probability of $X_1 = a_1, \cdots, X_k = a_k$ on the condition $\tilde{P}_n = P$ is the same as the probability of the following: given an urn containing n balls marked with symbols $a \in \mathcal{X}$, where the number of balls marked by a equals $nP(a)$, if k balls are drawn without replacement their consecutive marks will be $a_1, \cdots, a_k$. Clearly, this probability approaches that for drawing with replacement, uniformly in the sense that the difference is less than any fixed $\varepsilon > 0$ for $n \geq n_0$ sufficiently large depending on k and ε only. Thus

$$\left| \Pr\{X_1 = a_1, \cdots, X_k = a_k | \tilde{P}_n = P\} - \prod_{i=1}^{k} P(a_i) \right| < \varepsilon$$

if

$$n \geq n_0(k, \varepsilon). \qquad (\text{III}.26)$$

Let

$$U_\delta = \{P : |P(a) - P^*(a)| < \delta \quad \text{for each } a \in \mathcal{X}\} \qquad (\text{III}.27)$$

be a small neighborhood of P^*. As $\overline{\Pi} \cap U_\delta^c$ is closed there exists $P^{**} \in \overline{\Pi} \cap U_\delta^c$ with $D(P^{**} \| Q) = D(\overline{\Pi} \cap U_\delta^c \| Q)$, and by the assumed uniqueness of P^* this implies

$$D(\overline{\Pi} \cap U_\delta^c \| Q) = D(P^* \| Q) + \eta, \qquad \text{for some } \eta > 0. \qquad (\text{III}.28)$$

The Corollary follows since

$$\left| \Pr\{X_1 = a_1, \cdots, X_k = a_k | \tilde{P}_n \in \Pi\} - \prod_{i=1}^{k} P^*(a_i) \right|$$
$$\leq \sum_{P \in \Pi \cap \mathcal{P}_n} | \Pr\{X_1 = a_1, \cdots, X_k = a_k | \tilde{P}_n = P\}$$
$$- \prod_{i=1}^{k} P^*(a_i) | \Pr\{\tilde{P}_n = P | \tilde{P}_n \in \Pi\}$$

where for sufficiently large n the absolute value term is arbitrarily small if $P \in \Pi \cap U_\delta$ with δ small, by (III.26) and (III.27), while the conditional probability factor is less than $\exp(-n\eta/2)$ if $P \in \Pi \cap U_\delta^c$, by (III.28), Lemma II.2, and (III.22).

IV. Error Exponents for DMC's

A first major success of the method of types was to gain better insight into the error exponent problem for DMC's. Theorem IV.1, below, due to Csiszár, Körner, and Marton [32], shows that the "random coding" error exponent for constant composition codes is attainable universally, i.e., by the same encoder and decoder, for all DMC's for which it is positive. An important feature of the proof is that, rather than bounding the expectation of the error probability for an ensemble of codes (and conclude that some code in the ensemble meets the obtained bound), the error probability is bounded for a given codeword set and a given decoder. The role of "random coding" reduces to show the existence of a "good" codeword set. We will also reproduce the simple "method of types" proof of the "sphere packing" bound for constant composition codes (Theorem IV.2, cf. Csiszár and

Körner [30, p. 181]) establishing that the previous universally attainable error exponent is often (though not always) the best possible even for a known channel. This optimality holds among codes with a fixed codeword type, while the type yielding the best exponent depends on the actual channel.

Lemma IV.1: For any $R > 0$ and type $P \in \mathcal{P}_n(\mathcal{X})$, there exist $N \approx \exp(nR)$ sequences $\boldsymbol{x}_1, \cdots, \boldsymbol{x}_N$ in $\mathcal{T}_P^n$ such that for every joint type $P_{X\tilde{X}} \in \mathcal{P}_n(\mathcal{X} \times \mathcal{X})$ with $P_X = P_{\tilde{X}} = P$

$$|\{j : j \neq i, \quad (\boldsymbol{x}_i, \boldsymbol{x}_j) \in \mathcal{T}_{X\tilde{X}}^n\}| < \exp\{n(R - I(X \wedge \tilde{X}))\},$$
$$i = 1, \cdots, N \quad (\text{IV}.1)$$

(cf. Section II for notation).

Remark: Equation (IV.1) implies that $I(\boldsymbol{x}_i \wedge \boldsymbol{x}_j) \leq R$ for each $i \neq j$. In particular, $\boldsymbol{x}_1, \cdots, \boldsymbol{x}_N$ are distinct sequences if $R \leq H(P)$.

Proof: By a simple random coding argument. For completeness, the proof will be given in the Appendix.

Theorem IV.1: For any DMC $\{W : \mathcal{X} \to \mathcal{Y}\}$, a code with codeword set $\{\boldsymbol{x}_1, \cdots, \boldsymbol{x}_N\}$ as in Lemma IV.1 and decoder $\varphi : \mathcal{Y}^n \to \{0, 1, \cdots, N\}$ defined by

$$\varphi(\boldsymbol{y}) = \begin{cases} i, & \text{if } I(\boldsymbol{x}_i \wedge \boldsymbol{y}) > I(\boldsymbol{x}_j \wedge \boldsymbol{y}) \text{ for each } j \neq i \\ 0, & \text{if no such } i \text{ exists} \end{cases}$$
$$(\text{IV}.2)$$

has maximum probability of error satisfying

$$\max_{1 \leq i \leq N} e_i \lesssim \exp\{-nE_r(R, P, W)\} \qquad (\text{IV}.3)$$

where

$$e_i = W^n(\{\boldsymbol{y} : \varphi(\boldsymbol{y}) \neq i\} | \boldsymbol{x}_i) \qquad (\text{IV}.4)$$

and

$$E_r(R, P, W)$$
$$= \min_{\substack{P_{XY} \in \mathcal{P}(\mathcal{X} \times \mathcal{Y}) \\ P_X = P}} [D(P_{XY} \| W) + |I(X \wedge Y) - R|^+] \quad (\text{IV}.5)$$

is the "random coding" exponent for codeword type P.

Remarks:

i) Denote by $I(P, W)$ the mutual information $I(X \wedge Y)$ when $P_{XY} = P \times W$. Clearly, $E_r(R, P, W) > 0$ iff $R < I(P, W)$. Thus the channel-independent codes in Theorem IV.1 have exponentially decreasing error probability for every DMC with $I(P, W) > R$; it is well known that for channels with $I(P, W) < R$ no rate-R codes with codewords in $\mathcal{T}_P^n$ have small probability of error. The exponent $E_r(R, P, W)$ is best possible for many channels, namely, for those that satisfy $R_{cr}(P, W) \leq R < I(P, W)$, cf. Remark ii) to Theorem IV.2.

ii) It follows by a simple continuity argument that for any DMC

$$E_r(R, W) = \max_{P \in \mathcal{P}(\mathcal{X})} E_r(R, P, W)$$

466

is also an attainable error exponent with rate-R codes, though no longer channel-independent ones (as the maximizing P depends on W). This exponent is positive for every R less than the channel capacity $C(W) = \max_P I(P, W)$. It was first derived by Fano [44], and then in a simple way by Gallager [46], in algebraic forms different from that given above.

iii) The "empirical mutual information decoder" (IV.2) was first suggested by Goppa [48] as one not depending on the channel and still suitable to attain channel capacity. This decoder could be equivalently defined, perhaps more intuitively, by minimizing the "entropy distance" $H(\boldsymbol{x}_j|\boldsymbol{y})$ of the codewords from the received $\boldsymbol{y}$. Lemma IV.1 may be visualized as one asserting the existence of codes with good entropy distance distribution. As Blahut [16] observed, among sequences in a single type class the entropy distance satisfies the axioms of a metric, except that it may vanish for certain pairs of distinct sequences.

Proof of Theorem IV.1: As $W^n(\boldsymbol{y}|\boldsymbol{x}_i)$ is constant for $\boldsymbol{y} \in \mathcal{T}^n_{Y|X}(\boldsymbol{x}_i)$, we may write, using (II.7)

$$
\begin{aligned}
e_i &= \sum W^n(\mathcal{T}^n_{Y|X}(\boldsymbol{x}_i) \cap \{\boldsymbol{y}: \varphi(\boldsymbol{y}) \neq i\}|\boldsymbol{x}_i) \\
&\approx \sum \frac{|\mathcal{T}^n_{Y|X}(\boldsymbol{x}_i) \cap \{\boldsymbol{y}: \varphi(\boldsymbol{y}) \neq i\}|}{|\mathcal{T}^n_{Y|X}(\boldsymbol{x}_i)|} \\
&\quad \cdot \exp\{-nD(P_{XY}\|W)\}
\end{aligned}
\tag{IV.6}
$$

where the summation is for all joint types $P_{XY} \in \mathcal{P}_n(\mathcal{X} \times \mathcal{Y})$ with $P_X = P$.

This and other sums below will be bounded in the $\lesssim$ sense by the largest term, without explicitly saying so.

To bound the cardinality ratios in (IV.6), notice that by the definition (IV.2) of φ, $\varphi(\boldsymbol{y}) \neq i$ iff there exists $j \neq i$ such that the joint type of $(\boldsymbol{x}_i, \boldsymbol{x}_j, \boldsymbol{y})$ is represented by dummy RV's $X\tilde{X}Y$ with

$$
I(X \wedge Y) \leq I(\tilde{X} \wedge Y). \tag{IV.7}
$$

Thus, denoting by $\Pi_n(XY)$ the set of joint types

$$
P_{X\tilde{X}Y} \in \mathcal{P}_n(\mathcal{X} \times \mathcal{X} \times \mathcal{Y})
$$

with given P_{XY}, with $P_{\tilde{X}} = P$, and satisfying (IV.7),

$$
\begin{aligned}
&\mathcal{T}^n_{Y|X}(\boldsymbol{x}_i) \cap \{\boldsymbol{y}: \varphi(\boldsymbol{y}) \neq i\} \\
&= \bigcup_{P_{X\tilde{X}Y} \in \Pi_n(XY)} \bigcup_{j: j \neq i} \mathcal{T}^n_{Y|X\tilde{X}}(\boldsymbol{x}_i, \boldsymbol{x}_j).
\end{aligned}
\tag{IV.8}
$$

By Lemma II.3

$$
\begin{aligned}
\frac{|\mathcal{T}^n_{Y|X\tilde{X}}(\boldsymbol{x}_i, \boldsymbol{x}_j)|}{|\mathcal{T}^n_{Y|X}(\boldsymbol{x}_i)|} &\approx \frac{\exp\{nH(Y|X\tilde{X})\}}{\exp\{nH(Y|X)\}} \\
&= \exp\{-nI(\tilde{X} \wedge Y|X)\} \\
&= \exp\{-n[I(\tilde{X} \wedge XY) - I(X \wedge \tilde{X})]\} \\
&\leq \exp\{-n[I(\tilde{X} \wedge Y) - I(X \wedge \tilde{X})]\}.
\end{aligned}
\tag{IV.9}
$$

Since $\mathcal{T}^n_{Y|X\tilde{X}}(\boldsymbol{x}_i, \boldsymbol{x}_j) \neq \emptyset$ only when $(\boldsymbol{x}_i, \boldsymbol{x}_j) \in \mathcal{T}^n_{X\tilde{X}}$, (IV.1) and (IV.9) imply that

$$
\begin{aligned}
&\frac{\left|\bigcup_{j \neq i} \mathcal{T}^n_{Y|X\tilde{X}}(\boldsymbol{x}_i, \boldsymbol{x}_j)\right|}{|\mathcal{T}^n_{Y|X}(\boldsymbol{x}_i)|} \\
&\lesssim \sum_{\substack{P_{X\tilde{X}} \in \mathcal{P}_n(\mathcal{X} \times \mathcal{X}) \\ P_X = P_{\tilde{X}} = P}} |\{j: j \neq i, (\boldsymbol{x}_i, \boldsymbol{x}_j) \in \mathcal{T}^n_{X\tilde{X}}\}| \\
&\quad \cdot \exp\{-n[I(\tilde{X} \wedge Y) - I(X \wedge \tilde{X})]\} \\
&\lesssim \exp\{-n[I(\tilde{X} \wedge Y) - R]\}.
\end{aligned}
\tag{IV.10}
$$

This bound remains valid if $I(\tilde{X} \wedge Y) - R$ is replaced by $|I(\tilde{X} \wedge Y) - R|^+$, since the left-hand side is always ≤ 1. Hence (IV.8) gives

$$
\begin{aligned}
&\frac{|\mathcal{T}^n_{Y|X}(\boldsymbol{x}_i) \cap \{\boldsymbol{y}: \varphi(\boldsymbol{y}) \neq i\}|}{|\mathcal{T}^n_{Y|X}(\boldsymbol{x}_i)|} \\
&\lesssim \exp\left\{-n \min_{P_{X\tilde{X}Y} \in \Pi_n(XY)} |I(\tilde{X} \wedge Y) - R|^+\right\} \\
&\leq \exp\{-n|I(X \wedge Y) - R|^+\}
\end{aligned}
\tag{IV.11}
$$

where the last inequality holds by (IV.7). Substituting (IV.11) into (IV.6) gives (IV.3), completing the proof.

Theorem IV.2: Given arbitrary $R > 0$, $\delta > 0$, and DMC $\{W: \mathcal{X} \to \mathcal{Y}\}$, every code of sufficiently large blocklength n with $N \geq \exp\{n(R+\delta)\}$ codewords, each of the same type P, and with arbitrary decoder φ, has average probability of error

$$
\frac{1}{N} \sum_{i=1}^N e_i \geq \exp\{-n[E_{sp}(R, P, W) + \delta]\} \tag{IV.12}
$$

where

$$
E_{sp}(R, P, W) = \min_{\substack{P_{XY} \in \mathcal{P}(\mathcal{X} \times \mathcal{Y}) \\ P_X = P, I(X \wedge Y) \leq R}} D(P_{XY}\|W) \tag{IV.13}
$$

is the "sphere packing" exponent for codeword type P.

Remarks:

i) It follows from Theorem IV.2 that even if the codewords are not required to be of the same type, the lower bound (IV.12) to the average probability of error always holds with $E_{sp}(R, P, W)$ replaced by

$$
E_{sp}(R, W) = \max_P E_{sp}(R, P, W).
$$

The latter is equal to the exponent in the "sphere packing bound" first proved by Shannon, Gallager, and Berlekamp [74]. The first simple proof of the sphere packing bound was given by Haroutunian [52]. The author is indebted to Haroutunian for the information that he had been aware also of the proof reproduced below but published only his other proof because it was not restricted to the discrete case.

ii) Both $E_{sp}(R, P, W)$ and $E_r(R, P, W)$ are convex functions of R, positive in the same interval $[0, I(P, W))$; they are equal if $R \geq R_{cr}(P, W)$ where

467

$R_{cr}(P, W)$ is the abscissa of the leftmost point where the graph of $E_{sp}(R, P, W)$ as a functions of R meets its supporting line of slope -1. The same holds for $E_{sp}(R, W)$ and $E_r(R, W)$ which are (positive and) equal in an interval $[R_{cr}(W), C(W))$. For R in this interval, their common value is the exact error exponent for rate-R codes. For smaller rates, the exact error exponent is still unknown.

iii) Dueck and Körner [42] showed that for codes with codeword set $\{x_1, \cdots, x_N\} \subset \mathcal{T}_P^n$ and rate $(1/n) \log N > R + \delta$ with $R > I(P, W)$, the average probability of correct decoding goes to zero exponentially with exponent not smaller than the minimum of $D(P_{XY}\|W) + |R - I(X \wedge Y)|^+$ for $P_{XY} \in \mathcal{P}(\mathcal{X} \times \mathcal{Y})$ satisfying $P_X = P$. This result follows from (IV.16) by Lemma II.3. In [42] also its tightness was proved.

Proof of Theorem IV.2: Given a codeword set

$$\{x_1, \cdots, x_N\} \subset \mathcal{T}_P^n$$

and arbitrary decoder φ, write

$$D_i = \{y \colon \varphi(y) = i\}, \qquad i = 1, \cdots, N. \qquad \text{(IV.14)}$$

For every joint type $P_{XY} \in \mathcal{P}_n(\mathcal{X} \times \mathcal{Y})$ with $P_X = P$

$$\sum_{i=1}^N |\mathcal{T}_{Y|X}^n(x_i) \cap D_i| \leq \left| \bigcup_{i=1}^N \mathcal{T}_{Y|X}^n(x_i) \right| \leq |\mathcal{T}_Y^n|. \quad \text{(IV.15)}$$

Hence, supposing $N \geq \exp\{n(R + \delta)\}$, it follows by (II.6) and (II.7) that

$$\frac{1}{N} \sum_{i=1}^N \frac{|\mathcal{T}_{Y|X}^n(x_i) \cap D_i|}{|\mathcal{T}_{Y|X}^n(x_i)|} \lesssim \frac{1}{N} \frac{\exp\{nH(Y)\}}{\exp\{nH(Y|X)\}}$$
$$\leq \exp\{n(I(X \wedge Y) - R - \delta)\}. \tag{IV.16}$$

In particular, if $I(X \wedge Y) \leq R + \delta/2$ and $n \geq n(\delta)$ (sufficiently large), the left-hand side of (IV.16) is less than $1/2$, say, and hence

$$\frac{1}{N} \sum_{i=1}^N \frac{|\mathcal{T}_{Y|X}^n(x_i) \cap D_i^c|}{|\mathcal{T}_{Y|X}^n(x_i)|} \geq \frac{1}{2},$$
$$\text{if } I(X \wedge Y) \leq R + \frac{\delta}{2}, \ n \geq n_0(\delta). \quad \text{(IV.17)}$$

On account of (IV.4) and (IV.14), it follows from (IV.17) and Lemma II.3 that

$$\frac{1}{N} \sum_{i=1}^N e_i = \frac{1}{N} \sum_{i=1}^N W^n(D_i^c|x_i)$$
$$\geq \frac{1}{N} \sum_{i=1}^N W^n(\mathcal{T}_{Y|X}^n(x_i) \cap D_i^c|x_i)$$
$$= \frac{1}{N} \sum_{i=1}^N \frac{|\mathcal{T}_{Y|X}^n(x_i) \cap D_i^c|}{|\mathcal{T}_{Y|X}^n(x_i)|} W^n(\mathcal{T}_{Y|X}^n(x_i)|x_i)$$
$$\approx \exp\{-nD(P_{XY}\|W)\} \qquad \text{(IV.18)}$$

for joint types $P_{XY} \in \mathcal{P}_n(\mathcal{X} \times \mathcal{Y})$ with $I(X \wedge Y) \leq R + \delta/2$. A simple continuity argument shows that for sufficiently large n the minimum of $D(P_{XY}\|W)$ for these joint types is less than the minimum in (IV.13) plus δ, and this completes the proof.

Related Further Results

The proof technique of Theorem IV.1 has lead to various further results. Already in Csiszár, Körner, and Marton [32] a stronger result than Theorem IV.1 was proved, with an exponent better for "small rates" than $E_r(R, P, W)$. With the channel-dependent maximum-likelihood decoder, a similar derivation yields an even better exponent for small rates that, when optimized with respect to the codeword type, gives the exponent of Gallager's [46] "expurgated bound" (cf. [30, pp. 185, 193]). In [32] the problem of separately bounding the erasure and undetected error probabilities was also addressed; a decoder $\varphi \colon \mathcal{Y}^n \to \{0, 1, \cdots, N\}$ yields an erasure if $\varphi(y) = 0$, while an undetected error occurs if $\varphi(y)$ equals a message index $1 \leq i \leq N$ but not the correct one. Using a (still channel-independent) modification of the decoder (IV.2), jointly attainable exponents for erasure and undetected error probabilities were obtained (cf. [30, pp. 174–177]). Csiszár and Körner [28] derived exponential error bounds attainable with (a codeword set as in Lemma IV.1 and) decoders defined similarly to (IV.2) but with $\alpha(P_{xy})$ instead of $I(x \wedge y)$ for an arbitrary function α on $\mathcal{P}(\mathcal{X} \times \mathcal{Y})$, possibly channel-dependent. Recently Telatar and Gallager [77] used channel-dependent decoders of a somewhat more general kind to derive jointly attainable exponents for erasure and undetected error probabilities improving upon those in [32].

A particular class of α-decoders received considerable attention recently. They are the d-decoders defined by minimizing a "distance"

$$d(x, y) = \frac{1}{n} \sum_{i=1}^n d(x_i, y_i),$$
$$d(x, y) \text{ a given function on } \mathcal{X} \times \mathcal{Y} \quad \text{(IV.19)}$$

setting $\varphi(y) = i$ if $d(x_i, y) < d(x_j, y)$ for all $j \neq i$, and $\varphi(y) = 0$ if no such i exists. Here the term "distance" is used in the widest sense, no restriction on d is implied. In this context, even the capacity problem is open, in general. The d-capacity of a DMC is the supremum of rates of codes with a given d-decoder that yield arbitrarily small probability of error. In the special case when $d(x, y) = 0$ or 1 according as $W(y|x) > 0$ or $= 0$, d-capacity provides the "zero undetected error" capacity or "erasures-only" capacity. Shannon's zero-error capacity can also be regarded as a special case of d-capacity, and so can the graph-theoretic concept of Sperner capacity, cf. [35].

A lower bound to d-capacity follows as a special case of a result in [28]; this bound was obtained also by Hui [55]. Balakirsky [12] proved by delicate "type" arguments the tightness of that bound for channels with binary input alphabet. Csiszár and Narayan [35] showed that the mentioned bound is not tight in general but its positivity is necessary for positive d-capacity. Lapidoth [59] showed that d-capacity can equal the channel capacity $C(W)$ even if the above lower bound is strictly smaller. Other recent works addressing the problem of d-capacity or its special case of zero undetected error capacity include Merhav, Kaplan, Lapidoth, and Shamai [67], Ahlswede, Cai, and Zhang [9], as well as Telatar and Gallager [77].

V. Capacity of Arbitrarily Varying Channels

AVC's were introduced by Blackwell, Breiman, and Thomasian [15] to model communication situations where the channel statistics ("state") may vary in an unknown and arbitrary manner during the transmission of a codeword, perhaps caused by jamming. Formally, an AVC with (finite) input alphabet $\mathcal{X}$, output alphabet $\mathcal{Y}$, and set of possible states $\mathcal{S}$ is defined by the probabilities $W(y|x, s)$ of receiving $y \in \mathcal{Y}$ when $x \in \mathcal{X}$ is sent and $s \in \mathcal{S}$ is the state. The corresponding probabilities for n-length sequences are

$$W^n(\boldsymbol{y}|\boldsymbol{x}, \boldsymbol{s}) = \prod_{i=1}^{n} W(y_i|x_i, s_i). \qquad \text{(V.1)}$$

The capacity problem for AVC's has many variants according to sender's and receivers's knowledge about the states, the state selector's knowledge about the codeword, degree of randomization in encoding and decoding, etc. Here we concentrate on the situation when no information is available to the sender and receiver about the states, nor to the state selector about the codeword sent, and only *deterministic codes* are permissible.

For a code with codeword set $\{\boldsymbol{x}_1, \cdots, \boldsymbol{x}_N\}$ and decoder $\varphi \colon \mathcal{Y}^n \to \{0, 1, \cdots, N\}$, the maximum and average probability of error are defined as

$$e = \max_{\boldsymbol{s} \in \mathcal{S}^n} \max_{1 \leq i \leq N} e_i(\boldsymbol{s}) \qquad \overline{e} = \max_{\boldsymbol{s} \in \mathcal{S}^n} \frac{1}{N} \sum_{i=1}^{N} e_i(\boldsymbol{s}) \qquad \text{(V.2)}$$

where

$$e_i(\boldsymbol{s}) = W^n(\{\boldsymbol{y} \colon \varphi(\boldsymbol{y}) \neq i\}|\boldsymbol{x}_i, \boldsymbol{s}). \qquad \text{(V.3)}$$

The supremum of rates at which transmission with arbitrarily small maximum or average probability of error is possible, is called the m-capacity C_m or a-capacity C_a, respectively. Unlike for a DMC, $C_m < C_a$ is possible, and C_a may be zero when the "random coding capacity" C_r is positive. Here C_r is the supremum of rates for which ensembles of codes exists such that the expectation of $e_i(\boldsymbol{s})$ over the ensemble is arbitrarily small for $i = 1, \cdots, N$ and all $\boldsymbol{s} \in \mathcal{S}^n$. Already Blackwell, Breiman, and Thomasian [15] showed that

$$C_r = \max_{P_X \in \mathcal{P}(\mathcal{X})} \min_{P_S \in \mathcal{P}(\mathcal{S})} I(X \wedge Y)$$
$$\text{where } P_{XSY} = P_X \times P_S \times W \qquad \text{(V.4)}$$

and gave an example where $C_r > C_a = 0$.

Below we review the presently available best result about m-capacity (Theorem V.1; Csiszár and Körner [29]), and the single-letter characterization of a-capacity (Theorem V.2; Csiszár and Narayan [33]). Both follow the pattern of Theorem IV.1: for a "good" codeword set and "good" decoder, the

error probability is bounded via the method of types. A remarkable feature is that the very error-bounding process naturally suggests a good decoder.

Given an AVC defined by

$$\{W(y|x, s), x \in \mathcal{X}, s \in \mathcal{S}, y \in \mathcal{Y}\}$$

as above, for input symbols x and $\tilde{x}$ we write $x \sim \tilde{x}$ if there exists PD's Q and $\tilde{Q}$ on $\mathcal{S}$ such that

$$\sum_{s \in \mathcal{S}} W(y|x, s)Q(s) = \sum_{s \in \mathcal{S}} W(y|\tilde{x}, s)\tilde{Q}(s), \qquad \text{for all } y \in \mathcal{Y}. \qquad \text{(V.5)}$$

The AVC is symmetrizable if there exists a channel $U \colon \mathcal{X} \to \mathcal{S}$ such that

$$\sum_{s \in \mathcal{S}} W(y|x, s)U(s|\tilde{x}) = \sum_{s \in \mathcal{S}} W(y|\tilde{x}, s)U(s|x)$$
$$\text{for all } x, \tilde{x} \in \mathcal{X}, \ y \in \mathcal{Y}. \qquad \text{(V.6)}$$

It has long been known that $C_m = 0$ iff $x \sim \tilde{x}$ for all $x, \tilde{x}$ in $\mathcal{X}$ [57], and that the right-hand side of (V.9) below is always an upper bound to C_m [10]. Ericson [43] showed that symmetrizability implies $C_a = 0$.

Theorem V.1: For $P \in \mathcal{P}(\mathcal{X})$ write

$$C(P) = \min_{P_{XS} \in \mathcal{P}(\mathcal{X} \times \mathcal{S}), \, P_X = P} I(X \wedge Y)$$
$$\text{where } P_{XSY} = P_{XS} \times W \qquad \text{(V.7)}$$

and

$$D(P) = \min I(X \wedge \tilde{X})$$
$$\text{subject to } P_X = P_{\tilde{X}} = P, \Pr\{X \sim \tilde{X}\} = 1. \qquad \text{(V.8)}$$

Then $\min[C(P), D(P)]$ is an achievable rate for the maximum probability of error criterion, for each $P \in \mathcal{P}(\mathcal{X})$. Hence

$$C_m = \max_{P \in \mathcal{P}(\mathcal{X})} C(P) \qquad \text{(V.9)}$$

if the maximum is attained for some P with $C(P) \leq D(P)$.

Theorem V.2: For a nonsymmetrizable AVC, $C_a = C_r$.

Remarks: The first strong attack at a-capacity was that of Dobrushin and Stambler [40]. They were first to use large deviations arguments (including Chernoff bounding for dependent RV's) as well as "method of types" calculations to show that for randomly selected codes, the probability that $N^{-1} \sum_i e_i(\boldsymbol{s})$ is not small for a fixed $\boldsymbol{s} \in \mathcal{S}^n$ goes to zero doubly exponentially, implying the same also for $\overline{e}$. Unfortunately, as the method of types was not yet developed at that time, much effort had to be spent on technicalities. This diverted the authors' attention from what later turned out to be a key issue, viz., the choice of a good decoder, causing the results to fall short of a complete solution of the a-capacity problem. Not much later, Ahlswede [2] found a shortcut to that problem, proving by a clever trick that $C_a = C_r$ whenever $C_a > 0$; however, a single-letter necessary and sufficient condition for $C_a > 0$ remained elusive. Remarkably, the sufficiency of nonsymmetrizability for $C_a > 0$ does not seem

469

easier to prove than its sufficiency for $C_a = C_r$. The strongest result about m-capacity preceding [29] was that of Ahlswede [4] who proved (V.9) for AVC's such that $x \sim \tilde{x}$ never holds when $x \neq \tilde{x}$. He used large deviations arguments similar to those of Dobrushin and Stambler [40], and was first to use a sophisticated decoder (but not the one below). A full solution of the m-capacity problem appears a long way ahead; one of its special cases is Shannon's celebrated zero-error capacity problem.

Proof of Theorems V.1 and V.2: First one needs an analog of Lemma IV.1 about the existence of "good" codeword sets. This is the following

Lemma V.1: For any $\varepsilon > 0$, $R > \varepsilon$, and sufficiently large n, for each type $P \in \mathcal{P}_n(\mathcal{X})$ with $H(P) \geq R$ there exist $N \approx \exp(nR)$ sequences $\boldsymbol{x}_1, \cdots, \boldsymbol{x}_N$ in $\mathcal{T}_P^n$ such that for all joint types $P_{X\tilde{X}S} \in \mathcal{P}_n(\mathcal{X} \times \mathcal{X} \times \mathcal{Y})$ and all $\boldsymbol{s} \in \mathcal{S}^n$

$$|\{j: (\boldsymbol{x}_i, \boldsymbol{x}_j, \boldsymbol{s}) \in \mathcal{T}_{X\tilde{X}S}^n\}| \leq \exp\{n[|R - I(XS \wedge \tilde{X})|^+ + \varepsilon]\},$$
$$i = 1, \cdots, N \quad \text{(V.10)}$$

$$\frac{1}{N} |\{i: I(\boldsymbol{x}_i \wedge \boldsymbol{s}) > \varepsilon\}| \leq \exp(-n\varepsilon/2) \quad \text{(V.11)}$$

$$\frac{1}{N} |\{i: (\boldsymbol{x}_i, \boldsymbol{x}_j, \boldsymbol{s}) \in \mathcal{T}_{X\tilde{X}S}^n \text{ for some } j \neq i\}| \leq \exp(-n\varepsilon/2),$$
$$\text{if } I(X \wedge \tilde{X}S) > |R - I(\tilde{X} \wedge S)|^+ + \varepsilon \quad \text{(V.12)}$$

$$I(\boldsymbol{x}_i \wedge \boldsymbol{x}_j) \leq R, \quad \text{if } i \neq j. \quad \text{(V.13)}$$

This lemma can be proved by random selection, although more refined arguments are needed to get (V.10)–(V.12) than those in the proof of Lemma IV.1. One has to show that only with probability going to zero faster than exponentially will the randomly selected codewords violate (V.10)–(V.12), for any fixed $\boldsymbol{s} \in \mathcal{S}^n$, and i in (V.10). This can be done by Chernoff bounding. One difficulty is that in case of (V.12) dependent RV's have to be dealt with; this can be overcome using an idea of Dobrushin and Stambler [40]. For details, cf. [29] and [33].

We will use a codeword set as in Lemma V.1, with a decoder φ whose exact form will be suggested by the very error-bounding process.

Denote by $\Pi^m(\eta)$ and $\Pi^a(\eta)$ the family of those joint distributions $P_{XSY} \in \mathcal{P}(\mathcal{X} \times \mathcal{S} \times \mathcal{Y})$ that satisfy

$$D(P_{XSY} \| P_{XS} \times W) < \eta, \quad P_X = P \quad \text{(V.14)}$$

respectively,

$$D(P_{XSY} \| P_X \times P_S \times W) < \eta, \quad P_X = P. \quad \text{(V.15)}$$

Notice that $\Pi^a(\eta) \subset \Pi^m(\eta)$ since

$$D(P_{XSY} \| P_X \times P_S \times W)$$
$$= D(P_{XSY} \| P_{XS} \times W) + I(X \wedge S). \quad \text{(V.16)}$$

A codeword $\boldsymbol{x}_i$ and a received sequence $\boldsymbol{y}$ may be considered "jointly typical" if there exists $\boldsymbol{s} \in \mathcal{S}^n$ such that the joint type of $(\boldsymbol{x}_i, \boldsymbol{s}, \boldsymbol{y})$ belongs to $\Pi^m(\eta)$ or $\Pi^a(\eta)$. The contribution to the maximum or average probability of error of output sequences $\boldsymbol{y}$ not jointly typical in this sense with the

codeword sent is negligible. Indeed, we have by Lemmas II.1 and II.3, writing $\mathcal{P}_n$ as a shorthand for $\mathcal{P}_n(\mathcal{X} \times \mathcal{S} \times \mathcal{Y})$

$$W^n \left(\bigcup_{P_{XSY} \in \mathcal{P}_n \setminus \Pi^m(\eta)} \mathcal{T}_{Y|XS}^n(\boldsymbol{x}_i, \boldsymbol{s}) | \boldsymbol{x}_i, \boldsymbol{s} \right) \lesssim \exp(-n\eta) \quad \text{(V.17)}$$

and—using also (V.16) and (V.11)—

$$\frac{1}{N} \sum_{i=1}^N W^n \left(\bigcup_{P_{XSY} \in \mathcal{P}_n \setminus \Pi^a(\eta)} \mathcal{T}_{Y|XS}^n(\boldsymbol{x}_i, \boldsymbol{s}) | \boldsymbol{x}_i, \boldsymbol{s} \right)$$
$$\leq \frac{1}{N} |\{i: I(\boldsymbol{x}_i \wedge \boldsymbol{s}) > \varepsilon\}| + \frac{1}{N} \sum_{i: I(\boldsymbol{x}_i \wedge \boldsymbol{s}) \leq \varepsilon}$$
$$\cdot W^n \left(\bigcup_{P_{XSY} \in \mathcal{P}_n \setminus \Pi^m(\eta-\varepsilon)} \mathcal{T}_{Y|XS}^n(\boldsymbol{x}_i, \boldsymbol{s}) | \boldsymbol{x}_i, \boldsymbol{s} \right)$$
$$\lesssim \exp(-n\varepsilon/2) + \exp(-n(\eta - \varepsilon)). \quad \text{(V.18)}$$

Motivated by (V.17) and (V.18) we will consider

$$L(\boldsymbol{y}) = \{i: P_{\boldsymbol{x}_i \boldsymbol{s} \boldsymbol{y}} \in \Pi \text{ for some } \boldsymbol{s} \in \mathcal{S}^n\} \quad \text{(V.19)}$$

as the list of candidates for the decoder output $\varphi(\boldsymbol{y})$, where Π denotes $\Pi^m(\eta)$ or $\Pi^a(\eta)$ according as the maximum or average probability of error criterion is being considered.

Dobrushin and Stambler [40] used, effectively, a decoder whose output was i if i was the only candidate in the above sense (with $\Pi = \Pi^a(\eta)$), while otherwise an error was declared. This "joint typicality decoder" has been shown suitable to achieve the a-capacity C_a for some but not all AVC's. To obtain a more powerful decoder, when the list (V.19) contains several messages one may reject some of them by a suitable rule. If only one $i \in L(\boldsymbol{y})$ remains unrejected, that will be the decoder output. We will consider rejection rules corresponding to sets $\Psi \subset \mathcal{P}(\mathcal{X} \times \mathcal{X} \times \mathcal{S} \times \mathcal{Y})$ of joint distributions $P_{X\tilde{X}SY}$ as follows: a candidate $i \in L(\boldsymbol{y})$ is rejected if for every $\boldsymbol{s} \in \mathcal{S}^n$ with $P_{\boldsymbol{x}_i \boldsymbol{s} \boldsymbol{y}} \in \Pi$ there exists $j \neq i$ in $L(\boldsymbol{y})$ such that the joint type of $(\boldsymbol{x}_i, \boldsymbol{x}_j, \boldsymbol{s}, \boldsymbol{y})$ belongs to Ψ. To reflect that $P_{\boldsymbol{x}_i \boldsymbol{s} \boldsymbol{y}} \in \Pi$ and that $P_{\boldsymbol{x}_j \tilde{\boldsymbol{s}} \boldsymbol{y}} \in \Pi$ for some $\tilde{\boldsymbol{s}} \in \mathcal{S}^n$ (as $j \in L(\boldsymbol{y})$), we assume that Ψ consists of such joint distributions $P_{X\tilde{X}SY}$ whose marginals P_{XSY} and $P_{\tilde{X}Y}$ satisfy

$$P_{XSY} \in \Pi$$
$$P_{\tilde{X}Y} \text{ is the marginal of some } P_{\tilde{X}\tilde{S}Y} \in \Pi. \quad \text{(V.20)}$$

A set Ψ of joint distributions with the properties (V.20) will be called permissible if for each $\boldsymbol{y} \in \mathcal{Y}^n$, the rejection rule corresponding to Ψ leaves at most one $i \in L(\boldsymbol{y})$ unrejected. Then $\varphi(\boldsymbol{y})$ is set equal to the unrejected $i \in L(\boldsymbol{y})$, at 0 if no such i exists. For such a decoder φ, preliminarily with an unspecified $\Psi \subset \mathcal{P}(\mathcal{X} \times \mathcal{X} \times \mathcal{S} \times \mathcal{Y})$, the maximum or average probability of error can be bounded via standard "method of types" technique. The result will suggest a natural choice of Ψ that makes the bound exponentially small under the hypotheses of Theorems V.1 and V.2. The calculation is technical but instructive; it will be given in the Appendix.

Further Developments

By the above approach, Csiszár, and Narayan [33] also determined the a-capacity $C_a(\Lambda)$ for AVC's with state constraint Λ. The latter means that only those $\boldsymbol{s} \in \mathcal{S}^n$ are permissible state sequences that satisfy $n^{-1} \sum_i \ell(s_i) \leq \Lambda$ for a given cost function ℓ on $\mathcal{S}$. For this case, Ahlswede's [2] trick does not work and, indeed, $0 < C_a(\Lambda) < C_r(\Lambda)$ may happen. Specializing the result to the (noiseless) binary adder AVC ($\mathcal{X} = \mathcal{S} = \mathcal{Y} = \{0, 1\}$, $W(y|x, s) = 1$ if $y = x + s \bmod 2$) with $\ell(s) = s$, the intuitive but nontrivial result was obtained that for $\Lambda < 1/2$, the a-capacity $C_a(\Lambda)$ equals the capacity of the binary symmetric DMC with crossover probability Λ. Notice that the corresponding m-capacity is the maximum rate of codes admitting correction of each pattern of no more than Λn bit errors, whose determination is a central open problem of coding theory. The role of the decoding rule was further studied, and a-capacity for some simple cases was explicitly calculated in Csiszár and Narayan [34].

While symmetrizable AVC's have $C_a = 0$, if the decoder output is not required to be a single message index i but a list of k candidates $i_1, \cdots, i_k$, the resulting "list code capacity" may be nonzero already for $k = 2$. Pinsker conjectured in 1990 that the "list-size-k" a-capacity is always equal to C_r if k is sufficiently large. Contributions to this problem, establishing Pinsker's conjecture, include Ahlswede and Cai [7], Blinovsky, Narayan, and Pinsker [17], and Hughes [54]. The last paper follows and extends the approach in this section. For AVC's with $C_r > 0$, a number M called the symmetrizability is determined, and the list-size-k a-capacity is shown to be 0 for $k \leq M$ and equal to C_r for $k > M$. A partial analog of this result for list-size-k m-capacity is that the limit of the latter as $k \to \infty$ is always given by (V.9), cf. Ahlswede [6].

The approach in this section was extended to multiple-access AVC's by Gubner [50], although the full analog of Theorem V.2 was only conjectured by him. This conjecture was recently proved by Ahlswede and Cai [8]. Previously, Jahn [56] determined the a-capacity region of a multiple-access AVC under the condition that it had nonvoid interior, and showed that then the a-capacity region coincided with the random coding capacity region.

VI. OTHER TYPICAL APPLICATIONS

A. Rate-Distortion Theory

The usefulness for rate-distortion theory of partitioning n-length sequences into type classes was first demonstrated by Berger [13]. He established the following lemma, called the type covering lemma in [30].

Lemma VI.1: Given finite sets $\mathcal{X}$, $\mathcal{Y}$ and a nonnegative function $d(x, y)$ on $\mathcal{X} \times \mathcal{Y}$, for $P \in \mathcal{P}_n(\mathcal{X})$ and $D \geq 0$ let $N_n(P, D)$ denote the minimum number of "d-balls of radius D"

$$B(\boldsymbol{y}, D) = \{\boldsymbol{x}: d(\boldsymbol{x}, \boldsymbol{y}) \leq D\} \qquad \text{(VI.1)}$$

needed to cover the type class $\mathcal{T}_P^n \subset \mathcal{X}^n$, where $d(\boldsymbol{x}, \boldsymbol{y})$ is defined by (IV.19). Then

$$\max_{P \in \mathcal{P}_n(\mathcal{X})} \left| \frac{1}{n} \log N_n(P, D) - R(P, D) \right| \to 0, \qquad \text{as } n \to \infty \qquad \text{(VI.2)}$$

where

$$R(P, D) = \min I(X \wedge Y)$$
$$\text{subject to } P_X = P \quad Ed(X, Y) \leq D \qquad \text{(VI.3)}$$

is the "rate-distortion function."

This lemma is seen today as a consequence of a simple general result about coverings known as the Johnson–Stein–Lovász theorem, cf. Cohen *et al.* [21, p. 322]. The latter is useful in information theory also in other contexts, cf. Ahlswede [3].

An immediate consequence of Lemma VI.1 is that the minimum (asymptotic) rate of source block codes admitting the reproduction of each $\boldsymbol{x} \in \mathcal{X}^n$ by some $\boldsymbol{y} \in \mathcal{Y}^n$ with distortion $d(\boldsymbol{x}, \boldsymbol{y}) \leq D$, is equal to $\max_{P \in \mathcal{P}(\mathcal{X})} R(P, D)$. Berger [13] also used this lemma to derive the rate-distortion theorem for arbitrarily varying sources.

As another application of Lemma VI.1, Marton [64] determined the error exponent for the compression of memoryless sources with a fidelity criterion. In fact, her error exponent is attainable universally (with codes depending on the "distortion measure" d but not on the source distribution Q or the distortion threshold D). Thus the following extension of Theorem III.1 holds, cf. [30, p. 156]: Given

$$0 < R < \max_{P \in \mathcal{P}(\mathcal{X})} R(P, D)$$

there exist codeword sets $C_n \subset \mathcal{Y}^n$ such that

$$\frac{1}{n} \log |C_n| \to R \qquad \text{(VI.4)}$$

and for every PD $Q \in \mathcal{P}(\mathcal{X})$ and every $D \geq 0$

$$\frac{1}{n} \log Q^n \left(\left(\bigcup_{\boldsymbol{y} \in C_n} B(\boldsymbol{y}, D) \right)^c \right) \to -F(R, Q, D) \qquad \text{(VI.5)}$$

where

$$F(R, Q, D) = \inf_{P: \, R(P, D) > R} D(P \| Q). \qquad \text{(VI.6)}$$

Moreover, for any sequence of sets $C_n \subset \mathcal{Y}^n$ satisfying (VI.4) the liminf of the left-hand side of (VI.5) is $\geq -F(R, Q, D)$. Remarkably, the exponent (VI.6) is not necessarily a continuous function of R, cf. Ahlswede [5], although as Marton [64] showed, it is continuous when $d(\boldsymbol{x}, \boldsymbol{y})$ is the normalized Hamming distance (cf. also [30, p. 158]).

Recently, several papers have been devoted to the redundancy problem in rate-distortion theory, such as Yu and Speed [82], Linder, Lugosi, and Zeger [61], Merhav [65], Zhang, Yang, and Wei [83]. One version of the problem concerns the "rate redundancy" of D-semifaithful codes. A D-semifaithful code is defined by a mapping $f: \mathcal{X}^n \to \mathcal{Y}^n$ such that $d(\boldsymbol{x}, f(\boldsymbol{x})) \leq D$ for all $\boldsymbol{x} \in \mathcal{X}^n$, together with an assignment to each $\boldsymbol{y}$ in the range of f of a binary codeword of length

$\ell(\boldsymbol{y})$, subject to prefix condition. Yu and Speed [82] showed that for a memoryless source with generic distribution Q there exist D-semifaithful codes whose rate redundancy

$$\frac{1}{n} \sum_{\boldsymbol{x} \in \mathcal{X}^n} Q^n(\boldsymbol{x}) \ell(f(\boldsymbol{x})) - R(Q, D) \qquad \text{(VI.7)}$$

is less than a constant times $\log n / n$, moreover, such codes may be given universally (not depending on Q). They also conjectured that the rate redundancy (VI.7) can never be less than a constant times $\log n / n$, under a technical condition that excludes the case $D = 0$. Zhang, Yang, and Wei [83] proved that conjecture, and also determined the exact asymptotics of the "distortion redundancy" of the best rate-R block codes, again under some technical condition. This result of [83] says that for a memoryless source with generic distribution Q, the minimum of

$$\sum_{\boldsymbol{x} \in \mathcal{X}^n} Q^n(\boldsymbol{x}) d(\boldsymbol{x}, f(\boldsymbol{x})) - D(Q, R) \qquad \text{(VI.8)}$$

for mappings $f \colon \mathcal{X}^n \to C_n \subset \mathcal{Y}^n$ with $|C_n| \leq \exp(nR)$ is asymptotically equal to constant times $\log n / n$, with an explicitly given constant. Here $D(Q, R)$ is the inverse function of $R(Q, D)$ defined by (VI.3), with Q fixed. Both papers [82] and [83] heavily rely on the method of types. The latter represents one of the very few cases where the delicate calculations require more exact bounds on the cardinality and probability of a type class than the crude ones in Lemma II.2.

B. Source–Channel Error Exponent

When a memoryless source with alphabet $\mathcal{S}$ and generic distribution Q is transmitted over a DMC $\{W \colon \mathcal{X} \to \mathcal{Y}\}$ using a source-channel block code with encoder $f \colon \mathcal{S}^n \to \mathcal{X}^n$ and decoder $\varphi \colon \mathcal{Y}^n \to \mathcal{S}^n$, the probability of error is

$$\sum_{\boldsymbol{s} \in \mathcal{S}^n} Q^n(\boldsymbol{s}) W^n(\{\boldsymbol{y} \colon \varphi(\boldsymbol{y}) \neq \boldsymbol{s}\} | f(\boldsymbol{s})). \qquad \text{(VI.9)}$$

Using techniques as in the proof of Theorem IV.1, Csiszár [22] showed that by suitable source-channel codes of blocklength $n \to \infty$, not depending on Q, the error probability (VI.9) can be made exponentially small whenever $H(Q) < C(W)$, with exponent $\min_R [e_Q(R) + E_r(R, W)]$ (cf. (III.3) and the remarks to Theorems IV.1 and IV.2 for notation). This exponent is best possible if the minimum is attained for some $R \geq R_{cr}(W)$. For further results in this direction, including source-channel transmission with a distortion threshold, cf. Csiszár [24].

C. Multiterminal Source Coding

Historically, the first multiuser problem studied via the method of types was that of the error exponent for the Slepian–Wolf [76] problem, i.e., separate coding of (memoryless) correlated sources. Given a source pair with generic variables (X, Y), the error probability of an n-length block code with separate encoders f, g and common decoder φ is

$$\Pr\{\varphi(f(X^n), g(Y^n)) \neq (X^n, Y^n)\} \qquad \text{(VI.10)}$$

where (X^n, Y^n) represents n independent repetitions of (X, Y). Csiszár, Körner, and Marton proved in 1977 (published in [27], cf. also [30, pp. 264–266]) that for suitable codes as above, with encoders that map $\mathcal{X}^n$ and $\mathcal{Y}^n$ into codeword sets of sizes

$$\|f\| \approx \exp(nR_1) \qquad \|g\| \approx \exp(nR_2), \qquad \text{(VI.11)}$$

the error probability (VI.10) goes to zero exponentially as $n \to \infty$, with exponent

$$E_1(R_1, R_2, X, Y) = \min_{P_{\tilde{X}\tilde{Y}} \in \mathcal{P}(\mathcal{X} \times \mathcal{Y})} [D(P_{\tilde{X}\tilde{Y}} \| P_{XY})$$
$$+ |\min(R_1 - H(\tilde{X}|\tilde{Y}), R_2 - H(\tilde{Y}|\tilde{X}),$$
$$R_1 + R_2 - H(\tilde{X}\tilde{Y}))|^+]$$
$$\text{(VI.12)}$$

whenever (R_1, R_2) is in the interior of the achievable rate region [76]

$$\mathcal{R}(X, Y) = \{(R_1, R_2) \colon R_1 \geq H(X|Y), R_2 \geq H(Y|X),$$
$$R_1 + R_2 \geq H(X, Y)\}. \qquad \text{(VI.13)}$$

This assertion can be proved letting φ be the "minimum entropy decoder" that outputs for any pair of codewords that pair $(\boldsymbol{x}, \boldsymbol{y}) \in \mathcal{X}^n \times \mathcal{Y}^n$ whose nonprobabilistic entropy $H(\boldsymbol{x}, \boldsymbol{y})$ is minimum among those having the given codewords (ties may be broken arbitrarily). Using this φ, the incorrectly decoded pairs $(\boldsymbol{x}, \boldsymbol{y})$ belong to one of the following three sets:

$$D_1 = \{(\boldsymbol{x}, \boldsymbol{y}) \colon H(\boldsymbol{x}', \boldsymbol{y}) \leq H(\boldsymbol{x}, \boldsymbol{y})$$
$$\text{for some } \boldsymbol{x}' \neq \boldsymbol{x} \text{ with } f(\boldsymbol{x}') = f(\boldsymbol{x})\}$$
$$D_2 = \{(\boldsymbol{x}, \boldsymbol{y}) \colon H(\boldsymbol{x}, \boldsymbol{y}') \leq H(\boldsymbol{x}, \boldsymbol{y})$$
$$\text{for some } \boldsymbol{y}' \neq \boldsymbol{y} \text{ with } g(\boldsymbol{y}') = g(\boldsymbol{y})\}$$
$$D_3 = \{(\boldsymbol{x}, \boldsymbol{y}) \colon H(\boldsymbol{x}', \boldsymbol{y}') \leq H(\boldsymbol{x}, \boldsymbol{y})$$
$$\text{for some } \boldsymbol{x}' \neq \boldsymbol{x} \text{ and } \boldsymbol{y}' \neq \boldsymbol{y}$$
$$\text{with } f(\boldsymbol{x}') = f(\boldsymbol{x}), g(\boldsymbol{y}') = g(\boldsymbol{y})\}.$$

It can be seen by random selection that there exist f and g satisfying (VI.11) such that for each joint type $P_{\tilde{X}\tilde{Y}} \in \mathcal{P}_n(\mathcal{X} \times \mathcal{Y})$

$$\frac{|D_1 \cap \mathcal{T}_{\tilde{X}\tilde{Y}}^n|}{|\mathcal{T}_{\tilde{X}\tilde{Y}}^n|} \lesssim \exp\{-n|R_1 - H(\tilde{X}|\tilde{Y})|^+\}$$

$$\frac{|D_2 \cap \mathcal{T}_{\tilde{X}\tilde{Y}}^n|}{|\mathcal{T}_{\tilde{X}\tilde{Y}}^n|} \lesssim \exp\{-n|R_2 - H(\tilde{Y}|\tilde{X})|^+\}$$

$$\frac{|D_3 \cap \mathcal{T}_{\tilde{X}\tilde{Y}}^n|}{|\mathcal{T}_{\tilde{X}\tilde{Y}}^n|} \lesssim \exp\{-n|R_1 + R_2 - H(\tilde{X}\tilde{Y})|^+\}.$$

Hence the assertion follows by Lemmas II.1 and II.2.

The error exponent (VI.12) for the Slepian–Wolf problem is attainable universally, i.e., with codes not depending on the distribution of (X, Y). This result is a counterpart of Theorem IV.1 for DMC's. The counterpart of Theorem IV.2 was also established by Csiszár, Körner, and Marton, *loc cit:* For no source pair can the error probability of codes satisfying (VI.11) decrease faster than with exponent

$$E_2(R_1, R_2, X, Y) = \min_{P_{\tilde{X}\tilde{Y}} \colon (R_1, R_2) \notin \mathcal{R}(\tilde{X}, \tilde{Y})} D(P_{\tilde{X}\tilde{Y}} \| P_{XY}).$$
$$\text{(VI.14)}$$

The functions in (VI.12) and (VI.14) are equal if (R_1, R_2) is close to the boundary of $\mathcal{R}(X, Y)$. For such rate pairs, their common value gives the exact error exponent.

Remark: For the intrinsic relationship of source and channel problems, cf., e.g., Csiszár and Körner [30, Secs. III.1 and III.2], Csiszár and Körner [28], and Ahlswede [3, Part II].

The above results have been extended in various ways. Extensions to more than two correlated sources are straightforward, cf. [27], or [30, pp. 267, 268]. Csiszár and Körner [28] showed that good encoders can be obtained, instead of random selection, also by a graph-theoretic approach. Another contribution of [28], in retrospect the more important one, was to apply the method of types to study the performance of various decoders, and to improve the exponent (VI.12) for "large" rates. Csiszár [23] showed that the exponent (VI.12) is (universally) attainable also with linear codes, i.e., constraining f and g be linear maps (to this, $\mathcal{X}$ and $\mathcal{Y}$ have to be fields, but that can always be assumed, extending the alphabets by dummy symbols of zero probability if necessary). Also in [23], linear codes were shown to give better than the previously known best exponent for certain rate pairs. More recently, Oohama and Han [70] obtained another improvement for certain rate pairs, and Oohama [69] determined the exact exponent for a modified version of the problem. That modification admits partial cooperation of the encoders, which, however, does not affect the achievable rate region (VI.13) nor the upper bound (VI.14) to achievable error exponents. On the other hand, the modification makes the exponent in (VI.14) achievable for all rate pairs (R_1, R_2) in the interior of $\mathcal{R}(X, Y)$, even universally.

D. Multiterminal Channels

The first application of the method of types to a multiterminal channel coding problem was the paper of Körner and Sgarro [58]. Using the same idea as in Theorem IV.1, they derived an error exponent for the asymmetric broadcast channel, cf. [30, p. 359] for the definition of this channel.

Here let us concentrate on the multiple-access channel (MAC). A MAC with input alphabets $\mathcal{X}$, $\mathcal{Y}$, and output alphabet $\mathcal{Z}$ is formally a DMC $\{W: \mathcal{X} \times \mathcal{Y} \to \mathcal{Z}\}$, with the understanding that there are two (noncommunicating) senders, one selecting the $\mathcal{X}$-component the other the $\mathcal{Y}$-component of the input. Thus codes with two codewords sets $\{\boldsymbol{x}_1, \cdots, \boldsymbol{x}_M\} \subset \mathcal{X}^n$ and $\{\boldsymbol{y}_1, \cdots, \boldsymbol{y}_N\} \subset \mathcal{Y}^n$ are considered, the decoder φ assigns a pair of message indices i, j to each $\boldsymbol{z} \in \mathcal{Z}^n$, and the average probability of error is

$$\bar{e} = \frac{1}{MN} \sum_{i=1}^{M} \sum_{j=1}^{N} W^n(\{\boldsymbol{z}: \varphi(\boldsymbol{z}) \neq (i, j)\}|\boldsymbol{x}_i, \boldsymbol{y}_j). \quad \text{(VI.15)}$$

The capacity region, i.e., the closure $\mathcal{C}$ of the set of those rate pairs (R_1, R_2) to which codes with $M \approx \exp nR_1$, $N \approx \exp nR_2$, and $\bar{e} \to 0$ exist, is characterized as follows: $(R_1, R_2) \in \mathcal{C}$ iff there exist RV's U, X, Y, Z, with U taking values in an auxiliary set $\mathcal{U}$ of size $|\mathcal{U}| = 2$, whose joint

distribution is of form

$$\begin{aligned} P_{UXYZ}&(u, x, y, z) \\ &= P_U(u)P_{X|U}(x|u)P_{Y|U}(y|u)W(z|x, y) \quad \text{(VI.16)} \end{aligned}$$

and such that

$$\begin{aligned} R_1 &\leq I(X \wedge Z|YU) \\ R_2 &\leq I(Y \wedge Z|XU) \\ R_1 + R_2 &\leq I(XY \wedge Z|U). \end{aligned} \quad \text{(VI.17)}$$

The capacity region $\mathcal{C}$ was first determined (in a different algebraic form) by Ahlswede [1] and Liao [60]. The maximum probability of error criterion may give a smaller region, cf. Dueck [41]; a single-letter characterization of the latter is not known.

For (R_1, R_2) in the interior of $\mathcal{C}$, $\bar{e}$ can be made exponentially small; Gallager [47] gave an attainable exponent everywhere positive in the interior of $\mathcal{C}$. Pokorny and Wallmeier [71] were first to apply the method of types to this problem. They showed the existence of (universal) codes with codewords $\boldsymbol{x}_i$ and $\boldsymbol{y}_j$ whose joint types with a fixed $\boldsymbol{u} \in \mathcal{U}^n$ are arbitrarily given $P_{UX} \in \mathcal{P}_n(\mathcal{U} \times \mathcal{X})$ and $P_{UY} \in \mathcal{P}_n(\mathcal{U} \times \mathcal{Y})$ such that the average probability of error is bounded above exponentially, with exponent depending on P_{UX}, P_{UY}, and W; that exponent is positive for each W with the property that for P_{UXYZ} determined by (VI.16) with the given P_{UX} and P_{UY}, (VI.17) is satisfied with strict inequalities. Pokorny and Wallmeier [71] used the proof technique of Theorem IV.1 with a decoder maximizing $I(\boldsymbol{x}_i \boldsymbol{y}_j \wedge \boldsymbol{z}|\boldsymbol{u})$. Recently, Liu and Hughes [62] improved upon the exponent of [71], using a similar technique but with decoder minimizing $H(\boldsymbol{x}_i \boldsymbol{y}_j|\boldsymbol{z}\boldsymbol{u})$. The "maximum mutual information" and "minimum conditional entropy" decoding rules are equivalent for DMC's with codewords of the same type but not in the MAC context; by the result of [62], "minimum conditional entropy" appears the better one.

VII. EXTENSIONS

While the type concept is originally tailored to memoryless models, it has extensions suitable for more complex models, as well. So far, such extensions proved useful mainly in the context of source coding and hypothesis testing.

Abstractly, given any family of source models with alphabet $\mathcal{X}$, a partition of $\mathcal{X}^n$ into sets $A_1, \cdots, A_{N_n}$ can be regarded as a partition into "type classes" if sequences in the same A_i are equiprobable under each model in the family. Of course, a subexponential growth rate of N_n is desirable. This general concept can be applied, e.g., to variable-length universal source coding: assign to each $\boldsymbol{x} \in A_i$ a binary codeword of length $\ell(\boldsymbol{x}) = \lceil \log_2 N_n \rceil + \lceil \log_2 |A_i| \rceil$, the first $\lceil \log_2 N_n \rceil$ bits specifying the class index i, the last $\lceil \log_2 |A_i| \rceil$ bits identifying $\boldsymbol{x}$ within A_i. Clearly, $\ell(\boldsymbol{x})$ will exceed the "ideal codelength" $-\log_2 P(\boldsymbol{x})$ by less that $\lceil \log_2 N_n \rceil + 1$, for each source model in the family.

As an example, consider the model family $\mathcal{R}$ of renewal processes, i.e., binary sources such that the lengths of 0 runs preceeding the 1's are i.i.d. RV's. Define the renewal type of a sequence $\boldsymbol{x} \in \{0, 1\}^n$ as $(k_0, k_1, \cdots)$ where k_j denotes the number of 1's in $\boldsymbol{x}$ which are preceeded by exactly j consecutive 0's. Sequences $\boldsymbol{x} \in \{0, 1\}^n$ of the same renewal type are equiprobable under each model in $\mathcal{R}$, and renewal types can be used for the model family $\mathcal{R}$ much in the same way as standard types for memoryless sources. Csiszár and Shields [37] showed that there are $N_n = \exp(O(\sqrt{n}))$ renewal type classes, which implies the possibility of universal coding with redundancy $O(\sqrt{n})$ for the family of renewal processes. It was also shown in [37] that the redundancy bound $O(\sqrt{n})$ is best possible for this family, as opposed to finitely parametrizable model families for which the best attainable redundancy is typically $O(\log n)$.

Below we briefly discuss some more direct extensions of the standard type concept.

A. Second- and Higher Order Types

The type concept appropriate for Markov chains is "second-order type," defined for a sequence $\boldsymbol{x} = x_1 \cdots x_n \in \mathcal{X}^n$ as the PD $P_{\boldsymbol{x}}^{(2)} \in \mathcal{P}_{n-1}(\mathcal{X}^2)$ with

$$P_{\boldsymbol{x}}^{(2)}(a, b) = \frac{1}{n-1} |\{i : x_i = a, x_{i+1} = b\}|. \qquad \text{(VII.1)}$$

In other words, $P_{\boldsymbol{x}}^{(2)}$ is the joint type of $\boldsymbol{x}' = x_1 \cdots x_{n-1}$ and $\boldsymbol{x}'' = x_2 \cdots x_n$. Denote by $\mathcal{P}_n^{(2)}(\mathcal{X}, a)$ the set of all possible second-order types of sequences $\boldsymbol{x} \in \mathcal{X}^n$ with $x_1 = a$, and for dummy RV's X, Y representing such a second-order type (i.e., $P_{XY} \in \mathcal{P}_n^{(2)}(\mathcal{X}, a)$) let $\mathcal{T}_{XY, a}^{n, 2}$ denote the type class $\{\boldsymbol{x} : \boldsymbol{x} \in \mathcal{X}^n, P_{\boldsymbol{x}}^{(2)} = P_{XY}, x_1 = a\}$.

The analog of (II.1) for a Markov chain $X_1, X_2, \cdots$ with stationary transition probabilities given by a matrix W is that if $P_{\boldsymbol{x}}^{(2)} = P_{XY}$ and $x_1 = a$ (with $\Pr\{X_1 = a\} > 0$) then

$$\Pr\{X^n = \boldsymbol{x} | X_1 = a\}$$
$$= \prod_{(a, b) \in \mathcal{X}^2} W(b|a)^{(n-1)P_{XY}(a, b)}$$
$$= \exp\{-(n-1)[H(Y|X) + D(P_{XY}\|W)]\} \qquad \text{(VII.2)}$$

where $X^n = X_1 \cdots X_n$. The analog of Lemma II.2 is that for $P_{XY} \in \mathcal{P}_n^{(2)}(\mathcal{X}, a)$

$$|\mathcal{T}_{XY, a}^{n, 2}| \approx \exp\{nH(Y|X)\} \qquad \text{(VII.3)}$$

$$\Pr\{X^n \in \mathcal{T}_{XY, a}^{n, 2} | X_1 = a\} \approx \exp\{-nD(P_{XY}\|W)\}. \quad \text{(VII.4)}$$

Of course, (VII.4) is a consequence of (VII.2) and (VII.3). The simple idea in the proof of Lemma II.2 suffices only for the $\lesssim$ part of (VII.3), the $\gtrsim$ part is more delicate. One way to get it (Boza [19]) is via the exact formula for $|\mathcal{T}_{XY, a}^{n, 2}|$ due to Whittle [80], an elementary proof of which has been given by Billingsley [14]. An important property of second-order types is that they have (equal or) asymptotically equal marginals as $n \to \infty$. Indeed, for $\boldsymbol{x} = ax_2 \cdots x_{n-1}b \in \mathcal{T}_{XY, a}^{n, 2}$ the marginals P_X and P_Y of $P_{XY} = P_{\boldsymbol{x}}^{(2)}$ differ only at a and b, if $a \neq b$, both differences being $(n-1)^{-1}$. Moreover, denoting by $\mathcal{P}_e(\mathcal{X}^2)$ the set of those $P \in \mathcal{P}(\mathcal{X}^2)$ whose two marginals are equal, each irreducible $P \in \mathcal{P}_e(\mathcal{X}^2)$ can be arbitrarily approximated by second-order types $P' \in \mathcal{P}_n^{(2)}(\mathcal{X}, a)$ with $P' \ll P$ if n is sufficiently large

($P \in \mathcal{P}_e(\mathcal{X}^2)$ is called irreducible if the stationary Markov chain with two-dimensional distribution P is irreducible).

The above facts permit extensions of the results in Section III to Markov chains, cf. Boza [19], Davisson, Longo, and Sgarro [38], Natarajan [68], Csiszár, Cover, and Choi [26]. In particular, the following analog of Theorem III.3 and its Corollary holds, cf. [26].

Theorem VII.1: Given a Markov chain $X_1, X_2, \cdots$ with transition probability matrix W and $\Pr\{X_1 = a\} > 0$, and a set of PD's $\Pi \subset \mathcal{P}(\mathcal{X}^2)$ such that $P \ll W$ for each $P \in \Pi$, the second-order type $\hat{P}_n^{(2)}$ of $X_1, \cdots, X_n$ satisfies

$$\lim_{n \to \infty} \frac{1}{n} \log \Pr\{\hat{P}_n \in \Pi | X_1 = a\} = -\min_{P \in \overline{\Pi} \cap \mathcal{P}_e(\mathcal{X}^2)} D(P\|W)$$

(VII.5)

iff there exist second-order types $P_n \in \Pi \cap \mathcal{P}_n^{(2)}(\mathcal{X}, a)$ such that $D(P_n\|W)$ approaches the minimum in (VII.5). Further, if the minimum in (VII.5) is attained for a unique P^*, and $X_1^*, X_2^*, \cdots$ denotes a stationary Markov chain with $P_{X_1^* X_2^*} = P^*$, for $(a_1, \cdots, a_k) \in \mathcal{X}^k$ with $P_{X_1^*}(a_1) > 0$, we have

$$\lim_{n \to \infty} \Pr\{X_2 = a_2, \cdots, X_k = a_k | \hat{P}_n^{(2)} \in \Pi, X_1 = a_1\}$$
$$= \Pr\{X_2^* = a_2, \cdots, X_k^* = a_k | X_1^* = a_1\} \quad \text{(VII.6)}$$

whenever (VII.5) holds for $a = a_1$.

Remarks:
i) Let Π^i denote the set of those irreducible $P \in \Pi \cap \mathcal{P}_e(\mathcal{X}^2)$ for which all $P' \ll P$ in a sufficiently small neighborhood of P belong to Π. The first assertion of Theorem VII.1 gives that (VII.5) always holds if the closure of Π^i equals $\overline{\Pi} \cap \mathcal{P}_e(\mathcal{X}^2)$.
ii) Theorem VII.1 is of interest even if $X_1, X_2 \cdots$ are i.i.d.; the limiting conditional distribution in (VII.6) is Markov rather than i.i.d. also in that case.

As an immediate extension of (VII.1), the rth-order type of a sequence $\boldsymbol{x} \in \mathcal{X}^n$ is defined as the PD $P_{\boldsymbol{x}}^{(r)} \in \mathcal{P}(\mathcal{X}^r)$ with

$$P_{\boldsymbol{x}}^{(r)}(a_1, \cdots, a_r)$$
$$= \frac{1}{n-r+1} |\{i : x_i = a_1, \cdots, x_{i+r-1} = a_r\}|. \quad \text{(VII.7)}$$

This is the suitable type concept for order-$(r-1)$ Markov chains, in which conditional distributions given the past depend on the last $(r-1)$ symbols. All results about Markov chains and second-order types have immediate extensions to order-$(r-1)$ Markov chains and rth-order types.

Since order-k Markov chains are also order-ℓ ones if $\ell > k$, the analog of the hypothesis-testing result Theorem III.2 can be applied to test the hypothesis that a process known to be Markov of order k_0 is actually Markov of order k for a given $k < k_0$. Performing a multiple test (for each $k < k_0$) amounts to estimating the Markov order. A recent paper analyzing this approach to Markov order estimation is Finesso, Liu, and Narayan [45], cf. also prior works of Gutman [51] and Merhav, Gutman, and Ziv [66].

"Circular" versions of second- and higher order types are also often used as in [38]. The rth-order circular type of $x_1 \cdots x_n \in \mathcal{X}^n$ is the same as the rth-order type of $x_1 \cdots x_n x_1 \cdots x_{r-1} \in \mathcal{X}^{n+r-1}$, i.e., the joint type of the r sequences $x_1 \cdots x_n$, $x_2 \cdots x_n x_1$, $\cdots$, $x_r \cdots x_n \cdots x_{r-1}$. A technical advantage of circular types is compatibility: lower order circular types are marginals of the higher order ones. The price is that expressing probabilities in terms of circular types is more awkward.

B. Finite-State Types

A sequence of $\mathcal{X}$-valued RV's $X_1, X_2, \cdots$ is called a unifilar finite-state source if there exists a (finite) set $\mathcal{S}$ of "states," an initial state $s_1 \in \mathcal{S}$, and a mapping $f: \mathcal{S} \times \mathcal{X} \to \mathcal{S}$ that specifies the next state as a function of the present state and source output, such that

$$\Pr\{X^n = \boldsymbol{x}\} = \prod_{i=1}^{n} W(x_i|s_i), \quad s_{i+1} = f(s_i, x_i) \quad \text{(VII.8)}$$

where W is a stochastic matrix specifying the source output probabilities given the states. As the state sequence $\boldsymbol{s} = s_1 \cdots s_n$ is uniquely determined by $\boldsymbol{x} = x_1 \cdots x_n$ and the initial state s_1, so is the joint type $P_{\boldsymbol{s}\boldsymbol{x}}$. It will be called the finite state type $P_{\boldsymbol{x}}^{f, s_1}$ of $\boldsymbol{x}$, given the mapping f and the initial state s_1, cf. Weinberger, Merhav, and Feder [79]. Notice that the rth-order type (VII.7) of $\boldsymbol{x} = x_1 \cdots x_n$ is equal to the finite state type of $x_r \cdots x_n$ for $\mathcal{S} = \mathcal{X}^{r-1}$ and $f: \mathcal{S} \times \mathcal{X} \to \mathcal{S}$ defined by $f(a_1 \cdots a_{r-1}, a) = a_2 \cdots a_{r-1}a$, with $s_1 = x_1 \cdots x_{r-1}$.

Denote the set of finite-state types $P_{\boldsymbol{x}}^{f, s_1}$, $\boldsymbol{x} \in \mathcal{X}^n$, by $\mathcal{P}_n^f(\mathcal{X}, s_1)$, and let $\mathcal{T}_{SX, s_1}^{n, f}$ denote the class of sequences $\boldsymbol{x} \in \mathcal{X}^n$ with $P_{\boldsymbol{x}}^{f, s_1} = P_{SX}$. Then for $\boldsymbol{x} \in \mathcal{T}_{SX, s_1}^{n, f}$, (VII.8) gives

$$\Pr\{X^n = \boldsymbol{x}\} = \exp\{-n[H(X|S) + D(P_{SX}\|W)]\}. \quad \text{(VII.9)}$$

Further, for $P_{SX} \in \mathcal{P}_n^f(\mathcal{X}, s_1)$ the following analogs of (VII.3) and (VII.4) hold:

$$|\mathcal{T}_{SX, s_1}^{n, f}| \approx \exp\{nH(X|S)\} \quad \text{(VII.10)}$$

$$\Pr\{X^n \in \mathcal{T}_{SX, s_1}^{n, f}\} \approx \exp\{-nD(P_{SX}\|W)\}. \quad \text{(VII.11)}$$

These permit extensions of results about Markov chains and second-order types to unifilar finite-state sources and finite-state types. Weinberger, Merhav, and Feder [79] used this type concept to study the performance of universal sequential codes for individual sequences (rather than in the averaged sense). They established a lower bound to the codelength, valid for most sequences in any given type class $\mathcal{T}_{SX, s_1}^{n, f}$, except for a vanishingly small fraction of the finite-state types $P_{SX} \in \mathcal{P}_n^f(\mathcal{X}, s_1)$.

The finite-state model (VII.8) can be extended in various ways. Let us consider here the extension when the "next state" s_{i+1} depends on the past sequence $x^i = x_1 \cdots x_i$ not necessarily through s_i and x_i but, more generally, $s_{i+1} = F(x^i)$ where $F: \mathcal{X}^* \to \mathcal{S}$ is an arbitrary mapping. Here $\mathcal{X}^*$ denotes the set of all finite sequences of symbols from $\mathcal{X}$, including the void sequence λ; the initial state s_1 need not be explicitly specified in this model, as it is formally given by

$s_1 = F(\lambda)$. The type concept adequate for the source model

$$\Pr\{X^n = \boldsymbol{x}\} = \prod_{i=1}^{n} W(x_i|s_i), \quad s_{i+1} = F(x^i) \quad \text{(VII.12)}$$

is the F-type $P_{\boldsymbol{x}}^F$ defined as the joint type $P_{\boldsymbol{s}\boldsymbol{x}}$, where $\boldsymbol{s}$ is determined by $\boldsymbol{x}$ as in (VII.12). Of course, for the corresponding F-type classes $\mathcal{T}_{SX}^{n, F}$ we still have (VII.9) when $\boldsymbol{x} \in \mathcal{T}_{SX}^{n, F}$, and consequently also

$$|\mathcal{T}_{SX}^{n, F}| \le \exp\{nH(X|S)\}. \quad \text{(VII.13)}$$

Unlike for the finite-state type classes $\mathcal{T}_{SX, s_1}^{n, f}$, however, a lower bound counterpart of (VII.13) cannot be established in general.

An early appearance of this F-type concept, though not of the term, was in Csiszár and Körner [31], applied to DMC's with feedback. The encoder of a feedback code of blocklength n for N messages is defined by mappings $F_k = \mathcal{Y}^* \to \mathcal{X}$, $k = 1, \cdots, N$, that specify the input symbols $x_i = F_k(y^{i-1})$, $i = 1, \cdots, n$, depending on the previous received symbols $y^{i-1} = y_1 \cdots y_{i-1}$, when message k is to be transmitted. Then the received sequence $\boldsymbol{y} \in \mathcal{Y}^n$ in generated by a generalized finite-state model as in (VII.12), with alphabet $\mathcal{Y}$, state set $\mathcal{X}$, and $F = F_k$. In particular, the probability of receiving an $\boldsymbol{y} \in \mathcal{T}_{XY}^{n, F_k}$ equals $\exp\{-n[H(Y|X) + D(P_{XY}\|W)]\}$, cf. (VII.9). Hence a decoder φ will correctly decode message k with probability

$$\sum_{P_{XY} \in \mathcal{P}_n(\mathcal{X} \times \mathcal{Y})} |\mathcal{T}_{XY}^{n, F_k} \cap D_k| \exp\{-n[H(Y|X) + D(P_{XY}\|W)]\}$$
$$\text{(VII.14)}$$

where $D_k = \{\boldsymbol{y}: \varphi(\boldsymbol{y}) = k\}$. Similarly to (IV.16), we have

$$\sum_{k=1}^{N} |\mathcal{T}_{XY}^{n, F_k} \cap D_k| \le \left| \bigcup_{k=1}^{N} \mathcal{T}_{XY}^{n, F_k} \right|$$
$$\le |\mathcal{T}_Y^n| \le \exp\{nH(Y)\}. \quad \text{(VII.15)}$$

On account of (VII.13) (with (S, X) replaced by (X, Y)), the left-hand side of (VII.15) is also $\le N \exp\{nH(Y|X)\}$. It follows that if $N > \exp(nR)$ then

$$\frac{1}{N} \sum_{k=1}^{N} |\mathcal{T}_{XY}^{n, F_k} \cap D_k| \le \exp\{n[H(Y|X) - |R - I(X \wedge Y)|^+]\}.$$
$$\text{(VII.16)}$$

Averaging the probability of correct decoding (VII.14) over the messages $1 \le k \le N$, (VII.16) implies that the average probability of correct decoding is

$$\lesssim \exp\{-n \min[D(P_{XY}\|W) + |R - I(X \wedge Y)|^+]\}$$

where the minimum is for all $P_{XY} \in \mathcal{P}(\mathcal{X} \times \mathcal{Y})$. Comparing this with Remark iii) to Theorem IV.2 shows that feedback cannot exponentially improve the probability of correct decoding at rates above channel capacity.

A recent combinatorial result of Ahlswede, Yang, and Zhang [11] is also easiest to state in terms of F-types. Their "inherently typical subset lemma" says, effectively, that given $\mathcal{X}$ and $\varepsilon > 0$, there is a finite set $\mathcal{S}$ such that for sufficiently large n, to any $A \subset \mathcal{X}^n$ there exists a mapping $F\colon \mathcal{X}^* \to \mathcal{S}$ and an F-type P_{SX} such that

$$|A| \approx |A \cap \mathcal{T}_{SX}^{n,F}| \geq \exp\{n(H(X|S) - \varepsilon)\}. \quad \text{(VII.17)}$$

While this lemma is used in [11] to prove (the converse part of) a probabilistic result, it is claimed to also yield the asymptotic solution of the general isoperimetric problem for arbitrary finite alphabets and arbitrary distortion measures.

C. Continuous Alphabets

Extensions of the type concept to continuous alphabets are not known. Still, there are several continuous-alphabet problems whose simplest (or the only) available solution relies upon the method of types, via discrete approximations. For example, the capacity subject to a state constraint of an AVC with general alphabets and states, for deterministic codes and the average probability of error criterion, has been determined in this way, cf. [25].

At present, this approach seems necessary even for the following intuitive result.

Theorem VII.2 ([25]): Consider an AVC whose permissible n-length inputs $\boldsymbol{x} \in \mathbb{R}^n$ satisfy $\|\boldsymbol{x}\|^2 \leq n\Gamma$, and the output is $\boldsymbol{y} = \boldsymbol{x} + \boldsymbol{z} + Z^n$ where the deterministic sequence $\boldsymbol{z} \in \mathbb{R}^n$ and the random sequence Z^n with independent zero-mean components Z_i may be arbitrary subject to the power constraints $\|\boldsymbol{z}\|^2 \leq n\Lambda_1$, $\sum_{i=1}^n E(Z_i^2) \leq n\Lambda_2$. This AVC has the same a-capacity as the Gaussian one where the Z_i's are i.i.d. Gaussian RV's with variance Λ_2.

For the latter Gaussian case, Csiszár and Narayan [36] had previously shown that

$$C_a = \begin{cases} \dfrac{1}{2} \log\left(1 + \dfrac{\Gamma}{\Lambda_1 + \Lambda_2}\right), & \text{if } \Gamma > \Lambda_1 \\ 0, & \text{if } \Gamma \leq \Lambda_1. \end{cases} \quad \text{(VII.18)}$$

Discrete approximations combined with the method of types provide the simplest available proof of a general form of Sanov's theorem, for RV's with values in an arbitrary set $\mathcal{X}$ endowed with a σ-algebra $\mathcal{F}$ (the discrete case has been discussed in Section III).

For probability measures (pm's) P, Q on $(\mathcal{X}, \mathcal{F})$, the I-divergence $D(P\|Q)$ is defined as

$$D(P\|Q) = \sup_{\mathcal{A}} D(P^{\mathcal{A}}\|Q^{\mathcal{A}}) \quad \text{(VII.19)}$$

the supremum taken for partitions $\mathcal{A} = (A_1, \cdots, A_k)$ of $\mathcal{X}$ into sets $A_i \in \mathcal{F}$. Here $P^{\mathcal{A}}$ denotes the $\mathcal{A}$-quantization of P defined as the distribution $\{P(A_1), \cdots, P(A_k)\}$ on the finite set $\{1, \cdots, k\}$.

The τ-topology of pm's on $(\mathcal{X}, \mathcal{F})$ is the topology in which a pm P belongs to the interior of a set Π of pm's iff for some partition $\mathcal{A} = (A_1, \cdots, A_k)$ and $\varepsilon > 0$

$$\{P'\colon |P'(A_j) - P(A_j)| < \varepsilon, \quad j = 1, \cdots, k\} \subset \Pi. \quad \text{(VII.20)}$$

The empirical distribution $\hat{P}_n$ of an n-tuple $X^n = (X_1, \cdots, X_n)$ of $\mathcal{X}$-valued RV's is the random pm defined by

$$\hat{P}_n(A) = \frac{1}{n} |\{i\colon X_i \in A\}|, \qquad A \in \mathcal{F}. \quad \text{(VII.21)}$$

Theorem VII.3: Let $X_1, X_2, \cdots$ be independent $\mathcal{X}$-valued RV's with common distribution Q. Then

$$\liminf_{n \to \infty} \frac{1}{n} \log \Pr\{\hat{P}_n \in \Pi\} \geq - \inf_{P \in \Pi^0} D(P\|Q), \quad \text{(VII.22)}$$

$$\limsup_{n \to \infty} \frac{1}{n} \log \Pr\{\hat{P}_n \in \Pi\} \leq - \inf_{P \in \overline{\Pi}} D(P\|Q), \quad \text{(VII.23)}$$

for every set Π of pm's on $(\mathcal{X}, \mathcal{F})$ for which the probabilities $\Pr\{\hat{P}_n \in \Pi\}$ are defined. Here Π^0 and $\overline{\Pi}$ denote the interior and closure of Π in the τ-topology.

Theorem VII.3 is a general version of Sanov's theorem. In the parlance of large derivations theory (cf. Dembo and Zeitouni [39]) it says that $\{\hat{P}_n\}$ satisfies the large deviation principle with good rate function $D(\cdot\|Q)$ ("goodness" means that the sets $\{P\colon D(P\|Q) \leq \alpha\}$ are compact in the τ-topology; the easy proof of this property is omitted).

Proof: (Groeneboom, Oosterhoff, and Ruymgaart [49]) Pick any $P \in \Pi^0$, and $\mathcal{A}$ and ε satisfying (VII.20). Apply Theorem III.3 to the quantized RV's $X_i^{\mathcal{A}}$ with distribution $Q^{\mathcal{A}}$, where $X_i^{\mathcal{A}} = j$ if $X_i \in A_j$, and to the set of those distributions $\tilde{P}$ on $\{1, \cdots, k\}$ for which $|\tilde{P}(j) - P(A_j)| < \varepsilon$, $j = 1, \cdots, k$.

As the latter is an open set containing $P^{\mathcal{A}}$, it follows that

$$\lim_{n \to \infty} \frac{1}{n} \log \Pr\{|\hat{P}_n(A_j) - P(A_j)| < \varepsilon, j = 1, \cdots, k\}$$
$$\geq -D(P^{\mathcal{A}}\|Q^{\mathcal{A}}). \quad \text{(VII.24)}$$

The left hand side of (VII.24) is a lower bound to that of (VII.22), by (VII.20). Hence, as $P \in \Pi^0$ has been arbitrary, (VII.19) and (VII.24) imply (VII.22).

Notice next that for each partition $\mathcal{A}$, Theorem III.3 applied to the quantized RV's $X_i^{\mathcal{A}}$ as above and to $\Pi^{\mathcal{A}} = \{P^{\mathcal{A}}\colon P \in \Pi\}$ gives that

$$\limsup_{n \to \infty} \frac{1}{n} \log \Pr\{\hat{P}_n^{\mathcal{A}} \in \Pi^{\mathcal{A}}\} \leq - D(\Pi^{\mathcal{A}}\|Q^{\mathcal{A}})$$
$$= - \inf_{P \in \Pi} D(P^{\mathcal{A}}\|Q^{\mathcal{A}}). \quad \text{(VII.25)}$$

Clearly, (VII.23) follows from (VII.19) and (VII.25) if one shows that

$$\sup_{\mathcal{A}} \inf_{P \in \Pi} D(P^{\mathcal{A}}\|Q^{\mathcal{A}}) = \inf_{P \in \overline{\Pi}} \sup_{\mathcal{A}} D(P^{\mathcal{A}}\|Q^{\mathcal{A}}). \quad \text{(VII.26)}$$

The nontrivial but not too hard proof of (VII.26) is omitted.

The "discrete approximation plus method of types" approach works also for other problems that can not be entered here. For extensions of the hypothesis testing results in Section III, cf. Tusnády [78].

VIII. CONCLUSIONS

The method of types has been shown to be a powerful tool of the information theory of discrete memoryless systems. It affords extensions also to certain models with memory, and can be applied to continuous alphabet models via discrete approximations. The close links of the method of types to large deviations theory (primarily to Sanov's theorem) have also been established.

Sometimes it is claimed that "type" arguments, at least for models involving only one set of sequences as in hypothesis testing, could be replaced by referring to general results from large deviations theory. This is true for some applications (although the method of types gives more insight), but in other applications the explicit "type" bounds valid for all n afford stronger conclusions than the asymptotic bounds provided by large deviations theory. It is interesting to note in this respect that for the derivation of (VII.6) even the familiar type bound was not sufficient, rather, the exact formula (of Whittle [80]) for the size of second order type classes had to be used.

Of course, the heavy machinery of large deviations theory (cf. [39]) works for many problems for which type arguments do not. In particular, while that machinery is not needed for Sanov's theorem (Theorem VII.3), it appears necessary to derive the corresponding result for continuous alphabet Markov chains. Indeed, although the method of types does work for finite alphabet Markov chains (cf. Theorem VII.1), extension to general alphabets via discrete approximations does not seem feasible, since quantization destroys the Markov property.

APPENDIX

Proof of Lemma IV.1: Pick $2N$ sequences $\boldsymbol{x}_1, \cdots, \boldsymbol{x}_{2N}$ from $\mathcal{T}_P^n$ at random. Then, using Lemma II.2, we have for any joint type $P_{X\tilde{X}} \in \mathcal{P}_n(\mathcal{X} \times \mathcal{X})$ with $P_X = P_{\tilde{X}} = P$, and any $i \neq j$,

$$
\begin{aligned}
\Pr\{(\boldsymbol{x}_i, \boldsymbol{x}_j) \in \mathcal{T}_{X\tilde{X}}^n\} &= \frac{|\mathcal{T}_{X\tilde{X}}^n|}{|\mathcal{T}_P^n|^2} \\
&\leq \frac{\exp\{nH(X,\tilde{X})\}}{[|\mathcal{P}_n(\mathcal{X})|^{-1}\exp\{nH(P)\}]^2} \\
&= |\mathcal{P}_n(\mathcal{X})|^2 \exp\{-nI(X \wedge \tilde{X})\}. \quad \text{(A.1)}
\end{aligned}
$$

This implies that

$$
\begin{aligned}
E|\{j: j \neq i, (\boldsymbol{x}_i, \boldsymbol{x}_j) \in \mathcal{T}_{X\tilde{X}}^n\}| \\
\leq 2N|\mathcal{P}_n(\mathcal{X})|^2 \exp\{-nI(X \wedge \tilde{X})\}. \quad \text{(A.2)}
\end{aligned}
$$

Writing

$$
\begin{aligned}
&F_i(\boldsymbol{x}_1, \cdots, \boldsymbol{x}_{2N}) \\
&= \sum_{\substack{P_{X\tilde{X}} \in \mathcal{P}_n(\mathcal{X} \times \mathcal{X}) \\ P_X = P_{\tilde{X}} = P}} |\{j: j \neq i, (\boldsymbol{x}_i, \boldsymbol{x}_j) \in \mathcal{T}_{X\tilde{X}}^n\}| \\
&\quad \cdot \exp\{nI(X \wedge \tilde{X})\}, \quad \text{(A.3)}
\end{aligned}
$$

it follows from (A.2) that

$$
E \sum_{i=1}^{2N} F_i(\boldsymbol{x}_1, \cdots, \boldsymbol{x}_{2N}) \leq 4N^2 |\mathcal{P}_n(\mathcal{X})|^2 |\mathcal{P}_n(\mathcal{X} \times \mathcal{X})|. \quad \text{(A.4)}
$$

On account of (A.4), the same inequality must hold without the expectation sign for some choice of $\boldsymbol{x}_1, \cdots, \boldsymbol{x}_{2N}$, and then the latter satisfy

$$
F_i(\boldsymbol{x}_1, \cdots, \boldsymbol{x}_{2N}) \leq 4N|\mathcal{P}_n(\mathcal{X})|^2 |\mathcal{P}_n(\mathcal{X} \times \mathcal{X})| \quad \text{(A.5)}
$$

for at least N indices i. Assuming without any loss of generality that (A.5) holds for $i = 1, \cdots, N$, it follows by (A.3) that

$$
\begin{aligned}
&|\{j: j \neq i, (\boldsymbol{x}_i, \boldsymbol{x}_j) \in \mathcal{T}_{X\tilde{X}}^n\}| \\
&\quad \leq 4N|\mathcal{P}_n(\mathcal{X})|^2 |\mathcal{P}_n(\mathcal{X} \times \mathcal{X})| \exp\{-nI(X \wedge \tilde{X})\} \quad \text{(A.6)}
\end{aligned}
$$

for each $1 \leq i \leq N$ and $P_{X\tilde{X}} \in \mathcal{P}_n(\mathcal{X} \times \mathcal{X})$ with $P_X = P_{\tilde{X}} = P$. As $N \approx \exp(nR)$ may be chosen such that $4N|\mathcal{P}_n(\mathcal{X})|^2 |\mathcal{P}_n(\mathcal{X} \times \mathcal{X})| < \exp(nR)$, this completes the proof.

Proof of Theorems V.1, V.2 (continued): Consider a decoder as defined in Section V, with a preliminarily unspecified permissible set $\Psi \subset \mathcal{P}(\mathcal{X} \times \mathcal{X} \times \mathcal{S} \times \mathcal{Y})$. Recall that Π denotes $\Pi^m(\eta)$ or $\Pi^a(\eta)$ defined by (V.14) and (V.15), according as the maximum or average probability of error criterion is considered, and each $P_{X\tilde{X}SY} \in \Psi$ has to satisfy (V.20).

Clearly, for $\boldsymbol{y} \in \mathcal{T}_{Y|XS}^n(\boldsymbol{x}_i, \boldsymbol{s})$ with $P_{XSY} \in \Pi$ we can have $\varphi(\boldsymbol{y}) \neq i$ only if $\boldsymbol{y} \in \mathcal{T}_{Y|X\tilde{X}S}^n(\boldsymbol{x}_i, \boldsymbol{x}_j, \boldsymbol{s})$ for some $j \neq i$ and $P_{X\tilde{X}SY} \in \Psi \cap \mathcal{P}_n(\mathcal{X} \times \mathcal{X} \times \mathcal{S} \times \mathcal{Y})$. Using (II.7) and (V.10), it follows that the fraction of sequences in $\mathcal{T}_{Y|XS}^n(\boldsymbol{x}_i, \boldsymbol{s})$ with $\varphi(\boldsymbol{y}) \neq i$ is bounded, in the $\lesssim$ sense, by

$$
\begin{aligned}
&\exp\{-nH(Y|XS)\} \sum \exp\{nH(Y|X\tilde{X}S)\} \\
&\quad \cdot \exp\{n[|R - I(XS \wedge \tilde{X})|^+ + \varepsilon]\} \\
&\approx \max \exp\{-nI(\tilde{X} \wedge Y|XS) + n|R - I(XS \wedge \tilde{X})|^+ \\
&\qquad\qquad + n\varepsilon\}
\end{aligned}
$$

where the sum and max are for all joint types $P_{X\tilde{X}SY} \in \Psi \cap \mathcal{P}_n(\mathcal{X} \times \mathcal{X} \times \mathcal{S} \times \mathcal{Y})$ with the given marginal P_{XSY}. Except for an exponentially small fraction of the indices $1 \leq i \leq N$, it suffices to take the above sum and max for those joint types that satisfy the additional constraint

$$
I(X \wedge \tilde{X}S) \leq |R - I(\tilde{X} \wedge S)|^+ + \varepsilon. \quad \text{(A.7)}
$$

Indeed, the fraction of indices $1 \leq i \leq N$ to which a $j \neq i$ exists with $P_{\boldsymbol{x}_i \boldsymbol{x}_j \boldsymbol{s}} = P_{X\tilde{X}S}$ not satisfying (A.7), is exponentially small by (V.12).

If the fraction of incorrectly decoded $\boldsymbol{y}$'s within $\mathcal{T}_{Y|XS}^n(\boldsymbol{x}_i, \boldsymbol{s})$ is exponentially small for each $P_{XSY} \in \Pi^m(\eta) \cap \mathcal{P}_n(\mathcal{X} \times \mathcal{S} \times \mathcal{Y})$, it follows by (V.3) and (V.17) that $e_i(\boldsymbol{s})$ is exponentially small. Hence, writing

$$
F(X, \tilde{X}, S, Y) = I(\tilde{X} \wedge Y|XS) - |R - I(XS \wedge \tilde{X})|^+, \quad \text{(A.8)}
$$

the maximum probability of error e defined by (V.2) will be exponentially small if a $\xi > \varepsilon$ exists such that $F(X, \tilde{X}, S, Y) \geq \xi$ whenever $P_{X\tilde{X}SY} \in \Psi$.

Similarly, if the fraction of incorrectly decoded $\boldsymbol{y}$'s within $\mathcal{T}_{Y|XS}^n(\boldsymbol{x}_i, \boldsymbol{s})$ is exponentially small for each $P_{XSY} \in \Pi^a(\eta) \cap \mathcal{P}_n(\mathcal{X} \times \mathcal{S} \times \mathcal{Y})$, except perhaps for an exponentially small fraction of the indices $1 \leq i \leq N$, it follows by (V.18) that $N^{-1} \sum_i e_i(\boldsymbol{s})$ is exponentially small, supposing, of course, that $\varepsilon < \eta$. Hence the average probability of error $\bar{e}$ defined by (V.2) will be exponentially small if a $\xi > \varepsilon$ exists such that $F(X, \tilde{X}, S, Y) \geq \xi$ whenever (A.7) holds and $P_{X\tilde{X}SY} \in \Psi$.

Actually, in both cases $F(X, \tilde{X}, S, Y) \geq \xi > 0$ suffices, as $\varepsilon > 0$ in Lemma V.1 can always be chosen smaller than ξ.

To complete the proof, it suffices to find a permissible set of joint distributions $\Psi \subset \mathcal{P}(\mathcal{X} \times \mathcal{X} \times \mathcal{S} \times \mathcal{Y})$ such that

i) in case of Theorem V.1, $F(X, \tilde{X}, S, Y)$ has a positive lower bound subject to $P_{X\tilde{X}SY} \in \Psi$ if $R < \min[C(P), D(P)]$,

ii) in the case of Theorem V.2, $F(X, \tilde{X}, S, Y)$ has a positive lower bound subject to $P_{X\tilde{X}SY} \in \Psi$ and (A.7) if

$$R < \min_{P_S \in \mathcal{P}(\mathcal{S})} I(X \wedge Y) \text{ where } P_{XSY} = P \times P_S \times W, \tag{A.9}$$

cf. (V.4), and the AVC is nonsymmetrizable.

Now, from (A.8),

$$
\begin{aligned}
F(X, \tilde{X}, S, Y) &= I(\tilde{X} \wedge YXS) - R \\
&\geq I(\tilde{X} \wedge Y) - R \quad \text{if } I(XS \wedge \tilde{X}) \leq R.
\end{aligned}
\tag{A.10}
$$

Moreover, if (A.7) holds then $I(\tilde{X} \wedge S) \leq R$ implies $R + \varepsilon \geq I(X \wedge \tilde{X}S) + I(\tilde{X} \wedge S) = I(\tilde{X} \wedge XS) + I(X \wedge S) \geq I(\tilde{X} \wedge XS)$, hence

$$
\begin{aligned}
F(X, \tilde{X}, S, Y) &\geq I(\tilde{X} \wedge YXS) - R - \varepsilon \\
&\geq I(\tilde{X} \wedge Y) - R - \varepsilon \quad \text{if } I(\tilde{X} \wedge S) \leq R.
\end{aligned}
\tag{A.11}
$$

If $P_{X\tilde{X}SY} \in \Psi$ then $P_{\tilde{X}Y}$ is the marginal of some $P_{\tilde{X}\tilde{S}Y} \in \Pi$, cf. (V.20), where Π denotes $\Pi^m(\eta)$ or $\Pi^a(\eta)$. In the first case, $P_{\tilde{X}\tilde{S}Y} \in \Pi = \Pi^m(\eta)$ implies by (V.14) that $P_{\tilde{X}\tilde{S}Y}$ is arbitrarily close to $P_{\tilde{X}\tilde{S}} \times W$ and hence any number less than $C(P)$ defined by (V.7) is a lower bound to $I(\tilde{X} \wedge Y)$ if η is sufficiently small. Then (A.10) shows that the claim under i) always holds when $I(XS \wedge \tilde{X}) \leq R$. In the second case $P_{\tilde{X}\tilde{S}Y} \in \Pi = \Pi^a(\eta)$ implies by (V.15) that $P_{\tilde{X}\tilde{S}Y}$ is close to $P \times P_{\tilde{S}_s} \times W$ and hence any number less than the minimum in (A.9) is a lower bound to $I(\tilde{X} \wedge Y)$ if η is sufficiently small. Then (A.11) shows that the claim under ii) always holds when $I(\tilde{X} \wedge S) \leq R$.

So far, the choice of Ψ played no role. To make the claim under i) hold also when $I(XS \wedge \tilde{X}) > R$, chose Ψ as the set of joint distributions $P_{X\tilde{X}SY}$ satisfying $I(\tilde{X} \wedge Y | XS) \geq \xi > 0$, in addition to (V.20). It can be shown by rather straightforward calculation using (V.8) and (V.13) that this Ψ is permissible if $R < D(P)$, providing η and ξ are sufficiently small, cf. [29] for details.

Concerning the claim under ii) in the remaining case $I(\tilde{X} \wedge S) > R$, notice that then (A.8) gives

$$
\begin{aligned}
F(X, \tilde{X}, S, Y) &= I(\tilde{X} \wedge Y | XS) \\
&= I(\tilde{X} \wedge YX | S) - I(\tilde{X} \wedge X | S) \\
&\geq I(\tilde{X} \wedge YX | S) - \varepsilon
\end{aligned}
$$

because $I(\tilde{X} \wedge X | S) \leq I(X \wedge \tilde{X}S) \leq \varepsilon$ by (A.7). Hence the claim will hold if Ψ is chosen as the set of those joint distributions $P_{X\tilde{X}SY}$ that satisfy $I(\tilde{X} \wedge YX | S) \geq \xi > 0$ in addition to (V.20). It can be shown that this Ψ is permissible if

the AVC is nonsymmetrizable and η, ξ are sufficiently small, cf. [33] for details.

REFERENCES

[1] R. Ahlswede, "Multi-way communication channels," in *Proc. 2nd Int. Symp. Inform. Theory* (Tsahkadzor, Armenian SSR, 1971). Budapest, Hungary: Akadémiai Kiadó, 1973, pp. 23–52.

[2] ——, "Elimination of correlation in random codes for arbitrarily varying channels," *Z. Wahrscheinlichkeitsth. Verw. Gebiete*, vol. 44, pp. 159–175, 1978.

[3] ——, "Coloring hypergraphs: A new approach to multi-user source coding I–II," *J. Comb. Inform. Syst. Sci.*, vol. 4, pp. 76–115, 1979, and vol. 5, pp. 220–268, 1980.

[4] ——, A method of coding and an application to arbitrarily varying channels, *J. Comb. Inform. Systems Sci.*, vol. 5, pp. 10–35, 1980.

[5] ——, "Extremal properties of rate distortion functions," *IEEE Trans. Inform. Theory*, vol. 36, pp. 166–171, Jan. 1990.

[6] ——, "The maximal error capacity of arbitrarily varying channels for constant list sizes," *IEEE Trans. Inform. Theory*, vol. 39, pp. 1416–1417, 1993.

[7] R. Ahlswede and N. Cai, "Two proofs of Pinsker's conjecture concerning arbitrarily varying channels," *IEEE Trans. Inform. Theory*, vol. 37, pp. 1647–1649, Nov. 1991.

[8] ——, "Arbitrarily varying multiple-access channels, part 1. Ericson's symmetrizability is adequate, Gubner's conjecture is true," Preprint 96–068, Sonderforschungsbereich 343, Universität Bielefeld, Bielefeld, Germany.

[9] R. Ahlswede, N. Cai, and Z. Zhang, "Erasure, list, and detection zero-error capacities for low noise and a relation to identification," *IEEE Trans. Inform. Theory*, vol. 42, pp. 52–62, Jan. 1996.

[10] R. Ahlswede and J. Wolfowitz, "The capacity of a channel with arbitrarily varying cpf's and binary output alphabets," *Z. Wahrscheinlichkeitsth. Verw. Gebiete*, vol. 15, pp. 186–194, 1970.

[11] R. Ahlswede, E. Yang, and Z. Zhang, "Identification via compressed data," *IEEE Trans. Inform. Theory*, vol. 43, pp. 48–70, Jan. 1997.

[12] V. B. Balakirsky, "A converse coding theorem for mismatched decoding at the output of binary-input memoryless channels," *IEEE Trans. Inform. Theory*, vol. 41, pp. 1989–1902, Nov. 1995.

[13] T. Berger, *Rate Distortion Theory: A Mathematical Basis for Data Compression.* Englewood Cliffs, NJ: Prentice Hall, 1971.

[14] P. Billingsley, "Statistical methods in Markov chains," *Ann. Math. Statist.*, vol. 32, pp. 12–40; correction, p. 1343, 1961.

[15] D. Blackwell, L. Breiman, and A. J. Thomasian, "The capacities of certain channel classes under random coding," *Ann. Math. Statist.*, vol. 31, pp. 558–567, 1960.

[16] R. E. Blahut, "Composition bounds for channel block codes," *IEEE Trans. Inform. Theory*, vol. IT-23, pp. 656–674, 1977.

[17] V. Blinovsky, P. Narayan, and M. Pinsker, "Capacity of the arbitrarily varying channel under list decoding," *Probl. Pered. Inform.*, vol. 31, pp. 99–113, 1995.

[18] L. Boltzmann, "Beziehung zwischen dem zweiten Hauptsatze der mechanischen Wärmetheorie und der Wahrscheinlichkeitsrechnung respektive den Sätzen über das Wärmegleichgewicht," *Wien. Ber.*, vol. 76, pp. 373–435, 1877.

[19] L. B. Boza, "Asymptotically optimal tests for finite Markov chains," *Ann. Math. Statist.*, vol. 42, pp. 1992–2007, 1971.

[20] H. Chernoff, "A measure of asymptotic efficiency for tests of a hypothesis based on a sum of observations," *Ann. Math. Statist.*, vol. 23, pp. 493–507, 1952.

[21] G. Cohen, I. Honkala, S. Litsyn, and A. Lobstein, *Covering Codes.* Amsterdam, The Netherlands: North Holland, 1997.

[22] I. Csiszár, "Joint source-channel error exponent," *Probl. Contr. Inform. Theory*, vol. 9, pp. 315–328, 1980.

[23] ——, "Linear codes for sources and source networks: Error exponents, universal coding," *IEEE Trans. Inform. Theory*, vol. IT-28, pp. 585–592, July 1982.

[24] ——, "On the error exponent of source-channel transmission with a distortion threshold," *IEEE Trans. Inform. Theory*, vol. IT-28, pp. 823–828, Nov. 1982.

[25] ——, "Arbitrarily varying channels with general alphabets and states," *IEEE Trans. Inform. Theory*, vol. 38, pp. 1725–1742, 1992.

[26] I. Csiszár, T. M. Cover, and B. S. Choi, "Conditional limit theorems under Markov conditioning," *IEEE Trans. Inform. Theory*, vol. IT-33, pp. 788–801, Nov. 1987.

[27] I. Csiszár and J. Körner "Towards a general theory of source networks," *IEEE Trans. Inform. Theory*, vol. IT-26, pp. 155–165, Jan. 1980.

[28] ——, "Graph decomposition: A new key to coding theorems," *IEEE Trans. Inform. Theory*, vol. IT-27, pp. 5–11, Jan. 1981.

[29] ——, "On the capacity of the arbitrarily varying channel for maximum probability of error," *Z. Wahrscheinlichkeitsth. Verw. Gebiete*, vol. 57, pp. 87–101, 1981.

[30] ——, *Information Theory: Coding Theorems for Discrete Memoryless Systems*. New York: Academic, 1981.

[31] ——, "Feedback does not affect the reliability function of a DMC at rates above capacity," *IEEE Trans. Inform. Theory*, vol. IT-28, pp. 92–93, Jan. 1982.

[32] I. Csiszár, J. Körner, and K. Marton, "A new look at the error exponent of discrete memoryless channels," presented at the IEEE Int. Symp. Information Theory (Cornell Univ., Ithaca, NY, 1977), preprint.

[33] I. Csiszár and P. Narayan, "The capacity of the arbitrarily varying channel revisited: Positivity, constraints," *IEEE Trans. Inform. Theory*, vol. 34, pp. 181–193, Mar. 1988.

[34] ——, "Capacity and decoding rules for arbitrarily varying channels," *IEEE Trans. Inform. Theory*, vol. 35, pp. 752–769, July 1989.

[35] ——, "Channel capacity for a given decoding metric," *IEEE Trans. Inform. Theory*, vol. 41, pp. 35–43, Jan. 1995.

[36] ——, "Capacity of the Gaussian arbitrarily varying channel," *IEEE Trans. Inform. Theory*, vol. 37, pp. 18–26, Jan. 1991.

[37] I. Csiszár and P. C. Shields, "Redundancy rates for renewal and other processes," *IEEE Trans. Inform. Theory*, vol. 42, pp. 2065–2072, Nov. 1996.

[38] L. Davisson, G. Longo, and A. Sgarro, "The error exponent for the noiseless encoding of finite ergodic Markov sources," *IEEE Trans. Inform. Theory*, vol. IT-27, pp. 431–348, 1981.

[39] A. Dembo and O. Zeitouni, *Large Deviations Techniques and Applications*. Jones and Bartlett, 1993.

[40] R. L. Dobrushin and S. Z. Stambler, "Coding theorems for classes of arbitrarily varying discrete memoryless channels," *Probl. Pered. Inform.*, vol. 11, no. 2, pp. 3–22, 1975, English translation.

[41] G. Dueck, "Maximal error capacity regions are smaller than average error capacity regions for multi-user channels," *Probl. Contr. Inform. Theory*, vol. 7, pp. 11–19, 1978.

[42] G. Dueck and J. Körner, "Reliability function of a discrete memoryless channel at rates above capacity," *IEEE Trans. Inform. Theory*, vol. IT-25, pp. 82–85, Jan. 1979.

[43] T. Ericson, "Exponential error bounds for random codes in the arbitrarily varying channel," *IEEE Trans. Inform. Theory*, vol. IT-31, pp. 42–48, Jan. 1985.

[44] R. M. Fano, *Transmission of Information, A Statistical Theory of Communications*. New York: Wiley, 1961.

[45] L. Finesso, C. C. Liu, and P. Narayan, "The optimal error exponent for Markov order estimation," *IEEE Trans. Inform. Theory*, vol. 42, pp. 1488–1497, Sept. 1996.

[46] R. G. Gallager, "A simple derivation of the coding theorem and some applications," *IEEE Trans. Inform. Theory*, vol. IT-11, pp. 3–18, Jan. 1965.

[47] ——, "A perspective on multiaccess channels," *IEEE Trans. Inform. Theory*, vol. IT-31, pp. 124–142, Mar. 1985.

[48] V. D. Goppa, "Nonprobabilistic mutual information without memory," *Probl. Contr. Inform. Theory*, vol. 4, pp. 97–102, 1975.

[49] P. Groeneboom, J. Oosterhoff, and F. H. Ruymgaart, "Large deviation theorems for empirical probability measures," *Ann. Probab.*, vol. 7, pp. 553–586, 1979.

[50] J. A. Gubner, "On the deterministic-code capacity of the multiple-access arbitrarily varying channel," *IEEE Trans. Inform. Theory*, vol. 36, pp. 262–275, Mar. 1990.

[51] M. Gutman, "Asymptotically optimal classification for multiple tests with empirically observed statistics," *IEEE Trans. Inform. Theory*, vol. 35, pp. 401–408, Mar. 1989.

[52] E. A. Haroutunian, "Bounds on the error probability exponent for semicontinuous memoryless channels," *Probl. Pered. Inform.*, vol. 4, no. 4, pp. 37–48, 1968, in Russian.

[53] W. Hoeffding, "Asymptotically optimal tests for multinominal distributions," *Ann. Math. Statist.*, vol. 36, pp. 1916–1921, 1956.

[54] B. L. Hughes, "The smallest list for the arbitrarily varying channel," *IEEE Trans. Inform. Theory*, vol. 43, pp. 803–815, May 1997.

[55] J. Y. N. Hui, "Fundamental issues of multiple accessing," Ph.D. dissertation, MIT, Cambridge, MA, 1983.

[56] J. H. Jahn, "Coding for arbitrarily varying multiuser channels," *IEEE Trans. Inform. Theory*, vol. IT-27, pp. 212–226, Mar. 1981.

[57] J. Kiefer and J. Wolfowitz, "Channels with arbitrarily varying channel probability functions," *Inform. Contr.*, vol. 5, pp. 44–54, 1962.

[58] J. Körner and A. Sgarro, "Universally attainable error exponents for broadcast channels with degraded message sets," *IEEE Trans. Inform. Theory*, vol. IT-26, pp. 670–679, 1980.

[59] A. Lapidoth, "Mismatched decoding and the multiple-access channel," *IEEE Trans. Inform. Theory*, vol. 42, pp. 1439–1452, Sept. 1996.

[60] H. J. Liao, "Multiple access channels," Ph.D. dissertation, Univ. Hawaii, Honolulu, 1972.

[61] T. Linder, G. Lugosi, and K. Zeger, "Fixed-rate universal lossy source coding and rates of convergence for memoryless sources," *IEEE Trans. Inform. Theory*, vol. 41, pp. 665–676, May 1995.

[62] Y. S. Liu and B. L. Hughes, "A new universal random coding bound for the multiple-access channel," *IEEE Trans. Inform. Theory*, vol. 42, pp. 376–386, 1996.

[63] G. Longo and A. Sgarro, "The source coding theorem revisited: A combinatorial approach," *IEEE Trans. Inform. Theory*, vol. IT-25, pp. 544–548, May 1979.

[64] K. Marton, "Error exponent for source coding with a fidelity criterion," *IEEE Trans. Inform. Theory*, vol. IT-20, pp. 197–199, Mar. 1974.

[65] N. Merhav, "A comment on 'A rate of convergence result for a universal d-semifaithful code,'" *IEEE Trans. Inform. Theory*, vol. 41, pp. 1200–1202, July 1995.

[66] N. Merhav, M. Gutman, and J. Ziv, "On the estimation of the order of a Markov chain and universal data compression," *IEEE Trans. Inform. Theory*, vol. 35, pp. 1014–1019, Sept. 1989.

[67] N. Merhav, G. Kaplan, A. Lapidoth, and S. Shamai, "On information rates for mismatched decoders," *IEEE Trans. Inform. Theory*, vol. 40, pp. 1953–1967, Nov. 1994.

[68] S. Natarajan, "Large deviations, hypothesis testing, and source coding for finite Markov sources," *IEEE Trans. Inform. Theory*, vol. IT-31, pp. 360–365, 1985.

[69] Y. Oohama, "Universal coding for correlated sources with linked encoders," *IEEE Trans. Inform. Theory*, vol. 42, pp. 837–847, May 1996.

[70] Y. Oohama and T. S. Han, "Universal coding for the Slepian–Wolf data compression system and the strong converse theorem," *IEEE Trans. Inform. Theory*, vol. 40, pp. 1908–1919, 1994.

[71] J. Pokorny and H. M. Wallmeier, "Random coding bound and codes produced by permutations for the multiple-access channel," *IEEE Trans. Inform. Theory*, vol. IT-31, pp. 741–750, Nov. 1985.

[72] I. N. Sanov, "On the probability of large deviations of random variables," *Mat. Sbornik*, vol. 42, pp. 11–44, 1957, in Russian; English translation in *Select. Transl. Math. Statist. Probab.*, vol. 1, pp. 213–244, 1961.

[73] E. Schrödinger, "Über die Umkehrung der Naturgesetze," *Sitzungsber. Preuss. Akad. Wiss. Berlin Phys. Math. Klass.*, vols. 8/9, pp. 144–153, 1931.

[74] C. E. Shannon, R. G. Gallager, and E. R. Berlekamp, "Lower bounds to error probability for coding on discrete memoryless channels," *Inform. Contr.*, vol. 10, pp. 65–104 and 522–552, 1967.

[75] C. E. Shannon and W. Weaver, *The Mathematical Theory of Communication*. Urbana, IL: Univ. Illinois Press, 1949.

[76] D. Slepian and J. K. Wolf, "Noiseless coding of correlated information sources," *IEEE Trans. Inform. Theory*, vol. IT-19, pp. 471–480, 1973.

[77] İ. E. Telatar and R. G. Gallager, "New exponential upper bounds to error and erasure probabilities," in *Proc. IEEE Int. Symp. Information Theory* (Trondheim, Norway, 1994), p. 379.

[78] G. Tusnády, "On asymptotically optimal tests," *Ann. Statist.*, vol. 5, pp. 358–393, 1977.

[79] M. J. Weinberger, N. Merhav, and M. Feder, "Optimal sequential probability assignment for individual sequences," *IEEE Trans. Inform. Theory*, vol. 40, pp. 384–396, Mar. 1994.

[80] P. Whittle, "Some distributions and moment formulae for the Markov chain," *J. Roy. Stat. Soc.*, ser. B, vol. 17, pp. 235–242, 1955.

[81] J. Wolfowitz, *Coding Theorems of Information Theory*. Berlin, Germany: Springer, 1961.

[82] B. Yu and T. P. Speed, "A rate of convergence result for a universal d-semifaithful code," *IEEE Trans. Inform. Theory*, vol. 39, pp. 513–820, May 1993.

[83] Z. Zhang, E. Yang, and V. K. Wei, "The redundancy of source coding with a fidelity criterion—Part one: Known statistics," *IEEE Trans. Inform. Theory*, vol. 43, pp. 71–91, Jan. 1997.

Comments on Broadcast Channels

Thomas M. Cover, *Fellow, IEEE*

(Invited Paper)

Abstract— The key ideas in the theory of broadcast channels are illustrated by discussing some of the progress toward finding the capacity region. The capacity region is still unknown.

Index Terms— Binning, broadcast channel, capacity, degraded broadcast channel, feedback capacity, Slepian–Wolf, superposition.

I. INTRODUCTION

A broadcast channel has one sender and many receivers. The object is to broadcast information to the receivers. The information may be independent or nested. We shall treat broadcast channels with two receivers as shown in Fig. 1. Multiple receiver broadcast channels are defined similarly.

Definition: A *broadcast channel* consists of an input alphabet $\mathcal{X}$ and two output alphabets $\mathcal{Y}_1$ and $\mathcal{Y}_2$ and a probability transition function $p(y_1, y_2 | x)$. The broadcast channel is said to be *memoryless* if

$$p(y_1^n, y_2^n | x^n) = \prod_{i=1}^{n} p(y_{1i}, y_{2i} | x_i).$$

A $((2^{nR_1}, 2^{nR_2}), n)$ code for a broadcast channel with independent information consists of an encoder

$$x^n \colon 2^{nR_1} \times 2^{nR_2} \to \mathcal{X}^n,$$

and two decoders

$$\hat{W}_1 \colon \mathcal{Y}_1^n \to 2^{nR_1}$$
$$\hat{W}_2 \colon \mathcal{Y}_2^n \to 2^{nR_2}.$$

The probability of error $P_e^{(n)}$ is defined to be the probability the decoded message is not equal to the transmitted message, i.e.,

$$P_e^{(n)} = P(\hat{W}_1(Y_1^n) \neq W_1 \text{ or } \hat{W}_2(Y_2^n) \neq W_2)$$

where the message (W_1, W_2) is assumed to be uniformly distributed over $2^{nR_1} \times 2^{nR_2}$.

Definition: A rate pair (R_1, R_2) is said to be *achievable* for the broadcast channel if there exists a sequence of $((2^{nR_1}, 2^{nR_2}), n)$ codes with $P_e^{(n)} \to 0$.

Manuscript received December 15, 1997; revised May 1, 1998. This work was supported in part by NSF under Grant #NCR-9628193, by ARPA under Contract #J-FBI-94-218-2, and by JSEP under Grant #ARMY DAAG55-97-1-0115.

The author is with the Departments of Electrical Engineering and Statistics, Stanford University, Stanford, CA 94305 USA (e-mail: cover@isl.stanford.edu).

Publisher Item Identifier S 0018-9448(98)06081-7.

Fig. 1. Broadcast channel.

Definition: The *capacity region* of the broadcast channel is the closure of the set of achievable rates.

It is often the case in practice that one received signal is a degraded, or corrupted, version of the other. One receiver may be farther away or "downstream." When X, Y_1, Y_2 forms a Markov chain, i.e., when $p(y_1, y_2 | x) = p(y_1 | x) p(y_2 | y_1)$ we say that Y_2 is a *physically degraded* version of Y_1 and that $p(y_1, y_2 | x)$ is a *physically degraded* broadcast channel. We note that the probabilities of error $P(\hat{W}_1 \neq W_1)$ and $P(\hat{W}_2 \neq W_2)$ depend only on the marginals $p(y_1 | x)$ and $p(y_2 | x)$ and not on the joint. Thus we define a weaker notion of degraded.

Definition: A broadcast channel $p(y_1, y_2 | x)$ is said to be *degraded* if there exists a distribution $\tilde{p}(y_2 | y_1)$ such that

$$p(y_2 | x) = \sum_{y_1} p(y_1 | x) \tilde{p}(y_2 | y_1).$$

II. CAPACITY REGION FOR THE DEGRADED BROADCAST CHANNEL

Achievable rate regions for Gaussian broadcast channels, cascades of binary-symmetric channels (a special case of degraded broadcast channels), the push-to-talk channel, orthogonal broadcast channels, and product broadcast channels were found in Cover [16]. Surveys of multiuser theory, including broadcast channels, can be found in [19], [22], [23], [26], [35], [62], [69], [98], [99], [100], [107], and [108].

We first consider sending independent information over a degraded broadcast channel (Fig. 2) at rates R_1 to Y_1 and R_2 to Y_2. The capacity region, conjectured in [16], was proved to be achievable by Bergmans [9], and the converse was established by Bergmans [10] and Gallager [41].

Theorem 1: The capacity region for the degraded broadcast channel $X \to Y_1 \to Y_2$ is the convex hull of the closure of all (R_1, R_2) satisfying

$$R_2 \leq I(U; Y_2)$$
$$R_1 \leq I(X; Y_1 | U)$$

for some joint distribution $p(u)p(x|u)p(y, z|x)$, where the auxiliary random variable U has cardinality bounded by $|\mathcal{U}| \leq \min\{|\mathcal{X}|, |\mathcal{Y}_1|, |\mathcal{Y}_2|\}$.

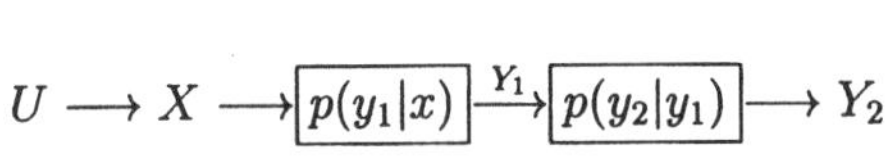

$$U \longrightarrow X \longrightarrow \boxed{p(y_1|x)} \xrightarrow{Y_1} \boxed{p(y_2|y_1)} \longrightarrow Y_2$$

Fig. 2. Degraded broadcast channel with auxiliary input U.

Proof (Outline of Achievability): We first give an outline of the basic idea of superposition coding for the broadcast channel. The auxiliary random variable U will serve as a cloud center distinguishable by both receivers Y_1 and Y_2. Each cloud consists of 2^{nR_1} codewords X^n distinguishable by receiver Y_1. The worst receiver Y_2 can only see the clouds, while the better receiver can see the individual codewords within the clouds.

Fix $p(u)$ and $p(x|u)$.

Random Codebook Generation. Generate 2^{nR_2} independent codewords of length n, $u^n(w_2)$, $w_2 \in \{1, 2, \cdots, 2^{nR_2}\}$, according to $\prod_{i=1}^{n} p(u_i)$.

For each codeword $u^n(w_2)$, generate 2^{nR_1} independent codewords $x^n(w_1, w_2)$ according to the conditional probability mass function $\prod_{i=1}^{n} p(x_i|u_i(w_2))$. Here $u^n(w_2)$ plays the role of the cloud center understandable to both Y_1 and Y_2, while $x^n(w_1, w_2)$ is the w_1th satellite codeword in the w_2th cloud. The cloud center $u^n(w_2)$ is never actually sent.

Encoding: To transmit the pair (W_1, W_2), send the corresponding codeword $x^n(W_1, W_2)$.

Decoding: Receiver Y_2 determines the unique $\hat{\hat{W}}_2$ such that $(u^n(\hat{\hat{W}}_2), y_2^n)$ is jointly typical. If there are none such or more than one such, an error is declared.

Receiver Y_1 looks for the unique $(\hat{W}_1, \hat{W}_2)$ such that $(u^n(\hat{W}_2), x^n(\hat{W}_1, \hat{W}_2), y_1^n)$ is jointly typical. If there are none such or more than one such, an error is declared.

Error Analysis (Outline): The condition

$$R_2 < I(U; Y_2)$$

guarantees that $\hat{\hat{W}}_2 = W_2$ with high probability because there are $2^{nI(U; Y_2)}$ distinguishable u^n's as observed by Y_2. The extra information in $x^n \sim p(x^n|u^n)$ is viewed as noise by Y_2. The condition $R_1 < I(X; Y_1|U)$ guarantees that receiver Y_1 can decode $\hat{W}_1 = W_1$ with high probability, given that the receiver has already decoded W_2. $\square$

Note that the proof uses a "subtract-off" or conditioning idea for receiver Y_1. Let Y_1 first determine $u^n(W_2)$. This can be done, because the inferior receiver Y_2 can also determine W_2. Then condition on u^n (or subtract it from the received signal for the Gaussian channel) and decode the refined message W_1 given u^n and Y_1^n.

This subtract-off method can also be used for the multiple-access channel, and its implementation is one of the challenges of code-division multiple access (CDMA). A treatment of code-division broadcasting (one sender and m receivers) and code division multiple access (m senders and one receiver) for the bandlimited additive white Gaussian noise channel is given in Bergmans and Cover [11], where it is proved that the CDMA rate region is strictly larger than the rate regions

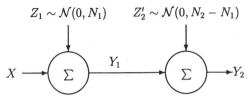

Fig. 3. Gaussian broadcast channel.

achievable by frequency-division multiple access (FDMA) and time-division multiple access (TDMA).

We now consider the Gaussian broadcast channel

$$Y_1 = X + Z_1$$
$$Y_2 = X + Z_2$$

where $Z_1 \sim \mathcal{N}(0, N_1)$ and $Z_2 \sim \mathcal{N}(0, N_2)$. This is a particular example of a degraded broadcast channel because the channel can be recharacterized as shown in Fig. 3, where $Z_2' \sim \mathcal{N}(0, N_2 - N_1)$.

Let

$$C(x) = \frac{1}{2} \log (1 + x)$$

denote the capacity in bits per transmission of a memoryless Gaussian channel with signal-to-noise ratio x.

Theorem 2: The capacity region for the Gaussian broadcast channel, with signal power constraint P, is given by

$$R_1 \leq C\left(\frac{\alpha P}{N_1}\right)$$
$$R_2 \leq C\left(\frac{(1-\alpha)P}{\alpha P + N_2}\right), \qquad \text{for } 0 \leq \alpha \leq 1.$$

This region is achieved by the coding scheme described in [16]. Choose 2^{nR_2} Gaussian codewords $u^n(i)$ independent and identically distributed (i.i.d.) $\sim \mathcal{N}(0, (1-\alpha)P)$. For each of these codewords $u^n(i)$, generate 2^{nR_1} satellite Gaussian codewords $v^n(j)$ of power αP and add them to form codewords $x^n(i, j) = u^n(i) + v^n(j)$. Thus, the fine information $v^n(j)$ is "superimposed" on the coarse information $u^n(i)$. Bermans [9], [10] proved the converse.

The achievability of the region in Theorem 1 for general degraded broadcast channels was established by Bergmans [9]. There followed a year of intense activity trying to prove the converse, i.e., to prove that the natural achievable rate region, was indeed the capacity region. Correspondences were exchanged between Aaron Wyner (Bell Labs), Patrick Bergmans (then at Cornell), and Robert Gallager (MIT). Finally, one day at the end of the year, Wyner received proofs of the converse by Bergmans [10] and by Gallager [41]. Gallager's proof successfully defined the role of the auxiliary random variable U in terms of the collection of all the outputs up to the current time. Bergmans' proof, on the other hand, held for the Gaussian channel. Gallager's proof did not apply to the Gaussian channel with a power constraint, nor did Bergmans' proof apply to the general unrestricted broadcast channel. Bergmans' proof, instead, used a conditional entropy power inequality, the first use of this inequality since Shannon (1948).

So the key ideas in the early papers were superposition coding, subtracting off (or conditioning on) message information layer by layer, identification of the superposition variable in the converse, and the use of the entropy power inequality.

III. THE DETERMINISTIC BROADCAST CHANNEL

Van der Meulen [97] and Cover [18] established an achievable rate region for sending common information at rate R_0 to both receivers and conditionally independent information at rates R_1 and R_2 to the two receivers. (Jahn [58] considered the arbitrarily varying broadcast channel counterpart.) The region was soon enlarged by ingenious work by Gelfand [42], Pinsker [43], [82], and Marton [74], [75]. Gelfand looked at a particular deterministic broadcast channel, known as the Blackwell channel, given by

$$Y_1 = \begin{cases} 1, & x = 1 \\ 0, & x = 2 \text{ or } 3 \end{cases}$$

$$Y_2 = \begin{cases} 1, & x = 1 \text{ or } 2 \\ 0, & x = 3. \end{cases}$$

Here one sees that one can send at one bit per transmission to receiver Y_1 or to receiver Y_2, but not simultaneously to both. What, then, is the set of achievable (R_1, R_2) pairs?

Gelfand found the capacity region in [42]. Soon thereafter, Marton [74] and Pinsker [82] independently established the capacity region for general deterministic broadcast channels. The extra ingredient in the deterministic broadcast channel investigation is the use of the Slepian–Wolf theorem [94] and a binning argument [17] used in its proof.

In the Slepian–Wolf theorem, one has two correlated random variables U and V, and i.i.d. copies (U_i, V_i) all drawn according to $p(u, v)$. How many bits of information R_1 does one need to say about U and how many bits R_2 does one need to say about V so that the combined description will recover U and V with negligible probability of error?

Theorem 3 (Slepian and Wolf [94]): Let $(U_i, V_i) i = 1, 2, \cdots$, be i.i.d. discrete random variables. There exist maps $i_n: \mathcal{U}^n \longrightarrow 2^{nR_1}$, $j_n: \mathcal{V}^n \longrightarrow 2^{nR_2}$, $|i_n(\cdot)| = 2^{nR_1}$, $|j_n(\cdot)| = 2^{nR_2}$, and reconstruction functions $\hat{u}^n(i_n, j_n)$, $\hat{v}^n(i_n, j_n)$, such that

$$\Pr\{(\hat{U}^n, \hat{V}^n) \neq (U^n, V^n)\} \longrightarrow 0$$

if and only if

$$R_1 > H(U|V)$$
$$R_2 > H(V|U)$$
$$R_1 + R_2 > H(U, V). \qquad (1)$$

One can achieve a rate pair in this region by a random binning argument. Suppose that one randomly throws all u^n sequences into 2^{nR_1} bins. Similarly, one randomly throws the v^n sequences into 2^{nR_2} bins. Describe U^n by its bin number $i(U^n)$ and V^n by its bin number $j(V^n)$, where $|i(\cdot)| = 2^{nR_1}$, and $|j(\cdot)| = 2^{nR_2}$. Then a common receiver will be given the bin numbers of U^n and V^n. If there is only one jointly typical

(U^n, V^n) pair in that bin, the receiver will make no mistake in reconstructing U^n and V^n. So the idea is to form a product partition of $2^{nR_1} \times 2^{nR_2}$ bins that is fine enough to isolate the typical (U^n, V^n) pairs. Rates (R_1, R_2) satisfying (1) suffice.

For the proof of the capacity of the deterministic broadcast channel, we use a product partition that is coarse enough so that with high probability any product bin will contain at least one typical (y_2^n, y_2^n) receiver sequence. To see how this is done we consider a channel in which $y_1 = f_1(x)$, $y_2 = f_2(x)$, where f_1 and f_2 are deterministic functions.

Suppose one wishes to send a pair of indices i and j to receivers 1 and 2, respectively. Fix a probability distribution $p(x)$, thus inducing a joint distribution $p(x, y_1, y_2)$. From this we can calculate the marginal distribution $p(y_1, y_2)$. The object here is to control Y_1 and Y_2 simultaneously by use of X. We first do a product binning of y_1^n and y_2^n, 2^{nR_1} bins for the y_1^n sequences and 2^{nR_2} bins for y_2^n. For what set of rates R_1 and R_2 will these bins contain at least one jointly typical (y_1^n, y_2^n)? Once we have answered that question, the problem is solved, because y_1^n and y_2^n are deterministic functions of x^n, so if there exists a jointly typical (y_1^n, y_2^n) in bin (i, j), say, one merely looks up the sequence x^n which results in y_1^n and y_2^n in order to send information i to Y_1 and j to Y_2. Thus rates R_1 and R_2 are achieved.

The partitioning of $\mathcal{Y}_1^n \times \mathcal{Y}_2^n$ is coarse enough so that a given (i, j) bin contains at least one jointly typical pair (X^n, Y^n), with high probability, if $R_1 < H(Y_1)$, $R_2 < H(Y_2)$, and $R_1 + R_2 < H(Y_1, Y_2)$. Thus we have the following theorem:

Theorem 4 [74], [82]: The capacity region of the deterministic memoryless broadcast channel with $y_1 = f_1(x)$, $y_2 = f_2(x)$, is given by the convex closure of the union of the rate pairs (R_1, R_2) satisfying

$$R_1 < H(Y_1)$$
$$R_2 < H(Y_2)$$
$$R_1 + R_2 < H(Y_1, Y_2).$$

Comment: Here $R_1 < H(Y_1)$ ensures that there is at least one typical y_1^n per bin, and $R_1 + R_2 \leq H(Y_1, Y_2)$ ensures there is at least one jointly typical (y_1^n, y_2^n) per product bin. We note the interesting complementary relationship of this rate region to the Slepian–Wolf region in Fig. 4.

Marton [75] then generalized this result to arbitrary broadcast channels by setting up a kind of determinism by selecting a subset of distinguishable input sequences. Soon thereafter El Gamal and Van der Meulen [36] gave a simpler proof.

In the following theorem, we outline a proof of a special case of Marton's general result, where it is assumed that the information is independent and there is no common message. This special case isolates a new coding idea involving a pair of auxiliary random variables. This, together with superposition, yields Marton's theorem. Papers referring to Marton's region include Gelfand [43], Hajek [51], Han [52], Heegard [56], and Jahn [58], as well as [22], [23], [35], and [36]. The outline of the proof of the following theorem is due to El Gamal and Van der Meulen [36].

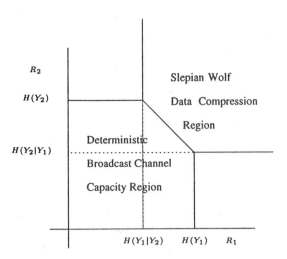

Fig. 4. The capacity regions for Slepian–Wolf data compression and for the deterministic broadcast channel, for the joint probability mass function $p(y_1, y_2)$ induced by $p(x)$.

Theorem 5 (Marton [75]): The rates (R_1, R_2) are achievable for the broadcast channel $\{\mathcal{X}, p(y_1, y_2|x), \mathcal{Y}_1 \times \mathcal{Y}_2\}$ if

$$R_1 \leq I(U; Y_1)$$
$$R_2 \leq I(V; Y_2)$$
$$R_1 + R_2 \leq I(U; Y_1) + I(V; Y_2) - I(U; V) \quad (2)$$

for some $p(u, v, x)$ on $\mathcal{U} \times \mathcal{V} \times \mathcal{X}$.

Comment: This achievable region is the capacity region if the broadcast channel has one deterministic component [75].

Proof (Outline): Fix $p(u, v)$, $p(x|u, v)$. The channel $p(y_1, y_2|x)$ is given. The idea is to send u to y_1 and v to y_2.
Random Coding: Generate $2^{nI(U; Y_1)}$ typical u's $\sim p(u)$. Generate $2^{nI(V; Y_2)}$ typical v's $\sim p(v)$. Randomly throw the u's into 2^{nR_1} bins and the v's into the 2^{nR_2} bins. For each product bin, find a *jointly* typical (u, v) pair. This can be done if

$$R_1 + R_2 < I(U; Y_1) + I(V; Y_2) - I(U; V).$$

To see this, recall that independent choices of u^n and v^n result in a jointly typical (u^n, v^n) with probability $2^{-nI(U; V)}$. Now there are $2^{n(I(U; Y_1) - R_1)}$ u^n's in any U bin, and $2^{n(I(V; Y_2) - R_2)}$ v^n's in any V bin. Thus the expected number of jointly typical (u^n, v^n) pairs in a given product $U \times V$ bin is

$$2^{n(I(U; Y_1) - R_1)} 2^{n(I(V; Y_2) - R_2)} 2^{-nI(U; V)}.$$

The desired jointly typical (u^n, v^n) pair can be found if this expected number is much greater than 1, which follows if (R_1, R_2) satisfies (2).
Continuing with the coding, for each $U \times V$ bin and its designated jointly typical (u^n, v^n) pair, generate $x^n(u^n, v^n)$ according to the conditional distribution $\prod_{k=1}^n p(x_k|u_k, v_k)$.

Encoding: To send i to Y_1 and j to Y_2, send $x^n(u^n, v^n)$, where (u^n, v^n) is the designated pair in the product bin (i, j).
Decoding: Receiver Y_1, upon receiving y_1^n, finds the u^n such that (u^n, y_1^n) is jointly typical. Thus it is necessary that $R_1 < I(U; Y_1)$. He then finds the index i of the bin in which u^n lies. Receiver Y_2 finds the v^n such that (v^n, y_2^n) is jointly typical. Thus we need $R_2 < I(V; Y_2)$. He then finds the index j of the bin in which v^n lies. $\square$

IV. RESULTS FOR SPECIFIC CHANNELS

El Gamal [30] showed that feedback cannot increase the capacity of the physically degraded broadcast channel, i.e., broadcast channels for which $p(y_1, y_2|x) = p(y_1|x)p(y_2|y_1)$. It was later shown by Dueck [29] and Ozarow [80], [81] that feedback can in fact increase the capacity of general broadcast channels, in contrast to the single-user channel, where Shannon [91] proved that feedback does not increase capacity.

Ozarow and Leung [81] showed a new way to achieve the capacity region for the Gaussian broadcast channel with feedback using the Kailath–Schalkwijk coding scheme, in which one uses feedback to attempt to correct the misperceptions of (Y_1, Y_2) as seen by the transmitter. Their method, however, does not generalize to more than two receivers. Work on feedback capacity for broadcast channels appears in [29]–[31], [34], [71], [72], [80], and [81].

Poltyrev [84]–[87] looked at the reversely degraded broadcast channel (see also Hughes-Hartogs [57] for the Gaussian channel and Ohkubo [75]). Later, El Gamal [33] furnished a proof of the converse, thus establishing the Poltyrev region for the reversely degraded broadcast channel as the capacity region.

Channels in which one receiver is superior to another and channels with nested information were studied by Marton, Körner, Csiszár, El Gamal, and others [24], [32], [39], [62]–[64].

V. AN ALTERNATIVE VIEW OF CAPACITY

In this section, we illustrate the delicacy of the definition of the capacity region for broadcast channels and multiuser channels in general.

We consider a memoryless broadcast channel with m receivers $Y_1, Y_2, \cdots, Y_m$. If we were to ignore the needs of all receivers but the kth, the sender could communicate to receiver k at capacity

$$C_k = \max_{p(x)} I(X; Y_k).$$

But an optimal code for receiver Y_k generally precludes transmission at capacity to the other receivers. We now argue that a single communication strategy can achieve communication at capacity C_k bits per transmission for all the receivers, $k = 1, 2, \cdots, m$. This seems to violate the known results bounding the capacity region. Nonetheless there is some truth to this assertion. What is going on?

Suppose, for example, that an advanced civilization wishes to transmit its knowledge to other stars. Having little idea of which stars are listening, when they started to listen, or the noise characteristics of the receivers, it is not clear at first what communication strategy to employ.

But the following process seems reasonable. From time to time send a brief beacon signal to get any newcomer's attention. For somewhat longer periods, send a simple description of the language. Then send several years of information. Follow it up with thousands of years of information, including previous information. Then repeat the cycle with longer periods and more information. If the time durations are appropriately chosen, each star can receive all the information at its own capacity from the time it comes on line.

More precisely, use a $\left(2^{n_{ik}C_k}, n_{ik}\right)$ code, for receiver k, for the kth segment of the ith cycle. Thus $n_{ik}C_k$ bits would be received by Y_k during its segment of n_{ik} transmissions. Let the blocklengths n_{ik} increase rapidly enough so that

$$n_{ik}/N_{ik} \longrightarrow 1, \quad \text{as } i \longrightarrow \infty$$

where

$$N_{ik} = \sum_{r \le i} \sum_{s \le k} n_{rs}$$

is the total communication time up through segment ik. Thus even if earlier information is discarded, the information rate for receiver k at time N_{ik} is

$$n_{ik}C_k/N_{ik} \longrightarrow C_k.$$

So capacity is achieved.

In fact, these remarks are applicable to time-invariant memoryless communication networks with, say, m senders and n receivers with arbitrary noise and feedback. Let C_{jk} be the capacity from transmitter j to receiver k when all the rest of the resources of the network are devoted to aiding the communication from j to k. The other senders will presumably act as facilitators, relays, or simply get out of the way. Then, by letting the blocklengths grow as before, the capacities C_{jk} are achieved.

By now it should be clear that the resolution of the apparent discrepancy in capacity regions is that the time at which the information becomes available is different for each transmitter–receiver pair. Capacity is ϵ-achieved at a different subset of times for each receiver.

If, however, we had asked for the set of achievable rates $\{R_{jk}\}$ for block n-codes with probability of error $P_e^{(n)}(j, k) \longrightarrow 0$, we would be confined to the classical capacity region. The resolution, then, is that the capacity region is the set of rates that can be achieved simultaneously.

VI. Concluding Remarks

One of the coding ideas used in achieving good rate regions is superposition, in which one layers, or superimposes, the information intended for each of the receivers. The receiver can then peel off the information in layers. To achieve superposition, one introduces auxiliary random variables that act as virtual signals. These virtual signals participate in the construction of the code, but are not actually sent. One useful idea used in the proof of capacity for the deterministic broadcast channel is random binning of the outputs Y_1 and Y_2. Another technique is Marton's introduction of correlated auxiliary random variables. Marton's region is the largest known achievable rate region for the general broadcast channel, but the capacity region remains unknown.

Acknowledgment

The comments of A. El Gamal and J. Thomas have been very helpful.

References

[1] R. Ahlswede, "Multi-way communication channels," in *Proc. 2nd Int. Symp. Inform Theory* (Tsahkadsor, Armenian S.S.R., 1971). Budapest, Hungary: Hungarian Acad. Sciences, 1973, pp. 23–52.

[2] _____, "The capacity region of a channel with two senders and two receivers," *Ann. Probab.*, vol. 2, pp. 805–814, Oct. 1974.

[3] R. F. Ahlswede and J. Körner, "Source coding with side information and a converse for degraded broadcast channels," *IEEE Trans. Inform. Theory*, vol. IT-21, pp. 629–637, Nov. 1975.

[4] M. Aref, "Information flow in relay networks," Ph.D. dissertation, Stanford Univ., Stanford, CA, Oct. 1980.

[5] L. A. Bassalygo, "Bound for permissible transmission rates in a broadcast channel with errors in both components," *Probl. Pered. Inform.*, vol. 17, no. 4, pp. 19–28, Oct.–Dec. 1981; translated in *Probl. Inform. Transm.*, vol. 17, no. 4, pp. 228–236, Oct.–Dec. 1981.

[6] L. A. Bassalygo and M. S. Pinsker, "Bounds on volume of error-correcting codes in a broadcast channel (generalized Blackwell channel)," *Probl. Pered. Inform.*, vol. 16, no. 3, pp. 3–16, July–Sept. 1980; translated in *Probl. Inform. Transm.*, vol. 16, no. 3, pp. 163–174, July–Sept. 1980.

[7] _____, "A comment on the paper of Kasami, Lin, Wei, and Yamamura, 'Coding for the binary symmetric broadcast channel with two receivers,'" *Probl. Pered. Inform.*, vol. 24, no. 3, pp. 102–106, July–Sept. 1988; translated in *Probl. Inform. Transm.*, vol. 24, no. 3, pp. 253–257, July–Sept. 1988.

[8] R. Benzel, "The capacity region of a class of discrete additive degraded interference channels," *IEEE Trans. Inform. Theory*, vol. IT-25, pp. 228–231, Mar. 1979.

[9] P. P. Bergmans, "Random coding theorem for broadcast channels with degraded components," *IEEE Trans. Inform. Theory*, vol. IT-19, pp. 197–207, Mar. 1973.

[10] _____, "A simple converse for broadcast channels with additive white Gaussian noise," *IEEE Trans. Inform. Theory*, vol. IT-20, pp. 279–280, Mar. 1974.

[11] P. P. Bergmans and T. M. Cover, "Cooperative broadcasting," *IEEE Trans. Inform. Theory*, vol. IT-20, pp. 317–324, May 1974.

[12] R. E. Blahut, *Principles and Practice of Information Theory*. Reading, MA: Addison-Wesley, 1987.

[13] L. Boutsikaris and R. Narayan, "An achievable rate region for a broadcast channel and its implications on signal design" in *IEEE Int. Symp. Information Theory* (St. Jovite, Que., Canada, Sept. 1983), p. 62.

[14] A. Carleial, "A case where interference does not reduce capacity," *IEEE Trans. Inform. Theory*, vol. IT-23, pp. 387–390, May 1977.

[15] S. C. Chang, "Coding for T-user binary symmetric broadcast channels," in *IEEE Int. Symp. Information Theory* (Santa Monica, CA, Feb. 1981), p. 34.

[16] T. M. Cover, "Broadcast channels," *IEEE Trans. Inform. Theory*, vol. IT-18, pp. 2–14, Jan. 1972.

[17] _____, "A proof of the data compression theorem of Slepian and Wolf for ergodic sources," *IEEE Trans. Inform. Theory*, vol. IT-22, pp. 226–278, Mar. 1975.

[18] _____, "An achievable rate region for the broadcast channel," *IEEE Trans. Inform. Theory*, vol. IT-21, pp. 399–404, July 1975.

[19] _____, "Some advances in broadcast channels," in *Advances in Communication Systems, Vol. 4, Theory and Applications*, A. Viterbi, Ed. New York: Academic, 1975, ch. 4.

[20] T. M. Cover and A. El Gamal, "Capacity theorems for the relay channel," *IEEE Trans. Inform. Theory*, vol. IT-25, Sept. 1979.

[21] T. M. Cover and S. K. Leung, "An achievable rate region for the multiple-access channel with feedback," *IEEE Trans. Inform. Theory*, vol. IT-27, pp. 292–298, Mar. 1981.

[22] T. M. Cover and J. A. Thomas, *Elements of Information Theory*. Wiley, 1991.

[23] I. Csiszár and J. Körner, *Information Theory: Coding Theorems for Discrete Memoryless Systems.* New York: Academic, 1981.

[24] ——, "Broadcast channels with confidential messages," *IEEE Trans. Inform. Theory*, vol. IT-24, pp. 339–348, May 1978.

[25] H. De Pedro, C. Heegard, and J. K. Wolf, "Permutation codes for the Gaussian broadcast channel," in *IEEE Int. Symp. Information Theory* (Ronneby, Sweden, June 1976), pp. 64–65.

[26] R. L. Dobrushin, "Survey of Soviet research in information theory," *IEEE Trans. Inform. Theory*, vol. IT-18, pp. 703–724, Nov. 1972.

[27] C. P. Downey and J. K. Karlof, "Group codes for the Gaussian broadcast channel with two receivers," *IEEE Trans. Inform. Theory*, vol. IT-26, pp. 406–411, July 1980.

[28] ——, "Group codes for the M-receiver Gaussian broadcast channel," *IEEE Trans. Inform. Theory*, vol. IT-29, pp. 595–597, July 1983; also, in *IEEE Int. Symp. Information Theory* (Santa Monica, CA, Feb. 1981), pp. 34–35.

[29] G. Dueck, "Partial feedback for two-way and broadcast channels," *Inform. Contr.*, vol. 46, no. 1, pp. 1–15, July 1980.

[30] A. El Gamal, "The feedback capacity of degraded broadcast channels," *IEEE Trans. Inform. Theory*, vol. IT-24, pp. 379–381, May 1978.

[31] ——, "Broadcast channels with and without feedback," in *11th Annu. Asilomar Conf. Circuits, Systems and Computers* (Pacific Grove, CA, Nov. 1977), pp. 180–183.

[32] ——, "The capacity of a class of broadcast channels," *IEEE Trans. Inform. Theory*, vol. IT-25, pp. 166–169, Mar. 1979.

[33] ——, "Capacity of the product and sum of two unmatched broadcast channels," *Probl. Pered. Inform.*, vol. 16, no. 1, pp. 3–23, Jan.–Mar. 1980; translated in *Probl. Inform. Transm.*, vol. 16, no. 1, pp. 1–16, Jan.–Mar. 1980.

[34] ——, "The capacity of the physically degraded Gaussian broadcast channel with feedback," *IEEE Trans. Inform. Theory*, vol. IT-27, p. 508, July 1981.

[35] A. El Gamal and T. M. Cover, "Multiple user information theory," *Proc. IEEE*, vol. 68, pp. 1466–1483, Dec. 1980.

[36] A. El Gamal and E. Van der Meulen, "A proof of Marton's coding theorem for the discrete memoryless broadcast channel," *IEEE Trans. Inform. Theory*, vol. IT-27, pp. 120–122, Jan. 1981.

[37] P. Estabrook and B. Jacobs, "Optimization of direct broadcast satellite system channel capacity," in *Int. Conf. Communications: Integrating Communication for World Progress (ICC'83)* (Boston, MA, June 1983), vol. 3, pp. 1416–1420.

[38] G. D. Forney, "Information theory," unpublished course notes, 1972.

[39] P. Gacs and J. Korner, "Common information is much less than mutual information," *Probl. Contr. Inform. Theory*, vol. 2, no. 2, pp. 149–162, 1973.

[40] R. G. Gallager, *Information Theory and Reliable Communication.* New York: Wiley, 1968.

[41] ——, "Capacity and coding for degraded broadcast channels," *Probl. Pered. Inform.*, vol. 10, no. 3, pp. 3–14, July–Sept. 1974; translated in *Probl. Inform. Transm.*, pp. 185–193, July–Sept. 1974.

[42] S. I. Gelfand, "Capacity of one broadcast channel," *Probl. Pered. Inform.*, vol. 13, no. 3, pp. 106–108, July–Sept. 1977; translated in *Probl. Inform. Transm.*, pp. 240–242, July–Sept. 1977.

[43] S. I. Gelfand and M. S. Pinsker, "Capacity of a broadcast channel with one deterministic component," *Probl. Pered. Inform.*, vol. 16, no. 1, pp. 24–34, Jan.–Mar. 1980; translated in *Probl. Inform. Transm.*, vol. 16, no. 1, pp. 17–25, Jan.–Mar. 1980.

[44] ——, "Coding for channel with random parameters," *Probl. Contr. Inform. Theory*, vol. 9, no. 1, pp. 19–31, 1980.

[45] L. Georgiadis and P. Papantoni-Kazakos, "Limited feedback sensing algorithms for the broadcast channel," in *IEEE Int. Conf. Communications* (Chicago, IL, June 1985), vol. 1, pp. 52–55.

[46] ——, "Limited feedback sensing algorithms for the packet broadcast channel," *IEEE Trans. Inform. Theory*, vol. IT-31, pp. 280–294, Mar. 1985.

[47] A. Goldsmith, "Capacity and dynamic resource allocation in broadcast fading channels," in *Proc. 33rd Annu. Allerton Conf. Communication, Control, and Computing,* (Monticello, IL, Oct. 1995), pp. 915–924.

[48] ——, "Capacity of broadcast fading channels with variable rate and power," in *IEEE GLOBECOM 1996, Communications: The Key to Global Prosperity* (London, UK, Nov. 1996), pp. 92–96.

[49] A. Goldsmith and M. Effros, "The capacity region of broadcast channels with memory," in *Proc. IEEE Int. Symp. Inform. Theory* (Ulm, Germany, June–July 1997), p. 28.

[50] I. Gopal and R. Rom, "Multicasting to multiple groups over broadcast channels," *IEEE Trans. Commun.*, vol. 42, pp. 2423–2431, July 1994.

[51] B. E. Hajek and M. B. Pursley, "Evaluation of an achievable rate region for the broadcast channel," *IEEE Trans. Inform. Theory*, vol. IT-25, pp. 36–46, Jan. 1979; also in *Proc. Int. Conf. Communications* (Chicago, IL, June 1977), pp. 249–253.

[52] T. S. Han, "The capacity region for the deterministic broadcast channel with a common message," *IEEE Trans. Inform. Theory*, vol. IT-27, pp. 122–125, Jan. 1981.

[53] ——, "A new achievable rate region for the interference channel," *IEEE Trans. Inform. Theory*, vol. IT-27, pp. 49–60, Jan. 1981.

[54] T. S. Han and M. H. M. Costa, "Broadcast channels with arbitrarily correlated sources," *IEEE Trans. Inform. Theory*, vol. IT-33, pp. 641–650, Sept. 1987.

[55] C. Heegard, H. E. DePedro, and J. K. Wolf, "Permutation codes for the Gaussian broadcast channel with two receivers," *IEEE Trans. Inform. Theory*, vol. IT-24, pp. 569–578, Sept. 1978.

[56] C. Heegard and A. El Gamal, "On the capacity of computer memory with defects," *IEEE Trans. Inform. Theory*, vol. IT-29, pp. 731–739, Sept. 1983.

[57] D. Hughes-Hartogs, "The capacity of the degraded spectral Gaussian broadcast channel," Ph.D. dissertation, Inform. Syst. Lab., Stanford Univ. Stanford, CA, Tech. Rep. 7002-2, July 1975; also in *Proc. Nat. Telecommun. Conf.* (Dallas, TX, Dec. 1976), p. 52.1/1–5.

[58] J. H. Jahn, "Coding of arbitrarily varying multiuser channels," *IEEE Trans. Inform. Theory*, vol. IT-27, pp. 212–226, Mar. 1981.

[59] T. Kasami, S. Lin, V. K. Wei, and S. Yamamura, "Coding for the binary symmetric broadcast channel with two receivers," *IEEE Trans. Inform. Theory*, vol. IT-31, pp. 616–625, Sept. 1985; also in *Proc. IEEE Int. Symp. Information Theory* (St. Jovite, Que., Canada, Sept. 1983), p. 61.

[60] C. Keilers, "The capacity of the spectral Gaussian multiple-access channel," Ph.D. dissertation, Dept. Elec. Eng., Stanford Univ., Stanford, CA, Apr. 1976.

[61] R. King, "Multiple access channels with generalized feedback," Ph.D. dissertation, Stanford Univ., Stanford, CA, Mar. 1978.

[62] J. Körner, "Some methods in multi-user communication," in *Information Theory, New Trends and Open Problems*, G. Longo, Ed. Vienna, Austria: Springer-Verlag, 1976, pp. 172–176.

[63] J. Körner and K. Marton, "General broadcast channels with degraded message sets," *IEEE Trans. Inform. Theory*, vol. IT-23, pp. 60–64, Jan. 1977.

[64] ——, "Comparison of two noisy channels," *Coll. Math. Sco. F. Boliya*, vol. 16, in *Topics of Information Theory.* Amsterdam, The Netherlands: North Holland, 1977, pp. 411–423.

[65] J. Körner and A. Sgarro, "Universally attainable error exponents for broadcast channels with degraded message sets," *IEEE Trans. Inform. Theory*, vol. IT-26, pp. 670–679, Nov. 1980.

[66] B. D. Kudryashov, "Upper bounds for decoding error probability in some broadcast channels," *Probl. Pered. Inform.*, vol. 15, no. 3, pp. 3–17, July–Sept. 1979; translated in *Probl. Inform. Transm.*, pp. 163–174, July–Sept. 1979.

[67] B. D. Kudryashov and G. S. Poltyrev, "Upper bounds for decoding error probability in some broadcast channels," *Probl. Pered. Inform.*, vol. 15, no. 3, pp. 3–17, July–Sept. 1979; translated in *Probl. Inform. Transm.*, vol. 15, no. 3, pp. 163–174, July–Sept. 1979.

[68] A. V. Kuznetsov, "Use of defect-correcting codes to restrict access to a broadcast channel," *Probl. Pered. Inform.*, vol. 17, no. 4, pp. 3–10, Oct.–Dec. 1981; translated in *Probl. Inform. Transm.*, pp. 217–222, Oct.–Dec. 1981.

[69] W. J. Leighton and H. H. Tan, "Broadcast channels: Some recent developments and open problems," in *Proc. Int. Telemetering Conf.* (Los Angeles, CA, Sept. 1976), pp. 284–293.

[70] ——, "Trellis coding for degraded broadcast channels," *Inform. Contr.*, vol. 39, no. 2, pp. 119–134, Nov. 1978; and in *Proc. IEEE Int. Symp. Inform. Theory* (Ithaca, NY, Oct. 1977), p. 54.

[71] ——, "Capacity region of degraded broadcast channels with feedback," *Inform.ation Sci.*, vol. 13, no. 2, pp. 167–177, 1977.

[72] C. Leung, "On the capacity of an n-receiver broadcast channel with partial feedback," in *IEEE Int. Symp. Inform. Theory* (Santa Monica, CA, Feb. 1981), p. 27.

[73] H. Liao, "A coding theorem for multiple access communication," in *Int. Symp. Information Theory* (Asilomar, 1972); also "Multiple access channels," Ph.D. dissertation, Dept. Elec. Eng., Univ. Hawaii, Honolulu, HI, 1972.

[74] K. Marton, "The capacity region of deterministic broadcast channels," in *Trans. Int. Symp. Inform. Theory* (Paris-Cachan, France, 1977).

[75] ——, "A coding theorem for the discrete memoryless broadcast channel," *IEEE Trans. Inform. Theory*, vol. IT-25, pp. 306–311, May 1979.

[76] R. J. McEliece and L. Swanson, "A note on the wide-band Gaussian broadcast channel," *IEEE Trans. Commun.*, vol. COM-35, pp. 452–453, Apr. 1987.

485

[77] F. Morii, H. Nakanishi, and Y. Tezuka, "Error probabilities for Gaussian broadcast channel," *Electron. and Commun. Japan*, vol. 59, no. 6, pp. 18–26, June 1976.

[78] M. Ohkubo, "A coding theorem for broadcast channels with degraded components," *Trans. Inst. Electron. Commun. Eng. Japan*, Section E (English), vol. E61, no. 12, p. 979, Dec. 1978.

[79] J. M. Ooi and G. W. Wornell, "Decentralized control of a multiple access broadcast channel: Performance bounds," in *Proc. 35th IEEE Conf. Decision and Control* (Kobe, Japan, Dec. 1996), vol. 1, pp. 293–298.

[80] L. Ozarow, "Coding and capacity for additive white Gaussian noise multi-user channels with feedback," Ph.D. dissertation, Dept. Elec. Eng. and Comp. Sci., MIT, Cambridge, MA, 1983.

[81] L. H. Ozarow and S. K. Leung-Yan-Cheong, "An achievable region and outer bound for the Gaussian broadcast channel with feedback," *IEEE Trans. Inform. Theory*, vol. IT-30, pp. 667–671, July 1984.

[82] M. S. Pinsker, "Capacity of noiseless broadcast channels," *Probl. Pered. Inform.*, vol. 14, no. 2, pp. 28–34, Apr.–June 1978; translated in *Probl. Inform. Transm.*, pp. 97–102, Apr.–June 1978.

[83] N. Pippenger, "Bounds on the performance of protocols for a multiple-access broadcast channel," *IEEE Trans. Inform.Theory*, vol. IT-27, pp. 145–151, Mar. 1981.

[84] G. S. Poltyrev, "Carrying capacity for parallel broadcast channels with degraded components," *Probl. Pered. Inform.*, vol. 13, no. 2, pp. 23–35, Apr.–June 1977; translated in *Probl. Inform. Transm.*, pp. 97–107, Apr.–June 1977.

[85] ———, "Capacity for a sum of broadcast channels," *Probl. Inform Transm.*, vol. 15, no. 2, pp. 111–114, Apr.–June 1979 (English translation).

[86] ———, "On accuracy of random coding bounds for broadcast channels," *Probl. Contr. Inform. Theory*, vol. 11, no. 5, pp. 1–11, 1982 (English translation of a Russian paper).

[87] ———, "Random-coding bounds for some broadcast channels," *Probl. Pered. Inform.*, vol. 19, no. 1, pp. 9–20, Jan.–Mar. 1983; translated in *Probl. Inform. Transm.*, vol. 19, no. 1, pp. 6–16, Jan.–Mar. 1983.

[88] H. Sari, G. Karam, and I. Jeanclaud, "Frequency-domain equalization of mobile radio and terrestrial broadcast channels," in *Proc. IEEE GLOBECOM* (San Francisco, CA, Nov.–Dec. 1994), vol. 1, pp. 1–5.

[89] H. Sato, "An outer bound to the capacity region of broadcast channels," *IEEE Trans. Inform. Theory*, vol. IT-24, p. 374, May 1978.

[90] S. Shamai, "A broadcast strategy for the Gaussian slowly fading channel," in *Proc. IEEE Int. Symp. Information Theory* (Ulm, Germany, June–July 1997), p. 150.

[91] C. E. Shannon, "The zero-error capacity of a noisy channel," *IRE Trans. Inform. Theory*, vol. IT-2, pp. 8–19, 1956.

[92] ———, "Two-way communication channels," in *Proc. 4th Berkeley Symp. Prob. Stat.* Berkeley, CA: Univ. California Press, 1961, vol. 1, pp. 611–644.

[93] B. D. Sharma and V. Priya, "On broadcast channels with side information under fidelity criteria," *Kybernetika*, vol. 19, no. 1, pp. 27–41, 1983.

[94] D. Slepian and J. K. Wolf, "Noiseless coding of corelated information sources," *IEEE Trans. Inform. Theory*, vol. IT-19, pp. 471–480, July 1973.

[95] B. S. Tsybakov and V. A. Mikhailov, "Free synchronous packet access in a broadcast channel with feedback," *Probl. Pered. Inform.*, vol. 14, no. 4, pp. 32–59, Oct.–Dec. 1978; translated in *Probl. Inform. Transm.*, pp. 259–280, Oct.–Dec. 1978.

[96] D. N. Tse, "Optimal power allocation over parallel Gaussian broadcast channels," in *Proc. IEEE Int. Symp. Information Theory* (Ulm, Germany, June–July 1997), p. 27.

[97] E. C. Van der Meulen, "Random coding theorems for the general discrete memoryless broadcast channel," *IEEE Trans. Inform. Theory*, vol. IT-21, pp. 180–190, Mar. 1975.

[98] ———, "A survey of multi-way channels in information theory: 1961–1976," *IEEE Trans. Inform. Theory*, vol. IT-23, pp. 1–37, Jan. 1977.

[99] ———, "Recent coding theorems for multi-way channels. Part I: The broadcast channel (1976–1980)," in *New Concepts in Multi-User Communication (NATO Advanced Study Institute Series)*, J. K. Skwyrzinsky, Ed. Groningen, The Netherlands: Sijthoff & Noordhof, 1981.

[100] ———, "Recent coding theorems and converses for multi-way channels. Part II: The multiple access channel (1976–1985)," Department Wiskunde, Katholieke Universiteit Leuven, Leuven, Belgium, 1985.

[101] M. Van Dijk, "The binary symmetric broadcast channel with confidential messages, with tampering," in *Proc. 1995 IEEE Int. Symp. Information Theory* (Whistler, BC, Canada, Sept. 1995), p. 487.

[102] ———, "On a special class of broadcast channels with confidential messages," *IEEE Trans. Inform. Theory*, vol. 43, pp. 712–714, Mar. 1997.

[103] P. Vanroose and E. C. Van der Meulen, "A new proof of the zero-error capacity region of the Blackwell broadcast channel," in *Proc. 10th Symp. Information Theory in the Benelux* (Houthalen, Belgium, May 1989), pp. 37–43.

[104] B. Verboven and E. Van der Meulen, "Capacity bounds for identification via broadcast channels that are optimal for the deterministic broadcast channel," *IEEE Trans. Inform. Theory*, vol. 36, pp. 1197–1205, Nov. 1990.

[105] N. D. Vvedenskaya and B. S. Tsybakov, "Stack algorithm in a broadcast channel with capture," *Probl. Pered. Inform.*, vol. 27, no. 2, pp. 25–34, Apr.–June 1991; translated in *Probl. Inform. Transm.*, pp. 107–116, Apr.–June 1991.

[106] F. M. J. Willems, "The maximal-error and average-error capacity region of the broadcast channel are identical," *Probl. Contr. Inform. Theory—Probl. Upravl. I Teorii Inform.*, vol. 19, no. 4, pp. 339–347, 1990.

[107] J. Wolf, "Multi-user communication networks," in *Commun. Syst. and Random Process Theory*, J. K. Skwirzynski, Ed. Alphen aan den Rijn, The Netherlands: Sijthoff & Norrdhoff, 1978, pp. 37–53.

[108] A. Wyner, "Recent results in the Shannon theory," *IEEE Trans. Inform. Theory*, vol. IT-20, pp. 2–10, Jan. 1974.

Applications of Error-Control Coding

Daniel J. Costello, Jr., *Fellow, IEEE*, Joachim Hagenauer, *Fellow, IEEE*,
Hideki Imai, *Fellow, IEEE*, and Stephen B. Wicker, *Senior Member, IEEE*

(Invited Paper)

Abstract—An overview of the many practical applications of channel coding theory in the past 50 years is presented. The following application areas are included: deep space communication, satellite communication, data transmission, data storage, mobile communication, file transfer, and digital audio/video transmission. Examples, both historical and current, are given that typify the different approaches used in each application area. Although no attempt is made to be comprehensive in our coverage, the examples chosen clearly illustrate the richness, variety, and importance of error-control coding methods in modern digital applications.

Index Terms— Block codes, channel coding, convolutional codes, error-control coding.

I. INTRODUCTION

WITH his 1948 paper, "A Mathematical Theory of Communication," Shannon [1] stimulated a body of research that has evolved into the two modern fields of Information Theory and Coding Theory. The fundamental philosophical contribution of [1] was the formal application of probability theory to the study and analysis of communication systems. The theoretical contribution of Shannon's work in the area of channel coding was a useful definition of "information" and several "channel coding theorems" which gave explicit upper bounds, called the channel capacity, on the rate at which "information" could be transmitted reliably on a given communication channel.

In the context of this paper, the result of primary interest is the "noisy channel coding theorem for continuous channels with average power limitations." This theorem states that the capacity C of a bandlimited additive white Gaussian noise (AWGN) channel with bandwidth W, a channel model that approximately represents many practical digital communication and storage systems, is given by

$$C = W \log_2(1 + E_s/N_0) \text{ bits per second (bps)} \quad (1)$$

Manuscript received March 2, 1998; revised June 1, 1998.

D. J. Costello, Jr. is with the Department of Electrical Engineering, University of Notre Dame, Notre Dame, IN 46556 USA (phone: +1-219-631-5480, fax: +1-219-631-4393, e-mail: Daniel.J.Costello.2@nd.edu).

J. Hagenauer is with the Institute of Communications Engineering (LNT), Munich University of Technology (TUM), 80290 Munich, Germany (phone: +49-89-28923467, fax: +49-89-28923490, e-mail: Hag@LNT.E-Technik.TU-Muenchen.DE).

H. Imai is with the Institute of Industrial Science, University of Tokyo, Minato-ku Tokyo, 106-8558, Japan (phone: +81-3-3402-6231, fax: +81-3-3402-6425, e-mail: imai@iis.u-tokyo.ac.jp).

S. B. Wicker is with the School of Electrical Engineering, Cornell University, Ithaca, NY 14853 USA (phone: +1-607-255-8817, fax: +1-607-255-9072, e-mail: wicker@ee.cornell.edu).

Publisher Item Identifier S 0018-9448(98)06086-6.

where we assume perfect Nyquist signaling, E_s is the average signal energy in each signaling interval of duration $T = 1/W$, and $N_0/2$ is the two-sided noise power spectral density. (In this formulation of the capacity theorem, one quadrature (two-dimensional) signal is transmitted in each T-second signaling interval, and the nominal channel bandwidth $W = 1/T$. See Wozencraft and Jacobs [2] for a more complete discussion of the concept of channel bandwidth.) The proof of the theorem demonstrates that for any transmission rate R less than or equal to the channel capacity C, there exists a coding scheme that achieves an arbitrarily small probability of error; conversely, if R is greater than C, no coding scheme can achieve reliable performance. However, since this is an existence theorem, it gives no guidance as to how to find appropriate coding schemes or how complex they may be to implement.

Beginning with the work of Hamming, which was published in 1950 [3] but was already known to Shannon in 1948, many communication engineers and coding theorists have developed numerous schemes for a variety of applications in an attempt to achieve performance close to what was promised by Shannon with reasonable implementation complexity. In this paper, we will survey the progress made in applying error-control coding techniques to digital communication and storage systems over the past 50 years and see that great advances have occurred in designing practical systems that narrow the gap between real system performance and channel capacity. In particular, we will focus on applications in six areas: space and satellite communications (Section II), data transmission (Section III), data storage (Section IV), digital audio/video transmission (Section V), mobile communications (Section VI), and file transfer (Section VII). Included among the applications covered in this survey are the Consultative Committee on Space Data Systems (CCSDS) standard coding scheme for space and satellite communications, trellis coding standards for high-speed data modems, the Reed–Solomon coding scheme used in compact discs, coding standards for mobile cellular communication, and the CRC codes used in HDLC protocols. The reader may wish to consult the paper published in 1974 by Jacobs [4], which reviewed applications of error-control coding over the first 25 years after the publication of Shannon's paper, to get an appreciation for the accelerated rate at which coding techniques have been applied to real systems in recent years.

The result in (1) can be put into a form more useful for the present discussion by introducing the parameter η, called the spectral (or bandwidth) efficiency. That is, η represents the

Spectral Efficiency, η, versus E_b/N_0

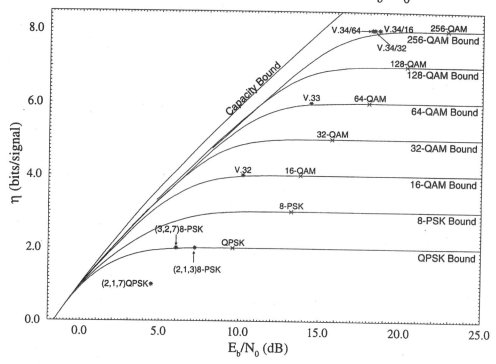

Fig. 1. Capacity curves and the performance of several coding schemes for data transmission applications.

average number of information bits transmitted per signaling interval of duration T seconds. Then

$$0 < \eta < C/W \qquad (2)$$

and

$$E_s/N_0 = \eta E_b/N_0 \qquad (3)$$

where E_b is the average energy per information bit. Substituting the above relations into (1) and performing some minor manipulations yields

$$E_b/N_0 > (2^\eta - 1)/\eta \qquad (4)$$

which relates the spectral efficiency η to the signal-to-noise ratio (SNR), represented by E_b/N_0. The bound of (4) expresses the fundamental tradeoff between the spectral efficiency η and the SNR E_b/N_0. That is, increased spectral efficiency can be reliably achieved only with a corresponding increase in the minimum required SNR. Conversely, the minimum required SNR can be reduced only by decreasing the spectral efficiency of the system.

The bound of (4) is shown plotted in Fig. 1 and is labeled the capacity bound. This curve represents the absolute best performance possible for a communication system on the AWGN channel. The performance of a particular system relative to the capacity bound may be interpreted in two distinct ways.

First, the capacity bound may be interpreted as giving the minimum SNR required to achieve a specific spectral efficiency with an arbitrarily small probability of error. For example, if one wants to transmit $\eta = 1$ information bit per signal, then there exists a coding scheme that operates reliably with an $E_b/N_0 = 0$ dB. Conversely, any coding

scheme, no matter how complex, sending $\eta = 1$ information bit per signal with an E_b/N_0 less than 0 dB will be unreliable. This interpretation indicates the maximum power reduction available using appropriate coding schemes compared to an uncoded system. As an illustration, consider that an uncoded quadrature phase-shift keyed (QPSK) system with coherent detection has a spectral efficiency of $\eta = 2$ and achieves a bit-error rate (BER) of 10^{-5} at an $E_b/N_0 = 9.6$ dB. Since coding can provide essentially error-free communication at the same spectral efficiency and an $E_b/N_0 = 1.8$ dB, we say that a maximum power (or coding) gain of 7.8 dB is available in this case.

Second, the capacity bound may be interpreted as giving the maximum spectral efficiency at which a system may operate reliably for a fixed SNR. For example, if an $E_b/N_0 = 0$ dB is available, then there exists a coding scheme that operates reliably with a bandwidth efficiency of $\eta = 1$ information bit per signal. Conversely, any coding scheme, no matter how complex, sending more than $\eta = 1$ information bit per signal will be unreliable if $E_b/N_0 = 0$ dB. This interpretation indicates the maximum spectral efficiency increase available using appropriate coding schemes compared to an uncoded system. As an illustration, again consider an uncoded QPSK system with coherent detection. Since a coded system operating at an $E_b/N_0 = 9.6$ dB can provide reliable communication at a spectral efficiency of $\eta = 5.7$ information bits per signal, we say that a maximum spectral efficiency (or rate) gain of 3.7 bits per signal is available in this case.

The capacity bound assumes that, for a given spectral efficiency, one is free to choose the signaling (modulation) scheme which results in the best possible performance. However, in real communication systems, there are many practical considerations that come into play in choosing a modulation scheme. For example, satellite communication systems that use nonlinear traveling-wave tube amplifiers (TWTA's) require constant envelope signaling such as M-ary phase-shift keying (M-PSK) in order to avoid signal distortion. Also, for data transmission over voice-grade telephone channels, the intersymbol interference caused by bandwidth limitations necessitates the use of large signal constellations that employ a combination of amplitude and phase modulation (AM/PM) to achieve high data rates. It is, therefore, instructive to compute the maximum spectral efficiency η required to achieve reliable communication given a particular modulation scheme and SNR.

For the discrete-input, continuous-output, memoryless AWGN channel with M-ary phase-shift-keyed (M-PSK) or quadrature amplitude modulation (M-QAM) modulation and assuming equiprobable signaling, the capacity bound becomes [2]

$$\eta^* < \log_2(M) - (1/M) \sum_{i=0}^{M-1}$$

$$E\left\{ \log_2 \sum_{j=0}^{M-1} \exp[(|a^i + n - a^j|^2 - |n|^2)/N_0] \right\} \quad (5)$$

where a^i is a channel signal, n is a Gaussian distributed noise random variable with mean 0 and variance $N_0/2$, and E is the expectation operator. The bound of (5) is plotted in Fig. 1 for equiprobable QPSK, 8-PSK, 16-QAM, 32-QAM, 64-QAM, 128-QAM, and 256-QAM modulation. (For M-QAM signal sets with large M, nonequiprobable signaling, called signal shaping, can improve performance by as much as 1.53 dB compared to equiprobable signaling [5].)

For a specified signaling method and SNR, the bound of (5) represents the maximum spectral efficiency required to achieve reliable communication. For example, a QPSK system operating with an $E_b/N_0 = 1.64$ dB can transmit a maximum of $\eta = 1.5$ bits per signal. This is 0.44 bit per signal less than an ideal system without any modulation constraints. Alternatively, to send $\eta = 1.5$ information bits per signal using QPSK modulation requires a minimum $E_b/N_0 = 1.64$ dB. This is 0.76 dB more than an ideal system without any modulation constraints.

In the sections that follow, we will have occasion to compare some of the coding systems discussed to the capacity curves in Fig. 1 in order to assess their relative power and/or spectral efficiency, at least in the cases where AWGN is the primary signal impairment. In other cases, such as mobile communications, where signal fading is the major source of errors, and data storage, where media contamination causes most of the problems, a clear view of optimum performance is not as readily available.

II. APPLICATIONS TO SPACE AND SATELLITE COMMUNICATIONS

Most of the early work in coding theory was directed at the low spectral efficiency, or power-limited, portion of the capacity curve. This was principally due to two factors. First,

many early applications of coding were developed for the National Aeronautics and Space Administration (NASA) and the European Space Agency (ESA) deep-space and satellite communication systems, where power was very expensive and bandwidth was plentiful. Second, no practical coding schemes existed that could provide meaningful power gains at higher spectral efficiencies. Thus our paper begins with a survey of applications of error-control coding to space and satellite communication systems.

The deep-space channel turned out to be the perfect link on which to first demonstrate the power of coding. There were several reasons for this, most notably those listed below.

1) The deep-space channel is almost exactly modeled as the memoryless AWGN channel that formed the basis for Shannon's noisy channel coding theorem. Thus all the theoretical and simulation studies conducted for this channel carried over almost exactly into practice.

2) Plenty of bandwidth is available on the deep-space channel, thus allowing the use of the low-spectral-efficiency codes and binary-modulation schemes that were most studied and best understood at the time.

3) Because of the large transmission distances involved, which caused severe signal attenuation, powerful, low-rate codes, with complex decoding methods, were required, resulting in very low data rates. However, since a deep-space mission is, by nature, a very time-consuming process, the low data rates realized in practice did not present a problem.

4) A deep-space mission is also, by nature, a very expensive undertaking, and thus the additional cost of developing and implementing complex encoding and decoding solutions can be tolerated, especially since each decibel of coding gain realized resulted in an overall savings of about $1 000 000 (in the 1960's) in transmitting and receiving equipment.

Thus it is no surprise that Massey, in a recent paper [6], called deep-space communication and coding a "marriage made in heaven."

As a starting point to understand the gains afforded by coding on the deep-space channel, we consider an uncoded BPSK system with coherent detection. (Throughout this section we assume BPSK modulation, which transmits uncoded information at a rate of 1.0 information bit per signal. If coding is used, the code rate r, in information bits per BPSK signal, then represents the spectral efficiency of the coded system.) Simulation results and analytical calculations have shown that uncoded BPSK achieves a BER of 10^{-5}, considered "reliable" in many applications, at an $E_b/N_0 = 9.6$ dB. This point is plotted in Fig. 2 with the label BPSK. (All the points in Figs. 1 and 2 are plotted for a BER of 10^{-5}. Actual BER requirements vary from system to system in deep-space applications depending on several factors, such as the nature and sensitivity of the data and whether it has been compressed on the spacecraft prior to transmission.)

From the capacity curve in Fig. 2, it can be seen that the minimum E_b/N_0 required to achieve error-free communication at a code rate $r = 1/2$ bit per signal is 0.0 dB, and

Code Rate, r, versus E_b/N_0

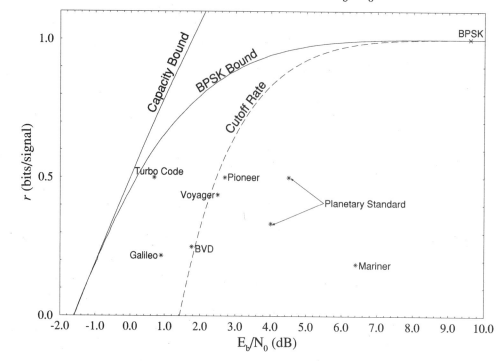

Fig. 2. Capacity and cutoff rate curves and the performance of several coding schemes for deep-space applications.

thus a power savings of 9.6 dB is theoretically possible with an appropriate rate $r = 1/2$ coding scheme. Looking at the BPSK capacity curve, however, reveals that to achieve a rate $r = 1/2$ with BPSK modulation requires only a slightly larger $E_b/N_0 = 0.2$ dB. Thus for code rates $r = 1/2$ or less, very little in potential coding gain is sacrificed by using BPSK modulation. This, combined with the difficulty in coherently detecting signal sets with more than two points and the relative abundance of bandwidth on the deep-space channel, resulted in the choice of BPSK modulation with code rates $r = 1/2$ bit/signal or below for deep-space communication.

One of the earliest attempts to improve on the performance of uncoded BPSK was the use of a rate $r = 6/32$ biorthogonal, Reed–Muller block code, also referred to as the (32, 6) RM code. This code was used on the 1969 Mariner and later Viking Mars missions in conjunction with BPSK modulation and soft-decision maximum-likelihood decoding. The code consisted of 64 codewords, each 32 bits long, with a minimum Hamming distance between codewords of $d_{\min} = 16$. The 64 codewords can be viewed as a set of 32 orthogonal vectors in 32-dimensional space, plus the complements of these 32 vectors, and thus the name "biorthogonal." Full soft-decision maximum-likelihood decoding (decoding using unquantized demodulator outputs) was achieved by using a correlation decoder, based on the Hadamard transform, developed by Green at the Jet Propulsion Laboratory (JPL) that subsequently became known as the "Green Machine" [7].

The Mariner system had code rate $r = 6/32 = 0.1875$ bit/signal and it achieved a BER of 10^{-5} with an $E_b/N_0 = 6.4$ dB. (Note that, since BPSK modulation is assumed, each BPSK signal represents one code bit, and thus the code rate r

is equivalent to the spectral efficiency.) This point is plotted in Fig. 2 with the label "Mariner." From Fig. 2, it is seen that the Mariner code requires 3.2 dB less power than uncoded BPSK for the same BER, but it requires more than five times the bandwidth and is still 7.5 dB away from the BPSK capacity curve at the same specrtral efficiency. It is important to note that even with its significant bandwidth expansion, the coding gain actually achieved by the Mariner code was rather modest. This is due to the fact that this code, as is typical of block codes in general, has a relatively large number of nearest neighbor codewords, thus substantially reducing the available coding gain at moderate BER's. (At lower BER's, a coding gain of up to 4.8 dB is achievable, but this is reduced to 3.2 dB at a BER of 10^{-5} by the code's 62 nearest neighbors.) In fact, most of the coding gain achieved by the Mariner code was due to the extra 2–3 dB obtained by using full soft-decision decoding, a lesson that has carried over to almost all practical coding implementations where coding gain is a primary consideration.

A significant advance in the application of coding to deep-space communication systems occurred later in the 1960's with the invention of sequential decoding [8] for convolutional codes and its subsequent refinement [9]. It was now possible to use powerful long-constraint-length convolutional codes with soft-decision decoding. Thus for the first time, practical communication systems were capable of achieving substantial coding gains over uncoded transmission.

Sequential decoding was first used in 1968 on an "experimental" basis. (This was actually a deliberate stratagem to circumvent lengthy NASA qualification procedures [6].) The Pioneer 9 solar orbit space mission used a modified version of a rate $r = 1/2$ systematic convolutional code originally constructed by Lin and Lyne [10], but the coding scheme was changed for subsequent missions. (A convolutional code is said to be in systematic form if the information sequence appears unchanged as one of the encoded sequences.) It is interesting to note that, even though the Mariner coding system was designed first, the Pioneer 9 was actually launched earlier, and thus the Lin–Lyne code was the first to fly in space. The Pioneer 10 Jupiter fly-by mission and the Pioneer 11 Saturn fly-by mission in 1972 and 1973, respectively, both used a rate $r = 1/2$, constraint length $K = 32$, i.e., a $(2, 1, 32)$ nonsystematic, quick-look-in (QLI) convolutional code constructed by Massey and Costello [11]. The two 32-bit code generator sequences used for this code are given in octal notation by

$$\boldsymbol{g}^{(1)} = 73353367672 \qquad \boldsymbol{g}^{(2)} = 53353367672. \qquad (6)$$

The code was chosen to be nonsystematic in order to give it a larger minimum free Hamming distance d_{free}, in this case $d_{\text{free}} = 21$, compared to the best systematic code of the same constraint length. This is true for convolutional codes in general, i.e., for a given constraint length, a measure of decoding complexity, more free distance, and thus better performance, can be achieved using a nonsystematic rather than a systematic code. The fact that the two generators differ in only one bit position gives the code the "quick-look" property, i.e., the capability of obtaining a reasonably accurate quick estimate of the information sequence from the noisy received sequence prior to actual decoding. This is an important capability in some situations that is always available with systematic codes, but not, in general, with nonsystematic codes. Requiring this capability does result in some reduction in free distance, however, and thus represents a compromise between choosing the best possible code and retaining the "quick-look" property. Nevertheless, the above code has had a long and distinguished career in space, having been used, in addition to the above two missions, on the Pioneer 12 Venus orbiter and the European Helios A and Helios B solar orbiter missions.

A sequential decoder using a modified version of the Fano tree-searching algorithm with 3-bit soft decisions (3-bit quantized demodulator outputs) was chosen for decoding. For lower speed operation, in the kilobit-per-second (kbps) range, decoding could be done in software. Faster hardware decoders were also developed for operation in the megabit-per-second (Mbps) range [12], [13]. This scheme had code rate $r = 1/2 = 0.5$ bit/signal and achieved a BER of 10^{-5} at an $E_b/N_0 = 2.7$ dB (see Fig. 2, "Pioneer"), thus achieving a 6.9-dB coding gain compared to uncoded BPSK, at the expense of a doubling in bandwidth requirements. This represented a significant improvement compared to the Mariner system and resulted in performance only 2.5 dB away from the BPSK capacity curve. An excellent discussion of the considerations that went into the design of these early deep-space coding systems is included in the paper by Massey [6].

Sequential decoding algorithms have a variable computation characteristic which results in large buffering requirements, and occasionally large decoding delays and/or incomplete decoding of the received sequence. In some situations, such as when almost error-free communication is required or when

retransmission is possible, this variable decoding delay property of sequential decoding can be an advantage. For example, when a long delay occurs in decoding, indicating a very noisy and therefore probably unreliable frame of data, the decoder can simply stop and erase the frame, not delivering anything to the user, or ask for a retransmission. A so-called "complete" decoder, on the other hand, would be forced to deliver a decoded estimate, which may very well be wrong in these cases, resulting in what has been termed a "fools rush in where angels fear to tread" phenomenon [11]. However, fixed delay is desirable in many situations, particularly when high-speed decoding is required. In addition, the performance of convolutional codes with sequential decoding is ultimately limited by the computational cutoff rate R_0 (the rate at which the average number of computations performed by a sequential decoder becomes unbounded), which requires SNR's higher than capacity to achieve reliable communication at a given code rate [2], as shown in Fig. 2. For example, to achieve reliable communication at a code rate of $r = 0.5$ bit/signal using sequential decoding and BPSK modulation on the AWGN channel requires an $E_b/N_0 = 2.4$ dB, whereas the capacity bound only requires an $E_b/N_0 = 0.2$ dB. The E_b/N_0 at which the Pioneer code achieves a BER of 10^{-5} is only 0.3 dB away from the cutoff rate, and thus there is little to be gained with longer constraint length codes and sequential decoding at this code rate and BER.

These undesirable characteristics of sequential decoding and the possibility of higher decoding speeds led to the use of maximum-likelihood Viterbi decoding [14] in the next generation of deep-space communication systems. The Viterbi algorithm, like sequential decoding, is compatible with a variety of modulation and quantization schemes. Unlike sequential decoding, though, the Viterbi algorithm has a fixed number of computations per decoded branch and thus does not suffer from incomplete decoding and, ultimately, is not limited by a computational cutoff rate.

The Voyager 1 and 2 space missions were launched in 1977 to explore Jupiter and Saturn. They both used a $(2, 1, 7)$ nonsystematic convolutional code with generator polynomials

$$\boldsymbol{G}^{(1)}(D) = 1 + D + D^3 + D^4 + D^6$$
$$\boldsymbol{G}^{(2)}(D) = 1 + D^3 + D^4 + D^5 + D^6 \qquad (7)$$

and $d_{\text{free}} = 10$. This code and a companion $(3, 1, 7)$ code with generators

$$\boldsymbol{G}^{(1)}(D) = 1 + D + D^3 + D^4 + D^6$$
$$\boldsymbol{G}^{(2)}(D) = 1 + D^3 + D^4 + D^5 + D^6 \qquad (8)$$
$$\boldsymbol{G}^{(3)}(D) = 1 + D^2 + D^4 + D^5 + D^6$$

and $d_{\text{free}} = 15$, were both adopted as NASA/ESA Planetary Standard Codes by the Consultative Committee on Space Data Systems (CCSDS). The $(2, 1, 7)$ code has also been employed in numerous other applications, including satellite communication and cellular telephony, and has become a *de facto* industry standard [15].

The above codes were decoded using a 3-bit soft-decision maximum-likelihood Viterbi decoder. Since the complexity

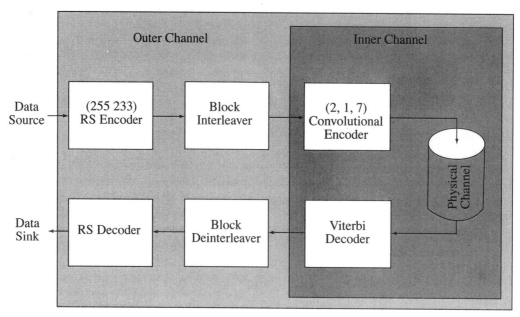

Fig. 3. The CCSDS concatenation standard.

of Viterbi decoding grows exponentially with code constraint length, it was necessary to choose these short constraint length codes rather than the long constraint length Pioneer codes used with sequential decoding. The $K = 7$ codes chosen have a decoding trellis containing 64 states, considered reasonable in terms of implementation complexity. The performance of these codes is plotted in Fig. 2 with the label "Planetary Standard". The $(2, 1, 7)$ code requires an $E_b/N_0 = 4.5$ dB to operate at a BER of 10^{-5}. Though this code results in a 5.1-dB power advantage compared to uncoded transmission, its performance is 1.8 dB worse than the Pioneer system, due to the short constraint length used. However, its decoder implementation complexity is simpler than a sequential decoder, it does not suffer the long buffering delays characteristic of sequential decoding, and, because of its regular trellis structure, it is adaptable to parallel implementation, resulting in decoding speeds in the 100's of Mbps [16].

The Planetary Standard also played a major role in military satellite communications well into the 1980's (as incorporated into the Satellite Data Link Standard (SDLS)). In general, convolutional encoding with Viterbi decoding will continue to be used in earth-orbiting satellite communication systems well into the next century. The Globalstar and Iridium systems use $K = 9$, rate $1/2$ and $K = 7$, rate $3/4$ convolutional codes, respectively. The rationale for the differing constraint lengths and rates lies with the nominal lengths (and consequent space loss) of the satellite-to-ground links for the two systems. Globalstar satellites operate at altitudes of approximately 1400 km, while Iridium operates at half that height [17].

Coding gain beyond that provided by the Planetary Standard can be achieved using code concatenation. Concatenation is a scheme first introduced by Forney [18] in which two codes, an "inner code" and an "outer code," are used in cascade. The inner code should be designed to produce a moderate BER (typically on the order of 10^{-3} to 10^{-4}) with modest complexity. The outer code can be more complex and should

be designed to correct almost all the residual errors from the inner decoder, resulting in nearly error-free performance (BER's, say, on the order of 10^{-10}). The most common arrangement is a combination of a short constraint length inner convolutional code with soft-decision Viterbi decoding and a powerful nonbinary Reed–Solomon (RS) outer code. This combination was eventually accepted in 1987 as the CCSDS Telemetry Standard [19].

In fact, though, several other concatenation schemes had been tried earlier. For example, on the 1971 Mariner mission, a $(6, 4)$ RS outer code with symbols drawn from GF(2^6) was used in conjunction with the $(32, 6)$ RM code as an inner code, and on the two 1977 Voyager missions, a $(24, 12)$ extended Golay outer code was used together with the $(2, 1, 7)$ Planetary Standard code as an inner code [20]. In both cases, the data to be transmitted consisted mostly of uncompressed image information, along with small amounts of sensitive scientific information. The outer codes were used only to give added protection to the scientific information, so that the overall coding rate was not reduced much below the inner-code rates. In the case of the Mariner system, each 6-bit symbol from the outer code is encoded into one 32-bit codeword in the inner code. This "matching" between the outer code symbol size and the information block size of the inner code means that each block error from the inner decoder causes only one symbol error for the outer decoder, a desirable property for a concatenation scheme consisting of two block codes. Finally, although both inner decoders made use of soft-decision inputs from the channel, the outer decoders were designed to work directly with the "hard decisions" made by the inner decoders. Outer decoders which also make use of soft-decision inputs will be considered later in this section.

The CCSDS Standard concatenation scheme consists of the $(2, 1, 7)$ Planetary Standard inner code along with a $(255, 223)$ RS outer code, as shown in Fig. 3. (Note that the CCSDS Standard assumes that all the data is protected by both codes, inner and outer, although it is clearly possible to protect some data using only the inner code or to send some data without any protection at all.) The RS code consists of 8-bit symbols chosen from the finite field $GF(2^8)$ based on the primitive polynomial

$$\boldsymbol{p}(x) = x^8 + x^7 + x^2 + x + 1. \tag{9}$$

The generator polynomial (in cyclic code form) is given by

$$\boldsymbol{g}(x) = \prod_{j=112}^{143} (x - \alpha^{11j}) \tag{10}$$

where α is a root of $\boldsymbol{p}(x)$. From (10), we see that $\boldsymbol{g}(x)$ has 32 first-order roots, giving it degree 32, and thus the code contains 32 redundant symbols. Since RS codes are maximum-distance separable (MDS), their minimum distance is always one more than the number of redundant symbols. Hence this code has $d_{\min} = 33$ and can correct any combination of 16 or fewer symbol errors within a block of 255 symbols (2040 bits). Hard-decision decoding of the outer code is performed using the Berlekamp–Massey algorithm [21], [22]. Finally, in order to break up possibly long bursts of errors from the inner decoder into separate blocks for the outer decoder, thus making them easier to decode, a symbol interleaver is inserted between the inner and outer codes. Interleaver depths of between two and eight outer-code blocks are typical [23].

With the CCSDS Standard concatenation scheme, the E_b/N_0 needed to achieve a BER of 10^{-5} is reduced by a full 2.0 dB compared to using the Planetary Standard code alone, with only a slight reduction in code rate (from $r = 0.5$ to $r = 0.44$). The performance of the $(2, 1, 7)$ code in a concatenated system with the $(255, 223)$ RS outer code is shown in Fig. 2 with the label "Voyager." The concatenated Voyager system operates in the same E_b/N_0 region as the Pioneer system, gaining about 0.2 dB with a 12.5% loss in rate. Thus short constraint length convolutional codes with Viterbi decoding in concatenated systems can be considered as alternatives to long constraint length codes with sequential decoding.

Variations on the concatenated CCSDS theme continue to be used at the end of the century in near-earth applications. For example, in 1998 the DirecTV satellite system was using a concatenated convolutional-Viterbi/Reed–Solomon system to bring television signals to three million subscribers.

Recently, technological advances have made it practical to build maximum-likelihood Viterbi decoders for larger constraint length convolutional codes. The culmination of this effort was the Big Viterbi Decoder (BVD) designed by Collins to decode a $(4, 1, 15)$ code. The BVD was constructed at JPL for use on the Galileo mission to Jupiter [24]. The decoder trellis has $2^{14} = 16\,384$ states, making internal decoder communication a formidable task, but decoding speeds up to 1 Mbps were still achieved. The code has octal generators

$$\boldsymbol{g}^{(1)} = 46321 \quad \boldsymbol{g}^{(2)} = 51271 \quad \boldsymbol{g}^{(3)} = 63667 \quad \boldsymbol{g}^{(4)} = 70535 \tag{11}$$

and $d_{\text{free}} = 35$, clearly a very powerful code. It achieves a BER of 10^{-5} at an $E_b/N_0 = 1.7$ dB, only 2.6 dB away from

the BPSK capacity curve. (See Fig. 2, "BVD.") Compared to the $(2, 1, 7)$ Planetary Standard code, it gains a full 2.8 dB. In a concatenated system with the $(255, 223)$ RS outer code, the $(4, 1, 15)$ code requires an E_b/N_0 of just 0.9 dB to achieve a BER of 10^{-5}, is within 2.0 dB of capacity, and is 1.6 dB more power efficient than the Voyager system. (See Fig. 2, "Galileo.") Although the above rate $1/4$ systems are 50% less bandwidth efficient than their rate $1/2$ counterparts, it should be recalled that bandwidth is plentiful in deep space, and thus it is common to sacrifice spectral efficiency for added power efficiency. In fact, an even less spectrally efficient $(6, 1, 15)$ code is currently scheduled to be flown aboard the Cassini mission to Saturn [25]. However, further bandwidth expansion may be difficult to achieve due to the fact that additional redundancy may reduce the energy per transmitted symbol below the level needed for reliable tracking by the phase-locked loops in the coherent demodulator.

As a further improvement on the CCSDS Concatenation Standard, errors-and-erasures decoding, a suboptimum form of soft-decision decoding, can be used to provide some performance improvement if erased symbols are available from the inner decoder. One method of providing erased symbols is based on two facts mentioned above: 1) a frame of several RS code blocks is interleaved prior to encoding by the inner code, and 2) decoding errors from the inner decoder are typically bursty, resulting in strings of consecutive error symbols. Although long strings of error symbols will usually cause problems for an RS decoder, after de-interleaving they are more spread out, making them easier to decode. In addition, once a symbol error has been corrected by the RS decoder, symbols in the corresponding positions of the other codewords in the same frame can be flagged as erasures, thus making them easier to decode. This technique is known as "error forecasting" and has been discussed in a paper by Paaske [26].

Another method of improving the CCSDS Concatenation Standard makes use of iterative decoding. In one approach, the RS codes in a given frame are assigned different rates, some higher that the $(255, 223)$ code and some lower, such that the average rate is unchanged. After an initial inner decoding of one frame, the most powerful (lowest rate) outer code is decoded, and then its decoded information bits (correct with very high probability) are fed back and treated as known information bits (side information) by the inner decoder in a second iteration of decoding. This procedure can be repeated until the entire frame is decoded, with each iteration using the lowest rate outer code not yet decoded. The use of known information bits by the inner decoder has been termed "state pinning," and the technique is discussed in a paper by Collins and Hizlan [27].

A more general approach to iterative decoding of concatenated codes was proposed by Hagenauer and Hoeher with the introduction of the Soft-Output Viterbi Algorithm (SOVA) [28]. In the SOVA, reliability information about each decoded bit is appended to the output of a Viterbi decoder. An outer decoder which accepts soft inputs can then use this reliability information to improve its performance. If the outer decoder also provides reliability information at its output, iterative decoding can proceed between the

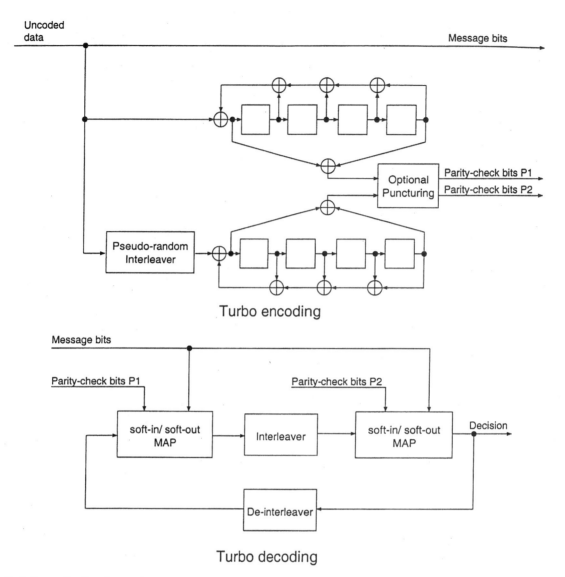

Turbo encoding

Turbo decoding

Fig. 4. The "turbo" encoding/decoding system.

inner and outer decoders. In general, such iterative decoding techniques for concatenated systems can result in additional coding gains of up to about 1.0 dB. In the CCSDS system, however, the outer RS decoder cannot make full use of such reliability information. Nevertheless, several combinations of error forecasting, state pinning, and iterative decoding have been applied to the CCSDS system by various researchers, resulting in an additional coding gain of about 0.5 dB [20], [23].

As our final topic in this section, we discuss a significant new discovery called "turbo codes," which is currently being considered as a software upgrade for the Cassini mission. Turbo codes, which are also known as parallel concatenated convolutional codes, were first introduced in a paper by Berrou, Glavieux, and Thitimajshima [29]. Turbo codes combine a convolutional code along with a pseudorandom interleaver and maximum *a posteriori* probability (MAP) iterative decoding to achieve performance very close to the Shannon limit. A block diagram of the turbo encoding/decoding system is shown in Fig. 4. The encoder employs a simple $(2, 1, 5)$ code in systematic feedback form, using two copies of the

parity generator separated by a pseudorandom interleaver. The generator matrix is given by

$$\boldsymbol{G}(D) = \begin{bmatrix} 1 & \dfrac{1+D^4}{1+D+D^2+D^3+D^4} \end{bmatrix}. \quad (12)$$

(The code is the same as that generated by a conventional non-systematic feedforward encoder with generator polynomials $\boldsymbol{G}^{(1)}(D) = 1+D+D^2+D^3+D^4$ and $\boldsymbol{G}^{(2)}(D) = 1+D^4$, but it is important that it be encoded in systematic feedback form because of the way the interleaver combines the two parity sequences.) The encoder output consists of the information sequence and two parity sequences, thus representing a code rate of $1/3$. Alternately puncturing (deleting) bits from the two parity sequences produces a code rate of $1/2$, and other code rates can be achieved by using additional parity generators and/or different puncturing patterns. The pseudorandom interleaver re-orders the information sequence before encoding by the second parity generator, thus producing two different parity sequences. In essence, the interleaver has the effect of matching "bad" (low-weight) parity sequences with "good" (higher weight) parity sequences in almost all cases, thus

494

generating a code with very few low-weight codewords. For large enough information sequence blocklengths, performance very close to the Shannon limit can be achieved at moderate BER's, even though the free distance of turbo codes is not large. In fact, for most interleavers, the free distance of the above code is only $d_{\text{free}} = 6$, even for very long blocklengths. The excellent performance at moderate BER's is due rather to a drastic reduction in the number of nearest neighbor codewords compared to a conventional convolutional code. In a paper by Benedetto and Montorsi [30], it was shown that the number of nearest neighbors is reduced by a factor of N, where N is the blocklength. This factor is referred to as the "interleaver gain."

The other important feature of turbo codes is the iterative decoder, which uses a soft-in/soft-out MAP decoding algorithm first applied to convolutional codes by Bahl, Cocke, Jelinek, and Raviv [31]. This algorithm is more complex than the Viterbi algorithm by about a factor of three, and for conventional convolutional codes it offers little performance advantage over Viterbi decoding. However, in turbo decoding, the fact that it gives the maximum MAP estimate of each individual information bit is crucial in allowing the iterative decoding procedure to converge at very low SNR's. Although the SOVA can also be used to decode turbo codes, significant improvement can be obtained with MAP decoding [32].

At almost any bandwidth efficiency, performance less than 1.0 dB away from capacity is achievable with short constraint length turbo codes, very long blocklengths, and 10–20 iterations of decoding. In Fig. 2, the point marked "Turbo Code" shows performance at a BER of 10^{-5} for rate $r = 1/2$ and information blocklength $N = 2^{16} = 65536$, with 18 iterations of decoding. This is a full 3.8 dB better than the Planetary Standard $(2, 1, 7)$ code, with roughly the same decoding complexity, and is also 1.0 dB better than the very complex BVD code, which operates at 50% less spectral efficiency! Using the same rate of $1/4$, the turbo code outperforms the BVD code by about 1.9 dB. The major disadvantages of a turbo code are its long decoding delay, due to the large blocklengths and iterative decoding, and its weaker performance at lower BER's, due to its low free distance. The long delays are not a major problem except in real-time applications such as voice transmission, and performance at lower BER's can be enhanced by using serial concatenation [33], so turbo codes seem to be ideally suited for use on many future deep-space missions.

A comprehensive survey of the application of coding to deep-space communication as the decade of the 1960's drew to a close was given in a paper by Forney [34]. For a more recent review of the subject, the article by Wicker [25] is an excellent source.

III. APPLICATIONS TO DATA TRANSMISSION

As mentioned previously in this paper, the focus of much of the early work in coding theory was on reducing power requirements at low spectral efficiencies. This was due, in part, to the fact that no practical coding schemes existed that could provide meaningful power gains at higher spectral efficiencies.

This changed dramatically with Ungerboeck's discovery of trellis-coded modulation (TCM) [35].

In his 1982 paper, Ungerboeck constructed trellis codes for amplitude modulation (AM), phase-shift-keyed (PSK), and quadrature amplitude modulation (QAM) modulation schemes. As an example, consider the simple four-state, 8-PSK code shown in Fig. 5 along with its trellis diagram. The encoder has two input bits, x^2 and x^1. The input bit x^2 is differentially encoded to produce the encoded bit y^2. (Differential encoding of this bit is needed to take advantage of the "rotational invariance" property of the code so that the correct information sequence can be recovered after decoding in the event the receiver demodulator locks onto the wrong phase. This is an important practical consideration which will be discussed further later in this section.) The input bit x^1 is encoded by a $(2, 1, 3)$ systematic feedback convolutional encoder with generator matrix

$$\boldsymbol{G}(D) = \left[1 \quad \frac{D}{1 + D^2}\right] \qquad (13)$$

producing the two encoded bits $y^1 = x'$ (an information bit) and y^2 (a parity bit). (It should be noted here that the reason for using systematic feedback encoders in TCM has nothing to do with the reason for using them in turbo coding. In TCM, nonsystematic feedforward encoders can be used with similar results, but systematic feedback encoders are preferred because they provide a convenient canonical representation for the high-rate codes, typically $r = k/(k + 1)$, commonly used in TCM and because the noisy received information bits can be directly accessed prior to decoding.) The signal mapper (modulator) then generates an 8-PSK signal according to the mapping shown in Fig. 5. Ignoring the differential encoding, at each time unit the mapper input consists of two information bits, y^2 and y^1, and one parity bit, y^0, and the mapper output consists of one 8-PSK signal. Thus the information rate, or spectral efficiency, of this scheme is $\eta = 2$ bits/signal, the same as an uncoded system using QPSK modulation. (The fact that only one information bit, y^1, enters the convolutional encoder and the other information bit, y^2, remains "uncoded" is a feature of many, but not all, TCM schemes. The best code design for a given situation may or may not contain uncoded information bits, depending on the signal constellation, code complexity, and spectral efficiency.) Decoding is performed by a conventional soft-decision Viterbi decoder operating directly on the noisy received 8-PSK signals. In this example, the decoding trellis has four states, as shown in Fig. 5. Because the code has one uncoded information bit, the trellis contains so-called "parallel transitions," i.e., parallel paths of length one branch each connecting pairs of states at different time units. Parallel transitions in the trellis diagram are characteristic of all TCM schemes that contain uncoded information bits.

The first important insight due to Ungerboeck was his realization that for the nonbinary signal constellations used in TCM, minimum free squared distance d_{free}^2 in Euclidean space, rather than minimum free Hamming distance d_{free}, is the primary parameter that determines code performance. His technique of "mapping by set partitioning," as opposed to the conventional Gray mapping used in uncoded modulation,

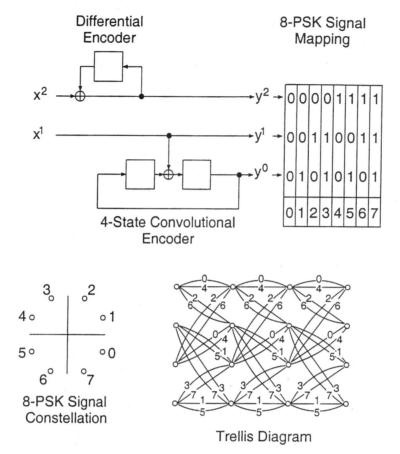

Differential Encoder

8-PSK Signal Mapping

	0	0	0	0	1	1	1	1
	0	0	1	1	0	0	1	1
	0	1	0	1	0	1	0	1
	0	1	2	3	4	5	6	7

4-State Convolutional Encoder

8-PSK Signal Constellation

Trellis Diagram

Fig. 5. The four-state 8-PSK Ungerboeck code.

turned out to be the key to achieving performance gains with TCM compared to uncoded modulation at high spectral efficiencies. One of the important goals of mapping by set partitioning is to insure that parallel transitions in the trellis are mapped into signals far apart in signal space, thus minimizing the probability of short, one-branch, error events due to uncoded bits. For the four-state, 8-PSK code considered above, $d_{\text{free}}^2 = 4$, whereas for uncoded QPSK, $d_{\text{free}}^2 = 2$, assuming unit energy signals in both cases. Hence this simple TCM scheme has a factor of 2, or 3 dB, asymptotic, i.e., high SNR, coding gain compared to uncoded QPSK. (The asymptotic coding gain of any code is always somewhat larger than its "real" coding gain at moderate BER's, due to the effect of nearest neighbor codewords. In this case, the coding gain at a 10^{-5} BER is 2.4 dB, as shown in Fig. 1 with the notation "(2, 1, 3) 8-PSK.") Also, unlike the case with binary modulation, where coding gains are achieved only at the expense of bandwidth expansion, the TCM scheme has the same spectral efficiency, viz., 2.0 bits/signal, as uncoded QPSK. Thus the 3-dB asymptotic coding gain is achieved without bandwidth expansion! In the case of TCM, it is expanding the size of the signal constellation, rather than expanding the bandwidth, that results in the possibility of coding gain. This fundamental realization by Ungerboeck has led to an entire new set of application areas for coding in the range of high spectral efficiencies.

Ungerboeck was able to construct a number of interesting codes as a result of his original work [36], [37]. For example, his 64-state, (2, 1, 7), 4-ary AM code requires an $E_b/N_0 = 6.2$ dB to achieve a BER of 10^{-5} with soft-decision Viterbi decoding. This code has the same spectral efficiency as uncoded BPSK and requires 3.4 dB less power to achieve the same BER! Note, however, that a (2, 1, 7) convolutional code can also be used with conventional Gray mapped QPSK modulation to achieve a BER of 10^{-5} with an $E_b/N_0 = 4.5$ dB, 1.7 dB less than the AM code, thus illustrating the advantage of using quadrature modulation when possible. (See Fig. 1, "(2, 1, 7) QPSK.") As another example, Ungerboeck's 64-state, (3, 2, 7), 8-PSK code has a spectral efficiency of $\eta = 2.0$ bits/signal and requires an E_b/N_0 of only 6.0 dB to reach a BER of 10^{-5} with soft-decision Viterbi decoding. (See Fig. 1, "(3, 2, 7) 8-PSK.") Thus the four-state and 64-state, 8-PSK Ungerboeck codes require 2.4 and 3.6 dB less power, respectively, than uncoded QPSK to achieve the same BER with the same spectral efficiency. Finally, the 64-state code is 3.3 dB away from the 8-PSK capacity curve, which means that more than half the potential gain of rate $r = 2/3$, 8-PSK TCM can be achieved with relatively modest complexity.

For spectral efficiencies of $\eta = 3.0$ bits/signal or greater, two-dimensional (2D) or multidimensional (MD) QAM signal sets offer better performance than PSK signal sets. (MD signal sets are formed by mapping encoded bits into more than one constituent 2D signal point at a time.) QAM signal sets more efficiently pack the 2D signal space and thus can achieve the same minimum distance between signal points, which effectively limits the performance of a trellis code, with less average energy per signal than a comparable PSK signal set. This performance advantage of QAM signal sets has led modem designers to choose QAM, and QAM-based trellis codes, for use in high-speed data transmission.

The performance of Ungerboeck's codes quickly dispelled the belief that power reduction is only attainable with a corresponding decrease in spectral efficiency, as is the case when we limit our choice of modulation to BPSK. This was a welcome result for modem designers, who had been frustrated in their attempts to go beyond data rates of 9600 bps [38]. Since the International Telecommunications Union's ITU-T V.29 modem standard was adopted in 1976, little progress was made in increasing the speed and quality of data transmission over voice-grade telephone lines until the appearance of the V.32 and V.33 standards in 1986, both of which included a TCM encoder/modulator. The V.29 standard used uncoded 16-QAM modulation and a 2400-symbol/s signaling rate to achieve a spectral efficiency of $\eta = 4.0$ bits/signal and a transmission speed of 9600 bps in a half-duplex (one-way) mode. Due to the bandwidth constraints of the channel, signaling rates higher than 2400 symbols/s were not considered feasible. Thus the only avenue to increased data rates was to expand the size of the signal constellation. However, due to the SNR constraints of the channel, this meant that signals had to be packed closer together, resulting in degraded performance. So a clear need developed for a scheme which would allow constellation expansion at the same signaling rate, thus achieving higher data rates, and yet provide a coding gain to at least recover the noise margin lost by the closer packing of signals. TCM proved to be just such a scheme and, combined with some sophisticated signal-processing techniques, has resulted in a series of improvements which have pushed modem speeds up to 33 600 bps full-duplex.

In the remainder of this section, we will limit our discussion to two examples: the eight-state, (3, 2, 4), nonlinear 2D code developed by Wei [39] and adopted by ITU-T for the V.32 and V.33 standards and the 16-state, (3, 2, 5), linear four-dimensional (4D) code also developed by Wei [40] and adopted by ITU-T as one of the codes for the V.34 standard. The V.32 standard uses two uncoded bits and a 32-CROSS signal constellation, for a spectral efficiency of $\eta = 4.0$ bits/signal and a 9600 bps data rate, and achieves about 3.5 dB better performance (due to trellis coding) and full-duplex operation (due to echo cancellation) compared to the uncoded V.29 standard operating at the same data rate. In the V.33 standard, four uncoded bits and a 128-CROSS constellation are used to achieve $\eta = 6.0$ bits/signal and a 14 400-bps data rate. The V.34 standard, considered the ultimate modem standard for the classic linear Gaussian model of the telephone channel [41], uses an MD mapping, a constituent 2D signal constellation containing a maximum of 1664 points, and as many as eight uncoded bits (ten information bits total) per symbol to achieve a spectral efficiency up to $\eta = 10.0$ bits/signal and data rates as high as 33 600 bps. Advanced line probing, adaptive equalization, and precoding techniques are used to increase the signaling rates to as high as 3429 symbols/s, compared to

the previous standard of 2400 symbols/s. (In V.34, the data rates are not necessarily integer multiples of the symbol rates, since the signal mapping technique, called shell mapping [42], allows the mapping of fractional bits per symbol.) The V.34 standard also includes two other codes which offer slightly better performance at a cost of increased complexity [41]. One is a 32-state, (4, 3, 6), linear 4D code developed by Williams [43] that gains 0.3 dB compared to the 16-state Wei code, but is four times more complex. The other is a variation of a 64-state, (5, 4, 7), nonlinear 4D code also developed by Wei [40] that gains an additional 0.15 dB over the 16-state code, but is 16 times as complex. In both these cases, more bits are encoded by the convolutional code, so fewer uncoded bits are needed to achieve a particular data rate.

A block diagram of the eight-state, nonlinear 2D code developed by Wei [39] is shown in Fig. 6, along with a sketch of the 32-CROSS constellation adopted for the ITU-T V.32 standard. Note that the encoder has four input information bits, x^1, x^2, x^3, and x^4. $x^3 = y^3$ and $x^4 = y^4$ are uncoded and directly enter the 32-CROSS signal mapper (modulator). x^1 and x^2 are first differentially encoded and then enter the (3, 2, 4) systematic feedback nonlinear convolutional encoder, producing three output bits: y^1 and y^2 (information bits) as well as y^0 (a parity bit). The five encoded bits y^0, y^1, y^2, y^3, and y^4 then enter the modulator and are mapped into one of the 32-CROSS signals, as shown in Fig. 6. Since one 32-CROSS signal is transmitted for every four information bits entering the encoder, the spectral efficiency of the code is $\eta = 4.0$ bits/signal. (The V.33 standard uses the same code along with four uncoded information bits and a 128-CROSS constellation to achieve a spectral efficiency of $\eta = 6.0$ bits/signal.) As noted in the above example, soft decision Viterbi decoding, using an eight-state trellis with four-fold (16-fold in the V.33 case) parallel transitions, is performed based on the noisy received symbols at the demodulator output. Since the encoder contains two AND gates, it is nonlinear and cannot be described using the usual generator sequence notation. The nonlinear encoder was needed to make the code invariant to 90° phase rotations, i.e., a rotation of the signal space by any multiple of 90° still results in a valid code sequence. For a code with this property, as long as the bits affected by the phase rotation are differentially encoded, the correct sequence can still be decoded if the demodulator locks onto the wrong phase by any multiple of 90°. For 2D signal constellations, it is impossible to achieve 90° invariance with linear codes (the best that can be done is 180° invariance), and hence nonlinear codes are needed for full rotational invariance. This was a crucial insight made by Wei [39] in the design of this code.

The eight-state, (3, 2, 4), nonlinear 2D Wei code used in the V.32 and V.33 standards has free distance $d_{\text{free}}^2 = 5$, number of nearest neighbors $N_{\text{free}} = 16$, and achieves a coding gain of 3.6 dB at a BER of 10^{-5} compared to uncoded 16-QAM ($\eta = 4.0$) and 64-QAM ($\eta = 6.0$) modulation, respectively. As in the other examples, this coding gain is achieved without bandwidth expansion. These points are shown in Fig. 1 with the designations "V.32" and "V.33."

A block diagram of the 16-state, (3, 2, 5), linear 4D code developed by Wei [40] is shown in Fig. 7, along with a

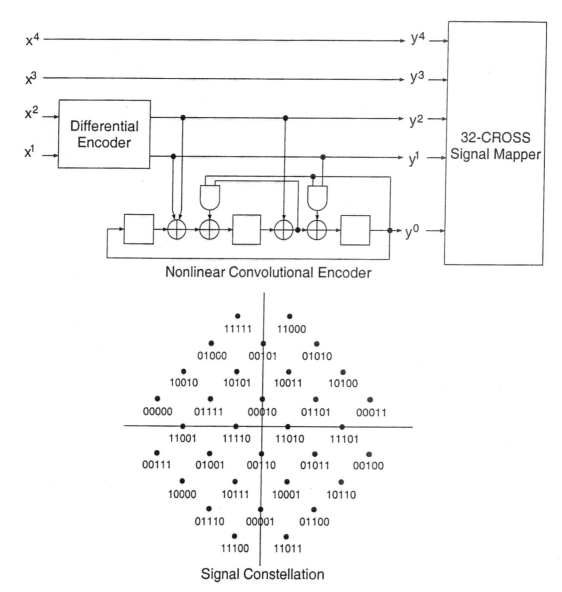

Fig. 6. The eight-state V.32 code.

sketch of a 224-point constellation which, along with its mirror inverse, forms a constituent 448-point 2D signal constellation consistent with the ITU-T V.34 standard. The TCM portion of the encoder has three input information bits: two coded (x^1 and x^2) and one uncoded (x^3). In addition, bits x^2 and x^3 are differentially encoded, since they are affected by phase rotations. Full 90° rotational invariance can be achieved with a linear code in this case since the signal constellation is 4D. (In general, it is possible to achieve full rotational invariance with linear codes using MD signal constellations, at least for code rates $r = k/(k + 1)$ with $k < 4$.) The $(3, 2, 5)$ systematic feedback linear convolutional encoder shown in Fig. 7 (a simplified form) is equivalent to an encoder with generator matrix

$$\boldsymbol{G}(D) = \begin{bmatrix} 1 & 0 & \frac{D^3}{1+D^4} \\ 0 & 1 & \frac{1+D}{1+D^4} \end{bmatrix} \quad (14)$$

and produces three output bits: y^1 and y^2 (information bits) as well as y^0 (a parity bit). Along with the differentially

encoded bit y^3, they enter the 4D signal mapper (modulator). The constituent 2D constellation is divided into four subsets, and thus there are 16 subsets in the 4D constellation. The four encoded bits y^0, y^1, y^2, and y^3 are mapped into one of the 16 subsets in the 4D constellation. In the most basic version of the standard, the additional uncoded information bits needed to achieve the desired spectral efficiency are then used to select the particular 4D signal point to be transmitted. For example, if a spectral efficiency of $\eta = 7.0$ bits/signal is desired using a constituent 192-point 2D signal constellation, an additional 11 uncoded information bits are needed in each 4D signaling interval. In this case, the ratio of the constellation size to the size of the uncoded constellation which would support the same spectral efficiency, i.e., the constellation expansion ratio (CER), is CER = $192/128 = 1.5$, or 50% less than that needed with 2D TCM. By choosing the constituent 2D constellation subsets and the mapping such that lower energy signal points (the "inner points" in the constellation) are used more often than higher energy points (the "outer

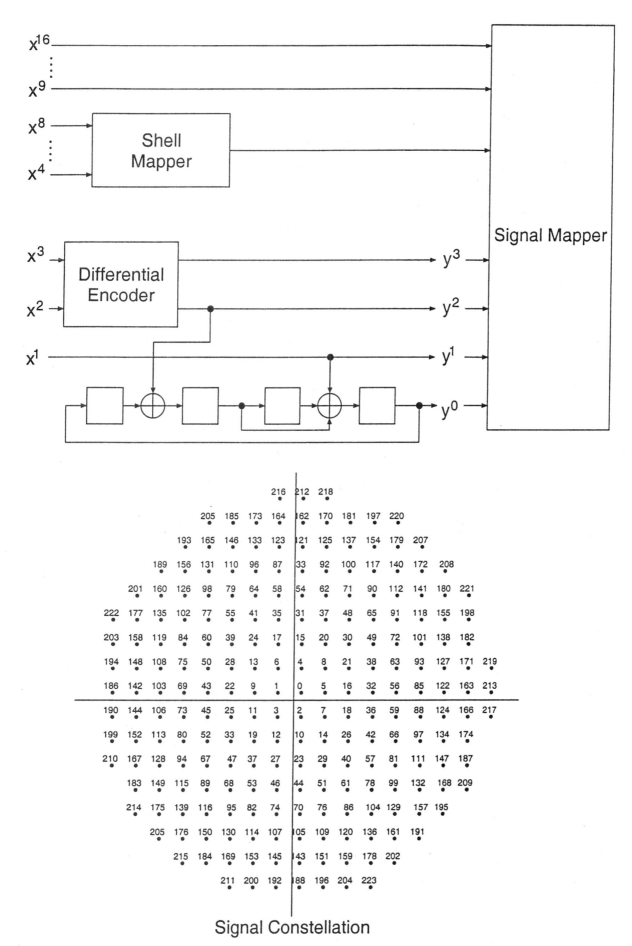

Fig. 7. The 16-state V.34 code.

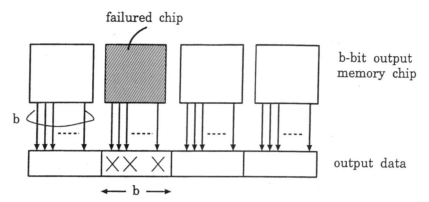

Fig. 8. The b-bit-per-chip semiconductor memory organization.

points" in the constellation) a technique called constellation shaping [44], an additional "shaping gain" is achieved. This concept can be extended by further expanding the basic 2D signal constellation beyond 192 points in conjunction with the shell mapping approach. In this approach, the signal selection (mapping) is done over several symbol intervals so that enough dimensions are included to produce an approximately spherical constellation, known to be optimal in high-dimensional spaces. In the V.34 standard, shell mapping is applied to a 16-dimensional constellation, i.e., eight 2D symbol intervals, to achieve up to 0.8 dB of shaping gain. For the constituent 448-point 2D signal constellation shown in Fig. 7, a total of 20 information bits over eight 2D symbols are devoted to shell mapping, and four information bits per symbol are left uncoded. This arrangement gives a total spectral efficiency of

$$\eta = 3/2 \text{ (coding)} + 20/8 \text{ (shaping)} + 4 \text{ (uncoded)}$$
$$= 8.0 \text{ bits/signal.} \tag{15}$$

The size of the constituent 2D signal set can vary depending on the desired shaping gain and CER. Usually, an additional CER due to shaping of about 25% is enough to approach 0.8-dB shaping gains. In this example, the constellation size of 448 yields a CER $= 448/256 = 1.75$, for a total of 75% constellation expansion, 50% due to coding and 25% due to shaping. Shaping was included in the standard because it was ultimately a simpler way of picking up an additional 0.8 dB than by using a more complex code. In theory, as much as 1.5 dB of shaping gain is available [5], but the methods needed to achieve the extra gain are quite complex.

The 16-state, $(3, 2, 5)$, linear 4D Wei code used in the V.34 standard has free distance $d_{\text{free}}^2 = 4$, number of nearest neighbors $N_{\text{free}} = 12$ per 2D signal, and achieves a coding gain of 4.2 dB at a BER of 10^{-5} compared to uncoded 256-QAM ($\eta = 8.0$) modulation. (Note that the smaller free distance here compared to the eight-state V.32 code does not translate into less coding gain, since the uncoded systems used to compute the coding gain are different). This point is shown in Fig. 1 with the designation "V.34/16." The slightly improved performance obtained by using 32- and 64-state codes is also indicated in Fig. 1 with the designations "V.34/32" and "V.34/64," respectively.

A good summary of the state-of-the-art in modem design circa 1990 was given in the review article by Forney [38]. A more thorough discussion of the considerations that went into the design of the V.34 modem can be found in [41].

IV. DATA STORAGE APPLICATIONS

In this section, we cover two applications of coding to data storage, high-speed computer memories and magnetic/optical discs. The use of RS codes in compact discs represents the most widely used and best known application of error-control coding over the 50-year time span covered by this review.

A. Error-Correcting Codes for High-Speed Computer Memories

Error-correcting codes are widely used to enhance the reliability of computer memories. In these storage applications, the codes have unique features not seen in most communication applications. This is due to the following conditions required for error control in computer memories.

1) Encoding and decoding must be very fast to maintain high throughput rates. Therefore, parallel encoding and decoding must be implemented with combinatorial logic instead of the linear feedback shift-register logic usually used in other applications.

2) Unique types of errors, such as byte errors, are caused by the organization of semiconductor memory systems. As memory systems become large, the b-bit-per-chip organization shown in Fig. 8 tends to be adopted. Then a chip failure causes the word read out to have errors in a b-bit block, called a b-bit byte or simply a byte.

3) Redundancy must be small, because the cost per bit of high-speed semiconductor memories is high compared with magnetic memories and other low-speed memories.

The best-known class of codes for semiconductor memories is the SEC/DED (single-error-correcting/double-error-detecting) codes. It can be viewed as a class of shortened versions of extended Hamming codes. These codes have minimum distance $d_{\text{min}} = 4$ and are capable of correcting single errors and detecting double errors. Usually, however, they can detect more than just double errors. Since the additional error-detection capability depends on the structure of the parity-check matrix, many proposals for enhanced error-detection properties have been presented.

Among the many proposed schemes, the SEC/DED/SbED (single-error-correcting/double-error-detecting/single b-bit byte error-detecting) codes have been put into practical use. These codes can correct a single bit error and detect any errors in a single b-bit byte as well as any two bit errors. Such detection capability is useful for the memory organization of Fig. 8, i.e., a b-bit per chip organization, where a chip failure causes a byte error.

As an example, let us consider the case of $b = 4$. An SEC/DED/S4ED code is constructed as follows. Let $p = 2^{m-1}$ and let $\{\boldsymbol{h}_i | i = 1, \cdots, p\}$ be the set of all binary m-dimensional column vectors of even weight if m is odd and of odd weight if m is even. For $i, j = 1, 2, \cdots, p$, the following $2m \times 4$ matrices $\boldsymbol{H}_{ij}$ are defined as

$$\boldsymbol{H}_{ij} = \begin{bmatrix} \boldsymbol{h}_i & \boldsymbol{h}_j & 1 + \boldsymbol{h}_i + \boldsymbol{h}_j & 1 + \boldsymbol{h}_i + \boldsymbol{h}_j \\ 1 + \boldsymbol{h}_i + \boldsymbol{h}_j & 1 + \boldsymbol{h}_i + \boldsymbol{h}_j & \boldsymbol{h}_i & \boldsymbol{h}_j \end{bmatrix} \tag{16}$$

where 1 denotes the m-dimensional column vector whose components are all ones. Letting $n = 2p(p - 1)$, we define a $2m \times n$ matrix $\boldsymbol{H}$ as

$$\boldsymbol{H} = [\boldsymbol{H}_{12} \boldsymbol{H}_{13} \cdots \boldsymbol{H}_{1p} \boldsymbol{H}_{23} \cdots \boldsymbol{H}_{2p} \boldsymbol{H}_{34} \cdots \boldsymbol{H}_{p-2,p} \boldsymbol{H}_{p-1,p}]. \tag{17}$$

Then it is easily seen that the $(n, n - 2m)$ code C having parity-check matrix $\boldsymbol{H}$ is an SEC/DED/S4ED code [45], [46]. For example, in the case of $m = 4$, an SEC/DED/S4ED code of length 112 with eight check bits is constructed. Shortening this code by 40 bits, we have a $(72, 64)$ SEC/DED/S4ED code. In order to have 64 information bits, SEC/DED codes require at least eight check bits. The construction method described above gives a code having the same redundancy as ordinary SEC/DED codes and, in addition, the capability of detecting any errors in a single 4-bit byte.

As high-speed semiconductor memories become larger, more powerful error-correcting codes are needed. This has made SbEC/DbED (single b-bit byte error correcting/double b-bit byte error-detecting) codes practical. Such codes are constructed from RS codes or Bose-Chaudhuri-Hocquengham (BCH) codes over $GF(2^b)$. If each symbol of $GF(2^b)$ is expressed as a b-bit byte, then RS codes or 2^b-ary BCH codes having minimum distance $d_{\min} = 4$ are SbEC/DbED codes. In applying these codes to semiconductor memories, they are usually substantially shortened to fit the number of information bits to the respective application. In such cases, we can sometimes obtain more efficient codes by slightly modifying RS codes [47].

Table I shows the minimum number of parity-check bits for the best known SEC/DED codes, SEC/DED/ SbED codes, and SbEC/DbED codes when the number of information bits is 32, 64, and 128 for $b = 4$ and 8 [48].

B. Error-Correcting Codes for Magnetic/Optical Discs

Error correction for magnetic-disc memories began with the application of Fire codes [49] in the 1960's. Later, RS codes

TABLE I
MINIMUM NUMBER OF PARITY-CHECK BITS FOR THE BEST KNOWN ERROR-CONTROL CODES FOR HIGH-SPEED MEMORIES

code	b	number of information bits		
		32	64	128
SEC/DED	–	7	8	9
SEC/DED/SbED	4	7	8	9
	8	10	10	11
SbEC/DbED	4	12	14	16
	8	24	24	24

assumed the major role in this area. On the other hand, RS codes have been the principal error-correcting codes used in optical-disc memories from the beginning. These applications were greatly expanded with the appearance of the compact disc (CD) and the CD–read-only memory (CD-ROM) at the beginning of the 1980's [46], [50].

The CD format uses a coding system called CIRC (cross-interleaved RS codes), which is a combination of two short-ened RS codes of minimum distance $d_{\min} = 5$ over $GF(2^8)$. The information sequence is first encoded by a $(28, 24)$ code and then by a $(32, 28)$ code. For audio signals, an error interpolating technique can be used to estimate the original signal values by interpolating or extrapolating from reliable values for those errors that cannot be corrected.

However, such a technique is not applicable for data stored in computer systems, and thus greater error correction ca-pability is required for the CD-ROM. Thus a CRC (cyclic redundancy check) code with 32 check bits and a product of two shortened RS codes with minimum distance $d_{\min} = 3$ over $GF(2^8)$ are used in addition to the CIRC. The encoder for a CD-ROM first appends four check bytes of a CRC to the user data of 2048 bytes with a 4-byte header and then adds eight bytes of all zeros for future extension. Alternate bytes are taken from the resulting sequence to produce two sequences of length 1032 bytes. Then, after rearranging the bytes, each sequence is encoded by a product of $(26, 24)$ and $(45, 43)$ RS codes to give a codeword of length 1170 bytes. Finally, the two codewords are combined and a synchronization pattern of 12 bytes is added to make one sector of a CD-ROM having 2352 bytes, as shown in Fig. 9, which is then applied to the CIRC encoder. A decoder for a CD-ROM is depicted in Fig. 10.

There are various ways of decoding the product code [51]. Reliability information for each symbol is obtained from the CIRC decoding process. Unreliable symbols are interpolated for audio CD's, but they are treated as erasures for CD-ROM's. If necessary, more detailed reliability information is available and soft-decision iterative decoding can be applied to make the decoding results as reliable as possible. However, the error rate of current CD's is not high, and the CIRC itself is an error-control coding scheme powerful enough for most CD's. Thus if the error probability of CIRC decoding is small enough, simple erasure decoding for the two RS codes can be adopted,

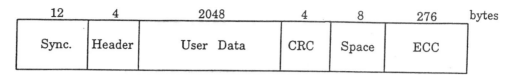

12	4	2048	4	8	276	bytes
Sync.	Header	User Data	CRC	Space	ECC	

CRC: check bytes of CRC

ECC: check bytes of two codewords of the product code

Fig. 9. The structure of one sector of a CD-ROM.

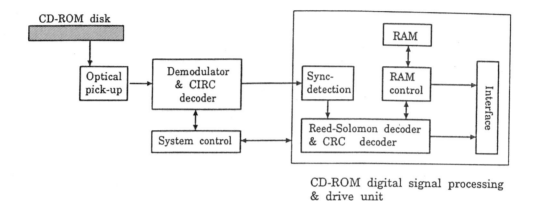

CD-ROM digital signal processing & drive unit

Fig. 10. The CD-ROM decoder.

as is the case for most CD-ROM drive units. With a single decoding of each of the two codes, all erasures in any eight or fewer positions can be corrected, since the minimum distance of the product code is $d_{\min} = 9$. But there exists at least one pattern of nine erasures that cannot be corrected by any decoder. If erasure decoding of the product code is iterated a few times, though, many patterns of nine or more erasures can be corrected.

Each of the RS codes in the CD and CD-ROM systems is decoded by directly calculating the coefficients of the error locator polynomial from the syndromes. This technique, which is simpler than other methods of decoding RS codes, can be applied whenever the minimum distance is no more than 7 or 8, as is the case for these RS codes.

Since the epoch-making success of the application of the CIRC system to CD's, the major error control roles for optical and magnetic discs have been monopolized by RS codes. This popularity is also supported by the progress of implementation techniques for codes with high error-correcting capability. Recently, it has become common to use RS codes over $GF(2^8)$ having very large minimum distances. For example, there exists a general purpose encoder/decoder chip for $(255, 255 - p)$ RS codes for which the number of check bytes p can be varied up to 36 [52]. This chip can correct up to s erasure bytes and t error bytes for any nonnegative integers s and t satisfying $2t + s \leq p$ at speeds of at least 33 Mbytes/s.

V. Applications in Digital Audio/Video Transmission

In this section, we present a specific example of an application of a cyclic code to digital audio broadcasting (DAB) and then discuss more generally the various coding systems used in DAB and digital video broadcasting (DVB) standards.

A. Difference Set Cyclic Codes for FM Multiplexed Digital Audio Broadcasting

There are many error-correcting codes that have been applied to DAB systems. Among them, the difference set cyclic code [53] adopted for an FM multiplexed DAB system is an example of an application involving a majority logic decodable code [54]. The initial use was for error correction in a TV teletext system [55]. For Western languages, the $(8, 4)$ extended Hamming code sufficed to keep the transmitted text readable. However, for the Japanese language this was not the case, because the language has ideograms called *kanji* (Chinese characters) and even one error may make the text unreadable or incorrect.

Hence more powerful codes were desired. However, the decoder had to be very simple, because it was to be installed in a TV set for home use. For these reasons, a $(273, 191)$ difference set cyclic code was adopted as a simply decodable code with high error-correction capability. This code has minimum distance $d_{\min} = 18$ and can correct eight or fewer errors. In practice, it was shortened by one bit to a $(272, 190)$ code to fit the data format of the teletext.

The $(273, 191)$ code is constructed on the basis of a perfect difference set

$$D = \{d_0, d_1, \cdots, d_{16}\}$$
$$= \{0, 18, 24, 46, 50, 67, 103, 112, 115, 126,$$
$$128, 159, 166, 167, 186, 196, 201\}.$$

Any codeword $\boldsymbol{x} = (x_0, x_1, \cdots, x_{272})$ in this code satisfies the following parity-check equations:

$$x_0 + x_{d_{i,0}} + \cdots + x_{d_{i,i-1}} + x_{d_{i,i+1}} + \cdots + x_{d_{i,16}} = 0,$$
$$i = 0, 1, \cdots, 16 \quad (18)$$

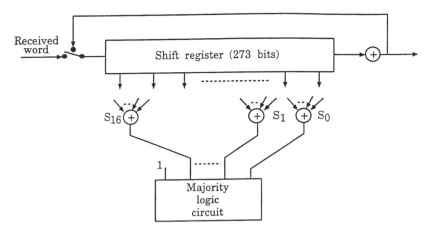

Fig. 11. Majority logic decoder for the (273, 191) code.

where $d_{ij} = d_i - d_j \bmod 273, 0 \leq d_{ij} < 273$. Every symbol of a codeword except x_0 appears once and only once in these equations, and x_0 is contained in all the equations. Let r_j be the received symbol for the jth bit x_j of the transmitted codeword, $j = 0, 1, \cdots, 272$. (r_j may be an analog symbol in the case of soft output demodulation.) We denote the result of a decision on r_j at a previous stage of decoding by $[r_j]$ and the error in $[r_j]$ by e_j, i.e., $e_j = x_j - [r_j] \bmod 2, e_j \in \{0, 1\}$. Initially, $[r_j]$ is taken to be the hard quantized version of r_j. Then, defining a syndrome bit s_i ($i = 0, 1, \cdots, 16$) for the received word $\boldsymbol{r} = (r_0, r_1, \cdots, r_{272})$ by

$$s_i = [r_0] + [r_{d_{i,0}}] + \cdots + [r_{d_{i,i-1}}] + [r_{d_{i,i+1}}] + \cdots + [r_{d_{i,16}}]$$
$$= e_0 + e_{d_{i,0}} + \cdots + e_{d_{i,i-1}} + e_{d_{i,i+1}} + \cdots + e_{d_{i,16}} \quad (19)$$

we can correctly estimate the error e_0 in $[r_0]$ as the majority element of $S = (s_0, s_1, \cdots, s_{16}, 1)$ when the number of errors is no more than eight, because at least ten components of S are 1 if $[r_0]$ is erroneous and at most eight components of S are 1 otherwise. The errors in the other bits are estimated in the same way after the received word is cyclically permuted. Fig. 11 shows a decoder based on this principle.

This majority logic decoder is much simpler than a BCH decoder of comparable length and error-correcting capability. In fact, a majority logic LSI decoder was fabricated with about one tenth the number of gates as a BCH decoder. For such a simple implementation, code efficiency must be compromised. However, considerable improvement in error-correcting capability is realized by introducing soft-decision decoding.

Optimal soft-decision decoding of the first bit x_0 in the transmitted codeword requires a MAP estimate of x_0, or equivalently the error bit e_0. In the remainder of this section, we consider MAP estimation of e_0, i.e., estimating e_0 as the value that maximizes the *a posteriori* probability (APP) $P(e_0|\boldsymbol{r})$, given the received word $\boldsymbol{r}$. It is difficult to calculate $P(e_0|\boldsymbol{r})$ exactly. Therefore, some assumptions on the independence of the received symbols are needed. For an AWGN channel, the MAP estimate of e_0 is approximated as

$$\hat{e}_0 = \begin{cases} 1, & \sum\limits_{i=0}^{16} s_i W_i > T \\ 0, & \sum\limits_{i=0}^{16} s_i W_i < T \end{cases} \quad (20)$$

where $\hat{e}_0$ denotes the estimate of e_0, T is a threshold given by

$$T = \frac{1}{2} \sum_{i=0}^{16} W_i, \quad (21)$$

and the weighting factor W_i is defined as

$$W_i = \frac{\log P_{ei}}{\log P_{oi}}. \quad (22)$$

P_{ei} and P_{oi} are the probabilities that the number of nonzero errors appearing in (19) is even and odd, respectively. This algorithm, which is called APP decoding [56], is near-optimal, but it is not practical because it demands too much complexity to compute W_i. Therefore, the following further approximation is commonly made [57].

Let $\boldsymbol{e}_i$ be an error pattern corresponding to a previous decision concerning the received symbols appearing in (19), i.e.,

$$\boldsymbol{e}_i = (e_0, e_{j_1}, e_{j_2}, \ldots, e_{j_{16}})$$

where

$$j_1 < j_2 < \cdots < j_{16}$$

and

$$\{j_1, j_2, \cdots, j_{16}\} = \{d_{i,0}, \cdots, d_{i,i-1}, d_{i,i+1}, \cdots, d_{i,16}\}.$$

We then approximate P_{ei} as the probability of the error pattern $\boldsymbol{e}_{ei}^*$ having maximum probability among all $\boldsymbol{e}_i$ of even weight. Similarly, we approximate P_{oi} by the probability of the error pattern $\boldsymbol{e}_{oi}^*$ having maximum probability among all $\boldsymbol{e}_i$ of odd weight. These $\boldsymbol{e}_{ei}^*$ and $\boldsymbol{e}_{oi}^*$ can be easily obtained by using the trellis shown in Fig. 12. Such an approximation of APP decoding for the difference set cyclic code is called APP trellis decoding.

The APP decoder is optimal if all 273-tuples $\boldsymbol{x} = (x_0, x_1, \cdots, x_{272})$ satisfying (18) are codewords. Since this is not true in general, the decoding performance of APP decoding can sometimes be improved by variable threshold decoding [58], which involves iterative decoding with a variable threshold. At first, the threshold T is set high to avoid miscorrection. The decoding result for a received symbol then replaces the previous decision in succeeding stages of APP decoding. This operation gives so-called extrinsic information

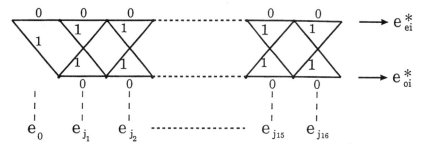

Fig. 12. The trellis for computing e^*_{ei} and e^*_{oi}.

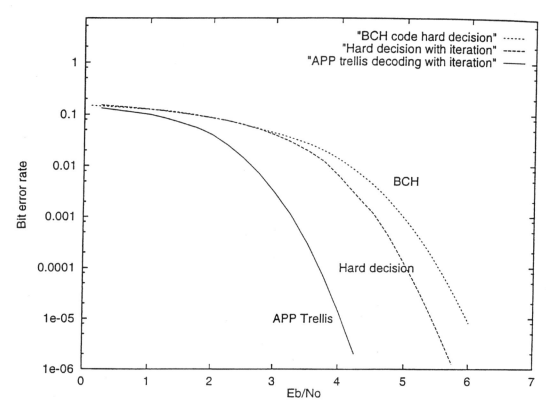

Fig. 13. Decoding performance of the $(273, 191)$ code and a $(273, 192)$ BCH code.

[32] to the decoding of the other symbols. After each iteration, T is decreased to correct additional bits. When T reaches the value given by (21), decoding is complete.

Fig. 13 shows the decoding performance of APP trellis decoding and hard decision decoding over an AWGN channel. In both cases, variable threshold decoding with three iterations was adopted. In the figure, the hard-decision decoding performance of a $(273, 192)$ shortened BCH code correcting nine or fewer errors is also shown for comparison. Variable-threshold APP trellis decoding shows excellent decoding performance in spite of the simplicity of its implementation. A decoder chip for this algorithm has been implemented for application to FM multiplexed DAB systems.

B. Rate-Compatible Punctured Codes for Digital Audio Broadcasting

The European DAB System, which will be also used for DVB and the MPEG audio system [59], makes extensive use of rate-compatible punctured convolutional (RCPC) coding

schemes. The basic principles of these schemes are described below.

1) Unequal and Adaptive Error Protection with RCPC Codes: Rate $r = 1/n$ convolutional nonsystematic feedforward or systematic feedback encoders have the advantage of a binary trellis and therefore employ a simple Viterbi or MAP decoder [32]. From a $(2, 1, 5)$ nonsystematic feedforward encoder with generator matrix

$$\boldsymbol{G}(D) = [1 + D + D^4, \quad 1 + D^3 + D^4] \qquad (23)$$

we obtain a systematic feedback encoder with a rational parity generator

$$\boldsymbol{G}(D) = \left[1 \quad \frac{1 + D + D^4}{1 + D^3 + D^4}\right]. \qquad (24)$$

Both encoders generate the same set of codewords, but they have slightly different BER performance. For very noisy channels, the BER curve of the feedback encoder is better than and approaches, but does not cross, the BER curve for uncoded performance.

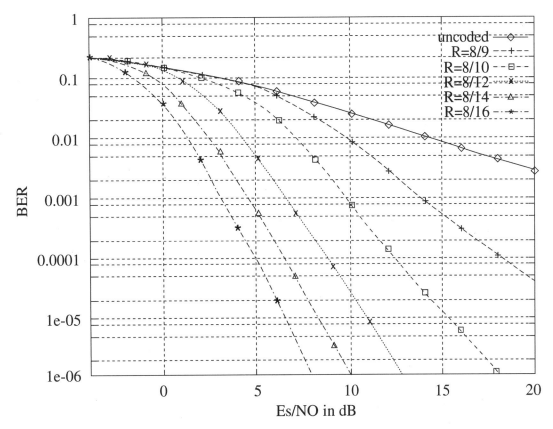

Fig. 14. BER performance of nonsystematic feedforward RCPC codes for $K = 5$ and $R = 8/9$ to $R = 1/2$ on the statistically independent Rayleigh fading channel.

Higher rate codes are easily obtained by puncturing. If this is done in a rate-compatible way, such that all the code bits in the higher rate code are also used for the lower rate codes, we obtain an RCPC code [60]. This code family, with a puncturing period of P, has rates equal to

$$r = \frac{P}{P + l}, \qquad \text{for } l = 1 \text{ to } P \cdot (n - 1). \qquad (25)$$

The lowest rate is the rate of the original rate $r = 1/n$ code, called the mother code. Puncturing tables for different rates are given in [60]. Even lower rates can be achieved by duplicating bits, i.e., by replacing "1" by "2" or some higher integer in the puncturing tables. On a multiplicative, fully interleaved Rayleigh fading channel these systematic codes perform as shown in Fig. 14. By puncturing all of the nonsystematic bits, the rate 1 (uncoded) system is easily incorporated. Therefore, we have a great variety of coding options which can be easily adapted to source and channel requirements because the encoder and the decoder are the same for the whole code family and can be adapted using only the puncturing control. At the receiver, punctured bits marked with "0" in the puncturing tables are stuffed with zero values and repeated bits are combined by adding their soft received values. Therefore, the decoder always operates with the mother code and its trellis remains unchanged.

2) The RCPC Coding Scheme for the European DAB System: The European DAB system [61] uses the source-coding system of ISO/MPEG Audio [59]. In this case, PCM Audio at 2 times 768 kbps is compressed, typically down to 2 times 128 kbps

or less. Using a psychoacoustic model of the human ear, the audio band is divided into 32 subbands which employ adaptive quantization. The data stream sent to the multiplexer contains headers, a scalefactor and scalefactor-select information, and quantized samples with bits of different significance. This format and the dynamic data rate require unequal and adaptive error protection. Therefore, the RCPC codes described above have been designed for three different rates (1/3, 4/9, and 8/15) using a constraint length $K = 7$ mother code with 64 states. Later, in [62], an even more sophisticated system was proposed, where the rate pattern of the RCPC codes can be changed almost continuously within the data frame, depending on the varying rate and protection requirements of the source bits. As a result, the resource "protection bits" are used according to the needs of the source bits and the variation of the audio signal. The overall system exhibits a more graceful degradation at the edge of coverage of the radio broadcast system where the SNR deteriorates.

C. Error-Correcting Codes for Digital Video Systems

Decoding speed is at the top of the list of requirements for error control in digital video systems. For this reason, powerful error-correcting codes had not been considered for this application until the 1990's. The first standardized error-correction method for digital video transmission, recommended as a part of the ITU-T H.261 standard in 1990, is very simple. It uses a (511, 493) BCH code, which has minimum distance $d_{\min} = 6$ and is capable of correcting two or fewer random errors and

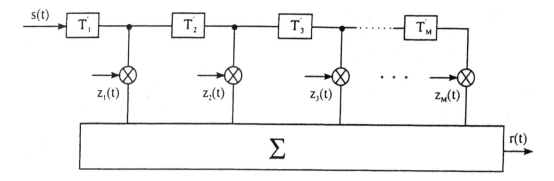

Fig. 15. Simplified model of the mobile communications channel.

detecting three random errors. In addition, it is designed to correct a burst error of length no longer than six.

Since then, however, more sophisticated error-correction schemes based on RS codes have been put into practical use with advanced video coding standards like MPEG2. For DVB, in particular, concatenated codes composed of an RS code as the outer code and a convolutional or trellis code as the inner code have been used. For example, a $(204, 188)$ code obtained by shortening the $(255, 239)$ RS code with minimum distance $d_{\min} = 17$ has been adopted as the outer code along with the $(2, 1, 7)$ CCSDS convolutional code (sometimes punctured) as the inner code in the European digital terrestrial TV broadcasting system.

Multilevel coding with multistage decoding [63] is a strong candidate for future DVB systems. By employing unconventional signal labeling (mapping), the large number of nearest neighbors associated with multistage decoding can be reduced significantly. This results in highly efficient transmission for multivalue modulation formats such as M-PSK and M-QAM with moderate complexity [64]. Also, because of its excellent error performance, turbo coding [29] may be considered as the inner code in a concatenated system for future applications. Both turbo coding and multilevel coding suffer from relatively long decoding delays, but this might be allowed in some DVB applications.

VI. APPLICATIONS IN MOBILE COMMUNICATIONS

The advent of digital mobile communications during the last 15 years has resulted in the frequent use of error-control coding because the mobile channel exhibits raw error rates of 5 to 10%, mainly due to fades, bursts, and interference from other users and other cells. This also means that decoders must work at low values of E_b/N_0. Consequently, all the features known to decoder designers must be used, such as interleaving, soft decisions, channel state information, and concatenation. On the other hand, bandwidth is scarce and expensive in a heavily booming cellular market. This means that the resource "redundancy" must be used with care, applying methods such as unequal and adaptive error protection. Of course, the dramatic increase in integrated circuit complexity has allowed the use of very sophisticated error-control methods. It is quite common to employ in a handheld mobile phone two Viterbi

algorithms in tandem, one for the equalizer and one for the FEC decoder, all on one chip, which also includes source compression for the speech signal, channel estimation, and other tasks.

In this section, we will give some Shannon theory background for the mobile channel, describe the most widely used FEC schemes in mobile communications, and conclude with some advanced FEC features currently being discussed for digital mobile systems.

A. The Mobile Radio Channel and the Shannon Limit

The mobile communications channel can be modeled as shown in Fig. 15, where the received complex equivalent baseband signal after multipath distortion is

$$r(t) = \sum_{m=1}^{M} s(t - T_m) \cdot z_m(t) \tag{26}$$

with complex time-varying factors $z_m(t)$. At the receiver we also have noise and interference, usually modeled as an additive AWGN component with one-sided power spectral density N_0. If the channel is nonfrequency-selective, i.e., if the delay $T_M = \sum_{m=2}^{M} T_m$ is less than the symbol duration, then the channel induces only multiplicative distortion with $z = x + jy$. The amplitude

$$|z| = a = \sqrt{x^2 + y^2} \tag{27}$$

is then Rayleigh- or Rician-distributed. For the Rayleigh case we have

$$f_a(a) = \frac{a}{\sigma^2} \cdot e^{-a^2/2\sigma^2} \tag{28}$$

and a uniformly distributed phase. If sufficient interleaving is applied, these random variables become statistically independent. For coherently detected BPSK modulation, only the amplitude fluctuations are relevant. These assumptions allow us to calculate Shannon's channel capacity for this mobile channel. The capacity C is calculated as a function of the channel SNR

$$E_s/N_0 = rE_b/N_0 \tag{29}$$

where r represents the code rate. If we transmit at the capacity limit we obtain from the parameter equation

$$r = C(rE_b/N_0) \tag{30}$$

506

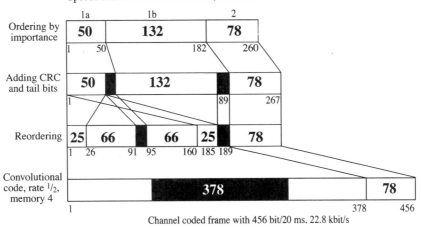

Speech Frame with 260 bit/20 ms, 13 kbit/s

Fig. 16. FEC scheme for the full rate GSM speech coder.

TABLE II
SHANNON LIMIT FOR THE RAYLEIGH FADING CHANNEL

Input	Output	Rate	$E_b/N_0|\min$ Rayleigh
binary	soft + CSI	$\to 0$	-1.6 dB
binary	soft	$\to 0$	-0.5 dB
binary	binary	$\to 0$	1.4 dB
binary	soft +CSI	0.5	1.8 dB
binary	soft	0.5	2.5 dB
binary	binary	0.5	4.9 dB

the Shannon limit

$$E_b/N_0|_{\min} = f(r). \qquad (31)$$

For an interleaved Rayleigh fading channel, depending on the use of soft decisions and channel state information (CSI), the Shannon SNR limits of Table II can be calculated [65].

This Shannon theory result tells the designer of an FEC system for such a mobile channel that

- for low-rate codes, the mobile Rayleigh channel is not worse than the Gaussian channel, because low-rate interleaved coding acts like a multiple diversity system which transforms independent Rayleigh channels into a Gaussian channel;
- for rate $1/2$ codes, the Rayleigh channel degrades the system by 2 to 3 dB, and
- soft decisions can gain up to 2.4 dB, and CSI, namely the fading amplitude, can gain roughly another decibel.

B. FEC Coding in the Global System for Mobile Communications (GSM)

With currently some 80 million mobile phones worldwide, the error-control system of GSM is probably the most widely used form of nontrivial FEC besides the compact disc and high-speed modems. The speech and data services of the GSM standard use a variety of FEC codes, including BCH codes and Fire codes, plus CRC codes for error detection and codes for synchronization, access, and data channels. These codes are used as outer codes in a concatenated scheme. We will concentrate here on the inner coding scheme, which is primarily used for the full rate speech traffic channel. A 20-ms slot of the 13-kbit/s full rate speech coder produces a block of 260 bits, split into three sensitivity classes. 78 bits are rather insensitive to errors and are unprotected. The 50 most significant bits are initially protected by a 3-bit CRC used for error detection. Then these 53 bits, along with the remaining 132 bits, or a total of 185 bits, are encoded with a $(2, 1, 5)$ nonsystematic convolutional code with generator matrix

$$\boldsymbol{G}(D) = [1 + D^3 + D^4, \quad 1 + D + D^3 + D^4]. \qquad (32)$$

In order to terminate the trellis, four known tail bits are added, as shown in Fig. 16. This leads to a total of 378 coded bits and, including the 78 uncoded speech bits, results in a block of 456 bits every 20 ms, for a rate of 22.8 kbit/s. Together with seven other users, these bits are interleaved in groups of 57 bits and spread over eight TDMA bursts, which are transmitted over the mobile channel using GMSK modulation. The bursts include a midamble of 26 bits (+ two signaling bits) used by the receiver to estimate the channel tap values corresponding to the multipath model shown in Fig. 15. Using the channel tap estimates, an MLSE equalizer employing the Viterbi algorithm outputs hard or soft values for the 456 bits in a block. After deinterleaving, the Viterbi decoder accepts 378 values and outputs 185 bits from the terminated 16-state trellis. If the check with the CRC code is positive, the 50 plus 132 decoded bits, together with the 78 unprotected bits, are delivered to the speech decoder. A negative CRC usually triggers a concealment procedure in the speech decoding algorithm, rather than accepting any errors in the 50 most important bits.

When, as defined in the GSM standard, frequency hopping is used on the bursts in an urban enviroment, statistically independent Rayleigh fading is a reasonable assumption. In this case, we notice from the Shannon limits in Table II that at a rate of $r = 1/2$ we can gain up to 3.1 dB in required SNR if the channel decoder uses CSI and soft values. Since a normal Viterbi equalizer delivers only hard decisions, a modification is necessary leading to a SOVA or MAP type soft-in/soft-out

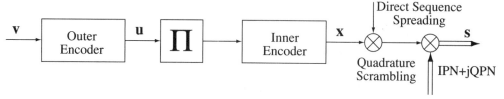

Fig. 17. A CDMA transmitter.

TABLE III
FEC CODES IN GSM SPEECH CODING

Service	Speech rate	constraint lengths	code rates
Full rate	13.0	5	1/2
Enhanced full rate	13.0	5	1/2
Half Rate	5.6	7	1/2, 1/3

equalizer. Most GSM terminals now use some kind of soft values from the equalizer as inputs to the decoder.

GSM is a good example how Shannon's theory can help a system designer. Although with such simple codes we are not operating at the absolute values of Shannon's limit given in Table II (GSM operates at approximately 7 dB), the relative gains between hard and soft decisions remain a good indicator.

Other FEC coding schemes used for the different speech options defined by GSM are summarized in Table III. For data services, the currently defined user data rates in GSM are 2.4, 4.8, and 9.6 kbit/s. When a full rate channel is used the respective code rates are 1/6, 1/3, and 1/2. It will be a difficult task to accomodate higher user data rates in one full rate slot.

C. FEC Coding in the CDMA Mobile System (IS-95)

In CDMA systems for mobile communication, FEC is very important in combating multiuser interference (MUI) and the influence of multipath fading. Therefore, most systems use a low-rate channel code followed by direct sequence (DS) spreading with a high processing gain. Others use a concatenation of two or more low-rate codes followed by DS spreading, which provides privacy (a signature sequence), but has a low processing gain. A well-known example of the latter type of system is the uplink of the Qualcomm system based on the IS-95(A) standard [66]. As shown in Fig. 17, this system consists of an outer convolutional code C^O with rate $r^O = 1/3$ and constraint length $K = 9$, a block interleaver (Π) with 32 rows and 18 columns, and a 64-ary orthogonal modulation scheme. The orthogonal modulation (the inner code C^I) is a so-called Hadamard code, or Walsh function, and can be viewed as a systematic block code of rate $r^I = 6/64$ and minimum distance $d_{\min} = 32$. The subsequent processing steps are: 1) DS spreading by a factor of 4, 2) quadrature scrambling of the in- and quadrature-phase components with different PN sequences (IPN and QPN), and 3) offset QPSK modulation (not shown in Fig. 17).

In the following, we describe two types of receiver structures. The first is a coherent receiver, where we must know the carrier phase, the delays of the multipath channel, and the complex factors of the different propagation paths (i.e., perfect CSI estimation). This leads to an M-finger RAKE receiver with *maximum ratio combining* (MRC) [67]. In each RAKE finger, the respective path delay is compensated, followed by a multiplication with the complex conjugate propagation coefficient z_m.

Classical demodulation after the coherent RAKE receiver involves maximum-likelihood (ML) detection of the transmitted Hadamard codeword by searching for the maximum value of the correlation vector, which is easily implemented with the fast Hadamard transform (FHT). The systematic bits (information bits) of the demodulated codeword are then weighted with the maximum value of the correlation vector. (The Hadamard code can also be decoded with a "soft-in/soft-out" decoder [32].) Afterwards, they are passed on to the deinterleaver and the outer soft-in/hard-out Viterbi decoder.

The other case is a noncoherent receiver design without any knowledge of the phase of the signal. Here, in each RAKE finger, the FHT must be performed for both the in-phase and quadrature-phase components after the delay compensation. After *square-law combining* (SLC) [67] of the $2M$ correlation vectors, classical ML detection is also performed to find the maximum value of the correlation vector. Further decoding of the outer code is straightforward, as in the coherent case.

D. Relations Between Source and Channel Coding for Mobile Channels

A basic result of Shannon's information theory is that source and channel coding can be treated separately. Of course, this is true in the information-theoretic sense: as long as the entropy of the source is less than the channel capacity, there exists a separable source and channel coding scheme that allows transmission over the channel with arbitrarily low error probability. Arising from this basic result, there has been a clear-cut interface between source and channel coding and decoding. However, on a transmission channel with extensive noise, interference, multipath, fading, and shadowing, it is too expensive in terms of bandwidth, delay, and complexity to implement perfect channel coding.

In a practical system, the different blocks of source coder, channel coder, transmission channel, channel decoder, and source decoder are linked in a variety of ways, as indicated in Fig. 18.

- Source significance information (SSI) is passed to the channel coder for static or dynamic unequal error protection. Unequal error protection can be easily performed

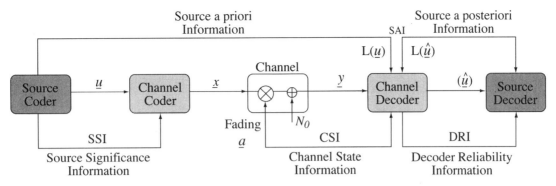

Fig. 18. Links between source and channel coding in a transmission over a mobile channel.

with block and convolutional codes, and in a very simple way by RCPC codes, as described in Section VII-B1).

- The channel decoder and the demodulator are not only connected by the hard decisions of the demodulator/detector. Soft decisions and channel state information (CSI) are also passed on.

- At the receiver, when the channel decoder makes errors and these errors can be detected by a CRC or by other means, it is common engineering practice to interpolate the source sample values. One also use more sophisticated methods to conceal errors by using the decision on the current bit and its reliability. This sophisticated concealment, however, requires channel decoders that deliver "soft outputs," i.e., decisions and "decision reliability information" (DRI) as shown in Fig. 18.

- Another approach links source and channel decoding to an even greater extent. Source-controlled channel decoding [68] uses *a priori* and *a posteriori* information about the source bits. For reasons of delay and complexity and because of highly nonstationary sources, many source coding schemes still contain redundancy and some bits are highly correlated, at least at times. Under these circumstances source and channel decoding should be linked more closely. In fact, Shannon mentioned this possibility in his 1948 paper [1]: "However, any redundancy in the source will usually help if it is utilized at the receiving point. In particular, if the source already has redundancy and no attempt is made to eliminate it in matching to the channel, this redundancy will help combat noise." Consequently, if some redundancy or bit correlation is left by the source coder, this should be utilized jointly by the channel and source decoder. The source *a priori/ a posteriori* information (SAI), as indicated in Fig. 18, tells the decoder with a certain probability the value of the next bit to be decoded. It is much better to give the channel decoder all the information known about the bits which are to be decoded, i.e., about correlation or bias values, than to allow it to make errors by blind decoding, thus causing it to conceal these errors later. The goal of source-controlled channel decoding is to reduce the channel decoder error rate by supplying the channel decoder with source information. Especially on mobile channels, gains of several decibels in channel SNR have

been achieved for speech, audio, still image, and video sources [68], [69], [70].

The last three items can be implemented in existing systems because they do not require changes at the transmitter. They are "value-added" devices to be used only when appropriate, for instance, in a bad channel environment. An example for GSM can be found in [69].

E. Turbo Decoding for Mobile Communications

In 1993, decoding of two or more product-like codes was proposed using iterative ("turbo") decoding [29]. (See also the end of Section II.) The basic concept of this new coding scheme is to use a parallel concatenation of at least two codes with an interleaver between the encoders. Decoding is based on alternately decoding the component codes and passing the so-called *extrinsic information* to the next decoding stage. For good soft-in/soft-out decoders this *extrinsic information* is an additional part of the soft output. Even though very simple component codes are used, the "turbo" coding scheme is able to achieve performance close to Shannon's bound, at least for large interleavers and at BER's of approximately 10^{-5}.

Moreover, it turned out that the turbo method originally applied to parallel concatenated codes is much more general [71] and can be sucessfully applied to many detection/decoding problems such as serial concatenation, equalization, coded modulation, multiuser detection, joint source and channel decoding, and others. We will mention here two applications for mobile communications to show the potential of turbo decoding.

1) Parallel Concatenated (Turbo) Codes for GSM Applications: The turbo decoding method was not available at the time of GSM standarization. But it is interesting to consider what can be gained in the GSM System with turbo decoding. In [72], the FEC system for GSM was redesigned with parallel concatenated codes, while keeping all the framing and the interlever as in the full rate GSM System. This means that a frame length of only 185 information bits could be used. This is different from the common usage of turbo codes, where several thousand bits are usually decoded in one frame. Nevertheless, it was shown that on GSM urban channels with frequency hopping, an improvement in channel SNR (i.e., an additional coding gain) of 0.8 to 1.0 dB is possible. Although several iterations of the turbo decoder are necessary to achieve

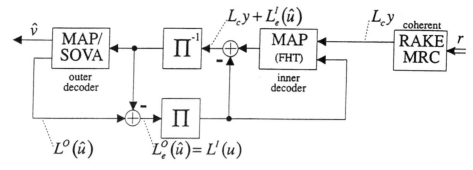

Fig. 19. Iterative decoding in a coherent receiver.

this gain, the total decoding complexity is comparable to the GSM system because the turbo component codes had only four states, compared to the 16-state code used in standard GSM.

2) Turbo Detection in the IS-95 Mobile System: In this section, we explain the principle of turbo detection for the IS-95 uplink when coherent demodulation is applied. An application to the noncoherent uplink can be found in [73]. For iterative decoding, it is necessary to replace the outer Viterbi decoder with a modified soft-output Viterbi algorithm (SOVA) or a MAP decoder which delivers soft-output information with each decoded bit. The soft information from the outer decoding stage is interleaved and then fed back as *a priori* information in a redecoding of the inner code. This leads to a serial turbo decoding scheme. A schematic overview of the receiver is given in Fig. 19.

From the L-finger RAKE receiver we obtain a vector $\boldsymbol{y}$. The received log-likelihood values $L(x|y) = L_c y + L_e^I(\hat{u})$, including the fed back *a priori* values $L^I(u)$ of the systematic bits, are correlated with the Hadamard codewords using the FHT. This results in the correlation vector $\boldsymbol{w}'$. The approximate MAP decoding rule then reduces to a simple expression

$$ L^I(0) \simeq \frac{1}{2} \cdot \max_{j, u=+1}(w_j') - \frac{1}{2} \cdot \max_{j, u=-1}(w_j'). \qquad (33) $$

To obtain the *a priori* information, we must decode the outer code with a SOVA or MAP decoder. The extrinsic part of the soft ouput for the outer decoded bits is then used as the *a priori* information $L^I(u)$ for the systematic bits of the inner code in the feedback loop shown in Fig. 19.

Simulation results for the AWGN channel show that an additional coding gain of about 1.0–1.5 dB can be achieved with iterative decoding after five iterations. If the simple approximation in (33) is applied, the resulting degradation is less than 0.1 dB.

VII. FILE TRANSFER APPLICATIONS

File transfer is the movement of digital information from one data terminal to another. This digital information is organized into characters, frames, and files. File transfer applications typically demand a very high level of reliability; unlike voice applications, a single erroneous bit can render a multimegabyte file useless to the end user. Communication links in wireless and wired file transfer systems are designed to be highly reliable. In many systems, the majority of data errors

result from single-event upsets caused by equipment transients. The error-control systems for these applications use error detection coupled with retransmission requests to maximize reliability at some cost to throughput. At their simplest, such error-control systems use parity-check bits or CRC codes to trigger retransmission requests. Since the retransmission requests occur well below the application layer, and are in a sense "automatic," such protocols are usually called *automatic repeat request* (ARQ) protocols. (The "RQ" in "ARQ" is taken from the Morse code designation for a retransmission request.) More complicated protocols include elements of FEC and packet combining to reduce the frequency of retransmission requests.

This section begins with a quick look at parity, CRC, and "pure" ARQ protocols. Several popular file-transfer protocols are provided as examples. Consideration is then given to hybrid protocols and packet combining.

A. Parity Bits and CRC's

In asynchronous file-transfer systems, each character is treated as a separate entity [74]. Seven-bit ASCII is the most ubiquitous example (where ASCII stands for "American Standards Committee for Information Interchange"). The 128 possible characters cover upper and lower case Roman letters, Arabic numerals, various punctuation marks, and several control characters. The standard error-control technique for asynchronous ASCII is the simplest possible: a single parity bit is appended to each ASCII character. The value of the appended bit is selected so that the sum of all eight transmitted bits is 0 modulo 2 (even parity) or 1 modulo 2 (odd parity). In either case, the resulting code can detect all single errors, as well as a large number of error patterns of higher weight. The encoding and decoding circuit is extremely simple, and can be constructed using a small number of exclusive-OR gates or a few lines of code. The *Kermit* data modem protocol is a typical example of an asynchronous file-transfer system that uses simple parity checks.

In synchronous transmission systems, error control can be expanded to cover entire frames of data. Since the frame is a larger transmission element than the character, the number of encoding and decoding operations is reduced, along with the number of potential requests for retransmission.

The most popular synchronous error-control techniques are based on shortened linear cyclic codes. Let C be an (n, k)

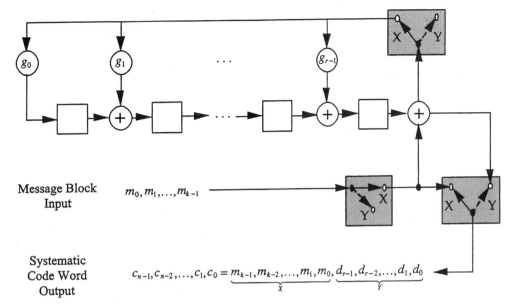

Fig. 20. A CRC encoder circuit.

Message Block Input $m_0, m_1, \ldots, m_{k-1}$

Systematic Code Word Output $c_{n-1}, c_{n-2}, \ldots, c_1, c_0 = \underbrace{m_{k-1}, m_{k-2}, \ldots, m_1, m_0}_{X}, \underbrace{d_{r-1}, d_{r-2}, \ldots, d_1, d_0}_{Y}$

cyclic code with a systematic encoder. Let S be the subset of codewords in C whose j high-order information coordinates (i.e., the j rightmost coordinates in the codeword) have the value zero. Let C' be the set of words obtained by deleting the j rightmost coordinates from all of the words in S. C' is an $(n - j, k - j)$ shortened systematic code that is usually referred to as a CRC, or *cyclic redundancy check*, code [75]. CRC codes are also called *polynomial codes*.

Note that CRC codes obtained from cyclic codes through shortening are almost always noncyclic. However, it is still possible to use the same shift-register encoders and decoders that are used with the original cyclic code. Consider the systematic cyclic encoder in Fig. 20. Before encoding begins, the shift-register memory elements are set to zero. If the first j high-order message symbols are equal to zero, their insertion into the encoding circuit does not change the state of the shift register, and results only in the output of j zeroes. The deletion of j high-order symbols from the message block thus has no impact on the encoding process except for the deletion of j zeroes in the corresponding message positions of the codeword.

The shift-register taps $\{g_0, g_1, \cdots, g_{r-1}\}$ in Fig. 20 are the coefficients of a degree-r CRC generator polynomial

$$g(x) = x^r + g_{r-1}x^{r-1} + \cdots + g_1 x + g_0.$$

Given a message block

$$\boldsymbol{m} = (m_0, m_1, \cdots, m_{k-1})$$

and the associated message polynomial

$$m(x) = m_{k-1}x^{k-1} + m_{k-2}x^{k-2} + \cdots + m_1 x + m_0$$

the encoder computes the remainder $d(x)$ obtained from the division of $x^r m(x)$ by $g(x)$. The remainder is appended to

the message bits to complete the systematic encoding. The resulting code polynomial has the form $c(x) = x^r m(x) + d(x)$.

The encoder can also be used as a decoder. Note that, by construction, $c(x) = x^r m(x) + d(x)$ must be divisible by $g(x)$ without remainder. If the encoded data is not corrupted during transmission, the "encoding" of the received version of $c(x)$ will result in a zero remainder. The detection of a nonzero remainder after the processing of the received data is the trigger for a retransmission request.

There are a variety of "rules of thumb" for selecting CRC generator polynomials. Bertsekas and Gallager [76] note that it is common practice to select $g(x) = (x + 1)b(x)$, where $b(x)$ is primitive. The $(x + 1)$ factor ensures that all odd-weight error patterns are detectable. Table IV contains several CRC codes of varying length that have been used in practice. Detailed examinations of various polynomials with different degrees are provided in [77]–[79].

The error-detecting capability of a CRC code is best measured in terms of the percentage of possible error patterns that are detectable. Channel errors tend to occur in bursts in the wired file-transfer applications that make the most use of CRC codes, so the memoryless channel assumption that underlies a Hamming distance analysis is not valid. An r-bit CRC can detect $100 \cdot (1 - 2^{-r})\%$ of all error patterns.

CRC codes are often altered in practice to avoid the possibility of confusing the check bits with protocol flag fields (frame delimiters, for example) or to maintain a minimum transition density (an important consideration in magnetic recording applications). The modification to the code typically involves complementing some or all of the check bits. Though the code is no longer linear, error-detection performance is unaffected.

In some applications it is easier to generate an r-bit checksum by simply segmenting the information to be protected into r-bit words and computing the sum (without carry). As with the unmodified CRC, the resulting code is linear and can detect $100 \cdot (1 - 2^{-r})\%$ of all error patterns.

TABLE IV

CRC Code	Generator Polynomial
CRC-4	$g_4(x) = x^4 + x^3 + x^2 + x + 1$
CRC-7	$g_7(x) = x^7 + x^6 + x^4 + 1 = (x^4 + x^3 + 1)(x^2 + x + 1)(x + 1)$
CRC-8	$g_8(x) = (x^5 + x^4 + x^3 + x^2 + 1)(x^2 + x + 1)(x + 1)$
CRC-12	$g_{12}(x) = x^{12} + x^{11} + x^3 + x^2 + x + 1 = (x^{11} + x^2 + 1)(x + 1)$
CRC-ANSI	$g_{ANSI}(x) = x^{16} + x^{15} + x^2 + 1 = (x^{15} + x + 1)(x + 1)$
CRC-CCITT	$g_{CCITT}(x) = x^{16} + x^{12} + x^5 + 1$
	$= (x^{15} + x^{14} + x^{13} + x^{12} + x^4 + x^3 + x^2 + x + 1)(x + 1)$
CRC-SDLC	$g_{SDLC}(x) = x^{16} + x^{15} + x^{13} + x^7 + x^4 + x^2 + x + 1$
	$= (x^{14} + x^{13} + x^{12} + x^{10} + x^8 + x^6 + x^5 + x^4 + x^3 + x + 1)(x + 1)^2$
CRC-24	$g_{24}(x) = x^{24} + x^{23} + x^{14} + x^{12} + x^8 + 1$
	$= (x^{10} + x^8 + x^7 + x^6 + x^5 + x^4 + x^3 + x + 1)(x^{10} + x^9 + x^6 + x^4 + 1)$
	$\cdot (x^3 + x^2 + 1)(x + 1)$
CRC-32$_A$ [80]	$g_{32_A}(x) = x^{32} + x^{30} + x^{22} + x^{15} + x^{12} + x^{11} + x^7 + x^6 + x^5 + x$
	$= (x^{10} + x^9 + x^8 + x^6 + x^2 + x + 1)(x^{10} + x^7 + x^6 + x^3 + 1)$
	$\cdot (x^{10} + x^8 + x^5 + x^4 + 1)(x + 1)(x)$
CRC-32$_B$ [78]	$g_{32_B}(x) = x^{32} + x^{26} + x^{23} + x^{22} + x^{16} + x^{12} + x^{11} + x^{10} + x^8 + x^7 + x^5 + x^4 + x^2 + x + 1$
CRC-32$_C$ [76]	$g_{32_C}(x) = x^{32} + x^{26} + x^{23} + x^{16} + x^{12} + x^{11} + x^{10} + x^8 + x^7 + x^5 + x^4 + x^2 + x + 1$

In the next section we consider the various means by which retransmission requests can be incorporated into a file-transfer protocol.

B. Retransmission Request Modes

In this section we derive the basic relations and design choices that determine the throughput performance of an ARQ protocol. We begin by determining the number of times that a given packet can expect to be transmitted before it is accepted by the receiver. Given the probability P_r that an error is detected and a retransmission request generated, the expected number of transmissions T_r is computed as follows:

$$T_r = (1 - P_r) + 2P_r(1 - P_r) + 3P_r^2(1 - P_r) + \cdots$$
$$+ kP_r^{k-1}(1 - P_r) + \cdots$$
$$= (1 - P_r)\sum_{k=1}^{\infty} kP_r^{k-1} = \frac{1}{1 - P_r}. \tag{34}$$

There are three basic modes that are used in the implementation of retransmission-request protocols: stop-and-wait (SW-ARQ), go-back-N (GBN-ARQ), and selective-repeat (SR-ARQ) [75], [80], [81]. These three modes provide varying levels of throughput by changing the amount of buffering required in the transmitter and/or receiver. Throughput (η) is defined here to be the average number of encoded data blocks (packets) accepted by the receiver in the time it takes the transmitter to send a single k-bit data packet.

SW-ARQ is by far the simplest of the three modes. In this mode, the transmitter sends a single packet and waits for an acknowledgment (ACK). If an ACK is received, the transmitter sends the next packet. Otherwise, the first packet is retransmitted. Since the transmitter is idle while waiting for the response, this mode of ARQ is often called "Idle RQ" [74]. Let Γ be the number of bits that the transmitter could have transmitted during this idle time. An SW-ARQ protocol based on a rate $R = k/n$ error-detecting code will provide the following throughput:

$$\eta_{SW} = \frac{k}{T_r(n + \Gamma)} = R\left(\frac{1 - P_r}{1 + \Gamma/n}\right). \tag{35}$$

SW-ARQ protocols require very little buffering in the transmitter, and virtually none in the receiver. For this reason such protocols are often used in simple data modems (the "Kermit" protocol is a typical example). The disadvantage, of course, lies in the inefficient use of the channel, an inefficiency that increases with the distance between transmitter and receiver.

GBN-ARQ protocols assume that the transmitter is capable of buffering N packets. When the transmitter is informed by the receiver of an error in some packet, say packet j, the transmitter "goes back" to that packet and resumes transmission from there. The parameter N is the number of packets that have been subsequently sent by the transmitter since the jth packet, and that must now be retransmitted. N is a function of the roundtrip propagation and processing delays for the transmitter and receiver and can be approximated by $\lceil \Gamma/n \rceil$. The throughput for a GBN-ARQ protocol based on a rate $R = k/n$ error-detecting code is as follows:

$$\eta_{GBN} = \left(\frac{k}{n}\right)\left(\frac{1}{1 + (T_r - 1)N}\right) = R\left(\frac{1 - P_r}{1 + P_r(N - 1)}\right). \tag{36}$$

Note that the transmitter in a GBN-ARQ protocol is continuously transmitting. GBN-ARQ protocols are thus often called "Continuous RQ" protocols [74].

SR-ARQ protocols are also Continuous RQ protocols. In this case the transmitter only retransmits the specific packets for which an ACK is not received. This requires significant buffering in both the transmitter and the receiver, but maximizes channel efficiency. The throughput in this case is no longer a function of channel delay. The throughput for a rate $R = k/n$ code is quickly computed as

$$\eta_{SR} = \left(\frac{k}{n}\right)\left(\frac{1}{T_r}\right) = R(1 - P_r). \tag{37}$$

In the next section we consider the means by which error detection retransmission requests are incorporated into two popular file-transfer applications.

C. High-Level Data-Link Control Protocol

The High-Level Data-Link Control (HDLC) protocol is a general-purpose protocol that operates at the data link layer of the OSI reference model [82]. It was created by the International Standards Organization (ISO) and is designated ISO 4335. HDLC uses the services of a synchronous physical layer and can provide a best effort or a reliable communications path between the transmitter and receiver (i.e., with acknowledged data transfer). The selected HDLC mode determines the type of service. HDLC is generally implemented using a Continuous RQ mode.

Link Access Procedure Version B (LAPB) is a subset of HDLC that is commonly used to control the transfer of information frames across point-to-point data links in public and private packet-switching networks. Such networks are generally referred to as X.25 networks [74].

The HDLC frame format has six basic elements [82].

- An 8-bit opening flag.
- An 8-bit address field (expandable in 8-bit increments).
- An 8-bit control field (expandable in 8-bit increments).
- An information field of arbitrary size.
- A 16-bit frame check field (32 bits optional).
- An 8-bit closing flag.

The bits in the 16-bit frame check field are computed using CRC-CCITT, as defined in Table IV. CRC-32$_C$ is the optional 32-bit code that is used in applications requiring an extremely high level of reliability (e.g., high-speed local-area networks).

In full-duplex mode, HDLC allows for the use of "piggyback acknowledgments"—a situation in which acknowledgments or requests for retransmission of packets on the forward channel are combined with other data transmitted on the return channel.

D. The Internet and TCP/IP

The key technology underlying the Internet (and many internets, intranets, and variations thereof) is the suite of protocols that go by the name *TCP/IP*. TCP/IP is named after two constituent protocols, the Transmission Control Protocol and the Internet Protocol, but the suite actually contains several dozen protocols [83]. TCP/IP allows for the internetworking of computer networks that are based on different networking technologies. For example, TCP/IP allows for the seamless interconnection of token rings (IEEE 802.5) with Ethernet-based systems (IEEE 802.3).

A TCP/IP internetworking architecture can be divided into four basic layers.

- An *Application Layer* consisting of user processes (TEL-NET, FTP, SMTP, etc.).
- A *Transport Layer* that provides end-to-end data transfer.
- An *Internetwork Layer* (also called the Internet layer) that provides the image of a single virtual network to upper layers by routing datagrams among the interconnected networks.

- A *Network Interface Layer* (also called the link or data-link layer) that provides the actual interface to the hardware of the individual networks (e.g. X.25, ATM, FDDI, and packet radio networks).

The Internet Protocol (IP) is the heart of the Internetwork layer. It is a connectionless protocol that does not assume or provide any measure of link reliability. The only error control incorporated into the IP datagram is a 16-bit checksum that only covers the header. The checksum is obtained by computing the 16-bit one's complement of the one's complement sum of all 16-bit words in the header (the checksum itself is assumed to be zero during this computation) [84]. If a received IP datagram has an incorrect checksum, the entire datagram is discarded. There is no provision for a retransmission request, in part because it would not be known from whom to request the retransmission. It should also be noted that IP does not provide a check on the data field within the datagram. This must be provided at the Transport layer.

There are two basic transport-layer protocols: the Transmission Control Protocol (TCP—connection oriented) and the User Datagram Protocol (UDP—connectionless). Both protocols "encapsulate" IP datagrams by appending transport-layer headers. UDP has an optional 16-bit checksum that, when used, is calculated in a manner similar to the IP datagram checksum. The UDP checksum is a 16-bit one's complement of the one's complement sum of the encapsulated IP header, the UDP header, and the UDP data. As with IP, UDP does not allow for acknowledgments. UDP simply arranges received packets in the proper order and passes them on to the application. Internet telephony is typical of the applications that use UDP in that it emphasizes latency over reliability.

TCP, on the other hand, makes full use of its 16-bit checksum. TCP assigns sequence numbers to each transmitted data block, and expects a positive acknowledgment from the transport layer of the receiving entity. If an acknowledgment is not received in a timely manner, the block is retransmitted. The full retransmission protocol is a variation of SR-ARQ that uses a window to control the number of pending acknowledgments. The transmitter is allowed to transmit all packets within the window, starting a retransmission clock for each. The window is moved to account for each received acknowledgment.

E. Hybrid-ARQ Protocols and Packet Combining

In 1960, Wozencraft and Horstein [85], [86] described and analyzed a system that allowed for both error correction and error detection with retransmission requests. Their system, now known as a type-I hybrid-ARQ protocol, provides significantly improved performance over "pure" ARQ protocols. The goal in designing such systems is to use FEC to handle the most frequently occurring error patterns. The less frequently occurring (those most likely to cause FEC decoder errors) are handled through error detection and the request of a retransmission.

Error-control protocols based on algebraic block codes (e.g., RS and BCH codes) and hard-decision decoding provide a natural form of type-I hybrid-ARQ protocol. The most commonly used hard-decision decoders for BCH and RS codes use bounded distance decoding algorithms that correct a number of errors up to some design distance t. If there is no codeword within distance t of the received word, the bounded distance decoding algorithm fails, providing an indication of uncorrectable errors. When decoder failures are used as a trigger for a retransmission request, the BCH- and RS-based systems become examples of type-I hybrid-ARQ protocols [87]. The ReFLEX and cellular digital packet data (CDPD) wireless data protocols are typical of the applications that use these strategies.

Type-I hybrid-ARQ protocols can also be based on complete decoders. Drukarev and Costello developed the "Time-Out" and "Slope Control" algorithms for type-I protocols based on convolutional codes with sequential decoding [88]. Yamamoto and Itoh [89] developed a similar protocol based on Viterbi decoding.

Pure ARQ and Type-I hybrid-ARQ protocols generally discard received packets that trigger retransmission requests. In 1977, Sindhu [90] discussed a scheme that made use of these packets. Sindhu's idea was that such packets can be stored and later combined with additional copies of the packet, creating a single packet that is more reliable than any of its constituent packets. Since 1977 there have been innumerable systems proposed that involve some form of packet combining. These packet-combining systems can be loosely arranged into two categories: code-combining systems and diversity-combining systems.

In code-combining systems, the packets are concatenated to form noise-corrupted codewords from increasingly longer and lower rate codes. Code combining was first discussed in a 1985 paper by Chase [91], who coined the term. Subsequent code-combining systems are exemplified by the work of Krishna, Morgera, and Odoul [92], [93]. An early version of a code-combining system was the type-II hybrid-ARQ protocol invented by Lin and Yu [94]. The type-II system allows for the combination of two packets, and is thus a truncated code-combining system. The system devised by Lin and Yu was developed for satellite channels. Type-II systems based on RS and RM codes were later developed by Pursley and Sandberg [95] and by Wicker and Bartz [96], [97], and similar systems which utilize RCPC codes were introduced by Hagenauer [60].

In diversity-combining systems, the individual symbols from multiple, identical copies of a packet are combined to create a single packet with more reliable constituent symbols. Diversity-combining systems are generally suboptimal with respect to code-combining systems, but are simpler to implement. These schemes are represented by the work of Sindhu [90], Benelli [98], [99], Metzner [100], [101], and Harvey and Wicker [102].

VIII. CONCLUSION

In this paper, we have presented a number of examples illustrating the way in which error-control coding, an outgrowth of Shannon's Information Theory, has contributed to the design of reliable digital transmission and storage systems over the past 50 years. Indeed, coding has become an integral part of almost any system involving the transmission or storage of digital information. And as we look to the future and the "digital revolution," with such innovations as digital cellular telephony, digital television, and high-density digital storage, it seems assured that the use of coding will become even more pervasive.

In trying to assess the impact that various advances in coding theory have had in the practical arena, some general trends become apparent. Although most of the early work in coding was based on algebraic constructions and decoding methods, recent trends definitely favor probabilistic, soft-decision decoding algorithms. With a few notable exceptions, such as the ubiquitous Reed–Solomon codes, the 2–3-dB loss associated with hard-decision decoding can no longer be tolerated in most applications. In fact, one of the most exciting current areas of coding research is the development of soft decoding methods for algebraically constructed block codes with good distance properties. Because of the relative ease of soft-decision decoding of convolutional codes (due to the development of sequential decoding, and later the Viterbi algorithm), convolutional codes became the preferred choice in most practical applications. The relative scarcity of nearest neighbor codewords in convolutional codes compared to block codes also tipped the scale in their favor, particularly in applications requiring only moderate BER's, where the number of nearest neighbors plays an important role in performance. On the other hand, in applications where data integrity is paramount, or when there is a strong tendency towards burst errors, powerful nonbinary error-correcting (e.g., Reed–Solomon) or binary error-detecting (e.g., CRC) block codes are still preferred.

Another noticeable trend is the relatively recent emergence of many commercial applications of coding. It is fair to say that the driving force behind almost all coding applications in the first 25 years after the publication of Shannon's paper was government scientific (e.g., NASA) programs or military applications. However, in the most recent 25 years, particularly with the emergence of the compact disc, high-speed data modems, and digital cellular telephony, commercial applications have proliferated. From our perspective, it seems fairly certain that this trend will not only continue but accelerate. Indeed, in this paper we have been able to touch on only a few of the many current activities involving the development of coding standards for various commercial applications. Thus it is clear that error-control coding has moved from being a mathematical curiosity to being a fundamental element in the design of digital communication and storage systems. One can no longer claim to be a communication or computer system engineer without knowing something about coding.

As we look towards the future, it seems clear that parallel and/or serial concatenated coding and iterative decoding (i.e., turbo coding) are destined to replace convolutional codes in many applications that require moderate BER's and can tolerate significant decoding delay. This is another illustration of the importance of minimizing the number of nearest neighbor codewords in applications requiring only moderate BER's. More generally, turbo coding has pointed the way towards more creative uses of code concatenation as a means of achieving exceptional performance with moderate decoding complexity. The need for almost error-free performance in many scientific applications and high-performance commercial systems, such as CD's and computer memories, seems certain to continue to spur interest in extremely powerful code designs with very large minimum distance, such as algebraic-geometry codes and multilevel construction techniques. And further advances in signal-processing technology are sure to speed the conversion of almost all decoding machines to the use of soft decisions. Finally, coding will continue to find use on increasingly difficult channels as demands for more reliable communications and data storage accelerate. The technical challenges inherent in designing appropriate codes for the many anticipated new mobile communication services, which must operate in severe multipath and fading conditions, and high-density data storage applications, with increasingly difficult read/write signal processing requirements, promise to keep coding theory an active research field well into the next century.

ACKNOWLEDGMENT

The authors wish to thank Dr. Lance C. Perez, Dr. G. David Forney, Jr., Dr. Shu Lin, Dr. Robert H. Morelos-Zaragoza, and Dr. Oscar Y. Takeshita as well as Hermano A. Cabral for valuable comments that contributed to the preparation of this paper.

REFERENCES

[1] C. E. Shannon, "A mathematical theory of communication," *Bell Syst. Tech. J.*, vol. 27, pp. 379–423, 1948.

[2] J. M. Wozencraft and I. M. Jacobs, *Principles of Communication Engineering*. New York: Wiley, 1965.

[3] R. W. Hamming, "Error detecting and error correcting codes," *Bell Syst. Tech. J.*, vol. 29, pp. 147–150, 1950.

[4] I. M. Jacobs, "Practical applications of coding," *IEEE Trans. Inform. Theory*, vol. IT-20, pp. 305–310, May 1974.

[5] G. D. Forney, Jr., and L. F. Wei, "Multidimensional constellations—Part I: Introduction, figures of merit, and generalized cross constellations," *IEEE J. Select. Areas Commun.*, vol. 7, pp. 877–892, Aug. 1989.

[6] J. L. Massey, "Deep-space communication and coding: A marriage made in heaven," in *Lecture Notes on Control and Information Sciences 82*, J. Hagenauer, Ed.. Bonn, Germany: Springer-Verlag, 1992.

[7] R. R. Green, "A serial orthogonal decoder," in *Jet Propulsion Laboratory Space Programs Summary*, vol. IV, no. 37–39, June 1966, pp. 247–251.

[8] J. M. Wozencraft and B. Reiffen, *Sequential Decoding*. Cambridge, MA: MIT Press, 1961.

[9] R. M. Fano, "A heuristic discussion of probabilistic decoding," *IEEE Trans. Inform. Theory*, vol. IT-9, pp. 64–74, Apr. 1963.

[10] S. Lin and H. Lyne, "Some results on binary convolutional code generators," *IEEE Trans. Inform. Theory*, vol. IT-13, pp. 134–139, Jan. 1967.

[11] J. L. Massey and D. J. Costello, Jr., "Nonsystematic convolutional codes for sequential decoding in space applications," *IEEE Trans. Commun. Technol.*, vol. COM-19, pp. 806–813, Oct. 1971.

[12] J. W. Layland and W. A. Lushbaugh, "A flexible high-speed sequential decoder for deep space channels," *IEEE Trans. Commun. Technol.*, vol. COM-19, pp. 813–820, Oct. 1971.

[13] G. D. Forney, Jr., and E. K. Bower, "A high-speed sequential decoder: Prototype design and test," *IEEE Trans. Commun. Technol.*, vol. COM-19, pp. 821–835, Oct. 1971.

[14] A. J. Viterbi, "Error bounds for convolutional codes and an asymptotically optimum decoding algorithm," *IEEE Trans. Inform. Theory*, vol. IT-13, pp. 260–269, Apr. 1967.

[15] A. J. Viterbi, J. K. Wolf, E. Zehavi, and R. Padovani, "A pragmatic approach to trellis-coded modulation," *IEEE Commun. Mag.*, vol. 27, pp. 11–19, July 1989.

[16] G. Fettweis and H. Meyr, "High-speed parallel viterbi decoding: Algorithm and VLSI-architecture," *IEEE Commun. Mag.*, vol. 29, pp. 46–55, May 1991.

[17] W. W. Wu, E. F. Miller, W. L. Pritchard, and R. L. Pickholtz, "Mobile satellite communications," *Proc. IEEE*, vol. 82, pp. 1431–1448, Sept. 1994.

[18] G. D. Forney, Jr., *Concatenated Codes*. Cambridge, MA: MIT Press, 1966.

[19] Consultative Committee for Space Data Systems, "Recommendations for space data standard: Telemetry channel coding," Blue Book Issue 2, CCSDS 101.0-B2, Jan. 1987.

[20] R. J. McEliece and L. Swanson, "Reed–Solomon codes and the exploration of the solar system," in *Reed–Solomon Codes and Their Applications*, S. B. Wicker and V. K. Bhargava, Eds. Piscataway, NJ: IEEE Press, 1994, pp. 25–40.

[21] E. R. Berlekamp, *Algebraic Coding Theory*. New York: McGraw-Hill, 1968. (Revised edition, Laguna Hills, CA: Aegean Park, 1984.)

[22] J. L. Massey, "Shift register synthesis and BCH decoding," *IEEE Trans. Inform. Theory*, vol. IT-15, pp. 122–127, Jan. 1969.

[23] J. Hagenauer, E. Offer, and L. Papke, "Matching Citerbi decoders and Reed–Solomon decoders in concatenated systems," in *Reed–Solomon Codes and Their Applications*, S. B. Wicker and V. K. Bhargava, Eds.Piscataway, NJ: IEEE Press, 1994, pp. 242–271.

[24] O. M. Collins, "The subleties and intracacies of building a constraint length 15 convolutional decoder," *IEEE Trans. Commun.*, vol. 40, pp. 1810–1819, Dec. 1992.

[25] S. B. Wicker, "Deep space applications," in *CRC Handbook on Coding Theory*, V. Pless, W. C. Huffman, and R. Brualdi, Eds. Boca Raton, FL: CRC, ch. 25, to be published in 1998.

[26] E. Paaske, "Improved decoding for a concatenated coding system recommended by CCSDS," *IEEE Trans. Commun.*, vol. COM-38, pp. 1138–1144, Aug. 1990.

[27] O. M. Collins and M. Hizlan, "Determinate state convolutional codes," *IEEE Trans. Commun.*, vol. 41, pp. 1785–1794, Dec. 1993.

[28] J. Hagenauer and P. Hoeher, "A Viterbi algorithm with soft-decision outputs and its applications," in *Proc. 1989 IEEE Global Communications Conference* (Dallas, TX, Nov. 1989), pp. 47.1.1–47.1.7.

[29] C. Berrou, A. Glavieux, and P. Thitimajshima, "Near Shannon limit error-correcting coding and decoding: Turbo codes," in *Proc. 1993 IEEE Int. Communications Conf.* (Geneva, Switzerland, May 1993), pp. 1064–1070.

[30] S. Benedetto and G. Montorsi, "Unveiling turbo codes: Some results on parallel concatenated coding schemes," *IEEE Trans. Inform. Theory*, vol. 42, pp. 409–428, Mar. 1996.

[31] L. R. Bahl, J. Cocke, F. Jelinek, and J. Raviv, "Optimal decoding of linear codes for minimizing symbol error rate," *IEEE Trans. Inform. Theory*, vol. IT-20, pp. 284–287, Mar. 1974.

[32] J. Hagenauer, E. Offer, and L. Papke, "Iterative decoding of binary block and convolutional codes," *IEEE Trans. Inform. Theory*, vol. 42, pp. 429–445, Mar. 1996.

[33] S. Benedetto, D. Divsalar, G. Montorsi, and F. Pollara, "Serial concatenation of interleaved codes: Performance analysis, design, and iterative decoding," *IEEE Trans. Inform. Theory*, vol. 44, pp. 909–926, May 1998.

[34] G. D. Forney, Jr., "Coding and its application in space communications," *IEEE Spectrum*, vol. 7, pp. 47–58, June 1970.

[35] G. Ungerboeck, "Channel coding with multilevel/phase signals," *IEEE Trans. Inform. Theory*, vol. IT-28, pp. 55–67, Jan. 1982.

[36] _____, "Trellis-coded modulation with redundant signal sets—Part I: Introduction," *IEEE Commun. Mag.*, vol. 25, pp. 5–11, Feb. 1987.

[37] _____, "Trellis-coded modulation with redendant signal sets—Part II: State of the art," *IEEE Commun. Mag.*, vol. 25, pp. 12–21, Feb. 1987.

[38] G. D. Forney, Jr., "Coded modulation for band-limited channels," *IEEE Inform. Theory Soc. Newslet.*, vol. 40, pp. 1–7, Dec. 1990.

[39] L. F. Wei, "Rotationally invariant convolutional channel coding with expanded signal space. Part II: Nonlinear codes," *IEEE J. Select. Areas Commun.*, vol. SAC-2, pp. 672–686, Sept. 1984.

[40] _____, "Trellis-coded modulation with multidimensional constellations," *IEEE Trans. Inform. Theory*, vol. IT-33, pp. 483–501, July 1987.

[41] M. V. Eyuboglu, G. D. Forney, Jr., P. Dong, and G. Long, "Advanced modulation techniques for V. fast," *Euro. Trans. Telecommun.*, vol. 4, pp. 243–256, May–June 1993.

[42] G. Lang and F. Longstaff, "A Leech lattice modem," *IEEE J. Select. Areas Commun.*, vol. 7, pp. 968–973, Aug. 1989.

[43] British Telecom, "Code choice for V. fast," Contribution D0, CCITT Study Group 14, Geneva, Switzerland, Aug. 1993.

[44] A. R. Calderbank and L. H. Ozarow, "Nonequiprobable signaling on the Gaussian channel," *IEEE Trans. Inform. Theory*, vol. 36, pp. 726–740, July 1990.

[45] T. R. N. Rao and E. Fujiwara, *Error-Control Coding for Computer Systems*. Englewood Cliffs, NJ: Prentice-Hall, 1989.

[46] H. Imai, Ed., *Essentials of Error-Control Coding Techniques*. San Diego, CA: Academic, 1990.

[47] C. L. Chen, "Symbol error-correcting codes for computer memory systems," *IEEE Trans. Comp.*, vol. 41, pp. 252–256, Feb. 1992.

[48] E. Fujiwara, "Application of coding theory to computer systems," in *Proc. 1997 IEICE General Conf.*, Mar. 1997, vol. TA-3-8, pp. 572–573.

[49] P. Fire, "A class of multiple-error-correcting binary codes for non-independent errors," Sylvania Rep. RSL-E-2, Sylvania Electronics Defense Lab., Reconnaissance Syst. Div., Mountain View, CA, Mar. 1959.

[50] K. A. S. Immink, "RS codes and the compact disc," in *Reed–Solomon Codes and Their Applications*, S. B. Wicker and V. K. Bhargava, Eds. Piscataway, NJ: IEEE Press, 1994, pp. 41–59.

[51] H. Imai and Y. Nagasaka, "On decoding methods for double-encoding systems," *Electron. Commun. Japan*, vol. 65-A, pp. 36–44, Dec. 1982.

[52] M. Hattori, N. Ohya, M. Sasano, K. Sato, and N. Shirota, "Improved general purpose Reed–Solomon erasure encoder/decoder chip," in *Proc. 1993 Picture Coding Symp.*, Mar. 1993.

[53] E. J. Weldon Jr., "Difference set cyclic codes," *Bell Syst. Tech. J.*, vol. 45, pp. 1045–1055, 1966.

[54] T. Kuroda, M. Takada, T. Isobe, and O. Yamada, "Transmission scheme of high-capacity FM multiplex broadcasting system," *IEEE Trans. Broadcasting*, vol. 42, pp. 245–250, Sept. 1996.

[55] O. Yamada, "Development of an error-correction method for data packet multiplexed with TV signals," *IEEE Trans. Commun.*, vol. COM-35, pp. 21–31, Jan. 1987.

[56] J. L. Massey, *Threshold Decoding*. Cambridge, MA: MIT Press, 1963.

[57] M. Takada and T. Kuroda, "Threshold decoding algorithm using trellis diagram for majority logic decodable codes," in *Proc. 1996 Int. Symp. Information Theory and Its Applications* (Victoria, BC, Canada, Sept. 1996), vol. 1, pp. 397–400.

[58] K. Yamaguchi, H. Iizuka, E. Nomura, and H. Imai, "Variable threshold soft decision decoding," *IEICE Trans.*, vol. 71-A, pp. 1607–1614, Aug. 1988 (in Japanese). English version available in *Electron. Commun. Japan*, vol. 72, pp. 65–74, Sept. 1989,.

[59] ISO-IEC, "Coding of moving pictures and associated audio up to about 1.5 Mbit/s," ISO-ICE, Std. CD 11172-3, Part 3–Audio.

[60] J. Hagenauer, "Rate-compatible punctured convolutional codes and their applications," *IEEE Trans. Commun.*, vol. 36, pp. 389–400, Apr. 1988.

[61] G. Plenge, "A new sound broadcasting system," *EBU Tech. Rev.*, vol. 246, pp. 87–112, Apr. 1991.

[62] C. Weck, "Unequal error protection for digital sound broadcasting—Principle and performance," presented at the 94th AES Conv., preprint 3459, Berlin, Germany, Mar. 1993.

[63] H. Imai and S. Hirakawa, "A new multilevel coding method using error-correcting codes," *IEEE Trans. Inform. Theory*, vol. IT-23, pp. 371–377, May 1977.

[64] R. H. Morelos-Zaragoza, M. P. C. Fossorier, S. Lin, and H. Imai, "Multilevel block coded modulation with unequal error protection," in *Proc. 1997 IEEE Int. Symp. Information Theory* (Ulm, Germany, July 1997), p. 441.

[65] J. Hagenauer, "Zur Kanalkapazitaet bei Nachrichtenkanaelen mit Fading und gebuendelten Fehlern," *AEU, Electron. Commun.*, vol. 34, pp. 229–237, 1980.

[66] Qualcomm Inc., "An overview of the application of code division multiple access to digital cellular systems and personal cellular networks," Qualcomm, Inc., San Diego, CA, May 1992.

[67] J. Proakis, *Digital Communications*. New York,: McGraw-Hill, 1989.

[68] J. Hagenauer, "Source controlled channel decoding," *IEEE Trans. Commun.*, vol. 43, pp. 2449–2457, Sept. 1995.

[69] C. Erben, T. Hindelang, and W. Xu, "Quality enhancement of coded and corrupted speeches in GSM mobile systems using residual redundancy," in *Proc. ICASSP97* (Munich, Germany, Apr. 1997), vol. 1, pp. 259–262.

[70] W. Xu, J. Hagenauer, and J. Hollmann, "Joint source-channel decoding using the residual redundancy in compressed images," in *Proc. 1996 Int. Conf. Communications* (Dallas, TX, June 1996), pp. 142–148.

[71] J. Hagenauer, "The turbo principle: Tutorial introduction and state of the art," in *Proc. Int. Symp. Turbo Codes* (Brest, France, Sept. 1997), pp. 1–11.

[72] F. Burkert, G. Caire, J. Hagenauer, T. Hindelang, and G. Lechner, "Turbo decoding with unequal error protection applied to GSM speech coding," in *Proc. 1996 IEEE Global Communications Conf.* (London, U.K., Nov. 1996), pp. 2044–2048.

[73] R. Herzog, A. Schmidbauer, and J. Hagenauer, "Iterative decoding and despreading improves CDMA-systems using M-ary orthogonal modulation and FEC," in *Proc. 1997 IEEE Int. Conf. Communications* (Montreal, Que., Canada, June 1997).

[74] F. Halsall, *Data Communications, Computer Networks, and Open Systems*, 4th ed. Wokingham, U.K.: Addison-Wesley, 1995.

[75] S. B. Wicker, *Error Control Systems for Digital Communication and Storage*. Englewood Cliffs, NJ: Prentice Hall, 1995.

[76] D. Bertsekas and R. Gallager, *Data Networks*. Englewood Cliffs, NJ: Prentice Hall, 1987.

[77] G. Castagnoli, J. Ganz, and P. Graber, "Optimum cyclic redundancy-check codes with 16-bit redundancy," *IEEE Trans. Commun.*, vol. 38, pp. 111–114, Jan. 1990.

[78] P. Merkey and E. C. Posner, "Optimum cyclic redundancy codes for noisy channels," *IEEE Trans. Inform. Theory*, vol. IT-30, pp. 865–867, Nov. 1984.

[79] K. A. Witzke and C. Leung, "A comparison of some error detecting CRC code standards," *IEEE Trans. Commun.*, vol. COM-33, pp. 996–998, Sept. 1985.

[80] R. J. Benice and A. H. Frey, "An analysis of retransmission systems," *IEEE Trans. Commun. Technol.*, vol. COM-12, pp. 135–145, Dec. 1964.

[81] S. Lin, D. J. Costello Jr., and M. J. Miller, "Automatic-repeat-request error control schemes," *IEEE Commun. Mag.*, vol. 22, pp. 5–17, Dec. 1984.

[82] R. L. Freeman, *Practical Data Communications*. New York: Wiley, 1995.

[83] D. E. Comer, *Internetworking with TCP/IP*, vol. I, 3rd ed. Englewood Cliffs, NJ: Prentice-Hall, 1995.

[84] E. Murphy, S. Hayes, and M. Enders, *TCP/IP, Tutorial and Technical Overview*, 5th ed. Upper Saddle River, NJ: Prentice-Hall, 1995.

[85] J. M. Wozencraft and M. Horstein, "Digitalised communication over two-way channels," presented at the Fourth London Symp. Information Theory, London, U.K., Sept. 1960.

[86] ——, "Coding for two-way channels," Tech. Rep. 383, Res. Lab. Electron., MIT, Cambridge, MA, Jan. 1961.

[87] S. B. Wicker, "Reed–Solomon error control coding for data transmission over Rayleigh fading channels with feedback," *IEEE Trans. Veh. Technol.*, vol. 41, pp. 124–133, May 1992.

[88] A. Drukarev and D. J. Costello Jr., "Hybrid ARQ error control using sequential decoding," *IEEE Trans. Inform. Theory*, vol. IT-29, pp. 521–535, July 1983.

[89] H. Yamamoto and K. Itoh, "Viterbi decoding algorithm for convolutional codes with repeat request," *IEEE Trans. Inform. Theory*, vol. IT-26, pp. 540–547, Sept. 1980.

[90] P. Sindhu, "Retransmission error control with memory," *IEEE Trans. Commun.*, vol. COM-25, pp. 473–479, May 1977.

[91] D. Chase, "Code combining—A maximum-likelihood decoding approach for combining an arbitrary number of noisy packets," *IEEE Trans. Commun.*, vol. COM-33, pp. 385–393, May 1985.

[92] H. Krishna and S. Morgera, "A new error control scheme for hybrid-ARQ systems," *IEEE Trans. Commun.*, vol. COM-35, pp. 981–990, Oct. 1987.

[93] S. Morgera and V. Oduol, "Soft decision decoding applied to the generalized type-II hybrid-ARQ scheme," *IEEE Trans. Commun.*, vol. 37, pp. 393–396, Apr. 1989.

[94] S. Lin and P. S. Yu, "A hybrid-ARQ scheme with parity retransmission for error control of satellite channels," *IEEE Trans. Commun.*, vol. COM-30, pp. 1701–1719, July 1982.

[95] M. B. Pursley and S. D. Sandberg, "Incremental redundancy transmission for meteor burst communications," *IEEE Trans. Commun.*, vol. 39, pp. 689–702, May 1991.

[96] S. B. Wicker and M. Bartz, "Type-II hybrid-ARQ protocols using punctured MDS codes," *IEEE Trans. Commun.*, vol. 42, pp. 1431–1440, Apr. 1994.

[97] ——, "The design and implementation of type-I and type-II hybrid-ARQ protocols based on first-order Reed-Muller codes," *IEEE Trans. Commun.*, vol. 42, pp. 979–987, Mar. 1994.

[98] G. Benelli, "An ARQ scheme with memory and soft error detectors," *IEEE Trans. Commun.*, vol. 33, pp. 285–288, Mar. 1985.

[99] ——, "An ARQ scheme with memory and integrated modulation," *IEEE Trans. Commun.*, vol. COM-35, pp. 689–697, July 1987.

[100] J. Metzner, "Improvements in block-retransmission schemes," *IEEE Trans. Commun.*, vol. COM-27, pp. 524–532, Feb. 1979.

[101] J. Metzner and D. Chang, "Efficient selective-repeat ARQ strategies for very noisy and fluctuating channels," *IEEE Trans. Commun.*, vol. COM-33, pp. 409–416, May 1985.

[102] B. A. Harvey and S. B. Wicker, "Packet combining systems based on the Viterbi decoder," *IEEE Trans. Commun.*, vol. 42, pp. 1544–1557, Apr. 1994.

The Art of Signaling: Fifty Years of Coding Theory

A. R. Calderbank, *Fellow, IEEE*

(Invited Paper)

Abstract—In 1948 Shannon developed fundamental limits on the efficiency of communication over noisy channels. The coding theorem asserts that there are block codes with code rates arbitrarily close to channel capacity and probabilities of error arbitrarily close to zero. Fifty years later, codes for the Gaussian channel have been discovered that come close to these fundamental limits. There is now a substantial algebraic theory of error-correcting codes with as many connections to mathematics as to engineering practice, and the last 20 years have seen the construction of algebraic-geometry codes that can be encoded and decoded in polynomial time, and that beat the Gilbert–Varshamov bound. Given the size of coding theory as a subject, this review is of necessity a personal perspective, and the focus is reliable communication, and not source coding or cryptography. The emphasis is on connecting coding theories for Hamming and Euclidean space and on future challenges, specifically in data networking, wireless communication, and quantum information theory.

Index Terms—Algebraic, information and coding theory, quantum and space–time codes, trellis.

I. A BRIEF PREHISTORY

BEFORE Shannon [187] it was commonly believed that the only way of achieving arbitrarily small probability of error on a communications channel was to reduce the transmission rate to zero. Today we are wiser. Information theory characterizes a channel by a single parameter; the channel capacity. Shannon demonstrated that it is possible to transmit information at any rate below capacity with an arbitrarily small probability of error. The method of proof is random coding, where the existence of a good code is shown by averaging over all possible codes. Now there were codes before there was a theory of coding, and the mathematical framework for decoding certain algebraic codes (Bose-Chaudhuri-Hocquengham (BCH) codes) was written down in the late 18th century (see Wolf [227] and Barg [5]). Nevertheless, it is fair to credit Shannon with creating coding theory in that he established fundamental limits on what was possible, and presented the challenge of finding specific families of codes that achieve capacity.

Classical coding theory is concerned with the representation of information that is to be transmitted over some noisy channel. There are many obstacles to reliable communication, including channel estimation, noise, synchronization, and interference from other users, but there are only two resources available to the code designer; memory and redundancy. The proper allocation of these resources to the different obstacles is fertile ground for information theory and coding, but for the past 50 years the focus of coding theory in particular has been reliable communication in the presence of noise. This general framework includes the algebraic theory of error-correcting codes, where codewords are strings of symbols taken from some finite field, and it includes data transmission over Gaussian channels, where codewords are vectors in Euclidean space. Compact disk players [168], [113], hard-disk drives [152], and high-speed modems [83] are examples of consumer products that make essential use of coding to improve reliability. The importance of these applications has served to focus the coding theory community on the complexity of coding techniques, for it is entirely appropriate that performance of a code should be valued as a function of delay and decoding complexity. Ever since Shannon's original paper, coding theorists have attempted to construct structured codes that achieve channel capacity, but this problem remains unsolved. It is in fact tempting to ask a slightly different question; to fix the complexity of decoding and to ask for the maximum transmission rate that is possible. There is a sense in which the journey is more important than the goal, for the challenge of coming close to capacity has generated many important coding techniques.

The notion of combined source/channel coding is present in the telegraph codebooks that were used from 1845 until about 1950 (see [120, Ch. 22]). These books, arranged like dictionaries, would list many useful phrases, or even sentences, each with its corresponding codeword. They were compiled by specialists who competed on the basis of compression (the ability to capture a specialist vocabulary in few words), ease of use, and resistance to errors (exclusion from the codebook of words obtained from codewords by single letter substitution or transposition of adjacent letters). An important motivation was the price per word on undersea cablegrams which was considerable (about $5 per word on a trans-Atlantic cable message in 1867, falling to 25 cents per word by 1915). The addition of adjacent transpositions to Hamming errors means that the universe of words makes for a more complicated metric space, so that determining efficiency or even optimality of a particular code is extremely complicated. This framework did not encourage the creation of coding theory but it did not prevent telegraph code makers from using linear codes over a variety of moduli, and from realizing that the more parity-check equations were used, the greater the minimum distance would be.

Manuscript received June 1, 1998; revised August 15, 1998.

The author is with the Information Sciences Research Center, AT&T Labs., Florham Park, NJ 07932 USA.

Publisher Item Identifier S 0018-9448(98)06887-4.

In exploring the beginnings of coding theory, it is important to be mindful of intent. In the early 1940's the famous statistician Fisher [71], [72] discovered certain remarkable configurations in Hamming space through his interest in factorial designs. Consider $2^N - 1$ factors taking values ± 1 that influence the yield of a process, and suppose pairwise interactions do not affect yield. We are led to an expression

$$f(X) = \sum_{a \in \mathbb{F}_2^N} \lambda_a X_a + E$$

where E captures error and imprecision in the model. We look to determine the coefficients λ_a by measuring $f(X)$ for a small number of binary vectors X called *experiments*. Further, we are interested in a collection of experiments that will allow us to distinguish the effect of factor X_a from that of $X_{a'}$; in the language of statistical design, these factors are not to be *confounded*. The 2^N experiments $X_a = (-1)^{a.v}$, for $v \in \mathbb{F}_2^N$, have this property, and correspond to codewords in the binary simplex code. The assertion that main effects X_a are not confounded is simply that the minimum weight in the Hamming code is at least 3. In classical statistical design the experiments are taken to be a linear code C, and large minimum weight in the dual code $C^{\perp}$ is important to ensure that potentially significant combinations of factors are not confounded. Since coding theory and statistical design share a common purpose we can understand why Fisher discovered the binary simplex code in 1942, and the generalization to arbitrary prime powers in 1945. However, it is important to remember his intention was not the transmission of information.

On an erasure channel, a decoding algorithm interpolates the symbols of a codeword that are not erased. In an algebraic error-correcting code the information in each encoded bit is diffused across all symbols of a codeword, and this motivates the development of decoding algorithms that interpolate. This notion is fundamental to the Berlekamp–Massey algorithm that is used for decoding a wide class of cyclic codes, and to the new list decoding algorithm of Sodan [203]. However Wolf [227] observed that as far back as 1795, de Prony [58] considered the problem of solving over the real field, the system of equations

$$\sum_{i=1}^{v} e_i X_i^k = S_i, \qquad k = 1, 2, \cdots, 2t$$

for the coefficients e_i, in the case where $v = t$. In algebraic coding theory this system of equations appears in the decoding of t-error-correcting BCH codes, but the underlying field is finite, the index v ($v \leq t$) is the number of errors, and the coefficients e_i are the error values. Nevertheless, the solutions proposed by de Prony [58] and Peterson [170], Gorenstein and Zierler [104] have the same form: all solve for the coefficients $\sigma_1, \cdots, \sigma_v$ of the *error-locator polynomial*

$$\sigma(x) = \prod_{i=1}^{v}(1 - xX_i)$$

by analyzing the recurrence relation

$$\sigma_1 S_{j+v-1} + \cdots + \sigma_v S_j = -S_{j+v}, \qquad j = 1, \cdots, v.$$

Algebraic coding theory calculates the determinant of this linear system for $v = t, t-1, \cdots$. It is zero if v exceeds the number of errors that occurred and nonzero if equality holds. Once the error-locator polynomial is known Chien search [40] can be used to find the error locations X_i, and then finding the errors e_i is simple linear algebra. By contrast, de Prony used Lagrange interpolation, and this corresponds to the refinement of the basic algorithm for decoding BCH codes that was suggested by Forney [73]. Berlekamp ([11, Ch. 7]) and Massey [153] expressed the problem of finding the coefficients of the error-locator polynomial as that of finding the shortest linear feedback shift register that generates the syndrome sequence. The Berlekamp–Massey algorithm has recently been generalized to more than one dimension, and used to decode algebraic-geometry codes. This story is told in more detail by Barg [5], but even this outline reveals considerable synergy between the discrete and the Euclidean world. This synergy is one of the strengths of the text by Blahut [14] and there is reason to resist any balkanization of coding theory into algebraic codes and codes for the Gaussian channel.

II. AN INTRODUCTION TO HAMMING SPACE

Let $\mathbb{F}_q$ denote the finite field with q elements, and let $\mathbb{F}_q^N$ denote the set of N-tuples $(a_1, \cdots, a_N)$, where $a_i \in \mathbb{F}_q$. The *Hamming weight* wt(x) of a vector $x \in \mathbb{F}_q^N$ is the number of nonzero entries. The *Hamming distance* $D(x, y)$ between two vectors $x, y \in \mathbb{F}_q^N$ is the number of places where x and y differ. Thus $D(x, y) = $ wt$(x + y)$. An (N, M, D) *code* C over the alphabet $\mathbb{F}_q$ is a collection of M vectors from $\mathbb{F}_q^N$ (called *codewords*) such that

$$D(x, y) \geq D, \qquad \text{for all distinct } x, y \in C$$

and D is the largest number with this property. The parameter D is called the *minimum distance* of the code.

Vector addition turns the set $\mathbb{F}_q^N$ into an N-dimensional vector space. A *linear code* is just a subspace of $\mathbb{F}_q^N$. The notation $[N, k, D]$ indicates a linear code with blocklength N, dimension k, and minimum distance D. The next result is both fundamental and elementary.

Theorem: The minimum distance of a linear code is the minimum weight of a nonzero codeword.

It is possible to describe any code by just listing the codewords, and if the code has no structure, then this may be the only way. What makes a linear code easier to discover is that it is completely determined by any choice of k linearly independent codewords. Perhaps ease of discovery is the main reason that coding theory emphasizes linear codes.

A *generator matrix* G for an $[N, k]$ linear code C is a $k \times N$ matrix with the property that every codeword of C is some linear combination of the rows of G. Given an $[N, k]$ linear code C, the *dual code* $C^{\perp}$ is the $[N, N-k]$ linear code given by

$$C^{\perp} = \left\{ x \in \mathbb{F}_q^N \mid (x, c) = 0 \text{ for all } c \in C \right\}$$

where

$$((x_1, \cdots, x_N), (y_1, \cdots, y_N)) = \sum_{i=1}^{N} x_i y_i$$

is the standard inner product. An $[N, k]$ linear code C is also completely determined by any choice of $N - k$ linearly independent codewords from $C^\perp$. A *parity-check matrix H* for an $[N, k]$ linear code C is an $(N - k) \times N$ matrix with the property that a vector $x \in \mathbb{F}_q^N$ is a codeword in C if and only if $Hx^T = 0$. Thus a generator matrix for C is a parity-check matrix for $C^\perp$ and vice versa. A linear code C is said to be *self-orthogonal* if $(x, y) = 0$ for all $x, y \in C$. If C is self-orthogonal, then $C \subseteq C^\perp$ and we can construct a parity-check matrix for C by adding rows to a generator matrix. If $C = C^\perp$, then C is said to be *self-dual*. In this case, a single matrix serves as both a generator matrix and a parity-check matrix.

It is interesting to look back on Blake [15] which is an annotated selection of 35 influential papers from the first 25 years of algebraic coding theory and to distinguish two larger themes; geometry and algorithms. Here the early work of Slepian [196]–[198] on the internal structure of vector spaces provides a geometric framework for code construction. By contrast, the emphasis of work on cyclic codes is on the decoding algorithm. In the last 25 years, the fear that good codes might turn out to be very difficult or impossible to decode effectively ("messy") has been proved to be unfounded.

Hamming distance is not changed by *monomial transformations* which consist of permutations of the coordinate positions followed by diagonal transformations $\mathrm{diag}\,[\lambda_1, \cdots, \lambda_N]$ that multiply coordinate i by the nonzero scalar λ_i. Monomial transformations preserve the Hamming metric and we shall say that two codes C_1 and C_2 are *equivalent* if one is obtained from the other by applying a monomial transformation. In her 1962 Harvard dissertation, MacWilliams [146] proved that two linear codes are equivalent if and only if there is an abstract linear isomorphism between them which preserves weights. Extensions of this result to linear codes over finite rings and to different weight functions (for example, Lee weight) have been derived recently by Wood [228].

A. The Sphere-Packing Bound

The sphere $S_e(a)$ of radius e centered at the vector $a \in \mathbb{F}_q^N$ is the set

$$S_e(a) = \left\{ x \in \mathbb{F}_q^N \mid D(x, a) \leq e \right\}.$$

Since there are $q - 1$ ways to change an individual entry we have

$$|S_e(a)| = \sum_{i=0}^{e} \binom{N}{i} (q - 1)^i.$$

Let C be a code in $\mathbb{F}_q^N$ with minimum Hamming distance D and let $e = \lfloor (D - 1)/2 \rfloor$. *The sphere-packing bound*

$$|C| \left(\sum_{i=0}^{e} \binom{N}{i} (q - 1)^i \right) \leq q^N.$$

expresses the fact that spheres of Hamming radius e centered at the codewords of C are disjoint, and the union of these spheres is a subset of $\mathbb{F}_q^N$. An e-error-correcting code C for which equality holds in the sphere-packing bound is said to be *perfect*. For perfect single-error-correcting *linear* codes, the sphere-packing bound gives

$$|C|(1 + (q - 1)N) = q^N.$$

Since C is linear, there is a dual code $C^\perp$ satisfying $|C^\perp| = q^N/|C| = q^s$ for some s, and so $N = (q^s - 1)/(q - 1)$. The columns h_i, $i = 1, 2, \cdots, N$ in a parity-check matrix H for C are vectors in $\mathbb{F}_q^s$. If $\lambda h_i = h_j$ for some $\lambda \in \mathbb{F}_q$, then $(e_i - \lambda e_j)H^T = 0$. This means $e_i - \lambda e_j \in C$, which contradicts the fact that C is a code with minimum Hamming weight $D = 3$. Hence different columns of H must determine different one-dimensional subspaces of $\mathbb{F}_q^s$. Since there are exactly $N = (q^s - 1)/(q - 1)$ distinct one-dimensional subspaces of $\mathbb{F}_q^s$, we must choose exactly one vector from each subspace. Note that given s, any two codes of length $(q^s - 1)/(q - 1)$ obtained in this way are equivalent. This completes the classification of perfect single-error-correcting linear codes, but even perfect single-error-correcting nonlinear codes are not yet completely understood.

It is natural to start the search for other perfect codes by looking for instances where $\sum_{i=0}^{e} \binom{N}{i}(q - 1)^i$ is a power of q. For $e = 2$, $q = 3$, $N = 11$ we find

$$3^6 \left(1 + 11 \cdot 2 + \binom{11}{2} \cdot 4 \right) = 3^{11}$$

and for $e = 3$, $q = 2$, $N = 23$ we find

$$2^{12} \left(1 + 23 + \binom{23}{2} + \binom{23}{3} \right) = 2^{23}.$$

In each case there was a code waiting to be found; the $[11, 6, 5]$ ternary Golay code, and the $[23, 12, 7]$ binary Golay code.

The ternary Golay code was discovered by Virtakallio in 1947 and communicated in issues 27, 28, and 33 of the Finnish football pool magazine *Veikaaja*. The ternary alphabet is associated with the possible outcomes of a soccer match (win, lose, or draw), and Virtakallio's aim was to approximate closely an arbitrary vector in Hamming space (the ternary Golay code has the property that given any $x \in \mathbb{F}_3^{11}$ there is a unique codeword c such that $d_H(x, c) \leq 2$).

The Golay codes [102] were discovered by Golay in 1949, but their rich algebraic structure was not revealed until much later. The $[24, 12, 8]$ binary Golay code is obtained from the perfect $[23, 12, 7]$ code by adding an overall parity check, and it is a most extraordinary code. The codewords of any given weight form beautiful geometric configurations that continue to fascinate combinatorial mathematicians. The symmetry group of this code plays a central role in finite group theory, for it is the Mathieu group M_{24}, which is perhaps the most important of the 26 sporadic simple groups.

In a perfect e-error-correcting code, the spheres of radius e about the codewords are disjoint and they cover the whole space. MacWilliams [146], [147] proved that an e-error-correcting linear code is perfect if and only if there are exactly e nonzero weights in the dual code. For example, the $[11, 6, 5]$

ternary Golay code is perfect, and nonzero codewords in the dual code have weight 6 or 9. Uniformly packed codes are a generalization of perfect codes that were introduced by Semakov, Zinoviev, and Zaitzev [183] in which the spheres of radius $e + 1$ about the codewords cover the whole space, and these spheres overlap in a very regular way. There are constants λ and μ (with $\lambda < (n - e)(q - 1)/e + 1$) such that vectors at distance e from the code are in $\lambda + 1$ spheres and vectors at distance $e + 1$ from the code are in μ spheres. If the restriction on λ were removed, a perfect code would also be uniformly packed. Goethals and van Tilborg [101] showed that an e-error-correcting linear code is uniformly packed if and only if there are exactly $e + 1$ nonzero weights in the dual code. For example, the $[24, 12, 8]$ binary Golay code is uniformly packed with $\lambda = 0$ and $\mu = 6$, and is self-dual with nonzero weights 8, 12, 16, and 24.

The connection between the metric properties of a linear code and the weight spectrum of the dual code is just one facet of the structural framework for algebraic coding theory that was introduced by Delsarte [48] in his Ph.D. dissertation, and this dissertation might well be the most important publication in algebraic coding theory over the past 30 years. The framework is that of association schemes derived from a group-theoretic decomposition of the Hamming metric space, and it will be described briefly in Section IV. The concept of an association scheme appears much earlier in the statistics literature, and Delsarte was able to connect bounds on orthogonal arrays from statistics with bounds for codes.

Of course, perfect codes are best possible since equality holds in the sphere-packing bound. However, Tietäväinen [212], van Lint [138], and Zinoviev and Leontiev [231] have shown that the only perfect multiple-error-correcting codes are the binary and ternary Golay codes, and the binary repetition codes. Critical to these classification results is a remarkable theorem of Lloyd [141] which states that a certain polynomial associated with a group-theoretic decomposition of the Hamming metric space must have integral zeros (for a perfect linear code these zeros are the weights that appear in the dual code).

B. The Gilbert–Varshamov Bound

We fix the transmission rate R, and we increase the block-length N in order to drive the error probability to zero. If the symbol error probability is p, then the average number of errors in a received vector of length N is Np. The minimum distance D must grow at least as fast as $2Np$. This explains the importance of the quantity $\alpha(\delta)$ which measures achievable rate, given by

$$\alpha(\delta) = \limsup_{N \to \infty} \frac{\log_q A_q(N, \delta N)}{N},$$

where $A_q(N, \delta N)$ is the maximum size of a code with minimum distance δN. To study $\alpha(\delta)$ we need to estimate the number of vectors $V_q(N, e)$ in a sphere of radius e in $\mathbb{F}_q^N$. If $0 \le \lambda \le (q - 1)/q$, then

$$\log_q \frac{V_q(N, \lfloor \lambda N \rfloor)}{N} = H_q(\lambda)$$

where $H_q(x)$ defined on $[0, (q - 1)/q]$ is the appropriate generalization of the binary entropy function, and is given by

$$H_q(0) = 0$$
$$H_q(x) = x \log_q(q - 1) - x \log_q x - (1 - x) \log_q(1 - x),$$
$$\text{for } 0 < x \le \frac{q-1}{q}.$$

Independently, Gilbert [95] and Varshamov [218] derived a lower bound on achievable rate that is surprisingly difficult to beat. In fact, Varshamov proved there exist linear codes C with

$$|C| \sum_{i=0}^{d-2} \binom{N-1}{i} (q-1)^i \ge q^N$$

which for particular values N, d is sometimes stronger.

Theorem (The Gilbert–Varshamov Bound): If $0 \le \delta \le (q-1)/q$, then

$$\alpha(\delta) \ge 1 - H_q(\delta).$$

Proof: It is sufficient to prove

$$A_q(N, D) \ge q^N / V_q(N, D - 1).$$

Let C be an (N, M, D) code in $\mathbb{F}_q^N$, where $M = A_q(N, D)$. Then, by definition, there is no vector in $\mathbb{F}_q^N$ with Hamming distance D or more to all codewords in C. This means that

$$\mathbb{F}_q^N = \bigcup_{c \in C} S_{D-1}(c)$$

which implies $|C| V_q(N, D - 1) \ge q^N$. $\square$

The proof shows it is possible to construct a code with at least $q^N / V_q(N, D - 1)$ codewords by adding vectors to a code with minimum distance D until no further vectors can be added. What is essential to the Gilbert–Varshamov (G-V) argument is an ensemble of codes, where for each vector v that appears in some code, we have control over the fraction λ_v of codes from the ensemble that contain v. In the original G-V argument, the ensemble consists of all linear codes of a certain dimension. The group of nonsingular linear transformations preserves this ensemble (though linear transformations do not, in general, preserve Hamming weight) and acts transitively on nonzero vectors, so that $\lambda_v = \lambda$ is constant. The G-V argument applies to more restrictive ensembles of codes, for example, to binary self-orthogonal codes with all Hamming weights divisible by 4 [149]. Here the function $Q(v) = \text{wt}(v)/2$ defines a quadratic form on the space of all binary vectors with even Hamming weight. Self-orthogonal codes correspond to totally singular subspaces and transitivity of the underlying orthogonal group leads to the G-V bound. Similar arguments provide lower bounds for quantum error-correcting codes [34] and for the minimum norm of certain lattices (see [142]), and there is a sense in which the classical bounds of Conway and Thompson are also obtained by averaging.

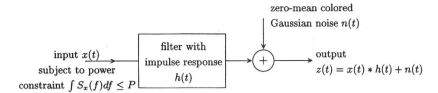

input $x(t)$
subject to power
constraint $\int S_x(f)df \le P$

filter with
impulse response
$h(t)$

zero-mean colored
Gaussian noise $n(t)$

$+$

output
$z(t) = x(t) * h(t) + n(t)$

Fig. 1. The Gaussian channel model.

III. EUCLIDEAN SPACE

A *Gaussian channel* combines a linear filter with additive Gaussian noise as shown in Fig. 1. In the time domain the output $z(t)$ is given by

$$z(t) = x(t) * h(t) + n(t)$$

where $x(t)$ is the input waveform, $h(t)$ is the *channel impulse response*, $x(t) * h(t)$ is the convolution of $x(t)$ with $h(t)$, and $n(t)$ is zero-mean-colored Gaussian noise.

The Fourier transform of $h(t)$ is the *frequency response* $H(f)$ of the channel, and the *power spectrum* $S_h(f)$ is given by $S_h(f) = |H(f)|^2$. In the frequency domain the signal $x(t)$ and the noise $n(t)$ are characterized by their Fourier transforms $X(f)$ and $N(f)$, respectively, and by their power spectra $S_x(f)$ and $S_n(f)$. An essential feature of the model is a power constraint

$$\int S_x(f)df \le P$$

on the power spectrum $S_x(f)$ of the input waveform $x(t)$. The *channel signal-to-noise function* $\mathrm{SNR}_h(f)$ is given by $\mathrm{SNR}_h(f) = S_h(f)/S_n(f)$, and is measured in decibels by taking $10 \log_{10} \mathrm{SNR}_h(f)$.

The model is limited in that the output $z(t)$ is assumed to depend linearly on the input $x(t)$, and to be time-invariant. In magnetic-recording applications, this linearity assumption becomes less valid once the recording density exceeds a certain threshold. In modem applications, the noise $n(t)$ starts to depend on the input $x(t)$ once the transmission rate exceeds a certain threshold. However, these caveats should not subtract from the importance of the basic model.

We think of the input $x(t)$ and the output $z(t)$ as random variables. The mutual information between $x(t)$ and $z(t)$ is the conditional entropy of $z(t)$ given $x(t)$. Channel capacity results from maximizing mutual information. Information-theoretic "waterfilling arguments" show that there is a constant K and a frequency band $\mathcal{W} = \{f \mid K \ge 1/\mathrm{SNR}_h(f)\}$, such that the capacity achieving input power spectrum $S_x^*(f)$ is given by

$$S_x^*(f) = \begin{cases} K - 1/\mathrm{SNR}_h(f), & \text{if } f \in \mathcal{W} \\ 0, & \text{if } f \notin \mathcal{W}. \end{cases}$$

The sampling theorem of Nyquist and Shannon allows us to replace a continuous function limited to the frequency band $\mathcal{W}$ by a discrete sequence of W equally spaced samples, without loss of any information. This allows us to convert our continuous channel to a discrete-time channel with signaling interval $T = 1/W$. The input $x(t)$ is generated as a filtered sequence $\sum x_k p(t - kT)$, where x_k is complex and the pulse

p has power spectrum proportional to $S_x^*(f)$ on $\mathcal{W}$. The output $z(t)$ is sampled every T seconds and the decoder operates on these samples.

Opportunity for coding theorists is a function of communications bandwidth. The capacity-achieving bandwidth of an optical fiber is approximately 10^9 Hz, which is too large for sophisticated signal processing. By contrast, the capacity achieving bandwidth of a telephone channel is approximately 3300 Hz. If a modem is to achieve data rates of 28.8 kb/s and above, then every time we signal, we must transmit multiple bits. Mathematics now has a role to play because there is time for sophisticated signal processing.

An *ideal band-limited Gaussian channel* is characterized by a "brickwall" linear filter $H(f)$ that is equal to a constant over some frequency band of width W hertz and equal to zero elsewhere, and by white Gaussian noise with a constant power spectrum over the channel bandwidth. The equivalent discrete-time ideal channel represents the complex output sequence z_k as

$$z_k = x_k + n_k$$

where (x_k) is the complex input sequence and (n_k) is a sequence of independent and identically distributed (i.i.d.) complex zero-mean Gaussian random variables. We let S_x denote the average energy of the input samples (x_k), and we let S_n denote the average energy of the noise samples. Shannon proved that the channel capacity of this ideal channel is given by

$$C = \log_2(1 + S_x/S_n) \text{ bits/Hz}$$

or

$$\tilde{C} = CW = W \log_2(1 + S_x/S_n) \text{ bits/s.}$$

We may transmit m bits per hertz by selecting x_k from a fixed constellation of 2^m points from the integer lattice $\mathbb{Z}^2$ in the complex plane. This method of signaling is called 2^m-*Quadrature Amplitude Modulation* (2^m-QAM), and this is uncoded transmission since there is no redundancy. There is a gap between capacity of this ideal channel and the rate that can be achieved by uncoded QAM transmission. The size of this gap varies with channel SNR and for sufficiently high SNR it is approximately 3 bits/Hz. This can also be expressed as a gap in SNR of approximately 9 dB since the extra rate changes S_x to $S_x/8$ and $10 \log_{10} 8 \approx 9$ dB.

Shannon recognized that signals input to a Gaussian channel should themselves be selected with a Gaussian distribution; the statistics of the signals should match that of the noise. We start by choosing a lattice Λ in real N-dimensional space $\mathbb{R}^N$.

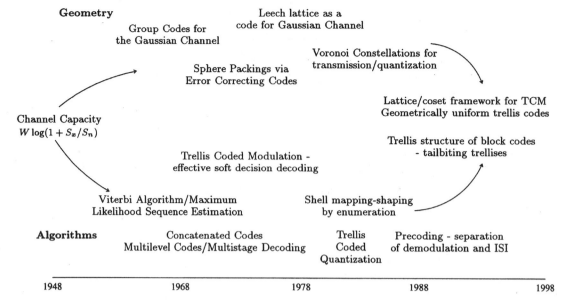

Group Codes for
the Gaussian Channel

Leech lattice as a
code for Gaussian Channel

Voronoi Constellations for
transmission/quantization

Sphere Packings via
Error Correcting Codes

Lattice/coset framework for TCM
Geometrically uniform trellis codes

Channel Capacity
$W \log(1 + S_x/S_n)$

Trellis structure of block codes
- tailbiting trellises

Trellis Coded Modulation -
effective soft decision decoding

Viterbi Algorithm/Maximum
Likelihood Sequence Estimation

Shell mapping-shaping
by enumeration

Algorithms

Concatenated Codes
Multilevel Codes/Multistage Decoding

Trellis
Coded
Quantization

Precoding - separation
of demodulation and ISI

| 1948 | 1968 | 1978 | 1988 | 1998 |

Fig. 2. Fifty years of information theory and coding for the power-constrained Gaussian channel.

Here the text by Conway and Sloane [44] is a treasury of information about sphere packings, lattices, and multidimensional Euclidean geometry. The signal constellation Ω consists of all lattice points within a region $\mathcal{R}$. The reason we consider signal constellations drawn from lattices is that signal points are distributed regularly throughout N-dimensional space. This means that the average signal power P of the constellation Ω is approximately the average power $P(\mathcal{R})$ of a probability distribution that is uniform within $\mathcal{R}$ and zero elsewhere. This approximation is called the *continuous approximation* and we shall use it extensively. If we fix the size of the signal constellation, then the average signal power depends on the choice of lattice and on the shape of the region that bounds the constellation. We obtain a Gaussian distribution by choosing the bounding region to be an N-dimensional sphere.

From the time that Shannon derived the capacity of the Gaussian channel there has been a divide between coding theory and coding practice. The upper track in Fig. 2 is the world of geometry and the lower track is the world of algorithms. We shall illustrate the differences by following an example, but a very positive development over the last five years is that these two tracks are converging.

A. Lattices

We begin with geometry. Formally, a *lattice* Λ in real N-dimensional space is a discrete additive subgroup of $\mathbb{R}^N$. A basis for the lattice Λ is a set of m vectors $v_1, \cdots, v_m$ such that

$$\Lambda = \left\{ \sum_{i=1}^{m} \lambda_i v_i \mid \lambda_i \in \mathbb{Z}, \; i = 1, \cdots, m \right\}.$$

The lattice Λ is said to be m-dimensional and usually we have $m = N$. If $w_1, \cdots, w_m$ is another choice of basis then there exists a unimodular integral matrix Q such that $w_i = Q v_i$ for all $i = 1, \cdots, m$. The Gosset lattice E_8 was discovered in the last third of the nineteenth century by the Russian mathematicians A. N. Korkin and E. I. Zolotaroff, and by the English lawyer and amateur mathematician Thorold Gosset:

$$E_8 = \{(z_1, \cdots, z_8) \mid z_i \in \mathbb{Z}, \; i = 1, \cdots, 8$$
$$\text{or } z_i \in \mathbb{Z} + 1/2, \; i = 1, \cdots, 8,$$
$$\text{and } z_1 + z_2 + \cdots + z_8 \in 2\mathbb{Z}\}.$$

A *fundamental region* $\mathcal{R}$ for a lattice Λ is a region of $\mathbb{R}^N$ that contains one and only one point from each equivalence class modulo Λ. In the language of mathematics, $\mathcal{R}$ is a complete system of coset representatives for Λ in $\mathbb{R}^N$. If $v_1, \cdots, v_m$ are a basis for a lattice Λ then the parallelotope consisting of the points

$$\mu_1 v_1 + \cdots + \mu_m v_m \qquad (0 \leq \mu_i < 1)$$

is an example of a fundamental region of Λ. This region is called a *fundamental parallelotope*. If $\Lambda \subseteq \mathbb{R}^N$ is a lattice, and $y \in \Lambda$ is a lattice point, then the *Voronoi region* $\mathcal{R}(y)$ consists of those points in $\mathbb{R}^N$ that are at least as close to y as to any other $y' \in \Lambda$. Thus

$$\mathcal{R}(y) = \{x \in \mathbb{R}^N \mid \|x - y\|^2 \leq \|x - y'\|^2 \text{ for all } y' \in \Lambda\}.$$

The interiors of different Voronoi regions are disjoint though two neighboring Voronoi regions may share a face. These faces lie in the hyperplanes midway between two neighboring lattice points. Translation by $y \in \Lambda$ maps the Voronoi region $\mathcal{R}(w)$ to the Voronoi region $\mathcal{R}(w + y)$, so that all Voronoi regions are congruent.

A maximum-likelihood decoding algorithm for the lattice Λ finds the Voronoi region $\mathcal{R}(y)$ that contains the received vector $v \in \mathbb{R}^N$. The Voronoi regions $\mathcal{R}(y)$ are the decision regions for this algorithm. We may create a fundamental region for the lattice Λ by deleting faces from a Voronoi region. Different ways of deleting faces correspond to different rules for resolving ties in a maximum-likelihood decoding algorithm.

Given a lattice $\Lambda \subseteq \mathbb{R}^N$, there are many ways to choose a fundamental region, but the volume of the fundamental region is uniquely determined by the lattice Λ. This volume is called the *fundamental volume* and we denote it by $V(\Lambda)$. There is a simple formula for the fundamental volume. Let $v_i = (v_{i1}, \cdots, v_{iN})$, $i = 1, \cdots, m$ be a basis for $V(\Lambda)$, and let $A = [v_{ij}]$. The fundamental volume $V(\Lambda)$ is given by $V(\Lambda)^2 = \det A^T$. It is easily verified that the fundamental volume of the Gosset lattice E_8 is equal to 1, the same as the integer lattice $\mathbb{Z}^8$.

Let Ω be an N-dimensional signal constellation consisting of all points from a lattice Λ that lie within a region $\mathcal{R}$, with centroid the origin. If signals are equiprobable, then the average signal power P is approximately the average power $P(\mathcal{R})$ of a continuous distribution that is uniform within $\mathcal{R}$ and zero elsewhere. Thus

$$P \approx P(\mathcal{R}) = \frac{1}{NV(\mathcal{R})} \int_{\mathcal{R}} \|x\|^2 \, dv$$
$$\approx G(\mathcal{R})V(\mathcal{R})^{2/N}$$

where

$$V(\mathcal{R}) = \int_{\mathcal{R}} dv$$

is the volume of the region $\mathcal{R}$, where

$$G(\mathcal{R}) = \frac{\int_{\mathcal{R}} \|x\|^2 \, dv}{NV(\mathcal{R})^{1+2/N}}$$

is the normalized or dimensionless second moment. The second moment $G(\mathcal{R})$ results from taking the average squared distance from a point in $\mathcal{R}$ to the centroid, and normalizing to obtain a dimensionless quantity.

We see that the average signal power P depends on the choice of lattice, and on the shape of the region that bounds the signal constellation. The formula $P \approx G(\mathcal{R})V(\mathcal{R})^{2/N}$ separates these two contributions. The volume $V(\mathcal{R}) = |\Omega|V(\Lambda)$, so that the second factor is determined by the choice of lattice. Since different lattices require different volumes to enclose the same number of signal points, it is possible to save on signal power by choosing the lattice appropriately. Since the second moment $G(\mathcal{R})$ is dimensionless, it is not changed by scaling the region $\mathcal{R}$. Therefore, the first factor $G(\mathcal{R})$ measures the effect of the shape of the region $\mathcal{R}$ on average signal power.

It is natural to compare the performance of E_8 as a code for the Gaussian channel with uncoded QAM transmission (the integer lattice $\mathbb{Z}^8$). Since the fundamental volumes coincide we may use the same region to bound both signal constellations. Performance gain is then determined by the minimum squared Euclidean distance $d^2(E_8)$ between two distinct points in the lattice E_8. We have $d^2(E_8)/d^2(\mathbb{Z}^8) = 2$ which corresponds to a coding gain of 3 dB.

B. Trellis Codes Based on Lattices and Cosets

Next we turn to algorithms. In 1976, Ungerboeck [215] constructed simple trellis codes for the Gaussian channel that provided coding gains of between 3 and 6 dB. His original paper has transformed the subject of coding for the Gaussian channel. Calderbank and Sloane [36] then abstracted the idea of redundant signaling based on lattices and cosets. The signal

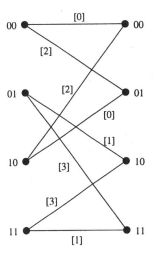

Fig. 3.   Labeling edges by cosets in $[\mathbb{Z} : 4\mathbb{Z}]$.

points are taken from an N-dimensional lattice Λ, and the signal constellation contains an equal number of points from each coset of a sublattice Λ'. One part of the binary data stream selects cosets of Λ' in Λ, and the other part selects points from these cosets. All the redundancy is in the coset-selection procedure, and the bits that select the signal point once the coset has been chosen are referred to as *uncoded bits*. Forney [79], [80] coined the name *coset code* to describe redundant signaling based on lattices and cosets, and this name captures the essential property of these signaling schemes. Coset coding provides a level of abstraction that makes it possible for a code designer to handle complicated codes and large signal constellations.

Switching from uncoded transmission using the integer lattice Λ to coded transmission using a coset code C based on the lattice partition Λ/Λ' requires that the N-dimensional signal constellation be expanded by a factor $2^{N\rho(C)}$, where $\rho(C)$ is the redundancy of the coset code C. Note that all redundancy is in the method of selecting cosets, so this quantity is easy to calculate. We assume that the constellation is expanded by scaling a bounding region, so that the power penalty incurred by expansion is $4^{\rho(C)}$. The coding gain $\gamma(C)$ of the coset code C is then given by

$$\gamma(C) = d^2(C)4^{-\rho(C)}.$$

This is the gain over uncoded transmission using the integer lattice (QAM signaling).

We introduce the method of trellis coding by means of an example where the lattice Λ is the integer lattice $\mathbb{Z}$, and the sublattice Λ' is $4\mathbb{Z}$. Fig. 3 shows the encoder trellis where the edges have been relabeled by the four residue classes modulo 4. All the redundancy is in the coset (residue class modulo Λ') selection procedure; one bit chooses from four cosets. The symbol $[i]$ represents the coset $\{z \mid z \equiv i \pmod 4\}$. For transmission all cosets are translated by $-1/2$. Since all redundancy is in the coset-selection procedure, we can achieve any transmission rate by just increasing the number of uncoded bits.

The power and simplicity of the lattice/coset viewpoint comes from viewing the signal constellation as a finite subset of an infinite lattice. By focusing on the infinite lattice, we eliminate the influence of constellation boundary effects on code structure and code performance.

It is not hard to prove that the minimum squared distance $d^2(C)$ between different signal sequences is given by $d^2(C) = 9$. To calculate the redundancy $\rho(C)$, we observe that every one-dimensional signaling interval, one input bit selects half of the integer lattice. The redundancy $\rho(C) = 1$, and the nominal coding gain $\gamma(C)$ is given by

$$\gamma(C) = 10 \log_{10} \frac{9}{4^1} = 3.3 \text{ dB}.$$

There is, however, a difference between the nominal coding gain calculated above and the coding gain observed in practice. For channels with high SNR the performance of a trellis code C is determined by the minimum squared distance $d^2(C)$ between output sequences corresponding to distinct input sequences. For coset codes this minimum squared distance is determined by the minimum nonzero norm in the sublattice Λ' and by the method of selecting cosets. For channels with moderate SNR (symbol error probability $\sim 10^{-6}$) performance is determined by the minimum squared distance $d^2(C)$, and by the number of nearest neighbors or path multiplicity. A telephone channel is an example of a channel with moderate SNR. Here Motorola Information Systems has proposed a rule of thumb that reducing the path multiplicity by a factor of two produces a coding gain of 0.2 dB. The result of discounting nominal coding gain by path multiplicity in this way is called *effective coding gain*.

Every lattice point in E_8 has 240 nearest neighbors; the neighbors of the origin (the point 0^8) are the 112 points $(\pm 1)^2 0^6$, and the 128 points $(\pm 1/2)^8$ where the number of minus signs is even. This means that E_8 offers a way of arranging unit spheres in eight-dimensional space so that 240 spheres touch any given sphere. Levenshtein [134] and Odlyzko and Sloane [165] proved that it is impossible to exceed this. We can start to appreciate that the lattice E_8 is a fascinating mathematical object, and this large *kissing number* contributes to its allure. When we apply the discounting rule to the lattice E_8 the path multiplicity (per dimension) is $240/8 = 30$, whereas for the trellis code the path multiplicity is 4. The difference is an important reason why high-speed modems employ trellis codes based on lattices and cosets, rather than lattices in their natural state.

Before the invention of trellis-coded modulation by Ungerboeck [215] researchers designed codes for the Gaussian channel using heuristics that approximated Euclidean distance. For example, Nakamura [161] designed codes for phase modulation by restricting the congruence of signals modulo 8. This approach was also used for QAM transmission by Nakamura, Saito, and Aikawa [162]. Their measure of distance was Lee distance, which is computed entry by entry as a sum of Lee weights. The *Lee weight* $\mathrm{wt}_L([i])$ of a coset in $[\mathbb{Z} : 8\mathbb{Z}]$ is the smallest absolute value $|x|$ of an integer x congruent to i modulo 8. This amounts to designing codes for the L^1 metric. The assumption that noise is Gaussian makes it more appropriate to follow Ungerboeck and work with the L^2 metric directly.

One reason that trellis-coded modulation has had an enormous impact on communications practice is that around 1982 digital electronics were sufficiently advanced to implement codes of the type proposed by Ungerboeck. And when it is not possible to build circuits the only recourse is geometry. A second reason, also very important, is that consumers were waiting for new products, like high-speed modems, that this invention made possible. With all the benefits of hindsight we may look back and find the principles of set partitioning in earlier mathematical work by Leech [131] at a time when digital electronics were not ready for this innovation. However, Leech's work lacked any vision of communications practice, and Ungerboeck made the link explicit between his mathematical theory of set partitioning and the transmission of information.

C. Sphere Packings and Codes

Leech [131] showed how to use error-correcting codes to construct dense sphere packings in N-dimensional space. The idea is to specify a set of vectors with integer entries by constraining the binary expansion of those entries.

The *Leech coordinate array* of a vector $x = (x_1, \cdots, x_N)$ with integer coordinates is obtained by writing the binary expansion of the coordinates x_i in columns starting with the least significant digit. The first row of the coordinate array is the 2^0 row, the second row is the 2^1 row, the third row is the 2^2 row, and so on. To find the binary expansion (a_l) of a negative number $-a$, simply write

$$-a = \sum_{l \geq 0} a_l 2^l$$

and for $i = 1, 2, \cdots$ solve the equation

$$-a \equiv \sum_{l \geq 0} a_l 2^l \pmod{2^i}.$$

In row 2^0, the entry 1 represents an odd integer, and the entry 0 represents an even integer. We define subsets of the integer lattice $\mathbb{Z}^N$ by constraining the first L rows of the coordinate array. Given L binary codes $C_1, \cdots, C_L$ with blocklength N, the sphere packing $\Lambda(C_1, \cdots, C_L)$ consists of all vectors $x \in \mathbb{Z}^N$ for which the ith row of the coordinate array of x is a codeword in C_i. If $L = 1$, and if C_1 is a binary linear code, then

$$\Lambda(C_1) = \{x \in \mathbb{Z}^N \mid x \equiv c \pmod{2}, \text{ for some } c \in C_1\}.$$

Here $\Lambda(C_1)$ is a lattice, since it is closed under addition. This construction is described by Leech and Sloane [132], where it is called *Construction A*, though Forney [80] uses the term *mod 2 lattice* to distinguish lattices constructed in this way. In general $\Lambda(C_1, \cdots, C_L)$ is not a lattice.

We make contact again with the Gosset lattice E_8 by taking C_1 to be the extended $[8, 4, 4]$ Hamming code C. The fundamental volume $V(\Lambda(C)) = 16$, and the minimum squared distance $d^2(\Lambda(C)) = 4$. The code C contains the zero vector, 14 codewords of weight 4, and the all-one vector $\mathbf{1}$ of weight 8. There are 14×2^4 vectors in $\Lambda(C)$ of type $(\pm 1)^4 0^4$, and 16 vectors in $\Lambda(C)$ of type $(\pm 2)0^7$. This gives 240 vectors

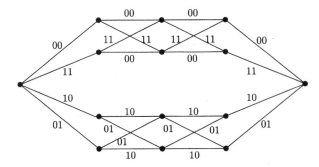

Fig. 4. A decoding trellis for the $[8, 4, 4]$ Hamming code.

TABLE I-A
MAXIMUM-LIKELIHOOD DECODING OF THE BINARY GOLAY CODE

When	Who	How	How many
1986	Conway and Sloane	128 cosets of $(1111) \otimes P_6$	1614
1986	Be'ery and Snyders	Fast Hadamard Transform	1551
1988	Forney	64-state trellis decoder via $|(8,7)/(8,4)/(8,1)|^3$	1351
1989	Snyders and Be'ery	generalized Wagner rule	827
1991	Vardy and Be'ery	ML decoding of $C_{24}^e \cup C_{24}^o$ using ML hexadecoder	651

TABLE I-B
MAXIMUM-LIKELILHOOD DECODING OF THE LEECH LATTICE

When	Who	How	How many
1986	Conway and Sloane	Turyn construction from E_8	55,968
1988	Forney	256-state trellis decoder via $|E_8/RE_8/2E_8|^3$	15,167
1989	Lang and Longstaff	Wagner decoding rule	~10,000
1989	Be'ery, Shahar, Snyders	generalized Wagner rule and look-up tables	6,129
1993	Vardy and Be'ery	ML decoding of $4 \times Q_{24}$ using ML hexadecoder	3,595

in $\Lambda(C)$ with minimum norm 4, and it is easily seen that there are no others. This second appearance of the number 240 is not happenstance. The lattice $\Lambda(C)$ is a realization of the Gosset lattice E_8 on a different scale. There is a norm-doubling linear transformation $\Phi : \mathbb{R}^8 \to \mathbb{R}^8$ satisfying $\|\Phi(x)\|^2 = 2\|x\|^2$ that transforms the original realization of E_8 into $\Lambda(C)$.

Conway and Sloane [44] describe more sophisticated variants of Construction A, but it may be more interesting to apply the original construction to codes defined over the ring $\mathbb{Z}_{2^a}$ of integers modulo 2^a. For example, extended cyclic codes over $\mathbb{Z}_{2^a}$ obtained from certain binary cyclic codes by Hensel lifting determine even unimodular lattices via Construction A. The binary Golay code determines the Leech lattice in this way, and this is perhaps the simplest construction for this remarkable lattice that is known. For more details see [108], [19], and [28].

D. Soft-Decision Decoding

The origin of the term *trellis code* is that the graph of state transitions looks like the structures used by gardeners to support climbing plants. Codewords are represented as paths through this trellis.

The decoder has a copy of the trellis. It processes the noisy samples and tries to find the path taken by the binary data. The decoding algorithm was proposed by Viterbi [219] and later shown to be a variant of dynamic programming. Every trellis stage, the decoder calculates and stores the most likely path terminating in a given state. The decoder also calculates the path metric, which measures distance from the partial received sequence to the partial codeword corresponding to the most likely path. Fig. 4 shows a decoding trellis for the $[8, 4, 4]$ Hamming code or for the lattice E_8 (in this interpretation the digits 0, 1 represent the cosets $2\mathbb{Z}, 2\mathbb{Z} + 1$ and the metric for an edge labeled $\epsilon\epsilon'$ is determined by the distances from the received signals r, r' to $2\mathbb{Z}+\epsilon, 2\mathbb{Z}+\epsilon'$). At time $\ell = 4$ in Fig. 4, the decoder only needs to update two path metrics and make one comparison to determine the most likely path terminating in a given state.

Viterbi [219] originally introduced this decoding method only as a proof technique, but it soon became apparent that it was really useful for decoding trellis codes of moderate complexity. The importance of this application is the reason the decoding method is called the Viterbi algorithm by communication theorists. Forney [77] recognized that the Viterbi algorithm is a recursive optimal solution to the problem of estimating the state sequence of a discrete time finite state Markov process observed in memoryless noise. Many problem in digital communication can be cast in this form.

Decoding algorithms are assembled from basic binary operations such as real addition, real subtraction, comparing two real numbers, and taking an absolute value. For simplicity, we might assign unit cost to each of these operations, and we might neglect the complexity of say multiplication by 2 (since this can be accomplished by merely shifting a binary expansion). It is then possible to compare different algorithms, and to show, for example, that the iterative decoding procedure for Reed–Muller codes based on the $|u \mid u + v|$ construction is less complex than the standard procedure using the fast Hadamard transform (see [80]). Quite recently there has been substantial interest in effective trellis-based decoding of codes and lattices. Tables I-A and I-B follow the progress that has been made in reducing the number of operations required for maximum-likelihood decoding of the Golay code and the Leech lattice (see [216] and [217] for details and additional references).

Decoding complexity can be reduced still further through bounded-distance decoding. Here the decoder corrects all error patterns in the Euclidean sphere of radius ρ about the transmitted point, where ρ is the packing radius of the code or lattice. This means that the error exponent of the bounded-distance decoder is the same as that of a maximum-likelihood decoder. Forney and Vardy [87] have shown that bounded-distance decoding of the binary Golay code and Leech lattice requires only 121 and 331 operations, respectively. The overall degradation in performance is about 0.1 dB over a wide range of SNR's.

It was Conway and Sloane [43] who revived the study of the complexity of soft-decision decoding algorithms for block codes and lattices. Their paper served to inspire a great deal of work, including the results reported in Table I. However, it is fair to say that this work was specific to particular families of codes, and fundamental asymptotic questions seemed out of reach. That changed with Tarokh's 1995 thesis [208] showing that decoding complexity grows exponentially with coding gain. The lower bound on complexity is established by means of an ingenious argument involving a differential equation, and the upper bound uses a sophisticated tensor product construction. Together the results show that the lower bound is asymptotically exact.

It is instructive to look back at the work of Slepian [199] who constructed codes for the Gaussian channel by taking a finite group of $N \times N$ matrices, and applying each matrix to a fixed vector in $\mathbb{R}^N$. It is remarkable that Ungerboeck codes are examples of Slepian signal sets (see [81]). One minor difference is that the group of isometries has become infinite. A more important difference is the emphasis today on the complexity of the group. This was not an issue that concerned Slepian, but it is of paramount importance today, because it determines the complexity of soft-decision decoding.

E. Multilevel Codes and Multistage Decoding

The coded-modulation schemes proposed by Ungerboeck make use of a partition Γ_L of the signal constellation into 2^L subsets sometimes corresponding to L levels in the Leech coordinate array. A rate $(L-1)/L$ convolutional code selects the subset, and the remaining uncoded bits select a signal from the chosen subset. Instead of coding across all levels at once, we might directly allocate system redundancy level by level, an idea that first appeared in the context of binary codes. In 1977, Imai and Hirakawa [112] presented their multilevel method for constructing binary block codes. Codewords from the component codes form the rows of a binary array, and the columns of this array are the codewords in the multilevel code. Imai and Hirakawa also described a multistage bounded-distance decoding algorithm, where the bits are decoded in order of decreasing sensitivity, starting with the bits protected by the most powerful error-correcting code. Subsequently, Calderbank [22] and Pottie and Taylor [173] described simple multilevel coset codes for the Gaussian channel, and quantified the performance/complexity advantages of multistage decoding over full maximum-likelihood decoding. Here the purpose of the parity check is to provide immunity against single symbol errors. Concerning theoretical limits, Wachsmann and Huber [220] have shown that multilevel codes with turbo code components come within 1 dB of the Shannon limit.

F. The Broadcast Channel

The flexibility inherent in multilevel coding and multistage decoding makes it easy to introduce unequal error protection when some bits are extremely sensitive to channel errors and others exhibit very little sensitivity. For example, Code Excited Linear Prediction (CELP) is a method of transmitting speech by first communicating a model of the vocal tract specified by parameters that depend on the speaker, and then exciting the model. This model includes pitch information, and an error here has much more impact on the reproduced speech quality, than an error at the input to the model. Specific speech/channel coding schemes for wireless channels are described by Cox, Hagenauer, Seshadri, and Sundberg [47]. This matching of speech and channel coding has become standard practice in the engineering of cellular voice services.

A second example is digital High-Definition Television (HDTV) that has been made possible by recent advances in video compression. Digital broadcast differs from digital point-to-point transmission in that different receivers have different signal-to-noise ratios, which decrease with distance from the broadcast transmitter. One concern with digital broadcast is its sensitivity to small variations in SNR at the various receiver locations. This sensitivity is manifested as an abrupt degradation in picture quality, which is generally considered unacceptable by the TV broadcast industry.

It is possible to achieve more graceful degradation by means of joint source and channel coding. There are algorithms for compressing video signals that output coarse information and fine information. The coarse information is sensitive because it provides a basic TV picture, and the fine information is less sensitive because it adds detail to the coarse picture. The channel-coding scheme is designed to provide greater error protection for the coarse information, so that the distant receiver always has access to the coarse picture. Receivers that are closer to the broadcast transmitter can obtain both the coarse picture, and the fine detail, so that, indeed, there is a more graceful decline in the quality of reception.

This philosophy of joint source and channel coding has its roots in the information-theoretic work of Cover [46] on broadcast channels. He considered a typical broadcast environment where a source wishes to transmit information over a Gaussian channel to a strong receiver with SNR S_2, and a weak receiver with SNR S_1. Cover established the efficiency of *superimposing information*; that is, broadcasting so that the detailed information meant for the stronger user includes the coarse information meant for the weaker user. The geometry of the achievable rate region makes it apparent that it is possible to achieve close to capacity $C_2 = \frac{1}{2}\log(1 + S_2)$ for the strong receiver at the cost of reducing the achievable rate for the weaker receiver only slightly below capacity $C_1 = \frac{1}{2}\log(1 + S_1)$. Specific multilevel codes that can be used in terrestrial broadcasting of HDTV to provide unequal error protection are described by Calderbank and Seshadri [34]. The data rate for HDTV is about 20–25 Mb/s in 6-MHz bandwidth, corresponding to transmission of 4 bits/symbol. It is possible to provide virtually error-free transmission (greater than 6-dB coding gain) for some fraction (for example, 25%) of the data, while providing a modest gain of 1–2 dB for the remaining data with respect to uncoded transmission. The connection with the information-theoretic work of Cover on broadcast channels is described by Ramchandran, Ortega, Uz, and Vetterli [175] in the context of their multiresolution joint source/channel coding scheme for this same application. Their paper proposes a complete system, and describes a particular source-coding algorithm that delivers bits with different sensitivity to channel errors.

G. Methods for Reducing Average Transmitted Signal Power

We consider signal constellations that consist of all lattice points that fall within some region $\mathcal{R}$. If the region $\mathcal{R}$ is an N-cube with faces parallel to the coordinate axes, then the induced probability distribution on an arbitrary M-dimensional projection is uniform. Changing the shape of the region $\mathcal{R}$ induces a nonuniform probability distribution on this M-dimensional projection. Thus gains derived from shaping a high-dimensional constellation can be achieved in a low-dimensional space by nonequiprobable signaling. The asymptotic shaping gain is $\pi e/6$ or 1.53 dB.

The problem of addressing a signal constellation is that of mapping a block of input data to a signal point. This problem enters into the design of both encoder and decoder; for the decoder needs to invert the mapping in order to recover the data stream corresponding to the estimate for the transmitted sequence of signals. The N-cube is a particularly simple Cartesian product for which the addressing problem is trivial, but here there is no shape gain. Spheres optimize the shape gain available in a given dimension but are hard to address. Conway and Sloane [42] proposed the use of Voronoi constellations based on a lattice partition Λ/Λ_S—the constellation consists of points from a translate of Λ that fall within a Voronoi region for the shaping lattice Λ_S. They showed how to use a decoding algorithm for Λ_S to address the constellation. Unfortunately, the ratio of peak-to-average power for Voronoi constellations (and spheres) is very high, precluding their use.

Calderbank and Ozarow [31] introduced the method of shaping on rings, where the region $\mathcal{R}$ is partitioned into T subregions so as to obtain T equal subconstellations with increasing average power. A shaping code then specifies sequences of subregions, and it is designed so that subconstellations with lower average power are more frequent. The purpose of the shaping code is to create a good approximation to the desired Gaussian distribution, and it is important to minimize the complexity of the shaping code. The shell mapping algorithm used in the V.34 modem standard enumerates all points in the Cartesian product of a basic two-dimensional constellation that are contained in a higher dimensional sphere. Laroia, Farvardin, and Tretter [130] show that it is possible to construct a 64-dimensional constellation from a 384-point two-dimensional constellation that supports uncoded transmission at 8 bits/symbol with a shaping gain of 1.20 dB and a peak-to-average power ratio (PAR) of 3.76. Alternatively, it is possible to achieve a shaping gain of 1 dB with a PAR of 2.9 (for comparison, the PAR of the two-dimensional sphere is 2).

1) Shaping by Searching a Trellis: A trellis code is an ensemble of codewords that can be searched efficiently. This search can be carried out with respect to any nonnegative measure that is calculated on a symbol-by-symbol basis. In Viterbi decoding this measure is distance from the received sequence. Here the measure is signal energy, but many other

applications are possible, for example, the reduction of peak to average power in OFDM systems. Trellis shaping is a method proposed by Forney [82] that selects a sequence with minimum power from an equivalence class of sequences, by means of a search through the trellis diagram of a code. The signal constellation is divided into rings labeled by the possible outputs of a binary convolutional code. Shaping information is transmitted by choosing a coset of the convolutional code, and a decoder selects the minimum-norm vector in the coset for transmission. Now data is transmitted in blocks of about 1000 symbols by periodically terminating the convolutional code. The delay would be unacceptable if it were only possible to recover information carried by the shaping code on a block-by-block basis. However, it is possible to specify cosets on a symbol-by-symbol basis using the theory of syndrome formers, developed by Forney [75] as part of his algebraic theory of convolutional codes. Forney ([75], [77], [78], [81]) has explored the algebraic structure of convolutional codes, and the connections with linear systems theory in some depth. Forney and Trott [85] have since shown that most of this structure theory extends to trellis codes based on lattices and cosets.

H. Precoding for ISI Channels

We begin with a brief account of the evolution in signal processing for magnetic-recording channels. Until quite recently, virtually all magnetic recording systems employed peak detection, where one sampled output is used to estimate the value of one symbol recorded on the disk. The reliability of peak detection depends on the minimum spacing between transitions. If two transitions are too close, the peaks are reduced in amplitude and shifted. Binary sequences input to magnetic recording systems that employ peak detection are required to meet certain runlength constraints in order to improve linear density and to improve system reliability. The (d, k) constraint requires that adjacent 1's be separated by at least d 0's and by at most k 0's. Here it is important to recall that in NRZI (nonreturn-to-zero-interleaved) recording the symbol 0 represents no transition, and the symbol 1 represents a transition. Long runs of 0's correspond to long stretches of constant magnetization. When the binary input satisfies a (d, k) constraint, it is possible to signal $(d+1)$ times as fast while maintaining the same spacing between transitions. If the code rate is R then the increase in linear density is given by the product $R(d+1)$. The k constraint aids timing recovery since timing is derived from transitions in the recorded data. Note that increasing the speed of circuitry is not without its challenges.

Peak detection looks at a signal sequence with respect to itself, not with respect to other signal sequences that could have been transmitted. The idea of using maximum-likelihood sequence estimation in magnetic-recording systems was suggested in 1971 by Kobayashi and Tang [125]. However, it has only recently become possible to implement partial response maximum likelihood (PRML) detection at sufficiently high speeds. PRML detection provides increases in linear density of about 30% by eliminating the d constraint. The resulting intersymbol interference (ISI) is equalized at the output of the channel to some tractable response such as PRIV $(1 - D^2)$ or EPRIV $((1 - D)(1 + D)^2)$. Maximum-likelihood (Viterbi) decoding is accomplished by tracking the state of the channel, as described in Kobayashi [124] or Forney [76].

A basic feature of telephone channels and certain optical memories (see [27]) is that they are linear subject to a peak constraint, and support a continuum of recording levels. This is fundamentally different from conventional magnetic-recording channels which are inherently nonlinear and where, to force linearity, the write current in the recording head has to be sufficient to ensure positive or negative saturation of the magnetic medium. Hence it is only possible to record the levels ± 1. The ability to write a continuum of levels at the input to this channel makes it possible to employ precoding techniques such as the one developed by Tomlinson [213], and by Miyakawa and Harashima [157], for Gaussian channels subject to ISI. The philosophy behind this precoding technique is that since the channel is known, it is possible to anticipate and correct for the effects of the channel at the input, so that a very simple decoder can be used at the output. It is not possible to use Tomlinson–Harashima precoding on conventional magnetic- and optical-recording systems where it is only possible to record a small discrete number of levels.

We consider transmission of A equally spaced analog levels $a_i \in \{0, 1, \cdots, A - 1\}$ over a discrete time channel with causal impulse response q_i, $i \geq 0$ for which $q_0 = 1$. The output v_i is given by

$$v_i = a_i + \sum_{j \geq 1} a_{i-j} q_j.$$

Tomlinson–Harashima precoding [157], [213] is a nonlinear method of precoding the data a_i that renders the output of the $Q(z)$ channel effectively free of intersymbol interference, and allows instantaneous symbol-by-symbol decoding of the data.

The Tomlinson filter does not transmit the data a_i directly, but instead transmits precoded data a_i', where

$$a_i' = a_i - \sum_{j \geq 1} a_{i-j}' q_j + A m_i$$

where m_i is the unique integer such that $a_i' \in [0, A]$. Now the output v_i is given by

$$\begin{aligned} v_i &= a_i - \sum_{j \geq 1} a_{i-j}' q_j + A m_i + \sum_{j \geq 1} a_{i-j}' q_j \\ &= a_i + A m_i \end{aligned}$$

and instantaneous symbol-by-symbol decoding is possible via congruence modulo A.

Precoding is a part of the V.34 modem standard [116] for communication over bandlimited Gaussian channels and variants thereof. In telephone-line modem applications it is important that the statistics of the channel symbols are Gaussian, so they match the statistics of the noise. Here Tomlinson–Harashima precoding is not appropriate since reduction modulo A seems to produce channel symbols a_i' that are uniformly distributed over the interval $[0, A]$. The ISI precoder [129] that forms a part of the V.34 standard is a more sophisticated alternative to Tomlinson–Harashima precoding. It achieves significant shaping gain (the saving in

average transmitted signal power provided by a Gaussian input distribution over a uniform distribution) without increasing the complexity of trellis decoding much beyond that of the baseline memoryless channel. The key idea is to separate the problem of decoding in the presence of additive white Gaussian noise (AWGN) from that of resolving intersymbol interference. This is captured geometrically in Fig. 5. Precoding modifies the input just enough to ensure that the output of the channel $Q(D)$ is a trellis codeword. A Viterbi decoder takes care of the noise, and inversion of the channel provides an approximation to the original input. The original input can be recognized from the approximation, since both lie in a common Voronoi region. There is a small power penalty connected with the power of the sequence that modifies the original input, but this penalty can be made insignificant. Running this precoded transmission system "backward" provides a system for quantizing an individual source with memory (cf. trellis-coded quantization [150]).

I. The AWGN Channel and the Public Switched Telephone Network

Trellis codes provide effective coding gains of about 4.5 dB on the AWGN channel, and a further 1 dB is available through shaping schemes of moderate complexity. Forney and Ungerboeck [86] observe that the cutoff role of a high-SNR channel corresponds to an effective coding gain (without shaping) of about 5.7 dB at error probabilities of about 10^{-6}. This is as high an effective coding gain as anyone has achieved with moderate complexity trellis codes.

The coset codes described in this paper select signal points from uniformly spaced constellations. When harmonic distortion and PCM noise (logarithmic quantization noise) are significant channel impairments it can be advantageous to distort the uniform spacing. Testing of high-speed voiceband modems has revealed a significant increase in distortion for points near the perimeter of a QAM signal constellation. This distortion increases with distance from the center of the constellation and limits performance at data rates above 19.2 kb/s. The perimeter distortion can be reduced by transforming the signal constellation so that points near the center are closer together, and points near the perimeter are further apart. When the channel SNR is high, such a transformation reduces immunity to Gaussian noise because points near the center of the transformed constellation are closer together than in a uniformly spaced constellation with the same average power. Betts, Calderbank, and Laroia [13] have demonstrated theoretically that for channel SNR's of practical interest, there is actually a small gain in immunity to Gaussian noise. In fact, an appropriate coded-modulation scheme can produce gains of about 0.25 dB. Experiments support the intuition that it is advantageous to employ trellis codes for which the dominant error is a trellis path error, and the longer that error the better.

In fact, the Public Switched Telephone Network is evolving toward the point where an analog voiceband channel will consist of short analog end links connected to PCM codes, with no intermediate tandem D/A or A/D transformations. This observation inspired development of the V.90 modem

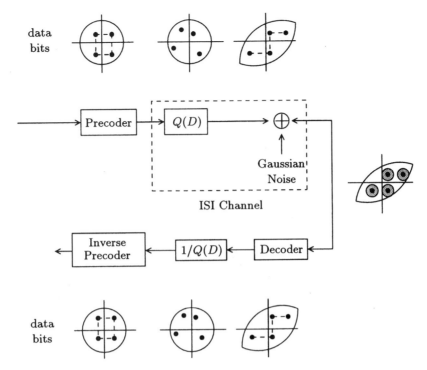

Fig. 5. A geometric rendering of a precoded transmission system.

standard, concluded in February 1998 which promises 56 kb/s downstream and delivers V.34 upstream.

J. The Potential of Iterated Decoding

In algebraic error-correcting block codes the information in each encoded bit is distributed across all symbols in a codeword. Information carried by concatenated codes is segmented, with some bits determining the encoding of a particular component subblock, and other bits the linkage between the different components. In decoding concatenated codes, initial estimates for component codewords are combined by decoding the code that links components together. In turbo codes the information in each bit is replicated in two different localities of a codeword. The original construction is to produce a first parity sequence by encoding an information sequence using a rate $1/2$ recursive systematic encoder, to permute the information bits using a very long interleaver (10^4–10^5 bits), and to produce a second parity sequence by encoding the permuted sequence using a second encoder of the same type as the first (possibly identical). Decoding is an iterative process where bit level soft decisions produced by one decoder are used to improve (hopefully) the decisions produced by the other decoder at the next step. The potential of this combination of local encoding and iterative decoding was revealed by Berrou, Glavieux, and Thitmajshima [12] who demonstrated that a 16-state rate $1/2$ turbo code can operate at an SNR 0.7 dB greater than capacity of the AWGN channel, with a decoded bit-error rate of 10^{-5}. For comparison, the Big Viterbi Decoder [41] designed to decode a 16 384-state convolutional code requires 2.4 dB to achieve the same bit-error rate. Like many revelations there was a period of initial scepticism, but now there are no doubts that this is a spectacular achievement. It is interesting to observe

that the search for theoretical understanding of turbo codes has transformed coding theorists into experimental scientists. One empirical discovery is the existence of an *error floor* at low error rates that depends on the size of the interleaver. Perhaps the most interesting theoretical connection is that between the *forward–backward algorithm* [6] (a.k.a. the *BCJR algorithm* [3]) used in decoding convolutional codes, and belief propagation in Bayesian networks [167], a technique used for training and system identification in the neural network community [90], [145].

The ideas of local encoding and iterative decoding were present in a classic paper of Gallager [91], [92] written some 30 years before the discovery of turbo codes. A low-density parity-check (LDPC) matrix is a binary array where the number of 1's in each row and column is kept small. Gallager suggested using the adjacency matrix of a randomly chosen low-degree bipartite graph as the parity-check matrix. Decoding is again an iterative process where bit-level soft decisions obtained at one stage are used to update bit-level soft decisions about a particular bit at the next stage by means of the parity-check equations involving that bit. Gallager distinguished two different types of information, *intrinsic* and *extrinsic*, and understood that only extrinsic information is useful for iterative decoding. He developed the geometric picture of a *support tree* where the influence of a bit fans out across all symbols in a controlled way as the iterations progress. Gallager was not able to show correctness of the proposed iterative algorithm but he showed long LDPC codes can achieve rates up to capacity on the binary-symmetric channel with maximum-likelihood decoding. Subsequently, Zyablov and Pinsker [232] showed that with high probability over the choice of graph, the codes proposed by Gallager could be decoded in $\log n$ rounds, where each decoding round

TABLE II
A GENERATOR MATRIX FOR THE $[24, 12, 8]$ BINARY GOLAY CODE

11	00	11	11	11	00	00	00	00	00	00	00
00	11	01	01	01	11	00	00	00	00	00	00
00	00	11	10	10	11	11	00	00	00	00	00
00	00	00	11	11	01	01	11	00	00	00	00
00	00	00	00	11	10	11	10	11	00	00	00
00	00	00	00	00	11	11	11	00	11	00	00
00	00	00	00	00	00	11	01	11	01	11	00
00	00	00	00	00	00	00	11	01	11	01	11
11	00	00	00	00	00	00	00	11	11	10	01
11	11	00	00	00	00	00	00	00	11	01	10
11	10	11	00	00	00	00	00	00	00	11	01
01	11	10	11	00	00	00	00	00	00	00	11

removes a constant fraction of errors. More recently, MacKay and Neal [145] demonstrated near Shannon-limit performance of LDPC codes with iterative decoding. If the art of simulation had been more advanced in 1963, the history of coding theory might look very different today.

Sipser and Spielman [192] only discovered Gallager's paper after deriving asymptotically good linear error-correcting codes with decoding complexity $O(\log N)$-linear time only under the uniform cost model where the complexity of adding two N-bit binary vectors is independent of N. The combinatorial objects at the heart of the Sipser–Spielman construction are *expander graphs* in which every vertex has an unusually large number of neighbors, and these codes are of the type proposed by Gallager. The machinery of expander graphs enabled Sipser and Spielman to prove that the sequential decoding algorithm proposed by Gallager was in fact correct for these expander codes, something Gallager had not been able to do 30 years earlier.

The idea that graphical models for codes provide a natural setting in which to describe iterative decoding techniques is present in Tanner [207] but has undergone a revival in recent years [221], [222]. One way this school of coding theory connects with the classical theory is through the study of tailbiting trellises for binary block codes. Solomon and van Tilborg [200] demonstrated that a tailbiting trellis for a binary block code can in fact have fewer states than a conventional trellis. Table II shows a generator matrix of the $[24, 12, 8]$ binary Golay code that provides a 16-state, 12-section tailbiting trellis [26], whereas a conventional trellis must have 256 states at its midpoint [158]. The specific discovery was motivated by a suggestion of Wiberg [221, Corollary 7.3], and by the general result that the number of states in a tailbiting trellis can be as few as the square root of the corresponding number for a conventional trellis at the midpoint [222]. The time axis for a tailbiting trellis is defined most naturally on the circle, though it can also be defined on an interval with the added restriction that valid paths begin and end in the same state. The *span* of a generator is the interval from the first to the last nonzero component, and the generator is said to be *active* in this interval. For the Golay code, we see from Table II that at every time slot only four generators are active, hence the $2^4 = 16$ states in the tailbiting trellis (see [26] for details). It is quite possible that other extremal self-dual block codes (notably the $[48, 24, 12]$ Quadratic Residue code) will also have generator matrices that correspond to low-complexity tailbiting representations.

In iterative decoding the focus is on understanding the domain of attraction for a codeword rather than understanding the boundaries of a Voronoi region. In the future we might well see a shift in emphasis within coding theory from static geometry to dynamical systems. Certainly it would be interesting to have a counterpart of turbo codes in the world of algebraic error-correcting codes.

K. On Duality Between Transmission and Quantization

The theory of communication and that of quantization overlap significantly, but there has been less cross pollination between the two communities than might be expected. Nevertheless, it is commonly understood that the problems of coding and quantization are in some sense dual.

The lattice-decoding algorithms described in previous sections can be used to represent a source sequence x as the sum of a lattice point v, and an error sequence $e = (e_i)$. In quantization the objective is the lattice point v, and the expected value $E(e_i^2)$ is the *mean-squared error* (mse) normalized per dimension. By contrast, the objective in transmission is not the lattice point v, but the error sequence e. The idea is to choose a suitable discrete set of source sequences x, so that the entries of the error sequence e have a distribution that is approximately Gaussian.

The error sequence e is distributed over the Voronoi region $\mathcal{R}$ of the lattice, and if this distribution is uniform, then the mean-squared error $E(e_i^2)$ is equal to the second moment $G(\mathcal{R})$. In quantization, the quantity $\gamma(\mathcal{R}) = 1/12G(\mathcal{R})$ is called the *granular gain*, and it measures the reduction in mean-squared error that comes from choosing the shape of the quantization cell. The baseline for comparison is uniform scalar quantization (using the integer lattice) where the quantization cell is the N-cube C_N with second moment $G(C_N) = 1/12$. Table III presents a correspondence between quantities of interest in communications and in quantization (with respect to Gaussian channels/sources). Successive refinement is a

530

Coding	Quantization
Transmission over AWGN channel (memoryless) subject to a power constraint	Quantization of a memoryless Gaussian source (mmse distortion) [143]
Coding Gain: The Voronoi cells should cover a region of appreciable noise probability	Boundary Gain: For a given mse the spheres of appropriate radius about the codewords should cover a region of appreciable source probability
Shaping Gain: Bounding region that minimizes second moment leads to minimum average transmitted signal power	Granular Gain: mse distortion favors Voronoi cells with the smallest second moment
Trellis Coded Modulation [215]	Trellis Coded Quantization [150]
Broadcast Channel [46]	Successive Refinement [127], [65]
Precoding for ISI Channels [129]	Quantization of Sources with Memory
Multiple Access Channels	Quantization of Correlated Sources [200]

particular case of multiple descriptions, where two channels connect the source to the destination (see [166], [64], and [214]). Either channel may fail and this failure is known to the decoder but not the encoder. The objective is to obtain good performance when both channels work and to degrade gracefully if either channel fails. The two channels may be considered equally important, and this is different in spirit from layered coding (successive refinement) where a high-priority channel transports important bits. The emergence of wireless systems employing multiple antennas, and of active networking in lossy packet networks represent an opportunity for the multiple descriptions coding paradigm.

L. The Notion of Frequency Domain

This is the idea of using constraints in the frequency domain to separate codewords in the time domain. We begin by considering integer valued sequences $p = (p_0, p_1, \cdots, p_{N-1})$ which we represent as polynomials $p(D) = \sum_{i=0}^{N-1} p_i D^i$. We shall say that the sequence $p(D)$ has a Kth-order spectral null at $\theta = 2\pi\ell/M$, if $p(D)$ is divisible by $(e^{i\theta} - D)^K$. A collection of sequences with this property is called a *spectral null code*. To show that it is possible to separate vectors in Euclidean space by placing spectral constraints in the frequency domain, we consider the case $\theta = 0$. We say that the sequence $p(D)$ has *a sign change at position* u if $p_u \neq 0$, and $\text{sign}(p_u) = -\text{sign}(p_t)$, where $t = \max\{i < u \mid p_i \neq 0\}$.

Theorem (Descartes Rule of Signs): Let $p(D)$ be a real polynomial with K positive real roots, not necessarily distinct. Then the number of sign changes in the sequence p of coefficients of $p(D)$ is at least K.

For a proof we refer the reader to Householder [111]. Now consider a code with a Kth-order spectral null at $\theta = 0$. It follows directly from Descartes Rule of Signs that the

minimum squared distance between codewords is at least $2K_d^2$, where d is the minimum distance of the integer alphabet employed (for the bipolar alphabet ± 1, this gives a bound of $8K$. This simple observation is the starting point for the construction of many codes used in magnetic recording applications; more details can be found in Immink and Beenker [115], Karabed and Siegel [121], Eleftheriou and Cideciyan [63], and the survey paper [152]. The objective in all these papers is to separate signals at the output of a partial-response channel by generating codewords at the input with spectral nulls that are matched to those of the channel. The special features of telephone channels and recording channels have also led to new connections between coding theory, dynamical systems, and linear systems theory [151].

M. Partial-Response Channels and Coding with Spectral Constraints

It is natural to try to devise coding schemes that meet both spectral null and minimum distance/coding gain objectives. Starting from an uncoded L-level data sequence (i_k) we want to generate a real-valued sequence (y_k) with nulls at certain prescribed frequencies in such a way that the data (i_k) can be recovered instantly from the sequence (y_k). Fig. 6 shows an input sequence $x(D)$ passing through a partial response channel with impulse response (transfer function) $p(D)$, resulting in an output $y(D) = x(D)p(D)$, which is called a partial-response-coded (PRC) sequence. A white-noise sequence $n(D)$ may be added to $y(D)$ to give a noisy PRC sequence $z(D)$, representing the output of a real channel. The input sequence $x(D)$ can be recovered from the PRC sequence $y(D)$ by passing $y(D)$ through a filter with transfer function $1/p(D)$. (We have to imagine that $x(D)$ "starts" at some finite time for this inverse filtering operation to be well-defined, and we assume the initial values are known.) Thus the sequence

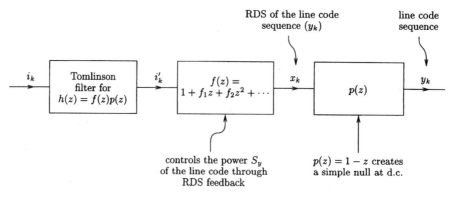

Fig. 6. Diagram for either partial-response signaling or signaling with spectral nulls.

$x(D)$ may be reconstructed as the "running digital sum" (RDS) of the PRC sequence $y(D)$. The spectra of the RDS sequence and PRC sequence are related by the partial-response transfer function expressed in the frequency domain. The order of the spectral null will be the order of the corresponding zero in $p(z)$. This number needs to be doubled to describe the order of the null in the actual power spectrum, which is proportional to $|p(e^{i\theta})|^2$.

We define the *RDS power* S_x as the sample variance of the RDS variables x_k, assuming sufficient stationarity (so that this notion is well-defined), and the *PRC power* S_y as the sample variance of the PRC variables y_k. Neither is necessarily larger than the other. Given $p(z)$, the problem is to choose $f(z)$ so as to minimize S_y subject to the requirement that S_x be held fixed. This will single out a one-parameter family of filters $f(z)$ indexed by the RDS power S_x. It is necessary to constrain $f(z)$, for otherwise the minimizing solution is $f(z) = 1/p(z)$ and the null disappears (the power S_x becomes infinite). Decreasing the width of a spectral null in the line-code spectrum requires a large peak at the appropriate frequency in $f(z)$, and hence large power S_x.

The new information in each symbol x_k is carried by the i.i.d. input i_k' to the filter $f(z)$. The power S of the sequence i_k' is the effective signal power at the output of a minimum mean-squared error (MMSE) predictor for the RDS sequence (x_k). For a single null at dc, Forney and Calderbank [84] show that the filter $f(z) = 1/(1 - \beta z)$ gives the best possible tradeoff between the RDS power S_x and the line code power S_y. The optimum tradeoff is shown in Fig. 7 and is given by

$$4\left(\frac{S_x}{S}\right)\left(\frac{S_y}{S} - 1\right) = \left(\frac{S_y}{S}\right)^2.$$

The corresponding PRC spectra are shown in Fig. 8. As S_y approaches S, S_x necessarily increases without bound, and $H_y(\theta)$ becomes flatter with a sharper and sharper null at dc. These power spectra $H_y(\theta)$ are called "first-order power spectra" by Justesen [118], who considers them to be an interesting representative class of simple spectra for sequences with dc nulls, in that they remain small up to some cutoff frequency f_0 and then become approximately constant over the rest of the band. He notes that if f_0 is defined as the frequency at which $H_y(f_0) = S_y/2$ (the "half-power" frequency), then,

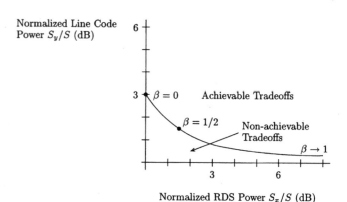

Fig. 7. Optimum tradeoff between S_x/S and S_y/S.

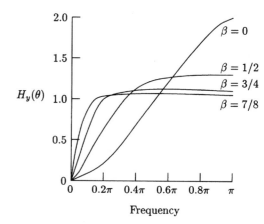

Fig. 8. PRC spectra for first-order autoregressive RDS sequences with parameter β.

for these first-order power spectra

$$\pi f_0 \simeq (S_y/2S_x)f_N$$

(where f_N is the upper Nyquist band-edge frequency), so that $\pi f_0/f_N \simeq 1 - \beta$ (or $\theta_0 \simeq 1 - \beta$), at least for $\beta \geq 1/2$.

The optimum tradeoff between S_x and S_y for sequences $\{x_k\}$ and $\{y_k\}$ that are related by $y(D) = x(D)p(D)$, where $p(D)$ is a response with arbitrary spectral nulls, was developed in subsequent work by Calderbank and Mazo [30]. Forney and Calderbank have shown that, at least for sequences supporting large numbers of bits per symbol, coset codes can be adapted to achieve effectively the same performance and complexity on

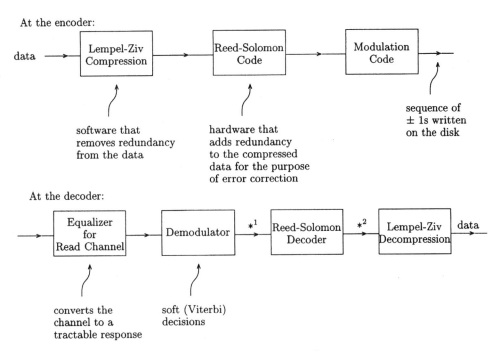

At the encoder:

At the decoder:

Fig. 9. Concatenation of an inner modulation code with an outer Reed–Solomon code. At $*^1$ the demodular provides a maximum-likelihood estimate of the $\pm$ valued sequence written on the disk, and the bit-error probability might be between 10^{-6} and 10^{-10} depending on the aggressiveness of the modulation strategy. At $*^2$ the bit-error probability needs to be 10^{-18}, that is, essentially error-free.

partial-response channels, or for sequences with spectral nulls, as they do in the ordinary memoryless case. This in addition to the optimum tradeoff between input and output powers.

N. Concatenated Codes

Applications of coding theory (see [45]) from deep-space communication to consumer electronics employ an inner modulation code with an outer algebraic error-correcting code (usually a Reed–Solomon code). Fig. 9 is a representation of a magnetic recording channel. For this application it is likely that in the next five years we will see full integration of demodulation and Reed–Solomon coding (a single-chip solution).

There are opportunities to use soft information calculated by the demodulator in Reed–Solomon decoding. For a small increase in decoder complexity it is possible either to provide reliability information about every demodulated data symbol, or to provide a list of the two or three best estimates of the ± 1-valued sequence written on the disk (see [184] and [106]). For the second alternative, the quantity of interest is the probability that the true write sequence is not among the list of two or three. This quantity may be recast as a decrease in bit-error probability; the old range $[10^{-10}, -10^{-6}]$ becomes $[10^{-14}, 10^{-8}]$, an improvement of about 1.5 dB for the list of three estimates. Both alternatives have the potential to simplify Reed–Solomon decoding, but it is not so easy in practice, and even the declaration of erasures is something of an art. It may in fact be more productive to focus on interpolating reliable symbols as in [203]. Staged decoding can provide additional coding gains of up to 1 dB in concatenated systems. For example, Hagenauer, Offer, and Papke [107] identify Reed–Solomon codewords that are

correct with very high probability, and have the inner decoder treat the corresponding information bits as side information in a second round of decoding (*state pinning*). Particularly in magnetic recording, it can be advantageous to reverse the order of modulation and Reed–Solomon encoding (a systematic encoder is required). This reduces error propagation and can result in coding efficiencies (see [17] and [114]).

The theoretical foundations of concatenated coding are found in Forney [74], who showed that for polynomial decoding complexity, the error rate could be made to decrease exponentially with blocklength at any rate less than capacity. The notion of concatenated codes has been pursued with enthusiasm in the Russian literature, and there is a substantial commonality to the generalized cascade codes of Zinoviev [230], and the multilevel codes of Imai and Hirakawa [112]. In algebraic coding theory, Justesen [117] provided an explicit construction of a sequence of codes for which the rate and the normalized distance d/N are both bounded away from zero. For a long time prior to his construction there had been serious doubt as to whether this was possible. Now it is easy to show there exist field elements $\alpha_m \in \mathbb{F}_{2^m}$, so that the binary concatenated codes determined by pairs $(c, \alpha_m c)$, $c \in \mathbb{F}_{2^m}$ meet the Gilbert–Varshamov bound as $m \to \infty$. However, this is not an explicit construction. Justesen's idea was to consider pairs $((c_j), (\alpha_j c_j))$ where the field element α_j depends explicitly on the symbol c_j, but where variation in α_j from symbol to symbol provides the kind of performance attributable to random coding.

IV. Two Important Developments
in Algebraic Coding Theory

Even in the 1977 edition of MacWilliams and Sloane there were 1478 references. Since it would be unwise to attempt a comprehensive array of algebraic coding theory in the space available, we have chosen instead to highlight two developments of particular importance. The first is the geometric-mathematical framework of association schemes presented by Delsarte [48] that provides a common language for coding theory, statistical design, and algebraic combinatorics. The second is grounded in algorithms, and follows developments in cyclic codes through to the creation of algebraic-geometry codes that beat the Gilbert–Varshamov bound.

The theory of association schemes was inspired in part by the MacWilliams Identities, though it is the nonnegativity of the MacWilliams transform that is important, rather than the identity connecting the weight distribution of a linear code to that of the dual code (see [51]). It is these MacWilliams Inequalities that lead to the MRRW linear programming bound on codes, and to lower bounds on combinatorial designs and orthogonal arrays. Many notions of regularity in group theory, combinatorics, and statistics are expressed very naturally in terms of association schemes. For example, the study of distance regular graphs, now a large subject in its own right (see [21]), is the study of association schemes with a particular (P-polynomial) property.

We begin with a section that emphasizes approximation in the theory of combinatorial designs. The notion of approximation is one reason the theoretical computer science community has made extensive use of coding theory in recent years. In particular, codes have been used to design small sample spaces that approximate the behavior of large sample spaces, leading to bounds on the number of random bits used by probabilistic algorithms and the communications complexity of cryptographic protocols. From the perspective of computational complexity it is natural to view random bits as a resource analogous to time and space, and to design algorithms that require as few as possible. For details on this and other applications of coding theory to computational complexity see Feigenbaum [67].

A. Approximation, Combinatorial Designs, and the Johnson Scheme

The concept of approximation is similar but slightly different from that of quantization. The purpose of a design is to capture with a small ensemble the regularity properties of a much larger universe. Designs are concerned with approximating a universe closely, whereas codes are concerned with separating an ensemble widely. Questions in coding theory are packing problems, whereas questions in design theory are covering problems. There is a duality between packing and covering that can be made mathematically precise using the theory of association schemes.

An *association scheme* is a set X together with a partition of the two-element subsets of X into N classes $\Gamma_1, \cdots, \Gamma_N$ satisfying the following conditions:

1) given $x \in X$, the number v_i of points $y \in X$ with $\{x, y\} \in \Gamma_i$ depends only on i;
2) given $x, y \in X$ with $\{x, y\} \in \Gamma_k$, the number of points $z \in X$ with $\{x, z\} \in \Gamma_i$ and $\{y, z\} \in \Gamma_j$ is a constant p_{ij}^k that depends only on i, j, and k.

We may think of an association scheme on X as a coloring of the complete graph on X with colors $c_1, \cdots, c_N$ where an edge has color c_i if it belongs to Γ_i. The first condition asserts that each monochromatic graph (X, Γ_i) is regular. The second condition asserts that the number of triangles with a given coloring on a given base depends only on the coloring and not on the base.

The Johnson scheme $J(v, d)$ offers an algebraic means of quantifying the duality between packing and covering properties of d-subsets of a v-set. The point set Ω of $J(v, d)$ is the set of d-subsets of a v-set, these subsets intersect in $d + 1$ possible ways, and the $d + 1$ relations

$$R_i = \{(x, y) \mid |x \cap y| = d - i\}, \qquad i = 0, 1, \cdots, d$$

determine an association scheme. Starting from this simple observation, Delsarte [48] used the representation theory of the symmetric group and orthogonal polynomials to derive an algebraic foundation for extremal set theory.

The vector space $\mathbb{R}^\Omega$ consists of all mappings ψ from Ω to $\mathbb{R}$, and is invariant under the natural action of the symmetric group S_v. The irreducible S_v-invariant subspaces under this action are the harmonic spaces $\text{harm}(i)$, $i = 0, 1, \cdots, d$, where $\dim(\text{harm}(i)) = \binom{v}{i} - \binom{v}{i-1}$. The adjacency matrix D_i of the graph (Ω, R_i) is symmetric, and the relations

$$D_i D_j = \sum_k p_{ij}^k D_k$$

imply that the matrices $D_0 = I, D_1, \cdots, D_d$ span a $(d+1)$-dimensional commutative real algebra called the *Bose–Mesner algebra* of the Johnson scheme [20]. The adjacency matrices D_i commute with the natural action of the symmetric group, and Delsarte [48] proved that the $d+1$ eigenspaces common to the matrices D_i are in fact the harmonic spaces. Calderbank, Delsarte, and Sloane [25] constructed an explicit spanning set for each harmonic space $\text{harm}(i)$. For every i-set A, let

$$f_A = \sum_{j=0}^i (-1)^j \binom{i}{j}^{-1} \binom{d-j}{i-j} \binom{v-i+1}{j} \sigma_j(A),$$

where $\sigma_j(A)$ is the sum of the characteristic functions of all j-subsets of A. As A ranges over every i-set the vectors f_A span $\text{harm}(i)$.

The harmonic spaces are of combinatorial importance, because if the characteristic function of a family of d-subsets of a v-set is orthogonal to a harmonic space $\text{harm}(j)$, then this family exhibits some regularity with respect to j-sets. To connect this viewpoint with classical design theory, we recall that a $t - (v, d, \lambda)$ design is a collection $\mathfrak{B}$ of subsets of a v-element set such that every member of $\mathfrak{B}$ contains d points and every subset of t points is in λ blocks. Here we are looking at the universe of d-point subsets, and we are approximating the regularity properties of this universe with respect to t-subsets of coordinates.

If ζ is an S_v-invariant subspace of $\mathbb{R}^\Omega$, then we can write

$$\zeta = \sum_{i \in T} \text{harm}(i)$$

for some subset T of $\{0, 1, \cdots, d\}$, where $\sum$ denotes orthogonal sum. There are 2^{d+1} such subspaces. Now let $\mathfrak{B}$ be a nonempty family of d-subsets of a v-set. A subspace ζ of $\mathbb{R}^{\Omega}$ will be said to be $\mathfrak{B}$-*regular* if it satisfies

$$\langle \pi(\mathfrak{B}), \psi \rangle = \frac{|\mathfrak{B}|}{|\Omega|} \langle \pi(\Omega), \psi \rangle, \qquad \text{for all } \psi \in \zeta$$

where $\pi(\ )$ is the characteristic function of a subset of Ω. Here we are thinking about a design as a way of approximating the statistics of the full ensemble Ω of d-subsets of a v-set, using only a proper subset $\mathfrak{B}$. The vector $\pi(\Omega)$ is the all-one function which spans harm (0). Orthogonality implies that the inner product $\langle \pi(\Omega), \psi \rangle$ vanishes for all $\psi \in$ harm (j) with $j \geq 1$. It follows from the definitions that if ζ is S_v-invariant and $\mathfrak{B}$-regular then

$$\langle \pi(\mathfrak{B}), \psi \rangle = 0, \qquad \text{for all } \psi \in \text{harm } (j), \text{ with } 0 \neq j \in T.$$

In this case we say $\mathfrak{B}$ is a T-*design* (when $0 \in T$, a T-design is defined to be a T'-design with $T' = T \setminus \{0\}$). The importance of this equation is that it shows the equivalence between the concepts of a T-design in $J(v, d)$ and an S_v-invariant $\mathfrak{B}$-regular subspace of $\mathbb{R}^{\Omega}$. The following theorem of Delsarte [48] makes the connection with classical design theory.

Theorem: A t-design in $J(v, d)$ is a T-design, where $T = \{1, 2, \cdots, t\}$.

Let $\mathfrak{B}$ be a family of d-subsets of a v-set. *The inner distribution* $a = (a_0, \cdots, a_d)$ of $\mathfrak{B}$ is given by

$$a_i = |\mathfrak{B}|^{-1} \sum_{x, y \in \mathfrak{B}} D_i(x, y)$$

which is the average valency of the relation R_i restricted to $\mathfrak{B}$. The information carried by the inner distribution is packing information about the family $\mathfrak{B}$. The $d+1$ numbers in the inner distribution are all that is necessary to calculate the norm of the projection of the characteristic function $\pi(\mathfrak{B})$ on the harmonic spaces harm (i). These norms carry information about how subsets in $\mathfrak{B}$ cover the v points. This is what is meant by quantifying the duality between packing and covering.

Since the Bose–Mesner algebra is semisimple, it has a unique basis of minimal mutually orthogonal idempotent matrices $J_0, \cdots, J_d$. Here $J_0 = J/\binom{v}{d}$, where J is the matrix with every entry 1, and the columns of J_i span the harmonic space harm (i). If

$$D_l = \sum_{i=0}^{d} P_l(i) J_i, \qquad \text{for } l = 0, 1, \cdots, d$$

then

$$D_l J_i = P_l(i) J_i$$

so that $P_l(i)$ is the eigenvalue of D_l on the harmonic space harm (i). The $(d+1) \times (d+1)$ matrix P with ilth entry $P_l(i)$ is called the *eigenmatrix* of the Johnson scheme. The eigenvalue $P_l(i) = E_l(i)$, where $E_l(x)$ is the Eberlein polynomial defined

by

$$E_l(x) = \sum_{j=0}^{l} (-1)^j \binom{x}{j} \binom{v-x}{l-j} \binom{v-d-x}{l-j},$$
$$l = 0, 1, \cdots, d.$$

For a proof, see Delsarte [48]. The matrix $Q = P^{-1}/\binom{v}{d}$, with ilth entry $Q_l(i)$ is called the *dual eigenmatrix*. Note that

$$J_l = \left(\sum_{i=0}^{d} Q_l(i) D_i \right) \Big/ \binom{v}{d}.$$

The entry $q_l(i) = H_l(i)$, where $H_l(x)$ is the Hahn polynomial defined by

$$H_l(x) = \left[\binom{v}{l} - \binom{v}{l-1} \right]$$
$$\times \sum_{i=0}^{l} \left\{ (-1)^i \binom{l}{i} \binom{v+1-l}{i} \binom{d}{i}^{-1} \binom{v-d}{i}^{-1} \right\} \binom{x}{i},$$
$$l = 0, 1, \cdots, d.$$

Again we refer the reader to Delsarte ([48] or [50]) for a proof.

Given a family $\mathfrak{B}$ of d-subsets of a v-set, the *dual distribution* $b = (b_0, b_1, \cdots, b_d)$ is given by

$$b_i = \frac{|\Omega|}{|\mathfrak{B}|^2} \pi(\mathfrak{B}) J_i \pi(\mathfrak{B})^T = \frac{|\Omega|}{|\mathfrak{B}|^2} \|\pi_i\|^2$$

where π_i is the orthogonal projection of $\pi(\mathfrak{B})$ onto the eigenspace harm (i).

Theorem ([48]): The inner distribution a, and the dual distribution b are related by

$$aQ = |\mathfrak{B}|b$$

where Q is the dual eigenmatrix of the Johnson scheme.

Proof: We have

$$\left(\frac{1}{|\mathfrak{B}|} aQ \right)_l = \frac{1}{|\mathfrak{B}|} \sum_{i=0}^{d} Q_l(i) a_i$$
$$= \frac{1}{|\mathfrak{B}|^2} \pi(\mathfrak{B}) \left(\sum_{i=0}^{d} Q_l(i) D_i \right) \pi(\mathfrak{B})^T = b_l,$$

as required. $\qquad \square$

It is also possible to capture the regularity properties of a design $\mathfrak{B}$ through analysis of invariant linear forms. With any t-subset x of V and any integer $i \in [0, t]$ we associate the number $D_i(x)$ that counts the blocks in $\mathfrak{B}$ meeting x in $t - i$ points. Suppose that for all t-subsets x, we have a linear relation

$$f_0 D_0(x) + f_1 D_1(x) + \cdots + f_t D_t(x) = c$$

where $f_0, f_1, \cdots, f_t$ and c are fixed real numbers. Then we say that the $(t+1)$-tuple $(f_t)_{i=0}^t$ is a t-*form* for $\mathfrak{B}$. The set of t-forms clearly is a vector space, which will be called the t-*form space* of $\mathfrak{B}$. The dimension of the t-form space measures regularity of $\mathfrak{B}$ with respect to t-subsets, and when $\mathfrak{B}$ is a classical t-design, the t-form space coincides with

$\mathbb{R}^{t+1}$. Calderbank and Delsarte [24] have shown that the t-form space is completely determined by the inner distribution of $\mathfrak{B}$, and that the invariant t-forms can be calculated via a matrix transform that involves a system of dual Hahn polynomials. For example, the inner distribution of octads in the binary Golay code is $(1,0,0,0,280,0,448,0,30)$ and the 7-form space can be generated from the particular 7-form

$$D_0(x) + D_1(x) = 1.$$

It is interesting to note that given any collection of 8-element subsets of a 24-set for which this particular 7-form is invariant, the linear span must be the binary Golay code.

The fundamental question in design theory is usually taken to be: Given v, d, λ does there exist a $t - (v, d, \lambda)$ design? This is certainly a natural question to ask from the perspective of small geometries, but it does not involve the idea of approximation in an essential way. Designs play an important role in applied mathematics and statistics and this author would suggest that questions involving fundamental limits on the quality of approximation are more important than questions involving existence of individual designs.

One of the strengths of the association scheme approach to designs is that it allows arbitrary vectors in $\mathbb{R}^{\Omega}$, not just the characteristic vectors of collections of d-sets, in particular it includes signed designs [177].

We mention briefly an elegant application to extremal set theory that was inspired by Delsarte's thesis. A family $\mathfrak{B}$ of d-element subsets of v-set is called t- intersecting if $|B \cap B'| \geq t$ for all $B, B' \in \mathfrak{B}$. The problem of determining the maximum size of t-intersecting families goes back to Erdős, Ko, and Rado [66] who proved the following theorem.

Theorem: Suppose that $\mathfrak{B}$ is a t-intersecting family with $v \geq v_0(d, t)$. Then

$$|\mathfrak{B}| \leq \binom{v - t}{d - t}.$$

The bound is obviously best possible, since we may take $\mathfrak{B}$ to be all d-subsets containing a fixed t-element subset. The best possible value of $v_0(d, t)$ is $(d - t + 1)(t + 1)$, as was shown by Frankl [89] for $t \geq 15$, and then by Wilson [225] for all t. The eigenvalues of the adjacency matrices D_i are a little difficult to work with, and Wilson used instead the matrices $S(j)$, with rows and columns indexed by d-sets, and where the (A, C) entry counts j-subset B for which $A \cap B = \emptyset$ and $B \subseteq C$. Thus $S(j)$ is a linear combination of $D_d, \cdots, D_{d-j}$ and the eigenvalues turn out to be

$$\lambda(i, j) = (-1)^i \binom{d - i}{j - i} \binom{v - j - i}{d - i}'$$

with multiplicity $\binom{v}{i} - \binom{v}{i-1}$. It is interesting to note that when $t = 1$, it is easy to prove the Erdős–Ko–Rado theorem using this algebraic framework. An intersecting family determines a principal submatrix of $B(0) = D_d$ that is identically zero, and the size of this submatrix is bounded above by $\binom{v}{d} - \max(l_+, l_-)$, where $l_+(l_-)$ is the number of positive

(negative) eigenvalues. We obtain

$$|\mathfrak{B}| \leq \binom{v}{d}$$
$$- \left[\binom{v}{d} - \binom{v}{d-1} + \binom{v}{d-2} - \binom{v}{d-3} + \cdots \right]$$
$$= \binom{v}{d} - \binom{v-1}{d}$$
$$= \binom{v-1}{d-1}$$

as required. □

We now consider 2-designs in greater detail. If b denotes the number of blocks, and if r denotes the number of blocks containing a given point, then the identities

$$bk = vr \quad \text{and} \quad r(k - 1) = (v - 1)\lambda$$

restrict the possible parameter sets. These identities are trivial in that they are obtained by elementary counting arguments. It is natural to impose the restriction $k < v$, and in this case we have Fisher's inequality $b \geq v$. Designs with $b = v$ are called symmetric designs. In a symmetric design there is just one intersection number; two distinct blocks always intersect in λ points. Conversely, it is easily shown that a 2-design with one intersection number is a symmetric design. The Bruck–Ryser–Chowla theorem provides a nontrivial restriction on the parameter sets of symmetric designs. Here "nontrivial" means an algebraic condition that is not a consequence of simple counting arguments. The Bruck–Ryser–Chowla theorem also provides a connection between the theory of designs and the algebraic theory of error-correcting codes. The row space of the incidence matrix of a symmetric design determines a self-dual code with respect to some nondegenerate scalar product. The restrictions provided by the theorem are necessary conditions for the existence of these self-dual codes (see Lander [128], Blokhuis and Calderbank [18]).

B. Algebraic Coding Theory and the Hamming Scheme

The Hamming scheme $H(N, q)$ is an association scheme with N classes. The point set X is $\mathbb{F}_q^N$, and a pair of vectors $\{x, y\}$ is in class Γ_i if the Hamming distance $D(x, y) = i$. The adjacency matrices D_i of the graph $(\mathbb{F}_q^N, \Gamma_i)$ generate the Bose–Mesner algebra of the scheme, and there is a second basis $J_0, \cdots, J_N$ of mutually orthogonal idempotent matrices. The two bases are related by

$$D_l = \sum_{i=0}^{N} K_l(i) J_i$$

$$q^N J_l = \sum_{i=0}^{N} K_l(i) D_i,$$

where

$$K_l(z) = \sum_{j=0}^{l} (-1)^j (q - 1)^{l-j} \binom{z}{j} \binom{n - z}{l - j}$$

is the lth Krawtchouk polynomial. Recall that $K_l(z)$ is the coefficient of λ^l in

$$(1 - \lambda)^x (1 + (q-1)\lambda)^{N-x}.$$

In this association scheme, the eigenmatrix P and the dual eigenmatrix Q are identical.

The inner distribution $a = (a_0, \cdots, a_N)$ of a code C is called the *distance distribution*, and the entry a_i is the average number of codewords at distance i from a given codeword. If C is linear then a is simply the weight distribution. The dual distribution $b = (b_0, \cdots, b_N)$ is given by $aQ = |C|b$ which we expand as

$$b_l = \frac{1}{|C|} \sum_{i=0}^{N} a_i K_l(i), \qquad l = 0, 1, \cdots, N.$$

For linear codes C we recognize these equations as the MacWilliams Identities [146], [147] that relate the weight enumerator of a linear code to that of the dual code $C^\perp$. A little rearrangement gives

$$|C^\perp| \sum_{x \in C^\perp} \lambda^{\mathrm{wt}(x)} = \sum_i \sum_l a_i K_l(i) \lambda^l$$
$$= \sum_i a_i (1-\lambda)^i (1 + (q-1)\lambda)^{N-i}$$

which is the single variable form of the MacWilliams Identities. It is sometimes more convenient to associate to a linear code C a weight enumerator in two variables. Then

$$W_C(x, y) = \sum_{c \in C} x^{N - \mathrm{wt}(c)} y^{\mathrm{wt}(c)}$$

and the MacWilliams Identities take the form

$$W_{C^\perp}(x, y) = \frac{1}{|C|} W_C(x + (q-1)y, x - y).$$

There are several families of nonlinear codes that have more codewords than any comparable linear code presently known. These are the Nordstrom–Robinson, Kerdock, Preparata, Goethals, and Delsarte–Goethals codes [52], [98], [99], [122], [164], and [174]. Aside from their excellent error-correcting capabilities, these pairs of codes (Kerdock/Preparata and Goethals/Delsarte–Goethals) are remarkable in the sense that although these codes are nonlinear, the weight distribution of one is the MacWilliams transform of the weight distribution of the other code in the pair. Hammons *et al.* [108] provide an algebraic explanation by showing that there is a natural definition of Kerdock and Preparata codes as linear codes over $\mathbb{Z}_4$, and that as $\mathbb{Z}_4$ codes they are duals. The mystery of the weight distributions is resolved by observing that $(\mathbb{Z}_4^N$, Lee distance) and $(\mathbb{F}_2^{2N}$, Hamming distance) are isometric (see Subsection IV-D), and that there is an analog of the standard MacWilliams Identities for codes in the Lee metric. There are in fact a number of different association schemes and MacWilliams Identities that are useful in coding theory. Delsarte and Levenshtein [55] mention five, including the association scheme relative to the split-weight enumerator.

There is a great deal of interesting mathematics associated with self-dual codes. The weight enumerator $W_C(x, y)$ of a binary self-dual code C with all weights divisible by 4 is invariant under the transformations

$$\begin{pmatrix} x \\ y \end{pmatrix} \rightarrow \frac{1}{\sqrt{2}} \begin{pmatrix} 1 & 1 \\ 1 & -1 \end{pmatrix} \begin{pmatrix} x \\ y \end{pmatrix}$$

and

$$\begin{pmatrix} x \\ y \end{pmatrix} \rightarrow \begin{pmatrix} 1 & 0 \\ 0 & i \end{pmatrix} \begin{pmatrix} x \\ y \end{pmatrix}.$$

These transformations generate a group containing 192 matrices, and Gleason [97] used a nineteenth century technique called invariant theory to prove that $W_C(x, y)$ is a polynomial in the weight enumerators of the $[8, 4, 4]$ Hamming and $[24, 12, 8]$ Golay codes. An immediate corollary is that the blocklength N is divisible by 8. More details and generalizations can be found in a very nice survey by Sloane [201]. There is also a very fruitful connection between self-dual binary codes with all weights divisible by 4 and even unimodular lattices. In fact, there are parallel theorems giving upper and lower bounds on the best codes and lattices, and parallel characterizations of the weight enumerator of the code and the theta series of the lattice (see [44, Ch. 7]).

The most important theorem relating codes and designs is the Assmus–Mattson theorem. The statement of this theorem given below differs from the statement given elsewhere (for example, in Assmus and Mattson [2] or MacWilliams and Sloane [148]) where the conclusion applies only to codewords of sufficiently low weight. This restriction is to exclude designs with repeated blocks. Since we mean to allow t-designs with repeated blocks, we may drop the extra restriction.

Theorem (Assmus–Mattson): Let C be a linear $[v, k, d]$ code over $\mathbb{F}_q$, where the weights of the nonzero codewords are $w_1 = d, w_2, \cdots, w_s$. Let $d', w_2', \cdots, w_{s'}'$ be the nonzero weights in $C^\perp$. Let t be the greatest integer in the range $0 < t < d$, such that there are at most $d - t$ weights w_i' with $0 < w_i' \leq v - t$. Then the codewords of any weight w_i in C form a t-design.

The theorem is proved using the MacWilliams Identities. We puncture the code by deleting coordinates $p_1, \cdots, p_t$ to obtain a code $\hat{C}$. The code $\hat{C}^\perp$ is obtained by taking codewords c in $C^\perp$ with $c_{p_1} = c_{p_2} = \cdots = c_{p_t} = 0$ and deleting these coordinates. The MacWilliams Identities allow us to solve for the weight distribution of $\hat{C}$ and the solution is independent of the choice of $p_1, \cdots, p_t$.

Delsarte [49] identified four fundamental properties of a code or more generally, a subset of an association scheme:

- the *minimum distance* d;
- the *degree* s, which is the number of nonzero entries a_i in the inner distribution, not counting $a_0 = 1$;
- the *dual distance* d', which is the index i of the first nonzero entry b_i in the dual distribution, not counting $b_0 = 1$;
- the *dual degree* s' (sometimes called the *external distance*), which is the number of nonzero entries b_i in the dual distribution, not counting $b_0 = 1$.

There is also the (maximum) strength t which is $d' - 1$. In the Johnson scheme, a subset of strength t is a t-design.

The combinatorial significance of the external distance s' is understood through the characteristic polynomial of a code C, which is given by

$$\alpha(\xi) = \frac{q^N}{|C|} \prod_{\substack{1 \leq i \leq N \\ b_i \neq 0}} \left(1 - \frac{\xi}{i}\right).$$

We expand the shifted polynomials $\xi^m \alpha(\xi)$ in terms of Krawtchouk polynomials

$$\xi^m \alpha(\xi) = \sum_{i=0}^{s'+m} \alpha_i^m K_i(\xi).$$

Now, given a vector $z \in \mathbb{F}_q^N$, let $\beta_i(z)$ be the number of codewords $c \in C$ for which $D(c, z) = i$. Delsarte [48] proved

$$\sum_{i=0}^{s'+m} \alpha_i^m \beta_i(z) = \begin{cases} 1, & \text{if } m = 0 \\ 0, & \text{otherwise.} \end{cases}$$

Taking $m = 0$, we see that the covering radius of C is bounded above by the external distance.

If the minimum distance d is greater than the external distance s', then the coefficients $\alpha_0^0 = \alpha_1^0 = \cdots = \alpha_{d-s'-1}^0 = 1$. For $i < d - s'$, this is proved by choosing $x \in \mathbb{F} - q^N$ at distance i from some $c \in C$. Then by the triangle inequality, every other $c' \in C$ is at distance greater than s' from x. Since $\mathfrak{B}_i(x) = 1$, and $\mathfrak{B}_j(x) = 0$ for $j \leq s'$, $j \neq i$ we have $\alpha_i = 1$. This leads to the famous characterization of perfect codes mentioned in Section II.

Theorem: Let C be a code with minimum distance d and external distance s', and let $e = \lfloor (d-1)/2 \rfloor$. Then

$$\sum_{i=0}^{e} \binom{N}{i}(q-1)^i \leq \frac{q^N}{|C|} \leq \sum_{i=0}^{s'} \binom{N}{i}(q-1)^i.$$

If one of the bounds is attained, then so is the other, the code is perfect, and its characteristic polynomial is

$$\psi_e(z) = \sum_{l=0}^{e} K_l(z).$$

This result is named for Lloyd who obtained the theorem for $q = 2$ by analytic methods prior to the discovery of the MacWilliams Identities. For comparison, the characteristic polynomial of a uniformly packed code is

$$\sum_{l=0}^{e-1} K_l(z) + (1 - \lambda/\mu)K_e(z) + 1/\mu K_{e+1}(z).$$

The problem of finding good upper bounds on the size of a code with minimum distance d can be expressed as a linear program. We treat the entries a_i of the inner distribution as real variables, and we look to maximize the sum $\sum_{i=0}^{N} a_i$ under the linear constraints

$$a_0 = 1, \; a_i = 0, \qquad \text{for } i = 1, \cdots, d-1$$
$$a_i \geq 0, \qquad \text{for } i = d, \cdots, N$$

$$\sum_{i=0}^{N} a_i K_l(i) \geq 0, \qquad \text{for } l = 1, \cdots, N.$$

It has in fact proved more convenient to attack the dual minimization problem. Here we look for a polynomial $F(z)$ of degree at most N, where the coefficient f_k in the Krawtchouk expansion

$$F(z) = \sum_{l=0}^{N} f_l K_l(z)$$

are nonnegative, where $f_0 > 0$, and where $F(i) \leq 0$ for $i = d, \cdots, N$. The size of any code with minimum distance d is bounded above by $F(0)/f_0$. The McEliece, Rodemich, Rumsey, Welch (MMRW) bound [156] results from polynomials

$$F(z) = \frac{1}{c-z}(K_t(c)K_{t+1}(z) - K_{t+1}(c)K_t(z))^2$$

where $1 \leq t \leq \lfloor (N-1)/2 \rfloor$, and c is an appropriately chosen real number. For binary codes the rate R satisfies

$$R \leq H_2\left(1/2 - \sqrt{\left[\frac{d}{N}\left(1 - \frac{d}{N}\right)\right]}\right)(1 + o(N)).$$

Strengthening the dual problem by requiring $F(x) \leq 0$ for $d \leq x \leq N$ gives a new problem where the minimizing polynomial can be found explicitly [136], [194]. However, the asymptotics of the solution coincide with the MRRW bound.

A second application of linear programming is to bounding zero-error capacity of a discrete memoryless channel, a concept introduced by Shannon [188] in 1956. Here the input alphabet becomes the vertex set of a graph, and two vertices are joined if the action of noise cannot result in the corresponding symbols being confused at the output of the channel. The problem of determining the zero-error capacity of the pentagon remained unsolved for some 20 years until the linear programming solution by Lovász [144].

The combinatorial significance of the dual distance d' is understood in terms of variation in the inner distribution of translates of C. For example, a code C is said to be *distance-invariant* if the number of codewords at distance i from a given codeword depends only on i and not on the codeword chosen. Linear codes are distance-invariant, as are the binary images of linear codes over $\mathbb{Z}_4$ after applying the Gray map (for example, the Kerdock and Preparata codes). Delsarte [48] proved that a sufficient condition for distance invariance is that the degree s is at most the dual distance d'. The argument rests on degrees of freedom in the MacWilliams transform. If $d' \geq s$ then there is no variance in the distance distribution of translates $C + x$ where $D(x, C) \leq d' - s$ is constant (for details see [55] or [38]).

We have seen how the dual degree s' and the minimum distance d can be used to provide upper bounds on the size of codes. We now describe how the degree s and the dual distance d' can be used to provide lower bounds on the size of designs. Given a subset Y of $\mathbb{F}_q^N$, we form the array where the rows are the words in Y. The subset Y is an *orthogonal array of strength t and index λ* if, in each t-tuple of distinct columns of the array, all t-tuples of symbols appear exactly λ

times. Clearly, $|Y| = \lambda q^t$. This what it means to be a design in the Hamming scheme. The two notions of strength coincide, and this is evident when Y is linear.

The counterpart to the characteristic polynomial is the *annihilator polynomial* given by

$$\gamma(\xi) = |Y| \prod_{\substack{1 \le i \le N \\ a_i \ne 0}} \left(1 - \frac{\xi}{i}\right)$$

which we expand in terms of Krawtchouk polynomials

$$\gamma(\xi) = \sum_{l=0}^{s} \gamma_l K_l(\xi).$$

If the maximum strength t is at least the degree s, then the coefficients $\gamma_0 = \cdots = \gamma_{t-s} = 1$. The counterpart of the previous theorem is the following.

Theorem: Let Y be a design with degree s and maximum strength t, and let $f = \lfloor t/2 \rfloor$. Then

$$\sum_{i=0}^{f} \binom{N}{i}(q-1)^i \le |Y| \le \sum_{i=0}^{s} \binom{N}{i}(q-1)^i.$$

If one of the bounds is attained, then so is the other, the design is called *tight* and the annihilator polynomial is

$$\psi_f(z) = \sum_{l=0}^{f} K_l(z).$$

This is the Rao bound [176] for orthogonal arrays of strength t. The corresponding theorem in the Johnson scheme is the Ray–Chaudhuri/Wilson bound for tight designs [178] ($2s$-designs with s different block intersection sizes). For $s > 1$ the only known example is the set of minimum-weight codewords in the perfect binary Golay code.

C. Spherical Codes and Spherical Designs

We begin in real Euclidean space with a mathematical criterion that measures how well a sphere is approximated by a finite point set. Let $\Omega = \{P_1, \cdots, P_M\}$ be a set of M points on the unit sphere

$$S^{N-1} = \{x = (x_1, \cdots, x_N) \in \mathbb{R}^N \mid x \cdot x = 1\}.$$

Then Ω is a *spherical t-design* if the identity

$$\int_{\Omega_d} f(x) d\mu(x) = \frac{1}{M} \sum_{i=1}^{N} f(P_i)$$

(where μ is uniform measure on S^{N-1} normalized to have total measure 1) holds for all polynomials f of degree $\le t$.

For example, a soccer ball is a truncated icosahedron rather than a perfect sphere, and the 60 vertices of the soccer ball form a spherical 5-design. Goethals and Seidel [100] improved upon the standard soccer ball by slightly perturbing the vertices so as to produce a spherical 9-design. This is a very particular spherical design. Seymour and Zaslavsky [186] proved that for any positive integers N and t, and for all sufficiently large M, there exist spherical t-designs of size M in $\mathbb{R}^N$. This result is a remarkable generalization of the mean value theorem and is not constructive.

There are strong structural similarities between the Euclidean sphere S^{N-1} and the Hamming and Johnson schemes. All are *distance-transitive* in the sense that given points x, y, x', y' the distances $D(x,y)$, $D(x',y')$ are equal if and only if there is an isometry g for which $x^g = x'$ and $y^g = y'$. For the Euclidean sphere, isometries are simply orthogonal transformations. Delsarte, Goethals, and Seidel [54] showed that the earlier method of deriving lower bounds on designs remains valid, though the particular orthogonal polynomials are different. Also see [55] for more details.

Delsarte, Goethals, and Seidel [53] also derived upper bounds on the cardinality of sets of lines having prescribed angles both in $\mathbb{R}^N$ and $\mathbb{C}^N$. The inner products between unit vectors in the different lines determine the inner distribution of these spherical codes. Given a spherical code Ω let $A = \{|(a,b)|^2 \mid a \ne b \in \Omega\}$. For $s \in \{0, 1\}$ and integers $k \ge 0$, the Jacobi polynomial $Q_{k,s}(x)$ in the real variable x is defined by a three-term recursion that depends on the choice of field.

Theorem [53]: For any $\epsilon > 0$, let $F(x)$ be a polynomial satisfying $\alpha^s F(\alpha) \le 0$ for all $\alpha \in A$, $f_{k,\epsilon} \ge 0$ for all $k \ge 1$, and $f_{0,\epsilon} > 0$, where $f_{k,s}$ is the coefficient of $Q_{k,s}$ in the Jacobi expansion of $F(x)$. Then

$$|\Omega| \le F(1)/f_{0,\epsilon}.$$

This theorem provides upper bounds on the size of families of sequences with favorable correlation properties that are used in spread-spectrum communication. For instance, there is an interesting example involving Kerdock codes. Cameron and Seidel [37] used quadratic forms on $\mathbb{Z}_2^{m+1}$ to construct a family of lines through the origin of $\mathbb{R}^N$, where $N = 2^{m+1}$, such that any two lines are perpendicular or at an angle θ where $\cos \theta = 1/\sqrt{N}$. These line sets are the union of $N/2$ frames corresponding to cosets of the first-order Reed–Muller code in the Kerdock code. König [126] and Levenshtein [135] observed that adding the standard coordinate frame did not increase the set of prescribed angles, and that the augmented system of lines met an upper bound derived from the above theorem. The $\mathbb{Z}_4$-linear Kerdock code determines an extremal system of lines in complex space (see [23]).

D. From Cyclic Codes to Algebraic-Geometry Codes

We take the perspective of frequency-domain techniques particular to finite fields. The notions of time and frequency domain for codes defined over finite fields, and the idea of using constraints in the frequency domain to separate codewords in the time domain are of fundamental importance. This is the foundation for the Reed–Solomon codes that are found everywhere today, from computer disk drives to CD players.

The early theory of cyclic codes was greatly influenced by a series of reports written mostly by Assmus, Mattson, and Turyn in the 1960's and early 1970's. They were much quoted and used extensively by van Lint [139] in his first book on coding theory. These reports were much influenced by the monthly meetings on coding theory held first at Hanscom Field then at Sylvania involving Assmus, Gleason, Mattson, Pierce, Pless, Prange, Turyn, and the occasional distinguished visitor.

We begin by observing that the binary $[2^m-1, 2^m-m-1, 3]$ Hamming code may be defined as the collection of binary vectors $(a_0, a_1, \cdots, a_{2^m-2})$ that satisfy

$$\sum_{i=0}^{2^m-2} a_i \alpha^i = 0$$

where α is a primitive (2^m-1)th root of unity in the extension field $\mathbb{F}_{2^m}$. (Recall that the Hamming code is the unique binary $[2^m-1, 2^m-m-1, 3]$ code, and the new definition certainly determines a code with these parameters.) We may think of the matrix

$$[1, \alpha, \alpha^2, \cdots, \alpha^{2^m-2}]$$

as a parity-check matrix for this Hamming code and increase minimum distance by adding a second spectral constraint:

$$\begin{bmatrix} 1 & \alpha & \alpha^2 & \cdots & \alpha^{2^m-2} \\ 1 & \alpha^3 & \alpha^6 & \cdots & \alpha^{3(2^m-2)} \end{bmatrix}.$$

This is the parity-check matrix for the two-error-correcting BCH code. More generally we may define a *BCH code with designed distance* d by means of the parity-check matrix

$$H = \begin{bmatrix} 1 & \alpha & \alpha^2 & \cdots & \alpha^{2^m-2} \\ 1 & \alpha^2 & \alpha^4 & \cdots & \alpha^{2(2^m-2)} \\ 1 & \alpha^3 & \alpha^6 & \cdots & \alpha^{3(2^m-2)} \\ \vdots & \vdots & \vdots & & \vdots \\ 1 & \alpha^{d-2} & \alpha^{2(d-2)} & \cdots & \alpha^{(d-2)(2^m-2)} \end{bmatrix}.$$

Note that the rows of H are not linearly independent: some spectral constraints are inferred by others: for example, $\sum_{i=0}^{2^m-2} a_i \alpha^i = 0$ implies $\sum_{i=0}^{2^m-2} a_i \alpha^{2i} = 0$. The assertion that the minimum distance is at least d amounts to proving that every set of $d-1$ columns is linearly independent. This is a Vandermonde argument.

The Hamming code and the BCH codes with designed distance d are examples of cyclic codes. These codes play an important role in coding practice, and are good in the sense that there are cyclic codes that meet the Gilbert–Varshamov bound. A linear code is *cyclic* if the set of codewords is fixed by a cyclic shift of the coordinates: if $(c_0, \cdots, c_{N-1})$ is a codeword, then so is $(c_{N-1}, c_0, \cdots, c_{N-2})$. To verify that the above codes are indeed cyclic, we apply the identity

$$\alpha^\ell \sum_{i=0}^{2^m-2} a_i \alpha^{\ell i} = \sum_{i=0}^{2^m-2} a_{i+1} \alpha^{\ell i}$$

where subscripts are read modulo 2^m-1. The theory of cyclic codes identifies the sequence $(a_0, a_1, \cdots, a_{N-1})$ with the polynomial $a_0 + a_1 x + \cdots + a_{N-1} x^{N-1}$. Cyclic codes then correspond to ideals in the residue class ring $\mathbb{F}_2[x]/(x^N-1)$, and the structure theory of principal ideal rings can be brought to bear. It is also possible to approach cyclic codes through a discrete analog of the Fourier transform called the *Mattson–Solomon polynomial* [154]. The vector

$$a(x) = a_0 + a_1 x + \cdots + a_{N-1} x^{N-1}$$

is represented by the polynomial $A(x) = \sum_{j=1}^{N} A_j X^N$ where

$$A_j = a(\alpha^j) = \sum_{i=0}^{N-1} a_i \alpha^{ij}.$$

The BCH code with designed distance $d = 2\delta$ is then the set of all vectors a for which $A_1 = A_2 = \cdots = A_{\delta-1} = 0$. VLSI implementation of Reed–Solomon decoding has inspired a great deal of creativity regarding effective computation in finite fields, for example Berlekamp's bit-serial multiplication circuits. For an introduction to this area see McEliece [155], and note the dedication to Solomon.

1) Cyclic Codes Obtained by Hensel Lifting: A binary cyclic code C is generated by a divisor $g_2(x)$ of x^N-1 in $\mathbb{F}_2[x]$. Hensel's Lemma allows us to refine a factorization $x^N - 1 = g_2(x)h_x(x)$ modulo 2, to a factorization $x^N - 1 = g_{2^a}(x)h_{2^a}(x)$ modulo 2^a, and to a factorization $x^N - 1 = g(x)h(x)$ over the 2-adic integers. The polynomial $g_{2^a}(x)$ generates a cyclic code C_{2^a} over the ring of integers $\mathbb{Z}_{2^a}$, and the polynomial $g(x)$ generates a cyclic code C_∞ over the 2-adic integers. The codes over $\mathbb{Z}_{2^a}$ can also be described in terms of parity checks involving Galois rings, and this is completely analogous to the construction of binary cyclic codes through parity checks involving finite fields.

A very striking theorem of McEliece (generalized to Abelian codes in [56]) characterizes the possible Hamming weights that can appear in a binary cyclic code C in terms of l, the smallest number such that l nonzeros of C (roots of $h_2(x)$) have product 1. The characterization is that all Hamming weights are divisible by 2^{l-1}, and there is a weight not divisible by 2^l. Though this theorem has been generalized to cyclic codes obtained by Hensel lifting [28] there remains the possibility of using the codes C_{2^a}, C_∞ to infer additional properties of C. We might, for example, hope to resolve the deceptively innocent question of given two m-sequences, whether or not -1 must appear as a crosscorrelation value.

A special case of particular interest is cyclic codes over $\mathbb{Z}_4$ that are obtained from binary cyclic codes by means of a single Hensel lift. It will be of interest to characterize the possible Lee weights that can appear in this cyclic code. Recall the the *Lee weights* of the elements $0, 1, 2, 3$ of $\mathbb{Z}_4$ are, respectively, $0, 1, 2, 1$ and that the Lee weight of a vector in $\mathbb{Z}_4^N$ is just the rational sum of the Lee weights of its components. This weight function defines the *Lee metric* on $\mathbb{Z}_4^N$. If we imagine $0, 1, 2, 3$ as labeling (clockwise) four equally spaced points on a circle, then Lee distance is distance around this circle. The Lee metric is important because there is a natural isometry from $(\mathbb{Z}_4^N$, Lee Metric) to $(\mathbb{F}_2^{2N}$, Hamming Metric) called the Gray map. This map ϕ is defined from $\mathbb{Z}_4$ to $\mathbb{Z}_2$ by

$$\phi(0) = (00) \quad \phi(1) = (01) \quad \phi(2) = (11) \quad \phi(3) = (10)$$

and is extended in the obvious way to a map ϕ from $\mathbb{Z}_4^N$ to $\mathbb{F}_2^{2N}$. It is evidently distance preserving. Hammons *et al.* [108] proved that the Gray image of the Hensel lift of the first-order Reed–Muller code RM$(1, m)$ is the Kerdock code [122]. The Gray image of the Hensel lift of the extended Hamming code differs slightly from the standard Preparata code [174], but shares the same distance structure. The Kerdock, Preparata, and Delsarte–Goethals codes are nonlinear binary codes, defined via quadratic forms, that contain more codewords than any linear code presently known. What remains mysterious is how to construct efficient linear codes over $\mathbb{Z}_4$ that correct more than three errors by specifying parity checks involving Galois rings. We do not have any counterpart to the BCH, Hartmann–Tzeng, and Roos bounds for classical cyclic codes (for a unified approach to these bounds see [140]).

2) Algebraic-Geometry Codes: The last 20 years have seen the construction of algebraic-geometry codes that can be encoded and decoded in time polynomial in the blocklength N, and with performance that matches or exceeds the Gilbert–Varshamov bound. This was proved by Tsfasman, Vlăduţ, and Zink [211] for finite fields $\mathbb{F}_q$, where q is a square and $q \geq 49$, but this numerical restriction on q may not be essential. It was and is a spectacular result, so spectacular that it motivated many mathematicians to learn some coding theory, and many engineers to learn some algebraic geometry. The consequence has been a fascinating combination of abstract geometry and efficient computational methods that has been described in a number of excellent surveys and introductory articles, for example, [110], [204], and [16].

We begin by describing the codes proposed by Reed and Solomon [179], that are now found everywhere from computer disk drives to CD players. Even these codes did not go into use immediately because fast digital electronics did not exist in 1960. Consider the vector space

$$L_r = \{f(z) \in \mathbb{F}_q[z] \mid \deg f \leq r\}$$

of polynomials with coefficients in the field $\mathbb{F}_q$ and degree at most r. Let $\alpha_1, \cdots, \alpha_N$ be distinct elements of $\mathbb{F}_q$, and define the evaluation map

$$\mathrm{ev}\,(f) = (f(\alpha_1), \cdots, f(\alpha_N)).$$

The evaluation map is linear, and if $r < N$ it is $1 - 1$. The image of L_r is a Reed–Solomon code with dimension $r + 1$ and minimum distance $d = N - r$. Reed–Solomon codes are optimal in the sense that they meet the Singleton bound $d \leq n - k + 1$. The only drawback is that the length N is constrained by the size of the field $\mathbb{F}_q$, though this constraint can be removed by passing to general BCH codes.

The construction of Reed–Solomon codes can be generalized by allowing polynomials $f(z_1, \cdots, z_m)$ in several variables, and by evaluating these polynomials on a subset of the affine space $\mathbb{A}^m$. In general, the result will be a code with a poor tradeoff between k/N and d/N. However, the Russian mathematician Goppa [103] made the inspired suggestion of choosing the subset of $\mathbb{A}^m$ to be points on a curve. Tsfasman, Vlăduţ and Zink recognized that existence of asymptotically good codes required curves over finite fields with many rational points, hence the entrance of modular curves. Table IV juxtaposes developments in algebraic geometry codes with the corresponding theory for BCH codes.

V. The Next Fifty Years

We have chosen to highlight two very different challenges, the creation of a quantum information theory, and the devel-

opment of coding techniques for data networks in general, and wireless networks in particular.

In 1948 the main thread connecting information theory and physics was understanding the new perspective on entropy and its relation to the laws of thermodynamics. Today the main thread is quantum mechanics, as methods in information theory and computing have been extended to treat the transmission and processing of intact quantum states, and the interaction of such "quantum information" with classical information. According to Bennett and Shor [10]

> It has become clear that an information theory based on quantum principles extends and completes classical information theory, somewhat as complex numbers extend and complete the reals. The new theory includes quantum generalizations of classical notions such as sources, channels and codes, and two complementary, quantifiable kinds of information—classical information and quantum entanglement.

In this perspective we focus on the development of quantum error-correcting codes.

We then turn to 21st century communication. Fifty years from now it will be disappointing if the focus of coding theory is point-to-point communication in the presence of noise. Telecommunications will likely be dominated by packet data/voice transmitted over wide-area networks like the Internet where network management is distributed. The reliability and even the nature of individual links will be of secondary importance, and the challenge will be to understand the network as a whole and to guarantee end-to-end quality of service.

A. Quantum Error-Correcting Codes

Classical bits take the values 0 or 1 at all times, but quantum bits or qubits occupy a superposition of the 0 and 1 states. This is not to say that the qubit has some intermediate value between 0 and 1. Rather, the qubit is in both the 0 state and the 1 state at the same time to varying extents. Mathematically, a qubit is a two-dimensional Hilbert space, and a quantum state is a vector

$$\alpha|0\rangle + \beta|1\rangle, \qquad \text{where } |\alpha|^2 + |\beta|^2 = 1.$$

A collection of N different two-state memory cells is then expressed as the tensor product of the individual two-dimensional Hilbert spaces, so we are led to vectors

$$\sum_{v \in V} \alpha_v |v\rangle, \qquad \text{where } V = \mathbb{Z}_2^N \text{ and } \sum_{v \in V} |\alpha_v|^2 = 1.$$

When the qubit $\alpha|0\rangle + \beta|1\rangle$ is measured with respect to the basis $|0\rangle$, $|1\rangle$ the probability that the qubit is found in a particular state is the square of the absolute value of the corresponding amplitude. The evolution of an isolated quantum system conserves superposition and distinguishability, and is described by a unitary transformation that is linear and preserves inner products. This is the analog in Hilbert space of rigid rotation in Euclidean space.

BCH Codes	Algebraic Geometry Codes
Flexibility in choice of code (block length N not constrained by field size as with RS codes)	Flexibility regarding block length requires curves with many rational points
	Block length of codes from plane curves (e.g. Hermitian curves) bounded by $q^2 + q + 1$
[137] Performance degrades with large block length (cannot bound both d/N and k/N away from zero asymptotically)	[211] Existence of codes from modular curves with polynomial complexity that exceed the GV bound for alphabets of size $q \geq 49$
	[93] Explicit curves (from here to codes is still a lot of work)
Gorenstein-Peterson-Zierler Algorithm: Complexity $O(N^3)$	Basic Algorithm [119]: Complexity $O(N^3)$, restricted to plane curves
	Modified Algorithm [195]: Arbitrary curves
	Porter's Algorithm [171], [172]: generalization of Euclidean algorithm for decoding classical Goppa codes — equivalent to modified algorithm
[60], [169] Error locating pairs of vector spaces — common framework for decoding cyclic codes up to and beyond the BCH bound, and the Basic Algorithm	
[70] Decoding beyond the BCH designed distance	[69], [59] Decoding up to the Goppa designed distance, using majority voting to find additional syndromes for the error vector
	[61] gives a different solution
	[123], [229] Decoding Hermitian codes up to the actual distance using special properties of the affine ring of the curve
1-dimensional Berlekamp-Massey Algorithm: Complexity $O(N^2)$	[180], [181] Multidimensional generalization of the Berlekamp-Massey Algorithm with complexity $O(N^{3-2/m+1})$ for curves in $\mathbb{A}^m$
	[182] Incorporates majority voting
[205] List decoding of Reed-Solomon codes	[189] List decoding of algebraic geometry codes

The first work connecting information theory and quantum mechanics was that of Landauer and Bennett who were looking to understand the implications of Moore's Law; every two years for the past 50 years, computers have become twice as fast while components have become twice as small. As the components of computer circuits become very small, their description must be given by quantum mechanics. Over time there developed a curiosity about the power of quantum computation, until in 1994 Shor [190] found a way of exploiting quantum superposition to provide a polynomial time algorithm for factoring integers. This was the first example of an important problem that a quantum computer could solve more efficiently than a classical computer. The design of quantum algorithms for different classes of problem, for instance finding short vectors in lattices, is currently an active area of research.

The effectiveness of quantum computing is founded on coherent quantum superposition or entanglement, which allows exponentially many instances to be processed simultaneously. However, no quantum system can be perfectly isolated from the rest of the world and this interaction with the environment causes decoherence. This error process is expressed mathematically in terms of Pauli matrices. A bit error in an individual qubit corresponds to applying the Pauli matrix $\sigma_x = \left(\begin{smallmatrix} 0 & 1 \\ 1 & 0 \end{smallmatrix}\right)$ to that qubit, and a phase error to the Pauli matrix $\sigma_z = \left(\begin{smallmatrix} 1 & 0 \\ 0 & -1 \end{smallmatrix}\right)$. The third Pauli matrix, $\sigma_y = \left(\begin{smallmatrix} 0 & -i \\ i & 0 \end{smallmatrix}\right) = i\sigma_x\sigma_z$, corresponds to a combination of bit and phase errors. The group E of tensor products $\pm w_1 \otimes \cdots \otimes w_N$ and $\pm i w_1 \otimes \cdots \otimes w_N$, where each w_j is one of $I, \sigma_x, \sigma_y, \sigma_z$, describes the possible errors in N qubits. The *Error Group* E is a subgroup of the unitary group $U(2^N)$. In general, there is a continuum of possible errors in qubits, and there are errors in sets of qubits which cannot be described by a product of errors in individual qubits. For the purposes of quantum error correction, however, we need consider only the three types of errors σ_x, σ_y, and σ_z, since any error-correcting code which connects t of these errors will be able to correct arbitrary errors in t qubits [62], [9]. We do not go into the details of this result, but essentially it follows from the fact that the matrices I, σ_x, σ_y, and σ_z form a basis for the space of all 2×2 matrices, and so the tensor products of t of these errors form a basis for the space of $2^t \times 2^t$ matrices.

In classical computing one can assemble computers that are much more reliable than any of their individual components by exploiting error-correcting codes. In quantum computing this was initially thought to be precluded by the Heisenberg Uncertainty Principle (HUP) which states that observations of a quantum system, no matter how delicately performed, cannot yield complete information on the system's state before observation. For example, we cannot learn more about a single photon's polarization by amplifying it into a clone of many photons—the HUP introduces just enough randomness into the polarizations of the daughter photons to nullify any advantage gained by having more photons to measure. At first, error correction was thought to be impossible in the quantum world because the HUP prevents duplication of quantum states. This is not so—only repetition codes are eliminated. The trick is to take quantum superposition + decoherence, to measure the decoherence in a way that gives no information about the original superposition, and then to correct the measured decoherence. The first codes were discovered quite recently [191], [203], [8], [35] but there is now a beautiful group-theoretic framework for code construction [32], [105], [33].

Commutative subgroups of the error group E play a special role. The quantum error-correcting code is the subspace fixed by the commutative subgroup—hence the name *stabilizer codes*. Errors move the fixed subspace to a different eigenspace of the original commutative subgroup. This eigenspace is identified by a process similar to that of calculating a syndrome in the classical world. Note that syndrome decoding identifies the coset of a linear code containing the received vector, and not an error pattern. However, given the coset, there is a coset leader that gives the most probable error pattern. Likewise, in the quantum world there is an error that is most probable given the eigenspace that has been identified.

The error group in classical theory is the subgroup B of bit errors. It is possible to describe classical linear codes as the fixed spaces of commutative subgroups of B, so the new framework is a graceful extension of the classical theory. Recent developments in quantum coding theory include a quantum analog of the MacWilliams Identities in classical coding theory [192].

B. The Changing Nature of Data Network Traffic

Today we lack fundamental understanding of network data traffic, and we need to replace network engineering methods developed for voice traffic. Information theory and coding may have an important role to play, but the first step must be to develop channel models through active and passive network measurement, that capture the interaction of applications, protocols, and end-to-end congestion control mechanisms.

A. K. Erlang (1878–1929) was the first person to study call blocking in telephone networks. By taking measurements in a small village telephone exchange he worked out a formula, now known as Erlang's formula, that expresses the fraction of callers that must wait because all lines are in use. Ever since Erlang, the nature of voice telephone traffic—exponentially distributed interarrival and holding times—has remained unchanged. However, Erlang did not anticipate fax, nor could he imagine the emergence of data networks where computers talk rather than humans. For voice networks the only statistic that matters is the mean traffic rate. By contrast, data traffic is extremely bursty and looks the same when viewed over a range of different time scales. More precisely, aggregate packet-level network traffic exhibits fractal-like scaling behavior over time scales on the order of a few hundred milliseconds and larger, if and only if the durations (in second) or sizes (in bytes) of the individual sessions or connections that generate the aggregate traffic have a heavy-tailed distribution with infinite variance. The self-similar nature of data network traffic was an empirical discovery made by Leland, Taqqu, Willinger, and Wilson [133] from extensive measurements on different local-area networks. The fact that heavy tails are found everywhere from sizes of files in a file system to bursts and idle periods of individual Ethernet connections, leads to self-similarity at the packet level across local- and wide-area networks (see [224] or [223] for a popular article). Above a certain time scale there are no surprises in voice traffic since everything reduces to the long-term arrival rate. For data traffic, significant variation on quite coarse time scales means that routers require large buffers, that safe operating points have to be set very conservatively, and that overall network performance is no longer a guarantee of individual quality of service. Absent new insights from coding and information theory, these variations are likely to be magnified on wireless channels by the rapidly changing nature of fading and interference.

The flow of packets at the different layers in the TCP/IP hierarchy is determined by Internet protocols and end-to-end congestion control mechanisms. The impact of the network on traffic shows up on small time scales, from a few hundred milliseconds and downwards. Feldmann, Gilbert, and Willinger [68] have proposed cascades (or multiplicative processes) as an explanation for the more complex (multifractal rather than monofractal) scaling behavior exhibited by measured TCP/IP and ATM wide-area network traffic. The thought is that cascades allow refinement of self-similarity (monofractal scaling) to account for local irregularities in WAN traffic that might be associated with networking mechanisms such as TCP flow control that operate on small time scales. Fig. 10 is taken from [68] and it compares local scaling behavior of exactly self-similar traffic with that of measured WAN traffic. This author would suggest that particularly on wireless channels, we need to change the metrics we use to evaluate systems, de-emphasizing long-term average packet loss statistics, and augmenting throughput with appropriate measures of delay.

C. It is Dangerous to Put Limits on Wireless

The heading is a quotation of Marconi from 1932. Fig. 11 superimposes research issues in wireless communication on

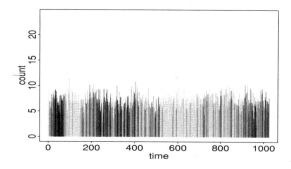

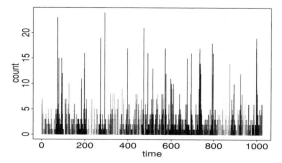

Fig. 10. Local scaling analysis of packet-level data traffic; different shades of gray indicate different magnitudes of the local scaling exponents at the different point in the traffic trace (black for small scaling exponents or "bursty" instants, light for large scaling exponents or "lull" periods). From top to bottom: (exactly) self-similar traffic, and WAN trace at the 1-ms time scale. The latter trace was gathered from an FDDI ring (with typical utilization levels of 5–10%) that connects about 420 modems to the Internet. It was collected between 22:00 and 23:00, July 22, 1997 and contains modem user as well as nonmodem user traffic totalling 8 910 014 packets.

a plot that displays the increasing size of the U.S. cellular market. Unlike the Gaussian channel, the wireless channel suffers from attenuation due to destructive addition of multipaths in the propagation media and due to interference from other users. Severe attenuation makes it impossible to determine the transmitted signal unless some less-attenuated replica of the transmitted signal is provided to the receiver. This resource is called *diversity* and it is the single most important contributor to reliable wireless communications. Examples of diversity techniques are (but are not restricted to) as follows.

- *Temporal Diversity:* Channel coding in connection with time interleaving is used. Thus replicas of the transmitted signal are provided to the receiver in the form of redundancy in temporal domain.

- *Frequency Diversity:* The fact that waves transmitted on different frequencies induce different multipath structure in the propagation media is exploited. Thus replicas of the transmitted signal are provided to the receiver in the form of redundancy in the frequency domain.

- *Antenna Diversity:* Spatially separated or differently polarized antennas are used. Replicas of the transmitted signal are provided to the receiver in the form of redundancy in spatial domain. This can be provided with no penalty in bandwidth efficiency.

When possible, cellular systems should be designed to encompass all forms of diversity to ensure adequate performance. For instance, cellular systems typically use channel coding

in combination with time interleaving to obtain some form of temporal diversity [206]. In TDMA systems, frequency diversity is obtained using a nonlinear equalizer [4] when multipath delays are a significant fraction of symbol interval. In DS-CDMA, RAKE receivers are used to obtain frequency diversity, and more general two-dimensional RAKE structures have been proposed [159] that exploit temporal and spatial structure in the received multipath signal. Antenna diversity is typically used in the uplink (mobile-to-base) direction to provide link margin and cochannel interference suppression. This is necessary to compensate for the low-power transmission from mobiles [96]. The focus here will be narrowband 30-kHz TDMA (IS-136) channels, specifically the design of channel codes for improving the data rate and/or the reliability of communications over fading channels using multiple transmit and receive antennas. Information-theoretic aspects of transmit diversity were addressed by Telatar [210] and by Foschini and Gans [88]. They derived the outage capacity curves shown in Fig. 12 under the assumption that fading is quasistatic, that is constant over a long period of time and then changing in an independent manner. Recall that 10% outage capacity is the transmission rate that can be achieved 90% of the time. With only two antennas at both the base station and the mobile there is the potential to increase the achievable data rate by a factor of 6.

Transmit diversity schemes use linear processing at the transmitter to spread the information across the antennas. At the receiver, the demodulator computes a decision statistic based on the received signals arriving at each receive antenna $1 \leq j \leq m$. The signal d_t^j received by antenna j at time t is given by

$$d_t^j = \sum_{i=1}^{n} \alpha_{i,j} c_t^i \sqrt{E_s} + \eta_t^j$$

where the noise η_t^j at time t is modeled as independent samples of a zero-mean complex Gaussian random variable with variance $N_0/2$ per dimension. The coefficient $\alpha_{i,j}$ is the path gain from transmit antenna i to receive antenna j. It is assumed that these path gains are constant during a frame and vary from one frame to another (quasistatic flat fading). Feedforward information (the path gains α_{ij}) is required to estimate the channel from the transmitter to the receiver. The first scheme of this type was proposed by Wittneben [226] and it includes the delay diversity schemes of Seshadri and Winters [185] as a special case. In delay diversity there are two transmit antennas, and a signal is transmitted from the first antenna, then delayed one time slot, and transmitted from the second antenna ($c_t^2 = c_{t-1}^1$). It has been shown by Wittneben that delay diversity schemes are optimal in providing diversity in the sense that the diversity advantage experienced by an optimal receiver is equal to the number of transmit antennas. There is, however, no "coding gain." For wireless systems employing small numbers of antennas, the space–time codes constructed by Tarokh, Seshadri, and Calderbank [209] provide both coding gain and diversity, and using only a 64-state decoder come within 2–3 dB of outage capacity. The general problem of combined coding and

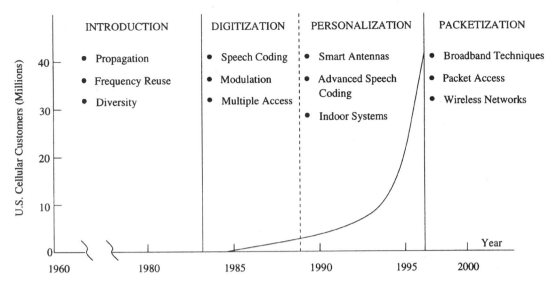

Fig. 11. Progress in wireless communications.

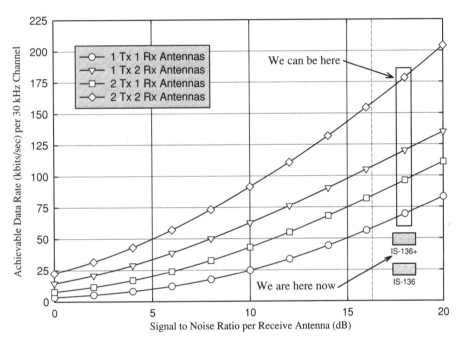

Fig. 12. Achievable data rates with multiple antennas at 10% outage capacity.

modulation for multi-input (multiple transmit antennas) multi-output (multiple receive antennas) fading channels is a new research area with great potential.

D. Interference Suppression

The challenge in designing cellular radio networks is to satisfy large demand with limited bandwidth. Limits on the available radio spectrum means that cochannel interference is inevitable when a cellular radio network is operating near capacity. The standard solution is to treat cochannel interference as Gaussian noise, and to employ powerful channel codes to mitigate its effect. This solution is far from optimal, since the decoder is using a mismatched metric. Interference is often due to a few dominant cochannel users, and this cannot be described as additive white Gaussian noise.

A second method of providing interference suppression is adaptive antenna array processing at the receiver. Here a substantial body of work by Winters and colleagues (see [96]) has shown that a receiver using N-branch spatial diversity can completely eliminate $N - 1$ interferers using optimal linear combining.

The challenge for coding theory is to provide immunity to multiple channel impairments, in this case fading and cochannel interference. This author advocates a divide-and-conquer strategy, specifically the development of concatenated coding schemes where an inner component code might enable interference suppression, and an appropriate outer code might provide additional immunity to fading. For narrowband 30-kHz TDMA channels it is possible to design very simple space–time block codes that provide diversity gain using only

545

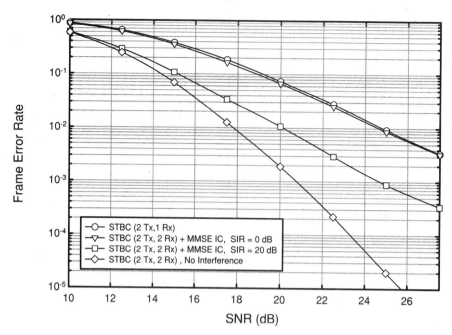

Fig. 13. Frame error rate performance of 8-PSK modulation with a space–time block code and interference suppression.

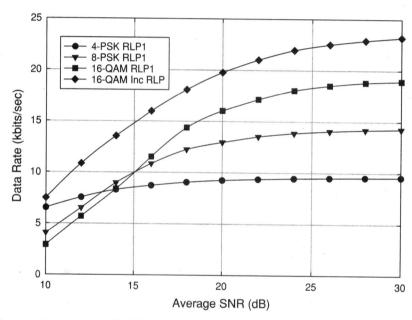

Fig. 14. Throughput of an incremental redundancy radio link protocol on a narrowband 30-kHz IS-136 channel.

transmit antennas. For example, Alamouti [1] presents the code

$$[c_1, c_2] \rightarrow \begin{bmatrix} c_1 & -c_2^* \\ c_2 & c_1^* \end{bmatrix}$$

where the signals r_1, r_2 received over two consecutive symbol periods are given by

$$\begin{pmatrix} r_1 \\ r_2^* \end{pmatrix} = \begin{pmatrix} h_1 & h_2 \\ h_2^* & -h_1^* \end{pmatrix} \begin{pmatrix} c_1 \\ c_2 \end{pmatrix} + \begin{pmatrix} n_1 \\ n_2 \end{pmatrix}.$$

Assuming that channel state information is known to the receiver, we may form

$$\begin{pmatrix} h_1^* & h_2 \\ h_2^* & -h_1 \end{pmatrix} \begin{pmatrix} r_1 \\ r_2^* \end{pmatrix} = (|h_1|^2 + |h_2|^2) \begin{pmatrix} c_1 \\ c_2 \end{pmatrix} + \begin{pmatrix} n_1' \\ n_2' \end{pmatrix}$$

where the noise vector (n_1', n_2') has zero mean and covariance $(|h_1|^2 + |h_2|^2)I_2$, and take the vector that results to a slicer. This code provides diversity gain (but no coding gain) and decoding is remarkably simple. The 2×2 matrix that describes transmission is a particularly simple example of an orthogonal design [94] and this rather arcane mathematical theory provides generalizations to more antennas.

If two antennas are available at the receiver, then Naguib and Seshadri [160] have shown that it is possible to suppress interference from a second space–time user by exploiting the special structure of the inner space–time block code. Fig. 13 shows the performance of their scheme with 8-PSK modulation. When the signal power of the interferer is equal to that of the desired signal, performance is the same as that of a system employing two transmit and one receive antenna. When there is no interference, the second antenna provides additional immunity to fading. The decoder does not require any information about the interference, and simply adapts automatically.

E. Radio Link Protocols

In wireless communication, coding theory is associated with the physical layer which lies at the bottom of the protocol stack. The next layer is radio link protocols which are designed to deliver error-free packets to the higher networking layers. The gains that come from joint optimization of the physical and radio link layers are substantial, and may well be essential to the engineering of attractive wireless data services.

A very interesting idea with great potential is that of incremental redundancy. Packets received in error are stored at the receiver, and additional parity packets are transmitted until the original packet is decoded successfully. The type of hybrid radio link protocol is extremely flexible and can be tuned to different delay/throughput characteristics by adjusting the coding strategy and packet size (see [163]). Fig. 14 shows the throughput that can be achieved on narrowband 30-kHz channels. An alternative method of increasing throughput is to measure the signal-to-noise ratio (SNR) at the receiver and adapt coding and modulation to the measured SNR. It is difficult to do this accurately (within 1 dB) in the presence of rapid fading, and changing interference. Furthermore, the SNR values that trigger changes in coding and modulation vary with mobile speed so that collection of second-order statistics is necessary. The incremental redundancy radio link protocol implicitly adapts to SNR and provides superior performance. The rise of the Internet shows the power of distributed control in communications systems, and lightweight engineering is another reason to prefer implicit adaptation to SNR over explicit measurement and adaptation to SNR. The radio link protocol described by van Nobelen [163] has been accepted as a standard for the IS-136 high-speed packet state mode, and has similar potential to improve the proposed GSM EDGE standard.

ACKNOWLEDGMENT

The author is grateful to Peter Cameron for information on Fisher and the Hamming codes, to Jim Reeds for historical detail on telegraph codebooks, to Alexander Vardy for the statistics in Table I on soft-decision decoding, and to Walter Willinger for education on data network traffic. He would also like to thank Alexander Barg, Ian Blake, Iwan Duursma, G. David Forney Jr., Jon Hall, Ayman Naguib, Colin Mallows, Nambi Seshadri, Emira Soljanin, and Vahid Tarokh for their advice on earlier drafts of the manuscript. The author takes full responsibility for the faults that remain.

REFERENCES

[1] S. Alamouti, "Space block coding: A simple transmitter diversity scheme for wireless communications," submitted to *IEEE J. Select. Areas Commun.*, 1997.

[2] E. F. Assmus Jr. and H. F. Mattson Jr., "New 5-designs," *J. Combin. Theory*, vol. 6, pp. 122–151, 1969.

[3] L. R. Bahl, J. Cocke, F. Jelinek, and J. Raviv, "Optimal decoding of linear codes for minimizing symbol error rate," *IEEE Trans. Inform. Theory*, vol. IT-20, pp. 284–287, 1974.

[4] N. Balaban and J. Salz, "Dual diversity combining and equalization in digital cellular mobile radio," *IEEE Trans. Veh. Tech.nol*, vol. 40, pp. 342–354, 1991.

[5] A. Barg, "At the dawn of the theory of codes," *Math. Intelligencer*, vol. 15, pp. 20–26, 1993.

[6] L. E. Baum and T. Petrie, "Statistical inference for probabilistic functions of finite-state Markov chains," *Ann. Math. Statist.*, vol. 37, pp. 1554–1563, 1966.

[7] S. Benedetto and G. Montorsi, "Unveiling turbo codes: Some results on parallel concatenated coding schemes," *IEEE Trans. Inform. Theory*, vol. 42, pp. 409–428, 1996.

[8] C. H. Bennett, G. Brassard, S. Popescu, B. Schumacher, J. A. Smolin, and W. K. Wootters, "Purification of noisy entanglement and faithful teleportation via noisy channels," *Phys. Rev. Lett.*, vol. 76, pp. 722–725, 1996; also LANL eprint quant-ph/9511027.

[9] C. H. Bennett, D. DiVincenzo, J. A. Smolin, and W. K. Wootters, "Mixed state entanglement and quantum error correction," *Phys. Rev. A*, vol. 54, pp. 3824–3851, 1996; also LANL eprint quant-ph/9604024.

[10] C. H. Bennett and P. W. Shor, "Quantum information theory," this issue, pp. 2724–2742.

[11] E. R. Berlekamp, *Algebraic Coding Theory.* New York: McGraw-Hill, 1968.

[12] C. Berrou, A. Glavieux, and P. Thitmajshima, "Near Shannon limit error correcting coding and decoding: Turbo codes," in *Proc. Int. Conf. Communications*, 1993, pp. 1063–1070.

[13] W. Betts, A. R. Calderbank, and R. Laroia, "Performance of nonuniform constellations on the Gaussian channel," *IEEE Trans. Inform. Theory*, vol. 40, pp. 1633–1638, 1994.

[14] R. E. Blahut, *Algebraic Methods for Signal Processing and Communications Codes.* New York: Springer-Verlag, 1991.

[15] I. F. Blake, *Algebraic Coding Theory; History and Development.* Stroudsburg, PA: Dowden, Hutchinson and Ross, 1973.

[16] I. Blake, C. Heegard, T. Høholdt, and V. K. Wei, "Algebraic-geometry codes," this issue, pp. 2596–2618.

[17] W. G. Bliss, "Circuitry for performing error correction calculations on baseband encoded data to eliminate error propagation," *IBM Tech. Discl. Bull.*, vol. 23, pp. 4633–4634, 1981.

[18] A. Blokhuis and A. R. Calderbank, "Quasisymmetric designs and the smith normal form," *Des., Codes Cryptogr.*, vol. 2, pp. 189–206, 1992.

[19] A. Bonnecaze, A. R. Calderbank, and P. Solé, "Quaternary quadratic residue codes and unimodular lattices," *IEEE Trans. Inform. Theory*, vol. 41, pp. 366–377, 1995.

[20] R. C. Bose and D. M. Mesner, "On linear associative algebras corresponding to association schemes of partially balanced designs," *Ann. Math. Statist.*, vol. 30, pp. 21–38, 1959.

[21] A. E. Brouwer, A. M. Cohen, and A. Neumaier, *Distance Regular Graphs.* Berlin, Germany: Springer-Verlag, 1989.

[22] A. R. Calderbank, "Multilevel codes and multistage decoding," *IEEE Trans Commun.*, vol. 37, pp. 222–229, 1989.

[23] A. R. Calderbank, P. J. Cameron, W. M. Kantor, and J. J. Seidel, "$\mathbb{Z}_4$-Kerdock codes, orthogonal spreads and extremal euclidean line sets," in *Proc. London Math. Soc.*, vol. 75, pp. 436–480, 1997.

[24] A. R. Calderbank and P. Delsarte, "Extending the t-design concept," *Trans. Amer. Math. Soc.*, vol. 338, pp. 941–962, 1993.

[25] A. R. Calderbank, P. Delsarte, and N. J. A. Sloane, "Strengthening of the Assmus–Mattson theorem," *IEEE Trans. Inform. Theory*, vol. 37, pp. 1261–1268, 1991.

[26] A. R. Calderbank, G. D. Forney, Jr., and A. Vardy, "Minimal tail-biting representations of the golay code and others," *IEEE Trans. Inform. Theory*, to be published.

[27] A. R. Calderbank, R. Laroia, and S. W. McLaughlin, "Partial response codes for electron trapping optical memories," *IEEE Trans. Commun.*, vol. 46, pp. 1011–1019, 1998.

[28] A. R. Calderbank, W.-C. W. Li, and B. Poonen, "A 2-adic approach to the analysis of cyclic codes," *IEEE Trans. Inform. Theory*, vol. 43, pp. 977–986, 1997.

[29] A. R. Calderbank, G. McGuire, P. V. Kumar, and T. Helleseth, "Cyclic codes over $\mathbb{Z}_4$, locator polynomials and Newton's identities," *IEEE Trans. Inform. Theory*, vol. 43, pp. 217–226, 1996.

[30] A. R. Calderbank and J. E. Mazo, "Baseband line codes via spectral factorization," *IEEE J. Select. Areas Commun.*, vol. 7, pp. 914–928, 1989.

[31] A. R. Calderbank and L. H. Ozarow, "Nonequiprobable signaling on the Gaussian channel," *IEEE Trans. Inform. Theory*, vol. 33, pp. 726–740, 1990.

[32] A. R. Calderbank, E. M. Rains, P. W. Shor, and N. J. A. Sloane, "Quantum error correction and orthogonal geometry," *Phys. Rev. Lett.*, vol. 78, pp. 405–409, 1997; also LANL eprint quant-ph/9605005.

[33] A. R. Calderbank, E. M. Rains, P. W. Shor, and N. J. A. Sloane, "Quantum error correction via codes over GF(4)," *IEEE Trans. Inform. Theory*, vol. 44, pp. 1369–1387, July 1998.

[34] A. R. Calderbank and N. Seshadri, "Multilevel codes for unequal error protection," *IEEE Trans. Inform. Theory*, vol. 39, pp. 1234–1248, 1993.

[35] A. R. Calderbank and P. W. Shor, "Good quantum error-correcting codes exist," *Phys. Rev. A*, vol. 54, pp. 1098–1105, 1996; also LANL eprint quant-ph/9512032.

[36] A. R. Calderbank and N. J. A. Sloane, "New trellis codes based on lattices and cosets," *IEEE Trans. Inform. Theory*, vol. 33, pp. 177–195, 1987.

[37] P. J. Cameron and J. J. Seidel, "Quadratic forms over GF(2)," *Indag. Math.*, vol. 35, pp. 1–8, 1973.

[38] P. Camion, "Codes and association schemes," in *Handbook of Coding Theory*, R. A. Brualdi, W. C. Huffman, and V. Pless, Eds. Amsterdam, The Netherlands: Elsevier, to be published.

[39] H. Chen, "On minimum Lee weights of Hensel lifts of some binary BCH codes," *IEEE Trans. Inform. Theory*, submitted for publication.

[40] R. T. Chien, "Cyclic decoding procedure for the Bose–Chaudhuri–Hocquenghem codes," *IEEE Trans. Inform. Theory*, vol. IT-10, pp. 357–363, 1964.

[41] O. M. Collins, "The subtleties and intricacies of building a constraint length 15 convolutional decoder," *IEEE Trans. Commun.*, vol. 40, pp. 1810–1819, 1992.

[42] J. H. Conway and N. J. A. Sloane, "A fast encoding method for lattice codes and quantizers," *IEEE Trans. Inform. Theory*, vol. IT-29, pp. 820–824, 1983.

[43] ———, "Soft decoding techniques for codes and lattices including the Golay code and the Leech lattice," *IEEE Trans. Inform. Theory*, vol. IT-32, pp. 41–50, 1986.

[44] ———, *Sphere Packings, Lattices and Groups*. New York: Springer-Verlag, 1988.

[45] D. J. Costello, Jr., J. Hagenauer, H. Imai, and S. B. Wicker, "Applications of error control coding," this issue, pp. 2531–2560.

[46] T. M. Cover, "Broadcast channels," *IEEE Trans. Inform. Theory*, vol. IT-18, pp. 2–14, 1972.

[47] R. V. Cox, J. Hagenauer, N. Seshadri, and C.-E. Sundberg, "Variable rate sub-band speech coding and matched convolutional channel coding for mobile radio channels," *IEEE Trans. Signal Processing*, vol. 39, pp. 1717–1731, 1991.

[48] P. Delsarte, "An algebraic approach to the association schemes of coding theory," *Philips Res. Rep. Suppl.*, no. 10, 1973.

[49] ———, "Four fundamental parameters of a code and their combinatorial significance," *Inform. Contr.*, vol. 23, pp. 407–438, 1973.

[50] ———, "Hahn polynomials, discrete harmonics and t-designs," *SIAM J. Appl. Math.*, vol. 34, pp. 157–166, 1978.

[51] ———, "Application and generalization of the MacWilliams transform in coding theory," in *Proc. 15th Symp. Information Theory in the Benelux* (Louvain-la-Neuve, Belgium, 1989), pp. 9–44.

[52] P. Delsarte and J.-M. Goethals, "Alternating bilinear forms over GF(q)," *J. Comb. Theory (A)*, vol. 19, pp. 26–50, 1975.

[53] P. Delsarte, J.-M. Goethals, and J. J. Seidel, "Bounds for systems of lines and Jacobi polynomials," *Philips Res. Rep.*, vol. 30, pp. 91–105, 1975.

[54] ———, "Spherical codes and designs," *Geom. Dedicata*, vol. 6, pp. 363–388, 1977.

[55] P. Delsarte and V. I. Levenshtein, "Association schemes and coding theory," this issue, pp. 2477–2504.

[56] P. Delsarte and R. J. McEliece, "Zeros of functions in finite abelian group algebras," *Amer. J. Math.*, vol. 98, pp. 197–224, 1976.

[57] P. Delsarte and J. J. Seidel, "Fisher type inequalities for euclidean t-designs," *Lin. Alg. Appl.*, vols. 114/115, pp. 213–230, 1989.

[58] M. R. de Prony, "Essai expérimentalle et analytique," *J. École Polytech. Paris*, vol. 1, pp. 24–76, 1795.

[59] I. Duursma, "Majority coset decoding," *IEEE Trans. Inform. Theory*, vol. 39, pp. 1067–1071, 1993.

[60] I. Duursma and R. Kötter, "Error-locating pairs for cyclic codes," *IEEE Trans. Inform. Theory*, vol. 40, pp. 1108–1121, 1994.

[61] D. Ehrhard, "Achieving the designed error capacity in decoding algebraic-geometric codes," *IEEE Trans. Inform. Theory*, vol. 39, pp. 743–751, 1993.

[62] A. Ekert and C. Macchiavello, "Error correction in quantum communication," *Phys. Rev. Lett.*, vol. 77, pp. 2585–2588, 1996; also LANL eprint quant-phi/9602022.

[63] E. Eleftheriou and R. Cideciyan, "On codes satisfying Mth order running digital sum constraints," *IEEE Trans. Inform. Theory*, vol. 37,

[64] A. A. El Gamal and T. M. Cover, "Achievable rates for multiple descriptions," *IEEE Trans. Inform. Theory*, vol. IT-28, pp. 851–857, 1982.

[65] W. H. R. Equitz and T. M. Cover, "Successive refinement of information," *IEEE Trans. Inform. Theory*, vol. 37, pp. 269–275, 1991.

[66] P. Erdős, C. Ko, and R. Rado, "Intersection theorems for systems of finite sets," *Quart. J. Math. Oxford*, vol. 12, pp. 313–320, 1961.

[67] J. Feigenbaum, "The use of coding theory in computational complexity," in *Different Aspects of Coding Theory, Proc. Symp. in Appl. Math.*, vol. 50. Providence, RI: Amer. Math. Soci., 1995, pp. 207–233.

[68] A. Feldmann, A. C. Gilbert, and W. Willinger, "Data networks as cascades: Investigating the multifractal nature of internet WAN traffic," to be published in *Proc. ACM/SIGCOMM'98*.

[69] G.-L. Feng and T. R. N. Rao, "Decoding of algebraic geometric codes up to the designed minimum distance," *IEEE Trans. Inform. Theory*, vol. 39, pp. 37–45, 1993.

[70] G.-L. Feng and K. K. Tzeng, "A new procedure for decoding cyclic and BCH codes to the actual minimum distance," *IEEE Trans. Inform. Theory*, vol. 40, pp. 1364–1374, 1994.

[71] R. A. Fisher, "The theory of confounding in factorial experiments in relation to the theory of groups," *Ann. Eugenics*, vol. 11, pp. 341–353, 1942.

[72] R. A. Fisher, "A system of confounding for factors with more than two alternatives, giving completely orthogonal cubes and higher powers," *Ann. Eugenics*, vol. 12, pp. 2283–2290, 1945.

[73] G. D. Forney, Jr., "On decoding BCH codes," *IEEE Trans. Inform. Theory*, vol. IT-11, pp. 549–557, 1965.

[74] ———, *Concatenated Codes*. Cambridge, MA: MIT Press, 1966.

[75] ———, "Convolutional codes I: Algebraic structure," *IEEE Trans. Inform. Theory*, vol. IT-16, pp. 720–738, 1970; correction in vol. IT-17, p. 360, 1971.

[76] ———, "Maximum likelihood sequence estimation in the presence of intersymbol interference," *IEEE Trans. Inform. Theory*, vol. IT-18, pp. 363–378, 1972.

[77] ———, "The Viterbi algorithm," *Proc. IEEE*, vol. 61, pp. 267–278, 1973.

[78] ———, "Minimal bases of rational vector spaces wtih applications to multivariable linear systems," *SIAM J. Contr.*, vol. 13, pp. 439–520, 1975.

[79] ———, "Coset codes—Part I: Introduction and geometrical classification," *IEEE Trans. Inform. Theory*, vol. 34, pp. 1123–1151, 1988.

[80] ———, "Coset codes—Part II: Binary lattices and related codes," *IEEE Trans. Inform. Theory*, vol. 34, pp. 1152–1187, 1988.

[81] ———, "Geometrically uniform codes," *IEEE Trans. Inform. Theory*, vol. 37, pp. 1241–1260, 1991.

[82] ———, "Trellis shaping," *IEEE Trans. Inform. Theory*, vol. 38, pp. 281–300, 1992.

[83] G. D. Forney, Jr., L. Brown, M. V. Eyuboglu, and J. L. Moran III, "The ′ 34 high-speed modem standard," *IEEE Commun. Mag.*, vol. 34, pp. 28–33, Dec. 1996.

[84] G. D. Forney, Jr. and A. R. Calderbank, "Coset codes for partial response channels; or coset codes with spectral nulls," *IEEE Trans. Inform. Theory*, vol. 35, pp. 925–943, 1989.

[85] G. D. Forney, Jr. and M. Trott, "The dynamics of group codes: State spaces, trellis diagrams and canonical encoders," *IEEE Trans. Inform. Theory*, vol. 39, pp. 1491–1513, 1993.

[86] G. D. Forney, Jr. and G. Ungerboeck, "Modulation and coding for linear Gaussian channels," this issue, pp. 2384–2415.

[87] G. D. Forney, Jr. and A. Vardy, "Generalized minimum distance decoding of euclidean-space codes and lattices," *IEEE Trans. Inform. Theory*, vol. 42, pp. 1992–2026, 1996.

[88] G. J. Foschini, Jr. and M. J. Gans, "On limits of wireless communication in a fading environment when using multiple antennas," *Wireless Personal Commun.*, to be published.

[89] P. Frankl, "The Erdős-Ko-Rado theorem is true for $n = ckt$," in *Combinatorics, Proc. 5th Hungarian Colloq. Combinatorics, Keszthely*. Amsterdam, The Netherlands: North-Holland, 1976, pp. 365–375.

[90] B. J. Frey and F. R. Kschischang, "Probability propagation and iterative decoding," in *Proc. 34th Allerton Conf. Communication, Control, and Computing*, 1996, pp. 482–493.

[91] R. G. Gallager, "Low-density parity-check codes," *IEEE Trans. Inform. Theory*, vol. IT-8, pp. 21–28, 1962.

[92] R. G. Gallager, *Low-Density Parity-Check Codes*. Cambridge MA: MIT Press, 1963.

[93] A. Garcia and H. Stichtenoth, "A tower of Artin-Schreier extensions of function fields attaining the Drinfeld-Vlădut bound," *Invent. Math.*, vol. 121, pp. 211–222, 1995.

[94] A. V. Geramita and J. Seberry, "Orthogonal designs, quadratic forms and Hadamard matrices," in *Lecture Notes in Pure and Applied Mathematics*,

vol. 43. New York and Basel: Marcel Decker, 1979.

[95] E. N. Gilbert, "A comparison of signalling alphabets," *Bell Syst. Tech. J.*, vol. 31, pp. 504–522, 1952.

[96] R. D. Gitlin, J. Salz, and J. H. Winters, "The capacity of wireless communications systems can be substantially increased by the use of antenna diversity," *IEEE J. Select. Areas Commun.*, to be published.

[97] A. M. Gleason, "Weight polynomials of self-dual codes and the MacWilliams identities," in *Actes Congrés Int. de Math.*, vol. 3, pp. 211–215, 1970.

[98] J.-M. Goethals, "Two dual families of nonlinear binary codes," *Electron. Lett.*, vol. 10, pp. 471–472, 1974.

[99] _____, "Nonlinear codes defined by quadratic forms over $GF(2)$," *Inform. Contr.*, vol. 31, pp. 43–74, 1976.

[100] J.-M. Goethals and J. J. Seidel, "The football," *Nieuw. Arch. Wiskunde*, vol. 29, pp. 50–58, 1981.

[101] J.-M. Goethals and H. C. A. van Tilborg, "Uniformly packed codes," *Philips Res. Rep.*, vol. 30, pp. 9–36, 1975.

[102] M. J. E. Golay, "Notes on digital coding," *Proc. IEEE*, vol. 37, p. 657, 1949.

[103] V. D. Goppa, "Codes on algebraic curves," *Sov. Math.–Dokl.*, vol. 24, pp. 170–172, 1981. Translation from *Dokl. Akad. Nauk S.S.S.R.*, vol. 259, pp. 1289–1290, 1981.

[104] D. C. Gorenstein and N. Zierler, "A class of error correcting codes in p^m symbols," *SIAM J.*, vol. 9, pp. 207–214, 1971.

[105] D. Gottesman, "A class of quantum error-correcting codes saturating the quantum Hamming bound," *Phys. Rev. A*, vol. 54, pp. 1862–1868, 1996; also LANL eprint quant-ph/9604038.

[106] J. Hagenauer and P. Hoeher, "A Viterbi algorithm with soft-decision outputs and its applications," in *IEEE Globecom'89*, 1989, pp. 1680–1685.

[107] J. Hagenauer, E. Offer, and L. Papke, "Matching Viterbi decoders and Reed–Solomon decoders in concatenated systems," in *Reed–Solomon Codes and Their Applications*, S. B. Wicker and V. K. Bhargava, Eds. Piscataway, NJ: IEEE Press, 1994, pp. 242–271.

[108] A. R. Hammons, Jr., P. V. Kumar, A. R. Calderbank, N. J. A. Sloane, and P. Solé, "The $\mathbb{Z}_4$-linearity of Kerdock, Preparata, Goethals and related codes," *IEEE Trans. Inform. Theory*, vol. 40, pp. 301–319, 1994.

[109] R. H. Hardin and N. J. A. Sloane, "Codes (spherical) and designs (experimental)," in *Different Aspects of Coding Theory, Proc. Symp. Applied Mathematics*, vol. 50. Providence RI: Amer. Math. Soc., 1995, pp. 179–206.

[110] T. Høholdt and R. Pellikaan, "On the decoding of algebraic-geometric codes," *IEEE Trans. Inform. Theory*, vol. 41, pp. 1589–1614, 1995.

[111] A. S. Householder, *Principles of Numerical Analysis*. New York: McGraw-Hill, 1953.

[112] H. Imai and S. Hirakawa, "A new multi-level coding method using error correcting codes," *IEEE Trans. Inform. Theory*, vol. IT-23, pp. 371–377, 1977.

[113] K. A. S. Immink, "RS codes and the compact disk," in *Reed–Solomon Codes and Their Applications*, S. B. Wicker and V. K. Bhargava, Eds. Piscataway, NJ: IEEE Press, 1994, pp. 41–59.

[114] _____, "A practical method for approaching the channel capacity of constrained channels," *IEEE Trans. Inform. Theory*, vol. 43, pp. 1389–1399, 1997.

[115] K. A. S. Immink and G. Beenker, "Binary transmission codes with higher order spectral nulls at zero frequency," *IEEE Trans. Inform. Theory*, vol. IT-33, pp. 452–454, 1987.

[116] International Telecommunication Union, ITU-T Recommendation V.34, "A modem operating at data signaling rates of up to 28,800 bits/s for use on the general switched telephone network and on leased point-to-point 2-wire telephone-type circuits," Sept. 1994.

[117] J. Justesen, "A class of constructive asymptotically good algebraic codes," *IEEE Trans. Inform. Theory*, vol. IT-18, pp. 652–656, 1972.

[118] _____, "Information rates and power spectra of digital codes," *IEEE Trans. Inform. Theory*, vol. IT-28, pp. 457–472, 1982.

[119] J. Justesen, K. J. Larsen, H. E. Jensen, A. Havemose, and T. Høholdt, "Construction and decoding of a class of algebraic geometry codes," *IEEE Trans. Inform. Theory*, vol. 35, pp. 811–821, 1989.

[120] D. Kahn, *The Codebreakers, The Story of Secret Writing*. New York: MacMillan, 1967.

[121] R. Karabed and P. H. Siegel, "Matched spectral null codes for partial response channels," *IEEE Trans. Inform. Theory*, vol. 37, pp. 818–855, 1991.

[122] A. M. Kerdock, "A class of low-rate nonlinear binary codes," *Inform. Contr.*, vol. 20, pp. 182–187, 1972.

[123] C. Kirfel and R. Pellikaan, "The minimum distance of codes in an array coming from telescopic subgroups," *IEEE Trans. Inform. Theory*, vol. 41, pp. 1720–1731, 1995.

[124] H. Kobayashi, "Correlative level coding and maximum likelihood decoding," *IEEE Trans. Inform. Theory*, vol. IT-17, pp. 586–594, 1971.

[125] H. Kobayashi and D. T. Tang, "Applications of partial response channel coding to magnetic recording systems," *IBM J. Res. Develop.*, vol. 14, pp. 368–375, 1970.

[126] H. König, *Isometric Embeddings of Euclidean Spaces into Finite-Dimensional lp-Spaces* (Banach Center Publications, vol. 34.). Warsaw, Poland: PWN, 1995, pp. 79–87.

[127] V. Koshélev, "Estimation of mean error for a discrete successive approximation scheme," *Probl. Inform. Transm.*, vol. 17, pp. 20–33, 1981.

[128] E. S. Lander, *Symmetric Designs: An Algebraic Approach* (London Math. Soc. Lecture Notes, vol. 74). London/New York: Cambridge Univ. Press, 1983.

[129] R. Laroia, "Coding for intersymbol interference channels—Combined coding and precoding," *IEEE Trans. Inform. Theory*, vol. 42, pp. 1053–1061, 1996.

[130] R. Laroia, N. Farvardin, and S. Tretter, "On optimal shaping of multidimensional constellations," *IEEE Trans. Inform. Theory*, vol. 40, pp. 1044–1056, 1994.

[131] J. Leech, "Notes on sphere packings," *Canadian J. Math.*, vol. 19, pp. 251–267, 1967.

[132] J. Leech and N. J. A. Sloane, "Sphere packings and error-correcting codes," *Canadian J. Math.*, vol. 23, pp. 718–745, 1971.

[133] W. E. Leland, M. S. Taqqu, W. Willinger, and D. V. Wilson, "On the self-similar nature of ethernet traffic (extended version)," *IEEE/ACM Trans. Networking*, vol. 2, pp. 1–15, 1994.

[134] V. I. Levenshtein, "On bounds for packings in n-dimensional euclidean space," *Sov. Math.–Dokl.*, vol. 20, no. 2, pp. 417–421, 1979.

[135] _____, "Bounds on the maximum cardinality of a code with bounded modulus of the inner product," *Sov. Math.–Dokl.*, vol. 25, pp. 526–531, 1982.

[136] _____, "Designs as maximum codes in polynomial metric spaces," *Acta Applic. Math.*, vol. 29, pp. 1–82, 1992.

[137] S. Lin and E. J. Weldon, Jr., "Long BCH codes are bad," *Inform. Contr.*, vol. 11, pp. 452–495, 1967.

[138] J. H. van Lint, "Nonexistence theorems for perfect error correcting codes," in *Computers in Algebraic Number Theory, SIAM-AMS Proc.*, vol. IV, 1971.

[139] _____, "Coding theory," in *Springer Lecture Notes*, vol. 201. Berlin-Heidelberg-New York: Springer, 1971.

[140] J. H. van Lint and R. M. Wilson, "On the minimum distance of cyclic codes," *IEEE Trans. Inform. Theory*, vol. IT-32, pp. 23–40, 1986.

[141] S. P. Lloyd, "Binary block coding," *Bell Syst. Tech. J.*, vol. 36, pp. 517–535, 1957.

[142] H.-A. Loeliger, "Averaging bounds for lattices and linear codes," *IEEE Trans. Inform. Theory*, vol. 43, pp. 1767–1773, 1997.

[143] T. D. Lookabaugh and R. M. Gray, "High-resolution quantization theory and the vector quantizer advantage," *IEEE Trans. Inform. Theory*, vol. 35, pp. 1020–1033, 1989.

[144] L. Lovász, "On the Shannon capacity of a graph," *IEEE Trans. Inform. Theory*, vol. IT-25, pp. 1–7, 1979.

[145] D. J. C. MacKay and R. M. Neil, "Near Shannon limit performance of low density parity check codes," *Electron. Lett.*, vol. 32, pp. 1645–1646, 1996 (reprinted vol. 33, pp. 457–458, 1997).

[146] F. J. MacWilliams, "Combinatorial properties of elementary abelian groups," Ph.D. dissertation, Harvard Univ., Cambridge, MA, 1962.

[147] _____, "A theorem on the distribution of weights in a systematic code," *Bell Syst. Tech. J.*, vol. 42, pp. 79–94, 1963.

[148] F. J. MacWilliams and N. J. A. Sloane, *The Theory of Error-Correcting Codes*. Amsterdam, The Netherlands: North Holland, 1977.

[149] F. J. MacWilliams, N. J. A. Sloane, and J. G. Thompson, "Good self-dual codes exist," *Discr. Math.*, vol. 3, pp. 153–162, 1972.

[150] M. W. Marcellin and T. R. Fischer, "Trellis-coded quantization of memoryless and Gauss-Markov sources," *IEEE Trans. Commun.*, vol. 38, pp. 82–93, 1993.

[151] B. Marcus, "Symbolic dynamics and connections to coding theory automata theory and system theory," in *Different Aspects of Coding Theory, Proc. Symp. Applied Mathematics*, vol. 50. Providence, RI: Amer. Math. Soc., 1995, pp. 95–108.

[152] B. H. Marcus, P. H. Siegel, and J. K. Wolf, "Finite-state modulation codes for data storage," *IEEE J. Select. Areas Commun.*, vol. 10, pp. 5–37, 1992.

[153] J. L. Massey, "Shift register synthesis and BCH decoding," *IEEE Trans. Inform. Theory*, vol. IT-15, pp. 122–127, 1969.

[154] H. F. Mattson, Jr. and G. Solomon, "A new treatment of Bose-Chaudhuri codes," *SIAM J.*, vol. 9, pp. 654–669, 1961.

[155] R. J. McEliece, *Finite Fields for Computer Scientists and Engineers*. Boston-Dordrecht-Lancaster: Kluwer, 1987.

[156] R. J. McEliece, E. R. Rodemich, H. Rumsey, Jr., and L. R. Welch, "New upper bounds on the rate of a code via the Delsarte-MacWilliams

inequalities," *IEEE Trans. Inform. Theory*, vol. IT-23, pp. 157–166, 1977.

[157] H. Miyakawa and H. Harashima, "Capacity of channels with matched transmitting technique for peak transmitting power limitation," in *Nat. Conv. Rec. IECE Japan*, 1969, pp. 1268–1264.

[158] D. J. Muder, "Minimal trellises for block codes," *IEEE Trans. Inform. Theory*, vol. 34, pp. 1049–1053, 1988.

[159] A. Naguib, "Adaptive antennas for CDMA wireless networks," Ph.D. dissertation, Stanford Univ., Stanford, CA, 1996.

[160] A. F. Naguib and N. Seshadri, "Combined interference cancellation and maximum likelihood decoding of space-time block codes," preprint, 1998.

[161] K. Nakamura, "A class of error correcting codes for DPSK channels," in *Proc. Int. Conf. Communication*, 1979, pp. 45.4.1–45.4.5.

[162] Y. Nakamura, Y. Saito, and S. Aikawa, "256-QAM modem for multicarrier 400 Mb/s digital radio," *IEEE J. Select. Areas. Commun.*, vol. JSAC-5, pp. 329–335, 1987.

[163] R. van Nobelen, "Toward higher data rates for IS-36," in *Proc. IEEE Vehicular Technology Conf.*, 1998, pp. 2403–2407.

[164] A. W. Nordstrom and J. P. Robinson, "An optimum nonlinear code," *Inform. Contr.*, vol. 11, pp. 613–616, 1967.

[165] A. M. Odlyzko and N. J. A. Sloane, "New bounds on the number of spheres that can touch a unit sphere in *n*-dimensions," *J. Combin. Theory*, vol. (A)26, pp. 210–214, 1979.

[166] L. H. Ozarow, "On a source coding problem with two channels and three receivers," *Bell Syst. Tech. J.*, vol. 59, pp. 1909–1921, 1980.

[167] J. Pearl, *Probabilistic Reasoning in Intelligent Systems: Networks of Plausible Inference*. San Francisco, CA: Morgan-Kaufmann, 1988.

[168] J. B. H. Peek, "Communications aspects of the compact disk digital audio system," *IEEE Commun. Mag.*, vol. 23, pp. 7–15, Feb. 1985.

[169] R. Pellikaan, "On the decoding by error location and the number of dependent error positions," *Discr. Math.*, vols. 106/107, pp. 369–381, 1992.

[170] W. W. Peterson, "Encoding and error correction procedures for the Bose-Chaudhuri codes," *IEEE Trans. Inform. Theory*, vol. 6, pp. 459–470, 1960.

[171] S. C. Porter, "Decoding codes arising from Goppa's construction on algebraic curves," Ph.D. dissertation, Yale Univ., New Haven, CT, 1988.

[172] S. C. Porter, B.-Z. Shen, and R. Pellikaan, "On decoding geometric Goppa codes using an extra place," *IEEE Trans. Inform. Theory*, vol. 38, pp. 1663–1676, 1992.

[173] G. J. Pottie and D. P. Taylor, "Multilevel codes based on partitioning," *IEEE Trans. Inform. Theory*, vol. 35, pp. 87–98, 1989.

[174] F. P. Preparata, "A class of optimum nonlinear double error correcting codes," *Inform. Contr.*, vol. 13, pp. 378–400, 1968.

[175] K. Ramchandran, A. Ortega, K. M. Uz, and M. Vetterli, "Multiresolution broadcast for digital HDTV using joint source/channel coding," *IEEE J. Select. Areas Commun.*, vol. 11, pp. 6–23, 1993.

[176] C. R. Rao, "Factorial experiments derivable from combinatorial arrangements of arrays," *J. Roy. Statist. Soc.*, vol. 9, pp. 128–139, 1947.

[177] D. K. Ray-Chaudhuri and N. M. Singhi, "On existence of *t*-designs with large *v* and λ," *SIAM J. Discr. Math.*, vol. 1, pp. 98–104, 1988.

[178] D. K. Ray-Chaudhuri and R. M. Wilson, "On *t*-designs," *Osaka J. Math.*, vol. 12, pp. 737–744, 1975.

[179] I. S. Reed and G. Solomon, "Polynomial codes over certain finite fields," *SIAM J.*, vol. 8, pp. 300–304, 1960.

[180] S. Sakata, "Finding a minimal set of linear recurring relations capable of generating a given finite two-dimensional array," *J. Symbolic Comput.*, vol. 5, pp. 321–337, 1988.

[181] S. Sakata, "Extension of the Berlekamp-Massey algorithm to *N* dimensions," *Inform. Comput.*, vol. 84, pp. 207–239, 1990.

[182] S. Sakata, J. Justesen, Y. Madelung, H. E. Jensen, and T. Høholdt, "Fast decoding of algebraic geometric codes up to the designed minimum distance," *IEEE Trans. Inform. Theory*, vol. 41, pp. 1672–1677, 1995.

[183] N. V. Semakov, V. A. Zinoviev, and G. V. Zaitzev, "Uniformly packed codes," *Probl. Pered. Inform.*, vol. 7, pp. 38–50, 1971 (in Russian).

[184] N. Seshadri and C.-E. Sundberg, "Generalized Viterbi detection with convolutional codes," in *IEEE Globecom'89*, 1989, pp. 1534–1538.

[185] N. Seshadri and J. H. Winters, "Two signaling schemes for improving the error performance of frequency-division-duplex (FDD) transmission systems using transmitter antenna diversity," *Int. J. Wireless Inform. Networks*, vol. 1, pp. 49–60, 1994.

[186] P. D. Seymour and T. Zaslavsky, "Averaging sets," *Adv. Math.*, vol. 52, pp. 213–240, 1984.

[187] C. E. Shannon, "A mathematical theory of communication I, II," *Bell Syst. Tech. J.*, vol. 27, pp. 379–423; 623–656, 1948; Reprinted in C. E. Shannon and W. Weaver, *A Mathematical Theory of Communication*. Urbana, IL: Univ. Illinois Press, 1949.

[188] _____, "The zero-error capacity of a noisy channel," *IRE Trans. Inform. Theory*, vol. IT-2, pp. 8–19, 1956.

[189] M. A. Shokorollahi and H. Wassermann, "Decoding algebraic-geometric codes beyond the error-correction bound," preprint, 1997.

[190] P. W. Shor, "Algorithms for quantum computation: Discrete logarithm and factoring," in *Proc. 35th Annu. Symp. Foundations of Computer Science*, 1994, pp. 124–134.

[191] _____, "Scheme for reducing deroherence in quantum computer memory," *Phys. Rev. A.*, vol. 52, pp. 2493–2496, 1995.

[192] P. W. Shor and R. Laflamme, "Quantum analog of the MacWilliams identities in classical coding theory," *Phys. Rev. Lett.*, vol. 78, pp. 1600–1602, 1997; also LANL eprint quant-ph/9610040.

[193] V. M. Sidel'nikov, "Extremal polynomials used in bounds of code volume," *Probl. Pered. Inform.*, vol. 16, pp. 17–39, 1980 (in Russian). English translation in *Probl. Inform. Transm.*, vol. 16, pp. 174–186, 1980.

[194] M. Sipser and D. A. Spielman, "Expander codes," *IEEE Trans. Inform. Theory*, vol. 42, pp. 1710–1722, 1996.

[195] A. N. Skorobogatov and S. G. Vlăduţ, "On the decoding of algebraic geometric codes," *IEEE Trans. Inform. Theory*, vol. 36, pp. 1461–1463, 1990.

[196] D. Slepian, "A class of binary signaling alphabets," *Bell Syst. Tech. J.*, vol. 35, pp. 203–234, 1956.

[197] _____, "A note on two binary signaling alphabets," *IRE Trans. Inform. Theory*, vol. IT-2, pp. 84–86, 1956.

[198] _____, "Some further theory of group codes," *Bell Syst. Tech. J.*, vol. 39, pp. 1219–1252, 1960.

[199] _____, "Group codes for the Gaussian channel," *Bell Syst. Tech. J.*, vol. 47, pp. 575–602, 1968.

[200] D. Slepian and J. K. Wolf, "Noiseless coding of correlated information," *IEEE Trans. Inform. Theory*, vol. IT-19, pp. 471–480, 1973.

[201] N. J. A. Sloane, "Error-correcting codes and invariant theory: New applications of a nineteenth century technique," *Amer. Math. Monthly*, vol. 84, pp. 82–107, 1977.

[202] G. Solomon and H. C. A. van Tilborg, "A connection between block and convolutional codes," *SIAM J. Appl. Math.*, vol. 37, pp. 358–369, 1979.

[203] A. M. Steane, "Error correcting codes in quantum theory," *Phys. Rev. Lett.*, vol. 77, pp. 793–797, 1996.

[204] H. Stichtenoth, "Algebraic geometric codes," in *Different Aspects of Coding Theory, Proc. Symp. App. Math.*, vol. 50. Providence, RI: Amer. Math. Soc., 1995,

[205] M. Sudan, "Decoding of Reed–Solomon codes beyond the error-correction bound," *J. Complexity*, vol. 13, pp. 180–193, 1997.

[206] C.-E. Sundberg and N. Seshadri, "Digital cellular systems for North America," in *IEEE Globecom'90*, 1990, pp. 533–537.

[207] R. M. Tanner, "A recursive approach to low complexity codes," *IEEE Trans. Inform. Theory*, vol. IT-27, pp. 533–547, 1981.

[208] V. Tarokh and I. F. Blake, "Trellis complexity versus the coding gain of lattices, parts I and II," *IEEE Trans. Inform. Theory*, vol. 42, pp. 1796–1807 and 1808–1816, 1996.

[209] V. Tarokh, N. Seshadri, and A. R. Calderbank, "Space-time codes for high data rate wireless communication: Performance criterion and code construction," *IEEE Trans. Inform. Theory*, vol. 44, pp. 744–765, 1998.

[210] E. Telatar, "Capacity of multi-antenna Gaussian channels," AT&T Bell Labs. Internal Tech. Memo, June 1995.

[211] M. A. Tsfasman, S. G. Vlăduţ, and T. Zink, "On Goppa codes which are better than the Varshamov-Gilbert bound," *Math. Nach.*, vol. 109, pp. 21–28, 1982.

[212] A. Tietäväinen, "On the nonexistence of perfect codes over finite fields," *SIAM J. Appl. Math.*, vol. 24, pp. 88–96, 1973.

[213] M. Tomlinson, "New automatic equalizer employing modulo arithmetic," *Electron. Lett.*, vol. 7, pp. 138–139, 1971.

[214] V. A. Vaishampayan, "Design of multiple description scalar quantizers," *IEEE Trans. Inform. Theory*, vol. 39, pp. 821–834, 1993.

[215] G. Ungerboeck, "Channel coding with multilevel/phase signals," *IEEE Trans. Inform. Theory*, vol. IT-28, pp. 55–67, 1982.

[216] A. Vardy and Y. Be'ery, "More efficient soft decoding of the Golay codes," *IEEE Trans. Inform. Theory*, vol. 37, pp. 667–672, 1991.

[217] _____, "Maximum-likelihood decoding of the Leech lattice," *IEEE Trans. Inform. Theory*, vol. 39, pp. 1435–1444, 1993.

[218] R. R. Varshamov, "Estimate of the number of signals in error correcting codes," *Dokl. Akad. Nauk. SSSR*, vol. 117, pp. 739–741, 1957.

[219] A. J. Viterbi, "Error bounds for convolutional codes and an asymptotically optimal decoding algorithm," *IEEE Trans. Inform. Theory*, vol. IT-13, pp. 260–269, 1967.

[220] U. Wachsmann and J. Huber, "Power and bandwidth efficient digital communication using turbo codes in multilevel codes," *Euro. Trans. Telecommun.*, vol. 6, pp. 557–567, 1995.

[221] N. Wiberg, "Codes and decoding on general graphs," Ph.D. dissertation, Linköping Univ., Linköping, Sweden, 1996.

[222] N. Wiberg, H.-A. Loeliger, and R. Kötter, "Codes and iterative decoding on general graphs," *Euro. Trans. Telecommun.*, vol. 6, pp. 513–525, 1995.

[223] W. Willinger and V. Paxson, "Where mathematics meets the internet," to be published in the *Notices Amer. Math. Soc.*

[224] W. Willinger, M. S. Taqqu, and A. Erramilli, "A bibliographical guide to self-similar traffic and performance modeling for modern high-speed networks," in *Stochastic Networks: Theory and Applications, Royal Statistical Lecture Note Series*, vol. 4, F. P. Kelly, S. Zachary, and I. Ziedins, Eds. Oxford, U.K.: Clarendon Press, 1996, pp. 339–366.

[225] R. M. Wilson, "The exact bound in the Erdős-Ko-Rado theorem," *Combinatorica*, vol. 4, pp. 247–257, 1984.

[226] A. Wittneben, "Base station modulation diversity for digital SIMUL-CAST," in *Proc. IEEE Vehicular Technology Conf.*, 1993, pp. 505–511.

[227] J. K. Wolf, "Decoding of Bose–Chaudhuri–Hocquenghem codes and Prony's method for curve fitting," *IEEE Trans. Inform. Theory*, vol. IT-3, p. 608, 1967.

[228] J. A. Wood, "Extension theorems for linear codes over finite rings," preprint 1997.

[229] K. Yang and P. V. Kumar, "On the true minimum distance of hermitian codes," in *Coding Theory and Algebraic Geometry* (Lecture Notes in Mathematics, vol. 1518). Berlin, Germany: Springer, 1992, pp. 99–107.

[230] V. A. Zinoviev, "Generalized cascade codes," *Probl. Pered. Inform.*, vol. 12, pp. 2–9, 1976 (in Russian).

[231] V. A. Zinoviev and V. K. Leontiev, "The nonexistence of perfect codes over Galois fields," *Probl. Contr. Inform. Theory*, vol. 2, pp. 123–132, 1973.

[232] V. V. Zyablov and M. S. Pinsker, "Estimates of the error-correction complexity of Gallager's low density codes," *Probl. Inform. Transm.*, vol. 11, pp. 18–28, 1976.

Algebraic-Geometry Codes

Ian Blake, *Fellow, IEEE*, Chris Heegard, *Fellow, IEEE*, Tom Høholdt, *Senior Member, IEEE*, and Victor Wei, *Fellow, IEEE*

(Invited Paper)

Abstract—The theory of error-correcting codes derived from curves in an algebraic geometry was initiated by the work of Goppa as generalizations of Bose-Chaudhuri-Hocquenghem (BCH), Reed–Solomon (RS), and Goppa codes. The development of the theory has received intense consideration since that time and the purpose of the paper is to review this work. Elements of the theory of algebraic curves, at a level sufficient to understand the code constructions and decoding algorithms, are introduced. Code constructions from particular classes of curves, including the Klein quartic, elliptic, and hyperelliptic curves, and Hermitian curves, are presented. Decoding algorithms for these classes of codes, and others, are considered. The construction of classes of asymptotically good codes using modular curves is also discussed.

Index Terms— Algebraic curves, algebraic-geometry codes, asymptotically good codes, decoding algorithms.

I. INTRODUCTION

THE origins of the subject of error-correcting codes are found in the classical papers of Shannon [79]. The subject developed rapidly, both in engineering practice and as a mathematical discipline. The notions of Bose–Chaudhuri–Hocquenghem (BCH), Reed–Solomon (RS), and Goppa codes, in particular, achieved prominence with extensive research contributions over a period of almost four decades. Along with a developing mathematical theory of codes, went intense research on the most efficient algorithms to decode them, an effort that continues.

From a theoretical point of view, a significant research objective was to construct asymptotically good codes, codes whose parameters achieved the Varshamov–Gilbert lower bound, introduced in the next section. Although there was much interesting work on the problem [48], the goal remained elusive.

While the construction of asymptotically good codes proved difficult, the construction of many other interesting classes of codes proceeded swiftly. Prominent among these are the

Manuscript received December 5, 1997; revised May 11, 1998. The work of C. Heegard was supported in part by the National Science Foundation under Grant NCR-9520981.

I. Blake is with Hewlett-Packard Laboratories, Palo Alto, CA 94304 USA (e-mail: ifblake@hpl.hp.com).

C. Heegard is with the School of Electrical Engineering, Cornell University, Ithaca, NY 14853 USA (e-mail: heegard@ee.cornell.edu) and with Alantro Communications, Santa Rosa, CA USA.

T. Høholdt is with the Mathematical Institute, Technical University of Denmark, DK 2800, Lyngby, Denmark (e-mail: tom@mat.dtu.dk).

V. Wei is with the Department of Information Engineering, The Chinese University of Hong Kong, Shatin, New Territory, Hong Kong (e-mail: kwwei@ie.cuhk.edu.hk).

Publisher Item Identifier S 0018-9448(98)05712-5.

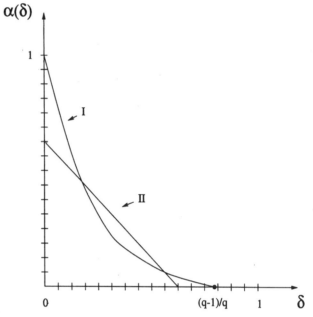

Fig. 1. I: Gilbert–Varshamov bound, II: Tsfasman–Vlăduţ–Zink bound, $q \geq 49$.

classes of BCH, RS, and Goppa codes, already mentioned, whose mathematical properties and decoding algorithms were widely studied. These classes of codes have codewords that can be viewed as either the evaluation of certain functions on a set of distinct elements in a finite field, or the evaluation of residues there, and these notions have proved to be important. While it was known [64] that there exists a sequence of Goppa codes that met the Varshamov–Gilbert bound, their actual construction proved more difficult. Goppa [33], [34] made the crucial observation in generalizing these notions by, in one instance, evaluating a set of rational functions at the points on an algebraic curve. In making this step, many of the tools needed to determine the important parameters of the code, or bounds on them, such as the code length, dimension, and minimum distance, already existed in the elegant theorems of algebraic geometry, notably the Hasse–Weil theorem and the Riemann–Roch theorem. Having evaluated the construction of codes in this manner, it quickly led Tsfasman, Vlăduţ, and Zink [91], [92], using modular curves, to show how asymptotically good codes could be constructed over alphabets of size $q \geq 49$, a truly remarkable achievement (see Fig. 1).

The theory of algebraic-geometry codes involves the relatively deep and fundamental results of algebraic geometry.

While there are now several books that attempt to give self-contained treatments of algebraic geometry and codes ([65], [83], [90]) it nonetheless requires effort on the part of the nonexpert to appreciate the significant developments of the area. The aim of this paper is not so much to give a survey of the rather large body of work that now exists in this area, but to trace the evolution of the subject over the past few decades from the earliest code constructions to the elegant and deep theory that exists today. In particular, an attempt is made to give some notion as to the role the properties of algebraic curves has played in the subject. While the review has been written for the nonexpert, some familiarity with the subject of error-correcting codes and algebra has been assumed. The aim has been to outline the construction of important classes of codes instrumental in the development. It is also intended to give a brief overview of those concepts from algebraic geometry needed to appreciate the development, in a relatively self-contained manner to allow such a nonexpert a glimpse into this development of the subject.

The next section reviews the constructions of certain basic classes of codes, RS, BCH, and Goppa, in such a manner that makes natural the critical step that was taken in extending these to constructions of codes from algebraic curves. The mathematical background needed to understand the application of algebraic geometry to coding is outlined in Section III. While no proofs are given, the theory is illustrated with examples and an informed reader should be able to appreciate the ideas involved. Section IV uses the ideas developed to outline the construction of codes that are derived from many of the more commonly used curves, including the Klein quartic, elliptic and hyperelliptic curves, and Hermitian curves. In addition, interesting constructions due to Feng and Rao ([22], [24]) are considered.

The study of decoding algorithms for codes from curves in an algebraic geometry has been intense over the last decade, meeting the challenge of extending the one-dimensional concepts of decoding BCH, RS, and Goppa codes, to two dimensions. This has involved consideration of the difficult problems encountered in extracting decoding information from the two-dimensional syndromes and the incorporation of the structure of the curves in the decoding process. Progress on this problem is covered in Section V.

Section VI outlines the use of modular curves in the construction of sequences of asymptotically good codes, a quest that started in the 1950's with the establishment of the Varshamov–Gilbert bound. The first step in this direction was taken with the interesting construction of Justesen [48]. The elegant and deep approach using the theory of modular curves holds promise for even greater insight into this challenging problem.

A few comments on the problems and challenges that might be of interest in the future are given in the final section of the paper. The introduction of algebraic geometry to the problem of constructing codes, and in particular, families of asymptotically good codes, has opened up fascinating possibilities of both a theoretical and practical nature for future research. It is hoped this paper might serve as a starting point from which these possibilities might be appreciated.

II. FROM REED–SOLOMON CODES TO ALGEBRAIC-GEOMETRY CODES

A setting that has proved fruitful for coding theory is to view a code C as a subset of the vector space of n-tuples over the finite field of q elements, $\mathbb{F}_q$, which we denote as $\mathbb{F}_q^n$. The (Hamming) distance between any two vectors of the space, $\boldsymbol{a}$, $\boldsymbol{b} \in \mathbb{F}_q^n$ is then the minimum number of coordinate positions in which they differ, denoted by $d(\boldsymbol{a}, \boldsymbol{b})$. The Hamming weight of a vector $\boldsymbol{a} \in \mathbb{F}_q^n$, $w(\boldsymbol{a})$, is the number of its coordinate positions which are nonzero. The minimum distance of a code is then

$$d = \min_{\boldsymbol{a}, \boldsymbol{b} \in C, \, \boldsymbol{a} \neq \boldsymbol{b}} d(\boldsymbol{a}, \boldsymbol{b}).$$

If $|C| = M$ and C has minimum distance d, it is referred to as an $(n, M, d)_q$ code.

Defining the sphere of radius r with center $\boldsymbol{x}$ as

$$S(\boldsymbol{x}, r) = \{\boldsymbol{a} \in \mathbb{F}_q^n | d(\boldsymbol{a}, \boldsymbol{x}) \leq r\}$$

it is immediately seen that it is possible to surround the codewords of a code C with minimum distance d, with nonintersecting spheres of radius $t = \lfloor (d-1)/2 \rfloor$ where $\lfloor \cdot \rfloor$ is the floor function. Since each sphere contains

$$\sum_{i=0}^{t} \binom{n}{i}(q-1)^i$$

vectors it follows that

$$|C| \left\{ \sum_{i=0}^{t} \binom{n}{i}(q-1)^i \right\} \leq q^n$$

a result referred to as the Hamming bound for the code C. A code that achieves this bound with equality is called perfect and the existence of perfect codes is now a settled problem [61].

Designing codes that have a large minimum distance for a given code size, and alphabet size, without more structure is challenging. The addition of linearity to the code set, i.e., requiring that the codewords or vectors of C form a linear subspace of $\mathbb{F}_q^n$, allows considerably more to be said about the code properties. A linear $(n, k, d)_q$ code C is a k-dimensional subspace of $\mathbb{F}_q^n$ with the property that any two distinct codewords are at least distance d apart. Notice that the addition of two codewords is also a codeword, and so the minimum distance of the code is the weight of the smallest weight nonzero codeword, i.e.,

$$d = \min_{\boldsymbol{a} \neq \boldsymbol{b}} d(\boldsymbol{a}, \boldsymbol{b}) = \min_{\boldsymbol{a} \in C, \, \boldsymbol{a} \neq 0} w(\boldsymbol{a}).$$

The linear code C, as a k-dimensional subspace, can be generated by a set of k linearly independent codewords, $\boldsymbol{g}_1, \cdots, \boldsymbol{g}_k \in \mathbb{F}_q^n$. If the codeword $\boldsymbol{g}_i$ is viewed as the row of a $k \times n$ matrix G, the code C is the rowspace of G, and G is referred to as a generator matrix of C. A possible encoding procedure for C is then to encode the message vector $\boldsymbol{m} \in \mathbb{F}_q^k$ to $\boldsymbol{m}G$. Indeed,

$$C = \{\boldsymbol{c} | \boldsymbol{c} = \boldsymbol{m}G, \, \boldsymbol{m} \in \mathbb{F}_q^k\}.$$

Corresponding to the subspace C is the orthogonal subspace

$$C^\perp = \{\boldsymbol{x} \in \mathbb{F}_q^n | (\boldsymbol{x}, \boldsymbol{c}) = 0, \ \forall \boldsymbol{c} \in C\}$$

where $(\boldsymbol{x}, \boldsymbol{c})$ is the usual inner product on $\mathbb{F}_q^n$. Such a subspace will have a generator matrix H and, by definition

$$GH^t = 0$$

where 0 is the $k \times (n-k)$ matrix of zeros. Alternatively, we can express the code as

$$C = \{\boldsymbol{c} \in \mathbb{F}_q^n | \boldsymbol{c}H^t = 0 \in \mathbb{F}_q^{n-k}\}.$$

Viewed in this manner, a codeword $\boldsymbol{c} \in C$ of weight w corresponds to a dependency relation among the w columns of the matrix H corresponding to nonzero coordinates of C. From this observation it follows immediately that the code C has minimum distance of at least d if and only if no subset of $d-1$ or fewer columns of H are linearly dependent over $\mathbb{F}_q$. Because the columns of H are $(n-k)$-tuples, and the maximum number of such independent columns is $n-k$, it follows that $d \leq n-k+1$. This is the Singleton bound for (n, k, d) linear codes. Codes which achieve equality are referred to as maximum-distance separable (MDS).

By similar reasoning, suppose it has been possible to construct a $(n-k) \times (n-1)$ matrix over $\mathbb{F}_q$ such that all sets of $(d-2)$ or fewer columns are linearly independent. In the "worst case" such sums give distinct $(n-k)$-tuples and hence if

$$q^{n-k} > \sum_{i=0}^{d-2} \binom{n-1}{i}(q-1)^i$$

then it is possible to add a column to the matrix which is linearly independent to any set of $d-2$ other columns and hence achieve an $(n, k, d)_q$ code. This is referred to as the Varshamov–Gilbert bound. An asymptotic version of it will be used in a later section.

It will be useful to recall a few elementary properties of polynomials. By a fundamental theorem of algebra, a polynomial of degree n over a field $\mathbb{F}$ has at most n zeros in that field. The smallest extension of $\mathbb{F}$ containing all the zeros of the polynomial is called its splitting field. The polynomial $f(x) \in \mathbb{F}[x]$ has a zero of order m at β if $(x-\beta)^m$ divides $f(x)$ while $(x-\beta)^{m+1}$ does not. A zero of order one is called a simple zero.

One construction of a Reed–Solomon (RS) code over the finite field $\mathbb{F}_q$ is as follows. Let $\{\alpha_0, \alpha_1, \cdots, \alpha_{n-1}\}$ be a set of n distinct elements from $\mathbb{F}_q$ and let $L \subset \mathbb{F}_q[x]$ denote the set of polynomials of degree less than $k \leq n$. Define the code C by

$$C = \{(f(\alpha_0), f(\alpha_1), \cdots, f(\alpha_{n-1})), \ f \in L\}$$

which has length n and dimension k, since a monomial basis easily leads to a generator matrix of rank k. Since a polynomial of degree less then k has at most $k-1$ zeros, each codeword has weight at least $n-(k-1) = n-k+1$. As it is easy to construct polynomials with exactly this many zeros, this is the minimum distance of the code, so the code is MDS. Cyclic

RS codes of length $q-1$ as well as extended noncyclic codes of length q can also be easily described.

Further, let $\{v_0, v_1, \cdots, v_{n-1}\}$ be a set of nonzero, not necessarily distinct elements from $\mathbb{F}_q$. The code

$$C' = \{(v_0 f(\alpha_0), v_1 f(\alpha_1), \cdots, v_{n-1} f(\alpha_{n-1})), \ f \in L\}$$

has the same parameters as the previous code and is referred to as a generalized RS (GRS) code with vector $\boldsymbol{v} = (v_0, v_1, \cdots, v_{n-1})$. This minor adjustment can be useful in some constructions.

The above code can be described in a slightly different manner which will provide a useful perspective for the subsequent transition to construction of codes from algebraic curves. Consider the set of pairs of elements (x_1, x_2), $x_i \in \mathbb{F}_q$. Pairs which are scalar multiples of each other are identified, i.e., the pairs $\beta(x_1, x_2) = (\beta x_1, \beta x_2)$ are identified for all $\beta \in \mathbb{F}_q^*$. Thus all pairs can be grouped into equivalence classes with representatives

$$(1, \alpha), \qquad \alpha \in \mathbb{F}_q \text{ and } (0, 1)$$

and such classes are identified as the projective line $\mathbb{P}^1$. The extension to higher dimensional projective spaces is immediate, constructing $\mathbb{P}^N$ from $N+1$-tuples over $\mathbb{F}_q$.

Consider the set of rational functions $a(x, y)/b(x, y)$ where $a(x, y)$ and $b(x, y)$ are homogeneous polynomials of the same degree. Define now L to be the vector space of all such rational functions over $\mathbb{F}_q$ with the additional property that they do not have poles on $\mathbb{P}^1$ except possibly at the point $(0, 1)$, a point we will subsequently refer to as the point at infinity. Furthermore, when the rational function does have a pole at the point at infinity, it is of order less than k. Clearly, a ratio of polynomials of the form $a(x, y)/x^l$, $l < k$ where $a(x, y)$ is homogeneous of degree l, has this property. The RS code can then be described as

$$C = \{(f(P_1), \cdots, f(P_n), \ f \in L\}$$

where the $P_1, \cdots, P_n$ are a subset of the projective points not at infinity. The process of evaluating rational functions at a sequence of points on a curve (so far only a line) will be of importance to our development.

The addition of the requirement that every cyclic shift of a codeword also be a codeword, has led to powerful techniques for the design of good linear codes. While cyclic codes will not be discussed in any detail here, the following construction of BCH codes will be of interest. Let α be a primitive nth root of unity in an extension field of $\mathbb{F}_q$, say $\mathbb{F}_{q^m}$, $n | q^m - 1$, and let $g(x) \in \mathbb{F}_q[x]$ be the polynomial of smallest degree with zeros $\{\alpha^i, i = 1, 2, \cdots, 2t\}$ for some integer $t \geq 1$. Let the degree of $g(x)$, referred to as the generator polynomial of the code, be $n-k$ and note that $n-k \leq 2tm$ since for general q, the maximum number of distinct cyclotomic cosets of these elements is $2t$, each containing at most m elements. Then

$$C = \{a(x)g(x) | \deg(a(x)) < k, \ a(x) \in \mathbb{F}_q[x]\}$$

is a BCH code of length n, dimension $k \geq n - 2tm$, and minimum distance $d \geq 2t+1$. The code can be viewed as the null space, over $\mathbb{F}_q$, of the rowspace of the parity-check matrix $H = (\alpha^{ij})$, $i = 1, 2, \cdots, 2t$, $j = 1, 2, \cdots, n$. The bound on the minimum distance follows from the fact that any $2t$ or fewer columns are independent, from a van der Monde argument.

Notice that if we take the polynomial

$$h(x) = \prod_{i=1}^{2t} (x - \alpha^i) \in \mathbb{F}_{q^m}[x]$$

then the above code, with $g(x)$ replaced by $h(x)$ and the field of definition, $\mathbb{F}_q$ replaced by $\mathbb{F}_{q^m}$, is an RS code C', of length n, dimension exactly k, and minimum distance exactly $d = 2t + 1$. The BCH code C is then a subfield subcode of C', i.e.,

$$C = C' \cap \mathbb{F}_q^n$$

i.e., the set of all codewords in C with all coordinates in the field $\mathbb{F}$. Such subfield subcodes have been of considerable interest in more general situations than the particular case of BCH codes described here, e.g., [83].

To prepare for a definition of Goppa codes, the definition of BCH codes is first recast. With the same notation as above, consider the computation

$$(x^n - 1) \sum_{i=0}^{n-1} \frac{c_i}{x - \alpha^{-i}}$$

$$= \sum_{i=0}^{n-1} c_i (x^n - 1) \frac{1}{x(1 - x^{-1}\alpha^{-i})}$$

$$= \sum_{i=0}^{n-1} c_i \frac{(x^n - 1)}{x} \cdot \{1 + x^{-1}\alpha^{-i} + x^{-2}\alpha^{-2i} + \cdots\}$$

$$= \sum_{i=0}^{n-1} c_i \sum_{j=0}^{n-1} x^j (\alpha^{-i})^{n-1-j}$$

$$= \sum_{j=0}^{n-1} x^j \sum_{i=0}^{n-1} c_i (\alpha^{j+1})^i.$$

For $j = 0, 1, \cdots, d - 2$ the inner summation is zero, by definition. Thus

$$(x^n - 1) \sum_{i=0}^{n-1} \frac{c_i}{x - \alpha^{-i}} = x^{d-1} f(x)$$

for some polynomial $f(x)$, i.e., the summation is divisible by x^{d-1}. Thus

$$\sum_{i=0}^{n-1} \frac{c_i}{x - \alpha^{-i}} \equiv 0 \bmod x^{2t}.$$

Consequently, a word $(c_0, c_1, \cdots, c_{n-1})$, $c_i \in \mathbb{F}_q$, is a codeword iff it satisfies the above equation. The construction yields either an RS or BCH code depending on the field of definition. Notice that the polynomial x^{2t} has a zero of order $2t$ at $x = 0$.

The passage from the above definition to that of Goppa codes will involve nothing more than replacing the sequence of nth roots of unity with an arbitrary set of distinct elements and the polynomial x^{2t} with a more general polynomial $g(x)$.

(Note that this is not the generator polynomial used in the BCH construction—it is conventional to use $g(x)$ in both cases.)

Definition 2.1: Let $L = \{\alpha_0, \alpha_1, \cdots, \alpha_{n-1}\}$ be a set of n distinct elements in $\mathbb{F}_{q^m}$ and $g(x) \in \mathbb{F}_{q^m}[x]$ be a monic polynomial such that $g(\alpha_i) \neq 0$, $i = 0, 1, \cdots, n-1$. Then the Goppa code $\Gamma(L, g)$ is the set of words $(c_0, c_1, \cdots, c_{n-1}) \in \mathbb{F}_q^n$ such that

$$\sum_{i=0}^{n-1} \frac{c_i}{x - \alpha_i} \equiv 0 \bmod g(x).$$

The polynomial $g(x)$ is referred to as the Goppa polynomial.

Comparing to the previous formulation, if $g(x) = x^{2t}$ and $L = \{\alpha^{-i}, 0 \leq i \leq n - 1\}$, α a primitive nth root of unity, then $\Gamma(L, g)$ is a BCH code with designed distance d, although it is noted that not all BCH codes are Goppa codes. By a simple manipulation of the definitions, it will be shown that $\Gamma(L, g)$ where g has degree t, has dimension at least $n - mt$ and minimum distance at least $t + 1$.

It is also noted that $\Gamma(L, g)$ is a subfield subcode of the dual of a generalized RS code. To see this, let $g(x) = \sum_{i=0}^{t} g_i x^i$. From the fact that

$$\frac{g(z) - g(x)}{z - x} = \sum_{k+j \leq t-1} g_{k+j+1} x^j z^k$$

it follows that, for any codeword $(c_0, \cdots, c_{n-1})$ we have

$$\sum_{i=0}^{n-1} c_i h_i \sum_{k+j \leq t-1} g_{k+j+1} (\alpha_i)^j z^k = 0$$

where $h_i = 1/g(\alpha_i)$. Since the coefficient of z^k must be zero for $0 \leq k \leq t - 1$, it follows that the inner product of the codeword with the rows of the following matrix must be zero:

$$\begin{bmatrix} h_0 g_t & \cdots & h_{n-1} g_t \\ h_0(g_{t-1} + g_t \alpha_0) & \cdots & h_{n-1}(g_{t-1} + g_t \alpha_{n-1}) \\ \vdots & \cdots & \vdots \\ h_0 \sum_{i=1}^{t} g_i \alpha_0^{i-1} & \cdots & h_{n-1} \left(\sum_{i=1}^{t} g_i \alpha_{n-1}^{i-1} \right) \end{bmatrix}.$$

Using elementary row operations, this is easily reduced to a parity-check matrix for the code $\Gamma(L, g)$ of the form

$$\begin{bmatrix} h_0 & h_1 & \cdots & h_{n-1} \\ h_0 \alpha_0 & h_1 \alpha_1 & \cdots & h_{n-1} \alpha_{n-1} \\ \vdots & \vdots & \cdots & \vdots \\ h_0 \alpha_0^{t-1} & h_1 \alpha_1^{t-1} & \cdots & h_{n-1} \alpha_{n-1}^{t-1} \end{bmatrix}$$

from which the properties of the code noted above follow readily. Thus the Goppa code $\Gamma(L, g)$ is the dual of a GRS code with vector $\boldsymbol{v} = (h_0, h_1, \cdots, h_{n-1})$. As the rank of this matrix over $\mathbb{F}_{q^m}$ is exactly t, the rank over $\mathbb{F}_q$ is at most mt. Thus the dimension of $\Gamma(L, g)$ is at least $n - mt$ and the minimum distance is at least $t + 1$.

To put the transition to codes from algebraic curves in perspective, it will be of interest to recast the definition of Goppa codes. Consider a polynomial corresponding to a codeword $(c_0, c_1, \cdots, c_{n-1})$

$$f(x) = \sum_{i=0}^{n-1} \frac{c_1}{(x - \alpha_i)} = \frac{\omega(x)}{\lambda(x)}$$

$$\lambda(x) = \prod_i (x - \alpha_i) \in \mathbb{F}_{q^m}[x]$$

and $\deg \omega(x) < \deg \lambda(x) = n$. Then

$$c_i = f(x)(x - \alpha_i)|_{x = \alpha_i}$$

is obtained by canceling the simple pole in $f(x)$ at α_i and evaluating the result at α_i, i.e., it is the residue of $f(x)$ at α_i. Let

$$\chi_j(x) = \prod_{i=1, i \neq j}^{n} (x - \alpha_i) = \frac{\lambda(x)}{(x - \alpha_j)}$$

and let

$$f(x) = \frac{\omega(x)}{\lambda(x)} = \frac{g(x)q(x)}{\lambda(x)}$$

since by definition $g(x)|f(x)$. Note that the residue of $f(x)$ at α_i can be expressed as

$$\text{Res}_{\alpha_i}(f) = \frac{\omega(x)(x - \alpha_i)}{\lambda(x)}\bigg|_{x = \alpha_i} = \frac{g(\alpha_i)}{\chi_i(\alpha_i)}q(\alpha_i)$$

which is zero only if $q(\alpha_i) = 0$ as $g(\alpha_i)$, $\chi_i(\alpha_i) \neq 0$ by definition. Thus much as was done for RS codes, define a vector space of rational functions $f(x)$, L, such that

i) $f(x)$ has zeros where $g(x)$ has zeros, with multiplicity at least those of $g(x)$;
ii) $f(x)$ has poles only contained in the set L and in that case only poles of order one.

Consider the set of n-tuples C' over $\mathbb{F}_{q^m}$ defined by

$$C' = \{(\text{Res}_{\alpha_0} f, \text{Res}_{\alpha_1} f, \cdots, \text{Res}_{\alpha_{n-1}} f), \, f \in L\}$$

where the residue of a rational function is defined in the usual manner. It is seen immediately that the Goppa code $\Gamma(L, g)$ is the subfield subcode of this set over $\mathbb{F}_q$.

The two important perspectives to be drawn from this section, perspectives that will survive the transition to codes from algebraic curves intact, are the notions of defining codewords in the first instance, as the evaluation of a rational function at a fixed set of distinct places, and in the second instance, as the set of residues of a rational function at a fixed set of places. In the setting of algebraic geometry, the fixed set of places will be drawn from the points on a curve in an algebraic geometry. The two code constructions, using evaluations and residues at this fixed set of places, will carry over. The determination of code parameters, however, will depend in crucial ways on the theory of algebraic curves. The next section will serve as an overview of this theory, in preparation for Section IV which considers classes of codes that use these notions for their construction.

III. BASIC THEORY OF ALGEBRAIC GEOMETRY

We introduce the basic notions of algebraic geometry, in order to extend the construction and properties of codes discussed in the previous section to algebraic-geometry codes, to be discussed in the next section. We will give no proofs but refer to the standard textbooks ([65], [83], [90]). The central concepts required are limited and the material is illustrated with examples. It attempts only to convey the central themes of what is required to appreciate their application to coding.

A. Affine and Projective Varieties

Definition 3.1: Let $\mathbb{F}_q$ be the finite field with q elements and $\overline{\mathbb{F}}_q$ its algebraic closure. The n-dimensional affine space $\mathbb{A}^n$ is the set $\mathbb{A}^n = \{(a_1, \cdots, a_n)|a_i \in \overline{\mathbb{F}}_q\}$.

An element $P \in \mathbb{A}^n$ is called an *affine point* and if $P = (a_1, \cdots, a_n)$ with $a_i \in \overline{\mathbb{F}}_q$ then the elements a_i are called the *coordinates* of the point P. If $\mathbb{G}$ is a subfield of $\overline{\mathbb{F}}_q$ that contains $\mathbb{F}_q$ and P is a point with coordinates in $\mathbb{G}$, then P is called a $\mathbb{G}$-*rational point* and the set of $\mathbb{G}$-rational points of $\mathbb{A}^n$ is denoted $\mathbb{A}^n(\mathbb{G})$.

On the set $\mathbb{A}^{n+1} \setminus \{(0, 0, \cdots, 0)\}$ an equivalence relation $\equiv$ is given by

$$(a_0, \cdots, a_n) \equiv (b_0, \cdots, b_n) \Leftrightarrow \exists \lambda \in \overline{\mathbb{F}}_q \setminus \{0\} \text{ s.t.}$$
$$b_i = \lambda a_i, \qquad i = 0, 1, \cdots, n.$$

The equivalence class of $(a_0, a_1, \cdots, a_n)$ is denoted $(a_0 : a_1 : \cdots : a_n)$.

Definition 3.2: The n-*dimensional projective space* $\mathbb{P}^n$ is the set of all equivalence classes $\{(a_0 : a_1 : \cdots : a_n)|a_i \in \overline{\mathbb{F}}_q$, not all $a_i = 0\}$. An element $P = (a_0 : a_1 : \cdots : a_n) \in \mathbb{P}^n$ is called a *point* and $(a_0 : a_1 : \cdots : a_n)$ are called homogeneous coordinates of P. If $\mathbb{G}$ is a subfield of $\overline{\mathbb{F}}_q$ which contains $\mathbb{F}_q$ and P is a point for which there exist homogeneous coordinates $a_0, \cdots, a_n \in \mathbb{G}$ is called a $\mathbb{G}$-*rational point* and the set of $\mathbb{G}$-rational points of $\mathbb{P}^n$ is denoted $\mathbb{P}^n(\mathbb{G})$.

The set $H = \{(0 : a_1 : \cdots : a_n) \in \mathbb{P}^n\}$ is called the *hyperplane at infinity* and the points $Q \in H$ are the *points at infinity*. The mapping $\varphi \colon \mathbb{A}^n \to \mathbb{P}^n \setminus H$ defined by $\varphi(a_1, a_2, \cdots, a_n) = (1 : a_1 \cdots, : a_n)$ embeds $\mathbb{A}^n$ in $\mathbb{P}^n$. As a matter of notation, Q will be reserved throughout to denote a point at infinity.

The one-dimensional projective space, also called the projective line, consists of the points $(1 : a_1)$, $a_1 \in \overline{\mathbb{F}}_q$ together with the point at infinity $(0 : 1)$ and this set has been used in the previous section for the construction of RS codes.

A polynomial $f \in \overline{\mathbb{F}}_q[x_1, x_2, \cdots, x_n]$ can be considered as a map $f \colon \mathbb{A}^n \to \overline{\mathbb{F}}_q$ defined by

$$f(P) = f(a_1, \cdots, a_n).$$

If $f(P) = 0$ we call P a *zero* of f.

More generally, with every $T \subseteq \overline{\mathbb{F}}_q[x_1, \cdots, x_n]$ we associate the *zero set of T*

$$Z(T) = \{P \in \mathbb{A}^n | f(P) = 0 \text{ for every } f \in T\}.$$

Definition 3.3: A subset V of $\mathbb{A}^n$ is called an *algebraic set* if there exists a $T \subset \overline{\mathbb{F}}_q[x_1, \cdots, x_n]$ such that

$$V = Z(T).$$

Definition 3.4: Let $V \subset \mathbb{A}^n$ be an algebraic set. The set

$$I(V) = \{f \in \overline{\mathbb{F}}_q[x_1, \cdots, x_n] | f(P) = 0 \text{ for every } P \in V\}$$

is called the ideal of V.

It is easy to see that $I(V)$ is indeed an ideal of $\overline{\mathbb{F}}_q[x_1, \cdots, x_n]$. The ring $\overline{\mathbb{F}}_q[x_1, \cdots, x_n]$ is Noetherian, that is, every ideal is finitely generated. An ideal I with a single generating element is called principal and an ideal is prime if it is not the whole ring and whenever $ab \in I$ then $a \in I$ or $b \in I$. An ideal I is maximal in a set A if there is no proper ideal of A that properly contains I.

Lemma 3.5. Hilbert Nullstellensatz: Every maximal ideal of $\overline{\mathbb{F}}_q[x_1, \cdots, x_n]$ is of the form $\langle x_1 - a_1, \cdots, x_n - a_n \rangle$ with $a_i \in \overline{\mathbb{F}}_q$, $i = 1, \cdots, n$. For every element $P = (a_1, \cdots, a_n) \in \mathbb{A}^n$ the singleton $\{P\}$ is an algebraic set with ideal $I(P) = \langle x_1 - a_1, \cdots, x_n - a_n \rangle$.

Definition 3.6: An *affine variety* V in $\mathbb{A}^n$ is an algebraic set where $I(V)$ is a prime ideal. The set of $\mathbb{G}$-rational points of V is denoted $V(\mathbb{G})$. If $I(V)$ has a set of generators in $\mathbb{G}[x_1, \cdots, x_n]$ we say that V is *defined over* $\mathbb{G}$ and denote that $V/\mathbb{G}$. In this case we associate with the variety $V/\mathbb{G}$ the ideal

$$I(V/\mathbb{G}) = I(V) \cap \mathbb{G}[x_1, \cdots, x_n].$$

Definition 3.7: Let V be an affine variety. The quotient ring

$$\overline{\mathbb{F}}_q[V] = \overline{\mathbb{F}}_q[x_1, \cdots, x_n]/I(V)$$

is called the *coordinate ring* of V.

If V is defined over $\mathbb{G}$ the quotient ring

$$\mathbb{G}[V] = \mathbb{G}[x_1, \cdots, x_n]/I(V/\mathbb{G})$$

is called the *coordinate ring* of $V/\mathbb{G}$.

Remark: The coordinate ring of a variety V can be considered as a set of polynomial functions with values in $\overline{\mathbb{F}}_q$ defined at every point of V: let $g \in \overline{\mathbb{F}}_q[V]$ and $G \in \overline{\mathbb{F}}_q[x_1, \cdots, x_n]$ such that $g = G + I(V)$. Put $g(P) = G(P)$. This definition is independent of the choice of the representative G: if $G' \in \overline{\mathbb{F}}_q[x_1, \cdots, x_n]$, and $G' + I(V) = G + I(V)$ then $G' - G \in I(V)$ and, therefore, $0 = (G'-G)(P) = G'(P) - G(P)$ hence $G'(P) = G(P)$.

Since the ideal $I(V)$ of the variety V is a prime ideal the coordinate ring $\overline{\mathbb{F}}_q[V]$ is a domain. The following definition is therefore possible.

Definition 3.8: Let V be an affine variety. The field of fractions of $\overline{\mathbb{F}}_q[V]$, denoted $\overline{\mathbb{F}}_q(V)$ is called the *function field* of V. If V is defined over $\mathbb{G}$ we define the function field of $V/\mathbb{G}$, denoted $\mathbb{G}(V)$, as the field of fractions of $\mathbb{G}[V]$.

It follows from the definition of the function field $\overline{\mathbb{F}}_q(V)$ that it is a finitely generated extension of $\overline{\mathbb{F}}_q$, that is, there

exists elements $x_1, \cdots, x_k \in \overline{\mathbb{F}}_q(V)$ such that $\overline{\mathbb{F}}_q(V) = \overline{\mathbb{F}}_q(x_1, x_2, \cdots, x_k)$.

The *dimension* of an affine variety is the transcendence degree of $\overline{\mathbb{F}}_q(V)$ over $\mathbb{F}_q$.

Definition 3.9: An *affine curve* $\chi \subseteq \mathbb{A}^n$ is a variety of dimension 1.

As a matter of notation we will use χ to denote a curve in an algebraic geometry. When it is defined by a polynomial, we will denote the polynomial by F_χ or simply F when the curve is understood.

Example 3.10: Let $F \in \overline{\mathbb{F}}_q[x, y]$ be an irreducible polynomial and let us consider the variety

$$\chi = \{F = 0\} = \{P \in \mathbb{A}^2 | C(P) = 0\}.$$

It is clear that the function field $\overline{\mathbb{F}}_q(\chi)$ has transcendence degree one, and therefore χ is an affine curve and since it is contained in $\mathbb{A}^2$ it is called an *affine plane curve*.

Example 3.11: In the affine plane, we consider the parabola V with equation $Y^2 = X$. Here the coordinate ring $\overline{\mathbb{F}}_q(V)$ consists of all the expressions of the form $A + By$, where A and B are in $\overline{\mathbb{F}}_q[x]$ and y satisfies $y^2 = x$. So, $\overline{\mathbb{F}}_q(V)$ is an algebraic extension of $\overline{\mathbb{F}}_q(x)$ by an element y, satisfying this equation of degree 2.

A point (x_0, y_0) on a curve χ, with equation $F(x, y) = 0$ is said to be *nonsingular* if the partial derivatives do not both vanish at the point. The *tangent line at a point* (x_0, y_0) is a *linear polynomial* (i.e., a polynomial of degree one) described by the equation

$$t_{(x_0, y_0)}(x, y) = F_x(x_0, y_0)(x - x_0) + F_y(x_0, y_0)(y - y_0)$$

where $F_x(x, y)$ and $F_y(x, y)$ are the partial derivatives of $F(x, y)$ with respect to x and y.

Example 3.12: The curve $F(x, y) = y^2 - x$ has a tangent line at the point $(x = 1, y = 1)$, $t_{(1, 1)}(x, y) = -x + 2y - 1$ since $F_x(x, y) = -1$ and $F_y(x, y) = 2y$. On the other hand, a singular point occurs on the curve $F(x, y) = y^2 - x^3 + 2x^2 - x$ at the point $(x = 1, y = 0)$ since both derivatives $F_x(x, y) = -3x^2 + 4x - 1$ and $F_y(x, y) = 2y$ have a common zero at $(x = 1, y = 0)$ [1]. In this case, the curve has two distinct tangent lines at the singular point.

Definition 3.13: A curve χ is said to be *nonsingular* (or *smooth* or *regular*) if all the points on the curve are nonsingular, otherwise the curve is *singular*.

A more general definition of singularity will be given later in the section. In the example above, $y^2 - x$ is nonsingular while $y^2 - x^3 + 2x^2 - x$ is singular. A test for singularity of a curve χ is the existence, or not, of common zeros in the two partial derivatives.

Example 3.14: As an example over a finite field, consider the *Hermitian curve* from which an important class of codes will be considered in the next section. These curves will be used in a sequence of examples in this section. Consider the finite field $\mathbb{F}_q$ where $q = r^2 = p^{2m}$. The Hermitian curve is described by the polynomial $F(x, y) = y^r + y - x^{r+1}$. The curve is nonsingular since the derivatives

$$F_x(x, y) = -(r+1)x^r = -x^r \quad (r = p = 0 \text{ in } \mathbb{F}_q)$$

and

$$F_y(x, y) = ry^{r-1} + 1 = 1$$

have no roots in common (F_y has no roots).

A *monomial* of degree d is a polynomial

$$G \in \overline{\mathbb{F}}_q[x_0, \cdots, x_n]$$

of the form $G = a \cdot \prod x_i^{d_i}$ with $a \neq 0$ and $\sum_{i=0}^n d_i = d$, and a polynomial F is a *homogeneous polynomial* if F is the sum of monomials of the same degree.

A homogeneous polynomial $F \in \overline{\mathbb{F}}_q[x_0, \cdots, x_n]$ is said to have a *zero* at a point $P = (a_0 : a_1 : \cdots : a_n) \in \mathbb{P}^n/\overline{\mathbb{F}}_q$ if $F(a_0, a_1, \cdots, a_n) = 0$. This makes sense since

$$F(\lambda a_0, \cdots, \lambda a_n) = \lambda^d F(a_0, \cdots, a_n)$$

if F is homogeneous of degree d.

For a polynomial $f(x) \in \mathbb{F}_q[x]$ of degree d, the polynomial $y^d f(x/y)$ will be homogeneous of degree d. Conversely, one can reduce a homogeneous polynomial of degree d in n variables to a (nonhomogeneous) polynomial in $n-1$ variables.

More generally, with every set T of homogeneous polynomials from $\overline{\mathbb{F}}_q[x_0, x_1, \cdots, x_n]$ we associate the zero set of T

$$Z(T) = \{P \in \mathbb{P}^n | f(P) = 0 \text{ for every } f \in T\}.$$

Definition 3.15: A subset V of $\mathbb{P}^n$ is called a projective algebraic set if there exists a set T of homogeneous polynomials such that

$$V = Z(T).$$

Definition 3.16: Let $V \subseteq \mathbb{P}^n$ be a projective algebraic set. The ideal in $\overline{\mathbb{F}}_q[x_0, \cdots, x_n]$ which is generated by all homogeneous polynomials F with $F(P) = 0$ for every $P \in V$ is called the ideal of V and is denoted $I(V)$.

Definition 3.17: A *projective variety* V in $\mathbb{P}^n$ is a projective algebraic set such that $I(V)$ is a prime ideal.

The set of $\mathbb{G}$-rational points of V is denoted $V(\mathbb{G})$. If $I(V)$ has a set of homogeneous polynomials from $\mathbb{G}[x_0, \cdots, x_n]$ as generators we say that V is *defined over* $\mathbb{G}$ and denote that $V/\mathbb{G}$. In this case we associate with $V/\mathbb{G}$ the ideal

$$I(V/\mathbb{G}) = I(V) \cap \mathbb{G}[x_0, \cdots, x_n].$$

Definition 3.18: Let $V \subseteq \mathbb{P}^n$ be a nonempty projective variety. The quotient ring

$$\Gamma_h(V) = \overline{\mathbb{F}}_q[x_0, \cdots, x_n]/I(V)$$

is called the homogeneous coordinate ring of V. If V is defined over $\mathbb{G}$ then $\Gamma_h(V/\mathbb{G}) = \mathbb{G}[x_0, \cdots, x_n]/I(V/\mathbb{G})$.

An element $f \in \Gamma_h(V)$ is said to be a *form* of degree d if $f = F + I(V)$ where F is a homogeneous polynomial of degree d.

The function field of V is defined by

$$\overline{\mathbb{F}}_q(V) = \left\{ \frac{g}{h} \Big| g, h \in \Gamma_h(V) \text{ are forms of the} \right.$$
$$\left. \text{same degree and } h \neq 0 \right\}$$

and

$$\mathbb{G}(V) = \left\{ \frac{g}{h} \Big| g, \quad h \in \Gamma_h(V/\mathbb{G}) \text{ are forms of the} \right.$$
$$\left. \text{same degree and } h \neq 0 \right\}.$$

The *dimension* of the projective variety V is the transcendence degree of $\overline{\mathbb{F}}_q(V)$ over $\mathbb{F}_q$.

Definition 3.19: A *projective curve* $\chi \subseteq \mathbb{P}^n$ is a projective variety of dimension 1.

Example 3.20: Let $F \in \overline{\mathbb{F}}_q[X, Y, Z]$ be an irreducible homogeneous polynomial and let us consider the variety

$$\chi = \{F = 0\} = \{P \in \mathbb{P}^2 | F(P) = 0\}.$$

It is clear that this is a curve and since it is contained in $\mathbb{P}^2$ it is called the *projective curve*.

We clarify the connection between projective and affine varieties. For a polynomial

$$F = F(x_1, \cdots, x_n) \in \overline{\mathbb{F}}_q[x_1, \cdots, x_n]$$

of degree d set

$$F^* = x_0^d F(x_1/x_0, \cdots, x_n/x_0) \in \overline{\mathbb{F}}_q[x_0, \cdots, x_n]$$

then F^* is a homogeneous polynomial of degree d in $n+1$ variables.

Consider now an affine variety $V \in \mathbb{A}^n$ and the corresponding ideal $I(V) \subset \overline{\mathbb{F}}_q[x_1, \cdots, x_n]$. Define the projective variety $\tilde{V} \subset \mathbb{P}^n$ as follows:

$$\tilde{V} = \{P \in \mathbb{P}^n | F^*(P) = 0 \text{ for all } F \in I(V)\}.$$

This variety is called the *projective closure* of V.

On the other hand, let $\tilde{V} \subset \mathbb{P}^n$ be a projective variety and suppose that

$$W = \tilde{V} \cap \{(c_0 : \cdots : c_n) \in \mathbb{P}^n | c_0 \neq 0\} \neq \emptyset.$$

Define $\varphi \colon \mathbb{A}^n \to \mathbb{P}^n$ by

$$\varphi(a_1, a_1, \cdots, a_n) = (1 : a_1 : \cdots, a_n).$$

Then

$$V = \varphi^{-1}(W)$$

is an affine variety and

$$I(V) = \{F(1 : x_1 : \cdots : x_n) | F \in I(\tilde{V})\}$$

and the projective closure of V is $\tilde{V}$.

If V is an affine variety and $\tilde{V}$ its projective closure, the function fields $\overline{\mathbb{F}}_q(V)$ and $\overline{\mathbb{F}}_q(\tilde{V})$ are isomorphic and V and $\tilde{V}$ have the same dimension.

Example 3.21: The projective closure of the Hermitian curve has the equation $y^r z + y z^r - x^{r+1} = 0$ and this curve has only one point at infinity, namely $(0 : 1 : 0)$.

B. The Local Ring at a Point

Let V be a variety and $P \in V$. If $f \in \overline{\mathbb{F}}_q(V)$ then $f = g/h$ with $g, h \in \overline{\mathbb{F}}_q[V]$ for an affine variety and $f = g/h$ with $g, h \in \Gamma_h(v)$ for a projective variety. If there exists a representative of $f = g/h$ and $h(P) \neq 0$, f is said to be *defined* at P.

The ring $O_P(V) = \{f \in \overline{\mathbb{F}}_q(V) | f \text{ is defined at } P\}$ is called the *local ring at* P.

The evaluation of an element $f \in O_P(V)$ is defined as $f(P) = g(P)/h(P)$ in the affine case and in the projective case let $g = G + I(V)$, $h = H + I(V) \in \Gamma_h(V)$ where G and H are homogeneous polynomials of degree d. Let $P = (a_0 : a_1 : \cdots : a_n)$. Since

$$\frac{G(\lambda a_0, \cdots, \lambda a_n)}{H(\lambda a_0, \cdots, \lambda a_n)} = \frac{\lambda^d G(a_0, \cdots, a_n)}{\lambda^d H(a_0, \cdots, a_n)} = \frac{G(a_0, \cdots, a_n)}{H(a_0, \cdots, a_n)}$$

we can put

$$f(P) = G(a_0, \cdots, a_n)/H(a_0, \cdots, a_n)$$

if $H(P) \neq 0$.

$O_P(V)$ is indeed a local ring, its maximal ideal is

$$M_P(V) = \{f \in O_p(V) | f(P) = 0\}.$$

Definition 3.22: A *valuation ring* of the function field $\overline{\mathbb{F}}_q(V)$ is a ring O with the properties

- $\overline{\mathbb{F}}_q \subset O \subset \overline{\mathbb{F}}_q(V)$.
- For any $z \in \overline{\mathbb{F}}_q(V)$, $z \in O$, or $z^{-1} \in O$.

Theorem 3.23: Let O be a valuation ring of the function field $\overline{\mathbb{F}}_q(V)$. Then

- O is a local ring and has as unique maximal ideal $P = O \setminus O^*$ where $O^* = \{z \in O | \exists w \in O: zw = 1\}$.
- For $0 \neq x \in \overline{\mathbb{F}}_q(V)$, $x \in \mathcal{P} \Leftrightarrow x^{-1} \notin O$.
- $\mathcal{P}$ is a principal ideal.
- If $\mathcal{P} = tO$ then any $0 \neq z \in F$ has a unique representation of the form $z = t^n u$ for some $n \in \mathbb{Z}$, $u \in O^*$.
- O is a principal ideal domain. If $\mathcal{P} = tO$ and $\{0\} \neq I \subseteq O$ is an ideal then $I = t^n O$ for some $n \in \mathbb{N}$.

Definition 3.24: Let O be a valuation ring of $\overline{\mathbb{F}}_q(V)$ and $\mathcal{P}$ its unique maximal ideal with $\mathcal{P} = tO$. Then $z \in \overline{\mathbb{F}}_q(V)$ has a unique representation $z = t^n u$ with $u \in O^*$, $n \in \mathbb{Z}$. We define $\nu_{\mathcal{P}}(z) = n$ and $\nu_{\mathcal{P}}(0) = \infty$.

Observe that this definition does not depend on the choice of generator t of $\mathcal{P}$.

Theorem 3.25: The function $\nu: \overline{\mathbb{F}}_q(V) \to \mathbb{Z} \cup \{\infty\}$ satisfies

- $\nu_{\mathcal{P}}(x) = \infty \Leftrightarrow x = 0$
- $\nu_{\mathcal{P}}(xy) = \nu_{\mathcal{P}}(x) + \nu_{\mathcal{P}}(y)$
- $\nu_{\mathcal{P}}(x + y) \geq \min\{\nu_{\mathcal{P}}(x), \nu_{\mathcal{P}}(y)\}$ with equality if $\nu_{\mathcal{P}}(x) \neq \nu_{\mathcal{P}}(y)$
- $\exists z$ s.t. $\nu_{\mathcal{P}}(z) = 1$
- $\nu_{\mathcal{P}}(a) = 0$ for any $0 \neq a \in \overline{\mathbb{F}}_q$
- $\mathcal{P} = \{z \in \overline{\mathbb{F}}_q(V) | \nu_{\mathcal{P}}(z) > 0\}$
- $O = \{z \in \overline{\mathbb{F}}_q(V) | \nu_{\mathcal{P}}(z) \geq 0\}$
- $O^* = \{z \in \overline{\mathbb{F}}_q(V) | \nu_{\mathcal{P}}(z) = 0\}$.

A function satisfying the first five of these is called a *discrete valuation* and the ring O a *discrete valuation ring*.

We will now connect the points of a variety with discrete valuation rings of its function field. A more general definition of the singularity of a curve or variety than the one given earlier, follows:

Definition 3.26: Let V be a variety and $I(V) = \langle G_1, G_2, \cdots, G_s \rangle$. Let P be a point of V and consider the matrix

$$J_{V, P} = \{a_{ij}\}$$

where

$$a_{ij} = (\partial G_i / \partial x_j)(P)$$

for $i = 1, \cdots, s$, and $j = 1, \cdots, n$ (affine case) or $j = 0, 1, \cdots, n$ (projective case).

P is called *nonsingular* if

$$\text{rank } J_{V, P} = n - \dim V$$

and *singular* otherwise. The variety V is called singular if it has at least one singular point and *regular* otherwise.

Theorem 3.27: Let χ be a curve (projective or affine) and P a point of χ. P is nonsingular if and only if $O_P(\chi)$ is a discrete valuation ring.

If the variety is defined over $\mathbb{G}$ one can also consider the function field $\mathbb{G}(V)$. The definitions and the theorems still hold when one exchanges $\overline{\mathbb{F}}_q$ and $\mathbb{G}$. If ν is a discrete valuation of $\mathbb{G}(V)$ with valuation ring O and maximal ideal $\mathcal{P}$ then the pair $(O, \mathcal{P})$ is called a *closed point* of V and $d = [O/\mathcal{P}: \mathbb{G}]$ is called the degree of the point. If $\mathbb{G} = \overline{\mathbb{F}}_q$ then the closed points correspond to the nonsingular points and all have degree 1.

Let $\mathcal{P}_\chi$ denote the set of closed points of the curve χ.

Example 3.28: We will consider the projective plane curve χ with equation $zy^2 + yz^2 = x^3$ over the field $\overline{\mathbb{F}}_2$. In $Q = (0 : 1 : 1)$, we can take $t = x/z$ as a local parameter. Let $f = x/(y + z)$. We will determine $\nu_Q(f)$. We have

$$\frac{x}{y + z} = \frac{x^3}{x^2 y + x^2 z} = \frac{zy^2 + z^2 y}{x^2 y + x^2 z} = \frac{zy}{x^2} = t^{-2} \frac{y}{z}$$

and the second factor is a unit in $O_Q(\chi)$ so $\nu_Q(f) = -2$.

C. Divisors, the Vector Space $L(G)$, and the Theorem of Riemann–Roch

Let χ be a regular projective curve defined over $\mathbb{F}_q$. A *divisor* of χ is a formal sum

$$D = \sum_{P \in \chi} n_P P$$

where $n_P \in \mathbb{Z}$ and all but finitely many n_P's are zero. The *degree* of D is

$$\deg D = \sum_{P \in \chi} n_P \deg P.$$

The divisors of χ form an additive group $D(\chi)$, the *divisor group* of χ.

Let $f \in \overline{\mathbb{F}}_q(\chi)$. The *order of f* at a point $P \in \chi$ is defined to be $\nu_P(f)$ where ν_P is the discrete valuation corresponding to the valuation ring $O_P(\chi)$. If $\nu_P(f) > 0$, f is said to have a *zero* at P, and if $\nu_P(f) < 0$, f is said to have a *pole* at P. The *principal divisor* (f) of an element $0 \neq f \in \overline{\mathbb{F}}_q(\chi)$ is defined as $\sum_{P \in \chi} \nu_P(f)P$, and the *zero divisor* of (f) is

$$(f)_0 = \sum_{\nu_P(f)>0} \nu_P(f)P$$

and the *pole divisor* of f is

$$(f)_\infty = - \sum_{\nu_P(f)<0} \nu_P(f)P.$$

The degree of a principal divisor is zero which gives that

$$-\sum_{\nu_P(f)<0} \nu_P(f)P = \sum_{\nu_P(f)>0} \nu_P(f)P.$$

On $D(\chi)$ we define a partial order by

$$D_1 = \sum_{P \in \mathcal{P}_\chi} m_P P \leq D_2$$

$$= \sum_{P \in \mathcal{P}_\chi} n_P P \Leftrightarrow m_P \leq n_P, \qquad \text{for all } P \in \chi.$$

Definition 3.29: If $G \in D(\chi)$ let

$$L(G) = \{f \in \mathbb{F}_q(\chi) | (f) + G \geq 0\} \cup \{0\}$$

be the set of rational functions with poles only at the zeros of the divisor G and have zeros at the poles of G.

Notice that the divisor of a product of two functions is the sum of the respective divisors, $(f \cdot h) = (f) + (h)$, and the divisor of the sum of two functions $(f + h)$ satisfies $(f + h) \geq \min\{(f), (h)\}$, i.e., the minimum coefficient is chosen, point by point. $L(G)$ is a finite-dimensional vector space over $\mathbb{F}_q$, its dimension is denoted $l(G)$. The *Theorem of Riemann* says that there exists a nonnegative integer m such that for every divisor G of χ

$$l(G) \geq \deg(G) + 1 - m$$

and the smallest nonnegative integer with this property is called the *genus* and is denoted by $g(\chi)$ or g.

In order to determine $l(G)$ one needs the so-called *differentials*. We can think of differentials as objects of the form $f \, dh$ where f and h are rational functions, i.e., elements of $\mathbb{F}_q(\chi)$, such that the map which sends h to dh is a *derivation*. A derivation is $\mathbb{F}_q$-linear and the *Leibnitz rule* $d(h_1 h_2) = h_1 dh_2 + h_2 dh_1$ holds. We denote the set of differentials on χ by Ω_χ. One can talk about zeros and poles of differentials. At every closed point P there exists a *local parameter* that is, a function u such that $\nu_P(u) = 1$, and for every differential ω there exists a function f such that $\omega = f \, du$. The valuation $\nu_P(\omega)$ is now by definition $\nu_P(f)$, so we say that ω has a zero of order ρ if $\rho = \nu_P(f) > 0$ and ω has a pole of order ρ if $\rho = -\nu_P(f) > 0$. The divisor of ω is by definition $(\omega) = \sum \nu_P(u)P$. The divisor of a differential is called *canonical* and always has degree $2g - 2$.

In the same way as we have defined $L(G)$ for functions we now define the vector space $\Omega(G)$ with zeros and poles prescribed by G as

$$\Omega(G) = \{\omega \in \Omega_\chi | w = 0 \text{ or } (\omega) \geq G\}.$$

One could have defined the genus as the dimension of the vector space of differentials without poles, that is, of $\Omega(O)$, where O is the divisor with coefficient 0 at every closed point. The dimension of $\Omega(G)$ is called the *index of speciality* of G and is denoted by $i(G)$.

Theorem 3.30. Riemann–Roch: For a divisor G of a curve of genus g

$$l(G) = \deg(G) + 1 - g + i(G).$$

Furthermore, $i(G) = l(K - G)$ for all divisors G and canonical divisors K.

Moreover it is a consequence of the Riemann–Roch theorem that

Theorem 3.31: For any divisor G with $\deg(G) > 2g - 2$,

$$l(G) = \deg(G) + 1 - g.$$

Let ω be a differential. If P is a closed point of degree m and u is a local parameter at P, then there exists a rational function f such that $\omega = f \, du$. This function f has a formal Laurent series $\sum_{i=\rho}^\infty a_i u^i$, where the coefficients $a_i \in \mathbb{F}_{q^m}$ and $\rho = \nu_P(\omega)$ and $a_P \neq 0$. The *residue of ω* at P is by definition $\text{Tr}(a_{-1})$ and is denoted by $\text{Res}_P(\omega)$, where Tr is the trace map from $\mathbb{F}_{q^m}$ to $\mathbb{F}_q$.

The *residue theorem* states that for $\omega \in \Omega_\chi$

$$\sum_{P \in \mathcal{P}_\chi} \text{Res}_P(\omega) = 0.$$

Let P be a point of degree one. An integer $n \geq 0$ is called a *pole number* of P iff there exists an $f \in \overline{\mathbb{F}}_q(\chi)$ with $(f)_\infty = nP$. Otherwise, n is called a *gap number* of P. Clearly, n is a pole number if $l(nP) > l((n-1)P)$. Moreover, the set of pole numbers form an additive semigroup since if $(f_1)_\infty = n_1 P$ and $(f_2)_\infty = n_2 P$ then $(f_1 \cdot f_2)_\infty = (n_1 + n_2)P$.

Theorem 3.32: Suppose $g > 0$ and P is a closed point of degree one. Then there are exactly g gap numbers $i_1 < i_2 < \cdots < i_g$ of P and $i_1 = 1$ and $i_g \leq 2g - 1$.

An important case from the perspective of algebraic-geometry codes is when the curve χ is nonsingular and intersects the line at infinity in a single point, Q say. In this case the elements of $R = \bigcup_{m=0}^\infty L(mQ)$ has a simple description, since the rational functions $X = x/z$ and $Y = y/z$ represent a monomial generating set for R.

Example 3.33: Consider the Hermitian curve with equation $x^{r+1} = y^r + y$ over the field $\mathbb{F}_{r^2}$. Here $Q = (0 : 1 : 0)$ and $X = x/z$, $Y = y/z$ is a monomial generating set for

$$R = \bigcup_{m=0}^\infty L(mQ).$$

It is obvious that the sets $\{X^i Y^j | 0 \leq i < r\}$ and $\{X^i Y^j | 0 \leq i < r + 1\}$ each describes bases for R.

TABLE I
Gaps for the Hermitian Curve at the Point Q

q ($= r^2$)	r	Number of points	genus g	gaps
4	2	9	1	$\{1\}$
9	3	28	3	$\{1, 2, 5\}$
16	4	65	6	$\{1, 2, 3, 6, 7, 11\}$
25	5	126	10	$\{1, 2, 3, 4, 7, 8, 9, 13, 14, 19\}$
64	8	513	23	$\{1, 2, 3, 4, 5, 6, 7, 10, 11, 12, 13, 14, 15, 19,$ $20, 21, 22, 23, 28, 29, 30, 31, 37, 38, 39, 46, 47, 55\}$

The notion of gaps and the genus of the curve are closely related in this situation. As before, let $X = x/z$ and $Y = y/z$ and let $o_X > 0$ and $o_Y > 0$ be the pole orders at Q of these two functions. The semigroup of gaps is then generated by o_X and o_Y, so the genus of the curve is the number of elements in $\mathbb{N}$ that are not of the form $io_X + jo_Y$, $i, j \in \mathbb{N}$. For example, if $o_X = 3$ and $o_Y = 4$ then the gaps are $\{1, 2, 5\}$, which in turn implies that there are no rational functions on the curve with these pole orders at Q.

Example 3.34: As an example, the Hermitian curve over $\mathbb{F}_q$, $q = r^2$ is regular and has genus $g = r(r - 1)/2$. The order of X and Y is r and $r + 1$, respectively. To see this first consider the function $X = (x/z)$. The equation $x = 0$ describes a line in the plane. The intersection with the Hermitian curve, described by $y^r z + y z^r - x^{r+1}$, are single points of the form $(0 : \beta : 1)$ where $\beta^r + \beta = 0$. There are exactly r solutions for $\beta \in \mathbb{F}_q$. These are the simple zeros of the function X over the curve. Thus we conclude that X has r zeros, and thus r poles at the point Q and so the degree of X is $o_X = r$. In the case of $Y = y/z$, the zeros in the plane correspond to the line $y = 0$, intersects the Hermitian curve at the single point $(0 : 0 : 1)$. However, the order of this single root is $r + 1$. This implies that the pole order at Q, and thus the degree of Y on the curve, is equal to $o_Y = r + 1$. Table I shows some of these results for small values of r. The discussion can be cast more algebraically by saying that at $Q = (0 : 1 : 0)$, the semigroup S of pole numbers are generated by the divisors rQ and $(r + 1)Q$, that is, $S = \{ar + b(r + 1) | a, b \in \mathbb{N}_0\}$, and it can be seen that $(x/z)_\infty = rQ$ and $(y/z)_\infty = (r + 1)Q$ which implies that $L(mQ)$ has the functions $\{(x/z)^a (y/z)^b | ar + b(r + 1) \le m\}$ as a basis. The above computation of the genus of the curve, noted above, follows from this basis.

Example 3.35: We can directly calculate the dimension of $L(aQ)$. We get

$$\dim(L(aQ)) = \begin{cases} 1, & a = 0 \\ 1 + a - m(a), & 0 < a < 2g \\ a - g + 1, & 2g \le a \end{cases}$$

where $m(a) = |\{i | i \text{ is a gap}, i \le a\}|$. Note that $m(a) = g$ for $a \ge 2g$.

D. Counting Points on Curves

Let χ be a regular curve defined over $\mathbb{F}_q$ and let N_m be the number of points on χ of degree one over $\mathbb{F}_{q^m}$.

Definition 3.36: The zeta function of χ is defined as

$$Z(t) = \exp \sum_{m=1}^{\infty} N_m \frac{t^m}{m}.$$

The zeta function contains information about the number of points in various extensions of $\mathbb{F}_q$. It has the following property.

Theorem 3.37. Hasse–Weil: Let g be the genus of χ. Then

$$Z(t) = \frac{P(t)}{(1 - t)(1 - qt)}$$

where

$$P(t) \in \mathbb{Z}[t], \qquad P(t) = \prod_{i=1}^{2g} (1 - \alpha_i t)$$

where

$$\alpha_i \in \mathbb{C}, \qquad |\alpha_i| = \sqrt{q}, \ \alpha_i \alpha_{2g+1-i} = q$$

and

$$N_m = q^m + 1 - \sum_{i=1}^{2g} \alpha_i^r$$

and the α_i are complex algebraic integers.

The proof of $|\alpha_i| = \sqrt{q}$ is difficult. It is an analog of the Riemann hypothesis for curves over finite fields and was proved by Weil. It has as a consequence the Hasse–Weil bound.

Corollary 3.38. The Hasse–Weil Bound:

$$|N_m - (1 + q^m)| \le 2g \sqrt{q^m}.$$

Example 3.39: The Hermitian curve considered in Example 3.34 has $1 + r^2 + r(r - 1)r = r^3 + 1$ points of degree one over $\mathbb{F}_q$ so $N_1 = 1 + q + 2g\sqrt{q}$ and is therefore optimal with respect to the Hasse–Weil bound. To calculate the number of points we first note that $(0 : 1 : 0)$ is the only point with $z = 0$. If $z = 1$ we have $x^{r+1} = y^r + y$. The right-hand side is the trace function from $\mathbb{F}_{r^2}$ to $\mathbb{F}_r$ so from each of the r values of y, where $y^r + y = 0$ we get one solution and from the $r^2 - r$ values of y where $y^r + y \ne 0$ we get $r + 1$ x's. This gives $r + (r + 1)(r^2 - r) + 1$ points, that is, $r^3 + 1$.

E. Algebraic-Geometry Codes

The two code constructions at the end of Section II, one consisting of evaluating rational functions at a sequence of points, such as the case for RS codes and polynomial functions, the other evaluating residues of rational functions at a sequence of points, such as for Goppa codes, will be emulated for the case when the sequence of points is obtained from curves in an algebraic geometry.

In the first instance, let χ be a nonsingular projective curve over $\mathbb{F}_q$ of genus g and let $P_1, P_2, \cdots, P_n$ be rational points on χ and $D = P_1 + P_2 + \cdots + P_n$, a divisor. Let G be a divisor with support disjoint from D as noted, and assume that $2g - 2 < \deg(G) < n$.

Define the linear code $C(D, G)$ over $\mathbb{F}_q$ as the image of the linear map

$$\alpha: L(G) \longrightarrow \mathbb{F}_q^n$$
$$f \longmapsto (f(P_1), f(P_2), \cdots, f(P_n))$$

where

$$L(G) = \{f \in \overline{\mathbb{F}}_q(C) | (f) + G \geq 0\} \cup \{0\}$$

where $\overline{\mathbb{F}}_q(\chi)$ is the function field of the curve χ and

$$(f) = \sum_P \operatorname{ord}_P(f) P.$$

The parameters of the code are established by using the properties discussed in the previous section. The kernel of the map is the set $L(G - D)$ and

$$k = \dim C(D, G) = \dim L(G) - \dim L(G - D)$$
$$= \deg(G) - g + 1$$

since $\dim(L(G - D)) = 0$ if $\deg G \leq n$. The minimum distance follows from the following theorem.

Theorem 3.40: The minimum distance d of the code $C(D, G)$ satisfies

$$d \geq d^* = n - \deg(G).$$

Proof: $F \in L(G)$ has at most $\deg(G)$ zeros. $\square$

Thus the designed minimum distance of $C(D, G)$ is within g of the Singleton bound.

To emulate the residue construction of the classical Goppa codes, choose G and D as in the previous construction and recall that for a divisor $D \in D(\chi)$ of the curve χ

$$\Omega(D) = \{\omega \in \Omega | \operatorname{div}(\omega) \geq D\} \cup 0$$

where Ω is the set of differentials. Define the map

$$\alpha^*: \Omega(G - D) \longrightarrow \mathbb{F}_q^n$$
$$\omega \longmapsto (\operatorname{Res}_{P_1}(\omega), \operatorname{Res}_{P_2}(\omega), \cdots, \operatorname{Res}_{P_n}(\omega)).$$

The code $C^*(D, G)$ is defined as the image under α^*. Again, from the properties developed in the previous section, in particular as a consequence of the Riemann–Roch theorem, it is straightforward to establish that

$$\dim(C^*(D, G)) = n - \deg(G) + g - 1$$
$$d^* \geq \deg(G) - 2g + 2$$

again within g of the Singleton bound.

It follows from the Residue theorem that the codes $C(D, G)$ and $C^*(D, G)$ are duals of each other. Furthermore, it is possible to show [97] that there exists a rational differential form ω with simple poles and with residue 1 at the points P_i, $i = 1, 2, \cdots, n$ so that

$$C^*(D, G) = C(D, K + D - G)$$

with K the divisor of ω. This implies that the residue construction gives exactly the same class of codes as the first construction. It is nonetheless useful to retain the two approaches to code construction.

The next section considers some particular classes of curves and constructions of codes by the methods given here.

IV. CLASSES OF ALGEBRAIC-GEOMETRY CODES AND THEIR PROPERTIES

The previous section has established constructions of codes from algebraic curves as a natural evolution from RS and Goppa codes. Some classes of codes of particular interest that arise from these constructions applied to specific classes of curves are considered here. As a matter of notation, let $N_q(g)$ be the maximum number of points possible on a curve of genus g over $\mathbb{F}_q$. As in the previous section, for a specific curve we will denote the number of rational points of the curve over $\mathbb{F}_{q^m}$ by N_m, where the genus and field size q are understood.

A. Codes from the Klein Quartic

The homogeneous curve χ

$$x^3 y + y^3 z + z^3 x = 0$$

is referred to as the Klein quartic [83] which can be considered over any field. Interest in this curve will often be for fields of characteristic two. Since the curve is nonsingular of degree $d = 4$ over fields of characteristic not equal to 7 (and the curve is singular in that case), the genus of the curve is, by the Plücker formula

$$g = \frac{1}{2}(d - 1)(d - 2) = 3.$$

Consider the number of points on such a curve over a field of characteristic 2. It can be seen from the zeta function in Section III, that to determine the number of points on the curve over any extension field, it is sufficient to determine the number of points over $\mathbb{F}_{2^r}$, $r = 1, 2, 3$.

Over $\mathbb{F}_2$ the homogeneous equation has the three solutions $P_0 = (1 : 0 : 0)$, $P_1 = (0 : 1 : 0)$, and $P_2 = (0 : 0 : 1)$. To determine the number of points over $\mathbb{F}_{2^2}$ argue as follows. For $z \neq 0$ convert the equation to projective coordinates and define $u = x/z$, $v = y/z$ to give

$$u^3 v + v^3 + u = 0.$$

Consider solutions of the form $(\beta, \gamma, 1)$, β, $\beta \in \mathbb{F}_4^*$, $\mathbb{F}_4 = \{0, 1, \alpha, \alpha^2\}$ where $\alpha^2 + \alpha + 1 = 0$. For a fixed $\beta \in \mathbb{F}_4^*$, the equation reduces to

$$v^3 + \beta^3 v + \beta = 0.$$

If $\beta = 1$, the polynomial is irreducible over $\mathbb{F}_4$ and there are no solutions. For $\beta = \alpha$, there is one solution $(\alpha, \alpha^2, 1)$ and for $\beta = \alpha^2$ the single solution is $(\alpha^2, \alpha, 1)$ giving $N_2 = 5$.

To obtain the points over $\mathbb{F}_{2^3} = \{0, 1, \alpha, \alpha^2, \cdots, \alpha^6\}$ where $\alpha^3 + \alpha + 1 = 0$, α primitive, it is readily checked that

$$\sigma_1 \colon (x, y, z) \longmapsto (\alpha x, \alpha^4 y, \alpha^2 z)$$

and

$$\sigma_2 \colon (x, y, z) \longmapsto (z, x, y)$$

are automorphisms of the set of points, σ_1 of order 7 and σ_2 of order 3. The point $P_0 = (1, \alpha^2, \alpha^4)$ is a solution as are

$$P_{ij} = \sigma_1^i \sigma_2^j P_0, \qquad i = 0, 1, \cdots, 6, \quad j = 0, 1, 2.$$

These 21 points plus the original three points yield $N_3 = 24$. The numerator of the zeta function for the Klein quartic is then obtained as

$$P_\chi(t) = 1 + 5t^3 + 8t^6$$

and the zeta function is

$$Z(t) = \frac{1 + 5t^3 + 8t^6}{(1 - t)(1 - 2t)}.$$

The number of points on the curve over $\mathbb{F}_{2^i}$, N_i, is the coefficient of t^i in the series expansion of $Z(t)$.

Codes of differing lengths can be defined with the Klein quartic. Following the work of Hansen [39], define a set of codes of length 21 over $\mathbb{F}_8$. Using the evaluation construction of the previous section, define $D = \sum P_{ij}$ and the divisor with disjoint support

$$G = m(P_0 + P_1 + P_2), \qquad 2 \le m \le 6.$$

The code is defined by the mapping

$$\alpha \colon L(G) \longrightarrow \mathbb{F}_8^{21}$$
$$f \longmapsto (f(P_{ij})), \qquad i = 0, 1, 2, \cdots, 6, \quad j = 0, 1, 2.$$

Using the results of previous sections it can be shown the dimension of $L(G)$ over $\mathbb{F}_8$ is $3m - 2$ and the minimum distance of the code is $\ge 21 - 3m$. The codes have the parameters

$$(21, 3m - 2, \ge 21 - 3m), \qquad 2 \le m \le 6$$

and in fact the lower bound on the minimum distance is achieved for all values of m in the range shown.

In a similar fashion, define a code of length 23 by choosing $G = 10P_0$ and D the sum of the other 23 points. In this case, the code has the parameters $n = 23$, $k = 8$, $d = 13$.

B. Codes from Elliptic and Hyperelliptic Curves

An elliptic curve in homogeneous coordinates over a field K (more formally taken to be the algebraic closure $\overline{K}$) is irreducible and of the form

$$u^2 w + a_1 uvw + a_3 vw^2 = u^3 + a_2 u^2 w + a_4 uw^2 + a_6 w^3,$$
$$a_i \in \overline{K}.$$

All such curves are of genus 1. Making the transformation $x = u/w$, $y = v/w$ yields

$$y^2 + a_1 xy + a_3 y = x^3 + a_2 x^2 + a_4 x + a_6, \qquad a_i \in \overline{K}. \quad (1)$$

In homogeneous coordinates, the point at infinity is $Q = (0 : 1 : 0)$. If the coordinates are in K, the elliptic curve $E(K)$ is said to be over K.

For any such curve, it is possible to define an addition of points by observing that the straight line through any two points P_1, P_2 intersects the curve in a unique third point P_3. The "addition" of P_1 and P_2 is then defined as $Q \oplus P_3$ where $\oplus$ represents addition of points on the curve. Such an addition of points is easy to appreciate over the reals and all the geometric notions involved have straightforward analogs over a finite field. Thus the points of the elliptic curve over $\mathbb{F}_q$, $E(\mathbb{F}_q)$, have the structure of an Abelian group under this operation of point addition. This structure is the basis of elliptic curve cryptosystems [53], [62] which has generated further interest in the subject, with its deep results and important connections to number theory and other areas of mathematics [81].

In terms of the coefficients in (1) [62, p. 19], two fundamental quantities for the curve can be defined, the discriminant Δ, and the j-invariant $j(E)$. The curve is nonsingular iff $\Delta \ne 0$ and, if two curves are isomorphic they have the same j-invariant. Elliptic curves are well classified in terms of their isomorphism classes and their group structure [81] but such information is more than is required for our objectives.

Let $P_1, P_2, \cdots, P_n$ be rational points of the elliptic curve and Q the point at infinity. Choose the divisor D as $D = P_1 + P_2 + \cdots, P_n$ and as $G = mQ$ for some positive integer m. The code $C(D, G)$ over $\mathbb{F}_q$ obtained has the parameters $(n, m, d \ge n - m)$ and

$$|n - (q + 1)| \le \lfloor 2\sqrt{q} \rfloor.$$

Almost all of these codes will have a minimum distance of $d = n - m$ falling short of the Singleton bound by one. Van der Geer [94, p. 32] gives an example, credited to R. Pellikaan, where a $(6, 3, 4)$ code over $\mathbb{F}_4$, obtained from an elliptic curve, is actually an MDS code.

In the case when $G = mQ$, it is known [14] that $L(mQ)$ has a basis of the polynomials

$$\{1, x, x^2, \cdots, x^\delta, y, yx, \cdots, yx^{\hat\delta}\}$$
$$\delta = \left\lfloor \frac{m}{2} \right\rfloor \qquad \hat\delta = \left\lfloor \frac{m-2}{2} \right\rfloor$$

to give a code dimension of $\delta + \hat\delta + 2 = \lfloor m/2 \rfloor + \lfloor (m-2)/2 \rfloor + 2$ which is $m + 1$ if m is even and m if m is odd. The minimum distance of the code is $n - m$.

To determine the number of points on the curve over $\mathbb{F}_{q^k}$, it is sufficient to determine the number of points over $\mathbb{F}_q$, since the curves are of genus 1. Thus if $t = q + 1 - |E(\mathbb{F}_q)|$ then

$$|E(\mathbb{F}_{q^k})| = q^k + 1 - \alpha^k - \beta^k$$

where α and β are solutions of the equation $x^2 - tx + q = 0$.

The weight enumerator of MDS codes is uniquely specified by the code parameters. Since for (most) codes from elliptic curves, $d = n - k$, it is not surprising that some information is available for such codes. The subject has been considered by Katsman and Tsfasman, [50] (and in the book [90]). Define the weight enumerator of such a code C by

$$W_C(x) = \sum_{i=0}^{n} A_{n-i} x^i$$

or

$$W_C(x, y) = x^n + y^d \sum_{i=0}^{n-d} A_{d+i} y^i x^{n-d-i}$$

and, by the MacWilliams identities,

$$W_{C^\perp}(x, y) = q^{-k} W_C(x + (q-1)y, x - y).$$

By applying these relationships to the case of an $(n, k, d = n - k)$ code, it is found that [90, p. 302]

$$W_C(x) = x^n + \sum_{i=0}^{k-1} \binom{n}{i} (q^{k-i} - 1)(x-1)^i + B_k(x-1)^k.$$

It is known that $B'_{n-k} = B_k$, where the prime indicates weights in the dual code. For $n = 2k$, $W_C(x) = W_{C^\perp}(x)$ and the codes are formally self-dual. If $B_k = 0$ the code is MDS. In general, it is possible to show that

$$0 < B_k = B'_{n-k} \le \binom{n}{k}(q-1), \qquad d = n - k$$

and the determination of B_k uniquely specifies the weight enumerator of the code and hence of its dual. It is possible to characterize B_k as $(q-1)M$ where M is an integer with a combinatorial interpretation in terms of curve parameters [90, p. 303] but this is beyond our interests.

Recent authors ([9], [21]) have defined the defect of an $(n, k, d = n - k + 1 - \delta)$ code to be $\delta > 0$, i.e., the amount by which the minimum distance of the code fails to meet the Singleton bound. Codes with defect $\delta = 1$ which includes most of the codes derived from elliptic curves, are referred to as quasi- or almost-MDS codes. Further structural properties of such curves can be established.

Clearly, curves with small genus and large numbers of points are of interest in constructing codes. The quantity $N_q(g)$, the largest number of points over $\mathbb{F}_q$ for any curve of genus g, has been studied by several authors (e.g., [16], [58]) and the results find implications in coding theory. These refinements of the Hasse–Weil bound (and the Serre improvement) are briefly discussed for curves of small genus.

For curves of genus one, let $q = p^e$, $p = \text{char}(\mathbb{F}_q)$. The maximum number of points of a genus one curve then is

$$N_q(1) = q + 1 + \lfloor 2\sqrt{q} \rfloor$$

unless $p | \lfloor 2\sqrt{q} \rfloor$ and e is an odd integer, in which case

$$N_q(1) = q + \lfloor 2\sqrt{q} \rfloor.$$

The case of genus 2 is a little more complicated but, interestingly, a complete answer is still possible [78]. If q is an even power of a prime, $q \ne 4, 9$, then

$$N_q(2) = q + 1 + 4\sqrt{q}$$

and $N_4(2) = 10$, $N_9(2) = 20$. If q is an odd power of a prime p call q special if $p | \lfloor 2\sqrt{q} \rfloor$ or if there is an integer l such that $q = l^2 + l + 1$ or $q = l^2 + l + 2$. If q is not special then

$$N_q(2) = q + 1 + 2\lfloor 2\sqrt{q} \rfloor$$

and if q is special then

$$N_q(2) = \begin{cases} q + 2\lfloor 2\sqrt{q} \rfloor, & \text{if } \{2\sqrt{q}\} > (\sqrt{5} - 1)/2 \\ q + 2\lfloor 2\sqrt{q} \rfloor - 1, & \text{if } \{2\sqrt{q}\} < (\sqrt{5} - 1)/2 \end{cases}$$

where $\{2\sqrt{q}\} = 2\sqrt{q} - \lfloor 2\sqrt{q} \rfloor$, the fractional part.

For $N_q(3)$ specific results are available. Thus [30] for $3 < q \le 19$, $N_q(3) = 2q + 6$ except for $q = 8, 9$ where $N_q(3) = 4q - 8$. Tables for such functions for $q \le 25$ are given ([2], [90]).

As a generalization of elliptic curves, consider the hyperelliptic curves, defined by an equation of the form

$$\mathcal{X}: y^2 + h(x)y = k(x), \qquad h(x), k(x) \in K[x]$$

where $h(x)$ is a polynomial of degree at most g and $k(x)$ is monic of degree exactly $2g + 1$. We require the curve to be nonsingular, i.e., have no singular points $(x, y) \in \overline{K}^2$ where both of the partial derivatives $2y + h(x) = 0$ and $h'y - k'(x) = 0$ vanish. In such a case the genus of the curve is g. Notice that for elliptic curves $h(x)$ is at most a linear polynomial and $k(x)$ a monic cubic, and the curve is of genus 1.

If $\text{char}(K) \ne 2$ then the change of variables

$$x \mapsto x, \ y \mapsto y - (h(x)/2)$$

transforms the equation to

$$y^2 = f(x) \qquad \deg f(x) = 2g + 1.$$

In this case, if $P = (x, y)$ is a point on the curve, then $(x, -y - h(x))$ is also a point on the curve, the sum (addition of points on the curve, $\oplus$) of P and the point at infinity. If $\text{char}(K) = 2$ and (x, y) is on the curve, then so also is $(x, y + h(x))$. In homogeneous coordinates the point at infinity is $(0 : 1 : 0)$ and has multiplicity $2g - 1$. The number of rational points on the curve N is bounded by

$$|N - (q+1)| \le g \lfloor 2\sqrt{q} \rfloor.$$

The following example [53], [94, p. 61], is instructive. Consider the curve

$$y^2 + y = x^5 + 1$$

of genus 2 over $\mathbb{F}_2$. It can be shown using the techniques established previously that the number of points on this curve over $\mathbb{F}_{2^k}$ is $2^k + 1$ unless $k = 4m$ in which case it is

$$2^{4m} + 1 + (-1)^{m+1} 2^{2m+2}.$$

One can use either of the code constructions for hyperelliptic curves to obtain codes. Continuing the previous example [94, p. 61], over $\mathbb{F}_{2^4}$ the curve has 33 points. Let D be the sum of the points not at infinity and $G = mQ$, Q the point at infinity. For the code $C^*(D, G)$ one obtains a sequence of codes $(32, k = 33 - m, d_m)$ over $\mathbb{F}_{16}$ with $d_m = m - 2$ for

$3 \leq m \leq 31$, $m \neq 3, 5$, $d_3 = 2$, $d_5 = 4$. The general question of the maximum length possible for a code over $\mathbb{F}_q$ from a curve of genus either one or two is examined in [6] and [66].

C. Codes from Hermitian Curves

The Hermitian curve in homogeneous coordinates is given by

$$u^{q+1} + v^{q+1} + w^{q+1} = 0$$

over $\mathbb{F}_{q^2}$, a special case of the Fermat curve

$$u^m + v^m + w^m = 0$$

for $(m, q) = 1$. The Hermitian curve is nonsingular and its genus is given by $g = q(q-1)/2$. It will be shown constructively that the number of rational points on the curve is given by $q^3 + 1$ and since, by the Hasse–Weil theorem

$$N_q \leq q^2 + 1 + 2g\sqrt{q^2} = q^3 + 1$$

all such curves are maximal. In projective coordinates the curve is written

$$u^{q+1} + v^{q+1} = 1.$$

Choose [30, p. 1558] $\gamma, \delta \in \mathbb{F}_{q^2}$ so that

$$\gamma^q + \gamma = \delta^{q+1} = -1$$

which is always possible (note that the left side is the trace over $\mathbb{F}_q$ and $\delta^{q+1} \in \mathbb{F}_q$). Make the transformations

$$x = \frac{1}{v - \delta u} \text{ and } y = \delta u x - \gamma$$

to yield the equation

$$y^q + y = x^{q+1}.$$

The common pole of x and y is the point at infinity.

To describe the q^3 rational points on the curve [83, p. 203] in slightly more detail than previously (Example 3.39), note that for each $\alpha \in \mathbb{F}_{q^2}$ there exists q distinct elements $\beta \in \mathbb{F}_{q^2}$ such that

$$\mathrm{Tr}\,(\beta) = \beta^q + \beta = \alpha^{q+1} \in \mathbb{F}_q$$

and the q^3 solutions are (α, β).

To form a code of length $n = q^3$ over $\mathbb{F}_{q^2}$, take D as the sum of the q^3 rational points and $G = mQ$ for a positive integer m. It can be shown [83] that the elements

$$\{x^i y^j, \ i \geq 0, \ 0 \leq j \leq q-1 \text{ and } iq + j(q+1) \leq m\}$$

forms a basis of $L(mQ)$. The above monomials can be used to construct a generator matrix of the code $C(D, mQ) = C_m$.

To determine the code parameters, define

$$A(m) = \{0 \leq l \leq m | i, j \in Z, \ l = iq + j(q+1),$$
$$i \geq 0, \ 0 \leq j \leq q-1\}$$

and let $\nu(m) = |A(m)|$.

To determine the dimension of the code C_m, note that for $m > 0$, C_m is empty, and for $m > q^3 + q^2 - q - 2$,

$\dim(C_m) = n = q^3$. Thus the interesting range for m is $0 \leq m \leq q^3 + q^2 - q - 2$.

It is first noted that the dual code to C_m is

$$C_m^\perp = C_{q^3 + q^2 - q - 2 - m}$$

and hence C_m is self-orthogonal if $2m \leq q^3 + q^2 - q - 2$ and self-dual iff $m = (q^3 + q^2 - q - 2)/2$, a case that is only possible if $q = 2^k$ for some positive integer k. The dimension of C_m is given by the cases

$$\dim(C_m) =$$
$$\begin{cases} m + 1 - (q^2 - q)/2, & \text{if } q^2 - q - 2 < m < q^3 \\ \nu(m), & \text{if } 0 \leq m \leq q^2 - q - 2 \\ q^3 - \nu(q^3 + q^2 - q - 2 - m), & \text{if } m > q^3. \end{cases}$$

The minimum distance of C_m satisfies

$$d \geq q^3 - m.$$

It can be shown that $d = q^3 - m$ when

$$q^2 - q \leq r \leq q^3 - q^2 + q.$$

Finally, it is noted [83] that the automorphism group of C_m is quite large. As before, let α, β be such that

$$\beta^q + \beta = \alpha^{q+1}, \qquad \alpha, \beta \in \mathbb{F}_{q^2}.$$

For each of the q^2 values of α there are exactly q values of β satisfying the equation. For $\epsilon \in \mathbb{F}_{q^2} \setminus \{0\}$ it is verified that if (x, y) is a point on the curve then so is $(\sigma(x), \sigma(y))$ where

$$\sigma(x) = \epsilon x + \delta \qquad \sigma(y) = \epsilon^{q+1} y + \epsilon \delta^q x + \mu.$$

Thus the automorphism group of the code contains a subgroup of size $q^3(q^2 - 1)$. More recently it has been shown by Xing [107] that, for $q + 1 \leq m \leq q^3 + q^2 - 2q - 3$, this is in fact, precisely the automorphism group. For either $0 \leq m \leq q - 1$ or $m \geq q^3 + q^2 - 2q - 1$

$$\mathrm{Aut}\,(C_m) \cong S_{q^3}$$

the symmetric group on q^3 letters. For the two cases of $m = q$ or $m = q^3 + q^2 - 2q - 2$ the group is slightly more complex, of the form

$$\mathrm{Aut}\,(C_m) \cong \mathrm{AGL}\,(2, q^2) \otimes S_q^{q^2}$$

where $\mathrm{AGL}\,(2, q^2)$ is the affine linear transformation of a line over $\mathbb{F}_{q^2}$ and $S_q^{q^2}$ is a copy of the q^2 symmetric group S_q. Notice that in the case $m = q$, $\dim(C_m) = 2$ and C_m is generated by the all-ones vector and

$$(x_1, \cdots, x_1, x_2, \cdots, x_2, \cdots, x_{q^2}, \cdots, x_{q^2})$$

from which the result follows. The case for $m = q^3 + q^2 - 2q - 2$ follows from duality.

The Hermitian codes clearly have interesting structure. Given their monomial basis of the form $x^i y^j$ with restrictions on the size of i and j, it is not surprising they can be expressed as catenated versions of generalized RS codes [105].

D. Other Constructions

Feng and Rao [22], [24] introduced two classes of codes, in some sense a generalization of previous classes, but in terms of methods used to establish their properties, quite novel. A brief introduction to their definition is given here. The two classes are given by

$$\text{Type I: } x^a + y^b + G(x, y) = 0$$

where $\deg(G) < b < a$, $\gcd(a, b) = 1$, and

$$\text{Type II: } x^a y^c + y^{b+c} + G(x, y) = 0$$

where $\deg(G) < \min(a + c, b + c)$, $\gcd(a, b) = 1$. This last type of curve is a generalization of the Klein curves with equation: $x^m y + y^m z + z^m x = 0$. The curves of Type I are always irreducible and have exactly one point at infinity which is regular iff $a = b + 1$. The properties of the evaluation codes derived from these curves depends very much on the form of the polynomials $G(x, y)$ and the method used for the code construction. Feng and Rao use the notion of a well-behaving sequence of monomials for the code construction. Høholdt *et al.* [44] analyze the properties of the codes using the notion of an order function. This approach is briefly described here. Let $\prec$ be an admissible order function on monomials and $f_i \prec f_{i+1}$. Every polynomial $f \in R$, R an $\mathbb{F}$-algebra, can be written in a unique manner as

$$f = \sum_{i=1}^{j} \alpha_i f_i, \qquad \alpha_i \in \mathbb{F}, \ \alpha_j \neq 0.$$

Define the mapping $\rho(.)$ from $\mathbb{F}[x_1, \cdots, x_m]$ to $N_0 \cup \{-\infty\}$ by $\rho(0) = -\infty$ and $\rho(f) = j - 1$ if j is the smallest positive integer for which f can be written as a linear combination of the first j monomials. The function $\rho(.)$ satisfies the following conditions:

i) $\rho(f) = -\infty$ iff $f = 0$;
ii) $\rho(\lambda f) = \rho(f)$ for all nonzero $\lambda \in \mathbb{F}$;
iii) $\rho(f + g) \leq \max\{\rho(f), \rho(g)\}$ with equality when $\rho(f) < \rho(g)$;
iv) if $\rho(f) < \rho(g)$ and $h \neq 0$ then $\rho(fh) < \rho(gh)$;
v) if $\rho(f) = \rho(g)$, then there exists $\lambda \in \mathbb{F}^*$ such that $\rho(f - \lambda g) < \rho(g)$

and any function satisfying these conditions is called an *order function* on R. A weight function is an order function satisfying the additional condition that $\rho(fg) = \rho(f) + \rho(g)$. It is not difficult to show that if there exists an order function on R then R is an integral domain.

If I is an ideal generated by the Type I polynomial $x^a + y^b + G(x, y)$, and $R = \mathbb{F}[x, y]/I$ then there exists a weight function ρ on R, R is an integral domain, and I is a prime ideal. Furthermore the set

$$\{x^\alpha y^\beta | 0 \leq \alpha < \beta\}$$

is a basis for R and $\rho(x) = a$ and $\rho(y) = b$.

For I an ideal generated by a Type II equation

$$x^a y^c + y^{b+c} + G(x, y)$$

then $\mathbb{F}[x, y]/I$ has a basis

$$\{x^\alpha y^\beta | 0 \leq \alpha < a, \text{ or } \beta < c\}.$$

In this case, an order function may not exist but when it does it must have the property that $\rho(x^a) = \rho(y^b)$.

Using the notion of an order function, codes of Types I and II, as evaluation codes, can be defined and bounds on their minimum distance established. Readers are referred to [44] for details on this approach.

V. Decoding of Algebraic-Geometry Codes

The decoding problem can be formulated as follows:

Definition 5.1: Let C be an (n, k)-code over the field $\mathbb{F}_q$ and $0 \leq \tau < n$. The function $\text{dec}_\tau \colon \mathbb{F}_q^n \to \mathcal{P}(C)$, $\mathcal{P}(C)$ the power set on C, where for any $y \in \mathbb{F}_q^n$

$$\text{dec}_\tau(y) = S(y, \tau) \cap C$$

is called a *decoder* with capability of correcting τ errors. Here $S(y, \tau)$ is the sphere with radius τ centered at y.

With this definition the following lemma is immediate.

Lemma 5.2: Let C be an (n, k)-code over the field $\mathbb{F}_q$ with minimum distance d and let $= \lfloor (d - 1)/2 \rfloor$. Then for any $y \in \mathbb{F}_q^n$, $|\text{dec}_t(y)| \leq 1$.

Proof: Suppose $c_1, c_2 \in S(y, t)$. Then

$$d(c_1, c_2) \leq d(c, y) + d(c_2, y) \leq t + t \leq d - 1$$

so $c_1 = c_2$. □

Most of the work in the constructions of decoders for algebraic-geometry codes has been focused on designing dec_t decoders with $t = \lfloor (d^* - 1)/2 \rfloor$ where d^* is some lower bound, e.g., the ones presented in Section III-E, on the minimum distance of the code, but recently Shokrollahi and Wassermann [80] have constructed dec_τ-decoders for larger τ by extending previous work of Sudan [88], who constructed such decoders for Reed–Solomon codes. For a survey on the decoding of algebraic-geometry codes and the history see Høholdt and Pellikaan [45].

In this section we will describe a decoding algorithm for algebraic-geometry codes of the form

$$C(m) = C(D, mG)^\perp = C^*(D, mG)$$

where $D = P_1 + \cdots + P_n$; $P_1, \cdots, P_n$, G distinct $\mathbb{F}_q$-rational points on a nonsingular absolutely irreducible curve χ of genus g defined over $\mathbb{F}_q$.

The decoder corrects up to $\lfloor (d_{\text{FR}} - 1)/2 \rfloor$ errors where d_{FR} is the Feng–Rao distance to be defined later. One has $d_{\text{FR}} \geq m - 2g + 2$ with equality if $m \geq 4g - 2$. The code $C(m)$ has length n and for any $y \in \mathbb{F}_q^n$ we have

$$y \in C(m) \Leftrightarrow \sum_{j=1}^{n} y_j f(P_j) = 0, \qquad \text{for all } f \in L(mQ).$$

When $2g - 2 < m < n$ the code $C(m)$ has dimension $k = n - (m - g + 1)$, since $L(mG)$ has dimension $m - g + 1$ from the Riemann–Roch theorem because $m > 2g - 2$ and the evaluation map $L(mG) \to \mathbb{F}_q^n$ which maps $f \in L(mG)$ into $(f(P_1), \cdots, f(P_n))$ is injective since $m < n$.

Recall that a number ρ_i is a nongap for G if $L(\rho_i G) \neq L((\rho_i - 1)G)$. In this case there exists a function

$$\varphi_i \in L(\rho_i G) \setminus L((\rho_{i-1})G)$$

which means that φ_i has a pole of order ρ_i at G and no other poles.

The nongaps satisfy

$$0 = \rho_1 < \rho_2 < \cdots < \rho_g < \rho_{g+1} = 2g$$

and $\rho_i = i + g - 1$ for $i \geq g + 1$, and the functions φ_i, $i = 1, 2, \cdots, m - g + 1$ provide a basis for $L(mG)$.

Let R denote the ring of all rational functions on X with poles only at G, that is,

$$R = \bigcup_{a=0}^{\infty} L(aG)$$

and let for $f \in R$, $\rho(f)$ denote the pole order of f at G, that is the smallest number b, such that $f \in L(bQ)$. If $f \in R$ and $\boldsymbol{y} \in \mathbb{F}_q^n$ we define the *syndrome* $S_{\boldsymbol{y}}(f)$ to be

$$S_{\boldsymbol{y}}(f) = \sum_{j=1}^{n} y_j f(P_j)$$

so we have

$$\boldsymbol{y} \in C(m) \Leftrightarrow S_{\boldsymbol{y}}(f) = 0, \qquad \text{for all } f \in R \text{ with } \rho(f) \leq m.$$

In the decoding situation we receive a vector $\boldsymbol{y}$ which is the sum of a codeword $\boldsymbol{c}$ and an error vector $\boldsymbol{e}$. We have $S_{\boldsymbol{e}}(f) = S_{\boldsymbol{y}}(f)$ if $\rho(f) \leq m$, so the syndromes $S_{\boldsymbol{e}}(f)$ can be calculated directly from the received word if $\rho(f) \leq m$. The standard decoding procedure for Reed–Solomon codes has the following five steps.

1) Syndrome calculation.
2) Obtaining a polynomial, called the error-locator polynomial, which has the error positions among its roots.
3) Obtaining error positions.
4) Calculating error magnitudes.
5) Recovering the codeword and the information symbols.

We will not discuss Steps 1) and 5) in detail since they are fairly easy once we have a basis for $L(mG)$, but we will demonstrate how Steps 2)–4) are generalized to the codes $C(m)$.

Let the error positions be $P_{i_1}, P_{i_2}, \cdots, P_{i_\tau}$. An element $h \in R$ satisfying $h(P_{i_1}) = h(P_{i_2}) = \cdots = h(P_{i_\tau}) = 0$

is called an *error locator*. We remark that it follows from the theorem of Riemann that the space $L((\tau + g)G)$ indeed contains a nonzero error locator since

$$\deg\left((\tau + g)Q - (P_{i_1} + \cdots + P_{i_\tau})\right) = g$$

so

dimension $L((\tau + g)G - (P_{i_1} + \cdots + P_{i_\tau})) \geq g - g + 1 = 1$. If h is an error locator we have $S_{\boldsymbol{e}}(fh) = 0$ for all $f \in R$ since

$$S_{\boldsymbol{e}}(fh) = \sum_{i \in I = \{i_1, \cdots, i_\tau\}} e_i f(P_i) h(P_i) = 0.$$

On the other hand, we can prove the following.

Theorem 5.3: Let $h \in L((\tau + g)G)$ satisfy $S_{\boldsymbol{e}}(fh) = 0$ for all $f \in R$ with $\rho(f) \leq \tau + 2g - 1$ then h is an error locator.

Proof: The condition implies that the vector $\boldsymbol{u}$ with coordinates $e_i h(P_i)$, $i = 1, \cdots, n$ is a codeword in $C(\tau + 2g - 1)$. But $\tau + 2g - 1 > 2g - 2$ so this code has minimum weight at least $\tau + 2g - 1 - 2g + 2 = \tau + 1$ which is greater than τ and, therefore, $\boldsymbol{u} = \boldsymbol{0}$ and hence $h(P_{i_j}) = 0, j = 1, \cdots, \tau$. $\qquad\square$

By combining the remark and the theorem one gets the idea of obtaining the error locator in the following way. Consider the following system of equations in the unknowns $\lambda_1, \lambda_2, \cdots, \lambda_{\tau+1}$:

$$\sum_{j=1}^{n} e_j \varphi_l(P_j) \sum_{i=1}^{\tau+1} \lambda_i \varphi_i(P_j) = 0, \qquad l = 1, 2, \cdots, \tau + g$$

or, equivalently,

$$\sum_{i=1}^{\tau+1} S_{\boldsymbol{e}}(\varphi_i \varphi_l) \lambda_i = 0, \qquad l = 1, 2, \cdots, \tau + g.$$

It then follows from the discussion above that this system indeed has a nontrivial solution and that $h = \sum_{i=1}^{\tau+1} \lambda_i \varphi_i$ is an error locator.

The problem is that we only know $S_{\boldsymbol{e}}(\varphi_i \varphi_j)$ if $\rho(\varphi_i \varphi_j) \leq m$, so in order to solve it we must have

$$(\tau + 1 + g - 1) + (\tau + g + g - 1) \leq m$$

that is, $2\tau + 3g - 1 \leq m$, with $d^* = m - 2g + 2$ we get $\tau \leq (d^* - g - 1)/2$.

i	1	2	3	4	5	6	7	8	9	10	11	12	13
φ_i	1	X	Y	X^2	XY	Y^2	X^3	X^2Y	XY^2	Y^3	X^4	X^3Y	X^2Y^2
ρ_i	0	4	5	8	9	10	12	13	14	15	16	17	18
$S(\varphi_i)$	α^9	α^{14}	0	α^5	α^9	α^9	α^7	α^{14}	α^{11}	α^6	α^2	α^{12}	0

i	14	15	16	17	18	19	20	21	22	23	24	25	26
φ_i	XY^3	Y^4	X^4Y	X^3Y^2	X^2Y^3	XY^4	Y^5	X^4Y^2	X^3Y^3	X^2Y^4	XY^5	Y^6	X^4Y^3
ρ_i	19	20	21	22	23	24	25	26	27	28	29	30	31
$S(\varphi_i)$	α^4	α^5	α^5	α^{12}	α^7	α^7	α^6	α^6	α^3	α^6	α^4	α^{11}	α^{10}

Example 5.4: The Hermitian curve over $\mathbb{F}_{16}$ has equation $x^5 + y^4 + y = 0$. It has genus $g = 6$, 64 $\mathbb{F}_q$-rational points in the affine part, and one point Q at infinity. As in Example 3.34 we have $\rho(X) = 4$, $\rho(Y) = 5$, and the functions $X^a Y^b$, $0 \le a < 5$, $0 \le b$, $4a + 5b \le m$ gives a basis for $L(mQ)$. Let $m = 31$ then we get a $(64, 38, 21)$ code over $\mathbb{F}_{16}$, so the algorithm described above corrects $(21 - 1 - 6)/2 = 7$ errors. Let α be a primitive element of $\mathbb{F}_{16}$ satisfying $\alpha^4 + \alpha + 1 = 0$. We consider a seven-error pattern where the errors are located at the points $P_1 = (1, \alpha)$, $P_2 = (\alpha^8, \alpha^3)$, $P_3 = (\alpha, \alpha^7)$, $P_4 = (\alpha^2, \alpha^3)$, $P_5 = (\alpha^{11}, \alpha^3)$, $P_6 = (\alpha^5, \alpha^3)$, $P_7 = (\alpha^{14}, \alpha^3)$, and the corresponding error values $e_1 = \alpha^6$, $e_2 = \alpha^8$, $e_3 = \alpha^7$, $e_4 = \alpha$, $e_5 = 1$, $e_6 = \alpha^6$, $e_7 = \alpha^{10}$. We get the table at the bottom of the preceding page. We want a locator of the form

$$\lambda_1 + \lambda_2 x + \lambda_3 y + \lambda_4 x^2 + \lambda_5 xy + \lambda_6 y^2 + \lambda_7 x^3 + \lambda_8 x^2 y$$

where the coefficients λ_i satisfy the equation

$$\begin{bmatrix} \alpha^9 & \alpha^{14} & 0 & \alpha^5 & \alpha^9 & \alpha^9 & \alpha^7 & \alpha^{14} \\ \alpha^{14} & \alpha^5 & \alpha^9 & \alpha^7 & \alpha^{14} & \alpha^{11} & \alpha^2 & \alpha^{12} \\ 0 & \alpha^9 & \alpha^9 & \alpha^{14} & \alpha^{11} & \alpha^6 & \alpha^{12} & 0 \\ \alpha^5 & \alpha^7 & \alpha^{14} & \alpha^2 & \alpha^{12} & 0 & \alpha^5 & \alpha^5 \\ \alpha^9 & \alpha^{14} & \alpha^{11} & \alpha^{12} & 0 & \alpha^4 & \alpha^5 & \alpha^{12} \\ \alpha^9 & \alpha^{11} & \alpha^6 & 0 & \alpha^4 & \alpha^5 & \alpha^{12} & \alpha^7 \\ \alpha^7 & \alpha^2 & \alpha^{12} & \alpha^5 & \alpha^5 & \alpha^{12} & 1 & \alpha^5 \\ \alpha^{14} & \alpha^{12} & 0 & \alpha^5 & \alpha^{12} & \alpha^7 & \alpha^5 & \alpha^6 \\ \alpha^{11} & 0 & \alpha^4 & \alpha^{12} & \alpha^7 & \alpha^7 & \alpha^6 & \alpha^3 \\ \alpha^6 & \alpha^4 & \alpha^5 & \alpha^7 & \alpha^7 & \alpha^6 & \alpha^3 & \alpha^6 \\ \alpha^2 & \alpha^5 & \alpha^5 & 1 & \alpha^5 & \alpha^6 & \alpha^8 & \alpha^{13} \\ \alpha^{12} & \alpha^5 & \alpha^{12} & \alpha^5 & \alpha^6 & \alpha^3 & \alpha^{13} & \alpha \\ 0 & \alpha^{12} & \alpha^7 & \alpha^6 & \alpha^3 & \alpha^6 & \alpha & \alpha^{10} \end{bmatrix} \begin{bmatrix} \lambda_1 \\ \lambda_2 \\ \lambda_3 \\ \lambda_4 \\ \lambda_5 \\ \lambda_6 \\ \lambda_7 \\ \lambda_8 \end{bmatrix} = \underline{0}.$$

Here we have used that $S(X^5) = S(Y^4 + Y) = \alpha^5 + 0 = \alpha^5$ and the corresponding expressions for $S(X^6)$, $S(X^5Y)$, $S(X^7)$, $S(X^6Y)$, and $S(X^5Y^2)$.

It can be seen that

$$(\lambda_1, \lambda_2, \cdots, \lambda_8) = (\alpha^{11}, \alpha^{13}, \alpha^{13}, 0, \alpha^{10}, 1, 0, 0)$$

is a solution so

$$h = \alpha^{11} + \alpha^{13} X + \alpha^{13} Y + \alpha^{10} XY + \alpha^2 X^2.$$

The zeros of this polynomial are $P_1, \cdots, P_7$ and $(\alpha^{11}, \alpha^{14})$; $(\alpha^{14}, \alpha^{12})$; (α^4, α^6).

Let $d^* = m - 2g + 2$, then we get

$$2\tau + 3g - 1 \le d^* + 2g - 2$$

so

$$\tau \le (d^* - 1 - g)/2.$$

This was the original approach of Justesen, Larsen, Havemose, Elbrønd Jensen, and Høholdt [47], and of Skorobogatov and Vlăduţ [82].

The calculation above makes it natural to look at the matrix of syndromes

$$\boldsymbol{S_e} = (S_{ij}(\boldsymbol{e})) = (S_e(\varphi_i \varphi_j)), \qquad 1 \le i, j \le N$$

where n is the smallest number such that $C(N) = \underline{0}$. We will first prove

Lemma 5.5: $\mathrm{rank}(\boldsymbol{S_e}) = \tau$.

Proof: Decompose $\boldsymbol{S}$ as a product of the three matrices $\boldsymbol{A}$ with elements $a_{ij} = \varphi_i(P_j)$, $i = 1, \cdots, N$, $j = 1, \cdots, n$, $\boldsymbol{B}$ a diagonal $n \times k$ matrix with $e_1, \cdots, e_n$ in the diagonal, and $\boldsymbol{A}^T$.

Then we have $\boldsymbol{S_e} = \boldsymbol{ABA}^T$ and

$$\mathrm{rank}(\boldsymbol{A}) = n = \mathrm{rank}(\boldsymbol{A}^T)$$

so

$$\mathrm{rank}(\boldsymbol{S}) = \mathrm{rank}(\boldsymbol{B}) = \mathrm{weight}(\boldsymbol{e}) = \tau. \qquad \square$$

Definition 5.6: For $l \in \mathbb{N}_0$ let

$$N_l = \{(i, j) \in \mathbb{N}_0^2 | \rho_i + \rho_j = l + 1\}$$

and let ν_l be the number of elements in N_l.

From the definition of the codes $C(m)$ we have that if $\boldsymbol{c} \in C(m)$ and $\rho_i + \rho_j \le m$ then $S_c(\varphi_i \varphi_j) = 0$ but if $\boldsymbol{c} \in C(m) \backslash C(m+1)$ and $\rho_i + \rho_j = m+1$ then $S_c(\varphi_i \varphi_j) \ne 0$ but this implies that

Lemma 5.7: If $\boldsymbol{c} \in C(m) \backslash C(m+1)$ then $\mathrm{weight}(\boldsymbol{c}) \ge \nu_m$.

Proof: We can repeat the decomposition of the syndrome matrix $\boldsymbol{S_c}$ so this has rank = weight $(\boldsymbol{c})$, but the nonzero elements appears in different rows and columns with zeros above, so this rank is at least ν_m. $\qquad \square$

Definition 5.8: For the code $C(m)$ we define

$$d_{\mathrm{FR}} = \min_{l \ge m} \{\nu_l\}.$$

Theorem 5.9: The minimum distance d of $C(m)$ satisfies

$$d \ge d_{\mathrm{FR}}.$$

Proof: This follows directly from the lemma. $\qquad \square$

Theorem 5.10: If $m \ge 4g - 2$ then $d_{\mathrm{FR}} = m - 2g + 2$.

Proof: If $m \ge 4g - 2$, $l \ge m$, and $\rho_i + \rho_j = l + 1$, we see that if $i \ge g + 1$ and $j \ge g + 1$ we get $l - 4g + 2$ solutions and if $i \le g$ or $j \le g$ we get $2g$ solutions so $\nu_l = l - 2g + 2$ from which the result follows. $\qquad \square$

We will now describe a procedure that, based on the known syndromes $S_e(\varphi_i \varphi_j)$, $\rho_i + \rho_j \le m$, determines the syndromes $S_e(\varphi_i \varphi_j)$, $\rho_i + \rho_j \le 2\tau + 3g - 1$ when $\tau \le \lfloor (d_{\mathrm{FR}} - 1)/2 \rfloor$. Combined with Theorem 5.3 this then gives a method to find an error locator. This is the brilliant idea of Feng and Rao [23], that was made precise by Duursma [17].

We first note that in the syndrome matrix the first unknown entries correspond to the indices $(i, j) \in N_m$ but as soon as we know one s_{ij} with $(i, j) \in N_m$ we know all $s_{i'j'}$ with $(i', j') \in N_m$ since $\rho(\varphi_i \varphi_j) = \rho(\varphi_{i'} \varphi_{j'})$ so

$$\varphi_i \varphi_j = \lambda \varphi_{i'} \varphi_{j'} + g \qquad (2)$$

where $\lambda \in \mathbb{F}_q^*$ and $\rho(f) \le m$ and this relation is independent of the error vector.

Consider the matrix

$$S(i, j) = \{s_{i'j'} | 1 \leq i' \leq i, 1 \leq j' \leq j\}.$$

If $\rho_i + \rho_j = m + 1$, then all entries of this matrix except s_{ij} are known

$$\begin{pmatrix} s_{1,1} & \cdots & s_{1,j-1} & s_{1,j} \\ \vdots & & \vdots & \vdots \\ s_{i-1,1} & \cdots & s_{i-1,j-1} & s_{i-1,j} \\ s_{i,1} & \cdots & s_{i,j-1} & ? \end{pmatrix}.$$

Definition 5.11: If $(i, j) \in N_m$, that is, $\rho_i + \rho_j = m + 1$ and the three matrices $S(i-1, j-1)$, $S(i-1, j)$, and $S(i, j-1)$ have equal rank, then (i, j) is called a *candidate* with respect to the code $C(m)$. If (i, j) is a candidate, then there is a unique value s'_{ij} to assign to the unknown entry s_{ij} such that the matrices $S(i, j)$ and $S(i - 1, j - 1)$ have equal rank. The element s'_{ij} is called the *candidate value* of the unknown syndrome s_{ij}. If $s'_{ij} = s_{ij}$ the candidate is called *true* and *false* otherwise.

Using the relation (2) every $(i', j') \in N_l$ gives a candidate value for s_{ij}. Denote the number of true candidates T and the number of false candidates F. An entry (i, j) is called a *discrepancy* if it is a candidate but the matrices $S(i, j)$ and $S(i - 1, j - 1)$ have different ranks.

Suppose now weight $(e) \leq \lfloor (d_{FR} - 1)/2 \rfloor$. Denote the number of discrepancies in the known part of the matrix by K. A candidate is incorrect if and only if it is a discrepancy, so

$$K + F \leq \text{total number of discrepancies} \leq \text{weight} (e).$$

If entry (r, s) is a known discrepancy, then all entries (r, s') is the rth row with $s' > s$ and all entries (r', s) the sth column with $r' > r$ are noncandidates. If $(i, j) \in N_m$ is not a candidate, then there is at least one known discrepancy in the same row or column. Thus the number of pairs $(i, j) \in N_m$ which are noncandidates is at most $2K$. The number of candidates is $T + F$, so

$$\nu_m = \#\text{candidates} + \#\text{noncandidates} \leq T + F + 2K.$$

Since weight $(e) \leq \lfloor (d_{FR} - 1)/2 \rfloor \leq (\nu_m - 1)/2$, we therefore get $K + F \leq (\nu_m - 1)/2 \leq (T + F + 2K - 1)/2$ and hence

$$F < T.$$

But this means that all true candidates give the same correct value for s_{ij}, so we have proven the following theorem.

Theorem 5.12: If the number of errors in a received word with respect to the code $C(m)$ is at most $(d_{FR} - 1)/2$, then the majority of the candidates vote for the correct value of $S(\varphi_i \varphi_j)$, $\rho_i + \rho_j = m + 1$.

Hence we can use this theorem until we have all the syndromes and then find the error locator. This completes Step 2). In this way we get an error locator h in $L((\tau + g)Q)$, so h has at most $\tau + g$ zeros. If $m \geq 4g - 2$ we have $\tau + g \leq d_{FR} - 1$. If $m < 4g - 2$, it is possible to extend the algorithm to get more error locators, with the property that the number of common zeros are $\leq d_{FR} - 1$. We can therefore find a set of at most $\tau + g$ points that contains the error positions by evaluating the function h at all the points $P_1, P_2, \cdots, P_n$, so this almost completes Step 3).

Example 5.13: We consider the Hermitian curve of Example 5.4 with $m = 25$, so we get a $(64, 44, 15)$ code over $\mathbb{F}_{16}$. We will correct the same seven-error pattern as in Example 5.4. The syndrome matrix is (in powers of α, with $*$ indicating a zero) as shown at the bottom of this page. Here $\times$ denotes the

	1	2	3	4	5	6	7	8	9	10	11	12	13	14	15	16	17	18	19	20	21
1	9	14	*	5	9	9	7	14	11	6	2	12	*	4	5	5	12	7	7	6	×
2	14	5	9	7	14	11	2	12	*	4	5	5	12	7	7	5	×				
3	*	9	9	14	11	6	12	*	4	5	5	12	7	7	6	×					
4	5	7	14	2	12	*	5	5	12	7	0	5	×								
5	9	14	11	12	*	4	5	12	7	7	5	×									
6	9	11	6	*	4	5	12	7	7	6	×										
7	7	2	12	5	5	12	0	5	×												
8	14	12	*	5	12	7	5	×													
9	11	*	4	12	7	7	×														
10	6	4	5	7	7	6															
11	2	5	5	0	5	×															
12	12	5	12	5	×																
13	*	12	7	×																	
14	4	7	7																		
15	5	7	6																		
16	5	5	×																		
17	12	×																			
18	7																				
19	7																				
20	6																				
21	×																				

syndrome corresponding to x^4y^2 with $\rho(x^4y^2) = 26$, which is the first unknown.

Using row operations one gets the matrix at the bottom of this page. From this it is seen that the positions $(6, 11)$, $(8, 8)$, and $(11, 6)$ are candidate positions and by keeping track of the performed row operations one sees also that the candidate values in all three cases are α^6, so this is the correct syndrome $S(f_{21})$. In the same manner one finds $S(f_{22}) = \alpha^3$, $S(f_{23}) = \alpha^6$, $S(f_{24}) = \alpha^4$, $S(f_{25}) = \alpha^{11}$, $S(f_{26}) = \alpha^{10}$, which corresponds to the results of Example 5.4 and we can now apply the basic algorithm for the code C_{26} as before.

However, since we now know at most $d_{\text{FR}} - 1$ positions $J \subseteq \{1, \cdots, n\}$ that include the error positions we can solve the system of linear equations given by

$$\boldsymbol{H}\boldsymbol{x}^T = \boldsymbol{H}\boldsymbol{y}^T, \quad x_j = 0, \qquad \text{for all } j \notin J$$

where $\boldsymbol{H}$ is the parity-check matrix of the code. It is clear that the error vector $\boldsymbol{e}$ is a solution and another solution $\boldsymbol{x}$ would give $\boldsymbol{H}(\boldsymbol{x} - \boldsymbol{e})^T = \underline{0}$ so $\boldsymbol{x} - \boldsymbol{e}$ would be a codeword of weight at most $d_{\text{FR}} - 1$ and hence must be zero. Therefore, $\boldsymbol{x} = \boldsymbol{e}$.

In this way we have found the error vector and Steps 3) and 4) are completed.

The way we have presented the solution to the decoding problem has the complexity of solving systems of linear equations, and is similar to the Peterson algorithm in using error-locator polynomials for decoding Reed–Solomon codes. It is possible to get lower complexity by using Sakata's generalization of the Berlekamp–Massey algorithm, as was done by Sakata, Elbrønd Jensen, and Høholdt in [77], O'Sullivan in [67], and Saints and Heegard in [71]. It is also possible to find the error values by using a generalization of the Forney formula, this was done by Leonard [56], Hansen, Jensen, and Kötter [40], and by O'Sullivan [68]. One could use the voting procedure described above to find all syndromes and then use a discrete Fourier-like transform to get the error values. This is the approach of Sakata, Jensen, and Høholdt [77].

VI. ASYMPTOTICS OF ALGEBRAIC-GEOMETRY CODES

One reason for the interest in algebraic-geometry codes is the fact that those codes can be used to give an asymptotically good sequence of codes with parameters better than the Varshamov–Gilbert bound in a certain range of the rate and for large enough alphabets. In this section we will review the construction.

Recall that a code C is called an (n, M, d)-code over $\mathbb{F}_q$ if C is a subset of $\mathbb{F}_q^n$ with minimum distance d and $|C| = M$. Let

$$A_q(n, d) = \max\{M \,|\, \text{there exists an } (n, M, d) \text{ code over } \mathbb{F}_q\}$$

and

$$\alpha(\delta) = \limsup_{n \to \infty} \frac{\log_q A_q(n, \delta_n)}{n}, \qquad \text{for } 0 \le \delta \le 1. \quad (3)$$

It is not hard to see that

$$\alpha(\delta) = 0, \qquad \text{for } 1 - \frac{1}{q} \le \delta \le 1 \quad (4)$$

and the Varshamov–Gilbert bound is the fact that

$$\alpha(\delta) \ge 1 - H_q(\delta), \qquad \text{for } 0 \le \delta \le 1 - \frac{1}{q} \quad (5)$$

	1	2	3	4	5	6	7	8	9	10	11	12	13	14	15	16	17	18	19	20	21
1	9	14	*	5	9	9	7	14	11	6	2	12	*	4	5	5	12	7	7	6	×
2	*	8	9	6	*	10	7	6	1	13	13	1	12	0	6	0	×				
3	*	*	13	1	11	1	9	7	10	12	12	7	5	14	10	×					
4	*	*	*	5	*	*	10	8	*	*	4	13	×								
5	*	*	*	*	*	*	5	*	*	*	8	×									
6	*	*	*	*	*	*	*	*	*	*	×										
7	*	*	*	*	5	0	*	10	×												
8	*	*	*	*	*	*	*	×													
9	*	*	*	*	*	*	×														
10	*	*	*	*	*	*															
11	*	*	*	*	*	×															
12	*	*	*	*	×																
13	*	*	*	×																	
14	*	*	*																		
15	*	*	*																		
16	*	*	×																		
17	*	×																			
18	*																				
19	*																				
20	*																				
21	×																				

where $H_q(x)$ is the q-ary entropy function defined by

$$H_q(0) = 0$$
$$H_q(x) = x \log_q(q-1) - x \log_q x - (1-x) \log_q(1-x),$$
$$0 < x \leq 1 - \frac{1}{q}.$$

In [91], it is shown that by using algebraic-geometry codes it is possible to prove that

$$\alpha(\delta) + \delta \geq 1 - \frac{1}{\sqrt{q} - 1} \qquad (6)$$

if q is a square.

It turns out that (6) gives an improvement of (5) if $q \geq 49$. The inequality (6) is the Tsfasman–Vlăduţ–Zink bound. Fig. 1 shows the two bounds for $q = 256$.

Let $R = k/n$ be the rate and $\delta = d/n$ the relative minimum distance of an algebraic-geometry code as defined in Section III. It then follows from the results in that section that

$$R + \delta \geq 1 - \frac{g-1}{n} \qquad (7)$$

where g is the genus of the curve involved in the construction.

In order to construct a sequence of good codes we therefore need curves with low genera and many $\mathbb{F}_q$-rational points. For a curve over $\mathbb{F}_q$ of genus g with N $\mathbb{F}_q$-rational points we get from the Hasse–Weil bound (3.38) that

$$N \leq q + 1 + 2g\sqrt{q}. \qquad (8)$$

Let

$$A(q) = \limsup_{g \to \infty} \frac{N(g)}{g}$$

where $N(g)$ is the maximal number of $\mathbb{F}_q$-rational points on a curve of genus g over $\mathbb{F}_q$. The Hasse–Weil bound implies that

$$A(q) \leq 2\sqrt{q}. \qquad (9)$$

In 1983, Vlăduţ and Drinfeld [16] improved on (9) by showing that

$$A(q) \leq \sqrt{q} - 1. \qquad (10)$$

When q is a square, Ihara in [46] and Tsfasman, Vlăduţ, and Zink [92] showed that

$$A(q) = \sqrt{q} - 1 \qquad (11)$$

by studying the so-called *modular curves* over finite fields.

This in turn means that there exists a sequence of codes satisfying

$$R + \delta \geq 1 - \frac{1}{\sqrt{q} - 1} \quad \text{when } q \text{ is a square} \qquad (12)$$

and, therefore, (6) follows.

The construction using modular curves is difficult. It is possible to do this with polynomial complexity but the actual construction of generator or parity-check matrices is intractable, so many researchers have tried to find a more simple construction. In [22], Feng and Rao suggested that one

could get asymptotically good codes by using the so-called generalized Klein curves, which are defined by the equations

$$x_{i+1}^3 x_i + x_i^3 + x_{i+1} = 0, \qquad i = 1, 2, \cdots, m-1$$

over $\mathbb{F}_8$.

Pellikaan tried to determine whether this claim was correct (the curves are asymptotically bad as recently proved by Garcia and Stichtenoth), and suggested using the curves with equations

$$x_{i+1}^2 x_i + x_i^2 + x_{i+1} = 0, \qquad i = 1, 2, \cdots, m-1$$

over $\mathbb{F}_4$. This led Garcia and Stichtenoth in [28] to study the affine variety χ_m over $\mathbb{F}_q$, $q = r^2$ given by the equations

$$x_i^{r-1} x_{i+1}^r + x_{i+1} = x_i^r, \qquad i = 1, 2, \cdots, m-1 \qquad (13)$$

and they showed that χ_m is indeed a curve and

$$\lim_{m \to \infty} \frac{N(\chi_m)}{g(\chi_m)} = r - 1 \qquad (14)$$

so in this way one can obtain an asymptotically good sequence of codes meeting the Tsfasman–Vlăduţ–Zink bound. Notice that the equations are of the following type:

$$F(x_i, x_{i+1}) = 0, \qquad \text{for } i = 1, \cdots, m-1$$

where

$$F(x, y) = x^{r-1} y^r + y - x^r.$$

The affine plane curve with equation $F(x, y) = 0$ has the property that for every nonzero element $x \in \mathbb{F}_q$ there are exactly r nonzero solutions in $\mathbb{F}_q$ of the equation $F(x, y) = 0$. This is seen by multiplying the equation with x and replacing xy with z. Then we get the equation $z^r + z = x^{r+1}$, which is an equation of the Hermitian curve over $\mathbb{F}_q$. For every given x in $\mathbb{F}_q$ the element x^{r+1} is in $\mathbb{F}_r$ and since the left side is the trace map from $\mathbb{F}_q$ to $\mathbb{F}_r$ we get r distinct z's such that $z^r + z = x^{r+1}$. If, furthermore, x is not zero, then $y = z/x$ is defined and is also nonzero. Therefore, the curve χ_2 has $(q-1)r$ points with nonzero coordinates in $\mathbb{F}_q$. Consider the map

$$\pi_m \colon \chi_m \to \chi_{m-1}$$

defined as

$$\pi_m(x_1, \cdots, x_{m-1}, x_m) = (x_1, \cdots, x_{m-1}).$$

If $(x_1, \cdots, x_{m-1})$ is a given $\mathbb{F}_q$-rational point of χ_{m-1} and $x_{m-1} \neq 0$, then there are exactly r possible nonzero values for $x_m \in \mathbb{F}_q$ such that $(x_1, \cdots, x_{m-1}, x_m)$ is a point of χ_m. Therefore, by induction, it is shown that

$$N(\chi_m) \geq (q-1)r^{m-1}.$$

The genus of the curve χ_m is more difficult to calculate. It is done by induction using the Hurwitz–Zeuthen formula [83] to the covering $\pi_m \colon \chi_m \to \chi_{m-1}$, which in this case is an Artin–Schreier covering. The result [30] is

$$g(\chi_m) = \begin{cases} r^m + r^{m-1} - r^{(m+1)/2} \\ \quad - 2r^{(m-1)/2} + 1, & \text{if } m \equiv 1 \bmod 2 \\ r^m + r^{m-1} - \frac{1}{2}r^{m/2+1} \\ \quad - \frac{3}{2}r^{m/2} - r^{m/2-1} + 1, & \text{if } m \equiv 1 \bmod 2 \end{cases} \quad (15)$$

from which (14) follows.

In order to make the codes really constructive one needs to find the right divisor G and the bases for the vector spaces $L(G)$. This seems to be very difficult. For the codes coming from χ_3 it has been done by Voß and Høholdt in [101].

Garcia and Stichtenoth [28] also presented another asymptotically good sequence of curves. Here the defining equations are

$$x_{i+1}^q + x_{i+1} = \frac{x_i^q}{x_i^{q-1}+1}, \qquad i = 1, \cdots, m-1 \quad (16)$$

over $\mathbb{F}_{q^2}$.

Here one also has

$$\lim_{n \to \infty} \frac{N(\chi_m)}{g(\chi_m)} = q - 1 \quad (17)$$

and, moreover, quite recently Pellikaan, Stichtenoth, and Torres in [69] succeed in calculating recursively the nongap sequence of Q, the point at infinity.

Let S_m denote the semigroup of nongaps at Q in χ_m. For $m \geq 1$ let

$$A_m = \begin{cases} q^m - q^{m/2}, & \text{if } m \text{ is even} \\ q^m - q^{(m+1)/2}, & \text{if } m \text{ is odd}. \end{cases} \quad (18)$$

Then $S_1 = \mathbb{N}_0$ and for $m \geq 1$

$$S_{m+1} = qS_m \cup \{x \in \mathbb{N}_0 | x \geq A_{m+1}\}. \quad (19)$$

One could hope that this will lead to a determination of the basis of $L(rQ)$ for χ_m.

The two sequences of curves given by (13) and (16) have recently been shown to be specific examples of modular curves by Elkies [20].

VII. CONCLUSIONS

The past fifteen years has seen extraordinary developments in the application of the ideas of algebraic geometry to the construction of codes and their decoding algorithms. While the highlight of these developments has been the construction of asymptotically good codes, very significant advances have been achieved in other directions. For all of the developments achieved to date, it is clear that many interesting challenges remain and other avenues yet to explore. These might include the following problems.

It is perhaps true that codes from geometries have yet to have an impact in practice. The development of classes of codes with the simplicity and efficiency of both encoding and decoding algorithms that rival those of Reed–Solomon codes, for example, will be required to break through current practice. While the development of asymptotically good codes over fields of size at least 49 is an impressive achievement, the development of asymptotically good binary codes, using ideas from algebraic geometry, remains an elusive and challenging goal.

The combinatorial structure of linear codes has been an interesting chapter in coding theory. Designs with excellent parameters often result from codes with exceptional structure, such as the Golay and quadratic residue codes and extremal self-dual codes [10]. With the superior properties of code classes developed from algebraic geometry, one might expect an investigation of their combinatorial properties would show promise. The investigation of such structure that utilizes the properties of the curves from which the codes are obtained, might prove interesting.

The intimate connections between codes and lattices, and more generally, sphere packings in Euclidean spaces, is now well established and a very active area of research [7]. The lattices and sphere packings derivable from codes in algebraic geometries where the resulting properties can be related to the properties of the curves used, might prove interesting. For example, lattices resulting from certain elliptic curves [18], [19], yield the best known packing densities for their dimensions. Perhaps further investigations in these directions will yield results of interest.

There is little doubt that future investigations of the ideas of algebraic geometry applied to these, and other, areas will reveal new and exciting results and directions. One cannot help but feel that the mathematical elegance of the ideas of algebraic geometry has yet to be fully exploited. It is hoped that this brief review has provided a look at where the subject stands today, as a platform for further work.

ACKNOWLEDGMENT

The authors would like to express their appreciation to Prof. R. E. Blahut and Prof. H. Stichtenoth, and to the anonymous reviewers, for their many helpful comments on the original draft of this paper. Their efforts are greatly appreciated.

REFERENCES

[1] S. S. Abhyankar, *Algebraic Geometry for Scientists and Engineers.* Providence, RI: Amer. Math. Soc., 1990.

[2] A. M. Barg, S. L. Katsman, and M. A. Tsfasman, "Algebraic geometric codes from curves of small genus," *Probl. Inform. Transm.*, vol. 23, pp. 34–38, 1987.

[3] E. R. Berlekamp, "On decoding binary Bose–Chaudhuri–Hocquenghem codes," *IEEE Trans. Inform. Theory*, vol. IT-11, pp. 577–580, Oct. 1965.

[4] R. C. Bose and D. K. Ray-Chaudhuri, "On a class of error correcting binary group codes," *Inform. Contr.*, vol. 3, pp. 68–79, Mar. 1960.

[5] B. Buchberger, "Multidimensional systems theory: Progress, directions and open problems in multidimensional systems," in *An Algorithmic Method in Polynomial Ideal Theory*, N. K. Bose, Ed. Dordrecht, The Netherlands: Reidel, 1985, ch. "Gröbner Bases."

[6] H. Chen and S.-T. Yau, "Contribution to Munuera's problem on the main conjecture of geometric hyperelliptic MDS codes," *IEEE Trans. Inform. Theory*, vol. 43, pp. 1349–1354, July 1997.

[7] J. H. Conway and N. J. A. Sloane, *Sphere Packings, Lattices and Groups.* Berlin, Germany: Springer-Verlag, 1993.

[8] D. Cox, J. Little, and D. O'Shea, *Ideals, Varieties, and Algorithms.* New York: Springer-Verlag, 1992.

[9] M. A. de Boer, "Almost MDS codes," *Desi., Codes Cryptogr.*, vol. 9, pp. 143–155, 1996.

[10] P. Delsarte, "An algebraic approach to the association schemes of coding theory," *Philips Res. Repts. Suppl.*, no. 10, 1973.

[11] ——, "On subfield subcodes of modified Reed–Solomon codes," *IEEE Trans. Inform. Theory*, vol. IT-21, pp. 575–576, 1975.

[12] Y. Driencourt and J. F. Michon, "Elliptic codes over fields of characteristic 2," *J. Pure and Appl. Alg.*, vol. 45, pp. 15–39, 1987.

[13] Y. Driencourt, "Some properties of elliptic codes over a field of characteristic 2," in *Lecture Notes in Computer Science*, vol. 229. Berlin: Springer-Verlag, 1985.

[14] Y. Driencourt and J. F. Michon, "Remarques sur les codes géométriques," *Compt. Rend.*, vol. 301, pp. 15–17, 1985.

[15] Y. Driencourt and H. Stichtenoth, "A criterion for self-duality of geometric codes," *Comm. in Alg.*, vol. 17, pp. 885–898, 1989.

[16] V. G. Drinfeld and S. G. Vlăduţ, "Number of points of an algebraic curve," *Func. Anal.*, vol. 17, pp. 53–54, 1993.

[17] I. M. Duursma, "Decoding codes from curves and cyclic codes," Ph.D. dissertation, Eindhoven Univ. Technol., Eindhoven, The Netherlands, Aug. 1993.

[18] N. D. Elkies, "Mordell–Weil lattices in characteristic 2 I: Construction and first properties," preprint.

[19] ——, "Mordell–Weil lattices in characteristic 2 II: The Leech lattice as a Mordell–Weil lattice," preprint.

[20] ——, "Beyond Coppa codes," in *Proc. 35th Allerton Conf. Communication, Control, and Computing* (Allerton House, Monticello, IL, 1997).

[21] A. Faldum and W. Willems, "Codes of small defect," *Des., Codes Cryptogr.*, vol. 10, pp. 341–350, 1997.

[22] G.-L. Feng and T. R. N. Rao, "Improved geometric Goppa codes, Part I: Basic theory," *IEEE Trans. Inform. Theory*, vol. 41, pp. 1678–1693, Nov. 1995.

[23] ——, "Decoding algebraic–geometric codes up to the designed minimum distance," *IEEE Trans. Inform. Theory*, vol. 39, pp. 37–45, Jan. 1993.

[24] ——, "A simple approach for construction of algebraic–geometric codes from affine plane curves," *IEEE Trans. Inform. Theory*, vol. 40, pp. 1003–1012, 1994.

[25] G.-L. Feng, V. K. Wei, T. R. N. Rao, and K. K. Tzeng, "Simplified understanding and efficient decoding of a class of algebraic–geometric codes," *IEEE Trans. Inform. Theory*, vol. 40, pp. 981–1002, 1994.

[26] P. Fitzpatrick, "A new derivation of an algorithm for solving the key equation," manuscript, 1993.

[27] W. Fulton, *Algebraic Curves*. New York: Benjamin, 1969.

[28] A. Garcia and H. Stichtenoth, "A tower of Artin–Schreier extensions of function fields attaining the Drinfeld–Vlăduţ bound," *Invent. Math.*, vol. 121, pp. 211–222, 1995.

[29] ——, "On the asymptotic behaviour of some towers of function fields over finite fields," *J. Number Theory,* vol. 61, pp. 248–273, 1996.

[30] ——, "Algebraic function fields over finite fields with many rational points," *IEEE Trans. Inform. Theory*, vol. 41, pp. 1548–1563, 1995.

[31] M. J. E. Golay, "Notes on digital coding," *Proc. IRE*, vol. 37, p. 657, June 1949.

[32] V. D. Goppa, "A new class of linear error-correcting codes," *Probl. Inform. Transm.*, vol. 6, pp. 207–212, Sept. 1970.

[33] ——, "Codes on algebraic curves," *Sov. Math.–Dokl.*, vol. 24, pp. 170–172, 1981, translation from *Dokl. Akad. Nauk S.S.S.R*, vol. 259, pp. 1289–1290, 1981.

[34] ——, "Codes associated with divisors," *Probl. Inform. Transm.*, vol. 13, pp. 22–27, 1977.

[35] ——, "Algebraico–geometric codes," *Math. USSR Izv.*, vol. 21, pp. 75–91, 1983.

[36] ——, *Geometry and Codes*. Dordrecht, The Netherlands: Kluwer, 1988.

[37] ——, "Rational representation of codes and (L, g)-codes," *Probl. Inform. Transm.*, vol. 7, pp. 223–229, 1971.

[38] R. W. Hamming, "Error detecting and error correcting codes," *Bell Syst. Tech. J.*, vol. 29, pp. 147–160, Apr. 1950.

[39] J. P. Hansen, "Codes on the Klein quartic, ideals and decoding," *IEEE Trans. Inform. Theory*, vol. IT-33, pp. 923–925, 1987.

[40] J. P. Hansen, H. E. Jensen, and R. Kötter, "Determination of error values for AG-codes and the Forney formula," *IEEE Trans. Inform. Theory*, vol. 42, pp. 1263–1269, July 1996.

[41] C. Heegard, J. H. Little, and K. Saints, "Systematic encoding via Gröbner bases for a class of algebraic geometric Goppa codes," *IEEE Trans. Inform. Theory*, vol. 41, pp. 1752–1761, Nov. 1995.

[42] J. W. P. Hirschfeld, M. A. Tsfasman, and S. G. Vlăduţ, "The weight hierarchy of higher dimensional Hermitian codes," *IEEE Trans. Inform. Theory*, vol. 40, pp. 275–278, 1994.

[43] A. Hocquenghem, "Codes correcteurs d'erreurs," *Chiffres*, vol. 2, pp. 147–156, 1959.

[44] T. Høholdt, J. H. van Lint, and R. Pellikaan, "Algebraic geometry codes," to be published.

[45] T. Høholdt and R. Pellikaan, "On the decoding of algebraic–geometric codes," *IEEE-Trans. Inform. Theory*, vol. 41, pp. 1589–1614, Nov. 1995.

[46] Y. Ihara, "Some remarks on the number of rational points of algebraic curves over finite fields," *J. Fac. Sci. Univ. Tokyo Japan*, vol. 28, pp. 721–724, 1981.

[47] J. Justesen, K. J. Larsen, H. E. Jensen, A. Havemose, and T. Høholdt, "Construction and decoding of a class of algebraic geometry codes," *IEEE Trans. Inform. Theory*, vol. 35, pp. 811–821, 1989.

[48] J. Justesen, "A class of constructive, asymptotically good algebraic codes," *IEEE Trans. Inform. Theory*, vol. IT-18, pp. 652–656, 1972.

[49] T. Kasami, S. Lin, and W. W. Petersen, "Some results on weight distributions of BCH codes," *IEEE Trans. Inform. Theory*, vol. IT-12, p. 274, Apr. 1966.

[50] G. L. Katsman and M. A. Tsfasman, "Spectra of algebraic geometry codes," *Probl. Inform. Transm.*, vol. 23, pp. 262–275, 1987.

[51] G. L. Katsman, M. A. Tsfasman, and S. G. Vlăduţ, "Modular curves and codes with a polynomial construction," *IEEE Trans. Inform. Theory*, vol. IT-30, pp. 353–355, 1984.

[52] C. Kirfel and R. Pelikaan, "The minimum distance of codes in an array coming from telescopic semigroups," *IEEE Trans. Inform. Theory*, vol. 41, pp. 1720–1732, 1995.

[53] N. Koblitz, "A course in number theory and cryptography," in *Graduate Texts in Mathematics*, vol. 114. Berlin, Germany: Springer-Verlag, 1994.

[54] G. Lachaud, "Les codes géométriques de Goppa," *Séminaire Bouraki*, no. 641, pp. 189–207, 1985.

[55] D. le Brigand, "Decoding of codes on hyperelliptic curves," in *Lecture Notes in Computer Science*, G. Cohen and P. Charpin Eds., vol. 514. Berlin: Springer-Verlag, 1990, pp. 126–134.

[56] ——, "A generalized Forney formula for AG-codes," *IEEE-Trans. Inform. Theory*, vol. 42, pp. 1263–1269, July 1996.

[57] R. Lidl and H. Niederreiter, "Finite fields," in *Encyclopedia of Mathematics and Its Applications*. Reading, MA: Addison-Wesley, 1983, vol. 20.

[58] Y. I. Manin, "What is the maximum number of points on a curve over F_2," *J. Fac. Sci. Univ. Tokyo*, vol. 28, pp. 715–720, 1981.

[59] F. J. MacWilliams and N. J. A. Sloane, *The Theory of Error-Correcting Codes*. Amsterdam, The Netherlands: North-Holland, 1977.

[60] R. J. McEliece, "The theory of information and coding," in *Encyclopedia of Mathematics and Its Applications*. Reading, MA: Addison-Wesley, 1977, vol. 3.

[61] F. J. MacWilliams and N. J. A. Sloane, *The Theory of Error-Correcting Codes*. Amsterdam, The Netherlands: North-Holland, 1997.

[62] A. J. Menezes, *Elliptic Curve Public Key Cryptosystems*. Dordrecht, The Netherlands: Kluwer, 1993.

[63] J. F. Michon, "Codes and curves," in *Lecture Notes in Mathematics*, H. Stichtenoth and M. A. Tsfasman, Eds., vol. 1518. Berlin, Germany: Springer-Verlag, 1988, pp. 22–30.

[64] C. Moreno, "Algebraic curves over finite fields," in *Cambridge Tracts in Mathematics 97*. Cambridge, U.K.: Cambridge Univ. Press, 1991.

[65] ——, "Algebraic curves over finite fields," in *Cambridge Tracts in Mathematics 97*. Cambridge, U.K.: Cambridge Univ. Press, 1993.

[66] C. Munuera, "On the main conjecture on geometric MDS codes," *IEEE Trans. Inform. Theory*, vol. 38, pp. 1573–1577, 1992.

[67] M. E. O'Sullivan, "Decoding of codes defined by a single point on a curve," *IEEE Trans. Inform. Theory*, vol. 41, pp. 1709–1719, 1995.

[68] ——, *The Key Equation for One-Point Codes and Efficient Error Evaluation,* Univ. Puerto Rico, Apr. 1998, preprint.

[69] R. Pellikaan, H. Sticthenoth, and F. Torres, "Weierstrass semigroups in an asymptotically good tower of function fields," *Finite Fields and Its Applications*, to be published.

[70] M. Perret, "Families of codes exceeding the Varshamov–Gilbert bound," in *Lecture Notes in Computer Science*, G. Cohen and P. Charpin, Eds., vol. 388. Berlin, Germany: Springer-Verlag, 1989, pp. 28–36.

[71] K. Saints and C. Heegard, "Algebraic geometric codes and multidimensional cyclic codes: A unified theory using Grøbner bases," *IEEE-Trans. Inform. Theory*, vol. 41, pp. 1733–1751, Nov. 1995.

[72] S. C. Porter, B.-Z. Shen, and R. Pellikaan, "Decoding geometric Goppa codes using an extra place," *IEEE Trans. Inform. Theory*, vol. 38, pp. 1663–1676, Nov. 1992.

[73] I. S. Reed and G. Solomon, "Polynomial codes over certain finite fields," *J. Soc. Ind. Appl. Math.*, vol. 9, pp. 300–304, June 1960.

[74] D. Rotillon and J. A. Thongly, "Decoding of codes on the Klein quartic," in *Lecture Notes in Computer Science,* G. Cohen and P. Charpin, Eds., vol. 514. Berlin, Germay: Springer-Verlag, 1990, pp. 135–149.

[75] K. Saints and C. Heegard, "Algebraic-geometric codes and multidimensional cyclic codes: A unified theory and algorithms for decoding using Grøbner bases," *IEEE Trans. Inform. Theory*, vol. 41, pp. 1733–1751, Nov. 1995.

[76] S. Sakata, "Extension of the Berlekamp–Massey algorithm to n dimensions," *Inform. Comp.*, vol. 84, pp. 207–239, 1989.

[77] S. Sakata, H. Elbrønd Jensen, and T. Høholdt, "Generalized Berlekamp–Massey decoding of algebraic–geometric codes up to half the Feng–Rao bound," *IEEE Trans. Inform. Theory*, vol. 41, pp. 1762–1768, Nov. 1995.

[78] J. P. Serre, "Sur les nombres des points rationnels d'une courbe algébrique sur un corps fini," *Compt. Rend. Acad. Sci. Paris*, vol. 297, sèr. I, pp. 397–401, 1983.

[79] C. E. Shannon, "A texinputematical theory of communication," *Bell Syst. Tech. J.*, vol. 27, pp. 379–423 and 623–656, 1948.

[80] M. A. Shokrollahi and H. Wassermann, "Decoding Algebraic–Geometric Codes Beyond the Error-Correction Bound," Berkeley, CA, 1997, preprint.

[81] J. Silverman, "The arithmetic of elliptic curves," in *Graduate Texts in Mathematics*, vol. 106. Berlin, Germany: Springer-Verlag, 1986.

[82] A. N. Skorobogatov and S. G. Vlăduţ, "On the decoding of algebraic–geometric codes," *IEEE Trans. Inform. Theory*, vol. 36, pp. 1461–1463, 1990.

[83] H. Stichtenoth, "Algebraic function fields and codes," in *Universitext*. Berlin, Germay: Springer-Verlag, 1993.

[84] ———, "A note on Hermitian codes over GF(q^2)," *IEE Trans. Inform. Theory*, vol. 34, pp. 1345–1348, 1988.

[85] H. Stichtenoth and C. Voß, "Generalized Hamming weights of trace codes," *IEEE Trans. Inform. Theory*, vol. 40, pp. 554–558, 1994.

[86] H. Stichtenoth, "On the dimension of subfield subcodes," *IEEE Trans. Inform. Theory*, vol. 36, pp. 90–93, 1990.

[87] ———, "Self-dual Goppa codes," *J. Pure Appl. Alg.*, vol. 55, pp. 199–211, 1988.

[88] M. Sudan, "Decoding of Reed–Solomon codes beyond the error-correction bound," *J. Complexity*, vol. 13, pp. 180–193, 1997.

[89] H. J. Tiersma, "Remarks on codes from Hermitian curves," *IEEE Trans. Inform. Theory*, vol. IT-33, pp. 605–609, 1987.

[90] M. A. Tsfasman and S. G. Vlăduţ, *Algebraic–Geometric Codes*. Dordrecht, The Netherlands: Kluwer, 1991.

[91] M. A. Tsfasman, S. G. Vlăduţ, and T. Zink, "On Goppa codes which are better than the Varshamov–Gilbert bound," *Math. Nachr.*, vol. 109, pp. 21–28, 1982.

[92] ———, "Modular curves, Shimura curves and Coppa codes, better than the Varshamov–Gilbert bound," *Math. Nachr.*, vol. 109, pp. 21–28, 1982.

[93] M. A. Tsfasman, "Goppa codes that are better than the Varshamov–Gilbert bound," *Probl. Inform. Transm.*, vol. 18, pp. 163–166, 1982.

[94] G. van der Geer, "Codes and elliptic curves," in *Effective Methods in Algebraic Geometry*, T. Mora and C. Traverso, Eds. Base, Switzerland: Birkhäuser, 1991, pp. 160–168.

[95] J. H. van Lint, "Introduction to coding theory," in *Gradate Texts in Mathematics*, vol. 86. Berlin, Germany: Springer-Verlag, 1982.

[96] J. H. van Lint and T. A. Springer, "Generalized Reed–Solomon codes from algebraic geometry," *IEEE Trans. Inform. Theory*, vol. IT-33, pp. 305–309, 1987.

[97] J. H. van Lint and G. van der Geer, *Introduction to Coding Theory and Algebraic Geometry*. Basel, Switzerland: Birkhäuser, 1988.

[98] J. H. van Lint, "Algebraic geometric codes," in *Coding Theory and Design Theory*, D. Ray-Chaudhuri, Ed. New York: Springer, 1990, pp. 137–162.

[99] S. G. Vlăduţ and Y. I. Manin, "Linear codes and modular curves," *J. Sov. Math.*, vol. 30, pp. 2611–2643, 1985.

[100] S. G. Vlăduţ, "An exhaustion bound for algebraic–geomeric 'modular' codes," *Probl. Inform. Transm.*, vol. 23, pp. 22–34, 1985.

[101] C. Voß and T. Høholdt, "An explicit construction of a sequence of codes attaining the Tsfasman–Vlăduţ–Zink bound. The first steps," *IEEE Trans. Inform. Theory*, vol. 43, pp. 128–135, Jan. 1997.

[102] S. B. Wicker and V. K. Bhargava, Eds., *Reed–Solomon Codes and Their Applications*. Piscataway, NJ: IEEE Press, 1994.

[103] J. K. Wolf, "Adding two information symbols to certian nonbinary BCH codes and some applications," *Bell Syst. Tech. J.*, vol. 49, no. 2, pp. 2405–2424, 1969.

[104] K. Yang and P. V. Kumar, "On the true minimum distance of Hermitian codes," in *Lecture Notes in Mathematics*, H. Stichtenoth and M. A. Tsfasman, Eds., vol. 1518. Berlin, Germany: Springer-Verlag, 1988, pp. 99–107.

[105] T. Yaghoobian and I. F. Blake, "Hermitian codes as generalized Reed–Solomon codes," *Des., Codes Cryptogr.*, vol. 2, pp. 5–17, 1992.

[106] ———, "Codes from hyperelliptic curves," in *Allerton Conf. Communication, Control and Computing*, 1992.

[107] C. Xing, "On automorphism groups of the Hermitian codes," *IEEE Trans. Inform. Theory*, vol. 41, pp. 1629–1635, 1995.

Fading Channels: Information-Theoretic and Communications Aspects

Ezio Biglieri, *Fellow, IEEE*, John Proakis, *Life Fellow, IEEE*, and Shlomo Shamai (Shitz), *Fellow, IEEE*

(Invited Paper)

Abstract— In this paper we review the most peculiar and interesting information-theoretic and communications features of fading channels. We first describe the statistical models of fading channels which are frequently used in the analysis and design of communication systems. Next, we focus on the information theory of fading channels, by emphasizing capacity as the most important performance measure. Both single-user and multiuser transmission are examined. Further, we describe how the structure of fading channels impacts code design, and finally overview equalization of fading multipath channels.

Index Terms—Capacity, coding, equalization, fading channels, information theory, multiuser communications, wireless systems.

I. INTRODUCTION

THE theory for Gaussian dispersive channels, whether time-invariant or variant, has been well established for decades with new touches motivated by practical technological achievements, reported systematically over the years (see [2], [62], [64], [94], [114], [122], [223], [225], [267] for some recent developments). Neither the treatment of statistical time-varying channels is new in information theory, and in fact by now this topic is considered as classic [64], with Shannon himself contributing to some of its aspects [261] (see [164] for a recent tutorial exposition, and references therein). Fading phenomena were also carefully studied by information-theoretic tools for a long time. However, it is only relatively recently that information-theoretic study of increasingly complicated fading channel models, under a variety of interesting and strongly practically related constraints has accelerated to a degree where its impact of the whole issue of communications in a fading regime is notable also by nonspecialists of information theory. Harnessing information-theoretic tools to the investigation of fading channels, in the widest sense of this notion, has not only resulted in an enhanced understanding of the potential and limitations of those channels, but in fact Information Theory provided in numerous occasions the right guidance to the specific design of efficient communications systems. Doubtless, the rapid advance in technology on the one hand and the exploding demand for efficient high-quality

and volume of digital wireless communications over almost every possible media and for a variety of purposes (be it cellular, personal, data networks, including the ambitious wireless high rate ATM networks, point-to-point microwave systems, underwater communications, satellite communications, etc.) plays a dramatic role in this trend. Evidently these technological developments and the digital wireless communications demand motivate and encourage vigorous information-theoretical studies of the most relevant issues in an effort to identify and assess the potential of optimal or close-to-optimal communications methods. This renaissance of studies bore fruits and has already led to interesting and very relevant results which matured to a large degree the understanding of communications through fading media, under a variety of constraints and models. The footprints of information-theoretic considerations are evidenced in many state-of-the-art coding systems. Typical examples are the space–time codes, which attempt to benefit from the dramatic increase in capacity of spatial diversity in transmission and reception, i.e., multiple transmit and receive antennas [92], [226], [280], [281], [283]. The recently introduced efficient turbo-coded multilevel modulation schemes [133] and the bit interleaved coded modulation (BICM) [42], as a special case, were motivated by information-theoretic arguments demonstrating remarkable close to the ultimate capacity limit performance in the Gaussian and fading channels. Equalization whether explicit or implicit is an inherent part of communications over time-varying fading channels, and information theory has a role here as well. This is mainly reflected by the sensitivity of the information-theoretic predictions to errors in the estimated channel parameters on one hand, and the extra effort (if any) ratewise, needed to track accurately the time-varying channel. Clearly, information theory provides also a yardstick by which the efficiency of equalization methods is to be measured, and that is by determining the ultimate limit of communications on the given channel model, under prescribed assumptions (say channel state parameters not available to either transmitter or receiver), without an explicit partition to equalization and decoding. In fact, the intimate relation among pure information-theoretic arguments, specific coding and equalization methods motivates the tripartite structure of this paper.

This intensive study, documented by our reference list, not only affected the understanding of ultimate limits and preferred communication techniques over these channels embracing a wide variety of communication media and models,

Manuscript received December 5, 1997; revised May 3, 1998.

E. Biglieri is with the Dipartimento di Elettronica, Politecnico di Torino, I-10129 Torino, Italy.

J. Proakis is with the Department of Electrical and Computer Engineering, Northeastern University, Boston, MA 02115 USA.

S. Shamai (Shitz) is with the Department of Electrical Engineering, Technion–Israel Institute of Technology, 32000 Haifa, Israel.

Publisher Item Identifier S 0018-9448(98)06815-1.

but has enriched information theory itself, and introduced interesting notions. This is illustrated by the notion of delay-limited capacity [127], [43], the polymatroidal property of the multiple-user capacity region [290], and the like. It is the practical constraints to which various communications systems are subjected which gave rise to new notions, as the "delay-limited capacity region" [127], capacity versus outage [210], generalized random TDMA accessing [155], and attached practical meaning to purely theoretical results, as capacity regions with mismatched nearest neighbor decoding [161] and many related techniques, and results derived for finite-state, compound, and arbitrarily varying channels. The body of the recently developed information-theoretic results not only enriched the field of information theory by introducing new techniques, useful also in other settings, and provided interesting, unexpected outcomes (as, for example, the beneficial effect of fading in certain simple cellular models [268]), but also made information theory a viable and relevant tool, not only to information theorists, scientists, and mathematicians, as it always was since its advent by C. E. Shannon 50 years ago, but also to the communication system engineer and designer. On the other hand, this extensive (maybe too extensive) information-theoretic study of this wide-ranging issue of fading channels, does not always bear worthy fruits. There is a substantial amount of overlap among studies, and not all contributions (mildly speaking) provide interesting, novel, and insightful results. One of the more important goals of this exposition is to try to minimize the overlap in research by providing a reasonable, even if only very partial, scan of directly relevant literature. There are also numerous misconceptions spread in the literature of some information-theoretic predictions and their implication on practical systems. In our exposition here we hope to dispel some of these, while drawing attention to the delicate interplay between central notions and their interpretation in the realm of practical systems operating on fading channels.

Our goal here is to review the most peculiar and interesting information-theoretic features of fading channels, and provide reference for other information-theoretic developments which follow a more standard classical line. We wish also to emphasize the inherent connection and direct implications of information-theoretic arguments on specific coding and equalization procedures for the wide class of fading channels [337]. This exposition certainly reflects subjective taste and inclinations, and we apologize to those readers and workers in the field with different preferences. The reference list here is by no means complete. It is enough to say that only a small fraction of the relevant classical Russian literature [73]–[76], [199], [203]–[209], [265], [293]–[295] usually overlooked by most Western workers in this specific topic, appears in our reference list. For more references, see the list in [75]. However, an effort has been made to make this reference list, as combined with the reference lists of all the hereby referenced papers, a rather extensive exposition of the literature (still not full, as many of the contributions are unpublished reports or theses. See [227] and [282] for examples). Therefore, and due to space limitations, we sometimes refrain from mentioning relevant references that can be found in the cited papers or by searching standard databases. Neither do we present references in their historical order of development, and in general, when relevant, we reference books or later references, where the original and older references can be traced, without giving the well-deserved credit to the original first contribution. Due to the extensive information-theoretic study of this subject, accelerating at an increased pace in recent years, no tutorial exposition and a reference list can be considered updated by the day it is published, and ours is no exception.

The paper is organized as follows. Section II introduces several models of fading multipath channels used in the subsequent sections of the paper. Section III focuses on information-theoretic aspects of communication through fading channels. Section IV deals with channel coding and decoding techniques and their performance. Finally, Section V focuses on equalization techniques for suppressing intersymbol interference and multiple-access interference.

II. CHANNEL MODELS

Statistical models for fading multipath channels are described in detail in [223], [441], and [459]. In this section we shall briefly describe the statistical models of fading multipath channels which are frequently used in the analysis and design of communication systems.

A. The Scattering Function and Related Channel Parameters

A fading multipath channel is generally characterized as a linear, time-varying system having an (equivalent lowpass) impulse response $c(t; \tau)$ (or a time-varying frequency response $C(t; f)$) which is a wide-sense stationary random process in the t-variable. Time variations in the channel impulse response or frequency response result in frequency spreading, generally called Doppler spreading, of the signal transmitted through the channel. Multipath propagation results in spreading the transmitted signal in time. Consequently, a fading multipath channel may be generally characterized as a doubly spread channel in time and frequency.

By assuming that the multipath signals propagating through the channel at different delays are uncorrelated (a wide-sense stationary uncorrelated scattering, or WSSUS, channel) a doubly spread channel may be characterized by the scattering function $S(\tau; \lambda)$, which is a measure of the power spectrum of the channel at delay τ and frequency offset λ (relative to the carrier frequency). From the scattering function, we obtain the *delay power spectrum* of the channel (also called the *multipath intensity profile*) by simply averaging $S(\tau; \lambda)$ over λ, i.e.,

$$S_c(\tau) = \int_{-\infty}^{\infty} S(\tau; \lambda) \, d\lambda. \qquad (2.1.1)$$

Similarly, the Doppler power spectrum is

$$S_c(\lambda) = \int_0^{\infty} S(\tau; \lambda) \, d\tau. \qquad (2.1.2)$$

The range of values over which the delay power spectrum $S_c(\tau)$ is nonzero is defined as the multipath spread T_m of the channel. Similarly, the range of values over which the

Doppler power spectrum $S_c(\lambda)$ is nonzero is defined as the Doppler spread B_d of the channel.

The value of the Doppler spread B_d provides a measure of how rapidly the channel impulse response varies in time. The larger the value of B_d, the more rapidly the channel impulse response is changing with time. This leads us to define another channel parameter, called the *channel coherence time* T_{coh} as

$$T_{\mathrm{coh}} = \frac{1}{B_d}. \tag{2.1.3}$$

Thus a slowly fading channel has a large coherence time and a fast fading channel has a small coherence time. The relationship in (2.1.3) is rigorously established in [223] from the channel correlation functions and the Doppler power spectrum.

In a similar manner, we define the *channel coherence bandwidth* B_{coh} as the reciprocal of the multipath spread, i.e.,

$$B_{\mathrm{coh}} = \frac{1}{T_m}. \tag{2.1.4}$$

B_{coh} provides us with a measure of the width of the band of frequencies which are similarly affected by the channel response, i.e., the width of the frequency band over which the fading is highly correlated.

The product $T_m B_d$ is called the *spread factor* of the channel. If $T_m B_d < 1$, the channel is said to be *underspread*; otherwise, it is *overspread*. Generally, if the spread factor $T_m B_d \ll 1$, the channel impulse response can be easily measured and that measurement can be used at the receiver in the demodulation of the received signal and at the transmitter to optimize the transmitted signal. Measurement of the channel impulse response is extremely difficult and unreliable, if not impossible, when the spread factor $T_m B_d > 1$.

B. Frequency-Nonselective Channel: Multiplicative Channel Model

Let us now consider the effect of the transmitted signal characteristics on the selection of the channel model that is appropriate for the specified signal. Let $x(t)$ be the equivalent lowpass signal transmitted over the channel and let $X(f)$ denote its frequency content. Then, the equivalent lowpass received signal, exclusive of additive noise, is

$$r(t) = \int_{-\infty}^{\infty} c(t;\tau)x(t-\tau)d\tau$$
$$= \int_{-\infty}^{\infty} C(t;f)X(f)e^{j2\pi ft}\,df. \tag{2.2.1}$$

Now, suppose that the bandwidth W of $X(f)$ is much smaller than the coherence bandwidth of the channel, i.e., $W \ll B_{\mathrm{coh}}$. Then all the frequency components in $X(f)$ undergo the same attenuation and phase shift in transmission through the channel. But this implies that, within the bandwidth W occupied by $X(f)$, the time-variant transfer function $C(t;f)$ of the channel is constant in the frequency variable. Such a channel is called *frequency-nonselective* or *flat fading*.

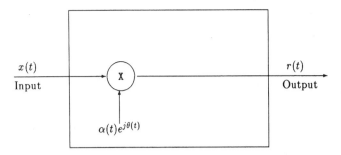

Fig. 1.   The multiplicative channel model.

For the frequency-nonselective channel, (2.2.1) simplifies to

$$r(t) = C(t;0)\int_{-\infty}^{\infty} X(f)e^{j2\pi ft}\,df$$
$$= C(t)x(t)$$
$$= \alpha(t)e^{j\theta(t)}x(t) \tag{2.2.2}$$

where, by definition, $C(t;0) = \alpha(t)e^{j\theta(t)}, \alpha(t)$ represents the envelope and $\theta(t)$ represents the phase of the equivalent lowpass channel response.

Thus a frequency-nonselective fading channel has a time-varying multiplicative effect on the transmitted signal. In this case, the multipath components of the channel are not resolvable because the signal bandwidth $W \ll B_{\mathrm{coh}} = 1/T_m$. Equivalently, $T_m \ll 1/W$. Fig. 1 illustrates the multiplicative channel model.

A frequency-nonselective channel is said to be *slowly fading* if the time duration of a transmitted symbol, defined as T_s, is much smaller than the coherence time of the channel, i.e., $T_s \ll T_{\mathrm{coh}}$. Equivalently, $T_s \ll 1/B_d$ or $B_d \ll 1/T_s$. Since, in general, the signal bandwidth $W \geq 1/T_s$, it follows that a slowly fading, frequency-nonselective channel is underspread.

We may also define a *rapidly fading channel* as one which satisfies the relation $T_s \geq T_{\mathrm{coh}}$.

C. Frequency-Selective Channel: The Tapped Delay Line Channel Model

When the transmitted signal $X(f)$ has a bandwidth W greater than the coherence bandwidth B_{coh} of the channel, the frequency components of $X(f)$ with frequency separation exceeding B_{coh} are subjected to different gains and phase shifts. In such a case, the channel is said to be *frequency-selective*. Additional distortion is caused by the time variations in $C(t;f)$, which is the fading effect that is evidenced as a time variation in the received signal strength of the frequency components in $X(f)$.

When $W \gg B_{\mathrm{coh}}$, the multipath components in the channel response that are separated in delay by at least $1/W$ are resolvable. In this case, the sampling theorem may be used to represent the resolvable received signal components. Such a development leads to a representation of the time-varying channel impulse response as [223]

$$c(t;\tau) = \sum_{n=1}^{L} c_n(t)\delta(\tau - n/W) \tag{2.3.1}$$

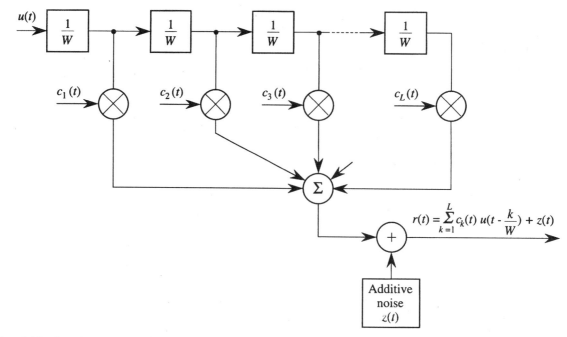

Fig. 2. Tapped-delay-line channel model.

and the corresponding time-variant transfer function as

$$C(t; f) = \sum_{n=1}^{L} c_n(t) e^{j2\pi fn/W} \qquad (2.3.2)$$

where $c_n(t)$ is the complex-valued channel gain of the nth multipath component and L is the number of resolvable multipath components. Since the multipath spread is T_m and the time resolution of the multipath is $1/W$, it follows that

$$L = \lfloor T_m W \rfloor + 1. \qquad (2.3.3)$$

A channel having the impulse response given by (2.3.1) may be represented by a tapped-delay line with L taps and complex-valued, time-varying tap coefficients $\{c_n(t)\}$. Fig. 2 illustrates the tapped-delay-line channel model that is appropriate for the frequency-selective channel. The randomly time-varying tap gains $\{c_n(t)\}$ may also be represented by

$$c_n(t) = \alpha_n(t) e^{j\theta_n(t)}, \qquad n = 1, 2, \cdots, L \qquad (2.3.4)$$

where $\{\alpha_n(t)\}$ represent the amplitudes and $\{\theta_n(t)\}$ represent the corresponding phases.

The tap gains $\{c_n(t)\}$ are usually modeled as stationary (wide-sense) mutually uncorrelated random processes having autorrelation functions

$$\phi_n(\tau) = E[\tfrac{1}{2} c_n^*(t) c_n(t + \tau)], \qquad n = 1, 2, \cdots, L \qquad (2.3.5)$$

and Doppler power spectra

$$S_n(\lambda) = \int_{-\infty}^{\infty} \phi_n(\tau) e^{-j2\pi\lambda\tau} \, d\tau. \qquad (2.3.6)$$

Thus each resolvable multipath component may be modeled with its own appropriate Doppler power spectrum and corresponding Doppler spread.

D. Statistical Models for the Fading Signal Components

There are several probability distributions that have been used to model the statistical characteristics of the fading channel. When there are a large number of scatterers in the channel that contribute to the signal at the receiver, as is the case in ionospheric or tropospheric signal propagation, application of the central limit theorem leads to a Gaussian process model for the channel impulse response. If the process is zero-mean, then the envelope of the channel impulse response at any time instant has a Rayleigh probability distribution and the phase is uniformly distributed in the interval $(0, 2\pi)$. That is, the envelope

$$R = |c(t; \tau)| \qquad (2.4.1)$$

has the probability density function (pdf)

$$p_R(r) = \frac{2r}{\Omega} e^{-r^2/\Omega}, \qquad r \geq 0 \qquad (2.4.2)$$

where

$$\Omega = E(R^2). \qquad (2.4.3)$$

We observe that the Rayleigh distribution is characterized by the single parameter Ω.

It should be noted that for the frequency-nonselective channel, the envelope is simply the magnitude of the channel multiplicative gain, i.e.,

$$R(t) = |C(t)| = \alpha(t) \qquad (2.4.4)$$

and for the frequency-selective (tapped-delay-line) channel model, each of the tap gains has a magnitude that is modeled as Rayleigh fading.

An alternative statistical model for the envelope of the channel response is the Nakagami-m distribution. The pdf for this distribution is

$$p_R(r) = \frac{2}{\Gamma(m)}\left(\frac{m}{\Omega}\right)^m r^{2m-1} e^{-mr^2/\Omega}, \qquad r \geq 0 \quad (2.4.5)$$

where Ω is defined as in (2.4.3) and the parameter m is defined as the ratio of moments, called the *fading figure*,

$$m = \frac{\Omega^2}{E[(R^2 - \Omega)^2]}, \qquad m \geq 1/2. \qquad (2.4.6)$$

In contrast to the Rayleigh distribution, which has a single parameter that can be used to match the fading-channel statistics, the Nakagami-m is a two-parameter distribution, with the parameters m and Ω. As a consequence, this distribution provides more flexibility and accuracy in matching the observed signal statistics. The Nakagami-m distribution can be used to model fading-channel conditions that are either more or less severe than the Rayleigh distribution, and it includes the Rayleigh distribution as a special case ($m = 1$). For example, Turin [518] and Suzuki [513] have shown that the Nakagami-m distribution provides the best fit for data signals received in urban radio channels.

The Rice distribution is also a two-parameter distribution that may be used to characterize the signal in a fading multipath channel. This distribution is appropriate for modeling a Gaussian fading channel in which the impulse response has a nonzero mean component, usually called a *specular component*. The pdf for the Rice distribution is

$$p_R(r) = \frac{r}{\sigma^2} e^{-(r^2+s^2)/2\sigma^2} I_0\left(\frac{rs}{\sigma^2}\right), \qquad r \geq 0 \qquad (2.4.7)$$

where s^2 represents the power in the nonfading (specular) signal components and σ^2 is the variance of the corresponding zero-mean Gaussian components. Note that when $s^2 = 0$, (2.4.7) reduces to the Rayleigh pdf with $\sigma^2 = \Omega/2$.

The Rice distribution is a particularly appropriate model for line-of-sight (LOS) communication links, where there is a direct propagating signal component (the specular component) and multipath components arising from secondary reflections from surrounding terrain that arrive with different delays.

In conclusion, the Rayleigh, Rice, and Nakagami-m distributions are the most widely used statistical models for signals transmitted through fading multipath channels.

III. Information-Theoretic Aspects

A. Introduction

This part of the paper focuses on information-theoretic concepts for the fading channel and emphasizes capacity, which is, however, only one information-theoretic measure, though the most important. We will not elaborate on other information-theoretic measures as the error exponents and cutoff rates; rather, we provide some comments on special features of these measures in certain situations in the examined fading models, and mainly present some references which the interested reader can use to track down the very extensive literature available on this subject.

The outline of the material to be discussed in this section is as follows: After a description of the channel model and signaling constraints, elaborating on the more special signaling constraints as delay, peak versus (short- or long-term) average power, we shall specialize to simple, though rather representative, cases. For these, results will be given. We also reference more general cases for which a conceptually similar treatment either has been reported, or can be done straightforwardly. Notions of the variability of the fading process during the transmitted block, and their strong implications on information-theoretic arguments, will be addressed, where emphasis will be placed on the *ergodic capacity, distribution of capacity* (giving rise to the "capacity-versus-outage" approach), *delay-limited capacity*, and the *broadcast* approach. Some of the latter notions are intimately connected to variants of compound channels. We shall give the flavor of the general unifying results by considering a simple single-user channel with statistically corrupted Channel State Information (CSI) available at both transmitting and receiving ends. We shall present some information-theoretic considerations related to the estimation of channel state information, and discuss the information-theoretic implications of wideband versus narrowband signaling in a realm of time-varying channels. The role of feedback of channel state information from receiver to transmitter will be mentioned. Robust decoders, universal detectors, efficient decoders based on mismatched metrics, primarily the variants of the nearest neighbor metric, and their information-theoretic implications, will mainly be referenced and accompanied by some guiding comments. Information-theory-inspired signaling and techniques, such as PAM, interleaving, precoding, DFE, orthogonalized systems, multicarrier, wideband, narrowband, and peaky signaling in time and frequency, will be examined from an information-theoretic viewpoint. (The coding and equalization aspects will be dealt with in the subsequent parts of the paper). Since one of the main implications of information theory in fading channels is the understanding of the full promise of diversity systems, and in particular transmitter diversity, this issue will be highlighted. Other information-theoretic measures as error exponents and cutoff rates will only be mentioned succinctly, emphasizing special aspects in fading channel.

While we start our treatment with the single-user case, the more important and interesting part is the multiple-user case. After extending most of the above-mentioned material to the multiple-user realm, we shall focus on features special to multiple-user systems. Strategies and accessing protocols, as code-division multiple access (CDMA), time-division multiple access (TDMA), frequency-division multiple access (FDMA), rate splitting [232], successive cancellation [62], and L-out-of-K models [48] will be addressed in connection to the fading environment. The notion of delay-limited capacity region will be introduced, adhering to the unifying compound-channel formulation, and its implication in certain fading models highlighted. Broadcast fading channels will then be briefly mentioned.

We shall pay special attention to cellular fading models, due to their ubiquitous global spread in current and future cellular-based communications systems [44], [113], [170], and [273]. Specific attention will be given to Wyner's model [331] and its fading variants [268]–[255], focusing on the information-theoretic aspects of channel accessing inter- and intracell protocols such as CDMA and TDMA. Inter/intracell and multicell cooperation, as time and frequency reuse are to be addressed emphasizing their emergence out of pure information-theoretic arguments. Signaling and accessing techniques spurred by information-theoretic arguments for the fading multiple-user case will be explicitly highlighted.

We end this section with concluding remarks and state briefly some interesting and relevant open problems related to the arbitrarily varying channel (AVC), compound channel, and finite-state channel, as they specialize to standard fading models. Further, unsolved and not fully understood issues, crucial to the understanding of communications networks operating over time-varying channels as aspects of combined queueing and information theory, interference channels, as well as random CDMA, will also be briefly mentioned.

B. Fading Channel Models, Signaling Constraints, and Their Information-Theoretic Aspects

In the previous section, general models for the time-varying fading channel were introduced. In this subsection we focus on those models and assumptions which are relevant for a standard information-theoretic approach and elaborate on those assumptions which lead to the required simplifications, giving rise to a rigorous mathematical treatment.

The general fading, time-varying information channels fall within the framework of multiway (network) multiple-user time-varying channels, where there are senders designated by indices belonging to a set $\mathcal{K}$ where sender $k \in \mathcal{K}$ has at its disposal $(M_t)_k$ transmitting antennas and it attempts to communicate with $\mathcal{M}_k$ receiving sites each of which is equipped with $(M_r)_{m,k}, m \in \mathcal{M}_k, k \in \mathcal{K}$, receiving antennas. The channel between a particular receiving antenna n_r and a particular transmitting n_t antenna, where n_r and n_t are determined by some ordering of the $\Sigma_{k \in \mathcal{K}} (M_t)_k$ transmitting antennas and the $\Sigma_{k \in \mathcal{K}} \Sigma_{m \in \mathcal{M}_k} (M_r)_{mk}$ receiving antennas, is characterized by a time-varying linear filter with an impulse response $c_{n_r, n_t}(t, \tau)$ modeled as in Section II. The assumption imposed on $c_{n_r, n_t}(t, \tau)$ and the constraints imposed on the transmitted signals of each of the users as well as the configuration and connectivity of the system dictates strongly the information-theoretic nature of the scheme which may vary drastically.

To demonstrate this point we first assume that $c(t, \tau)$ is given and fixed. The general framework here encompasses the multiple-user system with diversity at the transmitter and receiver. In fact, if the receiving sites cooperate and are supposed to reliably decode all users, then the resultant channel is the classical *multiple-access* channel [62]. If a user is to convey different information rates to various locations, the problem gives rise to a broadcast channel [62], when a single user is active, or to the combination of a multiple-access and broadcast channels when several users are transmitting simultaneously. This, however, is not the most general case of interest as not all the received signals at a given site (each equipped with many antennas) or group of receiving sites are to be decoded, and that

adds an interference ingredient into the problem turning it into a general multiple-access/broadcast/interference channel [62]. Needless to mention that even the simplest setting of this combination is not yet fully understood from the information-theoretic viewpoint, as even the capacity regions of simple interference and broadcast Gaussian channels are not yet known in general [191], [192]. In this setting, we have not explicitly stated the degree of cooperation of the users, if any, at all receiving sites. Within this framework, the network aspect, which has not been mentioned so far, plays a primary role. The availability of feedback between receiving and transmitting points on one hand, and the actual transmission demand by users, complicate the problem not only mathematically but conceptually, calling for a serious unification between information and network theory [95], [84] and so far only very rare pioneering efforts have been reported [285], [279], [17].

We have not yet touched upon signaling constraints, imposed on each user which transmits several signals through the available transmitting antennas. The standard constraints are as follows.

a) Average power applied to each of the transmitting antennas or averaged over all the transmitting antennas. Even here we should distinguish between average over the transmitted code block ("short-term" in the terminology of [43]) or average over many transmitted codewords ("long-term" average [43]).

b) Peak-power or amplitude constraints are common practice in information-theoretic analyses, (see [248] and references therein) as they provide a more faithful modeling of practical systems.

c) Bandwidth, being a natural resource, plays a major role in the set of constraints imposed on legitimate signaling, and as such is a major factor in the information-theoretic considerations of such systems. The bandwidth constraints can be given in terms of a distribution defining the percentage of time that a certain bandwidth (in any reasonable definition) is allocated to the system.

d) Delay constraints, which in fact pose a limitation on any practical system, dictate via the optimal error behavior (error exponent [399]), how close capacity can be approached in theory with finite-length codes. Here in cases where the channel is characterized by the collection of $\{c(t, \tau)\}$ which might be time-varying in a stochastic manner, the delay constraint is even more important dictating the very existence of the notions of Shannon capacity and giving rise to new information-theoretic expressions, as the capacity versus outage and delay-limited capacity.

The focus of this paper is on fading time-varying channels: in fact, the previous discussion treating $c(t, \tau)$ as a deterministic function should be reinterpreted, with $c_{n_r, n_t}(t, \tau)$ viewed as a *realization* of a random two-parameter process (random field) or a parametrized random process in the variable t (See Section II). This random approach opens a whole spectrum of avenues which refer to time-varying channels. What notions should be used depends on the knowledge available about all $c_{n_r,n_r}(t,\tau)$ and its statistical behavior.

We mainly refer to cases where the statistics of the two-parameter processes $c(t,\tau)$ (dropping the indices n_r, n_t for convenience) are known, which again gives rise to a whole collection of problems discriminated by specifying which information is available at the transmitting/receiving site. The spectrum of cases varies from ideal channel-state information (i.e., the realization of $c(t,\tau)$) available to both receiver/transmitter to the case of full ignorance of the specific realizations at both sides. In fact, in an information-theoretic setting there is in principle (but not always) a difference whether CSI information at the transmitter, even if ideal, is provided in a causal or noncausal mode. See [261] versus [101], respectively, for simple finite independent and identically distributed (i.i.d.) state channel models.

The case of unavailable realization of $c(t,\tau)$ at the receiving site gives rise also to various equalization procedures, which bear their own information-theoretic implications referring to the specific interpretation of the equalization method on one hand [16], [21], [58], [250], and the to information-theoretic role of the accuracy of the available channel parameters [185]–[186] on the other hand. This framework gives also rise to natural questions of how information-theoretically efficient are training sequence methods [140] and the like. This is the reason why we decided to introduce equalization, to be described in Section V, as an inherent part of this paper.

The precise statistical information on the behavior of $c(t,\tau)$ is not always available. This gives rise to the use of mismatched metrics and universal decoders [64], and makes classical notions of compound and arbitrarily variable channels [164], along with the large body of associated results, relevant to our setting. Central notions as random-versus-deterministic code books and maximum- versus average-error probabilities emerge naturally [164].

With the above discussion we hope to have made clear that the scope of information-theoretic framework of time-varying channels encompasses many of classical and recent ideas, as well as results developed in various subfields of information, communications, and signal processing theories. This is the reason why in this limited-scope paper we can only touch upon the most simple and elementary models and results. More general cases are left to the references. As noted before, our reference list, although it might look extensive, provides only a minuscule glimpse of the available and relevant theory, notions, and results. We will mainly address the simplest multipath fading model [223], as discussed in Section II, for $c(t,\tau)$, and, in fact, focus on the simplest cases of these models.

The specific implications of T_m and T_{coh} on a particular communication system depend on the constraints to which that system is subjected. Of particular relevance are the signaling bandwidth W and the transmission duration of the whole message (codeword) T. In the following, ΔT_c will denote T_{coh} measured in channel symbols.

In this section we discriminate between slow and fast fading by using time scales of channel symbols (of order W^{-1}), and between ergodic ($T \gg T_{\text{coh}}$) and nonergodic ($T \ll T_{\text{coh}}$)

channels according to the variability of the fading process in terms of the *whole codeword* transmission duration, assuming that $c(t,\tau)$ is indeed a nondegenerate random process. Clearly, for the deterministic, time-invariant channel, ergodicity does not depend on $\Delta T_c \to \infty$, as the channel exhibits the same realization $c(t,\tau)$ independent of t. While in general we assume slow fading here, implying a negligible effect of the Doppler spread, this will not be the case as far as ergodicity is concerned. The nonergodic case gives rise to interesting information-theoretic settings as capacity versus outage, broadcast interpretation, and delay-limited capacities, all relying on notions of compound channels [64], [164]. The fact that a specific channel is underspread in the terminology of Section II, i.e., $T_m B_d < 1$, implies that it can be treated as a flat slow-fading process, but nevertheless the total transmission duration T may be so large that $WT \gg 1$; thus the channel can overall be viewed as ergodic, giving rise to standard notions of the ergodic, or average, capacity. Although not mentioned here explicitly, the standard discrete-time interpretation is always possible either through classical sampling arguments, which account for the Doppler spread [186], when that is needed, or via orthogonalization techniques, as the Karhunen–Loève or similar [146], [147]. We shall not delve further in this issue: instead, we shall explicitly mention the basic assumptions for the information-theoretic results that we plan to present (and again give references for details not elaborated here). Throughout this paper we assume $WT \gg 1$, as otherwise there is no hope for reliable communication, even in nonfaded time-invariant channel as for example the additive white Gaussian noise (AWGN) channel.

C. Single User

In this subsection we address the single-user case, while the next one discusses multiple users.

1) General Finite-State Channel: In this subsection we resort to a simplified single-user finite-state channel where the channel states model the fading process. We shall restrict attention to flat fading, disregard intersymbol interference (ISI), and introduce different assumptions on the fading dynamics. The main goal of this subsection is to present in some detail a very simple case which will provide insight to the structure of the more general results. Here we basically follow the presentation in [41]. In case differentiation is needed the upper case letters (A) designate random variables, and lower case letters (a) indicate their values. Sequences of random variables or their realizations are denoted by A_n^m and a_n^m, where the subscripts and superscripts denote the starting and ending point of the sequence, respectively. Generic sequences are denoted by $\{A_n\}, \{a_n\}$. In cases where no confusion may arise, lower case letters are used also to denote random variables.

Consider the channel in Fig. 3, with channel input $x_n \in \mathcal{X}$ and output $y_n \in \mathcal{Y}$ and state $s_n \in \mathcal{S}$, where $\mathcal{X}, \mathcal{Y}$ and $\mathcal{S}$ denote the respective spaces. The channel states specify a conditional distribution $\{p(y|x,s), s \in \mathcal{S}\}$ where, given the states, the channel is assumed to be memoryless, that is,

$$p(y_1^N | x_1^N, s_1^N) = \prod_{n=1}^{N} p(y_n | x_n, s_n). \qquad (3.3.1)$$

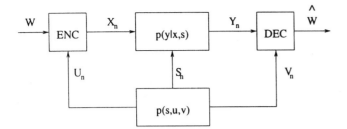

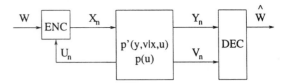

Fig. 3 Block diagram of the channel with time-varying state and transmitter and receiver CSI.

The transmitter and receiver are provided with the channel-state information, denoted by $u \in \mathcal{U}$ and $v \in \mathcal{V}$, via some conditional memoryless distribution

$$p(u_1^N, v_1^N | s_1^N) = \prod_{n=1}^{N} p(u_n, v_n | s_n). \qquad (3.3.2)$$

It is assumed that given x_n and s_n, the output y_n is statistically independent of $\{u_m\}$ and $\{v_m\}$ for any m. We further assume that s_n, u_n, and v_n are independent of past channel inputs (allowing for no ISI in this simple setting). The channel-state information is assumed to be perfect at the transmitter and/or receiver if u_n (respectively, v_n) equals s_n. No channel-state information is available to either transmitter or receiver if u_n (respectively, v_n) is independent of s_n. This model accounts for a variety of cases of known, unknown, or partially known (e.g., through noisy observations) of the channel-state information $u_n s_n v_n$ to the transmitter and/or receiver. For the framework so far we do not specify how the state s is related to the fading, and it may affect the observation in a rather general way.

Encoding and decoding on this channel can be described through a sequence of encoding functions $f_n: W \times U^n \to \chi$, for $n = 1, \cdots, N$, such that $x_n = f_n(\omega, u_1^n)$, where ω ranges over the set of possible source messages W and u_1^n is the realization of the transmitter CSI up to time n. It should be emphasized here that we assume that the channel states are revealed to the transmitter in a causal fashion, and therefore no predictive encoding is possible.[1] Decoding is done usually on the basis of the whole received signal and CSI at the receiver, that is, $\hat{\omega} = \phi(y_1^N, v_1^N)$ where $\hat{\omega}$ is the decoded message and $\phi: y^n \times v^n \to \omega$ the decoding function.

Shannon [261] has provided the capacity of this channel, where $\{s_i\}$ are i.i.d. and the CSI is available causally to the *transmitter only*. It is given in terms of

$$C^{(1)} = \max_{q(t)} I(\mathcal{T}; Y) \qquad (3.3.3)$$

where $\mathcal{T} = \{x_1, \cdots, x_{|\mathcal{S}|}\}$ is a random input vector of length equal to the cardinality $|\mathcal{S}|$ of S with elements in χ, where $q(t)$ is the probability distribution of $\mathcal{T}$. The transition probability of the associated channel with input $\mathcal{T}$ and output y is given by

$$p(y|\mathcal{T}) = \sum_{\ell=1}^{|\mathcal{S}|} p(y|x_\ell, s = \ell) p(s = \ell).$$

[1] If predictive encoding is allowed, that is, all the realizations of the i.i.d. channel states $\{s_i\}$ $i = 1, 2, \cdots, N$ are available to the transmitter only before encoding of the N-long block $(x_1, x_2, \cdots, x_N)$, the capacity results take a different form, as given in [101].

Fig. 4. Block diagram of the equivalent channel with transmitter CSI only and output (Y_n, V_n).

The setting described here, with noisy observations provided to the receiver/transmitter, was discussed in [237], but in [41] it has been proved to be a special case of Shannon's model. This is done by interpreting the problem as communicating over a channel with a state u and outputs y, v, where the associated conditional probability is

$$p'(y, v|x, u) = \sum_s p(y, v|x, u, s) p(s(x, u))$$
$$= \sum_s p(y|x, s) p(u, v|s) p(s)/p(u) \qquad (3.3.4)$$

as shown in Fig. 4.

As described in [261], [142], [143], and [69] coding on this channel, with state available to the transmitter, forms a strategy (we use here the terminology of [237]), as the coding operation $\mathcal{U} \to \chi$ is done on a function space. This might pose conceptual and complexity problems, especially for large values of $|\mathcal{U}|$. However, in a variety of cases, as specified below, there is no need to employ strategies, and standard coding over the original alphabet χ suffices.

a) General jointly stationary and ergodic $\{s_n\}, \{u_n\}, \{v_n\}$ with $u_n = g(v_n)$, where $g(\cdot)$ is a deterministic function $v \to u$. The channel capacity is given by

$$C^{(2)} = \sum_u p(u) \max_{q(x|u)} I(X; Y|V, u) \qquad (3.3.5)$$

where the optimization is over $q(x|u)$, and where $I(X; Y|V, u) = I(X; Y, V|u)$ is the corresponding mutual information with a given realization of $U = u$ [41].

b) No channel-state information at transmission and ergodic channel-state information at receiver

$$C^{(3)} = \max_{q(x)} I(X; Y|V). \qquad (3.3.6)$$

The special case of no CSI at the receiver is given by letting v be independent of s in (3.3.6).

c) Perfect channel state information at receiver and transmitter, assuming an ergodic state $\{S_i\} = \{U_i\}$

$$C^{(4)} = \sum_s p(s) \max_{q(x|s)} I(X; Y|s) \qquad (3.3.7)$$

where C^4 can be viewed as a special case of C^2.

d) Markov decomposable[2] ergodic [111], [41] with perfect state information at the receiver $v_n = s_n$ and a deterministic causal function of $\{s\}$ at the transmitter $u_n = g_n(s_1^n)$. The capacity is given by $C^{(2)}$ in (3.3.5), where $p(u)$ stands for the stationary distribution of U_n (see [41] for details).

Though we have restricted attention to a finite-state channel and, in fact, discrete input and output alphabets, imposing no further input constraints (like average and/or peak power), still the capacity expressions given here are insightful, and they provide the correct intuition into the specific expressions, as will be detailed in the following, resorting first to a very simple single-user flat-fading channel model [54], [85], [86], [119], [127], [210]. We notice that the assumption of joint ergodicity of $\{s_n, u_n, v_n\}$ plays a fundamental role: in fact, without it the Shannon sense capacity, where the decoded error probability can be driven to zero by increasing the blocklength, may essentially be zero. In this case, corresponding mutual information expressions can be treated as random entities, giving rise to capacity-versus-outage considerations. In this setting, power control, provided some CSI is given to the transmitter, plays a major role [43]. This is demonstrated in the case where full state information is available at the transmitter site. The transmitter may then attempt to invert the channel by eliminating the fading absolutely, which gives rise to the *delay-limited capacity* notion. This will be further addressed within the notions of compound and arbitrarily varying channels [64], [164], with constrained input and state spaces.

We shall demonstrate the general expression in the case of flat fading with inputs subjected to an average-power constraint, that is,

$$E(|x_n|^2) \le P_{\mathrm{av}} \qquad (3.3.8)$$

where E, the expectation operator, involves also U if a power-control strategy is employed at the transmitter.

Though the generalization to an infinite number of states and the introduction of an input constraint requires further justification, we use the natural extensions of the finite-state expressions, leaving the details to the references (in case these are available, which unfortunately might not always be so). See reference list in [164] and [41].

We shall demonstrate the general setting for the most simple model of a single-user, flat fading case where the signaling is subjected to an average-power constraint. The discrete-time channel, with k standing for the discrete-time index, is described by

$$y_k = a_k x_k + n_k \qquad (3.3.9)$$

where the complex transmitted sequence is a proper discrete-time process [171] satisfying the average-power constraint

---

[2] Here decomposability means that the channel is described by the one-step transition probability function $p(s_{n+1}, y_n | s_n, x_n)$, satisfying:

a) s_{n+1}, y_n are independent of all past states and inputs given s_n and x_n.

b) $\Sigma_{y_n} p(s_{n+1}, y_n | s_n, x_n) = r(s_{n+1}|s_n)$, where $r(\cdot|\cdot)$ is the transition probability of an indecomposable homogeneous Markov chain: $s_n \to s_{n+1}$.

(3.3.8). The circularly symmetric i.i.d. Gaussian noise samples are designated by $\{n_k\}$, where $E(|n_k|^2) = \sigma^2$. Here $\{y_n\}$ stand for the complex received signal samples. We assume that $\{a_k\}$ denote the samples of the complex circularly symmetric fading process with a single-dimensional distribution of the power $\nu_k = |a_k|^2$ designated by $p_\nu(\cdot)$, and uniformly in $[-\pi, \pi]$ and independently (of ν) distributed phase $\arg(a_k)$. We further assume that $E(\nu) = E|A|^2 = 1$. We will introduce further assumptions on the process $\{A_k\}$ for special cases to be detailed which fall, considering the above mentioned reservations, within the framework of the general results on finite-state channels presented in this subsection.

Perfect state information known to receiver only: This case has been treated by many [210], [111]–[112] and indeed is rather standard. Here we need to assume that $\{\nu_k\}$ is a stationary ergodic process, which gives rise to a capacity formula which turns out to be a special case of $C^{(3)}$ in (3.3.6)

$$C_{\mathrm{RCSI}} = E_\nu \log \left(1 + \frac{P_{\mathrm{av}} \nu}{\sigma^2}\right)$$
$$= \int_0^\infty p_\nu(\nu) \log \left(1 + \frac{P_{\mathrm{av}} \nu}{\sigma^2}\right) d\nu. \qquad (3.3.10)$$

It should be noted that there is no need to use variable-rate codes to achieve the capacity (3.3.10) (contrary to what is claimed in [118]). This is immediately reflected by the approach of [41], where the state is interpreted as part of the channel output (which happens to be statistically independent of the channel input). Hence, a simple standard (Gaussian) long codebook will be efficient in this case. However, we should emphasize that contrary to the standard additive Gaussian noise channel, obtained here by letting $a_k = 1 \ \forall k$, the length of the codebook dramatically depends on the dynamics of the fading process: in fact, it must be long enough for the fading to reflect its ergodic nature (i.e., $T \gg T_{\mathrm{coh}}$, or equivalently, $N \gg \Delta T_c$) [149].

Perfect channel-state information available to transmitter and receiver: Again, we assume that the channel state information $\{a_n\}$ is available to both receiver and transmitter in a causal manner. Equation (1.3.5) for $C^{(2)}$, under the input-power constraint (3.3.8), specializes here to the capacity formula

$$C_{\mathrm{TRCSI}} = E \sup \log \left(1 + \frac{P_w(\nu) \nu}{\sigma^2}\right) \qquad (3.3.11)$$

where the supremum is over all nonnegative power assignments $P_w(\nu)$ satisfying

$$E_\nu P_w(\nu) \le P_a. \qquad (3.3.11a)$$

The solution $(P_w^*(\nu))$, given in [112], is straightforward, and the optimal power assignment satisfies

$$\frac{P_w^*(\nu)}{P_{\mathrm{av}}} = \begin{cases} \dfrac{1}{\nu_0} - \dfrac{1}{\nu}, & \nu \ge \nu_0 \\ 0, & \nu < \nu_0 \end{cases} \qquad (3.3.12)$$

where the constant ν_0 is determined by the average power constraint and the specific distribution of the fading power $P_\nu(\nu)$. The capacity is given in terms of (3.3.11), with the optimal power control (3.1.12) substituted in. For compact expressions, which involve series of exponential integral function, see [155], specialized to the single-user case.

The optimal power control policy as in (3.1.12) gives rise to the time-water-pouring interpretation [112], that is, above a threshold ν_0 the lower the deleterious fading (ν is large), the larger the instantaneous transmitted power.

Clearly, the solution here advocates a variable-rate, variable-power communication technique [112], where different codebooks with rate $\log\left(1 + (P_w^*(\nu)\nu/\sigma^2)\right)$ are used when the fading realization is ν and the associated assigned power is $P_w^*(\nu)$.

What is more surprising is that also in this setting the full capacity is achieved by a fixed-rate coding system [41]. This is immediately realized by introducing at the input of the channel an (amplitude) amplifier, whose gain is $\sqrt{P_w^*(\nu)/P_{av}}$ controlled by the observed fading power ν. This amplifier is interpreted as part of the channel, the state of which is revealed now to the receiver only. That is, the effective power gain $P_w^*(\nu)/P_{av}$ replaces ν in the logarithmic term of (3.3.10), determining the capacity of the channel with states known to the receiver only. This implies that also in this case a standard Gaussian code can achieve capacity, provided it is long enough to reveal the ergodic properties of the channel, and hence put the averaging effect into action. Suboptimal power control strategies, as channel inversion and truncated channel inversion [112] may be useful in certain circumstances. These strategies are further discussed with reference to other cases in the following.

It is worth noting here that the availability of channel-state information at the transmitter in addition to the receiver gives only little advantage in terms of average reliable transmitted rate (see figures in [111] for lognormal, Rayleigh, and Nakagami fading examples), and this small advantage is in particular pronounced for low signal-to-noise ratio (SNR) values, where the unfaded Gaussian capacity $\log\left(1 + \text{SNR}\right)$ may be surpassed [111]. This occurs because the average received power, with the optimal power-control strategy, surpasses P_{av}, which is the average received power in the unfaded case. An obvious upper bound on C_{TRCSI} is given by applying Jensen inequality to $\log\left(1 + E(P_w^*(\nu)\nu)P_{av}/\sigma^2\right)$. This reflects the fact that with fixed received (rather than transmitted) power the fading effect is always deleterious.

Ideal CSI available to receiver with noiseless delayed feedback at the transmitter: A generalization of the previous case where perfect CSI was available to both transmitter and receiver takes place where delay is introduced and the CSI at the transmitter site, though unharmed, is available with a certain latency. This serves as a better model to common practice in those cases where CSI is fed back through another auxiliary channel (essentially noiseless, as it operates at very low rates), from the receiver to the transmitter.

We assume here that $\{S_k\}$ (returning here to the generic finite-state notations) is Markov, and that at time k, s_{k-d} is made available to the transmitter (the nonnegative integer d denotes the delay). For $d = 0$, no delay is introduced and the results given above hold (only ergodicity of $\{s_k\}$ is required for $d = 0$). This problem has been solved by [312]. In [41] the problem was shown to specialize to the Markov $\{S_k\}$ setting

treated in [142], where in this case of ideal CSI available to the receiver, no "strategies" are required and simple signaling over the original alphabet of the input achieves capacity. The capacity for the Gaussian complex fading channel with average input-power constraint is given by

$$C_{\text{DTRCSI}} = E_{\tilde{\nu}} \sup_{P_w(\tilde{\nu})} E_{\nu|\tilde{\nu}} \log\left(1 + \nu P_w(\tilde{\nu})\right) \qquad (3.3.13)$$

where we define $\nu = |a_k|^2$ and $\tilde{\nu} = |a_{k-d}|^2$, and the time index k is immaterial here. The operators $E_{\tilde{\nu}}$ and $E_{\nu|\tilde{\nu}}$ stand, respectively, for the expectations with respect to $\tilde{\nu}$ and the conditional expectation of ν with respect to $\tilde{\nu}$. The supremum is over all power assignments of $P_w(\tilde{\nu})$ (a function of $\tilde{\nu}$ which is available to the transmitter) satisfying the average power constraint

$$E_{\tilde{\nu}} P_w(\tilde{\nu}) \leq P_{av}. \qquad (3.3.14)$$

In (3.3.13) we have used the fact that the probability of $\nu = |a_k|^2$ when conditioned on a_{k-d} is a function of $|a_{k-d}|^2 = \tilde{\nu}$ only, for circularly symmetric (proper) Gaussian state process $\{a_k\}$.

Several sample examples have been worked out in [312] and [41], but no full solution has been found for C_{DTRCSI}, as an elegant analytical solution for $P_w^*(\tilde{\nu})$, the optimal power control, does not seem to exist. Clearly, bounds where suboptimal power-allocation strategy is applied are straightforward. A reasonable candidate is the optimal power-allocation strategy of the ideal no-feedback case $d = 0$, where in this case the suboptimal $P_w(\tilde{\nu})$ in (3.3.13) is based on the expected value of ν, that is, $P_w(\tilde{\nu}) = P_w^*(E(\nu|\tilde{\nu}))$, where $P_w^*(\cdot)$ is given by (3.1.12).

Unavailable channel-state information: In the case treated now, the channel-state information is not available to either transmitter and/or receiver. The case is conceptually simple, and for i.i.d. states $\{A_k\}$ the full solution is available for circularly complex distribution of $\{A_k\}$, that is, Rayleigh $|A|$ and correspondingly exponential ν. In fact, in [87] it is shown that the capacity-achieving distribution has a discrete i.i.d.[3] power $|X_k|$ and irrelevant phase. For relatively low values of the average signal-to-noise ratio (SNR) $= P_{av}/\sigma^2 < 8$ dB values, only two signaling levels $x = 0$ and $x = \sqrt{\alpha}$ with respective probabilities $(1 - p_\alpha, p_\alpha)$ suffice, where $\alpha p_\alpha = P_{av}$. For asymptotic behavior with P_{av}/σ^2 see [278]. Clearly, the capacity-achieving codes in this case deviate markedly from Gaussian codes, which achieve capacity when CSI is available either to the receiver or to both receiver and transmitter. This is evident from the fact that even the first-order statistics do not match the Gaussian statistics [253].

It is interesting to observe that the lower the SNR, the larger the amplitude α tends to be [87]. The intuition behind this result, already contained in [227], follows the observation that

$$I(X; Y) = I(X, A; Y) - I(A; Y|X).$$

For SNR $\to 0$, for a rather general class of peak- and average-power-constrained input distributions of X (including

---

[3] A discrete input distribution of the envelope $|X|$ is optimal also for other fading statistics (not necessarily Rayleigh), rising, for example, in diversity combining. See [87].

the binary two-level distribution)

$$I(X, A; Y) \xrightarrow[\text{SNR} \to 0]{} \log(1 + \text{SNR}).$$

The optimal distribution of $|X|$ should then minimize the expression

$$I(A; Y|X) = E_{|X|} \log \left(1 + \frac{|X|^2}{\text{SNR}} \cdot \text{SNR}\right) \qquad (3.3.15)$$

which results by noting that A is a unit-variance circularly symmetric Gaussian random variable independent of x. The minimization of (3.3.15) is carried over all distributions of $0 \le |X| \le \sqrt{\alpha}$ satisfying $E(|X|^2) = \text{SNR}$, and the straightforward solution is letting X be binary, taking on values 0 and $\sqrt{\alpha}$. This yields

$$I(A; Y|X) = \frac{\text{SNR}}{\alpha} \log(1 + \alpha).$$

The lower the SNR, the larger α gets. As $\text{SNR} \to 0$, the capacity yields $C_{\text{NCSI}} \xrightarrow[\text{SNR} \to 0]{} \text{SNR}$, the same as for perfect CSI available to the receiver only! While this occurs only at extremely low values of SNR [87], it takes place with markedly different signal structures. In the no-CSI case treated here, the specific signaling, "peaky" in time, alleviates the deleterious effect of unknown channel parameters, which drive $I(A; Y|X)$ to 0, by increasing the peak signaling value of α.

The case when the suitable model for the dynamics of the fading models is the block-fading channel [211], which occurs when $\{a_i\}$ are constant for a duration ΔT_c and the blocks of ΔT_c are chosen to be i.i.d., is treated in [176]. This recent beautiful result shows that the capacity-achieving distribution of the blockwise i.i.d. input vectors $X = (X_1, X_2, \cdots, X_{T_c})$ is given by $X = \mu \Phi$, where Φ is a ΔT_c-dimensional isotropically distributed unit vector, and μ is an independent nonnegative scalar random variable with $E(\mu^2) = P_{\text{av}}$. The numerical indication shows [176] that μ is discretely distributed, as in the case of $\Delta T_c = 1$ [87]. Coding and decoding in this case are standard: in fact, the scalar (for i.i.d. $\{A_k\}$) or ΔT_c-length vector (for i.i.d. ΔT_c block of $\{A_k\}$) channel is memoryless, assuming thus the standard information-theoretic characterization.

An intermediate situation, which bridges the full-CSI and no-CSI knowledge at the receiver, is modeled by partial side information available. This is a special case of the model of [41], [237] and the treatment is therefore standard: the corresponding result depends on the type and quality of that side information (see [176], [236], [149], and references therein).

Ideal CSI available to transmitter only: This model is attracting much less attention, probably due to its relatively rare occurrence in the real world. Extrapolating the results in [261], [41] for the continuous state distribution, we *conjecture* that for i.i.d. states the capacity here is given in terms of the capacity of a memoryless channel, whose input is a continuous waveform $v(t), t \in \mathbb{R}_+$ (the positive reals) and whose output

is a complex scalar y, with transition probability

$$p(y|v(\nu), \nu \ge 0)$$
$$= E_\nu p(y|v(\nu), \nu)$$
$$= \int_0^\infty p_\nu(\zeta) \frac{1}{2\pi\sigma^2} \left\{ \exp -\frac{1}{2\sigma^2} |y - \sqrt{\zeta}v(\zeta)|^2 \right\} d\zeta$$
$$(3.3.16)$$

and the input $v(\nu), \nu \ge 0$, is subjected to the average power constraint $E_\nu[v^2(\nu)] \le P_{\text{av}}$. With no loss of generality we have assumed that $a = \sqrt{\nu}$, that is zero phase of the fading process: in fact, since the transmitter has accurate access to the fading process, it can fully neutralize any phase shift by rotation at no additional power cost. While a general solution for the capacity with our conjecture seems difficult to obtain, as a complete time-continuous capacity-achieving strategy should be determined, nonetheless lower bounds can be derived by using suboptimal strategies. One of these, which calls for attention for its own sake, is the truncated channel inversion [112]. This is best described within the framework of fixed-rate signaling, where a Gaussian codebook is used and an amplitude amplifier at the transmitter is introduced with the power gain function

$$\frac{P_*(\nu)}{P_{\text{av}}} = \begin{cases} \dfrac{\alpha}{\nu}, & \nu \ge \nu_0 \\[2mm] 0, & \nu < \nu_0 \end{cases} \qquad (3.3.17)$$

where

$$\alpha^{-1} = \int_{\nu_0}^\infty \zeta^{-1} p_\nu(\zeta) \, d\zeta.$$

Thus the receiver sees an unfaded Gaussian channel

$$y = x + n \qquad (3.3.18)$$

with probability

$$p_G = \int_{\nu_0}^\infty p_\nu(\varepsilon) \, d\zeta$$

and a pure-noise channel

$$y = n \qquad (3.3.19)$$

with the complementary probability $1 - p_G$. The relevant transition probability for a receiver with no information about the channel state (which assumes a binary interpretation here) is

$$p(y|x) = p_G \frac{1}{2\pi\sigma^2} \exp\left\{ -\frac{|y - x|^2}{2\sigma^2} \right\}$$
$$+ (1 - p_G) \frac{1}{2\pi\sigma^2} \exp\left\{ -\frac{1}{2\sigma^2}|y|^2 \right\}. \qquad (3.3.20)$$

The threshold value ν_0 is chosen to optimize the corresponding capacity. In fact, if $\nu_0 = 0$ is legitimate, i.e., the channel is invertible with finite power, an obvious lower bound corresponds to the absolute channel inversion, where $p_G = 1$ and the corresponding capacity is

$$C_{\text{TCSI}} \ge C_{\text{CI}} = \log \left(1 + \frac{\text{SNR}}{E_\nu(1/\nu)}\right). \qquad (3.3.21)$$

An obvious upper bound in this case is the capacity in (3.3.7), where the channel-state information is made available also to the receiver. This capacity C_{CI} (where CI stands for Channel Inversion), is, in this case, also what is known as the delay-limited capacity [127]. This is a special case of the capacity-versus-outage framework in case of CSI available at the transmitter and receiver [43], as it will be briefly described later on. The difference between C_{CI} and C_{TRCSI} (3.3.11) can be seen in [112, Fig. 3] for the log-normal fading, and in [112, Fig. 5] for a Nakagami-distributed fading power with parameter $m = 2$. Indeed, these cases exhibit a remarkable difference. Optimizing for ν_0 in the truncated-inversion approach may diminish the difference for low SNR, as is the case when the channel states are available to the receiver as well. For Rayleigh-distributed fading amplitude, $C_{\text{CI}} = 0$, as no channel inversion is possible with finite transmitting power, as evidenced by the fact that $E_\nu(1/\nu) = \infty$. Improved upper bounds may take advantage of the fact (and its extensions) that on general Discrete Memoryless Channels (DMC) the cardinality of the capacity-achieving input is no larger than the cardinality of the output space [94]. Some information-theoretic notions to be treated in the following, as capacity-versus-outage, delay-limited capacity, and expected capacity, are intimately related with compound [164] and composite [61] channels, and they apply directly to the case where CSI is available to the transmitter only. This setting, when the fading CSI is available to the transmitter only, poses some interesting information-theoretic problems.

Concluding remarks: Although in this subsection we have only used simple channel models which cannot accommodate multipath, intersymbol interference, and the like, ([127], [146], [210], [290]), the basic structure of these capacity results is maintained also when they are extended to more general settings, as will be demonstrated succinctly in the following sections. We have also assumed that the fading coefficients $\{A_k\}$ are *ergodic* or even i.i.d. or Markov, which poses significant restrictions on the applicability of the results presented. We shall see that the basic structure is kept also in various cases where these restrictions are alleviated to some degree. For example, in the block-faded case with absolute no fading dynamics (that is, when the fading coefficient is essentially invariant during the whole transmission period T of the coded block) the expression of

$$\log \left(1 + \frac{p_w(\nu)\nu}{\sigma^2} \right) \tag{3.3.22}$$

for perfect CSI available to both receiver and transmitter (say) becomes a function of ν and a random variable itself, which under some conditions [210] leads to the notion of capacity-versus-outage. The interesting notion of delay-limited capacity becomes then a special case corresponding to the zero-outage result. In that case, power inversion (i.e., $P_w(\nu) = P_{\text{av}}/(\nu E(1/\nu)$, when possible) is used (see [43] for a full treatment). When CSI is available to the receiver only, the capacity-versus-outage results are obtained by no power adaptation, that is, $P_{\text{av}}(\nu) = P_{\text{av}}$.

The results here and in [69] will also be useful, though to a lesser extent, in the understanding of the extensive capacity

results in the multiple-access channel. In the next subsection we extend our treatment to some other important information-theoretic notions, which do not demand strict ergodicity of the fading process as in the case treated so far.

2) Information-Theoretic Notions in Fading Channels: In this section we review and demonstrate some of the more important information-theoretic notions as they manifest in fading channels. Again, our focus is on maximum rates, and hence capacities; the discussion of other important notions, as error exponents and cutoff rates, is deferred to a later section. Specifically, we address here the ergodic-capacity, capacity-versus-outage, delay-limited-capacity, and broadcast approach.

We will demonstrate the results in a unified fashion for simple single-user applications, while the multiple users, the more interesting case, will be discussed in the following subsection. We shall not elaborate much on the structure of the results, as these are essentially applications, manifestations, and/or extensions of the expressions in the general model of Subsection III-C.1). We shall conclude this subsection by mentioning the relevance of classical information-theoretic frameworks such as the compound and arbitrary-varying channels [164], where the compound channel, along with its variants form, in fact, the underlying models giving rise to the different notions of capacity to be addressed.

Ergodic capacity: The basic assumption here is that $T \gg T_{\text{coh}} = 1/B_d$, meaning that the transmission time is so long as to reveal the long-term ergodic properties of the fading process $c(t,\tau)$ which is assumed to be an ergodic process in t.

In this classical case, treated in the majority of references (see [41], [75], and references therein, [85], [112], [118], [119], [137], [155], [171], [210], [335]), standard capacity results in Shannon's sense are valid and coding theorems are proved by rather standard methods for time-varying and/or finite- (or infinite-) state channels [327], [310]. This means that, at rates lower than capacity, the error probability is exponentially decaying with the transmission length, for a good (or usually also random) code. We consider here the simple single-transmit/receive, single-user multipath channel with slow fading, that is, with $W \gg B_d$. The capacity, with channel state known to the receiver, is given by [210]

$$C_{\text{RCSI}} = E \int_{-\infty}^{\infty} \log \left(1 + \frac{P_{\text{av}}|C(t;f))|^2}{N_0} \right) df \tag{3.3.23}$$

where $C(t;f)$ is the frequency response at time t, given by

$$C(t;f) = \int_{-\infty}^{\infty} c(t,\tau)e^{-j2\pi f\tau} d\tau \tag{3.3.24}$$

and where N_0 stands for the additive white Gaussian noise (AWGN) spectral density. The expectation E is taken with respect to the statistics of the random process $C(t;f)$. Note that under the ergodic assumption these statistics are independent of either t or f, and the result is exactly as in (3.3.10) for the flat-fading case [210]. The same holds where the ideal channel-state information is available to both transmitter and receiver [112], [155] but the optimal power control should assign a different power level at each frequency according to the very same rule as in (3.1.12), correctly normalizing the total average power. For the ergodic case, multipath channels give no advantage for their inherent diversity: this rather surprising fact can be explained by considering the multipath case as a parallel channel generated by slicing the frequency band. The parallelism can be in time, frequency, or both, and, since the capacity in the ergodic case depends only on the first-order statistics of the fading state parameters, the equivalence is evident. In fact, also here, the ultimate capacity can be achieved by a fixed rate, variable-power scheme: it suffices to extend the same device used to deal with the flat-fading channel to the case at hand here, where now a frequency-shaping power amplifier is used by the transmitter to implement the optimal power-control strategy. The conclusion follows by viewing this amplifier as part of the channel, then by considering a resulting equivalent channel, whose states are known to the receiver only.

We have resorted here to the most simple case of a slowly fading ($W \gg B_d$), ergodic ($T \gg B_d^{-1}$) channel giving rise first to the very notion of Shannon's sense channel capacity on one hand and the decoupling of the time-varying and the frequency-selective features of the channel on the other. This decoupling is not at all mandatory, and capacity results for the more general case, where $W \ggg B_d$, can be rather straightforwardly evaluated [186], [146] using classical decomposition techniques to interpret the problem in terms of parallel channels, while accounting for the nonnegligible Doppler spread experienced here.

In general, it is rather easy to find the information capacities which are given by the appropriate averaged mutual information capacities. Showing that these expressions result also as outcomes of coding theorems (in the ergodic regime, of course) is a more subtle matter. Though straightforward techniques with clear extensions do work [94], [327], more elegant and quite general methods rely upon the recent concept of *information spectrum* [310], [124].

Capacity versus outage (capacity distribution): The ergodic assumption is not necessarily satisfied in practical communication systems operating on fading channels. In fact, if stringent delay constraints are demanded, as is the case in speech transmission over wireless channels, the ergodicity requirement $T \gg T_{\mathrm{coh}} = B_d^{-1}$ cannot be satisfied. In this case, where no significant channel variability occurs during the whole transmission, there may not be a classical Shannon meaning attached to capacity in typical situations. In fact, there may be a nonnegligible probability that the value of the actual transmitted rate, no matter how small, exceeds the instantaneous mutual information. This situation gives rise to error probabilities which *do not* decay with the increase of the blocklength. In these circumstances, the channel capacity is viewed as a random entity, as it depends on the instantaneous random channel parameters. The capacity-versus-outage performance is then determined by the probability that the channel cannot support a given rate: that is, we associate an outage probabilities to any given rate.

The above notion is strictly connected to the classical compound channel with *a priori* associated with its transition-probability-characterizing parameter θ. This is a standard approach: see [61]–[247]; in [83] this channel is called a *composite channel.* The capacity-versus-outage approach has the simple interpretation that follows. With any given rate R we associate a set Θ_R. That set is the largest possible set for which C_Θ, the capacity of the compound channel with parameter $\theta \in \Theta_R$, satisfies $C_\Theta \geq R$. The outage probability is then determined by $P_{\mathrm{out}} = \mathrm{Prob}\,(\theta \notin \Theta_R)$. (Note that the largest set might not be uniquely defined when the capacity-achieving distribution may vary with the parameter $\theta \in \Theta_R$; in this case the set is chosen as the one which minimizes the outage probability $\mathrm{Pr}\,(\theta \notin \Theta_R)$.)

Consider the simple case of a flat Rayleigh fading with no dynamics ($B_d = 0$), with channel-state information available to the receiver only. The channel capacity, viewed as a random variable, is given by

$$C(\nu) = W \log\left(1 + \nu\,\mathrm{SNR}\right) \qquad (3.3.25)$$

where $\mathrm{SNR} = P_{\mathrm{av}}/(N_0 W)$ is the signal-to-noise ratio and ν is exponentially distributed. The capacity R (nats per unit bandwidth) per outage probability P_{out} is given by

$$\begin{aligned} P_{\mathrm{out}} &\triangleq \mathrm{Pr}\,(C(\nu)/W \leq R) = \mathrm{Pr}\,(\ln\,(1 + \nu\,\mathrm{SNR}) \leq R) \\ &= 1 - \exp\left(-\mathrm{SNR}^{-1}\,(e^R - 1)\right). \qquad (3.3.26) \end{aligned}$$

In this case only the zero rate $R = 0$ is compatible with $P_{\mathrm{out}} = 0$, thus eliminating any reliable communication in Shannon's sense. It is instructive to note that the ergodic Shannon capacity is no more than the expectation of $C(\nu)$ [210]. In fact, when $B_d = 0$ the capacity-achieving distribution is Gaussian and remains fixed for all fading realizations, provided CSI is not available to the transmitter. The capacity of a compound channel is then given by the worst case capacity in the class Θ_R, and the largest set is then uniquely defined.

As mentioned above, ergodic capacities are invariant to the frequency-selective features of the channel in symmetrical cases (that is, when the single-dimensional statistics of $C(t; f)$ are invariant to the values of t and f). Now, a markedly different behavior is exhibited by the capacity-versus-outage notion. In [210], the two-ray propagation model has been analytically examined, and it was demonstrated that the inherent diversity provided by multipath fading is instrumental in dramatically improving the capacity-versus-outage performance. The general case where the fading does exhibit some time variability—though not yet satisfying the ergodic condition—is treated in [210] within the block-fading model. In this rather simplistic model the channel parameters are constant within a block while varying for different blocks (which, for example, can be transmitted blockwise-interleaved). The delay constraint to which the communication system is subjected determines the number of such blocks K_c that can be used (more on this in Section IV). The case $K_c = 1$ yields the fixed channel parameters discussed before, while $K_c \to \infty$ gives rise to the ergodic case. The parameter K_c is then used to comprehend the way the ergodic capacity is approached, while for finite K_c it provides the effective inherent diversity that improves considerably the capacity-versus-outage performance. For $K_c = 2$, optimal and suboptimal transmission techniques were examined and compared to the simple suboptimal repetition (twice for $K_c =$

2 transmission), while even the latter is shown to be rather efficient (at least in the same region of the parameters). The influence of correlation among the fading values in both blocks ($K_c = 2$) is also investigated, and it is shown that the significant advantage of $K_c = 2$ over $K_c = 1$ is maintained up to rather high values of the correlation coefficient. Space-diversity techniques, which also improve dramatically on the capacity-versus-outage performance, are also treated in [210] by reinterpreting the results for the block-fading channel. See also [93].

So far, we have addressed the case of side information available to the receiver only. For absolutely unavailable CSI, the capacity-versus-outage results may still be valid as is. The underlying argument which leads to this conclusion is the observation that the capacity of the compound channel does not depend on whether the transition–distribution governing parameter θ is available or not to the detector [64]. The rationale for this is the observation that since θ is constant, its rate for long codes, $n \to \infty$, goes to zero, and therefore it can be accurately estimated at the receiver site. Transmit, for example, a training sequence with length proportional to $\sqrt{n}$ [61] to facilitate the accurate estimation of θ, at no cost of rate as $n \to \infty$. In fact, the value of θ is not at all required at the receiver, which employs universal decoders [64], [88], [164, and references therein], [166], and [338]. The quantification of this rationale, rigorized in [216], is based on the observation that

$$\frac{1}{n}I(X;Y) = \frac{1}{n}I(X;Y|S) - \frac{1}{n}(I(S;Y|X) - I(S;Y)) \quad (3.3.27)$$

where, if the channel state process $\{S\}, n \to \infty$, is of asymptotically zero rate (or "strongly singular" in the terminology of [216])

$$\lim_{n \to \infty} \frac{1}{n}\{I(S;Y|X) - I(S;Y)\} \to 0.$$

Under the rather common "strong singularity" assumption, the ergodic capacity of the channel with or without states available to the receiver is the same. In some cases, we can even estimate the rate at which the capacity with perfect CSI available to the receiver is approached. See [176] for the single-user Rayleigh fading case, where the capacity is calculated for flat fading with strict coherence time T_{coh} (the block-fading model). The usefulness and relevance of the capacity-versus-outage results, as well as variants to the expected capacity [61] to be discussed later in the context of fading [247], are usually not emphasized explicitly in the literature in the context of unavailable CSI, in spite of their considerable theoretical importance and practical relevance. This has motivated the elaboration in our exposition.

For channel-state information available to both transmitter and receiver, the results are even more interesting, as the addition of a degree of freedom, the transmitter power control, may dramatically influence the tradeoff between capacity and outage. In some cases, power control may save the notion of Shannon capacity by yielding positive rates at zero outage, while this is inherently impossible for constant-transmit-power

techniques (which are usually optimal when no channel-state information is available at the transmitter).

The block flat-fading channel with channel-state information available to both receiver and transmitter is examined in [43] (which includes also the results of [313]). In this reference, under the assumption that the channel-state information of all K_c blocks is available to the transmitter prior to encoding, the optimal power-control (power-allocation) strategy which minimizes outage probability for a given rate is determined. It is shown that a Gaussian-like, fixed-rate code achieves optimal performance, where a state-dependent amplifier controls the power according to the optimal power-control assignment. The optimal power-control strategy depends on the fading statistics only through a threshold value, below which the transmission is turned off. The rate which corresponds to zero outage is associated with the delay-limited capacity [127]: in fact, the power-control strategy which gives rise to a zero outage probability gives also rise to the standard (Shannon-sense) capacity. For the case of $K_c = 1$ (single block) the optimal strategy is channel inversion, so that the transmitted power is

$$P_w(\nu) = P_{\text{av}}\nu^{-1}/E(1/\nu) \quad (3.3.28)$$

and the corresponding zero-outage capacity is

$$C_{\text{DL}} = \log\left(1 + \frac{P_{\text{av}}}{\sigma^2 E(1/\nu)}\right) \quad (3.3.29)$$

where P_{av} stands for the long-term average power constraint. In [43], a clear distinction is made between a short-term power constraint (bounding the power of the codebook) and a long-term power constraint (dictating a bound on the expected power, i.e., characterizing the average power of many transmitted codewords). Space-diversity systems are also examined and for that, in the Rayleigh fading regime, it is shown that

$$C_{\text{DL}} = \log\left(1 + \frac{D-1}{D}\frac{P_{\text{av}}}{\sigma^2}\right) \quad (3.3.30)$$

where the integer D designates the diversity level ($D = 1$ stands for no diversity). Note that in the absence of diversity, in the Rayleigh regime, $C_{\text{DL}} = 0$, as no channel inversion is possible with finite power, as implied by the fact that $E(\nu^{-1}) = \infty$.

For $K_c = 1$, the outage-minimizing power control is given by [43]

$$P_w(\nu) = \begin{cases} (e^R - 1)/\nu, & \nu > \nu^* \\ 0, & \text{otherwise} \end{cases} \quad (3.3.31)$$

where ν^* is the solution of

$$(e^R - 1)\operatorname{Ei}\left(1, \frac{e^R - 1}{\nu^*}\right) = P_{\text{av}} \quad (3.3.32)$$

and the corresponding outage is given by

$$P_{\text{out}} = 1 - \exp\left(-(e^{2R} - 1)/\nu^*\right). \quad (3.3.33)$$

Here

$$\operatorname{Ei}(n, x) \triangleq \int_1^\infty (e^{-xt}/t^n)\, dt, \qquad \text{for } \operatorname{Re}(x) > 0.$$

While, as seen before [43], [112], channel-state information gives little advantage, especially at low SNR, in terms of ergodic capacity (average rates), the performance enhancement exhibited in terms of capacity-versus-outage is *dramatic*. Suboptimal coding as repetition diversity was also examined in [43], and it has been determined that the optimal power-allocation strategy in this case is selection diversity. Further, it was shown that for the general K_c-block fading channel there is an optimal diversity order which minimizes outage. The latter conclusion may be interpreted as the existence of an optimal spreading/coding tradeoff in coded direct-sequence CDMA, where the direct-sequence spreading is equivalent (in a single-user regime) to a repetition code. Considerable advantage of channel-state information available to the transmitter, in terms of capacity versus outage, was demonstrated for the long-term average-power constraint. This advantage disappears almost entirely, when a short-term average-power constraint is dictated. The block-fading channel model with all channel-state information available also to the transmitter suits well multicarrier systems, where different carriers (frequency diversity) play the role of time-separated blocks (time diversity), and where the assumption in [43] that the CSI in all K_c blocks is available to transmitter beforehand is more realistic.

The capacity-versus-outage characteristics for a frequency-selective fading channel is studied in [41], where it is demonstrated that the inherent diversity present in the multipath fading model improves dramatically on capacity-versus-outage performance when compared to the flat-fading model. In fact, this diversity gives rise to a positive delay-limited capacity even in the Rayleigh fading regime (3.3.30). There are numerous interesting open problems in this category, some of which will be mentioned in our concluding remarks.

It is appropriate to mention here that the general results of [310] are also applicable to devise coding theorems in the setting of capacity versus outage. This is explained in [210], because the notion of ε-capacity is directly related to the capacity versus outage. This notion is treated within the framework of [310], as the transition probabilities for the code block transmitted are explicitly given and fully characterized statistically. See [83] for further discussion. See also [167] for coding theorems of compound channels with memory.

Delay-limited capacities: The notion of a delay-limited capacity has already been referred to before, in the context of capacity versus outage where the outage probability is set to zero. Any positive rate that corresponds to zero outage gives rise to a positive delay-limited capacity, as described in [43]. For single-user channels, this notion is associated with channel inversion when this is possible with channel-state information available at the transmitter (3.3.28). By using the terminology of [43], this gives rise to "fixed-rate" transmission.[4] The interpretation of [127] of the "delay-limited" capacity is associated with that reliable transmitted rate which is invariant and independent of the actual realization of the fading random phenomenon. Clearly, in the single-user case this policy leads to power inversion, thus making the observed channel absolutely independent of the realization of the fading

process. As concluded from (3.3.28), this policy cannot be applied unless the channel is invertible with finite power (that is, $E(1/\nu) < \infty$). So far, we have assumed full knowledge of the channel-state information at the transmitter. In case the transmitter is absolutely ignorant of such information while the receiver still maintains perfect knowledge of the CSI, the delay-limited capacity nullifies, unless the fading is bounded away from zero with probability 1. In such a case, say where $\nu \geq \nu_{\min}$ with probability 1, adhering to the simple model of Section III-B we find that

$$C_{\mathrm{DL}} = \log \left(1 + \frac{\nu_{\min} P_{\mathrm{av}}}{\sigma^2} \right). \qquad (3.3.34)$$

An interesting open problem is to determine under which general conditions the delay-limited capacity is positive with noisy CSI (in the framework of [41]) available to both transmitter and receiver. As discussed before, diversity gives rise to increased values of delay-limited capacity [43], and in the limit of infinite diversity delay-limited capacity equals the ergodic capacity. In fact, the channel is transformed to a Gaussian channel [43], for which both notions of delay-limited capacity and Shannon capacity coincide (see, e.g., (3.3.30) with $D \to \infty$). Multipath provides indeed inherent diversity, and, as demonstrated in [249], this diversity gives rise to a positive delay-limited capacity even in a Rayleigh regime, which otherwise would yield a zero delay-limited capacity.

It is appropriate to emphasize that the delay-limited capacity is to be fully interpreted within Shannon's framework as a rate for which the error probability can asymptotically be driven to zero. Hence it is precisely the capacity of a compound channel where the CSI associated with the fading is the parameter governing the transition probability of that channel. In this case, no prior (statistical characterization of these parameters) is needed, but for the determination of the optimal power control under long-term average-power constraints. It is also important to realize the significant advantage in having transmitter side information, in cases where a long-term average-power input constraint is in effect [43]. If CSI is available at the transmitter, then the capacity of the associated compound channel is the capacity of the worst case channel in the class, which might be larger than the capacity of a compound channel with no such information [164], as the transmitter can adapt its input statistics to the actual operating channel. For short-term power constraints, advantages, if at all present, are small, owing to the inability of coping with bad realizations of fading values [43]. In case of unvarying or very slowly varying channels, these results remain valid also when the receiver has no access to CSI.

As will shall elaborate further, interesting information-theoretic models result in the case of absolutely unknown statistical characterization of the fading process (say, for the sake of simplicity, discrete-time models). Here the notion of arbitrarily varying channel (AVC) is called for (see discussion of [164]), but we advocate the inclusion of further constraints on the states, in the AVC terminology, which account for the fading in our setting. This is to be discussed later.

The broadcast approach: The broadcast approach for a compound channel is introduced in Cover's original paper on

---

[4]Fixed rates achieve also the full capacity C_{RTCSI} [43] and do not necessarily imply channel inversion.

the broadcast channel [61]. The maximization of the expected capacity is advocated, attaching a prior to the unknown state that governs the compound channel transition probability. This class of channels with a prior was called composite channels in [83]. This approach inherently facilitates to deliver information rates which depend on the actual realization of the channel and that is without the transmitter being aware of what that realization is. As such, this approach is particularly appealing for block-fading channels where the Doppler bandwidth B_d is either strictly zero or small, that is, the channel exhibits only marginal dynamics. The application of the broadcast approach is advocated in [247] for this setting. In [236] it is applied for an interleaved scenario where the ergodic assumption is valid and hence the ergodic capacity can be achieved, undermining, to a large extent, the inherent advantage of this approach. In fact, as mentioned in [247], this approach is a matched candidate to successive-refinement source-coding techniques [228] where the transmitted rate and, therefore, the distortion of the decoded information depends inherently on the fading realization. In this setting, optimization of the expected distortion is of interest [247]. It should be noted that in the case where no channel dynamics are present (i.e., $B_d T = 0$ in the fading model), the results do not depend on whether side-information about the actual realization of the channel is provided to the receiver or not. This conclusion does not hold when the transmitter is equipped with this information, as in this case (rate- and power-) adapted transmission can be attempted.

This broadcast approach has been pursued in the case of a flat-fading Gaussian channel with no fading dynamics in [247]. In fact, as stated in [247], this strategy enables one to implement a continuum of capacity-versus-outage values rather than a single pair as in the case of the standard capacity-versus-outage approach discussed previously [210]. A continuum of parallel transmitted rates is implemented at the transmitter where an optimal infinitesimal power is associated with an infinitesimal rate. The expected rate was shown [247] to be given by

$$R_T(\Delta) = \int_\Delta^\infty (1 - F_\nu(u)) \frac{-u \, d\phi(u)}{1 + u\phi(u)} \qquad (3.3.35)$$

with $\Delta = 0$, where $\phi(u) = \int_u^\infty \mathrm{SNR}\,(s) \, ds$ is associated with the normalized ($\sigma^2 = 1$) power distribution $\mathrm{SNR}\,(s)$ of the infinitesimal transmitted rates. Here $F_\nu(\cdot)$ stands for the cumulative distribution function of the fading power and $\mathrm{SNR}\,(s) \, ds$ is the power assigned to the parallel transmitter rate indexed by s (a continuous-valued index). The optimal power distribution that maximizes $R_T(0)$ is found explicitly for Rayleigh fading, i.e., $F_\nu(u) = 1 - e^{-u}$. $R_T(s)$ stands for the expected rate conditioned on the realization of the fading power satisfying $s \geq \Delta$. Optimizing $R_T(s)$ over the input-power distribution $\mathrm{SNR}\,(s)$ combines in fact the broadcast approach which gives rise to expected capacities [61] with the capacity-versus-outage approach, which manifests itself with an associated outage probability of $F_\nu(\Delta)$. This original approach of [247], as well as the expected capacity of the broadcast approach [61], extends *straightforwardly* to a class of general channels [83].

Other information-theoretic models: In [164] classical information-theoretical models as the compound and arbitrarily varying channels are advocated for describing practical systems operating on fading time-varying channels, as are mobile wireless systems. The specific classification as indicated in [164] depends on some basic system parameters as detailed therein. For relatively slowly time-varying channels ($T \ll T_{\mathrm{coh}}$) compound models are suitable whether finite state, in case of frequency selectivity ($W > T_m^{-1}$), or regular DMC in case of flat fading. In cases of fast fading, the channel models advocated in [164] depend on the ergodicity behavior if $T_e < T$ (where T_e is the so-called "ergodic duration" [164]), a compound model with the set of states corresponding to the set of attenuation levels, is suggested. Otherwise, where $T_e > T$, an AVC memoryless or finite state, depending on the multipath spread factor, might be used. The latter as pointed out in [164], may though lead to overly conservative estimates. Using classical models can be of great value in cases where this setting provides insight to a preferred transmission/reception mechanism. Universal detectors [164], which were shown to approach optimal performance in terms of capacity and error exponents in a wide class of compound memoryless and finite-state channels, serve here as an excellent example to this point. So are randomized strategies in the AVC case, which may provide inherent advantages over fixed strategies. However, strict adherence to these classical models may lead to problematic, overpessimistic conclusions. This may be the case because transmission of useful information does not always demand classical Shannon-sense definitions of reliable communications. In many cases, practical systems can easily incorporate and cope with outages, high levels of distortion coming not in a stationary fashion, changing delays and priorities, and the like.

These variations carry instrumental information-theoretic implications, as they give rise to notions such as capacity versus outage and expected capacity. Further, in many cases, the available statistical characterization in practice is much richer than what is required for general models, such as compound channels and AVC. This feature is demonstrated, for example, in cases where the unknown parameter governing the transition probabilities of the channel is viewed as a random variable, the probability distribution of which is available. Input constraints entail also fundamental information-theoretic implications. In classical information-theoretic models these constraints are referred to as short-term constraints (that is, effective for each of the possible codewords) [94], while some practical systems may allow for long-term constraints, which are formulated in terms of expectations, and therefore are less stringent. This relaxed set of constraints is satisfied then in average sense, over many transmitted messages [43]. A similar situation exists in the AVC setting with randomized codes, where relaxed constraints are satisfied not for a particular codebook but for the expectation of all possible codebooks [164].

An example is the case, discussed before, where an average-power-constrained user (single user) operates over flat fading with essentially no dynamics (i.e., $B_d T \to 0$) and with a fading process $\{A_n\}$ which may assume values (a_n) arbitrarily close to zero (as, for instance, in the Rayleigh case). The strict notion of the compound channel capacity will yield null capacity: in fact, there is a chance, no matter how small, that the actual fading realization could not support any pre-assigned rate (irrespective of how small that may be). However, notions intimately connected to that of a compound (composite) channel, as of capacity versus outage on the one hand and expected capacities (with or without an associated outage) on the other, yield useful information-theoretic notions. These are not only applicable to the design and analysis of efficient communications systems over these relevant channels, but also may provide sharp insights on how to approach in practice (through suitable coding/decoding schemes) those ultimate theoretical predictions.

By no means do we imply that classical models as compound channels and/or AVC's are not valuable in deepening the understanding of the ultimate limitations and potential of communications systems over practical fading time-varying channels and provide fundamental insight into the actual coding/decoding methods that achieve those limits. On the contrary, as we have directly seen in the cases of capacity versus outage and expected capacity, these are valuable assets, that may grant just the right tools and techniques as to furnish valuable results in different interesting settings. This, however, may demand some adaptation mounted on the physical understanding of the problem at hand, which may manifest itself in a set of constraints of the coding/decoding and channel characteristics. Associating priors to the compound channel [61], [83] yielding the composite channel [83] and giving rise to capacity versus outage and expected capacity results, as discussed here, demonstrate this argument.

To further demonstrate this point, we consider once again our simple channel model of (3.3.9).

We assume an average-input-power constraint $E(|X|^2) \leq P_{\text{av}}$ and the fading variables A_i satisfy, as before, $E|\nu|^2 = 1$, where $\nu = |a|^2$, but we do not impose further assumptions on their time variability. Instead, we assume stationarity in terms of single-dimensional distribution $F_\nu(\alpha)$, which is assumed to be meaningful and available. Further, assume that $E(1/\nu) < \infty$.

Under ergodic conditions, the capacity with state available to the receiver only satisfies (3.3.10), i.e.,

$$C_{\text{RCSI}} = E_\nu \log \left(1 + \frac{\nu P_{\text{av}}}{\sigma^2}\right) \geq \log \left(1 + \frac{P_{\text{av}}}{\sigma^2 E\left(\frac{1}{\nu}\right)}\right)$$
(3.3.36)

where the right-hand-side (RHS) term follows from Jensen's inequality by observing that $\log\left(1 + c/x\right)$ is a convex function of x. Under no ergodic assumption and with CSI available to the receiver only, the capacity-versus-outage curve is given by (3.3.26)

$$P_{\text{out}} = F_\nu((e^R - 1)(P_{\text{av}}/\sigma^2)^{-1}).$$
(3.3.37)

The notions of expected capacity and expected capacity versus outage as in [247] are also directly applicable here. Note that,

as already mentioned, both of these notions apply without change to the case where CSI is available to none, either transmitter or receiver. In fact, under this model the channel is composite (unvarying with time), and hence the channel-state information rate is zero.

When channel-state information is available to the transmitter and then under the ergodic assumption, the capacity with optimal power control is given by (3.3.11). The delay-limited capacity equals here

$$C_{\text{DL}} = \log \left(1 + \frac{P_{\text{av}}}{\sigma^2 E(1/\nu)}\right).$$
(3.3.38)

Note that the delay-limited capacity is a viable notion irrespective of the time-variant properties of the channel (that is, irrespective of whether the ergodic assumption holds or not). Moreover, it does not require the availability of the CSI at the receiver (observing in this case a standard AWGN channel). Note that only a "long-term" average-input-power constraint gives rise to the C_{DL} (3.3.38) [43], as otherwise for short-term constraints marginal advantages in terms of the general capacity versus outage are evidenced. In the latter case, static ($B_d = 0$) fading is assumed.

The channel in the example gives, in fact, rise to an interesting formulation which falls under the purview of AVC. Consider the standard AVC formulation with additional (standard in AVC terminology [164]) state constraint, i.e.,

$$\frac{1}{n} \sum_{\ell=1}^{n} q(s_\ell) \leq \Lambda, \qquad \forall s_i \in \mathcal{S}$$
(3.3.39)

where $\mathcal{S}$ is the relevant state space, and $q(\cdot)$ is some nonnegative function. The input constraint is also given similarly, by

$$\frac{1}{n} \sum_{\ell=1}^{n} g(x_\ell) \leq \Gamma, \qquad \text{for almost all } \mathcal{M}$$
(3.3.40)

where (3.3.40) is satisfied for almost all possible messages in the message space $\mathcal{M}$ corresponding to the codeword $(x_1, x_2, \cdots, x_n)$, which may include a random mapping to account for randomized and stochastic encoders. Here $g(\cdot)$ is a nonnegative function, say $g(x) = |x|^2$, to account for the average power constraint. The AVC capacity[5] for a randomized code is given then by the classical single-letter equation

$$C_{\text{AVC}} = \max_{F_x:\, E(g(x)) \leq \Gamma} \min_{F_\nu(\cdot):\, E_\nu q(\nu) \leq \Lambda} I(Y; X)$$
$$= \min_{F_\nu(\cdot):\, E_\nu q(\nu) \leq \Lambda} \max_{F_x:\, E(g(x)) \leq \Gamma} I(Y; X)$$
(3.3.41)

which, in fact, looks for the worst case state distribution that satisfies constraint (3.3.39). What is also interesting here is that the input constraints take a "short-term" interpretation. Note that the AVC notion does not depend on any ergodic assumption and gives a robust model. In fact, when there is a stochastic characterization of the states, the notion can be combined with an "outage probability" approach, as then the

[5]We use here the extension of classical results for the continuous case which follows similarly to the results for the Gaussian AVC. Note that in case where the constraints are formulated in terms of expectations rather than on individual codewords and state sequences, no strong converse exists [164].

probability that the state constraint (3.3.39) is not satisfied and is associated with an *outage probability*. We do not imply here that the solution of a problem similar to (3.3.41) is simple. Usually it is not. Yet this approach, where state constraints are introduced, is interesting, and has a theoretical as well as a practical value. A special example, associated with the delay-limited approach, occurs when $q(x) = 1/x$, which, along with (3.3.39), implies that no fading variable can be extremely small and still the overall constraint is satisfied. The probability of this event can be computed or bounded. Associated with the AVC interpretation are all the settings which involve average and max error probability (as a performance measure), randomized and stochastic-versus-deterministic coding. All these notions are of interest in practice, and may provide insight to the preferred coding/decoding approaches: we wish only to note that, as the information-carrying signal appears in a product form with the fading variable (ax), which implies that the channel *is* symmetrizable[6] [164], thus providing theoretical support for a randomizing coding approach. This example demonstrates the value of general information-theoretic concepts when combined with relevant notions as the outage probability, giving all together an interesting communication model, which we believe to be of both theoretical and practical interest.

3) Information-Theoretic Inspired Signaling: Optimal Parameter Selection: In general, the capacity as well as the capacity-achieving distribution imply some underlying structure of optimal coding/signaling [253]. This is valid also in the realm of fading, and even more so, as information theory dictates some parameters of close-to-optimal coding systems. This is best demonstrated by the results for the case of CSI available to both the transmitter and the receiver, where information theory provides the precise optimal power-control strategy, and in addition indicates the exact transmitter structure that may approach the ultimate optimal performance with fixed-rate codes [43], [41]. The delay-limited capacity (3.3.38) where perfect channel inversion is attempted, exhibits (when applicable) for the receiver a classical AWGN channel for which, with modern coding techniques, capacity can be closely approached [27], [90], [60]. Here we will highlight some recent results of primary practical importance, in the case where no channel state information is available.

First, for the fast flat-fading model, (i.e., the fading coefficients $\{A_i\}$ are circularly symmetric i.i.d. Gaussian), the discreteness and peaky nature of the capacity-achieving inputs envelope gives rise to orthogonal coded pulse-position-like modulations (with efficient iterative detection as in [214]). Even more interesting is the case of the block-fading model, where the coherence time ΔT_c is some integer greater than 1, thus modeling slow fading. The elegant result in [176] not only gives the structure of the capacity-achieving signals, but in fact provides insight into the gradual tendency of the capacity to the ideal CSI available to the receiver with the increase of ΔT_c.

In the following we shall emphasize some recent insights into the peaky nature of capacity-achieving signaling in the realm of broadband time-varying channels, or more generally in cases where the channel characteristics incorporate a set of random parameters, the number of which is at least proportional to the transmission time (this entails a positive rate).

One of the more interesting models is that of "bandwidth-scaling" [187], [99], [286], where the random channel characterization implies that capacity-achieving signaling should be peaky in time and/or frequency. We shall demonstrate this feature adhering to an insightful formulation which is extended in [252] to account for many other models. Consider a simplified discrete-time channel model

$$y_{\ell,k} = a_{\ell,k}x_{\ell,k} + n_{\ell,k}, \quad \ell = 1, 2, \cdots, m, \; k = 1, 2, \cdots, n$$
$$(3.3.42)$$

where $y_{\ell,k}$ stands for the kth sample (out of nth blocklength) of the ℓth channel (out of m). The input $x_{\ell,k}$ is a complex variable which stands for the ℓth channel input at time k. The fading coefficients, designated by $\{a_{\ell,k}\}$, are assumed to be complex i.i.d. Gaussian random variables, satisfying $E|a_{\ell k}|^2 = 1 \; \forall \ell, k$. The corresponding i.i.d. Gaussian noise components with variance σ^2 per sample are $\{n_{\ell,k}$. The input is average-power constrained in the sense

$$\sum_{\ell=1}^{m} E(|x_{\ell k}|)^2 \leq P_{\text{av}}. \qquad (3.3.43)$$

This simple parallel-channel model can be interpreted as an orthogonal frequency division, where ℓ designates the ℓth frequency band. In this model, each frequency is subjected to independent fast flat fading and orthogonal ambient noise. Within this interpretation m is commensurate with the available bandwidth. Common sense advocates the use of the full bandwidth m with uniform power distribution per coordinate, and bounded inputs per coordinate. The boundedness is based on the "intuition" that for low signal-to-noise ratio (which is evident here for large m and finite P_{av} in (3.3.43)), peak limitation does not imply severe degradation in capacity [248].

We shall see not only why this "intuition" is misleading, but our viewpoint will immediately indicate the right way to go. The capacity here is given by

$$\sup_{\underline{X}: E|\underline{X}|^2 \leq P_{\text{av}}} I(\underline{X};\underline{Y}) \qquad (3.3.44)$$

where $\underline{X}, \underline{Y}$ are m-dimensional vectors with complex components. Now we use the same methodology that has already provided us the right insight[7] in the case of $m = 1$ [87]. Let

$$I(\underline{X};\underline{Y}) = I(\underline{A},\underline{X};\underline{Y}) - I(\underline{A};\underline{Y}|\underline{X}). \qquad (3.3.45)$$

Now

$$I(\underline{A},\underline{X};\underline{Y}) \leq m \log\left(1 + \frac{P_{\text{av}}}{m\sigma^2}\right) \qquad (3.3.46)$$

where this inequality follows by noting that

$$E\sum_{\ell=1}^{m}|a_{\ell,k}x_{\ell,k}|^2 = E\sum_{\ell=1}^{m}|a_{\ell,k}|^2|x_{\ell,k}|^2 \leq P_{\text{av}}. \qquad (3.3.47)$$

---

[6]Take the conditional distribution $U(s|x)\,ds$ in terminology of [164] to be $dF_G(s/x)$ where $F_G(\cdot)$ is some generic probability distribution.

[7]By this we already see that for $m = 1$, peak-limited signals cannot reach capacity, even at very small SNR values.

Recalling that the capacity in parallel channels with CSI available at the receiver only is achieved by equi-power Gaussian inputs, we have

$$I(\underline{A};\underline{Y}|\underline{X}) = \sum_{\ell=1}^{m} E \log \left(1 + \frac{|x_\ell|^2}{\sigma^2}\right) \quad (3.3.48)$$

where for the sake of clarity we omit the irrelevant time index. We first try equally spread signals, where $\{x_\ell\}$ are i.i.d., $E|x_\ell|^2 \le P_{\mathrm{av}}/m$, and where we assume that x_ℓ is not "peaky" in the sense of [99], that is, $E|x_\ell|^4 \le \alpha(P_{\mathrm{av}}/m)$ for some α (a relaxed feature as compared to strict peak-limitedness, that is $|x_\ell| \le \beta$ with probability 1, for some β). Since we take $m \to \infty$, modeling broadband systems, we conclude that

$$I(\underline{X};\underline{Y}) \le \lim_{m \to \infty} m \log \left(1 + \frac{P_{\mathrm{av}}}{m\sigma^2}\right)$$
$$- \sum_{\ell=1}^{m} E \log \left(1 + \frac{|x_\ell|^2}{\sigma^2}\right) \to \frac{P_{\mathrm{av}}}{\sigma^2} - \frac{P_{\mathrm{av}}}{\sigma^2} = 0$$

which demonstrates the absolute uselessness of this signaling strategy, in this setting.

Now, let us use orthogonal signaling with m orthogonal signals, that is, at each time k only one value of ℓ (out of m) of $x_{\ell,k}$ is active. Since orthogonal signaling is known to achieve capacity over the unlimited bandwidth AWGN, it is rather straightforward to show that for this signaling, as $m \to \infty$,

$$I(\underline{A},\underline{X};\underline{Y}) \to \frac{P_*}{\sigma^2} \quad (3.3.49)$$

where we assume for a moment that overall power P is used, that is,

$$\sum_{\ell=1}^{m} E|x_{\ell,k}|^2 = P_*.$$

The other term, however, is

$$I(\underline{A};\underline{Y}|\underline{X}) = \sum_{\ell=1}^{m} E \log \left(1 + \frac{|x_\ell|^2}{\sigma^2}\right) \le \log \left(1 + \frac{E|x_{\ell_*}|^2}{\sigma^2}\right)$$
$$= \log \left(1 + \frac{P_*}{\sigma^2}\right) \quad (3.3.50)$$

where we note here that only for one ℓ, say ℓ_*, the value of $|x_\ell|$ is not identically zero. These inequalities and (3.3.45) yield

$$I(\underline{X};\underline{Y}) \underset{m \to \infty}{\ge} \frac{P_*}{\sigma^2} - \log \left(1 + \frac{P_*}{\sigma^2}\right). \quad (3.3.51)$$

Note that this equation is no more than a special case[8] of [314].

Now instead of orthogonal signaling at each time epoch k, let us assume that signaling is done with a duty factor d, i.e., signaling is attempted only once per d epochs, where $P_* = d P_{\mathrm{av}}$ satisfies the overall average-power constraint. The relevant mutual information in this case follows by (3.3.51) and equals

$$I(\underline{X};\underline{Y}) = \frac{1}{d}\frac{d P_{\mathrm{av}}}{\sigma^2}\frac{1}{d} \log \left(1 + \frac{d P_{\mathrm{av}}}{\sigma^2}\right) \underset{d \to \infty}{\longrightarrow} \frac{P_{\mathrm{av}}}{\sigma^2} \quad (3.3.52)$$

where we recognize the familiar $(P_{\mathrm{av}}/\sigma^2)$ behavior. This behavior has been achieved however with a "peaky" signal, both in frequency (orthogonal signaling) and in time ($d \to \infty$). The same result could be achieved by using peakedness in time, only letting $\{x_{\ell,k}\}$ be all i.i.d. satisfying the peaky binary[9] capacity-achieving distribution. This distribution is naturally expected, as the m channels in (3.3.42) are independent and memoryless and, therefore, independent inputs over the index $\ell, \ell = 1, 2, \cdots, m$, should achieve capacity, which indeed is the case here, noting that the average-power constraint (3.3.43) does not impose additional restrictions regarding the statistical dependence of the signal components $\{x_\ell\}$.

This simple model is also well suited to address the case of correlated $\{a_\ell\}$, as is suggested in [99]. Assume block correlation, i.e., $a_{\ell,k} = a_{\ell',k}$ for $\ell, \ell' \in \mathcal{B}_q$, where $\mathcal{B}_q$, $q = 1, 2, \cdots, m/m'$, is the qth partition of the m possible indices into m/m' (assumed integer) groups of say consecutive indices. The fading coefficients in different groups are assumed i.i.d. This models a blockwise correlation. The capacity-achieving distribution can be found by adopting the results of [176], reviewed shortly in the following subsection in reference to diversity. That is, the input m'-vectors $\underline{x}_q = \{x_\ell\}$, with $\ell \in \mathcal{B}_q$, is distributed according to the result of [176], which reads $\underline{x}_q = \mu \Phi$, where Φ is an m'-dimensional isotropically distributed unit vector and μ is an independent scalar random variable. This scalar random variable is chosen so as to satisfy the average-power constraint per group $(P_{\mathrm{av}}/(m/m'))$. Over different groups the input vectors $\underline{x}_q$, for different values of q, are i.i.d. This model provides insight on how the standard AWGN capacity is approached.

Clearly, with $m/m' = 1$ and $m \gg 1$, we approach essentially a Gaussian behavior of the capacity-achieving signals [176], while for $m' = 1$ and $m \to \infty$, the peakiness in amplitude is evident. In all cases, of course, for $m \to \infty$, the classical capacity value P_{av}/σ^2 is attained, but the capacity-attaining signals have markedly different properties.

It is worth noting that the peakiness has nothing to do with multipath phenomena: in [286] it has been demonstrated that the same conclusion holds for a single-path channel even with a fixed gain but a random time-varying delay. The view taken in [252], which is mounted on a generalization of the relation (3.3.45) in the simple channel example treated here, attributes this behavior to general cases where the channel random features possess an effective "Shannon bandwidth" (we are borrowing this terminology form [177]) comparable to that of the information-conveying signal itself. The "peakiness" nature of capacity-achieving signals is essential in neutralizing the deleterious effect of the random behavior of those channel models, and that is in contrast to the intuition based on efficient signaling over the AWGN channel.

There is a variety of different wideband fading models, starting from classical works [153], [215], examining orthogonal signaling in a fading dispersive environment. In most settings the ultimate capacity P_{av}/N_0 is achievable, where N_0 is as before the AWGN power spectral density and where W, the signaling bandwidth, goes to infinity. This is the case

---

[8] In fact, Viterbi's result [314] follows immediately by the representation in [252] along with the classical Duncan–Kailath connection between average mutual information and causal minimum mean-square errors [81]. See [252] for details.

[9] For $m \to \infty$ the power per channel $P_{\mathrm{av}}/m \to 0$, and the capacity-achieving distribution is binary [87].

even for suboptimal energy-based detectors [215], [216]. See, for example, the orthogonal MFSK result in [314], which yields the limiting performance for M-frequency orthogonal signals of power P_*, each impaired by a complex random Gaussian fading process of power spectral density $S_{\mathrm{fad}}(f)$ (at all frequency translations) normalized to

$$\int_{-\infty}^{\infty} S_{\mathrm{fad}}(f)\,df = 1.$$

The result of Viterbi reads

$$C = \int_{-\infty}^{\infty} \frac{P_* S_{\mathrm{fad}}(f)}{N_0}\,df \int_{-\infty}^{\infty} \log\left(1 + \frac{P_* S_{\mathrm{fad}}(f)}{N_0}\right)df. \tag{3.3.53}$$

Again with the strategy as in (3.3.52), that is, transmitting at duty factor d with power $dP_{\mathrm{av}} = P_*$ while transmission takes place, one reaches the well-recognized relation

$$C \xrightarrow[d^{-1} \to 0]{} \frac{P_{\mathrm{av}}}{N_0}. \tag{3.3.54}$$

This P_{av}/N_0 result is not achievable when peak constraints are imposed on the signals. See [282] for the exact capacity and error-exponent formulas in the case of unrestricted-bandwidth communications in the fast-fading environment.

Clearly, even in the broad (infinite) bandwidth case when no dynamics is experienced by the fading process ($B_d = 0$), usually[10] no reliable communication in Shannon's sense is possible [63] and notions such as capacity-versus-outage and expected capacity emerge. Regretfully, in our exposition we could not elaborate on many relevant results, some developed decades ago [73]–[76], [199], [203]–[209], [227], [265], [293]–[295] as space limitations and the limited scope of this paper preclude a comprehensive treatment.

4) Other Information-Theoretic Inspired Signaling: In the preceding subsection we have focused on special features and in particular on the "peakiness" nature of the capacity-achieving signaling over special models of fading wideband channels. In fact, information theory provided over the last five decades much more than that, and here we succinctly scan some highlights, with particular attention paid to the fading regime.

Multicarrier modulation: This modulation method is motivated by Shannon's classical approach of calculating the capacity of a frequency-selective channel by slicing it to infinitesimal bands [262]. Shannon has demonstrated that this signaling strategy can approach capacity for a dispersive Gaussian channel. Multicarrier modulation has been considered rather extensively in connection to fading. See, for some recent examples [71], where multicarrier transmission is considered over multipath channels, with channel-state information given to both transmitter and receiver or just to the receiver. The loss of orthogonality and interchannel interference are considered. See also [103], where a multicarrier system is considered, and concatenated codes

are employed for each carrier. The inner repetition code is soft-decoded, while the outer code operates on hard decisions. The equivalent BSC capacity throughput is maximized over the number K of users and the number L of frequency repetitions. In [65] adaptive Orthogonal Frequency-Shift Keying (OFDM) is considered for a wideband channel. We have mentioned here very few of the more recent references and have left the rest of the extensive literature on this matter to the references and the reference lists within those references.

Interleaving: This is one of the major factors appearing in many practical communication systems which are designed to operate over approximately stationary memoryless channels. Information theory provides the relevant tools to assess the effects of such a practically appealing technique.

For example, insightful results in [41] indicate that, with ideal CSI available to the receiver or to both receiver and transmitter, interleaving entails no degradation, as the respective capacities are insensitive to the memory structure of the fading process. If perfect CSI is available to the receiver, information theory is used to devise very efficient signaling structures that have the potential, when combined with modern techniques such as "turbo" coding and iterative decoding, to approach channel capacity. This is demonstrated in the elegant Bit-Interleaved Coded Modulation technique [42] to be described in Section IV, as well as in multilevel coding with multistage decoding [133], [159], [321]. This case differs markedly when no CSI is available. Consider the block-fading model, the capacity of which with no interleaving and CSI is given by [176] and for relatively long blocks it equals essentially the capacity for a given channel state information at the receiver. Interleaving in this case inflicts an inherent degradation, whose severity increases with the blocklength over which the fading stays invariant. Full ideal interleaving results in the capacity of [87], which, as indicated above, may be markedly lower. In this case as well, the interleaving degradation disappears as $P_{\mathrm{av}}/\sigma^2 \to 0$.

Interleaving plays a major role also in other information-theoretic measures as cutoff rate and error exponents to be shortly discussed in what follows. In fact, the very block-fading model introduced in [210] is related to the obstacles in achieving efficient interleaving in the presence of stringent delay constraints.

Gaussian-like interference: Efficient signaling on the AWGN channel is by now well understood, and recent developments make it possible to come remarkably close to the ultimate capacity limits [90]. This is the primary motivation to make the deleterious interferers look Gaussian. While the classical known saddle-point argument proves that the Gaussian interference is in fact the worst average-power-constraint additive noise, a recent result by Lapidoth [161] proves that a Gaussian-based nearest neighbor decoder yields in the average of all Gaussian-distributed codebooks the Gaussian capacity irrespective of the statistical nature of the independent and ergodic noise. Thus in a sense one can guarantee the Gaussian performance even without trying to optimally utilize the noise statistics, which might not be available. We shall further elaborate on these results, which apply also for a flat-fading channel with full side-

---

[10]Unless channel inversion is possible with either long- or short-term average power constraints. Channel inversion is possible with short-term power constraint if the fading energy realization is bounded away from zero with probability 1.

information available to the receiver. In order to transform the multiplicative fading effect into an additive Gaussian-like noise one has to resort to some versions of central limit theorems. A recent idea uses spreading methods via filtering of the transmitted signal, spreading it in time, thus providing the diversity needed to mitigate the fading effect [328]. This serves as an alternative to interleaving, and this technique effectively transforms the fading channel into a marginally Gaussian channel over which standard coding methods are useful. A similar spreading effect is achieved by classical direct-sequence spread-spectrum methods with large processing gain factors [242], where again the time diversity makes performance depend on many independent fading realizations which by various variants of the central limit theorem manifest themselves in a constant gain factor with some penalty [328] which may not be too large. The diversity effect is not necessarily achieved in the time domain: the frequency domain serves this purpose equally well; so do combined time/frequency spreading methods, as these are based on variants of wavelet transforms [330]. Nevertheless, space-diversity methods, to be discussed later, also play a similar role providing the setting to average a reasonably large number of fading realizations. Some strategies employed in the multiple-user realm are left to the subsequent part of this section.

It is worth mentioning here (although this will be expanded upon in the next section) that coding provides inherently the necessary diversity to cope with fading, in a usually much more efficient way than various other diversity techniques, as direct-sequence spreading [177, and references therein]. The latter may be interpreted as an equivalent repetition code, which inherently points to its suboptimality. In certain cases, and in particular where no knowledge on the exact statistics and/or realizations of the fading variables at the receiver site is available, various time/frequency-spreading methods which transform the fading time-variable channel at hand into the familiar AWGN channel, are recommended, especially from the practical implementation point of view.

Spectrally efficient modulation: As for the AWGN channel, information theory provides fundamental guidelines for the design of such systems in the realm of a faded time-varying channel. One of the most typical recent examples is multilevel signaling, which is an appealing scheme [133] not only in the AWGN case, but also in the presence of fading. In fact, [159] uses the chain rule of mutual information to demonstrate that capacity for the flat-fading channel can be achieved with a multilevel modulation scheme using multistage decoding (with hard decisions). Interleavers are introduced on all stages, and rate selection is done, via an information-theoretic criterion (average mutual information for the stage conditioned on previously decoded stages), which if endowed with powerful binary codes, may achieve rates close to capacity, as inherent diversity is provided by the per-stage interleaver. (See also [241], [321], where multilevel coding with independent stage decoding in the realm of unfaded and faded channels is considered.) Rates are selected by mutual information criteria, and compared to the achievable results with multistage decoding.

In the contribution [42], the scheme originally advocated by Zehavi, where a coded-modulation signaling is bit-interleaved

and each channel is separately treated, is investigated via information-theoretic tools in the AWGN and flat-fading channel, with known and unknown channel-state information at the receiver. It is concluded that Gray labeling (or pseudo-Gray labeling if the former cannot be achieved) yields overall rates similar to the rates achieved by the signal set itself, while Ungerboeck's set partitioning inflicts significant degradation. (The cutoff rate is also investigated, and it is demonstrated that the cutoff rate, when exceeds 1, and with Gray or pseudo-Gray mapping, surpasses the corresponding cutoff rate of the signal set itself.) This is a remarkable observation which gives rise to parallel decoding of all stages with no side information passed between stages. This technique can also mitigate delay constraints, as each level is decoded on an individual basis. Further results are reported in [241] where multilevel coding with independent stage decoding in the realm of unfaded and faded channels is considered. Rates are selected by mutual information criteria, and performance is compared to the achievable results with multistage decoding. For a tutorial exposition on multilevel coding, see [133].

As we have already concluded, techniques and methods used for deterministic channels with or without dispersion are directly applicable to the time-varying framework, whether by taking one further expectation with respect to the random process characterizing this dispersive response or, alternatively, the final result is a random variable depending of course on the fact that channel characterization is treated as a random entity. Over the last five decades, information theory has been providing a solid theoretical ground and results motivating specific signaling methods with the goal of approaching capacity. We shall mention here only a few representative examples, while many others can be traced by scanning the information-theoretic literature. The classical orthogonalization which decomposes the original dispersive channel into parallel channels [94], [226], [132], [152] is fundamental not only for a conceptually rigorous derivation of capacity, but carries over basic insight into the very implementation of information-theoretic inspired signaling methods. The information-theoretic implications of tail-canceling and minimum mean-square error (MMSE) decision feedback as well as precoding techniques at the transmitter (cf. Tomlin-son–Harashima equalization and the like) are very thoroughly addressed [250], [58], [260], [57], [90]. While the results for fixed dispersive channels are directly applicable in the case where CSI is known both to the receiver and transmitter, this may not be valid in general for other cases. Clearly, many results, as that in [260], are applicable also to the case where CSI is available to the receiver only, as the transmitter employs a fixed strategy which is not channel-state adaptive. In fact, in a situation of slow time variations of the channel characteristics (that is, $B_d T \to 0$), those results are applicable also when no CSI is available, as this case falls within the compound-channel model, with the frequency response playing the role of the parameter characterizing the channel (i.e., its transition probability) [164].

These examples demonstrate clearly that most of the classical results developed over the last five decades of information-theoretic research are applicable as they are, or with some minor modifications, to the realm of faded time-varying channels [139]. This holds also for contributions which examine signaling used to communicate over a dispersive channel subject to constraints other than average power. References [248], [211], [256] and reference lists therein provide some examples, where the main signaling constraints are peak-power in many variations, combined or not with bandlimitedness.

5) Unavailable Channel-State Information: Information-Theoretic Aspects: In previous subsections we have addressed the capacity problem of a time-varying fading channel with a certain assumption about the availability, or nonavailability, of accurate CSI at the receiver and/or transmitter sites. The case of unavailable CSI accounts for the practical model and provides ultimate limits for cases where there are no separate channels to convey CSI to the receiver. Estimates of the degradation inflicted by lacking CSI are available (see, for example, [185]). Yet the receiver, if its structure requires such a CSI explicitly, must retrieve it from the received signal itself. Many approaches use different variants of training sequences to facilitate simple learning by the receiver of the CSI. As discussed in [164, and references therein], those approaches are in particular appealing for the case where $B_d T \to 0$, that is, the time-varying features of the channel are relatively slow. While having in such a case a negligible effect on capacity, as the training sequences are sent infrequently, yet the error exponent may suffer significant degradation [164]. Information theory does provide the tools to address such problems, and in a recent contribution [140] the information detection issue and CSI estimation are treated in a unified information-theoretic framework. Specifically, the optimal determination of CSI where side information or redundancy at a prescribed rate are available to the receiver is examined. Information-theoretic measures characterizing detection and estimation are presented, and associated bounds are found. It is concluded that in a variety of cases the above stated method of training sequences is suboptimal. Other papers, such as [287], use information-theoretic measures to compare different procedures to estimate the CSI, which is a dispersive vector channel in [287]. Full statistical characterization of the channel may not always exist, or even if it does exist, it might be unavailable. The compound or composite channels are classical examples, as once the transition statistics is determined, it characterizes performance through the whole transmission. While a whole class of decoders achieves the capacity of the compound channel and, primarily, that decoder matched to the saddle-point solution (3.3.41) of the worst case channel/best input statistics, a considerably more interesting class are universal decoders [164].

The universal decoder is able to achieve usually not only the capacity but the whole random-coding error exponent, which is associated with the optimal maximum-likelihood decoder matched to the actual channel, and this without any prior knowledge of the statistics of that operating channel. Indeed, universal decoders do not use the naive approach of decoupling the channel estimation and the decoding process. We shall reference here only a few such classical universal decoders as the maximizer of mutual information [64], the universal decoding based on Lempel/Ziv parsing [338], [166] applicable

to a variety of finite-state channels, and a recent contribution in [88] applicable to channels with memory. We leave the details to the excellent tutorial [164].

Mismatched decoding: An interesting information-theoretical problem (mismatched decoders) accounts for the fact that a matched and/or universal decoder might be very complex and in fact unfeasible, and addresses a whole spectrum of cases where either the channel statistics are not precisely known and/or implementation constraints dictate a given decoder. Here a receiver employs a given decoding metric irrespective of its suboptimality. The full extent of the information-theoretic problem, as reflected by the ultimate mismatched achievable rates, is not yet solved, but for binary inputs [22]. However, numerous bounds and fundamental insights into that problem have been reported. See [164] for a selected list of references and for further details.

One of the more interesting and relevant mismatched decoders is one that bases its decision on a Gaussian optimal minimum-distance metric. A class of results in [161] demonstrates that the Gaussian capacity cannot be surpassed for random Gaussian codes performance (performance is averaged over all codebooks), even if the additive noise departs considerably from the Gaussian statistics giving rise to a much higher *matched* capacity. In fact, with perfect CSI at the receiver [161], the same result holds for the ergodic fading channel with a general ergodic independent noise. That is, the associated capacity for the Gaussian case is attained, and cannot be surpassed by a random Gaussian code irrespective of the actual statistics of the additive noise. We shall further refer to similar results in the context of imperfect CSI at the receiver. The Gaussian-based mismatched metric has been applied for a variety of cases; see examples in [150] and [190].

In a variety of cases with special practical implications, the receiver has at its disposal imperfect channel-state information, which it uses to devise the associated decoding metric. Many works examine the associated reliable rate using different information-theoretic criteria as the mismatch capacity, mismatched cutoff rate (or generalized cutoff rate) [251], and error exponents [150, and references therein]. Even here there are many approaches which depend on the knowledge available at the receiving side. If the receiver is equipped with the full statistical description of the pair $(s, \hat{s})$ where $\hat{s}$ stands for the given or estimated state (relevant fading coefficients, for the case at hand) at the receiver, standard information-theoretic expressions apply, via the interpretation of $\hat{s}$ as part of the observables at the receiver. This however is seldom the case, and in most instances this statistical characterization is either unavailable or yields complex detectors. Here also, mismatch detection serves as an interesting viable option.

The mismatched decoder based on an integer metric, which is used on digital VLSI complexity-controlled implementations [238], has been considered in [33] in the binary-input fading channel with or without diversity. In such a setting the best space partition which maximizes the exact mismatched capacity has been found, and it has been shown to be reasonably robust to the optimizing criterion (either mismatch capacity or mismatched cutoff rate). Again, we shall refer to some other

596

relevant recent results [186], [165] and present some of the results in their most simple setting.

Consider the usual complex flat-fading channel (3.3.9), where it is assumed that the fading and the additive-noise processes $\{a_k\}$ and $\{n_k\}$ are independent and ergodic, and so is the input process $\{x_k\}$, assumed to be circularly symmetric Gaussian with power $E|X_k|^2 = P_{\text{av}}$. In our model we assume further that the receiver has an independent estimate $\hat{a}_k$ of a_k which is optimal in the sense that $E(\hat{A}_k|\hat{a}_k) = \hat{a}_k$ (for example, $\hat{a}_k$ is produced by a conditional expectation over a given sigma-algebra of measurements $\{z_j^k\}$ independent of $\{y_k\}$, that is, a side-information channel which conveys information on a_k via $\{z_j^k\}$, where j belongs to some set of indices). We assume that $\{\hat{a}_k, a_k\}$ are jointly ergodic. We interpret $\hat{a}_k$ as the known portion of the channel at the receiver, while the CSI estimation error is given by the sequence $e_k = (a_k - \hat{a}_k)$. The above assumption guarantees that $E(e_k|\hat{a}_k) = 0$, and it is straightforward to show that

$$
\begin{aligned}
I(Y, \hat{A}; X) &= I(\hat{A}; X) + I(Y; X|\hat{A}) \overset{a)}{=} I(Y; X|\hat{A}) \\
&= E_{\hat{a}} I(Y; X|\hat{A} = \hat{a}) \\
&\geq E_{\hat{a}} \log\left(1 + \frac{|\hat{a}|^2 P_{\text{av}}}{E_{a|\hat{a}}|a - \hat{a}|^2 P_{\text{av}} + E(|n|^2)}\right).
\end{aligned}
$$
(3.3.55)

Here a) results by noticing that $I(\hat{A}; X) = 0$, and the inequality follows by noticing that among the family of uncorrelated additive noises impairing a Gaussian input, the Gaussian noise with the same power yields the worst case [186]. This is a generalization of the result in [186], which considered the special case of real signals, Gaussian additive noise $\{n_k\}$ the estimate $\tilde{a} = E(a)$ where a stands for a nonnegative fading variable. In this case, the external expectation $E_{\hat{a}}$ in (3.3.55) is superfluous. While (3.3.55) provides a lower bound on the mutual information and due to the ergodic nature of the problem, this expression lower-bounds the capacity in this setting. The bound (3.3.55) depends on basic features[11] of the problem $|\tilde{a}|^2$ and the conditional error $E_{a|\tilde{a}}|a - \tilde{a}|^2$; yet to realize this bound, the decoder has to use the optimal statistics based on the channel transition probability

$$
\begin{aligned}
p(y, \tilde{a}|x) &= \int da\, p(y, \tilde{a}, a|x) \\
&= \int da\, p(\tilde{a}, a)\, p(y|x, a, \tilde{a}) \\
&= \int da\, p(\tilde{a}, a)\, p(y|x, a)
\end{aligned}
$$
(3.3.56)

where we notice by the channel setting that $p(y|x, a, \hat{a}) = p(y|x, a)$, where $p(\cdot)$ denote appropriate density or conditioned density.

An interesting result showed recently in [165] proves that the expression in (3.3.55) is in fact an upper bound on the achievable rates of a mismatched decoder which employs a matched metric for the Gaussian fading channel that assumes that the channel is $y = \tilde{a}x + n$. For the case of optimal phase

estimation, that is, $\arg(a) = \arg(\hat{a})$, which is evidently satisfied for the single-dimensional model where a is a nonnegative real fading variable [186], the bound (3.3.55) is strictly tight (i.e., equals the mismatched rate). This bound holds for the random Gaussian codebook and it demonstrates on one hand the usefulness of the mismatch decoding notion in practical applications and on the other hand it dictates, by noticing that the expression in (3.3.55) is power-limited and upper-bounded by

$$
E_{\tilde{a}} \log\left(1 + \frac{|\tilde{a}|^2}{E_{a|\tilde{a}}|a - \tilde{a}|^2}\right)
$$
(3.3.57)

that this model is extremely sensitive to the channel estimation error, which is contrary to common belief. In fact, [165] extends the treatment providing similar bounds on achievable rates for the mismatched nearest neighbor-based decoder in certain cases where the estimation $\tilde{a}$ of a is done *causally* by observing the received signals $\{y_k\}$. This extension serves to eliminate the assumption of an independent side-information channel, and allows for causal learning of the *a priori* unknown fading realizations. Therefore, its practical implications should be evident.

This concludes our very short review of some relevant information-theoretic considerations referred to suboptimal detection (as mismatched decoding) and the role of imprecise CSI. The material available in the literature for this case is especially rich (see relevant entries in our reference list, and references therein) and in general this forms a classical example where information-theoretic arguments provide valuable insights yielding a strong practical impact.

6) Diversity: Diversity, being a major means in coping with the deleterious effect of fading and time-varying characteristics of the channel, attracted naturally much information-theoretic attention. We do not intend here to provide a comprehensive review of these results (some of their practical implications to coding will be discussed in the next section), but rather mention just a few sample references putting the emphasis on the interesting case, catching of late much attention, of *transmitter diversity*. That is, transmitter diversity provides substantial enhancement of the achievable rates, which without any doubt will become extremely appealing in future communication systems [220]. As said, space diversity at the receiver is now common practice, which in fact has beenstudied for its information-theoretic aspects in many dozens of references in the literature. We shall, at best, mention only a small sample of those.

Diversity at the receiver with CSI available to the receiver is considered in [210], where capacities and capacity distributions are provided for two diversity branches with optimal (maximal-gain) or suboptimal (selection) combining, where both diversity branches may be correlated. It was demonstrated that the beneficial effect of diversity vanishes only at very high correlations. Capacity with CSI at the receiver for Ricean as well and Nakagami-m distributions with independent diversity reception is evaluated in [171] and [118]. Capacity close to Gaussian was evidenced for moderate degrees of diversity. Here channel-state information available to the receiver is assumed. In fact, in these models

---

[11] This is in particular evident in the special case [186] where the results depend only on the expectation $E(a)$ and the variance $E(a - E(a))^2$.

the receiver diversity manifests itself essentially in changing the distribution of fading. Tendency to Gaussianity with the increase of diversity is mentioned also in [153] and others. Some additional results are reported in [11], where capacity for Nakagami channels with or without diversity for different power strategies, as optimal power/rate adaptation, constant rate, and constant power, is evaluated. See also [12], where capacity is evaluated for three strategies: optimal power and rate adaptation, optimal rate adaptation, and channel inversion or constrained channel inversion. Maximal-ratio and selection combining techniques are examined, and the capacities are compared to the capacity of AWGN channels under similar conditions. It is concluded that, for moderate diversity, the channel inversion works very well and is almost optimal. As expected, capacity of the AWGN channel is approached with the increase of the number of diversity branches. See also [21], [302], [15], [72], [174], and many other references provided in the reference list here and reference lists of the cited papers. With no CSI, it has been demonstrated in [87] that for the Rayleigh fast flat-fading channel, the capacity-achieving distribution remains discrete in its input norm for receiver space diversity as well.

While space diversity at the receiver provides considerable gain in performance when the diversity branches are not too highly correlated, space diversity at the transmitter yields a dramatic increase in the reliable achievable rates provided that CSI is available at least to the receiver site, which also employs diversity. The unpublished report [239] considers the single-user multi-input multi-output Gaussian channel. Shannon capacity and also the capacity distributions are examined for the double-ray propagation channel model, and the implications of space diversity are explicitly pointed out. Much more recent literature, as in [326] where the capacity distribution for multiple transmit/receive antennas is considered, shows the substantial benefit of this diversity, which in fact may yield information rates that increase linearly with the number of (transmit/receive) antennas. See also [92], where capacity calculations of systems with $M_t = M_r$ transmitter and receiver antennas, with the receiver equipped with full CSI, is evaluated. A nice lower bound is presented, which gives rise to a suboptimal yet efficient signaling scheme [91]. Substantial gains are observed, pointing out to this diversity technique as a crucial part of future communications systems. In [198], information-theoretic calculations for the multiple-transmit antenna case, where channel-state information is available to receiver only is undertaken. Suboptimal schemes as in [326], where delayed versions of the same transmission are sent through different antennas, and Hiroike's method where phase shift replaces delay, are also considered. Asymptotically (with the number of antennas) with linear antenna processing it is shown that the nonselective fading channel is transformed into a white Gaussian channel with no ISI.

The case where CSI is provided also to the transmitter is considered in [43]. The optimal power control strategy for a single-user block-fading channel is found in the context of capacity versus outage. The major value of power control is put in evidence when capacity versus outage is considered, and this is much more pronounced when performance is measured in terms of capacity versus outage. The results apply to the multiple transmitting/receiving antennas case, thus facilitating the comparison of the performance of specific coding approaches (as the recently introduced space/time coding technique [281]), to the ultimate optimum. In [226], a discrete model for the time-invariant multipath fading, with L paths and, respectively, M_t and M_r transmit and receive antennas is considered. The information capacity is studied and forms of spatiotemporal codes are suggested. Contrary to what is claimed there, and as evidenced by our reference list, this is not the first observation of the dramatic improvement due to multiple transmit/receive antennas in a multipath fading channel. That paper demonstrates that for $L \geq \min(M_t, M_r)$, the capacity increases linearly with the minimum diversity supplied by the multiple transmit/receive antennas as is well known. The coding scheme advocated in the paper should be compared with that in [280] and [281]. Elegant rigorous analytical results are provided in [283], where the multi-input multi-output single-user fading Gaussian channel is investigated with CSI available to the receiver. Equations for the capacity, capacity distribution (i.e., capacity versus outage), and error exponents are provided. The methodology is based on the distribution of the eigenvalues of random matrices. The exact nonasymptotic distribution of the unordered eigenvalue is known [82] and used in [283] to compute the capacity of a single-user Gaussian channel with M_t transmitters and M_r receivers, where each transmitter reaches each receiver via an independent and identically distributed Rayleigh fading complex Gaussian channel. The capacity assumes the expression [283]

$$ C = \int_0^\infty \log\left(1 + \frac{P_{\text{av}}\lambda}{M_t}\right) \sum_{k=0}^{m_*-1} \frac{k!}{(k+n_*-m_*)!} $$
$$ \cdot (L_k^{n_*-m_*}(\lambda))^2 \lambda^{n_*-m_*} e^{-\lambda} d\lambda \qquad (3.3.58) $$

where $m_* = \min(M_r, M_t)$, $n_* = \max(M_r, M_t)$, P_{av} is the average transmitted power (all Rayleigh fading coefficients are normalized to unit power), and

$$ L_k^\ell(x) = \frac{1}{k!} e^x x^\ell \frac{d^k}{dx^k}(e^{-x} x^{\ell+k}) $$

is the associated Laguerre polynomial. Using the asymptotic eigenvalue distribution of [266] yields, for example, for $M_t = M_r \to \infty$, the result

$$ \frac{C}{M_t} \underset{M_t=M_r\to\infty}{\longrightarrow} \int_0^4 \log(1+P_{\text{av}}\nu) \frac{1}{\pi} \sqrt{\nu^{-1}-1/4}\, d\nu \quad (3.3.59) $$

which demonstrates the substantial *linear* (in M_t) increase in the reliable rate.

In fact [288], the result in (3.3.59) is invariant to the actual fading distribution as long as the i.i.d. rule is maintained, which is a direct outcome of the results in [266]. This makes the conclusions much more stable and interesting as far as practical applications and implications are concerned. The asymptotic result is easily extendible to the case where $M_t \to \infty$ while M_t/M_r is a fixed number, not necessarily unity, as in in the example above [283], [284]

While the results of [283] apply to the case where perfect CSI is available at the receiver, [288] examines also the asymptotic case (M_t very large) where perfect channel state is available to both the transmitter and receiver, and hence the transmitter employs the optimal "water-pouring" strategy to maximize capacity. It is concluded, as expected, that for low signal-to-noise ratio P_{av}/σ^2, there is a substantial four-fold increase in capacity, while, for $P_{av}/\sigma^2 \to \infty$, the advantage in revealing the CSI to the transmitter disappears. Reference [288] reports also some straightforward extensions to the frequency-selective fading channel.

The most interesting single-user diversity case is that of absolutely unavailable CSI to either transmitter and/or receiver. In this case, the time correlation of the fading coefficients (i.e., coherence time T_{coh}) is fundamental, as this dependence, if it exists, provides the mechanism through which one can cope with the fading process more efficiently as compared to the fully i.i.d. (or interleaved) case. The study of [176] examines this case for the block-fading model, that is, when complex Gaussian fading coefficients are kept fixed for the coherence time T_{coh} and selected independently for each coherence-time block interval. The insightful results of [176] characterize the capacity-attaining signal, which should take the forms of an isotropically distributed unitary matrix multiplied by an independent real nonnegative diagonal matrix. The striking conclusion of [176] is that there is no advantage in providing a transmit diversity which surpasses the coherence-time limits, that is, $M_t = \Delta T_c$ (assumed to be an integer) is optimum (though it may not be unique). This important conclusion places inherent limits on the actual benefit from increasing the transmit diversity in certain systems experiencing relatively fast fading. Clearly, if ΔT_c is large, the substantial gain of transmit diversity is attainable, as the ideal assumption of perfectly known CSI (say, at receiver only [283]) is realistic and can be closely approached in practice. Also, this striking outcome can be understood within the framework of the relation (3.3.27), which yields here

$$I(\underline{X}; \underline{Y}) = I(X; \underline{Y}|\underline{A}) - (I(\underline{A}; \underline{Y}|\underline{X}) - I(\underline{A}; \underline{Y})) \quad (3.3.60)$$

where $\underline{A}$ is the associated random fading parameter and $\underline{X}$ and $\underline{Y}$ are the transmitted M_t components and the receiver M_r components vectors, respectively.

Increasing M_t under a total average transmit-power constraint $E|\underline{X}|^2 \leq P_{av}$ yields no advantage, as the subtracting part in the RHS of (3.3.60) outbalances the increase (about linear in M_t for large enough M_r) in the expansion $I(\underline{X}; \underline{Y}|\underline{A})$ associated with the capacity of perfect CSI available to the receiver [283].

In [176] bounds on capacity are also given, by using specific signaling (lower bound) or letting the fading parameters be available to the receiver (upper bound). The capacity of the latter case (channel parameters known to receiver) is approached for increasing ΔT_c. The results are extended to cases with vanishing autocorrelation. The work in [87] deals with $\Delta T_c = 1$, and a single-antenna case, but allows for multiple receive antennas. Note that the results in [87] provide indications that the optimal random variables in the diagonal matrix in the capacity-achieving distribution of [176] should

take on discrete values, but no proof for this conjecture is yet available.

We conclude this subsection by emphasizing again that diversity is an instrumental tool in enhancing performance of communication systems in the realm of fading. The gain is substantial with transmit-diversity techniques when the coherence time of the fading process is adequately large as to allow for reasonable levels of transmit diversity.

7) Error Exponents and Cutoff Rates: While we put emphasis on different notions of capacity for the time-varying fading channel, much literature has been devoted to the investigation of other information-theoretic measures of primary importance; namely, error exponents and cutoff rates. The error exponent is one of the more important information-theoretic measures, as it sets ultimate bounds on the performance of communications systems employing codes of finite memory (say, block or constraint lengths). While only rarely is the exact error exponent known [282], classical bounds are available. The standard random coding error exponent serving as a lower bound on the optimal error exponent and the sphere-packing upper bound coincide for rates larger than the critical rate [94] thus giving the correct exponential behavior for these class of channels. (See [94] for extensions.) The cutoff rate [320], determining both an achievable rate and the magnitude of the random-coding error exponent, serves as another interesting information-theoretic notion. Although, contrary to past belief [178], it is no more considered as an upper bound on practically achievable rates, yet it provides a useful bound to the rates where sequential decoding can be practically used. In any case, it is a most valuable parameter, which may provide insight complementary to that acquired by the investigation of capacity.

Error exponents for fading channels have been addressed in [153] and [227] for various cases; in [227] the unknown CSI has been examined. In a recent work [282], the error exponent for the case of infinite bandwidth but finite power has been evaluated in the no-CSI scenario. This model, where performance is measured per-unit cost (power) as otherwise the system is unrestricted, is one of the few fading-channel models for which the exact capacity [304] and error exponent [96] can be evaluated. In [176] the random coding error exponent has been studied for the case of multiple transmit and receive antennas and for the block fading channel. In [85], the random-coding error exponent for a single-dimensional fading channel is evaluated with ideal CSI available to the receiver, and the corresponding error exponent for Gaussian-distributed inputs is given in the region above the critical rate through capacity. Reference [148] examines the block-fading model in terms of capacity, cutoff rates, and error exponents. It has been established that, though capacity is invariant in terms of the memory in the block-fading model, the error exponent suffers a dramatic decrease, indicating that the effective codelength is reduced by about the coherence blocklength ΔT_c factor. This phenomenon, resembling some previous observations made on the block interference channel [183], indicates the necessity to allow for large delay, that is, to use long block codes, in order to allow reasonable performance. In [148] it is concluded that with relaxed delay constraints, while the capacity characterizes the horizontal axis of the reliability function (rate), the vertical axis (magnitude) is better described by the cutoff rate in the block-fading model. The error-exponent distribution, giving rise to performance versus outage, has also been investigated, and commensurate behavior of both capacity and cutoff rate, which behave similarly in terms of the outage criterion, was demonstrated. Space- and time-diversity methods are investigated in [149], and shown to be most effective in the case of stringent delay constraints [149]. In [15], the random-coding error exponent for the quadrature fading Gaussian channel with perfectly known channel-state information at the receiver, is evaluated. Average- and peak-power constraints are examined, and bounds on the random-coding error exponent are provided. Also investigated are optimal (maximal-ratio combining) diversity schemes. It is demonstrated, as in [148], that the error exponent, in contrast to capacity, is largely reduced by the fading phenomenon. The case of correlated fading is also examined via a bound on the error exponent, and Monte Carlo simulation. For some additional references see the extensive reference list in [15].

In another work, [168], capacity and error exponents for Rayleigh fading channels with states known at receiver and fed back to transmitter are examined. Variable power and variable rate, controlled by means of varying the bit duration, are considered. The peak-power constraint, as well as feedback delays, are discussed, but the finite feedback capacity problem is solved correctly in [312]. The optimal power allocation suggested in [168], which is channel inversion, is misleading (see [112] for the correct solution).

In the nice contribution [175], upper and lower exponential (reliability type) bounds are derived for the block-fading channel with L diversity branches. The improved upper bound is found by letting the parameters (ρ in Gallager's notation [94]) to be channel-state-dependent. The lower bound hinges on the outage probability and the strong converse. Both bounds are shown to be rather close. The optimum diversity factor was found to depend also on the code rate and not only on the number L of available parallel independent channels (see [156] for a similar conclusion). Outages as well as cutoff rates are also considered.

In a recent contribution [31] the block-fading channel is considered, where CSI is available to both transmitter and receiver. The random-coding error exponent is investigated, and a practical power-control scheme is suggested. In this case, the channel is inverted just for the K' strongest fading values, and the result has the flavor of a delay-limited error exponent. A dramatic increase in the error exponent is reported (as expected). Further optimizing the Gallager parameter ρ [94], making it fading-vector-dependent, improves considerably the tightness, as has been already indicated in [175] for the binary case.

In [151], investigation of exponential bounds, as well as capacity and cutoff rates, in the realm of correlated fading with ideal CSI at the receiver is reported. Bounds are given, with and without a piecewise-constant approximation of the channel behavior.

In [283], the single-user channel with multiple transmit and receive additive Gaussian channels is examined also in terms of error exponents. It is shown that transmitter diversity has a substantial effect on the error exponent as well as on the capacity as discussed previously.

In the above we have scanned succinctly only very few of the contributions that address error exponents in the realm of random time-varying fading channels. However, this sample, small though it is, indicates the amount of effort invested into enhancing the understanding of performance of practical systems over this class of channels where more insight the mere reliable rate is sought. In fact, the results [148], [183], [15], [168], [175] for the error exponent reveal the need for considerable effective time diversity in any practical coding system, which dictates long delays for slow-varying fading models, as to achieve reliable communication in the classical Shannon's sense. The importance of CSI at the transmitter in terms of dramatic increase in the error exponent [31] similar to the capacity versus outage performance [43] also deserves special attention of practical-system designers, and that is opposed to the negligible increase in the ergodic capacity [112] in this setting. Cutoff rate, being a much easier notion to evaluate in the fading-channel realm, has been very thoroughly investigated for several decades. See [78] for example, and the reference list [122], [149]–[151], [182], [172], [302], [303], [201], [202], [19], [34], [77], [141], [67], [193], [160], [270], [274] which forms just a small unrepresentative sample of the available literature. As already said, cutoff rates were denied in recent years (especially with the advent of turbo codes and iterative decoding [27], [60]) their status as ultimate bounds on the practically achievable reliable communication. Yet, their importance as indicators of the error exponent behavior is maintained [148]. Since cutoff rates are relatively easy to evaluate in more or less closed forms, as compared to the full random-coding error exponent for example, current results in the literature are of interest, and further research addressing this notion in a variety of interesting settings in the fading time-varying channel is called for.

D. Multiple Users

In the previous subsection we have addressed only the single-user case: the main factor giving rise to the whole spectrum of information-theoretic notions, techniques, approaches, and results, was the randomly varying nature of the channel. With multiple-access communication, everything discussed so far extends conceptually, almost as is, to the multiple-user case. In addition, the existence of several users adds an extra significant dimension to the problem, which may modify not only the conclusions, but in some cases even the questions asked. Even for classical memoryless time-invariant channels, the realm of multiple-user communications affects in a most substantial way the methodology and information-theoretic approach. New notions as the multiple-access, broadcast, interference, relay, and general multiterminal network information theory emerge along with associated rate-regions, which replace the simple capacity notion used in the single-user case [62], [64]. The presence of fading in its general form affects in certain cases the problem at hand in a very substantial way which cannot be decoupled from its network (multiple-user) aspects. This is demonstrated (and described in some detail in the following) by the observation that in case of available CSI at receiver and average-power-constrained users, classical orthogonal TDMA can no more achieve the maximum throughput, in contrast to the unfaded case [62].

We will further see that the very presence of multiple users gives rise to new models that incorporate inherently the fading time-varying phenomenon into the multiple-user information-theoretic setting. Clearly, the wealth of the available material prevents any exhaustive, or even close-to-exhaustive, treatment of this topic. Here, to an extent even greater than before in this section, we shall discuss only a few select results, leaving the major part of results, techniques, and methodology to the references and reference lists therein. In essence, we shall follow the same path as in our previous exposition, by emphasizing only the information-theoretic aspects typical of multiple users operating in a fading regime. Though there are a variety of interesting multiple-user information-theoretic models, we shall focus on the multiple-access channel, and, to a lesser extent, on the broadcast channel, mentioning also some relevant features of the interference channel [62]. We shall put special emphasis on recently introduced cellular communication models, which have gained much attention lately.

1) The Multiple-Access Finite-State Channel: In parallel to the treatment in [41], providing a general framework which accounts for available/not available/partially available channel-state information (CSI) at transmitters and/or receivers, the preliminary results of [69] provide the framework and the general structure of the results in the multiple-access fading channel with/without CSI available to receiver/transmitter under the ergodic regime. The framework of [69] encompasses finite-state channels with finite-cardinality input, output, and state spaces, yet the structure of the results provides insight to the expressions derived for standard multiple-user (continuous) fading models with different degrees of CSI available at receivers/transmitters.

In fact, some of the results can be extended to continuous real-valued alphabets [69] and, in parallel to [41], in [69] some special cases are identified where "strategies" (in the terminology of [237]) are not needed, and signaling over the original input alphabet χ suffices to achieve capacity. Some of those specific cases, particularized to a simple ergodic flat-fading model, are presented in the following.

It is appropriate to mention here that the multiple-access channel, even in its simplistic memoryless setting, demonstrates some intricacies: for example, a possible difference between the capacity regions with average- or maximum-error criterion [80], which are equivalent in the single-user setting. We shall not address further these issues (see [164, and references therein]) but focus on the simplest cases, and in this respect on the average error probability criterion.

2) Ergodic Capacities: In parallel to the single-user case, the ergodic capacity region of the multiple-user (network) problem is well defined, and assumes the standard interpretation of Shannon capacity region. We shall scan here several cases with CSI available/nonavailable to receiver and/or transmitter. The issues treated here are special cases of the general

model stated in Section II and in Section III-B. We shall mainly focus on the multiple-access channel, and mention briefly the broadcast- and the interference-channel models.

Multiple-access fading channels: Consider the following channel model

$$y_k = \sum_{\ell=1}^{K} a_{\ell k} x_{\ell k} + n_k \qquad (3.4.1)$$

where x_k stands for the channel input of the ℓth (out-of-K) user and $a_{\ell k}$ designates the fading value at discrete-time instant k of user ℓ. The additive-noise sample is designated by n_k, while y_k represents the received signal at discrete-time instant k. We assume that all processes are complex circularly symmetric (proper). The ergodic assumption here means that we assume $\{a_{\ell k}\}$ to be jointly ergodic in the time index k and also independent from user to user (in the index ℓ). We assume that all the input is subjected to equal average-power constraints only, that is, $E|X_\ell|^2 \le P_{\mathrm{av}}, \forall \ell$. First we address the case where CSI is available to the receiver only. Here it means that all fading realizations $\{a_{\ell k}\}$ are available to the receiver, whose intention is to decode *all* K users. The achievable rate region is given here by

$$\sum_{\ell \in \mathcal{B}} R_\ell \le E_\nu \log \left(1 + \frac{\sum_{\ell \in \mathcal{B}} \nu_\ell P_{\mathrm{av}}}{\sigma^2} \right) \qquad (3.4.2)$$

where $\mathcal{B}$ is a subset of the set $\{1, 2, \cdots, K\}$ and where $\nu_\ell = |a_\ell|^2$ designates the received fading power and $\sigma^2 = E|n|^2$ is the noise variance. The irrelevant time index is suppressed here. The expectation E_ν operates over all fading powers $\{\nu_\ell\}$, $\ell \in \mathcal{B}$. The normalized sum rate per user indicates the maximum achievable equal rate per user and it is given by letting $\mathcal{B}$ be the whole set, yielding

$$R = \frac{1}{K} \sum_{\ell=1}^{K} R_\ell = E\nu \frac{1}{K} \log \left(1 + \frac{K P_{\mathrm{av}} \frac{1}{K} \sum_{\ell=1}^{K} \nu_\ell}{\sigma^2} \right). \qquad (3.4.3)$$

It is interesting to note that, by a careful use of the central limit theorem, as K increases we have [255]

$$R \underset{K \to \infty}{\longrightarrow} \frac{1}{K} \log \left(1 + \frac{K P_{\mathrm{av}}}{\sigma^2} \right) \qquad (3.4.4)$$

where the RHS is the result for the regular AWGN channel and, by Jensen's inequality, is an upper bound to R in (3.4.3). We see that the deleterious effect of fading is mitigated by the averaging inter-user effect, which is basically different from time/frequency/space averaging in the single-user case (see, for example, [329]). Equation (3.4.3) already demonstrates the advantage of CDMA channel access techniques over orthogonal TDMA or FDMA. In this simple setting, the orthogonal TDMA or FDMA give rise to a rate per user

$$R_{\mathrm{TDMA}} = E_\nu \frac{1}{K} \log \left(1 + \frac{K P_{\mathrm{av}} \nu}{\sigma^2} \right). \qquad (3.4.5)$$

With TDMA, a user transmits once per K slots with power KP_{av}, while with FDMA a user occupies $1/K$ of the frequency band with equivalent noise of power σ^2/K. We assume that either each frequency slice or time slot undergoes simple flat fading, hence giving rise to (3.4.5). By Jensen's inequality it follows immediately [255], [283] that

$$E \log \left(1 + \frac{1}{K} \sum_{\ell=1}^{K} \alpha_\ell \right)$$

is a nondecreasing function of K for i.i.d. nonnegative random variables $\{\alpha_\ell\}$, $\ell = 1, 2, \cdots, K$, thus establishing the advantage of CDMA over TDMA and FDMA under this fading model. For further details, see [97], [255], [48], [29], [86], and [298].

A natural question that arises here is how orthogonal CDMA compares to the optimum (3.4.3) and to orthogonal TDMA and FDMA (3.4.5). In orthogonal CDMA, all K users use orthogonal direct-sequence spreading (say, by Hadamard (Walsh) bipolar sequences). This method, assuming not only ergodic, but i.i.d. fading also in time, gives rise to the expression [255]

$$R_{OCDMA} = \frac{1}{K^2} E \log \left| \det \left(I^K + \frac{P_{av}}{\sigma^2} A^K A^{K_T} \right) \right| \quad (3.4.6)$$

where the entries of the $K \times K$ matrix A^K is the Schür (elementwise) product of an i.i.d. complex fading matrix and $K \times K$ an orthogonal (e.g., Hadamard) matrix. The $K \times K$ identity matrix is designated by I^K. A surprising result in [255] is that it is not necessarily true that $R_{OCDMA} \geq R_{TDMA}$ for all i.i.d. fading distributions, and an example, for a distribution of fading for which $R_{TDMA} > R_{CDM}$ for $K = 4$, is given in [255, Pt. II]. The reason is that the flat, discrete-time fading processes, *as modeled here*, can never destroy the inherent orthogonality of orthogonal FDMA or orthogonal TDMA, but can do so in the case of orthogonal CDMA. For further details on random CDMA in a flat-fading regime, see [254]. Another model, where orthogonal CDMA, TDMA, and FDMA are interpreted as different ways of using degrees of freedom in a fading regime, is considered in [86], where it is shown that, as far as aggregate rates (or equal rates) are concerned, with symmetric resources all the orthogonal methods (CDMA, TDMA, and FDMA) are equivalent. As it will be mentioned, orthogonal CDMA exhibits advantage over orthogonal TDMA and FDMA in terms of capacity versus outage. It is interesting to examine the model yielding (3.4.6) in terms of capacity versus outage.

We proceed now to the case where the CSI is available at all transmitter sites. That is, $\nu_\ell = |a_\ell|^2$, $\ell = 1, 2, \cdots, K$, is available at each of the transmitters. Here we have another optimization element, viz. power control. In view of the former result for CSI available at the receiver only, it is rather interesting that the optimal power control as found in [155] to optimize the throughput, dictates a TDMA-like approach. For equal average power P_{av} for all users, the user that transmits is the one that enjoys the best fading conditions, and the assigned power depends on that fading value. The instantaneous power assigned to the ℓth user, observing the realization of the fading

powers $\nu_1, \nu_2, \cdots, \nu_K$ is

$$P_{w\ell}(\nu_j, j = 1, 2, \cdots, K) = \begin{cases} \frac{1}{\lambda} - \frac{1}{\nu_\ell}, & \nu_\ell > \lambda, \nu_\ell > \nu_j \quad j \neq \ell \\ 0, & \text{otherwise} \end{cases} \quad (3.4.7)$$

and the associated average rate per user equals

$$C_{TRCSI} = \int_0^\infty \log \left(1 + \nu \left(\frac{1}{\lambda} - \frac{1}{\nu} \right)^+ \right) F^{K-1}(\nu) \, dF(\nu). \quad (3.4.8)$$

Clearly, if the best fading $\max(\nu_\ell, \ell = 1, \cdots, K)$ falls below the threshold λ no user transmits at all, where λ is a constant determined by the average-power constraint as follows:

$$\int_\lambda^\infty \left(\frac{1}{\lambda} - \frac{1}{\nu} \right)^+ F_\nu(\nu)^{K-1} \, dF_\nu(\nu) = P_{av}/\sigma^2. \quad (3.4.9)$$

The power control in (3.4.7) describes a randomized TDMA where indeed only one user at most transmits at each time slot, but the identity of this user is determined randomly by the realization of the fading process. This strategy does not depend on the fading statistics (as far as joint ergodicity is maintained), but for the constant λ which depends on the marginal distribution of the fading energy $F_\nu(\alpha)$, $\alpha \geq 0$, and this optimal strategy is valid also for nonequal average powers, where then the fading values should be properly normalized in (3.4.7) by the respective Lagrange coefficients [155].

In contrast to the single-user case [112], where optimal power control resulted in just a marginal increase in the average rate, here, in the multiple-users realm, the optimal power control yields a substantial growth in capacity, increasing with the number of users K, with respect to the fixed-transmitted-power case with the optimal CDMA strategy [97] also over the Gaussian classical unfaded maximum sum rate [62]. The intuition for this result [155] is that if K is large, then with high probability at least one of the i.i.d. fading powers will be large, providing thus an excellent channel for the respective user at that time instant. Such a channel is in fact advantageous even over the unfaded Gaussian channel with an average power gain.

The extension to frequency-selective channels is quite straightforward under the assumption that the Doppler spread is much smaller than the multipath bandwidth spread ($T_m B_d \ll 1$), decoupling in fact the frequency-selective features and the time variation (assumed to follow an ergodic pattern). The result, as determined in [157], is in fact exactly as in the flat-fading case: however, this strategy is employed per frequency slice (whose bandwidth is of the order of the coherence bandwidth). That is, at any time epoch many users may transmit, but at each band is occupied only by a single user, the one that enjoys the best (fading-wise) conditions at that particular band and time. As in the single-user case, since statistically all frequencies are equivalent, the ergodic capacity remains invariant to whether the channel exhibits flat- or selective-fading features. However, in the selective-fading case the average waiting time for a user to transmit reduces, as now for a wideband system there are many frequency bands (about the total bandwidth divided by the coherence bandwidth) over which transmission may take place. Algorithms to control the waiting time associated with this random TDMA accessing over the flat-fading channel are suggested and analyzed in [29] and discussed in the following. It is shown, contrary to the single-user case, that optimal power control, made possible when ideal CSI is available to all transmitters, yields considerable advantages with respect to the ergodic throughputs for many users, when fixed power is used (optimal for CSI available to receiver only). The optimal power allocation is no more than the extension of the "water filling" idea to this setting, where in the frequency-selective case water filling is done in both time and frequency. See also some results by [50] on this matter, and for the first extension (of water filling) to the multiple-user case over fixed intersymbol-affected Gaussian channels [56].

While [155], [157] considered the throughput (sum rate), in a remarkable work [43] the polymatroidal structure of the multiaccess Gaussian capacity region was exploited so as to provide an elegant characterization of the capacity region along with the optimal power allocation that achieves the boundary points of this region. The results are derived for the flat and frequency-dispersive cases, under the standard slow-time-variation assumption. A variety of other most interesting and multiple-access models exists [64], where one of the most relevant for practical applications is the "L-out-of-K multiple-access channel" model. Here out of K potential users, at most L are simultaneously active, and the achievable reliable rate region, irrespective of the identity of the active users, is of interest. The information-theoretic classification of this channel, in which the set of active users is random (but upper-bounded by L), is standard: in fact, it falls under the purview of normal channel networks (we adhere here to the terminology of [64]) (see also [217] for some additional results including error exponents). This model has been investigated in [64], [14], [48], [53], in combination with CDMA, where [48] focuses on the fading effect. Parallel to [97], it is demonstrated that CDMA is inherently advantageous over FDMA in the presence of fading.

Up to now we have assumed a fixed number of users transmitting to a receiver. In common models for communication (network) systems, a user accesses the channel randomly, as it gets a message to be transmitted [95], [28], [84]. The random access of users is a fundamental issue which is not yet satisfactorily treated in terms of information-theoretic concepts [95], [28],[84]. Indeed, the L-out-of-K model discussed is motivated here in a sense by random-access aspects, but it does not capture the fact that the number of transmitting users might itself be random and not fixed. Rather, it resorts to an upper bound to the number of active users (this is its maximum possible number L), which dictates in a sense of worst case achievable rates. Here we demonstrate originally this situation where it is assumed that K—the number of transmitting users—is an integer-valued positive random variable known both to the transmitters and the receiver.[12] We further resort to the case of CSI for all active users available at the receiver site

only. The achievable throughput TR_{RURCSI} (where RURCSI stands for Random Users Receiver Channel State Information) is given by

$$TR_{\mathrm{RURCSI}} = E_K E_{\underline{\nu}} \log \left(1 + \frac{P_{\mathrm{av}}}{\sigma_2} \sum_{i=1}^{K} \nu_i \right) \qquad (3.4.10)$$

where we have explicitly designated by E_K the expectation with respect to the number of users. By using [255, Pt. II, Appendix 2, Lemma] we see that

$$TR_{\mathrm{RURCSI}} \leq T_{\mathrm{RAURCSI}} = E_{\underline{\nu}} \log \left(1 + \frac{P_{\mathrm{av}}}{\sigma_2} \sum_{i=1}^{\overline{E(K)}} \nu_i \right) \qquad (3.4.11)$$

where T_{RAURCSI} stands for the throughput associated with the average[13] number of users $E(K)$.

In many situations we are interested in the average rate per user. While in the case of a fixed number of transmitting users, the maximum equal rate per user is given by the throughput divided by the number of users, this is no more the case when K is random. The maximal equal rate per user is given here by

$$R_{\mathrm{RURCSI}} = E_K E_{\underline{\nu}} \frac{1}{K} \log \left(1 + \frac{P_{\mathrm{av}}}{\sigma_2} \sum_{i=1}^{K} \nu_i \right). \qquad (3.4.12)$$

Now using the convexity of $x^{-1} \log (1+x)$, in a similar proof as in [255, Pt. II, Appendix 2, Lemma], it is verified that

$$R_{\mathrm{RURCSI}} \geq R_{\mathrm{AURCSI}} = E_{\underline{\nu}} \frac{1}{\overline{E(K)}} \log \left(1 + \frac{P_{\mathrm{av}}}{\sigma_2} \sum_{i=1}^{\overline{E(K)}} \nu_i \right). \qquad (3.4.13)$$

This demonstrates the rather surprising fact that random accessing helps in terms of average achievable rates per user when compared to average performance. This was also concluded in [255] for another setting where the random number of faded interfering users (other cell users) was considered. Clearly, it follows by (3.4.11) and (3.4.13) that

$$\overline{E(K)} R_{\mathrm{RURCSI}} \geq R_{\mathrm{AURCSI}}. \qquad (3.4.14)$$

Here we have demonstrated only a glimpse of the surprising features which are associated with information-theoretic consideration of random accessing in multiple-access channels in general and fading MAC in particular (for more examples see [255]). These interesting observations motivate serious study into this yet immature branch of information theory [95], [84]. Another possibility is to consider the average rate per a *specific* user, where this rate is measured only while that user is active. Under the assumption of all individual users independently accessing or not the channel, the average rate is given by (3.4.12) with K replaced by $K+1$, accounting for the fact that the inspected user is active by definition. There are different variants to the problem, and the expression to be used depends on the interpretation. See [9] for another simplistic model where other users are considered as additional noise.

The multiple-user case gives rise to different cases in terms of the available CSI. We shall demonstrate this by the

---

[12] This information is supplied, for example, by a control channel in cellular communication. This assumption can be mitigated for relatively long duration of transmission, which facilitates, for example, the transmission of a reliable "user identification" sequence to the receiver, at negligible cost in rate.

[13] $\overline{E(K)}$ stands for the upper bounding closest integer for $E(K)$, that is, $E(K) - 1 \leq E(K) \leq \overline{E(K)}$.

following example. The results of (3.4.7)–(3.4.9) describe the situation where full CSI is available to the receiver and to *each* of the user's transmitters facilitating thus a *centralized* power control strategy. Another case of interest, briefly studied in [331], considers the noncentralized power control. Here, each transmitter has access only to that fading variable that affects its own signal. Thus the power control can be based just on that knowledge. In [127], it was demonstrated that for the simple case of fading random variables that take on discrete values from a set of finite cardinality and for asymptotically many users, the optimal strategy tends to the extremal case that transmission takes place only if the fading power assumes its maximum possible value. It was also claimed that under these asymptotic conditions decentralized power control entails no inherent degradation (see also [126]). Randomized decentralized power control strategies are addressed in [249].

In general, no ideal CSI is available and only partial information is accessible to the decoder/encoder. This case can again be treated in a standard way in the multiple-user setting in parallel to the single-user situation, as has been discussed in the previous section. This falls within the framework treated in [69], for example, in case of partial CSI (denoted by $\hat{a}_{\ell k}$) available at the receiver only. The standard interpretation, where the received signal is interpreted as the tuple $\{y_k, \hat{a}_{\ell k}\}$, yields the desired results within the standard multiple-access Shannon theory [62] under ergodic assumptions.

The interesting and important case of multiple-access fading channel model, as given in (3.4.1), with no CSI available to either transmitter or receiver, gained relatively little attention, contrary to the single-user case. In [185] some inequalities of average mutual information were used to assess the effect of not knowing exactly the CSI for the single- and multiple-user case. For the multiple-user case, interference-cancellation techniques are advocated, even where CSI is not precise. In [186], the implications of unknown CSI are assessed via bounds. The lower bound is of the type of (3.3.55) with $\hat{a} = E(a)$, which associates the unknown part with equivalent additive Gaussian noise. Mismatched metric is often used in practice, where CSI is not precisely known or when the matched metric is too complicated to be efficiently implemented. For results on mismatched metric applied to the multiple-access channel, see [162], [161], and also [164]. In [161], the optimal Gaussian-based metric in a fading environment with ideal CSI at the receiver is studied, and the achievability of the Gaussian fading channel capacity region is established for non-Gaussian additive noise under some ergodic assumptions (see [164] for more details). In [23], the binary-input multiple-access channel is considered for a Rayleigh fading and the random phase impairments. The fading or random phase processes are assumed to be i.i.d., and it is shown that in both cases the sum rate (throughput) is bounded and does not increase logarithmically with the number of users (as is the case in the Gaussian multiple access channel). In [282], the i.i.d. Rayleigh fading multiple-access channel is considered, and the asymptotic (with the number of users) throughput is determined for the case of unrestricted bandwidth.

We focus now on the simple model in (3.4.1) with all fading CSI $\{a_{\ell k}\}$ i.i.d. in both $\ell = 1, 2, \cdots, K$, and the discrete-time

index k. As usual, we consider the average-power constraint and are interested here in the sum-rate (throughput), which is equivalent to K times the maximal equal rate per user. A rather surprising result is described in [259], based on reinterpreting the results of [176] where the number of transmit antennas is taken to be K—the number of users. This result demonstrates the optimality of the TDMA channel accessing technique here, where each user transmits $1/K$ of the time in its assigned time slot and when transmitting the average power used is KP_{av}. The throughput is then given by the solution of [87] where the per-user SNR is KP_{av}/σ^2, and where the optimal capacity-achieving input distribution is discrete. It is instructive to learn that, while for available CSI at the receiver the CDMA channel accessing technique is advantageous in a fading environment [97], TDMA prevails in the case of no CSI. If CSI is available both to transmitters and receiver (in a centralized manner), again a TDMA-like (i.e., randomized TDMA) becomes optimal [155], where the randomization is governed by the rule allowing only the one enjoying the most favorable fading conditions to transmit.

For ideal CSI available to the receiver and/or transmitters, the memory structure of the fading process is irrelevant for capacity calculations, which depend only on the single-dimensional marginal statistics. This is not the case when CSI is absent: here, the results depend strongly on the fading memory. The block-fading channel model, as introduced in [210], is readily extended to the multiple-user case by assuming that the fading coefficients stay unvaried for blocks of length ΔT_c and are independent for different blocks. In this case, the mixed CDMA/TDMA strategy where at each time epoch ΔT_c users are active simultaneously, is studied in [259], where for ΔT_c the CDMA technique takes over, and all K users transmit simultaneously.

3) Notion of Capacities and Related Properties: In parallel to the single-user case, the ergodic capacity or capacity region of the multiple-access channel, though important, comprises just a small part of the relevant information-theoretic treatment of meaningful expressions which indicate on the information transfer capabilities of the information network operating under fading conditions. We will first concisely extend the view of the single-user case to the multiple-access case, accounting specifically for capacity versus outage, delay-limited capacity, and a compound/broadcast approach. Then, the very nature of the multiterminal/multiple-user realm is shown to give rise to very relevant information-theoretic models, to be addressed briefly. Some of the examples to be considered are the broadcast and the interference channels, operating under fading conditions. Due to space and scope limitations, the presentation here will be very short and restricted to very few (mainly recent) works.

Capacity versus outage: The notion of capacity versus outage is easily extended to the multiple-access case. Some of the early references treating this problem are [49] and [50]. In [49], the outage probability for each user in the symmetric K-user setting is associated with the required average power for operation at a given rate. In [50], the corresponding outage probability of the optimized signature waveform is discussed, which turns out to be overlapping in frequency in the fading two-user case. Capacity versus outage for orthogonal accessing techniques (CDMA, TDMA, and FDMA) is discussed in [86], where the advantage of TDMA is demonstrated.

The multiple-access compound-channel model treated by [124] is fundamental in the interpretation of the capacity-versus-outage region as it is intimately connected with the ε-capacity region discussed in [124]. In parallel to the single-user case for invariant fading ($B_d = 0$), we associate with a rate vector $\underline{R}$ (whose dimension is equal to the number of users $-K$) a set $\Lambda_{\underline{R}}$. A vector parameter $\underline{A}$, standing for all relevant fading realizations, belongs to $\Lambda_{\underline{R}}$ provided that $\underline{A}$ gives rise to $\underline{R}$ using the standard multiple-access capacity-region equation. The associated outage probability for this vector $\underline{R}$ is designated by $P_{\text{outage}}(\underline{R}) = \text{Prob}(\underline{A} \notin \Lambda_{\underline{R}})$. For no channel dynamics ($B_d = 0$), the capacity-achieving distribution with CSI nonavailable to the transmitter is Gaussian, and remains the same for all fading realizations. Otherwise, in more general models of fading, or when partial CSI is available to the transmitter, Λ_R should be interpreted as the largest set, with a meaning similar to that of the single-user case discussed before. If ideal CSI is available to the transmitter, the associated compound channel capacity is the capacity with the worst case fading realization in the class Λ_R, as then the transmitter may adapt its input statistics to achieve the actual capacity per fading state realization. Further work on this notion in the realm of multiple-access fading channels is called for, so as to encompass cases of frequency selectivity and allowing for time variation of the fading parameters, yet not satisfying the ergodic assumptions. Studies paralleling [43], which treats the single-user case, are also needed as to assess theoretically the value, expected to be significant, of CSI at transmitter, given in terms of capacity region versus outage, in the multiple-user setting.

The capacity versus outage of the Knopp–Humblet [155] optimized accessing algorithm in the flat-fading MAC is discussed in [29], where it is assessed in terms of the distribution of the reliable transmitted rate in a window of L-time slots (say). A study of the capacity-versus-outage approach in the interesting L-out-of-K multiple-access channel model is conducted by [48]. It is demonstrated that the advantage of CDMA over FDMA in the symmetric two-user case is greater in terms of capacity versus outage than in terms of ergodic capacity. See also [86] for the capacity–outage performance of various orthogonal accessing methods in the fading regime.

Delay-limited capacity and related notions: The notion of delay-limited capacity is thoroughly investigated in [127], where a full solution is given for the case of CSI available to both receiver as well as transmitters. In parallel to the single-user case, the delay-limited capacity region is achievable irrespective of the dynamics of the fading. The polymatroid structure of the underlying problem is exploited to show that the optimal decoding is, in fact, successive interference cancellation [62], [315]. The optimal power allocation is such that it facilitates successive decoding with the proper ordering, which has explicitly been found in [128]. In a simple symmetrical case, where all users are subjected to the same average-power constraints and where we are interested in the delay-limited throughput (that is, equal rate C_{DL} per user),

the result for the complex fading channel (3.4.1) takes on a simple form

$$(e^{C_{\text{DL}}} - 1) \int_0^\infty [1 + F_\nu(\tau)(e^{C_{\text{DL}}} - 1)]^{K-1} \frac{dF_\nu(\tau)}{\tau} \, d\tau = \frac{P_{\text{av}}}{\sigma^2}$$

(3.4.15)

where $F_\nu(\tau)$ stands for the probability distribution function of the fading power $\nu = E|a|^2$ assumed to be independent for all K users. The optimal power allocation is geometric [315]

$$P_k(\nu_1, \nu_2, \cdots, \nu_K) = \frac{e^{(K-k)C_{\text{DL}}}}{\nu_k}$$

(3.4.16)

where we assume proper ordering of the user according to the fading power such that $\nu_1 > \nu_2 > \cdots > \nu_K$.

The study [127] introduces also a notion of a statistically based delay-limited multiple-user capacity. This notion requires no power control at the transmitters, and the achievable rate region is guaranteed via the statistical multiplexing of many independent users, which are affected by independent fading processes. For any desirable performance threshold as the average error probability, there exists a code of sufficient length n and a sufficiently large number of users, such that the average probability of a decoding error does not exceed the prescribed threshold (small though it may be), provided the rates belong to the statistical delay-limited capacity region. That limiting ($K \to \infty$) region is, in fact, independent of the realization of the fading process. Clearly, this notion inherently relies upon the existance of multiple users and has no single-user counterpart. A problem related to the delay-limited multiple-access capacity is the "call admission" and "minimum resource (power) distribution" problem [128]. In the latter context under given average power constraints and a desired bit rate vector $\underline{R}$ (which should be admissible—in the call admission problem—that is, it should belong to the associated delay-limited capacity region), the minimum possible power that achieves $\underline{R}$ is sought. The criteria to determine the minimum power is minmax, where the max is taken over the users and the min over respective powers. The algorithm in [128] for the optimal resource allocating solves simultaneously also the call admission problem. Related results in [197] address another criterion, the minimum transmit energy for a given rate vector and given realizations of the fading (referred to in [197] as channel attenuations). It is shown similarly to [128] that the best energy assignments give rise to successive decoding. This conclusion does not extend to receiver diversity.

While the ergodic capacity of the sample flat-fading MAC model with fading CSI available to both transmitters and receiver gives rise to the optimized centralized power controlled random TDMA approach [155], the random nature arises since only the user that enjoys the best fading conditions transmits, provided that the fading value is above a threshold. Yet, on the average, each of the K-users occupies exactly K^{-1} of the time slots, as in TDMA. Contrary to standard TDMA transmission is done in a random fashion, thus causing inherent increased delays: in fact, a certain user may wait a long time before he enjoys the most favorable fading conditions, and hence transmits. In the frequency-selective case [157], having more opportunities to transmit, this undesired prolonging of delay is mitigated to some extent. In [29], modified access algorithms were suggested to alleviate the increased delay associated with the optimized accessing [155]. The first version [29] defines a delay parameter of L slots, where it is demanded that all $K \leq L$ users should transmit within a window of L slots. If this is satisfied at a certain epoch, the transmitting user will be the one enjoying the best fading conditions as in [155], and if it is not satisfied, the transmitting user will be the one satisfying the maximum L-slot delay constraint independently of its fading realization..

Another version of a delay-reducing algorithm [29] examines a standard K-slot TDMA: in each time slot it is checked whether the user assigned to that slot has transmitted in a moving past L-slots delay window. If the answer is positive, then the user that enjoys the best fading condition, irrespective of its index as in [155], transmits. Otherwise, only the user with the same index as the current time slot (as in regular TDMA) is allowed to transmit. In [29] these variants of a delay-reducing algorithm are analyzed in terms of average rate versus the delay constraint L, relying on Markov and innovation properties of the channel-access algorithm. Power control is also incorporated and compared to the results of fixed transmitted power. The capacity versus outage of the proposed delay-reducing algorithms is discussed in [29], and compared to these features in the optimized (without any delay constraints) algorithm of [155]. As in the single-user case, the delay-limited capacity is associated with the multiple-access compound capacity [124], where the channel's statistical characterization is uniquely defined by the fading parameters, constituting here the parameter space of the compound channel.

The broadcast approach: While fading broadcast models are treated separately, the extensions of the expected capacity [61], [247] to the multiple-user case is of interest [247]. The basic model is a combined multiple-access and broadcast channel where several (K) users convey simultaneously information at different rates to M receivers. The general vector capacity region of the multiple-access/broadcast channel has not yet been fully characterized. In [247], a convenient suboptimal approach is taken, extending the single-user strategy. That is, each user transmits simultaneously a continuum of different information rates. The receiver is parametrized by a vector of K fading uses, where each affects independently the associated transmitted signal. The realization of this fading vector determines the instantaneous rate region (for the K users) that the receiver can reliably decode using the successive interference-cancellation technique. The power distribution of the transmitters having no access to the fading-coefficients realization can be optimized to maximize the expected capacity per user (all users are assumed symmetric), in a fashion similar to the single-user case [247]. In this model, as in the single-user case, no CSI is available to the transmitter, and the result holds for both given and unavailable CSI at the receiver when the fading parameters stay constant over the whole transmission. As commented before for the single-user case, this approach addresses the expected capacity region which combines broadcast and compound channels

[61], [247] when a prior on the compound-channel parameter set is available.

4) Other Information-Theoretic Models: The Compound, Composite, and Arbitrarily Varying Channel Models: In parallel to the single-user case, the compound and the composite MAC are useful notions and as such the rather rich material treating these models [164] is of direct relevance. The composite MAC gives rise to rigorous treatment of capacity region distributions (in the sense of broadcast approach [247]) and clearly coding theorems, in such a setting, are of interest. The results of [124] based on information spectrum provide a very appealing approach for deriving coding theorems in this kind of problems, the MAC being the natural extension of the single-user formalism.

In the multiple-access case, arbitrarily varying channels (AVC's) play an even greater role than their single-user counterpart, as here the existence of additional users induces new interesting dimensions. Also here, as in the single-user case, we advocate the introduction of state constraints in addition to the input-average-power (or other) constraints. This extension, formulated in a straightforward way similarly to the single-user case, is especially interesting in the multiple-access case. Not only may it give a better, i.e., less pessimistic, model for practical applications, but, as argued for the single-user case, this model also introduces the notion of AVC capacity region versus outage, where now the outage probability is associated with the probability that the state sequence (fading realizations in our setting) does not satisfy the assigned constraints. This example also demonstrates an interesting new features of this information-theoretic problem, as for example, the state-constrained AVC capacity region is nonconvex in general [117]. The possibly different results for deterministic versus random codes as well as average and maximum error probability criteria (see [164] for details) implies here operational practical insight of preferable signaling/coding approaches depending on the different service-quality measures and planning. As detailed in [164], there are many yet unresolved problems in the context of multiple-user AVC, even in the time-invariant unfaded regime.

5) Signaling Strategies and Channel-Accessing Protocols: As mentioned before, the network (multiple-user) information-theoretic approach to the fading channel inherently provides new facets to the problem as it highlights various options of channel accessing. This is not unique to the fading channel: in fact, many of the most interesting relatively recent techniques were developed for the classical multiple-access AWGN channel. In this subsection we shall briefly describe some of the interesting accessing techniques which have been attracting interest for the fading environment.

CDMA, TDMA, and FDMA: The classical techniques of CDMA, TDMA, and FDMA are commonplace in a multiple-access channel model without or with fading. While for nonfaded channels orthogonal channel accessing, which guarantees no interuser interference, meets the throughput capacity limit, under average-power constraints [62], as we have seen in the previous section, this is no more so when fading is present. It was demonstrated, for example, that CDMA is advantageous [97] for known CSI at the receiver, while

TDMA is preferred when no CSI is available [259]. Under the standard terminology, by CDMA we mean full coding, that is, all redundancy being used by coding. Other schemes, where direct-sequence spreading is combined with coding, that is, when the available redundancy is split between spreading and coding, are of primary theoretical and practical interest. Extensive study of this issue has been undertaken, as evidenced in the small sample of references [234], [179], [180], [235], [316], [305], [306], [134], [318], [181], [301], [307], [104], [299], [308], and references therein. Characterization of the properties of these schemes, which still maintain optimality in terms of throughput on the AWGN channel, was addressed in [234]. It was shown that under symmetric power allocation spreading with processing gain no larger than K—the number of users and sequences satisfying the Welch bound—preserves optimality. For the case where the processing gain is exactly K or larger, orthogonal spreading sequences maintain optimality. For general results with asymmetric power constraints, see [547].

The question now is, what happens in a fading regime? In [255] it is shown, for example, that when fading is present orthogonal DS-CDMA is not always (for any i.i.d. fading distribution) advantageous over TDMA, a somewhat counterintuitive result. In another model [86], where degrees of freedom are distributed in different fashions for orthogonal TDMA, FDMA, and CDMA, all three orthogonal accessing techniques remain equivalent under the fading regime. Many misconceptions appear in reference to fading, one of which is the conclusion that fading can be absolutely mitigated by adequately complex coding systems (see, for example, [25] and [36]). Fading can be mitigated only under special conditions, for example, in wideband systems [153], [94]. In [179] and [235], a pragmatic approach is suggested for coding for the multiple-access channel. The users employ in a sense a concatenated coding scheme where the outer code is in fact a modulation or "partial modulation" in the terminology of [180] and its function is to separate at the decoder the users into groups. In in each group, detection is made on the basis of a "single-user" approach. The classical example for this setting is direct-sequence spread spectrum (DS-SS) where the spreading acts as an inner "partial modulator," and the despreading as the corresponding decoder (pre-processor). In [179], it is argued that the partial modulator/demodulator central function is to create a good single-user channel for the coding system. Separating the burden of decoding the users between the demodulator, which demodulates (decodes) the inner modulation code which is to account for the presence of multiple users, and the standard decoder for the code, is the issue of [235], where the linear minimum mean-square-error demodulator is advocated (see also [254], [51], and references therein). Multiuser information-theoretic aspects of DS-SS coded systems has been thoroughly examined [254] (see also [308]). Many studies examine exactly the approach, advocated in [179], [134], and [235], where the simple multiuser decoding is used and a "single-user" channel is created for the desired user. In [254], for example, the matched filter, decorrelator, and minimum mean-square-error (MMSE) linear demodulators are considered, and the performance in terms of throughput or bandwidth efficiency is compared with the optimal detector. Random signature sequences modeling the practically appealing cases of long-signature sequences spreading many coded symbols are stressed. Other nonlinear front-end detectors, as decision-feedback decorrelator and MMSE processors, were also addressed (see [196] and [254, references]) and shown to be very efficient. The literature on the information-theoretic aspects of this issue is so vast that the references here, along with the reference lists therein, provide hardly more than a glimpse on this issue (see [308] and references therein for more details).

Much less work has been done on the fading regime. In [254], two fading models were addressed: the homogeneous model affects each chip independently, while the slow-fading model operates on the coded symbols, where that fading process is either correlative or i.i.d. (in case of ideal interleaving, for example). The results in [254] demonstrate the inherent asymptotic robustness of the random spreading coded system to any homogeneous fading, and this approach guarantees asymptotically full mitigation of the homogeneous fading effect. It is also pointed out that the difference between optimal spreading and random spreading measured by the information-theoretic predicted bandwidth efficiency diminishes even more in the homogeneous fading regime. There are many misconceptions relating to the information-theoretic aspects of coded DS-SS, random versus deterministic CDMA, the role of multiuser detection in this setting, and the like. Some of these misconceptions are dispelled in [307] (see also [254], [308], and references therein).

The struggle to achieve the full promise of information theory in the network multiple-user systems by adhering to the more familiar single-user techniques gave rise not only to the previously discussed combined coded DS-SS with essentially single-user decoder proceeded by simple multiple-user demodulators, but also led to a variety of novel interesting and stimulating channel-accessing techniques. These techniques, a small part of which will be shortly scanned in what follows, are not necessarily connected to fading channels. They do, however, operate in an optimal or at least a rather efficient fashion also in the presence of fading.

The single-user approach: The strong practical appeal of the single-user approach and the relatively large experience with capacity-approaching coding and modulation methods in an AWGN and fading environment [27], [90], [60] motivate vigorous search for efficient single-user coding techniques which do not compromise optimality in the multiple-access regime.

One of the first observations, which extends directly to the fading channel, is the successive-cancellation idea of [62] and [333]. This idea is based on the observation that the corner points (vertices) of the capacity region (a pentagon) are achieved by a single-user system and successive cancellation of the already reliable decoded data streams. The convex combination of the corner points can be achieved by time-sharing points in the capacity region, We shall present this well-known simple procedure for the two-user flat-fading ergodic model with channel-state information available at the receiver. This special case of (3.4.1) reads here as

$$y = a_1 x_1 + a_2 x_2 + n \qquad (3.4.17)$$

where $\nu_1 = |a_1|^2, \nu_2 = |a_2|^2$ are the corresponding fading powers, and $\sigma^2 = E(|n|^2)$ is the noise power. Both users are average power constrained to P_{av}. The two corner points are

$$R_1 = I(y, a_1, a_2; x_1) = E_{\nu_1, \nu_2} \log \left(1 + \frac{\nu_1 P}{\sigma^2 + \nu_2 P} \right)$$

$$R_2 = I(y, a_1, a_2; x_2 | x_1) = E_{\nu_2} \log \left(1 + \frac{\nu_2 P}{\sigma^2} \right)$$
$$\qquad (3.4.18)$$

$$R_1 = I(y, a_1, a_2; x_1 | x_2) = E_{\nu_1} \log \left(1 + \frac{\nu_1 P}{\sigma^2} \right)$$

$$R_2 = I(y, a_1, a_2; x_2) = E_{\nu_1, \nu_2} \log \left(1 + \frac{\nu_2 P}{\nu_1 P + \sigma^2} \right).$$
$$\qquad (3.4.19)$$

The corner points in (3.4.18) or (3.4.19) are achieved by a single-user approach where the first user (1 or 2 for (3.4.18) or (3.4.19), respectively) is decoded, interpreting the second user as Gaussian noise. Both users employ Gaussian codebooks, mandatory to achieve the pentagon capacity region [62]. After the first user has been reliably decoded, it is remodulated and fully canceled; then the second user, impaired only by the AWGN, is decoded. By time sharing between the two corner points (3.4.18) and (3.4.19), all the rate points on the capacity region pentagon are achievable

$$R_1 \le E_{\nu_1} \log \left(1 + \frac{\nu_1 P_{\mathrm{av}}}{\sigma^2} \right)$$

$$R_2 \le E_{\nu_2} \log \left(1 + \frac{\nu_2 P_{\mathrm{av}}}{\sigma^2} \right)$$

$$R_1 + R_2 \le E_{\nu_1, \nu_2} \log \left(1 + (\nu_1 + \nu_2) \frac{P_{\mathrm{av}}}{\sigma_2} \right). \qquad (3.4.20)$$

Time sharing requires mutual time-frame synchronization, which imposes undesirable restrictions on the system which are often physically impossible to meet, as in the case of the spatially spread communication system.

The elegant rate-splitting idea of [232] demonstrates that any point on the asynchronous capacity region (that is, the rate region, excluding the convex-hull operation [62]) without the need of time sharing and hence not requiring synchronism among users. The idea of [232] works as is for the fading channel with ideal CSI available to the receiver [230], [231]. This is demonstrated in the following for the simple case of the two-user fading-channel model given in (3.4.17), with known CSI at the receiver. The first user splits into two virtual users with corresponding power Δ and $P_{\mathrm{av}} - \Delta$, operating at rates $R_1^{(1)}$ and $R_1^{(2)}$ correspondingly. The second user operates regularly (no rate splitting) with power P_{av} at rate R_2. The successive cancellation mechanism first decodes the rate $R_1^{(1)}$ of user 1, then R_2 of user 2 following perfect cancellation of the interference of power Δ. Finally, rate $R_1^{(2)}$ of user 1 gets decoded after an ideal cancellation of the interference of power Δ and P_{av} corresponding to the rate streams $R_1^{(1)}$ and R_2 of users one and two, respectively. The corresponding equations

specify the rates

$$R_1^{(1)} = E_{\nu_1, \nu_2} \log \left(1 + \frac{\nu_1 \Delta}{\sigma^2 + \nu_2 P_{\mathrm{av}} + \nu_1 (P_{\mathrm{av}} - \Delta)} \right)$$

$$R_1^{(2)} = E_{\nu_1} \log \left(1 + \frac{\nu_1 (P_{\mathrm{av}} - \Delta)}{\sigma^2} \right)$$

$$R_2 = E_{\nu_1, \nu_2} \log \left(1 + \frac{\nu_2 P_{\mathrm{av}}}{\sigma^2 + \nu_1 (P_{\mathrm{av}} - \Delta)} \right). \qquad (3.4.21)$$

The combined rate of user one is $R_1^{(1)} + R_1^{(2)}$ and the rate of user two is R_2. It is easily verified, by picking $\Delta \in [0, P_{\mathrm{av}}]$, that the whole region as in (3.4.20) can be achieved. This is done with no interuser synchronism, which is an important feature in practical multiple-access channels. In [232] it is shown that in the K-user case all but one user have to split into virtual double users, thus transforming the problem to a $(2K - 1)$-user multiple-access channel, for which any rate in the region of the original K-user problem (3.4.21) is a vertex point in the $2K - 1$ capacity region, giving rise to successive cancellation. This important idea extends directly to dispersive channels with frequency-selective fading with perfect CSI at the receiver [230]. In fact, this idea motivates different power-control strategies in a multicell scenario [231], [45], [323] as will be discussed in reference to cellular communications models. The rate-splitting idea is extended in [115] to the general discrete memoryless channel, where in this case the two virtual users are combined via some general function to yield the channel input signal of each actual user. This idea impacts also the Gaussian channel with or without fading, and in fact gives rise to an interesting general intrauser time-sharing technique [116], [229] achieving again the asynchronous capacity region with no need for any interuser time synchronization. This interesting idea of [116] is demonstrated for our simple two-user AWGN fading channel. Again, the first user is split into two data streams which now access the channel *by time sharing*, and not in full synchronism as in the standard successive cancellation procedure [62]. The corresponding rates are

$$R_1^{(1)} = E_{\nu_1, \nu_2} \log \left(1 + \frac{\nu_1 P_{\mathrm{av}}}{\sigma^2 + \nu_2 P_{\mathrm{av}}} \right)$$

$$R_1^{(2)} = E_{\nu_1} \log \left(1 + \frac{\nu_1 P_{\mathrm{av}}}{\sigma^2} \right) \qquad (3.4.22)$$

which access the channel via time sharing at rates of $1 - \lambda$ and λ, respectively. The coded symbols corresponding to $R_1^{(1)}$ and $R_1^{(2)}$ are ideally interleaved according to their respective activity rate fractions $1 - \lambda$ and λ, respectively. The second user signals at the rate

$$R_2 = \lambda E_{\nu_1, \nu_2} \log \left(1 + \frac{\nu_2 P_{\mathrm{av}}}{\sigma^2 + \nu_1 P_{\mathrm{av}}} \right)$$

$$+ (1 - \lambda) E_{\nu_2} \log \left(1 + \frac{\nu_2 P_{\mathrm{av}}}{\sigma^2} \right). \qquad (3.4.23)$$

The first user operates at the rate

$$R_1 = (1 - \lambda) R_1^{(1)} + \lambda R_1^{(2)}$$

$$= (1 - \lambda) E_{\nu_1, \nu_2} \log \left(1 + \frac{\nu_1 P_{\mathrm{av}}}{\sigma^2 + \nu^2 P_{\mathrm{av}}} \right)$$

$$+ \lambda E_{\nu_1} \log \left(1 + \frac{\nu_1 P_{\mathrm{av}}}{\sigma^2} \right). \qquad (3.4.24)$$

608

The decoding is accomplished by first decoding the rate $R_1^{(1)}$ of user one during λ of the time where user two with its power P_{av} acts as an interferer. Then user two is decoded and that is possible by noticing that this user operates at two noise levels (interpreted as channel states). A fraction of $1 - \lambda$ is the only noise of the AWGN of power σ^2 (since the interference of power P_{av} which corresponds to $R_1^{(1)}$ is absolutely canceled) and a fraction of λ at noise level $\sigma^2 + P_{\text{av}}$ (as then user two is the first one to be decoded experiencing the full interference of user one operating at rate $R_1^{(2)}$). No synchronism between users is needed, as user two operates in a two-state noise channel where its states *are available to the receiver* only, and the ergodic conditions are in principle satisfied by the ideal interleaving employed for user one. Finally, the rate $R_1^{(2)}$ of user one is decoded, where the interference of the already reliably decoded user two is ideally canceled. This elegant idea facilitates achieving the full capacity region in (3.4.20), by changing the time-sharing parameter λ in the interval $\lambda \in [0, 1]$, and that without any common interuser time sharing. This contrasts with the original Cover–Wyner successive cancellation (see (3.4.18) and (3.4.19)), which requires interuser frame synchronization to achieve the full capacity region (3.4.20). This appealing method, which in fact can be viewed as a special case of the general function needed in [115], is extended in [229] to the K-user case, allowing for a generalized time-sharing modeled by a random switch, the position of which is revealed to the receiver. It is shown that also in the general case each of the $K - 1$ users should be split to no more than two virtual time-shared users, while one of the K users does not have to be split at all. The framework of [229] is straightforwardly applicable to the fading MAC. Another generalization, where only $\frac{1}{2} M \log_2 M + M$ single-user codes suffice to achieve any point of the AWGN M-user capacity region is reported in [334]. This is in contrast with the M^2 codes needed in the direct Wyner–Cover approach [333], and the idea extends straightforwardly to the fading channel with CSI available at the receiver.

Successive cancellation plays a major role in network information theory from both theoretical and practical viewpoints. So far we have addressed some works [62], [315], [116], [229], [297], [197], [232], [230], [231], [115], [333], [334] which demonstrate the theoretical optimality of this method in a rather general multiple-access framework, which also accounts for flat as well as dispersive fading channels [230], [231]. The practical appeal of these methods stems from their "single-user"-based rationale, and they provide an alternative to classical orthogonal channel-access techniques such as TDMA, FDMA, and orthogonal CDMA. As discussed before, in a fading environment the orthogonal accessing technique may exhibit performance inferior to fully wideband nonorthogonal (general CDMA) accessing techniques [97].

Successive cancellation plays a fundamental role in many other information-theoretic models, as in the L-out-of-K model introduced previously. For example, [53] discusses how the L-out-of-K capacity region can be achieved by successive cancellation (stripping) using M shells of rates. Each of the K possible users is divided into M data streams, transmitted in different shells, where each shell is detected with a single-user

detector, while successive interference cancellation is used for intershell interference reduction. While optimality is achieved for $M \to \infty$, performance close to optimal was demonstrated for finite M. This channel-accessing procedure is designed for cases where no interuser synchronization is present and no user ranking can be implemented. This precludes standard successive cancellation methods, as in [232], or time-sharing alternatives [116], [229]. These methods can be straightforwardly used in a fading regime, although this was not directly addressed in [53]. In [127], it has been shown that the optimal power control which achieves the delay-limited capacity region (with CSI available to transmitter and receiver) implies a successive interference cancellation configuration, which is a consequence of the underlying polymatroidal structure of the delay-limited capacity region. Successive cancellation is relevant to minimal-power regions which corresponds to given rates. In [128] such a power region is examined, where the rates are based on the delay-limited capacity notion, which are maintained at any fading realization, under a given average power constraint. It is shown that the optimal power strategy with a minmax power allocation criterion manifests itself so that the rates are amenable to successive decoding. A similar result is reported in [197], where the minimum transmit energy for a given rate vector with different and constant attenuation is considered. While for a single receiver the best energy assignment gives rise to successive decoding, this is no longer true in case of receiving diversity. In [284], successive cancellation is considered as a practical useful approach to attain the optimal performance as predicted by information theory in the case of spatial diversity. In [195], CDMA versus orthogonal channel accessing is examined in a slow-fading environment. Successive cancellation is considered for asymptotically many users. The transmitted powers are selected so as to yield the right distribution for successive cancellation of received power accounting for the statistics of the fading gain factors. Successive cancellation interpreted in terms of decision feedback in case of a vector correlated multiple channel is discussed in [297], where standard known procedures of linear estimation are used to evaluate the sum rate constraining average mutual information expressions. Though [297] evaluates the results for Gaussian additive noise only, the results extend directly to the fading regime with CSI available to the receiver only or to both transmitter and receiver. Successive cancellation with reference to cellular models is discussed in [45], [231], and [323] to be referred to in the following. Some practical implication of successive interference cancellation as the effect of imperfect cancellation and residual noise is addressed in [98], [306], [185], [188], [315], and [54]. The effect of successive cancellation on other information-theoretic measures, such as the cutoff rate is discussed in [68], where this measure does not seem to be a natural information-theoretic criterion to consider in combination with successive cancellation. Successive cancellation is an integral part of the information-theoretic reasoning associated with a broadcast-channel model [62]. This remains valid also for faded broadcast channels [106], as well as in certain interference channels to be addressed in the following.

We have here succinctly scanned a minute fraction of the available material about the information-theoretical as well as practical implications of successive cancellation on network communication systems. Generalizations to cases of frequency-selective channels and nonideal cancellation can be found in the cited references and references therein.

In parallel to the single-user case, also in the multiple-user network environment information theory provides strong clues to the preferred signaling/accessing techniques. We have already discussed much of the material related to channel-accessing methods. As for information-theoretic-inspired signaling, much of the material referred to in the single-user section extends to the multiple-user case, and that refers to multicarrier modulation, interleaving, Gaussian-like interference, spectrally efficient modulation, and the like. In fact, the single-user approaches, which are associated with either orthogonal techniques of coded DS-SS or successive cancellation, pave the way to adopt the results discussed so far in reference to the single-user case. This is the reason why here we shall restrict ourselves to mentioning only those results which do not follow directly from single-user information-theoretic results. Clearly, the multiple-user case dictates some profound dissimilarities and new features stemming directly from the existence of several noncooperative users giving another dimension to the information-theoretic problem. This feature is demonstrated, for example, when classical orthogonal methods (e.g. OFDM, orthogonal CDMA) are used. This signaling can either be associated with a single user, or with different users. This view is even more pronounced for the rate-splitting technique [315], [232], where a given user disguises into multiple users. The aggregate rate is invariant, whether groups of multiple users are in fact interpreted as a single user, or indeed they model absolutely different users. Stripping techniques in the L-out-of-K model, as in [53], where a user information to be transmitted is split among M-shells, thus mimicking M users with power disparities, also demonstrates this argument. Another example is the implication of interleaving, which more or less follows the discussion of the single-user case, yet with multiple users, interleaving may prove essential to achieve optimal performance with a given multiple-access strategy. This is demonstrated in the generalized per-user time sharing, which demands no interuser synchronization [116], [229], where interleaving (or interlacing) is essential to attain the optimum. Another example, where there is interplay between standard DFE procedures and the multiple-user regime, is the model of [297], where again it suits the standard vector single-user Gaussian channel [296], [131] with i.i.d. inputs of the multiple-user regime [297]. In all those examples, which were originally developed for Gaussian nonfading channels, the fading effect can be straightforwardly introduced and accounted for.

Unavailable channel-state information: In parallel to the single-user case, the model where CSI is unavailable is of great practical interest. Indeed, we have demonstrated the surprising result that for fast-varying (changing from symbol to symbol) fading, TDMA is optimal [259]. In practical models, the variability of the fading is much slower and the assumption $B_d T \to 0$ is, usually, well approximated. Estimates of the degradation are given in [185] via standard

information-theoretic inequalities. Also in the multiple-user case some appealing practical approaches are based on first estimating the CSI either by using training sequences or in a blind procedure. Then these estimates are used for the CSI parameters. Universal as well as fixed-decoding-metric receivers are of interest. For the multiple-access case, the literature on these issues is scarce (see [164, and references within]). Interesting results for the multiple-user achievable rate region with a given decoding metric are given in [162]. In fact, as to demonstrate the richness of the multiple-access channel model, the results in [162] extend in some cases the lower bounds on the mismatched-metric achievable rates of the single-user case, by treating it as a multiple-access channel. The techniques are directly applicable to operation in a fading environment. This is demonstrated in [161], where the multiple-access fading channel with CSI available to the receiver is considered. It is shown that the fading AWGN, MAC capacity region is in fact achieved with a random Gaussian codebook, for a general class of additive ergodic and independent noises. Indeed, this nice result finds application in the realm of multicell communication [255], where other cell users are modeled as not necessarily Gaussian independent noises.

Extending the results of the single-user case discussed previously, the results of [186] are evaluated also for the multiuser case while maintaining their basic flavor. In [165], the multiple-access fading model of (3.4.1) is investigated: Gaussian codebooks are used and the receiver substitutes estimates of the CSI $\hat{a}_{lk}$ for the actual unavailable a_{lk}, where it is assumed that $E(a_{lk}|\hat{a}_{lk}) = \hat{a}_{lk}$ for all $l = 1, 2, \cdots, K$ and an integer k. Under full joint ergodicity assumptions of $\{\hat{a}_{lk}, a_{lk}\}$, and $\{n_k\}$, it is shown in [165] that the standard Gaussian fading-channel capacity region upper-bounds the achievable mismatched capacity region. Here, $\{\hat{a}_{lk}\}$ are interpreted as the fading parameters, and the equivalent additive noise is, as in (3.3.55),

$$\sum_{j=1}^{K} E_{a_j|\hat{a}_j} |a_j - \hat{a}_j|^2 P_{\text{av}} + \sigma^2.$$

This bound is tight in the case of perfect phase estimation, which is equivalent to the assumption that $\{a_{lk}, \hat{a}_{lk}\}$ are nonnegative. The case where $\hat{a}_{lk} = E(a_{lk})$ is considered in [186], which shows that the above discussed Gaussian fading capacity region lower-bounds the achievable rate region with optimal decoding. This is problematic, as the receiver has usually no idea about the joint statistics of $\{a_{lk}, \hat{a}_{lk}\}$ needed to construct the optimal decoding metric. This result is inherently implied by [165] examining specific, clearly suboptimal, Euclidean-distance (nearest neighbor) based detectors. The results of [165] are applicable also to various models of CDMA, when successive cancellation is advocated using estimated fading CSI (assumed to be independent of channel observations, or under some further restrictive assumptions causally dependent on those observations) see [98].

Many more relevant results not explicitly elaborated on here can be found in our reference list and in the references therein.

$$\bigcup_{E[P_{\mathrm{av}1}(b^2,c^2)+P_{\mathrm{av}2}(c^2,b^2)]\leq P_{\mathrm{av}}} \left\{ \begin{array}{l} R_1 \leq E\dfrac{1}{2}\log\left(1+\dfrac{P_{\mathrm{av}1}(b^2,c^2)}{b^2\sigma^2+P_{\mathrm{av}2}(c^2,b^2)\mathbb{1}(b^2>c^2)}\right) \\[3mm] R_2 \leq E\dfrac{1}{2}\log\left(1+\dfrac{P_{\mathrm{av}2}(c^2,b^2)}{c^2\sigma^2+P_{\mathrm{av}1}(b^2,c^2)\mathbb{1}(c^2>b^2)}\right) \end{array} \right\} \qquad (3.4.29)$$

Diversity: Diversity plays a key role in the multiple-user case, as it does for the single-user scenario. While receiver diversity is straightforwardly accounted for within the standard multiple-access information-theoretic framework (see [255], [129], and references therein), recent interest was directed to the combined transmit/receive diversity in the presence of fading. This problem has been undertaken in [284], which extends the results of [283] to the multiple-access case. The model here is described by

$$\underline{y} = \sum_{j=1}^{K} A_j^T \underline{x}_j + \underline{n} \qquad (3.4.25)$$

where A_j is an $M_{t_j} \times M_r$ complex Gaussian matrix and $\underline{n}$ is an M_r-dimensional vector modeling AWGN noise. The M_{t_j}-dimensional vector $\underline{x}_j$ designates the transmitted signal of the jth user, which uses M_{t_j} antennas, and employs power $E|\underline{x}_j|^2 = P_{\mathrm{av}j}$. The vector $\underline{y}$ designates the received signal at the M_r receiving antennas. The matrix A_j stands then for the random independent fading process which accounts for the instantaneous attenuation from the lth transmit antenna to the jth received antenna.

The capacity region with perfect CSI available to the receiver is given by

$$\sum_{j\in\mathcal{K}} R_j \leq E\left\{ \log\det\left| I_r + \sum_{j\in\mathcal{K}} \frac{P_{\mathrm{av}j}}{M_{t_j}} A_j^T A_j \right| \right\} \qquad (3.4.26)$$

for all $\mathcal{K} \subset \{1, 2, \cdots, K\}$. In the above, E is the average operator and $\mathcal{K}$ designates a subset of the K users. It is demonstrated that, for a fixed M_r, with increased number of the transmit antennas $M_{t_j} \to \infty$, the fading is absolutely mitigated yielding the unfaded AWGN MAC capacity region

$$\sum_{j\in\mathcal{K}} R_j \leq M_r \log\left(1 + \sum_{j\in\mathcal{K}} P_{\mathrm{av}j}\right). \qquad (3.4.27)$$

The profound effect of the diversity is demonstrated here by the M_r factor in the above equation. For the symmetric case of equal power ($P_{\mathrm{av}j} = P_{\mathrm{av}}$) equal transmit antennas ($M_{t_j} = M_t$), and equal rate, the achievable sum-rate is given by C in (3.3.58), where now $m_* = \min(M_r, KM_t)$ and $n_* = \max(M_r, KM_t)$. The asymptotic case when both M_t and M_r grow to infinity while M_r/M_t is kept constant is also evaluated in [284]. The result specializes to (3.3.59) for the case of an equal number of transmit and receive antennas, i.e., $M_r/M_t = 1$.

6) Broadcast and Interference: Interesting models which are most relevant to cellular communications and communications networks are the broadcast and interference channels (see [62], [61], [191], and references therein). Of particular relevance are the broadcast and interference channels subjected

to fading. We shall describe some of the results and techniques by considering a simple two-user case under flat fading.

Fading broadcast channels: The model considered is described by

$$\begin{aligned} y_{1i} &= a_i x + b_i n_{1i} \\ y_{2i} &= d_i x + c_i n_{2i} \end{aligned} \qquad (3.4.28)$$

where $\{a_i, b_i, c_i, d_i\}$ are jointly ergodic processes, and n_{1i}, n_{2i} are independent Gaussian samples with respective variances σ_1^2, σ_2^2. The transmitted signal is denoted by x. For the sake of simplicity, we consider here the single-dimensional case where x and n are real-valued, and the fading variables $\{a_i, b_i, c_i, d_i\}$ are nonnegative. We shall assume, with no loss of generality when CSI is available at the receivers, that $a_i = d_i \equiv 1$ and $\sigma^2 = \sigma_2^2 = \sigma_1^2$, where the general case is absorbed into the statistics of $\{b_i, c_i\}$. The rate region with CSI $\{b_i, c_i\}$ given to the transmitter and receiver receiver is given by (3.4.29) at the top of this page, where $\mathbb{1}(x)$ denotes the indicator function. The case of CSI available to both receiver and transmitter is treated in [106], [107], [108], and then $P_{\mathrm{av}1}$ and $P_{\mathrm{av}2}$ may depend on the CSI (b and c here) as indicated explicitly in (3.4.29). The region given by the union in (3.4.29) is then maximized over all assignments of $P_{\mathrm{av}1}, P_{\mathrm{av}2}$ satisfying

$$E[P_{\mathrm{av}1}(b^2,c^2) + P_{\mathrm{av}2}(c^2,b^2)] \leq P_{\mathrm{av}}. \qquad (3.4.30)$$

In [106] and [108], the rate region of time (TDMA) and frequency (FDMA) division techniques for the fading broadcast channel was examined and compared to the optimal code-division (CDMA) approach. Note, however, that taking $P_{\mathrm{av}1}(b^2,c^2) = P_{\mathrm{av}1}(b^2)$, $P_{\mathrm{av}2}(c^2,b^2)) = P_{\mathrm{av}2}(c^2)$, as in [106] and [108], is a suboptimal selection. In fact, the optimality of time division for the broadband broadcast channel stems directly by [163]. The rate region of the broadcast channel with CSI available to the receiver only is more intricate, as the whole setting does not, in general, form a degraded broadcast channel [62]. This problem is under current research; interesting results on inner and outer regions have already been derived.

The parallel broadcast channels first addressed in [218] can be used to model the presence of memory (intersymbol interference); optimal power allocation, under average power constraint is addressed in [289] and [110]. For classical result on the capacity of spectrally shaped broadcast channels see [192], [100], and references therein. The broadcast channel is used to model downlinks in cellular communication (see [255], [108], and [158]), and this will further be addressed in the following.

The fading-interference channel: The interference channel [62], [191] is a very important model which accounts for the case where the transmitted signals of K users in a network interfere before being decoded at their respective destinations. Each decoder here is interested just in its respective user (or, in general, a group of users), while the other users, the codebooks of whom are available to all decoders, act as interferers. We examine here a flat-fading case of a simple symmetric version of the single-dimensional two-user interference channel with fading. Let the two received signals be respectively given by

$$y_{1i} = a_i x_{1i} + \alpha b_i x_{2i} + n_{1i}$$
$$y_{2i} = \alpha c_i x_{1i} + d_i x_{2i} + n_{2i} \qquad (3.4.31)$$

where $\{a_i, b_i, c_i, d_i\}$ denote nonnegative i.i.d. fading processes, and $\alpha \geq 0$ is the interference coefficient. The additive Gaussian noise samples are modeled by n_{1i} and n_{2i} having a given variance $E(n_{1i}^2) = E(n_{2i}^2) = \sigma^2$. User $j = 1, 2$, transmitting its own independent message via the codeword $\{x_{ji}\}$, is to be decoded separately by observing $\{y_{ji}\}$ only.

The capacity region for the interference channel is unknown in general even when no fading is present, that is, $a_i = b_i = c_i = d_i = 1$ (see [191] for a tutorial review). The case of strong interference $\alpha \geq 1$ is solved in the unfaded case [240], [59], and the rationale behind the solution [240] extends directly to the case where relevant CSI is available to the receiver only. Here receiver one, who processes $\{y_{1i}\}$, is aware of $\{a_i\}, \{b_i\}$ while the fading signals $\{c_i\}$ and $\{d_i\}$ are provided to the second receiver, who operates on the received samples $\{y_{2i}\}$. Here for $\alpha > 1$, the solution follows the same arguments as in the nonfaded case [240], that is: If user one (two) can be reliably decoded by receiver one (two), then it can also be reliably decoded by receiver two (one), which enjoys more favorable conditions ($\alpha \geq 1$) as far as user one (two) is concerned. In terms of average mutual information relations for $\alpha \geq 1$, we have, as in [240]

$$I(y_1; x_1 | x_2) < I(y_1; x_2 | x_1)$$

and

$$I(y_2; x_2 | x_1) > I(y_2; x_1 | x_2).$$

The corresponding rate region is then given by

$$R_1 \leq E_{\nu_1} \frac{1}{2} \log \left(1 + \frac{\nu_1 P_{av1}}{\sigma^2} \right)$$

$$R_2 \leq E_{\nu_2} \frac{1}{2} \log \left(1 + \frac{\nu_2 P_{av2}}{\sigma^2} \right)$$

$$R_1 + R_2 \leq \min \left\{ \begin{matrix} E_{\nu_1, \nu_2} \frac{1}{2} \log \left(1 + \frac{\nu_1 P_{av1} + \alpha^2 \nu_2 P_{av2}}{\sigma^2} \right) \\ E_{\nu_1, \nu_2} \frac{1}{2} \log \left(1 + \frac{\nu_1 \alpha^2 P_{av1} + \nu_2 P_{av2}}{\sigma^2} \right) \end{matrix} \right\}$$

$$(3.4.32)$$

where P_{av1} and P_{av2} are, respectively, the average powers of users one and two. The random variables $\nu_1 = a^2$ (or d^2) and $\nu_2 = b^2$ (or c^2) stand for the i.i.d. fading powers. In the nonfaded, symmetric case $P_{av1} = P_{av2} = P_{av}$, where $\nu = \nu_1 = \nu_2 = 1$, the rectangle uninterfered region (3.4.32) dominates for $\alpha^2 > 1 + (P_{av}/\sigma^2)$ [59]. In the faded case, however, the threshold value of α^2 depends on the fading statistics and is given by solving for α^2 the following:

$$E_{\nu_1, \nu_2} \log \left(1 + \frac{(\nu_1 + \alpha^2 \nu_2) P_{av}}{\sigma^2} \right)$$

$$\geq 2 E_{\nu_1} \log \left(1 + \frac{\nu_1 P_{av}}{\sigma^2} \right). \qquad (3.4.33)$$

If CSI is available to receivers and transmitters, the users may vary their powers P_{av1} and P_{av2} as functions of the fading variables, subjected to an overall average-power constraint. Note that, for CSI available to the receiver only, receivers one and two need only the realizations of the fading variables affecting them. If CSI is available to the transmitters as well, each transmitter may benefit from the knowledge of both fading coefficients: in fact, in this way, the two transmitters which know the fading coefficients can, in a sense, coordinate their powers. Both receivers have now also access to the fading power realization and hence are synchronized with the transmit-power variations. This procedure describes a centralized power control, while in the decentralized power control transmitters and receivers associated with a given user acquire access only to the fading power realization that affects the respective user.

In the following these interesting broadcast and interference channels models will be mentioned in reference to cellular communications (see [255], [108], and [158]).

7) Cellular Fading Models: The rapidly emerging cellular communications spurred much theoretical research into fading channels, as the time-varying fading response is the basic ingredient in different models of these systems [113], [44], [255]. Numerous information-theoretic studies of single-cell models emerged in recent years in an effort to identify, via a simple tractable model, the basic dominating parameters and capture their effect on the ultimate achievable performance.

Many of these models (see relevant references in [255]) are, in fact, standard multiple-access models, which are also referred to as single-cell models. Quite often, the multicell models are also described in a single-cell framework where other cell users are simply modeled as additional noise to be combined with the ambient Gaussian noise [255, and references therein]. For these purposes, the information-theoretic treatment of the models discussed so far suffices (see, for example, [97]). We shall put emphasis here on those information-theoretic treatments which address specifically the multicell structure in an intrinsic manner, and which inherently address the fading phenomenon. In particular, we elaborate on what is known as Wyner's [332] cellular model, where fading is also introduced [255], [268]. Some implications of the broadcast, interference, and L-out-of-K channel models, as well as successive cancellation, are also briefly addressed. References will be pointed out for many other information-theoretic studies of a variety of cellular communications models subjected to certain assumptions.

Wyner's cellular model with fading: In [331] Wyner introduced a single linear and planar multicell (receiver) configuration to model the uplink in cellular communication. This model captures the intercell interference by assuming that each cell is subjected to interference from its adjacent cells. In [331] no fading was considered, and the ultimate possible performance in terms of the symmetric achievable rate was assessed. A fully symmetric power-controlled system with a fixed number of users per cell and an optimal multicell receiver that optimally processes all received signals from all cells was assumed. Similar models were addressed in [129], [130], and [125]. Fading was introduced into Wyner's model by [255] and [268] where its simple linear real version reads

$$y_j^m = \sum_{k=1}^{K} a_{kj}^m x_{kj}^m + \alpha \sum_{k=1}^{K} b_{kj}^m x_{kj}^{m-1} + \alpha \sum_{k=1}^{K} c_{kj}^m x_{kj}^{m+1} + n_j^m$$

(3.4.34)

where y_j^m stands for the received signal at cell site m at time instant j and, all signals are assumed to be real-valued.[14] This signal is composed of K users of that cell (m) and $2K$ users of the two adjacent cells $(m-1), (m+1)$. Here x_{kj}^m stands for the coded signal of the kth user belonging to cell m at discrete time j. The Gaussian noise samples are designated by n_j^m. The random variables $\{a_{kj}^m, b_{kj}^m, c_{kj}^m\}$ model the independent flat-fading processes to which the users at cell m, $m-1$, and $m+1$ are subjected. We assume that fading processes for different users are independent, while for a given user the fadings are ergodic processes of time (index j). In the model, $\alpha \geq 0$ stands for the intercell interference attenuation factor, where for $\alpha = 0$ the model reduces to the single-cell scenario with no intercell interference. Wyner's unfaded model [331] results as a special case where $a_{kj}^m = b_{kj}^m = c_{kj}^m = 1$. It is assumed, unless otherwise stated, that K users, subjected to an average equal power constraint P_{av}, are active per each cell. The system is fully symbol- and frame-synchronized, giving rise to the discrete-time model in (3.4.34). Following Wyner, in order to assess the ultimate possible performance a "hyper-receiver," having a delayless ideal access to the received signals at all cell sites $\{y_j^m\}$, j, m integers, is assumed. In [268] this system is analyzed in terms of bounds on achievable equal rates. First, a TDMA intracell accessing technique is assumed where each of the K users in each cell accesses the channel in its respective slot and uses it when actively transmitting power KP_{av}. No intercell cooperation or coordination other than synchronism is assumed. While in the unfaded scenario [331] this accessing is optimal (not unique, however), this is no more the case in the fading regime [268].

Under some mild conditions on the fading moments, the achievable rate is expressed by [268]

$$C_{\text{TDMA}}(\alpha) = K^{-1} \int_0^\infty \frac{1}{2} \log\left(1 + \frac{KP_{av}}{\sigma^2} u\right) dP_{ev}(u)$$

(3.4.35)

where $P_{ev}(u)$ stands for the limit distribution of the unordered eigenvalue of the quadratic form of GG^T. The tridiagonal infinite-dimensional random matrix G has random entries

$$G = \{g_{nm}\} \quad g_{n,n} = a_n \quad g_{n,n-1} = \alpha b_n \quad g_{n,n+1} = \alpha c_n$$

where $\{a_n, b_n, c_n\}$ are i.i.d. fading coefficients. Unfortunately, the exact expression for $P_{ev}(u)$ is still unknown. In [268], two sets of bounds were introduced, viz., the entropy-based and moment bounds. For the special case of no fading, the result

reduces to Wyner's[15] case

$$C(\alpha) = K^{-1} \int_0^1 \frac{1}{2} \log\left\{1 + \frac{KP_{av}}{\sigma^2}(1 + 2\alpha \cos(2\pi\theta))^2\right\} d\theta.$$

(3.4.36)

The surprising results of [268] demonstrate that for $KP_{av}/\sigma^2 > 0$ dB and a certain range of relatively high intercell interference, the fading *improves* on performance as compared to the unfaded case [331]. These interesting results, demonstrating the efficiency of the time-variable *independent* nature in which a certain user is received in its own and adjacent cell sites, are attributed to the fact that the diversity provided by the multiple cell-sites receivers changes the interplay between the deleterious mutual interuser interference on one hand, and the SNR enhancement provided by the multisensor receiver on the other. This interplay acts in such a way that independently fluctuating receiving levels (in a way which is revealed to the receiver, while maintaining the average power) help, rather than degrade, the performance. This is observed despite the mentioned fact that intracell TDMA is optimal in the unfaded case [331], while it is suboptimal when fading is present [268]. Note that the advantage of fading in this setting [268] does not require a large number of users $(K \gg 1)$. The wide band (WB), that is CDMA intracell accessing, is also considered, demonstrating advantage over the TDMA intracell accessing. It was proved that WB accessing achieves the ultimate symmetric capacity (i.e., it maximizes the sum-rate) of the faded Wyner model [268]. Bounds on the achievable rates were found. The asymptotically tight (with the number of users K) upper bound

$$C_{\text{WB}}(\alpha) \underset{K \gg 1}{\approx} K^{-1} \int_0^1 \frac{1}{2} \log\left[1 + \frac{KP_{av}}{\sigma^2}\right.$$
$$\cdot \left\{E(a - E(a))^2 (2\alpha^2 + 1)\right.$$
$$\left.\left. + E^2(a)(1 + 2\alpha \cos 2\pi\theta)^2\right\}\right] d\theta$$

(3.4.37)

depends only on the variance $\text{Var}(a) = E(a - E(a))^2$ and the mean $E(a)$ of the fading process. It is demonstrated that $C_{\text{WB}}(\alpha)$ upperbounds the Wyner unfaded expression $(E(a^2) = 1, \text{Var}(a) = 0)$ for any value of α and P_{av}/σ^2, thus demonstrating the surprisingly beneficial effect of the fading in this cellular model. This advantage is maintained also nonasymptotically [268], but now the advantage is not necessarily uniform over P_{av}/σ^2 and α. It should be emphasized that the independence of the three fading processes associated with each user (that is, the fluctuating power which is received in the user's own cell and the two adjacent cells) is crucial for the advantage that fading can provide. This occurs because otherwise the transmitters could themselves mimic the fluctuating-fading effect (in synchronism with the receivers), without altering the average transmitted power, and gain on

---

[14]The results hold verbatim with obvious scaling of power and rate for the complex circularly symmetric case, where full-phase synchronism in the system is assumed.

[15]In [331], result (3.4.36) was found by interpreting different cell sites ordered by (m) as different time epochs which make this model with intracell TDMA equivalent to standard discrete-time ISI channels for which capacity and mutual information calculation is classical.

performance over (3.4.36) in the unfaded case. By the results of Wyner [331], this is clearly impossible.

The results in [331] and [268] extend to the planar configuration. The models, methodology, and techniques apply directly to cases where the intercell interference emerges not only from the adjacent cells but also from cells located further away. This interference is then weighted by a nonincreasing positive sequence α_j, where α_j is proportional to the relative attenuation factor of cells at level j from the interfered cell. We have demonstrated here the technique for $\alpha_0 = 1, \alpha_1 = \alpha$, and $\alpha_j = 0, j > 1$.

The Wyner fading model is also the focus of the wide-scope study reported in [255]. This study focuses on a practical method of a single cell-site receiver, where the K users assigned to a certain cell m (say) are decoded based only on the received signal at this cell site $\{y_j^m\}$. The adjacent-cells interfering users are interpreted as Gaussian noises (a worst case assumption, which is motivated also by the mismatched nearest neighbor-based detection of [161]). It is assumed that each cell-site receiver is aware of the fading realizations of its own assigned users, and thus the instantaneous signal-to-noise ratio is known at the receiving cell site. The transmitters do not have access to any CSI. The study [255] provides a general formulation for the achievable rate region (inner-bound) of which all other discussed intracell channel accessing methods as TDMA and CDMA (WB) are special cases. The notion of intercell time sharing (ICTS), which is equivalent in a sense to classical frequency reuse [273], rises as an inherent feature of the information characterization of the inner achievable rate region. The ICTS controls the amount of intercell interference from full interference (no ICTS) to no interference (full ICTS, where the even- and odd-number cells signal in nonoverlapped times). In the unfaded case, any orthogonal intercell channel accessing technique is optimal (albeit not unique), while the picture changes considerably when fading is present. With fading and nondominant intercell interference (small α) CDMA is advantageous; a conclusion consistent with the single-cell result [97]. This is since CDMA enjoys an inherent fading-averaging effect, where the averaging takes place over the different users. For an intercell interference factor above a given calculated threshold, TDMA intracell accessing technique is superior. (Under no fading, both approaches, CDMA and TDMA, are equivalent.) For the model examined, intercell sharing protocols (as fractional intercell time sharing (ICTS)) are desirable in cases of significant intercell interference, and those when optimized restore to a large extent the superiority of the CDMA intracell approach in fading conditions, also for the case of strong, intercell interference.

Extension to detection based on processing the received signal from two adjacent cell sites (two cell-site processing, or TCSP) is also considered. It is assumed that the receiver, processing both $\{y_j^m\}$ and $\{y_j^{m+1}\}$, is equipped with the codebooks as well as precise values of the instantaneous signal-to-noise ratios of all users in both cells $(m, m+1)$. This model serves as a compromise between the advantage of incorporating additional information from other cell sites on one hand, and the associated excess processing complexity on the other. The basic conclusions extend also to this case,

though the range of parameters (as the intercell interference factor α, and the total signal-to-noise ratio (KP_{av}/σ^2)) for which the relevant CDMA-versus-TDMA intracell accessing techniques and fractional intercell time sharing are relatively effective, changes. It is shown that for no ICTS and for $K \gg 1, \alpha \, \mathrm{SNR}_T \to \infty$ in TCSP, the intracell TDMA access is better than CDMA while the opposite is true for full ICTS giving rise to no intercell interference. The implications of space diversity with the two receiving antennas at the cell site, experiencing independent fading, are also considered. The intra- and intercell accessing protocols are characterized in terms of two auxiliary random variables which emerge in a general expression for an achievable rate region. The main results in [255], though evaluated under the flat-fading assumption, were shown to hold for the more realistic multipath fading propagation model, with CSI available at the receiver.

By relaxing the assumption of a fixed number of active users per cell, it has been demonstrated, using interesting convexity properties, that under certain conditions random users' activity is advantageous, in terms of throughput, over a fixed number of active users. Specific results were discussed for a Poisson-distributed users' activity. In the random-access model considered in [255], the random number of users affects the interference, while in the discussion in the previous section, similar conclusions given in terms of achievable rate per user are demonstrated for a fading single cell (no interference) scenario with a random number of simultaneously active users. This random user activity per cell models more closely real cellular communications. The information-theoretic features of orthogonal CDMA in an isolated cell and fading environment were addressed. In this regime, the way orthogonality between users is achieved (i.e., orthogonal TDMA, orthogonal frequency-shift multiple-access FDMA or OCDMA) plays a fundamental role contrary to the unfaded case where all orthogonal channel access techniques are equivalent to the optimal scheme under an average power constraint. The somewhat surprising, already mentioned, result for orthogonal DS-SS CDMA *not* being uniformly superior to orthogonal TDMA in terms of achievable throughput, has been demonstrated, and was attributed to the orthogonality destruction mechanism due to the fading process which may affect OCDMA but not orthogonal TDMA. See [86] for a different model where the equivalence of orthogonal accessing techniques (TDMA, FDMA, and CDMA) is maintained also in the fading regime.

Although [255] focuses mainly on TDMA and CDMA, in most cases equivalent results to TDMA can be formulated for FDMA using the well-known time-frequency duality.

In this work we have restricted our attention to the uplink channel. Yet, some conclusions can be drawn regarding the downlink channel as well [108], [158]. The results of [255] for a TDMA intracell accessing, yielding a single active transmission per cell, are relevant here. This is because all users are equivalent with respect to the downlink transmitter and, thus, if provided with the proper codebooks, each user can in principle access all the available information. The optimal rate per user is then given by the rate calculated in association with TDMA, where the total signal-to-noise-ratio is replaced by the normalized signal-to-noise ratio used by the downlink transmitter (see [108] for analysis of an isolated broadcast fading channel).

In [255], it was concluded that, with TCSP and a large number of users per cell, fading may actually be beneficial, which resembles the results of [268], where the ultimate receiver bases its decisions on the information received in all possible cell sites. Note, however, that for the TCSP case the advantage of fading was demonstrated for an asymptotically large number of users per cell ($K \gg 1$), while in [268], with an ultimate multicell processing receiver, the beneficial effect of fading is experienced also for nonasymptotic values of K.

A two-antenna microdiversity system under the assumption that the two cell-site receiving antennas experience independent fading is also considered in [255]. In (3.4.37), for the sake of simplicity, we have specialized to Wyner's linear model. Results for the more realistic planar model of [331] in the presence of fading are reported in [268] for the ultimate receiver and in [255] for the single cell-site processor.

Other cellular models: Many other models for cellular communication were studied via information-theoretic tools, and the reference list provided here includes dozens of relevant entries. See for example [139], [123], [32], [36], [40], [311], [324], [277], [70], [317], [196], [291], [145], and [169]. Some of the most interesting results concern the L-out-of-K model [53], which captures the fact that although there are many potential users per cell, only a relatively small part of them are actually active. The effect of random accessing has also been considered to some extent in [255], and here in Subsection III-D.2). Successive cancellation plays a key role not only in the L-out-of-K models, as well as in other multiple-user settings discussed so far, but this method when combined with rate splitting constitutes an interesting model for cellular communications [231]. In fact, various studies show that power control is not necessarily beneficial in a multicell system, [231], [45], [323]. By not controlling the power and properly ordering the users and their respective transmitted power, while all users are subjected to an average power constraint, the intercell interference is dramatically reduced. This stems from the fact that in a perfectly power-controlled system the major part of the interference is caused by those users assigned to other cells, located near the boundaries of the interfered cell and therefore transmitting with a relatively strong power. Abandoning the standard power control where the received power of all users at the cell site is kept fixed may improve dramatically [231] the performance predicted by information theory. This advantage is achieved without any use of the coded signaling structure of the interfering users at the cell site receiver, and treating those interferers just as additional noise. Certainly, optimized power control, which accounts for the intercell interference, will further enhance performance, and this calls for further theoretical efforts. In [45], the geometric power distribution is used, motivated by its optimality under average-power constraints, in the single-cell delay-limited capacity problem as well as under average transmit power constraints [197]. First, the proper ordering of the closest user to the cell-site receiver, operating at high power in the successive cancellation procedure, is decided

upon. Those in the vicinity of the cell boundary are decoded last, and therefore suffer from minimal interference from other users of the same cell site, the interference of which has already been canceled. This minimal interference permits their reception with weak power, which implies that the interference they inflict on other adjacent cells is small. The associated increase in capacity is remarkable, and this different power-control procedure undermines the arguments in [306] and [319] claiming limited incentive of employing optimal multiuser processing in case where intercell interference is present. Similar results can be deduced from [197] by reinterpreting the different attenuations to which different users are subjected and accounting also for the multiple-cell interference. The reference to Wyner's model in [197] is inappropriate, as it does not account for the interference from other cell users when also processing the signals of the other cell-site antennas. Rather, it is a standard receive diversity setting. The downlink cellular fading channel has been naturally modeled within the broadcast channel framework where a "single user," the cell site, transmits to many users (the mobiles). Usually a single-cell scenario is considered, while intercell interference, when accounted for, is added to the ambient Gaussian noise (see [158], [106], [107], [108], and [255]). In fact, a better model accounting in a more elementary way for the intercell interference is the broadcast/interference model. That is, since the cell site (the "single user") is interested to transmit information to a set of users assigned to this cell (possibly including some common control information directed to all users). The interference part of the model stems from the basic cellular structures, where the downlinks from different cell sites may interfere with each other. Little is known about rate regions of this model, even with no fading present. The same goes for the uplink, where the cell-site receiver should not necessarily treat the other cell users as interfering noise, provided that the receiver is equipped with the codebooks of the interfering users as well. As is well known [191], neither decoding of the interfering users is always optimal, but for the strong-interference case, nor treating it as pure ambient noise, but for the very-weak-interference case. It is of primary interest then to consider the case where the receiver is equipped with the codebooks of the adjacent cell users (a mild and practical assumption), though decoding is still based on a single cell-site processing as in [255]. The problem then falls within the classification of a multiple-access/interference channel where the multiple-access part stems from the (intracell) users to be decoded reliably and the interference part from the users assigned to other cells, the reliable decoding of which is not required. A comprehensive treatment of this interesting, albeit not easy, problem may shed light on the optimal intra- and intercell accessing protocols with or without fading. As demonstrated in [255], the interference-limited behavior (typical in cases when interference is interpreted as noise) is eliminated within this framework. To exemplify the intimate interplay between the multiple-access and interference features in a multicell model, consider the linear Wyner model, (3.4.34), with $\alpha = 1$. For a single cell-site processing due to the symmetry (in the case $\alpha = 1$) of all $3K$ users (of the mth cell and the two adjacent $m - 1$ and $m + 1$ cells), the interference-channel capacity equals the multiple-access channel capacity with $3K$ users [191], provided all users are active simultaneously in all cells. The achievable equal rate under symmetric power conditions is then given by

$$R = (3K)^{-1} E \frac{1}{2} \log \left(1 + \frac{3K P_{\mathrm{av}}}{\sigma^2} \frac{1}{3K} \sum_{i=1}^{3K} \nu_i \right). \quad (3.4.38)$$

Full ICTS, where odd and even cells (in the linear Wyner model [331]), transmit in different time zones gives rise to the rate R_*

$$R_* = \frac{1}{2K} E \frac{1}{2} \log \left(1 + \frac{2K P_{\mathrm{av}}}{\sigma^2} \frac{1}{K} \sum_{i=1}^{K} \nu_i \right) \quad (3.4.39)$$

where the equation accounts for the fact that the users of cell m transmit 50% of the time, and hence use, while transmitting, the power $2P_{\mathrm{av}}$ per user. It is clear that R_* might surpass R, as is the case for $K \gg 1$ where the fading effect is absolutely mitigated in both R (3.4.38) and R_* (3.4.39). In fact, in both cases $(1/K) \Sigma_{i=1}^{K} \nu_i \to 1$ [255]. This example demonstrates the intimate relation between multiple access, interference, and the cellular configuration (linear, with only adjacent-cell interference, in this case), and emphasizes the important role played by intercell cooperative protocols such as an optimized fractional ICTS considered by [255]. These intercell cooperative protocols emerged also in terms of the statistical dependence of auxiliary random variables, which appear in a general characterization of achievable rate regions [255].

E. Concluding Remarks

In this section we have tried to provide an overview of the information-theoretic approach to communications over fading channels. In our presentation an effort was made to describe not only results, but also concepts, insights, and techniques, with strong emphasis on recent results (some of which have even not yet been formally published). We preferred to emphasize nonclassical material, because the latter is by now well-documented in textbooks (see, for example, the classical techniques treating wideband fading channels reported in [153] and [94]). Even then, in view of the vast amount of recent studies, only those ideas and results which are more special and typical to these time-varying channels were elaborated to some extent. We have tried to put emphasis on new information-theoretic notions, such as the delay-limited capacity, on one hand, and to suggest an underlying unifying view on the other. Through the whole exposition, efforts were made to present ideas and results in their simplest form (as, for example, discrete-time flat-fading models). Extensions, when present, were only pointed out briefly by directing to relevant references.

First we have tried to unify the different cases of ergodic capacity (that is, when classical Shannon type of capacity definitions provide operative notions, substantiated via coding theorems). The different cases account for different degrees of channel-state information (CSI) available to

transmitter(s)/receiver(s). This unifying approach is based on Shannon's framework [261], as elaborated and further developed in [41] for the single-user case and in [69] for the multiple user problem. A complementary unifying view, which embraces notions as capacity versus outage [210], delay-limited capacity [127], and expected capacity based on a broadcast approach [247], hinges on the classical notion of a compound channel with a prior (when relevant) attached to its unknown state. This approach is advocated in many references, such as [150], [83], [61], and others, where in [83] the compound channels with a prior are called "composite channels." While coding theorems in this setting for the single-user case could be deduced from classical works (see [164, and references therein]), the spectral-information techniques provide strong tools to treat these models [310], and that is particularly pronounced for the multiple-user (network information theory) case [124]. In fact, this very approach gives rise to straightforward observations, not emphasized previously. For example, this view substantiates directly the validity of the capacity-versus-outage results (for the single- [210] and multiple-user [50] cases), developed originally for given channel-state information (CSI) to the receiver only, also for the case where CSI is not available (in case of static fading, that is, vanishing Doppler spread normalized to the transmission length $B_d T \to 0$).

Following [252], we have gained insight, based on elementary relations of average mutual information expressions, into the rather important implications on the capacity-achieving signaling properties in fast-time-varying channels with unavailable CSI. This kind of channels gives rise to "peaky" signals in time and/or frequency [286], [99]. In fact, interesting results on transmit/receive diversity [176], as well as TDMA optimality in multiple-access fast-varying channels [259], can also be interpreted within this framework, as well as classical, well-known results [314].

Numerous new results are scattered throughout this section, as exemplified by the optimality of TDMA in the fast dynamic multiple-access fast-fading channel, when CSI is unavailable, a result which comes in a sharp contrast with the optimality of CDMA (wide band) for the same model but with CSI given to the receiver [97], and the optimality of a fading controlled TDMA in case where CSI is available to both transmitter and receiver [155]. Preliminary treatment of achievable rates with CSI available to the transmitter only was attempted, in an effort to provide some further insight into the role played by the availability of the CSI. Certain new aspects of fading interference channels are also discussed, modifying the classical threshold value which defines a very strong interference for the Gaussian unfaded interference channel [59] (beyond which the interference effect is absolutely removed). Preliminary new results on random accessing in the MAC in presence of fading were also mentioned.

Although the flavor of our work is information-theoretic, we have made a special effort to emphasize practical implications and applications. This is because we believe that the insight provided by an information-theoretic approach has a direct and almost immediate impact on practical communications systems in view of the present and near-future technology. This synergy between information-theoretic reasoning and practical communications approaches, especially pronounced here for the time-varying fading channels, is the main motivation to combine, in our exposition, the parts on coding and equalization that follow. In view of this, we have devoted significant room to discuss issues as information-theoretic-inspired signaling and channel accessing, and discussed some of the information-theoretic implications of practical approaches which combine channel estimation and detection. See, for example, the discussion on the effect on nonideal (estimated) channel parameters, and on robust detectors, as the one based on nearest neighbor decoding [161], [165]. As for channel accessing, an interesting example to the practical implications of information-theoretic arguments, happens in Wyner's model [331] in which fading is introduced [255]. In this model, with a single cell-site processing (of the uplink cellular channel) the intercell sharing protocols emerge as a natural outcome, under certain conditions of relatively strong intercell interference. Sound theoretical basis for practical approaches such as frequency and/or time reuse is thus provided for practical cases, where only limited information processing is allowed.

We wish to mention again that our overall exposition of the information-theoretic aspects of fading channels is very limited. Many deserving topics were only mentioned cursorily. Error exponents and cutoff rates are two such examples; others occur in several applications supported by information-theoretic analyses (for example, a decision-feedback-based approach [297], multicarrier systems [71], and the like). Also important, practically appealing methods, such as coded spread spectrum (DS-CDMA) for example, enjoying intensive information-theoretic treatment, that account for fading aspects as well (see [254, and references therein]) were at best mentioned very briefly.

Our channel models and treatments are mainly motivated by the rapidly emerging cellular/personal/wireless network communications systems [113], [44], [114]; however, time-varying fading channels play a central part in many other applications. Also there, including, for example, satellite communications [274], [89], underwater channels, which exhibit particularly harsh conditions [290], [263], [136], [173][16] information-theoretic analysis is providing insight into the limitations and potentials of efficient communications. With this in mind, we have constructed a rather extensive additional reference list, focusing on information-theoretic approaches to time-varying channels. Some additional relevant references not cited in the text are [55], [2], [9], [3], [5], [105], [302], [336], [169], [184], [189], [120], [276], [271], [212], [244], [138], [20], [246], [30], [86], [121], [339], [269], [66], [46], [233], [275], [245], [264], [18], [213], [224], [3], [7], [8], [102], [272], [1]. By no means is this list complete or even close to complete: hundreds of directly relevant references were not included, but rather appear in the reference lists of the papers cited here. Only few of rather important unpublished technical reports (see for example [239], [227], and [282]) were mentioned, and the overall emphasis was put on recent literature. The reader interested in completing the picture of this interesting topic

is encouraged to access many additional documents, which can be traced either from the reference list or by accessing standard databases.

Indeed, the extension of these studies put in evidence the amount of recent interest of the scientific and technical community in a deeper understanding of the theoretical implications of communications over channel models which more accurately approximate current and future communication systems. (See, for example, work related to chaotic dynamical systems [330], [332].) These models cover a whole spectrum of classical media (as HF channels and meteor burst channels, used for many decades), and more recent channels and applications (as microwave wideband channels, wireless multimedia and ATM networks, cellular-based communication networks, underwater channels: see [220, and references therein]). Unfortunately, some misconceptions based on inaccurate information-theoretic analysis are scattered within these efforts. We hope that, by our short remarks or by providing or referencing correct treatments, we have contributed to dispel to some extent some of those.

This scope of studies gives the impression that we present here an account on a mature subject. This is certainly *not* our view. We believe, in fact, that the most interesting and profound information-theoretic problems in the area of time-varying fading channels are yet to be addressed. We have observed that some of the more interesting models, for, e.g., multicell cellular communications, can be formalized in terms of either the multiple-access/interference channel (uplink) or the broadcast/interference channel (downlink). Much is yet unknown for these models, as is evidenced by the yet open problems in reference to the general characterization of the capacity regions of broadcast and interference channels, even in the nonfading environment. These research endeavors are not only nice theoretical problems: on the contrary, when developed, the corresponding results will carry a strong impact on the understanding of efficient channel-accessing techniques. These implications were demonstrated in a small way via the emergence of intercell resource sharing for certain simplistic cellular fading communication models [255]. Fundamental aspects, as an intimate combinination of information and network (including queuing) theories, essential for a deep understanding of practical communications systems, is at best in its infancy stages [95], [84], [285], [17], [26]. Decisive results on the joint source-channel coding in time-varying channels are still needed, which would incorporate various decoding constraints (as delay, etc.) motivated by practical applications [322]. Also, there are common misconceptions about the validity of the source/channel separation theorem [154]. While with no restrictions on the source and channel coder separation holds for an ergodic source channel problem, this certainly is not the case where a per-state joint source and channel coding is attempted, for example, to reduce overall delay. Recent general results as in [300, and references therein] are useful in this setting. Models which account more closely for classical constraints such as the inherent lack of synchronization, presence of memory, and the associated information-theoretic implications (see, for example, [135], [219], [306], [309]) in the fading regime are yet to be studied.

---

[16]There are inaccurate conclusions in this paper due to an incorrect use of the Jensen inequality.

Arbitrarily varying channels and compound multiuser channels are intimately related to efficient communication over time-varying channels [164], and, as such, there are many relevant open problems with direct implications on communications in the presence of fading. So is the case with robust and mismatched decoders [164]. Within this class of channels, the issue of randomized versus deterministic coding rises in a natural way, and in the network setting this will bring up also the important issue of randomized channel accessing, treated however from purely information-theoretic viewpoint, and not just classical network/queuing theory. We have noticed that randomized channel accessing is a natural, sometimes advantageous, alternative for decentralized power control problems, and also that time-varying randomized multiuser coding may prove advantageous in an asynchronous environment and under a maximum (rather than average) error-probability criterion [52].

Throughout our paper we have scattered numerous much less ambitious information-theoretic problems, which intimately address the fading phenomenon, and the solution of which might considerably enhance the insight in this field.

A few such problems, some of which are currently under study, are listed as follows.

1) Capacities of the fading channel with CSI available to the transmitter only in either a causal or noncausal manner, for the single- and multiple-user cases.

2) The information-theoretic implications of optimal feedback, under constrained rate of the noiseless feedback channel.

3) Delayed feedback in the multiple-user environment, with specific application to the Markov–Rayleigh fading.

4) Constrained-states AVC interpretation of results related to the delay-limited capacity with states known or not known at the transmitter. Issues of maximum- and average-error criteria, as well as randomized and deterministic codes.

5) Conditions for positive delay-limited capacity with imperfect channel-state information available to transmitter, accounting also for diversity effects, as those provided by the frequency selectivity of the channel.

6) Determination of asymptotic eigenvalue density of quadratic forms of Toeplitz structured (for example, tridiagonal) matrices. This is directly related to the determination of the achievable rates in Wyner's cellular models [331], and their extensions with flat-fading present [268].

7) Optimal (location-dependent) power control in simple multiple-cellular models with limited cell-site processors, as to optimally balance between the desired effect of increased combined power and the associated deleterious interference.

8) Formal proofs for the discrete distribution of the scalar or diagonal random variables in reference to the ca-

pacity of block-fading channels with transmitter and receiver diversity [176].

9) Identification and evaluation of appropriate rates and information interrelations among certain information-theoretic characterizations of achievable rates for randomly activated users operating on a faded MAC.

10) Information-theoretic implications of a variety of channel-accessing methods such as TDMA, FDMA, CDMA, mixed orthogonal accessing methods for various fading models, and different information-theoretic criteria (such as ergodic capacity, capacity versus outage) with or without the presence of interfering users (multiple-cell scenario).

IV. CODING FOR FADING CHANNELS

In this section we review a few important issues in coding and modulation for the fading channel. Here we focus our attention to the flat Rayleigh fading channel, and we discuss how some paradigms commonly accepted for the design of coding and modulation for a Gaussian channel should be shifted when dealing with a fading channel. The results presented before in this paper in terms of capacity show the importance of coding on this channel, and the relevance of obtaining channel-state information (CSI) in the demodulation process. Our goal here is to complement the insight that information theory provides about the general features of the capacity-achieving long codes. We describe design rules which apply to relatively short codes, meeting the stringent delay constraints demanded in many an application, like personal and multimedia wireless communications.

A. General Considerations

For fading channels the paradigms developed for the Gaussian channel may not be valid anymore, and a fresh look at the coding and modulation design philosophies is called for. Specifically, in the past the choices of system designers were driven by their knowledge of the behavior of coding and modulation (C/M) over the Gaussian channel: that is, they tried to apply to radio channels solutions that were far from optimum on channels where nonlinearities, Doppler shifts, fading, shadowing, and interference from other users made the channel far from Gaussian.

Of late, a great deal of valuable scholarly work has gone into reversing this perspective, and it is now being widely accepted that C/M solutions for the fading channel may differ markedly from Gaussian solutions. One example of this is the design of "fading codes," i.e., C/M schemes that are specifically optimized for a Rayleigh channel, and hence do not attempt to maximize the Euclidean distance between error events, but rather, as we shall see soon, their Hamming distance.

In general, the channel model turns out to have a considerable impact on the choice of the preferred solution of the C/M schemes. If the channel model is uncertain, or not stable enough in time to design a C/M scheme closely matched to it, then the best proposition may be that of a "robust" solution, that is, a solution that provides suboptimum performance on a wide variety of channel models. For example, the use of antenna diversity with maximal-ratio combining provides good performance in a wide variety of fading environments. Another solution is offered by bit-interleaved coded modulation (BICM). Moreover, the availability of channel-state information (typically, in the form of the values of the attenuation introduced by the fading process) at the transmitter or at the receiver modifies the code design criteria.

The design of C/M schemes for the fading channel is further complicated when a multiuser environment has to be taken into account. The main problem here, and in general in communication systems that share channel resources, is the presence of multiple-access interference (MAI). This is generated by the fact that every user receives, besides the signal which is specifically directed to that user, some additional power from transmission to other users. This is true not only when CDMA is used, but also with space-division multiple access, in which intelligent antennas are directed toward the intended user. Earlier studies devoted to multiuser transmission simply neglected the presence of MAI. Typically, they were based on the naive assumption that, due to some version of the ubiquitous "central limit theorem," signals adding up from a variety of users would coalesce to a process resembling Gaussian noise. Thus the effect of MAI would be an increase of thermal noise, and any C/M scheme designed to cope with the latter would still be optimal, or at least near-optimal, for multiuser systems.

Of late, it was recognized that this assumption was groundless, and consequently several of the conclusions that it prompted were wrong. The central development of multiuser theory was the introduction of the optimum multiuser detector: rather than demodulating each user separately and independently, it demodulates all of them simultaneously. Multiuser detection was born in the context of terrestrial cellular communication, and hence implicitly assumed a MAI-limited environment where thermal noise is negligible with respect to MAI (high-SNR condition). For this reason coding was seldom considered, and hence most multiuser detection schemes known from the literature are concerned with symbol-by-symbol decisions.

Reasons of space prevent us from covering the topic of C/M for multiuser channels in detail. However, we should at least mention that multiuser detection has been studied for fading channels as well (see, e.g., [351], [352], and [354]). A recent approach to coding for fading channels uses an iterative decoding procedure which yields excellent performance in the realm of coded multiuser systems. (Also, noniterative multiuser schemes are well documented.) The interested reader is referred to [340]–[347].

Another relevant factor in the choice of a C/M scheme is the decoding delay that one should allow: in fact, recently proposed, extremely powerful codes (the "turbo codes" [359]) suffer from a considerable decoding delay, and hence their application might be useful for data transmission, but not for real-time speech. For real-time speech transmission, which imposes a strict decoding delay constraint, channel variations with time may be rather slow with respect to the maximum allowed delay. In this case, the channel may be modeled

as a "block-fading" channel, in which the fading is nearly constant for a number of symbol intervals. On such a channel, a single codeword may be transmitted after being split into several blocks, each suffering from a different attenuation, thus realizing an effective way of achieving diversity.

B. The Frequency-Flat, Slow Rayleigh Fading Channel

This channel model assumes that the duration of a modulated symbol is much greater than the delay spread caused by the multipath propagation. If this occurs, then all frequency components in the transmitted signal are affected by the same random attenuation and phase shift, and the channel is frequency-flat. If in addition the channel varies very slowly with respect the symbol duration, then the fading $R(t) \exp [j\Theta(t)]$ remains approximately constant during the transmission of several symbols (if this does not occur, the fading process is called *fast*).

The assumption of nonselectivity allows us to model the fading as a process affecting the transmitted signal in a multiplicative form. The assumption of slow fading allows us to model this process as a constant random variable during each symbol interval. In conclusion, if $x(t)$ denotes the complex envelope of the modulated signal transmitted during the interval $(0, T)$, then the complex envelope of the signal received at the output of a channel affected by slow, flat fading and additive white Gaussian noise can be expressed in the form

$$r(t) = Re^{j\Theta} x(t) + n(t) \qquad (4.2.1)$$

where $n(t)$ is a complex Gaussian noise, and $Re^{j\Theta}$ is a Gaussian random variable, with R having a Rice or Rayleigh pdf and unit second moment, i.e., $E[R^2] = 1$.

If we can further assume that the fading is so slow that we can estimate the phase Θ with sufficient accuracy, and hence compensate for it, then coherent detection is feasible. (If the phase cannot be easily tracked, then differential or noncoherent demodulation can be used: see, e.g., [382], [395], [396], [409], [433].) Thus model (4.2.1) can be further simplified to

$$r(t) = Rx(t) + n(t). \qquad (4.2.2)$$

It should be immediately apparent that with this simple model of fading channel the only difference with respect to an AWGN channel rests in the fact that R, instead of being a constant attenuation, is now a random variable, whose value affects the amplitude, and hence the power, of the received signal. If in addition to coherent detection we assume that the value taken by R is known at the receiver and/or at the transmitter, we say that we have *perfect CSI*. Channel-state information at the receiver front-end can be obtained, for example, by inserting a pilot tone in a notch of the spectrum of the transmitted signal, and by assuming that the signal is faded exactly in the same way as this tone.

Detection with perfect CSI at the receiver can be performed exactly in the same way as for the AWGN channel: in fact, the constellation shape is perfectly known, as is the attenuation incurred by the signal. The optimum decision rule in this case consists of minimizing the Euclidean distance between the received signal and the transmitted signal, rescaled by a factor R

$$\int_0^T [r(t) - Rx(t)]^2 \, dt \quad \text{or} \quad |\boldsymbol{r} - R\boldsymbol{x}|^2 \qquad (4.2.3)$$

with respect to the possible transmitted real signals $x(t)$ (or vectors $\boldsymbol{x}$).

A consequence of this fact is that the error probability with perfect CSI and coherent demodulation of signals affected by frequency-flat slow fading can be evaluated as follows. We first compute the error probability $P(e|R)$ obtained by assuming R constant in model (4.2.2), then we take the expectation of $P(e|R)$, with respect to the random variable R. The calculation of $P(e|R)$ is performed as if the channel were AWGN, but with the energy $\mathcal{E}$ changed to $R^2\mathcal{E}$. Notice finally that the assumptions of a noiseless channel-state information and a noiseless phase-shift estimate make the values of $P(e)$ thus obtained as yielding a limiting performance.

In the absence of CSI, one could pick a decision rule consisting of minimizing

$$\int_0^T [r(t) - x(t)]^2 \, dt \quad \text{or} \quad |\boldsymbol{r} - \boldsymbol{x}|^2. \qquad (4.2.4)$$

However, with constant envelope signals ($|\boldsymbol{x}|$ constant), the error probabilities obtained with (4.2.3) and (4.2.4) coincide. In fact, observe that the pairwise error probability between $\boldsymbol{x}$ and $\hat{\boldsymbol{x}}$, i.e., the probability that $\hat{\boldsymbol{x}}$ is preferred to $\boldsymbol{x}$ by the receiver when $\boldsymbol{x}$ is transmitted, is given by

$$\begin{aligned} P(\boldsymbol{x} \to \hat{\boldsymbol{x}}) &= P(|\boldsymbol{r} - R\hat{\boldsymbol{x}}|^2 < |\boldsymbol{r} - R\boldsymbol{x}|^2) \\ &= P(2R(\boldsymbol{r}, \boldsymbol{x} - \hat{\boldsymbol{x}}) < 0) \\ &= P((\boldsymbol{r}, \boldsymbol{x} - \hat{\boldsymbol{x}}) < 0). \end{aligned}$$

Comparison of error probabilities over the Gaussian channel with those over the Rayleigh fading channel with perfect CSI [358], [223] show that the loss in error probability is considerable. Coding can compensate for a substantial amount of this loss.

C. Designing Fading Codes: The Impact of Hamming Distance

A commonly approved design criterion is to design coded schemes such that their minimum Euclidean distance is maximized. This is correct on the Gaussian channel with high SNR (although not when the SNR is very low: see [419]), and is often accepted, *faute de mieux*, on channels that deviate little from the Gaussian model (e.g., channels with a moderate amount of intersymbol interference). However, the Euclidean-distance criterion should be outright rejected over the Rayleigh fading channel. In fact, analysis of coding for the Rayleigh fading channel proves that Hamming distance (also called "code diversity" in this context) plays the central role here.

It should be kept in mind that, as far as capacity-achieving codes are concerned, the minimum Euclidean distance has little relevance: it is the whole distance spectrum that counts [414]. This is classically demonstrated by the features of turbo codes [359], which exhibit a relatively poor minimum distance and yet approach capacity rather remarkably. In this sense, what we provide in this section is the fading-channel equivalent of the minimum-distance criterion, which is of direct relevance when short (and hence inherently not capacity-achieving) codes are to be designed for a rather high signal-to-noise environment.

Assume transmission of a coded sequence $\mathcal{X} = (\boldsymbol{x}_1, \boldsymbol{x}_2, \cdots, \boldsymbol{x}_n)$ where the components of $\mathcal{X}$ are signal vectors selected from a constellation $\mathcal{S}$. We do not distinguish here among block or convolutional codes (with soft decoding), or block- or trellis-coded modulation. We also assume that, thanks to perfect (i.e., infinite-depth) interleaving, the fading random variables affecting the various symbols $\boldsymbol{x}_k$ are independent. Hence we write, for the components of the received sequence $(\boldsymbol{r}_1, \boldsymbol{r}_2, \cdots, \boldsymbol{r}_n)$

$$\boldsymbol{r}_k = R_k \boldsymbol{x}_k + \boldsymbol{n}_k \qquad (4.3.1)$$

where the R_k are independent, and, under the assumption that the noise is white, the RV's n_k are also independent.

Coherent detection of the coded sequence, with the assumption of perfect channel-state information, is based upon the search for the coded sequence $\mathcal{X}$ that minimizes the distance

$$\sum_{k=1}^N |\boldsymbol{r}_k - R_k \boldsymbol{x}_k|^2. \qquad (4.3.2)$$

Thus the pairwise error probability can be expressed in this case as

$$P\{\mathcal{X} \to \hat{\mathcal{X}}\} \le \prod_{k \in \mathcal{K}} \frac{1}{1 + |\boldsymbol{x}_k - \hat{\boldsymbol{x}}_k|^2/4N_0} \qquad (4.3.3)$$

where $\mathcal{K}$ is the set of indices k such that $\boldsymbol{x}_k \ne \hat{\boldsymbol{x}}_k$.

An example: For illustration purposes, let us compute the Chernoff upper bound to the word error probability of a block code with rate R_c. Assume that binary antipodal modulation is used, with waveforms of energies $\mathcal{E}$, and that the demodulation is coherent with perfect CSI. Observe that for $\hat{\boldsymbol{x}}_k \ne \boldsymbol{x}_k$ we have

$$|\boldsymbol{x}_k - \hat{\boldsymbol{x}}_k|^2 = 4\mathcal{E} = 4R_c\mathcal{E}_b$$

where $\mathcal{E}_b$ denotes the average energy per bit. For two codewords $\mathcal{X}, \hat{\mathcal{X}}$ at Hamming distance $H(\mathcal{X}, \hat{\mathcal{X}})$ we have

$$P\{\mathcal{X} \to \hat{\mathcal{X}}\} \le \left(\frac{1}{1 + R_c\mathcal{E}_b/N_0} \right)^{H(\mathcal{X}, \hat{\mathcal{X}})}$$

and hence, for a linear code,

$$P(e) = P(e|\mathcal{X}) \le \sum_{w \in \mathcal{W}} \left(\frac{1}{1 + R_c\mathcal{E}_b/N_0} \right)^w$$

where $\mathcal{W}$ denotes the set of nonzero Hamming weights of the code, considered with their multiplicities. It can be seen that for high enough signal-to-noise ratio the dominant term in the expression of $P(e)$ is the one with exponent $d_{\min}$, the minimum Hamming distance of the code.

By recalling the above calculation, the fact that the probability of error decreases inversely with the signal-to-noise ratio raised to power $d_{\min}$ can be expressed by saying that we have introduced a *code diversity* $d_{\min}$.

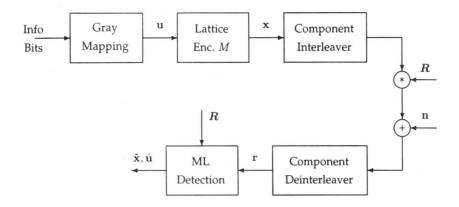

Fig. 5. System model.

We may further upper-bound the pairwise error probability by writing

$$P\{\mathcal{X} \to \hat{\mathcal{X}}\} \le \prod_{k \in \mathcal{K}} \frac{1}{|\boldsymbol{x}_k - \hat{\boldsymbol{x}}_k|^2/4N_0}$$
$$= \frac{1}{[\delta^2(\mathcal{X}, \hat{\mathcal{X}})/4N_0]^{H(\mathcal{X}, \hat{\mathcal{X}})}}$$

(4.3.4)

(which is close to the true Chernoff bound for small enough N_0). Here

$$\delta^2(\mathcal{X}, \hat{\mathcal{X}}) = \left[\prod_{k \in \mathcal{K}} |\boldsymbol{x}_k - \hat{\boldsymbol{x}}_k|^2 \right]^{1/H(\mathcal{X}, \hat{\mathcal{X}})}$$

is the geometric mean of the nonzero squared Euclidean distances between the components of $\mathcal{X}, \hat{\mathcal{X}}$. The latter result shows the important fact that the error probability is (approximately) inversely proportional to the *product* of the squared Euclidean distances between the components of $\boldsymbol{x}, \hat{\boldsymbol{x}}$ that differ, and, to a more relevant extent, to a power of the signal-to-noise ratio whose exponent is the Hamming distance between $\mathcal{X}$ and $\hat{\mathcal{X}}$. We stress again the fact that the above results hold when CSI is available to the receiver. With no such availability, the metric differs considerably from that leading to (4.3.4) (see [381]). This is in contrast to what was observed before for the case of constant-envelope signals.

Further, we know from the results referring to block codes, convolutional codes, and coded modulation that the union bound to error probability for a coded system can be obtained by summing up the pairwise error probabilities associated with all the different "error events." For high signal-to-noise ratios, a few equal terms will dominate the union bound. These correspond to error events with the smallest value of the Hamming distance $H(\mathcal{X}, \hat{\mathcal{X}})$. We denote this quantity by L_c to stress the fact that it reflects a diversity residing in the code. We have

$$P\{\mathcal{X} \to \hat{\mathcal{X}}\} \overset{\sim}{\ge} \frac{\nu}{[\delta^2(\mathcal{X}, \hat{\mathcal{X}})/4N_0]^{L_c}}$$

(4.3.5)

where ν is the number of dominant error events. For error events with the same Hamming distance, the values taken by $\delta^2(\mathcal{X}, \hat{\mathcal{X}})$, and by ν are also of importance. This observation may be used to design coding schemes for the Rayleigh fading channel: here no role is played by the Euclidean distance, which is the central parameter used in the design of coding schemes for the AWGN channel.

For uncoded systems ($n = 1$), the results above hold with the positions $L_c = 1$ and $\delta^2(\mathcal{X}, \hat{}) = |\boldsymbol{x} - \hat{\boldsymbol{x}}|^2$, which shows that the error probability decreases as N_0. A similar result could be obtained for maximal-ratio combining in a system with diversity L_c. This explains the name of this parameter. In this context, the various diversity schemes may be seen as implementations of the simplest among the coding schemes, the repetition code, which provides a diversity equal to the number of diversity branches (see [379], [380], [417], and [361, Chs. 9 and 10]).

From the discussion above, we have learned that over the perfectly interleaved Rayleigh fading channel the choice of a short code (in the sense elucidated above) should be based on the maximization of the code diversity, i.e., the minimum Hamming distance among pairs of error events. Since for the Gaussian channel code diversity does not play the same central role, coding schemes optimized for the Gaussian channel are likely to be suboptimum for the Rayleigh channel. We have noticed in the previous section that optimal (capacity-achieving) codes for the channel at hand (4.3.1) are in fact exactly the same codes as designed for the classical AWGN channel when CSI is available to receiver only [412] or to receiver and transmitter [376]. This is because those codes, being long, manage to achieve the averaging effect over the fading realizations. Here the conclusions are different, as we focus on short codes, whose different features, like code diversity, help improve performance.

1) Signal-Space Coding: Design of multidimensional constellations aimed at optimality on the Rayleigh fading channel has been recently developed into an active research area (see [362]–[364], [370], [389], [385], [429], [432], [398], and [431]).

This theory assumes the communication system model shown in Fig. 5. Here Rayleigh fading affects independently each signal dimension, and, as usual, perfect phase recovery and perfect (CSI) are available.

Let S be a finite n-dimensional signal constellation carved from the lattice $\{\boldsymbol{x} = \boldsymbol{u}M\}$, where $\boldsymbol{u}$ is an integer vector and M is the lattice-generator matrix. Let $\boldsymbol{x} = (x_1, x_2, \cdots, x_n)$ denote a transmitted signal vector from the constellation S. Received signal samples are then given by $\boldsymbol{r} = (y_1, y_2, \cdots, y_n)$ with $r_i = \alpha_i x_i + n_i$ for $i = 1, 2, \cdots, n$, where the α_i are independent real Rayleigh random variables with unit second moment (i.e., $E[\alpha_i^2] = 1$) and n_i are real Gaussian random variables with mean zero and variance $N_0/2$ representing the additive noise. With $\odot$ denoting component-wise product, we can then write $\boldsymbol{r} = \boldsymbol{R} \odot \boldsymbol{x} + \boldsymbol{n}$, with $\boldsymbol{R} = (R_1, R_2, \cdots, R_n)$, $\boldsymbol{n} = (n_1, n_2, \cdots, n_n)$, and $\boldsymbol{r} = (y_1, y_2, \cdots, y_n)$.

With perfect CSI, maximum-likelihood (ML) detection, which requires the minimization of the metric

$$m(\boldsymbol{x}|\boldsymbol{r}, \boldsymbol{\alpha}) = \sum_{k=1}^{n} |r_k - R_k x_k|^2 \qquad (4.3.6)$$

may be a very complex operation for an arbitrary signal set with a large number of points. A universal lattice decoder was suggested to obtain a more efficient ML detection of lattice constellations in fading channels [430], [429], [432], [364], [398], [431].

Signal-space diversity and product distance: With this channel model, the *diversity order* L_s of a multidimensional signal set is the minimum number of distinct components between any two constellation points. In other words, the diversity order is the minimum Hamming distance between any two coordinate vectors of the constellation points.

This type of diversity technique can be called *modulation*, or *signal-space diversity*. This definition applies to every modulation scheme and affects its performance over the fading channel in conjunction with component interleaving. By use of component interleaving, fading attenuations over different space dimensions become statistically independent. An attractive feature of these schemes is that we have an improvement of error performance without even requiring the use of conventional channel coding.

Two approaches were proposed to construct high modulation-diversity constellations (see [362], [363], [389], [385], [429], [432], [364], and [370]). The first was based on the design of high-diversity lattice constellations by applying the *canonical embedding* to the *ring of integers* of an *algebraic number field*. Only later was it realized that high modulation diversity could also be achieved by applying a certain rotation to a classical signal constellation in such a way that any two points achieve the maximum number of distinct components. Fig. 6 illustrates this idea applied to a 4-PSK. Two- and four-dimensional rotations were first found in [362] and [398], while the search for good high-dimensional rotations needs sophisticated mathematical tools, e.g., algebraic number theory [366].

An interesting feature of the rotation operation is that the rotated signal set has exactly the same performance than the nonrotated one when used over a pure AWGN channel, while as for other types of diversity such as space, time, frequency, and code diversity, the performance over Rayleigh fading channels, for increasingly high modulation diversity order, approaches that achievable over the Gaussian channel [371].

To give a better idea of the influence of L_s on the error probability, we estimate the error probability of the system described in Section IV-C1).

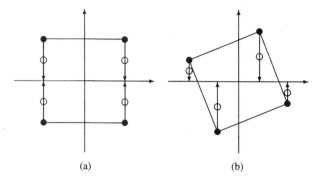

Fig. 6. Example of modulation diversity with 4-PSK. (a) $L_s = 1$. (b) $L_s = 2$.

Since a lattice is *geometrically uniform* [384], we may simply write that the error probability when transmitting a signal chosen from lattice Λ is the same for all signals, and in particular for the signal corresponding to the lattice point $\boldsymbol{0}$: $P_e(\Lambda) = P_e(\Lambda|\boldsymbol{0})$. The union bound to error probability yields

$$P_e(S) \le P_e(\Lambda) \le \sum_{\hat{\boldsymbol{x}} \ne \boldsymbol{x}} P(\boldsymbol{x} \to \hat{\boldsymbol{x}}) \qquad (4.3.7)$$

where $P(\boldsymbol{x} \to \hat{\boldsymbol{x}})$ is the pairwise error probability. The first inequality takes into account the edge effects of the finite constellation S compared to the infinite lattice Λ.

Let us apply the Chernoff bound to estimate the pairwise error probability. For large signal-to-noise ratios we have

$$
\begin{aligned}
P(\boldsymbol{x} \to \hat{\boldsymbol{x}}) &\le \frac{1}{2} \prod_{x_i \ne \hat{x}_i} \frac{1}{\dfrac{(x_i - \hat{x}_i)^2}{8N_0}} \\
&= \frac{1}{2} \frac{1}{\left(\dfrac{\eta}{8}\dfrac{\mathcal{E}_b}{N_0}\right)^l d_p^{(l)}(\boldsymbol{x}, \hat{\boldsymbol{x}})^2}
\end{aligned} \qquad (4.3.8)
$$

where $d_p^{(l)}(\boldsymbol{x}, \hat{\boldsymbol{x}})$ is the (normalized) *l-product distance* of $\boldsymbol{x}$ from $\hat{\boldsymbol{x}}$ when these two points differ in l components

$$d_p^{(l)}(\boldsymbol{x}, \hat{\boldsymbol{x}})^2 = \frac{\displaystyle\prod_{x_i \ne y_i} (x_i - y_i)^2}{(E/n)^l} \qquad (4.3.9)$$

η is the spectral efficiency (in bits per dimension pair), $\mathcal{E}_b$ is the average energy per bit, and $\mathcal{E}$ is the average signal energy. Asymptotically, (4.3.9) is dominated by the term $1/(\mathcal{E}_b/N_0)^{L_s}$ where $L_s = \min(l)$ is the diversity of the signal constellation. Rearranging (4.3.9) we obtain

$$P_e(\Lambda) \le \frac{1}{2} \sum_{l=L_s}^{n} \frac{K_l}{\left(\dfrac{\eta}{8}\dfrac{\mathcal{E}_b}{N_0}\right)^l} \qquad (4.3.10)$$

where $K_l = \Sigma_{d_p^{(l)}} A_{d_p^{(l)}} / (d_p^{(l)})^2$. $A_{d_p^{(l)}}$ is the number of points $\hat{\boldsymbol{x}}$ at l-product distance $d_p^{(l)}$ from $\boldsymbol{x}$ and with l different components, $L_s \le l \le n$. By analogy with the lattice theta series, $\tau_p = A_{d_p^{(L_s)}}$ is called the *product kissing number*.

This shows that the error probability is determined asymptotically by the diversity order L, the minimum product distance $d_{p,\min}^{(L_s)}$, and the kissing number τ_p. In particular, good signal sets have high L and $d_{p,\min}^{(L_s)}$, and small τ_p.

High-diversity integral lattices from algebraic number fields: The algebraic approach [363], [389], [386], [385], [429], [364], [365], [388], [370], [366], [372], [390], [378], [413], [415] allows one to build a generator matrix exhibiting a guaranteed diversity.

As a special case, high-diversity constellations can be generated by rotations [362], [432], [364], [365], [370]–[372]. First of all, note that if the lattice generator matrix M in Fig. 5 is a rotation matrix, then the signal constellation S can be viewed as a rotated cubic lattice constellation or a rotated multidimensional quadrature amplitude-modulation (QAM) constellation. This observation enables some of the previous results on high-diversity lattices to be applied to producing high-diversity rotated constellations.

One point has to be noted when using these rotated constellations: increasing the diversity does not necessarily increase to the same extent the performance: in fact, the minimum product distance $d_{p,\min}^{(L)}$ decreases and the product kissing number τ_p increases. Simulations show that most of the gain is obtained for diversity orders up to 16.

2) Block-Fading Channel: This channel model, introduced in [148] and [210] (see also [400] and [156]) belongs to the general class of block-interference channels described in [183]. It is motivated by the fact that, in many mobile radio situations, the channel coherence time is much longer than one symbol interval, and hence several transmitted symbols are affected by the same fading value. Use of this channel model allows one to introduce a delay constraint for transmission, which is realistic whenever infinite-depth interleaving is not a reasonable assumption.

This model assumes that a codeword of length $n = MN$ spans M blocks of length N (a group of M blocks will be referred to as a *frame*). The value of the fading in each block is constant, and each block is sent through an independent channel. An interleaver spreads the code symbols over the M blocks. M is a measure of the interleaving *delay* of the system: in fact, $M = 1$ (or $N = n$) corresponds to no interleaving, while $M = n$ (or $N = 1$) corresponds to perfect interleaving. Thus results obtained for different values of N illustrate the downside of nonideal interleaving, and hence of finite decoding delay.

For this channel, it is intuitive (and easy to prove) that the pairwise error probability decreases exponentially with exponent $d(M)$, the Hamming distance between codewords on a block basis (in other words, two nonequal blocks contribute to this block Hamming distance by one, irrespective of the symbols in which they differ). If a code with rate R_c bits per dimension is used over this channel in conjunction with an S-ary modulation scheme, then the Singleton bound [400], [156] upper-bounds the block Hamming distance

$$d(M) \leq 1 + \left\lfloor M\left(1 - \frac{R_c}{\log_2 S}\right)\right\rfloor. \qquad (4.3.11)$$

If this inequality is applied to a code with $r = 0.5, M = 8$, and $S = 2$ (the parameters that characterize the GSM standard of second-generation digital cellular systems), it shows that

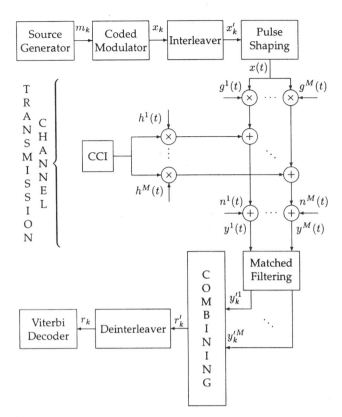

Fig. 7. Block diagram of the transmission scheme.

$d(8) \leq 5$. Now, the convolutional code selected for GSM achieves exactly this bound, and hence it can be proved to be optimum in the sense of maximizing the block Hamming distance [400]. The code was originally found by optimizing the Hamming distance, considering interleaving over eight time slots for full-rate GSM (and over four for half-rate) with one or two erasures. The result was a half-rate code which could decode even if three out of eight slots were bad (full-rate) [391], [407]. A larger upper bound would be obtained by choosing $S = 4$, in which case the challenge would be to find a code that achieves this bound.

Malkamäki and Leib [175] provide a fairly comprehensive analysis of coding for this class of channels, based on random-coding error bounds. Among the observations of [175], it is interesting to note that for high-rate codes the diversity afforded by the use of M blocks may not improve the average code performance: since the channel is constant during a block, it may be better to send the whole codeword in a single block rather than to divide it into several blocks.

D. Impact of Diversity

The design procedure described in the section above, and consisting of adapting the C/M scheme to the channel, may suffer from a basic weakness. If the channel model is not stationary, as may be the case, for example, in a mobile-radio environment where it fluctuates in time between the extremes of Rayleigh and AWGN, then a code designed to be optimum for a fixed channel model might perform poorly when the channel varies. Therefore, a code optimal for the AWGN channel may be actually suboptimum for a substantial

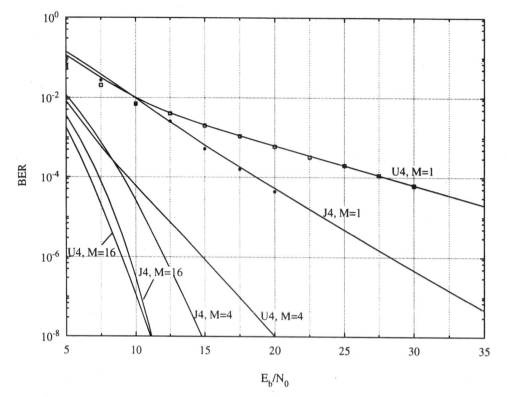

Fig. 8. Effect of antenna diversity on the performance of four-state TCM schemes over the flat, independent Rayleigh fading channel. **J4** is optimum for the Rayleigh channel, while **U4** is optimum for the Gaussian channel.

fraction of time.[17] An alternative solution consists of doing the opposite, i.e., *matching the channel to the coding scheme:* the latter is still designed for a Gaussian channel, while the former is transformed from a Rayleigh-fading channel (say) into a Gaussian one, thanks to the introduction of antenna diversity and maximal-ratio combining.

The standard approach to antenna diversity is based on the fact that, with several diversity branches, the probability that the signal will be simultaneously faded on all branches can be made small. Another approach, which was investigated by the authors in [302], [303], and [426], is philosophically different, as it is based upon the observation that, under fairly general conditions, a channel affected by fading can be turned into an additive white Gaussian noise (AWGN) channel by increasing the number of diversity branches. Consequently, it can be expected (and it was indeed verified by analyses and simulations) that a coded-modulation scheme designed to be optimal for the AWGN channel will perform asymptotically well also on a fading channel with diversity, at the cost of an increase in receiver complexity. An advantage of this solution is its robustness, since changes in the physical channel affect the reception very little.

This allows one to argue that the use of "Gaussian" codes along with diversity reception provides indeed a solution to the problem of designing robust coding schemes for the mobile radio channel.

Fig. 7 shows the block diagram of the transmission scheme with fading and cochannel interference.

The assumptions are [302], [303], and [426] as follows.

1) PSK modulation.
2) M independent diversity branches whose signal-to-noise ratio is inversely proportional to M (this assumption is made in order to disregard the SNR increase that actually occurs when multiple receive elements are used).
3) Flat, independent Rayleigh fading channel.
4) Coherent detection with perfect channel-state information.
5) Synchronous diversity branches.
6) Independent cochannel interference, and a single interferer.

The codes examined in [302], [303], and [426] are the following:

J4: Four-state, rate-2/3 TCM scheme based on 8-PSK and optimized for Rayleigh fading channels [397].
U4: Four-state rate-2/3 TCM scheme based on 8-PSK and optimized for the Gaussian channel.
U8: Same as above, with eight states.
Q64: "Pragmatic" concatenation of the "best" rate-1/2 64-state convolutional code with 4-PSK modulator and Gray mapping [428].

Fig. 8 compares the performance of **U4** and **J4** (two TCM schemes with the same complexity) over a Rayleigh fading channel with M-branch diversity.

It is seen that, as M increases, the performance of **U4** comes closer and closer to that of **J4**. Similar results hold for correlated fading: even for moderate correlation **J4** loses

---

[17] We recall that, as far as channel capacity is concerned, with CSI available to either the receiver or both receiver and transmitter, it is the capacity-achieving code which implicitly does time averaging, even when no diversity is present.

its edge on **U4**, and for M as low as 4 **U4** performs better than **J4** [302]. The effect of diversity is more marked when the code used is weaker. As an example, two-antenna diversity provides a gain of 10 dB at BER $= 10^{-6}$ when **U8** is used, and of 2.5 dB when **Q64** is used [302]. The assumption of branch independence, although important, is not critical: in effect, [302] shows that branch correlations as large as 0.5 degrade system BER only slightly. The complexity introduced by diversity can be traded for delay: as shown in [302], in some cases diversity makes interleaving less necessary, so that a lower interleaving depth (and, consequently, a lower overall delay) can be compensated by an increase of M.

When differential or pilot-tone, rather than coherent, detection is used [426], a BER floor occurs which can be reduced by introducing diversity. As for the effect of cochannel interference, even its BER floor is reduced as M is increased (although for its elimination multiuser detectors should be employed). This shows that antenna diversity with maximal-ratio combining is highly instrumental in making the fading channel closer to Gaussian.

1) Transmitter-Antenna Diversity: Multiple transmit antennas can also be used to provide diversity, and hence to improve the performance of a communication system in a fading environment; see, e.g., [393], [198], [434], [435], [436]. Transmitter diversity has been receiving in the recent past a fresh look. As observed in [198], "it is generally viewed as more difficult to exploit than receiver diversity, in part because the transmitter is assumed to know less about the channel than the receiver, and in part because of the challenging design problem: the transmitter is permitted to generate a different signal at each antenna."

The case with M transmit antennas and one receive antenna is relatively simple, and especially interesting for applications. A taxonomy of transmitter diversity schemes is proposed in [198]. In [410] and [198] each transmit antenna sees an independent fading channel. The receiver is assumed to have perfect knowledge of the vector R of the fading coefficients of the M channels, while the transmitter has access only to a random variable correlated with R. This variable represents side information which might be obtained from feedback from the receiver, reverse-path signal measurements, or approximate multipath directional information. The lack of channel knowledge at the transmitter results in a factor of M loss in signal-to-noise ratio relative to perfect channel knowledge.

General C/M design guidelines for transmit-antenna diversity in fading channels were considered by several authors (see, e.g., [383]).

2) Coding with Transmit- and Receive-Antenna Diversity: Space–Time Codes: As of today, the most promising coding schemes with transmit- and receive-antenna diversity seem to be offered by "space–time codes" [281]. These can be seen as a generalization of a coding scheme advocated in [418], where the same data are transmitted by two antennas with a delay of one-symbol interval introduced in the second path. This corresponds to using a repetition code. The diversity gain provided by space–time codes equals the rank of certain matrices, which translates the code design task into an elegant mathematical problem. Explicit designs are presented in [281],

based on 4-PSK, 8-PSK, and 16-QAM. They exhibit excellent performance, and can operate within 2–3 dB of the theoretical limits.

E. Coding with CSI at Transmitter and Receiver

An efficient coding strategy, which can also be used in conjunction with diversity, is based on the simple observation that if CSI is available at the transmitter as well as at the receiver the transmit power may be allocated on a symbol-by-symbol basis. Consider the simplest such strategy. Assume that the CSI R is known at the transmitter front-end, that is, the transmitter knows the value of R during the transmission (this assumption obviously requires that R is changing very slowly), and denote by $\gamma(R)$ the amplitude transmitted when the channel gain is R. One possible power-allocation criterion (constant error probability over each symbol) requires $\gamma(R)$ to be the inverse of the channel gain. This way, the channel is transformed into an equivalent additive white Gaussian noise channel. This technique ("channel inversion") is conceptually simple, since the encoder and decoder are designed for the AWGN channel, independent of the fading statistics: a version of it is common in spread-spectrum systems with near–far interference imbalances. However, it may suffer from a large capacity penalty. For example, with Rayleigh fading the transmitted power would be infinite, because $E[R^{-2}]$ diverges, and the channel capacity is zero.

To avoid divergence of the average power (or an inordinately large value thereof) a possible strategy consists of inverting the channel only if the power expenditure does not exceed a certain threshold; otherwise, we compensate only for a part of the channel attenuation. By appropriately choosing the value of the threshold we trade off a decrease of the average received power value for an increase of error probability.

A different perspective in taken in [43], where a coding strategy is studied which minimizes the outage rate of the M-block BF-AWGN. It is shown that minimum outage rate can be achieved by transmitting a fixed codebook, randomly generated with i.i.d. Gaussian components, and by suitably allocating the transmitted power to the blocks. The optimal power-allocation policy is derived under a constraint on the transmitted power. Specifically, two different power constraints are considered. The first one ("short-term" constraint) requires the average power *in each frame* to be less than a constant $\mathcal{P}$. The second one ("long-term" constraint) requires the average power *time-averaged over a sequence of infinitely many frames* to be less than $\mathcal{P}$.

In [111], the coding scheme advocated for a channel with CSI at both transmitter and receiver was based on multiplexing different codebooks with different rates and average powers, where the multiplexer and the corresponding demultiplexer are driven by the fading process. Reference [43] shows that the same capacity can also be achieved by a single codebook with i.i.d. Gaussian components, whose mth block of symbols is properly scaled before transmission. To see this, it is sufficient to replace the BF-AWGN channel with perfect transmitter and receiver CSI and gain α by a BF-AWGN channel with perfect receiver CSI only and gain $\beta = \alpha\gamma(\alpha)$, where $\gamma(\cdot)$ denotes the optimum power-control strategy. Since $\gamma(\cdot)$ is time-invariant, these channels have the same capacity irrespectively of the fading time correlation, as long as $\{\alpha\}$ forms an asymptotically ergodic process and no delay constraint is imposed (a rigorous proof, valid in a general setting, is provided in [41]).

A pragmatic power-allocation scheme for block-fading channels, simple but quite efficient, was proposed in [401]. It consists of inverting the channel only for a limited number of blocks, while no power is spent to transmit the others.

F. Bit-Interleaved Coded Modulation

Ever since 1982, when Ungerboeck published his landmark paper on trellis-coded modulation [424], it has been generally accepted that modulation and coding should be combined in a single entity for improved performance. Several results followed this line of thought, as documented by a considerable body of work aptly summarized and referenced in [397] (see also [361, Ch. 10]). Under the assumption that the symbols were interleaved with a depth exceeding the coherence time of the fading process, new codes were designed for the fading channel so as to maximize their diversity. This implied in particular that parallel transitions should be avoided in the code, and that any increase in diversity would be obtained by increasing the constraint length of the code. One should also observe that for non-Ungerboeck systems, i.e., those separating modulation and coding with binary modulation, Hamming distance is proportional to Euclidean distance, and hence a system optimized for the additive white Gaussian channel is also optimum for the Rayleigh fading channel.

A notable departure from Ungerboeck's paradigm was the core of [428]. Schemes were designed in which coded modulation is generated by pairing an M-ary signal set with a binary convolutional code with the largest minimum free Hamming distance. Decoding was achieved by designing a metric aimed at keeping as their basic engine an off-the-shelf Viterbi decoder for the *de facto* standard, 64-state rate-$1/2$ convolutional code. This implied giving up the joint decoder/demodulator in favor of two separate entities.

Based on the latter concept, Zehavi [437] first recognized that the code diversity, and hence the reliability of coded modulation over a Rayleigh fading channel, could be further improved. Zehavi's idea was to make the code diversity equal to the smallest number of distinct *bits* (rather than *channel symbols*) along any error event. This is achieved by bit-wise interleaving at the encoder output, and by using an appropriate soft-decision bit metric as an input to the Viterbi decoder.

One of Zehavi's findings, rather surprising *a priori*, was that on some channels there is a downside to combining demodulation and decoding. This prompted the investigation the results of which are presented in a comprehensive fashion in [42] (see also [357]).

An advantage of this solution is its robustness, since changes in the physical channel affect the reception very little. Thus it provides good performance with a fading channel as well as with an AWGN channel (and, consequently, with a Rice fading channel, which can be seen as intermediate between the latter two). This is due to the fact that BICM increases the Hamming distance at the price of a moderate reduction of the Euclidean distance: see Table I.

TABLE I
EUCLIDEAN AND HAMMING DISTANCES OF SELECTED BICM AND TCM SCHEMES FOR 16-QAM AND TRANSMISSION RATE 3 BITS PER DIMENSION PAIR (THE AVERAGE ENERGY IS NORMALIZED TO 1)

Encoder Memory	BICM		TCM	
	d_E^2	d_H	d_E^2	d_H
2	1.2	3	2.0	1
3	1.6	4	2.4	2
4	1.6	4	2.8	2
5	2.4	6	3.2	2
6	2.4	6	3.6	3
7	3.2	8	3.6	3
8	3.2	8	4.0	3

Recently, a scheme which combines bit-interleaved coded modulation with iterative ("turbo") decoding was analyzed [404], [405]. It was shown that iterative decoding results in a dramatic performance improvement, and even outperforms trellis-coded modulation over Gaussian channels.

G. Conclusions

This review was aimed at illustrating some concepts that make the design of short codes for the fading channel differ markedly from the same task applied to the Gaussian channel. In particular, we have examined the design of "fading codes," i.e., C/M schemes which maximize the Hamming, rather than the Euclidean, distance, the interaction of antenna diversity with coding (which makes the channel more Gaussian), and the effect of separating coding from modulation in favor of a more robust C/M scheme. The issue of optimality as contrasted to robustness was also discussed to some extent. The connections with the information-theoretic results for the previous section were also pointed out.

V. EQUALIZATION OF FADING MULTIPATH CHANNELS

Equalization is generally required to mitigate the effects of intersymbol interference (ISI) resulting from time-dispersive channels such as fading multipath channels which are frequency-selective. Equlization is also effective in reducing multiple-access interference (MAI) in multiuser communication systems. In this section, we focus our discussion on equalization techniques that are effective in combatting ISI caused by multipath in fading channels and MAI in multiuser communication systems. Many references to the literature are cited for the benefit of the interested reader who may wish to delve into these topics in greater depth. In reading this section, it should be kept in mind that the optimum coding/modulation/demodulation/decoding, as dictated by information-theoretic arguments, does not imply separation between equalization and decoding. However, the latter approach may yield robust systems with limited complexity, incurring in a small or even negligible loss of optimality. In this respect, we follow here the rationale of the previous section, that is, we attempt at complementing the information-theoretic insights with methods of primarily practical relevance. Thus in this section we shall not address explicitly the presence of code (which would be essential if

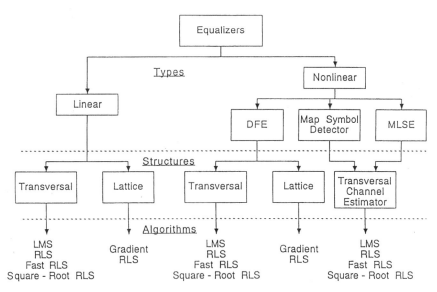

Fig. 9. Equalizer types, structures, and algorithms.

channel capacity were to be approached). A few remarks on this point will also be provided at the end of this section.

A. Channel Characteristics that Impact Equalization

As previously indicated, signals transmitted on wireless channels are corrupted by time-varying multipath signal propagation, additive noise disturbances, and interference from multiple users of the channel. Time-varying multipath generally results in signal fading.

The communication system engineer is faced with the task of designing the modulation/demodulation and coding/decoding techniques to achieve reliable communication that satisfies the system requirements, such as the desired data rates, transmitter power, and bandwidth constraints.

Not all system designs for wireless communications require the use of adaptive equalizers. In fact, if T_m is the channel multipath spread, the system designer may avoid the need for channel equalization by selecting the time duration T_s of the transmitted signaling waveforms to satisfy the condition $T_s \gg T_m$. As a consequence, the intersymbol interference (ISI) is negligible. This is indeed the case in the digital cellular system based on the IS-95 standard, which employs CDMA to accommodate multiple users. This is also the case in digital-audio broadcast (DAB) systems which employ multicarrier, orthogonal frequency-division multiplexing (OFDM) for modulation. On the other hand, if the system designer selects the symbol time duration T_s of the signaling waveforms such that $T_s < T_m$, then there is ISI present in the received signal which can be mitigated by use of an equalizer.

Another channel parameter that plays an important role in the effectiveness of an equalizer is the channel Doppler spread B_d or its reciprocal $1/B_d$, which is the channel coherence time. Since the use of an equalizer at the receiver implies the need to measure the channel characteristics, i.e., the channel impulse or frequency response, the channel time variations must be relatively slow compared to the transmitted symbol duration T_s and, more generally, compared to the multipath spread T_m. Consequently, $1/B_d \gg T_m$ or, equivalently, the

spread factor must satisfy the condition

$$T_m B_d \ll 1$$

that is, the channel must be underspread. Therefore, adaptive equalization is particularly applicable to reducing the effects of ISI in underspread wireless communications channels.

B. Equalization Methods

Equalization techniques for combatting intersymbol interference (ISI) on time-dispersive channels may be subdivided into two general types—linear equalization and nonlinear equalization. Associated with each type of equalizer is one or more structures for implementing the equalizer. Furthermore, for each structure there is a class of algorithms that may be employed to adaptively adjust the equalizer parameters according to some specified performance criterion. Fig. 9 provides an overall categorization of adaptive equalization techniques into types, structures, and algorithms. Linear equalizers find use in applications where the channel distortion is not too severe. In particular, the linear equalizer does not perform well on channels with spectral nulls in their frequency-response characteristics. In compensating for the channel distortion, the linear equalizer places a large gain in the vicinity of the spectral null and, as a consequence, significantly enhances the additive noise present in the received signal. Such is the case in fading multipath channels. Consequently, linear equalizers are generally avoided for fading multipath channels. Instead, nonlinear equalization methods, either decision-feedback equalization or maximum-likelihood sequence detection, are used.

Maximum-likelihood sequence detection (MLSD) is the optimum equalization technique in the sense that it minimizes the probability of a sequence error [223]. MLSD is efficiently implemented by means of the Viterbi algorithm [223], [454]. However, the computational complexity of MLSD grows exponentially with the number of symbols affected by ISI [223], [454]. Consequently, its application to practical communication systems is limited to channels for which the ISI spans

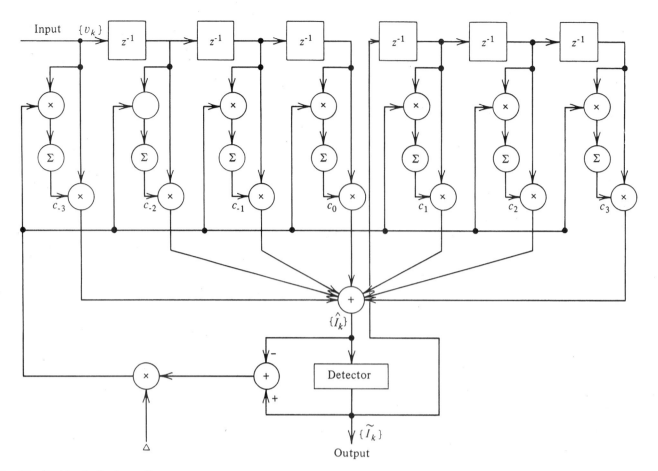

Fig. 10. Decision-feedback equalizer.

a relatively small number of symbols, e.g. fewer than ten. Such is the case for the GSM digital cellular system, where MLSD is widely used. This is also the case for the North America IS-54 or IS-136 digital cellular standard, where the ISI spans only two or three symbols [469].

On the other hand, there are wireless communication channels in which the ISI spans such a large number of symbols, e.g., 50–100 symbols, that the computational complexity of MLSD is practically prohibitive. In such cases, the decision-feedback equalizer (DFE) provides a computationally efficient albeit suboptimum, alternative [483]. The basic idea in decision-feedback equalization is that once an information symbol has been detected, the ISI that it causes on future symbols may be estimated and subtracted out prior to symbol detection. The DFE may be realized either in the direct form or as a lattice [223], [471], [504], [505]. The direct-form structure of the DFE is illustrated in Fig. 10.

It consists of a feedforward filter (FFF) and a feedback filter (FBF). The latter is driven by decisions at the output of the detector and its coefficients are adjusted to cancel the ISI on the current symbol that results from past detected symbols (postcursors).

The computational complexity of the DFE is a linear function of the number of taps of the feedforward and feedback filters, which are typically equal to twice the number of symbols (for $T/2$ fractional spacing) spanned by the ISI. The DFE has been shown to be **particularly** effective for equalizing

the ISI in underwater acoustic communication channels [510], [512]. It also provides a computationally simpler alternative to MLSD for use in the GSM digital cellular system, where the multipath spread of the channel may span up to six symbols [444]. The DFE has also been used in digital communication systems for troposcatter channels operating in the SHF (3–30-GHz) frequency band [223], [463] and ionospheric channels in the HF (3–30-MHz) frequency band [223], [463].

C. Fractionally Spaced Equalizers

It is well known [223] that the optimum receiver for a digital communication signal corrupted by additive white Gaussian noise (AWGN) consists of a matched filter which is sampled periodically at the symbol rate. These samples constitute a set of sufficient statistics for estimating the digital information that was transmitted. If the signal samples at the output of the matched filter are corrupted by intersymbol interference, the symbol-spaced samples are further processed by an equalizer.

In the presence of channel distortion, such as channel multipath, the matched filter prior to the equalizer must be matched to the channel corrupted signal. However, in practice, the channel impulse response is usually unknown. One approach is to estimate the channel impulse response from the transmission of a sequence of known symbols and to implement the matched filter to the received signal using the estimate of the channel impulse response. This is generally the approach used in the GSM digital cellular system, where digital voice and/or data is transmitted in packets, where each packet contains a sequence of known data symbols that are used to estimate the channel impulse response [449], [444]. A second approach is to employ a fractionally spaced equalizer, which in effect consists of a combination of the matched filter and a linear equalizer.

A fractionally spaced equalizer (FSE) is based on sampling the incoming signal at least as fast as the Nyquist rate [223], [457], [497], [520]. For example, if the transmitted signal consists of pulses having a raised cosine spectrum with rolloff factor β, its spectrum extends to $F_{\max} = (1 + \beta)/2T$. This signal may be sampled at the receiver at the minimum rate of

$$2F_{\max} = \frac{1 + \beta}{T}$$

and then passed through an equalizer with tap spacing of $T/(1 + \beta)$. For example, if $\beta = 1$, we require a $T/2$-spaced equalizer. If $\beta = 1/2$, we may use a $2T/3$-spaced equalizer, and so forth. In general, a digitally implemented FSE has tap spacings of KT/L, where K and L are integers and $K < L$. Often, a $T/2$-spaced equalizer is used in many applications, even in cases where a larger tap spacing is possible.

The frequency response of an FSE is

$$C_{T'}(f) = \sum_{k=0}^{N-1} c_k e^{-j2\pi f k T'}$$

where $\{c_k\}$ are the equalizer coefficients, N is the number of equalizer tap weights, and $T' = KT/L$. Hence, $C_{T'}(f)$ can equalize the received signal spectrum beyond the Nyquist frequency up to $f = L/KT$. The equalized spectrum is

$$C_{T'}(f)Y_{T'}(f) = C_{T'}(f) \sum_n X\left(f - \frac{n}{T'}\right) e^{j2\pi(f - n/T')\tau_0}$$

$$= C_{T'}(f) \sum_n X\left(f - \frac{nL}{KT}\right) e^{j2\pi(f - nL/KT)\tau_0}$$

where $X(f)$ is the input analog signal spectrum which is assumed to be bandlimited, $Y_{T'}(f)$ is the spectrum of the sampled signal, and τ_0 is a timing delay. Since $X(f) = 0$ for $|f| > L/KT$ by design, the above expression reduces to

$$C_{T'}(f)Y_{T'}(f) = C_{T'}(f)X(f)e^{j2\pi f\tau_0}, \qquad |f| \le \frac{1}{2T'}.$$

Thus the FSE compensates for the channel distortion in the received signal before aliasing effects occur due to symbol rate sampling. In addition, the equalizer with transfer function $C_{T'}(f)$ can compensate for any timing delay τ_0, i.e., for any arbitrary timing phase. In effect, the fractionally spaced equalizer incorporates the functions of matched filtering and equalization into a single filter structure.

The FSE output is sampled at the symbol rate $1/T$ and has a spectrum

$$\sum_k C_{T'}\left(f - \frac{k}{T}\right) X\left(f - \frac{k}{T}\right) e^{-j2\pi(f - k/T)\tau_0}.$$

Its tap coefficients may be adaptively adjusted once per symbol as in a T-spaced equalizer. There is no improvement in convergence rate by making adjustments at the input sampling

rate of the FSE. Results by Qureshi and Forney [497] and Gitlin and Weinstein [457] demonstrate the effectiveness of the FSE relative to a symbol rate equalizer in channels where the channel response is unknown.

In the implementation of the DFE, the feedforward filter should be fractionally spaced, e.g., $T/2$-spaced taps, and its length should span the total anticipated channel dispersion The feedback filter has T-spaced taps and its length should also span the anticipated channel dispersion [223].

D. Adaptive Algorithms and Lattice Equalizers

In linear and decision-feedback equalizers, the criterion most commonly used in the optimization of the equalizer coefficients is the minimization of the mean-square error (MSE) between the desired equalizer output and the actual equalizer output. The minimization of the MSE results in the optimum Wiener filter solution for the coefficient vector, which may be expressed as [223]

$$\boldsymbol{C}_{\mathrm{opt}} = \boldsymbol{\Gamma}^{-1}\boldsymbol{\xi} \qquad (5.4.1)$$

where $\boldsymbol{\Gamma}$ is the autocorrelation matrix of the vector of signal samples in the equalizer at any given time instant and $\boldsymbol{\xi}$ is the vector of cross correlations between the desired data symbol and the signal samples in the equalizer.

Alternatively, the minimization of the MSE may be accomplished recursively by use of the stochastic gradient algorithm introduced by Widrow and Hoff [534], [535], called the LMS algorithm. This algorithm is described by the coefficient update equation

$$\boldsymbol{C}_{k+1} = \boldsymbol{C}_k + \Delta e_k \boldsymbol{X}_k^*, \qquad k = 0, 1, \cdots \qquad (5.4.2)$$

where $\boldsymbol{C}_k$ is the vector of the equalizer coefficients at the kth iteration, $\boldsymbol{X}_k$ represents the signal vector for the signal samples stored in the equalizer at the kth iteration, e_k is the error signal, which is defined as the difference between the kth transmitted symbol I_k and its corresponding estimate $\hat{I}_k$ at the output of the equalizer, and Δ is the step-size parameter that controls the rate of adjustment. The asterisk on $\boldsymbol{X}_k^*$ signifies the complex conjugate of $\boldsymbol{X}_k$. Fig. 11 illustrates the linear FIR equalizer in which the coefficients are adjusted according to the LMS algorithm given by (5.4.2).

It is well known [223], [534], [535] that the step-size parameter Δ controls the rate of adaptation of the equalizer and the stability of the LMS algorithm. For stability, $0 < \Delta < 2/\lambda_{\max}$, where $\lambda_{\max}$ is the largest eigenvalue of the signal covariance matrix. A choice of Δ just below the upper limit provides rapid convergence, but it also introduces large fluctuations in the equalizer coefficients during steady-state operation. These fluctuations constitute a form of self-noise whose variance increases with an increase in Δ. Consequently, the choice of Δ involves tradeoff between rapid convergence and the desire to keep the variance of the self-noise small [223], [534], [535].

The convergence rate of the LMS algorithm is slow due to the fact that there is only a single parameter, namely Δ, that controls the rate of adaptation. A faster converging algorithm is obtained if we employ a recursive least squares (RLS) criterion for adjustment of the equalizer coefficients. The RLS

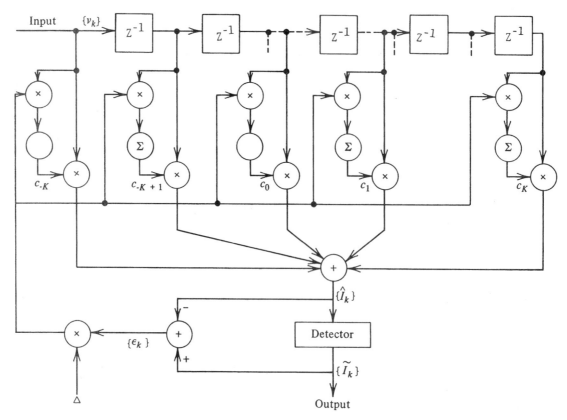

Fig. 11. Linear adaptive equalizer based on MSE criterion.

algorithm that is obtained for the minimization of the sum of exponentially weighted squared errors, i.e.,

$$\mathcal{E} = \sum_{n=0}^{k} w^{k-n} |I_n - \hat{I}_n|^2$$

$$= \sum_{n=0}^{k} w^{k-n} |I_n - \boldsymbol{C}_k' \boldsymbol{X}_n^*|^2$$

may be expressed as [223], [463]

$$\boldsymbol{C}_{k+1} = \boldsymbol{C}_k + \boldsymbol{P}_k \boldsymbol{X}_k^* e_k \qquad (5.4.3)$$

where $\hat{I}_k$ is the estimate of the kth symbol I_k at the output of the equalizer, $\boldsymbol{C}_k'$ denotes the transpose of $\boldsymbol{C}_k$, and

$$e_k = I_k - \hat{I}_k \qquad (5.4.4)$$

$$\boldsymbol{P}_k = \frac{1}{w} \left[\boldsymbol{P}_{k-1} - \frac{\boldsymbol{P}_{k-1} \boldsymbol{X}_k^* \boldsymbol{X}_k' \boldsymbol{P}_{k-1}}{w + \boldsymbol{X}_k' \boldsymbol{P}_{k-1} \boldsymbol{X}_k'} \right]. \qquad (5.4.5)$$

The exponential weighting factor w is selected to be in the range $0 < w < 1$. It provides a fading memory in the estimation of the optimum equalizer coefficients. $\boldsymbol{P}_k$ is an $(N \times N)$ square matrix which is the inverse of the data autocorrelation matrix

$$\boldsymbol{R}_k = \sum_{n=0}^{k} w^{k-n} \boldsymbol{X}_n^* \boldsymbol{X}_n'. \qquad (5.4.6)$$

Initially, $\boldsymbol{P}_0$ may be selected to be proportional to the identity matrix. Fig. 12 illustrates a comparison of the convergence rate of the RLS and the LMS algorithms for an equalizer of length the $N = 11$ and a channel with a small amount of ISI

[223], [505]. We note that the difference in convergence rate is very significant.

The recursive update equation for the matrix $\boldsymbol{P}_k$ given by (5.4.5) has poor numerical properties. For this reason, other algorithms with better numerical properties have been derived which are based on a square-root factorization of $\boldsymbol{P}_k$ as $\boldsymbol{P}_k = \boldsymbol{S}_k' \boldsymbol{S}_k$, where $\boldsymbol{S}_k$ is a lower triangular matrix. Such algorithms are called *square-root RLS algorithms* [463], [443]. These algorithms update the matrix $\boldsymbol{S}_k$ directly without computing $\boldsymbol{P}_k$ explicitly, and have a computational complexity proportional to N^2. Other types of RLS algorithms appropriate for transversal FIR equalizers have been devised with a computational complexity proportional to N [448], [508], [471]. These types of algorithms are called *fast RLS algorithms*.

The linear and decision-feedback equalizers based on the RLS criterion may also be implemented in the form of a lattice structure [471], [472]. The lattice structure and the RLS equations for updating the equalizer coefficients have been described in several references, for example, see [471]–[473]. The convergence rate is identical to that of the RLS algorithm for the adaptation of the direct form (transversal) structures. However, the computational complexity for the RLS lattice structure in proportional to N, but with a larger proportionality constant compared to the fast RLS algorithm for the direct form structure [223]. For example, Table II illustrates the computational complexity of an adaptive DFE employing complex-valued arithmetic for the in-phase and quadrature signal components. In this table, N_1 denotes the number of coefficients in the feedforward filter, N_2 denotes the number of coefficients in the feedback filter, and $N = N_1 + N_2$.

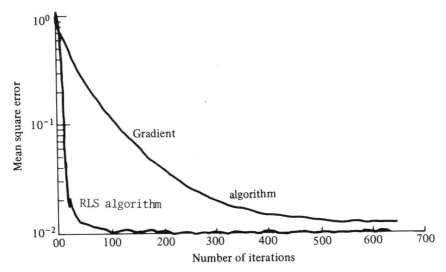

Fig. 12. Comparison of convergence rate for the RLS and LMS algorithms.

In general, the class of RLS algorithms provide faster convergence than the LMS algorithm. The convergence rate of the LMS algorithm is especially slow in channels which contain spectral nulls, whereas the convergence rate of the RLS algorithm is unaffected by the channel characteristics [223], [474].

E. Equalization of Interference in Multiuser Communication Systems

Adaptive equalizers are also effective in suppressing interference from other users of the channel. The interference may be in the form of either interchannel interference (ICI), or cochannel interference (CCI), or both. ICI frequently arises in multiple-access communication systems that employ either FDMA or TDMA. CCI is generally present in communication systems that employ CDMA, as in the IS-95 digital cellular system, as well as in FDMA or TDMA cellular systems that employ frequency reuse.

Verdú and many others [527], [528], [521]–[525] have done extensive research into various types of equalizers/detectors and their performance for multiuser systems employing CDMA. In a CDMA system, the channel is shared by K simultaneous users. Each user is assigned a signature waveform $g_k(t)$ of duration T_s, where T_s is the symbol interval. A signature waveform may be expressed as

$$g_k(t) = \sum_{n=0}^{M-1} a_k(n)p(t - nT_c), \qquad 0 \le t \le T_s \quad (5.5.1)$$

where $\{a_k(n), 0 \le n \le M - 1\}$ is a pseudo-noise (PN) code sequence consisting of M chips that take values $\{\pm 1\}$, $p(t)$ is a pulse of duration T_c, and T_c is the chip interval. Thus we have M chips per symbol and $T_s = MT_c$.

The transmitted signal waveform from the kth user may be expressed as

$$s_k(t) = A_k \sum_{i=-\infty}^{\infty} b_k(i)g_k(t - iT_s - \tau_k) \quad (5.5.2)$$

where $\{b_k(i)\}$ represents the sequence of information symbols, A_k is the signal amplitude, and τ_k is the signal delay of the kth user. The total transmitted signal for the K users is

$$
\begin{aligned}
x(t) &= \sum_{k=1}^{K} s_k(t) \\
&= \sum_{k=1}^{K} A_k \sum_{i=-\infty}^{\infty} b_k(i)g_k(t - iT_s - \tau_k). \quad (5.5.3)
\end{aligned}
$$

In the forward channel of a CDMA system, i.e., the transmission from the base station to the mobile receivers, the signals for all the users are transmitted synchronously, Hence, the delays $\tau_k = 0, 1 \le k \le K$.

As indicated in Section II, a frequency-selective fading multipath channel, which is modeled as a tapped delay line with time-varying tap coefficients, has an impulse response of the form

$$c_k(t; \tau) = \sum_{l=1}^{L_k} c_{lk}(t)\delta(\tau - t_{lk}) \quad (5.5.4)$$

where the $\{c_{lk}(t)\}$ denote the (complex-valued) amplitudes of the resolvable multipath components at the receiver of the kth user of the channel, L_k is the number of resolvable multipath components, and $\{t_{lk}\}$ are the L_k propagation delays.

For this channel model, the signal received by the kth mobile receiver in the forward channel may be expressed as

$$
\begin{aligned}
r_k(t) &= \sum_{l=1}^{L_k} c_{lk}(t)x(t - t_{lk}) + n_k(t) \\
&= \sum_{l=1}^{L_k} c_{lk}(t)s_k(t - t_{lk}) \\
&\quad + \sum_{\substack{j=1 \\ j\neq k}}^{K} \sum_{l=1}^{L_k} c_{lk}(t)s_j(t - t_{lk}) + n_k(t) \quad (5.5.5)
\end{aligned}
$$

where $n_k(t)$ represents the additive noise in the received signal. We observe that the received signal consists of the desired signal component, which is corrupted by the channel multipath, and channel-corrupted signals for the other $K - 1$

TABLE II
COMPUTATIONAL COMPLEXITY OF AN ADAPTIVE LSE

Algorithms	Total Number of Complex Operations	Number of Divisions
LMS	$2N + 1$	0
Fast RLS	$20N + 5$	3
Square-root RLS	$1.5N^2 + 6.5N$	N
Lattice RLLS	$18N_1 + 39N_2 - 39$	$2N_1$

channel users. The latter is usually called multiple-access interference (MAI).

An expression similar to (5.5.5) holds for the signal received at the base station from the transmissions of the K users.

The optimum multiuser receiver for the received signal given by (5.5.5) recovers the data symbols by use of the maximum-likelihood (ML) criterion. However, in the presence of multipath and multiuser interference, the computational complexity of the optimum receiver grows exponentially with the number of users. As a consequence, the focus of practical receiver design has been on suboptimum receivers whose computational complexity is significantly lower. The so-called "decorrelating detector" is a suboptimum receiver that is basically a linear type of equalizer which forces the CCI from other users in a CDMA system to zero [528]. The complete elimination of CCI among all the users of the channel is achieved at the expense of enhancing the power in the additive noise at the output of the equalizer. Another type of linear equalizer for mitigating the CCI in a CDMA system is based on the minimization of the mean-square error (MSE) between the equalizer outputs and the desired symbols [537]. By minimizing the total MSE, which includes the additive noise and CCI, one obtains a proper balance between these two errors and, as a consequence, the additive noise enhancement is lower.

In general, better performance against ISI and CCI in CDMA systems is achieved by employing a decision-feedback equalizer (DFE) in place of a linear equalizer. A number of papers have been published which illustrate the effectiveness of the DFE in combatting such interference. As examples of this work, we cite the papers by Falconer *et al.* [452], Abdulrahman *et al.* [438], and Duel Hallen [451].

The use of adaptive DFE's in TDMA and FDMA digital cellular systems have also been considered in the literature. For example, we cite the papers by D'Aria and Zingarelli [449], [450] Bjerke *et al.* [444], Uesugi *et al.* [519], and Baum *et al.* [439], which were focussed on TDMA cellular systems such as GSM and IS-54 (IS-136) systems.

The simultaneous suppression of narrowband interference (NBI) and (wideband) multiple-access interference (MAI) in CDMA systems is another problem that has been investigated recently. Poor and Wang [494], [495] developed an algorithm based on the linear minimum MSE (MMSE) criterion for multiuser detection which is effective in suppressing both NBI and MAI.

F. Iterative Interference Cancellation

In any multiple-access communication system, if the interference from other users is known at each of the user receivers, such interference can be subtracted from the received signal, thus leaving only the desired user's signal for detection. This basic approach, which is generally called *interference cancellation* is akin to the cancellation of the ISI from previously detected symbols in a DFE.

The idea of interference cancellation has been applied to the cancellation of MAI in CDMA systems. Basically, each receiver detects the symbols of every user, regenerates (remodulates) the users' signals, and subtracts them from the received signal to obtain the desired signal for the intended user.

The *successive interference canceler* (SIC) begins by acquiring and detecting the sequence of the strongest signal among the signals that it receives. Thus the strongest signal is regenerated and subtracted from the received signal. Once the strongest signal is canceled, the detector detects the symbol sequence of the second strongest signal. From this detected symbol sequence, the corresponding signal is regenerated and subtracted out. The procedure continues until all the MAI is canceled. When all the users are detected and canceled, a residual interference usually exists. This residual MAI may be used to perform a second stage of cancellation. This basic method of interference cancellation was investigated by Varanasi and Aazhang [522], [523] where they derived a multistage detector in which hard decisions are used to detect the symbols in the intermediate stages. Instead of hard decisions, one may employ soft decisions as proposed by Kechriotis and Manolakos [467]. Recently, Müller and Huber [484] have proposed an improvement in which an adaptive detector is employed that adapts to the decreasing interference power during the iterations. Such cancelers are called *iterative soft-decision interference cancelers* (ISDIC).

A major problem with the SIC or the ISDIC methods for MAI cancellation is the delay inherent in the implementation of the canceler. Furthermore, as with the DFE, the SIC and ISDIC are prone to error propagation, especially if there are symbol errors that occur in the detection of the strong users.

The problems of the detection delay in SIC or ISDIC may be alleviated to some extent by devising methods that perform parallel interference cancellation (PIC), as described by Patel and Holtzman [488] and others [445], [465].

The use of iterative methods for MAI cancellation and detection are akin to iterative methods for decoding turbo codes. Therefore, it is not surprising that these approaches have merged in some recent publications [458], [481], [500], [541].

G. Spatio-Temporal Equalization in Multiuser Communications

Multiple antennas provide additional degrees of freedom for suppressing ISI, CCI, and ICI. In general, the spatial dimension allows us to separate signals in multiple-access communication systems, thus reducing CCI and ICI. A communication system that uses multiple antennas at the transmitter and/or the receiver may be viewed as a *multichannel communication system*.

Multiple antennas at the transmitter allow the user to focus the transmitted signal in a desired direction and, thus, obtain

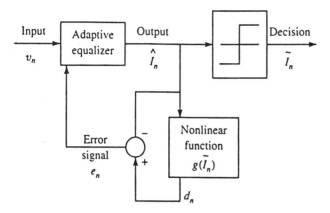

Fig. 13.   Adaptive blind equalization with stochastic gradient algorithm.

antenna gain and a reduction in CCI and ICI in areas off from the desired direction. Similarly, multiple antennas at the receiver allow the user to receive signals from desired directions and suppress unwanted signals, i.e., CCI and ICI, arriving from directions other than the desired directions. The use of multiple antennas also provides signal diversity and, thus, reduces the effect of signal fading.

Numerous papers have been published on the use multiple antennas for wireless communications. We cite a few representative papers below. For additional references, the reader may refer to the paper by Paulraj and Lindskog [489], which provides a taxonomy for space–time processing in wireless communication system.

Tidestav *et al.* [516], analyzed the performance of a multichannel DFE that performs combined temporal and spatial equalization, where the multiple antenna elements may be either at the base-station receiver or at the mobile receiver. The performance of the multichannel DFE was evaluated when the signal has a time slot structure similar to that of the GSM digital cellular system. In this paper, the performance of the multichannel DFE was also evaluated when used for multiuser detection in an asynchronous CDMA system with Rayleigh fading. The paper by Lindskog *et al.* [470] also treats the use of a multichannel DFE to equalize signals in an antenna array for a TDMA system.

Ratnavel *et al.* [501] investigate space–time equalization for GSM digital cellular systems based on the mean-square-error (MSE) criterion for optimizing the coefficients of the linear equalizer. Viterbi detection is employed for the ISI in the received signal.

Spatio-temporal equalization has also proved to be effective in digital communications through underwater acoustic channels [509], [511]. The underwater acoustic communication channel is a severely time-spread channel with ISI that spans many symbols. Due to the large delay spread, the only practical type of equalizer that has proved to be effective is the DFE. In such channels, spatial diversity is generally available through the use of multiple hydrophones at the receiver. In the case where a hydroplane array consists of a relatively large number of hydrophones, e.g., greater than five, Stojanovic *et al.* [511] demonstrated that a mutichannel DFE is especially effective in improving the performance of the receiver. In this paper, a reduced complexity receiver is described which consists

of a many-to-few K_1 to P, where $K_1 > P$ precombiner followed by a P-channel DFE. The precombiner is akin to a beamformer. The performance of the receiver is evaluated on experimental underwater acoustic data. The experimental results demonstrate the capability of the adaptive receiver to fully exploit the spatial variability of the multipath in the channel while keeping the system complexity to a minimum, thus allowing the efficient use of large hydrophone arrays.

Many other papers published in the literature treat spatio-temporal equalization of wireless channels. As examples, we cite the references [521], [525]. The majority of these papers are focused on spatio-temporal signal processing in CDMA systems.

H. Blind Equalization

In most applications where channel equalizers are used to suppress intersymbol interference, a known training sequence is transmitted to the receiver for the purpose of initially adjusting the equalizer coefficients. However, there are some applications, such as multipoint communication networks, where it is desirable for the receiver to synchronize to the received signal and to adjust the equalizer without having a known training sequence available. Equalization techniques based on initial adjustment of the equalizer coefficients without the benefit of a training sequence are said to be *self-recovering* or *blind*. It should be emphasized here that information-theoretic arguments address this situation in a natural setting of unavailable CSI. In general, the optimal information-theoretic approach does not depend on explicit extraction of CSI. Suboptimal, robust practical methods do however resort to algorithms which address explicitly the extraction of CSI, with or without the aid of training sequences.

There are basically three different classes of adaptive blind-equalization algorithms that have been developed over the past 25 years. One class of algorithms is based on the method of steepest descent for adaptation of the equalizer coefficients. Sato's paper [503] appears to be first published paper on blind equalization of PAM signals based on the method of steepest descent. Subsequently, Sato's work was generalized to two-dimensional (QAM) and multidimensional signal constellations in the papers by Godard [548], Benveniste and Goursat [442], Sato [549], Foschini [455], Picchi and Prati [491], and Shalvi and Weinstein [507].

Fig. 13 illustrates the basic structure of a linear blind equalizer whose coefficients are adjusted based on a steepest descent algorithm [223]. The sampled input sequence to the equalizer is denoted as $\{v_n\}$ and its output is a sequence of estimates of the information symbols, denoted by $\{\hat{I}_n\}$. For simplicity, we assume that the transmitted sequence of information symbols is binary, i.e., $\{\pm 1\}$. The output of the equalizer is passed through a memoryless nonlinear device whose output is the sequence $\{d_n \equiv g(\hat{I}_n)\}$. The sequence $\{d_n\}$ serves the role of the "desired symbols" and is used to generate an error signal, as shown in Fig. 13, for use in the LMS algorithm for adjusting the equalizer coefficients. The basic difference among the class of steepest descent algorithms is in the choice of the memoryless nonlinearity for generating

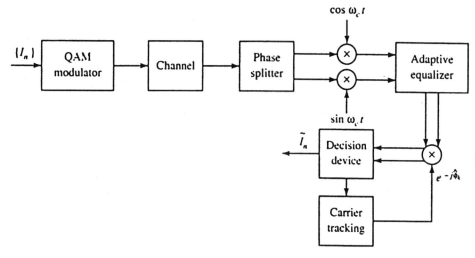

Fig. 14. Godard scheme for combined adaptive (blind) equalization and carrier phase tracking.

the sequence $\{d_n\}$. The most widely used algorithm in practice is the Godard algorithm [548], sometimes also called the constant-modulus algorithm (CMA). Fig. 14 shows a block diagram of Godard's scheme which includes carrier phase tracking.

It is apparent from Fig. 13 that the steepest descent algorithms are simple to implement, since they are basically LMS-type algorithms. As such, their basic limitation is their relative slow convergence. Consequently, their use in equalization of fading multipath channels is limited to extremely slow fading channels.

A second class of blind equalization algorithms is based on the use of second-order and higher order (usually, fourth-order) statistics of the received signal to estimate the channel characteristics and, then, to determine the equalizer coefficients based on the channel estimate.

It is well known that second-order statistics (autocorrelation) of the received signal sequence provide information on the magnitude of the channel characteristics, but not on the phase. However, this statement is not correct if the autocorrelation function of the received signal is periodic, as in the case for a digitally modulated signal. In such a case, it is possible to obtain a measurement of the amplitude and the phase of the channel response from the received signal. This cyclostationarity property of the received signal forms the basis for channel estimation algorithms devised by Tong *et al.* [517].

It is also possible to estimate the channel response from the received signal by using higher order statistical methods. In particular, the impulse response of a linear discrete time-invariant system can be obtained explicitly from cumulants of the received signal, provided that the channel input is non-Gaussian, as is the case when the information sequence is discrete and white. Based on this model, a simple method for estimating the channel impulse response from the received signal using fourth-order cumulants was devised by Giannakis and Hendel [456].

Another approach based on higher order statistics is due to Hatzinakos and Nikias [460]. They have introduced the first polyspectra-based adaptive blind-equalization method, named the tricepstrum equalization algorithm (TEA). This method estimates the channel magnitude and phase response by using the complex cepstrum of the fourth-order cumulants (tricepstrum) of the received signal sampled sequence $\{v_n\}$. From the fourth-order cumulants, TEA separately reconstructs the minimum-phase and maximum-phase characteristics of the channel. The channel equalizer coefficients are then computed from the measured channel characteristics.

By separating the channel estimation from the channel equalization of the received signal, it is possible to use any type of equalizer to suppress the ISI, i.e., either a linear equalizer or a nonlinear equalizer. The major disadvantage with the class of algorithms based on higher order statistics is the large amount of data required and the inherent computational comlexity involved in the estimation of the higher order moments (cumulants) of the received signal. Consequently, these algorithms are not generally applicable to fading multipath channels, unless the channel time variations are extremely slow.

More recently, a third class of blind-equalization algorithms based on the maximum-likelihood (ML) criterion have been developed. To describe the characteristics of the ML-based blind-equalization algorithms, it is convenient to use the discrete-time channel model described in [223]. The output of this channel model with ISI is

$$v_n = \sum_{k=0}^{L} f_k I_{n-k} + \eta_n \qquad (5.8.1)$$

where $\{f_k\}$ are the equivalent discrete-time channel coefficients, $\{I_n\}$ represents the information sequence, and $\{\eta_n\}$ is a white Gaussian noise sequence.

For a block of N received data points, the (joint) probability density function (pdf) of the received data vector $\boldsymbol{v} = [v_1 \ v_2 \ \cdots \ v_N]^t$ conditioned on knowing the impulse response vector $\boldsymbol{f} = [f_0 \ f_1 \ \cdots \ f_L]^t$ and the data vector $\boldsymbol{I} = [I_1 \ I_2 \ \cdots \ I_N]^t$ is

$$p(\boldsymbol{v}|\boldsymbol{f},\boldsymbol{I}) = \frac{1}{(2\pi\sigma^2)^N} \exp\left(-\frac{1}{2\sigma^2}\sum_{n=1}^{N}\left|v_n - \sum_{k=0}^{L} f_k I_{n-k}\right|^2\right).$$

$$(5.8.2)$$

The joint maximum-likelihood estimates of $\boldsymbol{f}$ and $\boldsymbol{I}$ are the values of these vectors that maximize the joint probability density function $p(\boldsymbol{v}|\boldsymbol{f},\boldsymbol{I})$ or, equivalently, the values of $\boldsymbol{f}$ and $\boldsymbol{I}$ that minimize the term in the exponent. Hence, the ML solution is simply the minimum over $\boldsymbol{f}$ and $\boldsymbol{I}$ of the metric

$$DM(\boldsymbol{I},\boldsymbol{f}) = \sum_{n=1}^{N} \left| v_n - \sum_{k=0}^{L} f_k \boldsymbol{I}_{n-k} \right|^2$$
$$= \|\boldsymbol{v} - \boldsymbol{A}\boldsymbol{f}\|^2 \qquad (5.8.3)$$

where the matrix $\boldsymbol{A}$ is called the *data matrix* and is defined as

$$\boldsymbol{A} = \begin{bmatrix} I_1 & 0 & 0 & \cdots & 0 \\ I_2 & I_1 & 0 & \cdots & 0 \\ I_3 & I_2 & I_1 & \cdots & 0 \\ \vdots & \vdots & \vdots & & \vdots \\ I_N & I_{N-1} & I_{N-2} & \cdots & I_{N-L} \end{bmatrix}. \qquad (5.8.4)$$

We make several observations. First of all, we note that when the data vector $\boldsymbol{I}$ (or the data matrix $\boldsymbol{A}$) is known, as is the case when a training sequence is available at the receiver, the ML channel impulse response estimate obtained by minimizing (5.8.3) over $\boldsymbol{f}$ is

$$\boldsymbol{f}_{\mathrm{ML}}(\boldsymbol{I}) = (\boldsymbol{A}^t \boldsymbol{A})^{-1} \boldsymbol{A}^t \boldsymbol{v}. \qquad (5.8.5)$$

On the other hand, when the channel impulse response $\boldsymbol{f}$ is known, the optimum ML detector for the data sequence $\boldsymbol{I}$ performs a trellis search (or tree search) by utilizing the Viterbi algorithm for the ISI channel.

When neither $\boldsymbol{I}$ nor $\boldsymbol{f}$ are known, the minimization of the performance index $DM(\boldsymbol{I},\boldsymbol{f})$ may be performed jointly over $\boldsymbol{I}$ and $\boldsymbol{f}$. Alternatively, $\boldsymbol{f}$ may be estimated from the probability density function $p(\boldsymbol{v}|\boldsymbol{f})$, which may be obtained by averaging $p(\boldsymbol{v},\boldsymbol{f}|\boldsymbol{I})$ over all possible data sequences. That is,

$$p(\boldsymbol{v}|\boldsymbol{f}) = \sum_m p(\boldsymbol{v},\boldsymbol{I}^{(m)}|\boldsymbol{f})$$
$$= \sum_m p(\boldsymbol{v}|\boldsymbol{I}^{(m)},\boldsymbol{f})P(\boldsymbol{I}^{(m)}) \qquad (5.8.6)$$

where $P(\boldsymbol{I}^{(m)})$ is the probability of the sequence $\boldsymbol{I} = \boldsymbol{I}^{(m)}$, for $m = 1, 2, \cdots, M$ and M is the size of the signal constellation. The latter method leads to a highly nonlinear equation for the channel estimate which is computationally intensive.

The joint estimation of the channel impulse response and the data can be performed by minimizing the metric $DM(\boldsymbol{I},\boldsymbol{f})$ given by (5.8.3). Since the elements of the impulse response vector $\boldsymbol{f}$ are continuous and the element of the data vector $\boldsymbol{I}$ are discrete, one approach is to determine the maximum-likelihood estimate of $\boldsymbol{f}$ for each possible data sequence and, then, to select the data sequence that minimizes $DM(\boldsymbol{I},\boldsymbol{f})$ for each corresponding channel estimate. Thus the channel estimate corresponding to the mth data sequence $\boldsymbol{I}^{(m)}$ is

$$\boldsymbol{f}_{\mathrm{ML}}(\boldsymbol{I}^{(m)}) = (\boldsymbol{A}^{(m)t} \boldsymbol{A}^{(m)})^{-1} \boldsymbol{A}^{(m)t} \boldsymbol{v}. \qquad (5.8.7)$$

For the mth data sequence, the metric $DM(\boldsymbol{I},\boldsymbol{f})$ becomes

$$DM(\boldsymbol{I}^{(m)},\boldsymbol{f}_{\mathrm{ML}}(\boldsymbol{I}^{(m)})) = \|\boldsymbol{v} - \boldsymbol{A}^{(m)}\boldsymbol{f}_{\mathrm{ML}}(\boldsymbol{I}^{(m)})\|^2. \qquad (5.8.8)$$

Then, from the set of M^N possible sequences, we select the data sequence that minimizes the cost function in (5.8.8), i.e., we determine

$$\min_{\boldsymbol{I}^{(m)}} DM(\boldsymbol{I}^{(m)},\boldsymbol{f}_{\mathrm{ML}}(\boldsymbol{I}^{(m)})). \qquad (5.8.9)$$

The approach described above is an exhaustive computational search method with a computational comlexity that grows exponentially with the length of the data block. We may select $N = L$, and, thus, we shall have one channel estimate for each of the M^L surviving sequences. Thereafter, we may continue to maintain a separate channel estimate for each surviving path of the Virtebi algorithm search through the trellis. This is basically the approach described by Raheli *et al.* [498] and by Chugg and Polydoros [447].

A similar approach was proposed by Seshadri [506]. In essence, Seshadri's algorithm is a type of generalized Viterbi algorithm (GVA) that retains $K \geq 1$ best estimates of the transmitted data sequence into each state of the trellis and the corresponding channel estimates. In Seshardi's GVA, the search is identical to the conventional VA from the beginning up to the L stage of the trellis, i.e., up to the point where the received sequence $(v_1, v_2, \cdots, v_L)$ has been processed. Hence, up to the L stage, an exhaustive search is performed. Associated with each data sequence $\boldsymbol{I}^{(m)}$, there is a corresponding channel estimate $\boldsymbol{f}_{\mathrm{ML}}(\boldsymbol{I}^{(m)})$. From this stage on, the search is modified, to retain $K \geq 1$ surviving sequences and associated channel estimates per state instead of only one sequence per state. Thus the GVA is used for processing the received-signal sequence $\{v_n, n \geq L+1\}$. The channel estimate is updated recursively at each stage using the LMS algorithm to further reduce the computational complexity. Simulation results given in the paper by Seshradri [506] indicate that this GVA blind-equalization algorithm performs rather well at moderate signal-to-noise ratio with $K = 4$. Hence, there is a modest increase in the computational complexity of the GVA compared with that for the conventional VA. However, there are additional computations involved with the estimation and updating of the channel estimates $\boldsymbol{f}(\boldsymbol{I}^{(m)})$ associated with each of the surviving data estimates.

An alternative joint estimation algorithm that avoids the least squares computation for channel estimation has been devised by Zervas *et al.* [539]. In this algorithm, the order for performing the joint minimization of the performance index $DM(\boldsymbol{I},\boldsymbol{f})$ is reversed. That is, a channel impulse response, say $\boldsymbol{f} = \boldsymbol{f}^{(1)}$, is selected and then the conventional VA is used to find the optimum sequence for this channel impulse response. Then, we may modify $\boldsymbol{f}^{(1)}$ in some manner to $\boldsymbol{f}^{(2)} = \boldsymbol{f}^{(1)} + \Delta \boldsymbol{f}^{(1)}$ and repeat the optimization over the data sequences $\{\boldsymbol{I}^{(m)}\}$.

Based on this general approach, Zervas developed a new ML blind-equalization algorithm, which is called a *quantized-channel algorithm*. The algorithm operates over a grid in the channel space, which becomes finer and finer by using the ML criterion to confine the estimated channel in the neighborhood of the original unknown channel. This algorithm leads to an efficient parallel implementation, and its storage requirements are only those of the VA.

Blind-equalization algorithms have also been developed for CDMA systems in which intersymbol interference (ISI) is present in the received signal in addition to MAI. Wang and Poor [530]–[533] have developed a subspace-based blind method for joint suppression of ISI and MAI for time-dispersive CDMA channels. The time-dispersive CDMA channel is first formulated as a multiple-input, multiple-output (MIMO) system. Based on this formulation and using the signature sequences of the users, the impulse response of each user's channel is identified by using a subspace method. From knowledge of the measured channel response and the identified signal subspace parameters, both the decorrelating (zero-forcing) multiuser detector and the linear MMSE multiuser detector can be constructed. The data is detected by passing the received signal through one or the other of these detectors. Other methods for performing blind multiuser detection have been developed by Honig *et al.* [461], Madhow [462], Talwar *et al.* [514], van de Veen *et al.* [526], Miyajima *et al.* [482], Juntti [466] and Paulraj *et al.* [490].

I. Concluding Remarks

In this section we have provided an overview of equalization techniques applied to fading dispersive channels. Of current interest is the use of equalizers for suppressing interference in multiuser systems and in time-varying channels. In view of the widespread developments in wireless communication systems, research on new adaptive equalization methods will continue to be an active area. The information-theoretic arguments provided before yield clear indications about the preferred coding/decoding method to be used in an effort to approach ultimate performance in a fading time-varying environment. Coding is the central ingredient in those schemes. Equalization, and in particular simple equalization algorithms, constitutes a practical method to cope with the frequency and time multiple user varying environment. In that respect, equalization, coding, and modulation should be inherently approached in a unified framework. This does not necessarily imply an increase in complexity that could not be handled in practice. This fact is documented by recent work which mostly resorts to iterative algorithms, and in which the coding part is inherent within the equalization process itself (which may cope also with multiuser interference). See [458], [481], [500], as well as [541], [47], [194] for some selected (and not necessarily representative) references to this area, which recently happened to be at focus of advanced research, and produced so far dozens of papers, not cited here. Although in the present section we have not addressed coding explicitly, it is important to realize that in efficient communication methods that strive for the optimum when operating on fading channels, coding and equalization are not to be treated separately, but intimately combined, as indeed is motivated by information-theoretic insight.

VI. Conclusions

In this paper we have reviewed some information-theoretic features of digital communications over fading channels. After describing the statistical models of fading channels which are frequently used in the analysis and design of communication systems, we have focused our attention on the information theory of fading channels, by emphasizing capacity as the most important performance measure and examining both single-user and multiuser transmission. Code design and equalization techniques were finally described.

The research trends in this area have been exhibiting a blessed, mutually productive interaction of theory and practice. On one hand, information-theoretic analyses provide insight or even sorts out the preferred techniques for implementation. On the other hand, practical constraints and applications supply the underlying models to be studied via information-theoretic techniques. A relevant example of this is the recent emergence of practical successive interference cancellation ([47], [194], and references therein) as well as equalization and decoding [450], [500] via iterative methods . These methods demonstrate remarkable performance in the multiple-access channel, and a deeper information-theoretic approach accounting for the basic ingredients of this procedure is called for (though not expected to be simple if the iterative procedure is also to be captured). To conclude, we hope that in this partly tutorial exposition we have managed to show to some extent the beauty and the relevance to practice of the information-theoretic framework as applied to the wide class of time-varying fading channels. We also hope that in a small way this overview will help to attract interest to information-theoretic considerations and to the many intriguing open problems remaining in this field.

Acknowledgment

The authors are grateful to Sergio Verdú for his continuous encouragement and stimulus during the preparation of this paper. Ezio Biglieri wishes to thank his colleagues Giuseppe Caire, Giorgio Taricco, and Emanuele Viterbo for education and support. Shlomo Shamai wishes to acknowledge interesting discussions he had with Emre Telatar.

References

[1] M. Abdel-Hafez and M. Safak, "Throughput of slotted ALOHA in Nakagami fading and correlated shadowing environment," *Electron. Lett.*, vol. 33, no. 12, pp. 1024–1025, June 5, 1997.

[2] F. Abrishamkar and E. Biglieri, "An overview of wireless communications," in *Proc. 1994 IEEE Military Communications Conf. (MILCOM'94)*, Oct. 2–5, 1994, pp. 900–905.

[3] M. S. Alencar, "The capacity region of the noncooperative multiple access channels with Rayleigh fading," in *Proc. Annu. Conf. Canadian Institute for Telecommunications Research* (Sainte Adele, Que., Canada, May 1992), pp. 45–46.

[4] M. S. Alencar and I. F. Blake, "The capacity for a discrete-state code division multiple-access channels," *IEEE J. Select. Areas Commun.*, vol. 12, pp. 925–927, June 1994.

[5] M. S. Alencar, "The effect of fading on the capacity of a CDMA channel," in *6th IEEE Int. Symp. Personal, Indoor and Mobile Radio Communications (PIMRC'95)* (Toronto, Ont., Canada, Sept. 26–29, 1995), pp. 1321–1325.

[6] _____, "The capacity for the Gaussian channel with random multipath," in *3rd IEEE Int. Symp. Personal, Indoor, and Mobile Radio Communications (PIMRC'92)* (Boston, MA, Oct. 19–21, 1992), pp. 483–487.

[7] _____, "The capacity region for the multiple access Gaussian channel with stochastic fading," in *3rd IEEE Int. Symp. Personal, Indoor, and Mobile Radio Communications (PIMRC'92)* (Boston, MA, Oct. 19–21, 1992), pp. 266–270.

[8] _____, "The Gaussian noncooperative multiple access channel with Rayleigh fading," in *Proc. IEEE Global Communications Conf. (GLOBECOM'92)*, Dec. 6–9, 1992, pp. 94–97.

[9] M. S. Alencar and I. F. Blake, "Analysis of the capacity region of noncooperative multiaccess channel with Rician fading," in *IEEE, Int. Conf. Communications, ICC '93* (Geneva, Switzerland, May 1993), pp. 282–286.

[10] ———,, "Analysis of the capacity for a Markovian multiple access channel," *IEEE Pacific Rim Conf. Communication, Computers, and Signal Processing* (Victoria, Ont., Canada, May 1993), pp. 81–84.

[11] M. S. Alouini and A. Goldsmith, "Capacity of Nakagami multipath fading channels," in *Proc. 1997 IEEE 47th Annu. Int. Vehicular Technology Conf. (VTC'97)* (Phoenix, AZ, May 4–7, 1997), pp. 358–362.

[12] ———, "Capacity of Rayleigh fading channels under different transmission and diversity-combining techniques," *IEEE Trans. Veh. Technol.*, submitted for publication.

[13] S. A. Al-Semari and T. E. Fuja, "I-Q TCM: Reliable communication over the Rayleigh fading channel close to the cutoff rate," *IEEE Trans. Inform. Theory*, vol. 43, pp. 250–262, Jan. 1997.

[14] A. A. Alsugair and R. S. Cheng, "Symmetric capacity and signal design for L-out-of-K symbol-synchronous CDMA Gaussian channels," *IEEE Trans. Inform. Theory*, vol. 41, pp. 1072–1082, July 1995.

[15] W. K. M. Ahmed and P. J. McLane, "Random coding error exponent for two-dimensional flat fading channels with complete channel state information," in *Proc. 1998 IEEE Int. Symp. Information Theory* (Cambridge, MA, Aug. 17–21, 1998), p. 394. See also: "The information theoretic reliability function for flat Rayleigh fading channels with space diversity," in *Proc. 18th Bienn. Symp. Communications*, 1996., and "The information theoretic reliability function for multipath fading channels with diversity," in *Proc. 5th Int. Conf. Universal Personal Communication* (Cambridge, MA, Sept. 29–Oct. 2, 1996), pp. 886–890.

[16] N. Amitay and J. Salz, "Linear equalization theory in digital data transmission over dually polarized fading radio channels," *Bell Syst. Tech. J.*, vol. 63, pp. 2215–2259, Dec. 1984.

[17] V. Anantharam and S. Verdú, "Bits through queues," *IEEE Trans. Inform. Theory*, vol. 42, pp. 4–18, Jan. 1996.

[18] J. C. Arnbak and W. Blitterswijk, "Capacity of slotted ALOHA in Rayleigh-fading channels," *J. Select. Areas Commun.*, vol. SAC-5, pp. 261–269, Feb. 1987.

[19] E. Baccarelli, "Performance bounds and cut-off rates for data channels affected by correlated random time-variant multipath fading," *IEEE Trans. Commun.*, to be published.

[20] E. Baccarelli, S. Galli, and A. Fasano, "Tight upper and lower bounds on the symmetric capacity and outage probability for bandwidth-efficient QAM transmission over Rayleigh-faded channels," in *Proc. 1998 IEEE Int. Symp. Information Theory* (Cambridge, MA, Aug. 17–21, 1998), p. 6. See also: E. Baccarelli, "Asymptotically tight bounds on the capacity and outage probability for QAM transmission over Raleigh-faded data channels with CSI," *IEEE Trans. Commun.*, submitted for publication.

[21] P. Balaban and J. Salz, "Optimum diversity combining and equalization in digital data transmission with applications to cellular mobile radio, Part I: Theoretical considerations, Part II: Numerical results," *IEEE Trans. Commun.*, vol. 40, pp. 885–907, May 1992.

[22] V. B. Balakirsky, "A converse coding theorem for mismatched decoding at the output of binary-input memoryless channels," *IEEE Trans. Inform. Theory*, vol. 41, pp. 1889–1902, Nov. 1995.

[23] I. Bar-David, E. Plotnik, and R. Rom, "Limitations of the capacity of the M-user binary Adder channel due to physical considerations," *IEEE Trans. Inform. Theory*, vol. 40, pp. 662–673, May 1994.

[24] J. R. Barry, E. A. Lee, and D. Messerschmitt, "Capacity penalty due to ideal zero-forcing decision-feedback equalization," in *Proc. Int. Conf. on Communications, ICC'93* (Geneva, Switzerland, May 23–26, 1993), pp. 422–427.

[25] G. Battail and J. Boutros, "On communication over fading channels," in *5th IEEE Int. Conf. Universal Personal Communications Rec. (ICUPC'96)* (Cambridge, MA, Sept. 29–Oct. 2, 1996), pp. 985–988.

[26] A. S. Bedekar and M. Azizoğlu, "The information-theoretic capacity of discrete-time queues," *IEEE Trans. Inform. Theory*, vol. 44, pp. 446–461, Mar. 1998.

[27] S. Benedetto, D. Divsalar, and J. Hagenauer, Eds., *J. Select. Areas Commun.* (Special Issue on Concatenated Coding Techniques and Iterative Decoding: Sailing Toward Channel Capacity), vol. 16, Feb. 1998.

[28] D. Bertsekas and R. Gallager, *Data Networks*. London, U.K.: Prentice-Hall, 1987.

[29] I. Bettesh and S. Shamai (Shitz), "A low delay algorithm for the multiple access channel with Rayleigh fading," in *9th IEEE Int. Symp. Personal Indoor and Mobile Radio Communication (PIMRC'98)* (Boston, MA, Sept. 8–11, 1998), to be published.

[30] S. Bhashyam, A. M. Sayeed, and B. Aazhang, "Time-selective signaling and reception for multiple fading channels," to be published in *1998 IEEE Int. Symp. Information Theory* (Cambridge, MA, Aug. 17–21,

[31] E. Biglieri, G. Caire, and G. Taricco, "Random coding bounds for the block-fading channel with simple power allocation schemes," presented at the Conf. on Information Sciences and Systems (CISS'98), Princeton Univ., Princeton, NJ, Mar. 18–20, 1998. See also: "Coding for the block-finding channel: Optimum and suboptimum power-allocation schemes," in *Proc. 1998 Information Theory Work.* (Killarney, Ireland, June 22–26, 1998), pp. 96–97.

[32] E. Biglieri, G. Caire, G. Taricco, and J. Ventura-Traveset, "Co-channel interference in cellular mobile radio systems with coded PSK and diversity," *Wireless Personal Commun.*, vol. 6, no. 1–2, pp. 39–68, Jan. 1998.

[33] N. Binshtock and S. Shamai, "Integer quantization for binary input symmetric output memoryless channels," *Euro. Trans. Telecommun.*, submitted for publication.

[34] K. L. Boullé and J. C. Belfiore, "The cut-off rate of time-correlated fading channels," *IEEE Trans. Inform. Theory*, vol. 39, pp. 612–617, Mar. 1993.

[35] K. Brayer, Ed., *J. Select. Areas Commun.* (Special Issue on Fading Multiplath Channel Communications), vol. SAC-5, Feb. 1987.

[36] A. G. Burr, "Bounds on spectral efficiency of CDMA and FDMA/TDMA in a cellular system," in *IEE Colloq. "Spread Spectrum Techniques for Radio Communication Systems"* (London, U.K., Apr. 1993), p. 80, 12/1–6.

[37] ———, "Bounds and estimates of the uplink capacity of cellular systems," in *IEEE 44th Veh. Technol. Conf.* (Stockholm, Sweden, June 8–10, 1994), pp. 1480–1484.

[38] ———, "On uplink pdf and capacity in cellular systems," in *Proc. Joint COST 231/235 Workshop* (Limerick, Ireland), pp. 435–442. See also "Bounds on the spectral efficiency of CDMA and FDMA/TDMA," COST, 231 TD(92), 125, Helsinki, Oct. 8–13, 1993.

[39] R. Buz, "Information theoretic limits on communication over multipath fading channels," Ph.D. dissertation, Dept. Elec. Comp. Eng., Queens Univ. 1994. See also in *Proc.s 1995 Int. Symp. Information Theory (ISIT'95)* (Whistler, BC, Canada, Sept. 17–22, 1995), p. 151.

[40] G. Caire, R. Knopp, and P. Humblet, "System capacity of F-TDMA cellular systems," in *GLOBECOM'97* (Phoenix, AZ, Nov. 3–8, 1997, pp. 1323–1327), to be published in *IEEE Trans. Commun.*

[41] G. Caire and S. Shamai (Shitz), "On the capacity of some channels with channel state information," in *Proc. 1998 IEEE Int. Symp. Information Theory* (Cambridge, MA, Aug. 17–21, 1998), p. 42.

[42] G. Caire, G. Taricco, and E. Biglieri, "Bit-interleaved coded modulation," *IEEE Trans. Inform. Theory*, vol. 44, pp. 927–947, May 1998. See also in *1997 IEEE Int. Conf. Communications (ICC'97)* (Montreal, Que., Canada, June 8–12, 1997), pp. 1463–1467.

[43] ———, "Optimum power control over fading channels," *IEEE Trans. Inform. Theory*, submitted for publication. See also "Minimum information outage rate for slowly-varying fading channels," in *Proc. IEEE Int. Symp. Inform. Theory (ISIT'98)* (Cambridge, MA, Aug. 16–21, 1998), p. 7. See also: "Power control for the fading channel: An information-theoretical approach," in *Proc. 35th Allerton Conf. on Communication, Control and Computing* (Allerton House, Monticello, IL, Sept. 30–Oct. 1, 1997), pp. 1023–1032.

[44] G. Calhoun, *Digital Cellular Radio*. Norwood, MA: Artech House, 1988.

[45] C. C. Chan and S. V. Hanly, "On the capacity of a cellular CDMA system with succcessive decoding," in *Int. Conf. of Telecom. 1997*. See also C. C. Chan and S. V. Hanly, "The capacity improvement of an integrated successive decoding and power control scheme," in *1997 IEEE 6th Int. Conf. Univ. Pers. Comm. Rec.* (San Diego, CA, Oct. 12–16, 1997), pp. 800–804.

[46] D. Chase and L. H. Ozarow, "Capacity limits for binary codes in the presence of interference," *IEEE Trans. Commun.*, vol. COM-27, pp. 441–448, Feb. 1979.

[47] N. Chayat and S. Shamai (Shitz), "Iterative soft peeling for multi-access and broadcast channels," in *9th IEEE Int. Symp. Personal Indoor and Mobile Radio Communication (PIMRC'98)* (Boston, MA, Sept. 8–11, 1998), to be published.

[48] K. S. Cheng, "Capacities of L-out-of-K and slowly time-varying fading Gaussian CDMA channels," in *Proc. 27th Annu. Conf. Information Sciences and Systems* (Baltimore, MD, The Johns Hopkins Univ., Mar. 24–26, 1993), pp. 744–749.

[49] R. S.-K. Cheng, "Optimal transmit power management on a fading multiple-access channel," in *1996 IEEE Information Theory Workshop (ITW'96)* (Haifa, Israel, June 9–13, 1996), p. 36.

[50] R. S. Cheng, "On capacity and signature waveform design for slowly fading CDMA channels," in *Proc. 31st Allerton Conf. Communication, Control, and Computing* (Monticello, IL, Allerton House, Sept. 29–Oct.

1, 1993), pp. 11–20.

[51] R. S.-K. Cheng, "Coded CDMA systems with and without MMSE multiuser equalizer," in *5th IEEE Int. Conf. Universal Personal Communication Rec. (ICUPC'96)* (Cambridge, MA, Sept. 29–Oct. 2, 1996), pp. 174–178.

[52] R. S. Cheng, "Randomization in multiuser coding summaries for the proceedings of workshop on information theory multiple access and queueing," in *Proc. Information Theory Workshop on Multiple Access and Queueing* (St. Louis, MO, Apr. 19–21, 1995), p. 48.

[53] R. S. K. Cheng, "Stripping CDMA—An asymptotically optimal coding scheme for L-out-of-K white Gaussian channels," in *IEEE Global Commun. Conf. (GLOBECOM '96)*, Nov. 18–22, 1996, pp. 142–146.

[54] R. G. Cheng, "On capacities of frequency nonselective slowly varying fading channels," in *Proc. 1993 IEEE Int. Symp. Information Theory* (San Antonio, TX, Jan. 17–22, 1993), p. 260.

[55] K.-C. Chen and D.-C. Twu, "On the multiuser information theory for wireless networks with interference," in *6h IEEE Int. Symp. Personal, Indoor, and Mobile Radio Communication PIMRC'95* (Toronto, Ont., Canada, Sept. 27–29, 1995), pp. 1313–1317.

[56] R. S. Cheng and S. Verdú, "Gaussian multiaccess channel with ISI: Capacity region and multiuser water-filling," *IEEE Trans. Inform. Theory*, vol. 39, pp. 773–785, May 1993.

[57] J. M. Cioffi, "On the separation of equalization and coding," in *Proc. 29th Allerton Conf. Communication, Control, and Computing* (Monticello, IL, Oct. 2–4, 1991), pp. 1–10. See also J. M. Cioffi and G. P. Dudevoir, "Data transmission with mean-square partial response," in *IEEE GLOBECOM'89*, Nov. 27–30, 1989, pp. 1687–1691, and C. E. Rohrs, "Decision feedback and capacity on the linear stationary Gaussian channel," in *IEEE GLOBECOM'95*, Nov. 13–17, 1995, pp. 871–873.

[58] J. M. Cioffi, G. P. Dudevoir, M. V. Eyuboglu, and G. D. Forney, "MMSE decision-feedback equalizers and coding—Part I: Equalization results, Part II: Coding results," *IEEE Trans. Commun.*, vol. 43, pp. 2582–2604, Oct. 1995.

[59] M. H. M. Costa, "On the Gaussian interference channel," *IEEE Trans. Inform. Theory*, vol. IT-31, pp. 607–615, Sept. 1985.

[60] D. J. Costello, Jr., J. Hagenauer, H. Imai, and S. B. Wicker, "Applications of error control coding," this issue, pp. 2531–2560.

[61] T. Cover, "Broadcast channels," *IEEE Trans. Inform. Theory*, vol. IT-18, pp. 2–14, Jan. 1972.

[62] T. M. Cover and J. A. Thomas, *Elements of Information Theory.* New York: Wiley, 1991.

[63] P. J. Crepeau, "Asymptotic performance of M-ary orthogonal modulation in generalized fading channels," *IEEE Trans. Commun.*, vol. 36, pp. 1246–1248, Nov. 1988.

[64] I. Csiszár and J. Körner, *Information Theory: Coding Theorems for Discrete Memoryless Systems.* New York: Academic, 1981.

[65] A. Czylwik, "Comparison of the channel capacity of wideband radio channels with achievable data rates using adaptive OFDM," in *Proc. ETH Euro. Conf. Fixed Radio Systems and Networks, ECRR'96* (Bologna, Italy, 1996), pp. 238–243.

[66] ——, "Temporal fluctuations of channel capacity in wideband radio channels," in *1997 IEEE Int. Symp. Information Theory (ISIT'97)* (Ulm, Germany, June 29–July 4, 1997), p. 468.

[67] W. C. Dam, D. P. Taylor, and L. Zhi-Quan, "Computational cutoff rate of BDPSK signaling over correlated Rayleigh fading channel," in *1995 Int. Symp. Information Theory* (Whistler, BC, Canada, Sept. 17–22, 1995), p. 152.

[68] A. D. Damnjanovic and B. R. Vojcic, "Coding-spreading trade-off in DS/CDMA successive interference cancellation," in *Proc. CISS'98* (Princeton, NJ, Mar. 18–20, 1998).

[69] A. Das and P. Narayan, "On the capacities pf a class state channels with side information," in *Proc. CISS'98* (Princeton, NJ, Mar. 18–20, 1998).

[70] C. L. Despins, G. Djelassem, and V. Roy, "Comparative evaluation of CDMA and FD-TDMA cellular system capacities with respect to radio link capacity," in *7th IEEE Int. Symp. Personal, Indoor, and Mobile Communication, PIMRC'96* (Taipei, Oct. 15–18, 1996), pp. 387–391.

[71] S. N. Diggavi, "Analysis of multicarrier transmission in time-varying channels," in *Proc. 1997 IEEE Int. Conf. Communications (ICC'97)* (Montreal, Que., Canada, June 8–12, 1997), pp. 1091–1095.

[72] S. N. Diggavi, "On achievable performance of diversity fading channels," in *Proc. 1998 IEEE Int. Symp. Information Theory* (Cambridge, MA, Aug. 17–21, 1998), p. 396.

[73] R. L. Dobrushin, "Information transmission over a channel with feedback," *Theory Probab. Appl.*, vol. 3, no. 4, pp. 395–419, 1958, secs. VII and IX.

[74] ——, "Mathematical problems in the Shannon theory of optimal coding on information," in *Proc. 4th Berkeley Symp. Mathematics,*

[75] ——, "Survey of Soviet research in information theory," *IEEE Trans. Inform. Theory*, vol. IT-18, pp. 703–724, Nov. 1972.

[76] R. L. Dobrushin, Ya. I. Khurgin, and B. S. Tsybakov, "Computation of the approximate capacities of random-parameter radio channels," in *3rd All-Union Conf. Theory of Probability and Mathematical Statistics* (Yerevan, Armenia, USSR, 1960), pp. 164–171, sec. VII.

[77] Dong-Kwan, P. Jae-Hong, and L. Hyuck-Jae, "Cutoff rate of 16-DAPSK over a Rayleigh fading channel," *Electron. Lett.*, vol. 33, no. 3, pp. 181–182, Jan. 30, 1997.

[78] B. Dorsch, "Forward-error-correction for time-varying channels," *Frequenz*, vol. 35, no. 3–4, pp. 96–106, Mar.–Apr. 1981. See also: "Performance and limits of coding for simple-time-varying channels," in *Int. Zurich Sem. Digital Communication*, 1980, pp. 61.1–61.8.

[79] B. G. Dorsch and F. Dolainsky, "Theoretical limits on channel coding under various constraints," in *Digital Commun. in Avionics, AGARD Conf. Proc.*, June 1979, no. 239, pp. 15-1–15-12.

[80] G. Dueck, "Maximal error capacity regions are smaller than average error capacity regions for multi-user channels," *Prob. Contr. Inform. Theory*, vol. 7, pp. 11–19, 1978.

[81] T. E. Duncan, "On the calculation of mutual information," *SIAM J. Appl. Math.*, vol. 19, pp. 215–220, July 1970.

[82] A. Edelman, "Eigenvalues and condition number of random matrices," Ph.D. dissertation, Dept. Math., Mass. Inst. Technol., Cambridge, MA, 1989.

[83] M. Effros and A. Goldsmith, "Capacity of general channels with receiver side information," in *Proc. 1998 IEEE Int. Symp. Information Theory* (Cambridge, MA, Aug. 17–21, 1998), p. 39.

[84] A. Ephremides and B. Hajek, "Information theory and communication networks: An unconsummated union," this issue, pp. 2416–2434.

[85] T. Ericson, "A Gaussian channel with slow fading," *IEEE Trans. Inform. Theory*, vol. IT-16, pp. 353–356, May 1970.

[86] E. Erkip, "Multiple access schemes over multipath fading channels," in *Proc. 1998 IEEE Int. Symp. Information Theory* (Cambridge, MA, Aug. 17–21, 1998), 216. See also "A comparison study of multiple accessing schemes," in *Proc. 31st Asilomar Conf. Signals, Systems, and Computers* (Pacific Grove, CA, Nov. 2–5, 1997), pp. 614–619.

[87] I. C. A. Faycal, M. D. Trott, and S. Shamai (Shitz), "The capacity of discrete time Rayleigh fading channels," in *IEEE Int. Symp. Information Theory (ISIT'97)* (Ulm, Germany, June 29–July 4, 1997), p. 473. (Submitted to *IEEE Trans. Inform. Theory*). See also: "A comparison study for multiple accessing schemes," in *Proc. 31st Asilomar Conf. Signals, Systems and Computers* (Pacific Grove, CA, Nov. 2–5, 1997), pp. 614–619.

[88] M. Feder and A. Lapidoth, "Universal decoding for channels with memory," *IEEE Trans. Inform. Theory*, vol. 44, pp. 1726–1745, Sept. 1998.

[89] M. Filip and E. Vilar, "Optimum utilization of the channel capacity of a satellite link in the presence of amplitude and rain attenuation," *IEEE Trans. Commun.*, vol. 38, pp. 1958–1965, Nov. 1990.

[90] D. G. Forney, Jr. and G. Ungerboeck, "Modulation and coding for linear Gaussian channels," this issue, pp. 2384–2415. See also: A. R. Caldebank, "The art of signaling: Fifty years of coding theory," this issue, pp. 2561–2595.

[91] G. J. Foschini, "Layered space-time architecture for wireless communication in a fading environment when using multiple-element antennas," AT&T-Bell Labs., Tech. Memo., Apr. 1996.

[92] G. J. Foschini and J. Gans, "On limits of wireless communication in a fading environment when using multiple antenna," *Wireless Personal Commun.*, vol. 6, no. 3, pp. 311–335, Mar. 1998.

[93] G. J. Foschini and J. Salz, "Digital communications over fading channels," *Bell Syst. Tech. J.*, vol. 62, pp. 429–456, Feb. 1983.

[94] R. G. Gallager, *Information Theory and Reliable Communication.* New York: Wiley, 1968.

[95] ——, "A perspective on multiaccess channels," *IEEE Trans. Inform. Theory*, vol. IT-31, pp. 124–142, Mar. 1985.

[96] ——, "Energy limited channels: Coding, multiaccess, and spread spectrum," Tech. Rep. LIDS-P-1714, Lab. Inform. Decision Syst., Mass. Inst. Technol., Nov. 1988. See also in *Proc. 1988 Conf. Information Science and Systems* (Princeton, NJ, Mar. 1988), p. 372.

[97] ——, "Perspective on wireless communications," unpublished manuscript. See also R. E. Blahut, D. J. Costello, Jr., U. Maurer, and T. Mittelholzer, Eds., "An inequality on the capacity region of multiaccess multipath channels," and "Perspective on wireless communications," in *Communication and Cryptography: Two Sides of One Tapestry.* Boston, MA: Kluwer, 1994, pp. 129–139.

[98] ——, "Residual noise after interference cancellation on fading multipath channels," in *Communication, Computation, Control, and Signal*

Processing (Tribute to Thomas Kailath). Boston, MA: Kluwer, 1997, pp. 67–77.

[99] R. Gallager and M. Medard, "Bandwidth scaling for fading channels," in *IEEE Int. Symp. Information Theory (ISIT'97)* (Ulm, Germany, June 29–July 4, 1997), p. 471 (reprint July 2, 1997).

[100] A. El. Gamal, "Capacity of the product and sum of two unmatched broadcast channel," *Probl. Pered. Inform.*, vol. 16, no. 1, pp. 3–23, Jan.–Mar. 1980.

[101] S. Gelfand and M. Pinsker, "Coding for channels with random parameters," *Probl. Contr. Inform. Theory*, vol. 9, no. 1, pp. 19–31, 1962.

[102] E. A. Geraniotis, "Channel capacity, cut-off rate, and coding for asynchronous frequency-hopped networks," in *Proc. MELECON'83, Mediterranean Electrotechnical Conf.* (Athens, Greece, May 24–26, 1983), p. 2.

[103] D. Goeckel and W. Stark, "Throughput optimization in faded multicarrier systems," in *Proc. Allerton Conf. Communication and Computers* (Monticello, IL, Allerton House, Oct. 4–6, 1995), pp. 815–825.

[104] _____, "Throughput optimization in multiple-access communication systems with decorrelator reception," in *Proc. 1996 IEEE Int. Symp. Information Theory and Its Applications (ISITA'96)* (Victoria, BC, Canada, Sept. 1996), pp. 653–656.

[105] J. G. Goh and S. V. Maric, "The capacities of frequency-hopped code-division multiple-access channles," *IEEE Trans. Inform. Theory*, vol. 44, pp. 1204–1214, May 1998.

[106] A. Goldsmith, "Capacity and dynamic resource allocation in broadcast fading channels," in *33th Annu. Allerton Conf. Communication, Control and Computing* (Monticello, IL, Allerton House, Oct. 4–6, 1995), pp. 915–924. See also, "Capacity of broadcast fading channels with variable rate and power," in *IEEE Global Communications Conf. (GLOBECOM'96)*, Nov. 18–22, 1996, pp. 92–96.

[107] _____, "Multiuser capacity of cellular time-varying channels," in *Conf. Rec., 28ht Asilomar Conf. on Signals, Systems and Computers* (Pacific Grove, CA, Oct. 30–Nov. 2, 1994), pp. 83–88.

[108] _____, "The capacity of downlink fading channels with variable rate and power," *IEEE Trans. Veh. Technol.*, vol. 46, pp. 569–580, Aug. 1997.

[109] A. J. Goldsmith and S. G. Chua, "Variable-rate variable-power MQAM for fading channels," *IEEE Trans. Commun.*, vol. 45, pp. 1218–1230, Oct. 1997.

[110] A. Goldsmith and M. Effros, "The capacity of broadcast channels with memory," in *IEEE Int. Symp. Information Theory (ISIT'97)* (Ulm Germany, June 29–July 4, 1997), p. 28.

[111] A. Goldsmith and P. Varaiya, "Capacity, mutual information, and coding for finite state Markov channels," *IEEE Trans. Inform. Theory*, vol. 42, pp. 868–886, May 1996.

[112] _____, "Capacity of fading channels with channel side information," *IEEE Trans. Inform. Theory*, vol. 43, pp. 1986–1992, Nov. 1997. See also "Increasing spectral efficiency through power control," in *Proc. 1993 Int. Conf. Communications* (Geneva, Switzerland, June 1993), pp. 600–604.

[113] D. J. Goodman, "Trends in cellular and cordless communications," *IEEE Commun. Mag.*, pp. 31–40, June 1991.

[114] V. K. Garg and J. E. Wilkes, *Wireless and Personal Communications Systems*. Upper Saddle River, NJ: Prentice-Hall, 1996.

[115] A. Grant, B. Rimoldi, R. Urbanke, and P. Whiting, "On single-user coding for discrete memorlyess multiple-access channel," *IEEE Trans. Inform. Theory*, to be published. See also in *IEEE Int. Symp. Information Theory* (Whistler, BC, Canada, Sept. 17–22, 1995), p. 448.

[116] A. J. Grant and L. K. Rasmussen, "A new coding method for the asynchronous multiple access channel," in *Proc. 33rd Allerton Conf. Communication, Control, and Computing* (Monticello, IL, Oct. 4–6, 1995), pp. 21–28.

[117] J. A. Gubner and B. L. Hughes, "Nonconvexity of the capacity region of the multiple-access arbitrarily varying channel subjected to constrains," *IEEE Trans. Inform. Theory*, vol. 41, pp. 3–13, Jan. 1995.

[118] C. G. Gunter, "Comment on "Estimate of channel capacity on a Rayleigh fading environment"," *IEEE Trans. Veh. Technol.*, vol. 45, pp. 401–403, May 1996.

[119] J. Hagenauer, "Zur Kanalkapazität bei Nachrichtenkanalen mit Fading und Gebundelten Fehlern," *Arch. Elek. Übertragungstech.*, vol. 34, no. 6, pp. S.229–237, June 1980.

[120] B. Hajek, "Recent models, issues, and results for dense wireless networks," in *Proc. Winter 1998 Information Theory Workshop* (San Diego, CA, Feb. 8–11, 1998), p. 26.

[121] E. K. Hall and S. G. Wilson, "Design and analysis of turbo codes on Rayleigh fading channles," *IEEE J. Select. Areas Commun.*, vol. 16, pp. 160–174, Feb. 1998.

[122] S. H. Jamali and T. Le-Ngoc, *Coded-Modulation Techniques for Fading Channels*. Boston, MA: Kluwer, 1994.

[123] J. S. Hammerschmidt, R. Hasholzner, and C. Drewes, "Shannon based capacity estimation of future microcellular wireless communication systems," in *IEEE Int. Symp. Information Theory (ISIT'97)* (Ulm Germany, June 29–July 4, 1997), p. 54.

[124] T. S. Han, "An information-spectrum approach to capacity theorems for the general multiple-access channel," *IEEE Trans, Inform. Theory*, to be published. See also "Information-spectrum methods in information theory," 1998, to be published.

[125] S. V. Hanly, "Capacity in a two cell spread spectrum network," in *Proc. 20th Annu. Allerton Conf. Communication, Control, and Computing* (Monticello, IL, Allerton House, 1992), pp. 426–435.

[126] _____, "Capacity and power control in spread spectrum macro diversity radio networks," *IEEE Trans. Commun.*, vol. 44, pp. 247–256, Feb. 1996.

[127] S. V. Hanly and D. N. Tse, "The multi-access fading channel: Shannon and delay limited capacities," in *33th Annu. Allerton Conf. Commun.ication Control, and Computing* (Monticello, IL, Allerton House, Oct. 4–6, 1995), pp. 786–795. To be published in: *IEEE Int. Symp. Information Theory (ISIT'98)* (Cambridge, MA, Aug. 16–21, 1998). See also "Multi-access fading channels: Part II: Delay-limited capacities," Memorandum no. UCB/ERL M96/69, Elec. Res. Lab., College of Eng., Univ. Calif., Berkeley, Nov. 1996.

[128] S. Hanly and D. Tse, "Min-max power allocation for successive decoding," in *Proc. IEEE Information Theory Work. (ITW'98)* (Killarney, Ireland, June 22–26, 1998), pp. 56–57.

[129] S. V. Hanly and P. Whiting, "Information-theoretic capacity of multi-receiver networks," *Telecommun. Syst.*, vol. 1, no. 1, pp. 1–42, 1993. See also "Information theory and the design of multi-receiver networks," in *Proc. IEEE 2nd Int. Symp. Spread Spectrum Techniques and Applications (ISSSTA'92)* (Yokohama, Japan, Nov. 30–Dec. 2, 1994), pp. 103–106 and "Asymptotic capacity of multi-receiver networks," in *Proc. Int. Symp. Information Theory (ISIT'94)* (Trondheim, Norway, June 27–July 1, 1994), p. 60.

[130] _____, "Information-theoretic capacity of random multi-receiver networks," in *Proc. 30th Annu. Allerton Conf. Communication, Control, and Computing* (Monticello, IL, Allerton House, 1992), pp. 782–791.

[131] W. Hirt and J. L. Massey, "Capacity of the discrete-time Gaussian channel with intersymbol interference," *IEEE Trans. Inform. Theory*, vol. 34, pp. 380–388, May 1988.

[132] J. L. Holsinger, "Digital communication over fixed time-continuous channels with memory, with special application to telephone channels," MIT Res. Lab. Electron., Tech. Rept. 430 (MIT Lincoln Lab. T.R. 366), 1964.

[133] J. Huber, U. Wachsmann, and R. Fischer, "Coded modulation by multilevel codes: Overview and state of the art," in *ITG-Fachberichte Conf. Rec.* (Aachen, Germany, Mar. 1998).

[134] J. Y. N. Hui, "Throughput analysis for code division multiple accessing of the spread spectrum channel," *IEEE J. Select. Areas Commun.*, vol. SAC-2, pp. 482–486, July 1984.

[135] J. Y. N. Hui and P. A. Humblet, "The capacity region of the totally asynchronous multiple-access channels," *IEEE Trans. Inform. Theory*, vol. IT-20, pp. 207–216, Mar. 1985.

[136] D. R. Hummels, "The capacity of a model for underwater acoustic channel," *IEEE Trans. Sonics Ultrason.*, vol. SC-19, pp. 350–353, July 1972.

[137] T. Huschka, M. Reinhart, and J. Linder, "Channel capacities of fading radio channels," in *7th IEEE Int. Symp. Personal, Indoor, and Mobile Radio Communication, PIMRC'96* (Taipei, Taiwan, Oct. 15–18, 1996), pp. 467–471.

[138] T. Inoue and Y. Karasawa, "Channel capacity improvement by means of two dimensional rake for DS/CDMA systems," to be presented at 48th Annu. Int. Vehicular Technology Conference (VTC'98), Ottawa, Canada, May 18–21, 1998.

[139] M. Izumi, M. I. Mandell, and R. J. McEliece, "Comparison of the capacities of CDMA, FH, and FDMA cellular systems," in *Proc. Conf. Selected Topics in Wireless Communication* (Vancouver, BC, Canada, June 1992).

[140] S. Jayaraman and H. Viswanathan, "Optimal detection and estimation of channel state information," *ETT*, submitted for publication. Also in *Proc. 1998 IEEE Int. Symp. Information Theory* (Cambridge, MA, Aug. 17–21, 1998), p. 40.

[141] B. D. Jeličić and S. Roy, "Cutoff rates for coordinate interleaved QAM over Rayleigh fading channels," *IEEE Trans. Commun.*, vol. 44, pp. 1231–1233, Oct. 1996.

[142] F. Jelinek, "Indecomposable channels with side information at the transmitter," *Infor. Contr.*, vol. 8, pp. 36–55, 1965.

[143] _____, "Determination of capacity achieving input probabilities for a class of finite state channels with side information," *Inform. Contr.*, vol.

9, pp. 101–129, 1966.

[144] P. Jung, P. W. Baier, and A. Steil, "Advantage of CDMA and spread spectrum techniques over FDMA and TDMA in cellular mobile radio applications," *IEEE Trans. Veh. Technol.*, vol. 42, pp. 357–364, Aug. 1993.

[145] P. Jung, P. Walter, and A. Dteil, "Advantages of CDMA and spread spectrum techniques over FDMA and TDMA in cellular mobile radio applications," *IEEE Trans. Veh. Technol.*, vol. 42, pp. 357–364, Aug. 1993.

[146] V. Kafedziski, "Capacity of frequency selective fading channels," in *Proc. IEEE Int. Symp. Information Theory* (Ulm, Germany, June 29–July 4, 1997), p. 339.

[147] ———, "Coding theorem for frequency selective fading channels," in *Proc. Winter 1998 Information Theory Workshop* (San Diego, CA, Feb. 8–11, 1998), p. 90.

[148] G. Kaplan and S. Shamai (Shitz), "Error probabilities for the block-fading Gaussian channel," *Arch. Electronik Übertragungstech.*, vol. 49, no. 4, pp. 192–205, 1995.

[149] ———, "On information rates in fading channels with partial side information," *Euro. Trans. Telecommun. and Related Topics (ETT)*, vol. 6, no. 6, pp. 665–669. Sept.–Oct. 1995.

[150] ———, "Information rates and error exponents of compound channels with application to antipodal signaling in a fading environment," *Arch. Electronik Übertragungstech.*, vol. 47, no. 4, pp. 228–239, 1993.

[151] G. Kaplan and S. Shamai, "Achievable performance over the correlated Rician channel," *IEEE Trans. Commun.*, vol. 42, pp. 2967–2978, Nov. 1994.

[152] S. Kasturia, J. T. Aslanis, and J. M. Cioffi, "Vector coding for partial response channels," *IEEE Trans. Inform. Theory*, vol. 36, pp. 741–762, July 1990.

[153] R. S. Kennedy, *Performance Estimation of Fading Dispersive Channels*. New York: Wiley, 1968.

[154] M. Khansari and M. Vetterli, "Source coding and transmission of signals over time-varying channel with side information," in *Int. Symp. Information Theory (ISIT'95)* (Whistler, BC, Canada, Sept. 17–22, 1995), p. 140. See also "Joint source and channel coding in time-varying channels," in *Proc. 1995 IEEE Information Theory Work., Information Theory, Multiple Access, and Queueing* (St. Louis, MI, Apr. 19–21, 1995), p. 9.

[155] R. Knopp and P. A. Humblet, "Information capacity and power control in single-cell multiuser communications," in *Proc. Int. Conf. Communications, ICC'95* (Seattle, WA, June 18–22, 1995), pp. 331–335.

[156] ———, "Maximizing diversity on block-fading channels," in *Proc. 1997 IEEE Int. Conf. Communication (ICC'97)* (Montreal, Que., Canada, June 8–12, 1997), pp. 647–651.

[157] ———, "Multiple-accessing over frequency-selective fading channels," in *6th IEEE Int. Symp. Personal, Indoor and Mobile Radio Communication (PIMRC'95)* (Toronto, Ont., Canada, Sept. 27–29, 1995), pp. 1326–1330.

[158] ———, "Improving down link performance in cellular radio communications," presented at GRETSI '95, Juan les Pins, Sept. 1995.

[159] Y. Kofman. E. Zehavi. and S. Shamai (Shitz), "A multilevel coded modulation scheme for fading channels," *Arch. Electronik Übertragungstech.*, vol. 46, no. 6, pp. 420–428, 1992.

[160] J. J. Komo and A. Aridgides, "Diversity cutoff rate evaluation of the Rayleigh and Rician fading channels," *IEEE Trans. Commun.*, vol. COM-35, pp. 762–764, July 1987.

[161] A. Lapidoth, "Nearest neighbor decoding for additive non-Gaussian channels," *IEEE Trans. Inform. Theory*, vol. 42, pp. 1520–1529, Sept. 1996. See also "Mismatched decoding of the fading multiple-access channel," in *Proc. 1995 IEEE IT Workshop Information Theory, Multiple Access, and Queueing* (St. Louis, MO, Apr. 19–21, 1995), p. 38. Also, "On information rates for mismatched decoders," in *Proc. 2nd Int. Winter Meet. Coding and Information Theory*, A. J. Han, Ed., p. 26, preprint no. 23, Insitut für Experimentelle Mathematik, Universität GH Essen, Essen, Germany, Dec. 12–15, 1993.

[162] ———, "Mismatch decoding and the multiple access channel," *IEEE Trans. Inform. Theory*, vol. 42, pp. 1439–1452, Sept. 1996.

[163] A. Lapidoth, E. Telatar, and R. Urbanke, "On broadband broadcast channels," in *1998 IEEE Int. Symp. Information Theory* (Cambridge, MA, Aug. 17–21, 1998), p. 188.

[164] A. Lapidoth and P. Narayan, "Reliable communication under channel uncertainty," this issue, pp. 2148–2177.

[165] A. Lapidoth and S. Shamai (Shitz), "Achievable rates with nearest neighbour decoding, for fading channels with estimated channel parameters," in preparation.

[166] A. Lapidoth and J. Ziv, "On the universality of the LZ-based decoding algorithm," *IEEE Trans. Inform. Theory*, vol. 44, pp. 1746–1755, Sept.

[167] A. Lapidoth and İ. E. Telatar, "The compound channel capacity of a class of finite-state channels," *IEEE Trans. Inform. Theory*, vol. 44, pp. 973–983, May 1998.

[168] V. K. N. Lau and S. V. Maric, "Adaptive channel coding for Rayleigh fading channels-feedback of channel states," submitted for publication. See also "Variable rate adaptive channel coding for coherent and noncoherent Rayleigh fading channel," in *Proc. Cryptography and Coding, 6th IMA Int. Conf.* (Cirencester, U.K., Dec. 1997), pp. 180–191.

[169] F. Lazarakis, G. S. Tombras, and K. Dangakis, "Average channel capacity in mobile radio environment with Rician statistics," *IEICE Trans. Commun.*, vol. E–77–B, no. 7, pp. 971–977, July 1994.

[170] W. C. Y. Lee, *Mobile Communications Design Fundamentals*, 2nd ed. New York: Wiley, 1993.

[171] ———, "Estimate of channel capacity in Rayleigh fading environment," *IEEE Trans. Veh. Technol.*, vol. 39, pp. 187–189, Aug. 1990.

[172] K. Leeuwin-Boullé and J. C. Belfiore, "The cut-off rate of the time correlated fading channels," *IEEE Trans. Inform. Theory*, vol. 38, pp. 612–617, Nov. 1992.

[173] H. A. Leinhos, "Capacity calculations for rapidly fading communications channel," *IEEE J. Oceanic Eng.*, vol. 21, pp. 137–142, Apr. 1996.

[174] M. D. Loundu, C. L. Despins, and J. Conan, "Estimating the capacity of a frequency-selective fading mobile radio channel with antenna diversity," in *IEEE 44th Vehicular Technology Conf.* (Stockholm, Sweden, June 8–10, 1994), pp. 1490–1493.

[175] E. Malkamäki and H. Leib, "Coded diversity block fading channels," submitted to *IEEE Trans. Commun.* See also, "Coded diversity of block fading Rayleigh channels," in *Proc. IEEE Int. Conf. Universal Personal Communications (ICUPC'97)* (San Diego, CA, Oct. 1997). See also, E. Malkamäki, "Performance of error control over block fading channels with ARQ applications," Ph.D. dissertation, Helsinki Univ. Technol., Commun. Lab., Helsinki, Finland, 1998.

[176] T. L. Marzetta and B. M. Hochwald, "Fundamental limitations on multiple-antenna wireless links in Rayleigh fading," in *Proc. IEEE Int. Symp. Information Theory (ISIT'98)* (Cambridge, MA, Aug. 16–21, 1998), p. 310. See also: "Multiple antenna communications when nobody knows the Rayleigh fading coefficients," in *Proc. 35th Allerton Conf. Communication, Control and Computing* Sept. 29–Oct. 1, 1997, pp. 1033–1042. See also in *Proc. 1995 Int. Symp. Information Theory (ISIT'95)* (Whistler, BC, Canada, Sept. 17–22, 1995), p. 151. See also "Capacity of mobile multiple antenna communication link in Rayleigh flat fading," *IEEE Trans. Inform. Theory*, submitted for publication.

[177] J. Massey, "Some information-theoretic aspects of spread spectrum communications," in *Proc. IEEE 3rd Int. Symp. Spread Spectrum Techniques and Applications (ISSSTA'94)* (Oulu, Finland, July 4–6, 1994), pp. 16–20. See also "Toward an information theory of spread-spectrum systems," in *Code Division Multiple Access Communications*, S. Glisic, Ed. Boston, Dordrecht, and London: Kluwer, 1995, pp. 29–46.

[178] ———, "Coding and modulation in digital communications," in *Proc. 1974 Zurich Sem. Digital Communications*, Mar. 1974, pp. E2(1)–E2(4).

[179] ———, "Coding and modulations for code-division multiple accessing," in *Proc. 3rd Int. Workshop Digital Signal Processing Techniques Applied to Space Communications* (ESTEC, Noordwijk, The Netherlands, Sept. 23–25 1992).

[180] ———, "Coding for multiple access communications," in *Proc. ITG-Fachtagung* (München, Germany, Oct. 1994), pp. 26–28.

[181] ———, "Spectrum spreading and multiple accessing," in *Proc. IEEE Information Theory Workshop, ITW '95* (Rydzyna, Poland, June 25–29, 1995), p. 31.

[182] T. Matsumpopo and F. Adachi, "Performance limits of coded multilevel DPSK in cellular mobile radio," *IEEE Trans. Veh. Technol.*, vol. 41, pp. 329–336, Nov. 1992.

[183] R. J. McEliece and W. E. Stark, "Channels with block interference," *IEEE Trans. Inform. Theory*, vol. 30, pp. 44–53, Jan. 1984.

[184] M. Medard, "Bound on mutual information for DS-CDMA spreading over independent fading channels," preprint.

[185] M. Medard and R. G. Gallager, "The effect of channel variations upon capacity," in *1996 IEEE 46th Vechicular Technology Conf.* (Atlanta, GA, Apr. 28–May 1, 1996), pp. 1781–1785.

[186] ———, "The effect upon channel capacity in wireless communications of perfect and imperfect knowledge of the channel," submitted to *IEEE Trans. Inform. Theory*.

[187] ———, "The issue of spreading in multipath time-varying channels," in *45th IEEE Vehicular Technology Conf.* (Chicago, IL, July 25–28, 1995), pp. 1–5.

[188] ———, "The effect of an randomly time-varying channel on mutual information," in *IEEE Int. Symp. Information Theory (ISIT'95)* (Whistler,

BC, Canada, Sept. 17–22, 1995), p. 139.

[189] M. Medard and A. Goldsmith, "Capacity of time-varying channels with channel side information," in *IEEE Int. Symp. Information Theory (ISIT'97)* (Ulm, Germany, June 29–July 4, 1997), p. 372.

[190] N. Merhav, G. Kaplan, A. Lapidoth, and S. Shamai (Shitz), "On information rates for mismatched decoders," *IEEE Trans. Inform. Theory*, vol. 40, pp. 1953–1967, Nov. 1994.

[191] E. C. van der Meulen, "Some reflections on the interference channel," in *Communications and Cryptography: Two Sides of One Tapestry*, R. E. Blahut, D. J. Costello, U. Maurer, and T. Mittelholzer, Eds. Boston, MA: Kluwer, 1994, pp. 409–421.

[192] ——, "A survey of multi-way channels in information theory," *IEEE Trans. Inform. Theory*, vol. IT–23, pp. 1–37, Jan. 1977.

[193] J. W. Modestino and S. N. Hulyalkar, "Cutoff rate performance of CPM schemes operating on the slow-fading Rician channel," in *Coded Modulation and Bandwidth-Efficient Transmission, Proc. 5th Tirrenia Int. Workshop*, E. Biglieri and M. Luise, Eds. New York: Elsevier, 1992, pp. 119–130.

[194] M. Moher, "An iterative multiuser decoder for Newr-capacity communications," *IEEE Trans. Commun.*, vol. 46, pp. 870–880, July 1998. See also: "Turbo-based multiuser detection," in *IEEE Int. Symp. Inform. Theory (ISIT '97)* (Ulm, Germany, June 29–July 4, 1997), p. 195.

[195] R. R. Muller, P. Gunreben, and J. B. Huber, "On the ability of CDMA to combat log-noraml fading," in *1988 Int. Zurich Seminar on Broadband Communications, Accessing, Transmission and Networking* (ETH, Zurich, Switzerland, Feb. 17–19, 1998), pp. 17–22.

[196] R. R. Muller and J. B. Huber, "Capacity of cellular CDMA systems applying interference cancellation and channel coding," in *Proc. Communication Theory Mini Conf. (CTMC) at IEEE Globecom* (Phoenix, AZ, Nov. 1997), pp. 179–184. See also: R. R. Muller, "Multiuser equalization for randomly spread ssignals: Fundamental limits with and without decision feedback," *IEEE Trans. Inform. Theory*, submitted for publication.

[197] R. R. Muller, A. Lampe, and J. B. Huber, "Gaussian multiple-access channels with weighted energy constraints," presented at the IEEE, Information Theory Workshop (ITW'98), Killarney, Ireland, June 22–26, 1998.

[198] A. Narula, M. T. Trott, and G. W. Wornell, "Information-theoretic analysis of multiple-antenna transmission diversity for fading channels," submitted to *IEEE Trans. Inform. Theory*. See also in *Proc. Int. Symp. Information Theory and Its Application, (ISITA'96)* (Victoria, BC, Canada, Sept. 1996).

[199] A. S. Nemirovsky, "On the capacity of a multipath channel which has dispersed reception with automatic selection," *Radiotekh.*, vol. 16, no. 9, pp. 34–38, 1961.

[200] F. D. Nesser and J. L. Massey, "Proper complex random processes with application to information theory," *IEEE Trans. Inform. Theory*, vol. 39, pp. 1293–1302, July 1993.

[201] T. Ohtsuki, "Cutoff rate performance for space diversity systems in Rayleigh fading channels without CSI," in *1997 IEEE 6th Int. Conf. Universal Personal Communications Rec.* (San Diego, CA, Oct. 12–16, 1997), pp. 396–400.

[202] ——, "Cutoff rate performance for space diversity systems in a correlated Rayleigh fading channel with CSI," in *Proc. IEEE Int. Symp. Information Theory* (Ulm Germany, June 29–July 4, 1997), p. 238.

[203] I. A. Ovseevich, "The capacity of a multipath system," *Probl. Inform. Transm.*, vol. 14, pp. 43–58, 1963.

[204] ——, "Capacity and transmission rate over channels with random parameters," *Probl. Inform. Transm.*, vol. 4, no. 4, pp. 72–75, 1968.

[205] I. A. Ovseevich and M. S. Pinsker, "Bounds on the capacity of a communication channel whose parameters are random functions of time," *Radiotekh.*, vol. 12, no. 10, pp. 40–46, 1957.

[206] ——, "Bounds on the capacities of some real communication channels," *Radiotekh.*, vol. 13, no. 4, pp. 15–25, 1958.

[207] ——, "On the capacity of a multipath communication system," *News Acad. Sci. USSR (Energ. Automat.)*, no. 1, pp. 133–135, 1959.

[208] ——, "The rate of information transmission, the capacity of a multipath system, and reception by the method of transformation by a linear operator," *Radiotekh.*, vol. 14, no. 3, pp. 9–21, 1959.

[209] ——, "The capacity of channels with general and selective fading," *Radiotekh.*, vol. 15, no. 12, pp. 3–9, 1960.

[210] L. H. Ozarow, S. Shamai (Shitz), and A. D. Wyner, "Information theoretic considerations for cellular mobile ratio," *IEEE Trans. Veh. Technol.*, vol. 43, pp. 359–378, May 1994.

[211] L. H. Ozarow, A. D. Wyner, and J. Ziv, "Achievable rates for a constrained Gaussian channel," *IEEE Trans. Inform. Theory*, vol. 34, pp. 365–370, May 1988.

[212] J. H. Park. Jr., "Two-user dispersive communication channels," *IEEE Trans. Inform. Theory*, vol. IT–27, pp. 502–505, July 1981.

[213] ——, "Non-uniform M-ary PSK for channel capacity expansion," in *2nd Asia-Pacific Conf. Communication (APCC'95)* (Osaka, Japan, June 13–16, 1995), pp. 469–473.

[214] M. Peleg and S. Shamai, "Reliable communication over the discrete-time memoryless Rayleigh fading channel using turbo codes," submitted to *IEEE Trans. Commun.*

[215] J. N. Pierce, "Ultimate performance of M-ary transmission on fading channels," *IEEE Trans. Inform. Theory*, vol. IT–12, pp. 2–5, Jan. 1966.

[216] M. S. Pinsker, V. V. Prelov, and E. C. Van der Meulen, "Information transmission over channels with additive-multiplicative noise," in *Proc. 1998 IEEE Int. Symp. Information Theory* (Cambridge, MA, Aug. 17–21, 1998), p. 332.

[217] E. Plotnik, "The capacity region of the random-multiple access channel," in *Proc. Int. Symp. Information Theory, ISIT'90* (San Diego, CA, Jan. 14–19, 1990), p. 73. See also E. Plotnik and A. Satt, "Decoding rule and error exponent for the random multiple access channel," in *IEEE Int. Symp. Information Theory (ISIT'91)* (Budapest, Hungary, June 24–28, 1991), p. 216.

[218] G. S. Poltyrev, "Carrying capacity for parallel broadcast channels with degraded components," *Probl. Pered. Inform.*, vol. 13, no. 2, pp. 23–35, Apr.–June 1977.

[219] ——, "Coding in an asynchronous multiple-access channel," *Probl. Inform. Transm.*, pp. 12–21, July–Sept. 1983.

[220] H. V. Poor and G. W. Wornell, Eds., *Wireless Communications: Signal Processing Prespectives* (Prentice-Hall Signal Processing Series). Englewood Cliffs, NJ: Prentice-Hall, 1998.

[221] R. Prasad, *CDMA for Wireless Personal Communications*. Boston, MA: Artech House, 1996.

[222] J. R. Price, "Nonlinearly feedback-equalized PAM versus capacity for noisy filter channels," in *Proc. Int. Conf. Communication*, June 1972, pp. 22-12–22-17.

[223] J. G. Proakis, *Digital Communications*, 3rd. ed. New York: McGraw-Hill, 1995.

[224] S. Qu and A. U. Sheikh, "Analysis of channel capacity of M-ary DPSK and D^2/PSK with time-selective Rician channel," in *42rd IEEE Vehicular Technology Conf (VTC'93)* (Secaucus, NJ, May 18–20, 1993), pp. 25–281.

[225] T. S. Rappaport, *Wireless Communications, Principles & Practice*. Englewood Cliffs, NJ: Prentice-Hall, 1996.

[226] G. G. Rayleigh and J. M. Cioffi, "Spatio-temporal coding for wireless communication," *IEEE Trans. Commun.*, vol. 46, pp. 357–366, Mar. 1998.

[227] J. S. Richters, "Communication over fading dispersive channels," MIT Res. Lab. Electron., Tech. Rep. 464, Nov. 30, 1967.

[228] B. Rimoldi, "Successive refinement of information: Characterization of the achievable rates," *IEEE Trans. Inform. Theory*, vol. 40, pp. 253–259, Jan. 1994.

[229] ——, "On the optimality of generalized time-sharing for M-ary multiple-access channels," presented at the IEEE, Information Theory Workshop (ITW'98), Killarney, Ireland, June 22–26, 1998. See also in *Proc. IEEE Int. Symp. Information Theory* (Ulm, Germany, June 29–July 4, 1997), p. 26.

[230] ——, "RDMA for multipath multiple access channels: An optimum asynchronous low complexity technique," in *7th Joint Swedish-Russian Int. Workshop Information Theory* (St. Petersburg, Russia, June 17–22, 1995), pp. 196–199.

[231] B. Rimoldi and Q. Li, "Potential impact of rate-splitting multiple access on cellular communications," in *IEEE Global Communications Conf. (GLOBECOM'96)*, Nov. 18–22, 1996, pp. 92–96. See also "Rate-splitting multiple access and cellular communication," in *1996 IEEE Information Theory Workshop (ITW'96)* (Haifa, Israel, June 9–13, 1996), p. 35.

[232] B. Rimoldi and R. Urbanke, "A rate-splitting approach to the Gaussian multiple-access channel," *IEEE Trans. Inform. Theory*, vol. 42, pp. 364–375, Mar. 1996.

[233] A. Rojas, J. L. Gorricho, and J. Parafells, "Capacity comparison for FH/FDMA, CDMA and FDMA/CDMA schemes," in *Proc. 48th Annu. Int. Vehicular Technnology Conf. (VTC'98)* (Ottawa, Ont., Canada, May 18–21, 1998), pp. 1517–1522.

[234] M. Rupf and J. L. Massey, "Optimum sequences multisets for synchronous code-division multiple-access channels," *IEEE Trans. Inform. Theory*, vol. 40, pp. 1261–1266, July 1994.

[235] M. Rupf, F. Tarkoy, and J. L. Massey, "User-separating demodulation for code-division multiple-access systems," *IEEE J. Select. Areas Commun.*, vol. 2, pp. 786–795, June 1994.

[236] M. Sajadieh, F. R. Kschischang, and A. Leon-Garcia, "Analysis of two-layered adaptive transmission systems," in *1996 IEEE 46th Vehicular*

Technology Conf. (VTC'96) (Atlanta, GA, Apr. 28–May 1, 1996), pp. 1771–1775.

[237] M. Salehi, "Capacity and coding for memories with real-time noisy defect information at encoder and decoder," *Proc. Inst. Elec. Eng.–I*, vol. 139, no. 2, pp. 113–117, Apr. 1992.

[238] J. Salz and E. Zehavi, "Decoding under integer metrics constraints," *IEEE Trans. Commun.*, vol. 43, pp. 307–317, Feb./Mar./Apr. 1995.

[239] J. Salz and A. D. Wyner, "On data transmission over cross coupled multi-input, multi-output linear channels with applications to mobile radio," AT&T Tech. Memo., May 1990.

[240] H. Sato, "The capacity of the Gaussian interference channel under strong interference," *IEEE Trans. Inform. Theory*, vol. IT–27, pp. 786–788, Nov. 1981.

[241] P. Schramm, "Multilevel coding with independent detection on levels for efficient communication on static and interleaved fading channels," in *Proc. IEEE Int. Symp. Personal, Indoor and Mobile Radio Communication (PIMRC'97)* (Helsinki, Finland, Sept. 1–4, 1997), pp. 1196–1200.

[242] H. Schwarte and H. Nick, "On the capacity of a direct-sequence spread-spectrum multiple-access system: Asymptotic results," in *6th Joint Swedish–Russian Int. Workshop Information Theory*, Aug. 22–27, 1993, pp. 97–101. See also H. Schwarte, "On weak convergence of probability measures and channel capacity with applications to code division spread-spectrum systems," in *Proc. Int. Symp. Information Theory, ISIT'94* (Trondheim, Norway, June 27–July 1, 1994), p. 468.

[243] R. Schweikert, "The two codeword exponent R_o for a slowly fading Rayleigh channel," in *5th Int. Symp. Information Theory* (Tbilisi, USSR, 1979).

[244] A. Sendonaris and B. Aazhang, "Total channel throughput of M-ary CDMA systems over fading channels," in *Proc. 31th Annu. Conf. Information Sciences and Systems* (Baltimore, MD, The Johns Hopkins University, Mar. 19–21, 1997), pp. 423–428.

[245] A. Seeger, "Hierarchical channel coding for Rayleigh and Rice fading," in *Communication Theory Miniconf., CTMC'97* (GLOBECOM'97, Phoenix, AZ, Nov. 1997), pp. 208–212.

[246] A. Sendonaris, E. Erkip, and B. Aazhang, "Increasing uplink capacity via user cooperation diversity," in *Proc. IEEE Int. Symp. Information Theory* (Cambridge, MA, Aug. 17–21, 1998), 156.

[247] S. Shamai (Shitz), "A broadcast strategy for the Gaussian slowly fading channel," in *IEEE Int. Symp. Information Theory (ISIT'97)* (Ulm, Germany, June 29–July 4, 1997), p. 150. See also "A broadcast transmission strategy for multiple users in slowly fading channels," in preparation.

[248] S. Shamai (Shitz) and I. Bar-David, "Capacity of peak and average power constrained-quadrature Gaussian channels," *IEEE Trans. Inform. Theory*, vol. 41, pp. 1333–1346, Sept. 1996.

[249] S. Shamai and G. Caire, "Some information theoretic aspects of frequency selective fading channels, with centralized and decentralized power control," in preparation.

[250] S. Shamai (Shitz) and R. Laroia, "The intersymbol interference channel: Lower bounds on capacity and precoding loss," *IEEE Trans. Inform. Theory*, vol. 42, pp. 1388–1404, Sept. 1996.

[251] S. Shamai (Shitz) and S. Raghavan, "On the generalized symmetric cut-off rate for finite-state channels," *IEEE Trans. Inform. Theory*, vol. 41, pp. 1333–1346, Sept. 1995.

[252] S. Shamai (Shitz), E. Telatar, and D. Tse, "Information theoretic aspects of capacity achieving signaling on Gaussian channels with rapidly varying parameters," in preparations.

[253] S. Shamai (Shitz) and S. Verdú, "The empirical distribution of good codes," *IEEE Tans. Inform. Theory*, vol. 43, pp. 836–846, May 1997.

[254] ——, "Spectral efficiency of CDMA with random spreading," *IEEE Trans. Inform. Theory*, to be published. See also "Multiuser detection with random spreading and error correcting codes: Fundamental limits," in *Proc. 1997 Allerton Conf. Commuication, Control, and Computing.*, Sept.–Oct. 1997, pp. 470–482; "Information theoretic apects of coded random direct-sequence spread-spectrum," in *9th Mediterranean Electrotechnical Conf. (MELECON'98)* (Tel Aviv, Israel, May 18–20, 1998), pp. 1328–1332.

[255] S. Shamai (Shitz) and A. A. Wyner, "Information theoretic considerations for symmetric, cellular multiple access fading channels—Part I, and Part II," *IEEE Trans. Inform. Theory*, vol. 43, pp. 1877–1911, Nov. 1997. See also "Information theoretic considerations for simple, multiple access cellular communication channels," in *Int. Symp. Information Theory and Its Application* (Sydney, Australia, Nov. 20–24, 1994), pp. 793–799; "Information considerations for cellular multiple access channels in the presence of fading and inter-cell interference," in *IEEE IT Workshop on Information Theory, Multiple Access, and Queueing* (St. Louis, MO, Apr. 19–21, 1995), p. 21, and "Information theoretic considerations for intra and inter cell multiple access protocols in mobile

fading channels," in *IEEE 1995 Information Theory Workshop (ITW'95)* (Rydzyna, Poland, June 15–19, 1995), p. 3.6.

[256] S. Shamai (Shitz), "On the capacity of a Gaussian channel with peak power and bandlimited input signals," *Arch. Electronik Übertragungstech.*, vol. 42, no. 6, pp. 340–346, 1988.

[257] S. Shamai (Shitz) and I. Bar-David, "Upper bounds on the capacity for a constrained Gaussian channel," *IEEE Trans. Inform. Theory*, vol. 35, pp. 1079–1084, Sept. 1989.

[258] S. Shamai (Shitz) and A. Dembo, "Bounds on the symmetric binary cut-off rate for dispersive Gaussian channels," *IEEE Trans. Commun.*, vol. 42, pp. 39-53, Jan. 1994.

[259] S. Shamai, T. Marzetta, and E. Telatar, "The throughput in a block fading multiple user channel," in preparation.

[260] S. Shamai (Shitz), L. H. Ozarow, and A. D. Wyner, "Information rates for a discrete-time Gaussian channel with intersymbol interference and stationary inputs," *IEEE Trans. Inform. Theory*, vol. 37, pp. 1527–1539, Nov. 1991.

[261] C. Shannon, "Channels with side information at the transmitter," *IBM J. Res. Develop.*, no. 2, pp. 289–293, 1958.

[262] C. E. Shannon, "Communication in the presence of noise," *Proc. IRE*, vol. 37, no. 1, pp. 10–21, Jan. 1949. See reprint (Classic Paper), *Proc. IEEE*, vol. 86, pp. 447–457, Feb. 1998.

[263] N. M. Shehadeh, A. Balghunem, T. O. Halvani, and M. M. Dawoud, "Capacity calculation of multipath fading channel (underwater acoustic communications)," in *Proc. MELECON'85, Mediterranean Electrotechnical Conf.* (Madrid, Spain, Oct. 8–10, 1985), pp. 181–185.

[264] W. H. Shen, "Finite-state modeling, capacity, and joint source/channel coding for time-varying channels," Ph.D. dissertation, Dept. Elec. Eng., Rutgers Univ., New Brunswick, NJ, 1992.

[265] V. I. Siforov, "On the capacity of communication channels with slowly varying random parameters," *Sci. Rep. Coll. Radiotekh. Elektron.*, no. 1, sec. VII, pp. 3–8, 1958.

[266] J. Silverstein, "Strong convergence of empirical distribution of eigenvalues of large dimensional random matrices," *J. Multivariate Anal.*, vol. 55, no. 2, pp. 331–339, 1995.

[267] B. Sklar, "Rayleigh fading channels in mobile digital communication systems, Part I: Characterization, Part II: Mitigation," *IEEE Commun. Mag.*, vol. 35, no. 9, pp. 136–146 (Pt. I), pp. 148–155 (Pt. II), Sept. 1997.

[268] O. Somekh and S. Shamai (Shitz), "Shannontheoretic approach to a Gaussian cellular multiple-access channel with fading," in *Proc. 1998 IEEE Int. Symp. Information Theory* (Cambridge, MA, Aug. 17–21, 1998), p. 393. See also: "Shannon theoretic considerations for a Gaussian cellular TDMA multiple-access channel with fading," in *Proc. 8th IEEE Int. Symp. Personal and Mobile Radio Communications (PIMRC'97)* (Helsinki, Finland, Sept. 1–4, 1997), pp. 276–280.

[269] A. F. Soysa and S. C. Sag, "Channel capacity limits for multiple-access channels with slow Rayleigh fading," *Electron Lett.*, vol. 32, no. 16, pp. 1435–1437, Aug. 1, 1996.

[270] W. E. Stark, "Capacity and cutoff rate of noncoherent FSK with nonselective Rician fading," *IEEE Trans. Commun.*, vol. 33, pp. 1153–1159, Nov. 1985. See also "Capacity and cutoff rate evaluation of the Rician fading channel," in *1983 IEEE Int. Symp. Information Theory*.

[271] W. E. Stark and M. V. Hegde, "Asymptotic performance of M-ary signals in worst-case partial-band interference and Rayleigh fading," *IEEE Trans. Commun.*, vol. 36, pp. 989–992, Aug. 1988.

[272] W. E. Stark and R. J. McEliece, "Capacity and coding in the 'presence of fading and jamming'," in *IEEE 1981 Nat. Telecommunications Conf. (NTC'81)* (New Orleans, LA, Nov. 29–Oct. 3, 1981), pp. B7.4.1–B7.4.5.

[273] R. Steele, Ed., *Mobile Radio Communications*. New York: Pentech and IEEE Press, 1992.

[274] Y. T. Su and C. Ju-Ya, "Cutoff rates of multichannel MFSK and DPSK in mobile satellite communications," *IEEE J. Select. Areas Commun.*, vol. 13, pp. 213–221, Feb. 1995.

[275] B. Suard, G. Xu, H. Liu, and T. Kailath, "Uplink channel capacity of space-division multiple-access schemes," *IEEE Trans. Inform. Theory*, vol. 44, pp. 1476–1486, 1998. See also: "Channel capacity of spatial division multiple access schemes," in *Conf. Rec., The 28th Asilomar Conf. Signals, Systems and Computers* (Pacific Grove, CA, Oct. 30–Nov. 2, 1994), pp. 1159–1163.

[276] G. Taricco, "On the capacity of the binary input Gaussian and Rayleigh fading channels," *Euro. Trans. Telecomm.*, vol. 7, pp. 201–208, Mar.–Apr. 1996.

[277] G. Taricco and F. Vatta, "Capacity of cellular mobile radio systems," *Electron. Lett.*, vol. 34, no. 6, pp. 517–518, Mar. 19, 1998.

[278] G. Taricco and M. Elia, "Capacity of fading channel with no side information," *Elecron. Lett.*, vol. 33, no. 16, pp. 1368–1370, July 31, 1997.

[279] F. Tarkoy, "Information theoretic aspects of spread ALOHA," in *6th IEEE Int. Symp. Personal, Indoor and Mobile Radio Communications, PIMRC'95* (Toronto, Ont., Canada, Sept. 27–29, 1995), pp. 1318–1320.

[280] V. Taroakh, N. Naugib, N. Seshadri, and A. R. Calderbank, "Space-time codes for wireless communications: Practical considerations," submitted to *IEEE Trans. Commun.*

[281] V. Tarokh, N. Seshadri, and A. R. Calderbank, "Space-time coding for high data rate wireless communication: Performance analysis and code construction," *IEEE Trans. Inform. Theory*, vol. 44, pp. 744–765, Mar. 1998. See also B. M. Hochwald and T. L. Marzetta, "Unitary space-time modulation antenna communications in Raleigh flat fading," Lucent Technologies, Bell Labs. Tech. Memo., 1998.

[282] E. Telatar, "Coding and multiaccess for the energy limited Rayleigh fading channel," Masters thesis, Dept. Elec. Eng. Comp. Sci., MIT, May 1988.

[283] _____, "Capacity of multi-antenna Gaussian channel," AT&T Bell Labs, Tech. Memo., 1995.

[284] _____, "Multi-antenna multi-user fading channels," submitted to *IEEE Trans. Inform. Theory.*; "Capacity of multi-antenna Gaussian channels," AT&T Tech. Memo, 1995.

[285] İ. E. Telatar and R. G. Gallager, "Combining queueing theory and information theory for multi access," *IEEE J. Select. Areas Commun.*, vol. 13, pp. 963–969, Aug. 1995.

[286] E. Telatar and D. Tse, "Capacity and mutual information of broadband multipath fading channels," in *Proc. 1998 IEEE Int. Symp. Information Theory* (Cambridge, MA, Aug. 17–21, 1998), 395. See also "Broadband multipath fading channels: Capacity, mutual information and detection," submitted for publication to *IEEE Trans. Inform. Theory.*

[287] J. Trager and U. Sorger, "Information theoretic comparison of different channel estimation rules for mobile radio channels," unpublished manuscript.

[288] D. Tse, "Capacity scaling in multi-antenna systems," to be published.

[289] D. N. Tse, "Optimal power allocation over parallel Gaussian broadcast channels," in *IEEE Int. Symp. Information Theory (ISIT'97)* (Ulm, Germany, June 29–July 4, 1997), p. 27.

[290] D. Tse and S. Hanly, "Capacity region of the multi-access fading channel under dynamic resource allocation and polymatroid optimization," in *1996 IEEE Information Theory Workshop (ITW'96)* (Haifa, Israel, June 9–13, 1996), p. 37. See also "Fading channels: Part I: Polymatroidal structure, optimal resource allocation and throughput capacities," Coll. Eng., Univ. Calif., Berkeley, CA, Nov. 1996.

[291] S. H. Tseng and V. K. Prabhu, "Channel capacity of optimum diversity combining and equalization with QAM modulation in cellular and PCS radio channel," in *2nd Conf. Universal Personal Communications* (Ottawa, Ont., Canada, Oct. 12–15, 1993), pp. 647–652.

[292] B. S. Tsybakov, "On the capacity of a two-way communication channel," *Radiotekh. Elektron.*, vol. 4, no. 7, pp. 1116–1123, 1959 (Section VII).

[293] _____,, "On the capacity of multipath channels," *Radiotekh. Elektron.*, vol. 4, no. 9, pp. 1427–1433, 1959 (Section VII).

[294] _____, "On the capacity of a single-path channel with randomly varying absorption," *Sci. Rep. Coll. Radiotekh. Elektron.*, vol. 2, pp. 44–51, 1959 (Section VII).

[295] _____, "The capacity of some multipath communication channels," *Radiotekh. Elektron.*, vol. 4, no. 10, pp. 1602–1608, 1959 (Section VII).

[296] _____, "Capacity of a discrete Gaussian channel with a filter," *Probl. Pered. Inform.*, vol. 6, pp. 78–82, 1970.

[297] K. Varanasi and T. Guess, "Optimum decision feedback multiuser equalization with successive decoding achieves the total capacity of the Gaussian multiple-access channel," in *Proc. Asilomar Conf.* (Pacific Grove, CA, Nov. 1997). See also "Achieving vertices of the capacity region of the synchronous Gaussian correlated-waveform multiple-access channel with decision feedback receivers," in *Proc. IEEE Int. Symp. Information Theory (ISIT'97)* (Ulm, Germany, June 29–July 4, 1997), p. 270. Also, T. Guess and K. Varanasi, "Multiuser decision feedback receivers for the general Gaussian multiple-access channel," in *Proc. 34th Allerton Conf. Communication, Control and Computing* (Monticello, IL, Oct. 1996), pp. 190–199.

[298] P. Varzakas and G. S. Tombras, "Comparative estimate of user capacity for FDMA and direct-sequence CDMA in mobile radio," *Int. J. Electron.*, vol. 83, no. 1, pp. 133–144, July 1997.

[299] V. V. Veeravalli and B. Aazhang, "On the coding-spreading tradeoff in CDMA systems," in *Proc. 1996 Conf. Information Scien. Syst.* (Princeton, NJ, Apr. 1996), pp. 1136–1146.

[300] S. Vembu, S. Verdú, and Y. Steinberg, "The source-channel separation theorem revisited," *IEEE Trans. Inform. Theory*, vol. 41, pp. 44–54, Jan. 1995.

[301] S. Vembu and A. J. Viterbi, "Two different philosophies in CDMA—A comparison," in *Proc. IEEE 46th Vehicular Technology Conf.* (Atlanta,

GA, Apr. 28–May 1, 1996), pp. 869–873.

[302] J. Ventura-Traveset, G. Caire, E. Biglieri, and G. Taricco, "Impact of diversity reception on fading channels with coded modulation—Part I: Coherent detection," *IEEE Trans. Commun.* vol. 45, pp. 563–572, May 1997.

[303] _____, "Impact of diversity reception on fading channels with coded modulation—Part III: Co-channel interference," *IEEE Trans. Commun.*, vol. 45, pp. 809–818, July 1997.

[304] S. Verdú, "On channel capacity per unit cost," *IEEE Trans. Inform. Theory*, vol. 36, pp. 1019–1030, Sept. 1990.

[305] _____, "Capacity region of Gaussian CDMA channels: The symbol-synchronous case," in *Proc. 24th Annu. Allerton Conf. Communication, Control, and Computing* (Monticello, IL, Allerton House, 1986), pp. 1025–1039.

[306] _____, "The capacity region of the symbol-asynchronous Gaussian multiple-access channel," *IEEE Trans. Inform. Theory*, vol. 35, pp. 733–751, July 1989.

[307] _____, "Demodulation in the presence of multiuser interference: Progress and misconceptions," in *Intelligent Methods in Signal Processing and Communications*, D. Docampo, A. Figueiras-Vidal, and F. Perez-Gonzales, Eds. Boston, MA: Birkhauser, 1997, pp. 15–44.

[308] _____, *Multiuser Detection*. New York: Cambridge Univ. Press, 1998.

[309] _____, "Multiple-access channels with memory with and without frame synchronization," *IEEE Trans. Inform. Theory*, vol. 35, pp. 605–619, May 1989.

[310] S. Verdú and T. S. Han, "A general formula for channel capacity," *IEEE Trans. Inform. Theory*, vol. 40, pp. 1147–1157, July 1994.

[311] P. Whiting, "Capacity bounds for a hierarchical CDMA cellular network," in *IEEE Int. Symp. Information Theory and Its Applications (ISITA '96)* (Victoria, BC, Canada, Sept. 1996), pp. 502–506.

[312] H. Viswanathan, "Capacity of time-varying channels with delayed feedback," submitted to *IEEE Trans, Inform. Theory.* See also in *1998 IEEE Int. Symp. Information Theory* (Cambridge, MA, Aug. 17–21, 1998), p. 238.

[313] H. Viswanathan and T. Berger, "Outage capacity with feedback," presented at the Conf. Information Siences and Systems (CISS'98), Princeton Univ., Princeton, NJ., Mar. 18–20, 1998.

[314] A. Viterbi, "Performance of an M-ary orthogonal communication system using stationary stochastic signals," *IEEE Trans. Inform. Theory*, vol. IT-13, pp. 414–421, July 1967.

[315] _____, "Very low rate convolutional codes for maximum theoretical performance of spread-spectrum multiple-access channels," *IEEE J. Select. Areas Commun.*, vol. 8, pp. 641–649, May 1990.

[316] _____, "Wireless digital communication: A view based on three lessons learned," *IEEE Commun. Mag.*, vol. 29, pp. 33–36, Sept. 1991.

[317] _____, "The orthogonal-random waveform dichotomy for digital mobile personal communications," *IEEE Personal Commun.*, 1st quart., pp. 18–24, 1994.

[318] A. J. Viterbi, "Error-correcting coding for CDMA systems," in *Proc. IEEE 3rd Int. Symp. Spread Spectrum Technology and Applications, ISSSTA'94* (Oulu, Finland, July 4–6, 1994), pp. 22–26. See also "Performance limits of error-correcting coding in multi-cellular CDMA systems with and without interference cancellation," in *Code Division Multiple Access Communications*, S. G. Glisic and P. A. Leppanen, Eds. Boston, MA: Kluwer, 1995, pp. 47–52.

[319] _____, *CDMA Principles of Spread Spectrum Communication.* New York: Addison-Wesley, 1995.

[320] A. J. Viterbi and J. K. Omura, *Principles of Digital Communication and Coding.* London, U.K.: McGraw-Hill, 1979.

[321] U. Wachsmann, P. Schramm, and J. Huber, "Comparison of coded modulation schemes for the AWGN and the Rayleigh fading channel," in *Proc. 1998 IEEE Int. Symp. Inform. Theory* (Cambridge, MA, August 17–21, 1998), p. 5.

[322] H. S. Wang and N. Moayeri, "Modeling, capacity, and joint source/channel coding for Rayleigh fading channels," in *42rd IEEE Vehicular Technology Conf.* (Secacus, NJ, May 18–20, 1993), pp. 473–479.

[323] D. Warrier and U. Madhow, "On the capacity of cellular CDMA with successive decoding and controlled power disparities," in *Proc. 48th Annu. Int. Vehicular Technology Conf. (VTC'98)* (Ottawa, Ont., Canada, May 18–21, 1998), pp. 1873–1877.

[324] _____, "On the capacity of cellular CDMA with successive decoding and controlled power disparities," presented at the 48th Annu. Int. Vehicular Technology (VTC'98), Ottawa, Ont., Canada, May 18–21, 1998.

[325] R. D. Wiesel and J. M. Cioffi, "Achievable rates for Tomlinson-Harashima precoding," *IEEE Trans. Inform. Theory*, vol. 44, pp. 825–831, Sept. 1998. See also "Precoding and the MMSE-DFE," in

Conf. Rec. 28th Asilomar Conf. Signals, Systems and Computers (Pacific Grove, CA, Oct. 30–Nov. 2, 1994), pp. 1144–1148.

[326] J. Winters, "On the capacity of radio communication systems with diversity in a Rayleigh fading environemt," *IEEE J. Select. Areas Commun.*, vol. SAC-5, pp. 871–878, June 1987.

[327] J. Wolfowitz, *Coding Theorems of Information Theory*, 3rd ed. Berlin, Germany: Springer-Verlag, 1978.

[328] G. W. Wornell, "Spread-response precoding for communication over fading channels," *IEEE Trans. Inform. Theory*, vol. 42, pp. 488–501, Mar. 1996.

[329] ――――, "Spread-signature CDMA: Efficient multiuser communication in presence of fading," *IEEE Trans. Inform. Theory*, vol. 41, pp. 1418–1438, Sept. 1995.

[330] G. W. Wornell and A. V. Oppenheim, "Wavelet-based representations for a class of self-similar signals with application to fractal modulation," *IEEE Trans. Inform. Theory*, vol. 38, pp. 785–800, Mar. 1992.

[331] A. D. Wyner, "Shannontheoretic approach to a Gaussian cellular multiple access channel," *IEEE Trans. Inform. Theory*, vol. 40, pp. 1713–1727, Nov. 1994.

[332] B. Chen and G. W. Wornell, "Analog error-correcting codes based on chaotic dynamical systems," *IEEE Trans. Commun.*, vol. 46, pp. 881–890, July 1998.

[333] A. D. Wyner, "Recent results in the Shannon theory," *IEEE Trans. Inform. Theory*, vol. IT-20, pp. 2–10, Jan. 1974.

[334] E. M. Yeh and R. G. Gallager, "Achieving the Gaussian multiple access capacity region using time-sharing of single-user codes," in *Proc. 1998 IEEE Int. Symp. Information Theory (ISIT'98)* (Cambridge, MA, Aug. 17–21, 1998), p. 213.

[335] Y. Yu-Dong and U. H. Sheikh, "Evaluation of channel capacity in a generalized fading channel," in *Proc. 43rd IEEE Vehicular Technology Conf.*, 1993, pp. 134–173.

[336] S. Zhou, S. Mei, X. Xu, and Y. Yao, "Channel capacity of fast fading channel," in *IEEE 47th Vehicular Technology Conf. Proc.* (Phoenix, AZ, May 4–7, 1997), pp. 421–425.

[337] R. E. Ziemer, Ed., "Fading channels and equalization," *J. Select. Areas Commun.* (Special Issue), vol. 10, no. 3, Apr. 1992.

[338] J. Ziv, "Universal decoding for finite-state channels," *IEEE Trans. Inform. Theory*, vol. IT-31, pp. 453–460, July 1985.

[339] ――――, "Probability of decoding error for random phase and Rayleigh fading channel," *IEEE Trans. Inform. Theory*, vol. IT–11, pp. 53–61, Jan. 1965.

[340] P. D. Alexander, L. K. Rasmussen, and C. B. Schlegel, "A linear receiver for coded CDMA," *IEEE Trans. Commun.*, vol. 45, pp. 605–610, May 1997.

[341] S. S. Beheshti and G. W. Wornell, "Iterative interference cancellation and decoding for spread-signature CDMA systems," in *IEEE 47th Vehicular Technology Conf. VTC'97* (Phoenix, AZ, May 4–7, 1997), pp. 26–30.

[342] M. C. Reed, P. D. Alexander, J. A. Asenstorfer, and C. B. Schlegel, "Near single user performance using iterative multi-user detection for CDMA with turbo-code decoders," in *Proc. PIMRC'97* (Helsinki, Finland, Sept. 1–4, 1997), pp. 740–744.

[343] T. R. Giallorenzi and S. G. Wilson, "Multiuser ML sequence estimator for convolutionally coded DS-CDMA systems," *IEEE Trans. Commun.*, vol. 44, pp. 997–1008, Aug. 1996.

[344] B. Vojcic, Y. Shama, and R. Pickholtz, "Optimum soft-output MAP for coded multi-user communications," in *Proc. IEEE Int. Symp. Information Theory (ISIT'97)* (Ulm, Germany, June 1997).

[345] Y. Shama and B. Vojcic, "Soft output algorithm for maximum likelihood multiuser detection of coded asynchronous communications," in *Proc. 30th Annu. Conf. Information Sciences and Systems* (Baltimore, MD, The Johns Hopkins Univ., Mar. 19–21, 1997), pp. 730–735.

[346] M. C. Reed, C. B. Schlegel, P. Alexander, and J. Asenstorfer, "Iterative multi-user detection for DS-CDMA with FEC," in *Proc. Int. Symp. Turbo Codes and Related Topics* (Brest, France, Sept. 3–5, 1997), pp. 162–165.

[347] M. Meiler, J. Hagenauer, A. Schmidbauer, and R. Herzog, "Iterative decoding in the uplink of the CDMA-system I-95 (A)," in *Proc. Int. Symp. Turbo Codes and Related Topics* (Brest, France, Sept. 3–5, 1997), pp. 208–211.

[348] B. Vucetic, "Bandwidth efficient concatenated coding schemes for fading channels," *IEEE Trans. Commun.*, vol. 41, pp. 50–61, Jan. 1993.

[349] E. Leonardo, L. Zhang, and B. Vucetic, "Multidimensional M-PSK trellis codes for fading channels," *IEEE Trans. Inform. Theory, vol. 43, pp. 1093–1108, July 1996.*

[350] J. Du, B. Vucetic, and L. Zhang, "Construction of new MPSK trellis codes for fading channels," *IEEE Trans. Commun.*, vol. 43, pp. 776–784, Feb./Mar./Apr. 1995.

[351] U. Fawer and B. Aazhang, "A multiuser receiver for code division

multiple access communications over multipath fading channels," *IEEE Trans. Commun.*, to be published.

[352] S. Vasudevan and M. K. Varanasi, "Optimum diversity combiner based multiuser detection for time-dispersive Rician fading CDMA channels," *IEEE J. Select. Areas Commun.*, vol. 12, pp. 580–592, May 1994.

[353] J. Du and B. Vucetic, "Trellis coded 16-QAM for fading channels," *Euro. Trans. Telecommun.*, vol. 4, no. 3, pp. 335–342, May–June 1992.

[354] Z. Zvonar and D. Brady, "Adaptive multiuser receivers with diversity reception for nonselective Rayleigh fading asynchronous CDMA channels," in *MILCOM '94* (Ft. Monmouth, NJ, Oct. 2–5, 1994), pp. 982–986.

[355] J. Du, Y. Kamio, H. Sasaoke, and B. Vucetic, "New 32-QAM trellis codes for fading channels," *Electron. Lett.*, vol. 29, no. 20, pp. 1745–1746, Sept. 30th, 1993.

[356] S. Wilson and Y. Leung, "Trellis-coded phase modulation on Rayleigh channels," in *Proc. Int. Conf. Communications* (Seattle, WA, June 7–11, 1987), pp. 21.3.1–12.3.5.

[357] S. A. Al-Semari and T. Fuja, "Bit interleaved I-Q TCM," in *Int. Symp. Information Theory and Its Applications (ISITA '96)* (Victoria, BC, Caqnada, Sept. 17–20, 1996).

[358] S. Benedetto and E. Biglieri, *Principles of Digital Transmission with Wireless Applications*. New York: Plenum, 1998.

[359] C. Berrou and A. Glavieux, "Near optimum error correcting coding and decoding: Turbo-codes," *IEEE Trans. Commun.*, vol. 44, pp. 1261–1271, Oct. 1996.

[360] E. Biglieri, G. Caire, and G. Taricco, "Error probability over fading channels: A unified approach," *Euro. Trans. Telecommun.*, pp. 15–25, Jan.-Feb. 1998.

[361] E. Biglieri, D. Divsalar, P. J. McLane, and M. K. Simon, *Introduction to Trellis-Coded Modulation with Applications*. New York: MacMillan, 1991.

[362] K. Boullé and J. C. Belfiore, "Modulation scheme designed for the Rayleigh fading channel," in *Proc. CISS'92* (Princeton, NJ, Mar. 1992), pp. 288–293.

[363] J. Boutros, "Constellations optimales par plongement canonique," *Mém. d'études, Ecole Nat. Supérieure Télécommun.*, Paris, France, June 1992.

[364] ――――, "Réseaux de points pour les canaux à evanouissements," Ph.D. dissertation, Ecole Nat. Supérieure Télécommun., Paris, France, May 1996.

[365] J. Boutros and E. Viterbo, "High diversity lattices for fading channels," in *Proc. 1995 IEEE Int. Symp. Information Theory* (Whistler, BC, Canada, Sept. 17–22, 1995).

[366] ――――, "Rotated multidimensional QAM constellations for Rayleigh fading channels," in *Proc. 1996 IEEE Information Theory Workshop* (Haifa, Israel, June 9–13, 1996), p. 23.

[367] ――――, "Rotated trellis coded lattices," in *Proc. XXVth General Assembly of the International Union of Radio Science, URSI* (Lille, France, Aug. 28–Sept. 5, 1996), p. 153.

[368] ――――, "New approach for transmission over fading channel," in *Proc. ICUPC'96* (Boston, MA, Sept. 29–Oct. 2, 1996), pp. 66–70.

[369] ――――, "Number fields and modulations for the fading channel," presented at the Workshop "Réseaux Euclidiens et Formes Modulaires, Colloque CIRM," Luminy, Marseille, France, Sept. 30–Oct. 4, 1996.

[370] J. Boutros, E. Viterbo, C. Rastello, and J. C. Belfiore, "Good lattice constellations for both Rayleigh fading and Gaussian channel," *IEEE Trans. Inform. Theory*, vol. 42, pp. 502–518, Mar. 1996.

[371] J. Boutros and M. Yubero, "Converting the Rayleigh fading channel into a Gaussian channel," presented at the Mediterranean Workshop on Coding and Information Integrity, Palma, Feb. 1996.

[372] J. Boutros and E. Viterbo, "Signal space diversity: A power- and bandwidth-efficient diversity technique for the Rayleigh fading channel," *IEEE Trans. Inform. Theory*, vol. 44, pp. 1453–1467, July 1998.

[373] G. Caire and G. Lechner, "Turbo-codes with unequal error protection," *IEE Electron. Lett.*, vol. 32 no. 7, p. 629, Mar. 1996.

[374] P. J. McLane, P. H. Wittke, P. K. M. Ho, and C. Loo, "Codes for fast fading shadowed mobile satellite communications channels," *IEEE Trans. Commun.*, vol. 36, pp. 1242–1246, Nov. 1988.

[375] D. Divsalar and M. K. Simon, "Trellis coded modulation for 4800–9600 bits/s transmission over a fading mobile satellite channel," *IEEE J. Select. Areas Commun.*, vol. SAC-5, pp. 162–175, Feb. 1987.

[376] M. K. Simon and D. Divsalar, "The performance of trellis coded multilevel DPSK on a fading mobile satellite channel," *IEEE Trans. Veh. Technol.*, vol. 37, pp. 79–91, May 1988.

[377] G. Caire, J. Ventura-Traveset, and E. Biglieri, "Coded and pragmatic-coded orthogonal modulation for the fading channel with noncoherent detection," in *Proc. IEEE Int. Conf. Communications (ICC'95)* (Seattle, WA, June 18–22, 1995).

[378] H. Cohen, *Computational Algebraic Number Theory*. New York: Springer-Verlag, 1993.

[379] D. Divsalar and M. K. Simon, "The design and performance of trellis coded MPSK for fading channels: Performance criteria," *IEEE Trans. Commun.*, vol. 36, pp. 1004–1011, Sept. 1988.

[380] _____, "The design and performance of trellis coded MPSK for fading channels: Set partitioning for optimum code design," *IEEE Trans. Commun.*, vol. 36, pp. 1013–1021, Sept. 1988.

[381] _____, "Maximum-likelihood differential detection of uncoded and trellis coded amplitude phase modulation over AWGN and fading channels—Metrics and performance," *IEEE Trans. Commun.*, vol. 42, pp. 76–89, Jan. 1994.

[382] F. Edbauer, "Performance of interleaved trellis-coded differential 8-PSK modulation over fading channels," *IEEE J. Select. Areas Commun.*, vol. 37, pp. 1340–1346, Dec. 1989.

[383] M. P. Fitz, J. Grimm, and J. V. Krogmeier, "Results on code design for transmitter diversity in fading," in *Proc. Int. Symp. Information Theory* (Ulm, Germany, June 29–July 4, 1997), p. 234.

[384] G. D. Forney, Jr., "Geometrically uniform codes," *IEEE Trans. Inform. Theory*, vol. 37, pp. 1241–1260, Sept. 1991.

[385] X. Giraud, "Constellations pour le canal à évanouissements," Ph.D. dissertation, Ecole Nat. Supérieure Télécommun., Paris, France, May 1994.

[386] X. Giraud and J. C. Belfiore, "Coset codes on constellations matched to the fading channel," in *Proc. Int. Symp. Information Theory (ISIT'94)* (Trondheim, Norway, June 1994), p. 26.

[387] _____, "Constellation design for Rayleigh fading channels," in *Proc. 1996 IEEE Information Theory Workshop* (Haifa, Israel, June 9–13, 1996), p. 25.

[388] _____, "Constellations matched to the Rayleigh fading channel," *IEEE Trans. Inform. Theory*, vol. 42, pp. 106–115, Jan. 1996.

[389] X. Giraud, K. Boullé, and J. C. Belfiore, "Constellations designed for the Rayleigh fading channel," in *Proc. Int. Symp. Information Theory (ISIT'93)* (San Antonio, TX, Jan. 1993), p. 342.

[390] X. Giraud, E. Boutillon, and J. C. Belfiore, "Algebraic tools to build modulation schemes for fading channels," *IEEE Trans. Inform. Theory*, vol. 43, pp. 938–952, May 1997.

[391] A. Gjerstad, "Sø king Etter Foldningskoder," Tech. Rep., Trondheim Univ., Trondheim, Norway, Sept. 1987 (in Norwegian).

[392] J. Hagenauer and E. Lutz, "Forward error correction coding for fading compensation in mobile satellite channels," *IEEE J. Select. Areas Commun.*, vol. SAC-5, pp. 215–225, Feb. 1987.

[393] A. Hiroike, F. Adachi, and N. Nakajima, "Combined effects of phase sweeping transmitter diversity and channel coding," *IEEE Trans. Veh. Technol.*, vol. 41, pp. 170–176, May 1992.

[394] P. Ho and D. Fung, "Error performance of interleaved trellis-coded PSK modulations in correlated Rayleigh fading channels," *IEEE Trans. Commun.*, vol. 40, pp. 1800–1809, Dec. 1992.

[395] L. Huang and L. L. Campbell, "Trellis coded MDPSK in correlated and shadowed Rician fading channels," *IEEE Trans. Veh. Technol.*, vol. 40, pp. 786–797, Nov. 1991.

[396] L. M. A. Jalloul and J. M. Holtzman, "Performance analysis of DS/CDMA with noncoherent M-ary orthogonal modulation in multipath fading channels," *IEEE J. Select. Areas Commun.*, vol. 37, pp. 1340–1346, Dec. 1989.

[397] S. H. Jamali and T. Le-Ngoc, *Coded-Modulation Techniques for Fading Channels*. New York: Kluwer, 1994.

[398] B. D. Jeličić and S. Roy, "Design of a trellis coded QAM for flat fading and AWGN channels," *IEEE Trans. Veh. Technol.*, vol. 44, Feb. 1995.

[399] B. Vucetic and J. Nicolas, "Construction and performance analysis of M-PSK trellis coded modulation on fading channels," in *Proc. Int. Conf. Communication (ICC'90)* (Atlanta, GA Apr. 1990), pp. 312.2.1–312.2.5.

[400] R. Knopp, *Coding and Multiple Access over Fading Channels*, Ph.D. dissertation, Ecole Polytech. Féd. Lausanne, Lausanne, Switzerland, 1997.

[401] R. Knopp and G. Caire, "Simple power-controlled modulation schemes for fixed-rate transmission over fading channels," submitted for publication, 1997.

[402] J. Nicolas and B. Vucetic, "Performance evaluation on M-PSK trellis codes over nonlinear fading mobile satellite channels," in *Proc. Int. Conf. Communication Systems (ICCA'88)* (Singapore, Nov. 1988), pp. 695–699.

[403] Y. S. Leung and S. G. Wilson, "Trellis coding for fading channels," in *Proc. Int. Communications Conf. (ICC'87)* (Seattle, WA, June 7–10, 1997), pp. 21.3.1–21.3.5.

[404] X. Li and J. A. Ritchey, "Bit-interleaved coded modulation with iterative decoding," *IEEE Commun. Lett.*, vol. 1, pp. 169–171, Nov. 1997.

[405] _____, "Bit-interleaved coded modulation with iterative decoding—Approaching turbo-TCM performance without code concatenation," in *Proc. CISS'98* (Princeton, NJ, Mar. 18–20, 1998).

[406] B. Vucetic and J. Du, "The effect of phase noise on trellis modulation codes on AWGN and fading channels," in *Proc. SITA'89* (Aichi, Japan, Dec. 1989), pp. 337–342.

[407] T. Maseng, personal communication to E. Biglieri.

[408] G. Stüber, *Principles of Mobile Communication*. Boston, MA: Kluwer, 1996.

[409] S. Y. Mui and J. Modestino, "Performance of DPSK with convolutional encoding on time-varying fading channels," *IEEE Trans. Commun.*, vol. 25, pp. 1075–1082, Oct. 1977.

[410] A. Narula and M. D. Trott, "Multiple-antenna transmission with partial side information," in *Proc. IEEE Int. Symp. Information Theory* (Ulm, Germany, June 29–July 4, 1997), p. 153.

[411] L. Zhang and B. Vucetic, "New MPSK BCM codes for Reileigh fading channels," in *Proc. ICCS&ISITA'92* (Singapore, Nov. 1992), pp. 857–861.

[412] R. G. McKay, P. J. McLane, and E. Biglieri, "Error bounds for trellis-coded MPSK ona fading mobile satellite channel," *IEEE Trans. Commun.*, vol. 39, pp. 1750–1761, Dec. 1991.

[413] M. E. Pohst, *Computational Algebraic Number Theory*, DMV Seminar, vol. 21. Basel, Switzerland: Birkhäuser Verlag, 1993.

[414] G. Battail, "A conceptual framework for understanding turbo-codes," *IEEE J. Select. Areas Commun.*, vol. 16, pp. 245–254, Feb. 1998.

[415] P. Samuel, *Algebraic Theory of Numbers*. Paris, France: Hermann, 1971.

[416] C. Schlegel and D. Costello, Jr., "Bandwidth efficient coding on a fading channel," *IEEE J. Select. Areas Commun.*, vol. 7, pp. 1356–1368, Dec. 1989.

[417] N. Seshadri and C.-E. W. Sundberg, "Coded modulations for fading channels—An overview," *Euro. Trans. Telecomm.*, vol. ET-4, no. 3, pp. 309–324, May–June 1993.

[418] N. Seshadri and J. H. Winters, "Two signaling schemes for improving the error performance of frequency-division-duplex (FDD) transmission systems using transmitter antenna diversity," *Int. J. Wireless Inform. Networks*, vol. 1, no. 1, 1994.

[419] M. Steiner, "The strong simplex conjecture is false," *IEEE Trans. Inform. Theory*, vol. 40, pp. 721–731, May 1994.

[420] G. Taricco and E. Viterbo, "Performance of component interleaved signal sets for fading channels," *Electron. Lett.*, vol. 32, no. 13, pp. 1170–1172, June 20, 1996.

[421] _____, "Performance of high diversity multidimensional constellations," in *Proc. IEEE Int. Symp. Information Theory* (Ulm, Germany, June 29–July 4, 1997), p. 167.

[422] _____, "Performance of high diversity multidimensional constellations," submitted to *IEEE Trans. Inform. Theory*, July 1996.

[423] K.-Y. Chan and A. Bateman, "The performance of reference-based M-ary PSK with trellis coded modulation in Rayleigh fading," *IEEE Trans. Veh. Technol.*, vol. 41, pp. 190–198, Apr. 1992.

[424] G. Ungerboeck, "Channel coding with multilevel/phase signals," *IEEE Trans. Inform. Theory*, vol. IT-28, pp. 56–67, Jan. 1982.

[425] D. L. Johnston and S. K. Jones, "Spectrally efficient communication via fading channels using coded multilevel DPSK," *IEEE Trans. Commun.*, vol. COM-29, pp. 276–284, Mar. 1981.

[426] J. Ventura-Traveset, G. Caire, E. Biglieri, and G. Taricco, "Impact of diversity reception on fading channels with coded modulation—Part II: Differential block detection," *IEEE Trans. Commun.*, vol. 45, pp. 676–687, June 1997.

[427] J. K. Cavers and P. Ho, "Analysis of the error performance of trellis-coded modulations in Rayleigh-fading channels," *IEEE Trans. Commun.*, vol. 40, pp. 74–83, Jan. 1992.

[428] A. J. Viterbi, J. K. Wolf, E. Zehavi, and R. Padovani, "A pragmatic approach to trellis-coded modulation," *IEEE Commun. Mag.*, vol. 27, no. 7, pp. 11–19, 1989.

[429] E. Viterbo, "Computational techniques for the analysis and design of lattice constellations," Ph.D. dissertation, Politec. Torino, Torino, Italy, Feb. 1995.

[430] E. Viterbo and E. Biglieri, "A universal lattice decoder," presented at the 14-ème Colloque GRETSI, Juan-les-Pins, France, Sept. 1993.

[431] E. Viterbo and J. Boutros, "A universal lattice code decoder for fading channels," submitted to *IEEE Trans. Inform. Theory*, Apr. 1996.

[432] M. A. Yubero, "Réseaux de points à haute diversité," Proyecto fin de carrera, Escuela Téc. Superior Ing. Telecomun., Madrid, Spain, May 1995.

[433] L. F. Wei, "Coded M-DPSK with built-in time diversity for fading channels," *IEEE Trans. Inform. Theory*, vol. 39, pp. 1820–1839, Nov. 1993.

[434] J. H. Winters, "The diversity gain of transmit diversity in wireless systems with Rayleigh fading," in *Proc. Int. Conf. Communication (ICC'94)*, May 1994, pp. 1121–1125.

[435] G. W. Wornell and M. D. Trott, "Efficient signal processing techniques for antenna diversity on fading channels," *IEEE Trans. Signal Proc.* (Special Issue on Signal Processing for Advanced Communications), Jan. 1997.

[436] ——, "Signal processing techniques for efficient use of transmit diversity in wireless communications," in *Proc. ICASSP-96* (Atlanta, GA, May 7–10).

[437] E. Zehavi, "8-PSK trellis codes for a Rayleigh channel," *IEEE Trans. Commun.*, vol. 40, pp. 873–884, May 1992.

[438] M. Abdulrahman, A. U. H. Sheikh, and D. D. Falconer, "Decision feedback equalization for CDMA in indoor wireless communications," *IEEE J. Select. Areas Commun.*, vol. 12, pp. 698–706, May 1994.

[439] K. L. Baum, D. E. Borth, and B. D. Mueller, "A comparison of nonlinear equalization methods for the U.S. digital cellular system," in *Proc. 1992 GLOBECOM*, pp. 291–295.

[440] J. Bellini, "Bussgang techniques for blind equalization," in *Proc. GLOBECOM'86* (Houston, TX, Dec. 1986), pp. 46.1.1–46.1.7.

[441] P. A. Bello, "Characterization of randomly time-variant linear channels," *IEEE Trans. Commun. Syst.*, vol. CS-11, pp. 360–393, Dec. 1963.

[442] A. Benveniste and M. Goursat, "Blind equalizers," *IEEE Trans. Commun.*, vol. COM-32, pp. 871–883, Aug. 1984.

[443] G. J. Bierman, *Factorization Methods for Discrete Sequential Estimation.* New York: Academic, 1977.

[444] B. Bjerke, J. G. Proakis, M. K. Lee, and Z. Zvonar, "A comparison of decision feedback equalization and data directed estimation techniques for the GSM system," in *Proc. ICUPC'97* (San Diego, CA, Oct. 13–15, 1997).

[445] R. M. Buehrer, A. Kaul, S. Stringlis, and B. D. Woerner, "Analysis of DS-CDMA parallel interference cancellation with phase and timing errors," *IEEE J. Select. Areas Commun.*, vol. 14, pp. 1522–1535, Oct. 1996.

[446] D. S. Chen and S. Roy, "An adaptive multiuser receiver for CDMA systems," *IEEE J. Select. Areas Commun.*, vol. 12, pp. 808–816, June 1994.

[447] K. Chugg and A. Polydoros, "MLSE for an unknown channel, Part I: Optimality considerations," *IEEE Trans. Commun.*, vol. 44, pp. 836–846, July 1996; "Part II: Tracking performance," Aug. 1996.

[448] J. M. Cioffi and T. Kailath, "Fast recursive least squares transversal filters for adaptive filtering," *IEEE Trans. Acoust., Speech Signal Processing*, vol. ASSP–32, pp. 304–337, Apr. 1984.

[449] G. D'Aria and V. Zingarelli, "Adaptive baseband equalizers for narrowband TDMA/FDMA mobile radio," *CSELT Tech. Repts.*, vol. 16, pp. 19–27, Feb. 1988.

[450] ——, "Fast Kalman and Viterbi adaptive equalizers for CEPT/GSM mobile radio," *CSELT Tech. Repts.*, vol. 17, pp. 13–18, Feb. 1989.

[451] A. Duel-Hallen, "Equalizers for multiple input/multiple output channels and PAM systems with cyclostationery input sequences," *IEEE J. Select. Areas Commun.*, vol. 10, pp. 630–639, Apr. 1992.

[452] D. D. Falconer, M. Abdulrahman, N. W. K. Lo, B. R. Peterson, and A. U. H. Sheikh, "Advances in equalization and diversity for portable wireless systems," *Digital Signal Processing*, vol. 3, pp. 148–162, Mar. 1993.

[453] U. Fawer and B. Aazhang, "A multiuser receiver for code division multiple access communications over multipath channels," *IEEE Trans. Commun.*, vol. 43, pp. 1556–1565, Feb./Mar./Apr. 1995.

[454] G. D. Forney, Jr., "Maximum likelihood sequence estimation of digital sequences in the presence of intersymbol interference," *IEEE Trans. Inform. Theory*, vol. IT-18, pp. 636–678, May 1972.

[455] G. J. Foschini, "Equalizing without altering or detecting data," *Bell Syst. Tech. J.*, vol. 64, pp. 1885–1911, Oct. 1985.

[456] G. B. Giannakis and J. M. Mendel, "Indentification of nonminimum phase systems using higher-order statistics," *IEEE Trans. Acoust, Speech Signal Processing*, vol. 37, pp. 360–377, Mar. 1989.

[457] R. D. Gitlin and S. B. Weinstein, "Fractionally-spaced equalization: An improved digital transversal equalizer," *Bell Syst. Tech. J.*, vol. 60, pp. 275–296, Feb. 1981.

[458] A. Glavieux, C. Laot, and J. Labat, "Turbo equalization over a frequency selective channel," in *Proc. Int. Symp. Turbo Codes and Related Topics* (Brest, France, Sept. 3–5, 1997), pp. 96–102.

[459] P. E. Green, Jr., "Radar astronomy measurement techniques," M.I.T. Lincoln Lab., Lexington, MA, Tech. Rep. 282, Dec. 1962.

[460] D. Hatzinakos and C. L. Nikias, "Blind equalization using a tricepstrum-based algorithm," *IEEE Trans. Commun.*, vol. 39, pp. 669–682, May 1991.

[461] M. Honig, U. Madhow, and S. Verdú, "Blind multiuser detection," *IEEE Trans. Inform. Theory*, vol. I41, pp. 944–960, July 1995.

[462] M. L. Honig, U. Madhow, and S. Verdú, "Blind adaptive interference suppression for near-far resistance CDMA," in *Proc. IEEE Global Telecommunications Conf.* (San Francisco, CA, 1994), pp. 379–384.

[463] F. M. Hsu, "Square-root Kalman filtering for high speed data received over fading dispersive HF channels," *IEEE Trans. Inform. Theory*, vol. IT-28, pp. 753–763, Sept. 1982.

[464] H. C. Huang and S. Schwartz, "A comparative analysis of linear multiuser detectors for fading multipath channels," in *Proc. 1994 GLOBECOM*, 1994, pp. 11–15.

[465] A. Johansson and A. Svensson, "Multistage interference cancellation in multi-rate DS/CDMA systems," in *Proc. PIMRC'95* (Toronto, Ont., Canada, Sept. 1995), pp. 965–969.

[466] M. J. Juntti, "Performance of decorrelating multiuser receiver with data-aided channel estimation," in *IEEE GLOBECOM Mini-Conf. Rec.* (Phoenix, AZ, Nov. 3–8, 1997), pp. 123–127.

[467] G. Kechriotis and E. Manolakos, "Hopfield neural network implementation of the optimal CDMA multiuser detector," *IEEE Trans. Neural Networks*, pp. 131–141, Jan. 1996.

[468] R. D. Koilpillai, S. Chennakeshu, and R. L. Toy, "Low complexity equalizers for the U.S. digital cellular systems," in *Proc. PIMRC'92* (Boston, MA, Oct. 19–21, 1992), pp. 744–747.

[469] J. Lin, F. Ling, and J. G. Proakis, "Joint data and channel estimation for TDMA mobile channels," in *Proc. PIMRC'92* (Boston, MA, Oct. 19–21, 1992), pp. 235–239.

[470] E. Lindskog, A. Ahlén, and M. Sternad, "Spatio-temporal equalization for multipath environments in mobile radio applications," in *Proc. IEEE 45th Vehicular Technology Conf.* (Chicago, IL, July 1995), pp. 399–403.

[471] F. Ling and J. G. Proakis, "Generalized least squares lattice and its application to DFE," in *Proc. 1982 IEEE Int. Conf. Acoustics, Speech, and Signal Processing* (Paris, France, May 1982).

[472] ——, "A generalized multichannel least-squares lattice algorithm with sequential processing stages," *IEEE Trans. Acoust., Speech, Signal Processing*, vol. ASSP–32, pp. 381–389, Apr. 1984.

[473] ——, "Adaptive lattice decision-feedback equalizers—Their performance and application to time-variant multipath channels," *IEEE Trans. Commun.*, vol. COM–33, pp. 348–356, Apr. 1985.

[474] ——, "Nonstationary learning characteristics of least squares adaptive estimation algorithm," in *Proc. Int. Conf. Acoustics, Speech and Signal Processing* (San Diego, CA, Mar. 1984), pp. 3.7.1–3.7.4.

[475] N. W. K. Lo, D. D. Falconer, and A. U. H. Sheikh, "Adaptive equalization for co-channel interference in multipath fading environment," *IEEE Trans. Commun.*, vol. 43, pp. 1441–1453, Feb./Mar./Apr. 1995.

[476] ——, "Adaptive equalizer MSE performance in the presence of multipath fading, interference and noise," in *1995 IEEE 45th Vehicular Technology Conf.* (Chicago, IL, July 25–28, 1995), pp. 409–413.

[477] ——, "Adaptive equalization for a multipath fading environment with interference and noise," in *44th IEEE Vehicular Technology Conf.* (Stockholm, Sweden, June 8–10, 1994), pp. 252–256.

[478] R. Lupas and S. Verdú, "Linear multiuser detectors for synchronous code-division multiple access channels," *IEEE Trans. Inform. Theory*, vol. IT-35, pp. 123–136, Jan. 1989.

[479] ——, "Near-far resistance of multiuser detectors in asynchronous channels," *IEEE Trans. Commun.*, vol. 38, pp. 496–508, Apr. 1990.

[480] U. Madhow, "Blind adaptive interference suppression for the near-far resistant acquisition and demodulation of direct-sequence CDMA signals," *IEEE Trans. Signal Processing*, vol. 45, pp. 124–136, Jan. 1997.

[481] I. D. Marsland, P. T. Mathiopoulos, and S. Kallal, "Noncoherent turbo equalization for frequency selective Rayleigh fast fading channels," in *Proc. Int. Symp. Turbo Codes and Related Topics* (Brest, France, Sept. 3–5, 1997), pp. 196–199.

[482] T. Miyajima, S. Micera, and K. Yamanaka, "Blind multiuser receivers for DS/CDMA systems," in *Proc. IEEE GLOBECOM Mini-Conf. Rec.* (Phoenix, AZ, Nov. 3–8, 1997), pp. 118–122.

[483] P. Monsen, "Feedback equalization for fading dispersive channels," *IEEE Trans. Inform. Theory*, vol. IT-17, pp. 56–64, Jan. 1971.

[484] R. R. Müller and J. B. Huber, "Iterated soft-decision interference cancellation," in *Proc. 9th Tyrhenian Workshop* (Lerici, Italy, Sept. 9–11, 1997).

[485] I. Oppermann and M. Latva-aho, "Adaptive LMMSE receiver for wideband CDMA systems," in *IEEE GLOBECOM Mini-Conf. Rec.* (Phoenix, AZ, Nov. 3–8, 1997), pp. 133–138.

[486] P. Orten and T. Ottosson, "Robustness of DS-CDMA multiuser detectors," in *IEEE GLOBECOM Mini-Conf. Rec.* (Phoenix, AZ, Nov. 3–8, 1997), pp. 144–148.

[487] H. C. Papadopoulos, "Equalization of multiuser channels," in *Wireless Communications*, V. Poor and G. Wornell, Eds. Englewood Cliffs, NJ: Prentice-Hall, 1998, ch. 3.

[488] P. Patel and J. Holtzman, "Analysis of a simple successive interference cancellation scheme in a DS/CDMA system," *IEEE J. Select. Areas Commun.*, vol. 12, pp. 796–807, June 1994.

[489] A. J. Paulraj and E. Lindskog, "A taxonomy of space-time processing for wireless networks," to be published in *IEEE Proc. Radar, Sonar, and Navigation.*

[490] A. J. Paulraj, C. B. Papadias, V. U. Reddy, and A. J. van der Veen, "Blind space-time signal processing," in *Wireless Communications*, V. Poor and G. Wornell, Eds. Englewood Cliffs, NJ: Prentice Hall, 1998, ch. 4.

[491] G. Picchi and G. Prati, "Blind equalization and carrier recovery using a stop-and-go decision directed algorithm," *IEEE Trans. Commun.*, vol. COM–35, pp. 877–887, Sept. 1987.

[492] H. V. Poor and L. A. Rusch, "Narrowband interference suppression in spread spectrum CDMA," *IEEE Personal Commun. Mag.*, vol. 1, pp. 14–27, Aug. 1994.

[493] H. V. Poor and S. Verdú, "Single-user detectors for multiuser channels," *IEEE Trans. Commun.*, vol. 36, pp. 50–60, Jan. 1988.

[494] H. V. Poor and X. Wang, "Code-aided interference suppression for DS/CDMA communications—Part I: Interference suppression capability," *IEEE Trans. Commun.*, vol. 45, pp. 1101–1111, Sept. 1997.

[495] ——, "Code-aided interference suppression for DS/CDMA communications, Part II: Parallel blind adaptive implementations," *IEEE Trans. Commun.*, vol. 45, pp. 1112–1122, Sept. 1997.

[496] G. Khachatrian, B. Cucetic, and L. Zhang, "M-PSK ring codes for Rayleigh channels," in *Proc. Int. Conf. Applied Algebra and Error Coding Codes (AAECC'90)* (Tokyo, Japan, Aug. 1990), p. 32.

[497] S. U. H. Qureshi and G. D. Forney, Jr., "Performance and properties of a $T/2$ equalizer," in *Nat. Telecommunications Conf. Rec.* (Los Angeles, CA, Dec. 1977), pp. 11.1.1–11.1.14.

[498] R. Raheli, A. Polydoros, and C. K. Tzou, "PSP: A general approach to MLSE in uncertain environments," *IEEE Trans. Commun.*, vol. 43, pp. 354–364, Mar. 1995.

[499] P. B. Rapajic and B. S. Vucetic, "Adaptive receiver structures for asynchronous CDMA systems," *IEEE J. Select. Areas Commun.*, vol. 12, pp. 685–697, May 1994.

[500] D. Raphaeli and Y. Zarai, "Combined turbo equalization and turbo decoding," in *Proc. Int. Symp. Turbo Codes and Related Topics* (Brest, France, Sept. 3–5, 1997), pp. 180–183. See also *IEEE Commun. Lett.*, vol. 2, pp. 107–109, Apr. 1998.

[501] S. Ratnavel, A. Paulraj, and A. G. Constantinides, "MMSE space-time equalization for GSM cellular systems," in *Proc. IEEE Vehicular Technology Conf.*, May 1996.

[502] L. A. Rusch and H. V. Poor, "Multiuser detection techniques for narrowband interference suppression in spread spectrum communication," *IEEE Trans. Commun.*, vol. 43, pp. 1725–1737, Feb./Mar./Apr. 1995.

[503] Y. Sato, "A method of self-recovering equalization for multilevel amplitude modulation systems," *IEEE Trans. Commun.*, vol. COM-23, pp. 679–682, June 1975.

[504] E. H. Satorius and S. T. Alexander, "Channel equalization using adaptive lattice algorithms," *IEEE Trans. Commun.*, vol. COM-27, pp. 899–905, June 1979.

[505] E. H. Satorius and J. D. Pack, "Application of least squares lattice algorithms to adaptive equalization," *IEEE Trans. Commun.*, vol. COM-29, pp. 136–142, Feb. 1981.

[506] N. Seshadri, "Joint data and channel estimation using fast blind trellis search techniques," *IEEE Trans. Commun.*, vol. 42, pp. 1000–1011, Mar. 1994.

[507] O. Shalvi and E. Weinstein, "New criteria for blind equalization of nonminimum phase systems and channels," *IEEE Trans. Inform. Theory*, vol. 36, pp. 312–321, Mar. 1990.

[508] D. T. M. Slock and T. Kailath, "Numerically fast transversal filters for recursive least-squares adaptive filtering," *IEEE Trans. Signal Processing*, vol. 39, pp. 92–114, Jan. 1991.

[509] M. Stojanovic, J. Catipovic, and J. G. Proakis, "Adaptive multichannel combining and equalization for underwater acoustic communications," *J. Acoust. Soc. Amer.*, vol. 94, pp. 1621–1631, Sept. 1993.

[510] ——, "Phase coherent digital communications for underwater acoustic channels," *IEEE J. Ocean. Eng.*, vol. 19, pp. 100–111, Jan. 1994.

[511] ——, "Reduced-complexity spatial and temporal processing of underwater acoustic communication signals," *J. Acoust. Soc. Amer.*, vol. 96, pp. 961–972, Aug. 1995.

[512] ——, "Performance of a high rate adaptive equalizer in a shallow water acoustic channel," *J. Acoust. Soc. Amer.*, vol. 97, pp. 2213–2219, Oct. 1996.

[513] H. Suzuki, "A statistical model for urban multipath channels with random delay," *IEEE Trans. Commun.*, vol. COM-25, pp. 673–680, July 1977.

[514] S. Talwar, M. Viberg, and A. Paulraj, "Blind estimation of multiple cochannel signals using an antenna array," *IEEE Signal Processing Lett.*, vol. 1, pp. 29–31, Feb. 1994.

[515] D. P. Taylor, G. M. Vitetta, B. D. Hart, and A. Mammela, "Wireless channel equalization," *Euro. Trans. Telecommun. (ETT)* (Special Issue on Signal Processing in Telecommunications), vol. 9, no. 2, pp. 117–143, Mar./Apr. 1998.

[516] C. Tidestav, A. Ahlén, and M. Sternad, "Narrowband and broadband multiuser detection using a multivariable DFE," in *Proc. 6th Int. Symp. Personal, Indoor and Mobile Radio Communications (PIMRC'95)* (Toronto, Ont., Canada, Sept. 27–29, 1995).

[517] L. Tong, G. Xu, and T. Kailath, "Blind identification and equalization based on second-order statistics," *IEEE Trans. Inform. Theory*, vol. 40, pp. 340–349, Mar. 1994.

[518] G. L. Turin *et al.*, "Simulation of urban vehicle monitoring systems," *IEEE Trans. Veh. Technol.*, pp. 9–16, Feb. 1972.

[519] M. Uesugi, K. Honma, and K. Tsubaki, "Adaptive equalization in TDMA digital mobile radio," in *Proc. 1989 GLOBECOM*, pp. 95–101.

[520] G. Ungerboeck, "Fractional tap-spacing equalizer and consequences for clock recovery in data modems," *IEEE Trans. Commun.*, vol. COM-24, pp. 856–864, Aug. 1976.

[521] M. K. Varanasi, "Group detection for synchronous CDMA communication over frequency-selective fading channels," in *31th Allerton Conf. Communication, Control and Computing* (Monticello, IL, Sept. 29–Oct. 1, 1993), pp. 849–857.

[522] M. K. Varanasi and B. Aazhang, "Multistage detection in asynchronous code-division multiple access communications," *IEEE Trans. Commun.*, vol. 38, pp. 509–519, Apr. 1990.

[523] ——, "Near-optimum detection in synchronous code division multiple access systems," *IEEE Trans. Commun.*, vol. 39, pp. 725–736, May 1991.

[524] M. K. Varanasi and S. Vasudevan, "Multiuser detectors for synchronous CDMA communication over nonselective Rician fading channels," *IEEE Trans. Commun.*, vol. 42, pp. 711–722, Feb./Mar./Apr. 1994.

[525] S. Vasudevan and M. K. Varanasi, "Optimum diversity combiner based multiuser detection for time-dispersive Rician fading CDMA channels," *IEEE J. Select. Areas Commun.*, vol. 12, pp. 580–592, May 1994.

[526] A van der Veen, S. Talwar, and A. Paulraj, "Blind identification of FIR channels carrying multiple finite alphabet signals," in *Proc. 1995 Int. Conf. Acoustics, Speech and Ssignal Processing*, May 1995, pp. II. 1213–I. 1216.

[527] S. Verdú, "Optimum multiuser asymptotic efficiency," *IEEE Trans. Commun.*, vol. COM-34, pp. 890–897, Sept. 1986.

[528] ——, "Recent progress in multiuser detection," in *Advances in Communication and Signal Processing*. Berlin, Germany: Springer-Verlag, 1989. (Reprinted in *Multiple Access Communications*, N. Abramson, Ed. New York: IEEE Press, 1993.)

[529] R. Vijayan and H. V. Poor, "Nonlinear techniques for interference suppression in spread spectrum systems," *IEEE Trans. Commun.*, vol. 38, pp. 1060–1065, July 1990.

[530] X. Wang and H. V. Poor, "Blind equalization and multiuser detection in dispersive CDMA channels," *IEEE Trans. Commun.*, vol. 46, pp. 91–103, Jan. 1998.

[531] ——, "Blind adaptive multiuser detection in multipath CDMA channels based on subspace tracking," *IEEE Trans. Signal Processing*, to be published.

[532] ——, "Blind multiuser detection: A subspace approach," *IEEE Trans. Inform. Theory*, vol. 44, pp. 677–690, Mar. 1998.

[533] ——, "Adaptive joint multiuser detection and channel estimation for multipath fading CDMA channels," to be published in *Wireless Networks* (Special Issue on Multiuser Detection in Wireless Communications).

[534] B. Widrow, "Adaptive filters, I: Fundamentals," Stanford Electron. Lab., Stanford Univ., Stanford, CA., Tech. Rep. 6764-6, Dec. 1966.

[535] B. Widrow and M. E. Hoff, Jr., "Adaptive switching circuits," in *IRE WESCON Conv. Rec.*, pt. 4, pp. 96–104, 1960.

[536] Z. Xie, C. K. Rushforth, and R. T. Short, "Multiuser signal detection using sequential decoding," *IEEE Trans. Commun.*, vol. 38, pp. 578–583, May 1990.

[537] Z. Xie, R. T. Short, and C. K. Rushforth, "A family of suboptimum detectors for coherent multiuser communications," *IEEE J. Select. Areas Commun.*, vol. JSAC-8, pp. 683–690, May.

[538] S. Yoshida, A. Ushirokawa, S. Yanagi, and Y. Furuya, "DS/CDMA adaptive interference canceller on differential detection in fast fading channel," in *44th IEEE Vehicular Technology Conf.* (Stockholm, Sweden, June 8–10, 1994).

[539] E. Zervas, J. G. Proakis, and V. Eyuboglu, "A quantized channel approach to blind equalization," in *Proc. ICC'91* (Chicago, IL, June 1991).

[540] X. Zhang and D. Brady, "Soft-decision multistage detection of asynchronous AWGN channels," in *Proc. 31st Allerton Conf. Communications, Control, and Computing* (Allerton, IL, Oct. 1993).

[541] S. Zhou, S. Mei, and Y. Yao, "Multi-carrier transmission combating slow fading using turbo code," in *Proc Int. Symp. Turbo Codes and Related Topic* (Brest, France, Sept. 3–5, 1997), pp. 151–153.

[542] K. Zhou, J. G. Proakis, and F. Ling, "Decision-feedback equalization of time-dispersive channels with coded modulation," *IEEE Trans. Commun.*, vol. 38, pp. 18–24, Jan. 1990.

[543] Z. Zvonar and D. Brady, "Multiuser detection in single-path fading channels," *IEEE Trans. Commun.*, vol. 42, pp. 1729–1739, Feb./Mar./Apr. 1994.

[544] _____, "Suboptimal multiuser detector for frequency selective fading synchronous CDMA channels," *IEEE Trans. Commun.*, vol. 43, pp. 154-157, Feb./Mar./Apr. 1995.

[545] _____, "Differentially coherent multiuser detection in asynchronous CDMA flat Raleigh fading channels," *IEEE Trans. Commun.*, vol. 43, pp. 1252–1254, Feb./Mar./Apr. 1995.

[546] _____, "Adaptive multiuser receivers with diversity reception for non-selective Rayleigh fading asynchronous CDMA channels," in *MILCOM '94* (Ft. Monmouth, NJ, Oct. 2–5, 1994), pp. 982–986.

[547] P. Viswanath, V. Anantharan, and D. Tse, "Optimal sequences, power control and capacity of synchronous CDMA systems with linear multiuser receivers," in *Proc. 1998 Information Theory Work.* (Killarney, Ireeland, June 22–26, 1998), pp. 134–135. See also "Optimal sequences and sum capacity of synchronous CDMA systems," submitted for publication to *IEEE Trans. Inform. Theory*, See also: J. Zhang and E. K. P. Chong, "CDMA systems in fading channels: Admissibility, network capacity and power control," priprint.

[548] D. N. Godard, "Self-recovering equations and carrier tracking in two-dimensional data communication systems," *IEEE Trans. Commun.*, vol. COM-28, pp. 1867–1875, Nov. 1980.

[549] Y. Sato, "Blind suppression of time dependence and its extension to multidimensional equalization," in *Proc. ICC'86*, pp. 46.4.1–46.4.5.

Lossy Source Coding

Toby Berger, *Fellow, IEEE*, and Jerry D. Gibson, *Fellow, IEEE*

(Invited Paper)

Abstract— Lossy coding of speech, high-quality audio, still images, and video is commonplace today. However, in 1948, few lossy compression systems were in service. Shannon introduced and developed the theory of source coding with a fidelity criterion, also called rate-distortion theory. For the first 25 years of its existence, rate-distortion theory had relatively little impact on the methods and systems actually used to compress real sources. Today, however, rate-distortion theoretic concepts are an important component of many lossy compression techniques and standards. We chronicle the development of rate-distortion theory and provide an overview of its influence on the practice of lossy source coding.

Index Terms—Data compression, image coding, speech coding, rate distortion theory, signal coding, source coding with a fidelity criterion, video coding.

I. INTRODUCTION AND PROLOGUE

THE concept of specifying the rate required to represent a source with some less-than-perfect fidelity was introduced by Shannon in his landmark 1948 paper. In Part V thereof, Shannon describes the idea of "continuous information" and defines "The Rate for a Source Relative to a Fidelity Evaluation." Furthermore, he states the first theorem concerning such lossy representations (his Theorem 21) and outlines its proof via an AEP-like argument. Shannon then writes the expression for the rate for the desired "valuation" (distortion) and poses the constrained optimization problem to be solved for the transition probabilities. Then he gives a general form of the solution to this optimization problem (now widely called the backward test channel), and specializes it to the important special case of difference distortion measures. In Theorem 22 he gives the exact rate for an ideal bandlimited Gaussian source relative to a mean-squared error (MSE) fidelity criterion, and in Theorem 23 he bounds the MSE information rate of a bandlimited non-Gaussian source in terms of now-classic expressions involving the source power and the entropy rate power. A most auspicious beginning indeed!

In 1948, although pulse-code modulation (PCM) was being developed for speech applications [259] and Dudley's vocoder had been around for about ten years [260], actual implementations of lossy digital compression systems were nonexistent. This testifies to the power of Shannon's insights but also helps explain why he would delay further consideration of lossy compression until 10 years later. By 1959, work in scalar quantization and PCM was well underway [196] and differential encoding had received considerable attention [180], [186], [215].

Shannon coined the term "rate-distortion function" when he revisited the source-coding problem in 1959 [2]. The insights and contributions in that paper are stunning. In particular, rate-distortion terminology is introduced, the rate-distortion function $R(D)$ is carefully defined, positive and negative coding theorems are proved, properties of $R(D)$ are investigated, the expression for $R(D)$ in several important cases is derived, some numerical examples are presented, the important lower bound to $R(D)$, now called the Shannon lower bound, is derived, and the duality between $R(D)$ and a capacity cost function is noted. A lifetime of results in two papers!

We treat Shannon's seminal contributions in greater detail below, also emphasizing how they inspired others to begin making significant contributions both to rate-distortion theory and to laying the groundwork for advances in the practice of lossy source coding. Specifically, we survey the history and significant results of rate-distortion theory and its impact on the development of lossy source-compression methods. A historical overview of rate-distortion theory is presented in the first part of the paper. This is followed by a discussion of techniques for lossy coding of speech, high-quality audio, still images, and video. The latter part of the paper is not intended as a comprehensive survey of compression methods and standards. Rather, its emphasis is on the influence of rate-distortion theory on the practice of lossy source coding.

There is both logic and historical precedent for separating the treatment of lossy source coding into a theory component and a practice component. Davisson and Gray took this approach in the Introduction of their 1976 compilation of papers on Data Compression [183]. Additionally, there is a continuity in the development of rate-distortion theory and, similarly but separately, in the development of the practice of lossy source coding. These continuities deserve preservation, since appreciation for research and development insights is enhanced when they are embedded in their proper historical contexts.

II. IN THE BEGINNING

Shannon's [1] motivations for writing "Section V: The Rate for a Continuous Source" likely included the following:

1) It provided the source coding complement to his treatment of the input-power limited AWGN channel.

Manuscript received December 1, 1997; revised July 1, 1998. This work was supported in part by NSF under Grants ECS-9632266 and NCR-9796255.

T. Berger is with the School of Electrical Engineering, Cornell University, Ithaca, NY 14853 USA.

J. D. Gibson is with the Department of Electrical Engineering, Southern Methodist University, Dallas, TX 75275 USA.

Publisher Item Identifier S 0018-9448(98)06886-2.

2) It provided the means by which to extend information theory to analog sources. Such an extension was necessary because all analog sources have infinite entropy by virtue of their amplitude continuity and, therefore, cannot be preserved error-free when stored in or transmitted through practical, finite-capacity media.
3) Shannon considered the results to have inherent significance independent of their analogies to and connections with channel theory.

A. A Brief Detour into Channel Theory

Shannon's most widely known and most widely abused result is his formula for the capacity of an ideal bandlimited channel with an average input power constraint and an impairment of additive, zero-mean, white Gaussian noise, namely,

$$C = W \log_2 (1 + P/N) \text{ bits/s}. \tag{1}$$

Here, P is the prescribed limitation on the average input power, W is the channel bandwidth in positive frequencies measured in hertz, and N is the power of the additive noise. Since the noise is white with one-sided power spectral density N_0 or two-sided power spectral density $N_0/2$, we have $N = N_0 W$. Of course, the result does not really require that the noise be truly white, just that its spectral density be constant over the channel's passband. Common abuses consist of applying (1) when

i) The noise is non-Gaussian.
ii) The noise is not independent of the signal and/or is not additive.
iii) Average power is not the (only) quantity that is constrained at the channel input.
iv) The noise is not white across the passband and/or the channel transfer function is not ideally bandlimited.

Abuse i) is conservative in that it underestimates capacity because Gaussian noise is the hardest additive noise to combat. Abuse ii) may lead to grossly underestimating or grossly overestimating capacity. A common instance of abuse iii) consists of failing to appreciate that it actually may be peak input power, or perhaps both peak and average input power, that are constrained. Abuse iv) leads to an avoidable error in that the so-called "water pouring" result [3], generalizing (1), yields the exact answer when the noise is not white, the channel is not bandlimited, and/or the channel's transfer function is not flat across the band. (See also [6] and [7].)

B. Coding for Continuous Amplitude Sources

There is a pervasive analogy between source-coding theory and channel-coding theory. The source-coding result that corresponds to (1) is

$$R = W \log_2(S/N) \text{ bits/s}. \tag{2}$$

It applies to situations in which the data source of interest is a white Gaussian signal bandlimited to $|f| \leq W$ that has power $S = S_0 W$, where S_0 denotes the signal's one-sided constant power spectral density for frequencies less than W. The symbol, N, although often referred to as a "noise," is actually an estimation error. It represents a specified level of mean-squared error (MSE) between the signal $\{X(t)\}$ and an estimate $\{\hat{X}(t)\}$ of the signal constructed on the basis of data about $\{X(t)\}$ provided at a rate of R bits per second. That is,

$$N = \lim_{T \to \infty} \frac{1}{2T} \int_{-T}^{T} dt E[\hat{X}(t) - X(t)]^2.$$

It was, and remains, popular to express MSE estimation accuracy as a "signal-to-noise ratio," S/N, as Shannon did in (2). It must be appreciated, however, that $\{\hat{X}(t) - X(t)\}$ is not noise in the sense of being an error process that is independent of $\{X(t)\}$ that nature adds to the signal of interest. Rather, it is a carefully contrived error signal, usually dependent on $\{X(t)\}$, that the information theorist endeavors to create in order to conform to a requirement that no more than R bits per second of information may be supplied about $\{X(t)\}$. In modern treatises on information theory, the symbol "D," a mnemonic for average distortion, usually is used in place of N. This results in an alternative form of (2), namely,

$$R(D) = W \log_2(S/D) \text{ bits/s} \tag{3}$$

which is referred to as the MSE rate-distortion function of the source.

Formula (3) gets abused less widely than formula (1), but probably only because it is less widely known. Abuses consist, analogously, of applying it to situations in which

i) The signal is non-Gaussian.
ii) Distortion does not depend simply on the difference of $\hat{X}(t)$ and $X(t)$.
iii) Distortion is measured by a function of $\hat{X}(t) - X(t)$ other than its square.
iv) The signal's spectral density is not flat across the band.

Again, abuse i) is conservative in that it results in an overestimate of the minimum rate R needed to achieve a specified MSE estimation accuracy because white Gaussian sources are the most difficult to handle in the sense of bit rate versus MSE. Abuses ii) and iii), which often stem in practice from lack of knowledge of a perceptually appropriate distortion measure, can result in gross underestimates or overestimates of R. Abuse iv) can be avoided by using a water-pouring generalization of (3) that we shall discuss subsequently. In anticipation of that discussion, we recast (3) in the form

$$R(D) = \max [0, W \log(S_0 W/D)]. \tag{4}$$

This form of the equation explicitly reflects the facts that i) the signal spectrum has been assumed to be constant at level S_0 across the band of width W in which it in nonzero, and ii) $R(D) = 0$ for $D \geq S_0 W$, because one can achieve an MSE of $S = S_0 W$ without sending any information simply by guessing that $X(t) = 0$. (If $\{X(t)\}$ has a nonzero mean $m(t)$, then of course one guesses $m(t)$ instead of zero. In general, adding a deterministic mean-value function to the signal process does not change its rate-distortion function with respect to any fidelity criterion that measures average distortion as some functional of the difference process $\{\hat{X}(t) - X(t)\}$.) The base of the logarithm in (4) determines the information unit—bits for $\log_2$ and nats for $\log_e$. When we deal with continuously distributed quantities, it is more "natural" to employ natural logs. When no log base appears, assume that a natural log is intended.

C. Deterministic Processes Have Nonzero Rate-Distortion Functions

It is appropriate at this juncture to comment on the relationship between rate-distortion theory and the theory of deterministic processes. The Wold decomposition theorem assures us, among other things, that any bandlimited random process is deterministic in the following sense: it can be predicted with zero MSE infinitely far into the future and infinitely far into the past once one knows the values it has assumed in an arbitrarily small open interval. This is because the sample paths of such processes are analytic functions with probability one, which implies that they have derivatives of all orders at every instant. Knowledge of the process over an arbitrarily small open interval allows each such derivative to be computed with perfect accuracy at any point within the interval by taking the limit of an appropriate difference quotient. This, in turn, permits using Taylor series or other techniques to extrapolate the process with perfect accuracy into the arbitrarily remote past and future. This suggests that the ideal bandlimited Gaussian process we have been studying should have an MSE rate-distortion function that is identically zero for all D because one needs to supply information about the process only during an arbitrarily short interval, after which it becomes known perfectly for all time. Yet, Shannon's formula $R(D) = W \log(S/D)$ says that one must keep supplying information about it for all time at a rate of $R(D) > 0$ in order to be able to reconstruct it with a MSE of $D < S$.

This apparent contradiction is readily resolved. The sticking point is that it requires an infinite amount of information to specify even a single continuously distributed random variable exactly, let alone the uncountable infinity of them indexed by all the points in an open interval. Accordingly, when information is provided at a finite rate, which is always the case in practice, one never learns the values in any interval perfectly no matter how long one gathers information about them. Determinism in the above sense thus is seen to be a purely mathematical concept that is devoid of practical significance. The operative, physically meaningful measure of the rate at which a random process, even a so-called deterministic random process, produces information subject to a fidelity criterion is prescribed by Shannon's rate-distortion theory.

D. The Basic Inequality

A basic inequality of information theory is

$$D \geq R^{-1}(C) \qquad (5)$$

sometimes referred to as the *information transmission inequality*. It says that, if you are trying to transmit data from a source with rate-distortion function $R(D)$ over a channel of capacity C, you can achieve only those average distortions that exceed the inverse of the rate-distortion function evaluated at C. (Not

surprisingly, the inverse rate-distortion function is called the distortion-rate function.)

Suppose, for example, that we wish to send data about the aforementioned bandlimited white Gaussian process $\{X(t)\}$ over an average-input-power-limited, ideally bandlimited AWGN channel. Assume our task is to construct on the basis of what we receive at the channel output an approximation $\{\hat{X}(t)\}$ that has the least possible MSE. The source and the channel have the same frequency band $|f| \leq W$. Since $R(D) = W \log_2(S/D)$, the distortion-rate function is

$$D(R) = S 2^{-R/W}$$

so (1) and (4) together tell us that

$$D \geq D(C) = S \exp\left[-\frac{W \log(1 + P/N)}{W}\right]$$

or

$$D/S \geq (1 + P/N)^{-1}. \qquad (6)$$

This tells us that the achievable error power per unit of source power (i.e., the achievable normalized MSE) is bounded from below by the reciprocal of one plus the channel signal-to-noise ratio (SNR).

E. An Optimum System via a Double Coincidence

There happens to be a trivial scheme for achieving equality in (6) when faced with the task of communicating the source of Section II-B over the channel of Section II-A. It consists of the following steps:

Step 1: Tranmit $X(t)$ scaled to have average power P; that is, put $\sqrt{P/S}X(t)$ into the channel.

Step 2: Set $\hat{X}(t)$ equal to the minimum mean-square error (MMSE) estimate of $X(t)$ based solely on the instantaneous channel output $\sqrt{P/S}X(t) + N(t)$ at time t.

Since the signal and the channel noise are jointly Gaussian and zero mean, the optimum estimate in Step 2 is simply a linear scaling of the received signal, namely,

$$\hat{X}(t) = \alpha[\sqrt{P/S}X(t) + N(t)].$$

The optimum α is found from the requirement that the error of the optimum estimator must be orthogonal to the data

$$E[\hat{X}(t) - X(t)][\sqrt{P/S}X(t) + N(t)] = 0.$$

This may be written as

$$E[(\alpha\sqrt{P/S} - 1)X(t) + \alpha N(t)][\sqrt{P/S}X(t) + N(t)] = 0.$$

Using $ES^2(t) = S$, $EN^2(t) = N$, and $EX(t)N(t) = 0$, we obtain $\alpha = \sqrt{PS}/(P + N)$. The resulting minimized normalized MSE is easily computed to be

$$D/S = (1 + P/N)^{-1} \qquad (7)$$

which means we have achieved equality in (6).

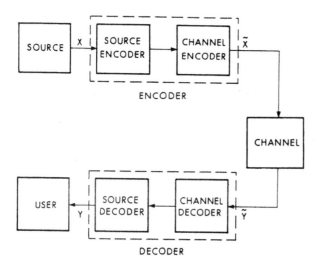

Fig. 1.

Thus the simple two-step scheme of instantaneously scaling at the input and at the output results in an end-to-end communication system that is optimum. No amount of source and/or channel coding could improve upon this in the MSE sense for the problem at hand. This fortuitous circumstance is attributable to a double coincidence. The first coincidence is that the source happens to be the random process that drives the channel at capacity. This is, the given source, scaled by $\sqrt{P/S}$, is that process of average power not exceeding P which maximizes the mutual information between the input and output of the channel. The second coincidence is that the channel just happens to provide precisely the transition probabilities that solve the MSE rate-distortion problem for the given source. That is, when the channel is driven by the scaled source, its output minimizes mutual information rate with the source over all processes from which one can calculate an approximation to the source that achieves a normalized MSE not in excess of $(1 + P/N)^{-1}$.

We are operating at a saddle point at which the mutual information rate is simultaneously maximized subject to the average power constraint and minimized subject to the average distortion constraint. The slightest perturbation in any aspect of the problem throws us out this saddle—unequal source and channel bandwidths, non-Gaussianness of the source or channel, an error criterion other than MSE, and so on. The result of any such perturbation is that, in order to recover optimality, it is in general necessary to code both for the source and for the channel as depicted in Fig. 1.

The source encoder and channel decoder usually have to implement complicated many-to-one mappings that depend on the values their inputs assume over long durations, not just at one instant. Hence, whereas a surface perusal of Shannon's founding treatise [1] might, via the key formulas discussed above, instill the illusion that all one ever has to do to build an optimum communication system is simply to insert into the channel a version of the given source trivially accommodated to whatever channel input constraints may prevail, nothing could be further from the truth. The goals of this tutorial paper include exorcising any such misconception and surveying the

major developments in rate-distortion theory over the fifty years from 1948 to 1998.

III. THE FIFTIES

A. The Russian School

From 1949 to 1958 no research was reported on rate-distortion theory in the United States or Europe. However, there was a stream of activity during the 1950's at Moscow University by members of Academician A. N. Kolmogorov's probability seminar. Kolmogorov, a renowned mathematician who founded axiomatic probability theory and contributed many of its fundamental limit laws, saw an application for Shannon's information theory in the long-standing isomorphism problem of ergodic theory. That problem concerns necessary and sufficient conditions for when two "shifts" can be placed in a one-to-one, measure-preserving correspondence. It includes as an important special case the question of whether or not two given random processes, or sources, can be viewed as perhaps intricately disguised rearrangements of the same information stream. Shannon's theory showed that each discrete-amplitude information source has an entropy rate H that measures in a fundamental way the rate at which it produces information, and that any two sources of the same entropy rate can be "coded" into one another losslessly. Thus entropy (more exactly, entropy rate) emerged as a promising candidate to serve as the long-sought invariant in the isomorphism problem. However, "coding" in Shannon theory differs from "coding" in ergodic theory. Shannon's coding concerns operations on possibly long but always finite blocks of information, thereby honoring a tie to practice, whereas the codes of ergodic theory operate on the entirety of each infinite sequence that constitutes a realization of an ergodic flow. Thus it was not a trivial matter to establish that entropy rate could indeed serve as an invariant in the sense of ergodic theory. Kolmogorov and Sinai [5], [8] succeeded in showing that equal entropy rates were a necessary condition for isomorphism. Years later, Ornstein [9] proved sufficiency within an appropriately defined broad class of random stationary processes comprising all finite-order Markov sources and their closure in a certain metric space that will not concern us here. With the Moscow probability seminar's attention thus turned to information theory, it is not surprising that some of its members also studied Section V, The Rate for a Continuous Source. Pinsker, Dobrushin, Iaglom, Tikhomirov, Oseeyevich, Erokhin, and others made contributions to a subject that has come to be called ϵ-entropy, a branch of mathematics that subsumes what we today call rate-distortion theory. ϵ-entropy is concerned with the minimal cardinality of covers of certain spaces by disks of radius ϵ. As such, it is a part of topology if a complete cover is desired. If, however, a probability measure is placed on the space being covered, then one can consider covering all but a set of measure δ, where $\delta = 0$ is also a value of considerable significance [10], [11], [1, p. 656]. It also becomes interesting to consider the expected distance from a point in the space to the closest disk center, which is the approach usually adopted in rate-distortion theory.

Most of the attention of scholars of ϵ-entropy was focused on the asymptotic case in which $\epsilon \to 0$. This doubtless accounts for why the symbol ϵ was selected instead of, say, D for distortion. It was appreciated that ϵ-entropy would diverge as $\epsilon \to 0$ in all continuous-amplitude scenarios. The problem was to determine the rate of divergence in particular cases of interest. Thus when invited to address an early information theory symposium, Kolmogorov [3] emphasized in the portion of his report dealing with ϵ-entropy Iaglom's expression for the limiting information rate of Wiener processes as $\epsilon \to 0$ and extensions thereof to more general diffusions. However, he also reported the exact answer for the ϵ-entropy of a stationary Gaussian process with respect to the squared L_2-norm for *all* ϵ, not just $\epsilon \to 0$ (his equations (17) and (18)). That result, and its counterpart for the capacity of a power-constrained channel with additive colored Gaussian noise, have come to be known as the "water-pouring" formulas of information theory. In this generality the channel formula is attributable to [12] and the source formula to Pinsker [13], [14]. We shall call them the Shannon–Kolmogorov–Pinsker (SKP) water-pouring formulas. They generalize the formulas given by Shannon in 1948 for the important case in which the spectrum of the source or of the channel noise is flat across a band and zero elsewhere. The water-pouring formulas were rediscovered independently by several investigators throughout the 1950's and 1960's.

B. The Water Table

Here is a simple way of obtaining the SKP water-pouring formula for the MSE information rate of a Gaussian source [12]. The spectral representation theorem lets us write any zero-mean stationary random process $\{X(t)\}$ for which $EX(t)^2 < \infty$ in the form

$$X(t) = \int_{-\infty}^{\infty} e^{itf} \, d\xi(f)$$

where $\xi(f)$ is a random process with zero mean, uncorrelated increments. Hence, if A and B are two disjoint sets of frequencies, the zero-mean random processes $\{X_A(t)\}$ and $\{X_B(t)\}$ defined by

$$X_A(t) = \int_A e^{itf} d\xi(f)$$

and

$$X_B(s) = \int_B e^{isg} d\xi(g)$$

satisfy $EX_A(t)X_B(t) = 0$ because $Ed\xi(f)d\xi(g) = 0$ when $f \in A$ and $g \in B$. That is, processes formed by bandlimiting a second-order stationary random processes to nonoverlapping frequency bands are uncorrelated with one another. In the case of a Gaussian process, this uncorrelatedness implies independence. Thus we can decompose a Gaussian process $\{X(t)\}$ with one-sided spectral density $S(f)$ into independent Gaussian processes $\{X_i(t)\}, i = 0, 1, \cdots$ with respective spectral densities $S_i(f)$ given by

$$S_i(f) = \begin{cases} S(f), & \text{if } i\Delta \le f < (i+1)\Delta \\ 0, & \text{otherwise.} \end{cases}$$

Let us now make Δ sufficiently small that $S_i(f)$ becomes effectively constant over the frequency interval in which it is nonzero, $S_i(f) \approx S_i, i\Delta \le f < (i+1)\Delta$.[1] Since the subprocesses $\{X_i(t)\}$ are independent of one another, it is best to approximate each of them independently. Moreover, given any such set of independent approximants, simply summing them yields the best MSE approximation of $\{X(t)\}$ that can be formed from them, the MSE of said sum being the sum of the MSE's of the subprocess approximants. Furthermore, the source-coding rate will be the sum of the rates used to approximate the subprocesses.

Subprocess $\{X_0(t)\}$ is an ideal bandlimited zero-mean Gaussian source with bandwidth Δ and spectral density $S(f) = S_0, 0 \le f < \Delta$. It follows from (4) that the minimum information rate needed to describe it with an MSE of D_0 or less is

$$R_0(D_0) = \max [0, \Delta \log (S_0 \Delta / D_0)].$$

Subprocess $\{X_i(t)\}$ for any $i > 0$ also is a bandlimited zero-mean Gaussian source with bandwidth Δ in positive frequencies, its frequency band being $[i\Delta, (i+1)\Delta)$ instead of $[0, \Delta)$. Consider any coded representation of it with rate R_i bits per second from which one can produce an approximation of it that has an MSE of D_i. Observe that we always can mimic this (R_i, D_i)-performance by by mixing down to baseband $[0, \Delta)$, performing the same coding and reconstruction operations on the result, and then mixing the approximation thus produced back into the band $[i\Delta, (i+1)\Delta)$. It follows that the best rate–distortion tradeoff we can achieve for subprocess $\{X_i(t)\}$ is

$$R_i(D_i) = \max [0, \Delta \log (S_i \Delta / D_i)].$$

By additively combining said approximations to all the subprocesses, we get an approximation to $\{X(t)\}$ that achieves an average distortion of

$$D = \sum_i D_i$$

and requires a total coding rate of

$$R = \sum_i R_i(D_i) = \sum_i \max [0, \Delta \log (S_i \Delta / D_i)].$$

In order to determine the MSE rate-distortion function of $\{X(t)\}$, it remains only to select those D_i's summing to D which minimize this R. Toward that end we set

$$d(R + \lambda^{-1}D)/dD_i = 0, \qquad i = 0, 1, 2, \cdots$$

where λ is a Lagrange multiplier subsequently selected to achieve a desired value of D or of R. Each D_i of course never exceeds $S_i \Delta$, the value that can be achieved by sending no information about $\{X_i(t)\}$ and then using $\hat{X}_i(t) = 0$ as the approximant. If the solution associated with a particular value

---

[1] There is some sacrifice of rigor here. Readers desirous of a careful derivation based on the Kac–Murdock–Szego theory of the asymptotic distribution of the eigenvalues of Toeplitz forms may consult Berger [26].

λ of the Lagrange multiplier is such that $D_i < S_i\Delta$, then the preceding equation requires that $-\Delta/D_i + \lambda^{-1} = 0$, or

$$D_i = \lambda\Delta.$$

The value $\lambda = 0$ corresponds to $D_i = 0$ for all i (hence, $D = 0$) and $R = \infty$. This expresses that fact that perfect reconstruction of a continuously distributed source cannot be achieved without infinite data rate, a result that is mathematically satisfying but devoid of physical usefulness. For finite values of λ, we deduce that

$$D_i = \begin{cases} \lambda\Delta, & \text{if } \lambda < S_i \\ S_i\Delta, & \text{if } \lambda \geq S_i. \end{cases}$$

It follows that the D and R values associated with parameter value λ are

$$D_\lambda = \sum_{\{i:S_i > \lambda\}} \lambda\Delta + \sum_{\{i:S_i \leq \lambda\}} S_i\Delta$$
$$= \sum_i \Delta \min(\lambda, S_i)$$

and

$$R_\lambda = \sum_i \max[0, \Delta \log(S_i/\lambda)].$$

We remark that the Lagrange solution tells us that to compute a point $(D, R(D))$ on the MSE rate-distortion function of $\{X(t)\}$, we should combine points on the rate-distortion functions $R_i(\cdot)$ of the subprocesses at points at which the slope $R_i'(\cdot)$ is the same for all i. That is, $R_i'(D_i)$ does not vary with i. This is a recurrent theme in rate-distortion theory. Constant slope means that the same marginal tradeoff is being drawn between rate and distortion for each of the independent components. Indeed, intuition suggests that this must be the case; otherwise it would be possible to lower the overall R for fixed D by devoting more bits to subprocesses being reproduced at points of lower slope and fewer bits to processes being reproduced at points of slope. In this connection the reader should observe that the slope of $R_i(D)$ is continuous everywhere except at $D = S_i\Delta$, where it jumps from $-1/S_i$ to 0. Hence, one can draw a tangent line to $R_i(\cdot)$ at $D = S_i\Delta$ with any slope between $-1/S_i$ and 0. For purposes of combining points in the sense of this paragraph, $R_i(\cdot)$ should be considered to have all slopes between $-1/S_i$ and 0 at $D = S_i\Delta$.

As $\Delta \to 0$ the above sums constituting our parametric representation of $R(D)$ become integrals over frequency, namely,

$$D_\lambda = \int_0^\infty \min[\lambda, S(f)]\, df$$

and

$$R_\lambda = \int_0^\infty \max[0, \log(S(f)/\lambda)]\, df.$$

Two-sided spectral densities with their attendant negative frequencies are less forbidding to engineers and scientists today than they were in the 1940's. Accordingly, the above result now usually is cast in terms of the two-sided spectral density $\Phi(f)$, an even function of frequency satisfying $\Phi(f) =$

$S(f)/2, f \geq 0$. Replacing the parameter λ by $\theta = \lambda/2$, we find that

$$D_\theta = \int_{-\infty}^\infty \min[\theta, \Phi(f)]\, df \tag{8}$$

$$R_\theta = \int_{-\infty}^\infty \max\left[0, \frac{1}{2}\log(\Phi(f)/\theta)\right] df. \tag{9}$$

Some practitioners prefer to use angular frequency $\omega = 2\pi f$ as the argument of $\Phi(\cdot)$; of course, df then gets replaced in (8) and (9) by $d\omega/(2\pi)$.

The parametric representation (8) of the MSE rate-distortion function of a stationary Gaussian source is the source-coding analog of the SKP "water-pouring" result for the capacity of an input-power-limited channel with additive stationary Gaussian noise. The source-coding result actually is better described in terms of a "water table," though people nonetheless usually refer to it as "water pouring." Specifically, in Fig. 2, the source's spectral density is shown as a heavy "mold" resting atop a reservoir. In those places where there is air between the surface of the water and the mold, the surface is at uniform height θ; elsewhere, the mold presses down to a depth lower than θ. The water height $\min[\theta, \Phi(f)]$ is the MSE distortion as a function of frequency. Equivalently, at each frequency the amount, if any, by which the height of the mold exceeds the water level, namely $\max[\Phi(f) - \theta, 0]$, is the portion of the signal power at that frequency that is preserved by the minimum-rate data stream based from which the source can be reconstructed with average distortion D_θ.

Equations (8) and (9) also specify the MSE rate-distortion function of a time-discrete Gaussian sequence provided we limit the range of integration to $|f| \leq 1/2$ or to $|\omega| \leq \pi$. In such cases, $\Phi(\omega)$ is the discrete-time power spectral density, a periodic function defined by

$$\Phi(\omega) = \sum_{k=-\infty}^\infty \phi(k)\exp(j\omega k)$$

where $\phi(k) = EX_j X_{j\pm k}$ is the correlation function of the source data. Note that when the parameter θ assumes a value less than the minimum[2] of $\Phi(\cdot)$, which minimum we shall denote by D^*, (8a) reduces to $D_\theta = \theta$, which eliminates the parameter and yields the explicit expression

$$R(D) = \frac{1}{4\pi}\int_{-\pi}^\pi \log[\Phi(\omega)/D]\, d\omega, \qquad D \leq D^*.$$

This may be recast in the form

$$R(D) = \frac{1}{2}\log(Q_0/D), \qquad D \leq D^*$$

where

$$Q_0 = \exp\left[\frac{1}{2\pi}\int_{-\pi}^\pi \log\Phi(\omega)\, d\omega\right]$$

is known in the information theory literature as the *entropy rate power* of $\{X_k\}$. We shall return to this result when discussing the literature of the 1960's.

[2] More precisely, less than the essential infimum.

654

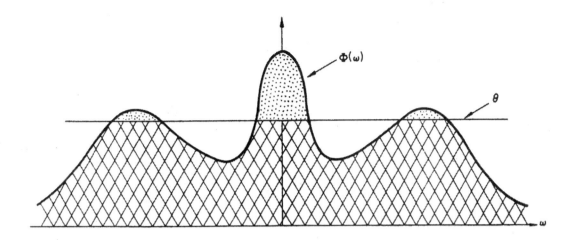

$\Phi(\omega)$

θ

ω

Fig. 2.

IV. SHANNON'S 1959 PAPER

In 1959, Shannon delivered a paper at the IRE Convention in New York City entitled "Coding Theorems for a Discrete Source with a Fidelity Criterion" [2]. This paper not only introduced the term "rate-distortion function" but also put lossy source coding on a firmer mathematical footing. Major contributions of the paper are as follows.

- Definition and properties of the rate-distortion function.
- Calculating and bounding of $R(D)$.
- Coding theorems.
- Insights into source–channel duality.

A. Definition and Properties of the Rate-Distortion Function

A *discrete information source* is a random sequence $\{X_k\}$. Each X_k assumes values in a discrete set $\mathcal{A}$ called the *source alphabet*. The elements of $\mathcal{A}$ are called the *letters* of the alphabet. We shall assume, until further notice, that there are finitely many distinct letters, say M of them, and shall write $\mathcal{A} = \{a(0), a(1), \cdots, a(M-1)\}$. Often we let $a(j) = j$ and hence $\mathcal{A} = \{0, 1, \cdots, M-1\}$; the binary case $\mathcal{A} = \{0, 1\}$ is particularly important.

The simplest case, to which we shall restrict attention for now, is that in which:

1) The X_k are independent and identically distributed (i.i.d.) with distribution $\{p(a), a \in \mathcal{A}\}$.
2) The distortion that results when the source produces the n-vector of letters $\underline{a} = (a_1, \cdots, a_n) \in \mathcal{A}^n$ and the communication system delivers the n-vector of letters $\underline{b} = (b_1, \cdots, b_n) \in \mathcal{B}^n$ to the destination as its representation of $\underline{a}$ is

$$d_n(\underline{a}, \underline{b}) = n^{-1} \sum_{k=1}^{n} d(a_k, b_k). \tag{10}$$

Here, $d(\cdot, \cdot) : \mathcal{A} \times \mathcal{B} \to [0, \infty)$ is called a *single-letter distortion measure*. The alphabet $\mathcal{B}$—variously called the reproduction alphabet, the user alphabet and the destination

alphabet—may be but need not be the same as $\mathcal{A}$. We shall write $\mathcal{B} = \{b(0), b(1), \cdots, b(N-1)\}$, where $N < M$, $N = M$, and $N > M$ all are cases of interest. When (10) applies, we say we have a *single-letter fidelity criterion* derived from $d(\cdot, \cdot)$.

Shannon defined the *rate-distortion function* $R(\cdot)$ as follows. First, let $Q = \{Q(b \mid a), a \in \mathcal{A}, b \in \mathcal{B}\}$ be a conditional probability distribution over the letters of the reproduction alphabet given a letter in the source alphabet.[3] Given a source distribution $\{p(j)\}$, we associate with any such Q two nonnegative quantities $d(Q)$ and $I(Q)$ defined by

$$d(Q) = \sum_{a \in \mathcal{A}} \sum_{b \in \mathcal{B}} p(a)Q(b \mid a)d(a, b)$$

and

$$I(Q) = \sum_{a \in \mathcal{A}} \sum_{b \in \mathcal{B}} p(a)Q(b \mid a) \log\left(\frac{Q(b \mid a)}{q(b)}\right)$$

where

$$q(b) = \sum_{a \in \mathcal{A}} p(a)Q(b \mid a).$$

The quantities $d(Q)$ and $I(Q)$ are, respectively, the average distortion and the average Shannon mutual information associated with Q.

The rate-distortion function of the i.i.d. source $\{X_k\}$ with letter distribution $\{p(a) = P[X_k = a]\}$ with respect to the single-letter fidelity criterion generated by $d(\cdot, \cdot)$ is defined by the following minimization problem:

$$R(D) = \min_{Q : d(Q) \le D} I(Q). \tag{11}$$

---

[3] Such a Q often is referred to as a *test channel*. However, it is preferable to call it a *test system* because it functions to describe a probabilistic transformation from one end of Fig. 1 to the other—from the source all the way to the user—not just across the channel. Indeed, the rate-distortion function has nothing to do with any channel *per se*. It is a descriptor of the combination of an information source and a user's way of measuring the distortion of approximations to that source.

Since the generally accepted object of communication is to maximize mutual information, not to minimize it, many people find the definition of the rate-distortion function counter-intuitive.[4] In this regard it often helps to interchange the independent and dependent variables, thus ending up with a *distortion-rate function* defined by

$$D(R) = \min_{Q:I(Q)\leq R} d(Q). \qquad (12)$$

Everyone considers that minimizing average distortion is desirable, so no one objects to this definition. Precisely the same curve results in the (D, R)-plane, except that now R is the independent variable instead of D. Distortion-rate functions are more convenient for certain purposes, and rate-distortion functions are more convenient for others. One should become comfortable with both.

Properties of the rate-distortion function include:

a) $R(D)$ is well defined for all $D \geq D_{\min}$, where

$$D_{\min} = \sum_{a \in \mathcal{A}} p(a) \min_{b \in \mathcal{B}} d(a, b).$$

The distortion measure can be modified to assure that $D_{\min} = 0$. This is done via the replacement $d(a, b) \leftarrow d(a, b) - \min_b d(a, b)$, whereupon the whole rate-distortion curve simply translates leftward on the D-axis by $D_{\min}$.

b) $R(D) = 0$ for $D \geq D_{\max}$, where

$$D_{\max} = \min_b \sum_a p(a)d(a, b).$$

$D_{\max}$ is the maximum value of D that is of interest, since $R(D) = 0$ for all larger D. It is the value of D associated with the best guess at $\{X_k\}$ in the absence of any information about it other than *a priori* statistical knowledge. For example, $D_{\max} = 1 - \max_a p(a)$ when $\mathcal{A} = \mathcal{B}$ and $d(a, b) = 1$ if $b \neq a$ and 0 if $b = a$.

c) $R(D)$ is nonincreasing in D and is strictly decreasing at every $D \in (D_{\min}, D_{\max})$.

d) $R(D)$ is convex downward. It is strictly convex in the range $(D_{\min}, D_{\max})$ provided $N \leq M$, where $N = |\mathcal{B}|$ and $M = |\mathcal{A}|$. In addition to the ever-present straight-line segment $R(D) = 0$, $D \geq D_{\max}$, if $N > M$ then $R(D)$ can possess one or more straight-line segments in the range $D_{\min} < D < D_{\max}$.

e) The slope of $R(D)$ is continuous in $(D_{\min}, D_{\max})$ and tends to $-\infty$ as $D \downarrow D_{\min}$. If there are straight-line

[4] Indeed, Shannon himself seems to have fallen prey to said information-maximizing mindset in the abstract of his 1959 paper, where he wrote (or someone typed):

In this paper a study is made of the problem of coding a discrete source of information, given a *fidelity criterion* or a *measure of the distortion* of the final recovered message at the receiving point relative to the actual transmitted message. In a particular case there might be a certain tolerable level of distortion as determined by this measure. It is desired to so encode the information that the maximum (sic) possible signaling rate is obtained without exceeding the tolerable distortion level.

The final sentence of this quote should be replaced by, say, "It is desired to minimize the signaling rate devoted to the encoded version of the information subject to the requirement that the tolerable distortion level is not exceeded."

segments in $(D_{\min}, D_{\max})$ (see d) above), no two of them share a common endpoint.

f) $R(D_{\min}) \leq H$, where

$$H = -\sum_{a \in \mathcal{A}} p(a) \log p(a)$$

is the source entropy. If for each $a \in \mathcal{A}$ there is a unique $b \in \mathcal{B}$ that minimizes $d(a, b)$, and each $b \in \mathcal{B}$ minimizes $d(a, b)$ for at most one $a \in \mathcal{A}$, then $R(D_{\min}) = H$.

Some of these properties were established by Shannon [2], including the essential convexity property d). For proofs of the others see Jelinek [27], Gallager [7], and Berger [26].

B. Calculating and Bounding of $R(D)$

1) Calculating Discrete Rate-Distortion Functions: The domain of variation of Q in the definition of $R(D)$ (see (11)) is contained in the $M(N-1)$-dimensional probability simplex defined by the equality constraints

$$\sum_b Q(b \mid a) = 1, \qquad \text{for every } a \in \mathcal{A}$$

and the inequality constraints

$$Q(b \mid a) \geq 0, \qquad \text{for all } (a, b) \in \mathcal{A} \times \mathcal{B}.$$

In addition, the variation is confined to those Q's that satisfy the constraint on the average distortion, namely,

$$d(Q) := \sum_a \sum_b p(a)Q(b \mid a)d(a, b) \leq D.$$

Moreover, the objective function $I(Q)$ is a convex function of Q.[5] Hence, determining $R(D)$ amounts to solving a convex mathematical programming problem. This justifies the following statements.

1) There are no local minima in the search region, just a lone global minimum. Hence, $R(D)$ exists despite the fact that a minimum rather than an infimum appears in its definition because this minimum always is achieved, not just closely approached. The minimum need not necessarily occur at a distinct point; it may be common to a subset of points that constitute a closed, convex subset of the domain.

2) Kuhn–Tucker theory provides necessary and sufficient conditions met by a test system Q that minimizes $I(Q)$ subject to the constraints (i.e., solves the minimization problem that defines $R(D)$).

3) The constraint $D(Q) \leq D$ always is satisfied with equality by the minimizing Q. Hence, all the constraints except $Q(b \mid a) \geq 0$ can be handled by Lagrange multiplier theory.

[5] That is,

$$I(\lambda Q_1 + (1 - \lambda)Q_2) \leq \lambda I(Q_1) + (1 - \lambda)I(Q_2)$$

for any $\lambda \in [0, 1]$ and any two test systems $\{Q_1(b \mid a)\}$ and $\{Q_2(b \mid a)\}$. See, for example, [7].

Because of the last item on this list, much insight can be gained into the problem of computing $R(D)$ by temporarily ignoring the constraints $Q(b \mid a) \geq 0$ and equating to zero the derivative of the Lagrangian functional $J(Q) = I(Q) + sd(Q)$ with respect to each component $Q(b \mid a)$ of Q. Following this approach, Shannon [2] showed that, for a fixed value s of the Lagrange multiplier, the minimizing Q, call it $\{Q_s(b \mid a)\}$, always is given in terms of a probability distribution $\{q_s(b), b \in \mathcal{B}\}$ by the prescription

$$Q_s(b \mid a) = \lambda_s(a) q_s(b) \exp [sd(a,b)]$$

where

$$\lambda_s^{-1}(a) = \sum_b q_s(b) \exp [sd(a,b)].$$

This reduces the problem of computing the point on the rate-distortion function parameterized by s to that of determining the unknown distribution $\{q_s(b)\}$. The hardest part of that is to determine for which values of b, if any, $q_s(b) = 0$. In certain problems with sufficient symmetry and/or small enough $|\mathcal{B}|$, $q_s(b)$ is strictly positive for all $b \in \mathcal{B}$ (except perhaps at $s = s_{\max}$, the value of s that corresponds to $D_{\max}$.) Shannon [2] used this circumstance to determine $R(D)$ in the special case of an equiprobable M-ary source with $d(a,b) = 1$ if $b \neq a$ and $d(a,b) = 0$ if $b = a$. The result is

$$R(D) = \log_2 M - h(D) - (1-d)\log_2(M-1),$$
$$0 \leq D \leq 1 - M^{-1} = D_{\max} \quad (13)$$

where $h(\cdot)$ is Shannon's binary entropy function

$$h(x) = -x \log_2 x - (1-x) \log_2(1-x).$$

The optimizing Q is

$$Q(b \mid a) = \begin{cases} 1 - D, & \text{if } b = a \\ D/(M-1), & \text{if } b \neq a \end{cases}$$

which says that the whole system should be constructed in such a way that its end-to-end probabilistic transition structure mimics that of an M-ary Hamming channel.

In the special case of a binary equiprobable source ($M = 2$), (13) reduces to

$$R(D) = 1 - h(D) = 1 + D \log_2 D + (1 - D \log_2(1-D)),$$
$$0 \leq D \leq 1/2 = D_{\max}.$$

The desired end-to-end system behavior then becomes that of a binary symmetric channel (BSC) with crossover probability D. It follows that, if one seeks to send a Bernoulli($\frac{1}{2}$) source over a BSC that is available once per source letter, then optimum performance with respect to the single-letter fidelity criterion generated by $d(a,b) = 1 - \delta_{a,b}$ can be obtained simply by connecting the source directly to the BSC and using the raw BSC output as the system output. There is need to do any source and/or channel coding. The average distortion will be $D = \epsilon$, where ϵ is the crossover probability of the BSC.

This is another instance of a double coincidence like that of Section II-E. The first coincidence is that a Bernoulli($\frac{1}{2}$) source drives every BSC at capacity, and the second coincidence is that BSC(ϵ) provides precisely the end-to-end system

transition probabilities that solve the rate-distortion problem for the Bernoulli($\frac{1}{2}$) source at $D = \epsilon$. Again, this double coincidence represents a precarious saddle point. If the channel were not available precisely once per source symbol, if the Bernoulli source were to have a bias $p \neq \frac{1}{2}$, if the channel were not perfectly symmetric, or if the distortion measure were not perfectly symmetric (i.e., if $d(0,1) \neq d(1,0)$), it would become necessary to employ source and channel codes of long memory and high complexity in order to closely approach performance that is ideal in the sense of achieving equality in the information transmission inequality (5). Shannon illustrated how algebraic codes could be "used backwards" to encode the equiprobable binary source efficiently with respect to the error frequency criterion for cases in which the medium connecting the source to the user is anything other than a BSC. This idea was extended by Goblick [29] who proved that ideally efficient algebraic codes exist for this problem in the limit of large blocklength.

To enhance appreciation for the fragility of the double-coincidence saddle point, let us replace the Bernoulli($\frac{1}{2}$) source with a Bernoulli(p) source, $p \neq \frac{1}{2}$. Calculations (see [26, pp. 46–47]) reveal that the rate-distortion function then becomes

$$R(D) = h(p) - h(D), \qquad 0 \leq D \leq \min(p, 1-p) = D_{\max}.$$

Although the optimum *backward* system transition probabilities $P(a \mid b)$ remain those of BSC(D), the optimum *forward* transition probabilities become those of a binary asymmetric channel. Hence, it is no longer possible to obtain an optimum system simply by connecting the source directly to the BSC and using the raw channel output as the system's reconstruction of the source. Not only does the asymmetric source fail to drive the BSC at capacity, but the BSC fails to provide the asymmetric system transition probabilities required in the $R(D)$ problem for $p \neq 1/2$. For example, suppose $p = 0.25$ so that $R(D) = 0.811 - h(D)$ bits per letter, $0 \leq D \leq 0.25 = D_{\max}$. Further suppose that $\epsilon = 0.15$ so that the channel capacity is $C = 1 - h(0.15) = 0.390$ bits per channel use. Direct connection of the source to the channel yields an error frequency of $D = \epsilon = 0.15$. However, evaluating the distortion-rate function at C in accordance with (5) shows that a substantially smaller error frequency of $R^{-1}(0.390) = 0.0855$ can be achieved using optimum source and channel coding.

The formula that Shannon provided for the rate-distortion function of an M-ary equiprobable source with distortion assessed by the single-letter distortion measure $d(a,b) = 1 - \delta_{a,b}$, namely (13), actually is a special case of a more general result published the preceding year by Erokhin [31], a student in Kolmogorov's seminar. At Kolmogorov's urging Erokhin considered a general i.i.d. discrete source with a finite or countably infinite alphabet and found a formula for what we would now call its rate-distortion function with respect to the error frequency criterion. Erokhin's result is that the rate-distortion function in question is given parametrically by the equations

$$D_\theta = 1 - S_\theta + \theta(N_\theta - 1)$$
$$R_\theta = -\sum_{a:p(a)>\theta} p(a)\log p(a) + (1 - D_\theta)\log(1 - D_\theta)$$
$$+ (N_\theta - 1)\theta\log\theta,$$

where N_θ is the number of source letters whose probability exceeds θ and S_θ is the sum of the probabilities of these N_θ letters. The parameter θ traverses the range $0 \le \theta \le p(a_2)$ as D varies from 0 to $D_{\max} = 1 - p(a_1)$, where $p(a_1) \ge p(a_2) \ge p(a)$ for all other $a \in \mathcal{A}$.

Moreover, the optimum output probability distribution $\{q(b)\}$ corresponding to parameter value θ is

$$q(b) = \frac{\max[0, p(b) - \theta]}{\sum_b \max[0, p(b) - \theta]}.$$

This, in turn, shows that said $\{q(b)\}$ is supported on a subset of letters assigned high probability by the source. In other words, more and more letters of low source probability are dropped out of use as reproduction letters as θ, and hence D, increases. Once a letter drops out of use, it never reappears for larger values of D, a property that is by no means common to all rate-distortion functions. For cases in which $|\mathcal{A}| < \infty$, the parameter θ can be eliminated when $0 \le \theta \le p_{\min}$, where $p_{\min}$ denotes the smallest of the $p(a)$, $a \in \mathcal{A}$. This results in the explicit formula

$$R(D) = H - h_b(D) - D\log(|\mathcal{A}| - 1),$$
$$0 \le D \le p_{\min}(|\mathcal{A}| - 1).$$

We shall later interpret this as an instance of tightness of a discrete version of the Shannon lower bound, with $p_{\min}(|\mathcal{A}| - 1)$ in the role of the associated critical value of distortion D^*.

2) The Shannon Lower Bound: Shannon then revisited the problem of continuous amplitude sources. Skeptics of Shannon's prowess in rigorous mathematics[6] should note that the paragraph introducing his treatment of "cases where the input and output alphabets are not restricted to finite sets but vary over arbitrary spaces" contains the phraseology "Further, we assume a probability measure P defined over a Borel field of subsets of the A space. Finally, we require that, for each z belonging to B, $d(m, z)$ is a measurable function with finite expectation." [2] For the case of a difference distortion measure $d(a, b) = d(b - a)$ and an i.i.d. time-discrete source producing absolutely continuous random variable (r.v.) with probability density $p(\cdot)$, Shannon used variational principles to derive a lower bound $R_L(D)$ to the rate-distortion function described parametrically as follows:

$$R(D_s) \ge R_L(D_s) := h(p) - h(g_s) \tag{14}$$

[6]There are none who doubt Shannon's insight and creativity. However, there are those who think that Shannon wrote his papers in a mathematically casual style not to make them more widely accessible but because he was not conversant with the measure-theoretic approach to probability and random processes. Those people are mistaken. That the renowned academician A. N. Kolmogorov referred to Shannon's conception of information coding in terms of the asymptotics of overlapping spheres in n-dimensional finite geometries in the limit as $n \to \infty$ as "incomparably deep" [4] should in itself have been enough to silence such skepticism, but alas it persists.

where

$$h(p) = -\int_{-\infty}^{\infty} p(x)\log p(x)\, dx$$

is the differential entropy of the instantaneous source density and $h(g_s)$ is the differential entropy of the "tilted" density

$$g_s(z) = \frac{\exp(sd(z))}{\int_{-\infty}^{\infty}\exp(sd(z))\, dz}$$

associated with the parameter s and the difference distortion measure $d(\cdot)$. The distortion coordinate D_s is given by

$$D_s = \int_{-\infty}^{\infty} d(z)\exp(sd(z))\, dz.$$

$R_L(D)$ of (14) has been named the Shannon lower bound [26].

In the case of squared error, $d(a, b) = (b - a)^2$, the parameter s can be eliminated and the Shannon lower bound can be expressed in the compact form

$$R_L(D) = \frac{1}{2}\log(Q_0/D)$$

where Q_0 is the entropy power of the source density. That is, Q_0 is the variance of a Gaussian r.v. that has the same differential entropy as does $p(\cdot)$, namely,

$$Q_0 = (2\pi e)^{-1}\exp(2h(p)).$$

If a typical source r.v. X_k can be expressed as the sum of two independent r.v.'s, one of which is $\mathcal{N}(0, D)$, then $R(D) = R_L(D)$. The largest value of D for which this can be done is called the *critical distortion* and is denoted by D^*. The critical distortion can be as small as 0, in which case the Shannon lower bound to the MSE rate-distortion function is nowhere tight. At the other extreme, if the source variables are themselves $\mathcal{N}(0, \sigma^2)$ r.v., then $Q_0 = D^* = \sigma^2 = D_{\max}$ so that the Shannon lower bound is everywhere tight and

$$R(D) = \max\left[0, \frac{1}{2}\log(\sigma^2/D)\right]. \tag{15}$$

This result is the time-discrete version of (4). It corresponds to taking samples of the ideal bandlimited Gaussian noise process $2W$ times per second and defining $\sigma^2 = S_0 W$. Its presence is in keeping with one of Shannon's avowed purposes for writing his 1959 paper, namely, to provide "an expansion and detailed elaboration of ideas presented in [1], with particular reference to the discrete case." (Interpreting "discrete" here to mean discrete amplitude and/or discrete time.)

It is noteworthy that, even when treating situations characterized by abstract reproduction alphabets, Shannon nonetheless meticulously employed discrete output random variables. "Consider a finite selection of points z_i $(i = 1, 2, \cdots, l)$ from the B space, and a measurable assignment of transition probabilities $q(z_i \mid m)$" [2]. Perhaps Shannon did this to insulate the reader from the theory of abstract spaces, but this seems unlikely given his accompanying use of the words "measurable assignment of transition probabilities." Also, providing the reader with such insulation was less a matter for concern in 1959 as it had been in 1948. A better explanation is that Shannon appreciated that the representation of the source would always have to be stored digitally; indeed, his major motivation for Section V in 1948 had been to overcome the challenge posed by the fact that continuous-amplitude data has infinite entropy. But, there is an even better explanation. It turns out that the output random variable $\hat{X}$ that results from solving the rate-distortion problem for a continuous-amplitude source usually is discrete! The region, if any, in which the Shannon lower bound is tight for distortions smaller than some positive D^* turns out to be the exception rather than the rule in that $\hat{X}$ is indeed continuous for each D in the range $[0, D^*)$. However, for $D \geq D^*$ Rose [158] recently has shown that the optimum $\hat{X}$ is discrete. (See also work of Fix [159] dealing with cases in which X has finite support.) In retrospect, it seems likely that Shannon knew this all along.

C. Source Coding and Information Transmission Theorems

Shannon did not state or prove any lossy source coding theorems in his classic 1948 paper. He did, however, state and sketch the proof of an end-to-end information transmission theorem for the system of Fig. 1, namely, his Theorem 21. Since the notation $R(D)$ did not exist in 1948, Shannon's theorem statement has v_1 in place of D and R_1 in place of $R(D)$. It reads:

> Theorem 21: If a source has a rate R_1 for a valuation v_1 it is possible to encode the output of the source and transmit it over a channel of capacity C with fidelity as near v_1 as desired provided $R_1 \leq C$. This is not possible if $R_1 > C$.

In 1959 Shannon included the word "Theorems" in the title of his article [2] and was true to his word.

He began by generalizing from a single-letter distortion measure to a *local distortion measure of span* g, denoted $d : \mathcal{A}^g \times \mathcal{B}^g \to [0, \infty)$, and then defining the distortion for blocks of length $m \geq g$ according to the prescription

$$d(\underline{a}, \underline{b}) = \frac{1}{m - g + 1} \sum_{k=1}^{m-g+1} d(a_k, a_{k+1}, \cdots, a_{k+g-1}; \\ b_k, b_{k+1}, \cdots, b_{k+g-1}).$$

Local distortion measures represent a significant improvement over single-letter distortion measures in many situations of interest. For example, if one is compressing a text that contains multidigit numbers, such as a company's annual report, a local distortion measure allows one to assign greater penalties to errors made in the more significant digits of such numbers than to errors in the less significant digits. Generalizing to a local distortion measure in no way complicates the proof of source coding theorems, but it significantly complicates the analytical determination of $R(D)$ curves [30].

Next he extended from i.i.d. sources to general ergodic sources.[7] This required generalizing the definition of $R(D)$ to

$$R(D) = \liminf_{m \to \infty} R_m(d)$$

<hr>

[7] Ergodic sources need not necessarily be stationary. It appears that Shannon intended his discussion to apply to stationary ergodic sources.

where $R_m(d)$ is to defined to be the minimum mutual information rate between a vector $\underline{X}$ of m successive source letters and any random vector $\underline{\hat{X}}$ jointly distributed with $\underline{X}$ in such a way that $Ed(\underline{X}, \underline{\hat{X}}) \leq D$, where $d(\cdot, \cdot)$ is the operative local distortion measure of span g. He then stated a "Positive Coding Theorem" and a "Converse Coding Theorem" and sketched their proofs. Both theorems were phrased in terms of what can and what cannot be accomplished when faced with the task of transmitting information about the given source over a given channel of capacity C and then generating a reproduction of the source based on the information available at the channel output. As such, they are examples of what we now call information transmission theorems or joint source–channel coding theorems. We summarize their content by using the first and second sentences of Theorem 21 of Shannon's 1948 paper quoted above, with the terminology appropriately revised to fit the current context.

Positive Theorem: If an ergodic source has a rate-distortion function $R(D)$ with respect to a fidelity criterion generated by a local distortion measure, then it is possible to encode the output of the source and transmit it over a channel of capacity C with fidelity as near D as desired provided $R(D) \leq C$.

Converse Theorem: Let $R(D)$ and C be as in the statement of the Positive Theorem. If $R(D) > C$ then it is not possible to transmit an encoded version of the source data over the channel and then reconstruct the source with fidelity D on the basis of what is received.

It is also possible to state and prove *source coding theorems* that depend only on the source and the distortion measure and have no connection to any channel.

Definition: A block source code of rate R and block-length n is a collection of $M = \lceil 2^{nR(D)} \rceil$ n-vectors $\mathcal{C} = \{\underline{b}_1, \cdots, \underline{b}_M\}$, where each $\underline{b}_i$ belongs to the nth-power $\mathcal{B}^n$ of the reproduction alphabet.

Definition: Given a block source code $\mathcal{C}$ and any $\underline{x} \in \mathcal{A}^n$, $\underline{b}(\underline{x}) \in \mathcal{C}$ is an *image* of $\underline{x}$ in $\mathcal{C}$ if $d(\underline{x}, \underline{b}(\underline{x})) \leq d(\underline{x}, \underline{b})$ for all $\underline{b} \in \mathcal{C}$; certain vectors $\underline{x}$ may have more than one image in $\mathcal{C}$.

The reader will appreciate that a block source code is simply a collection of vector quantizer "centroids," and that mapping each source word into an image of itself amounts to minimum-distortion vector quantization.

Positive Source Coding Theorem: Let $R(D)$ denote the rate-distortion function of an ergodic source with respect to a local distortion measure d. If $R > (R(D))$ then for sufficiently large n there exists a block source code $\mathcal{C}$ of rate R and blocklength n for which $Ed(\underline{X}, \underline{b}(\underline{X})) \leq D$.

Converse Source Coding Theorem: If $R < R(D)$ then for all n there does not exist a blocklength-n source code of rate R for which $Ed(\underline{X}, \underline{b}(X)) \leq D$.

The proof of the Converse Theorem given by Shannon is adequately rigorous. A corresponding proof of the Converse Source Coding Theorem can be obtained similarly by invoking the readily established facts that $R_n(\cdot)$ is monotonic nonincreasing and convex downward for every n at appropriate places in the argument.

The situation with respect to the Positive Theorem is more delicate. The nuance is that proving the theorem involves approximating the source by a sequence of sources the nth of which produces successive n-vectors independently of one another according to the n-dimensional marginal of the given stationary source. As $n \to \infty$ intuition suggests that the approximating sources will "converge" to the given source in the sense of mimicking its dependencies ever more closely, except perhaps in relatively narrow intervals near the boundaries of successive blocks. However, there are certain ergodic sources that exhibit extraordinarily long-range statistical dependencies. Initial efforts to prove the Positive Theorem rigorously in the generality stated by Shannon encountered obstacles imposed by the possibility of such long-range dependencies. Over the decades, a succession of increasingly general theorems were proved. First, it was proved only for finite-order Markov sources, then for strongly mixing sources [24], then for block-ergodic sources [25], then for weakly mixing sources, and finally for general stationary ergodic sources [7]. The extent to which Shannon knew, or at least intuited, that the Positive Theorem is true for general ergodic sources shall remain forever unresolved. Later, it was shown that even the ergodic assumption can be removed; stationariness is sufficient [15]. Also, a proof of the source coding theorem via large deviations theory was developed by Bucklew [16].

In 1993 Kieffer wrote an invited survey paper [17] concerning source coding with a fidelity criterion. This comprehensive and well-crafted article focused principally on source coding theorems, recapitulating how they were developed with increasing generality over time, including relatively recent emphases on universality, multiterminal models, and coding for sources modeled as random fields. Kieffer was selected for this task in considerable measure for his several contributions that proved source coding theorems with increasingly relaxed conditions in increasingly general contexts [18], [19], [20], [21], [22], [23]. Kieffer's survey article also contains an invaluable bibliography of 137 items.

It is not our purpose here to enter into the details of proofs of source coding theorems and information transmission theorems. Suffice it to say that at the heart of most proofs of positive theorems lies a random code selection argument, Shannon's hallmark. In the case of sources with memory, the achievability of average distortion D at coding rate $R_n(D)$ is established by choosing long codewords constructed of concatenations of "super-letters" from $\mathcal{B}^n$. Each super-letter is chosen independently of all the others in its own codeword and in the other codewords according to the output marginal $q(\underline{b})$ of the joint distribution $p(\underline{a})Q(\underline{b} \mid \underline{a})$ associated with the solution of the variational problem that defines $R_n(D)$.

D. Insights into Source-Channel Duality

Shannon concluded his 1959 paper on rate-distortion theory with some memorable, provocative remarks on the duality of source theory and channel theory. He mentions that, if costs are assigned to the use of its input letters of a channel,

then determining its capacity subject to a bound on expected transmission cost amounts to *maximizing* a mutual information subject to a linear inequality constraint and results in a capacity–cost function for the channel that is *concave* downward. He says, "Solving this problem corresponds, in a sense, to finding a source that is just right for the channel and the desired cost." He then recapitulates that finding a source's rate-distortion function is tantamount to *minimizing* a mutual information subject to a linear inequality constraint and results in a function that is *convex* downward. "Solving this problem," Shannon says, "corresponds to finding a channel that is just right for the source and allowed distortion level." He concludes this landmark paper with the following two provocative sentences:

> This duality can be pursued further and is related to a duality between past and future and the notions of control and knowledge. Thus we may have knowledge of the past but cannot control it; we may control the future but have no knowledge of it.

V. THE SIXTIES

With regard to rate distortion, the 1960's were a decade characterized principally by doctoral dissertations, conference presentations, and book sections. Centers of rate-distortion theory research were M.I.T. (to which Shannon had moved from Bell Labs), Yale, Harvard, Cornell, UC Berkeley, and USC. Columbia, Brooklyn Poly, Purdue, Stanford, and Caltech/JPL also were represented.

A. MIT

At M.I.T., Fano and later Gallager supervised doctoral dissertations that addressed aspects of rate distortion. Specifically, Goblick [29] wrote about algebraic source codes, about rate distortion for certain situations involving side-information, and about the rate at which the performance of block source codes could be made to converge to points on the $R(D)$ curve as blocklength increases. Another dissertation, by Pilc [32], [33] also bounded the performance of optimum source codes as a function of their blocklength. Recent research by Yang, Zhang, and Wei corrects the work of Pilc and extends it to sources with unknown statistics that possess memory [34], [35], [36]; see also related work by Linder, Lugosi, and Zeger [37], [38].

Pinkston wrote both a masters thesis [39] and a doctoral dissertation [40] concerning aspects of rate-distortion theory. The former concentrated on computing $R(D)$ and developing codes for situations in which $d(a, b) = \infty$ for certain (a, b)-pairs; this theory parallels analogous in some respects to the theory of the zero-error capacity of discrete channels. The latter also appeared in part as a journal paper [41].

B. Yale

At Yale, Schultheiss supervised a bevy of doctoral students who studied rate distortion. Gerrish [28] dissected the variational problem defining $R(D)$ in considerable detail. Although he did not use Kuhn–Tucker theory, Gerrish derived the necessary and sufficient conditions for optimality that application of that theory would have produced. Specifically, he showed that $Q_s(b \mid a)$, as given above in Section IV-B, is optimum for parameter value s if and only if the output distribution $q_s(b)$ that generates it satisfies the condition

$$c_s(b) := \sum_a p(a)\lambda_s(a)\exp[sd(a,b)] \begin{cases} =1, & \text{if } q_s(b) > 0 \\ \leq 1, & \text{if } q_s(b) = 0 \end{cases}$$

where

$$\lambda_s^{-1}(a) = \sum_b q_s(b)\exp[sd(a,b)].$$

Using this result Gerrish considerably expanded the class of discrete rate-distortion problems for which $R(D)$ could be determined analytically. He also concocted the famous example

$$\mathcal{A} = \mathcal{B} = \{0,1,2\} \qquad d(a,b) = |b-a|$$
$$p(1) = p \qquad p(0) = p(2) = (1-p)/2.$$

This example has the property that, if p is sufficiently small, then $q(1)$ is positive for a range of small D, is zero for slightly larger distortions, and then becomes nonzero for still larger distortions; at $D = D_{\max} = 1 - p$, $q(1) = 1$ regardless of the value of p. This example showed that even in a case with small alphabets and considerable symmetry, there is no simple behavior to the set $\{b : q(b) = 0\}$ as a function of distortion, in contrast to what Erokhin had established for the error frequency criterion $d(a,b) = 1 - \delta_{a,b}$. McDonald and Schultheiss [42]–[44] obtained results generalizing the Shannon–Pinsker water table result for Gaussian processes and MSE distortion to different sorts of constraints on the error spectrum. Huang, Spang, and Schultheiss [45], [46] derived enhanced vector quantization schemes with and without feedback by using orthogonal transformations inspired by considerations from rate-distortion theory.

C. Cornell

Research in rate-distortion theory at Cornell was spearheaded by Jelinek and subsequently by Berger. Jelinek analyzed the behavior of rate-distortion functions for small distortion [59]. Also, he used the theory of branching processes to show that performance arbitrarily close to the $R(D)$ curve could be achieved via tree codes [60]. (See also the paper by Davis and Hellman [58] in which a more precise analysis was conducted using branching processes with random environments.) Jelinek and Anderson [61] introduced the M-algorithm, an implementable procedure for encoding tree codes analogous to sequential decoding and stack decoding of tree and trellis channel codes, and documented its performance relative to bounds from rate-distortion theory. Under Berger's direction, information rates of sources modeled as dynamic systems were determined by Toms [64], tree encoding of Gaussian sources with memory was studied by Dick [65], and studies of complete decoding algorithms for triple-error-correcting algebraic source codes were initiated by Vanderhorst [62], [63]. Also, a paper on using Slepian's permutation codes as a mechanism for lossy source coding was written by Berger, Jelinek, and Wolf during a summer visit to Cornell by Wolf [66]. Solo papers by Berger during this period included a rate-distortion study of Wiener processes [67], [68] and a

treatment of coding for unknown sources varying over a class either randomly or under the control of an adversary [69]. It was shown, among other things, that the discrete-time Wiener process also exhibits a critical distortion phenomenon, the value of D^* being $\sigma^2/4$, where σ^2 is the variance of the increment between samples. Furthermore, it was established that the rate-distortion function of the Wiener sequence did indeed specify its MSE information rate despite the process being nonstationary. The treatment of unknown sources, like the work of Sakrison on classes of sources cited below, helped pave the way for subsequent studies of universal lossy source coding.

D. Harvard

At Harvard, Tufts supervised an active group of communication theorists including Ramamoorthy, Fine, Kellogg, Trafton, Leiter, Shnidman, and Proakis. Two others of Tufts's students, Berger and Gish, explicitly considered rate-distortion theory as a means for developing absolute performance limits against which to compare the communication and quantization schemes they analyzed [70], [71]. Berger's results showed that, although optimum PAM systems are quite efficient for communicating various types of data sources over filtered channels with additive Gaussian noise when the SNR is low, the gap between optimum PAM and information-theoretically optimum systems widens meaningfully as the SNR increases. This was among the insights that led Price and others to realize that dramatic gains in signaling rate still remained to be reaped in the transmission of digital data over clean telephone channels. Gish's results led to collaboration with Pierce on a theory of asymptotically efficient quantizing [72].

Studying the expression $\frac{1}{2}\log(Q_0/D)$ for the MSE rate-distortion function of a Gaussian sequence for $D \leq D^*$ (cf. Section III-B), Gish and Berger [73] noticed that the formula for the entropy rate power, namely,

$$Q_0 = \exp\left[\frac{1}{2\pi}\int_{-\pi}^{\pi}\log\Phi(\omega)\,d\omega\right]$$

is also the formula for the optimum one-step prediction error. That is, the entropy rate power Q_0 equals the variance of the minimum MSE estimate of X_k based on $\{X_j, j < k\}$. This is both intriguing and confounding. A confluence of fundamental quantities always is intriguing. Here is what is confounding. The sequence of successive one-step prediction errors, also called the *innovations process*, is stationary, zero-mean, uncorrelated, and Gaussian. Let us call it $\{I_k\}$. Rate-distortion theory tells us that $\{I_k\}$ can be encoded with an MSE of D using any data rate $R > \frac{1}{2}\log(Q_0/D)$ but no data rate smaller than this. Hence, in the range $0 \leq D \leq D^*$, the MSE rate-distortion function of $\{X_k\}$ is equal to that of $\{I_k\}$. This suggests that perhaps an optimum encoder should compute $\{I_k\}$ from $\{X_k\}$ and then use a code of rate $\frac{1}{2}\log(Q_0/D)$ to convey the memoryless sequence $\{I_k\}$ to the decoder with an MSE of D. However, it is unclear how the receiver could use these lossy one-step prediction errors to generate a D-admissible estimate of $\{X_k\}$. Furthermore, the rate-distortion problem does not impose a restriction to causal estimation procedures the way the one-step prediction problem does, so the apparent connection between them is enigmatic indeed.

E. UC Berkeley

Sakrison conducted and supervised research in rate-distortion at UC Berkeley. His initial papers [74]–[76] treated source coding in the presence of noisy disturbances, gave geometric insights into the source coding of Gaussian data, and treated the effects of frequency weighting in the distortion measure as part of an effort to deal with edge effects and other perceptual considerations in image coding. His paper with Algazi [77] dealt explicitly with two-dimensional coding techniques for images. In this connection, basic formulas for the information rates of Gaussian random fields were being developed contemporaneously at Purdue by Hayes, Habibi, and Wintz [80]. Sakrison also supervised an important dissertation in which Haskell [79] developed a new representation of the rate-distortion variational problem and used it to compute and bound rate-distortion functions in novel ways. Probably the most significant of Sakrison's contributions was his paper dealing with the information rate of a source that is known only to belong to a certain class of sources but is otherwise unspecified [78]. This paper contributed to setting the foundation for the study of universal lossy coding that flourished in succeeding decades.

F. USC

At USC, Gray [81] studied rate-distortion theory under the able tutelage of Scholtz and Welch. His doctoral dissertation contained many interesting results, perhaps the most startling of which was that the binary-symmetric Markov source exhibited a critical distortion phenomenon with respect to the error frequency distortion measure that was similar to that of MSE rate-distortion functions of stationary Gaussian sequences alluded to previously. Specifically, if $P(1 \mid 0) = P(0 \mid 1) = p$ describes the transition matrix of the binary-symmetric source, he showed that there exists a positive D^* such that

$$R(D) = h(p) - h(D), \qquad 0 \leq D \leq D^*.$$

What's more, using intricate methods involving Kronecker products of matrices and ordinary products of n matrices drawn in all possible ways from a certain pair of matrices, he found the explicit formula for D^* for this problem, namely,

$$D^* = \frac{1}{2}\left[1 - \sqrt{1 - \left(\frac{m}{1-m}\right)^2}\,\right], \qquad m = \min\left(p, 1-p\right).$$

He showed that similar behavior is exhibited by the rate-distortion functions of many autoregressive processes over real and finite alphabets, though explicit determination of D^* has proved elusive for any but the binary-symmetric case cited above. This work and extensions thereof were reported in a series of journal papers [82]–[84]. Gray continued research of his own on rate-distortion throughout succeeding decades and supervised many Stanford doctoral students in dissertations of

both theoretical and practical importance. Some of these will be dealt with in the portion of the paper dealing with the early 1970's.

G. Feedback Studies: Stanford, Columbia, Caltech/JPL

Schalkwijk and Kailath's celebrated work on capacity-achieving schemes for channels with feedback gave rise to studies of analogous problems for source coding. In this connection, Schalkwijk and Bluestein [48], Omura [49], and Butman [50] studied problems of efficient lossy coding for cases in which there is a feedback link from the user back to the source encoder.

H. The Soviet School

During the 1960's, Soviet scientists continued to contribute to the mathematical underpinnings of information theory in general and rate-distortion theory in particular; see Pinsker [52], Dobrushin [53], [54], and Tsybakov [51]. Also, Dobrushin and Tsybakov [55] wrote a paper extending rate-distortion theory to situations in which the encoder cannot observe the source directly and/or the user cannot observe the decoder output directly; see also Wolf and Ziv [56]. Like Jelinek, Lin'kov [57] provided tight bounds to $R(D)$ curves of memoryless sources for small D.

I. The First Textbooks

In 1968, the first treatments of rate-distortion theory in information theory texts appeared. Jelinek's [27, ch. 11] and Gallager's [7, ch. 9] were devoted exclusively to rate-distortion theory. Gallager's proved therein Shannon's 1959 claim that ergodicity sufficed for validity of the positive theorem for source coding with respect to a fidelity criterion. He also introduced the following dual to the convex mathematical programming problem that defines $R(D)$: Let $\underline{\lambda}$ denote a vector with components $\lambda(a)$ indexed by the letters of the source alphabet $\mathcal{A}$. Given any real s and any $\underline{\lambda} \geq \underline{0}$ let $\underline{c}$ denote the vector with components $c(b)$, $b \in \mathcal{B}$ defined by

$$c(b) = \sum_{a \in \mathcal{A}} \lambda(a) p(a) \exp\left[s d(a,b)\right].$$

Let

$$\Lambda_s = \{\underline{\lambda} \geq \underline{0} : \underline{c} \leq \underline{1}\}.$$

Gallager proved that

$$R(D) = \max_{s \leq 0, \underline{\lambda} \in \Lambda_s}\left[s D + \sum_{a \in \mathcal{A}} p(a) \log \lambda(a)\right].$$

Expressing $R(D)$ as a maximum rather than a minimum allows one to generate lower bounds to $R(D)$ readily. Just pick any $s \leq 0$ and any $\underline{\lambda} \geq \underline{0}$. Then evaluate $\underline{c}$. If the largest component of $\underline{c}$ exceeds 1, form a new $\underline{\lambda}$ by dividing the original $\underline{\lambda}$ by this largest $c(b)$. The new $\underline{\lambda}$ then belongs to Λ_s. It follows that the straight line $s D + \sum_a p(a) \log \lambda(a)$ in the (D, R)-plane underbounds $R(D)$. Not only are lower bounds to $R(D)$ produced aplenty this way, but we are assured that the upper envelope of all these lines actually *is* $R(D)$. This dual formulation is inspired by and capitalizes on the fact that a convex downward curve always equals the upper envelope of the family of all its tangent lines. It turns out that all known interesting families of lower bounds to $R(D)$ are special cases of this result. In particular, choosing the components of $\underline{\lambda}$ such that $\lambda(a)p(a)$ is constant yields the Shannon lower bound when the distortion measure is balanced (i.e., every row of the distortion matrix is a permutation of the first row and every column is a permutation of the first column) and yields a generalization of the Shannon lower bound when the distortion measure is not balanced.

VI. THE EARLY SEVENTIES

The period from 1970 to 1973 rounds out the first 25 years of rate-distortion theory. Although it may have appeared to those working in the field at that time that the subject was reaching maturity, it has turned out otherwise indeed. The seemingly "mined" area of computation of rate-distortion functions was thoroughly rejuvenated. Furthermore, foundations were laid that supported dramatic new developments on both the theoretical and practical fronts that have continued apace in the 25 years since.

Gallager's primary interests turned from information theory to computer science and networks during the 1970's. However, rate-distortion theory thrived at Stanford under Gray, at Cornell under Berger, who wrote a text devoted entirely to the subject [26], at JPL under Posner, at UCLA under Omura and Yao, and at Bell Labs under Wyner.[8]

A. Blahut's Algorithm

A Cornell seminar on the mathematics of population genetics and epidemiology somehow inspired Blahut to work on finding a fast numerical algorithm for the computation of rate-distortion functions. He soon thereafter reported that the point on an $R(D)$ curve parameterized by s could be determined by the following iterative procedure [85]:[9]

Step 0: Set $r = 0$. Choose any probability distribution $q_0(\cdot)$ over the destination alphabet that has only positive components, e.g., the uniform distribution $q_0(b) = 1/|\mathcal{B}|$.

Step 1: Compute

$$\lambda_r(a) = \left(\sum_b q_r(b) \exp \left[sd(a,b) \right] \right)^{-1}, \qquad a \in \mathcal{A}.$$

Step 2: Compute

$$c_r(b) = \sum_a \lambda_r(a)p(a) \exp \left[sd(a,b) \right], \qquad b \in \mathcal{B}.$$

If $\max_b c_r(b) < 1 + \epsilon$, halt.

Step 3: Compute $q_{r+1}(b) = c_r(b)q_r(b)$. $r \leftarrow r + 1$. Return to Step 1.

Blahut proved the following facts.

1) The algorithm terminates for any rate-distortion problem for any $\epsilon > 0$.
2) At termination, the distance from the point (D_r, I_r) defined by

$$D_r = \sum_{a,b} p(a)\lambda_r(a)q_r(b) \exp \left[sd(a,b) \right] d(a,b)$$

and

$$I_r = sD_r + \sum_a p(a) \log \lambda_r(a)$$

to the point $(D, R(D))$ parameterized by s (i.e., the point on the $R(D)$-curve at which $R'(D) = s$) goes to zero as $\epsilon \to 0$. Moreover, Blahut provided upper and lower bounds on the terminal value of $I_r - R(D_r)$ that vanish with ϵ.

Perhaps the most astonishing thing about Blahut's algorithm is that it does not explicitly compute the gradient of $R + sD$ during the iterations, nor does it compute the average distortion and average mutual information until after termination. In practice, the iterations proceed rapidly even for large alphabets. Convergence is quick initially but slows for large r; Newton–Raphson methods could be used to close the final gap faster, but practitioners usually have not found this to be necessary. The Blahut algorithm can be used to find points on rate-distortion functions of continuous-amplitude sources, too; one needs to use fine-grained discrete approximations to the source and user alphabets. See, however, the so-called "mapping method" recently introduced by Rose [158], which offers certain advantages especially in cases involving continuous alphabets; Rose uses reasoning from statistical mechanics to capitalize on the fact, alluded to earlier, that the support of the optimum distribution over the reproduction alphabet usually is finite even when $\mathcal{B}$ is continuous.

B. $R(D)$ Under Gray at Stanford

Following his seminal work on autoregressive sources and certain generalizations thereof, Gray joined the Stanford faculty. Since rate distortion is a generalization of the concept of entropy and conditional entropy plays many important roles, Gray sensed the likely fundamentality of a theory of conditional rate-distortion functions and proceeded to develop it [160] in conjunction with his student, Leiner [161], [162]. He defined

$$R_{X|Y}(D) = \min I(X; \hat{X}|Y)$$

where the minimum is over all r.v. $\hat{X}$ jointly distributed with (X, Y) in such a manner that $E_{X,Y,\hat{X}} d(X, \hat{X}) \leq D$. This not only proved of use *per se* but also led to new bounding results for classical rate-distortion functions. However, it did not treat what later turned out to be the more challenging problem of how to handle side-information $\{Y_k\}$ that was available to

---

[8] Centers of excellence in rate distortion emerged in Budapest under Csiszár, in Tokyo under Amari, in Osaka under Arimoto, in Israel under Ziv and his "descendants," in Illinois under Pursley, and at Princeton under Verdú, but those developments belong to the second 25 years of information theory.

[9] Blahut and, independently, Arimoto [86] found an analogous algorithm for computing the capacity of channels. Related algorithms have since been developed for computing other quantities of information-theoretic interest. For a treatment of the general theory of such max-max and min-min alternating optimization algorithms, see Csiszár and Tusnady [87].

$$R_{\mathrm{WZ}}(D) = \begin{cases} h(p) - h(p * D), & \text{if } 0 \le D \le D_c \\ \text{straight line from } (D_c, h(p) - h(p * D_c)) \text{ to } (p, 0), & \text{if } D_c \le D \le p \end{cases} \qquad (17)$$

the decoder only and not to the encoder. That had to await ground-breaking research by Wyner and Ziv [94].

Gray also began interactions with the mathematicians Ornstein and Shields during this period. The fruits of those collaborations matured some years later, culminating in a theory of sliding block codes for sources and channels that finally tied information theory and ergodic theory together in mutually beneficial and enlightening ways. Other collaborators of Gray in those efforts included Neuhoff, Omura, and Dobrushin [163]–[165]. The so-called *process definition* of the rate-distortion function was introduced and related to the performance achievable with sliding block codes with infinite window width (codes in the sense of ergodic theory). It was shown that the process definition agreed with Shannon's 1959 definition of the rate-distortion function $\liminf_{n \to \infty} R_n(D)$ for sources and/or distortion measures with memory. More importantly, it was proved that one could "back off" the window width from infinity to a large, finite value with only a negligible degradation in the tradeoff of coding rate versus distortion, thereby making the theory of sliding block codes practically significant.

Seeing that Slepian and Wolf [93] had conducted seminal research on lossless multiterminal source-coding problems analogous to the multiple-access channel models of Ahlswede [90] and Liao [91], Berger and Wyner agreed that research should be done on a lossy source-coding analog of the novel Cover–Bergmans [88], [89] theory of broadcast channels. Gray and Wyner were the first to collaborate successfully on such an endeavor, authoring what proved to be the first of many papers in the burgeoning subject of multiterminal lossy source coding [92].

C. The Wyner–Ziv Rate-Distortion Function

The seminal piece of research in multiterminal lossy source coding was the paper by Wyner and Ziv [94], who considered lossy source coding with side-information at the decoder. Suppose that in addition to the source $\{X_k\}$ that we seek to convey to the user, there is a statistically related source $\{Y_k\}$. If $\{Y_k\}$ can be observed both by the encoder and the decoder, then we get conditional rate-distortion theory *a la* Gray. The case in which neither the encoder nor the decoder sees $\{Y_k\}$, which perhaps is under the control of an adversary, corresponds to Berger's source-coding game [69]. The case in which the encoder sees $\{Y_k\}$ but the decoder does not was long known [29] to be no different from the case in which there is no $\{Y_k\}$. But the case in which the decoder is privy to $\{Y_k\}$ but the encoder is not proved to be both challenging and fascinating. For the case of a single-letter fidelity criterion and (X_k, Y_k)-pairs that are i.i.d. over the index k, Wyner and Ziv showed that the rate-distortion function, now widely denoted by $R_{\mathrm{WZ}}(D)$ in their honor, is given by

$$R_{\mathrm{WZ}}(D) = \min_{Z \in \mathcal{Z}_D} I(X; Z \mid Y) \qquad (16)$$

where $\mathcal{Z}_D$ is the set of auxiliary r.v. $Z \in \mathcal{Z}$ jointly distributed with a generic (X, Y) such that:

1) $Y - X - Z$ is a Markov chain; i.e.,

$$p_{Y,X,Z}(y, x, z) = p_Y(y) p_{X|Y}(x \mid y) p_{Z|X}(z \mid x).$$

2) There exists $g : \mathcal{Z} \times \mathcal{Y} \to \hat{\mathcal{X}}$ such that

$$E d(X, g(Z, Y)) \le D.$$

3) The cardinality of the alphabet $\mathcal{Z}$ may be constrained to satisfy $|\mathcal{Z}| \le |\mathcal{X}| + 1$.

Consider the special case in which $\{X_k\}$ and $\{Y_k\}$ are Bernoulli$(\frac{1}{2})$ and statistically related as if connected by a BSC of crossover probability $p \le 1/2$ and $d(a, b) = 1 - \delta_{a,b}$. $R_{\mathrm{WZ}}(D)$ for this case is shown in (17) at the top of this page, where $p * d = p(1 - D) + (1 - p)D$ and D_c is such that the sraight-line segment for $D \ge D_c$ is tangent to the curved segment for $D \le D_c$. Berger had used Bergmans [89] theory of "satellites and clouds" to show that (17) was an upper bound to $R(D)$ for this binary-symmetric case. The major contribution of Wyner and Ziv's paper resided in proving a converse to the unlikely effect that this performance cannot be improved upon, and then generalizing to (17) for arbitrary (X, Y) and $d(\cdot, \cdot)$.

The advent of Wyner–Ziv theory gave rise to a spate of papers on multiterminal lossy source coding, codified and summarized by Berger in 1977 [95]. Contributions described therein include works by Körner and Marton, [96]–[98], Berger and Tung [99], [100], Chang [101], Shohara [102], Omura and Housewright [103], Wolfowitz [104], and Sgarro [105]. In succeeding decades, further strides have been made on various side-information lossy coding problems [153], [154], [128], [155], [129], [130], and [156]. Furthermore, challenging new multiterminal rate-distortion problems have been tackled with considerable success, including the *multiple descriptions problem* [145], [150], [146]–[149], [151], [152], [157], [132], the *successive refinements problem* [133], and the *CEO problem* [134]–[136]. Applications of multiple descriptions to image, voice, audio, and video coding are currently in development, and practical schemes based on successive refinement theory are emerging that promise application to progressive transmission of images and other media.

D. Rate Distortion in Random Fields

In order for rate-distortion theory to be applied to images, video, and other multidimensional media, it is necessary to extend it from random processes to random fields (i.e., collections of random variables indexed by multidimensional parameters or, more generally, by the nodes of a graph). The work of Hayes, Habibi, and Wintz [80] extending the water-table result for Gaussian sources to Gaussian random fields already has been mentioned. A general theory of the information theory of random fields has been propounded [131], but we are more interested in results specific to rate distortion. Most of these have been concerned with extending the existence of critical distortion to the random field case and then bounding the critical distortion for specific models. The paper of Hajek and Berger [121] founded this subfield. Work inspired thereby included Bassalygo and Dobrushin [122], Newman [123], Newman and Baker [124] in which the critical distortion of the classic Ising model is computed exactly, and several papers by Berger and Ye [125], [126]. For a summary and expansion of all work in this arena, see [127].

E. Universal Lossy Data Compression

Work by Fitingof, Lynch, Davisson, and Ziv in the early 1970's showed that lossless coding could be done efficiently without prior knowledge of the statistics of the source being compressed, so-called *universal lossless coding*. This was followed by development of Lempel–Ziv coding [106], [107], arithmetic coding [108]–[110], and context-tree weighted encoding [111], [112], which have made universal lossless coding practical and, indeed, of great commercial value.

Universal lossy coding has proven more elusive as regards both theory and practice. General theories of universal lossy coding based on ensembles of block codes and tree codes were developed [138]–[144], but these lack sufficient structure and hence require encoder complexity too demanding to be considered as solving the problem in any practical sense. Recent developments are more attractive algorithmically [113]–[120]. The paper by Yang and Kieffer [117] is particularly intriguing; they show that a lossy source code exists that is universal not only with respect to the source statistics but also with respect to the distortion measure. Though Yang–Kieffer codes code can be selected *a priori* in the absence of any knowledge about the fidelity criterion, the way one actually does the encoding does, of course, depend on which fidelity criterion is appropriate to the situation at hand. All universal lossy coding schemes found to date lack the relative simplicity that imbues Lempel–Ziv coders and arithmetic coders with economic viability. Perhaps as a consequence of the fact that approximate matches abound whereas exact matches are unique, it is inherently much faster to look for an exact match than it is to search a plethora of approximate matches looking for the best, or even nearly the best, among them. The right way to trade off search effort in a poorly understood environment against the degree to which the product of the search possesses desired criteria has long been a human enigma. This suggests it is unlikely that the "holy grail" of implementable universal lossy source coding will be discovered soon.

VII. An Impact on Applications

After 25 years, in 1974, the theory of source coding with a fidelity criterion was well-developed, and extensive treatments were available in the literature, including a chapter in the book by Gallager [7] and the comprehensive text by Berger [26]. However, the impact of rate-distortion theory on the practice of lossy source coding, or data compression, was slight. Indeed,

Pierce in his 1973 paper states [221], "In general, I am content with the wisdom that information theory has given us, but sometimes I wish that the mathematical machine could provide a few more details."

To assess further the impact of Information Theory on lossy source coding 25 years after Shannon's original paper, we examine textbooks [222] and paper compendia [201], [183] from around that time. It is clearly evident that except for scalar quantization combined with entropy coding, and scalar quantization combined with transform coding for images, there was little in terms of concrete contributions.

Part of the reason for this elegant theory not influencing the practice of data compression can be traced to the observation that the practitioners of information theory and the designers of data compression systems formed mutually exclusive sets. A 1967 special issue of the PROCEEDINGS OF THE IEEE on Redundancy Removal, generally supports this conclusion, although the papers by Pearson [218] and O'Neal [216] directly incorporate some of Shannon's ideas and results. Perhaps a quote from Pearson's paper implies the gulf that existed: "The concept of a rate-distortion function, once grasped, is conceptually a very satisfying one;" the implication being that rate-distortion theory is not simple to comprehend, at least not at first reading.

However, even information theorists were not optimistic concerning the impact of rate-distortion theory on the practice of lossy source coding, but perhaps for much different reasons—they had a full grasp of the theory, its assumptions, and its implementation requirements, and the picture they saw was challenging. For example, rate-distortion theory requires an accurate source model, and such models for important sources were just being explored and were not well-known [7]. Second, fidelity criteria for important sources such as speech and images were not well-developed, although work was in progress [218]. Third, the AEP and random coding arguments used in proving information-theoretic results implied exponential growth in the codebook, and since, as stated by Wozencraft and Jacobs in their classic text, "One cannot trifle with exponential growth" [248, p. 387]; many outstanding researchers felt that implementation complexity might be the dominating issue [227], [228].

Happily, information theory has had a dramatic impact on lossy source coding, or data compression, in the last 25 years, although the three issues, source models, fidelity criteria, and complexity, remain major considerations.

In addition to the results, insights, and tools provided by Shannon's two original papers [1], [2], the legacy of the first 25 years included the results by Huang and Schultheiss [45] and Wintz and Kurtenbach [246] on bit allocation for scalar quantizers, the rate-distortion function for autoregressive (AR) processes and the MSE fidelity criterion as obtained by Gray [82] and Berger [26], and the tree coding theorem for Gaussian AR processes and the MSE fidelity criterion given by Berger [26]. These results served as a springboard to developing lossy coding techniques for sources with memory that explicitly exhibit information-theoretic concepts.

We start with a discussion of memoryless sources and then proceed to examine results for sources with memory. This is followed by developments of the several approaches to compression that have been useful for important sources such as speech, still images, high-quality audio, and video. The goal is to describe the contributions of information-theoretic results on the practice of lossy source coding without producing a voluminous survey of lossy source compression methods for the several sources.

VIII. MEMORYLESS SOURCES

Uniform and nonuniform scalar quantization was the primary technique for coding memoryless sources in 1974. These quantizers were usually implemented with an adaptive step size or scaling factor to allow the quantizer dynamic range to respond to rapid variations in source variance, and hence, to reduce the number of levels needed to cover this range with the allowable distortion. The adaptation was based upon tracking the input signal variance and was not motivated by any results from rate-distortion theory. The only real connection to information theory was through the idea of entropy coding the quantizer output alphabet. Subsequent work by Farvardin and Modestino [187] investigated the performance of entropy-constrained scalar quantizers for a variety of source input distributions. At the same time, information theorists were studying the encoding of memoryless sources using rate-distortion theory and began specifically drawing upon random coding arguments.

Random coding arguments are a staple in proving positive coding theorems, and hence, the existence of good source codes. However, many researchers and engineers, especially those interested in applications, find rate-distortion theory wanting in that only the existence of good codes is demonstrated and that no method for finding a good code is given. This view is somewhat myopic, though, because each random coding proof of the existence of a good code actually outlines a code construction. For example, the proof of the achievability of the rate-distortion function given in Cover and Thomas [252] begins by generating a codebook of 2^{NR} reproduction sequences and assigning each of them a codeword index. Then, each input sequence of length N is encoded by finding that sequence in the reproduction codebook that falls within the distortion typical set.

If we actually desire to encode i.i.d. Gaussian sequences of length N with average distortion D, we can then mimic this proof and generate a codebook consisting of 2^{NR} reproduction sequences of length N, where the individual components of each sequence are i.i.d. Gaussian random variables with zero mean and a variance of $\sigma^2 - D$. For a given input sequence of length N, the encoding procedure is to find that sequence in the codebook with the smallest distortion. Thus we see that exactly following the proof of achievability yields an explicit encoding procedure. Unfortunately, to accomplish this encoding step requires an exhaustive comparison of the current input sequence of length N with all sequences in the codebook, and subsequently repeating this comparison for all input sequences of length N to be encoded. Since there are 2^{NR} sequences in the codebook and N must be large to approach optimality, the encoding with such codebooks is arbitrarily complex.

An approach to combatting complexity in random codes is to add structure, and researchers did just this by proving coding theorems for tree and trellis codes that approach the rate-distortion bound arbitrarily closely. Results were obtained for tree coding of binary sources and the Hamming distortion measure by Jelinek and Anderson [61] and for tree coding of i.i.d. Gaussian sources and the MSE fidelity criterion by Dick, Berger, and Jelinek [65]. Viterbi and Omura [242] proved a trellis source coding theorem and Davis and Hellman [58] proved a tree coding theorem for source coding with a fidelity criterion, extending the work of Jelinek [60] and Gallager [190]. While this work did not directly impact applications, it did lay the groundwork for later research on coding sources with memory that has found widespread applications.

Likely, the most important lossy source-coding technique that has sprung directly from information theory is vector quantization. Only those who have a grasp of information theory can appreciate the motivation for studying vector quantizers (VQ's) for memoryless sources; additionally, there were many reasons for not pursuing VQ designs, even from an information theorist's viewpoint. Since performance grows asymptotically with vector length N and the number of input points grows proportionally to 2^{NR}, the exponential growth in encoding complexity seemed too daunting to overcome. Furthermore, there was the indication from rate-distortion theory that for Gaussian sources and the MSE distortion measure, only a 0.255-bit/sample reduction in rate, or a 1.53-dB reduction in distortion, with respect to entropy-coded scalar quantization, was available with vector quantization. Some of the best information theorists found this daunting [228]. However, in the late 1970's and the early 1980's, information theorists did turn their attention to vector quantization.

There were three main thrusts at that time. One centered on developing algorithms for the design of nonuniform VQ's, a second thrust examined uniform VQ performance and design, and a third studied the asymptotic performance (in block-length) of VQ's. Uniform VQ's were based upon lattices in N-dimensional space and this work drew upon algebraic structures and space-filling polytopes. Of course, the attraction to lattice (uniform) VQ's was that the regular structure should allow fast encoding methods to be developed and thus avoid the exponential growth in encoding complexity with vector length N. The study of VQ performance included the lattice VQ structures and extended to higher dimensions some of the approaches from scalar quantization. Algorithm development for nonuniform VQ design began with the algorithm by Linde, Buzo, and Gray [204], now called the LBG algorithm. This algorithm was built upon the k-means algorithm from pattern recognition and the scalar quantizer design methods developed by Lloyd [205]. Although it only guaranteed local optimality and the encoding stage was still exponentially complex in the NR product, the possibility of actually using a VQ and testing its performance became possible.

We leave further broad discussion of scalar and vector quantization to the excellent paper in this issue by Gray and Neuhoff [196]. However, later when discussing particular lossy source compression techniques, we will identify the role of vector quantization and the type of VQ employed.

In many applications, it was (and is) necessary to encode several independent memoryless sources subject to an overall rate or distortion constraint. Thus in those applications with a constraint on total rate, it becomes necessary to minimize total distortion by allocating rate across several scalar quantizers. Clearly evident in each of these contributions is the rate-distortion function for independent and identically distributed Gaussian sources and the MSE fidelity criterion as derived by Shannon [1], [2], or the distortion rate version $D = \sigma^2 2^{-2R}$.

In particular, the bit-allocation methods for scalar quantizers used the distortion rate version of Shannon's result with only a multiplicative scale factor on the variance, viz, as a criterion to be minimized by appropriate allocations of bits (rate). By adjusting this multiplicative factor, the rate distortion relationship could be made to approximate that of a distribution other than Gaussian, such as a Laplacian source.

Thus for M independent sources with respective variances σ_i^2, the individual distortions as a function of rate are $D_i = \gamma_i \sigma_i^2 2^{-2R_i}$ and the total distortion to be minimized is $D = \sum_{i=1}^{M} D_i$ subject to the overall rate constraint $\sum_{i=1}^{M} R_i \leq R$. The multiplier γ_i accounts for differences in distributions and for different encoding methods. We append the rate constraint using a Lagrange multiplier, so that the functional to be minimized is

$$J(R, \lambda) = D + \lambda R.$$

Letting γ_i be a constant, the resulting rate allocation is

$$R_i = R + \frac{1}{2} \log_2 \frac{\sigma_i^2}{\left[\prod_{j=1}^{M} \sigma_j^2 \right]^{1/M}}.$$

Although this approach often produces noninteger bit allocations for scalar quantizers, and *ad hoc* modifications are required to produce integer allocations and to achieve the desired total bit rate exactly, the coupling of coding independent sources with different scalar quantizers and "optimal" bit allocation was introduced and served as a framework for numerous future lossy coding techniques for both speech and images. Several other approaches to this bit-allocation problem that allow integer bit allocations and other constraints are now common. See Gersho and Gray [191] for a summary.

IX. SOURCES WITH MEMORY

An obvious approach to coding sources with memory when one already has numerous techniques for coding independent sources is to determine a transformation that models the source memory and then use this transformation to decompose the source with memory into several independent (or nearly independent) memoryless sources. Perhaps the most explicit delineation of this approach and the role of rate-distortion theory in coding sources with memory, in general, and transform image compression in particular, is given by Davisson [182]. Davisson decomposes a source with memory into an expansion of orthogonal components and allocates rate to each of these components according to their variance, an approach that was used previously by Gallager in proving a coding theorem for such Gaussian random process sources [7].

More specifically, Davisson [182] shows that the N-block rate-distortion function for a source with covariance matrix Φ_N and eigenvalues λ_i is given by

$$R_N(D) = \frac{1}{2N} [\log |\Phi_N| - \log D]$$

where the distortion is assumed to be small, $D \leq \min \lambda_i$.

These results amplify the work of Kolmogorov [3] and McDonald and Schultheiss [43]. Davisson also evaluates the rate-distortion function for a first-order Gauss–Markov source, a model often used for images, and expresses the result as a difference between the N-block rate-distortion function and the rate-distortion function asymptotic in N

$$R_N(D) - R(D) = \frac{1}{2N} \log \left(1 - \rho^2 \right)^{-1}.$$

Thus for $\rho = 0.95$, the N-block encoding requires $2.4/N$ more bits per sample than the best possible.

Tree and trellis coding theorems for structures involving transform decompositions are proved in [208], [217], and [209].

The rate-distortion function for AR sources, derived by Gray [82] and Berger [26], was a welcome addition since it came at a time when AR processes were finding their initial application to speech coding [170]–[172]. The elucidation of a tree-coding method for Gaussian AR sources and the proof of a tree-coding theorem for these sources, [26], gave impetus to the application of tree-coding techniques in speech-coding applications.

A. Predictive Coding

Predictive coding was a well-known technique for source compression based upon time-domain waveform-following by the time the second 25 years rolled around. In fact, there had been substantive contributions by the early 1950's [180], [186], [215], with the paper by Elias being significantly motivated by information theory ideas—primarily entropy. However, by 1976, predictive coding was an important practical approach to speech coding and also had applications to image coding [201]. The principal motivation behind this work, as well as its success, was the reduction in the dynamic range of the quantizer input and the decorrelation of the quantizer input by the predictor. Rate-distortion theory was just beginning to have an impact on predictive coders in 1976, and doubtless, Jayant [201] is correct in stating that, "... simple DPCM is still one of the classic triumphs of intuitional waveform coding." However, predictive coding was to become extraordinarily important in applications, and rate-distortion theory motivated coders were to play a major role.

1) Speech Compression: Interestingly, multipath-searched versions of differential encoders, such as delta modulation and DPCM, predated or paralleled the development of the tree-coding theorem by Berger, and were motivated by intuition and estimation theory. In particular, Irwin and O'Neal [199] studied multipath searching of a fixed DPCM system to depth 2, but found only modest increases in SNR. Cutler [181] investigated delayed encoding in a delta modulator with the goal of incorporating a more responsive (over-responsive) encoder to track the sudden onset of pitch pulses.

Anderson and Bodie [168] drawing directly on the theoretical results of Berger [26], and previous work on tree/trellis coding of i.i.d. sources, developed tree coders at 2 bits/sample for speech built around fixed DPCM code generators and the MSE distortion measure. Significant increases in SNR were obtained, but the reconstructed speech had a substantial "hissing" sound superimposed on the highly intelligible speech. Becker and Viterbi [175] considered bit rates of 1 bit/sample and took an approach that included a long-term predictor and a finite-state approximation to the AR model. Both the long- and short-term predictors were adaptive. They also reported work on an alternative excitation based upon a trellis. Stewart [236], [237] pursued trellis codes coupled with AR models and pushed the rates down below 1 bit/sample.

The primary result of these studies was an increase in output SNR, but the output speech quality still suffered from audible noise. To improve this speech quality and make tree coding a viable candidate for speech coding required adaptive code generators and perceptually based fidelity criteria. Wilson and Husain [245] examined 1-bit/sample tree coding of speech using a fixed-noise shaping motivated by the classical C noise weighting from telephony. Later work, using innovative adaptive code generators, perceptually weighted distortion measures, and new tree codes, achieved good-quality speech with tree coding at 8 kbits/s [261].

However, the major impetus for code-excited schemes in speech coding came from the paper by Atal and Schroeder [174] that demonstrated that high-quality speech could be generated by a predictive coder with a Gaussian populated codebook with 1024 entries, each of length 40 samples. The rate was estimated at 4 kbits/s, but the predictor coefficients were not quantized and the analysis-by-synthesis codebook search was accomplished by the use of a Cray computer! Thus this was very much a "proof-of-concept" paper, but a principal difference between this work and previous research by information-theoretic researchers on speech coding was that the authors used a perceptually weighted MSE to select the best codebook excitation sequence.

Atal and Schroeder [174] were aware of the earlier work on tree coding, but they were also motivated by the analysis-by-synthesis speech-coding method called multipulse linear predictive coding [173], where the codebook consisted of several impulses (say, 8 per frame of 40 samples or so) with arbitrary location and arbitrary magnitude. Multipulse linear predictive coding (multipulse LPC) produced good-quality highly intelligent speech, but the complexity of searching a relatively unstructured adaptive codebook was prohibitive. From this initial work, the tremendous effort on codebook-excited speech coders was spawned. The keys to producing high-quality highly intelligent speech with these coders are that the code generators, or predictors, are adaptive and the fidelity criterion includes perceptual weighting. The perceptual weighting attempts to keep the noise spectrum below that of the source spectrum at all frequencies of interest.

Complexity is always an issue in tree coding and codebook-excited approaches. In tree coding, complexity is addressed by nonexhaustive searching of the trees using depth-first, breadth-first, or metric-first techniques [169]. Nontree code-books typically contain many more samples per codeword than tree codes, so the search complexity for these codebooks is related to codebook structure and sparsity. A breakthrough in codebook excited techniques for speech has been the interleaved single pulse permutation (ISPP) codebook that consists of a few sparse impulse sequences that are phase-shifted versions of each other, where all of the pulses have the same magnitude [230]. Prior to this technique, codebooks were often designed off-line by using training mode vector quantization.

The impact of codebook-based approaches on speech coding standards has been dramatic. As shown in [179] and [194], many of the current standards for speech coding are code-excited predictive coding and the quality obtained by these techniques is much higher than might have been expected. For example, G.729 has a Mean Opinion Score (MOS) rating of 4.1, and G.728, a low-delay standard, has a quality rating of 4.0–4.1 [179]. G.728 employs a five-dimensional gain-shape vector quantizer (VQ) for its excitation vectors. Vector quantization for side-information is also commonly used and plays an important role in achieving the lowest possible transmitted data rate. The VQ's used for the coefficient representation are typically split VQ's so that the dimension of the VQ's can be kept as small as possible. These VQ's are designed using the training mode method and training the VQ's provides a substantial improvement in performance over any other VQ design technique.

2) Image Compression: Tree coding was also studied for image compression and some interesting results were obtained [211], [212]. The success of this approach for images has been much less than that for speech since a good image model is difficult to find and time-domain methods have not been able to keep pace with the much lower bit rates achievable in the transform domains.

B. Source Decompositions

Predictive coding is model-based and it works extremely well when the linear prediction, or autoregressive, model can adequately represent a source. Early on, however, speech and image compression researchers were drawn to frequency-domain decompositions to account for source memory. Of course, this is very much an electrical engineering way of thinking, namely, breaking a signal down into its constituent frequency components, and then coding these components separately. Two prominent examples of this approach are subband coding and transform coding.

In subband coding, the source to be compressed is passed through parallel filter banks that consist of bandpass filters, and the outputs of these filters are decimated and lowpass translated. Each of the resulting time-domain signals is coded using PCM (i.e., scalar quantization), DPCM, or some other time-domain compression technique. At the receiver, each signal is decoded and those signals that were not originally baseband are translated back to their appropriate filter band, all signals are interpolated (upsampled), and then all components are summed to yield the overall reconstructed source representation. One of the original challenges in subband coding was designing subband filters that provided good coverage of the desired frequency band without producing aliasing upon the reconstruction step due to the intermediate subsampling. The key advance was the development of quadrature mirror filters that, although they allow aliasing in the downsampling step at the encoder, these filters cancel the aliasing during the reconstruction at the receiver. These ideas continue to be generalized and extended. Allocating bits across the subbands is a critical step as well, and the approach differs depending upon the source and the application.

Transform coders take an M-block of input source samples and perform an M-point discrete transform on them. The principal idea is that a good transform will yield decorrelated or even independent components and will concentrate the signal energy into fewer significant components. Bit-allocation methods then discard unimportant frequency content and code each of the remaining components according to differing accuracies. The source can then be approximately reconstructed from the coded components via an inverse transform. Most transforms that are popular in compression are unitary and separable.

It can be shown that transform methods are a special case of subband techniques where the subband synthesis filters have impulse responses equal to the transform basis functions, the analysis filter impulse responses are the time-reversed basis functions, and the decimation factor in each band is the transform blocklength. Furthermore, wavelet methods allow for nonuniform tiling of the time–frequency plane, and therefore wavelet expansions generalize subband methods. In fact, any wavelet expansion has a corresponding perfect reconstruction filter bank interpretation. However, the differences between subband techniques and transform-domain techniques for coding are the frequency and time resolution, which leads to a preferred quantization approach.

In the following sections, we discuss subband, transform, and wavelet-based compression methods for speech, still images, video, and high-quality audio, with emphasis on information-theoretic influences.

1) Speech Compression: Interestingly, subband coding found its first applications to speech compression and then later to image compression, while transform coding had its first applications to image coding and later to speech/audio compression. The primary motivation for subband coding in speech compression was the ability to code the subbands with differing numbers of bits in order to isolate distortions to their individual bands and to achieve better perceptual coding performance. This turned out to be solid reasoning and subband coding of speech at 12 to 24 kbits/s is very competitive in performance and complexity. The bit allocations across the subbands can use the rate-distortion theory-motivated constrained optimization approach, but the existing subband speech coders employ experimentally determined allocations.

Most of the transform coders for speech have utilized the discrete cosine transform (DCT), although sinusoidal transforms and wavelets are also popular today. Transform-based coders can easily achieve high-quality speech at 16 kbits/s, and with perceptual coding and analysis-by-synthesis methods,

they generate good quality speech down to 4.8 kbits/s. Information theory has not had a major impact on these designs and further discussion of these techniques is left to the references [194], [202], [235].

The application of wavelets to speech coding is relatively new and has yet to produce speech coders that are competitive in rate, quality, and complexity with the predictive coding methods.

2) Image and Video Compression: Transform-based methods have been a dominant force in image compression at rates below 2 bits/pixel for over 30 years. The first rate distortion theoretic result to have an impact on image compression was the distortion rate expression for an i.i.d. Gaussian source subject to an MSE fidelity criterion that was used for bit-allocation calculations in transform coding. Typically, the transform coefficients were assumed to be independent and bits were allocated in proportion to the variances of the coefficients subject to an overall constraint on total bit rate. The solution to the resulting constrained optimization problem yields the bit allocation to achieve the minimum average total distortion.

The optimal transform in terms of energy compaction is the Karhunen-Loeve transform [166] which produces uncorrelated transform coefficients but requires the knowledge of the statistics of sources and often involves highly complicated computations. Among many practical transforms, the Discrete Cosine Transform (DCT) [223] is the one used the most, especially for two-dimensional signals. With good energy compactness and the existence of fast algorithms [176], [244], DCT-based transform coders are used in many applications and coding standards, such as H.320, JPEG [219], [243], and MPEG [178], [189].

Whatever transform is used, the transform itself does not compress the source, and the coding step comes after the transform, when transform coefficients are first quantized then entropy-coded under a certain bit budget. Therefore, how to design good quantizers and entropy coders for transform coefficients are a principal focus in transform coder design today.

Wavelets are becoming the decomposition of choice for most applications and new standards for still image and video coding today. Wavelets provide excellent energy compaction and the variable time scales allow the various features of an image to be well-reproduced [258]. Other advantages include easy adaptive coding, as described in the following sections.

3) Bit Allocation: In practical transform-coding schemes, different approaches have been used to achieve the coding limits. Using optimal bit allocation, the number of quantization bits devoted to a component is determined based on the average energy of the component. A simple yet effective way to allocate the available code bits to different components is described in [232], where code bits are assigned to transform components bit by bit in a recursive way. At each stage, one bit is assigned to the component with the highest energy, then this highest energy is reduced by half before going on to the next stage. The procedure ends when all the available code bits are assigned to the components.

A more sophisticated bit-allocation scheme was proposed by Shoham and Gersho in [234]. Based on the reverse water-filling results, all the components should have the same quantization error except for those with energy lower than the quantization error. For an individual component, the slope of its rate-distortion function is just the reciprocal of the quantization level d [26]. Therefore, this allocation scheme tries to find the slope that minimizes the total distortion for the rate-distortion functions of all the components. However, to find this minimum distortion, this scheme becomes computationally intensive since it has to estimate the rate-distortion function for every transform component so that the best slope can be found. This approach sometimes can achieve optimal performance for a given set of coefficients and a fixed set of quantizers. More discussions on bit allocation can be found in [191].

Using fixed bit allocation, the number of bits used for each component is fixed for all sample functions of the source, so the encoder only needs to send out the allocation information once and all other code bits are used to encode the coefficient values. When such schemes are used for two-dimensional signals, they are also called zonal coding schemes [201], [232] because the coded coefficients are in fixed region(s) in the two-dimensional data plane.

Optimal bit allocation is totally dependent on the statistical characteristics of the source; specifically, the variances of transform components are needed and in general, the source has to be stationary. There are drawbacks to such coding schemes. To get accurate estimates of the variances, a reasonably large number of sample functions have to be processed before actual coding starts, which introduces encoding delay. Further, in real-world applications, random sources are rarely truly stationary—the statistics of transform coefficients change either spatially or temporally, whereas estimation over a large number of sample functions can reflect only the average behavior of the source. While producing constant-rate code sequences, coders using fixed bit allocation cannot adapt to the spatial or temporal changes of the source, and thus coding distortion may vary from sample function to sample function due to changes of the source.

To deal with the random changes of a source, adaptive schemes are used, and one very old, yet useful, scheme is the threshold method [177], [222], which is actually the basis of today's JPEG standard. Using a threshold, the coder can determine if a coefficient needs to be coded by comparing its energy with a threshold. If the energy of the coefficient is higher than the threshold, the coefficient will be encoded, otherwise, it will be treated as zero and discarded. As opposed to zonal coding which has to determine the optimal quantization level under a fixed code rate, threshold coding is actually easier to approach: once a threshold is determined, there is no need to do bit allocation. Since a large number of transform coefficients will be quantized to zero, this method can greatly reduce the number of coefficients to be coded and has the ability to adapt itself to changes of the source, since which coefficients are coded can change from sample function to sample function. The drawback is that there is no control over the code rate, since whether a coefficient is coded or not depends only on its own local energy. Such coders usually produce variable rate code sequences.

From sample function to sample function, which coefficients are coded can change due to nonstationarity of the source;

therefore, information on which coefficients are coded for each sample function also must be provided to the decoder. Coding thus consists of two steps: one for the location of the coded coefficients, the other for their values.

We refer to the coefficient location information as side-information. For image coding, Ramchandran and Vetterli [224] proposed a thresholding method optimized in an operational rate-distortion sense that can be very effective in reducing the number of coefficients to be coded without sacrificing coding quality. In this method, whether a coefficient is coded or not depends not only on its local coefficient value with respect to a threshold, but also on the total cost of encoding a new coefficient. For each coefficient, the cost of coding is the total bits used for both the coefficient value and the coefficient location, and a decision strategy based on optimizing rate distortion performance for each data block is designed so that the coder can decide if a coefficient higher than the threshold is worth being coded. Therefore, this method is still a threshold-based coding scheme, but the focus is on how to reduce the number of coded coefficients without introducing significant error.

Although this method makes decisions in a rate-distortion sense, the statistical meaning of the rate-distortion function is lost. To calculate the coding cost, all data blocks are treated independently and the rate-distortion function of each data block is obtained as if each data block represented a different source [225]. The problem becomes how to merge all the different sources with rate-distortion optimality, and the basic idea is the same as in the optimal bit-allocation scheme described by Shoham and Gersho in [234], but in [234] the goal is to merge different transform components optimally, while here the goal is to merge different sample functions.

4) Side-Information and the Significance Map: In two-step coding schemes such as threshold coding, after determining which coefficients are to be coded, the encoder has to determine how to encode this information in addition to encoding the values of the chosen coefficients. A significance map is a representation of those transform coefficients with sufficient energy that they must be coded to achieve acceptable reconstructed signal quality. For transform coefficients of a sample function, and a fixed threshold t, a binary bitmap can be built to indicate which coefficients need to be coded. If a coefficient $|c_{ij}| > t$, then it is significant and will be encoded, so in the significance map, $b_{ij} = 1$, otherwise, $b_{ij} = 0$, indicating that the coefficient is not encoded. If a source can be decomposed into M components, then there are a total 2^M different patterns for the bitmap.

To encode the significance map, some practical coders make certain assumptions on the distribution of the significant coefficients. In threshold coding methods such as JPEG, to encode the significance map, a predetermined Huffman coder is used to encode the distance between two consecutive significant coefficients. The Huffman coder is designed based on the distributions of those distances obtained in experiments, such as was done in [177]. Since they are only experimental results, the coder may work very well for some images, but it is also possible that it may perform poorly for images with different statistical characteristics.

Another approach to coding both the significance map and the coefficient values is Shapiro's Embedded Zerotree coding method [233] based on the self-similarity assumption on wavelet transform coefficients. Shapiro's method is also called the EZW algorithm, since the embedded zerotree is used on the coefficients of a Discrete Wavelet Transform (DWT). The self-similarity assumption says that if a coefficient at a coarse scale (i.e., low frequency) is insignificant, then all the coefficients at the same location at finer scales (i.e., higher frequencies) are likely to be insignificant too. This means the significance of higher frequency coefficients can be predicted by the significance of a lower frequency coefficient at the same location. Since DWT coefficients have a natural tree structure, this makes it possible to use a quadtree to encode the significance map and achieve impressive coding performance.

Several related coding schemes have also been used based on analogous ideas, such as Said and Pearlman's set partitioning algorithm [226] which is basically similar to the EZW algorithm, in that they are all based on the self-similarity assumption, thus making these methods limited to certain types of transformations, such as the DWT.

In their three-dimensional (3-D) subband coding scheme, Taubman and Zakhor [238] used a more general approach to encoding the positions of coefficients, or the significance map. They tried to exploit the spatial correlation between coefficients to improve coding efficiency. Other approaches to encoding the significance map have also been attempted [214]. Although no statistical assumption is necessary, like all VQ schemes, this approach needs a training phase before it starts coding.

For image and video compression standards set in the last 10 years, the two-dimensional DCT is almost ubiquitous, appearing in the JPEG, H.261, MPEG1, MPEG2, H.263, and MPEG4 standards [184], [194]. Although bit-allocation methods drawing upon rate distortion theoretic results have been suggestive, many of the bit-allocation methods in the standards are based upon off-line perceptual experiments. The results are striking in that simple, uniform scalar quantizers can generate excellent perceptual results at rates of 0.5 bit/pixel and above. Lossless coding techniques, including Huffman coding and arithmetic coding, are important components of these standards as well.

Evolving standards, such as JPEG-2000 and MPEG4, have wavelet-based decompositions in place of or in addition to the DCT [184], [254].

C. High-Quality Audio Compression

Compression for high-quality audio is most often for playback applications that do not need real-time encoding; hence, relatively complicated techniques can be used for the encoding step. The basic approach has been to separate the input source material into blocks of time-domain samples and then decompose these samples into frequency-domain components for encoding. The importance of this approach is that results from auditory masking experiments in terms of the frequency-domain characteristics of the ear are available and can be incorporated in the distortion measure during the encoding process. Thus this method exhibits the concept of decomposing the source into several independent sources that are to be encoded subject to an overall limitation on rate. The distortion measure to be minimized in this case is very much a perceptual one and the achievement of the desired rate with the smallest audible distortion is done by iterative bit allocations until certain masking criteria are satisfied. Lossless coding techniques are also routinely employed.

Note that the approach for compression of high-quality audio is to devise a structure such that transparent perceptual quality is obtained, and whatever bit rate is necessary to achieve that goal is accepted (up to a point). Thus this compression problem is very much a rate-distortion problem—that is, minimize the rate for a specified distortion (perceptually transparent)—as opposed to a distortion-rate problem, as in many speech-coding applications [194], [255].

X. RECURRING THEMES

The influence of rate-distortion theory on lossy source coding can be seen in a few recurring themes for the optimization of specific source coders. The most common is to develop the operational rate distortion or distortion rate function for a particular source, source coder, and distortion measure, and then consider the constrained optimization problem that results by appending the appropriate rate or distortion constraint. The basis for this approach lies in considering Nth-order rate-distortion theory.

A. Nth-Order Rate Distortion Theory and Constrained Optimization

Let X^N denote the input source vector $(X_1, X_2, \cdots, X_N)$ and let its reconstruction be denoted by $\hat{X}^N$. The distortion between X^N and $\hat{X}^N$ is $d_N(X^N, \hat{X}^N)$ so that the average distortion over all source vectors and reproductions is given by

$$D_N = \frac{1}{N} E\{d_N(X^N, \hat{X}^N)\}.$$

The Nth-order distortion rate function can then be written as

$$D_N(R) = \inf_{p(\hat{X}^N | X^N)} \left\{ \frac{1}{N}[d_N(X^N, \hat{X}^N)] \mid \frac{1}{N} I(X^N; \hat{X}^N) \leq R \right\}$$

and asymptotically in blocklength

$$D(R) = \lim_{N \to \infty} D_N(R).$$

To find $D_N(R)$, we append the rate constraint with a Lagrange multiplier and minimize the functional

$$J(p(\hat{X}^N \mid X^N)) = E[d_N(X^N, \hat{X}^N)] + \lambda I(X^N; \hat{X}^N).$$

Let us define the length of the codeword that represents X^N to be $\ell_N(X^N)$ and so the average rate in bits per source symbol is

$$R_N = \frac{1}{N} E\{\ell_N(X^N)\}.$$

Then, for a given source encoder $\alpha_N(X^N)$, and decoder $\beta_N(X^N)$ that yields rate R_N and reconstruction $\hat{X}^N$, we can write the operational distortion rate function as

$$\hat{D}_N(R)$$
$$= \inf_{\alpha_N, \beta_N} \left\{ \frac{1}{N} E[d_N(X^N, \hat{X}^N)] \mid \frac{1}{N} E[\ell_N(X^N)] \le R \right\}.$$

$D_N(R)$ lower-bounds $\hat{D}_N(R)$ and the bound becomes tight as $N \to \infty$. We can pose a constrained optimization problem using the operational distortion rate function as

$$J(\alpha_N, \beta_N) = E[d_N(X_N, \hat{X}_N)] + \lambda E[\ell_N(X^N)]. \quad (18)$$

Since the operational distortion rate function is not necessarily convex or continuous, Lagrangian methods will not find $\hat{D}_N(R)$, however, we can use the Lagrangian formulation to find the convex hull.

Thus the approach is to iteratively minimize the functional in (18) using an algorithm similar to the generalized Lloyd method used for VQ design [191], [196].

B. Duality

An underutilized concept in obtaining lossy source compression methods is that of duality. Error-control coding and source coding are dual problems in the following sense: Decoding error-control codes consists of finding the best match to a received sequence given certain assumptions, a distortion criterion, and models. Alternatively, encoding for source compression entails the same steps. Further, decoding in source compression consists of receiving a particular transmitted sequence and mapping it into a unique output. Similarly, encoding for error-control coding maps a presented input directly into a particular transmitted sequence.

The development of trellis-coded quantization (TCQ) was spurred by this duality observation based upon results on trellis-coded modulation. In addition to providing good performance for speech coding at 16 kbits/s [253], TCQ is part of the verification model of JPEG-2000 at the time of this writing. In fact, TCQ combined with wavelets was the top-ranked coder in both objective and subjective performance at 0.125 and 0.25 bit/pixel (bpp) during the JPEG-2000 evaluations [254].

XI. RESEARCH CHALLENGES

A. Joint Source/Channel Coding

A fundamental result of information theory is that, assuming stationarity, optimal source coding and channel coding can be considered separately without loss of optimality. There are two caveats to this statement: First, separating source and channel coding may be more complex than a combined design [167], [207]; and second, both source and channel coding must be performing optimally, because if one is suboptimal, the other may be aided by incorporating the knowledge of this suboptimality.

Practitioners of lossy source coding for communications applications have always implemented coders that are robust to channel errors to some degree, with some attributable loss in source compression performance in the error-free case. This robustness is often obtained in waveform coding of speech by simply fading the memory of the encoder and decoder to "forget" channel errors and thus resynchronize the encoder and decoder adaptation. Another common approach to resynchronizing the source encoder and decoder in video-compression applications is to transmit an intracoded frame (no motion compensation) at some specified interval. For example, this happens every 132nd frame in the H.320 video conferencing standard and is accomplished in the MPEG1 and MPEG2 standards with I-frames. However, the I-frames in MPEG were inserted primarily for search-motivated applications more than error resilence.

Another way to achieve error robustness without implementing error-correction codes is to use natural source redundancy and/or models of the channel to detect and correct errors. For example, Sayood et al. [231] exploits known Markov properties of the source in an MAP search for the best match to a received sequence. Phamdo and Farvardin [220] take a similar approach.

For a given transmitted bit rate, splitting bits between source coding and channel coding has the expected result—namely, if bits are allocated to channel coding and the channel is ideal, there is a loss in performance compared to source coding alone. Similarly, if there are no bits allocated to channel coding and the channel is very noisy, there will be a loss in performance compared to using some error-protection coding. Numerous studies for speech, image, and video coding have investigated joint source–channel coding. These solutions specify the allocation of transmitted rate between source coding and channel coding for chosen sources, source compression methods, and channel models to achieve the best source reconstruction.

For many applications today, of which wireless communications is a prime example, channels are far from ideal and it is best to combine source and channel coding. The most common way this is evident in standards is by the use of unequal error protection (UEP). That is, some compressed source bits can have a much more profound effect on reconstructed source quality than others, so these bits must be error-protected. Thus the source and channel coding is joint in the sense that the channel coding uses knowledge of the source bit sensitivity as well as the channel, and that the source compression frees up a portion of the bit rate for the error protection function.

It is a recent trend in wireline and wireless applications to sense the quality of the channel or the channel SNR versus frequency by sending known sequences or tones and then using the channel quality information at the transmitter to optimize digital communications system performance. Examples of this method are precoding in V.34 modems, DMT-based ADSL modems, and SNR estimation in the IS-127 mobile standard. This same technique can be extended to joint source/channel coding where we could use channel quality measurements to determine how to partition the available transmitted bit rate between source and channel coding.

B. Background Impairments

One of the principal challenges to mobile speech compression today is the presence of unwanted sounds or other speakers at the handset or microphone input. In order for the speech coders to achieve the desired reconstructed quality at the low rates needed, the speech coders have incorporated source-specific and sink-specific models in the encoder. These models are based on the assumption that what is present at the source coder input is the source to be encoded, and the source alone. When other sounds are present, the source coder forces these assumptions on the input signal during the encoding process with sometimes disastrous results.

More specifically, users of voice communications devices are somewhat forgiving of naturally occurring sounds, but when the speech coder attempts to use its assumed models on signals that are not speech, the results of coding natural sounds may be unnatural sounding artifacts upon reconstruction. The usual approaches today are either to filter the incoming signal or to attempt to cancel unwanted signals at the input. Under appropriate assumptions, the filtering approach may be optimal.

Dobrushin and Tsybakov [55], Wolf and Ziv [56], and Berger [26] have investigated the mean-squared error encoding of a source with additive distortion. The general result is that, asympotically in blocklength, the optimal encoder/decoder pair consists of an optimal estimator followed by optimal encoding of the resulting estimate. An application and extension of this work is reported by Fischer, Gibson, and Koo [188], where results are presented for training mode vector quantization and speech sources. Gibson, Koo, and Gray [193] develop optimal filtering algorithms for additive colored noise with applications to speech coding. One of their algorithms is the optional noise canceller in the Japanese half-rate digital cellular standard. Neither filtering nor cancellation is entirely effective.

C. Error Concealment

When channel errors cannot be corrected, lossy source compression techniques depend on robustness properties of the source decoder to reconstruct an approximation of the source without catastrophic distortions. However, if entire frames or packets are lost, special modifications are required. Twenty-five years ago, when such modifications were first considered, they were labeled with the perhaps misleading term, soft-decision demodulation. Today, these modifications are called error-concealment techniques.

Error-concealment methods generally consist of estimation or interpolation techniques using decoded signals that had been received previously. In speech coding for mobile radio applications, when a frame is lost, the lost frame is often compensated for by repeating the data from the preceding frame along with some muting of the reconstructed speech.

In many image- and video-compression applications, the need for error concealment arises due to the loss of a block of data, such as the coded coefficients representing a block of pixels as in transform coding. For these situations, error concealment can be performed in the transform domain or in the pixel domain, using adjacent blocks.

Video applications that have low transmission rates can have the data for an entire frame in one packet. A lost packet in these situations requires temporal interpolation.

D. Variable-Rate Coding

In order to respond to the changing characteristics of the input source and hence be efficient in the utilization of the available bandwidth, there is a trend toward variable-rate coding of speech and video. The challenges here are to sense the changes in the source and adapt the source coder to these changes, and to make the variable-rate stream interoperate with the possibly fixed-rate transmission channel. Of course, the use of buffering to interface fixed-to-variable length lossless source codes to the channel is common; however, rate variations in these new lossy schemes can have a wide swing and hence amplify the challenges.

Variable-rate coders for speech and images have been studied for 25 years [206], [239]–[241], but key rate indicators are still difficult to determine. Rate indicators that have been used range from simple input energy calculations to measuring correlation or other spectral properties of the source, such as estimates of source spectral entropy [210]. It is expected that variable-rate coders will be the rule rather than the exception in future applications and standards.

E. Layered Coding or Scalability

To respond to changing network conditions, such as available bit rate or channel congestion, there is another clear trend toward layered or scalable compression schemes. The principal concept in scalability is that an improvement in source reproduction, namely, reduced distortion, can be achieved by sending only an incremental increase in rate over the current transmitted rate that is achieving a coarser reproduction of the source. SNR, spatial, and temporal scalability are all important in applications. It is evident that a source-compression method designed to operate at several lower rates cannot outperform the compression method designed for the overall total rate, so the question is when do optimal or near-optimal scalable compression methods exist?

SNR scalability has been addressed from the rate-distortion theory viewpoint by Koshelev [262]–[264] who called it divisibility, and by Equitz and Cover [133] under the heading of successive refinement of information. Equitz and Cover address the problem of starting out with a low rate but optimal source coder, that is, one that operates exactly on the rate-distortion bound, and then finding those conditions under which an incremental addition in rate also yields rate-distortion optimal encoding. It is shown that successive refinement in the rate-distortion optimal sense is not always possible and that a neessary and sufficient condition for successive refinement is that the individual encodings be expressible as a Markov chain. Rimoldi [265] generalizes these results and provides an insightful interpretation in terms of typical sequences.

Spatial and temporal scalability is nonstandard in terms of classical discrete-time rate-distortion theory since both involve changes in the underlying sampling rate. To address spatial and temporal scalability or layered coding, many researchers pose the operational rate distortion problem for their particular coder and optimize with respect to the convex hull of the performance curves.

Progressive coding has become important in image coding, since in a network environment, different users may have different access capability, such as different bandwidths, CPU power, etc., and may want to access the source at different levels of quality. In such circumstances, a coder that can provide a coded sequence in a progressive way has an advantage.

In transform coding, progressive coding can be accomplished in two basic ways: spectral selection and successive approximation. For example, in DCT-based image coders, an encoder using a spectral selection strategy can first encode all the dc coefficients, then the ac coefficients in the low-frequency region, and finally the high-frequency ac coefficients. Since for many common images, most activity is concentrated in the low-frequency area, if only limited code bits can be received, the decoder can still reconstruct the image at a lower quality using all the dc coefficients and some low-frequency ac coefficients. This is useful in browsing applications when a user only wants to get a rough picture of an image to decide if the selected image is the one needed.

The prioritized DCT method [197], [198] is a more advanced approach based on the same idea. In a prioritized DCT coder, the transmission order is determined by the coefficient energy, that is, coefficients with higher energy, i.e., containing more information, are transmitted first. This is intuitively quite straightforward, since the idea of transmitting the dc coefficients first in the above mentioned scheme is based on the observation that most of the time dc coefficients have the highest energy among all the transform coefficients. The prioritized DCT method adds some flexibility to the same strategy in the sense that the coder can decide which coefficients are to be transmitted first based on the actual values of the coefficients, instead of assuming that the dc coefficients and low-frequency ac coefficients will have higher energy. This is also an adaptive-coding scheme.

Another powerful progressive coding scheme is successive approximation. Instead of transmitting the low-frequency coefficients to their highest accuracy, the successive approximation method first sends only the most significant bits for all of the coefficients, then sends the next most significant bits, and so on. In contrast to spectral selection, which generates minimum distortion for selected coefficients but discards all of the other coefficients, successive approximation produces relatively constant distortion for all the coefficients, which is closer to the rate-distortion result.

Examples of coders that use successive approximation are the Embedded Zerotree algorithm (EZW) by Shapiro [233], and the modified version of the EZW algorithm proposed by Said and Pearlman [226]. In both methods, the Discrete Wavelet Transform (DWT) coefficients are encoded. One of the novelties of the two coders is the way the coder arranges the order of the DWT coefficients that enables the coder to efficiently encode the side-information as well as the coefficient values, as already discussed in Section IX-B2. A similar approach was also studied by Xiong et al. in a DCT-based image coder [249]. A modified version of the prioritized DCT scheme is proposed by Efstratiadis and Strintzis [185], in which DWT coefficients are considered and instead of

using a spectral selection strategy, this coder uses successive approximation to implement a hierarchical image coder.

Directly encoding DCT coefficients by layers can also be found in the literature [203]. Bit-plane encoding offers such easy functionality for progressive coding that it is widely adopted in new applications [254].

F. Multiterminal Source Coding

We have already noted the results on successive refinement of information (or divisibility) by Equitz and Cover [133], Koshelev [262]–[264], and Rimoldi [265] in Section XI-E, and their relationship to SNR scalability. Another multiterminal rate-distortion theoretic result that is finding applications in lossy source coding is the multiple descriptions problem [148], [150]. In this problem, the total available bit rate is split between (say) two channels and either channel may be subject to failure. It is desired to allocate rate and coded representations between the two channels, such that if one channel fails, an adequate reconstruction of the source is possible, but if both channels are available, an improved reconstruction over the single-channel reception results. Practical interest in this problem stems from packet-switched networks where the two channels can be realized by sequences of separately marked packets, and from diversity implementations in wireless applications. For recent results, see [266] and [267].

XII. STANDARDS

Standards-setting for compression of speech, high-quality audio, still images, and video has been a dominant force in compression research since the mid-1980's. Although some might criticize these standards activities as inhibiting research and stifling innovation, most would agree that these efforts have generated an incredible interest in lossy compression and have lead to extraordinary advances in performance. The principal effect on lossy compression research is to make the research problem multifaceted in that not only must compression rate versus distortion performance be evaluated, but background impairments, channel errors, implementation complexity, and functionality (such as scalable coding, searching, and backwards compatibility) also become important considerations for many applications.

A challenge for researchers is to define the problem well and to fold as many of these other constraints into the problem as necessary to address the application of interest. Because of the tremendous emphasis on standards, it is perhaps most important for those involved in basic research to avoid being limited by current trends and the constraints of the many standards in order to generate the new results and directions needed for substantial advances in performance.

For more details on lossy compression techniques and standards, the reader is referred to [179], [184], [194], and [254]–[257].

XIII. EPILOGUE

Rate-distortion theory and the practice of lossy source coding have become much more closely connected today than they were in the past. There is every reason to anticipate that a much tighter fusion of theory and practice will prevail in 2009 when we celebrate the fiftieth anniversary of Shannon's 1959 paper.

REFERENCES

[1] C. E. Shannon, "A mathematical theory of communication," *Bell Syst. Tech. J.*, vol. 27, pp. 379–423; 623–656, July and Oct. 1948. (Also in *Claude Elwood Shannon: Collected Papers*, N. J. A. Sloane and A. D. Wyner, Eds. Piscataway, NJ: IEEE Press, 1993, pp. 5–83.)

[2] _____, "Coding theorems for a discrete source with a fidelity criterion," in *IRE Conv. Rec.*, vol. 7, 1959, pp. 142–163. (Also in *Information and Decision Processes*, R. E. Machol, Ed. New York: McGraw-Hill, 1960, pp. 93–126, and in *Claude Elwood Shannon: Collected Papers*, N. J. A. Sloane and A. D. Wyner, Eds. Piscataway, NJ: IEEE Press, 1993, pp. 325–350.)

[3] A. N. Kolmogorov, "On the Shannon theory of information transmission in the case of continuous signals," *IRE Trans. Inform. Theory*, vol. IT-2, pp. 102–108, 1956.

[4] _____, "The theory of transmission of information, plenary session of the Academy of Sciences of the USSR on the automization of production" (Moscow, USSR, 1956), *Izv. Akad. Nauk SSSR*, pp. 66–99, 1957.

[5] _____, "A new metric invariant of transitive dynamic systems and automorphisms in Lebesgue spaces," *Dokl. Akad. Nauk. SSSR*, vol. 119, pp. 861–864, 1958.

[6] J. L. Holsinger, "Digital communication over fixed time-continuous channels with memory—With special application to telephone channels," Sc.D. dissertation, Dept. Elec. Eng., MIT, Cambridge, MA (Tech. Rep. TR 366, Lincoln Labs., Lexington, MA), 1968.

[7] R. G. Gallager, *Information Theory and Reliable Communication.* New York: Wiley, 1968.

[8] Y. G. Sinai, "On the concept of entropy of a dynamical system," *Dokl. Akad. Nauk. SSSR*, vol. 124, pp. 768–771, 1959.

[9] D. S. Ornstein, "Bernoulli shifts with the same entropy are isomorphic," *Adv. Math.*, vol. 4, pp. 337–352, 1970.

[10] E. C. Posner and E. R. Rodemich, "Epsilon entropy and data compression," *Ann. Math. Statist.*, vol. 42, pp. 2079–2125, 1971.

[11] R. J. McEliece and E. C. Posner, "Hiding and covering in a compact metric space," *Ann. Statist.*, vol. 1, pp. 729–739, 1973.

[12] C. E. Shannon, "Communication in the presence of noise," *Proc. IRE*, vol. 37, pp. 10–21, 1949.

[13] M. S. Pinsker, "Mutual information between a pair of stationary Gaussian random processes," *Dokl. Akad. Nauk. USSR*, vol. 99, no. 2, pp. 213–216, 1954.

[14] _____, "Computation of the message rate of a stationary random process and the capacity of a stationary channel," *Dokl. Akad. Nauk. USSR*, vol. 111, no. 4, pp. 753–756, 1956.

[15] R. M. Gray and L. D. Davisson, "Source coding theorems without the ergodic assumption," *IEEE Trans. Inform. Theory*, vol. IT-20, pp. 625–636, 1974.

[16] J. A. Bucklew, "The source coding theorem via Sanov's theorem," *IEEE Trans. Inform. Theory*, vol. IT-33, pp. 907–909, 1987.

[17] J. C. Kieffer, "A survey of the theory of source coding with a fidelity criterion," *IEEE Trans. Inform. Theory*, vol. 39, pp. 1473–1490, 1993.

[18] _____, "A unified approach to weak universal source coding," *IEEE Trans. Inform. Theory*, vol. IT-24, pp. 674–682, 1978.

[19] _____, "On the minimum rate for strong universal block coding of an class of ergodic sources," *IEEE Trans. Inform. Theory*, vol. IT-26, pp. 693–702, 1980.

[20] _____, "A method for proving multiterminal source coding theorems," *IEEE Trans. Inform. Theory*, vol. IT-27, pp. 565–570, 1981.

[21] _____, "Fixed-rate encoding of nonstationary information sources," *IEEE Trans. Inform. Theory*, vol. IT-33, pp. 651–655, 1987.

[22] _____, "Strong converses in source coding relative to a fidelity criterion," *IEEE Trans. Inform. Theory*, vol. 37, pp. 257–262, 1991.

[23] _____, "Sample converses in source coding theory," *IEEE Trans. Inform. Theory*, vol. 37, pp. 263–268, 1991.

[24] T. J. Goblick Jr., "A coding theorem for time-discrete analog data sources," *IEEE Trans. Inform. Theory*, vol. IT-15, pp. 401–407, May 1969.

[25] T. Berger, "Rate-distortion theory for sources with abstract alphabets and memory," *Inform. Contr.*, vol. 13, pp. 254–273, 1968.

[26] _____, *Rate Distortion Theory: A Mathematical Basis for Data Compression.* Englewood Cliffs, NJ: Prentice-Hall, 1971.

[27] F. Jelinek, *Probabilistic Information Theory.* New York: McGraw-Hill, 1968.

[28] A. M. Gerrish, "Estimation of information rates," Ph.D. dissertation, Dept. Elec. Eng., Yale Univ., New Haven, CT, 1963.

[29] T. J. Goblick Jr., "Coding for a discrete information source with a distortion measure," Ph.D. dissertation, Dept. Elec. Eng., MIT, Cambridge, MA, 1962.

[30] T. Berger and W. C. Yu, "Rate-distortion theory for context-dependent fidelity criteria," *IEEE Trans. Inform. Theory*, vol. IT-18, pp. 378–384, May 1972.

[31] V. Erokhin, "ϵ-entropy of a discrete random variable," *Theory Probab. Its Applic.*, vol. 3, pp. 97–101, 1958.

[32] R. Pilc, "Coding theorems for discrete source-channel pairs," Ph.D. dissertation, Dept. Elec. Eng., MIT, Cambridge, MA, 1967.

[33] _____, "The transmission distortion of a discrete source as a function of the encoding block length," *Bell Syst. Tech. J.*, vol. 47, pp. 827–885, 1968.

[34] Z. Zhang, E. H. Yang, and V. K. Wei, "The redundancy of source coding with a fidelity criterion—Part I: Known statistics," *IEEE Trans. Inform. Theory*, vol. 43, pp. 71–91, Jan. 1997.

[35] E.-h. Yang and Z. Zhang, "The redundancy of universal fixed rate source coding," presented at the 1998 IEEE Int. Symp. Information Theory, MIT, Cambridge, MA, Aug. 16–21, 1998.

[36] _____, "Abstract alphabet source coding theorem revisited: Redundancy analysis," presented at the 1998 IEEE Int. Symp. Information Theory, MIT, Cambridge, MA, Aug. 16–21, 1998.

[37] T. Linder, G. Lugosi, and K. Zeger, "Rates of convergence in the source coding theorem, in empirical quantizer design, and in universal lossy source coding," *IEEE Trans. Inform. Theory*, vol. 40, pp. 1728–1740, 1994.

[38] _____, "Fixed-rate universal lossy source coding and rates of convergence for memoryless sources," *IEEE Trans. Inform. Theory*, vol. 41, pp. 665–676, 1995.

[39] J. T. Pinkston, "Information rates of independent sample sources," M.S. thesis, Dept. Elec. Eng., MIT, Cambridge, MA, 1966.

[40] _____, "Encoding independent sample sources," Ph.D. dissertation, Dept. Elec. Eng., MIT, Cambridge, MA, 1967.

[41] _____, "An application of rate-distortion theory to a converse to the coding theorem," *IEEE Trans. Inform. Theory*, vol. IT-15, pp. 66–71, 1969.

[42] R. A. McDonald, "Information rates of Gaussian signals under criteria constraining the error spectrum," D. Eng. dissertation, Yale Univ. School Elec. Eng., New Haven, CT, 1961.

[43] R. A. McDonald and P. M. Schultheiss, "Information rates of Gaussian signals under criteria constraining the error spectrum," *Proc. IEEE*, vol. 52, pp. 415–416, 1964.

[44] _____, "Effective bandlimits of Gaussian processes under a mean square error criterion," *Proc. IEEE*, vol. 52, p. 517, 1964.

[45] J. J. Y. Huang and P. M. Schultheiss, "Block quantization of correlated Gaussian variables," *IRE Trans. Commun.*, vol. CS-11, pp. 289–296, 1963.

[46] H. A. Spang and P. M. Schultheiss, "Reduction of quantizing noise by use of feedback," *IRE Trans. Commun.*, vol. CS-12, pp. 373–380, 1964.

[47] B. Bunin, "Rate-distortion functions for correlated Gaussian sources," Ph.D. dissertation, Dept. Elec. Eng., Polytech. Inst. Brooklyn, Brooklyn, NY, 1969.

[48] J. P. M. Schalkwijk and L. I. Bluestein, "Transmission of analog waveforms through channels with feedback," *IEEE Trans. Inform. Theory*, vol. IT-13, pp. 617–619, 1967.

[49] J. K. Omura, "Optimum linear transmission of analog data for channels with feedback," *IEEE Trans. Inform. Theory*, vol. IT-14, pp. 38–43, 1968.

[50] S. Butman, "Rate-distortion over bandlimited feedback channels," *IEEE Trans. Inform. Theory*, vol. IT-17, pp. 110–112, 1971.

[51] B. S. Tsybakov, "ϵ-entropy of a vector message," presented at the IEEE Int. Symp. Information Theory, Ellenville, NY, 1969.

[52] M. S. Pinsker, "Sources of messages," *Probl. Pered. Inform.*, vol. 14, pp. 5–20, 1963.

[53] R. L. Dobrushin, "Individual methods for the transmission of information for discrete channels without memory and messages with independent components," *Sov. Math.*, vol. 4, pp. 253–256, 1963.

[54] _____, "Unified methods for transmission of information: The general case, *Sov. Math.*, vol. 4, pp. 289–292, 1963.

[55] R. L. Dobrushin and B. S. Tsybakov, "Information transmission with additional noise," *IRE Trans. Inform. Theory*, vol. IT-8, pp. 293–304, 1962.

[56] J. K. Wolf and J. Ziv, "Transmission of noisy information to a noisy receiver with minimum distortion," *IEEE Trans. Inform. Theory*, vol. IT-16, pp. 406–411, 1970.

[57] Y. N. Lin'kov, "Evaluation of ϵ-entropy of random variables for small ϵ," *Probl. Inform. Transm.*, vol. 1, pp. 12–18 (Russian pp. 12–18), 1965.

[58] C. R. Davis and M. E. Hellman, "On tree coding with a fidelity criterion," *IEEE Trans. Inform. Theory*, vol. IT-21, pp. 373–378, 1975.

[59] F. Jelinek, "Evaluation of distortion rate functions for low distortions," *Proc. IEEE*, vol. 55, pp. 2067–2068, 1967.

[60] _____, "Tree encoding of memoryless time-discrete sources with a fidelity criterion," *IEEE Trans. Inform. Theory*, vol. IT-15, pp. 584–590, 1969.

[61] F. Jelinek and J. B. Anderson, "Instrumentable tree encoding of information sources," *IEEE Trans. Inform. Theory*, vol. IT-17, pp. 118–119, 1971.

[62] J. A. Vanderhorst, "The error locator polynomial for binary and primitive triple error correcting BCH codes," M.S. thesis, School Elec. Eng., Cornell Univ., Ithaca, NY, Sept. 1971.

[63] _____, "Complete decoding of some binary BCH codes," Ph.D. dissertation, School Elec. Eng., Cornell Univ., Ithaca, NY, Aug. 1972.

[64] W. E. Toms and T. Berger, "Information rates of stochastically driven dynamic systems," *IEEE Trans. Inform. Theory*, vol. IT-17, pp. 113–114, 1971.

[65] R. J. Dick, "Tree coding for Gaussian sources," Ph.D. dissertation, School Elec. Eng., Cornell Univ., Ithaca, NY, May 1973. (See also R. J. Dick, T. Berger, and F. Jelinek, *IEEE Trans. Inform. Theory*, vol. IT-20, pp. 332–336, 1974.)

[66] T. Berger, F. Jelinek, and J. K. Wolf, "Permutation codes for sources," *IEEE Trans. Inform. Theory*, vol. IT-18, pp. 160–169, 1972.

[67] T. Berger, "Information rates of wiener sequences," presented at the IEEE Int. Symp. Information Theory, Ellenville, NY, Jan. 28–31, 1969.

[68] _____, "Information rates of Wiener processes," *IEEE Trans. Inform. Theory*, vol. IT-16, pp. 134–139, 1970.

[69] _____, "The source coding game," *IEEE Trans. Inform. Theory*, vol. IT-17, pp. 71–76, 1971.

[70] _____, "Nyquist's problem in data transmission," Ph.D. dissertation, Harvard Univ., Div. Eng. App. Phys., Harvard Univ., Cambridge, MA, 1966.

[71] H. Gish, "Optimum quantization of random sequences," Ph.D. dissertation, Harvard Univ., Div. Eng. Appl. Phys., Harvard Univ., Cambridge, MA, 1966.

[72] H. Gish and J. N. Pierce, "Asymptotically efficient quantizing," *IEEE Trans. Inform. Theory*, vol. IT-14, pp. 676–683, 1968.

[73] Private communication, 1967.

[74] D. J. Sakrison, "Source encoding in the presence of a random disturbance," *IEEE Trans. Inform. Theory*, vol. IT-14, pp. 165–167, 1968.

[75] _____, "A geometric treatment of the source encoding of a Gaussian random variable," *IEEE Trans. Inform. Theory*, vol. IT-14, pp. 481–486, 1968.

[76] _____, "The rate-distortion function of a Gaussian process with a weighted square error criterion," *IEEE Trans. Inform. Theory*, Addendum 610–611, vol. IT-14, pp. 506–508, 1968.

[77] D. J. Sakrison and V. R. Algazi, "Comparison of line-by-line and two-dimensional coding of random images," *IEEE Trans. Inform. Theory*, vol. IT-17, pp. 386–398, 1971.

[78] D. J. Sakrison, "The rate of a class of random processes," *IEEE Trans. Inform. Theory*, vol. IT-16, pp. 10–16, 1970.

[79] B. G. Haskell, "The computation and bounding of rate-distortion functions," *IEEE Trans. Inform. Theory*, vol. IT-15, pp. 525–531, 1969.

[80] J. F. Hayes, A. Habibi, and P. A. Wintz, "Rate-distortion function for a Gaussian source model of images," *IEEE Trans. Inform. Theory*, vol. IT-16, pp. 507–509, 1970.

[81] R. M. Gray, "Information rates of autoregressive sources," Ph.D. dissertation, Elec. Eng., Univ. South. Calif., Los Angeles, CA, 1969.

[82] _____, "Information rates of autoregressive processes," *IEEE Trans. Inform. Theory*, vol. IT-16, pp. 412–421, 1970.

[83] _____, "Rate-distortion functions for finite-state finite-alphabet Markov sources," *IEEE Trans. Inform. Theory*, vol. IT-17, pp. 127–134, 1971.

[84] _____, "Information rates of stationary ergodic finite-alphabet sources," *IEEE Trans. Inform. Theory*, vol. IT-17, pp. 516–523, 1971; Correction, vol. IT-19, p. 573, 1973.

[85] R. E. Blahut, "Computation of channel capacity and rate-distortion functions," *IEEE Trans. Inform. Theory*, vol. IT-18, pp. 460–473, 1972.

[86] S. Arimoto, "An algorithm for calculating the capacity of an arbitrary discrete memoryless channel," *IEEE Trans. Inform. Theory*, vol. IT-18, pp. 14–20, 1972.

[87] I. Csiszár and G. Tusnady, "Information geometry and alternating minimization procedures," in *Statistics and Decisions/Supplement Issue*, no. 1, E. J. Dudewicz, D. Plachky, and P. K. Sen, Eds. Munich, Germany: R. Oldenbourg Verlag, 1984, pp. 205–237. (Formerly entitled *On Alternating Minimization Procedures*, preprint of the Math. Inst. Hungarian Acad. Sci., no. 35/1981, 1981.)

[88] T. M. Cover, "Broadcast channels," *IEEE Trans. Inform. Theory*, vol. IT-18, pp. 2–14, 1972.

[89] P. Bergmans, "Random coding theorem for broadcast channels with degraded components," *IEEE Trans. Inform. Theory*, vol. IT-19, pp. 197–207, 1973.

[90] R. Ahlswede, "Multi-way communication channels," in *Proc. 2nd. Int. Symp. Information Theory* (Tsahkadsor, Armenian SSR), 1971, pp. 23–52.

[91] H. Liao, "Multiple access channels," Ph.D. dissertation, Dept. Elec. Eng., Univ. Hawaii, Honolulu, HI, 1972.

[92] R. M. Gray and A. D. Wyner, "Source coding for a simple network," *Bell Syst. Tech. J.*, vol. 58, pp. 1681–1721, 1974.

[93] D. Slepian and J. K. Wolf, "Noiseless coding of correlated information sources," *IEEE Trans. Inform. Theory*, vol. IT-19, pp. 471–480, 1973.

[94] A. D. Wyner and J. Ziv, "The rate-distortion function for source coding with side-information at the receiver," *IEEE Trans. Inform. Theory*, vol. IT-22, pp. 1–11, 1976.

[95] T. Berger, "Multiterminal source coding," in *The Information Theory Approach to Communications* (CISM Courses and Lectures, no. 229). Wien, New York: Springer-Verlag, 1977, pp. 171–231.

[96] J. Korner and K. Marton, "The comparison of two noisy channels," in *Trans. Keszthely Colloq. Information Theory* (Hungarian National Academy of Sciences, Keszthely, Hungary, Aug. 8–12), pp. 411–423.

[97] _____, "Images of a set via two channels and their role in multi-user communications," *IEEE Trans. Inform. Theory*, vol. IT-23, pp. 751–761, 1977.

[98] _____, "How to encode the modulo-two sum of binary sources," *IEEE Trans. Inform. Theory*, vol. IT-25, pp. 219–221, 1979.

[99] T. Berger and S. Y. Tung, "Encoding of correlated analog sources," in *Proc. 1975 IEEE–USSR Joint Work. Information Theory*. Piscataway, NJ: IEEE Press, Dec. 1975, pp. 7–10.

[100] S. Y. Tung, "Multiterminal rate-distortion theory," Ph.D. dissertation, Cornell Univ., Ithaca, NY, 1977.

[101] M. U. Chang, "Rate-distortion with a fully informed decoder and a partially informed encoder," Ph.D. dissertation, Cornell Univ., Ithaca, NY, 1978.

[102] A. Shohara, "Source coding theorems for information networks," Ph.D. dissertation, Univ. Calif. Los Angeles, Tech. Rep. UCLA-ENG-7445, 1974.

[103] J. K. Omura and K. B. Housewright, "Source coding studies for information networks," in *Proc. IEEE 1977 Int. Conf. Communications* (Chicago, Ill., June 13–15, 1977). New York: IEEE Press, 1997, pp. 237–240.

[104] T. Berger, K. B. Housewright, J. K. Omura, S. Y. Tung, and J. Wolfowitz, "An upper bound on the rate-distortion function for source coding with partial side information at the decoder," *IEEE Trans. Inform. Theory*, vol. IT-25, pp. 664–666, 1979.

[105] A. Sgarro, "Source coding with side information at several decoders," *IEEE Trans. Inform. Theory*, vol. IT-23, pp. 179–182, 1977.

[106] J. Ziv and A. Lempel, "A universal algorithm for sequential data compression," *IEEE Trans. Inform. Theory*, vol. IT-23, pp. 337–343, 1977.

[107] _____, "Compression of individual sequences via variable-rate coding," *IEEE Trans. Inform. Theory*, vol. IT-24, pp. 337–343, 1978.

[108] R. Pasco, "Source coding algorithms for fast data compression," Ph.D. dissertation, Stanford Univ., Stanford, CA, 1976.

[109] J. Rissanen, "Generalized Kraft inequality and arithmetic coding," *IBM J. Res. Develop.*, vol. 20, p. 198–, 1976.

[110] _____, "Universal coding, information, prediction and estimation," *IEEE Trans. Inform. Theory*, vol. IT-30, pp. 629–636, 1984.

[111] F. M. J. Willems, Y. M. Shtarkov, and T. J. Tjalkens, "The context-tree weighting method: Basic properties," *IEEE Trans. Inform. Theory*, vol. 41, pp. 653–664, 1995.

[112] _____, "Context weighting for general finite-context sources," *IEEE Trans. Inform. Theory*, vol. 42, pp. 1514–1520, 1996.

[113] Y. Steinberg and M. Gutman, "An algorithm for source coding subject to a fidelity criterion based on string matching," *IEEE Trans. Inform. Theory*, vol. 39, pp. 877–886, 1993.

[114] Z. Zhang and V. K. Wei, "An on-line universal lossy data compression algorithm by continuous codebook refinement," *IEEE Trans. Inform. Theory*, vol. 42, pp. 803–821, 1996.

[115] _____, "An on-line universal lossy data compression algorithm by continuous codebook refinement, Part II: Optimality for ϕ-mixing source models," *IEEE Trans. Inform. Theory*, vol. 42, pp. 822–836, 1996.

[116] I. Sadeh, "Universal compression algorithms based on approximate string matching," in *Proc. 1995 IEEE Int. Symp. Information Theory* (Whistler, BC, Canada, Sept. 17–22, 1995), p. 84.

[117] E. H. Yang and J. Kieffer, "Simple universal lossy data compression schemes derived from the Lempel–Ziv algorithm," *IEEE Trans. Inform. Theory*, vol. 42, pp. 239–245, 1996.

676

[118] E. H. Yang, Z. Zhang, and T. Berger, "Fixed-slope universal lossy data compression," *IEEE Trans. Inform. Theory*, vol. 43, pp. 1465–1476, 1997.

[119] I. Kontoyiannis, "An implementable lossy version of the Lempel-Ziv algorithm—Part I: Optimality for memoryless sources," NSF Tech. Rep. 99, Dept. Statist., Stanford Univ., Stanford, CA, Apr. 1998.

[120] ——, "Asymptotically optimal lossy Lempel-Ziv coding," presented at IEEE Int. Symp. Information Theory, MIT, Cambridge, MA, Aug. 16–21, 1998.

[121] "A decomposition theorem for binary Markov random fields," *Ann. Probab.*, vol. 15, pp. 1112–1125, 1987.

[122] L. A. Bassalygo and R. L. Dobrushin, "ϵ-entropy of the random field," *Probl. Pered. Inform.*, vol. 23, pp. 3–15, 1987.

[123] C. M. Newman, "Decomposition of binary random fields and zeros of partition functions," *Ann. Probab.*, vol. 15, pp. 1126–1130, 1978.

[124] C. M. Newman and G. A. Baker, "Decomposition of ising model and the mayer expansion," in *Ideas and Methods in Mathematics and Physics,—In Memory of Raphael Hoegh-Krohn (1938–1988)*, S. Albeverio *et al.*, Eds. Cambridge, U.K.: Cambridge Univ. Press, 1991.

[125] T. Berger and Z. Ye, "ϵ-entropy and critical distortion of random fields," *IEEE Trans. Inform. Theory*, vol. 36, pp. 717–725, 1990.

[126] Z. Ye and T. Berger, "A new method to estimate the critical distortion of random fields," *IEEE Trans. Inform. Theory*, vol. 38, pp. 152–157, 1992.

[127] ——, *Information Measures for Discrete Random Fields*. Beijing, China: Chinese Acad. Sci., 1998.

[128] A. H. Kaspi and T. Berger, "Rate-distortion for correlated sources with partially separated encoders," *IEEE Trans. Inform. Theory*, vol. IT-28, pp. 828–840, 1982.

[129] T. Berger and R. W. Yeung, "Multiterminal source encoding with one distortion criterion," *IEEE Trans. Inform. Theory*, vol. 35, pp. 228–236, Mar. 1989.

[130] ——, "Multiterminal source encoding with encoder breakdown," *IEEE Trans. Inform. Theory*, vol. 35, pp. 237–244, 1989.

[131] T. Berger, S. Y. Shen, and Z. Ye, "Some communication problems of random fields," *Int. J. Math. Statist. Sci.*, vol. 1, pp. 47–77, 1992.

[132] Z. Zhang and T. Berger, "Multiple description source coding with no excess marginal rate," *IEEE Trans. Inform. Theory*, vol. 41, pp. 349–357, 1995.

[133] W. E. Equitz and T. M. Cover, "Successive refinement of information," *IEEE Trans. Inform. Theory*, vol. 37, pp. 269–275, 1991. (See also W. E. Equitz and T. M. Cover, "Addendum to 'successive refinement of information'," *IEEE Trans. Inform. Theory*, vol. 39, pp. 1465–1466, 1993.)

[134] T. Berger, Z. Zhang, and H. Viswanathan, "The CEO problem," *IEEE Trans. Inform. Theory*, vol. 42, pp. 887–903, May 1996.

[135] H. Viswanathan and T. Berger, "The quadratic Gaussian CEO problem," *IEEE Trans. Inform. Theory*, vol. 43, pp. 1549–1561, 1997.

[136] Y. Oohama, "The rate distortion function for the quadratic Gaussian CEO problem," *IEEE Trans. Inform. Theory*, vol. 44, pp. 1057–1070, May 1998.

[137] E.-h. Yang, Z. Zhang, and T. Berger, "Fixed-slope universal lossy data compression," *IEEE Trans. Inform. Theory*, vol. 43, pp. 1465–1476, Sept. 1997.

[138] D. L. Neuhoff, R. M. Gray, and L. D. Davisson, "Fixed rate universal block source coding with a fidelity criterion," *IEEE Trans. Inform. Theory*, vol. IT-21, pp. 511–523, 1975.

[139] K. M. Mackenthum Jr. and M. B. Pursley, "Strongly and weakly universal source coding," in *Proc. 1977 Conf. Information Science and Systems* (The Johns Hopkins University, Baltimore, MD, 1977), pp. 286–291.

[140] M. B. Pursley and K. M. Mackenthum Jr., "Variable-rate source coding for classes of sources with generalized alphabets," *IEEE Trans. Inform. Theory*, vol. IT-23, pp. 592–597, 1977.

[141] K. M. Mackenthum Jr. and M. B. Pursley, "Variable-rate universal block source coding subject to a fidelity criterion," *IEEE Trans. Inform. Theory*, vol. IT-24, pp. 349–360, 1978.

[142] H. H. Tan, "Tree coding of discrete-time abstract alphabet stationary block-ergodic sources with a fidelity criterion," *IEEE Trans. Inform. Theory*, vol. IT-22, pp. 671–681, 1976.

[143] J. Ziv, "Coding of sources with unknown statistics—Part II: Distortion relative to a fidelity criterion," *IEEE Trans. Inform. Theory*, vol. IT-18, pp. 389–394, 1972.

[144] T. Hashimoto, "Tree coding of sources and channels," Ph.D. dissertation, Dept. Mech. Eng., Osaka Univ., Toyonaka, Osaka, Japan, 1981.

[145] A. Gersho and A. D. Wyner, "The multiple descriptions problem," presented by A. D. Wyner at the IEEE Information Theory Work., Seven Springs Conf. Ctr., Mt. Kisco, NY, Sept. 1979.

[146] H. S. Witsenhausen, "On source networks with minimal breakdown degradation," *Bell Syst. Tech. J.*, vol. 59, pp. 1083–1087, 1980.

[147] J. K. Wolf, A. D. Wyner, and J. Ziv, "Source coding for multiple descriptions," *Bell Syst. Tech. J.*, vol. 59, pp. 1417–1426, 1980.

[148] L. H. Ozarow, "On the source coding problem with two channels and three receivers," *Bell Syst. Tech. J.*, vol. 59, pp. 1909–1922, 1980.

[149] H. A. Witsenhausen and A. D. Wyner, "Source coding for multiple descriptions II: A binary source," *Bell Syst. Tech. J.*, vol. 60, pp. 2281–2292, 1981.

[150] A. E. Gamal and T. M. Cover, "Achievable rates for multiple descriptions," *IEEE Trans. Inform. Theory*, vol. IT-28, pp. 851–857, 1982.

[151] T. Berger and Z. Zhang, "Minimum breakdown degradation in binary source encoding," *IEEE Trans. Inform. Theory*, vol. IT-29, pp. 807–814, 1983.

[152] R. Ahlswede, "The rate-distortion region for multiple descriptions without excess rate," *IEEE Trans. Inform. Theory*, vol. IT-31, pp. 721–726, 1985.

[153] A. D. Wyner, "The rate-distortion function for source coding with side information at the decoder—II: General sources," *Inform. Contr.*, vol. 38, pp. 60–80, 1978.

[154] H. Yamamoto, "Source coding theory for cascade and branching communication systems," *IEEE Trans. Inform. Theory*, vol. IT-27, pp. 299–308, 1981.

[155] C. Heegard and T. Berger, "Rate distortion when side information may be absent," *IEEE Trans. Inform. Theory*, vol. IT-31, pp. 727–734, 1985.

[156] H. Yamamoto, "Source coding theory for a triangular communication system," *IEEE Trans. Inform. Theory*, vol. 42, pp. 848–853, 1996.

[157] Z. Zhang and T. Berger, "New results in binary multiple descriptions," *IEEE Trans. Inform. Theory*, vol. IT-33, pp. 502–521, July 1987.

[158] K. Rose, "A mapping approach to rate-distortion computation and analysis," *IEEE Trans. Inform. Theory*, vol. 42, pp. 1939–1952, 1996.

[159] S. L. Fix, "Rate-distortion functions for squared error distortion measures," in *Proc. 16th Annu. Allerton Conf. Communication, Control and Computers* (Monticello, IL, 1978).

[160] R. M. Gray, "A new class of lower bounds to information rates of stationary sources via conditional rate-distortion functions," *IEEE Trans. Inform. Theory*, vol. IT-19, pp. 480–489, 1973.

[161] B. M. Leiner, "Rate-distortion theory for sources with side information," Ph.D. dissertation, Stanford Univ., Stanford, CA, Aug. 1973.

[162] B. M. Leiner and R. M. Gray, "Rate-distortion for ergodic sources with side information," *IEEE Trans. Inform. Theory*, vol. IT-20, pp. 672–675, 1974.

[163] R. M. Gray, D. L. Neuhoff, and J. K. Omura, "Process definitions of distortion rate functions and source coding theorems," *IEEE Trans. Inform. Theory*, vol. IT-21, pp. 524–532, 1975.

[164] R. M. Gray, D. L. Neuhoff, and D. S. Ornstein, "Nonblock source coding with a fidelity criterion," *Ann. Probab.*, vol. 3, pp. 478–491, 1975.

[165] R. M. Gray, D. S. Ornstein, and R. L. Dobrushin, "Block synchronization, sliding-block coding, invulnerable sources and zero error codes for discrete noisy channels," *Ann. Probab.*, vol. 8, pp. 639–674, 1975.

[166] N. Ahmed and K. R. Rao, *Orthogonal Transforms for Digital Signal Processing*. New York: Springer-Verlag, 1975.

[167] T. C. Ancheta Jr., "Joint source channel coding," Ph.D. dissertation, Dept. Elec. Eng., Univ. Notre Dame, Notre Dame, IN, Aug. 1977.

[168] J. B. Anderson and J. B. Bodie, "Tree encoding of speech," *IEEE Trans. Inform. Theory*, vol. IT-21, pp. 379–387, July 1975.

[169] J. B. Anderson, "Recent advances in sequential encoding of analog waveforms," in *Conf. Rec., IEEE Nat. Telecommunications Conf.*, 1978, pp. 19.4.1–19.4.5.

[170] B. S. Atal and M. R. Schroeder, "Predictive coding of speech signals," in *WESCON Tech. Papers*, 1968, paper 8/2.

[171] ——, "Adaptive predictive coding of speech signals," *Bell Syst. Tech. J.*, vol. 49, pp. 1973–1986, Oct. 1970.

[172] B. S. Atal and S. L. Hanauer, "Speech analysis and synthesis by linear prediction of the speech wave," *J. Acoust. Soc. Amer.*, vol. 50, pp. 637–655, 1971.

[173] B. S. Atal and J. R. Remde, "A new model of LPC excitation for producing natural sounding speech at low bit rates," in *Proc. IEEE Int. Conf. Acoustics, Speech and Signal Processing*, 1982, pp. 614–617.

[174] B. S. Atal and M. R. Schroeder, "Stochastic coding of speech at very low bit rates," in *Proc. IEEE Int. Conf. Communications*, 1984, pp. 1610–1613.

[175] D. W. Becker and A. J. Viterbi, "Speech digitization and compression by adaptive predictive coding with delayed decision," in *Conf. Rec. Nat. Telecommunications Conf.*, 1975, pp. 46-18–46-23.

[176] W. Chen, C. H. Smith, and S. Fralick, "A fast computational algorithm for the discrete cosine transform," *IEEE Trans. Commun.*, vol. COM-25, pp. 1004–1009, Sept. 1977.

[177] W.-H. Chen and W. K. Pratt, "Scene adaptive coder," *IEEE Trans. Commun.*, vol. COM-32, pp. 225–232, Mar. 1984.

[178] L. Chiariglione, "MPEG and multimedia communications," *IEEE Trans. Circuits Syst. Video Technol.*, vol. 7, pp. 5–18, Feb. 1997.

[179] R. V. Cox, "Three new speech coders from the ITU cover a range of applications," *IEEE Commun. Mag.*, vol. 35, pp. 40–47, Sept. 1997.

[180] C. C. Cutler, "Differential quantization of communications," U.S. Patent 2 605 361, July 29, 1952.

[181] ———, "Delayed encoding: Stabilizer for adaptive coders," *IEEE Trans. Commun.*, vol. COM-19, pp. 898–907, Dec. 1971.

[182] L. D. Davisson, "Rate-distortion theory and application," *Proc. IEEE*, vol. 60, pp. 800–808, July 1972.

[183] L. D. Davisson and R. M. Gray, *Data Compression*. Dowden: Hutchinson & Ross, 1976.

[184] T. Ebrahimi and M. Kunt, "Visual data compression for multimedia applications," *Proc. IEEE*, vol. 86, pp. 1109–1125, June 1998.

[185] S. N. Efstratiadis and M. G. Strintizis, "Hierarchical prioritized predictive image coding," in *Proc. Int. Conf. Image Processing (ICIP '96)* (Switzerland, Sept. 1996), pp. 189–192.

[186] P. Elias, "Predictive coding—Parts I and II," *IRE Trans. Inform. Theory*, vol. IT-1, pp. 16–33, Mar. 1955.

[187] N. Farvardin and J. W. Modestino, "Optimal quantizer performance for a class of non-Gaussian memoryless sources," *IEEE Trans. Inform. Theory*, vol. 30, pp. 485–497, 1984.

[188] T. R. Fischer, J. D. Gibson, and B. Koo, "Estimation and noisy source coding," *IEEE Trans. Acoust., Speech, Signal Processing*, vol. 38, pp. 23–34, Jan. 1990.

[189] R. D. LeGall, "MPEG: A video compression standard for multimedia applications," *Commun. Assoc. Comput. Mach.*, vol. 34, pp. 60–64, Apr. 1991.

[190] R. G. Gallager, "Tree encoding for symmetric sources with a distortion measure," *IEEE Trans. Inform. Theory*, vol. IT-20, pp. 65–76, Jan. 1974.

[191] A. Gersho and R. M. Gray, *Vector Quantization and Signal Compression*. Boston, MA: Kluwer, 1992.

[192] I. A. Gerson and M. A. Jasiuk, "Vector sum excited linear prediction (VSELP) speech coding at 8 kbps," in *Proc. IEEE Int. Conf. Acoustics, Speech and Signal Processing*, Apr. 1994, pp. 461–464.

[193] J. D. Gibson, B. Koo, and S. D. Gray, "Filtering of colored noise for speech enhancement and coding," *IEEE Trans. Signal Processing*, vol. 39, pp. 1732–1742, Aug. 1991.

[194] J. D. Gibson, T. Berger, T. Lookabaugh, D. Lindbergh, and R. L. Baker, *Digital Compression for Multimedia: Principles and Standards*. San Francisco, CA: Morgan-Kaufmann, 1998.

[195] R. M. Gray, *Source Coding Theory*. Norwell, MA: Kluwer, 1990.

[196] R. M. Gray and D. L. Neuhoff, "Quantization," *IEEE Trans. Inform. Theory*, this issue, pp. 2325–2383.

[197] Y. Huang, N. P. Galatsanos, and H. M. Dreizen, "Priority DCT coding for image sequences," in *Proc. IEEE Int. Conf. Acoustics, Speech, and Signal Processing* (Toronto, Ont., Canada, 1991), pp. 2629–2632.

[198] Y. Huang, H. M. Dreizen, and N. P. Galatsanos, "Prioritized DCT for compression and progressive transmission of images," *IEEE Trans. Image Processing*, vol. 1, pp. 477–487, Oct. 1992.

[199] J. D. Irwin and J. B. O'Neal, "The design of optimum DPCM (Differential Pulse Code Modulation) encoding systems via the Kalman predictor," *1968 JACC Preprints*, pp. 130–136, 1968.

[200] N. S. Jayant and P. Noll, *Digital Coding of Waveforms*. Englewood Cliffs, NJ: Prentice-Hall, 1984.

[201] N. S. Jayant, Ed., *Waveform Quantization and Coding*. New York: IEEE Press, 1976.

[202] A. M. Kondoz, *Digital Speech: Coding for Low Bit Rate Communications Systems*. Chichester, U.K.: Wiley, 1994.

[203] J. Li and C.-C. J. Kuo, "An embedded DCT approach to progressive image compression," in *Proc. Int. Conf. Image Processing (ICIP '96)* (Switzerland, Sept. 1996), pp. 201–204.

[204] Y. Linde, A. Buzo, and R. M. Gray, "An algorithm for vector quantizer design," *IEEE Trans. Commun.*, vol. COM-28, pp. 84–95, Jan. 1980.

[205] S. P. Lloyd, "Least squares quantization in PCM," unpublished, Bell Lab. Tech. Note, 1957.

[206] D. T. Magill, "Adaptive speech compression for packet communication systems," in *Conf. Rec. Nat. Telecommunications Conf.*, Nov. 1973, pp. 29D-1–29D-5.

[207] J. L. Massey, "Joint source channel coding," in *Communication Systems and Random Process Theory*, J. K. Skwirzynski, Ed. Amsterdam, The Netherlands: Sijthoff and Nordhoff, 1978, pp. 279–293.

[208] B. Mazor and W. A. Pearlman, "A trellis code construction and coding theorem for stationary Gaussian sources," *IEEE Trans. Inform. Theory*, vol. IT-29, pp. 924–930, Nov. 1983.

[209] ———, "A tree coding theorem for stationary Gaussian sources and the squared-error distortion measure," *IEEE Trans. Inform. Theory*, vol. IT-32, pp. 156–165, Mar. 1986.

[210] S. McClellan and J. D. Gibson, "Variable-rate CELP based on subband flatness," *IEEE Trans. Speech Audio Processing*, vol. 5, pp. 120–130, Mar. 1997.

[211] J. W. Modestino and V. Bhaskaran, "Robust two-dimensional tree encoding of images," *IEEE Trans. Commun.*, vol. COM-29, pp. 1786–1798, Dec. 1981.

[212] J. W. Modestino, V. Bhaskaran, and J. B. Anderson, "Tree encoding of images in the presence of channel errors," *IEEE Trans. Inform. Theory*, vol. IT-27, pp. 667–697, Nov. 1981.

[213] P. Noll, "MPEG digital audio coding," *IEEE Signal Processing Mag.*, vol. 14, pp. 59–81, Sept. 1997.

[214] L. V. Oliveira and A. Alcaim, "Identification of dominant coefficients in DCT image coders using weighted vector quantization," in *Proc. 1st Int. Conf. Image Processing (ICIP '94)* (Austin, TX, Nov. 1994), vol. 1, pp. 110–113.

[215] B. M. Oliver, "Efficient coding," *Bell Syst. Tech. J.*, vol. 31, pp. 724–750, July 1952.

[216] J. B. O'Neal Jr., "A bound on signal-to-quantizing noise ratios for digital encoding systems," *Proc. IEEE*, vol. 55, pp. 287–292, Mar. 1967.

[217] W. A. Pearlman and P. Jakatdar, "A transform tree code for stationary Gaussian sources," *IEEE Trans. Inform. Theory*, vol. IT-21, pp. 761–768, 1985.

[218] D. E. Pearson, "A realistic model for visual communication systems," *Proc. IEEE*, vol. 55, pp. 380–389, Mar. 1967.

[219] W. B. Pennebaker and J. L. Mitchell, *JPEG Still Image Data Compression Standard*. New York: Van Nostrand Reinhold, 1988.

[220] N. Phamdo and N. Farvardin, "Optimal detection of discrete Markov sources over discrete memoryless channels—Applications to combined source-channel coding," *IEEE Trans. Inform. Theory*, vol. 40, pp. 186–193, Jan. 1994.

[221] J. R. Pierce, "The early days of information theory," *IEEE Trans. Inform. Theory*, vol. IT-19, pp. 3–8, Jan. 1973.

[222] W. K. Pratt, *Digital Image Processing*. New York: Wiley, 1978.

[223] K. Rao and P. Yip, *Discrete Cosine Transform*. Boston, MA: Academic, 1990.

[224] K. Ramchandran and M. Vetterli, "Rate-distortion optimal fast thresholding with complete JPEG/MPEG decoder compatibility," *IEEE Trans. Image Processing*, vol. 3, pp. 700–704, Sept. 1994.

[225] ———, "Best wavelet packet bases in a rate-distortion sense," *IEEE Trans. Image Processing*, vol. 2, pp. 160–175, Apr. 1993.

[226] A. Said and W. A. Pearlman, "A new, fast, and efficient image codec based on set partitioning in hierarchical trees," *IEEE Trans. Circuits Syst. Video Technol.*, vol. 6, pp. 243–250, June 1996.

[227] D. J. Sakrison, "A geometric treatment of the source encoding of a Gaussian random variable," *IEEE Trans. Inform. Theory*, vol. IT-14, pp. 481–486, 1968.

[228] ———, "Image coding applications of vision models," in *Image Transmission Techniques*, W. K. Pratt, Ed. New York: Academic, 1979, pp. 21–51.

[229] R. Salami *et al.*, "Design and description of CS-ACELP: A toll quality 8 kb/s speech coder," *IEEE Trans. Speech Audio Processing*, vol. 6, pp. 116–130, Mar. 1998.

[230] R. Salami *et al.*, "ITU-T G.729 Annex A: Reduced complexity 8 kb/s CS-ACELP codec for digital simultaneous voice and data," *IEEE Commun. Mag.*, vol. 35, pp. 56–63, Sept. 1997.

[231] K. Sayood *et al.*, "A constrained joint source/channel coder design," *IEEE J. Select. Areas Commun.*, vol. 12, pp. 1584–1593, Dec. 1994.

[232] K. Sayood, *Introduction to Data Compression*. San Francisco, CA: Morgan-Kaufmann, 1996.

[233] J. M. Shapiro, "Embedded image coding using zerotrees of wavelet coefficients," *IEEE Trans. Signal Processing*, vol. 41, pp. 3445–3462, Dec. 1993.

[234] Y. Shoham and A. Gersho, "Efficient bit allocation for an arbitrary set of quantizers," *IEEE Trans. Acoust., Speech, Signal Processing*, vol. 36, pp. 1445–1453, Sept. 1988.

[235] A. S. Spanias, "Speech coding: A tutorial review," *Proc. IEEE*, vol. 82, pp. 1541–1582, Oct. 1994.

[236] L. C. Stewart, "Trellis data compression," Ph.D. dissertation, Dept. Elec. Eng., Stanford Univ., Stanford, CA, June 1981.

[237] L. C. Stewart, R. M. Gray, and Y. Linde, "The design of trellis waveform coders," *IEEE Trans. Commun.*, vol. COM-30, pp. 702–710, Apr. 1982.

[238] D. Taubman and A. Zakhor, "Multirate 3-D subband coding of video," *IEEE Trans. Image Processing*, vol. 3, pp. 572–588, Sept. 1994.

[239] A. G. Tescher and R. V. Cox, "Image coding: Variable rate differential pulse modulation through fixed rate channel," *Proc. Soc. Photo-Optical Instr. Eng.*, vol. 119, pp. 147–154, Aug. 1977.

[240] A. G. Tescher, "Transform image coding," in *Advances in Electronics and Electron Physics*. New York: Academic, 1979, pp. 113–155.

[241] V. R. Viswanathan *et al.*, "Variable frame rate transmission: A review of methodology and application to narrowband LPC speech coding," *IEEE*

678

Trans. Commun., vol. COM-30, pp. 674–686, Apr. 1982.

[242] A. Viterbi and J. Omura, "Trellis encoding of memoryless discrete-time sources with a fidelity criterion," *IEEE Trans. Inform. Theory*, vol. IT-20, pp. 325–332, May 1974.

[243] G. K. Wallace, "The JPEG still picture compression standard," *Commun. Assoc. Comput. Mach.*, vol. 34, pp. 30–44, Apr. 1991.

[244] Z. Wang, "Reconsideration of a fast computational algorithm for the discrete cosine transform," *IEEE Trans. Commun.*, vol. COM-31, pp. 121–123, Jan. 1983.

[245] S. G. Wilson and S. Husain, "Adaptive tree encoding of speech at 8000 bps with a frequency-weighted error criterion," *IEEE Trans. Commun.*, vol. COM-27, pp. 165–170, Jan. 1979.

[246] P. A. Wintz and A. J. Kurtenbach, "Waveform error control in PCM telemetry," *IEEE Trans. Inform. Theory*, vol. IT-14, pp. 640–661, Sept. 1968.

[247] J. W. Woods, Ed., *Subband Image Coding*. New York: Kluwer, 1991.

[248] J. M. Wozencraft and I. M. Jacobs, *Principles of Communication Engineering*. New York: Wiley, 1965.

[249] Z. Xiong, O. G. Guleryuz, and M. T. Orchard, "A DCT-based embedded image coder," *IEEE Signal Processing Lett.*, vol. 3, pp. 289–290, Nov. 1996.

[250] R. Zelinski and P. Noll, "Adaptive transform coding of speech signals," *IEEE Trans. Acoust., Speech, Signal Processing*, vol. ASSP-25, pp. 299–309, Aug. 1977.

[251] ——, "Approaches to adaptive transform speech coding at low bit rate," *IEEE Trans. Acoust., Speech, Signal Processing*, vol. ASSP-27, pp. 89–95, Feb. 1979.

[252] T. M. Cover and J. A. Thomas, *Elements of Information Theory*. New York: Wiley, 1991.

[253] M. W. Marcellin, T. R. Fischer, and J. D. Gibson, "Predictive trellis coded quantization of speech," *IEEE Trans. Acoust., Speech Signal Processing*, vol. 38, pp. 46–55, Jan. 1990.

[254] P. J. Sementilli, A. Bilgin, J. H. Kasner, and M. W. Marcellin, "Wavelet TCQ: Submission to JPEG-2000 (keynote address)," in *Proc. SPIE* (San Diego, CA, July 1998), vol. 3460.

[255] P. Noll, "MPEG digital audio coding," *IEEE Signal Processing Mag.*, vol. 14, pp. 59–81, Sept. 1997.

[256] T. Sikora, "MPEG digital video-coding standards," *IEEE Signal Processing Mag.*, vol. 14, pp. 82–100, Sept. 1997.

[257] R. V. Cox, B. G. Haskell, Y. LeCun, B. Shahraray, and L. Rabiner, "On the applications of multimedia processing to communications," *Proc. IEEE*, vol. 86, pp. 755–824, May 1998.

[258] M. Vetterli and J. Kovacevic, *Wavelets and Subband Coding*. Englewood Cliffs, NJ: Prentice-Hall, 1995.

[259] B. M. Oliver, J. R. Pierce, and C. E. Shannon, "The philosophy of PCM," *Proc. IRE*, vol. 36, pp. 1324–1331, 1948.

[260] H. Dudley, "The vocoder," *Bell Lab. Rec.*, vol. 17, pp. 1221–1226, 1939.

[261] H. C. Woo and J. D. Gibson, "Low delay tree coding of speech at 8 kbits/s," *IEEE Trans. Speech Audio Processing*, vol. 2, pp. 361–370, July 1994.

[262] V. Koshelev, "Multilevel source coding and data-transmission theorem," in *Proc. VII All-Union Conf. Theory of Coding and Data Transmission* (Vilnius, USSR, 1978), pt. 1, pp. 85–92.

[263] ——, "Hierarchical coding of discrete sources," *Probl. Pered. Inform.*, vol. 16, pp. 31–49, 1980.

[264] ——, "An evaluation of the average distortion for discrete scheme of sequential approximation," *Probl. Pered. Inform.*, vol. 17, pp. 20–33, 1981.

[265] B. Rimoldi, "Successive refinement of information: Characterization of the achievable rates," *IEEE Trans. Inform. Theory*, vol. 40, pp. 253–259, Jan. 1994.

[266] V. Vaishampayan, J.-C. Batallo, and A. R. Calderbank, "On reducing granular distortion in multiple description quantization," presented at the 1998 IEEE Int. Symp. Information Theory, MIT, Cambridge, MA, Aug. 16–21, 1998.

[267] V. K. Goyal, J. Kovacevic, and M. Vetterli, "Multiple description transform coding: Robustness to erasures using tight frame expansions," presented at the 1998 IEEE Int. Symp. Information Theory, MIT, Cambridge, MA, Aug. 16–21, 1998.

Quantum Information Theory

Charles H. Bennett and Peter W. Shor

(Invited Paper)

Abstract—**We survey the field of quantum information theory. In particular, we discuss the fundamentals of the field, source coding, quantum error-correcting codes, capacities of quantum channels, measures of entanglement, and quantum cryptography.**

Index Terms— **Entanglement, quantum cryptography, quantum error-correcting codes, quantum information, quantum source coding.**

I. INTRODUCTION

RECENTLY, the historic connection between information and physics has been revitalized, as the methods of information and computation theory have been extended to treat the transmission and processing of intact quantum states, and the interaction of such "quantum information" with traditional "classical" information. Although many of the quantum results are similar to their classical analogs, there are notable differences. This new research has the potential to shed light both on quantum physics and on classical information theory.

In retrospect, this development seems somewhat belated, since quantum mechanics has long been thought to underlie all classical processes. But until recently, information itself had largely been thought of in classical terms, with quantum mechanics playing a supporting role of helping design the equipment used to process it, setting limits on the rate at which it could be sent through certain quantum channels. Now we know that a fully quantum theory of information and information processing offers, among other benefits, a brand of cryptography whose security rests on fundamental physics, and a reasonable hope of constructing quantum computers that could dramatically speed up the solution of certain mathematical problems. These feats depend on distinctively quantum properties such as uncertainty, interference, and entanglement.

At a more fundamental level, it has become clear that an information theory based on quantum principles extends and completes classical information theory, somewhat as complex numbers extend and complete the reals. The new theory includes quantum generalizations of classical notions such as sources, channels, and codes, as well as two complementary, quantifiable kinds of information—classical information and quantum entanglement. Classical information can be copied freely, but can only be transmitted forward in time, to a receiver in the sender's forward light cone. Entanglement, by contrast, cannot be copied, but can connect any two points in space–time. Conventional data-processing operations destroy entanglement, but quantum operations can create it, preserve it, and use it for various purposes, notably speeding up certain computations and assisting in the transmission of classical data ("quantum superdense coding") or intact quantum states ("quantum teleportation") from a sender to a receiver.

Any means, such as an optical fiber, for delivering quantum systems more or less intact from one place to another, may be viewed as a quantum channel. Unlike classical channels, such channels have three distinct capacities: a capacity C for transmitting classical data, a typically lower capacity Q for transmitting intact quantum states, and a third capacity Q_2, often between C and Q, for transmitting intact quantum states with the assistance of a two-way classical side-channel between sender and receiver.

How, then, does quantum information, and the operations that can be performed on it, differ from conventional digital data and data-processing operations? A classical bit (e.g., a memory element or wire carrying a binary signal) is generally a system containing many atoms, and is described by one or more continuous parameters such as voltages. Within this parameter space two well-separated regions are chosen by the designer to represent 0 and 1, and signals are periodically restored toward these standard regions to prevent them from drifting away due to environmental perturbations, manufacturing defects, etc. An n-bit memory can exist in any of 2^n logical states, labeled 000..0 to 111..1. Besides storing binary data, classical computers manipulate it, a sequence of Boolean operations (for example, NOT and AND) acting on the bits one or two at a time being sufficient to realize any deterministic transformation.

A quantum bit, or "qubit," by contrast is typically a microscopic system, such as an atom or nuclear spin or polarized photon. The Boolean states 0 and 1 are represented by a fixed pair of reliably distinguishable states of the qubit (for example, horizontal and vertical polarizations: $|0\rangle = \leftrightarrow$, $|1\rangle = \updownarrow$). A qubit can also exist in a continuum of intermediate states, or "superpositions," represented mathematically as unit vectors in a two-dimensional complex vector space (the "Hilbert space" $\mathcal{H}_2$) spanned by the basis vectors $|0\rangle$ and $|1\rangle$. For photons, these intermediate states correspond to other polarizations, for example,

$$\nearrow = \sqrt{\tfrac{1}{2}} \left(|0\rangle + |1\rangle \right)$$

$$\searrow = \sqrt{\tfrac{1}{2}} \left(|0\rangle - |1\rangle \right)$$

Manuscript received January 4, 1998; revised June 2, 1998.

C. H. Bennett is with the IBM Research Division, T. J. Watson Research Center, Yorktown Heights, NY 10598 USA (e-mail: bennetc@watson.ibm.com).

P. W. Shor is with the AT&T Labs–Research, Florham Park, NJ 07932 USA (e-mail: shor@research.att.com).

Publisher Item Identifier S 0018-9448(98)06316-0.

and

$$\curvearrowright = \sqrt{\frac{1}{2}}\left(|0\rangle + i|1\rangle\right)$$

(right circular polarization). Unlike the intermediate states of a classical bit (e.g., voltages between the standard 0 and 1 values), these intermediate states cannot be reliably distinguished, even in principle, from the basis states. With regard to any measurement which distinguishes the states $|0\rangle$ and $|1\rangle$, the superposition $|\psi\rangle = \psi_0|0\rangle + \psi_1|1\rangle$ behaves like $|0\rangle$ with probability $|\psi_0|^2$ and like $|1\rangle$ with probability $|\psi_1|^2$. More generally, two quantum states are reliably distinguishable if and only if their vector representations are orthogonal; thus $\leftrightarrow$ and $\updownarrow$ are reliably distinguishable by one type of measurement, and $\nearrow$ and $\nwarrow$ by another, but no measurement can reliably distinguish $\leftrightarrow$ from $\nearrow$. Multiplying a state vector by an arbitrary phase factor $e^{i\theta}$ does not change its physical significance: thus although they are usually represented by unit vectors, quantum states are more properly identified with *rays*, a ray being the equivalence class of a vector under multiplication by a complex constant.

It is convenient to use the so-called bracket or bra-ket notation, in which the inner product between two d-dimensional vectors $|\psi\rangle$ and $|\phi\rangle$ is denoted

$$\langle\psi|\phi\rangle = \sum_{x=1}^{d} \psi_x^* \phi_x$$

where the asterisk denotes complex conjugation. This may be thought of as matrix product of the row vector $\langle\psi| = (\psi_1^*, \cdots, \psi_d^*)$, by a column vector

$$|\phi\rangle = \begin{pmatrix} \phi_1 \\ \vdots \\ \phi_d \end{pmatrix}$$

where for any standard column (or "ket") vector $|\psi\rangle$, its row (or "bra") representation $\langle\psi|$ is obtained by transposing and taking the complex conjugate.

A pair of qubits (for example, two photons in different locations) is capable of existing in four basis states, $|00\rangle$, $|01\rangle$, $|10\rangle$, and $|11\rangle$, as well as all possible superpositions of them. States of a pair of qubits thus lie in a four-dimensional Hilbert space. This space contains states like

$$\sqrt{\frac{1}{2}}\left(|00\rangle + |01\rangle\right) = \sqrt{\frac{1}{2}}|0\rangle(|0\rangle + |1\rangle) = \leftrightarrow \nearrow$$

which can be interpreted in terms of individual polarizations for the two photons, as well as "entangled" states, i.e., states like

$$\sqrt{\frac{1}{2}}\left(|00\rangle + |11\rangle\right)$$

in which neither photon by itself has a definite state, even though the pair together does.

More generally, where a string of n classical bits could exist in any of 2^n Boolean states $x = 000\cdots0$ through $111\cdots1$, a string of n qubits can exist in any state of the form

$$\Psi = \sum_{x=00\cdots0}^{11\cdots1} \psi_x|x\rangle \tag{1}$$

where the ψ_x are complex numbers such that $\sum_x |\psi_x|^2 = 1$. In other words, a quantum state of n qubits is represented by a complex unit vector Ψ (more properly a ray, since multiplying Ψ by a phase factor does not change its physical meaning) in the 2^n-dimensional Hilbert space $\mathcal{H}^{2^n} = (\mathcal{H}_2)^n$, defined as the tensor product of n copies of the two-dimensional Hilbert space representing quantum states of a single qubit. The exponentially large dimensionality of this space distinguishes quantum computers from classical analog computers, whose state is described by a number of parameters that grows only linearly with the size of the system. This is because classical systems, whether digital or analog, can be completely described by separately describing the state of each part. The vast majority of quantum states, by contrast, are entangled, and admit no such description. The ability to preserve and manipulate entangled states is the distinguishing feature of quantum computers, responsible both for their power and for the difficulty of building them.

An isolated quantum system evolves in such a way as to preserve superpositions and distinguishability; mathematically, such evolution is a unitary (i.e., linear and inner-product-conserving) transformation, the Hilbert-space analog of rigid rotation in Euclidean space. Unitary evolution and superposition are the central principles of quantum mechanics.

Just as any classical computation can be expressed as a sequence of one- and two-bit operations (e.g., NOT and AND gates), any quantum computation can be expressed as a sequence of one- and two-qubit quantum gates, i.e., unitary operations acting on one or two qubits at a time [1] (cf. Fig. 1). The most general one-qubit gate is described by a 2×2 unitary matrix[1] $\begin{pmatrix} \alpha & \gamma \\ \beta & \delta \end{pmatrix}$ mapping $|0\rangle$ to $\alpha|0\rangle + \beta|1\rangle$ and $|1\rangle$ to $\gamma|0\rangle + \delta|1\rangle$. One-qubit gates are easily implementable physically, e.g., by quarter- and half-wave plates acting on polarized photons, or by radio-frequency tipping pulses acting on nuclear spins in a magnetic field.

The standard two-qubit gate is the controlled-NOT or XOR gate, which flips its second (or "target") input if its first ("control") input is $|1\rangle$ and does nothing if the first input is $|0\rangle$. In other words, it interchanges $|10\rangle$ and $|11\rangle$ while leaving $|00\rangle$ and $|01\rangle$ unchanged. The XOR gate is represented by the 4×4 unitary matrix

$$\begin{pmatrix} 1 & 0 & 0 & 0 \\ 0 & 1 & 0 & 0 \\ 0 & 0 & 0 & 1 \\ 0 & 0 & 1 & 0 \end{pmatrix}.$$

Unlike one-qubit gates, two-qubit gates are difficult to realize in the laboratory, because they require two separate quantum information carriers to be brought into strong and controlled interaction. The XOR gate, together with the set of one-bit gates, form a universal set of primitives for quantum computation; that is, any quantum computation can be performed using just this set of gates without an undue increase in the number of gates used [1].

[1] A complex matrix is called unitary and represents a unitary transformation, iff its rows are orthogonal unit vectors. The inverse of any unitary matrix U is given by its *adjoint*, or conjugate transpose $U^\dagger$.

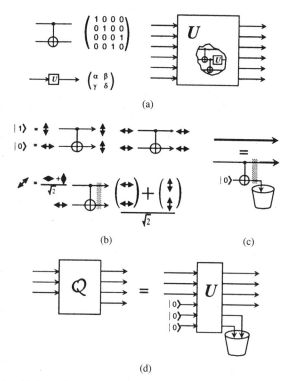

(a)

(b)   (c)

(d)

Fig. 1.   (a) Any unitary operation U on quantum data can be synthesized from the two-qubit XOR gate and one-qubit unitary operations (U). (b) The XOR can clone Boolean-valued inputs, but if one attempts to clone intermediate superposition, an entangled state (shading) results instead. (c) A classical wire (thick line) conducts 0 and 1 faithfully but not superpositions or entangled states. It may be defined as a quantum wire that interacts (via an XOR) with an ancillary 0 qubit which is then discarded. (d) The most general treatment, or superoperator, that can be applied to quantum data is a unitary interaction with one or more 0 qubits, followed by discarding some of the qubits. Superoperators are typically irreversible.

The XOR gate is a prototype interaction between two quantum systems, and illustrates several key features of quantum information, in particular the impossibility of "cloning" an unknown quantum state, and the way interaction produces entanglement. If the XOR is applied to Boolean data in which the second qubit is 0 and the first is 0 or 1 (cf. Fig. 1(b)) the effect is to leave the first qubit unchanged while the second becomes a copy of it: $U_{\mathrm{XOR}}|x, 0\rangle = |x, x\rangle$ for $x = 0$ or 1. One might suppose that the XOR operation could also be used to copy superpositions, such as $|\psi\rangle = \alpha|0\rangle + \beta|1\rangle$, so that $U_{\mathrm{XOR}}|\psi, 0\rangle$ would yield $|\psi, \psi\rangle$, but this is not so. The unitarity of quantum evolution requires that a superposition of input states evolve to a corresponding superposition of outputs. Thus the result of applying U_{XOR} to $|\psi, 0\rangle$ must be $\alpha|0, 0\rangle + \beta|1, 1\rangle$, an entangled state in which neither output qubit alone has definite state. If one of the entangled output qubits is lost (e.g., discarded, or allowed to escape into the environment), the other thenceforth behaves as if it had acquired a random classical value 0 (with probability $|\alpha|^2$) or 1 (with probability $|\beta|^2$). Unless the lost output is brought back into play, all record of the original superposition $|\psi\rangle$ will have been lost. This behavior is characteristic not only of the XOR gate but of unitary interactions generally: their typical effect is to map most unentangled initial states of the interacting systems into entangled final states, which from the viewpoint of either system alone causes an unpredictable disturbance.

Since quantum physics underlies classical, there should be a way to represent classical data and operations within the quantum formalism. If a classical bit is a qubit having the value $|0\rangle$ or $|1\rangle$, a classical wire should be a wire that conducts $|0\rangle$ and $|1\rangle$ reliably, but not superpositions. This can be implemented using the XOR gate as described above, with an initial $|0\rangle$ in the target position which is later discarded (Fig. 1(c)). In other words, from the viewpoint of quantum information, classical communication is an irreversible process in which the signal interacts enroute with an environment or eavesdropper in such a way that Boolean signals pass through undisturbed, but other states become entangled with the environment. If the environment is lost or discarded, the surviving signal behaves as if it had irreversibly collapsed onto one of the Boolean states. Having defined a classical wire, we can then go on to define a classical gate as a quantum gate with classical wires on its inputs and outputs. The classical wire of Fig. 1(c) is an example of quantum information processing in an open system. Any processing that can be applied to quantum data, including unitary processing as a special case, can be described (Fig. 1(d)) as a unitary interaction of the quantum data with some *ancillary qubits*, initially in a standard $|0\rangle$ state, followed by discarding some of the qubits. Such a general quantum data processing operation (also called a trace-preserving completely positive map or superoperator [47], [64]) can therefore have an output Hilbert space larger or smaller than its input space (for unitary operations, the input and output Hilbert spaces are, of course, equidimensional).

Paradoxically, entangling interactions with the environment are thought to be the main reason why the macroscopic world seems to behave classically and not quantum-mechanically [74]. Macroscopically different states, e.g., the different charge states representing 0 and 1 in a VLSI memory cell, interact so strongly with their environment that information rapidly leaks out as to which state the cell is in. Therefore, even if it were possible to prepare the cell in superposition of 0 and 1, the superposition would rapidly evolve into a complex entangled state involving the environment, which from the viewpoint of the memory cell would appear as a statistical mixture, rather than a superposition, of the two classical values. This spontaneous decay of superpositions into mixtures is called decoherence.

The quantum states we have been talking about so far, identified with rays in Hilbert space, are called *pure states*. They represent situations of minimal ignorance, in which, in principle, there is nothing more to be known about the system. Pure states are fundamental in that the quantum mechanics of a closed system can be completely described as a unitary evolution of pure states in an appropriately dimensioned Hilbert space, without need of further notions. However, a very useful notion, the *mixed state* has been introduced to deal with situations of greater ignorance, in particular

- an ensemble $\mathcal{E}$ in which the system in question may be in any of several pure states $|\psi_1\rangle$, $|\psi_2\rangle \cdots$, with specified probabilities $p_1, p_2 \cdots$;
- a situation in which the system in question (call it A) is part of larger system (call it AB), which itself is in an entangled pure state Ψ.

In open systems, a pure state may naturally evolve into a mixed state (which can also be described as a pure state of a larger system comprising the original system and its environment). Mathematically, a mixed state is represented by a positive-semidefinite, self-adjoint *density matrix* ρ, having unit trace, and being defined in the first situation by

$$\rho = \sum_i p_i |\psi_i\rangle\langle\psi_i| \qquad (2)$$

and in the second situation by

$$\rho = \mathrm{Tr}_B |\Psi\rangle\langle\Psi|. \qquad (3)$$

Here Tr_B denotes a partial trace over the indices of the B subsystem. A pure state ψ is represented in the density-matrix formalism by the rank-one projection matrix $|\psi\rangle\langle\psi|$.

It is evident, in the first situation, that infinitely many different ensembles can give rise to the same density matrix. For example, the density matrix

$$\begin{pmatrix} \frac{1}{2} & 0 \\ 0 & \frac{1}{2} \end{pmatrix}$$

may be viewed as an equal mixture of the pure states $|0\rangle$ and $|1\rangle$, or as an equal mixture of $(|0\rangle + |1\rangle)/\sqrt{2}$ and $(|0\rangle - |1\rangle)/\sqrt{2}$, or indeed as any other equal mixture of two orthogonal single-qubit pure states. Similarly, in the second situation, it is evident that infinitely many different pure states Ψ of the AB system can give rise to the same density matrix ρ for the A subsystem. One may therefore wonder in what sense a density matrix is an adequate description of a statistical ensemble of pure states, or of part of a larger system in a pure entangled state. The answer is that the density matrix ρ captures all and only that information that can be obtained by an observer allowed to examine infinitely many states sampled from the ensemble $\mathcal{E}$, or given infinitely many opportunities to examine part A of an AB system prepared in entangled pure state Ψ. This follows from the elementary fact that for any test vector ϕ, if a specimen drawn from ensemble $\mathcal{E} = \{\psi_i, p_i\}$ is tested for whether it is in state ϕ, the probability of a positive outcome is

$$\sum_i p_i |\langle\psi|\phi\rangle|^2 = \mathrm{Tr}\,(\rho|\phi\rangle\langle\phi|).$$

Similarly, for any test state ϕ of the A subsystem, the probability that an entangled state of the AB system having ρ as its partial trace will give a positive outcome is simply $\mathrm{Tr}\,(\rho|\phi\rangle\langle\phi|)$.

Perhaps more remarkable than the indistinguishability of the different ensembles compatible with ρ is the fact that any of them can be produced at will starting from any entangled state Ψ of the AB system having ρ as its partial trace. More specifically, if two parties (call them Alice and Bob) are in possession of the A and B parts, respectively, of a system in state Ψ, then for each compatible ensemble $\mathcal{E} = \{\psi_i, p_i\}$ that Bob might wish to create in Alice's hands, there is a measurement M he can perform on the B subsystem alone, without Alice's knowledge or cooperation, that will realize that ensemble in the sense that the measurement yields outcome i with probability p_i, and conditionally on that outcome having

occurred, Bob will know that Alice holds pure state ψ_i. Bob's ability to decide Alice's ensemble in this unilateral, *post facto* fashion, has an important bearing on quantum cryptography as will be discussed later.

Since a mixed state represents incomplete information, it is natural to associate with any mixed state an entropy, given by the von Neumann formula

$$S(\rho) = -\mathrm{Tr}\,\rho \log \rho. \qquad (4)$$

If the pure states Ψ_i comprising an ensemble are orthogonal, then they are mutually distinguishable, and can thus be treated as classical states. In this situation, the von Neumann entropy is equal to the Shannon entropy of the probabilities

$$H = -\sum_i p_i \log p_i.$$

When the pure states ψ_i are nonorthogonal, and thus not wholly distinguishable as physical states, the ensemble's von Neumann entropy is less than the Shannon entropy.

It is not hard to show that for any bipartite pure state Ψ, the density matrices ρ_A and ρ_B of its parts have equal rank and equal spectra of nonzero eigenvalues. Moreover, the original state has an especially simple expression in terms of these eigenvalues and eigenvectors

$$\Psi = \sum_k \sqrt{\lambda_k} |a_k\rangle \otimes |b_k\rangle \qquad (5)$$

where $|a_k\rangle$ and $|b_k\rangle$ are eigenvectors of ρ_A and ρ_B, respectively, corresponding to the positive eigenvalues λ_k. This expression, known as the Schmidt decomposition, unfortunately has no simple counterpart for tripartite and higher systems.

The recent rapid progress in the theory of quantum information processing can be divided into two related parts: quantum computation and quantum information theory. Although major practical questions remain concerning the physical realization of quantum computers, many of the most important theoretical questions in quantum computation have already been answered: quantum algorithms are known to provide an exponential speedup, compared to known classical algorithms, for integer factoring and a few other problems, a quadratic speedup for a broad range of search and optimization problems, and no significant speedup for such problems as iterated function evaluation. The discovery of quantum error-correcting codes and fault-tolerant gate arrays (reviewed in [59]) means that, in principle, finitely reliable components are sufficient to perform arbitrarily large reliable quantum computations, just as in the theory of classical computation. But there is a quantitative difference. Today's classical devices (e.g., CMOS transistors) are so intrinsically reliable that fault-tolerant circuits are rarely needed. By contrast, today's primitive quantum hardware is several orders too unreliable to be corrected by known fault-tolerant circuit designs. Fortunately, there appears to be no fundamental reason why this gap cannot be closed by future improvements in hardware and software.

Here we concentrate on the second area: quantum information theory, where the classical notions of source, channel, code, and capacity have been generalized to encompass the

TABLE I
CLASSICAL-QUANTUM COMPARISON

Property	Classical	Quantum
State representation	String of bits $x \in \{0, 1\}^n$	String of qubits $\psi = \sum_x c_x \lvert x \rangle$
Computation primitives	Deterministic or stochastic one- and two-bit operations	One- and two-qubit unitary transformations
Reliable computations from unreliable gates	Yes, by classical fault-tolerant gate arrays	Yes, by quantum fault-tolerant gate arrays
Quantum computational speedups		Factoring: exponential speedup Search: quadratic speedup Black-box iteration: no speedup
Communication primitives	Transmitting a classical bit	Transmitting a classical bit Transmitting a qubit Sharing an EPR pair
Source entropy	$H = -\sum p(x) \log p(x)$	$S = -\mathrm{Tr}\, \rho \log \rho$
Error-correction techniques	Error-correcting codes	Quantum error-correcting codes Entanglement distillation
Noisy channel capacities	Classical capacity C_1 equals maximum mutual information through a single channel use	Classical capacity $C \geq C_1$ Unassisted quantum capacity $Q \leq C$ Assisted quantum capacity $Q_2 \geq Q$
Entanglement-assisted communication		Superdense coding Quantum teleportation
Communication complexity	Bit communication cost of distributed computation	Qubit cost, or entanglement-assisted bit cost, can be less
Agreement on a secret cryptographic key	Insecure against unlimited computing power, or if $P = NP$	Secure against general quantum attack and unlimited computing
Two-party bit commitment	Insecure against unlimited computing power, or if $P = NP$	Insecure against attack by a quantum computer
Digital signatures	Insecure against unlimited computing power, or if $P = NP$	No known quantum realization

optimal use of various channels, noiseless and noisy, for communicating not only classical information but also intact quantum states, and for sharing entanglement between separated observers. Although the fundamental physics and mathematics on which it is based is over fifty years old, the new theory has taken shape mostly over the last five years. Quantum data compression [3], [45], superdense coding [16], quantum teleportation [10], and entanglement concentration [8], [53] exemplify nontrivial ways in which quantum channels can be used, alone or in combination with classical channels, to transmit quantum and classical information. More recently, quantum error-correcting codes [14], [19]–[23], [25], [28], [33], [46], [48], [58], [66], [68], [69] and entanglement distillation protocols [12], [14], [24], [40], [41] have been discovered which allow noisy quantum channels, if not too noisy, to be substituted for noiseless ones in these applications. Important problems still open include finding exact expressions, rather than upper and lower bounds, for the classical and quantum capacities of noisy quantum channels. Some of the main similarities and differences between classical and quantum information processing are summarized in Table I.

As noted earlier, entanglement plays a central role in this enlarged information theory, complementary in several respects to the role of classical information. One of the important tasks of quantum information theory is therefore to devise quantitative measures of entanglement for bipartite and multipartite systems, pure and mixed. More generally, the theory should characterize the efficiency with which multipartite states can be transformed into one another by local operations and classical communication alone, without the exchange of quantum information among the parties. A complementary question is the extent to which prior entanglement among separated parties can reduce "communication complexity," i.e., the amount of classical communication needed to evaluate functions of several inputs, one held by each party.

II. SOURCE AND CHANNEL CODING

A natural quantum analog of a (discrete, memoryless) information *source* is an ensemble $\mathcal{E}$ of pure or mixed states [2] $\rho_1, \rho_2, \cdots, \rho_k$, emitted with known probabilities $p_1 \cdots p_k$. The quantum analog of a (discrete noiseless) channel is any quantum system capable of existing in an arbitrary state in some finite-dimensional Hilbert space, of being entangled with other similar quantum systems, and of remaining stably in this entangled or superposed state while enroute from sender to receiver. Just as a sequence of n bits, sent through a classical channel, can be used to transmit any of up to 2^n distinct classical messages, so a sequence of n elementary 2-state quantum systems or *qubits* can be used to transmit an arbitrary quantum state in a Hilbert space of up to 2^n dimensions. The quantum analog of a noisy channel is a quantum system that interacts unitarily with an outside environment while enroute from sender to receiver. Noisy channels (including noiseless ones as a special case) may thus be described as superoperators.

If the states ρ_i of a quantum source are all orthogonal, the source can be considered purely classical, because complete information about the source state can be extracted by a measurement at the sending end, transmitted classically to the receiving end, and used there to make arbitrarily many faithful replicas of the source state. On the other hand, if the source states are pure and nonorthogonal, then no classical measurement can extract complete information about the source state, and, whenever a source state is sent through a quantum channel, at most one faithful copy of the source state can be produced at the receiving end, and then only if no faithful copy remains behind at the sending end. An interesting intermediate situation occurs when the source states are nonorthogonal but commuting mixed states (i.e., the density matrices of the states commute). Such a source can be "broadcast," i.e., given an unknown one of the source states ρ_i, two systems A and B can be prepared in a joint state $\boldsymbol{\rho}_i(AB)$, which is not a clone of the source state (i.e., $\boldsymbol{\rho}_i(AB) \neq \rho_i(A) \otimes \rho_i(B)$), but whose partial trace over either subsystem agrees with the source state

$$\rho_i = \mathrm{Tr}_A(\boldsymbol{\rho}_i(AB)) = \mathrm{Tr}_B(\boldsymbol{\rho}_i(AB)) = \rho_i.$$

This "broadcasting" is essentially the same as classically copying a random variable—the resulting copies each have the right distribution, but the joint distribution of the copies is not equal to the product distribution of several copies of the original source. If the density matrices of the source states do not commute (this includes the case of pure nonorthogonal states), then the source can neither be cloned nor broadcast [2].

Because quantum information cannot be read or copied without disturbing it, whatever encoding apparatus is used at the sending end of a quantum channel must function rather blindly. If the channel is to transmit nonorthogonal pure states faithfully, it must operate on the states that pass through without knowing or learning anything about them. For the same reasons, assessment of the quality of quantum data transmission is a somewhat delicate matter. If the source states are pure, and a quantum channel produces output W_i (in general a mixed state) on input ψ_i, then the transmission's *fidelity* [45] is defined as

$$F = \sum_i p_i \langle \psi_i | W_i | \psi_i \rangle. \tag{6}$$

This is the expectation, averaged over channel inputs, that the output would pass a test for being the same as the input, conducted by someone who knew what the input was. When even the source states ρ_i are mixed states, fidelity must be

defined [44] by a more complicated formula

$$F = \sum_i p_i \left(\mathrm{Tr} \sqrt{\sqrt{\rho_i} \, W_i \sqrt{\rho_i}} \right)^2 \tag{7}$$

which represents the maximum of (6) over "purifications" [44] of ρ_i, i.e., pure states ψ_i in a larger Hilbert space having ρ_i as their partial trace.

The two most important techniques of classical information theory are data compression and error correction. When the encoder and decoder are allowed to perform quantum operations, these techniques can be extended to quantum sources and channels, enabling data from a quantum source to be recovered with arbitrarily high fidelity after transmission through a noiseless or noisy quantum channel, provided the entropy of the source is less than the *quantum capacity* of the channel.

Classical data compression allows information from a redundant source, e.g., a binary source emitting 0 and 1 with unequal probability, to be compressed without distortion into a bulk asymptotically approaching the source's Shannon entropy. Similarly, quantum data compression (cf. Fig. 2(a)) allows signals from a redundant quantum source, e.g., one emitting horizontal ($\leftrightarrow$) and diagonal ($\nearrow$) photons with equal probability, to be compressed into a bulk approaching the source's von Neumann entropy, $S(\rho) = -\mathrm{Tr}\, \rho \log_2 \rho$, where $\rho = \sum_i p_i |\psi_i\rangle\langle\psi_i|$, with fidelity approaching 1 in the limit of large n. Quantum data compression [45] is performed essentially by projecting the state of a sequence of n source signals onto the subspace spanned by the $2^{n(H(\rho)+\epsilon)}$ most important eigenvectors of their joint density matrix (the n'th tensor power of ρ). This *typical subspace* is the subspace spanned by typical sequences of eigenvectors, where the probability associated with each eigenvector is its eigenvalue. For every positive ϵ and δ there exists an n such that for block size n or greater, the resulting projection has probability less that $\delta/2$ of failing (i.e., having the state not fall into the designated subspace when measured), and fidelity greater than $1 - \delta/2$ if it does succeed. Thus the overall fidelity exceeds $1 - \delta$.

Slightly generalizing this example, suppose the source emits two equiprobable states $| \leftrightarrow \rangle$ and $\cos \theta | \leftrightarrow \rangle + \sin \theta | \updownarrow \rangle$, i.e., two polarizations differing by an angle θ. The corresponding density matrix is

$$\frac{1}{2} \begin{pmatrix} 1 + \cos^2 \theta & \sin \theta \cos \theta \\ \sin \theta \cos \theta & \sin^2 \theta \end{pmatrix}. \tag{8}$$

This matrix has eigenvalues $\frac{1}{2}(1 \pm \cos \theta)$, so its von Neumann entropy, and the resulting compression factor, is $H_2(\frac{1}{2}(1 - \cos \theta))$, where H_2 is the dyadic entropy function

$$H_2(x) = -x \log_2 x - (1 - x) \log_2 (1 - x).$$

Though formally a close parallel to the classical noiseless coding theorem, quantum data compression is remarkable in that it can compress and re-expand each of 2^n distinct sequences of $\leftrightarrow$ and $\nearrow$ photons, with fidelity approaching 1 *for the entire sequence*, even though the sequences cannot be reliably distinguished from one another by any measurement.

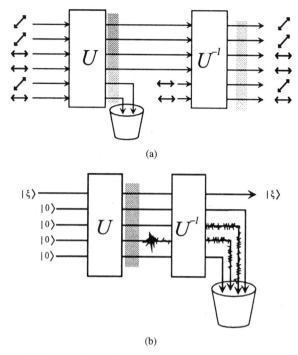

(a)

(b)

Fig. 2. (a) Quantum Data Compression: If classical data is redundant, due to unequal digit frequencies or correlations between the digits, it can be compressed to a smaller volume by techniques such as Huffman coding. Quantum data can be redundant in these ways but also in a third way: if the states in the data stream are nonorthogonal (e.g., a random stream of horizontal and 45° diagonal photons) and thus not wholly distinct as physical states. Such a data stream cannot be compressed by classical means, because the sending station would disturb the data by trying to read it. However, by performing unitary transformations on blocks of n incoming states, a quantum encoder can, without learning anything about the states, squeeze almost all their information into a smaller number of qubits, from which the original states can be reconstructed almost perfectly by an inverse transformation at the receiving station. The retained qubits leaving the encoder are heavily entangled (shading); the discarded qubits contain little information and are almost unentangled. The reconstruction approaches perfect fidelity, and the residual entanglement (pale shading) vanishes, in the limit of large n. (b) In a quantum error-correcting code, the encoder entangles the input state $|\xi\rangle$ with four standard qubits. The resulting entangled state can then withstand the corruption of any one of its qubits, and still allow recovery of the exact initial state by a decoder at the receiving end of the channel.

It is also quite interesting that the compression factor does not depend on the ensemble of states output by the source, but merely on the density matrix of these states. Although many different sources will give rise to the same density matrix, both the amount of compression achievable and the Schumacher–Jozsa algorithm for performing this compression depend only on the density matrix.

Quantum error-correcting codes [14], [19], [22], [23], [28], [33], [46], [48], [58], [66], [68], [69] have been the subject of intensive research since their discovery about three years ago. The idea that quantum error correction is possible is somewhat counterintuitive, because one familiar kind of classical error correction—in which the encoder makes several copies of the input and the decoder performs a majority vote over the channel outputs—cannot be used with quantum data because of the impossibility of accurately measuring or cloning an unknown quantum state. Nevertheless, quantum error-correcting codes (QECC) exist and are indeed a natural generalization of classical error-correcting codes ([cf. Fig. 2(b)). Rather than copying the input, the quantum encoder embeds it in a larger

Hilbert space in such a way that the error processes the code is designed to correct—here interaction of any one of the qubits with the environment—do not allow any information about the encoded state to leak out. This enables the quantum decoder to restore the data qubit to its exact original state without duplicating any quantum information, while funneling the effects of the error into ancillary qubits, which are then discarded.

To see how quantum error-correcting codes are constructed, consider the following example. Suppose we take the simplest classical error-correcting code, the threefold repetition code, and try to turn it into a quantum error-correcting code in the most obvious way. We obtain the following transformation:

$$|0\rangle \rightarrow |000\rangle$$
$$|1\rangle \rightarrow |111\rangle. \qquad (9)$$

This code does not represent a cloning of the original qubit, but rather an embedding of its two-dimensional Hilbert space into a particular two-dimensional subspace of the eight-dimensional space of three qubits, namely that spanned by the vectors $|000\rangle$ and $|111\rangle$.

The problem with this encoding is that, while it protects against any single bit flip (i.e., $\begin{pmatrix} 0 & 1 \\ 1 & 0 \end{pmatrix}$ or $|0\rangle \rightarrow |1\rangle$, $|1\rangle \rightarrow |0\rangle$), a phase flip (i.e., $\begin{pmatrix} 1 & 0 \\ 0 & -1 \end{pmatrix}$, or $|0\rangle \rightarrow |0\rangle$, $|1\rangle \rightarrow -|1\rangle$) in any one of the qubits will produce a phase flip in the encoded state. Thus protection against bit flips has been obtained at the expense of increasing the vulnerability to phase flips. Equivalently, we have protected the states $|0\rangle$ and $|1\rangle$ (encoded as $|000\rangle$ and $|111\rangle$) but we have made the states $\frac{1}{\sqrt{2}}(|0\rangle \pm |1\rangle)$—encoded as $\frac{1}{\sqrt{2}}(|000\rangle \pm |111\rangle)$—more vulnerable, as a phase error in any one of the three encoding qubits will induce a phase error in the encoded qubit. The difficulty arises because a successful quantum error-correcting code must protect the entire subspace generated by superpositions of encoded states $|0\rangle$ and $|1\rangle$. In general, quantum error-correcting codes cannot merely protect specific quantum states, but must protect an entire subspace.

There is a duality between the role of bits and phases, as can be seen by considering the so-called Hadamard transformation $H = \frac{1}{\sqrt{2}} \begin{pmatrix} 1 & 1 \\ 1 & -1 \end{pmatrix}$

$$|0\rangle \rightarrow \frac{1}{\sqrt{2}}(|0\rangle + |1\rangle)$$
$$|1\rangle \rightarrow \frac{1}{\sqrt{2}}(|0\rangle - |1\rangle). \qquad (10)$$

Under this transformation, bit flips become phase flips and *vice versa*. Applying the Hadamard transformation to the codewords of the triple-repetition code yields a code that protects against phase flips but not bit flips. This encoding is the following:

$$|0\rangle \rightarrow \frac{1}{2}(|000\rangle + |011\rangle + |101\rangle + |110\rangle)$$
$$|1\rangle \rightarrow \frac{1}{2}(|111\rangle + |100\rangle + |010\rangle + |001\rangle). \qquad (11)$$

Here phase flips can easily be seen to take an encoded $|0\rangle$ (or $|1\rangle$) to orthogonal states; for instance, a phase flip in the third qubit produces $\frac{1}{2}(|000\rangle - |011\rangle - |101\rangle + |110\rangle)$, orthogonal to both states in (11). Since the states resulting from a phase flip in any one of the three positions are all orthogonal to each other and to the original uncorrupted states, there is a von Neumann measurement to determine which phase flip has occurred, allowing it to be corrected. On the other hand, this encoding results in increased vulnerability to bit flips, as such an error in any qubit interchanges an encoded $|0\rangle$ and an encoded $|1\rangle$.

One objection that might be raised to the above analysis of the phase error-correcting code is phase flips are actually a very specific discrete form of error, while quantum-mechanical systems can undergo a continuous spectrum of errors. A general phase error is of the form $\left(\begin{smallmatrix} 1 & 0 \\ 0 & e^{i\theta} \end{smallmatrix}\right)$, whereas a phase flip corresponds to $\theta = \pi$. The answer to this objection is to show that the above code will correct any phase error. In fact, any quantum code-correcting phase flips will also correct general phase errors.

To see that it is enough to consider phase flips, we first use the fact that a quantum state can be multiplied by an arbitrary phase factor, so we can rewrite the phase error above as $\left(\begin{smallmatrix} e^{i\phi} & 0 \\ 0 & e^{-i\phi} \end{smallmatrix}\right)$ with $\phi = -\theta/2$. Consider what happens when this error is applied the first bit of the encoded state above. We obtain the mapping

$$|0\rangle \to e^{i\phi}(|000\rangle + |011\rangle) + e^{-i\phi}(|101\rangle + |110\rangle)$$
$$= \cos\phi(|000\rangle + |011\rangle + |101\rangle + |110\rangle)$$
$$+ \sin\phi(|000\rangle + |011\rangle - |101\rangle - |110\rangle). \quad (12)$$

Observe that this is a superposition of an encoded $|0\rangle$ with no error, with amplitude $\cos\phi$, and an encoded $|0\rangle$ with a phase flip in the first bit, with amplitude $\sin\phi$. When we measure which bit is wrong, a phase flip in bit 1 will be observed with probability $\sin^2\phi$, and no error observed with probability $\cos^2\phi$. In either case, the act of measurement has reduced the state vector, so the measured error corresponds to the actual error in the state. This error can subsequently be corrected.

The trick to obtaining a code that protects against both bit flips and phase flips in any one qubit is apply the two preceding codes in a nested fashion to obtain a nine-qubit concatenated code:

$$|0\rangle \to \frac{1}{2}\Big(|000000000\rangle + |111111000\rangle + |111000111\rangle$$
$$+ |000111111\rangle\Big)$$
$$|1\rangle \to \frac{1}{2}\Big(|111111111\rangle + |000000111\rangle + |000111000\rangle$$
$$+ |111000000\rangle\Big). \quad (13)$$

Bit flips are corrected by the inner code and phase flips are corrected by the outer code. It is easy to check that these correction processes do not interfere with each other—even if one of the qubits suffers both a bit flip and a phase flip, the error will be corrected properly.

We now have a code which protects against bit and/or phase flips in any single qubit. As noted before, quantum mechanics has a continuous space of errors and bit and phase flips are only two specific possibilities. However, just as the ability to correct phase flips sufficed to correct any phase error, so the ability to correct both phase and bit flips suffices to correct any single-qubit error. This follows from the fact that the identity

matrix I and the three Pauli matrices

$$\sigma_x = \begin{pmatrix} 0 & 1 \\ 1 & 0 \end{pmatrix} \quad \sigma_y = \begin{pmatrix} 0 & -i \\ i & 0 \end{pmatrix} \quad \sigma_z = \begin{pmatrix} 1 & 0 \\ 0 & -1 \end{pmatrix} \quad (14)$$

form a basis for the space of all 4×4 matrices. The Pauli matrix σ_x corresponds to a bit flip, σ_z corresponds to a phase flip, and σ_y corresponds to a qubit where both the value and the phase have been flipped. In general, if any tensor product of up to t of the Pauli matrices in different qubits can be corrected, a general error in up to t qubits can be corrected.

One way of understanding quantum codes is viewing the encoding process as a way of separating the space of encoded states and the space of possible few-bit errors into orthogonal dimensions of Hilbert space. This makes it possible to perform a measurement of the error without disturbing the encoded state, allowing a subsequent unitary transformation to correct the error. In actuality, it is not necessary to measure the error; one can accomplish error correction by unitary transformations which separate the Hilbert space into a tensor product of a space containing the encoded state and a space containing the error.

Shortly after the nine-bit code was discovered, a code protecting one bit by mapping it into seven bits was discovered independently by Andrew Steane [69] (who had not seen the nine-bit construction) and by Calderbank and Shor [22]. This was just the first representative of an infinite class of codes also presented in these papers. Subsequently, a five-bit was discovered [14], [49] by searching the space of possible codes. Several other codes followed [59], [70], as well as several papers on the general theory of quantum error-correcting codes [28], [47]. By analyzing these examples, a more general class of quantum codes was discovered [20], [33]. This led to the discovery of a method of turning certain additive GF(4) codes into quantum codes [21]. Using this connection between classical and quantum codes made it possible to find MacWilliams identities [68] and linear programming bounds [61], [62] that apply to quantum codes. Although we will not discuss this subject further, the area is still quite active.

Despite the rapid progress in quantum error-correcting codes, the notion of quantum channel capacity is more complicated and less well understood than its classical counterpart. As noted above, a quantum channel generally has three distinct capacities: an unassisted capacity Q for transmitting intact quantum states, a typically larger capacity C for transmitting classical information, and a classically assisted quantum capacity Q_2, for transmitting intact quantum states with the help of a two-way classical side-channel. Paralleling the definition of capacity for classical channels, the unassisted quantum capacity $Q(\mathcal{N})$ of a noisy channel $\mathcal{N}$ may defined as the greatest rate (transmitted qubits per channel use) at which, for arbitrarily large n and arbitrarily small ϵ, every state ψ of n qubits can be recovered with fidelity greater than $1 - \epsilon$ after block-encoding, transmission through the channel, and block-decoding. More precisely, $Q(\mathcal{N})$ is defined as

$$\lim_{\epsilon \to 0} \limsup_{n \to \infty} \left\{ \frac{n}{m} : \exists_{m, \mathcal{E}, \mathcal{D}} \forall_{\psi \in H_{2^n}} \langle \psi | \mathcal{D} \mathcal{N}^{\otimes m} \mathcal{E}(|\psi\rangle\langle\psi|) |\psi\rangle \right.$$
$$\left. > 1 - \epsilon \right\}. \quad (15)$$

Here $\mathcal{E}$ is an encoding superoperator from n qubits to m channel inputs and $\mathcal{D}$ is a decoding superoperator from m channel outputs to n qubits.

The classical capacity $C(\mathcal{N})$ of a noisy quantum channel is defined similarly as

$$\lim_{\epsilon \to 0} \limsup_{n \to \infty} \left\{ \frac{n}{m} : \exists_{m, \mathcal{E}, \mathcal{D}} \forall_{\psi \in \{|0\rangle, |1\rangle\}^n} \right.$$
$$\left. \langle \psi | \mathcal{D} \mathcal{N}^{\otimes m} \mathcal{E}(|\psi\rangle\langle\psi|) | \psi \rangle > 1 - \epsilon \right\}. \quad (16)$$

This is the same as the definition of Q except that here the universal quantification is over all Boolean states $\psi \in \{|0\rangle, |1\rangle\}^n$, rather than all possible states $\psi \in H_{2^n}$ of the n qubits, because classical communication does not require superpositions of the Boolean states to be transmitted faithfully. Clearly, $Q(\mathcal{N}) \leq C(\mathcal{N})$ for all $\mathcal{N}$.

Equation (15) is the so-called *protected subspace* definition of quantum capacity. Other definitions of quantum capacity, based on the channel's ability to faithfully convey entanglement, or coherent information (a quantum analog of mutual information to be discussed later) in the limit of large block sizes, have been proposed [4], but there is reason [5], [50] to believe they are equivalent to the protected-subspace capacity.

Both Q and C can be understood in terms of the block diagrams like Fig. 3(a), in which n qubits are encoded, sent through m instances of the channel, and then decoded to yield a more-or-less faithful approximation of the input state, either for all input states in the case of Q, or for all Boolean input states in the case of C. The classically assisted capacity $Q_2(\mathcal{N})$ is defined in terms of a more complicated protocol (Fig. 3(b)) in which the sender Alice initially receives n qubits, after which she and the receiver Bob can perform local quantum operations and exchange classical messages freely in both directions, interspersed with m forward uses of the noisy quantum channel $\mathcal{N}$, with the goal of ultimately enabling Bob to output a faithful approximation of the n-qubit input state. The capacity Q_2 is then defined by a limiting expression like (15), but with the encoder/decoder combination $\mathcal{E}, \mathcal{D}$ replaced by an interactive protocol of the form of Fig. 3(b). Clearly, $Q_2(\mathcal{N}) \geq Q(\mathcal{N})$ for any quantum channel $\mathcal{N}$, and channels are known for which this inequality is strict; an open question is whether there are channels for which $Q_2 > C$.

The assisted quantum capacity Q_2 will be discussed later in detail; here it suffices to indicate why it can exceed the unassisted capacity Q. In a typical Q_2 protocol, Alice does not use the noisy channel $\mathcal{N}$ to transmit the input state ψ to Bob directly; instead, she prepares a number m of EPR pairs in her laboratory and sends one member of each pair to Bob through the noisy channel. The result is a set of impure EPR pairs (i.e., entangled mixed states) shared between Alice and Bob. By performing local operations and measurements on these impure EPR pairs, and engaging in classical discussion of the measurement results, Alice and Bob can distill from the m impure EPR pairs a smaller number n of nearly pure pairs, even when the channel $\mathcal{N}$ through which the pairs were shared is so noisy as to have zero unassisted quantum capacity. The purified EPR pairs are then used, in conjunction with further classical communication, to "teleport" the input state ψ to Bob

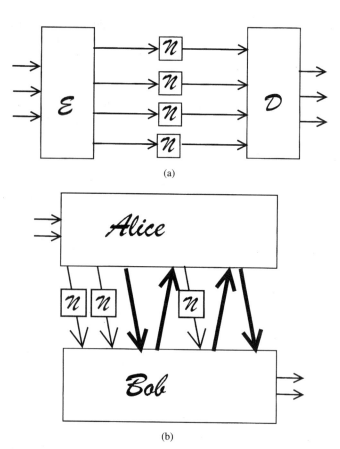

Fig. 3. (a) Unassisted quantum capacity Q of a noisy quantum channel is defined by the asymptotic performance of quantum error-correcting codes. (b) Classically assisted quantum capacity Q_2 is defined by the asymptotic performance of protocols involving forward uses of the noisy channel and unlimited classical communication between sender and receiver.

with high fidelity. Teleportation and entanglement distillation are discussed at length in subsequent sections.

For most noisy quantum channels $\mathcal{N}$, none of the three capacities is known exactly, though upper and lower bounds have been obtained. This is true, for example, of the *depolarizing channel*, a rough analog of the classical binary-symmetric channel. The depolarizing channel transmits the input qubit intact with probability $1 - p$ and replaces it by a random qubit with probability p. (Alternatively, the channel applies the identity operator to the input qubit with probability $1 - 3p/4$ and each of the three Pauli operators with probability $p/4$. The difference between $p/3$ and $p/4$ comes from the fact that applying at random one of the three Pauli operators or the identity operator effectively gives a random qubit.) A still simpler channel, whose capacities *are* known, is the *quantum erasure channel* [34], which transmits the input qubit intact with probability $1 - p$ and with probability p replaces it by a recognizable erasure symbol orthogonal to both $|0\rangle$ and $|1\rangle$. For this channel, the classical capacity C and the assisted quantum capacity Q_2 are both known to be $1 - p$ (the same as for a classical erasure channel) while the unassisted quantum capacity Q is known [13], [5] to be $\max\{1 - 2p, 0\}$.

The 50% erasure channel, for which $C = Q_2 = 1/2$ but $Q = 0$ nicely illustrates the difference between assisted and unassisted quantum capacities. The unassisted capacity Q of this channel must vanish by the following "no-cloning" argument, due to Smolin. Consider a (physically implementable) splitting device with one input port and two output ports which half the time sends the input qubit to the first output port and an erasure symbol to the second, the rest of the time sending the input qubit to the second and an erasure to the first. A recipient at either output port sees the source through a 50% erasure channel. Suppose there were a quantum error-correcting code by which an arbitrary unknown qubit could be encoded in such a way as to be reliably recoverable after transmission through a 50% erasure channel. Then each of the two recipients (call them Bob and Charlie) could recover a faithful copy of the unknown qubit, in effect cloning it. Since cloning is known to be impossible, a 50% erasure channel must have zero unassisted capacity. By the same token, a 50% depolarizing channel has zero unassisted quantum capacity. Nevertheless, either of these channels can still be used to transmit quantum information faithfully, when assisted by two-way classical communication in the manner of Fig. 3(b). In the case of the erasure channel, the sender shares EPR pairs through the channel, finds out by classical communication from the receiver which ones got through safely, and then uses the surviving EPR pairs to teleport the unknown qubits. Similar, but more complicated, arguments (cf. section on entanglement) show that the assisted quantum capacity of the depolarizing channel remains positive over the entire range $0 \leq p < 2/3$, while a stronger version of the no-cloning argument shows that its unassisted capacity vanishes for all $p \geq 1/3$. The no-cloning argument does not apply to Q_2 capacity because the classical communication breaks the symmetry between the two receivers, for example telling the sender, Alice, to perform different actions depending on whether she wants to send the input qubit to Bob or Charlie.

Mutual information between input and output plays an important role in classical theory, providing a nonasymptotic expression for the capacity, as the maximum (over input distributions) of the input:output mutual information for a single use of the channel, but this simplicity breaks down in the context of quantum channels. For none of the three capacities is there known a simple nonasymptotic quantity whose maximum for a single channel use equals the desired asymptotic capacity. Nevertheless, for both Q and C, mutual-information-like quantities have been devised that provide useful insight, and in some cases upper or lower bounds, on the asymptotic capacities. Here we discuss *coherent information* [4], a nonasymptotic quantity related to the unassisted quantum capacity Q. Later we will discuss the *Holevo bound*, a nonasymptotic quantity related to the classical capacity C of quantum channels. The Q_2 scenario, with its two-way communication, is obviously more complicated, and will not be discussed further in this context.

As noted earlier, a quantum channel, without loss of generality, may be viewed as a unitary interaction of the quantum information carrier q, enroute from sender to receiver, with an environment e initially in a standard state e_0. In order for the channel to carry intact quantum information, for example nonorthogonal states, or halves of EPR pairs, it is important that the environment not become too entangled with the quantum system passing through. At the other extreme, when

the environment interacts strongly, as in Fig. 1(c), the channel loses its capacity to carry quantum information, though its classical capacity may be unimpaired. Considerations of this sort motivated the definition of the coherent information as the difference $S(\rho(q')) - S(\rho(e'))$ between the von Neumann entropy $S(\rho(q'))$ of the information carrier's mixed state after it has passed through the channel (the prime denotes an after-interaction state), and the von Neumann entropy of the channel environment's after-interaction mixed state $S(\rho(e'))$. The coherent information is thus a function both of the channel interaction and the density matrix $\rho(q)$ characterizing the channel input before interaction. One would like to say that a channel's asymptotic unassisted quantum capacity Q is simply the maximum of its one-shot coherent information over input distributions $\rho(q)$, and in simple cases this is indeed correct. For example, for a noiseless qubit channel or quantum wire, the environment does not entangle at all; hence $S(\rho(e')) = 0$ and $\rho(q') = \rho(q)$, so that the coherent information attains its maximum value of one qubit when the channel is connected to a maximal-entropy input (which can be thought of as a random, unknown qubit state, or as half an EPR pair). On the other hand, whatever input state $\rho(q)$ is supplied to the classical wire of Fig. 3(b), the environment gains so much entropy that the coherent information $S(\rho(q')) - S(\rho(e'))$ is zero. Similarly, for the erasure channel, the maximal one-shot coherent information accurately predicts the asymptotic capacity Q. However, in more complicated cases, for example the depolarizing channel, the coherent information underestimates Q due to a failure of additivity [25]: because of the possibility of entangling inputs across multiple channel uses, more coherent information can be sent through n channel uses than n times the maximum that can be sent through through one use.

The oldest branch of quantum information theory [35], [37], [38] concerns the use of quantum channels to transmit *classical* information. The classical capacity C is defined as the maximum asymptotic rate at which classical bits can be sent through the quantum channel with arbitrarily high reliability.[2] Even this seemingly pedestrian capacity is not easy to calculate for quantum channels, because it may depend on using a quantum encoder to prepare inputs entangled over multiple uses of the channel, and/or a quantum decoder to perform coherent measurements on multiple channel outputs (cf. Fig. 4). Recent results [39], [65] have made it possible to calculate the capacity C_{CQ} with classical encoding and quantum decoding for many channels, and to show that in some cases this exceeds the maximum mutual information C_{CC} that can be sent through a single use of the channel [30], [63]. The effect of a quantum *encoding* is less well understood. In particular it is not known whether there are channels for which entangled inputs are needed to achieve full capacity [15].

---

[2]The term classical capacity is often used for the maximum rate at which classical information can be sent through a quantum channel using a *fixed alphabet* of input states. In this case, the capacity is a function both of the input alphabet and the channel. Here we define the capacity without such a constraint, optimizing over all input alphabets including states entangled among multiple uses of the channel. The capacity thus defined is a function only of the channel.

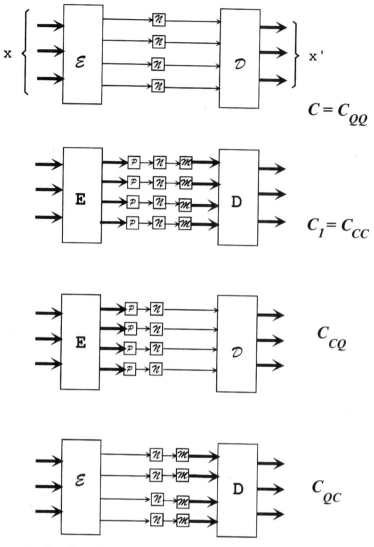

$$C = C_{QQ}$$

$$C_1 = C_{CC}$$

$$C_{CQ}$$

$$C_{QC}$$

Fig. 4. The unrestricted classical capacity, C or C_{QQ}, of a quantum channel is defined using a quantum encoder and a quantum decoder. The one-shot capacity $C_1 = C_{CC}$ uses a classical encoder to direct the preparation $\mathcal{P}$ of inputs to independent instances of the quantum channel, whose outputs are independently measured $\mathcal{M}$ and then decoded by a classical decoder. It is equal to the classical maximal mutual information transmissible through a single instance of the channel. C_{CQ} and C_{QC} are intermediate cases.

Even without considering channels and codes, a nontrivial problem arises because of the incomplete distinguishability among the states comprising a quantum source (classical source states are, of course, always distinguishable by definition). Suppose that a quantum source is known to emit states ρ_i with probabilities p_i. How much classical information about i can be obtained by an optimal measurement? One of the first results in quantum information theory, stated (with no published proof) by Levitin [49] and independently (with proof) by Holevo [37], gives an upper bound on this so-called "accessible information" I

$$I \le S\left(\sum_i p_i \rho_i\right) - \sum_i p_i S(\rho_i) \qquad (17)$$

which holds with equality only when the states ρ_i commute. In general, no nice formulas are known for computing the accessible information, although there are a variety of formulas giving upper and lower bounds [29].

Before we can discuss accessible information in detail, we must treat quantum measurement more fully, as accessible information requires us to find the measurement of a source producing the most classical information. So far, we have only dealt with von Neumann measurements, which are measurements distinguishing among d orthogonal vectors in $\mathcal{H}_d$ (or possibly among subsets of them). More general quantum-mechanical measurements are possible; these can be made by introducing an *ancilla* quantum system, making a unitary transformation on the combined systems, and then performing a von Neumann measurement on the resulting state of the ancilla. This is the most general type of measurement possible, and there is a more convenient way of describing these measurements. Any such measurement in a d-dimensional Hilbert space corresponds to a collection of positive-semidefinite Hermitian operators $E_1, E_2, \cdots, E_k$ with $\sum_{i=1}^k E_i = I$, and k may be greater than the dimension d of the original Hilbert space. If a system in state ρ is measured, the probability of obtaining the ith outcome is $\mathrm{Tr}\,(\rho E_i)$. Since the E_i are positive operators, these are called positive operator valued measurements (abbreviated POVM or POM).

There are several subtleties associated with accessible information. Some of these are illustrated by a beautiful example investigated by Peres and Wootters [58], which will also prove relevant to the classical capacity C. They consider a source emitting with equal probabilities the three signal states which correspond to polarizations of a photon at $0°$, $60°$, $120°$. These are

$$|a\rangle = |0\rangle$$
$$|b\rangle = \frac{1}{2}|0\rangle + \frac{\sqrt{3}}{2}|1\rangle$$
$$|c\rangle = \frac{1}{2}|0\rangle - \frac{\sqrt{3}}{2}|1\rangle. \tag{18}$$

The optimum measurement for these states is the POVM corresponding to $\frac{2}{3}|\bar{a}\rangle\langle\bar{a}|$, $\frac{2}{3}|\bar{b}\rangle\langle\bar{b}|$, $\frac{2}{3}|\bar{c}\rangle\langle\bar{c}|$, where the states $|\bar{a}\rangle$, $|\bar{b}\rangle$, $|\bar{c}\rangle$, are orthogonal to the original states $|a\rangle$, $|b\rangle$, $|c\rangle$, respectively; namely,

$$|\bar{a}\rangle = |1\rangle$$
$$|\bar{b}\rangle = \frac{1}{2}|1\rangle - \frac{\sqrt{3}}{2}|0\rangle$$
$$|\bar{c}\rangle = \frac{1}{2}|1\rangle + \frac{\sqrt{3}}{2}|0\rangle. \tag{19}$$

If the state $|a\rangle$, for example, is measured with respect to this POVM, the outcome $\bar{a}$ will never be observed, and there is probability $\frac{1}{2}$ of observing each of the outcomes $\bar{b}$ and $\bar{c}$. This gives accessible information of $\log_2 3 - 1 \approx 0.585$ bits.

If you consider two independent states output from the source above, and consider a joint measurement on them, this is equivalent to considering a source emitting the nine states $|aa\rangle$, $|ab\rangle$, $\cdots$, $|cc\rangle$, with equal probability. As might be expected, there is no way of gaining more than twice the information above, or 1.170 bits. However, the situation changes if you have a source emitting the three states $|aa\rangle$, $|bb\rangle$, $|cc\rangle$, with equal probability. We now describe a measurement that gives an accessible information of approximately 1.369 bits. The three states $|aa\rangle$, $|bb\rangle$, and $|cc\rangle$ span a three-dimensional vector space and are nearly orthogonal. Consider a von Neumann measurement which has axes close to these three states, namely, $|A\rangle$, $|B\rangle$, $|C\rangle$, where

$$|A\rangle = x|aa\rangle - y|bb\rangle - y|cc\rangle \tag{20}$$

and $|B\rangle$, $|C\rangle$ are defined similarly. Here x and y are chosen so that

$$\langle AB\rangle = \langle AC\rangle = \langle BC\rangle = 0$$

so

$$x = \left(4 + \sqrt{2}\right)/\sqrt{27} \approx 1.042$$

and

$$y = \left(2 - \sqrt{2}\right)/\sqrt{27} \approx 0.1127.$$

In this measurement, $|aa\rangle$ (for example) is measured as $|A\rangle$ with probability 0.9714 and as $|B\rangle$ and $|C\rangle$ with probability 0.0143 each. This gives an accessible information of 1.369 bits, producing more accessible information per qubit than the source emitting $|a\rangle$, $|b\rangle$, and $|c\rangle$ with equal probabilities.

After seeing this example, one might speculate that sources emitting more complicated codewords of length greater than two, and that joint measurements on these codewords could increase the accessible information still higher. This is indeed correct, and recently it was shown [39], [65] that Holevo's bound (17) is the correct formula for the limit of the maximum accessible information obtainable from tensor product sources having a marginal distribution equal to a given ensemble. Unlike the accessible information, the Holevo bound depends only on the density matrix of an ensemble and not the component states that make up this ensemble.

What does this example show? Suppose you are trying to communicate over a quantum channel, and are restricted to sending signals chosen from the three nonorthogonal states above. Achieving the largest capacity requires using codewords of length more than one and making joint (entangled) measurements on the signal. Now consider the problem of communicating classically over a general noisy quantum channel $\mathcal{N}$, where there is no restriction on the input alphabet, except that inputs are not allowed to be entangled across multiple channel uses. This is the situation of C_{CQ} in Fig. 4. If the marginal (one-shot) input ensemble consists of states ρ_i emitted with probabilities p_i, the corresponding output states (after passing through the channel) will be $\rho_i' = \mathcal{N}(\rho_i)$, and they will again occur with the probabilities p_i. Then the maximum C_{CQ} capacity achievable *with this input ensemble* is given by the Holevo bound

$$S\left(\sum_i p_i\rho_i'\right) - \sum_i p_i S(\rho_i') \tag{21}$$

and the unrestricted C_{CQ} is given by maximizing the above expression over the choice of input ensembles $\{\rho_i, p_i\}$. The ability to calculate the asymptotic capacity C_{CQ} by optimizing over the inputs to a single use of the channel have made it possible to show for a number of channels that C_{CQ} is greater than the one-shot capacity $C_1 = C_{CC}$ which is simply the maximum accessible information between input and output for a single channel use. Thus access to a quantum decoder spanning multiple channel outputs definitely increases the classical capacity of some quantum channels. It is not known whether access to a quantum encoder (allowing inputs to be entangled over multiple channel uses) increases the capacity. Thus of the four classical capacities depicted in Fig. 4, it is evident from the definitions that $C_{CC} \leq \{C_{CQ}, C_{QC}\} \leq C_{QQ}$. Specific examples are known where all four capacities are equal (e.g., the quantum erasure channel), and where C_{CQ} exceeds C_{CC}, but within these constraints the relation of C_{QC} and C_{QQ} to the other capacities is not known. Neither is the relation of these various classical capacities to the unassisted and assisted quantum capacities well understood. From the definitions it is clear that $C \geq Q$ for all channels, but is not known whether there are channels for which $C_1 < Q$.

III. Entanglement-Assisted Communication

While quantum source and channel codes optimize the use of one quantum resource—a quantum channel from sender to receiver—quantum teleportation [10] and quantum superdense

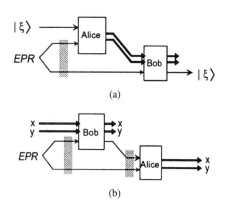

(a)

(b)

Fig. 5. (a) In quantum teleportation, prior sharing of an EPR pair, and transmission of a two-bit classical message from Alice to Bob, suffice to transmit an unknown quantum state even when nodirect quantum channel from Alice to Bob is available. (b) In quantum superdense coding, prior sharing of an EPR pair, and transmission of a qubit from Bob to Alice, suffices to transmit an arbitrary two-bit message (x, y).

coding [16] substitute a different quantum resource—namely, entanglement, in the form of entangled pairs of particles previously shared between sender and receiver—and use it to assist, respectively, in the performance of faithful quantum and classical communication.

In quantum teleportation (Fig. 5(a)) the sender (sometimes called "Alice") takes particle 1, whose unknown state $\xi_1 = \alpha \leftrightarrow_1 + \beta \updownarrow_1$ is to be teleported, and performs a joint measurement on it and particle 2, one member of the EPR pair. Particles 2 and 3 have been prepared beforehand in a maximally entangled EPR state, such as

$$\Phi^+_{23} = \sqrt{\tfrac{1}{2}} \left(\leftrightarrow_2 \leftrightarrow_3 + \updownarrow_2 \updownarrow_3 \right).$$

The original state is thus

$$(\alpha \leftrightarrow_1 + \beta \updownarrow_1) \Phi^+_{23}. \tag{22}$$

It is easy to verify that this state can be rewritten as

$$\begin{aligned} \tfrac{1}{2} (& \Phi^+_{12}(\alpha \leftrightarrow_3 + \beta \updownarrow_3) + \Phi^-_{12}(\alpha \leftrightarrow_3 - \beta \updownarrow_3) \\ & + \Psi^+_{12}(\alpha \updownarrow_3 + \beta \leftrightarrow_3) + \Psi^-_{12}(\alpha \updownarrow_3 - \beta \leftrightarrow_3)) \end{aligned} \tag{23}$$

where $\Phi^\pm$ and $\Psi^\pm$ are states in the so-called Bell basis, consisting of

$$\Phi^\pm_{12} = \sqrt{\tfrac{1}{2}} \left(\leftrightarrow_1 \leftrightarrow_2 \pm \updownarrow_1 \updownarrow_2 \right)$$

and

$$\Psi^\pm_{12} = \sqrt{\tfrac{1}{2}} \left(\leftrightarrow_1 \updownarrow_2 \pm \updownarrow_1 \leftrightarrow_2 \right) \tag{24}$$

four orthogonal maximally entangled states. The measurement on particles 1 and 2 projects them onto the Bell basis. The Bell measurement generates two bits of classical data, and leaves particle 3, now held by the receiver ("Bob"), in a residual state which can be unitarily transformed into a replica ξ_3 of the original quantum state ξ_1 which has been destroyed. This transformation is effected by subjecting particle 3 to one of four unitary operations 1, σ_z, σ_x, or σ_y according to which of the four outcomes, Φ^+, Φ^-, Ψ^+, or Ψ^- was obtained in the Bell measurement conducted by Alice.

Teleportation in effect splits the complete information in particle 1 into a classical part, carried by the two-bit message,

and a purely quantum part, carried by the prior entanglement between particles 2 and 3. It avoids both cloning (the state ξ is destroyed in particle 1 before it is recreated in particle 3) and faster-than-light communication (the two-bit classical message must arrive at the receiver before the replica can be created). Note that we have somehow transmitted a continuously parameterized quantum state accurately using only two classical bits. Since the Holevo bound (21) shows that only one classical bit can be extracted from a qubit, teleportation does not give rise to any paradoxes, but the process is still quite counterintuitive. It is possible due to the entanglement that was originally shared between Alice and Bob, and is an example of what Einstein called the "spooky action at a distance" present in quantum mechanics.

A closely related effect is *superdense coding* (Fig. 5(b)), a scheme due to Wiesner [16]. Here also Alice and Bob begin by sharing an EPR pair. The sender (whom we now call Bob because he performs the same actions as Bob in teleportation) then encodes a two-bit classical message by performing one of the four unitary operations mentioned above on his member of the pair, thereby placing the pair as a whole into a corresponding one of the four orthogonal Bell states. The treated particle is then sent to Alice, who by measuring the particles together can reliably recover both bits of the classical message. Thus the full classical information capacity of two particles is made available, even though only one is directly handled by the sender.

Although the Bell states are quintessentially nonlocal, in the sense of being maximally entangled, they have a number of useful local properties. They can be converted into one another by local operations, in particular by the Pauli operators. For example, σ_x, applied to either member of an EPR pair (but not both), interconverts $\Phi^\pm$ and $\Psi^\pm$, while σ_y interconverts $\Phi^\pm$ with $\Psi^\mp$. If Alice and Bob are given an unknown one of the four Bell states, neither Alice nor Bob alone can learn anything about which one it is by a unilateral local measurement, but if they each perform a measurement and share the results, they can then test whether their unknown state belongs to an arbitrary set of two Bell states. For example, to test whether it is a Ψ or a Φ state, they measure each qubit in the standard basis and compare the results. If the results agree, they had a Φ state; otherwise, they had a Ψ state. Of course, this is a rather destructive kind of testing, because after the measurement the Bell state is gone and cannot be brought back by any local actions. A Bell state can be conveniently indexed by two classical bits, the first or amplitude bit saying whether the Bell state is Φ or Ψ, and the second or phase bit saying whether it is of the $+$ or $-$ type. Bilateral local measurements of the type we have described have the effect of extracting one bit of information about an unknown Bell state while destroying the other. By choice of local measurement, Alice and Bob can ascertain the phase bit, the amplitude bit, or the XOR of the phase and amplitude bits (this amounts to determining whether the unknown state is in the subset $\{\Phi^+, \Psi^-\}$) but in all cases, the other bit is destroyed. More generally [14], if Alice and Bob share n Bell states (Alice holding one qubit of each pair and Bob the other), they can, by local actions, determine the parity of an arbitrary subset of bits in the $2n$-bit string describing their Bell states, at the cost of measuring (and therefore sacrificing) one of the pairs. This ability to manipulate and extract information from Bell states by local actions has important consequences for entanglement distillation, classically assisted (Q_2) quantum communication, and quantum cryptography.

IV. QUANTITATIVE THEORY OF ENTANGLEMENT

Since entanglement appears to be responsible for the remarkable behavior of information in quantum mechanics, a means of quantifying it would seem useful. We will discuss several such measures in this section. There is one "best" measure for entanglement of pure states, which is defined using entropy. However, there does not appear to be a unique best measure of entanglement for mixed states; which measure is best depends on what the measure is being used for. We will discuss several measures, all of which agree for pure quantum states.

Suppose Alice and Bob each hold one piece of a system in some quantum state. It is easy to define when these two pieces are entangled: this happens when the state of the entire system is not a mixture of tensor product states. More formally, the system is entangled iff its density matrix cannot be written in the form

$$\rho^{AB} = \sum_i p_i \, \rho_i^A \otimes \rho_i^B \qquad (25)$$

where ρ_i^A and ρ_i^B are states of Alice's and Bob's subsystems and p_i are probabilities. Any unentangled state can be prepared by Alice and Bob using only local quantum-state preparation and classical communication: first they choose the index i with probability p_i and then ρ_i^A and ρ_i^B can be prepared locally without further communication. Preparation of an entangled state, on the other hand, requires that Alice and Bob either share some pre-existing entanglement or acquire such entanglement by transmission of quantum states between them. Determining whether a given density matrix has nonzero entanglement is not easy, especially if Alice and Bob each have higher than two-dimensional Hilbert spaces to work with. We shall later discuss a test that addresses this question. However, we will first discuss measures of entanglement.

If ρ^{AB} is a pure state (i.e., a rank-1 matrix $|\Psi^{AB}\rangle\langle\Psi^{AB}|$), there is a unique entanglement measure which has the properties one might hope for, namely, the entropy of entanglement

$$E(\Psi^{AB}) = S(\mathrm{Tr}_B \, \rho^{AB}) = S(\mathrm{Tr}_A \, \rho^{AB}). \qquad (26)$$

This is the von Neumann entropy of the mixed state obtained when either Bob's or Alice's subsystem is disregarded. Why is this the right definition? To answer that, we need first decide what properties a good measure of entanglement must have. If entanglement is a resource, Alice and Bob ought not to be able to increase their entanglement by operations that involve only classical communication between them and local quantum operations. The ideal situation would then be if, whenever we are given two states ρ_1 and ρ_2 with entanglement E_1 and E_2, respectively, with $E_1 > E_2$, we could always reach the second state from the first state using only local quantum

operations and classical communication. Although this turns out to be too much to ask, an asymptotic version of this ideal situation holds when ρ_1 and ρ_2 are pure states. For any two pure bipartite states Ψ and Ψ' (since we will always be considering bipartite states we omit the superscript AB), in the large n limit, n independent copies of Ψ (in other words, the state $\Psi^{\otimes n}$) can be transformed by local actions and classical communication into a state arbitrarily close to $\Psi'^{\otimes n'}$, with the fidelity of the approximation tending to 1 and the yield n'/n tending to $E(\Psi)/E(\Psi')$ in the limit of large n [8], [32], [53]. An important property of this definition of entanglement is that it is *additive*. That is, if Alice and Bob share two independent systems with entanglement E_1 and E_2, respectively, the combined system will have entanglement $E_1 + E_2$.

For mixed states, it appears that the amount of pure-state entanglement asymptotically required to prepare a mixed state may, in general, be larger than the amount of pure-state entanglement that asymptotically can be extracted from that mixed state. We call the first quantity *entanglement of formation* and the second *distillable entanglement*. The formal definitions of these involve, for entanglement of formation, the number of EPR pairs required to create many copies of the state with high fidelity; and for distillable entanglement, the number of nearly perfect EPR pairs distillable with high fidelity from many copies of the state. It has been conjectured that the entanglement of formation of a mixed state can be strictly larger than the distillable entanglement. That we cannot prove or disprove this conjecture shows how much is still unknown in quantum information theory.

The entanglement of formation and distillable entanglement as defined above are asymptotic quantities. For the entanglement of formation, there is also a related natural nonasymptotic quantity. As we saw previously, mixed quantum states can, in general, be represented as probabilistic mixtures of pure states, and can be so represented in many different ways. The *one-shot* entanglement of formation can thus be defined as the average entanglement of the pure states in a mixture giving the desired mixed state most efficiently. That is,

$$E_F^{(1)}(\rho) = \min\left\{ \sum_i p_i E(\Psi_i) \,\Big|\, \rho = \sum_i p_i |\Psi_i\rangle\langle\Psi_i| \right\}. \qquad (27)$$

This quantity is clearly at least as large as the entanglement of formation, since the component pure states can asymptotically be created efficiently and then mixed together. It is not known whether the one-shot entanglement of formation is additive, that is, if

$$E_F^{(1)}(\rho_1 \otimes \rho_2) = E_F^{(1)}(\rho_1) + E_F^{(1)}(\rho_2). \qquad (28)$$

If it is additive, then it must agree with the asymptotic definition of entanglement of formation. Hill and Wootters have obtained an exact expression for the one-shot entanglement of formation for arbitrary states of two qubits [36], [73].[3]

To illustrate how pure EPR pairs can be distilled from partly entangled mixed states, we first define a particularly

---

[3] In [12], [14], [36], and [73] the term "entanglement of formation" is used for what we call here the one-shot entanglement of formation $E_F^{(1)}$.

simple kind of bipartite mixed state of two qubits, the so-called Werner state, which may be thought of as a partly depolarized EPR pair. A Werner state of *fidelity* F, denoted W_F, is a mixture of F parts of a canonical Bell state (without loss of generality the state $\Phi^+ = \sqrt{\frac{1}{2}}\,(|00\rangle + |11\rangle)$) with $(1-F)/3$ parts of the other three Bell states, that is,

$$W_F = F|\Psi^+\rangle\langle\Psi^+|$$
$$+ (1-F)/3(|\Psi^-\rangle\langle\Psi^-| + |\Psi^+\rangle\langle\Psi^+| + |\Psi^-\rangle\langle\Psi^-|). \tag{29}$$

There is a simple equivalence between p-depolarizing channels and Werner states W_F, where $F = 1 - 3p/4 \geq 1/4$: the Werner state W_F can be produced by transmitting a perfect Φ^+ pair through a p-depolarizing channel; conversely a p-depolarizing channel can be produced by performing teleportation with a Werner state W_F substituting for the perfect EPR pair called for in the teleportation protocol. This simple relation breaks down for other, less symmetric, channels and mixed states.

The final entanglement measure we wish to discuss is *relative entropy of entanglement,* introduced by Plenio and Vedral [72], [71] as a way of bounding the amount of distillable entanglement of a bipartite mixed state ρ. It is defined as

$$E_{RE}(\rho) = \min\{\mathrm{Tr}\,(\rho\log\rho - \rho\log\rho')|\rho' \text{ unentangled}\} \tag{30}$$

where the minimum is taken over all unentangled states ρ'. To explain why this gives a bound on distillable entanglement, we need to introduce the quantum analog of Sanov's theorem. Recall that Sanov's theorem expresses the distinguishability of two probability distributions in terms of relative entropy. The quantum Sanov's theorem [26] says that the probability of mistaking m copies of a quantum states ρ' for m copies of ρ after a measurement designed to test for ρ is at least $2^{-mS(\rho\|\rho')}$, where

$$S(\rho\|\rho') = \mathrm{Tr}\,(\rho(\log\rho - \log\rho'))$$

is the relative entropy. Further, there is a measurement that achieves this bound asymptotically. Now, if m copies of a state ρ can be purified to n EPR pairs, then the probability of distinguishing these n EPR pairs from a nonseparable state cannot be greater than the probability of distinguishing the m copies of the original state ρ from a nonseparable state, as the purification could be used as the first part of such a test. Using the projection onto the EPR state for distinguishing EPR pairs from unentangled states, we find that the probability of an unentangled state passing this test is at most 2^{-n}. This shows that the relative entropy of entanglement is an upper bound on the amount of distillable entanglement. It turns out that for Werner states $E_{RE} = 1 - H_2(F)$; more generally, for Bell-diagonal states $E_{RE} = 1 - H_2(\lambda)$ where λ is the largest eigenvalue in the density matrix. Rains [62] proved the same bound on distillable entanglement for Bell-diagonal states using a quite different method involving weight enumerators. E_{RE} is the best known upper bound on the distillable entanglement of Bell-diagonal states, and indeed for

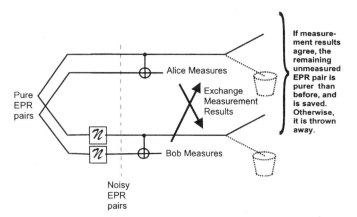

Fig. 6. One step of entanglement distillation by the iterative comparison method.

mixtures of *two* Bell states it gives the distillable entanglement exactly.

As noted earlier, one reason for wanting to distill good EPR pairs from Werner states, or other entangled mixed states, is in order to use a noisy quantum channel for reliable quantum communication. Given a depolarizing channel, Alice and Bob can use it to build up a supply of Werner states, distill some good EPR pairs from these, then use the EPR pairs, in conjunction with classical communication, to teleport the desired quantum information from Alice to Bob, or vice versa, even though no direct noiseless quantum channel is available, and even though the noisy quantum channel that is available may be too noisy to be salvaged by quantum error-correcting codes.

We now describe one way of distilling good EPR pairs from Werner states. Suppose that Alice and Bob share two EPR pairs. It is easily checked that if both Alice and Bob XOR their halves of the two perfect Φ^+ states together (this so-called bilateral XOR operation is shown in Fig. 6), they obtain two new Φ^+ states. More generally, if Alice and Bob bilaterally XOR any two Bell states together, the result will again be two Bell states, which depend on the initial Bell states in a simple reversible manner (the source Bell state's amplitude bit gets XORed into the target's amplitude bit, while the target's phase bit gets XORed into the source's phase bit, leaving the amplitude of the source and the phase of the target unchanged). Suppose Alice and Bob share two Werner states. When the halves of these are XOR'ed together, then if either EPR pair is imperfect (i.e., not a Φ^+ state), the impurity is likely to spread to both output pairs. One of the resulting pairs (say the target) can be measured in the standard basis, and the results compared to see whether they agree, as they should if both incoming pairs were good Φ^+ states. This destroys the measured pair, but gives an indication as to whether the surviving unmeasured pair is good or not. If the measurement results agree, then Alice and Bob keep the other pair, and if not, they throw it away. We can easily analyze the first-order efficiency of this process. When we XOR the two Werner pairs together, if we start with fidelity $1 - \epsilon$, then for small ϵ, the outgoing fidelity of each is roughly $1 - 2\epsilon$. Now, when one of the two impure EPR pairs is checked, the measurement process catches two of the three possible Bell state errors (Ψ^+, Ψ^-, Φ^-) thus leaving the unmeasured pair in a state with fidelity roughly $1 - \frac{2}{3}\epsilon$. Doing the calculations in detail, we find this process increases the fidelity of Werner states if the initial fidelity is better than 50%. On the other hand, any Werner state with less than 50% fidelity can be shown to be unentangled [12], so it is hopeless to try to extract entanglement from it.

This procedure is not the best distillation method known for Werner states. It can be improved in a number of ways. One improvement is to substitute a more intelligent iterative comparison procedure due to Macchiavello [24] (cf. also the explanation in [14]) which takes advantage of the fact that after the first iteration the output is no longer a Werner state, but a more structured mixture of Bell states. A second improvement is that when the Werner states' fidelity has been sufficiently improved (to above about 0.83), Alice and Bob should stop the iterative technique and finish the distillation by another technique, called hashing [14]. This involves taking a large number n of the partially purified pairs and locally operating on them to measure parities of random subsets of the $2n$ phase and amplitude bits. This hashing procedure (essentially the decoding of a random linear code), allows the remaining Bell-state errors to be efficiently found and corrected at a cost of discarding a number of pairs asymptotically approaching the entropy of the $2n$-bit sequence. The asymptotic yield of arbitrarily pure EPR pairs by hashing is thus $1 - S(\rho)$, where ρ is the density matrix of the input states to the hashing process.

The amount of noise an entanglement distillation protocol can tolerate depends on whether the protocol requires two-way communication between Alice and Bob (like the iterative comparison method), or can work with only one-way communication (like the hashing method). Protocols requiring only one-way communication are equivalent to quantum error-correcting codes, attaining the capacity Q in the limit of large n. Protocols depending on two-way communication, such as iterative comparison followed by hashing, give rise to the classically assisted Q_2 protocols of the type shown in Fig. 3(b). The yield of pure EPR pairs from Werner states, from hashing (D_H) and from the best known two-way (D_M) distillation protocol is shown in Fig. 7, along with the one-shot entanglement of formation E_F^1 and the relative entropy of entanglement E_{RE} of the Werner states. D_H vanishes for $F <$ 0.81071; the best known one-way protocol [25] is marginally better, having a cutoff at $F = 0.80944$. The other three quantities, D_M, E_{RE}, and E_F^1, all vanish at $F = \frac{1}{2}$. Because of the equivalence between Werner states and depolarizing channels, the two lower curves in this figure also give the best known lower bounds on the quantum capacities Q_2 and Q for the depolarizing channels with $p = 4(1 - F)/3$, while E_{RE} is the best known upper bound on Q_2.

We now discuss an elegant necessary condition for separability, the so-called partial transpose criterion of Peres [56]. Consider a density matrix ρ. Its transpose is also a density matrix. If a mixed state shared between two parties is unentangled, then it is a mixture of unentangled pure states, each of which is a tensor product of pure states of the two subsystems. Thus if the transformation corresponding to a

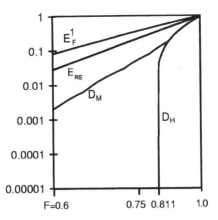

Fig. 7. Log plot of entanglement distillable from Werner states of fidelity F by hashing D_H and best known two-way protocol D_M, compared with their relative entropy of entanglement E_{RE} and their one-shot entanglement of formation E_F^1. (Abscissa is logarithmic in $F - \frac{1}{2}$.)

transpose by only one of the two parties is applied, the result, the so-called partial transpose $\tilde{\rho}$ will still be a density matrix. However, if the original mixed state ρ is entangled, then $\tilde{\rho}$ need not be a density matrix. It may, for example, have negative eigenvalues. To take a simple example, the density matrix corresponding to Bell state $\Psi^- = 1/\sqrt{2}\,(|01\rangle - |10\rangle)$, is

$$\frac{1}{2}\begin{pmatrix} 0 & 0 & 0 & 0 \\ 0 & 1 & -1 & 0 \\ 0 & -1 & 1 & 0 \\ 0 & 0 & 0 & 0 \end{pmatrix}.$$

The partial transpose of this matrix is

$$\frac{1}{2}\begin{pmatrix} 0 & 0 & 0 & -1 \\ 0 & 1 & 0 & 0 \\ 0 & 0 & 1 & 0 \\ -1 & 0 & 0 & 0 \end{pmatrix}$$

which has three eigenvalues of $\frac{1}{2}$ and one of $-\frac{1}{2}$, proving what we knew already, that Φ^- is entangled.

Subsequent work by the Horodecki family [40], [41] showed that positivity of the partial transpose is a necessary and sufficient condition for separability for mixed states of two qubits, and mixed states of a qubit with a three-state particle. Further research by the Hordeckis [42], [43] showed that no state with distillable entanglement, in any number of dimensions, can have a positive partial transpose, and led to the discovery of states with so-called "bound entanglement," i.e., entangled mixed states from which *no* pure entanglement can be distilled. These states (of which the simplest examples occur in $2 \otimes 4$- and $3 \otimes 3$-dimensional systems) are entangled in the sense that they are not mixtures of products states (in other words, their one-shot entanglement of formation is positive), yet their partial transposes are positive; hence they have no distillable entanglement.

V. Quantum Cryptography

Quantum cryptography is the art of applying the unique properties of quantum systems to cryptographic goals, that is, the protection of classical information from tampering or unauthorized disclosure in a multiparty setting where not all the parties trust one another.

This idea began with the proposal of quantum money by Wiesner [72]. Suppose that a piece of money has included with it some number n of quantum systems which are in a random sequence of nonorthogonal states, known only to the preparer, for example, a random sequence of the four polarizations $\leftrightarrow, \updownarrow, \nearrow, \searrow$. Then anybody who tries to duplicate the bill must clone nonorthogonal states, an impossible task. There are drawbacks of this scheme—available quantum information carriers have a decoherence time shorter than inflationary half-life of most currencies, and only the issuing bank (which would have a classical record of the secret sequence) can check the validity of the money, so a counterfeiter could indeed pass fake copies off to anybody else. However, this idea formed the basis of quantum key distribution or QKD. Quantum key distribution [6], [7], [9], [11], [24], [27], [52], [54] is a task involving both quantum and classical communication among three parties, the legitimate users Alice and Bob and an eavesdropper Eve. Alice and Bob's goal is to use quantum uncertainty to do something that would be impossible by purely classical public communication—agree on a secret random bit string K, called a cryptographic key, that is informationally secure in the sense that Eve has little or no information on it.[4] In the quantum protocol (cf. Fig. 8), Eve is allowed to interact with the quantum information carriers (e.g., photons) enroute from Alice to Bob—at the risk of disturbing them—and can also passively listen to all classical communication between Alice and Bob, but she cannot alter or suppress the classical messages. Sometimes (e.g., if Eve jams or interacts strongly with the quantum signals) Alice and Bob will conclude that the quantum signals have been excessively disturbed, and therefore that no key can safely be agreed upon (designated by a frown in the figure); but, conditionally on Alice and Bob's concluding that it is safe to agree on a key, Eve's expected information on that key should be negligible.

The practical implementation of quantum key distribution is much further advanced than other kinds of quantum information processing, owing to the fact that the standard QKD protocols require no two-qubit interactions, only preparation and measurement of simple quantum states, along with classical communication and computations. Optical prototypes working over tens of kilometers of fiber, or even through a kilometer of open air (at night), have been built and tested. In principle, however, a quantum key distribution protocol could involve quantum computations by Alice and Bob; and to be sure of its security, one ought to allow Eve the full power of a quantum computer, even though Alice and Bob do not need one for the standard protocols. Fig. 8 shows the most general situation, where Alice, Eve, and Bob each have a separate quantum computer.

Various proofs of security of quantum key distribution protocols, especially the four-state "BB84" protocol of [9], have

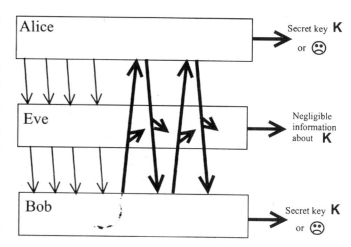

Fig. 8. In quantum key distribution, Alice and Bob, who trust each other but distrust Eve, wish to arrive at a secret key K of which Eve is ignorant. Alice and Bob have at their disposal a quantum channel on which Eve may eavesdrop actively, and a classical two-way channel on which she eavesdrops passively.

been offered. A complete security proof should encompass all attacks allowed by the laws of quantum mechanics, should be able to cope with noise, and should be applicable in realistic settings where noise arises not only from eavesdropping but also from noisy channels and detectors. Finally it should provide a way of calculating a safe rate of key generation as a function of the noise level observed by Alice and Bob. Early discussions of security treated only limited kinds of attacks, such as the interception and resending of individual photons. Subsequently [31] considered optimal eavesdropping strategies on individual qubits, while [17] considered a general collective attack on ancillas that have interacted separately with individual qubits. Most recently, Mayers and Yao [55] have given a security proof for BB84 against general quantum attacks, in the presence of finite channel and detector noise. Although they did not calculate an explicit noise threshold, their techniques can probably be used to show that BB84 still yields secure key in the presence of practical noise levels in the several percent range. The Mayers and Yao proof shows that QKD requires only current technology, yet is secure against attacks using any future technology consistent with the laws of quantum mechanics.

If we now allow Alice and Bob the full power of quantum computation, what further advantages do they gain? In contrast to BB84, such quantum-computational protocols for QKD, first proposed in [24] and rigorously developed in [52] are based on entanglement distillation, and require Alice and Bob to perform nontrivial gate operations on their quantum data. Aside from simplifying the proof of security, the main advantages of quantum-computational protocols for QKD are that they can tolerate more noise and, unlike BB84, can operate over arbitrarily great distances, using distributed quantum error correction along a chain of intermediate stations. In this approach to QKD, Alice and Bob use their insecure quantum channel to share a large number n of EPR pairs end-to-end, then distill a smaller number m of presumably good EPR pairs from the n distributed pairs, using the same sorts of distillation protocols they would use if they were distilling Werner states.

[4]Purely classical protocols for key agreement exist and are in widespread use, but these result in a key that is only computationally secure—an adversary with sufficient computing power could infer it from the messages exchanged between Alice and Bob. In particular, the most widely used classical key agreement protocols could be easily broken by a quantum computer, if one were available.

Finally, they use hashing to verify that the state of the m surviving pairs differs by only an exponentially small amount from a perfect product of EPR pairs such as $(\Phi^+)^{\otimes m}$. Now, if Alice and Bob actually possessed the perfect state $(\Phi^+)^{\otimes m}$, they could distill m bits of perfectly secret key from it by locally measuring each pair in the standard basis. Instead, they merely have a state approximating $(\Phi^+)^{\otimes m}$; but because the approximation is so good, they can go ahead as if it were perfect, and Eve's expected information on the resulting m bits of key will be bounded at an exponentially small fraction of bits.

Given the success of quantum key distribution, there was high hope that quantum techniques could help with another task, called two-party oblivious function evaluation. This is the problem, especially important in commerce and post-cold-war diplomacy, of enabling two mutually distrustful parties to cooperate in evaluating some publicly agreed function of private data held separately by each party, without compromising the private data any more than it would be compromised had they assigned the job of evaluating the function to a trusted intermediary. Initially Alice knows data x and Bob knows data y; when the protocol is finished, Alice and Bob should each also know $f(x, y)$, but neither party should know any more about the other party's private input than can logically be inferred from a knowledge of their own data and the common function value $f(x, y)$. Classical protocols for oblivious function evaluation exist, but like classical key agreement protocols they are only computationally secure, based on the assumption that certain problems are hard. Hopes for finding a secure quantum foundation for oblivious function evaluation were dampened last year by the proof that a different specific cryptographic problem, called bit commitment, is insecure in principle against quantum attacks [56], [52]. In bit commitment Alice has a bit which she does not wish to reveal to Bob. However, she wants to send some information to Bob which ensures that she can later reveal the value of her bit, and prove to him that it originally had the value she claims. A proposed protocol for quantum bit commitment [18] was found to have a flaw, and this flaw led to a proof that quantum bit commitment was impossible [52], [56]. This makes the design of quantum cryptographic protocols for tasks other than key distribution much more problematic, since bit commitment is a crucial ingredient in the classical implementations of many of them, and since many cryptographic primitives can be used to implement bit commitment, showing that they too are impossible.

ACKNOWLEDGMENT

The authors wish to thank numerous collaborators and colleagues for discussions of their work which is reviewed here, and A. R. Calderbank for helpful comments on a draft of this paper.

REFERENCES

[1] A. Barenco, C. H. Bennett, R. Cleve, D. DiVincenzo, N. Margolus, P. Shor, T. Sleator, J. Smolin, and H. Weinfurter, "Elementary gates for quantum computation," *Phys. Rev. A*, vol. 52, pp. 3457–3467, 1995.

[2] H. Barnum, C. M. Caves, C. A. Fuchs, R. Jozsa, and B. Schumacher, "Noncommuting mixed states cannot be broadcast," *Phys. Rev. Lett.*, vol. 76, pp. 2818–2821, 1996 (eprint quant-ph/9511010).

[3] H. Barnum, C. A. Fuchs, R. Jozsa, and B. Schumacher, "A general fidelity limit for quantum channels," 1996 (eprint quant-ph/9603014).

[4] H. Barnum, M. A. Nielsen, and B. Schumacher, "Information transmission through noisy quantum channels," 1997 (eprint quant-ph/9702049).

[5] H. Barnum, J. Smolin, and B. Terhal, "Results on quantum channel capacity," submitted to *Phys. Rev A* (eprint quant-ph/9711032).

[6] C. H. Bennett, "Quantum cryptography using any two nonorthogonal states," *Phys. Rev. Lett.*, vol. 68, pp. 3121–3124, 1992.

[7] C. H. Bennett, F. Bessette, G. Brassard, L. Salvail, and J. Smolin, "Experimental quantum cryptography," *J. Cryptol.*, vol. 5, pp. 3–28, 1992.

[8] C. H. Bennett, H. J. Bernstein, S. Popescu, and B. Schumacher, "Concentrating partial entanglement by local operations," *Phys. Rev. A*, vol. 53, pp. 2046–2052, 1996.

[9] C. H. Bennett and G. Brassard, "Quantum cryptography: Public key distribution and coin tossing," in *Proc. IEEE Int. Conf. Computers, Systems and Signal Processing* (Bangalore, India, 1984), pp. 175–179.

[10] C. H. Bennett, G. Brassard, C. Crépeau, R. Jozsa, A. Peres, and W. K. Wootters, "Teleporting an unknown quantum state via dual classical and Einstein–Podolsky–Rosen channels," *Phys. Rev. Lett.*, vol. 70, pp. 1895–1899, 1993.

[11] C. H. Bennett, G. Brassard, and D. Mermin, "Quantum cryptography without Bell's theorem," *Phys. Rev. Lett.*, vol. 68, pp. 557–559, 1992.

[12] C. H. Bennett, G. Brassard, B. Schumacher, S. Popescu, J. Smolin, and W. K. Wootters, "Purification of noisy entanglement and faithful teleportation via noisy channels," *Phys. Rev. Lett.*, vol. 76, pp. 722–725, 1996.

[13] C. H. Bennett, D. P. DiVincenzo, and J. A. Smolin, "Capacities of quantum erasure channels," *Phys. Rev. Lett.*, vol. 78, pp. 3217–3220, 1997.

[14] C. H. Bennett, D. P. DiVincenzo, J. Smolin, and W. K. Wootters, "Mixed state entanglement and quantum error correction," *Phys. Rev. A*, vol. 54, pp. 3824–3851, 1996 (eprint quant-ph/9604024).

[15] C. H. Bennett, C. A. Fuchs, and J. A. Smolin, "Entanglement-enhanced classical communication on a noisy quantum channel," 1996 (eprint quant-ph/9611006).

[16] C. H. Bennett and S. J. Wiesner, "Communication via one- and two-particle operators on Einstein–Podolsky–Rosen states," *Phys. Rev. Lett.*, vol. 69, pp. 2881–2884, 1992.

[17] E. Biham, M. Boyer, G. Brassard, J. van de Graaf, and T. Mor, "Security of quantum key distribution against all collective attacks" (eprint quant-ph/9801022).

[18] G. Brassard, C. Créepeau, R. Jozsa and D. Langlois, "A quantum bit commitment scheme provably unbreakable by both parties," in *Proc. 34th Annu. IEEE Symp. Foundations of Computer Science*, 1993, pp. 362–371.

[19] S. L. Braunstein, "Quantum error correction of dephasing in 3 qubits," 1996 (eprint quant-ph/9603024).

[20] A. R. Calderbank, E. Rains, P. W. Shor, and N. J. A. Sloane, "Quantum error correction and orthogonal geometry," *Phys. Rev. Lett.*, vol. 78, pp. 405–408, 1997 (eprint quant-ph/9605005).

[21] ——, "Quantum error correction via codes over GF(4), I" submitted to *IEEE Trans. Inform. Theory* (eprint quant-ph/9608006).

[22] A. R. Calderbank and P. W. Shor, "Good quantum error-correcting codes exist," *Phys. Rev. A*, vol. 54, pp. 1098–1106, 1995 (eprint quant-ph/9512032).

[23] I. L. Chuang and R. Laflamme, "Quantum error correction by coding," 1995 (eprint quant-ph/9511003).

[24] D. Deutsch, A. Ekert, R. Jozsa, C. Macchiavello, S. Popescu, and A. Sanpera, "Quantum privacy amplification and the security of quantum cryptography over noisy channels," *Phys. Rev. Lett.*, vol. 77, pp. 2818–2821, 1996. Erratum: vol. 80, p. 2022, 1998.

[25] D. P. DiVincenzo, P. W. Shor, and J. A. Smolin, "Quantum-channel capacity of very noisy channels," *Phys. Rev. A.*, vol. 57, pp. 830–839, 1998 (eprint quant-ph/9706061).

[26] M. J. Donald, "*A priori* probability and localized observers," *Found. Phys.*, vol. 22, pp. 1111–1172, 1992.

[27] A. Ekert "Quantum cryptography based on Bell's theorem," *Phys. Rev. Lett.*, vol. 67, pp. 661–663, 1991.

[28] A. Ekert and C. Machiavello, "Quantum error correction for communication," *Phys. Rev. Lett.*, vol. 77, pp. 2585–2588, 1996 (eprint quant-ph/9602022).

[29] C. A. Fuchs, "Distinguishability and accessible information in quantum theory," Ph.D. dissertation, Univ. New Mexico, Albuquerque, 1996 (eprint quant-ph/9601020).

[30] _____, "Nonorthogonal quantum states maximize classical information capacity," *Phys. Rev. Lett.*, vol. 79, pp. 1162–1165, 1997.

[31] C. A. Fuchs, N. Gisin, R. B. Griffiths, C.-S. Niu, and A. Peres "Optimal eavesdropping in quantum cryptography I," quant-ph/9701039.

[32] N. Gisin, "Nonlocality criteria for quantum teleportation," *Phys. Lett. A*, vol. 210, pp. 151–156, 1996.

[33] D. Gottesman, "A class of quantum error-correcting codes saturating the Hamming bound," *Phys. Rev. A*, vol. 54, pp. 1862–1868, 1996 (eprint quant-ph/9604038).

[34] M. Grassl, T. Beth, and T. Pellizzari, "Codes for the quantum erasure channel" (eprint quant-ph/9610042).

[35] C. W. Helstrom *Quantum Detection and Estimation Theory.* New York: Academic, 1976.

[36] S. Hill and W. K. Wootters "Entanglement of a pair of quantum bits," 1997 (eprint quant-ph/9703041).

[37] A. S. Holevo, "Information theoretical aspects of quantum measurement," *Probl. Pered. Inform.*, vol. 9, no. 2, pp. 31–42, 1973 (in Russian), translation in *Probl. Inform. Transm.*, vol. 9, pp. 177–183, 1973.

[38] _____, "Problems in the mathematical theory of quantum communication channels," *Rep. Math. Phys.*, vol. 12, pp. 273–278, 1977.

[39] _____, "The capacity of quantum channel with general signal states," submitted to *IEEE Trans. Inform. Theory* (eprint quant-ph/9611023).

[40] M. Horodecki, P. Horodecki, and R. Horodecki, "Separability of mixed states: Necessary and sufficient conditions," *Phys. Lett. A*, vol. 223, pp. 1–8 (eprint quant-ph/9605038).

[41] _____, "Distillability of inseparable quantum systems," 1996 (eprint quant-ph/9607009).

[42] M. Horodecki, P. Horodecki, and R. Horodecki "Mixed-state entanglement and distillation: Is there a 'bound' entanglement in nature?" 1998 (eprint quant-ph/9801069).

[43] P. Horodecki, "Separability criterion and inseparable mixed states with positive partial transposition," *Phys. Lett. A*, vol. 232, pp. 333–339, 1997 (eprint quant-ph/9703004).

[44] R. Jozsa, "Fidelity for mixed quantum states," *J. Modern Opt.*, vol. 41, 2315–2323, 1994.

[45] R. Jozsa and B. Schumacher, "A new proof of the quantum noiseless coding theorem," *J. Modern Opt.*, vol. 41, pp. 2343–2349, 1994.

[46] E. Knill and R. Laflamme, "A general theory of quantum error correction codes," *Phys. Rev. A*, vol. 55, pp. 900–911, 1997 (eprint quant-ph/9604034).

[47] K. Kraus, *States, Effects, and Operations: Fundamental Notions of Quantum Theory.* Berlin, Germany: Springer, 1983.

[48] R. Laflamme, C. Miquel, J.-P. Paz, and W. H. Zurek, "Perfect quantum error correction code," *Phys. Rev. Lett.*, vol. 77, pp. 198–201, 1996.

[49] L. B. Levitin, "On the quantum measure of information," in *Proc. 4th All-Union Conf. Information and Coding Theory* (Tashkent, 1969), in Russian.

[50] S. Lloyd, "The capacity of the noisy quantum channel," 1996 (eprint quant-ph/9604015).

[51] H.-K. Lo and H. F. Chau, "Why quantum bit commitment and ideal quantum coin tossing are impossible," 1997 (eprint quant-ph/9711065).

[52] _____, "Quantum computers render quantum key distribution unconditionally secure over arbitrarily long distance," 1998 (eprint quant-ph/9711065).

[53] H.-K. Lo and S. Popescu, "Concentrating entanglement by local actions—beyond mean values," 1997 (eprint quant-ph/9707038).

[54] D. Mayers and A. C. C. Yao, "Unconditional security in quantum cryptography," 1998 (eprint quant-ph/9802025).

[55] D. Mayers, "The trouble with quantum bit commitment," 1996 (eprint quant-ph/9603015).

[56] A. Peres, "Separability criterion for density matrices," *Phys. Rev. Lett.*, vol. 77, pp. 1413–1415, 1996.

[57] A. Peres and W. K. Wootters, "Optimal detection of quantum information," *Phys. Rev. Lett.*, vol. 66, pp. 1119–1122, 1991.

[58] M. B. Plenio, V. Vedral, and P. L. Knight, "Quantum error correction in the presence of spontaneous emission," *Phys. Rev. A*, vol. 55, pp. 67–72, 1997 (eprint 9603022).

[59] J. Preskill, "Reliable quantum computers," 1997 (eprint quant-ph/9705031).

[60] E. Rains,"Quantum weight enumerators" (eprint quant-ph 9611001).

[61] _____, "Quantum shadow enumerators," eprint quant-ph 9612015.

[62] _____, "Entanglement purification via separable superoperators," 1997 (eprint quant-ph/9707002).

[63] M. Sasaki, K. Kato, M. Izutsu, and O. Hirota "A simple quantum channel having superadditivity of channel capacity," 1997 (eprint quant-ph/9705043).

[64] B. Schumacher, "Sending entanglement through noisy channels," 1996 (eprint quant-ph/9604023).

[65] P. Hausladen, R. Jozsa, B. Schumacher, M. Westmoreland, and W. K. Wootters, *Phys Rev. A*, vol. 54, p. 1869, 1996.

[66] P. W. Shor, "Scheme for reducing decoherence in quantum computer memory," *Phys. Rev. A*, vol. 52, pp. 2493–2496, 1995.

[67] P. Shor and R. Laflamme, "Quantum analog of the MacWilliams identities in classical coding theory," *Phys. Rev. Lett.*, vol. 78, pp. 1600–1602, 1997.

[68] A. Steane, "Multiple particle interference and quantum error correction," in *Proc. Roy. Soc. London A*,vol. 452, pp. 2551–2577, 1996 (eprint quant-ph/9601029).

[69] L. Vaidman, L. Goldenberg, and S. Wiesner, "Error prevention scheme with four particles" (eprint quant-ph/9603031).

[70] V. Vedral and M. Plenio, "Entanglement measures and purification procedures" (quant-ph/9707035).

[71] V. Vedral, M. B. Plenio, M. A. Rippin, and P. L. Knight, "Quantifying entanglement," *Phys. Rev. Lett.*, vol. 78, pp. 2275–2279, 1997 (eprint quant-ph/9702027).

[72] S. Wiesner, "Conjugate coding," *Sigact News*, vol. 15, no. 1, pp. 78–88, 1983.

[73] W. K. Wootters, "Entanglement of formation of an arbitrary state of two qubits," 1997 (eprint quant-ph/9709029).

[74] W. H. Zurek, "Decoherence and the transition from quantum to classical," *Phys. Today*, vol. 44, pp. 36–44, 1991.

698

The Minimum Description Length Principle in Coding and Modeling

Andrew Barron, *Member, IEEE*, Jorma Rissanen, *Senior Member, IEEE*, and Bin Yu, *Senior Member, IEEE*

(Invited Paper)

Abstract—We review the principles of Minimum Description Length and Stochastic Complexity as used in data compression and statistical modeling. Stochastic complexity is formulated as the solution to optimum universal coding problems extending Shannon's basic source coding theorem. The normalized maximized likelihood, mixture, and predictive codings are each shown to achieve the stochastic complexity to within asymptotically vanishing terms. We assess the performance of the minimum description length criterion both from the vantage point of quality of data compression and accuracy of statistical inference. Context tree modeling, density estimation, and model selection in Gaussian linear regression serve as examples.

Index Terms—Complexity, compression, estimation, inference, universal modeling.

I. INTRODUCTION

IN this expository paper we discuss the so-called MDL (Minimum Description Length) principle for model selection and statistical inference in general. In broad terms the central idea of this principle is first to represent an entire class of probability distributions as models by a single "universal" representative model such that it would be able to imitate the behavior of any model in the class. The best model class for a set of observed data, then, is the one whose representative permits the shortest coding of the data.

There are a number of ways to construct representatives of model classes or, what is sufficient, to compute their codelength. The first and the crudest of them, Wallace and Boulton [52], Rissanen [38], is to encode the data with a (parametric) model defined by the maximum-likelihood estimates, quantized optimally to a finite precision, and then encode the estimates by a prefix code. For a reader with any knowledge of information theory there is nothing startling nor objectionable about such a procedure and the principle itself. After all, in order to design a good code for data, the code must capture the statistical characteristics of the

Manuscript received December 2, 1997; revised April 27, 1998. The work of A. Barron was supported in part by NSF under Grants ECE-9410760 and DMS-95-05168. The work of B. Yu was supported in part by ARO under Grant DAAH04-94-G-0232 and by NSF under Grant DMS-9322817.

A. Barron is with the Department of Statistics, Yale University, New Haven, CT 06520-8290 USA.

J. Rissanen is with IBM Research Division, Almaden Research Center, DPE-B2/802, San Jose, CA 95120-6099 USA.

B. Yu is with the Department of Statistics, University of California at Berkeley, Berkeley, CA 94720-3860 USA.

Publisher Item Identifier S 0018-9448(98)05284-5.

data, and in order to be able to decode, the decoder must be given this distribution, which permits the construction of the code, the "codebook," and the particular codeword for the observed data. It is the statisticians for whom the connection between probability distributions and codelengths tends to appear strange and on the surface of it nonexisting. And yet, even a statistician must admit, however grudgingly, that the principle seems to incorporate in a direct way some of the most fundamental, albeit elusive, ideas the founding fathers of statistical inference have been groping for, like the objective of statistics is to reduce data, Fisher [21], and that "we must not overfit data by too complex models." Perhaps, a statistician can take solace in the fact that by the fundamental Kraft inequality, stated below, a codelength is just another way to express a probability distribution, so that the MDL principle becomes the familiar Maximum Likelihood (ML) principle—albeit a global one.

Simple and natural as the MDL principle may be, it nevertheless provides a profound change in the way one should think about statistical problems. About the data themselves, it is not necessary to make the usual assumption that they form a sample from an imagined population, which is something that would be impossible to verify. After all, we are able to design codes for any data that on the whole can be finitely described. However, ever since Shannon's work we know how to design good codes for data generated by sampling a probability distribution, and the same codes will work reasonably well even for data which are not generated that way, provided that they have the kinds of restrictions predicated by the distribution, at least to some degree. Indeed, the greater this degree is the closer the resulting codelength for the data will be to the optimal for the distribution with which the code was designed. This seems to imply that we are just pushing the problem to the selection of the assumed probability distribution, which is exactly what we do. The probability distributions serve us as a means by which to express the regular features in the data; in other words, they serve as *models*. In fact, that ultimately is what all models do, including the deterministic "laws" of nature, which spell out the restrictions to such a high degree that the inevitable deviations between the data and the behavior dictated by the laws give rise to almost singular probability distributions. Prediction is certainly an important motivation for modeling, and one may ask why not use prediction error as a criterion for model selection. Fortunately, almost all the usual prediction

699

error criteria, be they in terms of probability of errors or some distance measure such as the absolute or squared errors, can be expressed in terms of codelength, and there is no conflict between the two [41], [44].

According to this program, the problems of modeling and inference, then, are not to estimate any "true" data generating distribution with which to do inference, but to search for good probability models for the data, where the goodness can be measured in terms of codelength. Such a view of statistics also conforms nicely with the theory of algorithmic complexity, Solomonoff [47], Kolmogorov [34], and can draw on its startling finding about the ultimate limitation on all statistical inference, namely, that there is no "mechanical," i.e., algorithmic, way to find the "best" model of data among all computable models (let alone the metaphysical "true" model).

Although the MDL principle stands on its own and cannot be tampered by findings in analysis, it still leaves a role for probability and coding theories albeit a different one: Analysis can provide support for the principle or pinpoint abnormal behavior, and help provide designs for good codes for data generated by various probability models and classes of them. It happens that such a code design follows a remarkably uniform pattern, which starts with Shannon's basic case of a fixed known data-generating probability distribution, say $P(\underline{x})$, where $\underline{x}$ denotes a data string to be encoded. In this case a meaningful optimization problem is to find a code that has the minimum mean length subject to the restriction that the codeword lengths $\ell(\underline{x})$ satisfy the fundamental Kraft inequality

$$\sum_{\underline{x}} 2^{-\ell(\underline{x})} \leq 1. \qquad (1)$$

If we dispose of the somewhat irrelevant restriction that the codeword lengths must be natural numbers, the minimization problem admits the remarkable solution that such *ideal* codeword lengths must coincide with the numbers $-\log P(\underline{x})$, giving the entropy as the minimized mean length. Hence, the optimal codelengths mimic the data generating distribution. Although the MDL principle requires us to find the length of the shortest codeword for the actually observed sequence, rather than a mean length, it is also true that no code exists where the probability of the set of codewords that are shorter than the optimal less c, $-\log P(\underline{x}) - c$, exceeds 2^{-c}. In other words, the codewords of the optimal code are practically the shortest for almost all "typical" strings generated by the distribution.

As stated above, the focus of interest in the MDL principle is in various classes of probability distributions as models, which together with the modeling problems they create are discussed first. For such classes we consider optimization problems that generalize the basic Shannon problem above. If $Q(\underline{x})$ denotes the sought-for universal representative of a model class $\{P(\underline{x}|\theta)\}$ under study, where θ is a parameter vector, the quantity of interest is the difference

$$\log \frac{1}{Q(\underline{x})} - \log \frac{1}{P(\underline{x}|\theta)} = \log \frac{P(\underline{x}|\theta)}{Q(\underline{x})}$$

between the codeword length of the representative and that obtained with Shannon's codes defined by the members $P(\underline{x}|\theta)$

in the class. The first problem calls for a code, defined by Q, which minimizes the difference given maximized over $\underline{x}$ and θ. In the second problem we seek $Q(\underline{x})$ which minimizes the mean difference. For smooth model classes the solutions to these two problems turn out to be virtually the same, and the minimized difference may be interpreted as the *parametric complexity* of the model class involved at the given data sequence of length n. Again generalizing Shannon's basic result the solutions will also be shortest possible for almost all typical strings generated by almost all models in the class. In analogy with the algorithmic or Kolmogorov complexity, the codelength that differs from the ideal by the parametric complexity is called *stochastic complexity*.

Although this paper is tutorial in nature we have decided not to restrict it to an elementary introduction, only, but also to survey some of the more advanced techniques inspired by the theory with the intent to demonstrate how the new ideas contribute to the analysis of the central problems arising in modeling. These include the demonstration of the desirable property of the MDL principle that, if we apply it to data generated by some unknown model in the considered class, then the MDL estimates of both the parameters and their number are consistent; i.e., that the estimates converge and the limit specifies the data generating model. We also discuss the close connection between statistical inference and an important predictive way to do coding, which lends itself to coding data relative to nonparametric models. We conclude the paper with applications of the MDL principle to universal coding, linear regression where the stochastic complexity can be calculated exactly, and density estimation.

II. MODELING PRELUDE

At two extremes of statistical modeling are issues of parametric inference in a given, perhaps small, finite-dimensional family or model class $\{P(\underline{x}|\theta): \theta \in \Theta \subset \Re^d\}$ and issues of nonparametric inference in infinite-dimensional function classes (e.g., of density or regression curves). The MDL principle has implications for each motivated by the aim of providing a good statistical summary of data. The principle is especially useful in the middle ground, where a variety of plausible families $\mathcal{M}_k = \{P_k(\underline{x}|\theta): \theta \in \Theta_k \subset \Re^{d_k}\}$ for $k \in \mathcal{K}$ are available, and one seeks to automate the selection of an estimate $\hat{k}$ based on data $\underline{x} = (x_1, \cdots, x_n)$. It is clear that both extremes of fixed small finite-dimensional or infinite-dimensional families have their limitations. Whereas in statistics these limitations and their resolutions via penalized risk criteria are often cast in terms of the bias and variance tradeoff, or the approximation and estimation tradeoff, we will seek here what we regard as a more intrinsic characterization of the quality of the summarization.

In the case that there is a sequence $\mathcal{M}_k, k \in \mathcal{K}$, of classes available for modeling the data, the MDL principle advocates a choice $\hat{k}$ that optimizes a codelength $\log 1/Q_k^*(\underline{x}) + l(k)$. Here $\log 1/Q_k^*(\underline{x})$ is a codelength for description of data using the model class $\mathcal{M}_k$ in accordance with optimal coding criteria discussed below, and $l(k)$ is a codelength for the description of the class k. For each model class, the codelength criterion involves in an intrinsic way a tradeoff between likelihood $\log 1/P_k(\underline{x}|\theta)$ and a parametric complexity associated with the class $\mathcal{M}_k$ that models data of the given length n. To optimize this tradeoff, we are led to the maximum-likelihood estimator $\hat{\theta} = \hat{\theta}(\underline{x})$ and a parametric complexity that is the minimum additional coding cost $c_{n,k}$ necessary for $\log 1/P_k(\underline{x}|\hat{\theta}) + c_{n,k}$ to be the length of a uniquely decodable code for $\underline{x} \in \mathcal{X}$. The MDL estimator $\hat{k}$ achieves minimum total codelength $\log 1/P_{\hat{k}}(\underline{x}|\hat{\theta}) + c_{n,\hat{k}} + l(\hat{k})$.

Rather than being interested in the bits of exact coding of the data, our interest in modeling is to provide quality summarization of the data through the estimated model. An ultimate or idealized summarization is captured by Kolmogorov's minimum sufficient statistic for description. Recall that the Kolmogorov complexity of a data sequence $\underline{x}$ is the length $K(\underline{x})$ of the shortest computer program that outputs $\underline{x}$ on a given universal computer. This complexity is a universal assignment for all strings $\underline{x}$ up to a constant (in the sense that for any given pair of universal computers there is a constant c of translation between computers such that for all sequences, no matter how long, the complexity assigned by the two computers differs by no more than c). Maximally complex sequences are those for which $K(\underline{x})$ equals $\log card(\mathcal{X})$ to within a constant. These are sequences which defy interesting summarization or compression.

To get at the idea of optimal summarization, Kolmogorov refined his notion of complexity (see [11, pp. 176, 182]). For each $\underline{x}$, there typically are a number of programs that are minimal in the sense of achieving within a given constant c the complexity $K(\underline{x})$. Among these minimal programs are those which describe the data in two parts. First, some property A (a subset $A \subset \mathcal{X}$), satisfied by the sequence $\underline{x} \in A$, is optimally described using $K(A)$ bits, and then $\log card(A)$ bits are used to give the index of $\underline{x} \in A$. When this description of $\underline{x}$ of length $K(A) + \log card(A)$ is minimal, $\log card(A)$ cannot be improved by using the length of any other encoding of $\underline{x}$ in A, and hence the $\log card(A)$ bits are maximally complex (uninteresting bits), conditionally given A. The *interesting part* arises in a property A that does not exactly represent, but rather summarizes the sequence. The best summary is provided by a program for a property A^* satisfied by $\underline{x}$ that has minimum $K(A^*)$ subject to $K(A^*) + \log card(A^*)$ agreeing with $K(\underline{x})$ (to within the specified constant). Such A^* may be called a *Kolmogorov minimal sufficient statistic* for the description of $\underline{x}$.

Our notion of summarization intended for statistical modeling differs from Kolmogorov's in two ways. We do not restrict the first part of the code to be the description of a set containing the sequence, but rather we allow it to be the description of a statistical model (where the counterpart to a set A becomes the uniform distribution on A), and corresponding to a statistical model we replace $\log card(A)$ by the length of Shannon's code for $\underline{x}$ using the model. Secondly, at the expense of ultimate idealism, we do not require that the descriptions of distributions be Kolmogorov optimal (which would be computationally unrealizable), but rather we make our codelength assignments on the basis of principles that

capture near optimality for most sequences. Neither do we seek the optimum among all computable distributions but only relative to a given list of models.

III. OPTIMAL CODING METHODS

A. Shannon Coding

Let $\underline{x} \in \mathcal{X}$ refer to data to be described and modeled, where $\mathcal{X}$ is a given countable set. Typically we have the set $\mathcal{X} = \mathcal{S}^n$ of length n sequences $\underline{x} = (x_1, \cdots, x_n)$ for $x_i \in \mathcal{S}$ from some discrete alphabet $\mathcal{S}$ such as English or ASCII characters or a discretization of real-valued variables.

Description of $\underline{x} \in \mathcal{X}$ is accomplished by means of a mapping into finite-length binary sequences, called *codewords*, where the map, called a (binary) *code*, is required to be one-to-one, and concatenations of codewords are also required to be in one-to-one correspondence with sequences of symbols $\underline{x}$, themselves sequences, from $\mathcal{X}$. That is the requirement of unique decodability. It is accomplished in particular by arranging the codewords to satisfy the property that no codeword is a prefix for a codeword of another $\underline{x} \in \mathcal{X}$. This yields a correspondence between codes and labeled binary trees, where the codeword for $\underline{x}$ is the sequence of zeros and ones that gives the path from the root to the leaf labeled $\underline{x}$. Given a code tree let $\ell(\underline{x})$ denote the length of the codeword (or path) that describes $\underline{x}$. According to the theory of Shannon, Kraft, and McMillan, see, e.g., [11], there exists a uniquely decodable code with lengths $\ell(\underline{x})$ for $\underline{x} \in \mathcal{X}$ if and only if the Kraft inequality (1) holds. Indeed, to each code there corresponds a subprobability mass function $Q(\underline{x}) = 2^{-\ell(\underline{x})}$. For a complete tree, in which every internal node has both descendants and all leaves are codewords, an interpretation is that a random walk starting at the root ends up at $\underline{x}$ with probability $Q(\underline{x}) = 2^{-\ell(\underline{x})}$, and hence $\Sigma_{\underline{x}} 2^{-\ell(\underline{x})} = 1$. Shannon gave an explicit construction of a code with length equal to $\log 1/Q(\underline{x})$, rounded up to an integer, as follows: Order the strings $\underline{x}$ by decreasing value of $Q(\underline{x})$ and define the codeword of $\underline{x}$ as the first $\ell(\underline{x})$ bits of the cumulative probability $\Sigma_{\underline{x}' < \underline{x}} Q(\underline{x}')$.

Shannon also posed the following optimization problem. If we are given a probability mass function $P(\underline{x})$ on $\mathcal{X}$, then what codelengths achieve the minimum expected value $E_P\ell(\underline{x})$? From the correspondence between codes and subprobability mass functions Q it is seen that the solution is to take $\ell(\underline{x}) = \log 1/P(\underline{x})$ if we ignore the integer codelength constraint. Indeed, with any other choice the excess codelength

$$\ell(\underline{x}) - \ell_P(\underline{x}) = \log 1/Q(\underline{x}) - \log 1/P(\underline{x}) = \log \frac{P(\underline{x})}{Q(\underline{x})}$$

has positive expected value, given by the relative entropy or Kullback–Leibler distance

$$E_P(\ell(\underline{x}) - \ell_P(\underline{x})) = E_P \log \frac{P(\underline{x})}{Q(\underline{x})} = D(P||Q)$$

which equals zero only if $Q = P$. Thus given P, the Shannon codelength $\ell_P(\underline{x}) = \log 1/P(\underline{x})$ is optimum, and $D(P||Q)$ is the expected codelength difference (redundancy) when Q is used in the absense of knowledge of P. This property, together with the simple probability inequality that $\ell(\underline{x}) - \ell_P(\underline{x})$ exceeds $-c$ except in a set of probability not greater than 2^{-c} for all $c > 0$, leads us to call $\ell_P(\underline{x}) = \log 1/P(\underline{x})$ the optimal or *ideal* codelength.

B. Coding with a Model Class

The subject of universal data compression deals with describing data when the source distribution P is unknown. A most useful coding theory, as an extension of Shannon's theory with P given, can be developed if the distributions P are, instead of being completely unknown, restricted to a class of parametric distributions $\mathcal{M}_k = \{P_k(\underline{x}|\theta) : \theta \in \Theta_k \subset \Re^{d_k}\}$, refered to above as a model class. The results also turn out to provide the codelengths required for the MDL criterion.

Suppose we are given a parametric family of probability mass functions $\mathcal{M} = \{P(\underline{x}|\theta) : \theta \in \Theta\}$, which have corresponding Shannon codelengths $\log 1/P(\underline{x}|\theta)$. There is a collection of data compressors, indexed by θ. With hindsight, after observation of $\underline{x}$, the shortest of these is $\log 1/P(\underline{x}|\hat{\theta})$, where $\hat{\theta} = \hat{\theta}(\underline{x})$ is the maximum-likelihood estimate (MLE) achieving $P(\underline{x}|\hat{\theta}) = \max_\theta P(\underline{x}|\theta)$. This is our target level of performance. Though its value can be computed, it is not available to us as a valid codelength, for without advance knowledge of $\hat{\theta}(\underline{x})$ we do not know which Shannon tree to decode. If we code data using a distribution $Q(\underline{x})$, the excess codelength, sometimes called regret, over the target value is

$$\log 1/Q(\underline{x}) - \log 1/P(\underline{x}|\hat{\theta}(\underline{x})) = \log \frac{P(\underline{x}|\hat{\theta})}{Q(\underline{x})} \quad (2)$$

which has the worst case value $\max_{\underline{x}} \log P(\underline{x}|\hat{\theta}(\underline{x}))/Q(\underline{x})$. Shtarkov [46] posed the problem of choosing $Q(\underline{x})$ to minimize the worst case regret, and he found the unique solution to be given by the maximized likelihood, normalized thus

$$Q^*(\underline{x}) = \frac{P(\underline{x}|\hat{\theta})}{C}$$
$$C = \sum_{\underline{x} \in \underline{X}} P(\underline{x}|\hat{\theta}(\underline{x})). \quad (3)$$

This distribution plays an important role in the MDL theory, and we refer to it as the normalized maximum-likelihood (NML) distribution. Notice that $C = C(\mathcal{M}, n)$ depends on the model class $\mathcal{M}$ and the size n of the sample space $\underline{X} = \mathcal{S}^n$. The corresponding codelength is

$$\log 1/Q^*(\underline{x}) = \log 1/P(\underline{x}|\hat{\theta}) + \log C(\mathcal{M}, n) \quad (4)$$

which gives the minimax regret

$$\min_Q \max_{\underline{x}} \log \frac{P(\underline{x}|\hat{\theta}(\underline{x}))}{Q(\underline{x})} = \log C(\mathcal{M}, n). \quad (5)$$

The proof of the optimality of Q^* is simply to note that $\log P(\underline{x}|\hat{\theta})/Q^*(\underline{x}) = \log C(\mathcal{M}, n)$ for all $\underline{x}$, and for any other subprobability mass function $Q(\underline{x})$ we have $Q(\underline{x}) < Q^*(\underline{x})$ for at least one $\underline{x}$, where $\log P(\underline{x}|\hat{\theta}(\underline{x}))/Q(\underline{x})$ is strictly worse.

This optimal codelength $\log 1/P(\underline{x}|\hat{\theta}) + c_n$ associated with the NML distribution is what we call the *stochastic complexity* of data relative to the model class $\mathcal{M}$. It exceeds the

log $1/maximized\ likelihood$ term by the additional coding cost

$$c_n = \log C(\mathcal{M}, n) = \log \Sigma_{\underline{x}} p(\underline{x}|\hat{\theta}(\underline{x})).$$

Because this additional cost rises due to the unknown parameter, we call it the *parametric complexity*. Also in support of this terminology we note that other coding schemes, such as two-part codes as in [43] (which first describe parameter estimates to an optimal precision and then the data conditional on the parameter estimates), achieve a similar complexity term expressed in terms of the length of the description of optimally discretized parameter estimates. We emphasize that in the case of the code with respect to the NML distribution, the normalization insures Kraft's inequality, and hence encoding of $\underline{x}$, can be done directly without the need for separate encoding of $\hat{\theta}$.

C. Codes Optimal for Average Regret

While we are interested in the regret defined in (2), we do not presume to be interested only in its worst case value. Thus we consider expected regrets with respect to distributions in $\mathcal{M}$ and with respect to mixtures of these distributions, and we discuss the behavior of the corresponding minimax and maximin values. A mixture that achieves an (asymptotic) minimax and maximin solution forms an alternative MDL coding procedure that will be related to the NML code. With respect to any distribution $P(\underline{x}|\theta) = P_\theta(\underline{x})$ in $\mathcal{M}$, the expected value of the regret of Q is

$$R_n(P_\theta, Q) = E_{P_\theta} \log \frac{P(\underline{x}|\hat{\theta}(\underline{x}))}{Q(\underline{x})}$$

where in the right side we left the dummy variable $\underline{x}$ over which the expectation is taken. Averaging the expected regret further with respect to any probability distribution w on Θ is the same as averaging with respect to the mixture (marginal)

$$Q^w(\underline{x}) = \int P(\underline{x}|\theta) \, dw(\theta)$$

and the resulting average regret is $E_{Q^w} \log P(\underline{x}|\hat{\theta})/Q(\underline{x})$, which equals

$$E_{Q^w} \log \frac{P(\underline{x}|\hat{\theta})}{Q^w(\underline{x})} + D(Q^w||Q).$$

Thus $Q = Q^w$ is the unique choice to minimize the average regret with respect to the distribution w. In decision-theoretic terminology, the Bayes optimal code is of length

$$\log 1/Q^w(\underline{x}) = \log 1/ \int P(\underline{x}|\theta) \, dw(\theta).$$

The expected regret has a minimax value

$$\overline{\mathcal{R}}_n(\mathcal{M}) = \min_Q \max_\theta E_{P_\theta} \log P(\underline{x}|\hat{\theta}(\underline{x}))/Q(\underline{x})$$

which agrees with the maximin value

$$\underline{\mathcal{R}}_n(\mathcal{M}) = \max_w \min_Q E_{Q^w} \log \frac{P(\underline{x}|\hat{\theta}(\underline{x}))}{Q(\underline{x})}$$
$$= \max_w E_{Q^w} \log \frac{P(\underline{x}|\hat{\theta}(\underline{x}))}{Q^w(\underline{x})} \quad (6)$$

where the maximization is enlarged from Θ to distributions on Θ, as is standard to allow equality of the minimax and maximin values. The maximization over w yields least favorable priors $\overline{w}$ for which the corresponding procedure, coding based on $Q^{\overline{w}}(\underline{x})$, is both maximin and minimax.

Related quantities studied in universal data compression are based on the expected codelength difference (redundancy)

$$D(P_\theta \| Q) = E_\theta \log \frac{P(\underline{x}|\theta)}{Q(\underline{x})}$$

which uses the unknown θ in the target value $\log 1/P(\underline{x}|\theta)$ rather than the MLE. The average redundancy with respect to a distribution on θ is equal to Shannon's mutual information $I(\theta; \underline{x})$ when the Bayes optimal code is used. Consequently, the maximin average redundancy is $\max_w I(\theta; \underline{x})$, which is recognized as the Shannon information capacity of the class $\{P(\underline{x}|\theta): \theta \in \Theta\}$ (Davisson [12]). The minimax value $\min_Q \max_\theta E_\theta \log P(\underline{x}|\theta)/Q(\underline{x})$ and the maximin value of the redundancy (i.e., the capacity) are equal (see Davisson et al. [14] and Haussler [28]). In subsequent sections we will have more to say about the Kullback–Leibler divergence $E_\theta \log P(\underline{x}|\theta)/Q(\underline{x})$, including interpretations in coding and prediction, its asymptotics, and useful finite sample bounds.

Both of the target values $\log 1/P(\underline{x}|\theta)$ and $\log 1/P(\underline{x}|\hat{\theta})$ are unrealizable as codelengths (because of lack of knowledge of θ in one case and because of failure of Kraft's inequality in the other) and an extra descriptional price is to be paid to encode $\underline{x}$. In this section we retain $\log 1/P(\underline{x}|\hat{\theta})$ as the idealized target value for several reasons, not the least of which is that (unlike the other choice) it can be evaluated from the data alone and so can be a basis for the MDL criterion. By use of the same quantity in pointwise, worst case, and average value analyses we achieve a better understanding of its properties. We identify that the parametric complexity $\log C(\mathcal{M}, n)$ (and its asymptotic expression) arises in characterization of the minimax regret, the minimax expected regret, and in pointwise bounds that hold for most sequences and most distributions in the model class.

Note that the minimax value of the expected regret, through its maximin characterization in (6), may be expressed as

$$\mathcal{R}_n(\mathcal{M}) = \max_w E_{Q^w} \log \frac{P(\underline{x}|\hat{\theta}(\underline{x}))}{Q^w(\underline{x})}$$
$$= \log C(\mathcal{M}, n) - \min_w D(Q^w(\underline{x}) \| Q^*(\underline{x})). \quad (7)$$

Thus optimization over w to yield a minimax and maximin procedure is equivalent to choosing a mixture $Q^{\overline{w}}(\underline{x})$ closest to the normalized maximum likelihood $Q^*(\underline{x})$ in the sense of Kullback–Leibler divergence (see also [56]). Moreover, this divergence $D(Q^{\overline{w}} \| Q^*)$ represents the gap between the minimax value of the regret and the minimax value of the expected regret. When the gap is small, optimization of the worst case value of the regret is not too different from optimization of the worst expected value over distributions in the class. In particular, if for some w the average regret $E_{Q^w} \log (P(\underline{x}|\hat{\theta}(\underline{x}))/Q^w(\underline{x}))$ and the NML regret $\log C(\mathcal{M}, n)$ agree asymptotically, then $D(Q^w(\underline{x}) \| Q^*(\underline{x})) \to 0$ and, consequently, w is asymptotically least favorable and

the asymptotic minimax regret and minimax expected regret coincide. Such asymptotic agreement of (average) regret for the NML and mixture distributions is addressed next.

D. Asymptotic Equivalence of Optimal Solutions in Average and Worst Cases

The solutions to the two related minimax problems in the preceding subsection, namely, the NML distribution $Q^*(\underline{x})$ and the mixture $Q^w(\underline{x})$ with respect to a distribution $w(\theta)$

$$Q^w(\underline{x}) = \int P(\underline{x}|\theta) \, dw(\theta)$$

both have merits as defining the codelength for the MDL principle, and deserve to be studied more closely. The mixtures, in particular, for a fixed-weight distribution $w(\theta)$ have the advantage, in addition to average regret optimality, that they extend to a distribution on infinite sequences when $P(\underline{x}|\theta)$ is defined consistently for all n, and hence they define a random process. To do the same for the NML distribution, a construct of the type

$$Q^*(x_{n+1}|x^n) = Q^*(x^{n+1})/\Sigma_u Q^*(x^n, u)$$

may be used.

We can study the asymptotic codelength of these distributions for smooth parametric families $\{P(\underline{x}|\theta): \theta \in \Theta \subset R^d\}$ on $\underline{x} = \mathcal{S}^n$ possessing an empirical Fisher information matrix $\hat{I}(\theta)$ of second derivatives of $(1/n) \log 1/P(\underline{x}|\theta)$. Let $I(\theta)$ be the corresponding Fisher information. We are interested both in the mean codelength and the pointwise codelength. We begin with the mixtures, for which the main technique is Laplace's approximation. Let $w(\theta)$ the prior density assumed to be continuous and positive. For smooth independent and identically distributed (i.i.d.) models, the expected regret is given by

$$E_{P(\underline{x}|\theta)}[\log 1/Q^w(\underline{x}) - \log 1/P(\underline{x}|\hat{\theta})]$$
$$= (d/2) \log \frac{n}{2\pi} + \log |I(\theta)|^{1/2}/w(\theta) + o(1)$$

where the remainder tends to zero uniformly in compact sets in the interior of Θ (see Clarke and Barron, [9, p. 454], where references are given for suitable conditions on the family to ensure the regularity of the MLE). This expected regret expression leads naturally to the choice of $w(\theta)$ equal to the Jeffreys prior proportional to $|I(\theta)|^{1/2}$ to achieve an approximately constant expected regret when $|I(\theta)|^{1/2}$ is integrable on Θ. The Jeffreys prior is

$$w_J(\theta) = |I(\theta)|^{1/2}/c_J$$

where $c_J = \int |I(\theta)|^{1/2} d\theta$. This gives, uniformly in sets interior to the parameter space, a value for the expected regret of

$$(d/2) \log \frac{n}{2\pi} + \log \int |I(\theta)|^{1/2} d\theta + o(1) \quad (8)$$

and, consequently, this is also the asymptotic value of the average regret $E_{Q^w} \log (P(\underline{x}|\hat{\theta}(\underline{x}))/Q^w(\underline{x}))$ with $w = w_J$. As discussed above, if the minimax regret has the same asymptotics as this average regret, then the minimax regret and minimax expected regret agree asymptotically and $D(Q^{w_J}(\underline{x})\|Q^*(\underline{x}))$ tends to zero. This asymptotic equivalence has been identified in the special case of the class of all discrete memoryless (i.i.d.) sources on a given finite alphabet in Xie and Barron [56]. Here we show it holds more generally.

The key property of Jeffreys prior [33] for statistics and information theory is that it is the locally invariant measure that makes small Kullback–Leibler balls have equal prior probability (see Hartigan [24, pp. 48–49]).

We next study the NML distribution and its asymptotic pointwise codelength. In Rissanen [43] conditions are given (without i.i.d. requirement) such that the code based on the NML distribution

$$Q^*(\underline{x}) = P(\underline{x}|\hat{\theta}(\underline{x}))/C_{\mathcal{M},n}$$

achieves regret that satisfies asymptotically

$$\log C(\mathcal{M},n) = (d/2)\log \frac{n}{2\pi} + \log \int |I(\theta)|^{1/2}\, d\theta + o(1).$$

That gives the asymptotics of what we have called the parametric complexity. The stochastic complexity is the associated codelength based on the NML distribution, which satisfies

$$\log 1/Q^*(\underline{x}) = \log 1/P(\underline{x}|\hat{\theta}) + (d/2)\log \frac{n}{2\pi}$$
$$+ \log \int |I(\theta)|^{1/2}\, d\theta + o(1) \qquad (9)$$

where the remainder does not depend on $\underline{x}$ and tends to zero as $n \to \infty$. The derivation in [43] directly examines the normalization factor in the NML code using a uniform central limit theorem assumption for the parameter estimates and does not involve Laplace's approximation.

The regret of this NML code is seen to agree with the average regret (8) of the mixture with Jeffreys' prior, in the sense that the difference tends to zero, which means that $D(Q^{w_J}(\underline{x})\|Q^*(\underline{x}))$ tends to zero as $n \to \infty$, providing the desired asymptotic equivalence of the Jeffreys mixture and normalized maximum likelihood.

Though $Q^{w_J}(\underline{x})$ and $Q^*(\underline{x})$ merge in the Kullback–Leibler sense, the ratio need not converge to one for every data sequence. Indeed, Laplace's approximation can be applied to obtain the pointwise codelength for the mixtures

$$\log 1/Q^w(\underline{x}) = \log 1/P(\underline{x}|\hat{\theta}) + \frac{d}{2}\log \frac{n}{2\pi}$$
$$+ \log \frac{|\hat{I}(\hat{\theta})|^{1/2}}{w(\hat{\theta})} + \epsilon_n(\underline{x}) \qquad (10)$$

where for the remainder to be small it is necessary that $\underline{x}$ be such that $\hat{\theta}(\underline{x})$ is in the interior of Θ. Here again a choice for $w(\theta)$ as Jeffreys' prior yields the same parametric cost as in (9), except for the remainder terms $\frac{1}{2}\log |\hat{I}(\hat{\theta})|/|I(\hat{\theta})| + \epsilon_n(\underline{x})$. These should have the desired stochastic behavior of converging to zero in probability for each P_θ with θ interior to Θ. By arranging for modifications to the mixture to better encode sequences with $\hat{\theta}$ near the boundary, or with $\hat{I}$ not close to I, it is possible to obtain codelengths under suitable conditions such that uniformly in $\underline{x}$ they do not exceed the

minimax regret asymptotically. See Xie and Barron [56] and Takeuchi and Barron [50].

E. Strong Optimality of Stochastic Complexity

We have seen that the solutions to the two minimax optimization problems behave in a similar manner, and the expressions (9) and (10) for the asymptotic codelength have the built-in terms we would like to see. First, there is the target value $\log 1/P(\underline{x}|\hat{\theta})$ that would be achievable only with advance knowledge of the maximum-likelihood estimate $\hat{\theta} = \hat{\theta}(\underline{x})$. Secondly, the remaining terms, dominated by the ubiquitous $(d/2)\log n$ penalty on the number of parameters, express the codelength price of our lack of advance knowledge of the best $\hat{\theta}$. Still, since the solutions are based on minimax criteria (for the regret or expected regret), a nagging suspicion remains that there might be another codelength which cannot be beaten except for some very rare sequences or a very small subset of the models. Reassuringly enough, it was shown in Rissanen [41] that the common behavior described above, in fact, is optimal for most models in the sense of the following theorem, which generalizes Shannon's noiseless coding theorem, by showing a positive lower bound on the redundancy of order $(k/2)\log n$ for most θ.

Assume that there exist estimates $\hat{\theta}(x^n)$ which satisfy the central limit theorem at each interior point of Θ, such that $\sqrt{n}(\hat{\theta}(x^n) - \theta)$ converges in distribution (or, more generally, such that $\sqrt{n}(\hat{\theta}(x^n) - \theta)$ is $O(1)$ in probability). Assume that the boundary of Θ has zero volume. If $Q(x^n)$ is any probability distribution for x^n, then (Rissanen [56]) for each positive number ϵ and for all $\theta \in \Theta$, except in a set whose volume goes to zero as $n \to \infty$

$$E_{P_\theta} \log \frac{P(x^n\|\theta)}{Q(x^n)} \geq \frac{k-\epsilon}{2}\log n.$$

Later Merhav and Feder [37] gave similar conclusions bounding the measure of the set of models for which the redundancy is a specified amount less than a target value. They use the minimax redundancy for the target value without recourse to parametric regularity assumptions, and they use any asymptotically least favorable (asymptotically capacity achieving) prior as the measure. Under the parametric assumptions, Rissanen [42], with later refinements by Barron and Hengartner [6], shows that the set of parameter values with $\overline{\lim}_n E_{P_\theta} \log P(x^n\|\theta)/Q(x^n)/\log n < (k/2)$ has volume equal to zero, and [6] shows how this conclusion may be used to strengthen classical statistical results on the negligibility of superefficient parameter estimation. Barron [2] obtained strong pointwise lower bounds that hold for almost every $\underline{x}$ sequence and almost every θ. Related almost sure results appear in Dawid [17].

Here we show that the technique in [2] yields asymptotic pointwise regret lower bounds for general codes that coincide (to within a small amount) with the asymptotic minimax regret including the constant terms.

Assume for the moment that $\underline{x}$ is distributed according to P and coded using Q. We recall the basic Markov-type inequality

$$P\{Q(\underline{x})/P(\underline{x}) \geq 2^c\} \leq 2^{-c}.$$

704

and the implication that the codelength difference $\log 1/Q(\underline{x}) - \log 1/P(\underline{x})$ is greater than $-c$ except in a set of probability less than 2^{-c} for all $c \geq 0$. We apply the inequality with P replaced by the mixture distribution

$$P^w(\underline{x}) = \int P_\theta(\underline{x}) \, dw(\theta)$$

to yield a conclusion for the codelength difference

$$d_n(\underline{x}) = \log 1/Q(\underline{x}) - \log 1/P^w(\underline{x}).$$

We find that for any choice of code distribution $Q(\underline{x})$, the P^w probability that $d_n \leq -2c$ is less than 2^{-2c}, so applying Markov's inequality to the prior probability

$$W\{\theta: P_\theta\{d_n \leq -2c\} > 2^{-c}\}$$

we find that it is not larger than 2^{-c}. The conclusion we will use is that the P_θ probability that $\log 1/Q(\underline{x})$ is less than $\log 1/P^w(\underline{x}) - 2c$ is less than 2^{-c}, except for a set B of θ with $w(B) \leq 2^{-c}$.

The Laplace approximation reveals under suitable conditions that

$$\log 1/P^w(\underline{x}) = \log 1/P(\underline{x}|\hat{\theta}) + \frac{d}{2} \log \frac{n}{2\pi}$$
$$+ \log |I(\theta)|^{1/2}/w(\theta) + o(1)$$

where the remainder $o(1)$ tends to zero in P_θ probability for each θ in the interior of the parameter space. Take w to be the Jeffreys prior density, which, because of its local invariance property for small information-theoretic balls, is natural to quantify the measure of exceptional sets of θ. The conclusion in this case becomes for any competing code distribution Q the code regret is lower-bounded by

$$\log 1/Q(\underline{x}) - \log 1/P(\underline{x}|\hat{\theta})$$
$$\geq \frac{d}{2} \log \frac{n}{2\pi} + \log \int |I(\theta)|^{1/2} \, d\theta - 2c + o(1)$$

where $o(1)$ tends to zero in P_θ-probability, for all θ in the interior of the parameter set, except for θ in a set B of Jeffreys probability less than 2^{-c}. This shows that asymptotically, the minimax regret cannot be beaten by much for most $\underline{x}$ with distribution P_θ for most θ.

Serendipitously, the basic inequality remains true with a uniformity over all n inside the probability. That is, $P\{\sup_n Q(\underline{x})/P(\underline{x}) \geq 2^c\}$ remains not greater than 2^{-c}, provided that the the sequences of distributions for $\underline{x} = x_1, x_2, \cdots, x_n$ remain compatible as n is increased (Barron [2, p. 28], Tulcea [51]). Consequently, setting

$$T = \sup_n \log^+ Q(\underline{x})/P(\underline{x})$$

we see that uniformly in n the excess codelength $\log 1/Q(\underline{x}) - \log 1/P(\underline{x})$ remains bigger than $-T$ where $T \geq 0$ has mean $E_P T$ not larger than $\log e$ and it is stochastically dominated by an exponential random variable $P\{T > c\} \leq 2^{-c}$. Using the Jeffreys mixture as the standard, it follows that for any competing compatible sequences of code distributions $Q(\underline{x})$ we have that for all n the codelength $\log 1/Q(\underline{x})$ is at least $\log 1/P^{w_J}(\underline{x}) - T$, which shows that the following strong

pointwise lower bound holds P^{w_J}-almost surely, and hence also P_θ-almost surely for w_J-almost every θ

$$\log 1/Q(\underline{x}) > \log 1/P(\underline{x}|\hat{\theta}) + \frac{d}{2} \log \frac{n}{2\pi}$$
$$+ \log \int |I(\theta)|^{1/2} \, d\theta - T + o(1)$$

provided the remainder in the Laplace approximation tends to zero P_θ-almost surely, for almost every θ. To quantify the behavior of T we note that $P^w\{T > 2c\} \leq 2^{-2c}$ and hence $P_\theta\{T > 2c\} \leq 2^{-c}$ except in a set B of θ with Jeffreys probability less than 2^{-c}.

In summary, these results provide a grand generalization of Shannon's noiseless coding theorem in setting the limit to the available codelength and also demonstrating coding techniques which achieve the limit. For such reasons and due to the accurate evaluation of the codelength in (9) it was called in [43] the *stochastic complexity* of the data string, given the model class involved.

F. Simplification via Sufficiency

Both the NML and mixture codes have a decomposition, based on likelihood factorization for sufficient statistics, that permits insightful simplification of the computations in some cases. In this section we change the notation for the members of the parametric family to $f_\theta(\underline{x})$ or $p_\theta(\underline{x})$ rather than $p(\underline{x}|\theta)$ so as to maintain a clearer distinction from conditional distributions, given estimators, or other functions of the data. In particular, in this section, $p(\underline{x}|\hat{\theta})$ refers to the conditional distribution given the maximum-likelihood estimator rather than the likelihood evaluated at the MLE.

For a sufficient statistic $S = S(\underline{x})$ the probability of sequences $\underline{x}$ factors as $f_\theta(\underline{x}) = p(\underline{x}|s)p_\theta(s)$ where $p(\underline{x}|s)$ is the conditional probability function for $\underline{x}$ given $S(\underline{x}) = s$ (independent of θ by sufficiency) and

$$p_\theta(s) = \sum_{\underline{x}: S(\underline{x})=s} f_\theta(\underline{x})$$

is the probability function for the statistic S. As a consequence of the factorization, the maximum-likelihood estimate $\hat{\theta} = \hat{\theta}(s)$ may be regarded as a function of the sufficient statistic. Consequently, the maximized likelihood is $f_{\hat{\theta}}(\underline{x}) = p(\underline{x}|s)p_{\hat{\theta}}(s)$ at $s = S(\underline{x})$, and the normalizing constant simplifies to

$$C = C(\mathcal{M}, n) = \sum_{\underline{x}} f_{\hat{\theta}(\underline{x})}(\underline{x}) = \sum_s p_{\hat{\theta}(s)}(s)$$

since

$$\sum_{\underline{x}: s(\underline{x})=s} p(\underline{x}|s) = 1.$$

Thus there is a close connection between the NML distribution for s, namely, $p^*(s) = p_{\hat{\theta}(s)}(s)/C$, and the NML distribution for $\underline{x}$

$$f^*(\underline{x}) = p(\underline{x}|s)p^*(s)$$

at $s = S(\underline{x})$. The stochastic complexity, then, splits as

$$\log 1/f^*(\underline{x}) = \log 1/p(\underline{x}|s) + \log 1/p^*(s)$$

into the complexity of s plus the Shannon codelength for $\underline{x}$ given s. In much the same manner, the Bayes mixtures factor as

$$f_w(\underline{x}) = p(\underline{x}|s)p_w(s)$$

where $p_w(s) = \int p_\theta(s)\,dw(\theta)$ and Bayes optimal codelengths split as

$$\log 1/f_w(\underline{x}) = \log 1/p(\underline{x}|s) + \log 1/p_w(s).$$

Of particular interest is the case (which holds true in exponential families) that the maximum-likelihood estimator is itself a sufficient statistic $s = \hat{\theta}(\underline{x})$. In this case, the NML distribution for $\underline{x}$ is

$$f^*(\underline{x}) = p(\underline{x}|\hat{\theta})p^*(\hat{\theta})$$

and the NML distribution for $S = \hat{\theta}$ becomes

$$p^*(s) = p_{\hat{\theta}}(\hat{\theta})/C = g(\hat{\theta})/C,$$

where $g(\theta) = p_\theta(\theta)$ which is obtained simply as a density on the range of the parameter estimator by plugging into the distribution of the estimator the same value for the estimate as for the parameter, with normalization constant $C = \Sigma_{\hat{\theta}}\, p_{\hat{\theta}}(\hat{\theta})$. For example, in the Bernoulli(p) model the NML distribution of the relative frequency of ones $\hat{p} = y/n$ is

$$\binom{n}{y}(y/n)^y(1 - y/n)^{n-y}/C_n$$

with

$$C_n = \sum_{y=0}^{n} \binom{n}{y}(y/n)^y(1 - y/n)^{n-y}$$

which by Stirling's formula can be shown to be close to the Jeffreys Beta $(1/2, 1/2)$ distribution for p internal to $(0, 1)$. In the Gaussian model studied in Section V, the NML distribution for the sufficient statistic subject to certain constraints on the parameters is shown to be exactly Jeffreys' distribution.

IV. Inference

A. Predictive Coding and Estimation

A given joint distribution $Q(\underline{x}) = Q(x^n)$ on n-tuples can be written in the predictive or sequential form

$$Q(x^n) = \prod_t^n Q(x_t|x^{t-1}). \qquad (11)$$

The converse is also true; that is, a joint distribution $Q(x^n)$ can be constructed by specifying the predictive distributions $\{Q(\cdot|x^{t-1})\}$.

For a given joint distribution Q, the factorization in (11) implies a predictive implementation of coding based on Q that encodes $x_1, x_2, \cdots, x_n$ one by one in that order. The codelength of x_1 is $-\log_2 Q(x_1)$. After the transmission of x_1, it will be known both to the sender and the receiver, and x_2 can be transmitted using the predictive distribution $Q(\cdot|x_1)$, which results in a codelength $-\log_2 Q(x_2|x_1)$. At time t the first $t - 1$ data points $x^{t-1} = (x_1, \cdots, x_{t-1})$ are known to the sender and the receiver, and $Q(\cdot|x^{t-1})$ can be used to transmit

x_t, which results in the codelength $-\log_2 Q(x_t|x^{t-1})$. In other words,

$$-\log_2 Q(x^n) = \sum_{t=1}^{n} -\log_2 Q(x_t|x^{t-1}) \qquad (12)$$

which means that the total codelength for encoding x^n using $Q(\cdot)$ is the same as encoding the symbols one by ony using the predictive or conditional distribution $Q(\cdot|x^{t-1})$.

If we now postulate that the underlying source distribution is $P(x^n)$, the expected redundancy of Q with respect to P, which is different from the expected regret considered in Section III, is the Kullback–Leibler divergence between P and Q

$$D(P(x^n)\|Q(x^n)) = E_P \log_2 \frac{P(x^n)}{Q(x^n)}$$

$$= E_P \log_2 \frac{\prod_t P(x_t|x^{t-1})}{\prod_t Q(x_t|x^{t-1})}$$

$$= \sum_{t=1}^{n} E_{P(x^n)} \log_2 \frac{P(x_t|x^{t-1})}{Q(x_t|x^{t-1})}$$

$$= \sum_{t=1}^{n} E_{P(x^{t-1})} E_{P(x_t|x^{t-1})}$$

$$\cdot \log_2 \frac{P(x_t|x^{t-1})}{Q(x_t|x^{t-1})}$$

$$= \sum_{t=1}^{n} E_{P(x^{t-1})} D(P(\cdot|x^{t-1})\,Q(\cdot|x^{t-1})).$$

This identity links the fundamental quantity, *expected redundancy*, from coding theory with statistical estimation, because the right-hand side is precisely the accumulated prediction error of the Kullback–Leibler risk of the sequence $\{Q(x_t|x^{t-1})\colon\ t = 1, \cdots, n\}$. This risk is equivalent to the mean squared error (MSE) when both P and Q are Gaussian distributions with the same covariance structure. In general, when P and Q are bounded away from zero, the Kullback–Leibler risk has a close connection with more traditional statistical estimation measures such as the square of the L^2 norm (MSE) and the Hellinger norm.

When Q is the mixture $Q(x^n) = \int P_\theta(x^n)\,dw(\theta)$ over a regular parametric family

$$\{P_\theta(x^n)\colon\ \theta \in \Theta \subset R^d\}$$

of d parameters with the mixing distribution or prior w, the tth summand in the accumulated risk is the risk of the Bayesian predictive distribution

$$Q(x_t|x^{t-1}) = \int P_\theta(x_t|x^{t-1}) P_w(\theta|x^{t-1})\,d\theta$$

where P_w is the posterior distribution of θ given x^{t-1}. In coding again, in order to build a code for x^n predictively, the predictive distribution $Q(\cdot|x^{t-1})$ allows us to revise the code in light of what we have learned from data prior to time t. For example, frequently appearing symbols should be assigned short codewords and less frequent ones long codewords. This predictive form lends itself naturally to the on-line adaptation of coding or estimation to the underlying source. Moreover, it has an intimate connection with the prequential approach to statistical inference as advocated by Dawid, [15], [16].

Let Q be built on the plug-in predictive distribution based on an estimator $\hat\theta(x^n)$, which often is a suitably modified maximum-likelihood estimator to avoid singular probabilities

$$Q(x_t|x^{t-1}) = P_{\hat\theta(x^{t-1})}(x_t|x^{t-1}).$$

Then the tth summand in the accumulated risk is

$$E_{P_\theta(x^{t-1})}D(P_\theta(x_t|x^{t-1})\|P_{\hat\theta(x^{t-1})}(x_t|x^{t-1}))$$

which is approximately $d/(2t)$ if $\hat\theta(x^t)$ is an efficient sequence of estimators. Summing up gives

$$\sum_{t=1}^{n} d/(2t) \approx \frac{d}{2}\log n$$

and this is exactly the leading term in the parametric complexity at sample size n. Hence, whether we consider estimation or predictive coding or, for that matter, any form of coding, we meet this same optimal leading term $(d/2)\log n$ in the regular parametric case, and it plays a fundamental role in both.

To bolster the connection given here between the individual risk of efficient estimators of order $d/2n$ and the optimal cumulative risk or redundancy of order $(d/2)\log n$, we mention here that classic results on negligibility of the set of parameter values for which an estimator is superefficient (LeCam [35] assuming bounded loss) are extended in Barron and Hengartner [6] to the Kullback–Leibler loss using results of Rissanen [42] on the negligibility of the set of parameter values with coding redundancy asymptotically less than $(1-\epsilon)(d/2)\log n$.

Frequently, we wish to fit models where the number of parameters is not fixed, such as the class of all histograms. For such the tth term in the accumulated risk

$$E_{P(x^{t-1})}D(P(x_t|x^{t-1})\|P_{\hat\theta^{\hat d}}(x_t|x^{t-1}))$$

where $\hat d = \hat d(x^{t-1})$ denotes the maximium-likelihood estimate of the number of parameters in $\hat\theta = \hat\theta(x^{t-1})$, behaves under suitable smoothness conditions as $t^{-\alpha}$ for some $0 < \alpha < 1$. Then the accumulated risk itself behaves as

$$\frac{1}{n}\sum_{t}^{n} t^{-\alpha} \approx n^{-\alpha}$$

and $n^{-\alpha}$ may be called the *nonparametric complexity per sample* at sample size n.

B. Consistency of the MDL Order Estimates

A test for any model selection and estimation procedure is to apply it to the selection of a model class and then analyze the result under the presumption that the data are generated by a model in one of the classes. It is to the credit of the MDL principle that the model-selection criteria derived from it are consistent although there are obviously other ways to devise directly consistent model-selection criteria, see, for example, Hannan [22] and Merhav and Ziv [36].

Consider first a family of parametric model classes, one for each k in a countable set K

$$\mathcal{M}_k = \{P(\underline{x}|\theta)\colon \theta \in \Theta_k \subset R^{d_k}\}.$$

If we use the mixture model for each $\mathcal{M}_k$ to represent the class, we need to minimize

$$\log 1/Q_k(\underline{x}) + l(k)$$

where

$$Q_k(\underline{x}) = \int_{\Theta_k} w_k(\theta) P_k(\underline{x}|\theta)\, d\theta$$

and

$$\sum_{k\in K} 2^{-l(k)} \le 1.$$

Denote the data-generating class by $\mathcal{M}_{k_0}$. The MDL principle identifies $\mathcal{M}_{k_0}$ with Q_{k_0} probability tending to 1. That is, the MDL prinple leads to consistent-order selection criteria, on average, provided that Q_k are singular relative to Q_{k_0} on the space of infinite sequences. This is true, for example, if the Q_k are distinct stationary and ergodic distributions, or they are mixtures of such distributions, provided that the priors induced on the space of distributions are mutually singular. For instance, we may have parametric families of i.i.d., or Markov, distributions, where the parameter spaces are of different dimensions and absolutely continuous prior densities are assigned to each dimension.

The proof is simple, [2], [5]. Let Q^* be the mixture of Q_k except for k_0

$$Q^*(\underline{x}) = c_l^{-1} \sum_{k\neq k_0} 2^{-l(k)} Q_k(\underline{x})$$

where

$$c_l = \sum_{k\neq k_0} 2^{-l(k)} \le 1.$$

Because all the models in the summation are singular relative to Q_{k_0}, Q^* must be mutually singular with Q_{k_0}. It follows that the log-likelihood ratio or redundancy

$$\log Q_{k_0}(X^n)/Q^*(X^n) = \log 1/Q^*(X^n) - \log 1/Q_{k_0}(X^n)$$

tends almost surely to infinity, Doob [20]. We find that with Q_{k_0} probability one, for n large

$$l(k_0) + \log 1/Q_{k_0}(X^n) < \log 1/Q^*(X^n)$$
$$\le \min_{k\neq k_0}\{1/Q_k(X^n) + l(k)\}.$$

The second inequality holds, because the sum

$$Q^*(X^n) = \sum_{k\neq k_0} 2^{-l(k)} Q_k(X^n)$$

is larger than the maximum of the summands. Thus the minimizing distribution is the distribution Q_{k_0} from the correct model class $\mathcal{M}_{k_0}$ as n tends to infinity and under probability Q_{k_0}, provided that Q_k are singular relative to Q_{k_0} on the infinite-sequence space, that is,

$$Q_{k_0}(\hat k = k_0) = \int w_{k_0}(\theta) P(\hat k = k_0|\theta)\, d\theta \to 1.$$

Moreover, $Q_{k_0}(\hat{k} = k_0$ for all large $n) = 1$. This implies that $P_\theta(\hat{k} = k_0$ for all large $n) = 1$ and hence that as $n \to \infty$

$$P(\hat{k} = k_0|\theta) \to 1$$

for w_{k_0}-almost all $\theta \in \mathcal{M}_{k_0}$.

In many situations, such as nested exponential families, the above result holds for all $\theta \in \mathcal{M}_{k_0}$. The proof is more involved, but gives more insight. Roughly speaking, the mixture version of the MDL is an approximate penalized likelihood criterion just as the two-stage MDL, which asymptotically behaves as the Bayesian Information Criterion (BIC) of Schwartz [49].

For n large, in probability or almost surely

$$\log 1/Q_k(X^n) = \log 1/P(X^n|\hat{\theta}_k) + \frac{d_k}{2}\log n + O(1).$$

From classical parametric estimation theory for regular families, such as nested exponential families, we have the following asymptotic expansion:

$$\log 1/P(X^n|\hat{\theta}_k) - \log 1/P(X^n|\hat{\theta}_{k_0})$$
$$\begin{cases} \Rightarrow \chi^2_{k-k_0}, & \text{if } k \geq k_0 \\ n||\theta_k - \theta_{k_0}||^2(1 + o(1)), & \text{if } k < k_0. \end{cases}$$

This gives the consistency of the mixture MDL for all θ_{k_0}.

Since other forms of the MDL share the same asymptotic expression with the mixture, they also identify the correct model with probability tending to 1 as the sample size gets large. Consistency results for the predictive MDL principle can be found in [15], [17], and [32] for regression models, [23], and [31] for time-series models, and [53] for stochastic regression models. For exponential families, [27] gives a consistency result for BIC. Predictive, two-stage, and mixture forms of the MDL principle are studied and compared in [48] in terms of misfit probabilities and in two prediction frameworks for the regression model. It is worth noting that searching through all the subsets to find codelengths $l(\cdot)$ can be a nontrivial task on its own.

We note that for consistency any $\ell(k)$ satisfying Kraft's inequality is acceptable. However, for good finite sample behavior, as well as asymptotic behavior of risk and redundancy, one should pay closer attention to the issue of choice of description length of the models. The index of resolvability provides a means to gauge, in advance of observing the data, what sort of accuracy of estimation and data compression is to be expected for various hypothetical distributions, and thereby yields guidance in the choice of the model descriptions.

C. Resolvability

Perhaps more relevant than consistency of a selected model, which as formulated above would presume that the data are actually generated by a model in one of the candidate classes, is the demonstration that the MDL criterion is expected to give a suitable tradeoff between accuracy and complexity relative to the sample size, whether or not the models considered provide an exact representation of a data generating distribution. The index of resolvability from Barron and Cover [5] provides a tool for this analysis.

Consider first the case that the description length entails multiple stages, yielding a minimum description length of the form

$$\log 1/P_{\hat{k}}(\underline{x}|\hat{\theta}) + L_{\hat{k}}(\hat{\theta}) + \ell(\hat{k})$$
$$= \min_{k \in K} \min_{\theta \in \Theta_{k,\delta}} \{\log 1/P_k(\underline{x}|\theta) + L_k(\theta) + \ell(k)\}$$

where $\ell(k)$ is the codelength for the class index k in K, the term $L_k(\theta)$ is the codelength for parameter values of precision δ in a quantized parameter space $\Theta_{k,\delta}$, and, finally, $\log 1/P_k(\underline{x}|\theta)$ is the codelength for the data given the described class index and parameter values. (Typically, the precision δ is taken to be of order $1/\sqrt{n}$ so as to optimize the tradeoff between the terms in the description length, yielding $(d_k/2)\log n$ as a key component of $L_k(\theta)$.) Minimizing the description length in such a multistage code yields both a model selection $\hat{k}$ by MDL and a parameter estimate $\hat{\theta}$ (close to the maximum-likelihood estimate) in the selected family.

As in [5], it can be conceptually simpler to think of the pair k and θ as together specifying a model index, say m. Selection and estimation of $\hat{k}, \hat{\theta}$ provides an estimate $\hat{m}$. Then the above minimization is a special case of the following minimum description length formulation, where $\Sigma_m 2^{-L(m)} \leq 1$:

$$B(\underline{x}) = \log 1/P_{\hat{m}}(\underline{x}) + L(\hat{m}) = \min_m \{\log 1/P_m(\underline{x}) + L(m)\}.$$

The corresponding *index of resolvability* of a distribution P by the list of models P_m with sample size n is defined by

$$R_n(P) = \min_m \{D(P(x^n)||P_m(x^n))/n + L(m)/n\}$$

which expresses, in the form of the minimum expected description length per sample, the intrinsic tradeoff between Kullback–Leibler approximation error and the complexity relative to the sample size.

It is easy to see that $R_n(P)$ upper-bounds the expected redundancy per sample, which is

$$(1/n)E_P(B(X^n) - \log 1/P(X^n)).$$

It is also shown in Barron and Cover [5] that if the models P_m are i.i.d. and the data are indeed i.i.d. with respect to P, then the cumulative distribution corresponding to $P_{\hat{m}}$ converges (weakly) to P in probability, provided $\inf_m D(P||P_m) = 0$. Moreover, if $L(m)$ are modified to satisfy a somewhat more stringent summability requirement $\Sigma_m 2^{-\alpha L(m)}$ for some positive $\alpha < 1$, then the rate of convergence of $P_{\hat{m}}$ to P is bounded by the index of resolvability, in the sense that

$$H^2(P, P_{\hat{m}}) \leq O(R_n(P)) \tag{13}$$

in probability, where

$$H^2(P, Q) = \int (\sqrt{p(x)} - \sqrt{q(x)})^2 \, dx$$

is the squared Hellinger norm between distributions with densities p and q. These bounds are used in [5] and [7] to derive convergence rates in nonparametric settings with the use of sequences of parametric models of size selected by MDL.

For description length based on a mixture model $Q^w(\underline{x}) = \int P(\underline{x}|\theta)\,dw(\theta)$ analogous performance bounds are available from a related quantity. In particular, the index of resolvability of a distribution $P(\underline{x})$ using the mixture of models $P(\underline{x}|\theta)$ with prior w and any parameter set A (usually chosen as a neighborhood around P) and sample size n is defined by

$$R_{n,A}(P) = \max_{\theta \in A}(1/n)D(P(\underline{x})||P(\underline{x}|\theta)) + (1/n)\log 1/w(A)$$

which when optimized over parameter sets A yields Kullback–Leibler balls

$$A_\epsilon = \{\theta\colon (1/n)D(P(\underline{x})||P(\underline{x}|\theta)) \le \epsilon^2\}$$

and index of resolvability

$$R_n(P) = \min_\epsilon \{\epsilon^2 + (1/n)\log 1/w(A_\epsilon)\}.$$

As shown in [3] (see also [4], [6], [29], and [57]), this quantity provides for the mixture code an upper bound to the expected redundancy per sample and thereby it also provides and upper bound to the Cesaro average of the Kullback–Leibler risk of the Bayes predictive estimators already discussed in Section IV-A.

Various parametric and nonparametric examples of determination of risk bounds of MDL estimators are possible as demonstrated in the cited literature; here we shall be content to give, in the next subsection, a general determination of the minimax rates in nonparametric settings.

D. Optimal Rate Minimax Estimation and Mixture Coding

In Section III we used Laplace's approximation method to obtain the behavior of the mixture distributions as solutions to the minimax mean redundancy problem for parametric models. In this subsection, we base our approach on a mixture code (or distribution) over a finite net to provide a unified approach to the upper and lower bounds on the optimal estimation rate in the minimax density estimation paradigm. However, the corresponding NML results in this nonparametric density estimation problem are yet to be developed, and NML's connection to the mixture distributions in this context is yet to be explored.

Fano's inequality from Information Theory has always been used to derive the lower bounds [8], [18], [25], [26], [58]. MDL-based density estimators now provide refinement to the lower bound and a matching upper bound as shown in Yang and Barron [57], revealing a Kolmogorov capacity characterization of the minimax values of risk and redundancy.

Consider a class $\mathcal{M}$ of i.i.d. densities, for which the distances between pairs of densities for x satisfy $D(f(\cdot)||g(\cdot)) \asymp H^2(f,g)$ for f and g in $\mathcal{M}$. This equivalence is satisfied by many, if not all, smooth function classes. The advantage of H^2 is that it satisfies the triangle inequality while D does not. However, D brings in clean information-theoretic identities and inequalities. Taking advantage of the equivalence of H^2 and D, we can switch between D and H^2 when appropriate to obtain a clear picture on optimal rate minimax estimation. Metric-entropy nets into which the estimation problem will be transferred turn out to be useful. Because such nets are finite, information-theoretic results such as Fano's inequality are easy to apply.

We are interested in the minimax estimation rates

$$\min_{\hat{f}}\max_{f \in \mathcal{M}} E_f H^2(f,\hat{f})$$

and

$$\min_{\hat{f}}\max_{f \in \mathcal{M}} E_f D(f(x)||\hat{f}(x))$$

where the minimum is over estimators $\hat{f}$ based on an i.i.d. sample of size n drawn from f, the divergence D is evaluated by averaging x with respect to f, independent of the sample, and E_f is taking the expected value of D as a function of the sample from f. Morever, we are interested in the minimax nonparametric complexity (redundancy)

$$\min_{Q}\max_{f \in \mathcal{M}} E_f D(f(x^n)||Q(x^n))$$

which, in accordance with Section IV-A, is the same as the minimax cumulative Kullback–Leibler risk. Here

$$f(x^n) = \prod_{i=1}^{n} f(x_i)$$

and the minimum is taken over all joint probability densities Q on $\mathcal{X}^n$ (which provide codes for x^n in $\mathcal{X}^n$). For a recent treatment of asymptotics and metric entropy characterization of the latter quantity see Haussler and Opper [30]. Here, following Yang and Barron [57], we focus on the relationship of the minimax risk to the nonparametric complexity and the Kolmogorov metric entropy as revealed through the resolvability and an improved application of Fano's inequality.

Let $V(\epsilon_n)$ be the Kolmogorov metric entropy of the ϵ_n-net $N(\epsilon_n)$ of $\mathcal{M}$ in terms of H or $\sqrt{D}$. That is, we need $N(\epsilon_n) = 2^{V(\epsilon_n)}$ number of ϵ_n balls to cover the class and no fewer. We use the code corresponding to the uniform mixture distribution $f_{\epsilon_n}(x^n)$ of the centers in the ϵ_n-cover. We examine the redundancy of the mixture with respect to the ϵ_n-net

$$R_n^{\epsilon_n}(f) = D(f(x^n)||f_{\epsilon_n}(x^n))$$

which from (13) is also the accumulated Kullback–Leibler prediction error of $f_{\epsilon_n}(x^n)$.

This is a crucial quantity in both upper and lower bounds on the minimax estimation error. It also bounds from above the risk of the mixture-induced density estimator $\hat{f}^{\epsilon_n}(x)$

$$E_f H^2(f,\hat{f}^{\epsilon_n}) \asymp ED(f||\hat{f}^{\epsilon_n}) \le \frac{1}{n}R_n^{\epsilon_n}(f),$$

where

$$\hat{f}^{\epsilon_n}(x) = (1/n)\sum_{i=0}^{n-1} f_{\epsilon_n}(x_{i+1}=x|x^i)$$

is the Cesaro average of the predictive density estimator induced by the mixture density $f_{\epsilon_n}(x^n)$ on the ϵ_n-net.

Moreover, there is a bound on $R_n^{\epsilon_n}(f)$ in terms of an index of resolvability. Let $g_f(x^n)$ be the closest member to

709

$f(x^n)$ in $N(\epsilon_n)$. Then $D(f(x^n)\|g_f(x^n)) \leq n\epsilon_n^2$, and

$$R_n^{\epsilon_n}(f) = D(f(x^n)\|f_{\epsilon_n}(x^n))$$

$$= E_f \log \left\{ f(x^n) / (2^{-V(\epsilon_n)} \sum_{g \in N(\epsilon_n)} g(x^n)) \right\}$$

$$\leq E_f \log \{ f(x^n) / (2^{-V(\epsilon_n)} g_f(x^n)) \}$$

$$= V(\epsilon_n^2) + D(f(x^n)\|g_f(x^n))$$

$$\leq V(\epsilon_n) + n\epsilon_n^2. \tag{14}$$

It follows that

$$E_f H^2(f, \hat{f}^{\epsilon_n}) \leq V(\epsilon_n)/n + \epsilon_n^2. \tag{15}$$

The same order upper bound holds for a minimum complexity estimator as shown in Barron and Cover [5], in which one minimizes a two-stage codelength over f in $N(\epsilon_n)$.

By adjusting the choice of ϵ_n these upper bounds yield the minimax rate for the redundancy and consequently for the cumulative Kullback–Leibler risk of predictive estimation.

If the function class $\mathcal{M}$ is sufficiently large (in the sense that $\tilde{\epsilon}$, achieving $V(\tilde{\epsilon}) = V(\epsilon)/4$, is of the same order as ϵ, as ϵ tends to zero), then the bounds here also yield the minimax rate for the estimation of f in the traditional noncumulative formulation.

Indeed, by a now standard Information Theory technique introduced to the statistics community by Hasminskii [25] (see also [8], [18], [26], [57], and [58]) the estimation error in terms of a metric can be bounded from below by Fano's inequality via the probability of testing error on the finite ϵ_n-net. Here we choose the net $N(\epsilon_n)$ as a maximal packing set in which we have the largest number of densities in $\mathcal{M}$ that can be separated by ϵ_n in the Hellinger metric (consequently, it is also a cover in the sense that every f in $\mathcal{M}$ is within ϵ_n of a density in the net). For any given estimator $\hat{f}$ of f, by consideration of the estimator $\tilde{f}$ which replaces $\hat{f}$ by the closest density in the ϵ_n net and use of the triangle inequality for Hellinger distance, one has that

$$\max_{f \in \mathcal{M}} E_f H^2(f, \hat{f}) \geq (\epsilon_n/2)^2 \max_{f \in N(\epsilon_n)} P_f(\tilde{f} \neq f).$$

Then by application of Fano's inequality there is a positive constant c such that for any estimator

$$\max_{f \in \mathcal{M}} E_f H^2(f, \hat{f}) \geq c\epsilon_n^2 (1 - (I_{\epsilon_n} + \log 2)/V(\epsilon_n))$$

where I_{ϵ_n} is the mutual information between Θ and X^n when Θ takes a uniform distribution on the ϵ_n-net and the conditional distribution of X^n, given a particular value f in the net, is $f(x^n) = \Pi_i f(x_i)$. Now as we recall this mutual information has been well studied, and ever since the development of Fano's inequality in the 1950's the precise nature of the capacity (the maximum value of the information over choices of input distribution) has played a central role in applications of Fano's inequality in Information Theory [11]. However, prior to reference [57], the mutual information in these statistical bounds had been bounded from above by the Kullback–Leibler diameter

$$n \times \max_{f, f'} D(f\|f').$$

To yield satisfactory rate bounds, from what would otherwise be a crude bound on mutual information, required first restricting f, f' to a subset of $\mathcal{M}$ of special structure in which the diameter is of the same order as the separation $n\epsilon_n^2$ and the same order as its log-cardinality (typically, via a hypercube construction), plus a hope that the minimax rate on the subset would be as large as on the original family $\mathcal{M}$, and the existence of such a special structure was a condition of the theory, so that application of that theory requires the invention of a hypercube-like construction in each case. However, the requirement of such construction can be easily bypassed.

Indeed, since I_{ϵ_n} is the minimum Bayes average redundancy with respect to a prior, it is not larger than the maximum redundancy of any given procedure. That is,

$$I_{\epsilon_n} = \min_Q (1/2^{V(\epsilon_n)}) \sum_{f \in N(\epsilon_n)} D(f(x^n)\|Q(x^n))$$

$$\leq \min_Q \max_{f \in N(\epsilon_n)} D(f(x^n)\|Q(x^n))$$

$$\leq \min_Q \max_{f \in \mathcal{M}} D(f(x^n)\|Q(x^n)).$$

Hence for any joint distribution Q on x^n

$$I_{\epsilon_n} \leq \max_{f \in \mathcal{M}} D(f(x^n)\|Q(x^n)).$$

For $\tilde{\epsilon}_n$ to be chosen later, take $Q(x^n) = f_{\tilde{\epsilon}_n}(x^n)$ as the uniform mixture over the net $N(\tilde{\epsilon}_n)$ to get

$$I_{\epsilon_n} \leq \max_{f \in \mathcal{M}} D(f(x^n)\|f_{\tilde{\epsilon}_n}(x^n)) = R_n^{\tilde{\epsilon}_n}(f).$$

It follows from the resolvability bound (14) that

$$I_{\epsilon_n} \leq V(\tilde{\epsilon}_n) + n\tilde{\epsilon}_n^2.$$

Hence

$$\max_{f \in \mathcal{M}} E_f H^2(f, \hat{f}) \geq c\epsilon_n^2 (1 - (V(\tilde{\epsilon}_n) + n\tilde{\epsilon}_n^2 + \log 2)/V(\epsilon_n)).$$

It is clear that the $V(\epsilon) + n\epsilon^2$ acts as the critical index of resolvability since it appears in both upper and lower bounds on the H^2 (or D) error in density estimation. It determines the minimax rate when $H^2 \asymp D$ as follows. Set $\tilde{\epsilon}_n$ to achieve $V(\tilde{\epsilon}_n) = n\tilde{\epsilon}_n^2$, thereby achieving the minimum order for $V(\epsilon) + n\epsilon^2$, and then choose ϵ_n somewhat smaller, but of the same order, such that

$$V(\tilde{\epsilon}_n) + n\tilde{\epsilon}_n^2 + \log 2 = V(\epsilon_n)/2.$$

Then we have

$$\max_{f \in \mathcal{M}} E_f H^2(f, \hat{f}) \geq c\epsilon_n^2/2.$$

Since the upper and lower bounds are of the same order we conclude that we have characterized the asymptotic rate of the minimax value.

Indeed, we find there is asymptotic agreement among several fundamental quantities: the nonparametric complexity (redundancy) per symbol

$$\min_g \max_{f \in \mathcal{M}} D(f(x^n)\|g(x^n))/n,$$

the Shannon capacity

$$\max_{w(\theta)\,\mathrm{on}\,\mathcal{M}} I(\Theta; X^n)/n,$$

the Kolmogorov capacity $V(\epsilon_n)/n$, the critical radius ϵ_n^2, the minimax Cesaro average prediction risk

$$\min_{\hat{f}_0,\hat{f}_1,\cdots,\hat{f}_{n-1}} \max_{f\in\mathcal{M}} (1/n) \sum_{t=0}^{n-1} E_f D(f\|\hat{f}_t),$$

the minimax Kullback–Leibler risk, and the minimax squared Hellinger risk based on a sample of size n.

These metric entropy characterizations of minimax rate in a nonparametric class $\mathcal{M}$ determine not only the minimax rate but also the rate achievable for most functions in the class, in the sense that for any sequence of estimators (or for any code distribution) the subclass of functions estimated at a better rate have a cover of asymptotically negligible size in comparison to $\mathcal{M}$. This is shown in Barron and Hengartner [6], extending the arguments of Rissanen [42] and in [45], and can also be shown by the methods of Merhav and Feder [37].

In the case of a Lipschitz or Sobolev class of functions on a bounded set, with s the order of smoothness, and several other function classes discussed in [57], the metric entropy is of order $V(\epsilon) \asymp \epsilon^{-1/s}$ for the L_2 metric and this remains the order of the metric entropy of the subclass of densities that are bounded and are bounded away from zero using H, $\sqrt{D}$, or L_2 for the distance. This leads to the optimal density estimation rate in terms of H^2 or D of $n^{-2/(2s+1)}$, which remains the optimal rate also in mean integrated squared error even if the densities are not bounded away from zero.

V. Applications

We discuss three applications of the MDL principle, the first on coding, the second on linear Gaussian regression, and the third on density estimation. As often is the case in nontrivial applications of the principle the model classes suggested by the nature of the applications turn out to be too large giving an infinite parametric or nonparametric complexity. A problem then arises regarding how to carve out a relevant subclass and how to construct a representative for it, the ideal being the stochastic complexity by the formula (9). However, computational issues often force us to use suitable mixtures or even combinations of the two perhaps together with the predictive method.

A. Universal Coding

Despite the close connection between the MDL principle and coding, the theory of universal coding and the code designs were developed without cognizance of the principle. This is perhaps because most universal codes, such as the widely used codes based on Lempel–Ziv incremental parsing, are predictive by nature, which means that there is no codebook that needs to be encoded, and hence the connection between the code redundancy and the number of bits needed to transmit the codebook was not made explicit until the emergence of a universal code based on context models, Rissanen [40]. We discuss briefly this latter type of universal codes.

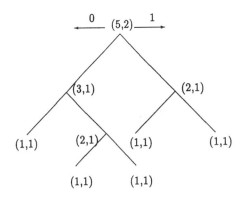

Fig. 1. Context tree for string 00100.

An obvious way to design a universal code for data modeled by a finite-state machine is to estimate the parameters from the data, including their number and the associated structure, and then use the result to encode the data. A particularly convenient way to do it is by an Arithmetic Code, see, e.g., Rissanen and Langdon [39], which is capable of encoding the individual symbols, even if they are binary, without the need to block them as required in the conventional Huffman codes. However, a direct execution of this program would require several passes through the data, which would result in an awkward code. In [40], an algorithm, called Context, was described which collects in a growing tree recursively, symbol for symbol, all the symbol occurrence counts in virtually all possible configurations of the immediately preceding symbols, called *contexts*, that the data string has. Hence, for instance, in the string 00100 the symbol value 0 of the fifth symbol x_5 occurs in the empty context λ four times. Out of these the preceding symbol is 0 twice, or, as we say, it occurs in the context 0 two times, and further out of these occurrences the symbol preceding the 0-context is 1 once. In other words, the substring 100 occurs once. Since extending the context to the left reduces the set of symbol occurrences it will be convenient to read the contexts from right to left. And this same phenomenon allows us to organize the nested sets of contexts in a binary tree, which can be grown recursively while also collecting the symbol occurrence counts. In such a representation, each node corresponds to a context, the root, in particular, to the empty context. We first spell out the relatively simple tree-growing algorithm, and show the tree obtained from the string 00100 in Fig. 1. We then describe how the special "encoding" nodes are chosen by use of the predictive version of the MDL principle described in Section IV, and, finally, we discuss to what extent the so-obtained universal model and data compression system achieve the ideal as defined in (9).

For the binary alphabet the tree-growing algorithm constructs a tree T_n for data string $x^n = x_1, \cdots, x_n$ with two counts c_0, c_1 at each node indicating the numbers of occurrences of the two symbols 0 and 1 at the context identified with the node, as follows.

1) Initialize T_0 as the 1-node tree with counts $(1, 1)$.
2) Having the tree T_{t-1}, read the next symbol $x_t = i$. "Climb" the tree along the path into the past x_{t-1}, $x_{t-2}, \cdots$ starting at the root and taking the branch

specified by x_{t-1}, and so on. At each node visited update the count c_i by 1. Climb until a node is reached whose count $c_i = 2$ after the update.

3) If the node is an internal node return to step 2). But if the node is a leaf, add two son nodes and initialize their counts to $(1, 1)$ and return to step 2).

Because of the initialization the counts exceed the real occurrence counts by unity, and they satisfy the important condition

$$c_i(s) = c_i(s0) + c_i(s1), \qquad i = 0, 1 \qquad (16)$$

where $s0$ and $s1$ are the son nodes of s, whenever the sons' counts $c_i(s0)$ and $c_i(s1)$ are greater than 1.

Suppose we have constructed the tree T_t and intend to encode the symbol x_{t+1}. The values of the past symbols $\cdots, x_{t-2}, x_{t-1}, x_t$, when read in reverse, define a path from the root through consecutive nodes, each having the two counts with which the symbol could be encoded. Which node along this path should we choose? A quite convenient way is to apply the MDL principle and to search for the earliest node s^* along this path where the sum of the sons' stochastic complexity of the substrings of x^t, defined by their symbol occurrences, is larger than that of s^*. Indeed, the stochastic complexity of the symbol occurrences at each node defines an ideal code length for the same symbols, and the node comparison is fair, because by the condition (16) each symbol occurring at the father node also occurs at one of the son nodes. The symbol occurrences at each node or context s may be viewed as having being generated by a Bernoulli source, and we can apply (9) to compute the stochastic complexity, written here as $L(s)$, to a good approximation as follows:

$$L(s) = c(s) \log c(s) - \sum_{i=0,1} c_i(s) \log c_i(s)$$
$$+ \frac{1}{2} \log \frac{c(s)\pi}{2} + O(1/c(s)). \qquad (17)$$

Instead of computing the stochastic complexities for every symbol occurrence by this formula it is much simpler to do it recursively as follows:

$$P(i|s) = \frac{c_i(s) + 1/2}{c(s) + 1} \qquad (18)$$

and the counts are the ones when the symbol i occurred at the node s. This recursive implementation, when cumulated over all the past symbol occurrences at this node, gives to within the last term the stochastic complexity in (17). To get a universal code we encode the symbol x_{t+1} with the ideal codelength $-\log P(i|s^*)$ at the selected node s^*, which can be approximated with an arithmetic code as well as desired.

Collectively, all the special "encoding" nodes s^* carve out from the tree T_t a complete subtree T_t^*, which defines a *Tree Machine* (Weinberger *et al.* [54]). If the data are generated by some *Tree Machine* in a class large enough to include the set of Markov chains as special *Tree Machines*, then with a somewhat more elaborated rule for selecting the encoding nodes the algorithm was shown to find the data-generating machine almost surely. (The algorithm given above differs slightly from the one in the cited reference but the results proven still hold.) Moreover, the ideal codelength for long strings defined by the resulting universal model, given as $L(x^n) = \Sigma_{s^*} L(s^*)$, differs from the stochastic complexity in (9) for the considered class of models by $o(\log n)$ or less. It cannot, however, agree with it completely, because the algorithm models the data as being generated by a collection of Bernoulli sources. In reality, the various Bernoulli processes at the states of a, say, Markov chain, are linked by the state transitions, which means that the stochastic complexity of a string, relative to Markov chains is smaller than the one defined by the ideal codelength of the universal Context algorithm. The same of course is true of the class of *Tree Machines*.

We conclude this subsection by mentioning another universal code (Willems *et al.* [55]), where no *Tree Machine* needs to be found. Instead, by an algorithm one can compute the weighted sum over all complete subtrees of T_t of the probabilities assigned to x^t by the leaves of the subtrees. When the weights are taken as "prior" probabilities we get a mixture of all *Tree Machine* models, each corresponding to a complete subtree. Again, since the codelengths defined by the complete subtrees differ from their stochastic complexities, the codelength of the mixture, which is comparable to that obtained with algorithm Context, will be larger than the stochastic complexity of data-generating *Tree Machines*.

B. Linear Regression

We consider the basic linear regression problem, where we have data of type $(y_t, x_{1t}, x_{2t}, \cdots)$ for $t = 1, 2, \cdots, n$, and we wish to learn how the values y_t of the *regression* variable y depend on the values $x_{it}, i = 1, 2, \cdots, K$, of the *regressor* variables $\{x_i\}$. There may be a large number of the regressor variables, and the problem of interest is to find out which subset of them may be regarded to be the most important. This is clearly a very difficult problem, because not only is it necessary to search through 2^K subsets but we must also be able to compare the performance of subsets of different sizes. Traditionally, the selection is done by hypothesis testing or by a variety of criteria such as AIC, BIC, [1], [49], and cross validation. They are approximations to prediction errors or to Bayes model selection criterion but they are not derived from any principle outside the model selection problem itself. We shall apply the MDL principle as the criterion, and the problem remains to find that subset of, say, k, regressor variables which permit the shortest encoding of the observed values of the regression variables y^n, given the values of the subset of the regressor variables.

For small values of K, a complete search of the $\binom{K}{k}$ subsets for $k = 1, \cdots, K$ is possible, but for a large value we have to settle for a locally optimal subset. One rather convenient way is to sort the variables by the so-called "greedy" algorithm, which finds first the best single regressor variable, then the best partner, and so on, one at a time. In order to simplify the notations we label the regressor variables so that the most important is x_1, the next most important x_2, and so on, so that we need to find the value k such that the subset $\{x_1, x_2, \cdots, x_k\}$ is the best as determined by the MDL criterion.

We fit a linear model of type

$$y_t = \beta' \underline{x}_t + \epsilon_t = \sum_{i=1}^{k} \beta_i x_{it} + \epsilon_t \qquad (19)$$

where the prime denotes transposition, and for the computation of the required codelengths the deviations ϵ_t are modeled as samples from an i.i.d. Gaussian process of zero mean and variance $\tau = \sigma^2$, also as a parameter. In such a model, the response data y^n, regarded as a column vector $y_1, \cdots, y_n$, is also normally distributed with the density function

$$f(y^n|X, \beta, \tau) = \frac{1}{(2\pi\tau)^{n/2}} e^{-(1/2\tau)\Sigma_t (y_t - \beta' \underline{x}_t)^2} \qquad (20)$$

where $X'_k = \{x_{it}\}$ is the $k \times n$ matrix defined by the values of the regressor variables. Write $Z_k = X'_k X_k = nS_k$, which is taken to be positive definite. The development until the very end will be for a fixed value of k, and we drop the subindex k in the matrices above as well as in the parameters. The maximum-likelihood solution of the parameters is given by

$$\hat{\beta}(y^n) = Z^{-1} X' y^n \qquad (21)$$

$$\hat{\tau}(y^n) = \frac{1}{n} \sum_t (y_t - \hat{\beta}'(y^n)\underline{x}_t)^2. \qquad (22)$$

We next consider the NML density function (3)

$$\hat{f}(y^n|X) = \frac{f(y^n|X, \hat{\beta}(y^n), \hat{\tau}(y^n))}{\int_{Y(\tau_0, R)} f(z^n|\hat{\beta}(z^n), \hat{\tau}(z^n)) dz^n} \qquad (23)$$

where y^n is restricted to the set

$$Y(\tau_{0,R}) = \{z^n | \hat{\tau}(z^n) \geq \tau_0\}. \qquad (24)$$

In this the lower bound τ_0 is determined by the precision with which the data are written. This is because we use the normal density function (20) to model the data and approximate the induced probability of a data point y, written to a precision δ, by δ times the density at y. For an adequate approximation, δ should be a fraction of the smallest value of σ of interest, namely, $\sqrt{\tau_0}$, which, in turn, has to be no larger than $\hat{\sigma}$. Put $R \geq \hat{\beta}'(y^n)S\hat{\beta}(y^n)$.

The numerator in (23) has a very simple form

$$f(y^n|X, \hat{\beta}(y^n), \hat{\tau}(y^n)) = 1/(2\pi e \hat{\tau}(y^n))^{n/2} \qquad (25)$$

and the problem is to evaluate the integral in the denominator. In [19], Dom evaluated such an integral in a domain that also restricts the range of the estimates $\hat{\beta}$ to a hypercube. He did the evaluation in a direct manner using a coordinate transformation with its Jacobian. As discussed in Subsection III-D we can do it more simply and, more importantly, for the given simpler domain by using the facts that $\hat{\beta}$ and $\hat{\tau}$ are sufficient statistics for the family of normal models given, and that they are independent by Fisher's lemma. Hence if we with $\theta = (\beta, \tau)$ rewrite $f(y^n|X, \beta, \tau) = f(y^n; \theta)$ in order to avoid confusion, then we have first the factorization of the joint density function for y^n and $\hat{\theta}(y^n)$, which, of course, is

still $f(y^n; \theta)$, as the product of the marginal density of $\hat{\theta}$ and the conditional density of y^n given $\hat{\theta}$

$$f(y^n; \theta) = p(y^n|\hat{\theta}(y^n); \theta)p(\hat{\theta}(y^n); \theta). \qquad (26)$$

By the sufficiency of the statistic $\hat{\theta}$ we also have

$$f(y^n; \theta) = h(y^n)p(\hat{\theta}(y^n); \theta) \qquad (27)$$

which shows that $p(y^n|\hat{\theta}(y^n); \theta) = h(y^n)$ is actually independent of θ. Moreover,

$$p(\hat{\theta}; \theta) = p_1(\hat{\beta}; \theta)p_2(\hat{\tau}; \tau) \qquad (28)$$

where p_1 is normal with mean β and covariance $(\tau/n)S^{-1}$ while p_2 is obtained from the χ^2 distribution for $n\hat{\tau}/\tau$ with $n - k$ degrees of freedom.

Integrating the conditional $p(y^n|\hat{\theta}(y^n); \theta) = h(y^n)$ over y^n such that $\hat{\theta}(y^n)$ equals any fixed value $\hat{\theta}$ yields unity. Therefore, with

$$p(\hat{\theta}; \hat{\theta}) \equiv g(\hat{\tau}) = p_1(\hat{\beta}; \hat{\theta})p_2(\hat{\tau}; \hat{\theta})$$

we get from the expression for the χ^2 density function in (28)

$$C = \int f(y^n|X, \hat{\theta}(y^n)) \, dy^n \qquad (29)$$

$$= A_{n,k} \int_{\tau_0, B}^{\infty} \tau^{-(k+2/2)} \, d\tau \, d\beta \qquad (30)$$

$$= \frac{A_{n,k}}{k/2} \tau_0^{-k/2} \cdot V \qquad (31)$$

where V is the volume of $B = \{\beta'S\beta \leq R\}$ and

$$A_{n,k} = \frac{|S|^{1/2}}{(2\pi)^{k/2}} \frac{\left(\dfrac{n-k}{2e}\right)^{n-k/2}}{\Gamma\left(\dfrac{n-k}{2}\right)}. \qquad (32)$$

We then have the NML density function itself

$$\hat{f}(y^n|X) = \frac{1}{(2\pi e\hat{\tau})^{n/2}C} = \frac{1}{(2\pi e\hat{\tau})^{n/2}g(\hat{\tau})}w(\hat{\tau}) \qquad (33)$$

$$w(\hat{\tau}) = g(\hat{\tau})/C. \qquad (34)$$

Equations (34) and (32) give the stochastic complexity in exact form. However, the evaluation of the gamma function has to be done from an approximation formula, such as Stirling's formula. When this is done the stochastic complexity reduces to the general formula (9) with a sharper estimate for the remainder term $o(1)$. For this the Fisher information is needed, which is given by $|I(\beta, \tau)| = |S|/(2\tau^{k+2})$ and the integral of its square root by

$$\int_{\tau_0}^{\infty} |I(\beta, \tau)|^{1/2} \, d\tau = \frac{\sqrt{2}}{k}|S|^{1/2}\tau_0^{-k/2}. \qquad (35)$$

We see in passing that the density function $w(\tau)$ agrees with

$$w(\tau) = |I(\beta, \tau)|^{1/2} \Big/ \int_{\tau_0, B}^{\infty} |I(\theta, \tau)|^{1/2} \, d\tau \, d\beta. \qquad (36)$$

If we then apply Stirling's formula to the gamma function in (32) we get

$$-\ln \hat{f}(y^n|X) = \frac{n}{2}\ln(2\pi e\hat{\tau}) + \frac{k+1}{2}\ln\frac{n}{2\pi} + \ln V$$
$$+ \ln \int_{\tau_0}^{\infty} |I(\theta,\tau)|^{1/2}\, d\tau + R(k,n) \quad (37)$$

where

$$R(k,n) = -1/(12(n-k)) - k/(2n)$$
$$+ O(k^2/n^2) + O(1/(n-k)^3)$$

in agreement with the general formula (9) except that the term $o(1)$ gets sharpened.

This formula can be used as a criterion for selecting k provided the regressor variables are already sorted so that we only want to find the first k most important ones. This is because we may safely encode each k with the fixed codelength $\log K$, or $\log n$ if no other upper bound exists. If by contrast the variables are not sorted by importance we have to add to the criterion the codelength $\log\binom{K}{k}$ needed to encode each subset considered.

It is of some interest to compare the stochastic complexity derived with the mixture density with respect to Jeffreys' prior $|I(\beta,\tau)|^{1/2}$ divided by its integral, which, however, cannot be taken as in (35) but it must be computed over a range of both β and τ. The latter can be taken as above, but the former will have to be a set such that it includes $\hat{\beta}$ in its interior. A natural choice is a k-dimensional hyperball B or an ellipsoid defined by the matrix S of volume V_k. Jeffreys' prior, then, is given by $\pi(\beta,\tau)$ in (34). We need to calculate the mixture

$$f_\pi(y^n|X) = \frac{k}{2V_k}\tau_0^{k/2}\int_B d\beta \int_{\tau_0}^{\infty} \frac{1}{(2\pi\tau)^{n/2}}$$
$$\cdot e^{(-n/2\tau)(\hat{\tau}+(\beta-\hat{\beta})'S(\beta-\hat{\beta}))}\tau^{-(k+2/2)}\, d\tau \quad (38)$$
$$< \frac{k}{2V_k(2\pi)^{n/2}}\tau_0^{k/2}|S|^{-1/2}\left(\frac{2\pi}{n}\right)^{-k/2}$$
$$\cdot \int_{\tau_0}^{\infty} e^{(-n/2\tau)\hat{\tau}}\tau^{-(n+2/2)}\, d\tau \quad (39)$$
$$< \frac{k}{2V_k(2\pi)^{n/2}}\tau_0^{k/2}|S|^{-1/2}\left(\frac{2\pi}{n}\right)^{-k/2}$$
$$\cdot \left(\frac{n\hat{\tau}}{2}\right)^{-n/2}\Gamma\left(\frac{n}{2}\right). \quad (40)$$

The first inequality comes from the fact that B does not capture all of the probability mass of the normal density. The second approximation is better; only the small probability mass falling in the initial interval $(0,\tau_0)$ of the inverse gamma distribution for τ is excluded. If we apply Stirling's formula to the gamma function we get

$$\ln\frac{\hat{f}(y^n|X)}{f_\pi(y^n|X)} > \ln V_k + Rem\,(k,n) \quad (41)$$

where $Rem\,(k,n)$ is a term similar to $R(k,n)$ in (37). For fixed k and large n the two criteria are essentially equivalent. This is because then the fixed set B will include virtually all of the

probability mass of the normal density function in the mixture centered at $\hat{\beta}$, and the left-hand side of (41) will exceed the right-hand side only slightly. However, for small n, the set B will have to be taken relatively large to capture most of the said probability mass, which means that $f_{\pi(y^n|X)}$ will be a lot smaller than $\hat{f}(y^n|X)$, and the mixture criterion will not be as sharp as the one provided by the NML density.

C. Density Estimation

In this section we discuss a simple density estimator based on histograms. Consider a histogram density function on the unit interval with m equal-length bins, defined by the m bin probabilities $p = p_1,\cdots,p_m$ satisfying $p_1 + \cdots + p_m = 1$

$$f(y|p,m) = mp_{i(y)} \quad (42)$$

where $i(y)$ denotes the index of the bin where y falls.

This extends to sequences x^n by independence. Write the resulting joint density function as $f(x^n|p,m)$. We are interested in calculating the NML density by use of (9). The Fisher information is given by $|I(p)| = \Pi_i p_i^{-1}$, and the integral of its square root, which is of Dirichlet's type, is given by $\pi^{m/2}/\Gamma(m/2)$. Equation (9) then gives

$$-\log \hat{f}(x^n|m) = -\log f(x^n|\hat{p},m) + \frac{m-1}{2}\log\frac{n}{2\pi}$$
$$+ \log\frac{\pi^{m/2}}{\Gamma(m/2)} + o(1) \quad (43)$$

where the components of $\hat{p} \equiv \hat{p}(x^n)$ are $c_j(x^n)/n$ and $c_j(x^n)$ denoting the number of data points from x^n that fall into the jth bin. Just as in the previous subsection one can obtain sharper estimates for the remainder than $o(1)$, but we will not need them.

Next, consider the mixture

$$\hat{f}(y|x^n) = \sum_{m=1}^{m(n)} w_n(m)\hat{f}(y|x^n,m) \quad (44)$$

where

$$w_n(m) = \frac{\hat{f}(x^n|m)}{\displaystyle\sum_{k=1}^{m(n)} \hat{f}(x^n|k)} \quad (45)$$

and $m(n) = \lceil n^{1/3}\rceil$ for large values of n. This number comes from analysis done in [45], where such a value for the number of bins was shown to be optimal asymptotically, when the ideal codelength for a predictive histogram estimator, equivalent to $\hat{f}(x^n|m)$, is minimized. For small values of n the choice of $m(n)$ could be made by the desired smoothness.

This estimator has rather remarkable properties. If the data are samples from some histogram with the number of bins less than $m(n)$, then the corresponding weight gets greatly emphasized, and the mixture behaves like the data-generating histogram. If again the data are generated by a smooth density function, then the mixture will also produce a surprisingly smooth estimate. To illustrate we took a test case and generated 400 data points by sampling a two-bin histogram on the unit

714

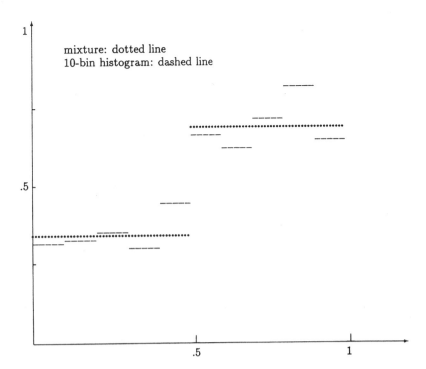

Fig. 2. Mixture and ten-bin histograms.

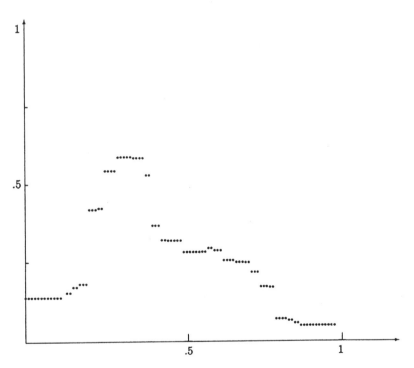

Fig. 3. A mixture histogram.

interval, where the first half has the probability mass 0.3 and the second 0.7, so that at the middle there is an abrupt change. We took $m(400) = 10$. Fig. 2 shows the result, dotted line, together with a ten-bin histogram, dashed line. The mixture nails down the two-bin data generating density just about perfectly, while the ten-bin histogram shows rather severe swings.

In Fig. 3 we have depicted the mixture density function with $m(n) = 10$ for another data set of size 76, not generated by any density function. The length of the steps is seen to be short in the rapidly changing regions of data density, which gives the illusion of smoothness and flexibility. Generating a continuous density function by connecting the dots with a curve would be easy, but to do so would require prior knowledge not present in the discrete data.

REFERENCES

[1] H. Akaike, "Information theory and an extension of the maximum likelihood principle," in *Proc. 2nd Int. Symp. Information Theory*, Petrov

and Csaki, Eds. Budapest: Akademia Kiado, 1973, pp. 267–281.

[2] A. R. Barron, "Logically smooth density estimation," Ph.D. dissertation, Dept. Elec. Eng., Stanford Univ., Stanford, CA, Sept. 1985.

[3] ——, "Are Bayes rules consistent in information?" in *Problems in Communications and Computation*, T. M. Cover and B. Gopinath, Eds. New York: Springer-Verlag, 1987, pp. 85–91.

[4] ——, "The exponential convergence of posterior probabilities with implications for Bayes estimators of density functions," Tech. Rep. 7, Dept. Statist., Univ. Illinois, Apr. 1988.

[5] A. R. Barron and T. M. Cover, "Minimum complexity density estimation," *IEEE Trans. Inform. Theory*, vol. 37, July 1991.

[6] A. R. Barron and N. Hengartner, "Information theory and superefficiency," *Ann. Statist.*, 1998, to be published.

[7] A. R. Barron, Y. Yang, and B. Yu, "Asymptotically optimal function estimation by minimum complexity criteria," in *Proc. 1994 IEEE Int. Symp. Information Theory*.

[8] L. Birgé, "Approximation dans les espaces metriques et theorie de l'estimation," *Z. Wahrscheinlichkeitstheor. Verw. Geb.*, vol. 65, pp. 181–237, 1983.

[9] B. S. Clarke and A. R. Barron "Information-theoretic asymptotics of Bayes methods," *IEEE Trans. Inform. Theory*, vol. 36, pp. 453–471, May 1990.

[10] ——, "Jeffreys' prior is asymptotically least favorable under entropy risk," *J. Statist. Planning and Infer.*, vol. 41, pp. 37–60, 1994.

[11] T. M. Cover and J. A. Thomas, *Elements of Information Theory*. New York: Wiley, 1991.

[12] L. D. Davisson, "Universal noiseless coding," *IEEE Trans. Inform. Theory*, vol. IT-19, pp. 783–795, Nov. 1973.

[13] ——, "Minimax noiseless universal coding for Markov sources," *IEEE Trans. Inform. Theory*, vol. IT-29, pp. 211–215, Mar. 1983.

[14] L. D. Davison and A. Leon-Garcia, "A source matching approach to finding minimax codes," *IEEE Trans. Inform. Theory*, vol. IT-26, pp. 166–174, 1980.

[15] A. P. Dawid, "Present position and potential developments: Some personal views, statistical theory, the prequential approach," *J. Roy. Statist. Soc. A*, vol. 147, pt. 2, pp. 278–292, 1984.

[16] ——, "Prequential analysis, stochastic complexity and Bayesian inference," presented at the Fourth Valencia International Meeting on Bayesian Statistics, Peniscola, Spain, Apr. 15–20, 1991.

[17] ——, "Prequential data analysis," *Current Issues in Statistical Inference: Essays in Honor of D. Basu, IMS Monograph 17*, M. Ghosh and P. K. Pathak, Eds., 1992.

[18] L. Devroye, *A Course in Density Estimation*. Basel, Switzerland: Birkhäuser-Verlag, 1987.

[19] B. Dom, "MDL estimation for small sample sizes and its application to linear regression," IBM Res. Rep. RJ 10030, June 13, 1996, also submitted for publication.

[20] J. L. Doob, *Stochastic Processes*. New York: Wiley, 1953.

[21] R. A. Fisher, "On the mathematical foundations of theoretical statistics," *Phil. Trans. Roy. Soc. London, Ser. A*, vol. 222, pp. 309–368, 1922.

[22] E. J. Hannan, "The estimation of the order of an ARMA process" *Ann. Statist.*, vol. 6, no. 2, pp. 461–464, 1978.

[23] E. J. Hannan, A. J. McDougall, and D. S. Poskitt, "The determination of the order of an autoregression," *J. Roy. Statist. Soc. Ser. B*, vol. 51, pp. 217–233, 1989.

[24] J. A. Hartigan, *Bayes Theory*. New York: Springer-Verlag, 1983.

[25] R. Z. Hasminskii, "A lower bound on the risks of nonparametric estimates of densities in the uniform metric." *Theory Probab. Its Applic.*, vol. 23, pp. 794–796, 1978.

[26] R. Z. Hasminsikii and I. A. Ibragimov, "On density estimation in the view of Kolmogorov's ideas in approximation theory," *Ann. Statist.*, vol. 18, pp. 999–1010, 1990.

[27] D. Haughton, "Size of the error in the choice of a model fit data from an exponential family," *Sankhya Ser. A*, vol. 51, pp. 45–58, 1989.

[28] D. Haussler, "A general minimax result for relative entropy," *IEEE Trans. Inform. Theory*, vol. 43, pp. 1276–1280, July 1997.

[29] D. Haussler and A. Barron, "How well do Bayes methods work for online prediction of $\{\pm 1\}$ values?" in *Proc. NEC Symp. Computation and Cognition*, 1992.

[30] D. Haussler and M. Opper, "Mutual information, metric entropy and cumulative relative entropy risk," *Ann. Statist.*, vol. 25, no. 6, 1997.

[31] E. M. Hemerly and M. H. A. Davis, "Strong consistency of the predictive least squares criterion for order determination of autoregressive processes," *Ann. Statist.*, vol. 17, pp. 941–946, 1989.

[32] U. Hjorth, "Model selection and forward validation," *Scand. J. Statist.*, vol. 9, pp. 95–105, 1982.

[33] J. Jeffreys, *Theory of Probability*, 3rd ed. Oxford, U.K.: Oxford Univ. Press, 1961.

[34] A. N. Kolmogorov, "Three approaches to the quantitative definition of information," *Probl. Inform. Transm.*, vol. 1, pp. 4–7, 1965.

[35] L. LeCam, "On some asymptotic properties of maximum likelihood and related Bayes' estimates," in *University of California Publications in Statistics*, J. Neyman, M. Loeve, and O. Struve, Eds. London, U.K.: Cambridge Univ. Press, 1953, pp. 277–329.

[36] N. Merhav and J. Ziv, "Estimating the number of states of a finite-state source," *IEEE Trans. Inform. Theory*, vol. 41, pp. 61–65, Jan. 1992.

[37] N. Merhav and M. Feder, "A strong version of the redundancy-capacity theory of universal coding," *IEEE Trans. Inform. Theory*, vol. 41, pp. 714–722, May 1995.

[38] J. Rissanen, "Modeling by shortest data description," *Automatica*, vol. 14, pp. 465–471, 1978.

[39] J. Rissanen and G. G. Langdon, Jr., "Universal modeling and coding," *IEEE Trans. Inform. Theory*, vol. IT-27, pp. 12–23, Jan. 1981.

[40] J. Rissanen, "A universal data compression system," *IEEE Trans. Inform. Theory*, vol. IT-29, pp. 656–664, Sept. 1983.

[41] ——, "Universal coding, information, prediction, and estimation," *IEEE Trans. Inform. Theory*, vol. IT-30, pp. 629–636, July 1984.

[42] ——, "Stochastic complexity and modeling," *Ann. Statist.*, vol. 14, pp. 1080–1100, 1986.

[43] ——, "Fisher information and stochastic complexity," *IEEE Trans. Inform. Theory*, vol. 42, pp. 40–47, Jan. 1996.

[44] ——, "Hypothesis selection and testing by the MDL principle," invited paper for the special issue of *Comp. J.* devoted to Kolmogorov complexity, 1997.

[45] J. Rissanen, T. Speed, and B. Yu, "Density estimation by stochastic complexity," *IEEE Trans. Inform. Theory*, vol. 38, pp. 315–323, Mar. 1992.

[46] Y. M. Shtarkov, "Universal sequential coding of single messages," *Probl. Inform. Transm.*, vol. 23, no. 3, pp. 3–17, July–Sept. 1987.

[47] R. J. Solomonoff, "A formal theory of inductive inference," Part I, *Inform. Contr.*, vol. 7, pp. 1–22; Part II, *Inform. Contr.*, vol. 7, pp. 224–254, 1964.

[48] T. P. Speed and B. Yu, "Model selection and prediction: Normal regression," *Ann. Inst. Statist. Math.*, vol. 45, pp. 35–54, 1994.

[49] G. Schwarz, "Estimation the dimension of a model" *Ann. Statist.*, vol. 6, no. 2, pp. 461–464, 1978.

[50] J. Takeuchi and A. R. Barron, "Asymptotically minimax regret for exponential and curved exponential families," in *Proc. IEEE 1998 Int. Symp. Information Theory* (Boston, MA, Aug. 1998).

[51] A. I. Tulcea, "Contributions to information theory for abstract alphabets," *Arkiv für Matematik*, vol. 4, no. 18, pp. 235–247, 1960.

[52] C. S. Wallace and D. M. Boulton, "An information measure for classification," *Comp. J.*, vol. 11, no. 2, pp. 185–195, 1968.

[53] C. Z. Wei, "On the predictive least squares principle," *Ann. Statist.*, vol. 20, pp. 1–42, 1992.

[54] M. J. Weinberger, J. Rissanen, and M. Feder, "A universal finite memory source," *IEEE Trans. Inform. Theory*, vol. 41, pp. 643–652, May 1995.

[55] F. M. J. Willems, Y. M. Shtarkov, and T. J. Tjalkens, "The context-tree weighting method: Basic properties," *IEEE Trans. Inform. Theory*, vol. 41, pp. 653–664, May 1995.

[56] Q. Xie and A. R. Barron, "Asymptotic minimax regret for data compression, gambling and prediction," *IEEE Trans. Inform. Theory*, submitted for publication, 1996.

[57] Y. H. Yang and A. R. Barron, "Information theoretic determination of minimax rates of convergence," *Annals of Statistics*, submitted for publication Oct. 1995, revised Mar. 1997.

[58] B. Yu, "Assouad, Fano, and Le Cam," *Festschrift in Honor of L. Le Cam on His 70th Birthday*, D. Pollard and G. Yang, Eds. Berlin, Germany: Springer-Verlag, 1997.

[59] B. Yu and T. P. Speed, "Data compression and histograms," *Probab. Theory Related Fields*, vol. 92, pp. 195–229, 1992.

Name Index

Attikiouzel, Y., **338** [492]
Auscher, P., **430** [3]
Auslander, L., **78** [46]
Ayanoglu, E., **330** [18] [19]
Azizoglu, M., **30** [195], **388** [34], **637** [26]

B

Babai, L., 181, **184** [113] [131] [134]
Babkin, V. F., 312, **339** [580] [581]
Baccarelli, E., **637** [19] [20]
Baggen, C. P. M. J., **255** [194]
Bahl, L. R., 227, **255** [188], **369** [5], **515** [31], **547** [3]
Baier, P. W., **640** [144]
Bailey, D. H., 91, **101** [6]
Bailey, D. W., 172, **184** [88]
Bailey, T., **157** [19]
Baker, C. R., **212** [1]
Baker, D., **389** [95]
Baker, G. A., 665, **677** [124]
Baker, R. L., **330** [20] [21], **334** [276], **678** [194]
Balaban, N., **547** [4]
Balaban, P., **637** [21]
Balakirsky, V. B., **31** [258], **131** [21] [22], 468, **478** [12], **637** [22]
Balakrishnan, M., **330** [22]
Balamesh, A. S., **330** [23] [24] [25] [26] [27] [28]
Baldi, P., **157** [20], **161** [283] [284]
Balghunem, A., **642** [263]
Ball, G. B., 293, **330** [29], **333** [230]
Bannai, E., 433, **458** [7] [8] [9] [10] [11]
Bar-David, I., **29** [167], **133** [101], 220, **252** [14], **255** [171], **637** [23], **642** [248] [257]
Barba, J., **339** [543]
Barbosa, L. C., **252** [13]
Barenco, A., **697** [1]
Barg, A. M., **547** [5], **572** [2]
Barlaud, M., **330** [12] [13] [14] [30]
Barlow, H. B., **430** [4]
Barndorff-Nielsen, O. E., **160** [230]
Barnes, C. F., **330** [31] [32] [33], **332** [177], **334** [297]
Barnes, C. W., **330** [34], **338** [499]
Barnes, E. S., **330** [35]
Barnum, H., **697** [2] [3] [4] [5]
Barnwell, T. P., **432** [88]
Barron, A. R., **28** [44] [95], **33** [390] [404] [406] [409], **48** [3], 87, **101** [15], **103** [111] [121] [122], 146, 153, 154, **131** [23], **157** [21] [22] [23] [24] [25] [26] [27] [28] [30], **162** [300], 707, 708, 711, **716** [2] [3] [4] [5] [9] [10] [29] [50] [56] [57]
Barron, R. L., **157** [27] [29]
Barry, J. R., **637** [24]
Bartlett, P. L., 152, 154, **157** [31] [32], **161** [244] [251] [252], **330** [36]
Barton, R. J., **213** [2] [3] [4]
Bartz, M., 514, **516** [96] [97]
Bashaw, M., **253** [80] [81]
Bashkirov, E. M., 140
Bashkirov, O., **157** [33]
Baskett, F., **332** [176]
Bassalygo, L. A., **32** [348], **33** [403], **131** [13], 386, **390** [101], **458** [12], **484** [5] [6] [7], 665, **677** [122]
Basseville, M., **213** [5]
Batallo, J.-C., **679** [266]
Bateman, A., **645** [423]
Bates, C. A., **254** [113]
Bath, W. G., **330** [37]
Batlo, J. C., **329**, **330** [38], **338** [510]

Battail, G., **637** [25], **645** [414]
Baum, E. B., 153, **157** [34] [35] [36] [37]
Baum, K. L., **646** [439]
Baum, L. E., **369** [6], **547** [6]
Bayes, T., **213** [6]
Beakley, G. W., **157** [38]
Beal, M.-P., **252** [15]
Beaudet, P., 142, **157** [17]
Beck, J., 138, **157** [39]
Becker, D. W., 668, **677** [175]
Bedekar, A. S., **30** [195], **388** [34], **637** [26]
Beenker, G. F. M., 233, **252** [16], **254** [108], **549** [115]
Be'ery, Y., **550** [216] [217]
Beheshti, S. S., **644** [341]
Behrens, R., **252** [17]
Bei, C. D., **330** [39] [40]
Beibel, M., 210, **213** [7] [8] [9]
Belevitch, V., **458** [13]
Belfiore, J. C., **336** [409], **637** [34], **640** [172], **644** [362], **645** [386] [387] [388] [389] [390]
Bell, A. G., 23
Bell, T. G., **213** [10]
Bellanger, M., **369** [7]
Bellini, J., **646** [440]
Bellman, R.1, **213** [11] [12]
Bello, P. A., **330** [41], **646** [441]
Belzer, B., **333** [185]
Benedek, G. M., **157** [40]
Benedetto, S., **369** [8] [9] [10] [11], **370** [101], **515** [30] [33], **547** [7], **637** [27], **644** [358]
Benelli, G., **516** [98] [99]
Benes, V. E., **389** [100]
Benice, R. J., **516** [80]
Benjamin, O. J., **331** [71]
Bennett, C. H., **34** [433], 541, 542, **547** [8] [9] [10], **697** [6] [7] [8] [9] [10] [11] [12] [13] [14] [15] [16]
Bennett, W. R., 284, 301, 316, **330** [43]
Benning, R. D., 141, **157** [12]
Bentley, J., **28** [91]
Bentley, J. L., **330** [44]
Benveniste, A., **646** [442]
Benzel, R., **484** [8]
Berge, C., 166, 174, **183** [19] [20] [77], **184** [92]
Berger, T., 26, **31** [272], **32** [323] [341] [344] [347], **33** [368] [373] [374] [378] [383] [387] [388] [389], **48** [4], **131** [25], 256, 259, 266, 268, **279** [1], **280** [12], 290, 294, 296, 329, **330** [45] [46] [47] [48] [49], **331** [96], **332** [132], **339** [558] [573], **430** [5], 462, **478** [13], **643** [313], 661, 664, 665, 666, 673, **675** [25] [26] [30], **676** [64] [66] [67] [68] [69] [70] [95] [99] [104], **677** [118] [125] [126] [127] [128] [129] [130] [131] [132] [135] [137] [134] [151] [157], **678** [194]
Berger, Y., **131** [24]
Berggren, M., **252** [7]
Bergmann, E. E., **252** [5]
Bergmans, P. P., 480, **484** [9] [10] [11], **676** [89]
Berkoff, M., 227, **252** [19]
Berlekamp, E. R., **30** [211] [212] [220], **133** [115], 163, **182** [1], 216, **252** [18], **369** [12], **370** [63], **459** [108], **479** [74], **515** [21], **547** [11], **572** [3]
Bernardo, J. M., **101** [7]
Bernstein, H. J., **697** [8]
Berrou, C., **369** [13], 429, 494, **515** [29], **547** [12], **644** [359]
Bertram, H. N., **252** [20] [21]
Bertsekas, D. P., 374, **388** [25] [26], **516** [76], **637** [28]
Besag, J., **77** [4]
Bessette, F., **697** [7]

Best, M. R., **458** [14]
Beth, T., **458** [15], **698** [34]
Betters, W., **547** [13]
Bettesh, I., **637** [29]
Betts, B., **369** [3] [4]
Betts, W., 528
Bhashayam, S., **637** [30]
Bhaskaran, V., **330** [50], **678** [211] [212]
Bhattacharya, P. K., 138, **157** [41]
Bickel, P. J., 138, **157** [42]
Biemond, J., **338** [526], **432** [101]
Bierbrauer, J., **458** [16]
Bierman, G. J., **646** [443]
Biggs, N. L., 136, 145, **157** [13], **161** [250], **458** [17] [18]
Biglieri, E., 30 [179], **131** [26], **369** [15], **636** [2], **637** [31] [32] [42], **643** [302] [303], **644** [359] [360] [361] [377], **645** [412] [426] [430]
Biham, E., **697** [17]
Bilgin, A., **679** [254]
Billingsley, P., 48 [5], **280** [21], **478** [14]
Bingham, J. A., **369** [14] [21]
Binshtock, N., **637** [33]
Birdsall, T. G., 188, **214** [86]
Birgé, L., 146, **157** [28], **430** [6], **431** [7], **716** [8]
Birman, M. S., **431** [8]
Bist, A., **339** [566]
Bjerke, B., **646** [444]
Blachman, N. M., 29 [170], **131** [27] [28]
Black, H. S., **330** [51]
Blackwell, D., 22, **31** [242] [248], **101** [8] [9], 112, **131** [29][30] [31], 167, **183** [38], **478** [15]
Blahut, R. E., 19, 21, 29 [149] [168], **30** [214], **77** [6], **131** [32], **255** [199], **330** [52], 462, **478** [16], **484** [12], **547** [14], 663, **676** [85]
Blake, A., **77** [5]
Blake, I. F., 519, **547** [15] [16], **550** [208], **574** [105] [106], **636** [4] [9] [10]
Blaum, M., **255** [195]
Bleakley, G. W., 141
Blichfeldt, H. F., 434, **458** [19]
Blinovsky, V., 30 [228], 117, **131** [33] [34], **132** [35], **478** [17]
Bliss, W. G., **252** [22] [23] [24], **547** [17]
Blitterswijk, W., **637** [18]
Blokhuis, A., 170, **183** [68], **547** [18]
Bloomberg, D. S., **254** [157]
Bluestein, L. I., 662, **675** [48]
Blum, A., **101** [10], **157** [43]
Blum, R. S., **213** [13]
Blumer, A. C., **101** [11], 145, **157** [44]
Bode, H. W., 199, **213** [14]
Bodie, J. B., **330** [10], **677** [168], 688
Boekee, D. E., **338** [526] [527], **432** [101]
Boeri, F., 294, **335** [353]
Boltzmann, L., 27 [29], 462, **478** [18]
Bonnecaze, A., **547** [19]
Bonnerot, G., **369** [7]
Boppana, R. B., **183** [80]
Borden, J. M., 29 [171], **132** [36]
Borth, D. E., **646** [439]
Bose, R. C., 433, **458** [20] [21] [22] [23], **547** [20], **572** [4]
Boser, B., **157** [45]
Botvich, D. D., **388** [45]
Bougoulias, D. P., **280** [37]
Boullé, K. L., **637** [34], **644** [362], **645** [389]
Boulton, D. M., 699, **716** [52]
Bouman, C. A., **336** [400]
Boutillon, E., **645** [390]

Boutros, J., **336** [409], **637** [25], **644** [363] [364] [365] [366] [367] [368] [369] [370] [371] [372]
Boutsikaris, L., **484** [13]
Bouwhuis, G., **252** [25]
Bouxas, B. H., **336** [387]
Bower, E. K., **515** [13]
Bowers, F. K., **252** [26]
Boyer, M., **697** [17]
Boyvalenkov, P. G., **458** [24] [25]
Boza, L. B., **478** [19]
Braat, J., **252** [25]
Brady, D., **644** [354], **647** [540], **648** [543] [544] [545] [546]
Brailovsky, V. L., 156, **160** [186]
Brassard, G., **547** [8], **697** [7] [9] [10] [11] [12] [17] [18]
Braun, V., **252** [27] [28]
Braunstein, S. L., **697** [19]
Braverman, E. M., 140, **157** [1] [2] [3] [4] [33] [46] [47]
Brayer, K., **637** [35]
Bregmen, L. M., **77** [7]
Breiman, L., 22, 27 [38], **31** [242] [248], 35, **48**[6], 112, **131** [29] [30] [31], 136, 138, 141, 142, 143, 154, **157** [42] [48] [49] [50], 167, **183** [38], 323, **330** [53], **478** [15]
Bremaud, P., 197–198, **213** [15]
Brickner, B., 243, **252** [29], **254** [154] [155]
Brinton, L. K., **330** [54]
Broomhead, D. S., 140, **157** [51]
Brouwer, A. E., **458** [14] [26] [27], **547** [21]
Brown, L., **369** [47], **548** [83]
Browne, J., **77** [8]
Bruce, J. D., **330** [55]
Bruck, J., **158** [52]
Buchberger, B., **572** [5]
Bucklew, J. A., **77** [9], 295, 312, 324, **330** [56] [57] [58] [59] [60] [61] [62] [63] [64], **333** [184], **335** [302], 660, **675** [16]
Bucy, R. S., 192, **213** [56]
Buehrer, R. M., **646** [445]
Buescher, K. L., **158** [53] [54]
Buhmann, J., **330** [65]
Bumova, S. P., **458** [24]
Bunin, B., **675** [47]
Burg, J. P., **77** [10], **337** [431]
Burkert, F., **516** [72]
Burnashev, M., 269, 270, **280** [14]
Burr, A. G., **637** [36] [37] [38]
Burrows, M., 28 [93]
Burshtein, D., 143, **157** [55]
Burt, P. J., **330** [66]
Bush, V., 25
Butler, C. S., **77** [11], **78** [60]
Butman, S., 662, **675** [50]
Buz, R., **637** [39]
Buzo, A., 294, 295, **331** [67] [68] [69], **333** [220], **335** [318], 666, **678** [204]
Byrne, C. L., 69, 71, **77** [12], **78** [52]

C

Cai, N., 29 [137], 117, **131** [14] [15] [16] [17], 176, 177, **184** [95] [120], **478** [7] [9]
Caire, G., **369** [15], **516** [72] [31] [32] [40] [41] [42] [43], **642** [249], **643** [302] [303], **644** [360] [373] [377], **645** [401] [426]
Calderbank, A. R., 29 [138], **32** [310], 170, **183** [67], **252** [30] [31], **253** [49] [55], **369** [16] [17], **458** [28] [29] [30] [31] [57], **515** [44], 523, 526, 527, 528, 532, **547** [13], **547** [18] [19] [22] [23] [24] [25] [26] [27] [28] [29] [30] [31], **548** [32] [33] [34] [35]

D

E

F

Hirt, W., **29** [165], **252** [39], **253** [87] [88], **639** [131]

Hizland, M., **515** [27]

Hjorth, U., **716** [32]

Ho, P., **645** [394] [427]

Ho, P.K.M., **644** [374]

Ho, Y. C., **159** [149]

Ho, Y. S., **334** [243]

Hoballah, I. Y., **280** [45] [46]

Hochwald, B. M., 328, **334** [244], **640** [176]

Hocquenghem, A., **573** [43]

Hodges, J. L., Jr., **158** [111] [112]

Hodges, P., **253** [44]

Hoeffding, W., 462, **479** [53]

Hoeher, P., **515** [28], **549** [106]

Hoff, M. E., Jr., **162** [298], **647** [535]

Hoggar, S. G., **458** [60]

Hoheisel, G., **459** [61]

Hoholdt, T., **547** [16], **549** [110] [119], **550** [182], 566, 572, **573** [44] [45] [47], **574** [77] [101]

Holden, S. B., 156, **159** [150]

Hole, J. K., **253** [89] [90]

Holevo, A. S., **698** [37] [38] [39]

Hollmann, H. D. L., 227, 236, **253** [91] [92] [93]

Hollmann, J., **516** [70]

Holsinger, J. L., **29** [160], 290, 292, **333** [205], **370** [57], **639** [132], **675** [6]

Holtzman, J. M., 632, **645** [396], **646** [488]

Holzman, R., 169, **183** [50]

Honig, M. L., **132** [76], **213** [40] [41], **646** [461] [462]

Honkala, I., **478** [21]

Honma, K., **647** [519]

Hopcroft, J. E., **253** [94]

Hopfield, J. J., **159** [151] [152], **338** [495]

Hornik, K., **159** [153] [154]

Horodecki, M., **698** [40] [41] [42]

Horodecki, P., **698** [40] [41] [42] [43]

Horodecki, R., **698** [40] [41] [42]

Horstein, M., **516** [85] [86]

Horvath, M., **159** [155]

Horwitz, H. M., **331** [112]

Hossain, S., **335** [334]

Householder, A. S., **549** 111

Housewright, K. B., **33** [373], **676** [103] [104]

Howe, R., **431** [54]

Howell, T. D., **255** [189]

Hsieh, C. H., **334** [245] [246]

Hsu, F. M., **646** [463]

Huang, H. C., **646** [464]

Huang, J. J. Y., 288, **334** [247] [248], 665, **431** [55], **675** [45]

Huang, J. Y., **334** [248]

Huang, L., **645** [395]

Huang, S. H., **334** [249]

Huang, T. S., **334** [250], **339** [555] [556]

Huang, Y., **678** [197] [198]

Huber, J. B., **369** [38], **370** [58] [59] [81], 526, 632, **371** [109] [110], **550** [220], **639** [133], **641** [195] [196] [197], **643** [321], **646** [484]

Hublet, P., **637** [40]

Hudson, J. M., **78** [49]

Huffman, D. A., 15, **28** [48], 164, **182** [5], 288, **334** [251]

Hughes, B. L., **31** [256] [297], 117, 129, **132** [75] [80] [81] [83] [95], **479** [54] [62], **639** [117]

Hughes, D. R., **459** [62]

Hughes-Hartogs, D., **485** [57]

Huhuet, J., **338** [500]

Hui, D., 313, **334** [252] [253] [254] [255] [256]

Hui, J. Y. N., **31** [293], **132** [84], **388** [41] [42], **389** [51], 468, **479** [55], **639** [134] [135]

Huijser, A., **252** [25]

Hulyalkar, S. N., **641** [193]

Humblet, P. A., **31** [293], **388** [31], **389** [72] [93], **639** [135], **640** [155] [156] [157] [158]

Hummels, D. M., **159** [119]

Hummels, D. R., **639** [136]

Hunter, R., **28** [50]

Hunter, S., **253** [95]

Husain, S., 668, **679** [245]

Huschka, T., **639** [137]

Hwang, C. R., **78** [35]

Hyuck-Jae, L., **638** [77]

I

Iasnogorodski, R., **389** [77]

Ibragimov, I. A., **716** [26]

Idier, J., **78** [68]

Ihara, S., **30** [173], **30** [239]

Ihara, Y., **573** [46]

Iizuka, H., **516** [58]

Imai, H., **253** [41], **369** [26], **370** [60], **516** [46] [51] [58] [63] [64], 526, 533, **549** [112], **638** [60]

Immink, K. A. S., **30** [201], 227, 233, 236, 238, 249, **252** [16] [25] [27], **253** [84] [96] [97] [98] [99] [100] [101] [102] [103] [104] [105] [106], **254** [107] [108] [109] [110] [111] [115] [118], **255** [202], **516** [50], **549** [113] [114] [115]

Inazumi, H., **102** [72]

Inoue, T., **639** [138]

Irwin, J. D., 667, **678** [199]

Ishizaki, O., **255** [176]

Isobe, T., **516** [54]

Itai, A., **157** [30]

Itakura, F., **78** [50], **334** [257] [258] [259]

Ito, K., **213** [42]

Ito, T., 433, **458** [10]

Itoh, K., **516** [89]

Itoh, N., **254** [135]

Ivanov, A. A., **458** [50]

Iwersen, J. E., **334** [260]

Izumi, M., **639** [139]

Izutsu, M., **698** [63]

J

Ja'Ja', J., 181, **184** [122]

Jacobs, B., **485** [37]

Jacobs, I. M., **30** [220], 64, **79** [104], 199, **214** [141], **370** [55] [63], **371** [118], **515** [2] [4], **679** [248]

Jacoby, G. V., 227, 233, **253** [40], **254** [112] [113]

Jacquet, P., **28** [107]

Jae-Hong, P., **638** [77]

Jaeger, F., **459** [63]

Jaffard, S., **431** [22]

Jahn, J. H., **132** [85], **479** [56], 482, **485** [58]

Jahns, J. G., **334** [285]

Jain, A. K., 156, **157** [19], **159** [122] [156], **161** [248], **334** [261]

Jakatdar, P., **678** [217]

Jalloul, L. M. A., **645** [396]

Jamali, S. H., **639** [122], **645** [397]

Janardhanan, E., **334** [262]

Jancey, R. C., 293, **334** [263]

Jansen, A., 249

Janssen, A. J. E. M., **252** [28], **254** [114] [115]

Rothschild, Lord, **255** [166]
Rotillon, D., **573** [74]
Roucos, S., **335** [342]
Rounds, E. M., 142, **161** [236]
Roussas, G., **157** [22] [24]
Roy, J. U., **336** [373]
Roy, R., **214** [99]
Roy, S., **639** [141], **645** [398], **646** [446]
Roy, V., **638** [70]
Royall, R. M., **161** [237]
Roychowdhury, V. R., **161** [238] [282], **185** [145] [146]
Roysam, B., **78** [61]
Rozonoer, L. I., 140, **157** [1] [2] [3] [4]
Rubin, D. B., 64, 69, **77** [27]
Rubin, G., **12** [36]
Rubin, I., **388** [11]
Ruderman, D. L., **432** [81]
Rudin, H., **388** [12]
Rudin, W., **161** [239]
Rudolph, D., **49** [47]
Rugar, D., **255** [167]
Ruiz, A., **370** [49] [87] [90]
Rumelhart, D. E., **161** [240]
Rumsey, H. C., Jr., 166, **183** [21], **337** [421], 434, **459** [90] [91], **460** [131], **549** [156]
Rupf, M., **641** [234] [235]
Rusch, L. A., **647** [492] [502]
Rushforth, C. K., **214** [142], **647** [536] [537]
Ruymgaart, F. H., **479** [49]
Ryabko, B. Y., 17, **28** [89] [90], **32** [317], **49** [54], 91, 99, 102, **102** [96] [97] [98]
Ryan, W. E., **255** [168]
Rydbeck, N., 328, **337** [448]
Rykov, V. V., **183** [34]
Ryu, B. K., **389** [48]

S

Sabin, M. J., **337** [449] [450] [451]
Sablatash, M., **32** [308]
Sacks, J., **161** [263]
Sadeh, I., **676** [116]
Sadjadi, F. A., **280** [35]
Safak, M., **636** [1]
Safra, S., 180, **184** [119]
Sag, S. C., **642** [269]
Said, A., **337** [457], **432** [82], 671, 674, **678** [226]
Saigal, R., 290, **336** [376]
Saints, K., **573** [41] [71] [75]
Saito, S., **78** [50], **334** [258] [259]
Saito, Y., **550** [162]
Sajadieh, M., **641** [236]
Sakata, S., **573** [76], **574** [77]
Sakrison, D. J., **32** [352], 329, **337** [452] [453] [454] [455] [456], 662, **676** [74] [75] [76] [77] [78], **678** [227] [228]
Sakurai, A., 152, **161** [241]
Salami, R., **678** [229] [230]
Salehi, M., **31** [299], **642** [237]
Sali, A., 169, 170, **183** [51] [70]
Salvail, L., **697** [7]
Salz, J., **133** [108], **547** [4], **549** [96], **637** [16] [21], **638** [93], **642** [238] [239]
Samarah, S., **431** [50]
Samuel, E., **102** [100]
Samuel, P., **645** [415]
Sandberg, S. D., **370** [91], 514, **516** [95]
Sandell, N. R., Jr., **280** [26]

Sanov, I. N., **78** [78], 462, **479** [72]
Sanpera, A., **697** [24]
Santha, M., **185** [147]
Sari, H., **486** [88]
Sarnak, P., **390** [105]
Sarvarayudu, G.P.R., 143, **161** [249]
Sarvis, J. P., **370** [92]
Sasaki, M., **698** [63]
Sasano, M., **516** [52]
Sasaoke, H., **644** [355]
Sathe, V., **28** [51]
Sato, H., **32** [305], **486** [89], **642** [240]
Sato, K., **516** [52]
Sato, Y., **647** [503], **648** [549]
Satorius, E. H., **647** [504] [505]
Sauve, A. C., 65, **78** [48]
Savari, S. A., **12** [13] [20], **28** [74], **102** [101]
Sayeed, A. M., **637** [30]
Sayiner, N., **255** [169], **280** [42]
Sayood, K., **332** [122], **333** [199], **337** [458], **678** [231] [232]
Sayrafianpour, K., **389** [90]
Scarpellini, B., **103** [102]
Schaefer, M., **388** [37]
Schalkwijk, J. P. M., **30** [232], **31** [270] [271] [272], 662, **675** [48]
Schapire, R. E., **102** [43] [55], 154, **161** [244]
Schatz, J. R., **458** [34]
Scheid, J., **388** [37]
Scheinerman, E. R., 165, **182** [8]
Schlaffli, L., **161** [245]
Schlegel, C. B., **644** [340] [342] [346], **645** [416]
Schmidbauer, A., **516** [73], **644** [347]
Schmidl, T., **337** [460]
Schmidt, R., **214** [100]
Schneider, K., **28** [72]
Schnitger, G., 180, **184** [114] [117]
Schocken, S., **160** [178]
Schoenberg, I., **459** [103]
Scholtz, R. A., **133** [117]
Schott, W., **252** [39]
Schramm, P., **642** [241], **643** [321]
Schrijver, A. A., **459** [104]
Schrödinger, E., **479** [73]
Schroeder, M. R., 668, **677** [170] [171] [174]
Schuchman, L., **337** [461]
Schulman, L. J., 181, **184** [127] [128]
Schultheiss, P. M., 288, **334** [248], **431** [55], 665, 667, **675** [43] [44] [45] [46]
Schulz, T. J., 69, 71, 76, **78** [72] [79] [80] [86], **79** [92]
Schumacher, B., **547** [8], **697** [2] [3] [4] [8] [12], **698** [45] [64] [65]
Schutzenberger, M. P., 311, **337** [462]
Schuurmans, D., 145, **161** [246]
Schwarte, H., **642** [242]
Schwartz, G., **103** [103], 708, **716** [49]
Schwartz, S., **646** [464]
Schweppe, F. C., 187, 191, 192, **214** [101]
Schwikert, R., **642** [243]
Seberry, J., **548** [94]
Sebestyen, G., 141, **161** [247]
Sedgewick, R., 178, **184** [106]
Seeger, A., **642** [245]
Segall, A., 197, **214** [102] [103], **389** [79]
Segan, M. I., 72
Seghers, J., **370** [84]
Seidel, J. J., **458** [44] [56], **459** [105], 539, **547** [23], **548** [37] [57], **549** [100]
Sekata, S., **550** [180] [181] [182]
Seldin, J. H., 76, **78** [81]

Warmuth, M. K., 95, **101** [12] [13], **102** [52] [69], 145, **157** [44], **159** [141]

Warrier, D., **643** [323] [324]

Wasan, M. T., **161** [293]

Wassermann, H., **550** [189], 566, **574** [80]

Watanabe, S., **158** [68], 196, 197, **213** [63]

Watkinson, J., **255** [196]

Watson, G. S., 140, **161** [294], **338** [525]

Weathers, A. D., 233, **255** [197] [198]

Weaver, W., **479** [75]

Webb, H., 72, **79** [108]

Webber, S. M., **331** [113]

Weber, J. H., **252** [1], **254** [140], **338** [514]

Weber, R., **389** [47]

Weck, C., **516** [62]

Weeks, W., IV, **255** [199]

Wegener, I., **34** [425]

Wegman, E. J., **157** [27]

Wegman, M., **101** [36]

Wei, C. Z., **716** [53]

Wei, L. F., **369** [48], **371** [112] [113] [114], **515** [5] [39] [40], **645** [433]

Wei, V. K., **28** [91], **33** [365], 181, **184** [125], 327, **332** [140], **339** [574] [576], 472, **479** [83], **485** [59], **547** [16], **573** [25], 660, **675** [34], **676** [114] [115]

Weigandt, T., **255** [200]

Weinberger, M. J., **12** [34], 94, 99, **102** [87], **103** [117] [118], **479** [79], **716** [54]

Weiner, N., 19

Weinert, H. L., **213** [52] [53], **214** [109] [135]

Weinfurter, H., **697** [1]

Weinstein, E., **647** [507]

Weinstein, S. B., **371** [115], **646** [457]

Weiss, A., **388** [44]

Weiss, B., **12** [9], **28** [43] [105], 38, 48, **49** [47] [50] [51] [52] [65], **103** [107]

Weiss, G., **430** [3], **431** [43]

Welch, L. R., 434, **459** [90], **460** [131], **549** [156]

Welch, T. A., **28** [99]

Weldon, E. J., Jr., **516** [53], **549** [137]

Weller, T., **389** [58]

Welsh, B., 76, **78** [77]

Wenger, D. L., **77** [10]

Wenocur, R. S., **161** [295]

Wentworth, R. H., **389** [59]

Westerlink, P. H., **338** [526] [527], **432** [101]

Westin, N., 294, **331** [74]

Westmoreland, M., **698** [65]

Wheeler, D. J., **28** [93]

White, H., 154, **159** [153], **162** [296] [297]

White, R. L., 77, **78** [87] [88]

Whiting, P., **31** [281], **132** [70], **639** [115] [129] [130], **643** [311]

Whittaker, E. T., **27** [7]

Whittaker, J. M., **27** [8]

Whittle, P., **479** [80]

Wiberg, N., **371** [116], 530, **551** [221] [222]

Wicker, S. B., **253** [41], **369** [26], 514, **515** [25], **516** [75] [87] [96] [97] [102], **548** [45], **638** [60]

Wickerhauser, G., **430** [3]

Wickerhauser, M. V., **331** [102], **431** [17]

Wicks, M. C., **280** [43]

Widmer, A. X., **255** [201]

Widrow, B., **162** [298], 286, 316, **338** [528], **339** [529], **647** [534] [535]

Wielandt, H., **460** [132]

Wiener, N., 14, **27** [11] [27], **103** [119], 186, **214** [136]

Wiesel, R. D., **643** [325]

Wieseltheir, J., **389** [95] [97]

Wiesner, S. J., **697** [16], **698** [69] [72]

Wigderson, A., 180, **184** [118] [119] [139] [141]

Wiggins, R. A., **280** [25]

Wilkes, J. E., **639** [114]

Willems, F. M. J., **12** [3] [5], 16, 17, **28** [73] [85] [103], **29** [110], **31** [273], 38, **49** [72], 100, **103** [120], **486** [106], **676** [111] [112], **716** [55]

Willems, W., **573** [21]

Williams, R. G. C., **371** [117]

Williamson, R. C., **161** [251] [252]

Willinger, W., **388** [40], 543, **548** [68], **549** [133], **551** [223] [224]

Wilson, D. V., 543, **549** [133]

Wilson, J., **458** [2]

Wilson, R. M., 164, 167, **182** [6], **459** [99], **460** [133] [134], 536, **549** [140], **550** [178], **551** [225]

Wilson, S. G., **339** [530] [531], **639** [121], **644** [343] [356], **645** [403], 668, **679** [245]

Wilton, A. P., **339** [532]

Winters, J. H., 544, **549** [96], **550** [185], **644** [326], **645** [418] [434]

Wintz, P. A., 328, **335** [304], **339** [533], 662, 665, **676** [80], **678** [246]

Wise, G. L., 295, 312, **329** [1], **330** [64]

Witsenhausen, H. S., 18, **29** [131], **33** [422], 172, 174, **184** [87], 295, 329, **333** [187], **339** [534] [535], **677** [146] [149]

Witten, I. H., **28** [63]

Wittke, P. H., **644** [374]

Wittneben, A., 544, **551** [226]

Witzke, K. A., **516** [79]

Woerner, B. D., **646** [445]

Woerz, T., **370** [89]

Wolf, J.,

Wolf, J. K., 17, **29** [126], **30** [201], **31** [283] [298], 172, 233, **184** [86], **252** [7] [32] [33], **253** [70] [128] [146] [147] [151], **255** [178] [179] [185] [197] [198] [203] [204] [212], 294, 329, **330** [49], **339** [536] [537], **371** [120], **388** [3], **479** [76], **485** [25] [55], **486** [94] [107], 518, **549** [152], **550** [200], **551** [227], **574** [103], **645** [428], 661, 664, 674, **675** [56], **676** [66] [93], **677** [147]

Wolfowitz, J., 20, 22, **30** [182], **31** [244] [247] [249], **33** [373], **131** [19] [20], **133** [124] [125] [126], 167, **183** [40], 211, **213** [25], 461, **478** [10], **479** [57] [81], **644** [327], **676** [104]

Wolverton, C. T., 140, **162** [299]

Wong, D., **339** [538]

Wong, E., 194, **214** [137] [138]

Woo, H. C., **679** [261]

Wood, J. A., **551** [228]

Wood, R., **253** [68]

Wood, R. C., 290, **339** [539]

Wood, R. W., **255** [205] [206]

Woodroofe, M., **214** [139]

Woods, J. W., 322, **333** [235], **339** [540] [541], **432** [101] [102], **679** [247]

Woods, R. C., **333** [208]

Woodward, P. M., 188, 189, **214** [140]

Wootters, W. K., **547** [8] [9], **697** [10] [12] [14], **698** [36] [57] [65] [73]

Wornell, G. W., **214** [85] [93], **486** [79], **641** [198] [220], **644** [328] [329] [330] [332] [341], **646** [435] [436]

Wozencraft, J. M., 64, **79** [104], 199, **214** [141], **371** [118] [119], **515** [2] [8], **516** [85] [86], **679** [248]

Wright, N., **339** [542]

Wu, H. S., **339** [543]

Wu, L., **339** [544] [544]

Wu, W. W., **515** [17]

Wu, X., **339** [546] [547]

Wu, Z. N., **255** [207]

Subject Index

Note: Page numbers listed in this Subject Index refer to the page numbers within this book. All entries were resourced from the *IEEE Transactions on Information Theory* issue from October 1998 (*IT-T Oct. 98*).

A

Access protocols

    inform. theory and commun. networks. *Ephremides, A., +, T-IT Oct 98* p. 372–390

Algebraic-geometric codes

    reliable commun., fifty yrs. of coding theory. *Calderbank, A.R., T-IT Oct 98* p. 517–551

Analog-digital conversion

    quantization theory, hist. *Gray, R.M., +, T-IT Oct 98* p. 281–339

Audio coding

    lossy source coding, rate-distortion theory impact. *Berger, T., +, T-IT Oct 98* p. 649–679

B

BCH codes

    alg.-geom. codes, review. *Blake, I., +, T-IT Oct 98* p. 552–574

Block codes

    data compression and harmonic anal. *Donoho, D.L., +, T-IT Oct 98* p. 391–432

    error-control coding appls., overview. *Costello, D.J., Jr., +, T-IT Oct 98* p. 487–516

    reliable commun., fifty yrs. of coding theory. *Calderbank, A.R., T-IT Oct 98* p. 517–551

C

Channel coding

    broadcast channels capacity region. *Cover, T.M., T-IT Oct 98* p. 480–486

    constrained codes for digital recorders. *Schouhamer Immink, K.A., +, T-IT Oct 98* p. 216–255

    fading channels, inform.-theoretic and commun. aspects. *Biglieri, E., +, T-IT Oct 98* p. 575–648

    Shannon theory, historical develop. *Verdú, S., T-IT Oct 98* p. 13–34

    Shannon theory, method of types. *Csiszár, I., T-IT Oct 98* p. 461–479

    zero-error inform. theory. *Körner, J., +, T-IT Oct 98* p. 163–185

Combinatorial mathematics

    assoc. schemes and coding theory. *Delsarte, P., +, T-IT Oct 98* p. 433–460

Communication channels

    reliable commun. under channel uncertainty. *Lapidoth, A., +, T-IT Oct 98* p. 104–133

Communication system reliability

    reliable commun. under channel uncertainty. *Lapidoth, A., +, T-IT Oct 98* p. 104–133

Communication systems

    inform. theory and commun. networks. *Ephremides, A., +, T-IT Oct 98* p. 372–390

Communication system signaling

    reliable commun., fifty yrs. of coding theory. *Calderbank, A.R., T-IT Oct 98* p. 517–551

Communication system traffic

    inform. theory and commun. networks. *Ephremides, A., +, T-IT Oct 98* p. 372–390

Complexity theory

    min. description length principle in coding/modeling. *Barron, A., +, T-IT Oct 98* p. 699–716

Convolutional codes

    error-control coding appls., overview. *Costello, D.J., Jr., +, T-IT Oct 98* p. 487–516

Correlation

    continuous-time stochastic procs. detect. *Kailath, T., +, T-IT Oct 98* p. 186–215

D

Data compression

    harmonic anal. and data compression. *Donoho, D.L., +, T-IT Oct 98* p. 391–432

    min. description length principle in coding/modeling. *Barron, A., +, T-IT Oct 98* p. 699–716

    pattern matching role in inform. theory. *Wyner, A.D., +, T-IT Oct 98* p. 1–12

    Shannon theory, historical develop. *Verdú, S., T-IT Oct 98* p. 13–34

    stat. inference under multiterminal data compression. *Te Sun Han, +, T-IT Oct 98* p. 256–280

Decoding

    alg.-geom. codes, review. *Blake, I., +, T-IT Oct 98* p. 552–574

    lin. Gaussian channels, modulation and coding. *Forney, G.D., Jr., +, T-IT Oct 98* p. 340–371

    reliable commun., fifty yrs. of coding theory. *Calderbank, A.R., T-IT Oct 98* p. 517–551

    reliable commun. under channel uncertainty. *Lapidoth, A., +, T-IT Oct 98* p. 104–133

Digital communication

    error-control coding appls., overview. *Costello, D.J., Jr., +, T-IT Oct 98* p. 487–516

M

Matched filters
continuous-time stochastic procs. detect. *Kailath, T., +, T-IT Oct 98* p. 186–215

Maximum likelihood detection
continuous-time stochastic procs. detect. *Kailath, T., +, T-IT Oct 98* p. 186–215

Maximum likelihood estimation
inform.-theoretic image form. *O'Sullivan, J.A., +, T-IT Oct 98* p. 50–79
min. description length principle in coding/modeling. *Barron, A., +, T-IT Oct 98* p. 699–716

Memories
error-control coding appls., overview. *Costello, D.J., Jr., +, T-IT Oct 98* p. 487–516

Memoryless systems
Shannon theory, method of types. *Csiszár, I., T-IT Oct 98* p. 461–479

Minimization methods
inform.-theoretic image form. *O'Sullivan, J.A., +, T-IT Oct 98* p. 50–79

Modeling
min. description length principle in coding/modeling. *Barron, A., +, T-IT Oct 98* p. 699–716

Modulation
lin. Gaussian channels, modulation and coding. *Forney, G.D., Jr., +, T-IT Oct 98* p. 340–371

Modulation coding
constrained codes for digital recorders. *Schouhamer Immink, K.A., +, T-IT Oct 98* p. 216–255

Multiaccess communication
inform. theory and commun. networks. *Ephremides, A., +, T-IT Oct 98* p. 372–390

Multipath channels
fading channels, inform.-theoretic and commun. aspects. *Biglieri, E., +, T-IT Oct 98* p. 575–648

N

Neural networks
learning pattern. class., review. *Kulkarni, S.R., +, T-IT Oct 98* p. 134–162

O

Optimization methods
continuous-time stochastic procs. detect. *Kailath, T., +, T-IT Oct 98* p. 186–215

P

Parameter estimation
stat. inference under multiterminal data compression. *Te Sun Han, +, T-IT Oct 98* p. 256–280

Pattern classification
learning pattern class., review. *Kulkarni, S.R., +, T-IT Oct 98* p. 134–162
stat. inference under multiterminal data compression. *Te Sun Han, +, T-IT Oct 98* p. 256–280

Pattern matching
inform. theory, role of pattern matching. *Wyner, A.D., +, T-IT Oct 98* p. 1–12

Polynomials
assoc. schemes and coding theory. *Delsarte, P., +, T-IT Oct 98* p. 433–460

Prediction methods
min. description length principle in coding/modeling. *Barron, A., +, T-IT Oct 98* p. 699–716
pattern matching role in inform. theory. *Wyner, A.D., +, T-IT Oct 98* p. 1–12
universal prediction from inform.-theoretic perspective, overview. *Merhav, N., +, T-IT Oct 98* p. 80–103

Probability
ergodic theory and inform. theory interacts. *Shields, P.C., T-IT Oct 98* p. 35–49
pattern matching role in inform. theory. *Wyner, A.D., +, T-IT Oct 98* p. 1–12
reliable commun. under channel uncertainty. *Lapidoth, A., +, T-IT Oct 98* p. 104–133

Pulse code modulation
quantization theory, hist. *Gray, R.M., +, T-IT Oct 98* p. 281–339

Q

Quantization
hist. of quantization theory. *Gray, R.M., +, T-IT Oct 98* p. 281–339

Quantum theory
inform. theory, survey. *Bennett, C.H., +, T-IT Oct 98* p. 680–698

Queuing analysis
inform. theory and commun. networks. *Ephremides, A., +, T-IT Oct 98* p. 372–390

R

Random noise
continuous-time stochastic procs. detect. *Kailath, T., +, T-IT Oct 98* p. 186–215

Rate distortion theory
lossy source coding, rate-distortion theory impact. *Berger, T., +, T-IT Oct 98* p. 649–679
quantization theory, hist. *Gray, R.M., +, T-IT Oct 98* p. 281–339
Shannon theory, historical develop. *Verdú, S., T-IT Oct 98* p. 13–34

Reviews
alg.-geom. codes. *Blake, I., +, T-IT Oct 98* p. 552–574
assoc. schemes and coding theory. *Delsarte, P., +, T-IT Oct 98* p. 433–460
broadcast channels capacity region. *Cover, T.M., T-IT Oct 98* p. 480–486
constrained codes for digital recorders. *Schouhamer Immink, K.A., +, T-IT Oct 98* p. 216–255
continuous-time stochastic procs. detect. *Kailath, T., +, T-IT Oct 98* p. 186–215
data compression and harmonic anal. *Donoho, D.L., +, T-IT Oct 98* p. 391–432
error-control coding appls., overview. *Costello, D.J., Jr., +, T-IT Oct 98* p. 487–516
fading channels, inform.-theoretic and commun. aspects. *Biglieri, E., +, T-IT Oct 98* p. 575–648
inform.-theoretic image form. *O'Sullivan, J.A., +, T-IT Oct 98* p. 50–79
inform. theory and commun. networks. *Ephremides, A., +, T-IT Oct 98* p. 372–390
learning pattern class. *Kulkarni, S.R., +, T-IT Oct 98* p. 134–162
lin. Gaussian channels, modulation and coding. *Forney, G.D., Jr., +, T-IT Oct 98* p. 340–371
lossy source coding, rate-distortion theory impact. *Berger, T., +, T-IT Oct 98* p. 649–679
min. description length principle in coding/modeling. *Barron, A., +, T-IT Oct 98* p. 699–716
quantization theory, hist. *Gray, R.M., +, T-IT Oct 98* p. 281–339
quantum inform. theory, survey. *Bennett, C.H., +, T-IT Oct 98* p. 680–698

Contributors

Shun-ichi Amari (M'88–SM'93–F'95) was born in Tokyo, Japan, on January 3, 1936. He graduated from the University of Tokyo in 1958, majoring in mathematical engineering, and received the Dr. Eng. degree from the University of Tokyo in 1963.

He was an Associate Professor at Kyushu University, and Associate and then Full Professor in the Department of Mathematical Engineering and Information Physics, University of Tokyo and is now Professor-Emeritus at the University of Tokyo. He is the Director of the Brain-Style Information Systems Group, RIKEN Brain Science Institute. He has been engaged in research in wide areas of mathematical engineering or applied mathematics, such as topological network theory, differential geometry of continuum mechanics, pattern recognition, mathematical foundations of neural networks, and information sciences.

Dr. Amari served as President of the International Neural Network Society, Council member of the Bernoulli Society for Mathematical Statistics and Probability Theory, Vice President of IEICE, among others, and is a founding Coeditor-in-Chief of *Neural Networks*. He received the Japan Academy Award, the IEEE Neural Network Pioneer Award, the IEEE Emanuel R. Piore Award, and many others.

Andrew R. Barron (S'81–M'85) was born in Trenton, NJ, on September 28, 1959. He received the B.S. degree in electrical engineering and mathematical sciences from Rice University, Houston, TX, in 1981, and the M.S. and Ph.D. degrees in electrical engineering from Stanford University, Stanford, CA, in 1982 and 1985, respectively.

From 1977 to 1982 he was a consultant and summer employee of Adaptronics, Inc., McLean, VA. From 1985 until 1992 he was a faculty member of the University of Illinois at Urbana-Champaign in the Department of Statistics and the Department of Electrical and Computer Engineering, as an Assistant Professor from 1985 to 1990, and Associate Professor from 1990 to 1992. He was a Visiting Research Scholar at the Berkeley Mathematical Sciences Research Institute in the Fall of 1991 and Barron Associates, Inc., Stanardsville, VA, in the Spring of 1992. In 1992 he joined Yale University, New Haven, CT, as a Professor of Statistics. His research interests include the study of information-theoretic properties in the topics of probability limit theory, statistical inference, nonparametric curve estimation, artificial neural networks, model selection, universal data compression, as well as prediction and investment theory.

Dr. Barron received (jointly with Bertrand S. Clarke) the 1991 Browder J. Thompson Prize (best paper in all IEEE TRANSACTIONS in 1990 by authors of age 30 and under) for the paper "Information-Theoretic Asymptotics of Bayes Methods." He has been serving on the Board of Governors of the IEEE Information Theory Society since 1995 and his term expires in 1999, and was Secretary of the Board of Governors during 1989–1990. He has served as an Associate Editor for the IEEE TRANSACTIONS ON INFORMATION THEORY from 1993 to 1995, and the *Annals of Statistics* for 1995–1997.

Charles H. Bennett was born in New York in 1943. He received the Ph.D. degree in chemical physics from Harvard University, Cambridge, MA, in 1970.

Publisher Item Identifier S 0018-9448(98)06658-9.

Since 1973 he has been with IBM Thomas J. Watson Research Center, Yorktown Heights, NY. He has worked on the thermodynamics of computation, the theory of reversible computation, computational complexity, quantum cryptography, and most recently quantum information and computation theory.

Dr. Bennett is an IBM Fellow and a member of the U.S. National Academy of Sciences.

Toby Berger (S'60–M'66–SM'74–F'78) was born in New York, NY, on September 4, 1940. He received the B.E. degree in electrical engineering from Yale University, New Haven, CT, in 1962, and the M.S. and Ph.D. degrees in applied mathematics from Harvard University, Cambridge, MA, in 1964 and 1966, respectively.

From 1962 to 1968 he was a Senior Scientist at Raytheon Company, Wayland, MA, specializing in communication theory, information theory, and coherent signal processing. In 1968 he joined the faculty of Cornell University, Ithaca, NY, where he is presently the J. Preston Levis Professor of Engineering. Since the 1997 Spring semester, he has been a Visiting Professor of Electrical Engineering at the University of Virginia, Charlottesville. His research interests include multiterminal coding theory, the information theory of random fields, communication networks, video compression, human signature compression and verification, and coherent signal processing. He is the author of the textbook *Rate Distortion Theory: A Mathematical Basis for Data Compression*.

Dr. Berger is a past president of the IEEE Information Theory Group and has served as Editor-in-Chief of the IEEE TRANSACTIONS ON INFORMATION THEORY. He has been a Fellow of the Guggenheim Foundation, the Japan Society for Promotion of Science, the Ministry of Education of the People's Republic of China, and the Fulbright Foundation. He received the 1982 Frederick E. Terman Award of the American Society for Engineering Education for outstanding contributions by a young electrical engineering educator. He is a member of Tau Beta Pi, and Sigma Xi.

Ezio Biglieri (M'73–SM'82–F'89) was born in Aosta, Italy. He studied electrical engineering at Politecnico di Torino, Torino, Italy, where he received the Dr. Eng. degree in 1967.

From 1968 to 1975 he was with the Istituto di Elettronica e Telecomunicazioni, Politecnico di Torino, first as a Research Engineer, then as an Associate Professor (jointly with Istituto Matematico). In 1975, he was named a Professor of Electrical Engineering at the Universitá di Napoli, Napoli, Italy. In 1977, he returned to Politecnico di Torino as a Professor in the Department of Electrical Engineering. From 1987 to 1989, he was a Professor of Electrical Engineering at the University of California, Los Angeles. Since 1990 he has been a Professor at the Politecnico di Torino. He has held visiting positions with the Department of System Science, UCLA, the Mathematical Research Center, Bell Laboratories, Murray Hill, NJ; the Bell Laboratories, Holmdel, NJ; the Department of Electrical Engineering, UCLA, the Telecommunication Department of the Ecole Nationale Supérieure de Télécommunications, Paris, France, and the University of Sydney, Australia. He has edited three books and coauthored four, among which is the recent *Principles of Digital Transmission with Wireless Applications* (New York: Plenum, 1998).

In 1988, 1992, and 1996, Dr. Biglieri was elected to the Board of Governors of the IEEE Information Theory Society, where he is now serving as its First Vice-President. From 1988 to 1991 he was an Editor of the IEEE TRANSACTIONS ON COMMUNICATIONS, from 1991 to 1994 an Associate Editor of the IEEE TRANSACTIONS ON INFORMATION THEORY, and since 1997 an Editor of the IEEE COMMUNICATIONS LETTERS. Since 1997, he has been the Editor-in-Chief of the *European Transactions on Telecommunications.*

Richard E. Blahut (S'71–M'71–SM'77–F'81) was born in Orange, NJ, on June 9, 1937. He received the B.S. degree in electrical engineering from the Massachusetts Institute of Technology, Cambridge, MA, the M.S. degree in physics from the Stevens Institute of Technology, Hoboken, NJ, and the Ph.D. degree in electrical engineering from Cornell University, Ithaca, NY.

From 1964 to 1994, he was employed in the Federal Systems Division of IBM. He has served as a Courtesy Professor of Electrical Engineering at Cornell University, where he taught from 1973 to 1994, and as a Consulting Professor at the South China University of Technology. He has also taught at Princeton University, Princeton, NJ, the Swiss Federal Institute of Technology, Zurich, and the NATO Advanced Study Institute. He is a Professor of Electrical and Computer Engineering at the University of Illinois and a Research Professor at the Coordinated Science Laboratory, Urbana, IL. He also serves as Engineering Consultant to ioptics Incorporated in the area of signal processing and communications theory, contributing to the design of optical storage systems. He has authored a series of advanced textbooks on the mathematical aspects of statistical information systems, including information theory, communications theory, surveillance theory, error-control codes, and digital signal processing.

Dr. Blahut served as President of the IEEE Information Theory Society in 1982 and was the Editor-in-Chief of the IEEE TRANSACTIONS ON INFORMATION THEORY from 1992 until 1995. Among other honors, he was named a Fellow of the IBM Corporation in 1980 and a member of the National Academy of Engineering in 1990. He is the 1998 recipient of the IEEE Alexander Graham Bell Medal.

Ian F. Blake (M'67–SM'81–F'91) received his undergraduate education at Queen's University in Kingston, Ont., Canada, and the Ph.D. degree from Princeton University, Princeton, NJ.

From 1967 to 1969, he was a Research Associate with the Jet Propulsion Laboratory, Pasadena, CA. From 1969 to 1996, he was with the Department of Electrical and Computer Engineering, University of Waterloo, Waterloo, Ont., Canada, where he was Chairman from 1978 to 1984. He has spent sabbatical leaves with the Mathematical Sciences section of the IBM Thomas J. Watson Research Center, Yorktown Heights, NY, the IBM Research Laboratories in Rüschlikon, Switzerland, and M/A-Com Linkabit in San Diego, CA. He is currently with the Hewlett-Packard Laboratories, Palo Alto, CA. His research interests are in the areas of algebraic coding theory, digital communication theory, finite fields, and cryptography.

Dr. Blake is a Fellow of the Institute for Combinatorics and its Applications, and a member of the Association of the Professional Engineers of Ontario.

A. R. Calderbank (M'89–F'98) received the B.S. degree in 1975 from Warwick University, U.K., the M.S. degree in 1976 from Oxford University, U.K., and the Ph.D. degree in 1980 from the California Institute of Technology, all in mathematics.

He joined AT&T Bell Laboratories in 1980, and prior to the split of AT&T and Lucent, he was a Department Head in the Mathematical Sciences Research Center at Murray Hill, NJ. He is now Director of the Information Sciences Research Center at AT&T Labs in Florham Park, NJ. His research interests range from algebraic coding theory to wireless communications to quantum computing. He has developed and taught an innovative course on bandwidth efficient communication at the University of Michigan and at Princeton University. He received the 1995 Prize Paper Award from the Information Theory Society for his work on the Z_4 linearity of the Kerdock and Preparata codes (jointly with R. Hammons Jr., P. V. Kumar, N. J. A. Sloane, and P. Solé).

From 1986 to 1989, Dr. Calderbank was Associate Editor for Coding Techniques, from 1995 to 1998 he was Editor-in-Chief for the IEEE TRANSACTIONS ON INFORMATION THEORY, and he was also Guest Editor for the Special Issue of the TRANSACTIONS dedicated to coding for storage devices. He served on the Board of Governors of the IEEE Information Theory Society from 1990 to 1996.

Daniel J. Costello, Jr. (S'62–M'69–SM'78–F'86) was born in Seattle, WA, on August 9, 1942. He received the B.S.E.E. degree from Seattle University in 1964 and the M.S. and Ph.D. degrees in electrical engineering from the University of Notre Dame, Notre Dame, IN, in 1966 and 1969, respectively.

In 1969 he joined the faculty of the Illinois Institute of Technology, Chicago, as Assistant Professor of Electrical Engineering. He was promoted to Associate Professor in 1973, and to Full Professor in 1980. In 1985 he became Professor of Electrical Engineering at the University of Notre Dame, and in 1989 was named Chairman of the Department of Electrical Engineering. He has served as a professional consultant for Western Electric, the Illinois Institute of Technology Research Institute, Motorola Communications, Digital Transmission Systems, and Tomorrow, Inc. In 1991 he was selected as one of 100 Seattle University alumni to receive the Centennial Alumni Award in recognition of alumni who have displayed outstanding service to others, exceptional leadership, or uncommon achievement. His research interests are in the area of digital communications, with special emphasis on error control coding and coded modulation. He has numerous technical publications in his field, and in 1983 coauthored a textbook entitled *Error Control Coding: Fundamentals and Applications.*

Since 1983, Dr. Costello has been a member of the IEEE Information Theory Society's Board of Governors, and in 1986 served as President of the BOG. From 1992 to 1995 he was Chair of the Conferences and Workshops Committee of the BOG. He has also served as Associate Editor for Communication Theory for the IEEE TRANSACTIONS ON COMMUNICATIONS, as Associate Editor for Coding Techniques for the IEEE TRANSACTIONS ON INFORMATION THEORY, and was Cochair of the 1988 IEEE International Symposium on Information Theory in Kobe, Japan, and the 1997 IEEE International Symposium on Information Theory in Ulm, Germany.

Thomas Cover (S'59–M'66–SM'72–F'74) received the B.S. degree from the Massachusetts Institute of Technology (MIT), Cambridge, MA, in 1960, and the M.S. and Ph.D. degrees in electrical engineering from Stanford University, Stanford, CA, in 1961 and 1964, respectively.

He teaches jointly in the Departments of Electrical Engineering and Statistics and holds the Kwoh-Ting Li chair in Engineering. He has been a faculty member at Stanford since 1964 and has served as a consultant to SRI, AT&T Bell Labs, Bellcore, and the California State Lottery. He served in the SIAM Visiting Lecturer Program in Statistics 1971–1974 and was a Distinguished Lecturer in Information Theory 1991–1993. During the academic year 1971–1972, he was a Visiting Associate Professor in Electrical Engineering at MIT and a Vinton Hayes Research Fellow at Harvard. He is a coauthor of *Open Problems in Communication and Computation* (New York: Springer-Verlag, 1987) and the textbook, *Elements of Information Theory* (New York: Wiley, 1991). His research interests include communication theory, information theory, portfolio theory, data compression, and the theory of gambling.

Dr. Cover is a member of the National Academy of Engineering, a Fellow of the Institute of Mathematical Statistics and the American Association for the Advancement of Science, and is a member of AMS, ACM, SIAM, IAPR, URSI, and Sigma Xi. He has served as Associate Editor for the IEEE Transactions on Information Theory, *Annals of Statistics*, *SIAM*, *PAMI*, and *Pattern Recognition*. He was President of the IEEE Information Theory Society in 1972. He received the 1972–1973 Information Theory Outstanding Paper Award (for the paper "Broadcast Channels") and received the 1990 Claude E. Shannon Award. In 1994 he was awarded the Pioneer Award from the IEEE Neural Networks Council for work on neural net capacity. He received the IEEE Richard W. Hamming Medal in 1997 for work in communication theory and pattern recognition.

Imre Csiszár (M'87–SM'91–F'92) was born in Miscolc, Hungary, on February 7, 1938. He received the diploma in mathematics from the L. Eötvös University, Budapest, Hungary, in 1961, and the Doctor of Mathematical Science degree from the Hungarian Academy of Sciences, Budapest, in 1977.

Since 1961, he has been with the Mathematical Institute of the Hungarian Academy of Sciences, and has been Head of the Information Theory Group there since 1968. He is also Professor of Mathematics at the L. Eötvös University. He has been Visiting Professor at various universities including the University of Bielefeld, Germany, the University of Maryland at College Park, Stanford University, Stanford, CA, University of Virginia, Charlottesville, and the University of Tokyo, Japan. His research interests are centered on Shannon theory and on application of information theory in mathematics, primarily in probability and statistics. He is coauthor of the book *Information Theory: Coding Theorems for Discrete Memoryless Systems* (New York: Academic Press, 1981).

Dr. Csiszár is President of the Hungarian Mathematical Society. In 1990 he was elected Corresponding Member and in 1995 Regular Member of the Hungarian Academy of Sciences. He was the recipient of the 1988 Paper Award of the IEEE Information Theory Society, the Academy Award for Interdisciplinary Research of the Hungarian Academy of Sciences in 1989, and the Shannon Award of the IEEE Information Theory Society in 1996.

Ingrid Daubechies (M'89–SM'97) received both the Bachelor's and Ph.D. degrees (in 1975 and 1980) from the Free University in Brussels, Belgium.

She held a research position at the Free University until 1987. From 1987 to 1994 she was a Member of the Technical Staff at AT&T Bell Laboratories, during which time she took leave to spend six months (in 1990) at the University of Michigan, and two years (1991–1993) at Rutgers University. She is now at the Mathematics Department and the Program in Applied and Computational Mathematics at Princeton University. Her research interests focus on the mathematical aspects of time-frequency analysis, in particular wavelets, as well as applications.

Dr. Daubechies is a member of the American Academy of Arts and Sciences (elected in 1993) and of the National Academy of Sciences (1998). The American Mathematical Society awarded her a Leroy P. Steele prize for exposition in 1994 for her book *Ten Lectures on Wavelets* (Philadelphia, PA: SIAM, 1992) as well as the 1997 Ruth Lyttle Satter Prize; the IEEE Information Theory Society awarded her a Golden Jubilee Technology Award in 1998. She is a member of the American Mathematical Society, the Mathematical Association of America, and the Society for Industrial and Applied Mathematics.

Philippe Delsarte was born in Brussels, Belgium, on April 27, 1942. He received the B.S. degree in electrical engineering, the M.S. degree in applied mathematics, and the doctoral degree in applied sciences, all from the Catholic University of Louvain, Belgium, in 1965, 1966, and 1973, respectively.

From 1966 to 1991, he was with Philips Research Laboratory Belgium. In 1991, he joined the Faculty of Applied Sciences of the Catholic University of Louvain, where he teaches mathematics and coding theory. His present interests include algebraic coding theory and combinatorial mathematics.

R. A. DeVore received the Ph.D. degree from Ohio State University, Columbus, in 1967.

He has been at the University of South Carolina, Columbia, since 1977, and is now the Robert L. Sumwalt Professor of Mathematics in the Department of Mathematics. He has published over 100 research articles and three research monographs in the areas of approximation theory, harmonic analysis, nonlinear partial differential equations, numerical analysis, and image processing. His recent research interests center on fast wavelet-based algorithms for image processing and numerical methods for nonlinear partial differential equations.

David L. Donoho, was born on March 5, 1957. He received the A.B. degree in statistics from Princeton University, Princeton, NJ, and the Ph.D degree in statistics from Harvard University, Cambridge, MA.

Before joining Stanford University, Stanford, CA, and the University of California at Berkeley, he worked in seismic exploration at Western Geophysical Co. He has been Professor of Statistics at Berkeley and Stanford. His research interests include signal recovery, robust statistical methods, asymptotic statistical theory, harmonic analysis, and wavelets.

Anthony Ephremides (S'68–M'71–SM'77–F'84) received the B.S. degree from the National Technical University of Athens, Athens, Greece, in 1967, and the M.S. and Ph.D. degrees in 1969 and 1971, respectively, from Princeton University, Princeton, NJ, all in electrical engineering.

He has been at the University of Maryland, College, Park, since 1971, and currently holds a joint appointment as Professor in the Electrical Engineering Department and the Institute of Systems Research (ISR). He is cofounder of the NASA Center for Commercial Development of Space on Hybrid and Satellite Communications Networks established in 1991 at Maryland as an offshoot of the ISR. He was a Visiting Professor in 1978 at the National Technical University in Athens, and in 1979 at the Electrical Engineering and Computer Science Department of the University of California, Berkeley, and at INRIA, France. During 1985–1986, he was on leave at MIT, Cambridge, MA, and ETH in Zurich, Switzerland. He has been the Director of the Fairchild Scholars and Doctoral Fellows Program, an academic and research partnership program in Satellite Communications between Fairchild Industries and the University of Maryland. His research interests are in the areas of communication theory, communication systems and networks, queuing systems, signal processing, and satellite communication.

Dr. Ephremides has served as Associate Editor for Communication Networks of the IEEE Transactions on Information Theory (1988–1991). He was the President of the IEEE Information Theory Society in 1987, has served on the Board of Governors of that Society for many years, and has been a member of the Board of the IEEE in 1989 and 1990. He was the General Chairman of the 1986 IEEE Conference on Decision and Control in Athens, Greece, and will be the Technical Program Chairman of the 1999 IEEE INFOCOM and the 2000 IEEE International Symposium on Information Theory. He won the IEEE Donald E. Fink Prize Paper Award in 1992.

Meir Feder (S'81–M'87–SM'93) received the B.Sc. and M.Sc. degrees from Tel-Aviv University, Tel-Aviv, Israel, and the Sc.D. degree from the Massachusetts Institute of Technology (MIT), Cambridge, and the Woods Hole Oceanographic Institution, Woods Hole, MA, all in electrical engineering, in 1980, 1984, and 1987, respectively.

After holding a position as a Research Associate and Lecturer at MIT, he joined in 1989 the Department of Electrical Engineering–Systems, Tel-Aviv University. He has also had visiting appointments at the Woods Hole Oceanographic Institution, Scripps Institute, and Bell Laboratories. During 1995–1996 he spend a sabbatical year as a Visiting Professor at the Electrical Engineering and Computer Science Department and the Laboratory of Information and Decision Systems at MIT.

During June 1993–June 1996, he served as an Associate Editor for Source Coding of the IEEE Transactions on Information Theory. He received the 1978 "Creative Thinking" award of the Israeli Defence Forces. He is the corecipient of the 1993 Information Theory Best Paper Award, for the paper "Universal Prediction of Individual Sequences." He also received the 1994 Tel-Aviv University prize for Excellent Young Scientists, the 1995 Research Prize of the Israeli Hi-Tech industry, and in October 1995 he received the research prize in applied electronics awarded by Ben-Gurion University, Beer-Sheva, Israel.

G. David Forney, Jr. (S'59–M'61–F'73) received the B.S.E. degree in electrical engineering from Princeton University, Princeton, NJ, in 1961, and the M.S. and Sc.D. degrees in electrical engineering from the Massachusetts Institute of Technology (MIT), Cambridge, MA, in 1963 and 1965, respectively.

Since 1965, he has been with the Codex Corporation, which was acquired by Motorola, Inc. in 1977, and its successor, the Motorola Information Systems Group, Mansfield, MA. He is currently a Vice President of the Technical Staff of Motorola and Bernard M. Gordon Adjunct Professor at MIT.

Dr. Forney was Editor of the IEEE Transactions on Information Theory from 1970 to 1973. He was a member of the Board of Governors of the IEEE Information Theory Society during 1970–1976 and 1986–1994, and was President in 1992. He has been awarded the 1970 IEEE Information Theory Group Prize Paper Award, the 1972 IEEE Browder J. Thompson Memorial Prize Paper Award, the 1990 IEEE Donald G. Fink Prize Paper

Award, the 1992 IEEE Edison Medal, the 1995 IEEE Information Theory Society Claude E. Shannon Award, the 1996 Christopher Columbus International Communications Award, and the 1997 Marconi International Fellowship. He was elected a member of the National Academy of Engineering (USA) in 1983, a Fellow of the American Association for the Advancement of Science in 1993, an honorary member of the Popov Society (Russia) in 1994, and a Fellow of the American Academy of Arts and Sciences in 1998.

Jerry D. Gibson (M'71–SM'83–F'92) currently serves as Chairman of the Department of Electrical Engineering at Southern Methodist University, Dallas, TX. He has held positions at General Dynamics, Ft. Worth, TX (1969–1972), the University of Notre Dame, Notre Dame, IN (1973–1974), and the University of Nebraska, Lincoln (1974–1976), and during the Fall of 1991, he was on sabbatical with the Information Systems Laboratory and the Telecommunications Program in the Department of Electrical Engineering at Stanford University, Stanford, CA. From 1987 to 1997, he held the J. W. Runyon, Jr. Professorship in the Department of Electrical Engineering at Texas A&M University, College Station. His research interests include data, speech, image, and video compression, multimedia over networks, wireless communications, information theory, and digital signal processing. He is coauthor of the book *Introduction to Nonparametric Detection with Applications* (New York: Academic, 1975 and IEEE Press, 1995), the author of the textbook *Principles of Digital and Analog Communications* (Englewood Cliffs, NJ: Prentice-Hall, 2nd. ed., 1993), and coauthor of the book *Digital Compression for Multimedia* (San Francisco, CA: Morgan-Kaufmann, 1998). He is Editor-in-Chief of *The Mobile Communications Handbook* (Boca Raton, FL: CRC Press, 1995) and Editor-in-Chief of *The Communications Handbook* (Boca Raton, FL: CRC Press, 1996).

Dr. Gibson was Associate Editor for Speech Processing for the IEEE Transactions on Communications from 1981 to 1985 and Associate Editor for Communications for the IEEE Transactions on Information Theory from 1988 to 1991. He has served as a member of the Speech Technical Committee of the IEEE Signal Processing Society from 1992 to 1995 and on the Editorial Board for the Proceedings of the IEEE from 1991 to 1997. He is currently a member of the IEEE Information Theory Society Board of Governors (1990–1998). He served as President of the IEEE Information Theory Society in 1996. He received The Frederick Emmons Terman Award from the American Society for Engineering Education, and in 1992, was elected Fellow of the IEEE "for contributions to the theory and practice of adaptive prediction and speech waveform coding." He was corecipient of the 1993 IEEE Signal Processing Society Senior Paper Award for the Speech Processing area.

Robert M. Gray (S'68–M'69–SM'77–F'80) was born in San Diego, CA, on November 1, 1943. He received the B.S. and M.S. degrees from the Massachusetts Institute of Technology, Cambridge, in 1966, and the Ph.D. degree from University of Southern California, Los Angeles, in 1969, all in electrical engineering.

Since 1969, he has been with Stanford University, Stanford, CA, where he is currently a Professor and Vice Chair of the Department of Electrical Engineering. His research interests are the theory and design of signal compression and classification systems. He is the coauthor with L. D. Davisson of *Random Processes* (Englewood Cliffs, NJ: Prentice-Hall, 1986) and *An Introduction to Statistical Signal Processing* available on the Web at http://www-isl.stanford.edu/˜gray/sp.html, with A. Gersho of *Vector Quantization and Signal Compression* (Boston, MA: Kluwer, 1992), and with J. W. Goodman of *Fourier Transforms* (Boston, MA: Kluwer, 1995). He is the author of *Probability, Random Processes, and Ergodic Properties* (New York: Springer-Verlag, 1988), *Source Coding Theory* (Boston, MA: Kluwer, 1990), and *Entropy and Information Theory* (New York: Springer-Verlag, 1990).

Dr. Gray is a member of Sigma Xi, Eta Kappa Nu, AAAS, AMS, and the Société des Ingénieurs et Scientifiques de France. He was a member of the Board of Governors of the IEEE Information Theory Group (1974–1980, 1985–1988) as well as an Associate Editor (1977–1980) and Editor-in-Chief (1980–1983) of the IEEE TRANSACTIONS ON INFORMATION THEORY. He was Co-Chair of the 1993 IEEE International Symposium on Information Theory and Program Co-Chair of the 1997 IEEE International Conference on Image Processing. He is an elected member of the of the of the IEEE Signal Processing Society Board of Governors and of the Image and Multidimensional Signal Processing Technical Committee of the IEEE Signal Processing Society. He is an appointed member of the Multimedia Signal Processing Technical Committee. He was corecipient with L. D. Davisson of the 1976 IEEE Information Theory Group Paper Award and corecipient with A. Buzo, A. H. Gray, and J. D. Markel of the 1983 IEEE ASSP Senior Award. He was awarded the IEEE Centennial Medal in 1984, the IEEE Signal Processing 1993 Society Award in 1994, and the IEEE Signal Processing Society Technical Achievement award in 1998. He was elected Fellow of the Institute of Mathematical Statistics (1992) and has fellowships from Japan Society for the Promotion of Science at the University of Osaka (1981), the Guggenheim Foundation at the University of Paris XI (1982), and NATO/Consiglio Nazionale delle Ricerche at the University of Naples (1990). During spring 1995 he was a Vinton Hayes Visiting Scholar at the Division of Applied Sciences of Harvard University.

Joachim Hagenauer (M'79–SM'87–F'92) received the Ing. (grad.) degree from Ohm-Polytechnic Nürnberg, Germany, in 1963, as well as the Dipl.-Ing. and Dr.-Ing. degrees in electrical engineering from the Technical University of Darmstadt, Darmstadt, Germany, in 1968 and 1974, respectively.

At Darmstadt University, he served as an Assistant Professor and "Dozent." From May 1975 to September 1976 he held a postdoctoral fellowship at the IBM Thomas J. Watson Research Center, Yorktown Heights, NY, working on error-correction coding for magnetic recording. Since 1977, he has been with the German Aerospace Center (DRL), Oberpfaffenholm, Germany, and since 1990, he has been the Director of the Institute of Communications Technology at DRL. During 1986–1987, he spent a sabbatical year as "Otto Lilenthal Fellow" at AT&T Bell Laboratories, Crawford Hill, NJ, working on joint source/channel coding and on trellis-coded modulation. Since April 1993 he has been Full Professor for Telecommunications at the University of Technology (TUM), Munich, where he teaches graduate courses on communication theory, mobile systems, as well as source and channel coding. His research interests include convolutional coding, data transmission via fading channels, and mobile communications.

Dr. Hagenauer served as Guest Editor for the IEEE JOURNAL ON SELECTED AREAS IN COMMUNICATIONS in 1989 and 1996 and as Program Cochairman of the 1997 International Symposium on Information Theory in Ulm, Germany, and is the Editor for Telecommunications Systems for the *European Transactions on Telecommunications (ETT)*. His awards include the Erich-Regener-Prize, the Otto-Lilienthal-Prize of the German Aerospace Research, and the 1996 E. H. Armstrong Award from the IEEE Communications Society.

Bruce Hajek (M'79–SM'84–F'89) received the B.S. degree in mathematics and the M.S. degree in electrical engineering from the University of Illinois,

Urbana-Champaign, in 1976 and 1977, and the Ph.D. degree in electrical engineering from the University of California at Berkeley in 1979.

He is a Professor in the Department of Electrical and Computer Engineering and in the Coordinated Science Laboratory at the University of Illinois at Urbana-Champaign, where he has been since 1979. He served as Editor-in-Chief for Communication Networks and Computer Networks for the IEEE TRANSACTIONS ON INFORMATION THEORY (1985–1988), as Editor-in-Chief of the same TRANSACTIONS (1989–19920, and as President of the IEEE Information Theory Society (1995). His research interests include wireless and high-speed communication networks, stochastic systems, combinatorial and nonlinear optimization, and information theory.

Te Sun Han (M'79–SM'88–F'90) received the B.Eng., M.Eng., and D.Eng. degrees in mathematical engineering from the University of Tokyo, Tokyo, Japan, in 1964, 1966, and 1971, respectively.

From 1972 to 1975 he was a Research Associate at the University of Tokyo, Tokyo, Japan. From 1975 to 1983 he was an Associate Professor in the Department of Information Sciences, Sagami Institute of Technology, Fujisawa, Japan. He was a Visiting Professor at the Faculty of Mathematics, University of Bielefeld, Bielefeld, Germany, in the Spring of 1980 and a Visiting Fellow at the Laboratory of Information Systems, Stanford University, Stanford, CA, during the Summer of 1981. From 1983 to 1985 he was a Professor in the Mathematics Department, Toho University Chiba, Japan. From 1985 to 1993 he was a Professor at the Department of Information Systems, Senshu University, Kawasaki, Japan. Since April of 1993 he has been a Professor at the Graduate School of Information Systems, University of Electro-Communications, Tokyo, Japan. From 1990 to 1991 he was a Visiting Fellow in the Department of Electrical Engineering, Princeton University, Princeton, NJ, and at the School of Electrical Engineering, Cornell University, Ithaca, NY. During the Summer of 1994 he was a Visiting Fellow with the Faculty of Mathematics, University of Bielefeld. His research interests include basic problems in Shannon Theory, multiuser source/channel coding systems, multiterminal hypothesis testing and parameter estimation under data compression, large-deviation approach to information-theoretic problems, and geometric structure of information systems.

From 1978 to 1990, Dr. Han was engaged in organizing the activities of the Board of Governors for the Society of Information Theory and Its Applications, Japan. He was a member of the program committee of the 1988 IEEE International Symposium on Information Theory, Kobe, Japan, a session organizer at the 1990 IEEE IT Workshop on Information Theory, Veldhoven, The Netherlands, a member of the organizing committee of the 1993 IEEE IT Workshop on Information Theory, Gotemba, Japan, and Co-Chairman of the 4th Benelux–Japan Workshop on Information Theory and Communication, Eindhoven, The Netherlands, in June 1994. From 1994 to 1996 he was Chairman of the Tokyo Chapter for the IEEE Information Theory Society and an Associate Editor for Shannon Theory for the IEEE TRANSACTIONS ON INFORMATION THEORY. He is a member of the Board of Governors for the IEEE Information Theory Society.

Chris Heegard (S'75–M'81–SM'92–F'95) was born in Pasadena, CA, on October 4, 1953. He received the B.S. and M.S. degrees in electrical and computer engineering from the University of Massachusetts, Amherst, in 1975 and 1976, respectively, and the Ph.D. degree in electrical engineering from Stanford University, Stanford, CA, in 1981.

From 1976 to 1978, he was an R&D Engineer at Linkabit Corp., San Diego, CA, where he worked on the development of a packet-switched satellite modem and several sequential decoders for the decoding of convolutional codes. In 1981, he joined the faculty of the School of

Electrical Engineering, Cornell University, Ithaca, NY, as an Assistant Professor; he was appointed to Associate Professor, with tenure, in 1987. At Cornell, he teaches courses in digital communications, error-control codes, information theory, detection and estimation theory, digital systems, and audio engineering. His current research interests include: information, coding, and communication theory, algorithms for digital communications, signal processing, and error control in optical and magnetic-recording systems, algebraic-geometric coding theory, and symbolic and numerical computer methods. Recently, he has become active in the topics of turbo coding and wireless communications. He is an active member of the consulting community. He has worked on problems of digital HDTV and cable TV transmission, DSP and hardware-based trellis-coded modems, modulation, and error control for optical LAN's, and modulation and coding for recording systems. He holds several patents in these areas.

In 1984, Dr. Heegard received the Presidential Young Investigator Award from the National Science Foundation and the IBM Faculty Development Award. He has ongoing research support from the NSF as well as ARO and NSA. He has been involved in the organization of several IEEE workshops and symposia. In 1986, he was elected to the Board of Governors of the Information Theory Society of the IEEE and re-elected in 1989. In 1994, he was the President of the Information Theory Society. He is a member of AES and Eta Kappa Nu.

Tom Høholdt (M'93–SM'96) was born in Copenhagen, Denmark, on April 26, 1945. He received the M.Sc. degree in mathematics from the University of Copenhagen in 1968.

He is Professor of Mathematics at the Technical University of Denmark, Lyngby. His research interests include coding theory, signal analysis, sequence design, and other areas of applied (discrete) mathematics. He served as Associate Editor for Coding Theory for the IEEE TRANSACTIONS ON INFORMATION THEORY from 1994 to 1996. He is coauthor of the paper that received the IEEE Information Theory Society 1991 Best Paper Award.

Hideki Imai (M'74–SM'88–F'92) was born in Shimane, Japan, on May 31, 1943. He received the B.E., M.E., and Ph.D. degrees in electrical engineering from the University of Tokyo, Tokyo, Japan, in 1966, 1968, and 1971, respectively.

From 1971 to 1992 he was on the faculty of Yokohama National University. In 1992 he joined the faculty of the University of Tokyo, where he is currently a Full Professor in the Institute of Industrial Science. His current research interests include information theory, coding theory, cryptography, spread spectrum systems and their applications.

Dr. Imai received Excellent Book Awards from the Institute of Electronics, Information and Communication Engineers (IEICE) in 1976 and 1991. He also received the Best Paper Award (Yonezawa Memorial Award) from IEICE in 1992, the Distinguished Services Award form the Association for Telecommunication Promotion Month in 1994, the Telecom System Technology Prize from the Telecommunication Advancement Foundation and the Achievement Award from IEICE in 1995. Recently, he received a Golden Jubilee Paper Award from the IEEE Information Theory Society. He was elected an IEEE Fellow for his contributions to the theory of coded modulation and two-dimensional codes in 1992. He chaired several committees of scientific societies such as the IEICE Professional Group on Information Theory. He served as the Editor for several scientific journals of IEICE, IEEE, etc. He chaired a lot of international conferences such as

the 1993 IEEE Information Theory Workshop and the 1994 International Symposium on Information Theory and its Applications (ISITA'94). He has been on the board of IEICE, the IEEE Information Theory Society, the Japan Society of Security Management (JSSM), and the Society of Information Theory and its Applications (SITA). At present he serves as President of the IEICE Engineering Sciences Society.

Kees A. Schouhamer Immink (M'81–SM'86–F'90) received the M.S. and Ph.D. degrees from the Eindhoven University of Technology, Eindhoven, The Netherlands.

He worked in industry for 30 years. Since 1995, has been an Adjunct Professor at the Institute of Experimental Mathematics, Essen University, Essen, Germany. He has contributed to the design and development of a wide variety of consumer-type audio and video recorders such as the LaserVision video disc, Compact Disc, Compact Disc Video, DAT, DV, DCC, and DVD. He holds 37 U.S. patents in various fields.

Dr. Immink is an elected member of the Royal Netherlands Academy of Sciences (KNAW) and holds fellowships of the AES, SMPTE, and IEE. For his contributions to the digital audio and video revolution, he received wide recognition, among others the IEEE Masaru Ibuka Consumer Electronics Award. He is Vice-President of the Audio Engineering Society and a Governor of the IEEE Information Theory Society and of the IEEE Consumer Electronics Society. He is a member of the IEEE Fellows Committee.

Thomas Kailath (S'77–M'62–F'70–LF'97) was born in Pune, India, on June 7, 1935. He received the B.E. (Telecom) degree from Pune University in 1956 and the S.M. and Sc.D. degrees in electrical engineering from the Massachusetts Institute of Technology, Cambridge, in 1959 and 1961.

He worked in the Communications Research Section of the Jet Propulsion Laboratories, Pasadena, CA, before joining Stanford University in January 1963 as an Associate Professor of Electrical Engineering. At Stanford he served as Director of the Information Systems Laboratory from 1971 through 1980, as Associate Chairman till 1987, and since then he has held the Hitachi Professorship in Engineering. His research has spanned a large number of disciplines, emphasizing information theory and communications in the 1960's, linear systems, estimation and control in the 1970's, and VLSI design and sensor array processing in the 1980's; concurrently, he contributed to several fields of mathematics, especially, stochastic processes, operator theory, and linear algebra. While he maintains all these interests to various degrees, his current research emphasizes their applications to problems of semiconductor manufacturing, especially microlithography.

Dr. Kailath has received outstanding paper prizes from the IEEE Information Theory Society, the American Control Council, the European Signal Processing Society, and the IEEE Signal Processing, Circuits and Systems, and Semiconductor Manufacturing Societies. He served as President of the IEEE Information Theory Society in 1975. He has also received the 1988 Technical Achievement and 1990 Society Awards of the IEEE Signal Processing Society, the 1995 IEEE Education Medal, and the 1996 Donald G. Fink Prizze. He has held Guggenheim and Churchill fellowships, among others, and was awarded honorary doctorates by Linköping University, Sweden, and Strathclyde University, Scotland. He is a Fellow of the Institute of Mathematical Statistics, and a member of the National Academy of Engineering, the American Academy of Arts and Sciences, and the Indian National Academy of Engineering.

János Körner was born in Budapest, Hungary, on November 30, 1946. He graduated in mathematics from Eötvös University, Budapest, in 1970.

After graduation he joined the Mathematical Institute of the Hungarian Academy of Sciences, Budapest, where he worked until he left Hungary, in 1989. From 1981 to 1983 he was on leave at Bell Laboratories, Murray Hill, NJ. At present, he is a Professor in the Department of Computer Science at the University "La Sapienza," Rome, Italy. He is the coauthor (with Imre Csiszár) of the book *Information Theory: Coding Theorems for Discrete Memoryless Systems*. His main research interests are in combinatorics, information theory, and their interplay.

Sanjeev R. Kulkarni (M'91–SM'96) received the B.S. degree in mathematics, the B.S. degree in electrical engineering, and the M.S. degree in mathematics from Clarkson University, Potsdam, NY, in 1983, 1984, and 1985, respectively; the M.S. degree in electrical engineering from Stanford University, Stanford, CA, in 1985; and the Ph.D. degree in electrical engineering from the Massachusetts Institute of Technology (MIT), Cambridge, in 1991.

From 1985 to 1991 he was a Member of the Technical Staff at MIT Lincoln Laboratory, Lexington, MA, working on the modeling and processing of laser radar measurements. In the spring of 1986, he was as a part-time faculty at the University of Massachusetts, Boston. Since 1991, he has been with Princeton University, Princeton, NJ, where he is currently Associate Professor of Electrical Engineering. His research interests include statistical pattern recognition, nonparametric estimation, adaptive systems, information theory, and image/video processing.

Dr. Kulkarni received an ARO Young Investigator Award in 1992 and an NSF Young Investigator Award in 1994.

Amos Lapidoth (S'89–M'95) was born in Jerusalem, Israel, on June 13, 1965. He received the B.A. degree in mathematics (*summa cum laude*) and the B.Sc. degree in electrical engineering (*summa cum laude*) concurrently in 1986, and the M.Sc. degree in electrical engineering in 1990, all from the Technion—Israel Institute of Technology, Haifa. He received the Ph.D. degree in electrical engineering from Stanford University, Stanford, CA, in 1995.

During 1987–1992, he conducted research and development in wireless communications in the Signal Corps Research Laboratories (IDF) and was twice awarded the Chief of the Signal Corps Award for Creative Thinking (1990, 1992). He has been with the Department of Electrical Engineering and Computer Science at the Massachusetts Institute of Technology, Cambridge, since 1995, and is the KDD Career Development Assistant Professor in Communications and Technology. His research interests are in digital communications and information theory.

Dr. Lapidoth is the recipient of the A. Finchey Prize for Outstanding Students of Electrical Engineering (1984), the Chief Scientist of the Ministry of Communication Fellowship for Research in the Field of Communication (1990), the Rothschild Fellowship for Graduate Studies (1992), and the NSF Career Development (CAREER) award (1997).

Vladimir I. Levenshtein (A'92) was born in Moscow, Russia, on May 20, 1935. He graduated from the Mechanical and Mathematical Faculty of the Moscow State University (MSU), Moscow, in 1958 and received the Candidate of Science degree in mathematics from the Institute of Applied Mathematics (IAM), Russian Academy of Sciences, Moscow, in 1963, and the Doctor of Science degree in mathematics from MSU in 1984.

Since 1958 he has been with IAM, where he is currently a leading scientific researcher. Since 1965 he has been teaching mathematics at MSU, where he also conducts a permanent seminar in coding theory. His research interests include extremum problems in discrete mathematics, coding theory, combinatorics, and the theory of orthogonal polynomials.

Gábor Lugosi was born in Budapest, Hungary, on July 13, 1964. He graduated in electrical engineering from the Technical University of Budapest in 1987, and received the Ph.D. degree from the Hungarian Academy of Sciences, Budapest, in 1991.

He taught at the Technical University of Budapest, and he spent some time as a Visiting Researcher at the University of Illinois at Urbana-Champaign. Since September 1996, he has been with the Department of Economics, Pompeu Fabra University, Barcelona, Spain. His research interest includes pattern recognition, nonparametric statistics, and information theory.

Neri Merhav (S'86–M'89–SM'93) was born in Haifa, Israel, on March 16, 1957. He received the B.Sc., M.Sc., and D.Sc. degrees from the Technion—Israel Institute of Technology, Haifa, Israel, in 1982, 1985, and 1988, respectively, all in electrical engineering.

From 1982 to 1985 he was a Research Associate with the Israel IBM Scientific Center in Haifa, where he developed algorithms for speech coding, speech synthesis, and adaptive filtering of speech signals in array sensors. From 1988 to 1990, he was with AT&T Bell Laboratories, Murray Hill, NJ, where he investigated and developed algorithms for speech recognition. Since 1990, he has been with the Electrical Engineering Department of the Technion, where he is a Professor. Since 1994 he has been also serving as Consultant to Hewlett-Packard Israel Science Center (HP-ISC). During 1995–1996 he was on sabbatical leave at Hewlett-Packard Laboratories, where he was involved in research topics associated with image and video compression. His current research interests are statistical signal processing, information theory, and statistical communications.

Dr. Merhav is a corecipient of the 1993 Paper Award of the IEEE Information Theory Society. Since 1996 he has served as an Associate Editor for Source Coding of the IEEE TRANSACTIONS ON INFORMATION THEORY.

Prakash Narayan (M'79–SM'94) received the B.Tech. degree in electrical engineering from the Indian Institute of Technology, Madras, in 1976, and the M.S. and D.Sc. degrees in systems science and mathematics, and electrical engineering, respectively, from Washington University, St. Louis, MO, in 1978 and 1981.

Since 1981, he has been on the faculty of the University of Maryland, College Park, where he is Professor of Electrical Engineering with a joint appointment at the Institute for Systems Research. He is a founding member of the Center for Satellite and Hybrid Communication Networks, a NASA Commercial Space Center, He has held visiting appointments at ETH, Zurich, Switzerland; the Technion, Haifa, Israel; the Mathematical Institute of the Hungarian Academy of Sciences, Budapest; Universität Bielefeld, Bielefeld, Germany; LADSEB, Padova, Italy; and the Indian Institute of Science, Bangalore. His current research interests are in information and communication theory, and performance evaluation issues in hybrid wideband terrestrial and satellite communication networks.

David L. Neuhoff (S'72–M'74–SM'83–F'94) was born in Rockville Centre, NY, in 1948. He received the B.S.E. degree from Cornell University, Ithaca, NY, in 1970, and the M.S. and Ph.D. degrees in electrical engineering from Stanford University, Stanford, CA, in 1972 and 1974, respectively.

In 1974, he joined the University of Michigan, Ann Arbor, where he is now Professor of Electrical Engineering and Computer Science. From 1984 to 1989 he was Associate Chairman of the Systems Science and Engineering Division of the EECS Department. He spent September 1989–June 1990 and January–May 1997 on leave at Bell Laboratories, Murray Hill, NJ. His research and teaching interests are in communications, information theory, and signal processing, especially data compression, quantization, image coding, Shannon theory, asymptotic quantization theory, and halftoning.

Dr. Neuhoff was Associate Editor for Source Coding for the IEEE TRANSACTIONS ON INFORMATION THEORY, 1986–1989. He served on the Board of Governors of the IEEE Information Theory Society, 1988–1990. He chaired the IEEE Southeastern Michigan Chapter of Division I in 1978, cochaired the 1986 IEEE International Symposium on Information Theory in Ann Arbor, and served as tutorial chair for ICASSP'95.

H. Vincent Poor (S'72–M'77–SM'82–F'87) received the Ph.D. degree in electrical engineering and computer science from Princeton University, Princeton, NJ, in 1977.

From 1977 until he joined the Princeton faculty in 1990, he was a faculty member at the University of Illinois at Urbana-Champaign. He has also held visiting and summer appointments at several universities and research institutions in the United States, Britain, and Australia. His research interests are primarily in the area of statistical signal processing and its applications. His publications in this area include the graduate textbook *An Introduction to Signal Detection and Estimation* published by Springer-Verlag in 1988 and 1994.

Dr. Poor is a Fellow of the Acoustical Society of America, and of the American Association for the Advancement of Science. He has been involved in a number of IEEE activities, including serving as President of the IEEE Information Theory Society in 1990 and as a member of the IEEE Board of Directors in 1991 and 1992. In 1992, he received the Terman Award from the American Society for Engineering Education, and in 1994, he received the Distinguished Member Award from the IEEE Control Systems Society.

Alon Orlitsky (M'91) was born on July 25, 1958. He received B.Sc. degrees in mathematics and electrical engineering from Ben Gurion University, Be'er Sheva, Israel, in 1980 and 1981, and M.Sc. and Ph.D. degrees in electrical engineering from Stanford University, Stanford, CA, in 1982 and 1986, respectively.

Between 1986 and 1996, he was with the Communications Analysis Research Department at AT&T Bell Laboratories (Lucent Technologies Bell Labs.), Murray Hill, NJ. From 1996 to 1997, he worked as a quantitative analyst at D. E. Shaw and Company, an investment firm in New York City. In 1997, he joined the University of California at San Diego, where he is currently a Professor of Electrical and Computer Engineering and of Computer Science and Engineering. His research concerns theoretical aspects of electrical engineering and computer science.

Dr. Orlitsky is a recipient of the 1981 ITT International Fellowship and the 1992 IEEE W. R. G. Baker Paper Award.

John Proakis (S'58–M'62–SM'82–F'84–LF'97) received the E.E. degree from the University of Cincinnati, Cincinnati, OH, in 1959, the S.M. degree from the Massachusetts Institute of Technology (MIT), Cambridge, in 1961, and the Ph.D. degree in engineering from Harvard University, Cambridge, MA, in 1966.

He was a staff member at the MIT Lincoln Laboratory, Lexington, MA, from 1961 to 1963, and a Member of the Technical Staff at GTE from 1966 to 1969. Since September 1969, he has been on the faculty of the Electrical and Computer Engineering Department, Northeastern University, Boston, MA, where he held the positions of Department Chair (1984–1997), Associate Dean and Director of the Graduate School of Engineering (1982–1984), and Acting Dean (1992–1993). His professional experience and interests are in the general area of digital communications and digital signal processing. He is the author of the book *Digital Communications* (New York: McGraw-Hill, 3rd ed., 1995), and the coauthor of *Introduction to Digital Signal Processing* (Englewood Cliffs, NJ: Prentice-Hall, 3rd ed., 1996), *Digital Signal Processing Laboratory* (Englewood Cliffs, NJ: Prentice-Hall, 1991), *Advanced Digital Signal Processing* (New York: Macmillan, 1992), *Digital Processing of Speech Signals* (New York: Macmillan, 1992), *Communication Systems Engineering* (Englewood Cliffs, NJ: Prentice-Hall, 1994), *Digital Signal Processing Using MATLAB* (Boston, MA: PWS , 1997), and *Contemporary Communication Systems Using MATLAB* (Boston, MA: PWS, 1998).

Joseph A. O'Sullivan (S'83–M'85–SM'92) was born in St. Louis, MO, on January 7, 1960. He received the B.S., M.S. and Ph.D. degrees in electrical engineering from the University of Notre Dame, Notre Dame, IN, in 1982, 1984, and 1986, respectively.

In 1986, he joined the faculty of the Department of Electrical Engineering at Washington University, St. Louis, MO, where he is now an Associate Professor. He is also Associate Professor of Radiology. He is a member of the Electronic Systems and Signals Research Laboratory, the Magnetics and Information Science Center, and the Center for Imaging Science at Washington University. He was Secretary of the Faculty Senate at Washington University and Faculty Representative to the Board of Trustees from 1985 to 1998. His research interests include information theory, estimation theory, and imaging science, with applications in object recognition, tomographic imaging, magnetic recording, radar, and formal languages.

Dr. O'Sullivan was Publications Editor for the IEEE TRANSACTIONS ON INFORMATION THEORY from 1992 to 1995, and is currently Associate Editor for Detection and Estimation. He was Chairman of the St. Louis Section of the IEEE in 1994. He has served on the organizing and program committees for several conferences and workshops, including being Cochair of the 1999 Information Theory Workshop on Detection, Estimation, Classification, and Imaging. He is a member of Eta Kappa Nu and SPIE.

Jorma J. Rissanen (A'89–SM'89) was born in Finland, on October 20, 1932. He received the Licentiate and Doctor of Technology degrees in control theory and mathematics from the Technical University of Helsinki, Helsinki, Finland, in 1960 and 1965, respectively.

He has been with IBM Research in San Jose, CA, since 1966, except for the academic year 1973–1974, when he held the Chair in Control Theory at Linkoping University, Linkoping, Sweden. He has done research in control, prediction, and system theories, relation theory, numerical mathematics, information and coding theory, and statistics. He has published more than 100 papers and a monograph *Stochastic Complexity in Statistical Inquiry*. He is also coholder of ten patents.

Dr. Rissanen received IBM Outstanding Innovation Awards in 1980 for the introduction of arithmetic codes; and in 1988 for work on statistical inference, information theory, and the theory of complexity; an IBM Corporate Award in 1991 for the MDL/PMDL principles and stochastic complexity; Best Paper Awards from IFAC in 1981 and from the IEEE Information Theory Group in 1986. He also received the IEEE 1993 Richard W. Hamming medal "For fundamental contributions to information theory, statistical inference, control theory, and the theory of complexity." Further, he received an Honorary Doctorate from the Technical University of Tampere, Finland, in 1992, He is an Advisory Editor of the *Journal of Statistical Planning and Inference*, an Associate Editor for *IMA Journal of Mathematical Control and Information*, and the *Journal of Computational and Applied Mathematics*. He is an Advisory Member for *IEICE Transactions on Fundamentals of Electronics, Communications and Computer Sciences*.

Shlomo Shamai (Shitz) (S'80–M'82–SM'89–F'94) received the B.Sc., M.Sc., and Ph.D. degrees in electrical engineering from the Technion–Israel Institute of Technology, Haifa, Israel, in 1975, 1981, and 1986, respectively.

During 1975–1985 he was with the Signal Corps Research Laboratories (Israel Defense Forces) in the capacity of a Senior Research Engineer. Since 1986, he has been with the Department of Electrical Engineering, Technion–Israel Institute of Technology, where he is now a Professor. His research interests include topics in information theory and digital and analog communications. He is especially interested in theoretical limits in communication with practical constraints, digital communication in optical channels, information-theoretic models for multiuser cellular radio systems and magnetic recording, channel coding, combined modulation and coding, turbo coding, and digital spectrally efficient modulation methods employing coherent and noncoherent detection.

Dr. Shamai (Shitz) is a member of the Union Radio Scientifique Internationale (URSI). He serves as Associate Editor for Shannon Theory for the IEEE TRANSACTIONS ON INFORMATION THEORY, and since 1995 has served on the Board of Governors of the IEEE Information Theory Society.

Paul C. Shields (M'70–SM'95–F'96) was born in South Haven, MI, in 1933. He received the B.A. degree in mathematics from Colorado College, Colorado Springs, in 1956, and the Ph.D. degree in mathematics from Yale University, New Haven, CT, in 1959.

He has held positions at MIT, Cambridge, MA; Boston University, Boston, MA; Wayne State University, Detroit, MI; and Warwick University; and has held visiting positions at Stanford University, Stanford, CA; Cornell University, Ithaca, NY; University of California, Berkeley, CA; University of Michigan, Ann Arbor; Eötvös Loránd University, Budapest, Hungary, TU Delft, Delft, The Netherlands, and CWI, Amsterdam, The Netherlands. He is now Professor of Mathematics at the University of Toledo, Toledo, OH, where he has been since 1974. He was a Fulbright Research Fellow at the Mathematics Institute of the Hungarian Academy of Sciences, Budapest, in 1985, and a Fulbright Teaching Fellow at Eötvös Loránd University in 1989. His research interests include linear algebra, ergodic theory, information theory, and statistics. His book *The Ergodic Theory of Discrete Sample Paths*, based on his recent lectures in Budapest, was recently published by the American Mathematics Society.

Peter Shor received the B.S. degree in mathematics from the California Institute of Technology, Pasadena, in 1981 and the Ph.D. degree in applied mathematics from the Massachusetts Institute of Technology, Cambridge.

The following year, he held a Post-Doctoral Fellowship at the Mathematical Sciences Research Institute, Berkeley, CA. Since 1986 he has been with AT&T Labs-Research, Florham Park, NJ. His research interests include quantum computing, combinatorial algorithms, and computational geometry.

In 1998, Dr. Shor was awarded the Nevanlinna prize. He is an AT&T Fellow.

Paul H. Siegel (M'82–SM'90–F'97) received the S.B. degree in mathematics in 1975 and the Ph.D. degree in mathematics in 1979, both from the Massachusetts Institute of technology. Cambridge, He held a Chaim Weizmann Post-Doctoral Fellowship at the Courant Institute, New York University.

He was with IBM Research in San Jose, CA, from 1980 to 1995, where he conducted and managed research on modulation, coding, and signal processing, primarily for data storage applications. He was a Visiting Associate Professor at the University of California, San Diego (UCSD), while at the Center for Magnetic Recording Research during the 1989–1990 academic year. He is currently Professor of Electrical and Computer Engineering at UCSD, and is affiliated with the Center for Magnetic Recording Research as well as the Center for Wireless Communications. His primary research interests lie in the areas of information theory and communications, particularly coding and modulation techniques, with applications to digital data storage and transmission. He holds seventeen patents in the area of coding and detection, and was named a Master Inventor at IBM Research in 1994.

Dr. Siegel was a member of the Board of Governors of the IEEE Information Theory Society from 1991 to 1996. He served as Co-Guest Editor of the May 1991 Special Issue on Coding for Storage Devices of the IEEE TRANSACTIONS ON INFORMATION THEORY, and served as Associate Editor for Coding Techniques from 1992 to 1995. He was corecipient, with R. Karabed, of the 1992 IEEE Information Theory Society Paper Award and shared the 1993 IEEE Communications Society Leonard G. Abraham Prize Paper Award with B. Marcus and J. K. Wolf. He is a member of Phi Beta Kappa.

Donald L. Snyder (S'60–M'62–SM'78–F'81) received the B.S.E.E. degree from the University of Southern California, Los Angeles, in 1961 and the M.S. and Ph.D. degrees in electrical engineering from the Massachusetts Institute of Technology (MIT), Cambridge, in 1963 and 1966, respectively.

From 1966 to 1969, he was on the faculty of MIT. Since 1969, he has been on the electrical engineering faculty of Washington University, St. Louis, MO. He served as Chairman of the Department of Electrical Engineering from 1976 to 1986 and as Associate Director of the Biomedical Computer Laboratory, Washington University School of Medicine. He is presently Director of the Electronic Systems and Signals Research Laboratory in the Department of Electrical Engineering and is the Samuel C. Sachs Professor of Electrical Engineering and Professor of Radiology. He is the author of papers on the theories of random processes, estimation, decision, and systems and the application of these theories to practical problems. Most recently, his interest has been in the development and application of random point process models in optical and radiological imaging. He is coauthor of *Random Point Processes in Time and Space*, published by Springer-Verlag.

Dr. Snyder served as Associate Editor for Random Processes for the IEEE TRANSACTIONS ON INFORMATION THEORY and was the 1981 President of the IEEE Information Theory Society.

Gottfried Ungerboeck (M'75–SM'82–F'85) received the Dipl. Ing. degree from the Technical University in Vienna, Vienna, Austria, in 1964 and the Ph.D. degree from the Swiss Federal Institute of Technology, Zurich, in 1970, both in electrical engineering.

In 1967, he became a Research Staff Member at the IBM Zurich Research Laboratory, Rueschlikon, Switzerland. His initial work dealt with digital speech processing and switching systems. Later he turned to research in communication and information theory. During the mid-1970's he began to work on combining coding and modulation. He also developed digital signal processors and engaged in their applications. His applied work concentrated on voiceband modems, satellite transmission, magnetic recording, and more recently on LAN transceivers and cable modems. Since 1978, he has managed signal-processing activities at the IBM Zurich Research Laboratory. He is presently a consultant working on "last mile" technologies.

Dr. Ungerboeck has been an IBM Fellow since 1984, and a Foreign Associate of the National Academy of Engineering (USA) since 1994. Throughout his career he has served for 14 years as an Associate Editor of IEEE TRANSACTIONS ON COMMUNICATIONS. He has been awarded the 1984 IEEE Information Theory Group Prize Paper Award. Recent recognitions include an honorary doctoral degree from the Technical University of Vienna (1993), the 1994 IEEE Richard W. Hamming Medal, the 1994 Eduard Rhein Basic Science Award (jointly with A. J. Viterbi), the 1996 Marconi International Fellowship Award, and the 1997 Australia Prize (jointly with A. Snyder and R. Tucker).

Santosh S. Venkatesh (S'81–M'85) was born in Trichur, India, on June 6, 1959. He received the B.Tech. degree with distinction from the Indian Institute of Technology, Bombay, India, in 1981, and the M.S. and Ph.D. degrees from the California Institute of Technology, Pasadena, in 1982 and 1986, respectively, all in electrical engineering.

Since 1986 he has been at the University of Pennsylvania, Philadelphia, where he is an Associate Professor of Electrical Engineering and the Neurosciences Graduate Group. He is also a member of the David Mahoney Institute for Neurological Sciences at the University of Pennsylvania. In 1994, he spent a 12-month sabbatical as a Visiting Associate Professor of Electrical Engineering and Computation and Neural Systems at the California Institute of Technology in Pasadena. He has also been a Visiting Research Fellow at Siemens Corporate Research, Princeton, NJ, and at AT&T Bell Laboratories, Murray Hill and Holmdel, NJ. He has also been a consultant for Dupont de Nemours, Inc., Wilmington, DE, and Microsoft Research, Seattle, WA. His research interests include Shannon theory, complexity theory, multiuser information theory, pattern recognition, computational learning theory, and neural networks. In the last few years he has been working on problems in the complexity of learning pattern classification using mixtures of labeled and unlabeled examples, multiuser communication theory, model selection and learning dynamics in supervised learning, and the characterization of threshold phenomena and phase transitions in neural networks.

Sergio Verdú (S'80–M'84–SM'88–F'93) was born in Barcelona, Spain, on August 15, 1958. He received the Telecommunications Engineering degree from the Polytechnic University of Barcelona, in 1980 and the Ph.D. degree in electrical engineering from the University of Illinois at Urbana-Champaign, in 1984.

In 1984 he joined the Faculty of Princeton University, Princeton, NJ, where he is a Professor of Electrical Engineering. His research interests are in information theory and multiuser communication. He has authored *Multiuser Detection* (Cambridge University Press, 1998). He has held visiting appointments at the Australian National University, the Technion–Israel Institute of Technology, the University of Tokyo, and the University of California, Berkeley.

Dr. Verdú served as Associate Editor for Shannon Theory of the IEEE TRANSACTIONS ON INFORMATION THEORY. He has served on the Board of Governors of the Information Theory Society since 1989, and was President of the Society in 1997. He was Cochairman of the Program Committee of the 1998 IEEE International Symposium on Information Theory, and is serving as Co-chairman of the 2000 IEEE International Symposium on Information Theory. He is a recipient of the NSF Presidential Young Investigator Award, the IEEE Donald Fink Paper Award, and a Golden Jubilee Paper Award from the Information Theory Society. He is also the corecipient (with V. Anantharam) of the 1998 Information Theory Society Paper Award.

Martin Vetterli (S'86–M'86–SM'90–F'95) received the Dipl. El.-Ing. degree from ETH Zürich (ETHZ), Switzerland, in 1981, the M.S. degree from Stanford University, Stanford, CA, in 1982, and the Doctoratés Science degree from EPF Lausanne (EPFL), Switzerland, in 1986.

He was a Research Assistant at Stanford and EPFL, and has worked for Siemens and AT&T Bell Laboratories. In 1986, he joined Columbia University, New York, NY, where he was last an Associate Professor of Electrical Engineering and co-director of the Image and Advanced Television Laboratory. In 1993, he joined the University of California at Berkeley where he was a Professor in the Department of Electrical Engineering and Computer Sciences. Since 1995, he has been a Professor of Communication Systems at EPF Lausanne, Switzerland, and since 1996, he has chaired the Communications Systems Division. His research interests include wavelets, multirate signal processing, computational complexity, signal processing for telecommunications, digital video processing and compression, and wireless video communications.

Dr. Vetterli is a member of SIAM, and was the Area Editor for Speech, Image, Video, and Signal Processing of the IEEE TRANSACTIONS ON COMMUNICATIONS. He received the Best Paper Award of EURASIP in 1984 for his paper on multidimensional subband coding, the Research Prize of the Brown Bovery Corporation (Switzerland) in 1986 for his thesis, the IEEE Signal Processing Society's 1991 and 1996 Senior Awards (with D. LeGall and K. Ramchandran, respectively), and the Swiss Latsis Prize in 1996. He was a plenary speaker at the 1992 IEEE ICASSP in San Francisco and is a coauthor, with J. Kovačević, of the book *Wavelets and Subband Coding* (Englewood Cliffs, NJ: Prentice-Hall, 1995).

Victor Wei (S'77–M'80–SM'93–F'95) received the B.S. degree in electrical engineering from National Taiwan University in 1976 and the Ph.D. degree in electrical engineering from the University of Hawaii in 1980.

From 1980 to 1983, he was with the Mathematics Research Center of Bell Laboratories, Murray Hill, NJ. From 1984 to 1994, he was with Bellcore, Morristown, NJ, becoming Director of Communication and Computation Principles Research in 1987. Since 1994, he has been with the Department of Information Engineering of the Chinese University of Hong Kong. His current research interests include error-correcting codes, cryptography, data compression, and communication VLSI.

Dr. Wei has been a Member of the Board of Governors (1991–1994) of the IEEE Information Theory Society, as well as Editor for Coding (1989–1992) and a Guest Editor for the Special Issue on Algebraic–Geometric Codes of the IEEE TRANSACTIONS ON INFORMATION THEORY.

Stephen B. Wicker (S'83–M'83–SM'93) received the B.S.E.E. degree with High Honors from the University of Virginia, Charlottesville, in 1982; the M.S.E.E. degree from Purdue University, West Lafayette, IN, in 1983; and the Ph.D. degree in electrical engineering from the University of Southern California, Los Angeles, in 1987.

From 1983 through 1987, he was a subsystem and system engineer with the Space and Communications Group of the Hughes Aircraft Company in El Segundo, CA. From 1987 through 1996, he was a member of the faculty of the School of Electrical and Computer Engineering at the Georgia Institute of Technology, Atlanta. Since then he has been a member of the faculty of the School of Electrical Engineering at Cornell University, Ithaca, NY. He has also served as a consultant in wireless telecommunication systems, error control coding, and cryptography for various companies and governments in North America, Europe, and Asia. He teaches and conducts research in wireless information networks, error control coding, and probabilistic network models. His research has focused on the development and application of advanced technologies for data links and multiple-access protocols in wireless networks. current emphases include the applications of Bayesian networks to problems of error control, mobility management, and resource allocation. He is the author of *Error Control Systems for Digital Communications and Storage* (Englewood Cliffs, NJ: Prentice-Hall, 1995) and coauthor of *Turbo-Coding* (Boston, MA: Kluwer, 1998). He is coeditor of *Reed–Solomon Codes and Their Applications* (New York: IEEE Press, 1994).

Dr. Wicker currently serves as the Editor for Coding Theory and Techniques for the IEEE TRANSACTIONS ON COMMUNICATIONS. His awards include the 1998 Cornell College of Engineering Michael Tien Teaching Award.

Jack K. Wolf (S'54–M'60–F'73) received the undergraduate degree from the Moore School of the Electrical Engineering at the University of Pennsylvania, Philadelphia, and the graduate degrees are from Princeton University, Princeton, NJ, where he received the Ph.D. degree in electrical engineering.

He is the Stephen O. Rice Professor of Magnetics in the Electrical and Computer Engineering Department and the Center for Magnetic Recording Research at the University of California, San Diego (UCSD). Also, he has a part-time appointment with QUALCOMM, Inc., San Diego. Prior to joining UCSD, he held full-time faculty appointments at New York University, the Polytechnic Institute of Brooklyn, and the University of Massachusetts at Amherst where he served as Chair of the Electrical and Computer Engineering Department. He was an officer in the U.S. Air Force stationed at the Rome Air Development Center, Rome, NY. He has worked at RCA Laboratories and Bell Laboratories and has consulted for many companies and government organizations. His present research interests at UCSD are concerned with the application of modern signal processing to high-density storage systems. At QUALCOMM, Inc., he is concerned with the design and development of wireless communication systems.

Dr. Wolf is a member of the National Academy of Engineering and a former President of the IEEE Information Theory Society. He has been an NSF Senior Postdoctoral Fellow and a Guggenheim Fellow. He was a recipient of the E. H. Armstrong Award of the IEEE Communications Society and was a corecipient of the Prize Paper Award of the IEEE Information Theory Society and the Leonard G. Abraham Prize Paper Award of the IEEE Communications Society. He received the 1998 Koji Kobayashi Computers and Communications Award for his contributions to multiuser communications and applications of coding theory to magnetic storage devices.

Aaron D. Wyner (F'75) (deceased) received the B.S. degree in 1960 from Queen's College, City University of New York, and the B.S.E.E. , M.S., and Ph.D. degrees from Columbia University, New York, NY, in 1960, 1961, and 1963, respectively.

From 1963 until his death he was doing research in various aspects of information and communication theory and related mathematical areas at Bell Laboratories, Murray Hill, NJ (formerly a division of AT&T and now a division of Lucent Technologies). From 1974 to 1993 he was Head of the Communications Analysis Research Department at Bell Laboratories, and later was a Distinguished Member of Technical Staff. He spent the year 1969–1970 visiting the Department of Applied Mathematics at the Weitzmann Institute of Science, Rehovot, Israel, and the Faculty of Electrical Engineering at the Technion–Israel Institute of Technology, Haifa, Israel, on a Guggenheim Foundation Fellowship. He has been a full- and part-time faculty member at Columbia University, Princeton University, and at the Polytechnic Institute of Brooklyn. He died on September 29, 1997.

Dr. Wyner was active in the IEEE Information Theory Society. He served on the Society's Board of Governors, as Chairman of its Metropolitan New York Chapter, as Associate Editor for Shannon Theory (1970–1972), and Editor-in-Chief (1983–1986) of the IEEE TRANSACTIONS ON INFORMATION THEORY, and Co-Chairman of two international symposia (1969 and 1972) and of a workshop (1984). In 1976 he served as President of the Society. In 1984 he received the IEEE Centennial Medal, and was the 1994 Shannon Lecturer at the International Symposium on Information Theory in Trondheim, Norway. He was also a member of URSI, having served as Chairman of U.S. Commission C from 1988 to 1990, and as Vice-Chairman of International Commission C from 1990 to 1993. In 1994 he was elected to the U.S. National Academy of Engineering.

Abraham J. Wyner (M'96) was born in New York City on April 8, 1967. He received the B.S. degree in mathematics from Yale University, New Haven, CT, in 1988 and the Ph.D. degree in statistics from Stanford University, Stanford, CA, in 1993.

From 1993 to 1995 he was Acting Assistant Professor of Statistics at Stanford University. In 1995 he became a Visiting Professor of Statistics at the University of California at Berkeley. His research interests include string matching, data compression, statistical modeling, entropy estimation, and genetics.

Dr. Wyner is a recipient of the National Science Foundation postdoctoral research fellowship in the Mathematical Science.

Bin Yu (A'92–SM'97) was born in Harbin, China, on March 18, 1963. She received the B.S. degree in mathematics from Peking University, Peking, China, in 1984, and the M.S. and Ph.D. degrees in statistics from the University of California at Berkeley in 1987 and 1990, respectively. Her doctoral research was on empirical processes for dependent data and Minimum Description Length (MDL) Principle.

She was an Assistant Professor of Statistics at the University of Wisconsin, Madison, from 1990 to 1992, a Post-Doctoral Fellow at the Mathematical Science Research Institute at Berkeley in the Fall of 1991, a Visiting Assistant Professor of Statistics at Yale University, New Haven, CT, in the Spring of 1993, and an Assistant Professor of Statistics at the University of California at Berkeley from July 1993 to June 1997. She is currently an Associate Professor of Statistics at the University of California at Berkeley. She is also a part-time Member of the Technical Staff at Bell Labs, Lucent Technologies. Her research interests are broad and currently include adaptive estimation and quantization in signal processing, classification problems in remote sensing, MDL principle and information theory, and Markov chain Monte Carlo methods. She has published over 20 technical papers in journals such as *The Annals of Statistics*, IEEE TRANSACTIONS ON INFORMATION THEORY, *The Annals of Probability*, *Probability Theory and Related Fields*, *Journal of American Statistical Association*, *Remote Sensing of Environment*, and *Genomics*.

757

Dr. Yu was in the S. S. Chern Mathematics Exchange Program between China and the United States in 1985; she is a recipient of George Martin Fellowship and Anthony Fellowship in 1985 and 1989; a recipient of the Evelyn Fix Memorial Medal and Citation in 1990, and a recipient of a Junior Faculty Award in 1993, and a CAREER Development Award in 1995, all at the University of California at Berkeley. She is serving as an Associate Editor for *The Annals of Statistics* and *Statistica Sinica* and is on the Board of Western Region of the International Biometrics Society. She is serving on the program committee of the IEEE International Symposium on Information Theory, Boston, MA, August 1998, and served for the 8th International Workshop on Algorithmic Learning Theory (ALT'97), Sendai, Japan, October 1997.

Jacob Ziv (A'57–F'73) was born in Tiberias, Israel, on November 27, 1931. He received the B.Sc., Dip. Eng., and M.Sc. degrees, all in electrical engineering, from the Technion—Israel Institute of Technology, Haifa, Israel, in 1954 and 1957, respectively, and the D.Sc. degree from the Massachusetts Institute of Technology (MIT), Cambridge, MA, in 1962.

From 1955 to 1959, he was a Senior Research Engineer in the Scientific Department, Israel Ministry of Defense, and was assigned to the research and development of communication systems. From 1961 to 1962, while studying for his doctorate at MIT, he joined the Applied Science Division of Melpar, Inc., Watertown, MA, where he was a Senior Research Engineer doing research in communication theory. In 1962 he returned to the Scientific Department, Israel Ministry of Defense, as Head of the Communications Division and was also an Adjunct of the Faculty of Electrical Engineering, Technion—Israel Institute of Technology. From 1968 to 1970 he was a Member of the Technical Staff of Bell Laboratories, Inc., Murray Hill, NJ. He joined the Technion in 1970 and is presently Herman Gross Professor of Electrical Engineering. He was Dean of the Faculty of Electrical Engineering from 1974 to 1976 and Vice President for Academic Affairs from 1978 to 1982. From 1977 to 1978, 1983 to 1984, and 1991 to 1992 he was on sabbatical leave at Bell Laboratories, Murray Hill, NJ. He has been Chairman of the Israeli Universities Planning and Grants Committee from 1985 to 1991. His research interests include general topics in data compression, information theory, and statistical communication.

Dr. Ziv is the President of the Israeli Academy of Science and the Humanities. In 1982 he was elected Member of the Israeli Academy of Sciences and was appointed as a Technion Distinguished Professor. In 1988 he was elected a Foreign Associate of the U.S. National Academy of Engineering. In 1993 he was awarded the Israel Prize in Exact Sciences (Engineering and Technology). He has twice been the recipient of the IEEE Information Theory Best Paper Award (for 1976 and 1979). He is the recipient of the 1995 IEEE Richard W. Hamming Medal and the 1995 Marconi International Award.